THE HISTORY OF PARLIAMENT

THE HOUSE OF COMMONS 1690–1715

Already published:

The House of Commons 1386–1421, ed. J. S. Roskell,
Linda Clark and Carole Rawcliffe (4 vols., 1992)

The House of Commons, 1509–1558, ed. S. T. Bindoff
(3 vols., 1982)

The House of Commons, 1559–1603, ed. P. W. Hasler
(3 vols., 1981)

The House of Commons, 1660–1690, ed. B. D. Henning
(3 vols., 1983)

The House of Commons, 1715–1754, ed. Romney Sedgwick
(2 vols., 1970)

The House of Commons, 1754–1790, ed. Sir Lewis Namier
and John Brooke (3 vols., 1964)

The House of Commons, 1790–1820, ed. R. G. Thorne
(5 vols., 1986)

In preparation:

The House of Commons, 1422–1504
The House of Commons, 1604–1629
The House of Commons, 1640–1660
The House of Commons, 1820–1832
The House of Lords, 1660–1832

In 1998, the History of Parliament Trust published in collaboration with Cambridge University Press, a CD-ROM, *The History of Parliament on CD-ROM*, which includes all the above published sections of the *History*, together with corrections, addenda and additional material.

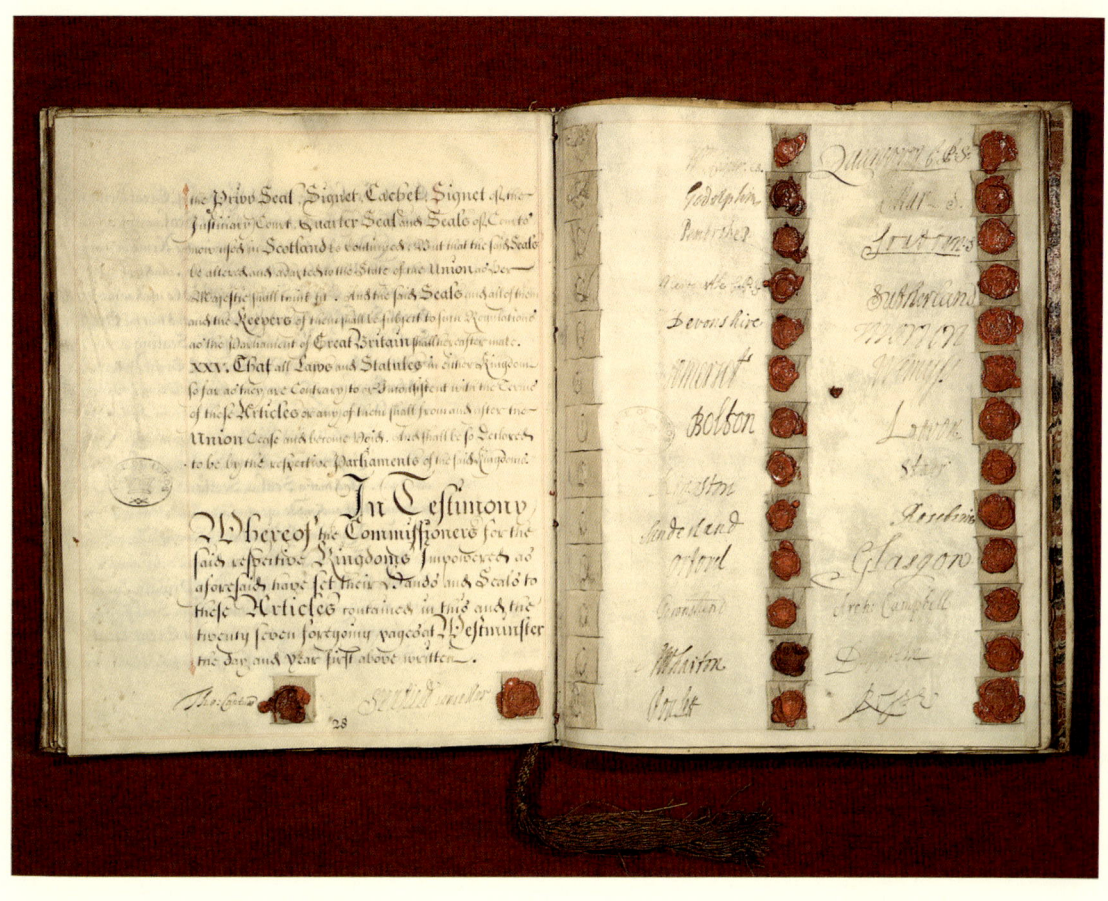

Treaty Articles of Act of Union between England and Scotland, 1706.
House of Lords Record Office

THE HISTORY OF PARLIAMENT

THE HOUSE OF COMMONS
1690–1715

*Eveline Cruickshanks, Stuart Handley
and D. W. Hayton*

III
MEMBERS
A–F

PUBLISHED FOR THE HISTORY OF PARLIAMENT TRUST
BY CAMBRIDGE UNIVERSITY PRESS
2002

PUBLISHED BY THE PRESS SYNDICATE OF THE UNIVERSITY OF CAMBRIDGE
The Pitt Building, Trumpington Street, Cambridge, United Kingdom

CAMBRIDGE UNIVERSITY PRESS
The Edinburgh Building, Cambridge CB2 2RU, UK
40 West 20th Street, New York NY 10011-4211, USA
477 Williamstown Road, Port Melbourne, VIC 3207, Australia
Ruiz de Alarcón 13, 28014 Madrid, Spain
Dock House, The Waterfront, Cape Town 8001, South Africa

http://www.cambridge.org

© History of Parliament Trust 2002

This book is in copyright. Subject to statutory exception
and to the provisions of relevant collective licensing agreements,
no reproduction of any part may take place without
the written permission of Cambridge University Press.

First published 2002

Printed in the United Kingdom at the University Press, Cambridge

Typeface Monotype Imprint 8.75/10.5 pt.   *System* QuarkXPress™   [SE]

A catalogue record for this book is available from the British Library

Library of Congress Cataloguing in Publication data

Cruickshanks, Eveline.
The history of the parliament : the House of Commons, 1690–1715 / Eveline
Cruickshanks, Stuart Handley, and D. W. Hayton.
v. ; cm.
Contents: v. 3. Members A–F
ISBN 0 521 77221 4
1. Great Britain. Parliament. House of Commons – History.   2. Great Britain – Politics
and government – 1660–1714.   I. Handley, Stuart.   II. Hayton, David, 1949–
JN673.C78   2001
328.441′072′09032–dc21   00-063092

ISBN 0 521 77221 4 five-volume set

Contents

List of contributors . . . . page vi
Editorial note vii
List of abbreviations viii
MEMBERS A–F 1

Contributors

E.C.	Eveline Cruickshanks
K.M.E.	Kathryn Ellis
P.L.G.	Perry Gauci
S.N.H.	Stuart Handley
A.A.H.	A. A. Hanham
R.D.H.	Richard Harrison
D.W.H.	D. W. Hayton
B.D.H.	Basil Duke Henning
M.J.K.	Mark Knights
H.J.L.	Henry Lancaster
C.I.M.	Ivar McGrath
E.R.	Ted Rowlands
P.W.	Paula Watson
D.W.	David Wilkinson
S.M.W.	Sonya Wynne

Editorial note

A raised asterisk (*) following a name denotes a Member of the House of Commons during the period covered by these volumes, where such inference is not apparent from the surrounding text. A raised dagger (†) against a name indicates a Member sitting outside the period and for whom an entry is to be found in earlier or later volumes. Where two (or more) Members bear exactly the same name and style they have been differentiated by the addition of roman numerals according to when they first entered Parliament, for instance Thomas Foley I, Thomas Foley II and Thomas Foley III. This numbering is specific to this section of the *History* only, and does not reflect a Member's seniority by age or within his family. For other conventions concerning the arrangement and content of biographies, the reader should refer to the section on 'Method' in Volume I (pp. 6–12).

Abbreviations

The following abbreviations are used in Volume III. They are arranged under three sections: I. preliminary paragraphs and text; II. endnotes; III. unpublished theses.

I. PRELIMINARY PARAGRAPHS AND TEXT

abp.	archbishop
adm.	admitted; admissions; admiral
adn.	archdeacon
adv.	advocate
aft.	after; afterwards
appr.	apprentice
b.	born
bap.	baptised
bd.	board
bp.	bishop
bro.	brother
bur.	buried
c.	circa; chief
called	called to the bar
capt.	captain
cdr.	commander
ch.	child(ren)
c.j.	chief justice
coh.	coheir(ess)
commdt.	commandant
commr.	commissioner
corp.	corporation
cos.	cousin
coy.	company in regiment
c.p.	common pleas
cr.	created
ct.	court
cttee.	committee
d.	died

viii

List of abbreviations

da.	daughter(s)
dep.	deputy
div.	divorced
d.s.p.	died *sine prole* (without issue)
d.v.p.	died *vita patris* (in the lifetime of his father)
E. I. Co.	East India Company
er.	elder
event.	eventual
fac.	faculty
f.m.	field marshal
gdda.	granddaughter
gdfa.	grandfather
gds.	grandson
gent.	gentleman
gov.	governor
Gren.	Grenadier
g.s.	grammar school
h.	heir; heiress
h.s.	high school
I.	Isle
[I]	Irish; Ireland
illegit.	illegitimate
j. Kb	justice King's bench
j.p.	justice of the peace
jt.	joint
KB	Knight of the Bath
Kb	King's bench
KC	King's Counsel
KG	Knight of the Garter
KS	King's scholar
KT	Knight of the Thistle
l.c.j.	lord chief justice
Ld.; ld.	Lord; lord
lic.	licence
lt., ltcy.	lieutenant; lieutenancy
m.	married
mar.	marriage
matric.	matriculated
Mq.	Marquess
nom.	nominated
o.	only
plenip.	plenipotentiary
posth.	posthumous
preb.	prebend; prebendary

pres.	president; presumably
Qb	Queen's bench
QC	Queen's Counsel
q.m.g.	quarter-master-general
R.	Royal
r.-adm.	rear admiral
rem.	removed
rep. peer [S]	representative peer of Scotland
res.	resigned
ret.	retired
s.	son(s)
[S]	Scottish; Scotland
SCJ	Senator of the College of Justices (Scotland)
s.p.	*sine prole* (without issue)
SPCK	Society for the Promotion of Christian Knowledge
SPG	Society for the Propagation of the Gospel in Foreign Parts
s.p.m.	*sine prole mascula* (without male issue)
s.p.s.	*sine prole superstite* (without surviving issue)
suc.	succeeded
summ.	summoned (to Lords)
surv.	surviving
tp.	troop
unm.	unmarried
v.-adm.	vice-admiral
vol.	volunteer
v.p.	*vita patris* (in the life of his father)
w.	wife
wid.	widow
yr.	younger
yst.	youngest

II. ENDNOTES

Add.	Additional mss, British Library
Add. ch.	Additional Charters, British Library
Addison Letters	*The Letters of Joseph Addison* ed. Graham (1941)
Ailesbury Mems.	*Memoirs of Thomas, Earl of Ailesbury* ed. Buckley (Roxburghe Club, 1890)
Al.	Alumni
Al. Westmon.	*List of Queen's Scholars of St Peter's College, Westminster* (1852)
AN	Archive Nationale, Paris
antiq.	antiquarian
AO	Archive(s) Office
app.	appendix

List of abbreviations

APS	Acts of the Parliament of Scotland
APC Col.	Acts of the Privy Council of England: Colonial
Arch.	Archaeological, Archaeologia
Arch. Ael.	Archaeologia Aeliana
Argyll Pprs.	The Argyll Papers ed. Maidment (1834)
ass. bks.	assembly books
Atterbury Epistolary Corresp.	The Epistolary Correspondence . . . of . . . Francis Atterbury ed. Nichols (1783–90)
Baillie Corresp.	The Correspondence of George Baillie of Jerviswood, 1702–8 ed. Kynynmond (Bannatyne Club, lxxii)
bdle.	bundle
BL	British Library
BN	Bibliothèque Nationale, Paris
Bodl.	Bodleian Library
Bodl. Rawl.	Rawlinson mss, Bodleian Library, Oxford
Bolingbroke Corresp.	Letters and Correspondence of Henry St. John, Viscount Bolingbroke ed. Parke (1754–98)
bor.	boroughs
Boyer, Anne Annals	Abel Boyer, The History of the Reign of Queen Anne Digested into Annals (1703–12)
Boyer, Anne Hist.	Abel Boyer, The History of Queen Anne (1735)
Bull. IHR	Bulletin of the Institute of Historical Research
Burnet	Bishop Burnet's History of His Own Time (1833)
Cal.	Calendar
Cam. Misc.	Camden Miscellany
Cam. Soc.	Camden Society
Campbell, Lives	John, Baron Campbell, The Lives of the Lord Chancellors (1845–69)
Chandler	Richard Chandler, The History and Proceedings of the House of Commons (1742–4)
CJ	Journals of the House of Commons
Clerk Mems.	Memoirs of . . . Sir John Clerk of Penicuik, 1676–1755 ed. Gray (Scot. Hist. Soc. xiii)
CLRO	City of London Record Office
Cocks Diary	The Parliamentary Diary of Sir Richard Cocks, 1698–1702 ed. Hayton (1996)
Colls.	Collections
Cowper, Diary	The Private Diary of William, First Earl Cowper (Roxburghe Club, 1833)
CP	G. E. C[okayne], Complete Peerage
Crossrigg Diary	Diary of the Proceedings of the Parliament and Privy Council of Scotland, 21 May 1700–7 Mar. 1707 by Sir David Hume of Crossrigg ed. Hope (Bannatyne Club, xxvii)
CSP Col.	Calendar of State Papers Colonial

List of abbreviations

CSP Dom.	*Calendar of State Papers Domestic*
Debates and Procs. 1694–5	*A Collection of the Debates and Proceedings in Parliament in 1694 and 1695* (1695)
dioc.	diocese
DNB	*Dictionary of National Biography*
Duchess of Marlborough Conduct	*An Account of the Conduct of the Dowager Duchess of Marlborough . . . to the year 1710* (1742)
Duchess of Marlborough Corresp.	*Private Correspondence of Sarah, Duchess of Marlborough* (1838)
Duchess of Marlborough Letters at Madresfield	*Letters of Sarah, Duchess of Marlborough . . . from the Original Manuscripts at Madresfield Court* (1875)
DWB	*Dictionary of Welsh Biography*
DZA	Deutsches Zentralarchiv, Merseburg (now Geheimes Staatsarchiv Preussischer Kulturbesitz, Berlin)
Ec. Hist. Rev.	*Economic History Review*
Egerton ch.	Egerton charters, British Library
Egerton	Egerton mss, British Library
EHR	*English Historical Review*
Evelyn Diary	*The Diary of John Evelyn* ed. de Beer (1955)
Fac. Off.	Faculty Office
Frag. Gen.	*Fragmenta Genealogica*
The Gen.	*The Genealogist*
Gent. Mag.	*Gentleman's Magazine*
Grey	Anchitell Grey, *Debates of the House of Commons 1667–94* (1769)
Hamilton Diary	*The Diary of Sir David Hamilton, 1709–14* ed. Roberts (1975)
Harl.	Harleian mss, British Library (also, as in Harleian Society)
HC Lib.	House of Commons Library
Hist. Parl. Scot.	*The Parliaments of Scotland* ed. Young (1992–3)
Hist. Reg. Chron.	*Historical Register* [Chronicle]
HLRO	House of Lords Record Office
HMC	*Historical Manuscripts Commission*
IGI	International Genealogical Index (Church of Latter-Day Saints)
Impartial View	*An Impartial View of the Two Late Parliaments . . .* (1711)
L. Inn Lib.	Lincoln's Inn Library, London
Lady Cowper, *Diary*	*Diary of Mary, Countess Cowper 1714–20* (1864)
Lady Mary Wortley Montagu Letters	*Letters of Lady Mary Wortley Montagu* ed. Halsband (1965–7)
Lansd.	Lansdowne mss, British Library
Lexington Pprs.	*The Lexington Papers* ed. Sutton (1851)
Life of Halifax	*The Works and Life of . . . Charles, Late Earl of Halifax* (1715)
LJ	*Journals of the House of Lords*
Lockhart Letters ed. Szechi	*Letters of George Lockhart of Carnwath, 1698–1732* ed. Szechi (Scot. Hist. Soc. ser. 5, ii)

List of abbreviations

Lockhart Mems. ed. Szechi	*'Scotland's Ruine': Lockhart of Carnwath's Memoirs of the Union* ed. Szechi (Assoc. Scot. Lit. Studies, xxv)
Lockhart Pprs.	*The Lockhart Papers* ed. Aufrere (1817)
Luttrell, *Brief Relation*	Narcissus Luttrell, *A Brief Historical Relation of State Affairs* (1857)
Luttrell Diary	*The Parliamentary Diary of Narcissus Luttrell, 1691–3* ed. Horwitz (1972)
Macky Mems.	*Memoirs of the Secret Services of John Macky* (1733)
Mar. Lic.	Marriage Licences
Marlborough–Godolphin Corresp.	*The Marlborough–Godolphin Correspondence* ed. Snyder (1975)
Mems.	Memoirs
MI	monumental inscription
mic.	microfilm
min.	minutes
Misc. Gen. et Her.	*Miscellanea Genealogica et Heraldica*
Morrice ent'ring bk.	Dr Williams' Library, London: Roger Morrice's Ent'ring Book
Mus.	Museum
N. and Q.	*Notes and Queries*
n.d.	no date
NLS	National Library of Scotland
NLW	National Library of Wales
NMM	National Maritime Museum
NRA	National Register of Archives, London
N. S.	New Style
n.s.	new series
NSA	Niedersächsisches Hauptstaatsarchiv, Hannover
OR	[Official] *Return of Members of Parliament compiled by the Public Record Office* (1878–91)
par.	parish
PCC	Prerogative Court of Canterbury
ped.	pedigree
Pittis, *Present Parl.*	[W. Pittis], *The History of the Present Parliament* (1711)
Portledge Pprs.	*The Portledge Papers* ed. Kerr and Duncan (1928)
PRO	Public Record Office (documents cited by class number only)
Procs. Occasional Conformity Bill	*The Proceedings of Both Houses of Parliament . . . upon the Bill to Prevent Occasional Conformity . . .* (1710)
RA	Royal Archives, Windsor Castle
Ranke	L. von Ranke, *A History of England* (1875)
RO	Record Office
Seafield Corresp.	*Seafield Correspondence from 1685 to 1708* ed. Grant (Scot. Hist. Soc. ser. 2, iii)
Seafield Letters	*Letters Relating to Scotland in the Reign of Queen Anne by James Ogilvy, First Earl of Seafield* ed. Hume Brown (Scot. Hist. Soc. ser. 2, xi)

Sel. Charters	*Select Charters* ed. Carr (Selden Soc. xxviii)
ser.	series
Shaftesbury Letters	*Letters from . . . the Late Earl of Shaftesbury to Robert Molesworth* ed. Toland (1721)
SHR	*Scottish Historical Review*
Shrewsbury Corresp.	*Private and Original Correspondence of Charles Talbot, Duke of Shrewsbury* ed. Coxe (1821)
Sloane	Sloane mss, British Library
SP	State Papers
sp.	special
SRO	Scottish Record Office (now the National Archives of Scotland)
Statutes	*Statutes of the Realm*
Stowe	Stowe mss, British Library
supp.	supplement
Swift v. Mainwaring	*Swift vs. Mainwaring: The Examiner and the Medley* ed. Ellis (1985)
Thoresby Diary	*The Diary of Ralph Thoresby* ed. Hunter (1830)
Thoresby Letters	*Letters of Eminent Men Addressed to Ralph Thoresby* (1832)
Tindal	Nicholas Tindal, *The Continuation of Mr Rapin de Thoyras's History of England from the Revolution to the Accession of King George II* (1751)
Top. and Gen.	*Topographer and Genealogist*
UCNW	University College of North Wales, Bangor
VCH	*Victoria County History*
Verney Letters 18th Century	*Verney Letters of the Eighteenth Century from the Manuscripts at Claydon House* ed. Lady M. Verney (1930)
Verney Mems.	*Memoirs of the Verney Family during the Seventeenth Century* ed. F. and M. Verney (1907)
Vernon–Shrewsbury Letters	*Letters Illustrative of the Reign of William III . . . Addressed to the Duke of Shrewsbury by James Vernon* ed. James (1841)
Vis.	Visitation
Wentworth Pprs.	*The Wentworth Papers 1705–39* ed. Cartwright (1883)
Wharton Mems.	*Memoirs of the Life of . . . Thomas, late Marquis of Wharton* (1715)
Wm. III State Tracts	*A Collection of State Tracts published . . . during the Reign of William III* (1705–7)
Wodrow, *Analecta*	Robert Wodrow, *Analecta* ed. Leishman (Maitland Club, lx)

III. UNPUBLISHED THESES

Barré thesis	D. C. Barré, 'Worcestershire Politics and Elections, 1679–1715' (Birmingham Univ. M.A. thesis, 1971)
Brooks thesis	C. Brooks, 'Taxation, Finance and Public Opinion, 1688–1714' (Cambridge Univ. Ph.D. thesis, 1971)

List of abbreviations

Challinor thesis	P. J. Challinor, 'The Structure of Politics in Cheshire, 1660–1715' (CNAA, Ph.D. thesis, 1983)
Clarke thesis	T. N. Clarke, 'The Scottish Episcopalians, 1688–1720' (Edinburgh Univ. Ph.D. thesis, 1987)
Craig thesis	A. G. Craig, 'The Movement for the Reformation of Manners, 1688–1715' (Edinburgh Univ. Ph.D. thesis, 1980)
De Krey thesis	G. S. De Krey, 'Trade, Religion and Politics in London in the Reign of William III' (Princeton Univ. Ph.D. thesis, 1978)
Doolittle thesis	I. G. Doolittle, 'The Government of the City of London, 1694–1767' (Oxford Univ. D.Phil. thesis, 1980)
Ellis thesis	E. L. Ellis, 'The Whig Junto in Relation to the Development of Party Politics and Party Organization from its Inception to 1714' (Oxford Univ. D.Phil. thesis, 1961)
Evans thesis	S. Evans, 'An Examination of Sir Humphrey Mackworth's Industrial Activities' (Wales Univ. M.A. thesis, 1950)
Ferguson thesis	W. Ferguson, 'Electoral Law and Procedure in 18th- and early 19th-century Scotland' (Glasgow Univ. Ph.D. thesis, 1957)
Hayton thesis	D. W. Hayton, 'Ireland and the English Ministers, 1707–16' (Oxford Univ. D.Phil. thesis, 1975)
Hopkins thesis	P. A. Hopkins, 'Aspects of Jacobite Conspiracy in England in the Reign of William III' (Cambridge Univ. Ph.D. thesis, 1981)
Hopkinson thesis	R. Hopkinson, 'Elections in Cumberland and Westmorland, 1695–1723' (Newcastle-upon-Tyne Univ. Ph.D. thesis, 1973)
Jones thesis	D. W. Jones, 'London Overseas Merchant Groups at the End of the 17th century, and the Move Against the East India Company' (Oxford Univ. D.Phil. thesis, 1970)
Macfarlane thesis	S. M. Macfarlane, 'Studies in Poverty and Poor Relief in London at the end of the 17th century' (Oxford Univ. D.Phil. thesis, 1983)
McGrath thesis	C. I. V. McGrath, 'The Irish Revenue System: Government and Administration 1689–1702' (London Univ. Ph.D. thesis, 1997)
Monod thesis	P. K. Monod, 'For the King to Enjoy his Own again: Jacobite Political Culture in England, 1688–1788' (Yale Univ. Ph.D. thesis, 1985)

Quinn thesis	J. F. Quinn, 'The Parliamentary Constituencies of Yorkshire from the Accession of Queen Anne to the Fall of Walpole' (Lancaster Univ. M.Litt. thesis, 1979)
Robbins thesis	C. A. Robbins, '"Honest Tom" Wharton: A Study in Political Organization, Party Politics, and Electioneering in England, 1679–1715' (Maryland Univ. Ph.D. thesis, 1990)
Speck thesis	W. A. Speck, 'The House of Commons, 1702–14: A Study in Political Organization' (Oxford Univ. D.Phil. thesis, 1965)
Sunter thesis	R. Sunter, 'Stirlingshire Politics, 1707–1832' (Edinburgh Univ. Ph.D. thesis, 1971)
Wahlstrand thesis	J. M. Wahlstrand, 'The Elections to Parliament in the County of Lancaster, 1688–1714' (Manchester Univ. M.A. thesis, 1956)
Ward thesis	P. W. U. Ward, 'Members of Parliament and Elections in Derbyshire, Leicestershire and Staffordshire between 1660 and 1714' (Manchester Univ. M.A. thesis, 1959)
Watson thesis	P. K. Watson, 'The Commission for Victualling the Navy, the Commission for Sick and Wounded Seamen and Prisoners of War and the Commission for Transport, 1702–14' (London Univ. Ph.D. thesis, 1965)

MEMBERS A–F

ABERCROMBY, Alexander (1678–1729), of Glassaugh, Fordyce, Banff.

SCOTLAND 1707–1708
BANFFSHIRE 1708–1727

b. 5 Nov. 1678, 3rd but 1st surv. s. of Alexander Abercromby (o.s. *d.v.p.* of John Abercromby of Glassaugh) by Katherine, da. of Sir Robert Dunbar, MP [S], of Grangehill, Elgin. *m.* by 1703, Helen (*d.* aft. 1744), da. and coh. of George Meldrum (*d.* 1692) of Crombie, Marnoch, Banff, minister of Glass, Banff, 2s. 4da. *suc.* gdfa. 1691.[1]

Commr. justiciary for Highlands [S] 1701, 1702; lt. 21 Ft. (R. Scots Fusiliers) 1706, capt. 1707, lt.-col. (half-pay) 1721; commr. Equivalent [S] 1707–19; a.d.c. to Duke of Marlborough (John Churchill†) in Low Countries 1711; lt. gov. Fort William 1726–?*d*.[2]

MP [S] Banffshire 1706–7.

Burgess, Edinburgh 1724.[3]

Falling into dependence on his Banffshire neighbour Lord Seafield (later 4th Earl of Findlater), Abercromby profited rather less than might have been expected from his patron's extended ministerial career under Queen Anne. But, although occasionally resentful in private, he always performed his public duty as befitted one unflatteringly described by an outside observer as Seafield's 'creature' and praised by the Earl's agent as 'the surest friend . . . that my lord has'. Descended from a younger son of Sir Alexander Abercromby of Birkenbog, grand falconer to King James VI, Abercromby had evidently inherited no strong religious or political principles, his immediate family background suggesting instead a survivor's pragmatism. In 1685 his father-in-law, a Presbyterian minister, had eventually been deprived after a lengthy period of conformity, but at the same time his own father and grandfather were demonstrating their pliability by taking the test; and each served both James II and William III as commissioners of supply for their county. Having entered into possession of the Glassaugh estate while still a boy, Abercromby complained soon after coming of age that his finances were in 'great disorder', a state of affairs for which his tutor, Sir James Abercromby of Birkenbog, may well have been at least partly responsible, since Birkenbog's management of his own property left something to be desired. Abercromby himself was no model of sobriety, for in January 1702 he was fined by the local Kirk authorities for 'scandalous conduct', but he took care to make himself an agreeable guest at Cullen House, providing the 3rd Earl of Findlater with books and obliging companionship. Through Findlater's influence he was nominated to the commission of the peace for Banffshire, and the commission of judiciary for the Highlands. Slower in coming was the salaried position in hope of which he had pledged his 'entire engagement' to Seafield's family. Advised in 1702 to 'change the plough for the sword', he set his mind on a military commission, but had to wait until February 1706 before he was made a lieutenant in the Royal Scots Fusiliers through Seafield's intercession, as part of that general gratification of the Court grouping in Scottish politics by which the ministry sought to pave the way for the Union.[4]

Abercromby was brought in by Seafield to the vacant parliamentary commissionership for Banffshire in 1706 in order to give a vote for Union. This he did, adhering to a straight Court line in all divisions, except for two unimportant absences. In the middle of the session he was able to purchase a captaincy for £1,000, and to make doubly sure of him, the ministry had included him in the Scottish civil list for a pension of £450, though whether this sum was ever paid must be open to question. Afterwards he was appointed to the commission on the Equivalent, again at Seafield's request. Predictably, he was also one of the Court contingent selected to represent Scotland in the first Parliament of Great Britain.[5]

Although the Equivalent commissionership remained disappointingly unremunerative, Abercromby gave no indication of dissatisfaction with the Court during his first session at Westminster. Indeed, until his departure for Scotland on active military service in mid-March 1708, he was surprisingly forward for someone so inexperienced. On 25 Feb. 1708 he told against a Junto- and Squadrone-inspired motion to alter the order of payments from the Equivalent; and his remaining appointment of significance, on 11 Mar., was to the drafting committee for a bill designed to counter the invasion threat by absolving Highland clansmen from their obligations to Jacobite chieftains.[6]

Abercromby was not only returned on Seafield's interest for Banffshire at the 1708 election, he acknowledged that the decision on whether he should stand at all belonged to his patron. Seafield was able to boast of him as one of 'my friends ... who, I hope, will serve her Majesty faithfully in the Parliament'. He was entrusted with carrying to Flanders the address of thanks from the House to the Duke of Marlborough, obtaining a leave of absence for this purpose on 25 Jan. 1709. He took the opportunity to solicit the Duke in person for military advancement, but to no avail. Returning to Westminster, he was nominated to draft a bill for the more effectual prohibition of wine imports on 9 Mar. 1709, and told on 31 Mar. against receiving the report of the Earl of Lindsey's (Robert Bertie, Lord Willoughby de Eresby*) estate bill, something of a party cause since Lindsey's turn to the Whigs, and thus a sign that Abercromby, as would be expected, was staying with the Court against the Junto and Squadrone. On 7 Apr. he told against the motion for a committee of the whole on the African Company bill, signalling his disapproval as a Scot for an initiative that appeared prejudicial to the equality of trade promised under the Union. Included in the renewed commission of the Equivalent in 1709, he continued to support the Court and voted for the impeachment of Dr Sacheverell in 1710. By this time he had set his eyes on another plum, the estate of James Douglas, an Aberdonian who had died intestate. Douglas' illegitimacy meant that, according to Scottish law, the property came to the crown, and it was customary in such cases for the discoverer to be granted either the whole estate or a substantial portion. Claiming to have 'discovered' the case, and citing his own 'good services' to the ministry as additional justification, Abercromby put in his request in March 1710. Initially, Seafield obtained a promise from Lord Treasurer Godolphin (Sidney†) that a grant would be made, but before the barons of the Scottish exchequer could send the necessary report a rival claimant emerged in the shape of the burgh council of Aberdeen. Exploiting the political leverage they derived from the imminent dissolution of Parliament, councillors enlisted in their cause such powerful advocates as the Earl of Mar and thereby succeeded in blocking prompt action, so that for Abercromby, abroad with his regiment, the summer of 1710 dragged by without the anticipated gratification from the Treasury. Moreover, Seafield's influence suffered considerably with the change in ministry. The best that could be done for Abercromby was to postpone a final judgment on the Douglas estate until another round of representations might be made.[7]

Abercromby's behaviour in the Parliament of 1710, to which he was returned unopposed with Seafield's blessing, faithfully reflected the political manoeuvring of his patron, who, starting from a position of loyalty to Godolphin, in due course made his peace with the new ministers. Abercromby appears as a Whig in the 'Hanover list', but as an episcopal Tory in the analysis of the Scottish returns by Richard Dongworth, episcopalian chaplain to the Duchess of Buccleuch. Neither classification bears much resemblance to reality. The first clue to Abercromby's political alignment in the new House was his vote on 10 Feb. 1711 in favour of the Squadrone Member, Mungo Graham, over the disputed election for Kinross-shire. This followed a fortnight's leave, granted on 26 Jan. 1711, and preceded a further prolonged absence on the Continent from May onwards, which seems to have lasted the entire campaigning season. According to Abercromby himself, he had intended to rejoin his troops earlier still, but 'my Lord Seafield, Mr Boscawen [Hugh, II*], and some others of my Lord Godolphin's friends ... advised my stay' to perform his duty in defence of the old ministry. When at last he did get away he applied himself immediately to Marlborough, armed with earnest recommendations from Seafield on his behalf. In reply, the Duke gave little more than promises: 'you may assure Lord Seafield', Marlborough told his Duchess, 'that whenever it is in my power I shall be glad to serve Captain Abercromby, for I know him to be a very honest and a good-tempered man'. All the Duke could do was appoint Abercromby as one of his aides-de-camp, but what was required was something altogether more substantial, especially since it now seemed less and less likely that the gift of Douglas' estate would materialize. In desperation Abercromby turned to Seafield:

> As my endeavouring to serve his Grace in Parliament or otherwise was upon your lordship's account, so it must be by your lordship's interest with him that I can expect anything. I therefore beg your lordship will write to him and use what arguments you think proper, in which you may represent the expense I have been at, as also my losing the gift of bastardy.

This letter also contained an ambiguous statement about promises made to him, via one Captain Middleton, of being 'better protected last year if I would join the new party'. Although in Scottish terminology the Squadrone was often dubbed the 'new party' it seems more likely (on the assumption that the Argylls' client, John Middleton II*, was the go-between) that Abercromby was referring to the new Scottish Court Tory interest supporting the Harley ministry.[8]

Returning to London for the beginning of the next session, Abercromby made a last effort to squeeze from Marlborough the performance of the various promises the Duke and the former lord treasurer had made. Having voted with the Whigs on 7 Dec. 1711 in favour of the 'No Peace without Spain' motion, he dispatched a letter two days later to one of Marlborough's confidants, declaring that unless he received some financial relief he would be obliged to quit London for his Scottish estates, such was the dismal appearance of his affairs. He concluded with the reproach that 'besides my expense and attendance my zeal and fidelity to his Grace's interest has made me refuse from others what I would [have] been proud of accepting from his hands'. Subsequent events were to expose the level of disingenuousness in these remarks. As far back as April 1711 there had been contact between Abercromby and Robert Harley*, and an assurance given by the new chief minister that the affair of Douglas' estate would be settled in Abercromby's favour. Nothing had happened, but towards the end of December, in the middle of the crisis over the Duke of Hamilton's patent and the peace terms, with Harley hunting every available Scottish supporter in the Lords, Seafield (now Earl of Findlater) renewed solicitations on his client's behalf. He wrote to Harley (now Lord Treasurer Oxford) to recommend Abercromby to his consideration:

> He is very willing to attend the Queen's service in Parliament and observe your lordship's directions in everything, for this I have earnestly recommended to him, but, having attended all the Parliaments and served all the campaigns since the Union without any assistance, he writes that he must return home unless your lordship do something for him . . . If your lordship do for him he will be very faithful to you and useful.

Harley must have responded with more promises, for on 18 Jan. 1712 Abercromby wrote to Findlater to assure him that he was 'fully resolved to support the Union' and that he had 'satisfied my lord treasurer of my inclination to serve the Queen and ministry in everything except what concerns private persons who are my old friends'. Absence from the House, rather than support for the government, ensued when Abercromby obtained two months' leave on 26 Jan. He therefore took no part in proceedings over the controversial Scottish Toleration Act. In the 1713 session he opposed the ongoing campaign by Sir Alexander Cumming* and Thomas Smith II* to regulate procedures for apportioning land tax in the convention of royal burghs, telling on 29 Apr. 1713 against an additional clause in the land tax bill for 'a rule whereby to tax the royal burghs of Scotland'. In this he was following the wishes of his patron, a pattern of behaviour equally evident during the malt tax crisis and the campaign to dissolve the Union. Abercromby told on 21 May against the obnoxious clause which charged malt produced in Scotland at 6d. a bushel, and attended the meeting of Scottish Members on 23 May calling for united action with Scottish peers. He acted as unofficial clerk at the ensuing meeting of lords and commoners where the proposal for a motion to dissolve the Union was broached and Findlater was named as the peer to introduce it in Parliament. Then, with his patron and the rest of the Scots courtiers, he returned to administration over the issue of the French commercial treaty, voting in favour of the bill confirming its 8th and 9th articles, both at the second reading on 4 June and again at the engrossment on the 18th.[9]

In spite of his loyalty to Findlater and Oxford, Abercromby was no better off financially: the Douglas estate grant still hung fire, and his salary as an Equivalent commissioner was hopelessly in arrears. By May 1713 his domestic affairs were moving towards a crisis. His wife delivered an ultimatum that if no preferment was forthcoming in the current session she would not be able to entertain the prospect of another expensive journey to Westminster, and might even have to 'sell his plate next Whitsunday'. Findlater, who had already spent substantial amounts of his own money in propping up Abercromby's estate, through the purchase of land and the redeeming of wadsets, felt obliged to intervene once more, with an advance of £1,000. 'I cannot see Glassaugh in distress', he wrote. But not even this sum seemed likely to afford more than temporary relief, for the problems were deep-set. One of the Earl's local agents reported:

> We have had a conference with Glassaugh anent his affairs and find the half and much more is gone. I am heartily sorry I have occasion to tell you this but there is no help for it but sell he must. He imputed a great deal of his loss to his serving my lord, which he [Findlater] is not now in a condition to repay by getting anything done for him . . .

What Findlater's assistance was able to achieve was to calm Mrs Abercromby's fears and keep the family afloat until the general election in which, with strong backing from his patron, Abercromby overawed a persistent challenger and secured another unopposed return. But Abercromby evidently failed to keep his promise to 'live upon his pay' and the year ended with Findlater expending more money to satisfy Abercromby's creditors and casting around desperately for some item of patronage on which to base a longer-term rescue. Several times Findlater applied to Oxford, pledging that Abercromby would 'serve with great fidelity' in the Commons, but received in return no more than repetitions of the old promise that £300 would be given of the Douglas estate.[10]

Abercromby's ultimate dependence was therefore on the lord treasurer, and with his re-election newly secured he approached Oxford directly:

> Being unanimously chosen, which I flatter myself I shall always be in this shire while I think it convenient or desirable, I take this opportunity to assure your lordship that in the Parliament you have not one more entirely devoted to your service than I shall be on all occasions and in everything to the utmost of my power. So you may acquaint the Earl of Findlater when my being in London can do you any service you shall find a ready compliance to testify what I do so sincerely profess, and since my Lord Findlater informed me how mindful you were of me after my departure from London, and the promises you were pleased to make there, I beg you to let the Earl or me know from whom I should receive your lordship's commands . . .

Still nothing was forthcoming, and after making the journey down to Westminster Abercromby tried again. In mid-April he sent Oxford a memorial setting out his claim to a grant from the Douglas property and reminding him of the many previous assurances,

> which . . . encouraged me, contrary to my own and friends' inclinations, to be at the expense of being returned this Parliament, notwithstanding I had ruined myself and family by the expense of attending, and by close adhering to every measure I judged most agreeable to your lordship forfeited all manner of reputation and expectation of friendship from those who had done me service formerly and still declared their willingness when able . . . it was upon the Earl of Findlater's call, and the late assurances he had from your lordship that I came up, and . . . as I have so will I strive to the utmost of my power to support every measure that may be agreeable and acceptable to your lordship; and lastly, had it not been upon the faith of these promises I could not have raised money to have brought me up, far less does my circumstances allow me to bear the charges of attending, and by trusting thereto both I and my numerous family must be reduced to great straits unless made good.

Not even these heartfelt pleas had any effect, a failure which may have helped to harden Abercromby's outlook. Already in Lord Polwarth's analysis of the Scottish returns he had been marked as a Hanoverian; and a tellership on 29 Apr. 1714 in favour of a Squadrone supporter over a Tory rival in the disputed election for Anstruther Easter Burghs was followed on 12 May by a vote for Robert Walpole II's wrecking motion to extend the scope of the schism bill to cover 'popery'. He was later described as a Whig in the Worsley list and, despite continued professions of service to the lord treasurer, may well have sided frequently with opposition. Early in June he had warned Oxford that, unless 'you will make good your repeated promises both last year and this', he would be forced to return to Scotland. The fact that he remained in attendance may indicate that at last he had penetrated the treasurer's defences. His contributions to the business of the House give no hint of his attitude to the ministry, since they dealt with matters of personal or Scottish interest. For example, on 24 June, on the third reading of the bill to discharge the commissioners of the Equivalent of the money they had already disbursed, he led the opposition to a clause proposed by George Lockhart* and others, which would have obliged the commissioners to account for the surplus moneys granted, in accordance with their legislative authority, to assist the wool-producing areas of Scotland. Having been the principal speaker against the clause, he told against it. Then on 2 July he was a teller again, with fellow Scotsman George Yeaman, against an amendment to the soap and paper duties bill which concerned the leather export bounty.[11]

Abercromby welcomed the Hanoverian succession, being one of the signatories to the proclamation of George 1 at St. James's on 1 Aug. 1714; and in November he presented a loyal address from Banffshire. Findlater secured his re-election the next year, and thereafter he voted consistently with the Court. After recovering financial solvency, he lost heavily in the South Sea and Mississippi Bubbles and was reduced once more to dejection and dependence. Petitions for preferment flowed from his pen. Some minor relief came through inclusion on the half-pay list, and a belated appointment as lieutenant-governor of Fort William. His sons were also provided for: one as a professional soldier, the other, an artist, with a life patent as King's limner in Scotland. Still a 'perfect friend' of Findlater, he followed the Earl into the Argyll connexion and at the 1727 election, although standing down himself, actively assisted Lord Ilay's burgh managers. He died on 23 Dec. 1728.[12]

[1]*Hist. Scot. Parl.* 2; C. D. Abercromby, *Fam. of Abercromby*, 87–88; *Diary of Brodie of Brodie* (Spalding Club), 351, 398, 406;

SRO Indexes, xviii. 7, 474; Shaw and Gordon, Hist. Province of Moray (1882), iii. 391; Recs. Co. Banff (New Spalding Club), 39. ²CSP Dom. 1700–2, p. 339; 1702–3, p. 354; Boyer, Anne Annals, vi. 234; Cal. Treas. Bks. xxiii. 234; xxix. 342; xxxi. 579; info. from Dr P. W. J. Riley on members of Scot. parl.; Cal. Treas. Pprs. 1714–19, p. 450. ³Scot. Rec. Soc. lxii. 1. ⁴HMC Portland, x. 333; SRO, Seafield mss GD248/561/49/17, John Philp to William Lorimer, 25 May 1713; GD248/561/50/2, Findlater to [–], 2 Nov. 1714; GD248/567/92/1, same to Lorimer, [1713]; Abercromby, 87–88; Diary of Brodie, 339; Reg. PC Scotland, 1684–5, pp. 164–6, 474–5; 1685–6, p. 357; APS, viii. 469; ix. 74; Seafield Corresp. 333–4, 338, 347–8, 354, 357, 368; Annals of Banff (New Spalding Club), ii. 73; Recs. Co. Banff, 232; Hist. Scot. Parl. 2; Fraser, Melvilles, ii. 196. ⁵Fraser, 196; info. from Dr Riley; Riley, Union, 331; Stowe 246, f. 17; Cal. Treas. Bks. xxii. 116; Riley, Eng. Ministers and Scotland, 209; R. Walcott, Pol. Early 18th Cent. 232. ⁶Cal. Treas. Bks. xxii. 79; Seafield Corresp. 466, 470–1.⁷Seafield Corresp. 470–1; Seafield Letters, 109; Marlborough–Godolphin Corresp. 1216–17, 1222, 1225–6; HMC 14th Rep. III, 208, 224; Cal. Treas. Bks. xxiv. 48, 196, 587; Cal. Treas. Pprs. 1708–14, pp. 174, 193–4, 207–8; HMC Portland, x. 333. ⁸G. Holmes, Pol. in Age of Anne, 357–8; SHR, lx. 64; SRO, Montrose mss GD220/5/808/18a-b, Graham to Montrose, 13 Feb. 1711; Add. 61136, f. 165; Marlborough–Godolphin Corresp. 1669–70; Seafield mss GD248/572/1/7/9, Abercromby to Seafield, 24 Sept. 1711. ⁹Stowe 246, f. 17; Add. 70051, memo. from Abercromby, 20 Apr. 1714; 70048, Findlater to Oxford, 22 Dec. 1711; Seafield mss GD248/572/1/7/10, Abercromby to Findlater, 18 Jan. 1712; NLS, ms 1392, f. 80; Aberdeen Univ. Lib. Duff House (Montcoffer) mss 3175/2380, 'Resolution of the Commons to Call a Meeting of the Lords', [23] May 1713; Lockhart Pprs. i. 424; Parlty. Hist. i. 69. ¹⁰Cal. Treas. Bks. 1708–14, pp. 594, 613; Seafield mss GD248/561/49/10, 16–17, 30–31, 43, 56, William Lorimer to [Findlater], 7 Feb., 26 Sept. 1713, John to William Lorimer, 16 May 1713, John Philp to same, 25 May 1713, Abercromby to [Findlater], 29 Sept. 1713, John Carnegy* to [same], 31 Oct. 1713, Findlater to William Lorimer, 17 Nov. 1713; GD248/561/48/36–37, 39, same to same, 30 Apr., 19 May 1713, John Lorimer to same, 13 May 1713; GD248/572/1/7/11, Abercromby to [Findlater], 12 Oct. 1713; GD248/566/86/10, John Philp to [Findlater?], n.d.; GD248/567/92/1, Findlater to William Lorimer, [1713]; HMC Portland, x. 211, 309; v. 351. ¹¹Add. 70048, Abercromby to Oxford, 29 Oct. 1713; 70051, memo. from Abercromby, 20 Apr. 1714; HMC Portland, x. 316, 318, 461–2; Lockhart Letters ed. Szechi, 107. ¹²Boyer, Pol. State, viii. 117–18; London Gazette, 6–10 Nov. 1714; Mystics of the North-East ed. Henderson (3rd Spalding Club), 169–72; Cal. Treas. Pprs. 1720–8, p. 262; J. S. Shaw, Management of Scot. Soc. 107–9.

D. W. H.

ABERCROMBY, James (d. 1724).

DYSART BURGHS 16 Jan.–21 Sept. 1710

illegit. s. of William Douglas Hamilton, 3rd Duke of Hamilton [S]. Prob. unm. cr. Bt. 8 Mar. 1710.¹

Ensign 1 Ft. (R. Scots) 1696, half-pay 1697, capt. 1701, brevet maj. 1706, lt.-col. 1709–Dec. 1710, Mar. 1711–17, brevet col. Nov. 1711; capt. and lt.-col. Coldstream Gds. Dec. 1710–Mar. 1711; a.d.c. to Earl of Orkney 1704–c.1709; town maj. Dunkirk 1712–?16; commr. inspecting demolition Dunkirk fortifications 1713–16.²

The illegitimate son of the 3rd Duke of Hamilton, Abercromby made his army career in the Royal Scots, the regiment commanded by his half-brother, George, 1st Earl of Orkney. As Orkney's aide-de-camp, he fought at Blenheim and Malplaquet, his deeds on the battlefield winning him a baronetcy. His brief appearance in Parliament was directly owing to Orkney and his elder brother, the 4th Duke of Hamilton. Abercromby was returned unanimously for Dysart Burghs at a by-election in 1710, but only after some convoluted manoeuvres. In the House Abercromby voted with the Court in order to earn the preferment he repeatedly solicited from the Duke of Marlborough (John Churchill†). According to Lockhart, he voted for the impeachment of Dr Sacheverell, notwithstanding the conflicting evidence in contemporary lists.³

Abercromby did not seek re-election in 1710, and although he contemplated standing for Dysart or Linlithgow Burghs in 1713, in the event contested neither seat. His professional fortunes, however, prospered under the Tories, as in the summer of 1712 he was appointed town major of Dunkirk under its new governor, John Hill*, a position that proved safe even against Hamilton's unexpected death at the end of the year. Having taken responsibility for the evacuation of French forces and the installation of an allied garrison, he subsequently supervised the withdrawal of those troops and the destruction of the fortress, accumulating in the process considerable arrears of pay and allowance. A memorial in his behalf was submitted to the Treasury in July 1714 and two years later he was still in pursuit of over £2,700 due to him. In 1717 he was obliged to dispose of his regiment to ease these 'hardships' and was granted £1,000 as royal bounty to tide him over. Abercromby died s.p. 'at his habitation in Charing Cross' on 14 Nov. 1724.⁴

¹SRO, Hamilton mss GD406/1/6507, Orkney to Hamilton, 1 May 1701. ²Cal. Treas. Bks. xxvii. 299; xxxi. 151, 397; Ailesbury Mems. 579–80. ³Boyer, Pol. State, xxviii. 529; EHR, xix. 310, 318; SRO, Montrose mss GD220/5/805/9, Mungo Graham* to Montrose, 15 Dec. 1709; Lockhart Mems. ed. Szechi, 287; Add. 61283, ff. 3, 5. ⁴HMC Portland, iv. 626–7; v. 101, 199; Boyer, Pol. State, iv. 22; Bolingbroke Corresp. ii. 411–12; Cal. Treas. Bks. xxviii. 104–5; Cal. Treas. Pprs. 1708–14, pp. 596–7; 1714–19, pp. 221, 287–8; Add. 61602, ff. 157–8; The Gen. n.s. vi. 106.

D. W. H.

ABNEY, Sir Edward (1631–1728), of Willesley Hall, Leics. and Portugal Row, Lincoln's Inn Fields.

LEICESTER 1690–1698

b. 6 Feb. 1631, 2nd but 1st surv. s. of James Abney of I. Temple and Willesley, sheriff of Derbys. 1656, by 1st w. Jane, da. of Edward Mainwaring of Whitmore, Staffs.; bro. of Sir Thomas Abney*. educ. Ashby-de-la-Zouche (Mr Porter) and Measham (Mr Houlton) schs.; Christ's,

Camb. 1649, BA 1652–3, MA 1656, LL.D. 1661, fellow 1655–?70. *m.* (1) 21 July 1661, Damaris (*d.*1687), da. of Thomas Andrewes, fellow of Christ's, Camb., 1s. (pres. *d.v.p.*) 3da.; (2) 18 Dec. 1688, Judith, da. and coh. of Peter Barr, merchant, of London, 2s. (1 *d.v.p.*). Kntd. 2 Aug. 1673; *suc.* fa. 1693.[1]

Clerk in Chancery 1670–82; commr. of public accts. 1694–5.[2]

Freeman, Leicester 1690; Fishmongers' Co. 1696.[3]

A branch of the Abney family had been established at Willesley since at least the early 15th century. Abney's father had participated in the Royalist defence of Ashby Castle in 1645. Before entering the House at the age of almost 60, Edward Abney's career was devoted to civil law. Initially he pursued an academic existence at Cambridge, having been allowed to retain his fellowship at Christ's after marrying the stepdaughter of the college's master, Dr Ralph Cudworth, the eminent Platonist theologian. Until 1662 his elder brother was still living and consequently the retention of this post was clearly of importance, especially as his marriage brought him no property. He was re-elected a fellow again in 1669, but in the year following obtained a highly lucrative place as one of the six clerks in Chancery.[4]

In 1685 Abney, a Presbyterian, stood for Leicestershire but was defeated. It was rumoured during the electoral preparations early in 1690 that he was to stand at Tamworth but in fact he stood for Leicester where initially his chances were considered doubtful, the corporation being dominated by Churchmen, 'the majority and best party'. He was returned, however, after a busy campaign in which he had the support of the earls of Stamford and Huntingdon, he being on particularly good terms with the latter as a family friend and legal adviser. Classed as a Whig by Lord Carmarthen (Sir Thomas Osborne†) in March 1690, he was noted in Robert Harley's* list, compiled c. April 1691, as a Court supporter. Grascome also classed him as such in a slightly later list. By 1694 Abney had obviously achieved sufficient prominence in the House, presumably through his committee work, to obtain election on 12 Apr. with 121 votes as one of the seven commissioners of accounts for 1694–5, with a salary of £500 p.a. It would appear that his candidacy was promoted by the Rose Club of which he was a member. He was not reappointed in 1695, and missed nomination in 1696 coming 11th in the ballot on 1 Feb. On 23 Apr. 1695 he was one of 24 MPs selected for the joint committee of both Houses to receive evidence from Sir Thomas Cooke* regarding bribes from the Old East India Company. Cooke's evidence led to the Commons' decision on the 27th to impeach the Duke of Leeds, and Abney was put on the committee charged to initiate the proceedings which were shortly afterwards aborted with the close of the session. Evidence for Abney's pro-Court stance can be found for the next Parliament to which he was re-elected in 1695. In January 1696 he was forecast as a Court supporter on the proposed council of trade; he took the Association at the end of February, voted in late March in favour of fixing the price of guineas at 22s. and on 25 Nov. supported the attainder of Sir John Fenwick. On 12 Feb. 1697 he was elected in the ballot for a new commission of accounts, coming second with 132 votes, but the appointing bill failed to pass.[5]

Abney stood down at the 1698 election when he was listed in about September as a former Court supporter. He died at his seat, Willesley Hall, on 3 Jan. 1728, having been blind for the last 20 years of his life. In drawing up his will in 1718 he excluded his eldest surviving, but mentally unfit, son, leaving his estates in Derbyshire, Leicestershire and Staffordshire to his youngest son Thomas, later a judge of the common pleas.[6]

[1] Nichols, *Leics.* iii. 1032; J. P. Yeatman, *Feudal Hist. Derbys.* v(9), p. 52; *The Gen.* v. 87. [2] *Chancery Procs. 1649–1714* (Index Lib. xxix), i. p. xxii. [3] *CJ*, xi. 154, 703; *Reg. Leicester Freemen*, i. 173; Guildhall Lib. mss 5587/1. [4] Yeatman, v(9), pp. 52, 93; Trinity, Dublin, Lyons (King) mss 2002/1105, Abney to Abp. King, 9 Aug. 1704; *CSP Dom.* 1668–9, p. 349. [5] *Parl. Hist.* v. 127; Bath mss at Longleat House, Thynne pprs. 24, ff. 134–5; Huntington Lib. Hastings mss HA10245, HA8, Thomas Piddocke to Earl of Huntingdon, 2 Feb. 1690, Abney to same, 1 Mar. 1690; Hereford and Worcester RO (Hereford), Harley mss C64/117; *HMC Kenyon*, 339. [6] *The Gen.* v. 87; n.s. vii. 156; Boyer, *Pol. State*, xxxv. 107; PCC 1 Brook; Foss, *Judges*, vii. 82.

A. A. H.

ABNEY, Sir Thomas (1640–1722), of Stoke Newington, Mdx. and Theobalds, Herts.

LONDON   1701 (Dec.)–1702

b. Jan. 1640, 4th but 3rd surv. s. of James Abney of I. Temple and Willesley, Leics., sheriff of Derbys. 1656, by his 1st w. Jane, da. of Edward Mainwaring of Whitmore, Staffs.; bro. of Sir Edward Abney*. *educ.* Loughborough, Leics. *m.* (1) lic. 24 Aug. 1668, Sarah (*d.* 1698), da. of Rev. Joseph Caryl, of Bury Street, London, 7ch. *d.v.p.*(at least 4s. 1da.); (2) 21 Aug. 1700, Mary (*d.* 1750), da. of John Gunston of Stoke Newington, 1s. *d.v.p.* 3da. Kntd. 2 Nov. 1693.[1]

Freeman, Fishmongers' Co. 1666, asst. 1691, prime warden 1704; common councilman, London 1689–90, alderman 1692, sheriff 1693, ld. mayor 1700–1.

Commr. taking subscriptions to Bank of Eng. 1694, 1709, Greenwich Hosp. 1695; dir. Bank of Eng. 1694–*d.*

(with statutory intervals); trustee, receiving loan to Emperor 1706.

Manager, Common Fund 1695; member, New England Co. by 1698; pres. St. Thomas' Hosp. 1707–d.[2]

Abney gained prominence as a leading spokesman for Dissenters, his piety leading his biographer to declare that 'the honour and service of God were his aim and business in life'. As the youngest son he moved to the capital to establish himself in trade, and quickly enjoyed a 'considerable increase' in fortune. He also became an important figure in Nonconformist circles, attending the Silver Street congregations of Presbyterian ministers Thomas Jacombe and John Howe. He also married a daughter of the ejected Independent divine Joseph Caryl, thereby proving that he was 'of a catholic spirit, and loved all true Christians rightly holding Christ the head'. However, he played no active role in the London corporation until after the Revolution, his acceptance of which can be gauged by his willingness to lend the government £800 in 1689.[3]

In October 1690 Abney demonstrated his support for his co-religionists by contributing a £10 subscription to the Nonconformist Common Fund, an organization of which he later became a gentleman manager. Under William he sought rapid promotion within the London corporation, briefly serving as a common councilman for St. Peter's Cornhill before becoming an alderman in December 1692. Only seven months later he was chosen as sheriff in an uncontested poll, and while serving in that office he received a knighthood. His standing within the City was further attested when he was appointed in June 1694 as one of the commissioners to take subscriptions for the Bank of England. He was duly elected one of its founding directors, and served intermittently in that capacity for the rest of his life. Another government scheme to receive his backing was the loan to circulate Exchequer bills, to which he subscribed £400 in May 1697. He also invested in the East India trade, but by the spring of 1698 had sold his £1,000 stake in the Old Company.[4]

In September 1699 Abney strongly contested the City's mayoral election, but although one of the two candidates to be returned to the court of aldermen, he failed to gain the chair. He stood again the following year, only to find himself at the centre of a bitter party dispute. His main rival on this occasion was the Tory (Sir) Charles Duncombe*, who topped the poll of freemen with 800 votes more than Abney. However, in the court of aldermen Sir Thomas achieved victory by 14 votes to 12, a result which infuriated the City Tories, who had been confident of gaining the majority there. Amid 'great animosities' in the capital, Sir Thomas Cooke* led a campaign to remove Abney, but all Tory efforts to undermine his election proved unsuccessful. At that time Abney was actually cited by the Prussian envoy Frederick Bonet as a 'bon Anglican', but he did not sever his ties with the Dissenters, qualifying himself for office by an occasional conformity to the Established Church.[5]

Abney's mayoralty proved as eventful as his election, his attendance at Dissenting meetings causing renewed controversy. Most significantly, he was cited as the catalyst for Daniel Defoe's *An Inquiry into the Occasional Conformity of Dissenters in Cases of Preferment*, which was prefaced by a direct challenge to John Howe to justify the presence of Nonconformists at Anglican services. The corporation itself was a scene of much party manoeuvring, and Abney was subjected to royal pressure when the London common council tried to petition the crown concerning the imprisonment of the Kentish petitioners. Although 'very zealous for the cause of liberty in opposition to illegal and arbitrary power', Abney bowed to the King's wishes and gave his casting vote to defeat the council's motion to address William. Later that year he led the City campaign to address the King to denounce Louis XIV's recognition of the Pretender. 'Though much opposed by a number of his brethren', Abney prevailed, and the wave of loyal addresses imitating London's example was reported to have given 'new life to the Whig interest at home and abroad'. He subsequently gained much credit for this political initiative, a 'considerable person' observing that Abney 'had done the King more service than if he had given him thousands, or raised him a million of money'.[6]

Such prominence led to Abney's candidature at the City election of November 1701, which saw an overwhelming victory for the Whigs. Not content with third place in the London poll, Abney also sought to thwart his Tory rival Sir Thomas Cooke at Colchester. In a letter to the aldermen of the Essex borough, Abney accused Cooke of opposing the recent London address, and then launched another attack 'which was worse than the former'. However, Cooke managed to secure an uncontested return. Abney proved an inconspicuous Member, his only significant contribution to Commons' business resting with an appointment to the drafting committee on a bill to employ the poor. Moreover, even though he clearly sat in the Whig interest, his name does not appear on any parliamentary list. The accession of Anne effectively ended his Commons career, since at the City election of July 1702 a resurgent Tory party managed to oust him and two of his fellow Whigs. Shortly before the contest his standing in the capital had been weakened by his removal from the colonelcy of a London militia regiment.[7]

Although destined never to sit in the House again, Abney petitioned the Commons on 7 Feb. 1704 in order to defend one of his Hertfordshire properties against the threat of a bill to resume royal grants. Thereafter his contribution to public life was largely confined to City affairs, for he was appointed in February 1706 as a trustee for receiving the loan to the Emperor, and three years later was chosen as a commissioner to enlarge the Bank's stock. He remained true to his political principles, voting in the Whig interest at the City elections of 1710 and 1713. Moreover, as a stubborn defender of Dissenting rights he found the Occasional Conformity Act of 1711 'one of the great trials' of his life. He chose to worship privately rather than lose his City office, a decision taken in consultation with 'several persons of distinction', and one which received the direct support of the Hanoverian court. Within the corporation he continued to play a prominent role, serving as acting mayor in September 1712, and featuring in May 1713 as one of the seven Whigs who withdrew from the court of aldermen to defer the aldermanic election of Tory Joseph Lawrence. A second clash with the Tory aldermen followed in December when Abney supported the publication of an anti-papist sermon, arguing that 'we are in a strange case now when no minister can preach against popery and slavery but it must be called sedition'.[8]

Having sacrificed public worship 'that he might be capable of serving his country and securing the interest of King George', Abney obviously welcomed the Hanoverian succession. He did not gain office under the new King, but remained politically active, attending a meeting of a Whig club in December 1716 to plan the party's strategy for the forthcoming common council elections. He was also said to have 'made several remonstrances to some of the ministers of state' concerning the repeal of the Occasional Conformity Act, and once the campaign had achieved its goal in 1719, he resumed his attendance at Dissenting meetings. For the previous seven years his religious needs had been administered by the great Nonconformist hymnodist Isaac Watts, who for over 30 years resided with the Abney family. Watts also led the widespread mourning which followed Abney's demise on 6 Feb. 1722, an event which was 'universally lamented'. The Father of the City at his death, he was praised as a wise and just magistrate who had encouraged 'all regular endeavours for the reformation of manners'. Moreover, his reputation for philanthropy 'without distinction of parties' had evidently earned him much respect. St. Thomas' Hospital remained his favourite charity, but two other causes to benefit from his support were the London corporation of the poor and the New England Company, both of which had close ties to Dissent. In the absence of a male heir, his 'very great estate' passed to his widow and three surviving daughters. Together they ensured that Abney House in Stoke Newington remained a mecca for Dissenters, and his widow Dame Mary Abney received special praise as 'a generous friend and succourer of gospel ministers'.[9]

[1] J. Nichols, *Leics*. iii. 1032; J. Smith, *Magistrate and Christian*, 37; *The Gen*. v. 90–92; Luttrell, *Brief Relation*, iii. 218. [2] Guildhall Lib. mss 5587/1; 5570/6, p. 145; Beaven, *Aldermen*, ii. 118; NLS, Advocates' mss, Bank of Eng. pprs. 31.1.7, f. 146; *Cal. Treas. Bks*. xxiii. 77; Add. 10120, ff. 232–6; Boyer, *Anne Annals*, iv. 126; Dr Williams' Lib. O. D. 68, f. 3; W. Kellaway, *New England Co*. 289. [3] Smith, 2, 37, 41, 66–67; *Cal. Treas. Bks*. ix. 1972, 1979. [4] Dr Williams' Lib. O. D. 67, f. 6; Luttrell, iii. 123; Univ. London mss 65/3; Bodl. Rawl. A.302, ff. 224–7. [5] Luttrell, iv. 566; *HMC Portland*, iii. 631; Centre Kentish Stud. Stanhope mss U1590/053/9, James Vernon I* to Alexander Stanhope, 4 Oct. 1700; *Vernon–Shrewsbury Letters*, iii. 139; Add. 30000D, f. 288. [6] E. Calamy, *Mems. of Life of John Howe* [1724], 210; Calamy, *Life*, i. 435–6; Smith, 62; G. S. De Krey, *Fractured Soc*. 201. [7] Add. 70075, Dyer's newsletter 27 Nov. 1701; Luttrell, v. 193. [8] *London Poll of 1710*; *London Rec. Soc*. xvii. 66; Smith, 49–50; Folger Shakespeare Lib. Newdigate newsletter 25 Sept. 1712; Beaven, i. 411; Huntington Lib. Hastings mss 44710, ff. 373–4. [9] Calamy, *Life*, ii. 245–6; *London Rec. Soc*. 39, 45; Smith, 51–52, 63; *DNB*; Boyer, *Pol. State*, xxiii. 234; Macfarlane thesis, 324; S. Price, *Funeral Sermon ... of Dame Mary Abney* [1750], 40.

P. L. G.

ACLAND, John (c.1674–1703), of Woodleigh, Devon.

CALLINGTON 1702–May 1703

b. c.1674, 1st s. of Sir Hugh Acland, 1st and 5th Bt.†, of Killerton, Devon by Anne, da. of Sir Thomas Daniel of Beswick Hall, Yorks. *educ*. Exeter, Oxf. matric. 12 May 1692, aged 17. *m*. 24 Mar. 1696, Elizabeth, da. of Richard Acland of Barnstaple, Devon and sis. of Richard Acland*, 5s. (1 *d.v.p*.) 1da.[1]

Acland was the son of a Tory baronet who had represented Barnstaple in the first Exclusion Parliament and Tiverton in the Parliament of James II. He was returned unopposed for Callington in 1702 on the interest of his kinsmen the Rolles, but made no significant contribution to the 1702–3 session. On 30 Oct. 1704 he was classed as a probable supporter of the Tack, but he had in fact died *v.p*. the previous year. He was buried at Broad Clyst 20 May 1703, aged 28, and was succeeded by his eldest son, Hugh†.[2]

[1] Vivian, *Vis. Devon*, 5. [2] Ibid.

E. C.

ACLAND, Richard (1679–1729), of Fremington, Devon.

BARNSTAPLE 1708–1713

bap. 22 Jan. 1679, 1st s. of Richard Acland of Barnstaple by his w. Mary. *educ.* Exeter, Oxf. 1697. *m.* 22 May 1700, Susanna (d. 1747), da. of John Lovering, merchant, of Barnstaple and Countisbury, Devon, 3s. (2 *d.v.p.*) 9da. (6 *d.v.p.*). *suc.* fa. 1703.[1]

Acland's father, a wealthy Barnstaple merchant, had purchased the manor of Fremington, three miles from the town, in 1683 and had been nominated mayor under the charter of 1688. His uncle Arthur sat for Barnstaple in the second Exclusion Parliament. Acland was returned for the borough in 1708, succeeding his wife's brother-in-law Samuel Rolle II, but left virtually no mark on proceedings. He voted against the impeachment of Dr Sacheverell early in 1710, and after his re-election later in the year was classed as a Tory in the 'Hanover list' of the new Parliament. On 19 Mar. 1711 he was given leave of absence for a month, though his behaviour had been sufficient to place him among the 'Tory patriots' opposed to the continuance of the war, and the 'worthy patriots' who contributed towards detecting the mismanagements of the late ministry. Another month's leave was accorded him on 21 Mar. 1712. He declined re-election in 1713 and made no subsequent attempt to regain his seat. He died in October 1729, his burial taking place at Barnstaple on the 16th.[2]

[1] *Trans. Devon Assoc.* xxxviii. 168, 182. [2] *CSP Dom.* 1687–9, p. 275; Lysons, *Devon*, 241; *Trans. Devon Assoc.* 168.

E. C.

A'COURT, Pierce (c.1677–1725), of Ivy Church, nr. Salisbury, Wilts. and Rodden, Som.

HEYTESBURY 1713–1715, 1722–7 Mar. 1725

b. c.1677, o. s. of John A'Court of Bath, Som. and Rodden, Som. by Mary, da. and h. of Robert Pierce, MD, of Bath. *educ.* Lincoln, Oxf. matric. 29 Mar. 1694, aged 16. *m.* 27 Nov. 1705, Elizabeth (d. 1746), da. and (in her issue) h. of William Ashe I*, 5s. (1 *d.v.p.*) 1da. *d.v.p. suc.* fa. 1701.[1]
Freeman, Wilton 1710–*d*.[2]

A'Court's family originally held land in Somerset and Bristol. He was defeated at by-elections for Bath in 1707 and 1708, but was eventually brought in by his Ashe relatives at Heytesbury. Although he made little recorded contribution to the work of the House, he proved himself a loyal Whig, voting on 18 Mar. 1714 against the expulsion of Richard Steele, and being classed as a Whig in the Worsley list.[3]

A'Court was dropped in 1715 in favour of another brother-in-law, William Ashe II*, but was returned again in 1722. He made his will on 20 Feb. 1723, bequeathing £200 to his wife and cousin and a further £100 to the caretaker of his house in Bath. His properties at Ivy Church and Almondsbury, Gloucestershire, were left to the trustees Edward Ashe* and Peter Bathurst* to pay outstanding debts and secure £150 p.a. for the education of his three surviving younger sons. A'Court died at Ivy Church on 7 Mar. 1725 and was buried next to his father in Haddon chapel, Rodden.[4]

[1] Hoare, *Wilts.* Heytesbury, 119, 121. [2] Wilts. RO, G25/1/22, pp. 15, 47, 49. [3] Hoare, 119. [4] *The Gen.* n.s. vi. 208; Hoare, 119; PCC 105 Romney.

D. W. H.

ACTON, Sir Edward, 3rd Bt. (c.1650–1716), of Aldenham Hall, nr. Bridgnorth, Salop.

BRIDGNORTH 1689–1705

b. c.1650, 1st s. of Sir Walter Acton, 2nd Bt.†, of Aldenham Hall by Catherine, da. of Richard Cressett of Upton Cressett and Cound, Salop. *educ.* Queen's, Oxf. matric. 4 May 1666, aged 16, MA 1667; I. Temple 1670. *m.* 8 Dec. 1674, Mary, da. and h. of John Walter of Elberton, Glos., 3s. 5da. *suc.* fa. 1665.[1]
Freeman, Bridgnorth 1673, recorder 1686–*d*.; freeman, Much Wenlock 1676, bailiff 1686–7; sheriff, Salop 1684–5; freeman, Ludlow 1697.[2]

On re-election in 1690 Acton was listed by Lord Carmarthen (Sir Thomas Osborne†) as a Tory and as a probable Court supporter, while in December Carmarthen again noted him as a likely supporter. The following April, Robert Harley* classed Acton as doubtful but possibly a Court supporter.[3]

The increasing influence of the Whigs moved Acton into opposition. He was removed from the Shropshire lieutenancy in 1693 through the influence of Hon. Richard Newport I*, and although he signed the Association in February 1696, he had been thought likely to vote against the Court over the proposed council of trade in January of that year, and in March voted against fixing the price of guineas at 22s. and in November against the attainder of Sir John Fenwick†. Acton's record of attendance in Parliament was noticeably poor: he was given leave of absence on 25 Jan. 1693 for 21 days, on 25 Jan. 1694 for his health, and again on 7 Mar. 1695 and 17 Dec. 1696. On 16 Dec. 1697 he was ordered into custody for non-attendance. Released on

12 Jan. 1698, he was granted leave of absence again on 21 Apr. following. In an analysis of the general election results compiled about September 1698, Acton was marked as a member of the Country party and was also forecast as likely to oppose a standing army. After 1700, his voting reflected the changes in the government: he was listed in February 1701 as likely to support the Court in agreeing with the committee of the supply's resolution to continue the 'Great Mortgage', and in the aftermath of that session was blacklisted as one who had opposed the making of preparations for war. He then voted on 26 Feb. 1702 in favour of the resolution vindicating the conduct of the Commons in the impeachments of the Junto ministers. In Anne's first Parliament he continued to vote with the High Tories, dividing on 13 Feb. 1703 against agreeing with the Lords' amendments to the bill for enlarging the time to take the oath of abjuration, was also forecast in March 1704 as a supporter of the government's actions in the Scotch Plot, and voted for the Tack on 28 Nov. 1704. His having been a 'Tacker' may have cost his family the seat, for although he possessed a considerable interest at Bridgnorth, his son Whitmore* was defeated there by two Whigs at the 1705 election. Acton died on 28 Sept. 1716.[4]

[1] *Trans. Salop Arch. Soc.* liv. 195–6; *Glos. N. and Q.* iii. 237. [2] Salop RO, Forester mss, copy of Much Wenlock corp. bk.; Ludlow bor. recs. min. bk. 1690–1712. [3] *Luttrell Diary*, 143; Luttrell, *Brief Relation*, iv. 319–20. [4] Add. 70235, Sir Edward Harley* to Robert Harley*, 28 July 1693; *HMC Portland*, iv. 271; *Trans. Salop Arch. Soc.* 195.

D. W. H.

ACTON, Whitmore (1678–1732), of Aldenham Hall, nr. Bridgnorth, Salop.

BRIDGNORTH   1710–1713

bap. 1 Apr. 1678, 1st s. of Sir Edward Acton, 3rd Bt.*, *educ.* St. Edmund Hall, Oxf. 1695; M. Temple 1699; *m.* c.1710, Elizabeth, da. of Matthew Gibbon of Putney, Surr., 1s. 3da. *suc.* fa. as 4th Bt. 28 Sept. 1716.[1]

Freeman, Much Wenlock 1695, Ludlow 1697; sheriff, Salop 1728–9.[2]

Thomas Hearne remembered the young Acton at Oxford:

He was a tall, handsome young man, and wore his own long hair. The daughter of Alderman Eustace of Oxford was a great companion of his, tho' she was married at the same time to a Gentleman Commoner (Mr Gower) of Merton College, and he used to entertain her in Edmund Hall, and to spend the nights with her and often walked out with her.[3]

A Tory like his father, Acton was defeated at Bridgnorth in 1705 but regained the seat for his family in 1710 after a stiff contest. Classed as a Tory in the 'Hanover list', he had entertained Sacheverell during the doctor's visit to Shropshire earlier that year, and in the first session of the new Parliament was one of the 'worthy patriots' who detected the mismanagements of the previous ministry. He was also a member of the October Club. Otherwise, however, he left no imprint on the proceedings of the Commons.[4]

Acton stood at Bridgnorth again in 1727 but was unsuccessful, and died at Aldenham on 9 Jan. 1732.[5]

[1] IGI, Salop; A. W. Gibbons, *Gibbons Fam. Notes*, 45; *Trans. Salop Arch. Soc.* ser. 4, v. 66. [2] Salop RO, Forester mss, copy of Much Wenlock corp. bk.; Ludlow bor. recs. min. bk. 1690–1712. [3] *Hearne Colls.* i. 118. [4] Forester mss, Sir William Forester to George Weld, 15 July 1710; G. Holmes, *Trial of Sacheverell*, 246. [5] *Hearne Colls.* xi. 21.

D. W. H.

ADDERLEY, William (*d.* 1693), of Lincoln's Inn, and East Burnham, Bucks.

NEW WINDSOR   17 May 1690–June 1693

3rd s. of William Adderley of Colney Hatch, Mdx. by Margaret, da. and h. of Edmund Eyre of East Burnham. *educ.* L. Inn 1658, called 1670. *m.* bef. 1666, Sarah, 4s. 2da. *suc.* fa. 1664.[1]

Collector sixpenny writs in Chancery 1668–9; cursitor, Beds. and Bucks. by 1671–?83; examiner in Chancery May 1685–Aug. 1691.[2]

Clerk of the peace, Mdx. 1673–83; commr. recusants, Bucks. 1675.[3]

Although only the third son, Adderley was heir to his father's property in Buckinghamshire and Berkshire, including lands at Burnham and New Windsor, because his elder brothers had taken the name Eyre in order to inherit the estates of their maternal grandfather, Edmund Eyre (*d.* 1650). Having trained as a lawyer, Adderley seems to have preferred a career in legal administration. In September 1668 he received a commission to collect the profits of sixpenny writs in Chancery at an annual rent of £1,400. This position only lasted for a year, but it was probably a mere adjunct to his Chancery office as cursitor for Bedfordshire and Buckinghamshire which he was recorded by Chamberlayne as holding in 1671, the first year such details were noticed. As these officials were responsible for making out the writs of course which kept the ordinary law courts functioning there was an obvious link with his role in 1668–9. In 1673 he was probably the William Adderley who was appointed clerk of the peace for Middlesex. Other activities included appointment to the commission of 1675 for seizing two-thirds of recusants' lands in Buckinghamshire, an activity entirely compatible with his willingness in 1679 to act as a surety for Richard Deerham, the receiver of recusant estates north of the Trent. Rather surprisingly, he is recorded as resigning from the clerkship of the peace in 1683, and it is possible that he relinquished his place as cursitor (worth as much as £1,300) at the same date because although Chamberlayne records him as *in situ* in 1682, he was out by 1687. In the early months of James II's reign he was named as an examiner in Chancery, a place he retained until 1691. His response to the events of James II's reign is unknown: indeed when the 'three questions' were asked in Buckinghamshire it was noted that, although a deputy-lieutenant, he had never been sworn into office.[4]

No evidence survives concerning Adderley's attitude to the Revolution of 1688, although he contested the elections for the Convention at New Windsor. He was probably a Tory, for when he petitioned Parliament his target was Henry Powle*, the Whig Speaker, rather than the other successful candidate, Sir Christopher Wren*. Some contemporary observers saw his challenge as inspired by Tory manoeuvres to remove Powle from the Chair, but Adderley chose to fight on the principle of a wide franchise for the borough. Although the House upheld Powle's election, Adderley was eventually to prove his point. On 17 Dec. 1689 he provided the Lords with information on the fees taken by the examiners in Chancery. Defeated again at New Windsor at the general election of 1690, he petitioned successfully on the issue of the franchise, being seated on 17 May 1690. His name appears on Lord Carmarthen's (Sir Thomas Osborne†) list of December 1690, probably indicating his support for the embattled chief minister in case of an opposition attack in the Commons. In April 1691 Robert Harley* classed Adderley as a Court supporter. However, Adderley's impact on the House was minimal and he made no recorded speeches. He was buried at East Burnham on 28 June 1693.[5]

[1] Lipscomb, *Bucks.* iii. 221; *VCH Bucks.* iii. 175; IGI, London; *Coll. Top. et Gen.* iv. 287. [2] *CSP Dom.* 1667–8, p. 588; 1668–9, p. 607; *HMC Lords*, ii. 327. [3] Stephens, *Clerks of Counties 1360–1960*, p. 127; *Cal. Treas. Bks.* iv. 788. [4] PCC 65 Grey, 110 Mico; *Coll. Top. et Gen.* 278; *CSP Dom.* 1667–8, p. 588; 1668–9, p. 607; *Cal. Treas. Bks.* ii. 439, 619; iii. 285; iv. 788; vi. 72; G. E. Aylmer, *King's Servants*, 223; Duckett, *Penal Laws and Test Act* (1883), 145. [5] *HMC Lords*, ii. 327; *Coll. Top. et Gen.* 287.

S. N. H.

ADDISON, Joseph (1672–1719), of Sandy End, Fulham, Mdx.; St. Margaret's, Westminster, and Bilton Hall, Warws.[1]

LOSTWITHIEL 1708–20 Dec. 1709
MALMESBURY 11 Mar. 1710–17 June 1719

b. 1 May 1672, 1st s. of Lancelot Addison, DD, chaplain in ordinary to Charles II and James II, and dean of Lichfield 1683–*d.*, by his 1st w. Jane, da. of Nathaniel Gulston, DD, rector of Wymondham, Leics., sis. of William Gulston, DD, bp. of Bristol. *educ.* Amesbury (Thomas Naish), Salisbury g.s., Lichfield g.s. 1683–6, Charterhouse 1686–7; Queen's, Oxf. 1687; Magdalen, Oxf. (demy) 1689–97, BA 1691, MA 1693, fellow 1697–1711; travelled abroad (France, Italy, Switzerland, Austria, Germany, United Provinces) 1699–1704. *m.* 9 Aug. 1716, Charlotte, dowager Countess of Warwick, da. and h. of Sir Thomas Myddelton, 2nd Bt.†, of Chirk Castle, Denb., sis. of Sir Richard Myddelton, 3rd Bt.*, wid. of Edward Rich, 6th Earl of Warwick and 3rd Earl of Holland, 1da. *suc.* fa. 1703.

Commr. appeals in excise 1704–June 1708; under-sec. of state 1705–Jan. 1709; sec. to Lord Halifax (Charles Montagu*) on mission to the United Provinces and Hanover Apr.–Aug. 1706; chief sec. [I] Jan. 1709–10, Sept. 1714–Aug. 1715; PC [I] 1709–*d.*; keeper of recs. in Bermingham tower, Dublin Castle 1709–15 June 1719 (apptd. for life Oct. 1715); sec. to lds. justices Aug.–Sept. 1714; ld. of Trade Dec. 1715–July 1717; PC 16 Apr. 1717; sec. of state (south) Apr. 1717–18.[2]

MP [I] 1709–13.
Freeman, Dublin 1709.[3]

Addison, the Whig *littérateur* and administrator, was born into genteel poverty as the son of a High Church clergyman whose hopes of preferment beyond his deanery of Lichfield had been effectively terminated by the Revolution of 1688. With both grandfathers parsons and an uncle a bishop, and having grown up in a bookish household, he began an academic career, being chosen a demy of Magdalen College, Oxford in the 'golden election' of 1689, and proceeding to a fellowship eight years later. However, neither scholarship, which he dismissed as narrow pedantry, nor a religious vocation held enough attractions for him, and he determined to make his way in the wider world, perhaps aiming at a classical ideal of citizenship, the combination of 'patriotism and urbanity'. He made his early reputation in Oxford as a Latin poet, and already by the time he became a fellow of Magdalen had gained admittance to the coterie of London wits that congregated at Will's coffee-house, and had even received praise from Dryden. He had also applied himself to seeking out patrons from among the leading Whig politicians, flattering Charles Montagu with inclusion in his 'account of the great

English poets', and dedicating poetry to Lord Somers (Sir John*). Despite his father's example, and the influence of High Tory tutors and friends at Magdalen, of whom the most notable was Henry Sacheverell (according to tradition, his room-mate), Addison had early shown himself a Whig, publishing in 1689 a tribute to the new regime, and in 1690 congratulatory verses on King William's safe return from Ireland. These convictions, in particular his faith in the Revolution of 1688, remained throughout his adult life. His partisanship was never of the strident kind, however. His correspondence, for example, betrayed few traces of his commitment to the Whig cause. This was partly a reflection of his natural diffidence, described somewhat acidly by Pope as

> Alike reserved to blame, or to commend,
> A timorous foe, and a suspicious friend;
> Dreading e'en fools, by flatterers besieg'd,
> And so obliging that he ne'er obliged.

Later, as the 'Spectator', Addison was to condemn 'a furious party spirit', which

> when it rages in its full violence, exerts itself in civil war and bloodshed; and when it is under its greatest restraints naturally breaks out in falsehood, distraction, calumny, and a partial administration of justice. In a word, it fills a nation with spleen and rancour, and extinguishes all the seeds of good nature, compassion and humanity.

This discreet temperament, allied to his talents and political reliability, recommended him to his Whig patrons, and in 1698, at the prompting of Montagu and Somers, he was granted £200 by the Treasury towards the expenses of a European tour, designed to help him prepare for the diplomatic service. Montagu also interceded with the authorities at Magdalen to obtain for him a dispensation from ordination, so that he could keep his college fellowship. Although he was able to meet many prominent European literary figures, travel, especially in France and Italy, confirmed Addison's prejudices, against Catholicism and against France: 'the French', he wrote, 'are certainly the most implacable, and the most dangerous enemies of the British constitution . . . we are thus in a natural state of war . . . with the French nation'.[4]

Addison arrived back from the Continent early in 1704 to a changing political climate, with his two protectors, Montagu (now Lord Halifax) and Somers, out of office but acquiring increasing weight with the Godolphin–Marlborough administration. There was no diplomatic posting for him, but he did not return to Magdalen, remaining in London to polish his account of his *Travels in Italy* and to join the Kit-Cat Club. At Halifax's suggestion, Lord Godolphin (Sidney†) approached him via the chancellor of the Exchequer, Hon. Henry Boyle*, to compose a public poem to celebrate Blenheim, and so successful was the outcome, 'The Campaign', that he was rewarded with a commissionership of appeals, to the value of £200 a year, with a promise of further advancement, which materialized the following year in the form of an appointment as under-secretary in the southern department. His smooth progress, interrupted only by the occasional sniping of Tory satirists, was much envied by Defoe, who wrote in 1705,

> Envy and party spleen h' has never known,
> No humbling jails has [sic] pulled his fancy down.

Having accompanied Halifax to Hanover in 1706, he published the next year a strong statement of the Whig case for the resolute pursuance of the war until the 'French and Spanish monarchies' were 'entirely disunited'. *The Present State of the War . . . Considered* drew upon personal experience to denounce France as a 'constant and most dangerous enemy to the British nation'. At the 1708 election he was brought in at Lostwithiel in a last-minute arrangement made by his master in the secretary's office, Lord Sunderland (Charles, Lord Spencer*), with a local Whig interest. Inevitably, he was listed as a Whig. Once elected, he promptly sold his excise place, presumably to prevent disqualification from sitting, and not, as his most recent biographer has argued, because he was short of money, a state of affairs which in any case seems highly unlikely. Then in January 1709 he was appointed as Lord Wharton's (Hon. Thomas*) chief secretary in Ireland, sailing to Dublin in April. According to the (admittedly suspect) testimony of his friend Swift, the behaviour of the Irish Whigs 'extremely offended' Addison's sensibilities: 'he told me they were a sort of people who seemed to think that the principles of a Whig consisted in nothing else but damning the Church, reviling the clergy, abetting the Dissenters, and speaking contemptibly [sic] of revealed religion'. In this office Addison proved a faithful servant and an assiduous correspondent, but he does not appear ever to have participated in the political management which was one of the Castle administration's most important functions. It went against his character, and in any case the viceroy's extrovert personality left little room. Likewise, although he attended debates in the Irish parliament, no evidence of any contribution survives, and there are apocryphal tales of his extraordinary bashfulness in this context. With Wharton his relationship was comfortable but never close, and some idea of his true feelings may be gleaned from his reaction to news of Tory plans to impeach the lord lieutenant in the 1709–10 session of the British Parliament. 'For my own part', Addison wrote, 'though perhaps I was not the most obliged person that was near his lordship, I shall think myself bound in honour to do him what right I can.' His 'obligation' consisted not only of the chief secretaryship, worth £2,000 a year, but a grant of the sinecure of keeper of the records in the Bermingham tower of Dublin Castle, 'an old obscure place', as Swift called it, to which an enhanced salary of £400 was then attached. Addison was subsequently to press Godolphin unsuccessfully to increase this sum by £100 and alter the tenure from pleasure to good behaviour. One of the incidental uses of the appointment may have been to oblige his resignation from the seat at Lostwithiel before the hearing of what was to be a very powerful petition against the return, and he made considerable efforts to prove his title to the office before the British parliamentary session of 1709–10 opened. In fact the Lostwithiel petition was heard, and he was unseated, before he had accomplished the proof, and he had to try to speed up the process again before a by-election arose in another suitable constituency. Fortunately he had succeeded when, in March 1710, a vacancy suddenly occurred in one of Wharton's boroughs, Malmesbury, where, coincidentally, the son of a former pupil of Addison was also lord of the manor. The by-election took place late enough for him to avoid any potential embarrassment over the impeachment of Henry Sacheverell, and he departed once more for Dublin in April, returning in August with, if Swift is to be believed, the praises of Irish Tories as well as Whigs ringing in his ears.[5]

Loss of office in the ministerial revolution of 1710 was a financial blow to Addison, but not a grievous one, especially since, through the favour of the new viceroy of Ireland, Ormond, he was able to keep his sinecure in the Dublin Castle muniment room. Always careful in money matters, he was sufficiently well off not to need to come to any arrangement with the Tory ministers. Indeed, his friendship with Swift cooled when the latter began to write for the incoming ministry, though, typically of Addison, there was no serious rupture. He was even able to pass a pleasant evening at table with Henry St. John II* and to 'talk in a friendly manner of party'. George Berkeley, a visitor to London, reported in 1713 that Addison and Richard Steele* had declared themselves 'entirely persuaded there is a design for bringing over the Pretender', though this particular conviction was short-lived. On the whole, Berkeley thought Addison 'more earnest in the Whig cause than Mr Steele', and indeed he was a dutiful member of the Hanover Club as well as the Kit-Cat. After his 'easy and undisputed' re-election at Malmesbury in 1710 he was classed as a Whig in the 'Hanover list', and on 7 Dec. 1711 voted for the 'No Peace without Spain' motion. In general, however, he took little or no part in parliamentary business, except for one occasion on 16 May 1713 when old loyalties obliged him to appear as a teller for an amendment intended to soften the terms of a resolution concerning Lord Wharton proposed in the aftermath of the report of the commissioners of accounts. Writing had now become his main preoccupation. Having collaborated with Steele on the *Tatler* in 1709–10 he began in March 1711 its successor, the *Spectator*, which for 18 months purveyed a hugely popular mixture of polite philosophy and gentle social satire, Addison's avowed aim being 'to bring philosophy out of closets and libraries, schools and colleges, to dwell in clubs and assemblies, at tea-tables and in coffee-houses'. Although the authors disclaimed any 'stroke of party', the general tone was distinctively, if mildly, Whiggish, an antidote to the furious polemic of the Tories. From time to time more obvious political propaganda crept in. As the presiding genius of the Whig wits at Button's, Addison could not entirely avoid the task of writing for his party. He had, in September 1710, endeavoured to answer the *Examiner* with his *Whig Examiner*. Later he offered a verse to lament the exile of a former hero, Marlborough (John Churchill†), in 1712:

O censure undeserved! Unequal fate!
Which strove to lessen Him who made Her great.

And following the defeat in 1713 of the French commerce bill, which he had voted against on 18 June, he contributed a 'playful Whig parable', *The Late Trial and Conviction of Count Tariff*, attacking the *Examiner* again, among other Tory targets. In private he assisted a Hanoverian minister in preparing official papers for submission to the British government. However, his most successful piece of writing in this period was his reworked play *Cato*, which was produced to great acclaim in 1713, proving to be 'so subtly ambiguous or strictly non-party' in its 'political innuendoes' that both sides 'applied' it 'to themselves' and, like the Whigs and Tories in Ireland, vied with each other in the volume of their applause of the author.[6]

Before the 1713 election Addison paid some £8,000 to purchase Bilton Hall, near Rugby, in order to make himself eligible for a parliamentary seat under the 1711 Landed Qualification Act, and also to acquire the rural retreat essential for any Augustan statesman. He continued to sit for Malmesbury, though, and did not attempt a Warwickshire constituency. Among several advisers consulted by Steele in the composition of *The Crisis*, in his case in the correction of drafts, he was one of those nominated by the Kit-Cat Club to prepare Steele's defence against the projected Commons' motion of expulsion. In the event, it was Robert Walpole II* who provided the basis for Steele's speech, though Addison prompted Steele from a nearby bench. Subsequently, as Steele recounted, Addison was 'sent out after me, from my friends, to bid me not be seen till I heard what will be the censure'. Naturally, Addison voted on 18 Mar. 1714 against Steele's expulsion, and was classified as a Whig both in the Worsley list and in a list of the Members re-elected in 1715.[7]

Addison was appointed, through Lord Halifax's intercession, as secretary to the regency upon Queen Anne's death. This office seemed to many to be an augury of immediate high preferment, possibly as a secretary of state. Addison himself looked forward to a place on the Board of Trade, and was bitterly disappointed to find himself once again chief secretary for Ireland, this time under his former superior as secretary of state, Lord Sunderland. He was, however, in the next few years to secure not only the post on the Board of Trade, but also the secretaryship of state for the southern department in Sunderland's administration. In neither capacity did he cut a figure in the Commons. He died on 17 June 1719.[8]

[1] Unless otherwise stated, this biography is based on P. Smithers, *Life of Joseph Addison* (1968) and *Addison Letters* ed. Graham. [2] SP 63/362/10–11; Add. 70677, Misc. 48; *Liber Munerum Publicorum Hiberniae* ed. Lascelles, i(2), 78–79. [3] *Cal. Ancient Recs. Dublin* ed. Gilbert, vi. 397. [4] G. Holmes, *Trial of Sacheverell*, 8; J. Carswell, *Old Cause*, 158; H. T. Dickinson, *Liberty and Property*, 100; W. L. Sachse, *Ld. Somers*, 195, 199. [5] G. M. Trevelyan, *Eng. under Queen Anne*, i. 422; *Poems on Affairs of State* ed. Ellis, vi. 666; vii. 166; *Cal. Treas. Bks.* xix. 400; Carswell, 106; *Swift Works* ed. Davis, x. 58; *Cal. Treas. Pprs.* 1708–14, p. 163; Hayton thesis, 192. [6] *Bolingbroke Corresp.* iv. 112–13; Add. 47027, ff. 13–14; *HMC 7th Rep.* 238; *Swift Stella* ed. Davis, 52; A. L. Rowse, *Early Churchills*, 316; *The Late Trial and Conviction of Count Tariff* (1713); Trevelyan, iii. 258; *Wentworth Pprs.* 330. [7] Cobbett, *Parlty. Hist.* vi. 1239, 1268; *Steele Corresp.* 295, 478; Coxe, *Walpole*, i. 45. [8] *Wentworth Pprs.* 410.

D. W. H.

AISLABIE, John (1670–1742), of Studley Royal, nr. Ripon, Yorks. and Red Lion Square, London.

RIPON 1695–1702
NORTHALLERTON 1702–1705
RIPON 1705–8 Mar. 1721

b. 4 Dec. 1670, 3rd s. of George Aislabie (*d.* 1675), registrar to abp. of York, by Mary, da. and h. of Sir John Mallory of Studley Royal. *educ.* York (Mr Tomlinson); St. John's, Camb. 1687; Trinity Hall, Camb. 1692, LL.B. 1692. *m.* (1) 2 June 1694 (with £5,000), Anne (*d.* 1700), da. of Sir William Rawlinson of Hendon, Mdx., 1s. 3da. (1 *d.v.p.*); (2) lic. 25 Apr. 1713, Judith, da. of Sir Thomas Vernon*, wid. of Dr. Stephen Waller of Hall Barn, Beaconsfield, Bucks. *s.p. suc.* bro. George 1693.[1]

?Registrar to abp. York ?c.1675; asst. Ripon Nov. 1698, alderman Dec. 1698, mayor 1702–3.[2]

Commr. Aire and Calder navigation 1699, building 50 new churches 1712–27.[3]

Ld. of Admiralty Oct. 1710–Apr. 1714; treasurer of navy Oct. 1714–18; PC 12 July 1716–21; chancellor of Exchequer, 1718–21.[4]

Originally Baltic merchants, the Aislabies were well established in York by the end of the 17th century. Aislabie's father very much enhanced their fortunes and status by marrying into one of the oldest landed families in the county, although in 1675 his marriage 'above himself' was to lead indirectly to his death in a duel with (Sir) Jonathan Jennings*, who had insulted Aislabie, calling him 'the scum of the county'. In 1693 John Aislabie inherited the estate of Studley Royal from his elder brother. The proximity of this estate to Ripon gave Aislabie a considerable interest in the borough, though in the 1690s he still relied upon the support of his wife's uncle, Archbishop Sharp, who had much influence in Ripon, to secure his return to Parliament. Prior to the 1695 election the Duke of Leeds (Sir Thomas Osborne†) informed the archbishop that he could do good at Ripon if he used his interest there to influence the election result: 'As Mr [Jonathan] Jennings* . . . will be sure of the first with a little of your Grace's countenance, so with your Grace's help Mr Aislabie may be the other member.' Although opposed to the idea of endeavouring to influence elections in general, the archbishop agreed to interpose at Ripon, and secured Aislabie's return. His ensuing political career was governed by voting patterns and party allegiances that 'defy classification', though he 'was taken by his contemporaries for a Tory'.[5]

Aislabie was the first member of his family to enter Parliament. His early career was relatively quiet, although from the outset a pattern of association with trade and revenue matters became apparent. In a probable forecast for the divisions of 31 Jan. 1696 on the proposed council of trade he was listed as likely to oppose the Court. He signed the Association promptly, though he was not recorded as voting in the division on the price of guineas in March. On the 28th he told against a motion for receiving an amendment from the Lords to the bill for encouraging the recruitment of seamen. In the 1696–7 session he voted on 25 Nov. for the attainder of Sir John Fenwick†. On 14 Jan. 1697 he was appointed to the drafting committee for a clause, or clauses, for better explaining the recoinage acts, the first of many pieces of legislation with which he was to be associated. In the 1697–8 session, following the presentation of a petition from the corporation and inhabitants of Ripon, Aislabie was appointed on 26 Jan. 1698 to the drafting committee for a bill for the more effectual prevention of the export of wool. Returned again for Ripon in the 1698 election, he was classed as a Court supporter in an analysis of the election results compiled in about September. However, he was included also on a forecast of those likely to oppose a standing army, and has been identified, from his absence from the Court side in the division on the disbanding bill on 18 Jan. 1699, as a Country Whig. Aislabie's affiliation with the Whigs during the last years of William III's reign appears to have been a temporary relationship. The following session, in 1699–1700, proved to be a distressing time for Aislabie. On 11 Dec. 1699 he was ordered into the custody of the serjeant-at-arms for being absent from a call of the House. Having been discharged on the 14th, personal tragedy struck when his wife and a daughter died in a fire at his house in Red Lion Square in January 1700. His son was only saved by being carried out of an upper window. The fire was said to have been started deliberately by a servant to conceal the theft of a casket of jewels.[6]

The death of his wife and daughter may have accounted in part for Aislabie's lack of political activity over the next few years. However, an analysis of the House into interests compiled in early 1700, while listing Aislabie under the interest of Archbishop Sharp, noted that this classification was 'doubtful'. This may have been due to Aislabie's successful endeavours to improve his personal interest in Ripon through the purchase of burgages, thereby releasing him from a dependence upon the archbishop. Aislabie was returned once again for Ripon in January 1701, and in February was listed as likely to support the Court in agreeing with the resolutions of the committee of supply to continue the 'Great Mortgage'. However, his absence from the House was noted on 6 June, when Thomas Frewen*, executor to the late Archbishop Frewen of York, presented a petition which required Aislabie's presence. Three days later Aislabie was in attendance at the House, when the petition was heard. He was returned again for Ripon in November in a contested election, and in keeping with his fluid party allegiances, was classed by Robert Harley* with the Tories in December. His parliamentary activity seems to have been hampered in 1702 by his election as mayor of Ripon, even though the corporation passed a resolution allowing him to dispense with the requirement to be resident in the borough during his term of office on account of his being an MP. His time as mayor, which may have excluded him from contesting the Ripon election, may also explain the accommodation reached between him and the Whig Sir William Hustler* for the 1702 election. Aislabie was returned for Northallerton, Hustler's normal constituency, while Hustler was returned in Aislabie's place at Ripon. The success of this arrangement suggests that Aislabie's interest in Ripon was already strong, though he improved it further when mayor, paying for the reconstruction of the market cross at a cost of about £500, restoring 'the wakeman's horn', and, 'besides other presents' to the corporation, presenting his fellow aldermen with a handsome silver cup for the use of future mayors. However, Aislabie did attend the House on occasion, and on 11 Feb. 1703, while dining at Archbishop Sharp's in the company of Bishop Nicolson, he informed the company of 'the long remonstrance of the Commons (this day) against the ministry in the last reign'.[7]

From 1704 onwards Aislabie became more active in Parliament and politics in general. Having had a quiet time during the 1703–4 session, in which he acted as a teller on 10 Jan. 1704 in favour of a motion for a second reading of the wine duties bill, Aislabie's Country Tory affiliations began to come to the fore during the 1704–5 session. In October 1704 he was forecast by Harley as a probable opponent of the Tack, and he did not vote for it on 28 Nov. On 7 Dec. he acted as a teller against committing the bill to regulate button-making, while on 13 Jan. 1705 he was appointed to the drafting committee for a bill to exclude those placemen from the House who held offices created since 1685. Aislabie's continuing interest in economic matters was signalled by his telling. On 23 Feb. he acted as a teller against an amendment to the bill prohibiting trade with France, which was designed to legitimize the importation of French wines through a friendly country, where such trade agreements were already contracted. In February and March he took an active part on behalf of the Commons in the Aylesbury case, serving on committees of inquiry and for managing a conference over the writs of error. On 13 Mar. he was named as a manager for a conference over the Lords' refusal of the Tory-inspired amendment to a naturalization bill, which aimed at denying voting rights to property-holding naturalized foreigners. However, even in this instance Aislabie has been identified as one of three managers 'of doubtful political leanings'.[8]

Returned once again for Ripon in 1705, and having been recorded by Bishop Nicolson in his diary as part of a 'throng' of MPs he met at Doncaster who were rushing to the new Parliament for the vote on the Speaker, Aislabie demonstrated his flexible allegiances by supporting the Court candidate in the division on 25 Oct. On 12 Nov. he was the first-named to the drafting committee for a bill for the ease of sheriffs in their office and in passing their accounts, which he saw through all its stages in the Commons. In a contribution to the debate on the Tories' 'Hanover motion' on 4 Dec. he again demonstrated his tendency to act independently, when he appeared to oppose the proposed address to bring over the Princess Sophia, observing that those who had previously been for an address were now against it. His Country credentials also came to the fore on the 13th when he was one of four Members appointed to prepare a bill for limiting the number of placemen in the House, while on the 19th, when the Tory Charles Caesar accused 'a great lord' [Lord Treasurer Godolphin (Sidney†)] of corresponding with St. Germain in the previous reign, Aislabie favoured showing 'compassion' to Caesar and advocated a reprimand rather than confinement in the Tower. In January 1706 Aislabie figured prominently among those who favoured the insertion of a place clause in the regency bill. Aislabie's contributions to the debates on this 'Whimsical clause' demonstrated his Country instincts. On 12 Jan. he argued that, without some such provision, 'all officers then in being may sit' in the Parliament which would convene at the Queen's death. He spoke again on the 15th, and on the 21st argued that the clause would 'perfect' the regency bill. On the 24th he told in favour of an amendment to the clause, which imposed a specific penalty on placemen who sat in Parliament, by making them ineligible to sit for ten years and fining them £500, instead of the non-specific reference to the punitive clauses of an act of Charles II's reign for excluding Catholics from Parliament. In keeping with his early speeches, he did not support the Court in the division on the place clause on 18 Feb. It was reported the next day that 'Aislabie is allowed by all, even the Whig Lords who heard the debate, to have spoke as well in it as ever anybody did in any'.[9]

In the summer of 1706 Aislabie was in contact with Secretary Harley, in relation to matters of an official nature. However, this contact also may have been the beginning of an endeavour on Aislabie's part to attach himself to a particular interest for the purposes of attaining government office. On 19 June he forwarded to Harley information received from the mayor of Ripon about a local lawyer who had allegedly declared that 'all who frequented any public worship where the Queen was prayed for were rebels and traitors', while on 15 July he sent him a loyal address from Ripon corporation for presentation to the Queen. The 1706–7 session saw Aislabie's involvement in a miscellany of legislative initiatives. First-named on 17 Dec. to the drafting committee for a bill for the sale of part of the Yorkshire estates of the late Christopher Lister* for the payment of debts, he presented this bill on 22 Jan. 1707. The following day he acted as a teller against a motion that the Whig Daniel Harvey* had been duly elected for Clitheroe. On 4 Feb. he was appointed to draft a Yorkshire estate bill. In the summer Aislabie was in contact with Harley once more, writing on 4 June to request some preferment in the navy for his kinsman Edward Blackett. On 11 Dec. he was first-named to the drafting committee for a bill concerning Irish forfeited estates, which he later presented to the House. He was also nominated on the 11th to the drafting committee for the bill to complete the Union, and on 21 Feb. he reported from the committee of inquiry into the representation of the commissioners for the Equivalent. Accordingly, on the 23rd, he was first-named to the body ordered to draft the bill for further directing payment of the Equivalent. The need for clarification of laws affected by the Union led to his appointment on the 27th to the drafting committee for the ease of Scottish Quakers. He also told on two occasions in March: on the 9th, when he told in favour of an amendment to Bishop Nicolson's cathedral bill, for allowing appeals from a bishop's local visitation, and on the 23rd, when he told against agreeing with a Lords' amendment to the East Riding land registry bill. The next day he was appointed to the drafting committee for a Yorkshire estate bill.[10]

In keeping with Aislabie's fluid political allegiances he was classed as a Tory in a parliamentary list of early 1708 and as a Whig in a later list of 1708. Returned again at Ripon in 1708, in the first session of the new Parliament he was noted for opposing certain expedients suggested by the Court party in the debates, following the Queen's Speech, on proposals for completing the Union. His occasional incarnation as a Tory was signalled on 15 Jan. 1709, when he told against the Whig Sir Cleave More, 2nd Bt.*, being declared duly elected for Bramber, and on 8 Mar. when he acted as a teller in favour of the Country Tory Robert Orme* being declared duly elected for Midhurst. However, despite his apparent affiliation with the Tory party, his continued adherence to Country principles was reported by John Pringle* in March when he included Aislabie among a group of Country Whigs who made occasional, although unsuccessful, attacks upon the ministry. Aislabie's role in the preparation of various economic and financial measures continued with his appointment to prepare a bill for the more effectual prohibition of imports of French wine and other goods (9 Mar.). His involvement in Scottish affairs included telling, on 8 Apr., for an amendment to the provisions for treason trials in Scotland in the bill for improving the Union, which represented a success on the part of his Country Whig associates. He also acted as a teller on the 18th against an amendment to the same bill. His Country principles were again visible in the 1709–10 session, when, on 25 Jan. 1710, he was one of the Members ordered to prepare a place bill. On 10 Feb. a complaint was made of a breach of privilege committed against Aislabie by a sheriff's bailiff, John Farrington, though by the 20th Aislabie was able to inform the House that Farrington 'had given him satisfaction', and the matter was dropped. On the 16th he was first-nominated to the drafting committee for a bill for the better security of rents and to prevent frauds by tenants, seeing the bill through all stages in the House. During the trial of Dr Sacheverell Aislabie displayed a dry sense of humour on 27 Feb. when the clerk was calling Members in alphabetical order of counties for proceeding to Westminster Hall. Several Scottish MPs objected to being relegated to the end, even after Wales, but Aislabie 'laughed off their protests that Aberdeenshire should have been called first by assuring them that when one of their own countrymen was impeached, they should have the precedency with pleasure'. Whether in keeping with his Country Tory affiliations or his independent nature, he voted against Sacheverell's impeachment.[11]

Following the fall of the Godolphin administration Aislabie again turned his attention to Harley, writing on 20 Aug. 'to congratulate you upon the happy turn of affairs, and to praise you the author of so great a revolution. I am not capable of advancing the public service except in respect of such elections as shall serve you.' It would appear Aislabie's intention was to procure a place in government through Harley's patronage, and by 21 Sept. rumours were spreading that Aislabie was to succeed Robert Walpole II* as treasurer of the navy. However, on the 24th, Lord Orrery (Hon. Charles Boyle II*) confirmed that no decision had been made, when he informed Harley that

> I find by Mr Aislabie that he would take it well if you would either say something to him yourself or commission me to say something to him before he goes into the country [for the elections], which I believe he designs to do in a few days. The town has given him a place which I perceive would not be so agreeable to him as another employment in the hands of the same gentleman whom it is reported he is to succeed, and as that employment would be more pleasing to him, so in my poor judgment he would be more fit for that than the other.

Despite Aislabie's interest in the office of treasurer of the navy, over the following days the rumours changed, with the prospective office now being that of a lord of the Admiralty. On the 29th Orrery again wrote to Harley requesting that he 'would endeavour to speak to Mr Aislabie as soon as possible, and make him some civil compliment of your inclination to him'. By the beginning of October it was confirmed that Aislabie was to be an Admiralty lord, which in view of his interest in the office of treasurer of the navy, appears to have been a disappointment to him. On 8 Oct. Sir Edward Blackett, 2nd Bt.*, wrote that

> Mr Aislabie is now with me and [I] perceive by him that he does not design to continue the Admiralty, and though he should, he tells me it does not lie in his way to give any manner of preferment to any one that is worth accepting. I believe in a very little time he will have another employment.

However, Aislabie did not display his dissatisfaction to Harley, and instead made the most of his involvement in the Yorkshire elections, not only securing his own return at Ripon, but also claiming in a letter to Harley on 27 Oct. that 'I have made use of the liberty you gave me to come down and have carried the county election triumphantly [for the Tory Sir Arthur Kaye, 3rd Bt.]: so there is an end of a Parliament bully [Sir William Strickland, 3rd Bt.]; no more lopping of heads and scandalous minorities'. He also requested that Harley 'take this county into your protection, and not suffer us to be governed by an old-fashioned interest; it is an easy matter to model it to your service and to make it yours'. In the 1710–11 session of the new Parliament, Aislabie partook in the Tory attacks on the Whigs on 19 Dec. over the 1708 charter for Bewdley. Lord Cowper (William*) noted in his diary that while certain Members had behaved well towards him when he attended the House in relation to the case, Henry St. John II and Aislabie had been 'particularly rude, both without any provocation'. However, Aislabie's Country instincts remained stronger than his official ties to the Tory ministry, as was noted by Kaye on 29 Jan. 1711, who recorded that 'the place bill was read the 3rd time and passed after long debate, by a majority of 235 to 143. All who have had, or now have, or are in hopes to have places, dividing against it, except for Sir William Drake, Mr [Robert] Benson, and Mr Aislabie'. Despite voting for the place bill, Aislabie remained in favour, and was made a justice for Westminster and Middlesex in February. On 31 Jan. he delivered information from the Admiralty on naval orders relating to the Palatines. At this time he was listed as a 'Tory patriot' who opposed the continuance of the war, and among the 'worthy patriots' who were said to have been responsible for detecting the mismanagements of the previous administration. He was also listed as one of the principal members of the newly founded High Church Tory October Club. These associations and activities kept him in favour with the ministry, St. John commending Aislabie to Harley on 19 Apr. for his behaviour towards the Queen.[12]

However, it was not long before Aislabie's independent nature asserted itself again. In the 1711–12 session he was to the fore among those Members who were dissatisfied with the government's attitude and policies, and who were to become known as the 'whimsicals', and later as the Hanoverian Tories. However, Aislabie was one of a few independent Tories who seem to have co-operated more openly with the Whigs than with any 'whimsical' group. He was also one of the first of these groups to express his concern, on 7 Dec. 1711, in the division over the 'No Peace without Spain' motion. According to the Dutch envoy, Aislabie was one of the proposers of the amendment to the Address. Thomas Smith II* noted that the clause was supported 'by all the considerable speakers of the Whigs . . . and by Mr Aislabie, who used to be on the other side'. It was also reported that Aislabie was one of several Tories who spoke against the peace negotiations during the debate. The peace issue also affected the October Club, with Aislabie being one of the first dissidents within it. However, Aislabie's dissidence did not interfere with his commitments of office in Parliament, and on 22 Dec. 1711 he presented the estimates of the navy debt, with an account of what part of the debt had been, and would be, satisfied by the South Sea stock. The lengthy debate on the barrier treaty on 14 Feb. 1712 kept him from dinner with Bishop Nicolson. He again distanced himself from the Tories on 25 Feb., when he successfully opposed a motion by Henry Campion which constituted part of the attack on the Duke of Marlborough (John Churchill†), wherein Campion proposed that a bill be prepared for forcing Marlborough to repay the 2.5 per cent deductions taken from the pay of foreign troops. Aislabie, along with Sir William Drake, countered this by saying that since the House had already put this affair before the Queen, it would not be very decent to take it out of her hands. Aislabie's involvement in financial matters continued during the session. He managed through all its stages in the House a bill for collecting and recovering the duties granted for the support of Greenwich Hospital, and on 24 May told in favour of implementing a resolution relating to marine pay arrears.[13]

Despite his tendency to oppose the ministry, Aislabie still seemed to remain in favour with Harley. He informed James Grahme* on 21 Oct. that 'I have not yet seen the Coll. [Harley], Captain [St. John], or Lieutenant [Robert Benson] but design to pay my homage tomorrow'. He also assured Grahme that he would 'do my endeavour', presumably at the Admiralty, to get arrears of pay for Grahme's friends. It was reported on 30 Dec. that Aislabie, in his capacity as an Admiralty Lord, was endeavouring to facilitate the Duchess of Marlborough's request for a yacht to take her to join her husband abroad. In the 1713 session Aislabie continued to fulfil his Admiralty role, presenting the ordinary naval estimates on 17 Apr., the estimates for sea officer half-pay on 20 May, and, on the 22nd, the estimates of naval officer half-pay. However, it was not long before his independent instincts came to the fore again, over the French commercial treaty. In the debate on the 8th and 9th articles of the new treaty on 18 June 'Sir Thomas Hanmer [4th Bt.], Mr Aislabie of the Admiralty . . . and divers others went with the Whigs against the Court', both Hanmer and Aislabie speaking and voting against the treaty. Aislabie was classified as a 'whimsical' in a list relating to the division. On 24 June a motion was made for an address, requesting an estimate of the half-pay for the marine regiments that were to be disbanded. Boyer attributes this motion to Aislabie.[14]

Despite siding against the ministry, Aislabie was continued in office following the 1713 session, Harley deciding against any purge of government. On Lord Chancellor Harcourt's (Simon I*) advice, Harley argued that it was 'best that Aislabie should be spared, and keep the rod over him'. He was included in the new Admiralty commission in January 1714, and, having been returned for Ripon once again, was still in office when the new Parliament met in February. On 18 Mar. he delivered information on the navy's strength and finances. He was not listed among those Members who voted against the expulsion of Richard Steele on that day. On the 24th he delivered information on naval expenditure and the sale of old ships and stores. However rumours of his pending removal from the Admiralty were confirmed in early April, after which he aligned himself squarely with the Whigs in opposition to the Tory ministry, as was evident from his inclusion as a Whig in the Worsley list. He was one of the chief speakers against the Court in the debate of 15 Apr. on whether the succession was in danger, his contribution being recorded thus:

On any attempts of Pretender he hoped messenger to Hanover would not be so long or mistake his way as of late. Well being of England now depends on mediation of France to all the courts of Europe. Such troops as these are only for this ministry. We are to procure amnesty to the Catalans and a better commerce for ourselves by prayers and fears. The first year of peace well worth six million and the 2nd year to cost us seven million. Did they mean the inability of the [kingdom] or of themselves to carry on the war? I won't say they forgot our trade to Portugal or Holland. The fondness of the Dutch in pressing so much to have but the half or that *asiento* which our South Sea Company would not take. I won't say our ministry gave up a Town in Flanders or a port in the South Sea for it.

He attacked the Court again on the 17th, over an address sent from the Lords relating to the treaties with France and Spain. He was reported to have said that

I hope it is not expected we should swallow down an address that has been cooked up above by the Lords and the ministry, 12 new-made peers and 16 Scotch pensioners, which would reduce us to a parlement of Paris. But rather that we should examine this peace step by step, for this is the only time for every honest man to speak, for as soon as this is got over we may expect to see five or six of the new garbled companies of the guards come and tell us 'this is your King'.

Consideration of the address was postponed until the 22nd, when Lord Downe (Hon. Henry Dawnay) and William Gore proposed the motion to fill up the blank in the address with the words 'and Commons'. In the following debate Aislabie supported (Sir) Peter King and other Whigs, speaking 'with great vehemence against the ministers, for having made so precarious a peace'. He was satirical and witty at first, insinuating that Downe and Gore would get peerages for their efforts, and that the address, like money supplies, was to be given as 'Plaister for [the] ministry's qualms, every sessions as long as they are in pain'. He also focused on the *asiento*, which he declared 'some took for a great country, others for the Golden Fleece, others for a bear skin ... if we are to thank the ministry we hope we shall do it especially for the *asiento*'. He then became serious, turning to the plight of the Catalans:

A people, that the Queen had said she thought herself obliged in honour and conscience to see they had their just rights and privileges, scandalously abandoned, but a Reverend Divine [Jonathan Swift] that was intimate with the ministry had let them into the secret, how it happened; for in his spirit of the Whigs, he treats them as a parcel of rebels, and as such not fit to be trusted with the privilege of giving money, which was very apt to put republican principle in them. If this doctrine prevailed it might in time be applied to them of that House. He concluded if the ministry could not sleep without such continual healing votes, to save the dignity of the House he would come into giving them an act of indemnity, but he dreaded a ministry that was too proud to ask one.

Another report described the opposition to the address as being part of the 'strugglings of the indefatigable party', but it was hoped that the debate had 'given a decisive period to their attempts', seeing as those 'against it' (Robert Walpole II, Aislabie and others) did not 'think fit to divide upon the question'. Aislabie continued to act in opposition, and in early May, when the House was considering doubling the taxes on soap and starch, he seconded Walpole's motion that the sum required be made up by the fourth part of the *asiento* which was reserved for the Queen.[15]

Aislabie's failure to toe the line within the Tory ministry had ultimately cost him his office, but his increasing identification with the Whigs was to prove beneficial following the Hanoverian succession. Whether his opposition to the Court during 1711–14 had been due to his disappointment over his place in 1710, or to his natural independent or Country instincts, his actions had 'ingratiated him very much with the Whigs', and resulted in his promotion in October 1714 as treasurer of the navy, which was the office he had originally desired. Unsurprisingly, Aislabie was classed as a Whig on two lists which compared the 1715 Parliament with its predecessor. However, his promotion under the Whigs and his previous actions gave some credence to the view expressed by Speaker Onslow (Arthur†), who wrote that Aislabie was regarded as a 'dark', 'cunning' man, 'suspected and low in all men's opinion', though he also acknowledged that Aislabie was a man of 'good understanding, no ill-speaker in Parliament, and very capable of business'. Aislabie's public career flourished under George I, when he rose to be chancellor of the Exchequer and Lord Sunderland's (Charles, Lord Spencer*) right-hand man in the South Sea affair. When the bubble burst in 1720, his deep involvement in the affair put an end to the rumours that he was to receive a peerage, and led to his resignation from office in January 1721 and expulsion from the Commons and temporary incarceration in the Tower in March. Subsequently, he was debarred from standing again. Still a wealthy man, Aislabie spent much of the remainder of his life developing Studley Royal and Fountains Abbey, which had come into his possession in 1716, with lavish buildings and landscaped gardens. His personal estate was such that he was able to give one daughter a portion of £13,000 in 1724. He continued to control the elections in Ripon until his death on 18 June 1742. By his will his son, William Aislabie†, inherited everything.[16]

[1] *Yorks. Arch. Jnl.* xxxvii. 263–4; W. Yorks. Archs. Vyner mss, 544–86, 5836, 5556, 5933 (*ex. inf.* Mr William Barber); *Fountains Abbey* (Surtees Soc. lxvii), 235–41. [2] *Yorks. Arch. Jnl.* 263, 267; *Ripon Millenary* ed. Harrison, 81, 83. [3] *HMC Lords*, n.s. iii. 204; E. G. W. Bill, *Q. Anne Churches*, pp. xxiii–xxiv. [4] Cobbett, *Parlty. Hist.* vi. 912; Add. 17677 DDD, f. 606; 42181, ff. 29–30; *Cal. Treas. Bks.* xxix. 20, 700; xxxii. 27–28; *HMC Var.* viii. 297, 299. [5] *Yorks. Arch. Jnl.* 263–7; *Ripon Millenary*, 67; W. A. Speck, *Tory and Whig*, 53; Glos. RO, Sharp mss 4/K27, Leeds to abp. of York, 10 Sept. 1695; Speck thesis, 97–98. [6] *Party and Management* ed. C. Jones, 76; *Yorks. Arch. Jnl.* 267; *Bull. IHR.* sp. supp. 7, p. 50; Luttrell, *Brief Relation*, iv. 605; *Fountains Abbey*, 240; *Yorks. Diaries* (Surtees Soc. lxv), 340. [7] Vyner mss, 231–4180, 5067–78, 5637, 5743–4, 5782 (*ex inf.* Mr William Barber); N. Yorks. RO, Swinton mss, Danby pprs. persons to be elected at Ripon, 24 Nov. 1701; *Fountains Abbey*, 238; *Ripon Millenary*, 83–86; *HMC Portland*, vi. 138; *Nicolson Diaries* ed. Jones and Holmes, 202. [8] *Bull. IHR.* xl. 157. [9] *Nicolson Diaries*, 282; *Bull. IHR.* xxxvii. 34; *Cam. Misc.* xxiii. 42, 54, 56, 63, 67, 79, 81; G. Holmes, *Pol. in Age of Anne*, 117; Centre Kentish Stud. Stanhope mss U1590/C9/31, Sir John Cropley, 2nd Bt.*, to James Stanhope*, 19 Feb. 1706; *Party and Management*, 80. [10] *HMC Portland*, iv. 313, 317, 417; *Yorks. Arch. Jnl.* 267–8. [11] Speck thesis, 97–98; Cunningham, *Hist. GB*, ii. 137; SRO, Ogilvy of Inverquharity mss GD205/34/4, Pringle to William Bennet*, 1 Mar. 1709; G. Holmes, *Trial of Sacheverell*, 124. [12] *HMC Portland*, iv. 570, 600, 604, 617, 676; J. Carswell, *S. Sea Bubble*, 50; Huntington Lib. Stowe mss 57(4) pp. 151, 161, 166; Churchill Coll. Camb. Erle mss 2/12, James Craggs I* to Thomas Erle*, 23 Sept. 1710; *Addison Letters*, 241; Add. 31143, f. 571; Northumb. RO, Blackett mss ZBL 189, Newby letter bk. Blackett to Edward Denniston, 8 Oct. [1710], same to John ?, 14 [Oct. 1710]; *Yorks. Arch. Jnl.* 268–70; Cowper, *Diary*, 50–51; *Cam. Misc.* xxxi. 329; Boyer, *Pol. State*, i–ii. 160, 117; Tindal, ii. 235. [13] Holmes, *Pol. in Age of Anne*, 280, 283; NSA, Kreienberg's despatches 7 Dec. 1711, 29 Feb. 1712; NLS, Advocates' mss, Wodrow pprs. letters Quarto 6, f. 45; Add. 47026, f. 103; *Bull. IHR.* xxxiii. 226–8; D. Szechi, *Jacobitism and Tory Pol.* 97–98; Boyer, *Anne Annals*, x. 298; *Nicolson Diaries*, 587. [14] Bagot mss at Levens Hall, Aislabie to Grahme, 12 Oct. 1712; Add. 22226, f. 257; 31144, f. 381; 17677 GGG, f. 230; Boyer, *Pol. State*, v. 233, 388–9, 393; vi. 103; Chandler, v. 1, 40–41; SRO, Cromartie mss GD305 addit./bdle. 15, [–] to [Earl of Cromarty], 20 June 1713; Cobbett, vi. 1223; Tindal, 320; *Yorks. Arch. Jnl.* 273–4. [15] *Bull. IHR.* xxxiii. 331; Add. 70382, Harley to Lord Harley (Edward*), 24 Oct. 1713; 31139, ff. 78, 91; 17677 HHH, f. 41; Boyer, *Pol. State*, vii. 56, 410; Stowe mss 57(10) p. 47; Szechi, 154; Wodrow pprs. letters Quarto 8, ff. 95–96; Douglas Diary (Hist. of Parl. trans.), 15, 22 Apr. 1714; Herts. RO, Panshanger mss, D/EP F35, p. 79; Cobbett, vi. 1348; Tindal, 355; *Wentworth Pprs.* 377–8; BL, Trumbull Alphab. mss 52, Thomas Bateman to Sir William Trumbull*, 23 Apr. 1714; Bodl. Ballard 25, f. 113; Glos. RO, Ducie mss, D340a/c20/9, [–] to Matthew Ducie Moreton*, [?1]9 May 1714. [16] *HMC 14th Rep. IX.* 510–11; *Wentworth Pprs.* 427, 430; *HMC Portland*, vi. 597, 606; vi. 137–8; Carswell, 70–71, 228–9, 242, 250, 259, 262–3, 268; Vyner mss, 6068, parcel T.30/2, indenture for repayments by Aislabie, 19 Mar. 1723; *Clerk Mems.* 148–9; *Fountains Abbey* (Surtees Soc. xli), 221; *Yorks. Diaries*, 254, 470; *HMC Hastings*, iii. 2; *Yorks. Arch. Jnl.* xxvii. 325; *Fountains Abbey* (Surtees Soc. lxvii), 239–41; *Ripon Millenary*, 85.

E. C./C. I. M.

ALCOCK(E), Lawrence (1677–1723), of Midhurst and Trotton Place, Suss.

MIDHURST 1701 (Feb.)–1713

bap. 25 June 1677, 1st s. of Lawrence Alcock, ?filazer, protonotary and exigenter for Monmouth 1692–*d.*, of Midhurst, by his w. Jane. *educ.* New Coll. Oxf. 1694; I. Temple 1694. *m.* lic. 6 May 1701, Anne (*d.* 1737), da. of Edward Fuller of Watford, Herts. 5s. (4 *d.v.p.*) 2da. *suc.* fa. 1699.[1]

Alcock's father had settled at Midhurst in the mid-17th century, when he began buying burgages there in alliance with the viscounts Montagu, lords of the borough, subsequently becoming steward there. Alcock himself was returned for Midhurst in February 1701 a few years after coming of age and continued to represent the borough until 1713. He was classed as a Tory by Robert Harley* in December 1701 though was not an active Member. In January 1703 he was given three weeks' leave of absence for his health. In October 1704 he was noted as a probable supporter of the Tack, but after being lobbied by Harley voted against it on 28 Nov. On 6 Nov. he had been given 14 days' absence due to his wife's illness. Classed as 'Low Church' on a list of about June 1705, he voted against the Court candidate for Speaker on 25 Oct. 1705 and was listed as a Tory in early 1708. In another list of 1708, updated with the election returns, he was also classed as a Tory, and in 1710 he voted against the impeachment of Dr Sacheverell. He was given leave of absence for his health in January 1710. Having as usual been returned for Midhurst in 1710, he subsequently appeared in published lists as one of the 'Tory patriots' who opposed the continuance of the war, and as one of the 'worthy patriots' who, in the first session of this Parliament, detected the mismanagements of the previous administration. He did not stand again after 1713 and died on 3 July 1723. Since all his own sons died without issue, the property passed to his daughter's second son, John Radcliffe, who was to sit for St. Albans in 1768.[2]

[1] Berry, *Suss. Gens.* 108; Add. 5699, f. 130; *London Mar. Lic.* ed. Foster, 12; PCC 66 Pott. [2] *Cowdray Archs.* ed. Dibben, 28; PCC 21 Richmond.

P. W.

ALDWORTH, Charles (c.1677–1714), of Frogmore, Berks. and Somerset House, Westminster.

NEW WINDSOR 21 Jan. 1712–21 Sept. 1714

b. c.1677, o. s. of William Aldworth† of Frogmore by his w. Anne. *educ.* King's, Camb. 1693; I. Temple 1695, called 1703. *unm. suc.* fa. 1700.[1]

Aldworth's father held several revenue offices during, Charles II's reign and was recommended by James II's agents for election to the proposed 1688 Parliament. In 1687 James II granted him a mansion house called Frogmore in New Windsor, and he later purchased the manor of Shaw in Old Windsor on a 99-year lease. In 1694, when James II was in 'great need' of money, William Aldworth was approached for funds by a Jacobite agent. Although Charles Aldworth entered the Inner Temple in 1695, in February 1696 he was granted a pass to go to Holland, from whence he went to the exiled court at St. Germain. In his absence his father fell into financial difficulties, partly over money owed him by the crown, but most of all through being defrauded by an attorney, Sir James Tillie, 'a villain' who had also cheated Christopher Vane*.[2]

Aldworth was still in France when his father died in 1700. The Earl of Manchester, English ambassador at Paris, wrote in December that 'Aldworth, a man of learning, who has been several years at St. Germain (he went there by the name of St. Bernard), is gone for England; he pretends he has leave from the government'. Aldworth had, in fact, been granted a licence to return on 26 Sept., under the Act of December 1697 for preventing correspondence with James II. Once in England Aldworth petitioned the Commons on 21 Mar. 1701 for his Windsor estates to be exempted from the bill to resume crown grants since 1684. In 1702 he obtained an Act of Parliament to enable him to sell part of his father's estates in Lincolnshire and Kent, as well as in Berkshire, to pay debts then amounting to £1,262 and provide portions of £4,000 and £3,500 for his two sisters.[3]

A protégé and correspondent of the Duke of Northumberland, Aldworth was part of the social circle of Queen Anne's favourite, Abigail, wife of Samuel Masham*. Aldworth also took a keen interest in parliamentary affairs, and was originally intended by Northumberland as the successor to William Paul at Windsor in May 1711. Instead, Masham took the seat himself. Aldworth continued to keep Northumberland apprised of parliamentary events, informing him on 18 Dec. 1711 about events in the Lords, while on the 22nd he recorded that the Commons had made a 'glorious representation' upon the peace, that the occasional conformity and land tax bills had passed, and that the Lords had made an address to the Queen to instruct her plenipotentiaries not to come to peace terms without consulting the allies. On the ennoblement of Masham later that month, Northumberland suggested that Aldworth replace him. Aldworth replied that

should the case in truth require the help of money to be spent, though I assure your Grace I have different accounts from Windsor, it is by no means what suits my circumstances. I thank God I have wherewithal to maintain me with comfort and some credit in the world, but to engage myself in debt by elections is what I cannot think of. I have too long felt the heaviness of debts and now I am upon the point of coming out of that very grievous condition, it would be thought madness for one upon uncertainties to venture again to that sea of miseries.

However, despite these sentiments he was returned unopposed on Northumberland's recommendation.[4]

Aldworth was an active Member in Parliament, attaching himself to the interest of Lord Bolingbroke (Henry St. John II*). On 9 Feb. 1712 Aldworth acted as a teller against receiving a Quaker petition desiring that they be allowed to affirm, while on 30 Mar. he told for a motion that Philip Bertie* was duly elected for Boston. On 12 Apr. he wrote to Northumberland reporting the day's debate and regretting that the adjournment seemed to mean that 'the popery bill' would be 'quite dropped'. He acted as a teller on 14 May against a Lords' amendment to the bill to prevent fraudulent conveyances before elections, for permitting Quakers to affirm, while on 3 June he told for the motion that William Cotesworth was not duly elected for Boston. In the 1713 session Aldworth acted as a teller on 9 May against adjourning the debate on the report of the commissioners of accounts. Aldworth was also a prominent supporter of the malt tax bill, and on the 20th he informed Northumberland of the proceedings in the House on this bill:

a motion was made for tacking the place bill to the malt bill. I thought it necessary to give my reasons as well as vote against it, and we carried it upon a division 160 to 111 and I am told by my friends that what I said was not altogether without weight... This day we recommitted a part of the report from the committee to whom the malt bill was committed, laying 8d. per bushel on malt in North Britain, upon a division 125 to 100. The Whigs to a man except Mr Smith were for recommitting.

On 11 June he presented a bill to make two prize ships free, and told for the bill's second reading, while on the 12th he intervened in the debate on the commercial treaty with France to contradict the assertion by Sir William Wyndham, 3rd Bt.*, that the opposition were attacking the treaty because they knew its success would spell their downfall. According to the Hanoverian envoy, Aldworth declared:

qu'il croyoit plutôt que la faction étoit croissante et, que si on n'employoit pas des remèdes bientôt d'une manière efficace elle seroit fort dangereuse, qu'on voyoit que la faction n'estoit pas encore ruinée, puis qu'elle avoit été capable de séduire tant de gens et produire tant de petitions contre le traité le plus avantageux qu'on eut jamais vu.

On the 16th he told against a motion for a second reading of the bill for continuing the Acts for the use of the Quaker affirmation, and on the 18th voted for the French commerce bill. In July he told in favour of reading a committee report on the bill for regulation of the land forces. Returned for New Windsor in a contested election in 1713, Aldworth acted as a teller on 5 Mar. 1714 in favour of hearing the Caernarvon Boroughs election case at the bar. In April he told against a resolution to confine the right of election at Brackley to the corporation and resident burgesses (20th), and against a motion that Sir John Anstruther, 1st Bt.*, had been duly elected for Anstruther Easter Burghs (29th). Aldworth spoke in the debate on 12 May in favour of the schism bill, and was appointed to the drafting committee. The following month he acted as a teller on 24 June against an amendment to the Earl of Ranelagh's (Richard Jones*) estate bill, and on the 29th against a motion to recommit the resolution that Hon. Benedict Leonard Calvert* had been duly elected for Harwich. Boyer recorded that on 13 Aug. Aldworth supported Horatio Walpole II's motion that the committee on the bill for support of the King's Household be instructed to include a clause for payment of the arrears owing to the Hanoverian troops. Aldworth was said to have stated on that occasion that

> for his part he had formerly been against that payment, because he had been given to understand in that very House, that the troops were deserters: but that he had since been informed that they were hired to fight, and had served well as long as there was fighting: and if, when they came in sight of the enemy, they who had hired them, would not suffer them to fight, he did not see the reason why they should be called deserters.

He was classed as a Tory in the Worsley list.[5]

Aldworth intended on standing for re-election to the 1715 Parliament, writing to the corporation of Windsor on 8 Sept.:

> I had long resolved not to serve any more in Parliament, a trouble and attendance I could hardly discharge as I ought, making a conscience of my duty, without neglecting too much my private affairs, which I am certain my true friends would not desire. It is with great pleasure I hear of the good inclinations of the town, shown in their dutiful address and hope Windsor will ever be represented by true Churchmen, faithful asserters of the constitution and dutiful subjects to the King.

However Aldworth was not to live long enough to contest the election. His death appears to have been due to his being 'a young rash gentleman' who had been 'so indiscreet as publicly to drink the Pretender's health, which drew upon him several unlucky quarrels'. On 21 Sept. Aldworth met at St. James's a Colonel Chudleigh of the foot guards, whom Aldworth had previously berated for drinking the health of the Duke of Marlborough (John Churchill†). Some bystanders expressed 'their wonder that a man who had publicly drunk the Pretender's health' should appear at the King's palace, which provoked a quarrel and a duel with Chudleigh, in which Aldworth was killed. Another report stated that Aldworth 'was insulted' by Chudleigh, who accused him of being a Jacobite, and that Aldworth's death in the duel was 'no great wonder, for he had such a weakness in both his arms that he could not stretch them, and this from being a child, and is supposed not to be a secret to' Chudleigh. Aldworth was buried at St. George's chapel, Windsor, on 28 Sept. His executor was his friend Sir Constantine Phipps, late lord chancellor of Ireland. With the deaths of Aldworth's two surviving sisters, both unmarried, the line died out.[6]

[1] *Misc. Gen. et Her.* n.s. iv. 173–4; ser. 3, v. 111–14. [2] PRO 30/50/12, 15–17, 20, 29; Berks. RO, Braybrooke mss D/EN/E10; *Orig. Pprs.* ed. Macpherson, i. 500; *CSP Dom.* 1696, p. 34; 1699–1700, p. 87. [3] *Regs. St. George's Chapel*, Windsor ed. Poyser, 210; 7th Duke of Manchester, *Court and Soc. Eliz. to Anne*, ii. 122; Cole, *Mems.* 265; *CSP Dom.* 1700–2, p. 123; *HMC Lords*, n.s. v. 208; Braybrooke mss D/EN/E10, L5. [4] Braybrooke mss D/EN/F23/2, Aldworth to [Northumberland], 18, 22 Dec. 1711; W. A. Speck, *Tory and Whig*, 60. [5] G. Holmes, *Pol. in Age of Anne*, 93, 255, 280; Braybrooke mss D/EN/F23/2, Aldworth to [Northumberland], 20 May 1713; NSA, Kreienberg's despatch 12 June 1713; Boyer, *Pol. State*, v. 388; vii. 461; viii. 155–6; Chandler, v. 41; D. Szechi, *Jacobitism and Tory Pol.* 122, 130, 137. [6] Braybrooke mss D/EN/F23/2, Aldworth to William Bigg, 8 Sept. 1714; Boyer, 262–3; Add. 22220, f. 126; *Reg. St. George's Chapel*, 213, 222, 226.

E. C.

ALLARDICE (ALLERDYCE), Sir George

(1672–1709), of Allardice, Kincardine.

SCOTLAND 1707–1708

bap. 17 Aug. 1672, 2nd s. of Sir John Allardice by Mary, da. of John Graham, Ld. Kinpont [S]. *educ.* 1688–92 Aberdeen Univ. (Marischal Coll.). *m. contr.* 20 Oct. 1692, Anna (*d.*1735), da. of James Ogilvy, 3rd Earl of Findlater [S], sis. of Hon. Patrick Ogilvy*, 3s. 5da. *suc.* bro. Dec. 1690; kntd. 1704.[1]

Commr. justiciary for Highlands [S] 1693, 1701, peace in the Highlands 1694; master of the mint [S] 1704.[2]

Burgess, Edinburgh 1696.[3]

MP [S], Kintore 1702–7.

An ancient Kincardineshire family, dating from at least the 15th century, the Allardices of that ilk had twice represented the county in the Scottish parliament. Allardice's father never sat in parliament, but made an advantageous match with the family of Graham, earls of Airth and Menteith. Allardice himself improved the family fortunes through trade, which facilitated his marriage to the Earl of Findlater's daughter in the autumn of 1692. This alliance was welcomed by Allardice's mother, but (according to a tradition preserved by the servants) the bride herself was not immediately enraptured, apparently shedding tears at 'the mean appearance of the house'. Upon the birth of his first child in 1693, Allardice reported proudly to his brother-in-law Sir James Ogilvy that 'I have made you both an uncle and a godfather'. Ogilvy, the future Lord Chancellor Seafield, proved the most important of Allardice's political connexions. In 1694 Ogilvy's legal expertise was largely responsible for resolving a disputed inheritance from the 2nd Earl of Airth and Menteith, Allardice acknowledging that he had been 'singularly obliged to his kindness in my affairs'. Seafield's appointment as secretary of state in 1696 made him an influential patron, Allardice reporting appreciatively to his father-in-law in August 1698 that 'there is none can know vacancies, or what may be done for a friend [better] than your son'.[4]

Returned to the Scottish parliament with Seafield's backing in 1702, Allardice followed his patron's lead in collaborating with the 'New Party' in 1704 and was rewarded with a knighthood and appointment as master of the mint. He voted solidly (apart from two insignificant abstentions) in favour of the Union and was included on the Court slate of representatives to the first Parliament of Great Britain. He did not, however, make his mark at Westminster though his attendance can nevertheless be deduced from several committee nominations during November and December. His only known vote was on 22 Jan. 1708 in support of the abortive attempt by the Court to defer the abolition of the Scottish privy council. He did not stand in 1708, not least because his former seat had been subsumed within Elgin Burghs, which was reserved for Seafield's brother, Patrick Ogilvy. Allardice was reported as terminally ill in September 1709, and died on 5 Oct.[5]

[1] *Hist. Scot. Parl.* 14-15; *Scots Peerage* ed. Paul, i. 141-3; *Recs. Marischal Coll. and Univ. of Aberdeen* (New Spalding Club), ii. 262; *Retours*, i. Kincardine, 174. [2] *Hist. Scot. Parl.* 14-15. [3] *Scot. Rec. Soc.* lix. 30. [4] *HMC 5th Rep.* 632; *Hist. Scot. Parl.* 14-15; *Seafield Corresp.* 90, 110, 125, 160, 243; *Scot. Hist. Soc.* ser. 3, v. 58-59; *Scots Peerage*, 141. [5] Info. from Dr P. W. J. Riley on members of Scot. parl.; NLS, ms 14498, ff. 82-83; Boyer, *Anne Annals*, iii. app. 44; Riley, *Union*, 331; SRO, Seafield mss GD248/566/85/46, Allardice to Findlater, 22 Jan. [1708]; Atholl mss at Blair Atholl, box 45, bdle. 8, no. 79, James Murray to Atholl, 8 Sept. 1709.

D. W.

ALLIN *alias* **ANGUISH, Sir Richard,** 1st Bt. (c.1659-1725), of Somerleyton Hall, Suff.

DUNWICH   5 Feb. 1709-1710

b. c.1659, ?2nd but 1st surv. s. of Edmund Anguish of Moulton, Norf. by Alice, da. of Sir Thomas Allin, 1st Bt., of Olderings House, Lowestoft, Suff. and Mark Lane, London, sis. (and in her issue h.) of Sir Thomas Allin, 2nd Bt.[†], of Somerleyton. *educ.* Great Yarmouth; St. John's, Camb. 30 Apr. 1695, aged 15. *m.* settlement c.19 Sept. 1699, Frances (*d.*1743), da. of Sir Henry Ashurst, 1st Bt.*, 5s. (2 *d.v.p.*) 1da. *suc.* uncle Sir Thomas Allin and assumed name of Allin 1696; fa. 1699; *cr.* Bt. as Sir Richard Allin 14 Dec. 1699.[1]

Jt.-customer, Great Yarmouth 1685-1708; customer 1708-9.[2]

Sheriff, Suff. 3-14 Dec. 1702; freeman, Dunwich 1709.[3]

Richard Anguish came of a family established in Norfolk since at least the early 16th century. Although the Somerleyton estate of the Allins, which he inherited in 1696, was somewhat encumbered, it was substantial enough for its acquisition to pitchfork him into the first rank of county society in Suffolk, and it also carried considerable electoral interest at Dunwich, where, under the influence of Sir Robert Rich, 2nd Bt.*, Allin (as he now for the most part called himself) acted with the Whig faction. After succeeding his father and marrying well, he was created a baronet in December 1699, but despite his new status he was reluctant to put up at Dunwich in a by-election the following month caused by Rich's death. Humphrey Prideaux reported that he was making

all the steps he can to get out of the [fanatic] interest now Sir R. Rich is dead, and his lady is as earnest in it as he. He hath refused to stand at Dunwich on the fanatic interest, and yet I do not find the gentry are very forward to give any regard to him.

In 1701 the young Sir John Perceval, 5th Bt.[†] (later 1st Earl of Egmont), found, on visiting Allin and his wife, a picture of domestic contentment: 'both have very good accomplishments and live happily together'.[4]

It may have been Allin's pressing debts that induced him to stand at Dunwich, as a Whig, in 1708. Seated on petition on 5 Feb. 1709, he was obliged to surrender his patent office in the customs in order to qualify himself, leaving his resignation until after a decision had been given on his return. On 9 Feb. the House was called upon to judge the legality of this manoeuvre, and resolved that he be admitted. He was among those listed as having supported in 1709 the naturalization of the Palatines, and a year later also voted in favour of the impeachment of Dr Sacheverell. He was defeated at Dunwich in 1710, and did not stand for Parliament again. His debts now totalled some £11,775, over £3,600 of which was due to the Treasury as part of the arrears owed by Samuel Pacy, a former receiver-general for Suffolk, for whom Allin had stood surety. In June 1710 and again at the end of the year he petitioned for time to pay, 'by reason he is only tenant for life and therefore can raise no money', a consequence of his marriage settlement, and eventually he was obliged to obtain in 1711 a private Act to enable him to sell off part of his estate. Allin died on 19 Oct. 1725. The baronetcy became extinct two generations later.[5]

[1] Carthew, *Hundred of Launditch*, iii. 318; Copinger, *Suff. Manors*, v. 6; *HMC Egmont*, ii. 198–9; *HMC Lords*, n.s. ix. 90. [2] *Cal. Treas. Bks.* viii. 198; xxiv. 275. [3] *HMC Var.* vii. 107. [4] *HMC Lords*, 90; *CSP Dom.* 1698, p. 342; *Prideaux Letters* (Cam. Soc. n.s xv), 193–4; Add. 47057, f. 6. [5] *CJ*, xvi. 532, 593, 607, 669; *HMC Lords*, 90; *Cal. Treas. Bks.* xxiv. 342, 564; xxv. 146.

D. W. H.

ALSTON, Sir Thomas, 3rd Bt. (c.1676–1714), of Odell, Beds.

BEDFORD   1698–1700

b. c.1676, 1st s. of Sir Rowland Alston, 2nd Bt., of Odell by Temperance, da. and coh. of Thomas Crew†, 2nd Baron Crew of Stene. *educ.* Trinity Coll. Camb. matric. 20 Apr. 1692, aged 16, MA 1693; I. Temple 1696. *unm. suc.* fa. as 3rd Bt. Sept. 1697.[1]

Burgess, Bedford 1698.[2]

Alston succeeded his father at about the same time as he attained his majority, and the very next year was returned for Bedford, replacing William Farrer*. This was a natural compliment to the proprietor of what was a very considerable local estate: Alston's mother had received some £20,000 from her father besides her share of his landed property, and the jointure settled upon her by her husband was worth at least £7,000. There was a strong Puritan tradition on both sides of the family. Alston's paternal grandfather, a brother-in-law of Chief Justice Oliver St. John†, had been active on the county committee and the committee of sequestrations for Bedfordshire during the Civil War, while the rectory of Odell was held successively from 1672 to 1703 by ministers who had been ejected in the Restoration Church settlement. His mother was a near relation of the Harleys, and indeed appealed successfully to Sir Edward Harley* for moral support during a period of estrangement from her husband in the last year of his life. The marriage had been a stormy one, and it may well be that Alston was a great deal closer to his mother than to his father, since the latter apparently made a habit of denying paternity, unofficially, to all of his children. The fact of being appointed to the county commission of the peace just prior to the 1698 general election might have suggested that Alston's political sympathies were Whiggish, but the Harley connexion was a complicating factor. The compiler of a comparative analysis of the old and new Parliaments did not know what to make of him, and he was eventually categorized as 'doubtful'. Nor did Alston provide during this Parliament sufficient further evidence of partisan allegiance. Indeed, he may not have been a particularly attentive Member: he was given a week's leave of absence on 17 Feb. 1699 and a dangerous illness the following summer probably reduced his parliamentary appearances in the second session, when he was again marked as 'doubtful' in an analysis of the Commons into various 'interests'.[3]

Alston appears not to have sought re-election in January 1701, and later that year embarked on a European tour, taking in Switzerland and Italy. He was thought of by Whigs in Bedfordshire as a possible candidate to succeed the ailing knight of the shire (Lord) Edward Russell shortly after the 1710 election, and at the next general election may have contemplated standing with the support of the Duke of Kent, but in neither case did anything transpire.[4]

Alston died, probably, in London, in December 1714. His will was dated 9 Dec. and he was buried at Odell on Christmas Day. The story that he had wasted his estate and at the time of his death was a prisoner in the Fleet is not borne out by his will, in which the Odell estate and other property in Bedfordshire was left intact and charged with numerous bequests amounting to over £1,000, together with annuities totalling £140 to his sisters. A friend in Bedford was given the choice of four books from his library, 'except Blow's atlas bound in velvet'. He did, however, request that all papers 'which concern only myself or my own private transactions', be destroyed immediately after his decease, and that his funeral take place 'after 'tis dark ... without any pallbearers or other attendance than my relations there with such of my tenants and the inhabitants of Odell as shall think fit to attend me'. His brother and principal heir, Sir Rowland, 4th Bt., sat for Bedfordshire as a Court Whig 1722–41.[5]

[1] L. Cresswell, *Stemmata Alstoniana*, 16. [2] Bedford Bor. Council, Bedford bor. recs. B2/3, corp. act bk. 1688–1718, f. 51. [3] *The Commons 1660–90*, ii. 169; PCC 39 Fagg; J. Godber, *Hist. Beds.* 248; *HMC Var.* vii. 346; A. G. Matthews, *Calamy Revised*, 164, 493; Add. 70112, Lady Alston to Sir Edward Harley, 4, 29 July, 8 Aug. 1697; Harley to Sir Rowland Alston, 13 Aug. 1697; Sir Rowland Alston to Harley, 22 Aug. 1697; L. K. J. Glassey, *Appt. JPs*, 128; *London Post*, 11–14 Aug. 1699. [4] *HMC Buccleuch*, ii. 752, 754,

757–8; Add. 29599, f. 121; Herts. RO, Panshanger mss, Ld. Cowper's (William*) diary, 3 Mar. 1712 (Speck trans.). [5]PCC 39 Fagg; *Beds. Par. Reg.* xi (Odell), 43; *VCH Beds.* iii. 73.

D. W. H.

ANDERTON, James (*b.* 1661), of the Inner Temple, London and Wigan, Lancs.

ILCHESTER 1701 (Feb.)–1705

bap. 22 Aug. 1661, 2nd s. of John Anderton of Wigan. *educ.* Barnard's Inn c.1678; I. Temple 1681, called 1686. *m.* Elizabeth, da. of Thomas Jennings of Burton, Som., 3da.[1]

Attorney and serjeant in Lancs. 1687–9; King's counsel of the duchy of Lancaster 1689–97; ?dep. custos rot. Lancs. 1698.[2]

Anderton was a practising lawyer. Little is known of his early life, though it seems that in 1688 he was serving Wigan corporation, which had been regulated by Lord Brandon (Charles Gerard*), in a legal capacity. The implication that Anderton collaborated with James II's policies is strengthened by his appointment in 1687 to legal office in the duchy of Lancaster by Robert Phelips[†], a supporter of James's policies and a non-juror after the Revolution. Anderton was removed from the duchy in April 1689, but in December the same year he obtained a different legal post within the duchy, and in July 1698 it became apparent that the Earl of Macclesfield (as Brandon had become) intended to nominate him as deputy custos of Lancashire. Macclesfield was piqued at the recent appointment of George Kenyon* as recorder of Wigan, despite attempts to blacken Kenyon as a Jacobite. Kenyon was also Lancashire's clerk of the peace by letters patent, and Peter Shakerley* perceptively noted that Anderton's proposed appointment was intended to 'nip' Kenyon 'of some profits'. Shakerley suggested that the Lancashire 'gentlemen' should 'remonstrate by petition to the King and Council' on the matter, and though it is unclear whether Anderton was appointed he unsuccessfully contested Wigan in 1698 in alliance with Sir Alexander Rigby*, a political ally of Macclesfield.[3]

The Somerset connexions of Anderton's wife led him to stand for Ilchester in the first 1701 election. After a hard-fought and notably venal election he was returned with a director of the New East India Company, but although Anderton had acted as counsel for the company, and despite his links with the Whig Macclesfield, he proved himself a committed Tory in the Commons. Blacklisted as having opposed during the 1701 session the preparations for war with France, he retained his seat at the second election of the year and, ironically, given the extensive bribes whereby he had obtained his return, was added on 20 Jan. 1702 to the committee drafting a bill for the better prevention of bribery at elections. The following month, on the 26th, he voted for the motion vindicating the Commons' proceedings in the last session against the former Whig ministers. Though sitting for a Somerset borough, Anderton's few significant committee nominations suggest his continuing concern for matters relating to the north-west, as he was appointed to examine the accounts of a late receiver of taxes for Cheshire and north Wales (25 Mar.), and reported upon the bill to vest lands of Whitworth parish, Cheshire in trustees (27 Mar.). When on 30 Mar. 1702 the Queen offered to return £100,000 from the civil list due to 'the great necessities of the nation' Anderton was among those who offered what Sir Richard Cocks, 2nd Bt.*, called 'nauseous and flattering expressions of thanks', proposing that Parliament give the Queen '£200,000 more to return the compliment'. Later in the session, on 12 May, Anderton seconded the petition, presented by Sir John Bolles, 4th Bt.*, of those imprisoned for the Assassination Plot, requesting that they be banished rather than have their imprisonment continued. His return for Ilchester in 1702 was complicated by a complaint against him of electoral bribery, though in January 1703 he was declared duly elected. In October 1704 he was forecast as a probable supporter of the Tack and either voted for it, or was absent, on 28 Nov. He did not stand for election again. The date of his death has not been ascertained.[4]

[1] IGI, Lancs.; Burke, *Commoners*, iv. 538. [2] Somerville, *Duchy of Lancaster Official Lists*, 56, 101. [3] *HMC Kenyon*, 196, 425. [4] *Cocks Diary*, 260, 288; Luttrell, *Brief Relation*, v. 254, 262.

P. W./R. D. H.

ANDREW, Thomas (c.1645–1722), of Great Addington and Harleston, Northants.

HIGHAM FERRERS 15 July 1689–1698
NORTHAMPTON 21 Feb. 1701–1702

b. c.1645, 1st s. of William Andrew of Great Addington. *educ.* ?Emmanuel, Camb. 1662; M. Temple 1675. *m.* 1 Mar. 1666, Anne (*d.* 1678), da. of Richard Kinnesman of Broughton, Northants., 2s. (1 *d.v.p.*) 2da. (1 *d.v.p.*). *suc.* uncle Robert Andrew[†] at Harleston 1674; fa. 1675.[1]

Commr. for rebuilding of Northampton 1675; sheriff, Northants. 1687–8, Mar.–Nov. 1689; steward, honor of Higham Ferrers 1701–2; receiver Apr.–June 1702.[2]

Thomas Andrew of Harleston should not be confused with a contemporary of the same name who flourished successfully in London as a merchant. After inactive service in the Convention, none of Andrew's subsequent ten years in Parliament was any busier, and all that can be traced are his fairly consistent political leanings. Lord Carmarthen (Sir Thomas Osborne†) marked him as a Whig in October 1690, and Robert Harley counted him a member of the Country party in around April 1691. By the spring of 1693 he was noted by Grascome as a Court supporter, an attribution confirmed in a further list of government supporters of 1694–5. Returned again for Higham Ferrers in 1695, he was predicted in January 1696 as likely to support the administration over the proposed council of trade, and at the end of the following month signed the Association. Late in March he voted for fixing the price of guineas at 22s., and on 25 Nov. for the attainder of Sir John Fenwick†. On 26 May 1698 he was given leave, possibly to allow him to prepare for the July election, but if this was his intention, he appears later to have subsequently withdrawn rather than stand a poll against a Tory rival, Thomas Ekins*. He was classed retrospectively as a supporter of the Court party in a post-electoral listing compiled in around September.

In the election of January 1701 Andrew stood unsuccessfully against Ekins at Higham Ferrers, but by the time his petition against Ekins had been presented, he had already secured the Northampton seat at a by-election towards the end of February. Returned again for Northampton in November, Andrew was considered a 'gain' for the Whigs in Lord Spencer's (Charles*) annotations on a list of the new Parliament. In April 1702 he was appointed to the receivership of Higham Ferrers in the duchy of Lancaster following the death of Thomas Ekins, the previous holder, but shortly before the summer election was dismissed with other Whig officials of the Duchy. Just after his appointment he had himself been criticized by Sir Justinian Isham, 4th Bt.*, one of Northamptonshire's leading Tories, for dismissing a subordinate official 'for no other reason but for voting honestly'. He played no part in the subsequent contest, and may thereafter have retired altogether from active politics. At the beginning of 1705 his household seems to have been afflicted with sickness: a daughter was close to death and he was himself 'very ill'. He none the less lived on until 1722, his burial at Harleston occurring on 19 Oct.[3]

[1] Baker, *Northampton*, i. 168; J. Isham, *Par. Reg. Extracts*, 10; PCC 21 Richmond. [2] *HMC Lords*, i. 187; Somerville, *Duchy of Lancaster*

Official Lists, 192, 194. [3] *Vis. London* (Harl. Soc. xcii), 4–5; *Northants. Past and Present*, vi. 30, 262; Baker, i. 168.

A. A. H.

ANDREWS, Sir Matthew (c.1630–1711), of Ashley House, Walton-on-Thames, Surr. and Mere, Wilts.

SHAFTESBURY   1679 (Oct.)–1681 (Mar.)
                             1689–1698

b. c.1630, 1st s. of Matthew Andrews, of Ironmonger Lane, London by Sarah, da. of Hugh Evance, clothworker, of London. m. bef. 1669, Anne (d. 1709), 1s. 3da. suc. fa. c.1643; kntd. 16 Apr. 1675.[1]

Freeman, Clothworkers' Co. 1652; member, Hon. Artillery Co. 1667, treasurer 1681–1703; freeman, E.I. Co. 1669, cttee. 1671–81 (with statutory intervals); er. bro. Trinity House 1680–d., master 1695–7, dep.–master 1697–9; gov. Christ's Hosp. by 1687.[2]

Sheriff, Wilts. 1676–7.

Commr. for preventing export of wool 1689–92; gent. of privy chamber 1689–1702; receiver of rents for manor of Mere 1693.[3]

Commr. public accts. 1691–4.

Andrews was a former merchant and shipowner who had started his career in India. His estate at Woodlands in Mere, some six miles from Shaftesbury, gave him an interest in the borough. Returned in 1690, he was classed as a Whig by Lord Carmarthen (Sir Thomas Osborne†). Andrews was appointed to many drafting committees in his career, often concerning matters of trade, especially those relating to the East India Company. He played a leading role in the abortive attempt to establish a commission of public accounts in 1690, being nominated to the drafting committee for a bill to appoint commissioners and reporting from the committee supervising their election by ballot (20 May). He himself was not chosen on this occasion, but when the bill was revived in the following session he came 5th in the poll with 119 votes. The commissionership carried a salary of £500 p.a. In December 1690 Andrews reported a bill to permit the employment of foreign seamen in English merchant ships, carrying it up to the Lords on the 23rd, and acted as a teller on 27 Dec. in favour of the bill for the speedier determination of elections. In April 1691 Robert Harley* classed him as a member of the Country party. In the 1691–2 session he helped to manage a local waterworks bill through the Commons, and told on 18 Feb. 1692 against the second reading of the Lords bill for the relief of London orphans. Appointed on 22 Feb. to examine

ANGUISH

William Fuller about his allegations of Jacobite plots, Andrews was sent to find Fuller's witnesses on the 23rd, reporting later the same day his failure to locate them. In the following session, during January and February 1693, he managed a bill to encourage the Greenland trade. In the 1693–4 session, he twice acted as a teller against the treason trials bill: on 14 Nov. against the first reading of the bill, and on 2 Jan. 1694 to terminate discussion in a committee of the whole by moving that the Speaker should resume the Chair. However, he was one of the Country Whigs who lost their places in the next ballot for commissioners of public accounts.[4]

Andrews successfully contested Shaftesbury in 1695, and continued to be involved in the preparation of legislation although he rarely managed any bills through the House. He was classed as 'doubtful' in a forecast of 31 Jan. 1696 over the proposed council of trade. He signed the Association in February, and in March voted with the Court to fix the price of guineas at 22s. On 25 Nov. he voted for the attainder of Sir John Fenwick†. Although involved in a local waterworks bill, in the 1697–8 session, his activity was curtailed by a leave of absence on 26 May 1698. He was listed as placeman in July 1698 and in another list in September was classed as a member of the Court party. He did not stand again for Parliament, probably because of advancing age. In 1710 he was listed as owning sufficient stock in the Bank of England to afford him a vote. Andrews died on 6 Mar. 1711 and was buried at Mere. A collector of paintings and china and something of a philanthropist, he had founded a school at Mere and made provision in his will for the salary of the schoolmaster and the upkeep of the premises.[5]

[1] Soc. of Genealogists, Boyd's London units 19529; PCC 32 Pile, 48 Young; *N. and Q.* ser. 10, v. 289; Hoare, *Wilts.* Mere, 24; *Le Neve's Knights* (Harl. Soc. viii), 298. [2] *Cal. Ct. Mins. E.I. Co.* ed. Sainsbury, viii. 209; ix. 30, 225; x. 302; xi. 40; W. R. Chaplin, *Trinity House*, 14–17, 58; G. A. Raikes, *Hist. Hon. Artillery Co.* ii. 477. [3] *Cal. Treas. Bks.* x. 350; Carlisle, *Privy Chamber*, 203; *Ancient Vellum Bk.* ed. Raikes, 109; info. from Prof. H. Horwitz. [4] Hoare, 24; *Cal. Treas. Bks.* x. 300–1, 1223; xviii. 134; xix. 114; *Cal. Treas. Pprs.* 1557–1696, p. 394; H. Horwitz, *Parl. and Pol. Wm. III*, 132, 140; Bath mss at Longleat House, Thynne pprs. 26, f. 341. [5] Hoare, 19; Egerton 3359 (unfol.); PCC 48 Young.

P. W.

ANGUISH see ALLIN

ANNESLEY

ANNESLEY, Hon. Arthur (c.1678–1737), of Farnborough, Hants; Bletchingdon, Oxon., and Knockgrenan, nr. Camolin, co. Wexford.

CAMBRIDGE UNIVERSITY 1702–18 Sept. 1710

b. c.1678, 3rd s. of James Annesley†, 2nd Earl of Anglesey, by Lady Elizabeth Manners, da. of John Manners†, 8th Earl of Rutland. *educ.* Eton c.1693–7; Magdalene, Camb. matric. 1698, MA 1699, fellow 1700. *m.* lic. 6 Jan. 1702, his cos. Mary (*d.* 1719), da. of Sir John Thompson, 1st Bt.*, 1st Baron Haversham, sis. of Maurice Thompson*, *s.p. suc.* bro. as 7th Earl of Anglesey and Visct. Valentia [I] 18 Sept. 1710.[1]

Gent. of privy chamber 1689–1702; jt. vice-treasurer and paymaster-gen. [I] Oct. 1710–16; PC 19 Oct. 1710; PC [I] 1711–*d.*; ld. justice Aug.–Sept. 1714.[2]

MP [I] 1703–10.

FRS 1704.

Commr. building 50 new churches 1711–15.[3]

Freeman, Drogheda 1712; high steward, Camb. Univ. 1722–*d.*; gov. co. Wexford 1727–*d.*[4]

Able, energetic, and ambitious to the point of ruthlessness, Annesley was also wilful and wayward: a formidable opponent but not always a reliable ally. In truth his talents were better suited to the political wilderness, which it was his ultimate destiny to inhabit, than the high office he evidently craved. In both the English and Irish Parliaments he proved to be a powerful orator with a simple message, giving trenchant expression to his party's prejudices, and making his name as 'the darling of the Church' and the scourge of Dissenters, the irony of which was not lost on those who remembered the Presbyterian sympathies of his grandfather and namesake, the 1st Earl of Anglesey. After a privileged upbringing in court circles, symbolized by service as a gentleman of the privy chamber, in which capacity he carried the canopy at King William's funeral, he made a brilliant reputation at Cambridge, publishing an edition of Catullus and other Latin poets while still an undergraduate. His political ideas may well have been formed at Magdalene, and before he had turned 25 he had already been chosen as one of the university's representatives in Parliament. Almost immediately he made his presence felt. Lord Spencer (Charles*) calculated his election as a 'loss' to the Whigs, a judgment borne out by Annesley's nomination on 4 Nov. 1702 to the drafting committee on the first occasional conformity bill. He was afterwards included in the committee of 10 Dec. to consider the seventh of the Lords' amendments to the bill, and on 13 Jan. 1703 was sent to the Upper House to request a conference on this subject. Although a teller on 9 Dec., with one of the

Members for the borough of Cambridge, against an amendment to the Cam navigation bill, most of his significant parliamentary activity in this first session concerned national rather than local issues. He reported on 7 Jan. 1703 from the committee to scrutinize the ballot for commissioners of accounts and the same day was a teller, on the Tory side, against recommitting the address in support of any increase in forces thought necessary, and to ask that the States General be required to put an end to all correspondence with France and Spain. Then on 13 Feb. 1703 he voted against agreeing with the Lords' amendments to the bill enlarging the time for taking the oath of abjuration. By the close of the session he was recognized as one of the more fluent and aggressive debaters among the younger generation of Tory Members, but, possibly because of a connexion with Secretary Nottingham (Daniel Finch†), to whom he looked for political leadership, his support seems to have been expected by the ministry.[5]

Prior to the resumption of Parliament in the autumn of 1703 Annesley went over to Ireland, where, returned to the house of commons in Dublin for his family's pocket borough, he took a prominent part in the early stages of the parliamentary session presided over by the new Tory viceroy, Ormond. As at Westminster he quickly achieved distinction among the spokesmen for the Church interest, harrying Whig politicians in revenge for the expulsion from the Irish parliament of his cousin Francis Annesley*, and making several telling interventions in debate, to denounce the Ulster Presbyterians as 'murderers' of Charles I, and to press for the revocation of the grant given by King William to Dissenting ministers, the *regium donum*. Back in London by 23 Nov. 1703, when he told against a motion for leave to print the Commons' votes, two days later he was named to the drafting committee for the second occasional conformity bill. On 7 Feb. 1704 he was appointed to the committee to prepare the address on Queen Anne's Bounty (subsequently reporting from the committee on 9 Feb.), and told in favour of going immediately into a committee of the whole House on the grants resumption bill. That he was now taking a position more openly critical of administration is suggested by his election (albeit in last place in the list) as a commissioner under the abortive public accounts bill of February 1704, and confirmed by his tellership on 10 Mar. against the recruiting bill. He had also served as a teller on 26 Feb. on a more private matter, for a clause on behalf of the bishop of Cloyne to be added as a rider to a bill for the relief of another Irish landowner from the effects of the Forfeitures Resumption Act, an example both of his willingness to promote the interests of his compatriots and of his devotion to the Anglican church in all its manifestations. He was forecast by Nottingham in March as a supporter of the government over its actions following the Scotch Plot. Given his history of enthusiasm for legislation to penalize Dissent, and in particular to put a stop to occasional conformity, he was named to the drafting committee for the third occasional conformity bill on 14 Nov., was naturally listed among those thought likely to support the Tack, voted for it or was absent on 28 Nov. and after the failure of this attempt, also told on 14 Dec. 1704 in favour of passing the bill. The ministerial reshuffle, by which Nottingham and other High Tories lost office, had long since freed him from any moral obligation to support Lord Godolphin's (Sidney†) ministry, and on 13 Jan. 1705 he was named to the drafting committee for a Tory place bill, 'that all persons, who are entitled by their offices to receive a benefit by public annual taxes to be granted, shall be incapable of sitting in this House, while they are in such offices'. A teller on the Tory side in a division on 26 Feb. 1705 on the Aylesbury case, he was appointed two days later as a manager for a conference with the Lords on this affair. Annesley's importance as a Tory politician was now such that efforts were mounted by the Whigs to impugn his loyalty to the Protestant succession, based on some alleged remarks of his in the Irish house of commons in 1703 to the effect that Parliament in England might at some future date decide to alter the Act of Settlement, to which he now retorted by claiming sole responsibility for the insertion into an address from the Dublin parliament of an affirmation of support for the succession of the Electress Sophia. More damaging, perhaps, were the attacks of satirists who denounced the violence of his speeches, his 'horrid language', 'raving throat' and 'bully tongue':

> A finished coxcomb, with assuming wit,
> In all but sense and manners he's complete;
> So furnished with the language of the town,
> He made our dunghill rhetoric all his own,
> All his endeavours to support the state,
> H' expresses in the style of Billingsgate.[6]

Annesley was one of the prime targets of the ministry's electioneering campaign in 1705. His place as a university representative was challenged by Godolphin's son Hon. Francis* and by none other than Isaac Newton*, who was knighted by the Queen when she visited Cambridge in May, an exercise interpreted by many observers to have been undertaken 'on purpose to turn Mr Annesley out'. The reason for this personal spite, according to one Tory, was that 'Mr Annesley last session made a speech in the House [of Commons] against my Lord Godolphin, and had the Parliament sat a week longer his lordship would certainly have been impeached'. At the general election itself no pains were spared by the treasurer, who sent down his own and the Queen's chaplain to vote for the ministerial candidates. Secretary of State Robert Harley* also canvassed college heads and fellows of his acquaintance, one of whom indignantly refuted allegations that Annesley was a 'turbulent' man: on the contrary, 'he is a scholar, and has been long of my acquaintance as such and has acquitted himself in all university business entrusted to him with great approbation'. The student body, too, reacted in Annesley's favour, and the election was marked by riotous undergraduates 'crying "No fanatic", "No occasional conformity"' against Godolphin and Newton. Annesley was returned in triumph at the top of the poll, and was duly classified as 'True Church' in a list of the new Parliament. The fact that cousin Francis was elected as well in 1705 makes it difficult henceforth always to be sure of Annesley's parliamentary activity. For example, we know that he voted against the Court candidate, John Smith I*, in the division on the Speaker, 25 Oct. 1705, but not whether he was the 'Mr Annesley' who had earlier spoken in favour of Smith's Tory opponent William Bromley II*, though given his greater prominence in the House he must count as the more likely of the two. In the same way he probably spoke on 4 Nov. on the bill from the Lords for the repeal of the Aliens Act, paving the way for the Tories' 'Hanover motion' (to invite over to England the heir presumptive to the throne) by pointing out the dangers of the succession not being yet decided in Scotland: it was, observed 'Annesley', 'not so easy to come from Han[over] as Scot[land]'. An Annesley was also a teller on the Tory side on 13 Nov. against a motion that the Coventry election petition be heard at the bar. On 8 Dec. 'Mr Annesley Irish', as Grey Neville* identified him, spoke in the debate on the Lords' resolution that the Church was not 'in danger' under the present administration. With heavy irony he agreed that 'the late Revol[ution]' had been 'a benefit': 'episco[pacy] in Scot[land]' had been 'abol[ished]', Presbyterianism had been 'restored' there and had moreover 'crept into Eng[land]'. Later in the same debate he intervened again, to answer a point raised by Lord Coningsby (Thomas*), a former Irish lord justice, who had reminded the House of the 800 loyal Ulster Presbyterian volunteers raised by Lord Granard for Charles II. Annesley acknowledged their contribution but wished to know the present 'designs' of 'the Scotch'. He then told against keeping the clause to stigmatize as an enemy to 'Queen, Church and kingdom' anyone 'going about to suggest' that the Church was in danger. The name Annesley figured frequently in the diarist's reports of the debates on the regency bill: on 11 Dec., during the controversy raised by Charles Caesar's* innuendoes against Lord Treasurer Godolphin; on 15 Jan. 1706, on a technical point arising from the arrangements proposed to be made on the Queen's death; and on 19 and 21 Jan., on further such details. One of the Annesleys had on 12 Jan. supported the motion for an instruction to the committee on the bill to insert a provision to secure the 'place clause' of the Act of Settlement, and over a month later, on 15 Feb., was a teller for postponing consideration of a Lords' amendment to this part of the bill, the so-called 'whimsical clause'. Other possible tellerships occurred on 13 Feb., for a Tory amendment to the recruiting bill, to prevent the 'irregular listing of men'; on 2 Mar., against a bill for the better regulation of charter and proprietary governments in America and for the encouragement of the Plantations trade; and on 8 Mar., against condemning the *Letter from Sir Rowland Gwynne* to the Earl of Stamford*, a pamphlet (in justification of the 'Hanover motion') which the ministry wished to burn. A much higher degree of probability attaches to his tellership against the Whig John Pedley in the Huntingdon election (22 Jan.), because of the possibility of a local (Cambridge) connexion with the case. Finally, both Annesleys were named as tellers, together, on 18 Mar., against proceeding on the report of the committee on the law reform bill. And responsibility for one bill may with confidence be assigned to Annesley rather than his cousin: that to make his Irish parliamentary constituency of New Ross a port for the exporting of wool to England, which he presented on 9 Jan. 1706 and subsequently managed through the House.[7]

In the next session, Annesley supported a Tory amendment moved on 6 Dec. 1706 which would have avoided committing Members to an acceptance of the Anglo-Scottish Union and would have 'left 'em free to argue against it' when the union bill was introduced. After two other Tories had proposed and seconded the amendment he 'more ingeniously spoke his and the sense of the other two in a few plain words', but without success. In the light of his loathing for Presbyterians, both in Ulster and in Scotland itself, it seems reasonable to credit him with consistent opposition to union, as manifested in three tellerships: on 28 Jan. 1707, in favour of an address requesting that the minutes of the 1702 union commission be laid before the House; on 22 Feb., for an instruction to the committee on the union bill to receive a clause guaranteeing that in future Englishmen would be free from any oath or test inconsistent with the religion and government of the Church of England, in the same way that the Scots had already been reassured as to their Kirk; and on 28 Feb., against passing the union bill in its final form. Two further tellerships probably belong in his biography: on 27 Jan. 1707, against a resolution approving the previous advancement of money under the heading 'extraordinary services', to go towards financing the war in Spain, one of many occasions on which Annesley's name appeared as a teller alongside that of his close political associate (Sir) Thomas Hanmer (4th Bt.)*, with whom he appears to have spoken in the debate; and on 1 Apr. following, against adjourning the report of the committee on the bill for securing the purchase of Cotton House for 'the public', in which again there was a Cambridgeshire connexion through the Cotton family. One speech was certainly his: in January, against the settlement on the Duke of Marlborough of a life annuity of £5,000. He 'spake mighty well against it in the House, and all sorts of people speaks well of him for it'.[8]

The last session of the 1705 Parliament was a particularly busy one for Annesley, as he was among the leaders of a powerful combined opposition to the ministry. He told on 10 Dec. 1707, when the land tax bill was reported, in a division over the inclusion of one John Brownell on the Cambridgeshire commission, and may have been a teller twice more during the proceedings on the bill on 12 Dec. In the crucial debate on 29 Jan. 1708 on the number of troops actually available in Spain at the time of the battle of Almanza, one of the Annesleys was a teller with Sir Thomas Hanmer against adjourning, and it was almost certainly Arthur who on 4 Mar. moved for a loyal address on the occasion of the Pretender's invasion attempt, to assure the Queen 'they would stand by her with their lives against the pretended Prince of Wales, and all other enemies at home and abroad', and who was then named to the committee for an address. This, however, was intended to dissociate the Tories from Jacobitism, not to demonstrate support for the ministry, and a month later Annesley was to be found vigorously opposing the motion for an address to thank Prince George as lord high admiral for his care in fitting out the fleet which had defeated the design of the invasion. Besides these high-political, set-piece debates, he also appears to have been involved in more mundane affairs. His many connexions with Oxford University make it likely that he was a teller on 19 Feb. against referring to a committee the petition of Sir Thomas Cookes Winford, 2nd Bt.*, for a bill to facilitate the charitable settlement in the will of the late Sir Thomas Cooke for the foundation of what was to become Worcester College, Oxford; and, despite the fact that his cousin Francis Annesley's legal training made Francis generally more useful as a sponsor of private bills, it may well have been Arthur who in February brought in a measure to assist one James Stopford to sell lands in Nottinghamshire, as this was the name of one of his neighbouring landowners in county Wexford and a fellow Tory member of the Irish parliament.[9]

Re-elected unopposed for the university in the general election of 1708, Annesley was marked as a Tory and as a Tacker respectively in two parliamentary lists of that year. There were two tellerships of considerable political significance, in which it is fair to assume that Arthur rather than Francis was the Annesley involved: on 20 Jan., in favour of (Sir) Simon Harcourt I* in the notorious Abingdon election case; and on 7 Mar., with Sir Thomas Hanmer, against passing the naturalization bill. He may also have told on 14 Apr., against an amendment to the bill preserving the rights of patrons to advowsons, and assisted in the management of the reintroduced private bill for James Stopford. In speeches he continued to bark defiance at the ministry. When Members were debating Treasury management but were showing some reluctance to criticize Godolphin explicitly, Annesley

> said he could not find why gentlemen should be shy in naming the T[reasure]r, for he would take it upon him to say, for all the great encomiums that some gentlemen were continually making upon him, that never was the Treasury worse managed. What, to have a million of money paid by the country, and not paid into the Treasury by the receivers, was strange management.

During the following summer he paid a lengthy visit to Lord Nottingham at Burley, where they were joined by Hanmer. Nottingham described Annesley's 'good company' as 'the best part of the entertainment here'. At the same time Annesley kept up his friendly acquaintance with Robert Harley, on one occasion writing from Burley to hint at the boredom his rustication had engendered, which showed the temperament of the politician. As might have been expected he was forward in defence of Dr Sacheverell. Whatever his views on the Revolution and the succession (and, unlike his elder brother, he was never seriously accounted a Jacobite by his own side), he would naturally come to the aid of an Anglican parson threatened by the Whigs. He had, after all, been one of the few

Tories in the Commons to defend Bishop Blackall's 1708 sermon in justification of the principle of non-resistance, and he took a similar stand in December 1709, when the notion of impeaching Sacheverell was first aired. He was, again, one of only a handful of Tories who opposed the motion to impeach, though at this stage very sparingly, none of them excusing the paragraphs, but desiring only that the matter might be referred to the committee of religion, or else one appointed on purpose, who might read the sermons at length; or else they did not think they could pass a fair judgment. Later, when opposition gathered strength, he spoke with other Tories on 11 Jan. in a more concerted effort to recommit the articles, and was listed among those who had voted against the impeachment. Probably the 'Mr Annesley' included on 25 Jan. 1710 in a drafting committee for a place bill, he was a teller with Hanmer on 15 Feb. against making an address to request the Queen to send over the Duke of Marlborough to attend the peace negotiations. In the debate on the motion for the address he had made 'a very warm speech' denouncing the Duke: to request his despatch to Holland would be 'exalting that man whose pride was already intolerable, setting him above the Crown, which would make us the most abject of slaves, and that 'twas insulting the sovereign to prescribe whom she should employ in the treaty of peace'. On 2 Mar. he was almost certainly the Annesley who told for an amendment to an address for the suppression of the 'present tumults' which would have added 'republicans' to the list of 'enemies to the Queen's table and government' who were held to be responsible for fomenting the disturbances. The following day he intervened to forestall a Whig proposal for a bill 'for the security of the Church'. Then on 24 Mar. he supported William Bromley II's motion for an address for a fast 'to deprecate the divine vengeance' to be apprehended from Parliament's failure to put a stop to what was viewed as the torrent of blasphemy, from the press and in some cases from the pulpit. He answered Whig comments to the effect that the ministry had more urgent things to do than 'meddle in matters of that nature' by commenting, 'it must give the world a strange idea of a ministry that thought it below them to show any concern for the honour of the great God'. His defence of Dr Sacheverell, of the Church of England, and of orthodox Christianity itself only served to increase his popularity among High Churchmen in Cambridge, and, conversely, the hostility of Whig sympathizers, as was shown by a curious incident in July 1710 when Annesley, supping with some university cronies in the course of a visit to his constituency, fell foul of a humourless Whig proctor, whose officious demands to the revellers to repair to their colleges were answered by banter and toasts to Dr Sacheverell, and who subsequently entered a formal complaint against their insouciant treatment of him. Although it made a stir in the pamphlet press, the affair came to nothing, and, as a dissolution loomed, Annesley's position in regard to his re-election seemed stronger than ever. Were he to stand again 'there was no probability that anyone would dare to oppose him'. At Westminster too, his prospects were rosy. As the likelihood of a ministerial revolution increased, his was one of the names that cropped up repeatedly when new appointments were rumoured, and Robert Harley certainly regarded him as one of the Tory Members for whom it would be essential to provide. He was, however, in this context still to some degree in the shadow of his elder brother, and while the Earl of Anglesey was being considered as a potential secretary of state, Annesley was thought of by Harley for some minor post, such as the mastership of the jewel office.[10]

His brother's sudden death in September 1710 changed Annesley's political status and his expectations. He succeeded to the title as Earl of Anglesey, and to the lucrative post of vice-treasurer of Ireland (albeit held jointly) which his brother had been given as a consolation prize for not achieving one of the great offices of state on the change of ministry. Anglesey could now conceive of himself as a candidate for the highest honours, and evidently did. Furthermore, although removed to the company of his seniors in the Upper House, he did not long remain a small fish in that bigger pool. His oratorical talents and sheer force of personality rapidly established him as a figure to be reckoned with. At the same time he did not lose his influence in the Commons. He 'took upon him the sole direction of the election' at Cambridge University, securing the return of 'his creature' Thomas Paske*, one of a number of Members in the Parliaments of 1710 and 1713 who can be regarded, and indeed were regarded by contemporaries, as followers of Anglesey. Like the majority of his fellow Tories, he seems to have been prepared at the outset of the 1710–14 ministry to give Robert Harley (subsequently Earl of Oxford) the benefit of any doubts he himself might have entertained. Though anxious to see the pursuance of a thoroughly Tory policy, in reference both to men and measures, he remained close to the ministers during the first session of the 1710 Parliament, being on particularly good terms with Henry St. John II*. He may have been privately sympathetic to the frustration felt by the October Club, and in February 1711 supported an abortive bill for the repeal of the Naturalization Act of 1709, but otherwise caused the ministry little public embarrassment. And after spending the autumn of 1711 at the Irish parliament he returned to Westminster almost as an enthusiastic ministerial loyalist, presumably as a result of observing the Duke of Ormond's failures as viceroy in Dublin and pluming himself as the natural and inevitable replacement. Indeed it seems likely that his ambition to be lord lieutenant more than any other factor dictated his political conduct over the next three years. During the winter of 1711–12 he canvassed and spoke for the administration, occasionally with excessive zeal, and the following year was brought into the inner circle of Oxford's cronies. He did not, however, receive any tangible reward for himself, and refused to regard a few favours for his friends and adherents as adequate compensation. In particular, Oxford's slowness in replacing Ormond in the Irish viceroyalty rankled with him, and when eventually it was decided that Ormond would be removed, the new lord lieutenant was not Anglesey after all but a moderate Whig, the Duke of Shrewsbury. Disappointed ambition was almost certainly behind his sharp turn away from the Court in June 1713, when he led the opposition in the Lords to the treaty of commerce with France and deployed his squadron of followers in the Commons against the treaty. Certainly he was not yet prepared to make a complete break with the ministry and follow Nottingham over to the Whigs. He listened to whatever offers Oxford and St. John (now Lord Bolingbroke) made to him without committing himself to either man, and in the autumn of 1713 did what he could to influence the direction of the ministry's Irish policy, attending Shrewsbury's Irish parliament, and both there and at the Irish privy council acted effectively to undermine the viceroy's management by encouraging the intransigence of hotter Tories, some of whom, most notably the Irish lord chancellor Sir Constantine Phipps, were almost open Jacobites. He returned to England the undisputed head of the Tory interest in Ireland, and courted by all factions at Westminster. Sir John Perceval, 5th Bt.[†], who had observed at close quarters his spoiling game in Ireland, depicted him at this time as avaricious and ambitious 'of power and honour', though 'very eloquent and enterprising' and possessed of a 'working head'. He also considered Anglesey 'violent' in party matters and one who would 'raise the prerogative to a high pitch'. This, however, may have been a somewhat unjust criticism, derived from Perceval's disgust at what was for Anglesey a political tactic rather than a point of principle, namely his assertion of the power of the Irish privy council to interfere in municipal affairs, especially in the case of the dispute over the Dublin mayoralty, on which Shrewsbury had vainly sought to reach a compromise. It might also be argued that Anglesey was always rather more concerned with honour than money *per se*, and indeed affected to despise mercenary motives when it suited him to do so. However, the overall accuracy of Perceval's description cannot seriously be questioned. He also summed up Anglesey's political position in early 1714:

> being at the head of the High Church clergy, he never would hearken to a coalition with the Whigs because the Dissenters were protected by them, and therefore though he resented the being by the ministry left out of their most private councils, yet he often concealed his temper, and left a door open for reunion with them.

In the 1714 Parliament Anglesey followed an erratic path, determined by his hope or despair at prospects of achieving the Irish viceroyalty for himself and the adoption of 'steady and vigorous measures' to strengthen 'the Church interest' in both kingdoms. Thus he 'tacked' first towards Lord Oxford; then early in April declared himself against the ministry in the 'succession in danger' debate and, for a spell, co-operated with the Whig and Nottinghamite opposition; and at last, after some wavering, joined with Bolingbroke, in the hope that Oxford 'was to have terms put upon him, and a junto'. Their alliance was symbolized by the schism bill, a measure dear to Anglesey's heart and made even more precious in his eyes by the addition of a clause extending the provisions to cover Ireland, an amendment Anglesey had brought in himself. His speech in favour of the bill was characteristic. He declared:

> that the Dissenters were equally dangerous both to Church and state; that they were irreconcilable enemies to the established Church . . . and . . . had rendered themselves unworthy of the indulgence the Church of England granted them at the Revolution.

Outside Parliament he expressed himself even more violently, reportedly saying in a coffee-house that there was no difference between Presbyterians and papists, and that 'jumbled together they would make an excellent salad for the devil'. From Bolingbroke, Anglesey was supposed to have received a promise of the lord lieutenancy of Ireland, but all that Bolingbroke was in fact able to procure was a commission for him to remodel the Irish army, presumably so as to give the Tories more of a chance to bargain with would-be successors when Queen Anne died. It came too late, however, and before he reached Dublin with his commission the Queen was dead.[11]

Fortunately for Anglesey, this last *volte-face* occurred too late to prevent him from taking his place as one of the regents appointed to govern the kingdom until the arrival of King George. His parliamentary stand over the succession in April had created an impression of him as the leader of the 'Hanoverian Tories', and also enabled him to secure the favour of the electoral family, to whom he had written in May 1714, probably with sincerity:

> The same principles of loyalty and obedience which made me a faithful and, I hope, good subject to her Majesty must needs tie me down a firm and zealous servant to the Hanover succession, as the only means (whenever we shall be deprived of our good and gracious sovereign) to repair so great a loss; and to secure and preserve to these nations our invaluable constitution in Church and state.

When the King arrived, Anglesey worked hard to cultivate this good opinion, and, unlike some other Hanoverian Tories, complied with whatever the new Whig ministry demanded. However, the cracks soon began to show. As early as 19 Aug. 1714 Defoe's letter in the *Flying Post* exposed the details of the commission to purge the Irish army and accused Anglesey of Jacobitism. Author and publisher were arrested and the story suppressed, but the seeds of suspicion had been planted. Harassment from Whig colleagues kept up the pressure and by March 1715 it was reported that Anglesey was 'out of court' and 'raging'. In July he made a speech in the Lords against Oxford's impeachment, recommending mercy and claiming, perhaps tactlessly, that 'such cruel proceedings would shake the sceptre in the King's hand'. The last straw, as far as the Court was concerned, would appear to have been some resolutions passed by the Irish house of commons in January 1716 condemning Anglesey as an enemy to the Protestant succession and a Jacobite, for his role in advising a prorogation of the Irish parliament in 1714 and the 'breaking' of the Irish army. Engineered by a faction among the Irish Whigs, these resolutions were brought in without any prior debate or inquiry, proceedings so irregular that, as one of the chief secretaries wrote, 'had it been against any person but one so generally hated and to that degree he is here, it must have miscarried'. As was expected, their communication to London was swiftly followed by Anglesey's dismissal from office. His own version of what had happened implied that he had left the administration voluntarily, but still admitted that he had been to some degree prepared to abandon his friends. If the court had called the servants of the late Queen to account and had stopped there (he told Bolingbroke) he must have considered himself a judge, and have acted according to his conscience on what should have appeared to him; but that war had been declared on the whole Tory party, and that now the state of things was altered.[12]

Anglesey remained a strong voice on the opposition benches after 1716, though very much as a Hanoverian Tory, and to begin with alongside Nottingham, whose anti-Socinian amendment to the bill of 1718 repealing the Occasional Conformity and Schism Acts he strongly supported. There was talk that he might return to office in a ministerial reconstruction in 1722, and he was approached again in 1725. The Jacobites in exile considered that he 'stands fairest to be at the head of the Tories' but were not encouraged to contact him. On the death of George I he appears to have recommended to the surviving body of Irish Tories that they come to terms with the Court, and himself secured the governorship of county Wexford, but nothing else. Nor did he lose his own influence at Cambridge University, where he was chosen high steward unanimously in 1722.[13]

Anglesey died on 31 Mar. 1737, at his house at Farnborough, and was buried in the parish church. 'He was esteemed the greatest orator of the present age', ran one public tribute, 'and whenever his lordship spoke ... the House of Lords was crowded to hear him'. Perceval, now Lord Egmont, whose earlier hostility had mellowed, wrote of him:

> He was in principle a High Churchman, but no Jacobite, and a man of strict virtue and honour, but a hard drinker, which very many years ago drew on the gout, of which he died at last. He had fine parts, was a remarkably good speaker in Parliament, and what he said was witty, bold and from the heart.

To his personal distress his entailed estates in Ireland and England, worth over £7,000 a year, and the Anglesey and Valentia titles were to descend to persons he despised: the lands to Charles Annesley, one of the 'Battle-axe guards' in Dublin; the earldoms and viscountcy to another cousin, Richard Annesley, Lord Altham, a half-pay officer and adventurer. At the same time 'what the law gave him the disposal of he would leave to the most worthy', and he therefore bequeathed his Oxfordshire estates and 'considerable' personalty to his cousin Francis. Minor beneficiaries under the will (which had been drawn up in 1735) included the brothers Hon. Andrews* and Hon. Dixie Windsor*, while another 'whimsical' or 'Hanoverian' Tory from Queen Anne's reign, Richard Shuttleworth*, had acted as a witness.[14]

[1] *Reg. of Deeds: Abstracts of Wills* (Irish Mss Commn.), i. 242; *Eton Coll. Reg.* ed. Sterry, 8. [2] Info. from Prof. R. O. Bucholz; *Cal. Treas. Bks.* xxv. 294; xxx. 105; Luttrell, *Brief Relation*, v. 635, 644. [3] E. G. W. Bill, *Q. Anne Churches*, p. xxiii; *Recs. R. Soc.* (1940), p. 389. [4] *Drogheda Corp. Council Bk.* ed. Gogarty, i. 315. [5] G. Holmes, *Pol.*

in Age of Anne, 278–9; Bodl. Ballard 36, f. 70; *Poems on Affairs of State* ed. Ellis, vii. 115–16; *Cal. Treas. Bks.* xvii. 198; *Hearne Colls.* xi. 435, 451; Boyer, *Anne Annals*, i. 138; Calamy, *Life*, i. 465; Bath mss at Longleat House, Portland misc. pprs. Ld. Godolphin to Robert Harley, 'Saturday at noon'. [6]*CSP Dom.* 1703–4, pp. 141, 198; Add. 28932, f. 101; Surr. RO (Guildford), Midleton mss 1248/2, ff. 129, 131–2, 197, 199; 1248/4, f. 360; *Poems on Affairs of State*, 115–16. [7]*Newton Corresp.* iv. 439; Trinity, Dublin, Lyons (King) mss 2002/1230, Francis Annesley to Abp. King [1705]; W. A. Speck, *Tory and Whig*, 101, 107; Bodl. Carte 244, f. 58; *HMC Portland*, iv. 179; J. Gascoigne, *Camb. in Age of Enlightenment*, 96–97; *Bull. IHR*, xxxvii. 29; Cobbett, *Parlty. Hist.* vi. 450; *Cam. Misc.* xxiii. 41, 45, 47–48, 53, 62, 70, 73, 81. [8]Anglesey mss at Plas Newydd, Roger Ackerley to Ld. Paget, 6 Dec. [1704]; Nottingham Univ. Lib. Mellish mss, [William Wrightson*] to Joseph Mellish, 16 Jan. 1706[–7]; G. Sitwell, *Letters of Sitwells and Sacheverells*, ii. 47. [9]Bodl. Ballard 10, f. 169; *Vernon–Shrewsbury Letters*, iii. 365; *HMC Portland*, iv. 480; *Addison Letters*, 106; Hayton thesis, 342. [10]*Wentworth Pprs*. 77–78, 110; Add. 61459, f. 163; *Hanmer Corresp.* 123; Leics. RO, Finch mss, Ld. Nottingham to Ld. Finch (Daniel*), 29 Aug. 1709; Add. 70282, Annesley to Harley, 6 Sept. 1709; 70332, memo. by Harley, 12 Sept. 1710; 70219, Thomas Conyers* to Harley, 18 June 1710; 57861, f. 151; Huntington Lib. Stowe mss 58(5), p. 124; 57(4), pp. 95–96; *Lockhart Pprs.* i. 318, 481; *Hearne Colls.* ii. 329; G. Holmes, *Trial of Sacheverell*, 90, 100–1; *HMC Portland*, iv. 539; Yale Univ. Beinecke Lib. Osborn mss, 'Acct. of Trial of Dr Sacheverell', 3 Mar. 1710; *Camb. under Q. Anne* ed. Mayor, 456–69; Nichols, *Lit. Anec.* i. 159; C. H. Cooper, *Annals of Camb.* iv. 99–100; *The Univ. of Camb. Vindicated* (1710), pp. 21–35; Bagot mss at Levens Hall, Edward Harvey* to James Grahme*, 12 July 1710; *HMC Mar and Kellie*, 484. [11]Churchill Coll. Camb. Erle mss 2/12, f. 33, James Craggs I* to [Thomas Erle*], 19 Sept. 1710; Boyer, ix. 243; *HMC Portland*, iv. 605–6; Holmes, *Pol. in Age of Anne*, 39–40, 278–81; K. Feiling, *Tory Party*, 435, 446, 450, 470; *Party and Management in Parl.* ed. C. Jones, 135, 143, 153; *Swift Stella*, i. 114, 240; ii. 584, 599; *Nicolson Diaries* ed. Jones and Holmes, 542; *Irish Hist. Stud.* xxii. 200–13; NSA, Kreienberg despatch 11 Dec. 1711; *Wentworth Pprs*. 254–5, 276–7, 357, 366–8, 371, 406; Cobbett, vi. 1037, 1330, 1335, 1352; H. Horwitz, *Revolution Politicks*, 236, 240, 242; Add. 70331, canvassing list [c. Jan. 1712]; 70262, Horatio Walpole I* to Oxford, 11 July [1712]; 70282, Anglesey to same, 8 July 1712; 47072, f. 86; 47087, ff. 56–57, 61–62, 64; Luttrell, vi. 715; *Hanmer Corresp.* 34; *HMC Portland*, v. 403, 467–8; Hayton thesis, 247, 252–4; *Swift Corresp.* ed. Williams, ii. 8–9; *Lockhart Letters* ed. Szechi, 93, 98; *HMC Polwarth*, i. 18; *HMC Kenyon*, 455–6; *Sir David Hamilton Diary* ed. Roberts, 63; Midleton mss 1248/3, f. 187. [12]G. M. Trevelyan, *Eng. under Q. Anne*, iii. 311; Burnet, v. 339; *Hanmer Corresp.* 57, 59–60; Stowe 227, f. 21; C. S. King, *A Great Abp. of Dublin*, 164; *Defoe Letters*, 447–8; L. Colley, *In Defiance of Oligarchy*, 181; *HMC Portland*, v. 508, 513; Hayton thesis, 305–6; Add. 61640, ff. 78, 81. [13]*HMC Portland*, v. 574; *HMC Carlisle*, 31; *HMC 5th Rep*. 189–90; Colley, 206; RA, Stuart mss 70/107, 71/137; *Penal Era and Golden Age* ed. Bartlett and Hayton, 46; *HMC Dartmouth*, iii. 55; Add. 32457, f. 5; Gascoigne, 96. [14]*Gent. Mag.* 1737, p. 252; Boyer, *Pol. State*, liii. 429; *HMC Egmont Diary*, iii. 387–8; T. Prior, *A List of the Absentees of Ire.* (1730), p. 5; Add. 28050, f. 149; *Reg. of Deeds: Abstracts of Wills*, 242.

D. W. H.

ANNESLEY, Francis (1663–1750), of Lincoln's Inn Fields, Mdx. and Thorganby, Yorks.

PRESTON	1705–1708
WESTBURY	1708–1715, 28 Mar.–1 June 1715, 1722–1734

bap. 24 Oct. 1663, 1st s. of Hon. Francis Annesley of Castlewellan, co. Down (6th s. of Francis Annesley†, 1st Visct. Valentia [I]) by Deborah, da. of Henry Jones, bp. of Meath. *educ*. Trinity, Dublin 1679, BA 1682, LL.B. and LL.D. 1725; I. Temple 1684, called 1690, bencher 1713. *m*. (1) 5 July 1695, Elizabeth, da. of Joseph Martin*, 7s. 2da.; (2) July 1732, Elizabeth (*d*. 20 May 1736), da. of John Cropley of Rochester, Kent, wid. of William Gomeldon of Summerfield Hall, Kent, *s.p.*; (3) 31 Aug. 1737, Sarah, da. of William Sloane of Portsmouth, Hants, wid. of Sir Richard Fowler, 2nd Bt., of Harnage Grange, Salop, *s.p. suc.* fa. aft. 1689; cos. Hon. Arthur Annesley* in personal and unentailed estates 1737.[1]

MP [I] 1692–9, 27 Aug.–28 Sept. 1703, 1713–14.

Commr. inquiry into forfeited estates in Ire. 1699–1700, trustee for sale 1700–3; commr. building 50 new churches 1711–15, 1727, taking subscriptions to S. Sea Co. 1711; public accts. 1711–14.[2]

Dir. New E.I. Co. 1700.

Freeman, Preston 1705.[3]

Trustee, Cottonian lib. by 1738.[4]

The share of his grandfather's estate that Annesley eventually inherited, though substantial enough in Irish terms to rank him among the greater gentry of county Down, was insufficient for the needs of an English country squire (being estimated at between £500 and £1,000 p.a.), and certainly did not deter him from seeking a fortune by other means. Marriage offered opportunities, and after unsuccessful negotiations with a neighbouring family, the Rawdons of Moira, he made an advantageous match in 1695 with the daughter of a rising London merchant, Joseph Martin. Legal education offered another avenue, especially inviting to a man of Annesley's quickness of mind and evident talent for public speaking, and after taking his degree at Trinity, Dublin, he was entered at an English inn of court. He then rapidly embarked upon a career at the bar, and in the public life of his native Ireland. His roots in the planter society of east Ulster determined the development of his political attitudes, which were a compound of strong sectarian prejudices: on the one hand fear and hatred of popery, on the other suspicion and resentment of the ever-increasing local influence of immigrant Scots Presbyterians. Thus he was at first a resolute Williamite, and in the Irish context a kind of 'Country Whig', but shifted towards a Tory position in the 1690s as the leading Irish Whigs abandoned their 'country' principles and he himself began to entertain serious apprehensions of an imminent Presbyterian coup. During the Revolution, while his father raised troops for the voluntary Protestant associations in the north of Ireland that kept up a resistance to King

James, Annesley himself seems to have remained in London, in contact with other exiled and temporarily impoverished Irish Protestants, whose bitter sense of grievance was to make them advocates of a vindictive anti-Jacobite and anti-Catholic strategy when they returned to Dublin after the war. In the short-lived Irish parliament of 1692 he joined his voice to those calling for a more vigorous promotion of Protestant interests and inquiries into corruption, and after the prorogation he attended the lord lieutenant, Lord Sidney (Henry†), together with other prominent parliamentary critics (several of them also from county Down) to request permission to go to England to place their various complaints before the King and Queen. He was not, however, among the Irish witnesses called by the English House of Commons inquiry in 1692–3 into mismanagements, or to give evidence in the impeachments at Westminster the following session of lords justices Porter (Sir Charles*) and Coningsby (Thomas*). The 'Francis Annesley' who was in attendance on both occasions was his cousin and namesake of Ballysonan, co. Kildare. As yet he seems to have had few contacts of his own in the English Parliament, relying instead on the connexions made by the more senior 'Country' politicians from his own locality, men like James Hamilton of Bangor and Hamilton's namesake of Tollymore, who were much nearer to the 'Country Whig' opposition than to the emergent Whig Junto. In consequence, he was not taken into office in 1694–5 along with the Junto's friends by the new Whig lord deputy, Lord Capell (Hon. Sir Henry*), and while some of his former comrades swallowed their principles and argued the ministerial line in the next Irish parliamentary session of 1695–6 he continued in opposition. Indeed, he was the unsuccessful 'Country' candidate for the speakership. The issue which exercised him most was the so-called 'sole right' of the Irish house of commons to initiate supply bills, and during this session he established himself as one of the leaders of the 'sole right party', so much so that Capell personally intervened to prevent his name being added to the Irish privy council as part of a further attempt to buy off opposition. According to the deputy, Annesley and one Colonel Eyre were 'the two noisy voters' in the entire session, 'and likewise the great promoters in the house of commons of all things that diminished the prerogatives of the crown and abated the King's revenue'.[5]

At this stage Annesley's connexions and political allies were still staunchly Whig. His closest collaborators in the Irish parliament were Hamilton of Tollymore, who was a relative of Lord Monmouth, and James Sloane*. He was also on good terms with Bishop King of Derry. Moreover, his marriage to the daughter of one of the merchants associated with the establishment of the New East India Company, into which Annesley was brought as a founding director, drew him into the circle of Whiggish 'moneyed men'. Nevertheless he moved gradually and inexorably towards the Tories. Still in opposition in the Irish parliament in 1697 and 1698, and occasionally 'violent' in his denunciations of the Court, he found himself working more and more with Irish Tories rather than Whigs, and in his pursuit of patriotic issues, such as the assertion of the appellate jurisdiction of the Irish house of lords in the case of the bishop of Derry against the Irish Society of London, in which he acted as counsel for the bishop, he came inevitably into open conflict with the Junto ministry. Although he resisted urgent requests to attend parliament in Dublin in the winter of 1698–9, he maintained his close connexions with 'patriots' like Bishop King and tried to persuade Irish MPs to send 'agents' to England to present their grievances. This whole process came to a head through his involvement in the resumption of the Irish forfeited estates. As a prominent 'patriot' in the Irish parliament, and one who had already broached the question of the resumption of the Irish grants (and Lord Portland's in particular) 'as a fund' for the use of 'the public', he was an obvious choice as one of the commissioners of inquiry chosen by the English Commons in February 1699, and indeed headed the ballot. Appropriately, it was he who eventually presented the commissioners' report on 15 Dec. following. In the parliamentary row which then ensued over party-political bias and English interference in the commissioners' work it emerged that he had been one of the most insistent advocates of the inclusion in the report of the grant of King James's personal estate to William's reputed mistress, Lady Orkney, and that he had received letters from various English MPs during his time as a commissioner, notably from Simon Harcourt I and Arthur Moore, encouraging him in his militancy. When trustees were elected in March 1700 to supervise the resumption and sale of the forfeitures he again headed the ballot, and proved himself not only diligent but 'pugnacious', the only trustee that the Whiggish lord chancellor of Ireland, John Methuen*, found personally difficult. Significantly, it was Annesley who brought over the trustees' report to Parliament in March 1701, and who attended the Commons both later that year and in February 1702 to answer questions and deliver further papers. While at Westminster he combined his official responsibilities as a trustee with a less formal role as adviser to and solicitor for various individuals with petitions to place before the Commons requesting legislative exemption from the effects of the Resumption Act, notably Anglican dignitaries such as the bishop of Cloyne, and of course Bishop King, whose pet scheme for a restoration to the Church of Ireland of the forfeited impropriations he did his best to forward. By 1702 he was exhausted: 'I own ingenuously to your lordship', he confessed to King in September of that year, 'that the three last years of my life have made me 15 years older than I otherwise should have been, and [have been] the least profitable to me in any respect.' The worst of it was that he had become identified not just with the Tory politicians in England who had been responsible for the passage of the Resumption Act and who continued to act as patrons of the trustees, but with the wave of anti-Irish sentiment that the controversy over the trust had aroused in England. When Queen Anne's first Irish parliament met in 1703 he felt that backlash personally, being expelled from the house of commons there on the grounds that a passage in the first paragraph of the trustees' report, for which he was held to be responsible, had 'misrepresented and traduced' the Protestant freeholders of Ireland. There was considerable irony in the fact that Annesley, himself a noted patriot in former sessions, had now fallen victim to an onset of patriotic enthusiasm, but party animosities also obtruded, and his Tory connexions proved a considerable liability, even his ties to the new viceroy, Ormond, who proved unable to protect him from the vindictiveness of Irish Whigs and of 'Country' members in general.[6]

Although Annesley continued to think of the Anglo-Irish rather than the English as his 'countrymen' and to maintain professional as well as personal interests in Ireland, the affair of the forfeitures trust marked a turning point in his career, and henceforth he made Westminster rather than Dublin the centre of his ambitions. At first he acted as an English agent for his Irish patrons, soliciting the passage of Irish bills through the Privy Council on behalf of Ormond's administration, and forwarding the parliamentary concerns of such long-standing clients as Bishop King and Bishop Crowe of Cloyne. Then in 1705 he secured election to the English House of Commons, obtaining the support of his old friend Lord Gower (Sir John Leveson Gower, 5th Bt.*) and, through the intercession of his cousin Lord Anglesey, that of the Duke of Hamilton, their combined support securing Annesley's return. He already had an English country seat, at Thorganby in the East Riding of Yorkshire, which his family had acquired in the 1640s, and before long began to make other purchases in the vicinity in order to establish himself more firmly in England. To observers at Westminster, however, and in particular Grey Neville* the parliamentary diarist of the 1705–6 session, he may well have been thought of as 'Mr Annesley Irish', if for no other reason than to distinguish him from Lord Anglesey's brother, Hon. Arthur Annesley, another High Tory with a powerful aversion to Dissenters, with whom his parliamentary career was to be closely entangled. In his first session Annesley, who had been listed as a 'Churchman' in an analysis of the new Parliament and whose election had been accounted a 'loss' by Lord Sunderland (Charles, Lord Spencer*), voted against John Smith I in the division on the Speaker, 25 Oct. 1705 and acted as a teller on 18 Mar. 1706, with his cousin Arthur, against proceeding on the report of the committee on the bill for reform of the legal process. The conclusion later that year of the negotiations for an Anglo-Scottish union raised his hackles. In part, he viewed it as a party-political job: the Scottish peers and Members at Westminster would represent 'so many dead votes one way', which would be 'a great stroke in the legislature'. Then there was the patent neglect of Irish interests, and the danger that preferential status for Scottish trade and manufacture would imperil the Irish economy. Finally, he feared the consequences for religion. Since the Kirk of Scotland was accepted as the establishment in North Britain, and indeed was termed in the bill of union 'the Protestant church', what, he asked a correspondent, 'is become of the mission?'. More particularly, he supposed that once the Union was passed, 'those of the established religion in Scotland' would have 'all imaginable countenance in Ireland as well as in England'. His own devotion to the Established Church, manifest at local level in his financing of the partial rebuilding of, and gifts of plate to, Thorganby parish church and in plans for rebuilding and for the foundation of a charity school in 'my own town' in county Down, was reflected in Parliament in his painstaking management of Bishop King's Irish forfeited impropriations bill, which he and Lord Coningsby successfully piloted through the Commons in March and April 1707, and this despite the fact that he was wounded in a duel during its progress. Overseas trade was another abiding concern, probably because of his father-in-law, and it is therefore likely that he rather than his cousin acted as a teller on 15 Apr. 1707 against an address to the Queen to act 'to recover' the Newfoundland trade. In the following session Annesley petitioned Parliament for relief in a dispute with the Irish MP Robert Dixon over the possession of an Irish forfeited estate Annesley had purchased in 1702. A bill for this purpose proceeded through the Commons, only to be rejected in the Lords in February 1708.[7]

In the less favourable political climate of 1708, with Leveson Gower replaced as chancellor of the duchy of Lancaster by the Whig 10th Earl of Derby (Hon. James Stanley*), Annesley switched to the Wiltshire constituency of Westbury, pocket borough of the Tory Earl of Abingdon (Montagu Venables-Bertie*), with whom he was for a long time both personally and professionally associated. He was classed as a Tory in a parliamentary list dating from early in the year, and, indeed, so pronounced had his High Church sympathies become that in September he wrote to Bishop King to appeal for financial assistance to the nonjuring bishop of Kilmore, Thomas Sheridan, whom he had discovered living in penury. On 5 Mar. 1709 he acted as a teller in a party matter, in favour of recommitting the report on an alleged breach of privilege committed against the Whig George Duckett. Having brought in a bill to make two Dutch-built vessels 'free ships', he told for the bill on 5 Apr., and his standing in the law points to his having served as a teller again ten days later, in favour of hearing a petition from the clerks of enrolment in Chancery against a bill to establish a public registry of deeds in Middlesex. Predictably, he was listed as having voted in early 1710 against the impeachment of Dr Sacheverell.[8]

Although re-elected without any real difficulty at Westbury in 1710, Annesley tried again at Preston in the same general election, but was unsuccessful. Marked as a Tory in the 'Hanover list', and recognized by fellow Tories as 'a very honest gentleman', he was optimistic as to what the incoming ministry might be able to achieve. 'I hope the power as it is again lodged in the crown will be there preserved from ever falling again into its merciless adversaries' hands' he wrote to an Irish correspondent. More particularly he hoped, as he had done since 1707, for 'a safe, honourable and lasting peace', concluded as quickly as possible so that the economy of the kingdom could recover and 'we shall once more see happy days'. At the same time, he recognized that, as he put it, 'a supply of treasure is the most difficult part of the ministry's work'. It was thought possible that he might be included in the new customs commission envisaged for Ireland, but nothing came of these rumours, and without an appointment of any kind other than his inclusion in a new commission of the peace for Middlesex, he quickly showed himself among the more aggressive of Tory back-benchers. As the only 'Mr Annesley' then in the Commons, his career there can be followed with more certainty. He acted as a teller on 2 Dec. 1710 in favour of hearing the merits of the Stafford election at the bar of the House. He was listed as one of the 'Tory patriots' voting for peace and also as a 'worthy patriot' exposing the mismanagements of the old ministry, and certainly his significant parliamentary activity for the most part involved inquiries into corruption of various kinds. March 1711 saw him elected to the revived commission of accounts, his previous service as an Irish forfeitures commissioner standing him in good stead. In April, with the backing of friends from the October Club, of which he was a member, he endeavoured to raise the issue of the Palatine immigration and to pass a censure on the Whig ministers who had encouraged it. His commercial experience made him a natural choice to spearhead investigations into corporate fraud. Having reported from the committee to consider the petitions of creditors of and proprietors in Sir Humphrey Mackworth's* Mine Adventurers' Company, he presented on 12 Mar. 1711 a bill for their relief, and in May chaired the committee of the whole House on the petitions of creditors of and subscribers to the Royal African Company. He also told, on 13 Mar., for a clause to be added to the bill obliging the Bank of England to redeem Exchequer bills on demand, which would have prevented anyone from being simultaneously a director of the Bank and the East India Company. Residual Irish patriotism led to his acting as a teller on 9 June in favour of reading the Lords' amendments to the bill to regulate the Scottish linen industry (which was in direct competition with the Irish). He was especially exercised by the scheme to build new churches in London and Westminster. The first-named Member of the committee appointed on 29 Mar. to draft the address in reply to the Queen's original message, he reported from this committee on 2 Apr., and, on 6 Apr., from a subsequent committee inquiring into petitions from Greenwich and other parishes proposing that funds remaining in the hands of the commissioners for the rebuilding of St. Paul's cathedral be applied to this new scheme. Then on 18 May he presented the bill to appropriate the coal duties to a fund for building 50 new churches, chaired the committee of the whole on the bill and later took a place on the commission appointed to oversee the project.[9]

Acknowledged as one of the leaders of the October Club by 1712, Annesley took a prominent part in the promulgation of the ministry's peace policy, being nominated to the committees of 17 Jan. 1712 and 6 June, which drew up separate addresses of thanks for the communication of the peace terms. Moreover, he chaired the committee of the whole House which considered the Barrier Treaty on 13 and 14 Feb. A trenchant critic of the Duke of Marlborough (John Churchill†), he had written to William, now archbishop, King in Dublin

I hope the dismission of the general from all his employments will be no ungrateful news to your Grace, or to others in Ireland, considering what has been proved against him in Parliament; had any other person been concerned in that of the poor soldiers' bread, the Commons would have called it notorious bribery and corruption, but you see what great regard is paid to a great man . . . I have great hopes of a peace, and that we shall have no further occasion for armies and generals abroad; if the war continues I know not which way we shall find funds for carrying it on.

Equally helpful to the administration was his conduct on 13 May in moving for a bill for the continuance of the South Sea Company, after which he was included in the drafting committee. He also concerned himself with two other bills which followed up his work in the preceding session. Having presented a bill to continue the commission for building 50 new churches on 29 Feb. he managed it through the House, a task which included chairing the committee of the whole on the bill. This concern for the Church probably also accounts for his appointment on 16 Apr. to draft a bill to ease the recovery of small legacies given to pious and charitable uses. The following month saw him pursue his interest of the previous session in the Royal African Company, as he was appointed to draft, and subsequently presented, a bill to make effectual agreements to be concluded between the Company and its creditors. He was also responsible for a private bill to enable the Duke of Ormond to convey to the crown the liberties of his palatinate of Tipperary in return for a cash equivalent.[10]

During the 1713 session Annesley shifted from a position of support for the Earl of Oxford's (Robert Harley*) ministry to one of open criticism and even occasionally outright opposition. Concern for the Hanoverian succession may have been one motive, and it does appear that by 1713 Annesley had left the October men to enlist in the pro-Hanoverian March Club. Another explanation may have been his association with prominent 'whimsicals' like Abingdon and his own cousin Arthur Annesley, now Earl of Anglesey. Some historians have regarded him as little more than Anglesey's lieutenant in the Commons, and the course he pursued in the last two parliamentary sessions of the reign seems to bear this out. He made the motion on 1 June 1713 for an address to the Queen to lay before the House the *asiento* contract, a proposal arising from a debate on the African trade, and was to the fore in proceedings on the French commercial treaty. On 18 June, he spoke and voted against the bill confirming the 8th and 9th articles of the treaty, being regarded as a 'whimsical'. At the same time he piloted through the Commons a bill, introduced on 29 June, to vest in the commissioners for building 50 new churches lands in the Strand, and another, brought in on 8 July, to enable Ormond's brother the Earl of Arran to take the oaths in England for his Irish office as master of the ordnance.[11]

Annesley was elected (as a Tory) to the Irish parliament held in the autumn of 1713 but did not accompany Lord Anglesey to Dublin, undertaking instead a 'progress' around the country seats of various leading English Tories. The new Parliament, to which he had been returned for Westbury, assembled in March 1714, and on 21 June 1714 he presented another bill to facilitate an agreement made by the commissioners for 50 new churches to purchase building land in the Strand. He was unwilling to let his name go forward for the ballot for commissioners of public accounts when a bill to renew the commission was brought forward in June, perhaps because he was now identified with Anglesey and the 'Hanoverian Tories'. On the basis of his voting record in this session he was classified in the Worsley list as a Tory who would often vote with the Whigs, while outside the House he solicited on behalf of the Irish privy council in the highly political dispute over the Dublin lord mayoralty, in which his cousin had taken a particular interest; he was even said to have negotiated the *rapprochement* in July 1714 between Anglesey and Lord Bolingbroke (Henry St. John II*); and was confidently predicted as the next lord chancellor of Ireland should Anglesey acquire the viceroyalty, which sadly for him never came to pass.[12]

In the aftermath of the Hanoverian succession Annesley guided through the Commons a bill to enable Irish office-holders in England to take the oaths to the new king without the necessity of travelling to Ireland. Re-elected to Parliament in 1715 as a Tory, he lost his seat on petition, a decision attributed to the fact that 'Mr Annesley has been long enough in this Parliament to show himself so true a friend to his country, and so obstinate an opposer of such who intend to make themselves rich by pillaging it'. He remained close to Abingdon, and to Lord Anglesey, who in 1719 recommended him, in case of a vacancy in the parliamentary representation of Cambridge University, as 'a person who would serve the university faithfully and not disreputable'. Annesley does in fact seem to have put up at a by-election there the following year, when he was praised as 'an honest Tory' and 'an honest Englishman', but did not stand a poll. Nevertheless he recaptured a seat at Westbury for the Bertie interest in 1722 and held it for two Parliaments, voting consistently against the administration. In 1732 he married as his third wife the niece of his old associate James Sloane and five years later inherited the unentailed English estates and 'very considerable' personalty of Lord Anglesey. He had long since abandoned Ireland and was now a permanent absentee. He died on 7 Apr. 1750.[13]

[1] Lodge, *Peerage of Ire.* (1754), ii. 284–5. [2] E. G. W. Bill, *Q. Anne Churches*, pp. xxiii–xxiv; W. Pittis, *Hist. Present Parl.* (1711), 348. [3] Lancs. RO, Preston bor. recs. CNP 3/1/1, p. 539. [4] Bodl. Carte 109, f. 353. [5] [T. Prior], *List of Absentees of Ire.* (1733), 3; *CSP Dom. 1703–4*, p. 131; Lodge, 284–5; E. St. J. Brooks, *Sir Hans Sloane*, 132–3, 151; *Davies Diary* (Cam. Soc. lxviii), 101; J. Hamilton, *Hamilton Mss* ed. Lowry, p. lxxviii; *Penal Era and Golden Age* ed. Bartlett and Hayton, 23, 25–26; Add. 28887, f. 392; 28879, f. 104; 70035, f. 154; *CJ*, x. 676, 688–9, 826, 832; xi. 34; *Cal. Treas. Bks.* ix. 1559; *HMC Buccleuch*, ii. 219; Nottingham Univ. Lib. Portland (Bentinck) mss PwA 267, Capell to Portland, 7 Mar. 1696. [6] *HMC Lords*, n.s. iv. 62, 65, 206; *CJ*, xi. 323; xiii. 65, 125, 273, 307, 395, 441, 714, 717, 764–5, 816; PRO NI, De Ros mss D638/1/15, John Hely to Ld. Coningsby, 28 Aug. 1697; *CSP Dom.* 1697, p. 342; 1700–2, p. 108; 1703–4, pp. 131–3, 140–1, 143; Northants. RO, Montagu (Boughton) mss 48/106, James Vernon I* to Shrewsbury, 3 Nov. 1698; *Bpric. of Derry and Irish Soc.* ed. Moody and Simms (Irish Mss Commn.), ii. 212, 214–15, 217, 234; Trinity, Dublin, King letterbks. 750/1, pp. 160, 206–7, 220; 750/2, ff. 18–19, 22–24, 48–49, 188–9, 205; 1489/1, pp. 129–30; 1489/92, p. 92; Lyons (King) mss 2001/874, Bp. Ashe to Bp. King, 7 Feb. 1701–2; 2001/909, Sir Robert Southwell to same, 5 May 1702; 2001/939, Annesley to same, 12 Sept. 1702; *HMC Buccleuch*, ii. 522; Portland (Bentinck) mss PwA 1012a, Ld. Winchester (Charles Powlett I*) to Portland, 10 Aug. 1697; J. G. Simms, *Williamite Confiscation in Ire.* 98–100, 103, 105, 116, 118, 121–2, 156–7; *Vernon–Shrewsbury Letters*, ii. 410; Chandler, iii. 113–14, 116–18, 121–2; Nat. Archs. Ire. Wyche mss 1/227, 233, 248, 250, Annesley to Sir Cyril Wyche*, 10, 24 June 1701, 19 Mar., 9 Apr. 1702; *HMC Ormonde*, n.s. viii. 41–42; Huntington Lib. Stowe mss 26(2), James Brydges'* diary, 19 Oct. 1701; *CJ Ire.* (1753), iii. 22–23; Add. 28891, ff. 104–5; 47072, ff. 16–17; Surr. RO (Guildford), Midleton mss 1248/2, ff. 84–85, 94. [7] Hayton thesis, 13; Add. 28893, ff. 22, 252; 28892, f. 437; *HMC Ormonde*, n.s. viii. 56–57; Lyons (King) mss 2002/1091, 1238, 1241, 1244, 1246, 1249, 1257, 1259, Annesley to King, 21 June 1704, 11 Jan., 11, 18 Feb., 8 Mar., [Mar.], 26 Apr., Apr., 10 May 1707; Bagot mss at Levens Hall, Hamilton to James Grahme*, 4, 8 Apr. 1705; *VCH Yorks. E. Riding*, iii. 93, 114, 119; *Cam. Misc.* xxiii. 45; C. S. King, *A Great Abp. of Dublin*, 117; Luttrell, *Brief Relation*, vi. 148. [8] Oxon. RO, Talbot III/ii/1; *HMC 2nd Rep.* 244. [9] Add. 70026, Hamilton to Robert Harley, 6 Oct. 1710; Lancs. RO, Kenyon mss DDKe 9/116/94, Nicholas Starkie to George Kenyon*, [22 Oct. 1710]; *HMC Kenyon*, 445; Lyons (King) mss 2002/1276, 2003/1382, 1392, Annesley to King, Oct. 1707, 2 Sept., 28 Nov. 1710; *HMC Downshire*, i. 890; Boyer, *Pol. State*, i–ii. 160; NSA, Kreienberg despatch 17 Apr. 1711; *London Rec. Soc.* xxiii. 2, 6, 8, 10–11. [10] Boyer, iii. 117; Lyons (King) mss 2008d/1420, Annesley to King, 12 Feb. 1711[–12]. [11] D. Szechi, *Jacobitism and Tory Pol.* 137, 143; G. Holmes, *Pol. in Age of Anne*, 278, 281–2; Chandler, v. 20; Cobbett, *Parlty. Hist.* vi. 1223. [12] Add. 47027, f. 59; 70236, Edward Harley* to Ld. Oxford, 26 Sept. 1713; Hayton thesis, 255, 315; Boyer, vii. 538; *HMC Portland*, vii. 192; *Swift Corresp.* ed. Williams, ii. 66. [13] Huntington Lib. Ellesmere mss EL 10742, Hon. James Bertie* to Ld. Cheyne (Hon. William*), 31 May 1715; Add. 22251, ff. 50, 54; 32457, f. 5; 34778, f. 44; 21553, f. 57; *HMC Portland*, v. 605, 611; vii. 447; Brooks, 215; *HMC Egmont Diary*, ii. 387–8; iii. 316; Prior, 3.

D. W. H.

ANSTIS, John (1669–1744), of West Duloe, Cornw. and Arundel Street, Norfolk Buildings, Westminster.[1]

ST. GERMANS   1702–1705
ST. MAWES   20 Jan. 1711–1713
LAUNCESTON   1713–1722

b. 28 Sept. 1669, 1st s. of John Anstis by Mary, da. and coh. of George Smith of Lantewy and Lunna, Cornw. *educ.* Exeter, Oxf. 1685; M. Temple 1690, called 1699, bencher 1722, treasurer 1730. *m.* 1695 (with £5,000), Elizabeth, da. and h. of Richard Cudlipp of Tavistock, Devon, 8s. (5 *d.v.p.*) 6da. (4 *d.v.p.*) *suc.* fa. 1692.[2]

High steward, Cornish tinners 1692–?*d.*[3]

Dep. gen. to auditors of imprest 1703–4; commr. prizes 1703–4; receiver-gen. of the stannaries, 1704–14; commr. to inspect and report on recs. 1704; keeper of recs. in Tower 1712; Garter king of arms 1718–*d.*[4]

An 18th-century account of Anstis' life claimed that he was 'said to be a natural son of the Scawen family by one Mrs Mary Smith, who being with child was married to John Anstis, a tenant of the Scawens'. The parish records, however, simply record that Anstis was the son of John Anstis. In 1670 Anstis' father purchased the office of registrar of the archdeaconry of Cornwall, and the following year bought land at West Duloe, Cornwall. Anstis trained for the law, which led in 1701 to his being one of two lawyers appointed by the Commons to draw up the impeachments of the Whig lords. He had also acquired the deep interest in heraldry and antiquarian study that was to dominate his later life. Returned for St. Germans on the accession of Queen Anne, he voted on 13 Feb. 1703 against agreeing with the Lords' amendments to the bill enlarging the time for taking the abjuration. Upon the death of the Garter king of arms in March 1703 he applied for the consequent vacancy, hoping that the support of the 13th Duke of Norfolk, the Earl Marshal, would be sufficient to gain the post. Norfolk, however, was still a minor and his desire to see Anstis appointed carried no weight against the opposition of the deputy Earl Marshal, the Earl of Carlisle (Charles Howard*). During the summer of 1703 Anstis received some compensation for this disappointment, in May being appointed deputy to the auditors of the imprest, an office he never executed, and in August he was included in the new commission for prizes, a post which carried a salary of £500 p.a. During the following year Anstis continued to receive marks of official favour, being granted in early 1704 a lease of duchy of Cornwall property in Kingsbear, Cornwall and later that year being appointed receiver-general of the stannaries and named to the commission to inspect and report upon the condition of the public records. In August Anstis' tenure as a prize commissioner was ended. The following October he was forecast by Robert Harley* as a likely supporter of the Tack, and though William Lowndes* was deputed to lobby Anstis on this matter he nevertheless voted for it on 28 Nov. Support for this measure did not lead to Anstis' removal from his post of receiver-general of the stannaries, and though he was not returned to the Commons in 1705 a contemporary reported that it was Anstis who 'declines standing'. There is no evidence of Court pressure being brought to bear to keep him out of the Commons.[5]

Anstis continued to crave the post of Garter king, and it was presumably in order to bolster his pretensions to this office that in 1707 he was nominated, but not created, Carlisle herald extraordinary and Norfolk herald. Within three years Anstis had begun a campaign to have the current Garter king, the aged Sir Henry St. George, surrender his grant of the office and to procure a new patent granting the office to St. George and Anstis jointly. Anstis enlisted George Granville* to write to Robert Harley in support of these claims and it is possible that Anstis' return, upon Francis Scobell's* interest, at the St. Mawes by-election of January 1711 was secured in order to advance his cause. Anstis made little contribution to the remainder of the 1710–11 session, but busied himself in carrying out an investigation into the conditions of various types of public records, and by the end of 1711 his involvement in such matters was said to have received the 'good liking' of the Earl of Oxford (as Harley had become). This approbation of Anstis' activity probably explains his appointment in 1712 as keeper of the records in the Tower. His loyalty to the ministry was made clear in the 1713 session when he voted on 18 June for the French commerce bill. At the 1713 election Anstis was returned for Launceston, having begun to treat the borough some months prior to the election, and though he made little impact upon the new Parliament, he made sufficient impression upon contemporaries to be classed as a Tory in the Worsley list and two further comparisons of the 1713 and 1715 Parliaments. His efforts continued to be focused upon obtaining a reversionary grant of the office of Garter king, and on 2 Apr. 1714 such a patent was issued. Six days later the Commons considered whether this grant required that Anstis should submit himself for re-election and resolved in the negative. Anstis retained his seat at the 1715 election, and, though he was arrested on suspicion of high treason later the same year, in 1718 he secured his appointment as Garter king. Anstis died at Mortlake, Surrey on 4 Mar. 1744, and was buried at Duloe on the 23rd.[6]

[1] Unless otherwise stated this account is based upon A. Wagner and A. L. Rowse, *John Anstis Garter King of Arms*. [2] Info. from Mr A. Ailes. [3] Boase and Courtney, *Bibl. Cornub.* 1030. [4] *DNB*; *Cal. Treas. Bks.* xviii. 284, 371; xix. 228, 336; xxix. 107; Boyer, *Pol. State*, iv. 64. [5] Polsue, *Complete Paroch. Hist. Cornw.* i. 302; *Cal. Treas. Bks.* xvi. 320; *Bull IHR*, xli. 182; Bodl. Ballard 20, f. 222. [6] *HMC Portland*, iv. 646; v. 225; *Cal. Treas. Bks.* xxv. 460–2, 590; Morice mss at Bank of Eng. Richard Blighe to Humphry Morice*, 19 Apr. 1713; *Bibl. Cornub.* 5, 1030.

E. C.

ANSTRUTHER, Sir John, 1st Bt. (c.1678–1753), of Anstruther and Elie House, Elie, Fife.

ANSTRUTHER EASTER B.	1708–10 Apr. 1712
	1713–1715
FIFESHIRE	1715–1741

b. c.1678, o. s. of Sir William Anstruther, MP [S], of Anstruther and Elie House, Ld. Anstruther SCJ by Lady Helen Hamilton, da. of John, 4th Earl of Haddington [S]; nephew of Sir Robert Anstruther, 1st Bt.* *m.* contr. 24 Jan. 1717, Lady Margaret Carmichael (*d.* 1721), da. of James, 2nd Earl of Hyndford [S], 2s. (1 *d.v.p.*) 1da. *d.v.p. cr.* Bt. 6 Jan. 1700; *suc.* fa. 1711.[1]

MP [S] Anstruther Easter 1702–7.

Burgess, Edinburgh 1708, Perth 1709, Ayr 1710; hereditary bailie, lordship of Pittenweem 1711–*d.*; hereditary searcher of customs and keeper of cocquets, Anstruther and Elie 1711–*d.*; commr. visitation, St. Andrews Univ. 1718.[2]

Hereditary carver and master of royal household [S] 1711–*d.*; master of works [S] 1717–43; commr. police [S] 1743–aft. 1744.[3]

Anstruther's father, a successful and occasionally formidable lawyer, provided his son with the landed endowment and political contacts necessary to launch him into Parliament. Although the two men may briefly have steered separate political courses at the time of the Union, the differences between them were never fundamental and Anstruther's later career as a Whig placeman faithfully reproduced his father's example. Sir William Anstruther, himself the younger son of a devoted cavalier, had secured a household office at the beginning of James II's reign but had subsequently struck out on a Presbyterian tack, and after the Revolution tied himself to the Melville interest, through whose influence he was made a lord of judiciary. He remained with the Court party under the Dalrymples, his loyalty secured by the grant of a sheaf of hereditary offices, but went into opposition with many of his colleagues in 1698 and did not return into the ministerial fold until some time after 1703. According to George Lockhart* his assistance to carry the Union was bought for £300.[4]

In the meantime Sir John Anstruther had entered

the Scottish parliament in 1702 for the burgh of Anstruther Easter. The family had been seated at Anstruther since the days of King David II, and Sir William had recently returned to live nearby at Elie, where he had purchased an estate and built an imposing house. Not unexpectedly, Sir John quickly associated himself with the Country opposition in the Scottish parliament, signing the protest in 1703 against the wine act. Through his mother he was connected with Lord Rothes, and according to Lockhart he followed Rothes and most of the Squadrone over to the Court in 1704. However, he gave his vote for the Duke of Hamilton's motion on the succession, the kind of behaviour which presumably led the Jacobite agent Scot to regard him as being of uncertain principles because his actions were variable. His mixed voting record on the Union would have done little to clear up the confusion. For the most part he abstained, notably on the crucial divisions on the first article and on ratification. In general he opposed the treaty, possibly on economic grounds since members of his family were actively engaged in trade in Anstruther itself and in the other small ports of east Fife. But Rothes persuaded him to be absent. Once the issue had been decided Anstruther fell into line with the Squadrone as they voted against the Court over the commissioners' allowances and over the Equivalent. A lingering uncertainty over his real opinions may well have been what deterred Court and Squadrone managers from including him among the Members returned to represent Scotland in the first Parliament of Great Britain. For all his own receptivity to Rothes' blandishments, his father was reported as late as December 1707 to be 'not . . . altogether for the measures of the Squadrone'.[5]

By the time of the 1708 election, Anstruther had firmly committed himself to Rothes' interest, on which he stood both for the burghs district and for knight of the shire. Even though he succeeded in the burghs, Rothes was so determined to secure the county seat, and so confident of the strength of his party's interest in the new Parliament, that a petition was duly put forward for Fifeshire. The death of the sitting member, Patrick Moncrieff*, before the case was heard in the House, prompted Anstruther to seek leave to withdraw in January 1709, perhaps as part of an electoral compact between Rothes and the Earl of Leven. Already possessing a seat in the Commons, Anstruther did not contest the ensuing by-election. He had not himself made much of an impression in the House as yet. He spoke and voted with his Squadrone colleagues, George Baillie and John Cockburn, against the ministry's conduct during the recent Jacobite invasion attempt, thereby keeping faith with the Hamilton pact, and he was considered by his party as a likely candidate for the place of clerk of the bills in a reshuffle of Scottish judicial appointments. His appearance on the Tory 'white list' of those who had voted against the impeachment of Dr Sacheverell was probably an error. When he was returned again in 1710 it was still as a Squadrone supporter, even though the Duchess of Buccleuch's chaplain, Richard Dongworth, classified him as a Court Tory.[6]

Anstruther's re-election was bitterly contested, and the involvement of a leading Tory, Sir Alexander Areskine, 2nd Bt.*, in the pre-election manoeuvres against him distinguished the affair as a party cause. The defeated candidate, George Hamilton*, petitioned the House, but before the case could be heard, Anstruther faced another, different, challenge to his right to sit, when on the death of his father early in 1711 he succeeded to a hereditary customs office at Anstruther and Elie, and thus came into jeopardy under the terms of the 1701 Act which excluded commissioners and other officers of the customs. He brought the matter to the House's notice himself on 26 Feb. 1711, requesting a judgment as to whether, through succeeding his father in this post, he was 'incapacitated from sitting'. After a sequence of adjournments the matter was finally debated on 10 Apr., by which time Anstruther's enemies had printed and distributed the arguments for disqualification. In a relatively thin House opinion was narrowly in his favour, the division being 61–57 on an amendment to the resolution. One of the tellers on his side was Robert Walpole II, while the two against were both High Tories, Henry Campion and William Shippen. In 1710–11 Anstruther twice attended the Anglo-Scottish dining group of Lord Ossulston, an informal association of a mixed political complexion. He was listed as one of the 'worthy patriots' who helped to expose the mismanagements of the previous administration, but probably retained his Squadrone affiliation.[7]

In the next session Anstruther voted with his Squadrone colleagues in favour of the 'No Peace without Spain' motion on 7 Dec. 1711, and likewise opposed the toleration bill on 7 Feb. 1712. He was himself a teller on 12 Mar., but on an issue of local rather than partisan significance, for an address to the Queen to lay before the House an estimate of the cost of completing the fortifications at Stirling. The very next day the report was made on Hamilton's election petition, but although the committee had found for Anstruther the House insisted the resolution be recommitted, in a division in which the tellers in favour of recommittal were both Argathelian Tories. On 10 Apr. the committee reported for the second time, changing its mind to endorse the petition, and Anstruther was unseated, Scottish Tories once more leading the hunt against him.

Anstruther now travelled abroad for the sake of his health, visiting his fellow Squadrone supporter Hon. William Kerr* at a military camp near Ghent in July 1712 and then travelling on to Aix-la-Chapelle in search of 'benefit by the waters'. In August he planned an excursion to Paris and intended there to meet the recent diplomatic appointee, the Duke of Hamilton, with whom he was on good terms notwithstanding their political differences. Their meeting was prevented, however, by the Duke's untimely death by duelling in November 1712, prior to his departure from England.[8]

Anstruther recovered his seat for the burghs at the 1713 general election, and was classified as a Hanoverian in Lord Polwarth's analysis of the Scottish returns. As before, his defeated opponent was Hamilton, whose petition was rejected on 29 Apr. 1714, thanks to a combination of Whig determination, Tory slackness, and the defection of some Court supporters. He had already voted on 18 Mar. 1714 against the expulsion of Richard Steele, and went on to divide on 12 May in favour of Robert Walpole II's amendment to extend the scope of the schism bill to cover Catholic education. His Whiggish sympathies were further in evidence during May, when he presented an address from Fifeshire on the Queen's recovery which took a distinctly Hanoverian line in contrast to that sponsored by his great rival Areskine, belittling the Jacobite threat. Areskine's subsequent reliance on non-juring (and therefore ineligible) voters backfired at the 1715 election, when Anstruther wrested the seat from him. He was simply listed as a Whig in the Worsley list.[9]

Anstruther was a target for Jacobite hostility during the Fifteen, his house being occupied for a time by rebel troops and his groom assaulted for refusing to divulge the whereabouts of hidden valuables. Re-elected to Parliament that year for the county as a Squadrone Whig, he voted consistently for administration, earning advancement in 1717 to the mastership of the works. His marriage tied him even more firmly into the Squadrone, especially since, by all accounts, his wife possessed considerable force of character. When he published a volume on *Drill Husbandry* a wag observed that 'no one could be better qualified to write on that subject, since there was not a better drilled husband in all Fife'. She was dead long before the Squadrone were ousted from power, so did not see Anstruther break ranks and align himself with the new Court managers. He kept to a ministerial line under Argyll until 1741, when he left Parliament. Two years later he exchanged his post for a pension and a place on the police commission.[10]

Anstruther died at Elie House on 27 Sept. 1753, leaving his only surviving son an estate in Fife that had expanded substantially through a series of purchases financed from the fruits of office.[11]

[1] *Hist. Scot. Parl.* 20–21; W. Wood, *East Neuk of Fife*, 245. [2] *Scot. Rec. Soc.* lxii. 8; Sandeman Lib. Perth, Perth burgh recs. B59/24/1/17, p.15; Carnegie Lib. Ayr, Ayr burgh recs. B6/18/8, council mins. 4 Oct. 1710; Brunton and Haig, *Senators Coll. of Justice*, 443–4. [3] *Cal. Treas. Bks.* xxxi. 413; *Cal. Treas. Bks. and Pprs.* 1742–5, p. 435. [4] *Reg. PC Scotland*, 1683–4, p. 137; 1685–6, p. 28; Wood, 187; *Balcarres Mems.* (Bannatyne Club, lxxi), 12; *Leven and Melville Pprs.* (Bannatyne Club, lxxvii), 305, 307, 321; Carstares, *State Pprs.* 257; *APS*, ix. 9, 20, 29; x. 246, 251, 269; xi. 102, 255; P. W. J. Riley, *King Wm. and Scot. Politicians*, 44, 170; *Cromartie Corresp.* i. 188. [5] Wood, 178, 243; R. Sibbald, *Hist. Sheriffdoms of Fife and Kinross* (1710), 131; info. from Dr P. W. J. Riley on members of Scot. parl.; *APS*, xi. 102, 417, 420, 423, 440; W. Fraser, *Earls of Haddington*, i. 251; *Lockhart Mems.* ed. Szechi, 67; Boyer, *Anne Annals*, iii. app. 42; *Orig. Pprs.* ed. Macpherson, ii. 15; Riley, *Union*, 329, 335; *Cromartie Corresp.* ii. 57. [6] SRO, Montrose mss GD220/5/159/5, Rothes to Montrose, 'Saturday at night' [1708]; GD220/5/202, Ormiston to same, 17 Mar. 1709; Scot. Hist. Soc. *Misc.* xii. 134; *SHR*, lx. 65. [7] L. Inn Lib. MP 100/166, *Reasons Why Sir John Anstruther Is Incapable of Sitting in the House of Commons* [1711]; *SHR*, lxxi. 125. [8] Roxburghe mss at Floors Castle, bdle. 1077, Kerr to his mother, 27 July 1712; Glos. RO, Blathwayt mss D1799/F172, passport, 1712. [9] *Lockhart Letters* ed. Szechi, 72–73; Add. 17677 HHH, ff. 205–6; *Scots Courant*, 7–10, 10–12 May 1714. [10] Wood, 188, 193; P. W. J. Riley, *Eng. Ministers and Scotland*, 266. [11] *Scot. Rec. Soc.* xxxi. 2; Wood, 185, 209.

D. W. H.

ANSTRUTHER, Sir Robert, 1st Bt. (1658–1737), of Wrae, Linlithgow, and Balcaskie, Fife.

FIFESHIRE   24 Mar.–21 Sept. 1710

bap. 24 Sept. 1658, 3rd s. of Sir Philip Anstruther, MP [S], of Anstruther, Fife, by Christian, da. of Sir James Lumsden of Innergellie, Fife, gov. of Newcastle-upon-Tyne 1645–7. *m.* (1) Sophia (*d.* 1686), da. and coh. of David Kinnear (*d.* 1684) of Kinnear, Kilmany, Fife, *s.p.*; (2) 12 Mar. 1687, Jean, da. and h. of William Monteith (*d.* by 1691) of Wrae, 5s. (2 *d.v.p.*) 2da.; (3) his cos. Marion (*d.* 1743), da. of Sir William Preston, 2nd Bt., of Valleyfield, Fife, 1s. 2da. Assumed name of Kinnear *c.*1684–6; *cr.* Bt. 28 Nov. 1694.[1]

MP [S] Anstruther Easter 1681–2, Anstruther Wester 1702–7.

Burgess and jt. receiver of customs, Anstruther Easter; burgess, Edinburgh 1689, Aberdeen 1698.

Jt. gen. receiver of supply and inland excise [S] 1691–1707; jt. farmer of excise [S] 1696–7; clerk and keeper of cocquet seal, Firth of Forth west of Queensferry 1697.[2]

Dir. Bank of Scotland 1696.[3]

After marrying two heiresses in succession, Anstruther completed his fortune with the help of a stint in government office after the Revolution and, almost certainly through the favour of his family's patrons the Melvilles, was raised to the baronetage. Of his first appearance in the Scottish parliament, as a 'merchant burgess' during the Duke of York's commissionership, nothing is known other than that he joined his brother William in subscribing the declaration against resistance. Their father, an old cavalier, still displayed enough loyalty to earn appointment in 1683 as a commissioner to administer the test and try recusants, but the two sons turned into a different path: William had opposed the Duke of York in 1681 and ranged himself with Presbyterian interests even before the Revolution. Robert showed a commitment to the Williamite regime in 1689-90 in his service on various local commissions, and although he failed to secure his seat in the convention of estates when a double return for Anstruther Easter was decided against him he was given a place as one of the general receivers of supply. Despite burning his fingers in the Darien venture (in which he invested at least £500), and in the ill-starred farm of the Scottish excise, he was able to purchase in 1698 an estate at Balcaskie, in his ancestral county of Fife, where he went on to build 'a very pretty . . . house, with all modish conveniences of terraces, park and planting'. The same year he served as a commissioner to the convention of royal burghs for the neighbouring burgh of Anstruther Easter. His family had long exercised an influence in the port of Anstruther and he had himself formerly represented the Easter burgh in parliament.[4]

Anstruther's opposition to union may have been determined by anxiety over the continuance of his office as general receiver; or, perhaps more likely, his trading interests may have made him nervous. He took part in the protests in 1705 against the treaty act, having been elected to Queen Anne's Scottish parliament for the other burgh at Anstruther, which he had represented since 1698 at the convention. His record in the parliamentary divisions on the Union was characterized by absenteeism. In all he registered only six votes (five of them on the opposition side), and he abstained in the crucial divisions on the first article and on ratification. It has been suggested that, like his nephew Sir John Anstruther, 1st Bt.*, he may have been subjected to pressure, but whereas Sir John was persuaded to abstain by the Squadrone lord, Rothes, Sir Robert almost certainly took his instruction from the Court Tory Lord Leven. He was at any rate insufficiently trusted either by the Court or the Squadrone managers to merit inclusion among the Scots representatives in the first Parliament of Great Britain.[5]

In the run-up to the 1708 election, Anstruther set himself against the interest of Lord Rothes in Fife. At a county meeting, called to prepare a loyal address, he argued strongly against making any mention of the Union, as Rothes had proposed, and instead offered an alternative draft 'wherein', as Rothes reported, 'there was not a word of the Union but a long ridiculous compliment to my Lord Leven for his courage, conduct and good success'. When Rothes and his supporters persisted with their version, Anstruther led a breakaway faction in drafting a 'counter-address'. However, the appearance of his nephew Sir John as Rothes' candidate necessitated some 'discreet conduct', and he seems to have avoided a public commitment to Leven's nominee. Even so, his return for the county at a by-election in March 1710 should probably be ascribed to Leven's influence. There was little opportunity for him to shine in the Commons, nor, so far as is recorded, did he make a speech. Anstruther died in March 1737. One of his sons was killed at Preston in 1715; another rose to the rank of general in the service of the Hanoverians.[6]

[1] *Scot. Rec. Soc.* viii. 192; W. Wood, *East Neuk of Fife*, 302; SRO Indexes, xxxi. 8; *Hist. Scot. Parl.* 21. [2] *Scot. Rec. Soc.* lix. 35; New Spalding Club, *Misc.* ii. 477; *APS*, xi. 156-7; *Hist. Scot. Parl.* 21; *Cal. Treas. Pprs.* 1720-8, pp. 68-69; *CSP Dom.* 1697, p. 539. [3] C. A. Malcolm, *Bank of Scotland*, 293. [4] Carstares, *State Pprs.* 257; *APS*, ix. 18, 29, 71, 141, 395; Wood, 186-7, 302; *Reg. PC Scotland*, 1681-2, pp. 705-6; 1683-4, p. 137; 1690, p. 570; R. Sibbald, *Hist. Sheriffdoms of Fife and Kinross* (1710), 131; *Darien Pprs.* (Bannatyne Club, xc), 391. [5] Info. from Dr P. W. J. Riley on members of Scot. parl.; P. W. J. Riley, *Union*, 335. [6] SRO, Montrose mss GD220/5/159/4, Rothes to Montrose, 30 Mar. 1708; ibid. GD220/5/159/5, same to same, 'Saturday at night' [1708].

D. W. H.

APPLEYARD, Matthew (c.1660-1700), of Kingston-upon-Hull, Yorks.

HEDON 1689-1695

b. c.1660, 3rd but 2nd surv. s. of Sir Matthew Appleyard† (d. 1670), by Frances, da. of Sir William Pelham of Brocklesby, Lincs. *educ.* Beverley sch.; St. John's, Camb. adm. 27 Apr. 1677, aged 16. *m.* 30 May 1682, Jane, da. of William Ramsden†, merchant, of Hull, 5s. (3 *d.v.p.*) 2da.[1]

Jt. customer, Kingston-upon-Hull 1661, sole 1670-May 1688, 1689-*d.*[2]

Appleyard had given evasive answers to James II's questions on the repeal of the Test Act and Penal Laws and was consequently removed in May 1688 from his long-standing position as customer of Hull. Following the Revolution he was reappointed as customer, with a salary of £39 p.a. However, such ancient customs offices were normally supplemented by substantial fees and perquisites. The duties of the office were carried out by a deputy, whose own salary of £20 a year remained unpaid until 1690, at which time Appleyard was ordered by the Treasury to settle the arrears. Appleyard had presented the corporation of Hedon with a 'handsome silver tankard', and after his return for the borough in 1690 was listed as a Tory and probable Court supporter by Lord Carmarthen (Sir Thomas Osborne†). The following year he was noted by Robert Harley* as a Court supporter, while during 1693–5 he was twice listed as a placeman. He was not an active Member, being given leave of absence on 6 Jan. 1694 and again on 31 Jan. 1695 for the recovery of his health. Presumably illness prevented him from standing again at the general election in 1695. He died at Lambeth early in June 1700 and was buried at Burstwick, Yorkshire.[3]

[1] *Lincs. Peds.* (Harl. Soc. l), 34. [2] *CSP Dom.* 1661–2, p. 39; *Cal. Treas. Bks.* viii. 1923, 2160; ix. 464; xv. 376. [3] Duckett, *Penal Laws and Test Act* (1882), 68–69; *Cal. Treas. Bks.* ix. 464, 730, 1076; G. R. Park, *Hedon*, 161; Luttrell, *Brief Relation*, iv. 656.

E. C./C. I. M.

APREECE, Robert (1638–1723), of Washingley Hall, Hunts.

HUNTINGDONSHIRE   22 Nov. 1673–1679 (July), 4 June–7 July 1698

b. c. Dec. 1638, 1st s. of Robert Apreece of Washingley Hall by Mary, da. of (Sir) Henry Bedingfield† of Oxburgh, Norf., half-bro. of Charles Orme† of Peterborough, Northants. *m.* 18 Apr. 1660, Frances, da. and h. of Henry Bexwell of Bexwell, Norf., 3s. 4da. (1 *d.v.p.*) 1 other ch. *suc.* fa. 1644.[1]

Commr. complaints, Bedford level 1663; appeals 1668.

Apreece was descended from the most prominent recusant family in Huntingdonshire. He himself admitted in 1688 that 'most of his relations' were 'Romanists', including two Benedictine monks who were to accompany James II into exile. Moreover his father had been martyred for allegiance to his religion and the Royalist cause during the Civil War, shot in cold blood at Lincoln in 1644 by parliamentarian troops on identifying himself to them as 'Apreece the papist'. His mother's second husband Humphrey Orme† was, however, a Protestant, who brought up Robert as an Anglican. Although his patrimony was depleted and encumbered because of recusancy fines during the Interregnum, his stepfather secured a composition for delinquency and at the Restoration married him off to an heiress of modest fortune, so that at least the Washingley estate was kept in the family's possession, even if it was no longer worth the £1,500 value put down when he was named to the abortive order of the Royal Oak. An active justice on the county bench, he was returned as knight of the shire at a by-election in 1673, and turned towards oppositionist politics in the later 1670s, eventually becoming a member of the Green Ribbon Club and voting for Exclusion. Presumably it was his manifold Catholic connexions that induced ministers to restore him as a justice and deputy lieutenant on James II's accession, and even though he gave essentially negative, and indeed almost impertinent, replies to questions over the repeal of the Penal Laws and Test Act, so that he was again removed from local office, he was still nominated as a court candidate for Huntingdonshire (where, admittedly, loyalists were relatively scarce) to the projected Parliament of 1688. He took no part in the Revolution but was restored once more to the bench by William III and in due course also as a deputy-lieutenant. 'Colonel' Apreece was a somewhat surprise candidate for Huntingdonshire in a by-election in 1698, quite possibly as a nominee of the 4th Earl of Manchester, since Manchester had appointed him as a deputy-lieutenant only two months before. Why he should have wished to resume a parliamentary career after such a lengthy interval is perhaps to be explained by an imminent crisis in his financial affairs, he having unwisely stood as surety for a defaulting land-tax receiver. After the briefest sojourn in the House, during which he supported the Court, according to a list compiled in about September that year, he lost the protection of parliamentary privilege and in 1702 was obliged to sell a considerable portion of his estate, obtaining a private Act for the purpose, in order to settle his debt of over £2,000 to the crown.[2]

Little more is heard of Apreece. His son, a gentleman of the privy chamber to George I, petitioned the crown successfully in 1718 for the office of bailiff of Norman Cross hundred, in Huntingdonshire. He himself died in 1723 and was buried at Fulham, where eventually his daughter Susanna was also laid to rest, the widow of Admiral Sir John Balchen.[3]

[1] Lansd. 921, f. 76; *Vis. Norf.* ed. Dashwood, i. 226. [2] Duckett, *Penal Laws and Test Act* (1883), 68; H. N. Birt, *Obit. Bk. of Eng. Benedictines*, 68, 73; R. Challoner, *Mems. Missionary Priests* ed. Pollen (1924), 456–7; *VCH Hunts.* i. 365; ii. 30–31; iii. 228; *Trans. Cambs. and Hunts. Arch. Soc.* v. 114; *CSP Dom.* 1698, p. 193; 1700–2, p. 254; Luttrell, *Brief Relation*, iv. 391; *Cal. Treas. Bks.* xiv. 382; xv. 47–48; xvii. 6, 54; xviii. 162. [3] *Cal. Treas. Bks.* xxxii. 216, 248; T. Faulkner, *Fulham and Hammersmith*, 115; Lysons, *Environs* (1792–6), ii. 375.

D. W. H.

ARCHDALE, John (1642–1717), of Temple Wycombe, Bucks.

CHIPPING WYCOMBE 1698–6 Jan. 1699

bap. 5 May 1642, 1st surv. s. of Thomas Archdale of Temple Wycombe by Mary, da. of John Neville, grocer and alderman of London. *m.* lic. 3 Dec. 1673, Anne Dobson (*d.* 1719), of High Wycombe, wid. of Walter Cary of High Wycombe 1s. 3da. *suc.* fa. 1676.[1]

Gov. N. Carolina 1695–7.

Archdale's grandfather, a vintner in Dowgate Street, London, acquired the manor of Loakes in Buckinghamshire in 1604 and that of Temple Wycombe in 1628. After holding office as sheriff in 1639–40 his father served with Edmund Waller†, the poet, on the county lieutenancy for Buckinghamshire in 1642. In 1664 Archdale went over to New England to try to make good the claims of his brother-in-law Ferdinando Gorges (who had married his sister, Mary) to the ownership of Maine, but his mission was unsuccessful. He returned to England in 1665 and in 1673 married a local widow, whose son, Thomas Cary, became a deputy-governor of Carolina. In 1674, Archdale became a member of the Society of Friends although the vicar of Wycombe tried to dissuade him by arguing the Church of England case with him for several days. The death of his father in September 1676, one month after that of his elder brother, saw Archdale inherit the family's Buckinghamshire properties. In 1678 he purchased Lord Berkeley of Stratton's share in Carolina, making over the title to his infant son, Thomas*. In 1682–3 he accepted a commission from the Carolina proprietors to collect rents from North Carolina, where a number of Quakers had settled, and thence he corresponded with George Fox. Although back home again in 1686, he returned in 1695 as governor, but two years later, after his son sold his share in the colony, he came back to England. As governor, he advocated freedom of conscience in the colony, declaring 'Dissenters could kill wolves and bears, fell trees and clear ground, as well as Churchmen', and was lenient to the Indians.[2]

Archdale's estate of around £500 p.a. provided him with a political interest in Wycombe, and he seems to have surprised the Wharton interest with his candidature in 1698. Subsequently, he was able to claim that he 'was chose by the majority of the Church of England without his own seeking', an inference, possibly, that he had Tory support. However, election to Parliament necessitated taking the oaths. One Quaker reported that:

Archdale intends to stand his choice this sessions. I am not easy at it for, first, I question if he can qualify himself . . . and yet keep within the verge of his principle as a Friend. But however it will cause many to imagine that we aim at that post, and to prevent us they may abridge us of the liberty they intended us.

Before the Commons met he was classed as a member of the Country party and forecast as likely to oppose the standing army. He did not take his seat, however, when Parliament sat in December 1698, and at the very beginning of January 1699 Lord Wharton's (Hon. Thomas*) agent reported from Wycombe:

The Quakers of this town held a general meeting, at which William Penn was president, and they considered whether Mr Archdale could in conscience take the oaths, in order to sit in the House of Commons as a Member, and after several debates, they resolved that he could not.

Thus, when the House was called over on 3 Jan. 1699 Archdale was absent, but he had given the Speaker a letter in which he said he had not opposed the desire of the burgesses to elect him 'believing that any declarations of fidelity . . . might in this case, as in others where the law requires an oath, be accepted'. Three days later he was called 'into the middle of the House, almost to the table', and there declared 'that it was not out of any disloyalty to the King or disaffection to the government that he had not qualified himself', but that he 'had advice of lawyers that his affirmation would stand good instead of an oath, which he could not take without prejudicing his party'. He then withdrew. After some debate in which it was agreed that the Affirmation Act was limited to actions in the law courts the House refused his request, and a new writ was issued.[3]

In 1700 Archdale and his son Thomas sold Temple Wycombe and Loakes to Lord Shelburne [I] (Henry Petty†). Five years later Archdale purchased Sir William Berkeley's share in Carolina and took an active part in the proprietary board, being called to the bar of the Lords in March 1706 to give evidence on a petition from Dissenters settled in Carolina against an attempt being made to enforce the Act of Uniformity there. Then in 1707 he published *A New Description of the Fertile and Pleasant Province of Carolina*. Having sold his proprietary share in Carolina to his son-in-law John Danson in 1708, Archdale seems to have retired to Wycombe, his abode when he wrote his will in 1714. He was buried on 4 July 1717. His grandson Thomas Archdale Rook inherited his estate in Oxfordshire and some houses in London; his granddaughter Mary Rook inherited his estate in Wycombe, worth £15 p.a., excepting 'the meeting-house of the people called

Quakers and the dwelling house adjoining', which was bequeathed to his son Thomas' two daughters. There were other small legacies, his daughter Anne receiving only £5, 'she having been well provided for in Carolina'.[4]

[1] H. B. Archdale, *Mems. of Archdales*, 79–82; PCC 142 Duke. [2] Lipscomb, *Bucks*. iii. 640; Archdale, 79–82; *Dict. Carolina Biog.* [3] *Bucks. Dissent and Parish Life 1669–1712* ed. Broad (Bucks. Rec. Soc. xxviii), 255; Bodl. Carte 233, f. 62; 228, f. 261; G. Locker Lampson, *A Quaker Post Bag*, 72–73; Suff. RO (Ipswich), Gurdon mss mic. 142, Sir William Cook* to Thornhagh Gurdon, 12 Jan. 1698[–9]; Luttrell, *Brief Relation*, iv. 469. [4] Lipscomb, 640; *Dict. Carolina Biog.*; HMC Lords, n.s. vi. 408, 410; Archdale, 82; PCC 72 Tenison.

E. C./S. N. H.

ARCHDALE, Thomas (c.1675–1711).

CHIPPING WYCOMBE   21 Jan. 1699–1700

b. c.1675, o. s. of John Archdale*. *educ*. Wadham, Oxf. matric. 11 Mar. 1692, aged 16. *m*. 20 Aug. 1699, Jane (d. 1722), da. of Charles Turner of King's Lynn, Norf., 2da.[1]

Freeman, Chipping Wycombe 1698.[2]

Capt. Roger Townshend's* Ft. 1706, R. Fusiliers 1707–bef. Mar. 1711.

Archdale, who did not share his father's Quaker outlook, was returned for Chipping Wycombe in his father's place at a by-election in 1699. He was granted leave of absence on 4 Apr. 1699. With the sale of the family's Buckinghamshire estates he did not stand again. His connexion through marriage with the Turners (his wife's cousin was Charles Turner*), and subsequent residence at Stanhow, Norfolk, explain his commission in Roger Townshend's newly raised regiment in 1706. However, after transferring to the Royal Fusiliers, he had left the army by March 1711. Archdale predeceased his father, dying on 9 Aug. 1711, aged 36, and was buried at High Wycombe.[3]

[1] H. B. Archdale, *Mems. of Archdales*, 82–83, 91; IGI, Norfolk; PCC 159 Young; *Blomefield's Norf. Supp.* ed. Ingleby, 161. [2] *Ledger Bk. of Chipping Wycombe* ed. Newall, 50. [3] Lipscomb, *Bucks*. iii. 640.

E. C./S. N. H.

ARCHER, Andrew (1659–1741), of Umberslade Hall, Tamworth, Warws.

WARWICKSHIRE   1690–1698
                28 Nov. 1705–1710
                1713–1722

bap. 2 Aug. 1659, 1st s. of Thomas Archer† by Anne (d. 1685), da. of Richard Leigh of London. *educ*. Trinity, Oxf. 1678; I. Temple 1680. *m*. lic. 15 June 1693, Elizabeth (d. 1704), da. of Sir Samuel Dashwood*, 4s. (1 d.v.p.) 4da (1 d.v.p.). *suc*. fa. 1685.[1]

Commr. rebuilding Warwick 1695; freeman Bath 1696.[2]

Commr. inquiry into forces and garrisons in Spain, Portugal and Italy 1711–12.[3]

The son of a parliamentarian commander in the Civil War and MP during the short Parliaments of 1659 and 1660, Archer inherited a well-run estate consisting of five manors centred on Umberslade and an iron mill near Stratford-on-Avon, all of which he managed according to his father's prudent economic maxims. In 1693, the year in which he married and began to plan the rebuilding of Umberslade, his income was £2,015. His match with Elizabeth Dashwood, the daughter of a wealthy City merchant, inevitably brought him into close proximity with the capital and its world of high finance, and in all probability awakened his own interest in the potential of investment. From at least 1708 until 1715 he had sizable stockholdings in the East India Company and in the Bank of England from which he supplemented his income. His marriage was equally advantageous in local terms since his wife's aunt was married to the 5th Lord Brooke (Fulke Greville†), a prominent figure among Warwickshire's Tory grandees.[4]

In 1690 he was returned for his county following a poll, but in the course of his first Parliament took no active part in proceedings. Lord Carmarthen (Sir Thomas Osborne†) was evidently under a misapprehension about his political colours, identifying him after the election as a Whig, though his partnership in the election with William Bromley II* and his subsequent behaviour clearly denote his Toryism. Carmarthen was on surer ground in noting him as a probable Court supporter, a promise Archer must have fulfilled for in December, towards the end of the second session, Carmarthen could class him as a likely supporter in connexion with the projected attack on him. The following April, Robert Harley* was inclined to view him as a Country supporter. He obtained a fortnight's leave on 7 Feb. 1694. At Kensington on 6 Apr. 1695 he and his friend and fellow Member Bromley presented an address condoling with the King on the death of Queen Mary. He polled in first place in the 1695 contest in Warwickshire, and in the recorded divisions of 1696 appeared unequivocally as an opponent of the Court: he was listed in January as likely to oppose the Court over the council of trade, refused at first to subscribe the Association, voted in March against fixing the price of guineas, and voted on 25 Nov. against the attainder of Sir John Fenwick†. On 16 Jan. 1697 he initiated a bill empowering magistrates to order the widening of highways, which he subsequently introduced and managed through all its stages. In the surprise motion on 15 Feb. to engross the bill for examining and stating the public accounts, he told for the opposing majority, not as an enemy of the commission in principle, but as a critic of the manner in which in late sessions it had been overtaken and manned by ministerialists. In what remained of the 1695 Parliament he was involved in no further proceedings: on 15 Jan. 1698 he was allowed a fortnight's leave to attend his pregnant wife.[5]

Archer's withdrawal from Parliament in 1698 was dictated by his antipathy to the Association two years before, though he had been fortunate enough to retain his place on the county commission of the peace. A comparative analysis of the old and new Houses of Commons compiled soon after the election noted him as a Country supporter. He continued to visit the capital, not least on account of his wealthy in-laws, and sent back reports on political developments. In March 1699, for example, he was writing to Sir Richard Newdigate[†] from Devonshire Square about the 'several long debates' concerning mismanagements in naval administration and in particular about the accusations of peculation levelled at Admiral Lord Orford (Edward Russell*). His approval of Country measures is again evident in January 1702 when he wrote to Sir John Mordaunt, 5th Bt., one of the county's Tory knights, expressing his pleasure at news that the House had 'chose their old Speaker and have showed their esteem of a man of so much integrity and honour as Mr Harley'. He hoped too that the tenor of proceedings in the new Parliament would not differ 'from what the last parliament did', and that despite the 'clamours' against it the nation would come to appreciate 'the truth of the matter of fact'. His circle of acquaintanceship among the Warwickshire gentry extended to Whigs as well as Tories, and, at least before he re-entered Parliament, he was on agreeable terms with Newdigate, who had stood against him in 1690 and 1695, and George Lucy, who in 1705 attempted unsuccessfully to breach the Tory monopoly over the county seats. Archer was much preoccupied during these years with the completion of a fine new country seat at Umberslade, which was finished in 1700. In the same year he was nominated to the lieutenancy by Lord Northampton, the county's lord lieutenant.[6]

Archer might never have re-entered Parliament but for the sudden death of Sir Charles Shuckburgh, 2nd Bt.*, in September 1705, shortly after having been re-elected for the county. In the haste to find a suitable Tory replacement, Archer, with his previous parliamentary experience, was an ideal choice, and willingly accepted the invitation to stand. Lord Digby (William*) reported to an acquaintance that at a meeting of gentlemen in October Archer had been agreed on 'unanimously'. Accordingly, he was returned unopposed at the by-election held at the end of November. In February and March 1707 he assisted in the promotion of Lord Digby's bill for providing Birmingham with a new church: he took charge of it in the House from the report stage, but the bill failed to emerge from the Lords. Early in 1708 he was classed as a Tory. On 19 Feb., at the report on the bribery bill, he told for the minority wanting to see a clause inserted for defining the 'inhabitant' franchise as in persons who had resided in, or whose family or household inhabited a borough for a given length of time. Re-elected in 1708, and classed once more as a Tory in a list of the returns, he continued to be active over the next two sessions. In a dispute on 24 Nov. over who should chair the supply committee, he told for the minority against the Whig favourite, William Farrer*; and on 3 Mar. 1709, when the merits of the Coventry election were reviewed, was teller against the Whig candidate, Sir Orlando Bridgman, 2nd Bt.* During February and March 1709 he steered fresh legislation for building the new church at Birmingham, and this time saw it pass both Houses. In the 1709–10 session he was teller on three occasions: on 25 Jan. 1710 for the minority against a Whig complaint that the town clerk of Beaumaris was in contempt of the elections committee for his failure to produce the town records; on 22 Mar., in the closing stages of the trial of Dr Sacheverell, for the minority opposing the motion demanding the Lords pass judgment against him; and two days later, to omit an adverse reflection on Sacheverell from a proposed address asking the Queen for a day of 'public fasting and humiliation'. He was also noted as having voted against the impeachment proceedings. On 24 Jan. he obtained leave to introduce another measure for improving highway maintenance which he subsequently introduced and saw through the House, only to see it fail once more in the Lords.[7]

Archer was in the Low Countries in August 1710 when he sent word of his intention not to stand in the forthcoming election. Bromley was immediately perturbed that Archer had chosen first to inform his steward, rather than his fellow Member Sir John Mordaunt, or himself, though regarding it as typical since 'he is no formalist'. When Archer did notify Bromley, it was to stress his resolve to remain out of England until after the election so that he could not be 'solicited' to change his mind. His reasons for standing down, however, are not apparent. His friend, the Amsterdam financier John Drummond, described him to Harley as 'a very hearty and staunch honest gentleman, and knows a great many good and useful things which I was ignorant of . . . He is still for the place bill, but that is a dispute betwixt him and me.' Archer's taste for foreign travel was given fresh rein in the summer of 1711 when he was named one of the three commissioners for inspecting 'the affairs of the armies' in Italy, Spain and Portugal, with a stipend of £5 a day, the main purpose of which was to inspect the accounting of provisions in the principal theatres of war and report on abuses. It is quite possible that his friend Bromley, now Speaker, had some part in the appointment, although Archer's mastery of Spanish was probably also a key consideration. At the end of June, Drummond informed the lord treasurer that Archer had written 'for some very useful instruction in the affair he is going about; . . . he is a real honest man for aught I could ever find, and scandalous abuses have been committed'. Embarking for Holland in November, Archer spent the next year or so 'in a continual fatigue of travelling and of business'. While touring through Holland and Germany at the beginning of 1712, on the way to Italy, he noted the general disposition against the peace, 'for they have more advantage by the war than we have'. He was particularly eager for news about how Whig placemen were voting at home upon the peace issue. From Genoa in April, at the end of a tour of inspection in Lombardy, he wrote optimistically to Mordaunt: 'as to the examination of accounts I believe we shall be able to do a great deal of service and I am very well pleased with my commission'. When the commissioners moved on to Spain and Portugal they uncovered a great many fraudulent practices, including monopolies operated by the governors of Gibraltar and Port Mahon. In December, as he and his two associates voyaged homewards, there was an unsubstantiated report that they had been captured by a Moroccan man-of-war. Archer seems to have been confident that his detailed findings would be recognized and rewarded by the ministry, and was chagrined when his ex-colleagues, Edward Stowell and Sir Henry Belasyse*, received preferment and was himself ignored. In the summer of 1713 he sought an interview with Lord Oxford and when his requests achieved nothing, wrote to him at length on 24 July, beginning:

> I have long been under apprehensions of having been misrepresented to your lordship and for that reason it was that I formally desired leave to wait on you. The general vogue of the town since the preferment of my colleagues gives me greater reason to fear that I am not well in your lordship's favour. Therefore in justice to myself I humbly beg leave to inform you of some of the services that have been done by me alone.

He strongly suspected that the other two commissioners had claimed credit for the report, which he believed would never have occurred if the ministry had urged Parliament to pay closer attention to the abuses uncovered. There is no trace of a response from the lord treasurer, and Archer was given no subsequent reward for his services. The reasons are not clear but it may be supposed that, as the allies proceeded towards a peace, Archer's eagerness to expose instances of fraud and abuse was considered ill-timed and tactless. At the general election held in September 1713 he accepted an invitation from the Warwickshire gentry to represent them again, and was returned unchallenged. He was apparently still determined to gain some advantage by his exertions in Spain, for at the beginning of October he was boldly asserting to such acquaintances as Thomas Carte in Oxford that when Parliament met there would be an exposé of the 'great number of intolerable abuses and cheats' he had helped to unearth, and that he would use 'his truest endeavours' to see that those concerned were punished. When Parliament did eventually reassemble, however, there was little inclination to pursue such matters. The Worsley list of the 1713 Parliament identified him as a Tory sometimes prone to vote with the Whigs, while the compilers of two similar lists labelled him simply as a Tory. His moderation is attested by the comment of a senior Whig, James Craggs I*, that 'Mr Archer and Mr [William] Colemore [II] . . . are with us in most of the questions'. He was teller in three divisions: on 31 Mar. 1714 against hearing the allegations made by the Whig disputant, Henry Grey*, in the Wallingford election case; on 20 May, at the report on the army bill, supporting the addition of a clause empowering j.p.s to inquire into 'fictitious names' in musters; and on 24 May in favour of outlawing the sale of reversions of ecclesiastical livings in a bill proposed for improving subsistence to curates. In June he was appropriately included on the 'Speaker's list' of moderate Tories canvassed for the new accounts commission, and in the ballot declared on the 18th he obtained 75 votes but was not elected.[8]

Archer was returned again in 1715, serving as a Tory member of the opposition until he stood down in 1722. In these later years he was burdened with increasing indebtedness. His finances never recovered from his purchase of another manor in 1716 for which he had to borrow, but which had been intended to improve the overall profitability of his estates. Away from public duties he seems to have devoted himself to his library, his will specifically bequeathing his collections of books and manuscripts to his eldest son Thomas. He lived to see both Thomas and his younger son Henry returned together on petition for Warwick against the Tory candidates in February 1735, and died at an advanced age on 31 Dec. 1741 at Umberslade. He asked in his will to be buried privately 'with my ancestors' at Tamworth church, and expressed regret that his legacies of £6,000 and £5,700 to his daughters could not be larger. Thomas Archer was elevated to the Lords as a baron in 1747.[9]

[1] J. Burman, *Story of Tamworth-in-Avon*, 51; Add. 27971, f. 12; Dugdale, *Warws.* 778, 781; *Mar. Lic. Vicar-Gen.* (Harl. Soc. xxxi), 260–1; J. R. Woodhead, *Rulers of London* (London and Mdx. Arch. Soc.), 56–57. [2] *Great Fire of Warwick* (Dugdale Soc. xxxvi), 121; Bath AO, Bath council bk. 3, p. 220. [3] *Cal. Treas. Bks.* xxv. 495. [4] *Univ. Birmingham Hist. Jnl.* ix. 130–43. [5] *Warws. Recs.* ix. p. xiv; H. Horwitz, *Parl. and Pol. Wm. III*, 191; Add. 27971, f. 12. [6] *Warws. Recs.* p. xxi; Warws. RO, Newdigate mss CR136/B/9, Archer to Newdigate, 16 Mar. 1698–9; Mordaunt of Walton mss CR1386/iii/53, same to Mordaunt, 5 Jan. 1701[-2]; Compton mss at Castle Ashby, 1090/49, Ld. Northampton to PC, 20 Apr. 1700; *CSP Dom.* 1700–2, p. 252. [7] Egerton 2540, f. 136. [8] Mordaunt mss CR1386/iii/12, 13, 55, 56, William Bromley to Sir John Mordaunt, 4, 8 Sept. 1710, Andrew Archer to same, 11 Jan., 16 Apr. 1712 N. S.; HMC Portland, iv. 583, v. 24, 460; *Cal. Treas. Bks.* xxv. 454, 495; *Post Boy*, 30 Oct.–1 Nov., 22–24 Nov. 1711; Folger Shakespeare Lib. Newdigate newsletter 25 Dec. 1712; Add. 70209, Archer to Ld. Oxford, 24 July 1713; Bodl. Ballard 18, f. 51; Fitzwilliam Mus. Lib. Camb. Perceval mss A21, Craggs to Anne Newsam, 22 Apr. 1714; NLS, Advocates' mss, Wodrow pprs. letters Quarto 8, f. 138. [9] *Univ. Birmingham Hist. Jnl.* 137, 139; PCC 108 Trenley.

A. A. H.

ARESKINE (ERSKINE), Sir Alexander, 2nd Bt. (c.1663–1727), of Cambo, Fife.

FIFESHIRE 1710–1715

b. c.1663, 1st s. of Sir Charles Erskine, 1st Bt., of Cambo by Penelope, da. of Arthur Barclay of Cothill, London, gent. privy chamber to Charles II. *m.* 1680, his cos. Lady Mary (*d.* aft. 1700), da. of Alexander Erskine, 3rd Earl of Kellie [S], 8s. (2 *d.v.p.*) 3da. *suc.* fa. as 2nd Bt. Feb. 1677.[1]

Jt. Lyon king of arms (with fa.) 1672–Feb. 1677, sole Feb. 1677 (crowned 1681)–Jan. 1703, jt. (with 2nd s. *d.v.p.*) Jan. 1703–by 1727, sole ?1727–?*d.*[2]

Burgess, Edinburgh 1708, Pittenweem by 1710; steward of Menteith, Perth (during incapacity of Charles Stuart, 21st Earl of Moray [S]) 1713–bef. 1719.[3]

It was a mixed inheritance that in 1677 descended to the young Areskine (as he himself preferred to spell his surname): a baronetcy, a place as the principal Scottish herald, and aristocratic connexions whose political allegiance suited the temper of the times; but on the debit side only a small and encumbered estate from which to support the crowd of siblings left unprovided for by his father. The fortune the first baronet had hoped to catch for him having eluded the family's clutches, he married a first cousin, the daughter of his uncle the Earl of Kellie, a match that was socially advantageous but in material respects relatively modest. His father's debts were such that Areskine's annual income – £300 salary as Lord Lyon, supplementing a rental of only £200 – proved insufficient to discharge them. Although the 'large, fine house' at Cambo was much admired, especially for its grounds, where the owner's horticultural expertise was much in evidence, Areskine was always a prey to 'necessities'.[4]

As early as 1681, when Areskine took the test imposed by the Scottish parliament, it was manifest that he harboured political sympathies proper to the offspring of an old cavalier, and to one whose sister was the daughter-in-law of the murdered Archbishop Sharp of St. Andrews. But financial straitening obliged him to restrain the expression of his prejudices and indeed to cut his principles according to circumstances. If continuance on local commissions in 1689–90 is any guide, Areskine accepted the Revolution, and in 1692 his appointment as Lord Lyon was ratified and regranted, tradition has it, through the influence of William Carstares, who had contracted an odd friendship with the family during Charles II's reign, when Sir Charles Erskine, as lieutenant-governor of Edinburgh castle, was for a time his gaoler. In 1703 the name of Areskine's son was added to the Lord Lyon's patent. But three years later an appeal came from Areskine to his distant kinsman Lord Mar, a long-standing patron of the family, for help in securing an increase in the fees exacted by the Lyon's office, pleading the further hardship wrought by the profusion of children from his own marriage. Thus although the Jacobite agent Scot relayed in 1706 a general report of Areskine's loyalty to the Pretender, another observer of the Scottish political scene claimed at this time that he was committed to the Protestant succession. The passage of the Union saw confirmation of his title as Lord Lyon, and the appointment of three younger sons as pursuivants in the office. He was pessimistic about the economic consequences of unification. 'I came from Edinburgh last week', he reported in October 1707,

a very desolate place already ... a great many were gone and going to London, and taking a great deal of money with them, which in all likelihood will not come back to us again. We will be certain of this loss every year, and I am afraid we shall never get an equivalent for it.[5]

The political revolution of 1710 at last opened the prospect of a ministry attuned to Areskine's sentiments. For the first time he appeared as a parliamentary candidate, egged on by Mar to contest Fife, in hopes of getting as a Member 'more ready payment of his bygone salaries and pensions'. Even with Mar to back him, he would not have been able to withstand the combined strength of Lords Rothes and Leven, hitherto the prevailing powers in the shire, had the contest been simply one of proprietorial interest. But in a flourish of party spirit the smaller lairds rallied to the cause of episcopalianism and returned its local champion. Areskine was also indefatigable in supporting men of like mind who were standing in the neighbouring burgh districts: 'I can hardly say I have been 24 hours at home since I saw you, and what with riding and drinking with the towns and country I think there shall be an end made of me.' Later he was to brag that he had been 'instrumental in bringing into the House of Commons as many honest gentlemen as any one subject of North Britain', and even when the election was over his enthusiasm remained undiminished, as he took upon himself the organization of the election petitions of his fellow Tories Sir John Malcolm* and George Hamilton*.[6]

Classed as a Tory in the 'Hanover list' and as an episcopal Tory in the analysis of Scottish election returns compiled by the Duchess of Buccleuch's chaplain, Richard Dongworth, Areskine was not long in showing his party colours, and was listed among the 'worthy patriots' who in the first session of this Parliament exposed the mismanagements of the previous ministry. Early impressions of the House were unfavourable. He observed that business was done 'after a very strange manner . . . very few thinking on it, or considering much how it goes, a very few having the management of all'. Shortly after the beginning of the session, he joined with four other Members, John Carnegie, Sir Alexander Cumming, 1st Bt., George Lockhart and Hon. James Murray, to create what one historian has described as an informal 'steering committee' to direct the pursuit of Scottish Tory ambitions. Its first priority was a toleration for Scottish episcopalians, and in the wake of the Greenshields case Lockhart and Areskine advocated a motion for a toleration bill. Anxious ministers lobbied against this, however, and persuaded them to stay their hands until a more favourable opportunity presented itself, to which they reluctantly agreed on condition that the Queen promise to sponsor the cause in due course.[7]

In April 1711 Henry St. John II* reminded Robert Harley* that Areskine, as a client of Lord Mar, was 'not to be forgotten' in any future round of preferments. The redemption of ministerial promises in September 1711, however, took a peculiar form. Areskine had been tipped to share in the new commission of the Scottish signet, but in fact he was not included with the two appointees; instead, by an informal arrangement, he was intended to receive a third of all the profits of the office. The agreement proved a nullity, for Areskine never received a penny from either of the two commissioners.[8]

As the 1711–12 session opened Areskine distinguished himself as a vocal defender of Scottish interests. In January 1712 he was a signatory to the representation to the attorney-general over the renewal of the Scottish staple at Campvere. He also followed Lockhart in an unsuccessful attempt to associate the Scots in the Lower House with the protests of their compatriots in the Lords over the Hamilton peerage case, and supported the tack of the land grants resumption bill, against the express wishes of Harley (now Lord Oxford). Moreover, he and his compatriots had been provoked by the Court's failure to promote toleration for Scottish episcopalian ministers. Lockhart's memory was that early in 1712 the 'steering committee' had renewed their 'concert' and decided to press not only for a toleration bill but a bill to resume rights of patronage over Scottish livings which had been taken over by local presbyteries from lay proprietors. Lockhart and Areskine apparently received notification of the Queen's consent to proceed, despite Oxford's continuing opposition. On 21 Jan. 1712 Areskine seconded the motion for leave to bring in the bill, and was appointed to the drafting committee. In the division of 7 Feb. Areskine naturally voted in favour, and remained closely associated with the bill's fortunes. When the Lords introduced an abjuration clause acceptable to the Kirk, Lockhart and Areskine were outraged. They 'cursed and blasphemed' but contented themselves with securing a further amendment to make the clause as objectionable to Presbyterians as it was to episcopalians. In October 1712 Areskine wrote to Oxford to recommend a 'moderate' Presbyterian to the chair of divinity at St. Andrews, against the candidate favoured by 'the violent party', and went on to endorse the request of 'the honest people' of the burgh of Burntisland for a royal presentation of a sympathetic minister to the kirk there, in order to forestall the wishes of the presbytery.[9]

In March 1713 Areskine signed the joint letter from Scottish Members and peers to Lord Dun, to urge that episcopalian ministers in Scotland be prevailed upon to take the oaths and pray for the Queen, in order that they might qualify themselves for the benefits of the Toleration Act and, more importantly, give the lie to insinuations of disloyalty coming from their

Presbyterian enemies. Soon afterwards he repeated the message in a private communication to his friend Harry Maule. Disappointed with the result of previous efforts, 'for as I understood there were not many of our clergy had scruple of conscience to do all we were expecting of them', he implored, 'for God's sake, advise them to go into what is expected of them, otherwise I don't doubt we shall not be able to get done what we wish'. As the events of the session unfolded, his attention was concentrated instead on the crisis over the malt tax and the motion for the repeal of the Union. He reported to Maule on 2 May that he had attended the Lords' debate on the malt tax, having been at first held up by 'a matter of moment for our country' in the Lower House. It was obvious to him then that the Whig Junto 'desire to make a handle of us', but in the conference of Scottish peers and Members afterwards he seconded Lockhart's proposal to seek the dissolution of the Union, speaking 'with his wonted warmth and zeal'. He abstained on the vote for the second reading of the French commerce bill on 4 June, but returned to supporting the Court at the engrossment on 18 June, apparently in accordance with instructions from the Pretender. That Areskine was 'highly Tory and Jacobite', or even 'ready to embrace a popish pretender', is attested by anecdotal evidence, but the extent of his commitment to the cause remains debatable. He was safely re-elected in 1713, and was also active in various burgh districts having taken care to urge his episcopalian contacts to 'bestir themselves now for the elections, as they see those that are not their friends diligent'. In Lord Polwarth's analysis of the Scottish returns Areskine was listed as 'Jacobite', in other words a Tory.[10]

The 1714 session saw Areskine draw more closely than ever towards Lockhart. At the outset he stood by his friend in the councils of the reconvened 'steering committee', when Lockhart's proposal for a renewed attack on the Union was reproved by their colleagues. The argument put forward by Carnegie, Cumming and Murray was that everything could safely be left in the hands of Secretary Bolingbroke (St. John), who had their best interests at heart. This was sharply rejected by Lockhart and Areskine who, with John Houstoun, 2nd Bt., Sir James Hamilton and several others splintered off from the main body of Scottish Tories. For seven to eight weeks there was no co-operation between the rival factions. Finally the five erstwhile comrades arranged a meeting at which, in order to re-establish the former working relationship, the ministerialist majority proposed a motion for a bill to resume the bishops' rents for the relief of those episcopalian clergy prepared to conform to the Toleration Act. To persuade Lockhart and Areskine, their friends made use of the names of Mar and Bolingbroke, and even of the Queen herself, and the two seceders allowed themselves to be talked round. It was not long before the Court grew alarmed, however, and pressed for the bill's abandonment. Areskine supported Lockhart in resisting this pressure, speaking his mind to Mar and condemning the 'intolerable usage' to which he and his colleagues had been subjected. The revival of the scheme at the hands of Carnegie, Cumming and Murray, created confusion and bitterness. At one stage it was thought Areskine might be nominated to the commission appointed to inquire into the bishops' revenues, but he was ultimately excluded. He continued, however, to vote with the Tories for the remainder of the session, opposing on 12 May Robert Walpole II's motion to extend the scope of the schism bill to cover Catholic education. He was named as a Tory on the Worsley list.[11]

Areskine was just as busy as ever in the 1715 election. He told Lord Cromartie's son that

> never was any time when there was more need for honest men to stick together and endeavour to make a good election for the next Parliament . . . If we are not able to assist the Tories here, we shall not have so good a title to their help and protection, and if we fall in the Whigs' mercy, what will [be]come of us?

This time Areskine's efforts passed unrewarded. He lost his seat in Fifeshire to a revitalized Rothes interest, allegedly because of his over-dependence on nonjuring voters, who were excluded when his opponent, Sir John Anstruther, called for the oaths to be tendered. In material terms, he had not suffered too much at the Hanoverian succession: he himself was still Lord Lyon, and his son Charles was advanced from a pursuivant's place to be Lyon clerk in June 1715. Only two of his sons had left the office, and one of these returned later. So when the Jacobite rising occurred Areskine pre-empted government action by racing to put himself in custody. He survived the wreck of Scottish Toryism and remained in place until his death on 4 Aug. 1727. Three of his sons spent time in France in 1716, where they made contact with Jacobite agents, but nothing of importance seems to have been transacted between them. Other sons besides the Lyon clerk were promoted within the office in the years after 1715. The youngest, however, went to Rome to study painting, married there and eventually fathered a cardinal.[12]

[1] *Scots Peerage* ed. Paul, v. 90–92; *Scot. Rec. Soc.* lxxvii. 16; N. Carlisle, *Gent. Privy Chamber*, 165. [2] *APS*, viii. 123–4; xi. 465; *CSP Dom.* 1703–4, p. 403 [3] *Scot. Rec. Soc.* lxii. 65; *State of Controverted Election . . . Pittenweem* [c.1710] [4] *HMC Mar and Kellie*, i. 262–3;

Lauder of Fountainhall, *Hist. Notices* (Bannatyne Club, lxxxvii), 164; *Cal. Treas. Bks.* xxii. 467; R. Sibbald, *Hist. Sheriffdoms of Fife and Kinross* (1710), 134; *Lockhart Letters* ed. Szechi, 53. ⁵*Reg. PC Scotland* 1676–8, p. 213; 1681–2, pp. 243, 723; 1683–4, p. 199; *Scots Peerage*, 90–92; *APS*, viii. 468; ix. 73, 143; *CSP Dom.* 1677–8, p. 397; 1691–2, p. 164; Carstares, *State Pprs.* 22; *Scot. Hist. Soc.* (ser. 1), xiv. 26; *Orig. Pprs.* ed. Macpherson, ii. 15; *HMC Portland*, viii. 206; Atholl mss at Blair Castle, box 45 bdle. 7, no.159, Areskine to [Atholl], 29 Oct. 1707. ⁶SRO, Mar and Kellie mss GD124/15/975/10, Mar to Ld. Grange (Hon. James Erskine†), 17 July 1710; GD124/15/943/5, Grange to Mar, 5 Feb. 1709; GD124/15/10/4, Ld. Bowhill (John Murray*) to same, 23 Sept. 1710; GD124/15/1011/1–2, Areskine to same, 7 Sept., 5 Dec. 1710; D. Szechi, *Jacobitism and Tory Pol.* 66; *HMC Portland*, iv. 558; SRO, Seafield mss GD248/560/45/58, Rothes to [Seafield], 20 Sept. 1710. ⁷*SHR*, lx. 64; Mar and Kellie mss GD124/15/1011/2, Areskine to Grange, 5 Dec. 1710; G. Holmes, *Pol. in Age of Anne*, 338; *Lockhart Letters*, pp. xxiv, xxvi; *Lockhart Pprs.* i. 338–9; SRO, Montrose mss GD220/5/808/18a–b, Mungo Graham* to Duke of Montrose, 13 Feb. 1711. ⁸*HMC Portland*, iv. 676; x. 462–3; SRO, Kennedy of Dalquharran mss GD27/5/2, Harry Maule to [Cornelius Kennedy], 24 Sept. 1711; P. W. J. Riley, *Eng. Ministers and Scotland*, 169–70. ⁹*Lockhart Letters*, 57; Szechi, 101–2, 111; *Lockhart Pprs.* 366; SRO, Breadalbane mss GD112/39/251/14, 'Letter from a Gent. in London', Mar. 1711; *HMC Portland*, v. 238; NLS, Advocates' mss, Wodrow pprs. letters Quarto 6, f. 93. ¹⁰Spalding Club, *Misc.* iv. 85–87; Aberdeen Univ. Lib. Duff House (Montcoffer) mss 3175/2380, 'Resolution of the Commons to Call a Meeting of the Lords', [23] May 1713; SRO, Dalhousie mss GD45/14/348/2–3, Areskine to Maule, 2 Apr., 2 May 1713; *Lockhart Pprs.* 423; *Parlty Hist.* i. 69; Szechi, 137–8, 200; Szechi thesis, app.; *Orig. Pprs.* 416; Wodrow pprs. letters Quarto 6, f. 19; *HMC Portland*, v. 140; Dalhousie mss GD45/14/348/5–7, Areskine to Harry Maule, 31 Aug., 2 Sept. [July] 1713. ¹¹*Lockhart Pprs.* 444–52; *Lockhart Letters*, 72–73, 101–3. ¹²*Cromartie Corresp.* ii. 153–4; Kennedy of Dalquharran mss GD27/3/24/4, Graham to Cornelius Kennedy, 12 Feb. 1715; *Scot. Rec. Soc.* lxxvii. 1–7, 16–17; *Scots Peerage*, 92–93.

D. W. H.

ARESKINE *see also* **ERSKINE**

ARNOLD, John (c.1635–1703), of Llanfihangel Crucorney, Mon.

MONMOUTH	26 Nov. 1680–1681 (Mar.)
SOUTHWARK	1689–1695
MONMOUTH	1695–1698

b. c.1635, o. s. of Nicholas Arnold† of Llanfihangel Crucorney by Letitia, da. and h. of Sir Edward Moore of Mellifont, co. Louth (1st s. *d.v.p.* of Gerald, 1st Visct. Moore of Drogheda [I]). *m.* by 1659 (with £1,500), Margaret, da. of William Cooke I* of Highnam Court, Glos., 1s. 4da. *suc.* fa. 1665.¹

Sheriff, Mon. 1668–9; commr. receiving subscriptions to land bank 1696; receiver, duchy of Lancaster estates, Mon. 1697–1702.²

The notoriety Arnold had acquired during the Exclusion Crisis as an extremist, addicted to political violence in the pursuit of Tory opponents and the persecution of Catholics in his native Monmouthshire, made it undesirable, not to say impossible, for King William to employ him after the Revolution. Arnold's first priority, however, was to obtain a reversal of the judgment given against him for *scandalum magnatum* in 1682 over an allegation that the then Marquess of Worcester (Henry Somerset†) was 'a papist and . . . deeply concerned in the Popish Plot', a defeat which had cost him £10,000 in damages and a spell in prison, and had left him in financial straits. A bill to debar the claim of Worcester, since created Duke of Beaufort, had been introduced into the Convention, where it had failed for lack of time. Further vain attempts were mounted in the 1690 Parliament before Arnold gave up the campaign and sought to salve his fortune by other means.³

Arnold was re-elected on the Whig interest at Southwark in 1690, believing that his enemies were also 'the enemies of England'. Naturally he was classed as a Whig in Lord Carmarthen's analysis of the new House, and on 22 Mar. he responded to Sir Thomas Clarges' motion to censure anti-Tory literature circulated at the last election by proposing a similar condemnation of anti-Whig blacklists. His appointment on 8 May to draft the bill for confirming the East India Company's charter prefigured a future interest in East Indian affairs. He told on 30 Apr. against a resolution of the elections committee pertaining to the Hertfordshire election, that refusal of the oaths should disqualify Quakers from voting; on 3 May over a constituency issue, to engross the bill to erect a court of conscience in Southwark; on 8 May on the Whig side against a clause, concerning the mayoralty, of the bill to restore the corporation of London; and on 17 May, on behalf of a fellow Whig in the Aldborough election case. But he was particularly exercised over his own bill, for reversing the 1682 judgment, which was introduced on 3 Apr. and received a first reading four days later, only for him to request and be granted leave to withdraw it on 1 May. The bill was reintroduced in the next session, on 21 Nov., and this time rapidly passed through its stages in the Commons, piloted through by Sir John Guise, 2nd Bt., and assisted in a division, on 1 Dec., on engrossment by two Whig tellers, Samuel Travers and Sir Walter Yonge, 3rd Bt. (in opposition to two Tories). However, Beaufort canvassed hard against the bill and secured its defeat in the Lords, on a division in which Lord Stamford told for Arnold. Added on 11 Oct. to the committee to draft a bill for examining public accounts, Arnold was also nominated on 22 Oct. to prepare a bill for attainting rebels. He told on 26 Nov., for committing the bill to reduce the interest of money; and, after being given leave of absence on 16

Dec., told again on 26 Dec. in favour of calling in counsel during the debate on the bill granting extensive reparations to Edmund Prideaux† out of the estate of Judge Jeffreys for sufferings at Jeffreys' hands at the time of the Monmouth rebellion. This parliamentary activity does not of itself connote a change of political orientation, but by April 1691 Robert Harley* was listing Arnold as a supporter of the Court.[4]

In the early stages of the 1691–2 session Arnold was especially active in promoting informations against smugglers and Jacobites, probably with the intention, at least in part, of embarrassing the ministers. On 14 Nov., he brought up a petition from one David Lashley, probably a merchant, alleging that a particular ship at Gravesend was bound for France with a cargo of lead and tin, but this story was repudiated by other Members. A similar allegation surfaced exactly a month later, when Arnold drew to the attention of the House an information he had received from a ship's captain concerning illicit trading to France 'for lead, etc.'. The informant, he claimed, had since been 'taken up' and held *incommunicado* by the secretary of state's messengers, who 'had refused to bring him up on a habeas corpus'. Once more the Members took no notice: they 'looked upon it as a trivial matter if true, but did not believe it'. On 16 Nov. Arnold spoke in support of a motion for an address to the King to lay before Parliament the examinations of Lord Preston (Sir Richard Grahme, 3rd Bt.†) and Matthew Crone relating to the so-called 'Preston Plot', and in a further such incident on 17 Feb. 1692 he presented a petition from an informer called Dodsworth 'desiring some consideration of his circumstances for discovering the design that was carrying on by the papists in Lancashire'. But his closest involvement was with the activities of the spy William Fuller. This, however, caused more embarrassment to Arnold than to the administration. On 1 Jan. his name cropped up in the House as one of six MPs requested specifically in a letter from Fuller to be appointed to confer with him and advise how best to 'bring over the two persons he spoke of', presumably conspirators willing to turn King's evidence. In the ensuing debate Arnold spoke in Fuller's defence, assuring the Commons that 'the only thing he desires is your protection'. Three days later he spoke again, during a discussion on Fuller's examination, his principal object being to discomfort some Tory Members accused of misleading the House. Then on 22 Feb. he raised Fuller's case once more. He reported to the House that he had visited the spy in prison, finding him 'in a bad condition'. Fuller apparently believed himself to be 'poisoned' and likely to die. A motion was proposed, in which Arnold joined, to appoint a small committee to attend Fuller and take his examination. Although nominated to this committee, he was subsequently entrusted by the House with a task on his own. Having declared that Fuller had told him where 'his two witnesses' could be found, he was ordered by the House to apprehend them. The following day he was obliged to admit that he 'had been abused in this matter and did therefore recommend it to the House to do what they thought fit, assuring them that what he did was for the service of the kingdom'. 'By a paper he met with at Fuller's', he added, 'he believed we were all abused, finding one which reflected highly on this House.' The House repeated its order that he should arrest the witnesses, this time naming two more MPs to accompany him. Again there was no result. Another instance of muckraking, although in this case aimed directly at two ministers and unconnected with specifically treasonous activities, had occurred on 29 Dec., when Arnold seconded Sir John Guise in presenting a petition against the Speaker, Sir John Trevor and Sir George Hutchins*, in their capacities as commissioners of the great seal. They were accused of having discouraged the reforming Middlesex justice Edward Stephens (a leading light in a local society for the reformation of manners) in Stephens' magisterial campaign against Sunday trading. Trevor's opposition to the reformation of manners movement had provoked particular hostility, and Arnold took a subsequent occasion to rebuke the Speaker on a procedural matter in a way that suggests he was pursuing a vendetta. He had moved on 2 Jan. 1692 the reading of the bill for the relief of debtors, a measure he had himself introduced on 18 Dec., when the Speaker intervened to oppose it. Arnold 'told him that he must not now think he was in Chancery but in the House of Commons, to whom he was but a servant, and that each Member had a liberty of speech in the House'. It is quite conceivable that Arnold's outrage over the Stephens case was genuine. His role as MP for Southwark, a hotbed of the reformation of manners movement, would in any case have made him a logical choice to present Stephens' petition, and some years afterwards, when approached by the Society for Promoting Christian Knowledge to act as a correspondent in Monmouthshire, he declared his zeal for 'promoting the business of reformation' and 'the suppression of vice and immorality'. Moreover, his name had been inserted into the Middlesex commission of the peace in 1690 at the King's specific request. His speech on 17 Feb. in support of a motion to refer a petition from the 'poor French Protestants' to a committee of the whole House would also tend to confirm this reforming outlook, since enthusiasm for the cause of the persecuted Huguenots was often a hallmark of the moral reformer. Besides his criticisms of individual ministers, his speeches on the subject of the supply tended towards making life difficult for the Court. On 1 Jan. 1692, for example, he intervened twice during discussion of the report of the committee of supply, the first time for agreeing to what was in effect an over-estimate of the yield of the hearth tax in Ireland; and then in favour of a motion to appoint a committee to receive proposals for raising money on the Irish forfeited estates, being afterwards named to that committee. He was, oddly enough, added to the committee subsequently, on 3 Feb., having two days earlier spoken against allowing the reception of a petition relating to the Irish forfeited estates bill, on the practical grounds that 'if you take the method of receiving petitions there will be no end'. He also told on 12 Feb. for a rider to this bill exempting Quakers from the requirement of taking the oaths stipulated in the bill, an issue on which he felt strongly, for ten days later he was speaking again for the Quakers' affirmation bill. In another contribution to a supply debate, on 12 Jan., he spoke against a proposal from Paul Foley I to secure an advance from 'the bankers' and the East India Company, secured on a perpetual fund: he opposed the idea that 'a public bank might be established for taking up of money'. Finally on 19 Jan., in a curiously non-partisan debate on the poll tax, he supported a 6*d*. rather than a shilling rate, arguing that 'you are now going for the sake perhaps of 100,000 shillings to disoblige and lose the hearts of 100,000 people'. The explanation of his speaking in this instance on the same side as Sir Christopher Musgrave, 4th Bt., and Sir John Lowther, 2nd Bt. II, may be that all three represented or hailed from poorer counties. A note of the Country Member's suspicion of the executive may also be heard in his denunciation on 20 Feb. of the Shadwell waterworks bill, 'for that it seemed to give a countenance to the Council board to hear matters of property between party and party'. At other times he was sharp in his defence of the rights and privileges of the Commons against invasion by the Lords, an attitude which cannot have been regarded in ministerial circles as conducive to political harmony. He attacked on 11 Dec. 1691 two of the Lords' amendments to the treason trials bill, one because it 'levelled impeachments by this House with indictments, giving the party the same advantages therein'; a second for providing that at the trial of any peer the entire Upper House should be summoned. Then on 13 Feb. 1692 in a debate on a conference with the Lords on the bill appointing commissioners of accounts he 'moved that, since the Lords were encroaching upon the privileges of this House, that we might remonstrate the same to the King and that it might be known where the fault lay'. His remaining speeches in the session were on 5 Jan. 1692, in favour of the bill to regulate the Thames Fishermen's Company; on 21 Jan., on the bill to prevent brewers from being maltsters, when he offered a clause 'to disable brewers from being justices of the peace in the same county where they were brewers', possibly to forestall any evasion of the alehouse licensing laws; and on 19 Feb., against the bill for confirming Cambridge University's charter. Two further tellerships occurred on 16 and 19 Feb., for a private bill and on an adjournment respectively.[5]

Arnold's appointment on 16 Nov. 1692 to the committees to examine the London merchants' petition over shipping losses and the paper submitted by the transports commissioners was indicative of a close interest in investigating reports of naval mismanagements during the preceding summer. In a debate on 30 Nov. on this very subject he was the only Whig to go beyond generalities and level specific criticisms at the secretary of state, Lord Nottingham (Daniel Finch[†]). After one Member had explicitly declined to single out any candidates for dismissal from high office, Arnold interjected:

> I will take liberty to name one, and that is the Lord Nottingham, who has beat two secretaries into one, who has prohibit[ed] the licensing some books writ in defence of this government, and has discouraged some witnesses in matters carrying on against this government.

His proposal on 8 Dec. 1692 for a conference with the Lords 'to consider of the state of the nation and the posture of our affairs' may have been an attempt to revive the naval inquiry, and later in the session he was appointed to inquire into the failure to intercept the French fleet (3 Feb. 1693). In debates on supply he seems to have spoken once in a vein critical of the administration, or at least at cross-purposes with the administration, when on 10 Feb. he called for 'a review of the poll bill'. Otherwise his contributions on issues of supply seem to have been influenced by non-political considerations or to have been concerned with details that were tangential to the main business of raising money, such as his motion on 10 Jan. for a clause in a supply bill to tax the King's bench prison in Southwark, a matter of constituency interest. A speech of 17 Jan. on the land tax bill once again showed his animosity towards the House of Lords: he opposed an amendment by the Lords to the bill which would have ensured that members of the Upper House were rated for the tax by their peers, 'for that the Lords by this means would pay very little to the tax'. And when he told, on 27 Jan., in favour of agreeing with a resolution of the committee of ways and means for an additional duty on exports of rabbit fur, his principal concern may well have been not the revenue but the regulation of this trade, for on the preceding 3 Dec. he had told for a bill to prevent frauds by the Hudson's Bay Company, and to prevent the export of rabbit and hare skins. He spoke again in this session for Quaker relief, supporting on 5 Dec. 1692 a petition from Quakers for exemption from the legal obligation to take oaths, and also revived his interest in the relief of debtors, a cause which he may have been led to espouse because of the location of the King's bench and Marshalsea prisons in his constituency, or conceivably because of his anxiety over the kind of social problems that the reformation of manners societies were tackling. On 19 Dec. he presented a petition from the 'poor prisoners' in the King's bench, and was the first-named Member of the committee appointed to consider it; on 23 Feb. 1693 he presented another, from the prisoners in the Fleet; and on 27 Feb. he tendered a rider to the bill for revising and continuing expired laws, to revive for one year the previous Act for the relief of 'poor prisoners', only for this to be rejected by the House as a dangerous precedent. More central to the aims of the moral reform campaign was the lotteries bill, which he moved on 10 Jan. and presented a week later. Its moralistic emphasis, as an attack on the vice of gaming, was heightened by Arnold's report to the House on 25 Feb. that he had been offered a bribe of as much as £100 p.a. to drop the bill. He was active too in legislation for the regulation of commerce, presenting on 9 Dec. 1692 a petition from the Poulterers' Company for a clause to be inserted into the bill against hawkers and pedlars, speaking on 2 Feb. 1693 against that bill, and serving as a teller on the same day for a clause in it 'that any person settling in a town, and paying to Church and poor, may carry goods'. He also acted as a teller on 18 Jan. in a procedural division over the East India bill. On the question of the Wye and Lugg navigation, which divided local opinion in Herefordshire and Monmouthshire, he separated from old friends like Lord Coningsby (Thomas), Sir Rowland Gwynne and the Harleys of Brampton Bryan, to tell against the bill on 13 Jan. Four days later came his one other tellership in this session, for postponing the report of the committee to regulate the privilege of Members in lawsuits. His last speech, in February, was a piece of partisan vindictiveness directed against the press licenser Edmund Bohun, a Tory for whose continued incarceration he successfully moved.[6]

Arnold's designation as a Court supporter with a place or a pension in Samuel Grascome's list in the spring of 1693 would have been more accurate if applied during and after the 1693–4 session of Parliament when Arnold's Whig party colleagues were more comfortably ensconced in the ministry. Indeed, in a satirical ballad written in 1694 Arnold was included among the members of the Court Whig Rose Club, an assumption borne out by his appointment on 29 Dec. 1693 to the committee to examine Sir Charles Meredith on the articles of impeachment against the Irish lords justices Lord Coningsby and Sir Charles Porter*, his tellership (with another Whig) on 16 Jan. 1694 in favour of an amendment to the land tax bill, and his nomination on 3 Feb. to the committee on the bill to prevent the export of bullion. The one aberration was his appearance as a teller on 20 Mar. against a rider offered to the salt duties bill. His colleague in the division was the Tory Sir Samuel Dashwood, while their opponents were the Court Whigs Edward Clarke I and Sir Walter Yonge, 3rd Bt. In purely party matters Arnold was heartily and consistently Whig. He intervened in the debate of 1 Mar. 1694 over the Bristol Tory MP Sir John Knight's published speech on the naturalization question, to request 'that the speech might be burnt at Bristol for the justification of the Member', while on 17 Apr. he acted as a teller in favour of the Whig Hon. Fitton Gerard* in the Clitheroe election case. Much of his parliamentary activity in this session concerned the affairs of the metropolis. He was a teller on 23 Dec. 1693 for a bill to erect a court of conscience for Holborn and Finsbury, and on 7 Mar. 1694 in favour of going into a committee of the whole House the next day on the London orphans' relief bill. On 17 Apr. he reported upon a petition from the 'traders and poor inhabitants' of London and Southwark, complaining about the quality of halfpence and farthings, and three days later reported from a further committee to draw up an address on the same theme. Familiar issues attracted his attention too: he and his parliamentary colleague at Southwark, Anthony Bowyer, were ordered on 28 Nov. 1693 to prepare another debtors' relief bill, and on 26 Feb. 1694 he told against another bill against hawkers and pedlars. He also told in a privilege case, and on three private bills, one of them concerning his distant connexion Sir Ralph Dutton, 1st Bt.* He was most active in the last session of the 1690 Parliament on what were distinctly party matters. The imposition of the oaths of allegiance and supremacy constituted one example. On 14 Jan. Arnold and Fitton Gerard were ordered to prepare a bill to disfranchise all those refusing 'the oaths to the government'. Later he told on 4 Feb. against an amendment to the land tax bill which would have omitted the necessity of tendering 'the oath' to the assessors, and on 11 Mar. in favour of a bill requiring 'certain persons' to take the oaths. His tellership on 20 Feb., against discharging from custody the mayor of Liverpool, who had been committed for irregularities in a recent by-election there, should probably be interpreted as a partisan gesture. He was active in pursuing the various inquiries into corruption instigated at this time: telling on 26 Feb. against recommitting the representation to the King over the abuses of army agents, on 18 Apr. against the bill of indemnity to Sir Thomas Cooke*, and on 1 May on a procedural motion relating to the impeachment of the Duke of Leeds. There may also have been partisan overtones to the division of 30 Apr. on the bill to reverse the attainder of the New York radical Jacob Leisler, Arnold acting as a teller for the bill. During this session he also reported, on 20 Apr., upon a private petition.[7]

In the 1695 general election Arnold succeeded in winning back his old seat at Monmouth, but only after prolonged negotiations with all the various principals in the county, both Whigs and Tories, ending in an agreement that he resign in turn at the next election to Henry Probert*. A teller on the Whig side on 16 Jan. 1696 in a division on the Hertfordshire election case, Arnold was forecast as likely to support the Court in the divisions of 31 Jan. 1696 on the proposed council of trade, and signed the Association promptly. He told for the Court on 3 Feb., in favour of a rider to the land tax bill to maintain the previous year's levels of assessment, and again on 17 Feb. for a motion to adjourn all committees. Support for the naturalization of foreign Protestants, evident in his speech in the 1690 Parliament against Sir John Knight, was evident in his presenting, on 29 Jan., a bill to naturalize, *inter alios*, the future Whig MP James Stanhope, and in his telling on 24 Apr. in favour of retaining a clause in the salt duties and land bank establishment bill for naturalizing subscribers to the bank. His interest in East Indian affairs was evident in a tellership on 2 Apr. to allow consideration of a merchants' petition objecting to any extension of the East India Company's monopoly to areas on the subcontinent not covered by the existing charter. Pet subjects which again engaged his interest were the regulation of street trading and the problem of debt. He was a teller on 12 Mar. for leave for a clause to be added to a further bill against hawkers and pedlars, on behalf of an interest-group he had represented before, the Poulterers' Company, to preserve their monopoly of the street trade in meat in London and Westminster. And on 23 Mar. he told in favour of the bill for improving the security enjoyed by creditors, and to prevent debtors from absconding. A subsequent tellership, on 18 Apr., against an amendment to the bill to stop Catholics disinheriting their Protestant heirs, which would have weakened the bill's provisions and allowed the testators more freedom of manoeuvre, in part reflected his old anti-papist bigotry. But there was a more immediate consideration, too, which may have motivated him – the involvement of his cousin Sir Henry Dutton Colt, 1st Bt.*, with whom he was still closely allied, in schemes to make money through the discovery of 'concealed' Catholic lands. The other teller against the amendment was Sir Henry's brother, John Dutton Colt*.[8]

From at least 1696 onwards Arnold became closely involved with these cousins' schemes to forward their search for preferment by the patronage and encouragement of various disreputable spies, informers and *agents provocateurs*, whose exposures of alleged Jacobite conspiracies were to serve both as a testimony to the Colts' and Arnold's loyalty and devotion to the Williamite regime and as a source of embarrassment and anxiety to ministers. The Duke of Shrewsbury seemed particularly vulnerable, given that he had been cited as a Jacobite sympathizer by Sir John Fenwick† and several informants at the time of the Assassination Plot, and he became the prime target. Towards the end of the 1696–7 session it was planned to bring before the House of Commons the informer Matthew Smith, who in himself represented one of the skeletons in Shrewsbury's cupboard, in so far as Smith's early information on the Assassination Plot had been unwisely discounted and ignored by Shrewsbury when secretary of state. The scheme, which came to nothing, was to introduce Smith's evidence into the deliberations of a committee, under Arnold's chairmanship, inquiring into abuses in the Mint. Arnold's appointment to the chair of this committee had been prefigured by his earlier involvement in complaints over the copper coinage, and by his appointment to the committee of 14 Jan. 1697 to draw up clauses to explain the Recoinage Acts. The first victim of the Mint committee was the engraver John Roettiers, denounced as a security risk in a report of 2 Feb. because he was himself a Catholic and allegedly 'kept an Irish papist in his house'. A further report dwelt on evidence of coin-clipping connived at or even committed by the officers of the Mint, and on 8 Apr. Arnold was named to a small drafting committee on a bill 'for regulating the corporation of moneyers'. Besides its general value as a means of ferreting out scandals, some with political overtones, the Mint committee had a more specific use as far as Arnold was concerned, for one of the places on which his cousin John Dutton Colt had fixed his ambition was that of master of the Mint, likely to fall vacant because of the ill-health of the occupant, Thomas Neale*. Arnold was also the probable instigator of another complaint of corruption in government, this time in the victualling office, for he gave evidence to a committee examining a petition on this matter from a protégé of his, John Tutchin, formerly a clerk in this office. The contents of Arnold's evidence was made clear to the House when this committee reported on 15 Apr. He claimed that in 1696 he had personally advanced a small sum of money to the purser of a man-of-war to facilitate the purchase of 'necessaries' for the ship's voyage, on a promise of reimbursement from the victualling commissioner Thomas Papillon*, but that Papillon had failed to fulfil his part of the agreement. The effect of this campaign of mischief-making could be seen in a recommendation from Sir William Trumbull* to the Earl of Sunderland in April 1697 that Arnold and John Dutton Colt might be considered for some reward in the light of their 'good service' in the Commons. Sunderland, however, informed Trumbull that though he was willing to find places for Dutton Colt and Arnold this could not be done 'without the Duke of Shrewsbury's consent'. Arnold received nothing more than a minor local office under the duchy of Lancaster, and it does seem that this should probably be attributed to the (justifiable) animosity of Shrewsbury, whose deputy James Vernon I* wrote in September 1697, 'I have a great contempt for the Arnolds, Colts, and all that would rise by accusations, and should have a stubbornness not to give way to them.' Arnold seems to have been fully aware of the opposition his pretensions had encountered in this quarter for in early December 1697 he and John Dutton Colt made approaches to Shrewsbury via Vernon, who reported that 'Mr Arnold has desired to make me a visit to tell me how he was put upon in relation to your grace'. Vernon added, with an air of considerable satisfaction, 'I can't but think you have done the world a great kindness in giving the occasion to these fellows to lay one another open. Here is a bag of poison now broken, and I hope it will be no more infectious.' Meanwhile, Sunderland had been able to overcome opposition from Shrewsbury, at least as far as to persuade the King to appoint Colt to a vacant commissionership in the excise, with Arnold to succeed the new commissioner in Colt's current post as customs collector in Bristol. This arrangement was, however, far from attractive. Vernon wrote again to Shrewsbury on 9 Dec.:

> Arnold came to me yesterday and would have made a merit of not making his report last sessions [on Smith's evidence to the Mint committee], but I was not of his opinion, and he had another book of Smith's, called his 'vindication', in manuscript, and asked me if I would read it . . . He said he came to ask my opinion whether he should have anything to do with him. I left him to his discretion . . . The mystery is unriddled tonight, for Colt hath desired me to excuse him from accepting a commissioner's place in the excise, if it should be intended, since he would rather wait for a vacancy in the customs, but added that his cousin Jack Arnold had rather be in the excise than anywhere. This is the reformation and zeal for the public that these rogues ever designed and I am glad it is out.

Five days later Vernon reported that he had been

> haunted again by Arnold, who would needs show me a petition of Smith's that was put into his hands to be presented to the House, but I refused to read it. And I should think he don't intend to present it, by giving me notice, but that he designs one should silence him by the promise of a place, which is more than I can undertake for, or think he deserves; and when he saw my indifference as to the stopping him, he asked me to acquaint the lord chancellor [Sir John Somers*] with it, whom he could satisfy that some in both Houses were concerned in that matter. That I think of doing . . . For my own particular, since one sees no end of this knavery, I had rather he should present his petition now than at another time. I don't think there is any disposition in the House to meddle with it, and I shall not spare letting them [the Commons] know what would have quieted them.

Vernon believed that 'all the use Mr Arnold would make' of Smith's 'papers' would be to 'recommend himself for an employment, which he was looking after, and when that was once secured he would discharge himself of them into some other hands, who should present them to the House'. He professed to dismiss the threat, thinking that Arnold's 'behaviour the last session would be remembered' by the House, 'when he had a report tending to this matter and kept out of the way the time it was called for'.[9]

Little was done at the beginning of the 1697–8 session to pursue Smith's case or any of the other information available for Arnold and his friends to exploit. He was named with John Perry* on 13 Dec. 1697 to prepare a bill to regulate the assize of bread, a response to the growing social problems with which Arnold, as a supporter of the movement for the reformation of manners, was deeply concerned. In the new year, on 9 Feb. 1698, Arnold spoke in support of (Sir) John Philipps' motion for an address to the King requesting the suppression of blasphemy and profaneness, and was nominated to the committee appointed upon this motion. On 6 Jan. there had occurred a strange incident, when he told for a minority of two against the bill to perpetuate the imprisonment of those accused of complicity in the Assassination Plot who were being held without trial, his colleague as a teller being the Lancashire Tory Thomas Brotherton. As late as the middle of January 1698 Vernon was ignorant of any attempt on the part of Arnold or the Colts to 'stir ... old matters', but within a month the cousins were back at their old game. Their instruments this time were William Chaloner and Aubrey Price, two informers who the previous year had fed information to the government through Sir Henry Dutton Colt about imaginary Jacobite plots. Unmasked, they had been committed to custody and temporarily disowned by their patron. On 18 Feb., however, Chaloner petitioned the House, claiming that his imprisonment was in itself the result of a conspiracy, on the part of 'some persons at the Mint', in revenge for previous disclosures of misdeeds. The petition was referred to a committee, of which Arnold was the first-named Member, his former chairmanship of the Mint committee of 1697 making him a natural choice. Vernon observed that during the cross-examination of Chaloner's witnesses by the committee Arnold showed 'too much regard for Chaloner's reputation'. Arnold was also rebuked for sending for 'examinations' and other papers without consulting the committee at large. When little progress was achieved along the lines Arnold and the Colts would have liked, they 'grew weary of it', and no report was made. But Arnold did not abandon the pursuit of scandal. In May it was said that he and Sir Rowland Gwynne were 'upon the hunt' for a copy of William Molyneux's *Case of Ireland ... Stated* in order to be able to complain about his assertions of Irish legislative independence before any representative of the Irish administration could do so, and thus imply negligence on the ministry's part. Less significant, perhaps, was his communication to James Vernon of evidence of coin-clipping in Exeter, which, if it had had any relevance to his quest for office, would only have served to underline his usefulness to government. His other parliamentary activity in what turned out to be his last session included the presentation of three bills: a multiple naturalization bill (1 Mar.), a measure to prevent the use of the King's ships for imports (19 Apr.), and a bill against gaming (2 May), the latter inspired by the societies for the reformation of manners. He told a further five times in this session: on 1 Feb. 1698, against committing the Don navigation bill; on 29 Mar. for nominating the Whig Edward Owen as a land tax commissioner for Coventry; on 19 Apr., in favour of a clause offered to the elections bill, to regulate the admission of honorary freemen; on 5 May, against receiving a petition from Northumberland concerning the halfpenny and farthing coinage; and on 17 May (with Sir Henry Dutton Colt) for committing yet another debtors' relief bill. He reported, on 25 Jan., upon a private petition and on 16 May was ordered (again with Sir Henry Dutton Colt) to prepare a second private bill on behalf of Sir Ralph Dutton.[10]

Arnold's claims to substantial preferment were still unrecognized at the end of the 1695 Parliament, although by way of some small compensation he was lent £200 by the Treasury in June 1698 and the following year received a further £200 as royal bounty. His financial circumstances were such that he was only able to repay half the loan before his death, and he only gave a portion to one of his four daughters, each of whom had been entitled to the sum of £1,000 on reaching the age of 17. It must be reckoned extremely unlikely, therefore, that he was the 'John Arnold' who himself lent £9,000 to the crown between March and July 1698. In accordance with the electoral treaty concluded at Monmouth three years before, he gave up his seat on the 1698 general election, being listed in an analysis of the old and new Parliaments as a member of the Court party 'left out'. Rumours that Thomas Morgan* of Tredegar would bring him in, to represent one of two constituencies for which Morgan expected to be returned, proved groundless. Arnold would appear to have retired to Monmouthshire during this Parliament, for when in December 1699 the House of Lords took up again the case of the informer Matthew Smith, and Arnold was shown to have 'employed' Smith, paid him money and corresponded with him when Smith was abroad, it was observed by Vernon that 'Mr Arnold is in the country and if he be sent for from Wales I know not whom he will be out of humour withal'. The Lords decided against summoning Arnold to hear his explanation, and when the matter was raised in the Commons the evidence against him was simply disbelieved. When early the following year a by-election for Monmouthshire seemed imminent, Arnold canvassed the county in opposition to Sir Charles, 3rd Bt.* No such election occurred, but Arnold held high hopes of returning to the Commons at the first election of 1701. According to the electoral treaty of 1695, he should have been returned for Monmouth again at this election, but by this time the political balance in the county had undergone several important shifts, and Arnold found himself frozen out by an alliance between the Morgans of Tredegar and the Williamses of Llangibby. He canvassed for the borough seat but did not force the issue to a poll, retiring with fulminations against those 'gentlemen' whose 'solemn promises' were, he said, no more to be relied upon than 'the King of France's'. He was not, however, by any means innocent himself, for the year before he had sought to contest a vacancy for knight of the shire against Sir Charles Kemys, 3rd Bt.*, the proper candidate for the county seat in 1701 according to the electoral compact. Ironically, he then tried to form an alliance with Kemys at the general election on the basis of their common grievances against the Morgans and Williamses, conveniently forgetting the bitterness of the by-election dispute, in which eventually both men had lost out.[11]

Arnold was still in good enough health to retain his place in the Monmouthshire lieutenancy in March 1701 but during the following year was replaced as duchy of Lancaster receiver, possibly as an act of party-political spite, and then as a county land tax commissioner, where he was succeeded by his only son. He died in 1703. After his son's death in 1726, *s.p.m.*, the estates were sold by his granddaughters to Edward Harley*.[12]

[1] Bradney, *Mon.* i. 219; Lodge, *Peerage of Ire.* (1754), i. 320; *Mar. Lic. Fac. Off.* (Harl. Soc. xxiv), 186; *HMC Lords*, n.s. vii. 348. [2] *CJ*, xii. 508; Somerville, *Duchy of Lancaster Official Lists*, 231. [3] *Hist. Jnl.* xxiii. 275, 282, 284, 287–8. [4] NLW, Penrice and Margam mss L1385, Arnold to [–], [c.1690]; Bodl. Ballard 22, f. 15; Wilts. RO, Ailesbury mss 1300/812A, Duchess of Beaufort to Earl of Ailesbury (Thomas Bruce†), [Dec. 1690]; Luttrell, *Brief Relation*, ii. 140; *HMC Lords*, iii. 208–9. [5] *Luttrell Diary*, 17, 23, 75, 78, 94, 102–4, 111, 125, 139, 146, 167, 184, 191–2, 194, 196, 198–9, 203; Grey, x. 225; Hopkins thesis, 216; *Chapter in Eng. Church Hist.* ed. McClure, 349; *CSP Dom.* 1689–90, p. 537. [6] H. Horwitz, *Revolution Politicks*, 137; *Luttrell Diary*, 275–6, 293, 302–3, 327, 357, 360, 379, 397, 417, 445, 448, 453; *Diary of Edmund Bohun* ed. Wilton Rix, 118. [7] *Poems on Affairs of State* ed. Cameron, v. 435; Bodl. Carte 130, f. 347. [8] *Hist. Jnl.* xxix. 566. [9] Hopkins, 222–3; H. Horwitz, *Parl. and Pol. Wm. III*, 192; *Vernon–Shrewsbury Letters*, i. 405, 440, 442, 445; BL, Trumbull Add. mss 125 (Trumbull's diary), pp. 8–9, 11; Northants. RO, Montagu (Boughton) mss 46/161–2, 164, 168, 181, James Vernon I to Shrewsbury, 7, 9, 14, 21 Dec. 1697, 18 Jan. 1697[–8]. [10] Montagu (Boughton) mss 46/181, 78–79, 81, 86, Vernon to Shrewsbury, 18 Jan., 11, 14, 18 Mar. 1697[–8]; Hopkins thesis, 226; *Vernon–Shrewsbury Letters*, ii. 83; Add. 40771, f. 167; 70019, f. 21. [11] *Cal. Treas. Bks.* xvii. 829, 860; xiv. 133; *HMC Lords*, n.s. vii. 348; *Vernon–Shrewsbury Letters*, ii. 152, 366, 392; Montagu (Boughton) mss 48/11, Vernon to Shrewsbury, 16 Dec. 1699; *Shrewsbury Corresp.* 597; *Hist. Jnl.* xxix. 566–7; NLW, Kemeys–Tynte mss 374, Charles Price to Sir Charles Kemys, 5 Mar. 1699–1700; 375, Edward Perkins to same, 9 Mar. 1699–1700; 377, Charles Hutchins to Tracy Catchmay, 11 Mar. 1699–1700; 384, Arnold to Kemys, 10 Jan. 1700[–1]. [12] *CSP Dom.* 1700–2, p. 254; Bradney, 215.

D. W. H.

ARTHINGTON, Cyril (c.1665–by 1724), of Arthington, Yorks. and Westminster.

ALDBOROUGH 1701 (Feb.)–1702

b. c.1665, 1st s. of Cyril Arthington of Milnthorpe, Yorks. by Anne, da. of Maj. Jonas Binns of Horbury, nr. Wakefield, Yorks. *educ.* Wakefield g.s.; Sidney Sussex, Camb. 29 June 1683, aged 17. *unm. suc.* 2nd cos. Henry Arthington† at Arthington 1682.[1]

FRS 1701.

The representative of a cadet branch of an old-established family of West Riding gentry, Arthington was brought in to inherit the ancestral manor on the failure of the direct male line. His own upbringing must have been comfortable, for he and his younger brother Sandford, a physician, were both given a university education, and when he succeeded his cousin at Arthington it was to property valued at some £2,200 p.a., which gave him a place among the greater gentry of the county, and enabled Sandford to be provided for with their father's estate. Arthington first confessed to parliamentary ambitions in January 1695, but though he considered entering the lists at the projected Aldborough by-election of 1697 he did not stand for Parliament until 1698, when he finally stood at Aldborough. In a bitterly contested election, during which Arthington was offered the support of the local vicar, tempers rose so sharply that he fought a duel with a rival candidate, Christopher Tancred*. Neither was wounded. Defeated at the poll, Arthington petitioned against another opponent, Sir Abstrupus Danby*, but without result. In the January 1701 election, however, he was unopposed. His cousin's political background and preferences had been Presbyterian and Whig, but he himself seems to have been a Tory. He may well have been influenced by his close friend and frequent companion Sir Godfrey Copley, 2nd Bt.*, whose interest at Aldborough had gone a long way towards procuring his return. Listed among those thought likely to support the Court in February 1701 in agreeing to continue the 'Great Mortgage', he told with Sir John Bolles, 4th Bt., on 10 June, for an amendment to the bill for appointing commissioners of accounts, designed to preserve powers granted under previous Acts to examine army and navy debts. Re-elected to the next Parliament in December, he was classified as a Tory by Robert Harley* and was listed as having favoured the motion of 26 Feb. 1702 vindicating the proceedings of the Commons in the impeachments of the Whig lords.[2]

Losing his seat at Aldborough in 1702, once the Duke of Newcastle (John Holles†) had secured complete control of the borough, he devoted much of his time thereafter to the study of antiquities and inventions, and to the activities of the Royal Society, at whose meetings he and Copley were regular attenders. They were in the habit of dining together 'every Wednesday at Pontack's and from thence go to Gresham College'. At home he developed his estate, building a canal to link his corn mill with the River Wharfe and to enable him to travel by water as far as Doncaster. He erected 'a noble hall' at Arthington, and 'furnished it with water conveyed in pipes of lead from an engine he has contrived at his mill . . . being an ingenious gentleman and well seen in hydrostatics'. Ralph Thoresby called him 'that observing gentleman'. Although Arthington did not stand for Parliament again until 1715, he attended the county elections of 1702 and 1708, and in January 1709 assisted West Riding woollen interests to lobby Parliament over 'the cloth bill'. In 1715 he put up as a Tory on the Slingsby interest at Knaresborough, was beaten into fourth place at the poll and petitioned unsuccessfully.[3]

Arthington adopted as his heir his brother's eldest son, who had been named Cyril in his honour and in expectation of this arrangement. It was anticipated in Sandford's will in 1705, which made no provision for the younger Cyril, and was formally confirmed in Arthington's own will in 1716. After a quarrel between uncle and nephew in 1720 had resulted in a temporary revocation of 'all bequests' in the nephew's favour, a second codicil on 2 Nov. 1723 recognized a reconciliation by restoring the status quo. The will was proved on 18 Dec. 1724.[4]

[1] R. Thoresby, *Ducatus Leodiensis* (1816), 7–8; Nichols, *Lit. Hist.* iv. 76; K. S. Bartlett, *Will of Horbury*, i. 42. [2] *Thoresby Diary*, i. 382, 411; Stowe 747, ff. 44, 70; T. Lawson-Tancred, *Recs. of a Yorks. Manor*, 220; *HMC Portland*, iii. 598; Huntington Lib. Stowe mss 26(1), Hon. James Brydges* diary, 20 Dec. 1698; Yorks. Arch. Soc. Copley mss, Robert Molesworth* to Sir Godfrey Copley, 19 Feb., 29 Mar. 1701; info. from Mr L. Fry. [3] *Thoresby Diary*, i. 143, 369, 373; ii. 6, 20; *Letters to Ralph Thoresby* (Thoresby Soc. xxi), 99; Stowe 748, f. 79; Nichols, 74–75; Thoresby, 7–8; App. 156. [4] Borthwick Inst. York, wills, Pont, Dec. 1705; Ainsty, Dec. 1724.

E. C./D. W. H.

ARUNDELL, Francis (1676–1712), of Stoke Park, Stoke Bruern, Northants.

NORTHAMPTON   2 Nov. 1704–1710

bap. 3 May 1676, 1st s. of Francis Arundell (*d.* 1736) of Stoke Park, sheriff Northants. 1693, by Felicia (*d.* 1710), da. of William Wilmer of Sywell, Northants. *educ.* Stoke Bruern sch.; Trinity Coll. Camb. 1693. *m.* lic. 1 July 1703 (with £5,000) Isabella (*d.* 1724), 4th da. of Sir William Wentworth† of Wakefield, Yorks., 1s. 2da. (1 *d.v.p.*).[1]

Surveyor of the outports 1711–*d.*[2]

The Arundells of Stoke Park came of ancient Cornish stock. Francis Arundell's grandfather and namesake, the son of a Cornish clergyman, inherited Stoke Park and its associated lands in 1645 on the death of his uncle, Sir Richard Crane, whose elder brother, Sir Francis, had been granted them by Charles I. In 1703 young Francis Arundell made his match with Isabella Wentworth, a maid of honour to the Queen, whose bestowal of a marriage portion of £3,000, in addition to the £2,000 settled by the Wentworths, was a signal mark of royal favour. Much later Arundell's distinguished soldier and diplomatist brother-in-law, Thomas Wentworth, Lord Raby (the future 3rd Earl of Strafford), was to claim that the marriage had taken place without his 'privity', he having just taken up his appointment as envoy at Berlin, which explains the coolness that always existed between them. When offering Strafford condolences upon Arundell's death in 1712, Lord Berkeley of Stratton was careful to add: 'though I know the intimacy between you was not great'.[3]

In November 1704 Arundell entered Parliament as a Tory after polling successfully at the Northampton by-election, but he was never active in proceedings. Within three weeks of his return he voted against the Tack on 28 Nov., and in a 1705 list relative to that division he was classed as a 'Churchman'. He also appears, erroneously, in a list of those opposed to the Lords' amendments to the abjuration bill in February 1703. On 21 Feb. 1705 he was teller against receipt of an additional clause to the bill for prohibiting all trade with France. Returned unopposed in 1705, he voted against the Court's candidate for the Speakership at the beginning of the new Parliament, 25 Oct. By December 1706 the Arundells had acquired a London residence of their own in Arlington Street, 'among the great people', as Lady Wentworth commented to her son Lord Raby. Yet pecuniary worries were never far away. Arundell's father had settled a yearly sum of £500 on the couple, but it was barely sufficient for their life-style in London's fashionable quarter. As his wife Isabella recalled later during her widowhood, debt was almost their constant preoccupation. In May 1709 when Isabella was pregnant and unable to travel she had to turn to her brother Raby for the means to allow herself and two servants to lodge with her mother at Twickenham, while Francis and the rest of their household returned to Northampton. Concluding her request, she confessed, 'Mr Arundell is very much ashamed I should be forced to beg this favour'. Arundell had been returned again in 1708, having withstood a contest, the expense of which may well have strained the family's resources. In August 1709 Isabella was disappointed in her hopes of rejoining the Queen's household as a woman of the bedchamber, and of the additional source of income the post would bring. The following summer Lady Wentworth pitied the fact that while Lord William

Powlett* had just obtained a place of £2,000 p.a., 'poor Mr Arundell can get nothing'.⁴

On 31 Jan. 1710, following a committee of the whole House on the place bill, Arundell told in favour of receiving the report the next morning. During the Sacheverell debates of February–March he opposed the impeachment, and several weeks after the acquittal wrote to Lord Raby in praise of the peers' 'great care for our reputation', which 'it has given us matter for addressing and showing our loyalty to the Queen and our steadiness to our Church'. In Northampton in 1710 his chances of re-election were placed in jeopardy by the active electioneering and expenditure of another Tory, William Wykes*, and by the expectation that one of the borough seats would automatically be taken by the Whig Montagu interest, thus ruling out a joint Tory candidature featuring Wykes and himself. Arundell did not accept his defeat immediately, however, for it was followed by a 'tedious scrutiny', almost certainly at his own instigation, but by the last week of October the result was confirmed. Waiting anxiously for the outcome, his wife wrote to her brother Lord Raby: 'I hope he will carry his election at last, for to be at great charges and lose it will be a double grief.' It was taken for granted in local Tory circles that Arundell would petition 'to prove indirect practices' and thereby to have the election declared void. He did so on 2 Dec. and though proceedings of some sort were evidently begun in the committee of elections, he was reporting to Raby early in March 1711 that 'at last I have made an end of my petition'. His timely appointment as surveyor of the outports, which brought him a salary of £366, now disqualified him from a parliamentary seat, 'so I hope to be at ease and shall be careful how I engage again in those affairs'. Strafford politely congratulated him on his post in May and hoped 'soon to congratulate you on a better'. But this ease to the Arundells' financial predicament was soon shattered. In November 1712 Arundell was struck down by smallpox. The low regard in which he was held by his in-laws was unconcealed in Lady Strafford's reference to the news in a letter to her husband: '[it] makes me defer making my men's surtout coat till I see whether he lives or dies, for, for a brother's mourning all people put their servants in grey'. Arundell was dead by the end of the month, predeceasing his father, and was buried at Stoke Bruern on 5 Dec. It was a cruel blow for Isabella. In January 1713 she confided to Strafford: 'poor Mr Arundell was a good man and no couple in the world thought themselves more happy than we did for many years'. Now responsible for two 'fatherless children', she was rescued from her unhappy plight by the Queen who in April appointed her a woman of the bedchamber with a salary of £500, but the comfort of the advancement was temporary. In October 1714, following the Hanoverian succession, she was 'warned' to vacate her lodgings in the royal apartments, and was thrown once more upon the goodwill of her immediate family.⁵

¹Baker, *Northants*. ii. 244, 249; *London Mar. Lic.* ed. Foster, 38; Add. 22228, f. 17. ²*Cal. Treas. Bks.* xxv. 13, 206. ³Vivian, *Vis. Cornw.* 12–13; Baker, 242–3; *Cal. Treas. Bks.* xviii. 346, 413; xix. 395; Add. 22228, f. 17. ⁴*Wentworth Pprs.* 59, 98, 122; Add. 22228, f. 17; 31144, ff. 327, 365. ⁵Add. 22228, ff. 5, 9, 11; 31143, ff. 478, 563, 582; 31144, ff. 20, 37, 327; *Verney Letters 18th Cent.* i. 306; *Cal. Treas. Bks.* xxv. 13, 206; xxvii. 273; *Wentworth Pprs.* 304, 307–8; Baker, 244.

A. A. H.

ASGILL, John (1659–1738), of London.

BRAMBER   1 Apr. 1699–1700, 1702–18 Dec. 1707

bap. 25 Mar. 1659, 2nd s. of Edward Asgill of Hanley Castle, Worcs. by his w. Hester. *educ.* M. Temple 1686, called 1692. *m.* Jane (*d.* 1708), da. of Sir Nicholas Browne, *s.p.*¹

Asst. R. Corp. of Eng. 1691, Merchant Adventurers' Co. 1691; commr. taking subscriptions to land bank 1696.²

MP [I] 21 Sept.–11 Oct. 1703.

Asgill, a prolific pamphleteer of eccentric views, trained as a lawyer. After qualifying, he quickly achieved success through the patronage of Robert Eyre*, and became a friend and legal adviser to Nicholas Barbon*, the builder and speculator. He and Barbon established a land bank in 1695, which the following year joined with John Briscoe's similar venture to advance to the Crown, a loan of £2,564,000, needed to establish a national land bank. He was a subscriber to the national bank and acted as its legal adviser, being one of the commissioners who negotiated with the Treasury. The scheme collapsed in June when the bank and the Treasury failed to agree terms, but Barbon and Asgill's enterprise continued to operate for another four years, despite increasing difficulties. Asgill justified the need for such an institution in a pamphlet entitled *Several Assertions Proved in Order to Create Another Species of Money than Gold or Silver* published in 1696, in which he advocated the creation of a new type of currency. Barbon died greatly in debt in 1698, naming Asgill as one of his executors. His death further weakened the bank, which finally collapsed in January 1700, when the *Flying Post* carried a notice that the trustees would be dividing the remaining effects. All this, and the growing confusion of Asgill's own affairs, made another of Barbon's legacies more welcome. Barbon had owned 16 burgages at Bramber, which Asgill evidently retained, as he was returned at a by-election there in 1699, thereby protecting himself from prosecution while the bank was wound up, and he doubtless hoped to use his seat to advance his legal career. An analysis of the House of January–May 1700, classifying Members into 'interests', listed Asgill with the Junto, but he was not an active Member, his own complicated concerns no doubt taking precedence over Commons' business.[3]

In June 1700 Asgill published a pamphlet in which he argued that true Christians had recovered in Christ all that they had lost in Adam and since natural death was the result of Adam's sin, believers were rendered immortal by Christ and could be 'translated' into eternal life without the necessity of dying first. He was henceforward named 'translation Asgill'. The pamphlet caused a stir and had unforeseen consequences for its author. Two months after its publication Bishop Burnet ordered the confiscation of all unsold copies, 'as containing things of dangerous consequence' and Defoe wrote a reply, 'An Enquiry into the Case of Mr Asgill's Translation: Shewing that 'Tis Not a Nearer Way to Heaven than the Grave', which he suppressed before publication, probably after reading a piece of doggerel 'The Way to Heaven in a String', which questioned Asgill's seriousness. Many contemporaries considered Asgill's pamphlet a joke.[4]

Meanwhile Asgill had decided to try his fortunes in Ireland, where the Forfeited Estates Act provided much work for an energetic lawyer. At first he prospered, amassing a fortune of, it was alleged, £10,000. He returned to England at least twice in 1701 to fight two unsuccessful elections at Bramber in February and November, finally succeeding in regaining the seat in 1702. But his main interests at this time remained in Ireland, where in 1703 he bought the forfeited estates of Sir Nicholas Browne (2nd Viscount Kenmare in the Jacobite peerage), who was living abroad in exile, for the term of Kenmare's life. He himself had married Kenmare's eldest daughter, who had been brought up as a Protestant. Over the following years his mismanagement of the properties, selling off leases at too low a price, double-letting and using the property as security for his increasingly shaky credit, ruined him and almost ruined the Browne family, and from 1708 onwards he was involved in innumerable lawsuits, not least with Anthony Hammond*, the trustee for Kenmare's children. At this time he was also acting as agent for the Hollow Sword Blades Company, a London corporation set up to buy Irish land cheaply from the trustees for forfeited estates. To further the company's interests, he secured his election to the Irish house of commons and on 9 Oct. 1703 presented a petition from the Company to be allowed to establish a credit in Ireland of £300,000, to be lent out at 6 per cent interest. Irish MPs showed considerable enthusiasm, but his parliamentary career in Ireland ended two days later. On the first day of the session, 25 Sept., Asgill's tract on death and translation had been brought before the Dublin house of commons when it had been voted 'wicked and blasphemous' and ordered to be burnt by the common hangman. Asgill made his defence on 11 Oct. and at first, it was reported to Lord Nottingham (Daniel Finch†),

> the character of the man and his generosity in his profession, together with several useful proposals he has for the improvement of the country, did at one time, seem to dispose the house very much to bring him off, or at least let the matter drop.

But when two pious members 'exposed the many indecent expressions in that book', he was expelled. On 10 Nov. a complaint by Anthony Hammond was heard against him. Hammond claimed that, while acting as a trustee for the Browne family, he had employed Asgill and that Asgill had then acted improperly in purchasing the Kenmare estates for himself, but the house acquitted him of a breach of trust.[5]

In England, Asgill was named as absent on 25 Nov. 1704, when the House took notice that he had not attended the Commons during this Parliament and decided to consider his case in a fortnight's time. Despite this threat, which in fact appears not to have been carried out, Asgill became only marginally more active: he was listed as voting against the Tack or absent on 28 Nov. and in February 1705 reported on a petition from the Hollow Sword Blades Company. Successful for Bramber in 1705, he was classed as a 'Churchman' in a list of the new Parliament, voted for the Court candidate for Speaker on 25 Oct., spoke twice for the Court on the regency bill in December and January, and was named in the list of those supporting the Court in the proceedings on the 'place clause' of the regency bill on 18 Feb. 1706. He also pushed through the House a bill granting him extra time in which to make the third and last payment for the Kenmare estates. On 7 Feb. 1706 the bishop of Salisbury moved to defeat this bill in the Lords because of Asgill's peculiar religious beliefs, 'but several noble lords observing that his family ought not to suffer for such a fault, 'twas ordered a second reading'. The bill received the Royal Assent on 16 Feb. On 4 Mar. Asgill spoke against the bill to prevent the growth of popery, on the grounds that it would offend

England's Catholic allies and appear to condone persecution of Protestants in France.[6]

During the prorogation, in the summer of 1707, three of Asgill's creditors obtained a judgment against him for a debt of nearly £10,000. He was arrested on 12 June and imprisoned in the Fleet. As soon as Parliament reassembled he wrote to the Speaker claiming his continued detention was a breach of privilege. A committee was set up on 10 Nov. 1707 to consider the complaint and to study precedents, and reported five days later. Because his opponents were at the same time attempting to raise the question of his pamphlet on death and translation, with a view to his eventual expulsion, consideration of the report was adjourned from 20 Nov. until the 25th when it was ordered to be recommitted. On the same day the complaint that his book was blasphemous was raised in the House and referred to a committee of inquiry. Edward Harley, a former associate in Barbon's land bank, presented the report on 29 Nov., but consideration was postponed until 9 Dec., when, according to James Vernon I,

> We sat till six to-night, because we had a long debate about Mr Asgill's report; some were for proceeding immediately to censure his book, others for delaying it till he could be heard according to his desire by letter, and, therefore, pressed that the matter of his privilege might be first determined, which was carried upon a division of 161 against 154.

Following this decision, the report on his privilege complaint was considered on 16 Dec., and upheld, resulting in an order for his release. He took his place in the House on 18 Dec. to defend himself against the charge of blasphemy, but failed and the book was ordered to be burnt by the common hangman. A motion to adjourn, presumably to give him time to escape the country, was then moved, but lost by 165 votes to 109. Without further delay he was expelled, although his name appears on one further parliamentary list, of early 1708, as a Whig. Having lost the protection of his privilege, Asgill was re-arrested and spent his remaining years within the rules of the Fleet and King's bench prisons, but was, however, able to publish several political pamphlets, particularly in support of the Hanoverian succession. In 1712 he published a long *Defence*, claiming that his opponents had misunderstood him, and that the real reason for his expulsion was to enable his creditors to prosecute him. Thomas Burnet, son of Bishop Burnet and a friend of Asgill, thought the *Defence* 'witty, but from it I am apt to think him somewhat cracked at present'. Asgill continued to be troubled over the Kenmare properties, and when the 3rd Viscount inherited in 1720 great problems were caused because of the claims of Asgill's creditors against the estate. After years of wrangling, his surviving interest, although of dubious legal validity, was bought out in return for a small annuity. He died on 10 Nov. 1738, aged 79.[7]

[1] *N. and Q.* ser. 4, v. 569; *Kenmare Mss* (Irish Mss Commn.), pp. 45, 467. [2] *CSP Dom.* 1691–2, pp. 422, 527; *CJ,* xii. 508. [3] *Biog. Britannica,* i. 218–19; R. D. Richards, *Early Hist. Banking in Eng.* 116–20; Add. 70155, jnl. of land bank commrs. 20 May–19 June 1696; PCC 19 Pott; *The Case of Bramber Election 1 May 1708.* [4] J. Asgill, *An Argument Proving that According to the Scriptures, Man May Be Translated from Hence into Eternal Life, without Passing through Death; Poems on Affairs of State* ed. Ellis, vi. 282. [5] Luttrell, *Brief Relation,* iv. 657; *CSP Dom.* 1703–4, pp. 130, 156–7, 195; *CJ Ire.* iii. 15, 45; *Kenmare Mss,* pp. x, 3, 6, 10–11, 21, 22, 24, 27, 45, 49, 127, 295 et seq. [6] *Cam. Misc.* xxiii. 54, 65, 76; *Nicolson Diaries* ed. Jones and Holmes, 372; Cobbett, *Parlty. Hist.* vi. 515. [7] Cobbett, vi. 600–1; *Vernon–Shrewsbury Letters,* iii. 290; *Biog. Britannica,* i. 221–3; *Burnet–Duckett Letters,* 14, 23–24, 25, 223; *Kenmare Mss,* 49; *Gent. Mag.* 1738, p. 605; *N. and Q.* 569.

P. W.

ASHBURNHAM, Hon. John (1687–1737).

HASTINGS   10 Feb.–16 June 1710

bap. 13 Mar. 1687, 2nd s. of John Ashburnham[†], 1st Lord Ashburnham by Bridget (*d.* 1719), da. and h. of Walter Vaughan of Porthamel House, Brec. *m.* (1) 21 Oct. 1710, Lady Mary Butler (*d.* 1713), da. of James, 2nd Duke of Ormond, *s.p*; (2) 24 July 1714, Lady Henrietta Maria Stanley (*d.* 1718), da. and coh. of William, 9th Earl of Derby, wid. of John Annesley[†], 6th Earl of Anglesey (*d.* 1710), 1da.; (3) 14 Mar. 1724, Lady Jemima de Grey (*d.* 1731), da. and coh. of Henry, 1st Duke of Kent, 1s. *suc.* bro. as 3rd Lord Ashburnham, 16 June 1710; *cr.* Earl of Ashburnham 14 May 1730.

Guidon and maj. 1 Horse Gds. 1707, col. 1713–15; col. of horse Duke of Ormond's regt. 1713; dep. gov. and dep. warden of Cinque Ports June 1713–14; ld. of bedchamber to Prince of Wales 1728–June 1731; capt. yeomen of the guard Nov. 1731–*d.*[1]

As early as 1702 Ashburnham's father had ordained that his second son should have a military career and in 1706 sought a commission for him from the Duke of Marlborough (John Churchill[†]) in the horse guards. He commended the 19-year-old to the duke, hoping 'his education is such as will never dishonour the near relation he has in blood to your Grace', and on a later occasion as having 'all the disposition in the world to serve, and if I may believe characters he is a pretty fellow both in languages and exercises becoming his age'. Accordingly, in January 1707, young Ashburnham was gazetted. In 1708 he stood unsuccessfully for Rye where his father had an interest, but in February 1710 he became MP for Hastings in succession to his elder brother William*, who the previous month had vacated the seat on succeeding to his father's peerage. His sojourn in the lower House lasted only until June when, upon William's death without issue, the barony passed to him. There is no indication of Ashburnham's political comportment in the Commons. Indeed, his army commission may have given him little chance to attend. In the summer, however, he so vehemently rebuffed Lord Poulett's attempt to induce him to join the Harleyite Tories in the Upper House as to leave no doubt that in spite of his Tory family background, his own sympathies were uncompromisingly Whig. During their encounter, Poulett tried to provoke Ashburnham on the subject of Lord Portland's recent promotion over him in the horse guards and trusted he would 'always be a zealous server of his country and join with the Queen and her party'.

The youth, with patience, heard him a full hour, then told him, 'My Lord, I am not sensible of any injury done me in my Lord Portland's preferment. Methinks 'tis an honour done the nation to have the guards commanded by one of his quality etc., and I think it an honour to serve under him, for which reason I will keep my commission. Indeed, had that empty-headed, ridiculous etc. Duke of Beaufort [a Tory] been preferred I should have took it for an affront and have thrown up the next day. As to the other part of your discourse [that] it tends to a vote, I will deal with you as an honest man. I design you none and, to prove myself sincere, may my estate sink under ground, my tenants be ruined, my family perish, and myself damned if ever I give you a vote.'

However, Ashburnham's words turn out to be those of an impressionable and politically undecided young man. His marriage just a few months later, in October, to a daughter of the Duke of Ormond, placed him firmly in the Tory orbit. That he subsequently acted as a Tory, or at least as a Court supporter, is indicated by the remark Ormond made to Jonathan Swift a few days after Lady Ashburnham's death in childbed early in January 1713, 'that he was afraid the Whigs would get him again'. Swift, who had been a devoted admirer and friend of Lady Mary, had little time for Ashburnham and alluded to his profligate nature: 'her lord's a puppy, and I shall never think it worth my while to be troubled with him now that he has lost all that was valuable in his possession'. Ormond's anxiety to sustain Ashburnham's support for the administration can be seen the same month, when he gave him the colonelcy of his own regiment of horse, and in June when he nominated him as his deputy as warden of the Cinque Ports.[2]

For a while, Ashburnham continued supporting the Tories in the Lords, and his younger brother Bertram stood, unsuccessfully, as a Tory candidate for Sussex in 1715. But in the early years of Hanoverian rule he drifted over to the establishment Whigs, and the conferment on him of court office at the opening of George II's reign, followed by his promotion in the peerage to earl, confirmed his political redemption. None the less, his enjoyment of these honours was clouded by ill-health and chronic financial problems. He squandered in play, and then in building, the fortune he had obtained through inheritance and his three marriages, and was twice forced to sell off considerable portions of landed property to offset escalating debt. At his death on 10 Mar. 1737, his estates much depleted, and huge debts remaining, his friend Lord Egmont (John Perceval†) mourned him as a 'shallow, good natured man'. He was buried in the family vault at Ashburnham and was succeeded as 2nd Earl by his only son, John.[3]

[1] *Edinburgh Courant*, 17–19 June 1713. [2] E. Suss. RO, Ashburnham mss 844, p. 75, Ld. Ashburnham to Duke of Ormond, 19 Oct. 1702; 846, same to Marlborough, [Feb. 1706]; Add. 61283, ff. 48, 50; *Clavering Corresp.* (Surtees Soc. clxxviii), 88–89; *Swift Stella*, 594–6. [3] G. Holmes, *Pol. in Age of Anne*, 425; Ashburnham mss 4190, 4201, 4202; *HMC Egmont Diary*, ii. 367.

A. A. H.

ASHBURNHAM, Hon. William (1679–1710).

HASTINGS 1702–21 Jan. 1710

b. 21 May 1679, 1st s. of John Ashburnham†, 1st Baron Ashburnham. *m.* 16 Oct. 1705, Catherine (*d.* 1710), da. and event. h. of Thomas Taylor of Clapham, Beds. *s.p.* *suc.* fa. as 2nd Lord Ashburnham 21 Jan. 1710.

Ashburnham, having recently come of age, was put up at Hastings by his father in the election of November 1701, though it was to Lord Ashburnham's immense chagrin that his interest in the town was of too little consequence at this particular time to forestall the election of a Whig outsider. On standing again, however, in 1702, and with political circumstances favouring the Tories, Ashburnham was returned unopposed, as he was to be during the next two elections. Only once did he perform any substantive task in proceedings, on 7 Dec. 1703, when he served as teller in favour of passing the occasional conformity bill. But though forecast at the end of October 1704 as likely to support the Tack, he either voted against it or was absent from the crucial division on 28 Nov., an indication of a vein of moderation in his Toryism. Notwithstanding, he featured as a 'Churchman' in an analysis of the House after the 1705 election. At the opening of the new Parliament on 25 Oct.

1705 he voted against the Court candidate for the Speakership. An analysis of the House produced early in 1708 notes him as a Tory, while another from around the same date indicates that he was also seen as a friend of the Court. In January 1710 he vacated his seat on succeeding his father to the Ashburnham barony. In June, however, he succumbed to smallpox and died on the 16th. He was buried at Ashburnham and just a month later was followed to the grave by his wife.[1]

[1] Luttrell, *Brief Relation*, vi. 592.

A. A. H.

ASHBURNHAM, Sir William, 2nd Bt. (1678–1755), of Broomham Park, Guestling, Suss.

HASTINGS   1710–1713
SEAFORD   1715–Feb. 1717
HASTINGS   1722–1741

bap. 1 Apr. 1678, 4th but 1st surv. s. of Sir Denny Ashburnham, 1st Bt.† of Broomham, being 1st s. by his 2nd w. Anne, da. of Sir David Watkins of The Piazza, Covent Garden, Westminster and Glos. *m.* 7 June 1701, Margaret (*d.* 1742), da. of Sir Nicholas Pelham*, *s.p. suc.* fa. as 2nd Bt. Dec. 1697.
    Chamberlain of the Exchequer 1710–*d.*; commr. of alienation office 1717–*d.*, receiver of fines 1735–*d.*[1]
    Freeman, Seaford 1715.[2]

The Ashburnhams of Broomham were a distant cadet branch of the main aristocratic line whose seat was at nearby Ashburnham. The two families had been brought into closer union in around 1650 with the marriage of Sir William's father to a daughter of John Ashburnham† whose nephew was created a baron in 1689. Sir Denny Ashburnham had been too sympathetic towards James II to be employed after the Revolution and had thereafter lived a retired existence, dying in 1697. It was left to his eldest surviving son and successor, William, to resurrect what had been lost of his family's social and political standing in the Hastings area. Even so, Sir William seems not to have been particularly ambitious for a seat in Parliament. His election in 1710 was primarily owing to the unforeseen death in June of his second cousin, the 2nd Lord Ashburnham (Hon. William*) whose younger brother, Hon. John Ashburnham*, on succeeding to the peerage, was forced to quit his parliamentary seat at Hastings. In agreeing to replace his cousin as MP, Sir William, whose father had represented Hastings in the 1680s, was ensuring that the seat remained firmly within the family's control. Earlier in the year, in May, he had become a sinecurist under the Whig ministry with his appointment as a chamberlain in the Exchequer court. He may have obtained the post through his father-in-law, Sir Nicholas Pelham, whose nephew (a son of his elder half-brother, Sir John Pelham, 3rd Bt.*) was Henry Pelham*, clerk of the pells since 1698.[3]

Ashburnham was brought in by the new Lord Ashburnham, a seeming Tory though connected with the previous ministry. Thus his political identity was not clear to the compiler of the 'Hanover list' of the 1710 Parliament who marked him as 'd[oubtful]'. But his antipathy to the Tory ministry can be seen in his vote in favour of the motion for 'No Peace without Spain' on 7 Dec. 1711, and on 18 June 1713 when he voted against the French commerce bill and was listed as a Whig. Despite his commitment to opposition, however, he was retained in his Exchequer post even though only held 'during pleasure'. In 1713, after an inactive three-year spell in the House, he did not stand for re-election. He was nominated by the future Duke of Newcastle to Seaford in 1715, only to resign in February 1717 on accepting another sinecure. Examining the 1715 returns, one parliamentary analyst mistook him for a Tory, assuming, evidently, that he was of the same political cast as his aristocratic cousin. Re-entering the House for Hastings again in 1722, he served uninterruptedly as a supporter of Walpole's administration until 1741 when ill-health forced him to stand down. He died without issue on 7 Nov. 1755 and was succeeded in the baronetcy by his younger brother Charles.

[1] IGI, London; J. C. Sainty, *Officers of the Exchequer* (List and Index Soc. sp. ser. xviii), 12; *Cal. Treas. Bks.* xxi. 158; *Cal. Treas. Bks. and Pprs.* 1735–8, p. 83; *Gent. Mag.* 1755, p. 523. [2] E. Suss. RO, Seaford ct. bk. p. 122. [3] Luttrell, *Brief Relation*, vi. 583.

A. A. H.

ASHBY, George (1656–1728), of Quenby, Leics.

LEICESTERSHIRE   1695–1698, 4 Dec. 1707–1708

b. 16 July 1656, 1st s. of George Ashby of Quenby, Leics. by Mary (*d.* 1721), da. of Euseby Shuckburgh of Naseby, Northants. *educ.* Trinity Coll. Camb. 1673, MA 1675; G. Inn 1674. *m.* 7 Nov. 1681 (with approx. £9,000) Hannah (*d.* 1733), da. and coh. of Edmund Waring of Umphriston, Salop, 7s. (3 *d.v.p.*) 4da. *suc.* fa. 1672.[1]
    Sheriff, Leics. 1688–9, 1698–9.

Ashby's ancestral connexion with Quenby dated from around the mid-15th century. His father died when he was still a minor, and his mother remarried another Leicestershire gentleman, George Hewitt of Rotherby. In 1676 Ashby's sister Elizabeth married the future lord keeper, Sir Nathan Wright, and since Wright himself was of low birth, the match played its due part in helping his political career to prosper. Ashby too was fortunate in the marriage stakes: his bride, the heiress Hannah Waring, was judged to be 'a very pretty woman' bringing "tis said £9,000 portion, but 'tis thought it will fall far short'. His funerary monument describes him as 'honest George Ashby, the Planter', an epithet applied to him on account of his arboreal interests. At Quenby he successfully cultivated a rare genus of cedar tree originating from Lebanon which attracted interest from, among others, the diarist John Evelyn, with whom Ashby was acquainted.[2]

In November 1695 Ashby was returned as a Whig for the county following a poll, but was then totally inactive in the ensuing three sessions of Parliament. A prospective supporter of the Court on the proposed council of trade in the forecast for the division on 31 Jan. 1696, he signed the Association at the end of February, voted in late March for fixing the price of guineas, and likewise on 25 Nov. for the attainder of Sir John Fenwick†. In the last session of this Parliament he was granted ten days' leave of absence (21 Mar. 1698). An analysis of the parties, compiled in about September 1698, counted him as a Court supporter in the former Parliament.

Ashby contested for re-election in 1698 but after a tough party struggle was very narrowly defeated. Despite his reputation as one of the 'dissenters' favourites' among the Leicestershire gentry, he seems to have played no active part in the election of January 1701, but in November, on behalf of the Whig candidates, Lords Roos (John Manners*) and Sherard (Bennet*), he engaged 'several . . . friends that were zealous . . . for me at my election'. With peace hanging in the balance, he strongly believed it was essential that the county's representation should rest with its aristocratic families and observed to Lord Rutland, 'it is the only expedient that could be proposed to prevent a division among us when unanimity is so requisite at home to preserve the peace of [E]urope'. Ashby re-emerges in December 1707 when after nearly ten years' absence from the Commons he captured the county seat vacated by the death of his one-time opponent John Verney*. A list compiled early in 1708 classed him as a Whig. Standing for re-election in May 1708, he was narrowly defeated after an intense campaign. At the January 1711 by-election he was thought of as a possible contender against Sir Thomas Cave, 3rd Bt.*, the Tory candidate, but Ashby himself made no move. Indeed, his originally Whig brother-in-law, Sir Nathan Wright, who had long since become politically detached from him and turned Tory, gave his blessing to Cave. Ashby actively engaged and failed at both the abortive February 1715 poll and its repeat in April, his last bid to return to Westminster. He died early in February 1728 and was buried on the 11th at Hungarton, Leicestershire. The inscription on his funerary monument declares that 'he had the honour of being twice chosen to represent this county in Parliament without any expense to himself or family. He then saved this county five thousand pounds one year in taxes; and procured several advantages to it, which it is hoped this county will long enjoy the benefit of.'[3]

[1] Nichols, *Leics*. iii. 300; *Verney Letters 18th Cent*. i. 66. [2] Nichols, iii. 216, 295; *Verney*, i. 66. [3] Rutland mss at Belvoir Castle, John Verney to Ld. Rutland, 28 May 1698, Ambrose Phillipps to same, 18 Nov. 1701, Ashby to same, 19 Nov. 1701, Thomas Sawbridge to same, 3 Mar. [1708]; *HMC Cowper*, ii. 418–19; *HMC Rutland*, ii. 168; BL, Verney mss mic. 636/53, Sir Thomas Cave to Ld. Fermanagh (John Verney*), 29 Feb. 1708; *CJ*, xvi. 22; Leics. RO, Braye mss 23D57/2858, Palmer to Cave, 10 Feb. 1711, 2861, Wright to same, 11 Feb. 1711; J. H. Plumb, *Growth of Pol. Stability*, 84; Nichols, iii. 285.

A. A. H.

ASHE, Edward (c.1673–1748), of Heytesbury, Wilts.

HEYTESBURY 1695–1747

b. c.1673, 1st s. of William Ashe I* by his 1st w.; bro. of William Ashe II*. *educ*. Wadham, Oxf. matric. 7 Apr. 1690, aged 16. *m*. 17 Aug. 1710, Frances, da. of Francis Luttrell*, wid. of Edward Harvey, jnr., of Coombe, Surr. (s. of Edward Harvey*), *s.p.s. suc*. fa. 1713.[1]

Storekeeper of the Ordnance Apr. 1710–12, clerk Dec. 1714–18; ld. of Trade 1720–46.[2]

'Ned' Ashe was put up for the family borough in the 1695 election, the first opportunity after his coming of age. The records of the House do not differentiate between Ashe and his father, but Ashe is likely to have been the more active. He may have been the 'Mr Ashe' who presented a petition from William Fowell on 9 Mar. 1696 praying to be heard on an estate bill, only for him to be given leave to withdraw the petition on the 16th when it transpired that it had not been signed, nor had it been presented by order of the petitioner. Ashe was forecast as likely to support the Court in the divisions of 31 Jan. 1696 on the proposed council of trade and signed the Association. In the second session he voted on 25 Nov. for the attainder of Sir John Fenwick†. It was certainly Edward who was given three weeks' leave of absence on 21 Jan. 1697, and he may have been the Member given leave on 17 May 1698, for an unlimited period.

Returned again for Heytesbury in 1698, Ashe was classed with the Court party on a comparative analysis of about September. In December 1701 Robert Harley* listed him as a Whig. From 1702 to 1708 Edward was the only 'Mr Ashe' in the Commons. During this period he acted as a teller on as many as 20 occasions. On 13 Feb. 1703 he voted in favour of agreeing with the Lords' amendments to the bill for enlarging the time for taking the oath of abjuration. Forecast as a probable opponent of the Tack, he did not vote for it on 28 Nov. 1704, and served as a teller on 5 Dec. against engrossing the occasional conformity bill itself.

In the 1705 election Ashe was returned not only at Heytesbury but also at Marlborough, on the Duke of Somerset's interest. His declared function at Marlborough, however, was to hold a seat until Somerset's heir, the Earl of Hertford (Algernon Seymour*), reached his majority in November, when Ashe switched his interest to Heytesbury. Ashe voted for the Court candidate as Speaker on 25 Oct. 1705, and, as well as telling on the Whig side on several election cases, he told on 8 Dec. against a proposal to go into a committee to consider the 'Church in danger' motion. He was also a teller against the motion on 12 Jan. 1706 to include in the regency bill a clause explaining the Act of Settlement, and he voted with the Court party on 18 Feb. in the proceedings over this 'place clause'. He had confided to his friend Lord Townshend in April 1708 that 'as to politics, I'm out of pain, I make no doubt that Whiggism will be triumphant'.[3]

Not surprisingly, Ashe was classed as a Whig in two analyses of the 1708 Parliament, one of them following the general election. However, his subsequent Commons career is not clearly distinguishable from that of his brother, William Ashe II, though again he was probably the more active and thus more often the 'Mr Ashe' named to tellerships. There were five such during the 1708–9 session, several on election cases. Ashe was also listed as having voted for the naturalization of the Palatines. In September 1709 Lord Treasurer Godolphin (Sidney†) recommended him to the vacant place of storekeeper of the Ordnance, as 'a very honest, well-tempered young gentleman' who 'has always been firm and right, and [has] waited too long for some opportunity of having a mark of the Queen's favour'. Godolphin added, 'this gentleman will have £2,000 a year'. The Duke of Marlborough (John Churchill†) quickly agreed to the nomination, as presumably did Ashe's friend Robert Walpole II*, but it was not until April 1710 that the Queen's consent could be obtained and the appointment made. He was also promised the governorship of Barbados when that place became vacant, although nothing came of this. Meanwhile Ashe had voted in favour of the impeachment of Dr Sacheverell, and may have acted as a teller on 2 Feb. 1710, for approving the text of the Commons' 'replication' to Sacheverell's 'answer'.[4]

The change of ministry in 1710 was not an immediate catastrophe for Ashe. In the past his kinsman Robert Harley, though failing to secure for him the posts he coveted, had nevertheless given him 'many expressions of . . . favour and esteem'. On hearing the news of Harley's appointment as chancellor of the Exchequer Ashe waited on him to offer congratulations, and received what he took to be a snub. 'Your porter denied you to me', he wrote to Harley,

though I knew you were at home. I can't doubt but he did it by your order, because he has formerly served me so several times. This is strong treatment to one that has the honour to be related to you. Perhaps you are apprehensive that I came to ask some favour of you, but I assure you that, as I never received the least friendship from any great man that ever I was acquainted with in my life, you shall never have any trouble in that kind.

He was, however, continued by Harley in his office in the Ordnance, and this despite refusing to modify his Whig politics, probably serving as a teller on 3 Apr. 1711 on the Whig side in the Cockermouth election case. His vote on 7 Dec. 1711 for the 'No Peace without Spain' motion may have been decisive, for a month later Harley (now Earl of Oxford) was canvassing candidates for his place. Even then he was not removed until June 1712. In the meantime he may well have been a Whig teller on 17 Jan. on a motion to adjourn during the debate on the expulsion of Walpole. He voted against the French commerce bill, as a Whig, on 18 June 1713, and in the following general election unsuccessfully contested the county with Thomas Pitt I* against two Tories. Although returned for Heytesbury, he still joined Pitt in petitioning. He voted on 18 Mar. 1714 against the expulsion of Richard Steele, and, as the only 'Mr Ashe' in the Commons, was a teller on 8 July 1714 for a motion to have the debts of the army stated. The previous month he had been paid £50 'as royal bounty'. He was classed as a Whig in the Worsley list and in a list of the Members re-elected in 1715.[5]

Ashe continued to sit for his family's borough until shortly before his death, and his subsequent fortunes mirrored those of his party. He was reinstated to the Ordnance in December 1714 and secured a place on the Board of Trade in 1720, which he held until frailty compelled him to retire. This latter post may have assisted him financially following losses incurred in the South Sea Company, for in July 1720 he wrote plaintively to Harley of his losses, asserting that 'I that have neither money nor friends have not been the better for it', and asking Harley to recommend him to Sir John Blunt, one of the directors of the Company, who he hoped would 'find out some way to enable me to provide for my family, who when I die might perish for want if he does not do it'. Ashe made his will on 25 Jan. 1744, leaving his wife Frances an annuity of £500 together with a life interest in the rental of Heytesbury and Knook parsonages, Wiltshire, leased by him since 1710. Bequests of £40 were made to the poor of the three parishes in which his principal property lay, further annuities and gifts were made to a number of servants, and £100 each was given to his nephews Edward, Pierce† and William A'Court†, the last of whom was made executor and principal beneficiary. Ashe died on 22 May 1748 and was buried at Heytesbury.[6]

[1] Hoare, *Wilts.* Heytesbury, 118, 150; *Burnet–Duckett Letters* ed. Nichol Smith, 157. [2] *CJ*, xvi. 427, 428; *Cal. Treas. Bks.* xxiv. 257; Boyer, *Pol. State*, i-ii. 387. [3] *HMC 15th Rep. VII*, 190; Wilts. RO, Ailesbury mss 1300/1317, Charles Becher to Hon. Robert Bruce*, 23 May, 13 Sept. 1705; *HMC Townshend*, 331–2. [4] *Marlborough–Godolphin Corresp.* 1366, 1381, 1455; Add. 38507, f. 83; *Cal. Treas. Bks.* xxiv. 257. [5] Add. 70209, Ashe to Harley, 9 Nov., n.d.; *HMC Portland*, v. 136; *Cal. Treas. Bks.* xxvi. 336; xxviii. 308; *HMC 15th Rep. VII*, 212; *Letters of Burnett to Duckett*, 59. [6] Add. 70209, Ashe to Harley, 30 July 1720; PCC 169 Strahan; Hoare, *Wilts.* Heytesbury, 150; Wilts. RO, 859/2.

D. W. H.

ASHE, Sir James, 2nd Bt. (1674–1733), of Twickenham, Mdx.

DOWNTON 1701 (Dec.)–1705

bap. 27 July 1674, 2nd but 1st surv. s. of Sir Joseph Ashe†, 1st Bt., of Twickenham by Mary, da. of Robert Wilson, Draper, of London. *m.* aft. June 1697, his cos. Elizabeth, da. of Sir Edmund Bowyer† of Camberwell, Surr., and half-sis. of Anthony Bowyer*, 1s. *d.v.p.* 4da. (3 *d.v.p.*). *suc.* fa. as 2nd Bt. 15 Apr. 1686.[1]

Sheriff, Wilts. 1706–7.

A minor at his father's death, and regarded as a 'very feeble' youth, Ashe was secured with an annuity of £200 to be paid by his mother from the family's extensive estates in Wiltshire and Yorkshire. His mother's property, however, remained under her own control, and while his stockholding in the East India Company in 1689 was estimated at £1,000, hers amounted to over £9,000. It was she who put him forward as a candidate for his father's old seat at Downton in 1695, as soon as he had reached his majority, but, partly through the duplicity of the family's agent, John Snow, nothing came of the attempt. Ashe's later marriage caused a rupture between mother and son, she complaining bitterly of 'his perverseness to me, and crossness in not marrying where I desired', but although she took pains to make sure that he should never come into possession of her fortune she could not prevent him from taking over his father's property; by 1697 he was in possession of Downton manor as well as a further 700 acres in neighbouring parishes. His lands in south Wiltshire were sufficiently extensive that in January 1700 he petitioned Parliament against a bill for making the Avon navigable between Christchurch, Dorset, and Salisbury, suggesting that the value of his properties there would fall as a result of such work. Regardless of his mother's antipathy towards him, manifested in her support of a rival candidate, Ashe made an interest at a by-election for Downton in May 1698. However, he was again unsuccessful and did not contest either of the two succeeding general elections, supporting John Eyre* and Carew Raleigh* at Downton in January 1701. Despite this failure, and an antipathy to 'the town [London] I hate so much', he took a great interest in parliamentary proceedings, sending down to Wiltshire in May 1701 a copy of the letter from the States General to King William appealing for assistance, and the Lords' address in response, with the covering comment, 'so now I hope we shall enjoy our liberties by entering into a war with France, which till now we had no hopes of'.[2]

Returned at last for Downton in November 1701, he was classed with the Whigs in Robert Harley's* analysis of this Parliament. He is not known to have spoken, but in a private letter of early April 1702 gave his opinion of the recent Commons' address as 'a wretched thing and dirty'. At the 1702 election he was prepared to 'relinquish' to John Eyre but was not called upon to do so. He voted on 13 Feb. 1703 for agreeing with the Lords' amendments to the bill for enlarging the time for taking the oath of abjuration, was forecast on 30 Oct. 1704 as likely to oppose the Tack, and did not vote for it on 28 Nov. In 1705 he did step down in favour of Eyre, although he was still included in a list of the new Parliament, as 'Low Church'. Ashe sought to advance himself again at Downton in 1708, but was squeezed out by the Eyre and Duncombe interests and by the freeholders' hostility towards him. He did not stand again. To compound his misfortune, in March 1709 his wife, for whom he had sacrificed his mother's local influence and from whom he was now 'living separately', successfully sought a legal judgment allowing her £300 a year in alimony.[3]

Ashe died at his house in Twickenham on 8 Nov. 1733, eight days after his younger surviving daughter. As he died intestate, his properties worth £4,000 p.a. together with £10,000 in cash devolved on his son-in-law Joseph Windham Ashe†, who was himself returned for Downton in the general election the following year.[4]

[1] *Le Neve's Knights* (Harl. Soc. viii), 2; Manning and Bray, *Surr.* iii. 409; R. S. Cobbett, *Memorials of Twickenham*, 64; PCC 41 North, 133 Pyne. [2] PCC 39 Lloyd; Add. 24120, f. 19; 22185, f. 12; R. W. Ketton-Cremer, *Felbrigg*, 76; Wilts RO, Radnor mss 490/909, Snow to Lady Ashe, 14 Sept., Lady Ashe to Snow, 24 Sept., 4 Oct., 11 Nov. 1695, Ashe to same, 10 May 1698, 30 Nov. 1700, May 1701; Sloane 4078, f. 263; *Wilts. N. and Q.* iii. 354; Wilts. RO, 906/W51; *CJ*, xiii. 125. [3] Radnor mss 490/909, Ashe to Snow, 6 Apr. 1702. [4] Luttrell, *Brief Relation*, vi. 412; *Gent. Mag.* 1733, p. 607; *Hist. Reg. Chron.* 1733, p. 43; Prob. 6/109, f. 77v.

D. W. H./H. J. L.

ASHE, Joseph (c.1684–1725), of Kensington Square, Westminster, and Langley Burrell, Wilts.

CHIPPENHAM   1710–17 Mar. 1711

b. c.1684, 2nd but o. surv. s. of Samuel Ashe† of Langley Burrell by Anne, da. of Oliver Pleydell of Shrivenham, Berks. *educ.* Christ Church, Oxf. matric. 4 Mar. 1702, aged 17; I. Temple 1703, called 1708. *m.* Elizabeth, da. of Sir John James of Heston, Mdx., at least 1s. *suc.* fa. 1708.[1]

Counsel, Marshalsea ct. ?–*d.*[2]

Returned at Chippenham in 1710, and classed as a Tory on the 'Hanover list', Ashe was unseated, on petition, in the following March. He was included, presumably by mistake, in the list of 'Tory patriots' who opposed the continuance of the war in 1711. Nevertheless, he was probably a Whig, for he was excluded from the Wiltshire commission of the peace in 1712. His parliamentary record is obscured in the Journal by the presence of Edward Ashe. In March 1716 he was recommended by the Treasury to the attorney-general to be a prosecuting counsel 'when the trial of the rebels comes on', as a barrister of whom they 'have a good character'. Little has been ascertained of his later years, although he presumably continued to work as a barrister. He died at his house in Kensington on 8 Oct. 1725, administration of his estate being granted to his widow.[3]

[1] PCC 240 Barrett; *Misc. Gen. et Her.* n.s. iv. 153; *Vis. Berks.* (Harl. Soc. lvii), 196; Lysons, *Environs* (1795), iii. 30–31. [2] *The Gen.* n.s. vi. 212. [3] L. K. J. Glassey, *Appt. JPs*, 215; *Cal. Treas. Bks.* xxx. 145; *The Gen.* 212; Boyer, *Pol. State.* xxx. 416.

D. W. H.

ASHE, William I (1647–1713), of Heytesbury, Wilts.

HEYTESBURY   8 Oct. 1668–1681 (Jan.)
                         1685–1687, 1689–1701 (Nov.)
WILTSHIRE   1701 (Dec.)–1702

b. 17 Nov. 1647, 1st surv. s. of Edward Ashe†, Draper, of Fenchurch Street, London and Halstead, Kent, being 1st by his 2nd w. Elizabeth, da. of William Jolliffe of Leek, Staffs., wid. of William Bowyer of Knippersley, Staffs.; bro. of Edward Ashe†. *educ.* I. Temple 1652, called Nov. 1653; St. Edmund Hall, Oxf. matric. 1664. *m.* (1) lic. 27 June 1670, Anne (*d.* 1684), da. of Alexander Popham† of Littlecote, Wilts., 4s. (2 *d.v.p.*), 1da.; (2) lic. 10 May 1694, Mary (*d.* 1721), da. of John Rivett, Skinner, of London and Beeston, Suffolk, wid. of Sir Henry Appleton, 4th Bt., of Jarvis Hall, South Benfleet, Essex, *s.p. suc.* fa. 1656.[1]

Capt. of ft. regt. of Mq. of Worcester 1673–4.

Ashe took full advantage of his family's controlling interest at Heytesbury, returning himself for the borough even before reaching his majority. A moderately active Member under Charles II and James II, at the beginning of the 1690 Parliament he was classed as a Whig by Lord Carmarthen (Sir Thomas Osborne†). In this Parliament his activity was usually limited to the occasional committee appointment. Robert Harley*, whom Ashe referred to as 'cousin', marked him down as a member of the Country party in April 1691. His only tellership in this Parliament occurred on 12 Nov. 1691 against giving leave for a bill to reduce the rate of interest. On Grascome's list he appeared on the Court side. His only drafting committee was on 1 Dec. 1694 to prepare a bill for the recovery of minors' debts.[2]

The Journals for Ashe's later Parliaments do not differentiate between him and his son Edward*, and most of his activity in the Commons has been attributed to Ashe jnr. However, he was forecast as a probable supporter of the Court in the division of 31 Jan. 1696 over the proposed council of trade and he signed the Association in the following month. He was listed as having voted against fixing the price of guineas at 22*s.*, but a later pamphlet claimed that he had been 'out of town' at the time. He was classed as a Court supporter in a comparative analysis of the old and new Parliaments in about September 1698, and was classed in February 1701 with those who were deemed likely to support the Court in continuing the 'Great Mortgage'. In December 1701 he graduated to the county seat, where his surprise election on the Whig interest was accounted a gain by Lord Spencer (Charles*); Harley also listed him as a Whig. He was defeated in 1705, whereupon he retired from the fray.[3]

A long sufferer from gout, Ashe made his will on 2 Oct. 1713 after becoming ill of the dropsy. He left £1,000 to his wife together with all the household goods from a residence in Bath, where he had evidently retired to recover his health. Generous legacies were made to his sons and named servants. By 20 Oct. it was noted that the dropsy had 'risen as high as his belly, and it is thought he cannot live long, which will be losing the worthiest gentleman . . . in the country'. He died two days later and was buried at Heytesbury on 29 Oct.[4]

[1] PCC 381 Berkeley; *Staffs. Peds.* (Harl. Soc. lxiii), 145; Hoare, *Wilts.* Heytesbury, i. 117–18, 150; *Mar. Lics. Vicar-Gen.* (Harl. Soc. xxxi), 290. [2] Add. 70209, Ashe to Harley, 8 July [?1701]. [3] *Bull. IHR.* sp. supp. vii. 19; *Wilts. Arch. Mag.* xlvi. 80; *HMC 15th Rep. VII*, 190; *Wilts. N. and Q.* i. 369. [4] *Letters of Burnet to Duckett* ed. Nichol Smith, 47–48; Wilts. RO, 859/2; Add. 70209, Ashe to Harley, 8 July [?1701]; PCC 44 Aston.

D. W. H./H. J. L.

ASHE, William II (c.1675–bef. Jan. 1732), of Ormond Street, London, and Heytesbury, Wilts.

HEYTESBURY   1708–1713, 1715–1722

b. c.1675, 2nd s. of William Ashe I* by his 1st w. and bro. of Edward Ashe*. *m.* bef. Oct. 1713, 1s.[1]

Returned on the family interest for Heytesbury, in a seat previously held by his father, Ashe was a reliable Whig. He was listed as having voted in 1709 for the naturalization of the Palatines, and the following year for the impeachment of Dr Sacheverell. In the next Parliament he voted on 7 Dec. 1711 for the 'No Peace without Spain' motion and on 18 June 1713 against the French commerce bill, again being classed as a Whig. He was also marked as a Whig in a list of the Members re-elected in 1715. Otherwise his parliamentary career is impossible to distinguish from that of his brother, Edward, though in all probability the latter was the more active. In his later years Ashe settled in London, where he was a merchant. He died without leaving a will, sometime before January 1732.

[1] Hoare, *Wilts*, Heytesbury, i. 150; PCC 44 Aston.

D. W. H.

ASHLEY, Anthony, Lord Ashley (1671–1713), of Wimborne St. Giles, Dorset.[1]

POOLE   21 May 1695–1698

b. 26 Feb. 1671, 1st s. of Anthony Ashley Cooper†, 2nd Earl of Shaftesbury, by Lady Dorothy, da. of John Manners†, 8th Earl of Rutland; bro. of Hon. Maurice Ashley*. *educ.* privately (Elizabeth Birch) 1675–9; Clapham sch. 1680; Winchester 1683–6; travelled abroad (France, Holland, Italy, Germany, Austria, Switzerland) 1686–9. *m.* 29 Aug. 1709 (with £3,000), Jane (*d.* 1721), da. of Thomas Ewer of Bushey Hall and the Leas, Watford, Herts., 1s. *suc.* fa. as 3rd Earl of Shaftesbury 2 Nov. 1699.

V.-adm. Dorset 1701–2.

Ashley was placed under the guardianship of his grandfather, the 1st Earl of Shaftesbury (Anthony Ashley Cooper†) in whose London house he was born, and hence at an early age came under the influence of the latter's close friend and secretary John Locke, the philosopher. Locke chose Ashley's first governess, the daughter of the prominent Nonconformist minister Samuel Birch, and on the death of her father in 1679, he appears to have followed her to a school in Clapham. He was then sent to Winchester where he suffered from the taunts of his schoolfellows on account of the first Earl's politics. In 1686 he started a European tour in the company of his tutor Daniel Denoue and Sir John Cropley, 2nd Bt.*, who became his lifelong friend. At least one permanent strand in his political thinking, hatred of France, was already clearly developed by this time, when in a letter to his father in May 1689, while on his return to England, he rejoiced in 'our late purge from those promoters of the interest that was to have enslaved us to the horridest of all religions and to the service of the usurpations and treacheries of that neighbouring crown that has aimed so long at the subjection of all Europe'. He refused offers to stand for Weymouth and for various Wiltshire boroughs in the 1690 election, explaining to Sir John Morton*, who had invited him to stand for Weymouth, that he as yet lacked the sufficient skills for political office and would gain 'greater experience by still looking on'. Indeed, he even journeyed to Wiltshire 'to prevent some gentlemen who were about to have promoted my interest there', arguing that the local gentry did not know him well enough.[2]

Ashley spent the next few years in study, and was also occupied with the family's estates and its interests in the Carolinas, where the 1st Earl had been a lord proprietor. It seems that Ashley inherited the proprietorship from his grandfather and was actively involved in meetings concerning the governance of the colony. However, he declined to become governor when the post was offered to him in 1695, and his inherited proprietorship was taken over by his brother, Maurice. During these years he remained on close and friendly terms with Locke, and he continued Locke's pension of £100 p.a. initiated by his grandfather. Looking back on the early 1690s he viewed 'two parties equally pretending service to the crown and government and equal merit in the Revolution'. However, the corrupt proceedings of Henry Guy*, Speaker Trevor and the Duke of Leeds (Sir Thomas Osborne†) convinced him of the merits of the Whigs. Two months after Trevor's expulsion 1695 Ashley entered the Commons for Poole on his family's interest at a by-election following the death of Sir John Trenchard. He was returned again at the general election held shortly afterwards.[3]

Ashley has been seen as 'that archetypal country Whig', and his short career in the Commons bears testimony to this interpretation. On 26 Nov. 1695 he made his maiden speech on the Country Whig bill to reform treason trials, when he was so overcome by nerves he broke down. The House, after giving him time to recover, urged him to continue, whereupon he said:

> If I, Sir, who rise only to speak my opinion on the bill now depending, am so confounded that I am unable to express the least of what I proposed to say, what must the condition of that man be who is pleading for his life, without assistance and under apprehension of being deprived of it?

Whether a premeditated oratorical device or not, this made a considerable impression upon the House. He was forecast as doubtful for the divisions of 31 Jan. 1696 over the proposed council of trade, he voted against the resolution barring Members of Parliament from being appointed to the new council, which the government favoured as a wrecking amendment, but he did support the Court motion for an abjuration oath for those chosen, an example of his willingness to take an independent line on matters, as one later encomium put it, 'when he apprehended it might in any way be beneficial to his country'. A document entitled 'some amendments proposed by Lord Ashley' in the papers of Sir William Williams demonstrates his role in supporting the Welshman's parliamentary qualifications bill, particularly in stipulating that the property qualification relate to real estate and that residency in a county, or near to a borough, also be a prerequisite for membership of the Commons. Commenting on legislative proposals was a regular activity as he seems to have done the same with Locke's ideas on the recoinage and on the Licensing Act. However, his espousal of 'Country' measures drew the wrath of the Court, as he wrote to Thomas Stringer on 15 Feb. 1696:

> You could, I believe, scarcely imagine with yourself ... who they are that are condemned for flying in the face of government as they call it, by being for such things as these are, and pressing such hard things on the prerogative or court. In short, you would hardly believe that your poor friend that now writes to you has sentence (and bitter sentence too) every day pressing upon him for going, as you may be sure he goes, and ever will go, on such occasions as these, whatever party it be that is in or out at Court, that is in possession of the places, and afraid of losing their daily bread by not being servile enough, or that are out of places, and think, by crossing the Court and siding with good and popular things against it, to get into those places of profit and management.

He was listed as voting against the Court on fixing the price of guineas at 22s., but this was challenged by another writer. He had, of course, signed the Association.[4]

In the next session Ashley continued his independent line by voting on 26 Jan. 1697 in favour of tacking Williams' qualification bill, which had been rejected by the Lords, to the capitation bill. He received leave of absence for a week on 22 Feb. James Vernon I* summed up the Court's attitude to his behaviour when he wrote to Shrewsbury on 17 Feb. 1698: 'I know not what my Lord Ashley's party is, or how far they have authorized him to make any proposals in their names, but I see there is but one sort of men the King can with safety depend upon, and many factions and interests are concurring to divide and pull them to pieces.' Unsurprisingly, he was classed as a member of the Country party in an analysis of about September 1698. Looking back on his time in the Commons, as recounted by his own son, Ashley explained his aims:

> the independent manner of acting my father observed himself he strove to increase in others ... as he was sensible that independency is the essence of freedom. Several gentlemen in the House ... formed a little society by the name of the Independent Club of which he was a member and had the chief hand in setting up (or in projecting) but this club was [of] no long duration.

However, by April 1698 his disillusionment was palpable as he wrote to Locke: 'I think it would have been altogether as well for my country and mankind, if I had done nothing, so fruitless have my endeavours been, and so little profit arisen from these years I have entirely given from myself to the public.' Even worse, his doctor later attributed his asthma to this period in the Commons: 'when in that House, he constantly attended the service of the House by day, and was late at night at the committees in a close room, with a crowd of people, where he was often carried into an eagerness of dispute, he contracted such a weakness of lungs, as to bring on a convulsive asthma'. Poor health gave him the ideal excuse to refuse to stand at the 1698 election. Indeed, following the death of his mother in June 1698, Ashley left for Holland, spending most of his time in Rotterdam with his friend Benjamin Furly, a Quaker merchant, and only returning to England in the following May. He re-entered Parliament as a peer, having succeeded his father in November 1699. Henceforth Shaftesbury's role was confined to the Lords, to electioneering in Wiltshire and Dorset, and, of course, to the publication of tracts dealing with political themes. He died at Naples from the effects of his asthma on 4 Feb. 1713, and his embalmed body was returned for burial in St. Giles's church, where an inscription was set up to his memory.[5]

[1] Unless otherwise stated this biography is based on R. Voitle, *3rd Earl of Shaftesbury* and B. Rand, *Shaftesbury Letters*. [2] PRO 30/24/22/2/108–9. [3] A. Salley, *Narratives of Early Carolina*, 296, 307; L. Klein, *Shaftesbury and the Culture of Politeness*, 131. [4] *Party and Management* ed. C. Jones, 44; Cobbett, *Parlty. Hist.* v. 966; H. Horwitz, *Parl. and Pol. Wm. III*, 165, 189; Centre Kentish Stud. Stanhope mss U1590/059/5, Robert Yard* to Alexander Stanhope, 11 Feb. 1696; NLW, Canon Trevor Owen mss 202; Klein, 136. [5] *Vernon–Shrewsbury Letters*, i. 189; ii. 15; PRO 30/24/21/222; *Locke Corresp.* vi. 369–70.

P. W./H. J. L.

ASHLEY, Hon. Maurice (c.1675–1726), of Bedford Row, Westminster.

WEYMOUTH AND
  MELCOMBE REGIS 1695–1698, 1701 (Feb.–Nov.)
WILTSHIRE 1701 (Dec.)–1702
WEYMOUTH AND
  MELCOMBE REGIS 1705–1713

b. 14 Apr. 1675, 3rd but 2nd surv. s. of Anthony Ashley Cooper†, 2nd Earl of Shaftesbury; bro. of Lord Ashley (Anthony Ashley*). *educ.* Winchester c.1682–9; Utrecht (private tutor). *m.* lic. 2 June 1709, Catherine (*d.* 1721), da. of William Popple of St. Clement Danes, London, *s.p.*[1]

After spending seven years at Winchester College, Ashley's attainments were such as to induce his brother, Lord Ashley, to write anxiously to their father in July 1689:

All that is called good breeding is . . . totally lost in him . . . The seven improving years of his life have been sacrificed at Winchester . . . in any other sort of reading he has no manner of tincture . . . There is nothing left to be lost in him, unless he were to be brought to lose some ill qualities that have grown up in the void that others have left, for here has been an acquisition indeed.

Lord Ashley's recommendation of a sojourn at Utrecht under the guidance of a tutor was accepted and by 1695 Ashley had so far improved that although still a minor he was returned at Weymouth on his father's interest and thus entered Parliament at the same time as his brother. He was classed as 'doubtful' in the forecast for the division on the proposed council of trade on 31 Jan. 1696, though he signed the Association promptly. He was, however, an inactive Member. He did not stand for re-election in 1698, and in a comparative analysis of the old and new Parliaments was classed as a Country supporter. Shortly after his father's death, his brother, now 3rd Earl of Shaftesbury, settled on him an estate of £1,000 p.a.[2]

At the first 1701 election Ashley was persuaded by Shaftesbury to stand again for Weymouth, and, assured of a 'secure interest', he was returned in a contested election. However, somewhat unexpectedly in November, as the next election approached, he was invited to stand for Wiltshire. His brother-in-law, Edward Hooper, wrote to Shaftesbury that he thought the offer should be accepted, because Ashley had 'heartily embraced this offer and if balked, I fear, will not be agreeable at all'. Ashley also stood at Weymouth once again, and was returned for both constituencies. In December he was classed as a Whig by Robert Harley*, and as a gain for the Whigs by Lord Spencer (Charles*). On 20 Jan. 1702 Ashley elected to sit for Wiltshire.[3]

Shaftesbury hoped to secure Ashley's return for Wiltshire a second time in 1702, but the accession of Queen Anne had reduced the Whigs' influence and Ashley was defeated in a contested election. Shaftesbury's agent, John Wheelock, informed the Earl on 29 Oct. 1703 that Ashley's expenses in the last three elections had been about £700, adding,

It is too much for him to spare yet not so much as it cost either of his opposers at the last election, as I am well assured, for which cause it's said both give out the next . . . I have been asked (and pressed for Mr Ashley's answer) both in the county of Wiltshire (by several) and by Mr Lewis for Dorsetshire, to know whether Mr Ashley designs to stand again for the first and by the latter whether he will decline that and stand for Dorsetshire . . . I would give no answer to either but that Mr Ashley would be wholly governed by the gentlemen.

The request from Wiltshire was seconded by Lord Somers (Sir John*) in a letter to Shaftesbury, who replied that having in the past 'with much difficulty . . . prevailed with' Maurice 'to act the candidate's part', he had now resolved to leave him to his own free choice. This attitude seems to have been the more necessary in that the brothers were on bad terms at this time, with one point at issue being Ashley's election expenses. He decided to stand for Weymouth instead of Wiltshire, to the annoyance of Shaftesbury, who implied that his choice would entail more expense for the family than if Wiltshire had been accepted. On 28 Dec. 1704 Ashley informed his brother that

I am sorry that my Lord Somers or any one has given you trouble upon my score; but the zeal of the people embarked in an interest to serve the public must excuse their setting any to solicit you. They were pleased to accept the offer of me when they had no reason to claim or think of me; and if in return they now claim me as having a sort of right to me since my first silly compliance in consenting to stand, I own I cannot blame them. Nor should anything but necessity hinder me from allowing their claim, submitting to it and acting accordingly.

Ashley was returned for Weymouth in a contested election in 1705, after which he was classed as a gain for the Whigs by Sunderland (Charles, Lord Spencer), while he was also noted as a 'Churchman' in another analysis of the new Parliament. He voted on 25 Oct. for the Court candidate as Speaker, though he was otherwise an inactive Member.[4]

Ashley's resentment against his brother seems to have run very deep, since no sooner was one cause of disagreement removed than another would appear. Shaftesbury had been out of favour with the Court since Anne's accession, and the ministerial changes since 1705 had not helped as much as he had expected. In the winter of 1707–8 Shaftesbury's friend Sir John Cropley, 2nd Bt.*, was attempting to use the Court's difficulties with both the Tories and the Junto to repair the Earl's relations with Lords Godolphin (Sidney†) and Marlborough (John Churchill†). Some success was achieved but the strategy was threatened by Ashley, of whom Cropley wrote to Shaftesbury on 15 Jan. 1708:

The only thing I am thinking of is your brother, his violence to the Court on your being obliged and considered. His behaviour, I know, will be outrageous, but . . . I am well prepared for this too. He shall lose his aim and not in the least hurt where he will intend it . . . I can plainly tell my lord treasurer his ill behaviour to you, for since he boasts of it, why I mayn't I can't see a reason.

However, Cropley's hope that Ashley would not stand in the forthcoming elections was disappointed, and he was returned again for Weymouth in a contested election. Classed as a Whig in two separate analyses of Parliament before and after the election, in the 1708–9 session he supported the naturalization of the Palatines, while in the following session he voted for the impeachment of Sacheverell.[5]

For several years Shaftesbury had been urging Ashley to marry, but without success. Finally, Shaftesbury himself decided to take a wife, whereupon Ashley also married, his wife being the daughter of a London merchant and dramatist, William Popple, the nephew of Andrew Marvell and friend of Locke. The licence was dated a month before his brother's wedding, but either there was some delay before the ceremony was held or he kept it a secret, since a year later Cropley informed James Stanhope* that Shaftesbury's 'monster of a brother, after eight years repeated ingratitude of all kinds, has married the old woman I told you of that my lord took to be the cause of all his misbehaviour'. In the same year Ashley successfully contested Weymouth once again. He was classed as a Whig in the 'Hanover list' and on 7 Dec. 1711 voted for the motion of 'No Peace without Spain'. He voted against the French commerce bill on 18 June 1713, but stood down at the election a few months later. Ashley died on 21 Oct. 1726, and was buried at Purton, Wiltshire.[6]

[1] Hutchins, *Dorset*, iii. 594; *Surtees Soc.* clxxviii. 127. [2] *Shaftesbury Letters*, 280–1; PRO 30/24/22/4, f. 325. [3] PRO 30/24/20/35, 38, 89, 91, 101–2; 30/24/21/14, 16, 36, 43, 44; 30/24/22/1, f. 91. [4] PRO 30/24/20/77, 87, 147, 186, 207; 30/24/21/231, 313–14; 30/24/22/1/67–68, 72; 30/24/22/2/155–6; 30/24/22/5/368. [5] *Shaftesbury Letters*, 383; PRO 30/24/20/144, 150; 30/24/21/1–5, 25–26; 30/24/22/1/61–62, 65; 30/24/22/4/318–19. [6] *Orig. Letters of Locke, Sidney and Shaftesbury* ed. Forster 237; *N. and Q.* ser. 4, vi. 222; Centre Kentish Stud. Stanhope mss U1590/C9/31, Cropley to Stanhope, 17 June 1710.

P. W.

ASHTON see **ASSHETON**

ASHURST, Sir Henry, 1st Bt. (1645–1711), of St. John's Street, Clerkenwell, Mdx. and Waterstock, Oxon.

TRURO   1681, 2 Feb. 1689–1695
WILTON   1698–1700, 1701 (Dec.)–1702

b. 8 Sept. 1645, 1st s. of Henry Ashurst, Merchant Taylor, alderman of London 1668, of Watling Street, London and Hackney, Mdx. by Judith, da. of William Reresby, merchant, of London; bro. of Sir William Ashurst*. *m.* lic. 26 Mar. 1670, Diana (*d.* 1707), da. of William, 6th Baron Paget, and sis. of Hon. Henry Paget*, 1s. 1da. *suc.* fa. 1680; *cr.* Bt. 21 July 1688.[1]

Freeman, Merchant Taylors' Co. 1668, asst. 1696; member, Levant Co. 1679, New Eng. Co. 1681; alderman, London Oct. 1688–9; freeman and bailiff, Oxford 1692; manager, Common Fund 1695.[2]

Agent, Massachusetts Bay by 1689–1701, Connecticut 1699–*d.*, New Hampshire by 1701–2.[3]

Commr. excise 1689–91, preventing export of wool 1689–92, receiving subscriptions to land bank 1696.

An important figure in Nonconformist circles, with strong links to the American colonies, Ashurst was lauded by one Dissenter as 'blessed with an inquisitive genius, a noble freedom of thought, and a generous love of truth'. His ancestors hailed from Lancashire, and since Elizabethan times had been imbued with a zealous Protestantism, most notably in the case of his father Henry, a close friend of Richard Baxter. Ashurst himself acted as executor for Baxter and Robert Boyle, and in his political career was ever keen to protect his co-religionists. His marriage into the family of Lord Paget enabled him to forge close links with other prominent Nonconformist sympathizers such as Philip Foley* and Richard Hampden I*, as well as with Robert Harley*, whom Ashurst once called 'my affectionate cousin'.[4]

Ashurst's first attempt to enter Parliament in 1670 proved unsuccessful, but he later gained election for Truro in 1681. He was subsequently an active supporter of the Whig cause, his prominence recognized by James II, who conferred a baronetcy on Ashurst in July 1688. A rapprochement with the Court may well have taken place over a year before, for in May 1687 William Cowper* had censured him for being 'a shuffler'. However, Ashurst was quick to recognize the Revolution, riding to William's headquarters at Windsor in December 1688, and accepting a place at the excise office four months later. This appointment reflected considerable personal wealth, Sir Henry having built upon his father's fortune by investing in the Levant and West Indies trades. Unlike his brother Sir William, he did not seek advancement in the City, resigning an alderman's seat early in 1689. Colonial affairs already appeared of greater personal concern, for in August 1689 he was reportedly acting for several North American governments. Moreover, he was said to have relished the task of presenting at court addresses from Massachusetts Bay, regarding the duty 'as if the Emperor had made him his envoy'.[5]

Although he had confided to a friend during the 1689 Parliament that 'I am forced to serve my dear country and the public to the neglect of my private affairs', at the election of March 1690 he was prepared to fight a contest to retain his Truro seat, and was subsequently identified as a Whig by Lord Carmarthen (Sir Thomas Osborne†). He was not particularly active in the House, although in the first session he was appointed to the committee to prepare the abjuration bill. In the next session he acted on 27 Dec. as a teller in support of an amendment to a bill to accelerate the determination of election disputes. Three months later he was removed from the excise commission, but there is no clear evidence to suggest that he was the victim of a political purge. He and his partners had demonstrated the value of their support to the new regime by advancing some £175,000 in loans to the crown. His removal may well have been voluntary, for in the course of that year he bought the manor of Waterstock at a cost of almost £16,000, an outlay perhaps reflecting a desire to spend less time in the capital. His father's purchase of the Oxfordshire manor of Emmington in 1665 had first established Ashurst influence in that county, and as early as 1686 Sir Henry had informed a friend of his wish to establish a country seat.[6]

His prominence in the Commons undiminished by these personal upheavals, on 18 Dec. 1691 Ashurst spoke against the East India Company. Most significantly, on 3 Feb. 1692 he joined with Hugh Boscawen I and Richard Hampden I in an unsuccessful attempt to defeat a proposal to render Nonconformist divines and teachers liable to a poll tax. Their argument focused on the fact that 'this was putting a mark upon these people and would rather widen the differences between us', a danger which Ashurst was evidently keen to avoid, having been charged by Baxter at the time of the Convention Parliament to work for the removal of the penal statutes. Later that year he was still hopeful that talks between Lord Nottingham (Daniel Finch†) and leading Dissenting ministers would have 'some good effect' towards the achievement of 'a comprehension the next sessions of Parliament'. Although Ashurst was obviously committed to the Nonconformist cause, Lord Carmarthen found difficulty in categorizing his political allegiance in the course of that year, querying his support for the Court.[7]

In the fourth session Ashurst made several contributions to Commons debates, beginning on 2 Dec. with a speech in favour of considering the government's credit before examining the military estimates. He was then prepared on 13 Dec. to support the motion of Sir Christopher Musgrave, 4th Bt.*, for the raising of a supply by monthly assessment. The next day he argued for the committal of an abjuration bill, taking the line that 'it would be very strange to throw out a bill that is for [the] preservation of their Majesties' persons'. On 30 Dec. he demonstrated his concern for the City's interest by moving on its behalf a rider to a bill to extend the contract for the capital's convex lights. A 'violent colic' curtailed his activity for the rest of the session, although he did act as a teller on 8 Jan. 1693 to block an adjournment of a hearing of the committee of the whole's report on a land tax bill. In the spring of 1693 Samuel Grascome listed him as a placeman, alluding to his former excise post, but indicated that he was not a supporter of the Court. Any animus against the ministry was certainly increased the following summer, for Ashurst lost over £3,000 in the Smyrna disaster, a misfortune which he blamed on the 'treachery of the Adm[iralty] and some in the Navy'. At the start of the new session he expressed grave reservations at the crisis the country found itself in, decrying the removal of Lord Nottingham and observing that 'most people tremble for fear' at the nation's prospects.[8]

His opposition to the administration was clearly signalled on 22 Dec. 1693 when he acted as a teller to pass a bill for more frequent Parliaments. In addition, on 29 Mar. 1694 he told against a motion to disagree with the Lords' amendments to a mutiny bill. Of far greater personal interest, on 18 Apr. he was ordered to carry up to the Lords a bill for the construction of 'good and defensible' ships. Also on 23 Apr. he acted as a teller against a clause in a bill to regulate hackney carriages which would have enabled them to ply their trade on Sundays. The next session saw him similarly conspicuous, for he alone was ordered on 21 Dec. 1694 to prepare a bill for the discovery of bankrupts' estates, a measure which he presented on 16 Jan. 1695. He continued to feature in connexion with government finance, acting as one of the committee to oversee the ballot for the commission of accounts, and telling on 16 Apr. in support of the House going into committee on a bill to levy duties on glassware and coal. His colonial interests subsequently recommended his close involvement with a bill to reverse the attainder of Jacob Leisler, the rebel executed for seizing the government of New York at the time of the Revolution. Eager to thwart the campaign of his rival Joseph Dudley* for the governorship of Massachusetts Bay, Ashurst promoted the bill to expose Dudley's arbitrary proceedings as the justice presiding over Leisler's trial. He twice reported from the committee on the bill, and boasted on 5 May that 'I shall never do New England so much good as by getting this bill passed'.[9]

Ashurst did not stand at the Truro election of 1695, a decision perhaps reflecting differences with his patron, Boscawen, who had remained loyal to the Court. Political disillusionment had certainly been suggested earlier in the year by the dedication he wrote to the Dissenting peer Lord Willoughby of Parham, for a biography of ejected minister Nathaniel Heywood. Echoing the views of the moral reformers, Ashurst railed against 'such a degenerate and licentious age', lamenting 'all the different parties we are so unhappily broken into'. His alienation from the ministry was further suggested by his appointment in 1696 as one of the commissioners to receive subscriptions to the land bank. Nonconformist divine Philip Henry, to whom he had entrusted the education of son Henry†, actually welcomed his removal from Westminster as 'a writ of ease to you from a great deal of trouble, which hath hitherto had too much influence upon the impairing of your bodily health'. Freed from parliamentary duties, however, Sir Henry dedicated even more of his energies to colonial affairs. In the summer of 1696 he organized with (Sir) Stephen Evance* a trial shipment of naval stores from New England, and the following year acted as the government's creditor for the Newfoundland campaign.[10]

Although Ashurst had no direct ties to the constituency of Wilton, his candidacy at the election of 1698 was welcomed there by an influential Dissenting interest. He was returned unopposed, unseating Sir John Hawles* in the process, but was unable to secure a victory for his son Henry at the Cornish borough of Fowey. At the outset of the new Parliament he was listed by one analyst as a Court supporter, an assessment which suggested a renewal of the alliance with his former Whig allies. He did not prove a prominent Member in the first session, his significant activity confined to the drafting and presentation of a private naturalization bill, and a tellership on 1 Mar. in support of the return of the Whig Hon. Thomas Newport* at Ludlow. He again acted as a teller in the next session, backing a motion on 1 Apr. 1700 to bring up a clause concerning the bill to apply the Irish forfeitures to public use. At that time he was listed by one political commentator as belonging to the Junto interest, but in December of that year he wrote to Robert Harley to offer his support in case Harley should wish to stand for the Speakership in the next Parliament. Most significantly, Ashurst alluded to 'our former difference in opinion about public matters', thereby supplying further evidence of his estrangement from erstwhile Country allies. Unfortunately for Ashurst, he was unable to fulfil his promise of support, for he subsequently failed to be returned for Wilton. He petitioned the House on 17 Jan. 1701, alleging bribery against his rival candidates, but the elections committee never reported on the matter.[11]

Having lost his seat, Ashurst could again devote his time to colonial affairs. In May he was appointed as agent for Connecticut, and for most of the year was involved in an unsuccessful battle to block the appointment of Dudley as governor of New Hampshire and Massachusetts Bay. In November 1701 he regained his seat at Wilton. His victory was regarded by Lord Spencer (Charles*) as a Whig gain, and at the outset of the new Parliament Harley concurred with this verdict, listing Ashurst with the Whigs. Sir Henry proved an inconspicuous Member once more, and his only recorded speech, in defence of parliamentary privileges on 17 Feb. 1702, was dismissed by Sir Richard

Cocks, 2nd Bt.*, as such 'a long and tedious oration that he nor anyone else knew what he meant'. The accession of Anne saw another downturn in his political fortunes, unable as he was to overcome two rival Whig candidates at Wilton, both of whom leant heavily on Nonconformist support. He petitioned the House on 27 Oct., accusing the mayor of gross irregularities in the return, but on 16 Nov. withdrew his protest.[12]

Thereafter Ashurst showed little enthusiasm for re-election, in contrast to his active participation in colonial matters. His vendetta against Dudley continued, reaching a climax in June 1708 when he wrote to the Duke of Marlborough (John Churchill†) to demand Dudley's dismissal as governor. Accompanying this request was *The Deplorable State of New England*, a pamphlet drafted overseas but with a dedication penned by Ashurst to Lord Sunderland (Charles, Lord Spencer). True to his spiritual priorities, he implored Sunderland to respect the colony's godly foundation, observing that 'if religion be worth anything, 'tis worth everything'. The campaign failed once again, and although Ashurst maintained his colonial links through his Connecticut office, ill-health restricted his activities from the time of his wife's death in 1707. Although languishing in 'a declining condition' in his final years, he continued to promote religion, appointing trustees in 1709 for the advowsons of Waterstock and Emmington, whom he admonished to choose ministers 'that believe and preach the old doctrinal articles commonly called Calvinistical'. The following year he predictably voted for the Whigs at the London poll, evidently concerned at the High Church campaign sparked by the trial of Dr Sacheverell. However, even an Anglican cleric lamented Ashurst's death on 13 Apr. 1711, Sir Henry's piety having earned him wide respect. Confessing himself to be 'unworthy to be remembered', he sought in his will to encourage 'serious religion', entrusting Nonconformist divines with various bequests for 'promoting Christianity here or abroad' and, more generally, for 'the glory of God'. His estate, which included the mansion he had erected at Waterstock after 1695, passed to his only son Henry, who subsequently sat for Windsor in the 1715 Parliament.[13]

[1] J. R. Woodhead, *Rulers of London* (London and Mdx. Arch. Soc.), 19. [2] Guildhall Lib. mss MF324; ex. inf. Prof. R. Walcott; W. Kellaway, *New England Co.* 289; Beaven, *Aldermen*, i. 213; *Oxford Council Acts* (Oxf. Hist. Soc. n.s. ii.), 231, 233; Dr Williams' Lib. mss O. D. 68, f. 3. [3] *CSP Col.* 1689–92, p. 212; 1700, p. 715; 1701, p. 115. [4] J. Dunton, *Life and Errors*, 350; *Bull. John Rylands Lib.* xiii. 309–10; Wood, *Life and Times*, ii. 137; Add. 70020, f. 33. [5] Herts. RO, Panshanger mss D/EP/F81, f. 11; Campbell, *Lives*, iv. 265; Luttrell, *Brief Relation*, i. 523; Woodhead, 19; *Recs. Col.*

Connecticut 1678–89, 470; *Sewall Diary* ed. Halsey Thomas, i. 232. [6] Bodl. mss Don. c. 169, f. 71; Som. RO, Sanford mss DD/SF 3110, John Freke to Edward Clarke I*, 31 Mar. 1691; *VCH Oxon.* vii. 223; viii. 93; Add. 45538, ff. 4–5. [7] *Luttrell Diary*, 88, 169; *Bull. John Rylands Lib.* 323–4; mss Don. c. 169, ff. 84–85. [8] *Luttrell Diary*, 285, 312, 318, 340; mss Don. c. 169, ff. 89–92. [9] T. Hutchinson, *Hist. Massachusetts Bay*, ii. 64; mss Don. c.169, f. 121. [10] *Remarks upon Life of Nathaniel Heywood* [1695]; *CJ*, xii. 508; Add. 45538, ff. 19–20, 22–23; *CSP Dom.* 1696, p. 309; *HMC Lords* n.s. iii. 159, 166. [11] Northants. RO, Montagu (Boughton) mss 47/63, James Vernon I* to Duke of Shrewsbury, 30 July 1698; Add. 70020, f. 33. [12] *CSP Dom.* 1700–2; p. 445; *Cocks Diary*, 217. [13] Add. 61366, f. 147; PCC 97 Young; *VCH Oxon.* vii. 221, 226; *London Poll of 1710*; *HMC Portland*, vii. 30.

P. L. G.

ASHURST, Henry (1669–1705), of St. Augustine's, London.

PRESTON 1698–1702

bap. 4 Mar. 1669, 1st s. of Sir William Ashurst*. *educ.* Wickhambrook, Suff. (Samuel Cradock); I. Temple 1685, called 1693. *m.* by 1699, Elizabeth, da. and h. of Edward Grace of Eltham, Kent, 2s.[1]

Commr. hackney carriages 1694–5; attorney and serjeant, duchy of Lancaster 1697–1702; High Easter steward, duchy of Lancaster 1697–1703.[2]

Freeman, Preston 1697; town clerk, London 1700–*d.*[3]

Member, New England Co. 1698.[4]

Although the son of a highly successful woollen-draper, Ashurst declined to enter business in preference to a legal career. However, he clearly shared his family's Nonconformist sympathies. He attended the academy of the ejected minister Samuel Cradock at Wickhambrook, and later joined the New England Company, an institution with strong Dissenting links. Possibly aided by his father's influence in the City, Ashurst gained his first public appointment in May 1694 as one of the commissioners to regulate hackney carriage licences. Within a year the commission had been rocked by allegations of corruption within its membership, but Ashurst denied involvement in corrupt practices and was cleared on 20 Mar. 1695 by the report of a Commons committee. Despite exoneration, only two months later he resigned office, reportedly in response to the government's decision to halve the commissioners' salaries.[5]

Ashurst's association with this scandal did not impede his advancement in legal circles. When the Whig Lord Stamford was appointed chancellor of the duchy of Lancaster in May 1697 he quickly appointed Ashurst attorney for the duchy, a post which proved to be the making of his political career. The chancellor's interest was clearly instrumental in Ashurst's victory at the Preston poll of August 1698, although his familial ties to the north-west may have smoothed his recommendation. Such success came in marked contrast to his cousin and namesake, Henry Ashurst† of Waterstock, Oxfordshire, who failed to be returned for the Cornish borough of Fowey.[6]

Soon after entering the House Ashurst was listed by one political commentator as a supporter of the Court, while another cited him as a placeman. Ashurst was an inactive Member. He told against referring to committee a petition to establish Norfolk and Hornsey land lotteries on 18 Dec. 1699, perhaps betraying a sympathy for the campaign for moral reform consistent with his Dissenting background in doing so, and on 13 Feb. 1700 spoke against the motion to resume all royal grants. In early 1700 he was classed by a parliamentary analyst as belonging to the interest of Lord Stamford. His opposition to the resumption suggested strong support for the Court, for neither Ashurst's patron nor family were beneficiaries of a royal grant. In July 1700 he emerged victorious from a keenly contested election for the town clerkship of London, an office reputedly worth £1,000 p.a., and he subsequently proved an active supporter of the City's interests, his name appearing on several petitions submitted to Parliament. Despite securing successive victories at the Preston contests of January and December 1701, however, Ashurst's contribution to parliamentary business was slight. The accession of Anne spelt the end of his parliamentary career. With his patron Stamford removed as chancellor of the duchy of Lancaster in May 1702 in favour of the Tory Sir John Leveson Gower, 5th Bt.*, Ashurst was dismissed as attorney in June 1702, and his lack of any personal interest at Preston meant that he was unable to mount any challenge at the Preston election the following month.[7]

Even though Ashurst had lost his seat, the responsibilities of his civic office ensured that he maintained some prominence at the centre of City affairs. Any political ambitions he may have harboured were, however, thwarted by his premature death at Bath on 30 Oct. 1705. His body was laid to rest in the family vault at St. Augustine's and his estate passed to his two sons, neither of whom aspired to enter Parliament.[8]

[1] IGI, London; *Le Neve's Knights* (Harl. Soc. viii), 414; Calamy, *Life*, i. 134–5. [2] *CSP Dom.* 1695, p. 254; Somerville, *Duchy of Lancaster Official Lists*, 51, 101, 207–8. [3] Lancs. RO, Preston bor. recs. CNP 3/1/1 p. 506. [4] W. Kellaway, *New England Co.* 289. [5] Cobbett, *Parlty. Hist.* v. 896; *Post Boy*, 4–6 June 1695. [6] Northants. RO, Montagu (Boughton) mss 47/63, James Vernon I* to Duke of Shrewsbury, 30 July 1698. [7] Som. RO, Sanford mss DD/SF4107(a), notes on debate, 15 [sic. 13] Feb. 1699[–1700]; *London Post*, 1–3 July 1700; Luttrell, *Brief Relation*, iv. 661; *HMC Lords*, n.s. iv. 158, 273; v. 8, 173, 229, 235, 238, 267. [8] *Post Man*, 1–3 Nov. 1705; Le Neve, *Mon. Ang.* 1700–15, p. 108; PCC 1 Eedes.

P. L. G.

ASHURST, Sir William (1647–1720), of Paternoster Row, London, and Highgate, Mdx.

LONDON 14 May 1689–1690, 1695–1702
1705–1710

bap. 2 May 1647, 2nd s. of Henry Ashurst, Merchant Taylor, of Watling Street and Hackney, Mdx. by Judith, da. of William Reresby, merchant, of London; bro. of Sir Henry Ashurst*. *m.* lic. 31 Aug. 1668, Elizabeth, da. of Robert Thompson, merchant, of Newington Green, Surr. 7s. (1 *d.v.p.*) 4 da.(1 *d.v.p.*). Kntd. 29 Oct. 1687.[1]

Freeman, Merchant Taylors' Co. 1668, asst. 1687, master 1687–8; common councilman, London 1678–83, auditor 1682–3, alderman 1687–Oct. 1688, Oct. 1688–*d.*, sheriff 1691–2, ld. mayor 1693–4; member and treasurer, New England Co. 1681, gov. 1696–*d.*; pres. Christ's Hosp. 1688; vice-pres. Hon. Artillery Co. 1689–1703, pres. 1708–*d.*; gov. Highgate sch. 1697–*d.*; St. Thomas' Hosp. by 1719.[2]

Commr. preventing export of wool 1689–92, Greenwich Hosp. 1694, 1704, excise 1698–1700, 1714–*d.*, relieve Vaudois, by 1701; trustee, Exchequer bills 1697; receiving loan to Emperor 1706; dir. Bank of Eng. (with statutory intervals) 1697–1714.

Proprietor, New Jersey by 1701.[3]

Ashurst remained a controversial figure throughout his career, an acquaintance observing that he never 'acted a little or mean thing in his whole life'. His known sympathy towards Dissent ensured him much opposition, reflecting as it did the upbringing of his 'holy father', a Presbyterian woollen-draper of Lancashire origin. However, although Ashurst followed his father's trade, there is no direct evidence of his regular attendance at a conventicle. He first came to prominence during the struggle over the London charter, a Tory observer opining in 1682 that 'naught' could be expected of him, and in June 1685 he was actually listed as one of the London lieutenancy commissioners to be disarmed for suspected disaffection towards the government. Under James II he was courted as a possible supporter for the royal policy of toleration, gaining election as alderman in August 1687 and receiving a knighthood three months later. His readiness to serve under James may well have earned him rebuke from several of his fellow Whigs, William Cowper* having earlier in the year described him as 'a knave and an ill man'. James's overtures failed to convert him, however, and he quickly accepted the Revolution. The strength of the City Whigs in the immediate aftermath of James's flight was attested by Ashurst's appointment in April 1689 as colonel in the City militia, as well as by his victory at a by-election held the following month. Such success rendered him a prime target for Tory attack, and in

January 1690 he was accused of having drunk a republican toast to 'our sovereign lord, or lords, the people'. The charge could not have helped his cause at the London contest of March 1690, where he finished a disappointing seventh, and within a few weeks he had also lost his colonelcy.[4]

Even though out of the House, Ashurst remained a powerful force within City politics, the Tory Sir Peter Rich† citing him in March 1690 as a leading Whig financier, and he certainly made at least one loan of £500 to the crown. Further proof of his influence came at the shrieval election of June 1691, where Ashurst gained a crushing victory, finishing nearly 1,400 votes ahead of his rivals. 'Both sides' were said to have agreed to support his nomination by the outgoing mayor, the Whig Sir Thomas Pilkington†, and among those who warmly greeted the result was Robert Harley*. Further proof of his links to Dissent was provided in January 1693, when the Nonconformist Common Fund actually wrote to him to request a donation, evidently confident of his sympathy to their cause. However, the Dissenting interest was unable to carry Ashurst to victory at the parliamentary by-election held two months later, since he finished some 200 votes behind Sir John Fleet*, a fellow alderman courted by both Whigs and Tories since the Revolution.[5]

Undaunted, later that year Ashurst fought a most successful campaign to gain the mayoralty, emerging with Sir John Houblon at the head of the Michaelmas poll, over 900 votes ahead of their nearest Tory challenger Sir Jonathan Raymond. On gaining the unanimous assent of the court of aldermen on 3 Oct., Ashurst made an impassioned speech against the dangers of current party divisions, warning that they threatened a possible return to popery and slavery. In particular, he vigorously defended himself against charges of republicanism, a London minister having already condemned his election as a prelude to the overthrow of Church and monarchy. The new lord mayor's allegiance to William and Mary could not be questioned, however, even though the exiled King James actually drafted a letter to Ashurst to request his support for a planned invasion. Indeed, on 30 Oct. he received a ringing endorsement from Lord Chief Baron Sir Robert Atkins, who, while 'reflecting much upon Lord Nottingham and the Church', recommended Ashurst as 'one every way so fitted and qualified for that great office', and assured him that he had 'the interests of all the Protestants in the world . . . on your side'. Four days later the new lord mayor received the personal congratulations of the King, having led a civic delegation to greet William on his return from campaign. In his year of office he proved a conscientious magistrate, reporting the movements of suspected persons, and conducting a campaign against prostitution.[6]

The government clearly saw Ashurst as an important ally in the City, for in June 1694 he was appointed one of the commissioners to receive the first subscriptions to the Bank. The following month he successfully petitioned for a grant from the Irish forfeitures as compensation for a debt of £1,200 owed by two Irish rebels, favouritism later described as a reward for 'his faithful services when lord mayor'. Such continuing prominence argued for his candidacy at the London election of October 1695, where he finished second as the Whigs regained three seats from their Tory rivals. His success was welcomed by Nonconformist minister Philip Henry, who confidently predicted that Ashurst's name 'will be precious to succeeding generations'. Sir William's support for the Court was demonstrated in the first session by a forecast for a division on 31 Jan. 1696 concerning the proposed Board of Trade, and on 27 Feb. he duly signed the Association. Having narrowly failed to become a commissioner for public accounts, finishing ninth in the ballot declared on 5 Feb., he proved an inconspicuous Member during that session, making no significant contribution to Commons business.[7]

During the next session, however, Ashurst was much more active, being closely involved with a local measure to repair the highways of Islington and St. Pancras, including a tellership on 4 Nov. in an unsuccessful attempt to commit the bill. Later that month he supported the attainder of Sir John Fenwick†, and his identification with the Court was further confirmed on 19 Dec. when he acted as a teller to block a bill to regulate elections. He again acted as a teller on 21 Jan. 1697 in order to oppose a clause submitted for addition to a land tax bill, and, returning to the capital's affairs, presented a bill to complete the building of St. Paul's cathedral. He was one of the two Members appointed to draft a bill to encourage the manufacture of woollens by a ban on the export of rival Irish produce. He was also named to the drafting committee on the Stour navigation bill, and his final important action in that session again concerned a supply measure as he told on 30 Mar. to block the committal of a bill to levy duties on wines and other commodities.

During the recess the government made further use of Ashurst's financial contacts, appointing him as one of the trustees for the circulation of Exchequer bills. He actually subscribed £1,000 to the scheme in May, but a fellow trustee later testified that Ashurst had 'never acted' in that office. The Bank's affairs clearly absorbed more of his energies, and although failing to mount any significant challenge for the governorship in July, he did become a director for the first time. In the ensuing session he was appointed on 7 Dec. to the committee to draft a bill to regulate the press, a measure revealing a possible concern for moral reform, especially since he was subsequently named to the committee to address the King to suppress profaneness and immorality. More predictably, he was one of the principal sponsors of a bill for the payment of inland bills of exchange, and, maintaining his interest in textile trade, managed a bill to enable two merchants to import Italian silk via Amsterdam. He later failed to block a bill to levy duties on coal and culm when acting as a teller on 3 May, his opposition perhaps stemming from the continuing hardship inflicted upon the capital's poor by high fuel prices. His distaste for this measure, however, did not prevent him from accepting a place on the excise commission in July 1698, a highly lucrative post which again signified his financial utility to the ministry. At the end of that month he finished a strong second at the London poll, a success emulated by his eldest son, Henry*, who was returned for Preston. Lord Stamford, chancellor of the duchy of Lancaster, was clearly instrumental in procuring the younger Ashurst's victory, and soon afterwards Secretary James Vernon I* sought to use Sir William's connexion with Stamford to further the electoral ambitions of Hon. Harry Mordaunt* at Bere Alston, although ultimately to no avail.[8]

Advancement to the excise commission was clearly seen to have influenced Ashurst's political outlook, for while one political observer bracketed him with the Court's opponents by forecasting shortly after the election that he would probably oppose the standing army, two other lists cited him as a placeman. His ties to the ministry had been strengthened even further by recent service as agent for the garrison at New York, his prominence within the New England Company acting as an obvious recommendation for that office. In the decisive division of the first session on 18 Jan. 1699 Ashurst voted in favour of the standing army, and subsequently became a prime target for the Country attack on royal influence in the Commons. On 17 Feb. the committee investigating royal revenue officials noted that he was an Exchequer bill trustee, but that he had 'declined to act in that trust since his being a Member of Parliament'. Only three days later the committee brought to the Commons' attention Ashurst's former commission for the first Bank subscription, but Sir William was able to retain his seat after 'so much' was said on his behalf. For the rest of the session he prudently refrained from any direct involvement in controversial issues, gaining nominations to drafting committees for measures to preserve game and to make free two ships, acting as teller on 24 Mar. against a bill to establish a corn-market at Westminster, and being named to the conference committee on the bill to make Billingsgate a free market.[9]

Ashurst also made little impression on the next session, with no significant contribution to business. Significantly, an analyst of the Commons in early 1700 was sufficiently unsure of Ashurst's political allegiance to query his identification with the Junto interest. However, the place legislation against excisemen passed during that session was clearly aimed at officers such as Ashurst. In June he decided to resign from the excise commission rather than cut short his parliamentary career, for which he was lauded in the press as one of the 'true patriots' who put the service of their country before self-interest. This decision was subsequently vindicated by his performance at the London election of January 1701, where he finished second as the Whigs took all four seats.[10]

In the new Parliament he initially revealed a willingness to support the new ministry, a list of 22 Feb. 1701 citing him as a probable supporter of the Court to agree with a resolution of the committee of supply to continue the 'Great Mortgage'. However, he may also have backed a Whig move to influence the passage of the Act of Settlement, since an affidavit for a Whig-inspired inquiry into the birth of the Pretender was signed at his Highgate home. Less controversially, he demonstrated concern for social issues, being named to drafting committees for bills to set the poor to work, and to redress abuses in hospitals and other charities. Personal affairs were also served in the course of this Parliament, the House taking notice on 19 May of Ashurst's petition to the trustees for Irish forfeitures to secure his grant against resumption. On 13 June it was reported that the petition was not to be transmitted to the trustees in Ireland, but the Parliament was dissolved before any resolution could be brought to the matter. His close interest in colonial affairs was subsequently demonstrated in August by his direct involvement with the surrender of the New Jersey charter. Moreover, three months later he was prepared to intervene on his brother Sir Henry's behalf in a dispute over the governorship of Massachusetts Bay and New Hampshire.[11]

Ashurst survived the London election of November 1701, finishing second in a closely contested poll. The following January he wrote to the

Electress Sophia to assure her of the City's support for the Hanoverian succession. He also appeared once more concerned for matters affecting the lower orders, gaining nominations to drafting committees for bills to set the poor to work, to settle a workhouse at Dorchester, and to punish felons and their accessories. He was also named to the committee to draft the bill to prevent clandestine imports from France. However, his attention was mainly focused on the confirmation of his grant from the Irish forfeitures. On 26 Mar. his petition to the trustees for the Irish forfeitures was read a second time, and a motion was carried for a bill to be brought in to relieve Sir William, although only after a division. Sir Rowland Gwynne*, a fellow Whig and associate of Lord Stamford, was the principal sponsor of the measure in the Commons, while Stamford himself acted as chairman of the committee in the Lords. Their aid ensured the bill a smooth progress, although the amendments made by the Upper House to the bill sparked fierce protests in the Commons on 15 May, several Members arguing that the Lords had altered a money bill. As Sir Richard Cocks, 2nd Bt.*, observed, 'this was more party than reason', and the measure was passed by a majority of 21.[12]

The accession of Anne promised a greater challenge to Ashurst's prospects, and at the London election of July 1702 he finished a lowly sixth as the Tories captured three of the City seats. The preceding month his London rivals had already engineered his removal as a colonel in the capital's militia, but he managed to retain the vice-presidency of the Honorary Artillery Company, commanding it in October on the occasion of the Queen's attendance at the Lord Mayor's Day celebrations. For the next three years, however, his political influence was largely confined to the court of aldermen. His colonial interests provided him with some leverage, and in 1705 he sought to persuade the Church hierarchy to employ Nonconformist ministers to convert the North American Indians, arguing that 'our ministers (though not episcopal) are capable of doing good'. Several years before he had clashed with the Earl of Bellomont [I] (Richard Coote*) over this issue, but the latter had evidently been impressed by Ashurst's missionary zeal, describing him as 'a right honest gentleman who will hearken to reason'.[13]

The London election of May 1705 saw a substantial rehabilitation of his party's fortunes, with Ashurst finishing third of the three Whig candidates to be returned. His political enemies greeted his return to Westminster with familiar attacks on his Nonconformist sympathies, a pamphleteer accusing him of having written to a friend that 'it's past 12 with the Church, so she must come down'. The Earl of Sunderland (Charles, Lord Spencer*) recognized his return as a Whig gain, and, having been predictably identified as 'No Church' by an analyst of the new Parliament, Ashurst voted on 25 Oct. for the Court candidate in the division on the Speakership. His significant activity in the first session was principally confined to the management of a bill to allow two London merchants to import a cargo of wine from Copenhagen, but he was also named to the conference committee on the bill to make an exemplification of Lord Conway's will. His allegiance to the Court was further demonstrated by his support on 18 Feb. for its proceedings concerning the place clause within the regency bill, a loyalty which recommended his appointment in the same month as a commissioner for receiving the loan to the Emperor.[14]

In the next session Ashurst was much more prominent, actively sponsoring a variety of measures, beginning with the management of a private estate bill. He was also one of the Members detailed to convey the thanks of the House to the bishop of Salisbury for preaching a sermon. More importantly, he was closely involved in the progress of a bill to encourage the Royal Lustring Company, having been closely involved with the scrutiny of the company's original petition for relief. Another corporation to benefit from his presence in the House was the London Gunmakers, whose petition for aid was reported to the House by Ashurst. He later became involved with a bill to curb the dangers of bringing gunpowder into the capital, and acted as a teller on 24 Apr. to read for a second time the Lords' amendments to the bill. Recalling earlier parliamentary interests, he was also nominated for the conference committee on the bill to continue the Vagrancy Act. He evidently backed the Court on the great issue of the Union, expressing warm approval for the measure on 6 Mar. to the Presbyterian Earl of Sutherland, and asking leave 'to call your lordship my countryman and to congratulate myself of being a Briton'. Several months before, he had actually sought to reassure Sutherland that the Union did not pose a commercial or religious threat to the Scots, at which time he insisted that (contrary to Jacobite rumours) English Dissenters lived 'amicably' with their Anglican neighbours.[15]

During the summer recess Ashurst had further cause for self-congratulation when he was restored in July as a colonel of the London militia. In the first session of the British Parliament he remained a conspicuous figure, principally in connexion with commercial and maritime affairs. On 6 Dec. 1707 he reported from the committee on a merchant petition complaining of the smuggling of French wine, and was one of the Members named to prevent such illegalities. He was also nominated to the drafting committee on a bill to prevent the import of cochineal, and on 26 Jan. 1708 acted as a teller to block the second reading of a bill to recruit seamen. Two more appointments to drafting committees followed in February, for measures to relieve three regiments and to regulate the militia. His allegiance to the Whig-dominated ministry was confirmed by two parliamentary lists of early 1708. In the remainder of the session he was a leading sponsor of a bill to regulate Bank elections, and was also named to the conference committee on a measure to amend the Highway Repair Act.[16]

The London Whigs again performed well at the City election of May 1708, at which Ashurst finished third. He did not prove as active as before in this Parliament. His support for the ministry was further suggested by an incident the following month, when he was duped by the Tory lord mayor (Sir) Charles Duncombe* into thinking that the allies had gained a major victory abroad. Evidently eager to boost support for the war effort, Ashurst hurried to Parliament to break the news, only to discover subsequently that no spectacular success had been gained. Edward Harley*, a recent convert to the opposition, enjoyed his humiliation, observing that the mayor had 'served that fellow well enough'. Maintaining his interest in commercial legislation, he was named to drafting committees on bills to ban the import of wrought marble, and to perpetuate acts against the forging of coins and promissory notes. In the next session he was again active, managing a bill to regulate the assize of bread, and being named to three drafting committees on commercial issues of obvious metropolitan interest. He remained loyal to his party during this Parliament, supporting the naturalization of the Palatines in early 1709, and voting for the impeachment of Dr Sacheverell a year later. The ministry's favourable impression of him was indirectly confirmed in early 1710 by his appointment as agent for Massachusetts Bay, the colonial assembly clearly viewing him as an influential ally in governing circles. However, despite his close connexion with the New England Company, Ashurst declined to serve the colony in an official capacity, pleading grounds of ill-health.[17]

The High Church campaign mounted before the general election of 1710 was an obvious threat to Ashurst's influence in London, and although polling over 3,000 votes at the City contest in October he finished bottom of the poll. This galling defeat was accompanied by the loss of his colonelcy, but as a senior alderman he remained an important figure in City circles, stubbornly opposing Tory efforts to gain control of the Honorary Artillery Company. In June 1711 it was even rumoured that his financial status might lead to reappointment as a revenue commissioner, but he did not gain preferment under Robert Harley's administration. Although he did not stand, or even vote, at the London election of October 1713, he was keen to maintain Whig dominance within the London corporation, prompting the mayor to adjourn a common council in March 1714 to thwart a Tory attempt to overturn the result of a ward election.[18]

Ashurst's loyalty to the Whig cause was rewarded on the accession of George I, for in November 1714 he was reappointed to the excise commission, a post which effectively precluded any ambition of a return to Westminster. He retained the office until his death on 12 Jan. 1720, which came 'after a very long indisposition', perhaps linked to an apoplectic seizure reported in November 1715. A most favourable epitaph was supplied by one of his colonial contacts, who lauded him as 'a hearty lover of our civil and religious liberties', but noted, somewhat surprisingly, that he had betrayed 'an extreme aversion to a court and the tedious ceremonies of attendance'. Although Ashurst had requested to be buried at St. Augustine's, London, his body was interred at Hedingham, Essex, the family's influence having been extended there in 1713 by the purchase of the manor of Castle Hedingham. His will revealed little concern for charitable causes, but prior beneficiaries of his benevolence included the London corporation of the poor and Greenwich Hospital, as well as several young Nonconformist ministers. His eldest son Henry having predeceased him, his principal estate, which included the 'beauteous pile of honour' he had built at Highgate in 1694, passed to his grandson William. Sir William's sons had already been well catered for, each having benefited from their father's wealth and influence, most notably William, who had become a comptroller at the stamp office. However, even though his son Robert succeeded him as governor of the New England Company, none of his surviving offspring attempted to emulate his parliamentary career.[19]

[1] *Le Neve's Knights* (Harl. Soc. viii), 414; IGI, London; F. C. Cass, *E. Barnet*, 68–69; *London Mar. Lic.* ed. Foster, 41; PCC 22 Shaller; J. P. Malcolm, *Londinium Redivivum*, ii. 94. [2] Guildhall Lib. ms MF324; Beaven, *Aldermen*, ii. 114; W. Kellaway, *New England Co.* 290; *Survey of London*, xvii. 61; J. Aubrey, *Surr.* v. 309. [3] Add. 10120, ff. 232–6; *Daily Courant*, 8 Aug. 1704; *CSP Dom.* 1700–2, p. 242. [4] J. Dunton, *Life and Errors*, 203; PCC 22 Shaller; SP29/418/199; Corp. London RO, lieutenancy min. bk. f. 24; Herts. RO, Panshanger mss D/EP/F81, f. 11, Cowper to his wife, 21 May 1687; Beddard, *Kingdom Without a King*, 71; Luttrell, *Brief Relation*, i. 516; ii. 25; *HMC Finch*, iii. 433–4. [5] Dorset RO, Fox-Strangways mss D124, box 235, bdle. 4, Rich to Sir Stephen Fox*,

17 Mar. 1690; Luttrell, ii. 250, 255; *Portledge Pprs.* 112; *HMC Portland*, iii. 469; Dr Williams' Lib. O. D. 67, f. 105. ⁶Luttrell, iii. 195–6, 217; Bodl. Carte 233, f. 285; 181, ff. 459–60; BL, Trumbull Misc. mss 28, Abraham Stanyan to Sir William Trumbull*, 4 July 1693; Add. 17677 NN, ff. 283, 289, 331; *Ld. Chief Baron's Speech to Sir William Ashurst* [1693]; *CSP Dom.* 1694–5, p. 127; Macfarlane thesis, 260. ⁷NLS, Advocates' mss 31.1.7, f. 146; *CSP Dom.* 1694–5, p. 139; *Cal. Treas. Bks.* x. 729; *Cal. Treas. Pprs.* 1557–1696, p. 441; Add. 45538, ff. 22–23; *HMC Kenyon*, 399. ⁸*Cal. Treas. Bks.* xii. 8; xiii. 393; Univ. London Lib. mss 65, item 3; *HMC Lords* n.s. iii. 150; Nottingham Univ. Lib. Portland (Bentinck) mss PwA 1466, James Vernon I to Ld. Portland, 16 July 1697; Add. 40772, f. 67. ⁹*Cal. Treas. Bks.* xiv. 151; *CSP Dom.* 1699–1700, p. 67. ¹⁰*Post Boy*, 13–15 June 1700. ¹¹Add. 70272, large acct. Revolution and succession; Luttrell, v. 82; *CSP Dom.* 1700–2, p. 445. ¹²Add. 17677 XX, f. 159; *HMC Lords* n.s. v. 33; *Cocks Diary*, 289. ¹³Luttrell, v. 193; Boyer, *Anne Annals*, i. 126; Kellaway, 234–5, 263; *CSP Col.* 1700, p. 609. ¹⁴*Coll. from Dyer's Letters Concerning Elections of Present Parl.* [1706]; Boyer, iv. 126. ¹⁵*Sutherland Bk.* ed. Fraser, ii. 203; NLS, Sutherland mss Dep. 313/529, Ashurst to Lord Sutherland, 20 Aug. 1706. ¹⁶Luttrell, vi. 188. ¹⁷*HMC Portland*, iv. 512; *CSP Col.* 1710–11, pp. 45, 91. ¹⁸Luttrell, vi. 640; G. S. De Krey, *Fractured Soc.* 263; *HMC Portland*, v. 15, 411–12. ¹⁹*Cal. Treas. Bks.* xxix. 149; Boyer, *Pol. State*, xix. 116; NMM, Vernon mss 1/1F, James Vernon I to Edward Vernon, 4 Nov. 1715; Kellaway, 167–8; Cass, 68–69; Morant, *Essex*, ii. 295; Macfarlane thesis, 324; *Evelyn Diary*, iii. 133; De Krey, 90; E. Settle, *Augusta Lacrimans* [1720]; *Survey of London*, 53.

P. L. G.

ASSHETON (ASHTON), Sir Ralph, 2nd Bt. (1652–1716), of Middleton, nr. Manchester, Lancs.

LIVERPOOL   9 Mar. 1677–1679 (Jan.)
LANCASHIRE   6 Feb. 1694–1698

b. 11 Feb. 1652, 1st s. of Sir Ralph Ashton, 1st Bt., of Middleton, by Anne, da. of Sir Ralph Assheton, 1st Bt., of Great Lever; bro. of Richard Assheton (Ashton)*. *educ.* privately; Brasenose, Oxf. 1668, MA 1669; travelled abroad 1673. *m.* (1) Mary (*d.* 1694), da. and h. of Thomas Vavasour of Spaldington, Yorks., 1s. *d.v.p.* 3da.; (2) 30 July 1696, Mary, da. and h. of Robert Hyde of Denton, Lancs., *s.p. suc.* fa. as 2nd Bt. 28 Apr. 1665; maternal uncle Sir John Assheton, 4th Bt., in Whalley Abbey estate 1697.¹
Freeman, Preston 1682.²

Assheton's family held extensive lands in the south of the county, and the family estates were augmented in 1697 when Assheton inherited the manor of Whalley, near Clitheroe. Raised as a Presbyterian, Assheton had conformed to the Church of England by 1673, but his Whiggish inclinations after the Revolution may have had their roots in his early religious allegiance. In the early 1690s Assheton was particularly active in supplying the government with information about suspected Jacobites, so much so that in 1690 Lord Brandon (Hon. Charles Gerard*) wrote to Secretary Shrewsbury of Assheton's 'zeal for his Majesty's service', and his loyalty to the new regime led Assheton to write to Roger Kenyon* in April 1690 in praise of the Commons' vote of supply, which would allow Ireland to 'be speedily reduced', thereby frustrating 'those that would destroy his Majesty and our happy government'. Assheton does not, however, appear to have been a violent partisan. He was the only man to serve on the Lancashire bench throughout the period 1689–1715, surviving numerous politically motivated regulations, and when Assheton stood for the county at the by-election of 1694, caused by Brandon's succession as Earl of Macclesfield, his candidacy was welcomed by all sides in the county and, after rumours of a contest, he was returned unchallenged.³

Assheton was an inactive Member, being granted leave of absence on 28 Mar. 1694 and 23 Mar. 1695, and in an analysis of the Commons Robert Harley* was able only to class him as 'doubtful'. His party loyalties were suggested by his support of the Whig (Sir) Alexander Rigby* at the Wigan election of 1695 and, having been returned unopposed for the county, he was forecast as a likely supporter of the ministry in the divisions of 31 Jan. 1696 on the proposed council of trade. He signed the Association the following month, and on 27 Mar. was granted a leave of absence. He was absent from the division on the attainder of Sir John Fenwick†, but had reached London by the end of January 1697 in order to guide through Parliament a bill to 'supply an omission . . . in his marriage settlement'. Despite opposition from Thomas Brotherton* and Sir William Williams, 1st Bt.*, the bill passed both Houses in February, but when the Commons was told that the Royal Assent had been granted Assheton had possibly already left London, having obtained leave of absence on 16 Feb. At the beginning of the following session Assheton was absent from the call of the House on 16 Dec. and was sent for and taken into custody. He was not released until 24 Jan. 1698, and on 12 Apr. he was granted a month's leave of absence. He did not stand for Parliament again, being classed as a member of the Court party 'out' of the 1698 Parliament, and he seems to have harboured no further parliamentary ambitions, as it was his younger brother Richard who was returned for the county at the by-election of 1703. His inheritance of the manor of Whalley had given him some influence at Clitheroe but he chose not to use this for his own advantage, though he was approached in 1710 by the Earl of Derby (Hon. James Stanley*) to lend his weight to the opposition to the Tory Edward Harvey*. Assheton died on 4 May 1716, being buried at Middleton six days later, and was succeeded in his title by his nephew Ralph. The Whalley estates passed to his three daughters, two of whom had married Thomas Lister II* and

Nathaniel Curzon†. Lister and Curzon were at this time in the process of consolidating their electoral interest at Clitheroe, and it may be that their wives' inheritance at Whalley aided their endeavours.[4]

[1] *Dorm. and Extinct Baronetcies*, 19–22; John Rylands Univ. Lib. Manchester, Legh of Lyme mss corresp. Anne Assheton to Richard Legh†, 29 Mar. [1673]. [2] *Preston Guild Rolls* (Lancs. and Cheshire Rec. Soc. ix), 180. [3] *VCH Lancs*. iv. 163; vi. 383; *Jacobite Trials at Manchester 1694* (Chetham Soc. ser. 1, xxviii), 48–49; *CSP Dom.* 1689–90, pp. 520, 541; 1691–2, p. 276; *HMC Kenyon*, 235–6, 238, 282, 284, 286; Lancs. RO, Hulton mss DDHu 48/45, Assheton to [William Hulton], 9 Jan 1693-4. [4] Liverpool RO, 920MD 174 Sir Willoughby Aston diaries, 7 Nov. 1695; *HMC Lords*, n.s. ii. 368; *HMC Kenyon*, 413; Lancs. RO, Kenyon mss DDKe/HMC/1031A, Richard Wroe to Roger Kenyon, 28 Jan. 1696–7; Norf. RO, Harbord mss (unsorted coll.), Derby to Assheton, 18 May 1710; *VCH Lancs*. iv. 167; *Dorm. and Extinct Baronetcies*, 22.

E. C./R. D. H.

ASSHETON (ASHTON), Richard (1654–1705), of Allerton and Gledhow, Yorks.

LANCASHIRE 11 Jan. 1703–1705

b. 4 May 1654, 2nd s. of Sir Ralph Ashton, 1st Bt., of Middleton, nr. Manchester, Lancs.; bro. of Sir Ralph, 2nd Bt.* *educ*. privately. *m*. Mary, da. of John Parker of Extwisle, Lancs., wid. of Benjamin Waddington of Allerton and Gledhow, 3s. 2da.[1]

After his father's death Assheton was brought up by his mother, a Presbyterian sympathizer, and for a time his tutor was a Dissenting minister who had been ejected in 1662. When Hon. James Stanley* succeeded as 10th Earl of Derby in November 1702 Assheton began canvassing support for the Lancashire seat left vacant and, with Derby's support and despite the protestations of the Tory Viscount Cornbury (Edward Hyde*) that Assheton 'cannot be acceptable under the rose at this time', he was returned unopposed. Assheton was an inactive Member, but in October 1704 he was classed as a probable opponent of the Tack, and in the division on 28 Nov. either approved the measure or was absent. He did not stand at the general election of 1705 and died in September the same year. His son succeeded to the baronetcy in 1716, but Assheton himself was the last member of his family to sit in Parliament.[2]

[1] *Vis. Lancs*. (Chetham Soc. ser. 1, lxxxiv), 15; *Dorm. and Extinct Baronetcies*, 19–22; *Life of Adam Martindale* (Chetham Soc. ser 1, iv), 196. [2] Greater Manchester RO, Legh of Lyme mss E17/89/25/2, Hyde to Peter Legh†, 23 Nov. 1702; John Rylands Univ. Lib. Manchester, Legh of Lyme mss corresp. Edward Allanson to same, 2 Dec. 1702.

E. C./R. D. H.

ASTLEY, Sir Jacob, 1st Bt. (c.1639–1729), of Melton Hall, Melton Constable, Norf.

NORFOLK 1685–1687, 1690–1701 (Nov.) 1702–1705, 1710–1722

b. c.1639, 1st s. of Sir Edward Astley of Hindolveston, Norf. by his 1st cos. Elizabeth, da. of Jacob, 1st Baron Astley of Reading. *educ*. King's, Camb. 1657; Christ Church, Oxf. matric. 1659. *m*. 6 Feb. 1661, Blanche (*d*. 1697), da. of Sir Philip Wodehouse, 3rd Bt.†, of Kimberley, Norf., 4s. 1da. *suc*. fa. 1653; uncle Sir Isaac Astley, 1st Bt., to Hillmorton, Warws. and Melton Constable 1659; cos. Jacob, 3rd Baron Astley to the entailed estates of 1st Baron Astley 1689; *cr*. Bt. 25 June 1660.[1]

Sheriff, Norf. 1663–4.

Ld. of Trade 1714–17.

Astley was the leading Tory in Norfolk in this period, but he was a careful man, a moderate, and moreover was never a very active Member. In 1690 Lord Carmarthen (Sir Thomas Osborne†) classed him as a Tory supporter of the Court. Carmarthen forecast in December that Astley would probably support him in the event of a Commons' attack on his ministerial position, also noting him as a Court supporter in another list compiled after 23 Dec. Robert Harley* also listed him as a supporter of the Court in April 1691. On 23 Jan. 1692 he was granted leave of absence for three weeks because his wife was ill. He was also given leave of absence on 12 Mar. 1695. He was forecast as a likely opponent of the Court on 31 Jan. 1696 over the proposed council of trade. He signed the Association promptly, and in March voted against fixing the price of guineas at 22*s*. On 25 Nov. he voted against the attainder of Sir John Fenwick†. Listed in about September 1698 as a member of the Country party, he was also forecast as likely to oppose the standing army. On 17 Dec. he was nominated to prepare a bill for the better preservation of game, and also on 7 Jan. 1699 was appointed to draft a private estate bill. He was listed in February 1701 as likely to support the Court over continuing the 'Great Mortgage', and was later blacklisted for having opposed making preparations for war with France. On 27 May he was appointed to the drafting committee for the Norwich court of conscience bill.[2]

In the election of December 1701 Astley did not declare himself a candidate for the county until quite late in the day, and was defeated by two Whigs. Having regained his seat at the next election, he probably spoke on the Court side in December 1702 in committee on a supply bill: 'the first thing I ever heard . . . [he] took notice of', observed a Norfolk Whig. On 20 Dec. 1703 he reported a private estate bill, and another bill on 14 Feb. 1704. In March 1704 Lord Nottingham (Daniel Finch†) listed him as likely to support the government in the anticipated proceedings on the Scotch Plot. Astley was forecast as an opponent of the Tack, and having also figured on Robert Harley's lobbying list, did not vote for the measure on 28 Nov. He told on 3 Feb. 1705 in favour of agreeing with the committee appointed to investigate the East Anglian coal trade in a resolution against the monopoly enjoyed by freemen of Great Yarmouth of the retailing of coal landed at that port, a monopoly denounced by the committee as a 'great grievance' to the inhabitants of Norwich and the surrounding countryside. His opposition to the Tack alienated some Tory support, and his taking up the grievances of Norwich probably cost him some Yarmouth votes, so that after an unsuccessful canvass he stood down at the 1705 election, allowing two Whigs to be returned. In 1706, when the two parties in Norfolk sent up rival addresses to the Queen, the Tories seeking by this means to re-establish their interest, Astley seems to have remained aloof. His support was looked for by the Whigs in vain, though there is no evidence that he associated himself with the Tory address either.[3]

Astley was returned again for Norfolk in 1710, with his nephew Sir John Wodehouse, 4th Bt.*, after a contest with two Whigs. He was classed as a Tory in the 'Hanover list'. In November 1710 he was reported to be 'dangerously ill'. In the 1710–11 session he was listed as one of the 'worthy patriots' who had exposed the mismanagements of the previous ministry. On 18 June 1713 he voted against the French commerce bill. In the Worsley list he appeared as a Tory, but another comparative analysis of the 1713 and 1715 Parliaments classed him as a Whig. After Queen Anne's death Robert Walpole II* certainly brought him over to the Whigs. Astley died on 17 Aug. 1729, aged 90, and was buried at Melton Constable.[4]

[1] PCC 256 Alchin. [2] *HMC Townshend*, 329. [3] Camb. Univ. Lib. Cholmondeley (Houghton) mss, John Turner* to Robert Walpole II, 16 Dec. 1702, 19 Feb. 1704-5; Charles Turner to Robert Walpole II, [c. May 1705]; W. Suss. RO, Shillinglee mss Acc. 454/853, Sir Edmund Bacon, 4th Bt. to Sir Edward Turnor, 21 Feb. 1704[-5]; 854, Thomas Peirson to same, 9 Mar. 1704[-5]; J. H. Plumb, *Walpole*, i. 45–46. [4] Add. 70421, newsletter 11 Nov. 1710.

D. W. H.

ATKINS, Sir Richard, 2nd Bt. (1654–96), of Clapham, Surr. and Tickford, Bucks.

BUCKINGHAMSHIRE 1695–28 Nov. 1696

bap. 27 Aug. 1654, 2nd but 1st surv. s. of Sir Richard Atkins, 1st Bt., of Clapham by Rebecca, da. and coh. of Sir Edmund Wright of Swakeleys, Mdx., ld. mayor of London. *educ.* ?M. Temple 1671. *m.* in or bef. 1684, Elizabeth, da. of Sir Thomas Byde† of Ware Park, Herts., 6s. (4 *d.v.p.*) 1da. *suc.* fa. 19 Aug. 1689.[1]

Col. of ft. 1694–*d.*
Commr. taking subscriptions to land bank 1696.[2]

Atkins' great-grandfather, Henry Atkins (*d*.1635), court physician to James I, purchased the manor of Tickford near Newport Pagnell from the crown, and also acquired the manor of Clapham for £6,000. Atkins' elder brother, Henry, died in 1677 (aged 24), leaving him as the heir. As a j.p. for Buckinghamshire in February 1688, he gave negative replies to the first two of James II's three questions on the repeal of the Test Act and Penal Laws and at the Revolution raised a troop for the Prince of Orange.[3]

Atkins' political allegiance at this time is somewhat perplexing. He was perceived as a Tory, yet he contested Buckingham in 1689 in alliance with Sir Peter Tyrell, 1st Bt.†, a Whig, against two Tories. When he stood there again in 1690, his stance was becoming clearer, at least in that the leading Buckinghamshire Whig, Hon. Thomas Wharton*, was prepared to back Atkins and Tyrell against the Temple interest. Certainly, Atkins was committed to the new regime, sending out warrants for the militia horse to assemble in July 1690 when a French invasion threatened. There seems little doubt that he was converted to the cause of Whiggery by Wharton, but the timing is difficult to pin-point. Richard Steele* later explained that Atkins had been one of the most active opponents of Wharton after the Revolution and had been

very zealous for promoting the Tory cause, assisted by the inferior clergy, but the thin appearance they made from time to time wearied Sir Richard at last, and he took a resolution to make his peace with my Lord [then Thomas] Wharton: accordingly he rode over to Winchendon, and told his Lordship with great frankness, he was come to dine with him and offer his friendship: for ... my Lord, says he, *I find 'tis in vain to be against you*. My Lord Wharton received him with such candour and kindness as entirely gained him over to his party.

However, Steele placed this conversion a few months before Atkins acquired his regiment in 1694. Thomas Chapman* likewise dated Atkins' conversion to some time after the Revolution and corroborated the story about the regiment. However, it was December 1693 before it was rumoured that Atkins would be given a horse regiment if any new levies were raised and April 1694 before he was actually given a commission to raise a foot regiment for service in Ireland. Meanwhile, despite being named first in the list, he possessed sufficient influence to avoid being pricked as sheriff of Buckinghamshire in November 1693.[4]

In the summer of 1695 Atkins was much in the news over a series of duels, apparently caused by the infidelity of his wife. He beat James Medlicott with his cane for talking about Lady Atkins, offered to fight Sir Edward Longueville with blunderbusses to compensate for the latter's physical disadvantages and exchanged a few passes with Lord James Howard*, who denied sleeping with Atkins' wife. Possibly finding his list of 15 men to confront a trifle overburdensome, Atkins took the matter up with his father-in-law, who 'being sensible of the provocation' agreed that his daughter should reside at Nottingham or in Buckinghamshire with £120 p.a. She duly took up residence in the 'parson's house near Newport Pagnell'. At the general election in October 1695, Wharton and Atkins were returned unopposed as knights of the shire, though Atkins possessed only a small estate in the county. However, Atkins also contested Buckingham, but again unsuccessfully. He was forecast as likely to support the Court on 31 Jan. 1696 in the division over the proposed council of trade, signed the Association, and voted in March for fixing the price of guineas at 22s. Despite his inexperience he was not averse to joining in party point-scoring, it being reported that on 13 Feb. 1696:

> some words passed ... in the committee [of the whole on the price of guineas] between Sir Richard Atkins and Sir Edward Seymour, that the House thought fit to interpose for preventing any quarrel. There being a question proposed for leaving the Chair, and Sir Edward Seymour being thought of in his debate to deviate from it, Sir Richard took him down to order, which he [Seymour] being surprised at, questioned whether he understood what order was; some others took notice of that as an improper reflection, and Sir Richard's reply to it was, that he should not apply to the House for satisfaction in any case where he could hope for it elsewhere.

Atkins was then brought back into the House and ordered not to prosecute the quarrel further. His final recorded intervention in debate occurred on 27 Feb. when he was one of 'two great courtiers' who opposed a motion to note that the French King and James II were promoters of the Assassination Plot.[5]

Atkins died on 28 Nov. 1696, and was buried at Newport Pagnell. The monument erected by his mother praised his accomplishments and service in Parliament before remarking that 'the latter part of his life [had] been clouded with some domestic troubles caused by the fault of others, not his own, which ought to be covered with a veil of silence', although they had 'hastened his end'.[6]

[1] IGI, Herts.; Manning and Bray, *Surr.* iii. 362. [2] *CJ*, xii. 510. [3] Manning and Bray, 361–2; *VCH Bucks.* iv. 417; T. C. Dale, *Our Clapham Forefathers*, 91; Duckett, *Penal Laws and Test Act* (1883), 143; Add. 70217, Chapman to [Ld. Oxford (Robert Harley*)], 22 Dec. 1711. [4] BL, Verney mss mic. 636/44, Sir Ralph Verney, 1st Bt.†, to John Verney* (Ld. Fermanagh), 6 July 1690; 636/47, same to same, 9, 11 Nov. 1693; *Wharton Mems.* 30; Add. 70217, Chapman to [Oxford], 22 Dec. 1711; Northants RO, Isham mss IC 1505, John to Sir Justinian Isham, 4th Bt.*, 10 Dec. 1693; *CSP Dom.* 1694–5, pp. 116–17; Luttrell, *Brief Relation*, iii. 293. [5] Verney mss 636/48, John to Sir Ralph Verney, 3, 4, 10, 11, 24 July, 7 Aug. 1695; Luttrell, 494, 506; *Lexington Pprs.* 168–9; *HMC Kenyon*, 405. [6] Manning and Bray, *Surr.* 362; *Clapham and the Clapham Sect* (Clapham Antiq. Soc.), 189–90.

E. C./S. N. H.

ATKINSON, Samuel (c.1645–1718), of Rotherhithe, Surr.

HARWICH   1698–14 Feb. 1699

b. c.1645, s. of Richard Atkinson, rector of Kessingland, Suff., by Judith, ?da. of Henry Fitzhugh of Great Barford, Beds. *m.* (1) [-]; (2) 2 May 1706, Mary (*d.*1746), da. of Edward Yallop, Merchant Taylor, of London, *s.p.*[1]

Gov. corp. of Sons of Clergy 1678; er. bro. Trinity House 1687, master 1700–1, dep. master 1706.[2]

Commr. licensing hawkers and pedlars 1698–?*d.*, transports 1689–1715.[3]

Freeman, Harwich and Portsmouth 1703.[4]

Atkinson's father had been appointed rector of Kessingland in 1641, but three years later was 'sequestered and distressed' during the Civil War and had the misfortune to die shortly after regaining his living at the Restoration. The children were consequently 'put to their shifts for a livelihood' and, as Samuel himself later recalled, it was his 'fortune to go very young to sea'. Through hard work he succeeded in rising out of impoverishment, and his knowledge of England's coast and maritime affairs proved highly useful. In 1665–6, at the time of the Second Dutch War, he acted as an agent for the transportation of goods from Bristol, possibly in an official capacity, since in 1708 he recalled having served the crown 'for the last 40 years'. Little is known of his peacetime activity, but he may well have been the Captain Atkinson who in 1676 commanded a ketch bound for Tangier, and was later described as a 'Guinea man'; and it is also likely that he traded with Turkey. His extensive experience made him an obvious appointment on 24 June 1689 to hire sufficient ships to transport and provision the army which was being sent to relieve the siege of Derry, and he was retained as a commissioner for transports until 1715. The post was, in theory at least, a lucrative one:

it paid £400 a year, and since huge sums of money were involved (in 1689–1702 the commissioners handled £577,000, and £1,336,000 in 1702–11) the possibilities existed for making a personal fortune, especially after Atkinson's appointment in 1703 as the agent for prizes in London and in 1705 as agent to sell prize ships and goods. He nevertheless had to work hard, and an indication of his devotion to do his work comes in a letter of 1704 in which he explained that despite bad weather and 'a great cold' he would 'if it pleased God . . . be carried on board' his ship to fulfil his duties. Some of his tireless skill at logistics also becomes apparent in his reports to the government (written in a style that exposes his lack of a formal education) which reveal him scurrying round the English coast in his efforts to secure a smooth passage for the troops. Always a man of energy, he was resourceful and inventive, co-patenting in 1691 'a new engine by which a man may stay and work for many hours at a considerable depth under water'.[5]

His strong connexion with the navy, and friendship with Under-Secretary of State John Ellis*, who was himself the son of a clergyman and a commissioner for transports, must have helped ensure Atkinson's return for Harwich in July 1698. Naturally listed as a placeman supporting the Court, and as voting on 18 Jan. 1699 against the third reading of the disbanding bill, he was nevertheless unable to serve the Court for long in Parliament. On 24 June 1698 he had been appointed as a commissioner for licensing hawkers and pedlars, with an annual salary of £100, thereby falling foul of a clause in the 1694 Lottery Act which barred holders of new financial offices from sitting in the Commons. This stipulation had been long neglected, and under normal circumstances Atkinson could have expected to have retained his seat. However, 'Country' antipathy to mismanagement and corruption at the Admiralty was running high, and it is tempting to suggest that Sir Thomas Davall I*, the other MP for Harwich, who was particularly incensed about the state of the navy, may have been involved in naming Atkinson as one of the 'disagreeable Members' who were to be expelled under the terms of the place clause. Moreover, the political atmosphere had become particularly charged at this time because of the rivalry between the Duke of Leeds (Sir Thomas Osborne†) and Charles Montagu*: the latter had secured the post of auditor of the Exchequer for his brother until he was ready to take it himself, much to the annoyance of Leeds, who had wanted the office conferred on his own son, Lord Carmarthen (Peregrine Osborne†). The matter of the place clause was therefore raised partly in the hope of embroiling Montagu in the affair, though the Duke's plan came to nothing and Atkinson was the unfortunate victim of circumstance: on 13 Feb. 1699 he was ordered to attend the House and the following day was deprived of his seat. Since the revenue from licensing hawkers and pedlars had been used towards the payment of interest on the transport debt, Atkinson had good cause to nurse a sense of grievance over his unseating.[6]

Atkinson's name nevertheless continues to appear in the Journals at the foot of accounts for the transport office, which was supplied out of the funds voted for the army and navy, although the cost was not included in their estimates. Problems about financing the department had soon become apparent. As early as 1691 Atkinson petitioned that he had 'undergone great difficulties in the service for want of seasonable supplies of money and is now in arrear above £900', and so deeply was he in debt for the state's expenditure that he feared prosecution by creditors. Another crisis arose in 1704, when the House had to vote £60,000 for transport provisions in an attempt to reduce the expanding naval debt. The financial position of the office had become even more fragile after 1702, when the commission was formally dissolved, leaving only a Treasury minute as the authority for Atkinson's disbursements, a vagary that was resolved only in 1710 when a new warrant for the commissioners' appointment retrospectively ratified their actions. This document was also the culmination of efforts to bring the office into line with the rest of the naval administration by regularizing the system of payments, though none of the impetus or ideas for the reform appears to have come from Atkinson himself. The accounting procedure adopted by the commissioners had been particularly open to abuse: a parliamentary report on 17 Mar. 1712 pointed out that they had never been asked for security for the money they spent, but had been 'left in liberty to make their payments in what manner they pleased, they neither numbered their bills, nor paid them in course, according to the method of the navy office'. Despite the ensuing reorganization, the settlement of accounts was still unfinished six years later. Atkinson stood unsuccessfully for Harwich at both 1701 elections, and as late as July 1704 was said to be one of the 'persons many of the corporation have their thoughts upon'. But he never regained his seat, and in any case would have been ineligible from 1707, when commissioners of transport were no longer allowed to sit in the Commons.[7]

In 1706 Atkinson married, apparently for the second time since his marriage allegation described him as a widower, and by then he was a rich man. In 1709 payments were defaulted on a mortgage of

£10,200 which Atkinson had funded for the Seckford family estates in Suffolk and Essex, and on 2 Nov. 1713 he formally acquired them. When he died on 13 Dec. 1718 these properties passed to his wife and then, since the couple were childless, to his grand-nephew Samuel. Mary also received £1,000 of South Sea Company stock, and property in Surrey and Middlesex was left to other relatives. He bequeathed £200 to Trinity House, where he had acted as master 1700–1, and made provision for the poor sons of the clergy, showing that success had not obscured the memory of his early struggles.[8]

[1] Guildhall Lib. mss 25803/2, f. 117 (*ex inf.* E. G. Richards). [2] BL, Dept. Printed Bks. 1865 c.13(6); W. R. Chaplin, *Corp. Trinity House*, index. [3] *Cal. Treas. Bks.* xiii. 365; Adm/1/5284 (*ex inf.* E. G. Richards); Watson thesis, 323. [4] Harwich bor. recs. 98/4, f. 138; R. East, *Portsmouth Recs.* 373. [5] Info. from E. G. Edwards; Add. 45516 B, accts. for 1665–6; Add. 28891, f. 348; *CSP Dom.* 1690–1, pp. 245, 252, 267, 292; 1702–3, p. 258; *CJ*, xvii. 70, 100. [6] Northants. RO, Montagu (Boughton) mss 47/143, James Vernon I* to Duke of Shrewsbury, 11 Feb. 1699; Add. 30000 C, f. 49; *CJ*, xii. 503-4. [7] Watson, 262, 273, 295, 325; *Cal. Treas. Bks.* ix. 1375; xviii. 461; xx. 255; xxiv. 376–7; xxix. 868; xxxi. 418; xxxii. 249; *CJ*, xiv. 424; xvii. 100; *Cal. Treas. Pprs.* 1557–1696, p. 186; Boyer, *Pol. State*, iii. 229–30; Add. 28886, ff. 158, 172, 195–6; 28889, ff. 13, 38, 72; 28893, f. 310; 28927, f. 180; Harwich bor. recs. 69/5, 69/6. [8] Guildhall Lib. mss 25803/2, f. 117 (*ex inf.* E. G. Richards); Copinger, *Suff. Manors*, iii. 7; Greater London RO, St. Mary, Rotherhithe par. reg. (*ex inf.* E. G. Richards); PCC 182 Browning.

M.J.K.

AUBREY, Sir John, 2nd Bt. (c.1650–1700), of Llantriddyd, Glam.

BRACKLEY 1698–15 Sept. 1700

b. c.1650, 2nd but o. surv. s. of Sir John Aubrey, 1st Bt., of Llantriddyd by Mary, da. and h. of Sir Richard South, Goldsmith, of Cheapside, London. *educ.* Jesus, Oxf. matric. 29 Oct. 1668, aged 18; M. Temple 1672. *m.* (1) 1 Mar. 1679, aged 27, Margaret (*d.* aft. 1680), da. of Sir John Lowther, 1st Bt.[†], of Lowther Hall, Westmld., 1s.; (2) c.1691–3, Mary (*d.* 1717), da. of William Lewis[†] of Bletchington, Oxon. and The Van, Glam., coh. to her bro. Edward Lewis[†] (*d.* 1674) and wid. of William Jephson* of Boarstall, Bucks., *s.p. suc.* fa. as 2nd Bt. Mar. 1679.[1]

Sheriff, Glam. 1685–6.

Aubrey's father was a man of some learning, who not only corresponded with, but from time to time made a home for, his poor relation and namesake, the noted antiquary. He was also a staunch cavalier, loyal to the King during the Civil War and a keen persecutor of Dissent and disaffection in the two decades after the Restoration, described in 1677 as 'a constant friend to the government in Church and state'. His son imitated him in both respects. A 'witty knight', he was likewise a correspondent of John Aubrey, and of Edward Lhuyd; and in politics he started out, at least, in the High Church tradition. He possessed influence enough to enable him to postpone shrieval duty in 1683–4, largely through the intercession of Sir Leoline Jenkins[†], the brilliant son of a 'copyholder' on the Aubrey estate, whose successful career had owed its origin to the patronage of the first baronet, and who put the case against his being pricked on the grounds, he told Aubrey, of 'the burthens on your estate'. Although obliged to undertake the office in 1685, his inclusion in the Glamorgan lieutenancy commissioned after James II's accession indicated the continuance of court favour, which he repaid in this instance by his active participation in the arrest of suspected plotters. He also managed to retain his place on the bench despite evading the King's questions on the repeal of the Test Act and Penal Laws. To the Duke of Beaufort's summons he replied that 'because of his crazy body, as he says, [he is] not able to undertake the journey'.[2]

Nothing is known of Aubrey's attitude to or involvement in the Revolution. Subsequently he repaired his fortunes by marrying the widow of William Jephson and rapidly divorcing her, or so it would appear, on terms which preserved for his family the 'very fair inheritance' she had brought, especially Jephson's Buckinghamshire estate, secured under the terms of the marriage settlement. By his death he was said to be worth £3,000 a year. His politics, like those of his kinsman and ally Sir Charles Kemys, 3rd Bt.* (and possibly influenced by them), may now have been veering somewhat towards Whiggery, as he was chosen at Brackley in 1698 on the interest of either the Egerton family or Kemys' brother-in-law Lord Wharton (Hon. Thomas*). It was, however, Aubrey's Country sympathies which were more obvious to contemporaries, as an analysis of the House prepared shortly after his election classed Aubrey as a Country supporter. He was also forecast as likely to oppose a standing army, and was not included upon the list of those who voted on 18 Jan. 1699 against the disbanding bill. A year later an analysis of the House into interests classed Aubrey as doubtful or, perhaps, opposition. Otherwise he seems not to have adorned his brief parliamentary career with any particular record of activity. Aubrey died on 15 Sept. 1700, aged 49, after a fall from his horse on his Buckinghamshire property. His body was transported to Llantriddyd for burial, where his memorial offered an ambiguous tribute to his wit and character: 'What he was, those who conversed with him best know.'[3]

[1] Lipscomb, *Bucks.* i. 75. [2] *NLW Jnl.* xxi. 168; Aubrey, *Brief Lives* ed. Clark, i. 315; ii. 7–8; Wood, *Life and Times*, ii. 117; P. Jenkins, *Making of a Ruling Class*, 118–20, 123, 138, 210, 222, 235; *CSP*

Dom. 1683–4, p. 108; 1685, p. 189; Duckett, *Penal Laws and Test Act* (1882), p. 280; J. R. S. Phillips, *Wales and Mon. JPs 1541–1689*, pp. 307–9. [3] *Index of Cases in Ct. of Arches* ed. Houston (Index Lib. lxxxv), 14; *Arch. Cambr.* (ser. 13), xiii. 210–11; *Top. and Gen.* iii. 35; *NLW Jnl.* 163; *Midland Hist.* iii. 30–31; Luttrell, *Brief Relation*, iv. 659; *Verney Letters 18th Cent.* i. 86; *Arch. Cambr.* 210–11.

D. W. H.

AUBREY, Sir John, 3rd Bt. (1680–1743), of Llantriddyd, Glam. and Boarstall, Bucks.

CARDIFF BOROUGHS   1 Feb. 1706–1710

b. 20 June 1680, o. s. of Sir John Aubrey, 2nd Bt.*, by his 1st w. *educ.* Jesus, Oxf. 1698. *m.* 20 June 1701, Mary Stealy (*d.* 1714), 2s. 2da.; (2) c.1716, Frances, da. of William Jephson* of Boarstall, 2 da.; (3) 1 Feb. 1725, Jane Thomas (*d.* bef.1741) of Boarstall, *s.p. suc.* fa. as 3rd Bt. 15 Sept. 1700.[1]

Sheriff, Glam. 1710–11.

Aubrey was intended for a lucrative marriage. His father had reputedly 'a much greater regard for the addition of four or five thousand pounds in a portion than for the alliance of any family whatsoever'. Sadly, within a year of succeeding to the baronetcy and the already substantial estate which had been accumulated by earlier shrewd matchmaking, he had been obliged to marry a 'waiting maid' of his mother whom he had made pregnant.[2]

Aubrey followed one family tradition in displaying an interest in antiquarian scholarship: he was one of the subscribers to Edward Lhuyd's *Archaeologia Britannica* (1707). His political attitudes, however, showed a more markedly Whiggish strain than had those of his father. In Glamorgan, where he was politically active, he sided with the Mansel interest, ex-Whig and now moderate Tory, against the High Tory coalition ranged against it, backing Thomas Mansel I* in the 1705 general election and being returned on Mansel's recommendation at a by-election in 1706, and again in 1708. Classed as a Whig in a list dating from early 1708, he voted the following year in favour of the naturalization of the Palatines, and he twice told with Whigs and against Tories, albeit on issues which were not obviously party causes: on 19 Apr., against a rider offered to the Middlesex registry bill; and the next day, to agree with the Lords in an amendment to the fire prevention bill. His most blatantly Whig act was his vote in favour of the impeachment of Dr Sacheverell, which would have made it impossible for Mansel to have nominated him for re-election even had he wished to do so.[3]

Although Aubrey transferred his residence to Buckinghamshire he does not seem to have participated in elections in his adopted county, but he continued to support the Whig cause in Glamorgan. In 1716 Thomas Hearne visited Boarstall, 'on purpose to look at a distance, at the great house there'. He added, 'I say at a distance, because I did not care to go in, the present family of the Aubreys that live there being great enemies to the hereditary succession, for the sake of which I am a sufferer.' In the merely domestic sphere, Aubrey's children provided echoes of his own adolescent waywardness: a son was disinherited for the same offence he had committed himself; and a daughter was 'debauched' by a clergyman 'perverted in his principles'. Aubrey died on 16 Apr. 1743, and was buried at Boarstall.[4]

[1] Lipscomb, *Bucks.* i. 75; Foster, *London Mar. Lics.* 55; IGI, Bucks.; *Cardiff Recs.* ed. Matthews, v. 498. [2] Cumbria RO (Carlisle), Lonsdale mss D/Lons/W2/2/2, James Lowther* to Sir John Lowther, 2nd Bt. I*, 25 Nov. 1699; P. Jenkins, *Making of a Ruling Class*, 260. [3] *Glam. Co. Hist.* iv. 401, 403, 408, 607; Jenkins, 148; *HMC Portland*, iv. 490. [4] *Hearne Colls.* v. 192; Jenkins, 260, 263.

D. W. H.

AUSTEN, Sir John, 2nd Bt. (1641–99), of Hall Place, Bexley, Kent; Stagenhoe, Herts.; and Bloomsbury Square, Mdx.

RYE   24 Oct. 1667–1679 (Jan.)
       1 Apr. 1689–c. Jan. 1699

bap. 1 Apr. 1641, 1st s. of Sir Robert Austen, 1st Bt., of Bexley by his 2nd w. Anne, da. of Thomas Muns, merchant, of London and Bearstead, Kent; bro. of Robert Austen I*. *educ.* G. Inn 1657; Padua 1660. *m.* lic. 6 Dec. 1661, Rose (*d.* 1695), da. and h. of Sir John Hale of Stagenhoe, 6s. (3 *d.v.p.*) 4da. (1 *d.v.p.*). *suc.* fa. as 2nd Bt.30 Oct. 1666.[1]

Commr. recusants 1675.
Commr. customs 1697–*d*.[2]

Austen's parliamentary career had come to a stop at the Exclusion Crisis, when despite his Country sympathies he did not stand for re-election. Regaining his seat for Rye in 1689, he was re-elected in 1690, outpolling the government-promoted candidates by the narrowest margin. During his years out of Parliament he appears to have spent little time in Kent, residing instead on the Hertfordshire estate of Stagenhoe which his wife had inherited on her father's death in 1672. On recovering his seat, however, Austen soon indicated his ambition to carve out a personal interest at Rye with government support, and succeeded in establishing a family interest which endured for the next ten years or so. Both he and his younger brother, Colonel Robert, consciously set out after the Revolution to further the local political influence of their family in Winchelsea and Rye, the Cinque Port towns which lay nearest their respective estates.³

On the eve of the 1690 Parliament Austen was categorized by Lord Carmarthen (Sir Thomas Osborne†) as a Whig. Whether in the first session he displayed the same initial independence as his brother is not clear, but in April 1691, several months after the close of the second session, Robert Harley* could classify him straightforwardly as a supporter of the Court. In the meantime he strove to consolidate his relationship with his constituents. The corporation of Rye, much concerned at this time with the vulnerability of their town to French attack, had applied to Lord Sydney (Hon. Henry Sidney†), the secretary of state, for improved security. Sydney sent assurances to the mayor in January 1691 that the matter was under close consideration, and stressed that Austen, 'who has solicited this matter with all the zeal and care imaginable, can inform you how far his Majesty has already condescended to your request'. This commendation of Austen to his corporation suggests that he was already proving his utility to the government in Parliament. The direction of Austen's aspirations was made even clearer in August when his brother, who was now on the Admiralty board, sought a vacant customs commissionership for him from Lord Sydney. The King, however, had already given the post away. Austen's attendance during the 1691–2 session may have been impaired by his recovery from a 'stroke of the apoplexy' which he suffered in mid-September.⁴

Unlike his younger brother, Austen was not at all conspicuous in the House. In the midst of the wave of Whig appointments which followed the close of the 1693–4 session, Lord Sunderland recommended Austen to Lord Portland as worthy of a customs commissionership, describing him as 'very honest and not troublesome'. Once again, however, he was passed over. His support for the national land bank projected in 1694 is suggested by the inclusion of his name in an undated published list of subscribers. After his re-election for Rye in 1695, his continued dependability as a Court supporter can be seen in the record of his conduct in 1696. He was forecast in January as likely to support the Court in the divisions over the proposed council of trade, was an early signatory to the Association, voted in March for fixing the price of guineas at 22s., and in the next session, on 25 Nov., voted for the attainder of Sir John Fenwick†. At the end of April 1697 he finally obtained the customs commissionership which had eluded him for so long and a salary of £1,000. The announcement caused ripples of disquiet among the 'Rose Club' Whigs who thought their 'chairman' Sir Henry Hobart, 4th Bt.*,

deserved the position much more than the quiescent Austen. By way of compromise, however, Austen was installed in the post while Hobart became an extra commissioner. In lists produced after the 1698 election His was duly noted both as Court supporter and placeman. His death occurred at his residence in Bloomsbury Square some time at the turn of the year, though the precise date has not been ascertained. After bequests of property to his younger surviving sons, the bulk of his estate passed to his heir, who also succeeded him at Rye.⁵

¹Berry, *Kent Fam. Peds.* 350; IGI, London; *Mar. Lic. Fac. Off.* (Harl. Soc. xxiv), 56; PCC 142 Pott; Le Neve, *Mon. Angl.* 1650–79, p. 117. ²*Cal. Treas. Bks.* xii. 158, 206. ³Duckett, *Penal Laws and Test Act* (1882), 359; Berry, *Herts. Fam. Peds.* 35. ⁴*CSP Dom.* 1690–1, pp. 239–40, 482; Add. 70015, f. 182. ⁵Nottingham Univ. Lib. Portland (Bentinck) mss PwA 1238b, Sunderland to Portland, 13 July 1694; 1256, same to the King [30 Apr. 1697]; NLS, Advocates' mss, Bank of Eng. pprs. 31.1.7, f. 95; Luttrell, *Brief Relation*, iv. 218, 468; *Cal. Treas. Bks.* xii. 158, 206; xiii. 406; H. Horwitz, *Parl. and Pol. Wm. III*, 192; *Top. and Gen.* iii. 30; PCC 142 Pott.

A. A. H.

AUSTEN, John (aft. 1673–1742), of Derehams, S. Mimms, and Highgate, Mdx.

MIDDLESEX   1701 (Dec.)–1702
                   3 Mar. 1709–1710, 1722–1727

b. aft. 1673, 1st s. of Thomas Austen of Derehams by Arabella, da. and h. of Edward Forsett of Ashford and Marylebone, Mdx. *unm. suc. fa.* 1701; *cr.* Bt. 16 Nov. 1714.¹

Although hailing from Mildenhall, Suffolk, the Austen family had settled at Hoxton in Shoreditch, Middlesex, before the end of the 16th century. Austen's early Stuart ancestors conducted business in the City, and his great-grandfather became a deputy of Billingsgate ward. However, following considerable growth in their landholdings, the Austens moved to the more rural setting of South Mimms, and their county standing was recognized in June 1693 when Austen's father was appointed a deputy-lieutenant for Middlesex. Austen snr. does not appear to have played any significant political role, but a 'Thomas Austin' was a member of the Middlesex jury which acquitted the Seven Bishops in the famous trial of June 1688, a Whiggish stance in accordance with the subsequent career of the Middlesex Member.²

Austen's date of birth remains elusive, but it is clear that he was under 30 at the time of the Middlesex election of December 1701, when he stood alongside Nicholas Wolstenholme in the Whig interest. Both were ridiculed by their opponents for their youth, and

Austen's campaign was also hampered by illness. However, he managed to secure second place in the poll, and his success was regarded as a Whig gain by Lord Spencer (Charles*). His activity in the House is unfortunately obscured by the presence of Robert Austen II, the Member for Winchelsea, who also shared his Whiggish principles. He may well have achieved some prominence in his first Parliament, for an Austen served as teller in three divisions. Following the death of King William, he again stood alongside Nicholas Wolstenholme for the county, but both were narrowly defeated.[3]

Austen did not contest the general elections of 1705 and 1708, when the Whigs reasserted their supremacy, but the death in February 1709 of sitting Member Sir John Wolstenholme, 3rd Bt., gave Austen the opportunity to regain a place at Westminster. The current weakness of the Middlesex Tories was subsequently demonstrated by his unopposed victory, which had been predicted well in advance. He quickly revealed his party loyalties, being listed as one of the supporters of the naturalization of the poor Palatines in early 1709, and a year later he voted for the impeachment of Dr Sacheverell. The presence in the House of Joseph Austin, MP for Perth Burghs, hinders analysis of Austen's activity, although neither appears to have made a substantial contribution to Commons business. Given the similarity of their political outlook, either Member may have been the 'Mr Austin' who acted as teller alongside the Whig Lord William Powlett on 18 Dec. 1709 in a division on the Cirencester election. However, the Middlesex MP can be plausibly identified as a member of the drafting committee chosen on 16 Feb. 1710 to regulate select vestries within the bills of mortality, a matter which reflected Whig concern to curb High Church influence in the capital. Consistent with this position, soon afterwards he signed a Whig address from the Middlesex justices and grand jury, which condemned recent disorders committed in the name of non-resistance and passive obedience.[4]

The Middlesex election of 1710 proved disastrous for the Whigs, and Austen finished bottom of the poll. He did not seek to regain his seat in 1713, but was restored to prominence after the Hanoverian succession, when he was raised to the dignity of baronet. Perhaps emboldened by this honour, he contested Middlesex in 1715, but could only manage third place. He tried again in 1722, and was successful, but decided not to seek re-election in 1727. Significantly, at that time he was in the process of selling off his real estate, and financial concerns may possibly have influenced his decision to retire from politics. As early as 1710 he had disposed of the manor of Tyburn for £17,000, and after the sale of Highbury in 1725 he appeared increasingly eager to realize his landed wealth. In 1729–30 he was ready to part with considerable property in Hoxton, and went on to find purchasers for Derehams in 1733, and for the manor of Ashford in 1741. Remaining unmarried, he contented himself with a residence at Highgate, and, aside from electioneering, his only conspicuous expense was an impressive art collection, probably inspired by his father's example. Following Austen's death on 22 Mar. 1742, his body was interred at South Mimms, and his fortune passed to Mary Wright, a spinster whom he described in November 1740 as 'living with me'. There is no evidence to suggest that she bore him any children, and, after her death in 1753, Austen's art treasures were put up for auction.[5]

[1] *London Mar. Lic.* ed. Foster, 53. [2] *Vis. London* (Harl. Soc. xv), 33; *List of Principal Inhabitants of London, 1640*, p. 2; *Survey of London*, viii. 60; *CSP Dom.* 1693, p. 181; Luttrell, *Brief Relation*, i. 446. [3] Bodl. Ballard 11, f. 168; *Post Boy*, 16–18 Dec. 1701. [4] Add. 70420, newsletter 15 Feb. 1709; Add. ch. 76111. [5] *VCH Mdx.* v. 284; viii. 56; *Survey of London*, viii. 74, 85; G. Clinch, *Marylebone and St Pancras*, 4; *HMC Portland*, v. 15; Lysons, *Hist. Acct. of Mdx. Parishes*, 2; *HMC 15th Rep. VII*, 179–82; PCC 73 Trenley; *Catalogue of Collection of Sir John Austen* [1755].

P.L.G.

AUSTEN, Robert I (1642–96), of Heronden, Tenterden, Kent.

WINCHELSEA   4 Oct. 1666–1679 (Jan.)
                 1689–22 Aug. 1696

bap. 3 Aug. 1642, 2nd s. of Sir Robert Austen, 1st Bt., by his 2nd w.; bro. of Sir John Austen, 2nd Bt.* *educ.* G. Inn 1657. *m.* lic. 29 Sept. 1669, Judith (*d.* 1716), da. and coh. of Ralph Freke of Hannington, Wilts., 4s. 2da. *suc.* uncle John Austen c.1655.[1]

Dep. mayor, Winchelsea, and speaker of the Guestling, Cinque Ports 1668.[2]
Ld. of Admiralty 1691–*d.*[3]
Commr. public accts. 1691–2.
Commr. Greenwich Hosp. 1695, taking subscriptions to land bank 1696.[4]

In his later parliamentary career Austen, who was invariably known by his militia rank of colonel, typified the dutiful courtier-MP. His non-committal stance over Exclusion had cost him his seat for Winchelsea in 1681 and there were occasions subsequently when his 'negligence' or caution in executing government orders caused ministerial irritation. But in May 1689, shortly after regaining his seat, he sought recognition from the new regime for having lately 'opposed the designs of popery and arbitrary power', and for doing 'what he could to promote the design of his present Majesty'. He petitioned the Treasury for the obsolete office of surveyor of the outports, and though the customs commissioners were instructed to consider the feasibility of reviving the office, nothing was done for him on this occasion. He was returned for Winchelsea a fifth time in 1690, as before, on the basis of personal interest, and his Whig credentials were noted in Lord Carmarthen's (Sir Thomas Osborne†) list of the new Parliament. Disappointed of office, he was at first an open critic of the ministry, particularly on supply matters. On 27 Mar. he expressed reservations about settling the revenue on the King and Queen for life, while the next day he couched these misgivings in the language of principled objections. One of King William's promises, he told the House, had been

> to secure us, that no successor be able to bring us again into our misfortunes. The great mischief being the revenue for lives, you will never do good in an ill prince's time – I am sure you will never tell him that he is an ill one. A Parliament will secure you from other ill persons, as well as ill kings; I mean the ministers. Granting it for life will prevent any ill ministers from being called in question, and you can never reach them. I hope the King will be as rich at the end of his time four years, as if he had the revenue for life.

He rejected, on the 31st, imputations that the Commons were obstructing progress on supply: the fault, he said lay with the King's servants, who 'yet do not tell us what is required'. But when management of the previous year's money was highlighted on 1 Apr. he defended the Court unequivocally, arguing in a somewhat blinkered fashion that it was more pertinent to ensure future prospects of better management than to inquire into last year's 'actions'. It was no doubt for his candid opinions on supply and expenditure that he was included on the committee of 14 Apr. to prepare a bill to establish a commission of public accounts. His Whig principles were clearly advertised on the 17th when he cautioned against rejecting proposals by leading City Whigs for remodelling London's municipal institutions, and he did not take it kindly when some Members scoffed at his suggestion that it was inadvisable to 'anger' City gentlemen in view of the government's pressing need for ready cash. On the 22nd, at the second reading of the bill to reverse the quo warranto against the City, he declared that no one who had failed to acknowledge William's government should be 'restored' under the bill's provisions. He did not wholly embrace the motion of the Court manager Sir Henry Goodricke, 2nd Bt.*, on the 24th for a Commons address of thanks for the King's solicitude towards the Church in his remodelling of the London lieutenancy. While allowing that the Anglican prelates were 'all very good men', he cast an oblique aspersion, observing that a generally-worded address would also include senior clerics who had 'wept for joy' at King James's return to Whitehall in December 1688; 'but as to thanking the King for any general kindness done to the Church of England, I am for it'. His Whiggish instincts led him to oppose an attempt on 26 Apr. to deprive non-jurors of their rights under habeas corpus. On 2 May, when complaint was raised against Anthony Rowe* for distributing an anti-government pamphlet, Austen was blocked by Sir Edward Seymour, 4th Bt., in his own attempt to order a censure upon another Tory Member, Hon. John Beaumont*. During the prolonged committee discussions on the regency bill on 5 May he suggested deferral of the matter until the King had intimated how much regnal power he was prepared to relinquish while in Ireland, and that a 'modest question' along these lines might be put to the King. The following day, as deliberations continued, he appeared less equivocal, declaring himself unconvinced of any necessity for the King's absence, though he thought that to 'advise' the King would be 'unmannerly' and would reduce him to the status of a 'doge of Venice'. On 12 May he was openly critical of Tory MPs who he felt made too much of the Lords' request to examine Sir Robert Clayton* and Sir George Treby* concerning the changes in the London lieutenancy: 'to suppose they [the Lords] shall shock you is more than you ought to do'. During committee proceedings on the 13th concerned with maintaining 'the peace of the nation' he protested at Sir Edmund Jennings'* insensitivity in proposing an adjournment motion so that MPs could 'go to dinner', and proceeded to support the arrangements for 'a management by council' which, he warned, if not endorsed by the House, would 'look ill abroad'. On 20 May he was declared in first place with 183 votes in the ballot for commissioners of public accounts, a reflection of the esteem in which Austen was held among MPs, to whom he evidently appealed widely as a man moderately critical of Court measures. Austen's aloofness towards the Court at this juncture was additionally apparent in his refusal to co-operate in the royal initiative early in June to establish a commission of accounts, following the failure of the Commons' bill, a commission which was to consist of the Members recently balloted. Indeed Austen's resistance on the issue seems to have been particularly prominent. Speaker Trevor* (Sir John) reported to the King that 'Col[onel] Austen, Sir Robert Rich, 2nd Bt.*, and the rest of that party [i.e.

the other Whig nominees] will not act', having been prey to 'all imaginable misconceptions on your good intentions of that commission'.[5]

During the 1690–1 session Austen adopted a more pro-Court attitude. This was noticeable, for example, in supply on 9 Nov. when he answered Paul Foley's outburst against heavy wartime expenditure with quiet moderation: 'I believe all are unanimous that a fleet is necessary. 'Tis a great charge, and necessary it should be so.' No doubt to the delight of Court managers, he deflected Sir Christopher Musgrave's attempt to fluster the government with a question about the escape of French ships blockaded at Dunkirk, unnoticed by the English fleet. Austen pointed out that the French fleet's departure had been no great secret, and had been unobserved because of its occurrence 'on the Dutch side and not ours'. In the renewed efforts to establish a commission of public accounts Austen was once again a popular choice, taking fourth place with 129 votes in the ballot for commissioners. This time the public accounts bill passed and he was enjoined to serve. At the same time, however, he was also made a lord of the Admiralty with a salary of £1,000, thus realizing his earlier ambition to be brought into administration. Given his respectability among the Whigs, the appointment was clearly a ploy to anchor Whig support for the government. But its timing would also suggest ministers' anxiety to prevent the accounts commission from being peopled entirely by critics of the Court. Austen's recruitment must have seriously compromised him in the eyes of his fellow commissioners. Analysing the House in April 1691, Robert Harley* labelled him as a Court supporter. Although he was an assiduous attender at the commission's meetings throughout the spring and summer months (despite trouble from a 'lame hand'), the nature of his contribution to its proceedings cannot be determined, and from September until the last meeting towards the end of January 1692 his appearances became less frequent.[6]

When supply business opened in the next session on 9 Nov., Austen defended the government's need for a navy of at least 30,000 men, arguing that 40,000 would be desirable. At the behest of his colleagues on the accounts commission, Sir Thomas Clarges, Paul Foley I and Robert Harley, a select committee was appointed to scrutinize the navy estimates on which he and his fellow Admiralty commissioners were necessarily included. On the 11th, in the wake of the unfolding attacks upon naval 'mismanagements', Austen moved that the Admiralty commissioners be allowed copies of Admiral Russell's (Edward*) personal account of the fleet's summer actions (presented to the Commons the previous day) to assist them in meeting the request for a statement of the orders issued to Russell. When Harley reported from the navy estimates committee on the 14th, Austen supported all the resolutions, including provision for four new fourth-rate ships at a cost of £28,864, though this final item was later dropped. On the 30th he saw no reason why the estimates for general officers should be referred to a 'particular' or select committee, as proposed by Clarges, rather than to the committee of the whole. He acquainted the House on 6 Dec. that the Lords had requested from the accounts commissioners a copy of their recent report to the Commons, together with their fault-finding 'observations'. It was agreed, however, that the Lords had no right to the latter, these having been specifically ordered by the Lower House. Though in 1689 he had held £1,400 of East India stock, he spoke against the Company on 18 Dec. in the committee of the whole on the East India trade, and on the 23rd moved that the company's proposal of a joint stock of £1,300,000 to facilitate its continued operation was 'unsatisfactory'. That Austen's credit among MPs had waned since his appointment to the Admiralty was apparent on 19 Jan. 1692, when an amendment was unanimously approved to the bill for the renewal of the accounts commission, omitting both himself and his Admiralty colleague Sir Robert Rich, 2nd Bt. In supply on the 12th he regarded with some scepticism Foley's scheme to secure a £1,000,000 loan from the bankers, the condition for which would be the establishment of a fund to repay the debt still outstanding on account of Charles II's stop of the Exchequer. He ventured that if the bankers had any concrete proposals in mind these should first be judged by the Treasury. Much more to his taste in ways and means was Henry Goldwell's* proposal on 18 Jan. for excises on specific commodities, a fiscal principle to which he gave his unqualified support:

> If you will reach all men and raise money by an equal tax, I know no better way . . . I find we shall try other ways till they are so oppressive that we must come to an excise at last as the equallest – that which will reach all men and no men farther than he pleases himself.

Austen was one of several Whigs who on 22 Jan. took issue with a motion not to place on record the Commons' verdict of guilty upon the Tory Sir Basil Firebrace* for having bribed his Chippenham electors in the recent by-election. Four days later, at the second reading of the bill for a new East India Company, an issue on which there were no clear political alignments, he backed Sir Edward Seymour's view that the measure could not be pursued until the existing company's stock commitments had been squared. Following the Lords' blockage of the Commons' bill to renew the accounts commission, Austen spoke against the 'tacking' of a clause for this purpose to the poll bill, from which his and Rich's names were again excluded. Since Luttrell did not record the substance of Austen's speech, it is not clear whether he was opposing the commission itself, or less fundamentally, the 'irregularity' of 'tacking'. Undaunted by the recent efforts to exclude them, Austen and Rich tried on 8 Mar. to take their places at the first meeting of the reconstituted accounts commission, justifying their continued presence on the basis of some ambiguity in the wording of the Poll Act. After discussion, however, they were denied admittance by the seven other commissioners, who minuted that they 'could not safely with respect to the trust reposed in them ... act with [them]'.[7]

In the early weeks of the 1692–3 session, Austen's official responsibilities compelled him to defend the Admiralty against the accusations of all-round incompetence and mismanagement from Country opponents. He made a forceful intervention for the government on 21 Nov. on the subject of mercantile losses, beginning with a direct rejoinder to the suggestion that naval affairs be entrusted to a new set of Admiralty commissioners: 'I will not confess myself so ignorant as some think me.' He then told the House that the complaints examined in a recent select committee on merchant losses had not been properly substantiated, and that blame for the losses suffered could be apportioned to the insurers, whose willingness to underwrite ships regardless of the availability of convoys encouraged merchants to undertake hazardous voyages. On 26 Nov. he responded to a complaint of breach of privilege instigated by George Churchill*, who had been called to the Admiralty in connexion with recent remarks in the House concerning the 'cowardice' of a naval captain serving in the West Indies. Austen gave immediate assurances that the purpose of summoning Churchill was to ascertain if the captain concerned was a fit object for the King's mercy. In supply on 2 Dec. he supported the government's move to consider the 'clause of credit' to meet the deficiency arising from the Poll Act, before proceeding upon the army and navy estimates, while the following day he advocated the government's line to consider the army estimates in their entirety rather than give priority to the needs of home defence, as desired by the Country party. In deliberations on the land tax on the 13th he favoured the proposal for a pound rate against a monthly assessment. On 19 Jan. 1693, at the report stage of the woollen bill, he opposed Robert Waller's* clause to preserve the monopoly of the Hamburg Company, opposition which may well have been tinged with personal animosity towards Waller, who in November had been among those who had roundly denounced the Admiralty commissioners. Some time in January, Austen and three other prominent, mainly pro-government, Whig MPs, John Dutton Colt, Sir Ralph Dutton, 1st Bt., and Sir Thomas Pope Blount, 1st Bt., were involved in the interrogation of a Jacobite suspect at Newgate. Samuel Grascome, who reported the episode in a pamphlet, stated that there had been some attempt by two of the Members (though he avoided saying which) to suborn the man into inventing an assassination plot. On the penultimate day of the session, 13 Mar., Austen 'was entirely for disagreeing' with a Lords' amendment to the privateers' bill concerning the award of prize money, since it created a precedent for the Upper House to 'order the manner of disposing money'.[8]

Thereafter, Austen made no further recorded speeches in the House. There were reports at the end of January 1694 that he and most of his colleagues were to be dropped from the Admiralty Board, but he was retained when it was eventually reconstructed in the spring. His steadfastness towards the Court was lampooned in a poetical satire upon the 'Rose Club' activists published in 1694. Here, he and Rich were described as 'those two precious beagles of state ... mightily overpaid for the prate'. However, his consistent support for the several schemes put forward for a national land bank during 1694–6 is apparent from the inclusion of his name in several published lists of subscribers. In one of these he also appears as one of the 'present directors'. Re-elected in 1695, he was forecast in January 1696 as likely to support the Court on the proposed council of trade. He was also an early signatory to the Association. By February 1696, Austen's infirmities were such as to prevent him from attending Admiralty business and probably also the House. He had indicated his willingness to resign in lieu of a pension, but in June, despite his declining condition, the lords justices were unwilling to replace him. A replacement had still not been found at the time of his death on 22 Aug. He was buried the following day in the family vault at Bexley. His disordered financial arrangements caused his widow and heir some vexation. Although he had provided his wife with a comfortable jointure of £450, he made no provision for his two grown-up daughters and youngest son, while his eldest son inherited an estate saddled with debts amounting to £3,000.[9]

[1] IGI, London; Berry, *Kent Fam. Peds.* 350; *The Gen.* n.s. xxxiii. 200; *Westminster Abbey Reg.* (Harl. Soc. x), 286; *Arch. Cant.* xvii. 97; *Elizabeth Freke Diary* ed. Carbery, 44; PCC 262 Berkeley; *Kentish*

MI (Tenterden) ed. Duncan, 57. ²Cal. Black and White Bks. (Kent Recs. xix), 520, 521. ³CSP Dom. 1690–1, p. 225. ⁴Add. 10120, f. 232; CJ, xii. 508. ⁵Cal. Treas. Pprs. 1557–1696, p. 40; Grey, x. 16–17, 21, 23, 32, 57, 61, 72, 108–9, 124, 129, 135; Bodl. Rawl. A. 79, f. 83; CSP Dom. 1690–1, p. 29. ⁶Grey, x. 168, 170; Luttrell, Brief Relation, ii. 15; CSP Dom. 1690–1, p. 225; Cal. Treas. Bks. ix. 1125; EHR, xci. 40; Some Remarks on Bill for Taking, Examining and Stating the Public Accounts of the Kingdom (1701); Harl. 1488–9, passim; HMC Portland, iii. 467. ⁷Luttrell Diary, 10, 13, 19–20, 52, 63, 87, 92, 125, 138, 150, 157, 187; Bodl. Carte 130, f. 328; Trinity, Dublin, Clarke mss 749/13/1329, Robert Yard* to George Clarke*, 12 Nov. 1691; Add. 22185, f. 12; PRO NI, De Ros mss D636/13/93, 111, John Pulteney* to Ld. Coningsby (Thomas*), 9 Jan., 16 Feb. 1691–2; Add. 70119, Robert to Sir Edward Harley*, 9 Jan. 1691–2; Centre Kentish Stud. Stanhope mss U1590/059/11, Robert Yard to Alexander Stanhope, [c.12 Mar. 1692]; Harl. 1489, f. 76. ⁸Luttrell Diary, 246–7, 261, 285, 289, 311, 375, 477; Grey, x. 272, 281; Samuel Grascome, New Court Contrivancies (1693). ⁹Luttrell Diary, iii. 262; CSP Dom. 1694–5, p. 114; 1696, pp. 232, 299; Poems on Affairs of State ed. Ellis, v. 435; NLS, Advocates' mss 31.1.7, ff. 95, 98–99; CJ, xii. 508; Stanhope mss U1590/059/5, Yard to Stanhope, 11 Feb. 1695–6; HMC Buccleuch, ii. 339, 367; Elizabeth Freke Diary, 44.

A. A. H.

AUSTEN, Robert II (c.1672–1728), of Heronden, Tenterden, Kent.

HASTINGS 1695–1698
WINCHELSEA 1701 (Dec.)–1702

b. c.1672, 1st s. of Robert Austen I*. m. lic. 30 Apr. 1703, aged 31, Jane, da. of William Strode† of Barrington, Som., 3s. (1 d.v.p.) 1da. suc. fa. 1696.¹

2nd lt. 1 marine regt. 1691, 1st lt. 1695; 2nd lt. of marines Col. Thomas Brudenell's regt. 1698; 2nd lt. of ft. Col. Thomas Stringer's* regt. (Gren. Gds.) 1702.

Commr. taking subscriptions to land bank, 1696.²

As a young man Austen served as a lieutenant in the Tenterden company of the Cinque Ports militia under the command of his father, before graduating in 1691 to a junior commission in Sir Richard Onslow's (3rd Bt.*) marine regiment. It was doubtless owing to his father's local associations and position as an Admiralty lord that the corporation of Hastings accepted him in 1695 as their representative. An additional factor would have been his family's business relations with the Ashburnhams, whose influence was well established in the Hastings area. There was also a family connexion in that the wife of Lord Ashburnham (John II*) was a relative of Austen. Austen quickly emerged, after his father's example, as a Court supporter: he was forecast in January 1696 as likely to support the Court in the divisions over the proposed council of trade, was an early signatory to the Association, voted in March for fixing the price of guineas at 22s., and voted for the attainder of Sir John Fenwick† on 25 Nov. There is some suggestion, however, that after his father's death in August 1696 he may not have been quite so consistent in his pro-Court sympathies: on 15 Feb. 1697 he was teller (with John Pulteney*, his fellow MP for Hastings) for the minority in favour of engrossing the bill to renew the commission of public accounts; while in a comparative analysis of the old and new Houses of Commons compiled shortly after the 1698 election, he was marked as a Court supporter.³

At the 1698 election Austen was defeated at Hastings, and failed to dislodge his supplanter in subsequent proceedings against the return. In January 1701, finding his prospects at Hastings unimproved, he focused attention on Winchelsea, his father's old constituency, only to be defeated as the result of the mayor's corrupt machinations in favour of other candidates. In consequence of Austen's petition the election was declared void, but for the time being he was denied the opportunity of submitting himself to a second election, since the House ordered that no new writ be issued for Winchelsea during the current session. His opportunity came in November, however, with the dissolution of Parliament, and this time he was returned. Analysing the new House of Commons, Robert Harley* noted him as a Whig. From this point, however, it is impossible to distinguish him in the Journals from the Middlesex MP of the same surname.

At the 1702 election Austen was generally expected to retain his seat, but was narrowly outvoted. His petition against the return was disregarded by the now Tory-dominated House. It was probably a sign of his family's waning influence in the port that he made no further attempts to recover the Winchelsea seat. These problems may well have been financially related, or at least partly so, for Austen's father died leaving no provision for his younger offspring and an estate heavily encumbered with debts, circumstances which required long-term frugal management. Austen's own death occurred in the summer of 1728, some time between 20 July, when his will was drawn up, and 5 Sept., when it was proved. He requested burial at Tenterden church 'with as little charge and expense as my quality and the way I have lived in will decently admit and allow of'. To his surviving younger son and daughter he left £1,500 charged on the mortgage of the Sussex manor of Cottingham, while the Heronden estate passed to his eldest son. Both sons, William and Robert, were eventually to succeed their cousins as the 6th and 7th baronets.⁴

¹Berry, Kent Fam. Peds. 350; London Mar. Lic. ed. Foster, 51; Frag. Gen. viii. 148; Add. 24120, f. 34; PCC 256 Brook. ²CJ, xii. 508. ³Southern Hist. ix., 67. ⁴Add. 29588, ff. 102, 104; Elizabeth Freke Diary ed. Carbery, 44; PCC 256 Brook.

A. A. H.

AUSTEN, Sir Robert, 3rd Bt. (1664–1706), of Hall Place, Bexley, Kent.

RYE   23 Jan. 1699–1701 (Nov.)

bap. 19 Mar. 1664, 1st surv. s. of Sir John Austen, 2nd Bt.* *educ.* St. Albans sch.; Peterhouse, Camb. 1680. *m.* c.1687, Elizabeth (*d.* 1725), da. and coh. of George Stawell of Cothelstone, Som., 5s. (2 *d.v.p.*) 6da. (1 *d.v.p.*). *suc.* fa. as 3rd Bt. c. Jan. 1699.[1]

The ease with which Austen was returned at Rye in 1699, less than a month after the death of his father, underlines the strength of the personal connexion which the family had established with the corporation. The new MP delayed his arrival at Westminster by a few weeks, being allowed a fortnight's leave on 2 Feb. There is no reason to doubt that he followed in the Whiggish tradition of his family, but his standpoint in relation to the Court is a matter of speculation. The only extant listing of MPs on which his name appears was the analysis of the House drawn up some time between January and May 1700 in which Members were marked according to 'interests' and 'connexions'. The fact that he was not marked as belonging to any particular group, but simply as 'Q[uery]', might suggest that he maintained a degree of independence, or was even an opponent of the Court.

Austen's concern to promote Rye's economic interests can be seen in the lead he took in 1701 in the initiation of a bill for the renovation of the town's badly silted-up harbour. It was probably Austen who moved for the bill on 3 May, as he was first-named of the three Members ordered to prepare it. However, the bill, which he introduced on 15 May, did not receive a first reading until the 24th and proceeded no further, having evidently become locked in difficulty. Austen did not stand for re-election at Rye later in the year, though it is not clear why. That another Whig was chosen in his place would imply that he had fallen foul of the corporation, possibly over the failure of the harbour bill. A serious breach is also suggested by the fact that the family made no attempt thereafter to recover their footing in the constituency. Austen none the less retained hopes of re-entering Parliament, and in 1705 came very close to being elected a knight of the shire for Kent. He died some time in late June or early July the following year, his burial taking place at Bexley on 5 July 1706. To his young heir (Sir Robert Austen, 4th Bt.†) he left an estate valued at £559 p.a. but encumbered with debts of £12,498 (which may have included legacies totalling £6,500 to his younger sons and daughters), so that in 1712 his widow was compelled to obtain an Act for the sale of one of the manors.[2]

[1] Berry, *Kent. Fam. Peds.* 350; *Arch. Cant.* xviii. 371–2; *The Gen.* n.s. i. 112, 227; PCC 160 Eedes. [2] *Post Man,* 26–29 May 1705; *Arch. Cant.* 371; *HMC Lords,* n.s. ix. 231.

A. A. H.

AUSTIN, Joseph (*d.*1735), of Kilspindie, Perth.

PERTH BURGHS   1708–1710

prob. yr. s. of Thomas Austin, candlemaker, of Perth. *m.* by c.1700. Ann(a) Waters, 4s. (?1 *d.v.p.*) 7da.[1]
Bailie, Perth 1704–6; burgess, Edinburgh 1708.[2]

Austin was almost certainly a younger son of Thomas Austin, an English soldier in the Cromwellian army, who settled at Perth and became 'the father of trade and navigation in the burgh', according to an early 19th-century panegyric. By 1676 this Thomas, described as a candlemaker, had made a name for himself as a violent opponent of the ruling loyalist clique on the town council, and after an election riot was fined and temporarily barred from taking any burgh appointment. One of his sons, William (*d.* 1724), held municipal office in Perth continuously from 1704 to 1712, and was the pro-Hanoverian provost in 1715.[3]

Austin himself first comes to notice in September 1700 when he stood unsuccessfully for election to Perth council as a representative for the merchants, gaining that office at the second attempt in October 1702. He was Perth's delegate to the first parliamentary election for the district in 1708, and as *praeses* engineered his own return, despite competition from Mungo Graham* and George Yeaman*. Not much can be said of his performance in the Commons, for he scarcely troubled the compilers of parliamentary records, and, so far as is known, did not contribute to any debate. A Presbyterian Whig, he was wrongly listed as having voted against the impeachment of Dr Sacheverell. In the run-up to the 1710 election he was criticized locally for his poor parliamentary performance. He did not stand in 1710, giving his interest to the Squadrone member John Haldane*. He died on 8 Nov. 1735, and was succeeded by his son, also called Joseph.[4]

[1] IGI, Perth. [2] *Memorabilia of Perth* (1806), 197–8; *Scot. Rec. Soc.* lxii. 9. [3] *Memorabilia of Perth,* 197–201; *SRO Indexes,* lxv. 8; lxx. 6; *Reg. PC Scotland,* 1673–6, pp. 552–70; 1678–80, p. 362; *Scot. Hist. Soc.* ser. 3, xxv. 70–71. [4] Perth burgh recs. B59/24/2/2/12.1, elections to council, 20 Sept. 1700, 5 Oct. 1702, memorial, n.d. [1710]; *Lockhart Mems.* ed. Szechi, 287; Calamy, *Life,* ii. 204–6, 208; *Services of Heirs* ser. 1, i. 1730–9, p. 2.

D. W. H.

AYLMER, Matthew (c.1650–1720), of Covent Garden, Westminster and Westcliffe, nr. Dover, Kent.

DOVER   15 Dec. 1697–1713, 1715–18 Aug. 1720

b. c.1650, 2nd s. of Sir Christopher Aylmer, 1st Bt., of Balrath, co. Meath by Margaret, da. of Matthew Plunkett, 5th Baron Louth [I]. *m.* bef. 1682, Sarah (*d.* 1710), da. of Edward Ellis of London, 2s. (1 *d.v.p.*), 4da. (2 *d.v.p.*). *cr.* Baron Aylmer of Balrath [I] 1 May 1718.[1]

Ensign of ft. Duke of Buckingham's regt. 1672–?3, Tangier regt. 1677, lt. 1678; capt. of horse, Queen Dowager's regt. 1686–?; lt.-col. of horse by 1690, marines 1697; ent. RN 1677, lt. 1678, capt. 1679, r.-adm. Feb. 1693, v.-adm. July 1693, adm. of fleet, 1709–1711, 1714–18, half-pay 1708–9, 1711–14; r.-adm. of Eng. 1718–d.; extra commr. Navy Board 1694–1702; ld. of Admiralty 1717–1718.[2]

Commr. Greenwich Hosp. 1695–?1703, gov. 1714–*d.*; keeper, Greenwich park and palace 1714–*d.*; gov. Deal Castle 1700–?4.[3]

Freeman, Portsmouth 1695, Dover 1697.[4]

Commr. registering seamen 1696–?1700.[5]

Long-established in Ireland, the Aylmers were Old English palesmen with estates in the counties of Meath and Louth. As Catholics they suffered during the Civil Wars, when Aylmer's grandfather was imprisoned, but were restored at least to some of their lands in 1661. Aylmer's father, who received a baronetcy at this time, showed a loyalty to King Charles II which extended to a willingness to compromise with the Protestant establishment: he subscribed to the 'protestation and remonstrance' of Catholic gentry in 1661 repudiating papal authority, and both his younger sons, Matthew and George, conformed to the Established Church. As a result, Christopher came into conflict both with his own father, and then with his eldest son, Gerald, who disputed title to the family inheritance before eventually succeeding as 2nd Bt. Gerald then jeopardized the family estates by joining James II in 1689. In October 1690 Matthew Aylmer petitioned for a grant of the property his brother had forfeited, but the outcome is not known.[6]

As the second son, Matthew embarked on a military career, as did his younger brother, George (*d.* 1689). He seems to have become a client of the 2nd Duke of Buckingham, in whose regiment he was commissioned. After the disbandment of the regiment, family history notes that Aylmer raised troops in Munster for the Dutch, before obtaining a commission in a Tangier regiment in 1677, and then switching to a naval career. While on active service at Tangier, he was raised to captain by Admiral Arthur Herbert†, and continued to serve until the evacuation of the garrison in 1683–4. In James II's reign Aylmer saw service at sea against Monmouth's rebels, before receiving promotion in the army. Given his Catholic antecedents, and his elder brother's commitment to Rome, Aylmer's position was fraught with possibilities and dangers; in July 1687 he received a dispensation from taking the oaths of allegiance and supremacy while acting as an army captain. However, in 1688 he showed unequivocal support for the Prince of Orange, and was a leading participant in the 'navy plot' against James II.[7]

Aylmer's main patron at this time appears to have been Edward Russell*. In February 1690, a report that John Hill had been appointed to the Navy Board brought a missive from Russell to Secretary Nottingham (Daniel Finch†), extolling Aylmer's qualifications for such a post and recalling previous service to the Williamite cause. He was considered for a flag as early as August 1690, but it was as a captain that he was given command of the Mediterranean fleet in 1690–1, although he was allowed to retain his lieutenant-colonelcy in the army. In August 1691 Aylmer sought command of the West Indies squadron, but had to wait until 1693 for a flag. He may have tried to take advantage of the Smyrna fleet debacle in 1693, because Sir Ralph Delaval* wrote acidly, 'there was not a flag at the council of war so very fond of coming into port as Mr Aylmer who I suppose doth all the good is in his nature but his hand is to every resolution of our councils of war which I hope to see him deny'. The following year saw his appointment to the Navy Board.[8]

Aylmer's first foray into electoral politics ended in a double return at the Portsmouth by-election of 1695 (after Russell himself had created the vacancy by opting to sit for Cambridgeshire). The Commons on 24 Jan. 1696 voted this a void election, and even with Russell's backing Aylmer's interest proved insufficient to overcome that of John Gibson, the town's lieutenant-governor, who was returned unopposed at the second by-election. Early in 1696, the deposition of the Assassination Plotter Peter Cook suggested that the Jacobites thought they could 'depend' upon Aylmer, but nothing incriminating was revealed. In May 1697 he subscribed £1,000 to the contract for lending money to circulate Exchequer bills. The death of James Chadwick* left a vacancy for Dover, a borough in which the navy could exercise considerable influence. Aylmer approached the corporation in June 1697 and, despite snide references by Philip Papillon* to Aylmer's Irishness and lack of any visible estate in the town or county, he was returned on 15 Dec., taking his seat on the 20th.[9]

In February 1698 Aylmer was given command of the squadron destined for the Mediterranean. At this point he was 'in town', and presumably attending Parliament. Delays in supplying the fleet, owing to a shortage of funds, meant that he did not sail until September, which may have allowed him to consolidate his position in Dover with timely applications to the government for money to repair Dover harbour. Before leaving England he was re-elected, and was listed as a placeman in September 1698 and as a placeman on a comparative analysis of the old and new Parliaments. In an addendum to this list he was marked as absent, and the House officially excused his attendance on 7 Mar. 1699 because of his duties at sea and as envoy to various North African states.[10]

During Aylmer's absence (he returned at the end of October 1699) there was a lengthy parliamentary inquiry into mismanagements at the Admiralty, one of the allegations being the delay in fitting out Aylmer's squadron. Other, more specific, charges against him included his detention of the *Centurion* at Cadiz in order to force its commander, Price, to concede a large share of his profits, and Aylmer's role as victualler of his own fleet while in the Mediterranean. Opinion divided on party lines as to his culpability. Sir Richard Cocks, 2nd Bt.*, thought Price's charges 'mere malice, nothing in it at all', while James Vernon I* reported that the House had considered, in regard to victualling, that Aylmer was 'too honest and too considerate' to have submitted false accounts and profit thereby. However, Robert Harley's* papers contain the draft of a resolution condemning Aylmer for corruption and breach of trust in detaining Price at Cadiz. This may well relate to the debate in the committee of the whole on 10 Mar. 1699, when Aylmer was blamed, but the matter was 'let fall before they came to any question'.[11]

While Aylmer was at sea during the summer of 1699 Orford resigned his place at the Admiralty. In discussions that followed there was talk of promoting George Churchill* to a flag senior to Aylmer, no doubt as part of the Earl of Marlborough's (John Churchill†) rapprochement with the Court. Vernon felt that Aylmer might resign over this matter, possibly 'to give a handle for finding fault with the partialities of this commission of Admiralty, and to show the case is not much mended in that respect', and that the appointment of Churchill would be difficult to defend on the grounds of experience and seniority. In the event, Churchill went to the Admiralty in place of Sir Robert Rich, 2nd Bt.*, while Aylmer continued at the Navy Board. An analysis of the House into 'interests' in early 1700 listed Aylmer as a member of the Bedford/Orford connexion. This affiliation did not help him to obtain one of the limited number of peacetime commands, although his name was linked with a squadron going to the Straits. In March 1701 he was listed among those flag officers 'unemployed at sea'. Aylmer's attention to constituency matters, such as his appointment on 12 Feb. 1700 to draft a bill to repair Dover harbour, ensured that he was returned at the election of January 1701; he even appears to have retained the naval interest at Dover although another Court supporter, Secretary of State Sir Charles Hedges*, was also returned. In the ensuing parliamentary session, Aylmer was listed among those thought likely to support the Court in February over the 'Great Mortgage'.[12]

When Dover corporation rebuffed Hedges in the run-up to the election of December 1701, it was mostly because of Aylmer's 'neglect' of their interests. In comparison, he had been more attentive, particularly over the harbour. Aylmer was also solicitous for his own interests: hence a petition he signed with three other navy commissioners on 31 Dec. 1701, for the continuance of an allowance of £80 p.a. for housing, in view of the fact that they could not be accommodated in government property. Aylmer had resided in the parish of St. Paul's, Covent Garden, since at least as early as 1694, moving from St. Martin's-in-the-Fields at some point after 1690, possibly coincidental with his appointment to the Navy Board in 1692. He had also purchased an estate near Dover, presumably by 1701 when he presented to an advowson at nearby East Langdon. On a list of the new Parliament, Harley classed him as a Whig. With fewer naval duties to perform, Aylmer was more active in the 1701–2 session, and was included on the drafting committee of a bill to encourage privateers. On a personal note he also assisted in the management of a private bill for the Fitzgerald and Plunkett families, with both of whom the Irish Aylmers were connected.[13]

Aylmer had been appointed vice-admiral of the red in January 1702, but the death of William III saw his naval career at a standstill, following the Queen's decision to employ George Churchill in that place, and the consequent dispute about seniority which Vernon had predicted three years before. Aylmer was also left out of a revamped Navy Board, for which the governorship of Deal and nomination to the Kentish lieutenancy and the bench were poor recompense. Re-elected for Dover in 1702, in July he petitioned the Queen for a pension, such as had been given by William III to Admirals Delaval and Killigrew (Henry*). Aylmer considered his position to be similar, in that he had been displaced from being vice-admiral of the red by Churchill and then removed from the Navy Board, whereas the official view was that Aylmer had declined to serve and had as a consequence also lost his post as a navy commissioner. Although L'Hermitage had described him in February 1702 as a Whig and a creature of Orford, Aylmer was spotted caballing in September with Lord Burlington (Hon. Charles Boyle I*), Lord Somers (Sir John*), Lord Halifax (Charles Montagu*), (Sir) Thomas Felton* (4th Bt.) and 'Mr Hopkins [?Thomas*]'. Nothing came of these discussions between overlooked politicians, but Aylmer remained a Whig, voting on 13 Feb. 1703 to agree with the Lords' amendments enlarging the time for taking the oaths of abjuration. Forecast as an opponent of the Tack, he did not vote for it on 28 Nov. 1704.[14]

In January 1705 there was a rumour that Aylmer would serve at sea again the following summer, and in a conciliatory move the Treasury ordered a stay of prosecution against Aylmer and Sir Basill Dixwell, 2nd Bt.*, for failure to account for money given to them to repair Dover harbour. Returned again at the 1705 election, Aylmer was described in an analysis of the new House as a 'High Church Courtier', and his name appears on a list of placemen for 1705, presumably because of his governorship at Deal. On 25 Oct. 1705 he voted for the Court candidate as Speaker, and later in the session, on 18 Feb. 1706, supported the Court in the proceedings on the 'place clause' of the regency bill. He was more active in the Commons in this Parliament, his committee appointments again reflecting his interest in naval affairs, and in 1706 he presented a memorial to the Treasury on the desirability of the Navy Board taking over responsibility for Dover harbour.[15]

Re-elected in 1708, Aylmer was classed as a Whig on two lists of that year. He sought to capitalize on the swing towards the Whigs at this time and gain further preferment. Thus on 25 May, only a few weeks after the general election, he wrote to Marlborough to remind the Duke of a memorial delivered the previous winter, in which Aylmer had asked for the governorship of Greenwich Hospital, 'or to be allowed a subsistence'. Since that post had been disposed of, Aylmer recounted the 'hardships under which I suffer, and not being conscious that I have done anything can deserve so particular a mark of severeness above all other officers'. Marlborough seems to have responded favourably to this letter, which was referred to Lord Treasurer Godolphin (Sidney†), although nothing was done immediately. In December 1708 a commission was made out for Aylmer as admiral of the fleet, which was superseded the following day. This was a device to provide Aylmer with a 'subsistence' on half pay at a high rank. In 1709 he supported the naturalization of the Palatines. With the Earl of Pembroke (Hon. Thomas Herbert†) as Lord High Admiral, rumours began to circulate as early as March that the Admiralty would be put into a commission which would include Aylmer. The same rumours recurred in October and November, but when Orford was brought back into the Admiralty Aylmer was not one of the commissioners; instead he was given command of the fleet. This did not please everyone: Sir John Jennings* felt rather as Aylmer had done in 1702 when Churchill had been appointed, and Arthur Maynwaring* noted that 'the officers have no real value for Mr Aylmer, nor indeed for anyone now but for Jennings'. As a consequence of his appointment Aylmer had to fight a by-election, but was returned unopposed. In the 1709–10 session he voted for the impeachment of Dr Sacheverell.[16]

Returned again at the 1710 election, Aylmer soon lost his position as admiral and commander-in-chief of the fleet. Indeed, at the committee of elections on 22 Feb. 1711, both Aylmer and Jennings were 'severely criticized' for interfering at the election for Weymouth by treating the corporation on board ship. However, when the report came before the House on 17 Mar. no resolution critical of Aylmer was passed. The end of the session saw Aylmer appealing to Harley for repayment of the contingency money he had spent while equipping himself for service at sea the previous year and referring again to the hardships he had undergone. In the following session Aylmer voted on 7 Dec. 1711 for the 'No Peace without Spain' motion, but otherwise was not very active. In the 1713 session he was not present in the Commons to vote in the divisions of 18 June over the French commerce bill because he had gone to Deal Castle with Sir John Norris* (his son-in-law) to celebrate the marriage of his younger daughter to Hugh Fortescue*.[17]

Not only was Aylmer defeated at the 1713 general election, it was even felt necessary to scotch a rumour in the following January that he was a Catholic. However, he was soon back in favour after the Hanoverian succession. In October 1714 he was reported to have been made governor of Greenwich Hospital, a post he had long coveted, which 'is a very pretty post, and has a very pleasant house to dwell in'. November saw him reappointed admiral of the fleet, and he regained his seat in the Commons at the 1715 general election. On a comparative analysis of the 1713 and 1715 Parliaments he was listed as a Whig. Aylmer continued as admiral until he exchanged the post for the honorific title of rear-admiral of England and an Irish peerage in 1718. He died at Greenwich on 18 Aug. 1720, although his will, dated in June that year, still gave his address as Covent Garden. In it he had appointed as executor his son Henry†, an equerry to the King. Swift wrote off his compatriot as a violent partisan, but Aylmer seems to have been skilled at exploiting the situations available to him. His early naval career was marked by the smooth facility with which he moved between patrons, yet he managed to retain his seat at Dover even after the original backing of the Navy interest had been lost.[18]

[1] F. J. Aylmer, *Aylmers of Ire.* 190, 194–5, 253; *Misc. Gen. et Her.* ser. 4, iv. 75–77; *Mariner's Mirror*, li. 178–9; *Addison Letters*, 80; IGI, London. [2] *CSP Dom.* 1676–7, p. 512; 1677–8, p. 337; 1690–1, p. 189; Luttrell, *Brief Relation*, iv. 191; vi. 684; *Mariner's Mirror*, lxxiii. 206; *CJ*, xvi. 225. [3] Add. 10120, f. 232; *Daily Courant*, 8 Aug. 1704. [4] R. East, *Portsmouth Recs.* 371; Add. 29625, f. 130. [5] J. Ehrman, *Navy in War of Wm. III*, 600. [6] Aylmer, 146–52, 154. [7] Ibid. 168–9; *CSP Dom.* 1687–9, p. 23; 1690–1, p. 147; *Cal. Treas. Pprs.* 1557–1696, p. 156; *By Force or By Default?* ed. Cruickshanks, 85–87; *Cam. Soc.* n.s. xlvi. 27. [8] *HMC Finch*, ii. 270; iii. 243, 386, 451; *CSP Dom.* 1690–1, p. 189; Centre Kentish Stud. Papillon mss U1015/O57/7, Delaval to Thomas Papillon*, 29 June 1693. [9] *CSP Dom.* 1696, p. 111; 1697, p. 525; Luttrell, iv. 59; Univ. of London mss 65, item 3; Papillon mss U1015/C44, p. 28. [10] Luttrell, iv. 344, 415, 418, 518; *CSP Dom.* 1698, pp. 104, 371; Add. 28123, f. 1; 28943, f. 76; *Vernon–Shrewsbury Letters*, ii. 151–2; *Cal. Treas. Pprs.* 1697–1702, p. 140; *Cal. Treas. Bks.* xiii. 65. [11] Luttrell, iv. 577; Add. 30000 C, f. 226; 40773, f. 152; 70044, f. 203v; H. Horwitz, *Parl. and Pol. Wm. III*, 252–3; *Cam. Misc.* xxix. 351, 390; *Cocks Diary*, 3; *Vernon–Shrewsbury Letters*, ii. 263, 266; *CSP Dom.* 1699–1700, p. 90. [12] Add. 40774, ff. 53–54; Luttrell, iv. 650; *CSP Dom.* 1700–2, p. 283; Bodl. Carte 228, f. 402. [13] Add. 28887, f. 374; *CSP Dom.* 1700–2, p. 283; IGI, London; Hasted, *Kent*, ix. 421; Aylmer, 190; *Jnl. Kildare Arch. Soc.* iii. 174–5. [14] *Navy Recs. Soc.* ix. 145; Luttrell, v. 152; *CSP Dom.* 1702–3, pp. 275–7, 394, 437; info. from Prof. N. Landau; Add. 29588, f. 196. [15] Folger Shakespeare Lib. Newdigate newsletter 6 Jan. 1705; *Cal. Treas. Pprs.* 1702–7, p. 460; *Cal. Treas. Bks.* xix. 377, 515, 519. [16] Add. 61111, ff. 204–5; 70420, newsletter 24 Feb. 1709; *Marlborough–Godolphin Corresp.* 1051; Luttrell, vi. 387, 501; *CJ*, xvi. 226; *HMC Downshire*, i. 871, 881; *Navy Recs. Soc.* liii. 341; *Duchess of Marlborough Corresp.* i. 279. [17] Luttrell, vi. 684; Bodl. Ballard 39, f. 34; Add. 70321, memo. Aylmer to Oxford, [c. Aug. 1711]; 70209, Aylmer to Oxford, 15 Aug. 1711; Papillon mss U1015/C45, p. 100. [18] Papillon mss U1015/C45, pp. 185, 353; *Navy Recs. Soc.* lxx. 383; *HMC Polwarth*, i. 462; PCC 188 Shaller; *Swift Works* ed. Davis, v. 261; G. Holmes, *Pol. in Age of Anne*, 363.

S. N. H.

AYSCOUGH, Sir Edward (1650–99), of South Kelsey, Lincs.

GREAT GRIMSBY 1685–1687, 1689–20 Oct. 1699

bap. 19 Nov. 1650, 1st s. of Sir Edward Ayscough† of South Kelsey by Isabel, da. of Sir John Bolles, 1st Bt., of Scampton, Lincs. *educ.* Melton, Lincs.; Sidney Sussex, Camb. 1667; Padua 1671; G. Inn 1671. *m.* (1) Bridget (*d.* 1684), da. of Edward Skinner of Thornton College, Lincs., 1s. *d.v.p.* 2da. (1 *d.v.p.*); (2) 1 Aug. 1685, Mary (*d.* 1715), da. and h. of William Harbord*, 1s. 7da. (3 *d.v.p.*) *suc.* fa. 1668; kntd. 17 Jan. 1672.[1]

Sheriff, Lincs. 1683–4; high steward, Gt. Grimsby 1686–Oct. 1688.[2]

Commr. prizes 1689–June 1699, drowned lands 1690.[3]

Although a very late convert to the ranks of Revolution supporters, after 1689 Ayscough adapted to the role of Court placeman. His family's tenure of the lordship of Stallingborough had secured his ancestors' electoral success at nearby Grimsby since 1529, and in 1690 he gained his third successive victory there. At the outset of the new Parliament he was classed by Lord Carmarthen (Sir Thomas Osborne†) as a Whig, but was not a prominent Member. In the spring of 1691 Robert Harley* marked him as a Court supporter. He was nominated to two drafting committees on 31 Oct. 1691, for bills to secure the rights of corporations, and to regulate parliamentary elections, he being doubtless familiar with corruption in his own notoriously venal constituency. In the fifth session he was granted a leave of absence on 11 Jan. 1694, but on 12 Jan. 1695 a motion was tabled that he should be placed into custody of the serjeant-at-arms for nonattendance. It was defeated, and instead the Speaker was ordered to write to him to require his presence. In 1693–5 his name appeared on several lists of placemen (as a commissioner of prizes) and Samuel Grascome classed him as a Court supporter.[4]

Ayscough gained an unopposed victory at Grimsby in 1695, and remained loyal to the Court. He was classed as a probable government supporter for a division on the proposed council of trade in January 1696, signed the Association, and in March voted to fix the price of guineas at 22*s*. However, he was prepared to invest £3,000 in the abortive land bank scheme, which was promoted by enemies of the Whig Junto. In the next session he supported the ministry with his vote on 25 Nov 1696. in favour of the attainder of Sir John Fenwick†. During the summer of 1698 he was twice identified as a placeman, and, following another unopposed return at Grimsby, was classed in about September of that year as a Court man. His backing for the government ensured his survival on the prize commission, but he and his colleagues could not escape close scrutiny by Parliament in the 1698–9 session. Although he managed to avoid censure himself, the commission was finally revoked on 10 June 1699. He died on 2 Oct. 1699 at Grasby, Lincolnshire, and was buried at Stallingborough. His only surviving son Charles did not long survive him, and his estates were shared by his daughters, to whom he had made bequests amounting to over £10,000.[5]

[1] *Lincs. Peds.* (Harl. Soc. l), 66–68. [2] *CSP Dom.* 1686–7, p. 223; 1687–9, p. 264. [3] *CSP Dom.* 1689–90, p. 146; *Cal. Treas. Bks.* ix. 794;

xiv. 401. [4] J. C. Walter, *Ayscough Fam.* 9–10. [5] NLS, Advocates' mss, Bank of Eng. pprs. 31.1.7, f. 95; Luttrell, *Brief Relation*, iv. 465; *Cal. Treas. Bks.* xiv. 401; *Lincs. Peds.* 67; PCC 1 Noel.

P. W./P. L. G.

BACKWELL, John (1654–1708), of Tyringham, Bucks.

WENDOVER   1685–1687, 1690–1701 (Nov.)

b. 20 Apr. 1654, 1st s. of Edward Backwell[†], banker, of St. Mary Woolnoth, Lombard Street, London by his 1st w. Sarah, da. of one Brett, merchant, of London. *educ.* I. Temple 1676, called 1680. *m.* 1678, Elizabeth, da. and h. of Sir William Tyrringham[†] of Tyringham, Bucks., 11s. (5 *d.v.p.*) 2da. (1 *d.v.p.*). *suc.* fa. 1683.[1]

Jt. comptroller of customs, London 1671–*d.*[2]
Member Hon. Artillery Co. 1675.[3]

The son of Charles II's banker, Backwell acquired the manor of Tyringham, near Newport Pagnell, by marriage, and inherited property near Wendover from his father, who claimed to have been born nearby and who 'purchased an estate' there. Unfortunately, the repercussions of the stop of the Exchequer were visited upon Backwell and it seems that a parliamentary seat was useful in dealing with his father's creditors. Upon his election in 1690, Lord Carmarthen (Sir Thomas Osborne[†]) classed him as a Tory and probable Court supporter, and as a member likely to support him in late December 1690 in case an attack was made on his ministerial position. In April 1691 Robert Harley* classed him as a Country supporter. However, most lists of the period merely record the fact that he was a placeman by virtue of his patent office in the customs of London. The main characteristic of his parliamentary career appears to have been absence, for one reason or another. On 31 Dec. 1691 he was given leave on health grounds, but was back in the Commons by 2 Feb. 1692 when he complained of a breach of privilege following the arrest of a menial servant. A further leave was granted on 12 Dec. 1693. In the 1694–5 session Henry Guy* thought him a 'friend', presumably in relation to the attacks upon Guy in the Commons. Backwell received leave of absence, again for health reasons, on 9 Mar. 1695.[4]

Re-elected in 1695, possibly after an intervention by the Marquess of Carmarthen's son (Peregrine Osborne[†]), Backwell was ordered on 26 Jan. 1696 to ask Dr Gregory Haskard to preach on the anniversary of Charles I's execution. He was forecast as likely to vote against the Court in the division of 31 Jan. on the proposed council of trade and received leave for a fortnight on 5 Feb. He signed the Association and voted in March against fixing the price of guineas at 22s. In the following session he was on hand to vote against the attainder of Sir John Fenwick[†] on 25 Nov. 1696 before obtaining ten days' leave on 3 Dec. because of an illness of his wife. The 1697–8 session saw the passage of a private act to satisfy his father's creditors. Despite allegations that he was fraudulently concealing an estate of £3,000 p.a. and that he had received £127,000 since his father's death, Backwell was able to secure an act whereby 235 creditors accepted only 21.5 per cent of what was owing to them. His opponents appear to have seen his parliamentary privilege as a bar to securing a better settlement.[5]

Returned again in 1698, Backwell was classed as a member of the Country party in about September 1698 and forecast as likely to oppose the standing army. He received leave again on 17 Feb. 1699 for two weeks. In July he wrote to John Ellis* that he had been indisposed before he had left town, although a second letter announced his intention of returning to London at the start of September. A correspondent of (Sir) John Verney* (Lord Fermanagh) also expected to find him at the customs house that month. Returned again in January 1701 he was listed as a supporter of the Court in February over the 'Great Mortgage'. On the strength of his activities in this session he was later blacklisted as having opposed the preparations for war with France. Backwell did not stand again, dying in 1708, his remains being buried at Tyringham on 15 Apr.[6]

[1] *Reg. St. Mary Woolnoth*, 52; Lipscomb, *Bucks.* iv. 376; Burke, *LG* (1952), 2575. [2] *Cal. Treas. Bks.* iii. 926; xxii. 206. [3] *Ancient Vellum Bk.* ed. Raikes, 105. [4] Stowe 304, ff. 132–3; *Luttrell Diary*, 167–8. [5] *HMC Lords* n.s. iii. 222–3. [6] Add. 28884, ff. 103, 206; BL, Verney mss mic. 636/51, Anne Nicholas to Verney, 23 Sept. 1699; Lipscomb, 376.

E. C./S. N. H.

BACON, Sir Edmund, 4th Bt. (1672–1721), of Gillingham, Norf.

ORFORD   10 Feb. 1700–1708

bap. 6 Apr. 1672, s. of Sir Henry Bacon, 3rd Bt., of Herringfleet, Suff. and Gillingham by Sarah, da. of Sir John Castleton, 2nd Bt., of Shipdham and Sturston, Norf. *educ.* Botesdale; St. John's, Camb. 1687. *m.* (1) c.25 Dec. 1688, Philippa (*d.* 1710), da. of Sir Edmund Bacon, 4th Bt., of Redgrave, Suff., 2s. other ch.; (2) 16 Apr. 1713, Mary, da. and coh. of John Castell (*d.* 1735), of Raveningham, Norf., 1s. 2da. *suc.* fa. c. Jan. 1686.

Freeman, Dunwich 1694–?1701, 1708; Orford 1695–1704, 1709–14.[1]

Never more than a half-hearted parliamentarian at best, Bacon spurned a good opportunity to stand at

Orford in 1695. His candidature for the borough in the following general election, though supported by the Tory 'gentlemen' of Suffolk and one faction in the bitterly divided corporation electorate, was not considered particularly promising even by those of the same political persuasion as himself. For if, as was expected, the outcome went to the adjudication of the House, his being a stranger to Westminster, 'and never . . . acquainted with the proceedings there', would, it was thought, count against him. In the event, he was seated on petition by one vote, in what was viewed by most observers, and not merely disgruntled Whigs, as a flagrantly partisan judgment. On 19 Feb. 1700 his name was added to the committee examining the proceedings in relation to charters and the granting of new charters during William's reign (a subject in which his warring constituents had a special interest). Re-elected in January 1701, in a repeat of the previous contest, he was forecast in February as likely to support the Court on agreeing with a resolution of the committee of supply to continue the 'Great Mortgage', and subsequently figured in the 'black list' of those opposed to the preparations for war.[2]

After at first 'neglecting' the Orford voters, Bacon eventually stirred himself in September 1701 and visited the borough, in the company of several friends and supporters. Treating and spending freely, he won back the allegiance of several key men, and by November had re-established sufficient influence over the corporation to be able to dictate the terms of the borough's loyal address. At the general election a month later he and his Tory partner Sir Edward Turnor* were safely returned by the majority of the corporators, though not without a challenge from their Whig opponents. Robert Harley* classed Bacon with the Tories in his analysis of the new House, and he was listed as having favoured the motion of 26 Feb. 1702 vindicating the Commons' conduct in the impeachments of the Whig ministers. On 17 Apr. he acted as a teller for an amendment to the land tax bill, and, after a more comfortable, though not unopposed, re-election at Orford, told again on 2 Nov., when the issue of the impeachments was reopened, this time in favour of a Tory resolution that the Commons had not received justice at the hands of the Upper House. He was also a teller on 28 Jan. 1703 on the Tory side in the disputed election for Plympton Erle. Although forecast on 30 Oct. 1704 as likely to vote against the Tack, he in fact voted for it in the critical division of 28 Nov. On 20 Dec., after presenting Orford's address to the Queen congratulating her on the victories of both the Duke of Marlborough (John Churchill†) and Sir George Rooke*, he was granted leave of absence on 20 Dec.

Late in January 1705 he wrote to his constituency colleague: 'I perceive the session is drawing to a conclusion as fast as may be and I hope I shall be excused for not coming up. It is very good hunting weather and I make the best of it I can.' Parallel to this indifference towards parliamentary affairs was his increasing inattentiveness to constituency matters. Initially, in the immediate aftermath of the 1702 general election, he had shown some energy in busying himself in pursuit of a new charter for the borough, but once the disputes within the corporation had been patched up he began to slip back into his old habits. One of his agents wrote in January 1705:

> I cannot tell what Sir E. B. means, unless it be to disoblige all his [friends], for he promised to contribute £10 towards the repair of the quay; now that has been finished some time, but no money comes, which causes a great murmuring; and then there was £4 4s. his p[ar]t of the dinner when my Lord [?Dysart (Lionel Tollemache*)] was sworn mayor, and 50s. he promised Mr Morgan towards Nat. Gooding's debt, and that not being paid causes great discontent there. I could wish that he would take some care about the payment of all these sums that he has promised, to prevent the ill effects that may arise from the not doing of it.

Suggestions that he might care to visit the borough and pay what he had promised were treated with disdain. 'As to your Orford affair', he told Sir Edward Turnor in February,

> I do not doubt but if the corporation [were] exposed to sale they may find purchasers enough and I am afraid a visit will not prevent it, and I can assure you I shall never come to the bidding point, for if they have not gratitude enough to accept my service next time I shall be very contented to stay at home. All the regret I shall have will be that parting with so good a partner . . .

In due course, however, he consented to mingle with the corporators, and after the customary treating was adopted again as member in the 1705 election, when he and Turnor were returned unopposed, though some voters still muttered regretfully of the counter-offers they had been prevailed upon to reject. Bacon, who himself wrote that he identified devotion to 'the public good' with 'zeal to promote the Church of England', was marked as 'True Church' in a list of the new Parliament. He was up at the beginning of the first session, in time to vote against the Court candidate for Speaker on 25 Oct. 1705, but may not have been particularly conscientious in his attendance thereafter. In December 1706 it was reported from Norfolk that his wife had parted from him, having 'quitted Gillingham for ever, and . . . gone this day in the coach for London and carried her infant with her', leaving the other children with her husband. Probably he had already decided to 'quit the service' of Orford in Parliament, for the corporation was choosing an intended replacement in January 1707. Certainly in February 1708 mention was being made of his determination to step down. In one parliamentary list of that year he was classed as a Tory, and in another as a Tacker.[3]

Although not a candidate himself in the 1708 election, Bacon voted for the Tory candidates in Ipswich, and maintained some involvement in the continuing affairs of Orford corporation. It was probably he rather than his namesake of Garboldisham who was seriously wounded in a duel with a Whig squire in Suffolk shortly after the general election in 1708, and who was admitted into the Duke of Beaufort's 'loyal brotherhood' in 1709, only to be expelled for non-attendance. He remained one of the principal Tories in Norfolk despite his reluctance to spend money in putting up for Parliament, and in 1721 was included in Christopher Layer's list of the 'loyal gentlemen' of the county, with an income estimated at £1,600 a year. Bacon died on 10 July 1721, being succeeded by his eldest son, another Sir Edmund, who became a client of Robert Walpole II* and, after contesting Orford unsuccessfully, sat for Thetford 1722–38.[4]

[1] Suff. RO (Ipswich), Dunwich assembly bks. EE6/1144/13, p. 82; EE6/1144/14 (19 Sept. 1701, 12 May 1708); Orford ct. bks. EE5/4/3, pp. 20, 77, 88, 107–8. [2] Murrell thesis, 285–318; W. Suss. RO, Shillinglee mss Ac.454/973–4, 839–40, 1024, 976, 1088, Nathaniel Gooding to Sir Edward Turnor, 18 July, 17 Oct. 1698, 16 Jan. 1698–9, Ld. Hereford to same, 19 July 1698, Turnor to Ld. Hereford, 21 July 1698, John Hooke to Turnor, 29 July 1698, June [?1699]; Add. 22186, f. 98; *Cocks Diary*, 47–48; Luttrell, *Brief Relation*, iv. 612; *Vernon-Shrewsbury Letters*, ii. 262; *Hervey Diary*, 31; Cumbria RO (Carlisle), Lonsdale mss D/Lons/W2/2/3, James* to Sir John Lowther, 2nd Bt. I*, 10 Feb. 1699[–1700]. [3] Shillinglee mss Ac.454/1182–5, 844–5, 1152, 1155, 1034, 1159, 1195, 856, 1039–41, 1044–6, 853, 1162, 878, 1949, Leicester Martin* to Turnor, 15, 26 Aug., 5 Sept. 1701, John Morgan to same, 26 Aug. 1701, 6 June 1704, John Sanders to same, 4 Sept. 1701, William Betts to same, 9 Sept. 1701, Thomas Palmer to same, 3 Nov. 1701, 25 Oct. 1702, 8 May 1704, 26 Feb. 1704–5, John Hooke to same, 9 Dec. 1702, 9 Oct., 1 Nov. 1704, 9 Jan., 6 Feb. 1704–5, 2, 30 Apr. 1705, 23 Jan. 1706–7, Ld. Dysart to same, 28 June 1704, Bacon to same, 21 Feb. 1704–5, 20 Mar. [?1705], Turnor and Clement Corrance* to mayor of Orford, 17 Feb. 1707–8; Murrell thesis, 317–18, 336–40. [4] Info. from Dr P. Murrell; Shillinglee mss Ac.454/1081, 1083, John Hooke to Turnor, 29 Aug., 28 Sept. 1709; Luttrell, vi. 317; Add. 49360, ff. 8–13; Camb. Univ. Lib. Cholmondeley (Houghton) mss, Horatio Walpole I* to Robert Walpole II, 27 July 1710; Nottingham Univ. Lib. Portland (Harley) mss, Pw2Hy 654, 'A copy of part of a letter from Sir Alganoun Potts . . .' [?c.1710]; P. S. Fritz, *Ministers and Jacobitism 1715–45*, p. 143.

D. W. H.

BACON, Sir Edmund, 6th Bt. (c.1680–1755), of Garboldisham, Norf.

THETFORD   12 Dec. 1710–1713
NORFOLK   1713–1715
            26 June 1728–1741

b. c.1680, 1st s. of Sir Robert Bacon, 5th Bt., of Redgrave, Suff. by Elizabeth, da. of Thomas Chandler of London. *educ.* Pembroke, Camb. 1697. *m.* (with £3,500) 27 Nov. 1712, Mary, da. of Sir Robert Kemp, 3rd Bt.*, 4da. *suc.* fa. as 6th Bt. 31 Jan. 1704.[1]

Bacon was the premier baronet of England. In his father's time the family estates had been loaded with debts, and in about 1703 Redgrave and other properties in Suffolk and Norfolk were sold to clear the encumbrances, the family removing to Garboldisham. Bacon was returned unopposed at a by-election shortly after the general election of 1710, in place of (Sir) Thomas Hanmer II* (4th Bt.), and probably with his help. He told on the Tory side in the disputed election for Cockermouth on 17 Mar. and 24 Apr. 1711. He was listed among the 'worthy patriots' who had exposed the mismanagements of the old ministry. On 7 Dec. 1711 he joined a Tory back-bench revolt and voted with the Whigs in favour of the 'No Peace without Spain' motion. He was a member of the March Club. On 11 Apr. he told in favour of taking into custody a Whig printer who had published a 'scandalous libel'. He was elected on 13 May 1712 to the abortive commission to examine King William's land grants. On 26 May he told against bringing in an East India bill. In the next session he was a teller on 7 May 1713 against a Whig motion to adjourn before the House had completed consideration of the report of the accounts commissioners.[2]

Bacon's marriage helped his finances, and in 1713 he was returned for Norfolk. No vote is recorded in this Parliament, but the Worsley list classed him as a Tory who had sometimes voted with the Whigs, an assessment which may indicate that he was a follower of Hanmer. Bacon did not stand in 1715. His name was included in the list of possible Jacobite sympathizers sent to the Pretender in 1721, and in Christopher Layer's list of the 'loyal' Norfolk gentlemen he was noted as having £1,500 a year. He was returned as a Tory knight of the shire at a by-election in 1728. Bacon died on 30 Apr. 1755, having in his will requested to be buried at Redgrave.[3]

[1] Blomefield, *Norf.* vii. 165; Add. 39219, f. 86. [2] *CSP Dom. 1703–4*, pp. 456–7; *Huntington Lib. Q.* xxxiii. 168–9. [3] *HMC Portland*, vi. 152; P. S. Fritz, *Ministers and Jacobitism 1715–45*, p. 143; PCC 155 Paul.

D. W. H.

BACON, Thomas see **SCLATER**

BACON, Waller (c.1669–1734), of Earlham, nr. Norwich.

NORWICH   6 Dec. 1705–1710, 1715–11 Nov. 1734

b. c.1669, o. surv. s. of Francis Bacon of Gray's Inn by Elizabeth, da. and h. of Thomas Waller† (*d.* 1682) of St. Andrew, Holborn, Mdx. and Earlham. *educ.* Christ Church, Oxf. matric. 23 Feb. 1686, aged 16; G. Inn 1679, called 1693, bencher 1709. *m.* (1) 4 Apr. 1695 (with £2,000), Mary (*d.* 1701), da. and coh. of Richard Porter of Framlingham, Suff., *s.p.s.*; (2) settlement 28 Aug. 1703, Frances, prob. da. of Edward Nosworthy, rector of Diptford, Devon, 3s. (1 *d.v.p.*). *suc.* fa. 1679; mother 1704.[1]

Commr. victualling 1714–17; commissary of musters and stores in Minorca 1722–*d.*

Freeman, Norwich 1718.[2]

Bacon was descended from a younger son of Lord Keeper Nathaniel Bacon. He leased the Earlham estate from his mother, succeeding to this and other property in 1704. He had been appointed a deputy-lieutenant for Norwich by December 1702. Backed by Lord Townshend, he stood on the Whig interest at Norwich in 1705 and, with his partner, John Chambers, carried the day against two Tories. However, there was a double return, and Bacon and Chambers had to wait to be seated until 12 days after the opening of Parliament. A steady Whig, Bacon was classed by Lord Sunderland (Charles, Lord Spencer*) as a 'gain'. He voted for the Court candidate for Speaker on 25 Oct. 1705. Another list of the new Parliament classed him as a 'Churchman'. On 19 Jan. 1706 he was appointed to the drafting committee for a bill to regulate duties on coal imported into Great Yarmouth, a measure undertaken in response to popular pressure from Norwich and the county. On 16 Feb. he reported a petition of some army officers for relief, being ordered the same day to bring in a bill to this end. He voted on 18 Feb. 1706 for the Court over the 'place clause' in the regency bill. He was appointed on 19 Dec. to draft another bill on Yarmouth coal duties, this time managing it successfully through the House. In two lists of 1708 he appeared as a Whig. On 12 Feb. he reported another petition of army officers for arrears of pay, subsequently introducing, on 3 Mar., a bill to state the accounts of the regiments concerned. Re-elected in 1708, he was appointed on 24 Jan. 1709 to the drafting committee on a bill to continue the Wymondham–Attleborough Road Act. He voted for the naturalization of the Palatines in 1709 and for the impeachment of Dr Sacheverell in 1710. In January 1710 he had assisted in the parliamentary management of a bill to regulate hackney coaches, and he reported a private estate bill on 9 Mar.

Defeated in 1710 and 1713, Bacon came back into Parliament in 1715. He was classed as a Whig in the Worsley list and proved a faithful supporter of Walpole. He died on 11 Nov. 1734.[3]

[1] Blomefield, *Norf.* iv. 195, 510, 515; PCC 93 Cottle, 258 Ockham; Sheffield Archs. Bacon Frank mss BFM 1041, 1247; *Norf. Arch.* xxxiii. 8, 92–93; Vivian, *Vis. Devon*, 782. [2] *Norf. Rec. Soc.* xxiii. 102. [3] Bacon Frank mss BFM 1043, 1247; *CSP Dom.* 1702–3, p. 397; Camb. Univ. Lib. Cholmondeley (Houghton) mss, Ld. Townshend to Robert Walpole II*, 8 Oct. 1705.

D.W.H.

BAGNOLD, John (c.1642–98), of Derby.

DERBY   1695–1 May 1698

b. c.1642, poss. s. of Walter Bagnold of Marston, Derbys. *m.* bef. 1670, Hannah, da. of Joseph Parker of Derby, 3s. 1da.[1]

Town clerk, coroner and steward of Derby 1676–*d.*; dep.-receiver assessment, Derby 1678; receiver-gen. assessment, Derby 1678–80.[2]

After the 1695 election Lady Anne Pye wrote of the election at Derby:

Bagnold the town clerk is one, a small estate, no quality nor good repute but so great an interest in the town as to make the Duke [of Devonshire, William Cavendish†] at last resolve that his son the Lord Henry Cavendish* should join with him.

Little is known about Bagnold apart from his tenure of various local offices. He may have been related to the Bagnall family of Staffordshire, which provided Newcastle-under-Lyme with two town clerks in the 17th century. Alternatively, his father may have been the Walter Bagnall of Marston who stood as one of his sureties when Bagnold was appointed receiver-general of taxes for the county in 1678. The Bagnolds certainly had a small estate at Marston in the early 18th century, an enclave among the lands acquired by the Cavendish family after the dissolution of the monasteries.[3]

During the 1680s Bagnold trod the political tightrope with some skill, managing to retain his municipal offices despite the frequent changes in direction of successive regimes. In 1683 he was clearly assisting the Tory reaction by deposing evidence against George Vernon I*, the fiercely pro-Exclusionist MP for Derby, noting that Vernon had threatened to lead armed resistance rather than accept James as King, although Bagnold was noticeably less hostile than the other witnesses. By 1687–8, when Vernon was back in favour as a leading Whig 'collaborator' and right-hand man of the absentee lord lieutenant, the Earl of Huntingdon, Bagnold attached himself to Vernon in the hope of keeping the office of town clerk of Derby. Bagnold was notably reticent at appearing in public for the surrender of the borough charter at the beginning of 1688 and for Vernon's court-sponsored candidacy at Derby in the ensuing parliamentary election. He was, however, willing to wait upon the lord lieutenant with a congratulatory address to the King on the birth of the Prince of Wales.[4]

The great interest which Vernon noted Bagnold as having in the town of Derby in 1688 was successfully put to the test in the 1695 election. Originally, it seemed that Bagnold and Vernon had divided up the town between them, but a late intervention by Lord Henry Cavendish persuaded Bagnold to join with the Chatsworth interest and the two carried it despite the free-spending tactics of their opponent. Bagnold even felt confident enough of his position to approach the Duke of Devonshire to finance his defence against an expected election petition from Vernon. However, if Bagnold felt that he owed his election to Cavendish influence, he did not show it in his parliamentary conduct. He was forecast as likely to oppose the Court in the divisions of 31 Jan. 1696 over the proposed council of trade and voted against the Court in March over fixing the price of guineas at 22s., on both occasions appearing on the opposite side to his fellow-Member Cavendish. He did however sign the Association. The only legislation with which he was associated was the Derwent navigation bill. On 12 Dec. 1695 he was the sole Member ordered to prepare it, presenting the bill on 18 Dec., but it never emerged from committee following a petitioning campaign against it. In the following session he voted on 25 Nov. 1696 against the attainder of Sir John Fenwick†, before being given leave of absence on 8 Mar. 1697.[5]

Bagnold died on 1 May 1698, aged 55, and was buried in All Saints' church, Derby, the only member of his immediate family to sit in Parliament. His son John was mayor of Derby in 1717.[6]

[1] Derbys. RO, D652/T2; R. Simpson, *Hist. Derby*, i. 355; W. Woolley, *Hist. Derbys.* (Derbys. Rec. Soc. vi), p. xiii; Lysons, *Derbys.* 117–18. [2] Info. from Derby Local Stud. Lib.; *CSP Dom*. 1676–7, p. 231; *Cal. Treas. Bks.* v. 949, 1098–9, vi. 644–5, 673. [3] *HMC Portland*, iii. 573; Woolley, p. xiii. [4] *The Commons 1660–90*, iii. 636–7; *CSP Dom*. July–Sept. 1683, p. 210; *HMC Hastings*, ii. 184; Huntington Lib. Hastings mss HA369–73, 3227–8, 12974–5, 12979, 12983, Bagnold to Huntingdon, 5 Mar. 1687[–8], 26 Mar., 16, 25 Apr., 30 Aug. 1688, G. Fletcher to same, 21 Mar. 1687[–8], 28 May 1688, Vernon to same, 31 Jan., 4 Mar., 1 July 1688, n.d. [5] Devonshire mss at Chatsworth House, Whildon pprs., John to James Whildon, 25 Oct. 1695, 'Monday afternoon'; C84–86, Aaron Kinton to same, 31 Oct., 9 Nov. 1695; *HMC Portland*, iii. 573; Hereford and Worcester RO (Hereford), Harley mss C64/117, ballot for commrs. of accts. [6] Lysons, 117–18; Simpson, 355; Woolley, 48.

S. N. H.

BAGOT, Charles (1681–1738), of Hanbury, Staffs.

STAFFORDSHIRE 7 Feb. 1712–1713

b. 5 Nov. 1681, 2nd surv. s. of Sir Walter Bagot, 3rd Bt.*, and bro. of Edward Bagot*. *unm.*[1]

Although he came from one of the leading Staffordshire families, nothing is known of Bagot's early career. He does not appear to have studied at Christ Church as his elder and younger brothers did, nor at an inn of court. He took a prominent part in the celebrations in July 1710 attending Sacheverell's Staffordshire progress. This may have been part of his campaign for the county elections as, with the backing of his elder brother, Bagot shortly afterwards announced his intention to stand for knight of the shire. However, support for him was far from unanimous, prompting one of Lady Gower's stewards to comment that some gentlemen refused Bagot their votes 'because he's a second brother and hath but a small estate and it's believed he will not carry it and others think he will decline standing'. In the event it took a gentry meeting to achieve a compromise, by which Bagot desisted in favour of Hon. William Ward* in return for the promise of a free run at the next election. The opportunity came at a by-election caused by Hon. Henry Paget's* elevation to the peerage at the beginning of 1712. Given his brother's interest and the prevailing climate of opinion, no Whig ventured to oppose his election. However, once in the House, Bagot does not appear to have been very active. Evidence upon which to judge his political stance is scarce, but loyalty to the ministry is indicated by his vote on 18 June 1713 for the French commerce bill. He did not stand for Parliament in 1713, the Bagot interest being eclipsed following the death of his brother in 1712 and the consequent minority of his nephew, Sir Walter Wagstaffe Bagot, 5th Bt.†[2]

In December 1714 Bagot was elected to the 'mock' corporation of Cheadle, an indication of Jacobite leanings. He died on 26 Apr. 1738 at his lodgings in Essex Street, near the Strand. In his will he left sizable sums of money, totalling £2,000, to his sister Anne and two nieces, and the remainder of his estate to the fifth baronet.[3]

[1] J. C. Wedgwood, *Staffs. Parl. Hist.* (Wm. Salt Arch. Soc.), ii. 206. [2] Staffs. RO, Sutherland mss D868/9/67, J. White to Lady Gower, 21 Aug. 1710; *HMC Portland*, iv. 608–9; *HMC 5th Rep.* 208.

[3] Monod thesis, 498; *Gent. Mag.* 1738, p. 276; *Hist. Reg. Chron.* 1738, p. 17; PCC 86 Brodrepp.

S. N. H.

BAGOT, Edward (1674–1712), of Blithfield, Staffs.

STAFFORDSHIRE 1698–1708

b. 21 Jan. 1674, 1st surv. s. of Sir Walter Bagot, 3rd Bt.*, and bro. of Charles Bagot*. *educ.* Christ Church, Oxf. 1691; M. Temple 1693. *m.* 15 Apr. 1697, Frances (*d.* 1714), da. and h. of Sir Thomas Wagstaffe*, 2s. (1 *d.v.p.*) 2da. *suc.* fa. as 4th Bt. 15 Feb. 1705.[1]

As heir to one of the most important families in Staffordshire, Bagot could expect to play a major role in county politics. During speculation about the negotiations for his marriage, he was reported to be worth £4,000 p.a., which would have placed him at the apex of county society. The chronic ill-health of his father accelerated his initiation into politics, and indeed he had replaced his father in the lieutenancy by May 1703. However, the future bishop of Bristol, George Smalridge, was surprised by his decision to seek election in 1698 as conversations at Oxford had led him to believe that Bagot 'entertained some notions which would not give him leave to qualify himself to be a Member of Parliament'. According to Sir John Leveson Gower, 5th Bt.*, Bagot's interest was too strong to be threatened: 'your relations are too numerous. Your family too considerable, and have lived with reputation too long in the country to be baffled should you resolve on it.' However, a contest was threatened by the intervention of Hon. Robert Shirley, heir to Lord Ferrers, who began to make an interest before the dissolution. Bagot countered by defending the Staffordshire tradition whereby prospective candidates merely informed the gentry of an intention to offer themselves for election and let a county meeting choose the candidates, in order to avoid acrimonious disputes. The sitting Member, Hon. Henry Paget*, agreed with this approach and then joined forces with Bagot against Shirley, who had resolved to continue to a poll. A meeting between the Bagots and the Shirleys at the last moment may possibly have avoided a poll on the understanding that Shirley would be unopposed at the next election, though this must be counted unlikely.[2]

To contemporaries Bagot's political stance was clear. His name appeared on a comparative analysis of about September 1698 of the old and new Commons as a Country supporter, and he was forecast as a likely opponent of a standing army. Following his re-election in January 1701 he was noted as likely to support the Court in February over the 'Great Mortgage'. On 16 May he was given leave to go into the country because his father was very ill. Bagot was re-elected unopposed in November 1701, and on a list of the new Parliament, Robert Harley* classed him as a Tory. Although the Journals do not show him as an active Member, there is evidence that he took his duties seriously. On 29 Jan. 1702 he wrote, 'we are more honest now than ever we were for we sit at it till two or three o'clock in the morning'. On 26 Feb. he voted with the Tories in favour of the resolution vindicating the Commons' proceedings the previous year on the impeachments of William III's ministers.[3]

Returned again without a contest in the 1702 election, Bagot was thought sufficiently important to be named by William Lowndes* when the latter wrote to the Lord Treasurer in support of Sir George Parker's* request to succeed William Campion* as sub-commissioner for prizes at Dover: 'your favour to him will be well taken by his brother Bagot and other gentlemen in the House'. In the first session of the new Parliament he voted with the Tories on 13 Feb. 1703, against the Lords' amendment enlarging the time for taking the Abjuration. In the following session, he was listed on Lord Nottingham's (Daniel Finch[†]) forecast of likely supporters in November 1703 over the Scotch Plot. However, in the next session he did not vote for the Tack on 28 Nov. 1704. Having recently succeeded to the baronetcy, he was again returned unopposed at the 1705 election. He also made a point of assuring another Tory, Sir Richard Myddelton, 3rd Bt.*, of his interest in Denbighshire. On a list of the 1705 Parliament he was marked 'Low Church', almost certainly due to his opposition to the Tack. He was, in fact, far more committed to the cause of the Church than this vote implied. Peter Shakerley* canvassed Bagot's vote for the Tory candidate, William Bromley II*, in the forthcoming Speaker's election, and despite being afflicted by gout, he set out for London and on 25 Oct. duly voted against the Court candidate. Two other lists confirm his adherence to the Tory cause: one compiled after the admission of the Scottish Members in 1707 and the other a list of the 1707 Parliament which included the returns for 1708.[4]

It was probably gout which compelled Bagot's retirement from Parliament at the 1708 election. He continued to espouse the Tory cause locally, most notably as a host to Dr Sacheverell during the doctor's triumphant tour through Staffordshire in 1710. Bagot almost certainly supported the election of the doctor's brother Charles as knight of the shire in February 1712 in succession to his own long-time partner Paget. He died in May of that year, being buried at Blithfield. His widow married (Sir) Adolphus Oughton[†] (1st Bt.), a strong Whig, leading to a major legal suit between her second husband and the Bagots over property she held in dower. The victor in this dispute was Sir Walter Wagstaffe Bagot, 5th Bt.†, a minor in 1712, who went on to reclaim the family's seat in Parliament, as a Tory, at a by-election in 1724.⁵

¹W. Bagot, *Hist. Fam. Bagot*, 80; J. C. Wedgwood, *Staffs. Parl. Hist.* (William Salt Arch. Soc.), ii. 183. ²Nichols, *Lit. Hist.* iii. 265-6, 269; *CSP Dom.* 1703-4, p. 278; Wm. Salt Lib. (Stafford), Bagot mss D/1721/3/291, Sir John Leveson Gower, 5th Bt.*, to Bagot, 10 Feb. 1697[-8]; Bagot to Sir Charles Skrymsher, 12 Feb. [1698]; same to [–] [Feb. 1698]; John Pershall* to [Bagot], 4 Aug. 1698 (Horwitz trans.). ³Warws. RO, Wagstaffe-Bagot mss MI 143, Bagot to wife, 29 Jan. 1702. ⁴*Cal. Treas. Bks.* xvii. 358; NLW, Chirk Castle mss E.998, Bagot to Myddelton, 30 May 1705; Cheshire RO, Shakerley mss, Shakerley to Bagot, 29 Aug. 1705; *Bull. IHR* xxxvii. 22. ⁵Anglesey mss at Plas Newydd, Bagot to Henry Paget, 10 May 1707; Add. 70421, newsletter 27 June 1710; Bagot, 80; *Verney Letters 18th Cent.* i. 275.

S. N. H.

BAGOT, Sir Walter, 3rd Bt. (1644–1705), of Blithfield, Staffs.

STAFFORDSHIRE 1679 (Mar.)–1681, 1685–1687
1689–1690
7 Dec. 1693–1695

b. 21 Mar. 1644, 3rd but 1st surv. s. of Sir Edward Bagot, 2nd Bt., by Mary, da. and h. of William Lambard of Buckingham. *educ.* Christ Church, Oxf. 1662; M. Temple 1666. *m.* lic. 25 June 1670, Jane (*d.* 1695), da. and h. of Charles Salusbury of Bachymbydd, Denb., 5s. (2 *d.v.p.*) 5da. (1 *d.v.p.*). *suc.* fa. as 3rd Bt. 30 Mar. 1673.¹

Commr. inquiry into offences in Needwood forest, 1687.²

Bagot was descended from a family which claimed to have held property in Staffordshire since the reign of William I. He sat for the county in five successive Parliaments between 1679 and 1690, but his service had been undistinguished, punctuated as it was by severe bouts of ill-health. Possibly for this reason he did not stand in the 1690 election. However, the death of Walter Chetwynd* in March 1693 forced him back into the political arena. A group of Whigs led by Philip Foley* attempted to set up Hon. Henry Paget* at the ensuing by-election. This manoeuvre was blocked by the Tories, who accused Paget of ignoring the tradition by which the candidates were agreed by the gentry at a county meeting. Bagot was set up at such a meeting in October 1693 and his candidacy widely publicized in a circular letter signed by many leading gentry. Faced by this show of strength, and unsure of being able to triumph at the poll, Paget desisted, leaving Bagot to be returned unopposed.³

Bagot is not mentioned in the Journals, nor does his name appear on the one parliamentary list extant from his period of service in the House, which named Court supporters. His attendance was probably limited by ill-health, which continued to trouble him. In April 1695 he was noted as one of a group of Denbighshire landowners opposing a grant to the Earl of Portland of crown lands in Wales, but he was not in London when the group's representatives lobbied the Treasury. He did not stand at the 1695 election. By 1698 he had obviously decided to transfer his interest to his son, Edward*, as he wrote in March of that year that he was 'so totally disabled that I can do my country no further service'. Although he was included in the lieutenancy commission of March 1701, he had resigned this to his son by May 1703. He died on 15 Feb. 1705, his remains being buried under the altar of Blithfield church.⁴

¹W. Bagot, *Hist. Fam. Bagot*, 75. ²Staffs. RO, Vernon mss D1790/A/4/3. ³G. Wrottesley, *Hist. Bagot Fam.* 2-5; Hereford and Worcester RO (Hereford), Foley mss Box E12/F/IV/BE, [–] to Philip Foley, n.d.; 'gents.' circular letter, 4 Oct. 1693; E12/IV/BE/273, 275, William Nabbs to Philip Foley, 17, 18 Oct. 1693. ⁴*Cal. Treas. Pprs.* 1557-1696, p.438; *Cal. Treas. Bks.* x. 1051, 1202; Wm. Salt Lib. (Stafford), Bagot mss D/1721/3/291, Edward Bagot to [–], 1 Mar. 1697-8 (Horwitz trans.); *CSP Dom.* 1700-2, p. 250; 1703-4, p. 278; Bagot, 79.

S. N. H.

BAILLIE, George (1664–1738) of Jerviswood, Lanark. and Mellerstain, Berwicks.

SCOTLAND 1707–1708
BERWICKSHIRE 1708–1734

b. 16 Mar. 1664, 1st s. of Robert Baillie of Jerviswood by Rachel, da. of Sir Archibald Johnston of Warriston, Edinburgh, Ld. Warriston SCJ and in Cromwellian Parl., sis. of James Johnston*. *educ.* Franeker 1682. *m.* 17 Sept. 1691, Grisell (*d.* 1746), da. of Sir Patrick Hume, 1st Earl of Marchmont [S], 1s. 2da. *suc.* fa. 1684, to estates 28 June 1690.¹

MP [S] Berwickshire 1691–1701, Lanarkshire 1702–7.
Burgess, Edinburgh 1692, Canongate 1693, Dumbarton 1697.²
Receiver gen. [S] 1693–1701; treasurer depute [S] 1704–5; PC [S] 1704, 1707; commr. treasury [S] 1704–7, exchequer [S] 1707, Equivalent [S] 1707–9; ld. of Trade 1710–12, of Admiralty 1714–17, of Treasury 1717–25.
Dir. Co. of Scotland 1696, Bank of Scotland 1699; extraord. dir. R. Bank of Scotland 1727–30.³

The Baillies became landed proprietors in the 17th century, when Baillie's grandfather, a prosperous

Edinburgh merchant, purchased the estate of Jerviswood in 1631 and that of Mellerstain 12 years later. In 1684, however, both were forfeited, as a consequence of the execution of Baillie's father on a charge of high treason. A Presbyterian opponent of the Restoration regime in Scotland, Robert Baillie had been arrested in 1683 under suspicion of involvement in the Rye House Plot. Before departing for the safety of Holland, Baillie visited the family estates, where 'his tenants out of great love to him, and to the memory of his father, most generously paid him up all the rents that were resting in their hands, and also advanced him half a year's rent, though they had then another master, the Duke of Gordon, to whom the estate was given'. The traumatic events surrounding his father's execution had a profound effect on Baillie's character, giving a 'grave, silent, thoughtful turn to his temper which before that time was not natural to him'. He was not embittered by his misfortunes, for having been, as he expressed it, 'bred in the school of affliction' he was convinced of 'both the reasonableness and necessity of showing mercy to others in the like circumstances'. Such sentiments stemmed from religious conviction, which was central to Baillie's character. Without unnecessary ostentation, he maintained a rigorous spiritual discipline, even during the hustle of political life. His personal integrity was acknowledged by opponents: the Jacobite George Lockhart* described him as 'morose, proud, and severe, but of a profound solid judgment'.[4]

Baillie resided in Holland from 1684 until the Revolution, when he returned with William of Orange's army and was thereafter restored to his inheritance. During his exile, Baillie had become closely involved with the family of Sir Patrick Hume of Polwarth, one of his father's associates, who had himself only narrowly escaped capture. Baillie became the boon companion of Hume's eldest son and fell in love with his daughter, Grisell. At the Revolution, she rejected an offer from the Princess of Orange to become a maid of honour, preferring to return to Scotland to be near Baillie. Her father initially entertained some doubts about the match, but soon altered his opinion and thoroughly endorsed the marriage. It proved a happy union, distinguished by deep affection and mutual confidence. During Baillie's absences in England, she fulfilled a vital role as conduit of sensitive information to his political associates in Scotland.[5]

Baillie's parliamentary career began in 1691, when he was returned for Berwickshire, in place of his father-in-law, who had recently been created Lord Polwarth. He did not commence attendance, however, until 1693, at which time he was also appointed receiver-general and nominated to the commission for building kirks. Thereafter he attended regularly and acted with his father-in-law, who was appointed lord chancellor in 1696 and raised to the earldom of Marchmont in 1697. The following year, however, marked a temporary split between them, with Marchmont deciding to remain in office under Queensberry, despite the removal of Tullibardine. Although Baillie was absent during the parliamentary session of 1698, upon his return he demonstrated that he was not prepared to support the Court simply because Marchmont remained in office. Baillie endorsed the Country party's attack over the mismanagement of the Darien affair, and as a director of the Company of Scotland, with a personal investment of £1,000, had ample grounds for dissatisfaction. During the sessions of 1700 and 1701, he voted consistently against the Court, and was consequently dismissed from office. From 1702 he was re-united with Marchmont, who was himself removed from the chancellorship shortly after the accession of Queen Anne. In the Scottish election of 1702 Baillie was returned, on a Country platform, for both Berwickshire and Lanarkshire, opting to sit for the latter.[6]

Baillie remained in the Country party until the split of 1704, in which he played a leading role. Following secret negotiations, a new system for managing Scotland was devised under the aegis of Lord Chancellor Seafield, involving co-operation between sections of the Court and Country parties. This system rapidly proved unworkable, and Baillie held office as treasurer-depute for only a few months. Out of this failed political experiment, however, the Squadrone emerged as an enduring connexion and Baillie became one of its leading lights. He helped mastermind Squadrone tactics over the Union, which involved a double game of supporting the wishes of the English Court by voting in favour of the Union itself, while continuing to oppose on selected subsidiary questions. These tactics were directed towards the twin objectives of securing the Hanoverian succession via the Union, while continuing to aim at the future reduction of Queensberry's domination of Scottish patronage. One of the questions upon which the Squadrone had opposed the Court was the disposal of the Equivalent, and Baillie was appointed to the Scottish committee overseeing its calculation. He was therefore a natural choice for the commission monitoring the disposal of the money, an appointment which must also be regarded as a placatory gesture from the

Court towards Marchmont. Baillie proved an inactive member, however, declining from the outset to become involved, and was quietly dropped when the commission was later reduced in size.[7]

The prominent role which Baillie had played in the Union debates ensured his selection among the Squadrone representatives to the first Parliament of Great Britain, but at one stage it appeared that ill-health would prevent his attendance. Indeed, it is probable that his participation in Scottish parliamentary affairs had also been disrupted by illness, for he was absent for no obvious political reason from more than half a dozen divisions. At the end of August 1707 his wife reported that he had 'recovered from a dangerous illness', but was 'now so deaf that he cannot converse with anybody' and, in mid-September, noted that 'his deafness increases daily' and that it was 'long since he laid aside thoughts of going to London'. The cause of this complaint has not been ascertained, but the condition was chronic, sometimes so severe as to incapacitate him completely. Yet, the personal accounts of debates which Baillie regularly transmitted from London to Scotland demonstrate that he enjoyed periods of good hearing and, even when suffering an attack, could usually find ways of circumventing his disability. Deafness did not seem to impair his confidence as a debater, and may, paradoxically, have been a contributory factor in his 'grave and weighty manner of speaking'. He had recovered sufficiently to take his seat for the beginning of the session and on 4 Dec. was appointed to the drafting committee for a bill to repeal the Scottish act of security. He was a frequent contributor to debate, and often assumed a leading role on Scottish affairs. On 29 Nov. 1707 he had opened the Squadrone attack upon the Scottish privy council, arguing that 'now since we are one people, our administration of government should be one'. He also pointed out that the council merited abolition on libertarian grounds. According to the contemporary historian Cunningham, Baillie 'eloquently and briefly exposed the immoderate power of the privy council in former times, the vigorous exercise of their authority, and what dreadful examples they had exhibited of all sorts of cruelties'. This line of argument was lent additional force by the well-known history of his father's execution. In the debate of 11 Dec., upon the report of the committee of the whole, Baillie once more spoke first in the debate and was first-named to the drafting committee for a bill to complete the Union. The Squadrone's enthusiasm for abolishing the council stemmed from the fact that it was an instrument of Queensberryite rule, both for its executive powers and electoral influence. With regard to the latter, Baillie played an important role in successfully countering a rearguard action by the Court to preserve the council until after the next election. He also supported the Squadrone attempt to unify the powers of j.p.s throughout Britain, though this was inevitably regarded as an attack upon the heritable jurisdictions which were protected by the 14th article of the Union. Baillie believed that Parliament had the power to 'explain the articles', but the Squadrone's controversial move alienated some former supporters of the bill for completing the Union. There was therefore some justice in the assessment of James Vernon I* that Baillie was 'a zealous promoter of reducing all to conformity with England, supposing everything practicable, and perhaps not enough considering how consistent his schemes may be with rights and privileges, reserved and made sacred by the articles of Union'. The interpretation of the articles of Union became a recurrent theme in Anglo-Scottish politics, and with some justification Baillie later came to the opinion that Parliament was 'sometimes for acting as if the two kingdoms were united and sometimes as if they were not so'. Nevertheless, his faith in the importance of the Union, particularly as a bulwark against Jacobitism, remained unshaken.[8]

During the invasion scare of 1708, Baillie supported measures to counter the Jacobite threat, but was unhappy about the means which were adopted, particularly the pre-emptive arrest of the Duke of Hamilton, the nominal head of the Scottish cavaliers. Following the duke's transportation to London, Baillie supported the combined Junto–Squadrone efforts to secure his release in return for an electoral pact. Although undoubtedly aware that many of Hamilton's followers were Jacobites, Baillie thought political co-operation was defensible, despite the fact that the association appeared to some as a 'Devil's compact'. There was a respectable precedent in their joint endeavours in the Scottish Country party before the Union, and both Hamilton and Baillie shared an abiding antipathy to Queensberry and the old Court party. Moreover, in both the Commons and peerage elections, Hamilton's influence would be of great use, particularly in the latter, where Squadrone peers were at risk of being entirely excluded. During the 1708 election, Baillie himself derived only marginal benefits from the pact. His election for Berwickshire was no doubt facilitated by Hamilton's support, but Marchmont's position as hereditary sheriff together with Baillie's own standing with the electors were much more significant. The implications of the alliance with the Junto were difficult to assess in the early stages, but the Squadrone clearly expected that their own pretensions to office would be supported by the Whig leaders. So, for example, Baillie's diplomatic skills were employed to encourage the recently dismissed William Bennet* to have faith that the Junto would soon be sufficiently powerful to demand his reinstatement. Moreover, Baillie was to ensure that the propaganda value of Bennet's case was exploited and, if possible, to return early to London to concert tactics for the coming session, for '[the Whig Lords] beg that you may be here a month or six weeks before the Parliament sits down'. Meanwhile, a tasteless rumour circulated in London in mid-July that Baillie might succeed to the office of lord register, 'in consideration that the last hanged his father'.[9]

Upon returning to London, in November 1708, Baillie was confident that 'things are like to turn in favour of the Whigs', but remained uncertain as to 'what influence this will have on Scots affairs'. On 11 Dec. he attended a Junto–Squadrone dinner to discuss parliamentary tactics. According to Rothes' report, Baillie and John Cockburn* (the only Scots Members present) were subjected to something of an inquisition by the Junto, from which they emerged with credit, having demonstrated 'a great deal of heartiness to go thoroughly to work'. On 20 Dec. Baillie was added to the drafting committee for a bill to prevent the embezzlement of shipwrecked goods and on the 23rd was nominated to that for a bill to improve recruitment, the latter being a topic upon which the Junto had laid particular stress at the recent meeting. Although Baillie agreed with the Whigs on major issues of principle, such as the succession, there were limits to his willingness to engage in party politics, particularly with regard to election cases, where he felt torn between the necessity of supporting the Whig cause and his pious expectation that cases would be heard essentially on their merits. On 16 and 18 Dec. he abstained over the Westminster election, in preference to joining almost all of the Scots, who were determined to victimize the sitting Member, a Court Whig, for some disparaging remarks about Scotland. Baillie was not satisfied with the practicalities of co-operating with the Whigs, and disliked the Junto's unwillingness to co-operate on an open and equal footing. He complained to his wife in mid-December that the Squadrone's expectations regarding petitions in the Scottish peerage elections were unlikely to be fulfilled:

[The Court] being resolved to stand by [Scots ministry] . . . I know not if [Whig Lords] have either courage or strength to oppose it . . . [Whig Lords] . . . have not treated [New Party] as might have been expected, after the advances that were made last summer, and all that has passed has had nothing of that frankness as is usual among men upon the same bottom. In short [New Party] is altogether ignorant of what is intended to be done. Whether this proceeds from want of power or from other causes, time must determine . . . Both on [Whig Lords'] part and [Squadrone] there is nothing but complaints of one another, the consequences whereof I dread . . . It is [Baillie's] chief business to keep them [together] . . . T'other day [Baillie] had a free communing with [Somers (Sir John*)] and which, though he thought necessary at this juncture, he could not discern how it took, nor does he [know] what effect it will have . . . Never were men so starved as [Squadrone] is at present, for [Church party] supposing him [sic] to be with [Whig Lords], scarcely pay them civilities; [Court Whigs] treat him after the same manner, and yet [Whig Lords] have no confidence in him and hardly take notice of him. I'm afraid at bottom there is too great a contempt for [Scotland] and that those are best liked who will troll without asking questions. In all the complaints on [Whig Lords'] side, I hear [Baillie] bears a large share of the blame . . . If [Whig Lords] throw off [New Party] you may expect me home in a short time and I doubt not but the rest will take the same course, for if I understand anything they will never come to [union] with [Tories] in opposition to [Whigs], which makes [New Party] case the more hard.

Given the results of the election petitions in the Lords, which produced only token victories in the disqualification of Queensberry's vote (as a British peer) and the seating of the politically unreliable Marquess of Annandale, Baillie's pessimistic forecast appeared accurate. Squadrone hopes were briefly revived by the Junto's efforts to obtain high office for the Duke of Montrose, but Baillie had recognized the inherent dangers in the Junto's strategy, as he later reported to Marchmont: 'they had proposed a third Secretary in order to get Scots business into the Cabinet' and 'were so fond of the thing as not to consider in time what might be the consequences of having a wrong person named'. Baillie's fears that Queensberry would become the unintended beneficiary of the Junto's efforts were justified, and Montrose was offered the lesser office of keeper of the Scottish privy seal. The Squadrone had been outmanoeuvred by the Court and kept in the dark by the Junto, with the result that Montrose and Roxburghe (who was to be made a Privy Councillor) were liable to cause offence whether they accepted or declined. Baillie was disgusted that instead of lending their support to a polite refusal by the Squadrone peers, the Junto unexpectedly swung their weight behind acceptance. Baffled at this sudden reversal, he was convinced that refusal would earn the Squadrone the label at Court of 'impracticable men', whereas acceptance would mortally offend the Duke of Hamilton, who had not even been treated with 'common civility' by the Junto, despite having 'acted most fairly and honestly'. To lose the connexion with Hamilton ('without whom we can signify nothing') would be disastrous not just for the Squadrone, but for the state of parties in general, 'for if we leave the Duke, he will certainly go over to some other side, and if the Treasurer [Sidney Godolphin†] take him up, prove useful to him even against the Whigs'. In the event, Roxburghe and Montrose accepted office. Baillie's mistrust of the Junto had only been confirmed by the circumstances of these appointments, and he came to realize that his own plain-speaking with Somers had been counter-productive. He was reliably informed in January 1709 that Somers deemed him 'an haughty man', who 'would not be satisfied with being eminent in the House of Commons', but aimed 'to be head of a party'. Baillie himself recalled that Somers had been

> uneasy while I talked to him, though I did it with all the softness and discretion I was capable of, 'tis true it was with plainness, which was absolutely necessary, but that they cannot bear and I have reason to believe he did not take it well, for from that time to this I could never meet with him, though I have called often, and I'm not like to be a favourite with any set here, only because I cannot bring myself to go along with everything proposed, particularly in the [Commons] elections, in which there is the greatest injustice done I ever saw; and if a man differs in any one thing, all he does goes for nought, to such a height is party business come. Where it will end God knows.

Baillie's scruples caused some friction with the other Squadrone leaders, and he confided to his wife that because he resisted 'going all lengths' in election cases, Roxburghe and Montrose had begun 'to take umbrage at my way, and to think it does them hurt'. Baillie had therefore threatened to retire to Scotland, but had compromised by feigning illness. 'I have kept to my chamber a week', he reported on 24 Jan. 1709, 'because I could not possibly go along with some things [that] were a-doing in the House of Commons and the opposing of which might have done them [the Junto] hurt. I was forced to pretend sickness, though I was ill only one day.' His absence coincided with Whig triumphs over the Bramber and Abingdon election cases. Baillie was unsure how long he would be able to tolerate the partisan atmosphere at Westminster, and asserted that 'if things do not change beyond expectation, this is like to be my last essay in public business for knavery is predominant here'.[10]

Baillie returned to attendance on 25 Jan. 1709 and three days later took an active part in the committee of the whole on improving the Union, and was appointed on the 29th to draft a bill to standardize treason law throughout Britain. This initiative had been prompted by the failure to convict a group of Stirlingshire lairds, who had been arrested for their suspicious conduct at the time of the attempted Jacobite invasion. Despite the provisions in the Union treaty which safeguarded the Scottish legal system, the ministry decided that it was necessary to strengthen the legal process in Scotland. Baillie's appointment to the drafting committee on this bill did not, however, signify wholehearted approval of this policy. Although evidence is scant, it appears that opposition from Scottish Members killed off the bill in committee. The ministry subsequently decided to reintroduce a similar bill in the Lords. Baillie played a key role in attempts to amend this second treason bill. One modern historian has inferred from the Squadrone's own abortive schemes for radical reform of the courts of session and judiciary, together with their earlier campaign against the Scottish privy council, that a treason bill was 'theoretically in accord' with their principles. In this interpretation the Squadrone are charged with adopting a more or less cynical strategy, designed to prevent a backlash in Scotland, where the bill would inevitably prove unpopular. Baillie's own explanation of his conduct does not accord with this analysis. While his enthusiasm for improving the Union remained unabated, he believed that if it could be demonstrated that Scottish procedure was superior to that of England, then the former should prevail. Although he misjudged the case, he was sincere in believing that as a consequence of the Scots' campaign against the bill, the ministry would 'wish they had not meddled with us, for a spirit is raised that will not be easily laid, and I'm convinced the Commons are so much possessed with the advantages of our form of procedure that sometime or other they will appropriate the same to themselves'. He hoped to preserve the mandatory provision in Scotland that the accused be given advance notice of the names of hostile witnesses. Not only would the unification of treason laws, in Baillie's view, 'break in upon our civil rights', but it also threatened to undermine 'the whole rights of property of Scotland' by amending the penalties of forfeiture. Baillie monitored the progress of the bill through both Houses, and at one stage tried to create procedural delays 'in order to have had the bill cast off for this session'. One consequence of this activity was an unwelcome postponement of his departure for Scotland. He had been appointed on 21 Feb. to a drafting committee for a bill to regulate export-allowances on Scottish fish; yet on the following day began arranging details of his journey home 'some time next month'. On 10 Mar. he voted against the government on a motion criticizing the measures taken during the late invasion scare, explaining to his wife that 'I could not have done otherwise, for by the papers which were laid before the House it appeared to me as clear as sunshine that due care had not been taken of Scotland'. Unfortunately, 'all our friends were on that side of the question I was against, or did leave the House without telling us, so that ten of us were left to join the Tories'. On 11 Mar. the new treason bill was presented to the Lords, and by the 22nd Baillie reluctantly conceded that 'the treason bill has broke my measures, for I cannot leave this [place] till . . . I see what fate it has . . . This vexes me exceedingly.' On 9 Apr. he feared that 'the matter may be drawn out in length by conferences' because the Commons had successfully carried amendments confining forfeitures to the life of the person attainted and for a ten-day notification period for prosecution witnesses. On 19 Apr., and much to Baillie's disappointment, the bill finally passed the Lords with these clauses nullified by a wrecking amendment postponing their implementation.[11]

Baillie's jaundiced view of the current state of politics was confirmed by a conversation with Hon. Sir David Dalrymple, 1st Bt.*, during May in which no hint was given that the Squadrone would be consulted about appointments to vacant legal places. Reporting to Marchmont that the pretensions of the Earl's son, Hon. Sir Andrew Hume*, to a place in the court of session were unlikely even to be considered, he concluded that 'those called the Scottish ministry did in Scots business what they pleased'. Nevertheless, the leading role which Baillie had taken in parliamentary proceedings had made a considerable impression. He was viewed as a valuable recruit, for Lord Coningsby (Thomas*) informed the Lord Treasurer, on 18 June, that of the Squadrone Members 'Baillie is the best speaker'. The Junto also sought a better understanding with Baillie, informing him on Godolphin's authority, that if he would '*freely and heartily enter into measures* . . . care should be taken to show that greater equality was meant for the future by doing something to *distinguish him*'. In some alarm, Roxburghe reported to Montrose, on 30 July, that 'Mr Baillie I find strikes at the words marked'. Montrose therefore attempted to persuade Baillie not to rebuff the offer, writing immediately with his opinion that the offending phrase could 'import no more to an honest man that to enter into honest measures with one's friends . . . if bad measures are proposed no honest man is bound . . . to go into them'. Montrose conceded that it was not 'good to bring in oneself for an example, but if it is to be pardoned in any case at all it may be in this'. Nothing came immediately of this initiative, but Baillie clearly did not offend the ministry by an outright refusal, for at the beginning of the second session he reported that 'when I came here I found the Court and Junto more favourably disposed to the Squadrone than last year, the former with a desire to have in Seafield, the latter from a desire to be rid of Queensberry'. As a result of negotiations that were kept a closely guarded secret, an arrangement was devised whereby the Squadrone would secure the inferior posts in Scotland, while Seafield would replace Queensberry as secretary of state and Hamilton would be 'pleased either by a place of name and show, or by calling him to the House [of Lords] and putting him in the [Privy] Council'. Neither Seafield nor Hamilton was involved in these initial negotiations, but Baillie insisted that the Junto accept 'the *whole* package and not just some parts of it'. In the meantime, the Whig Lords were to 'cajole' Hamilton to prevent him from allying with Queensberry 'for there is a tampering there and he is not so frank with us as formerly'. The Squadrone for their part accepted the Junto's assessment that no major changes could be accomplished safely until after the session. Since the principal objective was to undermine Queensberry's influence at the next election, there was no need to act immediately. Although the 1710 election took place under very different circumstances, Baillie's later conduct towards Hamilton should be understood in the light of his objectives in 1709. There is continuity in his attitude to Hamilton from the original pact of 1708 to the election of 1710. Likewise, Baillie's support of Hamilton's elevation to the British peerage in 1711 is more readily understandable, in view of the Squadrone's original suggestion of securing this dignity for him more than two years previously.[12]

Baillie was nominated, on 18 Jan. 1710, to draft a bill to discharge Scottish freeholders from attendance on lords justices, and was first-named, on 13 Feb., to the second reading committee on the same bill. On 20 Jan. he had been 'almost brought to the bar' during the committee of elections, for derogatory remarks about the manner in which the Roxburghshire election was determined. He voted against the place bill on 4 Feb., reporting that 'all our countrymen were against it, and

I and others that were for it till now were obliged to be on that side because the House refused to receive an order excepting places . . . which were desired to be allowed to sit in the House on the part of Scotland'. Only seven Scottish offices were enumerated, which Baillie thought 'equal to the number of 50 allowed on the part of England', but, owing to a combination of procedural objections and blatant English prejudice, this request was refused. Baillie felt let down by the managers of the bill, who 'had advised us it would be regular enough' to make belated changes to the bill. He did not keep his resentment hidden, for 'when things went as they did, I told this in the House, and that we were little obliged to them who had pretended to be our friends'. Baillie voted for the impeachment of Dr Sacheverell and assiduously attended the trial as a spectator, even to the detriment of his health. He was perplexed by the rumours of ministerial changes which abounded in the wake of the trial, but recognized that the Junto would now be unable to deliver their earlier promises regarding wide-scale changes. Nevertheless, Baillie was a beneficiary of a vacancy in the Board of Trade created by the death of Lord Herbert of Chirbury (Henry*) in January. The appointment did not take place till after the end of the session, but Baillie kissed hands for this office in late April and was formally added to the Board on 12 May. That he accepted office is unsurprising, since this prestigious post carried with it a salary of £1,000 p.a. Meanwhile he continued to promote the Squadrone's plan for co-operating with Hamilton at the next election. According to a third-hand report, Baillie approached Hamilton and 'assured him that he was more his than anybody's, with abundance of more compliments and desired his friendship and protection'. Hamilton agreed to support Baillie's re-election for Berwickshire, and it should be inferred that Baillie also sought some level of co-operation in the peerage elections. The agreement between Hamilton and Baillie over the county election gave rise to a complicated series of manoeuvres at court in September 1710, which stemmed directly from the Earl of Mar's attempts to prevent Baillie's re-election. Although a vigorous challenge was mounted, Baillie was once more returned. Mar was therefore unable to carry out his scheme for removing Baillie from office in favour of one of his own followers, Lord Northesk. In the peerage elections, Mar was more successful, and Baillie's hopes of assistance from Hamilton were dashed. Rather than face a humiliating poll, the Squadrone boycotted the election. The fact that no Squadrone peers were returned to the 1710 Parliament meant that Baillie's importance, particularly as a channel of information, increased. In the electoral analysis of the Duchess of Buccleuch's chaplain Richard Dongworth, Baillie was reckoned a Court Tory, thereby classifying him as one who was 'episcopal or Presbyterian upon occasion, who depend on or are moved by the Court ministers'. Baillie's status as an office-holder, and perhaps his recent electoral agreement with Hamilton, provide the only known grounds upon which such an assessment could have been made. It proved wide of the mark. On all ecclesiastical questions Baillie voted a strict Presbyterian line.[13]

In mid-December 1710 Baillie gave the following account of his daily routine in the new Parliament:

> I like . . . meddling with nothing but which is my proper business and do see very few company which I'm pleased with at present . . . I get up about eight, make a visit or two at most, not having time for more. Go to the Board [of Trade] at ten, from that to the House before one, after it rises home to dinner and never go abroad again unless it be to the committee of elections, and that but seldom. To bed about eleven and so round, if I'm not invited to dinner as I was most part last week.

One reason for his restricted social life was his peculiar status in the ministry of Robert Harley*. 'I have seen [Somers] and [Godolphin]', he informed his wife, 'who were exceeding kind, but have not been able to get discourse of [Harley], though I have attempted it.' He also reported that the Whigs in the Commons seemed 'to be jealous of me, and [Tories] there do not take notice of me, and few or none of my former friends have called to see me'. He was consequently unsure of what might happen in the near future. Although aware that 'some late attempts have been made against me', he had not sought a personal interview with the Queen 'upon pretence of my deafness, for it is so nice a point that the thought of it frightens me'. Even if he were to pay his respects at court, he remained convinced that 'this will not do without a hearty concurrence with the measures of [English ministry]'. He was naturally concerned about any attack upon Godolphin and the late ministry, but was 'resolved to do whatever I think right'. Baillie correctly perceived that it was Harley's intention to maintain a 'moderate party' and 'to have [Tories] rest satisfied with promises till the session is over that he may keep the Whigs in heart in order to balance the other'. On 21 Dec. Baillie voted in the minority against the committal of the place bill, 'being resolved to be against the bill, unless stronger reasons be given for it than any I have yet heard'. He therefore deemed it proper to oppose the bill at this early stage, and was convinced 'that many that were for it will be against the bill at long run'. On 18 Jan. 1711, in a letter to Montrose, he owned himself 'entirely ignorant, no body thinking it worth their while to speak to him, which makes him both easy and honest'.[14]

The record of Baillie's parliamentary activity in the Journals largely reflects his duties and interests as a lord of Trade. On 6 Mar. he presented papers to the House, relating to African trade; on 14 Mar. he was appointed to draft a bill to encourage naval stores; and on 8 May was nominated to a conference committee on a Lords' amendment to a bill preserving pine trees in America. He also paid particular attention to fiscal measures which would adversely affect Scottish interests. On 3 Mar. he had reported that, owing to his own intervention, the leather tax had been 'rectified on the particulars of most consequence to us . . . it is now put upon the weight and might have been rectified as to all if it had not been for the too great zeal of our people'. He regretted that some of the Scots Members had interfered with parts of the bill which had no bearing on Scotland, with the result that 'this made the House so impatient that they would not bear with reasoning'. Baillie himself had adopted a more subtle approach: 'before the report was made I had spoke to some of those who had the direction of that matter, which had a good effect'. His arguments therefore received a favourable hearing. Baillie asserted that, since foreign leather was to be taxed by weight, home-produced leather would in some cases be liable to a higher duty: 'the consequence of which would be a great discouragement to if not the utter ruin of the leather manufacture of Britain'. His efforts proved in vain, however, for the leather duty was rejected, on 26 Mar., with a projected loss of revenue of £120,000. This money 'with some other taxes already voted but not appropriated', Baillie thought, 'would have gone near to have raised the money yet wanting for this year's service'. According to the rules of procedure, the same tax could not be reintroduced in the same session. Therefore the wording was altered to a duty on 'all skins and hides'. Baillie realized that such a tax, though similar to the previous proposal, would be 'heavy upon our country, if the quota of the duty is made high' and consequently expected to be 'blamed for going into it'. He nevertheless supported the tax, being determined to 'prefer the public interest to the private concern of any corner of the country'. Since most of the funds were already engaged, and the alternative tax proposals were 'new and uncertain', this tax was necessary, and any failure of supply was equivalent to 'yielding the cudgel to our enemies'. On 29 Mar. he admitted privately that 'I begin to repent at most of the part I acted in it; for the House this day laid the tax so high . . . that it will be to us an unsupportable burden'. No regard was paid to 'the difference between the largeness of their skins and ours by which we shall be liable in payment of double yea triple to what they are liable'. Baillie therefore spoke in favour of apportioning the tax 'upon all sorts of skins and hides by the value and weight, as it is done in some cases', but felt that this line of argument was 'not much noticed, which made me speak only once'.[15]

Baillie also resented the poor treatment which the Scottish linen industry received at the hands of Parliament. During late January 1711 he had spoken in the committee of ways and means against the export duty on British linen:

> urging that besides the bad effects in general of imposing burdens on the native produce and manufacture of any country, this tax in a particular manner affected Scotland; for though little or no linen cloth was manufactured in and exported from England; and it was a wise and constant maxim never to impose any duty on English woollen cloth, it was equally just and to be expected that the Scots linen cloth, now that the two kingdoms were united, would meet with the same encouragement.

As a result of pressure from Scots Members, a clause was added to the supply bill, explaining the linen duty. This did not exempt Scottish linen, but rather imposed the full duty of 6d. only on linen of 40 ells, and allowed for the shorter lengths (which were common in Scotland) to pay a reduced duty *pro rata*. The Scottish linen industry was therefore already a controversial topic, prior to the introduction, on 7 Apr., of a bill for its further regulation. This measure had been designed to encourage Scotland's only real alternative to the woollen industry, which had been adversely affected by the Union. Among its provisions was a clause confirming the Scottish parliament's legislation, banning the export of flax and linen yarn to Ireland. Baillie had been unsure whether in the current climate it was wise to introduce such a bill, but defended it once it came before the Commons. He countered English arguments that it was unnecessary to reiterate the prohibition on exports to Ireland, by stating that it was standard parliamentary practice 'to revive and confirm old standing laws'. Nevertheless, when the bill returned from the Lords on 2 June, not only had the clause relating to exports been removed, but additional benefits had been accorded to the Irish linen industry. 'If these amendments are agreed to', he lamented, then all the advantage we had proposed by the Union to the linen trade of Scotland will be lost, for Ireland must carry it from us. We pay a duty upon exported linen, they pay none; besides they can work cheaper and, if they are allowed to buy up our flax and yarn, we shall have nothing to make linen of.

Baillie therefore directed his energies towards delaying tactics and was relieved that the lateness of the session prevented the passage of the bill. Perhaps the most worrying development was that the Junto had played a leading role in securing the detrimental amendments in the Lords. Baillie thought that 'if it had been for nothing else but their account, Scotland ought to have been treated by them more favourably. What the meaning of this can be I'm not able to guess unless it be that [Whig Lords] are weary of the Union'.[16]

Another alarming episode for Baillie and other Scottish supporters of the Union occurred towards the end of the session. On 9 May 1711 William Lowndes introduced a clause to the lottery bill, which proposed an alteration in the priority accorded to the payment of official salaries in Scotland over that of drawbacks and premiums on trade. Since Scotland had no right to English revenue for paying either drawbacks or premiums, the introduction of this clause (without prior notice in a thin House) was viewed suspiciously by the Scots Members. Although Baillie had not been present when the clause was first read, he played a prominent role in the subsequent Scottish attack upon it, arguing that as a consequence of the Union, 'the civil list of Scotland as well as that of England became part of the civil list of Great Britain, and that both should be upon the same footing'. He further observed that 'this clause tended to make a distinction, which on other occasions, where taxes were to be raised, was carefully avoided'. To enact such a clause 'was as much to say that if there should happen to be no produce of the customs of Scotland, or at least not sufficient for the ends, that country was to be deserted and no courts nor government maintained in it, or no drawbacks nor premiums to be paid'. Baillie's arguments gradually gained some support from English Members, who came to view the clause as a bad precedent, since drawbacks were a means whereby merchants received back their own property. If drawbacks were not paid, then Scottish merchants had no other recourse, whereas unpaid salaries would necessarily become debts on the civil list. As a result, the clause was withdrawn on 1 June. Even so, Baillie did not escape criticism for his conduct. Baillie defended his own actions on the grounds that the objectionable clause had been imperfectly explained. Moreover, the crown had the legal right to dispose of any surplus Scottish revenue in England, therefore 'it was but reasonable that what was deficient for defraying the public expense of Scotland should be supplied from the funds of England'. His justification ended with a plea for future assistance: 'if I was in the wrong', he told his wife, 'you may tell my friend the advocate [Dalrymple], he is to be charged with it for not being here, and I cannot tell how great a penance I would undergo, rather than to have another winter without him'. The session had been a mortifying experience, with successive events making it difficult for Baillie to maintain credibility. On 2 June he explained in a letter home that his recent correspondence had only related some of the reverses and insults which Scotland had suffered, adding that 'you can guess how much this must [fash Baillie], considering how much he was [for Union] and how well he has [stood] by [Whigs]. This may make him lose flesh.'[17]

Further changes took place over the summer which had a profound impact on Anglo-Scottish relations. At the tail end of the session Hamilton was created a British peer, but the trial of his right to sit in the Lords was deferred until after the prorogation. Baillie viewed this tactic by the Court with considerable suspicion and would have preferred Hamilton's right to have been tested immediately. The death of Queensberry in July 1711 also created uncertainty over whether Harley (now Lord Oxford) would renew the third secretaryship of state. It soon became clear that Hamilton's pretensions to succeed Queensberry would not be taken seriously. Baillie maintained a sympathetic but ambivalent attitude towards Hamilton. He was delighted at the original offer of the British dukedom, describing Hamilton as one of his closest friends, but nevertheless regarded his elevation as an unfortunate test case. Baillie confided privately to Montrose that Hamilton was 'certainly the most unfit person to have made the trial upon and therefore I could never think the Court in earnest'. He correctly perceived that the whole episode rapidly became a struggle between finely balanced political forces in the Lords, rather than an impartial determination of the principles involved. The aspect which most upset Baillie was the hostility of the Junto. As early as June, he was aware that the Junto was preparing to oppose Hamilton 'let the consequence be what it will, yea though it should break the Union'. Such an intention was, in Baillie's view, 'so inconsistent with last year's professions, that I shall think . . . [Squadrone] to be [disengaged] and at [liberty] to [act] as prudence directs'. The Hamilton case therefore presented

Baillie, once more, with a political dilemma. On most questions his sympathies lay with the Whigs, but he could not reconcile himself to their short-term political agenda. The Junto wished to prevent the ministry from raising Scottish representative peers to the British peerage and filling vacancies with its own nominees. Baillie not only suffered hostility from the Junto, but was also subject to a concerted campaign from Oxford's Scottish managers, Mar and Dupplin, who devised an attack upon the Squadrone, framed in ostensibly friendly terms. Without any consultation with Baillie, his son-in-law Alexander Murray* was included in the commission of chamberlainry and trade for Scotland. This was politically damaging because the commission was perceived by many as a means of ministerial bribery. Baillie reported to Montrose on 4 Dec. that

> the new commission of trade has lost us credit here, to that degree that I could not have thought it possible in so short a time, for people do not stick to say openly that the peers could not or would not come up till bribed, that those who have not got places are to have money and that the Parliament was prorogued till they should arrive.

Murray's appointment was therefore not respectable and, moreover, made Baillie's own status on the Board of Trade subject to criticism.

> Your friend has his share of contempt upon Mr Murray's being named in the commission, though I knew nothing of it. Yea, I believe it has been done with design to lessen my credit with my friends and to separate Murray from me, if not to make way to turn me out, for now there will be no need of a Scotsman upon the council of trade here; but that I value little in comparison of the way my friends have treated me.

An attack by Oxford's Scottish managers upon Montrose was equally well conceived, comprising an offer of an unsuitable diplomatic post, which was accompanied by disingenuous and contradictory rumours. To the Junto he was represented as a potential defector to the Court, whereas to the Tories his predictable refusal was used to revive the canard that the Squadrone were 'impracticable' men. Baillie therefore had his work cut out to 'set the matter in a true light', and it was against this complex background that he charted his course through the 1711–12 session. He summed up his dilemma thus:

> The Whigs and many of the Tories are to oppose the Duke of Hamilton's patent and I must own that to assist them goes against the grain with me, and yet for one to act from resentment against his country is so mighty a point, is a heavy thing, and what I cannot well think of, and I'm sure we owe no such favour to the ministry.

Baillie resolved this problem, much as he had previously done, by attempting to judge each issue on its merits without feeling constrained either to follow the Whigs in partisan measures, or to seek a closer relationship with the ministry. His greatest disappointment was in the lacklustre performance of the Scottish peers, who not only failed to make a full attendance in support of Hamilton, thereby contributing to his defeat, but also lacked the political willpower to seize 'some proper occasion in some [critical affair] to [break] the [neck] either of [Whig] or [Tory]'. The cause of this pusillanimity was obvious to Baillie: the last election had returned a docile contingent of representative peers, who lacked 'resolution' and were unable 'to resist money'. Baillie naturally viewed the exclusion of the Squadrone peers as a crucial factor in this situation. Despite the shortcomings of the current system, he was hostile to proposals made in the aftermath of the Hamilton case for abolishing peerage elections in favour of hereditary Scottish seats in the Lords. In addition to entertaining constitutional doubts over how such a change could be managed without damaging the Union settlement, Baillie also feared that, in the present political climate, the Squadrone peers might still find themselves excluded, and resolved therefore 'to use my credit to break any measure that must have such a tail'.[18]

In January 1712 Baillie reported to his wife that he was 'almost blind with want of sleep, for I have not been in bed this four nights till three in the morning. It was not debauching but about business, for this is no idle time.' He had assiduously attended the proceedings against Robert Walpole II* and the Duke of Marlborough (John Churchill†), voting against the censure of the latter on 24 Jan. On such questions, he generally followed the Whig line, and had voted on the opening day of the session in favour of 'No Peace without Spain', despite having earlier expressed the opinion that the Whigs went 'too far against the peace' and that it would have 'been better to have made the best of it, since it was to be'. He was also unhappy about Lord Nottingham's (Daniel Finch†) arrangement with the Junto for opposing the peace with the *quid pro quo* of an occasional conformity bill. He was convinced that by 'acting against principles' the Whigs would not simply lose the Dissenting interest, but also 'most of their friends in Scotland'. He did not accept the argument that Whig involvement was primarily designed to prevent a bill 'in worse terms', and thought that the Junto were angling for a new route to power. Scottish opposition to the bill was hamstrung by the fact that the bill might apply solely to England.

Although it could be amended with clauses respecting Scotland, this would inevitably raise the question of toleration for episcopalian clergy. In the early stages of the bill, Baillie mooted certain 'expedients . . . which were thought reasonable' but these were rejected by his Scottish co-adjutors, who thought they would make a toleration act 'unavoidable'. Baillie himself was not fundamentally hostile to toleration for episcopalians, but would have preferred the issue to remain dormant. He disliked religious persecution and thought the Kirk merely damaged its own position by an excessive insistence on its privileges. So, for example, he thought that the hard-line Presbyterians had mismanaged the Greenshields affair and thereby paved the way for legal toleration. Although Baillie disliked the Scottish toleration bill, he adopted a moderate line, speaking against it only as 'unseasonable and ill timed', while saying 'nothing against the thing itself'. On 26 Jan. 1712, he reported that the bill 'goes on apace, our own countrymen are most zealous in it' and that consequently it was necessary 'to make the best of it'. During the committee stage, he supported abortive amendments moved by 'those Scots who favoured Presbyterian government', none of which were 'against the toleration itself, but only to bring the Act as near the Toleration Act of England as was possible, and to make it consistent with the articles of the Union'. When the bill passed the Commons, on 7 Feb., Baillie voted against it without making a speech, owing to 'the heat on the other side' which had been created by Dalrymple's arguments against toleration.

> There was abundance to be said against it . . . But as things went it could not have been done without sharpness, which was not fit. In short, I was against dividing the House upon the question 'agree to the bill or not', for I saw we would make but a sad appearance; and it so happened; for there was only 13 against it, but zeal must carry it and I was obliged to show myself with that small number though contrary to my inclination; I mean of exposing ourselves, for I was really against the bill as it is passed.

The particular failings of the bill, in Baillie's opinion, were the curtailment of the powers of magistrates in enforcing Kirk discipline, and the failure to include a doctrinal test. Baillie did not, however, participate in the manoeuvres by the delegation from the Kirk that secured amendments to the bill in the Lords, although he did approve of these changes, which comprised restrictions on the use of the English liturgy and the reading of banns, and safeguards against intrusion into vacant churches. Particularly controversial was the addition of an abjuration clause. Baillie predicted that not many episcopalians would 'come to take the Abjuration for the uncertainty of meeting house', and noted that 'very few more amendments' would 'have satisfied me perfectly'. He predicted, however, that there would now be further debate on the bill in the Commons, but hoped that even this might be turned to account, by forcing the deferral of the bill for this session. In fact, the Scottish Tories made good use of the abjuration issue to create disarray in Presbyterian ranks.[19]

The clause which had been added to the bill in the Lords required that all Scottish ministers take an abjuration oath, similar (but not identical) to that used in England. The wording differed because some Presbyterians were known to object to swearing an oath in support of the succession 'as limited' by the English Act of Succession. This phrase was deemed 'relative and conditional' and therefore objectionable on theological and practical grounds. The theological argument was that the divine plan with respect to the succession had not yet been revealed and that the oath was therefore impious and presumptive. The practical objection was that the phrase implied thoroughgoing approval of the Act of Succession, including the stipulation that the monarch must be of the Church of England. Presbyterians were therefore being asked to swear to uphold a system of Church government which, in the terms of the Solemn League and Covenant, was inherently sinful. The net effect was that the equality of the two separate Church establishments, as enshrined in the Union, was being undermined. Presbyterians were however prepared to accept an oath which was, in their expression, purely 'narrative and descriptive'. Thus the oath which had been added to the bill in the Lords used the phrase 'which is limited' rather than 'as limited'. The existence of the English Act would thereby be acknowledged, but without creating any theological entanglements. Naturally, the Scottish Tories in the Commons (incensed at the introduction of an abjuration clause but recognizing that it would now be impossible to remove it) settled for rendering the oath as objectionable as possible to Presbyterians. They therefore moved that the oath be amended to bring it into exact conformity with the English one. Baillie found it difficult to explain Presbyterian objections to the phrase 'as limited'. There were two obvious pitfalls. First, to pose as the champion of a superior theology would prompt an Anglican backlash; and, second, to reveal the equivocal stance with regard to the Act of Succession undermined the oath itself. It might well be argued that one form of equivocation was as bad as another, rendering abjuration virtually useless as an anti-Jacobite measure. Baillie himself regarded the Presbyterian objections as 'groundless at best', but attempted, for the sake of harmony within the Kirk, to obtain an oath with the phrasing 'which is limited'. When this question was debated on 21 Feb., Baillie admitted that

> I had great difficulty to bring myself to explain this matter . . . however, I thought it necessary to say something, but it was not much, for it could bear no other argument save that of being upon a toleration it seemed reasonable to indulge the regular clergy in their scruple, since the security to the government and the Protestant succession was not in the least weakened by the Lords' amendment of the oath.

Not surprisingly, he found that such an approach 'signified little' and the offensive wording 'as limited' was included in the resultant Toleration Act. Baillie continued to be active in finding ways to make the oath acceptable to Presbyterians, the first priority being to secure time for the Kirk to consider its position. He managed a bill to extend the time-limit before the Toleration Act came into force, chairing a committee of the whole on 13 June, from which he reported the following day, carrying up the bill on the 16th. Baillie was later active in a commission appointed by the Kirk to examine this issue. He denounced non-jurors as schismatic and

> denied the design of the [Toleration] Act was to establish the Church of England, except insofar as it was established by the Protestant succession, and that was only . . . as a body of Protestants, and no further . . . The oath now came upon us upon another foot, viz. the Union, wherein our reserved rights were secured.[20]

As a Presbyterian, Baillie had also opposed the bill restoring lay patronage in Scotland. He spoke against the introduction of the bill on 13 Mar. 1712 and repeated his objections at the committal stage on the 29th. On the latter occasion he was the principal speaker against the measure, being 'forced to take more upon him than fell to his share' on account of the absence on legal business of Dalrymple. Baillie also continued to maintain a watchful eye on tax proposals which were unfair to Scotland, and joined in the opposition to the paper duty in April and May. He agreed with his fellow Scots that the proposed duties breached the proportion of taxes established by the Union, but refused to countenance Lockhart's suggestion that they either unite in opposition to the Court on every issue, or 'leave the House in a body'. Baillie argued that he could not join a secession 'without the concurrence of his constituents'. Lockhart simply replied that Baillie 'had done worse', referring to his conduct at the time of the Union. Without a secession, however, sufficient pressure was placed on the ministry to have 'several of the gravaminous things' dropped. Baillie's moderating influence on this occasion presaged his reaction to the crisis over the Union in the following session. Over the question of the war, he continued to vote with the Whigs, but remained unhappy about their tactical approach. He believed, for example, that the motion criticizing Ormond's restraining orders, on 28 May, was 'ill-timed and worse managed', for the paltry minority revealed the weakness of opposition and provided an opportunity for the ministry to carry its own address without difficulty. Baillie thought that 'the question might have been dropped, which would . . . have answered the one proposed better than what has happened'. He subsequently noted, on 7 June, that there was a 'profound silence' on the address thanking the Queen for communicating the peace terms because 'those gentlemen who had made a bustle all summer were unwilling to expose their numbers, for the vote would have gone against them by a great majority'.[21]

Baillie's opposition to the peace, together with the increasing influence of the Tories over the ministry, meant that he was a marked man. His removal from the Board of Trade was rumoured in late April, and he was duly dismissed after the end of the session. He was pessimistic about the future prospects of the Squadrone, describing the party in late June as 'quite forgot, if not despised'. Some comfort was derived from the appointment of Seafield (now Earl of Findlater) to a vacancy in the Scottish representative peerage, and Baillie wrote to the leading Squadrone peers encouraging them to 'fall in frankly with the measure'. He argued that this appointment 'must work a change that may turn to account', since Findlater was neither ill-disposed towards the Squadrone, nor firmly connected to either of the existing camps within the Scottish Court interest.[22]

Baillie spent the recess in Scotland, returning to London in January 1713. His journey south had been difficult because of the poor state of his health. Frustrated with waiting in London for the session to commence, he therefore decided to take a cure at Bath, spending a fortnight there from 21 Feb., but making sure that he was back for the first day of parliamentary business. The trip, from a medical point of view, had been a waste of time, for he reported on 9 Apr. that 'I am next to stone-deaf, in so much that I heard nothing so as to report what passed in the House this day'. The main question which occupied his attention was the imposition of the malt tax on Scotland, which was voted in a committee of the whole on 11 May. He gave little credence to reports that 'it will yet be modified as to Scotland... that we shall be obliged to pay less upon the same quantity of malt'. These proceedings had taken him slightly by surprise, for according to his own understanding of parliamentary procedure, another tax should have been considered prior to that on malt. As a consequence, his letters to his constituents alerting them of the likelihood of the tax were sent too late and arrived only after the event. In any case, he did not endorse the idea of consulting his constituents and was opposed to any idea of 'positive instructions' from them. He had consented to write only because he was being criticized by the Scots at Westminster for having failed to do so. Baillie considered that the defeat over the malt tax was partly a result of mismanagement. Some Scots had favoured 'joining with the Members of England who are against it', whereas others suggested 'offering an equivalent of two months' cess on the part of Scotland'. Baillie had objected to the strategy of offering any concession at the outset, deeming it 'most consistent with the article of Union settling our land tax proportionally to that of England, which if once broke in upon, especially from choice, no body knows how far it may be pushed on other occasions'. As befitted his character, he had favoured going 'squarely to work, though it should be lost this year, we may have a hit for it the next year'. Between this initial defeat and the subsequent passage of the tax, Baillie attempted to mitigate its effect by proposing a reduced duty for Scotland, and, when this failed, a deferral of the tax until the peace with France was ratified. He even supported an attempt to tack the place bill to the malt tax, not so much to support the former, as fatally to compromise the latter. Throughout these proceedings he felt that 'the Whigs have dealt basely with us', either by leaving the House or voting against the Scots. His familiar dilemma reappeared: the conduct of the Whigs 'is very hard on us who have gone along with them; to the prejudice of our probable interest at home if we leave them not; and yet how can that be done, in other matters, while we think them in the right'. He was disgusted at the hostile manner in which parliamentary procedure had been utilized against the Scots, and, by the time the bill passed the Commons on 22 May, described himself as 'so tired out... more with vexation than with toil'. A week later he was convinced of 'a dismal prospect... whether the Union is broke or continued, both must bring ruin on Scotland. Which of them will do it soonest or most effectually I cannot say.' He began, however, quietly to exert his influence, restraining one unnamed friend (probably Cockburn), 'who has talked so wildly to me upon it that I have been forced to check him'. Baillie subtly undermined the campaign to dissolve the Union. As one hostile observer expressed it, he was 'full of shifts'. These tactics included a disingenuous proposal, in a meeting of Scottish representatives on 26 May, 'not to advance too far until they knew the minds of their constituents', a suggestion which drew the expected riposte from Lockhart that 'the minds of their constituents were not asked in the making of the Union, and there was no need of asking it to dissolve it'. Having failed in his strategy of deferring any immediate action, Baillie then sought, on 27 May, to fracture Scottish unity by resisting a proposal that 'the Scots should as one man oppose every party in everything that would not come up with them to break the Union'. He refused point blank 'to give up his conscience', shunning with horror the idea of doing 'evil that good might come of it'. Baillie's prevarication thereby provided a respectable cover under which others chose to depart from collective action. Privately, Baillie admitted that though his declaration was 'honest in itself', he had 'other reasons for it, which were not fit to be mentioned at the meeting'. He realized that an effective attack on the ministry by the Scottish peers might prompt the Court to favour 'dissolving the Union... in order to be rid of them'. This would adversely affect the Squadrone, since the sitting peers would perhaps gain the approval of the Junto. Instead, it was far better to provide a rationale for some peers to remain loyal to the ministry, so that 'the Squadrone might have the means to ruin their credit at [the] next election, by laying the blame upon them for the failing of the dissolution, and at the same time might keep their own ground with the Whigs'. He was therefore greatly relieved at the subsequent fiasco in the Lords on 1 June over the motion to dissolve the Union.[23]

Baillie now turned his attention to the French commerce bill, speaking against the bill on 4 June, when his contribution was 'longer than... my custom, but the thing required it'. He also spoke against the engrossment of the bill on the 18th. The surviving drafts of his speeches reveal both his detailed knowledge of the tariffs and his close analysis of key clauses. His masterly exposition of these facts lent weight to his rebuttal of the government's argument that any consequent loss of revenue could be met by raising higher duties on other nations. Baillie maintained that

> the French have secured against [this] by the words... *exigitur et exigitur*, which plainly determines that no greater duties shall be paid by the French than is now

payable by other nations in goods of the same kind . . . We are tied down, for the duties presently payable by other nations is made the rule with respect to France, so that you cannot exceed them without a breach of the treaty.

The rejection of the bill he described as an 'unexpected' victory. Contemporary lists note Baillie not only as a speaker in the debate, but classify him as a Whig. Indeed, his problematic relationship with the Whigs was rapidly being resolved by the pressure of events.[24]

Baillie was re-elected without a contest for Berwickshire in 1713, and was listed as a Hanoverian in Lord Polwarth's analysis of Scottish Members. Despite such important events as the death of Hamilton and the political breach between the Duke of Argyll and Oxford, the Squadrone fared no better at the peerage election, and Baillie therefore continued the principal representative of the party at Westminster. Roxburghe informed him on 30 Jan. 1714 that it was 'downright expected' that Baillie should be in London in advance of the opening of Parliament, in order to concert measures with the Whigs, principally concerning the succession. Baillie duly complied with this request. He took a prominent part in defence of Richard Steele, speaking against his expulsion from the House on 18 Mar.

> Your friend took his share and after having endeavoured to justify Steele from the charge . . . mentioned as causes of our danger: the growth of popery in Scotland; the arming of the Jacobites; the late order to seize arms, whereby friends to the government could only suffer; the giving pensions to the heads of clans; and the pamphlets, not only those that were writ against the settlement, but such . . . as seemed to be writ of design to exasperate one part of her Majesty's subjects against the other to make way for the Pretender. He likewise took notice of the power of France . . . [and] our danger from the Pretender continuing at Bar Le Duc, notwithstanding of her Majesty's instances for his removal and upon the strength of his party within the kingdom . . . supposing their number not to be great, yet they were considerable because of their diligence.

He concluded that to expel Steele would be 'a discouragement to the friends of the establishment, and an encouragement to its enemies both abroad and at home, and . . . it might be constructed as a vote against the succession itself, it being against books writ expressly for it'. Despite losing the question, Baillie thought the opinions expressed in debate might have 'good effect' and asked his wife to pass on details of his own speech to Marchmont and Polwarth, 'lest it should be misrepresented'. In early April he complained that his attendance in the House was 'hard labour', but was determined to remain active, and wholeheartedly supported the Whigs over election cases, being resolved not to 'disoblige my friends'. He was not particularly alarmed by reports of divisions within the ministry, deducing that any change could not harm the security of the succession because of widespread diplomatic support and the divisions within Tory ranks on this question. Nevertheless, he conceded that 'matters go backwards and forwards', and that much would depend on the committee on the state of the nation tabled for 15 Apr. He was heartened by proceedings in this committee, being convinced of the wisdom of dividing on a procedural, rather than substantive, motion, for this allowed many Hanoverian Tories to make what amounted to 'an open declaration for the succession'. Two days later, however, in the wake of a Lords address approving all the ministry's actions over the peace, he described himself as 'never more down than at this minute'. When the Commons approved this address without a division on 22 Apr., Baillie conceded that it was 'not prudent' to divide the House, since 'our new friends . . . said nothing in the debate'. This result, he predicted, 'will probably put an end to further struggling this season, unless some new incident happens, or that the treaty of commerce with France be brought in again'. Although he was 'tired of sitting so long in a warm House' and keen to be back in Scotland 'clipping of sheep', he determined to remain at Westminster until the end of the session, unhappy at the thought of anything going awry in his absence. He voted on 12 May for extending the schism bill to cover Catholic education, and later the same month opposed two initiatives by Scottish Tories for the resumption of bishops' rents and the remodelling of the militia. On 19 June he attended the revived committee of elections, in support of the Whig Member in the controverted by-election for Harwich. After the hearing concluded, he fell in 'with some English gentlemen of my acquaintance, who summoned me to drink a bowl of punch, which was done in great sobriety but kept me late . . . This is only the second time that I have been in a public house at night since I came here.' He voted against adding a punitive clause to the bill for discharging the Equivalent commissioners on 24 June, despite having been involved in its preparation. On 12 July he departed for Scotland, but, shortly after arriving home, news of the Queen's death prompted him to return to London and attend the brief session during August, remaining in town to present a loyal address from Berwickshire in September.[25]

Baillie was rewarded for his loyalty to the Hanoverian succession with appointment, in October, to the Admiralty Board, transferring in 1717 to the

Treasury. Having been re-elected for Berwickshire in 1715, he continued to represent the county until 1734, though he was removed from office in 1725, an event which coincided with the Duke of Argyll's purge of the Squadrone. His willingness to leave office had been signalled two years previously, and he now received a pension equal to his salary of £1,600 p.a. Spiritual matters increasingly occupied his attention, for his retirement from Parliament (though partly a result of failing health) was the fulfilment of a vow he had made 'on his first entering business, that if he ever arrived to his grand climacteric, let his health or station be what it would, he would then retire' because 'he had a more immediate call to spend what remained to him in constant devotion'. Following a brief illness, he died 'with a calm serene countenance, and scarce a groan' at Oxford on 6 Aug. 1738, and was buried privately at Mellerstain. One obituarist described Baillie as 'a most zealous patriot, a very able statesman, and a most perfect Christian'; another commented on his 'deportment so full of dignity, and such an uncommon, one may say peculiar strength of thinking and speaking'. According to his daughter, 'he had the most tender and affectionate heart' and was always 'firm and steady in doing what he thought right'.[26]

[1] *Hist. Scot. Parl.* 30; *Album Studiosorum Academiae Franekerensis,* 229; *Scot. Hist. Soc.* ser. 3, xlvii. 217–90. [2] *Scot. Rec. Soc.* lix. 41; lxxxiii. 8; lxxiii. 10. [3] C. A. Malcolm, *Bank of Scotland,* 293; info. from Dr P. W. J. Riley on members of Scot. parl.; N. Munro, *Hist. R. Bank of Scotland,* 405. [4] *Scot. Hist. Soc.* ser. 2, i. pp. ix–xii, xxiii; *DNB* (Baillie, Robert); Lady Murray, *Mems. of George Baillie* (1824), 14–16, 20–22; Burnet, ii. 431–5; *Lockhart Pprs.* i. 95. [5] *Scot. Hist. Soc.* ser. 2, i., pp. xvi–xvii; *DNB* (Baillie, Grisell); *HMC 14th Rep. III,* 121; Murray, 83. [6] *Hist. Scot. Parl.* 30, 353–4; info. from Dr Riley; *Darien Pprs.* (Bannatyne Club, xc), 372; SRO, Ogilvy of Inverquharity mss GD205/31/1/146, Teviot to Bennet, 2 Aug. 1701. [7] Info. from Dr Riley; *HMC 14th Rep. III,* 194; Riley, *Union,* 334; Riley, *Eng. Ministers and Scotland,* 35, 215. [8] Ogilvy mss GD205/33/3/2/5, Grisell Baillie to Bennet, 30 Aug. 1707; Roxburghe mss at Floors Castle, bdle. 739, same to [Countess of Roxburghe], 19 Sept. 1707; Bennet to same, 16 Dec. 1707; Cumbria RO (Carlisle), Lonsdale mss D/Lons/L1/4/stray letters (Wharton), [?Sir Humphrey Mackworth*] to Ld. Wharton (Thomas*), [29 Nov. 1707]; Cunningham, *Hist. GB,* i. 414; ii. 74; Atholl mss at Blair Castle, box 45, bdle. 7, nos. 193, 198, Yester to Tullibardine, 7 Dec. 1707, James Murray to [Atholl], 15 Dec. 1707; W. A. Speck, *Birth of Britain,* 126; *Vernon–Shrewsbury Letters,* iii. 284; *Lockhart Pprs.* 335–6. [9] Riley, *Eng. Ministers,* 104–5; *Baillie Corresp.* 192–6; Ogilvy mss GD205/33/3/27, Baillie to Bennet, 29 July 1708; GD205/36/2, Grey Neville* to same, 11 July 1708. [10] Haddington mss at Mellerstain, 3, Baillie to wife, 13, 20 Nov., 18 Dec. 1708, 24 Jan. [1709] (Jones trans.); NLS, ms 14415, ff. 168–9; Ogilvy mss GD205/34/4, John Pringle* to Bennet, 18 Dec. 1708; SRO, Montrose mss GD220/5/804/2a, Mungo Graham* to [Montrose], 5 Jan. 1709; SRO, Hume of Marchmont mss GD158/1117/4, Baillie to Marchmont, 6 Feb. 1709. [11] Riley, *Eng. Ministers,* 119; Haddington mss, 3, Baillie to wife, 12 Mar. [1709], 19, 22, 24, 26, 29, 31, Mar., 5, 9, 7, 12, 14, 16, 19 Apr. 1709 (Jones trans.); *Nicolson Diaries* ed. Jones and Holmes, 493; Montrose mss GD220/5/203, Baillie to Montrose, 9 Apr. 1709; Speck, 155–6. [12] Hume of Marchmont mss GD158/1117/2, 3, Baillie to Marchmont, 1 June, 24 Dec. 1709; Add. 28055, f. 426; Montrose mss GD220/5/206/2, Roxburghe to Montrose, 30 July 1709. [13] NLS, ms 7021, f. 199; Haddington mss, 3, Baillie to wife, 4 Feb., 7, 9, 14, 16, 18 Mar. 1709[–10] (Jones trans.); *Scots Courant,* 28 Apr.–1 May 1710; SRO, Mar and Kellie mss GD124/15/975/19, Mar to Ld. Grange (Hon. James Erskine†), 14 Sept. 1710; Add. 70048, same to Robert Harley, 25 Aug. 1710; 70049, same to same, 8 Oct. [1710]; *HMC Portland,* x. 328–9; D. Szechi, *Jacobitism and Tory Pol.* 204–5; *SHR,* lx. 65. [14] Haddington mss, 4, Baillie to wife, 3, 19, 21 Dec. 1711 (Jones trans.); Montrose mss GD220/5/2/256/1, same to Montrose, 18 Jan. 1711. [15] Haddington mss, 4, Baillie to wife, 3, 27, 29 Mar. 1711 (Jones trans.). [16] *Lockhart Pprs.* 325–9; *Scot. Hist. Soc. Misc.* xii. 137; Haddington mss, 4, Baillie to wife, 2, 5, 9, 19 June 1711 (Jones trans.). [17] *Lockhart Pprs.* 335–6; Haddington mss, 4, Baillie to wife, 2, 14 June 1711 (Jones trans.). [18] Haddington mss, 4, Baillie to wife, 2 June 1711, same to Montrose, 4, 31 Dec. 1711, 19 Jan. 1711–12 (Jones trans.); *HMC 14th Rep III,* 172; Montrose mss GD220/5/256/6, 7, 8, Baillie to Montrose, 7, 12, 14 June 1712. [19] Haddington mss, 3, Baillie to Montrose, 16, 18 Feb. 1709[–10], 5, same to wife, 13 Nov., 13 Dec. 1711, 29 Jan., 2, 7 Feb. 1711–12 (Jones trans.); Montrose mss GD220/5/268/6, Baillie to Montrose, 26 Jan. 1711–12. [20] *Lockhart Pprs.* 381–2; Haddington mss, 5, Baillie to Montrose, 21 Feb. 1712 (Jones trans.); Wodrow, *Analecta,* ii. 93, 122. [21] Haddington mss, 5, Baillie to wife, 13, 29 Mar. 1712 (Jones trans.); Wodrow, 45; Montrose mss GD220/5/268/14, 15, Baillie to Montrose, 29 May, 7 June 1712. [22] BL, Trumbull Alphab. mss 54, Ralph Bridges to Sir William Trumbull*, 25 Apr. 1712; Haddington mss, 5, Baillie to Montrose, 1 July 1712, same to Tweeddale, 3 July 1712, same to Roxburghe, 4 July 1712 (Jones trans.). [23] Haddington mss, 5, Baillie to wife, n.d., 7 Jan., 10, 21 Feb., 9 Apr., 21, 28 May 1713, misc. pprs. 1/384, memo. [1713] (Jones trans.); *HMC Polwarth,* i. 7–9; *Scot. Hist. Soc. Misc.* xii. 153; *Lockhart Letters* ed. Szechi, 76, 80. [24] *Parlty. Hist.* i. 69; Haddington mss, 5, Baillie to wife, 4, 20 June 1713, misc. pprs. 1/359, draft speeches, [1713] (Jones trans.). [25] Haddington mss, 6, Baillie to wife, n.d., 20 Mar., 1, 3, 10, 17, 22, Apr., 22 May, 19 June, 10 July 1714, Roxburghe to Baillie, 30 Jan. 1714 (Jones trans.); *Lockhart Letters,* 106–8; NLS, Advocates' mss, Wodrow pprs. letters Quarto, 8, f. 144; *Flying Post,* 12–14 Aug., 28–30 Sept. 1714. [26] *HMC Polwarth,* 286; Add. 36125, f. 303; Murray, 3–6, 25–27, appendix, 'Character of Baillie'; BL, Dept. of Printed Bks. 1878.d.12 (24).

D. W.

BAKER, George (*d.* 1723), of Crook Hall and Elemore in Lanchester, co. Dur.

DURHAM 1713–1722

o. s. of George Baker of Crook Hall by Elizabeth, da. and h. of Samuel Davison of Wingate Grange, co. Dur. *m.* bef. 1713, Elizabeth, da. and coh. of Thomas Conyers*, 2s. (1 *d.v.p.*) 2da. (1 *d.v.p.*). *suc.* fa. 1699.[1]

Baker was the great-grandson of Sir George Baker, the recorder of Newcastle who had held the town for the Royalists and suffered severe losses during the Civil War. His father was a benefactor of St. John's College, Cambridge, and his uncle Thomas Baker, the celebrated antiquary, was a non-juror who found refuge at St. John's until being ejected for refusing to take the oaths to George I. Rather surprisingly, however, Baker himself was sent neither to Durham school nor to Cambridge, unlike the rest of his family. Returned unopposed for Durham in 1713, in partnership with his father-in-law Thomas Conyers, he was classed as a Tory in the Worsley list. Baker continued to sit for Durham in the 1715 Parliament but was defeated at the 1722 election. He died, at Bristol, on 1 June the following year, and was buried at Lanchester on the 12th.[2]

[1] Surtees, *Dur.* ii. 357–8. [2] Ibid.

E. C.

BAKER, John (1660–1716), of East Langdon, nr. Deal, Kent.

WEYMOUTH AND
MELCOMBE REGIS   1713–3 June 1714
                           1715–10 Nov. 1716

b. 1660, s. of James Baker of Deal by his w. Elizabeth, afterwards w. (lic. 28 Mar. 1666) of John Brett of Deal, carpenter. *unm.*[1]

Lt. RN 1688, capt. 1691, r.-adm. 1708, v.-adm. 1709.

Shortly after being made a captain Baker was serving in Sir George Rooke's* squadron, which was involved in the loss of the Smyrna convoy in 1693. He spent much of the rest of the war in the Mediterranean, remaining on active service during the peace. After the resumption of hostilities Baker returned to the Mediterranean, where he served in the main fleet at Cadiz and Vigo in 1702, and took part in the capture of Gibraltar and the battle of Malaga in 1704, in which he was wounded, and in the attempt on Toulon in 1707. In the autumn of 1707 he returned to England with the fleet under Sir Clowdesley Shovell*, when several of the ships, including the admiral's, were wrecked off the Scillies. Promoted rear-admiral in February 1708, he served under Sir George Byng* in the fleet that repelled the Jacobite invasion attempt. Early in 1709 he was put in command of an expedition to Port Royal, Newfoundland, but when this was abandoned because of the possibility of peace, he was sent back to the Mediterranean. Later in the year Baker was promoted to vice-admiral, a few days after the appointment of a Whig-dominated Admiralty commission, which included his friend and recent commander, Byng, and the Earl of Orford (Edward Russell*). Baker remained in the Mediterranean until the end of the war, capturing a rich French prize in 1712. With the coming of peace he was ordered to return home and was not given any further command during the Queen's reign.[2]

In 1713 Baker successfully contested Weymouth, voting against the expulsion of Richard Steele on 18 Mar. 1714. In June he was unseated on petition by the Tory majority in the House. Classed as a Whig in the Worsley list and two other comparative analyses of the 1713 and 1715 Parliaments, Baker sat for Weymouth until his death, which took place at Port Mahon on 10 Nov. 1716. He was buried in Westminster Abbey.

[1] *Westminster Abbey Reg.* (Harl. Soc. x), 288. [2] Charnock, *Biographia Navalis*, ii. 379–83; *Byng Pprs.* (Navy Recs. Soc. lxviii), ii. 3–138; *Marlborough–Godolphin Corresp.* 1044, 1269, 1275, 1287, 1319; Luttrell, *Brief Relation*, v. 465; vi. 339, 354, 409, 427, 467, 473, 491, 522, 599; Boyer, *Anne Annals*, vi. 241.

P. W.

BALCH, George (d. 1738), of Bridgwater, Som.

BRIDGWATER   1701 (Feb.)–1710

1st s. of Robert Balch*. *m.* 10 Dec. 1707, Hanna Ludlow (d. c.1730), 3s. *d.v.p.* 1da. *suc.* fa. 1705.[1]

Mayor, Bridgwater 1699–1700, 1708–9, ald. 1709–11.[2]

Like his father, Balch was in business as a 'merchant' and was a prominent member of Bridgwater's corporation. He was also an active member of the town's Dissenting community and a trustee of the Presbyterian Christ Church Chapel. Returned to Parliament in February 1701, he continued to represent the borough until 1710. On 13 Feb. 1703 he voted for agreeing with the Whig Lords' amendments to the bill extending the period in which the oath of abjuration was to be taken, while in October 1704 he was predicted as a likely opponent of the Tack and did not vote for it (or was absent) in the division of 28 Nov. He was otherwise wholly inactive and was regularly granted leave of absence for unspecified periods of time: 28 May 1701, 10 Apr. 1702, 7 Jan. 1703, and 8 Jan. 1704. Classed as 'Low Church' in 1705, he voted for the Court candidate for Speaker on 25 Oct., and was granted leave on 12 Jan. 1706, several of his family having fallen ill. Early in 1708 he was noted as a Whig. In 1709 he voted in favour of naturalizing the Palatines, and in 1710 in favour of the impeachment of Dr Sacheverell, obtaining three weeks' leave on 16 Mar. Despite his long association with Bridgwater, his interest was not sufficient to withstand the Tory attack levelled at him in the 1710 election. After that, his position appears to have gone into decline. He lost his place on the Somerset bench, and it is probable that he joined in the series of resignations from the corporation in the spring of 1712: he was certainly no longer a member of it in 1715. He died in 1738, and in his will, proved on 20 Jan. 1739, left the bulk of his property to his grandson, Robert Balch.[3]

[1] F. Brown, *Som. Wills*, v. 18; IGI, London; PCC 165 Gee, 3 Henchman. [2] A. H. Powell, *Ancient Borough of Bridgwater*, 288, 300; S. G. Jarmon, *Bridgwater*, 271; info. from Dr J. M. Triffitt. [3] Info. from Dr Triffitt; Huntington Lib. Stowe mss 58(6), p. 215; L. K. J. Glassey, *Appt. JPs*, 207; PCC 3 Henchman.

P. W.

BALCH, Robert (c.1651–1705), of Bridgwater, Som.

BRIDGWATER 24 Feb. 1692–1695

b. c.1651, s. of Thomas Balch of Dulverton, Som. *educ*. St. Alban Hall, Oxf. matric. 3 June 1668, aged 16. *m*. 26 Dec. 1678, Elizabeth Everard, 1s. 1da.[1]

Mayor, Bridgwater 1688–9, 1691–2.[2]

Balch set up as a merchant in Bridgwater, becoming a prominent member of the corporation. An active Presbyterian, he was a trustee of Brent's charity, established in the town to provide for the education of Dissenting ministers, and was closely involved in the life of the town meeting-house. Entering Parliament for Bridgwater following a closely contested by-election in February 1692, he was at first classed as 'doubtful', but was later categorized as a Court supporter. A largely inactive Member, his only contribution of note to proceedings was a speech on 10 Feb. 1693 in favour of adding Bridgwater to the list of ports legally able to import wool from Ireland. This undistinguished record was probably due, at least in part, to poor health. He was granted leave of absence on medical grounds twice in his second session, on 21 Jan. and on 15 Feb. 1693, and again on 29 Jan. 1694 and 12 Jan. 1695. He stood down at the 1695 election. The date of his death is not known, but his will was proved on 2 Nov. 1705. He was succeeded by his son, George*.[3]

[1] IGI, Somerset; PCC 165 Gee. [2] S. G. Jarmon, *Bridgwater*, 271. [3] Info. from Dr. J. M. Triffitt; *Luttrell Diary*, 378, 417, 485.

P. W.

BALDWYN, Acton (1681–1727), of Bockleton, Worcs.

LUDLOW 1705–1715, 1722–30 Jan. 1727

b. 27 June 1681, 1st s. of Charles Baldwyn*. *educ*. Balliol, Oxf. 1698; I. Temple 1701. *m*. 17 Oct. 1702, Eleanor, da. and coh. of Sir Charles Skrymsher (*d*.1709), of Norbury, Staffs., *s.p. suc*. fa. 1707.[1]

Freeman and common councilman, Ludlow 1710.[2]

Baldwyn's election in 1705, which was owing primarily to his family's strong interest at Ludlow, supplemented by strenuous efforts of his own, appeared in Lord Sunderland's (Charles, Lord Spencer*) calculations as a gain for the Whigs, but he was classified as a 'Churchman' in a list of the new Parliament, voted against the Court in the division on the Speaker, 25 Oct. 1705, and was classed as a Tory in early 1708. Described, somewhat imaginatively, as a Tacker in an analysis of the 1708 returns, when he stood successfully at Ludlow with Sir Thomas Powys*, he subsequently voted against the impeachment of Dr Sacheverell.[3]

At the 1710 election Baldwyn was at first confident of being re-elected at Ludlow, where his 'behaving himself so well' in the Sacheverell affair had secured his popularity, but was faced with three other candidates, the other outgoing Member, Powys, his own cousin Humphrey Walcot*, and Francis Herbert*, whom he described pejoratively as 'a thorough-paced Whig'. Each stood separately, and in this situation Baldwyn was reluctant to declare himself, only announcing his candidature at the last minute. After vain attempts to persuade 'an honest gentleman' to join with him, he eventually suggested to Robert Harley* (via an intermediary) that the resources of the new ministry be used to prevail upon Walcot to withdraw. When this had been accomplished, and Herbert had also withdrawn, Baldwyn and Powys were returned without effective opposition.[4]

Classed as a Tory in the 'Hanover list', Baldwyn was one of the 'worthy patriots' who in the first session of the 1710 Parliament exposed the mismanagements of the previous ministry and was listed as one of the 'Tory patriots' who opposed the continuance of the war. On 18 June 1713 Baldwyn spoke and voted for the French commerce bill. He was supported by Harley, now Earl of Oxford and Lord Treasurer, in his election in 1713, in which he was involved in a three-cornered contest with two other Tories. Following his heavy expenditure in 1710, some £200 in all, he was 'resolved to spend no money' on this occasion, and held onto his seat by dint of vigorous personal canvassing among the freemen. Perhaps this self-reliance in his constituency enhanced his independence of mind in the Commons: at any rate, he appeared in the Worsley list as a Tory who would sometimes vote with the Whigs.[5]

In February 1715 his brother reported that Baldwyn 'owned to Mr Kingdon and me the other night he had an inclination to be a Whig three months ago, but now seems well convinced he shall not be pleased with their measures'. Even though he had not suffered on his own account in the purge of Tories from central and local office after the Hanoverian succession, being retained on the commission of the peace, he put up as a Tory in the 1715 election. He was defeated then, but recovered the seat again on the Tory interest, in 1722. The previous year a 'Mr Baldwyn' had been included among the Shropshire contingent in the list of 'well-wishers' prepared for the Pretender. Baldwyn died on 30 Jan. 1727.[6]

[1] *Trans. Salop Arch. Soc.* ser. 4, ii. 344–7, 379–80; PCC 58 Farrant; *Top. and Gen.* iii. 269; *VCH Staffs.* iv. 157–8; IGI, Staffs. [2] Salop RO, Ludlow bor. recs. min. bk. 1690–1712. [3] *VCH Salop.* iii. 286–7; Staffs. RO, Aqualate mss, Ludlow poll 1708. [4] Salop RO, Bishop mss, Sir Thomas Powys to Henry Mitton, 29 July 1710; NLW, Ottley mss 2570, 2584, Charles Baldwyn to Adam Ottley, 25 July, 1 Nov. 1710; 2578, Acton Baldwyn to Adam Ottley, Sept. 1710; *VCH Salop*, 287; Huntington Lib. Stowe mss 57(4), p. 133; 58(5), pp. 218–19; 58(6), pp. 254–5; Add. 70263, Salwey Winnington* to Robert Harley, 25 Sept. 1710. [5] Chandler, v. 41; Aqualate mss, list of voters at Ludlow, 1713; Ottley mss 2578, Acton Baldwyn to [Adam Ottley], Sept. 1710; 2441, Charles Baldwyn to Adam Ottley, 21 Aug. 1713; Lincs. AO, Massingberd Mundy mss, Charles Baldwyn to Burrell Massingberd, [c. Sept. 1713]; *VCH Salop*, 287. [6] Ottley mss 1631, Charles Baldwyn to Adam Ottley, 17 Feb. 1714–15; L. K. J. Glassey, *Appt. JPs*, 247–8; Massingberd Mundy mss, Charles Baldwyn to Burrell Massingberd, 4 Jan. 1714[–15]; P. S. Fritz, *Ministers and Jacobitism 1715–45*, 153; *Trans. Salop Arch. Soc.* 347.

D. W. H.

BALDWYN, Charles (c.1652–1707), of Bockleton, Worcs. and Stokesay Castle, Salop.

LUDLOW   1681, 1689–1690, 1695–1698

b. c.1652, 4th but o. surv. s. of Sir Samuel Baldwyn† of Stokesay Castle by Elizabeth, da. of Richard Walcot, merchant, of London; cos. of George Walcot* and Humphrey Walcot*. *educ.* Shrewsbury sch. 1663; Queen's, Oxf. matric. 13 Dec. 1667, aged 15; I. Temple 1665, called 1674. *m.* lic. 11 May 1679, Elizabeth, da. and h. of Nicholas Acton of Bockleton, Worcs., 4s. 1da. *suc.* fa. 1683.[1]

Freeman, Ludlow 1679, common councilman 1681–5, 1690–1701, alderman 1701–*d*., recorder 1704–*d*.; freeman, Much Wenlock 1680; sheriff, Herefs. 1690–1; high steward, Leominster 1691–6; chancellor, dioc. of Hereford 1694–*d*.[2]

Baldwyn's marriage brought him a fortune, but his interest at Ludlow was derived from his own family's property nearby. Both his father and grandfather had sat for Ludlow, and Baldwyn himself, after having stood unsuccessfully in 1679, had been elected there in 1681, probably as an Exclusionist. Certainly he was not included in the Tory corporation named by the charter granted to the borough by James II in 1685. Afterwards he may have been one of the Whigs who 'collaborated' with King James II over the relaxation of the penal laws. He was returned to the Convention in January 1689 at an election held under the old charter, but took no part in the disputes between the rival corporations in 1690–2: he did not stand in the 1690 election, nor did he attend meetings of the common council after the old corporation had resumed the government of the borough in December of that year, nor join other members of the old corporation in signing a petition to the King and Queen for a new charter to re-affirm their authority. He began to appear again as a common councilman only a short time before the general election of 1695, when he was returned, probably with Tory support, in a contest with two Whigs.[3]

Originally marked as 'doubtful' in a forecast for the division on the proposed council of trade in January 1696, he was later reclassified as supporting the opposition, but signed the Association promptly and voted with the ministry in March over fixing the price of guineas at 22s. Baldwyn also reported and carried up four private bills in this session. In the same year he was appointed to the lieutenancy of the adjoining county of Herefordshire.[4]

Next session Baldwyn was a teller three times: on 19 Nov. 1696 against an opposition motion that the House, before going into the committee of ways and means, should first take into consideration the bill to regulate elections; on 17 Dec. against the bill for the relief of creditors; and on 6 Feb. 1697 against a motion to adjourn a debate on a harbour bill so that the House could proceed to the third reading of the bill to restrict the wearing of fabrics from Persia and the East Indies. He had been given a leave of absence on 19 Dec. and in February–March managed a private bill through the Commons from the report stage. In the 1697–8 session, Baldwyn's main task was the management of a bill for the execution of various judgments which had been saved in a clause in the Act of 1689 abolishing the council in the marches. Having been granted leave of absence for 21 days on 18 Mar. 1698, he appeared again in April to report a private bill and carry it up to the Lords.

In the 1698 election Baldwyn did not stand. Instead, he supported one of the Tory candidates, William Gower*, giving evidence on Gower's behalf at the hearing of a petition by the defeated Whig candidate, reported to the House on 1 Mar. 1699. Nor, despite being chosen as recorder of Ludlow in 1704, did he stand again. He left his interest in the borough to his eldest son, Acton Baldwyn, who was returned in 1705 not long after having come of age. Baldwyn died 4 Jan. 1707.[5]

[1] PCC 26 Poley; *London Mar. Lics.* (Harl. Soc. xxvi), 302; *Trans. Salop Arch. Soc.* ser. 2, vii. 34; ser. 4, ii. 135; vi. 64. [2] Salop RO, Ludlow bor. recs. admissions of freemen, min. bk. 1684–90, 1690–1712; Salop RO, Forester mss, copy of Much Wenlock corp. bk.; G. F. Townsend, *Leominster*, 291; *CSP Dom.* 1696, p. 282.

[3] Ludlow bor. recs. min. bk. 1690–1712, copy of petition to William and Mary. [4] *CSP Dom.* 1696, p. 488. [5] Ludlow bor. recs. min. bk. 1690–1712; *Trans. Salop Arch. Soc.* 34.

D. W. H.

BALE, Christopher (d. 1708), of Cathedral Close, Exeter.

EXETER   4 June 1689–1695

1st s. of Paul Bale, fuller, of Exeter by Mary Hooper of Exeter. *m.* (1) Margaret (*d.* 1675), da. of William Bruerton of Heavitree, Devon, 1s. *d.v.p.* 4da.; (2) lic. 21 Feb. 1677, Elizabeth, da. of William Stawell of Herebear, Bickington, Devon, 1s. *suc.* fa. c.1677.[1]

Freeman, Exeter 1675, common councilman 1675–84, alderman 1684–7, Nov. 1688–*d.*, mayor Dec. 1688–9, 1696–7; receiver, city revenues 1683–4; freeman, Salisbury 1681; receiver, land tax, Devon and Cornw. 1691–5.[2]

Bale was a leading member of Exeter's governing merchant class and closely associated with Sir Edward Seymour, 4th Bt.* Restored as a Tory alderman in early November 1688, he joined the then mayor and other aldermen in remaining loyal to James II and refusing to recognize the Prince of Orange's authority when the prince and his army entered Exeter in mid-November, an act of defiance resulting in his brief suspension; nor, in common with other members of the corporation, did he sign Seymour's Exeter association. Although not elected to the Convention until a by-election in June, his name was included in the published 'blacklist' of those who in February had opposed the transfer of the crown. Bale was returned for Exeter, this time unopposed, again with Seymour in the 1690 general election, following which he was classed as a Tory by Lord Carmarthen (Sir Thomas Osborne†) in an analysis of the new House, and in another list as a Court supporter. In December Carmarthen noted Bale as a supporter in anticipation of an attack on him in the Commons. Robert Harley's* list of around April 1691 also classified him as a Court supporter, and on his becoming a receiver of taxes, several later lists noted him as a placeman. This evidence of Bale's pro-Court inclinations is further borne out by his having spoken on 28 Nov. 1691 in favour of the army estimates. As teller on 20 Feb. 1693 he signified his opposition to a motion to enable Plymouth and Bridgwater to import Irish woollens. On 6 Dec. he presented a petition from Exeter merchants complaining of excessive rates charged by the prize office for salvage of retaken vessels. In March 1695 he supervised a private bill concerning the estates of Henry Northleigh, the late MP for Okehampton.[3]

Standing down at the general election of 1695, Bale became mayor of Exeter a second time the following year, and continued his efforts to recover from the Treasury a debt of £345 which the corporation had spent on the King's Dutch troops when they were quartered on the town in November 1688. In the later 1690s he led the corporation's campaign against the establishment of a corporation of the poor in Exeter, partly because it was an autonomous institution outside the control of the corporate body, and partly as a Tory reaction against what was regarded as a likely forum for Whiggish and Dissenting reformers. Once the corporation had been founded in 1698, he continued to harass its proceedings. Bale died overseas between 16 June 1707, when his will was drawn up, and 2 Dec. 1708, when it was proved.[4]

[1] *Trans. Devon Assoc.* lxii. 210; J. L. Vivian, *Exeter Mar. Lic.* 120; PCC 61 Reeve; Soc. of Geneal., Exeter mar. lic.; G. D. Stawell, *Quantock Fam.* 175. [2] *Exeter Freemen* (Devon and Cornw. Rec. Soc. extra ser. i), 167; *Trans. Devon Assoc.* 210; Hoare, *Wilts.* iv. 477; *Cal. Treas. Bks.* ix. 975; x. 465, 1299. [3] Add. 41805, ff. 65, 118, 122, 129, 161, 168, 207; *Luttrell Diary*, 48. [4] *HMC Exeter*, 219–21, 227; T. V. Hitchcock, 'The English Workhouse . . . 1696–1750' (Oxf. Univ. D.Phil. thesis, 1985), 61–62, 69; PCC 279 Barrett.

E. C.

BALLE, Robert (c.1639–aft.1731), of Mamhead, Devon; Campden House, Kensington, London; and Leghorn, Italy.

ASHBURTON   1708–1710

b. c.1639, 5th s. of Sir Peter Balle† (*d.*1680), of Mamhead, recorder of Exeter, by Ann, da. of William Cooke† of Highnam, Glos. *unm.*[1]

?Consul at Leghorn by 1689–?[2]

FRS 1708.

Balle was a younger son of Sir Peter Balle, who represented Tiverton in the early parliaments of Charles I and in the Short Parliament, and subsequently became a Royalist during the Civil War. After the Restoration Balle went to Leghorn, where he settled as a merchant (probably in partnership with his brother John Balle), and became a factor for the Levant Company. Two other brothers, Amos and Giles, were also merchants, based at Cadiz and Genoa respectively. In April 1689 he was reporting to Lord Nottingham (Daniel Finch†) from Leghorn, probably in the capacity of consul, on French naval movements in the Mediterranean, and expressed hope 'for the prosperous success of King William, who can only save us'. He was in England in 1696, when he was granted a pass to go to Ireland. In 1700 he joined with other London merchants in petitioning the Lords against a clause in the draft bill to prohibit trade with France relating to foreign bills of exchange as being 'very destructive' to trade. Sir Lambert Blackwell*, who encountered Balle at Leghorn in around 1702, found him the most troublesome of the merchants with whom he had to deal: 'he is known to be a turbulent sort of man, that never speaks well of any one behind their backs, but fawns to their faces'. He was put up and returned at Ashburton in 1708, and was noted by Lord Sunderland (Charles, Lord Spencer*) as a 'gain' for the Whigs. He voted in 1709 for the naturalization of the Palatines and a year later for the impeachment of Dr Sacheverell. But he did not seek re-election in 1710.[3]

Thereafter, Balle confined himself to his business and botanical interests and he created a famous garden at his house in Kensington. He frequently attended council meetings of the Royal Society to which he had been admitted as a fellow in 1708. During a sojourn at Paris in the winter of 1718–19, he wrote to Hans Sloane: 'this government at present lies under great difficulties from the Pope, the Devil and Spain, but the noble Whigs there with you have so bravely behaved themselves, that the Tories and High Church here seem quite confounded and disheartened'. He returned to Italy, settling permanently at Leghorn sometime after July 1720, but continued to correspond with the Royal Society through Sloane and (Sir) Isaac Newton*. Visiting him at Leghorn in February 1731, John Swinton, a fellow of Wadham College, Oxford, described him as:

> an old English gentleman of 97 years old [sic] who notwithstanding has his understanding and all his senses perfect and entire. He was formerly consul in this place, afterwards Member of Parliament for a borough in Devonshire and Fellow of the Royal Society. He has lived here 69 years, his first arrival there in the year 1662.

The date of his death has not been ascertained. His nephew Thomas Balle was MP for Exeter 1734–41.[4]

[1] Vivian, *Vis. Devon*, 37 Sloane 4047, f. 288. [2] *HMC Finch*, iii. 423. [3] Stowe 219, ff. 209–10, 254–5; info. from Mrs N. R. R. Fisher; *HMC Finch*, 423; *HMC Lords*, n.s. vi. 295; Add. 34356, f. 1. [4] Sloane 4045, ff. 165,181; 4046, f. 100; 4047, f. 288; 4068, f. 138; info. from Mrs Fisher; Wadham College, Oxf. mss travel jnl. of Swinton, 18 Feb. 1731 (*ex inf*. Prof. J. M. Black).

E. C.

BAMPFYLDE, Sir Coplestone Warwick, 3rd Bt. (c.1689–1727), of Poltimore, nr. Exeter, Devon.

EXETER 1710–1713
DEVON   1713–1727

b. c.1689, 1st s. of Col. Hugh Bampfylde of Warleigh, nr. Plymouth, Devon (*d.v.p.* s. of Sir Coplestone Bampfylde, 2nd Bt.†) by Mary, da. and h. of James Clifford of Kingsteignton, Devon. *educ.* Christ Church, Oxf. matric. 26 Jan. 1708, aged 18. *m.* June 1716, Gertrude, da. of Sir John Carew, 3rd Bt.*, wid. of Sir Godfrey Copley, 2nd Bt.*, 1s. 2da. *suc.* fa. 1691; gdfa. as 3rd Bt. 9 Feb. 1692; cos. Warwick Bampfylde to Hardington Park, Som. 1695.

Bampfylde's father, 'a young gentleman of the sweetest temper and the greatest hopes of any other in all those parts', attended Prince William soon after his landing in 1688, but the family subsequently refused to accept the Revolution settlement. Personal tragedy struck shortly afterwards: in 1691 the colonel rode 'hastily down a hill, fell from his horse and broke his neck'. Bampfylde's grandfather, Sir Coplestone Bampfylde, was so grief-stricken that he gave in to gout which attacked 'like an armed man surprising the castle of his heart'. Shortly before his death he had nevertheless 'called his family together and left this in strict charge with them, "that they should always continue faithful to the religion of the established Church of England and be sure to pay their allegiance to the right heirs of the crown"'. The infant Bampfylde, who had inherited the estate and title, was cared for by his mother, 'a lady of great worth and virtues', who protected her son from a number of lawsuits disputing his property rights. One case concerned the widow of the 2nd baronet, who had persuaded her husband to bequeath part of the estate by will even though it had been entailed to Bampfylde's father: a Chancery decision, made by Lord Somers (Sir John*), declared that Poltimore, which was 'the chief seat of the family', should remain in the hands of Bampfylde and his mother. A second case brought the family into conflict with Alexander Popham* over the estate of Henry Rogers, whose estate Popham had inherited, but which was held in trust by Warwick Bampfylde, whose estate had in turn passed to Sir Coplestone. When in 1696 a bill was introduced in the House to allow leases to be made during Bampfylde's minority, Popham petitioned against it and was joined by William Blathwayt*, whose wife Mary had also been one of the beneficiaries of Rogers' will. The estate bill therefore foundered, and had to be reintroduced in 1698 (again by fellow Devonian Nicholas Hooper*), this time successfully.[1]

Bampfylde entered Parliament as soon as his age made him eligible, representing Exeter, which lay only four miles from Poltimore. He was marked as a Tory on the 'Hanover list', and was included among the 'worthy patriots' who, in the first session, detected the mismanagements of the previous administration. On 27 Jan. 1711 he was granted leave of absence on health grounds. He was one of a group of High Tories, including Sir John Trevelyan, 2nd Bt.*, and Sir Francis Warre, 1st Bt.*, who were entertained by Henry Seymour Portman* that summer and, like them, had become a member of the October Club; but on 18 June 1713 he voted against the French commerce bill. The previous month he had also presented an address from his own locality of Bradninch, which thanked the Queen for her 'good intentions towards the House of Hanover', as well as fulminating against the 'groundless jealousies contrived by a faction'. This activity might suggest that he belonged to the Hanoverian wing of his party; but his opposition to the commerce bill may equally well have stemmed from Exeter's anxiety (as stated in the town's petition of 4 June) lest there be 'any obstruction to the exportation of woollen manufactures of this kingdom to Portugal'; and it may have been the influence of Francis Gwyn*, co-presenter of the Bradninch address, rather than Bampfylde's, that ensured the Hanoverian tone. Certainly the government suspected Bampfylde of Jacobite sympathies, for he was taken into custody during the Fifteen (though retained as a j.p.) and included in 1721 on a list sent to the Pretender of presumed sympathizers. He seemed to confirm such hopes in 1722, after the discovery of the 1722 plot, when he sheltered Atterbury's secretary, Thomas Carte.[2]

Elected for Devon in 1713, Bampfylde was classed as a Tory in both the Worsley list and another comparison of the 1713 and 1715 Parliaments. He continued to represent the county until 1727. In 1716 he married Gertrude, the sister of his close friend Sir William Carew, 5th Bt.*, who had also been placed in custody in 1715. Bampfylde died on 7 Oct. 1727, and provided in his will for a mourning ring to be given 'unto all and every clergyman' that attended his funeral. He left £2,500 to his wife, £20,000 to his daughter Mary, and the estate, in trust under his brother John†, Sir William Carew, John Worth* and Sir Hugh Acland, 6th Bt.†, to his son Richard, who was himself elected for Exeter in 1743.[3]

[1] J. Prince, *Worthies of Devon* (1701), 124–5; *HMC 7th Rep.* 416; Luttrell, *Brief Relation*, ii. 252; Vivian, *Vis. Devon*, 40; BL, Dept. of Printed Bks. 1560/4372, 4376; *HMC Lords*, i. 400; ii. 532; PCC 70 Irby. [2] Nottingham Univ. Lib. Manvers mss 4376, Gifford letterbk. Portman to Gifford, 19 Aug. 1711; *London Gazette*, 23–26 May 1713; Monod thesis, 523; L. K. J. Glassey, *Appt. JPs*, 250. [3] PCC 134 Brook; Morice mss at Bank of England, Sir Nicholas† to Humphrey Morice*, 14 Sept. 1708, 256, William Pole* to [–], 13 Nov. 1715.

M. J. K.

BANGHAM, Edward (c.1659–c.1712), of Leominster, Herefs.

LEOMINSTER 1710–c.1712

b. c.1659. *m.* Ann (*d.* Sept.1712), at least 2s. 2da. *d.v.p.*[1]
Bailiff, Leominster 1689, 1695.

A 'dyer' of Leominster, Bangham may well have been connected with the namesake who had been bailiff of the borough before him in 1672. He came into Parliament on the interest of his partner Edward Harley* in 1710, probably as a makeweight, since, as one observer noted, it was not in any way obvious 'what pleasure Ned Bangham can take in the House'. He had not always been associated with the Harleys, however. Indeed, in the January 1701 general election he had acted as the 'principal agent' of John Dutton Colt* in a contest against Edward Harley, implicated up to the hilt in Colt's alleged bribery, treating and menaces. It may be assumed that the appointment of Bangham's son Edward to be deputy to Edward Harley as an auditor of the imprest helped to swing the family over to the Harley side. Edward Bangham jnr. seems in turn to have served as his master's 'principal agent' in the Leominster constituency from 1710 onwards.[2]

Bangham was classed as a Tory in the 'Hanover list', and was subsequently listed as one of the 'worthy patriots' who in the first session exposed the mismanagements of the previous administration. In other respects, he realized the low expectations entertained of him. He made no speech of which there is a record, and was twice granted leave of absence, on 8 Feb. 1711 for a month, and on 1 Feb. 1712 for six weeks. The date of Bangham's death, aged 53, is recorded on a funerary monument as '1712'. Given that the House took no notice of a vacancy arising, an 'old style' reference to 1713 may well have been intended. His son continued as deputy auditor of the imprest until his death in 1760, when the Herefordshire estate of Stockton Bury, which his governmental service had enabled him to purchase, passed to a son-in-law, Hon. Thomas Harley†, himself a younger son of the 3rd Earl of Oxford and thus a grandson of Auditor Harley.[3]

[1] J. Price, *Hist. and Top. Acct. Leominster*, 69, 115, 117, 125; W. R. Williams, *Herefs. MPs*, 137; PCC 314 Lynch. [2] NLW, Ottley mss 2587, Charles Baldwyn* to Adam Ottley, 10 Oct. 1710; Price, 68; Add. 70216, James Caswall to Robert Harley*, 9 Oct. 1710; 70226, Thomas Foley I* to same, 25 Sept. 1710, 19 Aug. 1713; 70278, list of witnesses in Leominster election case [1701]; 70084, Ld. Coningsby (Thomas*) to bailiff of Leominster, 11 Dec. 1714; *CJ*, xiii. 471–3; Williams, 137; *Cal. Treas. Bks. and Pprs.* 1731–4, p. 587; *Cal. Treas. Pprs.* 1714–19, p. 378. [3] Price, 117; *Cal. Treas. Bks. and Pprs.* 1742–5, p. 803; *Gent. Mag.* 1760, p. 346; Williams, 137.

D. W. H.

BANKES, John (c.1668–1714), of Kingston Lacy and Corfe Castle, Dorset.

CORFE CASTLE 1698–1714

b. c.1668, 1st s. of Sir Ralph Bankes† of Kingston Lacy and Corfe Castle by Mary, da. and h. of John Brune of Athelhampton, Dorset. m. lic. 30 May 1691, Margaret, da. of Henry Parker*, sis. of Hugh Parker*, 5s. 2da. suc. fa. 1677.[1]

Hereditary constable, Corfe Castle; hereditary ld. lt. Isle of Purbeck.[2]

A High Tory, and related by marriage to the Earl of Rochester (Laurence Hyde†), Bankes sat for Corfe Castle, a constituency which his father and grandfather had also represented. Nothing is known about Bankes during his first Parliament, apart from an early prediction that he would oppose the standing army. In February 1701 he was listed as likely to support the Court over the 'Great Mortgage', and in December Robert Harley* classed him as a Tory. Bankes voted on 26 Feb. 1702 in favour of the resolution to vindicate the Commons over the impeachments of the previous session. Having been forecast as likely to support the Tack, he duly voted for it on 28 Nov. 1704. In an analysis of the 1705 Parliament he was listed as 'True Church'. On 25 Oct. 1705 he divided against the Court candidate for Speaker, and on 20 Dec. he received leave of absence for health reasons. Noted as a Tory in an early analysis of the 1708 Parliament, he later voted against the impeachment of Dr Sacheverell. The 'Hanover list' classified him as a Tory in 1710, and he appears both in the list of 'Tory patriots' who opposed the continuance of the war, and in the list of 'worthy patriots' who detected the mismanagements of the previous administration. Thereafter, he was probably suffering from ill-health, receiving leave for that reason on 24 Feb. 1711 and 31 May 1712. He was buried at Wimborne, Dorset, in 1714. Two of his sons sat for Corfe Castle after 1715.[3]

[1] Hutchins, Dorset, iii. 221, 239–40. [2] Bodl. Willis mss 48, ff. 225, 235. [3] Hutchins, 221.

P. W.

BANKS, Caleb (1659–96), of Aylesford, Kent.

QUEENBOROUGH	1685–1687
MAIDSTONE	1689–1690
ROCHESTER	27 Oct. 1691–1695
QUEENBOROUGH	1695–13 Sept. 1696

b. 18 Sept. 1659, 1st s. of Sir John Banks, 1st Bt.* educ. privately; Queens', Camb. 1675; G. Inn 1675; travelled abroad (France) 1677–9. m. Elizabeth, da. of Samuel Fortrey, clerk of the Ordnance, of Salesbury Court, London and Chatteris, Cambs., s.p.[1]

Freeman, Maidstone 1681; asst. Rochester bridge 1693–d.[2]

Cttee. E.I. Co. 1683–4.[3]

Despite a thorough education, complete with French tutor, a spell residing with Samuel Pepys, 'to wean him from home', and a French tour in the company of John Locke, Banks was destined to remain in his father's shadow. In part this must have been a question of finance, since he was dependent upon an allowance of about £700 p.a.; in part a matter of personality, for he was described by his father in 1677 as in need of encouragement 'to appear and converse with others'. As he was the heir to a fortune, Banks's place in local society was secure: indeed, he served as a militia captain from 1683 to 1688 and again after the Revolution when he also became a j.p. and deputy-lieutenant. However, while his father remained active he himself could not aspire to an independent role in politics. Having sat in James II's Parliament Banks joined the opposition to the King, being one of the officers in whose custody James was held at Faversham. He sat for Maidstone in the Convention of 1689 but lost his seat at the 1690 election. Efforts to intrude him at Rye also failed, where he was recommended to the corporation as 'one that is heir to a plentiful fortune and that my Lord Nottingham [Daniel Finch†] hath a particular respect for', so that Banks had to wait until a vacancy occurred at Rochester in 1691 before being able to return to the Commons.[4]

Back in the House, Banks made little impact. Samuel Grascome listed him as a placeman between 1693 and 1695, justifying his inclusion with the comment that both father and son were 'tally brokers, by which trade they have got above £20,000'. His name also appears on a list of 'friends' of Henry Guy* when the latter was under attack in the 1694–5 session. In the 1695 election Banks again switched seats, being returned for Queenborough. He was forecast as likely to oppose the Court in the division on 31 Jan. 1696 over the proposed council of trade; like his father, he refused to sign the Association, and he voted in March against fixing the price of guineas at 22s. It seems doubtful whether Banks was actually at Westminster when the Association was tendered to Members, because a newsletter of 31 Mar. numbered him among those 'in the country' who had not yet signed. If he was absent, ill-health was the reason, for on 29 Apr. he wrote in trepidation to his brother-in-law, Hon. Heneage Finch I*, asking him to intercede with Sir John Banks on behalf of his wife, in case 'it please God

I die under the course of physic I am going into'. Evidently his worst fears were realized, for on 22 Aug. Robert Crawford* wrote that 'Mr Banks continues as ill as one can live that has frequent, fainting convulsive fits, and cannot hold out many days'. By 3 Sept. even his father had given up hope, tipping off Sir George Rooke* of the impending vacancy, 'his son being so extremely ill that he thinks he can't last above four or five days longer'. Banks died on 13 Sept., predeceasing his mother by a few weeks. At least his father heeded the appeal for maintenance for his widow, allowing her £300 p.a. for life.[5]

[1] Centre Kentish Stud. U234 B2, fly-leaf; D. C. Coleman, *Sir John Banks*, 122, 127–8. [2] Coleman, 142; info. from Mr P. F. Cooper, Bridge Clerk, Rochester Bridge Trust. [3] Info. from Prof. H. Horwitz. [4] Coleman, 122, 127; *Locke Corresp.* ed. de Beer, i. 465, 493; info. from Prof. N. Landau; Add. 42596, f. 47; 42586, f. 85; *N. and Q.* ser. 3, vi. 23. [5] Bodl. Rawl. D. 846, ff. 1–2; Huntington Lib. HM 30659, newsletter 31 Mar. 1696; Luttrell, *Brief Relation*, iv. 37; Coleman, 133, 187; BL, Althorp mss, Crawford to Mq. of Halifax (William Savile*), 22 Aug. 1696, Rooke to same, 3 Sept. 1696.

S. N. H.

BANKS, Jacob (1662–1724), of Milton Abbas, Dorset and Somerford, Hants.

MINEHEAD 1698–1715

b. 22 Aug. 1662, 2nd s. of Lars Bengtsson Banck of Stockholm, Sweden by his w. Kristina Barckman. *m.* 1696, Mary, da. and h. of John Tregonwell of Milton Abbas, wid. of Francis Luttrell*, 2s. kntd. 6 or 7 Dec. 1698.[1]

Capt. RN 1690–7.[2]

Freeman, Bath 1707.[3]

Banks was a Swede by birth. His father was a supervisor at the 'packhouse' in Stockholm. Banks himself came to London in 1680 or 1681, joining his brother, Lars, who was secretary to their maternal uncle, Baron Johan Barckman Leijonberg, the Swedish ambassador to the English court. He subsequently made his home in England and entered the Royal Navy in 1681. Afterwards he saw active service in the West Indies, and at the battle of Beachy Head in 1690 assumed command of his ship when the captain was wounded. In the same year he was promoted to captain, and served inconspicuously in various commands throughout the war. After the Peace of Ryswick he was placed on half-pay, and, although his financial predicament was made considerably easier by his marriage to a wealthy widow, it became a matter of smouldering annoyance to him to that he was never again offered a commission. His wife brought him an estate in Dorset and a connexion with the family of her first husband, the Luttrells of Dunster Castle, who had a controlling interest at Minehead which was placed at Banks's disposal in 1698, and he was returned for the borough after a contest. A Tory, he was at first classed as a placeman and Court supporter, presumably because of his naval commission, and voted on 18 Jan. 1699 in favour of a standing army. In February 1701 he was noted as likely to support the Court in agreeing with the committee of supply's resolution to continue the 'Great Mortgage', and on 26 Feb. 1702 voted in favour of the Commons' proceedings in the impeachments of William III's Whig ministers.[4]

In Minehead, shortly after Anne's accession Banks made a bold display of his Toryism by donating to the town a statue of her. Classed by Lord Spencer (Charles*) as a 'loss' for the Whigs following the 1702 election, Banks's next recorded vote was on 13 Feb. 1703 against agreeing to the Whig Lords' amendments to the bill extending the period allowed for taking the oath of abjuration. He was forecast in October 1704 as a probable opponent of the Tack, and although included in Robert Harley's* lobbying list against the measure, actually voted in its favour on 28 Nov. Accordingly, he was noted as 'True Church' in a list published after the 1705 election. With fewer Tories in the Commons during the ensuing Parliament he became a more active figure in the House. In the first session he voted on 25 Oct. against the Court candidate for Speaker, and acted as a teller in two election cases: on 10 Nov. on a procedural question in connexion with the disputed Cheshire election; and on the 24th against declaring the Court Tory Henry Killigrew* duly elected for St. Albans. Banks was a teller again on 22 Feb. 1707 against going into committee on the bill for the Union with Scotland, and on three more occasions during the 1707–8 session, the most politically obvious question concerning the repeal of the game laws in which Banks told against. Classed as a Tory early in 1708, he was several times a teller in the opening session of the new Parliament, twice on procedural matters, and on 7 Dec. 1708 in support of Anthony Hammond* in a question to declare him ineligible for a seat in Parliament. A quarrel in the House between Banks and fellow Tory Gilbert Dolben on 22 Jan. 1709 resulted in their having to make a formal pledge to prosecute the matter no further. On 31 Jan. 1710 he was teller against the motion for the sermon given to the House on the anniversary of Charles I's execution to be printed, and later voted against the impeachment of Dr Sacheverell.

During his election campaign at Minehead in 1710 Banks expressed his support for Sacheverell by expounding the notion of passive obedience to the crown in all circumstances, which one of his Whig opponents, William Benson, dubbed the 'Minehead doctrine' in a pamphlet published the following year. Listed as a Tory in the 'Hanover list' of the new Parliament, Banks was classed as one of the 'worthy patriots' who in the first session detected the mismanagements of the previous administration. One political observer described him at this time as 'a Swede, one of the most violent Tories in the House. He procured one of the highest addresses last summer . . . He has a good estate, and he is very forward to speak in the House, though no foreigner speaks worse English.' Next session, on 24 May 1712, he was teller in connexion with a complaint from several marine officers. Although he was gaining in prominence among the High Tories, he was bitter at being constantly overlooked in naval promotions despite having 'constantly' offered his services to the Admiralty commissioners. He petitioned the Queen directly in May 1712, stating

> that he has not even obtained during your Majesty's happy and glorious reign what he was allowed to the death of his late Majesty King William, and as he hopes that no action of his life hath occasioned your Majesty's displeasure, . . . so does he humbly pray your Majesty's gracious direction that the arrears of his half-pay as captain may be paid him.

In a private letter to Lord Treasurer Oxford (Harley) some months later, by which time his claim for arrears was under active consideration, he attributed his lack of success in his naval career to many years of political victimization by the Whigs: 'your Lordship not being ignorant of those reasons for which I was debarred from it in the last administration'. By now a leading member of the October Club, he treated its members in June to a magnificent supper to celebrate the peace. His close friend Lord Strafford chose him to act as his proxy at his installation as a Knight of the Garter at Windsor on 4 Aug. 1713. Early in 1714 he was elected president of the October Club. In the last Parliament of the reign he acted as a teller on 15 June in proceedings on the disputed Southwark election. On the Worsley list he appeared as a Tory. He declined to stand for re-election after the accession of George I, but appears to have dabbled mildly in Jacobitism and in 1717 was a leading suspect in the Swedish Plot. He was arrested and interrogated, but the authorities, having failed to find proof of his guilt, released him on £5,000 bail. He died on 22 Dec. 1724.[5]

[1] Hutchins, *Dorset*, i. 161; iv. 385, 401; info. from Mr Bengt Nilsson. [2] Charnock, ii. 306. [3] Bath AO, Bath council bk. 3, p. 474. [4] Info. from Mr Nilsson; Charnock, *Biographia Navalis*, ii. 306; *CSP Dom.* 1697, p. 213; *CJ*, xv. 374; C. H. Firth and J. K. Chance, *Notes of Diplomatic Relations of England with N. of Europe*, 29; H. C.

Maxwell Lyte, *Dunster and its Lords*, 100; *Hist. Dunster*, 217; Luttrell, *Brief Relation*, iv. 142. [5] Hutchins, iv. 385, 401; *Bull. IHR*, xlvi. 177; NLS, Advocates' mss, Wodrow pprs, letters Quarto 5, f. 130; Add. 70317, Banks's memorial to Queen, May 1712; 70279, Banks to Oxford, 24 Feb. 1712–13; 31138, f. 274; NSA, Kreienberg despatch 10 June 1712; P. S. Fritz, *Ministers and Jacobitism 1715–45*, 23, 25; *The Gen.* n.s. vi. 181.

P. W./A. A. H.

BANKS, Sir John, 1st Bt. (1627–99), of The Friars, Aylesford, Kent and Arch Row, Lincoln's Inn Fields, Mdx.

MAIDSTONE	1654–1655, 1656–1658, 1659
WINCHELSEA	2 Feb. – 7 Mar. 1678
ROCHESTER	1679 (Mar.)–1681 (Mar.), 1685–1687 1689–1690
QUEENBOROUGH	1690–1695
MAIDSTONE	1695–1698

bap. 19 Aug. 1627, 1st s. of Caleb Banks of Maidstone, Kent by Martha, da. of Stephen Dann of Faversham, Kent. *educ.* Emmanuel, Camb. 1644. *m.* 28 Nov. 1654, Elizabeth (*d.* 1696), da. of Sir John Dethick of Tottenham, Mdx., ld. mayor of London 1655–6, 2s. *d.v.p.* 3da. (1 *d.v.p.*). *cr.* Bt. 25 July 1661; *suc.* fa. 1669.[1]

Freeman, Maidstone 1654, Rochester 1683; asst. Rochester bridge 1659–61, 1679–*d.*, warden 1680, 1687, 1694.[2]

Freeman, E.I. Co. 1657–92, cttee. 1658–9, 1669–72, 1674–5, 1677–9, 1680–1, 1682–3, 1685–6, gov. 1672–4, 1683–4; member, Levant Co. Aug. 1660–?*d.*; asst. R. African Co. 1672–4, 1676–8, sub.-gov. 1674–5; member, New England Co. 1673, R. Fishery Co. 1677.[3]

FRS 1668–*d.*

Commr. Greenwich Hosp. 1695; taking subscriptions to land bank 1696.[4]

By the time of the 1689 Revolution Banks was extremely wealthy, having made money from trade, government finance and investment in land. Although the last decade of his life saw him retreat from large-scale trading ventures and from heavy involvement in the land market, he continued to lend money to the government. Nor did the 1690s see a retreat from politics. He remained a Tory, keen to stay on good terms with the Treasury, which provided him with so many opportunities for profit. On matters other than financial, his family links with the Finches appear to have been most important. Thus, on the crucial issue of the right to the crown, Banks was firmly with those who regarded William and Mary as King and Queen *de facto* but not *de jure*.

At the 1690 election Banks was unable to retain his seat at Rochester, being forced to seek refuge at Queenborough. On a list of 1690 the Marquess of Carmarthen (Sir Thomas Osborne†) classed him as a

Court supporter. The opening session saw Banks appointed to a single drafting committee. One of his prime concerns during the next session was to further his son Caleb's* election petition for Rye, and to this end he called upon friends such as Sir Joseph Williamson*, to whom he wrote on 3 Nov. 1690 soliciting his attendance at the committee of elections. In December Carmarthen listed Banks as a supporter in case of an attack upon him in the Commons. However, in April 1691 Robert Harley* counted Banks as a Country supporter. He acted as a teller on 18 Feb. 1692 in favour of giving a second reading to the Lords' bill for the relief of the distressed orphans of the city of London. In February 1693 his younger daughter, Mary, married John Savile of Methley, with a portion of £18,000, which emphasized her father's material success. An anonymous list of 1693 placed Banks as an opponent of the East India Company. The reasons for his appearance on this list are unknown, but in 1692 he had divested himself of his remaining shares (he had retained £3,250 worth of stock in April 1689), and Lord Nottingham (Daniel Finch†) was also hostile to the company. Furthermore, from 1695 Banks was buying shares (often in other people's names) and lending money to the company. In the 1692-3 session he was named to a single drafting committee. His name also appears on a list of 'friends' of Henry Guy* between December 1694 and March 1695, at a time when Guy was under pressure in the Commons.[5]

At the 1695 general election Banks left Queenborough to his son, Caleb, coming in for Maidstone instead, where he owned some houses, and which lay only three miles from his estate at Aylesford. He was forecast as likely to oppose the Court in a division on 31 Jan. 1696 over the proposed council of trade. He refused to sign the Association in February, in common with his Finch relatives, and in March voted against fixing the price of guineas at 22s. In the following session on 25 Nov. 1696, he voted against the bill to attaint Sir John Fenwick†. Despite his Tory politics, in May 1697 his name appeared on a list of subscribers to the contract for lending money to circulate Exchequer bills. September 1697 offered two more examples of Banks's influence. On the 9th he obtained a proclamation with a reward for the discovery of those who had robbed his park in Kent. Later, on the 28th, Charles Montagu* wrote to William Blathwayt* of his hope that a substantial contribution towards the funds needed to pay off foreign troops would be forthcoming from Banks and Sir Joseph Herne*, who 'are to bring me a proposition'. The 1697-8 session witnessed Banks taking an interest in the parliamentary attack on Charles Duncombe* for falsely endorsing Exchequer bills. Thus, on 23 Feb. 1698, Banks recounted the proceedings in the Commons the previous day when the House had defeated a motion that 'receiving Exchequer bills . . . upon bills of exchange drawn payable in milled money and gold was contrary to law and a loss to the public', on the grounds that the practice 'was thought to be well done because it might encourage the passing of 'chequer bills'. On 3 Apr. Banks wrote to his son-in-law Hon. Heneage Finch I* that he was not well enough to visit, although this did not prevent him from commenting that 'the ways and means to raise money we find very difficult and have about four millions yet to raise', nor from discussing Duncombe's incarceration in the Tower.[6]

Banks was defeated at Maidstone in the general election of 1698, attributing this setback to the overconfidence of his friends. He also decided against the 'fatigue' of a petition. Having written as early as April 1697 that he found 'my age growing sensibly on me', Banks seemed almost relieved to have lost. However, he maintained an interest in politics, writing to Finch on 18 Nov. 1698 that 'Mr Grenville [Hon. John Granville*] will endeavour to be Speaker'. Banks may well have backed Granville, for on a list of September 1698, comparing the old and new Parliaments, he was classed as a Country supporter. By 9 Aug. 1699 he was clearly ailing, as he described the symptoms of his illness to his daughter: a 'sharpness of urine' and a 'weakness . . . in the parts about the fundamentals and sometimes a short, sharp pain there'. He died on 19 Oct. 1699, leaving net assets of approximately £170,000. The bulk of his estate, including Aylesford, passed through his eldest daughter, to the Finches, earls of Aylesford, although the Saviles obtained his London house.[7]

[1] D. C. Coleman, *Sir John Banks*, 4, 46, 120, 187-8. [2] Centre Kentish Stud. Md/RF2/1, list of freemen 1598-1721; info. from Medway Area Archs.; info. from Mr P. F. Cooper, Bridge Clerk, Rochester Bridge Trust. [3] Info. from Prof. H. Horwitz; Coleman, 25; K. G. Davies, *R. African Co.* 378; W. Kellaway, *New England Co.* 290; *Sel. Charters*, 198. [4] Add. 10120, f. 232; *CJ*, xii. 508. [5] *CSP Dom.* 1690-1, p. 156; Add. 22185, f. 12; Coleman, 92, 134, 161-2, 185. [6] Univ. of London Lib. ms 65, item 3, list of subscribers, 1697; Luttrell, *Brief Relation*, iv. 280; *CSP Dom.* 1697, pp. 359, 361; *Vernon-Shrewsbury Letters*, i. 356; Add. 34355, f. 55; Devonshire mss at Chatsworth House, Finch-Halifax pprs. Banks to Heneage Finch I, 23 Feb. 1697[-8], 3 Apr. 1698. [7] Finch-Halifax pprs. same to same, 26 July, 18 Nov. 1698; Coleman, 188-91.

S. N. H.

BANKS, Legh (1666–1703), of Gray's Inn, Mdx.

NEWTON 1695–1698

bap. 30 Aug 1666, 4th s. of William Banks I† of Winstanley, nr. Wigan, Lancs. by Frances, da. and event. h. of Peter Legh of Burch Hall, Lancs.; bro. of William Banks II†. *educ.* G. Inn 1685. *unm.*[1]

Burgess, Wigan 1695.[2]

Banks, whose father had sat for Newton and Liverpool, was a cousin and 'particular friend' of Peter Legh† of Lyme, the non-juring patron of Newton. When Legh was accused of high treason in the Lancashire Plot (1693–4) Banks was one of the few persons allowed to visit him in the Tower, and, with the assistance of the Irish informer Taaffe, Banks arranged a meeting with John Lunt, the chief witness against the accused. He persuaded Lunt that he wished to aid him in the conspiracy to take a share of the forfeited lands of the accused plotters, and Lunt revealed to Banks that his allegations were untrue, and that he had forged supposed Jacobite commissions to the alleged plotters. Banks testified against Lunt at the Manchester trials in October 1694, his testimony being vital to the acquittal of the six Catholic gentlemen tried there and to the release of Legh when his case was heard at Chester the same month. On 23 Nov. 1694 Banks repeated his account of Lunt's fabrications to the Commons' investigation into the Lancashire Plot. Banks's key role in Legh's acquittal prompted Legh to return Banks for Newton in 1695. He was forecast as likely to oppose the Court in the divisions of 31 Jan. 1696 over the proposed council of trade, and the following day it was reported that he had voted against the imposition of the abjuration oath for members of the new body. Banks was among those who initially refused to sign the Association and his opposition to the ministry continued in March when he voted against fixing the price of guineas at 22s., and into the following session when on 25 Nov. he voted against the attainder of Sir John Fenwick†. Banks did not stand at the 1698 election, following which he was listed as a member of the Country party 'out' of the new Parliament. His life came to a premature and unfortunate end in late October 1703 when he 'unhappily drowned crossing the river [Dee] near Chester'.[3]

[1] IGI, Lancs.; *Parl. Rep. Lancs.* 285. [2] Wigan RO, Wigan bor. recs. AB/MR/10. [3] *HMC Kenyon*, 366–7, 381–2, 387–94, 398–9; *Jacobite Trials Manchester 1694* (Chetham Soc. ser. 1, xxviii), 90–91; *CSP Dom.* 1694–5, pp. 322–7; *HMC Portland*, iii. 560; Add. 70075; Dyer's newsletter 28 Oct. 1703.

E. C./R. D. H.

BARBON, Nicholas (c.1637–98), of Crane Court, Fleet Street, London and Osterley Park, Mdx.

BRAMBER 1690–1698

b. c.1637, s. of Praisegod Barbon or Barebone†, Leatherseller, of Fleet Street, London by his w. Sarah ?Fenn. *educ.* ?Exeter Coll. Oxf. matric. 1656, BA 1659; Leyden 2 July 1661, aged 24; Utrecht 1661, MD 1661. *m.* lic. 26 Jan. 1670 aged 28, Margaret Hayes of St. Andrew's, Holborn, 1s. *d.v.p. suc.* fa. 1680.[1]

Fellow, College of Physicians 1664.[2]

Commr. taking subscriptions to land bank 1696.[3]

Barbon was said by Roger North† to be the son of the well-known Dissenting preacher, Praisegod Barbon, and there seems no reason to doubt his parentage. Parish registers show he must have been one of several children, but his early years remain obscure. He may have attended Oxford, and certainly went into medicine, attending the universities of Leyden and Utrecht. The choice of university was undoubtedly influenced by his father's difficult position in England after the Restoration, which saw him imprisoned in the Tower from November 1661 to July 1662. On his return to England Barbon set up in practice, but lack of success led him to abandon the pursuit of medicine for speculative building. The fire of 1666 gave him his chance and he soon established himself as one of the leading builders and property developers in London. He bought and cleared land, often demolishing properties in the process, and built in their stead large numbers of small houses and shops. He developed Mincing Lane, bought Essex House in the Strand to convert into small houses and tenements for shops, taverns and cookshops, built Red Lion Square, which provoked a riot between his workmen and the gentlemen of Gray's Inn, developed Chancery Lane and parts of Lincoln's Inn and began to rebuild the Temple (but failed to complete the work). He rebuilt a house in Crane Court in Fleet Street, where he 'lived as lord of the manor'. Despite the scale of his building enterprises, he always operated in an atmosphere of financial risk. According to North, Barbon would stave off his creditors until legal action was taken against him, at which time he compounded at 4 or 5 per cent.[4]

In addition to his activities as a developer, Barbon set up a fire insurance company in 1667, probably the first in London. At first he ran it as a purely personal business, but in 1680 it merged into a new joint-stock company, called the Fire Office. Among his partners in the new venture were Samuel Vincent, Sir John Parsons* and later, Felix Calvert*, the two latter Tory MPs. The company worked on the principle of making fixed payments in the event of loss, for fixed annual premiums, and it employed men in various parts of London to fight fires. Although the corporation of the city of London proposed to establish its own fire insurance company in 1681, it was not until 1684 that this rival, called the Friendly Society, was formed.[5]

Barbon had first considered entering Parliament in 1680, largely in order to avoid his creditors. He is reputed to have told Sir Thomas Draper, from whom he had leased land in Blackfriars, that 'he was likely to be a Member of Parliament and did intend to pay no rent'. He did not follow up his plan until 1690 when he entered Parliament for Bramber, where he had bought a number of burgages. Lord Carmarthen (Sir Thomas Osborne†) classed him as a Whig in a list of the new Parliament, but the Journals record no significant activity in this session. However, in 1690 he published his best-known work, *A Discourse of Trade*, in which he argued that the value of things was determined by use and quantity and the market was the best judge of value. He further maintained that money only represents produce, having no inherent value of its own.[6]

In the next session, in December 1690, Carmarthen listed Barbon as a probable supporter in case of an attack in the Commons on his position as chief minister. Barbon's motives for entering Parliament still seem to have been primarily concerned with promoting business projects and avoiding actions for debt. A few months after his election he and Parsons successfully claimed privilege in a case brought against them by other trustees of the fire insurance company for failing to build in Well Close, a site bought by Barbon from the crown, which buildings were to be security for the funds of the company. The suit was then dropped. In April 1691, Robert Harley* classed Barbon as a Court supporter.[7]

In the next session, it was appropriate that Barbon with his experience in building and property development should have reported on 9 Jan. 1692 from a committee on the 18th concerned with the condition of the roof of the chamber. He was named to a further committee on the 18th to inspect the building structure of the whole House. On 12 Feb. he acted as a teller in favour of allowing Quakers in Ireland to affirm instead of taking the oath and on 9 Jan. 1693 he told in favour of allowing the King to appoint commissioners of assessment for any county where an insufficient number had been nominated. In the spring of 1693 his name appeared on Grascome's list of placemen, not because he held an office, but because his 'privileges are worth to him £1,000 p.a.'. How useful his parliamentary privilege was to him was further shown when in May 1693 the inhabitants of Chancery Lane and Fickets Field presented a bill of indictment against him for obstructing their light and right of way by his building in Fickets Field (New Square, Lincoln's Inn). Barbon refused to answer, insisting on his privilege, and continued building as before. Classified as a Court supporter in another list from the spring of 1693, he gave qualified support to the ministry on 5 Dec. over the army estimates.[8]

In the 1694–5 session, Barbon was similarly inactive. On 18 Dec. 1694 in the committee of ways and means he proposed a chimney tax as an alternative to the tax on leather desired by the Court. One satire which attacked Barbon's endless building projects and his avoidance of his creditors by entering Parliament mentions this proposal: Barbon would

Revive damned chimney money and impose,
Gabels on children's warming hands and toes.

By 1694 Barbon had sold his interest in the Fire Office, possibly because of disputes with the other trustees over the buildings in Well Close. He started a new insurance scheme in order to exploit a patent he had obtained in December 1694 to develop an engine for raising water from the Thames to provide drinking water for the inhabitants of London. The patent was assigned to trustees to set up a company, including several MPs, Hon. Thomas Newport, Sir Edward Hussey, Thomas Foley and Robert Harley, but the plan came to nothing. In 1695 Barbon established a land bank in partnership with an enterprising lawyer, John Asgill*, one of four such ventures launched in 1695 and 1696. At first the bank flourished and numbered among its trustees Edward Harley* and Mordecai Abbot, a commissioner of the Bank of England.[9]

Having been returned again for Bramber in 1695, one of Barbon's first parliamentary actions was to promote a bill to have his Red Lion Square development made into a separate parish. A petition to this effect from the inhabitants was presented to the Commons on 13 Dec. 1695, whereupon Barbon was named to a drafting committee for a bill, which he presented on 11 Feb. 1696, but which fell at the committal stage. He had been forecast as a probable opponent of the Court in the divisions on 31 Jan. 1696 over the proposed council of trade, but signed the Association immediately. On 10 Feb. the House approved the unification of Barbon's bank with John Briscoe's land bank, to advance the money needed to establish a national land bank. An Act of Parliament (7 and 8 Gul. III, c.31) was passed, authorizing the establishment of the bank to raise a government loan of £2,564,000 at 5 per cent interest. Subscribers were to be incorporated as stockholders, lending money on the security of bonds to be vested in the bank. Commissioners were appointed and on 21 May 1696 a committee of 21, including Barbon, and with Asgill as legal adviser, was chosen to negotiate with the Treasury. The scheme collapsed because the 5 per cent interest offered was too low to attract sufficient subscriptions. At the beginning of July the committee tried to renegotiate terms with the Treasury, asking for a £300,000 discount on the £2,564,000. When this was refused the scheme was abandoned. Despite the failure, Barbon's own land bank continued to function separately, but with decreasing success, until it too was wound up in 1700. In the meantime Barbon was contributing to the debate about the recoinage. His pamphlet, *Coining the New Money Lighter* (1696), supported William Lowndes* against John Locke, arguing that because the metal content of money had no effect on its value, it was perfectly legitimate for it to be valued above the price of the metal it contained and that the government should fix this price as merchants did on their goods. He suggested increasing the price of silver and lowering that of the guinea. Not surprisingly he voted with the Court for fixing the price of guineas at 22s. in March 1696.[10]

In the 1696-7 session, on 29 Dec. 1696, Barbon presented a written proposal to the House for reforming the administration of tallies and increasing their value by setting up a transfer office to deal with them. The proposal received favourable attention and was ordered to lie on the table, but nothing further came of it. On 3 Feb. 1697 Barbon acted as a teller against a move to enlarge the Bank of England by a new subscription. He spoke against the standing army on 8 Jan. 1698 and on 13 Jan. brought in a bill to lower the rate of interest. In April he became so ill that several writers, including Narcissus Luttrell*, reported his death. In fact he recovered, but in other respects was less fortunate. His debts continued to mount and on 2 May he yet again invoked his parliamentary privilege against the seizure of his house and goods by the bailiffs. On the same day he was first-named to a second-reading committee for a bill to explain the Recoinage Acts.[11]

Barbon intended to fight the next election at Bramber and it was reported that he had been met on the way by the bailiffs and had been obliged to withdraw. In fact he had died, at the end of July 1698, before the election took place. His opposition to the army probably explains his classification as a Country supporter in a comparative list of the old and new Parliaments of September 1698 The story that he ordered his executor, Asgill, not to pay his debts, is contradicted by the explicit provision in his will that all his assets be used to pay creditors. In February 1698 one writer had estimated that Barbon had invested 'not less than £200,000' in building; for which . . . he deserves more of the public than any subject in England'. Others, however, were not so laudatory about his business activities and a rather more sceptical portrait of him comes from the pen of Roger North:

> He judged well of what he undertook, and had an inexpugnable pertinacity of pressing it through. He never proposed to tempt men to give way or join but by their interest, laid plainly before them . . . And he would endure all manner of affronts and be as tame as a lamb . . . He never failed to satisfy everyone in treaty and discourse, and if he had performed as well, had been a truly great man. His fault was that he knowingly overtraded his stock, and that he could not go through with undertakings without great disappointments to the concerned, especially in point of time. This exposed him to great and clamorous debts, and consequently to arrests and suits, wherein he would fence with much dexterity, with dilatories and injunctions.[12]

[1] *Lives of the Norths* ed. Jessop, iii. 53–54; Guildhall Lib. St. Bride's, Fleet Street par. reg. 26 Nov. 1670; *CSP Dom.* 1661–2, p. 447; PCC 137 Hoare; *Mar. Lic. Vicar-Gen.* (Harl. Soc. xxiii), 174. [2] Monk, *R. Coll. of Physicians*, i. 345. [3] *CJ*, xii. 508. [4] North, 53–60; St. Bride's, Fleet Street par. reg. 9 Dec. 1634, 4 Oct. 1636; J. T. Squire, *Regs. Par. of Wandsworth, Surr.* 306; *Cal. Treas. Bks.* vii. 35, 360, 362, 375, 381, 389, 398, 406; Luttrell, *Brief Relation*, i. 309–10; ii. 403; F. B. Relton, *Fire Insurance Cos.* 19–20. [5] Relton, 20–22, 27–47, 432; Luttrell, i. 135; *CSP Dom.* 1687–9, p. 137; *Cal. Treas. Bks.* ix. 819; *Sel. Charters*, 207–12. [6] R. D. Richards, *Early Hist. Banking in Eng.* 116–17; Palgrave, *Dictionary of Pol. Econ.* i. 119–21. [7] C 8/238/19; C 10/337/19; info. from A. F. Kelsall. [8] C 8/352/47; Grey, x. 340. [9] Add. 46527, f. 32; 54496, patent 338; *Poems on Affairs of State* ed. Cameron, v. 495; info. from A. F. Kelsall; *CSP Dom.* 1693, pp. 150, 207; C54/4776/20; Richards, 116–19; Luttrell, iii. 512. [10] H. Horwitz, *Parl. and Pol. Wm III*, 167; Richards, 119; Add. 70155, jnl. of commrs. for land bank, 20 May–7 July 1696. [11] A. E. Monroe, *Monetary Theory before Adam Smith*, 80, 82–83, 86, 115, 135, 142; Centre Kentish Stud. Stanhope mss U1590/O59/5, Robert Yard* to Alexander Stanhope, 29 Dec. 1696; Som. RO, Sanford mss DD/SF/4512, *A Proposal for Raising the Public Credit, by Setting up an Office for Transferring and Discounting Tallies*; *Cam. Misc.* xxix. 360; *Post Boy*, 5–7 Apr., 30 July–2 Aug. 1698; Luttrell, iv. 364; *Vernon–Shrewsbury Letters*, ii. 35. [12] Yale Univ. Beinecke Lib. Osborne coll. Biscoe-Maunsell newsletters 30 July 1698; Luttrell, iv. 409; *N. and Q.* ser. 1, vi. 3; PCC 19 Pott; *Lowther Corresp.* ed. Hainsworth, 510–11; North, 53–54.

P. W. / S. M. W.

BARKER, Sir John, 4th Bt. (c.1655–96), of Ipswich, Suff.

IPSWICH   14 Dec. 1680–1681 (Mar.), 1685–1687
1689–14 Aug. 1696

b. c.1655, 2nd s. of Sir John Barker, 2nd Bt., of Grimston Hall, Trimley, Suff. by Winifred, da. of Sir Philip Parker, 1st Bt.†, of Erwarton, Suff. *educ.* Merton, Oxf. matric. 10

Feb. 1674, aged 18. *m.* 2 June 1678, Bridget, da. of Sir Nicholas Bacon† of Shrubland, Barham, Suff., 1s. 1da. *suc.* bro. as 4th Bt. May 1665.¹

Portman, Ipswich 1685–Sept. 1688.²

Blacklisted by Anthony Rowe* as one who had voted in February 1689 against the transfer of the crown, Barker was nevertheless re-elected on the Tory interest at Ipswich in 1690. Lord Carmarthen (Sir Thomas Osborne†) listed him as a Tory and a supporter of the Court. He was unable to attend Parliament at its opening: writing at the end of February 1690 to excuse his having sent an agent to negotiate the sale of his timber to the navy, he described himself as 'but lately recovered from a long and dangerous sickness', which made him 'very unwilling to undertake a winter's journey'. On 21 Mar. he was still in Ipswich, but he had arrived at the House by 2 Apr. when he was nominated to an inquiry committee. The following month, on the 9th, Barker was nominated to prepare a bill upon the wine regulations. On 16 Dec. he told against Thomas Trenchard* in a disputed election for Dorchester. In the same month Carmarthen forecast that Barker would support him in the event of a Commons' attack on his ministerial position. In Robert Harley's* list of April 1691 he was classed with the Country party. He was appointed on 28 Oct. 1691 to draft a bill for the general improvement of highways. On 17 Dec. he was granted leave of absence for two weeks, his wife being ill, and in the following session he was again given leave of absence, for a week, on 3 Feb. 1693. He told on 24 Nov., probably on the opposition side, on an adjournment motion. On 15 Jan. 1694 he was once more given leave of absence, on this occasion for a fortnight. With his Ipswich colleague and fellow Tory Sir Charles Blois, 1st Bt., he escaped the Whig purge of the Suffolk commission of the peace in 1694 because he was a Member of Parliament. According to Edmund Bohun, who was no friend of his, he 'should have been' turned out 'but for that only consideration'. On 4 Dec. 1694 Barker was nominated to prepare a prison regulation bill, and later in the same session, on 4 Feb. 1695, he told with Blois against imposing an oath on land tax assessors. On 6 Mar. he was granted three weeks' leave of absence to recover his health. He was a teller twice more this session, on 13 and 16 Apr., both times against going into committee on the glass duty bill.³

Forecast as a probable opponent of the Court in the divisions of 31 Jan. 1696 on the proposed council of trade, Barker refused the Association and voted in March against fixing the price of guineas at 22s. He acted as a teller three times in February 1696: against leave for a bill to enable Quakers to affirm instead of swearing oaths (7 Feb.); for the Tory candidates in the Dunwich election (12 Feb.); and in favour of a Tory motion for an address to the King to postpone the assizes for two weeks (17 Feb.). Humphrey Prideaux reported on 20 July that Barker 'lies in a very languishing condition, not like to recover'. Barker died on 14 Aug. 1696. 'My worthy friend Sir Charles Blois' was named as a trustee in his will.⁴

¹*E. Anglian*, n.s. iv. 33; PCC 306 Pyne. ²R. Canning, *Ipswich Chs.* (1754), 52, 82. ³Add. 18986, ff. 473, 477; *Bohun Diary* ed. Wilton Rix, 103, 106, 121–2, 184. ⁴*Prideaux Letters* (Cam. Soc. n.s. xv), 181, 184; PCC 306 Pyne.

D. W. H.

BARKER, Samuel (c.1659–1708), of Fairford Park, Glos.

CRICKLADE 1702–1708

b. c.1659, o. s. of Andrew Barker of Fairford Park by Elizabeth, da. of William Robinson of Cheshunt, Herts. *educ.* Trinity, Oxf. matric. 13 Mar. 1676, aged 16. *m.* 7 July 1706, Francisca, da. of one Hubberd, upholsterer, of Bartholomew Lane, London, 2da. *suc.* fa. 1700.¹

Sheriff, Glos. Mar.–Nov. 1692.

Barker's family was originally from Shropshire, but his grandfather had been a merchant in and Member for Bristol and his father had purchased Fairford at the Restoration. Barker's first attempt at Cricklade, in 1690, ended in defeat, and five years later he rejected a proposal from Henry Ireton* to stand for Cirencester. When he was eventually returned in 1702, it was largely through his own efforts and on 'the Whig interest'. His relationship to the Tory Lord Leominster (Sir William Fermor†), whose first wife had been Barker's sister, meant nothing in political terms, and probably by this time little if anything socially. Nor was his fondness for Fairford parish church, which he was mainly responsible for 'beautifying', a reflection of any political commitment to 'the Church' in general. Forecast as a probable opponent of the Tack, he did not vote for it on 28 Nov. 1704. He is not known to have made any speeches. Re-elected in 1705, Barker voted for the Court candidate as Speaker on 25 Oct. 1705, and was listed as a Whig in early 1708. His other parliamentary activities are difficult to distinguish from those of Scorie Barker*.²

Barker was unable to put to political advantage the financial resources open to him as a result of his marriage in 1706 to 'a very considerable fortune in the City' for he died just before the next election, on 1 May 1708. His estate passed in due course to his longer-surviving daughter, the wife of James Lambe of Hackney. She, outliving her husband, willed it in turn to one John Raymond who, on inheriting, changed his name to Barker.[3]

[1] *Vis. Glos.* ed. Fenwick and Metcalfe, 10; Atkyns, *Glos.* 226; Rudder, *Glos.* 443; *Post Man*, 18–20 July 1706; PCC 8 Lane; Add. 40794, ff. 2–3; Le Neve, *Mon. Angl.* 1700–15, p. 21. [2] *Vis. Glos.* 10; *Guise Mems.* (Cam. Soc. ser. 3, xxviii), 162; Add. 40794, ff. 2–3; Atkyns, 227. [3] *Post Man*, 18–20 July 1706; Luttrell, *Brief Relation*, vi. 299; Rudder, 443; *An Acct. of Fairford* (1791), 14.

D. W. H.

BARKER, Scorie (c.1652–1713), of Grove House, Chiswick, Mdx.

WALLINGFORD   1679 (Mar.)–1681 (Mar.)
MIDDLESEX   1705–1710

b. c.1652, 1st s. of Henry Barker of Grove House, Chiswick by Anne, da. of Chaloner Chute† of Sutton Court, Chiswick. *educ.* M. Temple 1662, called 1675; Oriel, Oxf. matric. 17 May 1667, aged 15. *m.* lic. 19 May 1679, Anne, da. of Sir John Robinson, 1st Bt.†, of Milk Street, London and Nuneham Courtnay, Oxon., 8s. 5da. *suc.* fa. 1695.[1]

Freeman, Wallingford 1679; bencher, M. Temple 1691, reader 1693, treas. 1702–3.[2]

Of Berkshire origin, the Barkers had first established themselves in Chiswick in the mid-16th century, and by the time of the Restoration were one of the leading families in the parish. According to the evidence of his matriculation, Scorie was born in about 1652, but his marriage licence suggests that his birth came two years later. He derived his unusual Christian name from his maternal grandmother, Anne Skory, who had married the eminent lawyer and Speaker, Chaloner Chute. The family's respectability owed much to their long-standing association with the legal profession, and Scorie duly entered the Middle Temple, thereby following the example of three successive generations of Barkers. Moreover, enduring family influence in Berkshire, most notably their ownership of the manor of Clapcot, facilitated his return for Wallingford in 1679–81. Although his father held a clerkship of the crown in Chancery, Barker was prepared to oppose the Court, voting for Exclusion. However, despite his success at Wallingford, he did not seek to regain a place in the House until December 1701, when he stood for Middlesex 'singly upon his own interest', and finished a lowly fifth. There were reports that he put up only to transfer his votes to another candidate, which may partially account for his undistinguished performance at the poll.[3]

Barker did not contest the county election of July 1702, but subsequently demonstrated support for the war effort by advancing £3,000 to the crown. In 1705 he emerged as one of the Whig candidates for Middlesex, and finished top of the poll. Lord Sunderland (Charles, Lord Spencer*) regarded his return as a Whig gain, while another parliamentary analyst classed him as 'Low Church'. He also voted for the Court candidate as Speaker, and on 18 Feb. 1706 supported the Court during proceedings on the 'place' clause in the regency bill. Unfortunately, the presence in the House of fellow Whig Samuel Barker, Member for Cricklade, makes it difficult to delineate his Commons activity. However, in the first session he can be plausibly identified as the main sponsor of a bill to settle the estate of Thomas Gower of Edmonton, Middlesex. The politics of the Middlesex Member were far from obscure, since in 1708 two parliamentary lists classed him as a Whig.[4]

Barker enjoyed an unopposed return at the county election of May 1708, and proved an active Member, there being no possible confusion concerning entries for 'Mr Barker' in the Journals for that Parliament. Although selected for drafting committees for bills to give powers to the London commission for sewers, and to regulate the payment of seamen's wages, he was more prominently involved with the management of a bill to relieve creditors of the Royal African Company, and, not surprisingly, with a land registry bill for Middlesex. During this first session he was classed as one of the supporters of the poor Palatines, and in the next voted for the impeachment of Dr Sacheverell. Further proof of his party loyalties came in February 1710, when he played an important role in drafting the bill to regulate select vestries within the bills of mortality, a Whig measure aimed at limiting High Church influence within the capital. Soon afterwards he signed an address from the Westminster commission of the peace condemning recent disturbances by Church supporters, and supported a similar volley from the Middlesex sessions.[5]

Having emerged as an opponent of the High Tories, Barker paid the price at the county contest of October 1710, when both he and his running-mate John Austen* were well beaten. He did not get another chance to regain his seat, since he died shortly before the next general election, and was buried on 22 Aug. 1713 at Chiswick. His will revealed a surprising distaste for dynastic honours, directing that his funeral should not be accompanied by 'escutcheons, achievement, or anything else belonging to the useless science of heraldry'. His estate, which included gardens at Chiswick reputed to be 'the finest in England', passed to his eldest son Henry, who subsequently used the family interest to mount four unsuccessful campaigns for a county seat between 1715 and 1740.[6]

[1]PCC 201 Leeds. [2]Berks. RO, Wallingford statute bk. 1648–1766, f. 108. [3]*Vis. Berks.* (Harl. Soc. lvii), 64; *VCH Mdx.* vii. 76–77; W. P. W. Phillimore and W. H. Whitear, *Chiswick*, 251; *London Mar. Lic.* ed. Foster, 77; *VCH Bucks.* iii. 230, 549; *Post Boy*, 18–20 Nov. 1701. [4]*Cal. Treas. Bks.* xix. 338. [5]Add. ch. 76111, 76123. [6]*Mdx. and Herts. N. and Q.* iii. 159; PCC 201 Leeds; Phillimore and Whitear, 13.

P. L. G.

BARKER, Sir William, 5th Bt. (c.1685–1731), of Ipswich, Suff.

IPSWICH	1708–1713
THETFORD	1713–1715
SUFFOLK	31 Oct. 1722–23 July 1731

b. c.1685, o. s. of Sir John Barker, 4th Bt.*. *educ.* Ipswich sch.; Pembroke, Camb. 7 Apr. 1702, aged 16. *m.* (1) aft. 1713, Mary (*d.* 1716), da. and h. of John Bence*, 1s.; (2) 9 Feb. 1731, Anne, wid. of Edward Spencer of Rendlesham, Suff., *s.p.*; ?1s. illegit. *suc.* fa. as 5th Bt. 14 Aug. 1696.[1]

Freeman, Dunwich 1703, Orford 1709.[2]
Commr. public accts. June–Oct. 1714.

Returned as a Tory at Ipswich in 1708, and classed as such in a list of the new Parliament, Barker acted as a teller on 5 Feb. 1709 in favour of the Tory candidates in the disputed Dunwich election. He voted against the impeachment of Dr Sacheverell. In the 'Hanover list' he was classed as a Tory, following his re-election after a contest at Ipswich in 1710. Satisfied with the straightforward rejection of a petition against his return on 3 Feb. 1711, he spoke and told against a motion to condemn the attempt to unseat him as 'frivolous and vexatious'. A teller on 3 Apr. 1711 on the Tory side in a division on the Cockermouth election, and again on 19 May in favour of the coal trade bill, he was listed among the 'Tory patriots' who voted against the continuation of the war and among the 'worthy patriots' who in this session laid open the mismanagements of the previous ministry. He was also a member of the October Club. Writing to Lord Treasurer Oxford (Robert Harley*) on 29 May 1711 to request a local office for his uncle, he admitted 'that at this juncture I ought not to give your lordship another trouble upon so slight an occasion, but really not only my business but want of health will oblige me to quit the town shortly, and if I could obtain an early answer it would double the obligation'.[3]

A teller on 17 Jan. 1712 against a Whig attempt to adjourn the proceedings against Robert Walpole II before Walpole could be expelled the House, Barker was denied leave of absence on 21 Mar. when a motion to that effect was defeated. On 20 Apr. 1712 he led the October Club in defending the tack to the lottery bill of the inquiry into crown grants since 1689. His speech, prepared beforehand, was described by L'Hermitage as 'fort étudié . . . mais fort vif et fort échauffé'. In L'Hermitage's report,

> il dit qu'on avoit porté à diverses fois des bills pour rapeller les dons de la couronne, et qu'ils avoient toujours été rejettés, et qu'il n'y avoit pas d'autre moyen de faire passer celui-ci que de le joindre au bill de la lotterie, mais qu'on disoit que les seigneurs ne les passeroient pas ensemble qu'il etoit surprenant qu'on alleguast une telle raison et que si cela étoit à quoi dont il avoit servi à un grand homme d'avoir fait créer 12 pairs, s'il n'estoit pas presentement sur de cette chambre et que son credit ne put pas aller à faire passer une chose si utile et pourquoi on les avoit engagés à joindre ces 2 bills, si on ne vouloit pas les soutenir et si on pretendoit les faire passer et repasser tantôt d'un côté et tantôt de l'autre, qu'on s'étoit plaint de l'ancien ministre, mais que de la manière dont celui-ci agissoit on avoit encore moins lieu de s'en louer et il ajouta divers autres choses semblables.

On 6 May he told against separating the two bills, and after the defeat of the Tack he served as chairman of the committee appointed to supervise the election of commissioners under the now separate land grant bill. Negotiations for his marriage to the daughter of John Bence* revealed considerable financial difficulties. He admitted in January 1713 that his net income amounted to only about £830 and that he was £3,500 in debt, besides which his house and furniture were 'in so great decay' that it would 'cost a good deal of money to make them fit for the reception of a lady', so that he depended on a generous settlement from Bence: 'all my friends tell me, money is what I want'. The details of the eventual settlement have not been ascertained.[4]

Barker told on the Court side on 21 Apr. 1713 on a motion to go into ways and means, and in the 1713 election was chosen at Thetford, probably on the recommendation of (Sir) Thomas Hanmer II* (4th Bt.). He did not, however, follow Hanmer in the new Parliament. He acted as a teller on 18 Mar. 1714 in favour of condemning Richard Steele's* *Crisis* and *Englishman*, having taken part in the debate, in which he said that Steele both 'insinuates the Q[ueen] has enabled Savoy as her favourite to make his pretensions to this kingdom' and 'brings her Majesty into contempt as having broken her word with Parliament'. On 15 Apr. he spoke for the Court against the motion that the succession was in danger under the present ministry. Lord Bolingbroke (Henry St. John II*) recommended Barker strongly to Oxford as a candidate for office. He was elected on 18 June as one of the accounts commissioners and was a teller twice more: on 8 June, on a private bill, and on 21 June, to adjourn the hearing of the report on the bill amending the Woollen Act. He was marked as a Tory in the Worsley list.[5]

Barker died on 23 July 1731 at his house in East Street, 'near Red Lion Square'. In his will he left £500 to provide for the upbringing and apprenticeship 'to some good trade' of one Charles King, offspring of Mary King, who may have been his illegitimate son.[6]

[1] *Ipswich Sch. List*, comp. Murfey, 6; Copinger, *Suff. Manors*, ii. 340. [2] Suff. RO (Ipswich), Dunwich bor. recs. EE6/1144/14; W. Suss. RO, Shillinglee mss Ac.454/1083, John Hooke to Sir Edward Turnor*, 28 Sept. 1709. [3] Add. 70210, Barker to Oxford, 29 May 1711. [4] *Huntington Lib. Q.* xxxiii. 168; Add. 17677 FFF, f. 187; Shillinglee mss Ac. 454/1256, 1258, Barker to Turnor, 20 Dec. 1712, 17 Jan. 1712–13. [5] Douglas diary (Hist. of Parl. trans.), 18 Mar. 1714; NLS, Advocates' mss, Wodrow pprs. letters Quarto 8, f. 96; *HMC Portland*, v. 425. [6] Boyer, *Pol. State*, xlii. 102; PCC 203 Isham.

D. W. H.

BARLOW, Sir George, 2nd Bt. (c.1680–by 1726), of Slebech, Pemb.

CARDIGAN BOROUGHS 1713–1715
HAVERFORDWEST 3 May–4 July 1715

b. c.1680, 1st s. of Sir John Barlow, 1st Bt., of Slebech and Minwere, by his 2nd w. Katherine, da. of Christopher Middleton of Middleton Hall, Carm.; bro. of John Barlow*. *educ.* Eton. *m.* 31 May 1695, Winifred, da. of George Heneage of Hainton Hall, Lincs., 1s. *suc.* fa. as 2nd Bt. by 27 June 1695.[1]

Although their estate in Pembrokeshire had originally consisted of former monastic land, the Barlows of Slebech had remained Catholic well into the 17th century, and were still regarded as 'Church papists' in the early 1670s. The Member's uncle, William Barlow, knight of the shire in the 1685 Parliament, was almost certainly a recusant. He was also notorious for his Jacobite sympathies, being described in 1693 as 'a known enemy to their Majesties and their government'. The first baronet, his brother, was a little more cautious. A conformist, he seems to have tried to prove his loyalty in 1690 by informing the government of a Jacobite 'libel' in circulation locally. None the less, he too was presented by a Pembrokeshire grand jury three years later as one who had refused the oaths of supremacy and allegiance. He died between 17 Sept. 1694, the date of his will, and 27 June 1695, when it was proved. Possibly Sir George had succeeded as 2nd baronet by the time of his marriage. His Catholic bride brought him property in Lincolnshire, some of which he attempted in vain to dispose of in 1698, through a private bill, in order to pay off various 'debts and legacies'. Otherwise the match was a failure, the young Lady Barlow 'eloping from her husband' after the birth of their only child.[2]

Barlow was included in the Pembrokeshire commission of the peace on his coming of age in 1701, but did not stand for Parliament until the 1713 election, when he was brought in by the Jacobite Lewis Pryse* for Cardigan Boroughs. He is not known to have spoken in the Commons. On 25 May 1714 he was given a month's leave of absence because of ill-health. Reckoned to be 'the head of the Tory party' in Pembrokeshire, he was classed as a Tory in the Worsley list. Defeated at Pembroke Boroughs at the 1715 election, Barlow was chosen for Haverfordwest at a by-election later the same year but he was subsequently turned out on petition in favour of a Whig namesake, John Barlow†. His name was included in the list given in to the Pretender, 1721, presumably as a possible sympathizer. Barlow had died before 3 Mar. 1726, when administration of his estate was granted to his estranged wife. It is possible that in his last years he had made over Slebech to his brother John* and removed to Lincolnshire. Certainly by 1739 his heir, the third baronet, was reported as residing in that county.[3]

[1] M. Barlow, *Barlow Fam. Recs.* 45; *W. Wales Hist. Recs.* iii. 146–8; BL, Verney mss mic. 636/48, John Verney* (Ld. Fermanagh) to Sir Ralph Verney, 1st Bt.†, 5 June 1695. [2] *W. Wales Hist. Recs.* 117–22, 140–8; J. M. Cleary, *Catholic Recusancy of Barlow Fam.* (Newman Assoc. Cardiff Circle, Ppr. 1), 14–16; *CSP Dom.* 1689–90, pp.130, 445; *Trans. Cymmro. Soc.* 1947, pp. 219–20; Verney mss mic. 636/48, John to Sir Ralph Verney, 5 June 1695; *CJ*, xii. 118, 349. [3] L. K. J. Glassey, *Appt. JPs*, 148, 249–50; *Ceredigion*, v. 404; Hereford and Worcester RO (Worcester St. Helen's), Hampton mss 705:349/BA5117/3/xi/21, John Stephens to Lady Pakington, 29 Oct. 1714; P. S. Fritz, *Ministers and Jacobitism 1715–45*, p.153; Barlow, 45; Add. 24120, f. 36; 24121, f. 371.

D. W. H.

BARLOW, John (c.1682–1739), of Colby, Wiston, Pemb.

PEMBROKESHIRE 1710–1715

b. c.1682, 2nd s. of Sir John Barlow, 1st Bt., of Slebech and Minwere, Pemb. by his 2nd w., and bro. of Sir George Barlow, 2nd Bt.* *m.* (1) 1 May 1708 (with £5,000), Anne (*d.* 1733), da. of (Sir) Simon Harcourt I* of Stanton Harcourt, Oxon., 6s. (5 *d.v.p.*) 1da.; (2) c.1734, Anne, da. of Richard Skrine of Warleigh Manor, Som., 1da.[1]

?Pursebearer to ld. keeper 1710–aft. 1716 (to ld. chancellor from 1713).

Barlow presumably purchased the Colby estate well before his marriage, since he was included in the Pembrokeshire lieutenancy as early as 1701. 'As violent' a Tory as his elder brother, according to a local Whig, he appears to have deviated from the family's traditional recusancy so far as to become a staunch

Churchman: he was actively involved in the charity school movement in Wales, and took a close interest in ecclesiastical patronage, writing urgently to Bishop Ottley in 1715 to attempt to forestall the nomination of a 'Whig' parson to a vacant living. His victory in the 1710 county election was greatly assisted by 'the diligence of the clergy', 50 of whom polled for him as against a mere seven for his opponent.[2]

Barlow may have been appointed his father-in-law's pursebearer as lord keeper in October 1710 though, according to Chamberlayne, this 'Mr Barlow' still held the office under the Whig lord chancellor, William Cowper*, in 1716. Certainly it would appear that his marital connexions kept Barlow close to the Court during the ensuing Parliament. Despite being given leave of absence on 3 Mar. 1711, for health reasons, he was listed among the 'worthy patriots' who in the first session exposed the mismanagements of the old ministry, but he did not join the October Club. On 14 May 1713 he told against the place bill at its second reading. Little is known of his conduct in the 1714 Parliament, to which he was returned unopposed, other than that he was marked as a Tory in the Worsley list.[3]

Reports that local Whigs wanted Barlow to be chosen sheriff of Pembrokeshire in order to prevent his standing for Pembrokeshire in 1715 proved ill-founded, but he was defeated at this election and did not stand for Parliament again. Unlike Sir George he was not regarded by the Jacobites in 1721 as reliable: although he had been 'very forward and fit to be tried', he had 'become cautious, since he married Lord Harcourt's daughter'. He did, however, become a member of the Society of Sea Serjeants in 1726 during his uncle William Barlow's[†] presidency of the club. Barlow died on 29 Oct. 1739, aged 57. The Colby estate, together with property acquired from his deceased younger brother, went to the daughter of his second marriage. The sole surviving son of his former marriage, George, inherited the family home at Slebech, perhaps purchased by Barlow from his elder brother, and sat as MP for Haverfordwest 1743–7.[4]

[1] M. Barlow, *Barlow Fam. Recs.* 45; G. D. Barlow, *Barlow Fam. Recs.* 195; Add. 24120, f. 36; *W. Wales Hist. Recs.* iii. 149–51; IGI, London. [2] *W. Wales Hist. Recs.* 150; *CSP Dom.* 1700–2, p. 254; L. K. J. Glassey, *Appt. JPs*, 249–50; *SPCK Corresp.* ed. Clement (Univ. of Wales Bd. of Celtic Stud. Hist. and Law, ser. x), 329; *Pemb. Life 1572–1843* ed. B. E. and K. A. Howells (Pemb. Recs. Soc. 1972), 60; G. Holmes and W. A. Speck, *Divided Soc.* 71. [3] Luttrell, *Brief Relation*, vi. 644; HMC Portland, iv. 569. [4] Hereford and Worcester RO (Worcester St. Helen's), Hampton mss 705:349/BA5117/3/xi/21, John Stephens to Lady Pakington, 29 Oct. 1714; *Pemb. Life 1572–1843*, 58–59; P. S. Fritz, *Ministers and Jacobitism 1715–45*, p. 153; *Trans. Cymmro. Soc.* (1947), 221; (1967), 75; *Welsh Hist. Rev.* i. 290; *W. Wales Hist. Recs.* 150–1.

D. W. H.

BARNARDISTON, Sir Samuel, 1st Bt. (1620–1707), of Brightwell, Suff. and Bloomsbury Square, Mdx.

SUFFOLK   19 Feb. 1674–1681 (Mar.), 1690–1702

b. 23 June 1620, 3rd s. of Sir Nathaniel Barnardiston[†] of Kedington, Suff. by Jane, da. of Sir Stephen Soame[†] of London, ld. mayor 1598–9. *m.* (1) Thomasine (*d.*1654), da. of Joseph Brand[†] of Tower Street, London and Edwardstone, Suff., *s.p.*; (2) aft. 1679, Mary, da. of Sir Abraham Reynardson, Merchant Taylor, of Bishopsgate Street, London, ld. mayor 1648–9, wid. of Richard Onslow, merchant, of London, *s.p. cr.* Bt. 11 May 1663.

Freeman, Grocers' Co. 1654, Levant Co. 1654, asst. 1654–62, 1669–72, 1673–4, 1675–8; freeman, E.I. Co. 1657, cttee. 1661–8, 1670–6, 1677–83, dep. gov. 1668–70.[1]

Sheriff, Suff. 1666–7; freeman and alderman, Dunwich 1680–4.[2]

Commr. public accts. 1691–4.

Barnardiston, 'the old troubler of our Israel', as a Suffolk Tory described him, was returned for the county on the Whig interest in 1690, and was listed as a Whig by Lord Carmarthen (Sir Thomas Osborne[†]). Presumably because of his own previous involvement in and his family's present connexions with the Turkey trade he was one of several Members ordered on 29 Mar. 1690 to prepare a bill to restrict the import of thrown silk, following a petition from the Levant Company. He was nominated to the drafting committees for bills to regulate the East India trade (2 Apr.); to appoint commissioners of public accounts (14 Apr.); to draw up the oath of abjuration (24 Apr.); to prepare a test of fidelity to the government (29 Apr.); and to confirm the charter of the East India Company (8 May), in which he still owned considerable stock. On 15 May he told against a rider to the supply bill (forfeitures) extending the time for office-holders to take the oaths. He was elected, with the second lowest total of votes, in the ballot for commissioners of accounts under the abortive public accounts bill, and at the start of the next session, on 11 Oct. 1690, was named to the committee to bring in a second bill for examining public accounts. He was also appointed to the committee of 25 Oct. for examining the army and navy estimates (from which he reported on 5 Dec.). Much of his time in November and December was taken up with securing the passage of a private bill to relieve his estate from several 'encumbrances', the results of the fine of £10,000 imposed on him in 1684 for seditious libel, a judgment which had been reversed on appeal in 1689. In the election of commissioners of accounts on 26 Dec. he was again successful, reaching one place higher than before, and this time the bill passed. In the following April Robert Harley*, a fellow commissioner, listed him among the Country party.[3]

In a debate on 7 Nov. 1691 on the miscarriages of the fleet, Barnardiston seconded the motion of another commissioner, the Tory Sir Thomas Clarges*, that Admiral Russell (Edward*) be called upon to produce 'a journal of the transactions of the fleet'. During the year he had quarrelled with Sir Josiah Child, 2nd Bt.*, and in consequence had sold all his East India Company stock. In this and subsequent sessions he actively supported the moves to establish a new company. On 2 Dec. 1691, when Sir Edward Seymour, 4th Bt., presented 'heads' for the regulation of a company to be established by Act of Parliament, Barnardiston spoke in favour of setting a minimum of £1,500,000 stock, a proposal for which he also acted as a teller on 17 Dec. He is recorded as having spoken again on 16 Dec. in support of the introduction of a bill to encourage privateers against the French, which he said would be 'very useful to advance our trade, prevent the taking of our merchant ships, and in a great measure save our charge of taking a winter guard'. On 8 Jan. 1692 he spoke and told against the bill for lessening the interest of money, and four days later he followed Robert Harley and William Ettrick in advocating the setting up of a committee to study proposals introduced by Paul Foley I for carrying on the war against France upon a fund of perpetual interest. On 12 Feb. 1692 he reported the bill allowing English ships to be sailed with foreign seamen to and from the West Indies, carrying it up to the Lords four days later. His two remaining tellerships in this session were on 19 Feb., with his colleague as knight of the shire, Sir Gervase Elwes, 1st Bt., to adjourn rather than go into committee immediately on the bill against corresponding with their Majesties' enemies; and on 22 Feb. in favour of the Quakers' affirmation bill. In the same month he helped manage a private estate bill through the House.[4]

It was reported in October 1692 that Barnardiston was seriously ill, having had 'several fits of an ague'; but he had recovered by the beginning of the parliamentary session. On 17 Nov. he spoke in favour of bringing in a bill to establish a new East India Company, and on 24 Nov. he intervened in a debate in the committee considering the 'heads' of this bill, to declare his conviction that

> this trade cannot be carried on but in a joint-stock. I was formerly of this company, and remember in Oliver's time the trade was open, which had near endangered the loss of the trade, and so they were forced to get a charter for a joint-stock to preserve it.

On 17 Dec. he presented a bill to prevent abuses in the packing and weighing of butter and cheese. Harking back to the arguments he had used in support of the project for a new East India Company, he informed the House in a speech on 10 Jan. 1693 in favour of the bill to encourage and to regulate the Greenland trade that 'this was a very beneficial trade but lost to this nation, being engrossed by the Dutch and the Hamburgers, of whom we are forced to have the commodity at expensive rates'; and that the only way to regain this trade was to incorporate them in a company with a joint-stock exclusive to others. Narcissus Luttrell* noted that these comments were 'not liked of by some'. When the bill was eventually passed Barnardiston was ordered to carry it up to the Lords (2 Mar.). Two more speeches of his are recorded in this session: on 19 Jan. he spoke against the bill to encourage woollen manufactures, which its enemies said 'was a project driven on by the factors of Blackwell Hall for their own interest'; and on 8 Feb., following a complaint against the activities of press-gangs in Essex, he was one of the local Members who 'gave an account of divers great abuses committed by press-masters'. He was a teller seven times: against the bill for the importing of Italian silks, which threatened both the Turkey trade and the Suffolk woollen industry (11 Jan. 1693); for the opposition side on a procedural motion (17 Jan.); against the bill against hawkers and pedlars, which Robert Harley, Sir Thomas Clarges and other members of the Country party had opposed (2 Feb.); against giving leave of absence to Granado Pigot (10 Feb.); against the continuance of the Licensing Act (20 Feb.); for an additional clause to the bill continuing the Act against Trade with France, to encourage privateers to work the routes of the Levant and East India traders (2 Mar.); and against a rider to the lotteries bill, to preserve the annuity due to a Colonel Vaughan (6 Mar.). In Samuel Grascome's list in the spring of 1693 he was marked as doubtful.[5]

Discussing prospects for a new Parliament in November 1693 Humphrey Prideaux considered Barnardiston and Elwes certain to retain their seats: both, he claimed, were 'stiff republicarians'. In the 1693-4 session Barnardiston acted six times as a teller: on 24 Jan. 1694 against a bill to revive the Woollen Act; on 8 Mar. in favour of an additional clause to the bill for the relief of the London orphans; on 29 Mar. for the House insisting on its disagreement with the Lords' amendments to Sir John Maynard's* estate bill; on 31 Mar. against another bill against hawkers and pedlars; on 14 Apr. for a motion to fix at ¾d. in the pound the fees claimed by Exchequer officers in respect of provisions in the wine, beer and tunnage duties bill; and finally, on 17 Apr. in support of Hon. Fitton Gerard* in a disputed election case for

Clitheroe. When the accounts commissioners' report on payments for secret service and to Members was read on 9 Dec. Robert Harley took pains to explain the circumstances of a payment of £500 to Barnardiston. This had been part of the money remaining in the Exchequer at the Revolution, some £1,905 in all, out of the £10,000 fine levied on Barnardiston in 1684. Harley recapitulated the events in the case: 'His fine was brought into the Exchequer. He brought a writ of error, and ... in the Lords' House, reversed the judgments, *etc*. The interest of his fine came to more than £500 and he ought to have all.' In the ballot of 11 Apr. 1694 for a new commission, the first since 1690, Barnardiston was one of three members replaced by Court Whigs.[6]

Barnardiston was nominated on 12 Feb. 1695 to the drafting committee for a bill to deter highway robbery, and was a teller on the 20th in favour of allowing Nathaniel Palmer leave of absence. He was ordered on 12 Apr. to prepare and bring in a bill to explain the Act allowing a Bounty on the Export of Coin. His three other tellerships included two on points of procedure (26 and 29 Apr.), in which he appeared on the Whig side against Tories. In May his petition was allowed for full payment of the £1,905 owed him from the Exchequer, with the proviso that the King would pay the sum outstanding when 'in a condition' to do so. He was re-elected without opposition in 1695. He was numbered among the opposition in the forecast for the divisions on 31 Jan. 1696 on the proposed council of trade, and signed the Association promptly. He voted in March against fixing the price of guineas at 22*s*. He presented a bill on 10 Mar. to reform abuses in the 'garbling' of spices, drugs and other such goods, and two days later was a teller in favour of inserting into the bill against hawkers and pedlars a clause to safeguard the position of poulterers, in response to a petition from the Poulterers' Company. On two subsequent occasions in this session he acted as a teller: on 17 Apr., in the minority, against adjourning the report on his own garbling spices bill; and five days later against a Court-inspired amendment to the supply bill (salt duties and land bank), which sought to stipulate that receivers swear on oath that money they were paying over had actually been received 'for revenues and taxes'. No settlement of his debt from the Crown having yet been made, he attended at the Treasury board in May 1696 with a memorial estimating the sum due at over £2,400, including compound interest, less the £500 which had previously been paid him. Although the King's promise was reaffirmed and the amount of the debt admitted (excepting interest), the official letter of confirmation was apparently mislaid and no action was taken. In the next session Barnardiston voted on 25 Nov. 1696 against the attainder of Sir John Fenwick[†]. On 27 Nov. he told for rejecting a petition from Southwark against the landownership qualification in the bill regulating elections. In February 1697 he made an unsuccessful attempt to intrude himself into elections at Orford, where a vacancy had arisen. A member of the corporation wrote, 'there was ... a messenger from Sir Samuel Barnardiston to let us know if we would elect a friend of his he would do great things for us, but the answer he received ... was that whatsoever Lord Hereford agreed upon we would stand to'. Soon afterwards Barnardiston made a serious blunder in Parliament. A manager at a conference on 19 Mar. to discuss the Lords' amendments to a bill against the import of East Indian cloth, he so far departed from the instructions of the Commons as to argue against the bill. The next day a complaint was made against him and it was moved that he be sent to the Tower. He was attacked by Court Whigs and defended by Tories, and after a lengthy debate it was resolved that a Speaker's reprimand would be sufficient punishment 'in consideration of his great age and infirmities, and of his sufferings and services, formerly, in maintaining the rights of this House'. A year later, in February 1698, he was again in trouble. During investigations on 5 Feb. into irregularities in Exchequer bill payments, one of the witnesses, under pressure of cross-examination, claimed to have been told that some 'great men' were involved. This was in due course exposed as a lie but not before Barnardiston had 'reproached' another witness for contradicting the allegation, an intervention for which he 'was obliged to ask pardon of the House'. On 1 Feb. 1698 he reported a petition of officers, clothiers and innkeepers who had claimed they were owed money for the maintenance of the army in 1677–9. Also in this session he assisted his nephew, Sir Thomas Barnardiston, 2nd Bt.*, to prepare a bill to erect a workhouse and hospital at Sudbury.[7]

Returned again at the head of the poll in the 1698 election, Barnardiston was listed in about September 1698 as a supporter of the Country party. In June 1699 he petitioned the King for at least the third time for the payment of his debt. Although a warrant was ordered by the Treasury board in August no money was issued, and he was obliged to renew his petition in December. On this occasion the board minuted that payment was to be 'respited till there be some more money'. Six months later Barnardiston asked yet again. At last in April 1701, he was paid what was owing to him, but without any interest. At the head of the poll for Suffolk once more in January 1701, he was said at the beginning of February to have been 'very ill' but to be 'now on the mending hand, being past danger'. Included in the 'blacklist' of those who had opposed making preparations for war, he was one of the signatories to a published rejoinder, justifying the conduct of the Members named. In December 1701, after his re-election, he was listed by Harley with the Tories. On 26 Feb. 1702 he presented a private bill on behalf of a kinsman.[8]

After Queen Anne's accession Barnardiston pursued his claim to interest on the money repaid him in 1701. Twice, in June 1702 and March 1703, he presented petitions, and twice he was refused. In 1702 his ascendancy in Suffolk elections was suddenly broken, and he suffered the indignity of coming bottom of the poll, having in all probability fought the election as a Whig. In 1705 he certainly stood as a Whig, and came bottom of the poll for a second time. When making his will in July 1706 he declared himself to be 'of sound and perfect memory'. He asked to be 'decently interred, without pomp or ostentation', and among others named 'Edward Harley of Lincoln's Inn' as a trustee. Despite his claims to have lost some £20,000 over and above the £10,000 fine as a result of the 1684 judgment, he still possessed assets of more than £15,000 together with a house in Middlesex and extensive property in Suffolk, most of which he had purchased himself. Barnardiston died on 8 Nov. 1707 and was buried at Brightwell. The baronetcy passed to his nephew Samuel*, but a great-nephew, also called Samuel, a merchant in the Levant, inherited the bulk of his estate.[9]

[1] Info. from Miss S. P. Anderson; *Cal. Ct. Mins. E.I. Co.* ed. Sainsbury, v. 189; vi. 100, 200, 306; vii. 31, 141, 218, 316; viii. 55, 187, 322; ix. 122, 225; x. 46, 175, 302; xi. 40, 176, 268; Add. 38871, f. 7. [2] Suff. RO (Ipswich), Dunwich bor. recs. EE6/1144/13. [3] Bodl. Tanner 27, f. 110; Chandler, ii. 382, 388. [4] *Luttrell Diary*, 7, 56, 83, 117, 124; *DNB*. [5] Add. 70115, Abigail to Sir Edward Harley*, 8, 15 Oct. 1692; *Luttrell Diary*, 234, 259, 358, 374, 397, 411, 459, 460. [6] *Prideaux Letters* (Cam. Soc. n.s. xv), 156; Grey, x. 357; H. Horwitz, *Parl. and Pol. Wm. III*, 132, 140. [7] *Cal. Treas. Bks.* x. 1371; xi. 9, 151, 171; W. Suss. RO, Shillinglee mss Ac.454/971, Nathaniel Gooding to Sir Edward Turnor*, 22 Feb. 1696–7; Luttrell, *Brief Relation*, iv. 198; *CSP Dom.* 1698, p. 71. [8] *Cal. Treas. Bks.* xiv. 99, 404; xv. 2, 32, 103, 124; xvi. 59, 224; *Post Boy*, 4–6 Feb. 1701; *An Answer to the Black List, or the Vine Tavern Queries* (1701). [9] *Cal. Treas. Pprs.* 1702–7, pp. 13, 132–3, 418; *Cal. Treas. Bks.* xvii. 43; *CSP Dom.* 1702–3, p. 418; W. A. Speck, *Tory and Whig*, 104–5; PCC 254 Poley.

D. W. H.

BARNARDISTON, Samuel (1660–1710), of St. Peter's Hall, South Elmham St. Peter, Suff.

IPSWICH 1698–1700

b. 28 Jan. 1660, 4th but 1st surv. s. of Nathaniel Barnardiston of Shoreditch Place, Hackney, Mdx. by Elizabeth, da. of Nathaniel Bacon of Friston, Suff.; neph. of Sir Samuel Barnardiston, 1st Bt.*, cos. of Sir Thomas Barnardiston, 2nd Bt.* *educ.* G. Inn 1680. *m.* 13 Aug. 1709 (with £6,000) Martha, da. and coh. of Thomas Richmond, apothecary, of London, *s.p.* *suc.* fa. c.1680; uncle as 2nd Bt. 8 Nov. 1707.[1]

Barnardiston's father, probably a Turkey merchant like his brothers, acquired lands in Suffolk upon which his son was able to live as a country gentleman. If the preamble to his will is anything to go by, Nathaniel Barnardiston remained true to his Presbyterian upbringing. Nothing has been discovered of Samuel's religious beliefs, though in 1709 he is found ordering from a London bookseller a new printing of Foxe's *Martyrs* and 'six Bibles of a good and true impression . . . for children in the country'. In the 1698 election he and Richard Philips* combined to 'throw out' the Court Whig Charles Whitaker* at Ipswich. In a list of the new Parliament he was classed together with his uncle and cousin as a supporter of the Country party. A militia captain, he was added to the drafting committee for a militia bill on 8 Feb. 1699.[2]

Although Barnardiston succeeded to his uncle's baronetcy in 1707 he did not inherit any of the first baronet's estates. Barnardiston died on 3 Jan. 1710, being succeeded by his brother Pelatiah, who in turn died in May 1712 and was succeeded by a cousin, Nathaniel. With Nathaniel's death the following September, the baronetcy became extinct.[3]

[1] PCC 251 Young, 91 Bath. [2] PCC 91 Bath; D. R. Lacey, *Dissent and Parlty. Pol. 1661–89*, pp. 376–7; Stowe 748, f. 87; W. Suss. RO, Shillinglee mss Ac.454/1023, John Hooke to Sir Edward Turnor*, 26 July 1698. [3] PCC 254 Poley.

D. W. H.

BARNARDISTON, Sir Thomas, 2nd Bt. (c.1646–98), of Kedington, Suff. and Silk Willoughby, Lincs.

GREAT GRIMSBY 1685–1687, 1689–1690
SUDBURY 14 Oct. 1690–7 Oct. 1698

b. c.1646, 2nd but 1st surv. s. of Sir Thomas Barnardiston, 1st Bt.†, of Kedington by Anne, da. of Sir William Armine, 1st Bt.†, of Osgodby, Lincs. and coh. to her bro. Sir Michael, 3rd Bt. *educ.* St. Catharine's, Camb. 1664; G. Inn 1667. *m.* lic. 26 July 1670, Elizabeth, da. and h. of Sir Robert King of Boyle Abbey, co. Roscommon, 6s. (1 *d.v.p.*). *suc.* fa. as 2nd Bt. 4 Oct. 1669.

Freeman and alderman, Dunwich 1680–4; recorder, Gt. Grimsby 1686–?Oct. 1688; steward, honor of Clare 1689–91.[1]

A Whig who had inclined in 1688 towards collaboration with James II, Barnardiston had acted with his party in the Convention, though he had not been listed as voting for the disabling clause of the corporation bill. He supported his uncle, Sir Samuel Barnardiston,

1st Bt.*, and the other Whig candidate, Sir Gervase Elwes, 1st Bt.*, in the Suffolk election of 1690, when he was himself defeated at Grimsby. It was probably Elwes who brought him in for Sudbury at a subsequent by-election, perhaps in return for his having resigned the Clare stewardship. Barnardiston acted as a teller with Elwes on 1 Nov. 1690, for a motion that two men who had been accused of a breach of privilege against the Tory Thomas Christie should be allowed a hearing at the bar of the House, and on 5 Dec. he was again a teller, with a Whig and opposite two Tories, against granting Sir William Ellys, 2nd Bt., a fortnight's leave of absence. In April 1691 he was listed by Robert Harley* as a doubtful member of the Country party. On 14 Nov. 1691 Barnardiston was granted a fortnight's leave to attend his mother-in-law's funeral. He told on 16 Dec. for the bill to register servants going to the plantations. On 4 Jan. 1692 he was granted leave 'to attend the funeral of a near relation'. He had returned to the House by 12 Feb. when he told for a proviso on behalf of Simon Luttrell, to be added to the Irish forfeitures bill, telling again on 16 Feb. in favour of an extra clause to the poll tax bill. On 18 Nov. he was nominated to the drafting committee for a bill to extend the patent on convex lights. He was included in Samuel Grascome's list of 1693 as a Court supporter. Leave of absence was granted him on 5 Jan. 1694, on health grounds, and again on 26 Feb. 1695, and on 7 Jan. 1696 he was one of six Members ordered into custody for inexcusable absence. He was forecast as an opponent of the Court on the proposed council of trade on 31 Jan. 1696. He signed the Association and voted for fixing the price of guineas at 22s. in March. On 25 Nov. he voted for the attainder of Sir John Fenwick[†]. Further leave of absence was given him on 22 Dec. 1696 and on 1 Mar. 1698, and although he was named with his uncle on 5 Apr. 1698 to prepare a bill for a workhouse and hospital in Sudbury, no such bill was presented.

Re-elected for Sudbury in 1698, Barnardiston was listed as a member of the Country party and as an opponent of a standing army. But he did not live to take his seat, dying on 7 Oct. 1698, aged 52.

[1] Suff. RO (Ipswich), Dunwich bor. recs. EE6/1114/13; *CSP Dom.* 1686–7, p. 223; Somerville, *Duchy of Lancaster Official Lists*, 203.

D. W. H.

BARRELL, Francis (1663–1724), of Rochester, Kent.

ROCHESTER   1701 (Dec.)–1702

b. 26 Jan. 1663, 1st s. of Francis Barrell[†], serjeant-at-law, of St. Margaret's, Rochester, by Anne, da. of Richard Somer of Clifford's Inn and St. Margaret's. *educ.* Eton 1673–7; M. Temple 1675, called 1686; Brasenose, Oxf. matric. 1680. *m.* 29 May 1690, Anne (*d.* 1717), da. of William Kitchell of Canterbury and wid. of John Cropley of St. Margaret's, 4s. (3 *d.v.p.*) 5da. (1 *d.v.p.*). *suc.* fa. 1679.[1]

Freeman, Rochester 1689, recorder 1692–*d.*[2]

Barrell was from a clerical family, the grandson of a prominent Kentish clergyman. Two of his brothers held benefices attached to Rochester cathedral. He was himself a devout Anglican, but whereas his grandfather had been the most forthright Arminian preacher in the county, his own religious outlook was markedly different. His diary displays not only a profound piety, but a belief in the working of divine providence in his daily life, and a habit of spiritual self-examination in a traditionally Puritan vein. It was not unusual for him to invoke God's help, for example, 'to become a new creature, utterly forsaking every evil way and living in a constant, sincere and universal obedience all the rest of my life'. What is more, his theology smacked strongly of orthodox Calvinism, emphasizing the salvation of the 'elect'. His attachment to the Church of England, however, almost guaranteed that he would be a Tory, and he was returned as such to the Parliament of 1701–2 for his home town of Rochester, which his father had briefly represented in 1679. He wrote in his diary, apropos of his election:

O Lord, I beseech you, enable me by Thy grace faithfully to discharge this trust to the advancement of Thy glory, the safety, honour and welfare of my King and country, and . . . above all that it may not be prejudicial to me in that great affair of my life, the making my calling and election to a better world sure . . .

Barrell was appointed on 17 Jan. 1702 to a committee to prepare a bill to prevent bribery and corruption at elections, and he was listed as having favoured the motion of 26 Feb. 1702 vindicating the Commons' proceedings during the previous Parliament in the impeachments of King William's ministers.[3]

Barrell did not seek re-election after this Parliament. Little is known of the remainder of his public career, though at the Kent election of 1713 he voted for the Tory candidates and he was still active on the Tory side in borough politics in Rochester at the time of the 1715 election. On his 48th birthday, in 1709, he reflected 'how little time of these many years' he had 'employed in those works of piety and charity, for which alone we come into the world'. His foundation of three schools, in Rochester and nearby Strood, to teach poor boys reading, the Anglican catechism, psalms and hymns, may reflect this renewed commitment to the work of reformation. As recorder of

Rochester he was, despite his Tory sympathies, responsible for drafting various loyal addresses strongly deprecating disaffection and rebellion. His removal from the commission of the peace in 1719 is probably best explained by the increasing ill-health which was leading him to neglect the 'stewardship' of his offices. The death of his beloved wife less than two years previously had broken his spirit. However, there remained a sufficient sense of duty, whether partisan or official in nature, to induce him to visit 'the good bishop of Rochester', Francis Atterbury, in the Tower in February 1723. In that month, Barrell recorded, he 'first fell ill' of the 'long indisposition' which brought him to his death on 11 June 1724. He was buried in Rochester cathedral, where his epitaph recalled the overpowering sense of humility which dominated his character, and which not even his supposed outspokenness on the public stage could obstruct. He was 'holy in death, pious in life', with 'a craving for heaven' and 'a contempt for worldly things, of which for a long time he had sickened'.[4]

[1] Hasted, *Kent*, ii. 538; *Vis. Kent* (Harl. Soc. liv), 9; J. Thorpe, *Reg. Roff*. 707–8; *Rochester Cathedral Reg*. ed. Shindler, 44, 46; J. Thorpe, *Custumale Roff*. 244; *Eton Coll. Reg*. ed. Sterry, 23; Centre Kentish Stud. U145/F11, pp. 2–3, 7–9, 11–14, 17; *Mar. Lic. Vicar-Gen*. (Harl. Rec. Soc. lxvi), 51; PCC 147 Exton. [2] Info. from Mrs H. Ford, archivist, Medway Area Archs. [3] A. G. Matthews, *Walker Revised*, 210–11; P. Clark, *Eng. Provincial Soc. from Reformation to Rev*., 326, 361; A. Everitt, *Community of Kent and Gt. Rebellion*, 105; U145/F11, pp. 2, 4–6, 8, 10–11, 13, 15–19. [4] Add. 5443, f. 202; Centre Kentish Stud. U145/F11, pp. 15, 17–20, 22; Centre Kentish Stud. Q/RPe 1, poll bk.; *Repts. of Charity Commrs. Kent 1819–37*, 55; F. F. Smith, *Hist. Rochester*, 359–61; info. from Prof. N. Landau; Thorpe, 707–8.

D. W. H.

BARRINGTON, Sir Charles, 5th Bt. (c.1671–1715), of Barrington Hall, Hatfield Broad Oak, Essex.

ESSEX   23 Feb. 1694–1705, 1713–1715

b. c.1671, 2nd s. of Thomas Barrington (1st s. d.v.p. of Sir John Barrington, 3rd Bt.[†], of Hatfield Broad Oak), by Lady Anne Rich, da. and coh. of Robert, 3rd Earl of Warwick. *educ*. Felsted sch. *m*. (1) 20 Apr. 1693, Bridget (*d*. 1699), da. and h. of Sir John Monson of Broxbourne, Herts., *s.p*.; (2) 23 May 1700, Lady Anna Marie Fitzwilliam (*d*. 1717), da. of William, 1st Earl Fitzwilliam, of Milton, Northants., *s.p. suc*. bro. as 5th Bt. 26 Nov. 1691.[1]

Freeman, Maldon 1695, alderman 1701–*d*., bailiff 1702, 1706, 1710, 1714; freeman, Colchester 1700; v.-adm. Essex 1702–5, 1712–15.[2]

Despite a relatively long parliamentary career Barrington remains a somewhat faceless backbencher, 'a courteous affable gentleman' with a partiality for venison, 'as much esteemed as any in the county he lived in', and 'a constant stickler for the High Church party'. His family laid claim to being 'knights before English was in England', and to have been converted to Christianity by St. Augustine. The Barringtons' subsequent devotion to the Church was symbolized by the occupation of the Priory, a house attached to the east end of Hatfield Broad Oak parish church, though the structure was in such bad condition by the late 17th century that it had to be pulled down. Barrington's ancestors had been active Parliamentarians, and were related to both Oliver Cromwell and another leading Parliamentarian family in Essex, the Mashams. Sir Charles attended school locally, and it is very unlikely that he would have been old enough to have been the cornet of the same name listed for Ossory's regiment in 1685. In February 1694, three years after succeeding his brother to the baronetcy, he stood and was successful at a by-election for the county. Barrington's eagerness to enter Parliament at this time may have been due to a wish to safeguard the passage during the 1693–4 session of a bill enabling him to settle a jointure on his first wife, though it had already received its second reading before the election, and was granted the Royal Assent on 23 Mar. 1694.[3]

Barrington stood again at the 1695 general election, 'set up by the gentlemen' of the county and the Church party, and headed the poll. He was listed in January 1696 among those Members likely to oppose the Court on the proposed council of trade, and although on 8 Feb. was given leave of absence, he had returned by 27 Feb. to take the Association. Barrington nevertheless voted against the attainder of Sir John Fenwick[†] on 25 Nov. 1696, possibly indicating a sympathy for the supporters of the exiled James that is also suggested by his possession, and perhaps even authorship, of a manuscript tract written in the aftermath of the Revolution and called 'Second Thoughts'. He appears to have been totally inactive in the final session of the 1695 Parliament, but again contested the county in July 1698 on the Church interest. Listed as a Country supporter, he was also marked in August 1698 as likely to oppose a standing army. On 16 Feb. 1699 he acted in a local matter by presenting a private bill for the sale of an Essex estate, and subsequently reported it on 9 Mar. from committee. Described in a newspaper as being worth £6,000 p.a., he married again in 1700 and sought to renew private legislation to make provision for his second wife and any possible offspring. On 11 Apr. a bill to that effect was presented to the House, and passed rapidly through its three readings, receiving the Royal Assent on 12 June. Barrington had been listed in February among those likely to support the Court in agreeing with the committee of supply's resolution to continue the 'Great Mortgage', but his loyalties are difficult to pinpoint at this stage and another categorization of MPs marked him as of an unknown, or possibly opposition, interest.[4]

Barrington again secured a county seat in December 1701, and was at his most active in the ensuing session. On 27 Jan. 1702 he pursued local interests when he acted as teller in a debate over the Maldon election, in which agents of Irby Montagu* were found guilty of bribery and corruption. On 17 Feb. 1702 he acted as teller for the noes on a motion to proceed with consideration of forfeited estates in Ireland, activity perhaps explained by his family's connexions there, and by the fact that his grandfather, Sir Thomas Barrington†, had been a large purchaser of forfeited estates earlier in the century. A week later, on 24 Feb. 1702, he acted as teller for those against a motion that the house adjourn during its debate on the Coventry election, with the result that the officials who had supported the Whig Henry Neale's* candidature by 'illegal means' were punished. Barrington may have been prompted to act on the side of the Tory Sir Christopher Hales, 2nd Bt.*, in this dispute because they had both been blacklisted as opponents of the preparations for war during 1701. On 26 Feb. Barrington was among those who voted for the motion vindicating the Commons' impeachment proceedings against William's ministers, and on 5 Mar. he acted as teller on a motion that the House agree to an amendment on the malt tax bill. Perhaps as a reward for his industry on behalf of the Tories during the session he was appointed by the new ministry as vice-admiral of Essex.[5]

Barrington was again returned at the 1702 election, though the only information about his activities in the first session relates to his having voted on 13 Feb. 1703 with the Tories to extend the time for taking the oath of abjuration. On 10 Jan. 1704 he acted as teller for those who opposed a second reading of the wine duties bill, possibly in defence of his county's trade. In the middle of March he was listed as a supporter of the government's actions in the Scotch Plot. Until this time his career had attracted relatively little attention, but his support for the Tack on 28 Nov. 1704 did not escape his Whig opponents in Essex who soon began meeting to discuss ways to oust him at the next general election. Perhaps in order to counter this threat Barrington became busier in protecting his and his locality's interests in the Commons. On 23 Feb. 1705 he acted as teller for those who wished to grant certain exemptions from the ban on the importation of French wine, and a week later one Edmund Theobolds, who had evidently been active in the Whig campaign to discredit Sir Charles in preparation for an election, was found guilty of 'false and scandalous reflections' on the knight of the shire and of 'misrepresenting his voting and acting' in Parliament to the freeholders. This did not, however, prove enough to stave off defeat at the polls in May, though it was reported that Barrington's defeat was only achieved 'by a great deal of foul play from the fanatic party'. As proof of the vituperativeness of the campaign a tailor was prosecuted in July for having told one of Barrington's voters that Sir Charles was 'a traitor to the Queen and the country'.[6]

Barrington's vote for the Tack and the loss of his seat meant political eclipse. He was replaced as vice-admiral of Essex, and removed from the commission of the peace in Hertfordshire, though not in his own county. This experience seems to have been a sobering one, for he appears not to have sought re-election in 1707 or 1708, and devoted his energies instead to his parish, improving the fabric of the church and refurbishing almshouses. Although it was reported in April 1710 that he would stand, Child seems to have been unable to persuade Barrington to carry through his resolve at the polls in October, even though there was a surge of support for the Tories, Boyer reporting that 'both the Church men might have been chosen'. Perhaps encouraged by seeing the Tories once more in power and by his restoration to the post of vice-admiral, Barrington decided to stand again for election in July 1713. His campaign was successful. Listed as a Tory on the Worsley list, he may well have been a follower of Bolingbroke (Henry St. John II*), since he was approached in February 1714 by one patronage-seeker trying to reach the secretary, though his genealogy also linked him to Nottingham (Daniel Finch†). After the prorogation of Parliament on 25 Aug. 1714, following Anne's death, he sent a letter to the Essex freeholders soliciting votes, but the dissolution was not announced until 15 Jan. 1715, and although Dyer suggests that he had intended to stand as a candidate, Barrington died two weeks later, on 29 Jan. 1715. He left no direct heirs, and his sizable estate was divided between his cousin John Barrington and a son of his sister Anne, wife of Charles Shales, the Queen's goldsmith.[7]

[1] *VCH Essex*, ii. 535–6; viii. 167; Morant, *Essex*, ii. 505. [2] Essex RO, Maldon bor. recs. sessions bks. D/B3/1/24, ff. 64, 149, 155, 187, 201, 215, 235, 237, 267, 272, 303, 317, 326; *Oath Bk. of Colchester* ed. Benham, 234; Boyer, *Pol. State*, iv. 372; Luttrell, *Brief Relation*, v. 550. [3] *Fitzwilliam Corresp.* ed. Hainsworth and Walker (Northants. Rec. Soc. xxxvi), 73; Boyer, ix. 155; *VCH Essex*, ii. 243–4; viii. 167; *Trans. Essex Arch. Soc.* n.s. i. 251; *Vis. Essex* ed.

Howard, i. 87; *CSP Dom.* 1685, p. 76; Colchester Public Lib. mss E324/241, 'A True and Exact Cat. of the... Freeholders that voted for Sir Charles Barrington', 1694; W. Suss. RO, Shillinglee mss Ac.454/1138, [Yardley] to Sir Edward Turnor*, 12 Feb. 1694; *Bramston Autobiog.* (Cam. Soc. xxxii), 378. ⁴*Bramston Autobiog.* 391; Shillinglee mss Ac.454/833, Manyon to Turnor, 14 Oct. 1695; Egerton 2651, ff. 200–3; *Essex Review*, xxx. 41; *Post Boy*, 28–30 May 1700; Bodl. Ballard 10, f. 35. ⁵A. Barrington, *The Barringtons*, ch. v; *Trans. Essex Arch. Soc.* n.s. ii. 38. ⁶*Essex Review*, xx. 177; *Fitzwilliam Corresp.* 174; Essex RO, Q/SR524/1–2, recognizances, 12 May 1705. ⁷Luttrell, v. 567; L. K. J. Glassey, *Appt. JPs*, 176; *VCH Essex*, viii. 179, 181–2; BL, Trumbull Alphab. mss 54, Ralph Bridges to Sir William Trumbull*, 3 Apr. 1710; Add. 70421, Dyer's newsletter, 26 Oct. 1710; 5853, f. 106; Egerton 2651, f. 206; *Jnl. Brit. Stud.* vi(1), p. 50; R. Walcott, *Pol. Early 18th Cent.* 56; *Essex Review*, xxxi. 3; Boyer, ix. 155.

M. J. K.

BARRY, James, 4th Earl of Barrymore [I] (1667–1748), of Castle Lyons, co. Cork, Ire.

STOCKBRIDGE   1710–1713, 30 Apr. 1714–1715
WIGAN   1715–1727, 1734–1747

b. 1667, 2nd but 1st surv. s. of Richard Barry, 2nd Earl of Barrymore [I], by his 3rd w. Dorothy, da. and h. of John Ferrar of Dropmore, co. Down. *m.* (1) (with £10,000), Elizabeth (*d.* 1703), da. of Charles Boyle†, Ld. Clifford, 1s. *d.v.p.* 2da.; (2) June 1706, Lady Elizabeth (*d.* 1714), da. of Richard Savage*, 4th Earl Rivers, 1da.; (3) 12 July 1716, Lady Anne Chichester, da. of Arthur, 3rd Earl of Donegall [I], 4s. 2da. *suc.* half-bro. Lawrence as 4th Earl 17 Apr. 1699.¹

Capt. of ft. Col. Richard's regt. 1689–93; col. 13 Ft. 1702–15; brig.-gen. 1706, maj.-gen. 1709, lt.-gen. 1710.

Freeman, Cork 1700, Salisbury 1712; burgess, Wigan 1712, mayor 1725, 1734.²

PC [I] 1714–*d.*

Barry was descended from an ancient, somewhat impoverished, Irish family. His grandfather had died from a wound received at the battle of Liscarrol while fighting for the Royalists, and while Barry's father had sat in James II's Irish parliament of 1689 his elder half-brother Lawrence had been attainted for remaining in England. Possibly the family had wanted a foot in both camps until the result of the Revolution became clear. Once William III had emerged victorious Barry's father took his seat in the Irish house of lords in the parliament of 1692, and his half-brother signed the Irish Association in 1697. Barry's military career started in 1689, but came to an abrupt and unexplained halt in 1693, though the dowry of £10,000 he received from his first marriage may have removed the necessity of military service. After succeeding to the title, Barrymore was granted a pardon in March 1700 'for all crimes and offences by him committed against his Majesty', though these crimes were not specified, and in March 1702 he purchased a regiment of foot for 1,400 guineas from his brother-in-law, Sir John Jacobs. The regiment was sent to Spain in 1704, and Barrymore spent much of the next few years on active service in the Peninsula, though he had sufficient leave in London to contract a second advantageous marriage in June 1706 with Lady Elizabeth Savage, without the knowledge or consent of her father, Lord Rivers, who was informed of the event by Sir Roger Bradshaigh, 3rd Bt.*, in August 1706. On 12 Aug. Bradshaigh added the more reassuring information that 'I am told my Lord Barrymore has in present near £1,500, and I find he is generally well spoken of about the town and indeed seems more concerned for disobliging your lordship than those who have been most active in this affair'. Barrymore's regiment remained in the Peninsula, however, and in May 1709 he was captured at Caya, being exchanged in August that year and returning to England where he was promoted lieutenant-general in January 1710.³

Elected a member of the Board of Brothers in February 1710, Barrymore was returned for Stockbridge in October with the assistance of a fellow Board member, the Duke of Beaufort, and was classed as a Tory in the 'Hanover list'. Though he was added on 13 Mar. 1711 to the staff of the Duke of Argyll in Spain, he remained in England and was later listed among the 'worthy patriots' who had detected the mismanagements of the previous ministry during the session. Barrymore returned to Spain, where he acted as Argyll's second-in-command, assuming command at times during Argyll's absence, but was disillusioned by the lack of military success, writing in April 1712 to 'inform the Duke of Argyll and my Lord Dartmouth how near ruin we are', and that 'our miseries daily increase'. He returned to England in the autumn of 1712, but by February 1713 was again in Spain, writing to Lord Treasurer Oxford (Robert Harley*) that he would shortly be left 'to be baited by the officers of the three reduced regiments in Catalonia, who are without money or ships to carry them home'. Barrymore returned to England in time to be appointed on 10 Apr. 1713 to draft the Douglas navigation bill, and six days later was the first-named member of the second-reading committee on the bill. His vote on 18 June against the French commerce bill indicates that by this time his Toryism had taken on a 'whimsical' nature.⁴

Barrymore's father-in-law, Lord Rivers, had died in 1712, his will making no mention of his only legitimate daughter, Lady Barrymore, and leaving his estates in Lancashire, Cheshire, Yorkshire and Essex to his cousin, and the inheritor of the title, John Savage, a Roman Catholic priest, and after him to a natural daughter. Barrymore at once challenged the settlement and secured possession of Wardley in Lancashire and consequently control of the Rivers interest at Wigan. In the 1713 election, while still contesting Stockbridge, Barrymore stood at Wigan, utilizing the Rivers interest, together with the support of the Finches, but was defeated in both boroughs. In December 1713 Swift wrote to Oxford that 'the Earl of Barrymore's friends say he would take it kindly to be made a privy councillor' in Ireland, and the suggestion was acted upon the following January. When the 1713 Parliament opened Barrymore lodged petitions against the return of his opponents at Stockbridge and Wigan (3 Mar. 1714), but his failure to sign the petition concerning Wigan led to its dismissal by the House on 6 Apr., when leave to introduce a new petition was also refused. The expulsion of Richard Steele led, however, to Barrymore being seated for Stockbridge on 30 Apr., and a modern historian has noted that he was one of a number of Members who rallied under the banner of (Sir) Thomas Hanmer II* (4th Bt.) in this Parliament. The whimsical nature of his Toryism in the 1713 Parliament is clear from the fact that the Worsley list classed him as a Tory who would on occasion vote with the Whigs, while two further comparisons of the 1713 and 1715 Parliaments listed him as a Whig and a Tory respectively. Barrymore secured his interest at Wigan in December 1714, and was returned for the borough at the 1715 election. Following the Fifteen, Barrymore was removed from the colonelcy of his regiment, though he was one of the few Tories retained on the Lancashire bench in the aftermath of the rebellion. In the 1740s a disillusioned and elderly Barrymore was active in Jacobite intrigue. He died on 5 Jan. 1748 in his eightieth year, the family interest at the borough having been assumed by his son, Richard Barry†.[5]

[1] Lodge, *Peerage of Ire.* i. 307–10. [2] *Cork Corp. Council Bk.* ed. Caulfield, 282; Dorset RO, Strangways mss D124/Box 238 bdle. 11, William Waterman to Charles Fox*, 13 Nov. 1712; Wigan RO, Wigan bor. recs. AB/MR/10. [3] *LJ Ire.* i. 448, 479, 673; Lodge, 307, 311; *CSP Dom.* 1699–1700, p. 410; 1703–4, p. 522; *HMC Bath*, i. 87–89; *Cal. Treas. Bks.* xix. 515; Luttrell, *Brief Relation*, vi. 42, 76, 442, 473; Add. 61127, f. 7; 70420, Dyer's newsletters 17, 19 May 1709; *Edinburgh Courant*, 10–12 Aug. 1709. [4] Add. 49360, ff. 15, 17, 58; Beaufort mss at Badminton House, Duke of Beaufort to Henry Whitehead, 14 Sept. 1710; P. Dickson, *Red John of the Battles*, 135–6, 146–7; *HMC Portland*, v. 155, 270, 327. [5] PCC 219 Barnes; *Bull. John Rylands Lib.* xxxvii. 127–8; Add. 70146, Lady Oxford to Abigail Harley, 23 Aug. 1712; 70287, William Bromley II* to Oxford (Robert Harley*), 4 Sept. 1712; *HMC Kenyon*, 448, 453; *HMC Portland*, v. 270, 327; G. Holmes, *Pol. in Age of Anne*, 281; NLS, Crawford mss 47/2/281, George Kenyon* to Bradshaigh, 15 July 1713, 47/2/637, Barrymore to [–], 17 Nov. 1713; 47/3/38, Kenyon to Robert Hollinshead, 11 Dec. 1714; *Swift Corresp.* ed. Ball, vi. 243; L. K. J. Glassey, *Appt. JPs*, 293.

P. W./R. D. H.

BASSET, Francis (1674–1721), of Tehidy, Cornw.

MITCHELL 1702–1705

b. 10 Feb. 1674, o. s. of Francis Basset of Tehidy by Lucy, da. of John Hele, of Bennetts, Cornw. *educ.* Pembroke, Camb. 1693. *m.* (1) Elizabeth, da. and coh. of Sir Thomas Spencer, 3rd Bt.†, of Yarnton, Oxon., wid. of Sir William Gerrard, *s.p.*; (2) 1713, Mary, da. and h. of John Pendarves, rector of Drewsteignton, Devon and event. h. to her uncle Alexander Pendarves*, 2s. 4da. *suc.* fa. 1675.[1]

Stannator, Tywarnhaile, 1703; sheriff, Cornw. 1708–9.[2]

The Basset family had been seated at Tehidy since the 12th century. Basset was the great-grandson of Sir Francis Basset, a prominent Cornish Royalist who incurred great financial losses as a result of the Civil War. Basset nevertheless succeeded to a substantial estate, Thomas Tonkin* writing that Basset owned 'a considerable tin-works' out of which was raised 'above a hundred thousand pounds worth of tin' at Carnekye, the advowsons of the three considerable parishes of Tehidy, Camborne and Redruth, as well as 'royalties of wrecks' in these parishes. At the December 1701 election Basset had supported James Buller*, the Tory candidate for the county, and was himself successful in 1702 at Mitchell on the Tory interest. In October 1704 he was listed as a probable supporter of the Tack, but he did not vote for it on 28 Nov. This was, however, probably owing to absence rather than opposition to the measure, as Basset had defaulted at a call of the House on 25 Nov., was ordered into custody and not discharged until 8 Jan. 1705. Later the same month, on the 21st, he was granted a three-week leave of absence. He did not stand at any subsequent election.[3]

Basset married the niece and prospective heir of Alexander Pendarves, who 'offered to settle on him his whole estate, provided he would after his death take his name'. He refused to do so, whereupon Pendarves married Mary Granville, the young niece of Lord Lansdown (George Granville*) and the future Mrs Delany, in the hopes of siring an heir of his own. Delany later described Basset as a man with enough 'wit and cheerfulness' to make up for his 'despicable' figure, and recorded that shortly after a visit to Pendarves' house, he 'was seized with terrible fits that ended his life' on 11 Dec. 1721. His younger son and namesake sat for Penryn from 1766 to 1769.[4]

[1] Vivian, *Vis. Cornw.* 19; Polsue, *Complete Paroch. Hist. Cornw.* ii. 218. [2] Tregonning, *Stannary Laws*, 118. [3] Polsue, 218–20, 227–8; Cornw. RO, Buller mss BO/23/63, Basset to Buller, 24 Nov. 1701. [4] M. Delany, *Autobiog. and Corresp.* i. 23, 25, 38–40, 61; Vivian, 19.

E. C.

BASSETT, Sir William (1628–93), of Claverton, nr. Bath, Som.

BATH   27 Nov. 1669–1679 (July), 1681 (Mar.)
            1685–1687, 1689–25 Sept. 1693

bap. 17 Apr. 1628, 1st s. of William Bassett of Claverton by his 2nd w. Elizabeth, da. and h. of Sir Joseph Killigrew† of Lothbury, London and Landrake, Cornw. *m.* (1) Philadelphia, da. of James Campbell of Woodford, Essex and coh. to her bro. Sir John Campbell, 1st Bt., *s.p.*; (2) 28 Sept. 1685, Rachel, da. of Sir Theophilius Biddulph of Westcombe Park, Greenwich, Kent, *s.p. suc.* fa. 1656; kntd. 7 July 1660.[1]

Bassett had represented Bath in almost every Parliament since 1669, and his reputation for drunkenness and debt made him no less worthy a choice to the corporation in 1690. Lord Carmarthen (Sir Thomas Osborne†) listed him as a Court Tory in a list produced in March, and as a Court supporter in two further lists later in the year. An additional list among Robert Harley's* papers of Apr. 1691 also noted his pro-Court tendencies. He was, for the most part, an inactive Member. He was named on 28 Nov. 1691 to the committee ordered to draft a bill regarding the manufacture of saltpetre, and on 22 Nov. 1692 brought a complaint of privilege against two persons who had seized part of his estate, a verdict in his favour being reported on 28 Jan. 1693. Bassett died later that year on 25 Sept., and was buried at Claverton. He had already been forced to mortgage Claverton, and his will directed that the estate be sold by trustees to pay off his extensive debts, which was done in 1701.[2]

[1] *Som. and Dorset N. and Q.* iii. 62; PCC 414 Berkeley; *Le Neve's Knights* (Harl. Soc. viii), 89. [2] F. Brown, *Som. Wills*, iv. 20; Collinson, *Som.* i. 146.

P.W.

BATEMAN, Sir James (c.1660–1718), of Shobdon Court, nr. Leominster, Herefs. and Soho Square, London.

ILCHESTER   2 June 1711–1715
EAST LOOE   1715–9 Nov. 1718

bap. 29 Apr. 1660, 1st s. of Joas [?Johannes] Bateman, merchant, of Tooting, Surr., alderman of London, by his 2nd w. Judith (*d.* 1709), da. of John de la Barre, merchant, of Fenchurch Street, London. *m.* lic. 3 Dec. 1691, Esther (*d.* 1709), da. and coh. of John Searle, merchant, of Finchley, Mdx., 4s. 3da. Kntd. 14 Dec. 1698; *suc.* fa. 1704.[1]

Dir. Bank of England 1694–1711 (with statutory intervals), dep. gov. 1703–5, gov. 1705–7; receiver, subscriptions to Bank of Eng. 1695; dir. Co. of Scotland 1695; receiver, subscriptions to New E.I. Co. July 1698, dir. 1698–1700, 1703–4, 1707–9, (united) E.I. Co. 1709–10; receiver, Two Million loan, Oct. 1698; trustee, Exchequer bills 1697–1710, receiving loan to Emperor 1706; commr. enlarging capital stock of Bank of Eng. 1709; sub.-gov. S. Sea Co. 1711–*d.*; trustee, sale of S. Sea stock 1714–16.[2]

Commr. Greenwich Hosp. 1695, dir. 1703–?*d.*; commr. building 50 new churches 1712–15.[3]

Sheriff, London Feb.–Sept. 1702, alderman 1708, ld. mayor 1716–17; member, Lorimers' Co. until 1709, Fishmongers' Co. 1709–*d.*, prime warden 1710–12.[4]

One of the great merchant financiers of his time, Bateman built his success and colossal wealth upon the considerable mercantile business established by his father, a Flemish émigré naturalized in 1660. His Dutch Calvinist upbringing and his family's marriage links with several leading London Dissenters inevitably helped to shape his Whiggish outlook. From 1683 or 1684 he was resident at the Portuguese port of Alicante where he was engaged in the lucrative wine trade. He had returned to London by the early 1690s, and having already amassed a sizable fortune he continued to operate on a large scale as an Iberian wine importer. He quickly assumed a prominent position within the City, lending £10,250 on the land tax in 1693, and became a major subscriber to the Bank of England at its inception in 1694 and one of its founding directors. He was also involved at this juncture in the campaign for a new East India Company in rivalry to the existing Tory-dominated company, and was a signatory to an unsuccessful petition for this purpose presented to the Commons on 8 Jan. 1694. In the 1695 election he took the bold step of contesting Totnes against the Tory magnate, Sir Edward Seymour, 4th Bt.*, but suffered a humiliating defeat. The precise circumstances of his candidature in the borough remain unclear, but he clearly saw the acquisition of a parliamentary seat as a means of enhancing his status and influence. As a result of his involvement in the Company of Scotland in 1695, he came close to being impeached along with his fellow directors following the House of Commons' inquiry which concluded in January 1696. The inquiry's report, considered by the House on 21 Jan., spoke of Bateman's 'contradictory answers' and he was consequently declared guilty of high crimes and misdemeanours. Though a committee was ordered to prepare his and the other impeachments, it never reported and the issue lapsed with the close of the session. He was one of a consortium of businessmen who in 1697 was remitting money to the forces in Flanders, and in April that year was appointed one of the trustees for circulating

Exchequer bills, at a salary of £400 p.a., he himself having subscribed £2,000 towards funding the bills. The end of his first term as a Bank director in August, along with his colleagues Sir Henry Furnese* and Gilbert Heathcote*, was much regretted by government officials such as Secretary Vernon (James I*) who regarded them as 'useful men in their several kinds'. The following year he was chosen as a founding director of the New East India Company and in December he was knighted. A parliamentary seat still eluded him, however, and in the general election of January 1701 he failed again, this time at St. Mawes where he appears to have been a candidate on the New East India Company interest.[5]

It may have been Bateman's failure to enter Parliament that steered him into City politics. In February 1702 he was elected sheriff, and in March 1703 he stood for alderman of London, but although he was one of the two candidates elected, he was not nominated by the court. On his father's death in 1704 he inherited property in London, Hertfordshire and Kent, and the following year he purchased the manor of Shobdon in Herefordshire which became his principal country seat. It appears to have been this geographical proximity to the Harleys that brought him into a closer and, as events were to prove, beneficial acquaintanceship with Robert Harley*. He finally achieved his ambition of becoming a London alderman in 1708. At the time of the subscription for doubling the Bank's capital in March 1709, Bateman's stock amounted to £10,300, making him one of the select band of 24 City figures with stock at £10,000 or more; his subscription to the Bank on this occasion amounted to a further £10,000.[6]

After the dismissal of Lord Treasurer Godolphin (Sidney†), one of Harley's chief concerns was to ensure that his government had sufficient financial access in the City. His private correspondent John Drummond†, a prominent banker at Amsterdam who knew the workings of war finance intimately, advised Harley in August 1710 on the importance of securing 'such a man who has credit abroad as Sir James Bateman or Sir Theodore Janssen who, next to Furnese, and I may say Sir James preferable to him, has the best interest and credit abroad'. Drummond further advised in September that Bateman would be invaluable as the government's remittancer at Antwerp 'where the subsistences of the native British troops are paid' and where 'he is in great credit'. Moreover, Bateman's amenability could be guaranteed, Drummond felt, by virtue of his having been 'disobliged this year by the Whig cabal of the East India Company' which had apparently blocked his re-election to the company's board in April. His political outlook remained intact, however, and he proceeded to campaign, unsuccessfully, as a Whig candidate for London in the October general election. It is not clear if Harley made use of Bateman's financial services in the Low Countries, but the ministry's need for stronger support from the monied men of the City became acute during the winter when the Whig directors of the Bank attempted to wreck Harley's scheme to fund Exchequer bills. To this end, Harley, in April 1711, set out to capture the directorates of the City's two Whig strongholds, the Bank and East India Company, and headed the ministerial list with Bateman as candidate for the governorship of the Bank. In common with a number of Whigs, Bateman was evidently willing to accommodate himself to the new Tory government, but how much he was prepared to compromise his Whig background and principles can only be gauged from his later behaviour in the Commons. Harley's immediate plans were foiled when Bateman and the others on the ministerial ticket were defeated, but he kept Bateman well to the fore in his subsequent plans to ease the government's financial problems. Strings were pulled to have him promptly brought into Parliament. When a seat became available at the Somerset borough of Ilchester in mid-May, Harley instructed his Treasury colleague Lord Poulett, who controlled the seat, to ensure Bateman's return; this was accordingly done on 2 June without even requiring Bateman's presence. Lord Oxford (as Harley had since become) had probably by this time already allocated to him the central role of sub-governor of the newly established South Sea Company, the chief purpose of which was to assist in the recovery of government credit by funding public debts. Bateman helped in backing this new venture with a subscription of £9,000.[7]

On 13 May 1712 Bateman featured among the supporters of a bill proposed for continuing the South Sea trade as initially authorized under the recent legislation establishing the Company, and presented the bill himself next day. A rumour in March 1713 that he was to be elevated to the peerage proved without foundation. Having assisted the government with a loan of £65,000 for the navy in July 1712, in return for which he received the equivalent sum in South Sea stock, he was included on the naval estimates committee of 29 Apr. and made further substantial loans in 1713. On 14 May he helped to promote the ministerial line on the commercial aspects of the peace settlement by seconding Arthur Moore's motion for a bill for implementing the 8th and 9th articles of the commercial treaty with France, and duly voted for the bill at its report stage on

18 June. Earlier, on 2 June, he had acted as a teller in favour of preserving the Royal African Company's monopoly.[8]

Bateman was returned again for Ilchester in 1713. In his capacity as sub-governor of the South Sea Company, he was involved in the protracted negotiations over the division of the profits of the *asiento* between the Queen, the company and certain individuals believed to be acting for Bolingbroke (Henry St. John II*) and Bolingbroke's close associate, Arthur Moore. The matter was eventually settled to the company's satisfaction, but Bateman's suspicions of Moore's activities led him to alert the other directors to evidence that he was using one of the two *asiento* ships for his own private trading purposes. Bateman's exposure of Moore proved to be the preparatory step in the full-scale parliamentary attack launched late in the 1714 session, encouraged in part by friends of Lord Oxford in their efforts to discredit Bolingbroke. In the Worsley list Bateman was noted as a Tory who had sometimes voted with the Whigs during the 1713 Parliament, but after the Hanoverian succession he reverted to full Whig allegiance though supporting 'the Prince's party' in the first years of the 'schism'. He died of 'gout of the stomach' at his house in Soho Square on 9 Nov. 1718, and was buried at Tooting, leaving a fortune reputed to be worth £400,000, which besides property included £30,000 in cash. To his eldest son, William†, who was raised to the Irish peerage as Viscount Bateman in 1725, he left his Herefordshire estates valued at £14,000 p.a., while his two younger sons, James† and Richard, inherited his estates in Tooting, Kent and in Essex.[9]

[1] Info. from Dr P. L. Gauci; J. R Woodhead, *Rulers of London* (London and Mdx. Arch. Soc.), 25; *London Mar. Lic.* ed. Foster, 95; Lodge, *Peerage of Ire.* iii. 325–27. [2] *N. and Q.* clxxix. 39; *Cal. Treas. Bks.* x. 954; xii. 8; xiii. 102; xiv. 143; xxv. 456; xxix. 80–81; xxx. 4, 122; *CJ*, xi. 401; Beaven, *Aldermen*, ii. 121; Boyer, *Anne Annals*, iv. 126. [3] Add. 10120, ff. 232–6; J. Cooke and J. Maule, *Hist. Account of Royal Hospital . . . at Greenwich* (1789), 60; E. G. W. Bill, *Q. Anne Churches*, p. xxiii. [4] Beaven, 121. [5] G. S. De Krey, *Fractured Soc.* 226; P. G. M. Dickson, *Financial Revol.* 264, 429; info. from Dr Gauci; DZA, Bonet despatch 6/16 July 1694; *Cal. Treas. Bks.* xii. 3, 19, 32, 50, 62–3, 107, 270, 307; xiii. 86; Univ. of London, MS 65/3; Add. 34348, f. 70; *CSP Dom.* 1698, p. 370. [6] Add. 70075, newsletters 11, 20 Mar. 1703; 70210, Bateman to Harley, 17 Aug. 1708; Woodhead, 25; D. W. Jones, *War and Econ.* 331; Dickson, 261, 263–4. [7] *HMC Portland*, iv. 559, 583; Pittis, *Pres. Parl.* 80; De Krey, 240–2; Add. 70252, Poulett to Oxford, [4 June 1711]; 17677 EEE, f. 225. [8] Add. 17677 GGG, f. 94; *Cal. Treas. Bks.* xxvi. 373; xxvii. 7, 73, 91; Chandler, v. 11; *Wentworth Pprs.* 334. [9] *HMC Lords*, n.s. x. 435, 438–40, 443–4, 446–8, 455–60; *Hearne Colls.* vi. 253; info. from Prof. J. M. Black.

P. W./A. A. H.

BATHURST, Allen (1684–1775), of Oakley Park, nr. Cirencester, Glos.

CIRENCESTER   1705–10 Dec. 1709
                  23 Dec. 1709–1 Jan. 1712

b. 16 Nov. 1684, 3rd but 1st surv. s. of Sir Benjamin Bathurst*; bro. of Benjamin* and Peter Bathurst*. *educ*. privately (Abel Boyer); Trinity, Oxf. 1700. *m*. 6 July 1704, Catherine (*d*. 1768), da. of Sir Peter Apsley† of Westminster, Mdx., 4s. 5da. *suc*. fa. 1704; *cr*. Baron Bathurst 1 Jan. 1712, Earl Bathurst of Bathurst 27 Aug. 1772.[1]

Commr. taking subscriptions to S. Sea Co. 1711; PC 13 July 1742; capt. gent. pens. 1742–4; treasurer to Prince of Wales 1757–60.[2]

Bathurst was brought up in close proximity to the court, his father being financial comptroller to the Prince and Princess of Denmark and his mother a long-standing companion of both daughters of James II. His early education was under the charge of the journalist Abel Boyer who as a French Protestant refugee had fled France in 1685. In 1700 he went up to Trinity Hall, Oxford, where his uncle, the aged but much-respected Dean Ralph Bathurst, was still president. He soon proved to be a youthful rebel against the constraining effects of court life, telling his tutor in December 1702: 'do not judge me as a courtier . . . I partake nothing of the court, though I live in it, but the giddiness of it; and 'tis very hard for a weak brain not to be turned'. On his father's death in 1704 he inherited extensive estates in Northamptonshire and Gloucestershire, notably the manor of Cirencester where Sir Benjamin had built up a strong electoral interest.[3]

Bathurst was returned for Cirencester at the 1705 election six months before coming of age. He was an uncompromising Tory: his earlier anti-Court sentiments persisted and the ministry found him a difficult young man to dragoon. His mother had retired from London after her husband's death, her long friendship with Anne having cooled somewhat as a result of the Queen's refusal to pay a generous portion on the marriage in 1703 of Lady Bathurst's niece, the daughter of her sister Lady Wentworth, who had been a maid of honour to the Queen. Lord Treasurer Godolphin (Sidney†) wrote in September 1705 to the Duchess of Marlborough urging her to keep Lady Bathurst in humour, 'if she will make her son go right in the House'. On 23 Oct., with the Commons about to reconvene and vote on the Speakership, the Queen, almost certainly at the Duchess's prompting, wrote to Lady Bathurst requesting her son's vote for the Court candidate, John Smith I:

I look upon myself to have a particular concern for Mr Bathurst, both for his father's sake and the long acquaintance and friendship there has been between you and me, which makes me very desirous he may always behave himself rightly in everything. I do not at all doubt of his good inclinations to serve me, and, therefore hope, though it should be too late to recall his resolutions as to the other Speaker, he will be careful never to engage himself so far into any party as not to be at liberty to leave them when he sees them running into things that are unreasonable, for I shall always depend on his concurring in everything that is good for me and the public.

Bathurst, however, had already committed himself to supporting his kinsman William Bromley II, a leader of the High Tories whose intimacy with the Bathurst family went back over many years, and he duly voted against the Court candidate on the 25th. His continuing to act against the Court under Bromley's wing soon led to a final breach between the Duchess of Marlborough and his mother, relations having cooled since 1704 when the Duchess had flatly refused to countenance Lady Bathurst's proposed betrothal of Bathurst to one of the Duchess's daughters. In August 1706 the Duchess wrote to Lady Bathurst declining to perform some promised 'service' on account of her son's having acted 'very scandalously' against her the previous November in the proceedings on the disputed St. Albans election in which the Duchess had been involved in the Whig interest. Lady Bathurst responded that her son

> often professes to me a true sense of the obligations his family have had to your Grace . . . and he has or at least persuades me so, the most zealous intention to serve her Majesty and the public: how his actions have answered to these professions I have lived too much out of the world to make a right judgment of.[4]

Whilst Bathurst remained in opposition to the Godolphin ministry his recorded involvement in proceedings was slight. Before the 1708 election the only sign of any substantive activity was his inclusion on the drafting committee of a bill to end an embargo on cloth exports, a subject of particular concern to the wool-producing Gloucestershire districts. Bathurst's already extensive estates were further augmented when his wife inherited much of the Apsley property on the death of her bachelor brother in 1708. Classed as a Tory in two analyses of the House early in 1708, he successfully contested Cirencester in that year's general election. In the succeeding Parliament he began to show his mettle as a Tory activist. On 20 Jan. 1709 he was a teller for the Tory side in the disputed Abingdon election. His own return was declared void on 10 Dec. 1709, but he was re-elected a fortnight later. He voted against the impeachment of Dr Sacheverell early in 1710 and was teller in favour of an adjournment motion on 24 Mar. intended to prevent the House from proceeding against the Doctor's published *Answer* to the articles of his impeachment. On the 29th he presented to the Queen the Tory address from Gloucestershire of which she was reported to have taken 'little notice'. The change of administration in the summer of 1710 brought speculation that he would soon be granted a peerage, but this was not forthcoming and in the autumn general election he was re-elected for Cirencester.[5]

Under the new Tory administration Bathurst entered what was to be the busiest phase of his Commons career. He was duly noted as a Tory in the 'Hanover list' of the new Parliament. On 12 Dec. his 'country' inclinations were demonstrated once more when he joined a small group of Tories who secured authorization to prepare a bill for setting a minimum landed qualification for MPs. In January and February 1711 he was appointed to several of the committees set up to investigate areas of 'mismanagement' by the previous ministry, most notably abuses in victualling, tax collection and army administration. His membership of the October Club doubtless inspired his active participation in these inquiries: the Duchess of Marlborough recalled years later his particular efforts at this juncture to blacken her husband's reputation. He was nevertheless quick to alert his cousin Lord Raby when several fellow Octobrists threatened to initiate an inquiry into crown grants, believing Raby's own interests might be directly affected. On 15 May he was teller for a Tory motion laying blame for over-spending and the increased national debt squarely upon the former Whig ministers, and on the 24th was included on the committee ordered to draft a representation to the Queen on the various investigations. He had previously been teller on 27 Jan. against declaring the Whig Viscount Shannon (Richard Boyle*) elected for Hythe; and on 27 Feb. in favour of a petition seeking the renovation of St. Botolph's church, London. Though the entry of his younger brother Peter to the House in mid-March creates a problem of identity in subsequent Journal references to 'Mr Bathurst', it has been assumed that with regard to business concerning the 'mismanagements', it was the elder Bathurst who was concerned. In printed lists published after the session he featured as a 'Tory patriot' opposed to the continuance of the war, and as a 'worthy patriot' who participated in detecting the mismanagements of the previous administration. Closer to Henry St. John II* than Harley, he was one of the founder members of St. John's 'Society of Brothers' which began its meetings in June, and with Dean Swift was soon actively engaged in enlisting further recruits.[6]

In the next session it was probably Bathurst rather than his brother who acted as a teller for the ministry on 7 Dec. in the division on 'No Peace without Spain'. His Commons career came to an end, however, on 1 Jan. 1712 when, still only 27, he was made a peer, one of the 12 created to assist the passage of the peace through the Upper House. His ambitious Wentworth cousins privately observed among themselves how 'Mr Bathurst and all his family give themselves airs as [if] this grace and favour was her Majesty's goodness to them, and not at all their seeking', and that had it not been for the lord treasurer's urgent need 'they might yet be fed with promises'. In the crisis-ridden atmosphere of the Queen's last months Bathurst took the view that the quarrel between Bolingbroke and Oxford was not serious. But it was to Bolingbroke (St. John) that he remained loyal, and in July when it seemed that Bolingbroke might be asked to form a new administration, Bathurst was talked of as a possible commissioner of the Treasury. After the Queen's death he hoped to make an accommodation with the new ministry, expressing his anxiety that George I should listen to Tories as well as Whigs. Once it became clear that the new King had no intention of employing the Tories, Bathurst became a Jacobite, sending money and assurances of support to the old Pretender and vigorously opposing successive Whig ministries in the Lords. There was a restlessness about him which his brother Benjamin found annoying: 'he has more than once, in my opinion, quitted his best friends for those I think very indifferent. He flies about in life as in his journeys, still pursuing something new, without taking the least delight in anything he once has known.' During Pelhamite rule he was a member of Prince Frederick's 'Leicester House faction', and when the princely household was re-established in the later 1750s around Frederick's son, the future George III, Bathurst was appointed its treasurer. It was not until 1772, however, when he was almost 88, that these services were acknowledged with a long-awaited earldom. Two of Bathurst's sons had followed him into Parliament and he lived to see the elder, Henry†, become lord chancellor in 1771. He died on 16 Sept. 1775 and was buried at Cirencester where his monumental inscription records that 'in the legislative and judicial departments of the great council of the nation he served his country 69 years, with honour, ability and diligence'. His successor burned all his correspondence, to destroy evidence, it was thought, of Jacobite connexions.[7]

[1] B. Bathurst, *Letters of Two Queens*, 16; *Proc. Huguenot Soc. London*, xxiv. 46–47. [2] Pittis, *Present. Parl.* 348. [3] Bathurst, 253–5, 262–3; *DNB* (Bathurst, Ralph); NLW, Ottley mss 1988, Bathurst to Adam Ottley, 24 Dec. 1702. [4] *HMC Bathurst*, 4–6; *Letters of Queen Anne* ed. Curtis Brown, 174–5; *Marlborough–Godolphin Corresp.* 499; Bathurst, 262–3, 265–6; Add. 61455, ff. 90, 103. [5] Boyer, *Anne Annals*, ix. 159; Luttrell, *Brief Relation*, vi. 563; *Wentworth Pprs.* 137. [6] Add. 61415, ff. 89–90; *Wentworth Pprs.* 180; *Bolingbroke Corresp.* i. 246; *Swift Stella* ed. Davis, 423, 448. [7] *Wentworth Pprs.* 237, 382, 528; *Swift Corresp.* ed. Williams, ii. 78; iii. 371; *HMC Stuart*, iv. 453, 482; v. 380, 431, 484–5; *DNB*; *Cam. Misc.* xxiii. 106, 211, 213–14; *Bigland's Colls.* (Bristol Glos. Arch. Soc.: Glos. Rec. Ser. v. pt. i), 379.

P. W./A. A. H.

BATHURST, Sir Benjamin (1638–1704), of Paulerspury, Northants. and St. James's Sq., Westminster.

BERE ALSTON   1685–1687
NEW ROMNEY   1702–27 Apr. 1704

b. 3 Oct. 1638, 13th but 6th surv. s. of George Bathurst (d. 1651) of Theddingworth, Leics. by 1st w. Elizabeth, da. and coh. of Edward Villiers of Hothorpe, Northants. m. June 1682, Frances (d. 1727), da. of Sir Allen Apsley† of Westminster and Apsley, Suss., 6s. 2da. (3s. 1da. d.v.p.). Kntd. 17 Jan. 1682.[1]

Freeman, E.I. Co. 1676, cttee. 1684–6, 1690–5, 1696–8, dep. gov. 1686–8, 1695–6, gov. 1688–90; asst. R. African Co. 1677–9, 1684, 1687–8, 1690–5, 1700, dep. gov. 1680–1, sub. gov. 1682–3, 1685–6, 1689.[2]

Alderman, London 1677, 1683–6, 1703; freeman, New Romney 1685, Brackley Sept.–Oct. 1688.[3]

Commr. for Duke of York's revenue 1683–5; treasurer to Princess Anne 1683–1702, to Duke of York 1684–5, to Prince George of Denmark 1683–1702; treasurer and receiver-gen. to Duke of Gloucester 1698–1700; commr. of horse to Prince George 1687–1702, to Queen Anne Apr.–July 1702; cofferer of Household 1702–d.[4]

Commr. Christ's Hosp. by 1684, Greenwich Hosp. 1695, land bank 1696.[5]

Having amassed considerable wealth as a merchant, Bathurst had become a prominent figure in London's commercial world by the early 1680s, and his extensive loans to the government earned him a knighthood in 1682. His involvement in the financial affairs of the Duke of York gave him close proximity to the court and in 1682 he married a close friend of the Duke's daughters. Upon Princess Anne's marriage the following year, his wife had little difficulty in obtaining for him the post of treasurer in the princess's household, and with his City connexions and financial dexterity he quickly became one of the royal couple's small circle of intimate friends. He shouldered responsibility for the management of the household and was always addressed by Anne in her letters as 'your very affectionate friend'. Away from London he made Paulerspury, the Northamptonshire manor he purchased in or just before 1687, his principal country residence.[6]

In the 1690 election Bathurst offered his services to the mayor and jurats of New Romney where in 1685 he had become a freeman. As a man of proven Tory disposition he promised he would 'very heartily stick to the interest of the Church as well as to the preservation of all our liberties and properties as Englishmen'. But despite promises to use his City and court connexions to further the interests of the port or any member of its corporation, Bathurst's offer was not taken up. He remained particularly active in the East India Company after his period of governorship ended in 1690, standing security for £20,000 of their stock in 1691, while his personal stockholding was put at £7,250 in 1692. In November 1694 he was one of a committee of nine set up by the company to investigate charges that Sir Thomas Cooke* had, while governor, used the company's money to bribe MPs. When the allegations came before a Commons committee early in March 1695, Bathurst testified that Cooke had repeatedly sidestepped his requests for accounts of the expenditure, and that when he found £30,000 had been 'charged for secret services' he had had 'some warm discourse' with Cooke who had reminded Bathurst of his oath to the company to maintain their 'secrets'. To this Bathurst had replied that he 'was also bound by oath to be true to the interest of the company'. He alleged further that Cooke had told him that some £90,000 in cash was 'to gratify some persons in case the bill [for confirming the company's charter] should pass'. Bathurst himself appears to have been above suspicion, there having been but modest outlays from the company's funds during his own governorship.[7]

During the earlier part of 1695 Bathurst purchased from Lord Newburgh's (Charles Livingston†) widow the manor of Cirencester in Gloucestershire, seemingly with the intention of entering Parliament. When in the summer of that year a dissolution began to seem inevitable, his friend the Earl of Marlborough (John Churchill†) encouraged him to stand, telling him, 'I need say nothing to you how much it may happen to be for the Princess's service to have you of the House'. He initially proposed standing with another local gentleman, Henry Ireton*, against the existing MPs, but then withdrew. After the election he nevertheless took measures to gain popularity in the borough, including the procurement of a royal warrant allowing the inhabitants to hold two fairs each year.[8]

Soon after the recoinage in 1696 Sarah Marlborough notified Princess Anne that Bathurst 'did cheat her extremely' in the management of her financial affairs. He had apparently remitted to the princess and her husband some £7,000 or £8,000 of a larger sum he had been holding on their behalf, at the old rate of 30s. per guinea instead of at the new rate of 21s. 6d. By questioning Bathurst about these transactions and causing him some discomfiture, Lady Marlborough claimed to have prevented him from embezzling the princess further. Anne was obviously apprised of Bathurst's activities but cautioned Sarah to keep quiet, presumably not wanting to harm her friendship with Bathurst's wife.

However, in April 1697 she discovered that Bathurst was selling offices in her household 'in a most shameful manner, which has given me a much greater abhorrence of him than ever'. When confronted on the subject, Bathurst claimed that the money, amounting to several hundred pounds, had been given voluntarily, but the princess was not fooled: as she informed Sarah, 'it was very plain by his way of speaking to see that what he said was false'. Despite this humiliation, the question of Bathurst's dismissal did not arise, presumably on account of Anne's closeness to his wife, and he continued to feature in the princess's correspondence as 'your very affectionate friend'. More surprisingly still, he retained the confidence of the Marlboroughs, handling a large investment of theirs in the East India Company in November 1697.[9]

Soon after her accession Anne appointed Bathurst cofferer of the royal household, a place worth £2,000 p.a., while in May 1702 there was a report, albeit false, that he was to be created an earl. In June, amid preparations for the election, he joined with a fellow Tory, Sir Walter Clarges, 1st Bt.*, in the Westminster contest, only to desist when offered a safe seat in the Court interest at New Romney. Though he could invoke a considerable interest at Cirencester, he had been quite content to allow his steward, Charles Coxe*, to take advantage of it. During the Queen's visit to Oxford University in August he was one of the household members to receive the degree of Doctor of Civil Law. He retained 'a considerable stock' in the East India Company, but was by now far too preoccupied with his court duties to give much attention to the company's affairs. In March 1703 he stood proxy for Marlborough at the Duke's installation as a Knight of the Garter. In the Commons his activity was confined almost entirely to the role of spectator. In mid-March 1704 Secretary Lord Nottingham (Daniel Finch†) listed him as a potential supporter in the event of proceedings concerning the 'Scotch Plot'.[10]

Bathurst died after suffering a week of 'high fever' on 27 Apr. 1704. His sister-in-law Lady Wentworth commented that he had 'not been well a great while but thought to wrestle with it'. He left the bulk of his estates in Gloucestershire and Northamptonshire to his eldest son, Allen*, while to his two surviving younger sons he bequeathed lands in Wiltshire, Oxfordshire, Lincolnshire and Middlesex, and to his daughter he left £10,000. His executors included his kinsman (through his wife's Fortrey relations) William Bromley II* and his 'nephew' George Bohun* with whom he had been involved in the East India Company. The monumental inscription to him at Paulerspury, where he was buried, glossed over his lapses of honesty in managing the royal finances with a tribute to 'his singular prudence and economy'. Typically, however, the Duchess of Marlborough could not forget. In an *aide-mémoire* written some years later she recalled that Bathurst had left a fortune of

near £10,000 a year to his family, all raised from about fifteen hundred in the princess's service which is a full proof of his taking money and doing all the wrong things in his power, for he had a great many children to bring up and the lawful profits of his employment could not amount to above eight hundred or a thousand pounds a year.[11]

[1] IGI, Northants.; Baker, *Northants*. ii. 203, 207; B. Bathurst, *Letters of Two Queens*, 145–6, 277. [2] Info. from Prof. H. Horwitz; K. G. Davies, *R. African Co*. 378. [3] J. R. Woodhead, *Rulers of London* (London and Mdx. Arch. Soc.), 26; *CSP Dom*. 1685, p. 291; 1687–9, p. 269. [4] Add. 24927; Bathurst, 164–5; *CSP Dom*. 1683–4, p. 182; 1699–1700, p. 49; *Cal. Treas. Bks*. xiii. 440; Luttrell, *Brief Relation*, v. 160, 192. [5] *Cal. Treas. Bks*. vii. 1053; Add. 10129, f. 232; *CJ*, xii. 508. [6] Bathurst, 164–5, passim; BL, Loan 57/71; Baker, 202. [7] Centre Kentish Stud. New Romney bor. recs. NR/Aep/56/3, Bathurst to mayor and jurats, 15 Feb. 1690; *Luttrell Diary*, 96; Add. 22185, f. 53; *Debates and Procs. 1694–5*, pp. 8, 10, 68; *CJ*, xi. 268–9. [8] *Bigland's Colls*. (Bristol Glos. Arch. Soc.: Glos. Rec. Ser. ii. pt. i), 363; *HMC Bathurst*, 3–4; *Trans. Bristol and Glos. Arch. Soc*. vii. 271–2; *CSP Dom*. 1695, pp. 93, 117. [9] Add. 61455, f. 34; 61415, ff. 89–90; E. Gregg, *Queen Anne*, 109–10; Bathurst, 234–5. [10] Luttrell, *Brief Relation*, v. 276–7, 418; *Verney Letters 18th Cent*. i. 108; *Vernon–Shrewsbury Letters*, iii. 223; BL, Trumbull Alphab. mss 50, Thomas Bateman to Sir William Trumbull*, 15 June 1702; Boyer, *Anne Annals*, i. 77, ii. 2; Add. 22852, f. 123. [11] Bathurst, 256; PCC 87 Ash; J. A. Hankey, *Hist. Apsley and Bathurst Fams*. 55; Baker, 207; Add. 61415, f. 103.

P. W./A. A. H.

BATHURST, Benjamin (1692–1767), of Lydney, Glos. and Mixbury, Glos.

CIRENCESTER   1713–1727
GLOUCESTER   16 Feb. 1728–1754
MONMOUTH   1754–5 Nov. 1767

bap. 25 June 1692, 5th but 3rd surv. s. of Sir Benjamin Bathurst*; bro. of Allen* and Peter Bathurst*. *educ*. Eton 1699; Trinity, Oxf. 1708. *m*. (1) 17 Dec. 1713, Finetta (*d*. 1738), da. of Henry Poole of Kemble, Glos., 22ch.; (2) 22 Oct. 1741, Catherine (*d*. 1794), da. of Rev. Lawrence Brodrick, chaplain to the House of Commons and preb. Westminster, wid. of Dr William Whitfield, 14ch.[1]

FRS 1731.
Outranger, Windsor Forest 1763–*d*.[2]

By virtue of his father's position in the household of Princess Anne, Bathurst and his brother Peter were childhood companions to the princess's son, the Duke of Gloucester, and in 1697 Benjamin was included in a portrait of the Duke. Upon his father's death in 1704 he inherited the manors of Lydney, Gloucestershire and Mixbury, Oxfordshire. At the general election of 1713, just after coming of age, he was returned for the family seat at Cirencester. While he left no mark whatsoever on the recorded proceedings of the House, his early political behaviour and outlook appear to have foxed parliamentary analysts. Despite his family's strong Tory credentials, he was classed in the Worsley list of the 1713 Parliament as a Whig who would often vote with the Tories. He voted with the Whigs on 18 Mar. 1714 against the expulsion of Richard Steele, and was marked as a Whig in two other lists of this Parliament drawn up in 1715, but his Tory identity thereafter is confirmed by an analysis of the House compiled by Francis Gwyn* in 1723. The impression gained is that as a 'whimsical Tory' Bathurst may have acted with the Whigs more frequently than most of his brethren. He remained an MP for the rest of his life, dying on 5 Nov. 1767.[3]

[1] Baker, *Northants*. ii. 203; *Top. and Gen*. iii. 494; IGI, Wilts.; Burke, *Peerage* (1959), 233; *Westminster Abbey Regs*. (Harl. Soc. x), 85. [2] Collins, *Peerage*, v. 89. [3] B. Bathurst, *Letters of Two Queens*, 236; *Parlty. Hist*. xv. 349; PCC 87 Ash.

P. W./A. A. H.

BATHURST, Peter (1687–1748), of Greatworth, Northants. and Clarendon Park, nr. Salisbury, Wilts.

WILTON   1711–1713
CIRENCESTER   1727–1734
SALISBURY   1734–1741

b. 3 May 1687, 4th but 2nd surv. s. of Sir Benjamin Bathurst*; bro. of Allen* and Benjamin Bathurst*. *educ*. Eton c.1700; Trinity, Oxf. 1703. *m*. (1) 1709, Leonora-Maria (*d*. 1720), da. and h. of Charles Howe of Greatworth, 1s. (*d.v.p.*) 2da.; (2) 3 Oct. 1720, Lady Selina (*d*. 1779), da. of Robert Shirley, 1st Earl Ferrers, 5s. 10da.[1]

Bathurst spent his childhood at the court of Princess Anne, where he and his brother Benjamin were companions to the Duke of Gloucester. His father had left him lands in Lincolnshire, and on his marriage he acquired part of his father-in-law's estate in Northamptonshire. He had also at some stage acquired the Clarendon Park estate which he made his principal residence. He stood as a Tory for Wilton, a few miles westwards, in 1710 and during the course of an acrimonious campaign threatened to deny the town's flannel-makers their vital supply of blue clay from Clarendon Park. Although he was defeated, the Commons overturned the result in his favour, enabling him to take his seat alongside his elder brother. Most subsequent references in the Journals to 'Mr Bathurst' were almost certainly to the senior and more experienced brother. The younger Bathurst's limited activities come clearly into view from January 1712 when Allen was raised to the peerage. He was nevertheless listed as a 'worthy patriot' who in the 1710–11 session was involved in detecting the mismanagements of the previous Whig administration. He was also a member of the October Club. On 26 May he was teller against the East India Company's petition for a bill to extend their term. By June 1713 he was aligning himself with the 'whimsical' Tories, and on the 18th voted against the French commerce bill. He did not seek re-election in 1713, but on re-entering Parliament in 1727 he resumed his connexions with the Tories. Bathurst died on 25 Apr. 1748 and was buried at Laverstock where a fulsome monumental inscription describes him in private life as 'a lover of letters and liberal knowledge, affectionate and affable to a numerous family', and in the public sphere as 'a lover of his country, which he long and faithfully served in Parliament . . . without seeking or even expecting, any other reward than the honest consciousness of having acted as became him'. Clarendon went initially to his eldest son, Peter[†], but eventually reverted to the descendants of his eldest daughter, Selina.[2]

[1] Baker, *Northants.* i. 509, ii. 203; Hoare, *Wilts.* Alderbury, v. 108, 172; IGI, London, Wilts. [2] B. Bathurst, *Letters of Two Queens*, 236; PCC 87 Ash; *VCH Wilts.* vi. 26; Hoare, 108.

P. W./A. A. H.

BATHURST, Theodore (c.1646–97), of Leeds and Marske, Yorks.

RICHMOND 1690–1695

b. c.1646, 7th but 3rd surv. s. of John Bathurst[†], MD, of London and Marske by Elizabeth, da. and coh. of Brian Willance of Marske. *educ.* Trinity, Oxf. matric. 11 May 1665, aged 18; L. Inn 1668, called 1675. *m.* lic. 10 Apr. 1669, Lettice, da. of Sir John Repington of Leamington, Warws., 6s. (4 *d.v.p.*) 2da. *suc.* bro. by 1681.[1]

Bathurst's family were descended from the same Kentish stock as their distant kinsmen, the Bathursts of Northamptonshire and Gloucestershire. His father, who had been physician to Oliver Cromwell[†], acquired by marriage an estate in the manor of Marske in Yorkshire, just over four miles from Richmond, which he twice represented in Parliament. Bathurst made the law his profession, and, having qualified, returned to the north, buying a house in Leeds, which seems to have been his principal residence, although his father, who had died in 1659, had bequeathed him considerable estates, including property in Richmond, and several lead mines. It was doubtless at Leeds that he first made the acquaintance of Ralph Thoresby, the antiquarian and topographer, who described him as a 'learned and ingenious gentleman'. He appears to have inherited the family's principal seat at Clint's Hall in Marske from an elder brother by 1685. During that year he was indicted at York assizes for denouncing the King as a 'rogue', but the upshot of the case is unknown. He was in more trouble in 1689 when a suit was brought against him in Chancery concerning his title to the Yorkshire estates devised upon him by his father. He won the case, but his possession of the forest of Arkengarthdale, where there were valuable lead mines, was later challenged in the courts by the widow of Colonel Archibald Douglas, who claimed that her husband had been granted a 51-year lease of the forest by James II.[2]

The desire to escape the trouble and cost of threatened litigation may well have been Bathurst's chief motive for standing for Parliament in 1690, when he was returned for Richmond. He was classed as a Court supporter in lists compiled by Lord Carmarthen (Sir Thomas Osborne[†]) dating from March and December 1690, and in April 1691 was listed by Robert Harley* as a member of the Country opposition, becoming a frequent, though not outright, critic of the government on a broad range of measures. On 31 Oct. 1691 he was included among those appointed to draft a bill to regulate elections, and on 6 Nov. he 'inveighed' against the size of the Privy Council and argued for its reduction to 12. In a supply debate on the 18th he demanded that ministers reveal 'what sums of money have been sent to the Duke of Savoy, to the Dutch and to the beggarly princes of Germany', and on the 28th supported a move to exclude officers from the estimate of the land forces. On the 30th, however, he parted company with several leaders of the Country party over the Lords' clause in the Irish oaths bill by which Catholic lawyers were obliged to take only the oath of allegiance, and supported the solicitor-general's view that the Lords must first explain their justification of it in relation to the articles of the recent Treaty of Limerick. Earlier, on 9 Nov., he had supported the second reading of the treason trials bill, a favourite 'Country' measure, and spoke twice in favour of Lords' amendments to it (31 Dec. and 13 Jan. 1692). The next day he opposed a supply resolution engineered by the Country opposition to minimize the officering of the army in Ireland. His support for the monied interest was shown on the 15th when he opposed the bill for a reduction in the interest rate, although three days later he supported a proposal put forward in committee of supply by the financial projector Thomas Neale* for a 2 per cent tax on 'all money out at interest or invested in stock', and in a more punitive vein on the 29th suggested that the members of the corporation of London should be made personally responsible for the considerable debt owed to the London orphans. He spoke on 5 Feb. in favour of allowing the bill for establishing a new commission of accounts to complete its course despite being heavily amended by the Lords; on the 6th, for confirming the charter of the Tory-dominated old East India Company; on the 15th, for granting additional time to the existing commissioners of accounts; on the 16th against allowing the King to meet any shortfall in poll tax receipts by borrowing; on the 18th in favour of withholding the poll tax bill until the Lords had passed the forfeited estate bills; and on the 19th against the bill to make correspondence with enemy powers a treasonable offence.[3]

In the 1692–3 session Bathurst continued in the main to act with the Country wing of the Tory party. On 15 Nov. he supported Sir Thomas Clarges' demand that current alliances be laid before the House prior to consideration of supply, but two days later showed a complete change of mind over the East India trade by indicating his support for a new company. On the 18th he supported the new treason trials bill. When the progress of the war was debated on the 21st his 'blue-water' Toryism was demonstrated in his advocacy of a naval policy 'and let your confederates take care of the land for I think we get nothing by them'. He condemned the influence that 'the high and mighty [Dutch] deputies' were widely thought to exercise over the King when on campaign in Flanders and proposed that William be addressed to remain at home. On the 28th, in the committee on the treason trials bill, he supported the view that the measure should come into force at an early date rather than wait until the war had ended. He spoke twice in the heated debates on naval mismanagements. Commenting on 30 Nov. on the documentation relating to the failure to follow up the victory at La Hogue with a descent on the French coast, he took note that ministerial authorities had been keen to pursue the design despite the officers' belief that it was 'impracticable'. As it had been made the subject of 'great discourse' the previous session, it had evidently been a ploy 'to draw you in and pick your pockets'. He concluded that for Britain to prosecute the war with any success it was essential to safeguard trade and to attempt a full-scale landing in France. His second intervention came on 5 Dec., in support of Paul Foley I's censure motion that the naval strategists had botched the planned descent. In supply on 1 Dec. he opposed a request for a special grant to finish Plymouth naval yard on the grounds that this had not been presented according to form; and on the 13th opposed the suggested 4s. in the pound land tax as 'an uncertain tax' likely to produce arrears. He considered as ill-advised the bill for the punishment of treasonous utterances against the King and Queen, debated on the 14th, since it was 'not a time to encourage treasons, when perjuries and subornations thereof are so frequent'; as a Tory, however, he probably also harboured misgivings about the new oath proposed in the bill. During late December and early January he managed the passage of a private estate bill. On 9 Jan. 1693 he spoke in favour of increasing the number of the commissioners of accounts as a matter of necessity 'when so much money is given'; and on the 23rd joined in the Tory attack on Bishop Burnet's *Pastoral Letter*. While at first sight Bathurst's opposition on 28 Jan. to the triennial bill may seem paradoxical, it is probable that he shared the annoyance of several other opposing Tories with the Lords' presumption in seeking to interfere with the custom of the Commons.[4]

That Bathurst continued to speak frequently is borne out in a description of the debate on 1 Feb. 1694 on the King's rejection of the place bill, when the reporter noted that 'Mr Bathurst spoke as usual', but these later speeches have not been recorded. The spring of 1694 brought him fresh personal troubles, when a petition was presented to the Treasury on 1 Mar. effectively asking for government support against him in the dispute over his possession of Arkengarthdale forest, court proceedings having been halted by his election to Parliament. He was granted leave of the House on the 23rd, seemingly in order to attend to the matter. The Treasury took no action, but he seems by this time to have been in financial difficulties. He stood in the 1695 election, but failed to retain his seat. After his death early in 1697 administration of his estates was granted to a creditor. His legal troubles did not expire with him, for his son and heir, Charles, was involved in an unsuccessful lawsuit with Lord Wharton (Hon. Thomas*), over the possession of the lead mines in Arkengarthdale. A grandson, Charles Bathurst, was elected for Richmond in 1727.[5]

[1] *Yorks. Arch. Soc. Jnl.* vi. 267–69; *London Mar. Lic.* ed. Foster, 96. [2] *Yorks. Arch. Soc. Jnl.* 268–9; Thoresby, *Ducatus Leodiensis*, 16. [3] *Luttrell Diary*, 4, 8, 26, 47, 50, 99, 105, 128, 130, 133, 136, 164, 171, 174, 187, 190, 193, 195. [4] Ibid. 227, 234, 237, 243, 265, 271–2, 279, 294, 311, 316, 329, 356, 381, 391. [5] Grey, x. 383; *Cal. Treas. Bks.* x. 519, 581; xxv. 169; *Yorks. Arch. Soc. Jnl.* 267.

P. W./A. A. H.

BATTELEY, Samuel (c.1652–1714), of Horringer, nr. Bury St. Edmunds, Suff.

BURY ST. EDMUNDS   20 Feb. 1712–1713

b. c.1652, ?3rd s. of Nicholas Batteley (*d.* 1681), apothecary, of Bury St. Edmunds, alderman of Bury St. Edmunds 1668, 1680, by Anne. *educ.* Bury St. Edmunds g.s. *m.* (1) 21 Nov. 1682, Mary Bright (*d.* 1697) of Bury St. Edmunds, 2s. *d.v.p.* 3da. *d.v.p.*; (2) by 1699, Anne, at least 2s. *d.v.p.*

Common councilman, Bury St. Edmunds 1683–Mar. 1688, Oct. 1688–91, capital burgess 1691–*d.*, alderman 1695–6, 1707–8.[1]

Two elder brothers having entered the Church, it was Batteley who carried on his father's business as an apothecary. A loyal supporter of Lord Hervey's (John*) interest in Bury St. Edmunds, he agreed to be put up by the corporation at a by-election in 1712 in order to hold the vacant seat as 'trustee' for Hervey's son, Hon. Carr Hervey*, who was not quite of age and was in any case abroad at the time, and also to prevent Hervey's rival Sir Robert Davers, 2nd Bt.*, from capturing it. A further inducement to let his name go forward may have been the imminent prospect of an appeal to the Lords against him, in respect of some Irish property he owned jointly with Reynolds Calthorpe*. By April 1712 Batteley was critically ill: he was officially absent from the House from 12 May. At the next election he duly gave up his seat to Carr Hervey.[2]

On 15 July 1714 Lord Hervey recorded that 'my good friend and honest neighbour, Mr Samuel Batteley, died at his house in Horringer'. With no surviving children, Batteley's heir was his nephew John, son of his brother Nicholas, rector of Ivychurch, Kent, and like him also a clergyman.[3]

[1] *Bury St. Edmunds G. S. List* (Suff. Green Bks. xiii), 19–21; *St. James, Bury St. Edmunds Par. Reg.* (Suff. Green Bks. xvii), ii. 133, 212, 215, 223, 232, 235, 243; iii. 157, 172, 174, 185, 188–9, 193, 205, 216, 220; Gage, *Thingoe Hundred*, 501; Suff. RO (Bury St. Edmunds), Bury St. Edmunds bor. recs. EE500/D4/1/2, ff. 184, 219, 255; E500/D4/1/3(a), ff. 39, 244. [2] *Bury St. Edmunds G. S. List*, 19–20; *Hervey Letter Bks.* i. 238, 316–17, 319, 325, 327–8; *HMC Lords*, n.s. ix. 198. [3] *Hervey Diary*, 61; *Bury St. Edmunds G. S. List*, 19–20.

D. W. H.

BATTISCOMBE, Peter (*d.*1725), of Symondsbury, Dorset.

BRIDPORT   22 Dec. 1697–1700

2nd s. of Christopher Battiscombe of Symondsbury by Mary, da. of Peter Starre of Bradford Abbas. *educ.* M. Temple 1691. *unm. suc.* fa. to property in Bridport, Allington and Bradpole 1671; er. bro. at Symondsbury 1685.[1]

Battiscombe was descended from a family which had owned the farm of Vere's Wotton in Dorset since the reign of Henry VI. His father, a younger son, had settled at Symondsbury on the outskirts of Bridport, and by the terms of his will, proved in 1671, Peter inherited various tenements and houses in Bridport and other Dorset parishes. His elder brother, Christopher, was not mentioned in the will but presumably Symondsbury had already been settled on him and after his execution in 1685 for participation in the Monmouth rebellion, this estate too came to Peter. Battiscombe was returned for Bridport at a by-election in 1697 and again at the following general election. He was classed as a member of the Country party in about September 1698, and an analysis of the House into interests in early 1700 classed him as doubtful. Granted a fortnight's leave of absence on 13 Mar. 1700, he did not stand again. Sir Charles Hedges* had considered purchasing Symondsbury in 1698, but deemed its electoral influence 'insufficient in itself to induce me'. In March 1701 Battiscombe was granted tithes in Bestwell, Dorset and some small parcels of land in Yorkshire. He died in 1725, leaving the bulk of his property to a kinsman by marriage, George Sampson.[2]

[1] Hutchins, *Dorset*, ii. 240. [2] Add. 24107, f. 179; *Cal. Treas. Bks.* xvi. 230; Dorset RO, Battiscombe mss D198/5, 7; PCC 73 Duke.

P. W.

BAYLIS, Robert (1673–1748), of Watling Street, London.

THETFORD   1708–1710

b. 14 Nov. 1673, 1st s. of Robert Baylis of Watling Street by his 2nd w. Mary Blower of St. Andrew's, Holborn. *educ.* Merchant Taylors' 1685–6; Sidney Sussex, Camb.

1690; I. Temple 1691, called 1699. *unm. suc.* fa. 1697; kntd. 16 June 1727.[1]

Common councilman, London 1691–1710, alderman 1719–*d.*, sheriff 1724–5, ld. mayor 1728–9.[2]

Comptroller of the penny post by 1716–aft. 1720; commr. salt duty 1720, customs 1720–7, 1731–*d.*; receiver-gen. land tax, London, Mdx. and Suff. 1728, house duty, London by 1729–aft. 1744, Mdx. and Westminster by 1733–aft. 1744.[3]

Dir. E.I. Co. 1731–3; pres. St. Thomas' Hosp. 1745–*d.*

Baylis' father, who came of a Gloucestershire family, established himself in London as a tobacconist and served twice as a common councilman for the City (on the first occasion at least, as a Whig). Baylis himself probably followed the same trade; he certainly followed his father's politics. He was returned in 1708 for Thetford, where he was a 'stranger', with the support of the Duke of Grafton but principally by his own exertions, having reputedly spent some £3,000 among the voters. He was marked as a Whig in a list of the new Parliament, and his election was put down as a 'gain' by Lord Sunderland (Charles, Lord Spencer*). He was listed as having voted for the naturalization of the Palatines in 1709 and for the impeachment of Dr Sacheverell in 1710. Although the Norfolk Whigs wished him to put up for re-election at Thetford in 1710 he declined, and did not stand for Parliament again. He nevertheless played a prominent part in London politics, supporting Whig parliamentary candidates in several subsequent elections.[4]

Baylis died on 21 Nov. 1748 and was buried in the church of St. John the Evangelist, Friday Street, alongside his father and two brothers. By a will dated only a week before his death his entire estate was bequeathed to 'Mrs Mary Cash *alias* Carey, and Miss Caroline Carey her daughter, both now living with me', to be divided equally between them.[5]

[1] *Compleat Guide to . . . London* (1740), 118; *Merchant Taylors' Sch. Reg.* ed. Hart; J. R. Woodhead, *Rulers of London* (London and Mdx. Arch. Soc.), 27; PCC 109 Pyne, 353 Strahan; *Mar. Lic. Vicar-Gen.* (Harl. Soc. xxxiv), 38. [2] Beaven, *Aldermen*, i. 53; ii. 124. [3] Ibid.; *Cal. Treas. Bks. and Pprs.* 1729–30, pp. 89, 215, 223; 1731–4, p. 385; 1742–5, p. 549. [4] Woodhead, 27; *Prideaux Letters* (Cam. Soc. n.s. xv), 200; G. Holmes, *Pol. in Age of Anne*, 175–6; Norf. RO, Bradfer-Lawrence mss, Ashe Windham* to [Ld. Townshend], 8 June 1710; Beaven, i. 53, 291–2; *London Pollbk. 1713*. [5] *Merchant Taylors' Sch. Reg.*; PCC 353 Strahan.

D. W. H.

BAYNTUN, Edward (c.1659–1720), of Hardenhuish, Wilts.

CALNE 1705–1710

b. c.1659, o. s. of Henry Bayntun† of Bath, Som. and Bremhill, Wilts. by Joanna, da. of Edmund Trimnell of Hanger, Bremhill. *educ.* Trinity, Oxf. matric. 12 Mar. 1675, aged 15; L. Inn 1679. *m.* by 1692, his. cos. Lucy, da. of Sir Edward Bayntun† of Spye Park, Bromham, Wilts., sis. of Henry Bayntun*, 7s. (4 *d.v.p.*) 1da. *suc.* fa. 1672.[1]

Bayntun was from a cadet branch of the family settled at Spye Park, Wiltshire. He was plucked from obscurity partly as a result of his marriage to Lucy, sister of Henry Bayntun, the head of the family, and also by the fact that Henry's only son, John, showed no apparent interest in parliamentary service. Although it was left to Bayntun to sit for one of the family's traditional north Wiltshire boroughs, he was already in his mid-40s when elected, by which time there had been five consecutive Parliaments without a Bayntun present.

Although Calne was considered a safe seat for the family, Bayntun's election met with some difficulties. Having unsuccessfully contested the first Parliament of 1701, Bayntun petitioned, but without success. In the general election of November 1701, while active in support of the Whig candidates for Wiltshire, he again stood on the Whig interest at Calne with Henry Blaake*. While Blaake topped the poll, Bayntun was included in a double return with the Tory Sir Charles Hedges* for the second seat. The committee of elections declared the election void, and Bayntun did not contest the by-election. Meanwhile, Robert Harley had classed him as a Tory in a list of this Parliament, possibly because his late cousin and brother-in-law, Henry, had been a strong Tory. Bayntun was finally successful in 1705 after a contest. He was listed as a 'Churchman' in an analysis of the new Parliament, although his election was reckoned a gain for the Whigs by Lord Sunderland (Charles, Lord Spencer*). On 25 Oct. he voted for the Court candidate as Speaker. Marked as both a Whig and a Tory in a list of early 1708, he voted in 1709 for the naturalization of the Palatines, and in the following year for the impeachment of Dr Sacheverell. After another double return in 1710, his opponents were declared elected on 22 Dec.[2]

Bayntun wrote his will on 3 Oct. 1720. Describing himself as 'weak in body', he died shortly afterwards and was buried in the family vault at Bromham on 10 Oct. He did not detail his possessions or properties, but asked that his executors, Blaake and James Montagu III*, divide these equally between his four surviving children. None of his sons succeeded him in Parliament.[3]

[1] Wilts. RO, 518/3; PCC 216 Buckingham; Burke, *Commoners*, iv. 685; *Le Neve's Knights* (Harl. Soc. viii), 32. [2] *Wilts. Arch. Mag.* xlvi. 80. [3] PCC 216 Buckingham; Wilts. RO, 1046/1.

D. W. H./H. J. L.

BAYNTUN, Henry (1664–91), of Farleigh Castle, Som. and Spye Park, Bromham, Wilts.

CHIPPENHAM 1685–1687, 1689–1690
CALNE 1690–c. June 1691

bap. 17 Nov. 1664, 1st s. of Sir Edward Bayntun† of Spye Park by Stuarta, da. of Sir Thomas Thynne† of Richmond, Surr. *educ.* ?travelled abroad, 1678–?9. *m.* 1 Sept. 1685, Lady Anne, da. of John Wilmot, 2nd Earl of Rochester, coh. to her bro. Charles, 3rd Earl, 1s. 1da. *suc.* fa. 1679.[1]

Free burgess, Devizes 1682–1684, May 1689–*d.*[2]

Bayntun was descended from one of the most prominent gentry families of north Wiltshire, with estates concentrated in Bromham, Bremhill and neighbouring parishes. He was related to other local gentry families, including the Thynnes and the Danvers, and through his grandmother to Lord Carmarthen (Sir Thomas Osborne†). In 1674 a contract was drawn up for his marriage to Sophia, daughter of James, Lord Somerville, but the marriage did not take place. In 1678 he was granted a licence to travel abroad for three years with one Dr Brunel. It is not known whether he left England, but in the following year he was at Spye Park, having succeeded to his father's considerable properties. To these Bayntun later added £4,000 and several manors in Somerset secured through his marriage to the daughter and co-heir of John, Earl of Rochester. In addition, his family ties now encompassed the St. Johns of Lydiard Tregoze, Wiltshire, and the Hungerfords of Farleigh Castle.[3]

The Wiltshire properties guaranteed the Bayntuns parliamentary service in one of several local constituencies. Most conspicuous of these were Calne, Chippenham and Devizes, in at least one of which a Bayntun had sat for the previous five generations. Although his father had been one of the more radical MPs of the Long Parliament, Bayntun was classed as a Tory, and perhaps as a Court supporter, by Carmarthen in March 1690 after having been elected at Calne following a contest. In Robert Harley's* list of April 1691 he was classed as a Country supporter. He was not recorded as making a speech.[4]

On 2 July 1691 Luttrell reported Bayntun's death as having 'lately' occurred. He was buried the same day at Bromham. Leaving debts of at least £22,000, to satisfy his creditors he raised £42,000 by mortgaging his ancestral estates of Bromham and Bromham Bayntun together with the Farleigh estate which he had bought from Sir Edward Hungerford* only four years previously for £56,000. Despite these debts, Bayntun was able to settle his widow with a £3,000 jointure and bequeath £4,000 to his sister, Lucy. A petition for a private bill to secure a portion for his daughter and establish a trust for his only son, a minor, was presented on 10 Dec. 1692, and despite a petition against it from his widow and young son, it duly passed. Farleigh and other properties were devised to his executors, Walter Grubbe* and Sir Edmund Warneford†. These properties were sold to repay interest on loans running to £1,000 p.a. Bayntun's will also specified that should his son die without a male heir then his remaining estate was to descend to his daughter, Anne, on the condition that she married a Bayntun 'kindred of the fourth degree' or that her husband assume the Bayntun name. Anne, who married Edward Rolt†, duly inherited the larger part of the Wiltshire properties, and her son, also an MP, assumed the name Bayntun Rolt.[5]

[1] *Bayntun Commonplace Bk.* ed. Freeman (Wilts. Rec. Soc. xliii), 35; Burke, *Commoners*, iv. 685; *The Ancestor*, xi. 24–25; *Bromham Par. Reg.*; *Wilts. Arch. Mag.* iv. 248; *Mar. Lic. Vicar-Gen.* (Harl. Soc. xxiv), 176. [2] B. H. Cunnington, *Annals of Devizes*, 166; Devizes bor. recs. G20/1/18, 19. [3] PCC 405 Vere, 361 King, 365 North; *Bayntun Commonplace Bk.* 21, 33; *VCH Som.* vi. 96; Wilts. RO, 445/1, 415/134; *Vis. Wilts.* (Harl. Soc. cv–cvi), 168. [4] *Wilts. Arch. Mag.* xvi. 80; Hoare, *Wilts. Downton*, 7; Bath mss at Longleat House, Thynne pprs. 24, f. 164; G. Yule, *Independents in Eng. Civil War*, 131; Egerton 3359, ff. 27–28. [5] Luttrell, *Brief Relation*, ii. 259; Wilts. RO, Goldney mss 473/377, funeral bill 2 July 1691; *VCH Wilts.* vii. 72, 183; C. Clay, *Public Finance and Private Wealth*, 179–80; *Wilts. Arch. Mag.* iv. 248; xiii. 234; Collinson, *Hist. of Som.* lii. 356.

D.W.H./H.J.L.

BEAUMONT, Sir George, 4th Bt. (c.1664–1737), of Stoughton Grange, nr. Leicester.

LEICESTER 1702–9 Apr. 1737

b. c.1664, 2nd s. of Sir Henry Beaumont, 2nd Bt.†, of Stoughton Grange by Elizabeth, da. of George Farmer of Holbeach, Lincs., prothonotary of c.p. *educ.* New Coll. Oxf. matric. 9 Feb. 1683, aged 18, BCL 1690, fellow, DCL (by diploma) 1714. *unm. suc.* bro. as 4th Bt. 5 Dec. 1690; to the estates of his cos. Thomas, 3rd Visct. Beaumont of Swords [I] at Cole Orton, Leics. 1702.[1]

Commr. privy seal 1711–13; ld. of Admiralty Apr.–Oct. 1714.

Trustee, Radcliffe Lib. 1714–*d.*[2]

'Disinterested, just, steady, intrepid, he possessed every virtue that adorns a public station.' So runs the epitaph for Beaumont reputedly composed by his friend Swift. A second son, and not in expectation of title and estates, he obtained a fellowship at New College, Oxford, though he may have been one of the non-resident fellows of which the college had an exceptional number. At first Beaumont, a thoroughbred Tory, stirred reluctantly at the prospect of entering the Commons for Leicester, a short journey from his seat. John Verney* informed Lord Rutland (John Manners†): 'Sir George Beaumont has often writ me word that he has totally declined all thoughts of standing for burgess at Leicester, for which I am very sorry . . . and have used all the arguments I could to dissuade him from that resolution'. By 1701 his attitude had changed. In the January election he allowed himself to be put up for Oxford University by a group of younger dons who wished to challenge the pre-eminence of Christ Church in choosing the candidates, but soon afterwards withdrew. A by-election arising shortly afterwards in March, Beaumont was re-adopted by the discontented element, this time to stand against William Bromley II*. He saw the contest through to a finish, and though defeated he succeeded in attracting a respectable following. In the second 1701 election Beaumont campaigned with a fellow Tory, John Verney*, for the Leicestershire seats against two Whigs, but he and Verney stood down before the contest was brought to a poll. He was finally chosen for the borough of Leicester in 1702 which he represented for the rest of his life.[3]

During the next three parliaments Beaumont was largely inactive, though behind the scenes he was assiduous in cultivating and maintaining the political contacts in the midlands which later helped to single him out as one of his party's leading activists. Apart from members of the gentry, his expanding network of friendships included figures such as Dean Swift, whose mother lived at Leicester, while Swift also spent time with Beaumont at Stoughton Grange. On 13 Feb. 1703 he voted against agreement with the Whig Lords' amendments to the abjuration bill. His sole undertaking next session was a bill for selling off the Cheshire estate of a Leicestershire gentleman, the first of a series of similar measures he supervised for gentry, mainly of his home county. In October 1704 he was noted as a 'probable supporter' of the Tack, and despite Robert Harley's* noting him to be lobbied against the measure, he duly voted for it on 28 Nov. 1704. On 19 Dec. he was teller in favour of adding a clause for qualifying justices of the peace to the recruiting bill. Shortly after the 1705 election Beaumont was noted as 'True Church' in a published list of the new Parliament, and on the first day of the session voted against the Court candidate for the Speakership. He spoke on 19 Dec. 1705 in the debate on the second reading of the regency bill which he presumably opposed. On 13 Feb. 1706 he told for the losing Tory side on an amendment to the recruiting bill. In the meantime, between November and February, he took charge of a bill authorizing a Leicestershire land sale, though it failed to pass the Upper House. A more successful second version was managed by him in March–April 1707. The corporation of Leicester's intention early in 1708 to establish a workhouse in the town forced Beaumont to arbitrate in a local squabble. On presentation of the corporation's petition on 6 Feb., he and his co-Member, James Winstanley*, were immediately ordered to prepare a bill. Amendments to the bill in committee became the subject of dispute and Beaumont, reporting this development on 8 Mar., had to seek permission for a recommittal. Even so, once his further report was made on 16 Mar., followed by an order for engrossment, the project was pushed no further.[4]

Beaumont's Tory colours were noted in two published lists of early 1708. It was perhaps not surprising given his Tory zeal that the final, most Whiggish phase of Lord Godolphin's (Sidney†) ministry saw a complete lapse in Beaumont's recorded activity in the House: all that is known is his opposition to the impeachment of Dr Sacheverell in the early part of 1710. Following the Tory victory in the autumn of 1710, Beaumont immediately became more prominent among the rank and file of Tory MPs. Besides an increasing workload of party business he nevertheless found time to supervise the passage of an estate bill for a Leicestershire colleague, Geoffrey Palmer*. In the disputed return for Cockermouth on 7 Apr. he was teller for hearing evidence against General James Stanhope*, currently a prisoner-of-war in Spain. As one of the 'Tory patriots' who voted for the peace in April, he was classed a little later as a 'worthy patriot' who had in the first session assisted in detecting the mismanagements of the outgoing administration, and was also a member of the October Club. On 18 Apr. he told for adjourning debate on the general post office bill, and on 7 May against agreeing with Lords' amendments to the game bill, the effect of which was to make existing penalties harsher. He was then put on a committee to state the grounds of disagreement to the Upper House.[5]

By now Beaumont was an important cog in ministerial political organization. Collaborating with Speaker Bromley, another High Churchman, he kept in touch with Tories of the midland counties of Leicestershire, Northamptonshire, Warwickshire and occasionally Derbyshire, securing their attendance in the Commons. Not only did he operate by letter, he also toured these shires in person, thereby earning the nickname, 'the Sergeant'. He soon proved he was not one of the more full-blooded members of the October Club. In June it was publicly declared that he was to be one of four 'excellent' new lords commissioners of trade, although he was not in fact ambitious for office. On being sounded by Lord Treasurer Oxford (Robert Harley) through Bromley's agency, he was found to be pliable: 'I have had an opportunity also of speaking to Sir G. Beaumont', wrote Bromley,

> but cannot fix anything upon him, he does not care to take a sinecure, and had rather have an employment of some business, but professes himself to be very easy to wait till others more impatient for employment are provided for, and whether he has anything or nothing he will behave himself with all duty to her Majesty and with all due regards to those at the head of her affairs.

In conjunction with two other prominent midland Tories, Sir Thomas Cave, 3rd Bt.*, and Sir Justinian Isham, 4th Bt.*, Beaumont may well have had some part in the reconstitution of the commission of the peace for Leicestershire.[6]

On 6 Dec. 1711, the eve of the new session, Beaumont was summoned by Henry St. John II* to a meeting at the Speaker's house, presumably to finalize tactics for the Address debate and other vital business; and at the commencement of proceedings next day he was duly named to the committee to draft the Address. In late December he accepted office as one of the three commissioners of the privy seal acting for John Robinson, bishop of Bristol, during Robinson's mission as envoy at Utrecht, and was sworn on the 23rd. By January 1713, Beaumont was intensively involved in setting up the Tory campaign in the midlands for the forthcoming election. Before the dissolution he managed a bill for Sir William Langhorne relating to the exchange of a parsonage house in Kent (April); and was twice teller: agreeing to grant leave for a bill to implement articles 8 and 9 of the commercial treaty with France (14 May); and against the addition of a clause to the bill for freeing the Africa trade (2 June). All the while, Beaumont was active in his capacity as a regional 'whip', herding in Tories to support the administration's peace measures. He wrote to Sir Justinian Isham on 30 May: 'Mr Speaker desired I would tell you he hopes to see you in the House as soon as possible', and went on to stress the certainty of a revolt by the Scots Members. Predictably, he supported the commercial treaty with France in the crucial division on 18 June 1713, but not without losing some face at Leicester, where wool-growing interests inevitably regarded him as favouring the shipment of unwrought wool from France. Despite opposition to him on these grounds, he retained his seat.[7]

Beaumont's employment was terminated when the privy seal was taken out of commission in August 1713. The 1714 session was a period of intense activity for him on behalf of the ministry and began on 2 Mar. with him seconding the motion for the Address and his inclusion on its drafting committee. Many other committee appointments followed during the course of the session. He returned to the ministerial benches on 5 Apr. when he was appointed an Admiralty lord, in place of John Aislabie*, though at the time of his appointment he was actually 'taking his tour to fetch up the midland Members'. Beaumont's governmental and parliamentary commitments were now such as to prompt Sir Thomas Cave, still idling in Leicestershire, to remark early in June that he had 'not received my usual summons from Sir George, who never fails on all urgent occasions'. In the Commons he played a leading part in supervising the bill for reviving the commission of accounts. On moving for the bill on the 3rd, he was also teller for the ministerial majority approving a motion to empower the commissioners to scrutinize debts due to the army, transport service and the sick and wounded incurred under the previous administration. Beaumont introduced the bill on 11 June, and three days later moved that the forthcoming committee of the whole be instructed to introduce a clause reappointing the previous set of commissioners, with the exception of Francis Annesley*, and in the ensuing division told for the minority in favour. He went on to chair the committee (23 June), make its report (26 June), and convey the bill to the Lords on the 30th. On 11 June he was one of a team of MPs ordered to prepare the bill for settling a reward on the discoverer of a means of calculating longitude with greater precision. In the final weeks of the collapsing Oxford ministry Beaumont was one of the key players with other leading Church Tories in diverting their followers away from Bolingbroke (Henry St John II).[8]

A signatory to the proclamation of George I, Beaumont quickly set about summoning Tory MPs urgently to London. On the death of Dr John Radcliffe* in November, Beaumont and William Bromley were named in the doctor's will as trustees to administer his £80,000 bequest to Oxford University. At a ceremony on 7 Dec., at which Radcliffe's name was entered among the university's public benefactors, a doctorate of civil laws was conferred on Beaumont by diploma. His role in the Leicestershire election of April 1715 was described by Sir Thomas Cave as 'indefatigably active', providing an opportunity for one opposition lampoonist to mock 'Sir George Bombast' and his authority over the midland Tories: 'they [Sir Geoffrey Palmer and Sir Thomas

Cave] are both very quick sighted, and can take a sign from Sir George presently, so that there is no danger of their giving a wrong vote when Sir George is in the House'.

Beaumont died on 9 Apr. 1737.[9]

[1] Nichols, *Leics.* ii. 860; *Hist. Oxf. Univ.* ed. Sutherland and Mitchell, v. 55. [2] I. Guest, *Dr Radcliffe and his Trust*, 482. [3] Nichols, ii. 855; *Hist. Oxf. Univ.* v. 40, 55, 58–59; Rutland mss at Belvoir Castle, John Verney to Duke of Rutland, 28 May 1698, Ambrose Phillipps to same, 18 Nov. 1701. [4] *Cam. Misc.* xxiii. 51. [5] *Swift Corresp.* ed. Ball, i. 158. [6] G. Holmes, *Pol. in Age of Anne*, 300–1, 307; *Verney Letters 18th Cent.* i. 246; Add. 57861, f. 162; 70214, Bromley to Harley, June 1711; L. K. J. Glassey, *Appt. JPs*, 212. [7] Bodl. Rawl. A.286, f. 89; Boyer, *Anne Annals*, x. 303; Northants. RO, Isham mss IC1746, Justinian to Sir Justinian Isham, 20 Jan. 1713; IC2796, Beaumont to same, 30 May 1713; *VCH Leics.* iv. 121. [8] *Cal. Treas. Bks.* xxvii. 2, p. 335; NSA, Kreienberg despatch 5 Mar. 1714; Boyer, *Pol. State*, vii. 410; *Verney Letters 18th Cent.* i. 246; *Bull IHR*, xxxiv. 216; Douglas diary, [14] June 1714 (Hist. Parl. trans.). [9] Boyer, *Pol. State*, viii. 117; Leics. RO, Braye mss 23D57/2877, Beaumont to Sir Thomas Cave, 3 Aug. 1714; 3004 [printed squib, c.1715]; *Wentworth Pprs.* 434; *Hearne Colls.* (Oxford Hist. Soc.), v. 3–4; *Verney Letters 18th Cent.* i. 333.

A. A. H.

BEAUMONT, Hon. John (c.1636–1701), of St. Anne's, Westminster, Mdx.

NOTTINGHAM 1685–1687
HASTINGS 9 Aug. 1689–1695

b. c.1636, 2nd s. of Sapcote, 2nd Visct. Beaumont of Swords [I], of Cole Orton, Leics. by 1st w. Bridget, da. of Sir Thomas Monson, 1st Bt., of Carlton, Lincs. *educ.* Market Bosworth g.s.; Christ's, Camb. matric. 3 Nov. 1653, aged 17. *m.* (1) lic. 10 Sept. 1663, Felicia (*d.* 1687), da. of Thomas Pigott of Chetwynd, Salop, wid. of William Wilmer (*d.* 1660) of Sywell, Northants., and of Sir Charles Compton† (*d.* 1661) of Grendon, Northants. *s.p.*; (2) 3 Oct. 1693, Philippa, da. of Sir Nicholas Carew† of Beddington, Surr., *s.p.*[1]

Gent. of privy chamber by Dec. 1660, carver by 1679–?bef. 1682, equerry 1685–Sept. 1688.[2]

Capt. independent tp. of horse 1666–7; capt. of ft. Holland Regt. (later the Buffs) Jan.–Mar. 1674; capt. of gds. [I] 1676–7; capt. Anglo-Dutch brigade 1678–84; lt.-col. of ft. Princess Anne's Regt. (later 8 Ft.) 1685–Sept. 1688, col. Dec. 1688–95; lt.-gov. Dover Castle 1686–Sept. 1688, 1689–93/4.[3]

FRS 1685.

Freeman, Portsmouth Jan. 1688; commr. lodemanage court, Cinque Ports 1689.

Coming from an aristocratic background, Beaumont had embarked on a career as an army officer, although until 1685 most of his commands had been in the Dutch service. His prospects took a distinctly promising turn at the beginning of James II's reign when he was given the lieutenant-colonelcy of a new English regiment, an equerry's post in the royal household, and shortly afterwards the lieutenant-governorship of Dover Castle. He also obtained a seat in Parliament. Despite his close associations with the court, he did not see eye to eye with the King's religious policies, and in September 1688 his stout Anglican conscience came dramatically into conflict with royal designs when he along with five junior officers refused to admit Irish Catholics to their regiment. For this he was cashiered and lost his other appointments. His well-publicized stand against King James, and his active support for William in November, quickly established him in the new King's good opinions, and shortly after the coronation he was promoted colonel of his old regiment and reinstated as lieutenant-governor of Dover Castle.

Since the office of lord warden of the Cinque Ports remained vacant, Beaumont, as the next senior official, was forced in the summer of 1689 to defend his claims to the 'government' of the Ports over those of the Earl of Winchilsea. The King's unwillingness to grant Winchilsea the lord wardenship arose directly from a reluctance to disoblige Beaumont. With a new election in the offing, Secretary Nottingham (Daniel Finch†) may have felt that Beaumont was better motivated for the business of securing Court support from the Ports. Thus for the time being, the lord wardenship was kept vacant while Winchilsea was mollified with the lord lieutenancy of Kent and a pension. All electoral affairs concerning the Ports were left to Beaumont. A by-election arising at Hastings in August, he visited the town 'to find out a fit man to stand for that place', and in the process was himself chosen, much to the disdain of the sheriff and local gentry. In February 1690 it was to him that the election writs for the Ports were directed, and he set about promoting Court candidates in a number of the towns, most notably Hastings, Hythe, New Romney and Rye. His task was made especially awkward by the sensibilities aroused in the Convention Parliament on the subject of electoral interference by previous lord wardens and their agents. He assured local gentlemen such as Julius Deedes, the retiring Member for Hythe, whose interest Beaumont needed in support of a Court nominee, that though the King's predecessors 'have pretended some right to nominate one in every Port . . . that is not the way he intends to pursue'. Deedes was doubtless not the only one to whom Beaumont pointed out the benefits of serving the King's will: 'it may beget you an interest that may be useful to you'. Veiled threats of this order were not well received among the Ports, and during the first session complaints about Beaumont's electioneering activities led to the passage of a bill denying the lord warden any right to nominate to parliamentary seats.[4]

Re-elected for Hastings, Beaumont was noted by Lord Carmarthen (Sir Thomas Osborne†) as a Tory supporter of the Court. On 26 Apr. he declared himself 'totally against' the imposition of an abjuration oath on the premise that it was 'rather a snare than a security', but pledged his utter devotion to the new government. 'It is well known', he told the House, 'that I parted with my commands in his [King James's] time, because I would not transgress the laws, and thereby lost my bread; and rather than I will injure this government, but with all my power assist it, I will lose my life'. A few days later, he notified the House of a libellous pamphlet, and named the Member responsible for its publication. He was less than enthusiastic in September about joining the King's expedition to Ireland, pleading to Secretary Nottingham a whole string of excuses: an impending law suit, ill-health, his parliamentary duties, his responsibilities at Dover, as well as the necessity of raising new recruits for his regiment, which had recently suffered serious desertion. He was refused exemption, but was given permission to return early with Lord Marlborough (John Churchill†). While in Ireland, however, he took part in the siege of Kinsale. Once back in England he was complaining earnestly to Lord Nottingham at the end of November about the dilapidated and ill-stocked condition of Dover Castle and its vulnerability to French attack, and he emphasized, with reference to recent actions, the castle's importance in coastal defence.[5]

Beaumont appeared on Robert Harley's† list of April 1691 as a Court supporter and continued to figure in subsequent lists of placemen. His efforts to improve the defensibility of Dover Castle are reflected in his being given a week's leave of absence on 11 Jan. 1692 'to go to Dover on his Majesty's service'. During the summer he served in Flanders and was present at the siege of Namur. At the outset of supply proceedings on 22 Nov. he moved for presentation of the army and navy estimates, while on 16 Dec. his military experience placed him among those nominees ordered to draft the mutiny bill. By August 1694 Beaumont had been 'removed' from his Dover Castle command. It would appear that Lord Romney (Hon. Henry Sidney†), who had become lord warden in 1691, had for some time wanted the post for his nephew, Colonel Robert Smith, and it was he who was appointed in Beaumont's place. It may have been that Beaumont's recent remarriage had made him neglectful of his duties ('Colonel Beaumont is fond to an infinite degree and the happiest man in the world', it was reported in November), providing Romney with a suitable pretext for his dismissal. The last occasion on which Beaumont's name occurs in the Journals was on 30 Apr. 1695 when he complained of an insult he had received in the House the previous day from another Member, Sir William Forester. Before the House could properly investigate the incident, the two men met again, and on reopening their quarrel, proceeded to St. James' Square where in a duel Forester was 'disarmed'.[6]

Standing down at the autumn election, Beaumont resigned his regiment in December and thereafter took no further part in public or military affairs. In January 1696 he was granted the half-pay pension of a colonel 'in consideration of his long and faithful services', but found great difficulty in obtaining the money. In response to his complaint to the Treasury in May 1698 it was minuted that there 'was nothing to pay him out of at present', and his case was deferred until the next meeting of Parliament. Despite this shoddy treatment, Beaumont bore the ministers no malice, willingly supporting government financial measures, for instance, in May 1697 by subscribing £600 to a circulation of Exchequer bills. He died on 3 July 1701, having been for some time in 'a declining condition', and predeceasing his elder brother, Viscount Beaumont, whose heir presumptive he had been. Leaving no issue, he bequeathed an annuity to his distant cousin, 'my worthy kinsman', Sir George Beaumont, 4th Bt.*, while to his wife he left an estate in the East Riding of Yorkshire as well as the residue of his property elsewhere.[7]

[1] *London Mar. Lic.* ed. Foster, 106; Northants RO, Isham mss IC1490, John to Sir Justinian Isham*, 3 Oct. 1693. [2] N. Carlisle, *Privy Chamber*, 165. [3] J. Childs, *Nobles, Gent. and Profession of Arms* (Soc. for Army Hist. Res. Sp. Publn. xiii), 6; Luttrell, *Brief Relation*, ii. 224, 399. [4] *HMC Finch*, ii. 205, 221–2; *CSP Dom. 1689–90*, p. 219; Add. 42586, ff. 78–79, 81, 85; H. Horwitz, *Parl. and Pol. Wm. III*, 100. [5] Bodl. Rawl. A.79, f. 79; Grey, x. 109; *HMC Finch*, ii. 432, 458, 493. [6] *Luttrell Diary*, 249; Luttrell, ii. 224, 399, 491–2; iii. 354, 468; Northants. RO, Isham mss IC1490, 1501, John to Sir Justinian Isham, 3 Oct., 18 Nov. 1693; *Lexington Pprs.* 86. [7] Luttrell, iii. 564; *Cal. Treas. Bks.* x. 1281; *Cal. Treas. Pprs. 1697–1702*, p. 51; Univ. of London Lib. MS 65/3, 'List of subscribers . . . to circulate Exchequer bills, May 1697'; Nichols, *Leics.* iii. 744; PCC 91 Dyer.

A. A. H.

BEAW, William (c.1676–1738), of Doctors' Commons, London.

MITCHELL 1701 (Feb.–Nov.)

b. c.1676, 1st s. of William Beaw, bp. of Llandaff 1679–1706, by Frances, da. of Alexander Bowsier of Southampton, Hants. *educ.* Magdalen, Oxf. matric. 4

Nov. 1681 aged 15, BA 1685, BCL 1686, DCL 1695; Doctors' Commons 1696. *m*. bef. 1686, Margaret, da. of Richard Lyster of Rowton Castle, Salop, 3s. *suc*. fa. 1706.¹

Chancellor, dioc. of Llandaff 1687–*d*.

Beaw was descended from Guillaume Beau, who took part in the siege of Boulogne in 1544, and whose issue settled first in London and then in Berkshire. His father served as a Royalist major of horse in the Civil War before taking holy orders, eventually becoming bishop of the impoverished see of Llandaff. Beaw entered Oxford in 1681, where he trained for the civil law, and after leaving university he became his father's secretary before being appointed chancellor of Llandaff diocese in 1687, an office he held for the rest of his life. At the first general election of 1701 Beaw was elected at Mitchell, a return he probably owed to his sister's marriage to a Protestant branch of the Arundells, a Catholic family who were lords of the manor at Mitchell. Beaw's contribution to the first 1701 Parliament was negligible, though he was listed as one of those who in this Parliament had opposed the preparations for war against France. He was arrested for debt in 1703 and spent the rest of his life in the Fleet prison. His father had long complained that he could not support his own large family out of the income of such a 'scandalously poor' see as Llandaff, and indeed when he died in 1706 he left nothing but debts, his widow relying on a pension of £40 p.a. from the royal bounty to keep her from starvation. Beaw died in the Fleet on 6 Jan. 1738.²

¹ Bradney, *Mon*. iv. 68; G. D. Squibb, *Doctors' Commons*, 185. ² Bradney, 67–68; *HMC Lords*, iv. 15–17; Luttrell, *Brief Relation*, vi. 17; *HMC Portland*, iv. 166; *Cal. Treas. Bks*. xix. 31; xxi. 230; xxvii. 546; *Hist. Reg. Chron*. 1738, pp. 6–7.

E. C.

BEDINGFIELD, Daniel (?c.1636–1704), of King's Lynn, Norf.

KING'S LYNN 1690–1695

b. ?c.1636, 3rd s. of Humphrey Bedingfield of Wighton by Abigail, da. of William Hicks, scrivener, of London. *educ*. Queens', Camb. 1657; G. Inn 1659, called 1667, bencher 1689, treasurer 1698. *s.p*.¹

Jt. receiver of estates of duchy of Lancaster, Cambs., Norf. and Suff. 1664–86, receiver 1686–*d*.²

Freeman, King's Lynn Oct. 1688, recorder Nov. 1688–*d*.³

Bedingfield's family was a cadet branch of the Catholic Bedingfields of Oxburgh, and his uncle and namesake had served as clerk of the Parliaments in 1637. Returned in 1690 with Sir John Turner*, he was listed by Lord Carmarthen (Sir Thomas Osborne†) as a Tory. In December Carmarthen forecast that Bedingfield would support him in the event of a Commons attack. Robert Harley* listed Bedingfield as a Court supporter in April 1691. He was named to the drafting committees for three bills: for the more easy recovery of small tithes (11 Oct. 1692); to regulate King's Bench and Fleet prisons (18 Oct.); and to extend the patent for convex lights (18 Nov.). Samuel Grascome listed him as a Court supporter in 1693. Bedingfield presented a private estate bill on 3 Feb. 1694 on behalf of Charles Turner*, nephew of Sir John. On 19 Feb. he reported a bill for improvements to the Acts encouraging privateers. On 23 Mar. he was given leave of absence. He was appointed to the drafting committee for a prison bill on 4 Dec. In early 1695 he was listed as a friend of Henry Guy*, possibly in connexion with a likely attack upon Guy in the Commons. On 20 Feb. 1695 he told on the Tory side against giving leave of absence to Nathaniel Palmer. Bedingfield vacated his seat in 1695 in favour of Charles Turner. In a letter of February 1696 to the Norfolk non-juror Sir Nicholas L'Estrange, 4th Bt.†, he commented: 'I believe the reality of the design of assassinating the King. Several are taken, and all under disguises and endeavouring to escape. You and I remember a plot they did not do so in.'⁴

Bedingfield died on 13 Sept. 1704, having named his nephew Christopher Bedingfield of Wighton as his heir. Despite a challenge from his niece Elizabeth Bedingfield, Christopher's sister, the will was proved 30 Oct. 1704.⁵

¹ IGI, Norf.; PCC 194 Ashe; *Vis. Norf*. (Norf. Arch Soc.), i. 168–9. ² Somerville, *Duchy of Lancaster Official Lists*, 199. ³ *Cal. Freemen King's Lynn*, 199; H. Le Strange, *Norf. Official Lists*, 200. ⁴ *HMC 11th Rep. VII*, 112. ⁵ Le Neve, *Mon. Ang*. 1700–15, p. 92; PCC 194 Ash.

D. W. H.

BEDINGFIELD, Sir Robert (1637–1711), of Ludgate Street, London.

HEDON 1701 (Feb.–Nov.)

b. bef. 2 June 1637, 5th s. of John Bedingfield of Lincoln's Inn and Halesworth, Suff. by Joyce, da. of Edmund Morgan of Lambeth, Surr.; bro. of Henry Bedingfield†. *m*. (1) lic. 22 Dec. 1662, Elizabeth (*d*. 1688), da. and coh. of Martin Harvey of Weston Favell, Northants., *s.p*.; (2) 10 Oct. 1689, Anne, da. and coh. of William Strode (*d*. 1661) of Newhouse, Warws., wid. of Nicholas Reynardson of London, *s.p*. Kntd. 18 Nov. 1697.¹

Freeman, Merchant Taylors' Co., master 1697; common councilman, London 1682–3, 1688–97, alderman 1697–d., sheriff 1702–3, ld. mayor 1706–7.[2]

A woollen-draper, Bedingfield was a strong Tory and had at one time been a crony of Judge Jeffreys. He was brought in at Hedon by Henry Guy*, though he may well have been recommended by the borough's other patron, (Sir) Charles Duncombe*, with whom, as an alderman of London, he was presumably well acquainted. 'An understanding and true man', was how Guy described him. In May 1701 he petitioned the House for relief from the effects of the Act resuming forfeited estates in Ireland. Although generally inactive in Parliament, his single vote in the London common council forestalled a petition in support of the Kentish Petitioners. Having been blacklisted as one who had opposed preparations for war, he did not stand for re-election in November. In April 1702 the Commons rejected a motion for a private bill on his behalf pursuant to his petition. He was among six Tories named in October 1710 as colonels of the City militia, and supported the Tory candidates in the London parliamentary election a month later.[3]

Bedingfield died 'suddenly' on 2 May 1711, leaving as his principal heir his nephew Thomas Bedingfield 'of St. John's, Oxfordshire'. Another nephew received by his will 'the lease of my dwelling house and shop and the whole benefit and advantage of the same'.[4]

[1] A. Lumsden-Bedingfield, *Bedingfield Peds*. 37, 104, 168; *London Mar. Lic.* ed. Foster 108; *Mar. Reg. St. Dunstan's Stepney*, ii. 187; *Frag. Gen.* viii. 144. [2] J. R. Woodhead, *Rulers of London* (London and Mdx. Arch. Soc.), 28. [3] Luttrell, *Brief Relation*, i. 9; iv. 95; Beaven, *Aldermen*, i. 291, 303; ii. 195; *DNB* (Bedingfield, Henry); *De La Pryme Diary* (Surtees Soc. liv), 244; *HMC Portland*, iii. 640; Boyer, *Pol. State*, i–ii. 10. [4] Le Neve, *Mon. Angl.* 1700–15, p. 232; PCC 143 Young.

D. W. H.

BEKE, Richard (1630–1707), of Dinton, Bucks.

ELGIN AND NAIRN   1656
AMERSHAM   8 Feb. 1659
AYLESBURY   1689–1690
WENDOVER   1690–24 June 1700

bap. 8 Sept. 1630, 1st s. of Henry Beke of Haddenham, Bucks. by Frances, da. of John Billiard of Notts. *m.* (1) 7 Feb. 1656, Lavinia (*d.* 1658), da. of Roger Whetstone of Whittlesey, Cambs., *s.p.*; (2) lic. 1 July 1667, Jane, da. of Ld. Charles Powlett of Abbott's Anne, Hants, *s.p.*; (3) 10 Feb. 1684 (with £1,200), Elizabeth (*d.* 1737), da. of Sir Thomas Lee, 1st Bt.*, sis. of Thomas Lee*, 3da. *suc.* fa. 1654.[1]

Capt. of horse 1651, maj. 1656–9, lt.-col. Life Gds. 1659–60; lt.-col. of horse 1690; commr. appeals in excise 1689–d.[2]

Freeman, Chipping Wycombe 1691.[3]

Beke, whose first wife was Cromwell's niece, had been an officer in the New Model Army, and was known as 'Major Beke' for the rest of his life. He was probably a Dissenter and possessed sufficient political influence with some of the county's leading Whigs to ensure election to the Convention of 1689 and the following Parliament. At the Revolution he was granted a post in the excise, worth £200 p.a. Then in July 1690 he was commissioned in a regiment of horse raised in the city of London by the Marquess of Winchester (Charles Powlett I*). In the 1690 Parliament Lord Carmarthen (Sir Thomas Osborne†) classed him as a Whig. He was appointed to two committees of inquiry in October 1690, both relating to military matters. Robert Harley* classed him as a Country supporter in April 1691. He was listed as a government supporter in an analysis of March–December 1692 and by virtue of his office he appears as a placeman on various lists of 1692–3, including that by Samuel Grascome. There seems little doubt from snippets of correspondence that Beke's associates were local Whigs such as Hon. Thomas Wharton*, Richard Hampden I* and his 'cousin' and neighbour, Simon Mayne*. In the 1694–5 session Henry Guy* included him on a list of 'friends', which probably indicated his likely support for Guy, who was then under attack in the Commons. On 1 May 1695 he was teller against a motion to grant bail to Sir Thomas Cooke*.[4]

Re-elected in 1695, in the opening session of the new Parliament he was forecast as likely to support the Court in a division of 31 Jan. 1696 over the proposed council of trade, signed the Association, and voted for fixing the price of guineas at 22s. Returned again in 1698 he was classed as a member of the Court party and a placeman in about September 1698, and voted on 18 Jan. 1699 against the disbanding bill. In February 1700 it was noted that he had not come to London owing to ill-health and in June he was reported to be about to resign his place in the excise because place legislation had made it incompatible with a seat in the House. However, in the event he preferred to resign his seat in the Commons. He appears to have ceased to act as a j.p. at about this time, but presented a sacramental certificate to the quarter sessions in Buckinghamshire at the start of Anne's reign. In 1706 he was still residing at Dinton. He died on 29 Nov. 1707.[5]

[1] *Top. and Gen.* iii. 158–63, 172, 177; *London Mar. Lic.* ed. Foster, 110; *Bucks. Recs.* vi. 25. [2] *Treas. Bks.* ix. 110; xxi. 512. [3] *First*

Wycombe Ledger Bk. ed. Greaves (Bucks. Rec. Soc. xi), 233. [4]Add. 34730, f. 145; BL, Verney mss mic. 636/47, John Verney* (Ld. Fermanagh) to Sir Ralph Verney, 1st Bt.[†], 11 Nov. 1693.
[5] *Vernon–Shrewsbury Letters*, ii. 426; Luttrell, *Brief Relation*, iv. 661; *Bucks. Sess. Recs.* ii. 344, 454; *Bucks. Dissent and Par. Life 1669–1712* ed. Broad (Bucks. Rec. Soc. xxviii), 228; *Top. and Gen.* 163.

E. C./S. N. H.

BELASYSE, Sir Henry (c.1648–1717), of Potto, Yorks. and Brancepeth Castle, co. Dur.

MORPETH   1695–1701 (Nov.)
DURHAM   1701 (Dec.)–1708, 1710–15 Feb. 1712
MITCHELL   1713–1715

b. c.1648, 2nd s. of Sir Richard Belasyse of Ludworth, co. Dur. by his 2nd w. Margaret, da. of Sir William Lambton of Lambton, co. Dur. *educ.* Kepyer sch. Houghton-le-Spring, co. Dur.; Christ's, Camb. 1666; M. Temple 1668. *m.* (1) lic. 3 Mar. 1680, Dorothy (*d.* 1696), da. of Tobias Jenkins of Grimston, Yorks., sis. of Tobias Jenkins* and wid. of Robert Benson of Wrenthorpe, Yorks., 1s. *d.v.p.* 3da. *d.v.p.*; (2) 23 Apr. 1709, Fleetwood (*d.* 1733), da. of Nicholas Shuttleworth of Forcett, Yorks., 1s. *d.v.p.* 1da. *d.v.p.* Kntd. by 1681.[1]

Capt. Eng. regt. in Dutch service (later 6 Ft.) 1675–Oct. 1676, lt.-col. Oct. 1676–Mar. 1678, col. Mar. 1678–88; col. 22 Ft. 1689–June 1701, 2 Ft. June 1701–3; envoy, Bavaria 1694; brig.-gen. 1689, maj.-gen. 1692, lt.-gen. 1694; gov. Galway 1691–2, Berwick-upon-Tweed 1713–15; commr. inquiry into forces and garrisons in Italy, Portugal and Spain 1711–12.[2]

Freeman, Galway 1691, mayor 1691–2.[3]

Asst. R. Fishery Co. [I] 1692, Mines Co. 1693.[4]

MP [I] 1692–3.

For Belasyse, younger son of a Durham squire, soldiering was a profession in which he could make his fortune, and one to which he was physically and temperamentally suited. In 1674 he raised a company of musketeers for the service of the United Provinces, where he spent the next 14 years, seeing action in the war against France at Grave (1674), Maastricht (1676) and St. Denis (1678). He was probably knighted abroad, between January 1678 (when he sailed back to Holland from England as mere 'Colonel Belasyse') and March 1681 (when as Sir Henry he was given a licence to recruit volunteers for his Dutch regiment in the city of London). In 1685 he accompanied his men to England to assist in the suppression of the Monmouth rebellion. Some mystery attaches to his part in the preliminaries to Prince William's invasion in 1688. There is a story, emanating from an unknown source, that he incurred the Prince's displeasure in April 1687 and was forbidden the Dutch court. He did not, however, lose his regiment until April 1688, at which time he came over to England, making contact with Orangist conspirators in Yorkshire and in the words of Sir John Reresby, 2nd Bt.[†], a Jacobite loyalist, 'lurking' there until the Revolution broke out. It is possible that the rumour of his unpopularity with the Prince of Orange was a contrivance to enable him to conduct covert operations safely in England, and it may be significant that his regiment was only provided with a new colonel on the eve of its sailing with William's invasion fleet. The one piece of direct evidence is unclear, a letter from a Dutch official to William in January 1688 referring to Belasyse's recent illness and suggesting that his present weakened physical condition offered an occasion (perhaps a pretext) for him to discontinue his service in Holland. If he had fallen into disfavour with William, he doubtless redeemed himself in the Prince's eyes by his behaviour at the Revolution, when he assisted the northern rising under Lord Danby (Sir Thomas Osborne[†]), leading a detachment of troopers in the successful action to secure the city of York. By March 1689 he had been given a commission for a new regiment, which eventually materialized the following September, and he was raised to the rank of brigadier-general. He participated in the Irish campaigns from the very first, going over with the Duke of Schomberg in September 1689, serving at the Boyne and at the siege of Limerick the following year, and in 1691 at the crossing of the Shannon at Athlone and at the battle of Aughrim. Receiving some personal reward in the form of a grant of forfeited estates in county Galway, he served as military governor of Galway after the capitulation of the garrison in 1691, and in that capacity secured his own return for Galway city to the Irish parliament of 1692. However, he probably did not take his seat, since by the time the parliament met he was on military service elsewhere. Meanwhile, in January 1691, back in England during a break in the Irish war, he had been challenged to a duel by Colonel Richard Leveson*, 'upon an old quarrel that had happened between them in Ireland', and had been worsted, receiving 'a large wound' in the thigh, and other less serious injuries. Besides lending his sword to the new regime, he was also lending his money: £7,000 in 1689 on the security of the 12*d.* aid, and a further £6,000 by March 1691.[5]

When a descent on France was proposed in the spring of 1692, Belasyse asked the Queen if he might take part. The request was granted, and he was given the rank of major-general in that abortive expedition. The next year he was in Flanders, and took part in the battle of Landen. After Hon. Thomas Tollemache's* death at Camaret Bay in 1694 he applied for the succession to Tollemache's regiment but was overlooked.

However, he was employed by King William on a diplomatic mission to congratulate the Elector of Bavaria on the birth of a son. In 1695 he again saw action in the continental campaign, helping to repel Marshal Villeroi at Nieuport, and was a member of the court martial of the Danish general Ellenberg for alleged treachery at Dixmude.[6]

In 1693 his nephew Richard Belasyse* had released to him all rights to the family estates, encumbered as they were with debt, and in the 1695 election Sir Henry was elected for the borough of Morpeth, in the adjoining county. His old comrade, Lord Cutts (John*), the governor of the Isle of Wight, had been asked to find a seat for him in one of the island's boroughs, but claimed that this was impossible, and there was also talk that Belasyse might put up for the venal borough of Stockbridge, where, although he was not a candidate, he sought to promote an interest after the election through sponsoring a petition against those who had been returned. At Morpeth he had to combat malicious reports that he was disaffected with the Williamite regime, the story started by a barber in Drury Lane, who had tried unsuccessfully to interest the lords justices in information that Belasyse attended mass and was in contact with French agents. When a letter was intercepted conveying this tale to the Morpeth electors, Belasyse brought a legal action against the barber, and in due course won £5,000 damages. He had not attended the election himself, being still on campaign, but in November he requested permission to return to England before Parliament opened. At this stage, his family background (his father appears to have favoured Parliament during the Civil War), his record at the Revolution and his profession aligned him closely with the Whig ministry, and although he was forecast as likely to oppose the Court in the divisions of 31 Jan. 1696 on the proposed council of trade, he signed the Association promptly, voted for fixing the price of guineas at 22s. and subsequently, on 25 Nov. 1696, supported the bill of attainder against Sir John Fenwick†. In 1698, when he was re-elected without opposition at Morpeth, he was listed as a placeman and a Court supporter. Somewhat surprisingly he was also included in a list of likely opponents of the standing army, but on 18 Jan. 1699 he voted against the third reading of the disbanding bill. Although the bill passed, Belasyse's regiment avoided disbandment through being placed on the Irish establishment, when he was one of the colonels criticized for continuing to 'sell their vacancies' rather than fill places with experienced and deserving men. Belasyse was an inactive Member, and his only impact upon the records of the 1698 Parliament was his classification as a placeman in an analysis of the House into interests, dating from early 1700. The close friendship he had contracted with Lord Stamford drew him into a bitter quarrel in the summer of 1699 with Sir Basil Firebrace*. It was an episode in a long-running feud between Stamford and Lord Denbigh, centring on the disputed jurisdiction of Enfield Chase, where Denbigh was ranger but Stamford, as chancellor of the duchy of Lancaster, claimed overall authority. Firebrace was woodward under Denbigh and sought to impose restrictions on hunting in the Chase, restrictions that were to extend to Stamford and his underlings. The particular quarrel arose from an incident in which Firebrace's gamekeeper encountered one of Stamford's hunting parties and killed a greyhound belonging to Belasyse, who demanded that Firebrace dismiss the keeper or give satisfaction, threatening to pull the woodward's nose if he did not. Both men appealed to their patrons, and the affair was brought before Secretary Vernon (James I*), the lords justices, Privy Council and even, in 1701, the Commons, before subsiding. At one point Belasyse and Firebrace met one another by accident in Temple Lane and after spitting in each other's faces were narrowly prevented from drawing their swords. Firebrace had been frightened enough of his practised antagonist to have hired 'a kind of little guard' to attend him about town.[7]

The 1701 Parliament witnessed a shift in Belasyse's party-political affiliations. In common with Lord Cutts and other army officers, he offered some support to the new Tory ministry, being listed with those who supported the Court in February 1701 over the 'Great Mortgage'. That this amounted to a repudiation of his previous Whig loyalties became clear in the autumn of 1701 when James Lowther* reported that Lord Carlisle (Charles Howard*) intended to oppose Belasyse's continued return at Morpeth because Belasyse 'did not differ from Sir C[hristopher] M[usgrave] [4th Bt.*] two votes all the last session'. Belasyse prudently transferred to Durham City at the second election of the year, and though his return was calculated by Lord Sunderland (Charles, Lord Spencer*) as a gain for the Whigs, Robert Harley* listed him with the Tories. The accuracy of Harley's judgment is demonstrated by Belasyse's inclusion upon the list of those who had favoured the motion of 26 Feb. 1702 vindicating the Commons' proceedings in the impeachments of the previous session. The turn to the Tories paid off in terms of his career, for in the summer of 1702 he was chosen to act as second-in-command under the Duke of Ormond in a proposed landing at Cadiz. The Prussian envoy, reporting the appointment, dismissed Belasyse as a mediocre general and a covetous man, and events did not prove this judgment wrong. The success of the assault was marred by the behaviour of the troops under Belasyse's command, who landed at El Puerto de Santa Maria (Port St. Mary's) across the bay, and pillaged the town, ransacking churches as well as secular buildings, and allegedly raping the female inhabitants, including nuns. Belasyse apparently led the plundering himself. Directly Ormond heard of the outrage he placed his subordinate under arrest, the Imperial envoy, Count Wratislaw, urging the severest punishment. On arrival in England, however, Belasyse claimed parliamentary privilege. Immune from trial for misconduct in Spain, he was charged with breaking his arrest and was cashiered. The Queen's Speech to the newly elected Parliament on 21 Oct. 1702 referred publicly to reports of the 'disorders and abuses committed at Port St. Mary's'. In the House Belasyse voted on 13 Feb. 1703 against agreeing with the Lords' amendments to the bill extending the time for taking the abjuration oath. The following year he applied to Robert Harley, now secretary of state, for the Queen's recommendation to serve with the forces in Portugal, as a means of rehabilitating himself. After losing his regiment he had 'resolved the passing the remainder of my time in a retreat, but by the little experience I have had of that way of living I find it is not so agreeable to me, as I expected or could have wished'. The request was rejected. Listed in October 1704 as a probable supporter of the Tack, he was lobbied by Harley but still voted for it in the division on 28 Nov. 1704. As a result, he was classified as 'True Church' in a list of the Parliament elected in 1705. On 25 Oct. Belasyse voted against the Court candidate for Speaker. He made little impact upon the records of this Parliament, though on 23 Jan. 1706 he was nominated to draft a bill to allow the construction of a pier at the mouth of the Wear, county Durham. At the end of the Parliament he was described as a Tory in a parliamentary list.[8]

Despite having the backing of the Church interest at Durham in the 1708 election, Belasyse anticipated defeat and 'decamped' before the poll. In August 1710 he wrote once more to Harley to acquaint him with 'the great joy' with which 'the county received the news of your being at the head of the new ministry and that they will pay their taxes very cheerfully, since they now think their Church out of danger'. He accompanied these welcome tidings with an application for a renewed commission as lieutenant-general, to take rank from the date of his previous commission, arguing that such preferment 'would give me a further credit in my country and do me a further great service at my next election'. Although he was not reinstated, he won back his seat at Durham, with help from some of the clergy, and his own open purse, and after a bitter contest in which he and his wife were abused at the hustings. Marked as a Tory in the 'Hanover list', he figured among the 'worthy patriots' who in the first session of the 1710 Parliament exposed the mismanagements of the old ministry. It did not take him long to renew his solicitations to the chief ministers, first seeking in vain the governorship of Tynemouth Castle, near his Durham estate, and then applying to be sent back to Spain, whereupon Jonathan Swift remonstrated to Lord Treasurer Oxford (Robert Harley) that it would be shameful to return that 'most covetous cur' to the scene of his earlier disgrace. Oxford agreed in principle, but observed that it was not easy to find men who understood business and yet had no love for money; and so, late in 1711, Belasyse was appointed a commissioner to inquire into the state of the forces in the Peninsula and Italy, a move which had at least the political virtue of removing from Westminster a difficult and potentially disruptive individual, at a time when military men in general were developing doubts about the government's foreign policy. To complete the effect, Belasyse was expelled the House on 15 Feb. 1712, after a division, on the grounds that he had accepted an office of profit subsequent to his election, contrary to the 'place clause' of the 1706 Regency Act. By 1713 his spell as a commissioner was over, and, though still hankering after an army commission, he was appointed governor of Berwick. Taking refuge in a Cornish borough at the general election of that year, he seems to have followed an undeviating party line in the 1714 Parliament and in the Worsley list was marked as a Tory.[9]

Belasyse was turned out of his governor's post after the Hanoverian succession, and, although no longer in Parliament, was still recognized as a Tory, and thus as an enemy, by Whigs in Durham and Northumberland. He would not have had enough time to work his way into the favour of the new dynasty even if he had possessed the inclination and energy to do so, for he died on 16 Dec. 1717, aged 69. He was buried in Westminster Abbey.[10]

[1] Surtees, *Dur.* i. 158–60, 203; *Westminster Abbey Reg.* (Harl. Soc. x), 239–40, 290, 338, 411; *CSP Dom.* 1683–4, p. 191; *St. James Duke Place Mar. Reg.* iv. 90. [2] J. Childs, *Nobles, Gent. and Profession of Arms* (Soc. for Army Hist. Res. sp. publn. xiii), 7; F. J. G. ten Raa, *Het Staatsche Leger*, vi. 255; info. from Mr A. Exelby; *CSP Dom.* 1703–4, p. 266; Bodl. Rawl. C.393, f. 44; Folger Shakespeare Lib. Newdigate newsletter 25 Dec. 1712; *Post Boy*, 13–16 June 1713. [3] Univ. Coll. Galway, Galway corp. mss Liber D, pp. 1–2. [4] *CSP Dom.* 1691–2, p. 112; 1693, p. 207. [5] *CSP Dom.* 1677–8, p. 575; 1680–1, p. 226; 1689–90, p. 256; ten Raa, 107; J. Childs, *Army, Jas. II and Revolution*, 147–8; J. Carswell, *Descent on Eng.* 159, 169; Reresby

Mems. ed. Browning, 530, 585; *HMC 7th Rep.* 413, 420, 422; *Correspondentie* ed. Japikse, v. 4; Browning, *Danby*, i. 401, 413, 415; *HMC Portland*, iii. 431; *HMC Finch*, ii. 416; info. from Hist. Irish Parl.; PRO NI, De Ros mss D638/13/12, John Pulteney* to Thomas Coningsby*, 20 Jan. 1690–1; Trinity, Dublin, Clarke mss 749/3/407, William Blathwayt* to George Clarke*, 22 Jan. 1691; *Cal. Treas. Bks.* ix. 1061, 1979. [6] Luttrell, *Brief Relation*, ii. 498, 500; *Correspondentie*, ii. 202–3, 206; Trinity, Dublin, Lyons (King) mss 2008b/371, George Tollet to Abp. King, 11 Aug. 1694; *Cal. Treas. Bks.* x. 848; *HMC Downshire*, i. 512. [7] Surtees, 103; *Cam. Misc.* xxx. 399; Hants RO, Jervoise mss, Anthony Sturt* to [Thomas Jervoise*], 12 [Oct.] 1695, James Hooper to [same], 7 Dec. 1695; *CSP Dom.* 1695, pp. 39–40; Northants. RO, Montagu (Boughton) mss 46/33, Vernon to Shrewsbury, 5 Dec. 1696; 47/201, 207, same to same, 22 June, 6 July 1699; Add. 9731, f. 29; R. Howell, *Newcastle-upon-Tyne and Puritan Rev.* 193–4; *Vernon–Shrewsbury Letters*, ii. 58–59; Add. 40774, ff. 58–59, 62–64, 70–71; Boston Pub. Lib. Mass. mss K.5.3, Robert Yard* to Blathwayt, 23 June 1699; *Cocks Diary*, 149. [8] Cumbria RO (Carlisle), Lonsdale mss D/Lons/W2/2/4, James to Sir John Lowther, 2nd Bt. I*, 23 Sept., 18 Nov. 1701; Add. 30000 E, f. 236; 7074, f. 158; 40803, f. 65; *CSP Dom.* 1702–3, pp. 253–6; Dalrymple, *Mems.* iii(2), 275–6; G. M. Trevelyan, *Eng. under Q. Anne*, i. 265–6; *Poems on Affairs of State* ed. Ellis, vi. 477–8; Boyer, *Anne Annals*, i. 225–6; Luttrell, v. 237; *HMC Portland*, iv. 95–96. [9] *Arch. Ael.* ser. 4, xxxiv. 17; *HMC Portland*, iv. 570, 575, 645; v. 154; *Clavering Corresp.* (Surtees Soc. clxxviii), 101; *Swift Stella* ed. Davis, 306–7. [10] *Clavering Corresp.* 136; *Westminster Abbey Reg.* 290.

E. C./D. W. H.

BELASYSE, Richard (c.1670–1729), of Lincoln's Inn and Hampstead, Mdx.

MITCHELL 1710–1713

b. c.1670, o. s. of William Belasyse of Owton, co. Dur. by 2nd w. Catherine Brandling of Middleton, Yorks. *educ.* M. Temple 1689; I. Temple 1696; L. Inn 1699. *m.* lic. 14 Feb. 1701, aged 30, Margaret Marshall of St. Clement Dane, London, *s.p. suc.* fa. by 1681.[1]

Freeman, Durham 1702.[2]

?Groom porter at gate, 1702–*d.*[3]

Belasyse inherited an estate encumbered with debts and in 1693 released all his rights to Owton to his uncle Sir Henry Belasyse*. Thereafter he resided principally in London where, despite not being called to the bar of any of the three inns of court to which he was admitted, he established a legal practice, the success of which is suggested by his purchase in 1711 of over £3,000 of South Sea stock. Belasyse's parliamentary aspirations were first evident in 1702 when he stood for Morpeth, presumably on his uncle's interest, but he did not enter the Commons until returned for Mitchell in 1710. The 'Hanover list' classed him as a Tory, and in 1711 he was included among the 'worthy patriots' who had helped uncover the mismanagements of the previous ministry. On 3 Mar. 1711 he was granted a three-month leave of absence. He told on three occasions during the next session: against the expulsion of his uncle Sir Henry Belasyse (15 Feb. 1712); on the Tory side in the Carlisle election case (23 Feb.); and against the third reading of a rider, to exempt wills from being stamped, to the charitable uses bill (7 June). Belasyse was also involved in a more personal matter during this session, as he and his wife were signatories, in respect of their role as administrators of the deceased brother of Belasyse's wife, to a petition heard by the House on 4 Apr. requesting the payment of arrears owed to officers in a marine troop. Belasyse was the first-named Member appointed to the committee ordered to consider this petition, but though the committee's report recommending that the arrears be paid was agreed by the House on 24 May, no further action was taken. The matter was revived in the following session when a further petition, again signed by Belasyse and his wife, was heard by the Commons on 9 June 1713, but when the report upon this petition was considered ten days later it was ordered to lie on the table. Between April and June Belasyse managed through the House a bill for the ease of sheriffs. He appears to have become disillusioned with the ministry by this time, as on 6 May he voted against the French wines duty bill. Alternative versions of the list of the division of 18 June upon the French commerce bill have Belasyse voting both for and against this measure, the second of these lists classing him as 'whimsical'. In the light of his vote of 6 May it seems most likely that Belasyse opposed the French commerce bill, and such a vote may well explain why he was dropped from Mitchell in favour of his uncle at the 1713 election. He did not stand for election again and little more is known of his life. Belasyse died in 1729, being buried at Hampstead on 14 May, and four years later his wife was granted administration of his estate.[4]

[1] J. Foster, *Peds. of Yorks.* ii. (Belasyse); *London. Mar. Lic.* ed. Foster, 110. [2] Surtees, *Dur.* iv(2), 23. [3] Info. from Prof. R. O. Bucholz. [4] Surtees, i. 203; *HMC Lords*, n.s. vii. 339; ix. 107–8; *Hist. Jnl.* iv. 196; *HMC 13th Rep. VI*, 190; Foster, *Peds. of Yorks.*; Prob. 6/109.

E. C./R. D. H.

BELL, Ralph (*d.* 1733), of Sowerby, nr. Thirsk, Yorks.

THIRSK 1710–12 July 1717

1st s. of Robert Bell, of Sowerby by his w. Elizabeth. *m.* 3 Mar. 1697, Rachel, da. of Richard Windlow of Yarm, Yorks., 2s. *d.v.p.* 2da. *suc.* fa. 1711.[1]

Customer, Kingston-upon-Hull 1717–*d.*

Bell's family had been settled in Thirsk since the 16th century, and his father, who had a mansion house at Kirkgate, owned 22 of the borough's burgages. Bell himself, 'a mercer in Thirsk', was politically active in Yorkshire for many years before entering Parliament. His family's electoral interest was significant enough to place him in a position to nominate to one of the Thirsk seats. From 1695 onwards Bell supported the candidature of Sir Godfrey Copley, 2nd Bt., who represented the borough continuously until his death in 1709. Bell also took an interest in the county constituency, and on different occasions in 1701 and 1702 he advised the election agents of the Whig Lord Irwin (Arthur Ingram*), on the best strategy for winning the election. Bell himself was described in May 1702 as the 'agent' of the 9th Earl of Derby, whose family also had an interest in Thirsk.[2]

Following the death of Copley in 1709, Bell agreed to the return of Leonard Smelt, a nephew of Sir Thomas Frankland I*, at the ensuing by-election, on the understanding that the Franklands would 'agree to whom Mr Bell had a mind' to put forward at the next general election. In September 1710 it became apparent that Bell was considering standing for himself, Henry Frankland writing that Bell had 'in a manner resolved to stand . . . and I verily believe [he] will at last'. He was returned unopposed for the borough in 1710, and was classified as 'doubtful' in the 'Hanover list'. A Yorkshire correspondent of Robert Harley* reported in December 1710 that Bell

was . . . brought up a Churchman in his youth; but his father taking some distaste to a former minister of Thirsk set up a Dissenting congregation there, and has ever since adhered solely to it, but the son goes to church in the morning, and, (to humour his father) to the meeting in the afternoon. But since his election (or rather since Sir Thomas Frankland and he chose each other, for these two have much the greatest number of borough houses, and nobody can come in at Thirsk without their joint consent) he has stuck wholly to the Church, though some of his neighbours say he has been at the meeting . . . his capacity for a legislator will soon discover itself, if he offers to [speak] in the House, but I believe he will yet awhile be too modest to do that.

Harley's correspondent guessed that Bell would adhere to the Whigs. He voted on 18 June 1713 against the French commerce bill, on which occasion he was classed as a Whig. In the next Parliament he voted on 18 Mar. 1714 against the expulsion of Richard Steele. Bell was subsequently described as a Whig in the Worsley list.[3]

Re-elected in 1715, Bell was described as a Whig in two comparative analyses of the new Parliament with its predecessor. However, he agreed to leave Parliament in 1717 in return for a customs place. In 1722–3 he purchased the manor of Thirsk for £6,300 from the 10th Earl of Derby (Hon. James Stanley*), thereby adding to his stock of burgages. In 1726 Bell sold the manor to Frankland. However, he remained an important figure in the borough, being described by Browne Willis* as the 'lord of the town', who lived in 'a handsome new-built house' beside the church. He died on 3 Nov. 1733, and was buried in the churchyard at Thirsk. By his will he left his house in Sowerby to his wife for her life, along with the household goods and £100. His brother, John, was to receive an annuity of £50. However, his principal heir was his nephew Ralph Consett, who assumed the name of Bell. A descendant, John Bell, represented Thirsk from 1841 to 1851.[4]

[1] W. Grainge, *Vale of Mowbray*, 72–73; *LG* (1937). [2] *HMC Portland*, iv. 640; Sheffield Archs. Copley mss CD473, ff. 7–9, 11, 16; N. Yorks. RO, Swinton mss, Danby pprs. ZS, John Warcupp to Sir Abstrupus Danby*, 18 Aug. 1699; W. Yorks. Archs. (Leeds), Temple Newsam mss TN/C9/93, 243, Thomas Lumley to John Roades, 8 Sept. 1701, 2 May 1702. [3] N. Yorks. RO, Worsley mss ZON 13/1/310, Henry Frankland to Thomas Worsley I*, 20 Sept. 1710; Grainge, 72; *HMC Portland*, 640; G. Holmes, *Pol. in Age of Anne*, 17. [4] Bodl. Willis 15, ff. 123, 126; Borthwick Inst. York, wills, Prerog. Court. Dec. 1735; Grainge, 71.

E. C./C. I. M.

BELLEW, Richard, 3rd Baron Bellew [I] (*d.* 1715), of Duleek, co. Louth.

STEYNING   16 Feb.–8 May 1712

b. aft. 1664, 2nd s. of John Bellew, 1st Baron Bellew [I], of Duleek, co. Meath and Dundalk by Mary, da. of Walter Bermingham of Dunfert, co. Kildare. *m.* July 1695, Lady Frances Livingston, da. of Francis Brudenell, *styled* Lord Brudenell, wid. of Charles Livingston†, 2nd Earl of Newburgh [S], 1s. *suc.* bro. Walter as 3rd Baron Bellew 1694.[1]

Ensign, Sir Thomas Newcomen's regt. 1687.[2]

The Bellews were a Catholic Irish family and in 1690 and 1691 Bellew, his father and brother were all outlawed for fighting for James II and the family estates forfeited. Although entitled to the benefit of the Articles of Limerick, Bellew went abroad to France for health reasons. In 1694 he succeeded to the family title and fortune and spent the next three years struggling to have the outlawry reversed and regain the family estates. He gained powerful supporters, one of whom was his wife's kinsman, the Duke of Shrewsbury. Lord Wharton (Hon. Thomas*) also interested himself in the case, possibly out of spite against the Earl of Romney (Henry Sidney†) who had been granted the Bellew estates and was reluctant to part with them. William III also proved reluctant to co-operate but eventually Bellew was granted his pardon on 18 Mar. 1697. On 24 June 1698 Bellew was given leave to remain in England, but it took a further year before he regained his estates. The costs of obtaining his own and his father's pardon, the incumbrances on the estate, and the many claims outstanding against both himself and his father, left him heavily in debt and he spent the next few years fighting various law-suits and selling parts of the estate to pay his debts.[3]

In 1705 Bellew became a Protestant and was summoned to the Irish house of lords in 1707. In January 1709 he contested a by-election at Steyning on the interest of his brother-in-law, the 1st Duke of Richmond, probably on account of the parliamentary privileges he would gain if chosen. A double return was made. After a hearing at the bar on 15 Feb. 1709, the House decided in favour of Bellew's Whig opponent and adjourned further consideration of the election, at which point Bellew withdrew his petition. He successfully contested the borough a second time at a by-election in February 1712, but when the case was heard on petition, extensive bribery was proved against both candidates and the election was declared void. Bellew, then, had little opportunity to reveal any party political inclinations but, although he had campaigned on the interest of the Whiggish Duke of Richmond, he was probably perceived as a High Tory: in 1712 the tellers for Bellew were two October Club members, against two moderate Tories. Giving up Parliament as a means of repairing his fortune, Bellew petitioned for a pension in 1713 and on 13 Oct. was granted £300 p.a. His wife, disappointed at the size of this annuity, began to use her influence to get it increased, seeking assistance from, among others, Henry St. John II*, now Viscount Bolingbroke, who, while promising his own help, advised her to appeal to Shrewsbury. But no increase was forthcoming. After the accession of George I, Bellew's name appeared on a number of lists of Irish peers as a Whig, who had voted against the Court in the previous Irish parliament, but who would support the government if a new one was to be called. He died on 22 Mar. 1715 and was buried at Duleek.[4]

[1] *HMC Buccleuch*, ii. 201. [2] *CSP Dom.* 1686–7, p. 399. [3] *CSP Dom.* 1691–2, pp. 30, 307; 1694–5, p. 501; 1695, p. 82; 1696, pp. 61, 173, 240, 431, 470; 1697, pp. 64, 243–6, 251; 1698, p. 44; 1699–1700, pp. 86, 132, 173; *Cal. Treas. Bks.* x. 4, 132; xxii. 440; *Vernon–Shrewsbury Letters*, i. 66–9, 158, 477; ii. 331, 336–7; *Shrewsbury Corresp.* 120; J. G. Simms, *Williamite Confiscation in Ire.* 33, 35, 76, 84; Luttrell, *Brief Relation*, ii. 266; *HMC Buccleuch*, ii. 201, 209, 214, 244, 282, 285; Add. 61639, ff. 7–10; 40771, f. 294; *HMC Lords*, n.s. iv. 29, 32, 44; *HMC Ormonde*, n.s. viii. 240. [4] Luttrell, v. 621; *Cal. Treas. Bks.* xxvii. 382; *Bolingbroke Corresp.* iv. 384; Add. 61640, ff. 28, 30.

P.W.

BELLOMONT, Richard Coote, 1st Earl of [I] *see* **COOTE**

BELLOT, Renatus (c.1673–1710), of Bochym, Cornw.

MITCHELL 1702–1705

b. c.1673, o. s. of Christopher Bellot of Bochym by Bridget, da. of William Pendarves of Roskrow, Cornw. *educ.* M. Temple 1691; Pembroke, Camb. adm. 22 Apr. 1691, aged 17. *m.* bef. 1703, Mary, da. and h. of Edmond Spoure of Trebarthan Hall, Cornw. 1s.[1]

Stannator, Penwith and Kerrier 1703, 1710.[2]

A descendant of a family settled at Bochym since the reign of Elizabeth I, Bellot's father farmed the tin coinage jointly with Samuel Enys† from 1661 till 1664 and was sheriff of Cornwall in 1692. Bellot himself was recommended successfully at Mitchell in 1702 by the returning officer, Sir Richard Vyvyan, 3rd Bt.* Bellot made little impact upon the records of the Commons and made no recorded speeches. He was forecast in October 1704 as a probable supporter of the Tack but did not vote for it in the division on 28 Nov. 1704. Presumably as a consequence, he was dropped by Vyvyan at the next election. Bellot then went on to spend all his estate 'by riot and excess', and died 'of a fever' early in 1710, leaving an only son who died two years later, when Bochym was sold to George Robinson* for the payment of Bellot's debts.[3]

[1] Boase, *Coll. Cornub.* 823; Vivian, *Vis. Cornw.* 26, 356. [2] Tregoning, *Stannary Laws*, 118; R. Inst. Cornw. Tonkin's ms hist. Cornw. ii. 244. [3] Boase, 392; Polsue, *Complete Paroch. Hist. Cornw.* i. 288–9.

E.C.

BELLOT, Sir Thomas, 2nd Bt. (1651–99), of Moreton, Cheshire.

NEWCASTLE-UNDER-LYME
1679 (Mar.)–1681 (Mar.), 1690–1695
1698–Aug. 1699

b. 22 Oct. 1651, 1st s. of Sir John Bellot, 1st Bt., of Moreton and The Ashes, Endon, Staffs. by Anne, da. of Roger Wilbraham of Dorfold, Cheshire. *educ.* Christ Church, Oxf. 1668; L. Inn 1671. *m.* Feb. 1675, Susanna, da. of Christopher Packe†, Draper, of Basinghall Street, London and Cotes, Leics., 3s. (1 *d.v.p.*) 3da. *suc.* fa. as 2nd Bt. 14 July 1674.[1]

Freeman, Newcastle-under-Lyme 1678.[2]

The main estates of the Bellot family were at Moreton, Cheshire, eight miles from Newcastle, although they also owned half the lordship of the nearby manor of Horton. After sitting as an

Exclusionist, Bellot became a Whig 'collaborator' under James II. After the 1690 election, the Marquess of Carmarthen (Sir Thomas Osborne†) classed him as a Whig, and in April 1691 Robert Harley* listed him as a Country supporter, although with a qualification which may query this analysis. However, Bellot was not an active Member, so there is little other evidence on which to base an assessment of his politics. On Grascome's list of 1693 (extended to 1695) he was classed as a Court supporter, an analysis not inconsistent with Whiggery. Furthermore, he was mentioned as having canvassed support for Hon. Henry Paget* against the Tory critic of the Court, Sir Walter Bagot, 3rd Bt.*, in preparation for the Staffordshire by-election of 1693. There is no trace of him standing for re-election in 1695.[3]

Upon his return for Newcastle at the 1698 election, Bellot was forecast as likely to oppose the standing army and on an analysis of the old and new Parliaments, was classed as a Country supporter. Clearly, contemporaries expected him to adopt the stance of a Country Whig on this issue, but his loyalty to the Whig ministers may have proved stronger for in the crucial division of 18 Jan. 1699 he voted against the disbanding bill. Whether this vote represented an example of a move from Country to Court cannot be determined with any degree of certainty because Bellot died in August 1699. He was succeeded by his son, who represented Newcastle for two short periods in Anne's reign.[4]

[1] Ormerod, *Cheshire*, iii. 44; J. C. Wedgwood, *Staffs. Parl. Hist.* (Wm. Salt Arch. Soc.), ii. 140–1; *Staffs. Peds.* (Harl. Soc. lxiii), 21.
[2] T. Pape, *Newcastle-under-Lyme from Restoration to 1760*, p. 49.
[3] Wedgwood, 141; Hereford and Worcester RO (Hereford), Foley mss E12/F/IV, Philip Foley* to Henry Paget, 5 Oct. 1693.
[4] Wedgwood, 141.

S. N. H.

BELLOT, Sir Thomas, 3rd Bt. (1679–1709), of Moreton, Cheshire.

NEWCASTLE-UNDER-LYME   1705–27 Feb. 1706,
                                 1708–by 22 Jan. 1709

bap. 18 July 1679, 1st surv. s. of Sir Thomas Bellot, 2nd Bt.* *educ.* Chester sch.; Trinity Coll. Camb. 1699. *unm. suc.* fa. as 3rd Bt. 28 Nov. 1699.[1]
Freeman, Newcastle-under-Lyme 1704.[2]

Having succeeded to his father's political interest at Newcastle, Bellot did not find it easy to capture one of the borough's parliamentary seats. The reason was not any obvious personal incapacity, for he followed his father into the Cheshire lieutenancy, but rather the strength of the opposition. Furthermore, he may have been distracted from a parliamentary career by financial problems, caused by his father having acted as a surety for Morgan Whitley, the defaulting receiver-general of taxes for Cheshire and North Wales. Whitley's debts fell on to his sureties and in the case of Bellot led to a decision by the Treasury to proceed against his father's executors in October 1703.[3]

Bellot first stood as a candidate at Newcastle in the by-election of November 1703 caused by the elevation to the peerage of Sir John Leveson Gower, 5th Bt.* Following his defeat Bellot petitioned against the return of John Crewe Offley* and on 1 Feb. 1704 the election was declared void. At the ensuing by-election, held in November 1704, he was again defeated by Offley, but chose not to petition, and at the general election of 1705 was elected in partnership with his fellow Tory, Rowland Cotton, after reportedly assuring the electorate of both men's 'adhesion to the Church'. His political allegiance was clear to contemporaries: on one analysis of the 1705 Parliament he was classed as a 'Churchman'; while the Earl of Sunderland (Charles, Lord Spencer*) considered his return a loss for the Whigs. Bellot proved Sunderland right at the very beginning of the opening session by voting on 25 Oct. against the Court candidate for Speaker. His seat in the Commons was not secure, however, for he faced a challenge in the form of a petition against his return from Offley and John Lawton*. The need to prepare his defence may explain why he was granted leave to go into the country on 14 Dec. 1705. If so, it proved unavailing, for on 27 Feb. 1706 he was unseated by the House. Undeterred, Bellot was again returned at the 1708 election, whereupon Sunderland repeated his earlier calculation and marked the election a loss for the Whigs. However, Bellot did not remain in the Commons for long, being reported dead on 22 Jan. 1709, a few days before he and Cotton were again unseated on petition. Bellot was succeeded by his brother Sir John, 4th Bt., the last of the line.[4]

[1] Ormerod, *Cheshire*, iii. 44; *Staffs. Peds.* (Harl. Soc. lxiii), 21. [2] T. Pape, *Newcastle-under-Lyme from Restoration to 1760*, p. 50. [3] *CSP Dom.* 1700–2, p. 257; *Cal. Treas. Bks.* xvii. 285; xviii. 412; *Cal. Treas. Pprs.* 1702–7, p. 194. [4] *Dyer's newsletter* 15 May 1705 (Speck trans.); Bagot mss at Levens Hall, Ld. Gower to [?James Grahme*], 22 Jan. 1708[–9].

S. N. H.

BENCE, John (1670–1718), of Heveningham, Suff.

DUNWICH   8 Dec. 1691–1695
IPSWICH   1702–1708

bap. 27 Sept. 1670, 1st s. of Edmund Bence of Benhall, Suff. by Mary, da. of Robert Yallop of Thorpe next

Norwich, Norf. *educ*. St. Catharine's, Camb. 1685. *m*. by 1692, Catherine, da. of Sir Sackville Glemham of Glemham Hall, Little Glemham, Suff., sis. of Thomas Glemham*, 1da. *d.v.p. suc*. fa. 1702.[1]

Bailiff, Aldeburgh 1690; freeman, Dunwich 1691, bailiff 1691–2, alderman 1692–4, common councilman 1710; common councilman, Orford 1692.[2]

While still a minor, Bence served as bailiff of Aldeburgh and in that capacity assisted the brothers Sir Henry* and William Johnson* in the 1690 election. In return the Johnsons helped him in financial and business matters and probably supported him when he stood in 1691 against the Whig Henry Heveningham* in a by-election at Dunwich. There was a double return, but on 8 Dec. 1691 the House decided in Bence's favour. He proved an inactive Member, being ordered into custody on 2 Jan. 1693 for non-attendance, and lost his seat at the next election.[3]

Having bought the manor of Heveningham in about 1700, Bence came into Parliament again in 1702, for Ipswich. He voted for the Tack on 28 Nov. 1704, as had been forecast, and was granted leave of absence on 21 Dec. Classed as 'True Church' in an analysis of the 1705 Parliament, he gave his vote against the Court candidate for Speaker on 25 Oct. 1705. He was listed as a Tory in two lists of 1708, but did not stand at the general election of that year. Nevertheless, he 'was every day engaged in election work' on behalf of Tories in several corporations in Suffolk. He was still active the following year in support of Sir Edward Turnor's* interest in Orford, and the Tory cause in the county. He contested Aldeburgh in 1713 against his former friends the Johnsons but was well beaten.[4]

Bence died on 18 Oct. 1718 and was buried at Heveningham. Although survived by a grandson, he left the bulk of his property in Suffolk to his brother Alexander, together with legacies of over £3,000 to other members of his family and £1,500 to his 'friend' Miss Katherine Hooke, who had nursed him in his last illness. His son-in-law, Sir William Barker, 5th Bt.*, received 100 guineas; his grandson John, the future 6th Bt., £1,000. Heveningham was sold off.[5]

[1] T. S. Hill, *Recs. Thorington*, 102–3, 107–8, ped.; *Vis. Norf.* (Harl. Soc. lxxxvi), 250; Copinger, *Suff. Manors*, v. 128. [2] W. Suss. RO, Shillinglee mss Ac.454/893, 904, 906, 953, 956, Edward Pratt to Sir Edward Turnor*, 18 Mar. 1689[–90], 12 Nov. 1692, [1] Oct. 1693, Nathaniel Gooding to Turnor, 15 Nov., 10 Dec. 1692; Suff. RO (Ipswich), EE6 1144/13, pp. 72, 77; 1144/14; T. Gardner, *Dunwich* (1754), 85. [3] Shillinglee mss Ac.454/897, Pratt to Turnor, 29 Oct. 1691; Add. 22186, ff. 62–65, 69. [4] Copinger, ii. 96; Shillinglee mss Ac.454/1231, 1242, 1082, Bence to Turnor, 10 May 1708, 2 Sept. 1709, John Hooke to Turnor, 15 Sept. 1709; Add. 22248, ff. 13–14. [5] Hill, 108; PCC 77 Browning; Copinger, ii. 96.

D. W. H.

BENE, Robert (c.1652–1733), of Norwich and Frettenham, Norf.

NORWICH 1710–1715

b. c.1652, ?1st s. of Thomas Bene of Norwich by his w. Rebecca. *unm. suc*. fa. 1680.[1]

Freeman, Norwich 1674, sheriff 1694–5, alderman by 1708–*d*., mayor 1710–11.[2]

Bene, a brewer whose father seems to have established the family business, was returned for Norwich on the Tory interest in the year of his mayoralty and was classed as one of the 'worthy patriots' who exposed the mismanagements of the previous ministry. He was appointed to the drafting committee for a Norwich workhouse bill on 14 Dec. 1711, and was granted a month's leave of absence on 8 Apr. 1712. Re-elected in 1713 he was appointed, on 9 Mar. 1714, to the drafting committee for a bill to curb wool smuggling. He was defeated at the 1715 election and did not stand again for Parliament. He was listed by the Jacobite Christopher Layer as one of the 'loyal gentlemen' of Norfolk, with £1,000 a year.[3]

Bene died on 27 May 1733, aged 80, and was buried in the church of St. Martin-in-Coslany, Norwich, the parish in which his 'brewing office' was situated. His will mentioned property in two other city parishes and in several of the surrounding villages, and included specific bequests of £3,600 to be raised from the sale of land and some £2,400 from his personal estate. According to the inscription on his monument, 'his industry rendered him wealthy; his integrity, liberality and munificence, esteemed; his affection to his friends, and his benevolence to all men, beloved, and his death lamented'.[4]

[1] Norf. RO, NCC 36 Tetsall; Blomefield, *Norf.* iv. 482. [2] *Norwich Freemen*, 22; Rye, *Norf. Fams*. 270. [3] *Norwich Freemen*, 21; P. S. Fritz, *Ministers and Jacobitism 1715–45*, p. 145. [4] NCC 36 Tetsall; Blomefield, 482.

D. W. H.

BENNET, John (c.1656–1712), of Great and Little Abington, Cambs.

NEWTON 18 Dec. 1691–1695

b. c.1656, 1st s. of John Bennet† of Great Abington by Elizabeth, da. of Sir Thomas Whitmore, 1st Bt.†, of Apley Park, Salop. *educ*. Trinity Coll. Camb. 1673. *m*. 1681, Grace (*d*.1732), da. and coh. of Simon Bennet of Beachampton, Bucks., 1s. *suc*. fa. 1663.[1]

Bennet's father had acquired the manors of Great and Little Abington in 1652, and on his death Bennet inherited Little Abington, Great Abington being left to his mother. She released her interest to him in 1678, and the following year he purchased the advowson. A cousin of the 1st Earl of Arlington (Sir Henry Bennet†), and of Sir Levinus Bennet, 2nd Bt.*, Bennet sought to marry another cousin, Grace, of the Beachampton branch of the Bennet family. The bride's father agreed with the match, but wrote that

> my daughter Grace is more violent against him than her mother, and after she had given him five or six denials, she hath ever since locked herself up whenever he came to the house, both mother and daughter keep themselves very close from him, insomuch that he is forced to get a ladder to climb up to the window to them, but cannot see them when he hath done. Sometimes they fling a pail of water upon his head and wet him to the skin, the difference being so high among them; yet for all this he is not at all dismayed, but is fully resolved to stick by it and pursue his design, although it should last yet these seven years.

The wedding had taken place by 15 Oct. 1681, when Arlington reported the couple's return from France. Socially it was a good match for Bennet, as he became brother-in-law of Viscount Latimer (Edward Osborne†), and of the 4th Earl of Salisbury. Financially too, the rewards were promising: although the size of Grace's portion had yet to be fixed, her sister had received a dowry of at least £10,000. Domestic peace was not to be had, however, for Arlington reported on 29 Nov. that 'though the marriage be completed and allowed . . . the mother is not yet so appeased as to be quiet upon it'. In 1683 Bennet set about improving his landholdings around Abington, purchasing a large number of copyholds in the east and south of the parish and gradually creating a number of large enclosed fields. In 1686 he purchased the commons rights of the copyholders, and by 1687 he had completed the enclosure of his new lands. In 1690 Bennet embarked upon an ambitious project to install engines in Abington to power an irrigation system for his recently acquired lands, financing the project by mortgaging most of his Abington lands to Thomas Western, a London ironmonger.[2]

In 1688 a 'Mr John Bennet, a Dissenter' was recommended as a Court candidate for Cambridgeshire in the projected parliamentary elections. There is, however, no evidence that John Bennet of Abington had any Nonconformist sympathies, though when he stood for election at Cambridge University at the 1690 election Bennet drew most of his votes from the University's Whigs. When he finally entered the Commons in 1691, however, it was upon the interest of the non-juror Peter Legh† at Newton, Lancashire. Bennet's brother Thomas had been rector of Winwick, the parish containing Newton, since 1689, and he had further links to the borough through his relationship to Arlington, a close friend of the recently deceased Member Sir John Chicheley. Shortly after Chicheley's death Bennet wrote to the Tory Sir Richard Myddelton, 3rd Bt.*, asking him to intercede with Legh for his interest at the forthcoming by-election. Bennet pushed hard for Legh's backing, and his supporters promoted him as the man to defeat Thomas Brotherton*, who had been challenging Legh for a seat at Newton since 1685. The 9th Earl of Derby's approval clinched Legh's support for Bennet, who took his seat on 29 Dec. 1691, having already been solicited for his interest in a legal dispute then before the Lords concerning Lancashire estates. He proved to be an inactive Member, and at the 1695 election was squeezed out of Newton by the obligations Peter Legh had incurred defending himself from the accusations of the Lancashire Plot (1693–4). Having left Parliament, he soon ran into money troubles. Despite gaining, upon the violent death of his wife's mother in 1694, a third of his father-in-law's estate, Bennet had over-extended himself when improving his Abington estates, and in 1697 the mortgages Bennet had taken out in 1690 were foreclosed upon and his Abington lands were seized. This appears to have dealt Bennet's fortunes a mortal blow, and in 1712 he died in a debtor's prison, leaving a single son who died without issue in 1720, and a wife who lived in St. Martin-in-the-Fields until her death in 1732, when she was buried in Westminster Abbey.[3]

[1] *VCH Cambs.* vi. 5; *HMC Ormonde* n.s. vi. 190–1; Lipscomb, *Bucks.* ii. 529. [2] *VCH Cambs.* 5, 9, 14–15; *HMC Ormonde*, 54–55, 190–1, 242–3, 251–2. [3] Duckett, *Penal Laws and Test Act* (1883), 223; *VCH Lancs.* iii. 128; BL, Verney mss mic 636/45, John Verney* (Visct. Fermanagh) to Sir Ralph Verney, 1st Bt.†, 18 May 1692; *Lyme Letters* ed. Lady Newton, 20; NLW, Chirk Castle mss E1073, Bennet to Myddelton, 21 May 1691; John Rylands Univ. Lib. Manchester, Legh of Lyme mss corresp. Thomas† to Peter Legh, 24 May 1691, Derby to same, 2 June 1691, Thomas Hodgkinson to same, 22 Dec. 1691; *Luttrell Diary*, 94; Lipscomb, 529; *VCH Cambs.* 5; *Westminster Abbey Reg.* (Harl. Soc. x), 336.

E. C./R. D. H.

BENNET, Sir Levinus, 2nd Bt. (1631–93), of Babraham, Cambs.

CAMBRIDGESHIRE 1679 (Oct.)–1681 (Mar.)
1685–1687, 1689–5 Dec. 1693

bap. 18 Jan. 1631, 1st s. of Sir Thomas Bennet, 1st Bt., of Babraham by Mary, da. and coh. of Levinus Munck†, of London and Mortlake, Surr. *educ.* G. Inn 1644. *m.* 6 July 1653, Judith, da. of William Boevey, merchant, of Little Chelsea, Mdx. and Flaxley Abbey, Glos., 2s. (1 *d.v.p.*) 7da. *suc.* fa. as 2nd Bt. 28 June 1667.[1]

Sheriff, Cambs. and Hunts. 1652–3; commr. for

corporations 1662-3, complaints, Bedford level 1663, appeals 1668; freeman, Cambridge 1679.[2]

Ever since his first election as knight of the shire, to the first Exclusion Parliament, Bennet had played the part of a staunch but silent back-bench Tory, loyal to the Church but largely inactive. In his last Parliament, he raised his profile slightly while maintaining the same party-political stance. He and his colleague Sir Robert Cotton* overcame the handicap of being named on Anthony Rowe's* 'blacklist' of those who had voted in February 1689 against the transfer of the crown (a vote which in Bennet's case is questioned by a second contemporary division-list) to secure an apparently unopposed re-election as county Members, helped in part by a pamphlet written anonymously in their vindication. He was classed as a Tory and probably also a Court supporter in Lord Carmarthen's (Sir Thomas Osborne†) analysis of the new House of Commons in March 1690, and appeared in another ministerial calculation of support in the following December, possibly prepared in connexion with a projected parliamentary attack on Carmarthen. By April of the next year, however, Robert Harley* included him among the opponents of the government. He told on 3 Dec. 1692 against giving a second reading to a bill designed to protect the hat-manufacturing industry by enforcing the ban on sales of beaver fur by the Hudson's Bay Company, and preventing the export of rabbit and hare skins.[3]

Bennet died on 5 Dec. 1693. His one surviving son outlived him only by some eight years, and on his death the baronetcy became extinct, but the Babraham estate passed through a daughter to the Alexander family, who adopted the name of Bennet as an additional surname and eventually resumed the parliamentary tradition three generations on, in 1770, when Bennet's great-grandson, Richard Henry Alexander Bennet(t) was returned for Newport in Cornwall.[4]

[1] *Mortlake Par. Reg.* ed. Cockin 12. [2] *Camb. Antiq. Soc. Procs.* xvii. 105; C. H. Cooper, *Annals of Cambridge*, iii. 557, 582. [3] *Bull IHR*, lii. 42; *A Letter to a Gent. about the Election . . . for the County of Cambridge* (1690) [4] *M I Cambs.* ed. Palmer, 5.

D. W. H.

BENNET, Thomas (c.1640–1703), of Salthrop, Wroughton, Wilts.

MARLBOROUGH   1679 (Mar.)–1681 (Mar.)
24 Jan. 1695–1698

b. c.1640, o. s. of Sir Thomas Bennet, DCL, of Salthrop, master in Chancery 1635–*d*., by his 2nd w. Thomasine, da. and coh. of George Dethick of G. Inn and Poplar, Mdx. *m.* settlement 29 June 1659 (with £2,000), Martha (*d.* 1694), da. of John Smith of South Tidworth, Hants, sis. of John Smith I*, 2s. (1 *d.v.p.*) 5da. (1 *d.v.p.*). *suc.* fa. 1670.[1]

Bennet's family were longstanding north Wiltshire gentry whose seat at Salthrop had been leased from the governors of the Charterhouse from about 1612, when the family commissioned a survey of the estate. Succeeding generations accumulated a number of neighbouring manors, including Great Bupton, Clyffe Pypard and Costow. Although a cousin of the Earl of Arlington (Sir Henry Bennet†), Bennet voted for Exclusion. Out of Parliament, he took an interest in local affairs, being named in 1693 as one of three undertakers in the long-term project to make the Wiltshire Avon navigable from Salisbury to Christ Church, Dorset, which had thus far cost £3,500. Returned at a by-election in 1695 with the support of the Bruce interest, he was probably the 'Sir' Thomas Bennet given leave of absence on 9 Mar. He was also returned at the general election, although he demonstrated as little activity in this as in his previous Parliaments. Contemporaries seem to have been unsure what to make of him, and he was classed as 'doubtful' in the forecast for the division of 31 Jan. 1696 on the proposed council of trade. It did not help matters that he was listed both as having signed the Association at first and as having refused it. However, he voted against fixing the price of guineas at 22*s*., before being accorded leave of absence on 7 Apr. In the following session he opposed the attainder of Sir John Fenwick† on 25 Nov. 1696. A further grant of leave of absence, this time for three weeks, was made on 11 Apr. 1698. In a comparison of the old and new Parliaments in about September of that year he appeared among the members of the Country party 'left out', having been defeated at Marlborough in a three-cornered contest, again as the candidate of the Bruce family. His final attempt at Marlborough, in the general election of January 1701, also proved unsuccessful.[2]

Together with this lack of electoral success, Bennet may have been prompted to leave the political arena through illness, for he died on 29 June 1703. His wife having predeceased him, in his will he left all his personal and real estate to his surviving son, also Thomas, and portions of £1,500 to two daughters. Bennet was the last of his family to sit in Parliament; his son, who raised a plaque to his father's memory in Preshute church, received a reversion of the office of chirographer at the court of common pleas in 1699.[3]

[1] Wilts. RO, 551/6; *Wilts. Arch. Mag.* xxxvi. 286–7; *Le Neve's Knights* (Harl. Soc. viii), 145. [2] PCC 157 Penn; *VCH Wilts.* ix. 31;

xi. 241–2; HMC Var. iv. 249; CSP Dom. 1693, p. 33; Wilts. RO, Marlborough ct. bks G22/1/25, p. 41. [3] Wilts. RO, 551/5; PCC 180 Dogg; CSP Dom. 1699–1700, p. 160.

D. W. H.

BENNET, William (d. 1729), of Grubbet, Roxburgh.

SCOTLAND 1707–1708

1st s. of Sir William Bennet, 1st Bt., of Grubbet by Christian, da. of Alexander Morison of Prestongrange, Haddington. *educ.* ?Edinburgh, MA 1685. *m.* (1) Jean, da. of Sir John Kerr of Lochtour, Roxburgh. ?1s. (2) contract 18 Mar. 1692 (with 40,000 merks), Margaret (d. by 17 Aug. 1694) da. and h. of John Scougall of Whitekirk, Haddington. *s.p.* (3) Elizabeth, da. of Sir David Hay, MD, of Auchquhairney, ?1s. *suc.* fa. as 2nd Bt. 1710.[1]

Capt. own tp. of horse 1689–94, R. Scots drag. 1693; maj. Ld. Jedburgh's tp. of horse bef. 1697; half-pay 1698; muster master gen. [S] 1704–8; commr. excise 1714–25; ensign R. coy. Archers 1715.[2]

Burgess, Edinburgh 1691, Linlithgow 1693.[3]

MP [S], Roxburghshire 1693–1707.

From a solidly Presbyterian background, his grandfather a minister and his father suffering 'many hardships for conscience sake', Bennet was an enthusiastic supporter of the Revolution. He accompanied the Prince of Orange from Holland and 'made an offer to levy upon his own charge a troop of horse'. The Scottish parliament subsequently took responsibility for funding this force, but neglected to fulfil this engagement completely, leaving Bennet still claiming arrears after the Union. His military career, which included service abroad, continued until 1698, but was gradually superseded by his political activities. Having been returned to the Scottish parliament in 1693 for his native Roxburghshire, Bennet was initially associated with the Tweeddale–Johnston Court interest, but moved towards opposition as government came to be dominated by Queensberry and Argyll. The dismissal of Tullibardine in 1698 marked a turning point together with the failure of the Company of Scotland, in which Bennet had invested £300. He joined the Country party and by 1700 had become a leading activist, not only signing the opposition address calling for a meeting of parliament, but also travelling to London to present it. In the Scottish parliament he was appointed to the committee of security, presented the Roxburghshire petition on Darien, and voted in favour of an act to declare Caledonia a lawful colony. In addition to opposing the standing army, he was an advocate of extreme Presbyterian measures in order to sow divisions within the Court party. His religious beliefs were in fact moderate: he resisted any increase in the Kirk's supervision of individual morality, declaring that 'to be enslaved to the clergy' was a retrograde step from the liberty achieved by the Revolution (a viewpoint that was perhaps coloured by his own youthful experience of Kirk discipline on account of drunkenness).[4]

Bennet entered fully into the Country party's electoral campaign in 1702, closely observing national developments and playing a leading role in Roxburghshire, where he made clear that he favoured both written instructions from the constituency and the inauguration of a local committee to monitor the commissioners' conduct. During the 1703 parliament he continued active in the Country cause, being convinced that the components of the current ministry were 'so hard screwed up that some strings must crack and disorder the harmony of the present concert'. He was privately disillusioned, however, at the prospects of any fundamental change, since in his view all politicians behaved selfishly once in office and submitted to the dictates of their English overlords. Moreover, when opportunity offered, he was willing to take office, being appointed muster master as a consequence of the 'New Party' experiment of 1704. The failure of this coalition in 1705, and the return to opposition of those who formed an enduring political connexion as the Squadrone, marked another crisis in Bennet's political career. Although events were to transform him into a loyal member of the Squadrone, his permanent attachment was by no means a foregone conclusion. Under pressure from both sides he abstained on an important vote on 1 Aug. 1705 and proceeded to court both Queensberry and the 2nd Duke of Argyll. Unlike many of his Squadrone colleagues, he had avoided immediate dismissal and therefore found himself in an equivocal position until the Union, with private as well as public motives for supporting the government. In January 1706 he had received assurances from Queensberry that his place was secure, but rumours continued that Argyll might grant it instead to Sir Alexander Cumming, 1st Bt.* It was not until April 1706 that Bennet wrote to Queensberry, acknowledging that 'it is to your friendship that I owe the continuance in my post, and my gratitude shall ever attend my patron'. There is no reason to doubt Bennet's genuine conviction of the necessity of Union, but it is clear that the collective decision of the Squadrone to support this measure averted a political breach. Saved from the embarrassment of a complete separation, Bennet nevertheless took care to vote consistently with the Court, rather than following the Squadrone line of qualified approval. He was rewarded with a seat at Westminster as one of the Scottish representatives to the first Parliament of Great Britain.[5]

Following his arrival in London, Bennet was introduced to the Queen on 27 Oct. 1707, making her a short complimentary speech. Privately he was not impressed, having expected 'to have seen a splendid court at Kensington, but it had all the silence and solitude of a cloister'. The House itself was likewise a disappointment, Bennet having imagined it 'to be an auguster assembly' than it proved in reality. He soon came to realize, however, that 'a Member of the Commons is a person of respect during the session of Parliament'. Clearly a sociable individual, he kept company with fellow Scots and new-found English acquaintances, in particular establishing a close friendship with Grey Neville*. Shortly after the session opened, Bennet reported on 30 Oct. that Parliament had been adjourned for another week

> without any speech from her Majesty who cannot make her demand of supply until Marlborough [John Churchill†] show his conclusions with the allies as to the state of the war. The spirit of mutiny is predominant among the people of trade who seem to have a just pretence to grumble, from the intolerable losses they have sustained at sea ... The English are extremely courteous and civil and caress us on all occasions, and if the devil of division don't possess us we have it in our hands to cast the balance in conjunction with the northern counties which seem heartily to court our friendship as bound by the same interests.[6]

On 15 Nov. 1707 Bennet reported that parliamentary affairs 'now begin to be heartily in earnest, after having trifled away a great deal of time since we came here'. He was pleased that the Court was 'heartily alarmed at what has passed in both Houses, of calling to a severe account the bad conduct and mismanagement of the fleet'. This investigation was likely 'to run very deep', with 'scrutiny into all places, pensions, gifts, when, how and for what given'. Bennet hoped that unity among the Scottish Members would allow them to 'cast the balance, as we please', but doubted whether the adherents of the old Scottish Court party would be prepared to play such a game, 'having no free will'. No trace remained of recent professions of attachment to Queensberry. Bennet fully reverted to his allegiance to the Squadrone magnate, the Duke of Roxburghe, whom he described as 'our head and ears in the politics'. Bennet was extremely disdainful of the old Scottish Court party:

> Our sometime ministers of state make a very ordinary figure, and are quite out of countenance; people make it a jest here, that they who had the despotic government of a kingdom should so foolishly divest themselves of it, by advancing that [i.e. the Union] which was the only thing that could ruin them.

Bennet therefore endorsed one of the key aims of the Squadrone, namely breaking down the differences between English and Scottish administrations as a means of destroying the power of the Scottish Court party. The Queen's Speech had mentioned that Parliament should consider 'several matters' arising from the articles of Union, together with others which might 'reasonably produce those advantages that, with due care, must certainly arise from that treaty'. The formula was deliberately vague, designed to permit the ministry to set the agenda, but this strategy backfired when the Squadrone proposed the abolition of the Scottish privy council. This had not formed part of the ministerial plan, for the council was both a valuable executive branch of government and a means of maintaining the influence of the Court over elections. According to Bennet's account of events, a 'confederacy' was formed at Roxburghe's instigation which included Argyll and Montrose 'with all their friends and the whole Squadrone'. Bennet, motivated by the 'impulses of reason' and the desire to serve his patron, joined with this scheme, brushing aside the inevitable 'threatenings and promises' from the Court. Having participated in proceedings on this question in early December, he gave a detailed account of the debate of the 11th, upon the resolutions reported from the committee of the whole. After the passage of the motion for abolishing the Scottish privy council, Bennet spoke during a 'very intricate' debate on another resolution that j.p.s should have the same power in Scotland as in England. A number of lawyers who had formerly 'appeared for us in committee' now 'recanted their opinions in plain House', a betrayal which Bennet attributed to the efforts of Queensberry and Robert Harley*. With the initiative apparently slipping from the Squadrone, Roxburghe, who was observing proceedings from the gallery, decided to intervene.

> My Lord Duke beckoned me to the gallery, and told with great concern that he thought we had lost it, and his opinion was, we should make a fair retreat, by yielding to the clause they proposed ... for preserving the heritable jurisdictions. As I was returning with this advice to our friends ... the heads of the Tories, observing our conversation, and guessing what it meant, told me [that] ... if we would stand our ground they would give us a turn immediately, and that when we thought the House warmed for the question, that my speaking should be the signal for them to press it ... Bromley [William II] spoke like an angel, and after him six more of that kidney, which

turned the tide extremely, the solicitor-general [James Montagu I] summed up the whole argument ... which made us think the House in good humour for the question, which I proposed to be put, and was seconded with such a shout, that it was not in the Speaker's power to delay it.

The question was carried and the remaining resolutions passed without a division. Bennet was naturally appointed to the resultant drafting committee for a bill to complete the Union. He had earned respect from his colleagues for his role, albeit largely a fortuitous one, in co-ordinating this victory over the Court. At about this time Roxburghe's brother, Hon. William Kerr*, reported to his mother that Bennet had spoken in the House 'several times with great applause', whereas the Duke himself chose to celebrate Christmas with him, reporting that he 'behaved like himself ... and I think forgot no friend either in East Lothian or Teviotdale'.[7]

By now Bennet had learned that he would not be returned for Roxburghshire at the next election. It was decided that Kerr would stand instead, partly to ensure some parliamentary presence for the family should Roxburghe fail to secure a place as a representative peer. Bennet accepted this reverse with equanimity, the blow perhaps softened by his reported homesickness for Scotland. Somewhat surprisingly, given his impending retirement, Bennet actually increased his level of activity in the remainder of this Parliament.[8]

Having cast off the mask during the debates on the Scottish privy council, Bennet may have considered his dismissal from office to be inevitable unless there was a change of government. He apparently received assurances from Harley and Henry St. John II* that if he were to lose his place for opposing the ministry, he would be reinstated when their own plans for reconstructing it came to fruition. There is no doubt that Bennet was being pressurized by the Court and that his refusal to conform resulted in his removal. His crime was cumulative rather than a single transgression, certainly involving his attitude to the Scottish privy council and possibly to the government's proposals for a reform of the recruiting system. On 16 Jan. 1708 Bennet seconded Hon. James Brydges' proposal that the troops immediately required for Spain should be raised by some other means than the current recruiting acts. Although nominally supporting government, Bennet's speech created an unfortunate impression:

> Mr Bennet ... added that the men should be raised proportionably in all parts of the United Kingdom. He being called upon to explain ... he said they might take what rule they thought fittest, as the cess or any other. The cess being named by a Scotchman could not fail of being excepted against, for, that being the rate, they would raise but one man to our 40. He explained himself, that he did not mean that should be the measure between England and Scotland, but they would be willing to raise their proportion, according to the numbers of men that may be reasonably computed for each kingdom. The explanation did not take away the ill-impression of the first undigested proposition.

That Bennet, as muster master for Scotland, should have played a leading role in introducing the question is not in itself surprising, but the counter-productive effect of his speech is suggestive. On 22 Jan. the issue of the Scottish privy council was revived by a Court amendment for the deferral of abolition till after the next election. The Squadrone opposed and defeated this manoeuvre, allegedly with the assistance of Harley. Bennet may have played a part in securing Harley's support, in return contributing to the attack upon the Court. Certainly, when Harley finally achieved power in 1710, Bennet's Squadrone colleagues believed that he had a legitimate claim upon the new ministry, having surrendered 'a very good milch cow' in the service of Harley and St. John, who ought to feel 'obliged to restore you again'.[9]

Little is known of Bennet's parliamentary activities after Harley's fall in February 1708, or how frequently he opposed the Court in the remainder of the session. He joined his Squadrone colleagues John Cockburn and Hon. Sir Andrew Hume in an unsuccessful attempt on 26 Feb. to 'invert the classes of those to be paid out of the Equivalent', speaking 'most reflectingly and scurvily of the parliament of Scotland'; and on 17 Mar. told against a Tory amendment to the bill to secure American trade. After the session ended, Lord Seafield reported to Lord Godolphin (Sidney†) on 25 June that 'the Queen is resolved that Mr Bennet's commission of muster master shall cease now from this time'. The office was divided between two holders, which gave Bennet some small satisfaction that his enemies had gained 'but half a victory when the thing is split'. Meanwhile in London, Roxburghe was intent on making political capital out of the affair and sent word to Bennet that 'there's no fear but justice will be done him before long'. Prior to receiving word of his dismissal, Bennet had appealed to Sunderland (Charles, Lord Spencer*) for the 'blow to be staved off till the Parliament meets' and afterwards noted that the Junto were 'very hot on this business ... assuring a certain great man [Godolphin] that he should wish it undone ere he eat his Christmas goose'.[10]

In the 1708 election Bennet gave full support to Kerr's unsuccessful candidacy for Roxburghshire. Otherwise he retreated from political life. Roxburghe made sure that Bennet was not completely neglected, taking care to consult him on such questions as the county's commission of the peace. He continued to receive protestations of support for his reinstatement from a variety of figures, including Montrose and Sutherland. It was also reported in August 1709 that Sunderland was not only 'well disposed', but after speaking several times to Godolphin now had 'his promise for it'. Under-secretary Robert Pringle, the channel of this communication, himself believed that Bennet would never receive redress until the management of Scotland was placed in other hands. Roxburghe continued to press Bennet's case and in December 1709 sent a message via George Baillie's* wife that he had personally approached Seafield and Godolphin: the former having 'been as good as his promise' and the latter now conceding that if Bennet was not reinstated by the end of the session he 'should certainly have something else'. Nothing came of this, nor was likely to while Bennet remained outside Parliament. As one of his supporters had pointed out at the time of his dismissal, if he were 'to be a Parliament-man . . . there would be no question of keeping your post'. A return to Westminster appeared possible in 1710, when Kerr decided to stand elsewhere, but Bennet was defeated in a closely fought contest. He did not petition against the return, despite being convinced of the strength of his case, leaving the decision to Roxburghe and describing himself as perfectly willing to 'bask here in quiet and silence waiting the sunshine of a better day, which must come'.[11]

Bennet was forced to await the Hanoverian succession before receiving any mark of favour. His brother-in-law William Nisbet* was convinced that his former services would now be recognized, since 'most people know your share of the hazard and expense at the first Revolution and if that had not happened I think the present King would not have been so near the throne at this day'. He was not restored to his former office, which fell to another of Roxburghe's nominees. The Duke forewarned him of this turn of events in October 1714:

I cannot . . . tell you in a letter how this has happened, but you may depend upon it if the Duke of Montrose or I have any interest you will have a better place, for this was really not worth your having, being but about £150 a year, so that when some of your neighbours sneer upon your being baulked, as they think, pray let them sneer and don't say a word, for if you mention my having writ to you . . . I will truly take it ill . . . I have no doubt of procuring for you, and that very soon, a place in the customs or excise which is £500 a year. If you mention this to anyone you'll do me wrong and possibly yourself harm.

Appointment as a commissioner of excise duly followed, being confirmed after some complications in December. This place being incompatible with a seat in Parliament, Bennet had clearly abandoned any intention of reviving his parliamentary career.[12]

During the Fifteen, Bennet was active in countering the Jacobite threat in Roxburghshire, though his initiative in placing artillery at Kelso proved unwise when this fell into rebel hands before his scheme of fortification could be implemented. He spent the remainder of his life chiefly on his estates, devoting himself to agricultural improvements and to the composition of pastoral verse. In 1725 Bennet was removed from his excise post as part of the attack by Walpole (Robert II*) upon Roxburghe's influence in Scotland. Bennet was convinced that 'this cloud will blow over, who lives to see it'. He died on 23 Dec. 1729, being succeeded in turn by his sons, William and David, the baronetcy thereafter passing from the direct line and becoming extinct by mid-century. The estates passed to the Nisbet family, who subsequently sold them to the Marquess of Tweeddale.[13]

[1] *Hist. Scot. Parl.* 49; *Edinburgh Graduates*, 127; SRO, Biel mss GD6/1389/1-3, contract and discharge; *APS*, xi. app. 130-1; SRO, Cromartie mss GD305 addit./bdle. 14, Ld. Royston to [Cromarty], 6 Apr. 1710. [2] *Cal. Treas. Bks.* xxix. 198; SRO, Ogilvy of Inverquharity mss GD205/38/8, ensign's commn. [3] *Scot. Rec. Soc.* lix. 55; Ogilvy of Inverquharity mss GD205/38/8, burgess tickets. [4] A. Jeffrey, *Hist. Roxburgh*. iii. 337-40; info. from Dr P. W. J. Riley on members of Scot. parl.; P. W. J. Riley, *Wm. III and Scot. Politicians*, 170; *Scot. Hist. Soc.* ser. 3, xlvi. 52; *APS*, ix. 26, 59; x. 11, 193, 195, 207, 246, 269; *Reg. PC Scotland* 1686-9, pp. 489-91, 498; 1689, pp. 86, 156, 256, 381, 476, 767; 1690, pp. 195, 391, 429-30, 657; Fraser, *Melvilles*, ii. 121; *Cal. Treas. Bks.* xxii. 117, 145; *Darien Pprs.* (Bannatyne Club, xc), 402; *Crossrigg Diary*, 15-16, 25-26. [5] Roxburghe mss at Floors Castle, bdle. 726, Bennet to Countess of Roxburghe, 8 Oct. 1702; info. from Dr Riley; *APS*, xi. 72, 102; *Crossrigg Diary*, 139; Boyer, *Anne Annals*, iii. app. 43; *Orig. Pprs.* ed. Macpherson, ii. 10-11; P. W. J. Riley, *Union*, 45-46, 95, 118, 264-5, 334; *Intimate Soc. Letters of 18th Cent.* ed. J. D. S. Campbell, i. 29-30; Buccleuch mss at Drumlanrig Castle, bdle. 1152, no.30, Bennet to Queensberry, 12 Apr. 1706; Ogilvy of Inverquharity mss GD205/33/3/10/24, William Jamisone to Bennet, 29 Jan. 1705-6. [6] Roxburghe mss, bdle. 1069, Hon. William Kerr to Countess of Roxburghe, 28 Oct. 1707; bdle. 1079, Bennet to same, 30 Oct. 1707; Ogilvy of Inverquharity mss GD205/36/6, Neville to Bennet, 30 Dec. 1707, 4 Jan., 11 July, 14 Sept. 1708, 19 Mar., 19 May 1709; *SHR*, lxxi. 114. [7] Roxburghe mss, bdle. 795, Bennet to Countess of Roxburghe, 15 Nov. 1707; bdle. 739, same to same, 16 Dec. 1707; bdle. 1067, Kerr to same, n.d. [Dec. 1707]; bdle. 755, Roxburghe to same, 25 Dec. 1707. [8] Roxburghe mss, bdle. 739, Jamisone to Countess of Roxburghe, 15 Jan. 1707-8; bdle. 755, Roxburghe to same, 24 Jan. 1708. [9] P. W. J. Riley, *Eng. Ministers and Scotland*, 87-96; *EHR*, lxxx. 58; Ogilvy of Inverquharity mss GD205/36/6, St. John to Bennet, 12 Jan. 1707-8, J. Edmonstone to same, 6 Nov. 1710; *Vernon–Shrewsbury Letters*, iii. 309-10; Add. 61631, f. 63; 61632, f. 28; Cunningham, *Hist. GB*, ii. 138-40; DZA, Bonet

despatch 13/24 Feb. 1708. [10] *HMC Mar and Kellie*, i. 429; SRO, Seafield mss GD248/572/7/21, Seafield to Godolphin, 25 June 1708; Ogilvy of Inverquharity mss GD205/38/8, Bennet to Nisbet, 9 Aug. 1708; GD205/33/3/2/7, Baillie to Bennet, 29 July 1708; *Baillie Corresp.* 193-6. [11] Ogilvy of Inverquharity mss GD205/33/3/10/39, Jamisone to Bennet, 29 Oct. 1708; GD205/34/4, Charles Oliphant* to same, 11 Dec. 1708; GD205/36/6, Neville to same, 11 July, 14 Sept. 1708, 19 Mar. 1708-9, William Elliot to same, 8 June 1708, Robert Pringle to same, 11 Aug. 1709; GD205/31/1/1/13, Montrose to same, 15 Feb. 1709; GD205/33/3/2/7, Grisell Baillie to same, 4 Jan. 1710; Roxburghe mss, bdle. 1067, Kerr to Countess of Roxburghe, 18 Sept. 1710; bdle. 739, Bennet to same, 13 Dec. 1710. [12] Mss sold at Sothebys 14 Dec. 1976, lot 20, Nisbet to Bennet, 19 Aug. 1714; Ogilvy of Inverquharity mss GD205/31/1/17, Roxburghe to same, 12 Oct. 1714; *Cal. Treas. Bks.* xxix. 198; Roxburghe mss, bdle. 756, Roxburghe to mother, 9 Dec. 1714. [13] Jeffrey, 337-40; Jeffrey, *Historical and Descriptive Acct. Roxburgh.* 397-8; [P. Rae], *Hist. Late Rebellion* (1718), 185, 255, 269; *Hawick Arch. Soc. Trans.* (1911), 61; *HMC 14th Rep. III*, 53-55; *Works of Allan Ramsay* (1819), 18; G. Tancred, *Annals of a Border Club*, 251; Riley, *Eng. Ministers*, 258, 274; Boyer, *Pol. State*, xxxix. 166; *Services of Heirs*, i. 1730-9, p. 4.

D. W.

BENNETT, Sir John (c.1658-1723), of Essex Buildings, Essex Street, Westminster.

MORPETH 1708-1710

b. c.1658, 1st s. of John Bennett of St. Paul's, Covent Garden, Westminster and Witham, Essex by his w. Sarah. *educ.* G. Inn 1675, called 1683. *m.* 9 Jan. 1683 (with £1,000), Anne (*d.* 1722), da. of Sir Joseph Brand of Edwardstone, Suff., wid. of Thomas Dudson, woollendraper, of St. Benet's, Gracechurch Street, London, 4s. 2da. (1 *d.v.p.*). *suc.* fa. 1670; kntd. 10 July 1706.[1]

Attorney, duchy of Lancaster ct. 1678, clerk of council 1678-85; dep. south auditor, duchy of Lancaster 1678-84; clerk of revenue, duchy of Lancaster 1685-*d.*; steward, Essex, Herts. and Mdx. 1697-*d.*; judge of Marshalsea ct. 1699-*d.*; bailiff, Salford hundred 1699-*d.*; serjeant-at-law 1705.[2]

The ancestry of Bennett's father is obscure. Resident in London in the 1660s he purchased the manor of Witham, Essex in 1668, but otherwise little is known of his background save for the claim that he was descended from the same family as the Earl of Arlington (Henry Bennet†), and the 1st Lord Ossulston. This contention is perhaps supported by the numerous offices the young Bennett accrued in the duchy of Lancaster during the 1670s and 1680s, a period in which two of Arlington's political followers held the post of chancellor. After the Revolution Bennett retained office in the duchy and in the later 1690s gained a number of additional offices, mainly legal in character. The benefits he derived from his places were revealed to the Commons on 4 Feb. 1703 when the House was informed of a number of leases made to Bennett in the 1690s of lands, and a colliery, belonging to the duchy of Lancaster. If Bennett may have owed his initial administrative and legal advancement to the influence of Arlington, he certainly owed his parliamentary career to the interest of the 2nd Lord Ossulston. Ossulston had succeeded to Northumberland lands in 1706 and at the 1708 election forwarded Bennett's candidacy at Morpeth. Returned unopposed, Bennett proved himself to be a Whig, supporting in 1709 the naturalization of the Palatines and the following year voting for the impeachment of Dr Sacheverell. He was otherwise an inactive Member and did not stand in 1710 or subsequently. Bennett's sons followed him into the law, two of them becoming masters of chancery, one of whom was appointed clerk of the custodies in 1714. Little more is known of Bennett's career before his death on 21 Dec. 1723. Buried at Witham nine days later, he was succeeded by his eldest son. None of his sons entered the Commons, but Bennett's only surviving daughter married John Vaughan, 2nd Viscount Lisburne [I], who sat in George II's first Parliament.[3]

[1] *The Gen.* n.s. xx. 238; *Le Neve's Knights* (Harl. Soc. viii), 331, 493; *Vis. Mdx.* (Harl. Soc. xcii), 57. [2] Somerville, *Duchy of Lancaster Official Lists*, 39, 63, 71, 141, 206, 214. [3] Morant, *Essex*, ii. 107; Somerville, 3; C104/116, 21 Apr. 1708 (*ex inf.* Dr C. Jones); *HMC Portland*, v. 459; Boyer, *Pol. State*, xxvi. 675.

E. C.

BENSON, Robert (1676-1731), of Red Hall, nr. Wakefield; Bramham Hall, Yorks.; and Queen Street, Westminster.

THETFORD 1702-1705
YORK 1705-1713

bap. 25 Mar. 1676, 1st s. of Robert Benson of Wrenthorpe, Yorks. by Dorothy, da. of Tobias Jenkins of Grimston, sis. of Tobias Jenkins*. *educ.* ?London; Christ's, Camb. 1691; Padua 1694; travelled abroad (Italy). *m.* 21 Dec. 1703 (with £8,000), Elizabeth (*d.* 1757), da. of Hon. Heneage Finch I*, 1s. *d.v.p.* 1da.; 1da. illegit. *suc.* fa. 1676; *cr.* Baron Bingley 21 July 1713.[1]

? Capt. Sir Henry Belasyse* ft. reg. 1691.[2]

Freeman, York Apr. 1705, alderman May 1705-Sept. 1715.[3]

Ld. of Treasury Aug. 1710-May 1711; chancellor of Exchequer 14 June 1711-Aug. 1713; PC 14 June 1711-Sept. 1714, 11 June 1730-*d.*; ambassador to Spain 1713-14; treasurer of Household 1730-*d.*

Dir. S. Sea Co. July 1711-Feb. 1715.[4]

Trustee, West Riding Registry 1711; commr. building 50 new churches 1711-15, survey Westminster and St. James's manors 1712.[5]

? FRS 1699.[6]

Benson has long suffered from the dismissive verdict of historians unable to discern any merit in him beyond a moderate Toryism. Archdeacon Coxe predictably purveyed the Whig view that he was a mere 'cipher in office, and a dependant on his principal [i.e. Robert Harley*]'. Others have added little, describing him as 'a genial Tory nonentity', or as 'a watery Tory'. However, such comments fail to account for Benson's rise from relatively humble origins to the peerage in the course of his career. Admittedly, the foundations of his rise were laid by his father, who was, according to his rival for the Aldborough seat in 1673, Sir John Reresby, 2nd Bt.†,

> the most notable and formidable man for business of his time, one of no birth, and that had raised himself from being clerk to a country attorney to be clerk of the peace at the Old Bailiff, to clerk of assize of the northern circuit, and to an estate of £2,500 p.a., but not without suspicion of great frauds and oppressions. Besides, he was the great favourite of my Lord Dunblain [Sir Thomas Osborne†], then lord high treasurer.

Benson's father served as clerk of the peace for the West Riding 1637–46, when he was deprived of his office and later in the year compounded for £2,000. Undeterred by this setback Benson snr. entered the Inner Temple in 1654. As Reresby indicated, he rose through hard work, even transferring to Gray's Inn in 1664 where he kept chambers. After the Restoration he became clerk of the assizes in Yorkshire, his 11-year tenure ending in 1672 when he seems to have been employed by Danby as a Treasury official. Benson snr. seems to have laid plans to discover ways of improving the King's revenue and certainly cultivated Danby to whom 'he never failed once a day to make his court'. At his death in July 1676 he was said to have amassed an estate of '£3,000 p.a. in land and £120,000 in money'. Apart from Robert, he left a daughter, Elizabeth, and presumably both children were left in the care of his wife, who remarried in 1680, to Sir Henry Belasyse.[7]

Nothing is known of Benson's early life, but his connexion with Belasyse suggests that he may have been the 'Robert Benson' commissioned in 1691 a captain in Belasyse's foot regiment. It seems likely that he was the 'Robert Benson esq.' granted a pass to travel to Harwich and Holland in April 1693, although in August he petitioned successfully for four fairs and a weekly market to be held in Bingley, where he was lord of the manor. He was certainly abroad by September 1694 when he was in Italy. He was probably an accomplished young man for in December 1699 William Bridgeman proposed his election to the Royal Society, although there is a doubt as to whether his election was approved. Locally, too, he was beginning to make his mark because by April 1700, as 'Mr Benson of Stanley' (near Wrenthorpe), he was made a deputy-lieutenant of the West Riding and city of York. Parliamentary ambition was fulfilled through another family connexion. In 1700 his sister, Elizabeth, had married Sir John Wodehouse, 4th Bt.*, who was MP and recorder of Thetford. Although she died in January 1701, the link explains Benson's election at Thetford in 1702, especially as Wodehouse was originally thought of as a candidate for the county and did not stand for the borough on that occasion.[8]

In the Commons, Benson at first made little impression. He is not recorded as voting in the division on 18 Feb. 1703 on extending the time for taking the abjuration oath. Politically, however, he made a very astute marriage in December 1703 to the daughter of Lord Guernsey (Hon. Heneage Finch I*), younger brother of the Earl of Nottingham (Daniel Finch†). His first significant Commons activity occurred on 25 Jan. 1704 when he reported from the committee inquiring into the Lords' proceedings of the case of the Bathursts against Lord Wharton (Hon. Thomas*) over mining rights in Yorkshire. By April he was back in Yorkshire, where he reportedly came to blows in a quarrel with a son of Sir William Lowther*, a Yorkshire Whig. The only other indication of activity concerns a number of recommendations which he signed in company with other (mainly Yorkshire) Members for military commissions. In the following 1704–5 session he was forecast as likely to oppose the Tack and duly voted against it or was absent on 28 Nov. 1704. On 11 Jan. 1705 he was teller in favour of a motion that the House agree with a resolution that Protestants in the north of England be allowed to arm in order to secure themselves against the Scots.[9]

With Wodehouse again coming in for Thetford, Benson shifted his attention to York for the 1705 election. Again a family connexion paved the way, his uncle Tobias Jenkins standing down in his favour. Benson was admitted an alderman in the month preceding the election and was duly returned after a contest in May. Although absent from the crucial division on the Speakership on 25 Oct. 1705, he was listed as a 'Churchman' in one list and the Earl of Sunderland (Charles, Lord Spencer*) accounted his election a 'loss' for the Whigs. Benson adopted a higher profile in this Parliament, not least over the manoeuvres during the session to safeguard the Protestant succession. On 4 Dec. he seconded the Tory-inspired motion 'to bring over the Princess Sophia', a ploy to embarrass the ministry on account of the Queen's known opposition to it. The Whigs responded with the regency bill, which also engaged Benson's attention: he spoke in the committee of the whole on 15 Jan. 1706 to point out, apropos the summoning of Parliament, that he himself served for a constituency 150 miles from London and that the 'the Lords take upon 'em what House of Commons never allowed'. On 24 Jan. he told in favour of an amendment to the regency bill to ameliorate the penalties on those sitting in the House without taking the oaths. He was then named on 4 Feb. to the conference committee with the Lords over their amendments to the bill and during the subsequent disputes with the Lords he told on 18 Feb. against the bill becoming operative from the end of the Parliament, preferring the end of the session. Consequently, he was listed as opposing the Court over the place clause. He told twice concerning election petitions: on 17 Jan. for the motion on the Ludgershall election that Thomas Powell was not duly elected, thereby espousing the cause of the more moderate Tory candidate, John Richmond Webb, and on 8 Feb. against the motion that James Winstanley, another Tory, was not duly elected for Leicester.[10]

By contrast the 1706–7 session saw Benson's known involvement in the Commons limited to appointment in first place to the second-reading committee on the bill for establishing a land registry for the West Riding. In the next session he was a teller on 23 Mar. 1708 against an amendment to the bill establishing a registry for the East Riding that sought to limit the registry in the West Riding to transactions over £50. Benson's main activity in this session, however, was the procedural matter concerning the manner in which the Commons dealt with contested elections. On 18 Feb. he was added to the committee inquiring into this matter, and was sufficiently interested to make the report from it on the 21st. As James Vernon I* wrote:

> Mr Benson reported to-day the manner of balloting, which was received with laughter, but yet was agreed to. It consisted of several articles: first, that a balloting-box and balls should be provided; that it be carried about by the two clerks, one having the box, the other the balls; that the Speaker appoint two Members to attend the box; that the Member voting take a ball in his bare hand, and hold it up between his finger and thumb before he put it into the box; that the Members keep their places till the box be brought back to the table and the balls there told over.

Following his report Benson told in favour of accepting the committee's proposals and the remaining resolutions were agreed without a division. He acted as a teller on two further occasions: on 24 Feb. against an amendment to an Irish forfeitures bill and on 18 Mar. against instructing a drafting committee for a bill preserving public credit to explain a clause in an act from William III's reign that during the continuance of the Bank no other bank be set up by Act of Parliament. A list dating from early 1708 classed him as a Tory.[11]

Returned again in 1708, Benson was teller twice on the same day on 31 Mar. 1709: first, against receiving the report on the estate bill of the Marquess of Lindsey (Robert Bertie*), and then against the motion to commit the bill improving the Union. In 1709 Benson combined business acumen with philanthropy when he donated £250, 'being the moiety of a stock he has upon the profits of the locks made upon the rivers Aire and Calder', towards the boys' charity school in York, an action which could not but increase his local political influence. In the 1709–10 session Cunningham noted that Benson and Edward Wortley Montagu 'thought fit that one of them should move for a bill to restrain the military power in Parliament and the other for voting by ballot'. No mention is made in the Journals of a bill relating to balloting, but on 25 Jan. 1710 Benson was named to the drafting committee of the place bill. Other drafting committees included bills for the better security of rents and to prevent tenant fraud (16 Feb.) and for the relief of the Royal African Company's creditors (20th), which he presented on 13 Mar. Not surprisingly, he voted against the impeachment of Dr Sacheverell. His most important legislative work concerned the debts incurred by the Mine Adventurers' Company. He was first-named to the committee on the petition of the Company's creditors and proprietors (13 Feb.), reporting on the 25th and 13 Mar., and being charged on the latter date with drafting a bill for the relief of those concerned. Having presented this bill on 18 Mar. he became concerned to ensure that the end of the session was not used by Sir Humphrey Mackworth* as an opportunity to evade his responsibilities. Thus, on 31 Mar. he was first-named to draft a bill preventing Mackworth and his partners from leaving the kingdom before the end of the next session. He presented the bill on the following day and managed its rapid passage through the House, carrying it to the Lords on 5 Apr. By the 9th he was writing from Harwich en route for Holland to 'see how the peace goes on', which rather belies Cunningham's remark that following the failure of the place bill he went into Holland 'in great discontent'. He stayed in the Low Countries for some time, Lord Orrery (Lionel Boyle*) reporting on 10 June that Benson had been there for six weeks. Hon. James Brydges* informed John Drummond† in July that Benson was 'a very considerable gentleman', and his political stock was certainly rising as in mid-June his brother-in-law Dartmouth had been appointed secretary of state.[12]

Benson was clearly seen as a man likely to be

employed by the new Tory regime. In early August 1710 Drummond felt him an ideal replacement for the recently deceased envoy to Brunswick (Lionel Cresset) because he 'speaks all languages fit for that court and knows the world very well', but added perceptively, 'I believe he may be useful at home'. On 10 Aug. Benson was named to the new Treasury commission and began to attend the Board almost immediately. He may not have been the first choice for the post, but his appointment had the merit of helping to ensure the loyalty of the Finch clan, given Harley's aversion to employing the Earl of Nottingham, and L'Hermitage noted the significance of the appointment when he wrote that Benson was 'gendre de my Lord Guernsey'. He was also a moderate, so much so that Joseph Addison* called him a 'reputed Whig', who could not 'withstand the same temptation' as Richard Hampden II whom Harley had originally hoped to appoint. Others attributed Benson's promotion to the Duke of Argyll.[13]

Shortly after 10 Oct. 1710 Benson made a journey into Yorkshire, prompting his friend John Aislabie* to chide Harley that 'Benson may not be suffered to grow fat at Bramham', a reference to the new house which he was building some 13 miles or so from York. While he was absent rumours circulated that Lord Rochester (Laurence Hyde†) would serve as Lord Treasurer with Benson as chancellor of the Exchequer. He had returned to the Treasury by 25 Nov., the opening day of the parliamentary session. Henceforward, his attendance at the Treasury was very regular during the first five months of 1711. He was also the recipient of many requests for places, being adjudged by Sir Arthur Kaye, 3rd Bt.*, 'very civil and frank' in comparison to Harley. Classed as a Tory in the 'Hanover list', his name appeared among both the 'Tory patriots' who voted for the peace in April 1711 and the 'worthy patriots' who in this first session detected the mismanagements of the previous administration. Possibly owing to his administrative burden, Benson's activity in the House was limited. He was named on 15 Dec. to draft a bill enforcing quarantine regulations for ships. On 29 Jan. 1711 he voted for the place bill at its third reading, Kaye recording that 'all who have had, or now have, or are in hopes to have places, dividing against it, except Sir William Drake, Mr Benson and Mr Aislabie'. As if to confirm his stature within the administration in February he was named a justice for Westminster and Middlesex. On 27 Mar. he seconded Lowndes's ill-fated proposal for a leather tax.[14]

Following Harley's elevation to the lord treasurership, as Lord Oxford, Benson was named as chancellor of the Exchequer, attending the Board in that capacity until 19 June 1711, when he departed for the country, returning on 10 Aug. Meanwhile, in July he became a director of the South Sea Company, having subscribed £3,000. The decision to appoint Benson as chancellor was not universally applauded, George Lockhart* commenting that the post

> requires a man of great understanding, experience and activity, with an established character and reputation, as he is reckoned the first man of the House of Commons, when a member of it; whereas Mr Benson was one of the most confused speakers ever opened a mouth and was rather, or at least affected more to appear, a man of wit and pleasure than of parts and capacity of business. But the truth on it is, the Lord Oxford did not seem fond of employing men of great sense and eminent characters in the world.

Others were more circumspect, Swift contenting himself with the view that the chancellor 'eats the most elegantly of any man I know in town'.[15]

Whatever his abilities, Benson was more heavily engaged in parliamentary duties as a manager for the Court in the 1711–12 session. On 15 Dec. he proffered information to the Commons on the estimates for the army in the Low Countries, and the same day was named to prepare the land tax bill. On 23 Jan. 1712 he was named to draft another supply bill – this time for the malt duty. At least two commentators mentioned Benson's leading role on the 24th in the attack upon the Duke of Marlborough (John Churchill†) with Kreienberg noting 'mais tout n'étoit rien en comparison de la chaleur de Mr Benson'. On 18 Feb. he was among the appointees ordered to draw up a representation on the state of the war and in the days following attended several meetings with Swift, (Sir) Thomas Hanmer II and others to work on it, before it was reported by Hanmer on 1 Mar. On the 13th he informed the House of the Queen's agreement to represent to the king of Spain that only a reduced subsidy would be granted for the war in Spain. It was his presence at an October Club dinner, along with Henry St. John II*, which precipitated a group of more independently minded Members to split off and form the March Club. On 29 Mar. he was named to draft the lottery bill: unfortunately when the October Club successfully tacked the resumption bill to it at the committee stage, Benson 'ne se trouvant pas dans la chambre, on ne pouvoit pas bien juger de l'affaire'. However, he redeemed himself when the House separated the bills again on 6 May. On 13 May he was appointed to draft a bill continuing the South Sea Company and on the 22nd to draft a further supply bill. Earlier on the 22nd the House had attended the Queen in the Lords in expectation of hearing some news of the peace negotiations: when no news was forthcoming it was Benson who moved that the call of the House be delayed until 4 June and thereby initiated a warm debate in which 'notice was taken how long they had already waited in hopes of having the peace laid before them'.[16]

Benson remained at the Treasury Board until August, when he embarked on an extended sojourn in Yorkshire. On 20 Sept. he wrote to inform Oxford that he had 'a little of the new fever', and would be delaying his return to London. However, he was back at the Board on 14 Oct. With the political atmosphere tense in the run-up to the delayed 1713 session, denials appeared in the press in December 1712 refuting a rumour which saw Benson being made auditor of the imprest to make way for a Whig chancellor. With the prospect of a serious Whig assault on the peace when Parliament re-assembled, there were rumours in March 1713 of a new creation of peers, including Benson. However, with St. John now in the Upper House as Lord Bolingbroke, Benson presumably had to shoulder more of the management of the Commons. In one letter, probably dating from the eve of session, he advised Oxford to write to his father-in-law Lord Guernsey, 'for though he should not come to the meeting tomorrow yet the invitation will take away a pretence for complaint which his brother [Nottingham] would make use of'. Furthermore, he seems to have been the main conduit through which the Court passed information to the Commons. Thus, he presented information from the crown on 28 occasions, mostly concerning the peace and associated questions of trade. He was one of the Court spokesmen on the commercial questions which dominated much of the session: on 6 May he spoke in support of the bill suspending for two months the duties on French wines. Likewise, on 14 May he spoke for the Court in the debate on bringing in a bill to confirm the 8th and 9th articles of the French commercial treaty, being duly named to the drafting committee. May also saw him named to other drafting committees: to enable disbanded troops to resume work (2nd), and to continue the duties on malt, mum, cider and perry (12th). On 10 June, when the Commons received evidence hostile to the French commercial treaty, Benson objected to comments of Nathaniel Torriano which questioned the government's competence, calling for him 'to be turned out of their doors for talking [in] such a vilifying disrespectful manner of a treaty which her Majesty and her ministry had thought fit to make'. On the 18th, with the 8th and 9th articles under severe attack, he remained silent, though he did vote for the bill's passage. Also in June he was named to draft four other bills, but did not manage any of them.[17]

Following the end of the session Benson was raised to the peerage as Lord Bingley. This promotion was one that 'both sides are angry at'. Bolingbroke wished that Benson had stayed in the Commons and swapped jobs with Secretary Bromley (William II*). Dr Stratford at Oxford opined 'it was justly alleged in the late creation [January 1712] that all of them were of ancient families; no one I have met with is much acquainted with the new Lord's pedigree, nor are his merits in the House from whence he is removed sufficiently known'. Others, like Lord Berkeley of Stratton, felt that it was an affront to the dignity of the Upper House and told a story that Benson

> sent to the herald's office for supporters and they should send him word they could find no arms to be supported. He sent them word that Lord Somers [Sir John*] had no arms or supporters, till he was made a lord. They sent him word that was a mistake, for he [Somers] wisely foresaw what honour was coming to him, and a little before he had a privy seal from the King for the heralds to give him arms and after that he might have supporters.

Benson does not seem to have been bothered by such criticism, John Aislabie* reporting 'Lord Bingley looks with great glory, and the 12 peers die with envy', a reference to the mass creation at the beginning of the year. With Benson now forced to relinquish the chancellorship, thoughts ran to employing him in an ambassadorial role. Bolingbroke favoured France as 'his estate will bear it, and his obligations to the Queen will, if she requests it, I suppose make him willing', and Bingley sought advice from Dartmouth as to whether he should accept the post. In the event Bolingbroke opted to persuade both Bingley and Oxford that Spain was the ideal employment. However, as the negotiations over his equipage drew on, Bingley was still in England when Parliament re-assembled in February 1714 and was able to take his seat in the Lords. Soon after the Hanoverian succession he was mistaken for Lord Oxford and assaulted in a London street.[18]

Although shortly after being raised to the peerage Bingley was reported to be discontented with Oxford, it seems that he remained loyal to his former leader. Indeed, the same source has Bingley as involved in the negotiations in late August 1714 in which Oxford sought to persuade Lord Peterborough to join in an accusation against Bolingbroke. In November Bingley was again used as an intermediary by Oxford, this time to Bolingbroke. He continued to be allied to Oxford, voting against his impeachment in 1717 and opposing the repeal of the Occasional Conformity and Schism

Acts in 1718. He was heavily involved in promoting the shares of the South Sea Company, but after making considerable sums of money he may have sustained serious losses, having purchased stock when the price was falling, in the mistaken belief that the price would soon rise again. Consequently, he was still dealing in below par stocks in 1723–4. Whatever, the financial result he evidently enjoyed operating in the financial markets, having spent 'so much time among the brokers of Exchange Alley'. Bingley joined Lord Cowper's (William*) opposition to the Whig ministry in 1720–3, being the whip in 1721 for Lord Dartmouth and Lord Kinnoull (George Hay*), the latter being Oxford's son-in-law. Indeed, he continued in opposition until 1730, when he spoke for the Court on 27 Jan. in the debate on the Treaty of Seville. His reward for coming over to the Court was appointment as treasurer of the Household which he held until his death, 'of a pleurisy and a fever', on 9 Apr. 1731. He was buried on the 14th in Westminster Abbey. In his will he left his house in Queen's Street, 'where I formerly lived', to his wife. His executors, the Duke of Argyll, William Hamilton of Lincoln's Inn and Benjamin Hoare, 'goldsmith and banker', were to pay £7,000 to his natural daughter, Mary Johnson, who should take the name Benson after his death. To Anna Maria Burgoyne he gave £400 p.a. for life and the 'Nunnery' and estate in Hertfordshire, together with the lease of the house in Prospect Street where she lived. Further, the debts of her husband John Burgoyne were to be cancelled. The remainder of his estate went to his daughter, Harriet, who married in the following July George Fox[†], in his turn created Baron Bingley in 1762.[19] Boyer offered encomiums to Benson as chancellor,

> which office he executed with remarkable exactness and dexterity, being a man of very great natural abilities and thoroughly versed in business as well as all kinds of useful knowledge and polite literature and always remarkable for a firm adherence to the true interest and fundamental constitution of his country.

His most enduring monument was Bramham Park, a house he probably designed himself, albeit with the advice of professionals, which was universally admired.[20]

[1] IGI, Yorks.; *Wentworth Pprs.* 133; C107/89, m. settlement. [2] *CSP Dom.* 1690–1, p. 323. [3] J. Torr, *Antiq. York*, 142, 147. [4] J. Carswell, *S. Sea Bubble* (1993), 274. [5] *York Diaries II* (Surtees Soc. lxxvii.) 127–8; E. G. W. Bill, *Q. Anne Churches*, p. xxiii; *Cal. Treas. Bks.* xxvi. 137. [6] *Thoresby Letters* (Thoresby Soc. xxi.), 82; M. Hunter, *Royal Soc. and its Fellows*, 58, 60. [7] Coxe, *Marlborough*, vi. 36; E. Gregg, *Q. Anne*, 338; K. Feiling, *Hist. Tory Party*, 419; *Reresby Mems.* ed. Speck and Geiter, 90, 106; *Cal. Comm. Comp.* 1643–60, pp. 949–50; J. B. Walker, *Wakefield Its History and People*, 665–6; info. from Dr D. F. Lemmings; J. S. Cockburn, *Hist. English Assizes*, 76. [8] *CSP Dom.* 1690–1, p. 323; 1693, pp. 111, 253, 272; 1700–2, p. 31; *Wentworth Pprs.* 133; *Thoresby Letters* 82; Hunter, 58, 60; *HMC Var.* vii. 148. [9] Luttrell, *Brief Relation*, v. 416; Add. 61291, f. 44; 61294, f. 69; 61297, f. 64. [10] *Cam. Misc.* xxiii. 40, 67. [11] *Vernon–Shrewsbury Letters*, iii. 353–4. [12] York City Archs. Corpn. House Bk. 1706–19, f. 53; Cunningham, *Hist. GB*, ii. 284–5; Staffs. RO, Dartmouth mss D1778/V/811, Benson to Dartmouth, 9 Apr. [1710]; *HMC Portland*, iv. 544; Huntington Lib. Stowe mss 57(4), p. 60. [13] *HMC Portland*, iv. 560; *Cal. Treas. Bks.* xxiv. 34; Surr. RO (Guildford), Midleton mss 1248/3, f. 9; B. W. Hill, *Robert Harley*, 129; Add. 17677 DDD, f. 573; *Addison Letters*, 233; Bagot mss at Levens Hall, William Bromley II to James Grahme*, 1 Sept. 1710. [14] *Cal. Treas. Bks.* xxiv. 90, 102; xv. 1–65; *HMC Portland*, iv. 617; *Wentworth Pprs.* 133, 154, 189; *Yorks. Arch. Jnl.* xlvi. 107; *Cam. Misc.* xxxi. 329; *Post Boy*, 10[20]–22 Feb. 1711. [15] *Cal. Treas. Bks.* xxv. 66, 87; P. G. M. Dickson, *Financial Revol.* 450; Lockhart Pprs. 411–12; *Swift Stella*, 461. [16] BL, Trumbull Add. mss 136, bdle. 1, Ralph Bridges to Sir William Trumbull*, 25 Jan. 1711–12; NSA, Kreienberg despatches 25 Jan., 28 Mar., 25 Apr., 9, 23 May 1712 (Szechi trans.); *Swift Stella*, 494, 496; *Swift Works* ed. Davis, viii. 125–6; Add. 17677 FFF, f. 209; 61451, f. 151. [17] *Cal. Treas. Bks.* xxvi. 65, 77; Add. 70282, Benson to Oxford, 20 Sept. [1712], 'Sunday morning'; 17677 GGG, ff. 220, 230; *Post Boy*, 7–9 Aug., 29 Nov.–2 Dec. 1712; Kreienberg despatches 3 Mar., 8 May, 12 June 1713; *Letters of Burnet to Duckett* ed. Nichol Smith, 40; G. Holmes, *Pol. Relig. and Soc.* 128. [18] Cumbria RO (Carlisle), Lonsdale mss D/Lons/W2/3/13, Jane to James Lowther*, 25 July 1713; *HMC Portland*, v. 312, 324, 342, 360, 485; vii. 160; *Wentworth Pprs.* 347–8; Bagot mss, Aislabie to Grahme, n.d.; Dartmouth mss D1778/Iii/417, Bingley to Dartmouth, 5 Sept. [1713]; *HMC Lords*, n.s. x. 223; *Bolingbroke Corresp.* iv. 556; *Swift Corresp.* ed. Williams, ii. 103. [19] PRO 31/3/201, f. 77; 31/3/203, f. 69; L. Colley, *In Defiance of Oligarchy*, 64, 185, 209; *Bull. IHR*, lv. 80; *Parlty. Hist.* vii. 37; *HMC Dartmouth*, i. 325; *HMC Portland*, v. 613; C107/90; Add. 47127, f. 73; *Hist. Jnl.* xxxvi. 314, 329; Ld. Ilchester, *Ld. Hervey and His Friends*, 46; *HMC Egmont Diary*, ii. 11; *HMC Carlisle*, 67; *Westminster Abbey Regs.* (Harl. Soc. xliv) 331; PCC 86 Isham; IGI, London. [20] Boyer, *Pol. State*, xli. 411–12; Pevsner, *W. Riding*, 141, 622; *HMC Portland*, vi. 139.

E. C./S. N. H.

BENTINCK, Henry, Visct. Woodstock (c.1682–1726), of Titchfield, Hants.

SOUTHAMPTON 1705–1708
HAMPSHIRE 1708–23 Nov. 1709

b. c.1682, 2nd but 1st surv. s. of Hans Willem Bentinck, 1st Earl of Portland, by Anne, da. of Sir Edward Villiers of Richmond, Surr., knight marshal of the Household, sis. of Edward Villiers, 1st Earl of Jersey. *educ.* travelled abroad (Italy, Germany) 1701–3. *m.* 9 June 1704, Lady Elizabeth (d. 1733), da. and coh. of Wriothesley Baptist Noel[†], 2nd Earl of Gainsborough, 3s. 7da. *Styled* Visct. Woodstock 1689–1709; *suc.* fa. as 2nd Earl of Portland 23 Nov. 1709; *cr.* Duke of Portland 6 July 1716.[1]

Freeman, Southampton 1705.[2]

Capt. and brevet col. 1 Life Gds. 1710–13; ld. of bedchamber 1717–26; gov. and v.-adm. Jamaica 1721–d.[3]

The son of one of William III's closest friends and favourites, Lord Woodstock was heir to a large fortune and vast estates in England, which had been lavished on his father by the King. While still a child, he was shown a mark of favour by Queen Mary when she allowed him to carry the sword of state before her at a ceremonial attendance at church, a duty never before entrusted to one so young. The family usually spent a part of each year in Holland, and in January 1698 Woodstock, with his tutor, the historian Rapin de Thoyras, accompanied his father on his embassy to Paris. Although his father surrendered most of his offices in 1700 from jealous pique at the influence with the King of his rival, Arnold Joost van Keppel, he was still highly regarded and trusted by William. When the King visited Holland in 1701 he paid Woodstock flattering attentions, promising him command of his father's old cavalry regiment if Portland would permit him to return to England. Portland had other ideas, however, and in April 1701 Woodstock and his tutor set out on a grand tour, during which he was to pay his respects to the Electress Sophia of Hanover and her son. Sophia wrote to Portland that his son had been universally admired, while confiding to her niece that Woodstock had appeared to her to be very affected. Shortly after returning to England Woodstock married an heiress with a fortune of £60,000, who brought him the estate of Titchfield in Hampshire. At the same time, his father settled on him an income of £10,000 p.a.[4]

Woodstock first stood for Parliament at Southampton in 1705. Prior to the election it was reported that 'Lord Woodstock's friends in Hampton pretend they are sure of his election, he has already spent five hundred pounds'. This expenditure proved worthwhile, as he was returned in a contested election. His election was considered by Lord Sunderland (Charles, Lord Spencer*) as a gain for the Whigs. Woodstock was absent from the division on the Speaker on 25 Oct., though he was in the House on 8 Dec., when he was sent to desire a conference with the Lords on their resolution that anyone who suggested that the Church was 'in danger' was an enemy to the Queen. On 18 Feb. 1706 he was used as a messenger to the Lords once again, to desire a conference on the regency bill. However, he appears to have been inactive for the remainder of the 1705–8 Parliament. In 1708 he was noted as a Whig in two separate analyses of Parliament before and after the election of that year, at which he was returned for both Southampton and the county. He chose to sit for the county. On 30 Nov. he acted as a teller against a motion to adjourn further consideration of the merits of the double return for Dumfries Burghs, while on 5 Feb. 1709 he told against a motion that the Tory Sir Charles Blois, 1st Bt., had been duly elected for Dunwich, and on 29 Mar. he told in favour of the second reading of a bill from the Lords for improving the Union.[5]

A few days after the start of the next session Woodstock's succession to his father's earldom disabled him from sitting in the Commons. He was now in possession of the principal family seat of Bulstrode in Berkshire, and of estates in Cheshire, Cumberland, Hertfordshire, Norfolk, Sussex, Westminster and Yorkshire, worth in all some £850,150. His father also left him £10,000 p.a. in the bank of Holland. The Dutch properties went to a younger brother. In the Lords he sat as a Whig but was of little political importance. Advanced to a dukedom in 1716, he suffered losses in the South Sea Bubble, and was made governor of Jamaica, where he died on 4 July 1726, in his 45th year. His body was returned to England and was buried in Westminster Abbey, in the vault of the dukes of Ormond.[6]

[1] Boyer, *Anne Annals*, viii. 405; *Top. and Gen.* iii. 150, 377; Luttrell, *Brief Relation*, v. 433; F. Cundall, *Govs. of Jamaica in 18th Cent.* 104; M. E. Grew, *Wm. Bentinck and Wm. III*, 418. [2] Southampton RO, bor. recs. SC3/2, f. 41. [3] Cundall, 104, 115. [4] Grew, 198, 389–94, 399–402; Boyer, 399–405; Luttrell, 433. [5] Bath mss at Longleat House, Thynne pprs. 18, f. 50; *Bull. IHR*, xxxvii. 24; *Nicolson Diaries* ed. Jones and Holmes, 327, 404; PRO, 30/24/21/54–55. [6] Grew, 414–16; *Top. and Gen.* 377; Egerton 1708, f. 272; *HMC Laing*, ii. 207; Cundall, 115.

P. W./C. I. M.

BERE, Thomas (1652–1725), of Huntsham, nr. Tiverton, Devon.

TIVERTON 1690–1710, 1715–22 June 1725

bap. 23 May 1652, 1st s. of Thomas Bere of Huntsham by Margaret, da. of Sir John Davie, 1st Bt.†, of Creedy, Devon. *educ.* Exeter, Oxf. 1670. *m.* c.1686, Mary (*d.* 1700), da. of Robert Long of Stanton Prior, Dorset, wid. of George Stedman of Midsomer Norton, Som., 2s. *suc.* fa. 1680; fa.-in-law 1701.[1]

Commr. victualling the navy June 1706–*d.*

Coming from a family long associated with Tiverton, Bere was returned for the borough without opposition in 1690. He was classed as a Whig in Lord Carmarthen's (Sir Thomas Osborne†) analysis of the new Parliament. At the end of the year he applied unsuccessfully to the commissioners of customs for employment at Bristol. Robert Harley* classed him as a doubtful supporter of the Country party in April 1691. On 8 Jan. 1692 Bere presented to the Commons a petition from Tiverton complaining of the woollen manufactures in Ireland and that many workers from Devon had emigrated there. Samuel Grascome listed him as a Court supporter in 1693. Bere was granted three weeks' leave of absence on 20 Mar 1695. Re-elected in 1695, he was absent from a call of the House on 7 Jan. 1696, and was sent for in custody but discharged two days later. On 29 Jan. he told against a motion to adjourn all committees. He was forecast as a likely Court supporter over the proposed council of trade on 31 Jan., signed the Association the following month, and voted in March for fixing the price of guineas at 22s. He presented a bill to regulate the press on 2 Feb. 1697. Granted leave of absence on 22 Dec. for an unspecified reason, he was accorded further leave on 26 Feb. 1698 to attend his father-in-law's funeral.[2]

Bere was classed as a member of the Court party in September 1698, marked as query in an analysis of the House into interests in 1700, and listed as a Whig by Robert Harley* in December 1701. He presented a private estate bill on 19 Mar. 1702, carrying it up to the Lords on 6 May. He told on 20 May in favour of an amendment to provide maintenance for the Protestant children of Sir Anthony Mullady under the Irish forfeitures bill. On 13 Feb. 1703 he voted for agreeing with the Lords' amendments to the bill for enlarging the time for taking the oath of abjuration. The House was informed, in the report on King William's grants on 22 Dec., that he enjoyed a naval pension of £39 p.a. Forecast as a probable opponent of the Tack, he did not vote for it on 28 Nov. 1704. After the 1705 election, he was classed as 'Low Church' and voted for the Court candidate for Speaker on 25 Oct. He obtained a leave of absence for one month on 15 Dec. On 18 Feb. 1706 he supported the Court over the 'place clause' of the regency bill. A few months later his loyalty was rewarded with appointment to the victualling commission at a salary of £400 p.a. On 3 Apr. 1707 he told in favour of an amendment to a supply bill. He presented a private estate bill in favour of Roger Tuckfield* on 17 Jan. 1708. That session saw four more tellerships: against going into committee on a bill to encourage trade with America (14 Feb.); for recommitting the levy of a further duty on woollen yarn (25 Feb.); for an amendment to a supply bill (8 Mar.); and for extending beyond Europe a proposed duty exemption on linens (27 Mar.). Classed as a Whig before and after the 1708 election, Bere voted in 1709 for the naturalization of the Palatines and the following year for the impeachment of Dr Sacheverell. At the general election of 1710 he was subject to a double return for Tiverton, and was noted as such on the 'Hanover list'. The election having been declared void, Bere was defeated at the ensuing by-election. Somewhat surprisingly, in view of his Whig background, Bere was described to a senior Oxford don in 1711 as a 'good . . . Churchman and friend of Mrs Masham'. It was as a Whig, however, that he returned to the House in 1715, voting consistently with the administration until his death on 22 June 1725.[3]

[1] Vivian, *Vis. Devon*, 60; *Trans. Devon Assoc.* lxvii. 328; IGI, Somerset. [2] *Cal. Treas. Bks.* ix. 915; *Luttrell Diary*, 116. [3] Bodl. Ballard 21, f. 95.

E. C.

BERKELEY, Edward (c.1644–1707), of Pylle, nr. Wells, Som.

WELLS   1679 (Mar.)–27 Nov. 1680, 1685–1687, 1689–1700

b. c.1644, 1st s. of Edward Berkeley of Pylle by Phillippa, da. of George Speke of White Lackington, Som. *educ.* Wadham, Oxf. matric. 12 July 1661, aged 17; L. Inn 1665. *m.* c.1680, Elizabeth (*d.* 1724), da. and coh. of John Ryves of Ranston, Dorset, 3s. (1 *d.v.p.*) 3da. (2 *d.v.p.*). *suc.* fa. 1669.[1]

Usually known by his militia rank of colonel, Berkeley was second cousin to the Berkeleys of Bruton. His estate at Pylle was midway between Bruton and Wells where he had first been elected in 1679. He had been a Tory supporter of William of Orange in 1688, but during the Convention had opposed the notion that the throne was vacant. Re-elected for Wells in 1690, he was classed in one of Lord Carmarthen's (Sir Thomas Osborne†) lists as a Tory and in another as a probable Court supporter. That he fulfilled this expectation in the course of the first session is borne out in his being classed as pro-Court in Carmarthen's lists of October and December. He was first-named on 30 Nov. 1693 on a committee to consider an application for a bill to erect a bridge at Brean over the River Axe, but the rest of his Journal record relates only to grants of leave accorded him, in February–March 1694, January 1695, and March 1697. His early support for the Court gave way to opposition by the mid-1690s. In January 1696, on the proposed council of trade, he was forecast as a probable opponent of the Court, and late the following month he refused to sign the Association. In March he voted against the Court's preference for fixing the price of guineas at 22s., and in November voted against the attainder of Sir John Fenwick†. A list compiled shortly after the 1698 election identified him as one of the Country party, and he was forecast as likely to oppose the standing army during the 1698–9 session. He stood down at the January 1701 election, but made an unsuccessful bid for a county seat in 1702. He died in 1707 and was buried at Pylle. Besides his Somerset lands, his will mentions property in Gillingham, Dorset and in Gloucestershire but stated that it had taken 'lawsuits of great fatigue and expense to gain an estate' and he was particularly anxious that it be preserved intact by his elder son Maurice*. His younger son, William, was heir, and in 1728, eventual successor to the extensive west-country estates of Henry Seymour Portman*, Berkeley's first cousin once removed, and was thereby the founder of the wealthy Berkeley Portman dynasty.[2]

[1] *Vis. Eng. and Wales Notes* ed. Crisp, ix. 169–70; Collinson, *Som.* iii. 281–2; Hutchins, *Dorset*, i. 253–5. [2] Hutchins 253, 255; PCC 167 Poley.

P. W./A. A. H.

BERKELEY, James, Visct. Dursley (c.1680–1736), of Berkeley Castle, Glos.

GLOUCESTER 1701 (Dec.)–1702

b. c.1680, 2nd but 1st surv. s. of Charles Berkeley[†], 2nd Earl of Berkeley, by Elizabeth, da. of Baptist Noel[†], 3rd Visct. Camden, sis. of Edward Noel[†], 1st Earl of Gainsborough. *m.* c.13 Feb. 1711, Lady Louisa Lennox (*d.* 1717), da. of Charles, 1st Duke of Richmond, 1s. 1da. Styled Visct. Dursley 1699–1710; *summ.* to Lords in his fa.'s barony as Lord Berkeley of Berkeley 5 Mar. 1705; *suc.* fa. as 3rd Earl of Berkeley 24 Sept. 1710; KG 31 Mar. 1718.

Lt. RN 1699, capt. 1701, v.-adm. 1708, adm. Dec. 1708; v.-adm. of Great Britain 1718–*d.*, adm. of the fleet and c.-in-c. 13 Mar.–15 Apr. 1719; ld. of bedchamber 1714–27; first ld. of Admiralty 1717–27; PC 17 Apr. 1717; ld. justice 1719, 1720, 1726, 1727.[1]

Freeman, Gloucester 1701; ld. lt. Glos. 1710–12, 1714–*d.*; custos rot. Surr. 1710–*d.*; high steward, Gloucester 1710–12, 1714–*d.*; warden, Forest of Dean and constable of St. Briavel's Castle 1711–12, 1714–*d.*[2]

Er. bro. Trinity House 1715–*d.*, master 1715–19.

Lord Dursley, the heir to one of William III's middle-ranking politicians, began his career in the navy and was promoted captain of a frigate in April 1701 at the early age of 21. He successfully contested Gloucester in December 1701, when his return was counted as a gain for the Whigs by Lord Spencer (Charles*). Robert Harley* also classed him as a Whig in his list of the same date. He made no mark in proceedings, and his parliamentary career was cut short when his return to active service prevented his candidacy at the 1702 election. He was with Sir George Rooke* in the Mediterranean in 1704, distinguishing himself at the battle of Malaga. The following year he was summoned to the Upper House in his father's barony of Berkeley. His naval career continued to prosper, though his promotion to vice-admiral early in 1708 owed much to his political connexions, Lord Treasurer Godolphin (Sidney[†]) explaining to Marlborough (John Churchill[†]) that it had been done to please the Whigs who had been 'very pressing for him'. Further commands and promotion followed until his retirement from active service in May 1710, and in September he succeeded his father to the earldom of Berkeley and its estates. Despite the Tories' accession to power, he was appointed to succeed his father as lord lieutenant of Gloucestershire, but was replaced in January 1712 and at the same time removed from his rank of admiral of the red. He was recalled to active service in 1714 to command the fleet sent to meet King George I, who appointed him one of his lords of the bedchamber while still on board ship. For the next 13 years he played a central part in the Whig administration, taking charge of the Admiralty as first lord from 1717 until 1727 when his worsening relations with (Sir) Robert Walpole II* led to his dismissal. He died 17 Aug. 1736 at Aubigny in France, a seat of his brother-in-law the Duke of Richmond, and was buried at Berkeley. He was, as Lord Hervey (John[†]) recalled, 'born and educated a staunch Whig, and had never deviated a moment one step of his life from these principles'.[3]

[1] *Commissioned Sea Officers of RN* (Navy Recs. Soc., occ. pub. i), 31. [2] *Gloucester Freemen* (Glos. Rec. Ser. iv), 54; Bodl. Rawl. C.393, f. 52. [3] Charnock, *Biographia Navalis*, iii. 201–13; *Marlborough–Godolphin Corresp.* 1292; Luttrell, *Brief Relation*, vi. 715; *Hervey Mems.* 37.

P. W./A. A. H.

BERKELEY, John, 4th Visct. Fitzhardinge [I] (1650–1712), of Bruton, Som. and Pall Mall, Westminster.

HINDON 20 Apr. 1691–1695
NEW WINDSOR 1695–1710

bap. 18 Apr. 1650, 3rd but 2nd surv. s. of Charles Berkeley[†], 2nd Visct. Fitzhardinge, by Penelope, da. of Sir William Godolphin[†] of Godolphin, Cornw.; bro. of Charles[†] and Maurice*, 1st and 3rd Viscts. Fitzhardinge. *m.* Barbara (*d.* 1708), da. of Sir Edward Villiers, knight marshal of the Household, 3da. (1 *d.v.p.*). *suc.* bro. as 4th Visct. Fitzhardinge 13 June 1690.[1]

Page of honour to Charles II 1668–72; ensign Lord Le Power's Ft. 1673; capt. 1 Ft. Gds. 1675–85; lt.-col., Col. Edward Villiers' Ft. 1678; jt. searcher, Gravesend 1681–94; master of horse to Princess Anne 1685–1702; col. regt. of Dragoons [later 4 Queen's Hussars] 1685–24 Nov. 1688, 31 Dec. 1688–1 Sept. 1693; brig.-gen. 1690; gov. Kinsale 1692–3; keeper of Pall Mall 1692–*d.*; teller of Exchequer 1694–*d.*; treasurer of chamber to Queen Anne 1702–*d.*[2]

Custos rot. Som. 1690–*d.*; freeman, Kinsale 1692.[3]

Berkeley's father and elder brothers had become prominent figures in royal service during the early years of the Restoration. His older brother Charles was rewarded with an Irish viscountcy in 1663 which, by special remainder, passed firstly to his father in 1665, and then to his eldest brother Maurice. In 1668, the year of his father's death, he became a page to Charles II, and four years later joined the army. In June 1685, he fought at the battle of Sedgemoor and was shortly afterwards promoted colonel of his own regiment. At the beginning of 1685 he had entered the household of Princess Anne as master of the Horse, and the subsequent course of his career owed much to his wife's closeness to the princess. His kinship with Lord Godolphin (Sidney†), and his wife's intimacy with Sarah Churchill, helped to bind the connexion all the more. In the early hours of 24 Nov. 1688 Berkeley was a member of the small company consisting of Prince George of Denmark, the Duke of Grafton and Lord Churchill (John†) who defected to William of Orange. Berkeley was instantly deprived of his colonelcy by King James. Two days later, on the 26th, Berkeley's wife and Sarah Churchill were the only two of Princess Anne's ladies to accompany her on her secret flight from London. After the Revolution Berkeley was restored to his regiment, and in March 1690 was appointed to brigadier-general 'over all the horse'. In June he succeeded his brother as Viscount Fitzhardinge, although the family seat at Bruton remained in the hands of the dowager viscountess until her death in 1704. When Lord Nottingham (Daniel Finch†) immediately recommended that Fitzhardinge succeed his brother as lord lieutenant of Somerset, the new peer felt obliged to tell the Queen that, having no estate in the county, he feared he would not be 'so able to serve you as he ought' and was content with the office of custos. In February 1691 Godolphin put forward Fitzhardinge's name for the governorship of the Isle of Wight, but his expectations came to nothing as its incumbent, Sir Robert Holmes*, lingered on in the clutches of serious illness. By way of compensation Fitzhardinge was given a pension of £300 p.a.[4]

In April 1691 Fitzhardinge was returned at a by-election for Hindon. A Court Whig, his military experience gained him appointment in November to two committees concerned with expenditure on the army, and in February 1692 he was nominated a member of a conference committee on the mutiny bill. Generally speaking, however, he was not an active member of the House, and his next committee nominations did not occur until 1695. Furthermore, he made only one recorded speech. This was on 15 Dec. 1692 when he justified the grant of additional pay to the two regiments stationed in London on the basis of the 'dearer expense' there in comparison with towns elsewhere. Soon after Fitzhardinge's entry into Parliament, Marlborough's dismissal from his army commands was accompanied by rumours, said to have been initiated by the King, that Lady Fitzhardinge was partially responsible in having repeated a story about Marlborough's supposed communication with the Jacobite court-in-exile. In some quarters, she was thought to be a member of a cabal organized by her brother-in-law, the Earl of Portland, aimed at Marlborough's destruction. Whatever the truth behind this potentially damaging situation, Fitzhardinge's wife remained on close terms with both Lady Marlborough and the princess, and his own credibility survived apparently unscathed. Removed from the governorship of Kinsale in March 1693, it was on the strict understanding that he would be otherwise provided for as soon as possible. In less than a year he was granted a lucrative tellership of the Exchequer, valued at £1,500 p.a., although Godolphin saw this as part of a scheme by the King to lure the princess's servants and supporters from her service. Fitzhardinge had been classed as a placeman and Court supporter in two lists drawn up by Samuel Grascome in 1693. His name also appears on a list of 'friends' compiled by Henry Guy* during the 1694–5 session.[5]

In the 1695 election Fitzhardinge was returned on the Court interest for New Windsor and retained the seat until 1710. His continuing pro-Court stance is illustrated by his voting record in 1696; he was forecast as a probable Court supporter in the division of 31 Jan. over the proposed council of trade, in February he signed the Association, and in March voted with the administration on fixing the price of guineas at 22s. After the 1698 election a comparative analysis of the old and new Houses listed him once more as a placeman and Court supporter. On 31 Jan. 1699 he voted against the third reading of the disbanding bill, and in February 1701 he supported the Court on the question of continuing the 'Great Mortgage'. Robert Harley's* list of the following December classed him with the Whigs.

On her accession, Queen Anne appointed Fitzhardinge to the household office of treasurer of the chamber, valued at £1,200 p.a., while in 1703 his wife, who had been governess to the late Duke of Gloucester, was granted a pension of £600 p.a. He was recruited by Harley to lobby his son-in-law William Chetwynd against the Tack, and did not vote for it himself. Classed as a placeman and a 'High Church Courtier' after the 1705 election, he voted for the Court candidate for Speaker on 25 Oct. and supported the government on the 'place clause' in the regency bill in February 1706. He was listed as a Whig early in 1708. It is clear, however, that his activities in the

House rarely extended beyond quiet support for the ministry. He voted in favour of naturalizing the Palatines and the impeachment of Dr Sacheverell.[6]

Fitzhardinge retired at the 1710 election. Despite his wife's death in 1708 (soon followed by false rumours of his impending remarriage to a daughter of the Prussian ambassador), and the Tory ministry's eagerness to appropriate his offices after 1710, the Queen, out of tender regard for his past services, allowed him to retain his Exchequer and household posts. 'A man of wit and pleasant conversation', though said to be far too 'partial', he fancied himself as a man of letters and had written two rather mediocre plays. He died at Windsor of a palsy on 19 Dec. 1712 and was buried in Westminster Abbey. Having no male heir, his titles became extinct, and he left his estates at the disposal of his two surviving daughters.[7]

[1] *Vis. Eng. and Wales Notes* ed. Crisp, ix. 163–4; PCC 8 Leeds. [2] *Cal. Treas. Bks.* iii. 724, 815, 1327; iv. 862; vii. 174; viii. 12; ix. 88; x. 479, 597; xxvii. 538; *CSP Dom.* 1672, p. 662; 1684–5, p. 293; 1691–2, pp. 111, 426; 1693, p. 71; N. B. Leslie, *Suc. of Cols.* (Soc. Army Hist. Res. spec. pub. xi); 19; *Post Man*, 14–16 Apr. 1702; Luttrell, *Brief Relation*, v. 163. [3] *Kinsale Corp. Council Bk.* 195. [4] *Cal. Treas. Bks.* iii. 815; iv. 146, 274; *CSP Dom.* 1684–5, p. 293; F. Harris, *Passion for Govt.* 55, 67; E. Gregg, *Q. Anne*, 35, 64, 75; Burnet, iii. 335; *Hatton Corresp.* (Cam. Soc. n.s. xxiii), ii. 114; Dalrymple, *Mems.* iii(2), p. 72; *HMC Finch*, ii. 303; *CSP Dom.* 1690–1, p. 247; Bodl. Carte 130, ff. 330–1. [5] *Luttrell Diary*, 81; Coxe, *Marlborough* (1848), i. 34; Harris, 63; Luttrell, *Brief Relation*, iii. 58, 262; Gregg, 98. [6] Luttrell, v. 163; *Cal. Treas. Bks.* xviii. 211. [7] *Swift Corresp.* ed. Williams, i. 133; *Wentworth Pprs.* 311; *Westminster Abbey Regs.* (Harl. Soc. x), 275; PCC 8 Leeds.

P. W./A. A. H.

BERKELEY, John Symes (1663–1736), of Stoke Gifford, nr. Bristol, Glos.

GLOUCESTERSHIRE 1710–1715

bap. 1 Feb. 1663, 2nd s. of Richard Berkeley of Stoke Gifford by Elizabeth, da. of Henry Symes of Frampton Cotterel, Glos. *m.* (1) 28 Nov. 1695, Susan (*d.* 1696), da. and h. of Sir Thomas Fowles*, wid. of Jonathan Cope I*, *s.p.*; (2) 21 Feb. 1717, Elizabeth (*d.* 1742), da. and coh. of Walter Norborne of Calne, Wilts., wid. of Edward Devereux, 8th Visct. Hereford, 1s. 1da. *suc.* bro. 1685.[1]

Freeman, Gloucester 1712.[2]

That Berkeley took pride in the 'ancient' provenance of his family is apparent from his monumental inscription which recites that the manor of Stoke Gifford, a short distance from Bristol, had been 'enjoyed by the family some hundred years'. The manor had in fact been acquired by the 14th century, the family having some local pre-eminence by virtue of their distant connexions with their more august namesakes, the Berkeleys of Berkeley Castle and of Bruton, Somerset. John Berkeley inherited the family estates, unexpectedly, on the death of his elder brother in 1685, and later exploited their rich coal deposits. He was appointed to the Gloucestershire lieutenancy in October 1702, but did not emerge as a potential candidate for knight of the shire until 1710 when, as a Tory, his adoption was supported by the Duke of Beaufort. He achieved first place in the poll, and was shortly afterwards classed as a Tory in the 'Hanover list'. In the Commons his activities are difficult to sort from those of Maurice Berkeley, unless he was accorded his militia rank of colonel, or in cases where there was an obvious Gloucestershire interest. A published list noted him as one of the 'worthy patriots' who during the 1710–11 session assisted in exposing the mismanagements of the Godolphin administration, and at about the same time he became a member of the October Club. During February and March 1712 he supervised the passage of a bill, requested by the clothiers of Wootton-under-Edge, Gloucestershire, to prevent abuses in the manufacture of 'mixed broadcloth'. In the election of 1713 he retained his seat, again obtaining first place in the poll. He was possibly the 'Mr Berkeley' who acted as teller on 21 June 1714 in favour of postponing the report stage of a bill concerned with the encouragement of wool manufacture. In the Worsley list of the 1713 Parliament he appears as a Tory. He made no attempt, however, to remain in the House after the accession of George I. He died on 11 Dec. 1736 at Bath, and was buried at Stoke Gifford. His only son, Norborne Berkeley, sat for Gloucestershire from 1741 until raised to the peerage in 1763 as Lord Botetourt, and in 1740 his daughter married Lord Charles Noel Somerset†, a leading Tory and later 4th Duke of Beaufort.[3]

[1] Rudder, *Glos.* 698–9; IGI, Glos. and London; *CP*, ii. 234–5; vi. 481. [2] *Gloucester Freemen* (Glos. Rec. Ser. iv), 71. [3] Rudder, 698–9; Atkyns, *State of Glos.* 363; *CSP Dom.* 1702–3, p. 396; Huntington Lib. Stowe mss 58(6), p. 151; Boyer, *Pol. State*, lii. 648; PCC 1 Wake.

P. W./A. A. H.

BERKELEY, Maurice, 3rd Visct. Fitzhardinge [I] (1628–90), of Bruton, Som. and Pall Mall, Westminster.

WELLS 1661–1679 (Jan.)
BATH 1681 (Mar.), 1685–1687, 1689–13 June 1690

bap. 15 Dec. 1628, 1st s. of Charles Berkeley†, 2nd Visct. Fitzhardinge; bro. of John*, 4th Visct. Fitzhardinge. *m.* 1 Jan. 1649, Anne (*d.* 1704), da. of Sir Henry Lee, 1st Bt., of Quarrendon, Bucks., 2da.; 2s. illegit. by Mary Rutley. *cr.* Bt. 2 July 1660; *suc.* fa. as 3rd Visct. Fitzhardinge 12 June 1668.[1]

Servant to Duke of Gloucester May–Sept. 1660; gent. of privy chamber (extraordinary) June 1660, (ordinary) 1668–85; treasurer of Dunkirk garrison Dec. 1660–1; jt. agent for wine licences 1661–2; v.-pres. Connaught 1662–6; PC [I] 1663–?d.; commr. customs and excise accts. [I] 1666–7; capt. indep. tp. 1667, 1685, life gds. [I] 1676–85.[2]

MP [I] 1665–6.

FRS 1667.

Custos rot. Som. 1675–d., ld. lt. 1689–d.; freeman, Bath 1679, high steward 1685–Aug. 1688, Oct. 1688–d.[3]

A Court Tory with strong Irish attachments, Berkeley had been a sympathizer of the Duke of Monmouth and had taken a stand against James II's religious policies early in 1688. Later in the year he attended William of Orange during his progress through the West Country and entertained him at his seat at Bruton. He was rewarded with the lord lieutenancy of the county in 1689 and re-elected for Bath. On the eve of the 1690 session he was classed by Lord Carmarthen (Sir Thomas Osborne†) as a Tory, but made no mark in proceedings. He died on 13 June 1690 and was buried at St Mary's, Bruton. In his will he decreed that his estate, excluding his family seat, was to be sold off in order to raise cash for a series of bequests including £500 to his mistress Mary Rutley, and £500 to each of their two sons who also inherited his land in co. Westmeath in Ireland.[4]

[1] *Cal. Treas. Bks.* viii. 601; PCC 213 Dyke. [2] *SP* 29/20/55; LC 3/2; *CSP Dom.* 1660–1, p. 431; 1661–2, pp. 69, 132, 377; 1667, p. 182; 1676–7, p. 287; 1685, p. 209; *CSP Ire.* 1666–9, pp. 114, 349; *Cal. Clarendon SP*, v. 281, 544; *HMC Ormonde*, ii. 206, 208. [3] Bath AO, Bath council bk. 3, p. 69. [4] PCC 213 Dyke.

P. W./A. A. H.

BERKELEY, Maurice (c.1681–1717), of Pylle, nr. Wells, Som.

WELLS   1705–1708, 1710–30 May 1716

b. c.1681, 1st surv. s. of Edward Berkeley*. *educ.* Wadham, Oxf. matric. 15 June 1697, aged 16. *unm. suc.* fa. 1707.[1]

Berkeley was returned for Wells on his father's interest as a Tory in 1705 alongside his mother's cousin Henry Portman. He was classed as a 'Churchman' in a list drawn up after the general election and he duly voted against the Court candidate for Speaker on 25 Oct. It was perhaps due to his youth and inexperience that he featured not at all in proceedings, though his Tory sympathies were apparent to the compilers of two analyses of the House early in 1708. The death of his father in 1707 may have weakened his position and prevented him from standing in the 1708 election. He regained his seat in 1710, however, appearing as a Tory in the 'Hanover list' of the new Parliament. He featured in the 1710–11 session as one of the 'worthy patriots' who assisted in exposing the mismanagements of the Godolphin administration, and at about the same time became a member of the October Club. From 1710 the presence in the House of a second 'Mr Berkeley', his distant kinsman John Symes Berkeley, obscures from view any contributions he may have made to proceedings. He was classed as a Tory on the Worsley list of the 1713 Parliament. Contesting Wells successfully in 1715, he was unseated on petition in May 1716. His death probably occurred in the spring of 1717 (his will being proved in May), and the family estates passed to his younger brother William.[2]

[1] *Vis. Eng. and Wales Notes* ed. Crisp, ix. 169; Collinson, *Som.* iii. 281–2; Hutchins, *Dorset*, i. 253–5. [2] PCC 91 Whitfield.

P. W./A. A. H.

BERNERS, William (1679–1712), of Moore Place, Much Hadham, Herts.

HYTHE   27 Jan. 1711–c.19 June 1712

bap. 25 Aug. 1679, 1st s. and h. of James Berners of Moore Place, by Mary, da. of William Robinson of Bishop's Lane, Cheshunt, Herts, sis. of Samuel Robinson*. *educ.* Corpus, Camb. 1696. *m.* 1705, Elizabeth (*d.* 1725), da. of Robert Raworth, merchant, of London. 3s. *suc.* fa. 1692.[1]

Sheriff, Herts. 1710–11.

Berners' family had been merchants in London, but his father moved out of the city, establishing himself in a large 17th-century house, Moore Place, in Hertfordshire, where William was born. Berners inherited Moore Place from his father, together with a significant amount of land in Hertfordshire and London, a perpetual annuity of £20 on property in London and four shares in the New River Company which supplied water to London from Hertfordshire. Originally an investment made by Berners' grandfather, these shares proved a valuable inheritance, being worth about £4,000 each in 1698, and in 1700 they paid a dividend of £211. Moreover, Berners' four shares, being one-ninth of the total, gave him a significant stake in the Company.[2]

In 1705 Berners made a financially advantageous match with Elizabeth Raworth, daughter of a rich merchant. As well as being an East India merchant, Berners' father-in-law served on the lieutenancy of the City and as a director of the Bank of England during the 1690s. Raworth's sons, Henry, Robert and John, were also merchants. Berners, then, had close mercantile connexions but there is no evidence that he himself engaged in trade.[3]

In 1696 Berners signed the Hertfordshire Association. From 1703 to 1712 he was a justice in Hertfordshire, in which capacity he signed the 1706 Hertfordshire address congratulating the Queen on the victory at Ramillies. In August 1710 he was appointed sheriff. Although Berners had no known connexions with the area, he entered Parliament for the Cinque Port constituency of Hythe. Having unsuccessfully contested the 1710 election, he and John Boteler* petitioned against the return of the sitting Members. Although the committee of elections exposed bribery and treating on both sides, it recommended that the sitting Members be declared duly elected; a decision overturned by the House of Commons on 27 Jan. 1711. The mayor of Hythe, Henry Deedes, remained unreconciled to this defeat, refusing to confer on Berners the freedom of the borough.[4]

Berners' Toryism may have owed something to his maternal uncle Samuel Robinson, who was named a trustee in James Berners' will. It seems likely that Robinson played an important role in Berners' upbringing after James Berners' death, and it may be significant that they both sought to enter parliament in 1710. Berners was listed as one of the 'worthy patriots' who exposed the mismanagements of the previous administration in the 1710–11 session, and was also a member of the October Club. Local concerns probably prompted Berners' interest in the bill for repairing the road from Highgate in Middlesex to Barnet in Hertfordshire, on which he reported on 7 May 1712 and which he carried up to the Lords on 22 May and 4 June.[5]

Berners' parliamentary career was cut short by his death by 19 June 1712. He bequeathed most of his property to his eldest son and appointed his uncles, John Lockey and Samuel Robinson, and his brother-in-law, Henry Raworth, as trustees and executors.[6]

[1] IGI Herts. and London (Raworth, Elizabeth); Clutterbuck, *Herts.* iii. 406; Chauncy, *Herts.* i. 317; *Trans. East Herts. Arch. Soc.* iii. 144–5; Burke, *LG* (1937), 146; Bank of Eng. Berners/Raworth deposit, F16/8; *Trans. London and Mdx. Arch. Soc.* n.s. iv. 33–55; PCC admon. Dec. 1725; PCC 139 Fane. [2] *Trans. East Herts. Arch. Soc.* iii. 144–5; PCC 139 Fane, 128 Barnes; C 7/19/62; C 7/39/20; Scott, *Jt.-Stock Cos.* iii. 26. [3] PCC 213 Poley, 220 Shaller; *CSP Dom.* 1689–90, pp. 488–502; 1694–5, p. 21; 1697, pp. 269, 543; Add. 22851, ff. 133–4; 22852, ff. 39–40; 61620 f. 154. [4] *Hertford Co. Recs.* ed. Hardy, vii. 68, 373, 565; G. Wilks, *Barons of the Cinque Ports.* 92–93; *HMC Portland*, x. 70. [5] PCC 139 Fane, 128 Barnes; Boyer, *Pol. State*, iii. 117, 121. [6] *Post Boy*, 19–21 June 1712; PCC 128 Barnes.

S. M. W.

BERNEY, Richard (1674–c.1738), of Langley, Norf.

NORWICH 1710–1715

bap. 3 Aug. 1674, 2nd s. of John Berney of Westwick by Susan, da. of John Staines, prob. of Weston Longville, Norf. *educ.* G. Inn 1695. *m.* Mary, da. of Augustine Briggs of Norwich, mayor of Norwich 1695–6, 1da.

Steward, Norwich 1703–27, recorder 1727–*d.*; clerk of the peace, Norf. by 1730–*d.*[1]

Originally Norwich merchants, but established as country gentry since the 14th century and boasting one distant parliamentary ancestor, the Berneys had been 'the greatest family next the lords' in Norfolk in the early 17th century, when Richard Berney's grandfather had been created a baronet. The 1st baronet's fortune, estimated at '£7,000 p.a. and £50,000 in money' had however been left away from the title, to the Member's uncle and namesake, who had 'squandered' it all. A successful attorney in Norwich, Berney was returned on the Tory interest in 1710 (his elder brother appeared at the time to sympathize with the Whigs, but he too was later a Tory). Classed as a Tory in the 'Hanover list', he was noted among the 'worthy patriots' who exposed the mismanagements of the previous ministry. In January 1711 he reported the 'remarkable and famous victory' on the place bill in the Commons, in which 'we opposed the Court party in our own interest'. On 17 Dec. 1711 he presented a bill for establishing a workhouse in Norwich. Professional duties no doubt explain three leaves of absence during his tenure (14 Mar. 1711, 14 Mar. 1712 and 9 Mar. 1714). On 18 June 1713 he voted for the French commerce bill. In the Worsley list he was described as a Tory.[2]

Berney came bottom of the poll for Norwich in 1715 and was listed by the Jacobite Christopher Layer in 1721 as one of the 'loyal gentlemen' of Norfolk, with an income of £500 a year. He stood again in 1727, against the outgoing Whig Members, which caused some offence,

for he had lately been made recorder ... principally by their interest. They could not forbear thinking that some of the old leaven of the Tories still lodged in him, whose party he had formerly been of, but seems to have abandoned them for some time past.

In 1733 he married his daughter and heiress to Thomas Bramston†. Three years later Berney was bankrupt. Coming to a man 'who had a visible estate of £2,500 per annum', this caused a great stir in Norwich: it was reported in October 1736 that he

has made over all that he is worth to Mr Bramston ... for payment of his debts, and it is doubted whether there will be enough to pay everybody their own. He has got the Duke of Norfolk's [manorial] courts for Mr Bramston, who had with his wife £200 p.a. Surprising vanity of one who passed for a wise man, and a great lawyer, to affect the reputation of a great estate when he knew he was poor!

The following month:

Recorder Berney's affairs look darker and darker. Mr Bramston they say is very much crestfallen. Half a year ago he would not have given half a crown to have secured £40,000, and now, they say, except the Duke of Norfolk's courts, his wife will be worth nothing to him.

Berney's will, in which he described himself as 'weak in body', was dated 8 Dec. 1737 and proved 2 Mar. 1738.[34]

[1] H. Le Strange, *Norf. Official Lists*, 114–15, 127, 128; *HMC Townshend*, 349. [2] Rye, *Norf. Fams.* 43–46; Suff. RO (Ipswich), Gurdon mss mic. M142(1), Berney to Thornhagh Gurdon, 3 Jan. 1710[–11]; *Prideaux Letters* (Cam. Soc. n.s. xv), 166; *HMC Townshend*, 339; P. S. Fritz, *Ministers and Jacobitism 1715–45*, p. 143; Norf. RO, Dean Prideaux's diary, vol. 3, p. 19. [3] Fritz, 145; *VCH Norf.* ii. 520; R. W. Ketton-Cremer, *Country Neighbourhood*, 120, 126. [4] PCC 54 Brodrepp.

D. W. H.

BERTIE, Hon. Albemarle (c.1669–1742), of Swinstead, Lincs.

LINCOLNSHIRE   1705–1708
COCKERMOUTH   1708–1710
BOSTON   1734–1741

b. c.1669, 5th s. of Robert Bertie†, 3rd Earl of Lindsey, by 2nd w. Elizabeth, da. of Philip, 4th Baron Wharton; bro. of Hon. Peregrine II*, Hon. Philip* and Robert Bertie*, Lord Willoughby de Eresby; and half-bro. of Hon. Charles II*. *educ.* Univ. Coll. Oxf. matric. 3 July 1686, aged 17, BA 1689, MA 1691; All Souls, fellow 1694; M. Temple 1686. *unm.*[1]

Freeman, Appleby 1698.[2]

Auditor, duchy of Cornwall 1704–?13.[3]

Bertie first made his mark at Oxford, and by 1695 was of sufficient status to head the deputation which welcomed the Duke of Ormond prior to the royal visit of that year. Three years later he may well have been the 'Mr Bertie of University' touted as a possible candidate for the University election. With the support of his brother, Robert, 4th Earl of Lindsey, he successfully contested Lincolnshire for the Whigs in 1705. Prior to the poll Burrell Massingberd suggested that both the Whig candidates 'want estates sufficient to keep them out of temptation, it being confidently reported that Albemarle Bertie has nothing but an annuity for life under £200'. In fact he had rather more than this since the previous year he had replaced his elder brother, Philip Bertie, as auditor of the duchy of Cornwall. Classed as 'Low Church' in an analysis of the new Parliament, he was listed by Lord Sunderland (Charles, Lord Spencer*) as a gain for the Whigs. He voted for the Court candidate for Speaker on 25 Oct. 1705 and supported the administration over the 'place clause' in the regency bill the following February. His other parliamentary activities are impossible to disentangle from those of his many Bertie kinsmen in the House. However, he may plausibly be identified as the Member who managed a private bill to sell lands at Swinstead, and may have promoted a bill to improve river communications to Boston.[4]

In 1708 Bertie made way in Lincolnshire for his nephew, Lord Willoughby de Eresby (Peregrine Bertie*), and was himself returned for Cockermouth on the interest of his uncle, Lord Wharton (Hon. Thomas*). In 1709 he supported the naturalization of the Palatines, and although one parliamentary list suggested that he was absent at the time of the trial of Dr Sacheverell, others indicate that he voted for the impeachment. With no less than five Berties in the Parliament of 1708, it is again difficult to determine his Commons activity, although he may well have sponsored a bill to secure the estate of his brother Lord Lindsey. Prior to the election of 1710 he was tentatively identified as the Bertie candidate put forward by Lord Wharton (Hon. Thomas*) at Appleby. The Bertie in question withdrew before election day, having made it known that he 'was so tired of sitting in the House that he would not be in it again upon any consideration'. Despite the change of ministry Albemarle managed to retain his auditorship until at least November 1713, but it is unclear when he relinquished the post. Although he does not appear to have stood in 1713, nor in 1715, in January 1721 he did seek to re-enter the Commons at a by-election for Lincolnshire. He failed on that occasion, and it was not until 1734 that he returned to Westminster as Member for Boston, by courtesy of the influence of his nephew Peregrine, now 2nd Duke of Ancaster. He voted with the administration in that Parliament, but did not put up again, and died on 23 Jan. 1742.[5]

[1] PCC 42 Trenley; Collins, *Peerage*, ii. 20–21. [2] Cumbria RO (Kendal), Appleby bor. recs. WSMB/A min. bk. 3, 12 Sept. 1698. [3] *Cal. Treas. Bks.* xix. 239. [4] Bodl. Ballard 5, ff. 89–90; Tanner 22, f. 199; Lincs. AO, Massingberd mss 20/51, Burrell to Sir William Massingberd, 2nd Bt., 1 Feb. 1705. [5] Speck thesis, 73; *HMC Portland*, iv. 578; *Addison Letters*, 231; *Cal. Treas. Bks.* xxvii. 422.

P. W./P. L. G.

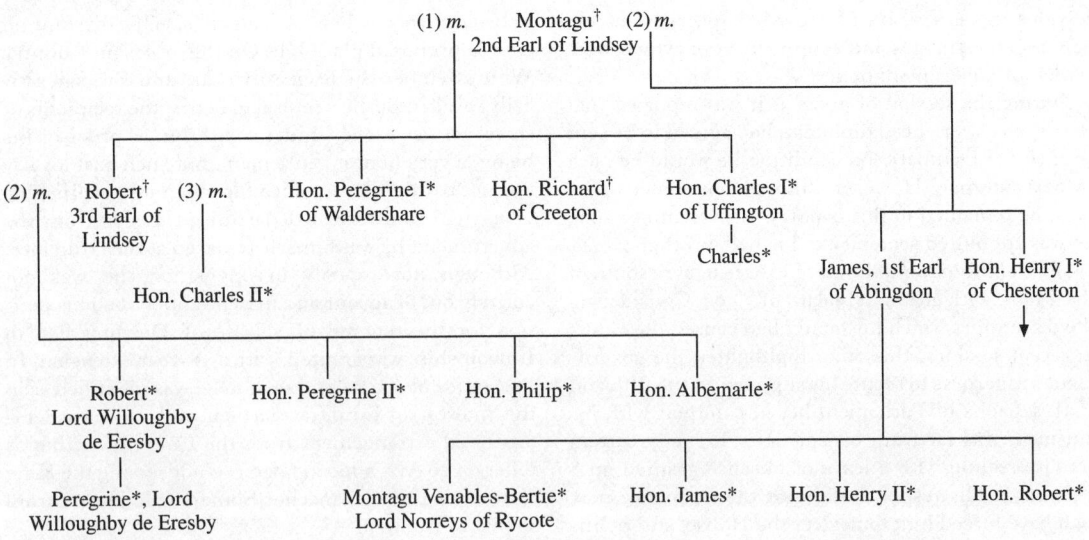

Note: This is not a complete pedigree, nor are children necessarily shown in correct order of precedence by age.

THE BERTIE FAMILY

BERTIE, Hon. Charles I (c.1640–1711), of Uffington, nr. Stamford, Lincs.

STAMFORD   4 Feb. 1678–1679 (Jan.), 1685–1687, 1689–22 Mar. 1711

b. c.1640, 5th s. of Montagu Bertie†, 2nd Earl of Lindsey, by his 1st w. Martha, da. of Sir William Cokayne, ld. mayor of London 1619–20, of Rushton, Northants., wid. of John Ramsey, 1st Earl of Holdernesse; bro. of Hon. Peregrine I* and half-bro. of Hon. Henry I*. *educ.* Westminster; Amersham sch. 1650; M. Temple 1658; MA Oxf. 1665, incorp. Camb. 1667; travelled abroad (France, Spain) 1660–5. *m.* 2 Sept. 1674, Mary, da. of Peter Tryon of Bulwick, Northants., wid. of Sir Samuel Jones† of Courteenhall, Northants., 1s. 1da.[1]

Lt. RN 1668; capt. 2 Ft. Gds. 1668–73; envoy extraordinary to Denmark 1671–2, to German States 1680–1; sec. to Treasury 1673–9; commr. Queen Mother's arrears 1677, appeals on excise duty 1677–9, inquiring into defects of the mint 1678–9; treasurer of Ordnance 1681–99, 1702–5; sec. to c.j. in eyre, south of Trent 1693–7; commr. Million Act 1694.[2]

Alderman, Stamford 1685–8, Boston 1685–Oct. 1688; conservator, draining and maintaining Deeping Fen 1685; freeman and bailiff, Oxford 1687.[3]

Asst. corp. to set poor to work 1691, N. W. America trading co. 1691; dir. Greenwich Hosp. 1703–?*d.*[4]

Although the last of the Berties to withdraw support for James II, Charles had taken an active part in the Revolution, and by 1690 had re-established himself at court. Most importantly, with the support of his powerful kinsman, the Marquess of Carmarthen (Sir Thomas Osborne†), he had managed to retain his office at the Ordnance under William and Mary. He had even less trouble in securing his parliamentary seat, having influenced the return at Stamford ever since his purchase of Uffington in 1673. Basking in victory after the Stamford election, he demonstrated strong High Tory principles by gloating over his defeat of a 'fanatic', which he thought 'the greatest service I can do my country'. He also confided his wish for 'a good Church of England Parliament'. At Westminster Carmarthen confirmed his Tory allegiance, and twice cited him as a Court supporter. He also marked him as an ally in December 1690, and the following April Robert Harley* listed him as a Court man. Unfortunately, his general contribution in this and other Parliaments is obscured by the presence of several kinsmen. None of his family had much of an impact on the first session, but in the second his status as a former secretary to the Treasury argues for his identification as a teller on 3 Jan. 1691 against amending an additional clause of appropriation to the bill to impose double excise duties.[5]

On the death in June 1691 of William Jephson*, secretary to the Treasury, Bertie lobbied to obtain his old place, but to no avail. This disappointment may have turned him against the Court, and it is tempting to identify him as the 'Mr Bertie' who in the ensuing two sessions made a series of recorded speeches during debates on estimates and supply, most of which were critical of government policy.

During the session of 1692-3, it was reported that Bertie, an experienced diplomat, had agreed to be sent as envoy to Denmark 'on condition he would be back by next summer'. However, although nominated to the post, he remained in this country. In November 1693 he was appointed secretary to his half-brother James, 1st Earl of Abingdon, the chief justice in eyre south of the Trent, with an annual salary of £500. Considering the discomfort which his family had caused the Court in recent sessions, this office highlighted the government's eagerness to secure his support. In the fifth and sixth sessions of Parliament he, in common with his kinsmen, was far from conspicuous, his only certain activity resting with a leave of absence granted on 8 Feb. 1694. His responsibilities at the Ordnance may well have forced him to neglect the House, and political analysts generally viewed him as a placeman, most notably Samuel Grascome, who in his list of 1693-5 classed him as a Court supporter as well. His name also appeared on a list drawn up in 1694-5 by Henry Guy*, who was possibly identifying likely allies in preparation to defend himself against attack at Westminster.[7]

Re-elected for Stamford in 1695, in December Bertie expressed concern for the position of his mentor Carmarthen (now Duke of Leeds), hoping that his affairs would 'sleep this session'. Alongside other followers of Leeds he was forecast in January 1696 as a probable opponent of the Court in connexion with the proposed council of trade, but signed the Association, and in March voted for fixing the price of guineas at 22s. However, the following November he joined with other 'Leeds Tories' in voting against the attainder of Sir John Fenwick†. In the spring of 1697 Abingdon was removed as chief justice in eyre, which dismissal probably terminated Bertie's lucrative secretaryship. Yet, despite differences with the increasingly Whig-dominated ministry, and the virtual exclusion of Leeds from the conduct of affairs, he retained his place at the Ordnance, his name appearing on lists of placemen and Court supporters in the summer of 1698. Residual tension between him and the Court was suggested by another political analyst, who forecast that he would oppose a standing army.[8]

Bertie's stance on disbandment in the ensuing Parliament is unclear, although he did not appear in the ranks of government supporters on that key issue. Tribute was paid to his standing in the House in February 1699 when he gained specific exemption from a proposed place bill. On this occasion Country Whig Member Sir Richard Cocks, 2nd Bt., sarcastically recalled Bertie's refusal to betray the recipients of secret service money under Charles II, as proof of his being 'a very honest gentleman', but such past loyalty did not secure him in office for much longer. In June 1699, with the formal departure of Leeds from the government, he was himself replaced at the Ordnance. Although now openly in opposition, he was not entirely out of favour and in September 1699 his petition for the renewal of a lease of Deeping Fen in Lincolnshire was granted, with a 48-year extension. In the course of the second session he was identified as in the 'interest' of Lord Carmarthen, and may have demonstrated estrangement from the Court by acting as teller on 10 Apr. 1700 in favour of addressing the King to remove Lord Chancellor Somers (Sir John*) from the Privy Council.[9]

Returned as usual for Stamford in February 1701, Bertie was noted as likely to support the Court over the committee of supply's resolution to continue the 'Great Mortgage'. Aside from an information concerning Ordnance accounts, his only definite action in that Parliament lay with a local measure of obvious personal import, a bill to drain Deeping Fen. More significantly, on 14 Feb. he may have told against a motion in support of the administration and its commitment to the peace of Europe. He may then have gone on the offensive against the King's former Whig ministers, since a Bertie was appointed on 1 Apr. to the committee to impeach the Earl of Portland, and told on 14 Apr. in favour of the motion that Lord Halifax (Charles Montagu*) was guilty of a high crime and misdemeanour. Charles Bertie was certainly on the attack on 29 Apr., lambasting government bribery, despite having previously 'given near £100,000 to corrupt Members', as Cocks acidly remarked. He was subsequently blacklisted as having opposed preparations for war, and at the second election of 1701 not only secured Stamford for the Tory interest, but also helped Sir Justinian Isham, 4th Bt.*, to gain a victory in Northamptonshire. In the ensuing Parliament he voted for the resolution of 26 Feb. 1702 vindicating the Commons' proceedings in the impeachments of the Whig lords.[10]

On the accession of Anne, Bertie was reappointed to his old office at the Ordnance, and wrote a letter of thanks to the Duke of Marlborough (John Churchill†), acknowledging his key role in securing him such preferment. Revelling in his restored favour, at the election of 1702 he again aided the Northamptonshire

Tories, assuring them that he was ready to 'bring all my guns with me from the Tower to level the ambition of that malevolent party'. In the first session of the Parliament he was one of the Members who thanked Dr Whincop for preaching to the House, and demonstrated Tory allegiance by voting on 13 Feb. 1703 against agreeing with the Lords' amendments to the bill to extend the time for taking the Abjuration. As a trustee for a royal estate given to the Duke of Leeds, in the next session he was probably the Charles Bertie who petitioned the House on 25 Jan. 1704 to ensure that the property would not be affected by the resumption bill, and a Bertie acted as a teller on 7 Feb. against the House going into committee on that bill. Also in the 1703–4 session, he was listed by Lord Nottingham (Daniel Finch†) as likely to support the Court in connexion with the proceedings envisaged on the Scotch Plot. In the next session he sponsored a private estate bill, and, having been forecast in October as a probable supporter of the Tack, duly voted for this High Tory measure on 28 Nov. 1704. At the end of this Parliament he lost his office, on which Dyer commented: 'the reason of the remove of this good old royalist is not said nor nobody knows but the Queen and one or two more, unless it be that for which the justices of the peace should have been removed'. Support for the Tack was almost certainly the immediate cause, as inferred by at least one observer, and Bertie himself was philosophical about his dismissal, reflecting, 'I am all obedience and resignation to her Majesty's pleasure and doubt not but she has pitched upon a more able successor than myself'.[11]

The Tack did not undermine Bertie's standing at Stamford, however, and after his return he was classed as 'True Church' in a list of 1705. He voted against the Court candidate for Speaker on 25 Oct., and his strident Anglicanism may have prompted him to speak on 8 Dec. in the debate about the dangers facing the Church. During the session of 1707–8 he was identified as a Tory, and in the succeeding Parliament he supported Robert Harley's plan to force the renewal of peace negotiations by withholding supply, writing on 28 Aug. 1709, 'the country longs for peace and thinks Tournai and its citadel are a dear bargain for six million a year, and the Dutch to reap the benefit thereof'. He opposed the impeachment of Dr Sacheverell and, after his tenth consecutive success at Stamford in 1710, was classed as a Tory on the 'Hanover list'.[12]

Bertie died on 22 Mar. 1711, in his 71st year, having suffered for nine months from a 'bad stomach'. He was buried at Uffington, where his monument paid tribute to the 'unspotted reputation' with which he had served Stamford for over 30 years. His seat in Parliament predictably passed to his son Charles, who represented the borough until 1727. Bertie's will testified to his political connexions and motivation, since he left £100 to the Duke of Leeds 'as a small instance of my gratitude and obligations', and expressed hope that his posterity would be 'firm and constant in the profession and practice of the true Protestant religion as established in the Church of England'.[13]

[1] Collins, *Peerage*, ii. 19; *Recs. Old Westminsters*, i. 83; *HMC Ancaster*, 425; *HMC Lindsey*, 269–70, 275–372; *The Ancestor*, ii. 181. [2] *CSP Dom.* 1673, p. 529; *Cal. Treas. Bks.* v. 486, 609, 663, 1204; vi. 158; x. 552; *Br. Dipl. Reps.* 1509–1688 (R. Hist. Soc.), 38, 150; H. Tomlinson, *Guns and Govt.* 225–6. [3] *CSP Dom.* 1685, pp. 39, 50; *HMC Lords*, i. 310; *Oxford Council Acts* (Oxford Hist. Soc. n.s. ii), 191. [4] *CSP Dom.* 1690–1, pp. 422, 527; 1703–4, p. 463. [5] F. E. D. Willis, *Hist. Uffington*, 43; Univ. Illinois, Misc. Eng. docs. Bertie to Edward Hubbard, 2 Mar. 1690. [6] Luttrell, *Brief Relation*, ii. 242; *Luttrell Diary*, 19, 24, 26, 32, 41, 59, 61, 75, 82, 99, 100, 103, 116, 129, 180, 182, 187, 190, 193, 197, 217, 224, 237, 254, 256, 265, 290, 386, 447. [7] Centre Kentish Stud. Stanhope mss U1590/059/2, Robert Yard* to Alexander Stanhope, 6 Dec. 1692, 31 Jan. 1693; Luttrell, iii. 231. [8] Rutland mss at Belvoir Castle, letters and pprs. xxi, Bertie to Ld. Rutland, 7 Dec. 1695. [9] *Cocks Diary*, 6; *Cal. Treas. Bks.* xiv. 56; xv. 173. [10] *Cocks Diary*, 104; Northants. RO, Isham mss IC 2718, Bertie to Isham, 17 Nov. 1701. [11] Add. 61283, f. 161; 17677 AAA, f. 213; Isham mss IC 2723A, 3712, Bertie to Isham, 27 July 1702, 16 May 1705; *HMC Portland*, iv. 190; Cumbria RO (Carlisle), Lonsdale mss D/Lons/W2/2/8, James Lowther* to Sir John Lowther, 2nd Bt. I*, 24, 27 Mar., 28 Apr. 1705. [12] *Cam. Misc.* xxiii. 48; Lincs. AO, Monson mss MM 7/12/136, Bertie to Sir John Newton, 28 Aug. 1709. [13] Boyer, *Pol. State*, i. 267; Sloane 4077, f. 84; Willis, 47–48; PCC 99 Auber.

P. W./P. L. G.

BERTIE, Hon. Charles II (1683–1727), of Chelsea, Mdx.

NEW WOODSTOCK 1705–1708

b. 1683, 6th s. of Robert Bertie†, 3rd Earl of Lindsey, being o. s. by his 3rd w. Elizabeth, da. and coh. of Thomas Pope, 2nd Earl of Downe [I], wid. of Sir Francis Henry Lee, 4th Bt.*, of Quarrendon, Bucks. and Ditchley, Oxon.; half-bro. of Hon. Albemarle*, Hon. Peregrine II*, Hon. Philip* and Robert Bertie*, Lord Willoughby de Eresby. *m.* (1) 29 Apr. 1714, Mary (*d.* 1725), da. of Thomas Browne of Addlethorpe, Lincs., and wid. of Nicholas Newcomen of Theddlethorpe, *s.p.*; (2) 13 Feb. 1726, Mary, da. of Henry Marshall, rector of Orby and Salmonby, Lincs. *s.p.*[1]

Freeman, Appleby 1698.[2]

Bertie was successful for New Woodstock in 1705 on the interest of his kinsman the 2nd Earl of Abingdon (Montagu Venables-Bertie*). Not surprisingly he espoused Abingdon's Tory principles, and voted against the Court candidate for Speaker on 25 Oct. 1705. Unfortunately, the presence of seven Berties in the House at this time makes it impossible to delineate his parliamentary activity. However, he appears to have maintained the party line, since in early 1708 two analysts identified him as a Tory. He did not stand in 1708, but at the next general election Lord Abingdon may well have made interest for him to contest Oxfordshire, although to no avail. Under Lord Oxford's (Robert Harley*) ministry he was keen for a captaincy in the foot guards, his mother reminding the treasurer that 'his principles are agreeable with yours'. He did not gain a commission, but his finances were improved by marriage to a rich widow, Mary Newcomen, on which occasion he was described as 'a gentleman remarkable for his adhesion to the loyal principles of his noble ancestors, both by father and mother, and [for] affection to her Majesty and the happy constitution in Church and state'. Neither of his wives produced an heir, and after his death on 15 Aug. 1727, his estates passed to Lord Albemarle Bertie, grandson of his half-brother Robert who was subsequently 1st Duke of Ancaster. He was buried 'decently but not pompously' at Theddlethorpe, near the resting-place of his first wife.[3]

[1]PCC 86 Auber; IGI, Lincs.; *HMC Portland*, v. 446; *Lincs. Peds.* (Harl. Soc. 51), 646, 719. [2]Cumbria RO (Kendal), Appleby bor. recs. WSMB/A min. bk. 3, 12 Sept. 1698. [3]BL, Trumbull Alphab. mss 54, Ralph Bridges to Sir William Trumbull*, 3 Apr. 1710; Add. 70177, Countess of Lindsey to Ld. Oxford, 18 Apr. [?1713]; *HMC Portland*, 446; *Hist. Reg. Chron.* 1727, p. 33; PCC 86 Auber; *Lincs. Peds.* 646.

P. W./P. L. G.

BERTIE, Charles (aft. 1674–1730), of Uffington, nr. Stamford, Lincs.

STAMFORD 2 Apr. 1711–1727

b. aft. 1674, o. s. of Hon. Charles Bertie I*. *m.* 14 Sept. 1704, Mary (with over £20,000), da. and h. of John Norborne of Great Stukeley, Hunts., 3s. 1da. *suc.* fa. 1711.[1]

Guided by his father, Bertie was politically active from at least 1702, when he became a freeholder of Northamptonshire in readiness for the county contest, and at the general election of 1705 he helped to mobilize support for the Tory candidates in that shire. It was not until 1711 that he gained a parliamentary seat, when returned on a family interest for Stamford at a by-election caused by the death of his father. The presence of several of his kinsmen in the Parliaments of 1710 and 1713 makes it impossible to establish his general contribution to Commons' business. However, he followed the lead of his kinsman, the 2nd Earl of Abingdon (Montagu Venables-Bertie*), in voting in June 1713 against the French commerce bill. He evidently did not sever all links with his party, for the Worsley list classed him as a Tory, and after 1715 he remained in opposition, voting against the septennial bill. He died on 12 Apr. 1730, leaving substantial inheritances to his younger offspring, and was succeeded by his son Charles, who did not choose a parliamentary career.[2]

[1]Luttrell, *Brief Relation*, v. 466. [2]Northants. RO, Isham mss IC 2749, 4221, Hon. Charles Bertie I to Sir Justinian Isham, 4th Bt.*, 27 July 1702, 15 May 1705; PCC 148 Auber.

P. W./P. L. G.

BERTIE, Hon. Henry I (c.1656–1734), of Chesterton, Oxon.

WESTBURY 18 Feb. 1678–1679 (Jan.)
 1679 (Oct.)–26 Nov. 1680
NEW WOODSTOCK 1681 (Mar.)
OXFORD 1685–1687, 1689–1695
WESTBURY 1701 (Dec.)–1702, 1 Dec. 1702–1715

b. c.1656, 8th s. of Montagu Bertie†, 2nd Earl of Lindsey, being 3rd s. by his 2nd w. Bridget, *suo jure* Baroness Norreys, da. and h. of Edward Wray of Rycote, groom of the bedchamber, wid. of Hon. Edward Sackville; half-bro. of Hon. Charles I* and Hon. Peregrine I*. *educ.* Padua 1674. *m.* (1) bef. 23 May 1687, Philadelphia, da. and coh. of Sir Edward Norreys*, 2s. (1 *d.v.p.*) 3da.; (2) Catherine (*d.* 1736), da. of Sir Heneage Fetherston, 1st Bt., of Stanford-le-Hope, Essex, *s.p.*[1]

Capt. Lord Gerard's Horse 1678–9; indep. tp. June–Dec. 1685; dep. constable of the Tower 1702–5.

Freeman, Oxford 1681–June 1688, Oct. 1688–?*d.*, Devizes ?–Mar. 1688.[2]

A Tory who had been unable to accept the pro-Catholic policies of James II, Bertie was returned for Oxford in 1690 on the interest of his brother, the 1st Earl of Abingdon. The continuing success of other family members at the polls hampers any attempt to determine his activity throughout his career at Westminster, and the Journals for the 1690 Parliament only specifically allude to him on the three occasions on which he was granted leave of absence. However, his politics are more certain, for at the outset of the first session he was cited by his kinsman, the Marquess of Carmarthen (Sir Thomas Osborne†) as a Tory and probable Court supporter, and Carmarthen listed him as an ally in December should he come under attack in the Commons. More equivocally, in April 1691 Robert Harley* tentatively identified him as a Country

Member. The following September Carmarthen was still willing to render him assistance, petitioning the King on his behalf:

> Sir Edmund Jennings* (who was a commissioner of prizes) is newly dead, and I know Lord Abingdon would take it as a favour to himself, if your Majesty would bestow that employment upon his brother, Mr Henry Bertie, who was at considerable expense in raising a troop of horse at your coming into England and nothing can be done more cheaply for him since it takes nothing out of your Exchequer; but it would be better for him if you would please to give him Mr [Robert] Ferguson's place [housekeeper of the excise office], who I suppose you will not think fit to continue longer in your service, after so many informations concerning him.

Unfortunately for Bertie, the letter produced no result, and he remained politically inconspicuous, although his name did appear in a list compiled by Henry Guy* in the 1694–5 session as a likely opponent of attacks on Guy in the House. Bertie did not seek re-election in 1695, not altogether surprisingly given his frequent requests to depart from the House. He did not stand in 1698 and January 1701, although he assisted (Sir) John Verney* (2nd Bt., later Viscount Fermanagh [I]) on his campaigns for election in Buckinghamshire, where Bertie was lord of the manor of Nutley. He was back at Westminster in December 1701, having been returned for Westbury on the interest of his nephew the 2nd Earl of Abingdon (Montagu Venables Bertie*). Classed as a Tory by Harley, in February 1702 Bertie supported the resolution vindicating the Commons' conduct in the impeachments of William III's Whig ministers during the preceding Parliament.[3]

On the accession of Anne, Bertie was appointed Abingdon's deputy as constable of the Tower. In the spring of 1703 he sought advancement at the Ordnance office, lobbying the Duke of Marlborough (John Churchill[†]) to become clerk of the deliveries. He was aided in this campaign by Abingdon, who thought Bertie's 'steadiness heretofore hath made it needless for anyone to answer for his truth and affection to this government', but all their efforts were in vain. Having only regained his Westbury seat on petition, he was forecast in October 1704 as a probable supporter of the Tack. However, doubts surround his vote in the division of 28 Nov., for although his name appears on two lists of Tackers, on another he is bracketed with opponents of the High Tory measure. Despite this confusion, it is clear that his identification with the Tackers brought about his dismissal in May 1705 from his office at the Tower. The controversy did not undermine his interest at Westbury, and following an unopposed victory he was classed as a 'Churchman' by an analyst of the new Parliament. He predictably voted against the Court candidate for Speaker on 25 Oct., and in the latter stages of the Parliament was twice cited as a Tory. In its successor he voted against the impeachment of Dr Sacheverell.[4]

Following victory at Westbury in 1710, Bertie was classified as a Tory in the 'Hanover list', and the following year his name appeared on the list of 'worthy patriots' who in the 1710–11 session had sought to expose the mismanagements of the previous administration. Moreover, he was celebrated as a Tory 'patriot' for opposing the continuance of the war. Having demonstrated such loyalty to the government, in October 1712 he lobbied Harley (now Lord Oxford) to promote his son James, who already had gained preferment as a manager of the lottery. However, towards the end of this Parliament Bertie followed his nephew, Abingdon, into opposition by voting on 18 June 1713 against the French commerce bill. He may well have remained in the ranks of the Hanoverian Tories, since all members of Abingdon's 'interest' were said to have opposed a motion on 15 Apr. 1714 that the Hanoverian succession was not in danger under the present ministry. On the other hand, he was later classed as a Tory *tout court* on the Worsley list. He did not put up in 1715, when his great-nephew Willoughby Bertie[†] contested Westbury, and retired from active politicking, despite having had his standing in Oxfordshire boosted by his wife's inheritance of the manor of Weston-on-the-Green. He died on 4 Dec. 1734, and although his only son Charles Montagu Bertie did not emulate his parliamentary success, his grandson Norreys Bertie[†] sat during the 1740s and 1750s.[5]

[1] PCC 258 Ockham; Collins, *Peerage*, iii. 629; *HMC Rutland*, ii. 114. [2] *Oxford Council Acts* (Oxford Hist. Soc. n.s. ii), 139; PC2/72, f. 632. [3] *CSP Dom*. 1690–1, pp. 516–17; *Verney Letters 18th Cent*. i. 161; *VCH Bucks*. iv. 42–43. [4] Add. 61283, f. 163; 61363, f. 57; Luttrell, *Brief Relation*, v. 164. [5] Add. 70279, Bertie to Oxford, 28 Oct. 1712; 47087, f. 69; *VCH Oxon*. vi. 349.

P. W./P. L. G.

BERTIE, Hon. Henry II (1675–1735).

BEAUMARIS 1705–1727

b. 4 May 1675, 3rd s. of James Bertie, 1st Earl of Abingdon, by 1st w. Eleanora, da. and h. of Sir Henry Lee, 3rd Bt., of Quarrendon, Bucks. and Ditchley, Oxon.; bro. of Hon. James*, Hon. Robert* and Montagu Venables-Bertie*, Lord Norreys. *m.* (1) 17 July 1708,

Annabella Susanna (d. 1708), da. of Hugh Hamilton, 1st Baron Hamilton of Glenawly [I], wid. of Sir John Magill, 1st Bt. [I], of Gill Hall, co. Down and Mark Trevor, 3rd Visct. Dungannon [I], s.p.; (2) 3 Oct. 1712 (with £10,000), Mary, da. of Hon. Peregrine Bertie I*, wid. of Anthony Henley*, 1da.[1]

Freeman and bailiff, Oxford 1702; ?freeman, Hertford 1703.[2]

Commr. public accts. 1711–14.

Although the younger son of a peer, Bertie was 'bred to the understanding of trade and merchandise' under the great merchant (Sir) Joseph Herne*. He does not, however, appear to have set up in business, and was returned under age for Beaumaris in 1705 on the interest of his brother-in-law the 4th Viscount Bulkeley [I] (Richard Bulkeley*). Sharing his family's Tory principles, he was appropriately classed as a 'Churchman' in a list of the new Parliament. As with all the Berties, it is difficult to trace his activity in the Commons due to the simultaneous presence of several family members, but he may be plausibly identified as a leading sponsor of Lord Bulkeley's estate bill in the first session. He voted against the Court candidate for Speaker on 25 Oct., and in early 1708 was identified as a Tory. He managed to survive an election hearing over his return at Beaumaris in 1708, and the following year was appointed 'register' for the Tory drinking club recently founded by the 2nd Duke of Beaufort, the 'Board of Brothers'. He predictably voted against the impeachment of Dr Sacheverell, and after his successful re-election at Beaumaris in 1710 was cited as a Tory on the 'Hanover list'.[3]

In March 1711 Bertie's kinsman, the Duke of Leeds (Sir Thomas Osborne†), wrote to Robert Harley* on his behalf, hoping to secure him a place on the customs commission or the Board of Trade. Significantly, Leeds was keen not 'to do him that injury as to get him nominated in the House of Commons for one of the commissioners of accounts which might perhaps be a bar to those other employments, but he is very fitly qualified for any of them'. No offer of a place being made, Bertie was duly chosen one of the commissioners on 19 Mar. 1711, taking first place in the ballot. A member of the October Club, he was listed as one of the 'worthy patriots' who in the 1710–11 session detected the mismanagements of the previous ministry. On 25 Jan. 1712, the day after the Tories had carried their vote of censure on the Duke of Marlborough (John Churchill†), he was one of the Members thanked by the Board of Brothers 'for their good attendance and service' in the House. He also distinguished himself by being the only commissioner of accounts not to vote on 6 May in favour of tacking a bill to examine royal grants onto a lottery bill. On a more personal note, he may well have carried up a bill to settle the estate of Anthony Henley, his wife's first husband. In the next session he may have put his mercantile grounding to good use by advancing economic legislation, possibly as the 'Mr Bertie' whom the Journals note as frequently involved with bills to encourage the tobacco trade and the manufacture of sail-cloth. In the key vote of 18 June 1713 he was the only Bertie who voted in favour of the French commerce bill.[4]

In the succeeding Parliament Bertie may have joined the rest of his family in voting against the Court in the 'succession in danger' debate of April 1714. Although possibly wavering in his political loyalties, he retained support within the House, finishing third on 18 June 1714 in the ballot for a new commission of accounts. Significantly, this election was seen as a victory for the October Club against the candidates promoted by (Sir) Thomas Hanmer II (4th Bt.)*. In that session Bertie may also have backed another bill to promote the tobacco trade. Soon after the accession of George I three parliamentary lists confirmed Bertie's Tory principles, but he was able to retain his seat while remaining in opposition until 1727, when he unsuccessfully challenged the Bulkeley interest. He died at Boulogne on 18 Dec. 1735.[5]

[1] Collins, *Peerage*, iii. 631; *Westminster Abbey Reg.* (Harl. Soc. x), 265; Folger Shakespeare Lib. Newdigate newsletter 7 Oct. 1712. [2] *Oxford Council Acts* (Oxf. Hist. Soc. n.s x), 12; Herts. RO, Hertford bor. recs. 25/105. [3] Add. 70250, Duke of Leeds to Robert Harley, 7 Mar. 1711; 49360, f. 3; PRO, HCA 13/81, p. 279. [4] Add. 70250, Leeds to Harley, 7 Mar. 1711; 49360, f. 100; BL, Trumbull Alphab. mss 54, John Bridges to Sir William Trumbull*, 9 May 1712. [5] Add. 47087, f. 69; NLS, Advocates' mss, Wodrow letters Quarto 8, f. 138; Boyer, *Pol. State*, l. 679.

P. W./P. L. G.

BERTIE, Hon. James (1674–1735), of Stanwell and Westminster, Mdx.

NEW WOODSTOCK   1695–1705
MIDDLESEX   1710–1734

b. 13 Mar. 1674, 2nd s. of James Bertie, 1st Earl of Abingdon by 1st w.; bro. of Hon. Henry II*, Hon. Robert* and Montagu Venables-Bertie*, Lord Norreys. m. (1) 5 Jan. 1692, Elizabeth (d. 1715), da. and event. h. of George, 7th Baron Willoughby of Parham, 10s. (5 d.v.p.) 4da. (3 d.v.p.); (2) Elizabeth, da. of Rev. George Calvert of Stanwell, s.p.[1]

Freeman and bailiff, Oxford 1695; freeman, Hertford 1704; commr. sewers, Tower Hamlets 1712, Trent navigation 1714; steward of Grosmont, Skenfrith and White Castle, duchy of Lancaster 1714–20.²

Commr. building 50 new churches 1711–15.³

Returned for New Woodstock on his father's interest, Bertie remained a Country Tory throughout the 1695 Parliament. He was forecast in January 1696 as a probable opponent of the Court in connexion with the proposed council of trade, refused the Association the following month, and voted in March against fixing the price of guineas at 22s. Furthermore, in the second session he opposed the attainder of Sir John Fenwick†. The presence of several Berties in this and all subsequent Parliaments renders difficult any attempt to delineate his Commons activity. However, in the third session Bertie gained much prominence by bringing a case before the Lords concerning property bequeathed to his wife by her great-uncle, John Cary, on condition that she married Francis North, 2nd Lord Guildford; if she did not, the estate, valued at some £2,000 p.a. and including the manor of Stanwell, Middlesex, was to go to Cary's great-nephew, the 6th Viscount Falkland. The case was heard in Chancery in February 1698 and a decree made in Falkland's favour. Bertie appealed to the Lords, who on 17 Mar. 1698 decided to grant the lands to Mrs Bertie for life, with the reversion to Lord Falkland, thereby providing Bertie with a proprietorial interest in Middlesex. Some observers clearly thought he had been fortunate to gain this settlement, and he was also lucky to avoid censure for the libellous paper which his brother Robert* had circulated to advance the Bertie cause. He had no difficulty in retaining his seat at the election of 1698, after which he was listed as a Country supporter, and was probably forecast as likely to oppose a standing army. Moreover, in the course of the second session he was predictably identified as a follower of his kinsman, the Duke of Leeds (Sir Thomas Osborne†).⁴

In February 1701 Bertie was noted as likely to support the Court in agreeing with the committee of supply's resolution to continue the 'Great Mortgage'. Re-elected at the end of the year despite being blacklisted as an opponent of preparations for war with France, he voted on 26 Feb. 1702 in favour of the resolution vindicating the Commons' proceedings in the impeachments of William III's ministers in the preceding Parliament. Having topped the Woodstock poll of 1702, he was later forecast as a probable supporter of the Tack, and duly voted for it on 28 Nov. 1704. He did not stand in 1705, apparently content to allow his kinsman Hon. Charles Bertie II to take over his seat at Woodstock, but cast his vote for the Tory candidates at the Middlesex contest. An analyst of the new Parliament, mistakenly identifying James as one of the Members for Woodstock, cited him as 'True Church', possibly confusing him with Charles Bertie. James did not put up in 1708 either, probably cowed by the growing influence of the Duke of Marlborough (John Churchill†) in the Oxfordshire borough.⁵

At the general election of 1710 Bertie successfully contested Middlesex in the High Church interest, and also voted Tory at the Hertford contest. He was duly classed as a Tory in the 'Hanover list', and his name later appeared among the 'worthy patriots' who in the session of 1710–11 had detected the mismanagements of the previous administration. In addition, he was lauded as a Tory 'patriot' for having opposed the continuance of the war. Given his politics and constituency, he may also have been the 'Mr Bertie' who was first-named to the Tory-backed petition of Southwark inhabitants complaining of the influx of Palatine refugees into their neighbourhood. In the succeeding session he was appointed to the drafting committee on a bill to repair a highway in Middlesex, which argues for his identification as the main sponsor of the Stanmore highway bill. In February 1712 he was listed as a member of the October Club, but in 1713 followed his brother, the 2nd Earl of Abingdon (Montagu Venables-Bertie) in voting against the ministry over the French commerce bill.⁶

Despite such apostasy, Bertie stood in the Tory interest at the Middlesex election of 1713, and achieved an unopposed victory. With three other 'Mr Berties' in the House, it is again difficult to trace his activity, but in the second session he may well have assisted legislation concerning the capital and its environs. In particular, on 5 Mar. 1714 he possibly told against a motion to hear the petition of the losing Whig candidates for London. Local connexions may have led him to act as a teller in two other election contests, on 16 Mar. against the return of the Whig (Sir) Thomas Wheate (1st Bt.) at New Woodstock, and on 3 July against the election at Southwark of John Lade, a recent convert to Whig ranks. He may also have sponsored a Kensington highway bill, and chaired committees of the whole on the navigation of the Thames.

Following a third successive victory for Middlesex in 1715, he was classed on the Worsley list as a Tory who had sometimes voted against his party, no doubt in reference to his vote on the French commerce bill. However, two other parliamentary lists bracketed him with the Tories, and he continued to oppose Whig policies. Although he lost his Stanwell estate on his wife's death in 1715, his personal interest in Middlesex was sufficiently strong to keep him at Westminster until the election before his death on 18 Oct. 1735. His heir, Willoughby, briefly sat for Westbury, and in 1743 succeeded as 3rd Earl of Abingdon.[7]

[1] F. G. Lee, *Church of Thame*, 445; Collins, *Peerage*, iii. 630; PCC 49 Derby; Lysons, *Hist. Acct. Mdx. Parishes*, 264–5. [2] *Oxford Council Acts* (Oxford Hist. Soc. n.s. ii), 257; Herts. RO, Hertford bor. recs. 25/106; *HMC Townshend*, 211; *HMC Lords*, n.s. x. 366; Somerville, *Duchy of Lancaster Official Lists*, 233. [3] *London Rec. Soc.* xxiii. 177. [4] *CSP Dom.* 1698, pp. 149, 150–1, 161; Luttrell, *Brief Relation*, iv. 337, 341, 356; *HMC Lords*, n.s. iii. 92–96; *The Gen.* xxiii. 202–6; Northants. RO, Montagu (Boughton) mss 46/84, James Vernon I* to Duke of Shrewsbury, 17 Mar. 1698. [5] *Mdx. Poll of 1705*. [6] Hertford bor. recs. 23/392b. [7] *VCH Mdx.* iii. 37.

P. W./P. L. G.

BERTIE, Montagu *see* **VENABLES-BERTIE, Montagu,** Ld. Norreys

BERTIE, Hon. Peregrine I (c.1634–1701), of York Buildings, Westminster, Mdx. and Waldershare, Kent.

STAMFORD	21 Oct. 1665–1679 (Jan.), 1685–1687
WESTBURY	1689–1695

b. c.1634, 2nd s. of Montagu Bertie[†], 2nd Earl of Lindsey, by 1st w.; bro. of Hon. Charles I* and half-bro. of Hon. Henry I*. *educ.* travelled abroad 1649–?54. *m.* lic. 23 Feb. 1674, aged 30, Susan (*d.* 1697), da. and coh. of Sir Edward Monyns, 2nd Bt., of Waldershare, 3da. (1 *d.v.p.*)[1]

Vol. (French army) 1654; cornet, R. Horse Gds. (The Blues) 1661, lt. 1667, capt. 1676–9.[2]

Commr. accts. loyal and indigent officers 1671, alienations 1675–*d.*[3]

Receiver of taxes, Kent 1677–8; alderman, Stamford and Boston 1685–Oct. 1688; freeman and bailiff, Oxford 1687.[4]

Bertie was returned for Westbury in 1690 on the interest of his half-brother, the 1st Earl of Abingdon, and in the course of the Parliament was thrice bracketed with supporters of the government by his brother-in-law, the Marquess of Carmarthen (Sir Thomas Osborne[†]), who also classed him as a Tory. Moreover, in December 1690 Carmarthen identified him as an ally in case of an attack on his own ministerial position in the Commons, and in the following April Robert Harley* listed him as a Court man. Unfortunately, the presence of so many Berties in this Parliament makes it impossible to delineate his Commons activity with any confidence. More generally, his career was overshadowed by that of his nephew Hon. Peregrine II, who was clearly a more prominent figure at Westminster. In the course of 1692–3 political observers classed him as a placeman, although in Samuel Grascome's list of 1693–5 he was cited as an office-holder who did not support the Court. Such a move into opposition mirrored that of his brother Hon. Charles Bertie I, and may be attributed to the influence of Carmarthen, who had drifted apart from other ministerial Tories. This breach was not permanent, however, judging by his advice to his brother, the 3rd Earl of Lindsey (Robert Bertie[†]), in November 1694 that Charles should use his interest at a Stamford by-election in the hope of making 'the Court look upon him with better eyes'. He did not stand again, allowing his nephew Hon. Robert Bertie to succeed to his seat at Westbury. He died on 3 Jan. 1701, and was buried at Waldershare. Significantly, his will suggests that he remained on good terms with the Duke of Leeds (formerly Carmarthen), and testifies to considerable wealth, he having provided each of his two surviving daughters with dowries of £10,000.[5]

[1] PCC 2 Dyer; Collins, *Peerage*, ii. 19; *CSP Dom.* 1649–50, p. 537; *The Topographer*, i. 16–17; *Canterbury Mar. Lics.* iii. 42. [2] *The Topographer*, 17; *CSP Dom.* 1679–80, p. 325. [3] *CSP Dom.* 1671, p. 255; *Cal. Treas. Bks.* iv. 326; xvi. 41. [4] *Cal. Treas. Bks.* v. 430; *CSP Dom.* 1685, pp. 39, 50; *Oxford Council Acts 1675–1701* (Oxford Hist. Soc. n.s. ii), 191. [5] *HMC Ancaster*, 436; Luttrell, *Brief Relation*, v. 2; PCC 2 Dyer.

P. W./P. L. G.

BERTIE, Hon. Peregrine II (c.1663–1711), of Great Marlborough Street, Westminster, Mdx.

BOSTON	1685–1687, 8 May 1690–1698
	1701 (Dec.)–1705
TRURO	30 Nov. 1705–1708
BOSTON	1708–10 July 1711

b. c.1663, 2nd s. of Robert Bertie[†], 3rd Earl of Lindsey, by his 2nd w.; bro. of Hon. Albemarle*, Hon. Philip* and Robert Bertie*, Lord Willoughby de Eresby, and half-bro. of Hon. Charles II*. *educ.* M. Temple 1679; Oxf. DCL 1702. *unm.* at least 2da. illegit. by 'Mrs Elizabeth Allen'.[1]

Cornet, indep. tp. of Horse 1685; vice-chamberlain to Queen Mary 1692–Feb. 1694, to King William Feb. 1694–1702, to Queen Anne 1702–6; PC 5 May 1695–*d.*; receiver, rents of duchy of Lancaster, Lincs. 1696–*d.*; teller of Exchequer 1706–*d.*[2]

Alderman, Boston 1685–Oct. 1688; ?freeman, Hertford 1703.[3]

Asst. Co. for making saltpetre 1692; commr. taking subscriptions to S. Sea Co. 1711.[4]

Bertie was a politician of independent mind, a placeman who often voted against the government, and ready to serve under Whig and Tory administrations. To observers such as Arthur Maynwaring*, he was an unscrupulous courtier, 'extreme envious and uneasy if anybody is taken notice of in any way whatever'. His political opportunism was exemplified by his return at a by-election at Boston in 1690, when, in order to consolidate the Tory interest of his father, he sought the aid of his kinsman, the Whig grandee Hon. Thomas Wharton*, to win Nonconformist votes. Another relation, the Marquess of Carmarthen (Sir Thomas Osborne†), listed him as a Court supporter at the outset of the Parliament, an assessment in which Robert Harley* concurred in April 1691. Bertie's contribution to the business of the House is less certain, thanks to the presence there of several relations, in particular his uncle Peregrine I. During the Parliament he was eager for office, and in August 1691 Carmarthen petitioned the King to secure him appointment as guidon in the guards. He does not appear to have obtained the post, but the Court's favour towards him was demonstrated in March 1692, when he replaced John Grobham Howe* as vice-chamberlain to Queen Mary. His name subsequently appeared on several lists of placemen.[5]

Despite his tenure of a crown office, Bertie often supported opposition measures in Parliament. In the 1692–3 session he took an active part in the debates on the naval failures of the previous summer, and only offered conditional support for the administration on 30 Nov., remarking:

> it is agreed by most that there is a coldness to this government, if not treachery. I doubt not there are several men in this King's councils that are not true to him, though I cannot name them. But such a general address I think not for your service, and, therefore, I am for searching into particulars.

During a debate on 20 Dec. on a motion of thanks to Admiral Edward Russell*, which developed into a Whig attack on Secretary Nottingham (Daniel Finch†), he recommended that since there were obviously divisions within the government, the House should advise the King 'to consult only with men of one principle and interest'. Earlier that month he had backed a motion to adjourn a committee on the supply, and had spoken against committing the bill for preserving their Majesties' persons and government. On 11 Jan. 1693 he broke with the placemen to speak in favour of a motion to address the King to appoint as Admiralty commissioners only men experienced in maritime affairs. Nine days later he joined Howe in drawing attention to Bishop Burnet's *Pastoral Letter*, as containing much dangerous matter, and subsequently spoke in favour of having the pamphlet burnt. He presumably was the 'Mr Bertie junior' who on 2 Feb. backed the motion of Sir Thomas Clarges* that pressing men into military service was against the rights of the subject. Moreover, on the same day he was probably the 'Mr Bertie (the younger)' who supported the triennial bill. In the remainder of the session Mr Bertie jnr. twice contributed to debate, backing on 8 Mar. the expulsion from the Commons of William Culliford, and two days later joining Hon. John Granville's call for the House to examine the appropriation of supplies granted in this session. This may have represented a significant switch of political loyalties on Bertie's part, for Granville's motion was aimed at exposing recent royal gifts to Carmarthen.[6]

In the next session Bertie continued to be a thorn in the government's side, speaking on 26 Jan. 1694 in favour of a motion that those who had advised the rejection of the place bill were enemies to King and country. Significantly, in Samuel Grascome's list of 1693–5 he was classed as a placeman who did not support the Court. Perhaps in an attempt to strengthen his wavering allegiance, or as a token of a more general reassurance to the Bertie family, in view of the Court's shift to the Whigs, he was appointed vice-chamberlain to the King in February 1694, with an additional £600 p.a. in salary. The following July it was reported that he fought a duel with the Whig peer Lord Cholmondeley, 'occasioned by some words' in public, but he continued to find favour at the increasingly Whig-dominated Court, being added in May 1695 to the Privy Council. Another sign of his rapprochement with the government was his membership of the Rose Club, which probably reflected his close connexion with its leader Thomas Wharton. His name also appeared in a list of 1694–5 compiled by Henry Guy* of his likely supporters in the Commons.[7]

Continuing to represent Boston in 1695, Bertie was classed as 'doubtful' in a forecast for the division of 31 Jan. 1696 on the proposed council of trade, although he was seen as more likely to oppose than support the Court. None the less, he signed the Association on 27 Feb., and may well have been one of 'two great courtiers' who spoke against a motion that Louis XIV and James II were behind the Assassination Plot, on grounds that 'it had not yet appeared so to the House'. The following month he voted with the Court on fixing the price of guineas at 22s., and in early April carried a message from the King for the House to attend him, a task he also fulfilled in the next session.[8]

The session of 1696–7 was most significant for the Bertie family, as Carmarthen led several of its members into opposition over the attainder of Sir John Fenwick†. However, the stance of the vice-chamberlain is less easy to discern. On 17 Nov. Bertie contributed to the debate on the best way of questioning Fenwick, but although one source suggests that he spoke in favour of the bill of attainder, he is recorded as voting against it in the key division of 25 Nov. More puzzlingly still, according to James Vernon I*, he simply 'went away' when the House divided. Whichever version was correct, the King was certainly displeased with him, for during a discussion with the Duke of Shrewsbury and Lord Sunderland in April 1697, William reportedly remarked that 'the whole family of the Berties were against him and declared himself not satisfied even with the vice-chamberlain, but Lord Sunderland excused him'. At that time L'Hermitage, the Dutch agent, expected him to lose his place, commenting:

> Le Sieur Bertie . . . sera ôté à ce qu'on dit de sa place; le roi n'en a point dit la raison, mais quoi qu'il fût au nombre des officiers de S. M[ajeste] il a paru si peu d'attachement à son service, en s'opposant dans la chambre des communes à tout ce qui lui étoit favorable, qu'on ne doute pas que cela n'en soit la cause.

The rumours of dismissal, however, appear to have influenced Bertie to change his ways. He managed to retain his office, and in about September 1698 he was listed as a member of the Court party. He did not stand in the election of that year or in February 1701, possibly due to differences with his father, who remained a Tory. However, following the death of the 3rd Earl, he came back to the House in December 1701, when his return was regarded by Lord Spencer (Charles*) as a gain for the Whigs. His only discernible action of note was to pass to the Commons the King's answer to an address concerning military quotas.[9]

Despite Bertie's Whiggish inclinations, Queen Anne retained him as her vice-chamberlain in 1702, although 'Jack' Howe was said to have refused the post, a report later corroborated by Maynwaring. In the first Parliament of her reign Bertie was forecast as a probable opponent of the Tack but did not vote in the division on 28 Nov. 1704. At the ensuing general election he was said to have 'lost' at Boston, and was brought in at a by-election for Truro on the interest of Hugh Boscawen II*. Once back in the House he was appointed to the committee for the conference on the Lords' address that the Church was not in danger, supported the Court in February 1706 on the 'place clause' of the regency bill, and in the latter stages of the Parliament was twice classed as a Whig. Outside the Commons he was busy politicking, exchanging his office of vice-chamberlain in December 1706 for a lucrative tellership of the Exchequer. According to Maynwaring, Bertie was not content with this post, and was constantly on the look-out for an appointment for life. Always critical of the activities of Bertie, whom he called 'Old Vice', Maynwaring was scornful of such endeavours, and was prepared to tell him to his face that

> if I should ever have any interest I would not for £3,000 employ it so ill as to put him out of the power of those that should oblige him, for I believed the next thing he would do would be to hang them if he could. That he would, to be sure, he said, if they deserved it: why else should he desire to be at liberty?

Bertie did not gain his objective, and also declined to purchase Maynwaring's office of auditor of the imprests, about which they negotiated for some time.[10]

At the general election of 1708 Bertie was able to regain his seat at Boston, a success which argues for his identification as the Member who in the first session aided the progress of the Boston church bill. Moreover, he may have managed a bill to confirm the title of his brother, the Marquess of Lindsey (formerly Robert Bertie, Lord Willoughby de Eresby), to part of Havering Park in Essex. He remained politically consistent, voting for the impeachment of Dr Sacheverell in early 1710. Shortly after the end of the session he was active in the campaign to raise his brother to a dukedom, making a personal plea to the Queen to advance him, but to no avail.[11]

Anticipating the end of the ailing Whig administration, as early as May 1710 Bertie claimed to be 'so far engaged' with the Tories. Worryingly for him, at that time rumours also circulated that he would be dismissed, but he did manage to keep his place. He cannot have endeared himself to Harley by acting for Lindsey in an unsuccessful attempt in 1711 to prevent the new lord treasurer taking the title of Earl of Oxford, which the Berties claimed to lie in their family. Maynwaring suggested that Bertie actually had designs on the title himself, 'but now his concern for his place keeps him silent'. Before the dispute could have any effect on his position at court, Bertie died 'suddenly' on 10 July 1711, 'being seized, as he was playing at cards, with a dead palsy'. Opinion was divided on his qualities, Macky thinking him 'a fine gentleman', who had 'both wit and learning', on which Swift commented, 'I never observed a grain of either'. His personal life was not without its controversy either, for he left his estate in trust for a Mrs Elizabeth Allen, 'commonly called Mrs Poltney', and his two daughters by her. Another report insisted that he had 'several children male and female', but none rose to prominence.[12]

[1] PCC 143 Young; Collins, *Peerage*, ii. 20. [2] Somerville, *Duchy of Lancaster Official Lists*, 190. [3] *CSP Dom.* 1685, p. 50; Herts. RO, Hertford bor. recs. 25/105. [4] *Sel. Charters*, 235; Pittis, *Present Parl.* 347. [5] Add. 61459, f. 97; Bodl. Rawl. lett. 51, f. 142; *CSP Dom.* 1690–1, p. 502; A. Browning, *Danby*, i. 497. [6] *Luttrell Diary*, 276, 287, 318, 331, 364, 377, 381, 397–8, 471, 475. [7] Grey, x. 377; Wood, *Life and Times*, iii. 444; *Cal. Treas. Bks.* x. 580; Centre Kentish Stud. Stanhope mss U1590/059/3, Robert Yard* to Alexander Stanhope, 17 July 1694; H. Horwitz, *Parl. and Pol. Wm. III*, 209, 220. [8] *HMC Kenyon*, 405. [9] Oldmixon, *Hist. Eng.* 152; *Vernon–Shrewsbury Letters*, i. 82; *Shrewsbury Corresp.* 479; Add. 17677 RR, f. 302. [10] DZA, Bonet despatch 17/28 Apr. 1702; Add. 61460, ff. 52, 202–3; 61459, f. 97; Northants. RO, Isham mss IC 2749, Hon. Charles Bertie I* to Sir Justinian Isham, 4th Bt.*, 13 May 1705; Luttrell, *Brief Relation*, vi. 113. [11] *Duchess of Marlborough Corresp.* i. 322. [12] Add. 61460, ff. 202–3; 61461, ff. 124–5; HMC Portland, iv. 689; *Top. and Gen.* iii. 383; *Hearne Colls.* iii. 193; *Macky Mems.* 73; *Swift Works* ed. Davis, v. 259; PCC 143 Young.

P. W./P. L. G.

BERTIE, Peregrine, Lord Willoughby de Eresby (1686–1742).

LINCOLNSHIRE 1708–1715

b. 29 Apr. 1686, 2nd but 1st surv. s. of Robert Bertie*, Lord Willoughby de Eresby (subsequently 4th Earl of Lindsey), by 1st w.; half-bro. of Lord Robert† and Lord Vere†. *m.* June 1711, Jane (with £40,000), da. and coh. of Sir John Brownlow, 3rd Bt.*, 3s. 4da. *summ.* to Lords in his fa.'s barony of Willoughby de Eresby 16 Mar. 1715; *suc.* fa. as 2nd Duke of Ancaster 26 July 1723.[1]

Ld. of bedchamber to George I 1719–27; ld. great chamberlain 1723–*d.*; receiver, duchy of Lancaster rents, Lincs. 1728–*d.*; ld. warden and c.j. in eyre north of Trent 1734–*d.*[2]

Ld. lt. Lincs. 1724–*d.*

Bertie did not become heir apparent to the earldom of Lindsey until 1704, on the death of his elder brother Robert. Quick to take advantage of his father's influence in Lincolnshire, at the age of 22 he successfully contested the county alongside the Whig George Whichcot. By 1708 his father (now Marquess of Lindsey) had switched allegiances to become a Whig supporter, but Bertie's subsequent parliamentary career suggests strong Tory loyalties. His activity in the first session reflected his party's principles, since he was appointed to the drafting committee on the Boston church bill, and to the committee of inquiry into the laws excluding placemen. In addition, he acted as a teller on two occasions, on 20 Jan. 1709 against the return of the Whig William Hucks* at Abingdon, and on 9 Mar. in favour of the House going into committee on the bill on the tobacco trade. In the second session he was nominated to the committee to examine the arrangements for the trial of Dr Sacheverell, and later voted against the impeachment.

Bertie's victory at the Lincolnshire election of 1710 clearly owed much to High Church support, and he was subsequently classed as a Tory in the 'Hanover list'. Furthermore, he was included among the 'worthy patriots' who in the first session detected the mismanagements of the previous administration, and was identified as a 'Tory patriot' for opposing the continuance of the war in 1711. He was also a member of the October Club. Remaining a fairly active Member, he told on 20 Dec. 1710 against an amendment to a supply bill. His concern to advance local issues is evident in his appointment to drafting committees for bills to erect a waterworks near Boston and to aid the drainage of Ancholme Level. On 13 June 1712 he delivered to the Commons a message from his father, the lord great chamberlain, concerning extra rooms to be fitted up for the service of the House.

Having gained an unopposed victory at the Lincolnshire election of 1713, Bertie made little contribution to Commons' business in the new Parliament. However, he appears to have joined with the Hanoverian Tories, voting in March 1714 against the expulsion of Richard Steele. Such a stance probably explains why the Worsley list bracketed him with the Whigs. He did not stand for the county at the general election of 1715, but on 16 Mar. 1715 was called to the Lords in his father's barony of Willoughby de Eresby. On the death of his father eight years later he became Duke of Ancaster, assumed the hereditary title of lord great chamberlain, and thereafter proved a steady supporter of the administration. From his ancestral seats at Grimsthorpe and Eresby he maintained extensive influence in Lincolnshire until his death on 1 Jan. 1742, and one of his younger sons subsequently sat for the county under George III.[3]

[1] Boyer, *Pol. State*, i–ii. 450; MI, Edenham par. ch. Lincs. [2] Somerville, *Duchy of Lancaster Official Lists*, 190; *Cal. Treas. Bks. and Pprs.* 1731–4, p. 567; 1742–5, p. 398. [3] Info. from Dr C. Jones.

P. W./P. L. G.

BERTIE, Hon. Philip (c.1665–1728), of Hayfield, Lancs.

Stamford   6 Dec. 1694–1698

b. c.1665, 3rd s. of Robert Bertie†, 3rd Earl of Lindsey by 2nd w.; bro. of Hon. Albemarle*, Hon. Peregrine II*, Robert Bertie*, Lord Willoughby de Eresby, and half-bro. of Hon. Charles II*. *educ.* Trinity, Oxf. matric. 7 Feb. 1683, aged 18, BA 1685. *m.* lic. 8 Aug. 1711, Lady Elizabeth, da. and coh. of William Brabazon, 3rd Earl of Meath [I], formerly w. of Sir Philips Coote of Mount Coote, co. Limerick, *s.p.*[1]

Capt. vol. ft. co. of scholars 1685; capt. Earl of Danby's (Peregrine Osborne†) vol. regt. Drag. 1690; gent. usher of privy chamber to Queen Mary by 1691–4; auditor, duchy of Cornwall 1692–1704; commr. Million Act 1694, to inspect the drawing of lots 1694.[2]

Asst. Co. for making saltpetre 1692.[3]

During the Monmouth rebellion Bertie demonstrated his allegiance to James II by training a foot company of scholars from Trinity, Lincoln and Wadham Colleges in Oxford. At that time he appears to have had designs on a fellowship at All Souls, and although unsuccessful, was commended by his proud father for 'his dutiful deportment and ... his industrious endeavours to make himself considerable'. In January 1686, on the death of his uncle Richard Bertie†, Lord Lindsey contacted Lord Abingdon about the possibility of Philip standing at New Woodstock, but no by-election occurred. At the Revolution he was involved in the northern rising with his kinsman, the Earl of Danby (Sir Thomas Osborne†), who described him in a letter to William as one of the Prince's own 'domestic servants'. This may refer to the place of gentleman usher to Queen Mary, which by 1691 was held by 'Philip Bertue'. In 1692 he was a contender for the office of vice-chamberlain to the Queen, but the post went to his brother Peregrine II. However, in the same year his loyalty to William was rewarded with the auditorship of the duchy of Cornwall. The standing of his brother, Lord Willoughby de Eresby, as chancellor of the duchy of Lancaster, encouraged him to make interest for a by-election at Clitheroe in 1693, although he desisted through lack of support. The following year he resolved to stand at Stamford, on the advice of his uncle, Peregrine Bertie I*, who wrote to his father, Lindsey, on 26 Nov.:

> I question not but your interest will help him to carry it, for my brother Charles [Bertie I*], though he has not declared yet, will be for him. It is a thing that if he carries, may be of great advantage to him, and make the court look upon him with better eyes ... Pray be not shy in this affair, for it will be the greatest advantage to your son in the world, and to yourself a no little one to put so many sons into the House.

He was duly returned, though not before having spent some £250 on entertaining the electorate, and, in common with the four other Berties in the House, failed to make an impact in the last session of the 1695 Parliament. However, soon after entering the House he was identified by Henry Guy* as one of his likely supporters against an attack in the Lower House. After Queen Mary's death Bertie's salary of £200 p.a. as one of her gentlemen ushers was continued as a pension, and he received further preferment as one of the managers of the Million Act, worth an annual £100.[4]

Re-elected for Stamford in 1695, Bertie was classed as doubtful in a forecast of one of the divisions on the proposed council of trade in January 1696, but, like the other Leeds Tories, he signed the Association in February and voted with the Court in March on fixing the price of guineas at 22*s*. However, the following November he voted against the attainder of Sir John Fenwick†. His attitude to the Court during the remainder of this Parliament is unclear, particularly as the presence of so many family members in the Commons obscures his parliamentary activity. Although the King showed his displeasure towards the Berties in 1697 by dismissing Bertie's brother, Lord Willoughby, and his father's half-brother, the 1st Earl of Abingdon, he himself retained office as auditor. He did not contest Stamford in 1698, when the Berties and the Cecils agreed to share the seats, but the auditorship may have prompted him to stand at Liskeard, where a Bertie finished fourth in the poll. Although outside Parliament, he was subsequently classed as a Court supporter by an analyst of the old and new Commons.[5]

In February 1699 Bertie was sued in King's bench by Sir Philips Coote upon 'an action of trespass for lying with his [Coote's] wife; and the jury found for the plaintiff and gave him £300 damages'. Bertie subsequently married the lady. He successfully petitioned in May 1701 for the continuation of his pension, after a cancelling order had been issued the previous January. He tried to re-enter Parliament in December 1701 for Mitchell, but the auditorship did not give him sufficient interest to carry the election. In May 1704 he was replaced as auditor by his Whig brother, Hon. Albemarle Bertie*, and later found 'difficulty' in receiving his pension, which fell into arrears. In

November 1711 he petitioned Lord Oxford (Robert Harley*) to set matters aright, hoping for 'better things from your lordship'. In order to further his cause, he reminded the lord treasurer of his candidacy at a forthcoming by-election at Boston, remarking how 'expense attends unpopularity', but then lost the contest, and was forced to petition the House. His stepmother, the dowager Countess of Lindsey, subsequently begged Viscount Fermanagh [I] (John Verney*), to be present at the elections committee hearing and

> to show him [Bertie] what kindness may be consistent with your own honour and justice. When his father was living, his principles were High Church, and he tells me he is so still ... If your lordship takes notice that I speak knowingly of Philip in his father's time, and only now say what he tells me of himself, the reason is, that the late differences between me and Lord Lindsey [Robert Bertie, Lord Willoughby de Eresby] made me, in kindness to him, advise him to compliment his brother so far, to keep at a distance with me, which was what I found he [Lindsey] expected from those who would be well with him, as it was necessary for his own younger brothers to be.

The committee decided in Bertie's favour, but the House declared the election void because of the intervention of Bertie's brother, Lindsey, lord lieutenant of the county. Bertie stood at the ensuing by-election, unsuccessfully, and again petitioned. The committee declared neither candidate elected, but the Commons disagreed and confirmed the return of the sitting Member, William Cotesworth.[6]

In November 1713 Bertie was still seeking the patronage of Lord Treasurer Oxford, enthusing: 'I am so happy now to be more and more an ally; you will please not to let me suffer with my own family (for want of either post or pension) in the vindicating your lordship's honour.' The letter produced no result. In March 1714 he passed to Oxford a memorial detailing alleged abuses in the Mint, at the same time requesting to be considered for the wardenship if it should become vacant as a result of these disclosures. This plea was likewise fruitless. He did not sit in Parliament after 1715 and died on 15 Apr. 1728. Having produced no heir, he left his brother Albemarle an estate in Liverpool, and bequeathed to charity 'a great interest' in the abortive Bootle waterworks of Sir Cleave More, 2nd Bt.*, as well as lands in Lincolnshire and Somerset.[7]

[1] Lodge, *Peerage of Ire*. i. 189; *Mar. Lic. Fac. Off.* (Brit. Rec. Soc. xxxiii), 263; PCC 139 Brook. [2]*Cal. Treas. Bks*. ix. 1817; x. 983, 1034; xvii. 727; xix. 239. [3]*Sel. Charters*, 235. [4]Wood, *Life and Times*, iii. 149; Bodl. Eng. Lett. e. 129, ff. 112, 118–19; *HMC 14th Rep. IX*, 453; Miege, *State of Great Britain* (1691), iii. 164; Luttrell, *Brief Relation*, ii. 390; *HMC Kenyon*, 273, 274, 275; Lincs. AO, Ancaster mss 3 ANC 8/1/17, Stamford election expenses, 6 Dec. 1694; *Cal. Treas. Bks*. x. 1034; *HMC 13th Rep. VI*, 250. [5]Carew mss at Antony House, BO/23/72/?, Liskeard poll 1698. [6]Luttrell, iv. 483; *Cal. Treas. Bks*. xvi. 41, 70; xix. 239; Add. 70278, Bertie to Oxford, 18 Nov. 1711; *Verney Letters 18th Cent*. i. 309. [7]Add. 70210, same to same, 17 Nov., 10 Dec. 1713, 27 Mar. 1714; Boyer, *Pol. State*, xxxv. 415; PCC 139 Brook.

P. W./P. L. G.

BERTIE, Robert, Lord Willoughby de Eresby (1660–1723).

BOSTON   1685–1687, 1689–1690
BOSTON AND PRESTON   1690–19 Apr. 1690

b. 20 Oct. 1660, 1st s. of Robert Bertie[†], 3rd Earl of Lindsey, by his 2nd w.; bro. of Hon. Albemarle*, Hon. Peregrine II* and Hon. Philip*, and half-bro. of Hon. Charles II*. *m*. (1) 30 July 1678, Mary (*d*. 1689), da. and h. of Sir Richard Wynn, 4th Bt.[†], of Gwydir, Caern., 5s. (1 *d.v.p*.) 3da.; (2) 6 July 1705, Albinia, da. of Thomas Farrington*, 4s. 1da. *summ*. to Lords in his fa.'s barony of Willoughby de Eresby 19 Apr. 1690; *suc*. fa. as 4th Earl of Lindsey 8 May 1701; *cr*. Mq. of Lindsey 21 Dec. 1706, Duke of Ancaster 26 July 1715.[1]

Freeman, Denbigh 1679; recorder, Boston 1685–Sept. 1688, Oct. 1688–*d*.; ld. lt. Lincs. 1700–*d*.[2]

Capt. Robert Werden's[†] Horse June–Dec. 1685.[3]

Chancellor, duchy of Lancaster 1689–97; ld. great chamberlain 1701–*d*.; PC 19 June 1701–*d*.; ld. justice 1715.[4]

Bertie had taken part in the northern rising led by his kinsman, the Earl of Danby (Sir Thomas Osborne[†]), in favour of William of Orange in 1688. His loyalty was duly rewarded with the chancellorship of the duchy of Lancaster, a post which enabled him to secure a seat at Preston at the general election of 1690. He was also returned for Boston on the interest of his father. During the first session he was classed as a Court supporter by Carmarthen (formerly Danby), but was only in the Commons a few weeks before being summoned to the Lords in his father's barony of Willoughby de Eresby to strengthen the Lord President's following there. He proved an ally of the Court in the Upper House, opposing the place bill in the 1692–3 session. He signed the Association, but went into opposition in 1696 during the controversy over the attainder of Sir John Fenwick[†], and was turned out of the chancellorship of the duchy of Lancaster the following year.[5]

In 1701 Bertie succeeded his father to the earldom,

and the hereditary office of lord great chamberlain. At the start of Anne's reign he was still a Tory, and remained so until at least December 1703, when he supported the second occasional conformity bill. 'Having of late taken up the profession of a Whig', at the general election of 1705 he turned his back on his former county allies, and was later rewarded with a marquessate. Despite this elevation he did not become a prominent politician, with Macky commenting that he 'doth not trouble himself with affairs of state'. However, he did make interest to secure a dukedom, and was ridiculed for such efforts by Arthur Maynwaring*, who described him as 'odious'. He did not return to Tory ranks after the ministerial changes of 1710, and later quarrelled with Robert Harley* over the rights to the earldom of Oxford, which Lindsey insisted lay dormant in his own family. His Whiggish allegiance eventually brought him a dukedom after the accession of George I. He died 26 July 1723, and was succeeded by his son, Lord Willoughby de Eresby (Peregrine Bertie*), who executed part of his grandiose plan for the rebuilding of Grimsthorpe. The family's enduring local influence ensured that two of his sons by his second marriage, Lord Robert and Lord Vere, gained seats at Boston.[6]

[1] MI Edenham par. ch. Lincs. [2] J. Williams, *Recs. of Denbigh*, 138; *CSP Dom.* 1685, p. 50. [3] *CSP Dom.* 1685, p. 412. [4] Somerville, *Duchy of Lancaster Official Lists*, 3. [5] A. Browning, *Danby*, i. 401, 538; *Peers, Pol. and Power* ed. C. and D. L. Jones, 109. [6] G. Holmes, *Pol. in Age of Anne*, 430; Lincs. AO, Massingberd mss 20/51, Burrell to Sir William Massingberd, 2nd Bt., 1 Feb. 1705; *Macky Mems.* 73; *Duchess of Marlborough Corresp.* i. 322; *HMC Ancaster*, 442–3; Pevsner, *Lincs.* 347–8.

P. W./P. L. G.

BERTIE, Hon. Robert (1677–1710), of Benham Valence, Berks.

WESTBURY 1695–1702, 1 Dec. 1702–1708

b. 28 Feb. 1677, 4th s. of James Bertie, 1st Earl of Abingdon, by 1st w.; bro. of Hon. Henry II*, Hon. James* and Montagu Venables-Bertie*, Lord Norreys. *educ.* New Coll. Oxf. 1693; M. Temple 1696, called 1700. *m.* lic. 13 Jan. 1709, Catherine, da. of Richard Wenman†, 4th Visct. Wenman of Tuam [I], *s.p.*[1]

Freeman and bailiff, Oxford 1699; recorder, Hertford 1701–*d.*, freeman 1703.[2]

Counsel for the duchy of Lancaster and steward in Oxon. and Berks. 1703–*d.*[3]

Bertie's enviable family connexions catapulted him into public life at the age of 19, when he was returned at Westbury on his father's interest. Until at least the following year he continued his studies in Oxford, whence an acquaintance enthused about his suitability for a career in the law, observing that 'he has capacity enough for it, and a steady resolution to pursue it'. The presence of no fewer than five Berties in the 1695 Parliament obscures his Commons activity, although occasionally the Journals do allude to his contribution. In his first session he was predictably keen to serve his university, carrying up a bill to secure the payment of impropriated tithes to Balliol College. A Tory in politics, he was listed as a probable opponent of the Court in a forecast of a division on 31 Jan. 1696 over the proposed council of trade, refused to sign the Association the following month, and in March voted against fixing the price of guineas at 22*s*. Moreover, in the next session he voted against the attainder of Sir John Fenwick†. No doubt at the behest of his constituents, soon afterwards he showed particular interest in the textile trade, sponsoring a bill for encouraging woollen manufacture, and acting as a teller on 20 Mar. 1697 on a question concerning a conference with the Lords on the bill to restrain the wearing of imported silks. He was also active in securing the services of Dr Lancaster to preach the sermon to mark the anniversary of the death of Charles I.[4]

In July 1697 Bertie fought a duel over a lady, but wrote to assure his father that he would never marry without his approval. He was involved in further trouble in March 1698, when he drew up a paper to aid his brother, James Bertie, in a dispute with Lord Falkland, which ultimately led to a hearing in the Lords. Robert's paper, an abstract of the case, contained an attack on Lord Chancellor Somers (Sir John*), who on 17 Mar. drew it to the attention of the Lords. The Upper House pronounced it to be a 'false, scandalous and malicious libel', and a message was sent to the Commons requesting leave for Bertie to appear before them. The Lower House decided that the Lords should first be requested to specify the grounds on which they wanted to examine him, and a dispute between the two Houses was only prevented by the Earl of Abingdon apologizing to the chancellor and the Lords on behalf of his son. This was accepted and the paper was ordered to be burnt by the common hangman.[5]

Bertie won re-election for Westbury in 1698, and soon afterwards was classified as a Country supporter, and probably forecast as likely to oppose a standing army. In the opening session he may well have played a prominent role in promoting the Blackwell Hall restoration bill, an issue of great significance for the Wiltshire cloth trade. During the next session he possibly played an important role in advancing the bill to repeal the Act banning the import of bone-lace, a measure desired by Salisbury clothiers. Not surprisingly, in early 1700 he was bracketed with the 'interest' of his kinsman, the Duke of Leeds (Sir Thomas Osborne†). Following another unopposed victory at Westbury, in February 1701 he was listed as likely to support the Court over the 'Great Mortgage', and was later blacklisted as having opposed preparations for war. Returned for Westbury alongside his uncle Hon. Henry Bertie I in November, he was classed by Robert Harley* as a Tory, and voted for the resolution vindicating the Commons' proceedings in the preceding Parliament over the impeachments of Whig ministers.[6]

Although defeated at Westbury in 1702, Bertie was seated on petition. His discernible contribution to Commons' business in that Parliament is confined to two drafting committees. In the third session he voted on 28 Nov. 1704 for the Tack, and was listed as 'True Church' in an analysis of the Membership in 1705. In the new Parliament he voted on 25 Oct. against the Court candidate for Speaker, and was the principal manager of a private bill to settle a cleric's estate. Moreover, he may have been the Bertie who on 23 Nov. acted as a teller in support of an adjournment of the committee on the Hertford election. In the latter stages of the Parliament he was identified as a Tory, but his political activity was curtailed by family matters, since on 4 Feb. 1708 he was granted a six-week leave of absence. Possibly still distracted by personal affairs, he reportedly did 'not care to stand' for Westbury in 1708. Uncertainty surrounds his subsequent parliamentary ambitions, for he died shortly before the next general election. Although the date of his demise is usually cited as 16 Aug. 1710, his death was actually noted by Dyer on 8 Aug., who recorded the cause to be 'a dead palsy'. His recent marriage had produced no offspring, and he left his estate to his wife, whom he praised for 'having been so extraordinary kind and civil to me'.[7]

[1] PCC 263 Smith; F. G. Lee, *Church of Thame*, 445; Collins, *Peerage*, iii. 631. [2] *Oxford Council Acts* (Oxford Hist. Soc. n.s. ii), 287; Herts. RO, Hertford bor. recs. 1/76, 25/105. [3] Somerville, *Duchy of Lancaster Official Lists*, 56, 220. [4] Bodl. Ballard 11, f. 135. [5] *HMC Var.* ii. 344; *LJ*, xvi. 236–8, 240, 241, 244, 246, 247–8; *CSP Dom.* 1698, pp. 149, 150–1, 154, 161, 236–8, 241–2; *HMC Lords*, n.s. iii. 92–96. [6] Ballard 39, f. 131. [7] Hertford bor. recs. 25/315; *HMC Bath*, i. 190; Add. 70421, Dyer's newsletter 8 Aug. 1710; PCC 263 Smith.

P. W./P. L. G.

BETHELL, Hugh (c.1648–1717), of Rise, Yorks.

HEDON 3 Dec. 1695–1700

b. c.1648, 2nd s. of John Bethell of Skirlaugh, Yorks. by Mary, da. of Richard Hildyard of Ottringham, Yorks. *m.* (1) Mary (*d.* 1684), da. of Edward Skinner of Thornton, Lincs., 3da. (2 *d.v.p.*); (2) settlement 17 Dec. 1690, Sarah, da. and coh. of William Dickenson of Watton Abbey, Yorks., 2s. (1 *d.v.p.*) 3da. (1 *d.v.p.*). *suc.* uncle Sir Hugh Bethell† at Rise 1679.[1]

Mayor, Hedon 1683–4.[2]

Bethell was the nephew of Sir Hugh Bethell, a Parliamentarian, who represented Hedon in the Convention of 1660 and in the Cavalier Parliament, and founded a charity for the poor of the borough. In August 1688 James II's agents considered that Bethell would be suitable to serve as a justice for the East Riding. He was returned for Hedon, in which borough his family had an interest, at a by-election in December 1695. However, Bethell was not an active Member, though his name was included in several parliamentary lists. He was classed as doubtful in the forecast of the divisions on the proposed council of trade on 31 Jan. 1696, and he signed the Association promptly. On 7 Apr. he was granted leave of absence. In the following session, on 25 Nov., he voted for the attainder of Sir John Fenwick†. Although he had initially been classed as a member of the Country party in a comparison of the old and new Commons in 1698, an addendum to the list queried this classification. In an analysis of the House into interests in early 1700 he was classed as an adherent of the Junto. Added to the East Riding lieutenancy in December 1699, he obtained from the crown in 1700 a fresh 99-year lease of the manor of Hempholme, which he had inherited from his uncle. He did not stand for election in 1701, seemingly due to opposition to his candidature from Henry Guy*, who represented the dominant interest in Hedon. Bethell did not sit in Parliament again, though he continued to be active in county commissions. He died on 2 Feb. 1717, aged 68, and was buried at Rise. By his will the sole heir to the estate was his son, Hugh. Apart from token bequests to his three surviving daughters, he left £200 to his cousin Robert Bethell, £500 to the poor of Rise, £5 to the poor of Walton, and, to the poor of 11 other parishes, at £12 per parish.[3]

[1] *Dugdale's Vis. Yorks.* ed. Clay, iii. 471–2; Poulson, *Holderness*, i. 409; Borthwick Inst. York, wills, prerog. court, Aug. 1717. [2] G. R. Park, *Hedon*, 96–97. [3] Duckett, *Penal Laws and Test Act* (1882), 59; *CSP Dom.* 1699–1700, p. 310; Nottingham Univ. Lib. Portland (Harley) mss Pw2 Hy819, Guy to [Robert Harley*], 9 Aug; *HMC Portland*, iv. 304; *Cal. Treas. Bks.* xv. 311, 327, 349; Clay, 472; Borthwick Inst. York, wills, prerog. court, Aug. 1717.

E. C./C. I. M.

BETTESWORTH, Peter (1676–1738), of Brockenhurst, Hants.

PETERSFIELD 1698–1700

bap. 21 Nov. 1676, o. s. of Peter Bettesworth of Chidden, Hants by his 2nd w. Elizabeth, da. of Elias Roberts of Hayes, Mdx. *educ.* travelled abroad (Holland) 1693. *m.* 14 July 1698, Sandys, da. of Sir James Worsley of Pylewell, Hants, sis. of Sir James Worsley, 5th Bt.*, 1s. *suc.* fa. 1689.[1]

Capt. William Evans' Ft. 1706–13, half-pay, 1713; a.d.c. to ld. lt. [I] 1716–17; maj. and capt. regt. of George, Lord Forrester (later 30 Ft.), 1717, lt.-col. 1718–32; dep. gov. Jersey by 1738.[2]

Freeman, Lymington 1705.[3]

Descended from a junior branch of the Bettesworths of Fyning, Sussex, Bettesworth's grandfather settled at Chidden about ten miles from Petersfield. Bettesworth's uncle, Thomas Bettesworth, was a captain in Colonel Richard Norton's* regiment in the Parliamentary army, and was appointed governor of Calshot Castle, near Southampton, in the 1650s. His father, a younger son, was admitted to Lincoln's Inn in 1649 and lived there until at least 1670, later returning to Chidden, and serving as a major in the Hampshire militia in the reign of Charles II. His will, dated 17 Dec. 1683 and proved 9 Jan. 1689, directed all his lands at Chidden and whatever of the personalty necessary to be sold to pay his debts, and named his good friends Lieutenant-Colonel Richard Norton and Richard Holt* as trustees of the will and guardians of his son. Although he was distantly related to the Bilson family of West Mapledurham, who possessed electoral influence in Petersfield, Bettesworth's connexion to Holt was probably the more important influence. In the summer of 1693, no doubt as part of his education, Bettesworth made a journey to Holland in the company of Holt and Charles Mompesson*. Holt may also have arranged Bettesworth's marriage into one of the more prominent Hampshire families in July 1698 and in the same year he retired in favour of Bettesworth at Petersfield.[4]

Returned unopposed, Bettesworth was classed as a member of the Country party in a comparative analysis of the old and new Parliaments drawn up in about September 1698 but did not vote on 8 Jan. 1699 for the bill for disbanding the army. No significant parliamentary activity is recorded for Bettesworth and an analysis of the House into interests in January–May 1700 could only mark him as doubtful, or, possibly, as opposition. However, his vote in the 1705 Hampshire elections, when he plumped for one Whig candidate, Thomas Jervoise*, indicates his political sympathies. He did not stand at any subsequent election, and thereafter seems to have run into financial difficulties. In 1706 he applied for an army captaincy, describing himself in a letter to the Duke of Marlborough (John Churchill†) as 'a gentleman of a good estate and family in the county of Southampton and who has served his country as MP and j.p. with good reputation'. The request was successful and he obtained a company in a regiment of foot. On 15 Dec. 1709 he successfully petitioned the Lords for a bill enabling him to sell lands in Hambledon which had been settled on his wife at their marriage, and to raise £1,600 out of the tithes of Kirdford in Sussex to discharge his debts and settle an estate at Kirdford on his family. The bill received the Royal Assent on 27 Feb. 1710. His regiment was disbanded in 1713 and he endured a spell on half pay until he was appointed in 1716 to the staff of the Irish lord justices and subsequently given the lieutenant-colonelcy of a foot regiment. He was eventually made deputy governor of Jersey, where he died on 13 Feb. 1738.[5]

[1] IGI, Hants; Berry, *Hants Gen.* 208; *Mar. Lic. Vicar-Gen.* (Harl. Soc. xxiii), 105, 174; *CSP. Dom.* 1693, p. 236; PCC admon. Apr. 1738; PCC 2 Ent. [2] *Gent. Mag.* 1738, p. 109. [3] E. King, *Old Times Revisited, Lymington*, 192. [4] Berry, 208; G. N. Godwin, *Civil War in Hampshire*, 232–3, 311–12, 318, 368, 378; *Black Bks. L. Inn*, ii. 404; *L. Inn Adm.* 259; *Mar. Lic. Vicar-Gen.* 105, 174; *CSP. Dom.* 1678–80, p. 60; 1693, p. 236; PCC 2 Ent; *Vis. Suss.* (Harl. Soc. lxxxix), 10–11. [5] *Hants Poll 1705* (IHR), 56; Dalton, *Army of Geo. I*, ii. 156n; *HMC Lords*, n.s. viii. 321; *LJ*, xix. 19–20; *Gent. Mag.* 1738, p. 109.

P. W./S. M. W.

BETTS, William (*d.*1738), of Epsom, Surr.

WEYMOUTH AND
MELCOMBE REGIS   1710–17 Mar. 1711,
18 Apr.–22 May 1711
1713–3 June 1714,
1715–7 May 1730

unm.

Dir. E.I. Co. 1709–11.

Nothing has been discovered of Betts's parentage. He was raised by the family of George Dodington* of Eastbury in Dorset. The reason for this circumstance, however, remains unclear. In adulthood Betts became a highly successful London merchant and financier. He was invited by local Whigs to contest Weymouth in 1710 and was returned after a contest, being classed in the 'Hanover list' as 'doubtful', although he was certainly a Whig. On 8 Feb. 1711 he told in the disputed election for Aberdeen Burghs. His own election was declared void on 17 Mar., following allegations of bribery and treating. He fought the ensuing by-election and came top of the poll, only to be unseated on petition. The same month he was one of the victorious Whig candidates in the elections to the directorate of the East India Company, and by this time held some £4,000 worth of Bank of England stock. In 1713 he contested Weymouth for the third time, being again elected at the poll and unseated on petition (3 June 1714). He had shown his party colours by voting against the expulsion of Richard Steele on 18 Mar. 1714. Classed as a Whig in the Worsley list and two other comparative analyses of the 1713 and 1715 Parliaments, Betts continued to represent Weymouth until 1730, when he lost his seat on a technicality. He died on 14 Mar. 1738, leaving £5,000 to George Bubb Dodington[†] and £2,000 to Thomas Wyndham of Tale, both of whom were nephews of George Dodington, and a further £1,000 to one of Dodington's closest political allies, John Tucker[†].[1]

[1] *Hist. Reg. Chron.* 1738, p. 11; *Cal. Treas. Bks.* xiv. 59; xx. 572; xxv. 614; Egerton 3357 (unfol).; PCC 56 Brodrepp.

P. W.

BICKERSTAFFE, Philip (1639–?1714), of Chirton, Northumb.

BERWICK-UPON-TWEED   1685–1687
NORTHUMBERLAND   1689–1698

bap. 28 Nov. 1639, 3rd s. of Haward Bickerstaffe of Chelsham, Surr. by Elizabeth, da. of Rowlands Watkins of Usk, Mon., wid. of Philip Barrett of Hampstead, Mdx. *m.* 24 Oct. 1675, Jane (*d.* 1694), wid. of John Clark[†] of Chirton, *s.p.*[1]

Clerk of the scullery by 1662, woodyard to 1683, poultry, ordinary 1683–5, supernumerary 1685–*d.*; ensign, Admiralty Regt. 1664, lt. 1665–78, capt. (Duke of York's Ft.) 1678–9.[2]

Freeman, Newcastle-upon-Tyne 1684; member, hostmen's co. of Newcastle-upon-Tyne 1684; common councilman, Berwick-upon-Tweed 1685–Oct. 1688.[3]

During the reign of Charles II Bickerstaffe made a career as a soldier and minor office-holder at court, and through a fortunate marriage acquired lands in Northumberland which, presumably, explains his resignation from the army in 1679. He continued to enjoy royal favour during the 1680s and responded with loyalty to both Charles and James II. At the Revolution he nevertheless played an important part on the Orangist side in securing the surrender of Tynemouth garrison, and kept his office as clerk of the poultry throughout the next two reigns. In 1690 Bickerstaffe retained the Northumberland seat he had held in the Convention, and in March was classed as a Tory and Court supporter by Lord Carmarthen (Sir Thomas Osborne[†]). Bickerstaffe proved to be an active Member of the 1690 Parliament, serving as teller on a wide range of issues. His partisan loyalties were clearly demonstrated in April. On the 14th he told on the Tory side in a division upon the Plympton Erle election case and later the same month, on the 24th, against a Whig amendment to the address thanking the King for the changes in the London lieutenancy. He also opposed the abjuration bill, one report of the debate of the 26th upon this measure recording that 'Captain Bickerstaffe [was] against it, because it will divide the nation'. After this bill had been rejected, he was nominated, on the 29th, to draft a bill to secure the government. However, Bickerstaffe's activity extended beyond party matters. On 15 May he reported from a committee concerned with a petition requesting payment of arrears owed for the quartering of the army in 1677. His interest in this issue possibly arose from the question of the debts owed to the Northumberland garrison towns of Tynemouth and Berwick-upon-Tweed. Bickerstaffe also reported, on two occasions, the bill to discourage the import of thrown silk, and was ordered to carry this measure to the Lords (10, 12, 13 May). The extent of his activity is clear from the fact that he told on a further seven occasions during this session, including for the second reading of the bill settling a charity for the maintenance of 'several scholars' at Oxford (23 Apr.); for passing the bill reversing the quo warranto against London (8 May); in favour of proceeding with the bill vesting the £500 forfeitures in the crown (9, 14 May); for an amendment to the bill vesting the hereditary revenue in the crown (16 May); and in favour of the Tory interpretation of the Aldborough franchise (17 May).[4]

In October 1690 Bickerstaffe assisted in the management of an estate bill (22, 28 Oct.), and his first tellership of the session came on the 28th when he told in favour of the House going into a committee of the whole upon the land tax. On 1 Nov. he told against hearing the counsel of those accused of breaching a Member's privilege and, after being appointed on 25 Nov. to consider another petition concerning arrears owed from the raising of the army in 1677, on 29 Nov. he told against amending the instruction to the committee on the bill attainting rebels so that it covered those Irish Protestants who since 8 July 1690 had acted under James II in civil as well as military offices. The following month his tellerships included those against engrossing the bill reversing the judgment of *scandalum magnatum* against John Arnold* (1 Dec.); against adjourning the debate upon a Tory petition complaining of the activities of the Whig lord mayor of London (11th); and for appropriating £100,000 of the yield of duties on East India goods to the use of the navy (15th). During December Bickerstaffe was included on a list of Lord Carmarthen's, probably of those likely to support the lord president in the event of a Commons' attack upon him, and he also chaired the committee concerned with the Earl of Ailesbury's (Thomas Bruce†) estate bill. A notable aspect of Bickerstaffe's activity in this session was his telling on the Tory side in five divisions upon disputed elections. His interest in the resolution of election cases was also evident in his tellerships against the engrossment and passage of the bill for the speedier determining of elections (27, 31 Dec.). His last significant act of the session was to tell, on 2 Jan. 1691, for the second reading of the bill establishing a court of inquiry for the relief of London orphans. In April 1691 he was classed as a Court supporter in Robert Harley's* analysis of the House.[5]

The 1691–2 session saw little let-up in Bickerstaffe's parliamentary activity. Before Christmas he was nominated to three drafting committees and twice told on the Tory side in divisions upon disputed elections. His first significant act of the new year was to tell, on 8 Jan. 1692, for the committal of the bill to reduce interest rates. During the debate five days later on the report from the conference concerning the Lords' amendments to the treason trials bill Bickerstaffe supported amending one of the measure's clauses in a manner which the Lords had suggested at this conference. Later the same month he told on the Tory side in the Chippenham election case (22nd), and for an amendment to the Dover harbour bill (25th). On the 28th his request to bring up a petition from an Irish Catholic office-holder who desired to be exempted from the Irish Oaths Act was refused. Having presented, on 2 Feb., another petition concerning arrears relating to the army raised in 1677, Bickerstaffe was appointed to the committee considering this petition. Three days later he told in favour of deleting from the bill vesting forfeited Irish estates in their Majesties a clause concerning entailed estates, and on 8 Feb. procured an additional clause to this bill intended to 'save the usher of the court of chancery' in Ireland. As the session drew to a close Bickerstaffe also demonstrated his support for it confirming the charters of Cambridge University, speaking for it on 19 Feb. and telling three days later for its passage.[6]

On 10 Nov. 1692 Bickerstaffe seconded the motion for the Address and was duly appointed to prepare it. Five days later he drew to the attention of the House an alleged breach of privilege against Sir John Bland, 4th Bt., and on 18 Nov. he told for the committal of the treason trials bill. His continuing support for the Court was evident on 8 Dec. during the debate of the committee on the advice to the King when he moved that a select committee be appointed to examine ways to supply the army abroad while reducing the outflow of the kingdom's coin, being named on the 12th to the resultant committee. During the sitting of the ways and means committee five days later it was his concern for Northumberland's best interest which was evident in his support for raising the land tax by monthly assessment rather than pound rate. Bickerstaffe's Toryism was demonstrated on 14 Dec. when he told against a Whig-promoted abjuration bill, and was again in evidence six days later when he spoke in opposition to John Smith I's motion praising Edward Russell's* actions as admiral, an implicit criticism of the Tory secretary of state Lord Nottingham (Daniel Finch†). In the new year Bickerstaffe paid further attention to the land tax bill. On 10 Jan. 1693 he spoke against a proposal from Sir William Strickland, 3rd Bt., to suspend the payment of pensions for the duration of the war, and later the same day told in favour of amending the clause of this bill relating to the payment of victualling office bills. Two days later he spoke against Hugh Boscawen I's proposal to disable land tax commissioners acting for parishes in which they were resident. His concern for financial legislation was also evident on 10 Feb. when he opposed Paul Foley I's proposal for a tax on shipping, informing Members of his opinion that 'there was enough upon shipping and trade already'. Bickerstaffe told on two further occasions in this session, for committing the bill to increase timber in the New Forest (8 Feb.), and in favour of passing an estate bill (1 Mar.). In the spring of 1693 he was listed as a placeman by Samuel Grascome, who also classed him as a Court supporter in an analysis of the House.[7]

Presumably as a consequence of his high level of parliamentary activity, Bickerstaffe was the third-named Member of the privileges and elections committee appointed on 7 Nov. 1693, and throughout the following two sessions frequently acted as teller. He told on nine occasions in the 1693–4 session, the most significant of which were against the clause of the triennial bill stating that a Parliament would be judged to have been held irrespective of the passage of any judgment or legislation (22 Dec.); against an amendment to the land tax bill relating to the payment of victuals (18 Jan. 1694); against retaining the words of oath upon payment of the salt duty (17 Mar.); and on the Tory side in the Clitheroe election case (17 Apr.). On 9 Feb. the House was informed, during consideration of William Jephson's* secret service accounts, that in 1692 Bickerstaffe had been paid £105 in respect of three and a half years' salary for his court place. His first tellership during the 1694-5 session came on 20 Dec. 1694 when he told against bringing up a clause to the tunnage and poundage bill, and in the new year he guided a bill for the recovery of small tithes through its early Commons stages. Otherwise, his recorded contribution to the Commons was again limited to tellerships. He told on three occasions during the passage of the glass duty bill (13, 19, 22 Apr.), and his Tory sentiments and support for the Court were evident in three further tellerships during April: against committing an abjuration bill to a committee of the whole (15th); against putting the question to expel Henry Guy (17th); and for recommitting the bill to reverse the attainder of the New York radical Jacob Leisler (30th).

In October 1695 it was suggested that 'anybody that might stand' would be able to defeat Bickerstaffe at the forthcoming Northumberland election, a conviction that probably stemmed from the mounting financial difficulties that earlier in the year had forced him to convey a significant part of his Northumberland estate to the holder of its mortgage. However, no electoral challenge was mounted and Bickerstaffe was returned unopposed. His first significant nomination of the Parliament came on 2 Dec. when he was appointed to draft another bill for the recovery of small tithes, a bill he subsequently guided through its Commons' stages. The 1695-6 session also saw him manage a bill to prevent theft and rapine in the north of England. Bickerstaffe told on nine occasions during this session, and both his Toryism and growing alienation from an increasingly Junto-dominated ministry are evident from a number of these tellerships. On 10 Dec. he told against a motion to recoin at both the old weight and fineness, indicating his support for a devaluation of the coinage. The significance of his next tellership on this issue, on 1 Jan. 1696, and in favour of appointing the following Friday for a committee of the whole to examine how to prevent the recoinage dislocating trade, is difficult to discern, but on 21 Jan. he acted against the Court by telling in favour of instructing the committee upon the bill to encourage milled money and plate to be brought to the Mint to consider the price of guineas. This opposition to the ministry was emphasized on 26 Mar., when he told against incorporating into this bill a clause setting the price of guineas at 22s. Bickerstaffe's political realignment was also made clear over another of the session's most pressing issues, the council of trade. He was forecast as likely to oppose the Court in the divisions of 31 Jan. upon this matter, and on this date told against Hon. Thomas Wharton's clause that Members be excluded from serving as commissioners of trade. That he had not taken his opposition to extremes was, however, evident from his prompt signing of the Association. During this session Bickerstaffe told a further four times including against an amendment, which would have undermined the joint-stock nature of the East India Company, to a resolution on the East India trade (11 Feb.); for an amendment to the affirmation bill requiring Quakers seeking the benefit of this measure to obtain a certificate from their congregation (10 Mar.); and for adjourning consideration of the bill regulating abuses relating to garbling spices (17 Apr.). The 1695-6 session was, however, to be the last in which Bickerstaffe played an active role in Commons' business. In the following session he voted, on 25 Nov., against the attainder of Sir John Fenwick†, but told on only three occasions: against reading the report on abuses in prisons (27 Jan. 1697); against committing the bill to admit merchants to the freedom of the Russian Company (15 Feb.); and against engrossing the wine duty bill (3 Apr.). The decline in his parliamentary profile may have been due to his alienation from the Court, but it may also have been a consequence of his increasing financial problems caused by his unsuccessful participation, in partnership with his elder brother, in the coal trade. In September 1697 he was called before the lords justices to account for money he had received to pay for the quartering of troops at Tynemouth but had failed to distribute, and in the following month it was noted that 'Capt. Bickerstaffe's interest re. Northum[berland] . . . is only valid and lasting as long as he meets with no opposition'. During the final session of the Parliament, Bickerstaffe was absent on 31 Mar. 1698 when a petition relating to him was presented to the House. He had returned to the Commons by 2 Apr. when the petition was read and Bickerstaffe was heard in response, and he told on three occasions in the later stages of the session: against a resolution calling for a coal duty (7 Apr.); for receiving a petition from Northumberland relating to copper coin (5 May); and for receiving a petition from the landlords of Suffolk Place, Southwark (6 May). Bickerstaffe did not contest the 1698 election, and a comparison of the old and new Houses in about September classed him as a Court supporter 'out' of the new House.[8]

Bickerstaffe never stood for election again, his energies probably being focused upon his financial difficulties. In September 1698 James Vernon I* reported that Bickerstaffe had 'had the misfortune to be seized in the Temple by bailiffs, who ran him into prison, and it will be hard for him to get out again, he having such a load of debts upon him'. It was no doubt to satisfy these debts that in 1699 Bickerstaffe sold his estate at Chirton to Sir William Blackett, 1st Bt.* Bickerstaffe's mining venture at Gateshead and Whickham, Durham continued to drain his coffers and was probably the main cause of his imprisonment in the Fleet for debt, recorded in 1710. At this time he was described as a merchant, perhaps indicating that he had diversified his economic activity in an attempt to improve his fortunes. This is also suggested by a petition to the crown in June 1714 from a man who had been imprisoned for five years having stood surety for Bickerstaffe in shipping salt from Berwick-upon-Tweed. The date of Bickerstaffe's death is unknown. He was alive in 1714 when his sister-in-law left him £10 to buy mourning, though a petition to the crown of June the same year refers to the 'late Captain Bickerstaffe'.[9]

[1] *Mems. St. Margaret's Westminster*, 162; PCC 14 Fairfax; Bradney, *Mon.* iii. 76; Manning and Bray, *Surr.* ii. 424; *New Hist. Northumb.* iv. 241. [2] SP 29/60/122; *HMC Ormonde*, n.s. iv. 659; vii. 185, 415; LS 13/231/5. [3] *Reg. of Freemen* (Newcastle-upon-Tyne Rec. Soc. iii), 103; *Newcastle-upon-Tyne Hostmen's Co.* (Surtees Soc. cv), 272; *CSP Dom.* 1685, p. 67; 1686–7, p. 231. [4] *New Hist. Northumb.* iv. 241; viii. 322; Bodl. Rawl. A.79, f. 79. [5] Wilts. RO, Ailesbury mss 1300/856 A2, cttee. list, 26 Dec. 1690. [6] *Luttrell Diary*, 128, 160, 168, 178, 194. [7] Ibid. 215, 302, 312, 359, 365, 417; Grey, x. 292. [8] Add. 70018, ff. 94–95, 217; *New Hist. Northumb.* iv. 241; H. Horwitz, *Parl. and Pol. Wm. III*, 164; E. Hughes, *N. Country Life*, i. 162–3; *CSP Dom.* 1697, p. 359. [9] Add. 40773, f. 28; *New Hist. Northumb.* viii. 322; Hughes, 162–3; *Le Neve's Knights* (Harl. Soc. viii), 378; PCC 166 Whitfield; *Cal. Treas. Bks.* xxviii. 309.

E. C./R. D. H.

BIDDULPH, Sir Michael, 2nd Bt. (1654–1718), of Elmshurst, Staffs. and Westcombe, Kent.

LICHFIELD 1679 (Mar.)–1681 (Mar.), 1689–1690
1695–1700, 1701 (Dec.)–1705
1708–1710

bap. 18 May 1654, 1st s. of Sir Theophilus Biddulph, 1st Bt.†, of Elmshurst, by Susanna, da. of Zachary Highlord, Skinner, of Hart Street, London and Morden, Surr. *educ.* St. Paul's; Christ's, Camb. adm. 2 Dec. 1670, aged 16. *m.* (1) 31 Dec. 1678 (with £8,000), Henrietta Maria (d. 1689), da. of Roger Whitley*, 1s. 2da.; (2) 7 Mar. 1698, Elizabeth (d. 1740), da. of William Doyley, Milliner, of St. Martin's-in-the-Fields, Westminster, 3da. *suc.* fa. as 2nd Bt. 25 Mar. 1683.[1]

Both Biddulph's father and uncle sat for Lichfield in the Restoration period. Biddulph succeeded to their interest and sat (as an inactive Member) during the three Exclusion Parliaments and the Convention of 1689. Locally he was more active, attending a meeting of gentry on 29 Nov. 1688 to consider how they should act in the wake of William's invasion and signing an address to James II on 4 Dec. asking him to remove all non-qualified people from civil and military posts. At the election of 1690 he was soundly defeated by the sitting Member, Robert Burdett, and Richard Dyott*, both of them vigorous Churchmen. However, he maintained an interest in Lichfield and was the first person to whom Secretary of State Nottingham (Daniel Finch†) wrote in 1692 to investigate a report of disaffection in the city. He regained his seat at the 1695 election, possibly as a result of an agreement, because Dyott did not stand.[2]

Back in Parliament, Biddulph was a consistent supporter of the Court, albeit once again an inactive one. Although originally classed as doubtful in the forecast of a division on 31 Jan. 1696 on the proposed council of trade, his name was later transferred to those supporting the Court. He signed the Association in February and voted for fixing the price of guineas at 22s. in March. In the following session he voted on 25 Nov. 1696 for the attainder of Sir John Fenwick†. After he had been re-elected in company with Dyott in 1698, the return was challenged by a more committed Whig, Humphrey Wyrley, but the petition never emerged from committee. On a comparative analysis of the old and new Parliaments undertaken in about September 1698 he was confirmed as a Court supporter. Rather intriguingly, on an analysis of the House undertaken between January and May 1700 he was not assigned to any interest, but marked with a query and the name of his brother-in-law Sir John Mainwaring, 2nd Bt.* The inference that he could be influenced by Mainwaring was reinforced by a comment made after the election of January 1701, that he was 'a poor weak man of very mean understanding and so consequently easily led away by the nose by his friends of whom Sir John Mainwaring, knight of the shire for Cheshire, has the most predominant power over him'. At this election Biddulph had suffered a surprise defeat in a four-way contest, possibly owing to his insufficient attention to essential electioneering tactics such as the provision of ale. Nevertheless, much confidence was expressed that the election of William Walmisley* would be overturned by the House and Biddulph returned at the ensuing by-election. The remark quoted above was made in the context of a manoeuvre to persuade Biddulph to desist in favour of Thomas Coke* or James Stanhope*. In the event, Walmisley survived, albeit fortuitously.³

Biddulph was certainly keen to re-enter the House, because following his defeat in January 1701 he promised that he would 'always vote as Dyott does'. This declaration was probably sufficient to unite Biddulph with Dyott for the election of November 1701. It may also explain why, in an analysis of the new Parliament, Robert Harley* marked him among those either of doubtful party allegiance or absent. A more plausible explanation is that he was unable or unwilling to attend the Commons due to the growing furore surrounding Morgan Whitley (his wife's cousin) and his debts to the crown as receiver-general of Cheshire and North Wales, for which Biddulph and Mainwaring were sureties. According to a report laid before the Commons by William Lowndes* on 19 Jan. 1702, the debt totalled £43,000, which even after deductions amounted to approximately £25,000. As early as July 1700 the Treasury had ordered an extent to be placed on Whitley's effects following information from Biddulph. Nevertheless, by February 1702 Biddulph was facing severe financial penalties for Whitley's failings, while in March some of Mainwaring's enemies in the House moved to examine Whitley in the hope that the receiver would implicate Mainwaring as the man holding the balance due to the crown.⁴

Despite facing a challenge from Sir Henry Gough* (presumably because he had broken his resolution to vote in the Commons 'with Dyott'), and an increasingly bleak financial future, Biddulph was re-elected for Lichfield on 6 Aug. 1702. At that time he was in gaol in Stafford, which forced the 'magistrates' of the city to visit the sheriff on the 8th 'to demand him for their Member'. His detention was probably the result of financial difficulties engendered by an agreement made between Biddulph, Mainwaring and the Treasury on 27 Feb. 1702 to secure Whitley's release in return for a payment of £3,850 into the Exchequer (plus a tally of £3,400) and for allowing judgment to be entered against their bonds. Lord Treasurer Godolphin (Sidney†) had confirmed this arrangement on 27 May. In August 1702 Biddulph petitioned the Treasury for a discharge from prison to enable him to raise £800 to pay off part of the debt. His major ally in this approach was the newly appointed chancellor of the duchy of Lancaster, Sir John Leveson Gower, 5th Bt.*, a Staffordshire landowner. Both (Sir) Charles Lyttelton† (3rd Bt.) and Lord Stanhope attributed Biddulph's eventual release in October 1702 to Leveson Gower's influence, Stanhope in critical terms, as it thwarted the hopes of Gough's early return to Parliament at a by-election. However, Biddulph evidently feared re-arrest, for Lyttelton reported on 16 Jan. 1703 that 'Sir Michael Biddulph though he be of the House, never comes there, and lodges incognito'. Nevertheless, he may have found it expedient to venture into the chamber on occasion, as he was recorded as voting with the Whigs on 13 Feb. 1703 in support of the Lords' amendment for enlarging the time for taking the abjuration oath.⁵

By the summer of 1703 Biddulph must have been in prison again, for in September he was released by the lord treasurer for 13 weeks in order to assist an inquiry into Whitley's accounts. His estates had also been taken over by the crown and his rents collected towards paying off his debt. However, this course was not very satisfactory from the Treasury viewpoint, because Biddulph only held a life interest in the estates and his death would liquidate the debt. Furthermore, long spells in prison had had a deleterious effect on his health. The solution was to apply to Parliament for a private Act to allow the lord treasurer to negotiate a composition for the remainder of the debt. Such a course had been suggested as early as August 1704 when the marriage of Biddulph's son, Theophilus, had provided sufficient funds to make the scheme practicable owing to his wife's portion. Accordingly, a petition was duly presented to the Commons on 20 Nov. 1704. When the report from the examining committee was read on 7 Dec. it revealed that the yearly value of the Staffordshire estates was £555 17s. 4d. and those in Kent £140 13s., and that a total of £1,105 4s. 9d. had been received from the former. A bill was introduced on 11 Dec. and passed its third reading on 24 Jan. 1705, which empowered the lord treasurer to compound with Biddulph before 25 Mar. 1706. The amount was duly set at £4,626 12s. and although it was necessary to extend the time limit, a report to the Commons on 12 Mar. 1708 indicated that the money had been paid into the Exchequer. During the passage of the Act, Biddulph did not vote for the Tack on 28 Nov. 1704.⁶

Although Biddulph did not sit in the 1705 Parliament, he was returned for Lichfield in 1708. His election was marked as a 'gain' for the Whigs by Lord Sunderland (Charles, Lord Spencer*). As in his earlier career, he seems now to have been an inactive Member. He did not stand again, dying on 2 Apr. 1718. He was succeeded by his son, Theophilus. In his will he left the unentailed part of his estate to his wife, plus the judgment for £10,000 he had received against Morgan Whitley.[7]

[1] IGI, London; J. C. Wedgwood, *Staffs. Parl. Hist.* (Wm. Salt Arch Soc.), ii. 141–2. [2] Wm. Salt Lib. (Stafford), Bagot mss, D/1721/3/291; *CSP Dom.* 1691–2, p. 269. [3] Centre Kentish Stud. Stanhope mss U1590/C9/9, Ld. Stanhope to [James] Stanhope, 26 Apr. [1701], same to 'my Ld.', 26 Apr. [1701], same to Coke, 8 Feb. 1700[-1]. [4] Stanhope mss U1590/C9/9, Ld. Stanhope to 'my Ld.', 26 Apr. [1701]; *HMC Cowper*, ii. 425; *Cal. Treas. Bks.* xv. 426; xvii. 16–17; *Cocks Diary*, 255–6. [5] *HMC Cowper*, ii. 451; Add. 29579, ff. 407, 416, 433; *Cal. Treas. Bks.* xvii. 17, 37, 361; BL, Lothian mss, Ld. Stanhope to Coke, 12 Oct. 1702. [6] *Cal. Treas. Bks.* xviii. 401; xx. 224–5, 603, 610; Bagot mss D(W)/1733/J1/2, ff. 8–9; Add. 29579, f. 497; *CJ*, xiv. 428, 448; xv. 603. [7] Wedgwood, 142.

S. N. H.

BIDDULPH, Michael (1661–97), of Polesworth, Warws.

TAMWORTH 1690–1695

b. 19 Nov. 1661, 1st s. of Michael Biddulph of Polesworth by Frances, da. and coh. of Dr John Kingston of London. *educ.* St. Catharine's, Camb. 1678. *m.* Lucy, da. and h. of George Wale of Radwinter, Essex, 2s. 2da. *suc.* fa. 1673.[1]

The Biddulphs were London merchants, although the elder branch of the family acquired an estate at Elmshurst, Staffordshire in the 17th century and Biddulph's father the manor of Polesworth in north Warwickshire through marriage. Little is known of Biddulph's public career until he stood for Tamworth in 1690, although a remark that 'the Presbyterians were for him the last time' to spite Viscount Weymouth (Thomas Thynne[†]) suggests that he may have made an interest there in the election to the Convention. He had the support of most of the corporation and the neighbouring gentry in 1690 as the only Churchman capable of joining with Sir Henry Gough* to defeat Thomas Guy* and Sir Charles Wolseley, 2nd Bt.[†] After receiving many letters on his behalf, Weymouth declared his support for Biddulph and Gough, who were returned ahead of Guy.[2]

At the beginning of the new Parliament Biddulph's name appears on a list marked by the Marquess of Carmarthen (Sir Thomas Osborne[†]) where he was classed as doubtful, probably because he was a new Member. In the 1690–1 session Biddulph was named in third place to the committee of elections and privileges. In a list of December 1690 Carmarthen noted him as a likely supporter, possibly in relation to a projected attack upon him in the Commons. In April 1691 Robert Harley* classed Biddulph as a Court supporter. On 15 Jan. 1692 he moved that the House desire the dean of St. Paul's to preach before them on the anniversary of Charles I's execution, and was duly deputed to make the request himself. In February he managed the Earl of Suffolk's estate bill through the House. When he carried the bill back to the Lords on 17 Feb. he also carried a message from the Commons to remind the Upper House of the bill for reducing interest. In the 1692–3 session he was appointed to another drafting committee. According to Samuel Grascome's list of spring 1693 he was a Court supporter with a place or pension. In the 1693–4 session he was appointed to two drafting committees and told on 16 Feb. 1694 against passing a resolution against Lord Falkland (Anthony Carey*).[3]

Biddulph did not stand at the election of 1695, although he appears to have remained active in local politics, for he took the Association to be subscribed at Tamworth along with John Chetwynd*. He died on 26 July 1697, leaving his estate to the eldest of his young children, with £1,000 each to his three other children. His cousin, Anthony Biddulph of Ledbury, Hertfordshire, was appointed their guardian.[4]

[1] J. C. Wedgwood, *Staffs. Parl. Hist.* (Wm. Salt Arch. Soc.), ii. 176–7. [2] *Vis. Warws.* (Harl. Soc. lxii), 21–22; *VCH Warws.* iv. 189; Bath mss at Longleat House, Thynne pprs. 28, ff. 266–7, 270, 274; 24, ff. 134–5, 144, 148. [3] *Luttrell Diary*, 130, 191. [4] Add. 29911, f. 97; Wedgwood, 177.

S. N. H.

BIGG, Richard (c.1675–1731), of Wallingford, Berks.

WALLINGFORD 1713–1715

b. c.1675, 1st s. of David Bigg of Wallingford by his w. Mary. *educ.* Corpus Christi, Oxf. matric. 8 Mar. 1692, aged 16, BA 1695, MA 1698. *m.* (1) Anne (d. 1711), da. and h. of Thomas Renda*, 1da.; (2) 28 Sept. 1730, Elizabeth Breedon, prob. da. of John Breedon of Bere Court, Pangbourne. *suc.* fa. ?1700.[1]

Alderman, Wallingford 1700, mayor 1702, 1711, 1722, 1725; freeman, Reading 1702.[2]

Bigg's paternal grandfather, Walter, served as Member for Wallingford in 1659, having previously had an active career as a major in the Parliamentarian army, a Presbyterian elder, sheriff of London and master of the Merchant Taylors' Company. Upon his death in 1659 he left his property in St. Giles-in-the-

Fields and in Berkshire to his elder son, David; the younger son, John†, inherited property in Huntingdonshire and sat for the county town in the Convention of 1689. David Bigg consolidated his position in Wallingford, serving as mayor on five occasions between 1672 and 1692, and as sheriff of the county in 1685. He was a Tory in politics, and his answers to King James's 'three questions' possibly reflect his Presbyterian background, as he agreed to support the repeal of the Penal Laws but equivocated over the Test Acts. During James II's reign he leased more land from the corporation in Wallingford and in 1690 secured a private Act which enabled him to sell most of his houses in St. Giles-in-the-Fields in order to make further purchases of property near his residence. This Act was managed in the Commons by Charles Hutchinson* and Simon Harcourt I*, the future Tory lord chancellor. Richard Bigg's associations were to be with the Tories when he entered Parliament.[3]

Having succeeded his father some time around the beginning of 1700, Bigg quickly established his own position in Wallingford, serving as mayor in 1702. His Tory contacts were further strengthened by his marriage to the heiress of Thomas Renda, lessee of Wallingford Castle. It seems probable that Renda supported Bigg's claims to a seat in 1713, as he did not then stand himself. Bigg was classed as a Tory on the Worsley list of 1713, but was inactive in the House. He lost his seat in 1715 and did not stand again. His will of November 1730 made provision for his mother and wife, most of his estates being placed in trust for the benefit of his only daughter and heiress, Elizabeth, the wife of John Cottingham.[4]

[1] PCC 20 Noel, 82 Richmond; IGI, Berks.; *VCH Berks.* iii. 304. [2] Berks. RO, Wallingford bor. statute bk. 1648–1766, f. 187v; R/AC1/1/19, f.64v; J. K. Hedges, *Hist. Wallingford*, ii. 230–1. [3] C. M. Clode, *Early Hist. Merchant Taylors' Co.* ii. 347; PCC 20 Noel, 514 Pell; *VCH Hunts.* ii. 235; iii. 63; Hedges, 230–1; Duckett, *Penal Laws and Test Act* (1883), 169; *CJ*, x. 433. [4] PCC 88 Isham; Hedges, 382.

S. N. H.

BILSON, Leonard (1681–1715), of West Mapledurham, nr. Petersfield, Hants.

PETERSFIELD 13 Jan. 1704–28 June 1715

bap. 25 Sept. 1681, 1st s. of Thomas Bilson† of West Mapledurham by Susanna, da. of Colonel William Legge† of the Minories, London, sis. of George†, 1st Baron Dartmouth, and William Legge†. *educ.* New Coll. Oxf. 1699. *unm. suc.* fa. 1692.[1]

Commr. Portsmouth and Sheet turnpike trust, 1711–*d.*; freeman, Portsmouth 1711.[2]

The ownership of estates in and near Petersfield and marriage into the Legge family had given Bilson's family an electoral interest in the borough which three successive generations of Bilsons had represented, the latest being Bilson's father in 1685 and 1689. Bilson followed the family tradition of education at Oxford where he had the honour of reciting a poem before Queen Anne during her visit to the university in August 1702.[3]

Bilson was returned to Petersfield at a by-election in 1704. In October he was reckoned doubtful in a forecast for the vote on the Tack, but his vote for the measure on 28 Nov. confirmed his solid Toryism, and an analysis of the 1705 Parliament (to which he was returned unopposed) identified him as 'True Church'. Having voted for the Tory candidate in the county elections, in Parliament Bilson voted against the Court candidate for Speaker on 25 Oct. 1705 and was given leave of absence for a month on 21 Dec. His next notable action was not until 1 Feb. 1707 when he was included among those named to draft a bill for a turnpike on the road between Petersfield and Butser Hill. Two lists of 1708 classed Bilson as a Tory and he continued true to form in the next Parliament. During the Sacheverell trial in 1710 he was a teller, on 2 Mar., in favour of a Tory motion to insert the word 'republican' into an address asking the Queen to take measures to suppress 'the present tumults set on foot and fomented by papists, non-jurors and other enemies'. Listed as having voted against the impeachment of Dr Sacheverell, February–March 1710, he told against a motion on 24 Mar. to burn a book to which Sacheverell had referred in his answer to the articles of impeachment.[4]

Bilson voted for the Tory candidates in the 1710 elections for Hampshire and was himself returned at Petersfield. Unsurprisingly he was classed as a Tory in the 'Hanover list'. He figured in the first session as one of the 'worthy patriots' who exposed the mismanagements of the previous administration, and was a member of the October Club. Since he was undoubtedly a High Tory, his membership of the club was probably genuine, although with his cousin Lord Dartmouth holding high office, it has been suggested that he may have acted as a Court spy. On 11 Jan. 1711 he was a teller in favour of extending the franchise at Lymington from the freemen to the inhabitants, a move aimed at ending the Whig monopoly of the borough. He was again named to the drafting committee for a bill for a turnpike on the Petersfield to Portsmouth road, 15 Feb., and twice, on 3 and 7 Apr., he acted as a teller on the Tory side in the contested election at Cockermouth. Bilson again voted for the Tory candidates in the 1713 county elections and was himself described as a Tory in the Worsley list and two other lists comparing the 1713 and 1715 Parliaments. Bilson continued to represent Petersfield until his death on 28 June 1715. His estates eventually passed to his cousin Henry Legge† who took the additional name of Bilson, as required by Bilson's will.[5]

[1] IGI, London; *Hants Vis.* (Harl. Soc. n.s. x), 133; *Hants Repository*, ii. 215. [2] *Portsmouth and Sheet Turnpike Commrs. Min. Bk.* (Portsmouth Rec. Ser. ii), 169; R. East, *Portsmouth Recs.* 375. [3] *VCH Hants*, iii. 89; Boyer, *Anne Annals*, i. 77. [4] *Hants Poll 1705* (IHR), 57. [5] *Hants Poll 1710* (IHR), 58; *1713*, p. 21; *Huntington Lib. Q.* xxxiii. 157; *Hants Repository*, ii. 215; PCC 232 Fagg.

P. W./S. M. W.

BINGHAM, Richard (c.1667–1735), of Melcombe Horsey (Melcombe Bingham), Dorset.

BRIDPORT   1702–1705
DORSET   25 Apr. 1711–1713

b. c.1667, s. of Strode Bingham of Henstridge, Som. by Cecily, da. of Thomas Chapman of Henstridge. *educ.* Exeter, Oxf. matric. 9 Mar. 1683, aged 15. *m.* 1695, Philadelphia, da. and h. of John Potenger of the Inner Temple, 6s. 7da. *suc.* uncle John Bingham† 1675.

Bingham, a Tory, was descended from an old Dorset family which had acquired the manor of Melcombe Bingham in the reign of Henry III. His father, a younger son, had settled at one of the family estates in Somerset, where Bingham himself spent his early years. He succeeded to the Dorset property in 1675 upon the death of his uncle, the Parliamentarian John Bingham. The estate which Bingham inherited was considerably encumbered with mortgages, however, and his financial prospects were not greatly improved by marriage in 1695 to the daughter of a minor author and poet. Returned for Bridport in 1702, Bingham assisted in the management of two private estate bills during his first Parliament, and voted, as had been forecast, in favour of the Tack on 28 Nov. 1704. He did not stand again until 1711, when returned at a by-election for the county. Bingham managed an estate bill through all its stages in April and May 1713 and voted on 18 June in favour of the French commerce bill. He retired at the dissolution, and is not known to have stood again. Bingham died in 1735.[1]

[1] Hutchins, *Dorset*, iv. 368–79; *Mems. John Potenger* ed. Bingham, pp. i, 38, 41, 59, 69.

P. W.

BIRCH, John I (1615–91), of The Homme, nr. Leominster and Garnstone Manor, nr. Weobley, Herefs.

LEOMINSTER   11 Sept. 1646–6 Dec. 1648
   1654–1655
   1656–1658, 1659, 1660
PENRYN   1661–1679 (Jan.)
WEOBLEY   1679 (Mar.)–1681 (Mar.)
   1689–10 May 1691

b. 7 Sept. 1615, 2nd but 1st surv. s. of Samuel Birch of Ardwick Manor, Manchester, Lancs. by Mary, da. of Ralph Smith of Doblane House, Manchester. *m.* (1) c.1643, Alice (d. 1675), da. of Thomas Deane of Bristol, wid. of Thomas Selfe, grocer, of Bristol, 2s. (1 *d.v.p.*) 3da.; (2) Winifred (d. 1717), da. of Matthew Norris of Weobley, 1s. *d.v.p. suc.* fa. 1669.[1]

Capt. of vol. ft. (parliamentary), Bristol 1643; lt.-col. of ft. (parliamentary) 1643–4, col. 1644–5; gov. Bath 1645, Hereford 1645–6; col. of horse 1646–8, ft. Feb.–Oct. 1660; commr. for indemnity 1647–9, to estates [S] 1648; councillor of State 25 Feb.–31 May 1660; commr. excise Feb. 1660–4, Admiralty Mar.–July 1660, disbandment Sept. 1660–1, 1679, maimed soldiers 1660–1; auditor of excise (for life) 1661; commr. for trade 1668–72, wine duties 1670–4; treasurer for loyal and indigent officers 1671.[2]

High steward, Leominster 1648–June 1660.[3]

Chairman, cttee. of privileges and elections 23 Jan.–21 Oct. 1689.

In his heyday 'the roughest and boldest speaker in the House', Birch was still a man to be reckoned with in the Commons when re-elected in 1690, in his 75th year. His keenness to secure his return for Weobley was such that he reneged on a promise to propose Thomas Foley II* to the borough, possibly fearing the outcome of a contest against the other declared candidate, Robert Price*. Classed as a Whig in Lord Carmarthen's (Sir Thomas Osborne†) analysis of the new Parliament, he made his first recorded speech of the opening session on 3 Apr. 1690, in the committee of supply, when he recalled to the attention of the House a suggestion offered in the previous Parliament for a tax on alehouses and brandy-cellars. In doing so he took the opportunity to make some criticisms of the conduct of public affairs:

I cannot easily swallow how we are brought into this necessity of money. I shall touch it very tenderly. Here is another year lost; but let us do what we can. Last year, by God's blessing, with hay and oats, you might have done your work. But it is more reasonable to provide the money than talk of things now; and nothing was so unseasonable as the prorogation of the last Parliament; that undid your business, and ... set you a year backward.

On 8 Apr. he was appointed to the drafting committee on a bill to reverse the quo warranto of 1683 against the city of London, a subject on which he spoke several times: he moved on 17 Apr. that the sheriffs of London be called in to present their petition; proposed on 22 Apr. that counsel be heard on the bill in committee, in order, as he said, to prevent a 'misunderstanding' between Parliament and the City; and on 24 Apr. intervened again in another debate on the bill. Also on the 24th he spoke against the motion for an address to thank the King for the changes that had been made in the London lieutenancy. 'Pray let this address alone', he begged, 'until we have beaten our enemies'. His main arguments, however, concerned the character of the alterations. He deplored factional vindictiveness, and reminded his audience of the unhappy events (as he saw them) that had followed the Restoration: 'one sort of people, who acted in a corner ... made men criminated in most corners of the kingdom; this brought us into a low condition'. Moreover, he urged the House to 'examine' what sort of men the new appointees were, 'and do not give thanks hand over hand for these men'. Later in the debate he put forward the idea that, rather than make an address, the House should vote for the imposition of an oath of abjuration. Full texts of his speeches do not survive, but at some point he evidently committed a slip of the tongue from which his enemies profited, in talking of 'overloading the cart', an image which inevitably recalled his own reputed origins as a carrier. He acted as a teller on 23 Apr., against the bill to settle John Snell's charity to maintain poor scholars at Oxford University. As it was reported, his speech on 28 Apr. against a clause in the bill of security, to lodge a power in the crown to commit into custody without bail persons suspected of treasonable correspondence with King James, was a masterpiece of ellipsis and innuendo, repeating attacks on the ministers that he had vented before. 'I am an ancient man', he began,

and I believe you will think me subject to jealousy ... This power (moved for) is in the King, and some choice Councillors. How has this grown a hard game before you, by some of great wisdom at the beginning of the game, else things could never go as they did in Ireland and at sea! I waited, and knew the conclusion would unriddle this business to you, and myself – some, when we parted last, were of my opinion, that if things were managed a second year, as we had done the first, we should not have a third. If we had gone in time into Ireland, it had been reduced without fighting; there was no way to bring in King James; and presently then, in the midst of this great business, to prorogue the Parliament! Then, as to the dissolution, this was done by the choice of Council; and what is to be done now? There is a great deal of tenderness and earnestness for the King to go into Ireland, and we are as ready for King James to come hither, as for King William to go thither. It must be the fidelity of the Privy Council that you must trust, and pray how has it been showed? The army is to come out of Flanders, and those that will, let them take it. I shall never be brought to an opinion to trust these Councillors who have so ill acquitted themselves.

The same broad theme was pursued in his speeches of 30 Apr. and 5 May on the regency bill, about which he expressed strong reservations. It was 'a most dangerous bill'. Should any dangers arise during the King's absence 'we have a brave army ... but so disappointed, that I fear the consequence ... And who must these commissioners be that must turn the whole in the King's absence? From what has been done, you may guess what will be done.' The other speeches attributed to him by Grey in this session were on 2 May, when he moved to adjourn the debate on the charge against Anthony Rowe* of publishing the *Letter to a Friend* ...; on 13 May, in the debate on providing for the peace of the kingdom in the King's absence; and on 15 May, on the report of the conference over the nomination of commissioners in the poll tax bill, when he declared his desire to 'follow the old way' and quoted a precedent from 1664–5. He acted as a teller three times: on 30 Apr., in a division arising from the Hertford election case regarding the entitlement of Quakers to vote without taking the oaths, which he supported; on 7 May, for referring the woollen manufacturers bill to a select committee; and on 16 May, against an amendment to the bill vesting the crown's hereditary revenues in William and Mary.[4]

The intimations of mortality that induced Birch to make his will in August 1690 and prescribe the form and wording for the imposing monument which was in its way to be his political testament, did not inhibit his parliamentary activity in the ensuing autumn. On 9 Dec. he presented a bill for the speedier determining of elections. In April 1691 he was listed by Robert Harley* as a Country party supporter. Birch died on 10 May 1691 and was buried at Weobley. Sir Edward Harley*, whose family had kept on cordial terms with Birch right up to his death, was distressed not to be able to attend the funeral of one he called 'my ancient friend and companion in arms for religion and liberty'. Birch's will declared that his property, in Herefordshire, Monmouthshire and Middlesex, was to go, not to his childless surviving son, but to his unmarried daughter Sarah, subject to the provision that she marry her cousin John Birch II*. The patrimonial estate in Lancashire had been sold for £4,300 the previous year. As Sarah fulfilled her father's wishes it was Birch's nephew upon whom the responsibility devolved to erect and maintain the monument in Weobley church. Its dimensions, and the phraseology of the inscription, so enraged the vicar and parishioners, especially after the younger Birch had surrounded it with a protective wooden screen which effectively shut off half the church, that an action was brought in the ecclesiastical court. Among other things, this suit alleged that the sentence in the inscription referring to Birch's Civil War service reflected on 'the justice of King Charles I of ever blessed memory' and justified 'the late iniquitous rebellion'. Bishop Ironside of Hereford ordered the removal of the screen and the effacement of the offending words, and despite threats of a counter-action, and physical attacks on the workmen employed in the task by 'several dependants of Colonel Birch's family', the sentence was carried out, only for the full inscription to be restored after the bishop's death in 1701.[5]

[1] *VCH Lancs.* iv. 280. [2] *Mil. Mem. of Col. Birch* (Cam. Soc. n.s. vii), 55, 94, 104, 120. [3] G. F. Townsend, *Leominster,* 291. [4] Burnet, *Own Time,* ii. 82; Add. 70014, f. 96; 42592, f. 138; Grey, x. 39–40, 54, 61, 64, 72, 74, 93–94, 100–1, 119, 138, 149–50. [5] E. Heath-Agnew, *Roundhead to Royalist,* 213–14, 216–20, 261; Add. 70234, Sir Edward to Robert Harley, 12 May 1691; *HMC 5th Rep.* 384–5; Wood, *Life and Times,* iii. 454; Bodl. Ballard 34, f. 132; Luttrell, *Brief Relation,* iii. 319.

D. W. H.

BIRCH, John II (c.1666–1735), of Garnstone Manor, Weobley, Herefs.

WEOBLEY   1701 (Feb.)–1702, 1705–1715
18 June 1715–30 Mar. 1732
1734–6 Oct. 1735

b. c.1666, 2nd s. of Rev. Thomas Birch, rector of Hampton Bishop, Herefs., afterwards vicar of Preston, Lancs. by his w. Mary. *educ.* G. Inn 1682; M. Temple 1687, called 1687. *m.* (1) bef. 14 July 1691, his cos. Sarah (*d.* 1702), da. and h. of John Birch I*, *s.p.*; (2) 26 Jan. 1704, Letitia, da. of John Hampden† of Great Hampden, Bucks., sis. of Richard Hampden II*, *s.p.*[1]

Attorney-gen. Brec., Glam. and Rad. 1695–1705; serjeant-at-law 1705; Queen's serjeant 1712; commr. forfeited estates 1716–25; cursitor baron of Exchequer 1729–*d.*[2]

Birch had been selected as the heir of his uncle John Birch I, inasmuch as the elder Birch had made his daughter's inheritance conditional upon marriage to her cousin. While the bridegroom was content to comply with this provision, and subsequently took pains to protect his uncle's funerary monument from Tory parishioners and ecclesiastical authorities enraged by its provocative references to the Civil War, he did not quite adhere in every respect to the religious and political tradition that old 'Colonel' Birch had exemplified. In campaigning to secure his uncle's parliamentary seat at Weobley, in the by-election held in 1691, he refused to accommodate himself to the wishes of the colonel's old political comrades, the Foleys and Harleys, and an acrimonious contest resulted. However, after the poll Birch agreed to withdraw a petition he was preferring in return for a promise by the Foleys and Robert Harley* to find him a seat elsewhere during this Parliament, or if they could not, to pay him £260. As he did not come into the House, he must have accepted the cash composition. At the following election he challenged again, but from a weaker position, which made the Harleys less concerned to interpose. If anything, feelings at this election ran even higher, with Birch relying on the 'Church interest' in his opposition to the Foleys. This reliance was understandable in the son of an Anglican parson, though it scarcely accorded with the Presbyterianism with which the name of John Birch had been associated in the preceding generation. Birch's relations in Bristol also displayed Tory sympathies in this period: their quarrel with the Whig John Dutton Colt* was attributed by Colt to party animosity. At the same time, Birch was himself involved in the movement for the reformation of manners, as a colleague of Edward Harley*, Robert's brother, in a pressure group in Middlesex, an interest which was characteristic of Presbyterians or those from Puritan backgrounds and which was also reflected perhaps in his abortive election campaign at Weobley in 1695, when he refused to pay money to the electors and moreover enjoyed support from Lord Weymouth (Thomas Thynne†), another active 'moral reformer'. Birch's political preferences cannot in fact be easily characterized at this point. In the 1698 election he went to a poll at Weobley against Thomas Foley II* and the Tory Robert Price*, but at the same time had been maintaining amicable relations with the Harleys since at least 1693 and seems to have given his interest in Radnorshire to Thomas Harley* against a Whig opponent.[3]

The election at Weobley in January 1701 was a complicated affair, characterized by shifting alliances, underhand dealings and wholesale bribery. However, on this occasion Birch seems to have overcome any scruples about spending money, and was successful at the election. His political sympathies are not readily apparent from his three tellerships during this Parliament: against giving a second reading to a private bill on behalf of Sir Walter Clarges, 1st Bt.* (2 May 1701); against adjourning a debate on the Lichfield election (10 May); and against an amendment to a motion to refer petitions on Irish forfeited estates to the trustees chosen under the Act of Resumption (31 May). However, his authorship of the bill to prevent the corrupting of jurors, which he presented on 13 Mar. 1701, and reported on 28 May, indicates a sympathy with the concerns of 'Country' Members. Re-elected in December 1701 after another contest, he was classed with the Tories in Robert Harley's list of the new Parliament, and, although a teller on 10 Feb. 1702 in favour of committing the abjuration bill, was included in the 'white list' of those who favoured the motion on 26 Feb. vindicating the Commons' proceedings in the impeachments of the four Whig lords. He was also one of several 'Country'-minded MPs who had promised to support Sir Richard Cocks, 2nd Bt., in his motion on 11 Feb. for the taxation of all crown grants since the Revolution, but who failed to appear in the House at the appropriate time. Of his other tellerships, two were on questions connected with the Irish forfeitures, against receiving or reading petitions from Lord Haversham (Sir John Thompson, 1st Bt.*) and Robert Edgworth respectively (20 Feb., 14 Mar.); one arose from the bill to regulate the King's Bench and Fleet prisons, against an instruction to the committee to state the 'encumbrances' on each institution (7 Mar.); and one was on a point of procedure, against a motion that all committees be adjourned (23 Jan.). During this Parliament he presented another bill on 5 Feb., for ascertaining the water-measure of fruit, and reported it on 7 Mar.[4]

After losing his seat in 1702, Birch was returned unopposed at Weobley in 1705. Uncertainty as to his party allegiance is reflected in the fact that he was described as a 'Churchman' in a printed analysis of the new Commons, while Lord Sunderland's (Charles, Lord Spencer*) private calculation of the election results accounted his return a 'gain' for the Whigs. In fact, he had already been recruited by Robert Harley to the ranks of the Court party by the offer of the coif, and although he had not been given the honour of Queen's serjeant, which he had himself considered 'the most acceptable', he had been permitted to name his brother to be his successor as attorney-general on the South Wales circuit, that office being 'incompatible' with the degree of serjeant. He voted on 25 Oct. for the Court candidate as Speaker, and supported the Court again on 18 Feb. 1706 in the proceedings over the 'place clause' in the regency bill, having contributed a comment on a matter of procedure to a debate on the clause on 21 Jan. On 12 Dec. 1706 he presented a bill for preventing the corrupting of jurors, while on 3 Mar. 1707 he was granted a leave of absence, the first of a series, which may well have been connected with the performance of professional or even official duties. That he was being considered for preferment is clear from a letter of Lord Coningsby (Thomas*) in May 1707, in which Coningsby reported (to Robert Harley) having spoken to the lord treasurer and lord chancellor in Birch's favour and found them 'both so inclinable that I cannot but conclude it done'. Whatever the intended appointment or favour may have been, nothing appears to have transpired. In the 1707–8 session Birch was the only Member in the House on 21 Nov. 1707 who 'had the boldness' to question whether the place clause of the Regency Act (which he had voted against less than two years before) should now be invoked as a result of the Act of Union rendering the Parliament technically a 'new' one. But on 16 Dec. he received another month's leave of absence. He was twice listed as a Whig in early 1708, but in a by-election for Weobley in December of that year gave his backing to a Tory, Henry Gorges*. Despite being granted an unlimited leave of absence on 15 Dec. 1708, he voted for the naturalization of the Palatines the following February. The next session, after his customary leave of absence had been granted on 17 Dec. 1709, this time for one month, he voted (before 16 Mar., when he was granted three weeks' leave of absence) for the impeachment of Dr Sacheverell. Returned unopposed at the 1710 election, and classed as a Whig in the 'Hanover list', Birch ceased to be a particularly active Member in this and the succeeding Parliament. He was given leave of absence again on 26 Feb. 1711, for a month, but was listed as voting on 7 Dec. 1711 in favour of the 'No Peace without Spain' motion, and on 18 June 1713 against the French commerce bill, on which latter occasion he was noted as a Whig. Returned at a by-election in 1715, he served successive Whig ministries as a loyal placeman, conveniently forgetting earlier 'Country' principles, until his death on 6 Oct. 1735, when he was succeeded in the Garnstone estate by his brother Samuel.[5]

[1] E. Heath-Agnew, *Roundhead to Royalist*, pp. xxiii, 215. [2] W. R. Williams, *Gt. Sessions in Wales*, 154–5; *HMC Portland*, iv. 216. [3] Heath-Agnew, 216–20; Bodl. Ballard 34, f. 132; *Trans. Woolhope Naturalists' Field Club*, xxxix. 128–9, 132–3; *HMC Portland*, iii. 469, 473, 478, 571; Nottingham Univ. Lib. Portland (Harley) mss

Pw2Hy 308, Robert Harley to Birch, 19 Sept. 1691; Craig thesis, 69–70; Harley mss at Brampton Bryan, Robert to Thomas Harley*, 30 July 1698. [4] *Trans. Woolhope Naturalists' Field Club*, 133–4; Add. 70019, ff. 270–1, 275; 29/190, f. 38; *HMC Portland*, iv. 11; Bath mss at Longleat House, Thynne pprs. 25, ff. 15, 17–18, 25, 27, 32, 46, 53–4, 58; *Cocks Diary*, 211. [5] Portland (Harley) mss Pw2Hy 513, Birch to Robert Harley, 24 Apr. 1705; *Cam. Misc.* xxiii. 81; *HMC Portland*, iv. 414, 513; *HMC Downshire*, i. 855–6.

D. W. H.

BLAAKE, Henry (c.1659–1731), of Pinnells, nr. Calne, Wilts. and Bristol, Glos.

CALNE 1695–1700, 1701 (Dec.)–1702

b. c.1659, 1st s. of Ambrose Blaake of Pinnells by Mary, da. of George Jaye of Hullavington, Wilts. *educ.* St. Edmund Hall, Oxf. matric. 3 July 1676, aged 17; I. Temple 1677; called 1688. *m.* ?1683 (with £2,000), Catherine, da. of Sir George Hungerford*, sis. of George* and Walter Hungerford*, 2s. (1 *d.v.p.*) 4da. (1 *d.v.p.*). *suc.* fa. 1682.[1]

Freeman, Wilton June–Oct. 1688; steward of sheriff's ct. Bristol 1712–21, town clerk 1721–*d.*[2]

Waiter, port of Bristol 1709–*d.*[3]

Blaake, whose family had been settled in the vicinity of Calne since at least the 14th century, inherited the moated estate of Pinnells in 1682. Shortly afterwards he secured £2,000 from his marriage to the daughter of his near neighbour, Sir George Hungerford, and in subsequent years was able to purchase other property in the county in Chippenham, Cherhill, Calston, Stoford and Quemerford.[4]

These properties put Blaake in good stead when he showed a local political interest; he had been active in elections in Calne, on the Whig side, as early as 1685. Returned unopposed in 1695 with his Tory brother-in-law George Hungerford, he was named to a single drafting committee before being granted leave of absence for ten days on 14 Jan. 1696. Upon his return he was more active. He was forecast as likely to support the Court in the division of 31 Jan. on the proposed council of trade, and signed the Association the following month. Also in February he demonstrated his links with Bristol, managing through all its stages in the Commons a bill to supply Bristol with fresh water, and acting as a teller on the 11th in favour of hearing a petition from the city regarding the East India trade. On 16 Mar. he reported from the committee on the bill for erecting hospitals and workhouses in Bristol and later in the month voted for fixing the price of guineas at 22*s*. In the next session he voted on 25 Nov. 1696 in favour of the attainder of Sir John Fenwick†. Given leave of absence on 19 Dec., this time for three weeks, he was back in London by 3 Mar. 1697 when he was a teller for agreeing to a resolution from the committee of ways and means to grant a further duty on cider and perry. Later in March he managed a bill to amend the laws for the relief of the poor through the House. In the following session he told on 22 Dec. 1697 against committing the bill to prevent the throwing of fireworks, before receiving leave on 8 Jan. 1698 owing to his wife's illness. Upon his return he told on two further occasions: on 10 Mar. 1698 for an amendment to the case prepared for a conference with the Lords on the bill of pains and penalties against Charles Duncombe*; and on 21 Apr. against an instruction to the committee on the coal duty bill to remove the duty on coal transported inland. He was allowed a further fortnight's leave on 27 Apr. in order to attend George Hungerford's funeral.[5]

Blaake was classed with the Court party in a comparative analysis of the new and old Parliaments in about September 1698, and soon gave further evidence to support such a conclusion. On 4 Jan. 1699 he wrote to Walter White* that he had 'signalized himself' by making 'a very violent speech in the House for a standing army and was so linked into the interest of the Court that they must not expect a good vote from me this session'. He then voted against the third reading of the disbanding bill on 18 Jan., prompting Henry Chivers* to write in a letter to some friends in Calne, 'I do really believe he will never give his country one vote, he is so linked in with the Court party', a 'reflection' for which Chivers was subsequently called to account before the House. Blaake himself spent several weeks in Wiltshire after being given a fortnight's leave of absence on 21 Jan., but he had returned in time to act as a teller on 8 Mar. 1699 against engrossing the place bill. He was a teller thrice more in this session: twice on the Malmesbury election case, and once regarding a petitioner's claims against the agent for two packet boats. During the next session he acted as a teller on 6 Jan. 1700 for a motion that the state of the navy be referred to the committee of supply, rather than left on the table to be perused by Members. His main legislative involvement in this session was to assist in the management of two measures through the House: a bill to improve the navigation of the Avon and Frome and for cleaning Bristol's streets, and an estate bill in favour of the Marquess of Tavistock. He was a teller on two further occasions: on 14 Mar. in favour of hearing the reports of the committee of privileges and on 4 Apr. for an additional clause to the bill imposing a duty on East Indian cloth imports.[6]

Blaake did not stand in the February 1701 election, but in the following November he co-operated with the electioneering efforts of Lord Wharton (Hon. Thomas*) in Wiltshire, and supported the Whig candidates for knight of the shire, William Ashe I* and Hon. Maurice Ashley*. He wrote to White:

> I need not tell you how much the fate of England, nay perhaps all Europe, depends on the proceedings of the approaching Parliament, nor how necessary it is for all honest men to take care in the choice of their representatives, but I beg you to be industrious against the election for our county. Ashe and Ashley is the word, and I am sure that you and I that have voted so many times together can't differ in that, for we both know 'em.

As regards White's election at Chippenham, where his own father-in-law was also concerned, he commented, 'I wish you joy of your deliverance from Squire Hungerford's opposition'. For his own part, he was able to come in again at Calne, in all probability through the good offices of his friend Edward Bayntun*, and was listed by Robert Harley* as a Whig. He spoke on 14 Feb. 1702 in defence of the Malmesbury election petitioners. He was a teller on 28 Apr. for leave for a bill for the relief of Ignatius Gould, a merchant, with respect to the resumption of the Irish forfeitures, and subsequently reported from committee three relief bills relating to the same issue.[7]

Blaake did not stand again, though he was still involved in Calne elections in 1710. Before long he sold Pinnells and went to live in Bristol, where in 1709 he had been given a small customs place worth £15 a year, and where he later held office in the corporation. He made his will a few days before his death on 10 July 1731, aged 72. Asking to be buried 'in the most private manner' in St. Mark's, the lord mayor's chapel in Bristol where a monument was raised to his memory, he left £200 to each of his surviving children. Neither of his sons succeeded him in Parliament.[8]

[1] *Wilts. N. and Q.* i. 452–4; iv. 515–17; v. 46; Add. 33412, f. 138; *Vis. Wilts.* ed. Phillipps, 30; R. C. Hoare, *Hungerfordiana*, 22–24; *Cal. Treas. Bks.* xxiii. 93; xxix. 335; *Cal. Treas. Pprs.* 1731–4, p. 522; PCC 82 Aston. [2] Wilts. RO, G25/1/21; A. B. Beaven, *Bristol Lists*, 323. [3] *Cal. Treas. Bks.* xxiii. 93. [4] Wilts. RO, 212B/1077; 546/38; *VCH Wilts.* xv. 219. [5] A. E. W. Marsh, *Hist. Calne*, 184–6; *Wilts. Arch. Mag.* xlvi. 70. [6] *Wilts. Arch. Mag.* 73–74, 77. [7] Ibid. 79–80; *Cocks Diary*, 213. [8] *Wilts. Arch. Mag.* 69; *Wilts. N. and Q.* i. 452–3; iv. 515–17; *Cal. Treas. Bks.* xxiii. 179; xxix. 369.

D. W. H.

BLACKETT, Sir Edward, 2nd Bt. (1649–1718), of Newby, Yorks. and Dartmouth Street, London.

RIPON 1689–1690
NORTHUMBERLAND 1698–1700

bap. 25 Oct. 1649, 2nd but 1st surv. s. of Sir William Blackett, 1st Bt.†, by Elizabeth, da. of Michael Kirkley, merchant, of Newcastle; bro. of Sir William Blackett, 1st Bt.* *m.* (1) settlement 28 Apr. 1674, Mary, da. and h. of Thomas Norton of Langthorne, Yorks., 1s. *d.v.p.*; (2) settlement 25 Nov. 1676, Mary (*d.* 1696), da. of Sir John Yorke† of Richmond, Yorks., 6s. 6da.; (3) 21 Oct. 1699, Diana (*d.* 1713), da. of Sir George Booth†, 1st Baron Delamere, of Dunham Massey, Cheshire, sis. of Hon. Henry Booth†, wid. of Sir Ralph Delaval, 2nd Bt., of Seaton Delaval, Northumb., 1s. *d.v.p.* *suc.* fa. as 2nd Bt. 16 May 1680.[1]

Member, merchant adventurers' co. of Newcastle-upon-Tyne 1672, hostmen's co. 1684; sheriff, Northumb. 1679–80; freeman, Ripon Sept. 1688.[2]

The son of a wealthy Newcastle merchant, Blackett inherited estates in Northumberland and Yorkshire. His first two marriages brought him further property in the latter county, the second bringing him lands worth £2,000 p.a., so that by the 1680s Blackett was a significant figure in both counties. He chose to emphasize his standing through the construction of Newby Hall at a cost of over £32,000. Contemporaries generally deemed this money well spent, two visitors to the house in 1703 describing Newby Hall as 'one of the most pleasant and most perfect that we ever saw', but this opinion was not universally held, as in 1701 one traveller carped that 'this house, were it not so cried up, might pass for a very good one, but the name it has got... prepares travellers to expect a much finer building'.[3]

Blackett had first entered public life during the Exclusion Crisis, pursuing the recusancy fines of Northumberland Catholics while sheriff, and when returned to the Convention for Ripon voted against declaring the throne vacant. Though Blackett was nominated in 1693 as one of three candidates for sheriff of Yorkshire, William III chose to ignore him. In 1697 he declared his intention of standing at the next election and, despite one observer's worry that he 'talks of more things than he puts into execution', he was returned unopposed for Northumberland the following year. The Tory sympathies suggested by what little is known of his prior political allegiance appear to be confirmed by an analysis of the new House classing Blackett as a likely opponent of a standing army. However, on 18 Jan. 1699 he voted against the third reading of the disbanding bill. His unexpected support for the Court is most explicable in terms of his brother Sir William's decision to oppose disbandment, but there is little evidence of his political allegiance following this vote. In early 1700 a classification of the Commons into interests listed Blackett under the independent Whig the 2nd Earl of Warrington, a judgment probably based upon Blackett's marriage in 1699 to Warrington's aunt. He decided against standing for Northumberland at the first 1701 election and, though urged in November 1701 and again in 1705 to forward his name for the county, he never stood for election again.[4]

Though he had resolved to live in retirement Blackett maintained electoral interests in a number of Yorkshire boroughs, most notably Ripon, as well as concerning himself in Yorkshire and Northumberland county elections, generally exercising his interest in favour of Tory candidates. He exerted himself in the election of his under-age nephew Sir William Blackett, 2nd Bt.*, at Newcastle in 1710, supporting his campaign and lobbying Yorkshire Members to be his 'friends' should a petition be presented against his nephew. His wealth was further augmented by his third marriage and by the marriage, with a portion of £8,000, of one of his sons to his third wife's only daughter, the heir to the Delaval lands at Seaton Delaval. Blackett, however, only obtained the portion in 1715 following protracted legal action, in which year he was awarded both the principal and interest amounting to £14,624. Blackett died on 22 Apr. 1718, and was buried in Ripon Minster. He was succeeded by his eldest surviving son Edward, whose son sat for Northumberland under George III.[5]

[1] *New Hist. Northumb.* xii. 277; NRA report 6531 (Blackett [Matfen] mss), p. 59; J. Hodgson, *Hist. Northumb.* pt. ii(1), 259.
[2] *Newcastle Merchant Adventurers* (Surtees Soc. ci), 98; *Newcastle Hostmen's Co.* (Surtees Soc. cv), 272; *Ripon Millenary Rec.* ed Harrison, 78. [3] *VCH N. Riding Yorks.* i. 296, 451; Hodgson, 259; *Blathwayt Diary* ed. Hardwick, 22–23; Add. 47057, ff. 31–32.
[4] L. Gooch, *The Desperate Faction?*, 3; Hull Univ. Lib. Bosville mss DDBM/32/1, [–] to Godfrey Bosville, 21 Nov. 1693; Luttrell, *Brief Relation*, iii. 395; Add. 70018, f. 217; 70019, f. 285; Huntington Lib. Stowe mss 58(1), pp. 17–18; Northumb. RO, Blackett (Matfen) mss, Bp. Moore of Norwich to Blackett, 13 Nov. 1701, Duke of Somerset to [same], 15 Mar. 1704–5. [5] N. Yorks. RO, Swinton mss, Danby pprs. 'persons to be elected', 24 Nov. 1701; Add. 24475, f. 138; Blackett (Matfen) mss ZBL 189, Blackett to Sir William Blackett, 2nd Bt., 3 Sept. [1710], same to [–], 4 Oct. 1710, same to Thomas Forster II*, 8 Oct. 1710 (Speck trans.); ZBL 190, same to Paul Foley II*, 27 Aug. 1713, same to Robert Fairfax*, 4 Sept. 1713 (Speck trans.); *New Hist. Northumb.* ix. 162–3; PCC 72 Tenison.

E. C./R. D. H.

BLACKETT, Sir William, 1st Bt. (1657–1705), of Greyfriars House, Newcastle-upon-Tyne and Wallington Hall, Northumb.

NEWCASTLE-UPON-TYNE 1685–1687
1689–1690
1695–1700
6 June–Dec. 1705

b. 14 June 1657, 5th but 3rd surv. s. of William Blackett† and bro. of Sir Edward Blackett, 2nd Bt.* the quartering of m. 27 Jan. 1685 (with £6,000), Julia (d. 1722), da. of Sir Christopher Conyers, 2nd Bt., of Horden, co. Dur., 2s. (1 d.v.p.) 8da. cr. Bt. 23 Jan. 1685.[1]

Freeman, Newcastle-upon-Tyne 1678, alderman by 1683–7, Oct. 1688–d., mayor 1683, 1698; member, merchant adventurers' co. of Newcastle-upon-Tyne 1679, hostmen's co. 1681, gov. 1684, 1691, 1692; sheriff, Northumb. Nov. 1689.[2]

Sub-farmer, coal duties 1680–Nov. 1688.[3]

Inheriting the bulk of his father's substantial estates and interest in the north-east coal industry, Blackett had become the region's second largest coal producer by the end of the 17th century. In 1689 his growing wealth allowed him to purchase further lands in Yorkshire and the Northumberland estates of Sir John Fenwick†. The latter cost £4,000 plus an annuity of £2,000 for the life of Fenwick and his wife, but the purchase also added to Blackett's mining interests. Not only did Blackett acquire further collieries by this transaction but he also found, as the Earl of Ailesbury (Thomas Bruce†) observed, 'as much lead on the estate as paid the purchase and more'. Blackett's good business sense and his burgeoning assets brought him a considerable income, estimated in 1705 at £10,000 p.a., and at his death he was described as one of the nation's 'richest commoners'.[4]

Following his uncontested return for Newcastle in 1695, Blackett was forecast as a likely opponent of the Court on the divisions of 31 Jan. 1696 upon the council of trade, and in March he voted against the Court on fixing the price of guineas at 22s. He was clearly not a Tory extremist, however, as he promptly signed the Association. A willingness to further both his own business interests and local concerns was twice demonstrated in this session. On 19 Feb. he was the sole Member appointed to draft a bill to settle the rents of coal wharves in Durham, Northumberland and Newcastle, and his promotion of this measure prompted the gratitude of Newcastle's hostmen's company, a group intimately connected to the coal trade of the Tyne and of which Blackett was a prominent member. It is clear from the minutes of this company that Blackett's efforts to facilitate this bill stemmed from his personal interests, as the need to settle these rents arose from increased transport costs for north-east coal owners caused by the exploitation of Northumberland coal deposits further from the banks of the Tyne. The session also saw Blackett nominated, on 9 Apr., to the committee considering the petition of the inhabitants of Hexham, Northumberland, where Blackett owned much of the land, against the quartering of troops upon them. Granted an indefinite leave of absence on 20 Apr., Blackett was called upon to deal with two issues of note during the recess. Sir John Fenwick's[†] arrest for his involvement in the Assassination Plot led Blackett to consult with the Treasury whether the annuity he was paying to Fenwick was still due, the treasury lords ordering that the annuity was payable only up to the time when Fenwick was accused of treason. Blackett's acceptance of this decision gave Fenwick the pretext to request, in July, a delay in his trial 'for want of money to make his defence', though the lords justices rejected Fenwick's petition. Blackett was also involved in quelling the disturbances at Newcastle occasioned by the recoinage, his role being to offer a crowd of 500 colliers, dissatisfied with the offer of 'papers of credit', gold in exchange for the 'old broad money', though Blackett's intervention only led to a short lull in the disturbances. At this time Blackett was in contact with the chancellor of the Exchequer Charles Montagu* concerning the latter's scheme to issue interest-bearing Exchequer bills, and it seems that Blackett had been a leading proponent of the decision to use these bills to satisfy the shortage of specie in Newcastle, the very policy that had prompted the public disturbances. At the beginning of the 1696–7 session Blackett absented himself from the division of 25 Nov. upon the Fenwick attainder, though whether this was on grounds of conscience or a feeling that given his financial involvement with Fenwick it was improper for him to vote on the issue, is unclear. It should be noted that in January 1697 Blackett renewed his agreement to pay an annuity of £2,000 to Fenwick's widow. Blackett's main concern during the remainder of the session was to renew attempts to resolve the issue of rents for coal wharves in the north-east, being the first-named Member appointed on 8 Dec. to draft such a bill and presenting it three days later. He was appointed, on 14 Jan. 1697, to draft a bill to explain the recoinage acts of the previous session and to inquire into miscarriages at the Mint. Granted a six-week leave of absence on 20 Feb., Blackett returned to London for the 1697–8 session. February and March saw him guide a bill to improve the supply of fresh water to Newcastle through its Commons stages.[5]

Blackett was returned unopposed at the 1698 election, and a comparison of the old and new Commons somewhat surprisingly classed him as a Court supporter, though a subsequent list queried this description. The reason for this shift in Blackett's political loyalties is difficult to discern, but it may be that his friendship with his fellow coal proprietor and northeast Member, Hon. Charles Montagu, drew him into the orbit of Chancellor of the Exchequer Charles Montagu. The shift in his political allegiance was clearly demonstrated in the debate of 18 Jan. 1699 on the disbanding bill, Blackett being one of a number of 'country gentlemen', including Whigs such as Sir John Mainwaring, 2nd Bt., Richard Norton and (Sir) John Philipps (4th Bt.), who 'zealously opposed the bill as leaving the nation naked and insecure'. Secretary of State James Vernon I* wrote that this opposition had occurred 'without any concert' with the Court and that Blackett had 'spoke very handsomely and close to the purpose'. He of course voted against the third reading of the disbanding bill. No more of Blackett's speeches are recorded for this session, but his actions upon the issue of the standing army appear to have been sufficient to bring him to the attention of the Court. With his Tory background and new-found willingness to join the Whigs in defending the Court, Blackett was in many ways an ideal candidate for office, given William III's inclination to remodel the ministry along less partisan lines, and in May Montagu wrote to Blackett to inform him of the King's decision to offer him a place on the restructured Treasury board. Montagu wrote of William's 'mighty inclination to have you about him' and assured Blackett that allowances would be made if personal business prevented him from attending London immediately. Blackett nevertheless declined the offer, a refusal which, Montagu reported, 'mightily concerned' the King and which William was not inclined to accept. Rather than press Blackett to accept immediately, however, Montagu explained that the King had 'resolved on this expedient (which may be a secret to other people), that he would keep Sir Stephen Fox* in the commission whom he had designed to put out, that if in the winter, upon discoursing all matters we can incline you to come in, there may be no difficulty in making room for you'. Blackett's high standing at this time is also indicated by a rumour in the following November that he was to be elevated to the peerage, but Blackett neither received this honour nor took a place on the Treasury commission. Blackett remained a Court supporter in this session. In the debate of 13 Feb. 1700 upon grants of forfeited estates to Whig ministers, for example, he was one of the Members who criticized John Grobham Howe's censure of these grants, pointing out that Howe himself had made a request for such a grant in 1689, and, after being nominated on 8 Apr. to manage the conference with the Lords upon the forfeitures bill, on 10 Apr. Blackett joined such Whigs as Lord Hartington (William Cavendish) and Richard Norton in opposing the motion of Sir Christopher Musgrave, 4th Bt., for an address requesting the dismissal of Lord Chancellor Somers (Sir John*). A parliamentary analysis dating from early 1700 listed Blackett as in the interest of the independent Whig the 2nd Earl of Warrington, a classification which though reflecting Blackett's political stance at this time may also have been due to the marriage of Blackett's brother, Sir Edward, to Warrington's aunt.[6]

It was reported in December 1700 that Blackett 'refuses to stand' for re-election, and he remained resolute in this determination until the 1705 election. Appearing to spend most of his time in Newcastle, Blackett occupied himself in pursuing a claim for a debt owed to his family, in respect of a loan his father had made to the king of Denmark in 1658, and keeping a watchful eye on the Scottish border and the northeast coast for possible Jacobite activity. He also busied himself in charitable activity, helping to establish both a charitable school and the keelmen's hospital in Newcastle while contributing towards the building of a chapel for colliers at Allenshead, Northumberland. Blackett ended his political retirement in 1705 when his return for Newcastle was again unopposed, but he was absent from the division of 25 Oct. upon the choice of the Speaker. He set off for London the following month, but his health went into a rapid decline and reports of his death were circulating by 4 Dec. His body was returned to Newcastle for burial, which took place on the 29th. He was succeeded by his eldest son, a Tory who sat for Newcastle from 1710 until his death.[7]

[1] *New Hist. Northumb.* xii. 377; J. Hodgson, *Hist. Northumb.* pt. ii(1), 259–60. [2] *Reg. of Freemen* (Newcastle Rec. Soc. iii), 95; *Arch. Ael.* ser. 4, xviii. 77, 82; *CSP Dom.* 1684–5, p. 205; 1687–9, p. 309; 1689–90, p. 116; *Newcastle Merchant Adventurers* (Surtees Soc. ci), 308; *Newcastle Hostmen's Co.* (Surtees Soc. cv), 263, 272. [3] *Cal. Treas. Bks.* viii. 230–1, 432. [4] R. Welford, *Men of Mark 'twixt Tyne and Tweed*, i. 302; J. Hatcher, *Hist. of British Coal Industry*, i. 253; *New Hist. Northumb.* ii. 62–63; iv. 327, 380; *VCH N. Riding Yorks.* i. 345, 351; *Ailesbury Mems.* 390; G. Holmes, *Pol. in Age of Anne*, 158; Luttrell, *Brief Relation*, v. 619. [5] *Newcastle Hostmen's Co.*, 151; *Cal. Treas. Bks.* xi. 4, 34, 192; *CSP Dom.* 1696, p. 260; Nottingham Univ. Lib. Portland (Bentinck) mss PwA 1461, Vernon to Portland, 7 July 1696; Bodl. Ballard 18, f. 16; Add. 34355, f. 7; Folger Shakespeare Lib. Newdigate newsletter 28 Jan. 1696–7. [6] Hatcher, 532; *Cam. Misc.* xxix. 376, 386; *CSP Dom.* 1699–1700, p. 27; *Vernon–Shrewsbury Letters*, ii. 253, 293; Add. 40773, f. 113; Northumb. RO, Blackett (Matfen) mss, Montagu to Blackett, 11, 27 May 1699; Luttrell, iv. 579; *Cocks Diary*, 51–52; H. Horwitz, *Parl. and Pol. Wm. III*, 268. [7] Add. 70019, f. 285; 28890, f. 303; 28947, f. 252; *CSP Dom.* 1700–2, pp. 523–4; 1703–4, pp. 225, 242, 489, 499, 504, 517–18, 524; *Cal. Treas. Bks.* xv. 450; *A Chapter in Eng. Church Hist.* ed. McClure, 207–8, 300, 303, 328; *Newcastle Hostmen's Co.* 158, 173, 253; *New Hist. Northumb.* iv. 100; Luttrell, v. 619; Welford, 305.

E. C./R. D. H.

BLACKETT, Sir William, 2nd Bt. (1690–1728), of Pilgrim Street, Newcastle-upon-Tyne and Wallington Hall, Northumb.

NEWCASTLE-UPON-TYNE 1710–25 Sept. 1728

b. 11 Feb. 1690, 1st s. of Sir William Blackett, 1st Bt.* educ. Univ. Coll. Oxf. 1705. m. 20 Sept. 1725, Lady Barbara (d. 1761), da. of William Villiers*, 2nd Earl of Jersey, s.p.; 1da. illegit. suc. fa. as 2nd Bt. 29 Dec. 1705.[1]

Freeman, Newcastle 1710; member, merchant adventurers' co. of Newcastle-upon-Tyne 1718, hostmen's co. 1722; gov., hostmen's co. 1726–8; mayor, Newcastle-upon-Tyne 1718.[2]

Blackett inherited his father's considerable estates and extensive mining interests, and his financial well-being was further enhanced in 1708 by the death of Sir John Fenwick's[†] widow, saving Blackett the £2,000 annuity which had been the cost of his father's purchase in 1689 of Fenwick's Northumberland estates. Despite the expectation that his minority would prevent him standing in 1710, Blackett was returned for Newcastle with the unequivocal support of both the corporation and the borough's Church interest, a song published after the election declaring that Blackett and William Wrightson* had stood for 'the Church, the Queen, for peace and the Protestant succession' against 'the Whigs and Dissenters'. He was an inactive Member, and no significant activity is recorded on his part in the 1710–11 session. As one of the cartel controlling the supply of north-east coal he was consulted in November 1710 about this group's response to the proposed bill to prevent combinations in the coal trade, but there is no evidence that he took an active part in opposition to the measure. Despite this lack of recorded activity, the end of the session saw Blackett included upon the list of 'worthy patriots' who had detected the mismanagements of the previous ministry. Having been appointed to the Northumberland bench in the summer of 1711, Blackett supported the attempt of the Newcastle corporation to pass a bill to regulate a hospital established in the borough by Newcastle's keelmen. He was appointed on 18 Jan. 1712 to draft such a bill, and six days later was the first-named Member of the measure's second-reading committee. Though the measure passed the Commons it was defeated in the upper House. In the following session he voted on 18 June 1713 for the French commerce bill, and later the same year was returned for Newcastle unopposed.

Blackett left no trace on the records of the 1713 Parliament, but was included on the Worsley list as a Tory and, having been returned for Newcastle in 1715, was similarly described in two comparisons of the old and new Parliaments. Contrary to common expectation he did not join the Jacobite rebels during the Fifteen and retained his seat until his death on 25 Sept. 1728. His burial, accompanied by a great deal of pomp and ceremony, took place at St. Nicholas', Newcastle on 7 Oct. His estates were left to his illegitimate daughter Elizabeth Ord upon condition that she marry Blackett's nephew Walter Calverley, who thereby inherited Blackett's interest at Newcastle, took the name Blackett in 1733, and sat for Newcastle for over four decades from 1734.[3]

[1] *Arch. Ael.* ser. 4, xviii. 86. [2] *Reg. of Freemen* (Newcastle Rec. Soc. vi), 3; *Newcastle Merchant Adventurers* (Surtees Soc. ci), 344; *Newcastle Hostmen's Co.* (Surtees Soc. cv), 264, 276; *Arch. Ael.* 86. [3] Folger Shakespeare Lib. Newdigate newsletter 2 Nov. 1708; *HMC Portland*, iv. 575; K. Wilson, *Sense of the People*, 138; E. Hughes, *N. Country Life*, i. 175; L. K. J. Glassey, *Appt. JPs*, 211; *HMC Lords*, ix. 230–1; *Barnes Mems.* (Surtees Soc. l), 478.

E. C./R. D. H.

BLACKMORE, Abraham (c.1677–1732), of the Inner Temple.

MITCHELL 1710–1713
NEWTON 1713–1715

b. c.1677, 2nd s. of Thomas Blackmore of St. Martin Pomeroy, London, common councilman of London 1683, 1688–91, by Elizabeth Meredith of St. Giles, Cripplegate, London. *educ.* Sherborne sch.; adm. Trinity Coll. Camb. 21 Jan. 1693, aged 15, BA 1697; I. Temple 1694, called 1700. *m.* lic. 26 July 1713, Edith Stutford of Selworthy, Som.[1]

Commr. public accts. 1714.

Blackmore's father, a distant relation of the physician Sir Richard Blackmore, had been a Tory common councilman of London who in 1690 was listed as one of those who should be consulted should the members of 'the Church party' be approached for a loan to finance the defence of a French invasion. Blackmore snr. had also been elected alderman in 1698 but passed over by the court. At his return for Mitchell in 1710, Abraham Blackmore was classed as a Tory in the 'Hanover list'. On 18 Apr. he told against the retention of the existing managers of the post office in the dominions. By this time Blackmore had joined the October Club, and on 20 Apr. he came fifth in the election of commissioners for the resumption of crown grants made since 1689, a measure sponsored by the Club. The bill, however, did not pass. Given this record it is no surprise that Blackmore was listed among the 'worthy patriots' who in the 1710–11 session detected the mismanagements of the previous administration. During the 1711–12 session he told on two occasions: the first in favour of the expulsion of Adam de Cardonnel for peculation while serving as the Duke of Marlborough's (John Churchill[†]) secretary (19 Feb.), and the second for a new duty upon the importation of black latten and prepared metals (29 Apr.). The 1713 session saw Blackmore tell, on 9 May 1713, against adjourning consideration of the report of the commissioners of accounts into the conduct of the Earl of Wharton (Hon. Thomas*), and six days later he told against the attempt to tack a place bill to the malt tax. The following day he was a teller against inserting a clause reflecting upon the family of the Scottish Jacobite George Lockhart* into a motion of censure against Wharton. His loyalty to the ministry was demonstrated on 18 June when he told in favour of engrossing the French commerce bill, being listed as a supporter of the bill in the printed division list.[2]

At the 1713 election Blackmore was 'handsomely and readily chosen' for Newton as part of the deal between Newton's patron Peter Legh[†] and the Earl of Oxford (Robert Harley*), by which Legh's brother Thomas II* received a place in return for granting Oxford the right to choose Legh's successor at Newton. Blackmore spoke on 18 Mar. 1714 for the motion that Richard Steele* be made to withdraw while the charges against him were heard, and subsequently told for the majority in favour of Steele's expulsion. He told on a further three occasions during this session: against allowing Lord Barrymore (James Barry*) to present a new petition on the Wigan election (6 Apr.); against adjourning the hearing of the Southwark election petition (15 June); and against the attempts of the Hanoverian Tories to recommit a motion that Thomas Heath II* had been duly elected for Harwich (29 June). On 17 June Blackmore had gained election, as one of the October Club's slate, as commissioner of accounts, finishing fifth in the poll with 184 votes. Inactive in the second session of 1714, Blackmore wrote to Peter Legh in December that he had 'determined with myself to quit the public scene', claiming that his withdrawal was due to 'a constitution that begins to feel the effects of living almost continually in this town [London]', and that he had resolved 'not only to leave the Parliament, but England too, for a year or two'. Blackmore instead pressed his political ally William Shippen* to apply to Legh for his seat, and Blackmore does not appear to have been a candidate at any subsequent election. He died in the Fleet prison on 18 May 1732, 'having cut his [own] throat'.[3]

[1] J. R. Woodhead, *Rulers of London* (London and Mdx. Arch. Soc.), 32; Soc. of Geneal. par. reg. index. [2] Woodhead, 32; Beaven, *Aldermen*, i. 151; Dorset RO, Fox-Strangways mss D124/box 235 bdle. 4, Peter Rich† to Sir Stephen Fox*, 17 Mar. 1690; *Huntington Lib. Q.* xxxiii. 171; D. Szechi, *Jacobitism and Tory Pol.* 77, 81–82, 130; *Daily Courant*, 7 Apr. 1712; *Bull. IHR*, xxxix. 64. [3] John Rylands Univ. Lib. Manchester, Legh of Lyme mss corresp. Peter Legh to John Ward III*, c.21 Aug. 1713, Blackmore to Legh, 9 Dec. 1714, Shippen to same, 9 Dec. 1714; *HMC Portland*, v. 331; Douglas diary (Hist. of Parl. trans.), 18 Mar. 1714; Add. 70305, ballot list, c. June 1714; NLS, Advocates' mss, Wodrow pprs. letters Quarto 8, f. 138; *Gent. Mag.* 1732, p. 775.

E. C./R. D. H.

BLACKWELL, Sir Lambert (*d.*1727), of St. James's, Westminster and Sprowston Hall, Norf.

WILTON 1708–1710

s. of John Blackwell, Grocer, of Bethnal Green, Mdx. and Mortlake, Surr. by his 2nd w. da. of Gen. John Lambert† of Calton, nr. Malham Tarn, Yorks. and Wimbledon, Surr. *m.* 17 Aug. 1697, Elizabeth, da. of Sir Joseph Herne*, 1s. 2da. (1 *d.v.p.*). Kntd. 23 Apr. 1697; *cr.* Bt. 16 July 1718.[1]

Member, Levant Co. 1672–?*d.*; director, S. Sea Co. 1715–21.[2]

Consul at Florence 1688–90, at Leghorn 1689–96, 1697–1705; agent for prizes and for droits and perquisites of Admiralty at Leghorn 1689–96, 1702–5; envoy extraordinary to Tuscany 1689–90, 1697–1705, to Genoa 1697–8, 1702–5, to Venice Feb.–Mar. 1702; surveyor-gen. of agents for prizes 1697; knight harbinger 1697–1701.[3]

Sheriff, Norf. 1719–20.

Blackwell's father, himself the son of a City merchant active in the Parliamentarian cause during the Civil War, was a captain in Cromwell's regiment in the New Model Army, subsequently serving as a treasurer for war under the Commonwealth and Protectorate. His first wife was distantly related to Cromwell; the second was a daughter of General Lambert. After the Restoration John Blackwell settled for a time in Ireland, where he had acquired property confiscated in the Cromwellian conquest, then emigrated to New England. Quickly developing landed and commercial interests there, he was appointed lieutenant-governor of Pennsylvania by William Penn in 1688 but quarrelled with the colonial assembly and threw up the office within a year. Lambert, a younger son, and possibly the first son of the second marriage, was 'bred a merchant' in the Turkey trade, and by the Revolution was well established at Leghorn. Employed by King William in consular and minor diplomatic work in Italy, he sought to improve his position by acquiring the patronage of the powerful, applying to the Duke of Shrewsbury among others. In 1697 his fortunes rose sharply. Returning to England, he was knighted, was named as knight harbinger and envoy to Genoa and Tuscany, and contracted a profitable marriage. He had embarked again by the end of the year, and arrived in Genoa in May 1698, having survived insults and violence from 'some persons belonging to the Duke of Berwick' encountered on the way. This second spell in Italy lasted seven years. He was not universally popular among the English merchants and gentlemen who applied to him for help, giving an impression of snobbishness, though Swift, for one, considered him 'a very good natured man'. Macky's *Memoirs* sketched him at this stage in his career:

> he affects much the gentleman in his dress, and the minister in his conversation; is very lofty, yet courteous, when he knows his people; much envied by his fellow merchants; of a sanguine complexion, taller than the ordinary size.[4]

Having in the summer of 1704 made approaches to friends in England for their help in moving him from his present 'troublesome, expensive employment' and effecting his reappointment as envoy to Venice, 'which will entitle me to an envoy's pay', Blackwell found himself instead recalled by letters dated November 1704, and took leave of the Grand Duke of Tuscany for the last time in February 1705. Back in England he continued his unsuccessful solicitations for senior ambassadorial postings and looked for a seat in Parliament, coming in for Wilton in 1708, where his mercantile interests, maintained throughout his stay in Florence and Genoa, were a distinct asset. Classed as a Whig in a list of 1708, his election reckoned a 'gain' by Lord Sunderland (Charles, Lord Spencer*), he voted in 1709 for the naturalization of the Palatines, and a year later for the impeachment of Dr Sacheverell. His one tellership occurred on 5 Apr. 1709, against a bill to make two Dutch-built vessels free ships. His ambitions and commitments made it easy to present him as one 'apt to follow the Court': during the 1708 Parliament he was petitioning the crown for a regrant of his father's estate in Ireland, and was awaiting payment of various expenses incurred as envoy. He found himself opposed by stauncher Whigs at Wilton and did not stand again.[5]

Blackwell was still of value to government after 1710 as a financier: he and a partner advanced some £60,000 to the crown in 1710–11, and under George I he acted as an intermediary in the raising of international loans, using his Genoese connexions. He was also prominent, though not especially active, in the South Sea Company, in which he had invested £13,000 at the outset, becoming a director in 1715. At about this time he began to acquire extensive property in east Norfolk, accumulating a rent roll of between £3,500 and £4,000 p.a. by 1720–1. This, together with his personal estate of around £30,000, became liable to sequestration under the terms of the South Sea Sufferers' Act of 1721. Although Blackwell, who pleaded that he had had no share in the 'secret management' of the scheme, and had been 'more weak than blameable', suffered less severely than others, his landed estate had to be dispersed.[6]

Blackwell died on 27 Oct. 1727, leaving not a will but two 'testamentary schedules', subsequently proved, which detailed the repayment of a £7,000 loan to his wife, and a bequest of £2,000 to his surviving daughter, the residue of the estate passing to his son, Sir Charles, 2nd Bt.[7]

[1] PCC 285 Farrant; J. R. Woodhead, *Rulers of London* (London and Mdx. Arch. Soc.), 32; G. E. Aylmer, *State's Servants*, 244; *Massachusetts Hist. Colls.* ser. 3, i. 63; *CSP Dom.* 1697, p. 321; *True and Exact Inventory . . . Sir Lambert Blackwell* (1721), pp. 11, 22. [2] Info. from Prof. R. Walcott; J. Carswell, *S. Sea Bubble*, 274. [3] Carswell, 274; Luttrell, *Brief Relation*, i. 603; iv. 248; Add. 28910, ff. 421–2; *Cal. Treas. Bks.* xi. 232; xii. 286; xvii. 1025; xix. 199, 483; xx. 590; xxi. 421; *Cal. Treas. Pprs.* 1702–7, p. 152; 1714–19, p. 89. [4] Woodhead, 32; Aylmer, 242–5; *Biog. Dict. 17th Cent. Brit. Radicals* ed. Greaves and Zaller, i. 68–69; J. Winsor, *Narrative and Critical Hist. America*, iii. 495; v. 207; C. P. Keith, *Chrons. Pennsylvania*, i. 184, 202; *Macky Mems.* (1733), 149; Add. 28897, f. 371; *HMC Buccleuch*, ii. 374; Luttrell, iv. 331, 346; *HMC Portland*, v. 71; *Swift Works* ed. Davis, v. 261. [5] *HMC 6th Rep.* 315; Add. 34356, ff. 61–62; 28056, f. 236; 28916, f. 119; *HMC Buccleuch*, ii. 707–8, 765; *HMC Portland*, iv. 344; *Duchess of Marlborough Corresp.* i. 123; Pembroke mss at Wilton House, R. Payne to James Harris, 10 Jan. 1707[-8], memo. 16 Feb. 1710; *Cal. Treas. Bks.* xxii. 295; xxiv. 22, 333. [6] *Cal. Treas. Bks.* xxix. 157; xxx. 123–4; *Case of Sir Lambert Blackwell* [?1721]; Add. 22221, f. 172; Carswell, 146, 218, 249, 255, 274–5; P. G. M. Dickson, *Financial Revol.* 119; Blomefield, *Norf.* vii. 217, 223, 227, 231, 254; x. 138; xi. 129, 136; *True and Exact Inventory*, 1–10, 27, 31, 33. [7] *Hist. Reg. Chron.* 1727, p. 49; PCC 285 Farrant.

D. W. H.

BLAGRAVE, Anthony (1680–1744), of Southcote, Reading, Berks.

READING 1701 (Dec.)–1702, 1708–1710
1722–1727

bap. 21 Sept. 1680, 1st s. of John Blagrave† of Southcote by Hester, da. of William Gore, merchant, of Barrow Gurney, Som. and London. *educ.* St. John's, Oxf. 1696. *m.* bef. 1706, his cos. Mary, da. of William Gore of Barrow Gurney (gds. of William Gore supra), 2s. 5da. (2 d.v.p.). *suc.* fa. 1704.[1]

Freeman, Reading 1701; sheriff, Berks. 1712–13.[2]

Blagrave came from a Whiggish family. His father, a Member of the Exclusion Parliaments, had been perceived as a possible collaborator of James II, and later was probably an investor in the Bank of England. Active after the Revolution as a justice and deputy-lieutenant in Berkshire, he was also consulted on county elections and by Reading corporation on some internal affairs. The basis of the Blagrave interest in Reading was property. Apart from Southcote, the family held a large number of houses (described unfavourably by Hearne in 1714), as well as other property leased from the crown in partnership with the Dalbys. Blagrave himself was admitted to the freedom of the borough on 13 Nov. 1701, just a few days prior to his election to the Commons. Lord Spencer (Charles*) failed to realize that Blagrave's victory over Sir Owen Buckingham* represented a loss for the Whigs, possibly because of the traditional political views of the Blagrave family. Robert Harley* was better informed, listing Blagrave with the Tories in an analysis of the newly elected Parliament. Blagrave was appointed to a single drafting committee in January 1702 and his name also appeared on the 'white list' of those who favoured the motion of 26 Feb. vindicating the proceedings of the Commons in the impeachment of William III's Whig ministers.[3]

Blagrave stood down at the 1702 election, for some unknown reason. His father died in March 1704 and it is likely that around this time he married his first cousin once removed, thereby acquiring considerable property in Somerset. He regained his seat in 1708, being classed as a Tory on a list of early 1708 with the returns added, an analysis confirmed by the Earl of Sunderland (Charles Spencer), who this time accounted his election a loss for the Whigs. His only recorded tellership occurred on 14 Apr. 1709, a vain effort to keep some words in the Lords' bill preserving the rights of patrons to advowsons. The tellers involved suggest that this view was held by Tory Churchmen. Not surprisingly, Blagrave voted in 1710 against the impeachment of Dr Sacheverell. He stood down again at the 1710 election, probably in favour of John Dalby*. He did not return to the Commons until 1722, by which time the Jacobites seem to have entertained hopes of his commitment to their cause, his name appearing on a list sent to the Pretender in 1721. After retiring from the Commons again in 1727 he had the pleasure of seeing his eldest son, John, returned for Reading in a by-election in 1739. By the time Blagrave was buried in December 1744 he had become a wealthy man, able to bequeath his estates in Berkshire and Somerset to John, £5,000 to his second son, and £4,000 apiece to his three surviving daughters.[4]

[1] *St. Mary's, Reading Par. Reg.* i. 88, 111, 114; ii. 146, 151; *Vis. Berks.* (Harl. Soc. lvi), 173. [2] Berks. RO, Reading corp. diary, 13 Nov. 1701. [3] Duckett, *Penal Laws and Test Act* (1883), 237; DZA, Bonet despatch 6/16 July 1694; *CSP Dom.* 1700–2, p. 249; *HMC*

Downshire, i. 558, 562; Reading corp. diary, 2 June 1690, 21 Dec. 1691; *Hearne Colls.* iv. 358–9; *Cal. Treas. Bks. and Pprs. 1742–5*, p. 124; *Bull. IHR*, xlv. 44. [4] J. Collinson, *Som.* ii. 206, 309; P. S. Fritz, *Ministers and Jacobitism 1715–45*, p.151; *St. Mary's, Reading Par. Reg.* ii. 174; PCC 3 Seymer.

S. N. H.

BLAKE, Sir Francis (1638–1718), of Ford Castle, Northumb.

BERWICK-UPON-TWEED 1689–1695, 1698–1700
NORTHUMBERLAND 1701 (Dec.)–1705

bap. 17 Oct. 1638, 2nd s. of Francis Blake of Highgate, Mdx. and Cogges, Oxon., registrar of fines in c.p. by 1646–*d.*, by his 1st w. Catherine, da. of Valentine Browne of Croft, Lincs. *m.* 13 Feb. 1662, Elizabeth, da. and coh. of Thomas Carr of Ford Castle, 1s. *d.v.p.* 7da. (2 *d.v.p.*). Kntd. 27 Aug. 1689; *suc.* bro. in Oxon. estate 1695.[1]

Though his mother had some connexion with Northumberland, Blake owed his estates in the county, including valuable collieries, to his marriage. His main seat was at Ford Castle, just ten miles outside Berwick-upon-Tweed, and, having represented the borough in the Convention, Blake retained his seat in 1690, and in March was classed as a Whig by Lord Carmarthen (Sir Thomas Osborne[†]). His first recorded speech came during a sitting of the supply committee on 31 Mar., when, in response to a plea from Sir Thomas Lee, 2nd Bt., for money to pay seamen's wages, Blake answered, in a somewhat disgruntled fashion, that 'they prorogued us and then dissolved us; surely they knew where money was to be had. It is so hot from the Mint that it has dropped through our hats.' Throughout the early sessions of this Parliament Blake's primary concern was the security of the new regime. This first became evident in the debate of 26 Apr. upon the abjuration bill, when Blake spoke in support of this measure and expressed the hope 'that those who refuse, may be clapt upon in safe hold'. Though this measure fell, Blake was nominated on 29 Apr. to draft a bill to secure the government, and on 20 May the Commons ordered him to obtain from the indisposed Sir James Rushout, 1st Bt.*, information concerning conspiracies against the government taking place in Worcestershire. Blake delivered this information to the House later the same day. No activity of Blake's has been recorded for the 1690-1 session, though in April 1691 he was listed by Robert Harley* as a Court supporter. More is known of his contribution to the 1691–2 session, when he proposed and carried amendments to the excise bill (14 Dec.) and the bill vesting the forfeited English estates in the crown (12 Feb.). His main interest, however, was the investigation of Jacobite plotting. On 16 Nov. he seconded Sir Edward Hussey's motion that the Commons address the King asking that the examinations and confessions of Matthew Crone and Lord Preston (Sir Richard Grahme[†]) be laid before the House. Three days later he queried whether the address had been delivered. Blake was also involved in the investigations into William Fuller's allegations that a number of prominent politicians had been involved in Jacobite intrigues. On 2 Dec. he and Sir Charles Sedley, 5th Bt.*, informed the House that they had received letters from Fuller claiming that he had information 'relating to the safety of the King and this government', and asked that Fuller be brought to the bar of the Commons to disclose this information. A week later Fuller was heard by the House, following which Blake moved for an address requesting that the King grant Fuller 'some allowance'. Though the ensuing debate decided against such an address it did resolve to grant Fuller an 'allowance for his maintenance' and to enable him to bring over from France two men who he claimed could substantiate his allegations. Consideration of Fuller's claims continued in the new year, and on 1 Jan. 1692 Fuller requested that Blake be one of six Members with whom he could confer on how to manage the bringing over of his two witnesses. Three days later Fuller again appeared before the House to request that these witnesses be granted the protection of the House for their journey to England. Though Blake noted the apparent contradictions in Fuller's statement, he nevertheless proposed that the House address the King to offer Fuller's witnesses such protection. Blake's close association with this case continued on 22 Feb., when Fuller's failure to attend the Commons led to Blake's inclusion upon a committee appointed to examine Fuller in his lodgings. Soon after this the House lost its patience with Fuller's procrastination and a legal prosecution against him was initiated. On 17 Nov. 1692 the House granted Blake permission to appear in the court of King's bench during Fuller's trial. Blake was less active in the 1692–3 session, though he spoke on three occasions: to support Paul Foley I's* proposal to raise £1,000,000 by a sale of annuities upon a tontine provision (15 Dec.); against the bill extending the patent for convex lights (30 Dec.); and unsuccessfully to propose a clause to the land tax bill which would have allowed mortgagees to deduct 4s. in the pound from interest paid on such loans (6 Jan. 1693). In the spring of 1693 he was classed as a Court supporter with a place or pension, though the nature of this emolument is uncertain. Thereafter he was less conspicuous in the House, though on 23 Apr. 1694 he told in the favour of the bill regulating Hackney coaches, and on 2 Jan. 1695 in favour of the ways and means committee being to sit the following day.[2]

Blake was defeated at Berwick in 1695, his petition against the return being unsuccessful, but he regained his seat in 1698 and in about September that year a comparison of the old and new Commons classed him as a Court supporter, though a later addition marked him as 'Q'. Blake proved such a qualification unnecessary, however, during the consideration of the disbanding bill. Though the contents of his speeches of 4 and 18 Jan. 1699 upon this bill are unknown, on the latter date he voted against this measure. Presumably in the expectation that this support for the ministry would bring some pecuniary reward, Blake lobbied the ministry after the end of the 1698–9 session for government office. Before embarking for the continent in the summer of 1699, the King informed the secretary of state, James Vernon I*, that the only place available was that of victualling commissioner, but Blake was unwilling to accept this post and thereby initiated summer-long discussions concerning his pretensions to government favour. According to Vernon, Blake's disinclination to accept the place of victualling commissioner stemmed from the belief that 'it was not worth his while to attend such an employment', and Vernon also reported that Blake would 'only accept it on condition that he may make it over to some other person'. The secretary of state regarded this as a statement that Blake would sell the place. He appealed to Blake to 'consider how infamous that would be' and recommended that Blake consult with Charles Montagu* and Lord Chancellor Somers (Sir John*). After discussions with the Junto, Blake offered to accept the office and exercise it himself, though Montagu had 'hinted' to Blake that payment of a sum of money would perhaps be more beneficial than the place. Montagu's advice was founded upon a desire to place other Members in the commission, and Vernon wrote to the King asking for advice on how to proceed, reminding William of 'Sir Francis' zeal, and I believe [you] would not have it checked, if nothing be done for him he is like to be uneasy'. Blake declared himself indifferent as to whether he should receive money, which he hoped would amount to £1,500 while Vernon wished to limit it to £500, or the place of victualling commissioner. Vernon was informed that the addition of the inexperienced Blake to this commission would not be welcomed by the Admiralty, and this consideration appears to have dictated that Blake receive money rather than a place. At the beginning of August Vernon was making preparations for 'the first payment' to Blake. Though the Court had gone to great lengths to secure Blake's loyalty, he was not an active Member in the 1699–1700 session. In early 1700 an analysis of the House according to 'interests' identified him as a follower of Lord Warrington, an obscure attribution that perhaps stemmed from the relationship between Warrington and Blake's fellow Northumbrian Member Sir Edward Blackett, 2nd Bt.[3]

Blake does not appear to have stood for election in January 1701, but at the second election of the year was returned for both Berwick and Northumberland. On 7 Jan. 1702 he informed the House of his decision to sit for the county, and on 7 Feb. seconded Emmanuel Scrope Howe's motion that the House investigate allegations that three Tory Members of the previous Parliament had, contrary to an order of the House, met with the French chargé d'affaires Poussin. Blake told on five occasions during this session. Three of these tellerships related to the Irish forfeitures, activity which may well have been prompted by the fact of his own family connexions in Ireland. He also told in favour of a Lords' amendment to the bill to secure the monarch and Protestant succession (6 May), and against an amendment to a bill requiring Jews to maintain and provide for such of their children as became Protestants (8 May). Blake retained his seat in 1702, and his Whig loyalties were again evident in this Parliament. On 13 Feb. 1703 he voted for agreeing with the Lords' amendments to the bill enlarging the time for taking the Abjuration, and, having been forecast in October 1704 as a likely opponent of the Tack, on 28 Nov. either voted against the measure or was absent from the House. His only other significant activity in this session was to assist in the management of two bills relating to Durham and Northumberland estates. Blake was defeated at the Northumberland election of 1705, though he was nevertheless included in an analysis of the new Parliament being classed as 'Low Church', and was also unsuccessful at the Berwick election of 1708. He does not appear to have stood for election again. He died on 8 Jan. 1718, and was succeeded in his estates by his daughters and his nephew Francis Delaval†.[4]

[1] *Kensington Par. Reg.* (Harl. Soc. Reg. xvi), 25, 31; *New Hist. Northumb.* xi. 402; *Lincs. Peds.* (Harl. Soc. l), 181; *Paroch. Colls.* (Oxf. Rec. Soc. ii), 100. [2] *New Hist. Northumb.* 403–9; Grey, x. 25, 225; Bodl. Rawl. A.89. f. 79; *Luttrell Diary*, 23, 28, 69, 78, 103, 110, 182, 199, 322, 340, 354. [3] *Vernon–Shrewsbury Letters*, ii. 300; Add. 40774, ff. 25, 34, 42, 52, 62–4, 70–71, 93, 97, 128. [4] *Cocks Diary*, 206; *New Hist. Northumb.* 408–9.

E. C./R. D. H.

BLANCH, John (c.1649–1725), of Wotton Court, nr. Gloucester and Eastington, Glos.

GLOUCESTER 1710–1713

b. c.1649. m. 25 Jan. 1688, Hannah (d. 1709), da. of William Mew, rector of Eastington, 1s. (d.v.p.) 1da.[1]

The identity of Blanch's parents has not been ascertained, but they were probably citizens of Gloucester. As a successful and wealthy clothier he purchased the Wotton Court estate in 1683 a short distance from the city. By the early 1690s he had become an important and well-informed lobbyist on behalf of the 'rich Gloucestershire clothiers', initially in their long-standing struggle to prevent the Blackwell Hall factors monopolizing the London cloth market and forcing clothiers to buy often inferior wool at inflated prices. A printed 'case' of 1699 mentions him as having been prominent in the attempts to place legislative restrictions on the factors in 1692 and 1693, a cause which he pursued again in 1699 when a new bill was initiated. In a pamphlet he published in 1694 he asserted that the suffering reputation of English wool in foreign markets arose from a decline in quality. He also advocated the regulation of mercantile activity in foreign markets wherever it undermined the trade in English wool. In 1698, for instance, he notified Edward Clarke I*, a commissioner of customs, that the East India merchants' intrusion into the Persian markets was upsetting the delicate reciprocal trade in silk and woollen cloth, and suggested that the situation could be remedied by uniting the East India and Levant companies into a single chartered body. He, of course, typified the protectionist opinions of his interest and its sometimes draconian extremes. In 1704, when a bill to hinder commerce with France was pending, he submitted a proposal to Secretary Harley (Robert*) to prohibit 'the wearing of hoods and scarves by all persons under such a degree of quality as your honourable House shall think fit, and by as strict an injunction of the wear of hats'.[2]

At the 1710 election Blanch was encouraged to stand for Gloucester and made a direct application for support to Harley. It was presumed by one observer that he stood purely 'in order to serve Mr Webb', a leading corporation Tory who was seeking re-election, as otherwise it was not apparent 'what pleasure he can take in the House'. But those well versed in Gloucester's affairs saw positive benefits in having 'honest John Blanch' as an MP and felt that he would 'prove a useful man in the affair of Blackwell Hall and the merchandise of our cloth, which has been for some time under a very disadvantageous management'. Following his election he was classed as a Tory in the 'Hanover list' of the new Parliament and was counted one of the 'worthy patriots' who during the first session helped to expose the mismanagements of the Godolphin administration. He was gratified to see the stimulus given to commerce by Harley's recovery from Guiscard's assassination attempt. Informing the chancellor at the end of March 1711 that 'bills of exchange that could not be discounted at 12 per cent may now be done at six per cent', he looked forward to telling him in person of the 'alteration in many other affairs', adding,

> it's plain to me that the chief heads of our faction will in a little time appear to be but slenderly supported, so that like Samson's riddle, sweet is like to come out of bitter, and a happy reconciliation of our unhappy divisions ... and as you have been signally instrumental in the happiest turn of affairs that may have ever happened to this kingdom, that the same good providence may still influence your actions to a peace which I think as our affairs now stand is highly needful.

Despite Blanch's consuming interest in commercial issues, he was not active in promoting measures in the House. He preferred instead to work 'behind the scenes' in persuading members of the government of the efficacy of various fiscal incentives to trade. As an MP he evidently felt he could now approach ministers with the weight of backbench opinion behind him. In January 1711 he submitted to Harley a detailed conspectus of proposals for the supply, designed to stimulate various branches of manufacture and trade; and repeated the exercise again in 1712. He enjoyed the position of an unofficial adviser whose expertise Harley periodically sought, and of being able to bend ministerial ears when necessary. In July 1711 he was consulted by the lord treasurer's brother Edward* on means of preventing the export of wool, and responded directly to Lord Oxford with his thoughts in full, the main thrust of which was that the laws 'lately made are very good, only ineffectual'. In 1713 he was active in sounding out MPs' views in relation to the restoration of full commercial links with France, and 'finding many Members that serve for clothing ports very pressing', proposed to Oxford the early repeal of laws prohibiting the admission of English woollen fabrics to France. At the election Blanch stood again, but his position had seriously weakened after the ministers had persuaded Thomas Webb, his fellow MP and main source of electoral support, to make way for another candidate. He none the less persisted, but lacking Webb's assistance came a poor third in the poll. He began canvassing again two weeks later, on hearing that one of the new Members was gravely ill, but the MP recovered, and he thereafter showed no further interest in recovering his seat. He subsequently devoted his energies to schemes for advancing Gloucester's position as a centre for the marketing and shipping of cloth, although an ambitious plan of 1723 could not overcome difficulties in the navigation of the lower Severn. He died on 10 July 1725, aged 76, and was buried at Gloucester's church of St Mary Magdalen. His only son having predeceased him, his estates passed to a nephew.[3]

[1] T. D. Fosbrooke, *Gloucester*, 154; *Mar. Lic. Vicar-Gen.* (Harl. Soc. xxxi), 42; *Misc. Gen. et Her.*, ser. 5, ii. 295–6. [2] *VCH Glos.* iv. 388; *The Blackwell Hall Factors' Case*... (1699); Blanch, *The Interest of England Considered in an Essay Upon Wool*... (1694); Som. RO, Sanford mss DD/SF 3839, Blanch to Clarke, 15 June 1698; Add. 70161, same to Harley, 20 Nov. 1704. [3] Add. 70211, Blanch to Harley, 18 Sept. 1710, 31 Mar. 1710[–11], 7 July 1711, 7 June 1713; 70226, Thomas Foley II* to same, 25 Sept. 1710; 70319, Blanch to same, 22 Jan. 1710[–11]; Christ Church, Oxf. Wake mss 23/209, Maurice Wheeler to Bp. Wake, 30 Oct. 1710; Bodl. Ballard 31, f. 120; *VCH Glos.* iv. 128, 388, 398; Fosbrooke, 154.

P. W./A. A. H.

BLAND, Sir John, 4th Bt. (1663–1715), of Kippax Park, Yorks. and Hulme Hall, Lancs.

APPLEBY   1681 (Mar.)
PONTEFRACT   1690–1695, 1698–1713

b. 2 Nov. 1663, 2nd s. of Sir Francis Bland, 2nd Bt., of Kippax Park by Jane, da. of Sir William Lowther[†] of Swillington, Yorks. *educ.* Univ. Coll. Oxf. 1679. *m.* 31 Mar. 1685, Anne (*d.* 1734), da. and h. of Sir Edward Mosley of Hulme Hall, 4s. (3 *d.v.p.*) 5da. (4 *d.v.p.*). *suc.* bro. as 4th Bt. 14 Dec. 1668.[1]

Alderman, Pontefract 1698–Sept. 1715, mayor 1703–4; commr. Aire and Calder Navigation, 1699; steward, Salford hundred and master forester, Simonswood and Croxteth, Lancs. 1702–6.[2]

Commr. revenue [I] 1704–6.[3]

Bland probably entered Parliament in 1681 at the behest of his maternal grandfather. Despite his marriage to the daughter of a Presbyterian sympathizer, Sir Edward Mosley (whose own wife and mother-in-law were certainly Dissenters), Bland's career was one of unwavering support for Anglicanism. He joined the 'true sons of the Church of England', a Lancashire group that volunteered to serve against Monmouth, and was clearly capable of violence over religious issues: in November 1687 he smashed the windows of a conventicle during a service. This incident perhaps reflected his rage at James II's Declaration of Indulgence and the reversal of political alliances which was eventually to lead to his own removal from the Lancashire bench in April 1688. Indeed, it is probable that the threat to the Church of England led Bland to become involved in Lord Delamere's plans for a north-western rising in support of the Prince of Orange. On 8 Oct. 1688, barely three weeks after Bland had been appointed a deputy-lieutenant of the West Riding, Lord Delamere was a guest at Hulme. When Delamere marched 'soldier-like' into Manchester on 16 Nov., one of Lord Middleton's informants heard Bland's name mentioned among a list of notables said to be supporting the rising. Indeed, on that same day it was reported that Bland had been 'taken at Rochdale going into Yorkshire' and forced to return to Manchester. Given Bland's Yorkshire connexion and his likely agreement with Delamere's manifesto on the need to defend Protestantism, it would seem likely that he was to be a link between Delamere and the revolt planned by Danby (Sir Thomas Osborne[†]) on the other side of the Pennines. After having his plans thwarted, Bland probably travelled westwards to join William, for on 4 Dec. he wrote a letter to his wife from Tewkesbury. Further evidence of a link with Delamere can be inferred from the latter's visit to Hulme on 24 Dec.[4]

Bland did not contest the elections to the Convention, but he was returned in 1690 for Pontefract, the borough closest to his seat at Kippax. Following his election he was classed by Danby, now Marquess of Carmarthen, as a Tory and probably as a supporter of the Court. During the summer of 1690, in conduct noticeably consistent with his earlier attitudes to religious minorities, he was active in Yorkshire, together with Sir Edmund Jennings*, in harrying Papists and others perceived to be disaffected to the government. Carmarthen included Bland on two lists dating from December 1690, one a calculation of those likely to support the Marquess in the event of a Commons attack upon his ministerial position, the other a more general list of Court supporters. On the other hand, in April 1691 Robert Harley* classed him as a Country supporter. If Bland was inclined to adopt a Country stance this did not preclude him from soliciting a place; thus, on 3 Aug. 1691, he wrote to George Clarke*, the secretary at war in Ireland, suggesting that 'if at the new modelling of your Irish government there be any idle employs fit for one that loves their ease as little as I do, there cannot be a fitter person and I believe I could have friends above to speak for me'. Although he was unsuccessful in this approach, the acquisition of a place become Bland's chief aim throughout his parliamentary career. On 15 Nov. 1692 Philip Bickerstaffe, Member for Northumberland, claimed that the actions of three men in suing Bland in the court of Exchequer constituted a breach of privilege. After Bland had himself confirmed that he had not sued them, the culprits were ordered into custody, being released on 6 Dec. after seeking pardon. From an early age Bland appears to have suffered periodic bouts of ill-health, particularly gout, which necessitated prolonged absences from the Commons: on 4 Jan. 1693 and 27 Jan. 1694 he was given leave of absence. On the second occasion he returned to the country only to be caught out by a call of the House on 14 Feb., whereupon he was ordered into custody. On his discharge on 25 Feb. he did not linger in London, and was back in the North by 9 Mar., where he wrote to Roger Kenyon* that 'these long sessions, I fancy, will incline a great many to be for the frequent calling of Parliaments, that were against it formerly'.[5]

Although Bland was still keen to remain in Parliament he was defeated at the 1695 election. He petitioned the Commons on 2 Nov. and travelled to London to press his case in person. No doubt the sharp eye he kept on the prospects of overturning his own defeat was responsible for his report to Kenyon on 31 Dec. 1695 that 'the last night was the first time there was any trial of skill betwixt Court and Country at the committee of elections this session, and it was a very full committee'. In the same letter Bland went on to discuss the bill for regulating the silver coin of the kingdom, which had passed the Commons on 27 Dec., and the accompanying proclamation on the deadlines for phasing out the old denominations. These measures had not only hit the West country particularly hard but 'guineas is now come to 30s. again, but half-crowns are now condemned quite, and it is the goldsmiths' trade to buy them at an underworth. Shillings and sixpences do pass pretty well, though not worth 2d. a piece, except at the market'. By 16 Jan. 1696 Bland had returned to Yorkshire, withdrawing his election petition officially on 10 Feb. According to the notes taken by the Earl of Bridgwater (John Egerton†), Bland was turned out of the Yorkshire commission of the peace for refusing to sign the Association. However, by April 1700 he was back serving as a deputy-lieutenant in the West Riding. In the last session of the 1695 Parliament he petitioned the Commons in the hope of forcing the undertakers of the Aire and Calder navigation to purchase or rent his mills, dams and weirs on the River Aire, which he foresaw being greatly damaged by their proposals. His petition was one of 21 against the bill as it stood unamended, and the opposition probably explains why the bill failed to pass both Houses before Parliament was prorogued.[6]

By 1698 Bland had become a major landowner in Lancashire as well as Yorkshire. Although he had enlarged his Yorkshire property through the purchase of lands in Allerton and Brigshaw, it was his wife's inheritance which formed the most significant addition to his property. Sir Edward Mosley's death in 1695 brought him control of the manors of Withington, Heaton Norris and Manchester, to which was added Hulme on the death of Lady Mosley in 1697. However, it was to Pontefract that Bland looked to regain his seat in the Commons, a feat he duly accomplished at the 1698 election, topping the poll. On an analysis of the old and new Commons, compiled in about September 1698, Bland was classed as a Country supporter, and he was also forecast as a likely opponent of a standing army. When the Aire and Calder navigation bill was reintroduced in the 1698–9 session, Bland emerged as one of its major supporters, reporting the measure to the House on 13 Mar. and being ordered eight days later to carry the bill to the Lords. The reason for his *volte-face* was the favourable settlement allowed him by the undertakers whereby he leased his mills on the river to them for 41 years at £97 10s. p.a. and was allowed to transport coal and lime from his pits, toll free, on part of the river. No wonder he subscribed £500 to the undertaking.[7]

Returned again for Pontefract in January 1701, Bland was listed in February as likely to support the Court in agreeing with the supply committee to continue the 'Great Mortgage'. Later, he was blacklisted for having in this Parliament opposed the preparations for war against France, although he left before the prorogation, being given leave of absence on 22 May. After the election of November 1701 he was listed with the Tories by Robert Harley, and as having favoured the motion of 26 Feb. 1702 vindicating the Commons' proceedings during the previous session in the impeachments of the Whig lords. By the beginning of Anne's reign his interest at Pontefract appeared more secure, no doubt because he was a generous benefactor to the town, one order of this period regarding the commencement of a suit on behalf of the corporation noting that an assessment would be levied 'in case Sir John Bland will not prosecute it at his own charge'. With such financial dependence, Bland's re-election in 1702 was unsurprising. The installation of the Tories in office by the Queen brought him scant reward, although Sir John Leveson Gower, 5th Bt.*, was probably instrumental in ensuring that he obtained the stewardship of Salford hundred, where Bland's Lancashire estates lay. Clearly he plied the leading ministerialists with requests for employment: in March 1703 the Duke of Marlborough (John Churchill†) reminded Lord Treasurer Godolphin (Sidney†) that Bland had been promised the first vacancy at the Board of Green

Cloth, excepting only a place belonging to Charles Scarborough, who was reported at that time to be ailing. Bland would no doubt have been a useful recruit for the Court, since he was certainly a High Tory, a fact demonstrated by his appearance in March 1704 on Lord Nottingham's (Daniel Finch†) forecast of support on the Scotch Plot. By the following month rumours were abroad concerning the demise of another of the officers of the Green Cloth, Scarborough having recovered. Marlborough was pressed to obtain the first vacancy for his own brother-in-law, Charles Godfrey*, who had earlier been promised Scarborough's place. In the event it was Godfrey who received the first vacancy, while in August 1704 Bland replaced Hon. Francis Robartes* as an Irish revenue commissioner. Meanwhile Bland had opened up a second front in his campaign for preferment, by entering into correspondence with the new secretary of state, Robert Harley. He foresaw a dissolution of Parliament following quickly upon Harley's appointment, in which case he cited his possession of the mayoralty of Pontefract as disabling him from seeking re-election, something which troubled him little as he had 'satisfied my curiosity enough, and had been at so much expense and trouble about elections and attending the Parliament', so that even if qualified he was resolved not to stand again. As the threat of an immediate dissolution disappeared, however, he changed his mind. At a council meeting in Pontefract in November 1704 (which, as usual, Bland failed to attend in person) the corporation was informed that he had 'a mind to give some money for the common good of the said borough', an offer which was accepted with alacrity, the corporation designating the rebuilding of the steeple of St. Giles' chapel as an appropriate object of his munificence. As a Tory office-holder, Bland occupied a pivotal position in the battle over the occasional conformity bill. On an initial forecast, he was noted as a probable opponent of the Tack, but he was also on Harley's lobbying list. He did not vote for the measure on 28 Nov. 1704. On 21 Dec. he received leave of absence and left London, probably for Yorkshire. By March 1705 he was in Lancashire, preparing his election campaign for Pontefract, and wrote to Harley expressing concern at the gloss being put on the defeat of the Tack:

> the Low Church party, as they call themselves, and the Dissenters of all kinds, join together in all places and have the assurance to say that they are the persons that the government approves of, and will countenance, and positively assert that when the House rises the Tackers will all be displaced.

Nevertheless, he was quick to note the possibility of exchanging his Irish office for an English equivalent if such a purge came about.[8]

Bland was re-elected in 1705, and, after informing Harley of a Whig plot to defeat Richard Shuttleworth* in the Lancashire county election, concentrated his attentions on avoiding the necessity of a journey to Ireland during the summer. His excuses ranged from the need to reorganize his estate administration after being cheated by three stewards, to a recent attack of gout in the stomach and the need to visit Bath or 'troop off'. On one analysis of the new Parliament he was classed as 'Low Church', an epithet he obviously rejected (although his wife may have found it acceptable). More accurately, on another list, he was described as a placeman. That being the case, he was one of the few placemen to vote on 25 Oct. 1705 against the Court candidate for Speaker, and in the following February in favour of the Tory Salwey Winnington* in the committee hearing on the Bewdley election. On this latter occasion he was joined by many other Tories associated with Robert Harley, much to the anger of the Whigs. He did, however, support the Court in the same month in the proceedings upon the 'place clause' of the regency bill. No doubt because of his failure to give the ministry consistent support, Bland was the first victim of Whig demands for more places following the prorogation of Parliament in March 1706. At the end of April he lost his position as an Irish revenue commissioner to William St. Quintin* and, further, when the Earl of Derby (Hon. James Stanley*) sealed his first commission of the peace as chancellor of the duchy of Lancaster in July, Bland found himself removed from the Lancashire bench. Out of office, he probably reverted to a more uncompromising Toryism, freed as he was from ministerial pressure. Not surprisingly, a list of early 1708 classed him as a Tory. On 23 Jan. 1708 the corporation of Pontefract asked him to procure an Act to make St. Giles's chapel the parish church. No bill was subsequently introduced, probably because Bland had received leave of absence on 19 Feb. for the recovery of his health. He went to Bath and in May 1708 reported to James Grahme* that upon his return he had been engaged in the elections for Yorkshire and Pontefract, the latter contest being 'the warmest we have had in these parts'.[9]

Having secured his re-election for Pontefract, Bland was classed as a Tory on a second list of early 1708 with the election returns added. His main interest in this session was probably the bill for building St. Ann's church in Manchester, which required his own consent and that of his wife, as lady of the manor. Although he was ill again, being given leave on 17 Jan. 1709 to stay in the country for a month, he was one of five Members ordered on 7 Feb. to prepare the bill. His poor health may have been the reason for some confusion among contemporaries over his voting record in the following session over the Sacheverell affair. Though one of the printed lists classed Bland as an opponent of the impeachment, most fail to mention him and he in fact may have been too ill to attend as he received leave of absence on 7 Mar. 1710, before the trial finished. Following the ministerial revolution and the ensuing dissolution, Bland was pressed by the Tories to contest Lancashire, no doubt in a bid to oust the Whig incumbent, Hon. Charles Stanley. However, he declined, on the grounds that 'neither my constitution nor purse was in order to undertake such a fatigue and expense'. He was returned for Pontefract and classed as a Tory on the 'Hanover list'. He wrote from Newark on his way to London complaining of ill-health and claiming the credit for Robert Frank's* return at Pontefract, whom he accused of entering the campaign late, so as to gain the support of Bland's voters without the attendant expense, a tactic 'which I would not have submitted to, if I had not preferred her Majesty's service above all things'. As one might expect, these comments were designed to prepare the way for an appeal for employment which, when it was sent to Harley, came with the full backing of Lord Carmarthen, now Duke of Leeds, who cited Bland's previous dismissal for opposing the Whigs, his constant expenses at Pontefract and the need for the Queen to encourage her friends. Bland seems to have hoped to regain his Irish post or the place he had previously coveted at the Green Cloth. No immediate rewards were forthcoming except for reinstatement on the Lancashire bench. At the start of 1711 his range of acceptable offices had expanded to include the Exchequer. In the Commons he certainly followed the Tory line in the 1710–11 session, being listed as a Tory patriot who opposed the continuance of the war and as a 'worthy patriot' who had helped detect the mismanagements of the previous administration. By June 1711, when Harley was considering a ministerial reshuffle, Bland's name appeared on a memorandum of possible appointees, although no office was specified and the current vacancy on the Irish revenue commission went instead to Sir Henry Bunbury, 3rd Bt.* Bland continued to pester Harley (now Earl of Oxford) throughout 1711 and into the summer of 1712, first to be made a teller of the Exchequer and then for something 'agreeable' in consideration of his 'long services in Parliament, expensive elections and eight years being displaced by the last ministry'. Because of his worsening health, these solicitations had to be conducted by post. Thus it was from Hulme in September 1712 that Bland reverted to his usual strategy in advance of an election: seeking to demonstrate to Oxford his usefulness to the ministry in the hope of future rewards. Preparations, he assured the lord treasurer, were well advanced to secure his son's election for Lancashire, along with Richard Shuttleworth. However, Bland was still at Bath early in June 1713, which probably explains why he failed to vote on the 18th of that month in the vital division on the French commerce bill.[10]

Bland did not stand at the 1713 general election, although his son was indeed successful for Lancashire. Retirement from the Commons seems to have presaged an entire withdrawal from local politics in Pontefract since, in December 1713, it appears that Bland's burgages in the borough were up for sale, together with other Yorkshire property. However, he remained an alderman of Pontefract until 23 Sept. 1715, when his letter of resignation was accepted. He died a little over a month later, on 25 Oct. 1715, while returning to Yorkshire from yet another sojourn at Bath. In his will he left his Lancashire estates and those he had purchased in Yorkshire in trust to his wife to pay his debts and a portion for his only surviving daughter.[11]

[1] N. Carlisle, *Colls. Bland Fam.* 41–44. [2] *HMC Lords*, n.s. iii. 204; *Pontefract Corp. Bk.* ed. Holmes, 422; Somerville, *Duchy of Lancaster Official Lists*, 140. [3] *Cal. Treas. Bks.* xix. 346; xx. 633. [4] *Newcome Autobiog.* ed. Parkinson (Chetham Soc. ser. 1, xxvi–xxvii), 259, 266–9; *HMC Kenyon*, 181; Cumbria RO (Kendal), Le Fleming mss WD/Ry 3190, Roger Kenyon to Sir Daniel Fleming†, 16 Apr. 1688; L. K. J. Glassey, *Appt. JPs*, 274–5; *CSP Dom.* 1687–9, p. 277; Add. 41805, f. 232. [5] Stowe 746, f. 129; *HMC Kenyon*, 374, 285, 289; Trinity, Dublin, Clarke mss 749/10/958, Bland to George Clarke, 3 Aug. 1691; *Luttrell Diary*, 227, 296. [6] *HMC Kenyon*, 386–7, 395; Huntington Lib. Ellesmere mss 9861, 'notes by Ld. Bridgwater'; *CSP Dom.* 1700–2, p. 30; *Bradford Antiquary*, n.s. xlii. 59, 63, 65. [7] Carlisle, 44; J. Booker, *Hist. Ancient Chapels of Didsbury and Chorlton* (Chetham Soc. ser. 1, xlii), 162–5; *Cam. Misc.* xx. 65–67; *Bradford Antiquary*, 71–72, 58. [8] *Pontefract Corp. Bk.* 250, 259; *Marlborough–Godolphin Corresp.* 162, 310, 331, 340, 356, 374; *HMC Portland*, iv. 84, 94, 149, 169–70; Add. 70249, Richard Musgrave to Harley, 1 Jan. 1704–5. [9] *HMC Portland*, 183, 203; *Newcome Diary* ed. Heywood (Chetham Soc. ser. 1, xviii), 91n.; *Bull. IHR*, xlv. 49; Coxe, *Walpole*, ii. 5; Glassey, 287; *Pontefract Corp. Bk.* 281; Bagot mss at Levens Hall, Bland to James Grahme, 25 May 1708. [10] *HMC Lords*, n.s. viii. 300; *HMC Portland*, iv. 576, 642–3; v. 221; Add. 70211, Bland to Harley, 14 Oct. 1710, 31 Dec. 1711, 1 July 1712; 70332, memo. 4 June 1711; Glassey, 289; Carlisle, 49; Lancs. RO, Kenyon mss DDKe 9/102/127, Nicholas Starkie to George Kenyon*, 6 June 1713. [11] Add. 22236, f. 67; *Pontefract Corp. Bk.* 328; Carlisle, 44–45; Le Neve, *Mon. Angl.* 1700–15, p. 302.

E. C./S. N. H.

BLAND, John (1691–1743), of Hulme Hall, Lancs. and Kippax Park, Yorks.

LANCASHIRE 1713–1727

bap. 10 Sept. 1691, o. surv. s. of Sir John Bland, 4th Bt.* educ. Christ Church, Oxf. 1707. m. 16 Oct. 1716 (with £8,000), Frances, da. of Hon. Heneage Finch I*, 1st Earl of Aylesford, sis. of Hon. Heneage Finch II* and Hon. John Finch†, 3s. (1 d.v.p.) 4da. suc. fa. as 5th Bt. 25 Oct. 1715.[1]

Bland's entry into public life would seem to have been an adjunct to his education, because in 1711 he joined the retinue of Britain's plenipotentiaries at Utrecht. By September 1712 his father was organizing his election for the county of Lancashire, which did indeed return him in the following year. The Worsley list and two further comparisons of the 1713 and 1715 Parliaments all classed Bland as a Tory. During the 1714 session he told, on 25 June, against a motion that a Southwark man had the right to vote, after having affirmed rather than take the oath of abjuration. After the death of Queen Anne he seems to have been much engaged in canvassing for the next election, suggesting to Legh that a worthy candidate at Newton might be Sir Christopher Musgrave, 5th Bt.*, in retreat from problems at Carlisle, and paying visits to places such as Preston in October 1714 in order to ensure his own re-election. Bland retained his seat until 1727 when he retired at the early age of 35. His reputation as a Jacobite had led to his arrest in November 1715 and also to his removal from the Lancashire bench. He seems to have shifted the centre of his political activity away from Yorkshire towards the Lancashire estates brought into the family by his mother. He was active in Manchester's affairs, exhibiting some of his father's distrust of non-Anglicans in a dispute in 1731 over a projected workhouse in the town. In a further echo of his father and his difficulties in obtaining employment, Bland set out in his will the hope that 'as it was his warmest desire that no son of his might have any dependence on the government, so he would wish to have a reversion of some patent place for life purchased for his said [second] son Hungerford'. The remainder of the will dwelt on strategies for paying off debts and raising portions for his younger children. He died at Bath on 9 Apr. 1743.[2]

[1] N. Carlisle, Colls. Bland Fam. 51–52. [2] Carlisle, 51; HMC Portland, v. 221; John Rylands Univ. Lib. Manchester, Legh of Lyme mss corresp. Bland to Peter Legh, 7 Sept. 1714; Devonshire mss at Chatsworth House, Finch–Halifax pprs. box. 3, no.107, Richard Assheton to [?Hon. Heneage Finch II], 15 Oct. 1714; CJ, xviii. 328; L. K. J. Glassey, Appt. JPs, 292; Lancs. RO, Kenyon mss DDKq/114/5, Bland to Thomas Kenyon and Thomas Pigot, n.d. [1730]; Carlisle, 51–55; Gent. Mag. 1743, p. 208.

E. C./S. N. H.

BLATHWAYT, William (1649–1717), of Little Wallingford House, Great Street, Westminster, and Dyrham Park, Glos.[1]

NEWTOWN I.o.W.   1685–1687
BATH   20 Nov. 1693–1710

bap. 2 Mar. 1649, o. s. of William Blathwayt, barrister, of the Middle Temple, by Anne, da. of Justinian Povey of Hounslow, Mdx., accountant-gen. to Queen Anne of Denmark. educ. M. Temple 1665; Padua Univ. 1672; travelled abroad (Sweden, Germany, Italy, Switzerland, France) 1672–3. m. 23 Dec. 1686, Mary (d. 1691), da. and h. of John Wynter of Dyrham Park, 4s. (2 d.v.p.) 1da. (d.v.p.). suc. fa. c.1650.[2]

Clerk of embassy, The Hague 1668–72, Copenhagen and Stockholm 1672; asst. sec. of trade and plantations 1675–9, sec. 1679–96; clerk of PC (extraordinary) 1678–86, (ordinary) 1686–d.; surveyor and auditor gen. of plantations 1680–d.; under-sec. of state (north) 1681–3; sec. at war 1683–Feb. 1689, May 1689–1704; ld. of trade 1696–1707.

Freeman, Bath 1693.[3]

Blathwayt's renown as a bureaucrat arises much less from any contribution he made to the perfection of the administrative machinery of state than from the sheer immensity of his workload and the ubiquity of his concerns. The height of his distinguished career came during the 1690s when, as acting secretary of state to William III while on campaign, he took charge of the diplomatic service and the running of the army under William's personal supervision. In this unique position he was, in effect, the King's chief executive servant, and enjoyed an omnipresence in the main spheres of administrative action. The diplomatist, George Stepney, a close friend and colleague of Blathwayt, saw him as an unabashed bureaucratic empire-builder, 'the patron of those who hold the quill and who takes pleasure in protecting generally whatever belongs to his province'. Though he was never a royal confidant after the fashion of Portland or Albemarle, his monopoly of information, his mastery of detail, precedent and form, and above all, his close proximity to the King, made him a singular influence within the processes of royal decision-making.[4]

Blathwayt's rise from a lowly clerkship in the diplomatic service to a series of senior posts at Whitehall was rapid, occurring within the space of a decade, 1668–78. Studious, cultured and linguistically adept, his diligence and organizational prowess won praise from several of the foremost of Charles II's and James II's administrators under whom he served, notably Sir William Temple† (in whose embassy at The Hague Blathwayt's career began), Sir Joseph Williamson*, Sir George Downing† and Sir Robert Southwell†. It was through Southwell's good offices that in 1683 he purchased the secretaryship at war. But for one short intermission in 1689, he held this office continuously until 1704, presiding over the running of the army during critical and formative years. Blathwayt's greatest sphere of independent initiative was in colonial administration, afforded through his office as secretary to the Privy Council committee for trade and plantations, and as auditor of plantation revenues. He was not averse to accepting sizable gratuities from colonial assemblies, and was involved in many colonial disputes. He became rich from his several salaries and the emoluments of office, and in 1686 married the heiress of the Dyrham Park estate in Gloucestershire, 'a very great fortune'. The knighthood, rumoured at this time to be in the offing, and which would have capped his professional success and prosperity, failed to materialize.[5]

Blathwayt had the good fortune to emerge unscathed from the 1688 Revolution. After William of Orange's invasion he remained loyal to James II, though at what point he went over to William is not clear. His last routine letter under King James appears to have been written on 8 Dec. A few days later, after William's entry into the capital, he was supplying the Prince with details of James's forces. Sometime in January or early February 1689, however, Blathwayt was required to quit the war office. He was replaced in April by John Temple, son of his old mentor, Sir William, but was promptly reinstated when shortly afterwards Temple committed suicide. The new King soon found him an indispensable asset in military organization. Although William thought him dull company, he acknowledged to Lord Halifax that Blathwayt had 'a good method'. Not only was he well informed, but he was the only English administrator who spoke fluent Dutch. The King was well aware that Blathwayt's modernizing imprint had helped to make the English army under James II one of the best in Europe. The Earl of Marlborough's (John Churchill[†]) appreciation of his soundness also helped to smooth his passage. The Whigs, however, were not prepared to forget Blathwayt's loyalty to the exiled Stuart, and in the early years of William's reign accusations of Jacobitism were frequently made against him. These cut no ice with William who valued him highly. The early years of the new reign saw Blathwayt working in close association with Lord Nottingham (Daniel Finch[†]), the secretary of state for the south under whose jurisdiction the war office came. Politically, he was an instinctive Tory with an obvious reverence for notions of prerogative power and executive discretion, and an impatience towards Whiggish concern for the rule of law. This, together with his unassailability and his extensive network of connexions, particularly in the realm of colonial patronage, where he engineered Tory appointments wherever possible, made him an object of scorn to Whig politicians. Their attitude to him was neatly encapsulated in Admiral Russell's (Edward*) sniping reference to him as 'that never-erring minister'.[6]

In February 1690, Blathwayt had objections to accompanying the King on campaign in Ireland, and it was widely understood that he was ready to resign his secretaryship to an official who was willing to go. William at first offered the post to George Clarke*, the army's judge-advocate, but such was his reluctance to part with Blathwayt that he retained him in the permanent secretaryship and instead appointed Clarke to attend him as temporary secretary in Ireland. The King's retention of Blathwayt in this manner irritated senior Whigs and puzzled even the Queen herself. In July Lord Monmouth confronted the Queen with allegations of Jacobitism in Lord Nottingham's office, and in particular 'fell upon Mr Blathwayt'. Reporting this discussion to the King, the Queen commented, 'I owned I wondered why you would let him serve here, since he would not go with you, but I said I supposed you know why you did it'. Suspicions about Blathwayt's loyalties must certainly have arisen, at least in part, from his activities in colonial matters. The King's commission to him as secretary at war explicitly extended his jurisdiction to the colonies where in the first years of the new reign he busied himself with the reappointment of every one of King James's Protestant governors. Blathwayt could ignore these charges by drawing attention to the far more urgent problems of poor co-ordination within the English administration and its inability to cope with the demands of the war in Ireland. 'Nobody', he complained in July to his old friend Sir Robert Southwell, 'has a particular charge of general matters so as to watch and pursue the dispatch of them in the several places.'[7]

The cost of the army was a prime target of the newly formed commission of accounts in March 1691, and it was hardly surprising that Blathwayt as the army's chief administrator should be examined at its very first meeting on the 13th. He was closely questioned in relation to the army accounts they had asked for, but, as one commissioner recorded, was not particularly co-operative and in certain respects appeared vague. In June he was mentioned as a possible successor to William Jephson* as Treasury secretary, on the assumption that Lords Nottingham and Carmarthen (Sir Thomas Osborne[†]) would recommend 'a friend of theirs'. The turning point in Blathwayt's career came in February 1692 when the King constituted him acting secretary of state to accompany him on campaign in the Low Countries. William's need was for a 'bureaucratic' rather than 'political' secretary, and Blathwayt, already directly responsible to the King in military administration, was ideally suited for his purpose. Blathwayt himself seems to have been none too enamoured of an arrangement that required him to endure the hardships of campaign, but his superior, Lord Nottingham, urged him to accept on the grounds that close proximity to the King would advance his prospects of appointment to the currently vacant northern secretaryship of state. He may also have been consoled by the thought that his discomforts would be limited to one or two campaigns at most. But as events turned out he attended the King on every one of his annual visits to the Low Countries until the last in 1701. As secretary at war he was effectively the King's secretary in all military matters, while as secretary of state he administered the diplomatic service under the King's direct supervision, acting as a vital filter for the huge amount of paperwork intended for the King's attention. He was never given a patent for the acting secretaryship but had charge of the signet by royal commission. On his return from the 1692 campaigning season, Blathwayt's hopes of the full secretaryship were disappointed. The eventual appointment of Sir John Trenchard* in March 1693 left him very bitter. Stepney wrote to an acquaintance in October:

> methinks Mr Blathwayt is not in the humour he ought to be and I apprehend his resentment of not being made secretary of state (as he expected and ought to have been) may make him lie down his other employment or at least no more follow the King in Flanders which is as bad for those who are abroad. For certainly no other man can be found out who can acquit himself with such capacity, honesty and diligence as he has done, which I apprehend his Majesty may perceive when it is too late.[8]

In November 1693, Blathwayt entered Parliament for Bath, less than ten miles from Dyrham Park. He remarked at the time to Richard Hill, deputy-paymaster of the forces in Flanders, that he had been 'for some time in Gloucestershire where my neighbours of Bath have made me a country gentleman'. Having declined the offer of a seat from the corporation of Newport on the Isle of Wight in December 1692 owing to 'the multiplicity of my business', he told Hill that although there were pressing reasons against accepting the Bath seat, he could not bear to 'see others run away with a burgess-ship under my nose and to which I have secured an everlasting title'. His wife had inherited Dyrham in November 1688, and died leaving Blathwayt in possession in 1691. He began rebuilding the house in the current fashionable 'Dutch' style in 1693. Owing to 'the multiplicity of my business' Blathwayt never became an active participant in parliamentary proceedings. Such interventions of his as are on record were brief and formal. He occasionally presented papers or reports on military and colonial matters, while his most frequent function, inevitably, was to illuminate information in estimates and accounts. At most, when the House was debating, he did no more than to clarify or correct information given by other MPs. Lord Raby was to recall that when Robert Harley* was in the House, 'Mr Blathwayt and others of the King's people were almost afraid to speak'. In the realm of legislation, however, he was certainly involved in the framing of more bills than he is credited with in the Journals. There are examples of colonial and trading measures in which, although he was not included among the drafting MPs, he contributed important clauses either on his own initiative or at the behest of others. His chief concern as a ministerial spectator was with the progress of supply proceedings, and the successes and failures of the government's efforts to raise money for the King's campaigns was a recurrent theme in his correspondence when in England. One of his most exacting and sensitive tasks was in liaising between the Treasury and the King over war expenditure. During his very first sojourn abroad in the summer of 1692 Lord Godolphin (Sidney†) was writing to him anxiously, warning that funds were 'falling extremely short'; and another letter implored him to represent to the King 'the consequences of loading his revenue with more anticipations'.[9]

On taking his seat in November 1693, Blathwayt found the House preoccupied with opposition attacks upon the ministry's handling of the naval war, and on 8 Dec. he informed Hill that 'we have cut down our admirals again after hanging, and there the gallows is remaining, so variable are our proceedings and may yet be more'. When Lord Falkland (Anthony Carey*) was disgraced in February 1694 and sent to the Tower for pocketing £2,000 of public money, Blathwayt felt that 'the fault was indeed but small but the crime great, the House resenting his partial and furious animosity in the business of the sea admirals and his sudden turning upon the toe'. Rarely in Blathwayt's voluminous correspondence, however, does one find much more than the occasional laconic comment about parliamentary proceedings. The same month, the Treasury finally agreed to his request of July the previous year to be paid the salary of a junior secretary of state for his services abroad. On this development he enthused to Stepney: 'the King denies me no advantages that belong to the office during my execution of it which is more satisfactory to me in the present juncture than another tenure'. On 5 Mar. 1694 he was teller for agreeing with the Lords' amendments to the mutiny bill. It was not long before senior opposition figures singled him out as a possible future focus of attack. In July, his friend Robert Henley* warned him that 'it is discoursed by some men very seriously that you occasion the carrying of money out of England to be distributed to the confederates whose agent you are in that matter, which they say shall be brought into Parliament'. Any thoughts of attacking Blathwayt had disappeared by the time Parliament reconvened for the 1694–5 session, and he was able to inform Hill on 23 Nov. that 'our Parliament has a very good countenance notwithstanding some frowns and moments of passion'. The following month he was reporting to Hill that 'our affairs go on merrily with relation to the land forces for which the gentlemen will have the triennial bill'. He was granted a fortnight's leave of absence on 21 Dec., but the 'most ungrateful and terrible news' of Queen Mary's death hastened his premature return to London. Early in February 1695, as Sir John Trenchard succumbed to serious illness, Blathwayt was among those spoken of as a possible successor as secretary of state, but for the time being no new appointment was made.[10]

Blathwayt's attentions were engrossed in a number of matters of direct interest to him during the 1695–6 session. On behalf of his corporation he initiated a bill for the navigation of the Avon between Bristol and Bath, obtaining leave for its introduction on 30 Dec. He presented it after some delay on 23 Jan. 1696, and only after a division, on the 27 Feb., in which Blathwayt served as a teller, was the bill consigned to a select committee where it was eventually dropped owing to the weight of landowner opposition. On 23 Jan. he supported a motion for a bill to prevent frauds and abuses in the plantation trade. Although this bill was subsequently steered through the House by a customs commissioner, James Chadwick, Blathwayt, who had gone down to Dyrham presumably in connexion with the navigation measure, kept in close touch with the bill's chief instigator, Edward Randolph, the surveyor-general of the customs in America, and at Randolph's request drafted an additional clause which declared that governors of proprietary colonies must first be approved by the crown. At the same time, his attention was engaged by the coinage crisis and the proposal for a council of trade. He remarked to Stepney at the end of December 1695 that, although he was gratified to see that the Commons 'makes good dispatch' with the supply, 'the business of the coin meets with greater difficulties and the Parliament's undertaking to appoint a council of trade by their own authority must needs be looked upon as a lessening of the power and influence of the crown'. Blathwayt's independence in colonial matters made the Privy Council committee on trade and plantations, which he had served as secretary for the previous 20 years, a prime political target to those who objected to the prospect of a council of trade handpicked by the King's ministers. Blathwayt regarded the passage of the bill establishing such a council as a foregone conclusion, and was duly forecast as a likely Court supporter in the division anticipated on 31 Jan. Although there is no specific evidence of Blathwayt's name being used by the opposition in the parliamentary struggle over the council of trade, the lord keeper, Sir John Somers*, and Admiral Russell were among his leading Whig detractors behind the scenes. But despite the implicit assault on Blathwayt's position in colonial administration, his vast experience could not so easily be dispensed with, and, when the Board of Trade was set up in May, the Assassination Plot scare having enabled the Court to win its way, Blathwayt was named as one of the new lords commissioners, and until 1698 was the only MP among them. He nevertheless had to struggle against continual Whig machinations to pare back his enormous influence in colonial affairs. The first signs of the new limitations he would be under came when Somers, to Blathwayt's intense annoyance, blocked the appointment of his cousin John Povey* as the Board's secretary. In the debates on the fixing of the price of guineas in March, Blathwayt, unusually, did not at first support the ministerial view which, prompted by the Bank of England's representations, favoured a fairly substantial lowering of the price of the guinea. He explained his position in a letter to Hill of 10 Apr.: 'It is very true I divided [on 20 Mar.] for fixing the price of guineas at 25s. which I knew was not in the interest of the Bank but of the King and old England, and let me tell you the country gentleman had then Mr [William] Lowndes* and other honest men in his company'. However, when the King made it known that he was prepared to countenance a reduction to 22s., Blathwayt voted in favour on 26 Mar. An enthusiastic supporter of the Association, he reported in April with reference to the bill for securing the government that 'we are doing great things in the House of Commons to strengthen the Association'.[11]

While Blathwayt was with the King during the summer of 1696, Charles Montagu*, the Junto Whig chancellor of the Exchequer, was careful to cultivate an acquaintanceship with him as a means of gaining the King's approval of his schemes for the alleviation of the liquidity crisis precipitated by the failure of the land bank. Early in June Blathwayt wrote to Montagu:

> You have done me a very great favour to entrust me with an account of transactions relating to the new [viz. land] bank wherein the part you have had has been so undeniably for his Majesty's service and preservation of the government that we could not but have had more dreadful effects of the contrary if the conspiracy had not intervened when nothing else could perhaps have saved us. I have made the proper use of the informations you have been pleased to give by laying them before the King, who is fully satisfied of the truth of your advices and holds you more than justified from all the disappointments or misfortunes that have happened or may yet happen by the different measures that have been taken. However, matters being as they are and our necessities like to be every day greater, especially now the new bank have by their extravagant demands put themselves almost out of a capacity of serving the government, his Majesty recommends it earnestly to your care if it be possible that we may not be ruined at home by the stoppage of the circulation of the species or abroad by the want of supplies where the whole army is brought to that necessity that they must have readily starved without his seasonable assistance, which in truth his Majesty takes to be so very great a service at this time from the Royal Bank [the Bank of England] which . . . his Majesty enjoins you to let them know his Majesty's sense of . . .

Following the Bank of England's refusal to remit further money to the army early in July, Blathwayt found himself in the unenviable position of having to coax the Treasury into finding other means of meeting the desperate shortage of cash. Towards the end of June, Montagu sent him his scheme for Exchequer bills 'that at your leisure you may correct it'. In his carefully worded response on 2 July Blathwayt praised the scheme as 'certainly very good' but believed that powerful City interests were bound to 'endeavour a defeat and disappoint it'. Blathwayt's tone quietly implied his belief that fanciful new schemes alone would do little to resolve the short-term crisis, and after expressing the King's satisfaction with the Bank of England and its efforts to restore credit, he ended with a general plea to find urgent means of providing desperately needed cash. Through Blathwayt, the King sent an urgent message to Godolphin on 9 July warning that if money were not quickly forthcoming, the army would have to be disbanded to avoid starvation. The same day Blathwayt penned a frantic personal plea to Montagu: 'Sir, I must repeat to you again, that our condition is such, that the army must inevitably perish if not relieved from England within a week or 10 days, so that for God's sake, for all our sakes, and for your own sake, find some means to help us.' Godolphin informed Blathwayt on the 14th that the Treasury could no longer supply the army and that if the King could not find credit abroad 'we must lie down and die'. The King's despatch of Lord Portland to London initiated the process whereby in mid-August the Bank furnished an additional £200,000, news which, as Blathwayt told Montagu, was received 'with all joy imaginable': though the 1696 campaign had achieved nothing, 'this relief brings us indeed into winter quarters'. The crisis drew Blathwayt and Montagu into a closer working relationship, and during the 1697 campaign Montagu was once again wholly reliant on Blathwayt in the transmission of his views on financial issues to the King. Blathwayt's faith in Montagu's financial skill was underlined in his subscription of £2,000 to the contract for loans to circulate Exchequer bills in 1697. They also had a common friend in George Stepney, whose career Blathwayt was keen to advance, and in 1698 Montagu was instrumental in bringing Stepney onto the Board of Trade. In September of that year, in the midst of the furore over Montagu's acquisition of the auditorship of the Exchequer, Blathwayt felt obliged to caution him not to betray any indication that he was taking the post as a possible refuge in the face of increasing adversity, advising him that 'it will be so far from advancing your just pretensions that it may be of greatest prejudice to you'.[12]

The 1696–7 session was an uneventful one for Blathwayt. On 25 Nov. he presented the Board of Trade's first report to the House, and the same day voted in favour of the attainder of Sir John Fenwick[†]. He presented the mutiny bill on 11 Jan. 1697. His later absence from proceedings, however, is indicated by a grant of leave accorded him on 20 Feb. During the summer Blathwayt was heavily involved in co-ordinating the completion of the Treaty of Ryswick, and was unable to escape blame for various last-minute hitches. James Vernon I* remarked to the Duke of Shrewsbury that 'the lords justices do not much admire this conduct; this is not like to recommend Mr Blathwayt to be secretary of state'. In the new session which opened in December he was greatly disturbed by the Country party's efforts to disband most of the army. 'This is uncomfortable news', he wrote to Hill on 10 Dec., 'to those that have served so well during the war.' By the 24th he was relieved to report that 'the Parliament are fallen into better humour and think to make amends . . . by providing a considerable fleet and for the King's civil list during life'. However, the figure of 10,000 men at a cost of £350,000 which the House finally agreed in committee on 11 Jan. 1698 seemed to him ludicrously short-sighted. He begged Hill, in Flanders, to 'lay this very gently before his highness [Prince de Vaudemont, the allied commander] and crave his pardon for our doings. So the brave army late under his command is like a shadow that fleeth away and is no more.' Blathwayt irritated Vernon with a small indiscretion in the House on 1 June over the question of a request for lists of the army so far, and as yet to be, disbanded. In a short debate on the matter, his disclosure that such papers would not be made available 'unless he had orders for it' was immediately seized upon by Sir Christopher Musgrave, 4th Bt., whose demand for them by way of an address threatened to raise the issue anew before the session closed.[13]

Towards the end of the 1690s Blathwayt began to grow impatient with the King's continuing to impose on him as a peripatetic bureaucrat, particularly now that the war was over, and he began to crave a settled position at Whitehall. After the 1698 election he was classed as a Court supporter and a placeman in a comparative analysis of the old and new House of Commons. Returning early in December 1698 from the congress on the Spanish succession problem, he plunged almost immediately into his activities at the Board of Trade, particularly in connexion with Sir Edward Seymour's bill to protect the English wool market by preventing the export of woollen manufactures and raw wool from Ireland. The Board considered the bill on 10 Jan. 1699, and it was largely on Blathwayt's initiative that the prohibition was extended to woollen exports from the American colonies. On the 18th he presented to the House the Board's representation in support of the bill including his proposed extension, and its referral to the bill's committee of the whole ensured that the clause was incorporated and became part of the statute. On 4 Jan. in a debate in committee on the disbanding bill, Blathwayt, fulfilling an earlier request, briefed the House on the minimum number of troops the government considered necessary in peacetime. After a wrangle over whether he should be allowed to quote his figures from memory, he pointed out that the total of 7,000 favoured by Country spokesmen was hardly sufficient. He warned against too low a reduction, reminding MPs that 'King Charles II had 9,919 men, and yet in King James' time there could be spared or got together no more than 2,232 men against [the Duke of] Monmouth'. It was pointed out, however, that his own estimate of just over 8,000 included the 3,000 marines on the navy establishment, half of whom would probably be kept for the maritime garrisons, which 'rather tended to satisfy the House that 7,000 would be sufficient for guards and garrisons'. He was no doubt relieved when the House eventually opted for the retention of 10,000, and he duly voted against the disbanding bill at its third reading on the 18th. On 14 Feb. in his capacity as the Board of Trade's spokesman in the House, he presented its representation on the value of guineas.[14]

Blathwayt must have privately delighted in presenting to the House the Board of Trade's report on 4 Dec. 1699 on the piracies committed by Captain William Kidd in the East Indies and his subsequent capture. Kidd had received a commission in 1697 to pursue troublesome buccaneers in whose captured booty his ministerial sponsors were to have a share. These backers had included Blathwayt's old Whig critics Admiral Russell (since made Lord Orford), Somers and the Earl of Bellomont [I] (Richard Coote*) who had been at pains to keep the commission from Blathwayt's knowledge as he was known to be on friendly terms with several colonial governors in league with the pirates whom Kidd was authorized to pursue. Kidd soon turned to piracy himself, however, and Blathwayt's report on the 4th, detailing the circumstances of his arrest by Bellomont, now governor of New York, was one of several presentations of papers preparatory to the full-scale debate on the affair on the 6th in which the Junto bore the brunt of attack. Towards the end of the session Blathwayt handled the later stages of a general bill for the suppression of piracy. Bellomont's antipathy to Blathwayt ran deeply. He held Blathwayt responsible for all the difficulties he encountered in fulfilling his governor's duties at New York, and in a letter of June 1700 to Lord Bridgwater (John Egerton†), Blathwayt's former colleague at the Board, spoke of him as an evil man so sinister that he could 'countermine and traverse all the honest endeavours of a number of men'. More parochial matters also found their way into Blathwayt's busy routine during the session, in the form of a new bill for the navigation of the Avon between Bristol and Bath. He moved for the bill on 9 Dec., presented it on the 16th and saw it committed on the 20th. But as with his previous bill, this measure, too, became hopelessly bogged down by opposition and failed to emerge from committee.[15]

In December 1700 it was rumoured that Blathwayt was to be created Earl of Bristol 'in consideration of his services to his Majesty', but apart from his salaries and the various emoluments of office he was never to receive any reward for his labours. Although Blathwayt shouldered a huge administrative burden, a burden which had tended to increase in the later 1690s as the King transferred his affections from Portland to the less adroit Albemarle, William plainly regarded him only as a working secretary and, as such, unworthy of an honour. Blathwayt's unflinchingly detached view of politics is well illustrated by his remarks on the dissolution of December 1700. The dissolution, he told George Stepney on the 19th, had

> caused the greatest heats imaginable among the parties, which, though they both say they will do the public business, seem resolved to treat one another unmercifully... if you would be secretary of state, now is the time. The two secretaries oppose one another in all their proceedings to please their respective friends.

During the new Parliament Blathwayt, a staunch enemy of chartered colonies and their 'great irregularities' of government, devoted much effort behind the scenes towards obtaining a bill for the annulment of the charters and uniting the colonies with the crown. The issue had been broached the previous session in a Board of Trade report delivered by Blathwayt, and on 29 Mar. 1701 he produced a lengthy representation embodying an extensive digest of complaints supplied by his chief associate in colonial matters, Edward Randolph. A bill was introduced in the Lords on 24 Apr. which Blathwayt did much to promote, strongly maintaining, for instance, that the crown was well within its right to demand the revocation of charters, but in June it was dropped owing to considerable Whig opposition. Besides presenting other army and colonial papers at various times, he is recorded as having supported the Court in a supply resolution to make good the deficiencies of funds since 1689.[16]

The pro-Whig ministerial changes at the end of 1701 prompted speculation in January 1702 that Blathwayt was to be replaced as secretary at war, one observer noting that it was unclear whether this was due specifically to his being 'obnoxious to the Lord Somers' party' or simply a piece of 'management'. On 28 Feb. he briefed the House regarding a petition concerning a complaint currently before the Board of Trade against Colonel Codrington, the governor of the Leeward Islands, and explained the Board's procedure for hearing affidavits. He spoke again on 2 May in answer to Thomas Coke's complaint that an army officer of foreign extraction had been promoted over the head of an English half-pay officer, and advised the House 'very plainly' that Coke had been misinformed. Blathwayt appears to have deliberately misled the House on this occasion, however, for his assertion that the English officer in question was not on half-pay was in fact patently untrue.[17]

With the death of William III in March 1702 Blathwayt suddenly found himself without the personal importance and prestige within the governmental machine which for so long he had derived from having close access to the monarch. He remained a member of the administration, being confirmed as secretary at war and as a lord of Trade in June and July. Marlborough, the newly appointed captain-general of the army, respected Blathwayt's abilities, but they were never close and the Duke quickly established his own secretariat. As Blathwayt had been so closely associated with the late King, Marlborough could not but regard him with some suspicion, and saw him as a rapacious schemer. When in August 1703 Godolphin proposed to increase the perquisites allowed Blathwayt in the war office, Marlborough replied: 'what you have in mind to do for Mr Blathwayt will never be opposed by me, but I can't forebear saying, that when he had the allowances he now pretends to, he was obliged to ten times the expense he now makes, and had also much more business'. Although he was now frequently bypassed in military matters, he was content after years of arduous activity to defer to his old friend and superior, Lord Nottingham, reappointed secretary of state, while in colonial affairs Nottingham appears to have allowed him continued free rein, enabling him to secure the appointment of several friends and allies to colonial governorships.[18]

On 5 Jan. 1704 Blathwayt moved for the mutiny bill which he presented on the 22nd. He was one of a number of Court Tories named to draft the recruiting bill on 7 Jan. but remained unconvinced that it would answer its purposes. Early in April he was removed from the secretaryship at war amid the dismissals of Nottingham and other High Tory ministers. The exact circumstances were an unfortunate example of a self-fulfilling prophecy. According to Marlborough's secretary Adam de Cardonnel*, Blathwayt's impending displacement had first been mentioned 'merely in jest' on 'St Taffy's Day' (1 Mar.) and Blathwayt himself had gone around merrily entertaining others with it 'till it came really to effect'. As a non-political associate of Lord Nottingham he was an easy target. He reassured Stepney on 11 Apr. that the Queen's disposal of his office to Henry St. John II* was

> in such a manner and with such assurances that I have no reason to be very sorry for the loss, having finished that long course without the least imputation of deserving blame and continuing in my other places which will allow me sufficient leisure to enjoy the rest of my life which I could not well do before.

Despite talk that he was also to lose his place on the Board of Trade, he retained his post as a commissioner.[19]

Blathwayt's association with Lord Nottingham did not extend so far as to support the Earl's line on occasional conformity, however. At the end of October 1704 he was forecast as a probable opponent of the Tack, and on 28 Nov. he either voted against it or was absent. On 17 Jan. 1705 he featured among the ministerialists required to draft a bill levying duties on certain goods re-exported to Ireland and the colonies, and on the 22nd he presented a bill to encourage the import of American naval stores. In an analysis of Parliament after the 1705 election he was classed as a 'High Church courtier', and in the division on the speakership on 25 Oct. duly voted with the Court. He presented papers on 19 Jan. 1706 concerning the Newfoundland trade and on the 24th was appointed to a committee to consider means to stimulate it. More important was his renewed attempt at a bill to tighten crown control over chartered and proprietary colonies. Seconding Secretary Hedges' (Sir Charles) motion for the bill on 14 Feb., he presented it himself on the 23rd, only to see it thrown out at second reading on 2 Mar. On 18 Feb. he supported the Court in proceedings on the 'place clause' of the regency bill.

In April 1707 Blathwayt lost his place on the Board, a sacrificial victim of Godolphin's need to bring more Whigs into the administration. Of the four commissioners dismissed, Blathwayt, with his detailed understanding of colonial issues, was by far the greatest loss. He went away deeply embittered, and his future dealings with the Board as auditor general of the plantations became acrimonious. His zest for public business and activity found other outlets, and on his constituents' behalf he moved for a bill on 20 Nov. to effect the repair of several highways leading into Bath, taking charge of all its subsequent stages, and finally conveying it to the Lords on 21 Jan. 1708. Early in 1708 one parliamentary analyst classed him somewhat incongruously as a Whig, while another identified him as a Court Whig. It would certainly appear that once released from his strict obligations to the Court he began to behave in key issues more as a Whig than as a Tory. On the Palatine question, for instance, during February–March 1709, he voted in favour of naturalization. He also appeared in a printed list as having voted for the impeachment of Dr Sacheverell early in 1710 although he was strenuously to deny having attended any of the debates, much less having participated in any division, owing to illness. It was indeed the publication of this vote which spelt the end of his parliamentary career. When it came to the Duke of Beaufort's notice amid the summer election campaign, the Duke immediately announced his recommendation of another candidate. Blathwayt endeavoured to defuse the situation by asking his former colleague on the Board of Trade, Lord Dartmouth, now secretary of state, to disabuse the Duke of his notions, but to no avail. He was also forced to deny a rumour in Bath of his intention to have the city's elections thrown open to all freemen in place of the corporation franchise if he were beaten. He virtually ensured his own defeat himself when just a few days before the election he sarcastically asked of General (John Richmond) Webb* in public 'whether the bullet that was lodged in him was a musket or a cannon bullet'. Angered by this further instance of Blathwayt's apparent tactlessness, members of the corporation were reported to have declared their resolution not to have 'such a blunderbuss' as their MP. His achievement of a poor third place in the poll was not unexpected, least of all by himself.[20]

Blathwayt was disappointed in his hopes that the Tory revival would restore him to ministerial favour. The new generation of Tory ministers had little liking for him. In 1712 Bolingbroke (Henry St. John II) derided the Hanoverian ministers as 'the poorest tools, next to Blathwayt, that ever dirtied paper'. He was particularly desirous to return to the Board of Trade, but, when this failed to occur, his acrimony towards the Board was vividly displayed when the commission of public accounts examined him in 1711 on the subject of colonial finances. From then on he lived mostly at Dyrham, plagued with rheumatism but still conscientiously performing his duties as auditor of the plantations, and never deviating from the scrupulous record-keeping that marked a lifetime of administrative activity. After a year of serious illness he died at Bath on 16 Aug. 1717 and was buried at Dyrham Church. The bulk of his estate, bequeathed to his eldest son, comprised Dyrham and several Somerset manors originally inherited by his wife and held in trust by him since her death in 1691. A share in the manor of Egham in Surrey passed to his younger son.[21]

[1] Unless otherwise stated, this biography is based on G. A. Jacobsen, *William Blathwayt*; *History*, xxxiv. 28–43. [2] IGI, London; Glos. RO, Blathwayt mss D2659/1, 3. [3] Bath AO, Bath council bk. 3, p. 172. [4] *Wm. and Mary Q.* ser. 3, xxxi. 404. [5] I. K. Steele, *Pol. of Colonial Policy*, 22. [6] *Shrewsbury Corresp.* 215. [7] *HMC Popham*, 270–1; Centre Kentish Stud. Stanhope mss U1590/053/1, James Vernon I to Alexander Stanhope, 27 May 1690; Dalrymple, *Mems.* iii. pt. 2, 94; *Age of Wm. III and Mary II*, eds. R. P. Maccubbin and M. Hamilton-Phillips, 66; *Wm. and Mary Q.* ser. 3, xxxvi. 380. [8] *EHR*, xci. 45; Bodl. Carte 79, ff. 368–9; Luttrell, *Brief Relation*, ii. 357, 601. [9] Add. 56241, ff. 7, 9; 9735, ff. 57, 59; Yale Univ. Beinecke Lib. Osborn Coll., Blathwayt mss box 5, Blathwayt to mayor and corp. of Newport, I.o.W., 6 Dec. 1692; *Wentworth Pprs.* 132. [10] Add. 56241, ff. 7, 10, 27, 29, 31; Christ Church, Oxf. Evelyn mss, William Draper to John Evelyn II*, 7 Feb. 1695. [11] Add. 34354, f. 8; 56241, ff. 70, 72; 9719, f. 95. [12] Add. 34355, ff. 1, 5, 7, 9, 20, 27; 37992, ff. 160, 161; Egerton 929, f. 22.

[13] Add. 56241, ff. 154, 160, 162. [14] *Irish Econ. and Soc. Hist.* vii. 40–1; *Cam. Misc.* xxix. 371–2, 381–3. [15] *Shrewsbury Corresp.* 136–7. [16] Luttrell, iv. 718; S. B. Baxter, *Wm. III*, 326; H. Horwitz, *Parl. and Pol. Wm. III*, 204; Osborn Coll. Blathwayt mss box 21, Blathwayt to Stepney, 11 Mar. [1701]. [17] Hereford and Worcester RO (Hereford), Brydges mss A81/IV/23/a, William to Francis Brydges, 27 Jan. 1701–2; *Cocks Diary*, 228–9, 279. [18] Boyer, *Anne Annals*, i. 51, 72, 78; Luttrell, v. 197; *Marlborough–Godolphin Corresp.* 226. [19] Add. 58221, f. 42; Luttrell, v. 411, 414; Blathwayt mss box 21, Blathwayt to Stepney, 11 Apr. [1704]. [20] Luttrell, vi. 163; *HMC Dartmouth*, i. 297; Glos. RO, Blathwayt mss D1799/X9, Blathwayt to mayor of Bath, 24 Aug. 1710; Huntington Lib. Stowe mss 58(7), pp. 4–5. [21] *Bolingbroke Corresp.* ii. 423; Boyer, *Pol. State*, xiv. 217.

A. A. H.

BLENCOWE, John (1642–1726), of Marston St. Lawrence, Northants.

BRACKLEY 1690–1695

b. 30 Nov. 1642, 1st s. of Thomas Blencowe of Marston St. Lawrence by his 2nd w. Mary (*d.* 1687), da. of Francis Savage, DD, of Ripple, Worcs. *educ.* Oriel, Oxf. 1661; I. Temple 1663, called 1670, bencher 1687. *m.* 23 Dec. 1675, Anne (*d.* 1718), da. of Rev. John Wallis, DD, FRS, fellow of New Coll. Oxf., 3s. (1 *d.v.p.*) 4da. (1 *d.v.p.*) *suc.* fa. 1674; kntd. 12 Dec. 1697.[1]

Asst. Banbury corp. 1683–4.[2]

Serjeant-at-law 1689; baron of Exchequer 1696–Nov. 1697; j.c.p. Nov. 1697–1722.[3]

Blencowe, whose ancestral connexion with Marston stretched back to the mid-15th century, appears to have displayed no more than an average talent for his chosen career in the law, but had the good fortune to acquire in Dr John Wallis a father-in-law ambitious to see him rise in his profession. Wallis was an outstanding mathematician and Oxford professor, employed after the Revolution by successive secretaries of state as a decipherer, and, as Wallis always considered his own services meagrely rewarded, he was not above using his contacts on Blencowe's behalf with great persistence. Elected in 1690 for Brackley, a short distance from his family seat, Blencowe's punctilious involvement in the debates and routine proceedings of the Commons, at least in the earlier sessions, reflected his own keenness to promote his chances of legal preferment. Early on, he was noted as a Whig by Lord Carmarthen (Sir Thomas Osborne†). On 30 Apr., at the second reading of the regency bill, when the validity of commissions in the monarch's absence came under discussion, Blencowe argued that the 'authorities' derived from them could not continue 'when the King is gone'. On 18 Dec. he reported from the committee to prepare a clause for disposing confiscations of rebels' estates as security towards war expenditure, and for apportioning some of the forfeitures to the King's own use. Around April 1691 Robert Harley* considered his attachment to the Country party as 'doubtful', an assessment that would appear to square with Wallis' own recommendation of him in the same month to Viscount Sydney (Hon. Henry Sidney†), secretary of state in the northern department, as 'cordially affected to their Majesties' service'. At the end of September Wallis pressed the case for Blencowe's appointment to the court of common pleas with Archbishop Tillotson:

> When I last waited on your Grace at London, I took the boldness to make a suggestion in the behalf of (my son-in-law) Mr Serjeant Blencowe (but without his privity) as a person so well known in Westminster Hall, and in the House of Commons, that I need not give any character of his abilities in his profession. I shall only say that I know him to be a person of great integrity, of temper and consideration and cordial to the Government. There are now two places void in the court of common pleas which will I presume be supplied on his Majesty's return. Both the secretaries have signified to me their Majesties' gracious inclination to be kind to me, and their own readiness to assist in it.[4]

Blencowe played a particularly vocal part in the third session. On 13 Nov. 1691 he made the first of several speeches in support of the Old East India Company, and later, on 2 Dec., he spoke against the proposal to establish a £1,500,000 stock for the company. On 11 Dec., when the House considered the Lords' amendments to the treason trials bill, Blencowe was among several lawyers who took issue with an added clause which raised sensitivity about the Lords' privilege of impeachment, although his own grounds for opposition are unrecorded. He supported the elections bill at third reading on the 12th, having assisted in its preparation the previous November, and spoke once more in favour of the Old East India Company on the 19th. He was able to reiterate his views on the Lords' amendments to the treason bill when the outcome of a conference between the two chambers was reported on the 31st. On 5 Feb. 1692 when the bill for vesting Irish forfeitures in the crown was reported, Blencowe objected to the committee's omission of a clause for forfeiting the remainder of estates in tail. In March a judicial vacancy on the King's bench prompted Wallis to put Tillotson again in mind of Blencowe's worthiness for the advancement which had already been 'signified by L[or]d Nottingham (Daniel Finch†) and others': in his recital of his son-in-law's qualities he stressed his attachment to 'those principles as to church and state which I am well assured your Grace would not dislike'. Wallis was careful to add that Blencowe himself was not 'solicitous' for the post. On 26 Aug. Nottingham was able to offer Wallis the deanery of Hereford, possibly in the belief that it would release him from having to fulfil promises to Blencowe, or possibly sensing that Wallis was obliquely angling for recognition of some kind for himself. Whatever the reasons behind Nottingham's offer, Wallis declined.[5]

Blencowe was less active in the 1692–3 session. According to Narcissus Luttrell's* record of proceedings in those months, he spoke in the House only three times: on 14 Dec. 1692, for committal of the bill 'for the preservation of their Majesties' person and government'; on 25 Feb. 1693, against addressing the King to dissolve the Old East India Company; and on 6 Mar. in favour of a private bill brought in on behalf of Lord Pembroke (Thomas Herbert†). In the course of January and February he managed through the Commons a similar measure for selling land belonging to a distant relative. The following session Blencowe unluckily incurred the displeasure of the House for absenteeism, although he does not seem to have been seriously in error: he had certainly been present in January 1694, obtaining nomination to a committee on the 12th, and was allowed leave of absence for an unspecified length of time on 23 Feb. However, less than three weeks then elapsed before on 14 Mar. he and 13 other Members were sent for into the custody of the serjeant-at-arms for disregarding a recent call of the House. He was discharged on payment of fees on the 31st. On 22 Feb. 1695 he was accorded a month's leave, but had returned by 22 Apr. when he was ordered to prepare a clause for a supply bill, requiring stage coachmen to renew their licences annually, which he presented later the same day. Grascome's analysis of the 1690 Parliament, reflecting the political situation current at some point between 1693 and 1695, indicates that during these later sessions Blencowe went through a phase of opposition: it is possible that this occurred during the 1693–4 session since the ministry was evidently unwilling to make any attempt in March 1694 to save him from the embarrassment of a committal into custody.[6]

Wallis renewed his solicitations for Blencowe in September 1695, suggesting on the 17th to the new secretary of state for the north, Sir William Trumbull*, that Blencowe be raised to the King's bench, and in another letter of the 30th denied any ambition of being 'made great' himself, but referring to his own son, John (Wallis*), and Blencowe, reminded Trumbull that 'a kindness to either of them would be so to me'. Blencowe would have stood for Brackley in 1695, but was 'prevailed upon' by Lords Sunderland and Monmouth to step aside in order that the latter's son, Hon. Harry Mordaunt*, might be chosen there instead. He did not put himself forward elsewhere. Informing Trumbull on 19 Nov. of this development, and observing that the latest vacancy among the judges had been filled, Wallis bemoaned the lot of his family: 'It seems hard that neither I, nor any of mine, are preferred.' But the following summer Blencowe's name was submitted to the King by the Duke of Shrewsbury as Lord Keeper Somers' (Sir John*) nominee to be appointed a baron of the Exchequer. In his memorandum to William, Shrewsbury described Blencowe as 'one who in former parliaments has seemed very well. Though not now in the House, he is an honest and able lawyer, and son-in-law to Dr Wallis of Oxford who deciphers the letters, and will think anything done for him at least as great an obligation, as if it were to himself.' Blencowe's patent for the office was issued on 17 Sept. 1696. Wallis, however, was not so easily satisfied and wrote stuffily to Trumbull on 23 Nov.:

> I begged that my son-in-law Mr Serjeant Blencowe might be made a judge of the common pleas rather than the exchequer, the perquisites there being inconsiderable compared with his practice, and (I doubt) the salary ill-paid. This being refused, I ask for myself. The same sagacity which serves to decipher a letter might be otherwise serviceable if thought worthy to be employed.

In November 1697 Wallis' wishes were met and Blencowe was moved to common pleas, but it is not clear if Wallis was directly responsible for the appointment. Early in 1701, when the chief justiceship of common pleas stood vacant, Wallis saw a further opportunity for his son-in-law's advancement even though Blencowe had positive reasons for not seeking the post himself, and tentatively broached the matter with Dr Humphrey Hody, Archbishop Tenison's domestic chaplain: 'I do not find that Mr Justice Blencowe thinks fit to seek it because it is thought some great man have an eye upon it for whom he hath a just esteem, and would not appear in opposition', but added, 'a promotion of my son-in-law would (on account of his lady my daughter) be a gracious favour to myself'. The 'great man' Wallis mentioned was probably the lord chief justice, Sir John Holt†, who was known to favour Sir Thomas Trevor* for the post. Wallis remained unrealistically hopeful that such obstacles might be surmounted and that the King might after all see fit to bestow the office on Blencowe. However, Blencowe was destined to progress no higher up the judicial ladder, presumably because he lacked substantial political connexions, and remained contentedly a puisne judge until his retirement. At the accession of Queen Anne there was some suggestion that he would be removed from common pleas, but in June 1702 a patent was issued for his reappointment. One of the more contentious legislative measures of this period upon which he was required to declare an opinion was the 1705–6 regency bill, at its committee stage in the Upper House. The judges were called in on 30 Nov. 1705 to pronounce on a clause for preventing the lords justices, who were to act in the sovereign's absence, from repealing Acts of Parliament. Blencowe was equivocal, submitting that since the bill vested regal power in the lords justices, that power might also be limited by the same statute, but at the same time he did not consider it possible to operate what would thereby amount to 'a qualified legislature'. He retired in June 1722, when in his 80th year, and as a mark of favour his full salary of £1,000 was continued until his death. Well before he left the bench he had become thoroughly convinced that he had ascertained the longitude and intended to lay his extensive writings on the subject before Parliament, though he never did so. It is possible that this was an early manifestation of the dementia which overcame him in his last years and gave rise to some bizarre behaviour. He died on 6 May 1726 and was buried at Brackley where a simple memorial tells that 'in every station, he excelled, and was beloved'.[7]

[1] *Vis. Northants.* (Harl. Soc. lxxxvii), 20–21; *DNB*; ibid. (Wallis, John). [2] *Banbury Corp. Recs.* (Banbury Hist. Soc. xv), 302. [3] *CSP Dom.* 1689–90, p. 76; *Cal. Treas. Bks.* xi. 268; xiii. 161, 366. [4] *DNB* (Wallis, John); Add. 32499, ff. 255, 291, 372; Grey, x. 101. [5] *Luttrell Diary*, 16, 56, 75–76, 88, 99, 172; Grey, x. 206–15; Add. 32499, ff. 297, 327; *DNB*. [6] *Luttrell Diary*, 319, 375, 449, 469; *Vis. Northants.* (Harl. Soc. lxxxvii), 248. [7] *HMC Downshire*, i. 551, 555, 586, 706; *HMC Lords*, n.s. vi. 325; *CSP Dom.* 1696, p. 216; Add. 32499, f. 372; H. Horwitz, *Parl. and Pol. Wm. III*, 294; *Cal. Treas. Bks.* xi. 268, 329; xiii. 161, 366; xvii. 258; Luttrell, *Brief Relation*, v. 183; Nichols, *Lit. Anecs.* ix. 273; Baker, *Northants.* i. 645.

A. A. H.

BLISS(E), Thomas (c.1647–1721), of Maidstone, Kent.

MAIDSTONE 1698–1702, 3 Nov. 1704–1708.

b. c.1647, ?s. of Thomas Blith of Maidstone and St. George's, Canterbury by Mary, da. of one Eastman of All Saints, Canterbury. *m.* bef. May 1695, Elizabeth (*d.* 1730), da. of John Kenward of Yalding, Kent, wid. of Ambrose Warde of Yalding, *s.p.*[1]

Chamberlain, Maidstone 1678–9, 1684; alderman 1682–88, 1710–11[2]

Bliss may have been the son of Thomas Blith, a brewer, whose marriage licence was issued at Canterbury in 1640. In 1662 a Thomas Blist took the oaths against the Solemn League and Covenant when the commissioners for corporations visited Maidstone. A man of that name leased a tenement in Maidstone in 1667. Rather confusingly, a 'Thomas Blist', a surgeon, aged 30, was licensed to marry a Maidstone widow, Ann Howting, in 1670. A widow of the same name actually married in 1674, implying that this Thomas Blist had died in the interim, or had not gone through with the ceremony. Interestingly, Bliss's house sported the arms of the barber surgeons' company and a deed of 1681 called him a surgeon. The date of Bliss's marriage to Elizabeth Kenward is not known, although it certainly took place before the will of her son by a previous marriage, Ambrose Warde, which was made in May 1695.[3]

Bliss had an extensive career as a local office-holder, beginning in 1674 when he took on the duties of churchwarden at All Saints' church in Maidstone. He served as chamberlain to the corporation in both 1678 and 1679, becoming an alderman in the charter granted in 1682 by Charles II, mayor in 1682–3 and chamberlain again in 1684. From this it seems clear that his sympathies lay with the local Tories, although his dismissal from the aldermanic bench in January 1688 is indicative of his refusal to support James II's religious policies. His attitude to the Revolution is unknown, but he may have been restored to the corporation. In 1691, Bliss acquired the lease of an alehouse in Maidstone which subsequently became known as the Globe. In July 1692 he became a j.p. for the county. Not surprisingly, in view of his Tory proclivities, his name appears on an undated list of subscribers to the land bank.[4]

Bliss entered the Commons at the 1698 election, being classed as a Country supporter on a comparative analysis of the old and new Parliaments. His name also appeared on a list which was probably a forecast of those Members likely to oppose a standing army. On 28 Jan. 1699 he received leave of absence for ten days to go into the country. In May 1699 his name was approved by the King as a deputy-lieutenant for Kent. By March 1701 he was listed as Captain Bliss, thereby indicating that he held a commission in the militia. Returned again in the election of January 1701, Bliss appears on a list of likely supporters of the Court over the 'Great Mortgage'. The appearance of Bliss's name on a 'blacklist' of those opposed to making preparations for war with France during the 1701 Parliament had significant repercussions at the Maidstone election the following November. Bliss's main opponent, Thomas Colepeper, distributed copies of the 'blacklist' as part of his campaign, implying that Bliss was a Jacobite. To support this contention he produced a witness who claimed that Bliss had called William III 'a usurper'. Thus, although Bliss won the election by two votes, he faced an election petition and a separate prosecution ordered by the attorney-general, which was instigated in December 1701. Bliss survived the accusations of Jacobitism which resurfaced in the Commons and was declared duly elected on 7 Feb. 1702. In the 1701-2 session his name occurs on a 'white list' of those who favoured the motion of 26 Feb. vindicating the Commons' proceedings in impeaching William III's ministers. Two days after the death of William III a 'Captain Bliss' lobbied Sir Charles Hedges* over whether the secretary had given orders to stop his prosecution. Bliss was right to be worried about this continuing saga for at the general election of 1702, allegations of his being in French pay and of Jacobitism were again made, and Bliss was defeated at the polls. Resort to petitioning saw the Commons make void the election on 8 Dec. 1702, but no new writ was issued. Thus the appearance of Bliss's name on a list of 13 Feb. 1703 of those Members who had voted against agreeing with the Lords' amendments to the bill enlarging the time to take the oath of abjuration is more likely to represent the compiler's conviction that Bliss would have voted with the Tories on this occasion.[5]

A new writ for Maidstone was eventually moved on 24 Oct. 1704. Bliss was elected on 3 Nov., in time to be the last name added to Robert Harley's* lobbying list for the Tack, which was originally composed on 30 Oct. Bliss was forecast as an opponent of the Tack, and on a subsequent list of 1705 in reference to the actual vote on 28 Nov. was described as a 'sneaker'. However he did not face difficulties at the 1705 election over his refusal to vote for the Tack. In the new Parliament he voted on 25 Oct. 1705 against the Court candidate in the division on the Speaker. Shortly afterwards, on 25 Nov., he received leave of absence for a fortnight. He seems to have been an inactive Member, but only one further leave of absence was granted to him, on 11 Feb. 1708, for a month. On two parliamentary lists in 1708 he was classed as a Tory, and he may have seen defeat looming in the 1708 election since he appears not to have put up on that occasion.[6]

Having retired from parliamentary politics, Bliss continued to play a role in local affairs. He was restored to the aldermanic bench in October 1710, but this decision was overturned in March 1711. He continued to accumulate property in Maidstone, taking a lease in 1714 of the rectorial tithes. He also set about securing a place for his family in the annals of the town, through small displays and charitable works. Thus in 1713 he presented a silver chalice, decorated with the Bliss coat of arms, to St. Martin's, Detling. In 1719-20 he spent £700 on a workhouse in Maidstone, which was subsequently finished and fitted out by the parish. He was removed from the commission of the peace in January 1719, but did not die until 8 Oct. 1721. In his will, he left his lands and personal estates to his wife, Elizabeth, whom he made his executor for carrying out the will and his bequests which totalled just over £1,800. She later married William Turner.[7]

[1] J. M. Russell, *Hist. Maidstone*, 351; *Canterbury Mar. Lic.* ii. 111; iii. 49; PCC 104 Bond. [2] Russell, 197, 351; *Recs. of Maidstone* ed. Martin, 164, 171; Centre Kentish Stud. md/ACm1/4, burghmote minutes, 30 Oct. 1710, 12 Mar. 1710-11. [3] *Canterbury Mar. Lic.* ii. 111; iii. 49, 143; *Recs. of Maidstone*, 146, 154; Russell, 350, 352; PCC 104 Bond. [4] Russell, 351; *Recs. of Maidstone*, 164; *Arch. Cant.* lxxii. 8; info. from Prof. N. Landau; NLS, Advocates' mss 31.1.7, f. 95, land bank subscribers, n.d. [5] *CSP Dom.* 1699-1700, p. 153; 1700-2, pp. 251, 454, 461; Add. 28885, f. 203. [6] Add. 70306, Harley's lobbying list. [7] Russell, 122, 351, 379; *Arch. Cant.* xxvi. 224; Hasted, *Kent*, iv. 316; info. from Prof. Landau; PCC 215 Buckingham.

S. N. H.

BLOFIELD, Thomas (c.1635-1708), of Norwich and Hoveton St. John, Norf.

NORWICH   1689-1701 (Nov.), 1702-1705

b. c.1635, 1st s. of Robert Blofield, rector of Westwick, Norf. 1636-44, 1653-d., Thorpe next Norwich 1642-4, 1660-d., by his 1st w. Mary, da. of Thomas Layer of Booton, Norf. *m.* by 1664, Elizabeth Watson, wid., da. of Henry Negus, merchant, of Norwich and Hoveton St. Peter, Norf., *s.p. suc.* fa. 1670.[1]

Freeman, Norwich 1661, sheriff 1685-6, alderman 1689, mayor 1691-2.[2]

Jt. receiver of poll tax, Norf. 1692.[3]

A Tory merchant, Blofield was classed by Lord Carmarthen (Sir Thomas Osborne†) in 1690 as a Court supporter. He was frequently involved in the preparation of bills concerning trade and commerce. On 9 May 1690, for example, he was appointed to prepare a bill for the regulation of wines, and on 6 Dec. was the first-named Member of the second-reading committee for an abortive bill to transfer this duty to customs. This session also saw Blofield nominated to draft bills for regulating the King's bench and Fleet prisons (18 Oct.); to prevent the export of wool (21 Oct.); and for maintaining the rights of corporations (31 Oct.). In December he was listed by Carmarthen as one who would give support in the event of a Commons' attack on his ministerial position. On 31 Oct. 1691 Blofield was nominated to the drafting committee for a bill to regulate abuses in parliamentary elections. On 2 Nov. 1691 he was first-named to draft another bill on the transfer of the duty, and five days later was among those ordered to prepare a poor relief bill. He was granted a fortnight's leave of absence on 11 Jan. 1692. During this session he was described to one Essex Tory as 'a very considerable man in the House and a very honest gentleman'. He was included in 1692 in two lists of placemen. On 15 Nov. 1692 he presented another duty bill, and three days later was appointed to draft a bill extending the patent for convex lights. He opposed the bill to renew the 1689 Woollen Act, speaking on 19 Jan. 1693 for the additional clause proposed by Robert Waller* to safeguard the position of the Hamburg Company, and on 17 Feb. against the bill itself at its third reading, when he confirmed, with evidence gained from conversations with the farmers of the duty, that the Act had considerably reduced the exports of woollens from provincial ports, presumably including Norwich. He also spoke on 2 Feb. in favour of the bill against hawkers and pedlars, protesting that 'these pedlars, who are generally Scotsmen, go away with a third part of the trade of the nation'. On 14 Nov. 1693 he was nominated to the drafting committee for a bill to encourage the clothing trade. He told on 12 Dec. against another attempt to revive the Woollen Act, and later in the session was appointed, on 14 Feb. 1694, to the drafting committee for a bill to regulate the wool trade in Norwich. During the 1694–5 session Blofield was listed as a friend of Henry Guy*, possibly in connexion with an attack on Guy in the Commons. He was also appointed, on 4 Dec., to prepare a bill relating to prisons and prisoners, and on 13 Apr. 1695 reported from the committee on the Royal African Company's charter. His interest in the latter issue probably stemmed from that committee's particular concern with a matter affecting the woollen industry.[4]

Returned again unopposed in 1695, he was nominated on 6 Dec. to a drafting committee for a bill to encourage woollen manufactures, presenting a bill to this end on 15 Feb. 1696. He had told on 16 Jan. on the Tory side in the Hertfordshire election case, and was forecast as likely to oppose the Court on 31 Jan. on the proposed council of trade. He signed the Association promptly, and voted against fixing the price of guineas at 22s. in March. He was again a teller on the Tory side on 17 Apr. 1696, on a procedural motion, and three days later was given leave of absence. During the summer he was asked by the lords of the Treasury to take charge of the recoinage operations at Norwich but declined, since to do so would have required his constant attendance, and recommended instead his cousin, who may have been appointed. For this refusal he was soon afterwards criticized by Lord Godolphin (Sidney†) when the Treasury received a complaint about 'the slow proceedings of the Norwich mint'. Chancellor of the Exchequer Charles Montagu* reported in July that Blofield was in favour of the Court's scheme for issuing interest-bearing Exchequer bills to alleviate the shortage of specie. On 25 Nov., after Parliament had reconvened, Blofield voted against the attainder of Sir John Fenwick†. Three days later he presented a bill to regulate the African trade, and during this session was nominated to draft bills to restrain the wearing of wrought silks and dyed calicoes (30 Nov.); to facilitate the restoration of 'decayed' harbours (19 Dec.); and for the more effectual prevention of the export of wool (17 Mar. 1697). Blofield told in favour of the silk and calico bill on 15 Jan., but could not prevent its being lost, and in the following session he and Sir Henry Hobart, 4th Bt.*, made another unsuccessful attempt to obtain such a bill. During this session of the 1695 Parliament he was appointed to prepare bills to restrain the wearing of East India stuffs (10 Jan. 1698) and for the more effectual prevention of robberies (29 Jan.). Blofield was listed in error as a placeman in July 1698, being credited with an office, that of receiver-general for the excise in Norfolk, held by his cousin Leonard Blofield.[5]

In a list of about September 1698 Blofield was classed as one of the Country party. He remained an active Member, being nominated in the preparation of bills to enlarge the Russian trade (9 Jan. 1699) and to regulate the militia (8 Feb. 1699). In the following session he was appointed, on 31 Jan. 1700, to prepare a bill to prohibit the wearing of silks and calicoes. In an analysis of the House into interests in early 1700 he was marked as a query or, perhaps, opposition. He supported the Court in February 1701 over continuing the 'Great Mortgage'. His attention to local interests was evident on 1 Apr. when he presented a bill to establish a court of conscience in Norwich, and his concern for trade was again manifested in his nomination, on 26 May, to draft a bill to establish a company for the export of woollens. Blofield was later blacklisted as one who had voted against preparing for war with France, and, according to a Norfolk Whig writing in April 1701, both Norwich Members, having 'voted for the peace of Europe', had 'mightily lost the good opinion of the city'. Despite Blofield's efforts to obtain a bill establishing a court of requests at Norwich, he lost his seat in the November election.[6]

Blofield was re-elected in 1702 after Lord Nottingham (Daniel Finch†) had interceded on his behalf with the new dean of Norwich, Humphrey Prideaux, for the cathedral interest. Though less active in legislative work than he had been previously, he nevertheless continued to take an interest in matters relating to trade and his locality. On 14 Jan. 1703 he presented a bill concerning the linen trade, and on 13 Feb. he voted against the Lords' amendments to the bill extending the time for taking the oath of abjuration. In the following session he was the sole Member appointed on 26 Nov. to draft a bill to enforce the Act requiring Norwich's shopkeepers to take up the freedom of the borough. On 8 Feb. 1704 he was nominated to prepare a bill to ban the wearing of calicoes. Having been forecast as a probable opponent of the Tack, he did not vote for it on 28 Nov. Blofield was nominated to draft two bills in this session, to enable one of the sureties of Norfolk's receiver-general for taxes to compound with the Treasury (7 Dec.), and to levy duties on imported wines and East India goods re-exported to Ireland or the colonies (17 Jan. 1705). He was subject to a double return at the 1705 election, losing his seat after a decision of the House on 6 Dec. The inclusion of Blofield in a list of those who had voted on 25 Oct. 1705 for Bromley as Speaker is an error.[7]

Blofield did not stand for Parliament again. He died on 17 Oct. 1708, in his 74th year, leaving his estate, consisting of property in Norwich and the parishes of Hoveton St. John, Hoveton St. Peter and Waxham, Norfolk, to his great-nephew Thomas Blofield, whose wife was also his own god-daughter and his wife's great-niece. There were bequests amounting to over £3,500, including several for charitable purposes. He was buried at Hoveton St. John, where his epitaph records that in his public life he

> signalized himself for his eminent zeal and steadiness to the Established Church, his loyal affection to his sovereign and the English monarchy, and an unwearied diligence in promoting the interest, trade and welfare of his country, his knowledge in which was equalled by few, his integrity exceeded by none.[8]

[1] PCC 25 Lane; *E. Anglian Peds.* (Harl. Soc. xci), 160. [2] *Norwich Freemen*, 88; H. Le Strange, *Norf. Official Lists*, 114, 115. [3] *Statutes*, vi. 40, 119; *Cal. Treas. Bks.* ix. 1539. [4] W. Suss. RO, Shillinglee mss Ac.454/904, Edward Pratt to Sir Edward Turnor*, 12 Nov. 1691; *Crisis and Order in English Towns* ed. Clark and Slack, 282–3; *Luttrell Diary*, 374, 396, 430. [5] *Cal. Treas. Pprs.* 1557–1696, p. 541; *CSP Dom.* 1696, p. 366; *Cal. Treas. Bks.* xi. 31; Add. 7121, f. 10. [6] Camb. Univ. Lib. Cholmondeley (Houghton) mss, Charles Turner to Robert Walpole II*, 9 Apr. 1701. [7] Add. 29588, f. 115; *Prideaux Letters* (Cam. Soc. n.s. xv), 195–6. [8] PCC 25 Lane; *E. Anglian Peds.* 160; W. Rye, *Norf. Fams.* 66.

D. W. H.

BLOIS, Sir Charles, 1st Bt. (1657–1738), of Grundisburgh Hall and Cockfield Hall, Yoxford, Suff.

IPSWICH   28 May 1689–1695
DUNWICH   29 Jan. 1700–5 Feb. 1709

bap. 14 Sept. 1657, 5th but o. surv. s. of Sir William Blois of Grundisburgh Hall by his 1st w. Martha, da. of Sir Robert Brooke† of Cockfield Hall and coh. to her bro. Sir Robert Brooke† (d. 1669) of Cockfield Hall and Wanstead House, Essex. *m.* (1) 11 May 1680, Mary (d. 1693), da. of Sir Robert Kemp, 2nd Bt.†, of Gissing Hall, Norf. and Ubbeston, Suff., sis. of Robert Kemp*, 3s. (2 *d.v.p.*) 1da.; (2) lic. 18 Apr. 1694, Anne, da. of Ralph Hawtrey*, 2s. (1 *d.v.p.*) 1da. *suc.* fa. 1675; *cr.* Bt. 15 Apr. 1686; *suc.* aunt Mary Brooke in Yoxford estate 1693.[1]

Alderman, Dunwich 1685–June 1688, 1692–4, 1700–*d.*, common councilman 1700, bailiff 1708, 1711–12; ?common councilman, Orford by 1698, ?portman 1709.[2]

Although his father was probably a Presbyterian, Blois himself was an Anglican and a staunch Tory: 'every way a gentleman' as a fellow Tory described him. Returned for Ipswich in 1690, he was listed by Lord Carmarthen (Sir Thomas Osborne†) as a Tory supporter of the Court. He was appointed on 2 Apr. to examine and prepare a bill upon the East India trade. In the next session he was appointed to the committee to draft the bills for regulating the militia (10 Oct.) and for attainting rebels in England and Ireland (22 Oct. 1690). On 2 Dec. he was a teller for Sir Thomas Grosvenor, 3rd Bt.*, in a disputed election for Chester. In December Carmarthen forecast that Blois would support him in the event of an attack on his ministerial position in the Commons. In April 1691 Robert Harley* listed him as a member of the Country party. Named on 28 Oct. to the drafting committee on a bill for the general improvement of highways, he was also nominated on 31 Oct. 1691 to draft bills for securing the rights of corporations, and for regulating abuses in elections. He was given three weeks' leave of absence on 21 Jan. 1692. On 31 Dec. he told in favour of committing the bill to prevent the exporting of gold and silver. He was again given leave of absence on 13 Jan. 1693, 'his lady being very ill'. On 14 Nov. he was appointed to a drafting committee for a bill to encourage the clothing trade. He was one of the few Tories to escape the purge of the Suffolk commission of the peace in 1693. In the 1694–5 session he told on 15 Jan. 1695, for the bill to exempt apothecaries from having to serve in parochial offices; on 4 Feb., on the Tory side, against including in the land tax bill the proposed oath for assessors; and on 8 Feb., again with the Tories, for agreeing with clause B of the treason trials bill as amended by the Lords and re-amended by the Commons. He was nominated on 11 Feb. to draft a bill for regulating printing and presses. Granted another three weeks' leave on 6 Mar., he had returned to the House by 16 Apr., when he told against going into committee on the glass duty bill. He told again on 19

Apr., this time probably for the Court, against putting off until the following Wednesday the hearing of the report on the glass duty bill.[3]

His succession in 1693 to the Brooke estate at Yoxford, which he thereafter made his principal residence, gave Blois an interest at Dunwich, and he was returned there unopposed at a by-election in 1700. Forecast in February 1701 as a likely supporter of the Court over agreeing to continue the 'Great Mortgage', he was later blacklisted as one who in this session had opposed the preparations for war with France. He was a teller on 17 June in favour of hearing the report on the bill for the relief of prisoners for debt. In Harley's list of the 1701–2 Parliament he was classed with the Tories. He voted on 26 Feb. 1702 for the resolution vindicating the proceedings of the Commons in the previous session over the impeachments of William III's ministers, and told the following day for the Tories against a motion to adjourn all committees. He was a teller on 16 Apr. against giving leave for a bill for the relief of Sir John Dillon from the effects of the clause for the resumption of the Irish forfeitures. In the 1702 Parliament he was nominated to the drafting committee on 10 Dec. 1702, to revise the Lords' 7th amendment to the occasional conformity bill. He told on 26 Nov. 1703 for leave for a bill requested by Norwich corporation, to oblige all 'traders' in the city to carry their share of the burdens of municipal office. He was again a teller on 24 Jan. 1704, on the Tory side on an adjournment motion concerning the bill to resume James II's grants, and on 3 Feb. in favour of agreeing with the committee investigating the East Anglian coal trade in a resolution sharply critical of the restrictive practices of Great Yarmouth corporation. Forecast as a likely supporter of the Tack, he voted for it on 28 Nov. 1704, and in consequence was classified as 'True Church' in a list of the House of Commons the following year. He voted against the Court candidate for Speaker on 25 Oct. 1705. Twice listed as a Tory in 1708, he was successful at the election of that year but was unseated on petition and did not stand for Parliament again. Blois died on 10 Apr. 1738 and was buried at Grundisburgh.[4]

[1] Add. 19185, ff. 192–3; Copinger, *Suff. Manors*, ii. 220. [2] Suff. RO (Ipswich), Dunwich bor. recs. EE6 1144/13, p. 76; 1144/14; T. Gardner, *Dunwich* (1754), 86, 142–3; *CSP Dom.* 1685, p. 15; *HMC Var.* vii. 104; *CJ*, xvi. 10; W. Suss. RO, Shillinglee mss Ac.454/973, 1083, Nathaniel Gooding to Sir Edward Turnor*, 18 July 1698, John Hooke to same, 28 Sept. 1709. [3] *HMC Egmont*, ii. 197; *Diary of Edmund Bohun* ed. Wilton Rix, 121. [4] Add. 19185, ff. 192–3.

D. W. H.

BLOUNT, Sir Thomas Pope, 1st Bt. (1649–97), of Tittenhanger, Ridge, Herts.

ST. ALBANS 1679 (Mar.)–1681 (Mar.)
HERTFORDSHIRE 1689–30 June 1697

b. 12 Sept. 1649, 1st s. of Sir Henry Blount of Tittenhanger by Hester, da. and h. of Christopher Wase of Islington, Mdx., wid. of Sir William Mainwaring of Chester, Cheshire. *educ.* at home; L. Inn 1668. *m.* 22 July 1669, Jane (*d.* 1726), da. of Sir Henry Caesar† of Bennington, Herts., 5s. (1 *d.v.p.*) 9da. *cr.* Bt. 27 Jan. 1680; *suc.* mother to Tittenhanger 1678, fa. to rest of estates 1682.

Commr. inquiry into recusancy fines, Herts. 1687–8, taking subscriptions to land bank 1696.[1]
Commr. for public accounts 1694–6.

As befitted the descendant of the founder of Trinity College, Oxford, Blount strove after that rare intellectual perfection which he described as 'true freedom and ingenuity of the mind'. In his *Essays*, published in 1691, he championed reason above superstition or custom. Like his brother and fellow author Charles, he attacked what he perceived as the irrationality of popery and the tyranny of sacerdotal priestcraft. Sympathetic to Dissent, he believed that men should not be forced into conformity with unnecessary ecclesiastical ceremonies, and that the 'Christian religion is a plain, simple, easy thing'. Aware that such views might antagonize the clergy, he prefaced his work with a characteristically frank declaration that he was 'unfeignedly . . . a true honourer of them, I mean such of them as live up to the honour of that holy profession, and of those that do not, I as little court their favour as I value their censure'. Again, like his brother, he disapproved of suppressing books, and argued that the wisest princes always granted the greatest liberty to their subjects. Accordingly he castigated the reigns of Charles II and James II, but thought it prudent to declare that 'of all sorts of governments, monarchy is the most agreeable to my genius'. Yet despite his wide-ranging learning and erudition, he was convinced that 'it is not a man's cloistering himself up in his study or his continual poring upon books' that made him wise, and accordingly he entered Parliament in 1679. Even at Westminster, however, he may have seen a struggle for reason and truth, for he wrote that 'a plurality of voices, 'tis true, carries the question in all our debates, but rather as an expedient for peace, than any eviction of right'. He was no party hack, refraining from 'no man's company because his opinion comes not up to mine', and self-righteously observed that 'when people once separate and rendezvous themselves into distinct sects and parties, they always confine their kindness to their own party, and look with a scornful and malignant aspect upon all the rest of mankind'.[2]

Blount joined the Green Ribbon Club in February 1679, evidently recruited in the aftermath of the Popish Plot, but he may not have been as radical in his outlook as his brother Charles, since he played a rather inconspicuous role during the Exclusion Crisis. Returned for Hertfordshire in 1689 and again in 1690, Blount was classed as a Whig by Lord Carmarthen (Sir Thomas Osborne[†]) and tended to side with the Court. He was therefore classified in December 1690 as one of those who might defend Carmarthen from attack, and was ranked in the Court party in the spring of 1693, though the marks by his name on Robert Harley's* list compiled in April 1691 suggest that this characterization of his views was not without doubt. In 1692 James II sent Blount's wife an invitation to witness the birth of his child at St. Germain, but Blount was so far from being a crypto-Jacobite that the following year the non-juror Samuel Grascome suggested that he was one of four Members whose visit to a robber in prison had produced a 'Williamite plot' against James' supporters. Although Blount's prior purpose on this occasion probably related to recent thefts from his house, in which he had lost £1,000 in money and plate, the incident seems further confirmation of his identification as a Court Whig.[3]

On 21 Jan. 1693 the House ordered the burning of a tract, *King William and Mary Conquerors*, which had been written by Charles Blount, either to ensnare the Tory licenser of books, Edmund Bohun, or, as has been alternatively suggested, genuinely to advance justification of the ideology of conquest for the transfer of the crown to William. It is difficult to tell, however, whether Sir Thomas' silence on the matter signifies embarrassment about the affair, or agreement with his brother's views. His independent mind nevertheless made him a natural choice on 12 Apr. 1694 for the commission of accounts, attracting as many votes as Paul Foley I*, and, despite his Court stance, he was on excellent terms with Robert Harley*, whom he assured 'that without anything of a compliment there is no person living more Mr Harley's humble servant'. On 7 Jan. 1695 he told against a motion to hear the report of the committee on the place bill, and although he came sixth on the ballot in March for the following year's commission of accounts, he won more votes than before. On 27 Mar. he was nominated to prepare the articles of impeachment against Lord Carmarthen, now Duke of Leeds.[4]

Re-elected for the county in 1695, Blount was preoccupied when Parliament assembled with a personal bill to provide for his large family after the marriage of his eldest son in December. Weddings were again his concern on 21 Apr. 1696 when he told in favour of the bill to enforce laws restraining marriages without licences. Blount was forecast as likely to support the Court in the divisions of 31 Jan. 1696 on the council of trade. Ten days earlier he had told against an instruction to the committee on clipped coin to consider the price of guineas, and in March duly voted for fixing the price at 22s. His closeness to the Court now lost him his place on the commission of accounts, though he headed the ministerial slate in the ballot, and at the start of the following session, on 3 Nov., he told against the referral of the commissioners' report on the deficiencies of funds. Having subscribed the Association earlier in the year, he voted on 25 Nov. 1696 for the attainder of Sir John Fenwick[†], and on 21 Jan. 1697 again told for the Court, against the clause exempting from the land tax the Queen Dowager's annuity. Six days later he told on a motion to read a report from the committee on abuses in prisons, acting with the leader of the Rose Club, Sir Henry Hobart, 4th Bt.* As one of the club's candidates, he topped the poll in February for commissioners of accounts, though the bill renewing the commission fell later the same month. He died 'of an apoplexy' on 30 June 1697. The main part of the estate passed to his eldest son Thomas, who was engaged in a suit against Ralph Freman I* and Charles Caesar*, the trustees of the estate of his great-grandmother, and at the 1697 and 1708 county elections the 2nd baronet voted for the Whig candidates.[5]

[1] *Cal. Treas. Bks.* viii. 1695–6; *CJ*, xii. 508. [2] T. Blount, *A Natural History* (1693); *Essays*, preface to 1691 ed.; *Essays* (3rd and enlarged edn, 1697), 63–65, 74, 87, 92, 200, 234, 253, 256, 267. [3] Magdalene, Camb. PL 2875, f. 470, Green Ribbon Club mins.; *CSP Dom.* 1692, p. 264; S. Grascome, *New Court Contrivances* (1693), 4–7; Add. 70116, Abigail to Robert Harley, 27 Aug. 1692. [4] *N and Q*, ccxxiii. 527–32; *HMC Portland*, iii. 556–7; H. Horwitz, *Parl. and Pol. Wm. III*, 132. [5] *HMC Kenyon*, 399; Horwitz, 191; Harl. 1492–5, passim; Add. 36242, f. 157; Herts. RO, Q/PE/1, f. 31, pollbk. 1697; D/EX/294/Z1, f. 97, pollbk. 1708.

M.J.K.

BOCLAND (BOCKLAND), Maurice (1648–1710), of Standlynch, nr. Downton. Wilts.

DOWNTON   30 Oct. 1678–1681 (Mar), 1685–1687
               1689–1695, 21 Feb.–7 July 1698

b. 20 Apr. 1648, 3rd but o. surv. s. of Walter Bocland (Bockland)[†] of Standlynch by Helen, da. of Hubert Hacon of Norwich, Norf. *educ.* Magdalen Coll. Oxf. 1664; I. Temple 1667; M. Temple 1669; Padua 1669. *m.* (1) 10 Feb. 1673, Joan (*d.* 1689), da. of John Penruddock of Compton Chamberlayne, Wilts., sis. of Thomas

Penruddock†, 3s. *d.v.p.* 6da. (1 *d.v.p.*); (2) by 1695, Mabel (with £2,000), da. of Sir Robert Dillington, 2nd Bt.†, of Knighton, I.o.W., sis. of Sir Tristram Dillington, 5th Bt.*, 2s., 1da. *suc.* fa. 1670.[1]

Freeman, Salisbury 1680–4, Oct. 1688–*d*.[2]

Bocland was able to return himself again at Downton in 1690 unchallenged by the other principal families who usually contended for the borough. Classed as a Whig by Lord Carmarthen (Sir Thomas Osborne†), on 24 Apr. 1690 he was nominated to prepare the bill for an oath of abjuration. Although marked by Robert Harley* as a possible supporter of the Country party in April 1691, he was described as 'Court' by the time Grascome drew up his list in 1693. In the 1692–3 session he reported from the committee on the bill dealing with the will of Henry Bayntun* and his estates in north Wiltshire (12 Jan.), and was named to the drafting committee on the bill to continue the Acts prohibiting trade with France (11 Feb.). On 6 Mar. he spoke against the bill to set aside amendments to the records of a fine and two recoveries in Glamorgan, brought in on behalf of Lord Pembroke (Thomas Herbert†). He was persuaded to step down at the 1695 election in favour of Charles Duncombe*, much to the chagrin of Lady Ashe, widow of Sir Joseph Ashe, 1st Bt.†, Bocland reappeared briefly in the Commons in 1698, being chosen at a by-election after Duncombe had been expelled. He was listed as a Court supporter in a comparative analysis of the old and new Parliaments in September 1698 but did not stand again, having been pushed aside at Downton by more powerful interests.[3]

Bocland made his will on 2 May 1710. The extensive coalmines, leadmines and quarries centred upon Shepton Mallet, Somerset, were settled on trustees, including his 'nephew' Thomas Freke*, to pay off his debts and secure £2,200 on his four younger daughters, who were also given the annuities of £800 invested in the Exchequer. He left £1,000 to his eldest daughter, Jane, and a similar sum together with the profits from the Shepton Mallet estate to his younger surviving son, Maurice†. Bocland had died by 28 Nov. 1710, when his will was proved. The Standlynch estate was sold by Maurice in 1726, who then migrated to Hampshire.[4]

[1] Hoare, *Wilts*. Downton, 50; *Misc. Gen. et Her*. ser. 2, ii. 125; ser. 5, ix. 110–11. [2] Hoare, *Wilts*. Salisbury, 477, 480, 487. [3] *Luttrell Diary*, 469. [4] Hoare, *Wilts*. Downton, 48; PCC 238 Smith.

D. W. H.

BODDINGTON, George (1646–1719), of Little St. Helen's, Bishopsgate, London.

WILTON 18 July–28 Nov. 1702

b. 15 Oct. 1646, 2nd but 1st surv. s. of George Boddington, Clothworker, of St. Margaret Lothbury, common councilman of London 1669, by Hannah, da. of Thomas Adams of Philpot Lane, St. Clement Eastcheap. *m*. (1) 19 Dec. 1671 (with £2,000), Mary (*d*. 1673), da. of William Steele† of Hatton Garden, Mdx., recorder of London 1649–55, ld. ch. baron of the Exchequer 1655–6, ld. chancellor [I] 1656–60, 1da. *d.v.p.*; (2) 2 July 1674 (with £3,000), Hannah (*d*. 1699), da. of John Cope, Haberdasher, of Cannon Street, 11s. (8 *d.v.p.*) 3da. (2 *d.v.p.*). *suc.* fa. 1671.[1]

Freeman, Clothworkers' Co. 1667, master 1705; member, Levant Co. 1667, asst. 1696, 1701, 1703; member, Eastland Co. 1676; common councilman, London 1689; gov. Greenland Co. 1693; dir. Bank of England 1694–5.[2]

Commr. taking subscriptions to land bank 1696.[3]

Boddington's grandfather 'wasted' a good estate at Brinklow in Warwickshire 'by gaming and extravagant living', and 'was thereby constrained to sell all he had to pay his debts, being then left in mean circumstances'. He put out his sons as apprentices in London and the eldest, George, father of the Member, succeeded in his trade as a packer sufficiently to repay this investment with financial support. Assisted by a maternal uncle, he established himself in a house in St. Margaret Lothbury, and by 1666 had acquired seven other properties in the vicinity. All were destroyed in the Great Fire, and although he was able to rebuild his business and his 'mansion house' his health was said to have been permanently impaired in the calamity, through 'his great exertions in removing his goods of trade'. A staunch Protestant, whose enthusiasm for the restored monarchy vanished within a year as he became convinced that the King and Duke of York were Catholics, he had married a lady of pronounced Puritan leanings. Their son recorded how his mother

> was of an excellent spirit, and . . . a great reader, and worker, and took all opportunities to instruct and instil good principles of religion and morals into us her children, and would often take us singly to her apartment and pray with us.

The young George, after demonstrating his ineptitude for more scholarly pursuits, was 'put . . . to a writing school' and, 'having made a small progress there in arithmetic', embarked in his father's business. A diligent youth, 'always first and last up in the house', he learnt 'merchants' accounts' and in 1664 began on his own, in a very small way. The next few years proved a time of crisis for the family, and for George in particular. In 1665 he underwent an experience of religious awakening, 'through the abounding grace of God', as he himself put it, and within a year or so attached himself to an Independent congregation, 'being under conviction that it was incumbent on me to be found walking in all the ordinances of God'. His career also took a new turn, as he was first apprenticed to a Flanders merchant and then, in the wake of the disaster wreaked by the Fire, set up in the Turkey trade, the initial capital of £1,000 somehow supplied by his father.[4]

Despite problems, as in 1681 when a consignment of 'country dressed cloths' that he intended for export to the Levant were seized 'for ill workmanship' and he was fined by the Clothworkers' Company, Boddington prospered. He was even able to cope with serious losses in the Smyrna convoy in 1693, in which he had risked 'the greatest part of my estate'. Happily, he wrote, 'the Lord of his great grace gave me a frame to praise him for taking away'. Earlier that year he had easily defeated Sir William Scawen* in an election for the governorship of the Greenland Company. Chosen one of the founding directors of the Bank, he soon found that this responsibility 'took up too much of my time', so disqualified himself in 1695 by selling his stock. His contribution of £500 the previous January to the loan on the security of the excise had not been among the more substantial. He remained a devout Nonconformist, although transferring his allegiance after his second marriage to the church ministered by John Collins, a Congregationalist and an associate of his new wife's stepfather Ralph Venning, also a Congregational pastor. Indeed, Boddington served as manager and treasurer of the Congregational fund. When elected to the common council of London in 1689 he lasted only two months before disqualification for refusing the Test. However, he may well have become an occasional conformist subsequently, since he acted as a churchwarden of St. Helen's, Bishopsgate in 1696 and 1700. Returned to Parliament for Wilton in 1702 with Sir John Hawles*, in a disputed election notorious for the participation of numerous Dissenting burgesses, he was unseated on petition and did not stand again.[5]

Boddington's later years were dominated by the twin preoccupations of business and family, and were marked by frequent visits to Bath, for his health. In 1704 he acquired from a bankrupt brother a house at Enfield, Middlesex, and went to live there. He died 10 May 1719, bequeathing in his will in addition to the £16,000 or so already made over to his children a further sum of more than £4,000, together with various leasehold properties in the City: his father's house in Lothbury to one son, his own 'mansion' in Little St. Helen's to another, the Sun Tavern in New Fish Street and other shops and houses.[6]

[1] *Fam. Min. Gent.* (Harl. Soc. xxxix), 1112–13; J. R. Woodhead, *Rulers of London* (London and Mdx. Arch. Soc.), pp. 33–34; Foss, *Judges*, vi. 489–92; *DNB* (Steele, William); Guildhall Lib. ms 10823/1, ff. 5–7, 26; 10823/2, ff. 8–11; *Misc. Gen. et Her.* n.s. ii. 547.
[2] Guildhall Lib. ms 10823/1, ff. 11, 21–23; info. from Prof. H. Horwitz; *N. and Q.* clxxix. 39. [3] *CJ*, xii. 509. [4] *Misc. Gen. et Her.* 545; *Fam. Min. Gent.* 1112; Guildhall Lib. ms 10823/1, ff. 3, 18–21.
[5] T. Girtin, *The Golden Ram*, 152; Guildhall Lib. ms 10823/1, ff. 11, 23; *Cal. Treas. Bks.* x. 913, 1452; xix. 294; xx. 125; info. from Prof. G. S. De Krey; J. E. Cox, *Annals St. Helen's, Bishopsgate*, 114, 119.
[6] Guildhall Lib. ms 10823, f. 23 and passim; *Fam. Min. Gent.* 1113; PCC 99 Browning.

D. W. H.

BOHUN, George (1642–1705), of Coundon and Newhouse, Warws. and Spitalfields, Mdx.

COVENTRY   1695–1698

bap. 23 Feb. 1642, 2nd s. of Abraham Bohun of Coundon (*d.* 1685), rector of Elmdon and vicar of Foleshill, Warws. by Elizabeth, da. of George Bathurst of Hothorpe, Northants. *m.* lic. 18 Oct. 1681, Mary, da. of Thomas Green of St. Martin's, London, 2s. *d.v.p.* 4da.[1]

Asst. R. African Co. 1684–6, 1689–92, 1695–7, dep. gov. 1687–8, sub-gov. 1693–4; cttee. E.I. Co. 1686–95, gov. 1696–8.[2]

Commr. taking subscriptions to land bank 1696.[3]

Bohun's ancestral line had been settled at Coundon since the 1570s, but before then the family's roots had lain in the area around Bakewell in Derbyshire. Unlike his elder brother Ralph, Bohun did not attend university, but embarked on what was to be a prosperous mercantile career in London. His trading interests were reflected in his rise to prominence in the African and East India Companies, and his stockholdings became considerable: in the latter company, for example, they stood at £3,300 in 1689. At the time of his marriage he was living at Wood Street in Cheapside, but on the death of a younger brother in 1690 he inherited property in Spitalfields which he later augmented. He was of sufficient standing to be nominated to the Middlesex lieutenancy in 1693. At the same time he maintained and cultivated his links with Coventry, although it was not until 1703 that he was added to the lieutenancy there. In 1692 he provided the town's principal church of St. Michael with two enormous iron candlesticks, but it was a gesture of generosity which may have seemed to flaunt his churchmanship too ostentatiously for the tastes of Presbyterian townsmen, who spread the rumour that the new lights were lit for the first time at the funeral of a lunatic who had overdosed himself with opium.[4]

Bohun, a Tory, was elected without opposition in 1695, and during his only term of parliamentary service his involvement in proceedings centred mainly upon the coinage and the affairs of the East India Company of which he was for most of the time the senior representative in the House. On 1 Jan. 1696 he was among those ordered to prepare a supply bill for extending the period for raising duties on East India merchandise. His likely support for the proposed council of trade in the divisions anticipated on 31 Jan. was regarded as 'doubtful', and in the following month he refused at first to sign the Association. He voted against the government on fixing the price of guineas in the division of either 20 or 26 Mar., while on 25 June he presented to the lords justices a petition from Coventry 'about the coin', but it was recorded that 'he did not stay for an answer'. On 31 Oct., in the next session, he was one of the Members appointed to prepare a bill 'for the relief of creditors'. He voted against the attainder of Sir John Fenwick† on 25 Nov. In a division on 13 Feb. 1697 he served as teller against a question to elect a new commissioner of accounts in place of Lord William Powlett*, who wished to be excused from serving.

During the early months of 1697 the East India Company, with Bohun as its governor, set itself against legislation to prohibit the growing importation of silks from the far east. The measure was promoted chiefly by the London silk-weavers, anxious to preserve their livelihoods against powerful competition. When on 19 Mar. they heard that the bill had been lost in the Lords an unruly crowd of weavers and other elements marched upon and assailed Bohun's residence in Spitalfields with 'iron bars, pick-axes and other instruments', threatening the lives of himself and his family. There was fierce resistance from members of his household, who fired shots, killing two protesters and wounding others, and the situation was only saved by the arrival of several companies of militia. The following day Bohun reported the incident to the House as a breach of privilege, and expressed apprehensions about the 'much greater number' that had since reassembled. It was agreed to address the King to deploy the militia 'or other forces' for the suppression of any further attacks on Bohun's property. Very soon afterwards Bohun became involved in a government initiative to provide the East India Company with the legislative recognition it had been seeking for several years for its monopoly over Asiatic trade. On 23 Mar. he was summoned to Whitehall, where it was proposed to him that the company should have a parliamentary 'settlement' in return for a loan to the crown of £400,000. The 'committees' (directors) concurred, but their decision to recommend the offer to the company's general court was taken no further. In the next parliamentary session, however, the matter was reopened. On 12 Apr., in ways and means, 'Mr Newport', possibly Hon. Thomas Newport*, said he had 'by chance' heard a suggestion that there was to be a loan from the company of £700,000 'upon a remote fund at 6 per cent' in return for an Act of Parliament, and called upon Bohun to verify whether such a scheme was intended. The company had indeed circularized Members with details of a proposal for making a £600,000 loan, but Bohun responded to Newport with due caution:

> Mr Bohun said he had no proposal to make of that kind, nor had any such thing been yet offered to their general court; there had been some discourses about it. Some against it absolutely, saying it would be to sell the trade of the nation and to ruin all manufacturers; some that if money were to be raised this way, a better bargain might be made, and for such an establishment the money should be given, not lent only; that if the company did not think fit to do it, there were others would for the sole benefit of the trade, and it was better to take a less sum without any after-reckoning or entailing a debt upon the nation.

It was agreed to defer further discussion until more information regarding the company's plans was available, though it was reported that 'Mr Bohun would have been glad to have had some better handle for bringing it under debate at this court'. Two days later the general court did agree to a loan of £700,000 and to a plan for bringing in the large number of interlopers in the East India trade. Bohun subsequently laid the offer before the King, who was willing that Parliament should consider it. Later in the month, however, Bohun stood down as a governor, succeeded by Sir John Fleet*, and so ceased to be officially involved in the negotiations. In the meantime, the interlopers' syndicate had put together, and the government had accepted, a rather more generous proposal to provide £2,000,000 at 8 per cent for the 'public service' which they would raise through a new subscription, and in return by statute they would be established as a new East India Company. When the enabling bill was before the House in June Bohun naturally stood in defence of the Old Company: on the 7th he 'insinuated that they had done the utmost that the public might be accommodated', and on the 10th he supported Fleet's somewhat desperate expression of the company's readiness to receive whatever proposal the House might make.[5]

Bohun did not stand for re-election in 1698. He died on 15 Nov. 1705 and was buried in the vault prepared for the family's use by his brother John Bohun in St. Michael's church. There being no surviving male issue, his principal estate at Coundon passed to his eldest daughter, Susanna, who married Gilbert

Clarke, the younger son and brother, respectively, of the Derbyshire MPs, Sir Gilbert and Godfrey Clarke.[6]

[1] IGI, Warws.; *Vis. Warws.* (Harl. Soc. lxii), pp. 40–41; Dugdale, *Warws.* 133–4; *Mar. Lic. Vicar-Gen.* (Harl. Soc. xxx), p. 76; T. W. Whitley, *Parl. Rep. Coventry*, 122–3. [2] K. G. Davies, *R. African Co.* 378; Add. 38871, ff. 9–11 [3] *CJ*, xii. 508. [4] *Vis. Warws.* (Harl. Soc. lxii), pp. 40–41; *VCH Warws.* viii. 52; Dugdale, 133; Add. 22185, f. 12; Harl. 7017, ff. 287, 297; PCC 263 Smith; *CSP Dom.* 1693, p. 181; 1703–4, p. 280. [5] *CSP Dom.* 1696, p. 245; 1698, pp. 188, 283, 289; *Jnl. Brit. Stud.* xvii(2), pp. 9–10; Luttrell, *Brief Relation*, iv. 199. [6] Whitley, 123; Harl. 7017, f. 287; PCC 263 Smith; *Fam. Min. Gent.* (Harl. Soc. xxxvii), 336.

A. A. H.

BOKENHAM, Hugh (c.1635–94), of Norwich.

NORWICH 1690–26 Apr. 1694

b. c.1635, 4th but 2nd surv. s. of Wiseman Bokenham of Thornham Magna, Suff. by Grace, da. of Paul D'Ewes of Stow Langtoft Hall, Suff., sis. of Sir Simonds D'Ewes, 1st Bt.† *m.* aft. 1664, Elizabeth (*d.* 1669), da. and h. of Christopher Flowerdew of Norwich and Hethersett, Norf., 1s. 1da.[1]

Freeman, Norwich 1661, sheriff 1673–4, alderman 1677, mayor 1681–2.[2]

Jt. receiver-gen. for poll tax, Norf. 1692.[3]

Bokenham, who had been apprenticed to a woollen-draper, was described during his mayoralty of Norwich, in 1681, as 'a gentleman of good family in Suffolk, and a very good estate, being reputed worth above £15,000'. He was also 'the gentlest and best behaved man in town'. Within days of this estimate of his fortune he came into a further 'estate of £700 *per annum* . . . his elder brother's family being extinct in [a] child which died last week'. As mayor of Norwich he was one of the leaders of the 'moderate' party in the city, men who were neither 'violent Whigs' nor 'violent Tories'; 'who are for the present government both in church and state but go soberly to work'. Together with the Whigs these moderates strongly opposed the surrender of the city's charter in 1682.[4]

Classed by Lord Carmarthen (Sir Thomas Osborne†) as a Whig in a list of the new Parliament in March 1690, Bokenham was also listed by Carmarthen in December as one who would support him in the event of a Commons' attack on his ministerial position. On 9 May he was nominated to the drafting committee for a bill to regulate wines. On 11 Oct. he was first-named to the committee of inquiry into abuses in the alnage duty, a matter of concern to his constituents. He appears on Robert Harley's* list of April 1691 and is marked with a 'd', which is perhaps a later annotation recording his death. Samuel Grascome classed him as a placeman in 1693 on account of his receivership of taxes. On 14 Feb. 1694 he was appointed to the drafting committee for a bill to regulate the wool trade in Norwich. Bokenham died on 26 Apr. 1694, aged 59. His will mentioned property in Hethersett, 'late of the Flowerdews', his wife's family, 'and what I bought myself'. It also noted estates in Suffolk, and money lent on the land of Sir Thomas Ogle in Lincolnshire.[5]

[1] PCC 91 Box, 171 Penn; H. Maudslay, *Buckenham Fam.* 35, 47, 246, 290, 297, 304–6, 314; Blomefield, *Norf.* v. 31; *Vis. Norf.* (Harl. Soc. lxxxv), 76. [2] *Norwich Freemen*, 153; H. Le Strange, *Norf. Official Lists*, 114; Maudslay, 47. [3] *Cal. Treas. Bks.* ix. 1539. [4] *Norwich Freemen*, 153; *Prideaux Letters* (Cam. Soc. n.s. xv), 121–2; *CSP Dom.* 1682, pp. 54, 274. [5] Maudslay, 47; PCC 91 Box.

D. W. H.

BOKENHAM, William (*d.* 1702), of St. Margaret's by Rochester, Kent.

ROCHESTER 1701 (Dec.)–1702

m. Frances, *s.p.*[1]

Lt. RN 1681, capt. 1689; ?ensign, Q. Dowager's Ft. 1685; capt. 2nd marine regt. 1691–8.

Nothing has come to light about Bokenham prior to his entry into the navy. His surname was common in East Anglia but he cannot be linked with any of the branches of the family there. It is noteworthy, however, that on one occasion in November 1701, in his role as a Kentish justice, he referred to a prisoner as a 'Suffolk or Norfolk man' whom he had known before the Revolution. Bokenham served under Admiral Arthur Herbert† in Tangier, being commissioned as a lieutenant in 1681 and commanding a ship in 1683 which was sent back to England. As he received captain's pay for this voyage it was counted as part of his commission when he was appointed to the rank of captain after the Revolution. Admiral Edward Russell* clearly entertained a favourable opinion of Bokenham's ability, informing Secretary Nottingham (Daniel Finch†) in May 1691, 'a better man I do not know in the fleet'. Between 1695 and 1697 Bokenham served as first captain to Admiral Sir George Rooke*, a post that was usually the precursor of a flag office. His landed estate was based in Rochester where, in 1693, he purchased Restoration House from the executors of Francis Clerke I*. In March 1699 he was appointed to the bench and the following year bought an estate at Westwell, near Ashford. Thus, when Bokenham was returned for Rochester in December 1701 he could point to his local property as well as his naval interest. The fact that at the poll he defeated a Tory, William Cage*, and in Parliament was not listed as voting on 26 Feb. 1702 for the motion vindicating the proceedings of the Commons in their impeachments of the Whig ministers, suggests that he was a Whig. He certainly attended the House, his name being rendered as 'Bockman' on 3 Feb. when the clerks recorded his appointment to a committee following a petition relating to nautical inventions.[2]

Bokenham did not contest the general election of 1702, being back at sea by June. That he was dropped from the new commission of the peace sealed in July 1702 is perhaps further evidence of Whiggish views. He died at sea on 10 Nov. 1702 Rooke recording in his journal on that date that 'Captain Bokenham died, and Captain Foulkes ordered to command the ship to Chatham'. His will, drawn up in May 1692, before his property acquisitions, left to his wife Frances all the money due to him for service at sea or on land. His property in Rochester may have descended at first to his brother Robert, another naval captain, but in the long run it passed to his brother Harry, whose daughter Anne, and her husband, John Dumaresque, sold it in 1719.[3]

[1] Prob. 10/1359, unreg. will. [2] *CSP Dom.* 1700–2, p. 442; *Mariner's Mirror*, lxxvi. 245; *HMC Finch*, iii. 71; J. Ehrman, *Navy in War of Wm. III*, 649; H. Maudslay, *Buckenham Fam.* 182; J. D. Davies, *Gents. and Tarpaulins*, 167; info. from Prof. N. Landau; *Arch. Cant.* xv. 114, 119; Hasted, *Kent*, vii. 422. [3] Info. from Prof. Landau; *Navy Rec. Soc.* ix. 162, 238; Prob. 10/1359; Maudslay, 207; *Arch. Cant.* 126.

S. N. H.

BOLD, Richard (1678–1704), of Bold Hall, Lancs.

LANCASHIRE   1701 (Feb.)–21 Mar. 1704

bap. 20 May 1678, 1st s. of Peter Bold† of Bold Hall, by Anne, da. of Adam Beaumont of Whitley, Yorks. *educ.* privately; Jesus, Camb. 1693. *m.* settlement 2 Nov. 1699, Elizabeth, da. of Thomas Norton of Barkisland, Yorks., 2s. 4da. *suc.* fa. 1692.[1]

Burgess, Wigan 1698; freeman, Lancaster 1702.[2]

Bold's father had been one of Lancashire's leading Tories from the late 1670s until his death in 1692, and Bold followed closely in his father's footsteps. Although his father's marriage settlement dates from December 1679, Bold had been born over a year prior to this so that, as his father had been, Bold was left fatherless while still a minor, and the Leghs of Lyme, in the person of Thomas Legh†, took charge of the young Bold. His education under Legh does not appear to have been strenuous and in 1692 it was reported as being regularly interrupted by the 9th Earl of Derby, a friend and political ally of Bold's father, taking Bold away from his tutor to attend various social events in Lancashire. After he left for university in 1693 nothing is known of Bold's activities until 1700, when his political ambitions came to the fore. Added to the commission of the peace in August 1700, Bold began to pursue a seat in Parliament, and he at first thought of sitting for Newton, a borough under the control of the Leghs of Lyme. Bold wrote to Peter Legh†, nephew of his former guardian, that 'I am resolved to applying myself as much as I can to the service of my country in general, my native county in particular, which I conceive cannot be better or more reasonably done than in the House of Commons'. He decided, however, to contest the county, writing to Sir Daniel Fleming† that his 'only design is to serve you and his country without the least prospect of advantage' and, with the support of Lord Derby, in January 1701 Bold was successful at the poll.[3]

Bold's Tory allegiance soon became evident, as he was subsequently blacklisted as having voted during the 1701 session against the preparations for the war with France. In June he attended a Lords' committee upon the estate bill of Sir Thomas Stanley, 4th Bt.*, in order to support the written consents of the concerned parties with verbal testimony. He was returned unopposed in the second 1701 election. His Toryism was confirmed by his favouring the motion of 26 Feb. vindicating the Commons' proceedings in the impeachment of William III's ministers in the previous session, and by April he was campaigning to retain his seat in Lancashire, complaining to one voter that 'I have had the misfortune to serve you when one election has just trod on the heels of another'. Chosen again in 1702 Bold was no more active in the new Parliament. When a Liverpool merchant requested Bold's assistance in dealing with the customs service, Liverpool's Whig Member Thomas Johnson complained that 'I never saw Mr B[old] two hours, nor I think once since I came except to serve some turn'. Bold died suddenly on 21 Mar. 1704, his early death mirroring that of his father. He left his estates in south Lancashire heavily encumbered with debts due to the need to find large sums to pay his mother's and wife's jointures and his sisters' dowries. His widow petitioned on 17 Dec. 1705 for a bill to vest the estate in trustees, and such a measure passed later in the session. Bold was succeeded by his son Peter, who sat for Wigan and Lancashire as a Tory in George II's reign.[4]

[1] IGI, Lancs.; *VCH Lancs.* iii. 403; NRA report 306 (De Hoghton mss), p. 6; John Rylands Univ. Lib. Manchester, Legh of Lyme mss corresp. James Liptrott to Thomas Legh, 18 Oct. 1692. [2] Wigan RO, Wigan bor. recs. AB/MR/10; *Lancaster Freeman Rolls* (Lancs. and Cheshire Rec. Soc. lxxxviii), 16. [3] Add. 22654, ff. 16–17; Legh of Lyme mss corresp. Liptrott to Legh, 18 Oct. 1692, Bold to Peter Legh, 27 Nov. 1700; L. K. J. Glassey, *Appt. JPs*, 284; Cumbria RO (Kendal), Le Fleming mss WD/Ry 5588, Bold to [Sir Daniel

Fleming], 6 Dec. 1700; Lancs. RO, Stanley mss DDK 15/22, copy letters of Ld. Derby, 15 Jan. 1700–1. ⁴Legh of Lyme mss corresp. Bold to Peter Legh, 20 June 1701; Lancs. RO, Kenyon mss DDKe/HMC/1036, same to George Kenyon*, 2 Apr. 1702; *Norris Pprs.* (Chetham Soc. ser. 1, ix), 124; Add. 27440, f. 138; *VCH Lancs.* 406.

E. C./R. D. H.

BOLLES, Sir John, 4th Bt. (1669–1714), of Scampton, Lincs.

LINCOLN 1690–1702

b. July 1669, o. surv. s. of Sir John Bolles, 3rd Bt., of Scampton by his 2nd w. Elizabeth, da. of Sir Vincent Corbet, 1st Bt.†, of Morton Corbet, Salop. *educ.* Christ Church, Oxf. matric. 1683; G. Inn 1680. *unm. suc.* fa. as 4th Bt. 3 Mar. 1686.

    Dir. land bank 1696.¹
    Commr. navigation of Aire and Calder 1699.²

Sir John was descended from a cadet branch of a family which had been settled in Lincolnshire since the 13th century, and had represented the county in the Parliaments of Edward III. Its fortune had been secured in the early 17th century by Sir George Bolles, alderman and lord mayor of London, who acquired by marriage the estate of Scampton, near Lincoln. By the reign of Charles II the Bolleses had also gained properties in Yorkshire, and were said to be worth £3,000 p.a. The Member's grandfather, Sir Robert, had stood successfully for Lincoln in 1661 and Bolles himself was returned there in 1690, although yet to reach his majority. At the outset of his career he was identified by Lord Carmarthen (Sir Thomas Osborne†) as a Whig, but soon established himself as a Country Tory, becoming an active committeeman and teller. Unfortunately, the madness which gripped him in later life has cast a shadow over his earlier political career, obscuring the fact that for a time he ranked among the most industrious of opposition members. For certain, the pro-Jacobite rantings which earned him notoriety in the last years of William's reign should not be regarded as proof of an enduring attachment to the exiled court. To some extent he was a victim of the party strife of that age, deliberately provoked into outbursts by both Whigs and Tories as they sought to score political points off each other.³

In the first session of the 1690 Parliament Bolles twice acted as a teller, in favour of the introduction of a bill to naturalize foreign Protestants, and against a bill to settle a private charity. Although only 20, on 2 May he was prepared to confront the parliamentary veteran Sir Edward Seymour, 4th Bt., over the published 'black list' of those who had voted against the transfer of the crown, an exchange which saw Seymour teasingly label the young Member 'a great original'. Sir John did not make any significant contribution to Commons' business in the second session, but in April 1691 was classed as a Country supporter by Robert Harley*. In the 1691–2 session he chaired a committee on a private bill, and on 27 Feb. 1692 spoke in favour of a measure allowing Quakers to affirm. In the next session he both argued and told on 27 Feb. 1693 against the bill to indemnify those who had ordered extraordinary measures in defence of the kingdom at the time of the threatened French invasion in 1692. Three days earlier he had moved for a postponement of the Newark election hearing, and on 9 Mar. presented a tradesmen's petition for an address to the King to enforce the laws against hawkers and pedlars. He was also involved with two private estate bills, and in the session of 1693–4 aided the passage of further such measures, plus a naturalization bill. He also served once as teller: on 23 Apr. 1694 when he made an unsuccessful attempt to block the bill to regulate hackney carriages.⁴

In the 1694–5 session Bolles played a more conspicuous role in promoting Country initiatives. Most notably, he was prominent in support of the place bill, telling on 28 Nov. in favour of committal, and chairing the ensuing committee of the whole in December. His eight other tellerships covered a wide range of issues, although principally relating to supply matters. Perhaps wishing to keep his political allies in the House, he told on 11 Feb. 1695 against granting a leave of absence for Country Member Salwey Winnington, and on 13 Apr. acted in favour of going into committee on the bills to punish several corrupt Members. On 1 May he was one of the unsuccessful tellers against a motion to adjourn all committees save that preparing articles of impeachment against Lord Carmarthen.

Bolles was re-elected for Lincoln in 1695 though he lost the county election. He petitioned the House against the shire return, but the matter was never reported by the elections committee. At the opening of the session he proposed Robert Harley for chairman of the committee of elections and privileges, but as the Country Whigs had already agreed with the Court to support (Sir) John Hawles*, the new solicitor-general, Harley left the chamber to avoid a contest. Bolles was very active in this session, as exemplified by his serving as teller on no less than 17 occasions. The measure which appears to have absorbed his greatest attention in the early part of the session was a bill for regulating elections, a matter of great concern for Country politicians. He also told against appointing a day to determine the double return at Mitchell.

Throughout the session he displayed interest in the regulation of the law, presenting a bill to reform courts of Equity, being first-named to a committee on a petition concerning the reduction of crime, and telling against a bill to enforce legislation relating to unlicensed marriages and the registration of births. He was also keen to contribute on coinage issues, and featured in proceedings against the Company of Scotland. Remaining fast to his political allies, he was the principal manager of a bill to reverse a former judgment against Sir William Williams, 1st Bt.*, and unsuccessfully told in favour of upholding the privilege complaint of the Tory Sir Nathaniel Napier, 2nd Bt. Moreover, he acted as a teller to block the inclusion of the Whig Sir William Scawen in the committee to investigate the East India Company's accounts. In January 1696 he was listed as a probable opponent of the government in a division on the proposed council of trade. Commercial matters preoccupied him during the rest of the session, for he chaired a committee on the petition of several Bristol merchants, was one of the Members detailed to review reactions to the bill to suppress hawkers and pedlars, and told against the engrossment of the bill to relieve creditors and prevent escapes. Furthermore, he was closely involved with the conferences sparked by the Lords' amendments to the bills to prohibit trade with France, and to encourage the Greenland trade. In February he chaired the committee on the bill appointing oaths for Ireland, and at the end of the month refused the Association. In March he was a teller in favour of an unsuccessful proposal to set the price of guineas at 24s., and was listed as voting against the Court on a motion to fix them at 22s. On 28 Mar. he carried up the mutiny bill, and told in support of considering amendments to the bill to encourage seamen. Three days later, for the second time this session, he told against the adjournment of committees, and on 1 Apr. acted as teller in support of their revival. He subsequently acted as teller against a clause offered to the bill to establish a land bank, and went on to become one of the directors of the abortive scheme, having invested £3,000. He piloted through the House a measure designed to prevent Catholics disinheriting their Protestant heirs, even though he had earlier acted as a teller against a motion for a supply to relieve poor French Protestants. He also featured in connexion with three private estate bills and a naturalization bill.[5]

In the session of 1696–7 Bolles was soon into his stride, telling on 26 Oct. against the House going into a committee of the whole to consider a supply for carrying on the war, and on 3 Nov. in favour of referring to the committee of supply the reports of the accounts commissioners on the deficiencies of funds. He predictably voted against the attainder of Sir John Fenwick†, and, no doubt resentful over the failure of the land bank, was active against the Bank of England. On 7 Nov. he told in favour of ordering the Bank to lay before the House an account of its debts, later chaired the committee inspecting its books, and was a teller again on 26 Mar. 1697 against passing a bill to enlarge its capital. He was also anxious to promote debate on the coinage, and told on 3 Mar. against amending a resolution concerning the cider duty. Somewhat surprisingly, he acted as a teller to deny a leave of absence to the Country Tory Sir Richard Temple, but this may have again been a move to maintain anti-Court strength in the Lower House. On 20 Mar. he told against naming the Member who had spoken in a conference against the bill to prohibit the wearing of wrought silks. Earlier that month he had chaired the committee on the Whitby harbour bill, probably eager to maintain the commercial viability of the North Sea ports, on which his county heavily depended. Displaying a habitual interest in estate bills, he oversaw the passage of three such measures, and was an obvious nominee for the committee to study procedure in the passage of private legislation. In April he chaired a committee of inquiry into abuses in the navy victualling board.

During the next session Bolles was once again a thorn in the Court's side, telling on 21 Dec. 1697 in favour of recommitting a resolution to vote the King a civil list of £700,000 for life. He was named to the drafting committee for a bill to regulate the militia, and was closely involved with fiscal legislation, chairing a committee of the whole on Acts relating to Exchequer bills, and being appointed to the committee to draft a bill to lessen interest rates, which he later presented. He also brought in a bill to appropriate the malt duty, and later told for adjourning the report on the bill to prevent the clipping of coin. On the 8th of that month he contributed to a debate on the instruction to the committee of supply to consider the charge of guards and garrisons. Prominent among his seven nominations to drafting committees in this session was that to prepare a bill for vacating all grants of Irish forfeitures made since 1688. However, on 20 Jan. he told against laying before the House an account of crown grants since 1660. Still a keen advocate of law and order, he was one of the committee to draft a bill to prevent robberies, and was later named to the inquiry into the security of post sent to Members. His partisan spirit was demonstrated on 4 Feb. when he told against a motion condemning a petition against the return of the Court Whig Sir Rushout Cullen, 3rd Bt., at

Cambridge. Seven days later he was a teller in support of the resolution fixing the debt owed to the Prince of Denmark. On 28 Mar. he told to obstruct the passage of a bill to preserve timber in the New Forest, having earlier backed a bill to enforce Acts prohibiting the destruction of enclosures. He subsequently acted as chairman over naval arrears. Trade again appeared a personal priority, since he was appointed to the drafting committee on a bill to prevent imports by royal vessels, chaired the committee of the whole on the bill confirming the privileges of the Hudson's Bay Company, and reported from the inquiry into the books of the East India Company. However, his main interest lay with the trial of the French merchants impeached for illegal trade with France during recent hostilities, and he gained nominations to several committees relating to that matter. He only concerned himself with one private estate bill in this session, but did advance local legislation in its last weeks, presiding over the speedy passage of a bill to establish a waterworks at Alverstoke, Hampshire.[6]

At the general election of 1698 Bolles not only campaigned at Lincoln, but also appeared at Newark to back John Rayner* against the Court Whig Sir Francis Molyneux, 4th Bt.* He only managed to secure his own return, after which he was classed as a Country supporter, and his name appeared in a probable forecast of opponents of the standing army. At the opening of the session he opposed the Court candidate for the Speakership, Sir Thomas Littleton, 3rd Bt., but to no avail. Once again conspicuous in Country ranks, he was appointed to the committee to prepare the disbanding bill, spoke on 23 Dec. in debate on its committal, and on 14 Jan. 1699 unsuccessfully moved the disbandment of 'the Scotch regiment'. Four days later he asserted that 'all without doors' were for reducing the military, observing that 'in the late war you were saved from an invasion without an army'. Moreover, on 16 Feb. he seconded Harley's motion to allow £4 for each man at sea. He again promoted electoral reform, being named to the committee to prepare the bill to examine the clerk of the crown's petition concerning the returns. He took a prominent part in the opposition attack on placemen, complaining on 10 Feb. that several Members were ineligible to sit under the terms of the 1694 Lottery Act. He later chaired the committee on the whole on the place bill, acted as a teller for its engrossment, and carried it up to the Lords. His animus against the ministry was also evident on 1 Mar., when he told to uphold the return of the Tory William Gower at Ludlow. As usual his legislative activity ranged widely, beginning with an appointment to the committee to draw up a bill to preserve game. Other drafting committees included those to prepare bills to regulate the militia, and to fix the determination of the Act prohibiting the import of bone-lace. Early in the session he had been approached to support a proposed scheme for the navigation of the Dee, but had refused. Nevertheless, he was appointed on 23 Mar. as a commissioner for the Aire and Calder Navigation Act. He thrice acted as a teller, against an amendment to the report on the state of the navy, to block the second reading of a private naturalization bill, and against changing a clause in a supply bill. More notably, he was named as one of the Members to manage the ballot for the commissioners to inquire into the Irish forfeitures, and was a predictable selection for the committee to draft the address against continuing the Dutch guards.[7]

Bolles seems always to have been regarded as something of an eccentric but during the summer of 1699 he began to betray symptoms of serious mental instability. At the Lincoln assizes he was sitting on the bench with Justice Gould

> and took upon him to govern the court, which the judge reprehending him for, he told him he was a Member of Parliament, that he stood up for the liberties of England, and would bring the judge upon his knees at the bar of the House of Commons. The judge committed him and ordered an indictment to be drawn up against him; but at the earnest intercession of the justices, it was let fall, who said no other bill could be found against him, but that he was distracted as sometimes happens when he falls into drinking and wants sleep.

The reaction of Secretary of State James Vernon I*, who in a letter to the King wished that Bolles' madness had 'appeared upon record as well as it does in many other places', indeed suggests that Sir John was already regarded as very unpredictable. His condition did not prevent him from returning to take his usual active part in the Commons in the ensuing session. During a debate on the Prince of Denmark's debt on 12 Dec., he finished a long speech by suggesting an address to the King to remove Bishop Burnet as tutor to the Duke of Gloucester, on the grounds that Burnet, in his *Pastoral Letter*, had 'hinted that his present Majesty came in by conquest'. Although this sally seems to have been greeted with much approval as well as laughter, an attempt to press the matter home on the following day failed, when he seconded the motion of Sir John Pakington, 4th Bt., to oust Burnet. On 18 Dec. Bolles acted as teller against a motion that the Whig placeman Foot Onslow had been duly elected for Guildford, and on 10 Feb. 1700 did so again to uphold the Tory interpretation of the franchise at Orford. Five days later he urged the House to put the motion of Sir Richard

Cocks, 2nd Bt., to resume all royal grants, observing that 'evil and wicked counsellors [are] about the King'. The following month he successfully moved an address asserting that no action should be taken in relation to Captain Kidd until the next session, which proposal was seen as 'in pique to my lord chancellor' (Sir John Somers*). He appeared to show great concern for social legislation, gaining nominations to committees to examine ways of setting the poor to work, and to search for precedents relating to petitions over prison abuses. Moreover, he twice acted as a teller in connexion with moves to prohibit the export of corn. His other principal interest was the bill to apply the Irish forfeitures to public use, twice telling against additional clauses, and being named on 8 Apr. to the conference committee on that measure.[8]

Bolles' political career reached a climax in the first Parliament of 1701. He was quick to show his party colours, telling on 14 Feb. against including an expression of commitment to European peace in an address to the King. On 21 Feb. was appointed to the drafting committee on a bill to resume crown grants made since 1684, and on the 28th presented a petition in support of the return of Sir Cleave More, 2nd Bt.*, at Liverpool, despite having previously advised More against such an appeal. During February he had also been listed among those likely to support the Court in agreeing with the committee of supply's resolution to continue the 'Great Mortgage'. But his moment of glory came on 11 Mar., when, during debates on the Act of Settlement, he was the first to name the Electress Sophia as successor, in a pre-emptive Tory strike to forestall the Whig Lord Spencer (Charles*). According to Burnet, the Tories chose Bolles specifically because he was known to be 'disordered in his senses . . . which seemed to make it less serious when moved by such a person'. Having thus 'stole the crown from his lordship', he was subsequently called to the chair of the committee on the bill. William Cowper* articulated Whig distaste for this move, observing that

> the King having . . . earnestly recommended that bill to Parliament in his speech from the throne, the Tories for fear of losing the King's favour did not endeavour to reject it, but set themselves to clog it . . . and to show their contempt and aversion whenever it came on . . . and by calling Sir J[ohn] B[olles] to the chair of the committee for that bill, who was then thought to be distracted, and was soon after confined for being so.

This opinion was confirmed by Bonet, who wrote that when the Tories

> n'ont pu le faire tomber sous quelque prétexte populaire ils l'ont traité d'une manière peu serieuse, et ils ont mis à la tête du comité qui devoit presider sur ce sujet un personage peu estimé afin de se moquer de ceux qui disoient que ce Bill étoit une pierre de touche pour connoître les Jacobites.

Very much at the forefront of the Tory offensive, on 17 Mar. Bolles joined with Seymour to lambast the Partition Treaties, likening their division of Europe to 'robbing on the highway'. On 15 Apr. he moved for the impeachment of Samuel Shepheard I*, who had been expelled from the House for his dubious electioneering activities on behalf of the New East India Company, and 'by his grin afterwards reflected upon the proceedings against Sir Charles Duncombe'. On 9 May he 'talked a long time foolishly against a war and our debts'. His six nominations to committees of inquiry gave him the opportunity to advance several Tory causes, he being named to committees to translate correspondence relating to the Partition Treaties, and to examine the destruction of woodland in Enfield Chase, doubtless hoping to embarrass the Whig Lord Stamford on the latter issue. Moreover, on 15 May he moved for an address to the King to ensure that cut timber remained on the Chase. However, only two days earlier he had told to uphold the return of the Whig William Walmisley at Lichfield. He resumed a more customary stance on 20 May, when he took the opportunity of a debate on the exclusion of customs commissioners from the House to reflect on the way in which Hon. Henry Boyle 'was altered by being a lord of the Treasury and chancellor of the Exchequer', for which observation Boyle 'jestingly' proffered thanks. In this month he again revealed an interest in prison reform, being nominated to the conference committee on the bill regulating the gaols of the Fleet and King's Bench. On 30 May, after he had made reference to charges formerly levelled against Lord Coningsby (Thomas*), the latter quipped that 'Bolles might do anything in any place safely, for he always carried his privilege about him'. In June Sir John was used by a section of the Tories to force a reconstitution of the commission of accounts, the absent Thomas Coke* being informed that during the committee hearings on the accounts bill on 6 June

> Musgrave [Sir Christopher, 4th Bt.] and the rest slunk off one after another: the committee was very thin at last: then it was gravely proposed by Lowndes [William] to throw aside the postponed clauses [constituting the general commission] and was seconded by others of the Court. This management being gross, we had no way left but to blow up Bolles, who went off like a bomb, to the amazement of Robin [Robert Harley] and Ranelagh [Richard Jones]. He told them of millions unaccounted for, and of bargains made to cover 'em.

Four days later Bolles told in favour of a clause for the accounts bill to maintain the powers of the commissioners to investigate military debts and prizes. He was later blacklisted with other High Tories for having opposed the preparations for war.[9]

Bolles' prominence over the Act of Settlement ensured him much publicity in the run-up to the second election of 1701, with both Whig and Tory propagandists casting him as a madman in order to satirize each other's policies. Successfully returned once more for Lincoln in November 1701, even by his own busy standards he had a most active Parliament. In January 1702, having chaired the committee on expiring laws, he was appointed to draft three separate bills to continue a miscellany of statutes. Interestingly, one of them was the Quaker Affirmation Act, and several Friends were ordered to attend him prior to his presentation of the aforementioned bill. The other bills concerned Acts to exempt apothecaries from parish offices, and for the punishment of vagrants, the first of which he steered through the House. Given his Tory credentials, he was a predictable selection to request the High Churchman Dr George Smalridge to preach to the House on the anniversary of Charles I's execution. On 28 Jan. he joined in the debate in committee on the abjuration bill, but delivered his most memorable political diatribe of the session at a Holborn tavern four days later. One witness, Cheek Gerard, testified that as he and two friends were drinking,

> about ten, Sir John Bolles ... came into their company; he appeared to have been drinking and pretty warm. Some discourse happening about elections, Sir John Bolles took occasion to say that there had been a letter intercepted, which was in order to turn him out of his corporation. This brought in some discourse about the King as if his Majesty endeavoured to hinder his election. Sir John being hot upon this subject said he did not value the King at all. Speaking of the pretended Prince of Wales, Sir John took occasion to commend him for a comely youth. Upon some discourse one of the company told Sir John he hoped there was nobody besides of his opinion, to which he replied, 'Yes, there was, the majority of the House of Commons'.

He was also said to have claimed that he had turned down an offer to become lord treasurer, prompting another observer to recall 'the ridicule of his expectation a year or two ago of being Speaker, and the great preparations he made towards it'. The information was forwarded to the secretary of state, but no action was taken.[10]

The scandal did not appear to diminish Bolles' contribution to Commons' business. He gained swift appointment to drafting committees on a private estate bill, and another bill to repair Whitby harbour, both of which he managed through the House. Despite his celebrated outburst at the Lincoln assizes, he was named to draft a bill to qualify j.p.s and deputy-lieutenants. Maintaining pressure on placemen, on 10 Feb. he moved that Sir Henry Furnese should not be allowed to sit in the House as a trustee for the circulation of Exchequer bills. However, the very next day, when Cocks moved for a supply from the pensions and lands granted by the crown since 1660, Bolles proposed that 4s. in the pound be raised instead. On 17 Feb. he raised the question of 'the impeachments' in a committee considering Commons' rights, and two days later unsuccessfully proposed an additional clause to the abjuration bill 'for the Church test'. Later on the 19th he spoke against the bill, arguing that it would disturb loyal subjects with tender consciences. Remaining true to his party, he voted on 26 Feb. 1702 for the resolution justifying the Lower House's proceedings on the impeachment of William's Whig ministers in the preceding Parliament. On 7 Mar. when it was known that the King was dying, he made 'many foolish, insolent' remarks 'as that the King was locked in a box and only in the hands of a few Dutch lords', and moved to adjourn for two days, a proposal construed as a Tory attempt to obstruct the passing of the abjuration and money bills. Outraged opponents demanded that he appear at the bar, and he was also interrupted by a message from the Lords requesting the House to continue sitting. Despite some Tory support, the motion was defeated, as was another attempt at adjournment later that day, which Bolles also favoured. The following day he 'talked at his usual mad rate' when the House discussed a conference with the Lords on the King's demise, and was appointed to the committee to draw up the address of condolence and congratulations to Queen Anne.[11]

The advent of the new reign saw Bolles quickly embrace the court. Whether the new ministry wished to accommodate him was an altogether different matter, his ranting during discussion on 9 Mar. of the chair of ways and means prompting yet more calls for him to be brought to the bar. When the House came to consider a supply for the new Queen he at first indicated privately to Cocks that he would oppose any attempt to grant her the civil list for life. However, when the matter was debated in committee on 16 Mar. Bolles 'proposed to continue the £50,000 she had and to give her for life what the King had', a notable shift in political stance. An exasperated Cocks noted two days later that Bolles 'talked like a fool' in debate on the Abjuration. On 30 Mar., he moved the Address, and on two consecutive days in April he was involved in scenes in the House. On the 17th, he clashed with John Smith I after the latter had criticized the drafting of an Irish bill brought in by Bolles concerning the entailing of estates on Protestants. Bolles replied that Smith's charges were false. This prompted calls for Sir John to be sent to the bar, but 'at last he was ordered and advised by his friends to ask pardon of Mr Smith and the House, which he did very awkwardly in his place, for he said if he had done anything to offend either the House or that gentleman he was sorry for it'. The following day 'in his foolish, mad way' he made a fierce attack on Lord Sunderland, castigating him for having changed his religion and calling him a pimp. He was stopped in midspeech by several Members, and was even rebuked by the Speaker. Sunderland's son, Lord Spencer, then rose to say that though in the past Bolles had 'often reflected upon his father', he had not thought 'anybody minded what he said', but now felt he must reply. There was a move to censure Bolles, but Musgrave came to his defence and moved the House to other business. Bolles was involved in yet another row on 1 May, this time with Seymour, who had urged the recommittal of the Albemarle Buildings bill on grounds that the business was so shady that a solicitor had to be taken out of Newgate to handle it. Bolles answered that

> he had known many an honest man kept in Newgate when those that deserved to go thither went at large. This occasioned a violent laughter and Sir Edward Seymour justly, though foolishly, took it to himself and said in answer . . . 'I have known men less mad in Bedlam than those that are out'. Up stood Bolles the second time and the House would have him speak and then he said out of the Proverbs, 'injustice and oppression make a wise man mad'.

In the latter stages of the session he was involved in no fewer than five private bills for relief from the Irish Forfeitures Resumption Act. Moreover, he was firstnamed to the committee on a private estate bill, and chaired the committee on a naturalization bill. He offered on 12 May a petition from the conspirators Counter and Bernardi pleading for banishment rather than imprisonment, but the bill to continue their incarceration was passed.[12]

On 1 June Bolles was arrested for speaking 'scandalous and treasonable words of the Queen', and soon afterwards an order was issued for a doctor to have regular access to him. The date of his release from custody is not known, but in late July it was reported that he had travelled to Lincolnshire in order to contest Lincoln against the Tory Sir Thomas Meres*. Such was his notoriety by this date that Defoe urged his defeat, observing

Blaspheming Bolles to his fen ditches sent
To bully justice with a Parliament.

He did not gain a seat, but was certainly at liberty the following August. Although free, his deteriorating mental health prevented him taking any further part in public life, and in April 1707 Sir Hans Sloane found him 'much disordered in his understanding and unable to hold discourse reasonably for any long time upon any subject without talking to himself or aloud of matters incoherent and impertinent'. Sloane considered there was little chance of his recovery and in 1709 an Act, describing Bolles as 'a lunatic', was passed to enable lands to be sold for the payment of his debts. He died intestate on 23 Dec. 1714, and was buried at St. Swithin's, London. He having remained a bachelor, his property passed to his only sister, Sarah Bolles, and was sold soon after her death in 1746.[13]

[1]NLS, Advocates' mss, Bank of Eng. pprs. 31.1.7, f. 98. [2]*CJ*, xii. 606. [3]C. Illingworth, *Scampton*, 41–43; *Her. and Gen.* ii. 120. [4]Grey, x. 112; *Luttrell Diary*, 198, 446, 450, 473. [5]Centre Kentish Stud. Stanhope mss U1590/059/4, Robert Yard* to Alexander Stanhope, 3 Dec. 1695; Advocates' mss, Bank of Eng. pprs. 31.1.7, f. 95. [6]*Cam. Misc.* xxix. 358. [7]*CJ*, xiii. 108; *Vernon–Shrewsbury Letters*, ii. 226; *Cam. Misc.* 380, 385, 394; Northants. RO, Montagu (Boughton) mss 47/132, Vernon to Duke of Shrewsbury, 14 Jan. 1699; Luttrell, *Brief Relation*, iv. 482; Chester RO, M/L/4/545, Peter Shakerley* to Henry Bennett, 19 Jan. 1699. [8]*Vernon–Shrewsbury Letters*, 337–8; *Cocks Diary*, 41–2; Luttrell, 592; Som. RO, Sanford mss DD/SF/1047a, notes of debate, 15 Feb. 1700; Montagu (Boughton) mss 48/46, Vernon to Shrewsbury, 16 Mar. 1700. [9]Liverpool RO, Norris mss 920NOR 1/78, 83, 86, William Clayton* to Richard Norris*, 6, 22, 28 Feb. 1701; Burnet, iv. 499–500; Yale Univ. Beinecke Lib. Osborn Coll. Blathwayt mss, box 21, William Blathwayt* to [?George Stepney], 11 Mar. 1701; G. Holmes, *Pol. in Age of Anne*, 89; Add. 30000 E, f. 183; Tindal, 451–2; *Cocks Diary*, 96, 188, 138, 154–5; *HMC Cowper*, ii. 428. [10]Tindal, 497; *Taunton-Dean Letter from E. C. to J. F. at Grecian Coffee-House* [1701]; Soc. of Friends Lib. mins. of meetings for sufferings, 253; *Cocks Diary*, 190; *CSP Dom.* 1700–2, pp. 499–501, 505. [11]*Cocks Diary*, 207, 211, 220, 235–6, 237; Strathmore mss at Glamis Castle, box 70, folder 1, bdle. 2, newsletter 19 Feb. 1702. [12]*Cocks Diary*, 241–2, 249, 269, 270–1, 276; Strathmore mss, box 75, bdle. 1, newsletter 31 Mar. 1702. [13]*CSP Dom.* 1702–3, pp. 119, 509; Northants. RO, Isham mss IC 4221, Hon. Charles Bertie I* to Sir Justinian Isham, 4th Bt.*, 27 July 1702; *Poems on Affairs of State*, ed. Ellis, vi. 424; Add. 4075, f. 241; 4078, f. 303; *HMC Lords*, n.s. viii. 273; Illingworth, 49–50.

P. W./P. L. G.

BOND, Denis (1676–1747), of Creech Grange, Dorset.

DORCHESTER   5 Dec. 1709–1710
CORFE CASTLE   1715–1727
POOLE   1727–30 Mar. 1732

b. 10 Dec. 1676, 1st s. of Nathaniel Bond* by his 2nd w. *educ.* I. Temple 1695, called 1703, bencher 1728, treasurer 1739. *m.* (settlement 2 July 1729) Leonora Sophia, 2nd da. of Sir William Dutton Colt, envoy to Hanover,

Hesse and Saxony 1689–93, bro. of Sir Henry Dutton Colt, 1st Bt.*, and John Dutton Colt*, and wid. of Edmund Dummer* of Swaythling, Hants, *s.p. suc.* fa. 1707.[1]

Freeman, Dorchester 1707, recorder 1707–15; freeman, Weymouth and Melcombe Regis 1707–*d.*, Poole 1719–*d.*, Wareham 1724–*d.*[2]

Carrier of the King's letters 1714–*d.*; commr. forfeited estates 1716–25; member, cttee. of management, Charitable Corp. 1725–32.[3]

A lawyer like his father, Bond was mooted as a candidate for Poole in February 1701 and a year later stood for Wareham, albeit unsuccessfully. In the run-up to the 1708 election, the Earl of Shaftesbury (Anthony Ashley*) described him as an ally of the 'deluded Whigs', by whom he meant the Junto. Returned for Dorchester at a by-election in 1709, Bond made no mark in the Commons during his brief tenure in this period and did not stand in 1713. Returned once more in 1715, he was classified as a Whig both in the Worsley list and in another comparative analysis of the two Parliaments. Bond continued to support the Whigs until he was expelled from the House in 1732 for his involvement in the frauds of the Charitable Corporation. He died on 30 Jan. 1747.[4]

[1] Hutchins, *Dorset*, i. 605. [2] Ibid. i. 36; ii. 361, 440; C. H. Mayo, *Dorchester Recs.* 429. [3] *Cal. Treas. Bks.* xxix. 344; xxxi. 83. [4] PRO 30/24/22/59–60; Hutchins, i. 605.

P. W.

BOND, Nathaniel (1634–1707), of Creech Grange, and Lutton, Steeple, Dorset.

CORFE CASTLE   1679 (Oct.)–1681 (Jan.)
DORCHESTER   1681 (Mar.), 1695–1698

b. 14 June 1634, 4th s. of Dennis Bond†, linen draper, of Dorchester and Lutton, Dorset, being 3rd s. by his 2nd w. Lucy, da. of William Lawrence of Winterbourne Steepleton, wid. of John Fley, vicar of Buckerell, Devon; half-bro. of John Bond† and bro. of Samuel Bond†. *educ.* Wadham, Oxf. 1650, BCL 1654, fellow, All Souls Oxf. 1648; incorp. Camb. 1659; I. Temple 1653, called 1661, bencher 1687. *m.* (1) 21 Dec. 1667, Elizabeth (*d.* 1674), da. and coh. of John Churchill, rector of Steeple, *s.p.*; (2) 3 Aug. 1675, Mary, da. of Lewis Williams of Bere Regis, Dorset, wid. of Thomas Browne of Frampton, Dorset, 2s.[1]

Recorder, Weymouth 1683–*d.*, Poole 1699–*d.*[2]
Serjeant-at-law 1689–*d.*; King's serjeant 1693–1702.

A Whig lawyer, Bond had failed to get a seat in the Convention and did not stand in 1690; but he was returned in 1695 for Dorchester, where he had property and family connexions. An interest in matters of trade and finance is indicated by his committee nominations. He was forecast as likely to support the Court in the divisions of 31 Jan. 1696 on the proposed council of trade and signed the Association promptly. Granted three weeks' leave of absence on 14 Feb., he returned to Westminster in March and voted for fixing the price of guineas at 22*s*. In October he assisted in the management of the bill for further remedying the ill state of the coinage. On 25 Nov. he was one of the Whigs who voted against the attainder of Sir John Fenwick†, possibly out of professional scruple. The remainder of Bond's parliamentary career as recorded in the Journals comprised nothing more than an occasional appointment to committee and two leaves of absence (5 Feb. 1697 and 1 Feb. 1698). Listed as a placeman in July, he was also noted in September as a courtier who had been 'left out' of the 1698 Parliament. Indeed, Bond had made no attempt to retain his seat. Although never returning to Parliament, he continued to play some part in local politics, particularly at Poole where he had been chosen recorder in 1699. At Queen Anne's accession he lost his place as King's serjeant. Bond died on 31 Aug. 1707 and was buried at Steeple. His eldest son Denis later sat for several Dorset boroughs.[3]

[1] Hutchins, *Dorset*, i. 602–3. [2] Ibid. i. 36; ii. 440; *CSP Dom. 1699–1700*, p.278. [3] Hutchins, i. 603.

P. W.

BOOTH, Hon. George (c.1655–1726), of Westminster.

DARTMOUTH   19 Sept.–28 Nov. 1689
MALMESBURY   3 Feb. 1692–1695
BOSSINEY   1695–1698
LOSTWITHIEL   1698–1700, 18 Apr. 1701–1702

b. c.1655, 4th but 2nd surv. s. of Sir George Booth†, Baron Delamer by 2nd w. Lady Elizabeth, da. of Henry Grey†, 1st Earl of Stamford; bro. of Henry Booth†, 1st Earl of Warrington. *educ.* G. Inn 1674. *m.* Lucy, da. of Hon. Robert Robartes† of Lanhydrock, Cornw., 1s.[1]

Freeman, Chester 1679; jt. clerk of the crown, Cheshire and Flints. Aug. 1689.[2]
Commr. customs Apr. 1689–94.[3]

Booth's role in the Revolution, as secretary to his brother Henry, Lord Delamer, was rewarded in 1689 with a place on the Board of Customs, at a salary of £1,000 p.a. It was presumably the influence of the customs that secured him a seat at the Dartmouth by-election of September 1689, but he was unseated on petition and defeated at this borough at the 1690 election. He was, however, successful upon the interest of Hon. Thomas Wharton* at the Malmesbury by-election of 1692, and took his seat on 8 Feb. Booth made little impact during his career in the Commons, but appeared on numerous lists of placemen and was classified by Samuel Grascome as a Court supporter with a place or pension. Booth was indeed in favour at court. In March 1692 he was added to the Middlesex commission of the peace on the orders of William III, and when he petitioned in 1693 for the reversion of the manor of West Ham after the death of the Queen Dowager, thought to be worth over £500 p.a., his request was granted 'by the King's express command'. Such favour did not, however, guarantee his place in the customs, and Booth was removed from this office in 1694. The Duke of Shrewsbury informed the King that 'Mr Booth is by all agreed to be a well-wisher to your government, but so highly charged with corruption as it is said he understands nor minds no other part of the place', and the Earl of Sunderland noted him more concisely as 'Mr Booth: a great Whig but an ill man'. In June 1694 Booth received some compensation for the loss of his place when the grant of the reversion of the manor of West Ham was confirmed, the rent initially levied upon Booth for this property being ordered in January 1695 to be waived, and his continued support for the ministry in the Commons is suggested by his inclusion during the 1694-5 session upon Henry Guy's* list of 'friends', probably in connexion with the Commons' attack upon Guy.[4]

At the 1695 election Booth was returned for Bossiney upon the interest of his brother-in-law the Earl of Radnor (Charles Bodvile Robartes†). Having been forecast as likely to support the Court in the divisions of 31 Jan. 1696 upon the council of trade, Booth signed the Association immediately and in March voted for fixing the price of guineas at 22s. This support for the ministry no doubt explains his failure in this session to be elected to the commission of accounts, his total of 134 votes falling well short of those actually chosen. Booth's Whiggery was clearly demonstrated in the following session by his vote on 25 Nov. for the attainder of Sir John Fenwick†. In February 1697 he was unsuccessful in his bid to fill the commissioner of accounts place vacated by Thomas Pelham I*, who had declined to serve this post, finishing a distant third in the ballot. That Booth would have been entirely unsuitable for such a post was suggested by the assessments of his performance in the customs commission. In the spring of 1697 he petitioned the government for a pension of £700 p.a. for 31 years, emphasizing that he had 'contributed his utmost to the safety, honour and interest of His Majesty's person and government'. His appeal was answered only in part as he was granted a £600 p.a. pension for seven years, backdated to December 1696. In July 1698 the same year he was included upon a list of placemen, in respect of the place in the customs he had lost four years previously. At the 1698 election Booth transferred to Lostwithiel, again with Radnor's support, and a comparison of the old and new Commons classed him as a Court supporter, a designation confirmed on 18 Jan. 1699 when he voted against the third reading of the disbanding bill. Shortly after the end of the 1698-9 session Booth petitioned to be allowed to surrender his pension in return for a grant of £600 p.a. for 21 years, a request granted in July. This grant and that of the manor of West Ham were notified to the Commons in the 1699-1700 session, during which he demonstrated his concern for the affairs of his native county by pledging not to support the proposed Weaver navigation bill. In the early months of 1700 an analysis of the Commons into interests listed Booth under that of Radnor, but Radnor's support was insufficient to secure Booth's return at the first election of 1701. Booth petitioned against his defeat, but upon the death of one of the successful candidates he withdrew this petition and was returned at the consequent by-election. He was re-elected at the second election of the year, being noted by Lord Spencer (Charles*) as a 'gain' and classed by Robert Harley* as a Whig. Booth again contributed little to parliamentary business, and he retired from the Commons at the 1702 election. Despite his substantial government pension, renewed in October 1710 and June 1711, it seems that he suffered financial difficulties. In 1711 his nephew the 2nd Earl of Warrington claimed in the court of Chancery that in 1701 Booth had retained for himself 1,000 guineas given him to pay two agents who had arranged Warrington's marriage to the daughter of a wealthy London merchant. The court found in Warrington's favour and ordered Booth to repay the money, a judgment confirmed in April 1714 when Booth appealed to the Lords against the verdict. It seems unlikely that repayment was made, though after the Hanoverian succession Booth's pension was again renewed. He died in June 1726, on either the 11th or the 12th, and was succeeded by his only son.[5]

[1] Ormerod, *Cheshire*, i. 534. [2] *Reg. Chester Freemen* (Lancs. and Cheshire Rec. Soc. li), 171; *CSP Dom.* 1689-90, p. 211. [3] *CSP Dom.* 1689-90, p. 53; *Cal. Treas. Bks.* x. 743. [4] *Luttrell Diary*, 177; *CSP Dom.* 1691-2, pp. 165, 220; 1693, p. 74; 1694-5, pp. 179, 181, 185; *Cal. Treas. Bks.* x. 112, 419, 486, 868; Nottingham Univ. Lib. Portland (Bentinck) mss PwA 1238a, [Sunderland] to [Portland], 13 July 1694. [5] *HMC Kenyon*, 399; Centre Kentish Stud. Stanhope mss U1590/059/6, Robert Yard* to Alexander Stanhope, 23 Feb. 1696-7; *Cal. Treas. Pprs.* 1697-1702, pp. 30-31, 297; *Cal. Treas. Bks.* xii. 16, 97, 120; xiv. 371, 408; Add. 36914, f. 11; *Bull. John Rylands Lib.* lv. 21-22; *HMC Lords*, n.s. x. 270-1; Boyer, *Pol. State*, xxxi. 647; *Hist. Reg. Chron.* 1726, p. 25.

E. C./R. D. H.

BOOTH, Hon. Langham (1684–1724), of Hawthorne, Cheshire.

CHESHIRE 1705–1710, 1715–1722
LIVERPOOL 2 Feb. 1723–7 May 1724

b. 8 June 1684, 3rd s. of Henry Booth†, 2nd Baron Delamer and 1st Earl of Warrington, by Mary, da. of Sir James Langham, 2nd Bt.†, of Cottesbrooke, Northants. *educ.* Christ Church, Oxf. 1701. *unm.*
   Burgess, Wigan 1708.[1]
   Groom of the bedchamber to Prince of Wales 1718–*d.*

The brother of the 2nd Earl of Warrington, an influential but needy Whig peer, Booth was returned for Cheshire in 1705, his election being reckoned by Lord Sunderland (Charles, Lord Spencer*) as a gain for the Whigs. He voted on 25 Oct. for the Court candidate for Speaker, and supported the Court in the following February on the 'place clause' of the regency bill. Sir George Warburton, 3rd Bt.*, Booth's opponent in 1705, twice petitioned against the Cheshire return on the basis that Booth had been a minor at the time of the election, but on 30 Jan. 1707 the elections committee voted him duly elected and on 10 Feb. the House confirmed this decision. On 21 Oct. Booth moved that John Smith I be re-elected as Speaker in the first Parliament of Great Britain, 'which was unanimously agreed to by the House', and in early 1708 an analysis of the House classed him as a Whig. Booth was unopposed in Cheshire at the election later that year, and on 29 Jan. 1709 he told against a motion designed to prevent the Commons proceeding on a Whig petition against a Tory Member, adjourning the hearing of the Orford election case. In early 1709 Booth also supported the naturalization of the Palatines. The following session saw moves to introduce a bill for the navigation of the Weaver, and in early December 1709 Peter Shakerley* reported that Booth was hostile to such a measure, as Shakerley claimed Booth had been in the previous session, and had told him that 'if he was in the House when the petition for leave to bring in the bill shall be offered he would oppose it'. Booth himself was slightly more equivocal when writing at the end of the month to an opponent of the bill, wondering 'how I can refuse delivering the petition to the House if it comes up signed by the gentlemen of the country', before stating that 'in my opinion I am against it [the bill]'. Extraparliamentary opposition to the projected navigation meant that no bill was brought before the House and Booth was spared having to make a public choice between his personal opposition to the scheme and his notions of the duty of a knight of the shire. It seems, however, that he had resolved this problem in favour of the former, as in February 1710 Shakerley wrote that 'I attend each morning to watch and oppose the petition for this project, our knights of the shire will not do it, and I think 'twill look very oddly for any other to present it'. The early months of 1710 also saw Booth vote for the impeachment of Dr Sacheverell. Defeated for the county in 1710 and turned out of the commission of the peace when the Tory tide was running high, he returned to Parliament and to the Lancashire bench following the Hanoverian succession. He died at Bath on 7 May 1724, leaving the bulk of his estate to his brother Lord Warrington but reserving a small 'part to Mrs Merryweather, a widow lady, of a considerable fortune'.[2]

[1] Wigan RO, Wigan bor. recs. AB/MR/10. [2] *Bull. John Rylands Lib.* lxv. 8–35; Luttrell, *Brief Relation*, v. 610, vi. 133, 226; L. K. J. Glassey, *Appt. JPs*, 174, 293; Add. 36914, ff. 34, 38, 44; Boyer, *Pol. State*, xxvii. 534.

E.C.

BORLASE, John (1667–1754), of Pendeen, St. Just, Cornw.

ST. IVES 1705–1710

bap. 24 Mar. 1667, 1st s. of John Borlase of Pendeen by Mary, da. of Richard Keigwin of Mousehole, Cornw. *educ.* Exeter, Oxf. matric. 1685; M. Temple 1685. *m.* 17 Mar. 1690, Lydia (*d.* 1725), da. of Christopher Harris of Hayne, Devon and Kenegie, Cornw., sis. of Christopher* and William Harris*, 9s. (4 *d.v.p.*), 4da. *suc.* fa. ?1694.[1]
   Stannator, Blackmore 1710; ?dep. recorder, St. Ives by 1710–aft. 1721.[2]

Borlase's grandfather, who was said to be descended from the Borlase family of Sithney, Cornwall, had purchased Pendeen, where the manor house was built in about 1670. The estate lay right in the heart of the tin mining district and Borlase's father 'greatly advanced his wealth by tin adventures'. However, he bequeathed quite a small patrimony to his son, and over £3,000 in portions to his younger children.[3]

It is unclear whether the local interest commanded by Borlase was sufficient to secure a seat at St. Ives in 1705 and 1708. However, his brother-in-law, William Harris, also had a local interest and he was also a distant relation of Lord Treasurer Godolphin (Sidney†) through his mother (a granddaughter of Nicholas Godolphin of Trewarthenick). Borlase was classed as 'Low Church' in a parliamentary list of 1705, and was recorded in the division list on the Speakership on 25 Oct. as voting for the Court candidate, though with a query beside his name. On 24 Jan. 1706 he was ordered to prepare a bill to enable the lord treasurer to compound for unpaid tobacco duties with two Falmouth merchants, presenting it on the 31st and managing it through all its stages in the House. He also supported the ministry on the 'place clause' of the regency bill on 18 Feb. Towards the end of the Parliament, he was listed as a Tory, possibly in error since after his re-election he voted in 1709 for the naturalization of the Palatines. However, he opposed Dr Sacheverell's impeachment in 1710. Despite this vote, he was defeated for St. Ives at the general election of 1710. He duly petitioned on 5 Dec. 1710, but to no avail and never stood again. Indeed, he was put out of the Cornish commission of the peace later in the year. He died in April 1754, aged 88. One of his sons was William Borlase, rector of Ludgvan, the celebrated Cornish antiquary, and another, Walter Borlase, vicar of Pendeen, was vice-warden of the Stannaries in 1750.[4]

[1] IGI, Cornw., Devon; C. S. Gilbert, *Hist. Survey Cornw.* ii. 44. [2] R. Inst. Cornw., Tonkin's ms hist. vol. 2, p. 244; J. H. Matthews, *St. Ives*, 299. [3] Polsue, *Complete Paroch. Hist. Cornw.* ii. 282; PCC 94 Box. [4] *Gent. Mag.* 1803, pp. 1114–15; L. K. J. Glassey, *Appt. JPs*, 207; Polsue, 285.

E. C./S. N. H.

BOSCAWEN, Hugh I (1625–1701), of Tregothnan, Cornw. and Greek Street, Westminster.

CORNWALL	1 Dec. 1646–6 Dec. 1648, 1659
	21 Feb.–16 Mar. 1660
GRAMPOUND	25 Apr.–12 July 1660
CORNWALL	12 July–29 Dec. 1660
TREGONY	1661–1681 (Mar.)
CORNWALL	1689–13 May 1701

bap. 21 Aug. 1625, 2nd s. of Hugh Boscawen of Tregothnan by Margaret, da. of Robert Rolle of Heanton Satchville, Devon, bro. of Charles† and Edward Boscawen†. *m.* (1) by 1649, Lady Margaret (*d.* 1688), da. of Theophilus Clinton, 4th Earl of Lincoln, 8s. *d.v.p.* 2da. (1 *d.v.p.*); (2) 7 Sept. 1693, Lady Mary (*d.* 1715), da. of Gilbert Holles†, 3rd Earl of Clare, sis. of John Holles†, 4th Earl of Clare, *s.p. suc.* bro. Nicholas 1645.[1]

Stannator, Blackmore, 1673; commr. recusants Cornw. 1675; Capt. St. Mawes Castle 1696–*d.*; recorder, Tregony by 1690–*d.*[2]

PC 14 Feb. 1689–*d.*; commr. appeal for prizes 1694–8; taking subscriptions to New E.I. Co. loan 1698.[3]

Commr. Greenwich Hosp. 1695; Member, New Eng. Co. by 1698.[4]

Boscawen was already a veteran parliamentarian in 1690, having served in the Long Parliament. In the Restoration period he had been seen as one of the leading Presbyterians in Cornwall, although as early as the 1670s he may have been conformable enough to retain local office as a j.p. He remained friendly with other Presbyterian families such as the Harleys, even giving Robert Harley* his entrée into the Commons for Tregony in 1689. As well as Tregony, where he was recorder, Boscawen had a strong interest at Truro and St. Mawes. However, he aspired to the county seat and reclaimed it at the elections to the Convention. As a strong supporter of the new regime he was made a Privy Councillor, but not given high office. He was returned again for the county in 1690, despite the opposition of Bishop Trelawny, whose endorsement of two other candidates suggested that he viewed Boscawen as overly sympathetic to Dissent. In the opening session of the new Parliament he was listed as a Whig by Lord Carmarthen (Sir Thomas Osborne†). As early as March 1690, Narcissus Luttrell* recorded a rumour that Boscawen would be raised to the peerage, but he remained in the Lower House. In the opening session of the 1690 Parliament Boscawen was named to two drafting committees, including that for damages to Edmund Prideaux† following a fine levied in 1685 by Judge Jeffreys.[5]

In a list drawn up to aid the Court's parliamentary management in the following session, Boscawen was noted as a Privy Councillor 'that ought to assist' the King's directions. If appointments to draft legislation are a guide he was certainly active in the 1690–1 session, when he was included in the nominations to prepare three bills. After the close of the session, in March 1691, Boscawen's brother-in-law, Lord Godolphin (Sidney†), put his name forward as a possible replacement for Sir Thomas Lee, 1st Bt.*, at the Admiralty, but without success. In April 1691 Harley classed him as a Court supporter.[6]

With the survival of more accounts of debates for the 1691–2 session, Boscawen's contribution to parliamentary business as a Court manager becomes clearer. In October he was named to three drafting committees. On 12 Nov. he seconded a motion for a bill suppressing hawkers and pedlars, but was dissatisfied with the bill as it emerged from committee on 16 Jan. 1692: although still in favour of legislation 'because it restrains a pernicious sort of people who carry about your treasonable libels, scandalous letters and papers', he felt that it should be left on the table and a new bill brought in. On the 13 Nov. he spoke in favour of a new East India Company (and was critical of the Old Company in debate on 18 Dec.). On 18 Nov. on the bill for abrogating the oath of supremacy in Ireland and appointing other oaths, he declared:

we that have estates in Ireland, are apprehensive that that clause [exempting lawyers inhabiting Irish-held towns when the articles of Limerick were signed] will spoil all the bill. Juries will be most Irish, and you cannot believe, but that Irish lawyers will be retained. Would you have these people live again to give a third rebellion in Ireland?

On 29 Dec. he moved for a committee of inquiry into precedents following Lord De La Warre's petition against Sir John Cutler's attempts to resume his privilege, but his advice was ignored.[7]

On 8 Jan. 1692 Boscawen declared that a petition from Cornish merchants asking for 'a free trade to all parts of the world' should be considered when the East India trade was settled. On the following day he was first-named to draft a bill reviving the Act encouraging shipbuilding, which he managed subsequently through most of its stages in the Commons, although it failed to pass the Lords. In the committee of the whole on ways and means on 15 Jan. he argued for continuing the excise longer than the one and a half years proposed by other Court spokesmen:

> there is great complaint by the merchants for want of convoys and by the Admiralty that that sort of ships – fourth and fifth rates – are more wanted than any, and therefore I desire we may continue it for two years and then there will be one half year to be applied to the building ships for convoys.

On the 19th he was first-named to consider the petition for charity from the exiled French Protestants. In the debate in ways and means on the merits of a poll tax on the same day, he spoke of the need for caution in case the measure encouraged disaffection. On the following day he pointed out that it was a tax upon gentlemen and commoners only, and that peers would appoint their own commissioners to fix rates for themselves. A second intervention saw him support levying the tax on those that kept a coach but who did not pay towards the militia. When the poll bill was discussed in committee of the whole on 3 Feb. he opposed a motion to tax Dissenting ministers and teachers because it would widen the differences between Protestants rather than unite them, a typical intervention from a man with a long-standing sympathy towards Dissent. On 5 Feb. he was first-named to the second-reading committee on the bill allowing the crown to make leases in the Duchy of Cornwall, subsequently managing the bill through the House, although it failed to pass the Lords. On the same day he was one of those Members who at the report stage of the bill vesting the Irish forfeited estates in the crown forced the reinstatement of a clause which had vested some of the estates in the crown in fee simple. At the third reading of the same bill on the 12th he opposed a rider that a third of the forfeited estates should be given to officers and soldiers who had served in Ireland, this time being on the losing side. On 13 Feb. he was named to draft a bill for the relief of the London orphans, which he presented on the 18th, but upon which no further action was taken in this session. At the report stage of the poll bill on the 15th he argued for a clause for commissioners to be appointed to assess the inns of court and chancery. Following a second petition from the French Protestants, this time forwarded by the King on the 17th, he supported moves to go into a committee of the whole since the issue involved money. When, three days later, the House went into committee on the bill against corresponding with their Majesties' enemies, 'some cried Mr Boscawen to the chair', but Secretary Trenchard was chosen instead. On 22 Feb. he was one of those who spoke for the committal of the Lords' bill for taking a solemn declaration from Quakers.[8]

In March 1692, Boscawen, together with the Earls of Bath and Radnor (Charles Bodvile Robartes†) and other Cornish gentlemen, subscribed £70,000 towards building two trading vessels under the terms of the grant made by Charles I to allow Cornwall to send two ships a year to India independently of the East India Company. He was classed as a placeman on two parliamentary lists of 1692 and in November was prepared to back his support for the government by lending £500 on the poll tax. He was again active in the 1692–3 session, beginning on 13 Dec. with a speech in the committee of the whole on ways and means in favour of a land tax levied by a pound rate. The following day he spoke for the committal of the abjuration bill. On the 19th he moved to bring in a bill repealing the Act prohibiting the export of copper, but had to be content with appointment (in 3rd place) to the resultant inquiry committee. On the same day he spoke in the second-reading debate on the bill regulating the East India trade. On the 22nd he proposed a rider at the third reading of the place bill to make the act temporary, but this move was negated. On the 30th he was one of those who opposed the bill extending the life of the patent concerning convex lights because it was against the public interest. Finally, on the 31st he spoke against the bill preventing the export of gold and silver and melting down the coin of the realm as 'it lessened so much of every man's estate as you lessened your money'.[9]

On 6 Jan. 1693 Boscawen was the sole Member named to draft a bill for rebuilding ships, which he managed through the House until the committee stage from which it failed to emerge. Significantly, he spoke on 11 Jan. at the report stage of the committee of the whole considering advice to the King, to oppose the resolution that the King should constitute his Admiralty commission of people with experience in maritime affairs. On the following day he offered a rider to the land tax bill to prohibit commissioners from having a role in the assessment of their resident parish. On the 17th he presented another bill allowing the crown to make leases of lands in the Duchy of Cornwall, which although he was first-named to the second-reading committee he did not report. However, following its amendment by the Lords, he objected on 8 Mar. to the Upper House changing the fees in the bill because it was a charge upon the subject, and was first-named to the resultant conference committee. On 19 Jan. at the report stage of the bill preventing the export of wool, he spoke against a clause promoted on behalf of the Hamburg Company because he felt it would hinder woollen exports. Again showing concern for the London orphans, he presented a petition on their behalf on 25 Jan. On 8 Feb. he was one of those who unsuccessfully pressed for the committal of the bill for preserving timber within the New Forest. On the 13th he opposed a clause of credit for dealing with a shortfall in the revenue, preferring only a review of the poll tax. Continuing his support for the bill preventing the export of wool at its third reading on 17 Feb., he argued that in order to encourage the export of woollens 'the more exporters the cheaper it would go out, and the cheaper it is the more you will send abroad and the better able to undersell your neighbours'. On 22 Feb. he intervened in the committee of the whole discussing the state of Ireland to note that 'Ireland is under a discontent but why I cannot tell', although the 'unseasonable' prorogation of parliament might have contributed to it. Thus, he thought further inquiry should be made rather than the anti-Court address which was eventually adopted. The following day he was one of those who successfully sought the rejection of a Lords' bill repealing a law for finding sureties for pardoned felons. On 1 Mar. he supported the bill for indemnifying persons giving evidence in treason cases. On 6 Mar. he was in favour of committing the bill setting aside amendments and alterations in the records of the Glamorgan grand sessions, in favour of the Earl of Pembroke (Hon. Thomas Herbert†).[10]

In 1693 Grascome classed Boscawen as a placeman. In August, together with Lord Keeper Somers (Sir John*), Sir John Trenchard, Richard Hampden I* and Lord Chief Justice Sir John Holt†, Boscawen was one of the Privy Councillors appointed to conduct an inquiry into the miscarriages of the Smyrna fleet. Somewhat surprisingly, given his age, he married in September the sister of the prominent Whig magnate the Earl of Clare (soon to be Duke of Newcastle) and hence into the Holles family which was noted for its Presbyterianism. After a sojourn in Tunbridge Wells, he was in London in September. Perhaps it was marriage which led him to solicit from Francis Tallents, the Nonconformist divine, the name of a person 'well qualified for a public living and of a quiet temper' to administer to St. Michael's Penkevel. Boscawen's chaplain, Joseph Halsey, had been ejected from the living in 1662, but 'is still desirous the place should be well supplied', and Boscawen hoped that Tallents 'may be acquainted with the best of those that conform upon that account'. Clearly, Boscawen still had extensive links with the 'moderate' Presbyterian elite, while himself conforming to the Church of England.[11]

In the new session of Parliament Boscawen was ordered on 14 Nov. 1693 to draft yet another bill for building 'defensible' ships, which this time reached the statute book. On 6 Dec. he presented a petition from Cornish merchants for the encouragement of privateers, and was named to a draft a bill after inquiry into the matter. Subsequently, he managed the bill through the House following its committal, carrying it to the Lords on 16 Apr. 1694. On 8 Dec. he was first-named to the second reading on the bill allowing the crown to grant leases in the Duchy of Cornwall, which, although he did not report, he carried up on 16 Apr. On 22 Dec. he was one of those Members who spoke against a clause in the triennial bill that 'a Parliament shall be understood to be holden, although no act of judgment shall pass within the time of their assembly'. On 29 Dec. he presented an estate bill on behalf of Thomas Vivian*, which he reported on 8 Jan. 1694. On 2 Jan. Boscawen was named to draft a bill to fix the assize of bread. On the 25th he was ordered to draft a bill to prevent abuses in the spoils of wrecks, which he managed until its committal stage from which it failed to emerge. On 1 Feb., during the debate on how the Commons should respond to the King's answer to their representation over the veto of the place bill, he advocated caution, suggesting that considering the posture of affairs Members should be satisfied with the royal answer. It was rumoured in February that Boscawen would replace the Earl of Bath as lord lieutenant of Cornwall, and a month later that he would be made a baron. Philip Foley* had also heard this rumour, noting on 1 Mar. that 'our great debate now is excise . . . Mr Bosca[wen] still remains for it; some say he is to be a baron'. Sir Christopher

Musgrave, 4th Bt.*, reported to Harley on 3 May 1694 that Boscawen was about to be made a peer, a promotion which in his view would have been 'a great loss' to the House, but though the rumour continued to circulate, Boscawen remained a commoner. However, from the tone of one of the Marquess of Normanby's complaints in May when he referred to 'Mr Boscawen or the last of the Privy Councillors', it would seem that he was regarded as one of its least important members. Financially, Boscawen's commitment to the new regime remained as strong as ever, as he invested over £4,000 in the newly established Bank of England.[12]

At the beginning of the 1694–5 session on 12 Nov. Boscawen was sympathetic about the need to give Members more time to arrive in London, but moved that the King's Speech should be taken into consideration on the 19th. He was again to the fore in the last week in November when he was one of those who spoke in favour of voting a supply as the House was 'bound in honour to a prosecution of the war with vigour and consequently to accord a substantial supply, otherwise it would be a great discouragement to the confederates'. He was named to three drafting committees, presenting a bill to prevent the import of pottery on 20 Dec. He was named to the committee ordered to draw up articles of impeachment against Carmarthen, now Duke of Leeds (27 Apr.). On 23 Apr. he was elected in 5th place with 100 votes to the committee charged with examining Sir Thomas Cooke*.[13]

Boscawen was heavily involved in the 1695 election campaign in Cornwall. Moves were again made to oppose him for the county, but in the event he was unopposed. He was also active at St. Mawes and Tregony. He was forecast as likely to support the Court in the division on 31 Jan. over the proposed council of trade, signed the Association promptly, and voted in March for fixing the price of guineas at 22s. During the summer he was active in London, sitting on prize disputes in June and attending the Privy Council in August.[14]

In the early days of the 1696–7 session Boscawen was summoned to a meeting of the leading Junto Whigs and ministerialists to decide how to proceed following Sir John Fenwick's† confession, although no resolutions were taken at that meeting. On 6 Nov. James Vernon I* reported that he had been one of those who in the debate on Fenwick had 'stood to it resolutely', defending Edward Russell*, the Duke of Shrewsbury and Marlborough (John Churchill†), as well no doubt as his brother-in-law, Lord Godolphin, and was thus instrumental in ensuring that the Commons ordered a bill of attainder against Fenwick. Following the first-reading debate on the 13th Vernon again praised him in a letter to Shrewsbury: 'Mr Boscawen is to be esteemed and commended for rousing the spirit of the House to that degree which afterwards kept itself up.' In his speech he was reported to have said

> The great thing, say some gentlemen, we must take care of, is the blood of a man: does anyone say he is innocent? No: but we must have some way or another that he must not be brought to his trial. I desire, as Englishmen, you will not only take care of the life of one man, but of the life of the King; of the lives of our wives and children, and all our families.

On 16 Nov. he argued in favour of admitting Goodman's evidence. On the 17th in a series of moves by those accused by Fenwick, he moved that Godolphin be heard at the bar to answer Fenwick's charges, according to Vernon pre-empting a similar motion from Lord Coningsby. Later in the day during the debate on committal, Boscawen's passion was again evident as he believed 'it is the consequence of bringing in a French army that is to be considered', and that the 'destruction of the people of England and the Protestant religion, will bring your people to go in wooden shoes'. At the third reading of the bill on the 25th he pronounced Fenwick guilty because he had fled and did not deny the fact of his crime and that even though there was not enough evidence to convict him in Westminster Hall, there was sufficient to satisfy his own conscience. Naturally, he voted for the attainder. Boscawen's main activity related to the grievances of the Cornish tinners. Having been first-named on 3 Mar. 1697 to a committee on a petition against the high duties on tin, he reported two resolutions from the committee on the 20th, being named to draft a bill to encourage the consumption of tin, which he presented on 6 Apr. The second resolution, being a matter of public finance, was referred to a committee of the whole, and upon a favourable report on 1 Apr. he was named to draft a bill to lessen the duty on tin which he helped to manage through the Commons.[15]

Boscawen was keenly interested in local appointments for the political influence they exerted. Thus, he warned in May 1697 that it was essential not to provoke Sir Francis Drake, 3rd Bt.*, to resign as recorder of Plymouth as it would result in electoral defeat for the Whigs in that borough. At the start of the new session, he seconded the motion for the Address on 3 Dec. 1697. Later that month he was named to bring in bills to prevent correspondence with King James and to remove certain payments associated with the shrievalty (both on the 7th), presenting the latter on the 14th and reporting it on 17 June 1698, although it fell in the Lords. His next legislative involvement concerned the will of (Sir) William Godolphin†, who had spent most of his later years in Spain. He was first-named to a committee on a petition relating to it and subsequently named to draft a bill which he presented on 10 Feb., the purpose of which was to ensure that Charles Godolphin* and other members of the Godolphin family would benefit rather than the Jesuits. On the question of disbanding the army, on 8 Jan. 1698 Boscawen moved to try to retrieve a situation lost for the Court in December by proposing an instruction to the committee of supply to consider the charge for guards and garrisons for 1698, with the aim of settling sufficient funds to provide for 15,000 men, but the opposition was strong enough to defeat him. On 29 Jan. he was appointed to draft a bill to prevent robberies and on 9 Feb. spoke in favour of an address for a proclamation to suppress profaneness, debauchery and the publication of blasphemous pamphlets, being nominated to the committee to draw it up. The remainder of the session saw him ordered to prepare three other bills. He also informed the Commons that the King would provide a list of persons licensed to return from abroad. Finally, he reported several times from a committee dealing with Molyneux's *Case of Ireland* and related issues.[16]

Boscawen was returned again for Cornwall in 1698, being classed as a placeman (in his capacity as governor of St. Mawes) and also as a Court supporter on a list comparing the old and new Parliaments. He spoke on 4 Jan. 1699, presumably supporting moves to allow the committee on the disbanding bill to alter the number of men allowed in England, although no evidence remains of what he said. Furthermore, at the third-reading stage of the disbanding bill on 18 Jan. he seemed to be arguing for a revision upwards of the number of men permitted from 7,000 to 10,000. His name appears on both lists of Members voting against the bill. His other activities in the Commons included nomination to two drafting committees, including a bill suppressing vice and immorality (23 Dec. 1698). Towards the end of the session there is evidence that his health was beginning to fail. On 8 Apr. Lady Anne Clinton reported that Boscawen was lodging at Kensington, 'having been very ill with a cold, but is now on a mending hand'. However, he fell ill again following a journey into Cornwall. Indeed, at the end of June Vernon was sufficiently concerned to tell Lord Coningsby that it would be 'a great loss' if Boscawen 'should go off'.[17]

In the 1699–1700 session Boscawen's legislative work was further reduced, resulting in just one drafting committee. However, he was active in February 1700 in defending Lord Chancellor Somers over a motion which sought to criticize ministers for procuring grants from the crown, referring to history in the process and citing the relationship between William Cecil† and Queen Elizabeth. Despite his advanced age, Boscawen still commanded the respect of the leading local politicians, Charles Trelawny* reporting that a plan to dispose of seats in Cornwall had foundered upon Lord Godolphin's refusal to 'disoblige old gurnet head'. Consequently, he was returned for the county again in January 1701.[18]

In the 1701 Parliament Boscawen was more active, being named to three drafting committees. As late as March he was being referred to by his brother-in-law, Newcastle, as someone to be applied to in case there was a problem over the investigation of his lieutenancy appointments. However, Boscawen died at his house in Greek Street on 13 May 1701. One contemporary thought him 'exhausted with age and laborious services for the public ... not only the oldest person, but also the oldest Member in the House, as being one that had sat in more Parliaments in the same capacity of knight of the shire, than any other representative whatever'. Rather less charitably the Earl of Ailesbury (Hon. Thomas Bruce†) considered him to have been one of those 'asserters of liberty and freedom of speech in Parliament, but were hindered into others' measures through ambition of being great and rich'. Most of his Cornish estates went to his nephew, Hugh Boscawen II*.[19]

[1] Vivian, *Vis. Cornw.* 47; Luttrell, *Brief Relation*, ii. 54; iii. 141; *Dorm. and Extinct Peerages*, 281; IGI, London; Le Neve, *Mon. Angl.* 1700–15, 301; *CSP Dom.* 1645–7, p. 150. [2] *Cal. Treas. Bks.* iv. 695; Add. 6713, f. 175; 70244, Henry Julian to Harley, 13 Feb. 1689–90; *Shrewsbury Corresp.* 117; *CSP Dom.* 1696, p. 162. [3] *CSP Dom.* 1694–5, p. 204; *Cal. Treas. Bks.* xiii. 386. [4] Add. 10120, f. 232; W. Kellaway, *New England Co.* 291. [5] 'Collectanea Trelawniana', 268 (Speck trans.); Luttrell, *Brief Relation*, iii. 280. [6] *CSP Dom.* 1690–1, p. 290. [7] *Luttrell Diary*, 14, 16, 88, 95, 133; Grey, x. 189. [8] *Luttrell Diary*, 118, 131, 141, 143, 145, 169, 171, 182, 185, 186, 192, 197, 198. [9] Luttrell, *Brief Relation*, ii. 375; *Luttrell Diary*, 312, 319, 327, 328, 336, 340, 343; *CJ*, x. 724. [10] *Luttrell Diary*, 364, 365, 374, 387, 410, 419, 429, 440, 443, 455, 469, 470. [11] Luttrell, *Brief Relation*, iii. 166; Carstares, *State Pprs.* 194; Add. 15857, f. 67. [12] Grey, 373, 385; Luttrell, *Brief Relation*, iii. 275; Wood, *Life and Times*, iii. 446; Add. 30013, f. 55; 42592, f. 40; *HMC Portland*, iii. 550; Nottingham Univ. Lib. Portland (Bentinck) mss, PwA 1151a, Normanby to Portland, 15 May 1694; DZA, Bonet despatch 6/16 June 1694. [13] Add. 46527, f. 22; Bodl. Carte 76, ff. 531–2; [14] Add. 70018, ff. 94–95; *HMC Downshire*, i. 675; *CJ*, xiii. 38–39. [15] Coxe, *Shrewsbury*, 417; *Vernon–Shrewsbury Letters*, i. 49, 64; Northants. RO, Montagu (Boughton) mss 46/21, Vernon to Shrewsbury, 13 Nov. 1696; Cobbett, *Parlty. Hist.* v. 1025, 1032, 1052, 1099–1101, 1140–1. [16] Add. 17677 SS, ff. 113, 115; *Cam. Misc.* xxix. 358; Horwitz, *Parl. and Pol. Wm. III*, 229; Add. 70019, Edward* to Sir Edward Harley*, 12 Feb. 1697[-8]. [17] *Cam. Misc.* xxix. 384–5; Add. 70113, Lady Clinton to Sir Edward Harley, 8 Apr. [1699]; 57861, f. 46; Montagu (Boughton) mss 47/204, Vernon to Shrewsbury, 29 June 1699; *Vernon–Shrewsbury Letters*, ii. 317. [18] Som. RO, Sanford mss DD/SF 410a, debates 13 Feb. 1699[-1700]; Add. 28052, f. 100. [19] Add. 33084, f. 165; 27440, f. 159; *English Post*, 12–14 May 1701; *Post Boy*, 13–15 May 1701; *Ailesbury Mems.* 359; PCC 151 Dyer.

E. C./S. N. H.

BOSCAWEN, Hugh II (c.1680–1734), of Tregothnan, Cornw.

TREGONY   1702–1705
CORNWALL   1705–1710
TRURO   1710–1713
PENRYN   1713–9 June 1720

b. c.1680, o. surv. s. of Edward Boscawen† of Wortherall and Roscarrock by Jael, da. of Sir Francis Godolphin†, sis. of Charles*, Sidney†, and Sir William Godolphin†, 1st Bt. *educ.* King's, Camb. 1697; travelled abroad (Low Countries, Austria) 1701. *m.* 23 Apr. 1700, Charlotte (*d.* 1754), da. and coh. of Charles Godfrey*, sis. of Francis Godfrey*, 8s. (1 *d.v.p.*), 10 da. (5 *d.v.p.*). *suc.* fa. 1685; uncle Hugh Boscawen I* at Tregothnan 1701; *cr.* Visct. Falmouth 9 June 1720.[1]

Groom of bedchamber to Duke of Gloucester 1698–1700; groom of bedchamber to Prince George of Denmark 1702–8; warden of the stannaries and high steward of duchy of Cornwall 1708–34; comptroller of the Household 1714–20; PC 12 Oct. 1714; jt. vice-treasurer [I] 1717–34.[2]

Capt. St. Mawes castle 1701–10, 1714–34; recorder, Penryn, Penzance and Tregony ?1701–?*d.*[3]

Boscawen's father, a wealthy Turkey merchant, left him a considerable fortune which included two Cornish manors. His mother, the sister of Lord Godolphin, and his uncle Hugh, a Privy Councillor under William III, provided him with important connexions. Thus, in September 1698 the King and his Dutch favourite Albemarle personally selected Boscawen as a member of the Duke of Gloucester's bedchamber at a salary of £200 p.a. This brought him into court circles and in 1700 he secretly married the daughter of Charles Godfrey, the master of the Jewel Office, the marriage not being made public until August. This marriage strengthened his connexions with Marlborough's (John Churchill†) circle. In May 1701 Boscawen was travelling abroad when his uncle died, leaving him Cornish estates worth £3,000 p.a., as well as extensive parliamentary interests. Almost immediately, his mother sought to secure the governorship of St. Mawes from her brother, although Godolphin felt that his age and absence might preclude his appointment. In any case Boscawen left Vienna, where he was studying French and learning 'the knowledge of men and business' under George Stepney, arriving at The Hague in July, possibly with a view to persuading Marlborough of his suitability for the post or in order to seek a commission. Godolphin informed his sister in August that Boscawen was not to accept the latter 'unless he designs to follow it the next year too, in case of a war'. In November 1701 he duly succeeded his uncle as captain of St. Mawes castle, and did not stand at the general election, possibly because he was under age. However, the new Parliament held some interest for him as in February 1702 a bill was passed naturalizing his wife.[4]

As a nephew of Lord Treasurer Godolphin and nephew by marriage of the Duke of Marlborough, Boscawen was soon given a place in Prince George's household worth £400 p.a. He duly entered Parliament for Tregony in 1702, his mother reporting in August that he had returned 'from Cornwall with as good success as he could expect at present from his affairs there'. In the new Parliament he supported the Court, voting on 13 Feb. 1703 for the Lords' amendments to the bill for enlarging the time for taking the oath of abjuration and on the 19th telling against adjourning the debate on the bill for better carrying on the war in the West Indies. In the 1703–4 session he received leave of absence on 15 Nov. for three weeks and acted as a teller on 14 Mar. 1704 against adjourning the debate on rewarding the heirs of a Colonel Baker for his services at Derry in 1690. In the following session he was forecast as a probable opponent of the Tack and was given the task of lobbying his fellow Cornish MP, Sir John Molesworth, 2nd Bt., on the issue. He did not vote for it on 28 Nov.[5]

By 1705 Boscawen, in league no doubt with Lord Treasurer Godolphin and Bishop Trelawny, had consolidated his electoral interest in Cornwall to such an extent that he was returned as knight of the shire at the top of the poll. Indeed, having secured his return for Truro as well, he was in the position of being solicited by his relatives for the borough seat when he elected to serve for the county. Further, Godolphin acknowledged his role in managing the government interest in the county when he informed Robert Harley* shortly before Parliament sat that 'having looked out this morning the list of the Cornish Members which I received from Mr Boscawen, with his letter in which it was enclosed, I send both to you, and if you want explanation of any part of it, Mr Boscawen will be glad to wait upon you'. Boscawen's own election was classed as a 'gain' by Lord Sunderland (Charles, Lord Spencer*), and he was marked as a placeman and a High Church courtier in two lists of that year. He duly voted for the Court candidate as Speaker on 25 Oct. On 15 Jan. 1706 he spoke on the regency bill, presumably on the government side, and voted for the Court on 18 Feb. over the 'place clause' in the bill. Like his father-in-law, he opposed the confiscation of Roman Catholic estates as proposed by the bill to prevent the growth of popery at its third reading on 4 Mar. 1706 because it would offend some of the allies and seemed to herald a policy of persecution as adopted in France. An indication of how Boscawen was perceived by his contemporaries can be seen by John Crewe Offley's* comment that Boscawen was 'a very good friend of mine and nephew to my Lord Treasurer'.[6]

In the 1706–7 session Boscawen managed an estate bill on behalf of the widow of the recently deceased Cornish MP, Henry Darell, through all its stages in the Commons. The 1707–8 session saw Boscawen identified as a 'Lord Treasurer's Whig', as opposed to a Junto Whig engaged in factious opposition to the ministry. On 19 Dec. he received leave of absence for six weeks, but had returned by 16 Jan. 1708 when he was named to draft a bill for 'the more effectual discovery of dead people pretended to be alive', presenting it on the 20th. On the 21st he was present to defend the ministry during the debate on the report of the committee considering more effective recruitment for the army. It was proposed that the resultant bill include a clause preventing the sale of commissions. Boscawen justified the practice

> in cases where officers were worn out in the service, or disabled by wounds; there being no other provision for them, it was a sure compassion to let them sell that they might have a little means of living rather than continue them their pay, when they were not able to serve.

Also on the 17th he reported from the committee on the Plymouth workhouse bill. On the 28 Jan. he spoke at the third reading of the bill to render the Union more complete in support of a rider forbidding judges to accept presents, suggesting that this measure should be extended to England. The fall of the Harleyites from office led to speculation that Boscawen would replace Thomas Mansel I* as comptroller of the household, but if he sought this office he was disappointed. On 16 Feb. he reported from the committee considering the petition of army aides-de-camp concerning arrears.[7]

No doubt as a reward for Boscawen's efforts in support of the lord treasurer and as a boost to his electoral interest in Cornwall, he was made warden of the Stannaries for life with an additional salary of £1,000 p.a. just before the general election of 1708. With his own as well as the Court's interest at his disposal he was active in many of the Cornish boroughs. James Craggs I* wrote on 7 May:

> Mr Boscawen has a very great command in this country and his new powers of warden of the stannaries will not a little improve it. We have been at several corporations a burgessing as they call it, where I do not see he is like to miscarry in any he pretends to.

When Parliament met, Boswcawen was appointed in December to draft bills on the prevention of embezzlement of shipwrecked goods (14th) and to encourage the fishery (18th). On 9 Feb. 1709 he told against adjourning the debate on the eligibility of Sir Richard Allin, 1st Bt., to sit in the Commons, which resulted in a resolution in his favour. On 23 Feb. he was added to the drafting committee on the bill ascertaining allowances for Scottish fish exports. In March he told twice: on the 3rd in favour of the election of Sir Orlando Bridgeman, 2nd Bt.*, for Coventry and on the 31st that a petition be brought up relating to the Earl of Clanricarde's estate bill. On 8 Mar. in a debate on papers concerning the treasonable activities of Harley's former clerk, William Greg, William Bromley II 'desired that since those papers were brought in as reflecting upon an honourable Member of the House [Harley], they might then go into consideration of them. At which Mr Boscawen was very angry and said he knew [of] nobody reflected upon.' His final important act of the session was on 18 Apr. 1709, when he told against adjourning the consideration of amendments to the bill improving the Union.[8]

On 9 Jan. 1710 Boscawen was given leave of absence for two months. In the event he remained away for longer, no doubt preparing for his quasi-regal progress through Cornwall on the way to the convocation of the Stannaries, and towards which he was given £1,100 by the government. Controversy followed when he was accused by opponents of organizing a mob of 5,000–6,000 from his tin mines near Truro to put pressure on the convocation to accept his terms for the tin contract with the government. In May Craggs felt that Boscawen was 'mistaken when he supposes that if this present Parliament be dissolved we shall be able to deal with the adversary in the next elections'. Craggs proved accurate in his forecast, with Boscawen unable to exercise his normal influence despite a life patent as warden of the stannaries, so much so that he even lost the county contest. Here the Sacheverell affair was crucial, even though Boscawen had been absent from the trial. As a correspondent of John Evelyn II* put it,

> though he was not at all concerned in his impeachment, as I satisfied many people yet they could not be persuaded, but he would have had a hand in it had he been in the House, so that mere surmises were looked on as matters of fact, and for this and no other reason he was so unfortunate as to miscarry.

Boscawen's candidates lost out to George Granville's*, and he himself took refuge at Truro.[9]

Boscawen was wrongly classed as a Tory in the

'Hanover list'. In the 1710–11 session he was one of the placemen voting on 7 Dec. 1711 for the motion 'No Peace without Spain'. He acted as a teller on 11 Apr. 1712 against a motion sending into custody the printer of the Dutch memorial opposing the peace, and on 21 Apr. against tacking to a supply bill legislation setting up a commission inquiring into crown grants. In the 1713 session his name appears on a list probably of those voting against the French wines duty bill on 6 May, but he is not recorded as voting on 18 June on the French commerce bill.[10]

At the general election of 1713 an agent of Lord Lansdown (George Granville*) complained that 'if honest men attack Mr Boscawen's friends, a means is found to discharge them, and give their posts to his agents', and deplored Harley's (now Lord Oxford) failure to remove 'Mr Boscawen's creatures'. Returned himself for Penryn, Boscawen was reported as criticizing the Address on 4 Mar. 1714 because it precluded further measures to secure the succession. He took part in the management of the bill for the relief of poor debtors, which he reported on 28 May and told in favour of passing on 28 June. He also voted against the expulsion of Richard Steele on 18 Mar. 1714. On 24 June he seconded the motion by Lord Hertford (Algernon Seymour) to place a reward of £100,000 on the Pretender's head, answering the criticism that it was an affront to the Queen's offer of £5,000 with the observation that £5,000 out of her private purse was equal to £100,000 from the nation. He told on 8 July in favour of allowing William Lowndes* and the South Sea Company committee men to attend the Lords in the investigation into the *asiento* treaty. Later that month he was involved in a controversy over the publication by the Whig journalist Abel Boyer of letters from the Queen and Lord Treasurer Oxford to the Elector of Hanover, which were said to compromise Bolingbroke (Henry St. John II*). The story was that

> the Elector communicated them to the Duke of Marlborough as a great secret; but that the Duchess accidentally lighting on them, thought it her duty to communicate a matter of so great consequence to one Mr Boscawen, a relation of hers in London, who was so generous as to communicate it to his friends, and they to theirs, and so on.

He was classed as a Whig in the Worsley list and on two lists classifying members returned in 1715.[11]

Boscawen was in high favour at court in the reign of George I, serving as comptroller of the household. In compensation for losing his office in 1720 he was made a peer. He died on 25 Oct. 1734 'of an apoplexy fit as he came down the stairs' at the seat of Robert Trefusis† in Cornwall.[12]

[1] Vivian, *Vis. Cornw.* 47–48; Collins, *Peerage*, vi. 68–70. [2] *Cal. Treas. Bks.* xxii. 366. [3] *CSP Dom.* 1700–2, p. 447. [4] *Vernon–Shrewsbury Letters*, ii. 177; Add. 40772, f. 102; Centre Kentish Stud. Stanhope mss U1590/O59/7, Robert Yard* to Alexander Stanhope, 18 Oct. 1698; HMC Cowper, ii. 403; BL, Evelyn mss, Godolphin to Mrs Boscawen, 17 May [1701]; *Marlborough–Godolphin Corresp.* 10, 21; S. Spens, *George Stepney*, 200; *CSP Dom.* 1700–2, p. 447. [5] Evelyn mss, Mrs Boscawen to John Evelyn II*, 14 Aug. 1702; *Bull. IHR*, xxxiv. 96. [6] *Marlborough–Godolphin Corresp.* 433, 469; *Parlty Lists Early 18th Cent.* ed. Newman, 65; *Cam. Misc.* xxiii. 68; Boyer, *Anne Annals*, iv. 225; Cobbett, *Parlty Hist.* vi. 515; Cheshire RO, Arderne mss DAR/H/14, Offley to Sir John Crewe, 18 Apr. 1706. [7] G. Holmes, *Pol. in the Age of Anne*, 229; *Vernon–Shrewsbury Letters*, iii. 320; Northants. RO, Montagu (Boughton) mss, 48/183, James Vernon I* to Shrewsbury, 29 Jan. 1707–8; Luttrell, *Brief Relation*, vi. 267; 7th Duke of Manchester, *Court and Soc. Eliz. to Anne*, ii. 280. [8] *Cal. Treas. Bks.* xxii. 366; Luttrell, *Brief Relation*, vi. 294; Add. 61164, f. 183; *Parlty. Lists Early 18th Cent.* 65; HMC Portland, iv. 521. [9] *Cal. Treas. Bks.* xxiv. 298–9; *Parls. Estates and Repn.* vi. 62–63; *Duchess of Marlborough Corresp.* i. 324; Evelyn mss, Sam. Thompson to Evelyn, 5 Jan. 1710–11. [10] *Bull. IHR*, xxxiii. 231. [11] HMC Cowper, iii. 107; NSA, Kreienberg despatch 5 Mar. 1714 (Szechi trans.); *Wentworth Pprs.* 392, 402. [12] HMC Polwarth, ii. 567; HMC Egmont Diary, ii. 131–2; *Gent. Mag.* 1734, p. 573.

E. C./S. N. H.

BOTELER, John (aft. 1668–1746), of Teston, Kent.

HYTHE   1701 (Jan.)–1710, 27 Jan. 1711–1715

b. aft. 1668, 2nd s. of Sir Oliver Boteler, 2nd Bt., of Teston, by his 1st w. Anne, da. of Sir Robert Austen, of Bexley, Kent, sis. of Sir John Austen, 2nd Bt.*, and Robert Austen I*; bro. of Sir Philip Boteler, 3rd Bt.* *educ.* M. Temple, 1685. ?*unm.*[1]

Cornet of drag. and horse, Col. John Berkeley's regt. 1685, Princess Anne's regt. 1687–92, Col. Francis Langston's regt. 1693–by 1702.

Lt.-gov. of Tilbury and Gravesend, 1702–?1715.[2]

Jurat, Hythe 1713–*d.*[3]

John Boteler's early life is rather more obscure than that of his younger brother, Sir Philip. He may have been the John Boteler who joined Colonel Berkeley's regiment as a cornet in 1685. Although it seems unlikely that he would have remained at this rank for so many years, a John Boteler appears in the lists as a cornet until about 1702. While in the army Boteler saw active service at the battle of Steenkerk in 1692.

Boteler's parliamentary career began in 1701 when he and his brother were elected for Hythe. He was classed as a Tory by Robert Harley* in December 1701. In May 1702 he was appointed lieutenant-governor of Tilbury and Gravesend. Almost immediately he became embroiled in a dispute with the governor, Major-General Hon. George Cholmondeley*. Sir

Philip Boteler evidently wrote to the secretary of state on the matter and received the rather curt reply that he would sort it out on his return from Bath but meanwhile, 'I think Mr. Boteler ought not to oppose the orders of the governor, but, if injured, ought to complain in the proper manner'. The dispute, over the perquisites of the governor and his lieutenant, was eventually decided in Boteler's favour.[4]

In 1704, Boteler was forecast as a probable opponent of the Tack, and the name Boteler (probably indicating both John and his brother) appears on Harley's lobbying list for the Tack, to be approached through Sir Thomas Hales, 2nd Bt.* Boteler did not vote for the Tack on 28 Nov. 1704. Re-elected in 1705, he was classed as a 'Churchman' in a list of the new Parliament. Although Boteler's name is missing from the division list of 25 Oct. 1705 over the Speakership, it seems likely that his omission was an oversight by the compiler because although only four Members are listed for the Cinque Ports as voting against John Smith I, the total at the bottom of the page is given as five. Moreover, Boteler was mentioned in a letter by John Bridges as one of a number of placemen voting against Smith. Surprisingly, a list of early 1708 classed Boteler as a Whig, but another list of early 1708 with the returns added marked him as a Tory. Boteler does not appear to have been an active Member, although he did vote against the impeachment of Dr Sacheverell in 1710. A John Boteler is also listed as holding stock in the Bank of England in 1710. Defeated in the election of 1710, Boteler was seated on 27 Jan. 1711 after a petition. He was listed as a 'worthy patriot' who in the 1710–11 session had helped to detect the mismanagements of the previous ministry, and as a member of the October Club in a Tory pamphlet of the same year. Boyer also listed him as a member of the club.[5]

Boteler's Toryism was confirmed by his appointment as a justice for Kent in 1711, a position he held until his death. His dispute with Cholmondeley flared up again in 1711 when, after Parliament had risen, Cholmondeley had Boteler arrested and imprisoned. He was still in prison in December 1711 when Parliament resumed, whereupon he complained to the House on the 10th of a breach of privilege, which led to his release. Finally, the Worsley list of the 1713 Parliament classed Boteler as a Tory. Having lost the 1715 election, he voted for the Tory candidates in the Kent county election, but then appears to have given up involvement in politics. At some point Boteler moved to St. James's parish, Westminster, where he wrote his will on 18 June 1745, naming as his main beneficiary his cousin John Austen of Bexley, who proved the will on 26 Feb. 1746.[6]

[1] Burke, *Ext. and Dorm. Baronetcies* (1838), 76; PCC 39 Edmunds. [2] Info. from Prof. R. Walcott. [3] Hythe Town Council, Hythe corporation mss, draft minutes of assembly, 1213–15. [4] *CSP. Dom*, 1702–3, pp. 239, 367; *HMC Portland*, x. 70. [5] *Bull. IHR*, xxxvii. 24, 36; Egerton 3359, unfol; Boyer, *Pol. State*. iii. 117. [6] Info. from Prof. N. Landau; *HMC Portland*, x. 70; *Cal. Treas. Bks*, xxvi. 345; *Hist. Jnl*. xxii. 572; G. Wilks, *Barons of the Cinque Ports*, 94; PCC 39 Edmunds.

S. M. W.

BOTELER, Sir Philip, 3rd Bt. (c.1667–1719), of Berham Court, Teston, Kent.

HYTHE 1690–1708

b. c.1667, 1st s. of Sir Oliver Boteler, 2nd Bt., by his 1st w.; bro. of John Boteler*. *m.* lic. 17 Dec. 1690 (with £8,000), Anne (*d.* 1717), da. of Sir Edward des Bouverie, merchant, of London and Cheshunt, Herts., sis. of Jacob des Bouverie*, 1s. *suc.* fa. as 3rd Bt. 17 Nov. 1689.[1]

Recorder, Hythe, 1690–?, jurat, 1698–*d.* and mayor, 1698–9.[2]

The Botelers had been established in Kent for four generations. Sir William Boteler, Sir Philip's grandfather, was created a baronet in 1641, raised a regiment for Charles I and was killed at the battle of Cropredy Bridge in 1644. His widow paid for this royalism in 1647 when she was fined for her late husband's delinquency. Boteler's father was a deputy-lieutenant for Kent from 1685 and although he answered in the affirmative to James II's 'three questions' in January 1688, he appears to have supported the Williamite regime, being appointed a j.p. for Kent in March 1690.[3]

Sir Oliver left his son extensive property in Kent (including Saltwood Castle which he sold in 1712) and in Bedfordshire. Boteler's inheritance was the source of dispute between himself and his stepmother, Anne. His relationship with her and other relatives was turbulent: on more than one occasion he accused them of trying to defraud him. The resulting court cases reveal an unhappy and violent family history. Boteler's parents had separated and Sir Oliver had then lived with Anne Uphill for several years, during which time they had two children, before marrying in 1684. The court case of October 1702, *Sir Philip Boteler* v. *Dame Anne Boteler*, reveals 1667 to be the approximate date of Boteler's birth.[4]

Boteler held several local offices. He was a militia colonel and a deputy-lieutenant for Kent in the 1690s. In an otherwise obscure incident in 1693 Boteler and several other gentlemen quitted their commands in the militia and consequently were required to resign their posts in the Kentish lieutenancy. However, Boteler was reappointed the next year and in fact was a deputy-lieutenant until at least 1702. He was also a justice for Kent from 1689 until his death.[5]

Boteler entered Parliament for Hythe in 1690, the same year he was made recorder. It seems likely that he co-operated with his fellow MP, William Brockman, in obstructing Hon. John Beaumont's* attempts to get government candidates into Cinque Port constituencies. Beaumont's letters to the mayor and corporation of Rye were apparently copied by Boteler and Sir John Austen, 2nd Bt.* These copies were probably taken for Brockman, who led the campaign against ministerial interference in the Cinque Ports.[6]

Boteler's Austen relations had Whig sympathies and he himself was classed as a Whig by the Marquess of Carmarthen (Sir Thomas Osborne†) in March 1690. The next year, April 1691, Robert Harley* listed him as doubtful, but possibly a Country supporter. On 17 Jan. 1693 he received leave of absence for a week. In the 1694–5 session he was listed among Henry Guy's supporters in connexion with the Commons' investigation of Guy for corruption, and he again received leave of absence for a week on 1 Feb. 1695. Re-elected in 1695, it was reported in the committee of the whole on the council of trade (probably on 20 or 28 Jan. 1696) that he had noted that if commissioners were unpaid and MPs passed a self-denying clause, then Members would merely exclude themselves from a task which no one else would be willing to undertake. He was forecast as likely to support the Court in the divisions on the proposed council of trade on 31 Jan. 1696, and indeed that day he spoke for an abjuration oath being applied to the proposed council's members. He signed the Association promptly and in March he voted with the Court on the fixing of the price of guineas at 22s. The 1696–7 session saw an increase in Boteler's activity in the Commons, although it is noteworthy that he is not recorded as having voted on 25 Nov. 1696 on the attainder of Sir John Fenwick†. He was named to three drafting committees, one of which, on 18 Jan. 1697, was to prevent the export of wool from England. This bill was partly prompted, it seems, by local interests as a petition on the clandestine trade in wool had been presented from Kent on 23 Dec. 1696. Boteler was then first-named on 18 Feb. 1697 to the second-reading committee on this bill before being granted leave of absence on 11 Mar. At the beginning of the following session he spoke on 10 Dec. 1697 in the committee of the whole on the King's Speech, seemingly in support of a standing army. He received leave of absence for a week on 28 Jan. 1698 but was back in the Commons by 9 Feb. when he was named to an address committee.[7]

Returned again in 1698, Boteler was queried as a Court supporter in a comparative analysis of the old and new Parliaments. He is not listed as voting against the bill to disband the army on 18 Jan. 1699, but was probably in London because he received leave of absence for ten days on 27 Jan. Further evidence of Boteler's keenness in protecting local interests occurred on 10 May 1699 when he, Sir Charles Sedley, 5th Bt.*, and William Campion* put a complaint to the Treasury Board against oppressive customs officers in Kent. In the following session, local interests were again to fore in his being the first-named, along with two fellow Cinque Port Members, to a drafting committee on 13 Feb. 1700 for a bill to prevent the sale in England of fish caught in foreign vessels, and on 5 Mar. he was the first-named to the second-reading committee on the resultant bill. On 13 Feb. Boteler spoke against putting a motion to condemn the procuring of crown grants by ministers, a question obviously aimed by Tory Members at Lord Somers (Sir John*). The pro-Whig stance of this speech contrasts with his failure to vote against the disbanding bill and may explain why the compiler of a list of early 1700, analysing the House into 'interests', listed Boteler as doubtful, or possibly as opposition.[8]

Elected with his younger brother for Hythe in the first election of 1701, Boteler was listed as one of those Members thought likely to support the Court in February over the 'Great Mortgage'. He received leave of absence on 9 May for two weeks. He was returned again in November 1701, and Robert Harley's analysis of this Parliament queried him as a Tory. This may indicate Harley's hope that Boteler could be accommodated within his own moderate brand of Toryism, or merely reflect changing circumstances such as the increasing influence of the Tories at Court as well as the death of Boteler's Whig uncles in 1696 and 1699. Boteler's speech on 16 Jan. 1702 in support of supplying the full quota of 40,000 men to the allies was contrary to the suggestions of the more extreme Tories such as Hon. Heneage Finch I and Sir Edward Seymour, 4th Bt., and may be seen as pursuing the kind of moderation espoused by Harley in an attempt to win over the King. Boteler was again active in the legislature in the 1701–2 session, but he was not listed among those voting on 26 Feb. 1702 to vindicate the Commons' proceedings in the impeachment of the Whig ministers, one of whom, Lord Somers, he had previously defended. Again unchallenged at the 1702 election, in 1704 Boteler was forecast as a probable opponent of the Tack, and the name Boteler (probably indicating both Sir Philip and his brother John) is on Harley's lobbying list as to be approached through Sir Thomas Hales, 2nd

Bt., knight of the shire for Kent. Boteler did not vote for the Tack on 28 Nov. 1704. He was re-elected in 1705, and an analysis of the new Parliament classed him as a 'Churchman'. In the division on the Speaker on 25 Oct. 1705, Boteler was listed as voting against the Court candidate. If he did, this was the first overt sign of committed Toryism. However, a list compiled in early 1708 still classed him as a Whig.⁹

A further indication that Boteler had changed his political standpoint occurs in the fact that there was a contest at Hythe in 1708 when, although his brother John was returned, Boteler himself lost out to Hon. John Fane. The configuration of candidates strongly suggests that the Botelers espoused the Tory side and were challenged by two Whigs, Fane and Brockman. Boteler petitioned against the return but eventually withdrew his complaint on 21 Dec. 1709, two days before a new writ was issued for Hythe, attendant on Fane accepting office. However, there is no evidence that Boteler contested the by-election, nor did he stand at the 1710 general election. Ill-health may have persuaded him to leave politics, but he voted for the Tory candidates in the 1713 Kent election. Having made his will as early as 28 Mar. 1708, he did not die until June 1719. He entrusted his property to his wife, his brother John and brothers-in-law William and Jacob des Bouverie, to convey to his only son Philip after payment of his debts. This son was included in a list of 1721 which estimated Jacobite strength in England and Wales in preparation for an uprising.¹⁰

¹Burke, *Ext. and Dorm. Baronetcies*, (1838), 76; C7/39/28; PCC admon. Oct. 1717; PCC 98 Browning, 45 Box. ²G. Wilks, *Barons of the Cinque Ports*, 90; Hythe Town Council, Hythe Corporation mss, draft minutes of Assembly, 1213–15. ³*CSP. Dom.* 1685, p. 165; June 1687–Feb. 1689, pp. 141, 228; 1689–90, p. 26; Duckett, *Penal Laws and Test Act* (1882), 347. ⁴Hasted, *Kent*, ii. 358, 443, 447, 450–1; iv. 207, 388, 396, 459; v. 123, 130–2, 577; vii. 577; viii. 224, 237, 363, 390; C7/54/107, C7/20/17, C7/39/28, C9/314/23. ⁵*CSP. Dom.* 1689–90, p. 206; 1693, p. 212; 1694–5, p. 19; 1700–2, p. 250; 1702–3, p. 394; *Arch. Cant.* vi. 76–7; Wilks, 90; info. from Prof. N. Landau. ⁶Wilks, 89; Add. 42586, ff. 78, 85. ⁷BL, Trumbull Misc. mss 32, debate, [31 Jan. 1696]; *HMC Hastings*, ii. 253; *Cam. Misc.* xxix. 356; Add. 70018, ff. 94–95. ⁸*CSP. Dom.* 1698–9, p. 78; Somerset RO, Sanford mss DD/SF 4107(a), debate 13 Feb. 1699[–1700]; W. L. Sachse, *Ld. Somers*, 160–1. ⁹Add. 17677 XX, f. 176; H. Horwitz, *Parl. and Pol. Wm. III*, 301; *Bull. IHR*, xxxvii. 36, 46. ¹⁰Wilks, 91; PCC 98 Browning; *Hist. Jnl.* xxii. 572; P. S. Fritz, *Ministers and Jacobitism 1715–45*, 150.

S. M. W./S. N. H.

BOUCHER, Thomas (c.1657–1708), of Heath Lane Lodge, Twickenham, Mdx. and Ogbourne St. George, Wilts.

MALMESBURY   21 Nov. 1702–1705

b. c.1657. *m.* (1) lic. 15 Jan. 1687 (aged about 30), Diana Hinderson of St. Martin-in-the-Fields, Mdx., *s.p.s.*; (2) Elizabeth, *s.p.s*; lastly, by 1701, Elizabeth (*d.* 1734), da. of Anthony Morris of Devonshire Street, Mdx., 1s. 1da., 2 or 3 ch. illegit.¹

?Cornet, Berkeley's drag. 1685.

It is possible that Boucher was originally a Wiltshireman, since the regiment of dragoons into which a namesake was commissioned in 1685 had been recruited mainly from the western parts of that county. However, his address at his first marriage (when he classed himself as a 'gentleman') was the same as his bride's, St. Martin-in-the-Fields. In 1694 a 'Thomas Boucher' was given a warrant to travel to Holland with three servants. A 'celebrated gamester', Boucher succeeded well enough in this profession to be able to make loans of some £8,500 to the crown in 1700, and his seat at Twickenham (on copyhold land) would, it was said, have passed in Italy for 'a delicate palace'. He was returned as the nominee of Sir Charles Hedges* in a by-election for Malmesbury in 1702, though later he may have cultivated some interest of his own there: in 1705 he paid £17,070 to Hedges' chief rival in the borough, Lord Wharton (Hon. Thomas*), for the manor of Christian Malford and other property in Wiltshire. Never known to have spoken in the House, he was forecast on 30 Oct. 1704 as a likely opponent of the Tack and did not vote for it on 28 Nov. He and his partner, Edward Pauncefort*, were defeated by Wharton's candidates at Malmesbury in 1705, and again in 1708, despite petitions ascribing their defeat to bribery.²

Boucher's fame as a gamester ensured that his misfortunes were given wide notice. In 1701 he nearly lost his sight as a result of a surgeon's blunder in attempting to clear his throat of a lodged bone, and shortly afterwards his family's visit to Bath was overshadowed with 'whispers' that he had lost a great deal of money. His death, at Bath, was reported by Luttrell on 2 Sept. 1708. The circumstances and aftermath proved a spicy item of gossip for one of his Twickenham neighbours. 'Poor Mr Boucher', she wrote,

went to the Bath . . . and died the week after . . . He made a great dinner for Sir John Germain [1st Bt.*] and some others, and, finding himself very ill, sent for [Dr] Garth, but when he came he told him, 'Doctor, you can do me no good, for I am just a dying', and so died. He was brought to this church [at Twickenham] and buried very privately under the communion table late at night. There was a paper put upon the church door in verse about his many wives: they say he has four. It's not known what he had left. Two old women were overheard to be very witty, saying, 'Why had he no [e]schutcheons? For he might have good arms, a pack of cards, a dice box and a quarter a pair of scissors'.

Reportedly having left a £12,000 marriage portion for his daughter, Boucher bequeathed his house and possessions in Twickenham to his wife Elizabeth, whom he referred to by her maiden name to avoid confusion with a former wife, and £1,000 to his niece Mary. He named William Clayton† and Richard Grantham* as guardians of two of his children. His son Thomas sat as MP for Chippenham 1723–7.[3]

[1] *Wilts. N. and Q.* v. 142–4; R. S. Cobbett, *Memorials of Twickenham*, 69, 354; *Mar. Lic. Vicar-Gen.* (Harl. Soc. xxx), 261; Add. 31143, f. 225. [2] *Wilts. N. and Q.* vii. 428–9; *CSP Dom.* 1694–5, p. 329; 1698, p. 200; *Cal. Treas. Bks.* xvi. 302; J. Macky, *Journey through Eng.* (1714–29), i. 36; Add. 27440, f. 147; 9100, f. 42; *Wilts. Arch. Mag.* xxviii. 43. [3] Add. 31443, f. 37; Herts. RO, Panshanger mss, D/EP F29, Lady Cowper's commonplace bk. p. 167; Luttrell, *Brief Relation*, vi. 346; *Wentworth Pprs.* 63; *Wilts. N. and Q.* v. 142–4.

D. W. H./H. J. L.

BOUGHTON, Sir William, 4th Bt. (1663–1716), of Lawford Hall, Newbold-on-Avon, Warws.

WARWICKSHIRE 31 Jan. 1712–1713

bap. 15 May 1663, o. s. of Sir William Boughton, 3rd Bt., of Lawford Hall by Mary (d. 1693), da. of Hastings Ingram of Little Woolford. *educ.* Magdalen Coll. Oxf., matric. 1681. *m.* (1) lic. 28 Feb. 1685, Mary (d. 1692), da. of John Ramsay, alderman, of London, 1s. 3da. (2 *d.v.p.*); (2) settlement 10 Aug. 1700, Catherine (d. 1725), da. of Sir Charles Shuckburgh, 2nd Bt.*, of Shuckburgh, Warws., 5s. (3 *d.v.p.*) 3da. *suc.* fa. as 4th Bt. 12 Aug. 1683.[1]

Sheriff, Warws. 1688–9.

Of an ancient lineage long settled on the borders of Warwickshire and Leicestershire, Boughton was 'far greater in personal worth than pedigree', an exemplar of 'provident' fatherhood, neighbourliness, hospitality and charity, at least according to the memorial inscription erected by his wife. These gentlemanly attributes had in fact been tempered in later life by a fondness for the bottle. His uncle, Sir Edward Boughton†, 2nd Bt., had represented Warwickshire, albeit inactively, in the two Exclusion Parliaments. He himself came into the baronetcy and family estates in the last years of his minority, and by his later twenties had already held the shrieval office, while in 1701 he was added to the lieutenancy. His second marriage to a daughter of Sir Charles Shuckburgh, 2nd Bt.*, allied him to one of the most prominent Tory families in the county. Another Tory family with whom he was in friendly association was his near neighbours, the Caves of Stanford: Boughton's will mentions a loan of £4,000 which he had at some point made to Sir Thomas Cave, 3rd Bt.* In the summer of 1710 Boughton entertained Dr Sacheverell at Lawford Hall, and in October appeared in support of the 'Church candidates' in the Coventry election. He was elected unopposed for the county at the by-election of January 1712, the year in which he was said to have refused a peerage, the offer possibly connected with the proposed 'mass' creation of Tory peers at that time. Later in the year his son and heir, Edward, was nominated high sheriff. The only record of any parliamentary activity whatsoever was his vote on 18 June 1713 in favour of the French commerce bill. His wife in her inscription to his memory nevertheless provided a glowing account of his service 'in the parliament of Q[ueen] Anne renowned for peace, where his steady and untainted principles, loyalty to his sovereign and zeal for the established Church of England eminently distinguished him'. He stood down in 1713. The final months of his life were clouded by tragedy. A disagreement within the family had distanced him from his younger daughter by his first wife, who in consequence went to reside in Lancashire with her elder sister and her brother-in-law, Sir Henry Hoghton, 5th Bt.*, where soon afterwards she died. Hearing the news in January 1716 Boughton fell ill with 'convulsions' and probably never recovered his health, dying on 22 July. Sir Thomas Cave attended the interment at Newbold and wrote shortly afterwards: 'I accompanied poor Sir Will[ia]m to the entrance of his Elysium, where I wished him a peaceful repose.'[2]

[1] IGI, Warws.; *Vis. Warws.* (Harl. Soc. lxii), 114; Nichols, *Leics.* iv. 302–3; Dugdale, *Warws.* 101; B. G. F. C. W. Boughton-Leigh, *Mems. of a Warws. Fam.* 60–61; NRA Rep. 9002, p. 111; *Verney Letters 18th Cent.* ii. 39. [2] Dugdale, 98; Nichols, 302–3; *CSP Dom.* 1700–2, p. 252; *Verney Letters 18th Cent.* 17, 39, 43, 44; G. Holmes, *Trial of Sacheverell*, 245; G. Holmes and W. A. Speck, *Divided Soc.* 71; PCC 158 Fox.

A. A. H.

BOULTER, Edmund (c.1630–1709), of Princes Street, London.[1]

BOSTON 1698–1701 (Nov.)

b. c.1630, ?1st s. of John Boulter of Abingdon by Susanna, da. of Edward Cutler, Salter, of London; sis. of Sir John Cutler, 1st Bt.* *unm.* *suc.* Sir John Cutler 1693, cos. Countess of Radnor, 1697.[2]

Freeman, Haberdashers' Co. 1656, livery, 1676, asst. 1686–1708; freeman, Boston 1698.[3]

Unmarried and of relatively humble origins, Boulter has slipped into obscurity and his identity has been the subject of some confusion. He was apprenticed to a London haberdasher on 23 July 1647, when his father was described in the company's register as a maltster of Abingdon. His father may have been the 'John Boulter' who was mayor of Abingdon in 1656 but evidently both he and his wife died while their children were still relatively young, leaving Boulter as head of the family. Boulter fulfilled his duty to his family, later paying the expenses of schooling the children of his three sisters. His care of his widowed sister Susanna and her son, John Fryer, later alderman, sheriff and lord mayor of London, was remembered by the latter with gratitude in his autobiography, written in the 18th century. The Boulters had close relations in the Dissenting community and although there is little evidence regarding Boulter's own religion, he was probably at least a sympathizer. One of his business partners was a Quaker and his sister Susanna married a man who was 'reputed . . . a lover of those now called Dissenters', and took her son to hear Dissenting preachers. Boulter's brother Robert, moreover, was well known to the authorities during the Restoration, being arrested for dispersing a seditious pamphlet in 1666. He wrote his will some 13 years later, in August 1679, wherein he left a legacy to Boulter, 'who hath rather been as an indulgent father unto me', and both he and Edmund signed the petition of December 1679 calling for a Parliament. Robert was again arrested for sedition in 1681 (the year in which he published the poems of Andrew Marvell), and had his house searched for treasonable papers after the Rye House Plot.[4]

Little is known of Boulter's activities during James II's reign, but he was evidently engaged in business as by April 1690 he was so successful as to attract the attention of the Grocers' Company, which decided on an approach to Boulter '(who is a member of the Haberdashers, but an eminent trader in the mystery of grocery) by such members as are acceptable to him', in order to persuade him to be 'translated' to their company. By October 1690, the agreement of the court of aldermen for Boulter's translation had been obtained and the Company was

> very sensible how much it may tend to the benefit and advantage of the Grocers in order to the future improvement of his Majesty's grace and favour in the privileges lately granted them to have so worthy and leading an example of his translation.

His uncle, Sir John Cutler, an eminent Grocer, was to be asked to influence Boulter in favour of the move, but nothing further came of it. The Boulters' political affiliations seem to have been in contrast to those of their uncle Cutler, but his influence may have altered Boulter's views and explain his appointment to the Tory-dominated London lieutenancy in 1690. Surviving the alterations of 1694 which removed many Tories, he was reappointed in 1694, 1704 and 1708. He was also chosen sheriff of London in July 1694 for the ensuing year but fined off.[5]

Boulter supported the Williamite regime with a loan of £2,000 in 1690 and a further £500 on the poll tax in 1692. Evidently already prosperous, he increased his fortunes considerably in 1693 on the death of Cutler, who named him residuary legatee and sole executor. It was widely reported that Cutler had left his estates in Yorkshire, Cambridgeshire and elsewhere, worth about £6,000 p.a., and half his personal estate, worth £60,000, to his daughter, the Countess of Radnor and her issue. In default of heirs the lands were remaindered to Boulter. Various other legacies were to be paid from the rest of the personal estate, with Boulter inheriting the residue. Some of these arrangements must have been made in earlier settlements, possibly at the time of the Countess's marriage as well as by a deed of 26 June 1690 mentioned in Cutler's will. Robert Yard* reported that the Earl of Radnor's (Charles Bodvile Robartes†) expectations of retaining his wife's inheritance were high, Boulter being a man 'of 64 years', unmarried and likely to leave everything to his cousin the Countess. In the event, however, the Countess predeceased him, dying childless in January 1697, and her share of her father's estate devolved on Boulter.[6]

A significant amount of Boulter's new wealth was in the form of debts owed to Cutler's estate. One such debt, of £18,000, was secured on the office of marshal of the King's bench prison, and in February 1697 Boulter successfully petitioned the Lords to protect the debt from provisions in the creditors' relief bill then passing through that House. Appropriate clauses were inserted on 15 Apr. 1697 to safeguard his interest, but the following year the security for this debt was once again threatened by another bill for the further relief of debtors. Boulter successfully petitioned the Commons for the insertion of protective clauses, but the bill did not complete all its stages before the dissolution.[7]

Although he lived in London, Boulter had some long-standing connexions with Boston. Corporation minutes record a gift from him in 1681 of books to the free school and it seems likely that he was the 'Mr Boulter' who had a warehouse in the town. His links with Boston stood him in good stead in 1698 when he was returned for the borough. His candidacy may have been motivated less by political interest than by the desire to evade a suit against him begun by the

Earl of Radnor, who possessed large claims on Cutler's estate. On 17 Feb. 1699 Radnor petitioned the Commons to order Boulter to waive his parliamentary privilege, stating that before the election he had promised to

> comply with the petitioner's demands; but being since chosen a Member of this House, he insists on his privilege; refusing to give it under his hand that he waives it, though he promised not to insist on privilege, before several witnesses.

After being referred to a committee on 20 Feb., the case was subsequently settled out of court and Radnor withdrew his petition on 18 Mar.[8]

Boulter was listed as a supporter of the Country party in an analysis of the new Parliament compiled about September 1698, forecast in October as likely to oppose a standing army and does not appear on the list naming those who voted against disbanding the army on 18 Jan. 1699. His name is found on a blacklist of Tories as having opposed preparations for war with France during the 1701 Parliament. Whether his age or the expectation of defeat influenced him, Boulter did not stand again. In his retirement he became more active in the Haberdashers' Company, frequently attending the meetings of the court of assistants, lending the Company £200 in 1707 and petitioning, though failing, to become clerk of the company in 1708. He was a benefactor to the poor, contributing £100 to the corporation for the poor of the city of London in 1702, and to the less agile riders of Lincolnshire, paying for the instalment of 'a great number of horsing-stones, each of three steps, inscribed E. B. 1708' on the road to Stamford. In 1703, he petitioned for and was granted the right to realize a large mortgage, previously owned by Cutler, on lands in Oxfordshire. Boulter died on 15 Feb. 1709. He left most of his property (estimated to be worth at least £150,000), which included extensive estates in Essex, Hampshire, Kent, Lincolnshire, London, Oxfordshire and Somerset, to be divided between his surviving brother, William, and three nephews.[9]

[1] Guildhall Lib. ms. 12017, p.25. [2] Soc. of Geneal. index of Berks. and Oxon. archdeaconry m. bonds and affidavits 1616–38, 1669–1710, i. unfol. bond, John Boulter and Susanna Cutler, 1633; Guildhall Lib. mss 15860/5, unfol.; Centre Kentish Stud. Stanhope mss U1590/059/2, Robert Yard to Alexander Stanhope, [Apr. 1693]; PCC 42 Coker. [3] Guildhall Lib. mss 15858/1, unfol; 15842/3, p. 142; 15842/4; Boston Corp. Minutes ed. Bailey, iv. 471. [4] Lincs. Past and Present, vii. 4–16; Guildhall Lib. ms 12017, pp. 8–11, 15, 17; 15860/5, unfol.; Municipal Chronicles of Abingdon ed. B. Challenor, 145; De Krey thesis, 536; CSP. Dom. 1665–6, p. 569; 1671, p. 565; 1680–1, pp. 382, 386; PCC 27 Hare; info. from Dr M. J. Knights; The Term Catalogues, 1668–1700 ed. E. Arber, i. 166. [5] Guildhall Lib. Cal. of Grocers' Co. Minutes, v. 915, 943; CSP. Dom. 1689–90, p. 502; 1694–5, p. 21; Luttrell, Brief Relation, iii. 343, 345. [6] Cal. Treas. Bks. ix. 1997; CJ, x. 724; PCC 42 Coker; Luttrell, iii. 81; HMC Ancaster, 433; Stanhope mss U1590/059/2, Yard to Stanhope, [Apr. 1693]; Harley mss at Brampton Bryan, bdle. 117, Robert Harley* to [–], 18, 25 Apr. 1693; Folger Shakespeare Lib. Newdigate newsletter 18 Apr. 1693. [7] HMC Lords, n.s. ii. 396–9, 406; 8 and 9 Gul. III, c. 27, sect. xix, xxii; Reasons Humbly Offered ... why the Bill ... Should Pass; without the Clause Proposed by Edmund Boulter... [8] Boston Corp. Minutes, 207, 314; The Case of Edmond Boulter, Esq; in Answer to the Petition of the Earl of Radnor. [9] Guildhall Lib. mss 12017, p. 25; 15842/4, pp. 83, 95 et seq.; E. Hatton, New View of London, 752–5; Thoresby Diary, ii. 13; CSP Dom. 1703–4, pp. 396, 455; Luttrell, vi. 408; PCC 1 Lane.

P. W./S. M. W.

BOUVERIE, Jacob des (1659–1722), of Allhallows, Barking, London and Terlingham, Kent.

HYTHE 1695–1700, 1713–1722

b. 1659, 3rd but 2nd surv. s. of Sir Edward des Bouverie, Mercer, Turkey and East India merchant, of Barking, London, and Cheshunt, Herts., by Anne, da. and coh. of Jacob de la Forterie, of London. unm.[1]

Commr. taking subscriptions to land bank 1696, S. Sea Co. 1711.[2]

Having fled religious persecution in Flanders, Bouverie's great-grandfather, a Huguenot, arrived in England in the 1560s and established himself at Canterbury. Bouverie's father moved to London and made his fortune as a merchant in the Levant and East India Companies. Although probably not one of the very richest merchants, he had sufficient wealth to pay £17,500 for lands in the hands of the Earl of Salisbury's trustees, lend £16,200 to the government in 1689–90 and, before his death, give his children some £24,000. Sir Edward has been identified by one historian as a Tory from his support for the Old East India Company and his election in 1690 to the Tory-dominated London common council. However, he was evidently acceptable to the Whig leadership, for in February 1694 he was appointed to the London lieutenancy at a time when many Tories were being purged. He died shortly afterwards in March, his estate being divided between his children, with Jacob des Bouverie inheriting half of the real estate (his elder brother William received the other moiety) and one-sixth of the personal estate. Two of Jacob's brothers, William and Christopher, were important Levant merchants, the former also serving as a director of the Bank of England and the latter as a director of the South Sea Company. Jacob himself was based in Aleppo in the 1680s as an agent for his father and other merchants.[3]

In 1695 Bouverie was elected as Member for Hythe with his brother-in-law Sir Philip Boteler, 3rd Bt.*, defeating the Whig William Brockman*. The previous year, Anne des Bouverie, having already brought Boteler a substantial portion, had also inherited a sixth of her father's personal estate, to be used by Boteler to buy land. Anne's marriage to Boteler was Bouverie's only link with Hythe at this time and it seems likely that Boteler influenced his election. In 1695 Bouverie was recorded as living in Barking, but in 1697 he bought the Dixwell estates in Kent, including the manor and hundred of Folkestone, whereby he became lord paramount of the hundred of Folkestone. This title carried with it certain local rights, the defence of which involved him in disputes with his neighbour, the lord of the manor of Cheriton, the same William Brockman he had defeated in election. In a further link with the Botelers, Bouverie charged his lands with an annuity of £300 for John Boteler* for life. Bouverie's position as a large landowner in Kent was recognized with his appointment as a deputy-lieutenant in December 1697 (a position he held until at least 1702) and as a justice in July 1700 until 1715. He was reappointed in 1716 and continued in office until his death in 1722.[4]

In the Commons Bouverie was forecast as likely to support the Court in the divisions on 31 Jan. 1696 on the proposed council of trade and was an early signatory of the Association. He continued this support for the government on 25 Nov. 1696 with a vote in favour of the attainder of Sir John Fenwick†. Bouverie was returned unopposed at the 1698 general election and in an analysis of the House in about September was queried as a possible Court supporter. However, he was then forecast as likely to oppose a standing army and was not listed as having voted against the disbanding bill on 18 Jan. 1699. An analysis of the House of early 1700 listed Bouverie as being in the Old East India Company 'interest', but although the Bouveries had in the past been closely associated with the Old Company, it is by no means clear that this was still the case. Bouverie's father and brother, William, were heavy investors in the Old Company and both had been assistants in the late 1680s and early 1690s. Bouverie himself had sold out his stock of £1,000 in 1698 and invested in the New East India Company. His last committee appointment for William's reign was on 13 Feb. 1700, to a drafting committee to prevent the sale in England of fish caught in foreign vessels, a matter of some significance in Kent. The committee was headed by his brother-in-law Boteler.[5]

Bouverie did not contest the January 1701 election, evidently making way for John Boteler. For much of Anne's reign Bouverie apparently retired to his estates and possibly continued with his merchant interests and investments. He had made a loan to the government in 1698 of £1,000, was a stockholder in the Bank of England in 1710 and by the end of his life held some £6,000 of stock in the South Sea Company.[6]

In contrast to his earlier career, Jacob des Bouverie's politics in the latter years of Anne's reign would appear to indicate Tory sympathies. Although he did not vote in the 1710 London poll, it is significant that he was appointed to the London lieutenancy commission of that year, when many Whigs were replaced by Tories. Moreover, Bouverie was elected for Hythe again in 1713, when he and John Boteler defeated William Brockman, and in the 1713 London poll he voted for all four Tory candidates. On 14 Apr. 1714 Bouverie was again involved in the issue of fish imports, being appointed to a drafting committee for a bill to prevent the import of fish by foreigners. The Worsley list identifies him as a Tory. Re-elected in 1715, he was described as a Tory on one list and as a Whig on another list of the 1713 and 1715 Parliaments. The Whig government also appears to have been uncertain as to his political views, dismissing him from the Kentish bench in July 1715, but reappointing him the following year. Thereafter he was apparently reconciled to the Whig government of George I, continuing as a Member for Hythe until his death.[7]

The changes in Bouverie's voting pattern and his classification in parliamentary lists from 1690 to 1722 would appear to indicate that he took a pragmatic view of politics. In 1698–9 he seems to have drifted away from his initial support for the Court. This may demonstrate a switch to the more Tory viewpoint which became apparent in 1710. However, his easy accommodation with the Hanoverian regime after 1716 implies that he held no strong ideological convictions. This is also suggested by the range of his investments, in companies which have been identified as being of various political inclinations, and it may also be significant that other members of his family seem to have taken an independent line in politics.[8]

Bouverie made his will on 7 June and died on 2 Sept. 1722, being described as 'an eminent London merchant'. He left most of his estate to his nephew Jacob, second son of Sir William des Bouverie. Jacob, created Viscount Folkestone in 1747, was Member for Salisbury, 1741–7, while his elder brother, Sir Edward des Bouverie, sat for Shaftesbury, 1719–34.[9]

[1]Hasted, *Kent*, viii. 152; Collins, *Peerage* (1812), v. 32; Add. 24120, f. 248; *Procs. Huguenot Soc. of London* xv. 49. [2]*CJ*, xii. 508; Pittis, *Present Parl.* 349. [3]Add. 24120, f. 248; *Procs. Huguenot Soc. of London* xv. 49; C9/281/48; C104/44, pts. i, ii; *Cal. Treas. Bks.* ix. 1972, 1977, 1981, 1985, 1988, 1989, 1995; PCC 45 Box; De Krey thesis, 460, 636; *CSP Dom.* 1694–5, p. 21; H. Horwitz, *Parl. and Pol. Wm. III.* 128;

Wood, *Life and Times*, iii. 448; *N. and Q.* clxxix. 59; J. Carswell, *S. Sea Bubble*, 277. [4]PCC 45 Box, 235 Marlbro'; *London Rec. Soc.* ii. 88; Hasted, 120, 136, 138-9, 149-50, 152, 164, 167, 181; Add. 42487, f. 123; 42588, ff. 66, 68; 70018, f. 104; Centre Kentish Stud. Pleydell-Bouverie mss, L19, L23-25; *CSP Dom.* 1697, p. 528; 1700-2, p. 251; 1702-3, p. 394; info. from Prof. N. Landau. [5]Add. 38871, unfol.; Bodl. Rawl. A.302, ff. 224-7. [6]*Cal. Treas. Bks.* xiv. 134; Egerton 3359, unfol.; PCC 235 Marlbro'. [7]*London Poll Book, 1710*; De Krey thesis, 482; *London Rec. Soc.* xvii. 82; info from Prof. N. Landau. [8]G. S. De Krey, *Fractured Soc.* 24-27, 141-4, 161, 242-3; De Krey thesis, 482. [9]PCC 235 Marlbro'; *Hist. Reg. Chron.* 1722, p. 41.

S. M. W.

BOWES, Sir William (1657–1707), of Streatlam Castle, co. Dur.

DURHAM CO. 1679 (Oct.)–1681 (Mar.)
              1695–1698
              1702–16 Jan. 1707

bap. 6 Jan. 1657, 4th but 1st surv. s. of Thomas Bowes of Streatlam Castle by Anne, da. and coh. of Anthony Maxton, BD, preb. of Durham and chaplain to Charles I. *educ.* Trinity Coll. Camb. 1672, MA 1675; G. Inn 1672. *m.* 17 Aug. 1691, Elizabeth (*d.* 1736), da. and h. of Sir Francis Blakiston, 3rd Bt., of Gibside, co. Dur., 4s. (1 *d.v.p.*) 4da. *suc.* fa. 1661; kntd. 13 Apr. 1684.[1]

Ranger, Teesdale forest and warden, Barnard forest 1685-9.[2]

Bowes's wealth and status in the north-east stemmed not only from his family's extensive estates but also from his involvement in Wearside's coal mining and metallurgical industries. He established a profile of modest loyalty under Charles II and in the early years of James II's reign, but had nevertheless been removed from the county Durham bench and militia by 1688, though no record survives of his answer to the three questions on the repeal of the Penal Laws and Test Acts. At the beginning of October 1688 the imminent landing of Prince William led to Bowes's being ordered to raise the Durham militia, the letter delivering this order also promising to restore him to his local offices, and though there is no further evidence of his attitude to the Revolution it is the case that, once raised, the Durham militia made no attempt to confront supporters of the Prince of Orange either upon their entry to Durham city or when they read a declaration in favour of free parliaments. Despite this apparent failure to support James during the Revolution, Bowes was removed in May 1689 from his post of ranger of Teesdale and in September that year was one of those who visited Lord Preston (Sir Richard Grahme[†]) in the Tower. Against this suggestion of Tory sympathies must be set the support Bowes received in 1695 from the Whig Christopher Vane* at the Durham county election, and it may be that the classification of Bowes as 'doubtful' in a forecast of the divisions of 31 Jan. 1696 upon the proposed council of trade stemmed as much from genuine confusion as to his partisan loyalties as from the uncertainty of classifying a recently elected Member. That Bowes was no extremist was indicated by his prompt signing of the Association, but the difficulty in classifying his political beliefs is made clear by his vote in March 1696 against the Court's proposal to fix the price of guineas at 22*s.* and his contrasting vote in the next session, on 25 Nov., for the attainder of Sir John Fenwick[†]. On 7 Jan. 1697 he was named to prepare a bill against 'unlawful weirs and dams, which take and destroy fish and the fry of fish', later presenting and reporting this measure, which was supported by a petition from Durham. The bill lapsed following the prorogation of April 1697, but in January 1698 Bowes introduced a bill for the preservation of the salmon fishery. He managed this measure until it was defeated on 9 Mar., shortly after which a cousin wrote that 'I am not only sorry, but the whole county is the same for the ill fate of your bill'. His only other significant activity in this session was to assist the passage of an estate bill, and on 15 Apr. he was granted an indefinite leave of absence.[3]

In March 1698 Bowes had been assured that his advocacy of the fishery bill 'has got you a good esteem in the county', but he did not stand in 1698 and was noted, in about September of that year, as having been a Country supporter. He devoted his energies towards his estate and other business affairs and declined standing at the first election of 1701, his cousin claiming that Bowes had 'neglected the best and fairest opportunity' to be elected. Such concern proved to be misplaced as Bowes was returned for Durham unopposed in 1702, but he remained an inconspicuous Member. His only significant contribution to the legislative business of the 1702 Parliament was to manage through the Commons a private bill, concerning an estate for which Lionel Vane* was a trustee, between January and February 1704. It has been suggested by a modern observer that during Queen Anne's reign Bowes should be listed among the Country Whigs. However, another modern historian's comment that 'little or nothing is known' of Bowes's political loyalties is more accurate, and what evidence there is does not create a clear picture of either Bowes's partisan loyalties or his attitude towards the ministry. That Bowes was not a Tory extremist can be seen from the forecast that he was a likely opponent of the Tack, and he either voted against this measure on 28 Nov. 1704 or was absent from the division. His opinion, recorded by

Bishop Nicolson in December that year, that 'had the Whigs been courtiers the Tack had been carried, because the Court could not have influenced so many High Churchmen', though perspicacious, reveals little of his own beliefs. More interestingly, Nicolson came away from this meeting assured that Bowes was 'a hearty well-wisher to the confederate union of the two kingdoms in succession and trade', an opinion incompatible with extreme Toryism and perhaps indicating Court and Whig sympathies. The former label would appear to be borne out by Bowes's actions following his unopposed election for Durham in 1705. Shortly after his election Bowes wrote to the Court Tory John Ellis* of his hope that 'we shall not differ (as sometimes we have done) in our votes', and, having been classed prior to the start of the 1705–6 session as 'Low Church', Bowes's support for the Court was apparently confirmed on 25 Oct. by his vote for the Court candidate for Speaker. Doubts as to Bowes's loyalty to the ministry, and the description of him as a Country supporter, stem from his absence from the list of those who supported the Court in February 1706 during the proceedings upon the place clause of the regency bill, but there is no indication if this was an act of conscience. Though Bowes's voting record is difficult to interpret, his recorded activity in the 1705–6 session reveals a clear concern for local interests, as January 1706 saw him appointed to draft bills for the better preservation of salmon (10th); to constitute the mayor of Newcastle-upon-Tyne governor of that borough's hospital for keelmen (16th); and to build a pier or piers at the mouth of the Wear (23rd). Having spent the summer of 1706 in the north-east, being foreman of the Durham grand jury which drew up a congratulatory address on Ramillies, by December Bowes had returned to London for the new session. On 16 Jan. 1707, however, he died. His body was returned to county Durham and on 7 Feb. he was buried at Barnard Castle.[4]

[1] Surtees, *Durham*, iv(1), p. 108. [2] *Cal. Treas. Bks.* viii. 260; ix. 102–3. [3] J. Nef, *Rise of Brit. Coal Industry*, i. 29; J. Hatcher, *Hist. of Brit. Coal. Industry*, i. 254; E. Hughes, *N. Country Life*, i. 63–64; Add. 40746, f. 137; 47047, f. 33; L. Gooch, *The Desperate Faction?* 8–10; V. L. Stater, *Noble Government*, 175; *CSP Dom.* 1689–90, p. 241; *CJ*, xi. 740. [4] Add. 47047, ff. 33, 41; 28884, f. 344; 28893, f. 137; 70221, Bp. Crewe to [Robert Harley*], 29 July 1706; G. Holmes, *Pol. in Age of Anne*, 222; *Party and Management* ed. Jones, 47, 80; *Nicolson Diaries* ed. Jones and Holmes, 261, 405.

E. C./R. D. H.

BOWYER, Anthony (1633–1709), of Camberwell Green, Surr. and the Inner Temple.

SOUTHWARK 1685–1687, 1690–1698

b. 4 Aug. 1633, 1st s. of Sir Edmund Bowyer† by his 1st w. Hester, da. of Sir Anthony Aucher† of Bishopsbourne, Kent. *educ.* Christ Church, Oxf. matric. 1651; I. Temple 1653, called 1661, bencher 1682, reader 1686, treasurer 1696–8. *m.* 14 Feb. 1673, Katherine, da. and h. of Henry St. John† of Beckenham, Kent, *s.p. suc.* fa. 1681.

Chairman, cttee. of elections and privileges 1694–5. Commr. Greenwich Hosp. 1695; gov. friendly soc. for widows 1696; cttee. charitable corp. 1707–*d*.

The Bowyer family was well established on the south bank of the Thames, having first settled in Camberwell in the mid-16th century. Bowyer's great-uncle, (Sir) Edmund†, had represented Southwark under Elizabeth, while Bowyer's father had wielded sufficient influence to become a Member for Surrey in the Cavalier Parliament. Although revealing a much closer attachment to Whig principles than his father, Bowyer was later acclaimed as a non-party figure, his epitaph citing him as 'generally esteemed in his lifetime and universally well-read, especially in the laws of his country, which gave him an equal aversion to tyranny and anarchy'. Despite his Whiggish leanings, Bowyer managed to secure an unopposed return to James II's Parliament, only to encounter a bitter reversal of fortune when finishing bottom of the poll at the election of 1689. This disappointment could be swiftly forgotten in the aftermath of his victory at Southwark in February 1690, when he was returned alongside the controversial Whig John Arnold*. In common with Arnold, Bowyer subsequently emerged as one of the most prominent Members in the campaign for moral reform, thereby displaying a crusading zeal which was reflected both in his work as a magistrate and through his generous local benefactions.[1]

At the outset of the 1690 Parliament Bowyer was identified by Lord Carmarthen (Sir Thomas Osborne†) as a Whig, and during the ensuing sessions he established himself as a most active Member. His metropolitan background was reflected in his close involvement in commercial issues, including appointment to the committee to prepare a bill to regulate the East India trade. He was also named to a drafting committee for the regulation of wines. Attentive to constituency affairs, he was nominated for a committee to draft a bill to improve the repair of highways and streets. In addition, he twice acted as a teller in the course of the session: on 13 May, in support of setting a seven-year limit to a bill to confirm the privileges of the Hudson's Bay Company; and three days later, to oppose the amendments made by the committee of the whole to a supply bill. In a matter of more obvious political significance, Bowyer had argued on 26 Apr. that the proposed abjuration oath was an indispensable safeguard during the King's absence. However, three days later, when the House discussed the potential threat posed by English Catholics, he seemed to adopt a more conciliatory stance by requesting clarification of the term, 'a reputed papist'.

Although there is no evidence to suggest a specific connexion with Ireland, Bowyer's anxiety over its future, particularly with regard to its Protestant communities, may have been increased by a visit to Ireland earlier in the year, an 'Anthony Bowyer' having been granted a pass on 7 Mar. to travel across the Irish Sea. Apart from appointment to committees on Irish issues, his other activity revolved around issues of more local significance, most notably his management of another bill to erect a court of conscience in Southwark. Selection for the committee to prepare a bill to regulate the King's Bench and Fleet prisons reflected his local magisterial responsibilities, and a concern for law and order was also suggested by a nomination to the drafting committee on a measure to secure the highways from robbers. He also sponsored a measure to incorporate the proprietors of the York Buildings waterworks in London. Although there could be little doubt concerning his metropolitan loyalties, his political allegiance was viewed with some suspicion by Robert Harley*, who, having initially listed Bowyer as a Country supporter in April 1691, later amended this assessment to 'doubtful'. Subsequent assessments of Bowyer's politics consistently bracketed him with the supporters of the Court, but his continued endorsement of reforming initiatives no doubt gave Court politicians grounds to suspect him.

The third session saw Bowyer pursue familiar interests, particularly a bill to improve the general standard of the highways, which he steered through the House. He also presented a measure to pave and clean the streets within the bills of mortality, was nominated to the drafting committee for a bill to explain the acts for the settlement of the poor, and chaired the committee of the whole on the London orphans bill (11 Feb. 1692). Such diligence did not deter him from more controversial issues. Focusing on Irish affairs, on 30 Nov. 1691 he successfully moved for provision to be made to enable Irish Quakers to signify their loyalty, thereby demonstrating his support for the Quaker affirmation championed by other moral reformers. His backing for electoral reform, a perennial Country cause, was also revealed when he was first-named to the committee on the bill to prevent false and double returns. He was also keen to voice his opinion over more politically charged matters of public finance. On 8 Jan. 1692 he spoke in favour of the bill to lessen interest rates, and 11 days later contributed to debate on a proposal to raise a 4s. poll tax. Although he may have shown some sympathy towards English Catholics in the first session, Bowyer revealed little compassion for the Irish rebels, opposing on 5 Feb. an attempt to omit from the Irish forfeitures bill a clause to enforce the surrender of remainders on entailed estates. Thereafter, the campaign to settle the debts owed to the London orphans absorbed most of his parliamentary energies, and on 18 Feb. he acted as a teller to block the reading of the Lords' bill for the orphans' relief. In a more factional guise, on 15 Feb. he had opposed a clause tacked to a poll tax bill which would have revived the bill of accounts. He subsequently played a prominent role in the House's examination of William Fuller, the spy languishing in King's Bench Prison. On 22 Feb. Bowyer reported to the House on Fuller's deteriorating health, and he was one of the Members subsequently ordered to take Fuller's information on oath. He reported back to the Commons the next day, on which occasion he suggested that Fuller was dying. However, his prognosis proved incorrect, and in the next session he was granted leave by the House to give evidence at Fuller's trial.

Bowyer's assiduity continued in the 1692–3 session, and included two appointments to drafting committees. On 18 Nov. he spoke against the second reading of a bill to prevent the sale of live cattle, his opposition rooted in a professional anxiety that its provisions 'altered the old ways of trial by jury'. In the following month he sought to block a bill from the Lords for halting abuses in the butter and cheese trade, although controversy over this commercial measure evidently rested with the decision of the Upper House to introduce a new levy with the bill. In the new year Bowyer twice acted as a teller: on 18 Jan. 1693, in support of a motion to introduce a private estate bill; and on 27 Jan., to agree with the resolution of the committee of the whole to levy a duty on the export of rabbit fur. In between these tellerships, he had attempted to block a motion to allow the Hamburg Company to export cloth to the Continent. There followed a series of important speeches from Bowyer, beginning on 28 Jan. when he rose to support the triennial bill, arguing that 'he thought long Parliaments very pernicious, and it was one of the articles of your bill of rights to have frequent Parliaments'. Expressing undoubted Country sympathies, he also sought to raise the issue of placemen, by observing, 'I have heard this present House said to be very well-officered, which I desire to prevent'. Given such political sentiments, it was no surprise that on 7 Feb. he spoke in favour of the clause which called for a Parliament to be held every year. In addition to these constitutional concerns, Bowyer remained closely involved in commercial matters, and spoke on 17 Feb. against the bill to encourage woollen manufacture, arguing that 'it would prejudice our navigation' by allowing foreign goods transported in English ships to evade import duties. He then acted as a teller on 20 Feb. in opposition to the revival of the Licensing Act, a stance which possibly reflected a lingering mistrust of the power of the executive. Moreover, three days later his concern for 'the security of the government' actually led him to support a motion to enable all Protestants to keep firearms. Similar anxiety over the Catholic threat probably lay behind his appointment on 24 Feb. to the committee to address the King over the mismanagement of Irish affairs. His final speech of the session, on 8 Mar., saw him take a predictably tough line over the disgraced commissioner for the Irish revenue, William Culliford, whose expulsion from the House Bowyer urged. Although evidently eager to expose governmental corruption, Bowyer was identified by Samuel Grascome soon after the end of the session as a supporter of the Court.[2]

At the beginning of the fifth session, constituency affairs again dominated Bowyer's concerns for, along with his fellow Southwark Member John Arnold, he was ordered on 28 Nov. to prepare a bill to answer the petition of poor prisoners held in King's Bench and the Fleet. Accordingly, he was subsequently the principal manager of the resultant measure to explain a recent Act to release poor prisoners. Magisterial interests to the fore once again, he was also closely involved with a bill concerning the registration of deeds. The new year saw Bowyer's parliamentary standing recognized by appointment to the chair of the committee of elections and privileges, his first report occurring on 18 Jan. Bowyer featured as a teller in four divisions: on 26 Feb., to block the engrossment of a bill to suppress hawkers and pedlars, a measure which he again tried to obstruct in a division on 31 Mar.; on 5 Apr., to reject a provision proposed for addition to a poll tax bill; and, finally, on 16 Apr., to counter a clause in a bill to encourage privateering against the French.

In the final session of the 1690 Parliament Bowyer sought to accelerate the campaign to regenerate the nation's morals, acting as the principal manager for a bill to suppress profane swearing. Moreover, his reforming zeal was suggested by appointments to drafting committees for bills to regulate the press, and to improve prisons. In the course of 1695 his reputation as a charitable benefactor was further enhanced by his selection as one of the commissioners for Greenwich Hospital. In the Commons itself, professional self-interest was the most likely cause of his close involvement in the House's debates over stamp duties, an association which led him to take the chair of the committee of the whole on that subject. He was subsequently one of the two Members ordered to prepare measures based on the committee's resolutions, and acted as the main sponsor of the resultant bill to explain the recent Stamp Act. His final recorded action in this Parliament occurred on 1 May when he was teller against a proposed amendment to a supply bill.

Although one report suggested that he might lose his seat to Sir George Meggot at the Southwark election of October 1695, Bowyer managed to maintain his place with some comfort, and later had the pleasure of seeing Meggot's petition against the return rejected by the House on 27 Dec. as 'vexatious, frivolous and groundless'. However, in the new Parliament Bowyer proved much less prominent, confining his activity in the first session to legal and electoral reform. In December he was named to the drafting committee to regulate proceedings in the courts of Equity, and the following month was one of only two MPs ordered to prepare a bill to prevent irregular proceedings by returning officers. His politics remained as consistent as his interests: he was cited as a likely supporter of the Court for the division over the proposed council of trade on 31 Jan. 1696, and voted in late March for fixing the price of guineas. He also found no difficulty in signing the Association.

However, prior to the next session Bowyer's reputation was threatened by allegations that the recent quartering of troops at Southwark had been obstructed by local magistrates. Fortunately for him, all the Southwark justices were acquitted 'with honour', and Bowyer subsequently proved his loyalty to the Court on 25 Nov. by voting in favour of the attainder of Sir John Fenwick[†]. Two days prior to that division Bowyer had maintained his reforming interests when acting as a teller to block the committal of a bill for the further regulation of elections. Before the session was over his good name had once again been tarnished by scandal, after an accusation was laid before the House on 28 Jan. 1697 that he had 'received a present to favour the prisons' in Parliament. This new charge, coming so soon after the controversy over the billeting of troops in Southwark, may well have been part of a deliberate campaign to discredit Bowyer, who had no doubt made many enemies in the course of his political and magisterial career. Whether co-ordinated or not, the attack was unsuccessful, for the House quickly voted the story 'false and scandalous', ordering the imprisonment of the accuser as well as the removal of the offending libel from the Journal. The only other significant duty Bowyer performed in the remainder of the 1695 Parliament concerned another personal crusade, reporting as he did on 6 Feb. from the committee on a bill for the relief and employment of the poor. By that time he had already established himself as one of the capital's leading philanthropists by becoming in November 1696 a founding governor of a fund to help poor widows.[3]

Having remained a largely anonymous figure in the final session of the 1695 Parliament, Bowyer decided not to stand at the Southwark election of July 1698, at which his seat was secured by the Whig brewer, John Cholmley*. Rumours subsequently circulated that a 'Bowyer' was likely to stand as a candidate at the Surrey election held a week later, but no member of the Camberwell family featured at that poll. Even though Bowyer was now out of the House, a parliamentary observer identified him soon afterwards as a Court supporter, thereby suggesting that his decision to retire was not motivated by political differences. A preference for local affairs, particularly charitable projects, provides a more likely explanation, especially since in April 1699 he confessed that he was 'so little an inquirer after news'. In his absence, his half-brother Edmund sought to emulate his success by standing for Southwark at the election of November 1701, but the challenge was easily rebuffed by the sitting Whig Members.[4]

Away from Westminster Bowyer found many avenues through which to channel his reforming energies. From the turn of the century he used the Surrey quarter sessions to prosecute immorality and profaneness, showing particular thoroughness with regard to Southwark and Rotherhithe. He also featured as one of the earliest subscribers to the SPCK, and in May 1701 was reported to have been willing to donate an annual £20 or £25 to fund local charity schools. The charitable corporation for the relief of poor debtors later became another favourite scheme, and Bowyer did not neglect to follow his ancestors' example by proving a generous patron to the poor of his native Camberwell. His will also bore witness to his concern for the care of the sick, prescribing that in the event of a complete failure of his line, the Bowyer estate was to go to Greenwich Hospital 'if there be any seamen actually in it', and, if it were empty, to St. Thomas' Hospital, Southwark. His epitaph, raised by his wife, did not fail to pay tribute to his generous nature, boasting that 'he did justice, showed mercy and was a friend to the poor'. After Bowyer's death on 28 June 1709, a pamphleteer was moved to publish a funeral oration in Bowyer's honour, taking the opportunity to launch a bitter attack on prevailing immorality and High Church zealotry. This broadside also left a convincing portrait of the high-mindedness of the deceased justice:

> severe in virtue and upright in mind,
> and so made fit to regulate mankind;
> he first reformed himself and then the state,
> a pattern for the modern magistrate.

Although the family mansions stood for over a century as lasting reminders of Bowyer's extensive influence in Camberwell and its environs, none of his successors achieved his prominence either locally or nationally.[5]

[1] Manning and Bray, *Surr.* iii. 406, 408–9; IGI, London; J. Aubrey, *Surr.* i. 181; *Surr. Arch. Colls.* iii. 220–6. [2] Bodl. Rawl. A.79, ff. 84–85, 89; *CSP Dom.* 1689–90, p. 499; *Luttrell Diary*, 50, 117, 141, 156, 172, 187, 201, 235, 320, 374, 391, 407, 430, 444, 471. [3] *Evelyn Diary*, v. 211; Add. 70070, newsletter 29 Oct. 1695; Luttrell, *Brief Relation*, iii. 565; iv. 120, 175; *Friendly Soc. for Widows* (1696). [4] Northants. RO, Isham mss IC1590, John Isham to Sir Justinian Isham, 4th Bt.*, 2 Aug. 1698; Som. RO, Sanford mss DD/SF/1093(6), Bowyer to Edward Clarke*, 5 Apr. 1699. [5] Surr. RO (Kingston), QS2/1/8, pp. 234, 271; QS2/1/9, pp. 53, 69; *Chapter in Eng. Church Hist.* ed. McClure, 3, 6, 7, 125, 131, 135; *Sel. Charters*, 257; Manning and Bray, 448; PCC 48 Smith; Aubrey, 181; *Funeral Satyr in Memory of ... the Late Mr Anthony Bowyer ... by a Friend of Dr Sacheverell's Club* (1709), p. 5; D. Allport, *Colls. of ... Camberwell*, 68–72.

P. L. G.

BOYLE, Hon. Charles I (1660–1704).

APPLEBY 1690–12 Oct. 1694

b. 30 Oct. 1660, 2nd but 1st surv. s. of Charles Boyle†, Baron Clifford of Lanesborough, Yorks. (2nd s. *d.v.p.* of Richard Boyle†, 2nd Earl of Cork [I] and 1st Earl of Burlington) by his 1st w. Lady Jane Seymour, da. of William Seymour†, 2nd Duke of Somerset; bro. of Hon. Henry Boyle*. *educ.* travelled abroad 1683–6. *m.* 26 Jan. 1688, Juliana (d. 1750), lady of the bedchamber to Queen Anne, da. and h. of Hon. Henry Noel† of North Luffenham, Rutland, 1s. 6da. (2 *d.v.p.*). *suc.* fa. as Visct. Dungarvan [I] and Baron Clifford of Lanesborough 12 Oct. 1694; *gdfa.* as 3rd Earl of Cork [I] and 2nd Earl of Burlington 15 Jan. 1698.[1]

Gov. co. Cork 1691; ld. lt. Yorks. (W. Riding) 1699–d.; v.-adm. Yorks. 1701–d.

Ld. treasurer [I] 1695–d.; gent. of the bedchamber 1697–1702; commr. union with Scotland 1702.[2]

PC [I] 1695–d.; PC 8 Jan. 1702.[3]

There was little in his character to distinguish Boyle from the other sparkish young aristocrats of his acquaintance. His pedigree was his greatest asset, obtaining for him a succession of honorific (and occasionally remunerative) appointments, and inducing in the minds of some unreflecting commentators the

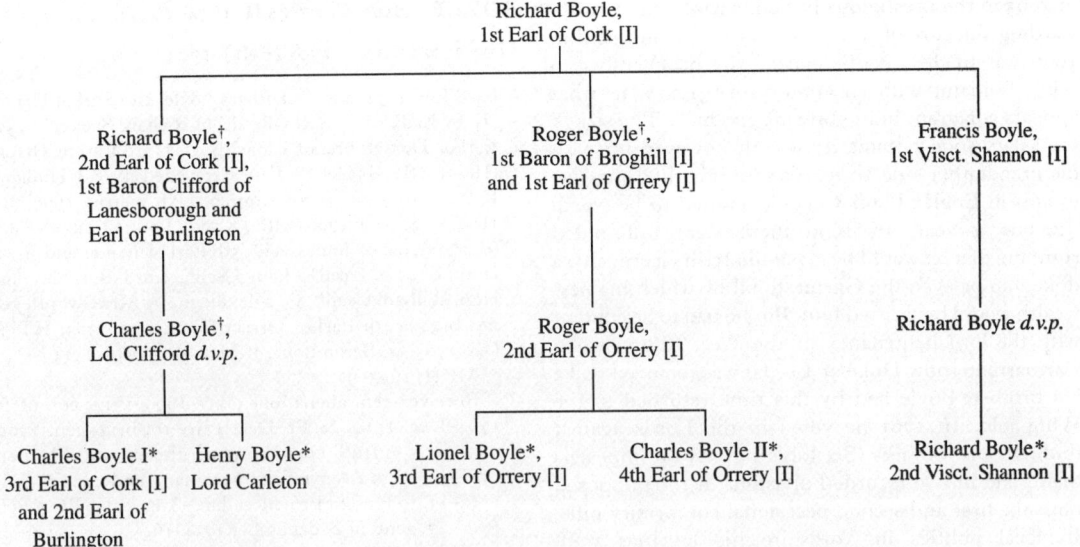

Note: This is not a full pedigree, nor are children necessarily shown in correct order of precedence by age.

THE BOYLE FAMILY

conventional opinion that he was 'one of the hopefullest young gentlemen in England'. In fact, his most famous exploit was probably his unsuccessful attempt in 1696 to seduce the actress Anne Bracegirdle, which for a time was something of a *cause célèbre* among the coffee-house wits.[4]

Boyle was returned for Appleby in 1690, almost certainly on the interest of Lord Thanet (Thomas Tufton[†]), to whom he was connected through the marriage of his aunt to Thanet's deceased elder brother, the 3rd Earl. Lord Carmarthen (Sir Thomas Osborne[†]), a fellow Yorkshireman, classed him as a Whig in an analysis of the new Parliament in March 1690, probably in reference to the moderate Whig sympathies of his father, Lord Clifford, and during the following winter considered him a potential recruit to the ranks of the Court managers in the Commons. He was 'to be spoken to by Lord Ranelagh [Richard Jones*]' but, Carmarthen noted, 'he is governed by Sir Thomas Lee [1st Bt.*]'. However, in Robert Harley's* list of April 1691 he appeared as a supporter of the Country party. His political associations were certainly Whiggish, and he may, like his brother Henry, have cultivated a pose of independence. In 1692 he stood bail for the Earl of Marlborough (John Churchill[†]), alongside his father's former mentor Lord Halifax (Sir George Savile[†]) and the Earl of Shrewsbury. Once his brother was returned to the House, on 21 Nov., it becomes impossible, on all but exceptional occasions, to separate out their parliamentary activity. Boyle appears under his full name in the Journals on 25 Feb. 1693 when he reported from the committee on a private bill on behalf of his great-uncle Francis, Lord Shannon. Narcissus Luttrell* noted that he was a teller on 7 Feb. 1693 in committee on the triennial bill against a Court amendment 'that nothing in the Act should extend to take away the King's prerogative to dissolve any Parliament sooner than three years'. However, in Grascome's list, compiled later that year, he was included on the Court side.[5]

After he succeeded to his father's titles in October 1694, Boyle seems to have become increasingly conscious of his own importance. He attended the Irish house of lords while in Dublin in 1695 and cherished pretensions to the highest offices in the Castle administration, so that failure to secure what he considered his due may explain his vote at Westminster in 1696 against the attainder of Sir John Fenwick[†]. In general during this Parliament he joined his brother Henry in opposition to the Whig ministry. He exhibited passive sympathy for the causes espoused by Irish 'patriots', and did what he could to help his friends Lords Coningsby (Thomas*) and Romney (Henry Sidney[†]) to obtain legislative confirmation in Ireland of their grants from the Irish forfeitures, against the intrigues of the Irish Court Whig faction linked to the Junto and led by the brothers Alan[†] and Thomas Brodrick*. He had already been permitted to succeed his grandfather in 1695 in the prestigious but otherwise largely unrewarding sinecure of lord treasurer of Ireland, and in 1697 was made a gentleman of the bedchamber to King William, with an annuity of £1,000, in what appears a flagrant bid to buy his goodwill. The size of the salary soon became irrelevant, however, for with his grandfather's death in 1698 he inherited massive estates in England and Ireland, reputed to be worth £22,000 a year. In 1699 there were unfounded rumours that he would be given the Irish viceroyalty, a dukedom or even the Garter, to all of which his new wealth would have fitted him. But he had to be content with the lord lieutenancy of the West Riding when Carmarthen (now Duke of Leeds) was removed. Like his brother, Boyle had by this time returned to the Whig fold. In 1701 he voted in the Lords against finding Lord Somers (Sir John*) guilty on impeachment, and in two recorded divisions in 1703 opposed both the first and second occasional conformity bills. In local politics in Yorkshire his loyalties were staunchly Whiggish. But his health was now failing, and after a brief illness he died at his house in Chiswick, Middlesex, on 9 Feb. 1704. As far as posterity was concerned, this relatively early death may not have been unfortunate, for he had already contracted such debts as would necessitate the subsequent disposal of entailed property (freed by Act of Parliament). According to one commentator, 'the sense of what he had done struck him so severely for the great wrong he had done his family, that he could not die in peace before he had obtained their pardon'. However, his only son could still inherit intact the bulk of the vast family estates, which financed his own later development into a celebrated virtuoso: collector, patron and even amateur architect, to whom the revival of Palladianism in England was principally due.[6]

[1] Devonshire mss at Chatsworth House, Lismore pprs. box 28, Countess of Cork's jnl. (*ex. inf.* Dr T. C. Barnard); Thoresby, *Ducatus Leodiensis*, i. 63; Lodge, *Peerage of Ire.* (1754), i. 100. [2] *Liber Munerum Publicorum Hiberniae* ed. Lascelles, ii. 42. [3] A. B. Beaven's list of Irish PCs, Hist. of Parl. [4] Wood, *Life and Times*, iii. 470; *Poems on Affairs of State* ed. Ellis, v. 370. [5] A. Browning, *Danby*, iii. 179; PRO NI, De Ros mss D638/13/162, John Pulteney* to Ld. Coningsby, 16 June 1692; H. C. Foxcroft, *Halifax*, ii. 152–3; *Luttrell Diary*, 408. [6] *CSP Dom.* 1696, p. 204; 1698, p. 36; 1699–1700, p. 137; H. Horwitz, *Parl. and Pol. Wm. III*, 336; Trinity, Dublin, Lyons (King) mss 1999/547, 557, Boyle to Abp. King, 30 Oct., 23 Nov. 1697; King letterbks. 750/1, pp. 138–40, King to Boyle, 4 Dec. 1697; *Cal. Treas. Bks.* xiii. 332; Luttrell, iv. 562, 573, 672; Browning, i. 548; G. Holmes, *Pol. in Age of Anne*, 426; *HMC Var.* viii. 85; *HMC Portland*, iii. 623; Nat. Lib. Ire., ms 6146; *HMC Lords*, n.s. vi. 289; Grosvenor mss at Eaton Hall, pprs. of 4th Bt.†, 'misc. pprs.', Sir Richard Grosvenor, 4th Bt.†, to Peter Shakerley*, 5 June 1705.

D. W. H.

BOYLE, Hon. Charles II (1674–1731).

HUNTINGDON 1701 (Feb.)–1705

b. 28 July 1674, 2nd s. of Roger Boyle, 2nd Earl of Orrery [I], by Lady Mary Sackville, da. of Richard Sackville†, 5th Earl of Dorset; bro. of Lionel Boyle*, 3rd Earl of Orrery [I]. *educ.* Sevenoaks; St. Paul's; travelled abroad (Holland, France) 1685–6; Christ Church, Oxf. matric. 1690, BA 1694. *m.* 30 Mar. 1706 (with £4,000), Lady Elizabeth Cecil (*d.* 1708), da. of John Cecil†, 5th Earl of Exeter and sis. of Hon. Charles Cecil*, John Cecil*, Lord Burghley and Hon. William Cecil*, 1s. 2 da. illegit. by Mrs Swordfeger. *suc.* bro. as 4th Earl of Orrery [I] 24 Aug. 1703; KT 30 Oct. 1705; *cr.* Baron Boyle of Marston 5 Sept. 1711.[1]

MP [I] 1695–9.

Receiver-gen. alienations office 1699–1717; col. of ft. 1704–Dec. 1710, 21 Ft. Dec. 1710–16; brig.-gen. 1709, maj.-gen. 1710; envoy extraordinary to Flanders 1711–July 1712, envoy extraordinary and plenip. July 1712–13, to United Provinces Jan.–Aug. 1711; PC 9 Feb. 1711–27; gent. of bedchamber 1714–16.[2]

FRS 1706.

Ld. lt. and custos rot. Som. Nov. 1714–15.

The beau ideal of 'politeness', Boyle embodied the new concept of civic virtue promoted by Augustan social philosophers, many of whom were his friends. He combined sophistication in his personal taste with distinction in the performance of his public duty, his talents enabling him to shine as a scholar and wit, soldier, diplomat and politician. However, he exhibited the weaknesses as well as the strengths of 'polite' culture. A prey to vanity and affectation, his brilliance was often merely superficial, his character itself essentially brittle, and his lasting achievements few.

In part at least, Boyle's powerful, and sometimes consuming, ambition may have derived from his early experience as a talented, yet relatively underprivileged, younger son, to whom the praise lavished by his tutors and the recognition afforded by the great were still inadequate compensation for his inferior position within his own family. Moreover, when eventually he was fortunate enough to succeed his elder brother it was to a depleted inheritance, though far from insubstantial in other men's eyes, with extensive property in Ireland and in Somerset, but no longer the mighty estate over which his grandfather had lorded. The great mansion at Charleville, county Cork, had been destroyed by Jacobite troops during the Irish wars, and the Cork estate as a whole, managed for the absentee earls in these years of economic depression by local agents of uncertain probity, yielded far less than the £4,000 nominal valuation of the rent-roll. To a nobleman with Boyle's *amour-propre*, and love of display, these were straitened circumstances.[3]

After a childhood spent in his elder brother's shadow, Boyle came into his own as an Oxford undergraduate. His father had envisaged for him, and had begun to provide, 'a pious and virtuous education, the objects of which are to fit a man to serve God, his king and his country', but at Christ Church his mentors were rather more worldly. Pre-eminent were his tutor, Francis Atterbury, under whom he studied not only classical authors but such moderns as Descartes and Locke, pronouncing the latter's *Essay Concerning Human Understanding* to contain 'a great deal of very good sense'; and the dean, Henry Aldrich, who 'conceived a particular esteem for him' and indeed nurtured him as 'the great ornament of our college'. Boyle evidently worked hard, and unlike his brother remained, as he said, 'firm' in his 'notions of morality', but his bent was literary rather than philosophical. Already by 1693 he had published translations of Plutarch and Lysander, and in that year was selected by Aldrich, as the college's star pupil, to prepare the edition which would, according to custom, be distributed to members as a Christmas gift and subsequently be offered for publication. The text chosen was the *Epistles* of 'Phalaris', of which Boyle produced a polished if undemanding version, skirting the knotty problems of authorship and authenticity. In passing he indulged his sarcasm in a jibe at the royal librarian, the formidable Dr Bentley, who had withheld from him access to a manuscript in the King's library, 'pro singulari sua humanitate' as Boyle put it in his preface. Stung by this insult from an undergraduate, Bentley turned his mind to the *Epistles* and produced a dissertation showing them to be spurious. Thus began a controversy which was to tarnish Boyle's golden reputation. A witty and effective riposte, published in his name, seemed at first to have carried the day, until it became known that this was not Boyle's work at all but had been produced by a team of Christ Church men, headed by Atterbury, who had been mobilized by Aldrich to vindicate the honour of the college. And in due course Bentley thundered out his second reply, a complete demolition of the case, which had been endorsed in Boyle's name, for the existence of 'Phalaris'. In the meantime the young man himself had left Oxford for a grander stage. He had written to Atterbury in 1693 that he viewed the alternatives proposed by his mother of remaining at Christ Church or removing to Ireland as equally unattractive. Instead, he intended to follow the King abroad:

> I am not obstinate (he protested) nor fond of being a soldier, nor by going to Flanders do I design to be one, but only to put myself in some way of getting bread . . . my pretensions are wholly at court . . . and not in the army, if I can make my way anywhere else.

Nothing would suit him better than a place as groom of the bedchamber. Unfortunately, the only post his connexions were able to find for him was a minor sinecure in Chancery. Deprived of the opportunity to glitter at Court, he pursued literary ambitions. Verses, epigrams and even a play, the comedy *As You Find It*, found their way into print, as he exchanged the tutelage of Atterbury for that of Dryden, to whose coffee-house circle he now belonged. There was some self-gratification in all this, but Boyle was also lampooned as 'a fine scholar sunk in wit', and his decision to publish a tragedy his grandfather had written proved another blunder. Lady Mary Wortley Montagu's devastating dismissal of his literary pretensions, though prompted by personal dislike and family animosities, reflected an opinion that was beginning to gain ground. Boyle had, she said,

> begun the world by giving his name to a treatise wrote by Atterbury and his club, which gained him great reputation, but (like Sir Martin Mar-all, who would fumble with his lute when the music was over) he published soon after a sad comedy of his own, and, what was worse, a dismal tragedy he had found among the first Earl of Orrery's papers. People could [more] easily forgive his being partial to his own silly works (as a common frailty) than the want of judgment in producing a piece that dishonoured his [grand]father's memory. Thus fell into dust a fame that had made a blaze by borrowed fire.[4]

A seat in the Commons formed a natural progression in such a career, and Boyle was duly put up at Huntingdon in the January 1701 general election on the Sandwich interest, as managed for the time being by the High Tory Lady Sandwich, a distant connexion of his by marriage. Besides being a party battle, the election contest was also a manifestation of a rancorous family dispute, for Lady Sandwich had determined to oppose what she saw as the baleful (and Whiggish) influence over her weak-minded husband of his uncle, Hon. Sidney Wortley Montagu*, patron of Boyle's opponents in the constituency. After some violence at the polls Boyle and one of the two Whig candidates were returned. The defeated Whig, John Pedley*, then petitioned, among other things accusing Lord Sandwich (though without naming him) of improper interference in an election. In Boyle's papers there survived a copy of a speech in defence of his own conduct and that of the unnamed peer, though whether it was ever delivered is far from certain. Having alleged that the petition was 'a shot that was particularly aimed at another', the speech observed that 'the violence of it comes from one that originally had no interest in the borough, but what he had from the very same place that I have mine, and, I doubt, has no interest in it now, but what he has from a much worse case'. Such comments were calculated to offend and led almost inevitably to a duel in which Boyle suffered serious wounds at the hand of Sidney Wortley Montagu and was *hors de combat* for several months. He was luckier in the outcome of the election case, however, where the petition was rejected. Because of his injuries he seems to have made less of an impact on proceedings in the Commons than might have been expected in view of the reputation that preceded him, though it must be said that his parliamentary activity, as reported in the Journals, is generally indistinguishable from that of his cousin, Hon. Henry Boyle*. He may have made an intervention in debate, for a draft of a speech in defence of his old university friend Christopher Codrington's governorship of the Leeward Islands was found in the manuscripts available to Boyle's biographer. After he had been returned again for Huntingdon in November 1701, this time unopposed, he was listed by Robert Harley* as a Tory, and indeed voted on 26 Feb. 1702 in favour of the motion vindicating the proceedings of the Commons in the impeachments of William's Whig ministers. In his third and last Parliament his succession to the earldom of Orrery makes him more readily identifiable in the Journals. By the 1704–5 session he had been drawn in to support the Court, by the gift of a colonelcy of foot. Forecast as an opponent of the Tack, he duly voted against it or was absent on 28 Nov. 1704. He was classed as a placeman in a list of the Commons the following year. His opposition to the Tack may have lost him Lady Sandwich's good opinion. Alternatively her influence over her husband may have failed, or Orrery himself simply grown tired of the House of Commons. Whatever the reason, he did not stand for re-election in 1705.[5]

For a time, Orrery seems to have applied his talents to the pursuit of martial honour; and, indeed, at the battle of Malplaquet he acquitted himself well. He was also pursuing patrons: first the Duke of Ormond, his commander-in-chief on the Irish establishment; then Marlborough, who helped him to a brigadier's commission; and finally Argyll, whose part he took against Marlborough in the great quarrel which began in the winter of 1709–10. It was through Argyll that Orrery was brought into the political intrigues of Robert Harley, and during 1710 he acted as an intermediary between Harley and Argyll. The responsibility nourished his self-esteem, so that in November 1710 he was moved to present his own list of terms to the new chief minister. His present post at the Treasury was, he believed, insufficient for a man of his abilities. Command of the yeomen of the guard would be an adequate promotion; he could also change his regiment from infantry to cavalry; and he would be pleased to be made a Privy Councillor. Probably as much to appease Argyll as to gratify his own vanity, he received promotion to major-general, was sworn of the Privy Council, and the following spring was sent on a prolonged diplomatic mission into Flanders. Despite his animosity towards Marlborough, the envoy's appointment was a good one. Orrery's peculiar qualities made him an ideal choice for any posting where polished and witty conversation was required rather more than an urgent attention to business. In both Brussels and The Hague he left a favourable impression of elegance and extravagance. When it became clear to him, however, that he had reached the limit of his advancement, he became resentful. Matters were not helped by Harley's failure to cover his (undoubtedly excessive) expenses. By the autumn of 1712 he had vowed not to go abroad again unless raised to ambassadorial dignity. The English barony he had been granted in 1711 was a forgotten obligation, and the loyal, if mute, supporter of the ministry in the House of Lords had become a 'whimsical'. He may even have enlisted in Lord Bolingbroke's (Henry St. John II*) 'combination' against Harley: the two had been close friends, and Orrery had been one of Bolingbroke's first choices for the dining-club, the 'Society of Brothers', he had established in 1711. But not even the friendship of two such 'philosophers' was proof against worldly disappointment, and by the autumn of 1713 Orrery was complaining of 'coldness and neglect' from Bolingbroke as well as Harley, and was turning instead to the Hanoverian court. Alongside Argyll, he was counted one of the Hanoverians' 'friends' in the Lords in the 1714 Parliament, spurning approaches from Harley and reassuring the Hanoverian resident of his fidelity. For this he was rewarded by George I, though perhaps not as amply as he thought he deserved: he retained his regiment and Exchequer sinecure, was admitted a lord of the bedchamber and appointed lord lieutenant of Somerset. In common with other 'Hanoverian' Tories the period of his honeymoon with the new dynasty lasted little more than two years, however, and in 1716–17, in the wake of Argyll's fall, he was dismissed from all his offices, though not as yet from the Privy Council.[6]

In the last phase of Orrery's career he emerged as a political figure in his own right, as patrons and mentors dropped away. Argyll, with whom he remained on good terms, was unable or unwilling to assist him when he returned to power in 1719. Halifax (Charles Montagu*), his other friend among the leading Whigs in 1714, had died. With Robert Harley (now Lord Oxford) he re-established cordial relations, yet still tinged with suspicion. Bolingbroke and Atterbury were more intimate friends, but he had outgrown pupillage of any kind. Guided by his own lights, he turned eventually to the Jacobite option, after the failure of the 'Leicester House' party. Contact was made by a Jacobite agent in the summer of 1717, with Orrery expected once again to act as a go-between with the Duke of Argyll. He gave several professions of goodwill, and for several years maintained a regular, though infrequent, correspondence with the exiled court, in which his principal themes were the impossibility of effecting anything of substance without the assistance of large numbers of foreign troops, and the equal necessity of the Pretender's taking steps to 'give satisfaction' about his religion. So notorious did his caution become in Jacobite circles that he was given the cant-name 'Jeremiah' in some secret correspondence. Partly at his own request and partly for tactical reasons he was kept ignorant of the crucial details of 'projects' prior to 1720, when he appears to have taken a more active role in Jacobite conspiracy, perhaps because like other Jacobites he saw in the ministry's difficulties a priceless opportunity, or perhaps because after Argyll's return to office, the ending of the Whig Schism and the reconciliation between the King and Prince of Wales, few other political avenues were open to him. There is some evidence that he was still 'visiting' the Prince in 1721, though without much hope. He was prevailed upon by the Pretender to travel to Paris in the summer of 1720, in order to join in persuading the Regent of the value of endorsing the Jacobite cause, but once again his 'excessive' caution got the better of him and he failed to raise the subject during his interview, to the chagrin, not to say disgust, of James's ministers. During the following winter and spring he continued to emphasize the need for foreign aid to effect any Jacobite restoration, and undertook negotiations with Lord Sunderland (Charles, Lord Spencer*) which came to nothing. Whether, like other leading Jacobites in England, he abandoned his belief in the impossibility of a purely domestic rising is unclear: for a spell money took the place of external assistance as the *sine qua non* of his strategy. What is certain is that he was not a party to the 'Atterbury Plot', though he was informed of its existence. He regarded it as at best a 'rash' attempt, suggesting instead that the money raised be spent on elections, to secure an 'honest' House of Commons and effect a restoration in a parliamentary way. Later he devised an alternative plan of his own, requiring 'patience' and French help. When news of the 'plot' broke, his comments were scathing: 'I hope your friends will take warning', he told the Pretender,

and not only go upon projects with a better foundation than this had which is now defeated, and which I told you, Sir, was very unlikely ever to succeed but will act in all respects with more caution than any have hitherto done. I believe now most of those forward people of whose characters as well as designs I dare say, Sir, you now think I gave you a pretty true account not long ago are convinced themselves that their scheme had not a solid foundation . . . The government now are put so much upon their guard that even the scheme that I sent you from myself cannot go on in all its parts but I think it may be reduced and made more plain and simple.

Subsequently he let it be known that he had indeed amended his alternative scheme, and requested commissions for himself as lieutenant-general and an unnamed friend to be a brigadier, with further commissions to come in due course. Meanwhile he advised the Pretender to concentrate on raising finance, and was himself entrusted with organizing the collection of funds from sympathizers in the city of London. It was this responsibility, and its attendant documentation, that made him vulnerable to ministerial accusations of complicity in the plot, based originally upon the dubious testimony of the Jacobite agents Layer and Plunkett, with whom Orrery or his secretary had had some dealings. Thus, although he had carefully kept apart from Bishop Atterbury, Lord North and the other 'forward' conspirators, who regarded him as 'a timorous fellow . . . always making difficulties, and schemes, out of his own brain', he was arrested and confined for six months in the Tower. His cousin Henry (now Lord Carleton) and Argyll were prepared, if need be, to 'form an interest in the House of Lords to save him' but eventually the ministry (warned of the danger to his health from continued imprisonment) were obliged to let him go for want of evidence. On his release he returned to the campaign of opposition in the Upper House in which he had for several years been a prominent figure. He also resumed his correspondence with the Pretender. Indeed he was now James's only correspondent of note in England, having taken over the direction of his affairs there. Not surprisingly, however, in view of recent experience, he was once again the 'excessively cautious' Orrery of old. Without a large force of regular troops from abroad, he opined, no rebellion would be feasible. 'People of reflection and fortunes will hardly venture their lives and estates unless they see they have some tolerable chance to succeed'. In a letter of 1727 he was more precise: at least 20,000 soldiers would be required for an invasion. Thus while he remained in regular contact with the Pretender, and was prepared on occasion to travel to France to give tentative assistance to renewed efforts at enlisting French help for a restoration, he was essentially a broken reed. Not even the unpleasant sensation of being struck off the Privy Council by George II could reinvigorate him, and this after he had gone to Court on the King's accession. Indeed he subsequently took a pension from the ministry, which according to Walpole he 'well earned'.[7]

Orrery died at his house in Downing Street, Whitehall, on 28 Aug. 1731, and was buried in Westminster Abbey. He had asked for 'a decent, not a costly, monument, with a proper inscription in Latin, describing my just character and behaviour, both in public and private, without any exaggeration or fulsome panegyric'. Despite his undoubted gifts, his lengthy public career and literary accomplishments, especially in the field of rendering classical texts, to which he returned late in his life with less renown but greater seriousness than in the days of the 'Phalaris' controversy, it may be fitting that he is commemorated in the name of an astronomical instrument invented, and dedicated to him, by someone else.[8]

[1] Lodge, *Peerage of Ire.* (1754), i. 294–5; Centre Kentish Stud. Sackville mss U269/A10/3; *Cal. Orrery Pprs.* ed. McLysaght (Irish Mss Commn.), 313–14; info. from L. B. Smith, jnr. [2] Luttrell, *Brief Relation*, iv. 580; *Cal. Treas. Bks.* xxxi. 417. [3] *Cal. Orrery Pprs.* 197; *Swift Corresp.* ed. Williams, iii. 475; iv. 91–92; [T. Prior], *A List of the Absentees of Ire.* . . . (1730), 2. [4] *Cal. Orrery Pprs.* 182; E. Budgell, *Mems. of Earl of Orrery and Boyle Fam.* (1732), 156–97; *Atterbury Epistolary Corresp.* ii. 1–23, 33; *Poems on Affairs of State* ed. Ellis, vi. 108, 136, 142; vii. 198; G. V. Bennett, *Tory Crisis*, 31–32, 38–43; *Hist. Oxf. Univ.* ed. Sutherland and Mitchell, v. 526; *Swift Works* ed. Davis, i. 5, 139; *Addison Letters*, 1; *Lady Mary Wortley Montagu Letters* ed. Halsband, iii. 58–59. [5] 7th Duke of Manchester, *Court and Soc. Eliz. to Anne*, ii. 85; *VCH Hunts.* ii. 35–36; Budgell, 198–208; Luttrell, v. 33. [6] Lodge, 295; Budgell, 209–10; *HMC Ormonde*, n.s. viii. 180; *Marlborough–Godolphin Corresp.* ed. Snyder, iii. 1288–9, 1301; *HMC Portland*, iv. 537–8, 544, 548, 553, 600, 605, 626, 635; v. 56, 100, 145, 216, 232–3, 348–9, 368–9, 467; G. Holmes, *Trial of Sacheverell*, 227; P. W. J. Riley, *Eng. Ministers and Scotland*, 147–8; *Cam. Misc.* xxvi. 148–9; Add. 37209, ff. 158–9, 179–80; *HMC 10th Rep. I*, 145–6; *Bolingbroke Corresp.* i. 35–36, 121, 169, 216, 246–7, 408; iii. 491–2; iv. 84, 157, 288–9; *Reasons which Induced Her Majesty to Create the Rt. Hon. Charles, Earl of Orrery, and James, Duke of Hamilton, Peers of Gt. Brit.* . . . (1711), 3; *Ailesbury Mems.* ii. 627–8, 645; *Swift Stella* ed. Davis, i. 99; ii. 423; G. Holmes, *Pols. in Age of Anne*, 426; Macpherson, *Orig. Pprs.* ii. 546; H. Horwitz, *2nd Earl of Nottingham*, 242. [7] Budgell, 212–16; Stowe 242, f. 194; *HMC Stuart*, iii. 290; iii. 259–60, 553–4; v. 122, 305–6, 336–7, 446–7, 456–8; vi. 137, 165–6, 260, 287; vii. 181–2, 261, 538, 626, 647; RA, Stuart mss 45/59; 46/93, 118, 128, 150; 47/35, 106; 48/17, 19, 23, 27, 71–72, 81, 107, 109; 49/4, 40; 51/53; 52/61, 100, 105; 53/13, 49, 87, 145; 54/77; 55/67; 57/111, 135; 58/127; 59/15, 55, 143; 60/127, 129–30; 63/33; 70/46, 107; 71/137; 100/45; *Rep. from the Cttee.* . . . *to Examine Christopher Layer* . . . (1722), 2–4, 13, 19, 22–23, 31–32; *Rep. from the Lords Cttees.* . . . *to Examine Christopher Layer* . . . (1723), 11, 13; Add. 62558, f. 26; Bennett, 225–9, 231, 233, 254, 260, 264; P. S. Fritz, *Ministers and Jacobitism 1715–45*, 69–70, 73, 77–78, 121, 126–7, 134–5; *Jacobite Challenge* ed. Cruickshanks and Black, 92, 94, 103–4; C. B. Realey, *Early Opposition to Walpole*, 82–83, 123; J. H. Glover, *Stuart Pprs.* i. 266, 276, 280, 321–2; ii. 59, 90; *Atterbury Epistolary Corresp.* v. 348; L. Colley, *In Defiance of Oligarchy*, 37, 63, 209; *The Commons 1715–54*, i. 67. [8] Countess of Cork and Orrery, *Orrery Pprs.* i. 99; Lodge, 296; Harvard Univ. Lib. Orrery mss 218/7.

D. W. H.

BOYLE, Hon. Henry (1669–1725), of Carleton House, Pall Mall, Westminster.

TAMWORTH	8 May 1689–1690
CAMBRIDGE UNIVERSITY	21 Nov. 1692–1705
WESTMINSTER	1705–1710

b. 12 July 1669, 3rd but 2nd surv. s. of Hon. Charles Boyle[†], Baron Clifford of Lanesborough, Yorks. by his 1st w.; bro. of Hon. Charles Boyle I*. *educ.* Westminster; travelled abroad 1685–8; Padua Univ. 1685; Trinity Coll. Camb. 1692, MA 1693, DCL 1720. *unm. cr.* Baron Carleton 19 Oct. 1714.[1]

Cornet, Queen's Horse (later 1 Drag. Gds.) 1685–Nov. 1688; cornet and maj. 2 Life Gds. by 1691–2; ld. of Treasury 1699–1702; keeper, royal garden at St. James's Palace 1701; chancellor of the Exchequer 1701–Apr. 1708; PC 27 Mar. 1701; ld. treasurer [I] 1704–15; commr. union with Scotland 1706, Trade and Plantations 1707; sec. of state (north) Feb. 1708–10; PC [I] Sept. 1714–?; ld. pres. 1721–*d.*[2]

MP [I] 1692–3; chairman cttee. supply Oct. 1692–?Nov. 1692.

Chairman cttee. of privileges and elections 1694–5, ways and means Mar. 1702, 1707; commr. public accts. 1695–7.

Ld. lt. and custos rot. Yorks. (W. Riding) 1704–15; v.-adm. Yorks. 1704–15.

Commr. Q. Anne's bounty 1704; trustee, Dr Busby's charity.[3]

A fine representative of a family which had been remarkable even among the Anglo-Irish planter aristocracy for talent, ambition and acquisitiveness, but which by the end of the 17th century was beginning to subside into pretentious complacency, 'Harry' Boyle was in many respects the perfect courtier to a parliamentary monarchy. The atmosphere of Whitehall and Westminster was his element. Urbane and raffish, he achieved equal popularity in the closet and in Parliament, and although his unfailing prudence and unruffled superiority irritated some satirists the public reputation he left among his contemporaries was largely without stain. His weakness was his tendency to self-indulgence, which in politics could manifest itself in an aversion to infighting and preference for well-remunerated ease, once such an alternative had become attainable. Early in his career, however, this failing was not apparent, since despite a 'substantial legacy' from his grandmother he was still obliged, as a younger son, to work to make his way.⁴

Boyle's multifarious connexions provided him with a quiverful of influential patrons. One of his aunts had married the Earl of Rochester (Laurence Hyde†), and prior to the Revolution Boyle occupied a privileged place in the Hyde circle. He may have owed his original military commission at least in part to Rochester's avuncular concern for his career, and in November 1688 he deserted to the Prince of Orange in company with Rochester's nephew by marriage, Prince George, and son-in-law, the Duke of Ormond, and his own brother-in-law, the Earl of Drumlanrig. After the Revolution he remained on good terms with the Hydes, who appear not to have greatly resented Boyle's alleged cuckolding of his cousin Lord Hyde (Henry*), but in politics he henceforth adopted his father's moderate Whiggery rather than Rochester's High Tory principles. He was returned to the Convention for Tamworth, a borough his father had represented in the Cavalier Parliament, and where the family still possessed some interest, exercised in conjunction with that of Lord Weymouth (Thomas Thynne†). Little is heard of Boyle during this first spell in the Commons, apart from the fact that at the dissolution he was blacklisted with the supporters of the disabling clause in the corporations bill, a distinction which may have hampered his efforts to secure re-election in 1690. Despite Weymouth's continued backing he was inhibited from contesting Tamworth again. Rochester was also involved in attempts to find an alternative seat, but did not prove particularly helpful. Boyle therefore looked elsewhere for assistance. He first took up a commission in Ormond's guards regiment; then, in the summer of 1692, evidently in some desperation, agreed to settle in Ireland and take over the management of his grandfather Lord Burlington's immense estate in counties Cork and Waterford. Burlington reassured his local agents that the young man was 'of a very excellent capacity and very apt to comprehend business as soon as he has been a little versed in it'. Elected to the Irish parliament, Boyle was, despite his inexperience, 'unanimously' voted into the chair of supply and apparently 'behaved himself . . . as if he had been at it ever since he was born . . . and nobody could have kept us to better order nor have managed the chair better than he did'. To his grandfather's disappointment, Boyle was soon rescued from the prospect of an extended Hibernian exile by news of a vacancy in the parliamentary representation of Cambridge University, of which his cousin the Duke of Somerset was chancellor. Hastily admitted to Trinity College, under the tutelage of Somerset's chaplain, Boyle was put up on Somerset's recommendation, the Duke actually serving as returning officer in the (probably diplomatic) absence of vice-chancellor George Oxenden*. Burlington protested that such a sudden change of plan was 'positively against my advice and directions' but could not dissuade his grandson from the course on which his heart was set.⁵

This time Boyle quickly made his mark in the House. Generally it is impossible to distinguish Boyle's parliamentary activity from that of his brother, Hon. Charles I, but it is probable that he was the 'Mr Boyle' who told on 29 Nov. 1692, just eight days after his election, against a Court-inspired motion that the committee of supply resume the following day, for his earliest recorded speech took place on 3 Dec., against another Court motion in the committee of supply to put the question on the total estimate for land forces. Because of his electoral dependence on Somerset it is fair to assume that he was the Boyle who managed the bill to settle various advowsons, including that of Petworth, Somerset's seat, through the House in January. Narcissus Luttrell* noted a 'Mr Boyle' offering a clause at the report of the mutiny bill on 11 Feb., 'against soldiers carrying their wives and children with them and quartering them upon the people', which would have been consistent with Henry's evident 'Country' stance, if somewhat disloyal to former comrades, and likewise speaking on 14 Feb. in favour of the public accounts bill at its second reading, 'because it gives satisfaction to the nation'. In the debate of 22 Feb. 1693 on the allegations of misgovernment in Ireland, Boyle disingenuously exploited his claim to specialist knowledge of, and particular concern for, a country to which he had only recently declined to remove:

if there have been miscarriages in Ireland (which I think few doubt of), now you are upon inquiring about them, unless you do something to prevent them you will but confirm them. I have spoke with gentlemen, and if what they tell me be true you will need neither an invasion nor a rebellion but the people will leave that kingdom – they are used so ill.

Later in the debate, however, when a motion was proposed for an address to recall the Irish parliament, Boyle 'was against it, for that he heard it was intended the parliament should sit very shortly' and moved instead for an adjournment of the debate to the 24th. On that day he tacked about again, joining prominent 'Country party' men in requesting an address that the King 'will be pleased to call' an Irish parliament, and being named to the drafting committee. Lastly in this session, on 27 Feb. 1693 he both spoke and probably told against the indemnity bill, which 'Country' Members had opposed because it provided for a suspension of habeas corpus. By now Boyle was already a well-known figure in the House, a noted 'Country' speaker and on intimate terms with leaders of all shades of opinion, from the Court Whig Hon. Charles Montagu*, whom he 'seduced . . . to keep the [summer] holidays at Epsom', to the 'Country' stalwart Robert Harley*, with whom he had quickly and shrewdly established a close friendship despite their striking differences of personality.[6]

After a brief visit to Ireland in the autumn of 1693 to make contact with the new lord justice Lord Capell (Hon. Sir Henry Capel*), probably with a view to involving himself in Irish politics and government in some capacity, Boyle was in attendance at the Commons by 22 Nov., when he contributed to the debate on the miscarriages of the fleet and was appointed to the committee to examine the merchants' petition on naval mismanagements. He was almost certainly the Boyle who told on the Country side on 28 Nov. against the passage of the triennial bill, after the failure to add a rider to secure frequent sessions, and who on 6 Dec. joined the Tory John Granville in telling against a motion blaming the admirals for the failures of the fleet in the last campaign. On 7 Dec. 'Mr Boyle' supported the motion to commit Lord Falkland (Anthony Carey*) to the Tower for alleged corruption: 'you have all the suspicion and ground to suspect something in the matter', he declared, and was a teller in favour. There were 11 other tellerships in this session ascribed to a Boyle, all in support of the Country party position and most of them on fiscal questions: on 20 Dec., in favour of a resolution of the committee of supply; 23 Dec., against an adjournment motion; 17 Jan. 1694 in two divisions on the land tax bill; 18 Jan., again on the land tax bill, against a clause offered at the report stage; 22 Jan., at the bill's third reading, against an amendment leaving out the clause to appoint cruising ships; 17 Feb., on another adjournment motion; 22 Feb., for John Cooke* in the Arundel election; 28 Feb., against the first resolution of ways and means, for collecting further money in addition to a land tax; 16 Mar., on a motion to adjourn the debate on the salt duty bill; and finally on 14 Apr., to adjourn debate on the bill for the incorporation of the Bank of England. It would seem reasonable to attribute most if not all to Henry Boyle. In the case of other parliamentary activity the ascription can sometimes be confirmed from other sources. We know that it was Henry rather than Charles who was assisted in the management of a bill concerning Irish forfeited estates, and given that Boyle was involved in the following session in promoting a treason trials bill, it seems reasonable to infer that he was the chairman of the committee of the whole in February 1694 on its predecessor, and similarly his later service as an accounts commissioner suggests that he may well have chaired the whole House committee on the accounts bill in April. That Henry was by far the more active parliamentarian is reinforced by the observation that Charles's resignation of his Commons seat in October 1694, on succeeding to his father's barony, made no appreciable difference to the frequency with which the name Boyle appeared in the Journals.[7]

Boyle's growing stature in the House is evident from his election to the chair of the committee of privileges and elections during the session of 1694–5. He had firmly identified himself with the 'Country' opposition to the emerging Whig ministry, and in particular had developed his close association with Robert Harley and Paul Foley I*, with whom, and with the Tory John Granville, he frequently acted. In addition to telling alongside Granville on 13 Dec. 1694, against a Court amendment to the triennial bill, Boyle managed the renewed treason trials bill through all its stages in the Commons. Other 'Country' causes in which he was involved were the place bill, telling on 26 Jan. 1695 in favour of an amendment, and the renewal of the accounts commission: having chaired and reported from the committee of the whole on the accounts bill (20, 21 Mar.), he was himself chosen a commissioner, reaching third place in the ballot. He was also appointed on 2 Apr. to the drafting committee for a clause in the mutiny bill to prevent army officers from extorting bribes from innkeepers to excuse them from quartering, a typical 'Country' grievance against the military. Particularly active on fiscal matters, he was a teller on 19 Jan., on a procedural motion concerning the petition of some City merchants against the Bank of England; on 13 Feb., against a leather tax; and on 12 Apr., in favour of going into a committee of the whole for supply. Together with Robert Harley he told on 6 Feb. for a qualifying amendment to a motion vindicating the Lancashire Plot trials, to declare there had been 'sufficient grounds' for the prosecutions only 'before the falsity of the witnesses was detected'. Significantly, when Paul Foley was elected as Speaker on 14 Mar., in place of Sir John Trevor, Boyle assisted Granville in conducting him to the Chair. He was included by Henry Guy in a list of 'friends' in connexion with the investigation by the Commons of Guy for corruption, and the remainder of Boyle's significant parliamentary activity in this session in fact related to inquiries into corruption, and being named to three committees in April concerning Sir Thomas Cooke's* alleged bribery by the Old East India Company, and on 27 Apr. to the committee to prepare articles of impeachment against the Duke of Leeds (Sir Thomas Osborne[†]). That he had become such a thorn in the Court's side probably accounts for the failure of Lord Capell's recommendation of him at this time for a seat on the Irish Privy Council. Capell was informed in May 1695 by the Duke of Shrewsbury, the secretary of state, that his list of new Councillors had been approved with one exception: 'the King defers doing it for Mr Boyle, he being lately made one of the commissioners for public accounts, and so not likely to go into Ireland this summer'.[8]

After a more difficult, three-cornered, contest at Cambridge University in the 1695 general election, in which Somerset's recommendation needed to be supplemented by some solicitation of college heads on Boyle's own part, he was returned to the Commons, to some disappointment, however, when as a result of a compromise between Speaker Foley and the ministerial Whigs Boyle was passed over for the chair of privileges and elections in favour of a courtier. In a limited display of resentment he pointedly absented himself from the committee's first meeting, but he was too self-disciplined to over-indulge his anger. Besides, other distinctions offered themselves in compensation. He reported from committees appointed to manage conferences with the Lords on the proceedings of the Scottish parliament on the East India trade (14, 16 Dec. 1695) and on the recoinage (11 Jan. 1696), and chaired the committee of the whole on the East India bill (4 Apr.), and on 5 Feb. was re-elected in third place (behind Harley and Foley) in the ballot for accounts commissioners. Forecast as likely to vote against the Court in the divisions of 31 Jan. 1696 on the proposed council of trade, Boyle was reported as speaking in the debate on that day against the resolution that MPs would not be eligible to sit on the council. He was teller on 15 Jan., on the opposition side on a motion to adjourn consideration of the coinage bill, on 17 Jan. in favour of the Lords' amendments to the treason trials bill, and again on 15 Feb. in a division on the recoinage issue, in favour of a resolution from the committee on the value of guineas to set a maximum of 28s., being listed among those who opposed ministerial proposals to fix the price at 22s in March. His other tellership on a question relating to financial and economic matters reflected not only his 'Country' allegiance but his position as a university representative. On 27 Jan. he told against a committee amendment to the land tax bill, concerning universities and hospitals. Constituency interests were again to the fore on 15 Feb., when he told in favour of an additional clause to the bill imposing a landed qualification on voters in parliamentary elections, a measure he had himself helped to draft, to exempt the two universities. It may have been in part this awareness of the need to nurse his reputation among the Cambridge colleges, as well as among Tories on the opposition benches, that led him into the occasional offence against Whig prejudices, as over the Quakers' affirmation bill, which he told against on 13 Mar., or the Association. He felt no qualms himself on taking the Association, being an early signatory, but was ready to oppose any attempt to exploit Tory scruples by making subscription a qualification for continued membership of the Commons, telling on 7 Apr. against a clause to this effect in the bill for the security of the King's person.[9]

Prior to the next session Boyle spent some time with the Hydes in Oxfordshire, enduring what were for him the privations of country life in return for the political dividends to be obtained from renewing his connexion with Rochester, and probably also the personal pleasures to be drawn from Lady Hyde's society. But he kept in regular correspondence with Robert Harley, remarking in one letter that he would be 'sorry to stay in the country till you wanted my assistance in town'. Indeed, as Parliament resumed he seemed politically inseparable from Harley. When Lord Somers (Sir John*) and the other leading ministers grew anxious of the possible parliamentary repercussions of the accusations contained in Sir John Fenwick's[†] confession, it was Boyle, along with Foley and Harley, whom they approached in order to head off difficulties. While Foley was willing to give assurances, Boyle followed Harley in treading more carefully. James Vernon I, deputed to undertake the negotiations, reported on 6 Nov. 1696 to the Duke of Shrewsbury (whose good name had been jeopardized by the confession) that he had spoken to Harley and Boyle,

> but I might as well have let them both alone; they were very well in their answers to me, but neither of them showed anything of it in the debate. Perhaps they thought it sufficient to be silent ... Mr Boyle would have made some kind of excuse to me, that he saw the business go on slowly, and nobody said anything that needed an answer, but Mr Howe's [John Grobham*] petulancy might have furnished occasion if he thought fit.

Four days later, in another debate on the bill, Harley took the opportunity to condemn Fenwick for 'falsely accusing persons of the greatest merit', but Boyle still remained silent. Eventually, on 17 Nov., he did 'make his compliments to the persons concerned' in Fenwick's examination, and Vernon was soon reporting that both Harley and Boyle were 'professing great respect' for Shrewsbury. As to the bill of attainder itself, Boyle consistently spoke and voted against it. At first he confined himself to procedural points, but in the debate on the committal he spoke out. For once a victim of nerves, so much so that he apologized for 'rambling' in his argument because of 'the awe I have upon me from this assembly', he was extremely careful to distinguish opposition to the bill from sympathy for its subject. The plot he regarded as heinous, and 'as to Sir John Fenwick, I know him not; as to his cause, I am sure I am against it; but how far I think him guilty or not, is not the single point to be considered'. Rather, the main issue was whether it could ever be right to condemn anyone to death for treason on the testimony of a single witness, a principle he had upheld before and which he now amplified with examples from the history of classical Rome and Renaissance Italy. He did, however, go so far as to question the danger allegedly presented by Fenwick himself to the King and to the state. Though 'a great offender', Sir John had not been accused of plotting William's assassination. Fenwick was 'foolish' rather than dangerous: 'when he walked about town, I never heard he was feared or regarded at that time'. And Boyle refuted the ministerial claim that to reject the bill would be to imperil the security of the realm:

> I hope, in this debate, gentlemen will be very cautious of using it as an argument, what application our votes shall have without doors, and with those we represent, when we are to give judgment . . . for the life and death of a man . . . the eagerness that is justifiable upon impeachments, may not look so well now we are judges upon a bill of attainder.

In the crucial division on the third reading of the bill, on 25 Nov. 1696, he gave his vote against. Later in the session, however, on 7 Jan. 1697, he was teller, with a Court Whig and against two Tories, in favour of passing the bill of attainder against those who had been involved in the Assassination Plot and had fled the country, and for retaining others in custody. This may have been an attempt to re-establish his credibility as an upholder of the Revolution settlement, or it may be the first sign of the shift in his politics that was to occur during the following year. At the outset of the session he had been as vigorous as ever in harrying the ministry and in the pursuit of 'Country' policies. In a debate on supply on 19 Nov. he had gone out of his way to attack the Court Whig Rose Club, calling them 'the lords of the articles' and had warned 'people not to receive questions that were brought them ready prepared'. Then on 3 Dec. he told in favour of engrossing the bill to regulate elections, a characteristic Country party obsession. It may be significant, however, that in this session he began to be markedly less active than before, and less closely involved with controversial questions. His one other tellership occurred on 25 Feb. 1697, against a Lords' amendment to the bill to restrain the wearing of East India cloths. The privileged position he occupied in the House is evident from the decision taken at the Rose Club in December 1696 to oppose the re-election of all the accounts commissioners 'except Mr Boyle', a decision subsequently reversed, but none the less significant. At the ballot in the following February, when the entire ministerial slate was adopted, Boyle was still in third position among the Country candidates, this time behind Robert Harley and Sir Christopher Musgrave, 4th Bt.* But the ministry may have begun to court him: rumours were rife in April 1697 that he would be included in the new commission of lords justices in Ireland. Such an appointment might have served two purposes. It could have won Boyle over to administration, or at least removed him from Westminster; and in Ireland it would have pacified those otherwise well-disposed political figures who resented the monopoly over power and patronage that the Junto's allies, Alan† and Thomas Brodrick*, had carved out for themselves. As one Irish 'Country Whig' noted, there was a 'universally great opinion' of Boyle's 'ability and integrity'. That nothing came of the speculation may testify to the strength of the Brodricks in resisting the appointment, or to Boyle's own unwillingness to leave the centre of affairs.[10]

It was the winter of 1697–8 which witnessed Boyle's crossing over from Country to Court, but while the timing of his *volte-face* can be established fairly precisely, its mainspring remains elusive. One historian has noted the coincidence of Boyle's change of direction with the death of his grandfather, Burlington, in January 1698, but there seems to be no logical connexion between the two events. Burlington had never exercised much influence over his grandson (witness the events of 1692) and the inheritance of £4,000 p.a. which Boyle drew from the Earl's estate should have disposed him towards independence rather than enlistment in the Court party. Conceivably the disparity between his legacy and the £22,000 p.a. inherited by his brother may have inspired him with envy. The evidence, however, suggests that Boyle had been preparing to abandon the Country interest for some time. Some curious meetings in the autumn of 1697 before Parliament reassembled, in which Boyle and his brother participated, together with Lord Rochester and the ministerialists Lord Coningsby (Thomas*) and Ranelagh (Richard Jones*), hint at an exploring of possibilities. When Parliament met, Boyle was at first as resolute an opponent of the Court as before. On 7 Dec. 1697 he seconded Robert Harley's motion that the House go into committee to consider the King's speech in general rather than only the supply in particular. But after the Christmas recess he appeared in support of the ministry on the controversial issue of the standing army, backing a Court party motion in the committee on the King's speech on 8 Jan. for an instruction to the committee of supply to consider in their provision for the military establishment the amount required for 'guards and garrisons', which would have had the effect of increasing the size of forces agreed by a previous vote. Nothing would give more encouragement to the French to invade, he claimed, than to see England deprived of the means to defend itself. The Dutch agent, L'Hermitage, who reported this speech, noted that it was the first time Boyle had spoken openly in support of the ministry. Country propagandists had already got wind of his transmogrification, however. A particularly vicious lampoon, which has been dated to December 1697, referred to him as 'our politician Boyle, that fawning arse-worm with his cringing smile', and, anticipating events somewhat, declared that he had 'grown an apostate' for 'sugar plums'. After a brief leave of absence granted on 22 Jan. 1698 to attend his grandfather's funeral, Boyle made another significant intervention on the Court side on 16 Feb., coming to the defence of Charles Montagu when the grant to Montagu's agent Thomas Railton was being attacked: Boyle spoke on Montagu's behalf and told against a motion made during the debate that Montagu should withdraw while the subject was being discussed. Not all his speeches were politically sensitive, however. His last recorded contribution in this Parliament was on the land tax bill but on an administrative issue, as he responded to the solicitations of a determined loyalist to oppose a clause in the bill which would have obliged the commissioners to 'pay as gentlemen'.[11]

The unfavourable publicity Boyle had suffered as a result of his turn towards the Court made it more important than ever that he should enjoy Somerset's express support at Cambridge in the general election of 1698, where there were two other strong candidates, including the young Tory Anthony Hammond*. Somerset duly obliged, with a personal recommendation of Boyle, 'my friend and relation', and he was returned comfortably, heading the poll by a wide margin. In a comparative analysis of the old and new Houses of Commons he was classed as a Court supporter, and indeed there was talk in September that he 'stood fair' to succeed to a likely vacancy on the Treasury commission. Not everyone in the Country party was convinced, however, that he was utterly lost to them. The ever-diplomatic Robert Harley despatched a pre-sessional letter of customary cordiality, which assumed that he and Boyle would continue to vote on the same side in the forthcoming Parliament, and the compiler of a forecast of the probable opposition to a standing army optimistically included Boyle in his list. Boyle's first experience of the political limelight in this Parliament came on 10 Jan. 1699, when he was elected to the chair of the committee of the whole on the state of the navy, a vehicle for the wide-ranging inquiries Harley and Paul Foley meant to launch into the administration of the first lord of the Admiralty, Lord Orford (Edward Russell*). Boyle may have been chosen for the chair as a compromise candidate acceptable to both Country and Court, but he eventually showed his colours, telling on 27 Mar. against a Country amendment to the committee's report, which would have urged a change in the personnel responsible for the management of naval affairs. In the meantime he had already made several interventions in debate in support of the ministerial position: on 18 Jan., against the disbanding bill, which he was then blacklisted for opposing; on 3 Feb., against John Grobham Howe's proposed amendment to the address of thanks for the King's speech giving his assent to the same bill, which would have denounced those criticizing the bill to the King; and on 16 Feb., in the committee of supply, on the naval estimates. He was also a teller on 6 Apr. on the Whig side against a motion to receive the committee report on the Corfe Castle election. Towards the end of the session, on 26 Apr., he told against the Court on a clause offered to the paper duty bill. This was a constituency matter, however, his fellow teller being the Oxonian Simon Harcourt I*, and shortly afterwards one university man was writing to another with tidings of 'our clause', which had allegedly been drawn up by Boyle and 'solicited' by Harcourt. In any case, Boyle was soon to receive his reward. Late in May the Prussian resident reported his appointment as a Treasury lord, remarking that he was still a young man but was none the less a person of merit and presently attached to the Court party. He was thus advanced to the front rank of Court spokesmen in the Commons, and with the handsome salary of £8,000 a year.[12]

Boyle was now a familiar figure at the pre-sessional gatherings of the Court Whig grandees. In August he joined Charles Montagu, the Duke of Shrewsbury and others at Boughton, possibly travelling on to Winchendon; then in September he visited Lord Chancellor Somers at Tunbridge Wells, before journeying on to pay his respects to Somerset at Petworth. Possibly it was this extensive high-political socializing that gave rise to reports at the time that he would be raised to the Irish peerage. He was certainly an asset to the ministry, both in his official capacity at the Treasury board, where Charles Montagu's retirement resulted in the weight of business falling on Boyle's shoulders, and in Parliament, where on 5 Dec. he was one of the principal Court spokesmen in a pre-concerted move to oppose Country party attempts to censure the patent granted to Captain Kidd's backers. Listed as having his own interest in the House in early 1700, he was again to the fore on 18 Jan., when he supported James Vernon's amendment to the Irish forfeitures resumption bill, to reserve a third to the King's own disposal, on 26 Jan. telling for the Court Whig James Sloane in the Thetford election dispute, and on 13 Feb., when he both spoke and told against an opposition motion to condemn the procurement of crown grants by ministers. He was also a teller on 18 Apr. against the motion for an address to request Somers' dismissal. Not surprisingly perhaps, during the following summer he was once more being touted as a possible Irish lord justice.[13]

Ever alert to changes in the political wind, Boyle was quick to renew contacts with the incoming Tory ministry when it finally became clear that the King could no longer retain the Junto in office, and in July 1700 he dined with Henry Guy*, Robert Harley and Lord Keeper Wright, a gathering which may have been called with some ulterior motive. His position in 1701 as a Whig member of a preponderantly Tory administration was a delicate one, the more so after he was advanced to the chancellorship of the Exchequer in April 1701 to fill a vacancy left by the resignation of another Court Whig. In these circumstances he chose to pursue a course of loyalty to the interests of the King, while being ready to defend former ministerial colleagues when their conduct in office came under censure. On 12 Feb. 1701, in a debate on the Address, he joined the then chancellor of the Exchequer, John Smith I*, in urging a form of words which would pledge the Commons to assist in measures to maintain the peace of Europe. He had now been joined in the House by his cousin, Hon. Charles Boyle II, and their parliamentary activity is usually difficult to distinguish. As chancellor, on 2 May Boyle spoke and then told on the 5th against a 'Country' motion, in ways and means, for leave to appropriate £100,000 from the civil list for the payment of the public debts. On 9 May during the debate on helping the Dutch, Boyle reportedly said that 'the fate of Europe was at stake, that we should resolve to maintain the balance of Europe and send the Dutch our men and ships according to the treaty'. During a further debate on ways and means, on 20 May, opposing a move to tack to a supply bill a clause preventing customs commissioners from sitting in the House, he 'said the hard passage the last tack [of the Irish forfeitures resumption bill of 1700] had and the unwillingness the Lords showed to it should in these times of danger show [u]s the inconveniency of pressing it', at which Sir John Bolles, 4th Bt.*, an outspoken Country Tory, 'told Boyle he was altered by being a lord of the Treasury and chancellor of the Exchequer. Boyle said jestingly he thanked that gent[leman] for his advice'. He had earlier spoken against the place clause in the bill of settlement at its report stage on 10 May. His defence of the Junto ministers had probably begun on 28 Mar., when Boyle told against another motion to condemn the grant to Captain Kidd's patentees. On 15 Apr., after the impeachments of Lord Somers and the three other Whig lords had been carried to the Upper House, the Tories moved for an address to the King to remove all four from his Council and presence for ever, to which Boyle answered that it 'was regular nor precedented that, now they were impeached, which was no more than accused, to put [a] censure upon them, which would be part of the sentence if they were found guilty'. The motion passed, however, and on 13 May Boyle both spoke and told against a second address for a reply from the King to the House's demand. Later, he made a strong speech in defence of Somers, when, on 16 May, the former chancellor's impeachment was debated. On the question of Somers' having accepted grants while in office, Boyle

> said this was never reckoned a fault before and that the Lord Southampton . . . had great grants and it was never esteemed a fault in him and that, considering the great post this lord was in and taken from it and made a lord, he could not think but there ought to be some recompense made him from the public, and that what he had done both in passing of grants and in taking of grants to himself was always practised, as it did appear to him, and that honourable gent[leman], meaning Seymour [Sir Edward, 4th Bt.*] had done the same thing.

Finally, on 4 June, at the report of the committee nominated to inspect precedents for the proceedings between the two Houses on the impeachments, he thanked Speaker Harley (Robert) for his remark that the Commons had gone 'out of the way' in not requesting a conference, amplifying Harley's observation and ending with a motion of his own 'for a conference'.[14]

Although remaining on close terms with Robert Harley, Boyle was still classed with the Whigs in

Harley's list of the second Parliament of 1701. On 21 Feb. he moved to forestall a Tory plan to pursue the question of the Irish land settlement by proposing instead that the House receive the report from the chairman of ways and means. After William III's death Boyle adapted quickly to the new political scene brought about by the change of monarch. The necessity of doing so was borne in upon him when the Tories turned him out of the chair of supply and ways and means, which he had briefly occupied in March 1702 in the temporary absence of the incumbent chairman, John Conyers*. On 9 Mar. he had defeated a Tory in an election to the vacant chair in ways and means, having himself been proposed and seconded by two Whigs and with 'hardly a negative' given against him. But two days later, in supply, the Tories opposed his continuance and successfully put up his quondam political comrade John Granville against him, who carried the vote on a division. Boyle, however, held the chair of the committee of the whole on the land tax bill, which would normally have gone with the chairmanship of supply and ways and means, on the procedural technicality that he had 'had it before'. Then on the 13th, the House divided on whether Granville should take the chair of supply, and carried the question by 25 votes. Boyle's response to this snub was a sharp *volte-face*. On 20 Mar., in a debate on the civil list bill, he followed Sir Edward Seymour in speaking to a motion, put forward by a Country Whig, 'to provide that what we . . . had given might not be begged by lords and ladies'. Almost immediately afterwards, the committee on the land tax bill resumed. John Conyers had now returned to Parliament and took the chair again, though 'some cried, "Boyle"'. It was observed at this time that in the work of procuring a supply the two most active Members on behalf of the Court were Granville and Boyle, and when, on 9 Apr, there was a contest for the chair of the committee of the whole on the bill appointing commissioners to treat for a union with Scotland, Boyle's name was proposed by Granville and seconded by Simon Harcourt I. His rival was a Whig, Sir Rowland Gwynne*, and this time Boyle was successful, though only after an intervention in his favour by Speaker Harley. Besides his official duties in the House, communicating papers and accounts, and messages from the Queen, his other noteworthy parliamentary activity at this time shows him giving assistance to the Court: in April he assisted in the management of the bill to enable the crown to appoint commissioners for a union with Scotland; and on 2 May he spoke against a Country Tory motion for the removal of foreign officers from the army, and was named to the committee for an address thanking the Queen for her announcement of an intention to declare war.[15]

Boyle's ability to adapt to the changing complexion of administrations in the political confusion of William's last years, and indeed his willingness to do so, proves that he had become a thorough courtier. Through assiduously 'paying court', as he himself put it, he won the trust and respect of Queen Anne, and this despite his rakish proclivities. His fellow ministers, especially Lord Treasurer Godolphin (Sidney†), found him an agreeable companion and more than useful as a man-of-business. To the satirists, on the other hand, he was now a perfect weathercock, renowned not just for his smooth manners and the pride he took in wearing his own hair, but for his 'complying with every reign'. Throughout the Parliament, his official position ensured he was appointed to many drafting committees on supply measures. On 16 Jan. 1703 he moved that the malt tax bill be carried to the Upper House, while on 13 Feb. he divided against the High Tories in favour of agreeing with the Lords' amendments to the bill for extending the time for taking the oath of abjuration. In the spring of 1704, in the wake of Lord Nottingham's (Daniel Finch†) fall and the ministerial reconstruction which brought in more moderate men, he was offered a secretaryship of state but declined, allegedly because he felt that such an advancement would expose him to envy. The chancellorship of the Exchequer was, in any case, more lucrative, less onerous, and held under a more secure tenure. Another rumour circulated in the following summer that he would be given a barony, but this too came to nothing: presumably the gain the ministry would have enjoyed in the Lords would have been counter-balanced by the loss to their debating strength in the Commons; or perhaps Boyle himself preferred to remain a big fish in the Lower House. The new offices he did receive in 1704 – the Irish lord treasurership, the lord lieutenancy of the West Riding and the vice-admiralty of Yorkshire – were all held in trust for his nephew, Lord Burlington, who had succeeded to his father's title while still a minor. In the 1704–5 session, Boyle was soon heavily involved in the ministry's efforts to defeat the Tack. Forecast as likely to oppose it, he spoke 'vehemently' and 'to admiration' on 14 Nov. 1704 against the motion for leave to reintroduce an occasional conformity bill, assisted Robert Harley's canvassing, and at the critical division on 28 Nov. spoke against the bill and was listed as either voting against or absent. In the debate he 'asked, whether any wise man among them would venture his whole estate upon a vote; and, answering himself in the negative, "then", added he, "shall we venture the safety of all England, nay of all Europe, upon this vote?"'. We also have a glimpse of his behind-the-scenes activity on another issue at about this time. Hearing that there were plans afoot to raise in the Commons the case of *Ashby* v. *White* (see AYLESBURY, Bucks.), he consulted the lord treasurer and convened a meeting of Court managers to discuss how best to put it off. Later, when the matter was brought up in the House, he was named to the committee (on 28 Feb. 1705) to confer with the Lords. He was also first-named to the committee to convey the thanks of the Commons to the Duke of Marlborough for his victory at Blenheim (14 Dec. 1704) and was entrusted with the chair of the committee on the bill to enable the Queen to make Marlborough a grant of the manor of Woodstock, thereby earning the gratitude and goodwill of the second of the 'duumvirs'. When the question of providing some reward for the Duke had first come before the House, in January 1705, Boyle had moved to proceed by way of an address to the Queen that she should propose the means and that Parliament should provide legislative endorsement of her wishes. In lists published after the dissolution he was, not surprisingly, stigmatized as a placeman, one compiler harking back to his Country party past in devising for him the peculiar (and essentially misleading) distinction of 'High Church courtier'.[16]

Having incurred the wrath of High Churchmen by his trenchant opposition to the Tack, Boyle wisely decided to forgo a contest for re-election in such an Anglican stronghold as Cambridge, and instead put up at Westminster, where royal officials traditionally enjoyed an interest. His success there was calculated by Lord Sunderland (Charles, Lord Spencer*) as a 'gain' for the Whigs, but it was essentially the Court rather than the Junto that benefited from his return. He was the host at a pre-sessional meeting of Court supporters organized by his old friend Robert Harley to settle on a candidate for the Chair, and duly voted as the ministry wished in the division on the Speakership, 25 Oct. 1705, in favour of John Smith I. His speech in favour of the Whig candidate in the Amersham election dispute earned praise from Lord Halifax (Charles Montagu), but here again he was in essence deferring to Godolphin's directions. On 12 Nov. one contemporary reported that Boyle 'would lose his credit' with the Whigs if they were to know the extent of his services to the Court. His other interventions in debate, as recorded in Grey Neville's* notes, were all in support of a ministerial rather than a partisan position. On 4 Dec. he opposed 'in plain terms' the Tory motion to invite over the Hanoverian heir to the throne, while tactfully conceding that the Elector was 'a gr[eat] prince'. In the proceedings over the Court's legislative riposte, the regency bill, he was particularly prominent. At the second reading on 19 Dec. 1705 he supported the commitment of the bill, in order that 'the succ[ession] may take place w[i]thout struggle', and when Charles Caesar* delivered himself of some innuendoes concerning Godolphin's loyalty to the Revolution settlement, Boyle was to the fore in pressing for action against such an abuse of parliamentary privilege. He also spoke three times in favour of the bill in committee, on various technical questions concerning the composition of the commission of regency and other arrangements to be followed after the Queen's death. Boyle was also closely involved in the struggle over the so-called 'whimsical clause' inserted by Country Whigs into the regency bill, to safeguard and amend the place provision of the Act of Settlement. He was consulted by Godolphin about the negotiations with leading proponents of the measure, was a teller on 15 Feb. for postponing consideration of the Lords' amendment, and was listed as having supported the Court in the proceedings on the clause on 18 Feb. 1706. Local rather than high-political considerations were also to the fore in January–February, Boyle managing a bill to settle the impropriate tithes of St. Bride's parish, London, through the House. From this session onwards has been dated Boyle's close involvement in the day-to-day management of Commons' business on behalf of the Godolphin ministry, with the leading echelon of 'Queen's servants' meeting regularly at his house in Pall Mall. His activity in the 1706–7 session was typical of this period. Having been a commissioner to negotiate the Anglo-Scottish Union, he was named on 11 Feb. 1707 to the committee to prepare the bill of union and told on 28 Feb. that the bill should pass. On 18 Mar. he again acted as a temporary replacement for an absent chairman of ways and means. The picture drawn of him in Macky's *Memoirs* may well apply to his person and character at this stage in his fortunes. Physically he was 'of middle stature, inclining to fat, dark complexion'; in behaviour

> a good companion in conversation, agreeable among the ladies, serves the Queen very assiduously in Council, makes a considerable figure in the House of Commons, by his prudent administration obliged everybody in the Exchequer, and in time may prove a great man.[17]

The crisis of the Godolphin–Marlborough ministry in the winter of 1707–8 was to provide Boyle with his opportunity to attain 'greatness', as he emerged as one of the leaders, if not the leader, of the group known as

'Lord Treasurer's Whigs': self-consciously moderate men, attached to the Court, who placed loyalty to Lord Godolphin, and beyond Godolphin loyalty to the Queen, above their obligations to party and to the Junto lords in particular. The allegiance of these 'Lord Treasurer's Whigs' was a crucial factor in Godolphin and Harley's efforts to reconstruct the ministry around a Court-centred coalition of moderate Tories and moderate Whigs, in order to resist the Junto's escalating demands for high office. Pledges of their cooperation, originally secured at a pre-sessional meeting in October, were confirmed at subsequent conferences, and when Parliament opened Boyle was chosen chairman of the committee on the Address. He was especially busy this session in his official capacity, submitting papers to the House and replying to addresses on the Queen's behalf. He also spoke frequently on behalf of the ministry, beginning, so far as the evidence indicates, with an 'extremely earnest' plea on 6 Dec. 1707 in favour of the continuance of the Scottish Privy Council, and following this five days later with a speech on the heritable jurisdictions in Scotland. At the same time his appointment on 22 Dec. to the drafting committee on the bill to prevent bribery and corruption at elections may have been intended to reaffirm his commitment to Country principles and thus reassure, and even help to win over, some of the Country Whigs, whose leaders had realigned themselves with the Junto in this session in order to put more pressure on the Court. One 'old Whig' was certainly convinced that Boyle was 'staunch', and remembered that he had been 'against the Court in K[ing] W[illia]m's time'. But his most important role was as a ministerial manager and spokesman, hosting the meetings at which tactics were discussed, as in January 1708 prior to the vital debate on 'the estimates for Spain', and then taking the lead in the Commons. On that particular occasion, in fact, he came to the rescue of the ministry from the embarrassment in which it had been landed by ill-considered remarks from Henry St. John II*, with an effective speech of his own, proposing 'that it should be first agreed what number of men were necessary, and then proceed to consider how they should be raised in the most easy and agreeable methods'. The issue was then transformed by the revelation that far fewer troops had been present in Spain at the battle of Almanza than had previously been agreed upon and provided for by Parliament, and Boyle once more laboured hard on the Court side to explain away the discrepancy. The debate on the scandal of the 'Spanish troops' may have been the occasion for Godolphin's break with Robert Harley, who had evidently been about some 'scheme' of his own, probably with the intention of replacing the Treasurer. Boyle's part in these obscure manoeuvres is no clearer than anyone else's: he had certainly been approached by Harley, who was of course an old friend, but when Harley fell he moved unhesitatingly into the vacancy as secretary of state. James Vernon commented: 'I am glad to think that Mr Boyle's changing his place did not arise from his own seeking, but in compliance with his friends, who judged very rightly that nobody else would have been so near acceptable.' Indeed, Boyle's popularity made his part in the reshuffle a smooth one. The staff in the secretary's office were assured that 'he is a very friendly gentleman, and you will be easy under him', and there was no opposition to his necessary re-election at Westminster. Speaker Onslow's retrospective assessment of his character is a good indication of the value placed on the appointment at the time. Noting that Boyle was 'in a particular confidence with the Lord Treasurer', Onslow went on:

> He was now at least very firm and acceptable to the Whigs, but without any party violence, and never engaged in mean things. He conducted the business of the government in the House of Commons with great dignity and wisdom, and was treated there and everywhere else with much personal respect and distinction.

Boyle himself was certainly intent on making the most of his opportunity. He threw himself into his work as secretary, hardly giving himself leisure to eat, and in the Commons seemed to take his place immediately at the head of the Court interest. On 24 Feb., in a debate on war strategy in the Peninsula, he opposed the views of Whig army officers like James Stanhope* and Thomas Erle*, that it would be better to transfer German forces from Italy rather than to send more troops from England, and indeed dissuaded the House from any motion on the subject, 'pressing the danger of such a question, that pointed only to confirm the former opinion of our troops not exceeding 8,600 men in Spain, which appeared not to be true in fact'. But it was an uphill struggle. The 'Lord Treasurer's Whigs', upon whom the entire burden of conducting government business now fell, were barely a match for the combined artillery of Junto Whigs, Country Whigs and Tories. Boyle therefore took steps to buttress his position. His first act as secretary of state was to appoint Horatio Walpole II* as his under-secretary, in the hope of cementing his friendship with Walpole's brother Robert (II*), the ablest of the other 'Lord Treasurer's Whigs'. He also put out feelers in the direction of the Country Whigs, some of whom were invited to a meeting at Boyle's house on 29 Mar., where a method was agreed upon of raising in the Commons the sensitive question of army recruitment. Their temporary backing may have extended to the debate on 1 Apr., when Boyle and his colleagues pressed a motion to thank Prince George as lord high admiral for his care in fitting out the fleet that had defeated the design of the attempted invasion. Towards the end of the session, the Whig Arthur Mainwaring made this assessment of Boyle

> he is of a temper to do what the ministers would have him ... and his genius seems rather filled for patchwork than for a great design, though he has a good understanding and is I believe very honest both in the private affairs of his office and in what relates to the public.[18]

Re-elected for Westminster in 1708, Boyle was twice listed as a Whig in that year. According to Boyle's friend and fellow 'Lord Treasurer's Whig', Lord Coningsby, the 'middle scheme', to preserve some freedom of manoeuvre for Godolphin by managing the Commons through a Court Whig vanguard largely independent of the Junto lords, was maintained until relatively late in 1709, although as Whig penetration of the ministry progressively deepened it became more difficult to distinguish a separate Court group on the Whig side. Boyle, ambitious and consumed by 'hatred to the Junto', was the key figure in this scheme. He it was who convened meetings of the Queen's servants to concert tactics, and who consistently led for the Court in debate. At the opening of the 1708 Parliament, rather than proceeding according to order by establishing the various grand committees, Boyle proposed that the House should first read the Queen's Speech, in view of the importance of demonstrating to the Allies the willingness of Parliament to keep up provision for the war. A member of the drafting committee set up on 29 Jan. 1709 to produce a bill for improving the Union, he himself introduced early in the next month a measure to protect the privileges enjoyed by foreign ministers and diplomats resident in Great Britain. Also in February, following a Commons' address, he laid before the House 'a state of the whole matter of the designed invasion' of the previous year. When, on 2 Mar., an address was sent down from the Lords to state the minimum conditions for any peace treaty with France, Boyle successfully moved an amendment to insist on the demolition of the fortifications and harbour of Dunkirk, observing that

> the British nation having been at a vast expense of blood and treasure for the prosecution of this unnecessary war, it was but just they should reap some benefit by the peace; and the town of Dunkirk being a nest of pirates, that infested the ocean, and did infinite mischief to trade.

In common with Whigs of every hue, he supported the bill to naturalize the Palatines, and he had two tellerships for the Court: on 23 Feb. in favour of retaining the original wording of a proposed address calling for an account of secret service expenditure, and on 26 Feb. for an amendment to a motion for another address requesting an account of arrears in the receipt of taxes. He also spoke for the Court during the debate of 15 Apr. on the bill for improving the Union (the treasons bill). But his most interesting intervention had occurred on 8 Mar. when some muck-raking Whigs, in pursuit of scandal concerning Robert Harley, were pressing for the House to examine the papers of William Greg. In reply Boyle 'said, there was nothing in them, and he was of opinion that the House should not be troubled'. This may have been more than a duty paid to old friendship. Far from dropping Harley when the former secretary's bid for power failed in February 1708, Boyle had remained on good terms with him and had cultivated the restoration of something approaching their previous intimacy, doubtless with an eye to expanding the base of his own support in the Commons. During the winter and spring of 1709–10 the strategic imperatives changed, but the desirability of Harley's friendship became in some respects even greater, and Boyle took continued pains to keep it, even though his principal hopes still lay elsewhere.[19]

The reappointment to the Admiralty of Lord Orford in November 1709 effectively marked Godolphin's capitulation to the Junto, and the end of Boyle's leadership of the Court Whigs. Though highly resentful, he did not withdraw from Court or Commons. Instead he swallowed his pride and agreed to co-operate with the Junto Whigs in Parliament, albeit without throwing himself quite as wholeheartedly into business as he had before. He was distinguished by being first-named to the committee of 14 Dec. 1709 to draw up the articles of impeachment against Dr Sacheverell, and in due course was named a manager for the impeachment, a subject on which Arthur Maynwaring* reported that he expressed himself 'with another sort of warmth than ever I heard him'. In the final debate on the articles, on 11 Jan. 1710, he spoke in general terms about 'Revolution principles' while avoiding points of detail, and at the impeachment itself was briefed to speak to the fourth article. Here again he spoke in generalities, and for once ineffectually, prompting some comments to the effect that he seemed to 'expect a change of affairs'. As the political crisis of 1710 unfolded step by step, Boyle was naturally the focus of speculation and the likelihood of his abandoning the ministry was widely discussed at every stage. Certainly Harley, who had transformed himself from wooed to wooer, did his best throughout 1710 to secure Boyle's goodwill, and at some points, notably in August, may have come close to winning him over. There was talk, too, of a scheme involving Lord Rochester in which Boyle may briefly have been involved. But despite an occasional slackening of his resolve, his conduct seems to have been remarkably consistent, and to have been governed by what was now a very close relationship with Godolphin, so much so that Maynwaring and other members of the Duchess of Marlborough's circle tended to judge Godolphin's intentions by Boyle's actions. Thus in January 1710, in the dispute over the appointment of Mrs Masham's brother to a colonelcy, Boyle's advice was sought by Godolphin, and the two joined in dissuading Marlborough from demanding Mrs Masham's dismissal, Boyle, it was said, out of fear that 'the remedy' would 'prove worse than the disease'. Such pusillanimity, as it appeared to the Duke and his Duchess, required all Godolphin's eloquence to excuse. He told Sarah he had 'never found' Boyle 'in a lie' and credited him with convincing the Queen of the necessity of 'satisfying' Marlborough, adding, in his accompanying letter to Marlborough, 'I am very glad anybody else has influence to do him [Boyle] justice, and I should be yet gladder if the same people who are always ready to give jealousies and suspicions, may have a little less influence for the future upon his account'. On 15 Feb., however, Boyle refrained from contributing to the debate on the motion to address for Marlborough to be sent to the peace negotiations in Holland, though he was subsequently named at the head of the committee to draw up the address. In June and July Harley's political courtship intensified. Significantly, he seems to have promised Boyle and John Smith I, who were acting together in these negotiations, that Godolphin would be retained in any reconstructed administration in which they would have a part. Harley's principal concern, despite these professions, was to keep in place moderate Whigs like Boyle once Godolphin had been dispensed with, and towards the end of August it appeared as if he would succeed in driving a wedge between the lord treasurer and the 'Lord Treasurer's Whigs'. Arthur Maynwaring reported in disgust to the Duchess of Marlborough that

> [Boyle], whom you are advised twice a day to admire, after having promised Mr [Edmund] Dunch* to dine with him yesterday, sent him word that it was a post day, and business pressed; and it is since come out that he dined with [Somerset], with L[or]d Dartmouth, and a great deal of such choice company; now I know a hundred of these accounts could make no impression, but [Lord Godolphin] and his confidants will always be in the right; but it will be hard to persuade anybody but [Godolphin] that [Boyle] is not the poorest wretch upon earth, to sneak to [Somerset], whom he always despised, and would never eat with, while [Godolphin] and [Marlborough] had power, and who dares not now come into Parliament, though he knows he shall be turned out of his place, lest any vote there should hinder his coming again to an employment, upon the first difficulty at court. But [Godolphin] will tell you, when you see him, that this is wise and right.

In fact, as Maynwaring hinted, Boyle had no intention of staying on in office, at least in the short term; his career was as yet bound to Godolphin's. Nor, on the other hand, was he willing to join other Whigs in fighting against the new ministry. In private, he and his friends were still as violent against the Junto as ever, but, along with Coningsby and Smith (to whose country home in Hampshire he retired at this crucial juncture), he had determined on a temporary withdrawal from politics, and had announced that he would not stand at any new election. In this decision he was proof against remonstrations from Marlborough and other Whigs. Some historians have viewed his refusal to put up for re-election as making a virtue of necessity: as one of the managers of Sacheverell's impeachment, he could have expected a rough ride wherever he was candidate. Maynwaring's explanation should not be discounted, that Boyle's self-abnegation was a Machiavellian ploy to leave him free to take up office again in the future, without being compromised by any action he would have been obliged to take in the new Parliament to vindicate his ministerial record. But it is equally possible that, in common with other 'Lord Treasurer's Whigs', Boyle was simply tired of politics: that he had disobliged too many of the influential in both parties, and left himself too few real friends, to be a credible figure, however highly respected he might be among those who merely observed the working of government and Parliament, and who, like Swift, were shocked at his eventual dismissal. But as the Queen herself observed, who had been most reluctant to part with him, his departure from administration on 20 Sept. 1710 was 'his own doing'.[20]

Boyle's correspondence in retirement affected to extol the pleasures of country life, and the charms of his new house, but he could not resist the temptations of the town for long, and he returned to London early in 1712 to play his part in the lionizing of Prince Eugene, at which time he confessed to Coningsby, 'I am retired from business, but not from the comforts and pleasures of this place'. He was also given to protestations of his innocence of any connexions or interests at court. Nevertheless, gossip continued to predict his imminent return to high office. That his reputation had not diminished was clear from Richard Steele's* decision to dedicate to him the third number of the *Spectator*, published in November 1712. So 'proper a patron' for the periodical, Steele wrote, would be hard to find, for in Boyle 'extraordinary talents' were embellished by 'that elegance and politeness, which appear in your private conversation'; 'that moderation in an high fortune, and that affability of manners, which are so conspicuous through all parts of your life'. But despite Boyle's abilities, not the least of which was to avoid making lasting enemies, there was no appropriate moment for Harley to give him an opportunity to return to office. He refused to stand at the 1713 general election, and shrewdly declined an offer to rejoin the Treasury commission after Harley's dismissal in July 1714, though the fact that Bolingbroke (Henry St. John II) and other High Tories were prepared to countenance his appointment speaks loudly of his general acceptability.[21]

With the death of Queen Anne Boyle seems to have felt the time right to reappear at centre-stage. He signed the proclamation of King George I, and in the first months of the new reign his name was frequently mentioned in connexion with such posts as secretary of state and first lord of the Treasury. In the end, he received only a coronation peerage in recognition of past services. One view was that he had declined office, 'perceiving that there would be a great fermentation in Parliament, on account of the maladministration at the latter end of Queen Anne's reign', and not himself being 'of a temper to act in troublesome times'. But the evidence seems to point only to an initial refusal to serve in the Treasury: subsequently he may well have involved himself in the factional struggles within the Whig party and on this account have expected the secretaryship. A later report was that he had 'gone into the country dissatisfied'. It would seem that he then began to forge a closer alliance with Hanoverian Tories like Caernarvon (Hon. James Brydges*) and Nottingham. Having at first sided with Townshend and Walpole during the Whig Schism, he involved himself in cabals with various Tories during the political crisis of 1720–1 and eventually returned to government in 1721, in the office of lord president, very much as an adherent of Lord Sunderland. So closely was he associated with Sunderland, in fact, that on the latter's death Boyle for once found himself almost isolated politically, 'Whigs' regarding him as an unwelcome colleague. That he was still the Boyle of old is indicated both by the promises that had to be made to him at different stages in these negotiations that he would have no difficulties to bear in his appointment, and by his eventual success in overcoming the resentments of disgruntled colleagues and settling down as a member of the Townshend–Walpole administration.[22]

Boyle died in office on 14 Mar. 1725, at Carleton House, and was buried in the family vault at Londesborough. His will revealed an estate approaching in size that of his grandfather, with landed property and substantial houses in Oxfordshire, Wiltshire and at Petersham in Surrey, and a personalty of well over £27,000, parcelled out among nieces and nephews in various aristocratic families. This wealth was largely the product of many years' profits of office, supplemented by investment in landed property. Though willing to do his duty as a member of the ministry and subscribe handsomely in 1706 to the loan to the Emperor, he seems to have eschewed any dabbling in funds or stocks. Those, like Lady Mary Wortley Montagu, who dealt in the tittle-tattle of the town, seized upon the fact that he had made the Duke of Queensberry his principal heir to resurrect the story that Queensberry's wife was Boyle's natural daughter by Lady Clarendon (the former Lady Hyde). 'He disposed of his estate as he did of his time', wrote Lady Mary,

> between Lady Clarendon and the Duchess of Queensberry. Jewels to a great value he has given, as he did his affections, first to the mother and then to the daughter. He was taken ill in my company at a consort at the [Duchess] of Marlborough's, and died two days after, holding the fair Duchess by the hand, and being fed at the same time with a fine fat chicken, thus dying, as he had lived, indulging his pleasures.

Irrespective of the truth of the Duchess of Queensberry's paternity, Lady Mary's malice did highlight the most important weakness in Boyle's character. Swift called it 'avarice'; Speaker Onslow, a trifle less bluntly, termed Boyle's private life 'too luxurious'. While no one could criticize him for indolence, his preference for comfort often made him reluctant to fight where the battle was hottest, and after his brief heyday at the head of the Court party in the Commons in 1708–9 he was happy to take a supporting role when he could find one, provided that it was sufficiently lucrative. Without this flaw, he would surely have achieved the 'greatness' once predicted for him. Speaker Onslow again:

> He had good natural abilities, with a very sound judgment; wary and modest in all his actions, even to a diffi-

dence of himself, that was often improper and hurtful to him. But on occasions which he thought required it, he showed no want either of spirit or steadiness, which the justice and honour of his nature and the decorum of his manner in everything, gave him a consideration and a weight in the opinion of those who knew his character far beyond what any other public person has acquired in our times. I have often thought him a . . . pattern for those who would govern this country well.[23]

[1] Devonshire mss at Chatsworth House, Lismore pprs. box 28, Countess of Cork's jnl. (*ex. inf.* Dr T. C. Barnard). [2] *Cal. Treas. Bks.* xviii. 237; xvi. 190; Lodge, *Peerage of Ire.* (1754), i. 99; *Liber Munerum Publicorum Hiberniae* ed. Lascelles, ii. 42; Boyer, *Anne Annals*, vi. 222; A. B. Beaven's list of Irish PCs, Hist. of Parl. [3] A. Savidge, *Q. Anne's Bounty*, 123–5; *Rec. Old Westminsters*, i. 113. [4] E. Budgell, *Mems. of Earl of Orrery and Boyle Fam.* (1732), pp. 149, 154; Burnet, v. 355–6; *Macky Mems.* 126; info. from Dr Barnard. [5] *Clarendon Corresp.* ed. Singer, ii. 167, 169–70; *HMC 7th Rep.* 418; *Orig. Letters* ed. Ellis (ser. 2), iv. 164; Bath mss at Longleat House, Thynne pprs. 24, ff. 136, 148, 150; Lancs. RO, Kenyon mss DDKe/9/72/19, Ld. Derby to Roger Kenyon, [1690]; Nat. Lib. Ire. Lismore mss 13226, Burlington to William Congreve, 9, 16, 23, 17 Aug., 1 Sept., 18 Oct., 17 Nov. 1692 (ex. inf. Dr Barnard); NLS ms 7014, f. 167, John Hayes* to Lord Tweeddale, 15 Oct. 1692; J. Gascoigne, *Camb. in Age of Enlightenment*, 90, 95; Add. 28931, f. 62; *Trinity Coll. Camb. Adm.* 1546–1700, p. 583; *Diary of Samuel Newton* (Camb. Antiq. Soc. Pubs. xxiii), 106. [6] *Luttrell Diary*, 290, 418, 421, 439, 442, 450; Add. 57861, f. 20; *HMC Portland*, iii. 542–3. [7] *HMC Portland*, iii. 542; Cobbett, *Parlty. Hist.* v. 785, 804; Add. 17677 OO, f. 168. [8] Add. 70212, Boyle to [Robert Harley], 'Wednesday'; D. Rubini, *Court and Country*, 125; Cobbett, v. 909, 914; *CSP Dom.* 1694–5, p. 462. [9] *HMC Portland*, iii. 571–2; Gascoigne, 90, 95; H. Horwitz, *Parl. and Pol. Wm. III*, 159; K. Feiling, *Tory Party*, 310; BL, Trumbull Misc. mss 33, [?(Sir) Gilbert Dolben*] to Sir William Trumbull*, n.d. [1696]. [10] *HMC Portland*, iii. 578–9; J. P. Kenyon, *Sunderland*, 285; *Vernon–Shrewsbury Letters*, i. 42, 48–49, 53, 63, 66, 112; Northants. RO, Montagu (Boughton) mss 46/17, 24, James Vernon to Shrewsbury, 6, 19 Nov. 1696; Cobbett, v. 1003–4, 1088–91; Add. 70306–9, list of votes for commn. of accts. [Feb. 1697]; Horwitz, 191; Nat. Archs. Ire. Wyche mss 1/143, A. Lucas to Sir Cyril Wyche*, 22 Apr. 1697; Luttrell, iv. 212; Trinity, Dublin, King letterbks. 750/1, pp. 138–40, Bp. King to Ld. Clifford (Hon. Charles Boyle I), 4 Dec. 1697. [11] Horwitz, 226, 229, 258; Luttrell, iv. 333; *CSP Dom.* 1697, p. 502; 1698, pp. 36, 96; Add. 70235, Sir Edward Harley* to Robert Harley, 4 Sept. 1697; 17677 SS, f. 114; Montagu (Boughton) mss 46/156, Vernon to Shrewsbury, 23 Oct. 1697; *Cam. Misc.* xxix. 360; *Poems on Affairs of State* ed. Ellis, iv. 24, 716; *HMC Le Fleming*, 351. [12] Devonshire mss at Chatsworth House, Robert Harley to Boyle, 16 Nov. 1698; Devonshire mss, Finch-Halifax pprs. Anthony Hammond to Sir John Banks, 1st Bt.*, 29 Mar. 1698; C. H. Cooper, *Annals Camb.* iv. 40; Camb. Univ. Lib. ms 3, f. 13; Luttrell, iv. 431; *Cam. Misc.* xxix. 379, 386, 395; Horwitz, 252; Bodl. Tanner 21, f. 10; Bodl. Ballard 4, f. 36; Add. 30000 C, f. 115. [13] Kenyon, 312; Nottingham Univ. Lib. Portland (Bentinck) mss PwA1499, Vernon to Portland, 11 Aug. 1699; Luttrell, iv. 555, 560, 562, 661; Add. 30000 C, f. 240; *Vernon–Shrewsbury Letters*, ii. 373, 375, 412, 431; Horwitz, 261–2; S. B. Baxter, *Wm. III*, 376. [14] *Vernon–Shrewsbury Letters*, iii. 110; Add. 17677 WW, ff. 202, 206; 30000 E, f. 165; Horwitz, 282, 284; *Cocks Diary*, 94, 118, 125–6, 130–1, 161. [15] Add. 70272, 'Large Acct. Revolution and Succession', pp. 16–17; 17677 XX, f. 253; *Cocks Diary*, 221, 241, 244, 253, 265, 279; *CJ*, xiii. 785–6, 794; Luttrell, v. 152, 161; Boyer, *Anne Annals*, i. 19. [16] *Duchess of Marlborough Corresp.* i. 312; Add. 61459, f. 93; 47025, f. 58; 17677 AAA, f. 62; *Poems on Affairs of State*, 523–4; *Norris Pprs.* (Chetham Soc. ix), 123; Folger Shakespeare Lib. Newdigate newsletters 29 Mar., 3 June 1704; *HMC Downshire*, i. 829; DZA, Bonet despatch 28 Apr./9 May 1704; *Procs. . . . upon Bill to Prevent Occasional Conformity* (1710), pp. 56, 59; *Bull. IHR*, xli. 179; xxxiv. 93, 95–96; Speck thesis, 124. [17] Gascoigne, 96; *Parlty. Lists Early 18th Cent.* ed. Newman, 72; *Bull IHR*, xlv. 47; *HMC Portland*, iv. 154–5; Univ. Kansas Kenneth Spencer Research Lib. Methuen–Simpson corresp. MS. C163, [?John Methuen] to Sir William Simpson, 12 Nov. 1705; *Cam. Misc.* xxiii. 42, 45, 49, 51, 53–54, 61, 70, 75; Add. 70284–5, Godolphin to Robert Harley, 'Friday morning', 'Friday at 12'; G. Holmes, *Pol. in Age of Anne*, 365; Bath mss, Portland misc. pprs. Godolphin to Harley, 'Tuesday, 10 at night', 27 Oct.; Cobbett, vi. 550; *Macky Mems*. 126. [18] *Archaeologia*, xxxviii. 8; *Huntington Lib. Q.* xv. 38; B. W. Hill, *Growth of Parlty. Parties 1689–1742*, pp. 105, 113; Add. 70338, memo. by Godolphin, 26 Oct. 1707; 70284–5, Godolphin to Harley, n.d.; 4291, f. 143; NLW, Plas-yn-Cefn mss 2740, Edmund Gibson to [?Bp. of Hereford], 6 Dec. 1707; *Vernon–Shrewsbury Letters*, iii. 291, 310, 347–8, 350, 354, 355; *Norris Pprs.* 167; Speck thesis, 202–3, 219, 220–1, 224–5; *EHR*, lxxx. 683–4, 686; DZA, Bonet despatch 6/17 Feb. 1708; Burnet, v. 355–6; *HMC Portland*, iv. 481; Cobbett, vi. 734; *Marlborough– Godolphin Corresp.* 943; 7th Duke of Manchester, *Court and Soc. Eliz. to Anne*, ii. 331; Add. 61459, f. 40. [19] Add. 57862, ff. 52–57; 17677 CCC. f. 646; 17677 DDD, ff. 65–66, 151; 70212, Boyle to Harley, 23 May, 3 Dec. 1709; Holmes, 365; Cobbett, vi. 774; Chandler, iv. 123; Boyer, *Anne Annals*, vii. 316–17; *HMC Portland*, iv. 510, 521. [20] Add. 57862, ff. 52–58; 61460, ff. 103, 166; 61461, ff. 80–81; 17677 DDD, f. 530; 61118, f. 122; 61608, f. 48; Holmes, 112, 224–5; Add. 70212, Boyle to Harley, 9 July, 10 Aug. 1710; G. Holmes, *Trial of Sacheverell*, 101, 149, 253; Boyer, viii. 226, 264; Yale Univ. Beinecke Lib. Osborn mss, 'Acct. of Trial of Dr Sacheverell' (1 Mar. 1710); *Impartial View of Two Late Parls.* (1711), p. 190; E. Gregg, *Q. Anne*, 304, 321, 323; B. W. Hill, *Robert Harley*, 129; Feiling, 419; *Wentworth Pprs.* 123; *Archaeologia*, xxxviii. 10, 15–17; *Marlborough–Godolphin Corresp.* 1416, 1417, 1509–10, 1541, 1625, 1627; Devonshire mss, Harley to Boyle, 11 Aug. 1710; *Duchess of Marlborough Corresp.* i. 342, 391, 396; *HMC Portland*, v. 650; Huntington Lib. Stowe mss 58(5), p. 127; 57(4), p. 191; Walpole mss at Wolterton Hall, Marlborough to Robert Walpole II, 15 Sept. 1710; Coxe, *Walpole*, ii. 35; PRO NI, De Ros mss D638/55/7, Boyle to Coningsby, 13 Oct. 1710; Cobbett, vi. 911; *Swift Stella* ed. Davis, i. 24, 174; *HMC Townshend*, 76; *Sir David Hamilton Diary* ed. Roberts, 17. [21] De Ros mss D638/55/8, 10, 12, Boyle to Coningsby, 5 Jan. 1711[-12], 26 May 1711, 22 Apr. 1712; Boyer, *Pol. State*, iii. 100 171; vii. 626; *Anne Annals*, x. 337; Hill, *Growth of Parlty. Parties*, 133; Add. 61461, f. 133; *HMC Var.* viii. 251; *Steele Corresp.* 463–4; Devonshire mss, Harley to Boyle, 11 Dec. 1713; Huntington Lib. HM44710, Kreienberg to Robethon, 28 Aug. 1713; Trinity, Dublin, Lyons (King) coll. 2004/1499, Ld. Mountjoy to Abp. King, 27 July 1714; G. M. Trevelyan, *Eng. under Q. Anne*, iii. 308–9. [22] Boyer, *Pol. State*, viii. 117; Macpherson, *Orig. Pprs.* ii. 638; *Wentworth Pprs.* 420, 427; Coxe, ii. 48; *HMC Stuart*, ii. 345; *HMC Townshend*, 106; L. Colley, *In Defiance of Oligarchy*, 188, 191, 199; Hill, *Growth of Parlty. Parties*, 183; Lady Cowper, *Diary*, 144; *HMC Portland*, v. 597, 614, 615, 622; *HMC Carlisle*, 31, 38. [23] *The Gen.* n.s. vi. 208; PCC 60 Romney; Boyer, *Anne Annals*, iv. 127; *Lady Mary Wortley Montagu Letters* ed. Halsband, ii. 48; iii. 48; *Hearne Colls.* viii. 17; *Swift Corresp.* ed. Williams, i. 174; Burnet, 355–6.

D. W. H.

BOYLE, Lionel, 3rd Earl of Orrery [I] (1671–1703).

EAST GRINSTEAD   26 Feb.–11 Oct. 1695
1698–1700
1701 (Dec.)–1702

bap. 11 July 1671, 1st s. of Roger Boyle, 2nd Earl of Orrery [I], by Lady Mary Sackville, da. of Richard Sackville, 5th

Earl of Dorset; bro. of Hon. Charles Boyle II*. *educ.* Eton c.1682–5; travelled abroad (France, Netherlands, United Provinces, Germany, Switzerland, Italy) 1685–9. *m.* c.23 Feb. 1693 (with £5,000), his 1st cos. Mary (*d.* 1714), illegit. da. of Charles Sackville†, 6th Earl of Dorset, *s.p.* Styled Lord Broghill 1679–82; *suc.* fa. as 3rd Earl 29 Mar. 1682.[1]

The financial decline of the Orrery family, largely brought about by an excess of conspicuous consumption over income, was arrested – though not reversed – in the person of the 3rd Earl. Lionel Boyle was still confronted by debt and obliged to become a supplicant for court favour. In making his appeals for relief he never tired of citing 'great losses and sufferings in the time of the late troubles in Ireland', though ironically enough the rationalization of his estate management consequent upon the devastation of his Irish property by Jacobite troops proved ultimately the saving of his fortunes. When the Revolution took place he was abroad, and by the time he returned to England he had been attainted by James II's Irish parliament as a 'rebel'. After spending the winter of 1689–90 in England, consorting with émigré Irish Protestants, he made his way to Ireland. In August 1690 he was at home in county Cork organizing local Williamite forces when a Jacobite detachment attacked and burned his mansion at Charleville, 'the best modern . . . built house in the kingdom' (costing between £20,000 and £40,000 to construct and furnish) and also 'laid waste' his plantation towns of Charleville and Askeaton (at a further financial loss to him of some £1,000). But he was left with an estate of his own which he was able to set after the peace at £1,300 p.a., and which his lawyer believed might be increased to £2,000 when the untenanted lands were let, together with a right in reversion to his mother's property, itself 'reasonably computed at £1,200 a year'. Rather than devote himself to the work of reconstruction, however, he retired to England and to the household of his maternal uncle, the 6th Duke of Dorset, who had already taken the family under his protection. Orrery's marriage not long afterwards to Dorset's illegitimate daughter 'made some noise abroad' and raised some eyebrows, for it was easy, though probably unjust, to assume that Dorset had imposed on his fatherless nephew. The more likely explanation was that Orrery, a complacent young man whose principal ambition was the continued enjoyment of high living among sociable companions, slipped readily into a matrimonial arrangement that would guarantee the retention of his uncle's goodwill.[2]

The benefits of Dorset's patronage extended to a parliamentary seat, and Orrery was returned at a by-election in 1695 for the pocket borough of East Grinstead. Dorset recommended him again at the general election of that year, but on the latter occasion Orrery and the other Sackville nominee, Hon. Spencer Compton*, were defeated by two Tories. They petitioned unsuccessfully. Before the next election Dorset apparently concluded an agreement with his chief rival in the borough, John Conyers*, to share the representation, and Orrery was returned unopposed with Conyers in 1698. In the meantime he had at last taken his seat in the Irish house of lords, where he may have used his position to promote his claim, first brought up in a petition to the Treasury in April 1697, to the share in the so-called Irish 'lapse money' granted to his grandfather by Charles II, that is to say the forfeited subscriptions of the English Adventurers in the 1640s, amounting now to £8,000. Perhaps in order to embarrass the Dublin administration, he moved during the debate on the ratification of the articles of Limerick to question the lords justices as to why they had altered the heads of the enabling bill before transmitting them to England. On another occasion, however, he voted with the Court, on the bill for the better security of the King's person and government. Whatever his tactics, they were adequate to ensure the granting of his request, and in January 1698 a warrant passed for the Irish treasury to levy Orrery's share of the 'lapse money' on all Catholic beneficiaries of the Restoration land settlement in Ireland. Subsequently his younger brother Charles Boyle II petitioned for a half-share for himself, and in November 1699 officials in Ireland were ordered to withhold a moiety of the receipts pending a decision on his claim, which, it would appear, was then rejected. Presumably because of this grant, Orrery was included in a list of placemen in about September 1698. He was also classed as a supporter of the Court in a comparative analysis of the old and new Houses of Commons. But he was an inactive Member, his name appearing in the clerk's list of 7 Mar. 1699 of those who had not attended at all during that session. In the following session he was given three months' leave of absence on 24 Jan. 1700 'to go into Ireland, his lady being very ill'. A list dating from about this time marked him as a follower of the Whig Junto, but after he had stood down at the general election of January 1701 in favour of Dorset's protégé Matthew Prior he made an approach to the new ministry, applying for a reversionary grant of some lands in Yorkshire worth £565 p.a. Dorset brought him back into Parliament for East Grinstead in December 1701, when his election was calculated as a 'gain' by Lord Spencer (Charles*) and he was classed as a Whig in Robert Harley's* list. His debts were now so considerable that he felt obliged to have a bill brought in to enable him to sell off entailed property. Sir Henry Dutton Colt, 1st Bt.*, took charge of the measure in February 1702 and succeeded in piloting it through Parliament. Orrery himself remained an inactive Member, with no recorded speech to his credit. He was defeated at East Grinstead in the 1702 election by John Conyers and another Tory, the previous understanding between Conyers and Dorset having broken down, and soon after he applied himself to a powerful Tory connexion, Lord Rochester (Laurence Hyde†), who had married one of his cousins. Rochester promised to do what he could to help Orrery's pretensions to office, whereupon he asked for a commissionership of trade, basing his request on 'my losses on the late Revolution, which were very great'. He disclaimed any notion that he was asking 'out of necessity', for 'God be thanked, I can live without it; but I am very ambitious and should be very proud of serving her [Majesty] and am very desirous of being particularly obliged to your excellency'. Nothing came forth.[3]

Orrery died at Earl's Court, Kensington on 24 Aug. 1703, and was buried with the Sackvilles at Withyham in Sussex. In his will, dated in May 1699, he had ordered that his grant of the 'lapse money' be used to pay his debts. Besides a bequest of £100 to a 'Mrs Susanna Louth', all his personal estate was left to his widow, who took as her second husband another Boyle, the 2nd Viscount Shannon (Richard*).[4]

[1] *Eton Coll. Reg.* ed. Sterry, 251; Centre Kentish Stud. Sackville mss U269/A10/3; U269/C139, St. John Brodrick to Simon Smith*, 1 June 1693; *Cal. Orrery Pprs.* ed. McLysaght (Irish Mss Commn.), pp. 313–70 passim; *CSP Dom.* 1686–7, p. 448; Luttrell, *Brief Relation*, iii. 41. [2] *Cork: Hist. and Soc.* ed. O'Flanagan and Buttimer, 316–33; *Cal. Orrery Pprs.* 317, 321, 372; Luttrell, ii. 121; *Evelyn Diary* ed. de Beer, v. 37; Sackville mss U269/A10/3; U269/C139; U269/C106, Lady Orrery to Dorset, 28 July; Add. 38847, f. 274; *Cal. Treas. Bks.* xiii. 221–3; *Cal. Treas. Pprs.* 1697–1702, p. 551; *Diary of Dean Davies* (Cam. Soc. lxviii), 91; Bodl. Carte 79, f. 490; E. Budgell, *Mems. Earl of Orrery and Boyle Fam.* (1732), 155. [3] Add. 70294, reply of Sir Thomas Dyke and John Conyers to case of Orrery and Compton, [1695]; *Cal. Treas. Bks.* xiii. 46, 221–3; xv. 213; *CSP Dom.* 1698, p. 26; 1699–1700, p. 297; J. G. Simms, *Williamite Confiscation in Ire.* 62; *HMC Hamilton (Supp.)*, 139; *Cal. Treas. Pprs.* 1697–1702, p. 551; *CJ*, xiii. 741–2, 747, 770, 774, 782; *HMC Lords*, n.s. iv. 417–18; Sackville mss U269/057; *Clarendon Corresp.* ed. Singer, ii. 444–5. [4] PCC 172 Dogg.

D. W. H.

BOYLE, Richard, 2nd Visct. Shannon [I] (c.1675–1740), of Shannon Park, co. Cork.

ARUNDEL	1708–1710
HYTHE	1710–27 Jan. 1711
	25 July 1712–1715
EAST GRINSTEAD	5 Apr. 1715–1722
	6 Nov. 1722–1734

b. c.1675, 1st s. of Richard Boyle (1st s. *d.v.p.* of Francis Boyle, 1st Visct. Shannon [I], of Shannon Park) by Elizabeth, da. of Sir John Ponsonby of Bessborough, co. Kilkenny. *educ.* Oxf. Univ. DCL 1695. *m.* (1) c.6 June 1704, Mary (*d.* 1714), illegit. da. of Charles Sackville†, 6th Earl of Dorset, wid. of his 2nd cos. Lionel Boyle*, 3rd Earl of Orrery [I], *s.p.*; (2) Jan. 1721, Grace (*d.* 1755), da. and h. of John Senhouse of Netherhall, Cumb., 1da. *suc.* gdfa. as 2nd Visct. Apr. 1699.[1]

Cornet, 2 tp. Horse Gds. 1693, guidon and maj. 1696–Feb. 1702; col. of Marines Feb. 1702–Jan. 1715; brig.-gen. 1704, maj.-gen. 1708; jt. comptroller for clothing the army 1708; dep. gov. Dover Castle 1709; lt.-gen. 1710; col. 25 Ft. Jan. 1715–June 1721; lt.-gen. [I] 1716, c.-in-c. [I] 1720–*d.*; col. 6 Drag. June 1721–Mar. 1727, 4 tp. Life Gds. Mar. 1727–*d.*; PC [I] 1721–*d.*; ld. justice [I] 1722–3, 1724; gen. 1735, f.m. 1739; gov. Portsmouth 1737–*d.*, Sheerness.[2]

Freeman, Cork 1722.[3]

Very much the poor relation of his grand Boyle cousins, Boyle inherited an estate of only £1,000 a year, and was, therefore, condemned to earn his living. His long and distinguished military career began, appropriately, with service as a volunteer at the battle of the Boyne. As a young guards officer in the Nine Years' War he saw action at Landen in 1693, but his first notable exploit occurred during the Cadiz expedition of 1702 when, in his capacity as colonel of a newly raised regiment of marines, he led the grenadiers in storming the fortifications at Vigo. He was then despatched to England with the news of the destruction of the French and Spanish fleets, for which he was rewarded by Queen Anne with a gratuity of £1,000. A similar experience awaited him three years later, as he again brought home tidings of a triumph in Spain, this time the taking of Barcelona, receiving another gratuity. Promotion, however, came more slowly. His political views may have been too Whiggish for the taste of Queen Anne's first ministry, and in January 1703 there was talk of his participation in a scandalous episode in St. James's Church, Piccadilly, both of which may have contributed to his lack of advancement after Vigo and an unsubstantiated rumour that he would lose his regiment. Prospects improved with the increasing Whig preponderance in government, and his own easier access to ministerial circles, through his brief membership of the Kit-Cat Club and marriage into the influential Sackville family. In 1708 he obtained a major-general's commission and a seat in Parliament for Arundel, the latter probably on the recommendation of the Earl of Scarbrough, a retired army officer and fellow Kit-Catter. Boyle's election was reckoned by the Earl of Sunderland (Charles, Lord Spencer*) as a 'gain' for the Whigs, and he was also classed as a Whig in a list of early 1708. He voted in 1709 in favour of the naturalization of the Palatines, and, having survived a contest and a petition at Arundel when he was obliged to seek re-election on accepting the deputy governorship of Dover Castle, was 'blacklisted' in 1710 as one who had supported the impeachment of Dr Sacheverell. He was not, however, a dedicated parliamentarian, placing his professional duty above his responsibilities as a Member: no speech of his is recorded, nor was he in this period named to any of the major committees. In 1708 he had pestered the Duke of Marlborough (John Churchill†) with his wish to return to Spain, and in 1710 he was entrusted with the leadership of the secret, and ultimately abortive, expedition to attack French Canada. Abandoning Arundel in the 1710 general election, since Scarbrough was no longer in a position to nominate both Members there, he was returned instead for Hythe, through the intercession of his brother-in-law Dorset, the lord warden of the Cinque Ports, and was classed as a Whig in the 'Hanover list' of this Parliament. Ousted on petition, he regained the seat at a by-election in 1712, and although voting as a Whig against the French commerce bill on 18 June 1713, retained both his regiment and his place in Parliament throughout the lifetime of the Tory administration. Under the Hanoverians his career flourished, both in England and in his native Ireland, where he was for many years commander-in-chief.[4]

Boyle died on 20 Dec. 1740, and was buried at Walton-on-Thames, Surrey, where he had purchased a substantial estate. He was commemorated in a splendid monument by Roubiliac, which portrayed him in full fig above an inscription of surpassing grandiloquence:

> By emulation excited to be a soldier, by enterprise ennobled as an officer, by experience matured into a commander, his birth adding lustre to his pretensions, his pretensions authorized by his merit, promoted swiftly, not undeservedly, to the command of various corps of foot, horse and horse-guards, and to the successive ranks of general officer during a long and continued peace, he attained by royal regard and just favour what he was ambitious to achieve by service.[5]

[1] Cottrell-Dormer mss at Rousham, Caesar mss misc. 'list of births, deaths, marriages'. [2] *CSP Dom.* 1696, p. 33; Boyer, *Anne Annals*, vii. 42; ix. 415; Luttrell, *Brief Relation*, vi. 270; *Cal. Treas. Bks.* xxx. 562; *Cal. Treas. Pprs.* 1720–8, p. 83; 1739–41, p. 598. [3] *Cork Corp. Council Bk.* ed. Caulfield, 478. [4] *Cork: Hist. and Soc.* ed. O'Flanagan and Buttimer, 321; Boyer, i. 126–7, 137; iv. 199; Luttrell, v. 233, 249; *HMC 12th Rep. IX*, 95; *Cal. Treas. Bks.* xx. 506; xxiv. 573; Herts. RO, Panshanger mss D/EP F30, p. 15; J. Caulfield, *Mems. Kit-Cat Club*, 131; *Marlborough–Godolphin Corresp.* 1067, 1448; G. Wilks, *Barons of Cinque Ports*, 92–93; *HMC Portland*, x. 70. [5] *Gent. Mag.* 1740, p. 622; Manning and Bray, *Surr.* ii. 772.

D. W. H.

BRACEBRIDGE, Samuel (1673–1735), of Lindley Hall and Fenny Drayton, Leics.

TAMWORTH 1710–23 Jan. 1723

b. 4 Apr. 1673, 1st s. of Abraham Bracebridge of Atherstone, Warws. by Mary, da. and coh. of Thomas Charnell of Snarestone, Leics. *educ.* Brasenose, Oxf. 1691; I. Temple 1690, called 1699, bencher 1721, reader 1731, treasurer 1734. *m.* Anne, da. of Thomas Savage of Malvern and Elmley Castle, Worcs., 6s. (2 *d.v.p.*) 3da. *suc.* fa. 1694.[1]

The Bracebridge estates were concentrated on the Warwickshire–Leicestershire border at Atherstone and Lindley. After succeeding his father (a former sheriff of Warwickshire), and embarking upon a legal career, Bracebridge rebuilt Lindley Hall in 1701 and purchased the adjacent manor of Fenny Drayton in 1706. Very little is known of his early life except for his involvement in local affairs as an active justice in Warwickshire in Anne's reign, and an interest in the parliamentary representation of nearby Tamworth dating back as far as January 1704 when it was reported that he was willing to stand there, although not in opposition to any 'honest country gentlemen'. According to Viscount Weymouth's (Thomas Thynne†) election agent 'the honest gentlemen of the county say he is an ingenious men, and of good principles, though his father had very ill ones'. Bracebridge does not seem to have taken his interest further until the highly propitious circumstances of 1710, when he was returned with his colleague from the Inner Temple, Joseph Girdler* (both had been called to the bar on the same day in June 1699).[2]

Once inside the House, Bracebridge proved to be a prime example of a lawyer-Member, relishing the work of legislation. His political perspective was clearly that of a Tory. He was classed as such on the 'Hanover list' of 1710, and was also noted as one of the 'worthy patriots' who during the 1710–11 session helped to detect the mismanagements of the previous administration. His views were given more personal expression in a letter he wrote in February 1711 to Sir Thomas Cave, 3rd Bt.*, encouraging him to stand in the forthcoming by-election for Leicestershire. It was couched in party terms, the main message being that if Cave 'should fail to stand a candidate it will be very fatal to the Church interest'. During the first session of the 1710 Parliament Bracebridge was involved in the management of at least four bills through the Commons. The first derived from his local connexions, as it concerned an estate bill to allow Viscount Cullen to sell a Leicestershire manor. Bracebridge presented the bill on 17 Feb. and, after a hiatus caused by a grant of leave for a month on 26 Feb., reported it from committee on 5 May. He also reported the bill for the better preservation of the fisheries on the river Thames (19 May), despite being omitted from the initial round of appointments to the second-reading committee and only being added on 30 Apr. In the case of the Brideoaks estate bill, concerning land in Oxfordshire, he reported on 26 May, despite having no discernible connexion with anyone directly involved. Finally, he seems to have been instrumental in reviving proceedings on the bill to alter the standard of plate, which was languishing until his name was added to the committee on 22 May. Eight days later he reported it to the House and the bill passed on 1 June.[3]

Bracebridge continued to be an active Member in the following session. He managed through the House a bill to make it easier for sheriffs to pass their accounts at the Exchequer, carrying it up to the Lords on 1 Mar. 1712. Following a fortnight's leave granted on the 24th, he returned to report twice from the committee dealing with the petition of two London wine merchants who wished to be excused the duty on Portuguese wine which they had accidentally sold retail instead of wholesale, and also from the committee dealing with a bill from the Lords involving the Warwickshire estate of Thomas Vyner. Bracebridge also acted as a teller on 24 May against a successful adjournment motion.

In the final session of the 1710 Parliament, Bracebridge continued to be active. He reported from committee two private bills dealing with bankruptcy and naturalization, and also on 3 July reported on the bill to explain the legislation licensing hackney chairs. He acted as a teller on 11 June 1713 in favour of giving a second reading to a bill allowing two prize ships to import cargoes into Britain. Continued loyalty to the Tory ministry is shown by his vote on 18 June 1713 for the French commerce bill.

Re-elected unopposed in 1713, Bracebridge was named to four drafting committees in the 1714 session, but only undertook the management of a naturalization bill, which he reported to the House on 7 May. His political views remained unaltered, for on the Worsley list and on two lists analysing the returns for 1715 through a comparison with the 1713 Parliament he was classed as a Tory. Bracebridge continued to represent Tamworth as a Tory until unseated on petition following the 1722 election. He appears to have been out of sympathy with the new regime, apparently prosecuting as rioters some people celebrating George I's coronation in November 1714. This may explain why he was left out of the Leicestershire commission of the peace on the Duke of Rutland's (John Manners*) recommendation in January 1715. In July 1715, he launched an attack on Lord Chancellor Cowper (William*) over the failure of local justices to put down riots in Wolverhampton, which probably explains why he was then removed from the Warwickshire bench as well in October 1715. Despite such personal setbacks, Bracebridge flourished financially, being obliged to add a codicil to his will in October 1718 because of his increasing fortune, estimated at £1,000 p.a. at his death. He was buried at Fenny Drayton on 11 Nov. 1735.[4]

[1] Nichols, Leics. iii. 1146. [2] Ibid.; Leics. Arch. Soc. xiv. 94; Add. 70213, Bracebridge to [Robert Harley*], 8 July 1704; Bath mss at Longleat House, Thynne pprs. 28, ff. 328–9; Cal. I. T. Recs. iii. 346. [3] Leics. RO, Braye mss 2850, Bracebridge to Cave, 6 Feb. 1710–11. [4] L. K. J. Glassey, Appt. JPs, 233, 238, 251; PCC 23 Derby; Gent. Mag. 1735, p. 682.

S. N. H.

BRADSHAIGH, Henry (1676–1712), of Haigh Hall, Lancs.

WIGAN 1708–July 1712

b. 6 Apr. 1676, 2nd s. of Sir Roger Bradshaigh, 2nd Bt.†, of Haigh by Mary, da. and coh. of Henry Murray of Berkhamsted, Herts., groom of the bedchamber to Charles I; bro. of Sir Roger Bradshaigh, 3rd Bt.* educ. privately (Mr Francis); Cartmel sch. unm.[1]

Capt. Visct. Shannon's (Richard Boyle*) marines 1702–d., maj. 1706–10; a.d.c. to Earl Rivers (Richard Savage*) in Spain 1706–8.[2]

Burgess, Wigan 1699, mayor 1709–10.[3]

Bradshaigh, a younger son, was left only £500 from family estates heavily encumbered with debts. His need to forge a career, and his brother Sir Roger's connexion with Earl Rivers (Richard Savage*), led him to purchase a commission in the marines in July 1702, and in 1706 Rivers promoted him while travelling to the Continent for active service. The return of Bradshaigh on the family interest at Wigan had been contemplated in 1705, but Sir Roger's defeat in the county election disrupted these plans, and he was not returned for Wigan until 1708. His only recorded parliamentary activity in the 1708 Parliament was his vote in favour of the impeachment of Dr Sacheverell in 1710. Returned unopposed in 1710, he was classed as a Whig in the 'Hanover list', but one observer noted that 'he is under Lord Rivers' power'. He was among the marine officers who petitioned for payment of arrears on 2 Apr. 1712, but by 7 July he had been visited by a London cleric concerned to ensure that Bradshaigh's temporal affairs were settled, and he had died by 14 July when he was removed from his regiment's listing.[4]

[1] IGI, Lancs.; info. from Mrs D. Backhouse. [2] NLS, Crawford mss 47/1/36, appointment as maj. 7 July 1706. [3] Wigan RO, Wigan bor. recs. AB/MR/10; AB/CL/102. [4] Lancs. RO, Kenyon mss DDKe 9/101/1, Thomas to George Kenyon*, 18 Jan 1704[-5]; *Bull. John Rylands Lib.* xxxvii. 18; *HMC Portland*, iv. 578–9; Crawford mss 47/1/37, memo. of W. Richardson, 20 Aug. 1712.

E. C./R. D. H.

BRADSHAIGH, Sir Roger, 3rd Bt. (1675–1747), of Haigh Hall, nr. Wigan, Lancs.

WIGAN 1695–25 Feb. 1747

bap. 29 Apr. 1675, 1st s. of Sir Roger Bradshaigh, 2nd Bt.†, of Haigh; bro. of Henry*. *educ.* privately (Mr Francis); Ruthin sch. *m.* 22 June 1697 (with £600 p.a.), Rachel, da. of Sir John Guise, 2nd Bt.*, sis. of Sir John Guise, 3rd Bt.*, 4s. (2 *d.v.p.*) 3da. *suc.* fa. as 3rd Bt. 17 June 1687.[1]

Burgess, Wigan 1695, mayor 1698–9, 1703–4, 1719–20, 1724–5, 1729–30.[2]

Col. of ft. 1706–9.

Elected while still a minor, Bradshaigh's parliamentary career is notable primarily for its longevity, a distinction achieved against a background of severe financial problems that on occasion threatened his interest at Wigan. Although the discovery of coal on the family's estates in the 16th century brought the Bradshaighs considerable income in the 18th century, the costs of developing the coal fields meant that Bradshaigh's father left the estate heavily encumbered with debts, a burden with which the 3rd baronet struggled. These financial difficulties became acute by the 1710s, and the high cost of maintaining an electoral interest in the quarrelsome borough of Wigan forced Bradshaigh into a client–patron relationship with Robert Harley*. Financial pressure forced Bradshaigh to trim his sails to the prevailing political wind in the hope of receiving patronage from the ministry, so that by Anne's reign he was one of a small number of Members who 'upheld the ministry of the day through all the fluctuations of party fortunes, supporting the Court whether it leaned to the Whigs or the Tories'.[3]

Bradshaigh was placed under the guardianship of Peter Shakerley* in 1687, and in 1690 he supported Shakerley's successful bid for a seat at Wigan. The first indication of Bradshaigh's political beliefs came in 1694, when, as one of only two surviving trustees for the grammar school at Blackrod, near Wigan, he rejected a list of new appointees, on the grounds that the majority of those proposed were Presbyterians, and instead proposed an alternative list dominated by local Tories. Bradshaigh successfully contested Wigan in alliance with Shakerley in 1695, and their opponent (Sir) Alexander Rigby* conceded that, although aged only 20, 'Sir Roger Bradshaigh had out-managed him'. Bradshaigh appears to have closely followed Shakerley's lead on first entering the House, being forecast as a likely opponent of the Court in the divisions of 31 Jan. 1696 on the proposed council of trade, duly voting against the imposition of an abjuration oath on that day, initially refusing to sign the Association, and in March voting against fixing the price of guineas at 22*s*. This impeccable Tory record was enhanced when in the second session of the 1695 Parliament he voted against the attainder of Sir John Fenwick†. The following year he married a wife of moderate fortune, and his good relations with Shakerley were demonstrated in the latter's assistance in drafting the marriage settlement.[4]

Bradshaigh was meticulous in maintaining his interest at Wigan, organizing the successful campaign to have George Kenyon* appointed recorder, and in 1698 was returned for the borough with Orlando Bridgeman* despite the opposition of Rigby. His name appears on an analysis of about September 1698 as a supporter of the Country party, and he was also forecast as a probable opponent of the standing army. In 1699 a disagreement over money led to a split with his mentor, Shakerley complaining about Bradshaigh's tardy repayment of loans, an accusation that Bradshaigh felt breached a previous agreement between the two. He informed Shakerley that

> your fast friendship I have acknowledged and always shall, but when a man is resolved to leave me I must endeavour to leave him to make my life easy . . . I am sure there was no one more desirous of continuing a friendship with you than myself, but I find it a thing not always to be relied upon.

This breach heralded a shift in Bradshaigh's political allegiances. From 1701 he formed a close alliance with the 4th Earl Rivers (Richard Savage*), following Rivers' political line until the Earl's death in 1712. In early 1700 Bradshaigh was classed as doubtful, or perhaps as opposition, in an analysis of the House, but at the first Wigan election of 1701 he stood in alliance with the Whig Emmanuel Scrope Howe*. He stood successfully on a joint interest with his former opponent Rigby (like Howe a Whig) at Wigan in December 1701. On 7 May 1702 Bradshaigh was teller against an amendment to apply one third of the revenues from forfeited Irish estates to public uses.[5]

The decisive shift in Bradshaigh's politics is indicated by the conduct of the 1702 Wigan election, when the Tory Bridgeman allied with Hon. Henry and Hon. Edward Finch*, younger brothers of Lord Nottingham (Daniel Finch*), to make strenuous if ultimately futile attempts to defeat Bradshaigh. The first session of the 1702 Parliament saw Bradshaigh tell, on 9 Dec. 1702, in favour of a motion to go into ways and means to settle the land tax, and in the following session, on 2 Mar. 1704, he told in favour of bringing up a petition relating to the Irish forfeitures bill. In the 1704–5 session he was forecast, in October 1704, as a probable opponent of the Tack. On 29 Jan. 1705 he was appointed to the committee to draft a bill to empower Thomas Kenyon, the brother of George, to compound with the Treasury for a debt incurred as executor for the late receiver of the land tax for Cheshire and North Wales, and Bradshaigh managed this bill through the Commons.[6]

Bradshaigh's alliance with north-western Whigs became clearer in the election of 1705, when he canvassed for the county with the support of the Junto Whig the Earl of Derby (Hon. James Stanley*), but defeat by two Tory candidates forced Bradshaigh to take the seat at Wigan he had originally intended for his brother Henry. Listed as 'Low Church' in an analysis of the 1705 Parliament, Bradshaigh voted for the Court candidate for Speaker on 25 Oct. 1705. He told against the Tacker Sir Samuel Garrard, 4th Bt.*, on 1 Dec., on the right of election at Amersham and in February 1706 again divided with the Court on the 'place clause' of the regency bill. In June Bradshaigh secured an address from his constituency praising the conduct of the war and not 'omitting the Church being out of danger'. Two months prior to this address he had been given a commission to form a new foot regiment. Whether this was a move to improve his financial position, a colonelcy in a foot regiment being worth approximately £800 p.a., is impossible to say, but Bradshaigh proved to be a poor soldier. His regiment, sent to Ireland in 1706, was said to be 'very thin of officers and soldiers' with (in the words of one observer) 'the worst' clothing 'I ever saw'. Bradshaigh's military career was, however, to be brief, as in March 1709 he sold the regiment for £2,700.[7]

Classed as a Whig in a parliamentary list of early 1708, Bradshaigh found his return at Wigan the following year challenged by Bridgeman and the Finches, but was able to secure his own election and that of his brother Henry. In 1709 he voted for the bill to naturalize foreign Protestants. His worsening financial position, the cost of maintaining his interest at Wigan adding to his inherited debts, led him to petition the Commons on 12 Jan. 1709 for a bill to enable him to sell the portion of the Countess of Oxford's estate inherited by his family, and to break the entail on his Lancashire estates in order to pay his father's debts and his siblings' portions. The bill, management of which was entrusted to Shakerley, Bradshaigh's brother-in-law, Sir John Guise, 3rd Bt., and (Sir) Gilbert Dolben, duly passed into law in April 1709, but Bradshaigh's financial problems continued. A protracted dispute with Edward Finch over the pulling down of the corporation's gallery in Wigan church, and the erection of an organ in its place, drained Bradshaigh's finances from 1709 onwards. Having voted in early 1710 for the impeachment of Dr Sacheverell, Bradshaigh's return for Wigan in 1710 was unchallenged, and he was classed as a Whig in the 'Hanover list' of the new Parliament. However, after the ministerial revolution of 1710 he followed the lead of his patron Rivers and joined with Harley. Bradshaigh told on 12 Dec. 1710 against a place bill, demonstrating a loyalty to the ministry that stemmed in large part from an increasing need for financial support. As the case over the Wigan gallery wound its expensive way through the courts Bradshaigh sent Harley a series of increasingly desperate requests for assistance. On 22 June 1711 he wrote to Harley, now Lord Treasurer Oxford, that

> The adjournment of the House for above 14 days has laid me open to the law, and I have already been sent to that unless I immediately pay my several debts upon which are obtained judgments, they will put into execution tomorrow or next day. Do but imagine the confusion I am in, and the reasons I have to hope for your favour before this time. My house will be rifled, myself and family exposed.

In November 1711 Bradshaigh requested that Oxford find him a place as a victualling commissioner, and on 17 Mar. 1712 he asked for £1,000, a request necessitated by 'the misfortune of a law suit I have long been engaged in for the benefit of my corporation and to keep up my interest there'. Bradshaigh's financial dependence upon the Court at this time may explain his telling on 2 Apr. 1712 against a petition that Arthur Moore* waive his privilege in a case involving a bad debt. On 7 Apr. he renewed his request to Oxford for the victualling commission place, begging the Lord Treasurer to 'find some way to assist me'. On 24 Apr. Bradshaigh, after prompting from Wigan braziers, told against laying a further duty on wrought brass. His requests for money were answered by Oxford in May 1712, and when he wrote to the lord treasurer regarding the Wigan by-election caused by the death of his brother, he assured Oxford that his own preferred candidate, George Kenyon, demonstrated 'affection to your Lordship's interest'. No doubt he expected such assurances to smooth the path of further requests for place or money; on 23 Feb. 1713 he assured Oxford that 'your Lordship has many friends, but none have been more zealous for your service than myself'. The 1713 session saw Bradshaigh present, on 13 Apr., a bill to make the River Douglas navigable, a scheme supported by the corporation of Wigan and which would have improved the transport links for his own coal pits at Haigh. His continuing support for the ministry, demonstrated by his vote on 18 June for the French commerce bill, yielded £1,000 from Oxford in August 1713.[8]

Bradshaigh's return for Wigan in 1713 was fiercely contested by Lord Barrymore (James Barry*), and although Bradshaigh secured the return of himself and Kenyon, the financial cost of victory was one he could not bear alone. Soon after the election he wrote requesting a further £400 from Oxford to defray his election expenses, and his financial problems gave Barrymore the opportunity to petition against Bradshaigh and Kenyon's return, alleging that they were not qualified to sit in the Commons under the terms of the Landed Qualification Act of 1711. Defending these claims entailed more expense for Bradshaigh, and he consequently renewed his requests for financial support from Oxford, who was assured that 'your Lordship may depend upon two sure friends' at Wigan. Bradshaigh told Oxford that such support 'shall not be like seed thrown on barren ground', and the requests were of some urgency as in February 1714 Bradshaigh feared 'an execution upon my goods in the country'. Bradshaigh would no doubt have been relieved at the Commons' rejection of the petition against Kenyon and himself on 6 Apr., but he was still under financial pressure from the costs of the legal case brought by Barrymore concerning the Wigan mayoral election of October 1713, and these demands led to further requests for financial assistance from Bradshaigh to Oxford. In July 1714 for example, Bradshaigh informed the lord treasurer that 'since the rising of the House I have had notice to expect the uttermost severity of the law from persons who have obtained judgments against me'. Self-interest probably accounted for Bradshaigh's distress at Oxford's dismissal in July 1714, though his surprise did not prevent him making one final request for financial aid. At the end of 1714 Bradshaigh came to an agreement with Barrymore by which they were to split the borough's representation at the forthcoming election. Although he was described as a Tory in the Worsley list and in two separate analyses comparing the 1713 and 1715 Parliaments, Bradshaigh's allegiance to the Court continued to be the primary, if not the sole, theme of his political career under the first two Georges. His financial problems did ease somewhat in the 1720s and 1730s, but when he died on 25 Feb. 1747, he still left debts amounting to £8,000.[9]

[1] NLS, Crawford mss 47/1/74, notebk. of Ralph Winstanley; info. from Mrs D. Backhouse. [2] Wigan RO, Wigan bor. recs. AB/MR/10; AB/CL/80, 90, 106. [3] J. U. Nef, *Rise of the British Coal Industry*, i. 61–63, 203; J. Langton, *Geographical Change and Industrial Revol.* 74, 88; Cheshire RO, Shakerley mss, draft of Bradshaigh Estate Act; *Bull. John Rylands Lib.* xxxvii. 123–5; Speck thesis, 95. [4] Crawford mss E3/6, Bradshaigh to William Hulton, 2 Jan. 1693[-4]; Liverpool RO, 920MD 174 Sir Willoughby Aston diaries, 7 Nov. 1695; Lancs. RO, Kenyon mss DDKe/66, brief for Mr Shakerley, c.1695; *HMC Kenyon*, 398–9; Shakerley mss, John Ward III* to Shakerley, 24 Sept. 1697. [5] *HMC Kenyon*, 423–4; PC 2/77, p. 160; Crawford mss 47/3/1 petition, c.1697; Kenyon mss DDKe 9/131/56, Bradshaigh to James Harvey, 12 Mar. 1697[-8]; Yale Univ. Beinecke Lib. Osborn coll. Blathwayt mss box 20, Robert Yard* to William Blathwayt*, 9 Aug. 1698; Shakerley mss, Bradshaigh to Shakerley, 28 Apr. 1699; 920MD 174 Aston diary, 22 Dec. 1701. [6] Cheshire RO, Arderne mss DAR/F/33, Samuel Daniell to [?], 31 July 1702. [7] Bagot mss at Levens Hall, Duke of Hamilton to James Grahme*, 16 Jan. 1704–5; Kenyon mss DDKe 9/101/1, Thomas to George Kenyon, 18 Jan. 1704[-5]; *HMC Kenyon*, 434, 437, 449; *Cal. Treas. Bks.* xx. 216, 738, 768; xxi. 450, 504; xxii. 15, 195; R. E. Scouller, *Armies of Q. Anne*, 126–47; *London Gazette*, 27 June–1 July 1706; *HMC Ormonde*, n.s. viii. 281; Add. 31143, f. 315. [8] Shakerley mss, Bradshaigh estate bill; Kenyon mss DDKe 9/132/41, Bradshaigh to Henry Mason, 7 Feb. 1710[-11]; Crawford mss 47/3/52, subscription, c.1711; *HMC Portland*, v. 18, 151; Add. 70213, Bradshaigh to Oxford, 7 Nov. 1711, 7 Apr., 14 May, 9 July, 8 Sept 1712, 23 Feb. 1712[-3], 18, 26 Aug 1713; *HMC Kenyon*, 450. [9] Add. 70213, Bradshaigh to Oxford, 6 Dec. 1713, 8 Jan., 9 Feb. 1713[-4], 26 Apr., 12 May, 17 July, 22 Aug. 1714; *HMC Kenyon*, 455; Crawford mss 47/3/38, Kenyon to Robert Hollinshead, 11 Dec. 1714.

E. C./R. D. H.

BRAMSTON, Thomas (1658–1737), of Waterhouse, Writtle, Essex.

MALDON 28 Jan. 1712–1727

bap. 10 Nov. 1658, 6th s. of Sir Mundeford Bramston, master in Chancery, and bro. of Sir John Bramston*, of Little Baddow by Alice, da. of Sir George Le Hunt of Little Bradley, Suff. *m.* 7 Aug. 1690, Grace (*d.* 1718), da. of Sir Henry Gregory, rector of Middleton Stoney, Oxon., 3s. (1 *d.v.p.*) 3da.[1]

Clerk in Chancery.

Freeman, Maldon 1679; capital burgess 1702, alderman 1713–d., bailiff 1716, 1720, 1724, 1728, 1732.[2]

Bramston's parliamentary career has frequently been conflated with that of his cousin and namesake, Thomas Bramston† of Skreens. The latter has been cited as having sat in Parliament from 1712 until 1747, but in fact could not easily have entered Parliament at the Maldon by-election in 1712, since he was born in September 1691, and would thus have been under 21 at the time, and ineligible to sit. Indeed, he was only made a freeman of the borough in December 1712, whereas the MP is described as a burgess at the time of his election. Nor was Bramston of Skreens chosen in

1715. In 1714 his father, Anthony Bramston of Skreens, referred to a 'cousin' standing for Maldon at the next election, by which he must have meant Thomas Bramston of Waterhouse. A notice of the latter's death in 1737 conclusively describes him as having represented the borough 'the last two Parliaments of Queen Anne and during the reign of his late Majesty'. It seems, therefore, that Thomas Bramston of Waterhouse sat from 1712 until the election in August 1727, when Thomas Bramston of Skreens took over the seat. This would explain the change in title on the official return for that year, to include the office of chief steward of Maldon, a post to which Bramston of Skreens had been appointed in 1722 on the death of his father, and also why 1727 seems to mark a dramatic increase in parliamentary activity recorded in the Journals and elsewhere. It would explain the younger Bramston's membership of Edward Harley's* 'Board', which began in 1727, a club in which Bramston of Waterhouse would have appeared a very old man.[3]

Thomas Bramston of Waterhouse was the youngest, and least talented, brother of George, a lawyer in the surrogate high court of Admiralty who had unsuccessfully contested Maldon in 1695, and William, fellow of Queens', Cambridge, and later prebendary of Worcester. It was presumably through the influence of his father, a master in Chancery, that Thomas became a clerk in the six clerks' office in Chancery Lane, near which he must have had lodgings, since his children were christened at St. Andrew's, Holborn. His uncle, Sir John Bramston, noted in a section of autobiography probably written between 1683 and 1685 that

> Sir William Parkins was very desirous the master of the rolls would have admitted him, and went with me to the master to prevail with him to do it, but he wanting a little time, Sir Harbottle Grimston† refused us both absolutely; he keeps the desk notwithstanding and is in good business, so that none of the chief clerks but are desirous he should come into their office.

In what must be an amendment to the text, made before his death in 1700, Sir John added that Thomas had been 'since admitted and sworn a clerk, and hath a desk in another office under another chief clerk'. Thomas was able to repay his uncle's interest in his advancement by acting for him as clerk in a Chancery suit over the estate of Sir John Berkenhead†. He does not, however, seem to have risen beyond this position, since Morant's 18th-century history of Essex describes him simply as 'of the six clerks' office', and his name appears on a petition of 1707 from its sworn clerks. Thomas was a frequent visitor at Skreens, where on 2 Sept. 1699 he dined with his brothers and his nephew, William Fytche*, who shared a prominent role in Maldon borough politics. Bramston was also intimate with like-minded Anglicans and fellow local office-holders, Sir Charles Barrington, 5th Bt.*, and John Comyns*. His own entry into politics came in 1699, when he gave evidence to the Commons' elections committee in support of Fytche's petition against Irby Montagu*, and he testified to the committee again in January 1702, this time in favour of Comyns, when he told MPs that he had been present the previous autumn 'all the time of the election, and there was not above one person that polled for Mr Fytche and Mr Comyns object[ed] to'. Standing on the Bramston interest at Maldon, he was returned at a by-election in January 1712, and although not recorded as having made any speeches, he voted for the French commerce bill on 18 June 1713, and was marked as a Tory on the Worsley and two other lists. In April 1713 he had become an alderman of Maldon, where he continued to hold prominent municipal office until his death, and attracted the attention of Lord Bolingbroke (Henry St. John II*), who inserted him into the commission of the peace for the county in March 1714. In October 1715 his cousin, Anthony Bramston, was arrested with others suspected of being disaffected to George I, and it may have been Thomas of Waterhouse who donated 'a sirloin of beef and a turkey' to those imprisoned, an act which would probably account for his removal as a j.p. in March of the following year. He was listed as a Tory in 1723 and continued to represent Maldon, probably until 1727. He may have retired due to ill-health, since his will is dated 1728, and he died on 30 May 1737, leaving the bulk of his estate to his son George, and establishing a trust fund, to be administered in part by Thomas Bramston of Skreens, for the provision of his daughters and younger son. His elder son, George, married the daughter of Lawrence Alcock*, and the eldest daughter married the third son of Sir Herbert Croft, 1st Bt.* In the light of Bramston's Chancery clerkship it is ironic that the will was so defaced with 'obliterations and interlineations' that it was not until August 1739 that George Bramston could satisfy the probate court that its terms had remained unaltered after his father's death.[4]

[1] IGI, London; Berry, *Essex Gens.* 51; *Bramston Autobiog.* (Cam. Soc. xxxii), ped. xx; *Le Neve's Knights* (Harl. Soc. viii), 14. [2] Essex RO, Maldon bor. recs. sessions bks. D/B3/1/23; D/B3/1/24, ff. 175, 319, 326, 346, 358–9; D/B3/1/25, ff. 33, 55, 81, 127, 179, 199, 239, 263, 295, 343, 364, 388, 504, 563, 578. [3] IGI, Essex (Bramston of Skreens); Maldon bor. recs. D/B3/1/16; D/B3/1/25, ff. 181, 312; Camb. Univ. Lib. Cholmondeley Houghton mss 683, Anthony Bramston to Robert Walpole II*, 1 Oct. 1714; *Hist. Reg. Chron.*

1737, p. 10; *Hist. Jnl.* xx. 95. [4]*Bramston Autobiog.* xx. 29, 361, 411; Morant, *Essex*, ii. 73; inf. from Prof. H. Horwitz; *VCH Essex*, ii. 535; L. K. J. Glassey, *Appt. JPs*, 224; *Essex Rev.* xxix. 103; *Gent. Mag.* 1737, p. 371; *Parlty. Hist.* xv. 349; PCC 170 Henchman.

M. J. K.

BRANDON, Charles Gerard, Visct. *see* GERARD

BRAY, Edmund (1678–1725), of Great Barrington, Glos.

TEWKESBURY 1701 (Feb.)–1708
GLOUCESTERSHIRE 22 June 1720–1722

bap. 7 Sept. 1678, 4th but 1st surv. s. of Reginald Bray of Great Barrington by Jane, da. of William Rainton of Shilton, Berks. *m.* 16 Dec. 1697, Frances, da. and h. of Sir Edward Morgan, 3rd Bt.[†], of Llantarnam, Mon., 3s. (1 *d.v.p.*) 3da. (1 *d.v.p.*). *suc. fa.* 1688.[1]

Freeman, Gloucester 1713.[2]

The fortunes of the Bray family had been founded in the late 15th century by Sir Reginald Bray, a favourite of Henry VII. One of Bray's younger nephews established a branch of the family in Gloucestershire, acquiring Great Barrington in 1553. Edmund Bray, having in 1697 married a considerable fortune, was returned as a Whig for Tewkesbury in the January 1701 election and retained his seat until 1708. He was wholly inactive in the House, however, and was several times granted long leaves of absence, on two occasions (20 Dec. 1704 and 29 Nov. 1707) for reasons of health. In the election of 1702 he successfully repelled a challenge at Tewkesbury from Sir Richard Cocks, 2nd Bt.* In the division on the Tack on 28 Nov. 1704 he either voted against or was absent. He successfully brought in a complaint of breach of privilege in February 1705 against attempts to eject some of the tenants on his wife's estates in Monmouthshire. Classed as 'Low Church' in a list of about June 1705, he voted for the Court candidate for Speaker on 25 Oct. His closeness to the Court is demonstrated in a letter to Secretary Robert Harley* of September 1706 in which he referred to 'the many obligations I lie under [to] you' and stressed his readiness to 'receive and obey your commands (upon all occasions) with the greatest pleasure'. He was noted as a Whig in a list of early 1708. He declined to stand for re-election at Tewkesbury in 1708, and when he stood for Cirencester in 1713 achieved only a poor fourth place in the poll. He was finally to return to the Commons in a county by-election in June 1720, when he continued to support the Whigs.[3]

Bray owned the quarries which provided some of the stone used in building Blenheim Palace, petitioning the government in 1717 for the payment of debts owing to him. He died on 6 Sept. 1725 and was buried at Great Barrington.[4]

[1] *Glos. N. and Q.* i. 241, 358–9; *Bristol and Glos. Arch. Soc. Trans.* lvii. 170–5; *Bigland's Colls.* (Glos. Rec. Ser. ii), 136. [2] *Gloucester Freemen* (Glos. Rec. Ser. iv), 73. [3] *Bristol and Glos. Arch. Soc. Trans.* lv. 298; lvii. 172–3; Add. 70213, Bray to Harley, 23 Sept. 1706. [4] *Cal. Treas. Pprs.* 1714–19, p. 323; *Bristol and Glos. Arch. Soc. Trans.* lvii. 173.

P. W.

BRENT, Edward (1656–1698), of Greenhithe, Kent and St. Olave's, Southwark, Surr.

SANDWICH 1690–28 Mar. 1698

bap. 18 Sept. 1656, 1st s. of Edward Brent of St. Olave's, Southwark, alderman of London 1668, by Christian, da. of Roger White of Dover, Kent. *unm. suc. fa.* 1677.[1]

Freeman, Sandwich 1690.[2]

In 1668 Brent's father was made an assistant of the shipwrights' company and the same year he fined for alderman of Cordwainers Ward. He had property interests in the City and Southwark, and in Kent where he owned hoys, chalk-pits and lime kilns, presumably shipping goods up to his wharves in Southwark. From his will it has been surmised that he was a Dissenter, a contention supported by the appearance of his son's name on a list of those to be inserted in February 1688 into the Kentish commission of the peace. Lacking property in the vicinity of Sandwich, Brent's main appeal to the freemen of the borough may well have been his Dissenting antecedents. He was admitted a freeman on the day of his election to Parliament in 1690, and added to the commission of the peace for the county in the following week.[3]

Further evidence, perhaps, of Brent's Nonconformist leanings can be found in the concern expressed by Roger Morrice over the petition presented against his election. The Whig Sir John Trenchard* saw Brent's triumph at the committee of elections as a victory for his party and the eventual division in the House on 31 Oct. 1690 was seen as a party cause. The Marquess of Carmarthen (Sir Thomas Osborne†) classed Brent as a Whig on an analysis of the 1690 Parliament, while Robert Harley* in April 1691 listed him as a doubtful but possible Court supporter. On 16 Dec. 1691 he was added to the drafting committee preparing a bill for making saltpetre in England, possibly in recognition of his own interests in mining and manufacturing. Nothing further of note occurs in the parliamentary record until the 1695 general election. On the very day of the poll, 22 Oct., John Freke informed Harley that 'Brent says he is sure'. In the event, his erstwhile partner, John Thurbarne*, petitioned against the result, but Brent's election was confirmed by the Commons on 31 Jan. 1696. Brent was forecast as likely to support the Court in the divisions over the proposed council of trade on 31 Jan., he signed the Association in February, and in March voted with the Court to fix the price of guineas at 22s. His only recorded tellership occurred on 18 Apr. 1696 when, at the report stage of a bill confirming a grant to the Earl of Torrington (Arthur Herbert†) of part of Bedford Level, Brent opposed a successful amendment obliging the Earl to perform all the covenants and agreements entered into by James II. In the following session he voted on 25 Nov. 1696 for the attainder of Sir John Fenwick†. He received leave of absence on 21 Jan. 1697 to go into the country to recover his health, and it may be that he was ailing at this date, for in October 1697, Thurbarne, although not a Member, was asked by the corporation to present its address to the King. On 8 Mar. 1698 a petition from George 'Etkyns' was presented to the Commons asking for liberty to sue Brent, notwithstanding his privilege, for failure to pay the purchase money for several pieces of land in Kent, including a chalk-cliff. Having been referred to the committee of privileges, it was still pending when Brent died on 28 Mar. 1698. Possibly the petition indicates that Brent was suffering financial troubles, a suggestion which may be supported by two petitions to the crown from an Edward Brent for permission to bring writs of error in two separate suits in 1695 and 1697, and a commission to 'Edward Brent' and others on 15 Mar. 1697 to investigate the estates of one John Strafford, outlawed for treason, preparatory to a grant of the estates if discovered. No will has been found.[4]

[1] IGI, London; *Vis. Surr.* (Harl. Soc. lx), 14. [2] Centre Kentish Stud. Sandwich bor. recs. Sa/Ac8, p. 279. [3] J. R. Woodhead, *Rulers of London* (London and Mdx. Arch. Soc.), 36; PCC 37 Hales; Duckett, *Penal Laws and Test Act* (1883), 288; info. from Prof. N. Landau. [4] Morrice ent'ring bk. 3, f. 218; Dorset RO, Lane (Trenchard) mss D60/F56, Trenchard to Henry Trenchard†, 21 Oct. 1690; Add. 70018, f. 94; *Post Boy*, 31 Mar.–2 Apr. 1698; *CSP Dom.* 1695, p. 79; 1697, p. 114; *Cal. Treas. Bks.* xi. 425.

S. N. H.

BRERETON, Edward (c.1642–1725), of Borras, Denb.

DENBIGH BOROUGHS 1689–1705

b. c.1642, 2nd s. of Edward Brereton (*d.v.p.* 1st s. of Owen Brereton of Borras) by Jane, da. of John Griffith† of Cefnamwlch, Lleyn, Caern. *educ.* Oriel, Oxf. matric. 1659; L. Inn 1660. *m.* (1) lic. 22 Nov. 1664 (with £3,500), Elizabeth (*d.* 1680), da. of Sir Thomas Lake† of Canons Park, Edgware, Mdx., 5s. (4 *d.v.p.*); (2) lic. 23 Dec. 1703, Elizabeth (*d.* aft. 1716), da. of Sir Hugh Owen, 2nd Bt.*, wid. of Lewis Anwyl, of Parc, Llanfrothan, Merion., *s.p. suc.* bro. 1657.[1]

Sheriff, Denb. 1675–6, 1677–8; freeman, Ruthin 1679, alderman 1692–3; mayor, Holt 1681–2, 1710–11; common councilman, Denbigh 1693–*d.*, alderman 1696–7.[2]

Commr. prizes June 1702–May 1706, salt May 1706–Dec. 1714.[3]

Although he possessed some influence of his own, deriving from his position as a country gentleman and his personal involvement in the municipal affairs of all three of the corporations which made up the Denbigh Boroughs constituency, Brereton owed his seat chiefly to the recommendation of Sir Richard Myddelton, 3rd Bt.* A decade earlier, in 1679, he had worked against the Myddelton interest in the county, but the 3rd baronet's politics were much closer to his own, and, until taking government office in 1702, he seems to have acted as a loyal dependant of Sir Richard, both nationally and locally. As befitted the stepson of an Anglican bishop (Humphrey Lloyd of Bangor), he was a Tory, voting in the Convention against the transfer of the crown, and he was listed as such in March 1690 by Lord Carmarthen (Sir Thomas Osborne†), who also marked him as a supporter of the Court. He served twice as a teller in May 1690: on the 15th, on the government side, in favour of passing the forfeited estates bill; and the following day, with another Tory, on an amendment to the bill vesting the hereditary revenue of the crown in William and Mary. In December 1690 Carmarthen included him in a list of supporters, probably drawn up in connexion with a projected attack on the Marquess in Parliament, but in April 1691 Robert Harley* classed Brereton as a supporter of the Country party. He was a teller again on 6 Mar. 1693, against a bill introduced on behalf of Lord Pembroke (Thomas Herbert†) to set aside amendments by Lord Chief Justice Jeffreys to the records of a fine and two recoveries in Wales: a party cause for Welsh Tories. Four more tellerships followed in the next session: on the Tory side in the Clitheroe and Worcester election cases (2, 7 Feb. 1694); against an amendment to the London orphans bill intended to safeguard the rights of one Samuel Hutchinson (8 Mar.); and against committing to custody Hugh Fortescue* for inattendance at the House (14 Mar.). In the following session he was listed among Henry Guy's* 'friends', in connexion with the Commons' attack upon Guy. With Myddelton 'in the country',

Brereton presented the original petition from the inhabitants of the lordship of Denbigh in April 1695, requesting a hearing at the Treasury against the proposed grants to Lord Portland. He later spoke on the petitioners' behalf to the Treasury board, seconding the objections raised by Sir William Williams, 1st Bt.*, though by all accounts not very effectively, and in January 1696 lent his weight to the petition to the Commons on the same subject. Forecast as likely to oppose the Court in the divisions of 31 Jan. 1696 on the council of trade, he followed Myddelton in refusing the Association and suffered the same retribution as his patron in being removed from the commission of the peace. He subsequently voted against fixing the price of guineas and, on 25 Nov. 1696, against the attainder of Sir John Fenwick†. Meanwhile in March and April 1696 he had managed through the Commons a bill to abolish the testamentary 'custom of Wales'. Given leave of absence for eight days on 5 Apr. 1698, he was back in the House by 26 May, when he told against an amendment to a resolution of the committee of ways and means concerning the establishment of the New East India Company, acting to protect the trading privileges of the Old Company. Further tellerships on the Old Company's behalf, against the second reading of the East India bill on 10 June 1698, against an amendment on 18 June to empower the Treasury to accept bank bills, and in favour of an additional clause on the 23rd, to retain parliamentary supervision of the trade, demonstrate a particular commitment over this issue.[4]

Re-elected in 1698 after a fierce contest with the son of the Country Whig Sir Robert Cotton, 1st Bt.*, Brereton was classified as a member of the Country party in a comparative analysis of the old and new Parliaments, and was included upon a forecast of likely opponents of a standing army. In the following three years Brereton closely supported Myddelton in the struggle with Cotton for control of Denbigh Boroughs, bringing a successful lawsuit against the pro-Cotton mayor of Holt over the illegal swearing of freemen there, and assisting Myddelton in a counter-active admission of freemen in Denbigh corporation, a controversial tactic which provoked a riot among the townsmen. In the Commons he was a teller once more on 1 Apr. 1700, against receiving a clause on behalf of a Mrs Wandesford as a rider to the land tax and Irish forfeitures resumption bill. The next general election saw another rancorous contest in Denbigh Boroughs, with Brereton winning a decisive victory. Brereton's support for the remodelled ministry was evident from his inclusion in February 1701 in a forecast of those likely to support the Court in the supply committee's resolution to continue the 'Great Mortgage'. On 11 Apr. Brereton was appointed to draft a bill, initiated following a petition from the brine salt producers of Cheshire, to prevent frauds and abuses in the salt duties. It was, however, the feud between the Myddelton and Cotton interests, fuelled by Brereton's attempt to succeed Cotton as steward of the lordship of Denbigh, which led to Brereton's most notable contribution to this Parliament. On 1 June 1701, in a debate on the land tax, Brereton queried the names of the new commissioners for Denbighshire: these, he said, were men mostly unknown to him, except for one who was Sir Robert Cotton's 'servant'. Cotton replied that

> they were men of account, and recommended to him by men of estates. Sir Robert was very angry, and when the House rose he struck Brereton over the head with a little cane just out of Westminster Hall. Brereton returned the compliment with two hard blows over the face with the head of his great cane.

Brereton was not blacklisted before the second election of 1701 as one who had opposed the preparations for war, but he was listed by Harley with the Tories in the 1701–2 Parliament, and he was listed as having favoured the motion of 26 Feb. 1702 vindicating the Commons' proceedings of the previous Parliament in the impeachments of the four Whig lords.[5]

Appointment in June 1702 as a commissioner of prizes at a salary of £500 a year, decried as it was by one Whig satirist who recalled Brereton's Country party record, did not at first make much difference to his voting in the Commons. He was a teller, for the last time, on 10 Nov. 1702, against taking into custody the under-sheriff of Merioneth for failure to return the election writ. In March 1704 Lord Nottingham (Daniel Finch†) forecast Brereton as a probable supporter in the proceedings upon the Scotch Plot. It was over the Tack, in 1704, that the break came. Forecast in late October as a likely opponent, he was included upon Harley's lobbying list and Lord Godolphin (Sidney†) deputed William Lowndes* to approach all commissioners for prizes, including Brereton, upon this matter. He was subsequently included upon a list, specifically excluding 'sneakers', of those who were either absent from the crucial division of 28 Nov., or had voted against this measure. Little is known of his subsequent parliamentary activity, other than that in 1705 he was listed as a placeman, but his failure to support the Tack cost him dear in Denbighshire. His occupancy of office had already raised doubts in the minds of locals as to his qualification to continue as a parliamentary candidate. Now he was informed that 'the temper and inclinations of the country gentlemen are not so favourable to me'. Such was the general feeling that he was obliged to abandon his campaign for re-election, though not before he had attempted to justify his conduct to Myddelton. 'I hear that some persons have aspersed me', he wrote,

and reported that I am turned a Whig. I cannot guess at the reason of it, unless it be that I did not stay in the House to vote for the tacking of the bill against occasional conformity to the land tax bill. I considered that the Lords had formerly published their resolution not to pass any bill that had another tacked to it, and that the former misunderstandings between both Houses were rather increased than diminished, and that it would be a dangerous experiment to try the success of that proposed tack, lest the miscarriage of the land tax bill might bring difficulties upon the nation; and delay the necessary supplies to the fleet and army.

But I must not forget to acquaint you, that I was heartily zealous for the bill itself against occasional conformity; and when the motion was made for leave to bring it into the House 'twas vigorously opposed, and I divided for it; and afterwards I appeared for the bill in all the steps which it made in the House (except in the tacking part) and now you have the history of my fanaticism; and I had rather be called a pickpocket than a Whig.[6]

Brereton's change of post in 1706 (which had been rumoured as early as the preceding October) may have been undertaken with an eye to qualifying himself for election again, since commissioners of prizes had been specifically excluded from Parliament under the terms of the recently passed Regency Act, and the commissionership of salt to which he was transferred carried exactly the same salary. However, although he was not on bad terms with Myddelton, joining his former patron in November 1705 in pressing to have a 'quiet, peaceable' non-juror excused from serving as sheriff of Denbigh, he does not appear to have been considered ever again as a parliamentary candidate. For the remainder of Anne's reign he presented a picture of a dutiful administrator, even becoming a voting stockholder in the Bank of England by 1710. But he was still dismissed on the Hanoverian succession.[7]

Brereton died on 10 Jan. 1725, aged 82, and was buried at Gresford, Denbighshire. His will noted purchases of lands in his home county, and the ownership of a house in St. James's, Westminster. It also advised the only surviving son to marry off his children to persons of good family and sober education hailing from within 50 miles of 'his mansion house of Borras'.[8]

[1] J. E. Griffith, *Peds. Anglesey and Caern. Fams.* 7, 58, 241; *London Mar. Lic.* ed. Foster, 177; A. N. Palmer, *Country Townships of Wrexham*, 164. [2] *Trans. Denb. Hist. Soc.* x. 37, 47; A. N. Palmer, *Town of Holt*, 149; J. Williams, *Recs. of Denbigh*, 142–3, 146. [3] *Cal. Treas. Bks.* xvii. 250; xx. 647, 650; xxix. 194. [4] *Cal. Treas. Bks.* x. 582, 1375; Cobbett, *Parlty. Hist.* v. 979; L. K. J. Glassey, *Appt. JPs*, 123. [5] *CJ*, xiii. 353–4; A. L. Cust, *Chrons. of Erthig*, i. 59–61; Luttrell, *Brief Relation*, iv. 533; *Cocks Diary*, 158. [6] *Cal. Treas. Bks.* xvii. 250; *Poems on Affairs of State* ed. Ellis, vi. 495–6; *Bull. IHR*, xli. 182; NLW, Chirk Castle mss E4204, Brereton to Myddelton, 3 Mar. 1704[-5]; E1010, 1000, 1012, Robert Wynne to same, 13, 21, 14 Mar. 1705; E6066, Myddelton to Wynne, 29 Mar. 1705; E6064, same to Sir William Williams, 2nd Bt.*, 7 Apr. 1705; E6065, Williams to Myddelton, 13 Apr. 1705; E979, William Robinson* to same, [1705]. [7] Folger Shakespeare Lib. Newdigate newsletter 30 Oct. 1705; *HMC Portland*, iv. 350; viii. 198; Egerton 3359 (unfol.). [8] Palmer, *Country Townships of Wrexham*, 162, 165.

D. W. H.

BRETT, Henry (1675–1724), of Cowley and Sandywell Park, nr. Dowdeswell, Glos.

BISHOP'S CASTLE   1701 (Dec.)–1708

b. 5 Dec. 1675, 1st s. of Henry Brett[†] of Down Hatherley, Glos. by Hester, da. of Richard Eynes of Enstone, Oxon. *educ.* Balliol, Oxf. 1693; M. Temple 1695. *m.* c.1701, Anne, da. of Sir Richard Mason[†] of Bishop's Castle, Salop and Sutton, Surr., div. w. of Charles Gerard*, Visct. Brandon, 2nd Earl of Macclesfield, 1da.[1]

Lt.-col. of ft. Sir Charles Hotham's* regt. 1705–6.

Country squire and man about town, Brett was a witty and charming companion, welcomed by the theatrical and literary celebrities whose society he sought. Colley Cibber, an intimate friend for many years, gives the following account of his early life. Brett's father, a Royalist during the Civil War,

coming early to his estate of about two thousand a year, by the usual negligences of young heirs had, before this his eldest son came of age, sunk it to about half that value, and that not wholly free from encumberances. Mr Brett . . . had his education, and I might say ended it, at the University of Oxford; for though he was settled some time after at the Temple, he so little followed the law there that his neglect of it made the law (like some of his fair and frail admirers) follow him. As he had an uncommon share of social wit, and a handsome person, with a sanguine bloom in his complexion, no wonder they persuaded him that he might have a better chance of fortune by throwing such accomplishments into the gayer world than by shutting them up in a study.

After living the life of a rake for many years, Brett finally took the advice of his friends and married an heiress, albeit a somewhat tarnished prize. Encouraged to set his sights on the divorced Lady Macclesfield, as a woman with 'enough in her power to disencumber him of the world and make him every way easy for life', he hurriedly wooed and wed her. His wife (who it is said first set eyes on him when he was fighting off some bailiffs in the street) brought him a fortune of between £12,000 and £25,000, which restored the family finances and enabled him to build a new house at Sandywell Park.²

Lady Macclesfield also possessed, by inheritance from her father, an interest at Bishop's Castle, which she had deployed in a previous election in favour of her brother-in-law Sir William Brownlow, 4th Bt.*, a Whig, against other Whig candidates supported by her ex-husband. After Lord Macclesfield's death in November 1701 Brett joined forces with one of the late Earl's followers, Charles Mason*, who was Lady Macclesfield's cousin, and both men were returned following a contest with a local Tory. Brett's election was put down by Lord Spencer (Charles*) as a gain for the Whigs, but he voted on 26 Feb. 1702 for the resolution vindicating the Commons' proceedings in the impeachment of the Junto ministers. He and Mason were returned without opposition at the next general election. In addition to managing a private bill through the Commons in December 1702, he was a teller on the Tory side on 23 Dec. 1702 against a proposal to resume all crown grants made in the reign of James II, but on the other hand told for the Whigs on 19 Jan. 1703, in favour of Lord James Russell* in a disputed election for Tavistock. His three tellerships during the 1703–4 session were all on the Whig side: on 9 Dec. to adjourn all committees; on 20 Jan. against an amendment to the West Riding land registry bill; and on 2 Mar. against bringing up a petition relating to the Irish forfeitures bill. Forecast as a probable opponent of the Tack, he voted against it or was absent on 28 Nov. 1704 and in the next month again acted as a teller with the Whigs, against a motion that the committee on the bill for recruiting be empowered to receive a clause concerning the qualification of magistrates. In November Henry St. John II* had recommended Brett to the Duke of Marlborough (John Churchill†) for an officer's commission and in March 1705 he was made lieutenant-colonel in a newly raised regiment commanded by Sir Charles Hotham, 4th Bt.*, being listed later that year as a placeman.³

In 1705 Brett and Charles Mason again stood successfully at Bishop's Castle in the Whig interest. Though classed as a 'High Church courtier' in a list of the new Parliament, Brett voted for the Court candidate for Speaker on 25 Oct. 1705, and on 24 Nov. 1705 was a teller on the Whig side in an election case for St. Albans. He supported the Court over the regency bill on 18 Feb. 1706. Not long afterwards, when his regiment was ordered to Portugal, he obtained leave to resign his commission and was succeeded in his company by a younger brother. Cibber explained his resignation by saying that 'his ambition extended not beyond the bounds of a park wall, and a pleasant retreat in the corner of it, which with too much expense he had just finished', while Godolphin had written on 13 June 1706 that Brett 'is very desirous to sell. I don't know whether the Queen will allow of it, but I think a man who goes so unwillingly is not like to do much service.' In 1707 Brett purchased from a friend, Sir Thomas Skipwith, 2nd Bt.*, a half-share in the patent for the Drury Lane theatre, and for a brief time involved himself in the politics of the theatrical world, exploiting his position as a patentee and his personal influence with the vice-chamberlain to bring to fruition a pet scheme of Colley Cibber for the union of the Drury Lane company with Cibber's company at the Haymarket. But Brett was making no profit from his share in the patent, and soon became weary of the vexation which it brought him. When Skipwith began a legal action in January 1708 for the recovery of his share, Brett lost no time in making it over to Cibber and some associates. Surprisingly, Brett was classed as a Tory in two parliamentary lists of 1708.⁴

Brett did not stand again, his interest at Bishop's Castle having apparently 'fallen', but he was a member of the coterie of Whig wits, gathered around Joseph Addison*, who met regularly at Will's, and later at Button's, coffee-house. In about 1712 he sold Sandywell Park to Lord Conway (Francis Seymour Conway*). His will was dated 14 Sept. 1724 and was proved two days later.⁵

¹ *Trans. Salop Arch. Soc.* ser. 2, x. 55; *Vis. Glos.* ed. Fenwick and Metcalfe, 25; *Bristol and Glos. Arch. Soc. Trans.* xxviii. 218; *Misc. Gen. et Her.* (ser. 4), v. 143. ² Atkyns, *Glos.* 211; *Apology for Life of Cibber* (1740), pp. 212–18; Spence, *Anecdotes* ed. Singer (1964), p. 205. ³ Add. 61131, f. 120. ⁴ *Apology for Life of Cibber*, 218–19, 227–9; *Marlborough–Godolphin Corresp.* 584; F. D. Senior, *Life and Times of Cibber*, 49, 55. ⁵ *HMC Portland*, iv. 455; Spence, 128; *Addison Letters*, 282; *Buildings of Eng.* ed. Pevsner, Glos. i. 218.

D. W. H.

BREWER, John (1654–1724), of Gray's Inn and West Farleigh, Kent.

NEW ROMNEY   1689–1710

bap. 9 Jan. 1654, 2nd but 1st surv. s. of Thomas Brewer of West Farleigh by 1st w. Jane, da. and coh. of Thomas Houghton of Mayfield, Suss. *educ.* Wadham, Oxf. matric 1669; G. Inn 1671, called 1678, ancient 1702. *m.* Jane (d. 1717), da. of George Baker of Maidstone, Kent. *suc.* fa. 1691.¹

Freeman, New Romney 1687, Rochester 1696,

Reading 1709; standing counsel, Tenterden, 1690–1, 1708–23, Cinque Ports 1691–d.; recorder, New Romney, 1687–1712, Deal 1699–d., Lydd 1702.[2]

Rec.-gen. of prizes 1702–7.[3]

Brewer was the second son of a barrister from a family which had been resident at West Farleigh since the reign of Henry VI. His elder brother died before 1681 (when the eldest son of his father's second marriage was also christened Thomas). Little is known of his father, who petitioned in 1660 for the royal imprimatur for the vacant recordership of Maidstone, which he finally obtained in 1667, but he was added to the Kentish commission of the peace in 1688 by James II's regulators. Brewer having been appointed recorder under James II's charter of 1687 and elected a freeman the same year, it was reported in September 1688 that New Romney was 'inclined' to choose him as one of its Members should James II call a new Parliament and he was duly returned to the Convention of 1689. Possibly owing to legal uncertainties, Brewer was again sworn a freeman and re-elected as recorder or 'assistant to the mayor and jurats ... at their courts and sessions'. Although called to the bar in 1678, he may have been the John Brewer appointed collector and surveyor of customs at Hythe, who was authorized to live at New Romney in 1682 (dismissed 1685). He may also have been the Mr Brewer jnr. of Maidstone (three and a half miles from West Farleigh) who was appointed in July 1688 to the commission in Kent investigating recusancy fines.[4]

Throughout his career Brewer seems to have been a moderate, hence his non-appearance on 'the black lists' of those in favour of agreeing on 5 Feb. 1689 with the Lords' amendment to the resolution that the throne was vacant, and of those in favour of the disabling clauses of the corporations bill in January 1690. Returned in 1690 Brewer was classed by the Marquess of Carmarthen (Sir Thomas Osborne†) as a Tory and a probable Court supporter, an assessment in keeping with the tenor of his remarks that New Romney corporation was made up of 'men eminently steady in the principles of our Established Church, which makes us not only the best Christians, but the best subjects'. As befitted a lawyer with many interests, Brewer was involved in a variety of legislative tasks, including the management of many bills through the Commons. In April 1690 he reported three bills from committee and carried them to the upper House. On 3 May he told against engrossing a bill setting up a court of conscience in Southwark; and on the same day also carried back to the Lords a bill ensuring that the Cinque Ports could hold elections free from the claims of the lord warden, the Commons having agreed to a Lords' amendment. This bill had failed in the preceding Parliament, but Brewer had clearly envisaged its reintroduction, reporting in January that 'for the future a short Act is prepared'. The 1690–1 session saw Brewer listed by Carmarthen in December as a likely supporter in event of an attack on him from the opposition. He was named to two drafting committees and reported two bills from committee. In April 1691 Robert Harley* classed him as doubtful but possibly a Court supporter, indicating an awareness that Brewer was not an easy man to categorize.[5]

The 1691–2 session saw Brewer again active in legislative matters. He defended the East India Company in the debate on 13 Nov. 1691 following the presentation of their accounts to the House. December saw him added to the drafting committee on the bill encouraging the manufacture of saltpetre in England. However, the resultant legislation was so unsatisfactory that he felt compelled to oppose it at second reading on 21 Jan., 'it being to establish a monopoly for the sole making of saltpetre to some persons when it appears others can make it. And why any should be excluded from making it when there is so great occasion for the thing I understand not.' On 2 Dec. he presented to the Commons another bill on the escape of prisoners, this time for the relief of creditors, and he was ordered to draft a bill on 22 Jan. 1692 for apprehending highwaymen, which he duly presented on the 29th. On 22 Feb. he spoke on the winning side against the passage of a bill confirming the charters of Cambridge University.[6]

As well as demonstrating an interest in criminal legislation, Brewer may well have been one of those lawyers with an interest in holding local courts. An interesting letter to William Brockman* in September 1692 illustrates the busy schedule Brewer was obliged to keep. Writing from New Romney on Saturday 24th, Brewer explained that on the Monday he had to attend 'the sessions and trials at Romney', returning to West Farleigh on the evening of the 27th, ready to travel to London on business the following day. In addition to local legal office, there were his duties as standing counsel for the Cinque Ports, an office to which he had been appointed in 1691, a previous occupant being his stepmother's father, Richard Kilburne of the Fowlers, Hawkhurst, Kent, an eminent solicitor in chancery and five times principal of Staple Inn.[7]

In the 1692–3 session, Brewer's main legislative activity centred on the bill he presented to the Commons on 26 Nov. 1692 for encouraging the apprehension of highwaymen. He reported this bill on 7 Feb. 1693 and also made a motion from the committee for leave to bring in another bill for the prevention of felonies. He carried up the highwaymen bill to the Lords on 11 Feb. Brewer intervened in three debates during the session. On 6 Jan., in the committee of the whole on the land tax, to oppose a clause empowering mortgagees to deduct 4s. in the pound out of the interest they paid; on 23 Feb., when presenting a rider at third reading to the bill for the preservation of game which provided for restraining 'inferior' tradesmen and apprentices from hunting, fishing or fowling, etc., which was amended and made part of the bill; and on 6 Mar. against the second reading of the Lords' bill setting aside amendments and alterations made in the legal records relating to recoveries in Wales. In 1693 Grascome listed 'John Brewer' as a placeman, having confused him with Richard Brewer, who had a colonelcy of a regiment of foot.[8]

In the 1693-4 session Brewer returned to a subject on which he had been active in the preceding session, being appointed on 18 Nov. 1693 to the drafting committee of a bill for apprehending highwaymen. No bill emerged but on 5 Jan. 1694 he was appointed to a committee of inquiry into the problem of highwaymen from which he reported on 15 Feb., being given sole responsibility for drafting a new measure punishing highwaymen by death, but again nothing happened. Having also been given sole responsibility for drafting a bill for regulating hackney coaches, he duly presented it on 13 Dec. 1693 only for it to be withdrawn, 'there being an appropriation of the money arising by the bill for which there is no order'. Having redrafted the bill, Brewer presented it again on the 16th, but despite orders for a second reading it proceeded no further. He told on one occasion (with the Tory, Peter Shakerley), on 6 Jan. 1694, against the motion that an opponent of the East India Company, Thomas Papillon, take the chair of the committee of the whole on the petition for a new company. His contributions to debate were confined to the discussion in the committee of the whole on 26 Jan. over the King's veto of the triennial bill, which, since it was 'liable to exceptions' and since 'I gave my vote to make the Prince of Orange king, but will never give my vote to unking him, I think it proper, in this case, for the King to exercise his negative voice'. May 1694 saw him attending the lord warden of the Cinque Ports, the Earl of Romney (Hon. Henry Sidney†), and seemingly in dispute with John Thurbarne* over his rights as counsel to the Cinque Ports, Thurbarne at one stage criticizing his rival's 'florid speech'.[9]

In the last session of the 1690 Parliament, Brewer was nominated to many drafting committees. The most important was his appointment on 4 Jan. 1695 as sole draftsman of a bill for the repair of churches and the more effectual recovery of church rates, which he then presented on the 16th, but which never emerged from committee. On 20 Dec. 1694 he had been appointed to the committee on a petition from hackney coachmen seeking relief from the recent Licensing Act, and he reported on 6 Feb. 1695 from the committee that a witness had refused to attend, whereupon the offender was ordered into custody. On 8 Mar. he reported from the same committee that the coachmen had proved their petition. A second resolution to the effect that some of the commissioners for licensing the coachmen had taken bribes was recommitted so that the committee could identify the offenders. The knowledge that the committee would reveal his brother Richard to be at fault explains the accusations made by Orlando Gee on the 7th that Brewer had accepted a bribe of 30 guineas for promoting a private bill. Brewer vindicated himself the next day, the accusations being voted 'scandalous' by the House. No doubt the need to clear his name explains why he did not immediately avail himself of the fortnight's leave of absence granted him on the 7th.[10]

Returned for New Romney at the 1695 election, Brewer faced a petition on 5 Dec. but no action resulted. Again he was active as a legislator. He was sole draftsman for a bill to prevent escapes and to relieve creditors, which he presented on 11 Jan. 1696 and reported from committee on 16 Mar. Brewer was also first-named to the committee on 28 Feb. to consider the petition from the weavers' company in Canterbury, expressing concern that their former economic troubles would return if the East India Company was established on a statutory basis without any restraint being placed upon their import of silks and bengals. Brewer was also involved in the management of several estate bills, some of which involved Kentish lands, including that of Sir William Barkham, 3rd Bt., for which he told in favour of giving a third reading on 13 Mar. Brewer received leave of absence on 19 Mar. for three weeks and there is no reason to assume he returned before the end of the session. He was one of numerous Members who stood on 1 Feb. in the ballot for commissioners of public accounts, but only obtained one vote. His political attitude was as ever not easy to fathom: he was forecast as likely to oppose the Court in the divisions on 31 Jan. 1696 on the proposed council of trade, but signed the Association promptly and voted in March for fixing the price of guineas at 22s.[11]

Brewer spent considerable time during each parliamentary recess in London, as can be seen from two items of correspondence in 1696. In June John Mascall of New Romney inquired of James Vernon I* about a reward for their apprehension of Sir John Fenwick†, noting that Brewer would wait on Secretary Shrewsbury about it. Similarly, when Richard Coffin made an inquiry in September about the price of hops, his correspondent consulted Brewer who had 'lately come out of Kent'. In the 1696–7 session, Brewer was only appointed to one committee in November, to draft a bill to prevent and prosecute escapes (a consistent interest of his), and he did not vote on the 25th in the division on Fenwick's attainder. Among the bills he was associated with were a bill to repair decayed havens, and following a petition on 23 Dec. from the Cinque Ports and adjacent areas, a bill for preventing the export of wool. Also, on 18 Feb., he was the sole Member appointed to prepare a bill to repeal a clause in the supply act relating to party guiles. This had originated from two petitions from Kentish brewers on 14 and 23 Feb., which were referred to a committee on a petition from the London brewers, to which Brewer had been nominated. The report found their grievances genuine. After Brewer had presented the resultant bill he took no further part in its management, receiving leave of absence on 6 Mar., the same day it was given a second reading.[12]

Somewhat surprisingly Brewer's first committee appointment in the 1697–8 session occurred as late as 26 Jan. 1698 when he was again named to draft a bill to prevent the export of wool. However, he was in London before this date, attending at the Treasury on the 18th about the purchase by Sir Francis Leigh* of the outlaw John Stafford's Kentish estate. Brewer was given leave of absence on 11 Mar. upon 'extraordinary occasions', presumably legal business outside London. He had returned before the end of March when he was again active in managing a private bill through the House. He was a teller on 28 Apr. at the report of the committee considering the Act levying a duty on births, marriages and burials, in favour of an unsuccessful resolution which would have obliged bachelors and widowers to supply a written account of themselves.[13]

Brewer may have joined forces with his erstwhile opponent, Sir Charles Sedley, 5th Bt.*, at the 1698 election for together they presented silver flagons to St. Nicholas' church, New Romney. Upon his return Brewer was classed as a Court supporter on a comparative analysis of the old and new Parliaments, but another list forecast him as likely to oppose a standing army. He confirmed the latter analysis on 23 Dec. 1698 when he intervened in the debate on the second reading of the disbanding bill to note that 'gentlemen whose interest is to keep up an arm[y] are for it; the number agreed to by him of 7,000, you may fill up the blanks', which is also consistent with his absence from those 'blacklisted' for voting against the disbanding bill on 18 Jan. 1699. He spoke in the debate on 9 Mar. 1699, against giving a second reading to the bill enabling the Old East India Company to continue trading for the remainder of the 21-year term it was granted in 1693. Having noted his original opposition to the Act setting up the New Company in 1698, Brewer continued that 'now it was an Act he was for maintaining of it since so many people had lent their money on it', an intervention which clearly coincided with the opinion of the House since the bill was rejected. Brewer's normal run of appointments does not occur in this session and he was given leave of absence on 16 Mar. The most likely explanation for Brewer's lack of involvement in the parliamentary session concerns his heavy involvement elsewhere, particularly as part of Deal's campaign to obtain a charter and thereby break free from Sandwich. His old antagonist, Thurbarne, was very critical of Brewer's actions, accusing him of betraying the Cinque Ports. When Brewer was debarred from appearing in the case as counsel in March, Thurbarne reported that 'the port's modest counsel is gravelled that his mouth is stopped'. Significantly, Brewer's activity in the Commons picked up from this point. His reward for promoting Deal's cause was to be named recorder in the town's first charter. Brewer was also involved in representing local grievances over the conduct of customs officers and the illegal export of wool. In May he asked the Treasury's leave to produce a scheme for preventing smuggling, but desired three weeks in which to write it 'because he must be in the country to hold courts'.[14]

The 1699–1700 session saw Brewer active in the Commons, mainly on matters of local concern. Three of the bills he was named to draft had identifiable Kentish interests. His one recorded contribution to debate occurred on 13 Feb., when Lord Somers (Sir John*) was attacked over his acquisition of fee farm rents in order to uphold the dignity of his peerage. Brewer stepped in to defend his legal contemporary: 'L[or]d Ch[ancellor's] behaviour hath been to the satisfaction of all even different parties, that the grants are not contrary to law nor oath', continuing with reference to Somers' service on behalf of the Seven Bishops and as attorney-general and noting that no one 'does love a poor lord, nor a poor H[ouse] of L[or]ds'. An analysis of the Commons into 'interests' undertaken in the first half of 1700 left Brewer as doubtful, or possibly as opposition, again signifying the difficulty contemporaries had in categorizing him.[15]

The dissolution of the Parliament saw Brewer

writing to New Romney in December 1700 to offer his services at the subsequent election. After citing his experience, he continued 'I do think 'tis more than probable that matters of the greatest consequence will be treated and transacted in this Parliament', and ended by excusing himself from personal attendance on the corporation owing to 'the ways and weather in some measure (but more the Act of Parliament that will not allow us to drink together)'. Duly elected, he was listed as likely to support the Court in February 1701 over the 'Great Mortgage'. Brewer's parliamentary activity in this session included drafting committees for a local initiative to erect a hospital and workhouse at Ashford in Kent and a similar measure to establish a corporation of the poor in the parish of St. James's, Westminster. He also managed three private bills through the Commons, including one in favour of Sir Robert Marsham, 4th Bt.* He made two recorded interventions in debate. On 14 Apr. he spoke at the report stage against the bill enacting Ryder's scheme for a waterworks at Deal on the grounds that it unjustly deprived another undertaker, who had spent £1,600 on a rival project. Although Brewer's role in the debate was clearly based on local considerations, Sir Richard Cocks, 2nd Bt.*, felt that the House favoured Ryder's bill because he was a 'Jacobite and a sportsman', thereby implying that Brewer was neither of these things. On 5 May, when the Court opposed a report from the committee of ways and means that since the Duke of Gloucester was dead £100,000 be appropriated from the civil list for the use of the public, 'Brewer said he was always for giving of taxes and for that reason was esteemed a courtier', but that since the reason for the £100,000 had now ceased with Gloucester's demise then it should be applied 'to the use of the public'.[16]

Returned after a contest at New Romney in November 1701, Brewer was classed by Robert Harley as a Tory. He was very active in the Commons in the 1701–2 session, especially in being nominated to drafting committees. After being first-named on 7 Feb. 1702 to a committee on the petition of hoymen and farmers in Kent and Essex, complaining of their difficulties in transporting corn and other inland provisions to London, he reported favourably, being one of two Members charged with drafting the necessary legislation for their relief. He managed the resultant legislation through the Commons. He also told on 21 May in favour of offering a rider to the Earl of Carlingford's relief bill concerning Trant's outlawry. Despite his defence of Somers two years before, Brewer was listed as supporting the motion on 26 Feb. vindicating the Commons' proceedings over the impeachments of the previous session. Extant contributions to debate show that on 7 Feb. Brewer disagreed with Cocks and Thomas Stringer while defending the conduct of Thomas Bliss*, the Tory candidate at the Maidstone election, and that on the 11th Brewer failed to appear as promised to support a motion sponsored by Cocks for raising revenue from all the grants made since the Revolution and from the sale of crown lands. On 6 Mar. it was reported that Brewer and Lord William Powlett had gone out of the House together to pursue a quarrel, thereby precipitating an adjournment. However, Cocks noted that Lord William had in fact remained in the Commons and the Journals do not mention the incident.[17]

Brewer applied to New Romney in April 1702 in preparation for the election necessitated by the death of William III. His letter stressed his experience and public service, rather pompously pronouncing: "tis of the greatest satisfaction to me that I have acquitted myself with such integrity and application of mind in your service'. The advent of a new regime also turned Brewer's thoughts towards advancement. From a letter penned to the Earl of Nottingham (Daniel Finch†) in June, it would seem that Brewer sought 'an honourable sinecure in the law', which although his 'present practice is more profitable than this office', would secure his financial independence and thereby allow him more time to devote to the Queen's service. Despite assurances of support from Nottingham, Sir Charles Hedges* (an Admiralty judge and a newly appointed secretary of state), Sir Edward Seymour, 4th Bt.*, the master of the rolls (Sir John Trevor*), Sir Benjamin Bathurst* (soon to partner him at Romney), and even, 'if I am not flattered', the Earl of Rochester (Laurence Hyde†), Brewer had been baulked of his desire by the intervention of a great minister, 'who hath more means of obliging friends' and one who had encroached on areas which were the 'right of others to prepare for the Royal Stamp' (possibly a reference to Lord Treasurer Godolphin [Sidney†]). In the event Brewer had to settle for the potentially lucrative post of receiver-general or treasurer of the prizes. With the Earl of Winchilsea reporting to Nottingham on 12 July that Bathurst and Brewer 'cannot fail' at Romney, they were duly returned ten days later.[18]

In the opening session of Queen Anne's first Parliament Brewer was appointed to six drafting committees. These included a bill to ascertain the tithes of hops (of obvious relevance to Kent), several estate bills, one of which concerned to Sir Thomas Stanley, 3rd Bt., who was related through marriage to Sir Stephen Lennard, 2nd Bt., the knight of the shire for

Kent, and a bill to prevent the export of wool, which he presented. He also managed the Lords' bill in favour of Hon. Mildmay Fane†, younger son of the 4th Earl of Westmorland, an influential Kentish figure.

Brewer was much busier in the 1703–4 session. On 9 Nov. 1703 Lord Godolphin wrote to Harley that he had spoken to Brewer, finding him 'convinced of the unseasonableness of this bill', presumably a reference to the second occasional conformity bill, leave for which was granted later that month. A sign of his stature (and Toryism) was his deputation, with John Sharp*, on 3 Mar. to ask the High Tory Francis Atterbury to preach before the House, and its corollary on the 9th, the Commons' message of thanks for the same. Brewer managed three bills through the House, two private measures involving first Sir Charles Bickerstaffe, a Kentish deputy-lieutenant in the 1690s, and, second Sir Thomas Style, 2nd Bt.†, formerly MP for Hythe, and, most important, a bill to continue the Dover Harbour Act, which necessitated his chairing a committee of the whole on 26 Jan. 1704, before the bill passed the Commons in February. On 17 Jan. he was the first-named to a committee of seven to search the Lords' Journals for their proceedings in the cases of *Ashby* v. *White* (see AYLESBURY, Bucks.) and *Soames* v. *Barnardiston*, a committee which was then given several related tasks and from which Brewer reported on 21 and 24 Jan. after inquiring into the proceedings in Queen's bench on the two cases. He was a teller on 18 Jan., successfully opposing the third reading of the bill establishing a land registry for the West Riding.[19]

It is possible that by this time Brewer had removed his residence out of his chambers in Coney Court, Gray's Inn, which were being used by the Pipe Office. He may have taken lodgings in Swallow Street, for on 28 Oct. 1704 Bishop Nicolson recorded a conversation with his 'fellow lodger, Mr Brewer of Kent' in which Brewer 'protests against the humour of consolidating', i.e. tacking. This evidence is consistent with a forecast that Brewer would probably oppose the Tack, although his name did appear on Harley's lobbying list as one to be approached by the chancellor of the Exchequer, Hon. Henry Boyle*. About this time Godolphin informed Harley that he had deputed William Lowndes* to lobby Brewer and the prize commissioners on the same issue, an effort which was evidently successful for on 26 Nov. Nicolson described Brewer as 'zealous against Tacking', and indeed he was not recorded as voting for it. On 17 Dec. Nicolson recorded Brewer's prediction that a similar measure must pass 'the next year', an indication that it was tacking to which he objected rather than legislation against the practice of occasional conformity. This may explain why one analysis of 1705 called him a 'sneaker'. Brewer's other actions in the 1704–5 session conformed to the same pattern. He was appointed to five drafting committees including one to waive duties on exported prize goods, which followed a petition from John Mascall, a prominent constituent who had served as mayor of New Romney on three occasions, and another on a supply bill continuing duties on low wines, coffee, etc. Brewer also chaired a committee of the whole on the bill to encourage the import of American naval stores, reporting it and carrying it to the Lords. On at least one occasion Brewer acted as a manager with a group of senior Tories including Sir Thomas Powys, Sir Humphrey Mackworth and William Bromley II at a conference on the vexed issue of the writ of error for the Aylesbury men.[20]

By virtue of his office as receiver of prizes, Brewer was classed as a placeman on a list of 1705. His letter to New Romney in March offering his services at the forthcoming general election made much of his office, and betrayed a certain unease that it might be used against him:

> I can't believe my being employed by her Majesty in office will put me under any disadvantage with any of you and the rather because 'tis wholly consistent with my duty to your trust which I have not neglected one day since I undertook it. I must say there is not one member of the House who with more diligence constantly attends the service of the House and when the bill against offices was first moved for I then openly declared in the House that I would quit my present or any other office, for the service of the public, if you would please to favour me in the next election.

Brewer was duly returned and after again being lobbied by Godolphin, voted for the Court candidate as Speaker. However, his Tory inclinations were revealed by Lord Halifax (Charles Montagu*) in a letter to the Duchess of Marlborough which named Brewer as one of 'about 20' who, although they had voted for John Smith I in the Speakership contest, had voted in December for the Tacker, Sir Samuel Garrard, 4th Bt.*, in the Amersham election case. Legislatively, Brewer managed three private bills through the Commons, all of which favoured people with Kentish connexions, and assisted in the management of others. Brewer's recorded interventions in debate in this session were limited to interventions during the regency bill. On 19 Dec., at second reading, he pronounced himself for the bill's committal and although he spoke on 12 Jan. 1706 over the instruction to the committee of the whole to receive amendments to explain the place clauses of the Act of Settlement, his comments were not recorded. Finally, on 19 Jan. on the composition of the regency Brewer was noted as saying that he 'would not have this bill drop in hopes of the expedient'. This is a trifle cryptic but probably indicates that Brewer was not part of the Tory attempts to obstruct the bill. Indeed, he duly supported the Court on 18 Feb. over the 'place clause'. The following day, he again upset the Whigs by joining other Court Tories in refusing to set a date for hearing the Bewdley election case, an action which favoured the Tory, Salwey Winnington*, over his Whig rival, Hon. Henry Herbert*.[21]

The 1706–7 session saw Brewer perhaps a little less active in the Commons. He had two tellerships: on 5 Dec. 1706 in favour of bringing up a petition from the six clerks in Chancery for relief against loss of fees, the success of which led to his appointment as first-named to the committee to consider their relief; and on 7 Jan. 1707 in favour of giving a second reading to a bill suppressing new glass-houses, etc., within one mile of Whitehall and St. James's. He was also appointed to four drafting committees, but did not manage any of the resultant legislation. By mid-April Brewer was attending the county sessions in Kent, but was unable to return to London as expected during May owing to ill-health. His absence makes it difficult to credit a report by Hon. James Brydges* on 8 May that

> by virtue of the Parliament being agreed to be a new Parliament the clause [under the Regency Act] for incapacitating such and such offices from being in the House hath taken place and thereupon Mr Mo[o]re [Arthur*] hath resigned his, with Brewer of prizes.

However, Brydges had defined the dilemma facing Brewer: whether to retain office or membership of the Commons. In the event, when the Commons took the matter into account on 18 Nov. 1707 a new writ was ordered for New Romney on the grounds that Brewer had 'been receiver of the prizes since the commencement of this present Parliament', the post-Union session being declared a new Parliament. Somewhat surprisingly, Brewer attended at the Treasury on the following day to resign his office. If this was in order to facilitate his success at the ensuing by-election, it certainly worked, because on 28 Nov. he was returned unopposed. There is no record of Brewer being given another office compatible with a seat at Westminster, which would have explained the otherwise surprising fact that he continued to support the Whig-dominated ministry. The reference to a Mr Brewer of the Escheat office in 1713 probably refers to his ownership of the building housing that office.[22]

An analysis of the Commons compiled after the Union marks Brewer as a Tory. He does not appear in a legislative capacity in the 1707–8 session until February 1708, possibly being involved in legal duties before then: Bishop Nicolson twice mentions visits to him in January and February, possibly concerning the cathedrals bill, which the bishop saw as a way of resolving his own conflict with Dean Atterbury. In March he chaired the committee of the whole on the bill extending the East India Company Act, and on 18 Mar. 1708 he took over the functions of the chair of ways and means, reporting the bill (which John Conyers had chaired) to continue half-subsidies.[23]

Re-elected again in 1708, Brewer was classed as a Tory in a list of the Commons with the 1708 returns added. In the opening session, he supported the naturalization of the Palatines, and was named to one drafting committee. There is little clue as to why his legislative activity should have fallen off so sharply, although he may have been active behind the scenes for in 1709 he was made a freeman of Reading 'in regard for the great service he hath done for this corporation'. Conceivably this involved legal and parliamentary work for the town and corporation in opposing the Kennet navigation bill which failed to pass the Commons. Brewer could plausibly have been interested in such work by his brother James, a medical man, who resided in Reading. The 1709–10 session saw Brewer's legislative involvement increase, but most of it concerned Kentish matters, for example the Sevenoaks to Tunbridge Wells road bill which he presented in December and subsequently managed through the Commons. He also voted for the impeachment of Dr Sacheverell.[24]

In the month before the dissolution of the Parliament, Edward Knatchbull* wrote to New Romney intimating that a number of the corporation had been unhappy with Brewer for some time: 'it having been discoursed in the county at the last election that if any neighbouring gentleman had offered his service he might probably have succeeded'. Certainly Brewer's Whiggish votes in 1709–10 would not have been favourably looked upon by Tories like Knatchbull. As if to confirm his vulnerability, Brewer's letter to Romney was a trifle defensive in that he admitted that after representing them for so long his conduct was bound to be excepted against by some, but that, if so, he was guilty of 'oversights not errors'. His reasons for standing were given as 'the security of our present happy establishment both in Church and state, together with the interest and prosperity of our town in general and everyone of you'. He ended ominously by saying that it was easy to set up against him and make promises. Brewer was defeated after a poll, petitioning on 1 Dec. 1710 against the return of Robert Furnese, but withdrawing his petition subsequently.[25]

Brewer continued to be active in politics despite being outside the Commons. In July 1712 Tenterden corporation returned Brewer's draft address for presentation to the Queen. Although discharged in May 1712 from his place as counsel and assistant to the corporation, ostensibly owing to lack of business, Brewer sought to return to the Commons at the New Romney by-election of 1713, writing to the corporation that after his previous defeat he had not solicited a seat elsewhere, but had retired from 'public' business. However, he was alarmed at reports which suggested he was over-confident of the corporation's support and explained his reticence in treating by saying that 'nothing but submission to an Act of Parliament could excuse me in not directing an entertainment'. Whether because of these faults or some others, there is no evidence that he stood at the by-election held in April 1713 or at the general election of August that year. This is perhaps strange, given that in June 1713 when he presented an address to the Queen from Deal, thanking her for the peace, he was able to procure an introduction into the royal presence from Lord Treasurer Oxford (Harley). Brewer continued to act in a legal capacity until the end of his life, serving as chairman of West Kent quarter sessions from at least as early as February 1712 until he was ousted in 1715, and retaining his place as counsel to the Cinque Ports until his death on 2 June 1724. In his will, written before his wife's death in 1717, he refers to the estate he had settled on his nephew Thomas (son of Dr James Brewer) on the latter's marriage. He mentioned rooms in New Court of Gray's Inn which he leased out and to others in use by the Pipe and Escheat Office. He also held £1,000 in Bank stock, valued at £1,300 and 'unsettled' real and personal estate of 'at least £4,000'.[26]

[1] IGI, Kent; PCC 21 Vere; *Vis. Kent* (Harl. Soc. liv), 26; Le Neve, *Mon. Angl.* 1650–79, p. 130; *Arch. Cant.* lxii. 80–81. [2] Centre Kentish Stud. New Romney bor. recs. NR/AC2, pp. 660, 662, 675–6; NR/AC3, p. 75; info. from Medway Area Archs.; Berks. RO, R/AC1/1/19, f. 105v.; *Arch. Cant.* xxxiii. 102; *Cal. White and Black Bks.* (Kent Recs. xix), 546, 555; *London Gazette*, 26–30 Mar. 1702. [3] *Cal. Treas. Bks.* xvii. 251; xxi. 51. [4] *G. Inn Pension Bk.* i. 368, 453; ii. 29; IGI, Kent; *CSP Dom.* 1660–1, p. 246; *Recs. of Maidstone* ed. Martin, 154; Duckett, *Penal Laws and Test Act* (1882), 359, 360; Add. 33923, f. 434; New Romney bor. recs. NR/AC2, pp. 660, 662, 673, 675; *Cal. Treas. Bks.* vi. 502, 537; vii. 444; viii. 280, 2028. [5] New Romney bor. recs. NR/AEp 56/1, Brewer to corporation, 8 Feb. 1689[-90]; Add. 33512, f. 118. [6] *Luttrell Diary*, 16, 146, 200. [7] *Stilling the Grumbling Hive* ed. Davison et al., 55, 59; G. Holmes, *Augustan Eng.* 138–42; Add. 42586, ff. 155–6, 190; *Cal. White and Black Bks.* 525, 535. [8] *Luttrell Diary*, 354, 444, 469. [9] Grey, x. 376; Add. 33512, ff. 132–4. [10] Som. RO, Sanford mss DD/SF 2980, Edward Clarke I* to Ld. Capell (Hon. Sir Henry Capel*), 23 Mar. 1695; Add. 17677 PP, f. 184; H. Horwitz, *Parl. and Pol. Wm. III*, 148–9. [11] Hereford and Worcester RO (Hereford), Harley mss C64/117, ballot of commrs. of accts. [12] *CSP Dom.* 1696, pp. 228–9; *Portledge Pprs.* 238. [13] *Cal. Treas. Bks.* xiii. 55–56; *Cam. Misc.* xx. 49–50. [14] *Arch. Cant.* xiii. 479; *Cam. Misc.* xxix. 380; *Cocks Diary*, 19; Add. 33512, ff. 158–60; *CSP Dom.* 1699–1700, p. 252; *Cal. Treas. Bks.* xiv. 78–79. [15] Horwitz, 265–6; Sanford mss DD/SF 4107(a), 'notes of the debate on my ld. Chancellor', 13 Feb. 1699[–1700]. [16] New Romney bor. recs. NR/AEp 59/1, Brewer to New Romney, 19 Dec. 1700; *Cocks Diary*, 97, 110. [17] *Cocks Diary*, 203, 211, 235. [18] New Romney bor. recs. NR/AEp 60/3, Brewer to corporation, 23 Apr. 1702; Add. 29568, ff. 79–80. [19] Bath mss at Longleat House, Portland misc. mss, ff. 209–10, [Godolphin] to [Harley], 9 Nov. [1703]; *Bull. IHR*, xli. 175. [20] *G. Inn Pension Bk.* ii. 143; *Nicolson Diaries* ed. Jones and Holmes, 215–16, 236, 256; *Bull. IHR*, xxxiv. 95; xli. 182; Portland misc. mss, ff. 196–7; *Arch. Cant.* xcv. 213, 220; Luttrell, *Brief Relation*, v. 529. [21] New Romney bor. recs. NR/AEp 60/1, Brewer to New Romney, 15 Mar. 1704[-5]; *HMC Bath*, i. 57; *Bull. IHR* xxxv. 28; xlv. 47, 48; *Cam. Misc.* xxiii. 50, 66, 74; G. Holmes, *Pol. in Age of Anne*, 91. [22] Huntington Lib. Stowe mss 58(1), pp. 143, 189; 57(1), p. 97; 57(2), pp. 104–5; *Cal. Treas. Bks.* xxi. 51. [23] *Nicolson Diaries*, 442, 448. [24] Berks. RO, R/AC1/1/19, f. 105v. [25] New Romney bor. recs. NR/AEp 63/1, Knatchbull to corporation, 14 Aug. [1710]; Brewer to same, 14 Sept. 1710. [26] *Arch. Cant.* xxxiii. 101; New Romney bor. recs. NR/AC3, p. 75; NR/AEp 64/2, Brewer to corporation, 3 Feb. 1712[-13]; N. Landau, *JPs*, 253, 280; *London Gazette*, 6–9 June 1713; Add. 62648, f. 67; PCC 132 Bolton; Boyer, *Pol. State*, xxvii. 623.

S. N. H.

BRIDGEMAN, John (c.1655–1729), of Prinknash Park, Glos.

GLOUCESTER 1701 (Feb.–Nov.)

b. c.1655, 1st s. of John Bridgeman of Prinknash Park by Margaret, da. of Sir Charles Berkeley†, 2nd Visct. Fitzhardinge [I] and Earl of Falmouth. *educ.* Wadham, Oxf. matric. 26 July 1672, aged 17; I. Temple 1673. *m.* c.1710, Catherine (*d.* 1744), da. of Richard Ockold of Upton St. Leonards, Glos. *s.p. suc.* fa. by 1663; uncle James Bridgeman 1694.[1]

Freeman, Gloucester 1702.[2]

Bridgeman's family had been established in Gloucestershire since at least the 15th century, acquiring Prinknash, some four miles from Gloucester, in about 1630. Orphaned by his mother's death in 1663, Bridgeman was placed under the guardianship of his uncle James Bridgeman, a barrister of the Inner Temple, who did all he could to keep him from wasting his fortune, going so far as to stipulate in his will of 1691 that, as a necessary condition of making Bridgeman his own heir, he abide by a previous property settlement. Even then trustees were appointed for this new inheritance, James 'finding by sad experience that John Bridgeman his nephew is not fit to have estates'. Bridgeman was returned for Gloucester in January 1701, although any activity during his brief sojourn in the House is concealed by the presence of another MP with the same surname, Orlando Bridgeman I. Moreover, there are only the vaguest clues as to his party sympathies which may have been Whiggish. He may have put up for the county at the second election of 1701 and in December 1702 contested Gloucester again at a by-election but was defeated, thereafter preferring to remain at Prinknash, where he enjoyed 'a large old house, and pleasant gardens, and a park of large extent, and distant prospects over the vale, and a great estate in this and other places'.[3]

Bridgeman was buried on 3 June 1729. He was succeeded by Henry Toye, the family solicitor, who thereupon changed his name to Bridgeman.[4]

[1] *Bristol and Glos. Arch. Soc. Trans.* vii. 296–9, 306. [2] *Gloucester Freemen* (Glos. Rec. Ser. iv), 58. [3] Ibid. 285–7, 297–8, 306; *HMC Portland*, iv. 27; Atkyns, *Glos.* 416. [4] *Bristol and Glos. Arch. Soc. Trans.* 299–300.

D. W. H.

BRIDGEMAN, Orlando I (1671–1721), of Clifton on Dunsmore, Warws. and Sherrard Street, Westminster.

WIGAN 1698–1701 (Nov.), 1702–1705

bap. 22 May 1671, 4th but 2nd surv. s. of Sir John Bridgeman, 2nd Bt., of Castle Bromwich, Warws. by Mary, da. and coh. of George Cradock of Caverswall Castle, Staffs. *educ.* Oriel, Oxf. matric. 1688, BA 1691; I. Temple 1694, called 1697. *m.* 20 Apr. 1697 (with £4,000), his 2nd cos. Catherine, da. of William Bridgeman† of Pall Mall, Westminster and Combs, Suff., sis. of Orlando Bridgeman II*, 1da. *d.v.p.*[1]

Freeman, Wigan 1698.[2]

Bridgeman was a grandson of Charles II's lord keeper (Sir Orlando Bridgeman, 1st Bt.†) and a first cousin of Sir Orlando Bridgeman, 2nd Bt.* His prospective father-in-law, William Bridgeman, thought that he would 'prove a man for business' and expected Bridgeman's father, Sir John Bridgeman, to take steps to 'further his coming into the school (the House of Commons)'. Bridgeman duly put up in 1698 at Wigan, where his family had some interest, and with Sir Roger Bradshaigh, 3rd Bt.*, succeeded in throwing out a Court Whig. He was listed in about September 1698 as a member of the Country party, but was not active in the ensuing Parliament. By the next election, Bradshaigh, having assumed a Whig stance in the House, had turned against Bridgeman, almost certainly because of his commitment to Toryism, but failed to oust him in the contest. In the November election he was defeated, despite strenuous efforts within the corporation, and the support of the 9th Earl of Derby. He regained his seat in 1702 after another contest, largely through the efforts of Lord Nottingham's (Daniel Finch†) younger brothers, the rectors of Wigan and nearby Winwick. In August he was severely injured in a carriage accident, and was even reported by Luttrell to be dead. His recovery was complete by February 1703, however, when on the 18th he acted as a teller against an additional clause, on behalf of one Robert Leigh, in the bill to facilitate the sale of Irish forfeited estates. During December and January 1704 he managed through the House a private bill for the Earl of Warwick, and he was again a teller on 18 Mar. 1704, against reading the reports of the Irish forfeiture trustees. Soon after the opening of the next session he was forecast as a likely supporter of the Tack, voting in its favour on 28 Nov. He did not stand in 1705, while in 1708 not even the backing of the chancellor of the duchy of Lancaster, Lord Gower (Sir John Leveson Gower, 5th Bt.*), could enable him to get the better of Sir Roger Bradshaigh and his brother Henry Bradshaigh*. At the 1713 election Bridgeman half-heartedly joined with Lord Barrymore (James Barry*) against Sir Roger and his candidate, but achieved little more than a handful of votes. This was his last attempt: from 1715 onwards the *rapprochement* and electoral alliance between Barrymore and Bradshaigh shut him out completely.

Bridgeman died on 14 Aug. 1721, leaving Clifton, which he had inherited from his father, to his widow.[3]

[1] *Wm. Salt Arch. Soc. Colls.* n.s. ii. 238; *Cal. I. Temple Recs.* iii. 303, 338; IGI, London; Staffs. RO, Bradford mss D.1287/18/15, C. Cratford to Sir John Bridgeman, 9 Mar. 1697, John Bridgeman to Wm. Lewis, 6 May 1701; D.1287/18/14, same to same, 22 Apr. 1697. [2] Wigan RO, Wigan bor. recs. AB/MR/10. [3] Bradford mss D.1287/18/15, Cratford to Sir John Bridgeman, 9 Mar. 1697; John Bridgeman to same, 2 May 1701; same to Orlando Bridgeman, 6 May, 4 Nov. 1701; same to Mr Taylor, 7 June 1701; *HMC Kenyon*, 425, 429, 442, 453, 455; *Bull. John Rylands Lib.* xxxvii. 125–6, 128–37; *Norris Pprs.* (Chetham Soc. ix), 60; Luttrell, *Brief Relation*, v. 202; *Hist. Reg. Chron.* 1721, p. 33; *Wm. Salt Arch. Soc. Colls.* 253, 255; PCC 156 Buckingham.

D. W. H.

BRIDGEMAN, Sir Orlando, 2nd Bt. (1678–1746), of Bloomsbury Square, Mdx.; Coventry, Warws. and Bowood, nr. Calne, Wilts.

COVENTRY	25 Feb. 1707–1710
CALNE	1715–1722
LOSTWITHIEL	25 Feb. 1724–1727
BLETCHINGLEY	1727–1734
DUNWICH	1734–Feb. 1738

bap. 27 Apr. 1678, o. s. of Sir Orlando Bridgeman, 1st Bt.†, of Little Park Street, Coventry and Ridley, Cheshire, by Mary, da. of Sir Thomas Cave, 1st Bt., of Stanford Hall, Northants. *educ.* Rugby 1689; Trinity, Oxf. 1694. *m.* lic. 15 Apr. 1702 (with £10,000), Susannah (*d.* 1747), da. of Sir Francis Dashwood, 1st Bt.*, 3s. (2 *d.v.p.*) 2da. (1 *d.v.p.*). *suc.* fa. as 2nd Bt. 20 Apr. 1701.[1]

Clerk of household to the Prince of Wales 1716–27; ld. of Trade 1727–37; gov. Barbados 1737–8.

Bridgeman, a grandson of Charles II's lord keeper, succeeded to his father's baronetcy and estates in 1701, a year or so after attaining his majority, and in 1702 made a financially advantageous match with a daughter of the wealthy City merchant, Sir Francis Dashwood. As part of the marriage settlement Bridgeman acquired Wanstead, one of Dashwood's manors in Essex, which for a while he used as his main country residence but later sold. From his father he had inherited Bowood, a lease from the crown which was renewed in 1702. His father had been a well-known figure in Coventry where the family had an appreciable interest, and in 1705 Bridgeman himself put up as a Whig candidate there. Though defeated, he and his partner petitioned and succeeded in having the election declared void. Despite a 'very vigorous opposition', they succeeded in reversing the previous result in a second contest in February 1707. Bridgeman was classed as a Whig in two lists of early 1708, and was re-elected at Coventry in the election of May that year. The losing Tory candidates petitioned, and when the matter was considered before the elections committee in March 1709 he was confronted with accusations of bribery and a compromising report that he had told the sheriffs that 'could he be returned by any majority, there would be a Parliament would do anything for him'. Notwithstanding, the opinion of the House carried in his favour. He was listed as having voted both for the naturalization of the Palatines and for the impeachment of Dr Sacheverell. Defeated at Coventry in 1710 as a result of the Tory resurgence in the city, he did not stand in 1713. In 1715 he was successful at the Wiltshire borough of Calne, where he exercised some influence by virtue of his seat at nearby Bowood.[2]

Bridgeman was afterwards a close supporter of Walpole and in 1727 was rewarded with a place on the Board of Trade. However, his building activities at Bowood, on which he had acquired the fee simple in 1727, brought escalating financial difficulty upon him. In 1738, shortly after obtaining the governorship of Barbados, he feigned his own suicide by drowning. He was later found, however, in October at an inn at Slough where he had taken refuge. He was buried on 5 Dec. 1746, having died in Gloucester gaol.[3]

[1] IGI, Warws.; *Colls. Wm. Salt Arch. Soc.* n.s. ii. 238, 250–1; *Wilts. Arch. Mag.* xli. 503–6; *Rugby Sch. Reg.* ed. Solly, i. 11; Bodl. D. D. Dashwood (Bucks.) mss A2, f. 15; *St. Botolph Bishopsgate Regs.* ii. 362, 427. [2] *Colls. Wm. Salt Arch. Soc.* 251; *Wilts. Arch. Mag.* xli. 412, 423, 504; Beaufort mss at Badminton House, Edward Hopkins* to [Ld. Coventry], 20 Feb. 1707; Add. 36868, ff. 9–10. [3] *HMC Egmont Diary*, ii. 510; *Wilts. Arch. Mag.* 505; *Gent. Mag.* (1746), p. 668.

D. W. H.

BRIDGEMAN, Orlando II (1680–1731), of Combs Hall, Suff.

IPSWICH 1 Apr. 1714–1715

bap. 22 June 1680, 1st and o. surv. s. of William Bridgeman† of Pall Mall, Westminster and Combs, under-sec. of state c.1667–81, 1683–94, sec. to the Admiralty 1694–8, by Diana, da. of Peter Vernatti. *m.* (1) 16 Apr. 1697, Catherine (*d.* 1711), 2s. (1 *d.v.p.*) 1da.; (2) 16 June 1716, Alice (*d.* 1731), da. of William Shawe of St. Clement's, Ipswich, Suff., wid. of Mileson Edgar of Red House, nr. Ipswich, *s.p. suc.* fa. 1699.[1]

Freeman, Dunwich 1705; portman, Orford by 1709.[2] Patentee to commrs. of bankrupts by *d.*[3]

In common with his Warwickshire kinsmen, Bridgeman was descended from John Bridgeman who became bishop of Chester in 1619. His great uncle, the bishop's son Sir Orlando Bridgeman, 1st Bt.†, achieved distinction as a lawyer and served as Charles II's lord keeper during 1667–72, while his father enjoyed a long career in the senior ranks of government bureaucracy. These two branches of the family were brought closer in 1697 through the marriage of Bridgeman's sister to his second cousin and namesake (Orlando I*). A local Tory gentleman whose seat stood within the vicinity of Ipswich, Bridgeman took part in a noisy protest early in 1709 against the town's Whig mayor for corruptly discharging his duties as a recruiting commissioner, and in consequence found himself, together with Leicester Martin* and several other local Tories, charged before the Privy Council in March with obstructing recruitment. As a result, he was removed from the commission of the peace and ordered to be prosecuted, but eventually, after an appeal, three of the offenders, including Bridgeman, were restored in March 1710 'by her Majesty's special command', Bridgeman and another riding in triumph to their first sessions, accompanied (according to Dyer) 'by the high sheriff and above 400 gentlemen and freeholders'. He stood for Parliament at Ipswich in 1710, but came bottom of the poll, and in 1713 was defeated again.

Though awarded the seat on petition in April 1714, he afterwards made no more ventures into electoral politics, confining himself instead to the adornment of Combs Hall which he had begun to rebuild after 1710. He died on 24 Apr. 1731, leaving Combs to his surviving son. In framing his testamentary statement of devotion to the Church, he expressed particular abhorrence of 'the present fashionable opinions of deism and, as it is called, freethinking'.[4]

[1] IGI, London; *Wm. Salt Arch. Soc. Colls.* n.s. ii. 237-8; Le Neve, *Mon. Angl.*, 1700-15, p. 264. [2] E. Suff. RO, EE6/1144/14; W. Suss. RO, Shillinglee mss, John Hooke to Sir Edward Turnor*, 28 Sept. 1709. [3] *Hist. Reg. Chron.* 1731, p. 21. [4] Bodl. Rawl. B.428, passim; Boyer, *Anne Annals*, viii. 158-9; L. K. J. Glassey, *Appt. JPs*, 189; Add. 70421, newsletter 10 June 1710; *Wm. Salt Arch. Soc. Colls.* 238; info. from Mr E. Martin.

D. W. H.

BRIDGER, Richard (1620-99), of Coombe Place, Hamsey, Suss.

LEWES   1679 (Mar.)-1681 (Mar.)
         1685-1687
         1689-1695

bap. 13 Feb. 1620, 1st s. of Henry Bridger of Ashurst by Jane, da. of John Ravenscroft of Horsham. *educ.* Magdalen Hall, Oxf. 1638; I. Temple 1640. *m.* settlement 23 Mar. 1652 (with £1,300), Frances (*d.* 1680), da. of Walter Burrell of Cuckfield, 3s. (1 *d.v.p.*) 5da. *suc.* fa. 1657.[1]

Bridger owned a sizable estate near Lewes and was returned again for the borough in 1690 on his own interest. He was classed as a Whig in Lord Carmarthen's (Sir Thomas Osborne†) analysis of the new Parliament and as a Country supporter in Robert Harley's* list of April 1691, but he was evidently not an active Member. Given leave of absence on 10 Jan. 1694 for health reasons, Bridger did not seek re-election in 1695. He was buried on 8 Jan. 1699 at Warminghurst in Sussex, one of his daughters later marrying Charles Goring*.[2]

[1] *Vis. Suss.* (Harl. Soc. lxxxix), 17; F. W. Steer, *Shiffner Archs.* pp. xviii, 10-11. [2] *Vis. Suss.* 17.

P. W.

BRIDGES *see also* **BRYDGES**

BRIDGES, William (*d.* 1714), of Wallington, Surr. and the Tower of London.

LISKEARD   1695-30 Oct. 1714

s. of Robert Bridges by his w. Mary Woodcock. Prob. *unm.*[1]

Farmer, hearth tax by 1681-4; clerk of deliveries, Ordnance 1682-Aug. 1683, storekeeper Aug. 1683-5, surveyor-gen. 1702-d.; ?sec. to commrs. of accts. and council of trade [I] 1683; commr. excise and hearth money 1684-5.[2]

Freeman, Portsmouth 1702; stannator, Foymore 1703; commr. Greenwich Hosp. 1704, fortifying Chatham, Harwich and Portsmouth 1709.[3]

Bridges was one of four brothers, offspring of the younger son of a minor Warwickshire landowner, and first cousins of John Bridges, the county historian of Northamptonshire, all of whom gained wealth and regained social position through active careers in business and subsequently in government service. The first of the quartet to establish himself in office was Robert Bridges, who worked under Lord Ranelagh (Richard Jones*) during the 1670s in the farm of the Irish revenue, before serving as a revenue commissioner in Ireland from 1682 until removed in 1687 at the behest of Lord Tyrconnel, as 'a damned fanatic'. William, whom we first encounter in 1671, lending the crown the sum of £200, partnered Robert in 1677 in advancing a much greater loan to the Irish military establishment, and in 1679 was granted a licence in his own right to import arms into Ireland. Four years later he seems to have bought a minor place in the Irish administration. The fact that a copy of his will was to be proved in Dublin indicates that he retained interests there. But thenceforth he pursued his career chiefly in England, where there were other connexions to be exploited, perhaps most notably his cousin Brook Bridges, auditor of the imprest and a founding director of the Bank of England. To begin with, however, brother Robert's help was crucial. Having acted as clerk to one of Robert's closest associates, Lemuel Kingdon†, as paymaster of the forces in England, Bridges joined the farmers of the hearth tax in about 1680, alongside Kingdon and another of Robert Bridges' Dublin colleagues, Patrick Trant. He took a leading part in managing that farm, and was named to the joint commission on the excise and hearth money in 1684 when the King resumed direct administration of the collection of the tax. By this time he had also acquired a place in the Ordnance office, possibly through Kingdon's influence, only to lose both these English posts in February 1685, after investigations into the conduct of the hearth money farm exposed corruption. Bridges and his colleagues were pardoned in March 1688, and after the Revolution he resurfaced as a contractor supplying transport and provisions to the troops on the Irish campaigns, and later still as a regimental agent. Although he was pursuing payment of arrears on Ordnance office payments, and another debt persisting since the days of the hearth-tax farm, he was sufficiently prosperous to become an early subscriber to the Bank.[4]

Bridges came into Parliament in 1695 through his friendship with Edward Dennis, a Cornish attorney (father of George Dennis, MP for Liskeard 1734–40), who 'governed', or claimed to be able to 'govern', the borough of Liskeard. During the greater part of his parliamentary career Bridges' activities in the Commons can seldom be distinguished from those of the several members of the Brydges family (with whom he seems to have been distantly connected), except for his appearances on parliamentary lists. He was classed as likely to oppose the Court in the forecast for the division on the proposed council of trade on 31 Jan. 1696, but he signed the Association promptly, and seems to have gravitated towards government. In the 1697–8 session he evidently opposed Country party manoeuvres to reduce the size of the standing army, dividing against the motion of 10 Dec. 1697 for the disbandment of all forces raised since 1680, a political indiscretion (so far as the voters in his constituency were concerned) that was thrown in his face when he sought re-election at Liskeard in 1698. He had also been included in a 'black list' of office-holders and Court pensioners published before the poll, but this was an error, the result of confusion with a 'William Brydges, jnr.', who held the post of secretary to the stamp duty commissioners. Though evidently one of Nature's placemen, Bridges' personal circumstances promoted a certain ambivalence at this time in his dealings with administration. His position as a regimental agent, and his dependence at the 1698 general election on the backing of the Trelawny interest at Liskeard, inclined him towards the Court, and especially a defence of the standing army, since his principal advocates at the hustings had been the brothers Charles* and Henry Trelawny*, both of them serving officers. At the same time he held no significant government appointment himself as yet, and indeed was still seeking the settlement of the debts due to him from his earlier involvement in the service of the crown. In a comparative analysis of the old and new Parliaments drawn up in about September 1698 he was classed as a Court supporter, but with some reservations, and he was also forecast as likely to oppose a standing army. In an analysis of the House into 'interests' in 1700 he was classed as doubtful or opposition, but after an unopposed re-election at Liskeard in January 1701 he supported the Court in February over the 'Great Mortgage'. He headed the list of defeated candidates for the abortive accounts commission in June. In Robert Harley's* analysis of the new Parliament of December 1701 he was classed with the Tories, and he voted on 26 Feb. 1702 in favour of the motion to vindicate the proceedings of the Commons in the impeachments of the four Whig lords.[5]

With the new reign Bridges at last returned to office; more specifically he returned to the Ordnance, where he was appointed surveyor-general, with an additional allowance of £200 p.a. over and above his salary (itself augmented by £100), and a residence in the Tower. He regularly presented accounts, estimates and papers to the House on behalf of the Ordnance office, and as a placeman served the Court with a faithfulness that rarely faltered. He was forecast as likely to oppose the Tack, and indeed did not vote for it on 28 Nov. 1704. On 24 Feb. 1705 he reported on a private bill. He was described as 'Low Church' in an analysis of the 1705 Parliament. He voted on 25 Oct. for the Court candidate as Speaker, and supported the Court in the proceedings on 18 Feb. 1706 over the 'place clause' in the regency bill. Although described as a Tory in early 1708, he was classed as a Whig in 1710 in the 'Hanover list' of the newly elected Parliament, but subsequently changed sides once more, being included in 1711 among the 'worthy patriots' who in the 1710–11 session exposed the mismanagements of the previous ministry. After presenting Liskeard's loyal address on the peace in 1713, he was marked as a Tory in the Worsley list.[6]

In failing health since at least the summer of 1712, when he had spent five months convalescing in the country, Bridges died on 30 Oct. 1714, and was buried in the church of St. Peter-within-the-Tower. His entire estate, including the manor of Wallington, purchased at some point after 1683, and at least £4,000 in Bank stock, passed to his unmarried sister Elizabeth, and eventually (in 1745) from her to a great-nephew, Sir Brook Bridges, 3rd Bt.† The monument raised by Elizabeth to William's memory noted in particular his tenure of the surveyor-generalship of the Ordnance, and added that he had been

in that and other considerable offices, through which he passed at different times, a diligent and faithful servant to the crown and to his country in Parliament; assiduous in public business, and in his private life possessing an happy equality of temper, adorned with exemplary sobriety and virtue.[7]

[1] Playfair, *Brit. Fam. Antiquity*, vi. 797–8; Manning and Bray, *Surr*. i. 270 (cf. *Mar. Lic. Vicar-Gen*. (Harl. Soc. xxx), 87); *St. Paul's, Covent Garden* (Harl. Soc. Reg. xxxv), 67. [2] *Cal. Treas. Bks*. vii. 297, 1074, 1485; xxiii. 224; H. C. Tomlinson, *Guns and Govt*. 224–5; *CSP Dom*. Jan.–June 1683, p. 6; 1684–5, pp. 302, 309; Luttrell, *Brief Relation*, i. 326. [3] R. East, *Portsmouth Recs*. 373; J. Tregoning, *Laws of the Stannaries*, 118; *Daily Courant*, 8 Aug. 1704. [4] *Cal. Treas.*

Bks. iii. 634, 808; iv. 603; v. 744, 746, 748, 966; vi. 202, 626; vii. 297, 1074, 1447, 1485, 1517; viii. 4–5, 11, 265, 747, 1607, 1817; ix. 1089, 1092, 1100, 1114, 1139; x. 1046; xv. 132; xvi. 507–10, 1194; *Cal. Orrery Pprs.* ed. Maclysaght (Irish Mss Commn.), 197; *HMC 11th Rep. VII*, 41; *HMC Ormonde*, ii. 274–5; n.s. iv. 49, 103, 124, 133, 154, 363; v. 438; vi. 10, 226, 233; viii. 349; *Liber Munerum Publicorum Hiberniae* ed. Lascelles, i(2), p.133; *Clarendon Corresp.* ed. Singer, i. 311, 323, 332, 513; ii. 138; *Index to Prerog. Wills in Ire.* ed. Vicars, 53; Luttrell, i. 326; C. D. Chandaman, *Eng. Public Revenue 1660–88*, p. 105; *HMC Lords*, n.s. i. 333–4; *CSP Dom. 1687–9*, p. 167; 1690–1, pp. 264, 270, 279; *HMC Finch*, ii. 389, 398; Nottingham Univ. Lib. Portland (Harley) mss Pw2 Hy 455, list of regimental agents; *Cal. Treas. Pprs.* 1557–1696, p. 202; DZA, Bonet's despatch 6/16 July 1694. [5] C. H. C. Baker and M. I. Baker, *James Brydges, 1st Duke of Chandos*, 116; Cobbett, *Parlty. Hist.* v. p.clxxi; *Cal. Treas. Bks.* x. 618; xv. 132; G. Holmes, *Pol. in Age of Anne*, 356; *Cal. Treas. Pprs.* 1557–1696, p. 202; Yorks. Arch. Soc. Copley mss DD38, box H–J, poll for commrs. of public accts. [16 June 1701]. [6] *CSP Dom.* 1703–4, p. 470; *Cal. Treas. Pprs.* 1708–14, pp. 144–5; *London Gazette*, 23–26 May 1713. [7] Tomlinson, 68; Le Neve, *Mon. Angl.* 1700–15, p. 393; Manning and Bray, 270; Egerton 3359 (unfol.); PCC Aston; Maitland, *Hist. London* (1756), i. 150.

D. W. H.

BRIGGS, Sir Humphrey, 4th Bt. (c.1670–1734), of Haughton, Salop.

SHROPSHIRE	1701 (Feb.–Nov.)
BRIDGNORTH	1702–1710
MUCH WENLOCK	13 July 1716–1727

b. c.1670, 1st s. of Sir Humphrey Briggs, 3rd Bt., of Haughton and Ernstrey Park, nr. Diddlebury, Salop by Barbara, da. of Sir Wadham Wyndham of Norrington, Wilts., j. Kb. *educ.* Wadham, Oxf. matric. 2 July 1687, aged 17; L. Inn 1687. *unm. suc.* fa. as 4th Bt. 31 Jan. 1700.[1]

Freeman, Much Wenlock 1708.[2]

Briggs was descended from a family which had come to Shropshire in the mid-16th century, and his grandfather had sat for Much Wenlock from 1646 until 1648. A staunch Whig, he was returned unopposed for Shropshire in January 1701, and was included in the county lieutenancy in March. Having been defeated at the next election, when he stood for the county with Richard Corbet* against two Tories, he was considered for a recommendation by the Howard interest at a by-election for Castle Rising in February 1702, but had to wait until the general election of that year to be returned again on the Whitmore interest at Bridgnorth. On 13 Feb. 1703 he voted for agreeing with the Lords' amendments to the bill for enlarging the time for taking the oath of abjuration, and he acted as a teller on 7 Mar. 1704 against a Tory motion to recommit the bill for recruiting. Forecast as a probable opponent of the Tack, he figured on Robert Harley's* lobbying list and voted against the measure or was absent on 28 Nov. 1704. Chosen again in 1705 after an election in which his opposition to the Tack may have been of advantage to him, he was classed as a 'Churchman' in a list of the new Parliament. He voted for John Smith I* in the election of a Speaker on 25 Oct. 1705, supported the Court over the regency bill on 18 Feb. 1706 and was listed as both a Whig and a Tory, the latter classification clearly a mistake, in early 1708. On 7 Jan. 1708 he was given leave to go into the country for a month. He supported the measures of the Whig administration, voting for the naturalization of the Palatines in 1709 and subsequently for the impeachment of Dr Sacheverell, an action which may have damaged his prospects for re-election, for in 1710 he and the other Whig Member for Bridgnorth, William Whitmore, were narrowly defeated by two Tories in a fierce contest dominated by the issue of the impeachment.[3]

Returning to England just before the Queen's death in 1714, Briggs wrote soon afterwards to a French correspondent that he was comforted to find the country well disposed towards King George, and that he hoped the King would soon see through the claim of the Tories always to have been supporters of the Hanoverian succession. He also confided that he had taken a decision not to seek re-election to Parliament, and was not returned in 1715. The following year, however, he came in at a by-election at Much Wenlock. Briggs died on 8 Dec. 1734 and was succeeded by his brother.[4]

[1] *Post Boy*, 3–6 Feb. 1700. [2] Salop RO, Forester mss, copy of Much Wenlock corp. bk. [3] *CSP Dom.* 1700–2, p. 249; Bradford mss at Weston Park, John Bridgeman to Sir John Bridgeman, 29 Nov. 1701; Norf. RO, Howard (Castle Rising) mss, Robert Walpole II* to Lady Diana Howard, 11 Jan. 1702; G. Holmes, *Pol. in Age of Anne*, 38. [4] Add. 39167, f. 122.

D. W. H.

BRIGHT (formerly Liddell), John (1671–1735), of Badsworth, Yorks.

PONTEFRACT	1698–17 Jan. 1700
	1 Feb. 1700–1701 (Nov.)

b. 23 Mar. 1671, 2nd s. of Henry Liddell*. *educ.* Christ's, Camb. 1689, MA 1690; M. Temple 1689. *m.* Cordelia, da. of Samuel Clutterbuck, of Hydes, Ingatestone, Essex, common councilman of London, 4s. (3 *d.v.p.*) 3da. (2 *d.v.p.*). *suc.* maternal gdfa. at Badsworth and assumed name of Bright 1688.[1]

Settled in the neighbourhood of Pontefract since the 15th century, the Brights were a wealthy West Riding family. In the early 17th century their Yorkshire estates were said to be worth £1,000 p.a. During the Civil Wars John Bright† had been one of the West Riding's leading Parliamentarians, and his loyalty to the Commonwealth extended to assisting the suppression of Sir George Booth's† rising of 1659. The following year, however, Bright supported the Restoration and in July 1660 was granted a baronetcy. The death of his only son six years later meant that when the baronet died in September 1688 he was succeeded in his estates by the second and third sons of his eldest daughter, who had married the leading Durham colliery owner Henry Liddell. The Carbrook estates were settled upon Henry, while the remainder of the estate was inherited by John. Upon gaining his grandfather's estate John Liddell assumed the surname Bright.[2]

John Bright (as he was now known) successfully contested Pontefract in 1698. In about September a comparison of the old and new Commons classed him as a Country party supporter, but on 18 Jan. 1699 he voted against the third reading of the disbanding bill. He was otherwise an inactive Member, and on 11 Dec. was sent for in custody, having been absent from a call of the House. He was discharged the following day. At the beginning of this session Robert Monckton* had renewed his petition against Bright's election at Pontefract, and when on 17 Jan. 1700 the House considered the report Bright's election was voided and a new writ ordered. At the consequent by-election Bright again defeated Monckton. He continued to make little impression upon the records of the House, though an analysis of the House dating from early 1700 listed him in the interest of the Junto. Bright retained his seat at the first election of 1701, his only recorded activity in this Parliament being to tell on 15 Apr. 1701 in favour of a Whig attempt to delay consideration of the report upon the East Retford election.

Bright 'declined standing' at the second 1701 election, and does not appear to have stood for Parliament again. He was, however, active in the Whig interest at the 1708 Pontefract election, Bright and his former adversary Monckton being 'sent' to the borough by the Duke of Newcastle (John Holles†) to assist attempts to unseat Sir John Bland, 4th Bt.* His continuing partisan loyalties were also evident in February 1715. Lord Carlisle (Charles Howard*) requested that Bright investigate allegations that the Tory Sir Arthur Kaye, 3rd Bt.*, had circulated copies of *The English Advice to Freeholders of England* at the West Riding's quarter sessions. Carlisle hoped that if Bright could prove the charge Kaye would be expelled from the Commons. Little more is known of Bright until his death. Family and local historians have customarily fixed the date of this as 1737, but two contemporary obituaries state that Bright died at Badsworth on 6 Oct. 1735. He was succeeded by his only surviving son, Thomas.[3]

[1] J. Foster, *Peds. of Yorks. Fams.* i. (Bright); Surtees, *Dur.* ii. 213; J.R. Woodhead, *Rulers of London* (London and Mdx. Arch. Soc.), 49; J. Hunter, *Hallamshire* ed. A. Gatty, 417–18. [2] W. S. Porter, *Notes on Hallamshire Fam. of Bright*, 2–7; *DNB* (Bright, Sir John). [3] W. Yorks. Archs. (Leeds), Temple Newsam mss TN/C9/150, William Lowther II* to Ld. Irwin (Arthur Ingram*), 17 Nov. 1701; Bagot mss at Levens Hall, Bland to James Grahme*, 25 May 1708; *HMC Portland*, v. 507–8; Boyer, *Pol. State*, l. 447; *London Mag.* 1735, p. 571.

E. C./R. D. H.

BRIGSTOCKE, Owen (1679–1746), of Llechdwnni, Kidwelly, Carm. and Queen's Square, Mdx.

CARDIGAN BOROUGHS   17 Mar. 1712–1713
CARDIGANSHIRE   29 Jan. 1717–1722

bap. 3 Apr. 1679, 1st s. of William Brigstocke of Llechdwnni by Winifred, da. and coh. of Robert Byrt of Llwydyrys, Card. *educ.* Eton bef. 1695; Jesus, Oxf. 1695; M. Temple 1697, called 1705; travelled abroad (Holland, France) 1700. *m.* Anne (*d.* 1746), da. of Edward Browne, MD, of Northfleet, Kent and h. to her bro. Thomas Browne, MD, of Northfleet, *s.p. suc.* fa. 1713.[1]
FRS 1710.[2]

Brigstocke, whose ancestors, formerly based in Surrey, had acquired a Carmarthenshire estate early in the 17th century, was returned for Cardigan Boroughs at a by-election in 1712 on the Tory interest of his relations the Pryses. His contribution to the remainder of the 1711–12 session was slight, though in June he carried to the Lords a bill to allow the easier recovery of small debts and legacies given to 'pious and charitable uses', and another concerning the estate of Lord Bellew [I] (Richard*). His antiquarian pursuits brought him into the orbit of Lord Treasurer Oxford (Robert Harley*), who in November 1712 encouraged him to apply for a minor customs place for a kinsman. In May 1713 Brigstocke was nominated to draft, and subsequently reported, a naturalization bill. Though dropped at the election of that year, he was nominated by Lewis Pryse* as knight of the shire in 1717, after Pryse had himself been expelled the House, but again seems to have been no more than a stop-gap. He voted in 1719 against the repeal of the Occasional Conformity and Schism Acts and stood down in 1722, never to put up for election again. By 1731 he was describing himself, in a letter to Sir Hans Sloane, as 'an old rusticated acquaintance'. Towards the end of his life he approached (Sir) Robert Walpole II* for a crumb of patronage for a nephew, recalling his and Walpole's schooldays together, and 'the frequent civilities you have shown me since'. Brigstocke died on 4 May 1746, and was buried at Kidwelly. His nephew succeeded him.[3]

[1]*Carmarthen Antiquary*, i. 40; *SPCK Corresp.* (Univ. of Wales Bd. of Celtic Studies, Hist. and Law ser. x), 45; *CSP Dom.* 1699–1700, p. 364; *DNB* (Browne, Thomas). [2]*Recs. R. Soc.* 391. [3]*Ceredigion*, v. 402–4; Harl. 3777, ff. 243–4; Add. 70213, Brigstocke to Ld. Oxford, 1 Nov. 1712; Sloane 4052, f. 52; Camb. Univ. Lib. Cholmondeley (Houghton) mss, Brigstocke to Walpole, 11 May [?1744]; *SPCK Corresp.* 45.

D. W. H.

BRISTOW, Robert I (1662–1706), of Micheldever, Hants, and St. Dunstan-in-the-East, London.

WINCHELSEA 1698–27 Feb. 1701

b. Dec. 1662, o. s. of Robert Bristow, Grocer and merchant, of Virginia and St. Gabriel, Fenchurch Street, London, alderman of London 1687–8, by his 1st w. Averilla (*d.* by 1680), da. of Thomas Curtis of Ware, Gloucester co., Virginia. *m.* 1 Jan. 1685, Katherine (*d.* 1751), da. of Robert Woolley, Vintner, merchant and broker, of St. Dunstan-in-the-East, London and East Sheen, Surr. common councilman of London 1682, 6s. (3 *d.v.p.*) 6da.[1]

Dir. Bank of Eng. 1698, 1701–3, 1706.[2]
Freeman, Winchelsea 1698, London by 1706.[3]

In the early 17th century Bristow's forebears were little more than well-off yeoman farmers living at Binsted in Hampshire. His father began as an apprentice, but in around 1660 migrated to Virginia and during the next 16 years made a handsome fortune as a merchant, acquiring estates in several Virginian counties. In the eyes of the colony's governors he was esteemed 'a man of good understanding in the Virginia affairs and one of integrity and moderation', but the shock of a violent local rebellion in 1676, in which he and his property were principal targets of attack, brought him back to England. Settling in London, where he invested in property, he maintained his valuable trading connexions with Virginia and the West Indies and was gradually absorbed into the upper echelons of mercantile society in the City. His only son Robert, the future Member for Winchelsea, was born in Virginia and in due course became his business associate. In 1685 Robert Bristow jnr. married a daughter of the wealthy London vintner Robert Woolley, a union that helped consolidate his family's emerging prominence among the merchant-financier elite. Bristow and his father were numbered among the original subscribers to the Bank of England pursuant to its incorporation in July 1694, but owing to the confusion which arises from their identical first names it is not clear whether it was he or his father who was elected a director of the Bank in April 1697. The Bank's records show Bristow and his father serving as director for alternating terms between 1697 and 1706, the younger Bristow being listed as a director in 1698, during 1701–3 and again in 1706.[4]

Though Bristow's country seat was at Micheldever in Hampshire, which his father bestowed on him at the time of his marriage, his electoral ambitions were focused upon Winchelsea, one of several Sussex towns in which he had purchased property. He was elected for the port without challenge in 1698 but in political terms he remains an elusive figure. Beyond the fact that during the 1698–9 session he was broadly sympathetic towards the Country viewpoint, being noted during the proceedings over disbandment as a probable opponent of the standing army, nothing more can be said of his politics: his party loyalties remain obscure. He served as a teller only once, on 10 Jan. 1700, concerning an amendment to the wording of a bill to free the market at Blackwell Hall from the restrictive practices of factors. His support for the Old East India Company, in which he was a major shareholder, as noted in a list identifying Members by 'interests' compiled between January and May 1700, may also suggest a degree of sympathy with the Country party in the late 1690s.[5]

Bristow's service as an MP for Winchelsea came to an abrupt and undignified end shortly after he was returned in the January election of 1701. The town's handful of voters had been the centre of a more than usually sordid and venal contest in which Bristow's agent was involved with the mayor in bribery and malpractice. Bristow was forced to give account of himself at the bar of the House when the case brought by the losing candidates was heard on 27 Feb., but in the face of overwhelming evidence of corruption on his and his partner's behalf the election was declared void. This humiliating exit evidently deterred Bristow from any future attempt to recover his seat or to seek re-election elsewhere. He fell critically ill during the summer of 1706, describing himself in the will he signed on 10 Aug. as 'weak in body'. He died, predeceasing his father, about a fortnight later and was buried on the 27th in his parish church of St. Dunstan. To his eldest son, Robert*, he bequeathed the manor of Micheldever, while to his wife he left the bulk of his land in the Rochford area of Essex. He also took steps to ensure the disposal of his proprietorial interest at Winchelsea, decreeing that all his Sussex property was to be sold by trustees for the benefit of his younger children.

[1]Hoare, *Wilts.* v. Frustfield, 33–34; *Misc. Gen. et Her.* (ser. 5), vii. 3–8, 51–53; J. R. Woodhead, *Rulers of London* (London and Mdx. Arch. Soc.) 38, 180; *St. Dunstan-in-the East* (Harl. Soc. Reg. lxxxiv–lxxxv), 63. [2]Bank of Eng. unpub. list of directors, 1694–1961. [3]E. Suss. RO, Winchelsea ct. bk. WIN 60, p. 58. [4]*Misc.*

Gen. et Her. 3–4, 12–13, 56; *CSP Dom.* 1697, p. 269; DZA, Bonet despatch 6/16 July 1694. [5] *Misc. Gen. et Her.* 51.

A. A. H.

BRISTOW, Robert II (1687–1737), of Micheldever, Hants, and Coleman Street, London.

WINCHELSEA 20 Dec. 1708–3 Nov. 1737

bap. 20 Oct. 1687, 2nd but 1st surv. s. of Robert Bristow I*; bro. of John Bristow†. *m.* 1 Dec. 1709, Sarah, da. of (Sir) John Ward II* of Squerryes, Kent, 4s. *suc.* fa. 1706, gdfa. 1707.[1]
  Freeman, Winchelsea 1708.[2]
  Dir. Bank of Eng. 1713–20 (with statutory intervals), E.I. Co. 1716–18; commr. stating army debts 1716–21; clerk of Bd. of Green Cloth 1720–*d.*[3]
  Gov. St. Thomas' Hosp. by 1719.[4]

Bristow's involvement in City financial circles began soon after he came of age. He had the twin advantages of belonging to a respected City dynasty and of wealth recently inherited from both his father and grandfather. Under the latter's will he received the Virginian lands which had formed the basis of the family fortune. Encouragement to maintain the family's interests in the City no doubt came additionally from his father-in-law John Ward II, an influential City figure who had been governor of the Bank in the early 1700s when Bristow's father was serving as a director. Bristow's Bank stockholding amounted to some £2,000 by March 1710, and within a few years his reputation among the Bank's investors was to earn him a place on its directorate. In December 1708, at the age of just 21, he was brought into Parliament for Winchelsea after the sitting Member George Dodington chose to make his election for Bridgwater. Bristow was presumably elected on what had been the family's old interest in the town which, despite his father's dying wish, had not been sold off, though his return may not have been possible without Dodington's nomination. It is quite likely that Dodington, with manifold government and business interests of his own in the City, had been acquainted with Bristow's father and grandfather and could vouch for him as a suitable successor in the seat.[5]

As his recorded votes show, and as later analyses of the House confirm, Bristow was a committed Whig, though never conspicuous in parliamentary proceedings. He performed his first substantive task on 20 Apr. 1709 as a teller in favour of amendments made by the Lords to a bill for preventing fire risks. During February and March 1709 he followed his party line in registering support for the naturalization of the Palatines, and in February and March 1710 voted in support of the impeachment proceedings against Dr Sacheverell. Despite these unequivocal demonstrations of Whiggery, his political identity eluded the compiler of the 'Hanover list' of the 1710 Parliament, who classed him as 'doubtful'. But his Whig outlook is clearly substantiated by a series of other recorded votes. On 7 Dec. 1711 he supported the 'No Peace without Spain' motion, while on 24 Jan. 1712, during the censure proceedings against the Duke of Marlborough (John Churchill†), he was a teller for the Whig minority on the central motion that the Duke had illegally accepted money from bread contractors during his command in the Low Countries. On 18 June he voted against the French commerce bill, and on 14 Mar. 1714 against the expulsion of Richard Steele. Other lists of the Commons compiled in 1713 and 1715, including the Worsley list, also consistently identify Bristow as a Whig.

Bristow was among the earliest to demonstrate his support for George I in taking his place among the signatories to the proclamation at St. James's Palace on 1 Aug. 1714. He continued to represent Winchelsea and was actively involved in the City until 1720. Appointed that year to the Board of Green Cloth, he was for the rest of his life an unswerving adherent of Whig government. He died on 3 Nov. 1737.[6]

[1] *Misc. Gen. et Her.* (ser. 5), vii. 5–7; *St. Dunstan-in-the-East* (Harl. Soc. Reg. lxxxiv–lxxxv), 37; IGI, London. [2] E. Suss. RO, Winchelsea ct. bk. WIN 60, p. 123. [3] Info. from Prof. H. G. Horwitz. [4] J. Aubrey, *Surr.* (1719), v. 311. [5] *Misc. Gen. et Her.* 5–7, 51–53; Egerton 3359 (unfol.). [6] Boyer, *Pol. State*, viii. 118; *Gent. Mag.* 1737, p. 701.

A. A. H.

BROCKMAN, William (1658–by 1742), of Beachborough, Kent.

HYTHE 1690–1695

bap. 2 Sept. 1658, s. and h. of James Brockman, of Beachborough, by Lucy, da. of James Young, merchant, of London. *educ.* Canterbury; M. Temple, 1674; St. John's, Camb. 1674; travelled abroad (Germany, Netherlands) 1686. *m.* settlement 15 Dec. 1692, Anne (*d.*1730), da. and coh. of Richard Glyd of Pendhill, Surr.; sis. of John Glyd†, 3s. (2 *d.v.p.*) *suc.* fa. 1684.[1]
  Commr. Dover Harbour, 1706?–1725.[2]
  Member, SPCK.[3]

Most of the lands eventually inherited by Brockman were purchased by his great-grandfather, but the Brockmans could count themselves a truly local family, tracing their connexion with Kent back to the time of Richard I. Brockman's grandfather, Sir William Brockman, gained local fame during the Civil

War. A staunch Royalist, Sir William was imprisoned from 1642 to 1645, and in 1648 he came with a troop of 800 men to the aid of Maidstone, under siege from General Thomas Fairfax's[†] Parliamentary army. Sir William and his brother Zouch were fined for their delinquency in 1651. In an apparent break with this Royalist tradition, Brockman's father, James, made known his desire to stand as a Whig candidate for Hythe in the second 1679 election, although in the event he stood aside in favour of Edward Hales[†].[4]

Brockman's own Whig inclinations were well enough known that in 1683, after the discovery of the Rye House Plot, his house was searched for arms. In 1685 he made a trip to France when the persecution of Protestants there was at its height and, assisted by the English envoy in Paris, Sir William Trumbull[*], by clandestine means successfully conveyed a Protestant refugee to England. Brockman left for Europe again in May 1686, returning by September. This second trip seems to have been a conventional sightseeing tour through Germany and the Netherlands.[5]

Brockman's political ambitions were endorsed in September 1688 when, at a meeting of East Kent gentlemen to decide on candidates for James II's abortive Parliament, he and James Chadwick[*] were nominated to stand for New Romney in case John Brewer[*] did not stand. In December Brockman travelled around Kent carrying messages about the capture of James II at Feversham. His enthusiasm for the Revolution swept Sir John Knatchbull, 2nd Bt.[*], further into the affair than he would have wished when, on Brockman's information, he was ordered to bring his troop of horse into Feversham after having resolved to stop at Ashford. At the end of December Knatchbull sent Brockman the Kent Association to sign, which no doubt he did readily. In 1689 Brockman was actively involved in the local election campaigns for the Convention Parliament, being closely associated with the attempts by (Sir) Edward Dering[†] (3rd Bt.) to stand for Kent. Brockman himself did not sit in the 1689 Parliament, and Hon. Anchitell Grey's[*] attribution to him of a speech on 4 June in the debate on the indemnity bill must be mistaken.[6]

Brockman was active in the county elections of March 1690 and entered Parliament himself, defeating three other candidates for Hythe. The retiring Member, Julius Deedes, gave his interest to his good friend Brockman. Brockman also attempted to enlist Hon. John Beaumont's[*] support, but without success because Beaumont was in the process of attempting to assert the right of the lord warden to nominate one of the candidates for each of the Cinque Ports and did not have Brockman in mind. Indeed, Beaumont asked Deedes to explain his support of Brockman, which he did, replying that he could not be more useful to the King

> than by endeavouring to send such a Member to Parliament who hath shown himself as forward for the bringing in the King, and hath been as careful for their Majesties' interest since their accession to the throne in all matters, especially in the due levying of money granted, as any man whatsoever.[7]

Brockman's parliamentary activity belies the fact that he was only to sit for five years. The true extent of his undertakings went far beyond the official record of his committee appointments and tellerships and is revealed in the large quantity of papers that he left. Much of this archive relates to his business as a local dignitary: a justice for Kent from 1688, he was removed in July 1702, reappointed in July 1705 and remained on the bench until his death. He was also active in local assemblies, such as that regularly held by the lords of Romney Marsh, and he was a deputy-lieutenant for Kent from May 1689 until at least 1703. In what can only be described as an obsession with his 'rights' (mainly to do with property), he conducted many lengthy court battles, the correspondence for which is also among his papers. Local affairs and moral reform were very much a part of Brockman's parliamentary concerns and his political papers reveal a man who was the very image of a Country Whig.[8]

Brockman's Whig credentials were, then, well known by 1690 and it is not surprising to find him marked as a Whig in Lord Carmarthen's (Sir Thomas Osborne[†]) list of Members of the new Parliament. He started his parliamentary career with high hopes. After the debate on the Plympton election on 27 Mar. he wrote to Julius Deedes that 'the King's friends are many, and I believe it will be hard to carry a point that shall favour any ministers more than the constitution'. He looked forward to the 'doubtful' elections being satisfactorily resolved so that the important issues could be tackled, 'and I would not have the public business interrupted, if I could help it, by private bills or other concerns'. This letter illustrates a characteristic tetchiness at unnecessary delay and another theme, that of freedom of elections on a local and national level, which was to preoccupy him throughout his life. Brockman's first action as a Member was to pursue the question of freedom of elections for the Cinque Ports. A bill had been introduced in January 1690 and Brockman was very much involved when it reappeared in March. It was not put into committee but there seems to have been a group which met and discussed how to get the bill through. With the help of other

Cinque Ports Members, Brockman collected evidence of Court intervention in the election, particularly letters sent by Beaumont to the relevant corporations putting forward the lord warden's claims to one seat. When Julius Deedes protested feebly that Beaumont's letter to him had been private, Brockman persisted until he obtained a copy. The bill was passed in May 1690.[9]

On 24 Apr. 1690 Brockman was appointed to a committee for drafting an abjuration oath, an unsuccessful Whig move proposed by Hon. Thomas Wharton*. In the debate on the bill, 26 Apr., Brockman took notes on what was said by Members who opposed, and then made a speech himself in reply. He said that the Act of Recognition having passed so readily and King William having been acknowledged king, he could not see how any could scruple to abjure King James. He used the occasion for irony at the expence of the Churchmen who had pressed an address of thanks to the King on the change of the London lieutenancy with great eagerness; 'this zeal I say should be extended to other instances'. He also vigorously attacked the idea that the clergy should be exempt from the oath, expressing his view that the clergy were no more than the most eminent part of the Church of England and that they should demonstrate their loyalty and lead by example. A table of the fees of Commons officers in Brockman's hand suggests that he was interested in the inquiry into the House's fees, although he was not named to the committees on 23 and 30 April. Somewhat quixotically, Brockman spoke against King William going to Ireland after the bill to make Mary regent had been passed in both Houses by 13 May. Raising the issue of the danger to King William, he proposed that a committee be appointed to draw up an address to express the 'sense of the House' on William's going, a suggestion which was not taken up. He also queried what the legal situation would be in Scotland as no provision had been made for a regency there.[10]

During the summer of 1690 Brockman's political activities did not cease, and after the naval debacle at Beachy Head he acquired copies of letters on the case against Admiral Torrington (Arthur Herbert[†]). In the second session Brockman became even busier. By this time he seems to have acquired a reputation for industry and was sent proposals by other Members on various subjects, particularly on raising revenue through different taxes. On 28 Nov. he told for the Whig side in the vote on the disputed Cardiganshire election, and on 1 Dec. was added to a drafting committee of a bill for preventing the export of wool. This was a matter of particular importance in Kent and Brockman received advice about possible remedies from such men as Julius Deedes and Sir James Oxenden, 2nd Bt.* An act was not passed at this time, progress being swamped by endless representations from special interest groups. Brockman also told on 2 Dec. against the question of whether to receive the London common council petition promoted by the Tories in an attempt to close loopholes in an earlier act which had allowed the Whigs to retain control of the bench of aldermen and the mayoralty.[11]

Brockman was listed as a Country party supporter by Robert Harley* in April 1691. On 31 Oct. he was the first-named to a committee to prepare a bill for maintaining and securing the rights and privileges of corporations. Brockman worked hard on this bill, attending committee meetings and preparing drafts, and presented it on 1 Jan. 1692. On 21 Dec. 1691 he presented a rider to the land tax bill, regulating and limiting the fees of Exchequer officers, which was accepted. On 8 Jan. 1692 he was appointed to an inquiry into ways to encourage the fisheries, another matter of local importance. On the same day he spoke for the bill for lessening the interest rate from 6 to 4 per cent, a measure promoted by another Country Whig, Sir Edward Hussey, 3rd Bt.* Notes made by Brockman on a paper objecting to the proposal are similar to the arguments put forward by the promoters of the bill: that such a move would keep up rents and land values and would help farmers to pay wages, and would encourage trade. Brockman's notes also reveal his belief in the importance of land, which 'principally preserves property and supports the government'. Ten days later, in the debate on supply, it was suggested that the salaries and fees of crown officials should go towards the war effort. Brockman, in a compliment with more than a hint of sarcasm, moved that since men who had places had made such a generous offer it should be supported.[12]

Brockman was granted leave for a month from 26 January. In Lord Carmarthen's list of March–December 1692 he was marked as a possible Court supporter, to be approached through Colonel Robert Austen I*. This may seem surprising given Brockman's obvious distrust of all ministries, but Carmarthen's optimism may have been founded on Brockman's support for the war. On 2 Feb. 1693 he voted for an unsuccessful bill for frequent Parliaments, and in the debate on 10 Feb. he supported the view that the measure was not an encroachment on the King's prerogative: 'it is better for the King to rely on his people, than on a ministry, not excepting the present ministry'. His proposed amendment, which is left somewhat obscure by Grey's report, seems to have been a call for the bill to be better drawn so that there would indeed be annual sessions. Another leave of absence was granted for a fortnight on 17 Feb.[13]

In the 1693–4 session Brockman concentrated on two measures. One was a bill for more frequent Parliaments, which he presented on 14 Nov. but had to withdraw and re-submit on 16 Nov., without a specified date of dissolution for the present Parliament. On 28 Nov. he told against the vote on a clause allowing an unspecified number of years before a session need be held, presumably because he supported annual sessions. The bill itself was voted down on the same day. The other issue to occupy Brockman was that of the mismanagement of the fleet in June 1693. The Whigs pursued several Tory admirals for the disasters which had struck the Smyrna convoy and Brockman's copious notes from the examinations of the admirals and their answers at the bar of the House, together with his own memoranda and questions interspersed, indicate both his Country and Whig sympathies. His written 'opinions' on the affair were threefold: that it had been the duty of the admirals to gain intelligence on the Brest fleet before they parted with the Turkey fleet, that they had neglected their duty and betrayed their trust in not doing so and that such neglect and treachery had been the cause of loss and dishonour to the English nation. These opinions were echoed in a vote which passed the House on 17 Nov. 1693 that 'upon the examination of the mismanagement of the fleet, and the loss the Turkey Company sustained this summer, there hath been a notorious and treacherous mismanagement of the fleet this year'. Brockman was a successful teller for the question of whether there was enough beer on board to have enabled the fleet to have conveyed the merchant ships out of danger of the French fleet, rather than returning for more supplies. If he needed any encouragement to pursue the matter, Brockman received an anonymous and threatening letter the same day to the effect that failure to punish those who were responsible would be a betrayal of the nation and lead to suspicions of treachery. The fact that the extremely partisan nature of the proceedings had left some Whigs disinclined to pursue the admirals does not seem to have deterred him.[14]

After these highly controversial debates Brockman was on leave of absence for three weeks from 12 Dec., during which time it is likely that he married Anne Glyd, the settlement being made on 15 Dec. Anne apparently held the same Whig ideals as her husband, as her letter to her brother of 10 Feb. 1689 indicates: 'it is high time to mingle our joy with yours, applauding that providence which has brought things to so happy a union, we all most zealously espoused your cause as far as words and wishes would reach'. Back in the House, on 14 Mar. 1694 Brockman told successfully on the question of sending Hugh Fortescue* into custody for continual absence. Brockman's hopes of a reward 'in the county where I distinguished myself with the earliest and forwardest actions for the support of this Revolution' were disappointed that summer when he was not given the governorship of Sandgate Castle in Kent.[15]

In the 1694–5 session, Brockman was the sole Member appointed to draft a bill for the improvement of freehold estates and the encouragement of trade, presenting it and being first-named to the second-reading committee. Brockman was also involved in one of the major issues of the session, that of bribery and corruption. He was particularly concerned at the bribery of Members. Recalling in his notes the Commons' resolution of 4 Jan. 1693, that no Member accept entertainments for the carrying on any matter under the consideration of the House, on pain of censure, he wrote that 'if a small bribe suffice to vacate an election, shall not the like serve for expulsion'. If not, then the practice seemed 'a crime only without and not within doors, and that it's the privilege of a Member only to be corrupt and make the House his sanctuary'. On 19 Apr. he told for the motion to delay the report on the supply bill until 24 Apr. (a measure probably designed to allow time to prepare for the examination of Sir Thomas Cooke* about the allegations), and on the 23rd was elected one of the committee charged with the examination of Cooke. He was then appointed to the committee to draw up the articles of impeachment against the Duke of Leeds (formerly Carmarthen). Brockman's papers contain a draft of the articles, with alterations in his own hand. On 30 Apr. Brockman was a teller in a successful party vote against the question of recommitting the bill to reverse the attainder of Jacob Leisler, the radical who had taken over the government of New York in 1689.[16]

In July 1695 Dr Richard Kingston wrote from Kent to Trumbull, 'here is in this neighbourhood one Mr Brockman, a justice of the peace, a Member of Parliament, an over busy man of "the '48 size and cut"'. This scathing (but accurate) description was prompted by Brockman having spoken against Trumbull. He had apparently 'made very sad prognostications of ill things that are to happen upon the management of so great a Tory', which could be a reference to Trumbull's appointment as secretary of state in May 1695. Kingston hoped that he would be able to counteract Brockman's campaign against

Trumbull. The letter also indicates Brockman's local influence: in conjunction with Sir Basil Dixwell, 2nd Bt.*, he 'has a great hand in placing and displacing officers of all sorts'. This influence, however, did not ensure his success in the October 1695 elections when he was defeated by Jacob des Bouverie*.[17]

Despite being out of the House, Brockman's interest in politics did not diminish. He defended the 1696 proposal for a land bank in an 'Advertisement', the militia bill of 1698 was evidently sent to him at the draft stage for his comments, and he signed the highly controversial Kentish Petition of May 1701. In December 1699 he had written to Robert Harley with suggestions to prevent the 'vexatious' and 'frivolous' seizures of wool by customs commissioners in Kent and to alleviate the land taxes on non-jurors who had since sworn the oaths. The land tax was a source of grievance for Brockman himself in 1707 when he again wrote to Harley to protest at the burden it placed on one of his estates. In May 1708 Brockman again stood for Hythe, in conjunction with Hon. John Fane*, but was defeated. His election expenses reveal that he was not averse to treating the corporation, although the sums involved were so small that he may have thought this practice did not conflict with his anti-corruption stance. Brockman also wrote several drafts of addresses to local politicians which attest to his continued concern for 'Whig principles'. One of these drafts, in October 1710, protested at the dissolution, played down the idea of the 'Church in danger' and called for vigorous prosecution of the war; another in July 1712 protested at the peace; and in October 1714 there was a loyal address to King George. Brockman was also a subscriber to the SPCK. He stood unsuccessfully in the Hythe election of 1715 and his 'Remarks' on a letter from the Duke of Dorset of October 1727 reveal that the campaign to oust the sitting Tory Members had cost approximately £1,000. Thereafter, Brockman's political hopes rested on his son, James, and he was very bitter at Dorset's refusal to support James at a by-election in Hythe in February 1728, when he was defeated.[18]

Brockman lived in London for five years from December 1724, during which time he prosecuted a case on behalf of the lords of Romney Marsh about water rights in the marsh. 'Retiring' in 1733, he made over his estates to his son and began drafting political tracts. With campaigns for the repeal of the Test and Corporation Acts gathering pace in the early 1730s, Brockman's writings included various proposals concerning the possibility of full civil rights for Dissenters; further addresses to Parliament urging, among other things, the reconciliation of differences between the parties; such material as 'a Friendly Address from an old Revolution Whig' in 1734; and considerations of the relationship between church and state in 1739–40.[19]

In his will, written on 5 July 1739, Brockman gave precise instructions for his burial, which was to be very private and plain and, while maintaining his preference for the Church of England, he expressed his sympathy for Dissenters and bequeathed £5 for the poor of each Dissenting congregation in his locality. In a final protest about the rejection of his son's candidacy for Hythe (and in an attempt to control elections from beyond the grave), Brockman railed against 'a certain Duke' (i.e. Dorset) who, despite being obligated to Brockman for his interest in Hythe, had turned several members of the corporation against Brockman's son. These members, 'more from zeal to foster a separate Court ministerial administration than to strengthen our happy Revolution establishment by a conjunction of Court and Country interest', had told Brockman that they would frustrate James's hopes at any cost. Brockman went on to enjoin James never to stand again for Hythe but, if ever it appeared that there had been a free and fair election, then James was to pay £100 to the majority,

in such a manner as shall appear to him most beneficial in ... recovering the native rights and liberties of the said corporation ... which have been so ignominiously ... trucked away by some ... members thereof, making merchandize of their personal public faith and trust for private present spells of filthy lucre since the said thrice happy Revolution.

Brockman died between 8 Sept. 1740 when the last codicil to his will was written and 21 Apr. 1742 when the will was proved. James Brockman, whose papers reveal a similar temperament and political outlook to that of his father, was faithful to the latter's wishes and a rather more polite version of the clause in Brockman's will about Hythe elections was read out at the town council meeting of 2 Feb. 1743.[20]

[1] IGI, Kent; Burke, *Commoners*, iii. 367–9; Add. 42691, ff. 61–79; 42603, f. 110. [2] Add. 42650, ff. 92–159. [3] SPCK Archs. Abstract letter book 3, item no. 2904. [4] Hasted, *Kent*. viii. 191, 196–7, 202–3, 208–9, 226, 262, 267, 320, 389, 392–4; Add. 42618, ff. 4–8, 12–17, 22–24; Burke, 368; *Cal. Comm. Comp.* 1643–60, p. 457; Stowe 746, f. 20. [5] *CSP Dom.* July–Sept. 1683, p. 117; Add. 42618, f. 34; BL, Trumbull Add. mss 23, Brockman to Trumbull, 22 Dec. 1685; Som. RO, Bouverie of Brymore mss, DD/BR 3/10, (Sir) Thomas Hales* to Thomas Hales, 20 Jan. 1685–6. [6] Add. 33923, ff. 462, 434; *N. and Q.* (ser. 3) vi. 23, 41, 121; Grey, ix. 286. [7] Add. 33923, f. 480; 42596. ff. 79, 81–82; G. Wilks, *Barons of the Cinque Ports*, 89. [8] Info. from Prof. N. Landau; Add. 42596–42600, passim; ff. 33–36, 47;

42621–42649, passim; 42653, passim; *CSP Dom.* 1694–5, p. 20; 1702–3, p. 394. [9]Add. 42586, ff. 78–80, 85–87; 42592, ff. 98–99. [10]Add. 42592, ff. 134–8. [11]Ibid. ff. 107–15, 123, 126, 154; H. Horwitz, *Parl. and Pol. Wm. III*, 64. [12]Add. 42592, ff. 167–8, 170; 42593, ff. 102–4; *Luttrell Diary*, 93, 117, 136. [13]Horwitz, 124; *Luttrell Diary*, 398; Grey, x. 307. [14]Add. 42592, ff. 198–201; 42593, ff. 11–31, 33; Horwitz, 12, 125. [15]Add. 42586, f. 65; 42587, f. 157; 42601, ff. 61–98; *CSP Dom.* 1694–5, p. 271. [16]Add. 42593, ff. 50, 55–56, 78; Horwitz, 152; G. B. Nash, *Urban Crucible*, 24–28. [17]*HMC Downshire*, i. 505; Add. 70018, ff. 94–95, 104. [18]Add. 42593, ff. 38–39, 80–84, 88, 93, 118–23, 136–7; 42612, f. 4; 42707, ff. 12–13; 70161, Brockman to Harley, 20 Dec. 1699; 70156, same to same, 30 Oct. 1707; SPCK Archs. Abstract letter book 3, item no. 2904. [19]Add. 42589, ff. 77–215; 42593, ff. 140–2, 144–53; 45198, f. 184; 42613, ff. 1–2, 8–11, 15–110. [20]PCC 111 Trenley; Wilks, 96–97.

S. M. W.

BRODRICK, Thomas (1654–1730), of Wandsworth, Surr. and Ballyannan, Midleton, co. Cork.[1]

STOCKBRIDGE   1713–1722
GUILDFORD   1722–1727

b. 4 Aug. 1654, 1st s. of Sir St. John Brodrick of Ballyannan, by Alice, da. of Laurence Clayton of Mallow, co. Cork; bro. of Alan Brodrick†, 1st Baron Brodrick [I] and Visct. Midleton [I]. *educ.* Trinity Hall, Camb. 1670, LLB 1677; M. Temple 1670. *m.* Anne, da. of Alexander Pigott of Innishannon, co. Cork, 1s. *suc.* uncle Sir Allen Brodrick† 1680; bro. St. John at Reigate 1707; fa. 1712.[2]

MP [I] 1692–1713, 1715–27.

PC [I] 1695–1711, 1714; comptroller of the salt 1706; jt. comptroller of army accts. 1708–11.[3]

Brodrick's family had been seated at Wandsworth in Surrey since the early 17th century, but their fortunes had really been made by his father, an officer in the parliamentary army during the Civil War, who received a large grant of lands in county Cork. Brodrick succeeded his uncle to the family seat at Wandsworth in 1680, and on his marriage his father settled on him some of the Irish estates. After the Revolution he spent most of his time in England – in London or indulging his passion for horse-racing at Newmarket; he came back to Ireland only to attend sessions of the Irish parliament. In the first parliament held there under William and Mary, in 1692, he and his younger brother, Alan, quickly emerged as leaders of the 'Country' opposition. In 1694–5 they established good relations with the new lord deputy, Lord Capell (Hon. Sir Henry Capel*), and were appointed to office, Alan as solicitor-general and Thomas to the Irish privy council. In the session of the Irish parliament held during the autumn of 1695 they acted as 'managers' for the lord deputy and, with his tacit consent, led an attack on the Tory lord chancellor, Sir Charles Porter*. Rumours that this might lead to their dismissal brought an anxious letter from Capell to the Duke of Shrewsbury, in which the lord deputy praised the brothers' 'credit . . . affection and abilities to serve his Majesty'. They stayed in office, and in 1697, when new lords justices were appointed, continued to manage affairs for Dublin Castle in the Irish house of commons. Thomas acted as agent for Lord Albemarle and Lady Orkney in respect of forfeited lands which the King had granted them in Ireland, and in 1699 narrowly escaped being censured by the English Commons for his activities in this connexion.[4]

After Anne's accession and the appointment of Ormond as lord lieutenant, Brodrick, although still an Irish privy councillor, went into active opposition in Ireland, both in the Irish parliament and in the council itself, and with his brother was one of the leaders of the Whig faction in the Irish house of commons. In England he became friendly with several important Whig politicians, including Lord Wharton (Hon. Thomas*), connexions which brought him office first as comptroller of the salt and later as joint comptroller of army accounts. He was renowned for his anticlerical views: Swift, in a pamphlet published in 1709, wrote of him:

> an honest bellwether [Brodrick] of your house (you have him now in England, I wish you would keep him there) had the impudence, some years ago, in parliament-time, to shake my lord bishop of Killaloe by his lawn sleeve, and tell him in a threatening manner that he hoped to live to see the day, when there should not be one of his order in the kingdom.

When his brother Alan heard this story, however, he refused to believe it.[5]

Dismissed both from his office of joint comptroller of army accounts and from the Irish privy council in 1711 by the Tory administration, Brodrick did not stand for re-election to the new Irish parliament in 1713, being returned instead to the British Parliament for Stockbridge with Richard Steele*, an election which caused Swift to write, as if addressing the bailiff of the borough, notorious for its venality: 'never was borough more happy in suitable representatives than you are in Mr Steele and his colleague, nor were ever representatives more happy in a suitable borough'. Predictably, Brodrick voted on 18 Mar. 1714 against the expulsion of Steele. He spoke on 15 Apr. against a motion that the succession was not in danger, and on 29 June told against upholding the Tory interpretation of the Southwark franchise. Classed as a Whig in the Worsley list, and in a further comparison of the 1713 and 1715 Parliaments, Brodrick continued to sit as a Whig after 1715, but although restored to the Irish privy council in 1714 he received no further marks of official favour. He died at Wandsworth on 3 Oct. 1730 and was buried there.[6]

[1] Unless otherwise stated, this biography is based on the Midleton mss in the Surr. RO (Guildford). [2] *Misc. Gen. et Her.* ser. 1, ii. 364–5; Manning and Bray, *Surr.* ii. 32–33. [3] *CSP Dom.* 1694–5, p. 469; 1702–3, pp. 143–4; Folger Shakespeare Lib. Newdigate newsletter 25 May 1706; *Cal. Treas. Bks.* xxii. 416; Boyer, *Pol. State*, i–ii. 452. [4] *CSP Dom.* 1694–5, p. 500; HMC *Buccleuch*, ii. 233, 248, 256, 257, 259–63, 271, 272–4, 279, 298–9, 521; Surr. RO (Kingston), Somers mss 371/14/F13, Capell to Shrewsbury, 7 Oct. 1695; Nottingham Univ. Lib. Portland (Bentinck) mss PwA 252, Capell to Portland, 6 Nov. 1695. [5] *CSP Dom.* 1703–4, pp. 159, 186, 501; *Addison Letters*, 144; *Swift Works* ed. Davis, ii. 117. [6] *Swift Works*, viii. 12; Douglas diary (Hist. of Parl. trans.), 18 Mar. 1714; *Reg. Wandsworth*, 361.

D. W. H.

BROMLEY, Clobery (1685–1711), of St. James's, Westminster and Baginton, Warws.

COVENTRY   26 Dec. 1710–20 Mar. 1711

bap. 18 Dec. 1685, 1st s. of William Bromley II* of Baginton by his 1st w. Catherine, da. of Sir John Cloberry† of Upper Eldon, King's Somborne and Parliament Street, Winchester, Hants; half-bro. of William Bromley†. *educ.* Rugby 1694; Christ Church, Oxf. matric. 1703. *m.* 25 Mar. 1708, Dorothy, da. of William Bromley I* of Holt Castle, Worcs., *s.p.*[1]

Commr. public accts. 19 Mar. 1711–*d.*

Bromley continued his studies at Oxford as a gentleman commoner for at least four years after matriculating. Despite his having reached his majority a year or so before the 1710 election, no arrangements were made on that occasion for him to join the Tory forces in the Commons. Very soon afterwards, however, he took the opportunity presented by a sudden vacancy at Coventry, a few miles from his family's principal seat at Baginton. With his father as the new occupant of the Speaker's chair, he was virtually assured of being returned. He took his seat after the Christmas recess and had within a short time thrown himself wholeheartedly into the activities of the October Club, in which he became a leading light: indeed, it is quite possible that he was involved in its inception. But his part in 'intrigues' to promote 'Country' measures that were anathema to the ministry was a source of embarrassment to his father, and on several occasions Robert Harley* was driven to complain to Bromley snr. about young Clobery's behaviour. On 19 Mar. 1711 Bromley jnr. was elected a commissioner of public accounts, taking fifth place in the ballot. By then, however, he had succumbed to smallpox, and expired during the morning of the next day. The House saw fit to adjourn until the 26th to allow the Speaker 'to perform the funeral rites, and to indulge his just affliction'. Swift thought the gesture 'handsomely done' but believed, as did other cynical minds, that the adjournment also provided a much needed breathing-space in proceedings in view of Harley's continued absence and recovery from Guiscard's assassination attempt. Bromley was interred at Baginton. In the will he had made five days before he died he bequeathed to his father all his 'lands and farms' in Warwickshire, Hampshire, Wiltshire and Dorset. Laments on Bromley's unfulfilled promise duly flowed from the pens of Tory writers: Swift, in the *Examiner*, spoke of his having 'already acquired so great a reputation for every amiable quality; and who might have lived to be so great an honour and ornament to his ancient family'; while in the *History of the Present Parliament* (1711), William Pittis sighed that 'expectation could not but accompany so promising a genius, bright intellects, and acquired understanding'.[2]

[1] IGI, Warws. and London; Vivian, *Vis. Devon*, 201; Dugdale, *Warws.* i. 232–3; PCC 99 Young. [2] *Hearne Colls.* iii. 135; NSA, Kreienberg despatch 23 Mar. 1711; *Parl. Hist.* v. 3; Huntington Lib. Q. xxxiii. 162–3; *Post Boy*, 20–22, 22–24 Mar. 1711; Cobbett, *Parlty. Hist.* vi. 1012; *Swift Stella* ed. Davis, 220–1; PCC 99 Young; *Swift Works* ed. Davis, iii. 121; Pittis, *Present Parl.* 169.

A. A. H.

BROMLEY, John I (c.1652–1707), of White River, St. Philip's, Barbados, and Horseheath Hall, Cambs.

CAMBRIDGESHIRE   1705–7 Oct. 1707

b. c.1652. *m.* by 1682, Dorothy (*d.* 1709), da. of Thomas White of Fittleford, Dorset, 2s.[1]

Member of assembly, Montserrat 1678, Barbados 1685–90, speaker 1689–June 1690, member of council June 1690–3, 1696–aft. 1698.[2]

So considerable was the fortune made by Bromley in the West Indies, and so precipitous the social ascent achieved by his family, reaching the peerage in the third generation, that, as with many another self-made man, the obscurity of his origins became the stuff of legend. Whether in fact he had ever been a 'pedlar' in Barbados, as the 1st Lord Egmont (John Perceval†) was later to allege, must be regarded as highly questionable. By his own account his father 'was of Hertfordshire and of the Bromleys of that country', and the pedigree unearthed for the college of arms identified him as the only surviving son of George Bromley of Westmills, near Ware, and Waterford Hall in Hertfordshire. 'I question the truth of this', observed the Norroy king of arms, Peter Le Neve, 'but dare not deny it.' In fact the descent was quite impossible, since Bromley was himself a year older than his putative father. There may have been some connexion between the families, and Bromley's eventual purchase of a Cambridgeshire estate may have reflected a desire to return to the vicinity of his paternal home. But equally suggestive is the fact that the Bromleys of Westmills were a family in financial decline in the late 17th century, and had indeed sold off their Hertfordshire property in the 1690s. If Bromley had been intent on manufacturing an armigerous descent for himself, a recently ruined family in a neighbouring county would have been an obvious choice. Whatever his real origins, he can first be traced as a member of the colonial assembly of Montserrat in 1678, bearing the title of 'captain'. Some years later he was elected to the Barbados assembly, serving as its speaker for a spell after the Revolution until appointed to the island's council. Having been suspended in 1693 by Governor James King for failure to take the sacrament in the Anglican church, he was saved from prosecution by the Privy Council's order and was restored in 1696. Not long afterwards he returned to England, settling first at Bookham in Surrey and then in 1700 paying Lord Alington £42,000 for the Horseheath estate, upon which he lavished a further £30,000 in 'improvements'. Far from abandoning his West Indian interests, he acted as an informal agent in England for Barbadian planters and merchants and in 1704–5 subscribed two petitions to the crown on behalf of the colony, the first requesting more troops to be garrisoned there on grounds of 'security' and the second in support of the governor, Sir Bevill Granville*, who found himself harassed by a faction in the assembly. At the same time he continued the process of acquiring gentility for himself and his family. He entered his elder son at Cambridge and in 1704 married him off to one of the daughters of William Bromley I*, for which occasion the pedigree was required. He himself embarked upon the country gentleman's *cursus honorum*: a deputy-lieutenant for Cambridgeshire in 1701, j.p. the following year, and, at the 1705 general election, one of the knights of the shire.[3]

Bromley had been returned on the Whig interest after a close contest, only ten votes separating him from the nearer of his Tory opponents, and possibly with the backing of the Junto Lord Orford (Edward Russell*). Classed as a 'Churchman' in one analysis of the new House, he was listed by Lord Sunderland (Charles, Lord Spencer*) as a 'gain' for the Whigs, and duly voted for the Court candidate, John Smith I*, in the division on the Speaker on 25 Oct. 1705. He was given leave of absence after little over a month, on 4 Dec. 1705, to recover his health, but was listed again as having voted for the Court on 18 Feb. 1706 over the 'place clause' of the regency bill. Perhaps because of poor health, he made little mark during the rest of his short parliamentary career, and no speech of his is recorded. A list of early 1708 named Bromley as a Whig, though he had in fact died on 7 Oct. 1707, aged 55, being buried at Horseheath, and leaving his elder son to succeed him in both the estates and his seat in Parliament.[4]

[1] *Camb. Antiq. Soc. Procs.* xli. 26–28; Cambs. RO, Horseheath par. reg.; PCC 220 Poley. [2] *CSP Col.* 1677–80, p. 264; 1685–8, pp. 48, 225; 1689–92, pp. 7, 77, 210, 237, 282; 1693–6, pp. 121, 127; 1696–7, pp. 67, 94, 451; 1697–8, pp. 37, 124; 1700, p. 114. [3] *HMC Egmont Diary*, iii. 260; Add. 29579, f. 496; *Camb. Antiq. Soc. Procs.* 26–28; Harl. 6775, f. 115; 7512, f. 9; Clutterbuck, *Herts.* ii. 215; iii. 304; *VCH Herts.* ii. 35; *Coll. Top. et Gen.* iv. 47; *CSP Col.* 1693–6, p. 277; 1704–5, pp. 267, 350, 370; 1706–8, pp. 1, 292; *APC Col.* 1680–1720, p. 268; *CSP Dom.* 1700–2, p. 225. [4] Camb. Univ. Lib. Cholmondeley (Houghton) mss Corresp. 405, John Turner* to Robert Walpole II*, 19 Feb. 1704–5; *Bull. IHR*, xxxvii. 34; Cambs. RO, Horseheath par. reg.; PCC 220 Poley.

D. W. H.

BROMLEY, John II (c.1682–1718), of Horseheath Hall, Cambs.

CAMBRIDGESHIRE   4 Dec. 1707–20 Oct. 1718

b. c.1682, 1st s. of John Bromley I*. *educ.* Clare, Camb. 1700. *m.* 10 Aug. 1704, Mercy, da. and in her issue h. of William Bromley I*, 1s. *suc.* fa. 1707.[1]

Sheriff, Cambs. and Hunts. 1704–5.

Besides the Barbadian plantations and substantial landed estate in Cambridgeshire which he inherited from his father, Bromley also secured control of his father-in-law's extensive property in Worcestershire and Shropshire under the terms of his marriage settlement. His riches probably deterred prospective opponents at the by-election for Cambridgeshire occasioned by his father's death in 1707, and he succeeded to the seat without a contest. Although in general it is difficult to distinguish his parliamentary activity from that of his namesakes in the House, notably Speaker Bromley of Baginton (William II) and William Bromley III, he evidently divided consistently with the Tories during the first session and was classed as a Tory in two lists from 1708. At the general election of that year he was again returned unopposed as knight of the shire, and this despite the fact that the local Whigs were 'disgusted' with him for 'having voted contrary to their interest', looking on him as 'one who has fallen off from Revolution principles'.

He did not improve in their eyes during this Parliament, voting early in 1710 against the impeachment of Dr Sacheverell, and at the next election was obliged to fight off a Whig candidate.[2]

Marked as a Tory in the 'Hanover list' of the 1710 Parliament, Bromley began it as a staunch Tory; indeed as one of the 'worthy patriots' who in the 1710–11 session exposed the mismanagements of the previous ministry. He was also a member of the October Club. However, although he had been listed in the previous April as one of the 'Tory patriots' who favoured peace, he participated in the first significant back-bench Tory revolt against the new ministry's foreign policy, when on 7 Dec. 1711 he voted with the Whigs on the 'No Peace without Spain' motion. It may well be that on this issue Bromley's West Indian and other mercantile interests induced in him a greater caution than the bulk of his party exhibited in their determination to put an end to the war. By 1713 it appears that he was taking a decidedly independent line from that of his party. In the division of 18 June 1713 on the French commerce bill he was listed as a Whig who both spoke and voted against the ministry. The possibility of some local connexion has led historians to suggest that he may now have been acting as a follower of the Hanoverian Tory Lord Anglesey (Hon. Arthur Annesley*) but his deviant voting pattern had been initiated before Annesley's own break from the Court. In the 1714 Parliament, to which he was re-elected unopposed, he voted against the expulsion of Richard Steele, and was classified in the Worsley list as a Whig who would sometimes vote with the Tories, though his correspondence makes clear that he was still a Tory. Indeed in Cambridgeshire the Whigs claimed that he was 'for bringing in the Pretender'.[3]

Bromley was listed as a Whig when he was returned to the 1715 Parliament, but this appears to have been an error. He voted against the ministry in 1716 over the septennial bill and a year later over the movement of Dutch troops, when he was inexplicably included among the 'civil' office-holders listed as acting with the opposition. In his will, drawn up only four days before his death, he pointedly bequeathed 200 guineas to William Bromley II* of Baginton, 'which I desire he would be pleased to receive as a testimony of my respect to his person and virtues'. There were also legacies to his 'worthy friend' Francis Shepheard* and Shepheard's brother Samuel* (another 'Hanoverian Tory' from 1713–14), who with Bromley of Baginton was made a guardian of his son Henry, later knight of the shire himself and 1st Lord Montfort. He specifically asked that the buildings and gardens he had begun at Horseheath should be completed in accordance with the plans he had laid down. It was there that he died, on 20 Oct. 1718, aged 36, and was buried in the parish church.[4]

[1] *Cal. Treas. Bks.* xxi. 243. [2] *HMC Lords*, n.s. vii. 539–41; *Cal. Le Neve Corresp.* 142, 145; Bodl. Rawl. B.281, f. 199; Add. 5847, f. 181. [3] *Bull. IHR*, xxxiii. 226, 228, 234; Huntington Lib. Q. xxxiii. 165; Boyer, *Pol. State*, iii. 117; G. Holmes, *Pol. in Age of Anne*, 282; Bodl. North b.2, Bromley to Ld. North and Grey, 30 [-]; North c.9, f. 5. [4] PCC 231 Tenison; *Hearne Colls.* vi. 249; *Procs. Camb. Antiq. Soc.* xli. 29.

D. W. H.

BROMLEY, William I (1656–1707), of Holt Castle, Worcs.

WORCESTER   1685–1700
WORCESTERSHIRE   1701 (Dec.)–1702
                           1705–5 Aug. 1707

b. 26 June 1656, 2nd but o. surv. s. of Henry Bromley† of Holt Castle by Mercy, da. of Edward Pytts† of Kyre Park, Worcs. *educ.* Christ Church, Oxf. 1673; M. Temple 1674. *m.* lic. 25 Apr. 1675, Margaret (*d.* 1707), da. and coh. of Sir Rowland Berkeley† of Cotheridge, 3da. (2 *d.v.p.*). *suc.* fa. 1670.[1]

Freeman, Worcester 1681.[2]

Bromley's career after 1690 has been overshadowed by that of his more illustrious contemporary, William Bromley II*, Speaker of the Commons 1710–13. Unlike his namesake, however, this Member was a Whig. Judging by his leases, Bromley owned considerable property in Worcester city as well as estates at Holt and Wick in the county and the manor of Shrawardine in Shropshire. Having sat for Worcester in the Convention in 1689, he was returned unopposed with Sir John Somers* in 1690, much to the chagrin of local Tory observers. As the Journals rarely differentiate between the various 'Mr Bromleys' in the House most committee appointments and tellerships probably refer to William Bromley II, especially as their frequency does not diminish when the Warwickshire Member was the only Bromley in the House. Fortunately, the political career of William Bromley of Holt can be traced through extant parliamentary lists and election correspondence. Lord Carmarthen (Sir Thomas Osborne†) classed him as a Whig in his analysis of the Parliament elected in 1690, but somewhat surprisingly his name appears on a list dating from December 1690 that probably indicates support for Carmarthen in the event of an attack on the minister in the Commons. By April 1691 Robert Harley* considered him to be a Country party supporter, although marked with a query. Grascome in an analysis in the spring of 1693 (extended to 1695) saw him as an adherent of the Court. In the confused alignments of the period these assessments suggest a Whig more inclined to follow the lead of the Court as the Whigs gained influence within the ministry. In local politics Bromley was a shrewd operator. Despite continued appeals from Charles Cocks*, he stayed aloof from the violent by-election held at Worcester in December 1693 to select a replacement for Somers. Thus, it must be extremely unlikely (though not impossible) that he was the 'Mr Bromley' who acted as a teller for Swift in the series of votes which saw Cocks seated on petition on 7 Feb. 1694. Bromley's position remained strong, however, for at the 1695 election it was Cocks who was obliged to seek another seat, while Bromley was returned with Swift. The rivalry between Bromley and Cocks was not ideological, for even Mrs Cocks admitted that Bromley 'will I suppose make a very good Member'. Furthermore, Bromley would have desisted in 1695 if he had been asked to do so by Somers (Cocks's brother-in-law), but the matter was not pressed. The only alternative seat upon which Bromley had a legitimate claim was the county where, in the opinion of Sir James Rushout, 1st Bt.*, he could not fail if allied with Thomas Foley I*.[3]

In the new Parliament Bromley was a consistent supporter of the ministry, now increasingly dominated by the Junto. On the proposal for a council of trade he was forecast as likely to support the Court in the divisions of 31 Jan. 1696. He signed the voluntary Association and voted in March 1696 for fixing the price of guineas at 22s. In the following session he voted on 25 Nov. 1696 for Sir John Fenwick's[†] attainder. In the 1698 election Bromley struggled to secure his re-election, facing stiff competition from Swift and Thomas Wylde*, a Whig with a residence in the city. Bromley was also active at Droitwich in securing votes for Cocks. On a comparative analysis of the old and new Parliaments he was listed as a Court supporter, although an addendum to the list added a query. However, his name also appeared on another list which was probably a forecast of those likely to oppose a standing army, and he was not blacklisted as voting against the disbanding bill on 31 Jan. 1699. Given his Court Whig associations, it is unclear whether this attitude was a survival of the Country attitudes which had characterized his party before 1688, or merely a response to political opinion in Worcester. His views on the issue of the standing army did not prevent his being assigned to the Junto interest in a further analysis of the House between January and May 1700. Bromley declined to contest Worcester at the general election of January 1701, possibly owing to the strength of Wylde's interest. Sir Charles Lyttelton, 3rd Bt.[†], discounted another possibility when he informed a correspondent that his decision was not 'on account of the Association for he was of the list and gave his vote to make it that before'.[4]

With the end of Bromley's parliamentary association with Worcester it is appropriate to assess his position in the county generally, before he became knight of the shire. He had been active in lieutenancy business as early as July 1690, seizing the horses of Roman Catholics. By 1697 he was captain of one of the two companies of militia horse, and was still in the lieutenancy in March 1701. Similarly, he was active in local fiscal administration, being named first commissioner in the Act for the 12d. aid in 1689, acting as surety for Philip Bearcroft, the collector of a series of central government taxes in Worcestershire in 1690–2, and recommending Thomas Albert as receiver-general of the land tax in April 1698. He certainly merited a county seat in terms of activity and landed wealth, for Lyttelton estimated his estate in 1703 at about £2,500 p.a. A month before the general election of November 1701 William Walsh* was still advancing the view that Bromley's position in Worcester was very strong, but in the event Bromley topped the poll for Worcestershire, with Walsh relegated to third place. Bromley's short absence from the Commons does not seem to have altered his political position, for he was classed as a Whig on Harley's list of December 1701. Although Lyttelton called Bromley and Walsh 'creatures' of Lord Somers, the two men were unable to secure an acceptable conjunction of interests at the 1702 election, with Bromley being defeated on this occasion. There seems little doubt that he was perceived as being much more moderate than Walsh, but that Tory voters did not wish to risk defeat by abandoning their tactic of plumping for Pakington. Bromley pronounced himself 'in a melancholy way since the election', blaming poor Whig management for his defeat.[5]

However, Bromley made a triumphant return to the Commons in 1705 as knight of the shire. An analysis of the new House listed him then as 'True Church', which may indicate confusion with his namesake. Somers did express some concern over Bromley's voting intentions on the crucial issue of the Speakership, but Lord Orford (Edward Russell*) attempted to quieten these fears by noting that 'I have all the reason that a man can expect that he will be honest in every particular. Before he went into Worcestershire I discoursed with him about Mr Smith [John I*]; he was not only for him but flaming against his namesake [William Bromley II].' Orford proved correct in his assessment, as Bromley duly voted for the Court candidate on 25 Oct. 1705. In late November he was bemoaning the late sittings of the House and attendance at committees, which have 'rendered me incapable of anything'. He voted on 18 Feb. 1706 to support the Court on the 'place clause' in the regency bill, although this battle over he was reported to be talking of leaving town on the 21st. In the following session he was ordered on 14 Feb. 1707, in company with Charles Cocks, to prepare a bill for the better preserving the ancient salt springs at Droitwich, and duly presented it on the 17th. The Duke of Shrewsbury confirmed his management when he referred to Sir John Talbot[†] putting the bill into 'Mr Bromley's hands', but it never emerged from the committee. Private papers suggest further involvement, in that Bromley was to be a trustee charged with overseeing the measure. His name appears on one final parliamentary list, an analysis from early in 1708, which classed him as a Tory. By this time, however, he had been dead for over six months.[6]

Bromley died on 5 Aug. 1707. On 25 July 1707, he had arrived at Horseheath in Cambridgeshire to visit his son-in-law, John Bromley II*. Although ill on arrival he was perceived to be in no immediate danger. However, by 5 Aug. he was clearly declining and was advised to set his affairs in order. To this end he issued some verbal instructions on behalf of his unmarried daughter, Dorothy, but died before these could be put into legal form. As a consequence, his will, made in 1703, was not the final settlement of his estate. This required a private Act as the proposals made to benefit Dorothy could not be implemented in view of the fact that both she and John Bromley II's son Henry[†] (1st Lord Montfort) were under age. Henry Bromley eventually inherited Holt Castle.[7]

[1] *Vis. Worcs.* ed. Metcalfe, 24–25; Nash, *Worcs.* i. 595, 600; *The Gen.* vii. 89; Collins, *Peerage*, vii. 254. [2] Hereford and Worcester RO (Worcester, St. Helen's), Worcester chamber order bk. 1679–1721, f. 97. [3] Add. 5842, ff. 136–41; Bodl. Ballard 35, ff. 48, 50; Surr. RO (Kingston), Somers mss 371/14/B6, 8–11, Cocks to Somers, 13 Nov., 9, 11, 12, 16 Dec. 1693; B7, Philip Bearcroft to same, 25 Nov. 1693; 01/19, Mary Cocks to same, n.d. [31 Aug. 1695]; J5, Rushout to same, 10 Aug. 1695. [4] *Shrewsbury Corresp.* 554; Add. 5842, f. 139; 29579, ff. 248, 256. [5] *Epistolary Curiosities* ed. Warner, i. 144–6; Egerton 1626, f. 52; *CSP Dom.* 1700–2, p. 256; *Cal. Treas. Bks.* ix. 234, 604, 974, 1473; xiii. 79; Add. 29579, ff. 367, 407, 443; Somers mss 371/14/B20, Walsh to Somers, 26 Oct. 1701; Hereford and Worcester RO (Worcester, St. Helen's), Cal. Wm. Lygon letters, 65, Bromley to Lygon, 6 Dec. [1702]. [6] Add. 34521, f. 63; 40776, ff. 40–41; Cal. Wm. Lygon letters, 150, 166, Bromley to Lygon, 29 Nov. 1705, Ann Bull to same, 19 Feb. 1705–6; Northants. RO, Montagu (Boughton) mss 77/80, Talbot to Shrewsbury, 11 Feb. 1706–7. [7] PCC 54 Barrett; *HMC Lords*, n.s. vii. 539–41.

S. N. H.

BROMLEY, William II (1663–1732), of Baginton, Warws. and St. James's, Westminster.

WARWICKSHIRE 1690–1698
OXFORD UNIVERSITY 21 Mar. 1701–13 Feb. 1732

bap. 31 Aug. 1663, 1st s. of Sir William Bromley KB of Baginton by Ursula, da. of Thomas Leigh[†], 1st Baron Leigh, of Stoneleigh, Warws. *educ.* Christ Church, Oxf. matric. 1679, BA 1681, DCL 1702; M. Temple 1683; travelled abroad (France, Italy) 1688. *m.* (1) by 1685 Catherine (*d.* 1688), da. and coh. of Sir John Cloberry[†] of Westminster, and King's Somborne, Hants, 1s. *d.v.p.*; (2) 21 Nov. 1689, Trevor [or Trever] (*d.* c.1691), da. of Samuel Fortrey of St. Giles-in-the-Fields, Mdx., *s.p.*; (3) by 1692, Cecilia (*d.* bef. 1698), da. of Sir William Swan, 1st Bt., of Southfleet, Kent, 1s. *d.v.p.*; (4) lic. 12 Jan. 1698, Elizabeth, da. of Ralph Stawell[†], 1st Baron Stawell, of Low Ham, Som. 2s. 3da (1 *d.v.p.*). *suc.* fa. 1682.[1]

Commr. for rebuilding Warwick 1695.[2]

Commr. public accts. 1702–4; chmn. cttee. of privileges and elections 1702–5; Speaker of the House of Commons 1710–13.

PC 23 June 1711; Sec. of state 1713–14.[3]

Commr. building 50 new churches 1711–15, taking subscriptions to S. Sea Co. 1711; trustee, Radcliffe Lib. 1714–*d.*[4]

Freeman, Portsmouth 1711.[5]

Bromley stands out as one of the paladins of Toryism in the reign of Queen Anne. Widely respected among his party brethren for his 'great honour and integrity', he was a 'grave' man of exemplary piety, morals and public spirit. He was an unwavering and unflagging proponent of High Church principles, though as one contemporary observed he was 'perhaps of no very shining parts'. His lack of originality was amply compensated for by a rigidity of purpose which made him an ideal party leader. One of his chief political assets was a 'short and clear manner of speaking' and this directness of approach enabled him to sustain his authority among the Tory squires. A leading historian has pointed out that the essence of Bromley's influence in the party had little to do with 'ties of blood and marriage', but was based almost entirely on 'comradeships forged through years of fighting common parliamentary campaigns'. As he made his way to the forefront of politics it became his abiding preoccupation to maintain Tory unity in the face of ministerial factionalism and exploitation. The fissiparous nature of the Tory party after 1710 made this task complicated in the extreme, but in his capacity, first as Speaker, and then briefly as secretary of state, he shouldered much of the burden of inspiring back-bench loyalty and support for an administration whose attitudes and policies often diverged from party zeal.[6]

Bromley was descended from a Staffordshire family whose ancestry could be traced back to the time of King John. In 1618 his grandfather had moved to Warwickshire, having purchased Sir Henry Goodere's† seat at Baginton. There seems little doubt that Bromley's ardent Toryism was inherited from his father, a Royalist commander in the Civil War who had been held captive for 15 months and forced to compound for £10,000. Bromley succeeded his father at the end of 1682, and in 1685, a year after coming of age, was added to the magisterial bench. His rise in the county elite was further underwritten in July 1686 when he was appointed to the lieutenancy. The death of his first wife in 1688 seems to have encouraged him to undertake a tour through France and Italy. While in Rome he was said to have 'heard there of the Prince of Orange's invasion before it was heard of in England'. He had returned, however, before January 1689, by which time he was once more engrossed in magisterial duties.[7]

In the approach to the 1690 general election Bromley emerged as a Tory candidate for knight of the shire. Although inexperienced in public affairs, he had already acquired the reputation of 'a very good man', and his recent spell of foreign travel had marked him as one whose horizons and interests extended beyond the parochial. Bromley won his seat, and Lord Carmarthen (Sir Thomas Osborne†), in noting him as a Tory, felt he might be counted upon to support the Court. He took time to gain his footing as an MP and was largely inactive during the first three sessions of the 1690 Parliament. Evidently he did not fulfil Carmarthen's expectations, as in April 1691 Robert Harley* saw him as a supporter of the Country party. Though he was not elected for Oxford University until 1701, his concern for its interests and privileges appeared in January 1692 when he commiserated with one college principal over a draconian clause in the land tax bill requiring all dons to take the oaths of allegiance on pain of a hefty imposition on their salaries and stipends. The publication of Bromley's travel memoirs in February (*Remarks on the Grand Tour of France and Italy*) provoked so much speculation about his loyalty to William III that he was quickly forced to withdraw all unsold copies. The space and attention he gave to descriptions of Catholic institutions and places of worship, the hospitality shown him by the English Cardinal Howard, and his having been admitted to kiss the Pope's slipper, were regarded by some as indicating a distinct preference for the Roman faith. Most damningly of all, he referred to William and Mary by their non-regal title as 'the Prince and Princess of Orange' while the exiled Stuarts were styled as 'King James and his queen'. By the end of the year stories were circulating that Bromley had even dined with the exiled king. Doubts about his loyalty to the new monarchs cannot have been allayed by the tone of his comments in the House on 14 Dec. 1692, when, in his first recorded intervention, he joined other Churchmen in opposing a bill 'for the preservation of their Majesties' sacred persons and government' on the grounds that the new oath to be imposed on office-holders 'would only prove to catch good, conscientious men and will not hold the bad'. He was teller, for the first time, on 9 Jan. 1693 in favour of exempting university property from the land tax bill. His attack later in the month on Bishop Burnet's *Pastoral Letter* as a 'dangerous' example of several recent tracts which sought to justify William III's title by right of conquest, seems to have been motivated by general Tory malice towards the bishop. His vigorous demands that the book be publicly burnt led to his acting as teller on this question on 23 Jan.; while the opportunity to exercise his views further came two days later when participating in conference proceedings with the Lords on Charles Blount's *King William and Queen Mary Conquerors*, which had declared the conquest argument to be 'inconsistent' with the principles of the Revolution settlement.[8]

From the 1693–4 session onwards Bromley acquired a higher profile in the Commons, a fact reflected in his nomination to an increased number of select committees. Although there is the possibility of confusion with William Bromley I, it can be assumed that most references in the Journals are to the Warwickshire Member on the strength of his election in 1696 to the commission of accounts, for which a necessary prerequisite was a track-record of work on major committees. In November he helped sponsor bills concerning the encouragement of the clothing trade and the registration of deeds, and on two later occasions was a teller on supply questions. On 7 Feb. in the debate on the Worcester election he was teller in favour of the sitting Tory Member. His attachment to 'Country' principles, and thus his disposition to oppose the government, was demonstrated during the debate on 7 Dec. concerning a grant of £2,000 to Lord Falkland (Anthony Carey*), one of the Admiralty commissioners. He warned the House that if they accepted the ministry's defence that payments to individuals by way of pensions were the norm, 'you must never expect discoveries'; and, while loath to commit Falkland to the Tower, was willing to see him expelled the House. Similarly, on 26 Jan. 1694 he was outspoken on the King's veto of the place bill. While careful not to reflect directly upon the King's right to exercise his prerogative powers, he maintained that the need to eradicate corruption provided a powerful case for such legislation: 'the bill offers remedy, but we are denied it, which speaks this language, "that the King will have us still corrupt"'. Concluding his speech, he declared: 'we have done well for religion, but all in vain if we enjoy not our liberties'.[9]

Bromley's 'Country' objections to the financial burdens of a standing army were apparent early in the 1694–5 session when he acted on 23 Nov. as teller against proceeding with the customary address for the army estimates. He was teller on two further occasions late in the session regarding a supply bill, and participated in several conferences with the Lords. Among other items of business, the bill for rebuilding Warwick in the aftermath of the devastating fire there in September 1694 almost certainly engaged much of his attention. His efforts on behalf of the town were acknowledged in his being named in the bill as one of the commissioners to oversee the rebuilding works. He was particularly active during the commissioners' most important work in the months immediately following the bill's enactment, and even as late as 1704 he was instrumental in obtaining a grant of £1,000 from the government 'towards finishing the church and relieving the sufferers'. Already, Bromley could be seen emerging as an energetic backbencher with wide-ranging interests.[10]

Though faced with a contest in Warwickshire in 1695, Bromley retained his seat with little difficulty. The worsening coinage crisis was one of the first matters the new House considered when it met in November. Bromley's involvement in issues relating to the coinage can be traced back to 1693 when his concern over the great quantities of farthings in circulation in his native county, and the local tax collectors' refusal to accept them in payment, induced him to take the problem to the Privy Council. Since then he had been nominated to committees on the export of coin and coin clipping. In the debates on the crisis towards the end of 1695, Bromley was one of several Churchmen who opposed the government's proposals for a recoinage of silver money as likely to prove too damaging to trade in the present circumstances of war. He was a member of the Commons' delegation which conferred with the Lords on 5 Dec. 1695 over the drafting of a joint address pressing for a speedy resolution of the situation. With the new year, Bromley's attention moved to issues with a stronger 'Country' focus. On 14 Jan. 1696 he capitalized on the unpopularity of the King's intended grant of several Welsh estates to the Earl of Portland by presenting a petition against it from representatives of the Welsh gentry.

This bold solo initiative prompted the appointment of a committee to address William not to proceed, which Bromley himself reported on the 17th. Later in the month he was forecast as likely to oppose the Court on the proposed council of trade. He made detailed reports from a committee, to which he had been appointed in December, to investigate areas of uncertainty in the levy of certain duties specified in a supply measure enacted the previous session. The estimation in which Bromley was by this time held by both the Church Tories and the Foley–Harley connexion was apparent in his inclusion on the 'Country' list for the ballot on the new commission of accounts, which, when declared on 5 Feb., placed him fifth with 200 votes. On the 24th, following disclosure of the Assassination Plot, he was appointed to a committee to confer with the Lords in drafting a joint address congratulating the King on his safe deliverance, but was one of the 80 or so Churchmen who subsequently refused to subscribe to the Association on the grounds that it was a 'Whig trick'. The following month Bromley was involved in the proceedings to establish a price level for the guinea. On 20 Mar. he was teller in favour of fixing it at 25s., and afterwards voted a further reduction to 22s. as preferred by the King. During February and March he took responsibility for two local bills, one relating to the estates of his Warwickshire neighbour Sir Thomas Wagstaffe*. In two election cases earlier in the session he had acted as teller in favour of Tories, and on 14 Apr. at the conclusion of one of the debates on the royal veto of the qualifications bill, he was a teller in favour of the motion that whoever had advised such a course was 'an enemy to the King and kingdom'.[11]

The Association presented a serious dilemma for Bromley, not least since his refusal to sign meant that he could not serve on the commission of accounts, and since three other recently balloted commissioners also withheld their signatures, the commission was rendered inquorate, thus jeopardizing the Country party's plans to exploit the commission in its forthcoming assaults on the ministry. In a letter of 25 Apr., Bromley told Robert Harley, the leader of the Country alliance, that he would be 'very glad' to meet the other commissioners in view of 'the greatest satisfaction I had in the honours the House did me to that employment, being in the company they joined me with', but could not comply with 'the terms since imposed'. Harley responded almost immediately with a carefully couched appeal, the crux of which was that many non-Associators had decided to comply with the law, having shown their principles by not signing voluntarily, and that the oath therefore had only a limited legal importance. After summarizing the legal authorities on this point, Harley begged 'pardon for all this stuff to a person of so great reading, good sense and well poised judgement as Mr Bromley, whose love for his country and the public good . . . supersedes all the arguments of just resentments', and ended with a plea:

> I am sure you will sacrifice more than that to the preserving the whole and keeping the nation from the power of a party who can have no strength but what is given them by such a refusal. Therefore I hope we shall be preserved by you from having stripes by scourges cut out of our own skins.

The urgency behind Harley's entreaty demonstrates Bromley's perceived importance as a rising Tory leader. Initially it seemed to one of the other non-subscribing commissioners, Francis Gwyn*, that Bromley might relent, but it was Gwyn himself who signed the Association, thereby establishing the necessary quorum for the commission to begin business. Although Bromley did eventually sign the Association, he did not participate in the accounts commission's proceedings. Towards the end of July he resigned his place on the Warwickshire lieutenancy, possibly in anticipation of his removal by the Privy Council, but remained a j.p. The reason for Bromley's reluctance to fall in with Harley's designs at this point is not exactly clear, but it raised his prominence among the Churchmen, his personal resistance to the Association giving him the character of a 'violent' Tory.[12]

The attainder proceedings against Sir John Fenwick† dominated the opening month or so of the 1696–7 session. On 9 Nov. Bromley was a teller against the motion to give a second reading to the attainder bill, and at the third reading on the 25th spoke at length against the measure. He added his voice to the assertions of other Tories that, though the power of Parliament was 'so transcendent and absolute', it ought to follow 'the rules of Westminster Hall, especially when they are founded upon common justice'. In Fenwick's case the government's use of defective evidence deviated from principles which he felt 'ought to be universal'. He dismissed ministerial apprehensions that Fenwick would constitute a danger to the government if allowed to go unpunished, and asked why it was that nothing had been done to attaint those whom the Declaration of Rights described as James II's 'evil counsellors'. In the division at the end of the debate he duly voted against passing the bill. Bromley's refusal to act as a commissioner of public accounts seems to have had a marked effect on the pattern of his activity during this session, and, more important, accentuated his standing as a party figure.

By refusing to act on the commission of accounts, he appears to have forfeited his usual place on the kinds of select committees to which he had usually been nominated. He was, however, much more frequently called upon to serve as a teller. After the Fenwick bill, he performed the task on 11 subsequent occasions, the majority of which dealt with politically orientated questions. On 27 Nov. he was teller against a Court-inspired amendment which sought to tone down a motion for a committee of the whole 'to consider the grievances of the nation' to one with the more temperate instruction to consider 'the state of the nation'. In proceedings on the Aldborough election on 27 Jan. 1697 he was teller against the issue of a writ for a by-election, presumably on account of the borough's reputation for venality. His Tory prejudices against a bill 'to secure debts and establish credit' were registered on 10 Feb. when he told against its committal. He told twice against the Whig-sponsored general naturalization bill, and on other occasions in relation to economic or supply questions.[13]

During the 1697–8 session the pattern of Bromley's recorded activity was much more along the lines seen during the 1695–6 session. His legislative concerns were restricted to a bill for the regulation of the militia, being appointed on 17 Dec. 1697 to its drafting committee, and two personal estate bills which absorbed much of his attention later in the session. He was teller on five occasions. On 19 Apr. he told in favour of adding to the elections bill a clause requiring all 'honorary freemen' of boroughs to be elected by vote in open court. Three more tellerships undertaken towards the end of the session show his dislike for the proposed new East India Company: on 26 May he was teller against a resolution from ways and means for conferring exclusive trading privileges on the new company; on 23 June, in favour of a clause offered to the 'two million fund' bill restricting the East India trade to those already entitled under the bill's provisions; and on the 25th against the motion for it to pass. At the 1698 election Bromley declined to stand, having in effect been precluded by his conduct in 1696. Many years later, in 1726, when he came to devise an account of his career for a memorial to be erected in Baginton church after his death, he chose to gloss over the circumstances, simply stating that 'I declined to serve any longer though it was unanimously desired at a meeting of the lords and gentlemen'. A two-year interlude ensued in his political career during which he was able to devote himself more fully to his scholarly interests. He had already contributed to an English version of Tacitus' *Annals*, begun in 1693 and published in 1698. It was a project which chimed in well with

Bromley's Country notions, given Tacitus' obsessions with deceit and dishonesty in the political arena and his warnings about arbitrary power.[14]

In the weeks prior to the January election of 1701 it was expected that Bromley, 'who would not stand in the last Parliament because of the Association', would return to the Commons. However, Bromley's intentions were otherwise. On congratulating Harley on his election as Speaker, he wrote from Baginton on 17 Feb., 'I have never till now had any reason to regret my being out of the House ... We that are in the country look upon your having the chair as a very good omen in this critical juncture.' Early in March, however, one of the Oxford University seats was declared vacant, and Bromley seems to have been easily prevailed upon to stand by the University's leading fixer in parliamentary matters, Dr Arthur Charlett. A good deal of support for Bromley was generated around the colleges, not least in Christ Church where he had been a student, but collegial in-fighting saw a rival candidate enter the lists in the form of another Midland Tory, Sir George Beaumont, 4th Bt.*, and there followed some scurrilous campaigning in which doubt was poured on Bromley's High Church credentials. None the less, at the poll on the 21st Bromley succeeded in defeating Beaumont, though not as overwhelmingly as Charlett had hoped.[15]

Once back in the House, Bromley quickly recovered his former standing as a Tory activist, becoming almost immediately immersed in the partisan attacks on the ministry. He was actively involved in his party's drive to impeach Lord Portland and the Junto lords, Somers (Sir John*), Orford (Hon. Edward Russell*) and Halifax (Charles Montagu*), for their role in the first Partition Treaty. On 14 Apr. he was a teller in favour of the motion declaring Orford guilty of advising the King to accede to the treaty, and on the 15th was added to the committee for preparing the articles of impeachment against all four lords. The next day he reported the terms of the same committee's address requesting the lords' removal 'for ever' from the King's counsels, and over the next fortnight or so was active in the committee's work of finalizing the impeachment articles. Bromley also seems to have played an active part in the Commons' inquiry into the despoliation of Enfield Chase, which was intended as the pretext for an attack on the chancellor of the duchy of Lancaster, the Whig Earl of Stamford. In the report which Bromley made to the House on 26 May, the Earl was found guilty of dereliction of duty, but though the matter was ordered to be referred to the King, no further action was taken. On the 28th, in proceedings on the disputed Winchester election, Bromley was a teller against a resolution in favour of the Junto supporter Lord William Powlett*. In the midst of these preoccupations, Bromley was forced to monitor the progress of a bill to establish the Cottonian Library at Westminster, in which Dr Charlett had requested him to insert an additional clause 'for regulating printing'. However, owing to the limited scope of the bill there was little Bromley could do to accommodate Charlett's desire for a 'general saving of the university privileges' and he advised that the best alternative 'was to watch for and get particular savings as there shall be occasion'. Following the hostilities between the Tories and the ministry, there ensued a four-week respite from the end of April in which no further progress was made with the Whig impeachments. Towards the end of May, however, the Whigs in the Lords began to pressurize the Commons into proceeding, in order to clear the names of Orford and Somers, and it was Bromley who conveyed the Commons' dismissive response to the Upper House. In a further debate touching these exchanges with the Lords on 4 June, he joined the many MPs to speak in defence of Commons privileges in impeachment proceedings; and was subsequently a teller against giving immediate approval to the Commons 'replication' to Somers concerning the impeachment articles against him. On 12 June he reported the terms of an address to thank the King for his recent speech requesting support for his alliances and promising assistance therein. Some time before the 1702 election, however, he was blacklisted as having in this session opposed preparations for war with France. Acknowledgment of Bromley's energies was made in the ballot for new commissioners of public accounts, declared on 17 June, in which he achieved third place with 168 votes. The bill for establishing a new commission failed, however, when Parliament was prorogued a few days later.[16]

In the second election of 1701 Bromley was returned for Oxford University unopposed. He was teller on 5 Jan. 1702 against appointing a day for hearing the Whig petitioners in the disputed Norwich election. During the opening month of business he was involved in several legislative initiatives, one for setting up a new commission of public accounts, another against bribery and corruption at elections, and a third, of importance to his academic constituents, to enforce existing laws vesting in the universities the presentation of benefices belonging to Catholics. On 7 Feb. he successfully proposed to the House an address urging on the King the expedient of employing half-pay officers in recruiting the new army. On the 17th the House engaged in a major debate instigated by Hon. Heneage Finch I, one of Bromley's High

Tory compatriots, concerning the 'rights, liberties and privileges of the Commons', issues lately provoked by the Kentish Petition. Three resolutions protective of Commons' rights put forward by the Tories excited very little debate, but a fourth proposed by Bromley stating that to address for a dissolution was 'tending to sedition' produced long and heated exchanges which ended in confusion. Following the report on the Coventry election on the 24th he moved to have the Whig sheriff taken into custody for gross partiality. Two days later he voted in favour of the motion vindicating the Commons' proceedings during the previous Parliament in the impeachments of William III's ministers. On 5 Mar. he was teller in favour of alleviating the 'malt rent' paid by university colleges. Two days later, he was among the main supporters, all Tories, of a motion to adjourn the House in view of the King's deteriorating condition, and on William's death the next day he was appointed to draft an address of condolence and congratulation to Queen Anne. On the 9th Bromley was involved in an incident in the Commons, which though unseemly, indicated his rising stature. In the absence of John Conyers a stand-in was sought for the chair of the ways and means committee. Upon MPs severally calling for both Bromley and Hon. Henry Boyle, Bromley went down to take the chair before it had been properly offered, and when the question for him was subsequently put, he lost to Boyle, quitting the chamber, shamefaced and 'baffled'. In another dispute over the chair on the 13th, Bromley was a teller in favour of John Granville, another staunch Churchman. He obtained second place in the ballot for the new commission of accounts, its thorough Tory membership having been preconcerted at a private meeting of Tory MPs. His work with the commission began on 6 Apr. and continued until it was wound up in April 1704. During March and April he took responsibility for a private Irish forfeitures bill and a bill for improving the 'government' of the hospital at Balsall in Warwickshire. On the penultimate day of the session, 23 May, he was teller in favour of an address recommending the chaplain of the House, Dr Francis Gastrell, for an ecclesiastical place.[17]

The new era of Toryism heralded by Queen Anne's accession soon drew Bromley into playing a more central role in a House of Commons now dominated by the Tories. As Tory hopes were raised, his position as a representative of the chief seminary of Anglicanism naturally placed him at the forefront of his High Church colleagues. In the 1702 general election he and Heneage Finch, the brother of Lord Nottingham (Daniel Finch†), received the approbation of Lord Rochester (Laurence Hyde†), one of the principal Anglican leaders recently appointed to the ministry. He was, of course, conspicuous during the Queen's visit to the university in August when a doctorate of civil law was conferred on him. Before the opening of the new Parliament Lord Nottingham procured the Queen's approval for the introduction of a bill to outlaw the practice of 'occasional communion' by Dissenters, and prevailed on Bromley to steer the measure through the Lower House. Bromley was enthusiastic about the prospect of putting a stop to what he described to Dr Charlett on 22 Oct. as 'that abominable hypocrisy, that inexcusable immorality of occasional conformity'; if the bill could be obtained 'it will probably cure most of the evils we labour under'. As the session began, he reported on the 26th from the Address committee and was teller against a Whig motion designed to remove a calculated slur upon the late King's name. Evidence suggests that Bromley took the lead in this committee, a university don who encountered him a day or two later being shown the original draft of the address 'in his own handwriting'. In the evening, at the first meeting of the committee of privileges and elections, Bromley was chosen its chairman, a position he retained for the duration of the Parliament. Over the next three months he presided over and reported on 19 disputed election cases. On 11 Nov. he read a report from the commission of accounts relating evidence of gross financial malpractice by Lord Ranelagh (Richard Jones*) as paymaster of the forces, which led to Ranelagh's resignation early the next month. Bromley presented the first bill against occasional conformity on 14 Nov., having moved for its introduction on the 4th. Backed by the Queen, the bill seems to have encountered little resistance during its passage through the Commons. He reported its committee stage on the 25th, and carried it to the Lords on 2 Dec. Almost immediately, however, the measure became heavily ensnared by wrecking amendments orchestrated by Lord Somers. From mid-December Bromley was deeply involved in efforts to resolve the deadlock, and was a leading participant in conferences with the Upper House on 17 Dec., 9 and 16 Jan. and 1 Feb. 1703. As these proceedings dragged on, however, prospects of the bill reaching the statute book began to fade, not helped by Tory attitudes on other matters such as the Queen's request for a £5,000 annuity for Marlborough (John Churchill†) which Bromley and fellow High Churchmen took a leading part in opposing on 15 Dec. He joined other Tories on 13 Feb. 1703 in voting against agreeing with the Lords' amendments to the bill for enlarging the time allowed for taking the oath of abjuration. At the end of the month, however, he was forced to abandon his political activities as he recovered from a life-threatening fever to which the strains of his parliamentary work during the session may well have contributed.[18]

Bromley and his associates had been sorely provoked by the mauling given the occasional conformity bill in the Lords and strongly suspected the ministers of complicity in its failure. Robert Harley spent most of the summer recess doing what he could to secure Tory support for the forthcoming session, but knowing that the angry High Tories would be most difficult of all to placate. In September he consulted Bromley with a view to obtaining his acquiescence in a 'scheme' for raising the supply in the coming session. Bromley's response that 'it is you only can raise a building suitable to this foundation', indicated that support would be forthcoming if Harley backed a new occasional conformity bill. In any event, Bromley was already set upon bringing in a new bill. By the time the session opened it was apparent to Lord Treasurer Godolphin (Sidney†) that 'the matter is too far engaged' and that Bromley 'is obstinate to the last degree'. On 25 Nov. Bromley successfully moved to reintroduce the occasional conformity bill, his oratory receiving particular acclaim. After presenting the bill two days later, he managed it through the House, chairing the committee of the whole on 2 Dec. and reporting on the 3rd. However, so rapid had been the bill's progress that many Tory peers had yet to arrive in town and it raised the possibility that the temporary Whig majority would throw it out. Bromley endeavoured to forestall this threat by feigning illness on 8 Dec., when he was due to carry the bill to the Lords, and he did not deliver it until the 13th. Two days later it was rejected outright on the motion for a second reading. Bromley was one of the chief movers behind an address ordered on 17 Dec. (which he reported next day) implicitly expressing the Commons' confidence in Secretary Nottingham, then under attack over his handling of the Scotch Plot.[19]

Since there were only five election cases and two privilege complaints in 1704, Bromley was left with a freer hand to deal with other legislative interests. One of these originated in the Queen's message of 7 Feb. promising provision for increasing the stipends of the poorer clergy. The establishment of what became known as Queen Anne's Bounty was Harley's way of mollifying Tory MPs, following the loss of the second occasional conformity bill. The measure, which Bromley took through all its Commons stages, enabled the crown to surrender to the Church its traditional income from first fruits and tenths, thereby providing a fund of £17,000 from which clerical incomes could be supplemented. Bromley likewise dealt with a private bill confirming a property agreement entered into by the authorities at Christ Church, Oxford, although the measure failed after its report stage. On 25 Feb. he came third in the ballot for a new commission of accounts with 195 votes. However, at the end of March, when the bill for appointing the new commission was sent up to the Lords, both Bromley and St. John asked to be left out 'that they might be capable of better employments, as is supposed'. To Dr Charlett, two days later, Bromley expressed pleasure at being relieved from the burdens of the commission and at the prospect of a long summer away from London, especially since 'too constant an application' had once again impaired his health.[20]

In October, as the new session approached, there was considerable speculation that the Tories would attempt to displace Harley as Speaker on the premise that this office and his secretaryship were wholly incompatible. Bromley had been touted as a likely successor as early as May and had remained a favourite choice throughout the summer months. A large meeting of Tory MPs, of which Bromley was a chief convenor, was planned to take place a week before the session opened, fuelling the likelihood of an all-out parliamentary attack on Harley, but in the event the expected attack failed to materialize, possibly because of an insufficient Tory attendance. To onlookers, it seemed for a short while that Bromley had been bought off by the ministry, it being reported at the beginning of November that he had accepted a clerkship of the Green Cloth. In fact, he was proceeding with plans to confront the ministry with a third bill against occasional conformity and, if necessary, to 'tack' it to a money bill to guarantee its passage through the Lords. His Oxford University constituents had urged him in the strongest terms to reintroduce the measure. Bromley successfully moved for the bill on 14 Nov. The crucial stage in its progress was reached on 28 Nov. when he moved for it to be tacked to the land tax bill. Introducing this motion, Bromley described occasional conformity as a 'scandalous hypocrisy . . . no way to be excused upon any pretence whatsoever'. He maintained that the practice was condemned even by 'the better sort of Dissenters', and that no 'wise government' countenanced the employment of persons in public offices whose religion differed from that established by law, and that this was not even allowed in Holland. Further, the Established Church now stood as much in danger from Dissenters as from papists. He then sought to justify the 'ancient practice' of tacking, saying that the great necessity there was for the money bill's passing was rather an argument for than against this proceeding. For what danger could there be that the Lords, who pretended to be such great patriots, should rather lose the necessary supplies, than pass an act so requisite for the preservation of the Church?

The tacking motion was lost however, Bromley himself serving as a teller for the minority in a division which saw over 100 Tories desert the High Church cause. In forcing the issue Bromley and his associates had taken the amazingly shortsighted course of requiring their prospective supporters among the office-holding and moderate Tories to put supply measures at risk, and to endorse the constitutionally dubious device of tacking. Under his supervision the occasional conformity bill continued its passage through the House, which was completed on 15 Dec. when Bromley carried it to the Lords, who rejected it later the same day. Opinion at Oxford was outraged, but when the House adjourned for the Christmas recess Bromley could do little more than express himself 'satisfied, after the disappointments we have met with, to find my endeavours to serve the Church and religion, are acceptable to those I have the honour to represent'. His continuing interest in 'Country' measures was signified in the support he gave for the introduction of two place bills on 13 Jan. 1705. In the remainder of the session his recorded activities were confined mainly to steering two private estate bills through the Commons and to proceedings relating to the Aylesbury case in which he reported the outcome of several conferences with the Lords. However, the burdens of the session again told on his health, leading in April to a serious fever which brought him close to death. The anonymous author of a newsletter commented that 'the death of this gentleman would have been a great loss to the Church party, he being one of the chief propagators for them in the House of Commons'.[21]

At Oxford Bromley was now very much the champion of the Anglican cause and in a three-cornered contest in the 1705 election received the first votes of every MA. As thoughts turned to the new Parliament during the summer Bromley was proposed by his Tory brethren as a candidate for the Speakership. Even some of the 'warm Whigs' were inclined towards him 'as the fittest man to pursue the sentiments of the House' instead of Harley, whom they could no longer endure. Throughout August Bromley was engaged in 'frequent meetings' with Rochester and Nottingham, and the forthcoming contest for the Chair was high on the agenda. In the early autumn his supporters spoke and wrote optimistically, although some shrewd Whigs, such as James Craggs II*, felt that the promises claimed by Bromley's 'cocksure' campaigners, claimed to be around 250, could not be put 'above 200' and that the Court candidate, John Smith I, would obtain the lion's share of votes from the Queen's servants. Harley, according to the historian John Oldmixon, was the instigator of a dirty tricks campaign against Bromley in which a republished version of Bromley's *Grand Tour of France and Italy*, highlighting passages that suggested the author's Jacobite and pro-Catholic leanings, was distributed among MPs. On his own copy of the work Bromley noted: 'this edition is a specimen of the good nature and good manners of the Whigs, and, I have reason to believe, of one of the ministry, very conversant in this sort of calumny'. He felt that if anything had been 'improper' and any 'observations trifling or impertinent', allowance ought to have been made for his being 'very young' at the time. Against his own account of this episode, Bishop Burnet described Bromley as 'a great favourer of Jacobites'. When the Commons assembled on 25 Oct. Bromley was proposed for the Chair by Lord Dysart (Lionel Tollemache) and seconded by (Sir) Thomas Hanmer II, both of whom had been active supporters of the occasional conformity bill, but Smith was elected by 248 votes to 205. Bromley cast his own vote politely for the Court candidate.[22]

As age and death removed older High Tory leaders from the parliamentary scene, so their places were taken by younger men, of whom Bromley was one of the most prominent by 1705. The set-backs of recent years at ministerial hands had embittered him to a degree which was now particularly noticeable. His sense of exasperation found an outlet in November during the committee proceedings on the disputed St. Albans election. When it emerged that the Duchess of Marlborough, an owner of property in the town, had written to the corporation recommending the Whig candidate Admiral Henry Killigrew*, several Tories 'reflected very indecently against her', but none more so than Bromley, who compared her to Edward III's mistress, Alice Perrers. On 4 Dec. he assisted Hanmer in a preconcerted manoeuvre against the ministry over the agitated question of the Scottish succession. Aware that Hanmer was ready to trip up the ministry with an unwelcome motion to invite the Electress Sophia of Hanover to reside in England (a similar motion having been made in the Lords on 15 Nov.), Bromley neatly cleared the way by moving the scheduled second reading of the 'Scotch bill', repealing the Alien Act that had been passed at Westminster in retaliation for the Scots' earlier intransigence over the succession. Thus, when the House in committee began to consider the Scottish parliament's most recent proceedings, Hanmer was able to launch his motion concerning the Electress Sophia. Bromley gave his support with a key speech pointing out that the proposal had in fact been necessitated by the advice Godolphin had given the Queen in August 1704 to approve the Scottish Act of Security whereby the Scottish parliament undertook to choose their own successor to the Scottish throne. During the debate on the 8th on the Lords' resolution that the Church was 'in danger', he gave a wide-ranging speech delineating the many fronts on which the Anglican Church stood exposed, some of which had been aired in the debate on the 4th: the power of the Presbyterians in Scotland; the absence of the next Protestant heir should the Queen die; the failure to legislate against occasional conformity; the proliferation of Dissenting schools and seminaries; the prevalence of profaneness, immorality and irreligion; the threat posed by the Scottish Act of Security; and the abuses already apparent in the administration of Queen Anne's bounty. It seems to have been during this debate, too, that he aspersed Godolphin as a crypto-Jacobite, accusing him of having been a signatory to the warrant for the imprisonment of the Seven Bishops, and adding 'that he had been named in all the plots etc. since the Revolution'. Bromley was fortunate to have had no action taken against him: a fellow Tory, Charles Caesar, was sent to the Tower for making similar insinuations against the Treasurer on the 19th. On 11 Dec. Bromley spoke again in favour of the ministry's bill for repealing the Alien Act as a necessary prelude to ministerial negotiations for a treaty of union with Scotland, though in committee proceedings on the 15th he and the rest of his party 'sat mute'. As a riposte to the Tory 'Hanover motion' the ministry initiated in the Lords a regency bill to safeguard the succession. At second reading in the Commons on the 19th Bromley opposed the proposal of a regency council to govern after the Queen's death until the arrival of her successor, arguing that the bill, while having a laudable purpose, was at the same time 'dangerous to the succession' on the premise that it would be possible for ministers to dictate the composition of the regency group. Tory efforts to stifle the bill continued during the committee stage: on 12 Jan. 1706 Bromley appears to have backed the Whig-sponsored 'whimsical' clause safeguarding the provision in the Act of Settlement which excluded all placemen from the Commons upon the Queen's death. Further, on the 15th, he stressed the necessity of making adequate provision for convening Parliament during a regency as a vital 'check' on the lords justices of whom 'none [could] have a worse opinion...than himself'. He returned to this theme in committee on the 19th in discussions on the composition of the regency, exposing the possibility that the new prince might be 'ruined by treacherous ministers' riven 'by animosities against one another'.[23]

During the summer the position of the Harley–St. John group of Court Tories began to weaken as differences over foreign policy arose between them and the Junto, and as the latter began to push for additional appointments in recognition of the parliamentary support they had lately given to the ministry. In consequence, Harley, St. John and their confrères began to look for a resumption of contact with the Tory leaders, particularly with Bromley and Hanmer, whom they regarded as leaders of the Tory rank and file, and several meetings were apparently held during the month or so before the 1706–7 session. Nothing seems to have come of these negotiations, however, the Tories continuing their usual course in opposition, and the Harleyites continuing their working relationship with Marlborough and Godolphin. When the session opened on 3 Dec. Bromley was named to the Address committee. Personal disaster struck towards the end of the month when fire gutted his seat at Baginton, destroying most of its contents including his 'large library of books and manuscripts'. During one of the committee sittings on the articles of Union in February 1707 Bromley opposed the 1st article stipulating that the Union was to take effect from 1 May 1707. On 22 Feb., as the House was about to go into committee on the bill to ratify the Union, Bromley, mindful of his constituents' interests, moved that consideration be given to an additional clause protecting Oxford and Cambridge universities, that they 'may continue for ever, as they are now by law established'. In March, at the request of Dr Charlett, he monitored the progress of a bill for regulating the printing of books, ensuring that 'sufficient care' was taken to see that the university libraries received copies of all new and reprinted volumes. The bill was to fail, however, before reaching the Lords. The same month he promoted a private estate bill on behalf of the Duke of Beaufort, a leading Tory peer.[24]

Despite the complaints he heard from country gentlemen about the burdens of war, Bromley saw that backbenchers had little alternative but to acquiesce in the financial demands for the coming year. Shortly after the new session began on 10 Nov. Bromley caused offence to the Court and most Whigs by proposing that the House, in accordance with directions in the Queen's speech, should give priority to measures to ensure 'the completion of the Union'. Godolphin was anxious to avoid adjustments to the Union that would upset ministerial ability to command the support of the Scots Members, but had to accede to discussions. At the report of the committee of the whole on 11 Dec. the resolution to standardize the powers of English and Scots j.p.s, favoured by the Squadrone, proved particularly contentious and received 'a broadside' from the Court. The resolution was passed when Bromley, followed by other principal Tories, joined the debate and helped to defeat the ministry's amendment allowing a different magisterial system north of the border. By mid-December it was clear that Bromley and other Tory activists had been preparing the groundwork for a major attack on the ministry over its conduct of the war in Spain. On the 18th, after the House had approved James Grahme's motion for a full-scale inquiry into the state of the war in Spain, Bromley, assisted by Ralph Freman II, moved for papers relating to the alleged deficiency of English forces at the battle of Almanza. On 21 Jan. 1708 he was among the leading Tory obstructors of the ministry's bill to step up conscription, taking notice of the 'abuses and hardships' mentioned in previous debates on army affairs and proposing a clause to prevent the selling of army commissions. He was subsequently named among the group of MPs directed to draft the bill. Harley's resignation from the administration on 11 Feb. made no immediate difference to the position of Bromley and his supporters, who continued to oppose Godolphin in the Commons. He took notice on 19 Feb. of the ministry's failure to present the papers he had asked for on 18 Dec., and moved for them again. On the 24th he took his party line in opposition to the government-sponsored bill to establish the validity of the Henrician statutes of cathedral and collegiate churches, opposing the measure again in committee of the whole on 9 Mar.[25]

The Whig victory at the polls in 1708, coupled with the Whigs' increased pressure on the duumvirs for more places, prompted Godolphin to seek support from the Tories in the coming session. However, Bromley adamantly refused to enter any arrangement with the lord treasurer when the latter made approaches in mid-July. Godolphin's suggestion that Harley be Speaker in the new Parliament was too much for Bromley to contemplate, since if put into effect it would immediately give Harley an advantageous position within the government, but by the later weeks of August contacts between Bromley and Harley were beginning to develop. On 20 Aug. Harley fulsomely addressed himself to Bromley: 'I can assure you, sir, that those who you conversed with last winter are resolved most heartily to enter into measures with you.' Initially, Harley's long disquisition on the need for political unification and renewal met with a polite but censorious response on 18 Sept. Bromley brushed aside Harley's contention that 'present difficulties' could be imputed to 'the mistakes of others' and made no bones about the fact that much of the blame rested with Harley himself. He also expressed his belief that the former secretary had been far too general about the 'public points' which they would pursue. He did not, however, rule out the possibility of further 'discourse' before Parliament convened, 'which will be necessary to unite us, and to create that confidence that I desire may be among us'. Late in September Bromley took a leading part in a series of Tory meetings, the outcome of which he reported to his mentor Lord Nottingham. It was agreed 'to get a full appearance' in time for the beginning of the new session and to push for a Tory Speaker. It was soon suggested that Bromley himself might stand for the Chair, a scheme which Harley readily embraced. As Harley wrote to Dr William Stratford of Christ Church on 10 Oct.: 'there can remain no room for doubt but that I will most readily and heartily espouse his interest, and particularly upon this occasion I will do my utmost to show him the regard I have for his person'. Two days later Bromley assured Harley 'that I truly value your friendship and . . . on all occasions [will] use my utmost endeavours to disappoint all arts that may be used to prevent our coming to a good understanding'. Bromley's main anxiety was the lack of wholehearted support shown at this juncture by Lord Nottingham who refused to appear in town to rally hesitant friends. In the event, however, the Speakership issue was resolved by the admission of the Junto lords Somers and Wharton (Hon. Thomas*) to the ministry, thereby guaranteeing Whig support for the Court candidate, Sir Richard Onslow, 3rd Bt. Though Bromley did not contest the Chair, it remained to be seen how fruitful his new rapport with Harley would be. On the eve of the new Parliament, Nottingham wrote to him sounding a cautionary note: 'As much as I wish an increase in our number by any just ways and would not therefore refuse the concurrence of Mr H[arley], yet to deal freely I do not expect any assistance from him; il y a something of a mystery in that affair and I can't help my jealousy.'[26]

On 22 Nov. 1708, a week after the new Parliament commenced, Bromley was chosen in first place on 22 Nov. to a committee to draw up the condolences of the House on the death of Prince George. This he reported the following day. On 13 Dec. he reflected damningly against the Duke of Marlborough following a vote of thanks to General John Richmond Webb* for his victory at Wynendael. He told the House that he did not disapprove the custom of thanking commanders who had performed eminent services, especially when such compliments were 'modestly' received. But he grieved the fact that 'a certain commander, on whom not only the thanks of the House, but also great rewards had been bestowed, appeared yet unsatisfied'. This thinly veiled attack on Marlborough 'scandalously surprised' the ministry for its 'malice' and was a topic of conversation for several weeks afterwards. In the meantime, Bromley was expressing doubts about Harley's reliability as an ally. On 7 Dec. he confided in a letter to Nottingham that Harley 'proposes schemes which, if they are pursued, may perhaps save a penny', but which were largely ineffectual. It was certainly within Harley's powers to propose 'more material and serviceable' ones, but if he did not soon do so, 'I think he may be justly suspected for the future'. Nottingham replied on the 20th: 'what you say of Mr H[arley] confirms me in my opinion . . . He is indeed in appearance more modest, humble and affable; but he steadily prosecutes his ends, which are plain set (though he be very reserved) to show him to be very ambitious and implacable.' Writing at the end of December, Bromley could see little prospect of a change in the current political situation despite intimations of the Queen's 'fixed resolution of changing the present measures, notwithstanding the greater difficulties that are now to be struggled with', and admitted that 'I do not build upon such an expectation'. While privately expressing these innermost doubts and apprehensions to Nottingham, and seeking the Earl's approval and guidance on issues such as the recent 'invasion' scare, Bromley none the less collaborated closely with Harley, asking him early in January 1709 for a briefing on the foreign situation and the invasion crisis 'and your instructions how to treat them and manage both to our common interest'. Even so, their plans, when carried into effect, made limited impact. On 12 Jan. Bromley seconded Harley's motion for accounts of army and navy expenditure for the war in Spain and Portugal, but the implied threat of a major inquiry failed to materialize. By early February it was reported that the 'Church side' had fallen into lassitude and that 'neither Bromley nor Hanmer open their mouths'. It may well have been at Bromley's instigation that a committee was formed on 16 Feb. to investigate the problem of land tax arrears, he being the first-named appointee. Reporting the committee's findings on the 26th, he was critical of receivers who retained in their hands considerable sums and thus burdened the public with the interest due on them. He was afterwards teller for the Tory minority in favour of a strongly worded address condemning these practices. During February he had also joined in opposing proposals for a bill removing the ancient requirement that fellows of Oxford and Cambridge take holy orders. On 5 Mar. he frustrated the ministry's expressed disinclination to proceed further on the 'Gregg case', which early in 1708 had implicated Harley in treasonous activity, by insisting that 'since those papers were brought in as reflecting upon an honourable Member of the House' they merited the due consideration of the House. Five days later the 'show' he had concerted 'with three or four others' for the proceedings on the recent invasion scare came to nothing owing to the thinness of the House.[27]

The ministers' determination to impeach Dr Sacheverell in the next session proved a turning point in Tory fortunes. Bromley's championship of the doctor's cause was distinctly ironic given his refusal earlier in the year to support Sacheverell for a chaplaincy at St. Saviour's, Southwark. At Oxford Sacheverell was much disliked owing to his extremism and maliciousness, and was particularly antagonistic towards Bromley's old college, Christ Church. Despite his personal feelings, however, Bromley quickly recognized the enormous political capital to be gained from taking on the doctor's defence. When the House was formally notified on 13 Dec. 1709 of the seditious content of Sacheverell's two contentious sermons, the Tory response was somewhat muted, Bromley being among several who spoke, 'but very sparingly'. Later, however, when the vote of censure passed and the cry of 'impeach' went up from the Whigs, he took the lead in securing a 'respite' in the proceedings until Sacheverell could be brought to the bar of the House. In the following day's debate, Bromley's arguments that the case should be heard before either a church court or the Queen's bench made no headway, and it was eventually resolved to proceed by impeachment. He also opposed a motion afterwards offered by the Whigs to address the Queen recommending ecclesiastical preferment for Benjamin Hoadly, the outspoken Low Church polemicist, in recognition of a recent sermon against Bishop Blackall of Exeter who had preached on passive obedience and non-resistance in the presence of the Queen. Bromley could not but see 'that it might be looked upon as an affront to the Queen, to desire her to prefer him for writing against a sermon which she had ordered to be printed'. On 22 Dec. Bromley was a teller in favour of admitting Sacheverell to bail. On 9 Jan. 1710 he was driven to complain of the ministry's delay in laying the impeachment articles before the House. Two days later, after these had been presented, he and other prominent Church Tories spoke 'very well' in support of Harley's criticism of the articles as loosely conceived and requiring further detailed consideration. A motion for recommitment was eventually lost, however. At the beginning of February the House received and considered Sacheverell's 'answer' to the impeachment articles, and on the 2nd Bromley told for the Tory minority against the proposed statement of reply. When the Commons received the Lords' message two days later appointing the trial to be heard at the bar of their House on 9 Feb., Bromley caught the ministry entirely off-guard with a proposal that swung the whole course of the Sacheverell episode decisively to the Tories' great advantage. No special provision had been made for MPs to attend the proceedings apart from the Commons' managers. However, Bromley moved that the Commons should attend the trial 'in a body' as a committee of the whole on the premise that the usual impeachment procedure allowed MPs to vote on whether to demand judgment, thus giving them a right to hear the the case in full. The motion was put to a division, Bromley serving as as teller, and narrowly passed. Thereupon, he was ordered to request the Lords to ensure 'convenient accommodation' for MPs, with Westminster Hall the obvious venue for the trial. The trial was consequently transformed into a great public spectacle. The Sacheverell proceedings had the effect of generating Tory obstructionism on other issues. On 15 Feb. Bromley helped lead the barrage of criticism 'fired' at a Whig motion to send the Duke of Marlborough to assist at the peace negotiations at Gertruydenberg. Bromley took grave exception to the fact that news of the negotiations had filtered through to the House via one of its merchant Members and not through proper ministerial channels. He sparked another major debate on 24 Mar. with a motion to address the Queen to appoint a day of public fasting 'to deprecate the divine vengeance ... on account of those horrid blasphemies which have been vented, published and printed in this kingdom'. However, the ministerial side succeeded in carrying a wrecking amendment referring specifically to the 'blasphemies' lately disseminated by Sacheverell.[28]

In the months of June and July, as the fate of Godolphin's ministry hung in the balance, Bromley went about his social and magisterial duties in Warwickshire. Towards the end of June he and other members of the county elite played host to Sacheverell. The doctor, Bromley informed Dr Charlett, 'was very welcome to us in Warwickshire. The prosecution of him has taken such a turn as must be of great service to our common interest if those that have it in their power will make the right use of it.' Paying careful attention to opinion among his wide Tory acquaintance, Bromley found expectations of a general election running high by the beginning of July. It was widely rumoured during these weeks that senior Tory MPs were to be drafted into the ministry, with Bromley either as treasurer of the navy or in the more exalted position of chancellor of the Exchequer. Once Godolphin had resigned on 8 Aug. Bromley could only assume that Parliament would be dissolved as a matter of course. He confessed to Charlett that 'dilatory proceedings have given some strength as well as courage to our enemies, and have wearied and disheartened our friends', and hoped that the appointment of a Harleyite Treasury Board would facilitate a recovery of lost ground: 'it is a juncture that concerns us all to be active'. Bromley resisted the urgings of many friends to go to London, a step which he felt would be highly indecent in view of persistent reports that he was about to be given high office. By the beginning of September, however, the summer impasse appeared to be drawing to a close as Bromley received 'repeated assurances', quite possibly from Harley himself, that 'no interest will be considered but the Church's'. He was also informed that the new ministers were anxious 'to make their bottom as wide as they can and to receive those who are of distinction, and have no blemish, provided they will come in on the same interest'. Bromley was now at least able to reassure restive Tory friends of a satisfactory outcome to the prolonged intrigues which had preceded, and for some weeks followed, the downfall of Godolphin's ministry. He was still in Warwickshire later in September when news reached him of the dissolution. Though this gave him great satisfaction, Harley's neglect of the Tory faithful still rankled, while the fact that many Whigs remained in the lieutenancies and commissions of the peace gave him cause to ponder the new chancellor's future intentions.[29]

Until the election it was widely assumed that Bromley would replace Robert Walpole II* as treasurer of the navy. As the extent of the Tory victory became clear, however, he emerged overnight as the principal contender for the Chair. Late in October and early November he was in London to concert tactics with other senior High Church colleagues, among them Hanmer, John Ward III, and Lord Anglesey (Hon. Arthur Annesley*). Despite the Whigs' talk of setting up their own candidate, the huge Tory majority guaranteed Bromley's success. When Parliament met on 25 Nov. he was proposed by Hanmer, who told the House:

> it was necessary to choose a man who had given signal proofs of his abilities and willingness to serve his country; one who had given evident proof of his affection to the constitution and goverment of the nation, who had been earnest in the prosecution of the war, and who would contribute to the support of the public credit; one who had distinguished himself for his zeal for the Protestant succession and was hearty for establishing the same in the illustrious House of Hanover and who would contribute to do everything for extinguishing all the hopes of the Pretender; and lastly who was well-affected to the Church of England.

Bromley was chosen 'without a negative'. He was nationally known and respected as a resolute leader of the Church party, a reputation consolidated by memories of his stubborn crusade against occasional conformity earlier in the Queen's reign. Indeed, to the many Tory newcomers in the House he was a much revered figure. Behind him he had many years' experience of parliamentary procedure which in recent years had included the chairmanship of the privileges and elections committee. Harley must have surmised that in the Chair he could be depended on to exercise a disciplining influence over the Tory ranks and help contain the extremism of which Harley was so apprehensive. He was an essential line of communication with the more responsible element of the High Church Tories. His connexions in the Commons were based largely upon bonds of friendship forged in political campaigns of former years, and embraced key Tory figures in many counties, not least the midland shires surrounding his native Warwickshire. One of Bromley's first acts was to appoint as his chaplain Dr Jonathan Kimberley, the rector of St. Michael's in Coventry, who according to Defoe was the author of a piece of 'High Church poison' and was one of the originators of the movement against occasional conformity.[30]

Bromley appears to have largely convinced himself that Harley was probably the best man to lead the Tories in power, even though Lord Nottingham clearly did not. As Bromley wrote to the chancellor on 14 Nov.: 'I had rather our friends at this time had obligations to you for what favours they receive than to any one else.' He was also ready to concede the need for moderate measures, but only as long as the members of the 'honest party' received their due share of favour and place. There was still a strong need, as he saw it, for encouragement to be given to those 'who by principle have the greatest zeal and affection for the establishment in Church and state'. Bromley trod a wary course as Speaker during the 1710–11 session, not least since there were so many new Tory Members of whom he had no personal knowledge or acquaintanceship. Though he was not at this stage hand in glove with Harley in managing the House, he did assist the chancellor's need for 'diversionary' measures in the Commons during sensitive proceedings on taxation, while at the same time continuing to serve his party's cause. His conduct in this latter respect is particularly well illustrated by the way he promoted the High Tory concern for the provision of churches in London. Bromley had become a willing accessory to the scheme elaborated by his friend Francis Atterbury for a working relationship between the Commons and the lower house of Convocation, of which Atterbury was prolocutor, that would inaugurate a programme of Anglican 'reformation', and thus lay the foundations for a new era of High Church endeavour. However, the ambitious scheme to provide London with additional churches was the only legislative venture which emerged. He secured the appointment on 14 Feb. 1711 of a Commons committee to investigate the shortage of churches in London and its suburbs, and despite his preoccupations as Speaker, appears to have taken considerable interest in its proceedings. On 1 Mar. he received a delegation of London clergy to thank him for his initiative; and on the 9th Atterbury provided him with 'a scheme' showing where new churches were most needed. Bromley presented this to the House next day. At the end of the month the Queen commended the project to the Commons and a bill for the building of 50 new churches in the metropolis passed soon afterwards. Bromley was temporarily incapacitated from taking the Chair following the death on 20 Mar. of his eldest son Clobery*. On thanking the House that day 'for their great kindness' in agreeing to adjourn until the 26th he broke down and had to be led away, unable to finish his speech. But to cynical minds, the adjournment was merely a tactic to create further delays following Guiscard's attempt on Harley's life on 8 Mar.[31]

As the 1710–11 session wore on, High Church Tories became increasingly impatient with Harley's constant hedging and his efforts to thwart their schemes. Amid financial crisis, supply business ran into trouble in February and by late March senior Tory MPs were concerting plans for disruptive action in the Commons. Bromley was very much at the centre of this activity, the impetus for which came in the first instance from Lord Nottingham who was still trying to put himself at the head of the High Church malcontents with Bromley in tow. Bromley appears to have been the convenor of a crucial meeting held on 2 Apr. to decide on tactics for the remainder of the session. In a letter which clearly indicates the depth of backbench Tory discontent, one Tory activist, John Ward III, informed Nottingham of the proceedings:

> Last night some of us met with the Speaker and came to a resolution to bring on the notice of the invasion, to force on the account of the customs and stamp office and what other mismanagements the Court can lay open without tedious inquiry and to make two representations, the one of the money matters, the other of the Church and State, and in the latter to expose the mask of moderation by which we have so much suffered and the trimming measures we fear and this in the boldest lively colours.

Harley's inability to supervise the House personally during his recuperation from Guiscard's attack enabled Tory activists to carry out much of this programme, evidently with Bromley's tacit support. However, the approbation which greeted Harley's much-awaited scheme to restore public credit, which he had unveiled at the beginning of May, effectively prevented Tory back-benchers from pushing to further extremes. It would appear that Harley at this point saw more clearly the pressing need to exercise greater discipline over the Church Tories. Thus signs of a closer relationship between Bromley and the ministry were apparent early in May when it was reported that Bromley had 'absolutely refused' membership of the October Club. And as the session drew to a close Harley took care to sound Bromley about the content and form of the Queen's closing speech. Bromley, as his summer correspondence shows, seems to have realized that it was now necessary to swim with the tide of Tory aspirations; the scenes of Tory consensus during the last month or so of the session had convinced him at last of Harley's probity.[32]

After the prorogation Harley (now Earl of Oxford and lord high treasurer) carried out a series of ministerial changes among which were a number of High Church appointments. Oxford chose to use Bromley as a go-between in his offer of the chancellorship of the Exchequer to Hanmer, though Hanmer was far too wary to take it. On the disposition of the senior ministerial offices it remained a matter of great personal regret to Bromley that Lord Nottingham was kept from public service. Yet the summer months saw Bromley on far better terms with Oxford than ever before. His attitudes to Oxford's policies had been transformed to the point of complete devotion, so much so that at the end of July he sharply chastised those Tories who remained critical of the lord treasurer. And when Oxford confided in him his hope that a 'good peace' would result from the preliminaries currently under negotiation, Bromley responded effusively on 18 Aug.:

> When I consider what you have done, I conclude nothing is impossible to your lordship; and I shall be heartily glad to see this effected, because as nothing is more wanted so nothing can be more acceptable to the people who now languish under the pressure of this heavy war, and consequently nothing can tend more to the establishment of your lordship's ministry.

He took care to announce his new-found optimism to his constituents. In a letter clearly meant for wide circulation he wrote: 'I shall be very glad to have Lord Treasurer think rightly of me. I look upon it we are embarked upon the same bottom, engaged in the same interests, and I am therefore very sincerely and unfeignedly his humble servant.' He briefed Lord Oxford at length on 25 Nov. on the problems he anticipated in managing Tory Members during the approaching session. Confident that they could be assuaged with respect to the ongoing peace negotiations, Bromley felt that a far greater cause of 'uneasiness' would arise from

> the expectations of those that sent them thither, to act as becomes a House of Commons chosen by a spirit raised from an opinion of great corruption in the late administration, that it would now be detected and punished, and that something would be done to secure our constitution in Church and state against the vile principles and practices that had been countenanced to the endangering of both.

As Bromley perceived it, the task of overcoming Tory obstreperousness would be exacting:

> The commission of accounts, I take it, will produce what will for the present entertain and satisfy them in the one, but the other is only to be done by putting the power into the hands of our friends, and by wholesome laws, if any are wanting and can be framed, that will be proper. The first is entirely in your lordship's province; the last too many think themselves proficient for, and will be prescribing those remedies, and no one can tell how far their well-meant zeal may carry them within those bounds which is truly my concern they should not exceed. I should be sorry to have anything peevishly said or attempted by our friends, and will not fail using my utmost endeavours to prevent it, but all I can do will be ineffectual without your assistance. They were pretty quiet last session, expecting great advantages from the representation [of grievances against the old ministry], which they now complain has been so little regarded that it only truly serves to bring them and their proceedings into contempt. I hear so much of this that I think I should not deserve any the least of those favours I receive

from you if I did not plainly lay it before you; and there is nothing can give me greater pleasure than to be instrumental in any degree in preserving among our friends the esteem and confidence, nay the gratitude, due to your lordship from them.

Oxford took seriously Bromley's advice to strengthen his relationship with the High Churchmen. Early in December, on the eve of the 1711–12 session, he held talks, arranged by Bromley, with senior Tories apparently to indicate his willingness to accept legislation against occasional conformity. At the end of the month Bromley was again deputed to coax Hanmer into accepting high office, but again without success. On 17 Jan. 1712 Bromley was forced to rally faint-hearted Tories during the committee proceedings on the peculation offences alleged against Robert Walpole II, declaring to those who could find little evidence of Walpole's guilt that his expulsion was an 'unum necessarium' and that business could not be carried on if he remained in the House. Greater difficulties materialized in connexion with the charges against the Duke of Marlborough due for consideration on the 25th. Bromley had to forewarn Oxford that the Duke's sympathizers were liable to outnumber his enemies in a vote of censure, whereupon the lord treasurer signified his intention of pursuing the matter no further. Towards the end of April pressure from Bromley's university constituents concerning a disadvantageous supply measure levying a duty on paper used for books obliged him to urge Oxford to modify the proposal. As he explained to the treasurer on 29 Apr., his being Speaker and his close association with the ministry imposed a strain on his relationship with the university authorities:

> they think they shall have cause to be more concerned for any hardship brought upon them while I have the honour to be in the Chair and under your lordship's ministry, whom they look upon as the patron of learning and their best friend and protector than at another time; and therefore I must beg your assistance to make this matter easy, but by allowing them a certain quantity of paper yearly free from the duty, and that one thousand reams will answer their ordinary expense.

At the same time he was also apprehensive about the effects of a bill to establish the value of crown grants made since 1688, a 'Country' project sponsored by the October Club. Bromley cautioned Oxford to take special care over this potentially divisive issue for the Tories and agree to allow the valuation to be undertaken by a commission of MPs: 'if they [the bill's supporters] can attain their end, it is certainly more desirable to attain it in a manner that will not distress and discompose affairs at this juncture'. For all his professions of loyalty, Bromley was dissatisfied with Oxford's languorous progress in 'serving and establishing our common interest' and warned him that 'there only wants a confidence which will unavoidably increase, the longer the making those thorough changes is delayed'. By early June the imminence of peace began to work euphoric effects on the backbenches. On 6 June when the peace terms were communicated Bromley witnessed an attendance of over 400 Members agree unanimously to a loyal address, a spectacle which he described as 'wonderful'. In July he and Oxford parted on excellent terms, Bromley convinced 'that your lordship is pursuing the interest of our country in Church and state . . . you have the hearts of the people at home.'[33]

The next parliamentary session was delayed until the signing of the peace treaties at the end of March 1713. By February, as Bromley alerted Oxford, Tory annoyance at being kept in 'uncertain attendance' was increasing. He himself was irritated by the 'unprecedented delays' in disposing ecclesiastical vacancies and at the neglect shown towards his recommendations of various university dons for preferment. Late in May, as the session progressed, Bromley, Hanmer and several other senior Tories failed in an attempt to halt George Lockhart's scheme to push for the dissolution of the Union with Scotland. Bromley, according to Lockhart, declared at their meeting that 'he was not very fond of the Union in all respects, but since there were some advantages to England from it, and that they had catched hold of Scotland, they would keep her fast'. It was inevitable that Bromley's combination of the Speakership with his management of the Tory back-benchers should provoke outbursts of Whig fury. On one such occasion during a debate on the bill of commerce on 9 June 'artful and unjust insinuations' were hurled at him by the Whig General James Stanhope, but as one Tory MP marvelled, 'our worthy Speaker . . . behaved himself answerable to his character, showing a warm and becoming resentment with (I think) more good nature than the party desired.' Bromley played a vital role in reconciling those Tories, including Hanmer, who had ensured the defeat of the French commerce bill on 18 June, and was no doubt influential in urging Oxford to recast the ministry on strictly Tory lines in order to satisfy the diehard critics of 'moderation'.[34]

Bromley was an obvious choice for promotion in Oxford's subsequent plans. By the end of July he was pressed by the treasurer to accept a secretaryship of state. Although his incorporation into the administration at almost the highest level was a concession to the Church party, Bromley was also regarded as one of the few who might help to conciliate the 'whimsicals'. Furthermore, the presence of a secretary in the Commons would help to alleviate some of the recent difficulties of controlling the House. Bromley felt very strongly that it was Hanmer's inclusion in the ministry that was most needed, and tried to persuade Hanmer to accept the secretaryship instead, but without success. Thus Bromley was sworn in on 17 Aug., and shortly afterwards left for Baginton 'to settle his private affairs', returning early in September. He was gratified to see that the new House would contain 'a vast majority of gentlemen of the same principles as in the last'. In view of the administration's indecision over policy the ministers delayed the opening of Parliament until the new year. The Queen's near-fatal illness during December renewed the struggle between Oxford, himself in ill-health and unable to see the Queen, and Bolingbroke. Early in the new year, Bromley's name was being linked with Bolingbroke and Sir William Wyndham, 3rd Bt.*, in projections for a possible new administration, and not surprisingly, despite Bromley's official links with Hanover as secretary of state for the 'northern department', the elector's envoy Schütz was left wondering about Bromley's true commitment to the Hanoverian succession. According to his own account, Schütz got an acquaintance to ask Hanmer 'to sound' Bromley about his 'intentions':

> He [Hanmer] did so; and Bromley protested to him that he had it as much in his heart as he was against the Pretender. He went still further and discovered his suspicions against some of the ministry; but Bromley affirmed he was not just to them; at least, he assured them, that he did not observe any such thing in their words or actions. This, together with his sending his son to Hanover, may be a reason for believing what he says, at least with regard to himself.

On the eve of the opening of Parliament Bromley appeared to be associated with Oxford's 'safe' if unfriendly adherence to Hanover. One report in mid-February had him supporting Oxford's view that an invitation to the electoral prince to take his seat in the Lords 'would be liable to a thousand inconveniencies'. However, Kreienberg was informed soon after that not only had the Queen authorized an invitation but that Bromley would propose it in the Commons and deliver the Queen's message in person at Hanover. But at a pre-sessional meeting of Tory MPs to discuss the content of the Address, at which Hanmer proposed the inclusion of a request to invite either the Electress Sophia or the electoral prince to England, Bromley dismissed the suggestion in 'plain terms', leading Hanmer to complain that he had been 'duped'.[35]

On the 16th, Bromley spoke handsomely in favour of Hanmer's nomination to the Chair. The occasion was marred, however, when Whig MPs accused Bromley of partiality, though he showed statesmanlike restraint in calming the Tory hotheads who leaped to his defence. (Not that all critics of Bromley's Speakership were Whigs: the Jacobite MP George Lockhart claimed in his memoirs that Bromley had regularly obstructed Scottish business and showed 'an unwillingness' in allowing Scots Members to speak.) When proceedings began properly on 2 Mar. Bromley obtained his usual place on the Address committee. The same month he supported the Court in the question of expelling Richard Steele*. As the conflict between Oxford and Bolingbroke continued during the spring, Bromley avoided taking sides. Amid rumours of Oxford's intention to resign, Schütz described his conduct as 'neuter'. By mid-March, according to another account, Oxford no longer consulted him. Bromley's prime concern in the midst of these ministerial feuds was to ensure that the ministry retained sufficient backing in the Commons. On his initiative Oxford, Bolingbroke, Speaker Hanmer and Lord Chancellor Harcourt (Simon I*) conferred on 4 Apr. with some 30 leading Tory MPs, when it was agreed 'that we should exert ourselves and not let a majority in Parliament slip through our hands, and that we should meet twice a week for a mutual confidence'. However, Bromley's efforts to maintain Tory unity had only limited success. On 15 Apr. the House in a committee on the state of the nation debated the Whig motion that the Hanoverian succession was 'in danger' under the present government. Bromley had the unenviable task of defending the ministry's recent record, and in particular of explaining the diplomatic problems entailed in forcing the Pretender's removal from Lorraine. He assured the House that 'our whole kingdom is an army against him'. Although the motion was defeated, over 50 Hanoverian Tory followers voted with the Whigs. Bromley convened another meeting on the evening of 21 Apr., preparing the ground for the following day's debate on the proposition (set out in a joint address) that the peace was 'safe, honourable and advantageous'. In the debate on the 22nd he answered criticisms of the ministry's 'narrative' of the peace negotiations and justified the superiority of the terms recently signed over those negotiated by the Whig administration in 1709. In May an intimation by Bromley that the electoral prince would not be sent to England was said to have 'thrown the Pretender's faction into transports of joy, and the friends of Hanover, both Whigs and Tories, into the utmost despair'. Over the next few weeks he appears to have identified himself more openly with Bolingbroke. He no doubt sensed that the treasurer's remaining days in office were numbered and that the Tory party was no longer safe while Oxford remained at the head of the ministry. Even so, on Swift's testimony he was one of the last of Oxford's ministerial followers to desert him: sometime earlier in the year, Swift had noted that with the exception of the Duke of Ormond, Lord Trevor (Sir Thomas*) and Bromley, the lord treasurer had not one friend 'of any consequence' in the administration. On 12 May Bromley supported Sir William Wyndham's motion seeking leave to introduce the so-called 'schism' bill, it being Bolingbroke's intention to rally the Tories in a way that would ruin the treasurer's remaining credit with the Church party. He also opposed a Whig wrecking ploy to extend the bill to include Catholic seminaries, and was subsequently among those named to prepare the bill. At the third reading on 1 June, he declared that he was prepared to let the bill drop if another was introduced to disenfranchise the Dissenters. Further confirmation of Bromley's alignment with Bolingbroke appeared on 24 June in the debate on the proposal to increase the reward for apprehending the Pretender from £5,000 to the prodigious sum of £100,000. Observers noted that he spoke as one of 'Bolingbroke's party' against the resolution as distinct from 'the lord treasurer's friends' who supported it. As well as causing a large shortfall in the sum voted for the supply, Bromley argued, it was an insult to the Queen to tell her 'that she did not take care enough of her people'. In the final month of the Queen's life there was some uncertainty about Bromley's ministerial future. Bolingbroke, it seems, did not want him in a senior capacity in any ministry of which he was the head, and had plans to replace him as secretary of state with Wyndham. On the other hand, it was thought that if the Duke of Ormond and Lord Anglesey were brought into a Bolingbroke government, Bromley might also be induced to join. He remained aloof, however, from the crisis leading up to and following Oxford's fall at the end of July.[36]

On 1 Aug., after the Queen's demise, Bromley was among the Privy Councillors who signed the proclamation of her successor. When on the same day the Commons met briefly, he moved to adjourn until Speaker Hanmer arrived in London. Bromley was particularly embittered by the reports that he was 'one who endeavoured to make the administration difficult by insinuating to all people that the Protestant succession was in danger'. On the 5th he moved an Address to King George, the text of which he reported the next day. Bromley did not necessarily accept, at least at first, that the Queen's death and the Hanoverian succession had put paid to Tory prospects. In the days ahead, the Tories appeared 'most forward to do the King's business', Bromley and Wyndham taking the lead in proposing a generous civil list. 'God be thanked,' he wrote to James Grahme on the 10th, 'all things are quiet . . . and there is not the least appearance they will be otherwise.' Towards the end of August he appears to have featured in a fanciful scheme of Lord Oxford's for a 'moderate' coalition involving the Whigs. But as the summer weeks passed it become more obvious to Bromley that the future did not favour his party, and at the end of September he was relieved of his office. Having been complimented by the King on his 'fidelity' as secretary of state, he turned down the accompanying offer of a teller's place in the Exchequer which he regarded as a demotion, particularly as it meant subordination to the Whigs. At first he and Hanmer 'were prevailed on by the tempting ambition of appearing generals of their party'. But other senior Tories felt 'that he did well in refusing a mark of favour unequal to what he had deserved at a time when his friends for no better reason are laid aside with him'. One consideration which doubtless weighed with him was the certainty that he would 'lose his reputation' with his university constituents if he accepted a place associated more with profit than with public service. By January 1715 his interest in politics had reached a low point. From Baginton he wrote to Grahme: 'I have been so long here and the dissolution of the Parliament so long delayed that I began to hope it would have died a natural death, and no other called at present. A year's intermission of a session of Parliament would be very welcome to the country.'[37]

Bromley remained one of Oxford University's MPs until his death in 1732. A significant new area of his involvement with the university began in November 1714 when, under the will of his friend Dr John Radcliffe*, he became a member of the trust set up to administer the doctor's magnificent benefaction to the university. Until the early 1720s he maintained his position among the leaders of a Tory party which he saw dwindle to fewer than 130 by 1727. Thereafter, his importance gradually faded, though he continued to be vigilant and active in debates and proceedings. His reputed inclination towards the Jacobite cause after the Hanoverian succession must be questioned. He is alleged to have had a minor part in the Jacobite 'Swedish Plot' of 1716, but the assertion rests on spurious evidence. He considered Jacobite intrigue harmful to the unity of his party and in 1717 was reported by Lord Harcourt to have persuaded many

Tory MPs of the pointlessness of such subterfuge. Moreover, he was subsequently never among the Tory MPs whose names featured in correspondence with the Stuart court. He died 'unexpectedly' at his New Bond Street lodgings on 13 Feb. 1732. In his will he had requested burial at Baginton 'without any funeral pomp which I have never approved of, it not benefitting the dead and disturbing the living'. He was buried in his Speaker's robes. Having settled his 'real estate' on his eldest surviving son William[†] on his marriage, he left portions to his younger children amounting to £18,000, and spoke of the poor relationship which had existed for many years between himself and his wife.[38]

[1] *Procs. in Quarter Sessions* (Warwick County Recs. viii), p. xxiii; (ix), p. xxxvii; *Hearne Colls.* i. 144; *Vis. Warwicks.* (Harl. Soc. lxii), 11–12; Vivian, *Vis. Devon*, 201; *London Mar. Lic.* ed. Foster, 191; R. E. C. Waters, *Genealogical Memoirs of Chester Families*, 48–9; PCC 33 Bedford. [2] *Great Fire of Warwick 1694* (Dugdale Soc. xxxvi), 121. [3] Boyer, *Pol. State*, ii. 445. [4] E. G. W. Bill, *Q. Anne Churches*, p. xxiii; *Cal. Treas. Bks.* xxv. 321; Pittis, *Present Parl.* 347; I. Guest, *Dr John Radcliffe and his Trust*, 482. [5] R. East, *Portsmouth Recs.* 375. [6] *HMC Portland*, v. 651; Burnet, v. 228; Cunningham, *Hist. GB*, ii. 135; *Hearne Colls.* i. 232; *Wentworth Pprs.* 429; G. Holmes, *Pol. in Age of Anne*, 277. [7] Dugdale, *Warws.* i. 233; *VCH Warws.* vi. 23; Hearne, i. 140; *Procs. in Quarter Sessions* (Warwick County Recs. viii), pp. xxiii, 249; *CSP Dom.* 1686–7, p. 203; Wood, *Athenae*, iv. 664–5. [8] Bodl. Ballard 35, f. 48; Wood, *Life and Times*, iii. 380–1; [W. Bromley], *Remarks on the Grand Tour...* (1692), 140, 158, 219 and passim; A. L. Manning, *Lives of the Speakers*, 419–20; Nichols, *Lit. Hist.* iii. 242; *Luttrell Diary*, 314, 380, 381–2. [9] Cobbett, *Parlty. Hist.* v. 805, 829. [10] *Procs. in Quarter Sessions* (Warwick County Recs. ix), p. xxvi; *Great Fire of Warwick of 1694* (Dugdale Soc. xxxvi), pp. xxviii–xxix, 121. [11] Halifax, *Life*, 30; H. Horwitz, *Parl. and Pol. Wm. III*, 164, 166. [12] Add. 70018, ff. 119, 120, 125; 29578, f.579; Luttrell, *Brief Relation*, iv. 74; *Cal. Treas. Bks.* xv. 304–5; L. K. J. Glassey, *Appt. JPs*, 122. [13] Cobbett, v. 1134. [14] PCC 33 Bedford; *Huntington Lib. Q.* lii. 319, 322–3; Hearne, i. 193. [15] SRO, Hamilton mss GD/406/1/4657, Gawin Mason to Duke of Hamilton, 2 Jan. 1700[-1]; *HMC Portland*, iv. 15; *Hist. Oxf. Univ.* ed. Sutherland and Mitchell, 59. [16] Huntington Lib. Stowe mss 26(2), James Brydges* diary, 26 Apr. 1701; Ballard 38, f. 131; *Cocks Diary*, 160, 162; Add. 70044, f.186. [17] *Cocks Diary*, 179; Horwitz, 302; Lambeth Palace Lib. mss 2564, p. 407; Brydges diary, 4 Mar. 1702; Add. 36859, f. 3. [18] *Hist. Oxf. Univ.* 62; Boyer, *Anne Annals*, i. 77; Burnet, v. 49; H. Horwitz, *Revolution Politicks*, 186; Ballard 38, f. 137; 21, f. 29; Luttrell, v. 229, 234; *Nicolson Diaries*, ed. Jones and Holmes, 137, 146; Add. 42176, f. 11; *Atterbury Epistolary Corresp.* iv. 381. [19] *HMC Portland*, iv. 67; Bath mss at Longleat House, Portland music. pprs., ff. 209–10, Godolphin to Harley, 9 Nov. [1703]; Luttrell, v. 362; *Atterbury Epistolary Corresp.* iii. 140; G. Holmes and W. A. Speck, *Div. Soc.* 162; 31/3/191, f. 16; G. V. Bennett, *Tory Crisis 1688–1730*, 71. [20] Univ. Kansas Spencer Research Lib. Methuen–Simpson corresp. C163, John Methuen* to Sir William Simpson, 28 Mar. 1704; Ballard 38, ff. 140, 153–4. [21] Methuen–Simpson corresp. Methuen to Simpson, 3, 10, 24 Oct. 1704; BL, Trumbull Alphab. mss 50, Thomas Bateman to Sir William Trumbull*, 23 May 1704; Bagot mss at Levens Hall, John Ward to James Grahme, 3 Oct. 1704, 12 Apr. 1705; Camb. Univ. Lib., Cholmondeley (Houghton) mss 358, 359, Spencer Compton* to Robert Walpole II, 12 Oct. 1704; Folger Shakespeare Lib. Newdigate newsletter 2 Nov. 1704; *Marlborough–Godolphin Corresp.* 275; Add. 17677 ZZ, f. 497; *Hist. Oxf. Univ.* 74, 75; Cobbett, vi. 359, 386, 402; Speck thesis, 134; *Nicolson Diaries*, 253; Luttrell, v. 529, 530; Strathmore mss at Glamis Castle, box 72, bdle. 3, newsletter 14 Apr. 1705. [22] *Hist. Oxf. Univ.* 76; Nottingham Univ. Lib. Portland (Bentinck) mss PwA 410, [–] to Portland, 27 July 1705; *Marlborough–Godolphin Corresp.* 481, 502; Bagot mss, Ld. Thanet to Grahme, 11 Sept. [1705]; Anglesey mss at Plas Newydd, box 16c, John Turton to [Ld. Paget], 10 Oct. 1705; Methuen–Simpson corresp., Methuen to Simpson, 16 Oct. 1705; Add. 61164, f. 169; Burnet, v. 228–9; Manning, *Speakers*, 420; Hearne, i. 69; Trumbull Alphab. mss 53, John Bridges to Trumbull, 26 Oct. 1705. [23] Horwitz, *Revolution Politicks*, 268–9; Add. 61474, ff. 131–2; Burnet, v. 230; *Duchess of Marlborough Corresp.* ii. 221; *Cam. Misc.* xxiii. 31, 39, 41, 49–50, 61, 70, 72; Cobbett, vi. 473, 508; Methuen–Simpson corresp. Methuen to Simpson, 11 Dec. 1705; SRO, Mar and Kellie mss GD 124/15/259/4, William Cleland to James Erskine, 18 Dec. 1705. [24] *HMC Bath*, i. 121; Burnet, v. 340; H. T. Dickinson, *Bolingbroke*, 53; Luttrell, v. 121; Dugdale, *Warws.* i. 233; *Nicolson Diaries*, 393; Chandler, iv. 57; *Hearne Colls.* i. 340, ii. 1. [25] Bagot mss, Bromley to Grahme, 11 Oct. 1707; Cunningham, *Hist. GB*, ii. 135; Roxburghe mss at Floors Castle, bdle. 739, William Bennet* to [Countess of Roxburghe], 16 Dec. 1707; P. W. J. Riley, *Eng. Ministers and Scotland*, 91; *Vernon–Shrewsbury Letters*, iii. 298, 320, 352; *Nicolson Diaries*, 461. [26] Speck thesis, 239; Add. 70214, Harley to Bromley [draft], 20 Aug. 1708, Bromley to Harley, 12 Oct. 1708; 70419, Harley to Stratford, 10 Oct. 1708; *HMC Portland*, iv. 504–5; Leics. RO, Finch mss box 6, bdle. 23, Bromley to Nottingham, 2, 23 Oct., 11 Nov. 1708, Nottingham to Bromley, 15 Nov. 1708; Horwitz, *Revolution Politicks*, 215; *HMC Bath*, i. 192–3, 194. [27] Cobbett, vi. 761; Trumbull Misc. mss 53, James Johnston* to Trumbull, 24 Dec. 1708, 4 [Feb.], 18 Mar. 1708–9; *Addison Letters*, 123–4; Stowe mss 57(3), p. 139, Brydges to Marlborough, 2 Jan. 1708–9; *Wentworth Pprs.* 69; Add. 33225, f. 13; 70214, Bromley to Harley, 5 Jan. 1708[-9]; *Marlborough–Godolphin Corresp.* 1185, 1201–2; Finch mss, box 6, bdle. 23, Bromley to Nottingham, 7, 31 Dec. 1708, Nottingham to Bromley [draft], 20 Dec. 1708; W. R. Ward, *Georgian Oxf.*, 33; Ballard 7, f.31; *HMC Portland*, iv. 521. [28] *Hist. Oxf. Univ.* 83; G. Holmes, *Trial of Sacheverell*, 57, 90, 111–12; Trumbull Alphab. mss 53, Ralph Bridges to Trumbull, 14 Dec. 1709; 54, same to same, 9, 13 Jan., 28 Mar. 1710; *Wentworth Pprs.* 99, 110; *HMC Portland*, iv. 531; Boyer, *Anne Annals*, viii. 256; Stowe mss 58(5), Robert Walpole II to Brydges, 15 Feb. 1709–10; Wodrow, *Analecta*, i. 259–60. [29] Warws. RO, Mordaunt mss C1368/iii/10, Bromley to Sir John Mordaunt, 5th Bt.*, 12 June 1710; Ballard 38, ff.147, 150–1; *Div. Soc.* 175–6; Add. 70421, newsletter 11 July 1710; Luttrell, v. 604; *Wentworth Pprs.* 128; Bagot mss, Bromley to Grahme, 13 Aug., 1 Sept. 1710; *Atterbury Epistolary Corresp.* i. 26. [30] Luttrell, v. 633, 659; Add. 38501, f. 114; 31143, f. 571; Horwitz, *Revolution Politicks*, 223; Stowe mss 57(4), p. 178, Brydges to [–], 12 Oct. 1710; Trumbull Alphab. mss 54, Ralph Bridges to Trumbull, 13 Nov. 1710; SRO, Montrose mss GD 220/5/807/2, Mungo Graham* to Duke of Montrose, 25 Nov. 1710; Boyer, *Pol. State*, i. 29; *Defoe Letters*, 129. [31] Add. 70281, Bromley to Harley, 14 Nov. 1710; *HMC Portland*, iv. 696, v. 116; Bennett, 133; Trumbull Alphab. mss 54, Ralph Bridges to Trumbull, 10 Mar. 1710–11. [32] Finch mss box 6, bdle. 24, John Ward [III] to Nottingham, 3 Apr. 1711; Trumbull Alphab. mss 54, Ralph Bridges to Trumbull, 9 May 1711. [33] Add. 70214, Bromley to Harley, [June], 18 Aug., 3 Dec. 1711, 30 July 1712; 70395, Stratford to Edward Harley*, 20 July 1712; *HMC Portland*, iv. 116, 133, 139, 167–8, vii. 40, 50; Finch mss, box 6, bdle. 24, Bromley to Nottingham, 27 Aug. 1711; Cobbett, vi. 1070; Mordaunt mss C1368/iii/15, Bromley to Mordaunt, 7 June 1712. [34] *HMC Portland*, v. 267; *Lockhart Pprs.* i. 426–7; Bodl., Rawl. lett. 92, f. 563. [35] *Hanmer Corresp.* 145–6, 150; *HMC Portland*, v. 321, 660–1; Boyer, *Pol. State*, vi. 123; *Bolingbroke Corresp.* iv. 239; Bagot mss, Bromley to Grahme, 8 Sept. 1713; Cobbett, vi. 1238; *Orig. Pprs.* ed. Macpherson, ii. 552, 564, 565, 577. [36] Cobbett, vi. 1254, 1346, 1350, 1358; Kreienberg despatch 19 Feb. 1714; Lockhart, i. 544–5; *Div. Soc.* 76, 112; Add. 47087, ff. 61–62; 47027, f. 133; NLS, Advocates'

mss, Wodrow pprs. letters Quarto 8, ff. 60, 118, 139; *Bull. IHR*, xxxiv. 213; Douglas diary (Hist. of Parl. trans.), 15, 22 Apr. 1714; Trumbull Alphab. mss 54, Ralph Bridges to Trumbull, 23 Apr., 14 May 1714; 52, Thomas Bateman to same, 21 Apr. 1714; *Swift Works* ed. Davis, vii. 156; *Orig. Pprs.* ii. 631, 634; *Wentworth Pprs.* 392; K. Feiling, *Tory Party*, 473. [37] Boyer, *Pol. State*, viii. 114; Coxe, *Walpole*, ii. 58; *HMC Portland*, vii. 198, v. 484; Add. 22221, f. 127; 47027, ff. 171–9; Bagot mss, Bromley to Grahme, 10 Aug. 1714, 26 Jan. 1714[–15]; Feiling, 478; Leics. RO, Braye mss 2890, Sir George Beaumont, 4th Bt.*, to Sir Thomas Cave, 3rd Bt.*, Oct. 1714; Ballard 31, f. 129. [38] L. Colley, *In Defiance of Oligarchy*, 189; *HMC Popham*, 289; PCC 33 Bedford; *ex inf.* Dr Kenneth Milne.

A. A. H.

BROMLEY, William III (1685–1756), of Upton-on-Severn, Worcs.

TEWKESBURY 1710–1713

b. 28 Apr. 1685, o. s. of Henry Bromley by Elizabeth, da. and h. of John Lench of Doverdale, Worcs. *educ.* Oriel, Oxf. 1701; M. Temple 1703, called 1710. *m.* (1) 2 May 1720, Mary (*d.* 1737[–?8]), da. and coh. of Joseph Moore, banker, of London, *s.p.*; (2) c.1733, Judith (*d.* 1770), da. of one Hanbury, 1da. *suc.* fa. 1686.[1]

Freeman, Worcester 1729; recorder, Tewkesbury 1735–*d.*[2]

The Bromleys of Upton were distant relatives of the Bromleys of Holt, both families being descended from Sir Henry Bromley (*d.* 1615), the eldest son of Thomas Bromley, the Elizabethan lord chancellor. Sir Henry purchased Upton and settled it on his younger son, by which route it passed to this Member. Although his father's will of January 1686 made no mention of him, it is probable that Bromley was brought up by his mother, who had been given full power to manage the family estates. He embarked upon a successful legal career, but seems to have been interested in politics almost from the time he came of age. In August 1707 he was undoubtedly the 'Mr Bromley of Upton' who, along with Thomas Vernon†, Richard Dowdeswell* and Anthony Lechmere* (all reputed friends of William Bromley I*), refused to engage for Samuel Pytts* in the contest for the vacant county seat in Worcestershire. This would place him among the influential group of moderate Whigs in the county who had formed the basis of William Bromley I's electoral interest. His own parliamentary ambitions centred on Tewkesbury, five and a half miles from Upton. In September 1710 he informed William Lygon (another friend of William Bromley I) that he 'had for some time a design of offering myself a candidate at this town and have made a private interest'. By early October he was predicting 'as great a struggle as has been known', as the two outgoing Members, Richard Dowdeswell and Henry Ireton, were standing against him with the support of the corporation. Dyer depicted Bromley's victory as the result of the Tory commonalty throwing off the Whig yoke. Thus Bromley was sent off to London in November by a crowd brandishing Dr Sacheverell's portrait. Henry Brydges may have been closer to the mark when he supplied his brother James* with the information that Bromley 'was set up by the Tories in opposition to Mr Ireton', but had thrown out the other Whig, Dowdeswell.[3]

Unfortunately, the evidence of Bromley's parliamentary activities does little to clarify his political views. He was classed as a Tory on the 'Hanover list' of 1710, and as a 'worthy patriot' who during the 1710–11 session detected the mismanagements of the previous administration. However, he voted against an amendment to the South Sea bill on 25 May 1711 in company with a group of committed Whigs, including two with Worcestershire connexions, Nicholas Lechmere* and John Rudge*. The tenor of his remarks on politics in letters to Lygon suggests a disposition to criticize the previous Whig ministry, as when he described the Commons' 'humble representation' to the Queen on 31 May 1711 as a request 'never to make use of any of those concerned in the late ministry'. In his letter of this date, Bromley wrote at length on his desire to marry Lygon's daughter. Somewhat defensively he alluded to a fear that his prospective father-in-law had 'censured my conduct and management and might suspect I might not be duly careful for the future'. In his own defence he declared: 'I have seen a good deal of the world by going about in it and have partaken of its pleasures as far as has been consistent with the rules of prudence or virtue.' On a more practical level he estimated his estate at about £450 p.a. in rents and about £150 'out in copyholds upon lives'. Nothing came of the proposal. In the 1713 session he may have been the 'Mr Bromley' who acted as a teller on 4 May in favour of an early second reading for the bill suspending for two months the duties on French wines. On 18 June he voted against the French commerce bill, being classed as a Whig at the same time. However, no Member for Gloucestershire dared to vote for the bill. He did not contest the seat again. Neither his admission to the freedom of Worcester nor his election as recorder of Tewkesbury can be taken as unequivocal proof of his political position, as both boroughs were then split between representatives of the government and opposition. He died on 7 Feb. 1756, being succeeded by his only daughter, the wife of John Martin of Overbury, possibly a relative of the John Martin who sat for Tewkesbury during George II's reign.[4]

[1] Nash, *Worcs.* ii. 445; *Vis. Worcs.* ed. Metcalfe, 25–26; IGI, London. [2] W. R. Williams, *Parl. Hist. Glos.* 245. [3] *Vis. Worcs.* 25–26; PCC 39 Lloyd; Surr. RO (Kingston), Somers mss 371/14/L29, William Walsh* to Ld. Somers (Sir John*), 18 Aug. 1707; Hereford and Worcester RO (Worcester), Cal. Wm. Lygon Letters, 345, 355, Bromley to Lygon, 8 Sept., 5 Oct. 1710; Add. 70421, newsletters, 14 Oct., 23 Nov. 1703; G. Holmes, *Trial of Sacheverell*, 253–4; Huntington Lib. Stowe mss 58(7), p. 4. [4] *Hist. Jnl.* iv. 202; Cal. Wm. Lygon Letters, 428, Bromley to Lygon, 31 May 1711; Williams, 245; PCC 60 Glazier; J. Bennett, *Hist. Tewkesbury*, 256.

S. N. H.

BROTHERTON, Thomas (c.1656–1702), of Chancery Lane, Mdx. and the Hey, Newton, Lancs.

LIVERPOOL   4 Dec. 1694–11 Jan. 1695
NEWTON   1695–1701 (Nov.)

b. c.1656, 2nd s. of John Brotherton (Bretherton) of the Hey and the Inner Temple by Margaret, da. of Thomas Blackburn of Orford, Lancs. *educ.* G. Inn 1676, called 1683; Jesus, Camb. 1677. *m.* lic. 5 June 1693, Margaret, da. and coh. of Thomas Gunter of Aldbourne, Wilts., 3s. 3da. *suc.* bro. John 1679.[1]

Brotherton's family had been settled at the Hey, in the barony of Newton, Lancashire, since at least 1573, and as a younger son Brotherton was put to the law and became a practising barrister. In 1685 he stood at Newton against Peter Legh† of Lyme, then 15 years old, whose family had the chief interest in the borough, but was comprehensively defeated, and his petition was one of the many not heard by the Parliament. When the sitting Member for Newton, Francis Cholmondeley†, refused to take the oaths to William and Mary in 1690 rumours spread in Newton that Brotherton would contest the seat again, and, though the Convention was dissolved before a writ could be issued, Brotherton made a strong bid for the seat at the general election of 1690. Supported by prominent Whigs such as Lord Brandon (Charles Gerard*), Roger Kirkby* and Thomas Norris*, Brotherton fought a vigorous but ultimately unsuccessful campaign, and followed this with an equally fruitless petition.[2]

When Brotherton finally entered Parliament his success was due to the support of a very different interest. Since the beginning of 1694 Brotherton had been gathering support at Liverpool, and in March the basis of this interest became apparent when a Lancashire cleric wrote to Clitheroe's Tory MP Roger Kenyon that 'Mr Brotherton is my friend and an honest churchman, to whom I entreat you to forwardly reconcile yourself'. Brotherton had transferred his allegiance to the Lancashire Tories, a switch emphasized in October 1694 when he acted as defence counsel at the trial of those accused in the Lancashire Plot. Wholeheartedly supported by the Lancashire Tory hierarchy at the Liverpool by-election of December 1694, Brotherton was returned when the mayor claimed that his opponent Jasper Maudit* was ineligible to stand due to his position as borough coroner. Brotherton was consequently elected, but Maudit was in no mood to accept this result and pressed his petition hard, a local Tory commenting, 'God grant Mr Brotherton may continue the sitting Member, for if it be judged a void election, we Churchmen shall have but a melancholy prospect at Liverpool'. Brotherton was unseated on 11 Jan. 1695, but he had established his Tory credentials following his flirtation with Lancashire's Whig interest, and he remained true to this creed for the remainder of his life.[3]

In October 1695 Brotherton wrote to Peter Legh asking him to 'pass by all our former misunderstandings' and to return him for Newton. Grateful for Brotherton's role in the acquittal of the accused Jacobites a year earlier as well as fearful of any renewed challenge from Brotherton, Legh agreed to this request. Brotherton assured Legh that he would 'with zeal preserve the established Church of England, with sincerity serve my borough and country, and with integrity promote your interest', and he fulfilled these promises throughout his active parliamentary career. Brotherton was a frequent nominee to significant committees, and teller upon a wide range of subjects. The first sign of his extensive legislative involvement came on 4 Dec. when his experience of the prolonged process of selecting the jury at the Jacobite trials the previous year seems to have led to his being the only Member appointed to draft a bill to supply the defects of an act of Edward I concerning the challenging of juries, a measure he subsequently presented on 5 Feb. 1696. His legal experience seems likely to account for his appointment, on 5 Dec. 1695, to draft a bill to regulate proceedings in the court of Equity. On 7 Jan. 1696 he told in favour of excusing Henry Priestman for being absent at the call of the House, and this month also saw him report from the committee which investigated the petition of the shipwrights of the naval dockyards. His opposition to the ministry was made clear in early 1696. He was forecast as likely to oppose the government in the divisions of 31 Jan. on the proposed council of trade, and Peter Shakerley* reported that on this date Brotherton voted against the imposition of an abjuration oath on members of the proposed council. On 4 Feb. he spoke in favour of Ambrose

Pudsay* in the debate on the Clitheroe election petition. On 19 Mar. he was nominated to the committee on expiring laws. He subsequently reported from this committee, and on 13 Apr. carried the resulting bill to the Lords. On 23 Mar. he told for engrossing a bill to prevent the escape of debtors, and to ensure the better security and relief of creditors. The same month saw him dismissed from the Lancashire bench for his initial refusal to take the Association, and his opposition to the ministry was confirmed in March when he voted against fixing the price of guineas at 22s. His final significant acts of the session were to report from the committee considering the bill confirming the grant of Bedford Level to the Earl of Torrington (Arthur Herbert†), and to tell in favour of this measure.[4]

Given his defence of accused Jacobites in Lancashire in 1694 it comes as no surprise that in the early weeks of the 1696-7 session Brotherton was active in the debates on the attainder of Sir John Fenwick†. At the opening of the proceedings on 13 Nov. he claimed that 'the Mace ought to be upon the table, because the bill is to be read', and then went on:

> I take the question to be now, whether the King's counsel should give evidence of any other matter than what is alleged in the bill. As to that I must observe to you that this bill does not set forth any particular charge against him; it is only the recital of an indictment, and it does not say the particular time and place where the fact was done . . . I am of opinion they ought to give evidence of nothing but what is in the bill.

Three days later Brotherton again protested the irregularity of the whole procedure:

> it has been objected there ought to be two witnesses by the late statute [Treasons Act] . . . But I must put you in mind, that it was so by the Statute of Edward VI and so was the common law before and my Lord Coke says there must be two witnesses and they brought face to face.

Later the same day he told against a motion that the prosecution counsel be allowed to examine witnesses upon the evidence of Cooke's trial. He returned to his point on witnesses on 17 Nov., arguing that 'if there be but one witness in case of treason, he shall be tried before the constable and marshal', at which point Brotherton was 'interrupted by the great noise the House made upon the novelty of the argument', and was unable to finish. He told on 24 Nov. for an amendment to the bill for bringing in plate to be coined at the Mint, and the following day voted against Fenwick's attainder. His concern for due process in cases of alleged treason was again evident when he chaired a committee of inquiry into the complaint made by the wife of a Conrad Griebe. Griebe had been arrested under a warrant from Sir William Trumbull* for treasonable practices, and, even though a habeas corpus had been granted, deported to the Netherlands. Trumbull's unwillingness to produce the original warrant led Brotherton, when reporting to the House on 8 Dec., to claim that the committee had been unable to examine the matter fully. Though the Commons ordered Trumbull to release the document to the committee, the issue was killed by a written statement from the King read to the Commons, informing the House that King William had ordered Griebe's removal from the country as he posed a danger to national security. During December Brotherton also managed through the House the bill for the relief of creditors. Brotherton told on six further occasions during this session: in favour of adding a clause to the land tax bill to make receivers responsible for paying for the billeting of soldiers in their locality (21 Jan.); for adjourning all committees (22 Jan.); on the Tory side in a division on the Tavistock election case (4 Feb.); against a motion to proceed immediately to elect a commissioner of accounts to replace Lord William Powlett* (13 Feb.); for an amendment to the cider duty bill (3 Mar.); and against passing a bill to void the annulment of the marriage of an infant female (7 Apr.). He also took an interest in a number of bills. In January, for example, he was consulted, at the behest of Liverpool corporation, on proposals for the navigation of the Irwell, and later in the month, on the 28th, opposed the second reading of Sir Ralph Assheton, 2nd Bt.'s* estate bill. During March he guided through the House a bill to continue the act for preventing delays at quarter sessions, taking steps to inform the Lancashire clerk of the peace, Roger Kenyon, of this measure. Brotherton's appetite for parliamentary business is emphasized by the fact that in addition he managed three estate bills through the Commons during this session.[5]

This appetite did not diminish in the 1697-8 session, even though he was granted ten days' leave of absence on 23 Dec. 'to bury a relation'. When, on 6 Jan. 1698, a clause was proposed to the bill to perpetuate the imprisonment of persons accused in the Assassination Plot, allowing the detention of individuals upon the evidence of one witness, it was reported that 'some opposition was made', and Brotherton predictably joined the protests. One newsletter claimed that

> when the question was put, whether the bill should pass, there were some noes and Mr Brotherton demanded a division, but the number was so small that everybody went out with the yeas, except Mr Brotherton, Sir

George Hungerford and Sir Edward Williams, who were left alone in the House, for which they were not a little laughed at.

The Journals record that Brotherton merely told against the clause, an opposition gaining only two votes. On 3 Feb. he was appointed to draft a bill to repeal the Elizabethan statute preventing the overproduction of malt, subsequently guiding the bill through the Commons, and on 9 Mar. told for the engrossing of a bill to preserve salmon in English rivers. In April he told on five occasions: against imposing further duties on coal (7th); in favour of adjourning the hearing of the report on counterfeiting the coin (15th); for instructing the committee of supply to take off all duties on inland coal transported overland (21st); against passing the bill to prevent counterfeiting the coin (27th); and against forcing bachelors and widowers to give their names and addresses in order to facilitate the collection of taxes imposed on them (28th). During the same month he also guided a naturalization bill through the Commons. Brotherton told a further five times in June: for freeing the looms of lustring weavers from being distrained for unpaid rent (1st); for an amendment to the tonnage and poundage (civil list) bill, to preserve the rights of the bankers to their debt (9th); to reject a motion to vest in Greenwich Hospital estates given to 'superstitious' uses (17th); against a clause specifying the interest rate at which the East India Company could undertake further borrowing (22nd); and against engrossing the bill to set up a new East India Company (23rd). The extent of his parliamentary activity in this session is indicated by the fact that he had also guided three estates bills through the House and chaired the committee upon another such measure.[6]

Returned for Newton again in 1698, Brotherton was, around September, classed as a member of the Country party in a comparison of the old and new Commons, and also forecast as a likely opponent of the standing army. On 18 Feb. 1699 he told in favour of amending the report of the supply committee in order to reduce the naval establishment from 15,000 to 12,000. He told on five occasions in March: in favour of the right of election at Ludlow being in 'sons and son-in-laws of freemen' (1st); against a call of the House (6th); in favour of giving a second reading to the East India Company bill (9th); against issuing more Exchequer bills (23rd); and for passing the Westminster corn market bill (24th). In March and April Brotherton had guided through the House a bill for the better apprehension of burglars, and on 4 May he told for a motion to bring in a bill to prevent abuses in the King's bench and the Fleet prisons. Brotherton was again active in respect of estate bills in this session, chairing the committees of two and guiding another two through the Commons.[7]

In the 1699–1700 session Brotherton's parliamentary activity continued apace. He told on the Tory side when the Ludlow election petition was heard on 18 Dec., before telling in favour of a call of the House on 22 Dec. On 8 Jan. 1700 he again acted as teller, in favour of excusing Ralph Freman II for being absent from a call of the House, and on 23 Jan. told in favour of leave being granted for a bill to prolong the act prohibiting the export of grain. He told on 2 Feb. in favour of the second reading of this bill. He was appointed on 13 Feb. to the committee upon the bill to improve the passage between Chancery Lane and Lincoln's Inn Fields, subsequently managing this measure through the Commons in March, and the same day spoke against the legality of grants made by the monarch to ministers of the crown during the war. On 26 Feb. he told against a motion that the *Dolphin* should trade as a free ship, and on 4 Mar. in favour of a motion that a committee of the whole examine the bill for the public resumption of all grants made since William's accession. March saw Brotherton guide through the House an estate bill and a bill to enable j.p.s to repair their county gaols. He was active in the debates over the forfeited land grants in March and April, telling in three divisions relating to this matter. Brotherton also told in favour of bringing up the petition of Richard Burdett (4 Apr.); for postponing reports from the committee of privileges and elections (5 Apr.); and against adjourning the House (10 Apr.).

In August 1700 Brotherton was restored to the Lancashire bench, and his Toryism and pretensions were satirized at the end of the year in a libel headed 'the titles of several Acts agreed in the Cabal', which included 'an Act to make Lord Romney and Lord Jersey two able ministers of state to be moved by Mr Brotherton'. After he had been returned for Newton in January 1701, Brotherton's attachment to the reconstructed ministry is suggested by his inclusion in February upon a list of likely supporters of the Court in agreeing with the supply committee's resolution to continue the 'Great Mortgage'. Reports then began to circulate of Brotherton's death, or that at the very least he was dying of a 'violent fever'. Applications to Peter Legh for Brotherton's seat proved, however, to be premature, and after his recovery Brotherton told, on 15 Apr., against adjourning the report of the East Retford election. His hostility to the recently removed Whig ministers was evident the same day when he was appointed to draw up the impeachment of Lord Halifax (Charles Montagu*). During May he managed through the Commons bills on the regulation of new mints, and for supplying the deficiency of funds for the path between Chancery Lane and Lincoln's Inn Fields. He told on four occasions in June: for applying to public uses money accruing from defalcations by the paymasters of the Navy (3rd); against making an appointment to the land tax commission for Suffolk (5th); for an amendment to a supply bill (16th); and in favour of taking the report of the committee on insolvent debtors (17th). In the same month he also managed through the Commons the estate bill of Sir Thomas Stanley, 4th Bt.* Included on the 'black list' of those who had opposed preparations for the war with France in the previous session, Brotherton was dropped from Newton in December 1701 to make way for Peter Legh's brother Thomas II*, with the prospect of being returned for the borough at a later election. Before he could press his claims for his return at Newton, however, he died on 11 Jan. 1702, aged 45.[8]

[1] *VCH Lancs.* iv. 134–5; *Vis. Lancs.* (Chetham Soc. ser. 1, lxxxiv), 56; *Mar. Lic. Vicar-Gen.* (Harl. Soc. xxxi), 259; *Moore Rental* (Chetham Soc. ser. 1, xii), 145. [2] John Rylands Univ. Lib. Manchester, Legh of Lyme mss corresp. Francis Cholmondeley to Peter Legh, 11 Jan. 1690[–90], Thomas Legh† to same, 6 Sept. 1690, George Cholmondeley* to Visct. Cholmondeley, c.1690; Lancs. RO, Kenyon mss DDKe 9/63/7, Thomas Legh† to Roger Kenyon, 2 Mar. 1689–90. [3] *HMC Kenyon*, 284, 320–1; Kenyon mss DDKe 9/67/37, Thomas Marsden to Kenyon, 27 Mar. 1693[–4]; DDKe 9/68/9, Richard Richmond to same, 4 Jan. 1694[–5]; *CSP Dom.* 1694–5, p. 325; Egerton 920, ff. 79–80; *Portledge Pprs.* 192. [4] Legh of Lyme mss corresp. Brotherton to Peter Legh, 10 Oct. [1695], 31 Oct. 1695, same to Edward Allanson, 10 Oct. 1695; *HMC Kenyon*, 398–401; L. K. J. Glassey, *Appt. JPs*, 282. [5] Cobbett, *Parlty. Hist.* v. 1013, 1039, 1101–2; Northants. RO, Montagu (Boughton) mss 46/32, Vernon to Shrewsbury, 3 Dec. 1696; *Norris Pprs.* (Chetham Soc. ser. 1, ix), 37–39; Kenyon mss, DDKe/HMC/1031A, Richard Wroe to Kenyon, 28 Jan. 1696–7; 1039, Peter Shakerley* to same, 6 Mar. 1696[-7]. [6] *CSP Dom.* 1698, p. 19; *Cam. Misc.* xx. 50. [7] *Cam. Misc.* 74, 78. [8] Nottingham Univ. Lib. Portland (Bentinck) mss PwA 2714, 'Titles of several public acts agreed to in the cabal', 7 Dec. [1700]; BL, Lothian mss, bdle. 95, Ld. Stanhope to Thomas Coke*, 24 Feb. 1700[-1], Coke to Stanhope, 26, 27 Feb. 1700[-1]; *HMC Cowper*, ii. 420–1; Add. 70020, f. 120.

E. C./R. D. H.

BROWNE, Thomas (1640–1713), of Arlesey, Beds.

BEDFORDSHIRE 1690–1695

bap. 3 Dec. 1640, 5th but 1st surv. s. of (Sir) Samuel Browne† of Arlesey, serjeant-at-law and j.c.p., by Elizabeth, da. of John Meade of Nortofts, Finchingfield, Essex. *educ.* Wratting, Suff.; St. John's, Camb. 1659; L. Inn 1660, called 1667. *m.* (1) 23 Feb. 1669, Cicely (*d.* 1675), da. of Sir William Poley† of Boxted, Suff. and sis. of Sir John Poley†, 2s. *d.v.p.* 2da.; (2) lic. 9 Oct. 1682, Mary (*d.* 1704), da. of Sir John Bernard, 2nd Bt.†, of Brampton Park, Hunts., 2s. 5da. (1 *d.v.p.*). *suc.* fa. 1668.[1] ?Gent. privy chamber 1670.[2]

Browne's father, a distinguished lawyer and a cousin of Chief Justice Oliver St. John†, had been a vigorous proponent of the Parliamentarian cause during the Civil War and had been appointed chief baron of the Exchequer in 1648. After Pride's Purge, however, he refused to act, and held no office under the Commonwealth and Protectorate, returning to the bench at the Restoration. Formerly a Presbyterian elder, he conformed after 1660 but assisted the Calvinist vicar of his parish of Arlesey to remain in his living despite the Act of Uniformity. His son continued this patronage and may have been a 'Whig collaborator' under James II, if his appointment to the county lieutenancy in February 1688 is anything to go by.[3]

Returned to the 1690 Parliament with Hon. Edward Russell*, Browne was classed as a Whig in Lord Carmarthen's (Sir Thomas Osborne†) analysis of the new House. Robert Harley's* list of April 1691 classed him as a supporter of the Country opposition but by the spring of 1693, according to Samuel Grascome, he had followed other Whigs in crossing over to the Court. He was given leave of absence on 23 Jan. 1694 for two weeks. Apart from this, little is known of his parliamentary career. In 1695, probably standing in partnership with Russell, he was defeated for the second county seat by William Duncombe*. He did not stand again.

Browne was buried at Arlesey on 27 June 1713. The legacies to younger children in his will, amounting to some £6,000, appear to show that he had not significantly depleted the fortune left him by his father. Among those appointed trustees to his heir was the Whig John Pedley*.[4]

[1] *Beds. Hist. Rec. Soc.* ii. 140–8; F. A. Blaydes, *Genealogia Bedfordiensis*, 6–7. [2] N. Carlisle, *Gent. Privy Chamber*, 187. [3] A. G. Matthews, *Calamy Revised*, 16; *CSP Dom.* 1687–9, p. 141. [4] *Beds. Hist. Rec. Soc.* 148–9.

D. W. H.

BROWNE (aft. **DUNCOMBE**), **Thomas** *see* **DUNCOMBE**

BROWNLOW, Sir John, 3rd Bt. (1659–97), of Hammersmith; Pall Mall, London, and Belton, Lincs.[1]

GRANTHAM 1689–16 July 1697

b. 26 June 1659, 1st s. of Sir Richard Brownlow, 2nd Bt., of Humby by Elizabeth, da. of John Freke† of Cerne Abbas, Dorset; bro. of William Brownlow*. *educ.* Westminster 1675; I. Temple 1676. *m.* 27 Mar. 1676, Alice (*d.* 1721), da. of Richard Sherard of Lobthorpe, Lincs., 1s. *d.v.p.* 6da. (1 *d.v.p*). *suc.* fa. as 3rd Bt. 1668; gt.-uncle Sir John Brownlow, 1st Bt., to Belton 1679.[2]

Treasurer of Marshalsea, 1686–7.
Sheriff, Lincs., Nov. 1688–Mar. 1689.
Commr. Greenwich Hospital, 1695.[3]

Brownlow succeeded his father when only nine years old, living with his mother until 1675 when his great-uncle Sir John Brownlow, 1st Bt., took over all his expenses, sent him to school at Westminster, and arranged a marriage with his cousin. As the principal heir of his great-uncle in 1679, he became a wealthy man with an annual income of £9,000 p.a., whereupon he bought a house for £5,000 in Southampton Square, London, and from 1685 to 1688 rebuilt Belton, his main seat, situated only two miles from Grantham. In 1689 he may have already been suffering from gout and the stone (afflictions which severely limited his parliamentary activity), as in July he made a detailed settlement of his property and wrote his will.[4]

The Brownlows were Parliamentarians during the Civil War and office-holders during the Interregnum but quickly reconciled themselves to the Restoration regime. Brownlow himself apparently had some Tory sympathies under Charles II and James II and in the Convention was listed as voting to agree with the Lords that the throne was not vacant but also as voting for the disabling clause in the corporation bill of January 1690. The latter vote is usually said to be a mistake for his brother William, a definite Whig, but on Brownlow's re-election for Grantham in 1690, he was classed first as 'doubtful' and finally as a Whig in the Marquess of Carmarthen's (Sir Thomas Osborne†) list of the new Parliament. On 26 Apr. 1690 he was given leave of absence for 21 days. In April 1691 he was classed as a Country party supporter by Robert Harley*. He spoke on 8 Jan. 1692 against the bill for lessening the interest on money, and received leave of absence six days later for a month to recover his health.[5]

In the 1692–3 session, Brownlow was appointed on 16 Dec. to the drafting committee of a bill for the better regulation and payment of quarters and the punishment of mutineers and deserters. On 6 Feb. 1693 he presented a petition from the inhabitants of Newark against the election of the Court Whig Sir Francis Molyneux, 4th Bt.*, whose opponent, Sir Richard Earle, was from a Parliamentarian family. On 9 Feb. he made a speech in support of the triennial bill and on the 17th Luttrell records that he had leave to go into the country, although this is not to be found in the Journals. He appeared in the House at the beginning of the 1694–5 session, but by 18 Dec. was seriously ill, his brother being given leave to visit him, and he probably took little further part in parliamentary activities that session.[6]

Despite Brownlow's opposition to the Court in Parliament, he entertained William 'very nobly' at Belton during the King's tour of Lincolnshire in October 1695, when he

> killed 12 fat oxen and 60 sheep, besides other victuals, for his entertainment, and made the most of him and his followers that can be imagined. The King was exceeding merry there, and drank very freely . . . The King said Brownlow entertained him like a prince . . . and has sent for him to London, to honour him the more, and to requite him for his kindness.

If William had any hopes that personal attention would change Brownlow's political stance he was soon disappointed, since Brownlow was forecast as likely to oppose the Court on 31 Jan. 1696 over the proposed council of trade. He did, however, sign the Association in February and his name was missing from the lists on the divisions on the price of guineas in March and the attainder of Sir John Fenwick† in November: it is possible that, although he still could not bring himself to support the Court, he did not wish to appear with opposition after the discovery of the Assassination Plot. In June that year, the 'country people', including local 'officers, constables and churchwardens', marched on Brownlow's house, shouting loyal slogans and demanding his help, they and their families 'being all fit to starve'. The crowd was not entirely satisfied with Brownlow's first offering of £15 of 'old milled money', being 'thankful but . . . it was so little, they might be forced out of necessity to come and see him again', Brownlow then threw open his cellars and many loyal toasts were drunk.[7]

Brownlow's suffering from gout and the stone finally became unbearable and, on 16 July 1697, while staying with his uncle, Thomas Freke I*, in Dorset, he shot himself. The coroner's jury found him *non compos mentis*, to enable the estates to stay in the family. By his marriage settlement, Belton was retained by his widow for her life and then entailed on his brother, William. The remainder of Brownlow's fortune, estimated at £10,000 p.a. and £60,000 in ready money, was left to his five surviving daughters, one of whom married her cousin, Sir John Brownlow, 5th Bt.*, while another three married into the nobility. His monument described him as 'a great ornament to his country in his public capacity and no less conspicuous in his private one'.[8]

[1] E. Cust, *Recs. Cust Fam.* ii. 148; Nottingham Univ. Lib. Portland (Bentinck) mss PwA 161b, Gaultier to Earl of Portland, 23 July/2 Aug. 1697. [2] *Cust*, 72, 140–4. [3] *Add*. 10120, ff. 232–6. [4] *Cust*, 143–7. [5] Ibid. 60, 113–14, 127–8, 148; *Luttrell Diary*, 117. [6] *Luttrell Diary*, 402, 415, 427. [7] *Pryme Diary* (Surtees Soc. liv), 73–74, 95–96; Add. 28879, f. 250. [8] *Cust*, 146, 150–1, 155; *CSP Dom.* 1697, pp. 264, 293–4; Portland (Bentinck) mss PwA 161b, Gaultier to Portland, 23 July/2 Aug. 1697; BL, Trumbull Misc. mss 58, John Ellis* to Sir William Trumbull*, 20, 22 July 1697; Centre Kentish Stud. Stanhope mss U1590/059/6 Robert Yard* to Alexander Stanhope, 27 July 1697.

P. W./S. M. W.

BROWNLOW, Sir John, 5th Bt. (1690–1754), of Arlington Street, London.

GRANTHAM 1713–1715
LINCOLNSHIRE 1715–1722
GRANTHAM 1722–1741

b. 16 Nov. 1690, 1st surv. s. of (Sir) William Brownlow*, (4th Bt.), by his 1st w. *educ.* ?Padua, 1710; *m.* (1) 12 Aug. 1712, his cos. Eleanor (*d.* 1730), da. and coh. of Sir John Brownlow, 3rd Bt.*, *s.p.*; (2) 24 Jan. 1732 (with £2,500), Elizabeth, da. of William Cartwright of Marnum, Notts., *s.p. suc.* fa. as 5th Bt. 6 Mar. 1701; uncle Sir John Brownlow, 3rd Bt., to Belton on *d.* of Lady Brownlow 1721; *cr.* Visct. Tyrconnel [I] 23 June 1718; KB 27 May 1725.[1]

Commr. to inquire into losses and damage sustained during Fifteen, 1716.[2]

Both Brownlow's parents died before he reached the age of 11 and he was thereafter brought up by his maternal grandmother, Lady Mason, who had assumed administration of his father's affairs. When he came of age he found great fault with the management of his property and the resulting coolness between himself and his grandmother was exacerbated by his possession of the manor of Sutton in Surrey, which he had inherited from his mother, but which Lady Mason believed rightly belonged to the children of her other daughter, Anne, formerly Countess of Macclesfield and now wife of Henry Brett*. With an income of £3,000 p.a., inherited from his father, Brownlow then made a fortunate first marriage to his cousin, one of the daughters and coheiresses of his uncle, Sir John Brownlow, 3rd Bt., who brought him £12,000 in money and a share of her father's estates, which were divided by Act of Parliament in 1713, Brownlow thereby obtaining four manors in Lincolnshire and property in London. He also purchased much of the remaining lands from the other heiresses for about £16,000. Brownlow was returned to Parliament in 1713 on his own interest. He voted on 18 Mar. against the expulsion of Richard Steele and was subsequently classed as a Whig in the Worsley list and two other lists analysing the 1713 and 1715 Parliaments.

Brownlow continued to sit in Parliament after 1715 as a Whig. Despite his considerable wealth, he lived above his income for many years and by the end of 1715 had shut up his house in Arlington Street. Created Viscount Tyrconnel in 1718, he retired from active politics in 1741, and his nephew, Sir John Cust, 3rd Bt.†, took over the parliamentary seat at Grantham in 1743. In 1745 Tyrconnel rhapsodized about the English victory at Culloden in a letter to Cust. Without a hint of irony, he wrote that he hoped that Parliament,

> who so liberally rewarded the great Duke of Marlborough [John Churchill†], will not fall short in their gratitude to the Duke [of Cumberland] but restore palaces at the public expense and a princely revenue to our glorious William, the second of the name, deliverer of this nation from popery, slavery and arbitrary power, and who I believe, if the government takes right measures, has forever quell'd that Jacobite, rebellious and turbulent people whom none but Oliver in any degree vanquished.

He died intestate 27 Feb. 1754, when his property went to his sister, the wife of Sir Richard Cust, 2nd Bt.†, who erected a monument to Brownlow praising both his '30 years of public service' and 'his considerate attention to the poor . . . whose lives were by his compassion rescued from idleness'.[3]

[1] Unless otherwise indicated, this biography is based on E. Cust, *Recs. Cust Fam.* ii. 72, 185–222. [2] *Cal. Treas. Bks.* xxx. 425. [3] *HMC Lords*, n.s. x. 90.

P. W./S. M. W.

BROWNLOW, William (1665–1701), of Humby, Lincs. and Arlington Street, Westminster, Mdx.

PETERBOROUGH 28 Dec. 1689–1698
BISHOP'S CASTLE 1698–3 Feb. 1700

b. 5 Nov. 1665, 2nd s. of Sir Richard Brownlow, 2nd Bt.; bro. of Sir John Brownlow, 3rd Bt.* *educ.* Sidney Sussex, Camb. 1680; I. Temple 1684. *m.* (1) lic. 27 July 1688 (with £10,000), Dorothy (*d.* 1700), da. and coh. of Sir Richard Mason† of Bishop's Castle, Salop and Sutton, Surr., 3s. (1 *d.v.p.*) 2da.; (2) 21 Dec. 1700, Henrietta, da. of Henry Brett† of Down Hatherley, Glos. and sis. of Henry Brett*, *s.p. suc.* bro. as 4th Bt. 16 July 1697.[1]

Although a younger son, Brownlow had a large income of about £3,000 p.a. from estates in Huntingdonshire and Somerset, together with personal property of £10,000 left to him by his great-uncle, Sir John Brownlow, 1st Bt., in 1679. In 1690 he was returned for Peterborough, which he had first represented for a short time in the Convention as a Whig. The borough was only one mile from his estate at Stanground in Huntingdonshire, which presumably gave him an interest. Classed as a Whig in Lord Carmarthen's (Sir Thomas Osborne†) list of the new Parliament, he was on 31 Oct. among the appointees to draft a bill suspending part of the Navigation Act to permit the employment of foreign seamen during the war with France. In April 1691 he was classed as a Country party supporter in Robert Harley's* list. On 4 Jan. 1692 he acted as a teller for Hon. John Granville's motion in favour of a supply of £6,000 for army hospitals, rather than the larger sum of £8,000 desired by the Court. Brownlow seems to have been a supporter of the government's bill 'for the preservation of their Majesties' persons and government' as, when a motion was proposed on 14 Dec. 1692 to reject the bill, he, no doubt ironically, 'stood up and desired instead of that they would put the question for rejecting King William and Queen Mary'. A few days later, the House refused him leave to go into the country, after which Brownlow contributed little further to this Parliament. In the spring of 1693 he was noted by Grascome as a government supporter. In 1694 he was listed as having subscribed between £4,000 and £10,000 to the Bank of England, and on 18 Dec. he was given leave of absence for 21 days to attend his brother, who was very ill.²

Brownlow was returned again for Peterborough in 1695, when he confirmed Grascome's earlier classification, being forecast as likely to support the Court in the division on 31 Jan. 1696 over the council of trade. On 1 Feb. he received a derisory two votes in the ballot for commissioners of public accounts. He was an early signatory of the Association, voting with the government in March for fixing the price of guineas at 22s. and in the following November for the attainder of Sir John Fenwick†. In June 1697 Brownlow succeeded his brother to the baronetcy, but to little else since the main family seat at Belton had been settled on the widow for her life and the rest of his brother's large fortune was divided among Sir John's daughters. In 1698 he abandoned his Peterborough seat to contest Bishop's Castle on the interest of his mother-in-law, Lady Mason. As the opposing interest at Bishop's Castle was headed by the 2nd Earl of Macclesfield (Charles Gerard*), the contest was doubtless embittered by the friendly relations between the Brownlows and Macclesfield's recently divorced wife, Lady Brownlow's sister. Lady Macclesfield had been a frequent visitor to the house in Arlington Street during her estrangement from Macclesfield and the Brownlows probably knew of her attachment to the 4th Earl Rivers (Richard Savage*). With the help of a section of the Mason family and some Tory support, Brownlow was successful. In the dispute over the election which followed, Lady Brownlow endeavoured to gain the support of James Vernon I*, who readily gave it, writing to the Duke of Shrewsbury, 'Sir William Brownlow has behaved himself so harmlessly, and is so right in voting that I do not think the House will or ought to part with him'.³

Listed again as a Court supporter in about September 1698 in a comparative analysis of the old and new Parliaments, Brownlow was then marked as a query in October on what was probably a list of those likely to oppose the standing army, but on 18 Jan. 1699 voted against disbanding. He subsequently caused comment, however, by his behaviour in the House on 18 Mar. during the reading of a message from the King, suggesting the House might consider the possibility of retaining his Dutch guards. An observer wrote, 'when it was read, all the House except the King of Bantam (Sir William Brownlow), sat uncovered, but he gave his brother audience with his hat on'. Apart from apparently showing disrespect for the King, the significance of his action, as well as the nickname, is unclear. Brownlow's election at Bishop's Castle was declared void on 3 Feb. 1700 on the grounds of bribery and no new writ was issued. In December that year he married Henrietta Brett. Her brother, Henry, had recently married Brownlow's sister-in-law, the former Countess of Macclesfield, and was to represent Bishop's Castle in the next two Parliaments. Brownlow unsuccessfully contested the borough in February 1701 in alliance with a Tory candidate but, although his petition was successful, he had died on 6 Mar. 1701, before the hearing could take place. He made no will, leaving his affairs in considerable confusion. Eventually letters of administration were taken out by his mother-in-law, Lady Mason.⁴

¹E. Cust, *Recs. Cust Fam.* ii. 72, 171–5. ²Ibid. 171–2; *Luttrell Diary*, 108, 320, 327; Add. 42593, f. 40. ³Cust, 146–7, 179; Add. 40771, ff. 300, 313; *Vernon–Shrewsbury Letters*, i. 468; ii. 146. ⁴*Recs. Cust Fam.* ii. 171–84; *Vernon–Shrewsbury Letters*, ii. 145; Bodl. Tanner 22, f. 6; *HMC Lords*, n.s. iii. 58.

P. W./S. M. W.

BRUCE, Charles, Lord Bruce (1682–1747), of Ampthill, Beds. and Savernake Park, Wilts.

GREAT BEDWYN   7 Dec. 1705–1710
MARLBOROUGH   1710–29 Dec. 1711

b. 29 May 1682, 2nd but o. surv. s. of Thomas Bruce†, 2nd Earl of Ailesbury and 3rd Earl of Elgin [S], by his 1st w. Elizabeth, da. of Henry Seymour, Lord Beauchamp, and

h. to her bro. William. *educ.* privately; academy at Brussels 1698. *m.* (1) 7 Feb. 1706 (with approx. £45,000), Lady Anne (*d.* 1717), da. and coh. of William Savile*, 2nd Mq. of Halifax, 2s. *d.v.p.*; (2) 2 Feb. 1720, Lady Juliana (*d.* 1739), da. of Charles Boyle I*, 2nd Earl of Burlington, *s.p.*; (3) 18 June 1739, Caroline (*d.* 1747), da. of John Campbell*, later 4th Duke of Argyll [S], 1da. *summ.* to House of Lords in fa.'s barony as Lord Bruce of Whorlton 29 Dec. 1711; *suc.* fa. 16 Dec. 1741; *cr.* Baron Bruce of Tottenham, Wilts. 17 Apr. 1746.[1]

Recorder, Bedford 1711–*d.*; burgess 1711.[2]

Lord Bruce, for whom Charles II had stood godfather, was left under the guardianship of his uncle Hon. Robert Bruce* on his father's exile in 1698, and eventually, on attaining his majority, assumed responsibility for his family's interests. For all the expanse of the Bruce estates, spread over several counties, he faced very considerable problems, with debts of some £70,000. Encouraged by his uncle Robert, he put to his father in 1703 a set of detailed proposals for future management, involving the sale of outlying properties, the reserving of the profits of the Bedfordshire and Yorkshire estates to provide an income for the Earl, and his own removal to Wiltshire, to the lands acquired from his mother's family, which he asked be made over to him in fee simple. He hoped thereby to put himself in the way of marrying and acquiring 'such a portion . . . as may save the Wiltshire estate'. Ailesbury seems to have agreed, and by 1705 Bruce had made enough progress with his plans to permit himself to risk matrimony. He found a bride, Lady Anne Savile, with a fortune variously estimated at between £50,000 and £60,000, and which he himself counted on as amounting to at least £45,000. The arrangements were almost finalized in the spring of 1705, but there were hitches, and this 'great match which has been so long depending' was not concluded until February of the following year. Still, however, he complained of the 'great . . . load of debt' weighing upon him. Evidently not all his earlier proposals had been carried out: the Somerset estates, expected to raise £15,000, had yet to be sold, and neither had he left the family seat at Ampthill in Bedfordshire. It was for reasons of sentiment and filial piety that he clung to Ampthill, but at last, in 1707, he was obliged to inform his father regretfully that, while he had done all he could to

> bring my affairs to such a compass that I might have been able to have continued at this place, both for your lordship's sake and my own, until such times as you had returned into England . . . I find it impossible to support my manner of living here . . . all this will force me to leave a place I very much love, to seek some other place where I may live at a much less expense.

After apparently residing for some time in another of the Bruce houses, Henley Park near Guildford, he eventually settled on the former Seymour estate at Savernake in Wiltshire.[3]

With the reform of the family finances came a reassertion of electoral influence, principally if not solely in the three Wiltshire boroughs of Great Bedwyn, Ludgershall and Marlborough, where the Bruces had long since taken over the old Seymour interest. Lord Bruce, when he became qualified to stand in 1705, seems to have thought of himself first as a county knight, and for Wiltshire rather than Bedfordshire, in spite of efforts to persuade him to contest the latter: in June 1705 Anne, Lady Nottingham, had written to him 'wishing . . . your Lordship would make your appearance, where I cannot but think you would have success, for though bribery has mightily prevailed in corporations, . . . yet a county will not be so managed, where so many gentlemen are concerned'. Nevertheless, Bruce reverted to Bedwyn, where he and uncle James were both defeated. Halifax, Bruce's future father-in-law, commented dryly that the family 'are of no consequence here, but I think abroad they will believe the election has not gone favourably to them, when neither Lord Ailesbury's son or brother could be chosen'. Their petition was soon withdrawn when a vacancy occurred, and Lord Bruce came in unopposed at the by-election. Like his uncles he probably inclined to the moderate wing of the Tory party, for all his new connexions with Lord Nottingham (Daniel Finch[†]), his wife's great-uncle. His father's friendship with the Duke of Marlborough (John Churchill[†]), and the family's desire to secure Ailesbury's return from exile, drew them at this time towards the Court. In 1703 Bruce had solicited Lord Treasurer Godolphin's (Sidney[†]) help in promoting a petition from his father to the Queen, and even though this attempt had failed, Godolphin had offered hope for the future. Bruce is not known to have made a speech in his first Parliament, but was nominated to bring in a Wiltshire estate bill. He gave an indication of his other parliamentary activity in a letter to his father in which he explained his attitude to the 1706 popery bill. Far from sympathizing with Ailesbury's conversion to Rome, he had himself remained staunch to the Protestantism in which he had been reared, and had reacted bitterly to signs from his sister that she might follow their father's path. Her clandestine courtship by the Duke of Norfolk had aroused his particular wrath. But he could not, for all this, bring himself to acquiesce in a measure which he felt to be 'in some points too severe' and 'resolved not to be there, but coming into the House unknowingly just as the question was putting [for passing the bill on 4 Mar. 1706], divided against it'. In a list of early 1708 he was marked as a Tory. By the time of the general election of that year he had made himself a force in Ludgershall as well as at Bedwyn and Marlborough. He received much encouragement from the mayor of Marlborough, who throughout April 1708 was anxious for Bruce to accept a seat for the borough. Farewell Perry, minister at St. Peter's, Marlborough, who worked closely with Charles Becher, Bruce's principal agent, asserted that Bruce's consent to contest the election would 'establish your interest so firmly in this town, as that it would be out of the power of any person for the future to shake it'. Bruce did not immediately reply, at which Perry warned him to write to the mayor, 'especially considering how matters now stand at Great Bedwyn where I am afraid your Lordship will meet with greater difficulties than in this town'. However, he chose to sit for Bedwyn, where he was easily re-elected, and secured the return of one uncle at Ludgershall and the other at Marlborough. Although Godolphin made good the earlier promise and in May 1709 obtained, at Bruce's request, a licence for Ailesbury to return to England, the family was not persuaded to go against its Tory principles, and all three Bruces voted against the impeachment of Dr Sacheverell. However, perhaps on account of their earlier voting record over the Tack, which Robert and James had opposed, a 'scandalous' and mischievous report that Lord Bruce and his uncles had supported the impeachment received credence in Wiltshire and required strenuous denials from their election agents: given the evident popularity of Dr Sacheverell in Marlborough and surrounding towns, it was suggested by Perry that Bruce give him some money to 'convince all gainsayers that his lordship is still in earnest for that cause which his accusers say he deserted'.[4]

The 1710 election in fact saw Bruce returned in two constituencies, Bedwyn and Marlborough, and on his behalf his uncle James quickly offered Robert Harley* the nomination to the spare seat. Classed as a Tory in the 'Hanover list' of this Parliament, Bruce was listed among the 'worthy patriots', who in the first session helped to detect the mismanagements of the previous ministry, but he did not join the October Club. At the end of December he was summoned to the Upper House in his father's barony as one of Harley's 'dozen' new peers. According to Ailesbury he would have preferred to stay in the Commons, and only accepted the honour in deference to the Earl's opinion. Although regarded by one authority as possibly a Jacobite at this time, there is no actual evidence as to his views on the succession.[5]

Bruce remained an active Tory partisan after his translation to the Lords, both in Parliament itself and at elections, financing Thomas Gibson[†] at Marlborough and Viscount Lewisham (George Legge[†]) at Bedwyn in the 1720s. Although he had moved to Wiltshire, where he consolidated his family's holdings by a series of purchases and sales, he also retained an interest in Bedfordshire elections, promoting Sir Pynsent Chernock, 3rd Bt.*, and John Harvey* for the county seat there, as well as in Yorkshire where he managed the return of the Tory Sir Miles Stapylton[†]. In 1721 his name figured at the head of the Wiltshiremen listed for the Pretender as likely sympathizers to the Jacobite cause. A sober individual, not much given to social gatherings, he was something of a bibliophile and dilettante antiquarian, corresponding with, among others, Thomas Hearne. He wrote his will on 15 May 1746, leaving a marriage portion of £15,000 to his only daughter, Mary, together with £1,800 to named relatives, miscellaneous legacies to a number of servants, and a stipulation that occupiers of Tottenham Park give £20 annually to the poor of Great Bedwyn. His wife was left his London house in Warwick St. All other property was secured to trustees, including the 3rd Earl of Oxford (Edward Harley[†]), Edward Popham[†] and John Ivory Talbot[†]. After his death, on 10 Feb. 1747, his remains were conveyed back to the family vault at Maulden, near Ampthill, for burial. His English titles were now extinct, save for the recently created barony of Bruce of Tottenham, which passed by a special remainder to his nephew and principal heir, Thomas Bruce-Brudenell, later Earl of Ailesbury by a subsequent creation. The Scottish earldom of Elgin went to a distant cousin, while his Scottish barony of Kinloss lay dormant until successfully claimed in the 19th century.[6]

[1] C. S. C. B. Bruce, *Life and Loyalties of Thomas Bruce*, 225, 298; *HMC Egmont*, ii. 215. [2] J. Godber, *Hist. Beds.* 324; N. Beds. Bor. Council, Bedford bor. recs. B2/3, corp. act bk. 1688–1718, ff. 111–12. [3] Bruce, 68, 225, 238–9, 245; *HMC 15th Rep. VII*, 189, 198–200; Luttrell, *Brief Relation*, v. 566; vi. 14; Add. 17677 AAA, ff. 223, 349; 17677 BBB, f.103; 4291, f. 48; Wilts. RO, Ailesbury mss 1300/1000, 1013, 1019, Ld. Bruce to Ailesbury, 6 Apr. 1705, 8 Aug. 1706, Oct. 1707; Northants. RO, Isham mss IC 2349, Philip Craig to Justinian Isham, 18 Feb. 1706; *Top. and Gen.* iii. 261; Roxburghe mss at Floors Castle, bdle. 738, S. Clerke to the Countess of Roxburghe, 28 Apr. 1705. [4] Bruce, 212, 235–9, 243–8, 252–6, 261; *HMC 15th Rep. VII*, 188, 192, 197, 201; Ailesbury mss add. Lady Nottingham to Ld. Bruce, 16 June 1705; 1300/1309, Charles Becher to Ld. Bruce, 6 July 1704; 9/19/919/3505, Perry to Ld. Bruce, 3, 7, 10 Apr. 1708; H. Horwitz, *Revolution Politicks*, 263; Add. 61458, f. 163. [5] *HMC Portland*, iv. 614; *Ailesbury Mems.* 562; E. Gregg, *Queen Anne*, 350; *Swift Stella* ed. Davis, 448. [6] Wilts. RO, 9/9/920; 9/35/287, 288, 291; 9/3/374/3513, Edward Dupplin to Ld. Bruce, 18 Nov. 1714; G. Holmes, *Pol. in Age of Anne*, 426; Christ Church, Oxf. Wake mss 5, f. 111; *HMC 15th Rep. VII*, 202, 204–13; L. Colley, *In*

Defiance of Oligarchy, 66, 217, 229; P. S. Fritz, *Ministers and Jacobitism 1715-45,* p. 149; *Ailesbury Mems.* 489; *Hearne Colls.* iv. 186; v. 70, 74, 79–80, 151; viii. 209, 244, 391; ix. 194, 402; *A Cat. of Bks. of Rt. Hon. Charles, Visct. Bruce . . . in Lib. at Tottenham . . .* (1733); PCC 87 Potter; *VCH Wilts.* xi. 109.

D. W. H.

BRUCE, Hon. James (c.1670–c.1732).

GREAT BEDWYN   1702–1705
MARLBOROUGH   1708–1710

b. c.1670, 8th but 3rd surv. s. of Robert Bruce†, 1st Earl of Ailesbury and 2nd Earl of Elgin [S], by Lady Diana, da. of Henry Grey†, 1st Earl of Stamford; bro. of Thomas†, 2nd Earl of Ailesbury, and Hon. Robert Bruce*. *educ.* Queens', Camb. fell. comm. 1684. *unm.*

Burgess, Bedford 1705.[1]
Commr. equivalent, 1707, R. Hosp. Chelsea 1711–*d*; jt. comptroller of army accts. 1711–*d*.[2]

James and Robert Bruce, younger brothers of the 2nd Earl of Ailesbury, had both served as volunteers against William of Orange in 1688. After Ailesbury's exile in 1698 James assisted Robert in attempting in vain to find some legal means by which the Earl might be enabled to return to England. Both brothers were elected to the 1702 Parliament through family influence, and for the most part their parliamentary careers are indistinguishable. It is highly likely, however, that in the House, as outside, the brothers acted together, High Tories to begin with but by early 1704 occupying places on the Court wing of the party, their 'moderation' perhaps to be explained by the difficult circumstances in which the family found itself, both financially and in respect of Ailesbury's continued exile, or perhaps by their brother's friendship with the Duke of Marlborough (John Churchill†), which had survived the events of the 1690s. Forecast as a likely opponent of the Tack, James Bruce figured on Robert Harley's* lobbying list, and on 25 Nov. 1704 Harley was reassured by Lord Treasurer Godolphin (Sidney†) that 'the two Bruces' would 'not easily . . . fail us'. Nor did they, as neither voted for the Tack in the crucial division three days later.[3]

Defeated at Great Bedwyn in 1705, despite being reassured of the support of Sir Edward Seymour, 4th Bt.*, Bruce briefly turned his attention to Ludgershall, where he was advised by Charles Becher, Lord Bruce's (Charles*) agent, to spend money generously if he hoped to carry a seat. Encouraged by Becher's report in December 1707 that he 'yet stands fair with the people, and there seems a general inclination to choose him', Bruce nevertheless retired in favour of his elder brother, Robert. He had also considered standing again at Great Bedwyn, and was advised how much he should spend on each vote, but was returned instead for another borough in which his family had a strong interest, Marlborough. Classified as a Tory on a list of early 1708 with the election returns added, he voted against the impeachment of Dr Sacheverell, and in October 1710, though he had not sought re-election himself, wrote to Harley to offer his services to the new ministry in some capacity. The offer of employment, when it came in late June 1711, was as joint comptroller of army accounts, with a salary of £1,500 p.a. By accepting this post Bruce might conceivably have imperilled the family's cordial relations with Marlborough, yet, as Ailesbury was to recall, 'although in his heart [James] wished well to the Duke of Marlborough, yet he refused not the task they gave him', and he succeeded so well in retaining the Duke's goodwill that, again according to Ailesbury, it was thanks to Marlborough that Bruce kept his office on the Hanoverian succession. While apparently 'esteemed by all for his integrity and good conduct in the execution of his office', his private life was less salubrious, and in 1727 he had reached the brink of bankruptcy, with gambling debts of around £12,000. To evade imprisonment for debt he was obliged to join Ailesbury in Brussels, beyond extradition. The crisis had come suddenly, before he could perfect his own scheme of escape by marrying the 'discreet, elderly' lady with a fortune of £9,000 p.a. whom he had cynically been pursuing, and he had instead to be extricated by the skill of his brother Robert, in negotiating a settlement with his creditors. No more was heard of marriage.[4]

Bruce was reappointed joint comptroller in September 1731, by which time he was living in St. Martin's-in-the-Fields. He may have died by August 1732, when the paymaster of the forces was ordered to make over his arrears to his colleague. The first unambiguous reference to his being deceased occurs in a Treasury warrant of 26 Jan. 1733. As he died intestate, the Prerogative Court of Canterbury appointed an administrator to his estate. By his death, he had been unable to complete a £20,000 bond with the Earl of Cardigan, which he had secured on the lease of manors in Yorkshire at Cardigan's marriage to Bruce's niece, Elizabeth, in 1707.[5]

[1] N. Beds. Bor. Council, Bedford bor. recs. B2/3, corp. act bk. 1688–1718, f. 69. [2] C. S. C. B. Bruce, *Life and Loyalties of Thomas Bruce,* 20; Boyer, *Pol. State,* i–ii. 452; *Cal. Treas. Bks. and Pprs. 1731–4,* p. 426; Add. 17677 EEE, f. 235v; *CJ,* xv. 419. [3] Bruce, 131, 212, 220, 261; Wilts. RO, Ailesbury mss 1300/1010, Ld. Bruce to Ailesbury, 14 Apr. 1706; *HMC 15th Rep. VII,* 200; *Bull. IHR,* xli. 182. [4] *HMC Portland,* iv. 614; Add. 17677 EEE, f. 235; 61458, f. 163; *Newton Corresp.* v. 326n, 341–3; *Ailesbury Mems.* 648; Bruce, 281–5;

HMC *15th Rep. VII*, 189, 199, 200–1, 230, 232. [5]*Cal. Treas. Bks. and Pprs.* 1731–4, pp. 307, 426, 516; PROB 6/112, pp. 107–11.

D. W. H.

BRUCE, John (*d*.1711), of Kinross House, Kinross.

SCOTLAND 1707–1708

o. s. of Sir William Bruce, 1st Bt., MP [S], of Balcaskie, Fife, clerk of bills [S] 1660–81 and master of works [S] 1671–*c*.1680, by his 1st w. Mary, da. of Sir James Halkett of Pitfirrane, Fife, MP [S]. *educ.* travelled abroad (France, Low Countries). *m.* contr. 3 May 1687 (with £6,000 Scots), Lady Christian (*d.* 1710), da. and coh. of John Leslie, 1st Duke of Rothes [S] and wid. of James Graham, 3rd Mq. of Montrose [S], *s.p. suc.* fa. 1 Jan. 1710.[1]

MP [S] Kinross-shire 1702–7.

Burgess, Glasgow 1702; hereditary sheriff, Kinross ?1702–*d.*

Commr. Equivalent [S] 1707–*d.*[2]

The most significant event in Bruce's political life was his marriage, which brought him eventually into the following of his stepson, the 1st Duke of Montrose, and thus into the ranks of the Squadrone. Like others in Montrose's connexion, his family had been strongly attached to the Stuart court, and his father found it difficult to abandon traditional loyalties after the Revolution. An eminent architect ('the Kit Wren of North Britain' according to Defoe) Sir William Bruce boasted in 1702 that he had served Charles II and James II faithfully for half a century. He had played a part in promoting the Restoration, by acting as a channel of communication between the King and General Monck (George[†]), and was rewarded with offices and a baronetcy. In the 1670s, at the height of his prestige and influence, he purchased the Kinross barony, upon which, and upon the town of Kinross, he lavished improvements. He built Kinross House, 'a stately building', in the words of Sir Robert Sibbald, 'which for situation, contrivance, prospects . . . parks and planting, is surpassed by few in this country'. The mansion was intended as a residence for the Duke of York in the event of the passage of the Exclusion bill. Bruce was appointed to the Scottish privy council at the accession of James II, but removed a little over a year later for his inflexibility on the issue of Catholic toleration. But he kept the sheriffdom of Kinross, granted by Charles I, in the face of hostile interest from more pliant courtiers, and evidently retained his devotion to King James. Although he passed through the Revolution with estate and office intact, there were soon signs of restlessness, most notably in a dispute with the local presbytery over the appointment of a minister for Kinross, where he had sought to intrude deprived episcopalian preachers. He became for a time the 'chief organizer' of the Scottish Jacobites, and during the scare over the Assassination Plot in 1696 was briefly interned. An appeal in 1702 to the new Scottish secretary, Lord Tarbat, for assistance in recovering his former post as master of the works showed that Sir William still kept an eye to the main chance, but shortly afterwards, in December 1702, he was 'declared a rebel' and his goods (though not his real property) confiscated. Thereafter the Pretender's agents took his zeal for the Jacobite cause as axiomatic.[3]

Of Bruce himself, it was said that like his father he was 'a man of parts', and that, 'as he had got a liberal education, [he] was looked upon as one of the finest gentlemen in the kingdom when he returned from his travels' abroad. He was active in countering the Earl of Argyll's rebellion in 1685, marching with government troops to Glasgow only to be summoned home by his anxious father. Relations between father and son deteriorated after the Revolution, an event the younger Bruce thoroughly welcomed. An avid Presbyterian, he informed his father in June 1690 that he would have no truck with 'liberty of conscience to all Protestants', preferring rather that the Scottish parliament should demonstrate its 'zeal for the true Protestant and Presbyterian religion by allowing no other to be professed'. Financial problems increased the tension in the relationship between father and son. Sir William's estate, estimated at 22,000 merks p.a. in the late 1680s, was to have been divided equally with his son as part of his marriage settlement. The arrangement was not properly implemented, however, and it emerged that Sir William had concealed the true extent of his debts.[4]

Bruce was returned to the Scottish parliament for Kinross-shire in 1702, and may already have assumed the hereditary sheriffdom. An investor of £500 in the Darien scheme, he joined the Country party, remaining in opposition during the 'New Party' experiment of 1704 and following Montrose's line of voting for the Duke of Hamilton's motion for postponing a decision on the succession. George Lockhart's* retrospective assessment that Bruce had supported his future Squadrone colleagues in office was mistaken. Bruce did, however, vote with the Squadrone over the Union, with only one or two absences, and was nominated for a seat in the first Parliament of Great Britain and a place on the Equivalent commission.[5]

Bruce seems to have been moderately useful to the Squadrone in the Commons, even though he did not cut much of a figure. He joined his fellow Equivalent commissioners in petitioning the Treasury over the non-payment of their salaries, and on 11 Mar. 1708 was nominated to draft a bill to discharge Highlanders from their obligations to disloyal clan chiefs. His father, by contrast, was placed in preventive detention during the invasion scare. Bruce did not stand in 1708, when the family's electoral interest was in any case divided: Sir William was 'running about' to assist the Tory cause wherever he could, while Bruce himself remained loyal to Montrose and the Squadrone, whose members, he felt, ought to try to 'get themselves into posts by all the means they can'. He was content to remain an Equivalent commissioner for the time being, though the conditions of the appointment, especially the absence of remuneration, made it an 'unhappy' one. The fact that he was simultaneously putting forward to Montrose proposals for reform of the Scottish customs suggests that he did not despair of alternative employment. In 1710 he gave his backing to the candidacy of Montrose's factor, Mungo Graham* in Kinross-shire, bending the rules to such a degree in his conduct of the freeholders' courts that he was fortunate to escape censure when the House overturned Graham's election on petition.[6]

After apparently recovering from illness in the winter of 1710–11, Bruce died on 19 Mar. 1711. The baronetcy became extinct, but his estates passed to a sister, and eventually to her son, John Hope, who represented the county under George II.[7]

[1] *Hist. Scot. Parl.* 75, 79; Lauder of Fountainhall, *Hist. Notices* (Bannatyne Club, lxxxvii), 344; SRO, Kinross House mss GD29/1220, contr. [2] *Scot. Rec. Soc.* lvi. 251; Boyer, *Anne Annals*, vi. 234; *Cal. Treas. Bks.* xxiii. 234. [3] *DNB* (Bruce, Sir William); *Hist. Scot. Parl.* 75; Defoe, *Tour* ed. Cole, 777–8; R. Sibbald, *Hist. of Sheriffdoms of Fife and Kinross* (1710), 107–8; Fountainhall, 633, 724, 730, 750; *Reg. PC Scotland*, 1685–6, p. 13; 1686, p. 221; 1690, p. 496; 1691, p. 135; *CSP Dom.* 1684–5, p. 113; 1696, p. 19; 1703–4, p. 399; *HMC Mar and Kellie*, i. 219; P. A. Hopkins, *Glencoe*, 423; *HMC Le Fleming*, 323; *HMC 12th Rep. VIII*, 51–52; Fraser, *Melvilles*, i. 272; *Cromartie Corresp.* i. 161–4; *Hooke Corresp.* (Roxburghe Club), i. 230, 440; ii. 26, 141; *Orig. Pprs.* ed. Macpherson, ii. 14–15, 19. [4] *DNB* (Bruce, Sir William); Kinross House mss catalogue (GD29), p. 160; GD29/1918/2–4, 8, 16, 24–25, John to Sir William Bruce, 1, 14, 15 June [1685], 9 June 1690, 9 Sept., 2 Nov. 1700, Sir William to John Bruce, 27 Sept. 1704. [5] *Darien Pprs.* (Bannatyne Club, xc), 372; info. from Dr P. W. J. Riley on members of Scot. parl.; SRO, Ogilvy of Inverquharity mss, letter of Sir William Bennet, 28 Jan. 1703, *ex inf*. Dr Riley; *Lockhart Mems.* ed. Szechi 67; Boyer, *Anne Annals*, iii. app. 42; *HMC 4th Rep.* 511; W. Fraser, *Earls of Haddington*, i. 244; *Hooke Corresp.* i. 440; *Orig. Pprs.* 19; *Baillie Corresp.* 104; Riley, *Union*, 334; R. Walcott, *Pol. Early 18th Cent.* 234. [6] SRO, Montrose mss GD220/5/142/2, Rothes to Montrose, 16 Dec. 1707; GD220/5/159/5, same to same, [?1708]; GD220/5/196/1–2, 4a, Bruce to same, 8, 17 Feb., 1 Mar. 1709; GD220/5/807/5–6, Graham to same, 2, 7 Dec. 1710; GD220/5/808/18a–b, same to same, 13 Feb. 1711; *HMC Mar and Kellie*, 435, 475–7; Luttrell, *Brief Relation*, vi. 291; *Cal. Treas. Bks.* xxii. 79; L. Inn Lib, MP100/145, *Controverted Election for . . . Kinross* [1711]. [7] Montrose mss GD220/5/808/1a,

Graham to Montrose, 2 Jan. 1711; *Hist. Scot. Parl.* 79; Scot. Hist. Soc. *Misc*. i. 484.

D. W. H.

BRUCE, Hon. Robert (1668–1729).

MARLBOROUGH	1702–1705
LUDGERSHALL	1708–1710
MARLBOROUGH	1710–1715
GREAT BEDWYN	1722–1727

bap. 11 Feb. 1668, 7th but 2nd surv. s. of Robert Bruce†, 1st Earl of Ailesbury; bro. of Thomas†, 2nd Earl of Ailesbury, and Hon. James Bruce*. *educ*. Queens', Camb. fell. comm. 1684; M. Coulon's acad. Paris 1685. *unm*.

Burgess, Bedford 1702.[1]

As the senior and more prudent of Lord Ailesbury's two surviving brothers, Robert Bruce took charge of the family's affairs when Ailesbury went into exile in 1698, and later counselled and assisted his nephew Lord Bruce (Charles*). He may have been implicated himself in the Assassination Plot, the testimony of Peter Cook mentioning a 'Mr Bruce', a Jacobite sympathizer, as attending a meeting at a Holborn tavern, but no further notice was taken of this evidence. Then in September 1699 he embarked for France with various other 'persons of quality' in order, it was said, 'to go [to] see the jubilee at Rome'. He did not, however, follow Ailesbury into the Catholic church, initially regarding reports of his brother's conversion as a 'ridiculous' calumny.[2]

Elected on the family interest at Marlborough in 1702, it is probable that, with his brother James, Bruce modified his political stance from an original High Toryism to accommodate himself to the Court. As the Journals fail to distinguish between the brothers, it is impossible to be sure of the identity of 'Mr Bruce'. In the 1702–3 session a 'Mr Bruce' acted as a teller twice, including on 23 Dec. 1702, in favour of the Tories' wrecking amendment to a motion by Sir John Holland, 2nd Bt., for a bill to provide that no placeman should sit in the House. In the next session 'Mr Bruce' acted as a teller on five occasions, all on the Court side, and in the third session he was recorded as a teller on two further occasions. Certainly Robert may be described as a 'moderate' Tory by 28 Nov. 1704, when, having been forecast as a likely opponent of the Tack and been lobbied by Robert Harley*, he did not vote for it.

Defeated at Marlborough in the 1705 general election, and in a by-election soon afterwards, Bruce turned his attention to Ludgershall, where with his nephew's help he was victorious in a contest in 1708. Classed as a Tory on a list of early 1708 with the election returns added, he voted against the impeachment of Dr Sacheverell, though a malicious rumour that all the Bruces had supported the impeachment was subsequently circulated in Wiltshire, and, probably because of his and James's earlier opposition to the Tack, was for a time widely believed. Both Robert and his nephew hedged their bets in the 1710 election by standing in two constituencies. He himself was returned at Marlborough after a close call, while losing narrowly at Ludgershall. Classed as a Tory in an analysis of the new House, he was listed among the 'Tory patriots' opposed to the war and the 'worthy patriots' who helped to detect the mismanagements of the previous administration. As the only 'Mr Bruce' in this Parliament, he can be positively identified as a teller in three divisions: on 17 Jan. 1712, in favour of the motion to declare Robert Walpole II* guilty of 'corruption'; on 23 May 1712, for leave for a private bill; and on 14 May 1713, against the second reading of the place bill.[3]

Bruce signed the proclamation of George I at St. James's on 1 Aug. 1714, as one of the 'other principal gentlemen of quality' joining with the peers and Privy Councillors. He was not a candidate at the 1715 election but was returned again on Ailesbury's recommendation in 1722. On the accession of George II he 'applied to' Walpole and was for that reason dropped by his brother at Bedwyn. But his abilities were still useful to the family, as he showed that year in extricating James from a morass of debt, and in 1728 Ailesbury was seeking to provide for him once more in the Commons. He died before any seat could be secured, on 19 May 1729. In his will, written in May 1725, he gave his address as Dover Street, St. Martin's-in-the-Fields and bequeathed all his estate to his nephew Charles, Lord Bruce, who was named the sole executor.[4]

[1] N. Beds. Bor. Council, Bedford bor. recs. B2/3, corp. act bk. 1688–1718, f. 69. [2] C. S. C. B. Bruce, *Life and Loyalties of Thomas Bruce*, 211–12, 219–20, 245, 252; *CSP Dom.* 1696, p. 110; Luttrell, *Brief Relation*, iv. 564. [3] *HMC 15th Rep. VII*, 201–2; Herts. RO, Panshanger mss DEP F56, ff. 66–67, Somerset to William Cowper*, 22 Nov. 1705. [4] Boyer, *Pol. State*, viii. 118; Bruce, 281–2, 284, 287; *HMC 15th Rep. VII*, 228–33; PCC 126 Abbott.

D. W. H.

BRUDENELL, Hon. James (c.1687–1746), of Luffenham, Rutland.

CHICHESTER 1713–1715
ANDOVER 1 Apr. 1715–1734
CHICHESTER 1734–9 Aug. 1746

b. c.1687, 2nd s. of Francis Brudenell, Ld. Brudenell (1st s. *d.v.p.* of Robert Brudenell, 2nd Earl of Cardigan), by Lady Frances, da. of Thomas Savile†, 1st Earl of Sussex. *educ.* travelled abroad (Italy) 1703–6; Padua 1704. *m.* Mar. 1725, Susan, da. of Bartholomew Burton of Ashwell, Rutland, sis. of William† and Bartholomew Burton†, 2s. 2da.[1]

Master of jewel office 1716–30; ld. of trade 1730–*d.*; groom of bedchamber 1733–*d.*

Recorder, Chichester 1730–*d.*

Like all his family, Brudenell had been brought up a Roman Catholic, but while he was visiting Italy with his brother George, 3rd Earl of Cardigan, they were both converted to Anglicanism, probably by the Duke of Shrewsbury, although Cardigan did not publicly renounce Catholicism until 1709. The young Brudenells lived a wild life and while they were still in Rome, Shrewsbury, at the request of their tutor, 'called at Lord Cardigan's and preached to Mr [James] Brudenell about his neglecting his studies'. Despite being ordered back to England in the autumn of 1704 by their guardian, Robert Constable, 3rd Earl of Dunbar [S], the two young men went on to Venice. Shortly after their arrival, Cardigan wrote to Shrewsbury that James had 'brought an ugly strain from Rome'. This may have been a reference to the smallpox, which he developed before Christmas. The brothers finally returned to England at the end of April 1706.[2]

Brudenell successfully contested Chichester in 1713 on the interest of his brother-in-law, the 1st Duke of Richmond. In contrast to his Tory brother, but like his patron Richmond, Brudenell was a Whig, voting on 18 Mar. 1714 against the expulsion of Richard Steele, and being classified as a Whig in the Worsley list. He continued to sit after 1715, voting consistently on the government side, until his death from apoplexy on 9 Aug. 1746.

[1] J. Wake, *Brudenells of Deene*, 189–90; *Hearne Colls.* viii. 348. [2] Wake, 190–7, 219, 258.

P. W.

BRUERE, George (aft.1673–1743), of Covent Garden, Westminster, and Great Marlow, Bucks.

GREAT MARLOW 9 Dec. 1710–1722

b. aft.1673, 1st s. of George Bruere *alias* Brewer of M. Temple, London, dep. auditor of the excise, by Mary, da. of Alexander Weld of Wildbury Hill, Herts. *m.* bef. 1701, Frediswede (*d.* 1740), da. of Sir William Goulston† of Whitechapel, Mdx. and Fairfield, Kent, 4s. (1 *d.v.p.*) 1 da., 6 o. ch. *suc.* fa. 1713.[1]

Bruere's father served as deputy auditor of the excise and had chambers in the Middle Temple until they were sold in 1700 to pay debts, but managed to retain his office until his death in June 1713. Bruere himself owed his election at Great Marlow to his close relationship to Sir James Etheridge*, his wife's stepfather. (A secondary relationship was that Bruere's mother was the daughter of Etheridge's stepfather.) Bruere probably came to reside in Marlow after his marriage to Etheridge's stepdaughter.[2]

Bruere was certainly prominent enough to accompany Etheridge in 1702 in presenting the borough's address of congratulation on the accession of Queen Anne, a role he performed again in 1704 and 1706. At the general election of 1710 he stood for Marlow on Etheridge's interest, and tied for the second seat with James Chase*. Although there was a double return, Chase waived his claims and Bruere was seated on 9 Dec. Classed as a Tory on the 'Hanover list', Bruere was also named as one of the 'worthy patriots' who helped detect the mismanagements of the late administration during the opening session of the Parliament. He was appointed to the drafting committee of the Aylesbury–Bicester road bill early in 1712. In July following, with Etheridge, he presented the Marlow address asking for peace and an end to Whig warmongering. He voted on 18 June 1713 for the French commerce bill. Re-elected in 1713, he appeared as a Tory in the Worsley list. Having presented the borough's address on the accession of George I, he was left out of the commission of the peace, despite taking the oaths in October 1714.[3]

Etheridge seems to have stood down in Bruere's favour in 1715 and after his return he was described as a 'whimsical' Tory on a list classifying those MPs who had been re-elected. Bruere continued to sit until 1722, by which time Etheridge had sold his main estate to Sir John Guise, 3rd Bt.* Bruere voted for the Tory candidates for the county in 1722, although in 1727 he appears to have acted for Robert Walpole II* in Great Marlow. It was the beneficiary of his intervention on that occasion, John Clavering†, who ensured that he regained his place on the county bench in March 1728. Bruere was buried on 1 Feb. 1743 at Great Marlow.[4]

[1] *Mar. Lic. Vicar-Gen.* (Harl. Soc. xxiii), 215; *Misc. Gen. et Her.* n.s. i. 213; i. 326–7; *Cal. Treas. Bks.* xxix. 649. [2] *Cal. Treas. Bks.* ix. 1227, 1274; xvii. 49; xxix. 649; *M. Temple Mins.* iii. 1474; *Misc. Gen. et Her.* n.s. i. 213. [3] *London Gazette*, 30 Apr.–4 May 1702, 12–16 Oct. 1704, 29 July–1 Aug. 1706; *Post Boy*, 8–10 July 1712; *Misc. Gen. et Her.* n.s. i. 215; *Bucks. Sess. Recs.* iv. 90. [4] Add. 61602, ff. 104, 108, 114; *Misc. Gen. et Her.* n.s. i. 215; *Bucks. Poll 1722* (IHR), 67.

E. C./S. N. H.

BRYDGES (BRIDGES), George (1678–1751), of Avington, Hants.

WHITCHURCH   21 Dec. 1708–1710
WINCHESTER   15 Mar. 1714–13 May 1751

b. July 1678, o. s. of George Rodney Brydges (Bridges)*. educ. ?Winchester 1686–91; ?travelled abroad (Holland) 1696. m. lic. 2 Dec. 1712, Anne, da. and coh. of Sir Joseph Woolfe (d. 1711), Mercer, of Hackney, Mdx., sheriff of London 1703–4 and alderman 1705–d., s.p. suc. fa. 1714; uncle Harry Brydges at Keynsham, Som. 1728.[1]

Freeman, Lymington 1701, Winchester 1701, Portsmouth 1710.[2]

Master keeper of south bailiwick, New Forest by 1704–aft.1720.[3]

Assured by his parentage of a privileged place in the first rank of Hampshire Whigs, Brydges represented his party at the Whitchurch election of 1708 and, although defeated at the poll after a stiff contest, was subsequently seated on petition by the Whig majority in the House. For the most part it has proved impossible to disentangle the record of his parliamentary activity from those of his various namesakes in the Commons, including his father. The exceptional instances are his support for the naturalization of the Palatines in 1709, his vote the following year in favour of the impeachment of Dr Sacheverell, and a grant of leave of absence (for ten days) made to him on 16 Feb. 1710. He did not stand at the 1710 general election, when he is found tendering moral support to Whig candidates at Andover, nor in 1713, but, having presented a statue of Queen Anne to the corporation of Winchester, he succeeded his father as Member there in a by-election in March 1714, and afterwards converted the seat into a lifetime possession with comparatively little difficulty. Although mistakenly classed as a Tory in a list of the 1715 Parliament, he remained, as he had indeed always been, a staunch Whig, and under the Hanoverians 'served . . . Administration long and . . . affectionately'.[4]

Brydges died on 13 May 1751. He was 'found drowned in the canal of his gardens at Avington . . . supposed by accident, [he] being 72 and paralytic', and was buried in the parish church. The bulk of his estate, the value of which was now estimated at £6,000 p.a., and which comprised his father's property in Hampshire, Middlesex (in Covent Garden) and Wiltshire, with property in Ireland, together with the family's ancestral estates in Somerset, inherited from an uncle, was entailed upon his distant cousin the 2nd Duke of Chandos (Henry Brydges†), whose father, Hon. James Brydges*, had spent many years in cultivating the connexion in expectation of just such an eventuality. A portion, however, was reserved for another cousin, the naval captain George Brydges Rodney[†], whom Brydges had helped to bring up and who was to go on to win fame as an admiral and in consequence a peerage as Lord Rodney.[5]

[1] *HMC Bath*, iii. 167; *Winchester Long Rolls 1653–1721* ed. Holgate, 53, 56, 58, 61, 63, 65–66; *CSP Dom.* 1696, pp. 43, 53; *Fac. Off. Mar. Lic.* (Index Lib. xxxiii), 275; Beaven, *Aldermen*, ii. 120; PCC 223 Young; *GEC Baronetage*, i. 132; *St. Helen's Bishopsgate* (Harl. Soc. Reg. xxxi), 57, 354; Lysons, *Environs* (1792–6), iii. 287, 299. [2] E. King, *Old Times Revisited*, 192; Hants RO, Winchester bor. recs. ordnance bk. 7, f. 174; R. East, *Portsmouth Recs.* 376. [3] *Cal. Treas. Bks.* xix. 440; *Cal. Treas. Pprs.* 1720–8, p. 36. [4] Hants RO, Jervoise mss, Stephen Barton to [Thomas Jervoise*], 24 Aug. 1710; Wilks, *Hants*, i. 16, 20; W. A. Speck, *Tory and Whig*, 125. [5] *Gent. Mag.* 1751, p. 236; C. H. C. and M. I. Baker, *James Brydges, 1st Duke of Chandos*, 218, 455; Pevsner, *Buildings of Eng.* Hants, 84; Wilks, 42; *DNB* (Rodney, George Brydges).

D. W. H.

BRYDGES (BRIDGES), George Rodney (aft. 1649–1714), of Avington, Hants.

HASLEMERE   1690–1698
WINCHESTER   1701 (Feb.)–Feb. 1714

b. aft. 1649, at least 3rd but 2nd surv. s. of Sir Thomas Bridges (*d.* 1707) of Keynsham, Som. by Anne, da. and coh. of Sir Edward Rodney[†] of Stoke Rodney, Som. *m.* 1677, Lady Anna Maria Brudenell (*d.* 1702), da. of Robert, 2nd Earl of Cardigan, and wid. of Francis Talbot, 11th Earl of Shrewsbury, 1s.[1]

Capt. Duke of York's indep. coy. 1673–aft.1675; groom of bedchamber 1678–85.[2]

Freeman, Portsmouth 1675, Winchester by 1701, Lymington 1701.[3]

The younger son of a noted Somerset Cavalier who had been Royalist governor of Bath during the Civil War (and an unsuccessful parliamentary candidate three times between 1666 and 1673), Brydges was one of the young 'gallants' of the Restoration court. After a spell as a captain in the Portsmouth garrison, during which he ran up debts and was reduced to borrowing from London goldsmiths, he had secured his fortune at the expense of what remained of his reputation by marriage to the notorious Countess of Shrewsbury, the former lover of the 2nd Duke of Buckingham, a domestic rearrangement which entailed his bringing an action in the court of arches for jactitation of marriage against his own previous mistress, Ann Smith, a shopkeeper in the New Exchange in the Strand, with whom he had evidently cohabited for some years. The Countess paid £4,500 to buy him a place as groom of the bedchamber, and it was almost certainly through her influence that he was appointed to the Staffordshire lieutenancy in 1680 and stood at Lichfield in the election to the Oxford Parliament. Although he enjoyed the support of 'the dean and churchmen there', the principal thrust of his campaign was an attack on the Tory lawyer Daniel Finch[†] (later 2nd Earl of Nottingham), whom he hoped thus to blackmail into providing him with a seat elsewhere, though without success. He seems to have remained loyal to the Court during the 'Stuart revenge', and even entertained Charles II at his new house in Hampshire while the King's house at nearby Winchester was under construction. In 1683 Lord Sunderland recommended him for a keepership in the New Forest. Although evidently not reappointed a groom of the bedchamber by James II, he was still a faithful courtier: having given satisfactory answers to the King's questions on the repeal of the Penal Laws and Test Act, he was recommended by the royal agents for inclusion in the Hampshire commission of the peace, and himself proposed to stand at Petersfield in the elections to the King's abortive Parliament of 1688, though a subsequent report stated that he had 'wholly left his interest and declines standing'. Of his conduct at the Revolution little is known: he was given a pass by King James to go down to Salisbury in November 1688, and another on 1 Dec. to travel to and from his seat at Avington. He does not seem to have been a candidate in the elections to the Convention, and then in March 1689 was granted an exemption, along with the Earl of Middleton, from having to quarter troops or suffer the requisition of his horses, evidence from which one may infer that he was still regarded as in some degree King James's man. Possibly of significance in this connexion is the fact that payment of his wife's pension of £1,600 p.a. on the Irish establishment, granted in 1672, was discontinued at the Revolution.[4]

By the time of the 1690 general election Brydges had succeeded in establishing his credentials as a Williamite: a *volte-face* doubtless achieved with the help of his powerful Whig connexions, in particular his stepson the 12th Earl (later 1st Duke) of Shrewsbury, and probably also his old friend Lord Brandon (Hon. Charles Gerard*). He was classed as a Whig by Lord Carmarthen (Sir Thomas Osborne[†]) in an analysis of the new Parliament, to which he had been returned for the Surrey constituency of Haslemere, possibly on the Onslow interest. In Robert Harley's* list of April 1691 he was classed as a Country party supporter, though with an additional comment of 'd[oubtful]', that may have been added much later. His involvement in a debate on naval affairs on 14 Nov. 1691 can conceivably be attributed in some measure to the fact that Sir Richard Onslow*, brother of Denzil*, his colleague at Haslemere, was at this point one of the lords of Admiralty. In the debate Brydges reported to the House information vouchsafed to him by a captain in the fleet that Admiral Sir Ralph Delaval* had lately captured a French ship containing documents that were 'of dangerous consequence' to the government. On the 16th he was ordered to name the captain and identified him as Carmarthen's son Lord Danby (Hon. Peregrine Osborne*). As a Member with Irish estates (at Skirk, Queen's co.) and considerable Irish connexions, he was a natural choice to be named on 1 Jan. 1692 to the committee to receive proposals for raising funds on the Irish forfeited estates; oddly, he was later added, on 20 Jan., to the same committee. When the ensuing Irish forfeitures bill was reported, on 9 Feb., he presented a clause on behalf of the Duke of Ormond. Almost certainly by this time he had penetrated the inner circle of Hampshire Whigs headed by the Duke of Bolton (Charles Powlett†), with whom he was to be closely associated in the future; and on 8 Feb. 1693 he spoke alongside other 'friends to the Duke of Bolton' in opposition to the bill to preserve timber in the New Forest. He was again active in Irish business on 22 Feb., introducing Irish witnesses to give evidence before the Commons in the debate on the charges of maladministration and corruption against the government in Dublin, and moving for the recall of the Irish parliament. Little is heard of him during the 1693–4 session, aside from a fortnight's leave of absence, granted on 8 Feb. 1694. Grascome's list now classified him as a Court supporter, however, and on 29 Nov. he was ordered to bring in another bill to vest the Irish forfeited estates in their Majesties, a measure he duly introduced on 3 Dec. After a second grant of leave, in February 1695, also for two weeks, he returned to the House by 26 Mar., when he was appointed to bring in a bill to oblige Sir Thomas Cooke* to disclose how he had distributed the sums, amounting to £87,000, detailed in the report of the committee of inquiry into the affairs of the East India Company. He introduced the bill on the 28th, chaired the committee of the whole House to which it was referred, and the committee on the Lords' bill to indemnify Cooke. He also took a prominent part in the impeachment of Carmarthen, now Duke of Leeds, for which the East India inquiry had paved the way.[5]

After the 1695 general election, and the arrival in the Commons first of Hon. James Brydges* and then of other namesakes, it becomes progressively more difficult to distinguish the parliamentary activity of the various 'Mr Brydges' recorded in the Journals. To some degree, however, Brydges' adopted Whiggism conveniently sets him apart, until the election of his own son in 1708. Classed as likely to support the Court in a forecast for the division on the proposed council of trade on 31 Jan. 1696, he signed the Association promptly, and in March voted for fixing the price of guineas at 22s. Because of his local interest, he was almost certainly the Brydges who told on 27 Feb. 1696 against the Avon navigation bill. His conduct over the attainder of Sir John Fenwick† in the following autumn seems to have been determined for the most part by his anxiety to protect the reputation of his stepson, Shrewsbury, whom Fenwick's confession had implicated in Jacobite intrigues. Even before Parliament met, Brydges was busy on Shrewsbury's behalf behind the scenes, and in the first debate on the affair, on 6 Nov., Shrewsbury was informed by James Vernon I* that Brydges had 'employed both industry and judgment'. He was clearly acting as his stepson's agent, attending high-level ministerial conferences to concert parliamentary strategy, and sending Shrewsbury regular progress reports. In the House he intervened whenever possible to forward the attainder, speaking on 13 Nov. to oppose any suggestion that Fenwick be allowed more time to produce witnesses, and, on a subsequent occasion, in favour of admitting as evidence the examination of the absconded witness, Cardell Goodman, when he observed acidly, 'if you do not read this affidavit I do not say but it is a kindness to Sir J. F., but what kindness will it be to the country and government?' On 17 Nov., before Fenwick was to be called in for examination, Brydges proposed a question to be asked him on Shrewsbury's behalf, namely what proof Fenwick possessed for his claim that 'Shrewsbury came into the office of Secretary of State again, by the operation and consent of King James'. Later in the same debate he suggested, to the general disapprobation of the House, that Fenwick also be required to confirm that the statement denouncing Shrewsbury and the rest was indeed in his own hand. He canvassed support for the bill as the crucial division came nearer, and on 25 Nov. voted for it himself. But the successful passage of the bill did not mark the end of Shrewsbury's personal danger, for, as Brydges reported, there were still those, like the Earl of Monmouth and 'the cabal in Dover Street', whose enmity to Shrewsbury was such that they were determined to pursue any scandal. In December and January 1697 Brydges continued to act for the Duke in this matter, gathering information and offering advice. The other issue in which he was active in the House in this session was the bill to naturalize the sons of the Earl of Athlone: he brought in the bill, and on 29 Dec. reported from the second-reading committee. This too would have done him no harm at court, and he moved quickly to cash in on whatever gratitude he had earned from the great men, asking Shrewsbury in January 1697 to use his influence with Lord Albemarle to secure a nomination to the new commission of lords justices to be named for Ireland, adding that Athlone too might be willing to help in return for Brydges' efforts over the naturalization bill. This was in fact to pitch his claims rather too high, and nothing came of it: he had more success with a petition for a renewal of payment of his wife's Irish pension, which was duly granted in April 1697, the pension being secured as before to Lord Rochester (Laurence Hyde†) as trustee, though this time Brydges rather than his wife was named as beneficiary. He was not, however, granted payment of the arrears which had accumulated since 1688. In the one remaining session of the Parliament he seems to have been less active than previously. He told Vernon in December 1697 that he intended to absent himself from the House when the rumoured attack on Sunderland eventually materialized, since past obligations to the Earl made it impossible for him to appear against Sunderland 'and he knew not how to be for him'; and on 7 Apr. 1698 he was officially granted two weeks' leave of absence. There had been no change in his political allegiance, however, for in a comparative analysis of the old and new Parliaments drawn up after the 1698 general election he was still ranked with the Court party.[6]

Despite the endorsement of his influential Whig friends, and of members of the administration like Vernon, Brydges failed to secure his re-election in 1698 at Haslemere, and may also have unsuccessfully contested a seat at Winchester, not far from his residence at Avington. He petitioned on 12 Dec., but his evidence (of bribery) was so feeble that on 9 Feb. 1699 the Commons not only rejected the petition but went on to vote it 'frivolous and vexatious'. He had not given up his efforts to obtain office, even without a vote in Parliament, and in January 1699 it was reported that he entertained hopes of a customs commissionership through the intercession of Lord Portland. In the first election of 1701 Brydges concentrated his attention on Winchester, where his own proprietorial interest and the help of the Powlett family stood him in better stead than at Haslemere. He topped the poll in a contested election. Now, in a time of adversity for the Whigs, he once more took a prominent part in parliamentary proceedings. He acted as a teller on 19 Feb. 1701 against the Tory attempt to expel Sir Henry Furnese* from the House on the basis of the clause in the Salt Duty Act excluding those concerned in the management of the revenue, again on 14 Apr., against the motion declaring Lord Orford (Edward Russell*) guilty of high crimes and misdemeanours, and, after a fortnight's leave of absence, granted on the 14th, was possibly a teller once more on 14 June, for an additional clause to the wine duty bill which would have 'respited' the sale of the Irish forfeited estates, a move opposed by leading Tories of the kind with whom James Brydges habitually associated. Returned unopposed at Winchester in November, he was grouped with the Whigs in Harley's list of this Parliament. His Irish connexions make it feasible that he was the Brydges involved in April–May 1702 in putting through a number of private bills arising from the resumption of the Irish forfeited estates, and who acted as a teller against leave for a bill on behalf of two Protestant ladies, Elizabeth Foulke and Elizabeth Wandesford (10 Mar.). He may also have been the 'Mr Brydges' who on 16 May moved an additional clause at the third reading of the bill to relieve the 'Protestant purchasers' of Irish forfeited estates from the effects of the resumption, a clause designed to 'encourage the sale' of the forfeitures and at the same time 'quieten the minds' of previous purchasers.[7]

In Queen Anne's first Parliament Brydges served in all probability as a teller in a division on the Plympton election on 28 Jan. 1703, in favour of the Whig Richard Edgcumbe*, and voted on 13 Feb. 1703 for agreeing with the Lords' amendments to the bill to enlarge the time for taking the oath of abjuration. On 19 Feb. 1704 he resumed his earlier practice of obtaining leave of absence early in the year, on this occasion for three weeks. Forecast as a probable opponent of the Tack at the beginning of the 1704–5 session, on 28 Nov. he either voted against it or was absent. Later in that session he evidently joined other Members with Irish interests or associations in working to forward the bill to permit the export of linen cloth to the Plantations and to prevent its importation from Scotland into Ireland. His Irish pension qualified him for inclusion in a 'blacklist' of placemen drawn up prior to the 1705 election, and, having been listed as a 'Churchman' in an analysis of the new Parliament, he voted on 25 Oct. 1705 for the Court candidate as Speaker, and supported the Court on 18 Feb. 1706 in the proceedings on the 'place clause' in the regency bill. His loyalty was rewarded in 1707 by a further rearrangement of his pension, Rochester now withdrawing from the trusteeship, so that the money was paid directly to Brydges. Meanwhile he had fulfilled a family obligation in the 1705–6 session of Parliament by managing through the House in February the bill to naturalize the Duchess of Shrewsbury, and probably also an obligation of friendship by introducing the bill on 26 Jan. to empower the Treasury to compound for the debt of a former receiver-general for Hampshire, who had been a client of the Powletts. Further leave of absence was granted on 21 Feb. 1707, and on 7 Jan. 1708, the latter restricted to three weeks, but even so he was probably still the Member who told on 17 Feb. 1708 against his former electoral opponent Frederick Tylney* in the Whitchurch election, and on the 19th in favour of committing the petition of Sir Thomas Cookes Winford, 2nd Bt.*, for a bill to settle the bequest of Sir Thomas Cooke to establish what was to become Worcester College, Oxford.[8]

Brydges was marked as a Whig in two parliamentary lists from early 1708, and in the next Parliament was probably a teller in two election cases: on 2 Dec. 1708, against a Tory amendment to a resolution of the committee over the Reading election; and on 29 Jan. 1709, again on the Whig side, in a division over the notorious Abingdon dispute. He supported the naturalization of the Palatines in 1709, and may well be credited with a further tellership, on 29 Mar. 1709, for giving a second reading to the bill for improving the union with Scotland. That month it was reported that he was at odds with his Winchester colleague, Lord William Powlett, over the bill to permit the importing of French wines, but on 28 Jan. 1710 he and Lord William told together in favour of a motion to thank Richard West, a canon of Winchester, for his sermon to the Commons, there being some Tory opposition to the motion on the grounds that West had declared the Civil War to have been the product of 'faults on both sides'. Predictably, Brydges voted for Dr Sacheverell's impeachment.[9]

Overcoming strong opposition from Tories at Winchester in the 1710 election, Brydges was noticeably less active during the ensuing Parliament. He was marked as a Whig in the 'Hanover list'. Either he or his son was a teller on 3 Feb. 1711 against referring to a committee a petition against a Hampshire enclosure Act, but he appeared on no further parliamentary lists. Nothing has been discovered of his relationship with the Tory administration other than an unsuccessful petition which he preferred in 1712–13 for the payment of the £13,600 arrears on his pension (accumulated between 1688 and its regranting in 1697), and for which he sought James Brydges' assistance.[10]

Brydges was returned again for Winchester in 1713 but two days before the election he had clumsily doctored an ingrowing toenail, which swiftly gangrened. On the advice of the royal physician his foot was amputated 'and such was his courage', ran one account, that he was able 'to tell the surgeon he had spoiled his dancing. But soon after the same was done to his leg above the knee.' After this his death was widely reported, but in fact he lingered over the winter, and was buried on 9 Feb. at St. Giles-in-the-Fields, his son succeeding him both in his estate and in his parliamentary seat.[11]

[1] *Vernon–Shrewsbury Letters*, i. 45, 49, 58, 64, 81, 113, 137, 143, 452–3; HMC *Buccleuch*, ii. 422, 429–30, 434–5, 438–9, 441–2; J. Oldmixon, *Hist. Eng.* (1735), 152; Cobbett, *Parlty. Hist.* v. 1014, 1032, 1051, 1055; *Shrewsbury Corresp.* 528–9; *CSP Dom.* 1697, pp. 74, 119; *Cal. Treas. Bks.* xii. 123. [2]*CSP Dom.* 1672–3, p. 587; 1675–6, p. 407; 1678, pp. 301, 336; Jan.–June 1683, p. 293; *Cal. Treas. Bks.* vii. 908; viii. 222. [3]R. East, *Portsmouth Recs.* 361; Hants RO, Winchester bor. recs. ordnance bk. 7, f. 166; E. King, *Old Times Revisited*, 192. [4]D. Underdown, *Som. in Civil War and Interregnum*, 69, 111, 128; P. R. Newman, *Royalist Officers in Eng. and Wales 1642–60*, p. 43; Lambeth Palace Lib. ct. of Arches recs. A12 (20 June 1677), E6/64, 112; E6, ff. 181–2; F8, f. 148; *CSP Dom.* 1679–80, p. 377; Jan.–June 1683, p. 293; 1683–4, pp. 24, 128, 142; 1685, p. 160; 1687–9, pp. 406, 415; 1689–90, pp. 32, 36; 1697, p. 74; *VCH Hants*, iii. 307; Wilks, *Hants*, ii. 41; Duckett, *Penal Laws and Test Act* (1882), pp. 419, 423–4, 429, 432. [5]*HMC Finch*, ii. 406; Rapin, *Hist.* i. 192; *Luttrell Diary*, 22, 409–10, 440; *HMC Lords*, n.s. viii. 275–6; Bolton mss at Bolton Hall, Thomas Cobbe to Bolton, 16 May 1698, Brydges to same, 8 Nov. 1698, Bolton to Ld. Winchester (Charles Powlett I*), 2 Dec. 1698, 2nd Duke of Bolton (Charles Powlett I) to Thomas Coward, 13 June 1710. [6]*Vernon–Shrewsbury Letters*, i. 45, 49, 58, 64, 81, 113, 137, 143, 452–3; HMC *Buccleuch*, ii. 422, 429–30, 434–5, 438–9, 441–2; Oldmixon, 152; Cobbett, 1014, 1032, 1051, 1055; *Shrewsbury Corresp.* 528–9; *CSP Dom.* 1697, pp. 74, 119; *Cal. Treas. Bks.* xii. 123. [7]Northants. RO, Montagu (Boughton) mss 47/63, Vernon to Shrewsbury, 30 July 1698; *Vernon–Shrewsbury Letters*, ii. 173, 250, 260; Add. 40773, f. 140; P. J. Le Fevre, 'Three Surrey Bors. 1660–1714' (Univ. of East Anglia MA thesis, 1981), p. 136. [8]Add. 28893, f. 84; *Cal. Treas. Bks.* xxi. 475. [9]Add. 28052, f. 130; Luttrell, *Brief Relation*, vi. 541. [10]Huntington Lib. Stowe mss 58(6), p. 242; 57(9), pp. 45, 67–68, 100; *Cal. Treas. Pprs.* 1708–14, p. 392; *Cal. Treas. Bks.* xxvi. 273. [11]Herts. RO, Panshanger mss D/EP F35, p. 16; Bodl. Carte 211, f. 137; BL, Trumbull Alphab. mss 51, Thomas Bateman to Sir William Trumbull*, 2 Sept. 1713; *Wentworth Pprs.* 352; *CP*, xi. 720.

D. W. H.

BRYDGES, Hon. James (1674–1744).[1]

HEREFORD   1698–16 Oct. 1714

b. 6 Jan. 1674, 4th but 1st surv. s. of James Brydges, 8th Baron Chandos of Sudeley, by Elizabeth, da. and coh. of Sir Henry Barnard (*d.* 1680), Mercer and Turkey merchant, of St. Dunstan-in-the-East, London and Bridgnorth, Salop, alderman of London 1661. *educ.* Westminster 1686; New Coll. Oxf. 1690–2; Wolfenbüttel acad. 1692–4; I. Temple 1710. *m.* (1) 27 Feb. 1696, Mary (*d.* 15 Dec. 1712), da. of Sir Thomas Lake† of Canons Park, Edgware, Mdx., bro. of Warwick Lake*, 6s. (5 *d.v.p.*) 3da. *d.v.p.*; (2) 4 Aug. 1713, his 2nd cos. Cassandra (*d.* 1735), da. of Francis Willoughby of Wollaton, Notts. and Middleton, Warws., sis. of Sir Thomas Willoughby, 2nd Bt.*, *s.p.*; (3) 18 Apr. 1736, Lydia Catherine, da. of John van Hattem of St. Swithin's, London and wid. of Sir Thomas Davall II*, *s.p. suc.* fa. as 9th Baron Chandos

16 Oct. 1714; *cr.* Earl of Carnarvon 19 Oct. 1714, Duke of Chandos 29 Apr. 1719.²

Freeman, Ludlow 1697, Old E.I. Co. 1700; commr. taking subscriptions to S. Sea Co. 1711; gov. Levant Co. 1718–36, Charterhouse by 1721–*d.*, Foundling Hosp. 1739; ld. lt. Herefs. and Rad. 1721–*d.*; steward of crown manors, Rad. 1721; chancellor, St. Andrews Univ. 1724–*d.*; ranger, Enfield chase 1737–*d.*³

Commr. public accts. 1702–3; member, council of ld. high adm. 1703–Apr. 1705; paymaster of forces abroad Apr. 1705–13; jt. clerk of hanaper (in reversion) Nov. 1714; PC 11 Nov. 1721.⁴

Brydges' climb to vast riches and a dukedom was agreed to have been 'the most surprising instance of a change of fortune raised by a man himself, that has happened . . . in any age', the details of which form an undeviating narrative of opportunism and corruption. At the height of his prosperity the parading of wealth in grandiose building projects and in patronage of the arts gave a spurious polish to what had been a grimy reputation. As a young man on the make, he showed a readiness to compromise past allegiances, personal loyalties and the ethics of public duty that was notorious even among his contemporaries. In the House of Commons, which he made the springboard for his official career, he was an indifferent speaker, with a delivery that one parliamentary reporter rendered as 'rat-a-tat', and an occasional insensitivity to the mood of the House, but was hard-working, clubbable and possessed of the saving quality of shamelessness, which prevented him from being intimidated by scandal or seriously embarrassed by failure.⁵

In so far as his principles extended beyond personal ambition, Brydges always demonstrated a strong attachment to *de facto* authority. A regular churchgoer, whose private papers reveal an unexpected interest in scriptural study, he was able to separate his spiritual from his material life, and unlike his High Tory father experienced no qualms over the Revolution: indeed, in March 1697 he and his family 'talked of the present government, and I defended the justice of it'. Whether or not his sojourn in Germany from 1692 to 1694 was planned upon any calculation of the dynastic prospects of the Hanoverian house, as one biography has suggested, he returned to England eager to announce himself a staunch Williamite, and from at least the beginning of 1697, when his surviving diary opens, he besieged the Whig administration with daily attendance at the levees of Charles Montagu*, Sir Thomas Littleton, 3rd Bt.*, and Lord Somers (Sir John*), begging a place in the excise, or the jewel office, or wherever room could be found for him. His argument on these occasions was that 'his father was a Jacobite and used him hardly by reason he was of contrary principles', though the reality of his family's finances was that Chandos did not possess the resources to spoil his son even if he had wanted to, and while Brydges was never impoverished he certainly needed the emoluments of office. A few years later, when he had firmly aligned himself with their opponents, the Whigs' recollections of his morning visits were maliciously sharp. Littleton related a conversation in which Brydges had said, of the excise commission, 'that he knew these places were disposed of to none but Parliament-men, that tho' he was not now one he was sure he should [be] the next session . . . and that he would deserve his place by voting', to which Littleton claimed to have replied, '"Sir, I don't know that the King expects any man's vote at the price of his place, but I believe this is an offer of the first impression, to promise how [you] will vote before you are chosen."' Montagu bid an acquaintance 'observe the stinking of his [Brydges] breath, which was very offensive to him in a morning'. At the same time, Brydges was also in contact with the leaders of the Country opposition, in particular Speaker Paul Foley I* and Robert Harley*, whose local influence was a factor in his chances of obtaining a parliamentary seat in his own county of Herefordshire. But for friendship, as distinct from advantage, he seems to have favoured the society of men of antiquarian and scientific interests, like Sir Godfrey Copley, 2nd Bt.*, and Anthony Hammond*, through whom he was introduced to the circle of 'commonwealthmen' at the Grecian tavern, and to such advanced political reading as Harrington's *Oceana*, Sir Thomas Pope Blount's* *Letters* and Locke's 'Disputes', though without making much of it.⁶

In preparation for the 1698 general election Brydges took pains to cultivate every political interest in Herefordshire, Whig or Tory, that might be useful. Even so, he faced a potentially difficult contest for the county, and was only rescued by the last-minute withdrawal of one of the outgoing Members from the election in Hereford, where he was returned unopposed. An interesting sidelight on the election was that, while canvassing for knight of the shire, he was obliged to counter rumours that he was 'a great courtier, a great creature of the Earl of Portland, and one that had received considerable advantages already from the Court on that account, and would certainly be a pensioner if once chose Parliament-man'. He denied this vigorously, but when he came up to London for the session one of his first calls was on Charles Montagu. Neither Montagu nor Littleton was at home, and significantly, a fortnight or so later, Brydges went instead to the levee of the Tory leader, Lord Rochester (Laurence Hyde†), after which he took his place in the House in the ranks of the Country opposition. Soon after the election he had been marked as a Court supporter in a comparative analysis of the old and new Commons, though this classification was queried in a subsequent list. He was also forecast as likely to oppose a standing army, and, though this may have been no more than an inference from the fact that he had been chosen at Hereford alongside Paul Foley, it proved accurate, for his name did not figure on the 'black list' of those who voted on 18 Jan. 1699 against the disbanding bill at a time when his diary records regular attendance at debates and committees. His dining companions were almost exclusively Tory, and the political clubs he attended were the Tory gatherings at the Fountain and the Vine. It may be that he had taken umbrage at the Junto lords' failure to make good their promises, but he was, on the whole, not a man to take serious offence at anything, and it seems more likely that his sensitive political antennae had detected a hint of change, and that he saw more prospect of advancement in hitching himself to the Tories, and in particular to Robert Harley, to whom he edged closer during this session. His first recorded speech was in the committee of supply on 2 Mar. 1699: after Charles Montagu had proposed granting £312,000 to cover the army estimates, Brydges moved an amendment to reduce this sum by £50,000, the difference to be made up by removing from the civil list the money provided for Queen Mary of Modena. On 14 Apr. he was elected to the chair of the committee on the bill to raise the militia, the Country party's preferred method of national defence, from which he reported on the 17th. He was one of the small knot of Country party activists responsible for preparing the bill to state the public accounts, but his contributions to parliamentary business were not confined to the major issues. On 3 Mar. he attended the committee on the bill to amend the previous Act to regulate the working of the wholesale cloth market at Blackwell Hall, and on 26 Apr. recorded that he had received the thanks of the Stationers' Company for efforts in securing an additional clause in the paper duty bill on the Company's behalf.[7]

Prior to the next session Brydges was to be found attending the levees of Rochester and the Duke of Leeds (Sir Thomas Osborne†), and when Parliament reassembled he once again kept company with Tories, at their club at the Goat tavern, and with his cronies from the Royal Society, men like Copley, Hammond, Charles Davenant* and Cyril Arthington*. He was also on social terms, though not especially close, with Robert Harley, occasionally dining at Harley's house. In the Commons he was anxious to make an impression as an energetic man-of-business and as an aggressive speaker on the Country side in the set-piece debates. In committee on 5 Feb. 1700 he took the lead in seeking to expose flaws in the accounting of the paymaster-general, Lord Ranelagh (Richard Jones*), a sublime irony in the light of his own later career: tactics had been concerted beforehand with Copley, Hammond and others, and Brydges had been chosen, or had chosen himself, to raise the matter, but, as James Vernon I* reported, 'my lord was too hard for him at figures'. Ten days later, in the committee of the whole House on the state of the nation, he thrust himself forward again. Sir Richard Cocks, 2nd Bt.*, wrote that Brydges 'downright railed against the government'. After denouncing the 'luxury' and 'avarice' of 'evil counsellors', he concentrated his fire on the issue of crown grants, bringing in the affair of Captain Kidd, and concluded with a motion to condemn the passing by ministers of grants to themselves. He was immediately challenged by Sir Rowland Gwynne*, for 'reflecting' by implication on Lord Somers, which 'occasioned some warmth between these gentlemen'. The general feeling of the House, even of oppositionists like John Grobham Howe*, was to vindicate Somers' good name, and Brydges was obliged first to deny that his motion 'aimed at' the chancellor, and then to apologize at the bar for expressions used in his reply to Gwynne. Neither this nor his earlier *faux pas* disconcerted him, however, and he was one of the Country MPs who hoped to serve on the commission to examine the debts due to the army, navy and transport service. When the House decided against allowing its Members to be appointed commissioners Brydges made sure that he and Copley participated in the gathering of Tory back-benchers at the Vine which agreed on the Country party's slate for the ballot. But perhaps his most particular concern at this time was the situation of the Old East India Company. Already connected with overseas merchants through his father's involvement in the Levant Company, he was approached on 10 Jan. by several 'gentlemen' to give his support to the Old Company's petition, and he entered wholeheartedly into their parliamentary schemes, being ordered on 19 Jan. to bring in the bill to continue the Company. An analysis of the House into interests in early 1700 identified him with the Old Company, and in March he was consulted on the parliamentary affairs of one of the Company's men, William Johnson, then absent on a voyage to the Indies, who wished to signify by letter his choice of constituency between the two for which he had been returned. The following month Brydges cemented his own relationship with the company by taking out his freedom, and in May he made his first purchase of Old Company stock. His participation in company cabals was at this time so intense that during the summer he attended discussions over municipal politics in the city of London with directors and their Tory allies.[8]

At this point in his career it would have been natural for Brydges to have formed a much closer association with Harley, who was not only the coming man in national politics but exercised considerable influence in Brydges' own locality. But the two men were never entirely compatible: Harley was too shrewd to be taken in by Brydges' flattery, and there was always a wariness, even an underlying coolness, in their relations. Perhaps, too, the very fact of Harley's involvement in Herefordshire politics formed a barrier: the two men were potential rivals, and Brydges in particular was never eager to ally himself too closely with any other interest in the county. At the general election of January 1701, for example, although he was returned together with Thomas Foley II*, he resisted joining Foley until forced into the partnership by an attack on his own position by a third candidate. In political outlook, however, he was closer to Harley than to many High Tory colleagues in the Country party, and he found no difficulty in moving over from opposition to support the new Tory administration. In his view of the situation in Europe, for example, commitment to the Revolution and concern for the safety of long-distance trade meant that he did not share the more extreme Tories' aversion to military action against France, even though he was highly critical of the second Partition Treaty. 'In my poor opinion', he told Thomas Coke*,

> had anyone studied to have disposed of that monarchy more to the disadvantage of Europe in general, and us in particular, it would have required, I fancy, a better headpiece than any of the two plenipotentiaries is master of, to have compassed it. Had they given that crown entire to France, the knavery would have been too gross, and we should quickly, I doubt not, have had another confederacy as strong as the last to have opposed it. But thus giving the greatest part, in appearance, to the house of Austria they think, I suppose, to lull the world asleep, though they cannot but be conscious to themselves at the same time they have given France not only the best and richest part, but that which will enable him to be master of the rest whenever he pleaseth, and puts him into immediate possession, if he hath a mind to it, of all the Mediterranean trade.

None the less, when Brydges arrived in London on 26 Jan. 1701 his first port of call was the house of Sir Bartholomew Shower*, where he met other Tories to discuss the election results. From there he went to the Thatched House tavern, 'to inquire for Colonel Granville [Hon. John*] and the club that used to be there on Sunday nights'. He now spent his mornings visiting Rochester, Sir Edward Seymour, 4th Bt.*, and Harley. At some point in February Brydges was listed with those likely to support the Court in agreeing with the committee of supply's resolution to continue the 'Great Mortgage'. A speech on 2 Apr., in the debate on the King's message relating the answer that had been given by the French ambassador to the demands of the States General, besides giving what was undoubtedly a genuine opinion as to the best course to be followed in foreign policy, revealed the part Brydges was playing as one of Harley's under-managers in the Commons. Starting off the debate, he

> said he first opened, as the youngest, to give others the cue, and that the wiser might be kept to sum all up at last. He lightly reflected upon all miscarriages, and said he would not say anything to widen our breaches when we should unite; he spoke of our debts, of our inabilities, and at last concluded with the danger of having France in possession of all Spain.

It was as a spokesman for the new Court party as much as a Tory tribune that he was to the forefront of the proceedings to impeach Lord Halifax (Charles Montagu*) and the other Whig lords. An active member of the committee nominated on 1 Apr. to draw up the articles against Lord Portland, which was later extended to prepare the articles against Halifax, Orford (Edward Russell*) and Somers, and to manage the ensuing conferences with the Lords, he also served on the subcommittee to translate into English Portland's letters on the second Partition Treaty and on 15 Apr. was chosen by the Commons to carry Halifax's impeachment to the Upper House, an act Halifax regarded as a gross personal betrayal. Significantly, on that day Brydges dined with Harley. He acted as a teller on 13 May for an address to the King requesting an answer to the previous address for the removal of the impeached lords from his 'counsel and presence'; made the report from the impeachments committee when the articles against Halifax were agreed on 9 June, and carried them to the Lords; and on 20 June reported from the committee to inspect the Lords' Journals concerning the impeachment proceedings. Complementing the impeachments in Tory strategy was the harassment of the old ministers through the re-establishment of a commission of public accounts. On 10 Apr. Brydges' diary noted that he had spent the evening at Shower's, 'where we finished the Act for stating the accounts', and a week afterwards he himself introduced the bill into the House. More acceptable to the King were the new Court party's efforts to forward supply. Brydges was a member of the committee to receive proposals for the payment of the public debts, and advancing the credit of the nation (10 Apr.), which, with 'the committee on the half-pay', he made a point of attending. On 2 May, in ways and means, he 'offered at many things' by way of fiscal expedients, which he had presumably discussed with Lord Godolphin (Sidney†) when he met him on 27 Apr., 'about the raising of what we had voted'. Cocks observed sourly that Brydges 'had taken great pains to inform himself of them, unless they were done for him', but detailed only one of his suggestions, the removal of the prohibition on the import of Indian silks, a move which would obviously have benefited both East India companies. Members greeted this with 'disdain, thinking this gent[leman] was not in the interest of his country'. After the next meeting of the committee Brydges and other Court Tories broke with the more violent members of their party in opposing a motion to cut £100,000 from the civil list, Brydges telling against a resolution to this effect when it was reported on 5 May, and finding himself on the opposite side to John Granville and Sir Charles Shuckburgh, 2nd Bt. To recover the situation, Sir Edward Seymour put forward a compromise in committee on the 21st, whereby the King would receive the civil list in full but would contribute a weekly sum of £3,000 to be used as security to raise a fund of £700,000. Brydges joined other courtiers in speaking for it. In the meantime his appetite for routine parliamentary business had not diminished: he reported a private naturalization bill on 4 June, and was frequently pressed to take up individual petitions relating to the Irish forfeited estates, from financial speculators and aggrieved ex-proprietors. For him the session ended very much as it had begun, as he supported the King's intention to go to war, and was named to the committee of 12 June to draft the Commons' address pledging support for any actions in defence of the allies and the liberties of Europe. This accorded with his own views on foreign policy as well as what he presumably gauged to be his personal advantage. He now regarded war as inevitable, and indeed essential to 'our preservation', though, as he confided to Thomas Coke, he felt the delay had been 'the greatest advantage imaginable to us', enabling the Dutch to put themselves 'in a posture of defence', and he hoped for economic reasons that hostilities would be brief, an outcome which in his view could only be achieved through 'vigorous' military action. In these circumstances it was hard that he should find himself blacklisted by the Whigs as one who had, among other things, allegedly opposed the making of preparations for war; and perhaps harder still that his strenuous attempts to earn himself some office, through assisting administration in the House, should meet with rebuffs from the King. Perhaps sensing that Harley had neither the personal interest nor the will to persuade William of his merits, Brydges had applied himself to other patrons, principally to the Earl of Marlborough (John Churchill†) and to Admiral Sir George Rooke*. His regular meetings with officers of the Admiralty and navy board suggest that he was seeking to qualify himself for a post in naval administration, but he seems to have pinned his hopes above all on Marlborough, whose influence may perhaps be detected in the bullishness of some of Brydges' statements on foreign policy during the summer of 1701. Marlborough was already praising him to the King, without effect, and perhaps also receiving direct requests for assistance in patronage matters.[9]

The second general election of 1701, in which Brydges again overcame a challenge from a third candidate at Hereford, this time by a crushing majority, was an eventful one for him, ending in a duel fought with a hot-tempered Herefordshire squire, James Morgan*, over remarks Morgan had passed concerning Lord Chandos. Before the Parliament met, Brydges spent an hour with Speaker Harley, who had, naturally, classed him with the Tories in his list of the new Parliament. Brydges was appointed on 2 Jan. 1702 to the committee on the Address, whose meetings he records attending, and was also soon active in promoting a measure to regulate the practice of stock-jobbing, which had been a peculiar concern of his for several years. He probably acted as a teller on 5 Jan. 1702, on the Tory side, against appointing a day for the elections committee to hear the Norwich petition; on 10 Feb. 1702, against a Whig amendment to the oath of abjuration included in the bill for the security of the King's person and the succession; and on 19 Mar., against leave for a bill to enable the appointment of commissioners to negotiate an Anglo-Scottish union. Apart from the bill to provide for the Protestant children of the Earl of Clanricarde and Lord Bourke of Bophin, which he presented on 7 Mar. and took a major share in managing, he seems to have been bothered less often in this session by Irish petitioners requiring assistance with saving bills concerning the forfeited estates. However, he may have been a teller on a number of divisions on Irish business: on 25 Feb., for a Tory-inspired instruction to the drafting committee on the bill to relieve Captain Bellew, to oblige Lord Romney (Henry Sidney†) to repay to the forfeiture trustees two-thirds of the purchase money received from Bellew; on 26 Mar., again with a Tory and in opposition to two Whig tellers, for a bill to relieve the Jacobite banker Sir Daniel Arthur; on 9 Apr., against committing a bill for the relief of Robert Edgworth; on 28 Apr., on an instruction to the committee on Ignatius Gould's bill; and finally on 7 May, for an instruction on the bill to relieve the 'Protestant purchasers' of forfeited estates, to provide that a third of the purchase money designed to be repaid them be instead vested in the trustees, 'for the use of the public'. With other Tories, he was listed as having voted on 26 Feb. in favour of the motion vindicating the Commons' proceedings in the impeachments of the Junto lords. He was an active member of the committee of 8 Mar. to draw up the address of condolence on the death of King William and congratulation on the accession of Queen Anne. The one speech recorded by Cocks in this session occurred on 31 Mar. when Brydges and Sir Thomas Powys* vainly opposed a motion to take into custody the Shropshire Tory George Walcot* following the hearing of an election case in which Walcot had been found guilty of 'notorious bribery'. His chief interest, however, seems to have been in the further attempt, this time successful, to reconstitute a plenary commission of accounts in order to pursue inquiries into alleged corruption by the previous Whig administration. As early as 14 Jan. he was at Simon Harcourt I's house where, he reported, 'we talked about commiss[ioners] of accounts', and as the ballot for commissioners approached, he dined with Thomas Coke, Arthur Moore*, Sir Christopher Musgrave, 4th Bt.*, and others at the Thatched House, where a slate of six candidates was agreed. He himself was chosen in fourth place when the outcome of the ballot was announced on 8 Mar., and from early April his diary shows him to have been preoccupied with the work of the commission to the exclusion of parliamentary business.[10]

With Queen Anne's accession Brydges' cultivation of Marlborough's friendship yielded dividends. Already in May 1702, Marlborough had 'begged' Lord Treasurer Godolphin to reserve Brydges a place on the council of the lord high admiral, Prince George of Denmark, 'against the next year'. By December there were rumours of his imminent appointment, though these were not confirmed until the following March, after Marlborough (now a duke) had renewed his solicitations. In Parliament there seems little doubt that he was the Brydges who in January and February 1703 chaired the committee of the whole on the mutiny bill, and served as a teller twice in the 1702–3 session, in favour of John Grobham Howe at the hearing of the Gloucestershire election (19 Nov. 1702), and apparently for the Tory side on an adjournment motion (23 Dec.). The impact of his appointment to office, however, was immediately observable in his parliamentary conduct in the next session. He opened the debate on 26 Nov. against the motion for leave for the introduction of an occasional conformity bill, and was soon entrusted with the task of presenting to the House, on behalf of the Admiralty council, the estimates for the navy. He may again have chaired the committee on the mutiny bill and have been a teller twice in February 1704: on the 21st, against committing the bill for setting the poor to work; and eight days later, to agree with the committee resolution in favour of an address urging an inquiry into the Scotch Plot. But although he seems to have settled into the part of a loyal 'Queen's servant', he did not regard his present post as sufficiently lucrative. In March 1704 he approached Godolphin for the vacant place of paymaster of marines, thereby disgusting his friend and confidant Charles Davenant, who was more conscious than he was himself of the dignity, as opposed to the profits, of office. Undeterred by his failure in this instance, he continued to bombard Godolphin and Marlborough with requests for a transfer from the Admiralty – to be chancellor of the Exchequer, lieutenant of the Ordnance, paymaster of the forces, and so on – on the specious grounds, not hitherto admitted, that he lacked experience in naval affairs. The tone of these letters was uniformly obsequious, and his behaviour in the Commons was equally servile and obliging. At the beginning of the 1704–5 session he was forecast as a probable opponent of the Tack; he did not vote for it on 28 Nov. By now the complexion of the ministry was changing, and Brydges was anxious that his indiscretions over the impeachments (as they now appeared to have been) should not be held against him. He wrote to Godolphin to beg him to intercede with the Junto lords, explaining that what had happened in 1701 was that

> my natural temper carrying me to pursue with warmth their measures and interest with whom I am engaged, I made some steps which may be remembered hereafter to my disadvantage, but I can say this for myself, that I was a knight adventurer without the least malice to any of the adverse party, though I might think my credit concerned to decline no part of the action to which I was assigned by those whose side I then happened to espouse; I was pitched upon by the House of Commons to carry up their impeachment against my Lord Halifax.

As if sheltering more closely behind the 'duumvirs' for protection, he now identified himself as their client. L'Hermitage might reckon Brydges' longed-for advancement in April 1705 to the office of paymaster of the forces abroad as a ministerial gain for the 'moderate Tories', but its partisan significance was minimal. Brydges spent the summer of 1705 on campaign with Marlborough, in order to secure himself in the Duke's favour (a stratagem he repeated the following year), and moved quickly to establish close personal relations with Marlborough's most trusted subordinates, as part of the same process.[11]

Re-elected without opposition in 1705, and marked as a placeman and as 'Low Church' in published preliminary assessments of the Parliament, he wrote optimistically to Marlborough before the session opened that 'the warm heads of either side will find it their interest to be quiet, and not disturb the Queen's affairs'. He voted on 25 Oct. for the Court candidate as Speaker. At about this time he was also acting as an intermediary between the lord treasurer and leading lights in the lower house of Convocation, like Francis Atterbury, whom he sought to persuade of the usefulness of inserting into Convocation's loyal address a clause complimenting Godolphin on his management of the revenue. In Parliament, Grey Neville* recorded a speech of his on 4 Dec., in the debate on the proposed union with Scotland, though without giving details, and further interventions on 19 Dec., at the second reading of the regency bill, to support calls to censure the Tory MP Charles Caesar for innuendoes against the lord treasurer, and to call for Caesar's confinement in the Tower. He may have spoken again in a subsequent debate on the regency bill on 12 Jan. 1706, and appears to have made a substantial contribution to the Court party's resistance to extensions to place legislation. A 'Mr Brydges' was a teller on 13 Dec. 1705 against leave for bringing in a place bill, and on 18 Feb. 1706 against a 'Country' counter-amendment to one of the Lords' amendments to the 'place clause' of the regency bill. Brydges was blacklisted as one who had supported the Court during these proceedings. Before he departed for the Low Countries in May he was also recorded as presenting official papers to the House concerning the payment of troops (22 Jan.), and, perhaps, reporting from the committee on a private naturalization bill. When he returned to England in the autumn he found the administration divided, and Harley making the first, secret and tentative, moves in a scheme to resist the drift towards the Junto, by 'raising a third party' of moderate men to join instead with the 'more reasonable' elements among the Tories. Brydges recounted this to Godolphin with the utmost care, expressing no direct personal opinion other than that he was himself entirely devoted to the treasurer's interest, but implying some sympathy for Harley's objectives. Nothing came of these approaches, however. In the 1706–7 session Brydges presented papers to the House on 22 Jan. 1707 in his capacity as paymaster. Either he or a namesake introduced the French wines bill in December 1706, and took charge in February 1707 of a bill to make the vessel *Supply* a free ship.[12]

The ministerial crisis foreshadowed by Harley's manoeuvres the year before came to a head in the winter of 1707–8. Brydges' correspondence at this time shows him identifying himself with the Court and especially with the 'duumvirs', deprecating the violence of party faction, and initially sympathetic to Harley's renewed schemes for a coalition of 'moderate Tories' and lord treasurer's Whigs. In Parliament he found himself as paymaster propelled into the spotlight during the controversial inquiries into the lack of available troops at the battle of Almanza, and also during the debates on recruiting which oppositionists from both parties opened up in the wake of the 'Spanish troops' scandal. He was repeatedly obliged to submit papers to the House, on 13 Nov., 13 Dec. (accounts of expenditure in Spain), 8 and 16 Jan. 1708 (accounts of money received for the Spanish service), made the motion for an alternative method of recruitment in committee on 16 Jan., and on 29 Jan., in the principal debate on 'Spanish troops', supported the secretary at war, Henry St. John II*, in expounding the ministry's explanation of the shortfall. More generally too, he seems to have taken an active part in the scheme of Court management organized by Harley, but he was not himself a Harleyite, as some contemporaries were beginning to describe him, and when Harley's alliance with Godolphin and Marlborough suddenly broke up at the beginning of February Brydges did not resign alongside the secretary. Instead, he remained loyal to the 'duumvirs', accepting their version of events and continuing in his post in an even more Whiggishly-inclined administration. Part of the explanation for his decision must lie in a rare instance of personal loyalty, reinforced by an awareness that, via his confidant William Cadogan*, Marlborough had been fully informed of the details of Brydges' shady dealings as paymaster – the manipulation of foreign exchange rates, wagering on the course of the war with the benefit of privileged information, insider trading in stocks, and other expedients from which vast profits were derived for Brydges and his accomplices, including Cadogan and perhaps Marlborough too. These profits must also in themselves have constituted a powerful inducement to stay: as paymaster, Brydges had at long last, and precipitately, made his fortune. He was in the process of buying his wife's family estate at Canons, which he finally acquired in 1713, and was casting about for other likely property, as well as investing large sums in shares and securities. So he drew even closer to Godolphin and Marlborough. Without the Harleyites there was more for the remaining Court managers to do, and by the end of the session Brydges was complaining not only of the workload of his office but of the fatigue of parliamentary attendance. His anomalous political position at this time is captured in two parliamentary lists drawn up early in 1708, which label him respectively as a Whig and a Tory, and reflected too in his preparations for the general election in May, in which he was anxious to be returned again to the Commons, 'where at least I have room to show my zeal and affection to that government by which I have [been] countenanced so much beyond my merit' (as he told Marlborough). Refusing Harley's assistance in Herefordshire, and fighting shy of any specific arrangement with Thomas Foley II in Hereford itself, he was forced to rely on his own interest in the town, and even with the benefit of government patronage was still sufficiently fearful to avail himself of Godolphin's recommendation to the Boscawen-controlled borough of Truro, where he was returned unopposed. In the event, however, he surmounted opposition in Hereford, and so the insurance was not required.[13]

Before the 1708 Parliament Brydges reassured both Godolphin and Marlborough of his loyalty, and indeed his complete reliance on their protection against the new 'scheme' he feared would arise: 'I shall never covet or seek any other patronage', he informed the lord treasurer,

> than that of your lordship and the Duke of Marlborough. I hope I have for some years behaved myself so among those with whom I desire to live well, as that no rancour remains on the score of past division, and while I cheerfully co-operate with such as your lordship judges fittest in this juncture to serve her Majesty, I flatter myself that your lordship's and my lord Duke's favours will continue to shine upon [me].

Once in the House he supported government consistently, and, as far as he could, unobtrusively, aligning himself with 'lord treasurer's Whigs' like Hon. Henry Boyle* and an old Herefordshire opponent Lord Coningsby (Thomas*). Typical of his attitude was the account he gave of the replacement of the Tory John Conyers as chairman of supply: 'I must confess (tho' I contributed to it) I am sorry for it, but there was no avoiding it; the Whigs were bent upon having favour, and the Court thought it not worthwhile to make a division among themselves.' He was prepared to back such partisan measures if he had to, and was, for example, listed among those who supported the naturalization of the Palatines, but he does not seem to have been anywhere near the vanguard. His significant Commons activity in the 1708–9 session consisted largely of presenting departmental papers as paymaster (11 Dec., 1 Feb., 21 Mar. 1709), though he may have been the Member who on 18 Feb. brought in a bill for encouraging the export of tobacco. The one issue which animated him was, not surprisingly, the defence of Marlborough's reputation from the snide attacks of some Tories, which he described as stemming from 'the impotent anger of a few discontented men'. He had recently been given further reason to be grateful to the Duke, as recurrent rumours of his own dismissal, in December and January, had been brought to nothing, probably as a result of Marlborough's intervention. As one cynical commentator had observed, when this talk had come to the surface, 'I fancy Mr Br[ydges] will scarcely be outed, because he has been at the bottom of all the cheating of a certain great man'. Brydges carried his low-key support for the ministry over into the next session, helping to whip in Court Whig voters for the crucial early days. He took a ministerial view of the decision to impeach Dr Sacheverell, writing in December 1709:

> I am clearly of opinion if there is not a stop put to the liberty some gentlemen of his coat take in their pulpits 'twill be in vain to think either the Queen can sit safe on the throne or the Members meet in peace and quietness in either House of Parliament.

And in January 1710 he was still convinced that 'the liberty of the pulpit was grown so high that it was time to take notice of it and put a stop to it'; so that although he was absent from the House around the middle of February his inclusion in the list of those who had voted for Sacheverell's impeachment was probably justified.[14]

The strength of popular reaction against the impeachment, however, gave Brydges pause. Aversion to any such outbreak of passion in politics led him to regard the trial as 'unfortunate', and in the immediate aftermath he wrote, 'I heartily wish it had never been meddled with, for I am very much afraid it will have the effect on our friends that the occasional bill formerly produced to the Tories . . . it hath revived old and forgotten disputes and raised such heats and jealousies of one another in the kingdom as will take up no little time to allay'. In his own borough he could do no more than seek to moderate the tone of the corporation's Sacheverellite address. He was also sensitive to the rising clamour against the war, considering peace to be ever more a necessity on political grounds, though to one correspondent in July he observed, 'I know not whether we ought to desire it [a peace] or not, since if the continuance of the war did not prevent and keep us in a [?little] I cannot tell what extremities the violence of parties might not drive us into'. By this time the prospect of a 'revolution' at Court and in the ministry was leading him to reconsider his position, and the changes in the political scene enabled him to demonstrate some characteristically deft footwork, after an initial blunder when he had pressed to be appointed to succeed his ailing superior, John Grobham Howe, in the paymaster's office and had been dissuaded by the Marlboroughs. He contrived to rebuild his links with Harley and 'moderate' Tories, and to distance himself from the Whigs and even from his erstwhile patron Godolphin, while retaining the confidence of Marlborough, whose military prowess would be needed by the incoming administration and who in any case knew too much about Brydges' past activities. His reinterpretation of the Sacheverell episode, for instance, was that the offending sermon had been a 'nonsensical' piece of 'Billingsgate' scarcely worthy of notice, and that the furore against the impeachment had been a justified reaction to the Whigs' open assertion of republican notions: 'The point is not', he wrote, 'how far resistance in cases of necessity is lawful (where a constitution is manifestly attempted to be subverted)', that question having been settled at the Revolution; rather,

> what gave offence was the endeavours to establish such a position by a new law [the bill 'for the better security of crown and Church'], which could serve only for a groundwork for any opposite to the Court, and which should happen to have a majority in Parliament, to form a rebellion.

As the months went by his correspondence shows him relocating his position on the party-political spectrum. In June 'our friends' were still the Whigs, but by September he was telling a Shropshire connexion that to join with a Whig faction in his election would not be 'agreeable' to his 'principles'. The reality seems to have been that he did not consider himself as truly belonging to either party, and his private observations were written from a Court or ministerial viewpoint. But for public consumption he was presenting himself as having always been at bottom a Tory. As his friend Charles Davenant pointed out, he could justify this by harking back to his early career in the House, and could claim it as a merit in the eyes of the Tories that he had 'meddled so little in the affairs of Parliament . . . these last three years'. As far as the party as a whole was concerned, and especially those who coveted his office, his failure to resign in 1708 had left an indelible stain. Harley, however, who had arguably the greatest reason to be aggrieved at his having remained in the ministry in 1708, was readily persuadable, and before the end of August was reassuring Brydges of the Queen's satisfaction with his service. Nor, in the end, did Brydges find it too painful to go back on his earlier pledges to Godolphin to resign 'cheerfully' should the treasurer be dismissed. His own rationalization was set out in a letter to his subordinate John Drummond, following Harley's message: he could reasonably claim, he wrote, to have kept faith with the 'duumvirs'

> in everything that regards them . . . personally . . . but, whatever I shall do for their service, I know no reason I have to sacrifice myself and fortunes to promote the interest of others from whom I have never received even so much as common civility, during the time I have been looked upon as one of them, and whose aims, I am persuaded, are to gain power enough to govern without control, not only those two, but the whole kingdom, and this in opposition to those I have, as 'twere, been bred up with, who are of the same principles with me, and who, notwithstanding my having differed with them of late, are willing to receive me with open arms.

Such arguments were accepted without question both by Marlborough, and, perhaps more surprisingly, by his Duchess, who commended, without sarcasm, Brydges' 'steady behaviour upon all occasions'. What remained was to secure his re-election at Hereford, where there had been reports of a weakening in his interest, and of treachery on the part of his agent. Paying rather more attention to the constituency than he had done in recent elections, he was able to win a substantial victory at the polls, even *in absentia*, and he approached the forthcoming Parliament in a confident mood, pleased with the Tory majority as a guarantee of stability, and sure of Harley's ability to retain control, and to raise funds for the maintenance of the war.[15]

Unembarrassed by his own change of tack, Brydges proved to be a visible rather than a reticent supporter of Harley's administration during the 1710–11 session. He served in all probability as a teller on 10 Mar. 1711 in favour of the bill to permit the importation of French wines, and frequently communicated papers to the House relating to the payment of troops. He himself recorded a vote with the Court party on 27 Mar. for the imposition of a leather duty. Despite having been noted as a Whig in the 'Hanover list', he was included among the 'worthy patriots' who detected the mismanagements of the previous ministry (a surprising inclusion since he was himself a prime object of Tory back-bench interest on this score) and the 'Tory patriots' who favoured peace. Behind the scenes he was useful to Harley as an intermediary with Marlborough, and with some financial interests in the City. All this encouraged ministers, and even some individual Tory back-benchers whom he had taken pains to cultivate, to come to his defence when the inevitable attempt was made, as he put it, to 'blow me up'. The occasion was the report of the commissioners of accounts, one of whose most spectacular findings was the sum of £6,500,000 unaccounted for on his part, with no accounts in fact having been passed or even made up in his office since 1707. The attack was led by the October Club, with the avowed purpose of obtaining his dismissal. The timing of the revelations coincided with Harley's spell of convalescence from the wound inflicted by Guiscard, and it thus fell to Brydges' 'cousin', as he called him, Henry St. John II*, to speak on his behalf. Whether St. John valued Brydges' gratitude for its own sake, or whether he saw this as a way to ingratiate himself even further with Marlborough and thus steal a march on his temporarily bedridden rival, is unclear. Whatever the reason, St. John made a spirited and successful defence, to Brydges' relief. Harley's rather cool reaction, however, was a complicating factor, and Brydges felt it necessary to write to him with an offer of resignation and a request for his full and unequivocal backing in order to deter any further assaults. On neither point did Harley reply directly, and although Brydges continued to recommend to Lord Treasurer Oxford (as Harley became) his own and his clients' and kinsmen's requests for favour and patronage, the two men did not recover anything approaching intimacy thenceforth but co-operated on the basis of mutual need. When Brydges applied to be appointed a director of the South Sea Company in June 1711 Oxford ignored him. The next crisis in his affairs took place in January 1712. This time it was not the renewed investigations of the accounts commissioners that troubled him, for he had not provided them with any further information on which to build a case and he could count on strong Whig support as well as the backing of ministerialists. The Whig tract *A State of the Five and Thirty Millions . . .*, published after the 1710–11 session, and allegedly the work of Robert Walpole II*, had taken pains to defend Brydges' official record in particular, and the members of the Hanover Club rallied round him when the affair of his delayed and incomplete accounts was raised again in the House in May 1712. Instead, his difficulty was a more general one: the focusing of High Tory hostility brought about by his own vigorous defence of Marlborough, first in the censure debate of January 1712 and then a month later, by implication at least, when on the report of the commissioners of accounts he intervened to discount any suggestions of irregularities in the bread contracts, a speech which, as much as his official interest, probably explains his appointment on 18 Feb. to the committee to investigate abuses in the musters, the clothing of the army and in military hospitals abroad. The first of these two contributions was the more important: it was by some way the most striking and effective of his parliamentary speeches, and a rare example of his crossing the current of popular opinion in the House. Some surprised observers gave him credit for courage, but most Tories were simply enraged, and rumours flew, even as far as Hereford, that his dismissal was imminent, for this time he had defied not only back-bench prejudice but also the declared interest of the ministry. However, Brydges had been nothing if not careful in preparing the ground. He was in close touch with Marlborough throughout the winter – may even have sought to dissuade the Duke from pursuing a public vindication – and when at last it became inevitable that Marlborough's reputation would be assailed directly in Parliament, Brydges wrote to Oxford to put his own case, shrewdly prefacing this with a letter of explanation to Lady Masham, whom he had already been flattering for some time. 'The Duke of Marlborough's business in Parliament has put me under very great difficulty', he began:

> The obligations I have to his Grace are known all over the world. His favour first raised me to what I am and I cannot leave him in his present troubles without incurring the censure of ingratitude. On the other hand, to appear in the defence of one who is so unfortunate as to lie under the Queen's displeasure, while I am actually in her service, carries with it such an air of indecency, as every gentleman ought to avoid.

He omitted to mention that he depended on Oxford's personal goodwill to continue to protect him from Treasury demands that he bring up to date his paymaster's accounts. Although Oxford may well have resented the adverse publicity thus given to his efforts at 'moderation', he none the less accepted the difficulties of Brydges' position and promised him indemnity, a fact that was quickly advertised to Brydges' parliamentary colleagues and even as far away as his constituency.[16]

Less than nine months after receiving these assurances from Oxford, Brydges wrote to the treasurer in November 1712 to beg leave to resign, on the grounds that, with the imminent conclusion of a general peace treaty, his office would be regarded as 'new' and would thus fall under the terms of the disqualification clauses of the 1706 Regency Act. He repeated the request in February 1713, before Parliament reassembled, suggesting that he would be better able to serve the Queen if he did not appear to have any 'immediate dependence' on her, but even after the Treaty of Utrecht was signed in March Oxford took no action. No challenge was offered to Brydges' position when the session opened, and in May Oxford promised that he would be permitted to resign, prompting an outpouring of gratitude and a renewed display of support for administration, which had already seen Brydges subscribing heavily to the £200,000 loan and encouraging local thanksgiving for the peace, and which now issued in the Commons in his vote on 18 June in favour of the French commerce bill. The accounts commissioners were still hunting him, and their report in this session criticized him personally for delay and prevarication, but he had become accustomed to shrugging off their attacks. Of more concern, as the session drew to a close, was Oxford's failure to make good the promise to relieve him of his post, and enable him to settle the affairs of the office. At last, in August, his patent was suspended, though there was still a great deal of unfinished business, and in the 1714 Parliament he was still to be found presenting various sets of departmental papers to the House.[17]

The last year of the Queen's reign necessitated another prolonged balancing act, as Brydges sought on the one hand the goodwill, or at least the neutrality, of both Oxford and Bolingbroke (the former Henry St. John), if for nothing else than to protect him from further inquiries into his accounts, which were now the subject of persistent Treasury investigations as well as being a prime target of the Commons' commissioners, and on the other the favour of the reversionary interest, which was approachable via the Marlboroughs. He had kept up his correspondence with Marlborough during the Duke's exile, with letters that recalled their past associations and pledged future service, while advising the Marlboroughs against returning to England before the Tories' rancour against them had abated. The events surrounding the Hanoverian succession demonstrated how skilfully Brydges' recent political course had been steered. When Oxford was dismissed from the treasurership in July, Brydges was widely reported to be among the leading candidates for the commission that was expected to take over from him; yet he had friends among the Whigs, such as Robert Walpole II, who had defended him from the accounts commissioners in the House in May, and he had so successfully paid court to Hanover that he was offered the comptrollership of the Household when the new King arrived, and succeeded in converting this proposal into a coronation earldom.[18]

Brydges never returned to office, though he did rise higher in the peerage in 1719, and he was considered on several occasions for the most prestigious places in government. After 1714 he found his way back to the Tories, having been described as a Whig in the Worsley list, and took up a position as one of the leaders of the 'moderate' or 'Hanoverian' wing of the Tory party. Certainly his attachment to the Protestant succession was never in doubt, and among his many improvements to his principal estate at Canons was the erection there in 1722 of an equestrian statue of George I. He played an important role in politics early in the reign, with a reputation enhanced by his wealth, his experience, and his connexions with the Marlboroughs, and during the Whig Schism was even talked of as a possible lord treasurer. But his heavy losses in the Mississippi and South Sea bubbles weakened his standing and perhaps sapped his will to pursue an active parliamentary and political career. He was far from pauperized, however, by these or other financial disasters, and at his death, on 9 Aug. 1744, left encumbrances of only £14,000 on his extensive properties. The ruin of his estate, and the consequent demolition of Canons, were instead the work of his son, the 2nd Duke of Chandos, Hervey's 'hot-headed, passionate, half-witted coxcomb'.[19]

Brydges' epitaph on the Chandos monument at Whitchurch, Hampshire, spoke of the 'patience, resignation and piety' of his last years, which other witnesses attest; of his great acts of 'humanity and charity', which are open to question; and of his public service, tending 'more to the good of his country and friends than his own', which defies belief. Yet the inscription's earlier reference to his 'constant application to business' did do him justice. As a Parliamentarian, Brydges' prime virtue was diligence, his cast of mind managerial. 'A great complier with every court', as Swift described him, he deplored the 'little narrow effects of party and faction', the violence which weakened the prerogatives of the monarchy and even the influence of the constituency patron over dependent voters, introducing in each case an unwonted popular element. His commitment to the Revolution and to the Hanoverian succession thus reflected above all a reverence for power. That his career should have prospered in a time of party rage is not only ironical, but a tribute to political skills that contemporaries recognized: according to Speaker Arthur Onslow[†], for example, he had parts of understanding and knowledge, experience of men and business, with a sedateness of mind and gravity of deportment, which more qualified him for a wise man, than what the wisest men have generally been possessed with.[20]

[1] Unless otherwise stated, this biography is based on C. H. C. and M. I. Baker, *James Brydges, 1st Duke of Chandos*. [2] J. R. Woodhead, *Rulers of London* (London and Mdx. Arch. Soc.), 24; *Rec. Old Westminsters*, i. 134; *CSP Dom.* 1691–2, p. 184; Lipscomb, *Bucks*. ii. 77; Lysons, *Environs of London* (1792–6), iii. 414; *Mar. Lic. Vicar-Gen.* (Harl. Soc. xxx), 155; *VCH Essex*, viii. 43, 45, 50; Morant, *Essex*, i. 492; *The Gen.* xxxi. 238. [3] Salop RO, Ludlow bor. recs. adm. of freemen; Pittis, *Present Parl.* 348; *Al. Carth.* 84, 118; Nichols and Wray, *Foundling Hosp.* 345; *Hearne Colls.* vii. 309; Somerville, *Duchy of Lancaster Official Lists*, 209–10. [4] *Cal. Treas. Bks.* xx. 236. [5] Burnet, vi. 47; *Cam. Misc.* xxiii. 42, 69. [6] Huntington Lib. Stowe mss 26(1), Brydges' diary 1697–9, 16 Jan., 13, 23 Mar. 1697, 12 Feb., 21 Apr., 26 Aug. 1698 and passim; *Vernon–Shrewsbury Letters*, ii. 17; *Cocks Diary*, 95, 168; M. Hunter, *R. Soc. and Its Fellows* (Brit. Soc. for Hist. of Science Monographs, 4), p. 85. [7] Stowe mss 26(1), 7, 8 Feb., 21 Nov., 6 Dec. 1698, 21 Jan., 13–14, 23, 27 Feb., 3, 14, 17, 19–21, 25 Mar., 26 Apr. 1699 and passim; 57(1), pp. 22–3; Add. 70019, f. 20; *Cam. Misc.* xxix. 397. [8] Stowe mss 26(2), Brydges' diary 1699–1702, 12 Nov., 21, 27 Dec. 1699, 10, 13, 26 Jan., 8, 22 Feb., 15, 19 Mar., 4, 24 Apr., 3 May, 1, 13, 31 Aug. 1700 and passim; Northants. RO, Montagu (Boughton) mss 48/29, 51, Vernon to Shrewsbury, 6 Feb., 28 Mar. 1700; *Cocks Diary*, 50–51; Som. RO, Sanford mss DD/SF 4107(a), notes of debate, 15 Feb. 1700; Yale Univ. Beinecke Lib. Osborn coll. Manchester mss, Robert Yard* to Ld. Manchester, 15 Feb. 1700; Macaulay, vi. 2956. [9] *HMC Cowper*, ii. 400–1, 410, 424–5, 433–4, 438; Stowe mss 26(2), 26 Jan., 2 Feb., 12 Mar., 10, 12, 14–15, 17, 26, 27 Apr., 1, 16 May 1701; 58(1), p. 25; 57(1), p. 34; *Cocks Diary*, 95, 97, 107, 167–8, 171, 181. [10] Stowe mss 26(2), 22 Dec. 1701, 2, 12, 14 Jan., 21–22 Feb., 3, 4, 8, 17 Mar., 4 Apr.–9 May 1702; 26(1), 3 Apr. 1697; *Cocks Diary* 250, 260; K. Feiling, *Tory Party*, 385. [11] Stowe mss 57(2), p. 1; 58(1), pp. 31, 42; *Marlborough–Godolphin Corresp.* i. 60, 159; *Post Boy*, 24–26 Dec. 1702; Add. 17677 WW, f. 138; ZZ, f. 497; AAA, f. 212; *Atterbury Epistolary Corresp.* iii. 140; *Huntington Lib. Q.* iv. 313, 316; xxx. 21–44. [12] *Bull. IHR*, xlv. 45; *HMC Portland*, iv. 274; *Cam. Misc.* xxiii. 31–32, 53, 56, 69; *HMC Popham*, 284; Boyer, *Anne Annals*, v. 432; Stowe mss 57(1), pp. 7, 46–47; *EHR*, lxxxii. 734; Add. 40776, f. 24. [13] Stowe mss 57(1), p. 225; 57(2), pp. 6, 18, 26, 29, 33–35, 112, 114, 123, 225; 58(2), pp. 243–4, 254, 262; 58(3), pp. 98–99; *Huntington Lib. Q.* xxx. 21–44, 264; i. 460; Luttrell, *Brief Relation*, vi. 253, 262; *Vernon–Shrewsbury Letters*, ii. 309; *EHR*, lxvi. 249–50; lxxx. 697–8; Add. 70338, list 26 Oct. 1707; *Swift Corresp.* ed. Williams, i. 69; DZA, Bonet despatch 10/21 Feb. 1707–8; Speck thesis, 24; Egerton 3359 (unfol.); *HMC Portland*, iv. 485. [14] Speck thesis, p. 97; Stowe mss 57(2), pp. 69, 86, 103–5, 135, 139, 178; 57(3), pp. 122, 127, 135, 167; 58(5), p. 124; *HMC Portland*, iv. 512–15; *Wentworth Pprs.* 69; G. Holmes, *Trial of Sacheverell*, 86. [15] *Huntington Lib. Q.* xxx. 43; iii. 238; iv. 335–6; Stowe mss 57(3), pp. 173, 186, 226, 274–5; 57(4), pp. 3, 30–31, 53–54, 88, 90, 109–10, 114, 133, 152, 178; 58(5), p. 198; 58(6), pp. 107, 177–8, 213; 58(8), pp. 130–1; G. Holmes, *Pol. in the Age of Anne*, 50; *Swift Stella* ed. Davis, i. 21–22; W. A. Speck, *Tory and Whig*, 57, 68–69; Add. 70226, Thomas Foley II to Harley, 30 Sept. 1710. [16] Stowe mss 57(4), p. 158; 57(5), pp. 52, 74–75, 133–4, 154–5; 57(6), pp. 152–3, 165–6, 171, 217–18; 58(7), p. 195; 58(8), pp. 3–4, 100, 139, 173–4, 236; 58(10), pp. 10, 128, 209–10, 225, 230; 58(11), p. 180; Pittis, 182–4; Cobbett, *Parlty. Hist.* vi. 1016, 1019; *HMC Cowper*, iii. 32; G. M. Trevelyan, *Eng. under Q. Anne*, iii. 128; H. T. Dickinson, *Bolingbroke*, 83; *Swift Stella*, i. 252–3; *Huntington Lib. Q.* i. 462–3; *Hist. Jnl.* iv. 190; Boyer, x. app. p. 56; Oldmixon, *Hist. Eng.* (1735), p. 488; Add. 17677 FFF, f. 36; NSA, Kreienberg despatch 25 Jan. 1712; *Cal. Treas. Bks.* xxv. 97. [17] Stowe mss 57(8), p. 111; 57(9), pp. 82, 114–15, 158–9; *Huntington Lib. Q.* 466–71; Add. 17677 GGG, ff. 84, 113; Chandler, iv. 341–2, 374; Boyer, *Pol. State*, v. 232–3; vi. 123; *Cal. Treas. Bks.* xxxi. 97–98. [18] *Huntington Lib. Q.* 471–2; iv. 340; *Cal. Treas. Bks.* xxviii. 155, 254, 397; Boyer, v. 136; vii. 361, 377, 626; Stowe mss 57(9), pp. 123–7, 168–9; 57(10), pp. 28–30, 189–91, 237–9; Macpherson, *Orig. Pprs.* ii. 638; *Swift Corresp.* ii. 78; *HMC Portland*, v. 436, 475; Trinity, Dublin, Lyons (King) mss 2004/1499, Ld. Mountjoy to Abp. King, 27 July 1714. [19] *Hearne Colls.* vii. 401; *HMC Stuart*, v. 187; L. Colley, *In Defiance of Oligarchy*, 188, 191–2; *Bull. IHR*, lv. 69, 81. [20] Burnet, vi. 47; *Hearne Colls.* ix. 68; *Swift Works* ed. Davis, v. 268; *Huntington Lib. Q.* xxx. 43; Stowe mss 57(2), p. 29; 57(4), p. 111; 57(10), pp. 28–30.

D. W. H.

BUBB, Jeremiah (*d.* 1692), of Foy, Herefs. and Carlisle, Cumb.[1]

CARLISLE 1689–27 Feb. 1692

m. (1) lic. 14 May 1677, Mary (*d.* 1689), da. and h. of George Abrahall, vicar of Foy, and wid. of Paul Abrahall of Ingestone, Herefs., 1s. *d.v.p.* 2da.; (2) by 1691, Alicia (*d.* 1721), da. of John Doddington of Doddington, Som., 1s.[2]

Gent. usher by 1677–*d.*[3]
Capt. regt. of Henry Cornewall* (later 9 Ft.) 1685–9; lt. gov. Carlisle 1689, gov. 1689–*d.*[4]
Freeman, Carlisle 1689.

Bubb's early life remains obscure, no evidence having come to light relating to his career before 1677. Having been appointed governor of Carlisle in December 1689, Bubb was able to deploy the electoral interest associated with this post to secure his return for the borough at the head of the poll at the 1690 election. Given his employments at Carlisle and at court, the classification of Bubb as a Court supporter in Lord Carmarthen's (Sir Thomas Osborne†) analysis of the new House is unsurprising, but this list makes it unclear whether the lord president regarded Bubb as a Tory or as 'doubtful'. Bubb's duties at Carlisle prevented him from attending the spring 1690 session. Between March and July he was engaged in seizing those in Cumberland suspected of disaffection, and it may be that a similar priority prevailed during the 1690–1 session as Bubb has left no record of any significant activity. His recorded contribution to Commons' business was similarly non-existent for the following session, but his attendance at Westminster is clear from his being called to the Lords on 2 Jan. 1692 'as a witness in a cause depending there'. He made no further impression on the records of the House, however, before his death on 27 Feb. 1692. He was buried at St. Giles-in-the-Fields, and his son by his second marriage, George, was brought up in the care of Bubb's Whig brother-in-law George Doddington*. George Bubb became a leading Whig Member under the first two Hanoverian monarchs, succeeding to his uncle's sizable estates in 1720 and adopting the surname Bubb Doddington.[5]

[1] J. Carswell, *Old Cause*, 138. [2] C. J. Robinson, *Mansions and Manors of Herefs.* 125; J. H. Matthews, *Hundred of Wormelow*, i. 122. [3] LS 13/231/6; Bodl. Carte 76, f. 63. [4] SP 44/165/165, 408. [5] Cumbria RO (Kendal), Le Fleming mss WD/Ry 3754, Sir Christopher Musgrave, 4th Bt.*, to Sir Daniel Fleming†, 6 Mar. [1690]; 3875, Fleming to [?], 18 July 1690; *CSP Dom.* 1689–90, p. 526; 1690–1, p. 77; *Luttrell Diary*, 107; Luttrell, *Brief Relation*, ii. 372; Soc. of Genealogists, Boyd's London Burials.

R. D. H.

BUCKINGHAM, Sir Owen (c.1649–1713), of Bread Street, London and Erleigh Court, Earley, Berks.

READING 1698–1701 (Nov.), 1702–1708

b. c.1649, 2nd s. of George Buckingham of Stanwell, Mdx., prob. by his 3rd w. Anne. *m.* (1) bef. 1673, Elizabeth (*d.* 1680), 3s. (2 *d.v.p.*) 2da.; (2) 10 Nov. 1681, aged 32, Mary (*d.* 1687), da. of Nathaniel Maxy, Vintner, wid. of Henry Warner (*d.* 1680), merchant, 2s. *d.v.p.* 3da. *d.v.p.*; (3) 10 July 1690, Hannah (*d.* 1691), da. of Peter de Lannoy of St. Olave and St. Saviour's, Southwark, wid. of John Curtis (*d.* 1688), grocer, of All Hallows, Bread Street, London, *s.p.*; (4) 21 Nov. 1693, Mary (*d.* 1694), da. and h. of Richard Franklin of New Windsor, Berks., *s.p.*; (5) 4 Feb. 1702, Dorothy (*d.* 1704), da. of Henry Cornish, Haberdasher, of London, and alderman of London 1680–3, sis. of Henry Cornish*, and wid. of Joseph Ashurst, Merchant Taylor, of London, *s.p.*; (6) 10 Jan. 1706, Frances (*d.* 1720), da. of Thomas Manley of St. Margaret's next Rochester, Kent, and wid. of one Buckley, E. India capt., *s.p.* Kntd. 14 Oct. 1695.[1]

Livery, Butchers' Co. by 1680–5, 1687–92, Salters' Co. 1692–*d.*; common councilman, London 1689–90, 1691–6, alderman 1696–*d.*, sheriff 1695–6, ld. mayor 1704–5; col. trained bands 1697–1702, 1707–10; freeman, Reading 1698; vice-pres. Hon. Artillery Co. 1708–11.[2]

Commr. taking subscriptions to land bank 1696, New E.I. Co. loan 1698; trustee, receiving loan to Emperor 1706.[3]

The younger son of an innkeeper, Buckingham was left only a small amount of freehold land in Middlesex by his father. He appears to have risen by dint of his own ability and a series of judicious marriages. By 1680 he was a liveryman in the Butchers' Company and about this time his name becomes common in records relating to City politics. He served on two Whig grand juries of minor importance in December 1680 and August 1681. At his second marriage in November 1681 his profession was given as 'salter'. His commitment to the Whig cause was probably based upon his religious connexions, for he was allowing conventicles to be held in his house in 1683 and acted as a surety for a Baptist in 1684–5. The government obviously suspected his loyalty, for he was arrested following Monmouth's rebellion in 1685. As a Whig Nonconformist he appears to have been seen by James II's advisers as a possible 'collaborator' in the policy reversal of 1687 which saw the government cultivating support among Dissenters. Thus, when the Butchers' Company was purged in 1687 Buckingham was restored to the livery (having been left out when a new charter was granted in 1685), but he refused to serve as an assistant, paying a fine of £10 instead. Buckingham's attitude to the Revolution was presumably favourable as he was able to catch the political tide to secure election to the common council in the Whig landslide of 1689, although he lost his seat temporarily in 1690. By 1692 he was lending money to the government. The same year he transferred to the Salters' Company. In February 1694 he was included in the new Whiggish lieutenancy commission for London. A year later he was described as a 'flaxman' following his election as sheriff, a victory which ended a dispute between the Whig aldermen, who wished to fine sheriffs-elect to raise revenue, and the liverymen who objected to such interference with the popular will. In his new office he went with other corporation officials in October to welcome back the King from abroad and received a knighthood in return. Then in 1696 he was elected to replace Sir Jonathan Raymond* as alderman for Bishopsgate, a wealthy inner-London ward. Since the qualification for such office was £10,000, he must now have been an extremely wealthy man.[4]

The basis of Buckingham's interest at Reading was his involvement in a large-scale venture for manufacturing sailcloth. The *Flying Post* recorded in January 1699 that 'Sir Owen Buckingham and some others have made proposals for employing a great number of poor in the linen manufacture and in making sailcloth, for which his Majesty has been at great charges for some years past'. Since this was after the 1698 election, which saw Buckingham returned for Reading, one must assume that the proposal was his fulfilment of a pledge made before the election. Reading received a massive injection of investment, and correspondingly reduced poor rates in return for electing Buckingham. He in turn found an outlet for his expertise as a hemp merchant, supplemented by research into Dutch and French production methods, and a seat in the Commons. The navy was also afforded a source of supply for sailcloth. By 1708 Buckingham was complaining of being out of pocket as the Navy Board did not take enough of his cloth, while he continued his manufactory at levels of full employment as a matter of 'honour', but the scheme gained him a seat at every election for ten years, bar that of November 1701. Buckingham had other interests in commerce, including the Russia Company's plan to sell tobacco to the Tsar's dominions in return for naval stores, and also trading ventures to the Canaries and Barbados. By 1706 he had also taken over much of the Fettiplace estates near Reading, as well as owning part of the old abbey.[5]

At the outset of his parliamentary career Buckingham was classed as a Court supporter on a comparative analysis of the old and new Houses of Commons compiled in about September 1698. This assessment was subsequently queried, but it seems accurate, since on the important division of 18 Jan. 1699 he was listed as voting against the disbanding bill. Possibly his propensity to support moral reform legislation, shared with others from Nonconformist backgrounds, caused some to associate him with Country Whiggery, but he does not seem to have connected such activities to more general party political concerns. Indeed, he even gave money to the nonjuror, Jeremy Collier, in recognition of his work attacking the stage. Buckingham survived a contested election in January 1701 and again showed his zeal for the Whig cause by acting as a teller on 10 May against a resolution prejudicial to the Whig candidates' case in the Lichfield election. In October 1701, as the only Whig alderman yet to serve, he was set up as his party's candidate for lord mayor of London but came third in the popular vote. He also lost his parliamentary election at Reading in November 1701.[6]

If Buckingham had wished to play down his Whiggish and Nonconformist credentials his marriage in February 1702 would have had the opposite effect. His fifth bride was the daughter of the Whig 'martyr', Alderman Henry Cornish, and widow of a prominent City Whig, Joseph Ashurst, the brother of Sir Henry Ashurst, 1st Bt.*, and Sir William Ashurst*, both highly visible Presbyterians. In July Buckingham regained his seat at Reading and continued to toe the Whig line in the Commons. On 13 Feb. 1703 he voted for agreeing to the Lords' amendments to the bill enlarging the time for taking the oath of abjuration. He was named in January 1704 to draft a bill relating to the employment of London's poor. By now his reputation for marrying widows and heiresses made for good newspaper copy, so that in October 1704, eight months after the death of his fifth wife, he was reported to have married 'an apothecary's widow in King Street, Cheapside, with whom he had £180,000 fortune'. If this was indeed the case it did not detract from his efforts to be elected lord mayor, backed this time by his claims of seniority, which also finally succeeded in October 1704. Given his religious affiliations he was, not surprisingly, forecast on 30 Oct. 1704 as an opponent of the Tack and did not vote for it on 28 Nov. His importance to the Whigs was emphasized at the end of October when he was sworn into office. At the celebratory dinner held afterwards at Drapers' Hall very few aldermen attended. This Tory snub 'was sufficiently made up by the honour the Duke of Somerset, Lords Somers [Sir John*] and Halifax [Charles Montagu*], and some others did his lordship in dining with him'. During his mayoralty he hosted a dinner on 6 Jan. 1705 for the Duke of Marlborough (John Churchill†). On 30 Jan. he requested the Queen's leave to go into the country to get rid of a 'very great cough', a request which must have meant an absence from Parliament. Finally, he was involved in a controversy in September 1705 over the election for a president of Bridewell Hospital, which he wished to refer to the court of aldermen even though the popular election had yielded a clear majority for the Tory candidate, Sir Thomas Rawlinson.[7]

In the midst of his mayoralty Buckingham had to seek re-election in 1705 at Reading. Having accomplished this he was classed as 'no Church' on a list analysing the new Parliament. He voted for the Court candidate for Speaker on 25 Oct. 1705, and on 18 Feb. 1706 supported the Court during the proceedings on the 'place clause' of the regency bill. During the 1705–6 session he was involved in promoting a private bill on behalf of the widow of Tanfield Vachell*. He received leave of absence on 21 Feb. 1706 for eight days, possibly in connexion with his marriage the previous month. Evidence of his involvement in the Commons on mercantile questions is scarce, but he clearly kept a keen eye on commercial matters, as is testified by his response on 26 Feb. 1707 to reports of fraud by wine and tobacco merchants exploiting a loophole in the Act of Union. According to (Sir) Thomas Johnson*, 'Buckingham yesterday morning would need move the House to come to some resolution to prevent it, but I heard Lord Coningsby [Thomas*] tell him, "What, are you mad? You will destroy the Union."' Whether disillusionment over the Union prompted a political rethink is uncertain, but Thomas Hearne wrote in April 1707 that Mr Francis Fox (Buckingham's chaplain when lord mayor) 'is turned from his Whiggish principles, and that he has prevailed in some measure with Sir Owen Buckingham to do the same'. Buckingham was also becoming dissatisfied with the arrangement whereby he employed the Reading poor on work commissioned by the Navy Board and gained a seat in the Commons as a consequence. Since 1706 his contract had been reduced from a half to a third of the navy's needs, causing over-production. In March 1708 he wrote to Lord Coningsby asking for a larger share in the next contract or else 'he must throw up the work, and take the disgrace of not being able to provide for the poor'. The response to his request is unknown. His last important committee nomination was in February 1708 to draft the repeal of a Spices Act. Buckingham retired from Reading in favour of his son at the 1708 election. Two lists from early 1708, however, confirm that he was still regarded as a Whig.[8]

In his retirement Buckingham continued to be a stalwart of the Whig cause in London, particularly as an alderman. Thus it was he, together with Sir John Houblon* and Sir Richard Levett, who reported to Secretary Sunderland (Charles, Lord Spencer*) on 8 Apr. 1710, in the wake of the Sacheverell riots. Later, he was criticized in the press in 1711 after Dr Sacheverell had been rudely treated at the annual elections for directors at the Bank of England. Buckingham died on 20 Mar. 1713, being succeeded by his son.[9]

[1] *Genealogists' Mag.* xiv. 146–56; *St. Mildred, Bread Street* (Harl. Soc. Reg. xlii), 65, 68–69, 71; Lipscomb, *Bucks.* iv. 491–2; Folger Shakespeare Lib. Newdigate newsletter 12 Jan. 1706. [2] Guildhall Lib. mss 6441/6–9; J. S. Watson, *Hist. Salters' Co.* 100; Beaven, *Aldermen,* ii. 119; J. R. Woodhead, *Rulers of London* (London and Mdx. Arch. Soc.), 40; Luttrell, *Brief Relation,* v. 193; vi. 186; Berks. RO, Reading corp. diary, 24 June 1698. [3] *CJ,* xii. 508; *Trans. Amer. Phil. Soc.* n.s. li. 34–35; Boyer, *Anne Annals,* iv. 126. [4] PCC 520 Ruthen; Guildhall Lib. mss 6441/6–9; info. from Dr M. J. Knights; *Genealogists' Mag.* 154; P. E. Jones, *Butchers of London,* 37; Beaven, 119; *Cal. Treas. Bks.* ix. 1653; Watson, 100; *CSP Dom.* 1694–5, p. 21; H. Horwitz, *Parl. and Pol. Wm. III,* 128; BL, Verney mss mic. 636/48, John Verney* (Ld. Fermanagh) to Sir Ralph Verney, 1st Bt.†, 21 Sept. 1695; G. S. De Krey, *Fractured Soc.* 183, 199, 10; Luttrell, iii. 537. [5] *Flying Post,* 26–28 Jan. 1699; *Cal. Treas. Pprs.* 1708–14, pp. 14–15; 1697–1702, p. 439; *Trans. Amer. Phil. Soc.* 29, 36, 84; *Cal. Treas. Bks.* xix. 531; *VCH Berks.* iii. 216; E. W. Dormer, *Erleigh Court,* 37. [6] *Past and Present,* cxxviii. 75, 90; J. Oldmixon, *Hist. Eng.* 192; De Krey, 200; Yale Univ. Beinecke Lib. Osborn coll. Blathwayt mss, Robert Yard* to William Blathwayt*, 2 Oct. 1701; Luttrell, v. 95. [7] Newdigate newsletter 19 Oct. 1704; De Krey, 204; *HMC Portland,* iv. 146, 158; R. Sharpe, *London and the Kingdom,* ii. 617; *HMC Ormonde,* n.s. viii. 132; Bodl. Rawl. D.863, ff. 89–90. [8] Liverpool RO, Norris mss 920NOR 2/453, Johnson to [Richard Norris*], 27 Feb. 1706[–7]; *Hearne Colls.* ii. 6; *Cal. Treas. Pprs.* 1708–14, pp. 14–15. [9] Add. 61610, f. 21; *Post Boy,* 19–21 Apr. 1711; *Genealogists' Mag.* 151.

S. N. H.

BUCKINGHAM, Owen (1674–1720), of Moulsford, Berks. and the Gatehouse, Reading Abbey.[1]

READING 1708–1713, 6 June 1716–5 Mar. 1720

b. 16 Dec. 1674, 2nd but 1st surv. s. of Sir Owen Buckingham* by 1st w. *educ.* travelled abroad (Austria, Italy), Padua Univ. 1706. *unm. suc.* fa. 20 Mar. 1713.[2]

Member, Russia Co. 1698.[3]

Gent. of privy chamber 1714–d.; commr. victualling 1717–d.[4]

Although Buckingham was admitted into the Russia Company in 1698 (as a matter of 'intrafamily bookkeeping'), and probably continued his father's sailcloth manufactory in Reading for a time, he does not seem to have been primarily concerned with industry and commerce. He was probably the 'Mr Buckingham' who accompanied Sunderland (Charles, Lord Spencer*) on his mission to Vienna in 1705 and in the following year was in Italy. On his return home he was elected to represent Reading following his father's retirement in 1708. Surviving tellerships and parliamentary lists indicate a commitment to the Whigs. A list of early 1708 with the returns from the election held later that year classed him as a Whig, and in the 1708–9 session he supported the naturalization of the Palatines. On 20 Apr. 1709 he acted as a teller on a more local matter, against an amendment by the Lords to a bill for the better prevention of mischiefs caused by fire, which allowed a still and furnace built by Daniel Tombes to be excepted from the Act's provisions. In the following session he voted for the impeachment of Dr Sacheverell. On 24 Mar. he acted as a teller against an adjournment, the House then proceeding to order Sacheverell's printed answers to his impeachment to be burnt.[5]

Re-elected in 1710, Buckingham was classed as a Whig on the 'Hanover list'. On 7 Apr. 1711 he acted as a teller on a procedural point during the hearing of the Cockermouth election, which led to the witnesses for the petitioner against James Stanhope* being heard. On 25 May 1711 he voted with a small group of committed Whigs against an amendment to the South Sea bill, possibly owing to the financial interests of his father. In the following session, on 17 Jan. 1712, he acted as a teller against the expulsion from the Commons of Robert Walpole II. On the crucial question of the 1713 session, trade with France, he was an active opponent of the ministry's policy. On 6 May his name appears on a parliamentary list which probably details votes against the French wines bill, and on 18 June he divided against the French commerce bill, when he was also classed as a Whig.[6]

Defeated at the 1713 election, he remained out of the Commons until 1716. Having already received office at court, he then became a commissioner for victualling the navy in 1717, a place held until his death in a duel on 5 Mar. 1720. This event occurred at the birthday party of his friend and, on this occasion, antagonist, Richard Aldworth who, according to the surgeon called to the scene, inflicted a wound on him seven inches deep. Most of Buckingham's Berkshire estate seems to have devolved upon his niece Elizabeth, who married Richard Manley, an unsuccessful candidate at Reading in 1739.[7]

[1] *Hearne Colls.* vi. 277. [2] *Genealogists' Mag.* xiv. 151–2; S. Spens, *George Stepney*, 257. [3] *Trans. Amer. Phil. Soc.* n.s. li. 105. [4] N. Carlisle, *Gent. Privy Chamber*, 223; *Navy Recs. Soc.* lxx. 497. [5] *Trans. Amer. Phil. Soc.* 29; E. W. Dormer, *Erleigh Court*, 37; Spens, 257. [6] *Hist. Jnl.* iv. 197. [7] Boyer, *Pol. State*, xix. 316; *Genealogists' Mag.* 152; Berks. RO, Braybrooke mss D/EN/L6, deposition of John Thorpe.

S. N. H.

BUCKNALL, Sir John (1658–1713), of Oxhey Place, Watford, Herts., and Bloomsbury Square, St. Giles-in-the-Fields, Mdx.

MIDDLESEX   8 Jan. 1696–1698

bap. 30 Jan. 1658, 1st s. of Sir William Bucknall† of Oxhey Place by Sarah, da. of Thomas Chits, Woodmonger, of St. Michael, Queenhithe, London; nephew of Ralph Bucknall*. *m.* (1) 9 Feb. 1686, Elizabeth, da. of Thomas Graham of St. Peter-le-Poer, London, 1s. 2da. (1 *d.v.p.*); (2) 1 Oct. 1694 (with £13,500), Mary, da. of Sir John Reade, 1st Bt., of Brockett Hall, Herts. *suc.* fa. 1676; kntd. 23 Feb. 1686.

Sheriff, Herts. 1692–3.

Commr. taking subscriptions to Bank 1694; gov. York Buildings Waterworks Co. 1700.[1]

The son of a wealthy tax farmer and commissioner, whose estate was valued at £113,000 shortly before his death, Bucknall was ideally placed to pursue a career in public life. He was described as a London merchant when knighted by James II in 1686, but does not appear to have sought civic advancement. However, he did invest heavily in City projects such as the waterworks at York Buildings, since his name headed a petition from its proprietors to the Commons on 1 Nov. 1690 for leave to bring in a bill to encourage that scheme, and he was cited as its governor in May 1700. He first obtained public office in his home county, becoming a deputy-lieutenant and sheriff, but was evidently spending much time in the capital, judging by his petition of April 1693 to reside outside Hertfordshire during his shrievalty. Moreover, his appointment as a commissioner to take subscriptions for the first Bank issue suggests that he remained an important contact in financial circles.[2]

Although Bucknall had inherited property in Harrow from his father, his candidacy for the Middlesex by-election of January 1696 did not reflect a significant personal influence in that county, and his narrow victory must be largely attributed to the strength of the local Whigs, who had scored a comfortable victory at the preceding general election. Indeed, it was only after his victory that he became a deputy-lieutenant for Middlesex. At Westminster he quickly established himself as a Court supporter, being forecast as one of its allies for a division on 31 Jan. concerning the proposed council of trade, signing the Association promptly, and voting in late March for fixing the price of guineas at 22s. Although he did not make any significant contribution to Commons' business in that session, his familial background in tax farming and brewing probably recommended his appointment in October 1696 as a commissioner to inquire into the estate of traitor Sir John Friend†. In the ensuing session he pursued a direct interest when first-named to the committee to examine the petition of the Brewers' Company against unjust exactions by the excise commissioners. In addition, on 5 Jan. 1697 he was allowed to return to the country for unspecified 'extraordinary occasions'. Shortly after that session he acted as foreman of the Middlesex grand jury, denouncing as scandalous recent religious works by Francis Atterbury, John Toland and John Locke. In the third session, following a period of leave granted in January 1698, Bucknall was more prominent, being nominated to two drafting committees on bills to promote navigation and to extend the qualification period for tax officials. He presented the navigation bill on 7 Apr.[3]

On the eve of the Middlesex general election of August 1698, Secretary of State James Vernon I* described Bucknall as 'a very honest, sensible man', but he lost his seat to the Tory Warwick Lake*. Soon afterwards an analyst of the old and new Parliaments confirmed Bucknall's politics by classing him as a Court supporter. His continued support for the Whig cause was subsequently testified by his unsuccessful candidacy at the first election of 1701. However, at the second election of that year he chose to stand on his own interest as 'a person of known integrity to the interest of the King and nation'. On the eve of the contest it was reported that the votes of other Whig candidates might be transferred to him, but at the poll he suffered the ignominy of finishing last. Thereafter he strove for a seat in Hertfordshire, standing unsuccessfully for the county in 1705 and 1708. He did not neglect the Middlesex Whigs, voting for their candidates at the shire election of 1705, and signing two addresses in 1710 which attacked High Churchmen for inciting disorder. The exact date of his death has not been ascertained, but may have been shortly after he signed his will on 2 Feb. 1713, when he confessed to being 'troubled with a sleepy distemper which very often ends in an apoplexy'. The will was not proved until the following August, and his body was interred at Oxhey. His estate passed to his son William, who emulated him as far as becoming sheriff of Hertfordshire in 1716, but did not aspire to Parliament.[4]

[1]*Post Boy*, 29 Nov.–2 Dec. 1701; IGI, London; J. R. Woodhead, *Rulers of London* (London and Mdx. Arch. Soc.), 40; *Westminster Abbey* (Harl. Soc. Reg. x), 26; *Le Neve's Knights* (Harl Soc. viii), 241. [2]Woodhead, 40; *Le Neve's Knights*, 401; *Cal. Treas. Pprs.* 1697–1702, p. 396; *CSP Dom.* 1691, p. 351; 1693, p. 98; NLS, Advocates' mss, Bank of Eng. pprs. 31. 1.7, f. 146. [3]*VCH Mdx.* iv. 204; *CSP Dom.* 1696, p. 56; *Cal. Treas. Bks.* xi. 282; Luttrell, *Brief Relation*, iv. 226. [4]*Vernon–Shrewsbury Letters*, ii. 144–5; *Post Man*, 11–13 Nov. 1701; *HMC Portland*, iv. 27; *Mdx. Poll 1705*; Add. Ch. 76111, 76123; PCC 183 Leeds; *Westminster Abbey*, 26.

P. L. G.

BUCKNALL, Ralph (*d.* c.1711), of Buriton, Hants, and St. Giles-in-the-Fields, Mdx.

PETERSFIELD 1701 (Feb.–Nov.)

Bro. of Sir William Bucknall[†], uncle of Sir John Bucknall*. *m.* (1) bef. 1664, 1da.; (2) lic. 30 Apr. 1670, Elizabeth, da. of John Birch I* of Whitbourne, Herefs., ?1s. *d.v.p.* ?3da.[1]

Jt. farmer of revenue [I] 1668–75.

Bro. Brewers' Co. 1672; gov. co. for carrying on manufacture of linen and paper in Jersey and Guernsey 1691, Saltpetre makers' co. 1692; cttee. R. Fishery Co. [I] 1691; asst. Miners Adventurers' Co. 1693; commr. taking subscriptions to land bank 1696.[2]

In common with his brother Sir William, Bucknall made his fortune as a tax farmer and brewer. Both were members of the cartel which undertook a seven-year farm of the Irish revenue from 1668 to 1675, and in 1671 were partners in the group headed by Lord St. John (Charles Powlett[†], later 1st Duke of Bolton), which had its grant of the farm of the customs cancelled after trying unsuccessfully to raise the terms. Also in 1671, Ralph was appointed excise farmer for Yorkshire and Sussex, although he assigned that responsibility to another financier. In the course of his career he displayed a more general entrepreneurial flair, becoming one of the founders of the York Buildings waterworks in 1675. Moreover, after the Revolution he was associated with a wide variety of commercial projects, most notably the manufacture of saltpetre, on account of which he was moved to petition the Commons on 27 Nov. 1691. Significantly, he could count on a small circle of investors to support these schemes, most notable among whom were his sons-in-law Thomas Powell* and William Gulston*.[3]

Bucknall first stood as a parliamentary candidate at the Great Marlow election of 1690. He appears to have had little connexion with the borough, but prevailed so far as to have his name included on one of the two indentures produced by this contest. However, the House ruled against there being a double return, thereby forcing him to petition. He subsequently made strong claims to have been duly elected on an extended franchise of inhabitant voters, but was unable to overturn the result. In 1693 he purchased the Hampshire manors of Mapledurham and Petersfield, and two years later was reported to have made interest to gain a seat at Petersfield. However, he does not seem to have offered a challenge to the sitting Members on election day, and it was not until January 1701 that his proprietorial influence secured him a place at Westminster. In the meantime he had been appointed as a commissioner for taking subcriptions to the abortive land bank, but it is unclear whether he shared the Tory sentiments of the major promoters of that scheme. On 2 May he acted as a teller against a bill to enable Sir Walter Clarges, 2nd Bt.*, to sell a piece of ground in Piccadilly. Frustratingly, his name does not appear on any parliamentary list, but on 23 May he was sufficiently roused to make 'a long-winded speech' against the proliferation of revenue officials, and argued that the yield of the excise should be higher. This oration met with the approval of Tory leader Sir Edward Seymour, 4th Bt.*, who commended him for having spoken against his own interest as a brewer.[4]

Despite considerable influence at Petersfield, Bucknall did not stand again. However, he did not neglect political affairs, signing two petitions in the spring of 1710 to condemn the recent excesses of High Tory supporters. Such Whiggish sentiments should not obscure his attachment to the church, he having taken the lead 'in almost all the parish business of consequence' as vestryman at St. Giles-in-the-Fields from 1675 until his death. The actual date of his demise remains uncertain, but probate evidence suggests that it lay between 9 Dec. 1710 and 15 Feb. 1711. His only son having predeceased him, he left his daughters real estate in Herefordshire and London, as well as fee-farms in Yorkshire, Middlesex and the capital. Probably recognizing their electoral value, he ordered the Hampshire properties to be put up for sale, and they subsequently passed to Edward Gibbon, grandfather of the historian.[5]

[1]*Mar. Lic. Fac. Off.* (Harl. Soc. xxiv), 172; *London Mar. Lics.* ed. Foster, 210; PCC 21 Young. [2]Guildhall Lib. ms 5445/21, p. 197; *CSP Dom.* 1690–1, p. 474; 1691–2, pp. 3–4, 249; 1693, p. 207. [3]*Cal.*

Treas. Bks. iii. 235, 833, 1122; vi. 408; Survey of London, xviii. 48. ⁴T. C. Wilks, Hist. Hants, iii. 320; Add. 70018, ff. 94–95; CJ, xii. 509; Cocks Diary, 145. ⁵Add. ch. 76111, 76123; J. Parton, Acct. of Hosp. and Parish of St. Giles-in-the-Fields, 384; PCC 21 Young; VCH Hants, iii. 87.

P. W./P. L. G.

BULKELEY, Richard, 3rd Visct. Bulkeley of Cashel [I] (c.1658–1704), of Baron Hill, Anglesey.

BEAUMARIS 1679 (Feb.)
ANGLESEY 1680–1681 (Mar.), 1690–9 Aug. 1704

b. c.1658, 1st s. of Robert Bulkeley†, 2nd Visct. Bulkeley of Cashel [I], by Sarah, da. of Daniel Harvey, Grocer and merchant, of Lawrence Pountney Hill, London and Croydon, Surr., sis. of Daniel Harvey† of Coombe, Surr.; bro. of Hon. Robert Bulkeley*. *educ.* travelled abroad (France, Italy) 1675–7. *m.* (1) 23 May 1681 (with £8,000), Mary, da. of Sir Philip Egerton† of Oulton, Cheshire, 1s.; (2) 1 Mar. 1688, Elizabeth (d. 1752), da. of Henry White of Penllan, Pemb., wid. of Thomas Lort of Stackpole, Pemb., *s.p. suc.* fa. as 3rd Visct. 18 Oct. 1688.

Custos rot. Caern. 1679–Apr. 1688, Anglesey 1690–d.; chancellor and chamberlain of Anglesey, Caern. and Merion. Oct.–?Dec. 1688, Apr. 1689–d.; mayor, Beaumaris 1689–90; constable of Beaumaris Castle and capt. of Beaumaris May 1689–1702; v.-adm. N. Wales 1701–2, N. Cornw. c.1702–d.[1]

Bulkeley had lost his place as custos rotulorum for Anglesey in 1688, and had even been turned out of the commission of the peace for his unwillingness to acquiesce in the repeal of the Penal Laws and Test Act. By way of reparation, James II named him to succeed his father as chancellor and chamberlain of the North Wales circuit in late October 1688, an appointment which may have lapsed at the Revolution. Despite the fact that his uncle Henry†, King James's master of the Household, joined the Jacobite court in exile, Bulkeley quickly accommodated himself to the new regime. The discovery of a Jacobite officer at Holyhead, one Captain Bellew, seeking a passage to Ireland, gave him an opportunity to display his loyalty to King William. Having ordered the captain's detention, he informed the secretary of state, Lord Nottingham (Daniel Finch†), and probably in the same letter inserted a petition for his own reinstatement in his local offices. Although he had to wait a year to be restored as custos, the chancellorship was given immediately, and coupled with a new post, that of constable of Beaumaris Castle. He had kept himself out of Parliament in 1689, bringing in his uncle for the county of Anglesey and nominating at Beaumaris Sir William Williams, 1st Bt.*, with whom he may have contracted a political *mariage de convenance* in order to survive the Revolution, but came back as knight of the shire at the 1690 election, and thenceforth held the seat unopposed. He was classed as a Tory, and possibly as a Court supporter, by Lord Carmarthen (Sir Thomas Osborne†) in March 1690, and in December was listed as a probable supporter in the event of a Commons' attack upon Carmarthen. In March 1691 a Jacobite agent included Bulkeley upon a list of 'persons well inclined' to James II. The following month Robert Harley* classed him as a Country party supporter, and in the 1694–5 session Henry Guy* listed him as a 'friend'. By 1696 he was firmly in opposition, being forecast as a likely opponent of the projected council of trade in the division on 31 Jan. Bulkeley was still a man of residual Jacobite sympathies, according to information sent to Abbé Renaudot at about this time, for the Speaker informed the House on 31 Mar. that he was one of the Members in the country who had refused to subscribe the Association. On 15 Apr. the House was informed that Bulkeley had at last signed. Listed as a member of the Country party in an analysis of the 1698 Parliament, he was also forecast as likely to oppose a standing army. In a list of February 1701 he was named as likely to support the Court in agreeing with the committee of supply's resolution to continue the 'Great Mortgage', and was classed with the Tories in the second Parliament of that year. He was listed as having favoured the motion of 26 Feb. 1702 vindicating the Commons' proceedings in the impeachments of the four Whig lords, and on 13 Feb. 1703 voted against the House of Lords' amendments to the bill to enlarge the time for taking the oath of abjuration. In March 1704 Nottingham listed him as a likely supporter in the proceedings upon the Scotch Plot. Bulkeley died 9 Aug. 1704, aged 46, and was buried at Beaumaris.[2]

[1] UCNW, Baron Hill mss 159; Cal. Treas. Bks. viii. 2109; ix. 107; xvii. 232; CSP Dom. 1689–90, p. 67. [2] L. K. J. Glassey, Appt. JPs, 88; CSP Dom. 1689–90, pp. 34, 67–68, 471; 1700–2, p. 539; Westminster Diocesan Archs. Old Brotherhood mss iii/3/232, memo. by Capt. Lloyd, 23 Mar. 1691; Ideology and Conspiracy ed. Cruickshanks, 125; A. Browning, Danby, iii. 212; Bolton mss at Bolton Hall D/20, Ld. William Powlett* to Mq. of Winchester (Charles Powlett I*), 11 Sept. 1698.

D. W. H.

BULKELEY, Richard, 4th Visct. Bulkeley of Cashel [I] (1682–1724), of Baron Hill, Anglesey.

ANGLESEY 30 Nov. 1704–1715, 1722–4 June 1724

b. 19 Sept. 1682, o. s. of Richard Bulkeley*, 3rd Visct. Bulkeley of Cashel [I], by his 1st w. *educ.* Christ's, Camb. 1698–1701, MA 1700. *m.* 13 Feb. 1703 (with £8,000),

Lady Bridget Bertie (*d.* 1753), da. of James, 1st Earl of Abingdon, sis. of Hon. Henry Bertie II*, Hon. James Bertie*, Hon. Robert Bertie* and Montagu Venables-Bertie, Lord Norreys*, 2s. 5da. *suc.* fa. as 4th Visct. 9 Aug. 1704.[1]

Constable, Beaumaris Castle and capt. of Beaumaris May 1702–16; chancellor and chamberlain of Anglesey, Caern. and Merion. 1704–Oct. 1715; custos rot. Anglesey 1706–Dec. 1715; v.-adm. N. Wales 1707–10, 1711–15; constable, Caernarvon Castle, chief ranger, forest of Snowdon and steward of the manors of Bardsey monastery, Caern. 1713–Nov. 1714.[2]

Bulkeley's father professed himself highly satisfied with his son's progress when reluctantly 'taking him from college' in order to introduce him to some of his responsibilities as heir apparent to the most powerful landed interest in Anglesey and Caernarvonshire. While the 3rd Viscount was still alive, the young man was entrusted with one of the clutch of important local offices under the family's control, that of constable of Beaumaris Castle, and in due course he succeeded to the rest: chancellor and chamberlain of Anglesey, Caernarvonshire and Merionethshire in 1704; custos of Anglesey in 1706; vice-admiral of North Wales a year later, and this despite his political antipathy to the then ministry. He had been returned unopposed as knight of the shire for Anglesey in his father's place at a by-election in 1704 and again at the general election in 1705. At first he was taken for a moderate, being listed as having voted against, or having been absent from the division on the Tack on 28 Nov., though he was not actually returned until two days after this division. In consequence he was classed as a 'Churchman' rather than as 'True Church' in an analysis of the 1705 Parliament. But he voted on 25 Oct. 1705 against the Court candidate for Speaker, and was twice listed as a Tory in 1708.[3]

This sharpening partisanship may in part have been a reflection of heightening political tension in Anglesey, where the Bulkeley interest was coming under a sustained attack, and partisan and personal antagonisms were spilling over from elections into social and economic relations. A Whig candidate, Owen Meyrick[†], had canvassed the county in 1705 but had not pressed his cause so far as a poll. In 1708, however, Meyrick stood against Bulkeley while another Whig, (Sir) Arthur Owen II, (3rd Bt.*), contested Beaumaris against the outgoing Member there, Bulkeley's brother-in-law Henry Bertie. By this time a series of quarrels had broken out, fuelled by Bulkeley's own arrogance and violence of temper, between his family and the leading supporters of the Whig interest in Anglesey, in particular Owen Hughes*, a Beaumaris attorney who had been the first to challenge the Bulkeley ascendancy in the borough constituency in 1698, and whose hand was still behind all manoeuvres against the Bulkeley family. When in 1706 Hughes's application for a renewal of his lease of the Abermenai ferry was disputed by the descendants of the lessees of two rival ferries and by the heir of another who, it was alleged, had been defrauded by Hughes at the original granting of the lease nearly 30 years before, both sets of claimants could count on backing from Baron Hill. Indeed, Bulkeley took a special interest in the latter case, which was to continue for several years beyond Hughes's death in 1708. The petition to the Treasury over the two rival ferries was decided against Hughes around the time of the 1708 election. Hughes and his friends had retaliated by promoting a complaint against Bulkeley for neglecting the maintenance of Beaumaris Castle and allegedly removing materials from the castle for his own use. This was heard by the Treasury in March 1708 and resulted in a mild reprimand for Bulkeley. At the same time Bulkeley suffered a partial defeat on a complaint he had in turn brought against another of his enemies, Serjeant John Hooke, the chief justice of the North Wales circuit. Long-standing enmity between the Whiggish Hooke and the dominant pro-Bulkeley faction in Beaumaris corporation had come to a head in 1706 when the new mayor, 'a pragmatical man' according to Hooke, refused the customary present of coals to the bench and was fined. Bulkeley brought this matter to the attention of the House on 28 Jan. 1708 and it was referred to the 'grand committee for courts of justice', meeting for the first time since the days of the Long Parliament. On the report, on 9 Mar., the House agreed only with a general resolution against the practice of judges demanding presents, and after a division threw out the specific censure of Hooke. These setbacks, and the Whig successes in the general election at large, though not in Anglesey itself, encouraged Bulkeley's opponents to pursue their campaign. A petition over the Beaumaris election was rejected by the Commons in 1710, after a committee hearing in which Bulkeley had come to blows with the Whig petitioner, (Sir) Arthur Owen II; and the charges arising from Bulkeley's governorship of Beaumaris Castle resurfaced, first in an attempt in April 1708 to secure a presentment against him by the Anglesey grand jury, frustrated amid scenes of considerable disorder, and then in 1709 in a printed 'memorial' to Lord Treasurer Godolphin (Sidney[†]), which widened the scope of the attack to take in accusations of corruption and bias on Bulkeley's part in respect of his other offices, as chancellor, vice-admiral and custos. There were even allegations of misconduct in his capacity as a land tax commissioner, and complaints of the undue influence he exerted over Beaumaris corporation. The memorial, intended to furnish reasons for Bulkeley to be deprived of all these offices, seems to have won little or no serious consideration in ministerial circles, but it did spark off a bitter propaganda war in Anglesey. A display of loyalty to the Bulkeley standard at a county meeting in 1709 intimidated Sir Arthur Owen, a prime mover of the memorial, into an apology, and after the hotter Whigs had in response dispatched a letter to Godolphin reaffirming their previous statements, Bulkeley's supporters organized a fuller meeting, which produced counter-resolutions. Their published account of the meeting made great play with Owen's retraction and stigmatized Hooke as the ringleader on the Whig side. Further eruptions ensued, and the ramifications of the affair were to stretch beyond the 1710 election, though without producing any concrete result. Meanwhile, Bulkeley was behaving in the Commons as befitted a high Tory, voting, for example, against the impeachment of Dr Sacheverell. He was still a far from active Member, however, emulating his father in that regard, and on 17 Mar. 1710 was granted leave of absence on the grounds of ill-health.[4]

During the ministerial revolution of 1710 Robert Harley* appears to have considered appointing Bulkeley to government office in Ireland, but it appears that no such post was offered. The Tory landslide in the 1710 election, reflected in Anglesey in an election in which Whig opposition was easily shrugged off, left Bulkeley in a position to be revenged on his foes. Hooke, whom Bulkeley considered a malicious 'fanatic', and against whom he had for some time been planning retribution, was dismissed; and a new lease of the Abermenai ferry, once the preserve of Owen Hughes and his kinsmen, was granted to Bulkeley through Robert Harley's* personal intervention. Bulkeley's only disappointment was the failure of his libel suit against Lloyd Bodvel, Hughes's nephew by marriage and political heir, and this despite counting once again on Harley's good offices. Following his election in 1710 Bulkeley had been classed in the 'Hanover list' as a Tory, and shortly before the start of the 1710–11 session he attended a meeting of Tory Members at the Fountain, one report stating that he was to be 'steward' of the next such meeting. During this session Bulkeley took the part of a typical backbench Tory, being listed as one of the 'worthy patriots' who exposed the mismanagements of the previous ministry, as one of the 'Tory patriots' who opposed the continuance of the war, and as a member of the October Club. He was absent from Parliament at the beginning of the 1711–12 session, thus forfeiting, according to one correspondent, his chance to be among Robert Harley's dozen new peers, although it is unlikely that Harley had seriously considered promoting to the Upper House someone as headstrong and fiery. His Jacobite connexions, most notably via his great-aunt Lady Sophia Bulkeley, one of whose children had married the Duke of Berwick, and his attested Jacobite sentiments in later life, have led to his being cited as a 'probable Jacobite' in the years 1710–14. Certainly his enemies thought he was 'for bringing in the Pretender', and his private papers contain copies of Jacobite poems and pamphlets dating from 1714 and some unsigned correspondence from 1713 which is pro-Jacobite in tone. Whether as a Jacobite or simply as a ministerial Tory, he voted on 18 June 1713 in favour of the French commerce bill, and not long afterwards was rewarded with a grant of the office of constable of Caernarvon Castle, which he had been soliciting for at least nine months. In the Worsley list he was classed as a Tory.[5]

Despite appealing to an unnamed intermediary for help in retaining his local 'honorary' offices under the new dynasty, Bulkeley lost them all within two years of the Hanoverian succession and was even obliged to acquiesce in the return of a Whig knight of the shire for Anglesey in the 1715 election. His disgruntlement revealed itself in a letter of September 1715 in which he prized 'retirement into the country' as 'the only happiness nowadays'. The recipient of a discreet Jacobite correspondence at the time of the Fifteen, he may have fostered Stuart loyalism in his own locality, for in 1717 informations were laid against several of his servants for drinking the Pretender's health. His name was one of those sent to the Stuart court in 1721 as a likely sympathizer, and in the following year he and his friend Sir Watkin Williams Wynn, 3rd Bt.†, 'audaciously burnt the King's picture and the several pictures of all the royal family'. With Wynn's help, he regained his parliamentary seat in 1722 but died just over two years later, at Bath, on 4 June 1724.[6]

[1] *Christ's Coll. Reg.* ii. 144; UCNW, Baron Hill mss 185, 189. [2] *Cal. Treas. Bks.* xvii. 232; xxvii. 325–7; xxix. 147, 777. [3] Add. 22910, f. 517. [4] *Trans. Anglesey Antiq. Soc.* (1930), p. 63; (1962), pp. 35–36, 37–44; H. R. Davies, *The Conway and Menai Ferries* (Univ. of Wales Bd. of Celtic Studies, Hist. and Law ser. viii), 179–83, 185; *Cal. Treas. Pprs.* 1702–7, pp. 558–9; *Cal. Treas. Bks.* xxii. 3–4, 9–10; Northants. RO, Montagu (Boughton) mss 48/183, James Vernon I* to Duke of Shrewsbury, 29 Jan. 1707–8; *Vernon–Shrewsbury Letters*, iii. 343, 359–60; Luttrell, *Brief Relation*, vi. 538; Add. 61607, ff. 199–203; Baron Hill mss 5529, memorial of Sir Arthur Owen and Bodvel, 21 Mar. 1708–9; 5533, *A Memorial to the Lord Treasurer against Lord Bulkeley*, 7 June 1709; 5534–5, Owen to Bulkeley, 26, 28 May 1709; 5538, affidavit of William Griffith, 27 Feb. 1710[-11];

5541, draft memorial to Ld. Godolphin, [1709]. [5]Add. 70331, memo., [1710]; *Trans. Anglesey Antiq. Soc.* (1962), pp. 45–46; Baron Hill mss 5576, case of Ld. Bulkeley, July 1709; 5577, Bulkeley to Robert Price*, 7 July 1709; 5581, 5584, Price to Bulkeley, 1 Aug., 15 Nov. 1709; 6772, [–] to same, 23 Oct. 1712; 6779, 'A letter by Mr Leslie to a Member of Parliament', 23 Apr. 1714; 6777, speech given at Plombières by James Stuart, 29 Aug. 1714; 6778, [–] to [–], 3 Jan. 1714[-5]; Baron Hill mss 216; Davies, 185–7, 304; BL, Verney mss mic. 636/54, Ld. Fermanagh (John Verney*) to Ralph Verney[†], 30 Nov. 1710; *Cal. Treas. Bks.* xxv. 80, 82, 156–7, 368; xxvii. 295; *Ideology and Conspiracy* ed. Cruickshanks, 168; G. V. Bennett, *Tory Crisis in Church and State*, 303–4; G. Holmes, *Pol. in Age of Anne*, 90; Szechi thesis, 264; *Welsh Hist. Rev.* i. 285–6. [6]Baron Hill mss 219; *Trans. Anglesey Antiq. Soc.* (1930), p. 64; (1962), pp. 46–48; A. Llwyd, *Hist. Mona*, 158; *Welsh Hist. Rev.* i. 286, 288–9; *Ideology and Conspiracy*, 84; P. S. Fritz, *Ministers and Jacobitism 1715–45*, p. 154; *The Gen.* n.s. vi. 104.

D. W. H.

BULKELEY, Hon. Robert (c.1662–1702).

BEAUMARIS 1701 (Dec.)–23 Dec. 1702

b. c.1662, 3rd s. of Robert Bulkeley[†], 2nd Visct. Bulkeley of Cashel [I]; bro. of Richard Bulkeley*, 3rd Visct. *educ.* Christ Church, Oxf. matric. 12 May 1679, aged 17, DCL 1683; I. Temple 1679. *unm.*[1]

Cornet, Queen Dowager's regt. of horse Dec. 1688–?1689; purveyor of hay and straw for royal stables 1696–*d.*; equerry to Queen Anne, May 1702–*d.*[2]

Bulkeley, whose uncle Henry[†] was master of the Household to both Charles II and James II before going into exile after the Glorious Revolution, received his doctorate at Oxford in 1683 as a member of 'the retinue of the Duke of York' but gained no further material advantage from his royal connexions until the last days of James's reign, when, having approached the Duke of Ormond to intercede for him, he was given a commission in a cavalry regiment. This lapsed at, or soon after, the Revolution, and in the early 1690s he appears to have harboured Jacobite sympathies as in March 1691 he was included upon a list sent to James II of those 'well inclined to his Majesty's interest'. It was a further five years before Bulkeley could share in the fruits of his elder brother's deft accommodation to the Williamite regime, acquiring a minor Household post in 1696. The family nominee at Beaumaris in the general elections of December 1701 and 1702, he was classed with the Tories in Robert Harley's* list of the former Parliament, and was listed as having favoured the motion of 26 Feb. 1702 vindicating the Commons' proceedings in the impeachments of William III's Whig ministers. Appointed an equerry to the new Queen in June 1702, he died in London on 23 Dec. following.[3]

[1]J. E. Griffith, *Peds. Anglesey and Caern. Fams.* 42; W. R. Williams, *Parl. Rep. Wales*, 11. [2]*CSP Dom.* 1687–9, p. 379; info. from Prof. R. O. Bucholz. [3]Wood, *Life and Times*, iii. 46; Lodge, *Peerage of Ire.* rev. Archdall, v. 27; *HMC Ormonde*, n.s. viii. 6; Westminster Diocesan Archs. Old Brotherhood mss iii/3/232, memo. by Capt. Lloyd, 23 Mar. 1691; Luttrell, *Brief Relation*, v. 180; Griffith, 42.

D. W. H.

BULKELEY, Hon. Thomas (c.1633–1708), of Dinas, Caern.

CAERNARVONSHIRE	1679–1681 (Mar.)
	1685–1687
ANGLESEY	1689–1690
BEAUMARIS	1690–1695
CAERNARVONSHIRE	10 Feb. 1697–1705
CAERNARVON BOROUGHS	1705–23 Mar. 1708

b. c.1633, 4th but 2nd surv. s. of Thomas Bulkeley, 1st Visct. Bulkeley of Cashel [I], by Blanche, da. of Robert Coytmore of Coytmore; bro. of Henry Bulkeley[†] and Robert Bulkeley[†], 2nd Visct. *educ.* Jesus, Oxf. 1652; G. Inn 1654. *m.* Jane, da. and coh. of Griffith Jones of Castellmarch, Caern., wid. of Thomas Williams of Dinas, *s.p.*[1]

Sheriff, Caern. Jan.–Nov. 1688; freeman, Caernarvon by 1692.[2]

Like his nephew the 2nd Viscount (Richard[†]), Thomas Bulkeley had lost his local offices in 1688 through refusing to consent to the repeal of the Penal Laws and Test Act. He had even been pricked as sheriff to prevent him from standing for re-election to Parliament. The family candidate for knight of the shire for Anglesey in the Convention, he was brought in by the 3rd Viscount again in 1690 at Beaumaris, leaving the Caernarvonshire seat free for another nephew, Sir William Williams, 6th Bt.*, who was also the 2nd Viscount's son-in-law. Relations with Williams later came under strain, Thomas Bulkeley fighting a duel in 1692 with Williams' close friend Sir Bourchier Wrey, 4th Bt.*, but this quarrel does not seem to have extended to any attempt against Williams at the polls in Caernarvonshire. An old Tory and anti-Exclusionist, Bulkeley had evidently behaved with as much tact as his nephew Lord Bulkeley in 1689, for he was not listed as voting against the transfer of the crown. Lord Carmarthen (Sir Thomas Osborne[†]) classed him as a Tory, and possibly a Court supporter, in March 1690, and in the following December he was listed as a likely supporter in the event of a Commons attack upon Carmarthen. In April 1691 Robert Harley* listed Bulkeley with the Country party opposition. During the 1694–5 session he was included on Henry Guy's* list of 'friends', probably in connexion with the Commons' investigation of Guy.[3]

Bulkeley did not put up in the 1695 election but was returned again for Caernarvonshire two years later at a by-election following the death of Sir William Williams. In September 1698 he was listed as a member of the Country party, and the following month was included in a list of likely opponents of a standing army. Bulkeley was now much less involved in the work of the House. In the 1701 Parliament he was forecast as likely to support the Court in agreeing with the supply committee's resolution to continue the 'Great Mortgage', but he made little further impact upon the record of this Parliament and on 31 May he was granted leave of absence. Classified with the Tories by Harley in December 1701, he was listed as having favoured the motion of 26 Feb. 1702 vindicating the Commons' proceedings in the previous Parliament on the impeachments of the four Whig lords. On the death of another nephew, Hon. Robert Bulkeley*, in 1702 there was a rumour that he would succeed to Robert's Household office as equerry to Queen Anne, but this would seem to have been without foundation. He introduced a private bill in February 1704, and in November of that year bore out a forecast by voting on the 28th for the Tack. Transferring to Caernarvon Boroughs in 1705 he voted on 25 Oct. against the Court candidate for Speaker, and remained a Tory to the end, being classed as such in a list dating from shortly before his death, which occurred on 23 Mar. 1708, by which time he had reached the age of 75.[4]

[1] J. E. Griffith, *Peds. Anglesey and Caern. Fams.* 42. [2] *Trans. Caern. Hist. Soc.* viii. 78. [3] Luttrell, *Brief Relation*, ii. 351; Norf. RO, Le Neve mss, [?Peter Le Neve] to John Millecent, 5 Feb. 1691[-2]. [4] Luttrell, v. 251.

D. W. H.

BULL, Henry (1630–92), of Shapwick, Som.

WELLS 1660–1679 (Jan.)
MILBORNE PORT 1679 (Oct.)–1681, 1685–1687
BRIDGWATER 1689–28 Jan. 1692

bap. 8 Oct. 1630, 3rd but 1st surv. s. of William Bull of the Middle Temple and Shapwick by Jane, da. and coh. of Henry Southworth, mercer, of London and Wells, Som. *educ.* I. Temple 1651, called 1658. *m.* 14 Apr. 1658, Elizabeth (*d.* 1712), da. of Robert Hunt† of Compton Pauncefoot, Som., 3s. *d.v.p.* 2da. *suc.* fa. 1676.[1]
Sheriff, Som. 1683–4.

A barrister of the Inner Temple, Bull was re-elected for Bridgwater in 1690, and was listed by Lord Carmarthen (Sir Thomas Osborne†) as a Whig, probably in error since he had been a Tory in the Convention. He was nevertheless noted as a supporter of the Court in two more of Carmarthen's 1690 lists, but in April 1691 appeared as a Country party supporter in Robert Harley's* list. A senior figure among the county gentry, he was reappointed a deputy-lieutenant in June 1690, having been first appointed the previous year. He was granted leave of absence for the recovery of his health on 17 Dec. 1691 but may not have returned to Westminster since he died 'suddenly' of diabetes on 28 Jan. 1692 and was buried at Shapwick. His elder daughter being deaf and dumb, his estates passed to his younger daughter, the future wife of George Dodington*.[2]

[1] Collinson, *Som.* iii. 428; A. J. Jewers, *Wells Cathedral*, 49. [2] Jewers, 49; Luttrell, *Brief Relation*, ii. 347; Add. 70016, f. 18.

P. W.

BULLER, Benjamin (*d.* 1702), of Exeter and St. Margaret's, Westminster.

SALTASH 5 Feb.–19 Dec. 1702

Poss. 2nd s. of Richard Buller (*d.*1691), Portuguese merchant, by 1st w. Leonor.[1]
Capt. of ft. Northcote's regt. 1696–7, 31 Ft. Mar. 1702–*d.*[2]

Buller may have been the 2nd son of a Lisbon merchant, who left 1.5 million Reis to him, his elder brother, also Richard, continuing in the trade. Buller joined the army, but was placed on half pay in 1697 when his regiment was disbanded. He was probably a kinsman of John Buller I* and James Buller*, who were presumably responsible for his candidature at the Saltash by-election in 1702. His one parliamentary action of note was to vote on 26 Feb. for the resolution vindicating the Commons' proceedings of the previous year over the impeachment of William's Whig ministers. In March 1702 he was given a new commission in a marine regiment. He was returned for Saltash unopposed at the general election of 1702, whereupon according to one contemporary, 'he attended diligently the service of the House, when it was sitting, but in the little recess they made for the better celebration of Christmas' he died. This was not the exact truth for Parliament did not adjourn until 23 Dec. and his 'much lamented' death had occurred on the 19th. He was replaced in his regiment on the 21st. Sentence was taken out on his will in February 1704.[3]

BULLER, Francis (aft.1670–98), of Shillingham, Cornw. and Isleham, Cambs.

SALTASH   1695–5 Feb. 1698

b. aft. 1670, 1st s. of Francis Buller (d. 1679, 1st s. of Francis Buller†) of Shillingham and Isleham by Mary, da. and h. of Sir John Maynard*; bro. of James Buller*. *unm. suc.* gdfa. 1682.[1]

Attorney-gen. to duchy of Cornwall ?–d.[2]

His father's estate having been damaged by a heavy fine for misprision of treason, Buller was invested with Shillingham and the Saltash property in 1676 in order to preserve the family's interest. However, he seems to have resided at Isleham as did his grandfather. Interestingly, his grandfather's will was not proved until 1694, which may indicate Buller's coming of age as his mother had been only 13 at her marriage in December 1670. It would also tie in with the revival of the Buller interest at Saltash, based on property in the parish of St. Stephen's by Saltash, for which he was returned at the 1695 election. In Parliament Buller was forecast as likely to oppose the government in the division on 31 Jan. 1696 over the proposed council of trade, signed the Association (but may have initially refused to do so), voted in March against fixing the price of guineas at 22s. and on 25 Nov. against Sir John Fenwick's† attainder. He received leave of absence on 2 Mar. 1697 to recover his health. On 1 Feb. 1698 Robert Harley* reported that 'Mr Buller a Member of our House, very young, hath the smallpox, not like to live, he was a very honest gentleman', and four days later Edward Harley* reported his death. In his will made a few days before his death, Buller left two trustees, Sir Rushout Cullen, 3rd Bt.*, and his great-uncle John Buller I*, who were each to receive £600 in trust to buy land for his sister Katherine's children. Legacies included £100 to his 'friend' Salwey Winnington*. The remainder of his estate went to his brother James.[3]

[1] Vivian, *Vis. Cornw.* 57–58; *London Mar. Lic.* ed. Chester, 213. [2] *Post Boy*, 31 Mar.–2 Apr. 1698. [3] Polsue, *Complete Paroch. Hist. Cornw.* iv. 170–1; PCC 78 King, 114 Lort, 210 Box; Add. 70019, ff. 16–17.

E. C./S. N. H.

[1] PCC 94 Vere. [2] *CSP Dom.* 1696, pp. 1–2; 1702–3, pp. 364, 388. [3] *Cal. Treas. Bks.* xv. 450; Add. 27440, f. 141; *Post Boy*, 22–24 Dec. 1702; PCC 218 Ash.

E. C./S. N. H.

BULLER, James (1678–1710), of Shillingham, Cornw.

SALTASH   25 Jan. 1699–1701 (Nov.)
CORNWALL   1701 (Dec.)–1705
SALTASH   1705–1708
CORNWALL   1708–14 Sept. 1710

bap. 8 Jan. 1678, 2nd s. of Francis Buller of Shillingham and Isleham, Cambs.; bro. of Francis Buller*. *educ.* New Coll. Oxf. 1695; M. Temple 1695. *unm. suc.* bro. 1698.[1]

Stannator, Foymore 1703, 1710; speaker, convocation of Stannaries 1703, 1710.[2]

Barely a fortnight after attaining his majority in January 1699, Buller was returned at a by-election at Saltash, one elected Member conveniently opting to sit for the county. Buller was absent from a call of the House on 11 Dec. 1699 and was sent for into custody, being discharged two days later. He was re-elected for the borough in January 1701. As if to underline his family's stature in the county, he transferred to the shire seat in December 1701. In the new House Robert Harley* listed him as a Tory, a classification borne out by his subsequent vote on 26 Feb. 1702 in favour of the motion vindicating the Commons' proceedings in the impeachment of William's Whig ministers. On 8 Apr. following he was granted leave of absence to recover his health.

At the general election of 1702 Buller and Hon. John Granville were chosen unopposed as knights of the shire. He was reported to be 'very much indisposed' at the end of January 1703, but voted on 13 Feb. against agreeing with the Lords' amendments to the bill for enlarging the time for taking the oath of abjuration. In September he attended the convocation of tinners, where he was chosen speaker and helped negotiate the pre-emption contract with the crown. In March 1704 he was listed among the supporters of Lord Nottingham (Daniel Finch†) over the Scotch Plot. In October he was forecast as likely to support the Tack and duly did so on 28 Nov. 1704.[3]

Possibly Buller's reputation as a 'Tacker' caused his defeat in the county election in 1705, but he was able to secure his return for Saltash instead. He was listed as 'True Church' and voted on 25 Oct. against the Court candidate for Speaker. In early 1708 he was listed as a Tory and in the general election of that year was chosen both for Saltash and the county, choosing to sit for the latter. In February 1709 Buller was arrested in a tavern in company with Lords Craven and Denbigh, Thomas Legh II* and Sir Cholmley Dering, 4th Bt.*, and committed to the Poultry Counter. Subsequently they brought actions against the offending constables who were forced to admit their fault publicly.[4]

In the summer of 1709 Buller was admitted as a member of the Board of Brothers (a Tory drinking club whose membership included Lords Craven and Denbigh). He attended the Board fairly regularly in the winter of 1709–10 and consequently was on hand to vote against the impeachment of Dr Sacheverell. Earlier on 8 Feb. 1710 a motion granting him leave of absence to attend the parliament of tinners turned into an attempt to address the Queen to ensure that it did not convene during the sitting of Parliament. Thus he was still in London after the prorogation on 5 Apr. and on hand a few days later to present a pro-Sacheverell address from Cornwall. He then left for the meeting of the Stannaries, being chosen its speaker on 20 Apr., and this time led the opposition to the terms proposed by the Whig lord warden, Hugh Boscawen II*, for a new pre-emption contract. As the parliament adjourned for the weekend, Buller rode to Truro and was thrown from his horse injuring his head. This necessitated the choice of a deputy-speaker on the 27th, but Buller was back in the chair on the 29th. Whether this fall had any long-term consequences is uncertain, but rumours of his death had reached London by 19 Sept., and it was later confirmed that he had died on the 14th. Coming as it did on the eve of a dissolution, Hon. James Brydges* believed that the Tories had 'lost a considerable support and indeed the greatest of their interest in Cornwall by the death of Mr Buller'. In his will he vested his estates in trust to 'such person or persons as shall be entitled to my capital mansion of Shillingham', which turned out to be his great-uncle, John Buller I*.[5]

[1] Vivian, *Vis. Cornw.* 57–58; IGI, Cambs. [2] Tregoning, *Stannary Laws*, 118. [3] *Post Boy*, 26–28 Jan. 1703; Boyer, *Anne Annals*, ii. 160; *Parlts. Estates and Rep.* vi. 61. [4] Add. 70420, newsletter 8 Feb. 1708–9. [5] Add. 49360, ff. 3, 6, 9–20; Boyer, ix. 160; R. Inst. Cornw., Tonkin's ms hist. vol. ii. 244; *Parlts. Estates and Rep.* 62–63; Add. 70421, newsletter 19, 28 Sept. 1710; *Huntington Lib. Q.* iii. 240; PCC 45 Young.

E. C./S. N. H.

BULLER, John I (c.1632–1716), of Morval, Cornw.

EAST AND WEST LOOE	1656–1658
EAST LOOE	1659
WEST LOOE	1660
SALTASH	1661–1679 (Jan.)
LISKEARD	1679 (Mar.)–1681 (Mar.), 1689–1690
GRAMPOUND	24 Nov. 1692–1695

b. c.1632, 2nd s. of Francis Buller† of Shillingham by Thomasine, da. of Sir Thomas Honeywood of Elmstead, Kent. *educ.* M. Temple 1646; Trinity Coll. Camb. 1647. *m.* (1) 22 Dec. 1659, Anne, da. and h. of John Coode of Morval, 1s. *d.v.p.* 4da.; (2) Jane, da. and h. of Walter Langdon† of Keveral, Cornw., 1s. 1da. *suc.* gt.-nephew James Buller* at Shillingham 1710.[1]

Recorder, West Looe Apr. 1660, Saltash by 1661–2, ?1710–*d.*; sheriff, Cornw. Nov. 1688–Mar. 1689; freeman, Liskeard c. Oct. 1688–?*d.*[2]

Buller, whose estate at Morval lay near the boroughs of Looe and Liskeard, owned the advowson of St. Stephen-by-Saltash. He acquired the estate at Keveral through his second marriage. In early life he had been a Presbyterian opponent of the Court, and in 1687 James II's agents still described him as a Dissenter. However, in the Convention he voted against the transfer of the crown. Returned for Grampound at a by-election in November 1692 he took his seat on 3 Dec. and was classed as a Court supporter by Grascome. He was not an active Member. On 2 Jan. 1694 a 'Mr Buller' was wounded in a duel following a quarrel between some Cornish gentlemen in a tavern in Holborn. Buller stood down in 1695, being content to foster his son's parliamentary ambitions at Liskeard in 1698 and at Lostwithiel in 1701. Having succeeded his great-nephew to the Shillingham estates at the very least he acquiesced in the candidature of William Shippen*, an extreme Tory, at Saltash in 1713. Buller died in 1716. In his will he founded charity schools for boys at Morval, Saltash, Liskeard, Looe, Penzance and Grampound to teach basic literacy, numeracy and the Church of England catechism. He placed his lands in the Isle of Thanet in the hands of trustees to sell in order to buy property in Devon and Cornwall for the benefit of his heir, his grandson John Francis Buller†, and in order to raise £6,000 to be divided between his four daughters.[3]

[1] Vivian, *Vis. Cornw.* 57; IGI, Cornw. [2] J. Allen, *Hist. Liskeard*, 271–2. [3] B. H. Williams, *Ancient W. Country Fams.* 39; Duckett, *Penal Laws and Test Act* (1882), 379; *Luttrell Diary*, 286; PCC 210 Box, 131 Fox; Luttrell, *Brief Relation* iii. 249; Allen, 178–9.

E. C./S. N. H.

BULLER, John II (1668–1701), of Keveral, Cornw.

LOSTWITHIEL   15 Jan.–17 Mar. 1701

bap. 15 Dec. 1668, o. s. of John Buller I* by 2nd w. *educ.* Christ Church, Oxf. matric. 19 Mar. 1686. *m.* 9 June 1691 (with £4,000), Mary (*d.* 1722), da. and coh. of Sir Henry Pollexfen†, l.c.j.c.p., of Woodbury, Devon, 1s. 2da.[1]

Sheriff, Cornw. 1691–2.

Upon Buller's marriage his father settled on him the estate of Keveral, five miles from Morval and worth £700 p.a. Almost immediately Buller was embroiled in the affairs of the Pollexfen and Drake families because on his death-bed (a few days after the wedding) his father-in-law named him as an executor in a codicil to his will made on 14 June 1691. Furthermore, no doubt as a consequence of his new-found independence, Buller was nominated as sheriff later in the year. His first foray into electoral politics appears to have been at Liskeard in 1698, when he was defeated. After taking legal advice he brought a civil action for £500 damages against the mayor for making a false return, on which no judgment was recorded (see LISKEARD, Cornw.). Buller was returned for Lostwithiel in January 1701 and attended the opening of Parliament. However, he died of the smallpox on 17 Mar. 1701. According to his will he made his father executor. However, it seems that Buller had 'involved himself in a great debt', so that his father refused to act, although he remained guardian of his grandchildren. Indeed, Buller snr. even sued his daughter-in-law for an allowance for undertaking this task. Buller's son, John Francis Buller, subsequently inherited both the Morval and Shillingham estates from his grandfather and sat as a Tory under George I.[2]

[1] IGI, Cornw.; Vivian, *Vis. Cornw.* 58; Egerton 2750, f. 17; E. F. Eliott-Drake, *Fam. and Heirs of Drake*, ii. 73–74, 148. [2] C 6/32/33; B. H. Williams, *Ancient W. Country Fams.* 39; Eliott-Drake, 79; Add. 27440, f. 156; *Post Boy*, 15–18 Mar. 1701.

E. C./S. N. H.

BULLOCK, Edward (1663–1705), of Faulkbourne Hall, Faulkbourne, Essex.

ESSEX 1698–1700
COLCHESTER 8 May–6 Dec. 1705

bap. 24 Jun. 1663, 1st s. of Edward Bullock of Faulkbourne Hall by Elizabeth, da. and h. of William Bolton of Ullenhall, Warws. *educ.* ?privately (John Ray) 1677–9; Newport sch. Essex; Trinity Coll. Camb. 1679; G. Inn 1682. *m.* (1) Elizabeth (*d.* 1691), da. and coh. of Sir Mark Guyon of Coggeshall, Essex, 1da. *d.v.p.*; (2) 11 Feb. 1693, Mary (*d.* 1748), da. of Sir Josiah Child, 1st Bt.†, of Wanstead, Essex, sis. of Sir Josiah Child, 2nd Bt.†, and of Sir Richard Child, 3rd Bt.*, 5s. (?1 *d.v.p.*) 2da. *suc.* fa. ?1671.[1]

Freeman, Maldon 1690, Colchester 1698.[2]

Bullock's political influence stemmed almost entirely from his two marriages to wealthy heiresses. His first wife, who died in childbirth, was heir to the best part of Sir Mark Guyon's extensive Essex estates, and the second was the daughter of Sir Josiah Child, the hugely wealthy governor of the East India Company. Bullock seems to have thought about exploiting his new alliance with Child to contest a by-election in Essex in 1694. He may well have hoped to win the support of Low Churchmen and Dissenters, since he had in early life probably come under the influence of John Ray, the naturalist, who refused to comply with the 1662 Act of Uniformity while remaining 'a strict as well as pious and exemplary conformist to the established church'. Nevertheless, Sir John Marshall's speculation that Bullock might be 'persuaded to desist and not espouse the fanatic interest' evidently proved correct. Marshall in fact believed that Child's Whiggishness was curbing Bullock's wish to support the candidates of the Church party, commenting that while he 'durst not be active for us . . . he won't appear against us', and would adopt the stance of studied neutrality that he had apparently shown at the last election. Perhaps because of this half-hearted support for his father-in-law, Child's 'rant', that he and Bullock could 'carry the election for whom they please', proved inaccurate, and the successful candidate was the High Church Tory Sir Charles Barrington, 5th Bt.*[3]

Bullock continued to lack the resolve to enter the fray of local or national politics, for he fined off from holding the county shrievalty when nominated in December 1694, a reluctance to accept the office that was repeated in 1695, 1701 and 1703. His hesitancy was again evident at the time of the 1695 election when, although 'he had said if the gentlemen [of the county] set him up he would stand', he refused to offer himself as a candidate when asked to do so, presumably because he was unwilling to offend Child. However, the fact that he was even considered as a colleague for Barrington against two Whigs suggests that he had been, and still was, involved in a delicate balancing act between the county's factions, and that his own politics were of a very moderate nature. Nevertheless, by the 1698 election he had reconsidered his position and decided to stand with Barrington, although it was observed by Sir John Bramston† that the Church party backed him, in part to recognize his acquired wealth and status, but also to use them to 'overbalance the interest of Sir Francis Masham, 3rd Bt.*, and Mr [Benjamin] Mildmay'. Since Bullock also had the official support of Bishop Compton of London, the plan 'took effect' and he was duly elected.[4]

Following the 1698 election Bullock was listed as a Country supporter on the comparative analysis of the old and new Houses of Commons, and was probably forecast in August 1698 as likely to oppose a standing army. It is very likely that he was the Mr Bullock who twice accompanied Hon. James Brydges* to the Tory club at the Vine in February 1699, yet he was also careful to maintain good relations with his father-in-law since it was no doubt on Child's behalf that on 27 Feb. he was among those ordered to prepare and bring in a bill for the continuation of the Old East India Company. Bullock must therefore have felt slightly aggrieved when, having performed this service, his wife was not left a legacy on Sir Josiah's death in June. Bullock was, however, marked as being of the East India Company's interest in a categorization of MPs drawn up early in 1700, along with his frequent companion Brydges, who may have seen in his friendship a way into the company's concerns. Bullock's brother John had by this time entered Parliament, so that it is difficult to be certain that it was Edward who presented a bill to the House on 5 Feb. 1700 for suspending the bounty money granted on the exportation of corn, which received the Royal Assent only four days later.[5]

Bullock's indecisiveness about his loyalties helped lose him his seat at the next election. At the beginning of December 1700 it had been reported that he would 'leave off Sir Charles Barrington' and join Masham, 'so that he does unite with the Dissenting party'; but on 7 Jan. 1701 Bishop Compton officially backed the combination of Barrington and Bullock for the Church interest. The rivalry between the Old and New East India companies, which was 'the greatest distinction in and about London', further damaged his campaign. It was noted that in Essex the supporters of the Old Company were 'great sufferers', and Bullock, who was known to be 'zealous for the cause', failed to secure re-election. He tried to regain his seat in the second election of 1701, once more with the sanction of Bishop Compton, who emphasized that the honour and safety of the nation depended on the return of 'good men', but was unsuccessful, perhaps because a rumour that he intended to 'run in harness' with the Whig Masham had characteristically blurred his position.[6]

By December 1704 Bullock seems finally to have deserted the High Church Tories and joined the Whigs since he is most likely to have been the Mr Bullock who met with others in Essex to agree on the joint ticket of Masham and Lord Walden (Henry Howard*) in order to oust Barrington. No longer seeking to represent the county himself, he was returned for Colchester in May 1705. Marked as a 'gain' for the Whigs by the Earl of Sunderland (Charles, Lord Spencer*), he justified the ascription by voting on 25 Oct. for the Court candidate as Speaker, and his 'Low Church' sympathies were also noted on another analysis of MPs. He died some six weeks later on 6 Dec. His will conveyed the estate of Dynes Hall to his brother, who had occupied it for some time, and several of his outlying properties were sold to discharge debts that may have been incurred by his own extensive building work on the east front of Faulkbourne Hall. His eldest son, Edward, dying without issue, the estate passed to the next son, Josiah, who, as befitted his name, took advantage of the family's links with the Childs to develop mercantile interests, marrying the youngest daughter of Sir Thomas Cooke*, governor of the East India Company and himself a former MP for Colchester.[7]

[1] IGI; *Vis. Essex* ed. Metcalfe, ii. 646–7; Morant, *Essex*, ii. 118; Burke, *Commoners*, ii. 622; *Essex Review*, xxxvi. 131; L. C. Bullock, *Mem. Fam. Bullock* (1905), ped. A; *London Mar. Lic.* ed. Foster, 214. [2] Essex RO, Maldon bor. recs. sessions bk. D/B3/1/23, entry for 20 Oct. 1690; *Oath Bk. of Colchester* ed. Benham, 232. [3] *DNB* (Ray, John); W. Suss. RO, Shillinglee mss Ac. 454/558–60, Sir John Marshall to Sir Edward Turnor*, 22 Jan., 15, ?21 Feb. 1694. [4] *CSP Dom.* 1702–3, p. 523; *Bramston Autobiog.* (Cam. Soc. xxxii), 392, 406; Camb. Univ. Lib. Add. mss 5, f. 209. [5] Huntington Lib. Stowe mss 28(1–2), James Brydges' diary (unfol.), 13, 17 Feb. 1699; Add. 40774, ff. 70–71. [6] Essex RO, Barrett-Lennard mss D/DL C48, C. Clarke to Dacre Barrett, 5 Dec. [1700]; Camb. Univ. Lib. Add. mss 5, ff. 215, 219; Bodl. Ballard 6, f. 35; Bodl. Locke c12, f. 158. [7] *Essex Review*, xx. 173; Bullock, 34, 38.

M. J. K.

BULLOCK, John (c.1671–1740), of Dynes Hall, Great Maplestead, Essex.

MALDON 14 Mar. 1699–1700

b. c.1671, 5th but 2nd surv. s. of Edward Bullock of Faulkbourne Hall and bro. of Edward Bullock*. educ. Halstead sch.; Peterhouse, Camb. adm. 27 Mar. 1690, aged 18; I. Temple 1687. m. (1) Rachel, da. and coh. of Sir Mark Guyon, wid. of Thomas Guyon, 1s. d.v.p. 1da.; (2) Hannah-Maria, da. and coh. of Samuel Keck, master in Chancery, s.p.[1]

Freeman, Colchester 1698, Maldon 1699.[2]

Bullock had much in common, both personally and politically, with his elder brother Edward. Both had married daughters of Sir Mark Guyon, and although the manor at Great Maplestead was not part of the inheritance of John's wife, Edward allowed them to live in the property, conveying it to them by his will in 1705. It was probably owing to the influence of his brother and the Child family of Wanstead (into which his brother had married) that Bullock was elected for Maldon at a by-election in 1699, though Sir John Bramston† condescendingly suggested that he was chosen because the gentry at that time 'had nobody that cared to be in the House, but he, writing a civil letter, submitting to the freemen, and offering to join with them in any other choice, wrought so on our good nature that we fixed on him'. Either he or his brother presented a bill to the Commons on 5 Feb. 1700 for suspending the bounty money given on the exportation of corn; and, no doubt influenced by the connexion with the Childs, Bullock was marked as being of the Old East India Company's interest at the beginning of that year. His memorial inscription claimed that, having sat once as an MP, 'he always afterward declined' to stand for election, though it was in fact reported just before Parliament was dissolved in December 1700 that he would 'not quit his intent of standing for Maldon for any man', and that he had joined with William Fytche*. Bullock must indeed have pressed for re-election, since on 9 Jan. 1701 it was reported that he had been 'left out' because of his links with the Old Company, and this defeat appears to have put an end to his parliamentary ambitions. Although he inherited Dynes Hall from his brother, he spent the latter part of his life at Clapham in Surrey, where he died sometime in 1740. Since his son John had predeceased him his estates passed to his daughter Rachel, who subsequently sold the manor.[3]

[1] Burke, *Commoners*, ii. 622; L. C. Bullock, *Mem. Fam. Bullock* (1905), p. 34; info. from Dr D. F. Lemmings. [2] *Oath Bk. of Colchester* ed. Benham, 232; Essex RO, Maldon bor. recs. sessions bk. D/B3/1/24, f. 108. [3] *Bramston Autobiog.* (Cam. Soc. xxxii), 406; Bullock, 34, 36; Essex RO, Barrett-Lennard mss D/DL C48, C. Clarke to Dacre Barrett, 5 Dec. [1700]; Bodl. Ballard 6, f. 35.

M. J. K.

BULTEEL, James (c.1676–1757), of Tavistock, Devon.

TAVISTOCK 26 Nov. 1703–1708, 3 Feb. 1711–1715

b. c.1676, 2nd s. of Samuel Bulteel (d. 1682) of Tavistock. *educ.* I. Temple 1694. *m.* 1 Oct. 1718, Mary, da. and h. of Courtenay Croker*, 1s. 1da. *suc.* John Modyford Hele at Flete 1716.[1]

Commr. public accts. 1714.

A Tory lawyer of Huguenot descent, Bulteel was a legal adviser to several landed families in Devon. He stood unsuccessfully for Tavistock in the two elections of 1701, but was returned unopposed at a by-election in November 1703. He was wrongly listed as having voted on 13 Feb. 1703 against agreeing with the Lords' amendments to the bill for enlarging the time for taking the oath of abjuration. Forecast as a probable supporter of the Tack, he did not vote for it on 28 Nov. 1704. On 15 Jan. 1705 he was appointed to the drafting committee on a private bill, managing it through all subsequent stages in the House. Re-elected without opposition in 1705, he was classed as 'Low Church' in an analysis of the new Parliament, and voted against the Court candidate for Speaker on 25 Oct. He spoke in defence of Charles Caesar* during a debate on the regency bill on 19 Dec. He managed another private bill through the House, having been appointed to its drafting committee on 14 Jan. 1706. He told on the Tory side over the disputed election for Coventry on 5 Feb. 1707, and on the 15th in favour of an instruction to a committee to name the Corporation Act in a bill from the Lords for the security of the Church. During March, he managed a private bill for the relief of Alexander Pendarves*. He told on 5 Apr. in favour of putting the question for an address to the crown on the Newfoundland fishery. On 14 Feb. 1708 he told against going into committee on the bill to secure American trade, again telling on 8 Mar. on an amendment to a supply bill. On 15 Mar. he told in favour of an amendment to the East India Company bill, which would have made it impossible to hold a directorship simultaneously of the company and the Bank of England. He presented a bill to impose further duties on imported yarn on 16 Mar., telling in favour of its second reading on 22 Mar. His final tellership of this Parliament was against the adjournment of a debate on a legal reform bill on 30 Mar.

Classed as a Tory in early 1708, Bulteel did not stand at the general election of that year. He contested Tavistock in 1710 and was seated on petition on 3 Feb. 1711. A member of the October Club and one of the 'worthy patriots' who exposed the mismanagements of the previous administration, he was chosen by ballot to the abortive commission for the resumption of King William's grants on 17 Apr. 1711. He managed two private bills through the House in April and May. On 12 May 1712 he was again elected to the grants resumption commission, an initiative which once again failed, as previously. He told on 26 May in favour of granting leave to bring in a bill to extend the charter of the East India Company. During June he assisted in the management of two more private bills. On 18 June 1713 he spoke and voted in support of the Court over the French commerce bill.[2]

Re-elected in 1713, Bulteel was nominated to the committee on the Address on 2 Mar. 1714. He managed three private bills through the House in this session. He told on 15 Mar. on a procedural motion over an address on the demolition of fortifications at Dunkirk. On 15 Apr. he seconded the motion that the Protestant succession was not in danger under her Majesty's government. During his speech he made an attack on Robert Walpole II*. He told on 14 May 1714 in favour of a resolution for a 2d. duty on London coal imports as part of the financing of repairs to a breach in the bank of the Thames. He was nominated on 10 June to the drafting committee for a bill to discharge the commissioners of the Scottish Equivalent from liability for money already disbursed. After chairing a committee of the whole on the Equivalent accounts on 21 June, he carried up to the Lords on 1 July the bill in favour of the commissioners. The previous day he had been elected a commissioner of public accounts. Listed as a Tory on the Worsley list, Bulteel retired from the House at the dissolution.³

In 1716 Bulteel, although no relation by blood, succeeded John Modyford Hele to Flete House and other Devon estates under the will of Hele's father, Richard*. Bulteel was named as a 'dubious' Jacobite sympathizer in a list sent to the Pretender in 1721. He died in 1757.⁴

¹Burke, *LG* (1952); *Trans. Devon Assoc.* xliii. 396; lxiv. 495; *Her. and Gen.* viii. 380; Vivian, *Vis. Devon*, 466. ²*Misc. Gen. et Her.* ser. 5, iii. 17–18; *Cam. Misc.* xxiii. 53. ³*Huntington Lib. Q.* xxxiii. 168; NSA Kreienberg despatch 16 May 1712; *HMC Lords*, n.s. x. 275; *Wentworth Pprs.* 370; Douglas diary (Hist. of Parl. trans.), 15 Apr. 1714; NLS, Advocates' mss, Wodrow pprs. letters Quarto 8, ff. 95, 138. ⁴P. S. Fritz, *Ministers and Jacobitism 1715–45*, p. 148; Vivian, 466.

E. C.

BUNBURY, Sir Henry, 3rd Bt. (1676–1733), of Bunbury and Stanney, nr. Chester.

CHESTER 1701 (Feb.)–1727

b. 29 Nov. 1676, 1st surv. s. of Sir Henry Bunbury, 2nd Bt., by Mary, da. of Sir Kenrick Eyton† of Lower Eyton, Denb. *educ.* St. Catharine's, Camb. 1694. *m.* 15 May 1699, Susannah, da. of William Hanmer of Bettisfield, Flints., sis. of Thomas Hanmer II*, 4s. (2 *d.v.p.*) 5da. *suc.* fa. as 3rd Bt. 20 Dec. 1687.¹

Sheriff, Cheshire 1699–1700; freeman, Chester 1700, 1701.²

Commr. revenue [I] 1711–15.³

Though the first member of his family to enter the Commons, Bunbury was descended from a gentry family which had been established at Stanney since the 12th century. His family gained the manor of Little Stanney by marriage during the 14th century and gradually expanded their landholdings in the county so that by the reign of Elizabeth I they owned land in 13 townships, including the borough of Chester. Bunbury's great-grandfather was an active Royalist, being imprisoned by Parliament's forces for 18 months before compounding in 1646 for £1,700, and it was later claimed that the family's support for the King during the Civil Wars cost it £10,000. The family's political activity following the Restoration is obscure, but in 1681 Bunbury's grandfather was awarded a baronetcy which Bunbury inherited aged only 11, following the death of his grandfather and father in 1682 and 1687 respectively. Some indication of Bunbury's character as a young man is given by the claim of his 19th-century descendant that the playwright George Farquhar based the character of 'Sir Harry Wildair' upon Bunbury. Farquhar described Wildair as 'an airy gentleman, affecting humorous gaiety and freedom in his behaviour', and though there is no contemporary confirmation that Wildair was modelled upon Bunbury it is the case that the play of 1699 in which Wildair first appeared was dedicated to the Cheshire Tory Sir Roger Mostyn, 3rd Bt.*, suggesting that Farquhar may have been acquainted with Bunbury. It is clear that Bunbury played a full role in the busy social life of the Cheshire elite, and once he had entered the Commons he frequently preferred the company of a bottle of claret and his Cheshire circle to attendance at the early weeks of parliamentary sessions. Bunbury's decision to enter Parliament suggests, however, that his nature was not entirely frivolous. This aspiration was first suggested in October 1700 by his admission to the freedom of Chester, and following his success at the contested election of January 1701 Bunbury held his seat until the death of George I.⁴

Bunbury maintained a low profile for much of his early parliamentary career. His only notable activity in the first 1701 Parliament was to report on 10 May upon a Cheshire estate bill, and six days later he obtained an indefinite leave of absence. Having been classed as a Tory in Robert Harley's* list of the 1701–2 Parliament, Bunbury made only a slight contribution to the business of the House. In January 1702 he promised to pursue the claim of Chester merchants for money owed them in respect of the transport they had provided in the early 1690s to aid the war in Ireland, but though he informed the corporation at the same time that 'I have not yet missed an hour in the House' his only notable activity was his nomination to draft the estate bill of the Cheshire Tory Sir Thomas Stanley, 3rd Bt., and his appointment to carry to the Lords a bill continuing the act exempting apothecaries from selected parochial offices. On 2 Mar. he was granted a three-week leave of absence. Bunbury's efforts to secure his interest at Chester, evident from his gift in March 1702 of £100 to the borough to clear debts accrued in the building of a new town hall, bore fruit in his uncontested re-election in 1702, and though his parliamentary profile remained low his partisan loyalties and concern to advance local interests were clear during the 1702 Parliament. In early 1703, for example, he twice petitioned the Treasury on behalf of Chester's merchants, while on 4 Feb. 1704 he was ordered to carry to the Lords a bill concerned with the estates of the deceased Thomas Legh I*. Concern for the privileges of the Anglican church was indicated later the same month when he told in favour of adding to a bill concerned with Irish forfeited lands a rider on behalf of the bishop of Cloyne, and his Tory sympathies are clear from his inclusion upon a list drawn up in March by Lord Nottingham (Daniel Finch†), probably a forecast of support on the Scotch Plot. The depth of these convictions was evident in a letter written in the summer of 1704 in response to rumours of a possible dissolution, in which Bunbury stated that his desire to remain in the Commons stemmed from a desire to do 'the service of my country . . . and that I only think this can be performed by heartily espousing the Church of England as by law established in opposition both to popery and presbytery'. Given such sentiments, it is unsurprising that on 28 Nov. Bunbury voted for the Tack. His only other notable activity in the 1704–5 session saw him tell in favour of referring to a select committee a bill, supported by Cheshire's button-makers, to encourage the manufacture of needle-work buttons, and in favour of accepting an additional clause to the bill to levy duties on imported wine and East India goods re-exported to Ireland or the colonies.[5]

Following his unchallenged return for Chester Bunbury spent much of the summer of 1705 in the company of his brother-in-law Hanmer (now 4th Bt.). Bunbury's Toryism was clearly evident at the start of the 1705–6 session. He was listed as True Church in an analysis of the new House and voted on 25 Oct. against the Court candidate for Speaker. During the 1705–6 session he adopted a higher parliamentary profile. In the debate in the committee of the whole on 4 Dec. on the Scottish parliament's actions relating to the succession Bunbury, described as 'a young Member not known before', was reported to have made 'a very applauded long speech' as part of the Tory attack upon the ministry. During the debate four days later on the 'Church in danger' resolution Bunbury emphasized the growth of Dissent, the general 'contempt' with which the Anglican clergy were viewed, and the ill-effects of the failure of the occasional conformity bills. He also figured in the debates upon the regency bill. The bill's second reading on 19 Dec., for example, saw him oppose the motion of censure against Charles Caesar*, while on 15 Jan. 1706 he was one of a number of Tories who objected to the bill's provision that Parliament was to meet 'immediately' following the death of the Queen, suggesting that this clause was only supported by those 'gent[lemen] about town and in offices' whose influence would thereby be increased relative to gentlemen normally resident in the country. During the consideration on 19 Jan. of the composition of the regency Bunbury ventured to query the possible problems of including specified office-holders on the regency council, citing the 'inconveniences which may arise if impeached persons may be in those places'. His interest in the regency bill is also evident from his appointment on 4 Feb. to prepare reasons for disagreeing with the Lords' amendments to this measure. His only other significant activity in the session came two days later when he told against fixing the days upon which matters of privilege were to be heard. Bunbury's burst of activity in the 1705–6 session was not sustained for the entire Parliament. Illness delayed his departure from Cheshire for the 1706–7 session until after Christmas, prompting a letter from the Speaker to Chester corporation informing them of a call of the House due in the new year. His only important act was to tell on the Tory side in the division of 5 Feb. 1707 on the Coventry election case. In the autumn of 1707 his journey to Parliament was again postponed, on this occasion until the end of November, but he had arrived in London by 9 Dec. when he was added to a committee. At the beginning of 1708 Bunbury was classed as a Tory, and it seems that he was among those Tories approached by Robert Harley* at this time in an attempt by the secretary of state to bolster his interest with the Tory party. That this was the case is suggested by a letter written in 1713 in which it was claimed that in early 1708 Bunbury, Hanmer and Peter Shakerley* were confident enough of their interest with Harley to assure a Cheshire resident seeking a place that 'they believed they had interest enough to recommend' him for a place in Harley's office. Whatever Bunbury imagined his influence to be at this time, he was an inactive Member, making no significant contribution to the 1707–8 session.[6]

In a break with his recent behaviour Bunbury was keen to leave Cheshire in October 1708 to attend the opening stages of the session, ignoring the requests of his friends to remain in the county until his wife was able to travel with him. This eagerness is most explicable in terms of the efforts of Hanmer and Shakerley to ensure a large attendance of the north-west's Tory Members at the beginning of the session when, in Hanmer's words, 'some matters of great moment are likely to be offered'. A list of Members dating from early 1708 classed Bunbury as a Tory, and he twice told in this interest upon disputed elections cases: on

16 Dec. in favour of declaring the tendering of the abjuration oath at the Westminster election a high crime and misdemeanour, and on 29 Jan. 1709 in favour of adjourning consideration of the Orford election case and thereby delaying consideration of the claims of the defeated Whig candidates. On both occasions Bunbury told in the minority, and at the beginning of February he complained to a Cheshire Tory of 'the distraction and confusion of all transactions here' and 'the violence with which everything is carried'. He went on:

> the business of Parliament is extremely tedious and vexatious this sessions, we try our elections at the bar and generally sit [on] them till one or two in the morning and then we can not convince people that 30 are more than three . . . this must end in the worst confusion and will at one time or other [result] in our quitting the House in a body, and then how public credit or the good of the kingdom will go on everybody may judge.

For the remainder of the session Bunbury showed some interest in minor mercantile affairs. On 10 Feb. he was nominated to draft a bill to encourage tobacco exports, telling on 9 Mar. in favour of setting a date for consideration of the bill by a committee of the whole, and on 7 Apr. he was appointed to consider a petition from merchants concerning a transport debt owing since the 1690s. He reported from this committee two days later. It seems, however, that the disillusionment with Parliament which had been evident as the 1708–9 session progressed may have lessened Bunbury's enthusiasm for the Commons, as, having arrived in Cheshire in May 1709, he remained there until the beginning of January 1710. Having at last travelled to London, he told on 25 Jan. in favour of granting leave for the introduction of a place bill. Bunbury's alarm at the proceedings against Dr Sacheverell is clear from a letter to his wife in which he was reported to have claimed that 'the main design in Parliament after Dr Sacheverell's trial is to make a new test whereby it is to be declared, that resistance against the king *de facto* or *de jure* is lawful and consentaneous to scripture'. Naturally he voted against the impeachment of Sacheverell.[7]

Following his return for Chester in 1710 Bunbury was listed as a Tory in the 'Hanover list'. In October Hanmer wrote to the Duke of Ormond to thank him for his 'kind inclination' towards Bunbury, and the reason for Hanmer's gratitude had become apparent by the end of the year when it was reported that Bunbury was to be added to the Irish revenue commission. No appointment was, however, made during the 1710–11 session. Bunbury was inactive in Parliament until February 1711 when he and Shakerley were consulted by Chester's tanners concerning rumours that new leather duties were intended by the ministry. The Chester Members wrote a joint reply, but it seems that following the introduction in March of a bill to establish such duties it was Shakerley who was the more active on the tanners' behalf. On 7 Mar. Bunbury did assist Shakerley in effecting the defeat of the Weaver navigation bill, a proposal felt to be injurious to the interests of Cheshire's brine salt trade, but otherwise Bunbury's attention was focused on less parochial matters. Having been the first-named Member appointed on 9 Mar. to prepare the Commons' address on the attempted assassination of Harley, later that day Bunbury reported from this committee and twice reported from conferences with the Lords on the address. His support for peace with France is clear from his telling the following day in favour of repealing the bill prohibiting the import of French wine, and his Toryism was demonstrated in two tellerships upon the Weymouth and Melcombe Regis election case. Bunbury was classed as both a 'Tory patriot' who had opposed the continuation of the war, and a 'worthy patriot' who had helped detect the mismanagements of the previous ministry in this session. He was also listed as a member of the October Club. Bunbury's behaviour at Westminster had done nothing to jeopardize his prospects of office, and his stay in Cheshire at the end of the session was brief. Prior to his return north Bunbury had been introduced to the Queen by Lord Oxford (as Harley had become) and less than a month after Bunbury's arrival at Chester in June it had become public knowledge that he was to succeed a recently deceased Irish revenue commissioner. At the end of July Bunbury set sail for Ireland. Following his return in November a writ was issued for the by-election necessary upon his taking office, and, having been re-elected unopposed, Bunbury left Chester for London on 7 Jan. 1712 and was at Westminster by the 17th. A week later Bunbury spoke for the censure of the Duke of Marlborough (John Churchill[†]), but otherwise he made little impact in the House. In February he was lobbied by representatives of Chester's tanners who hoped to persuade him to use his influence to obtain an act prohibiting the export of bark, a crucial raw material for the tanning of leather, the export of which had allowed the Irish leather industry to develop to such an extent that Chester's tanners viewed it as a threat to their livelihoods. The concerns of Chester's leather industry were, however, again pursued more by Shakerley than by Bunbury; it may have been that Bunbury's Irish office constrained him from promoting a bill intended to hinder an Irish industry. Concern for Irish interests was evident on 20

Mar. when he reported and carried to the Lords a bill regarding the estates of an Irish peer. Bunbury returned to Ireland in the summer to resume his duties, and though in February 1713 Oxford granted him leave to return to England, Bunbury remained in Ireland, probably as his departure would have left the revenue commission there inquorate. He was therefore absent from the 1713 session, and at the election of that year was forced to entrust the management of his interest at Chester to Shakerley. He was nevertheless returned unopposed.[8]

Bunbury had returned to England by January 1714 and appears to have been in London for the beginning of the new Parliament. His speech of 18 Mar. against Richard Steele* was described by Kreienberg as being in the interest of the Court, but in the following month's debate of the 15th on the succession Bunbury spoke against the ministry, being described as one of those who followed the lead of Hanmer in refusing to support the contention that the Protestant succession was not in danger. There is, however, little evidence that this speech indicated a general hostility on his part to the ministry. On 19 Apr. he told against an amendment to the bill to reduce the drawback on Irish tobacco imports, and on 6 May told on the Tory side in a division upon the Colchester election petition. He also told on 20 May against the second reading of a clause to the bill regulating the armed forces that would have given j.p.s the right to investigate fictitious names on army musters. That Bunbury had remained, in general, loyal to the ministry was suggested in June when he secured his requests for his revenue commissioner's salary to be backdated to the death of his predecessor in April 1711, and that he be granted further expenses in respect of the costs of his first journey to Ireland. Both the Worsley list and a comparison of the 1713 and 1715 Parliaments classed him unequivocally as a Tory. Bunbury remained a Tory following the Hanoverian succession, but his speech of April 1714 and his association with such leading Hanoverian Tories as Hanmer appear to have stood him in good stead as he initially retained his Irish place. Despite this mark of favour from the new ministry, however, Bunbury's support for the new regime appears to have diminished, as in May 1715 he was found to be engaged in Jacobite correspondence and in possession of seditious pamphlets. In September he was therefore removed from the revenue commission. Bunbury died on 12 Feb. 1733.[9]

[1] *Prescott Diary*, 99, 606, 933; Ormerod, *Cheshire*, ii. 395–6. [2] Chester RO, Chester bor. recs. assembly bks. A/B/3, f. 82; *Chester Freeman Rolls* ed. J. H. E. Bennet (Lancs. and Cheshire Rec. Soc. lv), 207. [3] *Cal. Treas. Bks.* xxv. 432; xxvi. 340; xxvii. 91; xxix. 185–6, 740. [4] Ormerod, 392–6; J. S. Morrill, *Cheshire 1603–60*, 53; *Cal. Comm. Comp.* 1643–60, p. 1139; *Works of George Farquhar* ed. Kenny, i. 135; Chester bor. recs. assembly bks. A/B/3, f. 96. [5] Chester bor. recs. mayor's letters M/L/574, Bunbury to Chester corporation, 22 Jan. 1701–2; *Cal. Treas. Bks.* xviii. 113; Northants. RO, Finch-Hatton mss FH 280 p. 17, Nottingham to John Methuen*, 11 Feb. 1702–3; John Rylands Univ. Lib. Manchester, Legh of Lyme corresp. Bunbury to Peter Legh†, 15 Aug. 1704. [6] *Prescott Diary*, 61, 63, 74, 128–9, 938–9; SRO, Mar and Kellie mss GD124/15/259/3, William Cleland to Hon. James Erskine†, 6 Dec. 1705; *Cam. Misc.* xxiii. 48, 55, 68, 76; Chester bor. recs. M/L/597, John Smith I* to Chester corporation, 24 Dec. 1706, Chester corporation to Smith, 28 Dec. 1706; *EHR*, lxxx. 684, 692. [7] *Prescott Diary*, 197, 234, 262–3, 270–1; G. Holmes and W. A. Speck, *Divided Soc.* 163; Legh of Lyme mss corresp. Bunbury to Legh, 1 Feb. 1708[-9]. [8] *HMC Ormonde*, n.s. viii. 320; Luttrell, *Brief Relation*, vi. 665; *Jnl. of Chester and N. Wales Architectural, Arch. and Hist. Soc.* xliv. 41–44; Chester bor. recs. M/L/4/640, Shakerley to Sir Thomas Aston, 3rd Bt., 8 Mar. 1710[-1]; 652, Bunbury to Chester corporation, 27 June 1713; *Prescott Diary*, 313, 316, 339–40; Add. 47026, f. 70; *HMC Portland*, v. 30–31; Oldmixon, *Hist. Eng.* (1735), 488; *Cal. Treas. Bks.* xxvii. 132; Legh of Lyme mss corresp. Bunbury to Legh, 21 Feb. 1712[-3]; NLW, Chirk Castle mss E5996, Bunbury to Sir Richard Myddelton, 1st Bt.*, 6 May 1713; Cheshire RO, Shakerley mss, Bunbury to Shakerley, 30 July 1713. [9] *Prescott Diary*, 374, 425, 427, 429; Douglas diary (Hist. of Parl. trans.), 18 Mar. 1714; NLS, Advocates' mss, Wodrow pprs. letters Quarto 8, ff. 69, 96; NSA, Kreienberg despatch 19 Mar. 1714; Holmes and Speck, 113; *Cal. Treas. Bks.* xxviii. 325; *Parlty. Hist.* xiv. 271.

R. D. H.

BURCHETT, Josiah (c.1666–1746), of St. Martin's-in-the-Fields, Mdx.

SANDWICH   1705–1713, 1722–1741

b. c.1666, prob. 1st surv. s. of John Burchett of Sandwich by his 2nd w. Katherine. *m.* (1) 24 Dec. 1695, Thomasine (*d.* 1713), da. of Sir William Honywood, 2nd Bt.*, 1s. 2da. (1 *d.v.p.*); (2) 22 July 1721, Margaret (*d.* 1740), wid. of Capt. Robert Arris, *?s.p.*; (3) 10 June 1740, Isabella (*d.* 1756), da. of John Robinson*, wid. of Mr. Wood, *?s.p.*[1]

Clerk to Samuel Pepys, as sec. to Admiralty, c.1680–Aug. 1687; clerk in the Admiralty Mar. ?1689–?Jan. 1691, by July 1693–?Apr. 1694; sec. to adm. of the Fleet Jan. 1691–by July 1693, ?Apr. 1694–Sept. 1694; sec. to Admiralty Sept. 1694–Oct. 1742; dep. judge advocate of Fleet July 1693–Aug. 1694; sec. of marines Feb. 1708–1713.[2]

Commr. Greenwich Hosp. 1695–?1704; er. bro. Trinity House 1707–22.[3]

A native of Sandwich, Burchett entered the service of Samuel Pepys around 1680, although he may not have graduated into employment in the Admiralty Office until 1685. In 1687 he was dismissed by Pepys, allegedly for accepting bribes, and in the years following made numerous attempts to regain a post in naval administration or, alternatively, to take ship to Jamaica. He may have been partially restored to favour following a letter to Pepys in February 1688 because he found work with William Hewer†, a member of the

Navy Board closely linked to Pepys, and in September 1688 was allowed to enlist on the *Portsmouth*. In October he found himself among the retinue of Admiral Lord Dartmouth (George Legge†), and through the good offices of Dartmouth's secretary, Phineas Bowles, when the latter was appointed secretary to the Admiralty under Torrington (Arthur Herbert†) in March 1689, Burchett was employed as a clerk. Promotion quickly followed and in June 1691 he was appointed secretary to Admiral Edward Russell*. He then alternated employment at the Admiralty Board with active service when Russell was at sea, until the place as secretary of the Admiralty became vacant in August 1694, although he had to wait until January 1695, when he returned from the Mediterranean, to take up his new office. After the 'fatigue' of the post persuaded his co-secretary, William Bridgeman, to retire in 1698, Burchett served as sole secretary until 1702. This period was probably crucial in allowing him time to establish his reputation; by 1700 a contemporary tract was describing the secretary as 'the spring that moves the clockwork of the whole board, the oracle that is to be consulted on all occasions'. He continued there, as either sole or joint secretary until 1742.[4]

In July 1694 Francis Gwyn* had informed Robert Harley* that 'Admiral Russell's Birket' had been appointed joint secretary, and for some years afterwards Burchett was seen as Russell's creature. In his published memoirs, notable for their discretion, Burchett did on occasion laud Russell's abilities, but his later career suggests that Burchett was adept at keeping on good terms with whoever exercised power at the Admiralty. Although he had married into a family of Kentish Whigs, Burchett's opportunity to enter Parliament appears to have come as a result of his contacts with his native port of Sandwich. The corporation certainly approached Burchett over Sandwich harbour and although he had indicated in January 1704 that only an Act of Parliament could solve their problems, some of the townsmen were sufficiently impressed to offer him one of the seats in the borough. He duly topped the poll at the 1705 election. One analysis of the 1705 Parliament considered Burchett 'a High Church courtier', but the Earl of Sunderland (Charles, Lord Spencer*) counted his election as a gain for the Whigs. He voted on 25 Oct. 1705 for the Court candidate as Speaker, and supported the Court on 18 Feb. 1706 in the proceedings on the 'place clause' of the regency bill. Burchett's knowledge of naval affairs made him invaluable to Sandwich, and in January 1706 he was advising the corporation on the correct procedure regarding court martials. He was also used by the corporation in March 1706 to approach Lord Keeper Cowper (William*) to recommend the minister of the Dutch congregation in the town for the living of St. Peter's, Sandwich. His solicitation was followed by a letter to Sandwich requesting details of the value of the benefice, Cowper being loath to part with a prize living which might suit one of the Queen's chaplains. March 1706 also saw Burchett elevated on to the Kentish commission of the peace. In 1707 the corporation of Trinity House elected him an elder brother in place of the Earl of Pembroke (Hon. Thomas Herbert†) on the grounds that to be the Earl's messenger was an implicit nomination to the corporation. In February 1708, Burchett's appointment as secretary to the marines (in succession to Henry St. John II*) necessitated a by-election in which he was returned unopposed. Not surprisingly, he was also returned at the general election held in May 1708 and was twice during the year listed as a Whig.[5]

The 1708 Parliament saw Burchett at his most active in this period in Admiralty matters. In the previous Parliament his role had been limited to behind-the-scenes preparation, with the presentation of papers to the Commons being left to Admiral George Churchill* as the leading light of the Prince's council. However, on 24 Nov. 1708 it was Burchett who presented to the House the statutory account of the activities of cruisers and convoys, and, who, two days later, presented the naval estimates. Indeed, for a short time after the death of Prince George, the navy was run in the Queen's name, with orders being countersigned by Burchett. With the appointment in November of Pembroke as lord high admiral, Burchett must have maintained his influence, because there was no advisory council to contend with. Rumours of his dismissal in March 1709 were misplaced and in June he was rewarded with £1,200 for his extraordinary service during the Queen's tenure of the office of lord admiral. Further evidence of royal favour followed in December 1709 when the Queen gave him a gift of plate to celebrate the christening of one of his children. With Pembroke's departure from the Admiralty imminent, Burchett wrote to Lord Treasurer Godolphin (Sidney†) in October 1709, concerned about his 'fate', not knowing 'how I may stand with those who are to succeed', and even offering to retire so long as his family would be provided for. Burchett need not have worried, as he presided over a smooth transition when Russell (now Earl of Orford) was named to head a new Admiralty commission in November. Indeed, Burchett again laid the estimates before the Commons, and continued to present papers until January 1710 despite the presence in the House of four Admiralty commissioners. He voted with the Whig ministry in 1709 in support of the naturalization of the Palatines and the following year for the impeachment of Dr Sacheverell. Despite this record, he survived the ministerial revolution of 1710.[6]

Burchett's election address to Sandwich corporation in 1710 was admirably understated; he admitted to being 'conscious' that he had 'not acquitted myself so as to deserve your future regard, but yet hope you will favourably believe that it has wholly arisen from want of power'. He was duly returned with a comfortable majority. As befitted a civil servant, whose first loyalty was to the ministry of the day, Burchett was classed as doubtful on the 'Hanover list' of 1710. However, he no longer presented Admiralty papers to the Commons, that task being performed in the 1710–11 session by Sir John Leake*. Correspondence exists from Burchett to the Earl of Strafford (first lord of the Admiralty, 1712–14), who for much of his tenure of office was abroad serving as ambassador at The Hague. In his letters Burchett was considerably more informative about the politics of the navy than would have been the case had Strafford been resident in England. Indeed, on one occasion in December 1712 he apologized 'for taking on me so much of the statesman, for I am sensible that I ought to confine myself to my daily drudgery without meddling with these matters'. Strafford was also called into action (as was John Michel II*) in April 1713 to pressurize Lord Treasurer Oxford (Harley) to enable Burchett to sit in the following Parliament. Burchett had been caught out by the provisions of the Landed Qualification Act of 1711, but as early as October 1712 had proposed that Lord Treasurer Oxford facilitate the acquisition of an estate which would enable him to sit in the next Parliament. The request was couched in terms of his long service and the manner in which his income had been adversely affected by the abolition of certain fees. Oxford appeared to have responded favourably, but put the onus on Burchett to find an estate which the crown could grant him. By January 1713 Burchett had solved that problem: 'the estate of one Robert Wise a tobacconist in London, called Stadham near Oxford, is ordered to be seized for customs due to her Majesty'. This was a property which, combined with the purchase of an adjacent estate, would make over £300 p.a. The plan fell through, as did his approach to his father-in-law for '£300 a year in Kent', and eventually he had to withdraw his candidature at Sandwich. On the parliamentary lists of the 1713 session, Burchett was not listed as voting on 18 June on the vital question of the French commerce bill. Fortunately, his correspondence informs us that he had 'readily and heartily' come into the peace, 'although the printer of the list of Members who voted for and against the treaty of commerce has been so good natured or forgetful to leave me out'. Indeed, to Strafford he had described the debate on the issue as a 'very hard tug'. Thus, not only did the 1713 election see Burchett disabled from sitting in the Commons, but the end of the war meant the loss of £400 p.a. when the marine regiments were disbanded. To make matters worse, in August he reported that his wife was 'either already dead or dying at the Bath', although she did not die until October.[7]

January 1714 saw Burchett recovering from illness, but continuing to keep Strafford informed of Admiralty affairs. On 23 Apr. 1714 he reported that the decision of the Commons the previous day to join with the Lords in an address to the crown had, he hoped, ended 'the dreadful fears which some people have shown for the Protestant succession'. The death of the Queen found him over-worked and in a quandary about his future, believing that

> notwithstanding the pains I am now taking, and what I have for many years undergone, with a hearty zeal for my country, I know not how my lot will fall upon this change, though possibly it may be to eat bread and cheese with my children, for all that I have been able to save these 30 years past will hardly give them more.

Burchett need not have worried, for the new first lord was none other than Orford, who of course had a keen appreciation of Burchett's administrative abilities. If there was any doubt about his loyalty after 1715, Burchett assuaged it by launching into print in 1716 with a poem entitled *Strife and Envy since the Fall of Man*, the last lines of which clearly distanced him from the previous Tory ministry. He returned to the Commons in 1722 and held his seat until 1741.[8]

Burchett died on 2 Oct. 1746, at the house in Hampstead to which he had retired. However, in his will he described himself as 'of St. Martin's-in-the-Fields'. It would seem that he left considerable funds in government stock, but the will gives no indication of the precise amount. Both his second and third marriages had been to widows, the first of whom was the sole beneficiary of her deceased husband's will in 1719. Burchett's main achievement was to remain in office despite frequent ministerial changes, and thereby help to establish the principle that civil servants should not be dismissed along with their political masters. There is some evidence that he felt an affinity with other such servants of the state: he once began a business letter to Under-Secretary John Ellis* with the words, 'we men of the quill'. However, in common with bureaucrats like Ellis and William Lowndes*, Burchett felt the need for a seat in the Commons. He certainly demonstrated considerable political skill in maintaining good relations with his superiors, while managing to distance himself from them when they fell from office. Only in hindsight does the longevity of his official career seem assured, but it was doubtless his administrative ability which commended him to successive politicians, some of whom, like Strafford, had great need of the man whose 'memory and knowledge of sea affairs is the best in Europe'.[9]

[1] *Mariner's Mirror*, xxiii. 479, 489, 492; Add. 31139, f.56; *Navy Recs. Soc.* cxx. 56; PCC 158 Glazier; *London Mar. Lic.* ed. Foster, 1144. [2] Luttrell, *Brief Relation*, vi. 268. [3] Add. 10120, f. 233; W. R. Chaplin, *Trinity House*, 188. [4] Add. 33512, f. 193; *Mariner's Mirror*, 480–4; Bodl. Rawl. A.189, f. 1; *Life, Jnls. and Corresp. of Pepys* ed. Smith, ii. 105; *CSP Dom.* 1698, p. 335; J. Ehrman, *Navy in War of Wm. III*, 561. [5] *HMC Portland*, iii. 551; Ehrman, 559–60; *N. and Q.* clxxvi. 56–57; Add. 33512, ff. 187–8; Centre Kentish Stud. Sandwich bor. recs. Sa/ZB2/164–5, Burchett to corp., 18 Jan., 25 Mar. 1705/6; Herts. RO, Panshanger mss D/EP/F173, f. 57, Burchett to Ld. Cowper, 23 Mar. 1705/6; info. from Prof. N. Landau; Chaplin, 64. [6] *HMC Portland*, iv. 510; *HMC Downshire*, i. 871; *Cal. Treas. Bks.* xxiii. 204, 454; Add. 61114, f. 218. [7] Add. 33512, ff. 191, 197–8; 31137, ff. 424–5; 31138, ff. 154–5, 198–9, 245–6, 270–1; 70203, Michel to Oxford, 27 June 1713; 70310-11, Burchett to Oxford, 10 Oct. 1712, 29 Jan., 30 May, 8 Aug. 1713. [8] Add. 31139, ff. 56, 128, 299; *N. and Q.* clxxvi. 57. [9] *Mariner's Mirror*, 493; PCC 286 Edmunds, 40 Browning; Add. 28891, f. 189; 31139, f. 64; G. Holmes, *Pol. in Age of Anne*, 356; G. Holmes, *Pol., Relig. and Soc.* 312.

S. N. H.

BURDETT, Robert (1640–1716), of Bramcote, Warws.

WARWICKSHIRE   1679 (Mar.)–1681 (Mar.)
LICHFIELD   1689–1698

b. 11 Jan. 1640, 1st s. of Sir Francis Burdett, 2nd Bt., of Foremark, Derbys. by Elizabeth, da. of Sir John Walter† of Sarsden, Oxon., c. baron of Exchequer 1625–30. *educ.* Queen's, Oxf. 1659; G. Inn 1662. *m.* (1) 1666, Mary (d. 1668), da. of Gervase Piggot of Thrumpton, Notts., 1s. d.v.p. 1da.; (2) 1676, Magdalen, da. of Sir Thomas Aston† of Aston, Cheshire, 4s. (3 d.v.p.) 4da. (2 d.v.p.); (3) aft. 1700, Mary, da. of Thomas Brome of Croxhall, Derbys., *s.p. suc.* fa. as 3rd Bt. 30 Dec. 1696.[1]

Asst. Linen Corp. 1690.[2]

The Burdett family had been settled in Warwickshire since the 11th century. By the late 17th century, however, their estates extended into Derbyshire, where the manor of Foremark had been acquired through marriage by Robert's grandfather. The family seem to have alternated between their two estates, with Robert's brother Walter living at Foremark and looking after the family's electoral interests in that county. After opposing the Exclusion bill Robert Burdett was added to the Warwickshire bench in 1681, where he proved an inactive justice. Although opposing James II's religious policies and attending Princess Anne at Nottingham, he also voted in the Convention against the transfer of the crown to William and Mary, and thus it is no surprise to find that he was left off the bench after the Revolution.[3]

Burdett was re-elected for Lichfield in 1690, the Marquess of Carmarthen (Sir Thomas Osborne†) classing him on a list of the new Parliament as a Tory and probable supporter of the Court. However, he does not appear to have been very active. His local political sympathies clearly lay with the Tories, for during the King's progress around the Midlands in the summer of 1690 Burdett dined in the royal presence together with Lord Digby (William*) and Sir Charles Holte, 3rd Bt.†, to the exclusion of Sir Richard Newdigate, 2nd Bt.†, a zealous partisan of the Whig cause. In the 1690–1 session, on 10 Oct he was sent to desire Dr Charles Hickman to preach before the Commons. In December Carmarthen listed him as a probable supporter in case of an attack upon his ministerial position in the Commons and in April 1691 Robert Harley* classed him as a Country party supporter. In this and in subsequent sessions he was named in the drafting of several bills and was given leave of absence for three weeks on 8 Feb. 1695 owing to his wife's illness.[4]

At the general election of 1695 Burdett was returned with Biddulph after the intervention of a 'Mr Combes' had been thwarted. In the first session of the new Parliament, he was forecast as likely to oppose the Court in the divisions on 31 Jan. 1696 over the council of trade; refused to sign the Association in February (reportedly sending back his lieutenancy commission to Lord Northampton in July); and voted in March against fixing the price of guineas at 22s. He acted as a teller on the Tory side on 10 Mar. 1696, against the engrossment of the Quaker affirmation bill. He adopted a much higher profile in the Commons during the following session. He voted on 25 Nov. 1696 against the attainder of Sir John Fenwick†, and acted as a teller on four occasions: on 28 Nov. in favour of a motion that the arrest of Sir Isaac Rebow's steward was a breach of privilege; on 10 Feb. 1697 against the committal of a bill for better securing debts and establishing credit, which scraped through by five votes; three days later against excusing Lord William

Powlett* from being a commissioner of accounts; and finally on 25 Feb. 1697, against allowing the committee of ways and means to consider a supply for the civil list at the same time as supply for the war. This record of activity is all the more surprising given that he received leave of absence twice during the session, on 2 Jan. 1697 owing to his father's illness (he was in fact already dead), and on 10 Mar. He also protested to the House that one of his servants had been arrested at the instigation of an attorney in breach of privilege, a complaint referred to the committee of privileges on 3 Mar. 1698, but with no result. He acted as a teller on three occasions: on 24 Mar. in favour of a motion to proceed with the bill for suppressing blasphemy and profanity; on 19 Apr. in favour of an amendment to the bill regulating elections, that all persons with the power of making freemen in parliamentary boroughs could, notwithstanding this act, create burgesses provided that they were natural born subjects living within five miles of the borough and with an estate worth £200 p.a. (clearly Burdett favoured retaining the gentry's ability to influence elections in neighbouring boroughs); and finally, on 18 May, for reading the order of the day to consider the Lords' amendments to the bill suppressing profanity. A comparative analysis of the old and new Houses of Commons in September 1698 classed him as a Country supporter, a stance wholly compatible with his Tory views.[5]

Somewhat unexpectedly, Burdett retired from Parliament in 1698. Nevertheless, he retained a keen interest in public affairs, both locally and nationally. For example, he opposed the Derwent navigation bill put forward in the 1698–9 session, and twice petitioned the Commons, on 15 May 1701 and 24 Nov. 1702, over land tax assessments for Hemlingford hundred in Warwickshire. He supported the Tory candidate Thomas Coke* in the Derbyshire election of December 1701, and felt able to call on Coke to help him avoid being pricked as sheriff in 1704. By 1704 he had been made a deputy-lieutenant for Warwickshire. Increasingly, his son Robert took an important role in family matters, especially in Derbyshire, where he was named a deputy-lieutenant in 1702, and even in Warwickshire, where in January 1704 he was being discussed as a possible parliamentary candidate for Tamworth. Robert jnr. died on 2 Jan. 1716, predeceasing his father, who himself died on 18 Jan. The heir was yet another Robert†, born posthumously, who later sat for Tamworth as a Tory.[6]

[1] Nichols, *Leics.* iii. 352; IGI, Notts., Derbys. [2] *Sel. Charters*, 213. [3] S. Erdeswicke, *Survey of Staffs*. 462; W. Woolley, *Hist. Derbys.* (Derbys. Rec. Soc. vi), 146; *Warws. Co. Recs.* viii. pp. xxxiii, xx; Duckett, *Penal Laws and Test Act* (1882), 167; D. Hosford, *Nottingham, Nobles and the North*, 108. [4] Bodl. Ballard 25, f. 16. [5] Add. 29578, f. 579. [6] BL, Lothian mss, Burdett to Coke, n.d.; HMC Cowper, ii. 442; iii. 51; *CSP Dom.* 1703–4, p. 279; 1702, p. 397; Bath mss at Longleat House, Thynne pprs. 28, ff. 328–9.

S. N. H.

BURGH, John (1673–1740), of Troy House, Mitchel Troy, Mon.

BRACKLEY 27 Jan. 1711–1713, 20 Apr. 1714–1715

b. 1673, 4th s. of Ulysses Burgh, DD, of Dromkeen, co. Limerick, bp. of Ardagh, by Mary, da. of Col. William Kingsmill, MP [I], of Ballybeg Abbey, co. Cork. *m.* Lydia (*d.* 1718), da. of Henry Clark of Mousley, Surr., 6s. (2 *d.v.p.*) 5da.[1]

Lt. of ft. Thomas Brudenell's regt. half-pay 1698.[2]

It is almost certain that this Member was the same John Burgh who became steward to two dukes of Beaufort and who had been born into the Burgh family of Dromkeen, co. Limerick, of Anglo-Norman descent. His grandfather, Richard Bourke, had converted from Catholicism and, on taking orders in the Anglican church, changed his name to Burgh. His father Ulysses Burgh, also an Anglican clergyman, had deserted James II for the Williamite cause, an apostasy which had led to the loyalist sacking of his property at Dromkeen. For these personal sufferings he was rewarded with a minor Irish bishopric in 1692, but died the same year shortly after his consecration. John Burgh saw military service during the 1690s as a lieutenant in Colonel Thomas Brudenell's foot regiment and was placed on the establishment of half-pay officers in this rank in 1698. In later life he was often referred to as 'Captain' Burgh, though this was probably his militia rank. He entered the service of the 2nd Duke of Beaufort as the Duke's chief steward, in 1703. It would seem very likely that he came to the young Duke's notice through the recommendation of the Duke of Ormond, the Duke's brother-in-law, possibly through the offices of Burgh's elder brothers, William and Thomas, either of whom, through their positions in the Irish administration, might have interceded with Ormond on his behalf. In the latter respect it is at least noteworthy that the timing of Burgh's appointment to Beaufort's service dovetails with Ormond's as lord lieutenant of Ireland in 1703. In common with his predecessors, Burgh resided at and administered the Beaufort estates from Troy House in Monmouthshire. In 1708 he became involved with the Treasury in sorting out the badly disordered finances of Michael Wicks, Member for Malmesbury in the 1698 Parliament. Wicks thought of Burgh as his 'nephew', though there was no familial connexion between them: Burgh's eldest brother Richard had married Wicks's ward, Elizabeth Griffin, in 1690. Wicks died in 1708 in a state of chronic indebtedness to the crown, incurred in his capacity as receiver of customs duties for the plantations, and in his will appointed Burgh his executor. This responsibility involved him over several years in the onerous task of straightening the financial chaos Wicks had left behind and in negotiating a settlement with the Treasury. In 1712 he had to petition the Commons, of which by this time he himself was a Member, to revive legislation secured by Wicks in 1705, enabling him to compound with the Treasury. A settlement was eventually agreed in 1714.[3]

In 1710 Burgh stood for Brackley with the support of Tory interests, although there is no indication that he ever held property in or near the borough, or indeed anywhere else in Northamptonshire. His entrée into the constituency seems to have come through Henry Watkins*, who since 1699 had served in several civilian capacities within the military administration and was shortly to become Ormond's private secretary, and whose brother, an Oxford don, had access to Magdalen College's extensive interest in and around Brackley. Though Watkins himself was later to sit for the constituency with Burgh, he did not do so in 1710. Burgh's own candidature in that year embroiled him in the bitter quarrels then subsisting between the Whig and Tory factions within the town corporation. Though narrowly defeated, he gained the seat in January 1711 after his petition, alleging partiality by the Whig mayor, had been considered by the elections committee. He was duly classed as a Tory in the 'Hanover list' of the 1710 Parliament, featured as a 'worthy patriot' who in the 1710–11 session helped to detect the mismanagements of the old ministry, and at about the same time was noted as a member of the October Club. When on 10 May 1711 the House considered the committee report on a supply bill levying an impost on hops, he told against provision for a lower duty on damaged hops. He told again on 13 May 1712 during the report stage of another supply bill, opposed to an allowance of drawback to Scottish university presses on the duties on paper used in the printing of learned works. On 18 June 1713 he voted for the French commerce bill. At the 1713 election he stood again for Brackley, this time joined by Watkins. Upon being defeated they both petitioned, taking advantage of the continuing strife within the corporate body which now played upon the question of the borough's franchise. A decision against them in the elections committee was later reversed in the Commons. Burgh's only recorded act in the new Parliament was to tell on 22 June 1714 for the Court majority in favour of an additional duty on soap.[4]

Burgh appears to have made no move to stand again at Brackley in 1715. This was probably due to the increase in his responsibilities on the Beaufort estates with the early death of the profligate 2nd Duke in May 1714 and the succession of his infant son. The control Burgh was able to exercise over the Beaufort demesne during the 3rd Duke's minority resulted in an enhancement of his personal influence and prestige both in Monmouthshire and in neighbouring parts of Gloucestershire. His purchases of several manors and leaseholds date from this period. His local prominence was indicated by his inclusion with a number of other Gloucestershire figures in a list of putative supporters sent to the Pretender in 1721. However, he had never been a member of the 2nd Duke's 'Board of Brothers'. In 1720, when a by-election became necessary for the Beaufort seat at Monmouth, Burgh seized the opportunity to resume a parliamentary career and announced his candidacy, having obtained the consent of the young Duke's two guardians, Hon. James Bertie* and Hon. Dodington Greville*, with whom he had worked very closely since 1714. However, he soon found his path blocked by a candidate, Hon. Andrews Windsor*, nominated by the 13-year-old Duke himself at the insistence of his meddlesome aunt, the Duchess of Grafton. It is quite conceivable that the Duchess was irritated by what she may rightly have visualized as Burgh's growing personal ascendancy in local affairs, based as it was on the Beaufort estate, and so pressed Windsor's prior claims to the seat for which he had stood unsuccessfully in 1715. Without delay, Burgh withdrew, explaining on 2 May to Sir Charles Kemys, 4th Bt.*, a leading Beaufort ally in Monmouthshire who had guaranteed Burgh his support:

> His Grace being but 13 years of age and under guardianship, I did not think he would so soon attempt the management of his own affairs, but that the consent of his guardians was sufficient. But since his Grace is prevailed upon to think himself better able to judge of his affairs and interest in this county than I am, I think myself obliged to return to you my most hearty thanks.

Bertie, with whom Burgh was on cordial terms, was equally nonplussed, and pledged for the future to shield his young charge from the aunt's designs; hoping, in effect, that this episode had not dampened Burgh's dedication to the family's interests.[5]

Burgh died a comparatively wealthy man at Troy on

25 Apr. 1740. He left the four farms, which he held leasehold of the Duke of Beaufort, to each of his four surviving sons, and £1,200 to each of four younger daughters, while the eldest was to receive the balance owing on her marriage portion, which amounted to an equal sum. He was buried in the churchyard at Mitchel Troy where in a monumental inscription he was remembered as 'a man of singular esteem both in public and private life, whose ruling passion was to do good and whose whole conduct spoke him the generous, humane and honest man'.[6]

[1] Burke's Irish Fam. Recs. 338; Bradney, Mon. ii. 168, 177. [2] Cal. Treas. Bks. iii. 274. [3] Bradney, 164; Cal. Treas. Bks. iii. 274; Mar. Lic. Vicar-Gen. (Harl. Soc. xxxi), 135; CJ, xvi. 408; xvii. 174, 182. [4] HMC Portland, vii. 165; Luttrell, Brief Relation, vi. 726; Add. 70280, Henry Watkins to 'Mr Harley', 2 Apr. 1714. [5] Bradney, 86, 166–8; RA, Stuart mss 65/16; Cal. Treas. Bks. xxix. 620. [6] Bradney, 168, 177.

A. A. H.

BURGHLEY, John Cecil, Ld. *see* **CECIL**

BURNABY, Anthony (*d.* 1708), of the Middle Temple.

STOCKBRIDGE   1701 (Dec.)–1705

1st s. of William Burnaby (*d.* 1693) of St. Clement Danes, Mdx. by his w. Isabella. *educ.* M. Temple 1695. *m.* 1s.[1]

Sec. to prize office 1702–d.[2]

The son of a London brewer, Burnaby was probably intended for the law, but never qualified. Having received his share of his patrimony during his father's life-time, he was left only £600 in his father's will with instructions that this was not to be placed at his own disposal, but was to be used to purchase a settlement approved by his mother, to whom everything else had been left. When she died shortly afterwards, she left the brewhouse and other properties to her younger sons and only £100 to Burnaby. With little money and no career, he hoped to make his fortune in government service and set about obtaining office by exposing abuses, beginning in July 1695, when he sent in a list of proposals for discovering and preventing the excise frauds of the brewers. The following March he suggested a bill to amend defects in the Excise Acts, and in May 1697 recommended the substitution of riding commissioners for supervisors to detect frauds in the excise, at the same time suggesting the appointment of an additional commissioner of excise for which post 'he humbly thinks himself qualified'. Unsuccessful in these efforts, he turned his attention to Parliament. He unsuccessfully contested Wilton in February 1701, but was returned for Stockbridge in December of that year, and was classed as a Tory in an analysis of the new Parliament by Robert Harley*. On 27 Jan. 1702 a petition was presented to the House asking for his parliamentary privilege to be set aside to enable the petitioners to proceed with a case against him concerning a disputed estate, but no action was taken before the end of the session. When the informer William Fuller was censured by the House on 5 Feb., Burnaby proposed a motion that a bill be brought in for having Fuller whipped 'in every coun[ty] town in England'. However, no one seconded the motion. In the same month Burnaby was included in the 'white list' of those Members who favoured the motion for vindicating the Commons' proceedings on the impeachments of the King's ministers in the previous Parliament. In April–May he managed a private bill through the House relating to the Irish forfeitures.[3]

In June 1702 Burnaby was appointed secretary to the prize commissioners with a salary of £400 p.a. for himself and his clerks, and the following month he was returned for Stockbridge in the general election. By the autumn of 1703 he found himself in trouble at the prize office. The commissioners, discovering 'the business was in great confusion and Mr Burnaby had not application equal to the employment', had appointed an extra clerk to take the minutes and answer letters. In response Burnaby had seized the new clerk's books, refusing to surrender them until the Board withdrew an order abolishing his fees. In May 1704 the Board applied to the lord treasurer for the return of the books, but despite the criticisms of the commissioners Burnaby kept his office and in 1705 even managed to secure employment for his brother, William, as sub-commissioner of prizes at Hull, who showed his gratitude by leaving Anthony 1s. in his will. Although inactive in Parliament, at the beginning of the 1704–5 session Burnaby was noted as a probable opponent of the Tack, and did not vote for it on 28 Nov. 1704. He stood for election again at Stockbridge in 1705, but was defeated. In June 1708 a former clerk in the prize office, James Gibbon, petitioned for his arrears of salary, which he claimed Burnaby had received from the Treasury but had not passed on. Burnaby's inglorious career in the prize office ended with his death on 14 Aug. 1708.[4]

[1] PCC 41, 136 Coker. [2] Cal. Treas. Bks. xvii. 250; xxiii. 105. [3] Cal. Treas. Bks. x. 1392, 1438; xii. 20, 187; Cal. Treas. Pprs. 1697–1702, p. 30; T 1/44/55; Cocks Diary, 200–1. [4] Cal. Treas. Bks. xvii. 250; xx. 219, 422; xxii. 283; Cal. Treas. Pprs. 1702–7, p. 266; T 1/90/103; Folger Shakespeare Lib. Newdigate newsletter 17 Aug. 1708.

P. W./C. I. M.

BURNETT, Sir Thomas, 3rd Bt. (aft. 1656–1714), of Crathes Castle and Leys, Kincardine.

SCOTLAND 1707–1708

b. aft. 1656, 1st s. of Sir Alexander Burnett, 2nd Bt., of Crathes Castle and Leys by Elizabeth, da. of (?William) Coutts of Auchtercoull, Aberdeen. *m.* 1677, his cos. Margaret (*d.* 1744), da. of Robert, 2nd Visct. Arbuthnott [S], 9s. (4 *d.v.p.*) 7da. (?5 o.ch. *d.v.p.*). *suc.* fa. as 3rd Bt. by 8 May 1663; uncle to Pittenkeirie and Sauchen, Aberdeen 1691.[1]

Burgess, Aberdeen 1674; rector, King's Coll. Aberdeen Univ. 1698–1705.[2]

MP [S] Kincardineshire 1689–1707.

PC [S] 1690–?1702, 1707–8; commr. reg. clerk [S] 1689–aft. 1690, visitation of schs. and colls. [S] 1690–aft. 1697, justiciary for Highlands [S] 1693, 1697, 1701, 1702, Equivalent [S] 1707–*d.*, exchequer [S] 1707–8.[3]

Burnett restored the political fortunes of the lairds of Leys, both locally and nationally, to something approaching the reputation his Covenanting grandfather had enjoyed, but the family's financial health continued to decline, and a constant tension between ambition and straitening means may be one explanation for his having been regarded as awkward and unpredictable. Indebtedness had accelerated steeply during his father's possession of the estate, a man whom the diarist Brodie of Brodie had deplored as 'profane, dissolute and naughty', but Burnett bore considerable responsibility for his own difficulties, his extravagance extinguishing the temporary recovery secured by the prudent management of his guardian, the 7th Earl Marischal, appointed when he had inherited as a minor. That he flouted Marischal's disapproval in order to marry while still in his nonage, also seems to indicate a headstrong personality.[4]

Despite manifold episcopalian and loyalist connexions, Burnett was true to his grandfather's political heritage. Enthusiastic for the Revolution, he was elected by his county to the Scottish convention, where he subscribed the act declaring the legality of proceedings and the letter of congratulation to King William, and in 1689–90 was chosen to several significant committees, including those for the security of the kingdom, for supply, for the plantation of kirks and for the visitation of schools and colleges. His value to the Revolution interest received prompt recognition from the government in appointment to the privy council and the commission entrusted with the office of register clerk. He was associated with the Tweeddale–Johnston faction in 1693–6, and, following the successive dismissals of Lord Tweeddale, James Johnston*, and Lord Tullibardine, moved into opposition in 1698. His motives were the usual combination of support for the former ministers and anger at personal losses in the Darien scheme, in his case an investment of £1,000. Although there was a rumour in June 1701 that Burnett was to be offered a peerage, his role as a prominent opposition member meant that he was not reappointed a privy councillor at Queen Anne's accession, and may indeed have already been dismissed.[5]

As an 'undoubted Revolution man' Burnett acted in concert with the Squadrone but kept a degree of independence. In September 1703 he argued in the Scottish parliament in favour of reading Lord Marchmont's proposal for an act to declare the succession in the Electress Sophia, subject to 'several weighty conditions', but only if this was not recorded in the minutes. He did not secede from opposition at the formation of the 'New Party' ministry in 1704, voting with the Duke of Hamilton in favour of postponing a decision on the succession. Otherwise, however, he was prepared to give limited co-operation to the Court over supply. Early in 1705 George Baillie* considered him to be a catch the ministry might well be able to land with an appropriate bait: 'the making Sir Thomas Burnett a councillor would gain him entirely'. The passing of a grant to the Duke of Queensberry (whose presence at the head of the Scottish ministry Burnett had long opposed) postponed a *rapprochement*, however, and it was as an opposition candidate that Burnett became a member of the committee of trade in 1705. The leaders of the cavaliers were convinced of his continuing 'honesty', and in 1706 the Pretender was informed that although Burnett

> was very wrong at the Revolution, and sometimes varies in parliament . . . he has for these last three sessions been for the most with the Country party, particularly for the grand resolves, and spoke boldly against the Hanoverian succession when proposed by Polwarth [i.e. Lord Marchmont]; and told myself, a week or two before I came from Scotland, that he would to the utmost of his power oppose the Union.

Nevertheless, when the treaty came before the Scottish parliament he went along with the Squadrone. After some early statements of 'Country' principle (that members should consult their constituents before voting, and that the English Act of Settlement – with its express limitations on royal power – should be read out) he stuck to a Squadrone line, his one quirk being to join the protest against the use of troops in Edinburgh. The rewards were readmission to the privy council and nomination to two commissions: the exchequer and the Equivalent. Without a salary he remained 'uneasy' for a time, but was chosen for a seat in the first Parliament of Great Britain.[6]

Self-interest prompted Burnett to oppose his Squadrone colleagues, in his only known speech at Westminster, over the motion to abolish the Scottish privy council on 11 December 1707. He was nominated the following day to the drafting committee for the bill to repeal the Scottish act of security and the act anent peace and war. He is known to have approved of the cathedrals bill, possibly influenced by his 'cousin german', the bishop of Salisbury. Evidently regarded as a Court supporter, Burnett was promised some further 'consideration', only to be informed by Lord Mar in May 1708 that his 'concern' had miscarried, for the present, but that Lord Treasurer Godolphin (Sidney†) had pledged that 'you should be taken care of another way as much to your advantage'. Nothing came of this, however.[7]

A victim of anti-unionist sentiment in Kincardineshire in 1708, Burnett did not even bother to register a vote let alone put himself forward as a candidate. He also boycotted the Aberdeenshire election, signing the petition against the return of Lord Haddo (William Gordon*) as the eldest son of a Scottish peer. More enthusiastic for a seat in 1710, he canvassed both in Kincardineshire and Aberdeenshire, albeit unsuccessfully. Burnett died in January 1714, leaving to his eldest son a 'well built' house and a 'well planted' estate, but financial affairs that were 'difficulted', with extensive debts and encumbrances, and unpaid bills. The 4th baronet was forced into further sales of land, and the sacrifice of part of his wife's jointure for the education of their children.[8]

[1] *Fam. of Burnett of Leys* (New Spalding Club), 60, 73, 79, 84–85; SRO Indexes, vii. 85; C. Rogers, *Fams. of Colt and Coutts*, 13; *Scots Peerage* ed. Paul, i. 308. [2] New Spalding Club, *Misc.* ii. 441; *Officers and Graduates of Univ. and King's Coll. Aberdeen 1495–1860* (New Spalding Club), 12. [3] *Reg. PC Scotland* 1690, pp. 19–20; *Fam. of Burnett*, 80–81; *CSP Dom.* 1689–90, p. 349; 1691–2, p. 167; 1696, p.168; 1697, p. 80; 1700–2, p. 338; 1702–3, p. 353; Luttrell, *Brief Relation*, ii. 9; *APS*, ix. 164; *Recs. Glasgow Univ.* (Maitland Club lxxii), ii. 552; *Cal. Treas. Bks.* xxiii. 234; xxix. 342; Sir J. Clerk and J. Scrope, *Hist. View of Forms and Powers of Ct. of Exchequer in Scotland* (1820), 120–3. [4] *Fam. of Burnett*, 72, 78–79, 85, 91–92; *Diary of Brodie of Brodie* (Spalding Club), 122; *HMC Portland*, iv. 199. [5] Info. from Dr P. W. J. Riley on members of Scot. parl.; *APS*, ix. 9, 20, 164, 188, 201; ix. (supp.). 56; x. 246, 269, 294; *Scot. Hist. Soc.* ser. 3, xlvii. 160; NLS, ms 7029, f. 88; *Darien Pprs.* (Bannatyne Club, xc), 400, 408; *Fam. of Burnett*, 80; Carstares, *State Pprs.* 387, 396. [6] Info. from Dr Riley; *APS*, xi. 72, 102, 222; *Crossrigg Diary*, 122, 131, 138, 174; P. W. J. Riley, *King Wm. and Scot. Politicians*, 142; *HMC Portland*, iv. 342; viii. 207; Boyer, *Anne Annals*, iii. app. 42; *HMC Laing*, ii. 80; *Baillie Corresp.* 49, 59; *Lockhart Letters* ed. Szechi, 14; *Orig. Pprs.* ed. Macpherson, ii. 16–17; *EHR*, lxxxiv. 521; P. W. J. Riley, *Union*, 334; *Fam. of Burnett*, 81; *HMC Mar and Kellie*, i. 404. [7] R. Walcott, *Pol. Early 18th Cent.* 233; *Nicolson Diaries* ed. Jones and Holmes, 459; Burnet, vi. 252; *Fam. of Burnett*, 82. [8] *Fam. of Burnett*, 84–85, 91–92; *Colls. Aberdeen and Banff* (Spalding Club), i. 33; *James Gordon's Diary* (3rd Spalding Club), 158, 161; NRA [S], Rep. 0024 (Burnett of Leys mss), pp. 21–23.

D. W. H.

BURRARD, George (aft.1653–1720), of Lyon's Inn and Lymington, Hants.

LYMINGTON 1698–1700

b. aft. 1653, 1st s. of George Burrard of Lymington by Katherine Gates of Rotherhithe, Surr. *educ*. Lyon's Inn 1673; I. Temple 1685. *unm*.[1]
Freeman, Lymington 1682, Winchester by 1701.[2]

Burrard was cousin to the Burrards of Walhampton. An attorney of Lyon's Inn, he acted for the borough of Lymington in 1687 during the quo warranto proceedings against the town's charter. He seems to have prospered, since in 1694 he was able to lend the government £400 and was one of the sureties, with the 2nd Duke of Bolton (Charles Powlett I*), of Thomas Cobb, receiver-general of taxes for Hampshire.[3]

After the death of his kinsman John Burrard* in 1698, Burrard took over the family seat at Lymington for one Parliament. He was classed as a Court supporter in a list of about September 1698 and voted against the disbanding bill on 18 Jan. 1699. An analysis of the House of early 1700 listed him as doubtful or possibly as opposition. Thereafter he took no further active part in politics, although he voted for the two Whig candidates in the parliamentary election at Lymington in February 1701. Some time later he gave up his law practice and retired to Lymington, where he was living at the time of his death in 1720. In his will, proved on 19 Jan. 1721, he mentions estates in Lymington and the neighbouring parishes of Boldre and Brockenhurst, leasehold property in Plymouth, and tenements and houses in Whitechapel, Middlesex. Most of this, together with his holdings in the Bank of England, the East India and South Sea Companies, he left to his nieces, the daughters of his sister.[4]

[1] S. G. Burrard, *Fams. of Borard and Burrard*, pp. x, xii. [2] E. King, *Old Times Revisited, Lymington*, 191; Hants RO, Winchester bor. recs. ordnance bk. 7, f. 214. [3] *Cal. Treas. Bks.* x. 907; xx. 649; King, 79–80. [4] King, 86, 214; PCC 3 Buckingham.

P. W.

BURRARD, John (c.1646–98), of Lymington, Hants.

LYMINGTON 22 May 1679–1681 (Mar.)
1685–1687
1689–14 May 1698

bap. 9 Jan. 1646, 3rd but 1st surv. s. of Thomas Burrard of Lymington and Old Palace Yard, Westminster by Elizabeth, da. of Gregory Isham of Barby, Northants. and h. to her bro. Arthur Isham; bro. of Paul Burrard I*. *educ*. M. Temple 1663. *m*. (1) 9 Jan. 1667, Elizabeth (*d*. 1676), da. and coh. of John Button† of Buckland,

Lymington, 2s. *d.v.p.* 5da.; (2) Alicia (*d.* 1703), da. of Richard Herbert†, 2nd Baron Herbert of Chirbury, *s.p. suc.* fa. 1661.[1]

Gent. of the privy chamber 1666–85.[2]

Freeman, Lymington 1667, mayor, 1672–3, 1692–5; freeman, Winchester by 1695; commr. spoils, New Forest 1679, ranger 1689–*d.*; gov. of Hurst Castle, Lymington by 1698–*d.*[3]

In the general election of 1690 Burrard successfully contested Lymington, which he controlled in alliance with the Powletts, dukes of Bolton, and was classed by Lord Carmarthen (Sir Thomas Osborne†) as a Whig in his list of the new Parliament. On 14 May he told against a motion to read the bill for vesting in their Majesties the £500 forfeitures. In the next session, in December 1690 Carmarthen listed Burrard as a probable supporter in case of an attack in the Commons against Carmarthen's ministerial position, and the following April Robert Harley* classed him as a Court supporter. On 23 Jan. 1692 he was granted leave to go into the country after a previous request, on the 2nd, had been refused. On 7 Feb. 1693 he spoke against a bill to increase and preserve timber in the New Forest, prompted by loyalty to his political and electoral ally, the Duke of Bolton (Charles Powlett†), then warden of the forest, and consideration for his constituents, whom the bill would have deprived of their common rights. On 6 Jan. 1694 he was given leave from the House for ten days, and on 5 Apr. 1694 acted as teller for a motion connected with the poll bill. Grascome's list of spring 1693, extended to 1695, classed him as a Court supporter with a place or pension.[4]

Again successful for Lymington in 1695, Burrard was given leave for two weeks on 9 Jan. 1696, was forecast as likely to support the government in the division of 31 Jan. 1696 on the proposed council of trade, and signed the Association promptly. In the 1696–7 session, he voted on 25 Nov. 1696 for the attainder of Sir John Fenwick† and was given leave of absence for three weeks on 26 Feb. 1697. Burrard died shortly before the end of this Parliament, on 14 May 1698 of a 'most violent fever sickness', his name appearing on a list of placemen compiled shortly after this date. Most of his property around Lymington was so heavily mortgaged it had to be sold after his death, with the exception of his share of the manor of Buckland, acquired by his first marriage, which was divided among his surviving daughters.[5]

[1] *Mems. St. Margaret's Westminster*, 196; Berry, *Hants Gens.* 153–4; S. G. Burrard, *Fams. of Borard and Burrard*, 66–67; S. Burrard, *Annals of Walhampton*, 23–24. [2] N. Carlisle, *Gent. Privy Chamber*, 177, 197. [3] E. King, *Old Times Revisited, Lymington*, 184, 190; Hants RO, Winchester bor. recs. ordnance bk. 7, f. 128; *Cal. Treas. Bks.* vi. 199; xvii. 951; *CSP Dom.* 1689–90, p. 32; Cobbett,

Parlty. Hist. v. p. clxxi. [4] *Luttrell Diary*, 105, 409. [5] Bolton mss at Bolton Hall, D/18, Thomas Cobbe to Bolton, 16 May 1698; S. G. Burrard, 66–67; S. Burrard, 23.

P. W.

BURRARD, Paul I (c.1651–1706), of Walhampton, nr. Lymington, Hants.

LYMINGTON   1701 (Feb.)–1705

b. c.1651, 4th but 2nd surv. s. of Thomas Burrard of Lymington; bro. of John Burrard*. *m.* 20 Mar. 1676, Anne (*d.* 1680), da. and coh. of John Button† of Buckland, Lymington, 3s. (2 *d.v.p.*). *suc.* mother to Walhampton 1680.[1]

Freeman, Lymington 1672, mayor, 1678–9, 1699–1700; freeman, Winchester by 1691.[2]

On the death of his mother in 1680 Burrard inherited estates at Walhampton and Old Palace Yard, Westminster, to which he added a moiety of the manor of Buckland in Lymington acquired by his marriage to the sister of his brother John's wife. He continued the electoral compact at Lymington with the 2nd Duke of Bolton (Charles Powlett I*), and in the second election of 1701 took over what had been John's seat for the borough, being listed as a Whig by Robert Harley*. Re-elected in 1702, he voted on 13 Feb. 1703 for agreeing with the Lords' amendments to the bill for enlarging the time for taking the oath of abjuration, and, having been forecast as a probable opponent of the Tack, voted against it or was absent on 28 Nov. 1704. He was given leave of absence for his health on 18 Dec. 1704. The Journals record no notable parliamentary activity for him. In the 1705 election he made way for his son, Paul Burrard II, possibly because of failing health, since he died in 1706, aged 55.[3]

[1] S. G. Burrard, *Fams. of Borard and Burrard*, 67–68. [2] E. King, *Old Times Revisited, Lymington*, 184, 190; Hants RO, Winchester bor. recs. ordnance bk. 7, f. 61. [3] Burrard, 66–68.

P. W.

BURRARD, Paul II (1678–1735), of Walhampton, nr. Lymington, Hants.

LYMINGTON   1705–1713, 1722–1727
YARMOUTH I.o.W.   1727–30 May 1735

b. 29 May 1678, 1st s. of Paul Burrard I*. *m.* 17 Oct. 1704, Lucy (*d.* 1750), da. and coh. of Sir William Dutton Colt, envoy to the courts of Hanover, Dresden, Celle and Brunswick, 4s. (1 *d.v.p.*) 1da. *d.v.p. suc.* fa. 1706.[1]

Freeman, Lymington 1699, mayor 1708–9, 1711–12, 1716–17, 1726–7, 1729–30, 1733–4; ranger of New Forest 1722–?*d.*[2]

Sub-commr. prizes, Portsmouth 1706–7; commr. leather duty Dec. 1714–18, taxes 1714–22.[3]

Returned for the family seat at Lymington in 1705, Burrard was a Whig like his father and equally inactive in the House. He was classed as a 'Churchman' in a list of the new Parliament, duly voted for the Court candidate for Speaker on 25 Oct. 1705 and supported the Court again in the proceedings over the 'place clause' of the regency bill on 18 Feb. 1706. Shortly afterwards he was appointed a sub-commissioner of prizes at Portsmouth but resigned that office in November 1707. Two lists of 1708 classed him as a Whig and, re-elected for Lymington that year, he supported the naturalization of the Palatines in 1709 and voted in 1710 for the impeachment of Dr Sacheverell. Classed as a Whig in the 'Hanover list' of the 1710 Parliament, he voted on 7 Dec. 1711 for the 'No Peace without Spain' motion. He was given leave of absence on 3 Feb. 1711, again on 14 Apr. for his health, and for 42 days on 7 Mar. 1712. He did not contest the 1713 election, but at the end of the following year was appointed a commissioner for taxes and the duties on leather with a salary of £500 p.a. He returned to Parliament in 1722, and thereafter consistently voted with the administration. He died on 30 May 1735.[4]

[1] Berry, *Hants Gens.* 154; S. G. Burrard, *Fams. of Borard and Burrard*, 68. [2] E. King, *Old Times Revisited, Lymington*, 184, 192; S. Burrard, *Annals of Walhampton*, 35. [3] *Cal. Treas. Bks.* xx. 648; xxi. 52; xxix. 193, 835; xxxii. 512, 600. [4] *Cal. Treas. Bks.* xx. 648; xxi. 52; xxxix. 338; *Gent. Mag.* 1735, p. 332.

P. W.

BURRIDGE, John I (c.1651–1733), of Lyme Regis, Dorset.

LYME REGIS 1689–1695, 1701 (Dec.)–1710

b. c.1651, 1st s. of Robert Burridge, merchant, of Lyme Regis by Elizabeth, sis. of John Cogan of Bristol. *educ.* Wadham, Oxf. 13 Mar. 1668, aged 18. *unm. suc.* fa. 1676.[1]

Freeman, Lyme Regis 1676, capital burgess by 1679, mayor 1680–1, 1696–7, 1715–16.[2]

Burridge, a merchant in Lyme Regis engaged in the import of wine and linen, was one of the Dissenters who had supported James II's attempt to introduce toleration. In the 1690 Parliament, he was listed by Lord Carmarthen (Sir Thomas Osborne†) as a Whig and in December 1690 as one of those who would probably support him in the event of an attack in the Commons. Robert Harley* classified him as a doubtful supporter of the Country party in April 1691. In the spring of 1693 Samuel Grascome listed Burridge as a Court supporter with a place or pension, but no known office may be attributed to him. He stood down in 1695 and did not return to the House until the second general election of 1701, when he was listed as a Whig by Harley. He continued to represent Lyme Regis in the next three Parliaments. Forecast as liable to oppose the Tack, he did not vote for it on 28 Nov. 1704. An analysis of the 1705 Parliament classed him as a 'Churchman', and he voted against the Court candidate for Speaker on 25 Oct. Classed as a Whig both before and after the election of 1708, he voted the following year for the naturalization of the Palatines. On 21 Dec. 1709 he obtained a leave of absence of one month. He voted for the impeachment of Dr Sacheverell in 1710.

During these years Burridge seems to have become financially embarrassed and at least one reason for his second spell in Parliament was to secure immunity from imprisonment for debt. It was alleged that at one election, either in 1702 or 1705, some sheriff's officers had lain in ambush at his house to arrest him, but that his supporters had intervened, beaten off the sheriff's men and escorted him to the guildhall, where he was unanimously elected. By 1710 his position had improved sufficiently to enable him to withdraw in favour of his nephew, John Burridge II*. He died on 6 Sept. 1733, aged 82, and was buried in Lyme parish church. In his will he left most of his property to his brother Robert and to Robert's elder son.[3]

[1] Hutchins, *Dorset*, ii. 71; PCC 1 Ent, 252 Price. [2] Hutchins, 49; PCC 252 Price; Dorset RO, Lyme Regis mss B6/11, p. 29. [3] G. Robert, *Hist. and Antiquities of Lyme Regis*, 295–6.

P. W.

BURRIDGE, John II (c.1681–1753), of London and Lyme Regis, Dorset.

LYME REGIS 1710–28 Feb. 1728

b. c.1681, 2nd s. of Robert Burridge of Lyme Regis, merchant, by his w. Mary. *m.* 1695, Martha, da. and h. of Warwick Ledgingham of Ottery St. Mary, Devon, *s.p.*[1]

Freeman, Lyme Regis 1704, mayor 1726–7.[2]

Burridge broke with the tradition of his family, whose mercantile activities had hitherto been centred on Lyme Regis, by establishing himself as a London merchant and shipowner, trading to the West Indies, Spain and America. He retained some interest in the West country, however, where his wife had inherited the manor of Ottery St. Mary in Devon and he himself had a reversionary life interest in the manor of Thorn Falcon in Somerset, settled on him at the time of his marriage by his uncle, John Burridge I*. He later bought from his father the reversion of Charmouth in Dorset. In the winter of 1707–8 Burridge was one of the merchants whose complaints about shipping losses led to a Junto-inspired inquiry in the Lords into the shortage of cruisers and convoys, the main object of which was to oust George Churchill* from the Admiralty. In 1710 Burridge succeeded to what had virtually become the family seat at Lyme, where he had in addition obtained an interest of his own by making a loan of £300 to the corporation and securing a mortgage on the town's waterworks. Classed as doubtful in the 'Hanover list' of the new Parliament, he soon made his political allegiance clear by voting for the motion of 'No Peace without Spain' on 7 Dec. 1711. On 6 June 1712 he told in favour of a bill to continue the Act enabling Quakers to affirm. He voted against the French wines duties bill on 6 May 1713. Marked as a Whig who was engaged in trade, Burridge also voted against the French commerce bill on 18 June 1713. In Queen Anne's last Parliament he voted on 18 Mar. 1714 against the expulsion of Richard Steele. He was listed as a Whig in the Worsley list and two comparative analyses of the 1713 and 1715 Parliaments. He remained an MP until he was unseated in 1728, and died on 2 Feb. 1753.[3]

[1] Add. 32707, f. 405; PCC 1 Ent, 252 Price; C. D. Whetham, *Manor Bk. of Ottery St. Mary*, 65; Dorset RO, Burridge mss B7/B6/10. [2] Dorset RO, Lyme Regis mss B6/14, 23 Oct. 1704; G. Roberts, *Hist. and Antiquities of Lyme Regis* (1834), p. 383. [3] *LJ*, xviii. 390; Burridge mss B7/B6/10.

P. W.

BURRIDGE, Robert (1656–1717), of Peter Street, Tiverton, Devon.

TIVERTON 28 Nov. 1702–1708

b. 1656. *m.* lic. 4 June 1678, Margaret (*d.* 1700), da. and coh. of Samuel Foote*, 2s. 6da.; (2) ?Martha Mompesson, wid. of Samuel Foote.[1]

Freeman, Lyme Regis 1688; receiver-gen. of taxes, Devon and Exeter 1696–1702; alderman, Tiverton, bef. 1698, mayor 1698–9, 1709–10.[2]

Burridge, a merchant engaged in the serge trade at Tiverton, had married a daughter and coheir of Samuel Foote, one of the town's leading merchants and its Member of Parliament. It was doubtless Foote's influence which was responsible for his election to the corporation. In 1682 Burridge was one of the common councilmen pardoned by the King for performing his duties without first having taken the Test. In the same year he and his father-in-law were accused of gun-running, but no action was taken against them. In 1689 he stood security for his brother-in-law John Cruwys upon his appointment as receiver of taxes for Devon. Burridge himself succeeded to this office in 1696, resigning in favour of his son in 1702. Meanwhile Burridge's business had prospered to such an extent that in one year he was estimated to have made a profit of £10,500, some of which was invested in the purchase of the manor of Hensleigh in Somerset. A Whig, Burridge was returned for Tiverton at a by-election in 1702. He voted on 13 Feb. 1703 in favour of agreeing with the Lords' amendments to the bill for enlarging the time for taking the oath of abjuration. On 28 Nov. 1704 he either voted against the Tack or was absent from the House. Re-elected in 1705 he was classed as 'Low Church' and voted for the Court candidate for Speaker on 25 Oct. He again supported the Court on 18 Feb. 1706 over the 'place clause' in the regency bill. He did not stand for any subsequent Parliament, dying in 1717. By his will, dated 13 Mar. and proved 24 Sept., he left most of his property to his eldest son, Samuel.[3]

[1] *Trans. Devon Assoc.* lxvii. 328; lxxxiv. 10; M. Dunsford, *Hist. Mems. Tiverton*, 316; PCC 165 Whitfield. [2] Dunsford, 449, 450; Bodl. mss Eng. misc. e 4, f. 13; *Cal. Treas. Bks.* x. 1308; xvii. 368, 370; Dorset RO, Lyme Regis mss B6/11, p. 34. [3] W. Harding, *Hist. Tiverton*, i. 80; iv. 185; *CSP Dom.* 1682, p. 69; *Trans. Devon Assoc.* 10; Dunsford, 450; PCC 165 Whitfield.

P. W.

BURRINGTON, John (1634–bef. 1708), of Sandford, Crediton, Devon.

OKEHAMPTON 23 Feb. 1694–1698

bap. 1 May 1634, 1st s. of John Burrington of Chudleigh and Holliscombe, Devon, by Susan Taylor. *m.* Mary (*d.* 1708), 1s. 2da. *suc.* fa. 1643.[1]

Commr. victualling the Navy 1695–1702.[2]

A member of an old-established Devon family, Burrington had removed his seat to Sandford in that county. At the Prince of Orange's landing in 1688, he played a decisive part in persuading the gentlemen of Devon to join the Prince by being the first to come forward himself, in his capacity as a major in the militia. He was returned for Okehampton at a by-election in February 1694, and in May the following year was appointed a victualling commissioner. At the next general election he was unopposed. Despite his nominal position as a Court Whig, his support for the government on major questions was equivocal. In January 1696 he was forecast as 'doubtful' on the question of the proposed council of trade, and though adding his signature promptly to the Association at the end of February, he voted in March against fixing the price of guineas at 22s. On 25 Nov., however, he supported the attainder of Sir John Fenwick†. On 15 Feb. 1697 he was teller against passing the bill to admit merchants to the freedom of the Russia Company, and on 3 Mar. 1698 for a motion that the servants of Arthur Owen II* had committed a breach of privilege against Sir Bourchier Wrey, 5th Bt.* In March 1698 he handled the latter stages of a bill to provide Crediton, near his estate, with a workhouse. In April he told for excusing Simon Harcourt I*, a Member absent at a call of the House; for a motion to lay a further duty on coal; for a motion that no one should be forced to accept guineas at 22s. or at a higher value than their worth in standard bullion; and (on the bill for regulating elections) against a clause to make void the admission of any new freemen in corporate boroughs, unless these were made on the day of the election of the chief magistrate, in open court, and with the consent of a majority of qualified voters. Finally, in June he supervised the passage of a private bill. He did not stand in 1698 when he was listed as a placeman (by virtue of his commissionership, worth £400 p.a.) and a Court supporter 'left out' of that Parliament. Two months after Queen Anne's accession he was dismissed from his post. The date of his death has not been ascertained: his consent to a private bill in the Upper House was recorded early in 1705, but he was dead by the time of his wife's burial in March 1708.[3]

[1] Vivian, *Vis. Devon*, 120–1. [2] Luttrell, *Brief Relation*, iii. 468; v. 171. [3] A. Jenkins, *Hist. Exeter*, 185–6; *CSP Dom.* 1699–1700, p. 255; *CJ*, xiv. 421; *HMC Lords*, n.s. vi. 265.

E. C.

BURSLEM, William (1662–1716), of Newcastle-under-Lyme, Staffs.

NEWCASTLE-UNDER-LYME 1710–1715

bap. 14 Oct. 1662, 2nd but o. surv. s. of James Burslem, of Newcastle-under-Lyme by Rebecca, da. of Humphrey Warnor of Abbots Bromley, Staffs. *m.* 28 July 1681, Dorothy (*d.* 1699), da. of Daniel Watson† of Nether Hall, Burton-upon-Trent, Staffs. 7s. (2 *d.v.p.*) 4da. (2 *d.v.p.*). *suc.* fa. 1675.[1]

Burgess, Newcastle-under-Lyme 1681, capital burgess 1685–1708, 1712–*d.*, mayor 1690–1, 1696–7; receiver-gen. Staffs. 1700–6.[2]

Burslem, as his surname suggests, came from a family with close connexions to the area around Newcastle-under-Lyme. He inherited property in nearby Wolstanton and in the borough itself. His grandfather had served as mayor twice in the early 1660s and he himself became an alderman during James II's reign, at about the same time cementing his local connexions with a marriage to the daughter of Daniel Watson, the borough's recorder from 1660 to 1683.[3]

Very little is known about Burslem's career before the turn of the century apart from the fact that he had begun practising as an attorney in Newcastle in 1682, a profession entirely consistent with the evidence of his will (made in 1699) which indicated that he was not a wealthy man, at least not so by the standards of those who aspired to parliamentary election. In 1700 he was appointed receiver-general of Staffordshire, a position apparently procured for him through the influence of Sir John Leveson Gower, 5th Bt.*, who took advantage of the indebtedness and then death of the previous incumbent, Thomas Spendelow, the nominee of John Lawton*, an important local Whig. Burslem used his new post to extend Tory influence in the county, particularly in Newcastle where he became Leveson Gower's main agent. To facilitate this work he acquired the place of deputy-steward of Newcastle manor (under Rowland Cotton*), and leases of the castle (from the crown) and, most importantly, of Leveson Gower's property in the borough, worth £90 p.a., which he sub-let to electoral advantage.[4]

Burslem first came to prominence in national politics after the disputed election at Newcastle in 1705, which resulted in the Commons unseating Cotton and another Tory, Sir Thomas Bellot, 3rd Bt., on 27 Feb. 1706 in favour of Lawton and his Whig partner, Crewe Offley*. In addition the House found Burslem guilty of bribery in endeavouring to procure votes for the Tory candidates and resolved to address the Queen to discharge him from office as receiver-general. Despite being dismissed in 1706, he played a similar role in the 1708 election. On this occasion, after the Tory candidates had been unseated on 1 Feb. 1709, Burslem was sent for into custody by the Commons and his actions used as a pretext to remove him from Newcastle corporation. Despite these setbacks, he was in a strong position to benefit from the Tory revival following the Sacheverell trial. The death of Lord Gower (as Leveson Gower had become) in 1709 had left him with an even greater role in the management and preservation of the Tory interest in the borough. Lady Gower, in particular, was keen to see him succeed in 1710 as a means of keeping at least one seat safe for her younger sons. With the death of Bellot also in 1709, he was the obvious partner for Cotton at the 1710 election. Given the enthusiasm of Newcastle's reception of Dr Sacheverell in July 1710, Burslem's return in October was scarcely surprising, even though one observer referred to his 'inconsiderable estate' and that he had been 'twice before the House of Commons called to account for what he did for Lord Gower'.[5]

On the 'Hanover list' of the 1710 Parliament Burslem was classed as a Tory, an analysis borne out by the appearance of his name among those 'worthy patriots' who had helped to detect the mismanagements of the previous ministry during the 1710–11 session. On 3 Feb. 1711 he intervened in the debate on the report of the Ipswich election case to refute Sir Joseph Jekyll's defence of the fairness of the previous Parliament because 'for far less crime, or rather no crime at all, he was by the last Parliament 11 weeks in custody of the serjeant, having as he said a very just petition'. In February 1712 he managed through its stages in the Commons the bill from the Lords enabling the young 2nd Lord Gower to make a settlement upon his marriage. He showed himself to be a firm supporter of the ministry by voting on 18 June for the bill confirming the 8th and 9th articles of the commercial treaty with France. Burslem was also active outside the House during this Parliament in order to rectify the perceived injustices of Whig partisanship between 1706 and 1708. First, shortly after his election, in December 1710, he received an allowance for extraordinary charges relating to his period as receiver-general, and then, in May 1711, he secured the appointment of his son, Thomas, in that post. More pleasing still was the decision in December 1712 of the corporation of Newcastle to restore him to the aldermanic bench while removing his Whig rival John Lawton.[6]

With the corporation more completely under Tory control Burslem was returned with Cotton at the general election of 1713. Crewe Offley petitioned against the return on 5 Mar. 1714 on the grounds that Burslem's estate was insufficient to meet the requirements of the recent Landed Qualification Act, but made no headway in a Tory-dominated House. Burslem's most important task in the 1714 session was the management through the Commons of a local turnpike bill, which he carried up to the Lords on 13 May 1714. He was classed as a Tory on the Worsley list. Burslem did not stand at the general election of 1715, preferring to back Cotton and a new partner, Henry Vernon II*, who were returned only to be unseated on petition. This was the end of Burslem's involvement in Newcastle elections, for he died on 17 Apr. 1716 at Oxford (according to Boyer), only four days after attending a council meeting. After his death his executors sold some of his property in Newcastle to Lord Gower.[7]

[1] P. W. L. Adams, *Hist. Adams Fam.* 77–78; IGI, Staffs.; *Newcastle-under-Lyme Par. Reg.* pt.2, pp. 129, 145, 197, 249, 252.
[2] R. W. Bridgett, 'Hist. Newcastle-under-Lyme, 1661–1760' (Keele Univ. M.A. thesis, 1982), 177; *N. Staffs. J. Field Stud.* xiv. 78; J. C. Wedgwood, *Staffs. Parl. Hist.* (Wm. Salt Arch. Soc.), ii. 207; *Cal. Treas. Bks.* xv. 98; xx. 606; J. Ward, *Bor. of Stoke-upon-Trent*, 336.
[3] Wedgwood, 207; Adams, 77–78. [4] T. Pape, *Newcastle-under-Lyme from Restoration to 1760*, p. 30; PCC 89 Fox; *Cal. Treas. Bks.* xv. 98; Nottingham Univ. Lib. Portland (Harley) mss Pw2 Hy 234, Philip Foley* to Thomas Foley (?II*), 7 Feb. 1701[-2]; *VCH Staffs.* viii. 15, 185; J. R. Wordie, *Estate Management in 18th Cent. Eng.* 234–5.
[5] *Cal. Treas. Bks.* xx. 606; Adams, 78–79; NRA Rep. 10699, viii. 64; Glos. RO, Hardwicke Court mss, Lloyd pprs. box 74, Dan. Tottie to Dr William Lloyd, 8 July 1710; Surr. RO (Kingston), Somers mss 371/14/O2/100, Mrs Rogers to [Mrs Mary Cocks], n.d., [1710].
[6] SRO, Mar and Kellie mss GD124/15/1020/9, Sir James Dunbar, 1st Bt.* to Ld. Grange (Hon. James Erskine†), 3 Feb. 1711; *Cal. Treas. Pprs.* 1708–14, p. 227; *Cal. Treas. Bks.* xxiv. 522; xxv. 59; Adams, 78–79. [7] Newcastle pollbk. 1714 (Hist. of Parl.); Boyer, *Pol. State*, xi. 506; Bridgett, 218; Wordie, 235.

S. N. H.

BURTON, John (1646–1703), of Great Yarmouth, Norf.

GREAT YARMOUTH 1701 (Dec.)–1702

bap. 20 Dec. 1646, 2nd but 1st surv. s. of William Burton†, merchant, of Great Yarmouth by his 2nd w. Martha. m. lic. 29 Mar. 1675, Anne, da. of John Desborough of Hackney, Mdx., 6s. (1 d.v.p.) 3da. suc. fa. 1673.

Freeman, Gt. Yarmouth 1672, alderman Jan.–Oct. 1688.[1]

The most prominent figure in Yarmouth's Dissenting community, Burton was a merchant by trade and an Independent in religion. He was the son of a loyal Cromwellian and had himself married the daughter of General Desborough, the brother-in-law of Oliver Cromwell†. Burton was one of James II's Whig 'collaborators' at Yarmouth and was returned in 1701 on the Dissenting interest. During his brief tenure he is not known to have given a speech, neither is any vote by him recorded. Defeated in 1702, he died on 22 Nov. 1703.[2]

[1] *Norf. Rec. Soc.* xxii. 10, 23–26; Gt. Yarmouth bor. recs. assembly bk. 1680–1701. [2] P. Gauci, *Pol. and Soc. in Gt. Yarmouth*, 207; Bodl. Ballard 4, f. 61; C. J. Palmer, *Hist. Gt. Yarmouth*, 129, 212, 244, 307; *Norf. Rec. Soc.* 34.

D. W. H.

BUTLER, James I (c.1651–96), of Patcham, Suss.

ARUNDEL 1679 (Mar.)–1681 (Mar.), 1690–1695

b. c.1651, 1st s. of James Butler, Clothworker, of St. Benet Fink, London and Amberley, nr. Arundel, Suss. by his 2nd w. Prudence, da. of John Vanacker, merchant, of London. educ. St. Edmund Hall, Oxf. matric. 5 May 1668, aged 17; travelled abroad c.1669. m. 1673, Grace (d. 1734), da. and coh. of Richard Caldicott of Sherrington, Selmeston, Suss., 1s. 4da. suc. fa. 1660.[1]

Commr. enclosures, Ashdown forest 1691.[2]

The son of a wealthy London merchant, Butler acquired an estate at Patcham in Sussex through his marriage and made this his principal seat. At the same time he retained some interests in the City and in 1689 held stock worth £1,500 in the East India Company. Probably a nonconformist in the Restoration period, Butler had represented Arundel in the Exclusion Parliaments, and successfully contested the borough again in 1690 when he was classed as a Court supporter in a list of March 1690 and as a Whig in Lord Carmarthen's (Sir Thomas Osborne†) list of the new Parliament. He was again classed as a Court supporter in a list of about October 1690 and in December as a probable supporter against an attack on Carmarthen in the Commons. Robert Harley* listed Butler as a Country party supporter in April 1691, but Grascome followed the more usual course in classifying him as a Court supporter in his list of spring 1693 extended to 1695. Butler was not active in the House, being sent for in custody on 2 Jan. 1693 for being absent at a call of the House, and then being granted leave of absence for 14 days on 19 Dec. 1693 and for 21 days on 23 Feb. 1694. On 22 Feb. 1694 he gave evidence for and acted as a teller in support of John Cooke*, the Whig candidate in the disputed by-election at Arundel. He did not stand again and died 11 July 1696, aged 45. He was buried at Thakeham in Sussex, his only son James later sitting for Arundel and Sussex.[3]

[1] *Vis. Suss.* (Harl. Soc. lxxxix), 22–23, 119; *Dorm. and Ext. Baronetcies*, 540–1; *Inhabitants of London in 1638* ed. Dale, i. 39. [2] *Suss. Arch. Colls.* xiv. 59. [3] Add. 22185, ff. 12–13; *Vis. Suss.* (Harl. Soc. lxxxix), 119.

P. W.

BUTLER, James II (c.1680–1741), of Warminghurst Park, Suss.

ARUNDEL 1705–1708
SUSSEX 1715–1722, 29 Feb. 1728–17 May 1741

b. c.1680, o. s. of James Butler I*. *educ.* ?Trinity Hall, Camb. 1698. *m.* 31 Jan. 1704, Elizabeth, da. of Sir Charles Caesar† of Benington, Herts., sis. of Charles Caesar*, and wid. of Sir Richard Bennet, 3rd Bt., of Babraham, Cambs., 3s. (2 *d.v.p.*) 1 da. (*d.v.p.*). *suc.* fa. 1696.[1]

Butler had bought the estate of Warminghurst from William Penn in 1702, and was returned for Arundel in 1705, when his election was reckoned by Lord Sunderland (Charles, Lord Spencer*) as a gain for the Whigs. He was classed as a 'Churchman' in an analysis of this Parliament. One of Butler's few actions in parliament was on 6 Mar. 1706 when he acted as a teller on the Whig side during the debate on the bill for preventing frauds by bankrupts, telling for a clause giving the benefit of the Act to those bankrupts who voluntarily surrendered themselves by a certain date. He was again classed as a Whig in a list of early 1708. In 1710 he owned £2,000 worth of stock in the Bank of England. He did not stand again until 1713, when he was unsuccessful in contesting the county in the Whig interest, but after the accession of George I he represented Sussex for many years, being classed as a Whig in a comparative analysis of the 1713 and 1715 Parliaments, and voting with the Whigs until his death from smallpox on 17 May 1741, aged 61. His only son John sat for East Grinstead and Sussex under George II and George III.[2]

[1] Berry, *Suss. Gen.* 176; *Suss. Arch. Colls.* lxxii. 228. [2] D. G. C. Elwes, *Castles, Mansions and Manors of W. Suss.* 250–1; Berry, 176; Egerton 3359 (unfol.).

P. W.

BYERLEY, Robert (1660–1714), of Middridge Grange, Heighington, co. Dur., and Goldsborough, Yorks.

DURHAM CO. 1685–1687
KNARESBOROUGH 1689–1690, 1695–c. May 1714

bap. 27 Mar. 1660, 4th but 2nd surv. s. of Anthony Byerley (*d.* 1667) of Middridge Grange by Anne, da. and coh. of Sir Richard Hutton† of Goldsborough. *educ.* Queen's, Oxf. 1677. *m.* 17 Mar. 1692, Mary (*d.* 1727), da. and h. of Philip Wharton (*d.* 1685) of Edlington, Yorks., warden of the Mint 1680–5, div. w. of Hon. James Campbell*, 2s. 3da. *suc.* bro. 1674.[1]

Freeman, Durham 1680; commr. Aire and Calder navigation 1699.[2]

Capt. indep. tp. 1685, 6 Drag. Gds. 1685–7, lt.-col. 1689, col. 1689–92; commr. privy seal Dec. 1711–13.[3]

Commr. taking subscriptions to land bank 1696, public accts. 1702–4.[4]

Though an inconspicuous Member of the 1685 and Convention Parliaments, by 1689 Byerley had clearly established his Tory credentials and by the early 1700s he had become 'a leading figure among the High Church gentry in Yorkshire'. He also established for himself a role of some significance at Westminster as a Tory zealot, primarily through his pursuit of the perceived misapplication of public monies. Although his actions were in part attributable to a partisan desire to pursue Whig ministers in and out of office, they also stemmed from Country beliefs typical of a man of his background. The Byerleys had possessed lands in both Yorkshire and Durham from the 16th century, and though his father's estate was valued at only £600 p.a. at the Restoration, the family gained further lands in Yorkshire following the death of a maternal uncle. Byerley took up the profession of arms, initially fighting for the King at Sedgemoor in an independent troop but quickly joining the regular army, and in 1689, having fought for William and Mary in Ireland earlier in the year, was given his own regiment upon the recommendation of Schomberg. Byerley returned to Ireland in the following two years, but while he was on duty there in November 1690 Mary Wharton, who one observer noted was 'designed' for Byerley, was kidnapped and forcibly married by Hon. James Campbell. The niece of Byerley's mother and heir to considerable Yorkshire estates, the 13-year-old Mary was said to be worth £1,500 p.a. Following the death of Mary's father in 1685 Byerley's mother had taken a close interest in her niece's welfare, possibly even taking responsibility for her upbringing, and the two were travelling together when she was kidnapped. Within two days of Wharton's marriage she was taken from Campbell's custody by order of the lord chief justice, and in March 1692, following an Act annulling the forced marriage, Byerley himself married her, thereby gaining further Yorkshire estates. The same month also saw Byerley arrested at Dover on suspicion of being a Jacobite going to the Continent, presumably travelling with his bride. It may be that he had been confused with the Jacobite Captain Joseph Byerley of Belgrave, Leicestershire, and he was promptly released on the orders of Secretary Nottingham (Daniel Finch[†]). The prospect of increased wealth through marriage may have prompted him to surrender his commission at the end of January 1692, but for a considerable part of the following two years Byerley was embroiled in a dispute regarding the accounts of his regiment for the Irish campaign, his claim for arrears being complicated by the allegation of his successor Colonel Hugh Wyndham that Byerley was considerably indebted to the regiment. He eventually received some of his arrears but the issue was to resurface during his parliamentary career, on one occasion causing him acute political embarrassment.[5]

In 1695 Byerley was returned unopposed for Knaresborough, the seat for which his grandfather had sat in the early 17th century and where he had inherited lands at his marriage, and was subsequently returned there at every election until his death. Though he was inactive in the first session, his Toryism soon became evident. Forecast as a likely opponent of the Court in the divisions of 31 Jan. 1696 over the council of trade, Byerley initially refused the Association and in March voted against the Court on fixing the price of guineas at 22s. Byerley took the Association in the court of King's bench in May but was nevertheless removed from Yorkshire's commission of the peace for his initial refusal. A further demonstration of Byerley's Tory beliefs came early in the following session, when on 25 Nov. he voted against the attainder of Sir John Fenwick[†]. He remained an inactive Member, however, his only significant committee nomination coming on 17 Mar. 1697 when he was named to draft an additional clause to the bill to repair the pier at Bridlington, Yorkshire. Of more note was a dispute over the accounts for Byerley's former regiment. On 14 Dec. 1696 the petition of soldiers from this regiment was ordered to lie on the table because of Byerley's absence, and on 15 Jan. 1697 their claim for arrears accrued during the Irish campaigns, and their contention that Byerley had failed to make up his accounts, was heard by the House. Byerley responded that his accounts were before the commission of accounts, and his request that the commissioners be asked to report to the Commons was granted by the House. On 30 Mar. the commissioners reported that Byerley's claim to be owed £467 17s. 3½d. had to be seen in the light of several inconsistencies in his accounts, pointed out by his successor Colonel Wyndham, so that he was owed no more than £39 13s. 1½d. The confused state of Byerley's accounts was also indicated by the commissioners' querying a payment of £2,000 for clothing the regiment, but on the general question of whether Byerley was liable for the arrears due to his former troops the commission stated that Wyndham had been colonel of the regiment when the King had ordered the Treasury to provide funds to satisfy such arrears. A letter written in early December 1697 demonstrated that Byerley's opposition sympathies remained strong, as he commented caustically upon the calls to disband the army that 'some great ones are much offended and would persuade some to believe the towns throughout England will petition for its continuance'. He made his first recorded speech on 17 Dec. in support of a motion by Sir John Kaye, 2nd Bt., for a writ for a by-election at the Yorkshire borough of Aldborough. The question of the arrears due to Byerley's former regiment was revived in the new year by a petition read on 3 Jan. and referred to the joint paymasters general of Ireland. On 4 Feb. the House ordered the commission of accounts to return Byerley's papers relating to his former regiment, and on 4 May it was reported that though arrears were due to what had been Byerley's regiment neither he nor his successor had received this money.[6]

Shortly before the opening of the 1698 Parliament Byerley was classed as a Country party supporter and a probable opponent of a standing army, and he confirmed his hostility to the Court during the debate of 6 Dec. on the choice of Speaker. James Vernon I* reported that Byerley spoke 'virulently' against the Court candidate and Treasury lord Sir Thomas Littleton, 3rd Bt., making 'reflections upon the Treasury'. Though Byerley's speech followed that of the leading Tory Sir John Bolles, 4th Bt., and his opposition was echoed by other prominent members of the opposition such as Sir Edward Seymour, 4th Bt., and Anthony Hammond, another report of the debate stated that such arguments were 'overpowered in reason' by Court speakers. Little more can be said of Byerley's activity in this session, though it appears that he took a more active role in the 1699–1700 session. Between January and March he managed a bill to allow justices to raise money to build and repair gaols. More significantly, Byerley played a part in the opposition harassment of the Whigs. On 2 Feb., for example, he took a leading role in the attack upon Lord Orford (Edward Russell*), reminding the House of its vote of the previous session condemning mismanagement of the naval accounts and moving that accounts dating back to February 1689 be laid before the House. His hostility to the Junto was further demonstrated in the debate of the 13th upon grants of forfeited land made to Lord Somers (Sir John*), opining 'that robbing by the great seal is worse than robbing on the h[igh]way'. His concern to pursue the alleged abuses of Whig ministers had a clear partisan motivation and in March he was among those Tories who supported John Grobham Howe's proposal to revive the commission of accounts and to appoint, without a salary, seven commissioners.[7]

Shortly after his return at the first election of 1701 Byerley wrote to Hon. James Brydges* that his intention to stay in the country 'two months longer than usual' had been unaffected by the death of the king of Spain, claiming that he was not 'a jot concerned' with the consequences for the disposition of the Spanish throne and its effect upon the state of Europe. His name does not appear in the Journals until 20 Feb. when he was the first-named Member nominated to investigate abuses in hospital revenues, his interest in this topic demonstrated by his reporting from this committee (9 Apr.) and being the first-named Member appointed to draft a bill to redress such abuses (24 Apr.). His support of the remodelled ministry became clear early in the session as he was listed as one of those prepared to support the Court in agreeing to the resolution of the supply committee to continue the 'Great Mortgage'. Byerley's concern to pursue partisan aims was, however, undiminished, so much so that by May the Whig Sir Richard Cocks, 2nd Bt.*, described him as 'the most party and ill-natured man in the House'. Tory and Country sympathies may explain his nomination on 20 Mar. to draft a bill to regulate parliamentary elections, but it was his enthusiastic participation in the attempted impeachment of former Whig ministers that was the most notable feature of his parliamentary activity. The concern evident in the previous session to pursue the alleged abuses of Orford at the Admiralty was again demonstrated with his nomination on 28 Mar. to examine the behaviour of the Admiralty solicitor, and on 14 Apr. Byerley was ordered to inform the Lords of the Commons' intention to impeach Orford. The following day he reported this matter to the House and was added to the committee drawing up the articles of impeachment against the Earl of Portland and the Junto lords. On 9 May Byerley carried to the Lords the articles of impeachment against Orford, and on the 23rd he moved that the select committee on the impeachment be instructed to search for precedents for the answers of the Junto lords to the impeachment articles. His particular hostility to Orford was again in evidence at the end of the month when, on either the 27th or the 30th, he moved that the Commons read its vote of 27 Mar. 1699 condemning the former cashier to the navy George Dodington*, and on the 31st Byerley was nominated to search for precedents for the Lords' appointing a date for Orford's trial. Though his activity in the final months of the session was dominated by the impeachments, Byerley was also nominated to manage a conference with the Lords (15 May) and to prepare an address promising to support the King's alliances for preserving the liberties of Europe (12 June). He also told against an additional clause to the bill appropriating part of the excise (16 June).[8]

Classed as a Tory by Robert Harley in December 1701, Byerley was an active Member of the second 1701 Parliament. Prior to the death of William in early March Byerley was nominated to draft bills for the employment of the poor and encouragement of privateers (6, 10 Jan.); told against allowing a petition relating to a forfeited Irish estate to lie on the table (23 Feb.); and presented a bill relating to a forfeited Irish estate (3 Mar.). He supported the motion of 26 Feb. vindicating the Commons' proceedings in the previous Parliament against the Whig ministers, and the approbation of his Tory peers for his recent parliamentary activity was indicated early in March by his inclusion on the Tory slate for the ballot for the revived commission of accounts. His partisan loyalty led to his attempt on 7 Mar. to make use of what was to prove to be the fatal illness of the King to propose an adjournment of the Commons which would have delayed the passage of the abjuration and malt tax bills. Tory success in the ballot for commissioners of accounts later that month saw Byerley elected in fifth place. His hostility towards union with Scotland was evident on 19 Mar. when he told against putting the motion for a bill to appoint commissioners to treat for such a union. A concern to further Yorkshire interests was evident on 2 Apr., when he told against exempting Great Yarmouth from the tolls levied by the bill to repair piers at Whitby. He also told against recommitting a bill concerned with an Irish forfeited estate (8 Apr.).[9]

Given Byerley's clearly demonstrated hostility to the Junto, it is likely that he took some pleasure, for partisan as well as pecuniary reasons, over the defeat in November 1702 of Lord Wharton's (Hon. Thomas*) judicial challenge against the right of Byerley and 12 others to land in Yorkshire containing 'a lead mine of great value', and his animosity both to the Junto lords and those who had served with them in the ministries of the 1690s was evident in the 1702–3 session. He had been a signatory to the accounts commission's report, presented to the House on 9 Nov., which condemned the former paymaster general Lord Ranelagh (Richard Jones*) for failing to prepare proper accounts, obstructing the investigation of the commissioners, and for alleged corruption. As a commissioner of accounts he was also involved in investigating Lord Halifax's (Charles Montagu*) alleged circumvention of Exchequer procedures, presenting a report on 26 Jan. which claimed that a failure to complete and transmit proper accounts amounted to a mismanagement of public funds. The Lords' response to this attack was prompt. On 3 Feb. they voted to ask the commissioners of accounts to attend the Lords' committee on their report, which prompted the Commons to nominate a committee, including Byerley, to investigate the precedents for such requests. Byerley's partisan loyalties were demonstrated by his vote of 13 Feb. to disagree with the Lords' amendments to the bill enlarging the time for taking the abjuration.[10]

Appointed on 9 Nov. 1703 to prepare the Address, Byerley's standing among Tory back-benchers by the 1703–4 session was indicated when he was included in a list of Members drawn up by Sir William Trumbull* described as the 'secret committee' of the Commons. This list may have been drawn up in connexion with the controversy over the Scotch Plot, and Byerley was nominated to draw up three addresses relating to this matter. In mid-March 1704 he was listed as a supporter of Secretary Nottingham on this issue. Though Byerley took an interest in various minor issues which came before the House, his parliamentary activity was again dominated by the commission of accounts. On 10 Jan. he moved that an information filed by the attorney-general relating to the charges levelled by the commissioners in the previous session against Halifax be read to the House, and on two further occasions he presented information from the commissioners to the Commons. On 25 Feb. it was announced that Byerley had again been elected a commissioner, but the bill to renew the commission was subject to a concerted attempt by Whig peers to sabotage the body which had spent much of the last two parliamentary sessions censuring former Whig ministers. Continuing claims for arrears due to Byerley's former regiment had been under investigation by the commissioners for military debts since the spring of 1703, and in March 1704 they reported to the Commons on the 10th and to a committee of the Lords six days later that they had not, owing to disputes between Wyndham and Byerley, received 'in the form they prescribed' accounts covering the years of the Irish campaigns. Byerley's involvement in this failure to produce correct accounts, one of the main charges made by the commission of accounts against Ranelagh and Halifax, presented peers hostile to the commission of accounts with the ideal pretext to torpedo the bill for the commission's renewal. Thus, on the 16th the Lords removed Byerley's name from the list of commissioners and added three of their own nominees. The following day the Commons appointed a committee, including Byerley, to investigate the Lords' amendments to the public accounts bill. The committee reported on the 20th, and the following day it was resolved, without a division, to appoint a committee to draw up reasons to disagree with the Lords' amendments. This committee's report of the 24th strongly endorsed both the right of the Commons to appoint commissioners and the election of Byerley in 'whose abilities and integrity, in the discharge of this trust, they have so much experience'. The Commons ordered that a conference be requested to inform the Lords of the Lower House's disagreement to the amendments, but the issue was not resolved before the end of the session so that the bill fell. However, the difficulties that Byerley experienced did not diminish his concern to condemn what he perceived as a misuse of public money, and on 31 Mar. he criticized James Vernon I for receiving 'four years' salary for nothing' while commissioner for prizes in the 1690s.[11]

At the beginning of the 1704–5 session Byerley was named, on 24 Oct., to prepare the Address, and it is clear from his actions concerning the Tack that his partisan ardour had in no way cooled. As early as 27 Oct. it had become known that Byerley was 'strongly for consolidating the bill against occasional conformity with the first money bill', and three days later he was forecast as a probable supporter of the Tack. He duly voted for it on 28 Nov., and it was probably the failure of the Tack that led Byerley to complain to Bishop Nicolson in early January 1705 of 'the unsteadiness of his friends'. He also appears to have taken an interest in a number of miscellaneous issues. As well as being nominated to draft three bills, to prevent outlawries being obtained via personal legal actions (24 Oct.), to prohibit trade with France (11 Nov.) and to introduce an alternative to cheek-burning as a punishment for theft (18 Dec.), he told against the introduction of a bill to enforce the Act encouraging the use of needlework buttons (21 Nov.) and against reading a bill concerned with duties upon East India goods re-exported to Ireland (22 Feb.). Any remaining doubts over Byerley's reputation for financial rectitude were lifted when the report of the commissioners for military debts concluded that Byerley had not been guilty of any corruption in the handling of the finances of his former regiment, and a Commons' resolution of 22 Feb. affirmed the propriety of his actions. Tory loyalties are the likely explanation of Byerley's activity in the final months of the session as in February he was nominated to three committees concerned with the Aylesbury case, and on 13 Mar. was appointed to manage a conference concerning a disagreement with the Lords over Tory attempts to add to a naturalization bill a clause preventing those naturalized from voting in parliamentary elections.[12]

Though Byerley remained in the House for the rest of his life and continued to promote and support Tory measures, his parliamentary career had passed its zenith. Classed as 'True Church' in an analysis of the 1705 Parliament, on 25 Oct. he voted against the Court candidate for Speaker. Byerley's only recorded speech of the session came in a debate on the regency bill on 19 Dec. when he defended Charles Caesar from attempts to have him removed to the Tower for Caesar's allusions to Lord Godolphin's (Sidney†) former contact with the Jacobite court. On 11 Mar. 1706 he told against a Lords amendment to a private bill, though no further significant activity is recorded for him until the first Parliament of Great Britain. Listed in early 1708 as a Tory, Byerley managed a bill in this session concerning the estates of Christopher Lister*, initiated by a petition from the Yorkshire Tory Sir Arthur Kaye, 3rd Bt.*, in addition to being nominated to draft bills for the regulation of servants (16 Feb. 1708) and to revive the Act on naval discipline (2 Mar.). Classed as a Tory shortly after the 1708 election, Byerley's only significant action in the 1708 Parliament was his opposition in early 1710 to the impeachment of Dr Sacheverell.[13]

With the revival of Tory fortunes in 1710, however, Byerley again took a more prominent role, returning with vigour to the attack on the alleged corruption of former Whig ministers. On 2 Dec. he moved for a statement of the number of troops in Spain and Portugal at the time of the battle of Alamanza, thereby reopening the controversy surrounding this issue, while on 19 Jan. 1711 he was sharply critical of the failure to produce an account of the previous year's contingencies. He even suggested 'that no supply should be granted till a satisfying account should be laid before them of these contingencies', but was unable to find a seconder. Suggestions in March 1711 that Byerley's right to sit in the House was to be challenged under the terms of the Landed Qualification Act came to nothing. At the end of the session Byerley was classed as a Tory patriot who had opposed the continuation of the war, as a 'worthy patriot' who had detected the mismanagements of the previous administration, and as a leading member of the October Club. To the surprise of at least one observer, who in February had described Byerley as one of the 'old Tories (who are not yet provided, and who have shown a great uneasiness all this session)', Byerley had initially kept his distance from the October Club, yet his appointment to office later in the year may be explained in part by his membership of the club, for at this time the Earl of Oxford (as Harley had become) was eager to improve his relations with the Octobrists. When rumours of a ministerial reshuffle were circulating in June 1711 it was suggested that Byerley's nomination as a lord of trade was imminent, though these reports proved inaccurate. Having moved the Address on 7 Dec. Byerley was the first-named Member appointed the same day to prepare it, reporting the following day. On 21 Dec. he was named a commissioner of the privy seal, an appointment characterized by one modern historian as part of the ministry's *rapprochement* with the October Club, and on the 22nd a writ was ordered for the by-election consequent upon this appointment. The *Official Returns* state that this election did not take place until January 1713, but the appointment in February 1712 of Byerley to two committees and to prepare a representation on the state of the war (18th) suggests that the election must have taken place in

January 1712, as did those of the two other commissioners of the privy seal appointed at the same time as Byerley. The possibility of Byerley being appointed a commissioner of trade was rumoured in the spring of 1712 but again came to nothing. The 1713 session saw Byerley nominated to draft a bill to open up the African trade (2 May). His loyalty to the ministry was evident during the passage of the French commerce bill, as on the 18th he spoke and voted for this measure. Re-elected in 1713 and classed as a Tory in the Worsley list, Byerley died during the 1714 session and on 3 May was buried at Goldsborough. He was succeeded by his eldest son, but all of Byerley's children died without issue and none entered the Commons.[14]

[1] Surtees, *Dur.* iii. 313; Luttrell, *Brief Relation*, ii. 394. [2] Surtees, iv(2), 22; *HMC Lords*, n.s. iii. 204. [3] *CSP Dom.* 1686–7, p. 374; *Cal. Treas. Bks.* xxv. 600; xxvii. 335. [4] *CJ*, xii. 508. [5] G. Holmes, *Pol. in Age of Anne*, 278; *VCH N. Riding Yorks.* i. 90, 360–1, 379; *HMC Le Fleming*, 263; *CSP Dom.* 1689–90, p. 347; 1691–2, pp. 117, 205; *Davies Diary* (Cam. Soc. ser. 1, lxvii), 122, 146; *HMC Finch*, ii. 423; Trinity, Dublin, Clarke mss 749/3/296, T. Maule to George Clarke*, 15 Nov. 1690; E. R. Wharton, *Whartons of Wharton Hall*, 31–33; *Docs. Relating to the Swaledale Estates of Ld. Wharton* (N. Yorks. RO Publ. 36), 11–12, 262–5; Luttrell, 128, 328; *Cal. Treas. Bks.* x. 270, 272, 279, 282, 286, 294, 299; *Cal. Treas. Pprs.* 1557–1696, p. 306. [6] Luttrell, iv. 60; Add. 70155, jnl. of land bank commrs.; L. K. J. Glassey, *Appt. JPs*, 123; T. Lawson-Tancred, *Recs. of a Yorks. Manor*, 218. [7] *Vernon–Shrewsbury Letters*, ii. 226–7, 424; *CSP Dom.* 1698, p. 424; Som. RO, Sanford mss DD/SF 4107(a), notes on debate, 15 [*recte* 13] Feb. 1699[–1700]; Northants. RO, Montagu (Boughton) mss 48/51, Vernon to Shrewsbury, 28 Mar. 1700. [8] Huntington Lib. Stowe mss 58(1), pp. 17–18; *Cocks Diary*, 144, 166. [9] Stowe mss 26(2), James Brydges' diary, 4 Mar. 1702; *Cocks Diary*, 237. [10] Luttrell, v. 235; *LJ*, xvii. 267. [11] *HMC Downshire*, i. 817; *HMC Lords*. n.s. v. 449–52; Luttrell, v. 402; *Vernon–Shrewsbury Letters*, iii. 254. [12] *Nicolson Diaries* ed. Jones and Holmes, 216, 267; *HMC Lords*, n.s. vi. 290–1; *Bull. IHR*, xl. 157. [13] *Cam. Misc.* xxiii. 52, 55. [14] NSA, Kreienberg despatch 5 Dec. 1710; NLS, Advocates' mss, Wodrow pprs. letters Quarto 5, ff. 107–8; *Nicolson Diaries*, 554; SRO, Montrose mss GD220/5/808/15, Mungo Graham* to Ld. Montrose, 6 Feb. 1711; GD220/5/256/20, George Baillie* to same, 8 Dec. 1711; *Scots Courant*, 8–11 June 1711; Add. 57861, f. 162; Huntington Lib. Q. xxxiii. 164; BL, Trumbull Alphab. mss 54, Ralph Bridges to Sir William Trumbull, 25 Apr. 1712; Chandler, iv. 41.

E. C./R. D. H.

BYNG, Sir George (1663–1733), of Southill, Beds.

PLYMOUTH   1705–21 Sept. 1721

b. 27 Jan. 1663, 1st s. of John Byng of Wrotham, Kent by Philadelphia Johnson of Loans, Surr. *m.* 5 Mar. 1691, Margaret, da. of James Master of East Langdon, Kent, 11s. (6 *d.v.p.*) 4da. (3 *d.v.p.*). *suc.* fa. 1683. Kntd. 22 Oct. 1704; *cr.* Bt. 15 Nov. 1715, Visct. Torrington 21 Sept. 1721; KB 27 May 1725.[1]

Ent. RN May 1678, lt. 1683, capt. 1687, r.-adm. 1703, v.-adm. 1706, adm. 1708, r.-adm. of G. Britain 1720, adm. of Eng. 1727–*d.*; cadet, grenadiers at Tangier May 1681; ensign 4 Ft. 1681, lt. 1683, capt. of grenadiers 1688; lt. horse gds. 1690–92; muster master of marines, 1698–9; special envoy to Dey of Algiers, 1703, plenip. to Fez of Morocco 1718, Italian states 1718–20; ld. of Admiralty Nov. 1709–Jan. 1714, Oct. 1714–Sept. 1721, 1st ld. 1727–*d.*; treasurer of navy Oct. 1720–Apr. 1724; PC 3 Jan. 1721–*d.*[2]

Commr. registry of seamen 1696–9, claims for coronation of Geo. II 1727, Greenwich Hosp.; er. bro. Trinity House 1698–*d.*, master 1711–13; freeman, Portsmouth 1703, Kinsale 1705, Edinburgh 1708.[3]

Two of Byng's ancestors sat in Parliament during the 15th and early 16th centuries, but his father was forced to sell the family estates at Wrotham in Kent. An attempt to settle in Ireland ended in flight to England to avoid creditors. In such penury Byng's education was entrusted to the Countess of Middleton, a family friend (who, as Lady Martha Carey, had lived at Moor Park, near to the residence at Rickmansworth of the family of Byng's grandmother, Katherine Hewit), although a comment recorded by Thomas Hearne in 1708 refers to Byng being her page boy. Given the family's straitened circumstances it was decided to send Byng to sea at the earliest opportunity and in 1678, as a result of the influence of the 2nd Earl of Peterborough, he entered the navy. Subsequently he served at Tangier (where his maternal uncle was a member of the garrison), and between 1684 and 1687 was in the East Indies pursuing pirates and interlopers. Back home he played a key role during the winter of 1688 in the Orangist conspiracy to undermine Lord Dartmouth's (George Legge†) control of the fleet. Suitably rewarded with a captaincy, a rank he had first attained in 1687, he served at Beachy Head in June 1690. An analysis of naval officers in 1691 described Byng as 'a young man, but a very good man', and a list of the following year 'makes it clear that Torrington [Arthur Herbert†] was his patron'. If this was the case, Byng quickly shifted his allegiance to Edward Russell*, declining to serve as first captain to the joint admirals in the spring of 1693, but accepting the post under Russell in September. After two spells in this post in the Mediterranean, Byng returned home in 1696 and was appointed a commissioner under the Act for registering seamen, and commissary of the marine regiments. Around this time he probably moved his family into Southill, as December 1697 saw the last baptism of one of his children at St. Paul's Covent Garden. Other honours followed, such as election as an elder brother of Trinity House, but no active command came his way until his appointment as first captain at the beginning of March 1702 under the new lord high admiral, the Earl of Pembroke (Hon. Thomas Herbert†), a promotion attributed to Whig influence. Only a week later William III died, thereby precipitating a change of personnel at the Admiralty.[4]

Byng's career prospects looked bleak on the accession of Anne: Prince George became lord high admiral and Byng failed to receive a flag, the accepted promotion due to a first captain. Indeed, in May 1702 he was reduced to petitioning for a rear-admiral's allowance (that traditionally paid to first captains), until employment could be found for him. At least one historian has attributed Byng's difficulties to the perception that he was a Whig and protégé of Russell. However, Byng received his flag in 1703 and served with distinction in the Mediterranean, being knighted on his return in October 1704. Sailing with the Channel fleet in 1705 provided Byng with an opportunity to enter Parliament as it enabled him to travel ashore rather than be confined to a foreign station. A flavour of his activities can perhaps be gleaned from the comment of one of Arthur Charlett's correspondents, who wrote that some people were angry at Byng for 'appearing at so many places'. He was returned in two constituencies, but his election at Great Bedwyn was threatened from the very first by a petition, so it was not surprising that Byng opted on 1 Dec. to sit for Plymouth, a borough more susceptible to navy influence. On one list of the 1705 Parliament he was classed as a 'High Church courtier', but the Earl of Sunderland (Charles, Lord Spencer*) correctly assessed his return as a gain for the Whigs. On 25 Oct. 1705 he voted for the Court candidate for Speaker, and on 18 Feb. 1706 supported the Court over the 'place clause' of the regency bill. Unsurprisingly, his other contributions to parliamentary affairs reflected his acknowledged expertise on naval matters. On 9 Jan. 1706 he was given leave to attend the Lords' committee investigating the manning of the fleet (actually attending on the 14th) and on 23 Jan. was appointed to the drafting committee of a bill to increase seamen. By early March, however, Luttrell reported that he was preparing to sail for Lisbon, his naval career taking precedence over duties at Westminster.[5]

Letters to Lord Cowper (William*) in December 1706 show that the Whigs were prepared to watch over Byng's interest at Plymouth during his extended absence. Byng returned to England in October 1707, narrowly avoiding the fate of his superior, Sir Clowdesley Shovell*, whose ship was lost off the Scilly Isles. In December 1707 he was appointed to two drafting committees: on the 8th, to prepare a bill for the better security and encouragement of the American trade; and on the 16th, to establish a workhouse in Plymouth. Finally, his expertise was used by the Lords when he was called to give evidence to a committee on the inconveniences of legislation regulating the coal trade as it related to the protections issued to seamen. On 5 Feb. 1708 he was given leave to attend the Lords regarding their investigations into the war in Spain. However, his parliamentary duties were cut short by the news of the attempted invasion by the Pretender in Scotland, which saw Byng dispatched northwards to prevent a landing. Byng accomplished his task, receiving the freedom of Edinburgh as a reward, but some people felt that he had allowed the Jacobite fleet to escape. He was unequivocal in rebutting that accusation, contending that the clean French ships were much faster than his own 'foul ships', and that 'my predecessor himself had he been at the head of us could neither have counselled or contrived how to have worked foul ships better'. In such circumstances the gesture from Edinburgh was eagerly seized upon by Byng to pronounce that 'calumny itself must now be silent, since you have given so open a proof to the world that my endeavours have not been unacceptable to you'. The state of the fleet was the pretext for a Whig attack on the Admiralty under Prince George, but the Commons voted an address of thanks on 1 Apr. to the Lord High Admiral, together with an addition from Richard Hampden II* praising Byng's conduct.[6]

Following his success in Scotland, Byng was perceived as a natural addition to the Prince's Council, but as Lord Treasurer Godolphin (Sidney†) wrote to the Duke of Marlborough (John Churchill†) on 19 Apr., 'the vacancies . . . will not (I believe) be well filled'. Thus, when Byng arrived in London later in April, Godolphin reported that he 'has not yet had that countenance shown him, which either his past diligence, or the hopes of his future behaviour in this summer's service might naturally lead him to expect'. The stumbling block appeared to be George Churchill*, who encouraged the 'natural, but very inconvenient averseness' the Queen and Prince George felt towards '[the Whigs] in general, and to Sir George Byng in particular'. The Queen's perception of Byng as a Whig was confirmed in two analyses of the post-Union Parliament in early 1708. Byng was able to achieve his re-election for Plymouth, having secured in April an invitation to stand, before naval duties intervened. While awaiting the wind at Spithead in August Byng described himself, albeit in jest, as an 'abandoned admiral'. In October he set sail for Lisbon, returning to England a year later. However, as early as February 1709 his recall was being canvassed as a replacement for Josiah Burchett* as secretary to a revamped Admiralty board. As the summer of 1709 wore on, the need to reorganize the Admiralty became more acute and the Whigs more animated against royal resistance to the demands of office for Orford and his friends. Arthur Maynwaring* thought that Byng was one man whom 'everybody would have . . . in this commission', because although he was an officer raised by Orford, he had been preferred on merit. Luttrell reported Byng's appointment as an Admiralty lord in October 1709, but it required continuous pressure well into November before the commission was settled, with Godolphin being accused of encouraging the Queen's resistance, despite protestations to the contrary. In the event Byng was forced to renege on an agreement with fellow admiral Sir John Jennings* that 'neither of them should come into the commission without the other'. A new writ was moved on 15 Nov. 1709 consequent upon his appointment, an office worth £1,000 p.a.[7]

Byng faced no opposition at Plymouth when returned at the by-election held on 2 Dec. 1709. On 16 Dec. he was nominated to the committee considering a petition for a bill for the preservation of Catwater harbour in Plymouth, and on the 20th was appointed to the committee preparing the resultant legislation. A list of Bank of England stockholders for March 1710 reveals that he then held between £500 and £2,000 worth of stock. Byng voted in the Commons in 1710 in favour of the impeachment of Dr Sacheverell, and appears to have attended regularly at the Admiralty board during the first six months of 1710. Despite his association with the Whigs, he retained his post at the Admiralty when a new commission was sealed in October 1710. Indeed, from a letter Byng wrote to Sir John Osborn of Chicksands on 28 Sept. it would seem that he had attempted to resign his post rather than serve with the 3rd Earl of Peterborough, but in the event the Earl had been employed instead on an embassy to Italy. Byng was returned again for Plymouth and was classed as a Whig on the 'Hanover list' of 1710. On 5 Jan. 1711 he presented to the Commons the accounts for the sick and wounded and a statement of the victualling debt, being appointed on the same day to the committee charged with investigating abuses in victualling. His only other significant action in the Commons during this session was on 28 Apr., when he acted as a teller in favour of referring the petition on the Weymouth by-election to the committee of privileges and elections, rather than hearing the cause at the bar. If anything, this was a vote on the Whig side, for the Tory House quickly unseated the Whig sitting Members. During the year Byng increased his power on the Admiralty board as Sir John Leake* stayed away, in protest at the failure to fill the place of first commissioner. Byng took the chair in Leake's absence, and 'being an artful designing man, and well qualified to fish in troubled waters, improved every circumstance to his own advantage'. Possibly because of his Whiggish views, he kept a low profile in Parliament, being given leave of absence for a month on 15 Apr. 1712 on health grounds. Others certainly felt his position to be anomalous, for Thomas Corbet[†], Byng's former secretary, now at Utrecht, wrote in June 1712, 'if to mention your name with the honour I owe you, is to be a Whig, I shall so far glory in the name'.[8]

In May 1713 Byng again showed signs of Whiggish sympathies when he became involved in a fracas at the Blue Posts, a hostelry frequented by Scottish Members, and wounded 'lieutenant-colonel' Stewart's [?Hon. John*] footman. In turn he himself was then beaten so badly by the man's friends that he had to be carried to his lodgings. Byng also came under verbal attack in June 1713 from both Sir James Wishart* and Lord North and Grey for his treatment of a local tax collector at Portsmouth, whom Byng, in his capacity as master of Trinity House, had dismissed for failing to vote for Sir Charles Wager* and a general 'firmness to the Church interest'. In view of this pressure, Byng did not vote in the division of 18 June 1713 on the French commerce bill. In January 1714 he was left out of the Admiralty commission, in what some historians have seen as a purge of officers inclined to support the Hanoverian succession. He was allowed half-pay as admiral of the white. Certainly, L'Hermitage still considered Byng to be a Whig. Days after his dismissal Byng declared to Osborn his wish to leave the 'crowd of knaves and fools' and become a j.p. at Southill. However, he did not depart from London immediately, showing his political colours when voting on 18 Mar. against the expulsion of Richard Steele. On 19 Mar. he asked and received permission from the Admiralty to follow his family into Bedfordshire.[9]

The Hanoverian succession saw Byng restored to favour and reappointed to the Admiralty board in October 1714, after an absence of just a few months, one commentator remarking that he 'always fell on his feet'. On the Worsley list Byng was noted as a Whig who would often vote with the Tories (as he was obliged to do as a placeman), but on two analyses comparing the 1713 and 1715 Parliaments he was deemed a Whig without qualification. In 1715 he commanded the Channel fleet which prevented the French from succouring the Jacobite rebels, despite rumours of an 'understanding' between Byng and the Pretender to allow the French fleet across the channel. Letters do exist, purporting to be from Byng to Ormond, and promoting a design for a Jacobite invasion, but as Byng's actions had been fundamental to securing the Hanoverians on the throne, this evidence may best be understood as a ruse, to which Byng was party, to entrap Ormond. Periodically, the Jacobites continued to cherish hopes that Byng would assist them, often linking his name with that of Orford. Byng continued to be active in naval administration until his death, honours being heaped upon him by George I (who found Byng a willing instrument for his foreign policy in the Baltic), including a baronetcy and a peerage. He died on 17 Jan. 1733, at his house in the Admiralty, of 'an asthma', part of 'the epidemic distemper that rages in London . . . but few die except such as have bad lungs, consumptive and asthmatical persons'. He was succeeded by his eldest surviving son, Hon. Pattee†, on whom at his marriage he had already settled his Bedfordshire estate, and who also received Byng's 'dwelling house' in Whitehall. The house he built at Southill was later disparaged by his grandson as in the 'vile taste' of a London tradesman.[10]

[1] *Navy Recs. Soc.* lxvii. pp. xv–xvi; *Mar. Lic. Vicar-Gen.* (Harl Soc. xxxi), 175; IGI, London. [2] *Cal. Treas. Bks.* xiv. 287. [3] W. R. Chaplin, *Trinity House*, 16, 188; R. East, *Portsmouth Recs.* 373; *Kinsale Corp. Council Bk.* ed. Caulfield, 208; Boyer, *Anne Annals,* vii. 41. [4] *Navy Recs. Soc.* lxvii. pp. xvi–xviii, xx, xxiii, xxv, xxix, lii. 77; Hasted, *Kent,* v. 12; D. Pope, *At Twelve Mr Byng was Shot,* 8–9; *Hearne Colls.* ii. 107; *Torrington Mems.* (Cam. Soc. n.s. xlvi.), 27–36, 80–81; J. D. Davies, *Gents. and Tarpaulins,* 209, 212; Folger Shakespeare Lib. Rich mss X d. 451 (98), list of capts. 1691; *Mariner's Mirror,* lxxiii. 188; IGI, London. [5] *CSP Dom.* 1702–3, pp. 129–30; G. M. Trevelyan, *Eng. under Q. Anne,* i. 271; Bodl. Ballard 21, f. 222; Wilts. RO, Aylesbury mss 1300/1317, 1327, 1324, 1326, Charles Becher to Ld. Bruce (Charles*), 13 Sept. 1705, 'Sat. night', same to Hon. Robert Bruce*, 29 Oct. 1705, info. 3 Nov. 1705; *Nicolson Diaries,* ed. Jones and Holmes, 352; Luttrell, *Brief Relation,* vi. 23. [6] Herts. RO, Panshanger mss D/EP/F54, ff. 69, 71, Sir Francis Drake, 3rd Bt.*, to Ld. Cowper, 13, 30 Dec. 1706; Boyer, vi. 241; Luttrell, vi. 228; *HMC Lords,* n.s. vii. 522; *Navy Recs. Soc.* lxviii. pp. xi–xii, 149; Camb. Univ. Lib. Cholmondeley (Houghton) mss 587a, Byng to Horatio Walpole II*, 21 Mar. 1708; 7th Duke of Manchester, *Court and Soc. Eliz. to Anne,* ii. 331. [7] *Marlborough–Godolphin Corresp.* 957, 963, 1028, 1405; *Navy Recs. Soc.* lxviii. 150; Cholmondeley (Houghton) mss 589, Byng to Walpole, 31 Aug. 1708; Add. 70420, newsletter 24 Feb. 1708–9; 61460, ff. 101–4; *HMC Downshire,* i. 871, 881; *Duchess of Marlborough Corresp.* i. 205, 278–9; Luttrell, vi. 501; *Cal. Treas. Bks.* xxiii. 462. [8] Egerton 3359; Add. 61580, ff. 192–220; *Navy Recs. Soc.* liii. 370, lxx. 45; NRA, Rep. 23370, Osborn of Chicksands mss O/185/5, Byng to Osborn, 28 Sept. 1710 [9] *HMC Laing,* ii. 171; SRO Dalhousie mss GD45/14/352/17, [Ld. Balmerino] to [–], 26 May [1713]; NLS, Advocates' mss, Wodrow pprs. letters Quarto 7, f. 158; Add. 31138, f. 211; 22222, f. 135; 17677 HHH, f. 41; Boyer, *Pol. State,* vii. 56; G. M. Trevelyan, *Eng. under Q. Anne,* iii. 315; *Navy Recs. Soc.* lxx. 71–72; NRA, Rep. 23370, O/185/7, Byng to Osborn, 16 Jan. 1714 [10] *Navy Recs, Soc.* liii. 409, lxx. 72–73; *HMC Stuart,* ii. 454, iv. 198, 388–9, 401, v. 556, vi. 302, 398; Stowe 742, f. 199; *VCH Beds.* iii. 253, 258, 261; Boyer, *Pol. State,* xlv. 98; *London Mag.* 1733, p. 45; *HMC Egmont Diary,* i. 309; PCC 188 Price; *Torrington Diaries,* ed. Andrews, iii. 318.

S. N. H.

BYROM, John (1659–95), of Byrom and Parr Hall, Lancs.

WIGAN 24 Jan. 1694–Mar. 1695

bap. 19 July 1659, 1st s. of Samuel Byrom of Byrom and Parr Hall by Margery, da. of George Venables of Agden, Cheshire. *educ.* G. Inn 1676. *m.* July 1682, Elizabeth, da. of Sir John Otway† of Ingmire Hall, Sedbergh, Yorks., 1s. 5da. (3 *d.v.p.*). *suc.* fa. 1686.[1]

Byrom's family had been settled in Lancashire since the 13th century, and an ancestor had served as knight of the shire in 1421 and 1429. Byrom was an avowed foe of the local Presbyterians, and in 1687 he pressed Bishop Cartwright of Chester to remove the Presbyterian congregation that had taken possession of St. Helen's chapel, a chapel of ease in Prescott parish, and to install an Anglican curate. Throughout the 1690s Byrom continued to pursue this issue. In 1691 he successfully removed the Presbyterian trustees of St. Helen's chapel, and then in 1692 he prevented the chapel being registered, under the terms of the Toleration Act, as a Dissenting meeting place. Byrom's strenuous activities in this field proved unsuccessful however, as the Presbyterians were able to register the chapel in 1696, and retained possession of it until 1710.[2]

In December 1693 Byrom entered the lists at the Wigan by-election occasioned by the death of Sir Richard Standish, 1st Bt.* Campaigning with support of Sir Roger Bradshaigh, 3rd Bt.*, Byrom was 'neither niggard of his purse nor far fetched', and was said to stand 'very fair with the generality of the townsmen'. He comfortably defeated his rivals for the vacant seat, but soon after his return he informed his cousin Roger Kenyon* that he would not be able to attend Parliament for 'some seasonable time' as his private affairs needed 'some settling', and it seems Byrom may never have taken his seat. He died between 28 Feb. 1695, when he made his will (at Parr), and 3 Mar. 1695, when he was buried. Byrom's only son Samuel, 'Beau Byrom', was a spendthrift who in 1710 sold Byrom Hall for £1,200 to the father of John Byrom of Manchester, the Jacobite poet.[3]

[1] M. Byron, *Byrom Chron.* 106–7; *Vis. Lancs.* (Chetham Soc. ser. 1, lxxxiv), 66–67. [2] *Cartwright Diary* (Cam. Soc. ser. 1, xxii), 77; *HMC Kenyon,* 246, 262; *Trans. Lancs. and Cheshire Antiq. Soc.* lxxv. 150–2; *VCH Lancs.* iii. 375. [3] Lancs. RO, Kenyon mss DDKe 9/66/25, Thomas to Roger Kenyon 15 Jan. 1693[-4]; Byrom, 108–9; *HMC Kenyon,* 278, 282–3; J. Byron, *Byrom's Manchester,* ii. 21–25.

E. C./R. D. H.

CADOGAN, William (c.1671–1726), of Caversham, Berks. and Jermyn Street, Westminster.

NEW WOODSTOCK   1705–16 Mar. 1714
                          24 Mar. 1714–21 June 1716

b. c.1671, 1st s. of Henry Cadogan, barrister, of Dublin and Liscarton, co. Meath, high sheriff of co. Meath 1700, by Bridget (*d.* 1721), da. of Sir Hardress Waller† of Castletown, co. Limerick, and bro. of Charles Cadogan†. *educ.* Westminster; Trinity, Dublin, 28 Mar. 1687, aged 15. *m.* c.1703, Margaretta Cecilia (*d.* 1749), da. of William Munter, councillor of supreme court of Holland, and niece of Adam Tripp, burgomaster, regent of Amsterdam, 2da. *suc.* fa. 1714. *cr.* Baron Cadogan of Reading 21 June 1716; Earl Cadogan 8 May 1718; KT 22 June 1716.[1]

Capt., Thomas Erle's* ft. regt. 1694–8; maj. Inniskilling Drag. Gds. 1698; brevet col. of ft. 1701; q.m.g. 1701–12; commissary for Danish and Württemburg forces 1701; col. 6 Horse 1703–12; brig.-gen. 1704, maj.-gen. 1707, lt.-gen. 1709; lt. Tower of London 1706–13; col. 2 Ft. Gds. (Coldstream) 1714–June 1722, 1 Ft. Gds. (Grenadiers) June 1722–*d.*; gov. I. o. W. 1715–*d.*; c.-in-c. Scotland Feb.–May 1716; gen. 1717; master-gen. of the Ordnance 1722–5.[2]

Special envoy to Vienna and Hanover 1706; envoy to Brussels 1707–11, 1714–15, United Provinces 1707–10, 1714–July 1716, ambassador July 1716–21; master of the robes 1714–*d.*; PC 30 Mar. 1717; ambassador to Vienna 1719–20; ld. justice (regency) 1723.

High steward, Reading 1716; freeman, Portsmouth 1721.

Commr. Chelsea Hosp. 1722–*d.*[3]

Through his expertise in logistics Cadogan became the most trusted staff officer of the Earl (later Duke) of Marlborough (John Churchill†), a position which afforded him considerable power and influence in his own right, and from which eventually he launched his own career in high politics. He came of Welsh ancestry, though army service under the Earl of Strafford (Thomas Wentworth†) had taken his grandfather (William Cadogan†) to Ireland where he had settled and later proved an equally dutiful servant of the Parliament and Commonwealth as governor of Trim, co. Meath. Cadogan's father, a prosperous Dublin lawyer, augmented the family estates in that county, particularly at Liscarton where he obtained the castle lands that William III had confiscated from the Talbot family which had formed part of the resumption of 1700. At his first election to Parliament in 1705, Cadogan was aspersed by the Tory newswriter John Dyer as a Whiggish upstart of questionable gentility: 'on his father's side his pedigree was proved by an epitaph that was made last summer by one at the herald's office and was never yet upon a tomb'. The young Cadogan first made an impression on Marlborough during the Irish campaigns early in William's reign, though it seems to have been the King himself who later prevailed on the Earl to give Cadogan a troop of horse. In April 1702 Marlborough was appointed to lead the allied armies and chose Cadogan, by then a proven military organizer, as his quartermaster-general. For the next ten years Cadogan was an integral part of the military high command, and was confided in by Marlborough almost as an equal.[4]

In January 1705 Marlborough was granted the royal manor of Woodstock and resolved to breach the interest of the Tory Earl of Abingdon (Montagu Venables-Bertie*) in the borough at the next electoral opportunity. Accordingly, at the general election four months later he proposed Cadogan as his own candidate. Marlborough's choice of Cadogan for the Woodstock seat was a distinctive sign of his esteem for the gifted brigadier and was doubtless meant as a reward for his contribution to the recent military successes. But Cadogan's presence in the Commons also gave Marlborough the practical advantage of having a personal representative there who could reliably report the moods of Members on matters touching the progress and cost of the war. Since Cadogan could not be released from duty abroad, Marlborough entrusted the management of the election to Henry St. John II*, the recently appointed secretary at war, and James Craggs I*, Marlborough's chief 'man of business'. Cadogan's close acquaintanceship with both men, and others of the 'Marlborough connexion' such as James Stanhope*, Henry Watkins* and Adam Cardonnel*, was naturally dictated by his all-embracing military responsibilities. He was returned for Woodstock but only after a brisk and at times uncertain contest. Though he sat for the borough almost without intermission until his ennoblement in 1716, he rarely, if ever, had time to concern himself with the politics of his constituency, and though Marlborough gave him the use of North Lodge in Woodstock Park, he seems to have been a rare visitor. In an analysis of the new Parliament Lord Sunderland (Charles, Lord Spencer*) noted Cadogan's election as a 'gain' for the Whigs. He was prevented, however, from taking his seat at the opening proceedings in October, Marlborough informing Lord Treasurer Godolphin (Sidney†) on the 9th that it was impossible for Cadogan's departure from headquarters to precede his own. His first recorded appearance in parliamentary proceedings was soon after the Christmas recess, on 7 Jan. 1706, when appropriately he was appointed to a small committee of MPs directed to convey the thanks of the House to Marlborough 'for his great services... in the last campaign', the high point of which had been the victory at Blenheim. On 18 Feb. Cadogan voted with the Court against the 'whimsical' place clause of the regency bill. He returned to Holland at the beginning of April, and the following month was present at the battle of Ramillies. In August, much to Marlborough's consternation, he was captured on a foraging expedition at Tournai. The Duke lost no time in arranging for an exchange, writing anxiously to Godolphin that Cadogan was 'absolutely necessary for my ease'. Cadogan attended the Commons on 3 Dec., the first day of the new session, but by February 1707 had returned to the Low Countries to brief Dutch politicians on the forthcoming campaign.[5]

Cadogan's multifarious responsibilities in running Marlborough's campaigns provided him with ample opportunity to indulge in unscrupulous profiteering ventures. He was particularly close in his collaboration with Hon. James Brydges*, the paymaster-general. The two men may initially have concocted various money-making schemes when Brydges joined Marlborough on campaign in the summer of 1705, shortly after being appointed paymaster. Cadogan was soon one of Brydges' leading accomplices in playing the gold market in the Low Countries, taking advantage of the varying exchange rates in different cities. With money remitted by Brydges, he bought cheaply, paid the army at higher rates and, with Brydges, pocketed the difference. These profitable operations were supplemented by purchases of gold which he later sold at profit to the army, and also investments in stocks on the basis of informed predictions about the likelihood of, and timing of peace. His full powers over forage-buying gave him ready access to other army funds for these and similar purposes. The gambler's lust for quick gain, which had consumed Cadogan as a young officer in Ireland, had by no means left him: he was now in a position to play for far greater stakes, laying enormous wagers on the outcome of various military operations on the basis of his privileged insider's knowledge. He was not always successful, however, and in 1707 lost heavily in a bet that Prince Eugene of Savoy would capture Toulon. His personal gains from these dubious enterprises were undoubtedly substantial. In 1707 he purchased the manor of Oakley in Buckinghamshire, within striking distance of Woodstock. This was followed in 1709 by the purchase of Caversham in Berkshire, an estate of over 1,000 acres, secured for him by Brydges, and in the same year he laid out a further £6,000 in Bank of England stock, thereby becoming one of the Bank's principal stockholders. He also lent large sums to Holland during the course of the war, which he demanded back almost as soon as peace was concluded.[6]

Cadogan's appointments in November 1707 as envoy extraordinary to Brussels and to The Hague were intended to complement his work as Marlborough's adjutant. When not on campaign he spent most of his time at Brussels as the English representative in the Anglo-Dutch 'condominium' which governed the Spanish Netherlands from 1706 following its recapture from the French. He was thus well placed to ensure close co-operation with the Brussels government in all matters concerning the war's progress, as well as to represent the commander's views and interests. Initially, the arrangement was meant only to be temporary, but at Marlborough's behest he was continued, having, as the Duke informed Godolphin in April 1708, 'behaved himself so well this winter at Brussels'. These new responsibilities, however, allowed Cadogan even less time to attend the Commons. He seems to have made no appearance in the House during the winter months of 1707–8, and was certainly absent from the crucial 'No Peace without Spain' division on 19 Dec. 1707. In February 1708 he earned the ministry's gratitude for his prompt despatch of regiments from Holland in readiness for the rumoured French invasion of Scotland. It was with evident dismay, however, that he learned of St. John's resignation later the same month. 'I am beyond expression concerned and surprised', he wrote to Brydges. 'I had a letter from him on that subject to justify the resolution he had taken. I am sorry he thought he had reason for it.' To those such as Cadogan, deeply immersed in the prosecution of the war, the Harleyite resignations can only have spelt an escalation of domestic opposition to its continuance. At the general election in May he was re-elected at Woodstock in his absence, and in a subsequent list of the new House was classed as a Whig. In July he was with Marlborough at Oudenarde, but in November was too overstretched to leave his duties to attend the new Parliament. By March 1709 complaints from the army's paymasters were evidently filtering through to him via Brydges about his mishandling of army money, whereupon he asked Brydges 'to put a stop to the continuing our project of buying up gold in Holland'. It was probably to this criticism that he alluded in a highly disingenuous letter of 12 Mar. to Lord Raby at Berlin:

> Blame and envy are the only fruits I have gathered out of the post I am still in, which I never asked for, nor desired to remain in, and to this minute I am a stranger to the reason why 'twas given me, or why 'tis not taken from me, since it creates so much offence.

He was apt to draw a veil over the growing anti-war opinion among the Tories in England, and thought the situation not very different from that prevailing in the United Provinces. 'They have their Bromleys and their Hanmers here [The Hague]', he wrote, 'as well as we have in England, but the greater number of those which govern are in the true interests of their country and believe with us no peace can be secure without obtaining the whole monarchy of Spain.' He was present at Malplaquet in September, but in a separate engagement a few days later was seriously wounded in the neck. Marlborough was in despair, not only for Cadogan's life, as surgeons failed to locate the ball, but also because, as he told Sarah, 'it will oblige me to do many things, by which I shall have but little rest'.[7]

The disintegration of Godolphin's ministry in August 1710 brought in the Harleyite Tories dedicated to ending both the war and the ubiquitous Marlborough influence in politics. Cadogan could do little but watch developments at a distance and allow Marlborough's fate to take its course. He professed himself willing to share the fortunes, whatever they might be, of 'the great man to whom I am under such infinite obligations . . . I would be a monster if I did otherwise'. Certain that Parliament would be dissolved in the coming months, Marlborough requested his wife to ensure Cadogan's re-election, anticipating Tory attacks on his conduct of the war when the House reassembled. He felt that Cadogan and Stanhope were the only MPs in his military entourage on whom he could rely for support, 'for they have both honesty and courage to speak truth'. Appropriately enough, at Reading, a short distance from his newly acquired estate at Caversham, the Tory election slogan was 'no Hanover, no Cadogan'. In December, Cadogan was perhaps not surprised to receive notice of dismissal from his diplomatic posts, an initial step in the 'mortification' of Marlborough. It was rumoured at this time that he had participated several times with, and even hosted, Generals Meredith* (Thomas), Macartney and Honeywood in drinking 'confusion to the ministry', and there was some belief that like them he would lose his military appointments, but the accusations against Cadogan were not pursued by the Court. By the end of December it was generally understood that he was to keep his posts 'out of consideration for Marlborough, who cannot dispense with him', dispelling the assumption then current that his lucrative lieutenancy of the Tower would go to Jack Hill, the brother of the Queen's new favourite, Abigail Masham. After visiting England briefly in January 1711, Cadogan returned to the Continent for what proved his last campaign as Marlborough's subaltern. Despite recent party recrimination Cadogan was cautious enough to maintain his old civility towards St. John, now secretary of state. The secretary was gratified that 'you remember an old friend who never did anything to be forgot'.[8]

On 31 Dec. 1711 Marlborough was finally dismissed as commander-in-chief of the forces in the Low Countries. He informed Cadogan by letter the following day, but this did not reach The Hague until 8 Jan. This delay, and the difficulty in obtaining a passport, prevented Cadogan from complying with the Duke's request to be in England by the 10th in connexion with the investigation by the commissioners of public accounts into Marlborough's alleged peculations concerning bread contracts and the pay of the foreign troops. Cadogan was, however, able to furnish Marlborough's urgent request for vital documentation illustrating his entitlement, in accordance with custom, to gratuities from bread contractors. Replying to the Duke on the 9th, he expressed profound 'concern and astonishment at the fatal news' and his own determination to quit the army, supposing 'the favour of giving up my employments will be readily granted'. Cadogan poured out his despondency a few days later to Henry Watkins, the army's judge-advocate and another of Marlborough's devoted retainers:

We have, dear judge, in the course of our long acquaintance generally agreed in our opinions of men and things; this makes it easy for me to guess at the indisposition of mind you complain of, and the cause of it. I am deeply affected in the same part, and by the same distemper, and am so far gone in it, as not only to be tired of business and employments, but even weary of life itself. You know the bottom of my heart, therefore can better imagine than I describe the affliction and weight of grief I am under. I am uncertain, and I assure you unconcerned as to what becomes of myself. I shall act according to the strictest rules of gratitude, duty and honour in relation to our great, unfortunate benefactor, and my zeal, inclination and desire to serve and suffer for him are equal to the vast obligations and favours I have received from him. As to the rest I shall do as people at sea when the violence of the storm obliges them to abandon the helm and cut down the masts, I commit myself to the mercy of the winds and waves. Whether they force me to split on rocks, or whether my good fortune may throw a plank in my way to carry me ashore, I am grown so insensible or so resigned as to be no longer in pain about.

Despite his professions of total submission to Marlborough's commands, Cadogan did not journey to England to participate on the Duke's behalf in the censure debate on 24 Jan. which centred on the commissioners' findings and which it was believed would be the prelude to impeachment. As the debate on the report approached, Marlborough may well have realized that his trusty lieutenant was almost as much a sitting target as himself, and that his presence in the House on so sensitive an occasion might easily spark calls for further inquiries. Cadogan's own record of chicanery with army funds would hardly have helped Marlborough's own predicament. Cadogan thus remained with the army in Flanders as its caretaker until a new commander was appointed. There were fresh predictions that he himself was about to fall from grace and lose the lieutenancy of the Tower, but while the Utrecht negotiations dragged on, his retention in the high command was seen as imperative. Cadogan's value as a field commander was even trumpeted in a spate of Tory pamphlets in which Marlborough's military genius was denigrated and ascribed to the acumen of subordinates, the principal of whom was Cadogan. In April, Cadogan's name was omitted from the list of lieutenant-generals selected to serve under the newly appointed generalissimo, the Duke of Ormond, but, at Ormond's express wish, for which St. John obtained the Queen's approval, Cadogan joined the 1712 campaign as quartermaster general. Despite these continuing signs of favour, Cadogan's retirement to Holland at the end of the campaigning season was evidently closely linked to Marlborough's own decision, taken soon after Lord Godolphin's death in September, to live abroad. On 1 Dec. he welcomed Marlborough to Ostend. Wishing still to appear in the good opinion of Lord Treasurer Oxford (Robert Harley*), Cadogan wrote in the most obsequious terms asking formal leave to attend the Duke in consideration of his 'ill-health, the inconvenience a winter's journey exposes him to, and his being without any one friend to accompany him'. The substance of Oxford's reply, if any there was, is not known, but in the weeks following, Cadogan was required to sell his regiment, doing so to his second-in-command, Lieutenant-Colonel George Kellum, for £3,500, and was finally replaced as lieutenant of the Tower of London. There is also some suggestion that in January 1713 Oxford considered bringing separate censures against Cadogan for his endeavours to protect Marlborough, though Lord Strafford, the former Lord Raby, counselled moderation and advised Oxford

> that it may be necessary to give him some encouragement, and to keep him in, since no man knows the Spanish Low Countries better than he does, nor is more expert in the affair of quarter-master general; and really without partiality, to one side or the other, I do believe the greatest part of Lord Marlborough's victories are owing to him, and even the Pensionary said to me: 'si vous voulez avoir un duc de Marlborough un Cadogan est nécessaire'. It would be well to keep him a little under, though you keep him still employed, and if you will let me know your sentiments as to my behaviour towards him I will be sure to observe them.

Oxford seems to have accepted the tenor of this advice, though if only to placate Dutch concern about the ministry's apparent vindictiveness towards Marlborough, which Strafford evidently encountered at the peace negotiations. None the less, by the time the Lord Treasurer had received Strafford's letter Cadogan had been dismissed from his remaining employments. This ostensible intervention by Strafford did nothing to allay Cadogan's developing hatred of his former friend, whom he was willing to condemn alongside Oxford in 1715.[9]

Until the death of Queen Anne in August 1714 Cadogan was engaged almost constantly in a round of quasi-diplomatic activity, as Marlborough's principal knight-errant in schemes to secure the Protestant succession in the Hanoverian dynasty. It says much for Cadogan's continued attachment to the ageing and ill ex-commander-in-chief that he was prepared to seek the acquiescence of allied statesmen in warlike schemes that were largely impracticable and bordered on the hare-brained. Yet Cadogan shared the Duke's obsessive belief that the Oxford ministry was preparing for a Jacobite restoration, and was joined by such other associates of Marlborough as the Duke's son-in-law, the Earl of Sunderland, and James Craggs I, still his agent in London. Cadogan's role in this covert, if inconclusive, activity was crucial. Foreign ministers, many of whom he knew personally, were more willing to meet him since he was less conspicuous than Marlborough. He also maintained contacts between the Duke and the leading Whigs in London, a process which quickly raised his own importance within the Whig party. During the first months of 1713 Cadogan worked assiduously to obtain support for Marlborough's somewhat far-fetched plan for an allied invasion of England that would usher in an 'honest' administration to preserve the Protestant succession. But neither Hanover, the Dutch nor the Emperor, the intended participants, regarded the proposal with any seriousness. It was soon superseded by another, put forward by Bernstorff, the principal Hanoverian minister, to establish a pro-Hanoverian defensive superiority in England upon the Queen's death. Cadogan himself was to take command of forces in London. In March he was able to report Marlborough's endorsement of the plan to Bothmer, the Elector's envoy at The Hague. It was plain, however, that the entire plan was contingent upon the Queen's death, of which there seemed no immediate prospect. Marlborough and Cadogan thus pursued their own quest for Imperial support for an invasion to overset the Tory government. They also spent much time goading the Hanoverian ministers to take positive action against the Oxford ministry and to send the electoral prince to London. In the summer Cadogan had high hopes that the impending general election would restore Whig fortunes, but he badly miscalculated the national mood. News of the Whigs' failure at the polls brought him to England early in September for consultations at Althorp with Sunderland, Craggs and others about future tactics. John Drummond*, the government's agent at The Hague, informed the lord treasurer that Cadogan had announced his intention of taking an active part in the new Parliament, 'and his being chosen at Woodstock makes people believe that his party is grown strong'. The Althorp gathering may well have discussed means of exploiting the disenchantment some Tory MPs bore towards the ministry, for shortly afterwards Cadogan was advocating to Schütz, the Hanoverian envoy in London, that the motions the Hanoverians had proposed for the ensuing parliamentary session might be made by amenable Tories, such as Archibald Hutcheson*, rather than by Whig Members. Cadogan, along with Marlborough, was even prepared to lend the Elector £20,000 for the purposes of building up a pro-Hanoverian faction among the 'poor lords' in the Upper House. He still believed, as he made clear to the Hanoverian ministers, that a continuance of 'the war of the Empire against France' would be of the 'greatest advantage' to the Whig party.[10]

The Queen's serious illness at the end of 1713 inspired a more ambitious plan from Marlborough for launching a Hanoverian invasion at her demise. Cadogan once again served as the Duke's emissary in seeking promises of Dutch and Imperial assistance. But from mid-March 1714 the pattern of Cadogan's exertions radically changed. The Pretender's refusal at this juncture to renounce his Roman faith extinguished any ministerial designs of offering him the crown. Henceforward, Cadogan's involvement in efforts to ensure the peaceable accession of the Hanoverian dynasty narrowed to the domestic front. Both he and Stanhope were active, for example, in enlisting the support of key domestic interests such as the merchants and monied men of the City. Cadogan had returned to London from The Hague towards the end of February for the new parliamentary session, not least because the validity of his own election at Woodstock the previous summer had been challenged by Tory petitioners. The election was declared void on 16 Mar. but he was re-elected without opposition eight days later. On 22 Apr. he spoke against the Tory motion to agree with the Lords' address setting out Parliament's confidence in the Utrecht peace. He replied to William Bromley II's* assertion that there had been a difference of opinion among the allies in 1711 about the cessation of arms, and that the States General had been at variance with Marlborough in their wish to avoid fighting. Cadogan pointed out that in fact all the generals bar one (unnamed) had on that occasion thought it unnecessary to give battle. He then went on to criticize the continuing vulnerability of the barrier between French and Dutch territory, and refuted Bromley's acclamation of the Utrecht peace settlement, pointing out that though there had been consistent allied success, much had been sacrificed at the negotiating table, before venturing his opinion that had the war been continued a little longer, the allies would have arrived at 'the heart of France'. From the end of April Cadogan acted as intermediary in the lord treasurer's negotiations with Marlborough, by which the former hoped to rescue his beleaguered ministry through an accommodation with the Whigs. Progress was effectively halted, however, in July when Oxford's duplicitous intentions towards the Whigs were exposed. It is quite conceivable that by the end of the month, with Marlborough poised to return, in all probability to form a new Whig ministry, Cadogan harboured real expectations of high ministerial office. But any such pretensions were cut short by the Queen's death on 1 Aug. and the inauguration of the pre-arranged Council of State from which Marlborough's and Sunderland's names had been omitted.[11]

In his subsequent career, Cadogan was a loyal, if ham-handed, servant of the Sunderland–Stanhope ministry. He remained MP for Woodstock until raised to the peerage in 1716. At the 1715 election he stood both at Woodstock and at Reading, having declined the chance of being returned for the more populous constituency of Westminster to which he had been warmly pressed. Almost from its beginning, the new reign offered him opportunities which amply fed a swelling ambition. Though he had come into his own as a Whig politician, his reputation was too obviously built upon the fame of the 'great man'. With his gauche ebullience, matched by his bulky appearance, he cut a somewhat implausible figure among subtler ministerial minds. His schooling and experience in domestic politics had been minimal. Entrusted with sensitive diplomatic tasks essential to the preservation of European peace, his want of tact and finesse only irritated such thoroughbred diplomatists as Horace Walpole II*. His old friend Lord Stanhope could not but note with amusement in 1719 Cadogan's overmighty 'notion of being *premier ministre*'. The Townshend–Walpole faction despised him for the unshakeable esteem in which he was regarded by the King. He knew the German language, shared the King's views on military and diplomatic affairs, and was well acquainted with the King's Hanoverian ministers. Following Marlborough's debilitating stroke in 1716 the command of the army passed to Cadogan, and on the Duke's death in 1722, he was appointed in succession as master-general of the Ordnance. Despite his clumsy attempt in 1723 to assume Marlborough's title of commander-in-chief, it was another two years before Sunderland's ministerial successors, Robert Walpole II* and Lord Townshend, succeeded in having him replaced with his old arch-enemy, the Duke of Argyll. This was undoubtedly the deepest of humiliations for Cadogan, who saw Argyll's ambitions as rival to his own. Moreover, he had never forgotten Argyll's part, as one of the powerful 'middle party', in the destruction of the Godolphin ministry, which in turn had led to the downfall of his own master.[12]

Cadogan died on 17 July 1726 at his residence at Kensington Gravelpits, Surrey, in his 57th year, and was buried at Westminster Abbey. In the absence of a male heir, the earldom became extinct, but the barony awarded under the 1718 patent passed by special remainder to his younger brother Charles.[13]

[1] PCC 223 Plymouth; Burke, *Peerage* (1939) 458; *Recs. Old Westminsters*, i. 155–6; *Al. Dub.* 126; *Saint-Simon Mems.* ed. Boislisle, xxxiv. 87. [2] *DNB*; *HMC 3rd Rep.* 189–90; Add. 39860, f. 90. [3] *DNB*; R. East, *Portsmouth Recs.* 377. [4] Lipscomb, *Bucks.* i. 353; *DNB* (Cadogan, William [1601–61]); K. S. Bottigheimer, *Eng. Money and Irish Land*, 200; *Repts. Commrs. Pub. Recs. Ire.* 1821–5, p. 356; *Coll. of Several Paragraphs out of Mr Dyer's Letters* (Bodl. Rawl. D.863, f. 89); W. S. Churchill, *Marlborough*, i. 535; Cunningham, *Hist. GB*, i. 246. [5] *Marlborough–Godolphin Corresp.* 417, 426, 503, 645, 647, 648; Add. 61131, f. 126; *VCH Oxon.* xii. 465; Luttrell, *Brief Relation*, vi. 34. [6] *Huntington Lib. Q.* xv. 21–44; Add. 22196, f. 99; 47025, ff. 69–70; Lipscomb, i. 354; E. P. Thompson, *Whigs and Hunters*, 100; Egerton 3359 (unfol.); *HMC Portland*, v. 426. [7] *Marlborough–Godolphin Corresp.* 926, 927, 961, 1376, 1377, 1378, 1380; *Studs. in Dipl. Hist.* eds. Hatton and Anderson, 61; H. T. Dickinson, *Bolingbroke*, 59; *Huntington Lib. Q.* xv. 30; Add. 22196, f. 194. [8] *DNB*; *Marlborough–Godolphin Corresp.* 1590, 1591, 1596, 1603; Monod thesis, 211; *Bolingbroke Corresp.* i. 62, 118; *Wentworth Pprs.* 162, 164, 165; *Swift Stella*, 121; *HMC Var.* ix. 355. [9] Add. 61160, f. 140; 47026, f. 110; Churchill, iv. 509–10; *Bolingbroke Corresp.* ii. 136, 258, 275; Boyer, *Pol. State*, iii. 249; iv. 331; *HMC Portland*, v. 257–8; ix. 323; G. M. Trevelyan, *Eng. under Q. Anne*, ii. 120; *Jnl. Soc. Army Hist. Res.* xxxix. 5. [10] *Hist. Jnl.* xv. 593–618; Boyer, *Pol. State*, vi. 184; G. Holmes, *Pol. in Age of Anne*, 291; *HMC Portland*, v. 330; *Orig. Pprs.* ed. Macpherson, ii. 502, 521. [11] *Hist. Jnl.* xv. 609–18; Rapin, *Hist. Eng.* ii. 347; *Orig. Pprs.* ii. 570; Boyer, *Pol. State*, vii. 244–5; Add. 70293, Henry Watkins to 'Mr Harley', 2 Apr. 1714; *Wentworth Pprs.* 378; Oley Douglas* diary (Hist. of Parl. trans.), 22 Apr. 1714. [12] Coxe, *Ld. Walpole*, i. 19; *Wentworth Pprs.* 441; Add. 61161, f. 43; *DNB*; J. H. Plumb, *Walpole*, i. 282; Thompson, 202–3; A. J. Guy, *Oeconomy and Discipline*, 28; *Orig. Pprs.* ii. 502. [13] *Westminster Abbey Reg.* (Harl. Soc. x), 318; *The Gen.* n.s. vii. 45.

A. A. H.

CAESAR, Charles (1673–1741), of Bennington, Herts.

HERTFORD	1701 (Jan.)–1708,
	1710–24 May 1715,
	1722–22 Jan. 1723
HERTFORDSHIRE	1727–1734,
	29 Apr. 1736–2 Apr. 1741

b. 21 Nov. 1673, 1st. s. of Sir Charles Caesar† of Bennington by Susanna, da. and coh. of Sir Thomas Bonfoy, merchant of London. *educ.* St. Catharine's, Camb. 1689, MA 1690; M. Temple 1690. *m.* 24 Nov. 1702 (with £5,000), Mary, da. of Ralph Freman I*, 2s. 2da. *suc.* fa. 1694.

Freeman, Hertford 1698, St. Albans 1704.[1]

Treasurer of the navy 1711–14.

The family's historian claimed that Charles Caesar of Great Hadham, Hertfordshire, and of Great Gransden, Huntingdonshire, represented Hertford until 1723 (*d.* 1726), and that Charles Caesar of Bennington sat for the county after 1727. In fact, the former seems never to have entered Parliament. The confusion may have arisen because both men shared similar political and religious allegiances, both had financial difficulties, and a commonplace book belonging to Caesar of Great Hadham noted a number of proceedings in the Commons relating to Caesar of Bennington. Moreover, Charles of Great Hadham was, like his kinsman, educated at Cambridge and the Middle Temple.[2]

Charles Caesar of Bennington was the son of Sir Charles Caesar, who had first been elected at Hertford in 1679, and who was chosen on a double return for the county in 1690, although the House decided against seating him. Sir Charles died in 1694, leaving his young son an estate worth £3,500, but Caesar inherited very few of his father's moderate characteristics. Whereas Sir Charles, like his Country Whig brother-in-law Sir Thomas Pope Blount, 1st Bt.*, 'would not willingly quarrel with his neighbours', his son, at least until after the Hanoverian succession, indulged in an intemperate feud at Hertford with William Cowper*; and while Sir Charles was 'very regular in his life and orderly in his family', his son was allegedly only a 'pretending zealot for High Church' who was at the same time notorious 'for lying with other men's wives'. Nevertheless, both Caesars were prepared to make use of the local Quaker interest to ensure electoral victory – indeed in 1727 Charles was advised to suppress a rumour that he wished Dissenters of all sorts to be rooted out – and both shared a belief in not sparing 'any cost or charge to obtain' their point, a resolution that ultimately ruined the family's fortunes. Charles 'espoused with great warmth the party called the Country party: in support of which he lavished away great sums of money, which brought on pecuniary embarrassment'.[3]

Caesar allied himself with the Hertford Tories who struggled against the Cowper interest in the borough. Though he was defeated when he stood for Hertford in 1698, Caesar was successful at the first election of 1701, the Cowper interest having been weakened by the loss of Quaker support after the trial in 1699 of Spencer Cowper* for the murder of Sarah Stout, a female Quaker 'friend'. At first his career was that of an undistinguished back-bencher: in February 1701 he was listed as likely to support the Court in agreeing with the committee of supply's resolution to continue the 'Great Mortgage'; and on 10 May acted as teller on the disputed franchise at Lichfield, following the lead of other Country Tories, including Ralph Freman II*, who was soon to become his brother-in-law. He was later blacklisted as having opposed during the 1701 session the preparations for war with France, but this did not prevent his re-election in the autumn. Caesar's activity in the new Parliament fully justified Robert Harley's* ranking of him as a Tory. On 20 Jan. 1702 he told against making the abjuration oath voluntary, a move designed to salve the conscience of those Tories who would only submit to a mandatory oath. Caesar also showed a concern to ensure the return of Tories in disputed election cases, telling with his friend Richard Goulston on 29 Jan. against the adjournment of the Malmesbury election case, and on 17 Mar. against the Whig Thomas White II*. Listed as having favoured the motion of 26 Feb. vindicating the Commons' proceedings in impeaching the King's Whig ministers, Caesar told the following day on another partisan issue, against the second reading of the bill authorizing the appointment of commissioners to negotiate a union with Scotland.[4]

Maintaining his hostility to the Cowpers – it was said in January 1702 that he would present the Quakers' appeal against the verdict of acquittal of Spencer Cowper – Caesar was re-elected in July 1702. On 10 Dec. 1702 he told against the introduction of a petition from the London Merchant Taylors' Company, an antipathy to trade not unusual in a country gentleman but also evidence of a particular hostility to that company, since he had earlier opposed the right of its members to vote at Lichfield. On 19 Jan. 1703 he joined with another Member who had been concerned in the Lichfield decision, Sir Willoughby Hickman, 3rd Bt., in telling on the right of election at Tavistock, against the Russell interest. On 13 Feb. he voted against agreeing with the Lords' amendment to the bill for enlarging the time for taking the abjuration oath, and four days later gave the first indication of an interest in naval affairs when he joined with his borough partner Goulston in telling against a motion to introduce (into the bill to revive the commission to investigate military and naval debts) a clause relating to the marines.[5]

At the start of the next session Caesar made clear his High Church allegiance, despite his local understanding with the Quakers, when he told on 25 Nov. 1703 in favour of introducing the second occasional conformity bill. His concern about the dangers threatening the Church may also explain his tellership on 18 Jan. 1704 in favour of the committal of the bill to restrain the licentiousness of the press. The remainder of his significant activity concerned the management of the war. On 7 Mar. he acted as teller in favour of recommitting the bill for recruiting forces, and three days later told against its passage, though his opposition to it may have been related to the fact that the bill dispensed with part of the Act for encouraging the increase of shipping. On 24 Mar. he was sent to the Lords to desire a conference on the amendments made by the peers to the bill for stating the public accounts, an indication of his growing stature within the House, though he had not been appointed to the committee to manage the conference itself. During March he was also listed by Lord Nottingham (Daniel Finch†) as a likely supporter in the proceedings on the Scotch Plot.

Caesar's rising status was again recognized at the beginning of the next session by appointment on 24 Oct. to prepare the Address. During this session he assisted in the management of two private bills through the Commons, but the most notable aspect of his significant activity was his growing disillusionment with the conciliatory tone of the ministry. On 14 Nov. he spoke and told in favour of the introduction of the third occasional conformity bill, and a month later was granted leave to make a motion after one o'clock, presumably to allow the bill a third reading, which took place later that day. Forecast as a supporter of the Tack, he duly voted for it on 28 Nov. He also supported his tacking brother-in-law, Ralph Freman II, in his attempt to pass a place bill, a measure largely promoted in reaction to the loss of the occasional conformity bill but which nevertheless brought Caesar into an unlikely partnership with his local rival, William Cowper*, whom in mid-November he and other Tories had attacked in the House. Both Cowper and Caesar were named on 13 Jan. 1705 to the bill's drafting committee, and two weeks later Caesar told for the passage of this measure. The following month, on the 14th, he told in favour of one of the Lords' amendments to Peter King's* moderate place bill, which would have excluded commissioners and officials of the Prize Office, yet another matter connected with Caesar's hobby-horse of naval administration. He told on 16 Jan. 1705 against the committal of the bill to appoint commissioners to treat for a union with Scotland, and further opposed Whig projects on 26 Feb. by telling with (Sir) Thomas Hanmer II* (2nd Bt.) on a motion to resume the debate on the Aylesbury election case later that day. On the 28th he was nominated to the committee to manage the ensuing conference with the Lords on the writs of error.6

The appointment in October of his rival, Cowper, to high office, which confirmed the ministry's shift towards the Whigs, may have been enough to push Caesar into more open hostility towards the Court. Certainly his actions in the new Parliament were dramatic. Marked as one of the 'True Church', he had already given a warning of his future conduct by voting on 25 Oct. against the Court's candidate for Speaker. His tellerships on 24 Nov. 1705 on the franchise at St. Albans, in favour of John Gape*, and twice on 6 Dec. (both times with Freman) in favour of Richard Goulston's election at his own borough, indicated that at first Caesar was concerned with securing the seats of Tories within his own county. National issues, however, soon predominated. On 8 Dec. he declared that the Church was 'now in more danger' than ever, an assertion 'confirmed by the last Parliament' and reinforced with reference to the occasional conformity bills. On 13 Dec. he and Freman were appointed to draft a new place bill, and on 19 Dec. he told, again with Freman, against the second reading of the regency bill. During a debate full of 'the foulest Billingsgate language', Caesar also made a highly charged but in Harley's opinion 'a long and tedious speech of railing' against the regency bill, which Harley thought did 'not answer the end' intended, since it vested 'power in men that may be bad'. In the heat of his argument he had claimed that 'there is a noble lord [meaning Sidney Godolphin†], without whose advice the Queen does nothing who, in the late reign, was known to keep a constant correspondence with the Court at St. Germain'. Although he quickly endeavoured to excuse himself, the House ordered him to withdraw, and on concluding that his comments had been 'highly dishonourable to her Majesty's person and government', committed him to the Tower. Grey Neville's* diary nevertheless suggests that while still provocative, Caesar's words had been conditional rather than positive, rhetorically suggesting that *if* there was such a traitor in the regency the matter should be set 'all aside'. The speech immediately provoked hostility from both sides of the House, with (Sir) Simon Harcourt I* calling it 'insufferable', but Caesar insisted that the words officially recorded were not accurate, and it was on this basis that his friends tried to clear him. As a result of a battery of Tories claiming 'that the word if was put in', even Foley (either Thomas I or II), who had been the first to call for the words to be written down, thought a reprimand the most suitable punishment; but the Whigs refused to give way and Caesar was taken into custody, the Tories apparently feeling it wiser to allow this than protest further and risk Caesar's permanent expulsion. The unrepentant Caesar spent the rest of the session kicking his heels in the Tower 'rather than submit to the House', but his confinement was hardly isolation, for he 'was visited by the Tories of both Houses, the Earl of Rochester (Laurence Hyde†) excepted, who sent Mr [Francis] Gwyn* to make his compliment and to tell him the nearness of his relation to the Queen made him not think it was decent to come in person'. The implication was that Caesar, described by Bonet as a young man 'qui a plus de vivacité que de prudence', had voiced what many others secretly thought but dared not express in public. Indeed, in the short term Caesar emerged from the incident with greater local popularity, being 'met by the country' on his return home, though the Cowpers privately rejoiced 'at the discomfiture of their enemy'.7

Caesar was only to feel the full consequences of his rash words the following summer. Despite having refused to sign a county address congratulating the Queen on the recent military victories 'because, he said, it applauded the administration', he carried up an address from Hertford, and waited at the Council chamber seeking admission, 'to the great surprise of all there, who wondered what could put him on doing so assured a thing, which could not be easy to the most confident'. According to Lady Cowper, Caesar had hoped that the address 'would make him welcome and chose that time to show his courage, but the Queen refused to see him, and sent word she would receive an address from Hertford but not from his hands'. She even told him that she did not 'desire his presence in her court'. William Cowper, now lord keeper, may have been responsible for the snub, since the Queen had at first expressed her willingness to receive the address on her way to church, but sent a countermanding message a quarter of an hour later, prompting Francis Annesley* to remark sarcastically that this showed how 'moderation steers the helm'. Caesar nevertheless 'pressed it on Secretary Hedges [Sir Charles*]' and tried to seek the intercession of Lord Rochester, who 'told him nothing could be done while the Queen continued in those hands'. To make the rebuff even more publicly humiliating, Caesar was removed from the Hertfordshire lieutenancy and the commission of the peace but, perhaps on Lord Keeper Cowper's initiative, the Queen 'let it not be known till the very time of the sessions, which made him depart there in great confusion'. Caesar was not the only one to suffer, for a Cambridge don was dismissed after he had implied that Anne was more prepared to listen to Presbyterians than to Churchmen.[8]

Undaunted by his recent ordeals, Caesar returned to the attack in the second session of Parliament, where his continuing credit was indicated by his nomination on 3 Dec. 1706 to the Address committee, though he was now prepared to talk more 'modestly'. He made his only reported speech of the 1706–7 session on 7 Jan. 1707, opposing a settlement upon the Duke of Marlborough (John Churchill†) and his heirs to 'accompany the title and house of Woodstock'. He was a teller on two motions concerned with the Church, the first on 7 Feb. 1707 in favour of a committee of the whole to discuss measures for its security, and the second, three days later, against adding words to the ensuing bill implying that the corporations were well provided for in the draft. The threat to the Church posed by integration with Presbyterianism in Scotland also explains his two tellerships on the bill of union, first on 22 Feb. against a motion for a committee of the whole to discuss the matter, and again six days later against the passage of the bill itself. He further harried the government on 19 Feb. by telling against the recommendation of the committee of ways and means about a further issue of Exchequer bills. His dislike of the union with Scotland was again immediately apparent. On 4 Dec. 1707 he opened a debate by raising 'some scruples against the union', and a week later told in favour of a clause in the supply bill which prevented the East India Company from any trading privilege until it had repaid the capital stock of the Scottish Company. He was again teller on 23 Jan. 1708 (with Sir Richard Onslow, 3rd Bt.) in favour of agreeing to a date for the dissolution of the Scottish Privy Council, a move designed by both Country Tories and Whigs to squeeze the ministry. On 12 Feb. he told against the committal of the Tone navigation bill, perhaps motivated by nothing more than a desire to frustrate the Whig Edward Clarke*, whose bill it was. Caesar's name appears for three more tellerships: on 16 Feb. against an amendment to allow the Earl of Ranelagh (Richard Jones*) to pay Col. John Savery for services in Ireland, further indication of his hostility to both the Whigs; on 19 Feb. against referring a petition from Sir Thomas Cookes Winford, 2nd Bt.*, to resolve the impasse about the foundation of Worcester College, Oxford, partly on party grounds but perhaps also because his own family was saddled with difficulties about endowing a university college; and on 9 Mar. in favour of a clause to clarify Church statutes concerning the jurisdiction of episcopal visitations. All this activity confirmed his categorization as a Tory on lists compiled that year.[9]

Indeed, despite his clamorous local welcome only two years before, Caesar found that his support at Hertford had withered to such an extent that he no longer felt able to contest the seat. Although this made him even more bitter against his 'professed enemy' Cowper, now lord chancellor, Caesar was reluctant to remain out of Parliament, and contested the by-election at Weobley in December, on the interest of Hon. Henry Thynne*, who had decided to sit for Weymouth and who preferred to nominate Caesar to the vacancy rather than Henry St. John II*. The Herefordshire Whigs believed that Caesar's candidacy was 'as great an affront as could be offered to our county', and despite arriving before other candidates to canvass support, he was unable to mobilize enough voters. He remained out of the political limelight until swept back into Parliament with the Tory landslide at the 1710 general election.

> And now Mr Harley coming into power, Mr Caesar applied to him to reinstate him in the Queen's favour. He did it so effectively that on 9 June 1710 he was able to write to Mr Caesar that the Duke of Shrewsbury . . . had laid before her Majesty in the manner he wished, namely an instance of his duty and regard to the Queen. It had the desired effect and there now remained no objection to his bringing an address. This was done and he was received very graciously.

Caesar was duly restored to the commission of the peace in December 1710. But it was not until the following June that Harley 'carried Mr Caesar into the Queen's closet at Kensington, where after many marks of his friendship and her favour, he kissed her hand to be treasurer of the navy'. This account, from the pen of Caesar's wife, glosses over some of the details of his appointment. First, Harley's derogatory remarks about Caesar in 1706 suggest that he was forced to accommodate him out of political pressure, despite his protestations of friendship. Certainly, Caesar was noted in 1714 as waiting to see Harley's rival, Bolingbroke, and Freman later recalled that his brother-in-law 'had gone all my Lord Bolingbroke's length in Queen Anne's reign'. It was only after the Hanoverian succession that Harley and Caesar became intimates. Second, although destined for some office, Caesar benefited from Freman's squeamishness about accepting a place. On 16 Sept. 1710 Caesar, in response to Harley's inquiry about what 'would be most agreeable', had only asked for 'Sir John Holland's* staff [as comptroller of the Household] or a teller's place in the Exchequer, if either can be obtained for me'. By 28 Sept. Harley had still not resolved what place he should offer, and Caesar wrote again, pleading for a decision before his election, though he felt confident about 'being put into some place'. Caesar was in fact left waiting until June 1711, perhaps so that in the meantime he could prove his effectiveness in the House, but also because it was unclear whether Freman would join the Court. In January 1711 it was reported that Freman would be made treasurer of the navy and Caesar comptroller of the Household, but the compromise worked out in the following months centred on the idea of a joint commission as treasurer 'to be taken out in Mr Caesar's name, and Mr Freman to have half pay without having his very clear estate subjected for security of great sums which that place requires'. Caesar thus gained status and high office, even though he was in some senses a front-man for his brother-in-law, a politician closer to Harley's taste. This is not to say that Caesar took his new responsibilities lightly. His interest in matters naval and financial had already been made clear, and there seems to have been no complaint about his competence to undertake the job.[10]

Labelled, not surprisingly, as a Tory on the 'Hanover list' of 1710, Caesar became a leading member of the October Club. Yet despite, and indeed partly because of, this allegiance to the Country wing of the party, Caesar set out to advertise himself for the navy office by forcing Harley to take notice of its mismanagement. He was noted in early January as joining with Freman in making daily harangues against the previous ministry. On one occasion, probably in connexion with the disputed Carlisle election, he even 'decoyed' (Sir) James Montagu I* into the House. On 5 Jan. 1711 he was first-named to the committee of inquiry into the abuses in victualling, and, as its chairman, reported on 12 Jan. about a prevaricating witness. The full report was made on 7 Feb., and included accusations against Thomas Ridge*, one of the contractors supplying the navy with beer, but the investigation was so detailed that consideration of it was deferred for a week. On 15 Feb., however, the designs of the October Club were broken when, after

> Caesar (as the Whigs term it) had put forth his commentaries, Mr Harley in a short speech asked the opinion of the House, at that time very full, whether they would be pleased to proceed immediately into a further inquiry into abuses? or first take care of the business of the public? . . .it was resolved *nemine contradicente* to go on with the supply, so that it is thought things will go quietly enough this session.

The naval contractors were nevertheless censured, and Ridge expelled from the House. All this was sufficient for him to be later listed as one of the 'worthy patriots' who had detected the mismanagement of the last administration. Yet after the failure of the attack on victualling abuses, Caesar seems to have changed tack, and did little to alienate the Court and jeopardize his chances of office. After the attempted assassination of Harley, he secured leave on 14 Mar. to introduce a bill making it a felony to attempt the lives of privy councillors. He told twice during May: on the 10th, against a clause in the supply bill reducing the duty on hops, and on the 30th in favour of deferring the consideration of the Lords' amendments to the bill for encouraging the transport of naval stores from Scotland.[11]

Appointment to office meant that Caesar was, ironically, a victim of the place legislation which he had himself supported, though the expense of his by-election victory in June 1711 must have been reduced by the fact that no candidate stood in opposition to him. He told against a Whig amendment relating to the need for the continuation of the war in Spain and the West Indies. When on 1 May the order was read for a call of the House, Caesar proposed to defer the review for a fortnight on the grounds that 'les affaires de la paix n'étant pas encore assez avancées, elle pourra l'être vers ce temps là et qu'alors le projet de paix pouvait être communiqué'. However, his speech apparently annoyed the House, and though the motion for an immediate call, which Caesar told against, was defeated, only a week's deferral was granted. Still with the war in mind, on 24 Jan. Caesar attacked Marlborough, telling with William Shippen* in favour of a motion censuring the Duke's alleged corruption. The rest of his activity that session consisted of informing the House about the navy and its finances, though the burdens of office did not prevent him entertaining at his house in the city. The guests included Jonathan Swift, who praised the classical Brutus in Caesar's presence, a 'blunder' that caused much merriment.[12]

With the Tories in full control of the House, the 1713 session proved to be one of the easiest for the new treasurer of the navy. On 10 Apr. 1713 Caesar told in favour of retaining a wording in the Address which allowed some flexibility to the Privy Council in negotiating the terms of the peace. The main concern of the session was to pass the French commerce bill, for which two tellerships reveal Caesar to have been an enthusiastic supporter: on 30 May he told in favour of an immediate reading of the bill, and on 4 June to commit it. On 18 June he both spoke and voted for this measure, though one report linked him to Freman and other Tories who opposed the bill. On the 23rd he told against putting a spoiling question to instruct the address committee to insist on liberty of trade to all parts of the French empire. During the course of the session Caesar had once again set before the House a number of naval estimates and accounts, and in May he defended Whig attacks on the pensions paid out of naval funds to Lord Strafford and Sir Francis Masham, 3rd Bt.*, planning to wrong-foot opponents by laying before the House the details of Lord Orford's (Edward Russell*) similar warrant.[13]

Having been re-elected for Hertford in August 1713, Caesar twice served as teller in the first session in connexion with the determination of disputed elections, the first occasion on 6 Apr. in favour of dropping consideration of Lord Barrymore's (James Barry*) petition concerning the Wigan election, and the second on 27 Apr. to secure the return of his local colleague John Gape at St. Albans. He made two recorded speeches that session, the first on 18 Mar. in favour of the expulsion of Richard Steele, and the second on 15 Apr. against the motion that the succession was in danger. On 7 May his animus against the union with Scotland was again apparent with his appointment to the committee to examine the debts of the Equivalent, though the committee may also have valued his financial expertise and his link with the ministry. His reconciliation with the Queen now seems to have been complete, for shortly before her death Anne 'gave him her picture by Sir Godfrey Kneller, and was pleased with its being to hang by Queen Elizabeth given to Sir Julius Caesar'. Caesar was too closely associated with the Tory administration to retain office for long after the Hanoverian succession. He nevertheless hung on to his post much longer than most people expected, largely because of a dispute about who should replace him. Thus the termination of his official career as well as its beginning was determined by internal Court politics, and as late as December 1714 Caesar was left in the commission of the peace.[14]

Although re-elected in 1715, and ranked as a Tory on all comparative lists with the 1713 Parliament, Caesar was unseated on petition. He subsequently became involved in Jacobite plots, but recovered his seat at Hertford and subsequently sat for the county, which he represented until his death at his house in New Bond Street on 2 Apr. 1741. He had enjoyed a very affectionate marriage to a woman admired by Pope and Swift, and her illness and recuperation in 1730 had prompted letters which not only show Caesar's rustication but also some of his charm and wit. When he was not in his fields, he told her, he 'went about all day long with my spade and don't suffer a weed to peep his head up without immediately cutting it off', and he likened himself to

> Adam before Eve was created, spending my time with the beasts in the field, the fowls of the air and the fish in the waters, tho' he had this advantage over me, that not having experienced how happy a loving and beloved wife makes her husband, he could not be so sensible of his want as I am who have for so many years been blessed with one, but I trust in God you will come from the Bath hither in perfect health, and then Bennington will be a paradise to me.

Yet his Eden was not to remain unspoilt, for he left large debts, part of which must have been the result of his ill-fated rebuilding of his seat as 'a palace of modern fashion, which was burnt to ashes immediately after it was completed and before it had been inhabited'. An obituary described him as

> a gentleman whose memory must be ever dear to all who have the love of their country at heart. He was a gentleman of unshaken loyalty to his prince, unmoved at the frowns of ministers, and one who dared in the worst of times, with a greatness of soul worthy of himself, assert and maintain the rights of his fellow subjects and liberties of his country. His generosity and humanity of temper were equal to the steadiness of his principles, and the sentiments he ever expressed, both in public and private life, were such as could only flow from a heart dedicated to virtue, and incapable of corruption.

He signed his will as 'Charles Adelmare otherwise Caesar', a reference to his family's Italian origins, but the faded grandeur of his name was virtually all he had to bequeath his son, for the estate was burdened with heavy debts.[15]

[1] Herts. RO, Hertford bor. recs. 25/100; St. Albans Pub. Lib. St. Albans bor. recs. 299. [2] E. Lodge, *Life of Sir Julius Caesar*, 62–74. [3] Lodge, 70; Chauncy, *Herts*. ii. 82; Herts. RO, Panshanger mss D/EP F31, Lady Cowper's commonplace bk. p. 259; Cottrell-Dormer mss

at Rousham, Caesar letterbk. B, William Plummer to Caesar, 22 Aug. 1727; Clutterbuck, *Herts*. ii. 285. [4] Add. 70036, f. 98; Bodl. Rawl. lett. 92, f. 72. [5] Panshanger mss D/EP F29, Lady Cowper's commonplace bk. p. 182. [6] *Bull. IHR*, xxxix. 52; Panshanger mss D/EP F30, Lady Cowper's commonplace bk. p. 313. [7] *Nicolson Diaries* ed. Jones and Holmes, 332; Coxe, *Marlborough*, i. 353; *Cam. Misc.* xxiii. 34, 45, 50–56; Add. 17677 BBB, ff. 28–29, 194; 62558, f. 1; DZA, Bonet despatch 20 Dec. 1705/1 Jan. 1706; Panshanger mss D/EP F31, p. 258. [8] Panshanger mss D/EP F31, pp. 258–9; Northants. RO, Isham mss IC 3726, John to Sir Justinian Isham, 4th Bt.*, 6 July 1706; Trinity, Dublin, Lyons (King) mss 2002/1216, Francis Annesley to Bp. King, 6 July 1706; *HMC Portland*, ii. 194; Staffs. RO, Paget mss D603/k/3/6, R. Acherley to Ld. Paget, 4 July 1706; Luttrell, *Brief Relation*, v. 77. [9] Lot 455 sold at Sotheby's, 21 July 1980, Joseph Addison* to George Stepney, 7 Jan. 1706[-7]; Chandler, iv. 54. [10] *HMC Portland*, iv. 513, 515, 595, 602; Huntington Lib. Stowe mss 57(2), p. 120; 57(3), p. 152; Add. 62558, f. 2; 70421, Dyer's newsletter 15 June 1710; Cottrell-Dormer mss, Caesar letterbk. A, Harley to Caesar, 9, 28 June 1710; *Orig. Pprs.* ed. Macpherson, ii. 533; *HMC Egmont Diary*, ii. 165; BL, Trumbull Alphab. mss 54, John Bridges to Sir William Trumbull*, 5 Jan. 1711; Ralph Bridges to same, 8 June 1711; Add. 57861, f. 102. [11] NSA, Kreienberg despatch 9 Jan. 1711; *Nicolson Diaries*, 545; Pittis, *Present Parl*. 67; Trumbull Alphab. mss 54, Bridges to Trumbull, 19 Feb. 1711; Boyer, *Pol. State*, i. 191. [12] Kreienberg despatch 2 May 1712; Add. 17677 FFF, f. 178; *Swift Stella* ed. Davis, 245, 602. [13] Hereford and Worcester RO (Hereford), Brydges mss A.81/iv/23/b, William Brydges to Francis Brydges, 21 June 1713; Add. 31144, f. 372. [14] NLS, Advocates' mss, Wodrow pprs. letters Quarto 8, f. 96; G. Holmes and W. A. Speck, *Div. Soc.* 76; Add. 62558, f. 3; *Wentworth Pprs*. 427; L. K. J. Glassey, *Appt. JPs*, 242. [15] Cottrell-Dormer mss, Caesar letterbk. F, Caesar to Mary Caesar, 13, 20 Sept. 1730; Clutterbuck, ii. 285; *Daily Post*, 3 Apr. 1741; PCC 80 Spurway.

M. J. K.

CAGE, William (1665/6–1738), of Milgate, Bearsted, Kent.

ROCHESTER 1702–1705, 1710–1715

bap. 28 Mar. 1665/6, o. s. of William Cage (*d.v.p.* 1676, 1st s. of William Cage of Milgate) of Hollingbourne, Kent by Cicely, da. and h. of Sir Cheney Culpeper (*d.* 1663) of Hollingbourne. *m.* bef. 1690, Catherine, 3s. (2 *d.v.p.*) 4da. (2 *d.v.p.*). *suc.* gdfa. at Milgate 1677.[1]

Sheriff, Kent 1694–5; freeman Rochester, 1702.[2]

Rather surprisingly for someone from a family dominated by lawyers, Cage did not follow his grandfather and father to an inn of court or university. The will of his grandfather, William Cage of Milgate, left the care of the records securing his grandson's estate with his cousin, Katharine Harlockenden, presumably trusting her more than his two younger sons and cousins. From the point at which he inherited his grandfather's estates, Cage's life remains obscure until he took on the shrievalty in December 1694. He was dismissed from the justices' bench in December 1695 and arrested the following February, presumably on suspicion of disloyalty to the regime. Rehabilitation must have occurred fairly quickly, as before the accession of Anne he was a deputy-lieutenant and militia colonel.[3] Nevertheless, Cage's doubtful loyalty provided ammunition for electoral opponents when he stood for Parliament in December 1701. Printed tracts appeared accusing him of speaking 'very slighting words of King William and his government and said there would be an alteration of the government in a little time'. Although this was probably effective as propaganda, since Cage lost the contest at Rochester, a report by the attorney-general, Sir Edward Northey*, found the evidence too flimsy to warrant a prosecution. In the absence of such tactics Cage was duly returned in 1702. He was not an active member, being given leave for three weeks on 23 Jan. 1703. However, he was recorded as voting on 13 Feb. against agreeing with the Lords' amendments enlarging the time for taking the oath of abjuration. He voted for the Tack on 28 Nov. 1704. No doubt it was his stance on the question of occasional conformity which explains Lord Halifax's (Charles Montagu*) description of him after his election defeat in 1705 as a 'violent man'.[4]

After a five-year absence Cage was re-elected to Parliament in the Tory landslide of 1710. Unfamiliarity may explain the uncertainty shown by the compiler of the 'Hanover list' as to his party affiliation. Any doubts must have been dispelled quickly, for Cage was among those named as 'worthy' patriots in the 1710–11 session for helping detect the mismanagements of the previous administration. He was granted a leave of ten days on 29 Mar. 1711. An October Club member, he voted on 18 June 1713 for the French commerce bill. Returned again in 1713, he was classed as a Tory on the Worsley list. His only nomination to a drafting committee occurred on 9 Mar. 1714, to the bill curbing wool smuggling. The death of Queen Anne and the subsequent reversal in Tory fortunes saw Cage decline to contest the 1715 election. Hence he began a long retirement from politics which only ended with his death on 21 Jan. 1738. His will left the family estates in Kent and Hampshire to his grandson, Lewis, while most of those properties purchased in his lifetime went to his son John.[5]

[1] IGI, Kent (gives 28 Mar. 1665 and 1666); Berry, *Kent Gens*. 273. [2] Info. from Medway Area Archs. [3] PCC 47 Hale; info. from Prof. N. Landau; *HMC Downshire*, i. 626; *CSP Dom*. 1700–2, p. 251. [4] *CSP Dom*. 1700–2, pp. 454–5; [*H*]*ail the Enemies of the King . . . that appear on the Behalf of Colonel Cage*; Add. 61458, f. 159. [5] Add. 5443, f. 202; PCC 31 Brodrepp.

S. N. H.

CALTHORPE, Reynolds I (1655–1720), of Elvetham, Hants.

HINDON 1698–13 May 1701
 1701 (Dec.)–1702
 1705–1708
 12 Feb. 1709–1710
 1715–12 Apr. 1720

b. 12 Aug. 1655, 3rd s. of Sir James Calthorpe of Ampton, Suff. by Dorothy, da. of Sir James Reynolds of Castle Camps, Cambs. *educ.* Bury St. Edmunds g.s.; Caius, Camb. 1673; M. Temple 1675. *m.* (1) 11 Apr. 1681, his cos. Priscilla (*d.* 1709), da. and h. of Sir Robert Reynolds† of Elvetham, wid. of Sir Richard Knight of Chawton, Hants, 1s. *d.v.p.*; (2) lic. 11 June 1715, Barbara (*d.* 1724), da. of Henry Yelverton, 1st Visct. de Longueville and 15th Ld. Grey of Ruthin, sis. of Talbot, 1st Earl of Sussex, 1s. 1da.[1]

On both sides Calthorpe's family had strong associations with the Parliamentarian cause: his father's knighthood had been conferred by Oliver Cromwell†; his father-in-law had been the Commonwealth's solicitor-general; and another maternal uncle, Sir John Reynolds†, had been a prominent Roundhead soldier and at one stage commissary-general in Ireland. Little has been discovered of Calthorpe's early life, though some connexion with the world of commerce may perhaps be inferred from his participation in loans to the government in the early 1690s to the tune of £7,500, and his subscription to the tontine in 1693. His first parliamentary candidature was in 1697 at a by-election for Hindon, where his wife's family had an interest. He was defeated on that occasion but succeeded in the general election the following year, when, probably standing as a Whig, he made a cross-party alliance with the man who had 'set up' his opponent in 1697, Sir James Howe, 2nd Bt.*, to throw off the challenge of two other Tories. Like his colleague, however, Calthorpe seems to have followed a Country tack, being forecast as likely to support the disbanding bill. In early 1700 an analysis of the House listed him as being in the Old East India Company interest, though no other connexion with the Company is known. Having held his seat at the first election of 1701 he was removed in May on a Tory petition, but when chosen again in November was classed with the Tories in Robert Harley's* list, and supported the motion of 26 Feb. 1702 vindicating the proceedings of the Commons in the impeachments of the Whig ministers.[2]

Calthorpe did not put up in 1702, giving his interest instead to his friend Thomas Jervoise*. In the 1705 election he persuaded Jervoise to contest Hampshire, where Calthorpe had also promised his backing to George Pitt*, and was himself returned at Hindon. This time he was listed as 'Low Church' in an analysis of the new Parliament, and he voted for the Court candidate in the division on the Speaker. For whatever reason, he was suddenly a more active Member in this Parliament, He was also no longer a Country Whig, supporting the Court on 18 Feb. 1706 in the proceedings on the 'place clause'. He was listed as a Whig in early 1708, and in the general election that year he stood at Hindon with Howe and another Tory, Edmund Lambert. Pushed into third place, he petitioned against both sitting Members, and was seated in place of Howe. A teller on 6 Apr. 1709 against a further duty on woollen yarn, he supported the naturalization of the Palatines in 1709 and voted for the impeachment of Dr Sacheverell in 1710. He was certainly present in the House in January 1710, when he warned Jervoise of a forthcoming call, and was chosen again as a Whig in the following October, being classified as a Whig in the 'Hanover list'. However, this election was the subject of a double return, and the Tory majority in the new House found against him. His elder son was the family representative at the 1713 election but died during the session so that Calthorpe was obliged to stand himself in 1715. Calthorpe died on 12 Apr. 1720.[3]

[1] *Gent. Mag.* 1832, i. 310. [2] *CJ*, x. 724; P. G. M. Dickson, *Financial Revol.* 305–6. [3] Hants RO, Jervoise mss, Calthorpe to Jervoise, 31 May 1702, 20 Jan. 1704, 10 Jan. 1710.

D. W. H.

CALTHORPE, Reynolds II (1689–1714), of Elvetham, Hants.

HINDON 1713–10 Apr. 1714

b. 6 Nov. 1689, 1st s. of Reynolds Calthorpe I*, being o. s. by his 1st w. *educ.* ?Bury St. Edmunds g.s. *unm.*[1]

Calthorpe took over his father's seat in the 1713 Parliament, surviving a contest and a petition. Welcomed by the *Flying Post* as a 'good patriot', he voted on 18 Mar. 1714 against the expulsion of Richard Steele and was classed as a Whig in the Worsley list and two other lists of the 1713 and 1715 Parliaments, but his parliamentary career was tragically brief. He died, *v.p.*, of smallpox on 10 Apr. 1714, and was buried at Elvetham.[2]

[1] *Gent. Mag.* 1832, p. 110; *Bury St. Edmunds G. S. List* (Suff. Green Bks. xiii), 58. [2] *Flying Post*, 10–13 Sept. 1713; Boyer, *Pol. State*, vii. 411; Le Neve, *Mon. Angl.* 1700–15, pp. 282–3.

D. W. H.

CALVERT, Hon. Benedict Leonard (1679–1715), of Woodcote Park, Epsom, Surr.

HARWICH   29 June 1714–1715

b. 21 Mar. 1679, 2nd but 1st surv. s. of Charles Calvert, 3rd Baron Baltimore [I], by Jane, da. of Vincent Lowe of Denby, Derbys., wid. of Henry Sewall, of Mattapary, Maryland. *educ.* G. Inn 1690; travelled abroad (France). *m.* 2 Jan. 1699, Lady Charlotte Lee (separated 1705), da. of Edward Henry, 1st Earl of Lichfield, 4s. 2da.; 2 illegit. ch. by one Groves. *suc.* fa. as 4th Baron Baltimore [I] 26 Feb. 1715.[1]

Gov. Maryland 1684–9; ranger, Woodstock park 1699–1705.[2]

Freeman, Harwich 1714.[3]

The Calverts, barons Baltimore, a Roman Catholic family, were founders and hereditary proprietors of Maryland, where they resided in St. Mary's county. The Member himself was made governor of Maryland at the age of five, a customary appointment for the eldest son of the proprietor. A deputy having then been appointed, Calvert returned to England with his father the following year. However, Lord Baltimore lost his rights in Maryland at the Revolution, and with them went the governorship. As a cavalry officer in Lord Salisbury's regiment Baltimore was outlawed by the new regime, even though he had not been in arms for James II. But afterwards he succeeded in having the outlawry reversed.[4]

Calvert's name was entered at Gray's Inn in 1690, but as a Catholic he probably did not attend. Instead, he spent some years at St. Germain. He secured on 26 Jan. 1698 a licence to return from France, under the Act of 1697. The following year he married a daughter of Lord Lichfield, on which occasion his father settled £1,000 a year on him, and Lord Lichfield gave him the rangership of his own park at Woodstock. Lichfield was displeased, however, when Lady Charlotte turned 'papist' in October 1699 after the birth of her first son, despite his 'utmost care to have her well grounded in the Protestant religion'. The couple separated in 1705, in which year Calvert received an unexpected windfall when the Duke of Marlborough (John Churchill†), who had been granted Woodstock by Queen Anne, had the rangership purchased for him for £6,450 by the Treasury. Calvert's father, who still received rents from the planters in Maryland, though with a diminished income as his house there had been plundered and his accounts and papers destroyed, was still allowing him £600 a year and paying for the education of his six children in Catholic schools abroad. In February 1711 Calvert sought a divorce from his wife in the Lords on the grounds of her 'open adultery', having obtained 'a sentence of divorce in the Arches Court of Canterbury without any proof of recrimination'. However, the bill did not succeed.[5]

In the autumn of 1713 Calvert began to ingratiate himself with Lord Oxford (Robert Harley*), sending him presents of venison, pheasants and partridges, reminding him that his family had had an income of 2s. per hodd of tobacco exported from Maryland until the Revolution, and informing him of his 'inclinations . . . to embrace the Protestant religion, which I have become hitherto deterred from by the apprehensions that my father would withdraw my subsistence'. Despite the efforts of his father, Calvert was received into the Church of England by the bishop of Hereford at the end of the year, which finally provoked Calvert's father into severing his allowance. Calvert stood at a contested by-election at Harwich in 1714, on the recommendation of its recorder, Lord Bolingbroke (Henry St. John II*). Despite being defeated, Calvert was seated on petition on 29 June, though Hanoverian Tories and some Country Tories would not vote for him. He was not included in any division lists for this Parliament, and was an inactive Member. He had placed his children in Protestant schools in the charge of Protestant tutors, under the care and advice of Oxford, and had obtained a pension of £300 a year from the Queen, as well as the appointment of Captain John Hart as governor of Maryland, who was to pay him a further £500 a year out of the profits of the office. He had also received an estimated £1,500 in arrears of customs duties from Maryland. On the Hanoverian succession he obtained the continuation of his pension from George I, and after his father's death in February 1715 he petitioned for the restoration of his rights as proprietor of Maryland, but did not live to enjoy them as he died on 16 Apr. 1715. His son, the 5th Lord, sat for St. Germans and for Surrey under George II. His grandson, the 6th and last baron, pursued a career of profligacy and extravagance, being tried for rape at Kingston, selling what remained of the English estates to a Soho upholsterer and dying in Naples in 1771.[6]

[1] Manning and Bray, *Surr.* i. 613; Boyer, *Anne Annals*, viii. 394. [2] *Biog. Dict. of Maryland Legislature*, i. 187; ii. 724; *Cal. Treas. Pprs.* 1702–7, pp. 318–19; *Cal. Treas. Bks.* xix. 511. [3] Harwich bor. recs. 98/5, f. 138. [4] C. C. Hall, *The Lords Baltimore and the Maryland Palatinate*, 118; *Cal. Treas. Bks.* xiv. 25; Luttrell, *Brief Relation*, ii. 140, 249; *CSP Dom.* 1689–90, pp. 522–3; 1690–1, p. 376; 1691–2, p. 111. [5] *HMC Buccleuch*, ii. 91; *HMC Lords*, n.s. ix. 98; *Cal. Treas. Pprs.* 1702–7, pp. 318–19; *Verney Letters*, i. 41; *Cal. Treas. Bks.* xix. 511; *CSP Col.* 1706–8, pp. 676–7; *Archives of Maryland*, xxv. 271. [6] Add. 70215, Ld. Baltimore to Calvert, 7 Aug., 14 Oct. 1713, Calvert to Oxford, 17 Sept., 20 Oct., 30 Dec. 1713, 6, 11 Jan., 19 Feb., 5 Mar. 1714; *Top. and Gen.* iii. 508; *HMC Portland*, v. 378; D. Szechi, *Jacobitism and Tory Pol.* 154, 159; *Archives of Maryland*, 271–2; *Cal.*

Treas. Bks. xxviii. 117, 187; Biog. Dict. of Maryland Legislature, 187.

E. C.

CALVERT, Felix (1664–1736), of Albury, Herts. and White Cross Street, St. Giles without Cripplegate, London.

READING   1713–30 May 1716

bap. 9 May 1664, 2nd s. of Thomas Calvert of St. Giles without Cripplegate by Anne, da. of William Ambrose of Reading, Berks. m. lic. 28 May 1689, Mary, da. of Sir Francis Winnington*, sis. of Salwey* and Edward Winnington*, 10s. (4 d.v.p.) 6da. (3 d.v.p.). suc. bro. bef.1672.[1]

Freeman, Hertford 1698; sheriff, Berks. 1707–8.[2]

Calvert was a member of a large family of London brewers that dominated the trade in the capital. The dynasty began with Calvert's grandfather, also Felix, whose three sons Felix jnr. (d. 1699), Thomas (d. 1668) and Peter (d. 1676) were concerned in brewing and in farming the excise during the Protectorate and Restoration, an association which only ended with Felix jnr.'s dismissal as an excise commissioner in February 1688. Calvert's father may have been a Dissenter, including in his will a Calvinist preamble which spoke of inheriting 'among the elect the joys . . . of eternal life'. Calvert himself seems to have taken over his father's interest in the Peacock brewery in White Cross Street, which in turn provided the centre of operations for his sons and grandsons. He should not be confused with his uncle Felix whose brewing activities centred on Thames Street and who was involved in various fire insurance ventures, or with his cousin, Felix (son of his uncle Peter), another brewer. During the 1690s Calvert lived near his brewery, as is attested by the annual record of his children's baptisms in the parish register. But around 1700 he purchased from Sir Thomas Brograve, 3rd Bt., the manor of Albury in Hertfordshire (previously half-owned by his uncle Felix) where he may have resided for part of the year, as in 1713 one of his children was baptized there. His Berkshire interests centred on property in Reading, presumably inherited from his mother and the manor of Marcham near Abingdon, which he purchased in 1691. Judicious cultivation of the Reading electors led to his return at the general election of 1713.[3]

Calvert was a Tory, being described as such on both the Worsley list and on an analysis of Members of the 1713 Parliament re-elected in 1715. His only contribution of note to the business of the Commons was to manage the Reading Turnpike Act through all its stages in the Commons. Although he was returned in 1715, his election was declared void, and he lost the subsequent by-election. In 1720 he made another, unsuccessful, attempt to regain his seat at Reading. According to Abel Boyer he died on 29 Dec. 1736 at his house in White Cross Street, leaving the bulk of his property to his eldest son, yet another Felix, plus substantial sums to his sons Peter and John (all of whom were subsequently partners in the brewery), and annuities to three younger sons. His grandson, John Calvert, sat for various boroughs between 1754 and 1802.[4]

[1] IGI, Berks.; VCH Herts. Fams. 55–56, 65. [2] Herts. RO, Hertford bor. recs. 25/100. [3] P. Mathias, Brewing Industry in Eng. 23, 313; VCH Herts. Fams. 55–77; C. D. Chandaman, Eng. Public Revenue, 60, 63, 73, 123; Cal. Treas. Bks. viii. 10, 1929; PCC 123 Hone; F. B. Relton, Acct. of Fire Insurance Cos. 27; IGI, London, Herts.; Clutterbuck, Herts. iii. 335; VCH Berks. iv. 356; Hearne Colls. iv. 313. [4] Boyer, Pol. State, liii. 103; PCC 2 Wake.

S. N. H.

CAMPBELL, Daniel (c.1672–1753), of Saltmarket, Glasgow; Shawfield, Lanark; and Ardentinny, Argyll.

SCOTLAND   1707–1708
GLASGOW BURGHS   24 Feb. 1716–1727
28 Mar. 1728–1734

b. c.1672, 3rd s. of Walter Campbell, 'captain of Skipness', Argyll, and bro. of John Campbell†. m. (1) 1695, Margaret, da. of John Leckie, merchant, of Newlands, Renfrew and Glasgow, Lanark, 3s. (1 d.v.p.) 3da.; (2) 4 Apr. 1714, Catherine (d. aft. 1722), da. of Henry Erskine, 3rd Ld. Cardross [S], wid. of Sir William Denholm, 1st Bt., MP [S], of Westshields, Lanark, 1da.[1]

Burgess, Glasgow 1694, ?Dumbarton 1703, Edinburgh 1706.[2]

Collector of customs, Port Glasgow 1701–7; commr. union with England 1706, Equivalent [S] 1707–9.[3]

MP [S] Inveraray 1702–7.

Campbell, a grandson of Walter Campbell, the heroic 'captain of Skipness' who fought and died for the Covenant against Montrose, was apprenticed to Robert Campbell, a noted Glasgow merchant, and made a modest fortune in transatlantic commerce. Having sailed to Boston in 1692 as part-owner of a cargo, he spent two years in America, trading with the colonies and in the West Indies, before returning to Glasgow, where he married into another important merchant family and resumed his business career, often in partnership with his brother Matthew, trading to the Baltic and even to Spain. Seeking to diversify his investments, he began to advance money to needy lairds, including his clan chief the 1st Duke of Argyll, with whose family he was henceforth to be closely associated in the capacity of a private banker and man of business. He was responsible for organizing and paying for the funeral of the 1st Duke in 1703. Foreclosing on loans drew him into the acquisition of landed property on his own account, culminating in the purchase in 1706 of the estate of Shawfield, just outside Glasgow, where he began to construct an imposing house.[4]

Argyll's influence must have played some part in Campbell's entrance in 1701 into the farm of the Scottish customs, as collector at Port Glasgow, a post that offered interesting possibilities to an unscrupulous merchant. And it was certainly by virtue of Argyll's nomination that in the 1702 election he was returned as commissioner for Inveraray. In the Scottish parliament he slavishly followed the 1st and 2nd dukes, with one possible exception, in September 1703, when he joined the larger burghs' protest against the act continuing the prohibition on the export of English and Irish wool. He represented the Argathelian interest on the union commission, and in the 1706–7 parliamentary session voted completely in accordance with the Court line, earning not only selection as a Scottish representative to the first Parliament of Great Britain, but inclusion in the Equivalent commission. This appointment may have been in part a recompense for his having forfeited his place in the customs in anticipation of administrative reconstruction after the Union. The presence of two other Campbells in the Commons makes it impossible to be certain of his appearances in the Journals.[5]

At the end of the Parliament no less than at its beginning, Campbell placed his reliance on the 2nd Duke of Argyll, and Argyll's brother Lord Ilay. It was to their influence that he resorted in March and April 1708 in an attempt to secure the appointment of two of his nominees to tidewaiters' places at Port Glasgow, in the face of resistance from the commissioners of the Scottish customs. But after the misfiring of his attempt on the Glasgow Burghs district in the general election of 1708 he found that he needed other patronage as well. There had been two returns. Campbell, in his capacity as commissioner for Rutherglen, had returned himself, supported by the commissioner for Renfrew. On the other side the presiding commissioner, Provost Robert Rodger of Glasgow, had returned himself, supported by the commissioner for Dumbarton. Campbell appealed to Anne, Duchess of Hamilton, as possessor of the hereditary sheriffdom of Lanarkshire, to ensure that he was 'first returned', promising to support her son Lord Archibald Hamilton* in the county election. But, although he made an 'appearance' for Lord Archibald at the Lanarkshire electoral court, it was Rodger who was returned for the burghs and Campbell who was obliged to petition. Shortage of time, and perhaps also the influence wielded on Rodger's behalf by the Duke of Montrose, prevented a hearing in either of the two sessions of this Parliament, and Campbell's own high-handedness ruined any possibility of a compromise at local level. The disappointment was compounded in 1709 when Campbell found himself omitted from the renewed commission on the Equivalent, and a year later, when a recommendation from Hon. Sir David Dalrymple, 1st Bt.*, failed to secure for him a place on the new Scottish customs board, Treasury appreciation of his experience in collection having doubtless been offset by remembrance of the difficulties he had caused the commissioners in 1708 over the tidewaiters' appointments.[6]

Campbell was deterred from standing at the 1710 election, but put up for Lanarkshire in 1713, with support from Glasgow corporation and especially from the Presbyterian ministers 'who pretend to govern the gentlemen of the shire'. Unfortunately for him, the Hamilton interest and the 'loyal gentlemen' proved the stronger, and he was defeated by Sir James Hamilton, 2nd Bt.* His desire to return to Westminster had probably been sharpened by the Treasury's renewed pursuit of the accounts of the customs farmers, still not delivered seven years after the Union, and by the more serious threat that the accounts commissioners would expose Campbell's own corrupt dealings in the Glasgow collectorship. In the event, he and the other farmers reached a composition with the Treasury in 1714, and the accounts commissioners' report, delivered to the Commons in April of that year, did no more than retail the evidence given of Campbell having abused his position to bring in brandy for himself duty-free, without stating an opinion of its reliability or making any recommendation.[7]

In 1715 Campbell stood again in the Glasgow Burghs district, this time against the express wishes of Argyll, who would have preferred Thomas Smith II* not to have been challenged. With only one of the four commissioners on his side, Campbell probably did not pursue the contest as far as the main election. He also made a desperate bid in Lanarkshire, where he combined with, of all people, the Jacobite George Lockhart* of Carnwath, in an effort to unseat a Whig, James Lockhart† of Lee. Here again he seems to have made a tactical retreat before the court met. Smith's death in 1716, however, furnished him at last with a better opportunity. The open endorsement of Argyll, corresponding inaction on the part of Montrose, and his own skilful canvassing in Glasgow corporation, were enough to give him the burghs seat at the ensuing by-election, almost by default. He returned to the Commons as a member of the Argyll connexion but one whose wealth made him increasingly independent. Campbell died on 8 June 1753, being succeeded by his grandson and namesake, who represented Lanarkshire 1760–8.[8]

[1] Mitchell Lib. Glasgow, Campbell of Shawfield mss (mic. in NLS, ms 15525); *Scot. Rec. Soc.* vii. 74; xxxv. 87; Wodrow, *Analecta*, iv. 171. [2] *Scot. Rec. Soc.* lvi. 232; lxii. 31; NLS, ms 15525. [3] *CSP Dom.* 1703–4, p. 409; *Cal. Treas. Pprs.* 1708–14, p. 22; *Cal. Treas. Bks.* xxii. 79; xxiii. 234. [4] C. Rogers, *Monuments and MIs in Scotland*, ii. 8; NLS, ms 15525; *Scot. Rec. Soc.* lvi. 232; *Extracts Glasgow Burgh Recs.* iv. 330, 484–5; B. Lenman, *Jacobite Risings in Britain*, 207–8. [5] Info. from Dr P. W. J. Riley on members of Scot. parl.; *APS*, xi. 101; P. W. J. Riley, *Union*, 331. [6] SRO, Mar and Kellie mss GD124/831/9, Sir David Nairne to Mar, 1 June 1708; *Cal. Treas. Pprs.* 1708–14, pp. 26–27, 41; *Edinburgh Courant*, 26–28 May 1708; SRO, Hamilton mss GD406/1/5492, 7866, [–] to dowager Duchess of Hamilton, 27 May 1708, Duke of Hamilton to same, 23 June 1708; Add. 61628, ff. 144–5; 61632, f. 70; SRO, Montrose mss GD220/5/219, John Grahame to Duke of Montrose, 22 Dec. 1709; GD220/5/805/2, Mungo Graham* to [same], 4 Aug. 1709; SRO, Stair mss GD135/140, f. 3. [7] *Scots Courant*, 2–5 Oct. 1713; NLS, Advocates' mss, Wodrow pprs. letters Quarto 5, f. 189; *Cal. Treas. Bks.* xxviii. 92; *HMC Portland*, x. 168; *HMC Lords*, n.s. vii. 575; Boyer, *Pol. State*, vii. 374–6. [8] R. M. Sunter, *Patronage and Pol. in Scotland*, 199–209; SRO, Kennedy of Dalquharran mss GD27/3/24/5, Mungo Graham* to Cornelius Kennedy, 1 Mar. 1715; Wodrow, *Analecta*, 68; J. S. Shaw, *Management of Scot. Soc.* 92–93; Lenman, 208–9.

D. W. H.

CAMPBELL, Sir James, 5th Bt. (c.1679–1756), of Auchinbreck, Argyll.

SCOTLAND 1707–1708

b. c.1679, 1st s. of Sir Duncan Campbell, MP [S], 4th Bt., of Auchinbreck by Lady Henrietta, da. of Alexander Crawford, 1st Earl of Balcarres [S] (whose wid. married Archibald Campbell, 9th Earl of Argyll [S]). *educ.* Glasgow Univ. 1695. *m.* (1) by 1696 (with 20,000 merks), Janet, da. of John (Ian Breac) Macleod of Dunvegan Castle, Skye, Inverness, 16th chief of clan Macleod, MP [S], 2s. (1 *d.v.p.*) 1da.; (2) c.1718, his 'cousin' Susanna, da. of Sir Alexander Campbell of Cawdor (Calder), Nairn, MP [S], 4s. 4da.; (3) Margaret, da. of Donald Campbell of Carradale or Glencarradale, Argyll, 2s. 2da. *suc.* fa. as 5th Bt. bef. 28 Nov. 1700.[1]

Commr. justiciary for Highlands [S] 1701, 1702; capt. 25 Ft. 1707–11.

MP [S] Argyllshire 1703–7.

Burgess, Edinburgh 1704, Inveraray 1716.[2]

The lairds of Auchinbreck, once among the most 'considerable branches' of clan Campbell, had been brought low by a combination of their own indiscretions and what they came to consider the base ingratitude of successive earls and dukes of Argyll, who allegedly rewarded exemplary loyalty with careless exploitation. During the civil wars the 2nd baronet commanded the Marquess (and 8th Earl) of Argyll's regiment in Ireland and in Scotland, dying at Inverlochy in 1645. His son, who had also been in arms for the Covenant, received compensation for losses in Montrose's rebellion of 1649, but at the Restoration was obliged

> to pay near £3,000 sterling on his entry into his estate, though he was forced to sell part to pay £8,000 sterling of the Marquess his debts for which he had been engaged with him, without any relief from the [9th] Earl, he not being obliged to it in law, being restored by the King's donative.

The next baronet, the Member's father, 'being young and giddy', was 'the only considerable man of the family who joined' the 9th Earl of Argyll in 1685. During the rising his castle at Carnassary in west Argyll was burnt by his local enemies the Macleans, and he suffered forfeiture as a rebel, though obtaining a remission in 1687 and eventual rescindment of the sentence in 1690 after he had taken an active part in the Revolution. The Argylls' enemies claimed that otherwise Auchinbreck snr. was 'ill rewarded' for these strenuous efforts: although he was given a captaincy in Argyll's regiment in 1689, and the following year participated in the commission appointed to carry out the functions of the lord clerk register, he was denied his real ambition of a peerage. The scraps of patronage that came his way did nothing to rescue his shaky finances, and he was only able to settle a debt of £40,000 Scots to a Campbell kinsman in the early 1690s by pressing a claim to the estates of the Macleods of Dunvegan, which he promptly sold off to his creditor. Relations with Argyll had broken down as early as August 1689, and there is no indication that they were subsequently repaired. Steadily declining health eventually induced Sir Duncan Campbell to demit his commission to the Scottish estates in 1700, and on a petition from various freeholders, supported by the evidence of the local minister and apothecary, the seat was declared vacant. It would seem that Sir Duncan's troubles were as much mental as physiological, for there was also testimony that he had publicly declared himself a papist, a curious twist to a long career of apparent devotion to the Presbyterian interest, and sufficient proof for some that he had gone mad. Conversion would certainly have been at odds with his subscription to the association only two years before, and his son's subsequent appearance as a Presbyterian elder in 1705.[3]

The 5th baronet himself seems to have repaired relations sufficiently to have begun his parliamentary career in 1703 in the retinue of the house of Argyll: in that year he joined the 1st Duke in protesting against the passage of the Scottish act of security; in 1704 he toed the Court line, as Argathelians were obliged to do, in opposing Hamilton's motion to postpone settlement of the succession; and a year later he was one of a covey of Campbells and other dependants who were admitted as burgesses of Edinburgh in the train of the 2nd Duke. In the Union parliament he again followed the Court voting pattern, supporting the treaty in the critical divisions on the 1st article and on ratification, and indeed consistently throughout the debates, with one important exception: the division on shire and burgh representation. This show of independence provoked Argyll's wrath. 'As to the Duke of Argyll's present business', reported Auchinbreck to the Earl of Breadalbane in February 1707,

> I know nothing but that he is much disobliged at Ardkinglass [James Campbell*] and my voting for the barons. He sent a message to us both that if we did not come to the house and vote against the barons and vote with himself [he] would never see our faces, and accordingly I have not seen his grace.

A truce of some kind must have been patched up to enable Auchinbreck to obtain a place in the Court contingent returned to the first Parliament of Great Britain. At some point in 1708 he was also granted a captaincy of foot, presumably at Argyll's recommendation.[4]

One of the Scottish Members welcomed to Westminster with appointment on 10 Nov. 1707 to the committee on the Address, Campbell proved surprisingly active in what was to be his only parliamentary session. He took charge of two bills, the earlier and more important to repeal the Scottish act of security, a measure he proposed on 4 Dec. and presented on the 9th. He told on 12 Dec. against a Squadrone motion to commit the bill to the whole House, and shepherded it through its remaining stages in the Commons. He was involved in various schemes of electoral reform, being nominated on 22 Dec. 1707 to the drafting committee for the bill to prevent corruption in parliamentary elections. Otherwise his more significant appearances in the Journals tended to be concerned with specifically Scottish business: drafting committees on the bill to regulate the linen manufacture (21 Jan. 1708), the salmon fishery (2 Feb.) and to direct payment of the Equivalent (23 Feb.). His opposition to the bill to complete the Union (which provided for the abolition of the Scottish privy council and of the heritable jurisdictions) at first incurred yet another rupture with Argyll, who had misguidedly declared himself in favour, but by the time of the division of 23 Jan., in which Campbell told for agreeing with a committee amendment, Argyll had come to realize that the attack on the jurisdictions was an ill-concealed plot against himself. Campbell's subsequent adoption of responsibility for the East Tarbert harbour bill, which he managed through the House, would seem to indicate that he was back in the Duke's good graces.[5]

Campbell's presence at the Argyllshire election of 1708, when he served as *praeses* for the unopposed election of James Campbell of Ardkinglass, marks the last point at which he can be said to have co-operated with the Argathelian interest. He did not attend the two subsequent elections, and at one or the other was even rumoured to be planning to stand against Ardkinglass, Argyll's brother Lord Ilay commenting that Auchinbreck 'is playing the devil and all against us'. At about this time it was reported that Auchinbreck had suffered 'great hardships' at Argyll's hands, in particular being passed over for a colonelcy in favour of John Middleton II*.[6]

The estrangement proved irrevocable. Auchinbreck reaped no benefit from the return to power of Argyll after the Hanoverian succession, and although he did not participate in the Fifteen, he was in contact with the Pretender within two years, expressing 'warm intentions' and even agreeing to attempt some liaison with Argyll. His new-found Jacobite loyalty drew him further on to ruin. By 1740 he was described by the Murray of Broughton as a man 'of desperate fortune and little interest'. So 'low' was his 'situation' that, although an old man, he determined to go to Jamaica to repair his finances when his house was destroyed by fire and he and his family thus 'reduced to the utmost straits'. Then the Jacobite 'association', into which he was drawn by his son-in-law Cameron of Lochiel, offered a renewed opportunity to solicit a subvention from the Pretender. Promised a pension of £300 in return for his so-called 'influence' in the western Highlands, he was a constant correspondent of the Jacobites until 1745, when, considering himself too old to fight, he was arrested and imprisoned. After the suppression of the rising, he found himself specifically excluded from the indemnity, and condemned to exist thereafter on the sparse remittances of Jacobite agents. He died at Lochgair in Argyll on 14 Oct. 1756, aged 77.[7]

[1] *Hist. Scot. Parl.* 92; *Recs. Glasgow Univ.* (Maitland Club, lxxii), iii. 157, 204; *SRO Indexes*, iii. 155; ix. 220–1, 275; R. C. Macleod, *Macleods of Dunvegan*, 168; *HMC Stuart*, v. 521; *APS*, xi. 147; *Services of Heirs* (ser. 1), i. 1710–19, pp. 4–5. [2] *CSP Dom.* 1702–3, p.

354; *Scot. Rec. Soc.* lxii. 31; n.s. xiv. 15. ³*Hist. Scot. Parl.* 91–92; *APS*, vi(2), 275, 499, 713; ix. 9, 20, 28, 166; ix. app. 10, 17, 53, 68; x. 209; Harley mss at Brampton Bryan, 'The Present State of the Family of Campbell', [?c.1713]; Lauder of Fountainhall, *Hist. Notices* (Bannatyne Club, lxxxvii), 642, 683, 692; *Reg. PC Scotland*, 1686–9, pp. 382, 402; 1690, p. 61; *HMC Stuart*, iv. 44, 46–48; *HMC Mar and Kellie*, i. 320; *Leven and Melville Pprs.* (Bannatyne Club, lxxvii), 252, 323; *Bk. of Dunvegan* (3rd Spalding Club), i. 97–98; *Crossrigg Diary*, 14; *Acts of Gen. Assembly of Church of Scotland*, 388. ⁴*Lockhart Mems.* ed. Szechi, 78; Boyer, *Anne Annals*, iii. app. 43; P. Dickson, *Red John of the Battles*, 64; info. from Dr P. W. J. Riley on members of Scot. parl.; P. W. J. Riley, *Union*, 331; SRO, Breadalbane mss GD112/39/204/ 8–9, Campbell to [Breadalbane], 10, 14 Feb. 1707. ⁵*HMC Mar and Kellie*, 424; SRO, GD112/39/210/13, Hon. John Campbell* to [Breadalbane], 1707; GD112/39/211/27, same to [same], 27 Jan. 1708. ⁶SRO, Inveraray sheriff ct. recs. SC54/21/1, pp. 1–8, Argyll. electoral ct. mins. 1708–13; NRA [S], Rep. 631, p. 706; Harley mss, 'State of the family of Campbell'. ⁷*HMC Stuart*, iv. 187; v. 520–1, 529; vi. 385; vii. 164–8; *Scot. Hist. Soc.* xxvii. 8–9, 22, 33–34, 137, 377–8, 441; (ser. 3), vii. 168; xiv. 94–95; *More Culloden Pprs.* ed. Warrand, v. 161–2; *Hist. Scot. Parl.* 92.

D. W. H.

CAMPBELL, James (c.1666–1752), of Ardkinglas, Argyll.

SCOTLAND	1707–1708
ARGYLLSHIRE	1708–1734
STIRLINGSHIRE	1734–1741

b. c.1666, 1st s. of Sir Colin Campbell, 1st Bt., MP [S], of Ardkinglas by Helen, da. of Patrick Maxwell, MP [S], of Newark, Renfrew. *m.* (1) by 1697, Margaret, da. and coh. of Adam Campbell (*d.*1704) of Gargunnock, Stirling, 1s. *d.v.p.* 8da. (at least 1 *d.v.p.*); (2) contract 23 Aug. 1731, Anne, da. of John Callendar of Craigforth, St. Ninian's, Stirling, wid. of Lt.-Col. John Blackadder, dep. gov. Stirling castle 1717–*d.*, *s.p. suc.* fa. as 2nd Bt. Apr. 1709.¹

Commr. justiciary for Highlands [S] 1701, 1702; lt. and brig. 4 Life Gds. (Scots Life Gds.) 1704, exempt and capt. Mar. 1708, guidon and maj. June 1708, cornet and maj. 1710, lt. and lt.-col. 1711–15; dep. gov. Stirling Castle 1715–17; muster master [S] 1734–?42.²

MP [S] Argyllshire 1703–7.
Burgess, Edinburgh 1704.³

The most faithful of Argyll's Campbell dependants in the Commons, Ardkinglas was returned unopposed for Argyllshire at each general election in this period. Earlier in the 17th century his family had given exemplary loyalty to their clan chief: Campbell's grandfather had served as colonel of a Highland regiment during the Civil Wars, and been excepted from the act of indemnity in 1662; his father, the first baronet, arrested in 1684 on suspicion of corresponding with the fugitive 9th Earl of Argyll, had suffered forfeiture and lengthy imprisonment upon admitting that he had sent Argyll money, and by the time of his eventual release, after the abortive rising of 1685, claimed to have exhausted his 'little fortune and estate'. At the Revolution Sir Colin Campbell was appointed sheriff depute of Argyllshire. Whether the crown met his claim for compensation for past sufferings is not known. Returned as a commissioner to the estates in 1693, he supported the Court, and the 1st Duke of Argyll, in the 1698 parliament and again in 1700–1. He also joined other courtiers in attendance at the 'rump' parliament of 1702.⁴

James Campbell succeeded his father as commissioner for Argyllshire at the general election of 1702 and was listed as a Court supporter. He appears to have performed his service in the Scottish estates as a moderately unquestioning follower of the 1st and 2nd dukes of Argyll, being present at a selective meeting of Court party men in 1702, and voting in 1704 against the Duke of Hamilton's motion on the succession. In return he received a commission in the Life Guards, and in 1705 he was admitted to his burgess-ship of Edinburgh in the 2nd Duke's retinue. In the Union parliament he generally followed the Court line, with few absences. His one vote against occurred on the question of shire and burgh representation, an act of self-assertion which drew down upon him the full wrath of his patron. As Sir James Campbell, 5th Bt.*, of Auchinbreck reported:

> The vote about writers [to the signet] being capable to be lords of session was the first thing disobliged [the] D[uke of] Argyll at Ardkinglas, and the barons' vote allowing no peer's son to represent them was what entirely disobliged him. He sent Ronald Campbell to Ardkinglas and me to inform us that if we did not vote with him against the barons we should never see him, and hitherto we have not.⁵

Reconciliation came swiftly, however: Campbell was included on the Court slate as one of the Scottish MPs in the first Parliament of Great Britain, where he was the only one of Argyll's dependants to remain obedient throughout the session, even supporting the bill to complete the Union (which abolished the Scottish privy council and the heritable jurisdictions) when other Campbells opposed it. He also received promotion in the army. Judging by the frequency with which he was mentioned in the Journals after he had succeeded his father in the baronetcy, it seems reasonable to suppose that he was more often than not the 'Mr Campbell' named in 1707–9. In his first session, local interest guaranteed his presence on the drafting committee on the East Tarbert harbour bill (18 Feb.). In 1710, now distinguishable by his baronet's title, he was named on 16 Feb. to the committee to prepare the bill to explain and enlarge the Act for better securing her Majesty's person and government. As would be expected of a leading Presbyterian elder, Campbell voted for the impeachment of Dr Sacheverell.[6]

Campbell's adherence to Argyll led him to be classified as a Court Tory in the list of the newly elected Scottish Members compiled in the autumn of 1710 by the Duchess of Buccleuch's episcopalian chaplain Richard Dongworth, but he was enough of a Whig to divide for the Squadrone Member Mungo Graham* in the division on 10 Feb. 1711 on the Kinross-shire election. He was markedly less active in this session, but was named on 14 Mar. to draft the bill to encourage the provision of naval stores in North Britain. In 1711–12 he may have been absent entirely: he was certainly in Scotland at the time of the critical division in February 1712 on the toleration bill. He was back at Westminster the following year, when he participated in manoeuvres by Scottish representatives in both Houses to promote the dissolution of the Union in the wake of the malt tax crisis. He told on two occasions in this session: on 7 May 1713 to adjourn the debate on the public accounts, and on 2 June in favour of putting the question to condemn the Royal African Company's trading monopoly. He voted on 4 June against giving a second reading to the French commerce bill, but was absent at the vote on engrossment on the 18th, possibly reflecting Argyll's ambiguous relationship with the ministry at this time and on this issue.[7]

By the time Parliament met again in 1714, Argyll and his brother Ilay had taken up a stance of unequivocal opposition to the Court, and Ardkinglas (who had been marked as a 'Hanoverian' in Lord Polwarth's analysis of Scottish returns) displayed strongly Whiggish colours. He voted on 18 Mar. 1714 against the expulsion of Richard Steele, and on 15 Apr. made a powerful speech in the debate on the succession, arguing that 'we cannot be out of danger while it is a test and a crime to say we are so', and describing the 'gentry of Scotland' as 'professed Jacobites'. He then voted on 12 May in favour of the motion of Robert Walpole II to extend the scope of the schism bill to include papists. Aside from the drafting committee on a bill to curb wool smuggling (9 Mar.), his significant parliamentary activity in this Parliament centred upon Scottish affairs. He was named to the committee charged on 28 May with drawing up a bill to explain the Linen Act and was a teller on 24 June against adding a clause to the bill discharging the Equivalent commissioners.[8]

Campbell may have been a signatory to the Edinburgh proclamation of George I, and was certainly one of the loyal Scottish Members 'expected in town' for the short parliamentary session in August 1714. He naturally appeared as a Whig on the Worsley list, having been returned once more on the Argathelian interest in 1715. Meanwhile he had transferred from the Life Guards to the deputy governorship of Stirling Castle, again presumably through his patron's influence. Although removed in the purge of Argyll's followers 1717, he remained a steady supporter of the Duke in the years that followed, and eventually secured his reward in 1734 with appointment to the office of muster master for Scotland.[9]

Campbell died at Gargunnock on 5 July 1752, aged 86. Lacking a surviving son, he left his estates to his grandson James Livingston, afterwards Sir James Campbell, who sat for Stirlingshire 1747–68.

[1] *Hist. Scot. Parl.* 90–91; *SRO Indexes*, iii. 731; ix. 248; *Services of Heirs* (ser. 1), i. 1700–9, p. 5; *Scot. Rec. Soc.* xxii. 17, 30; xxxv. 48; *HMC Stuart*, iv. 155; *Stirling Burgh Recs. 1667–1752*, 219, 224. [2] *CSP Dom.* 1702–3, p. 354. [3] *Scot. Rec. Soc.* lxii. 31. [4] NRA [S] Rep. 631, p. 706; *APS*, vi(1), 673; vi(2), 625; vii. 416; viii. app. p. 32; ix. app. p. 92; *Reg. PC Scotland*, 1684–5, pp. 27, 46, 97; 1685–6, pp. 33, 533, 558; 1689, p. 472; Lauder of Fountainhall, *Hist. Notices* (Bannatyne Club, lxxxvii), 553, 556; *HMC 12th Rep. VIII*, 13; P. W. J. Riley, *King Wm. and Scot. Politicians*, 170. [5] NLS, ms 14498, ff. 82–83; info. from Dr P. W. J. Riley on members of Scot. parl.; SRO, Clerk of Penicuik mss GD18/3124/119 (*ex inf.* Dr Riley); P. W. J. Riley, *Union*, 331; SRO, Breadalbane mss GD112/39/204/8–9, Campbell of Auchinbreck to [Breadalbane], 10, 14 Feb. 1707. [6] Breadalbane mss GD112/39/210/13, Hon. John Campbell* to [Breadalbane], n.d. [1707/8]; *Acts of Gen. Assembly of Church of Scotland*, 388. [7] *SHR*, lx. 63; SRO, Montrose mss GD220/5/808/18a-b, Graham to Montrose, 13 Feb. 1711; NLS, ms 1392, f. 80; Aberdeen Univ. Lib. Duff House (Montcoffer) mss 3175/2380, 'Resolution of the Commons to Call a Meeting of the Lords', May 1713; *Parlty. Hist.* i. 65, 69. [8] NLS, Advocates' mss, Wodrow pprs. letters Quarto 8, ff. 95–96; Douglas diary (Hist. of Parl. trans.), 15 Apr. 1714. [9] Boyer, *Pol. State*, viii. 125.

D. W. H.

CAMPBELL, Hon. James (aft. c.1660–?1713).

AYR BURGHS 1708–1710

b. aft. c.1660, 4th s. of Archibald Campbell, 9th Earl of Argyll [S] by his 1st w. Lady Mary, da. of James Stewart, 4th Earl of Moray [S]; bro. of Archibald Campbell, 1st Duke of Argyll [S] and Hon. John Campbell*. *educ.* Glasgow Univ. 1678. *m.* 10 Nov. 1690, Mary (annulled by Act of Parl. 20 Dec. 1690), da. and h. of Philip Wharton (*d.* 1685) of Edlington, Yorks.; (2) 1694, Margaret (*d.* 1755), da. of David Leslie, 1st Ld. Newark [S], 2s. 3da. (1 *d.v.p.*).[1]

Capt. of ft. Earl of Argyll's regt. 1689–bef. 1692; lt.-col. of ft. ?–c.1709.[2]

MP [S] Renfrew 1699–1702.

Dir. Bank of Scotland 1702.[3]

Burgess, Rothesay, Ayr, Edinburgh 1708.[4]

Preventive detention in Edinburgh Castle saved Campbell from the inevitable penalties which would have ensued had he been free to join his father's rising in 1685, but although he did not undergo the ordeal of forfeiture and restoration his economic circumstances were not much less straitened than those of most younger sons of Scottish peers. This may help to account for the desperation of his actions in 1690 when he made the mistake of practising the Highland custom of forced marriage on an English heiress (worth allegedly some £1,500 p.a.), whom he and two other Scottish army officers abducted from her carriage in Great Queen Street, Westminster. Within two days she had been restored to her family, by order of the lord chief justice, and a little over a month later the marriage was annulled by Act of Parliament. (She was later to marry Robert Byerley*.) Campbell himself escaped scot-free, even though one of his accomplices, Sir John Johnston, went to the scaffold. Campbell's subsequent marriage to the daughter of Lord Newark was socially advantageous but may not have been exceptionally profitable. His prospects were not furthered by the pall that descended upon relations with his brother, the 10th Earl (and later 1st Duke) of Argyll, when Campbell took the Countess's side in their bitter matrimonial disputes, although as one of her creditors Campbell derived some material benefit, in that she ensured rapid settlement of her debts. He evidently possessed some disposable capital, for he was able to subscribe £500 to the Darien venture in 1696, and in 1702 was a director of the Bank of Scotland. By 1699 he had patched up relations with Argyll in order to secure a seat in the Scottish parliament for Renfrew and he followed Argyll, and the Court, in the session of 1700–1 and again in 1702, when he joined the 'rump' of courtiers in attendance. He was not, however, returned at the subsequent general election.[5]

By the time Campbell resumed his parliamentary career, in 1708, he had obtained and given up again (or been about to give up) another army commission, almost certainly a colonelcy of foot, though the details remain elusive. In December 1710, long after he had sold out, he wrote to his nephew's wife, Margaret, Duchess of Argyll, to secure her assistance to recover his rank in a new commission, recalling her 'favour' in obtaining the original grant (though the responsibility may equally well have lain with her husband, the 2nd Duke, who as a boy had supposedly regarded Campbell as his favourite uncle, because of his loyalty to his mother). Campbell noted that 'I did a small piece of service at the time of the Union parliament, when I went with the detachments to the west', to quell the disturbances at Glasgow in 1706. But despite having himself disarmed the leader of the mob by running him through the shoulder, and having also been 'at a considerable charge at that time for intelligence which I was never considered [i.e. reimbursed] for', he had suffered the mortification of seeing 'Colonel George Douglas*, though he was under my command ... recommended by the Duke of Queensberry to her Majesty as having done good service upon that expedition, for which he got a col[onelcy] etc., and had 10s. a day added to his pay'. The poor return Campbell had received probably resulted from the relative weakness of his nephew's position at Court rather than any unwillingness on Argyll's part to serve him, for Campbell's successful candidature in the Ayr burghs district in the 1708 election owed much to Argyll's influence. For some unexplained reason (possibly connected with the earlier abduction episode), news of his return caused disquiet in royal circles. It was reported that the Queen 'is much surprised at the election of Colonel James Campbell. She thinks it puts her on a hard [?tack] and ... will make a cruel breach with somebody.' Once in the House, he does not seem to have been particularly prominent in parliamentary business, though it is in any case impossible to distinguish his appearances in the Journals from those of his various kinsmen. He was subsequently blacklisted for having supported Dr Sacheverell's impeachment, a vote which could be interpreted as a statement of loyalty to the Court, but which also probably represented a fundamental commitment to the 'Revolution interest': certainly Campbell's comments later in the year over the disciplinary action taken against Thomas Meredyth* and other Whig officers for anti-ministerial toast-drinking make it clear that, while deprecating any impiety or lèse-majesté on their part, he still regarded himself as a Whig. His financial preoccupations would certainly have been such as to draw him over to the administration, and in 1709 he had made a tentative approach to the ministry for some renewed military preferment. As he told the Duchess of Argyll the following year,

> my Lord Leven did last summer write to the secretary-at-war, Mr Walpole [Robert II*] to recommend me to the Duke of Marlborough [John Churchill†], that I might have a brigadier's commission of the same date with those of the last promotion, that thereby I might keep my rank in the army, in case I had the good fortune to get a post in the army again; and I see Mr Walpole's return to my Lord Leven, which was, that he had writ to the Duke of Marlborough in my favour, and some other officers who were neglected to be advanced at the last promotion of general officers, and that his grace promised to do us justice when he came to England, but a recommendation now by his Grace in my favour is not now to be expected.

In fact, neither Marlborough's influence, nor Argyll's after 1710, was sufficient to secure his reinstatement. At about the same time he had begun what were to prove tortuous negotiations with a namesake, James Campbell, for the purchase of the estate of Burnbank in Perthshire. Burnbank, a dissolute character, had already acquired a reputation for foul dealing in business matters, and it was thus no surprise that the affair became protracted and difficult, involving considerable legal costs before its eventual conclusion in January 1712. (Confusingly, the vendor retained his designation 'of Burnbank' throughout a spectacular moral decline thereafter which culminated in a sentence to transportation in 1720 for his part in the notorious murder of Mrs Nichol Muschet.) Meanwhile Campbell himself had relinquished his seat in Parliament at the 1710 election.[6]

According to an unpublished pedigree of the Fletchers of Saltoun, cited by the 19th-century Scots antiquary James Maidment, Campbell died in January 1713. This would not be absolutely incompatible with the evidence that a younger son and daughter were served as heirs to their portions of his estate as late as 1738, but the two facts are not easy to square. What is indisputable, however, is that Campbell's principal heir was his eldest son John.[7]

[1] *Scots Peerage* ed. Paul, i. 367–8; *Hist. Scot. Parl.* 92; *Recs. Glasgow Univ.* (Maitland Club, lxxii), iii. 134; E. R. Wharton, *Whartons of Wharton Hall*, 31; *LJ*, xiv. 600; *Scot. Hist. Soc.* xxxiv. 439. [2] *CSP Dom.* 1691–2, p. 175. [3] C. A. Malcolm, *Bank of Scotland*, 294. [4] Carnegie Lib. Ayr, Ayr burgh recs. B6/39/29, commn. 17 May 1708; B6/18/8, council mins. 27 May 1708; *Scot. Rec. Soc.* lxii. 31. [5] *Hist. Scot. Parl.* 92; Douglas, 367–8; Wharton, 31–32; *CSP Dom.* 1690–1, pp. 64–65; *A Brief Hist. of . . . the Unfortunate Sir John Johnston* (1690); *Argyle Pprs.* 43–57, 61–62; *Darien Pprs.* (Bannatyne Club, xc), 372; P. W. J. Riley, *King Wm. and Scot. Politicians*, 175. [6] *Argyle Pprs.* pp. xvii–xxii, xxv–xxxiii, 61–62, 160–5, 167, 171–5, 178, 180, 183, 198; Boyer, *Anne Annals*, v. 401; SRO, Mar and Kellie mss GD124/15/831/14, Sir David Nairne to Mar, 8 June 1708; SRO, Breadalbane mss GD112/39/254/7, James Campbell of Lawers to Breadalbane, 22 June 1711; *The Confession of Nichol Muschet of Boghal* (1818); *Elegy on the Mournful Banishment of James Campbell of Burnbank to the West Indies*, n.d. [7] *Argyle Pprs.* p. xviii; *Services of Heirs* (ser. 1), i. 1730–9, p. 6; 1740–9, p. 6.

D. W. H.

CAMPBELL, Hon. John (c.1660–1729), of Mamore, Dunbarton.

SCOTLAND   1707–1708
DUNBARTONSHIRE   1708–1722, 23 Jan. 1725–1727

b. c.1660, 2nd s. of Archibald Campbell, 9th Earl of Argyll [S]; bro. of Archibald, 1st Duke of Argyll [S] and Hon. James Campbell*. *educ.* Glasgow 1676. *m.* 1692 (with 18,000 merks), Elizabeth (*d.* 1758), da. of John, 8th Ld. Elphinstone [S], 7s. (3 *d.v.p.*) 6 da.[1]

?Capt. of ft. Earl of Argyll's regt. 1689–aft. 1690; commr. justiciary for Highlands [S] 1701, 1702; jt. master of King's works [S] 1705–Nov. 1714, sole Nov. 1714–17.[2]
MP [S] Argyllshire 1700–7.
Burgess, Edinburgh 1708, Ayr 1718.[3]

Except for one brief episode shortly after the Union, Campbell did not separate from the Argathelian interest no matter how far family loyalty was stretched. Having participated, albeit reluctantly, in his father's disastrous rising against James II, he suffered forfeiture and banishment after the commutation of his original capital conviction. Although restored at the Revolution, he remained in financial difficulties. 'Being a Scots younger brother', he explained to Lord Lauderdale, 'and forced to purchase lands even in several remote shires to undertake payment of one half to get the other allowed in payment of my patrimony from my brother Argyll, straitens me so much that unless I get in the debts that are owing me I must ruin.' He entered the Scottish parliament in 1700 as a Court supporter and attended the 'rump' parliament of 1702 alongside Argyll. The succession of his nephew to the dukedom made no appreciable difference to his attitude, even though he bore the brunt of a legal action brought by one Margaret Alison in pursuit of a debt owed by the deceased 1st Duke, suffering arrest and incarceration before he was bailed. In 1704 he followed his nephew in supporting the 'New Party' administration, and voted against the Duke of Hamilton's motion to postpone the settlement of the succession. He was granted a share in the office of master of the King's works in Scotland (at a salary of £200 Scots p.a.) on Argyll's formal entry into the ministry in 1705. It was probably just as well that he was unaware that in the preceding discussions Argyll had been willing to sacrifice his uncle's pretensions for an improvement in his own position.[4]

Campbell voted with the Court over the Union, with occasional absences, the most significant of which occurred over the issue of shire and burgh representation. He was regarded by the Court as safe enough to be chosen to the first Parliament of Great Britain, and may have been the 'Mr Campbell' whose arrival in Westminster was greeted with nomination on 10 Nov. 1707 to the committee on the Address. Apart from this, his appearances in the Journals in this session are impossible to distinguish from namesakes. He opposed the Squadrone campaign for the abolition of the Scottish privy council, a measure which Argyll had favoured until realizing that his own hereditary powers were threatened by a related scheme to unify the powers of j.p.s throughout Britain. Campbell reported to the Earl of Breadalbane on 27 Jan. 1708 that

> his Grace now finds [the] Squadrone intends to lay him low, for the bill about the council, justices of peace and circuit courts is passed our House, though we struggled all we could. This has calmed him, and after some reasonings he is to give me a scheme how he intends to have my son educated.[5]

In April 1708 Campbell made strong representations to the Scottish customs commissioners in favour of two Campbells removed from office in Port Glasgow, sending a 'blustering' letter in which among other things he claimed to be on very good terms personally with Lord Treasurer Godolphin (Sidney†). He encountered no difficulties at the general election, and was returned unanimously for Dunbartonshire. His subsequent attendance may have been impaired by ill-health, however. He voted for the impeachment of Dr Sacheverell, and when re-elected in 1710 was classed as a Whig by the Duchess of Buccleuch's chaplain, Richard Dongworth. He made no significant impact on the parliamentary record in this Parliament, and was noted as being absent in Scotland at the time of the division on the toleration bill in February 1712, and for both divisions on the French commerce bill (4 and 18 June 1713). Argyll's involvement with the ministry safeguarded his share of the mastership of the works, and in 1711, when the Duke was still in favour at Court, Campbell received a grant of £100 as royal bounty in response to a petition for arrears of salary. The money came at an opportune time, as he was anxiously engaged in the pursuit of his debts while at the same time being under threat of horning from his own creditors. Re-elected for Dunbartonshire in 1713, Campbell also served as *praeses* at the Argyllshire election. Predictably described by Lord Polwarth as a 'Hanoverian', he was up at Westminster in time to vote on 12 May 1714 in favour of extending the schism bill to cover Catholic education. Given his previous record of attendance, it seems more likely that his eldest son, John, newly returned for Buteshire, was the more active Member in this session. John snr. was subsequently classified as a Whig both in the Worsley list and in a list of the Members re-elected in 1715.[6]

Shortly after the Hanoverian succession Campbell was promoted to sole master of works, with his salary raised by half. During the Fifteen he took a leading part in local preparations to secure Dunbartonshire against the Jacobites. Upon going into opposition with Argyll in 1717 he lost his office, and though he was not compensated personally when Argyll returned to power in 1725, he remained faithful to his chief after regaining a Commons seat in a by-election that year. He stood down in favour of his eldest son in 1727 and died on 9 Apr. 1729.[7]

[1] *Scots Peerage* ed. Paul, i. 318–19; *Recs. Glasgow Univ.* (Maitland Club, lxxii), iii. 132; W. Fraser, *Lds. Elphinstone of Elphinstone*, i. 234. [2] *Reg. PC Scotland*, 1690, p. 649; 1691, p. 477; *CSP Dom. 1700–2*, p. 338; 1702–3, p. 354; *Cal. Treas. Bks.* xxix. 689. [3] *Scot. Rec. Soc.* lxii. 32; Carnegie Lib. Ayr, Ayr burgh recs. B6/18/9, council mins. 4 Apr. 1718. [4] *Hist. Scot. Parl.* 100; *Reg. PC Scotland*, 1685–6, pp. 164, 592–3; *APS*, ix. 166; Lauderdale mss at Thirlestane Castle, Campbell to [Lauderdale], 29 Apr. 1701; info. from Dr P. W. J. Riley on members of Scot. parl.; P. W. J. Riley, *King Wm. and Scot. Politicians*, 166, 170; *Argyle Pprs.* 101–2; P. W. J. Riley, *Union*, 127–8; Boyer, *Anne Annals*, iii. app. 43; Fraser, *Melvilles*, i. 278–9. [5] *Orig. Pprs.* ed. Macpherson, ii. 18; info. from Dr Riley; Riley, *Union*, 331; SRO, Breadalbane mss GD112/39/210/13, Campbell of Mamore to [Breadalbane], n.d. [1707/8]; GD112/39/211/27, same to [same], 27 Jan. 1708. [6] SRO, Inveraray sheriff ct. recs. SC54/21/1, pp. 1–9, Argyll electoral ct. mins. 1708–13; *Edinburgh Courant*, 18–21 June 1708; *Cal. Treas. Pprs.* 1708–14, pp. 26–27, 287; Breadalbane mss GD112/39/232/7, Campbell of Mamore to [Breadalbane], 15 Sept. 1709; GD112/39/210/14, Breadalbane to Ld. Glenorchy and Colin Campbell, n.d.; NLS, ms 1392, f. 80; Advocates' mss, Wodrow letters Quarto 7, f. 126; *Parlty. Hist.* i. 69; Lauderdale mss, Campbell to Lauderdale, 13 Aug. 1709, 1 Apr. 1710. [7] *Cal. Treas. Bks.* 784; *Bk. of Dumbartonshire*, i. 297–8, 303; P. W. J. Riley, *Eng. Ministers and Scotland*, 266; *Hist. Scot. Parl.* 100.

D. W. H.

CAMPBELL, John (c.1693–1770), of Mamore, Dunbarton.

BUTESHIRE	1713–1715
ELGIN BURGHS	7 Apr. 1715–1722
	25 Jan. 1725–1727
DUNBARTONSHIRE	1727–1761

b. c.1693, 1st s. of Hon. John Campbell*; bro. of Charles† and William Campbell†. *m.* c. 22 Oct. 1720, Mary (*d.* 1736), da. of John, 2nd Ld. Bellenden [S], maid of honour to Caroline, Princess of Wales, 5s.(2 *d.v.p.*) 1da. *suc.* fa. 1729, cos. Archibald Campbell as 4th Duke of Argyll [S] 15 Apr. 1761; KT 7 Aug. 1765.[1]

Ens. 3 Ft. Gds. (Scots Gds.) Oct. 1710, capt.-lt. and lt.-col. 1712–Aug. 1715; groom of bedchamber to George II as Prince of Wales and King 1714–61, to George III 1761–?d.; a.d.c. to 2nd Duke of Argyll Sept. 1715–17; lt.-col. 9 Ft. 1720–2, 27 Ft. 1735–7, col. 39 Ft. 1737–8, 21 Ft. (R. Scots Fusiliers) 1738–52, 2 Drags. 1752–*d.*; gov. Milford Haven 1734–61, Limerick 1761–*d.*; brig.-gen. 1743, maj.-gen. 1744, lt.-gen. 1747, gen. 1765; PC 2 Jan. 1762.[2]

Burgess, Glasgow 1716, ?Edinburgh 1720.[3]

Rep. peer [S] 1761–*d.*

The decision to send the young Campbell of Mamore for a soldier was imposed by his cousins Argyll and Ilay, whom he was to succeed many years later in the dukedom. It was through their combined influence that his foot was placed on the first rung of the ladder of preferment, with the acquisition in 1710 of an ensign's commission in the Scots Guards. But at one stage it had looked as if Argyll's patronage would be withheld. During the winter of 1707–8, with the Duke's political interest in some disarray, Campbell's father went to attend his clan chief with a request for a recommendation to office on his own account, only to be refused peremptorily for having disregarded Argyll's wishes in a Commons debate. 'In the same breath', he reported,

[Argyll] asked my son John of me to be educated as he thought fit, with a certification if I refused he would dispose of what he had as he pleased, and bid me not give a hasty answer, my son being the nearest of blood, and for whom he had a kindness, and bid me give my positive answer as soon as I could.

Mamore was nonplussed, and opted to do nothing. Fortunately, the difference was made up when the Duke realized that the bill to abolish the Scottish privy council and heritable jurisdictions, which he himself had supported but Campbell snr. and his other clansmen had opposed, was at least in part a stratagem devised by the Squadrone 'to lay him low'. Not surprisingly, this discovery had a calming effect, wrote Mamore, 'and after some reasoning he is to give me a scheme how he intends to have my son educated, and I am to give him to him'. The notion of a military career seems to have come later, and from Ilay, whose powers of cajolery were brought into play in the autumn of 1709 to 'cement his brother's friends' as Argyll turned to a political alliance with Robert Harley* and the Tories. Mamore reported on this occasion a visit to Ilay, who appeared 'in very good humour', and arranged for Campbell jnr. to be sent to him 'to try his inclinations. I am for breeding him a lawyer, and Ilay is for a commission in the army. I think both may be.'[4]

Having served in the Peninsula, and in command of the guards detachment sent to oversee the destruction of the fortifications at Dunkirk, Campbell entered Parliament at the 1713 general election while in all probability still a minor. His unopposed return on the Isle of Bute was owing to Argyll's influence, and was part of a campaign to increase the Argathelian presence in the Commons in this Parliament. Lord Polwarth's list of the Scottish representation marked him as a 'Hanoverian', that is to say a Whig, and he duly voted on 18 Mar. 1714 against the expulsion of Richard Steele. Either he or his father told on 7 May in favour of deferring the committee stage on the Scottish militia bill, an issue of particular concern to Argyll, whose hereditary rights were destined for abolition. This procedural manoeuvre, devised by George Lockhart*, effectively killed off the bill. Co-operation with Lockhart was merely tactical, however, and marked no shift in political allegiance. Campbell voted on 12 May for the Whig wrecking amendment to extend the schism bill to cover Catholic education.[5]

Campbell secured a seat in the 1715 Parliament for Elgin Burghs through Argyll's personal intervention, and even then only on petition, following an election marked by the physical intimidation of his opponents in at least one council in the district. Listed as a Whig in the Worsley list and other analyses of the new House, he proved a loyal client of Argyll. After a long military career, which culminated in his appointment in the Forty-Five as general commanding in the western Highlands, and an equally prolonged stint of parliamentary service in the Argathelian cause, he succeeded to the dukedom himself in 1761, by which time he had become, in the words of a modern historian, 'old and stupid'. He died on 9 Nov. 1770.[6]

[1] *Hist. Reg. Chron.* 1720, p. 36; *Scots Peerage* ed. Paul, i. 383–6. [2] *Cal. Treas. Pprs.* 1731–4, p. 682. [3] *Scot. Rec. Soc.* lvi. 316; lxii. 32. [4] SRO, Breadalbane mss GD112/39/210/13, Hon. John Campbell to [Breadalbane], n.d. 1707; GD112/39/112/27, same to [same], 27 Jan. 1708. [5] *Scots Courant*, 21–23 Sept. 1713; NLS, Advocates' mss, Wodrow pprs. letters Quarto 8, f. 118. [6] *More Culloden Pprs.* ed. Warrand, ii. 60; iii. 161; R. M. Sunter, *Patronage and Pol. in Scotland*, 47–48, 77–78, 188; A. Murdoch, *People Above*, 109.

D.W.H.

CAMPION, Henry (c.1680–1761), of Combwell, Goudhurst, Kent.

EAST GRINSTEAD	1708–1710
BOSSINEY	2 Dec. 1710–1713
SUSSEX	1713–1715

b. c.1680, 2nd but 1st surv. s. of William Campion*. *educ.* Trinity Coll. Camb. adm. 2 Dec. 1697, aged 17; L. Inn 1698. *m.* 8 June 1702 (with £5,000), Barbara (*d.* 1755), da. and h. of Peter Courthorpe of Danny Park, Suss., 4s. (3 *d.v.p.*) 4da. (3 *d.v.p.*). *suc.* fa. 1702.[1]

Commr. public accts. 1711–13.[2]

Campion proved to have quite different political sympathies from those of his father. Successful for East Grinstead in 1708, he was classed as a Tory in a list of the returns and soon confirmed this analysis by his actions in the House. On 4 Feb. 1709 he urged that if the bill to naturalize foreign Protestants was passed, a clause should be added insisting that naturalization be made conditional on the immigrant becoming a communicating Anglican, and on 7 Mar. acted as a teller in favour of such an amendment. He acted as a teller twice more: against passing a bill concerning

Smithfield market (29 Jan.), and in support of William Thompson III*'s election for Orford (22 Feb.).³

In the next session Campion told on 10 Dec. 1709, in favour of the Tory, Charles Coxe*, in the Cirencester election, and again on 8 Feb. 1710, for an address that the convocation of tinners not sit until after the end of the session. He was named to two drafting committees, one for a bill to regulate button manufacture (21 Jan.) and the other to bring in a bill to prevent bribery at elections (14 Feb.). He voted against the impeachment of Dr Sacheverell, and told on 21 Mar. against giving the thanks of the House to the managers of the trial.

In 1710 Campion did not stand at East Grinstead, but came in at a by-election for Bossiney, when Hon. Francis Robartes chose to sit for Bodmin. His election probably had the support of Robartes and George Granville*. As the session developed he, who previously 'n'a guère été connu hors de sa province', emerged as a spokesman for those Tories disillusioned with Robert Harley's* 'moderation' and duly became one of the leading members of the October Club. One of his first actions was against the Palatines, when he was first-named on 15 Jan. 1711 to the drafting committee for a bill to repeal the General Naturalization Act. He managed the resulting bill through the Commons in January, only for it to fail in the Lords. He was later appointed to the committee for drafting a qualifying bill for justices of the peace (6 Mar.). Campion was involved in the confrontation between the Court and the October Club over the disputed election at Carlisle, in which the Octobrists were trying to unseat the Whig, (Sir) James Montagu I, against the wishes of the ministry. On 20 Feb. he told in favour of resuming consideration of the case in three weeks, thus allowing time for the collection of evidence, and on 14 Mar. for the motion condemning Bishop Nicolson's intervention in the election. Campion also continued to pursue awkward questions concerning the Godolphin ministry, being chosen a commissioner of accounts on 9 Apr., and not surprisingly, he was classed as one of the 'worthy patriots' who had detected the mismanagements of the previous administration. On 5 Apr. he told on the Tory side in favour of an amendment to the bill for preventing bribery at elections, and on 10 Apr. he again told for the Tories against an amendment to a motion allowing the place-holder Sir John Anstruther to continue to sit in the House. He was also involved in two private bills, dealing with estates in Kent and Sussex, and managed one of them through the Commons.⁴

In the 1711–12 session Campion was one of a trio of MPs appointed to bring in a second bill to repeal the General Naturalization Act (22 Dec). Joining in the attack on the Duke of Marlborough (John Churchill†), on 25 Feb. he urged that the 2.5 per cent deductions taken by the Duke on money issued for foreign troops should be repaid. During the spring of 1712 the October Club was split by the defection of a number of Hanoverian Tories to form the March Club. The remainder, some of whom were appointed to office, formed an uneasy alliance with the Court, and, although Campion himself was not given a place, he was transformed from a strong critic of the administration into one of its defenders. On 2 Apr. 1712 he acted as a teller in favour of a motion to declare a petition against Arthur Moore frivolous and vexatious, and he successfully moved on 8 Apr. that the *Daily Courant*'s printing of the Dutch envoy's reply to parliamentary censures was a scandalous and malicious libel, being first-named to the resulting committee of inquiry into its publication. He also acted as a teller on 21 Apr. in favour of committing the bill to appoint commissioners of inquiry into crown grants, a measure dear to the hearts of the October Club, and was named to the committee to scrutinize the ballot of commissioners (13 May). Campion was a teller for the Tories in the Steyning election dispute on 8 May, and, in an apparent division within the October Club over tactics, on 17 May he and another Club member, Thomas Paske, told in opposition to fellow Octobrists John Hynde Cotton and John Carnegie for adjourning a debate on supply. Campion was shocked at Lord Treasurer Oxford's (Robert Harley) failure to get the bill inquiring into crown grants through the Lords, and when news of the defeat reached the Commons on 20 May, he

> stood up and in a very disorderly manner took notice of the speech of Lord Nottingham [Daniel Finch†], and almost repeated it, adding that he hoped the House would have in their immediate thoughts the resumption itself and think no more of inquiries: especially since that noble lord had declared he would be as much for the resumption as any person and only disliked the last bill, because it left room for partiality and favour. But all this was no more than an empty sally, and went off without being seconded.

Despite this disappointment, on 22 May he supported a Court motion to put off a call of the House and took the opportunity to cast aspersions on those who he claimed were obstructing a peace treaty. On 28 May he defended the ministry when the Whigs attacked the Duke of Ormond's refusal to engage the French, telling against an address to express concern at his restraint. When *A Letter from the States General to the Queen of Great Britain* was published, criticizing the peace negotiations, he moved a motion on 13 June condemning it as a scandalous libel. By this stage he was described by L'Hermitage as 'fort dévoué au parti de la cour'. On 17 June he was a teller against a Whig resolution that the Protestant succession should be guaranteed in the peace treaty. His other activities in this session included a drafting committee to help erect a chapel of ease in Deal (15 Feb.), and the management through the Commons in May of a bill from the Lords covering an estate in Kent and Sussex.[5]

In the last session of this Parliament, in June and July 1713, Campion managed through the House the bill for raising the militia, reporting it from the committee of the whole on 1 July. However, most of his activity was devoted to helping the ministry secure the passage of the French commerce bill. As a precursor, on 2 May he was a teller in favour of bringing in a bill to suspend the duties on French wines; on 30 May he told against a Whig attempt to delay the first reading of the bill confirming the 8th and 9th articles; and on 18 June he both spoke and voted in the bill's favour. In other business, he presented information to the House from the commission of accounts (16 May).[6]

Successful for Sussex in 1713, Campion continued to play his part in defence of the ministry. He spoke on 18 Mar. 1714 in favour of Richard Steele withdrawing from the House before the charge against him was made and for his expulsion (for which Campion duly voted). He also spoke on 15 Apr. for the Court motion that the Protestant succession was not in danger, and on 22 Apr. in support of an address of thanks for the peace. However, as the split within the Tory ministry developed, Campion supported Bolingbroke (Henry St John II*), which became clear in a committee of supply on 19 Apr., when he led the October Club in strongly opposing a ministerial motion to order payment of arrears to the Hanoverian troops. Furthermore, early in June he moved that a supply to clear the army's debts should exclude Hanoverian arrears. Then, when Bolingbroke encouraged the introduction of a schism bill, Campion warmly supported it. On 12 May he moved that Sir William Wyndham, 3rd Bt., have leave to make a motion, the latter then proposed the schism bill and Campion was named to the committee to draft it. In the debate of 18 June he replied to Robert Walpole II's suggestion that, as the bill was to extend to the Dissenters in Ireland, another measure should be brought in to enable them to enjoy toleration: his riposte was that if leave were to be given for such a bill it should be accompanied by one to incapacitate Dissenters from voting in parliamentary elections. Campion was a teller on 14 May for a duty to be imposed on coal coming into London to pay for maintenance of the Thames waterway, and on 21 May for a motion to debate the African slave trade. On 22 May he was named to the drafting committee for a bill to vest Scottish episcopal revenues in the crown, another measure promoted by Bolingbroke. On 24 June, Campion opposed the address of thanks to the Queen for publishing a reward for the capture of the Pretender and when the Earl of Hertford (Algernon Seymour) suggested the reward be raised from £5,000 to £100,000, 'Mr Campion very seriously said it would seem a downright affront to her Majesty to vote £100,000 reward after she had thought fit to propose but £5,000'. He told against addressing the Queen for an account of the army's debts on 8 July. His other activities included drafting committees to prepare heads for a bill to curb wool smuggling (9 Mar.), a matter of considerable local interest, and then to prepare the bill itself (15th); two tellerships on the Tory side in the disputed elections of Wigan (6 Apr.) and Southwark (3 July); and membership of the committee for counting the ballot for commissioners of accounts (17 June). Given this record the compiler of the Worsley list had no difficulty in classing him as a Tory.[7]

At the end of June 1714 rumours of Oxford's dismissal were accompanied by reports that in the resultant reshuffle Campion would be appointed chancellor of the Exchequer in a Bolingbroke-led administration. These rumours continued until the end of July, but Queen Anne's death ended all such speculation and effectively put an end to his parliamentary career. On 15 Aug. Campion opposed another attempt to introduce a £100,000 reward for the capture of the Pretender.[8]

After 1715 Campion was an active Jacobite, acting as a messenger and helping to organize the intended rising in the West in 1715. Although never arrested, he spent much of the next few years abroad, returning to England by 1720 and continuing to correspond with the Jacobite court. In 1725 he came into possession of Danny Park, Sussex, where he lived until his death on 17 Apr. 1761.[9]

[1] *Misc. Gen. et Her.* ser. 4, ii. 264; *Danny Archives* ed. J. A. Wooldridge, 13. [2] *Cal. Treas. Bks.* xxv. 360. [3] Cobbett, *Parlty. Hist.* vi. 780. [4] NSA, Kreienberg despatch 16 Jan. 1711; *Huntington Lib. Q.* xxxiii. 159. [5] D. Szechi, *Jacobitism and Tory Pol.* 108, 114; *Huntington Lib. Q.* 169–70; Kreienberg despatches 8 Apr., 23, 30 May, 13 Jun. 1712; SRO, Leven and Melville mss GD/26/13/149/2, acct. of proceedings, 22 May 1712; Add. 17677 FFF, f. 243. [6] Chandler, v. 41. [7] Douglas diary (Hist. of Parl. trans.), 18 Mar., 15 Apr. 1714; Cobbett, 1347, 1348, 1356; Boyer, *Pol. State*, vii. 461, 532; Holmes, *Pol. in Age of Anne*, 270; NLS, Wodrow papers, letters Quarto 8, ff. 118, 120–1, 131, 139; *Wentworth Pprs.* 392; DZA, Bonet despatch 28 June/1 July 1714. [8] *Wentworth Pprs.* 391; Wodrow papers, letters Quarto 8, f. 138; NLS, ms 6409/70, James to John

Macfarlane, 29 July 1714; Boyer, viii. 156. [9]*HMC Stuart*, i. 395; vii. 444; RA, Stuart mss 46/129, 'James III' to Ormond, 12 May 1720; 55/110, Campion to 'James III', 13 Nov. 1721; Wooldridge, p. xvi; *Misc. Gen. et Her.* 264.

P. W./S. M. W.

CAMPION, William (1640–1702), of Combwell, Goudhurst, Kent.

SEAFORD   1689–1698, 31 Dec. 1698–1700
KENT   1701 (Dec.)–1702

bap. 6 Feb. 1640, 1st s. of Sir William Campion of Combwell by Grace, da. of Sir Thomas Parker[†] of Ratton, Suss. *educ.* Trinity Coll. Camb. 1655; M. Temple 1657; Padua 1660. *m.* lic. 1 Nov. 1662, Frances, da. of Sir John Glynne[†], 2s. (1 *d.v.p.*) 7da. *suc.* fa. 1648.[1]

Sub-commr. prizes, Dover 1689–98, June 1702–*d.*[2]
Asst. Mines Co. 1693.[3]

Campion's royalist father having been killed during the Civil War, his own political identity seems to owe more to his uncle, the Court Whig Sir William Thomas, 1st Bt.*, on whose interest he entered Parliament for Seaford. Returned again in 1690, he was listed as a Whig by the Marquess of Carmarthen (Sir Thomas Osborne[†]), and opposed the Tories' proposed address of thanks to the King for the changes in the lieutenancy of London, saying in the debate on 24 Apr. 1690:

I am for the Church of England men to be employed in this lieutenancy. I know not whether it be true or no, but I have heard that several of them would not take the oaths to the government. I would know what this lieutenancy is before I give my consent to thank the King.

However, he opposed Comptroller Wharton's abjuration bill on 26 Apr., saying 'I am not for new oaths'. In April 1691 he was classed by Robert Harley* as a Court supporter and, as a sub-commissioner of prizes, his name appeared as a placeman on several lists in 1692 and 1693. In the 1691–2 session he was added to the drafting committee for a bill on the manufacture of saltpetre (2 Dec. 1691), and was given leave of absence on 14 Jan. 1692 for 14 days. In the next session, in January 1693, he managed a bill from the Lords allowing Sir George Parker, 2nd Bt.*, to make a settlement upon his marriage. In the 1693–4 session he was given leave of absence for 14 days twice, on 21 Dec. 1693 and 14 Feb. 1694.[4]

Returned again for Seaford in 1695, Campion was forecast as a probable supporter of the Court in the division on the proposed council of trade on 31 Jan. 1696, being given leave of absence on the same day for two weeks. He signed the Association in February, and voted in March with the Court in favour of fixing the price of guineas at 22s. In the following session, he voted on 25 Nov. 1696 for the attainder of Sir John Fenwick[†]. He was also nominated to a drafting committee for a private estate bill on behalf of a London scrivener (31 Dec.), and told in favour of referring a petition from the Royal African Company to the committee for regulating the Africa trade (11 Mar. 1697). In the next session he was given leave of absence for 21 days on 21 Dec. 1697.

Listed as a court placeman in a comparative analysis of the old and new Houses of about September 1698, he stood down at Seaford to make way for Sir William Thomas, but came back at a by-election in December when Thomas opted to sit for Sussex. He voted on 18 Jan. 1699 against disbanding the army. He was added on 8 Feb. to the committee drafting a bill for regulating the militia, and carried up a private estate bill to the Lords on 21 Apr. He was a teller on two occasions: once on 21 Apr. in favour of the censure of the Tory Henry Chivers for reflecting on other Members, and again on 27 Apr. 1699 for an amendment to the bill suppressing lotteries, which sought to extend the time allowed for a lottery to dispose of Sir Charles Bickerstaffe's estate. Given leave of absence again for 21 days on 21 Dec. 1699, he was back in the House on 15 Jan. 1700 when he was first-named to draft a bill for the repair of the Sevenoaks–Tonbridge highway, presenting the resulting bill on 27 Jan.

Campion did not stand in the first 1701 election but in the second successfully contested Kent, at which point he was listed by Harley as a Whig. On 14 Jan. 1702 he was given leave of absence for 14 days to recover his health. He died 20 Sept. 1702 and was buried at Goudhurst.[5]

[1]*Suss. Arch. Colls.* x. 3, 34–35; *Misc. Gen. et Her.* ser. 4, ii. 264. [2]*CSP Dom.* 1689–90, p. 172; *Cal. Treas. Bks.* xvii. 364. [3]*CSP Dom.* 1693, p. 207. [4]Grey, x. 67; Bodl. Rawl. A.79, f. 83. [5]*Suss. Arch. Colls.* 34–35.

P. W./S. M. W.

CAPEL, Hon. Sir Henry (1638–96), of Kew, Surr.

TEWKESBURY   1660–1681 (Mar.)
COCKERMOUTH   1689–1690
TEWKESBURY   1690–11 Apr. 1692

bap. 6 Mar. 1638, 3rd s. of Arthur Capel[†], 1st Baron Capell of Hadham (*d.* 1649), by Elizabeth, da. and coh. of Sir Charles Morrison, 1st Bt.[†], of Cassiobridge, Herts. *m.* settlement 16 Feb. 1659, Dorothy (*d.* 1721), da. and coh. of Richard Bennet of Chancery Lane, London and Kew, *s.p.* KB 23 Apr. 1661; *cr.* Baron Capell of Tewkesbury 11 Apr. 1692.

Steward of Ogmore, Glam. 1662–93; chief steward, manor of Richmond 1690–?92; high steward, Tewkesbury by 1695–d.; freeman, Dublin 1695.[1]

PC [I] 1673–85, 1693–d.; ld. of Admiralty 1679–80; PC 21 Apr. 1679–31 Jan. 1680, 14 Feb. 1689–d.; ld. of Treasury 1689–90; ld. justice [I] 1693–May 1695, ld. dep. [I] May 1695–d.; commr. appeals in prizes 1694–d.[2]

Gov. Society of Mineral and Battery Works 1689–d.; member, Society of Mines Royal 1690.[3]

An Exclusionist and staunch Whig, Capel had come to occupy a leading position among the parliamentary Whigs and had been appointed to the Treasury Board in 1689. In the 1690 election he switched seats from Cockermouth to Tewkesbury, where his extensive estates gave him a commanding interest. Lord Carmarthen (Sir Thomas Osborne†) classed him as a Whig on the list of the new Parliament, but his prospective support for the government was placed in question soon after the election when he was removed from the Treasury in accordance with a promise made by the King to Lord Halifax (Sir George Savile†), Capel having been one of Halifax's fiercest opponents in 1689. He did, however, receive a promise of future compensation and was evidently still expected to play his part in the management of government support, being listed at about this time as a 'Privy Councillor that ought to assist' in Parliament. His participation is recorded in several key debates of the first session. On 17 Apr. 1690, in the attack by the Churchmen on the recent alterations in the London lieutenancy, he spoke in favour of allowing the sheriffs to petition the House against them, and on the 24th against the Tory motion for an address of thanks to the King for the 'great care' he had shown towards the Church in making the changes, saying:

> Suppose you make this address, and you find those put in are not of the Church of England and have been of the bloody juries? When you address the King, do you not take every part of his speech into consideration, before you draw up your address? I never saw the list of this lieutenancy, but I have heard an ill character of some of them. I have seen the Church of England set forwards and backwards by Lord Clifford, who did head the declaration; and here we are set one against another and all for the interests of the papists . . . Another Parliament will find fault for this address as not consistent with reason.

He subsequently proposed that any address be couched in 'general' terms and should omit mentioning the lieutenancy altogether, but his counter-motion for a committee to report on the new appointments was unsuccessful. Two days later, on the 26th, he supported Hon. Thomas Wharton's* abjuration bill, declaring it to be 'a test, who are for King James and the French king, and thereby for popery, that we may know then if we must not secure this government'. On 13 May he was nominated a manager of a conference with the Lords on the Queen's regency bill.[4]

In the 1690–1 session Capel was active, at the request of his sister, the Duchess of Beaufort, in organizing opposition on behalf of their niece Elizabeth, Lady Ailesbury to a bill enabling her husband the Earl of Ailesbury (Thomas Bruce†) to dispose of some of the estates in Wiltshire which she had inherited from her late brother, the 3rd Duke of Somerset. His efforts were unavailing however, and the bill was passed. In lists drawn up between December 1690 and February 1691 he was still classified as a Court supporter, and by Robert Harley* in April 1691 as a Country party supporter. He evidently missed no opportunity of stating his strong Whiggish views. On 19 Nov. 1691 he spoke in favour of the Court's wish to deal with the army estimates 'in a lump' rather than item by item, stressing the imprudence of such action in the event of unexpected attacks from the French in Ireland or elsewhere: 'who would be so bold to advise his Majesty to withdraw any of his forces from the other parts of his kingdom, thereby to lessen what the Commons have thought fit to establish for the defence of those kingdoms?'. On the 28th he opposed the attempt to reduce the number of men voted for the army by including the officers in the estimate, further to which on the 30th he was named to the committee to consider lists of forces and garrisons needed by the King. During November he also participated in two conferences with the Lords. At the beginning of December he involved himself on behalf of the Duchess of Beaufort in further unsuccessful attempts to block another estate bill for the Earl of Ailesbury. He spoke three times in December and January against the Lords' efforts to tone down the treason trials bill; on 2 Jan. 1692 opposed reductions in the army in Ireland; and in ways and means on the 20th, supported the proposal for a quarterly poll, pointing out that the inclusion of peers within its scope was a particularly attractive feature. On 22 Jan. he spoke in favour of printing the vote which declared Sir Basil Firebrace* guilty of bribery; on the 28th, saw no reason for the Lords to have their own nominees on the commission of accounts, 'for what end should they have an account of the monies given and issued?'; and on 15 Feb. opposed the attempt to revive the commission of accounts by the back-door process of tacking a clause for this purpose to the poll bill.[5]

The promise of recompense given to Capel at the time of his dismissal from the Treasury was honoured in April 1692, when he was raised to the peerage (as Lord Capell), and a greater reward followed in May 1693 when he was appointed one of three lords justices to govern Ireland. Shortly afterwards he wrote to Admiral Edward Russell* of his disappointment at his friend and fellow Whig Lord Shrewsbury's refusal to accept a similar high office as it gave the impression that the Whigs were 'men contented with nothing', but was delighted when the Earl finally accepted the seals as secretary of state in March 1694. Meanwhile in Ireland all was not well. It had been hoped that the new dispensation, replacing the discredited Lord Sydney (Hon. Henry Sidney†) with a more balanced administration, in which Capell's Whig zeal would be balanced by the moderation of Sir Cyril Wyche* and William Duncombe*, would bring stability, but the experiment was not a success. Capell soon distanced himself from his fellow justices and concentrated on forging an alliance with the extreme Protestant party led by Thomas* and Alan Brodrick† and Robert Rochfort, at the same time urging the government to recall the Irish parliament. Wyche and Duncombe continually warned of the dangers and difficulties of such a course, but their influence waned as Capell's increased, thanks to the growing dominance of his Junto allies in England. Eventually the King, acting on the advice of Lord Sunderland, gave Capell sole responsibility for the government of Ireland in May 1695 by making him lord deputy. Having reshuffled the Dublin administration in accordance with the wishes of his Irish allies, Capell then summoned a new parliament, where with the help of the Brodricks and Rochfort he managed to achieve a satisfactory compromise on the claim of the Irish house of commons to possess a sole right to initiate supply bills; he also secured additional taxation, the annulment of all the proceedings of James II's Irish parliament, and the confirmation of the Act of Settlement. Within the Irish ministry he faced covert opposition from the lord chancellor, Sir Charles Porter*, who was anxious to secure the ratification of the Treaty of Limerick, something also desired by William, but about which Capell and his supporters were unenthusiastic. The breach came to a head when Capell's faction tried, unsuccessfully, to impeach Porter in the Irish parliament. Capell denied responsibility himself, although his refusal to intervene on Porter's behalf led many to suppose that he had tacitly countenanced the proceedings. The King urged a reconciliation, but little progress had been made by the time of Capell's death on 30 May 1696. His body was returned to England and buried at Little Hadham in Hertfordshire. Lord Dartmouth considered Capell 'very weak, formal [and] conceited', one who had 'no other merit than being a violent party man', but Shrewsbury and other Whigs naturally expressed a very different view.[6]

[1] Somerville, *Duchy of Lancaster Official Lists*, 228; *Cal. Treas. Bks.* ix. 627, 1682–3; *CSP Dom.* 1694–5, p. 462; *Cal. Ancient Recs. Dublin* ed. Gilbert, vi. 103. [2] *CSP Dom.* 1693, p. 134; 1694–5, pp. 204, 460; 1695, pp. 111–12, 331. [3] *Cal. Treas. Bks.* ix. 1460. [4] Foxcroft, *Halifax*, ii. 124; *CSP Dom.* 1690–1, p. 211; Cobbett, *Parlty. Hist.* v. 586, 592, 594; Bodl. Rawl. A.79, f. 78. [5] Wilts. RO, Ailesbury mss 1300/784, Lord Clarendon (Henry Hyde†) to Lady Beaufort, 13 Dec. 1690; 1300/787, Godfrey Harcourt to same, 1 Jan. 1690[–1]; 1300/788–90, Capell to same, 7 Jan. 1690–1, 4, 29 Dec. 1691; *Luttrell Diary*, 32, 48, 75, 105, 128–9, 143, 150, 153, 162, 187. [6] *Penal Era and Golden Age* ed. Bartlett and Hayton, 27–29, 40; H. Horwitz, *Parl. and Pol. Wm. III*, 118, 132; D. H. Somerville, *King of Hearts*, 184–8.

P. W./A. A. H.

CARDONNEL, Adam de (1663–1719), of Duke St., St. Margaret's, Westminster.[1]

SOUTHAMPTON 1701 (Dec.)–19 Feb. 1712

bap. 1 Nov. 1663, 2nd s. of Adam de Cardonnel, collector of customs, Southampton, of Southampton, Hants by Mary, da. and coh. of Nicholas Pescod of Holbury Cadland, Hants. *m.* (1) 26 Nov. 1711, Elizabeth (*d.* 1713), wid. of Isaac Teale, apothecary-general of the army, of St. Margaret's, Westminster, *s.p.*; (2) aft. Nov. 1714, Elizabeth, da. of René Baudowin of London, merchant, wid. of William Frankland, consul at Biscay (2nd s. of Sir Thomas Frankland, 2nd Bt.*), 1s. 1da.[2]

Agent, Col. John Hales's regt. of ft. 1688–?1693; chief clerk to sec. at war by 1692–1702; treasurer, hosp. for soldiers, overseas 1693–?1711, purveyor to the Household c.1700–2; sec. to Duke of Marlborough 1701–?*d*; secretary at war to the foreign forces 1702–1711; sec. at war Jan.–Sept. 1710.[3]

Freeman, Southampton 1699.[4]

Cardonnel's family were Protestant refugees from the neighbourhood of Caen in France, where his grandfather had owned the chateau de Cardonnel. It is unclear when the family arrived in England but the earliest records relate to Cardonnel's uncle, Peter de Cardonnel, and his father, also called Adam, who were granted letters of denization in 1641. Peter, the elder of the two, was a merchant trading in Southampton in the early 1640s. The brothers married two sisters, daughters of Peter's trading partner, Nicholas Pescod. Adam de Cardonnel senior's marriage was probably in 1656, the year he was naturalized. The family wealth seems to have been largely lost during the Civil War, when Peter apparently lent Charles I some £20,000, which was never repaid. Adam was given some reward for 'his good services' at the Restoration with the post of customer and later collector of customs at

Southampton, an office he held for nearly 50 years. He appears to have recovered his finances only very gradually, being imprisoned for debt in the 1660s, while his house consisted of only four hearths in 1662, though this had risen to nine by 1670. He was an elder in the French Church at Southampton for almost 50 years.[5]

Cardonnel's father evidently had modest hopes for his second son, one of four surviving brothers and three sisters, as in 1676 he unsuccessfully attempted to obtain the reversion of his post at Southampton for him. Cardonnel is next heard of in 1688 when he purchased a place as agent to Colonel Hales's new regiment of foot for £200. Sometime afterwards (the exact date is unknown), he entered the office of the secretary at war, William Blathwayt*, and by 1692 had risen to be one of the two chief clerks, thenceforward accompanying the secretary and the King to Flanders for every campaign. After the peace in 1697 Blathwayt continued to go with the King to Holland each summer as acting secretary of state, taking Cardonnel with him. Cardonnel's post evidently made him some profit as in May 1697 he subscribed £1,000 to the contract for lending money to circulate Exchequer bills. He wrote from Het Loo in July 1699 of his surprise, and disappointment, at the revival in Charles Duncombe's* fortunes, believing that 'the City have been very much mistaken in the choice they have made' for sheriff of London. In 1701 the Duke of Marlborough (John Churchill†), on being appointed commander-in-chief of the allied forces, made Cardonnel his secretary, one of his chief advantages, besides his experience of the details of military administration, being his fluent command of French (although apparently his talents did not extend to Latin). For the next ten years he accompanied Marlborough on campaign.[6]

Meanwhile, during the time spent in England Cardonnel tried to obtain a seat in Parliament, to which end he contested Southampton unsuccessfully in December 1699 and January 1701 and finally won a seat there in November 1701, when his return was reckoned by Lord Spencer (Charles*) as a gain for the Whigs and he was listed as a Whig by Robert Harley*. The following year Cardonnel succeeded Blathwayt as secretary at war to the foreign forces, on which Francis Nicholson, governor of Virginia, congratulated him, and hoped that Blathwayt would soon resign his entire post to Cardonnel, which apparently would complete a pact made sometime previously: that Josiah Burchett* would be secretary of the Admiralty, Nicholson governor of Virginia and Cardonnel secretary at war. Cardonnel continued to represent Southampton in 1702, although his absences from England prevented him from playing a very active part in the Commons. He was always acutely aware of the impact on domestic politics of the success or failure of the war and wrote to John Ellis* in October 1702 that the expedition to Cadiz should have landed 'coûte que coûte' and, anticipating events, complained that Sir George Rooke* should have surprised the French–Spanish fleet at Vigo, 'which would have made some amends for this disgrace and have calmed people's minds a little in England'. In a subsequent letter the news of the success at Vigo had reached him and he hoped it 'will make our miscarriages there pass over the more easily at home, so as to give no disturbance to the public business'. Returning to England in November, he informed Ellis that his main concern that session was to find a way to get an increase in the estimates for the troops, as many had gone unpaid during the last campaign and Marlborough had promised they would be paid this year. The next summer, when the course of the war appeared to be going badly, Cardonnel was 'apprehensive it will not answer the expectation of our friends in England, and that we will have foul weather at home this winter'. News of Sir Stephen Fox's* marriage in old age gave him further cause for reflection, and he wrote to Ellis, 'you and I must plead for old people's marrying, for neither of us can do it young'. Back in the House in November 1703, he was again concerned with the estimates for the army and, having inserted additional pay for the general officers and forage and waggon money, had distributed to the managers of the Commons arguments to be used in support of these figures. He then accompanied Marlborough on what was planned as a short trip to Holland to discuss the next campaign at the end of December, but contrary winds prevented their return until 15 Feb. 1704. The delay irritated Cardonnel, who ended one of his letters to Ellis with an outburst, 'these people are so stupid and are so little sensible of the danger at their doors that one would believe by the little regard they have to their own safety, they were predestined for ruin'. His mood the next summer was no better when he wrote to his friend Matthew Prior* at the end of July, 'I wish to God it were well over, that I might get safe out of this country'. He seems to have kept on good terms with the Court Tory, Sir Christopher Musgrave, 4th Bt.*, who 'generally meant very well', and lamented his death in July. The campaign continued into October and Cardonnel wrote again of his desire to be home, ending 'I am so starved with cold I can hardly hold a pen'. He would no doubt have voted against the occasional conformity bill and the Tack, but was absent in Europe, having at the end of November accompanied Marlborough to

Berlin, where he was given a present of 740 ducats by the Prussian king. On his return to The Hague he wrote to Ellis on 16 Dec., thanking him for 'the best news we have had of a long time, for we were in no little concern on account of the occasional bill'. Back at Whitehall in January, he wrote to his former colleague at the war office, Henry Watkins*, about the plans for Queen Anne's Bounty and promised that he would use all his influence to have Watkins 'employed in its distribution'. On campaign again in June 1705, he commiserated with Ellis, who had been sacked from his job as under-secretary of state, 'for my part, though I have the honour to serve the best of masters and am resolved never to serve another I could heartily wish to be my own man, that I might once in my lifetime have one hour to myself'.[7]

Re-elected in 1705, Cardonnel was listed as a placeman and a High Church courtier. He was absent from the division on the Speaker in October 1705, being still on the Continent. In November he was at Vienna attending to the business of Marlborough's grant of the principality of Mindelheim, with some reservations, as he wrote to Watkins: 'you know I was always of the opinion it would have been much more for his Grace's honour and interest, at least at home, no such thing had ever been thought of. I cannot help being still of the same mind.' Once back in England he voted with the Court over the 'place clause' of the regency bill on 18 Feb. 1706. Further showing his zeal, on the 20th he attended a committee of elections until past 2 o'clock in the morning.[8]

The allied armies' victories in 1706 raised Cardonnel's morale, and he wrote to Prior, 'believe me the Devil has no hand in what we are doing; we are guided by a better genius, which I hope, will still help us to mumble and humble the rogues till their great monarch is brought to know himself'. In October of that year he was accused by Sir Henry Furnese* of combining with Paymaster Hon. James Brydges* and William Cadogan* to alter, illegally, the method of paying the army. The charges were not followed up, although they may have given him some alarm, as he wrote on 30 Nov. to Watkins that the 'treasury' had dined with him and said that the deputy-paymaster of the forces in Amsterdam, Mr Sweet, was coming over to England, but he had been assured that it was only to assist in settling Lord Ranelagh's (Richard Jones*) accounts. Brydges and Cadogan certainly colluded in profiteering from the war but it is unclear whether Cardonnel was ever involved in their schemes. A letter from Brydges to Cadogan in the spring of 1707 may indicate that Cardonnel was not involved in one particular plan. Brydges had informed Sweet not to settle the account for forage for the Prussian troops but to leave it to Cardonnel or Cadogan: 'I added his name that Sweet might not suspect there was any bargain for you alone for it.' Cardonnel seems to have been suffering from war-weariness by this time, having written to Watkins in January of his discontent with their allies, 'and could heartily wish we were both well rid of them, one good successful campaign more I hope will [see] us at home for good and all to reap a little quiet fruit of our labours'. But there was to be no rest for Cardonnel and as ever he was inundated with army business. 'God preserve us from such allies' he wrote of the Germans in October 1707 and in the same month Marlborough wrote that the bulk of correspondence he was receiving from Sir Charles Hedges* was so great he had handed it all over to Cardonnel.[9]

Back in England for the next session, Cardonnel again hoped for a quiet life, writing to Watkins on 18 Nov. 1707, 'our friends the Whigs are very angry at that administration of the Admiralty and are making a bustle in both Houses. I wish it may soon blow over.' A month later he wrote again, that 'we seem to be in a sort of lethargy, but I hope our friends will find means to extricate themselves and set all to rights again'. Again his main concern was the army and on 6 Jan. 1708 he informed Watkins that they hoped to succeed in getting an Act for each county to provide a certain number of recruits. Ten days later he had been sitting until 6 o'clock in the evening in the debate on this bill and lamented the lack of progress. On 20 Jan. the bill was thrown out and he wrote, 'we are in great affliction for the miscarriage of our project'. Further frustration followed and on 3 Feb., after having sat until 8 o'clock in the evening, he wrote that they had been 'baffled in our affairs of Spain'. The apparent hostility of the House may have influenced the 'mislaying' of the papers concerning the claims for losses of horses by the Hanoverian troops, of which Cardonnel informed Watkins the same day. It appears that there had been some debate as to whether they should present these claims, Marlborough believing that not having made similar claims for the English troops this year, it would not have 'looked well to have taken more care of foreigners than our own people'. A government reshuffle in February 1708 included the removal of Harley, which Cardonnel hoped 'will set all to rights again', and the resignation a few days later of Henry St. John II* as secretary at war. Cardonnel informed Watkins on 13 Feb. that he would not be succeeding St. John, but if he entertained any secret hopes of promotion, he was disappointed. He wrote to Watkins on 2 Mar., 'our alterations at Court are but three days' wonder and are no more thought of, your humble servant neither thought nor would have accepted of any part of them'. On campaign that year, Cardonnel was pleased with the election results (which included his own uncontested return), but cautious about whether this could be translated to an untroubled session, writing to James Stanhope* in June, 'our friends pretend they will have a great majority in Parliament; that will depend in a good measure on what we are able to do here this campaign'. Two lists of early 1708, one with the returns for 1708 added, classified Cardonnel as a Whig. In September the same year it was apparently Cardonnel's report of the action to rescue the relief convoy for the besieged town of Lille which caused Marlborough to ascribe its success to his favourite, Cadogan, who had not arrived until the action was almost over, thereby infuriating General John Richmond Webb*, the real hero of the operation.[10]

In the winter of 1708–9 Marlborough wrote to the French on the possibility of peace negotiations, mentioning a bribe of 2 million livres, promised to him two years earlier by a French envoy if he would support a peace attempt. While considering this letter the French produced a memorandum dated November 1708 in which the importance of Cardonnel's influence on Marlborough was mentioned:

> Le crédit que Cardonnel a sur son esprit est tel, qu'il est absolument nécessaire de persuader le secrétaire pour réussir auprès du maître. Une somme de 300 mille livres serait utilement employée à cet effet, et le roi consent que M. le duc de Berwick la fasse proposer par celui qu'il choisera pour parler au duc de Marlborough.

Nothing came of these moves. Cardonnel appears to have played little further part in the session, being overseas in January and February 1709.[11]

Cardonnel anticipated a satisfactory session, writing on 15 Nov. 1709, 'our sessions opened today with the appearance of a good quiet winter's campaign'. In January 1710 he was in the middle of high-political intrigues, acting as an intermediary in negotiations between the Court and the Junto in London and Marlborough at Windsor, who was threatening to resign if Abigail Masham was not removed. His own career seemed on the rise in January, when Robert Walpole II* transferred to the treasurership of the navy and Cardonnel was at last made secretary at war, although immediately before the appointment he claimed to be in doubt as to whether he should accept the post or not. The peace negotiations broke down and Cardonnel was needed to serve another campaign in Flanders, so it was arranged that he should continue to act as Marlborough's secretary while leaving the duties of his new office to be handled by Walpole. Cardonnel was uneasy at this arrangement and now had his own interest in a peace. He wrote to Watkins on 31 Jan. 1710:

> between you and me, I should have been as well pleased with a fair quietus. I shall only kiss the Queen's hand and leave the management of the office to Mr Walpole till I return . . . our affairs here require a peace as much as they do on your side . . . I should be glad to yield something rather than prolong the war.

In Parliament he voted for the impeachment of Dr Sacheverell before returning to the Continent in late February. No sooner had he gone than it was rumoured that he would be replaced by St. John, who, however, disdained to succeed Cardonnel. That spring Brydges and Cadogan involved Cardonnel in their attempts to make money by speculating in stocks with the benefit of inside knowledge of the progress of the peace negotiations. On 26 Mar. 1710 Cadogan wrote to Brydges: 'Before my leaving The Hague, I took measures with Mr Cardonnel for his writing to you early, regularly and at large what passes in relation to the peace.' It is, however, unclear whether Cardonnel knew the use to which this information was being put and there is no evidence as to whether or not he himself was playing the market in this way.[12]

During the summer of 1710 Cardonnel wrote several letters mentioning his longing for peace, and also suffered a serious illness in July and August and was moved from camp to Lille. Marlborough wrote on 2 Aug. to his duchess: 'poor Cardonnel is very ill at Lille; if he should die, I should have a very great loss'. A subsequent letter containing news of Cardonnel's recovery expressed Marlborough's pleasure:

> For not only his having my business in his hands, which must have been very inconvenient to have changed, but he is also a very moral, honest man in an age when one meets with so many villains, which makes him the more valuable.

No sooner had Cardonnel recovered his health than a fresh anxiety arose from the political changes in England. On 8 Sept. he wrote to Brydges, thanking him for some news regarding payments for the army: 'it gives us a little life to see some care is taken of us, after the loss of my Lord Godolphin [Sidney†]', but he had begun to be inured to the changes as 'nothing could happen worse after so great a blow'. He also wrote to Horatio Walpole II* that he had heard the Tories 'are falling out among themselves . . . 'tis the way for honest men to come by their goods again'. His hopes were in vain and it was soon apparent that his post of secretary at war was also at risk. He made some attempt to save the situation, writing to the secretary of state on 11 Sept.:

my lord Duke is pleased to write to you this post to pray that upon the dissolution of Parliament, you will lay a commission before the Queen for me to be secretary at war, having, as you may please to remember, had the honour to kiss her Majesty's hand for it before my coming away, with her approbation of Mr Walpole's continuing to act till my return, and as I am in hopes that out of consideration to his Grace, it may be thought fit to continue me in that post, I would be glad to save the trouble of a new election; and, therefore, humbly entreat your favour that the commission may be despatched the first opportunity without any date and remain in your hands till I come home, when the blank may be filled up as it shall be thought proper.

Brydges hoped that Cardonnel would be continued as that would be a means of prevailing on Marlborough not to resign, but Cardonnel's application was in vain. At the end of September he was dismissed, much to Marlborough's mortification. St. John, now secretary of state, maintained a polite public face with Cardonnel but on 28 Nov. wrote that Marlborough,

lays great weight on Mr [George] Granville's* being put into Cardonnel's employment; has he forgot Britain enough to imagine so little a creature as the latter is capable of filling at this time of day, that post? The Queen's service would become ridiculous in such hands, and I will adventure to affirm that the state of the war could never be carried through the House of Commons by his secretary. Faction, indeed, will fit any man for any rank, and where that prevails, Cardonnel might be secretary at war.

Cardonnel himself reportedly considered his removal was 'in revenge' for the Duke's 'neglect' of Harley's 'proposals of commencing a correspondence'.[13]

Despite these setbacks, Cardonnel was again elected for Southampton in 1710, but his position remained very uncertain. In January he was inclined to believe that Marlborough would not be able to continue in office and wrote that he himself wanted nothing more than to retire. On 11 Jan. Marlborough and Harley met for the first time that session, 'tête à tête' at the former's lodgings, a meeting which Cardonnel hoped would 'tend toward healing over our unhappy divisions'. Marlborough remained at the head of the army and Cardonnel accompanied him on his last campaign in 1711. Despite the successes of the campaign, it was clear that the Tories were determined to bring down Marlborough, and Cardonnel with him. In August Cardonnel was thought to be 'under some uneasiness'. By the time he was due to return in November the army was already under investigation by the commission of public accounts and he seemed resigned to whatever fate would bring, writing 'everything begins to grow so indifferent to me that I shall have very little curiosity how matters go, my only aim . . . will be to retire quietly out of the noise of the world'. Back in England, Cardonnel married the widow of his long-time neighbour in Duke Street, Isaac Teale. On 7 Dec. 1711 he voted for the Whig motion of 'No Peace without Spain'. Two weeks later, on 21 Dec., the commissioners of public accounts laid before the House their report containing allegations from Sir Solomon de Medina, the army bread contractor from 1707 to 1711, that he 'gave yearly, on signing the said contracts, a gratuity of 500 gold ducats to Mr Cardonnel, secretary to the Duke of Marlborough, for his trouble and pains in translating the Dutch contracts; and putting the English contracts into form'. The allegation was part of a general attack on Marlborough. In his evidence to the commission Cardonnel had admitted that he had received about £200 on each contract, 'but would rather have been without anything'. The commissioners also claimed that he had sworn on oath that he had never heard of any gratuities paid by the bread contractor to Marlborough. This was seized on by the commissioners in their report as proof of the falsehood of Marlborough's claim that such perquisites were customary, since Cardonnel's ignorance or pretended ignorance showed 'the great caution and secrecy with which this money was constantly received' which 'gives reason to suspect that it was not thought a justifiable perquisite'. Marlborough later refuted, in a published vindication of himself, that Cardonnel had ever sworn any such thing. Three days after the report had been presented, Cardonnel wrote to Cadogan in Holland:

Sir Solomon in the affidavit he has taken declares that he was induced to make this present from what he knew had been practised by his predecessors and this is what my lord Duke's friends must endeavour to make appear, being, as you remember, the same his Grace mentioned himself in the letters he wrote to the commissioners from The Hague.

Cadogan was instructed to go immediately to The Hague to procure papers from previous bread contractors proving that such gratuities to commanders in chief had been customarily paid. He did not mention the accusation against himself. Cardonnel wrote to Watkins on 25 Dec., sending him a copy of the letter to Cadogan and directing him also to get papers which would prove their case. They 'must leave no stone unturned':

You will see by the votes that the commissioners of accounts have since brought their report into the House and that our master and your humble servant are in a manner condemned before they are heard, by which 'tis easy to guess how the stream runs . . . As for myself, if I have common justice even without any favour I can't think it can have any great consequence, however I am prepared for the worst.

Presumably this refers to the commissioners' presentation of the depositions on 22 Dec., for further consideration of the report had been put off till January. Cardonnel's own case was not taken up until February. In the meantime it appears that Marlborough and Cardonnel were badly let down: Watkins was away and did not return in time to be of much help, and, as Cardonnel wrote bitterly in January, 'I have had not one syllable of answer' from Cadogan. He wrote to Watkins on 18 Jan. 1712:

> If I suffer I take it rather to be an imputation upon my lord Duke than myself, for in all the actions of my life I can never accuse myself of having any way wronged the public, but on the contrary have created myself many enemies by endeavouring to prevent others doing it.

Enclosed in this letter he sent a copy of his defence, in which he wrote: 'I have served 21 years successively abroad without the least imputation of blame that I am sensible of, and therefore am the more concerned that any reflection should be made upon me in this House.' He admitted receiving a gratuity from Medina, but 'for the first three years, not so much as he mentions'. He claimed that he had not received the money for translating or putting the contents into form, since that was done entirely by the Treasury, nor was he the auditor of the bread account, but if in

> every campaign from the first day to the last, I am daily employed in procuring orders and letters from the general for the contractor's service, for escorts for his corn, meal and bread to and from the army and other services and that I never claimed or received the least fee from the contractor, though I was at charge in keeping my own clerks, I hope if on these considerations the contractor freely made me a present, the receiving of it for my daily care and pains will not be imputed to me as a crime.

It is not clear whether this reply was submitted in writing to the Commons or whether it was a draft of the speech Cardonnel made when his case was considered on 19 Feb. In either case his defence was not accepted by the House, which resolved by 128 votes to 100 that his taking a gratuity of 500 ducats annually from the bread contractor was 'unwarrantable and corrupt' and by a further vote of 125 to 99 he was expelled the House.[14]

Cardonnel was particularly incensed by the part played in his downfall by his former employer, Blathwayt. He wrote to Watkins on the day of his expulsion, 'our friend Blathwayt was pleased to give his helping hand' and again on 3 Mar. that despite his denials he was 'positive our master Blathwayt received a present yearly' from previous bread contractors. He asked Watkins to get certificates from the contractors in The Hague proving this, 'that I might have it in my power at least to mortify him a little'. His plan was to have the certificates and Blathwayt's deposition denying he received gratuities inserted in the newspapers in Holland, 'from whence we might have the better handle to print it here, for everybody concluded that lying declaration did me the most mischief in the House, though right or wrong they were resolved to have me out for my lord Duke's sake'. Nothing seems to have come of this scheme.[15]

Presumably Cardonnel did not consider it worthwhile to stand in the 1713 election but, despite his earlier protestations, he did unsuccessfully contest Southampton in 1715. He remained Marlborough's loyal secretary and in 1715 gave him advice on how to rectify fraud in a clothing contract for the army which had been made public and reflected badly on Marlborough. He died 22 Feb. 1719 and was buried at Chiswick, leaving £35,000 to his son and £10,000 to his daughter.[16]

[1] Add. 61411, ff. 1, 69. [2] D. C. A. Agnew, *Protestant Exiles from France*, i. 51, 199–200; ii. 371; *CSP Dom*. 1675–6, pp. 189, 241, 573; IGI, London; W. S. C. Copeman, *Apothecaries of London*, 53. [3] *HMC Lords*, iii. 432; Luttrell, *Brief Relation*, ii. 458; iii. 38; vi. 335; Coxe, *Marlborough*, i. p. xxii; v. 340; Add. 61412, f. 81. [4] Southampton RO, SC3/1/1, f. 249. [5] Agnew, 199; *Letters of Denization and Acts of Naturalization* (Huguenot Soc. of Lond. Pubns. xvii), 64, 70; *Bk. of Examinations and Depositions*, iv. 1639–44 (Southampton Rec. Soc. Pubns. 1936), 36; *Hants Mar. Lic. 1607–1640* ed. Willis, 150; *VCH Hants*, iii. 293–4; *CSP Dom*. 1661–2, pp. 504–5; 1665–6, p. 144; 1670, pp. 37, 102; *Hants Hearth Tax, 1665* (Hants Rec. Ser. xi), 288, 297; *Minute Bk. of the French Church at Southampton* (Southampton Rec. Soc. ser. xxiii), 1–51. [6] Add. 33618, ff. 27–33; 29555, ff. 25, 64; 28917, f. 222; *HMC Lords*, iii. 432; I. F. Burton, 'Secretary at War' (London Univ. Ph.D. thesis, 1960), 42–3; Add. 28917 *passim*; Univ. of London, Ms 65, item 3, subscribers to the contract for circulating Exchequer bills, May 1697; Coxe, i. p. xxii; *Wentworth Pprs*. 190. [7] *HMC Portland*, iv. 11, 613; Bodl. Carte 288, f. 344; Add 28917, f. 307; 61412, f. 81; 28918, ff. 89, 99, 105, 192, 257, 300, 331, 359; 42176, ff. 59–60, 65, 69; *Epistolary Curiosities* ed. Warner, 78; *HMC Bath*, iii. 433–4; *Wentworth Pprs*. 12. [8] Add. 42176, ff. 103, 125. [9] *HMC Bath*, iii. 433–4; *Huntington Lib. Q*. xv. 22, 35; Add. 42176, ff. 154, 171; *HMC 8th Rept*. pt. 2 (1881), 91; Coxe, iii. 41. [10] Add. 42176, ff. 194, 197, 201, 207, 209, 217, 219, 221, 227; Centre Kentish Stud. Stanhope mss U1590/0138/16, Cardonnel to Stanhope, 27 June 1708; Burnet, v. 378n. [11] PRO 31/3/195; Add. 61329, ff. 64–67. [12] Add. 42176, ff. 267, 285, 287, 293; Coxe, v. 135–8; *HMC Portland*, iv. 536; *Huntington Lib. Q*. xv. 42. [13] Add. 38500, ff. 49, 359; 38501, f. 71; 61413, f. 153; Coxe, v. 311, 340; Huntington Lib. Stowe mss 58(6) pp. 212–13; 57(4), p. 119; Burton, 264–5; *Duchess of Marlborough Corresp*. i. 405; *Bolingbroke Corresp*. i. 25; *HMC Portland*, iv. 635. [14] Add. 42176, ff. 315, 327, 331–2, 335–6, 341, 343, 345–7; 61411, ff. 1, 23; *Bolingbroke Corresp*. i. 307; Coxe, 149–61; Cobbett, *Parlty. Hist*. v. 1049–94. [15] Add. 42176, ff. 351–2, 355–6, 361. [16] Add. 37362, ff. 167, 175; 61315, ff. 223–4; 33618, ff. 27–33; *Hist. Reg. Chron*. 1719, p. 10.

P. W./S. M. W.

CAREW, Sir John, 3rd Bt. (1635–92), of Antony, nr. Saltash, Cornw.

CORNWALL	1660
BODMIN	16 May 1661–1679 (Jan.)
LOSTWITHIEL	1679 (Mar.)–1681 (Mar.)
CORNWALL	1689–1690
SALTASH	1690–1 Aug. 1692

bap. 6 Nov. 1635, 3rd but 1st surv. s. of Sir Alexander Carew, 2nd Bt.†, of Antony by Jane, da. of Robert Rolle of Heanton Satchville, Devon; bro. of Richard Carew*. *m.* (1) bef. 1664, Sarah (*d.* 1671), da. of Anthony Hungerford of Blackbourton, Oxon., 2s. *d.v.p.* 2da.; (2) Elizabeth (*d.* 1679), da. of Richard Norton I*, 2da. (*d.v.p.*); (3) by 21 Oct. 1682, Mary (*d.* 1698), da. of Sir William Morice, 1st Bt.†, of Werrington, Devon, and sis. of Sir Nicholas Morice, 2nd Bt.*, 2s. 1da. *suc.* fa. 23 Dec. 1644, bro. Richard 1691.[1]

Stannator, Penwith and Kerrier 1686.[2]
Sheriff, Cornw. 8–24 Nov. 1688.
Commr. drowned lands 1690.[3]

Carew, who had been a Presbyterian and an Exclusionist, was returned for Saltash in 1690, and classed as a Whig by the Marquess of Carmarthen (Sir Thomas Osborne†), and in April 1691 as a Country supporter by Robert Harley*. In June 1690 Carew petitioned for a renewal of a lease under the duchy of Cornwall of Trematon Castle in Saltash, which was then in his possession, but which expired in 1692. Although an extension was granted in May 1692, Carew had not taken it out at his death and with his executors unwilling to undertake the burden of upkeeping 'an old ruinous building', it reverted to the crown. In March 1692, together with the Earls of Bath and Radnor (Charles Bodvile Robartes†), Hugh Boscawen I* and other Cornish gentlemen, he subscribed £70,000 to build two ships to trade from Cornwall to India independently of the East India Company, under a grant from Charles I. Dying on 1 Aug. 1692, Carew was buried at Antony on the 6th. In his will, made in 'perfect' health on 29 Oct. 1691, he left £100 to be invested by Saltash corporation for the use of the poor. He left his estate at Antony to his wife, and in case she should die before his children came of age (as in fact she did), their custody and education was entrusted to the three surviving trustees of his post-nuptial marriage settlement of October 1682, namely Boscawen, Jonathan Rashleigh* and Nicholas Morice†, who were also made custodians of his lands in Devon and Cornwall to raise £3,000 apiece for his younger children, Gertrude and William. He was succeeded by his sons in turn, Sir Richard, 4th Bt. (*d.* 1703), and Sir William, 5th Bt.*[4]

[1] Vivian, *Vis. Devon*, 142–3; *The Gen.* xxiv. 23; PCC 220 Fane. [2] J. Tregoning, *Laws of the Stannaries*, 57. [3] *Cal. Treas. Bks.* ix. 794. [4] Ibid. 587, 1632; x. 209; Luttrell, *Brief Relation*, ii. 375; *Trans. Plymouth Inst.* ix. 293; PCC 103 Ash, 220 Fane.

E. C./S. N. H.

CAREW, Nicholas (1686–1727), of Beddington, Surr. and Dover Street, Piccadilly, London.

HASLEMERE	13 Dec. 1708–1710
	18 Mar. 1714–1722
SURREY	1722–18 Mar. 1727

bap. 26 Dec. 1686, 2nd but 1st surv. s. of Sir Francis Carew of Beddington by Anne, da. of William Boteler. *educ.* St. Catharine's, Camb. 1703. *m.* 2 Feb. 1709 (with £2,000), Elizabeth (*d.* 1740), da. of Nicholas Hackett of North Crawley, Bucks., 2s. 2da. *suc.* fa. 1689. *cr.* Bt. 11 Jan. 1715.

One of the most venerable dynasties in Surrey, the Carews had first settled at Beddington in the second half of the 14th century. Indeed, according to Aubrey's account, Beddington was 'noted for little else but the family and name of Carew'. Having gained recognition as knights of the shire as early as 1361, the family had periodically represented several of the Surrey constituencies, and their most recent parliamentarian, Carew's grandfather, Sir Nicholas†, had distinguished himself as a leading Exclusionist while sitting for Gatton between 1664 and 1681. However, by the time Carew succeeded his father in 1689, 'debauchery and neglect' had allowed the Beddington mansion to fall into temporary decay, and during his minority the estate was 'only kept by a servant or two from dilapidation'. Nevertheless, Carew's uncle Nicholas ensured that the family remained a political force within Surrey. Although ultimately failing to gain entrance to Parliament, the elder Carew stood for election at the county contests of 1698 and December 1701, and endeavoured to secure his return at Gatton in 1698, as well as at Bletchingley in 1695 and 1702. His political ambition may even have caused him in January 1701 to seek electoral success at the Cornish borough of St. Mawes, a constituency which later favoured the Onslow family, one of the Carews' staunchest Whig allies in Surrey. The younger Carew's own parliamentary aspirations were suggested by his attendance at the Bedfordshire election of 1705, a presence which reflected his family's territorial influence in that county. However, with extensive proprietorial interests in the north-east of Surrey, he was clearly capable of playing a significant role in the politics of his home county.[1]

Having recently visited such leading local politicians as Sir Richard Onslow, 3rd Bt.*, Sir William Scawen* and Sir John Parsons*, Carew eagerly sought to gain entrance to Parliament at the Haslemere by-election of December 1708. Even though Haslemere stood at the opposite end of the shire to his own residence, Carew took the seat vacated by fellow Whig Thomas Onslow* without a contest, thereby replicating the success of an early Stuart ancestor, Sir Francis[†]. In the House itself Carew proved far from conspicuous, his only significant contribution to the business of the House in his first Parliament resting with an appointment in the second session to the drafting committee on a bill to establish a land registry in Surrey. However, his Whiggish sympathies were clearly in evidence, for he supported the naturalization of the Palatines in early 1709 and a year later voted in favour of the impeachment of Dr Sacheverell.

The Haslemere election of October 1710 proved a bitter disappointment for Carew. Less than a week before the poll he was fairly confident of securing one of the seats, although he felt it prudent to send for an additional 100 guineas in order to improve his electoral chances. However, these extra funds did not prevent his finishing behind the two Tory candidates, a defeat rendered even more galling when a subsequent scrutiny disqualified nearly half of Carew's votes. Although he petitioned the House on 5 Dec. 1710 against the return of his Tory rival Theophilus Oglethorpe*, the elections committee never reported on his allegations. He did not stand at the next general election, where the Haslemere seats were shared between the two parties, but he scored a second by-election victory there after Thomas Onslow had again opted to stand for Bletchingley. In the short remainder of the session he twice acted as a teller on election matters: on 23 Mar. 1714, to instruct the elections committee to appoint a day to discuss the London return; and, on 25 June, to adjourn debate on the Southwark election. Given his presence at Westminster, he can probably be identified as the 'Nicholas Carew' who on 1 Aug. was in attendance at St. James's palace for the proclamation of the accession of George I.

The advent of the new royal dynasty proved a particular blessing for Carew, for he was honoured with a baronetcy in January 1715, and within weeks had achieved his first victory at a general election. A parliamentary list confirmed his Whiggish allegiance soon afterwards, and thereafter he proved a steady supporter of the ministry, although he did oppose the peerage bill. At the election of 1722 he managed to secure a prestigious county seat, taking advantage of the temporary absence of an Onslow candidate. He died on 18 Mar. 1727, shortly before he had a chance to seek re-election, but Arthur Onslow[†] later paid tribute to his political interest by earnestly soliciting the support of his widow, Lady Elizabeth, who subsequently married William Chetwynd[†], Member for Wootton Bassett between 1722 and 1727. Although Carew had succeeded in temporarily re-establishing the family's influence in local political circles, his principal achievement lay with the development of Beddington, the estate being transformed within his lifetime into a 'magnificently great' house with 'exquisitely fine' gardens. Although his heir, Sir Nicholas Hackett Carew, 2nd Bt., was not politically inclined, and was destined to be the last baronet, the Carew name remained indissolubly linked with Beddington for the rest of the 18th century.[2]

[1] Add. 29599, ff. 98, 131, 149; IGI, London; Manning and Bray, *Surr.* ii. 522–3, 527; J. Aubrey, *Surr.* ii. 159–60; *Evelyn Diary*, v. 427; *Surr. Arch. Colls.* x. 258. [2] *Surr. Arch. Colls.* 266, 270–1; Add. 29598, f. 18; 29599, f. 256; Boyer, *Pol. State*, viii. 117; *Cal. Treas. Bks.* xxix. 394; Defoe, *Tour* ed. Cole, i. 158.

P. L. G.

CAREW, Richard (1641–91), of Abertanat, Salop.

CALLINGTON   1679 (Oct.)–1681 (Mar.)
SALTASH   1690–c.Sept. 1691

bap. 21 Apr. 1641, 6th but 4th surv. s. of Sir Alexander Carew, 2nd Bt.[†]; bro. of Sir John Carew, 3rd Bt.* *m.* lic. 31 July 1674, Penelope, da. and coh. of Rice Tanat of Abertanat, *s.p.*[1]

Sub-commr. prizes, Plymouth ?1689–*d.*[2]

Returned for Saltash on his family's interest in 1690, Carew was listed as a Whig by Lord Carmarthen (Sir Thomas Osborne[†]) in March 1690, and by Robert Harley* in April 1691 as a Court supporter. His one parliamentary action of note was consistent with this as on 17 May he acted as a teller for the motion that the right of election for New Windsor lay in the mayor, bailiffs and select burgesses only, a franchise which favoured the Court Whig candidates. He made his will at Plymouth on 22 Aug. 1691, leaving most of his property to his brother. He was replaced as a sub-commissioner at Plymouth on 15 Sept. and buried at Antony on the 18th. After his death a dispute arose over the property he had inherited through his wife in Denbighshire, Montgomeryshire and Shropshire, which it was claimed should have reverted to his sisters-in-law upon payment of £4,000 by his executors, rather than go to his heir, his nephew, Sir Richard Carew, 4th Bt. In the event, in January 1698 the House of Lords reversed a decree in the 4th baronet's favour.[3]

[1]Vivian, *Vis. Devon*, 142; *The Gen*. xxv. 154. [2]*Cal. Treas. Bks*. ix. 1307. [3]Vivian, 142; *Cal. Treas. Bks*. 1307; PCC 5 Fane; *HMC Lords*, n.s. iii. 6–7.

E. C./S. N. H.

CAREW, Thomas (1664–1705), of Barley, nr. Exeter, Devon.

SALTASH   22 Mar. 1701–1705

bap. 31 Mar. 1664, 2nd but 1st surv. s. of Sir Thomas Carew† of Barley by Elizabeth, da. of John Cooper of Bowhill, Exeter. *educ.* M. Temple 1684. *unm. suc.* fa. 1681.[1]

?Sub-commr. prizes, Plymouth 1689.[2]

Capt. 10 Ft. by 1690–4; maj. and capt. of ft. Northcote's regt. 1694–7, 31 Ft. 1702, lt.-col. 1703–*d*.[3]

Carew was an army officer in the 1st Earl of Bath's regiment, which was composed mainly of Cornishmen. In 1694 he transferred to another regiment, but was placed on half-pay when it disbanded in 1697. He acted as executor in 1699 to his brother Henry, a teller of the Exchequer, who had been involved in the false endorsement of Exchequer bills (see DUNCOMBE, Charles). Returned for Saltash at a by-election in 1701 and again at the general election in December, presumably on the interest of his kinsman Sir Richard Carew, 4th Bt., of Antony, he was classed as a Tory by Robert Harley* and voted on 26 Feb. 1702 in favour of the motion to vindicate the Commons proceedings in the impeachments of William III's ministers. At the 1702 general election he was again elected for Saltash, but must have been abroad for most of that year since he served with his new regiment on the expedition to Cadiz and took part in the capture of the Spanish galleons in Vigo Bay. Sir Richard Carew, upon his death in 1703, bequeathed his personal estate to Thomas' brother, Richard, also of Barley, no doubt owing to financial disputes with Nicholas Morice†, his surviving trustee. In 1704 Carew was forecast as a probable supporter of the Tack, but did not vote for it on 28 Nov. His army commission explains his appearance on a list of placemen for 1705. He died on 7 Apr. 1705, two days after the dissolution, and was buried at St. Thomas the Apostle's, Exeter. He left each of his three sisters £100, and the same amount to his native parish; the remainder of his estate went to his brother, Richard.[4]

[1]IGI, Devon; Vivian, *Vis. Devon*, 142; *The Gen*. xxv. 155; Le Neve's *Knights* (Harl. Soc. viii), 264. [2]*CSP Dom*. 1689–90, p. 172. [3]Ibid. 1690–1, p. 3. [4]*CJ*, xii. 574; *Cal. Treas. Bks*. xiv. 349; xv. 450; PCC 85 Gee.

E. C./S. N. H.

CAREW, Sir William, 5th Bt. (1690–1744), of Antony, nr. Saltash, Cornw.

SALTASH   17 Jan. 1711–1713
CORNWALL   1713–8 Mar. 1744

bap. 24 Jan. 1690, 2nd s. of Sir John Carew, 3rd Bt.*, by his 3rd w. *educ.* Exeter, Oxf. 1707. *m.* 5 Jan. 1714 (with £3,000), Lady Anne, da. and h. of Gilbert, 4th Earl of Coventry, 1s. 1da. *d.v.p. suc.* bro. as 5th Bt. 24 Sept. 1703.[1]

Carew, whose father died when he was very young, was cared for by his mother until her death in 1698. His maternal uncle, Nicholas Morice†, then acted as guardian for both Carew and his elder brother, Sir Richard, the 4th baronet. Following his brother's death, Carew succeeded to the baronetcy. In 1707 he went up to Oxford, where he had trouble in extracting money from his guardian. Morice complained that Carew 'cannot want money without much ill husbandry and profuseness', especially as he had spent most of his time at the home of his brother-in-law, Sir Godfrey Copley, 2nd Bt.* Money problems underlined a difficult relationship, with Morice even complaining that his medical advice had been rejected, Carew having 'a very ill habit of body, and without giving vent to those ill humours wherewith he so much abounds, they will prove pernicious and fatal to him'. Political differences did not help matters, for as with his brother, growing maturity saw Carew begin to flex his muscles in the family's traditional area of influence at Saltash. Thus, in 1708 the Whiggish Morice had found that his nephew had his own ideas about the forthcoming election and was willing to join with the Bullers in favour of a Tory.[2]

It is likely that as soon as Carew came of age he entered Parliament for Saltash. This would explain why he did not contest the by-election held in December 1710, but rather waited for Alexander Pendarves to choose Penryn, which he did on 23 Dec. 1710, thereby precipitating a by-election in January 1711. Significantly, Carew gave Morice his 'absolute quietus and discharge' in November 1711, which had been delayed following disputes about the management of the estate and Carew's desire to retain Morice's agent, Richard Blighe, as his steward. Carew was not an active Member, being given leave of absence on 26 May 1712 for five weeks, but he was present on 18 June 1713 to vote for the French commerce bill. In July his influence was recognized by the government manager for the Cornish boroughs, Lord Lansdown (George Granville*), who asked Lord Treasurer Oxford (Robert Harley*) to oblige Carew by appointing a near relation of his to be post-master at Camelford. Having returned home to Cornwall in mid-August 1713, Carew was returned for the county at the ensuing general election. He was classified as a Tory in the Worsley list and on two lists comparing the Parliaments of 1713 and 1715.[3]

In November 1714 Carew was reported to be ready to spend heavily in the Tory cause at Liskeard and Saltash and to be confident of carrying the county contest. He was imprisoned during the Fifteen, and as a consequence lost his place on the bench the following year. However, he retained his county seat until his death on 8 Mar. 1744. His contemporary Thomas Tonkin* described him as 'a gentleman that in every respect comes up to the merits of the greatest of his ancestors'.[4]

[1] Vivian, *Vis. Devon*, 143; *Top. and Gen*. iii. 509; Boyer, *Pol. State*, vii. 55; Polsue, *Complete Paroch. Hist. Cornw*. i. 23, 26; *Trans. Plymouth Inst*. ix. 293. [2] *HMC Lords*, n.s. iii. 7; Morice mss at Bank of Eng. Nicholas to Humphry Morice*, 5 Oct. 1707, 5, 21 Mar. 1707[-8], 7 Oct. 1709. [3] Morice mss, Richard Blighe to Humphry Morice, 22 Sept., 9 Nov. 1711, same to ?Joseph Moyle*, 17 Aug. 1713; *HMC Portland*, v. 307. [4] Bodl. Ballard 18, ff. 71–72; Morice mss, (Sir) William Pole (4th Bt.*) to [?], 13 Nov. 1715; L. K. J. Glassey, *Appt. JPs*. 253; *Gent. Mag*. 1744, p. 168; Polsue, 23.

E. C./S. N. H.

CAREY *see also* **CARY**

CAREY, Anthony, 5th Visct. Falkland [S] (1656–94), of Great Tew, Oxon.

OXFORDSHIRE	1685–1687
GREAT MARLOW	1689–1690
GREAT BEDWYN	1690–24 May 1694

b. 15 Feb. 1656, o. s. of Henry Carey†, 4th Visct. Falkland, by Rachel, da. of Anthony Hungerford† of Blackbourton. *educ*. Winchester 1668; Christ Church, Oxf. 1672. *m*. June 1681, Rebecca (*d*. 1709), da. of Sir Rowland Lytton† of Knebworth, Herts., 1da. *d.v.p. suc*. fa. 2 Apr. 1663.[1]

Treasurer of the navy 1681–9; groom of the stole to Prince George 1687–90; ld. of the Admiralty 1691–Apr. 1693, first ld. Apr. 1693–Apr. 1694; PC 17 Mar. 1692–*d*.; envoy extraordinary to States General c.May 1694–*d*.[2]

Freeman, Portsmouth 1682–*d*., Wallingford 1685.[3]

Lord Falkland had rescued himself from debt by marrying 'a very great fortune', and had had the further good luck to invest in 1686–7 in a highly profitable expedition for the recovery of sunken treasure. Not all his ventures were so opportune, however: a trading voyage to the West Indies and South Seas, in which he participated, lost almost £43,000. Partly because of this, his finances were not robust enough in 1690 for him to afford to forgo the remuneration of office; nor, indeed, for him to contemplate an expensive county election when he could be brought into Parliament more cheaply elsewhere. The offer from an 'old friend', possibly Francis Stonehouse*, of a 'secure' return at Great Bedwyn easily dissuaded him from seeking re-election in Oxfordshire, where a contest was in prospect. Classified as a Tory and Court supporter in one of Lord Carmarthen's (Sir Thomas Osborne†) lists of the new Parliament, and again as a Court supporter in another Carmarthen list, he spoke on 9 Apr. 1690 against committing the recognition bill, and on 26 Apr. against the abjuration bill at its second reading, although on both occasions he took pains to proclaim his loyalty to the Williamite regime. 'I am as much for the interest of this bill as anybody', he declared of the former, and while he regarded the abjuration bill as at best futile and at worst counter-productive – 'destructive to the government' – he added the disclaimer, 'I have suffered too much in the last government ever to desire it to come back'. Early in June he lost his place as groom of the stole to Prince George, having asked permission to remain in England rather than attend the Prince on the Irish campaign, 'upon the score . . . of private business'. At first the Prince had granted him leave, but when his colleague Lord Cornbury (Edward Hyde*) made a similar request, an angry Princess Anne intervened, and prevailed with her husband to replace both men. It was presumably not long after his dismissal, and as a consequence, that Falkland figured on a list of 'managers of the King's directions' in the Commons, as one who was 'discontented'. In October, after Parliament had reopened, he sent a promise of support to Robert Harley* over his election petition for New Radnor. His support for Whigs against Tories in several election disputes in late October and early November, in which he was accompanied by Sir Edward Seymour, 4th Bt.*, aroused considerable comment. This separation from the rest of his party culminated in his telling on two occasions (on 4 and 25 Nov.) for John Grobham Howe* in the Cirencester election, which was popularly explained as arising from an antipathy to one of Howe's opponents, Henry Powle*. More important may have been the fact that Howe was the courtier among the three candidates. Falkland could already have received some prior assurance of his imminent re-employment, in the Admiralty commission, to which he was officially appointed in January 1691, although news writers had the story by 20 Dec. At any rate he was included in another list compiled by Carmarthen in December, probably of Members on whose loyalty Carmarthen could rely in the event of a Commons attack on his ministerial position.[4]

Falkland proved a conscientious placeman, giving an early instance of his dutifulness in the hostility with which he responded in March 1691 to the investigations of the commissioners of accounts. In the 1691-2 session he was named to four drafting committees, and on 9 Nov. to a committee to inspect the naval estimates, having spoken for the Court in the preceding debate. On 14 Nov., having delivered to the House copies of Admiral Russell's (Edward*) orders for the summer's expedition, he made several further interventions on the Court side in the adjourned debate on the estimates, and a week later spoke in defence of Sir Ralph Delaval*, and the Admiralty commission, in the affair of the intercepted French documents. He was one of the Court speakers on 15 Dec. when it was the turn of the army estimates to be scrutinized, supporting the resolution of the select committee that Dutch forces on the English establishment be paid according to English rates. He also twice defended the East India Company, in debates on 17 and 18 Dec. He told on 7 Jan. 1692 against agreeing with the Lords' request for a further conference on the treason trials bill, and again on 12 Feb. against a proposed rider to the Irish forfeitures bill that would have reserved a third of those lands for veterans of the Irish campaigns. Two days after he had opposed Hon. John Granville's* motion of 15 Feb. to tack to the poll tax bill a clause reviving the commission of accounts, he presented on behalf of the Court the excise loan bill. His reward for the session's work came the following month, when he was sworn a Privy Councillor.[5]

Twice listed as a placeman in 1692, once by Carmarthen, in parliamentary terms Falkland was the most active and prominent of the Admiralty commissioners, presenting various papers and estimates in November and early December, and was always to the fore when naval matters were discussed. After joining other Court party men on 15 Nov. in pressing for immediate consideration of the King's Speech, against Country party delaying tactics, he made a stout defence of the Admiralty on 21 Nov. in a debate on advice to be tendered to the King. This included calls for a new commission to be constituted of men with some practical experience, which would supersede the present 'land admirals', as Falkland and the other commissioners were nicknamed. His opinion was that 'the true cause of these mischiefs complained of proceeds from the want of cruisers and convoys', and reminded the House that 'I told you so the last year that your service would suffer ... when you denied the building of four':

Then his lordship reflected on the merchants' petition and the report from the committee thereon, took notice of some omissions therein and reflected on the same, and concluded he doubted not but the chairman [John Granville] had made a report according to his ability. So there was some contest between Colonel Granville and the Lord Falkland about it, on which Sir Thomas Clarges* called to the orders of the House – that when a matter is reported from a committee and the House hath approved it, it is not very usual to have the chairman or committee arraigned as that noble lord hath.

Despite the 'pleading' of Falkland and his fellow commissioner Sir Richard Onslow, 3rd Bt.*, the address was voted. Falkland's reaction was that 'if this committee be of opinion that I am not fit I will submit, but it is hard to be condemned upon common fame'. He continued his opposition when the resolution to address was reported, speaking 'very handsomely' and in particular answering points made by Colonel George Churchill* to such good effect that Churchill exempted him from further criticism, 'as having better experience than the ignorant major part which govern'. Two more interventions of his in debates on naval affairs are recorded this session. On 29 Nov., having first informed the House as to the disposition of men in the service, he spoke in favour of the motion to build eight new fourth-rate ships, 'as necessary as any in the estimate', adding, with a reference back to his previous claims regarding losses, 'for want of which you suffered much this summer'. He repeated this recommendation two days later. His other contributions were as befitting a placeman. He opposed on 21 Nov. 1692 demands for the removal of foreign general officers, arguing that any such decisions ought to be left to the King, 'who I doubt not will care therein'. He was a teller on 28 Nov. on an amendment to the treason trials bill. He spoke for the Court on 3 and 13 Dec. in the committee of supply and ways and means. He supported the abjuration bill at its second reading on 14 Dec., in a sharp *volte-face* from his opinion of two years before, on the grounds that now 'there is [an] absolute need to settle this government' and that to reject the bill would have 'ill consequences' abroad and greatly encourage 'the enemies of the government' at home. He served again as a teller on 2 Jan., against calling over the House. He spoke against the place bill at its third reading on 22 Dec.; and he both spoke and told against the triennial bill when it was reported on 9 Feb. 1693, because, he said, of his concern for the King's prerogative and his having observed that 'your enemies without doors and such as refuse the oaths to this government are best pleased with this bill – nay, I am told some of them are making interests to be chosen in your new Parliament'. His last known speech of the session occurred on 6 Mar., when he gave his support to a bill to set aside amendments in the records of a fine and two recoveries in Wales, on behalf of Lord Pembroke (Thomas Herbert†). Once more he was rewarded for his efforts, being promoted to first lord in April 1693, and he was included in three lists of placemen during the year, including that of Samuel Grascome.[6]

As first lord, Falkland was busier than ever in the House on naval affairs. In the first weeks of the 1693–4 session he laid before the House a series of papers, accounts, estimates and lists. On the question of naval mismanagements he adopted a very aggressive approach, and sought to excuse his own board by throwing all blame for the loss of the Smyrna convoy on admirals Delaval, Killigrew (Henry*) and Shovell (Sir Clowdesley*). He had already clashed with Killigrew during the Privy Council inquiry, the admiral having objected that in reading out a letter from Killigrew and his colleagues Falkland had suppressed a crucial passage which would have helped their cause, and Falkland in turn protesting when one of Killigrew's friends made this allegation public. In Parliament he took a place in the vanguard of the Whig attack on the admirals, his speech of 20 Nov. making a trenchant statement of the board's case, and insinuating in broad terms worse than incompetence on the part of those responsible for the summer's catastrophe:

> The commissioners of the Admiralty sent for an account of the execution of their orders; and that account was not sent for a long time after. They ought either to have executed their orders, or sent word why they did not . . . If orders were found impracticable, with respect to the board, they ought to have had notice. The council of war thought them impracticable: if they were ill orders, why was it not represented? If good, why not obeyed? The loss was a great misfortune to the nation, and all by mismanagement. It was a great charge for Sir George Rooke* to be sent away without orders – such a chain of causes all along, that I cannot think all this was done by chance. If some course be not taken, all will be lost, and it is nowhere to be done but here. These that sit at the helm, how can they serve the kingdom and King James too?

Two days later, after Killigrew had replied to Falkland's charges, and the three admirals had been examined at the bar, Falkland reopened the onslaught against them, pouring scorn on their claims not to have had orders in time: 'we could not know whether the French fleet was got out, but they should have known it'. But it was his speech on 27 Nov. that created the greatest stir. A foreign observer reported that

> Mylord Falkland . . . qui de Tory est devenu Whig et ennemi des Amiraux cassés fit une forte harangue contre leur conduite et même contre les ministres d'état Toris sans les nommer, qui ont eu la direction des affaires pendant trois ou quatre ans et dont la négligence est cause qu'on n'a rien fait d'utile pour leur Majestés et pour la nation: que si l'on ne faisoit pas mieux à l'avenir ce seroit encore un argent perdu que celui des subsides qu'on va donner, mais qu'il y a tout sujet d'espérer que la conduite sera dorénavant meilleure puis qu'on a changé de mains et que les nouveaux directeurs ne négligeront pas le bien de l'état et ne favoriseront pas l'intérêt des Jacobites, prenant a témoin les Membres des provinces éloignées si les Jacobites n'y sont pas devenus insolens depuis que quelques seigneurs du gouvernement les favorisent . . . il a loué la conduite de Mylord Torrington [Arthur Herbert†] lors qu'il se laissa battre par les Français, ou pour mieux dire lors qu'il laissa battre les Hollandais sans les secourir. Il dit qu'ayant sauvé la flotte il fut au hazard de perdre sa vie parce qu'un secrétaire d'état soit son ennemi. Il loua ensuite la conduite de l'Amiral Russell à la bataille de l'année dernière mais que cela n'avoit point empêché la même secrétaire de lui être contraire afin qu'il ne commandât pas la flotte cette année. En un mot il dit tous de choses et si différentes qu'on a de la peine à comprendre quel a été son but si ce n'est pas de se faire des amis nouveaux pour se mieux soutenir dans son emploi.

Any mystery surrounding Falkland's donning Whig colours, his desire for new political friends and his anxiety to retain his place would soon be dispelled when the commissioners of accounts reported on 7 Dec. Meanwhile he spoke on 28 Nov. against an amendment proposed by Harley to the triennial bill, and on 6 Dec. made another, less spectacular contribution to the debate on the miscarriages at sea. The accounts commissioners' report depicted him as still in need of funds, and as having made himself vulnerable by resort to irregular means to obtain them. It transpired that in the previous March he had approached Francis Rainsford, the Admiralty receiver, with a demand from the King for the payment of £4,000 in banker's notes, £2,000 in the name of Randolph Keine, a Dutch usher in the King's household, and £2,000 in various other names, the transaction to be kept secret. Keine's money had been accounted for, but not the rest. At first Falkland provided little or no evidence as to its ultimate destination, other than to tell the Commons that he had attended the King in April 1693 and had been promised directions, and to declare that he had not made any of the bills over to MPs. He relied on having acted by the King's order. However, when it was proposed on 7 Dec. that he withdraw and the sense of the House be taken, he volunteered the further evidence that he believed the money to have been intended for the King's 'immediate use' and that he had in fact been told to pay it over to the clerk of the closet for this purpose. But at this stage the Commons' concern was less with the demand for and payment of the money itself, which, though shady and irregular, was not obviously criminal, given that the King had authorized it, than with Falkland's suppression of evidence, to which Rainsford had testified and which he himself had admitted. While the accounts commissioners' investigations were under way Falkland had sent for Rainsford and on being shown the original of the letter in which the demand for the money had been made, had taken hold of it and kept it. As Falkland waited at the door of the House, visibly 'dans une grande inquiétude', his conduct was debated for two hours. Only the staunch backing of the leading Court Whigs, and in particular a strong statement on his behalf by Edward Russell, prevented him from being sent to the Tower, a motion for his committal being defeated by 38 votes in a House of over 300. Instead he was reprimanded. He also survived further revelations by the accounts commission of having received secret service money, claiming that it had been given for 'important considerations' and disposed of for the King's service. But on 9 Feb. 1694 the affair of the missing £2,000 reared up again. The accounts commissioners reported evidence Falkland had given them on 8 Dec., the day after his censure by the House, in which for the first time he acknowledged that the names on the bills, other than Keine's, were fictitious; that he had only recently informed the King of his receipt of the bills; and, most damaging of all, that at the outset of the business he had made a proposition to the Speaker (Sir John Trevor*) to join with him in procuring a sum of money by this means. It was now undeniable that the extra £2,000 had been destined for his own pocket, though he refused to say whether the King had promised it to him, and when asked if he had expected it replied, 'I have deserved more than that from this government, having been a great loser since the Revolution, and served it faithfully'. This time Russell could not save him, and on 16 Feb. 1694 he was sent to the Tower for 'a high misdemeanour and breach of trust' in 'begging and procuring' the £2,000 from the King 'contrary to the ordinary method of issuing ... money'. After three days, and on a petition presented by Thomas Erle*, he was discharged.[7]

King William had little choice but to remove Falkland when the Admiralty commission was remodelled in April 1694, but although discredited he was not abandoned. Rumour had it that he would be raised to the English peerage, and, a new departure for him, be appointed an ambassador. Early in May he was indeed named envoy to the States General, and his appointment must have been confirmed by 21 May when the King signed a warrant for his allowances. Already, however, he was 'very ill' with smallpox, and he died on the night of 24 May, being buried in Westminster Abbey. Despite Falkland's recent disgrace, John Evelyn, a family friend, could write of him as 'a pretty brisk, understanding, industrious young man, had formerly been faulty, now very much reclaimed ... Had been advancing extremely in the new court. All this now gone in a moment.' To Evelyn and to other less well-informed commentators, Falkland's signal achievement appeared to have been his reconstruction of the family fortune. But while his wife was satisfactorily provided for, from her own property and from the manor of Great Tew, settled on her and her heirs at marriage after her mother had bought out a previous mortgage, his own personal estate was insufficient to cover his debts, including the amount he still owed the crown from his treasurership of the navy. His successor in the viscountcy, a second cousin, became a Jacobite peer, and no member of the family sat again in Parliament until Lucius Ferdinand Cary, MP for Bridport 1774–80.[8]

[1] *CJ*, xiv. 118; *Her. and Gen.* iii. 40. [2] *CSP Dom.* 1694–5, p. 114. [3] R. East, *Portsmouth Recs.* 366; J. K. Hedges, *Hist. Wallingford*, ii. 239. [4] *CJ*, 118; *Evelyn Diary*, v. 182–3; *HMC Lords*, n.s. vi. 59; *Cal. Treas. Pprs. 1557–1696*, pp. 335–6, 457; *HMC Portland*, viii. 28; Newberry Lib. Chicago, case mss E5, C5434, f. 31, Clarendon to Abingdon, 15 Feb. 1690; Grey, x. 45, 77; Bodl. Rawl. A.79, ff. 71–72, 84; *Clarendon Corresp.* ii. 315; A. Browning, *Danby*, iii. 179; Add. 70230, John Hampden† to Harley, 15 Oct. 1690; Morrice ent'ring bk. 3, p. 218; H. Horwitz, *Parl. and Pol. Wm. III*, 81; *CSP Dom.* 1690–1, p. 225; Wood, *Life and Times*, iii. 348–9; Luttrell, *Brief Relation*, ii. 150. [5] *EHR*, xci. 45; *Luttrell Diary*, 10, 19, 82, 87–88, 187; Bodl. Carte 130, f. 328; Grey, 183; Luttrell, ii. 387, 390. [6] *Luttrell Diary*, 228, 245–6, 252, 265, 267, 282, 287, 290–1, 312, 315–16, 335, 415, 469; Nottingham Univ. Lib. Portland (Bentinck) mss PwA 2389, rep. of debate, 21 Nov. 1692; Carte 130, f. 340; Grey, 253–4, 270, 296. [7] Horwitz, 118, 125, 128; Luttrell, iii. 210, 214; *HMC Lords*, n.s. i. 251–2; Add. 17677 NN, ff. 320–1, 324–5; Grey, 319, 323–4, 329–30, 347–56; Cobbett, *Parlty. Hist.* v. 786; *HMC 7th Rep.* 215, 218; Ranke, vi. 225; Wood, 444. [8] Horwitz, 132; Wood, 446, 453; Luttrell, iii. 280, 299–300, 314, 317; *HMC Buccleuch*, ii. 65, 68; *CSP Dom.* 1694–5, p. 144; *Evelyn Diary*, v. 182–3; *CJ*, 118; *Cal. Treas. Bks.* x. 838.

D. W. H.

CAREY, Nicholas (c.1651–1697), of Up Cerne, Dorset and Hackney, Mdx.

BRIDPORT   1695–Apr./May 1697

b. c.1651, s. of Nicholas Carey, 'practitioner of physic', of St. Giles Cripplegate, London, by one Aimée. m. Susan, 1s. 2da.[1]

Apprentice, Goldsmiths' Co. 1663, freeman 1671, rentor 1689, prime warden 1695.[2]

Little is known of Carey's genealogy, other than that his father was an unlicensed London physician, and his mother was probably a French Huguenot. His father had achieved notoriety in 1676 when he undertook to publish *The Long Parliament Dissolved*, a tract written by Denzil Holles†. He was arrested and spent several months in the Tower after refusing to state whether he was acting on behalf of Holles, only confirming that the author had been his patient. It may have been from this episode that Carey developed a long friendship with Roger Morrice, the divine who was successively chaplain to Sir John Maynard† and Holles. Carey himself became a London goldsmith and banker, setting up in partnership with (Sir) Thomas Cooke* at the *Griffin* in Exchange Alley. In addition to their banking operations, both men jointly owned Hackney manor.³

Carey was pricked as one of the sheriffs of London in 1694, but instead chose to fine off. In the following year he was returned as Member for Bridport. Since his parliamentary colleague was another banker, Stephen Evance, a business connexion between the two men might explain Carey's choice of constituency. Nevertheless, at his election he may have depended upon his local association with Bridport, for he had already begun to set himself up as a country gentleman in 1685 with his purchase, for £11,000, of the manor of Up Cerne, 15 miles north-east of the borough. He had also solicited the help of his friend Morrice, who in September 1695 wrote to an anonymous party to acknowledge Carey's thanks 'for your readiness to devolve your interest upon him at such places as you think fit, and in one he has some little acquaintance'. Forecast as likely to support the government in the divisions of 31 Jan. 1696 over the proposed council of trade, he signed the Association in February and voted in March in favour of fixing the price of guineas at 22s. and on 25 Nov. for the attainder of Sir John Fenwick†.⁴

Carey wrote his will on 6 May 1696, giving Hackney as his address. He gave his wife a life interest in his houses in Southwark and St. Clement Danes, Westminster, and his property in Dorset to his son, also named Nicholas. His two daughters were secured with £5,000 marriage portions, friends and relations were bequeathed £1,650 and several sums of £30 were granted to the poor of Up Cerne, Stepney and Hackney. He also set aside £100 towards poor French Protestants and 'poor ministers not of the Church of England'. Carey probably died between 16 Apr. 1697, when Parliament was prorogued, and 17 May, when his will was proved. In the 1697–8 session a bill was passed for vesting a moiety of his messuages and lands in Hackney in trustees for the benefit of his son and widow.⁵

¹*HMC Lords*, n.s. iii. 172; Goldsmiths' Hall, apprenticeship bk. 2, f. 139; *CSP Dom.* 1676–7, p. 565. ²Goldsmiths' Hall, apprenticeship and freedom index, ct. bk. 10, f. 30; *Wardens and Members Ct. of Goldsmiths' Co.* 1. ³*CSP Dom.* 1675–6, pp. 547, 563; 1677–8, p. 47; *LJ*, xiii. 54–56. ⁴Luttrell, *Brief Relation*, iii. 325; *Portledge Pprs.* 180; Hutchins, *Dorset*, iv. 151; Lysons, *Environs* (1792–6), ii. 452; Dr Williams' Lib. Morrice mss 10, x. f. 5. ⁵PCC 90 Pyne.

P. W./H. J. L.

CARMICHAEL, Sir James, 4th Bt. (c.1690–1727), of Bonnington, Lanark.

LINLITHGOWSHIRE and LINLITHGOW BURGHS 1713–8 Apr. 1714
LINLITHGOW BURGHS 8 Apr. 1714–1715

b. c.1690, 2nd s. of Sir John Carmichael, 2nd Bt., of Bonnington, by Lady Henrietta, da. of James Johnstone, 1st Earl of Annandale [S]. *m.* contract 7 Jan. 1715, Margaret (*d.* 1759), da. and coh. of William Maxwell (aft. Baillie, *d.* 1725), MP [S], of Lamington, Lanark, 1s. 1da. *suc.* er. bro. as 4th Bt. 5 June 1691.

Burgess, Glasgow 1704, Edinburgh 1705, Lanark 1713.¹

Although undoubtedly the great-grandson of the 1st Lord Carmichael, this Member has a somewhat confusing genealogy. His grandfather, Sir James Carmichael of Bonnington (or Bonnytown), became a baronet in or about 1676. The mode was indirect: he bought, for £100, a blank warrant of baronetcy from John Bannatine, tutor to the Duchess of Hamilton's sons, who had obtained the warrant as a reward from his patroness. No formal record of Carmichael's elevation survives, but Sir James was reputedly accorded the rank of baronet by contemporaries. In later documents relating to the family's estates, however, he was styled *miles* or knight, which has caused confusion in the enumeration of the baronetcy. This usage, which was applied to other known baronets, should nevertheless be discounted and Sir James regarded as the 1st baronet. His eldest son, also James, who died in his father's lifetime, is sometimes wrongly dubbed the 2nd baronet, whereas this designation properly belongs to the second son, John, the Member's father. Sir John Carmichael died in January 1691, and was succeeded by his infant son, William, who survived his father by a mere five months. His younger brother, James, thus became the 4th baronet when he was less than two years old. Carmichael inherited a substantial landed estate spread across three Scottish counties: Ayrshire, Dumfriesshire and Lanarkshire.²

The most significant political influence within Carmichael's immediate family was his maternal uncle, the 1st Marquess of Annandale, and it was through him that Carmichael was introduced to

London society. In 1710–11, he became a member of the informal Anglo-Scottish dining club of Annandale's friend, Lord Ossulston. Supported by the Marquess, Carmichael stood for the shire and burghs district of Linlithgow in 1713. Successful for both, he was unseated on petition from the county but retained Linlithgow Burghs, which he had captured by virtue of a pact with Hon. George Douglas*. During his canvass, Carmichael had also enjoyed Squadrone support and was endorsed by Presbyterian ministers as a thoroughgoing Whig. In Lord Polwarth's analysis of the Scottish returns for 1713, he was listed as a Hanoverian.[3]

Carmichael made little impression at Westminster. He voted against the expulsion of Richard Steele on 18 Mar. 1714, and was later classified as a Whig in the Worsley list. With his kinsmen the Earl of Hyndford and Lord Carmichael, he played a prominent role in celebrations of the proclamation of George I at Lanark in August 1714. In honour of the pact with Douglas, Carmichael did not stand for the burghs district in 1715 and declined to make a second bid for the county. Although he did not stand for Parliament on any subsequent occasion, he continued to be active in public affairs in his locality, and, having been commissioned as a deputy-lieutenant, played a part in his county's resistance to the Fifteen. He subsequently discharged his duties conscientiously on the Lanarkshire commission of the peace.[4]

Carmichael died, aged 37, at Edinburgh on 16 July 1727 and was buried at Lamington, an estate (reportedly worth 20,000 merks p.a.) which his wife had recently inherited from her father. In expectation of succeeding to Lamington, Carmichael's eldest son, William, adopted the surname Baillie-Carmichael, but died in 1738, during his mother's lifetime, whereupon the baronetcy became extinct and the estates passed to his sister, Henrietta. In 1741, she married Robert Dundas† of Arniston, half-brother to the great Henry Dundas†, bringing with her then (so it was said) a fortune of £2,000 p.a.[5]

[1] *Scots Peerage* ed. Paul, iv. 587; *Hist. Scot. Parl.* 32; *Scot. Rec. Soc.* lvi. 477; lxii. 33; W. MacGill, *Old Ross-shire and Scotland*, ii. 69–70. [2] *Retours of Heirs*, ii. Lanark, 354, 401–2; *Services of Heirs*, i. 1710–19, p. 5; Irving, *Upper Ward of Lanark*. i. 243, 479; ii. 330–1; *N. and Q.* ser. 6, vii. 77; *Scots Peerage*, 586–7. [3] *SHR*, lxxi. 127. [4] *Scots Courant*, 11–13 Aug. 1714; *Scot. Hist. Soc.* ser. 3, xvii. 161, 180–204 passim; [P. Rae], *Hist. Late Rebellion* (1718), 232. [5] *Hist. Scot. Parl.* 32; *Sheriffdoms of Lanark and Renfrew* (Maitland Club, xii), 59; *Services of Heirs*, i. 1720–9, p. 6; 1730–9, p. 7; 1740–9, p. 6.

D. W. H.

CARNEGIE, John (c.1679–bef.1750), of Boysack, Inverkeillor, Forfar.

FORFARSHIRE   1708–30 July 1716

b. c.1679, 1st s. of John Carnegie of Boysack by Jean, da. of David Fotheringham, MP[S], of Powrie, Forfar. *educ.* Aberdeen Univ. (Marischal Coll.) 1696–8, Leyden 1700, aged 20; adv. 1703. *m.* 6 Nov. 1707, Margaret, da. of James Skene of Grange and Kirkcaldy, Fife, 2s. *suc.* fa. by 1683.[1]

Jt. curator, fac. adv. lib. [S] 1708–?1714.[2]
Burgess, Perth 1709, Dundee by 1713, Glasgow 1723.[3]
Sol.-gen. [S] Mar.–Oct. 1714.

Carnegie, whose grandfather, a younger son of the 1st Earl of Northesk, had sat for Forfarshire in the Scottish parliament in 1661–3, succeeded to the barony of Boysack at a very early age. As an advocate he demonstrated not only ability but an occasional stridency of expression, in one incident in January 1708 denouncing Scottish customs officers as 'land robbers or privateers'. Carnegie was almost predestined towards a cavalier bent in politics by his family background and connexions. One of his professional patrons was Lord Dun SCJ, a determined opponent of union, while his acquaintances prior to election to Parliament were men like his kinsman the 4th Earl of Northesk, and the Earl of Mar's brother Lord Grange SCJ (Hon. James Erskine†), whose distaste for the Duke of Hamilton's electoral pact with the Squadrone in 1708 Carnegie shared.[4]

After his election for Forfarshire in 1708 Carnegie was granted the early distinction of appointment on 22 Nov. 1708 to the committee on the Address. On 29 Jan. 1709 he was nominated to the drafting committee for a bill to unify treason laws throughout Great Britain. This was a proposal, however, that in common with other Scottish Members of varying political persuasions he opposed. On 10 Mar. 1709 he spoke against the ministry's conduct during the late invasion attempt, and the following year he voted against the impeachment of Dr Sacheverell.[5]

Re-elected after a contest in 1710, Carnegie was wrongly classed as a Whig in the 'Hanover list'. Richard Dongworth, the Duchess of Buccleuch's chaplain, correctly listed him as an episcopal Tory, and it was with other Scottish Tories that on 10 Feb. 1711 he maintained an awkward silence during the hearing of his compatriot Mungo Graham's* disputed election for Kinross-shire. At first, Graham (factor to the Squadrone Duke of Montrose) reported that Carnegie 'never opened his mouth neither for me nor against me, but he divided against me'. In his next communication this account was amended: Graham wrote that Carnegie and some other Tories 'who had been resolved to be against me, could not prevail with themselves to go the length to vote against me, so they went up to the galleries and skulked there'. On 5 Apr. Carnegie had been appointed to the drafting committee for George Lockhart's elections bill and on 19 May he spoke in defence of George Yeaman's linen bill. By this time Carnegie had been recruited into what one modern commentator has termed an informal 'steering committee' of Scottish Tory MPs, comprising Lockhart, Sir Alexander Areskine, 2nd Bt., Sir Alexander Cumming, 1st Bt., and Hon. James Murray. All except Cumming were Jacobite sympathizers, although their priority at this stage seems rather to have been the advancement of episcopalianism in Scotland. However, when Lockhart first put forward in the 1710–11 session the idea of a Scottish toleration bill he found Cumming, Murray and Carnegie ready with objections of the kind that ministerialists were also airing, an early indication that Carnegie, for one, was susceptible to the pull of the Court. Indeed, there had been rumours earlier in the year that Carnegie might obtain a judgeship in the court of session.[6]

At the start of the following session the five Members renewed their association, now resolving to bring forward the deferred toleration bill. 'The Scots are most zealous in it', reported George Baillie*, 'and none more than Mr Carnegie.' Nominated to the drafting committee on 21 Jan. 1712, he naturally voted for the bill on 7 Feb. Carnegie was equally active in other measures promoted by the 'steering-committee': on 13 Mar. he seconded the proposal to restore lay patronage in Scotland, and having acted as a teller was appointed to the drafting committee for the bill, also telling for its committal on the 28th. In the same month he managed the bill to repeal a Presbyterian-inspired act suppressing the Christmas recess of the court of session (Yule vacance). Scottish economic interests attracted his attention too. In January he had subscribed to a memorial signed by various Scots MPs to the attorney-general to represent the 'universal concern' to the people of Scotland of the proposed reconsideration by government of the staple contract; and on 29 Apr. he told in favour of a clause to be added to the land tax bill 'for a rule whereby to tax the royal burghs of Scotland' (see GLASGOW BURGHS). A tellership on 17 May against adjourning a session of the committee of ways and means shows him participating in a procedural dispute between back-bench Tories, though its significance remains unclear. The following month he managed a private bill for the relief of Lieutenant-General Sir William Douglas.[7]

Prior to the 1713 session Carnegie joined other Scottish episcopalian MPs and peers in signing a letter to Bishop Rose of Edinburgh, urging that non-juring clergy be prevailed upon to take the oaths, in order to give the lie to Presbyterian insinuations about their loyalty. At Westminster on 29 Apr. Carnegie once again told on the issue of the apportionment of land tax among the royal burghs. During this session his attention, like that of most Scottish Members, was principally directed towards the malt tax crisis and its sequel, the motion to dissolve the Union. A teller on 21 May against the original amendment from the committee on the malt duty bill to set the tax in Scotland at 6d. per bushel, he was one of those deputed by a meeting of Scottish Members in the evening after the debate to represent to Lord Treasurer Oxford (Robert Harley*) the nation's grievance over the vote. He participated also in joint meetings with Scottish peers, and when it was agreed to move for the dissolution of the Union, it was Carnegie, along with Cumming, Lockhart and Murray, who was summoned by 'a great man' to be plied with counter-arguments. He did not, however, maintain for long any distance between himself and administration. He voted with the Court in the divisions of 4 and 18 June 1713 on the French commerce bill. He continued to angle for appointment to the court of session, and may have enjoyed the backing of the Duke of Argyll's brother Lord Ilay. In December 1713, after Carnegie had been safely re-elected for Forfarshire, he wrote to Oxford, setting out his 'pretensions to preferment'.[8]

Listed as a 'Jacobite' (i.e. a Tory) in Lord Polwarth's analysis of the Scottish election results, Carnegie was increasingly associated in this Parliament with Lord Bolingbroke (Henry St. John II*). When Lockhart suggested that the campaign to dissolve the Union should be revived, Carnegie sided with Cumming and Murray in declaring that Bolingbroke was 'a good man and a wise man, and knew what was to be done and when to do it'. On 4 Mar. 1714 he told on the Tory side in the disputed election for Anstruther Easter Burghs, and spoke likewise on 18 Mar. in favour of the expulsion of Richard Steele. Later that month, upon the removal of Sir James Stewart, 1st Bt.*, for voting with the Whigs over the Steele case, Carnegie was appointed Scottish solicitor-general, at a salary of £200 a year. The good news was conveyed to Carnegie by Mar, who made a point of inviting him to dine before his formal audience at court. He supported Bolingbroke over the schism bill, voting on 12 May against the Whig wrecking amendment to extend its provisions to Catholic education. Relations with Lockhart and Areskine were soured by a convoluted dispute during May and June over a bill to resume the bishops' rents in Scotland in the crown as a fund for the maintenance of episcopalian clergy. Fears at court over the sweeping nature of Lockhart's draft bill and the lobbying of interested parties caused ministers to change their minds, a decision with which Carnegie, Cumming and Murray concurred. Carnegie approved of a watered-down proposal to appoint commissioners to investigate these revenues, but the enabling bill ran out of time in this session. Carnegie and Lockhart took opposite sides over the Scottish militia bill in May and June. This division within Scottish Tory ranks caused at least one Whig commentator to suspect a double game. In fact Carnegie had assumed the management of the bill at Bolingbroke's behest, presenting it on 26 May. Lockhart objected to it, however, as an English measure that would increase Scottish divisions and therefore took up the cause of the Duke of Argyll, whose hereditary rights were threatened by the bill. Lockhart proved the more astute parliamentarian and thwarted Carnegie's management by creating procedural delay. Carnegie told on two further occasions in this session: on 8 June, for an additional clause in the bill explaining the 1696 Bristol Workhouse Act, which may well have been part of a High Church attack on the financing of the institution; and on the 22nd, for an amendment to a resolution from ways and means, in order to exempt calicos and linens from the duty proposed to be levied on dyed and printed stuffs, a move to protect one of Scotland's major industries, on behalf of which Carnegie had already spoken in the debate on the reintroduced bill to regulate the Scottish linen manufacture.[9]

Although Carnegie signed the proclamation of George I in Edinburgh, he was promptly, and somewhat brusquely, removed from office in October 1714. Returned again for Forfarshire in the general election of 1715, he was put down as a Tory on the Worsley list and on an analysis of the new House, but abandoned parliamentary politics in favour of armed rebellion. After the failure of the Fifteen he fled to France, via Norway, with his 'very good friend Lord Pitsligo', and in his absence was expelled from the House and ordered to be prosecuted for high treason. The Pretender found some use for him in 1717 as envoy to the Swiss states, but exile did not prove congenial. In 1719 he was said to 'depend too much on Mr M[urra]y' and by 1726, allegedly because his private affairs were 'in great confusion', he returned to live in Scotland. Earlier he had advised other distressed Jacobite fugitives to do the same, on the pretext that they would be of more use to their master at home. He was accused, however, by Jacobites abroad of being 'attached to [the] Duke of Mar, in opposition to the King's present measures'. After persuading his old friend Lockhart to help him send a letter to the Pretender protesting innocence of these charges (in circumstances which make it clear that he was not himself in regular correspondence with James), he embroiled himself the very next year in the 'usager' controversy, encouraging dissident episcopalian clergy to resist the Pretender's interference in their affairs, in a way that Lockhart interpreted as 'basely' contravening his earlier 'solemn professions' of loyalty. An old man by the 1740s, he played no role in the Forty-Five, though a nephew, Sir John Wedderburn, was executed for taking part in the rising.[10]

Carnegie was dead by 14 May 1750, when his elder son was served as heir.

[1]*Scots Peerage* ed. Paul, vi. 495–6; *Recs. Marischal Coll. and Univ. of Aberdeen* (New Spalding Club), ii. 272–3; *Mems. Fam. of Skene* (New Spalding Club), 53–54; *Scot. Rec. Soc.* lxxvi. 32; viii. 67; *Album Studiosorum Academiciae Lugduno Batavae*, ed. Du Rieu, 758. [2]*Stair Soc.* xxix. 272; xxxii. 4. [3]Sandeman Lib. Perth, Perth Burgh Recs. B59/24/1/17, p. 14; Dundee City Archives, Dundee burgh recs. treasurer's accts. 1712–13 (unfol.); *Scot. Rec. Soc.* lvi. 366. [4]W. Fraser, *Hist. Carnegies*, i. p. lxxxvi; *Cal. Treas. Bks.* xxii. 90; xxvi. 275; *Cromartie Corresp.* ii. 57. [5]Scot. Cath. Archs. Blairs Coll. mss BL2/158/3, James Carnegy to Scots Coll. n.d. [1709]. [6]G. Holmes, *Pol. in Age of Anne*, 338; *SHR*, lx. 63; SRO, Montrose mss GD220/5/808/17, 18a–b, Graham to Montrose, 10, 13 Feb. 1711; *Lockhart Pprs.* i. 329, 338–9; D. Szechi, *Jacobitism and Tory Pol.* 102; SRO, Seafield mss GD248/560/46/18, John Philp to Seafield, 22 Jan. 1711. [7]*Lockhart Pprs.* 378; Montrose mss GD220/5/268/6, 8, Baillie to Montrose, 26 Jan., 15 Mar. 1711–12; NSA, Kreienberg despatch 14 Mar. 1712; *Lockhart Letters* ed. Szechi, 56–57. [8]Spalding Club, *Misc.* iv. 84–87; *Lockhart Letters*, 73, 75–76; Aberdeen Univ. Lib. Duff House (Montcoffer) mss 3175/2380, 'Resolution of the Commons to Call a Meeting of the Lords', [23] May 1713; *Parlty. Hist.* i. 69; *HMC Portland*, v. 183; x. 273, 443. [9]*Orig. Pprs.* ed. Macpherson, ii. 561; Holmes, 280; P. W. J. Riley, *Eng. Ministers and Scotland*, 252–3; *Lockhart Pprs.* 444–7, 449, 451–2, 458–9, 536; Douglas diary (Hist. Parl. trans.), 18 Mar. 1714; Kreienberg despatch 19 Mar. 1714; SP55/1, p. 39; *HMC Portland*, x. 217; *Cal. Treas. Bks.* xxix. 358; *Lockhart Letters*, 101; NLS, Advocates' mss, Wodrow pprs. letters Quarto 8, ff. 133–4. [10]Boyer, *Pol. State*, viii. 124; SP55/3, p. 10; *Scot. Hist. Soc.* (ser. 3), xxi. 302; xxxi. 87; *HMC Stuart*, iii. 270–1; iv. 458–9; *Lockhart Letters*, 285–6, 296, 301–2, 308, 334; Fraser, p. lxxxvi.

D. W. H.

CARR, Sir Ralph (1634–1710), of Newcastle-upon-Tyne, Northumb. and Coken, Houghton-le-Spring, co. Dur.

NEWCASTLE-UPON-TYNE 1679 (Oct.)–1681 (Mar.)
1689–1695

b. 14 July 1634, 1st s. of William Carr, merchant, of Newcastle-upon-Tyne by Jane, da. and coh. of Ralph Cock, merchant, of Newcastle-upon-Tyne. educ. Houghton-le-Spring, co. Dur.; St. John's, Camb. 1652;

G. Inn 1654. *m.* (1) Jane (*d.* 1667), da. of Sir Francis Anderson† of Newcastle-upon-Tyne, 1s. *d.v.p.* 2da. (1 *d.v.p.*); (2) Isabella, da. of Hon. James Darcy† of Sedbury Park, Yorks., 1s. *d.v.p. suc.* fa. 1666; kntd. 26 June 1676.[1]

Freeman, Newcastle-upon-Tyne 1660, alderman, by 1677–87, Oct. 1688–*d.*, mayor, 1677–8, 1693–4, 1705–6.[2]

Member, hostmen's co. Newcastle-upon-Tyne 1661, merchant adventurers of Newcastle-upon-Tyne, 1663; gov., hostmen's co. of Newcastle-upon-Tyne 1677–83, 1705–7.[3]

Commr. for carriage of coals 1679.[4]

Carr's family had been part of Newcastle's merchant elite since the 14th century, and his status and wealth were demonstrated by his purchase of an estate in Durham in 1665. Six years later he bought the mineral rights to this estate and in the 1670s became a prominent member of the corporate oligarchy which dominated Newcastle politics. His support for the Court during the Exclusion crisis and the 1680s came to an abrupt end in 1687 when he refused to support the repeal of the Penal Laws and Test Act, and when the Newcastle corporation refused to act upon William of Orange's writ for the Convention Carr was returned for the borough with the support of Newcastle's sheriff. During the Convention Carr nevertheless voted that the throne was not vacant, and the Toryism this suggests was confirmed when, after his unchallenged return for Newcastle in 1690, Lord Carmarthen (Sir Thomas Osborne†) classified him as a Tory and Court supporter.[5]

Carr told on two occasions during the 1690 session: against adjourning consideration of proposals vesting forfeited estates in the crown (9 May), and in favour of the sitting Tory Members in a division upon the Aldborough election (17 May). During the 1690–1 session Carmarthen listed him as a likely supporter in the event of a parliamentary attack upon himself but, though no significant activity of Carr's is recorded for this session, an analysis of the House among Robert Harley's* papers dating from April 1691 classified him as a Country party supporter. More is known of his contribution to the 1691–2 session in which Carr made at least three speeches. On 16 Jan. 1692 he spoke in favour of the bill to suppress hawkers and pedlars, joining Sir John Somers in arguing that 'they are a vagrant, wandering people, beneficial to none but themselves' and that the measure was 'for the interest of the nation because it is solicited by all the corporations of England'. Three days later he spoke in favour of the proposal that office-holders with places worth more than £500 p.a. should apply the excess to the cost of the war, and his concern for supply matters was also in evidence later the same day when he supported the raising of money upon a fund of perpetual interest, expressing the belief that 'when it hath gained credit ... it will be as good as the bank in Holland'. On the 20th Carr argued that the proposal of Sir Christopher Musgrave, 4th Bt., to rate every man charged with raising a horse for the militia at £1 10s. for the poll tax was too high. Given his merchant background it is hardly surprising that an interest in trade was evident in Carr's activity in the 1692–3 session. On 8 Dec. he presented a petition from London merchants opposing the bill to prohibit the export of woollen manufactures. When this measure was reported on 18 Jan. 1693, Carr supported, unsuccessfully, the addition of a clause preserving the right of the Hamburg Company to export wool to certain German states. On 2 Feb. he told in favour of engrossing the bill to prevent the decay of trade in towns and cities, and five days later was granted a month's leave of absence. He was classed as a Court supporter by Samuel Grascome in the spring of 1693. Less than a month into the next session, on 4 Dec., Carr was found to be absent without permission from a call of the House. He was excused, however, and granted a seven-day leave of absence. He was more conspicuous during this session. Having told on 23 Dec. against an adjournment, the new year saw him take an interest in four bills. His hostility to legislation restricting the wool trade was evident in his telling against both the second reading and committal of the bill to prevent wool exports and encourage woollen manufactures (11, 24 Jan. 1694), while on 16 Jan. he was nominated to draft a bill for measuring keels and other boats transporting coal on the Tyne. Carr presented this measure on 3 Feb. and two weeks later was the first-named Member of its second-reading committee. His concern for the interests of the north-east coal industry may account for his tellerships on 7 and 8 Mar. against the bill to relieve the London orphans, which proposed placing a duty on all coal transported to London. On 21 Mar. he told against engrossing a bill to make more effectual an Act regulating leather cutting, and six days later he was granted a leave of absence. In the final session of the 1690 Parliament Carr again promoted a bill to measure keels operating on the Tyne, being appointed on 6 Mar. 1695 to draft the bill, presenting it three days later, and on 21 Mar. was first-named to the second-reading committee. He was also included among a list of 'friends' of Henry Guy*, possibly in relation to parliamentary proceedings against Guy.[6]

Carr decided against standing at the 1695 election, and though in December 1700 he was reported to be standing at Newcastle, his parliamentary career had in fact ended. He remained active in local affairs, most notably as one of the members of the cartel founded in 1708 to regulate the production and price of north-east coal, until his death on 5 Mar. 1710. His eldest son Ralph had died four years previously, and it seems likely that Carr was succeeded by a grandson of the same name.[7]

[1] Surtees, *Durham*, i. 209. [2] *Reg. of Freemen* (Newcastle Rec. Soc. iii), 76; H. Bourne, *Hist. Newcastle*, 243–4. [3] *Newcastle Hostmen's Co.* (Surtees Soc. cv), 263, 270; *Newcastle Merchant Adventurers* (Surtees Soc. ci), 289. [4] *Cal. Treas. Bks.* v. 1205. [5] L. Gooch, *The Desperate Faction?*, 12. [6] *Luttrell Diary*, 132–3, 136, 140, 143, 301, 374, 397. [7] Add. 70018, ff. 94–95; *HMC Portland*, iii. 640; E. Hughes, *N. Country Life*, i. 167–8; Surtees, 209.

E. C./R. D. H.

CARR, Thomas (1658–1721), of Chichester, Suss.

CHICHESTER 1708–1710

bap. 14 July 1658, 1st s. of Alan or Allen Carr of Chichester by Anne, da. of William Elson of Barnham and Oving, Suss., sis. of William Elson I*. *unm. suc.* fa. 1668.[1]

Alderman, Chichester by 1698, mayor 1708–9.[2]

Carr's grandfather Thomas, the younger son of a Yorkshire squire, had been installed as parish incumbent of Oving in 1623 and had held on to his living throughout the Civil War, Interregnum and Restoration, until his death in 1663. Carr's father bequeathed his son £1,000 and some property in Petersfield on his death in 1668. The ten-year-old Thomas may then have come under the influence of his mother's family, the Elsons, for his mature politics reflected their Tory leanings. Indeed, he was allegedly a non-juror, refused the Association at first in 1696 and was ordered to be arrested, though he presumably subscribed later since he retained his place as captain of foot in the Sussex militia. He was returned to Parliament for Chichester in 1708 on the corporation interest and presumably with the support of the Elsons, and was classed as a Tory in a list of Parliament of early 1708. His election was reckoned a 'loss' by Lord Sunderland (Charles, Lord Spencer*). It seems more than a little surprising, therefore, to find him blacklisted in 1710 as one who had voted for the impeachment of Dr Sacheverell. Carr seems to have been left off the commission of the peace for Sussex in 1714. The following year he was nominated as a trustee in the will of the Catholic Anthony Kemp of Slindon. Carr was buried on 23 June 1721.[3]

[1] *Vis. Suss.* (Harl. Soc. lxxxix), 23; *Suss. Arch. Colls.* xxxiv. 189–90; Elwes and Robinson, *Castles and Mansions of Western Suss.* 161.
[2] Centre Kentish Stud. U269/O56, 'A short acct. of the behaviour of the corporation of Chichester', [n.d.]; A. Hay, *Hist. Chichester*, 571.
[3] Info. from Dr P. J. Le Fevre; *Suss. Arch. Colls.* 206; U269/O56, 'A short acct.'; PC 2/76, f. 192; Prob. 11/548/66 (*ex inf.* Dr Le Fevre).

E. C.

CARR, William (1664–1720), of Newcastle-upon-Tyne, Northumb.

NEWCASTLE-UPON-TYNE 1690–1710

b. 8 Dec. 1664, 2nd s. of William Carr, merchant, of Newcastle-upon-Tyne, by Mary. *educ.* Univ. Coll. Oxf. matric. 1683; Lincoln's Inn, 1692. *m.* Elizabeth, 1s.[1]

Member, Eastland co. 1687; member, hostmen's co. of Newcastle-upon-Tyne 1689, gov. 1690; member merchant adventurers' co. of Newcastle-upon-Tyne 1699.[2]

Alderman, Newcastle-upon-Tyne Nov. 1688–*d.*, mayor, 1689–90, 1702–3, 1705–6.[3]

Commr. of excise 1698–1700, 1714–*d.*[4]

Carr owed his parliamentary career to his family's position among the mercantile, coal-owning elite which dominated the corporation of Newcastle. He was created an alderman when Newcastle's charter was restored in late 1688, and his standing within the borough was confirmed the following year when he was appointed mayor. His swift rise through the corporation ranks was illustrated in 1690 when he was returned unopposed for Newcastle with his uncle Sir Ralph Carr, and in March he was listed by Lord Carmarthen (Sir Thomas Osborne†) as a Tory and Court supporter. An inconspicuous Member of the 1690 Parliament, he was listed by Carmarthen in December 1690 as one of his likely supporters against the attack anticipated in the Commons, while in April the following year Robert Harley* classed Carr as a possible, though not certain, supporter of the Country party. Grascome's analysis of the Commons dating from spring 1693 categorized him as a Court supporter. Returned unopposed for Newcastle in 1695, Carr was apparently hostile to the ministry in the 1695–6 session, as he was forecast as likely to oppose the Court in the divisions of 31 Jan. 1696 upon the council of trade and in March voted against fixing the price of guineas at 22*s*. That he was not an extremist, however, is evident from his prompt signing of the Association, and in the following session he absented himself from the division of 25 Nov. on the attainder of Sir John Fenwick†. His contribution to the business of the 1695 Parliament appears to have been slight. On 8 Dec. 1696 he was nominated to draft a bill to settle rents on coal wharves in the north-east, and his one recorded speech of the Parliament came on 18 Mar. 1697 when he successfully opposed a petition calling on him to waive his privilege in a suit concerning the possession of a Northumberland colliery. The summer of 1698 clearly demonstrated that Carr had abandoned his previous opposition to the ministry as in July he was appointed to the excise commission, with a salary of £800 p.a., but this change of political tack appears to have been no obstacle to his return for Newcastle in the 1698 election. Included in September 1698 upon a list of placemen and classed in a comparison of the old and new Commons as a Court supporter, Carr demonstrated his loyalty to the ministry on 18 Jan. 1699 by voting against the disbanding bill. His contribution to parliamentary business remained small, his only significant act being to tell on 2 May 1700 against allowing the import of cowries from Holland into London and other ports. An analysis of the House dating from between January and May 1700 listed Carr as in the influence of the independent Whig peer Lord Warrington, a classification perhaps explicable in terms of the relationship between Warrington and Carr's fellow Newcastle Member Sir William Blackett, 1st Bt. In June the same year Carr resigned his place in the excise, which had become incompatible with a seat in the Commons, and the failure to include Carr among the placemen listed in the analysis of the Commons from early 1700 may suggest that he had indicated his intentions in this matter some time before actually tendering his resignation. Returned for Newcastle in January 1701, Carr was listed in February among those thought likely to support the Court in agreeing with the committee of supply's resolution to continue the 'Great Mortgage'. His most significant activity in the 1701–2 Parliament was his involvement in preparing a bill to safeguard Newcastle's water supply, being nominated to its drafting committee on 25 Feb. 1702.[5]

Carr was re-elected for Newcastle to the first three Parliaments of Queen Anne's reign. On 13 Feb. 1703 he voted for agreeing with the Lords' amendments to the bill enlarging the time for taking the abjuration, the first indication that, as well as supporting the Court, he had embraced Whiggery. In the 1704–5 session he was forecast as likely to oppose the Tack and on 28 Nov. either voted against it or was absent from the division. Despite his failure to support the Tack, he was listed as a 'Churchman' in an analysis of the 1705 Parliament. On 25 Oct. 1705 he voted for the Court candidate for Speaker. After being nominated to draft an estate bill (6, 21 Dec.) and a bill to constitute Newcastle's mayor as governor of the town's keelmen's hospital (16 Jan. 1706), he was one of the Whigs absent from the Court side in the division of 18 Feb. upon the 'place clause' of the regency bill. Carr was included among those named on 27 Feb. 1707 to draft a bill to equalize English and Scottish export allowances, and a list of the Commons dating from early 1708 classed him as a Whig. The veracity of this judgment was borne out in the 1708 Parliament when he supported the naturalization of the Palatines, and the impeachment of Dr Sacheverell.[6]

Carr was opposed by two Tory candidates at Newcastle in 1710. His vote against Sacheverell had undermined his electoral interest and he was defeated. Despite suggestions in September 1712 that he was plotting to regain his seat he never stood again, but did not retire from public life. Following the Hanoverian succession he was restored to the excise commission and during the Fifteen was active in the government interest. A contemporary detailed the claims Carr was making for his efforts:

> He talks much of his indefatigable pains, such as his lying whole nights at the gates of the town ready to receive expresses as they came from this town [London], and giving despatches to the scouts he sent out whenever they returned, with much more of this nature to ingratiate himself. This a friend of ours had from a friend who heard it told to the Prince himself.

Carr retained his post in the excise until his death on 4 June 1720. He was succeeded by his infant son. The following year Carr's widow petitioned the Treasury for financial relief, claiming that her husband's actions at the Revolution, his maintaining an interest at Newcastle, his exertions during the Fifteen and his resignation in 1700 had meant that 'his fortune ... was so reduced that he had sold part of his estate'. She requested 'royal compassion for herself and infant son', and in November 1721 a warrant was ordered to pay her £200 p.a.[7]

[1] IGI, Northumb.; Surtees, *Durham*, i.209; *Arch. Ael.* ser. 3, xii. 5; *Cal. Treas. Pprs.* 1720–8, p. 91. [2] *Newcastle Merchant Adventurers* (Surtees Soc. ci), 319; *Newcastle Hostmen's Co.* (Surtees Soc. cv), 263, 273. [3] *North Country Diaries* (Surtees Soc. cxxiv), 188; H. Bourne, *Hist. Newcastle*, 244. [4] *Cal. Treas. Bks.* xiii. 393; xv. 96; xxix. 149, 835; Boyer, *Pol. State*, xix. 669. [5] *North Country Diaries*, 188; Centre Kentish Stud. Stanhope mss U1590/059/7, Robert Yard* to Alexander Stanhope, 26 July 1698; Luttrell, *Brief Relation*, iv. 410; Northants RO, Montagu (Boughton) mss 48/82, James Vernon I* to Duke of Shrewsbury, 15 June 1700; *Vernon–Shrewsbury Letters*, iii. 92–93. [6] *Party and Management* ed. Jones, 80. [7] Add. 70297, George Flint to [Ld. Oxford], 13 Sept. 1712; *Liddell-Cotesworth Letters* (Surtees Soc. cxcvii), 201, 208; Boyer, 669; *Cal. Treas. Pprs.* 1720–8, p. 91.

E. C./R. D. H.

CARTER, Lawrence I (c.1641–1710), of Clement's Inn and The Newarke, Leicester.

LEICESTER   1689–1695, 1701 (Dec.)–1702

b. June 1641, 1st s. of Lawrence Carter of Paulerspury, Northants. by Eleanor, da. and h. of John Pollard, yeoman, of Leckhampstead, Bucks. *educ.* Clement's Inn. *m.* (1) by 1667, Elizabeth (*d.* 1671), da. and coh. of Thomas Wadland, attorney, of The Newarke, 2s.; (2) lic. 5 July 1675, Mary, da. of Thomas Potter of London, 2s. 4da. *suc.* fa. 1669.[1]

Freeman, Leicester 1689; steward, honor of Leicester 1697–1702.[2]

Receiver-gen. duchy of Lancaster Mar.–July 1702.[3]

Carter, a prominent Leicester townsman, served his parliamentary apprenticeship as an active member of the Convention and was returned again for the borough in 1690 without opposition. In Lord Carmarthen's (Sir Thomas Osborne†) list he was identified as a Whig and in Grascome's as a Court supporter. His level of involvement during the new Parliament was very modest: there is no record of any contribution to debates and he was only occasionally required to serve on committees of any significance. During December 1691 and January 1692 he took charge of two private bills introduced in the Lords concerning the estates of two Leicestershire gentlemen, Richard Roberts and Sir Thomas Burton.[4]

Carter did not stand in the 1695 election. He probably owed his appointment in June 1697 to the stewardship of Leicester (within the duchy of Lancaster) to his patron, the Earl of Stamford, who had become the chancellor of the duchy the previous month. In March 1701, by which time his son Lawrence II was sitting for Leicester, Carter petitioned the House for an exemption from the bill then pending for the resumption of grants made since the accession of James II. As Leicester was part of the crown lands, he had been under the necessity of obtaining a licence from King James allowing him to implement a scheme to provide the town with a water supply which the projected resumption legislation would have nullified, but the bill did not in fact pass. During the same year he appears to have earned some local displeasure on account of an alleged underhand attempt to retain administration of the Huntingdon manorial courts under the new earl, while in the House of Commons he was aspersed for taking a bribe: John Wilkins, Member for Leicestershire, informed Thomas Coke*:

> Lord Huntingdon . . . is fallen into ill hands, namely Carter of Leicester. He hath tricked him and got a paper under his hand to keep his courts and what not. 'Tis an ill step; pray let him be dissuaded, for he's a rascal, and will ruin his reputation in the country. He is hinted at for taking 80 guineas in our House: you know a friend of yours that will hunt it out.[5]

Notwithstanding, Carter re-entered Parliament in place of his son in November 1701, although the reason for this arrangement is not clear. In his final brief spell in the Commons Carter was fairly active. Apart from various committee appointments, he was among those charged to prepare an ultimately unsuccessful bill against bribery and corruption at elections (17 Jan. 1702). Then, on 14 Feb., he was teller in favour of discharging from custody the authors of a petition which had condemned the election at Malmesbury, and again on the 23rd to allow a petition relating to Irish forfeitures to be earmarked for further consideration. During April and May he managed an estate bill on behalf of a Leicestershire gentleman, Abraham Barnwell. Consequent upon the Tory revival after Anne's accession, Carter was dismissed from his duchy posts once Stamford had been removed from the duchy chancellorship, and did not seek re-election to Parliament. In June he petitioned Parliament once more in respect of the licence for his water supply in Leicester upon the appearance of another resumption bill, but the measure was later discontinued. He died on 1 June 1710.

[1] IGI, Northants.; *Leckhampstead Par. Reg.* 11; H. R. Moulton, *Cat.* (1930), p. 91; Baker, *Northants.* ii. 206; Nichols, *Leics.* i. 318; *London Mar. Lic.* ed. Foster, 248; *Recs. Bor. Leicester* ed. Stocks, iv. 379. [2] *Reg. Leicester Freemen*, i. 172; Somerville, *Duchy of Lancaster Official Lists*, 180. [3] Somerville, 19. [4] *Luttrell Diary*, 130. [5] Somerville, 4, 180; *HMC Cowper*, ii. 429.

A. A. H.

CARTER, Lawrence II (1671–1744), of The Newarke, Leicester.

LEICESTER   1698–1701 (Nov.)
BERE ALSTON   1710–1722
LEICESTER   1722–7 Sept. 1726

bap. 30 Sept. 1671, 1st s. of Lawrence Carter I* by his 1st w. *educ.* Trinity, Oxf. 1688; I. Temple, adm. 1689, called 1694; L. Inn 1702. *unm.* Kntd. 4 May 1724.[1]

Recorder, Leicester 1697–1729.[2]

Solicitor-gen. to Prince of Wales 1715–26; KC 1715; serjeant-at-law 1724; baron of the Exchequer 1726–*d.*

Carter's standing within Leicester's ruling elite was overshadowed, at least initially, by that of his father. His almost unanimous election as recorder in 1697, just three years after qualifying at the bar, paved the way for his unopposed election at the next election. He also benefited from the assistance of his father's patron, the Earl of Stamford, to whose 'interest'

Carter was also stated to belong in a list of early 1700. Carter quickly became a regular participant in Commons proceedings and earned nomination to committees on a wide range of business. A Whig, he was identified with the Country party in a list of about September 1698. In February 1699 he managed a private naturalization bill through the House. On the 20th he was teller against committing the Derwent navigation bill which Leicester's corporation had resolved to oppose, being 'injurious to the trade and market of Leicester': it was probably Carter who had presented their petition (3 Feb.) and who subsequently led the case against the bill which resulted in its rejection. He was granted leave of absence on the 28th, though was back in attendance before the session closed.[3]

In the opening weeks of the next session Carter piloted through the House a private bill for selling part of an estate in Leicestershire. He was a teller on 15 Jan. 1700 against adjourning a debate on the Company of Scotland, and on 10 Feb. reported from the committee on a bill setting up a 'judicature' to deal with cases of hardship and arrears of pay among military personnel. On 15 Feb. he spoke against a motion for the resumption of grants, possibly not without some thoughts of the fate of his father's licence from the duchy of Lancaster for piping a water supply in Leicester. On 28 Feb. he reported from the committee on the petition of Sir Nathaniel Curzon and John Kent alleging their right, against the corporation of London, to establish a market under grants made to them by James II. Returned in January 1701, he was included in a list, probably of those likely to support the Court in agreeing with the committee of supply's resolution to continue the 'Great Mortgage'. He presented an unsuccessful bill on 2 June designed to apply the proceeds from sequestrated Catholic lands to the maintenance of Greenwich Hospital, of which his patron, Lord Stamford, was a commissioner.[4]

Carter's consuming preoccupation during the 1698 Parliament was the problem of abuse and malpractice in the running of two of London's debtor prisons, the Fleet and King's Bench. His involvement originated with the case of John Goodall, a prominent Leicester tradesman and former mayor, who had petitioned about the fate of his legal pursuit of a bankrupt. On being arrested, the man had been removed to King's Bench where, owing to the notorious liberties allowed inmates, he escaped before the bankruptcy commissioners could ascertain his estate. As a result Goodall himself was arrested and incarcerated in Leicester gaol for failing to satisfy his own creditors. Carter was a member of the committee appointed on 2 Jan. 1699 to examine Goodall's petition and look into 'the ill practices and abuses' of the Fleet and King's Bench. The inquiry took four months to complete, and a report was made on the final day of the session, 4 May. Other complaints, similar to Goodall's, came before the committee, and it emerged that creditors who brought 'actions of escape' against the principal officials of either gaol could obtain judgment only to be confronted with judicial refusal to grant a sequestration. It was a well-established practice for the owners of these two gaolerships to use them as security for loans or mortgages, and in cases of escape these 'incumbrances' left creditors entirely without further remedy at law, which made a nonsense of recently enacted laws for the ease of creditors. A legislative solution was proposed to prevent habeas corpus removals to the London debtor prisons, to discharge existing encumbrances, and to outlaw such practices for the future. With the session about to close, there was a gesture of endorsement for the committee's recommendations in an order for a bill, which Carter and two other MPs were to prepare.[5]

Early in the new session the matter was revived, probably at Carter's instigation, for it was he who took the chair of a committee to recapitulate the outcome of the inquiry. Carter made further reports, in December 1699 and January 1700, giving fuller details of the existing encumbrances. In the meantime, on 20 and 26 Jan. he presented separate bills for each gaol, to discharge all encumbrances, and, more drastically, abolishing the two prisons completely. Both measures were committed on 17 Feb., but not surprisingly failed to re-emerge. Another bill was presented by Carter on 27 Jan., with the broader intention of regulating all prisons, but in this too, following its committee stage, he was unable to make further headway. Undeterred, he repeated his efforts in the next session, presenting a single rationalized version of his previous bills, still directed at the Fleet and King's Bench, which completed its Commons stages on 22 Mar. 1701. In the Lords the bill was altered beyond recognition: one of its two other sponsors, Sir Richard Cocks, 2nd Bt.*, recorded on 15 May in his diary:

> The Lords desired a conference about the bill for regulating the prisons in which they would give their reasons for the amendments drawn by the judges: and indeed there were amendments, for nothing but the preamble of our bill was left: and the amendments were unjust and impracticable: *Nota*, the judges spoiled our bill for fear they should lose their new year gifts of £200 from the keepers of the King's Bench and Fleet.

The amendments were never considered and Carter's initiative lapsed.[6]

Replaced at Leicester by his father in the second general election of 1701, Carter stood again in 1702, with assistance from the Earl of Rutland (John Manners†), but was defeated. He was shortly afterwards reported as intending to rendezvous with Lord Stamford at Hanover. Failing again in the 1705 election, he petitioned against James Winstanley*, and after a lengthy and bitter hearing the committee found in his favour on 29 Jan. 1706 (by 113 votes to 107), only for the Commons to overturn the verdict. During the ensuing nine-year interlude in his parliamentary career, Carter continued his legal practice in London, where his business included acting as counsel in several appeal cases before the House of Lords.[7]

In the 1710 election Carter was returned by Lord Stamford for Bere Alston, a seat he held until 1722, Stamford having died two years before. The next three sessions saw him much less active than he had been as Member for Leicester. His position in relation to the new Tory government was noted as 'doubtful' in the 'Hanover list' of the 1710 Parliament. On 21 Dec. he acted as a teller for committing a place bill, and on 28 Feb. 1711 obtained a leave of absence. He voted for the 'No Peace without Spain' motion on 7 Dec. but earlier in 1711 his name had been included in a list of 'worthy patriots' who had exposed the mismanagements of the last administration. On 6 Mar. 1712, in a debate on the King's Lynn election, he told for the Whig minority against a motion that the expulsion of Robert Walpole II* debarred Walpole from re-election. In May Carter took charge of a private bill for selling part of a Kentish estate, and on the 12th was one of a group of lawyer-MPs who moved for a bill against duelling. On 5 June he was teller against an amendment to a bill enabling the son of a receiver-general to compound with the lord treasurer for his father's debts. Towards the end of the following session, on 18 June 1713, he voted against the French commerce bill, and was noted as a Whig on the Worsley list of the next Parliament. He reported on 30 Apr. 1714 from a committee investigating the management and application of turnpike dues. He was classed as a Whig in two lists of MPs re-elected in 1715.[8]

Carter's legal career flourished under the Whig regime from 1715, culminating in a knighthood and his appointment in 1726 as a baron of the Exchequer. He died on 14 Mar. 1744 and was buried at St Mary de Castro, Leicester, where a monumental inscription attests that 'in every station of his life [he] acquitted himself with integrity and honour'.[9]

[1] IGI, Leics.; Nichols, *Leics.* i. 319. [2] Nichols, 319. [3] *Leicester Bor. Recs.* ed. Chinnery, v. 27, 518. [4] Som. RO, Sanford mss DD/SF 4107(a) notes of debate, 15 Feb. 1700; *CP*, xii. 222. [5] Hartopp, *Mayors of Leicester*, 113. [6] *Cocks Diary*, 128–29. [7] *HMC Rutland*, ii. 171; BL, Trumbull Add. mss 133, Henry St. John II* to Sir William Trumbull*, 14 Aug. 1702; Luttrell, *Brief Relation*, vi. 6, 10–11, 14; *HMC Lords*, n.s. vi. 4; vii. 4, 35, 338. [8] *HMC Lords*, n.s. x. 366. [9] Nichols, 319.

A. A. H.

CARTERET, Sir Charles (1667–1719), of Toomer, Som. and Trinity Manor, Jersey.

MILBORNE PORT   1690–1700

bap. 24 July 1667, 2nd but 1st surv. s. of Sir Edward de Carteret of Toomer, Som., Whitehall and Trinity Manor, Jersey, gent. usher of the Black Rod, by Elizabeth, da. of Robert Johnson (*d.* 1660), Grocer and alderman of London. *m.* Aug. 1687, Mary Anne, da. of Hon. Nicholas Fairfax, at least 5s. 2da. *suc.* fa. 1683; kntd. 25 Oct. 1687.[1]

Cornet, indep. tp. of horse 1685; capt. lt. of horse Earl of Arran's regt. (4 Drag. Gds.) 1687–9.

It was hardly surprising that a history of the Carteret family, published in 1756 in celebration of the Whig politician Earl Granville, the former Lord Carteret, should quietly omit details of the life and career of his distant relative Sir Charles Carteret, an authentic Jacobite who had spent his later years in the service of the Stuart court-in-exile. The Carterets (also known as the de Carterets) were a leading Jersey family who had been prominent in the government of the island since the Middle Ages. Sir Charles's immediate forebears were of Trinity Manor, a junior branch of the de Carterets of St. Ouen, Jersey on whom a baronetcy had been bestowed in 1670. The two families became more closely linked in 1676 through the marriage of Sir Philip, 2nd Bt., with Sir Charles's sister. Carteret's father, a Royalist during the Civil War, shared Charles II's exile, served as Black Rod from 1676 until his death six years later, and although non-resident bailiff of Jersey was placed by James II in charge of the island's defence as major of the militia there.[2]

Carteret himself served in a troop of horse against Monmouth's rebellion and was later promoted to one of the regiments of guards. His early years were spent at the palace of Whitehall, where his father had lodgings and he was in high favour with James II. In 1687 he married Mary Anne Fairfax, a maid of honour to Mary of Modena, and a granddaughter of the 2nd Viscount Fairfax [I]. The King gave a marriage portion of £2,000 and it is possible that Carteret converted, at least temporarily, to Catholicism in line with his wife's faith. On receipt of his knighthood in October he was excused the usual fees. Carteret had already inherited the manor of Toomer, near

Milborne Port, which his father had purchased in 1679. In December 1687, before he had come of age, the King's agents reported that he had 'the best interest of anyone' at Milborne Port and added in September 1688 that not only would he be elected but he had influence enough to carry the second seat. He supported the King after the Dutch invasion and he and four servants were given a pass on 16 Nov. to visit King James at Salisbury. Though he did not stand for election to the Convention, he was making interest in the borough in July 1689, planning to stand jointly with Sir Thomas Travell*, a Whig merchant. In 1690, aged only 23, he was returned unopposed for the borough, and was classed by Lord Carmarthen (Sir Thomas Osborne†) as a Tory and in another list as a Court supporter. His attendance during the first session was foreshortened by a grant of leave on 21 Apr. In December Carmarthen saw him as a likely Court supporter, but in April 1691 he was noted by Robert Harley* as a Country supporter. There is no evidence, however, of any noteworthy involvement in parliamentary business.[3]

Returned in 1695, Carteret became more active in 1696, most notably as a teller. His political conduct in the House was consistently against the government. In January 1696 he was forecast as likely to oppose the Court over the proposed council of trade, and at the end of February was among the Tories who initially refused to sign the Association. However, he soon afterwards asked the pardon of the House and signed. In March he voted against fixing the price of guineas at 22s. In the next session he played an active part in the defence of Sir John Fenwick†, acting as teller on 6 Nov. with John Granville against authorizing the bill of attainder, and at the bill's third reading on the 25th he outlined his belief that the case was insufficiently proven. He also voted against the bill in the closing division. Two days later he was teller in favour of a motion that the 'grievances of the kingdom', rather than the 'state of the nation', should be considered by a committee of the whole. On 23 Nov. he had been teller in favour of giving a second reading to the bill for improving the regulation of elections. In July 1697 it was brought to the attention of the lords justices that Carteret's wife had been going about the streets of London in disguise distributing printed 'libels' sent from France, and orders were issued to the Post Office to intercept her letters. Returned again in 1698, Carteret was listed as a Country supporter, appeared in the forecast of those likely to oppose the standing army, and on 18 Jan. 1699 was one of the tellers (again with Granville) in favour of the disbanding bill. On 15 Mar. he conveyed a private naturalization bill to the Lords. He was given three weeks' leave of absence on 16 Dec., and was teller on 10 Apr. 1700 against adjourning the debate on an address for the removal of Lord Chancellor Somers (Sir John*) from the King's presence and councils.[4]

Carteret did not stand at the first general election of 1701 but instead left England for the Stuart court at St. Germain where, in November 1701, he was appointed gentleman usher of the Black Rod, the office his father had previously held under Charles II. He continued to serve the Old Pretender in this capacity until his death in July 1719 when he was buried at St. Germain-en-Laye in the presence of his son James and William Dicconson, treasurer to the Stuart Court.[5]

[1] A. Collins, *Hist. Carteret Fam.* 32; J. B. Payne, *Armorial of Jersey*, 64–65, 111; C. E. Lart, *Jacobite Extracts*, ii. 45; *Recusant Hist.* v. 72–74; info. from Dr A. Barclay. [2] Collins, 32; *Soc. Jersiaise Bull.* xii. 163. [3] *Pepys Diary*, viii. 115; *Cal. Treas. Bks.* viii. 1524; *Recusant Hist.* 72–73; *CSP Dom.* 1687–8, pp. 156, 409; 1690–1, p. 358; Feet of Fines, Som. Trinity term, 31 Car. II; Duckett, *Penal Laws and Test Act* (1883), 18, 230; Add. 28876, f. 210. [4] Add. 30000A, f. 27; Cobbett, *Parlty. Hist.* v. 1120; Boyer, *Wm. III*, iii. 224–5; *CSP Dom.* 1697, p. 252. [5] *HMC Stuart*, i. 166; Lart, 45; RA Stuart mss, 51/19, Joseph Ronchi to David Nairne, 9 Jan. 1721.

E. C.

CARTERET, Edward (1671–1739), of St. Clement Danes, Mdx.

HUNTINGDON   1698–1700
BEDFORD   1702–1705
BERE ALSTON   9 Dec. 1717–4 Apr. 1721

bap. 28 Nov. 1671, 3rd s. of Sir Philip Carteret of Haynes, Beds. by Lady Jemima, da. of Edward Montagu†, 1st Earl of Sandwich, and sis. of Hon. Charles Montagu* and Hon. Sidney Wortley Montagu*. *educ.* Brentwood; Trinity Coll. Camb. 1688; M. Temple 1688, called 1702. *m.* 21 Nov. 1699, Bridget (*d.* 1735), da. of Sir Thomas Exton†, LL.D., of Trinity Hall, Camb., dean of the Arches and chancellor, London dioc., wid. of Sir John Sudbury, 1st Bt., of Eldon, co. Dur. and of Thomas Clutterbuck of Ingatestone, Essex, 3s. *d.v.p.* 3da. (1 *d.v.p.*). *suc.* Mrs Ann Rider at Dagenhams, Romford, Essex 1732.[1]

Burgess, Bedford 1699, dep. recorder 1711–aft. 1718; prothonotary, palatinate of Durham 1712.[2]

Jt. postmaster-gen. 1721–Nov. 1732, sole Nov. 1732–June 1733, jt. June 1733–*d.*[3]

Carteret's father, having formerly distinguished himself on the Royalist side in the Civil War as governor of Mount Orgueil Castle in Jersey, had perished with his father-in-law and patron, Lord Sandwich, at the battle of Sole Bay in 1672. As a younger son, Carteret himself was put to the law, but his best hope for preferment rested on the influence of his mother's family, the Montagus, and it was as the nominee of his uncle, Sidney Wortley Montagu, that he was returned to Parliament for Huntingdon in the 1698 general election. On the basis of this family connexion he was classed as a supporter of the Court party in a comparative analysis of the old and new Parliaments, and he bore out this assessment by voting on 18 Jan. 1699 against the third reading of the disbanding bill. He also told on 27 Mar. on a matter of merely local interest (though some way from his own constituency), against committing a bill for the repair of a highway in Berkshire. An analysis of the House during the following session into various 'interests' listed him among the followers of his kinsman Charles Montagu*. His tenure of a parliamentary seat was interrupted, however, because of the difficulties encountered by Wortley Montagu at Huntingdon, and he did not stand for re-election in January 1701.[4]

In the 1702 general election Carteret was chosen at Bedford, the borough closest to his ancestral seat. Although he effectively replaced a Whig, William Farrer*, there is no reason to suppose that his political allegiance had changed. He told on 17 Feb. 1703 against a clause on behalf of Colonel Luke Lillingston, proposed to be added to the bill to continue the Act appointing commissioners to examine the debts of the army, navy and transports. Although Carteret sometimes consorted with clergymen on social occasions he was forecast as likely to oppose the Tack, and did not vote for it on 28 Nov. 1704. He was a teller on 3 Feb. 1705 in favour of a resolution condemning a local customs charge on coal levied at the port of King's Lynn as a grievance and an oppression to the inhabitants of Bedfordshire and Huntingdonshire. That same day he was appointed to the committee for a bill to reduce coal duties at all ports, which he presented to the House four days later. He was also a teller on 21 Feb. for agreeing with an amendment to the bill prohibiting commerce with France. Despite his vigilance on behalf of his constituents' interests in the business of the coal trade he was not re-elected in 1705, when Farrer resumed the seat: whether voluntarily or not, he relinquished his candidature. At his next appearance on the electoral scene, in 1710, when he unsuccessfully challenged Farrer and another Whig in Bedford, he probably relied on Tory support, for the following year he was appointed deputy-recorder under the Tory Lord Bruce (Charles*) 'by the recommendation of the loyal interest of the town', and in 1712 and 1713 he assisted in the presentation of pro-ministerial addresses on the peace. The prominence which this post gave him in the politics of the borough did not, however, enable him to relaunch his parliamentary ambitions, and he was not involved in the contest at the 1713 election.[5]

Carteret returned to Parliament in a by-election in 1717. Having obtained a post in the Post Office, in the last stage of his career he separated from his nephew, Lord Carteret, becoming, through the unscrupulous and partisan exercise of his official powers to monitor the royal mails, an important instrument of Walpole's ministry. Bequeathed a substantial estate in Essex by a female 'friend and relation' in 1732, he spent several years in improving the house and even built a private chapel there, while continuing to reside for the most part 'at the Post Office in Paul's churchyard'.[6]

Carteret died on 15 Apr. 1739 and was buried at Hornchurch in Essex. He had suffered for some time from the stone and had only recently been pronounced cured by a quack doctor to whose ministrations he had in desperation submitted himself. Thus the discovery of 'two white, smooth stones, the size of chestnuts' in his bladder was a 'triumph' for the sceptics and as such was reported in the press. Since he died intestate administration was granted to his two surviving daughters, one of them the wife of Edward Harvey*, and in due course they sold off the estate.[7]

[1] A. Collins, *Hist. Carteret Fam.* 64–65; *Mar. Lic. Fac. Off.* (Harl. Soc. xxiv), 234; F. A. Blaydes, *Genealogia Bedfordiensis*, 135; *Westminster Abbey Reg.* (Harl. Soc. x), 36, 293; Morant, *Essex*, ii. 568; *VCH Essex*, vii. 66. [2] Bedford Bor. Council, Bedford bor. recs. B2/3, corp. act bk. 1688–1718, ff. 56, 116; *Post Boy*, 1–4 Dec. 1711, 5–7 June 1712. [3] *Cal. Treas. Bks. and Pprs.* 1731–4, p. 521; 1739–41, p. 200. [4] Collins, 63–64; *VCH Hunts.* ii. 35. [5] *Nicolson Diaries* ed. Jones and Holmes, 255; Add. 29599, f. 119; *Post Boy*, 1–4 Dec. 1711; *London Gazette*, 10–12 July 1712, 30 May–2 June 1713; Bedford bor. recs. B2/3, ff. 113, 117. [6] P. S. Fritz, *Ministers and Jacobitism 1715–45*, p. 109; Lysons, *Environs* (1792–6), iv. 191; Morant, i. 62; *VCH Essex*, 67; *Autobiog. and Corresp. of Mrs Delany*, i. 447. [7] *Westminster Abbey Reg.* 36; *HMC 14th Rep. IX*, 245; *Gent. Mag.* 1739, p. 217; Lysons, 191.

D. W. H.

CARTWRIGHT, Thomas (1671–1748), of Aynho Park, Northants.

NORTHAMPTONSHIRE   1695–1698
                               1701 (Dec.)–10 Mar. 1748

b. 1671, o. surv. s. of William Cartwright† of Bloxham, Oxon. by his 2nd w. Ursula (*d.* 1702), da. of Ferdinando Fairfax†, 2nd Ld. Fairfax [S]. *educ.* St. Catharine's, Camb. 1687. *m.* 30 Mar. 1699, Armine (*d.* 1728), da. and coh. of Thomas Crew†, 2nd Baron Crew of Stene, 2s. 3da. *suc.* fa. and gdfa. 1676.

Sheriff, Northants. 1693–4, Oxon. 1699–1700.[1]

Thomas Cartwright's great-grandfather originated from Cheshire and purchased the manor of Aynho in

1616 from the profits of a successful career at the bar. It appears that the family's initial support for the parliamentarian cause waned in the 1650s, and by the early 1660s they had become staunchly Royalist. Cartwright was still a minor when he inherited his father's estates in Northamptonshire and Oxfordshire. Only two years after coming of age he was pricked for sheriff of Northamptonshire. It was his comfortable financial situation that made him a suitable Tory candidate in the election of 1695 in which one of the Whig opponents was the Earl of Sunderland's son, Lord Spencer (Charles*). Otherwise, as a young and still comparatively unknown quantity, Cartwright was seen as 'the least evil'. However, Spencer's unwillingness 'to set his pocket at stake ag[ain]st Mr Cartwright's' induced him to withdraw midway through the campaign, and Cartwright went on to poll second place in an election which cost him a princely £1,320 17s.11d.[2]

Cartwright was forecast in January 1696 as likely to support the Court on the proposed council of trade, refused at first to sign the Association before doing so early in March at the second time of asking, and towards the end of the same month opposed the government over fixing the price of guineas at 22s. He was then granted leave of absence on 3 Apr. In the next session recovery from serious illness seems to have caused him to miss the division on Sir John Fenwick's[†] attainder on 25 Nov., while on 23 Jan. 1697 he was granted a fortnight's leave, a call of the House being scheduled for the 25th. His name appeared on a list of reputed adherents of James II brought to the attention of James Vernon I* in June, though the imputation of Jacobitism in his case was not taken seriously. In 1698 Cartwright declined an invitation from Sir Justinian Isham, 4th Bt.*, to make an electoral partnership and stood singly. He was defeated in a three-cornered contest. An analysis of the parties drawn up in about September classed him retrospectively as one of the Country party. During what proved to be only a brief interlude out of Parliament he maintained his links with Tory MPs and continued to fraternize with them in their back-bench activities, dining, for instance, on 13 Jan. 1700 with Sir Godfrey Copley, 2nd Bt.*, Anthony Hammond* and Hon. James Brydges* at The Goat, a Tory venue in Bloomsbury Square, and 'concerting about Lord Ranelagh's (Richard Jones*) accounts'; and on 22 Feb. he met other gentlemen at Brydges' residence to discuss the same subject. Appointed high sheriff of Oxfordshire in 1699, he was granted special dispensation to hold the office *in absentia*, and at the end of 1700 was variously mentioned as an intending candidate for Northamptonshire, Oxfordshire and Banbury, though in fact he entered none of these contests. At the second election of 1701 he partnered Isham in the Northamptonshire election and polled second place. He was thereafter returned for the county at every subsequent election until his death in 1748.[3]

Cartwright's re-entry to the Commons in December 1701 was regarded by Lord Spencer as a 'loss' for the Whigs, and on 26 Feb. 1702 he voted for the resolution vindicating the Commons' proceedings in the impeachments of the King's ministers. A badly 'sprained foot' sustained in a hunting accident prevented him from attending much, and possibly all, of the 1703–4 session, and he asked Sir John Mordaunt, 5th Bt., to convey his excuses in case the House was called over. In mid-March 1704 Lord Nottingham (Daniel Finch[†]) listed him as a likely supporter in the event of an attack on his handling of the Scotch Plot, and in October Cartwright was identified as a probable supporter of the Tack, but in fact he abstained in the division of 28 Nov., being afterwards blacklisted as a 'sneaker'. In January 1705 he was party to a piece of Tory trickery in which John Parkhurst*, a former Whig knight of the shire for Northamptonshire, was censured for accounting irregularities at the Prize Office: Parkhurst alleged that Cartwright, Isham and William Bromley II* deliberately engineered the Commons' vote against him in a 'thin House' despite the fact that the Treasury secretary William Lowndes* had previously cleared Parkhurst of any malfeasance. In the contest of 1705 Cartwright polled second place to Isham, though only by five votes. At the opening of the new Parliament he voted against the Court candidate for the Speakership. Towards the autumn of 1706, he took the initiative of organizing an emergency meeting of the county's Tory gentlemen in response to early Whig preparations to mount a major offensive against Cartwright and Isham at the next election, though the effort of doing so left him in some doubt as to whether he wished to seek future re-election.[4]

During February and March 1707 Cartwright partly managed a private estate bill on behalf of an Oxfordshire gentleman, John Weedon. In a published list of early 1708 he was listed as a Tory. As the next session drew near in November, he had to be pressed by William Bromley II to attend the opening of the session punctually in order to participate in a projected bid to elect a Tory Speaker. In early 1710 he voted against the impeachment of Dr Sacheverell. His modest level of parliamentary activity did not noticeably increase under Harley's Tory administration. He was later noted as one of the 'worthy patriots' who during the 1710–11 session approved the exposure of the previous ministry's mismanagements, and as a 'Tory patriot' who in 1711 voted for peace. He also became a member of the October Club. In February–March 1712 he managed a private bill to confer the status of 'free ship' on a vessel belonging to a London merchant. Cartwright made regular visits to Bath where he enjoyed the company of such prominent Tory families as the Harleys, Foleys and Winningtons, though his presence there in July 1712 ruled him out as a suitable choice to present the Queen with his county's address on the peace negotiations. Evidence of some 'whimsical' moderation in his Tory outlook can be found in the Worsley list, in which he was classed as a Tory who sometimes sided with the Whigs. His major preoccupation during the 1714 session was his supervision of a bill for the navigation of the Nene.[5]

Returned again in 1715, Cartwright continued to represent his county as a Tory until his death on 10 Mar. 1748, aged 77.

[1] *VCH Northants. Fams.* 13; *Vis. Northants.* (Harl. Soc. lxxxii), 42. [2] *VCH Northants. Fams.* 11–12; E. G. Forrester, *Northants. Elections and Electioneering, 1695–1832*, p. 18; Northants. RO, Isham mss IC 1498, John to Sir Justinian Isham, 4 Nov. 1693; 1524, Henry Benson to same, 10 Aug. 1695. [3] Luttrell, *Brief Relation*, iv. 25; *Vernon–Shrewsbury Letters*, i. 268; Huntington Lib. Stowe mss 26(1), James Brydges'* diary (13 Jan., 22 Feb. 1700); Bodl. Tanner 22, f. 107; *CSP Dom.* 1699–1700, p. 328; Isham mss IC 1643, Thomas Tryst to Sir Justinian Isham, 31 Dec. 1700; 2708, Sir Matthew Dudley, 2nd Bt.*, to same, 20 Dec. 1700; 2716, Thomas Ekins* to same, 16 Nov. 1701; Add. 29568, ff. 37–38; Forrester, 24. [4] G. Holmes, *Pol. in Age of Anne*, 305; Add. 27740, f. 92; Isham mss IC 1665–6, Lady Isham to Sir Justinian Isham, 12, 17 Feb. 1704–5; 3702, Henry Benson to same, 22 Feb. 1704–5; 2754, Hon. Charles Bertie I* to same, 29 Aug. 1706; 2944, Cartwright to same, 31 Aug. 1706; Forrester, 30–31. [5] Isham mss IC 1705, William Bromley II to Sir Justinian Isham, 15 Oct. 1708; 3802, 2135, Sir Justinian to Justinian Isham, 20 July 1712, 13 June 1713; 1760, Justinian to Sir Justinian Isham, 11 June 1713; Bodl. Ballard 18, ff. 53–54; Northants. RO, Cartwright of Aynho mss C(A) 54, Aynho par. reg.

A. A. H.

CARY (CAREY), Edward (1656–92), of St. James's, Westminster and Caldicot, Mon.

COLCHESTER 1690–Aug. 1692

bap. 25 Apr. 1656, 2nd s. of Hon. Patrick Cary (Carey) of Horton, Dorset by Susan, da. of Francis Uvedale of Wickham, Hants. *educ.* Christ Church, Oxf. matric. 27 June 1673 (aged 17); L. Inn 1675. *m.* by 1687, Anne (*d.* by 1701), da. and coh. of Charles, 2nd Baron Lucas, of Shenfield, Essex, 1s. 1da.[1]

High bailiff, Westminster by 1684–*d.*; v.-adm. Essex 1691–2.[2]

Freeman, Colchester 1689.[3]

Cary's father, the youngest son of the 1st Viscount Falkland [S], had been brought up a Catholic in Ireland and spent a brief time as a monk at Douai before settling in England. From this unpromising background Edward's fortunes were improved by his inheritance in 1685 of the Caldicot manor in Monmouthshire, together with lands in Kent and Lincolnshire, under the will of John Cary of Stanwell, Middlesex. At about that time he married his cousin Anne Lucas, and took up residence in Westminster, where he had been appointed high bailiff, a post to which he had been nominated by the high steward, the 1st Duke of Ormond, and for which he was forced to substantiate his claim after the Revolution. It was presumably from his wife's interest at Lexden that he successfully contested the election for Colchester in 1690, and he can have been no novice to the scrutiny of the poll that overturned Sir Isaac Rebow's majority to give him the seat, since one of the functions of his Westminster post was to act as a returning officer. His other duties there were similar to those of the London sheriffs, albeit performed by a deputy, and recompensed by a right to all fines and forfeitures ordered in his court. Cary's claim that this right also included clipped money was disputed by the warden of the Mint, a disagreement that featured until after Cary's death when a verdict was finally given against his widow.[4]

Cary's activity in Parliament is sometimes difficult to distinguish from that of William Cary, MP for Okehampton, who sat at the same time, particularly as the two men shared a Tory allegiance. Both had also been educated at Oxford, and one acted as teller on 23 Apr. 1690 for a bill settling a private charity at the university. Presumably because Edward had never sat before, Lord Carmarthen (Sir Thomas Osborne†) marked him as 'doubtful' on a printed list of MPs in March 1690, but he soon showed himself to be under the influence of his cousin the 5th Viscount Falkland (Anthony Carey*), when on 26 Apr. he and Falkland spoke against the abjuration bill at its second reading. Edward declared that although he was 'so much a friend to the government that, when this was first proposed I was for it, and ready to take any engagement', he now believed that 'those who offer this abjuration oath, as a further security to the government, do make the government precarious, as if it needed somewhat to strengthen it'. Three days later he pushed the same line, arguing that it was 'better to accept of men's obedience upon any easy terms than impose on them'. On 30 Apr. one of the two namesakes acted as teller against resolving into a committee of the whole House to consider a bill discouraging the importation of thrown silk, and on 8 May Edward assisted the London Tories by acting as teller in favour of an amendment to the bill for reversing the quo warranto against the City of London. The same day he was asked to enforce an order that the streets between Temple Bar and Westminster Hall be kept clear, though the request had to be repeated in the next session. It may have been Edward who on 24 Oct. reported a private estate bill, acted as teller on 10 Nov. on a procedural motion to adjourn, and again on 26 Nov. on a bill for reducing the rate of interest from six to four per cent. As a prominent London office-holder he is likely to have been the 'Mr Cary' who acted as a teller on 2 Dec. 1690 for those who wished to read the petition of grievances from London's Tory common councilmen.[5]

Viscount Falkland was appointed to the Admiralty commission in January 1691, and it was presumably as a result of his influence that Cary was made vice-admiral of Essex on 28 Feb. 1691, earning him the classification of Court supporter on a list drawn up by Robert Harley* and dated April 1691. When Parliament reopened in October of that year Cary was consequently even closer to his cousin's politics. On 19 Nov., during a debate on supply, Cary spoke strongly in favour of 'a hearty prosecution of the war' and, noting the time 'to be the critical moment of our happiness or misery', moved for a vote that an army of 65,000 men was necessary. On 14 Nov., during a debate on the navy, he acted as teller on the Court side for money to build new ships, and on 28 Nov. spoke and once more told on behalf of the Court in a debate on the army estimates, arguing that the figure of 65,000 should not be reduced to include the number of officers. On 2 Jan. 1692 he was again a teller for the government, which wished to keep up the number of dragoons in Ireland, and on 15 Feb. acted twice as a teller opposing amendments to the poll bill. It was probably his Westminster rather than his Court stance that prompted Cary to act as teller on 2 Feb. on a proviso in the bill for preventing gunpowder being kept near the Tower of London, and as teller on 20 Feb. for a second reading of the bill for the relief of orphans in London. Given Falkland's defence of the East India Company it is likely that it was he who supported the Company on 13 Nov. 1691, and served as teller on 6 Feb. 1692 on the wording of an address about it; but either Edward or William Cary may have been a teller on 7 and 25 Jan. 1692 on motions concerning the bill for regulating trials in cases of treason, and on 16 Feb. for a private estate bill.[6]

Cary's death, which probably accounts for the addition of the letter 'd' to the Harley list of 1691, was reported by Luttrell on 9 Aug. 1692, and was possibly sudden and unexpected since he left no will, an administration order being granted for the estate on 24 Nov. 1692. His son, Lucius Henry Cary, succeeded as the 6th Viscount Falkland in 1694, and was created an earl in 1722 by the titular James III.[7]

[1] IGI, Mon; *Her. and Gen.* iii. 38–41; info. from Dr D. F. Lemmings. [2] *Cal. Treas. Bks.* viii. 1464; *EHR*, xxiii. 743. [3] *Oath Bk. . . . of Colchester* ed. Benham, 234. [4] *Her. and Gen.* 38–41, 133; W. H. Manchee, *The Westminster City Fathers*, 16–17; *Stow's Survey of London* ed. Strype (1720), ii(2), p. 58; *Cal. Treas. Bks.* ix. 415, 1251, 1386, 1683; x. 843; *Cal. Treas. Pprs.* 1557–1696, p. 436. [5] Grey, x. 76; Bodl. Rawl. A.79, ff. 71, 89. [6] *Luttrell Diary*, 16, 19, 30, 47, 188–9. [7] Luttrell, *Brief Relation*, ii. 535.

M. J. K.

CARY, William (c.1661–1710), of Clovelly, Devon.

OKEHAMPTON   1685–1687, 1689–1695
LAUNCESTON   1695–1710

b. c.1661, 2nd s. of George Cary, DD, dean of Exeter, by Mary, da. of William Hancock of Combe Martin, Devon; bro. of Sir George Cary† of Clovelly. *educ.* Queen's, Oxf. matric. 23 Mar. 1678, aged 16; M. Temple 1679. *m.* (1) aft. 1683, Joan (*d.* 1687), da. of Sir William Wyndham†, 1st Bt., of Orchard Wyndham, St. Decuman's, Som., *s.p.*; (2) settlement 28 Mar. 1694 (with £5,000), Mary (*d.* 1701), da. of Thomas Mansel† of Briton Ferry, Glam., sis. of Thomas Mansel II*, 3s. (1 *d.v.p.*) 2da. *suc.* bro. 1685.[1]

Recorder, Okehampton 1685–?Jan. 1688, 1689–*d*; freeman, Exeter 1697.[2]

Commr. drowned lands 1690.[3]

Cary, who had joined William of Orange after the Prince's landing in the West, was returned for Okehampton in 1690, following which he was classed as a Court supporter and a Tory by Lord Carmarthen (Sir Thomas Osborne†). His parliamentary activity is impossible to distinguish from that of his namesake Edward Cary* (Carey), and the disappearance of the surname 'Cary' from significant parliamentary activity after the death of Edward Cary in August 1692 strongly suggests that William was by some way the less prominent of the two. The only comment that can be made as to Cary's contribution to the 1690 Parliament is that he was included in December 1690 in Carmarthen's list of likely supporters in the event of a Commons attack upon his ministerial position. In 1695 Cary transferred to Launceston, which he then represented until his death. His contribution to the 1695 Parliament is again complicated by the presence of a namesake, on this occasion Nicholas Carey. Forecast as likely to oppose the Court in the divisions of 31 Jan. upon the council of trade, Cary initially refused to sign the Association and was subsequently removed from the commission of the peace. On 25 Nov. he voted against the attainder of Sir John Fenwick†, and the only other matter of note concerning him in this Parliament was the leave of absence he was granted on 11 May 1698. Classed as a Country supporter in about September in a comparison of the old and new Commons, he was included on 7 Mar. 1699 upon a list of Members who had not attended that session but were excused by reason of sickness or infirmity. In February 1701 he was listed as likely to support the Court over the 'Great Mortgage', and in December was listed as a Tory by Robert Harley*. He was included on the list of those who favoured the motion of 26 Feb. 1702 vindicating the Commons' proceedings in the previous session in the impeachments of the Whig lords. His only other notable parliamentary activity was to tell on 13 Mar. 1702 against the second reading of the bill for punishing felons and their accomplices.[4]

During Queen Anne's reign Cary remained consistent in his Tory sympathies. On 13 Feb. 1703 he voted against agreeing with the Lords' amendments to the bill enlarging the time for taking the abjuration, and in March 1704 Lord Nottingham (Daniel Finch†) included him upon a list of probable supporters over the Scotch Plot. The previous month a bill was passed to allow Cary to sell lands in Somerset and settle his Devon estates in order to pay debts and make provision for his younger children. That this act was occasioned by growing financial problems became clear in the summer when he was in correspondence with Harley concerning the possibility of being given a place of profit under the crown. He explained to Harley that

> by 16 or 17 years of war my estate, which mostly lies near the sea, has felt more than ordinary calamities of it, and hath been lessened in its income beyond most of my neighbours living in the inland country, and that a considerable jointure upon it, and four small children and the Act of Parliament procured last session for dismembering it, are motives which concur with my ambition to serve her Majesty.

Harley assured Cary of both his own and Lord Treasurer Godolphin's (Sidney†) 'goodwill', and his hope that 'a little patience . . . will present somewhat which may be consistent with your being a Member'. No place was forthcoming, however, and it is difficult to determine if this failure was occasioned by, or was the result of, Cary's support for the Tack. Forecast on 30 Oct. as likely to support this measure, on 28 Nov. he voted for it. An analysis of the 1705 Parliament classed Cary as 'True Church', and on 25 Oct. he voted against the Court candidate for Speaker. In early 1708 he was listed as a Tory and in 1710 he voted against the impeachment of Dr Sacheverell. Cary's only other significant activity in the 1708 Parliament was to tell, on 25 Jan. 1710, against the second reading of a bill relating to the making of buttons. Cary had died by 3 Oct. 1710, before the general election, and his will, drawn up the previous September, was proved in January 1711.[5]

[1] Vivian, *Vis. Devon*, 159; Collinson, *Som.* iii. 495; *Cat. Penrice and Margam MSS*, ser. 4, iii. 144. [2] W. K. H. Wright, *Okehampton*, 105; PC 2/76, f. 263; *Exeter Freemen* (Devon and Cornw. Rec. Soc. ex. ser. i), 201. [3] *Cal. Treas. Bks.* ix. 794. [4] Luttrell, *Brief Relation*, i. 477; H. Horwitz, *Parl. and Pol. Wm. III*, 338; L. K. J. Glassey, *Appt. JPs*, 123. [5] *HMC Portland*, iv. 99; Add. 70276, Harley to Cary, 28 July 1704; Morice mss at Bank of Eng. Sir Nicholas Morice, 2nd Bt.*, to Humphry Morice*, 3 Oct. 1710; PCC 4 Young.

E. C.

CASS, John (1661–1718) of Grove Street, Hackney, Mdx.

LONDON 1710–1715

b. 28 Feb. 1661, s. of Thomas Cass, Carpenter, of St. Botolph without Aldgate, London, and Hackney, by his 1st w. Martha Johnson. *m.* 7 Jan. 1684, Elizabeth Franklyn (*d.* 1732), of Wapping, Mdx. *d.v.p.* suc. fa. 1699. Kntd. 16 June 1712.[1]

Freeman, Carpenters' Co. 1687, asst. and master 1711, transferred to Skinners' Co. 1713, master 1714; alderman, London 1711, sheriff 1711.

Asst. R. African Co. 1705–8.

Treasurer, Bethlehem and Bridewell Hosp. 1709–14.

Commr. building 50 new churches 1711, 1712.[2]

Although described by his parish priest as 'a haughty, reserved man, neither loving nor beloved', Cass gained much popularity as one of London's High Church leaders. His father was a Hackney carpenter of possible French ancestry, who had built up a respectable fortune as a major building contractor to the Ordnance, which led to election in 1688 as master of the Carpenters' Company, and appointment as an officer of the Tower Hamlets militia. Fellow Hackney resident Sir John Friend† was a close associate, and thus at the time of the Assassination Plot of 1696 the Cass household came under much suspicion. It was later claimed that the traitor Friend was actually apprehended at Cass's house, and 'Col. Cash' was among the suspects rounded up following the discovery of the plot. Even though Thomas Cass was not prosecuted, the family subsequently faced a battle to recover a debt of £1,300 from Friend's confiscated estate. A royal grant to this end was achieved in February 1700, by which time the future Member had also succeeded to his father's fortune.[3]

As early as September 1701 Cass demonstrated his

political ambition by mounting his first, albeit unsuccessful, campaign to become alderman for Portsoken, the ward of his birth. Nevertheless, in October 1702 he reportedly absented himself from the Lord Mayor's Day celebrations on hearing that the Queen might knight him amid these festivities. He subsequently achieved greater prominence in City circles by becoming in 1705 an assistant in the Royal African Company, and his Tory outlook was confirmed by his votes in the Middlesex election of that year. After an unsuccessful candidacy at an aldermanic contest for Tower ward in December 1707, he concentrated his efforts on his native Portsoken, establishing his reputation there as one of the City's leading philanthropists. Displaying a particular concern for the education of the poor, in May 1709 he drew up a will to provide for the founding of schools in Hackney and in the Portsoken parish of St. Botolph without Aldgate. Although his plans for Hackney were never realized, the Portsoken school was soon put into operation, thereby fulfilling Cass's hopes that local children would be educated 'in the knowledge of the Christian religion according to the principles of the Church of England'.[4]

The determination with which the Whig aldermen fought to block his election for Portsoken in October 1709 clearly indicated that Cass had emerged as an important Tory figure in the City. Although his name was returned to the court alongside fellow Tory William Andrew, it was rejected by the aldermen 'after a long debate', and he was then overlooked a second time after Andrew had declined to serve on grounds of insufficient estate. The aldermen even refused to call another election, causing a storm of protest which evidently raised Cass's standing. In late September 1710 the City Tories put him forward as a parliamentary candidate, reportedly in place of (Sir) Charles Duncombe*. The subsequent poll proved very close, and Cass only gained the fourth seat by a 16-vote majority over the Whig, John Ward II*. Some observers predicted that Cass would lose the seat after the scrutiny, but his return was upheld, 'to the great mortification of the Whig party'. However, his success failed to impress the Whig aldermen, who rejected him as alderman for Portsoken on two further occasions. Tory indignation at the arbitrary behaviour of the bench led to a campaign to reform the City constitution, and the agitation eventually prevailed in January 1711 so far as to secure Cass an alderman's place.[5]

In the new Parliament Cass was lauded as a 'worthy patriot' for helping to discover in the first session the mismanagements of the previous ministry, and he was also cited as a 'Tory patriot' for opposing the continuation of the war, but proved an inactive Member. However, he achieved much publicity outside the House when his charity school was opened on 8 Mar. 1711, the anniversary of Anne's accession. A large assembly of peers and Members attended a thanksgiving service conducted by Dr Sacheverell, and a subsequent dinner was attended by 'a great number of the loyal true sons of the Church'. His support for the Anglican cause was further demonstrated that same year when he was appointed to the commission to build 50 new London churches.[6]

Despite recent Tory success in the capital, Cass and his allies were unable to make any gains at the elections for the Honorary Artillery Company in 1711 and 1712. In June 1711 he was elected sheriff 'by a great majority', but this victory was marred by reports suggesting that his success was welcomed by Jacobite supporters. Such slurs had evidently dogged his family ever since the time of the Assassination Plot, for a Tory pamphlet of 1710, *London's Happiness in Four Loyal Members*, had depicted Cass proclaiming 'No Perkin', thereby indicating his sensitivity to charges of abetting the Pretender. However, there is no evidence to suggest that he bore any allegiance to the exiled Stuarts, and Abel Boyer dismissed such claims as 'foolish presumption'.[7]

In the second session of the 1710 Parliament Cass was again inconspicuous, although he was nominated to two committees concerning bankruptcy legislation. He was identified in February 1712 as a Member of the October Club, and at the end of the session he received a knighthood when attending the presentation of the City's address of thanks for the Queen's promise to communicate the peace terms. Three months later he was one of the two Tories to be returned to the court of aldermen for the choice of mayor, but Sir Richard Hoare*, as the senior alderman, was chosen ahead of him. Though failing in this ambition, Cass was still an active party protagonist, leading a delegation of the Tower Hamlets lieutenancy to address the Queen on 27 Apr. with thanks for 'an advantageous peace'. However, he was prepared to break with the ministry over the French commerce bill, presenting a petition to the House against the measure, and on 18 June 1713 voting against the bill. Later that month he was named to the drafting committee on a bill to protect the privileges of London freemen.[8]

At the City election of October 1713 Cass again achieved a narrow victory, finishing third, with only 70 votes more than the fifth-placed John Ward II. The poll reveals that he actually voted for Robert Heysham*, a Tory who at that contest stood on the Whig 'merchant' interest. In the ensuing Parliament he remained anonymous, although he was nominated to the drafting committee for a bill to prevent the covert importation of aliens' goods, an issue of obvious metropolitan concern. He was still an active figure in civic affairs, and in December was awarded the colonelcy of a militia regiment. The same month he transferred from the Carpenters' to the Skinners' Company, probably with the design of gaining the mayoralty. However, despite becoming master of his new company, he never achieved the chair. Ill-health may have blocked his promotion, for in April 1714 he was reported to have travelled to Bristol 'to drink the waters of St. Vincent's Rock for the diabetes'.[9]

Identified as a Tory in the Worsley list, Cass found the Hanoverian succession a further impediment to advancement, losing his colonelcy and only managing fifth place at the City election of January 1715. However, in February 1716 the leaders of a Whig club testified to his continuing stature by proposing that he should retain his place on two City committees. He died at his Hackney home on 5 July 1718, 'leaving his lady childless and most of his estates to charitable uses'. While he gave generously to the Carpenters' Company and the Bethlehem Hospital, his charity school remained the principal beneficiary of his largesse. The board of trustees which he appointed to administer the school's affairs confirmed his commitment to the Established Church, its officers including Francis Atterbury, bishop of Rochester, and the Tory MP Sir William Withers. However, although the school proved a lasting achievement, its early years were dominated by legal wrangling over Cass's last, half-signed will. A bill to resolve the matter was rejected by the Commons in 1726, and not until 1748 was the school's future secured.[10]

[1] D. A. Brunning, 'Short Acct. of Sir John Cass and His Foundation' (T/S in Guildhall Lib.), 3; IGI, London; *Mar. Lic. Vicar-Gen.* (Harl. Soc. xxx), 156; *Gent. Mag.* 1732, p. 876. [2] Guildhall Lib. ms 21742/1; Beaven, *Aldermen*, ii. 122; K. G. Davies, *R. African Co.* 379; *London Rec. Soc.* xxiii. 178. [3] Brunning, 3–4; Guildhall Lib. ms 21742/1; *Cal. Treas. Bks.* ix. 562; xv. 268; Add. 22187, f. 116; HMC *Downshire*, i. 658. [4] Beaven, i. 185; Strathmore mss at Glamis Castle, box 70, folder 2, bdle. 3, newsletter 31 Oct. 1702; *Mdx. Poll of 1705*; Luttrell, *Brief Relation*, vi. 250; Brunning, 6; *Post Boy*, 3–6 Mar. 1711. [5] Luttrell, 506, 509, 634; BL, Trumbull Alphab. mss 54, Ralph Bridges to Sir William Trumbull*, 8, 13 Nov. 1710; Add. 70421, newsletters 16 Nov., 21 Dec. 1710; Beaven, i. 185. [6] *Post Boy*, 3–6 Mar. 1711; J. P. Malcolm, *Londinium Redivivum*, iv. 463. [7] G. S. De Krey, *Fractured Soc.* 263; Boyer, *Pol. State*, i. 450–1; *Cat. of Prints and Drawings in BM: Pol. and Personal Satires* ed. George, ii. 340–1. [8] Boyer, iii. 368; iv. 197; *London Gazette*, 28 Apr.–2 May 1713; Brunning, 4. [9] *London Rec. Soc.* xvii. 76; *Post Boy*, 22–24 Dec. 1713; HMC *Portland*, v. 411. [10] *London Rec. Soc.* xvii. 39; Brunning, 4, 7; PCC 210 Tenison.

P. L. G.

CASTLECOMER, Christopher Wandesford, 2nd Visct. [I] *see* **WANDESFORD**

CASTLETON, George Saunderson, 5th Visct. [I] *see* **SAUNDERSON**

CATER, John (1672–1734), of Kempston Hall, Beds.

BEDFORD 1710–1715
BEDFORDSHIRE 19 July 1715–1722

b. 1672, 1st s. of Samuel Cater of Kempston Hall and Harrold, sheriff of Beds. 1689–90, by Anne, da. of John Kendall of Bassingbourn, Cambs. *educ.* Wadham, Oxf. 1689. m. 10 July 1694, Mary (d. 1718), da. of Sir Thomas Middleton*, sis. of Thomas Middleton*, 3s. (2 *d.v.p.*) 1da. *d.v.p. suc.* fa. 1704.[1]
Burgess, Bedford 1707.[2]

Cater was descended from William Cater, the offspring of a younger son of a Leicestershire gentleman, who purchased an estate at Kempston, just outside Bedford, in about 1624 and served as sheriff of Bedfordshire in 1630–1. Little is known of the family's participation in politics prior to 1705, when Cater himself appears as voting for the two Whig candidates, Sir William Gostwick, 4th Bt.*, and (Lord) Edward Russell* in the Bedfordshire election. However, his father's exclusion from the county commission of the peace in 1687–8, appointment as sheriff before the general election of 1690, and support for the Bedford interest in the 1698 county election strongly suggest Whig sympathies. In his debut as a parliamentary candidate, for Bedford in 1710, Cater topped the poll, but his first reward was to be struck off as a j.p. in Surrey as part of the new ministry's purge of the local commissions. He was kept on for Bedfordshire, however, where he was a stalwart of the bench. After a three-week leave of absence granted on 6 Mar. 1711, he told on 28 Apr. against a Tory motion of censure on the previous Treasury commissioners for failing to compel the imprest accountants to pass their accounts. His inclusion in the list of 'worthy patriots' who in this session exposed the mismanagements of the old ministry must therefore be an error. He subsequently voted on 7 Dec. 1711 in favour of the 'No Peace without Spain' motion, and on 18 June 1713 against the French commerce bill, as a Whig. In the 1713 general election he retained his seat for Bedford while failing in a simultaneous candidature for knight of the shire on the Whig interest. Having voted on 18 Mar. 1714 against the expulsion of Richard Steele, he was a teller twice this session on election cases: on 20 Apr. against John Burgh* on the Brackley petition; and on 25 May in favour of a motion, arising from the debate on the Southwark election, that Quakers making their solemn affirmation instead of taking the oath of abjuration were entitled to vote. He was marked in the Worsley list as a Whig.[3]

Seated on petition in 1715, Cater proved himself a solid supporter of administration during this Parliament but did not seek re-election. He died on 16 Mar. 1734. The death of his one surviving son within two years meant that the estate passed to a brother-in-law, Robert Kendall, an alderman of London, who changed his name to Cater.[4]

[1] F. A. Blaydes, *Genealogia Bedfordiensis*, 164, 403; *Beds. N. and Q.* ii. 215; C. R. Parrott, *All Saints Par. Ch. Kempston*, 25–26; *Beds. Par. Reg.* xxxix. 19, 81–83, 85, 87. [2] Bedford Bor. Council, Bedford bor. recs. B2/3, corp. act. bk. 1688–1718, f. 91. [3] *Vis. Beds.* (Harl. Soc. xix), 89–90; *VCH Beds.* iii. 300–1; Beds. RO, OR 1823, *Beds. Pollbk. 1705*; Duckett, *Penal Laws and Test Act* (1883), 57; Add. 29599, f. 119; L. K. J. Glassey, *Appt. JPs*, 207; J. Godber, *Hist. Beds.* 370. [4] *VCH Beds.* 301; *Gent. Mag.* 1734, p. 164; 1736, p. 55.

D. W. H.

CAVE, Sir Thomas, 3rd Bt. (1681–1719), of Stanford Hall, Leics.

LEICESTERSHIRE 22 Feb. 1711–21 Apr. 1719

bap. 9 Apr. 1681, 1st s. of Sir Roger Cave, 2nd Bt.†, by his 1st w. Martha, da. and h. of John Browne of Eydon, Northants., clerk of the Parliaments. *educ.* Rugby 1690; Christ Church, Oxf. 1699 *m.* 20 Feb. 1703 (with £3,000), Margaret (*d.* 1774), da. of John Verney*, 1st Visct. Fermanagh [I], 2s. 2da. *suc.* fa. as 3rd Bt. 11 Oct. 1703.[1]

Sir Thomas Cave was in many ways the archetypal Tory country gentleman in terms of lifestyle and prejudices. A high-minded Anglican, he regarded himself as a political spectator rather than a participant, judging himself 'no tame politician'. Barely out of his youth, he inherited financially robust estates straddling the Leicestershire–Northamptonshire border from a father who never reconciled himself to his son's choice of bride. Sir Roger's own marriage had brought into the family a fortune of £30,000, and not unnaturally he wished his son and heir to marry equally advantageously. Cave's marriage to Margaret Verney in February 1703 was performed in London without his father's knowledge, a fact which momentarily 'filled the town with fresh discourse'. Neither did this *fait accompli* help to soften the elder Cave, who allowed his son a niggardly £80 a year 'to keep him from starving'. The young couple were made welcome at the Verneys' Buckinghamshire seat at Claydon, until Sir Roger's timely death in October. Cave very soon came to value a warm relationship with his father-in-law, and the two families exchanged visits regularly every year. On taking title and estates he quickly settled into the routines and responsibilities of a country gentleman. His letters to the Verneys reveal a companionable and sportsmanlike personality, dedicated to horse-racing, the chase and shooting, although his diminutive stature was not an asset: once, Lord Fermanagh observed, 'the little baronet hath much ado to get clear of the black thorns, or brussle through the tall underwood'. Besides the Tory Verneys, his social milieu included two leading Midlands gentry families, also of Tory stock: the Bromleys of Warwickshire, with whom he was connected through his father's second marriage, Cave's stepmother being the sister of William Bromley II*; and the Ishams of Northamptonshire, whom he invariably assisted at elections.[2]

Though not elected until 1711, Cave had by then gained some familiarity with the ways of the House, having attended debates in several sessions, probably at the invitation of Members in his acquaintance. In January 1705 he was present at the debates on a place bill, informing Fermanagh of the rejection of another bill, 'which I was in hopes might have passed', to incapacitate peers from holding public office or benefiting financially from taking their seats. At the same time he concurred with Fermanagh's desire to see a bill to compel army officer-MPs 'to be with their men, and not suffered to loiter in England when the campaign is begun', as 'equal and just'. Although the lateness of the session would not permit such a bill, he expressed a youthful determination to broach the idea with Members known to him. However, the design was soon forgotten. At the end of January he shared the homeward journey with Sir Justinian Isham, 4th Bt.*, and 'others of our countrymen', whose immediate task was to prepare for the forthcoming Northamptonshire election. His appointment in February as a deputy-lieutenant for Northamptonshire by its Whig lord lieutenant, the Earl of Peterborough, was made, so one gentleman speculated, 'to sweeten him'. During polling in May Cave energetically handled the problems of transporting distant freeholders by hiring all available horses and using his own coach to convey the elderly. The poll was given up, however, before his own contingent of voters could reach Northampton.[3]

In November 1705, Cave was in London to watch over a private bill initiated on his behalf in the House of Lords, enabling him to dispose of land at Eydon in Northamptonshire to raise portions for his brother and sisters, and which received the Royal Assent in mid-February. Some property was evidently retained at Eydon, since Cave's stepmother and sisters were still living there in 1711. In January he also took the opportunity to attend the Commons' proceedings on the disputed return for Leicester. In July 1707 Cave was one of the j.p.s dismissed during Lord Chancellor Cowper's (William*) extensive remodelling of the Leicestershire bench. Following John Verney's death in October, he canvassed busily for the Tory Geoffrey Palmer* in the ensuing by-election in November. On hearing of the motion made on 17 Nov. to repeal the Game Act he saw its use as a possible election gambit, and asked Fermanagh to find out 'who first motioned it in the House, and whether Churchman or Fanatick; if the first the information may be of service to us'. A few months later Cave was promoting the Tory cause again at the 1708 general election. As the new Parliament of 1710 assembled for its first session he reflected sceptically on the nation's euphoric mood of expectation: 'the ignorant country rejoyceth much, and seemeth to expect great alter[ati]ons from your house'.[4]

The accession of Lord Granby (John Manners*, Lord Roos) to his father's dukedom in January 1711 precipitated discussion about who might replace him as Member for Leicestershire. There was almost complete unanimity among the county's leading Tories, meeting in London early in February, that it should be Cave. They pressed him to resolve immediately, 'thinking you the fittest to represent the county'. Unenthusiastic at first, he merely told his father-in-law he had 'complied'. One of his strongest advocates was the former shire knight John Wilkins, who seems to have suggested his name to the county's leading Tory peer, Lord Denbigh, even before the by-election had materialized, and it was Wilkins who took on the task of organizing Cave's campaign. The appearance of a Tory rival, Henry Tate, to whom several of Cave's friends had already pledged themselves threatened an unnecessarily divisive campaign, which, as he himself recognized, would be damaging to the party. He explained his predicament to Fermanagh:

> the sudden resolution of some of my former friends must give the county a great deal of trouble and make the election more strange to see some before my friends now my opponents, and others formerly my opposites now my side bearers, for by losing my old I'm obliged to make new friends. I must confess 'twould be unhappy to have the Ch[urch] interest once divided which would be difficult to unite. I can't honourably recede from my engagem[en]t nor the worthy gents that desired my standing desire it.

By mid-February, however, Tate's withdrawal had retrieved the situation and Cave was returned without opposition. During his first session Cave was noted as a 'worthy patriot' who supported the initiatives to expose the previous ministry's mismanagements, but did not belong to any Tory back-bench group. He shared his party's irritation at the expense of maintaining troops abroad during lulls in campaigning, grumbling, 'I fear we shall pay 'em extravagantly dear for their quiet.' In the summer he was reinstated on the county bench by Lord Chancellor Harcourt (Simon I*). London proved thoroughly uncongenial to him, and he once compared 'stinking London' to his 'paradise' at home. He seems never to have spent longer than one month there at a time. Singularly inactive in the House throughout his parliamentary career, he became progressively less conscientious about his attendance. In his first session he was up at the House as late as June 1712, reporting to Fermanagh the embittered debates on the conduct of the war in which 'the Whigs raved very violently'. The following year, however, he left Claydon for London in mid-April, and was soon reporting that the 2s. reduction in the land tax 'no doubt will be highly acceptable to the country and all landed men'. A little over a month elapsed before he was again back at Stanford. Finding no opponents in the next general election, he had sufficient leisure to invite himself to Claydon, 'as we Leicestershire beanbullies apprehend no opposition, you may command my attendance on you'. Early in September he and Lord Tamworth (Robert Shirley*) were returned unchallenged.[5]

At the beginning of 1714 Cave expressed relief at news of the Queen's improving health, 'especially from the reflections of the ill consequences of her death, and what confusion it must have created, while affairs are so unsettled'. He was in no doubt that during her illness the Whigs had been 'very uppish' and the Tories 'as much dejected'. After the new session had opened he spent a token two or three weeks in London, returning comfortably before the House recessed for Easter on 24 Mar. Anticipating a summons from Sir George Beaumont, 4th Bt.*, 'the sergeant', he travelled south again in mid-April and for a few weeks was deeply absorbed in 'the excessive hurry and fatigue' of 'a continued close attendance' during the debates on the peace 'and never dined more than two days before six at night'. He was appalled at the attitude of the Whigs, referring to them with irony as the 'religious party', for espousing far more confidence in the Emperor as a guarantor of the Protestant succession than 'to our present good Protestant Queen', when persecutions of German Protestants under the late Emperor Joseph I were still 'very fresh' and there being no sign of change in imperial policy: "'tis monstrous to see what lies and impossibilities they suggest to us; I can equal their practices at best to nothing but the snake in the grass'. Within a few more weeks in mid-May he had reserved his place on the Aylesbury coach, having stayed in town longer than he had originally intended. Early in June news reached him that the House was to be called over, but he decided to remain until called up by Beaumont and 'take another mouthful of agreeable Leicestershire air'. He had little time for the 'whimsical' sentiments that were emerging in his party. Towards the end of June, further deferral of the call had caused him to give up the prospect of visiting London again in the session. He teased his father-in-law about the death of the Electress Sophia, jesting, 'I wish to know if you was at old Sophy's burial'. At the beginning of August the jokes were laid aside, however. Cave instantly responded to news of the Queen's death, and probably left for town even before receiving Beaumont's summons of the 3rd. At the Commons on the 4th he joined 'a great concourse of the members to prevent any Whiggish play after so great a loss of the Queen'. The Whigs appeared to him in buoyant, 'uppish' mood, 'and threatened hard'. He was back at Stanford on the 10th.[6]

Soon afterwards Cave came in for criticism from some of Leicestershire's county gentry for his indecisiveness upon the question of his candidacy in the forthcoming election. He may well have thought twice before embarking on what he must have apprehended would be a strenuous and expensive contest. He was certainly under no delusions about the newly exposed condition of the Tories: 'we are threatened in all our employs when the King comes over'. Having decided to press forward, he was smartly rebuked by Beaumont for neglecting to publicize his intentions:

> to do your brother [i.e. (Sir) Geoffrey Palmer (3rd Bt.)] and you justice you have done your parts to promote an opposition, in running out of the county and not condescending so much as to let your countrymen know you offer your services to them. We meet with Leicestershire men almost daily in town, who from the neglect of the former kn[igh]ts of the shire conclude they are to have new ones.

For the rest of the year Cave campaigned unstintingly, touring the county regularly on horseback in company with his fellow candidate, Palmer. Against his own inclination, he had been goaded by experienced electioneers such as Beaumont, James Winstanley* and John Wilkins into initiating an orchestrated campaign well before the Whig contestants appeared on the scene. In consequence of this protracted ordeal, quite unlike his previous unopposed elections, he became weighed down by the pressure of overcoming 'the vast Armada equipped with the great peers'. To his father-in-law he ruled out all question of a compromise with the Whigs, not wishing to 'yield to any degenerate terms of compromise of those spawners of iniquity', but the very next day, 19 Oct., confessed wearily to his brother-in-law, Ralph Verney†, 'I have taken more pains than I ever had thoughts of.' He was eventually returned in April 1715 following the Whig sheriff's refusal to make a return in February.[7]

Cave was still at an early age when he died on 21 Apr. 1719; he was buried at Stanford. His funerary monument, erected by his wife, described him as 'a gentleman of steadfast principles to Church and state'.[8]

[1] *Verney Letters 18th Cent.* i. 140. [2] Ibid. 131–3, 136–7, 139, 236, 255. [3] Ibid. 222–5; BL, Verney mss mic. 636/52, Fermanagh to Cave, 4 Feb. 1705, Cave to Fermanagh, 6 Feb., same to Ralph Verney, 22 May 1705; Northants. RO, Isham mss IC 3702, Henry Benson to Sir Justinian Isham, 22 Feb. 1705. [4] Verney mss mic. 636/53, Fermanagh to Penelope Vickers [c.Dec. 1705], Cave to Fermanagh, 24 Nov. 1705, 17 Jan. 1706, 10 Nov., 24 Nov. 1707, 5 Apr. 1708, 2 Dec. 1710; Nichols, *Leics.* iv. 352–3; *Verney Letters 18th Cent.* 229, 238, 322; L. K. J. Glassey, *Appt. JPs*, 180, 212. [5] Leics. RO, Braye mss 23D57/2846, Denbigh *et al.* to Cave, 6 Feb. 1711; 2845, Denbigh to same, 6 Feb.; 2843, 2852, Wilkins to Cave, 5 Feb., [7–9 Feb. 1711]; Verney mss mic. 636/54, Cave to Fermanagh, 11, 22 Feb. 1711; 636/55, same to same, July, 5 Sept. 1713, 27 Apr. 1714, Ralph Verney to Cave, 23 Apr. 1713; Isham mss IC 4441, Cave to Sir Justinian Isham, 19 Feb. 1711; *Verney Letters 18th Cent.* 216, 238, 310–11; G. Holmes, *Pol. in Age of Anne*, 250–1. [6] Verney mss mic. 636/55, Cave to Fermanagh, 16 Jan., 17 Mar., 13, 24 Apr., 11 May, 7, 26 June, 5, 14 Aug. 1714; Braye mss 2877, Beaumont to Cave, 3 Aug. 1714; *Verney Letters 18th Cent.* 246. [7] Braye mss 2878–9, Beaumont to Denbigh, 19, 21 Aug. 1714; 2881, Denbigh to Cave, 28 Aug. 1714; 2886, 2890, Beaumont to same, 16 Sept., Oct. 1714; Verney mss mic. 636/55, Cave to Fermanagh, 15 Sept., 18, 19 Oct., 6, 11 Dec., same to Ralph Verney, 19 Oct. 1714. [8] Nichols, 358.

A. A. H.

CAVENDISH, Lord Henry (1673–1700), of Soho Square, Mdx. and Latimer, Bucks.

DERBY   1695–10 May 1700

b. 1673, 3rd but 2nd surv. s. of William Cavendish†, 1st Duke of Devonshire, by Lady Mary, da. of James Butler, 1st Duke of Ormond; bro. of Ld. James* and William Cavendish*, Mq. of Hartington. *educ.* travelled abroad (Austria, Germany, Low Countries) 1690–?1; Padua Univ. 1691. *m.* 3 Aug. 1696 (with £20,000), Rhoda (*d.* 1730), da. of William Cartwright† of Bloxham, Oxon. and sis. of Thomas Cartwright*, 1da.[1]

As the son of a leading Whig magnate, Cavendish was soon involved in county affairs, having received his commission to act as a deputy-lieutenant for

Derbyshire by July 1690. His first experience of parliamentary proceedings probably occurred in 1694, before he entered the Commons, when a private bill was promoted to alter a family settlement so as to increase his maintenance and to provide a jointure for a future wife. Passed by the Lords, the bill was rejected at its third reading in the Commons on 9 Apr. Cavendish's income during his father's lifetime was therefore limited to £600 p.a., until he reached the age of 24, rising to £1,200 thereafter. A large part of the estate which provided this income was located in Leicestershire, which may account for Devonshire's initial plan that Cavendish should represent that county in the 1695 Parliament. However, the idea was dropped, probably on the advice of the Earl of Rutland (John Manners†), to whom Devonshire had applied for support. Instead Cavendish was returned for Derby, standing on a joint interest with the town clerk John Bagnold*, in a contest the costliness of which displeased his father.[2]

Cavendish was not very active during his parliamentary career. He was forecast as likely to support the Court in the divisions of 31 Jan. 1696 over the proposed council of trade, signed the Association in February, and although he was listed as voting against fixing the price of guineas at 22s., a later pamphlet specifically denied this to have been the case. In the interval before the second session he contracted a lucrative marriage to the daughter of a wealthy merchant, a young lady reported to be on the verge of becoming a great heiress since her only brother was then very ill (he survived until 1748). Subsequently, in the 1696-7 session, Cavendish followed a more independent line, voting on 25 Nov. 1696 against the attainder of Sir John Fenwick† (as did Devonshire, to whom Fenwick had divulged the most controversial accusations), and on 26 Jan. 1697 supporting the tack of the parliamentary qualifications clause to the capitation bill. On 11 Dec. 1697 he again joined the opposition, voting against recommitting a resolution from the committee of the whole House to disband all the land forces raised since September 1680. He was also named to several committees connected to the bill to punish Charles Duncombe*, which was under his brother's management.[3]

Cavendish was returned again for Derby in 1698. On a list prepared before the beginning of the 1698-9 session he was classified as a supporter of the Country party and he was not recorded as voting against the third reading of the disbanding bill on 18 Jan. 1699. Indeed, the King rebuked his father for allowing both sons to support disbanding. The only important legislative activity which he undertook during this session was to prepare and present the Derwent navigation bill also in January 1699. This was eventually rejected amid a welter of petitions in February. He died after the end of the next session, Edward Southwell* reporting on 11 May 1700 that 'my Lord Henry Cavendish, after suffering above a fortnight violently under a dead palsy died yesterday morning'. He was buried at Chatsworth on the 19th. According to one newspaper he was 'much lamented, he being one of the most accomplished gentlemen in England'. He died intestate. His personal estate was reputed to be worth over £10,000 and an inventory valued his goods at nearly £5,000, which was to be set against debts of £3,000.[4]

[1] IGI, London; Collins, *Peerage*, i. 353–4; Bodl. D.D. Dashwood C.3.7–8; BL, Althorp mss, Halifax pprs. Francis Gwyn* to Mq. of Halifax (William Savile*, Ld. Eland), 3 Aug. 1696; *Top. and Gen.* iii. 29; *CSP Dom.* 1689–90, p. 559; Devonshire mss at Chatsworth House, Cavendish pprs. Berand to Devonshire, ?6 Aug. 1690. [2] *HMC Cowper*, ii. 358; *CJ*, xi. 113, 147, 154; *HMC Lords*, n.s. i. 349–50; Rutland mss at Belvoir Castle, Devonshire to [?Rutland], 19 Sept. 1695; Devonshire mss, Whildon pprs. John to James Whildon, 25 Oct. 1695, Monday afternoon, 3 Mar. 1695[–6]; *HMC Portland*, iii. 573. [3] *Reflections upon a Scandalous Libel* (1697); Bodl. Carte 233, f. 18; Northants. RO, Montagu (Boughton) mss 46/59, James Vernon I* to Shrewsbury, 26 Jan. 1697. [4] Grimblot, *Letters*, ii. 321; Leics. RO, Finch mss box 4950, Southwell to Lord Nottingham (Daniel Finch†), 11 May 1700; Luttrell, *Brief Relation*, iv. 643; *Post Man*, 11 May 1700; BL, Lothian mss, Robert Harding to [Thomas Coke*], 20 May 1700; D.D. Dashwood C.3.1, 7–8.

S. N. H.

CAVENDISH, Lord James (c.1678–1751), of Staveley, Derbys. and Latimer, Bucks.

DERBY 1701 (Feb.)–1702, 1705–1710
 1715–16 Mar. 1742

b. c.1678, 4th but 3rd surv. s. of William Cavendish†, 1st Duke of Devonshire; bro. of Ld. Henry Cavendish* and William Cavendish*, Mq. of Hartington. *educ.* travelled abroad (France, Italy) 1696–8; Padua Univ. 1697. *m.* 6 July 1708 (with £8,000), Anne (*d.* 1721), da. of Elihu Yale of London, gov. of Fort St. George 1687–92 and founder of Yale University.[1]

Auditor of foreign revenues [I] 1742–d.

Upon the conclusion of the peace at Ryswick, Cavendish was able to travel abroad to complete his education. His adventures included an encounter with the exiled James II at the wedding of the Duke of Burgundy in December 1697 and a dinner at Count Grammont's where the Duke of Berwick was among the guests.[2]

Cavendish inherited the family interest at Derby on the death of his brother Lord Henry, being returned in January 1701 in partnership with Sir Charles Pye, 2nd Bt.* Re-elected in November, he was classed with the

Whigs in Robert Harley's* list of December 1701. On 28 Apr. 1702 he acted as a teller in favour of increasing the relief to be given to Ignatius Gould out of his forfeited estate in Ireland. Following the blow to Cavendish prestige at the county election of November 1701, James was set up for Westminster in July 1702 on a joint interest with Sir Henry Dutton Colt, 1st Bt.* On finishing bottom of the poll he challenged one of his opponents, Thomas Cross*, to a duel 'which is looked on as an act very rash, but his youth excuses him'. During his enforced absence from the House in the first Parliament of Anne's reign, an Act was passed to enable his father and elder brother to break a settlement his grandfather had made in 1683 guaranteeing him an income of £600 p.a. from lands in Suffolk. James no doubt consented to this measure because he had been the chief beneficiary of his brother Henry's death, inheriting his Buckinghamshire estate.[3]

After much preparation, Cavendish was returned for Derby in 1705 together with his partner Sir Thomas Parker*, unseating two Tories. He confirmed both his classification as a Low Churchman on a list of 1705 and Lord Sunderland's (Charles, Lord Spencer*) assessment that his election meant a gain for the Whigs, by supporting the Court candidate in the contest for Speaker on 25 Oct. 1705. He again supported the Court on the regency bill proceedings on 18 Feb. 1706 and was classified as a Whig on two lists compiled before and after the 1708 election. At the election of 1708 he was again returned with Parker, this time without a contest, although some of his supporters had been rather keen that he did not attend in person. Soon after this election he married the daughter of a merchant, despite some adverse comments that his bride was 'not handsome, and all his relations against the match', and that he 'has a fair prospect to be unhappy'. In the first session of the new Parliament he acted as a teller on 1 Feb. 1709 in support of the defeated Whig candidates at Coventry and later voted for the naturalization bill. In the following session he voted for the impeachment of Dr Sacheverell.[4]

Defeated at the election of 1710, Cavendish declined to stand in 1713 despite solicitations to join his interest to that of James Stanhope*. He was returned in 1715, being classified on a list of the new Parliament as a Whig, and continued to sit until accepting office in 1742. He died on 14 Dec. 1751, aged 73.[5]

[1] *Derby Mercury*, 20–27 Dec. 1751; Devonshire mss at Chatsworth House, Whildon pprs. Aaron Kinton to James Whildon, 24 Aug. 1697; *CSP Dom.* 1698, p. 278; Luttrell, *Brief Relation*, iv. 324; Boyer, *Anne Annals*, vii. 343; 7th Duke of Manchester, *Court and Soc. Eliz. to Anne*, ii. 366. [2] Luttrell, 324; *HMC Hastings*, ii. 305; *Vernon–Shrewsbury Letters*, ii. 111. [3] BL, Lothian mss, Robert Harding to [Thomas Coke*], 20 May 1700; *HMC Portland*, iv. 29; xiv. 467; *Vernon–Shrewsbury Letters*, iii. 233; Add. 70020, Thomas Bateman to Harley, 23 July 1702; Cumbria RO (Carlisle), Lonsdale mss D/Lons/W2/2/5, James Lowther* to Sir John Lowther, 2nd Bt. I*, 23 July 1702; *Verney Letters 18th Cent.* i. 167. [4] G. Sitwell, *Letters of Sitwells and Sacheverells*, ii. 83; Whildon pprs. Kinton to Whildon, 23 Nov., 30 Dec. 1704; Nottingham Univ. Lib. Mellish pprs. Me144–83/57, Edmund Parker to Parker, 3 Apr. 1708; Add. 70149, Anne Pye to Abigail Harley, 9 June 1708; 7th Duke of Manchester, 366; *Clavering Corresp.* (Surtees Soc. clxxiii), 10. [5] *HMC Portland*, iv. 612; Centre Kentish Stud. Stanhope mss U1590/C9/28, Thomas Gisborne to [James Stanhope*], 11 Apr. 1713.

S. N. H.

CAVENDISH, William, Mq. of Hartington (1672–1729).

DERBYSHIRE 1695–1701 (Nov.)
CASTLE RISING 2 Feb. 1702–July 1702
YORKSHIRE 1702–18 Aug. 1707

b. 1672, 2nd but 1st surv. s. of William Cavendish†, 1st Duke of Devonshire; bro. of Ld. Henry* and Ld. James Cavendish*. *educ.* privately; travelled abroad (Austria, Germany, Low Countries, Italy) 1690–1; Padua Univ. 1691. *m.* 21 June 1688 (with £25,000), Rachel (*d.* 1725), da. of William, Ld. Russell†, 4s. 3da. Styled Ld. Cavendish 1684–94, Mq. of Hartington 1694–1707; *suc.* fa. as 2nd Duke 18 Aug. 1707; KG 22 Mar. 1710.[1]

Col. 10 Horse 1688–90; capt. yeomen of gd. Jan. 1702–7; commr. union with Scotland 1706; ld. steward 1707–Sept. 1710, Sept. 1714–July 1716; PC 8 Sept. 1707–*d.*; ld. justice 1714, 1720–5, 1727; ld. pres. July 1716–17, 1725–*d.*

Freeman, Beverley 1703, Winchester by 1701; custos rot. Derbys. 1707–?; ld. lt. 1707–Sept. 1710, ?Aug. 1714–*d.*; c.j. in eyre, north of Trent 1707–?Sept. 1710; steward, honor of Tutbury 1707–*d.*, High Peak 1708–*d.*, Derby by 1712.[2]

Gov. Charterhouse 1727–*d.*

Hartington's father had sat in all of Charles II's Parliaments before succeeding to the earldom of Devonshire in 1684. By 1688 he had become sufficiently disenchanted with James II's rule to sign the invitation to William of Orange to intervene in English affairs. As the eldest son, Cavendish was given command of the regiment raised by his father to support the Dutch invasion of that year. He does not appear to have been an active colonel and was relieved of the command in April 1690, by which time he was travelling in Europe with his brother Henry. He had returned to England by October 1691 in readiness to contest a by-election at Westminster, but stood down because his father was unwilling for him to risk defeat 'at his first entrance into the world'. By May 1692 he had returned to the Continent to serve as a volunteer in Flanders.[3]

In the election of October 1695 the strength of the Cavendish interest ensured that Lord Hartington was returned unopposed for Derbyshire. He was not very active during his first session in the Commons, being granted leave of absence on 8 Feb. and not returning to London until after 25 Feb. 1696. Nevertheless, he was sufficiently motivated to attend and vote on most important occasions, as is indicated by his presence on the extant parliamentary lists for this session: he was forecast as likely to support the Court in the division of 31 Jan. 1696 over the proposed council of trade, and in February he signed the Association, which his father had presented in the Lords. The following month he voted to fix the price of guineas at 22s. He appears to have been inactive for much of the 1696–7 session, and hence missed the vote on the attainder of Sir John Fenwick[†], while both his father and brother voted against it. He showed his tendency towards opposition on 26 Jan. 1697 when he voted against 'tacking' a parliamentary qualifications clause to the capitation bill. At the start of the 1697–8 session, he again demonstrated his propensity towards independence from the Court by voting with the majority on 11 Dec. not to recommit a resolution from the committee of the whole House that all troops raised since 1680 be disbanded. Later in the session he took a leading role in the pursuit of Charles Duncombe*, Knight and Burton for falsely endorsing Exchequer bills. On 7 Feb. 1698 he presented three separate bills to punish the offenders; and on 18 Feb. chaired the committee of the whole on Duncombe's bill, reporting it three days later. Completion of the Commons stages did not signal the end of his involvement in Duncombe's case, as the Lords were dissatisfied with the proofs and on 7 Mar. Hartington was appointed to lead the managers for the Lower House at a conference on the bill. He reported that the Lords wished to have the case laid out more fully so that they could proceed. On 9 Mar. a committee was appointed to state the matters of fact, from which Hartington reported the following day. He was then deputed to manage the conference at which reasons were delivered to the Lords. The Upper Chamber remained dissatisfied and rejected the bill on 15 Mar., ordering Duncombe to be released. This raised the spectre of the Lords challenging the rights of the Commons, so on the following day Hartington was appointed to a committee to inspect the Lords' Journals to discover their proceedings on the bill. On 18 Mar. he reported that Duncombe had been released by order of the Lords, and he was immediately appointed to another committee to search for precedents of the Commons asserting its rights in like cases. On 22 Mar. he reported from this committee: it was resolved that no person committed into custody by the House could be discharged by another authority, and Duncombe was ordered to be taken into custody again. Finally, on 31 Mar., Hartington moved that Duncombe be transferred from the custody of the serjeant-at-arms to the Tower. During this episode Hartington showed himself to be both a tenacious defender of the rights of the House and an implacable foe of those Tories who had originally revealed the fraud in the hope of implicating Charles Montagu*. Hartington also chaired the committee on the bills to punish Knight and Burton which were also rejected by the Lords in favour of an address to the King to prosecute all three offenders through the law courts.[4]

Hartington was again returned for Derbyshire without a contest in the 1698 election, when his prospective opponent, John Curzon*, declined to force a contest. A comparative analysis of the old and new Parliaments classified him as a supporter of the Court, but a subsequent calculation left him as a query. On the opening day of the session he appeared to confirm the original forecast by proposing Sir Thomas Littleton, 3rd Bt., for Speaker, a candidate sponsored by the Junto and acceptable to the King. However, his subsequent actions were sometimes in contradiction, none more obviously than his opposition to a standing army. The Commons originally voted on 17 Dec. to reduce the army to 7,000 men and ordered a disbanding bill to be brought in. In response to the King's wishes, ministers attempted on 4 Jan. 1699 to instruct the committee on the bill to reconsider the number in the hope of increasing it to 10,000. Hartington was one of several influential Whigs who firmly opposed this manoeuvre, preventing the Court from even venturing a decision. Three days later he further demonstrated his support for disbandment by proposing that a supply be granted to the King to enable the troops to be paid off. A final effort by the Court to defeat the bill was lost on 18 Jan., by 67 votes, with Hartington again a prominent speaker on the Country side. Indeed, the King reproached Hartington's father over William's conduct (and that of his brother) concerning the army, only to be told that 'they had advanced nothing but what was reasonable, nothing but what he would have said himself if he had been in their place'. However, Hartington was not drawn exclusively to controversial measures to the neglect of more mundane legislation, since between January and March 1699 he managed through the House the naturalization bill of Philip Chenevix and others. Indeed, his stature had risen sufficiently for Lord Orford (Edward Russell*), his wife's great-uncle, to press him upon the King as a possible successor in the treasurership of the navy. William's preference for Littleton in this office was one of the reasons behind Orford's precipitate resignation in May 1699. Hartington's relative independence did not go unnoticed, for at the beginning of 1700 a list purporting to assign MPs to various interests could only mark him with a query.[5]

Hartington began the 1699–1700 session quietly, but eventually became embroiled in the legislation over Irish forfeitures. On 18 Jan. 1700, in the second-reading debate, Hartington proposed a motion to instruct the committee of the whole on the bill to receive a clause saving the lands granted to Sir Thomas Prendergast, an Irish Jacobite who had changed sides, and then provided information concerning the Assassination Plot of 1696, for which he had been rewarded with an Irish estate. There was opposition, on the grounds that the Commons 'would admit of no saving in this bill', and when the House agreed to reward Prendergast in another way Hartington withdrew the motion. He was then probably away from the House for a short time, being granted leave for a fortnight on 3 Feb. Hartington returned to the Commons to support those Whig ministers, especially Lord Chancellor Somers (Sir John*), who had been attacked over their role in the procurement of royal grants. On 13 Feb. he intervened twice in the debate on the state of the nation, opposing the systematic campaign to destroy the ministry on the issue of royal grants, asking who would be appointed in their stead; 'he hoped none of the ministry of K[ing] C[harles], none that were for the regency, none that had refused the Association, none behind the curtain'. In March Hartington chaired a meeting of 40–50 Whigs at which it was decided to exclude MPs from the Irish forfeitures commission. When the Irish forfeitures bill was reported on the 20th Hartington again applied to have Prendergast exempted from the resumption bill, his success reportedly opening the flood-gates to many other similar applications. When the ballot for forfeited estates commissioners took place on the 28 Mar. it was believed that Hartington and John Grobham Howe had 'concerted their lists' in favour of the four existing commissioners. This bill was then tacked to the land tax bill and burdened with several controversial amendments, including a clause excluding excise officers from the House. The Lords returned the bill to the Commons heavily amended, despite the fact that it was a money bill, thus provoking a constitutional conflict. Hartington was sent on 8 Apr. to desire a conference on the Lords' amendments. Before the end of the session he was again in the forefront of the Whigs defending Somers. On 10 Apr. a direct attack was made on the lord chancellor for accepting grants from the crown. A motion to address for his removal from the royal presence and councils forever was defeated, with Hartington prominent in the debate. According to James Vernon I* a Court-inspired adjournment motion was then lost, because 'some of our people had a mind to have a fling at the foreigners'. Hartington led this attack with a motion that all foreigners (except Prince George) be removed from the King's Councils in England and Ireland, and placing the blame for the conflict between the Houses over the Irish resumption bill firmly on the King's foreign favourites who had grants to protect. After the end of the session the Court tried to draw Hartington more securely into the ministerial fold. He was earmarked for a post in the bedchamber on the initiative of Lord Sunderland, who was anxious to put the Whigs in a better temper. However, the man appointed to make the initial approach reported that, although there was a time when Hartington would have been glad of an appointment, at present 'he was so much a friend of my Lord Somers that he would not now be obliged', presumably because he felt that Somers had been abandoned by the Court. Indeed, when Somers had taken leave of the King at Hampton Court, Hartington had been one of the 'cortege', along with Charles Montagu and Orford.[6]

In January 1701 Hartington was again returned for Derbyshire, this time on a joint interest with Lord Roos, although Thomas Coke*, his partner in the previous Parliament, forced a contest. On the opening day of the new session, Hartington proposed Sir Richard Onslow, 3rd Bt., an ally in the previous debates on the standing army, for Speaker in opposition to Robert Harley*, noting that Littleton had been commanded by the King not to attend (in order to clear the way for Harley) and that this represented an infringement on the rights of the House. The continuing rise in Hartington's stature in the House was confirmed by his role in the two key issues facing the Commons during the session: the deteriorating situation in Europe and the succession question. On the delicate international situation he was one of a number of Whigs who brushed aside Tory objections on 20 Feb. 1701 to ensure an address was adopted, asking the King to enter into negotiations with the States General to secure their mutual safety and the peace of Europe. On 26 Feb. he moved that a committee of the whole consider the problem of the succession, thus setting in train the proceedings which led to the Act of

Settlement. Similarly, on 2 Apr. he seconded an amendment made by Lord Cutts (John) to another address, adding the observation that the Treaty of Ryswick did not offer either England or the States a sufficient guarantee of security; a position which was interpreted as making the address significantly more hostile to France and thus abandoned for the sake of unanimity.[7]

Hartington was also deeply involved in the other partisan clashes which marked the session. As before, he was concerned to protect the Whig members of William's last administration. On 11 Apr. during the questioning of James Vernon over papers relating to the Partition Treaties, Hartington accused Sir Christopher Musgrave, 4th Bt., of being disaffected to the state and summoned him outside, an action widely interpreted as a challenge despite Musgrave's advanced age. The intervention of the Speaker prevented the quarrel from proceeding any further. This inquiry into the Partition Treaties led to another attack on Somers. The attack reached its height on 14 Apr. when, in a preconcerted move to disarm Somers' enemies, Hartington informed the House that the former lord chancellor was outside the chamber ready to answer any charges. Despite the success of this plan to gain a hearing, Somers was impeached later in the day. On 16 Apr. Hartington proposed an amendment to the address requesting the removal of the four impeached peers from the King's councils, referring to the ill consequences for the peace of Europe of the union of crowns between France and Spain. This was defeated by 208 votes to 120 on a procedural motion. Hartington was also involved in an abortive counter-attack against the Tories: on 16 May he seconded Maurice Thompson's motion to impeach Lord Jersey, a signatory to the Partition Treaty, but this was blocked by the Speaker who ruled it out of order. On 19 May Hartington and Thompson again attempted to carry the attack to their opponents, this time charging Sir Edward Seymour, 4th Bt., with corrupt proceedings in the Totnes election. To support their allegations they produced some letters written by Seymour and his fellow Member, Thomas Coulson, to one James Buckley and arranged for the recipient to be in attendance to prove them. Seymour and Coulson, however, satisfied the Commons as to their probity and instead Buckley was ordered into custody for breach of privilege. Hartington continued the fight against the impending impeachments. On 27 May he moved successfully to send to the Lords the Commons' reply to Orford's answer to the articles laid against him, thus enabling the trial to begin earlier, and reflecting the Junto's confidence that they could ensure an acquittal. Then on 20 June he told against a motion which blamed the ill consequence attendant upon the delay in supply on those who had engineered a breach between the Houses as a means of blocking the impeachments.[8]

Another of Hartington's interests during this session was finance, particularly the effects of the innovations forced on Parliament and the Treasury by the exigencies of war. When on 17 May the Old East India Company offered to take over the £2 million loan advanced by the New Company, at 5 per cent instead of the current 8 per cent, Hartington argued that although it was prudent to reduce the interest, this particular plan was unjust to the New Company, a speech which helped to shelve the project. He also spoke in committee on 21 May when the Court managers attempted to circumvent an earlier decision of the House to reduce the civil list by £100,000, with an ingenious scheme to take £3,000 each week from the civil list, mortgage it for three or four years and thereby raise the money to restore the cut. Hartington was among those who successfully moved a blocking amendment, that the public should be entitled to any surplus of the receipts over £6,000. He also intervened to defend the practice of issuing Exchequer bills, in a debate on 6 May over the ill usage of seamen. After 'Jack' Howe had attacked the bills as bringing ruin on future ministries, Hartington replied that when they had been introduced they 'were of great use and service to pay off the fleet and army when there was no money'. Although nominated to many of the most important inquiry committees during this session, Hartington's legislative activity was limited to three drafting committees in the earlier part of the session. In July he demonstrated his continuing Whig partisanship by attending a feast in the City in honour of the Kentish petitioners. On the dissolution of Parliament in November 1701, Hartington faced a difficult contest in Derbyshire. The outcome of a hard-fought campaign was defeat for Hartington, who petitioned against the return of his opponents. By February 1702, he had found refuge at a by-election at Castle Rising, on the interest of Lady Diana Howard, after Lord Ranelagh (Richard Jones) had opted to sit for West Looe. He then withdrew his petition and never stood for Derbyshire again.[9]

Hartington's prominence in the Lower House had led to speculation that he would replace Sir Charles Hedges* as secretary of state. However, in January 1702 he was appointed captain of the yeomen of the guard, a ceremonial post worth £1,000 p.a. At the time he re-entered Parliament the Commons were still debating the events of the previous session. On the subject of petitioning, renewed disturbances from Kent led to an order for a committee of the whole to consider the rights, liberties and privileges of the Commons, as a prelude to some resolutions criticizing the Whigs' tactics of the previous year. On 24 Feb. Hartington led a Whig counter-attack, successfully moving that the committee also consider the rights and liberties of the commons of England. When the committee met, two days later, a Tory motion that the Commons had not had right done by them in the late impeachments was defeated, whereupon Hartington took advantage of the situation to move that it was the undoubted right of the people of England to petition or address the King for the calling, sitting or dissolving of Parliaments. On 5 Mar. he presented to the House a bill for the relief of the Countess of Tyrconnel, concerning the Irish forfeited estates. On 11 Mar. Hartington moved that the statute of mortmain be repealed to 'enable persons to endow poor vicarages', but the matter dropped. The new reign altered Hartington's perception of politics, so that when Sir Richard Cocks, 2nd Bt.*, approached him in March to support a cut in the civil list he replied by noting the changed situation, especially the Queen's attitude, and said 'that we were represented as enemies and that this would make her believe so'; therefore, 'if anybody began the debate he would come into it but would not begin'. At the same time his own position must have improved at Court, where his wife became a lady of the bedchamber. On 2 May, Hartington gave a demonstration of his Whig loyalties by opposing a Tory motion that no person should be an officer in the new regiments unless they had been born in the Queen's dominions, had English parents, or were already on the half-pay list. He spoke particularly 'in behalf of the French refugees, alleging what a reflection it would be on England to abandon people, who upon so many occasions had ventured their lives for its safety and defence'. On 5 May, he illustrated his zeal for the Protestant succession by moving an address to thank the Queen for ordering that the Electress Sophia be prayed for in church services.[10]

In the 1702 election Hartington accepted an invitation to stand for Yorkshire, despite persistent rumours that he would put up again in his home county. After much manoeuvring, Hartington was returned unopposed with Sir John Kaye, 2nd Bt. On 26 Oct. 1702 he moved an amendment to the Address which sought to describe the success of the Earl of Marlborough (John Churchill†) as 'maintaining' rather than 'retrieving' England's honour. He was involved in several legislative projects during the session, presenting on 9 Dec. a bill to encourage and improve the production of sailcloth in England and reporting a bill to confirm the division of some lands in Burton Dasset, Warwickshire. He was also appointed on 23 Dec. to the committee to prepare a place bill. On 10 Dec. he was named to the committee to re-amend a Lords' amendment on the occasional conformity bill, and on 13 Feb. voted for the Lords' amendments to the bill enlarging the time for taking the abjuration oath.[11]

In the following session Hartington was early in the field, helping to organize Whig ranks for the forthcoming parliamentary battles. On 28 Oct. 1703 James Stanhope* wrote to Robert Walpole II* urging him to attend the House as early as possible, and specifically naming Hartington in a list of leading Whigs who joined in his request. His position on the main question of the session was made abundantly clear on 30 Nov., when he acted as a teller against the committal of the occasional conformity bill. As a knight for Yorkshire, he took full charge of piloting through the Lower House a bill for the public registration of all conveyances, mortgages and other securities in the West Riding, which passed the Commons on 20 Jan. 1704. He was also firmly engaged on the Whig side in the *Ashby* v. *White* case (see AYLESBURY, Bucks.). When, on 25 Jan., the Commons considered the Lords' verdict, Hartington spoke against the notion that bringing a lawsuit over the franchise would constitute a breach of privilege, arguing that 'the liberty of the cobbler ought to be as much regarded as of anyone else' and adding that an aggrieved voter had no other recourse but to the law which, 'if giving judgment upon it be contrary to the privileges of this House, then it is pretty plain that our privileges do interfere with the rights of the people that elected us'. Despite his intervention a series of hostile resolutions was ordered to be reported to the House the following day, when Hartington spoke again to stress the constitutional dangers contained in the resolutions:

> I think it will be very dangerous to the very being of this House: if this maxim had been allowed formerly, I think there would have been no need of taking away of charters, and of quo warrantos; by the influence of officers they might have filled this House with what members they had pleased, and then they could have voted themselves duly elected.

The Commons accordingly confirmed the committee's resolutions. After this debate, Hartington does not appear to have been very active in the Commons, possibly due to the imminent birth of a child (a son) on 18 Mar. 1704.[12]

After a sojourn in Yorkshire during the summer of 1704, possibly with an eye to the next election, due in

1705, Hartington returned to London to help whip in Whig Members for the forthcoming session. On 12 Oct. he was reported to be ill of the gout, and consequently an appeal was sent to Robert Walpole II to come up to London for the start of the session so that the Whigs in the Lower House would not be left entirely without a leader. Hartington was not inactive, however, as on 14 Oct., he sent directions to the north urging Members to come up in case Harley should resign the Speakership and cause a trial of strength early in the session. His absence from the committee on the Address is probably evidence that ill-health prevented his attendance at the beginning of the session, especially as there is no proof of his presence until 14 Nov., when he spoke against giving leave to introduce the occasional conformity bill. His attitude on the issue was sufficiently well known that in a forecast in October he was classed as a likely opponent of the Tack. He did indeed vote against it on 30 Nov., even being used by the Court to lobby his colleague Kaye. In December Doncaster 'entrusted' him with a bill to make the Don navigable, which he presented on the 7th, and on the 9th he presented a bill to encourage inventions to improve the manufacture of clocks, watches and other engines. As befitted one of his social and political standing he was one of those MPs deputed to attend Marlborough with the thanks of the House on 14 Dec. After the Christmas recess, he was able to monitor, if not direct, a private estate bill designed to break the settlement on the Cavendishes' Suffolk estates to vest them in trustees for the payment of debts. His final task of importance in this session related to the case of *Ashby v. White*, which had revived when one of the Aylesbury voters had returned to the law courts. On 28 Feb. Hartington helped to manage a conference with the Lords, to help maintain a good correspondence between the two Houses, at which the Lords proffered some resolutions relating to the ancient, fundamental liberties of the kingdom. The issue rapidly developed into a party battle, with the Tory majority defending the rights of the Commons, which precluded Whigs from being delegated to represent the Lower House.[13]

As early as November 1703 there were rumours that Hartington was working to undermine Coke's interest in Derbyshire in preparation for the 1705 election. However, he decided to stand again for Yorkshire on a joint interest with Hon. Thomas Watson Wentworth* against Kaye. Despite some optimism among Derbyshire Tories that he might be defeated, he was returned with Kaye when Wentworth gave up the poll. On two lists compiled around this time Hartington was noted as, respectively, a placeman and a Low Churchman. On the opening day of the session, 25 Oct. 1705, he spoke in support of John Smith I* in the contest for Speaker, taking 'occasion to reflect upon the universities, calling 'em the trumpeters of rebellion', and was duly recorded as voting for the Court's candidate in the division. On 3 Nov. he reported from the committee on the Address. Much of his activity during this session centred on the succession question. On 4 Dec., in response to the Tories' 'Hanover motion', offered in committee of the whole, which left Whigs the choice of offending either the present or future monarch, by respectively supporting or opposing an invitation to the heir presumptive to reside in England, Hartington supported a successful proposal that the chairman leave the chair without putting the question, thus avoiding the issue. Four days later he was again involved in party exchanges when the Commons considered a resolution from the Lords that the Church was in a flourishing condition and that whoever suggested otherwise was 'an enemy to the Queen, the church and the kingdom'. In the ensuing debate, in which the Tories attempted to delete this partisan observation, Hartington spoke twice: first to oppose the motion that the resolution be considered in committee of the whole, on the grounds that there was no precedent for such a move; and later to dispute the view that occasional conformity posed a danger to the Church, suggesting that, on the contrary, bills to penalize the practice would ruin the Church by dividing it. He then assisted in managing the conference with the Lords to inform them of the Commons' agreement to their resolution. On 19 Dec. he moved the committal of the regency bill, 'to provide in case of the Queen's death for people to get in possession by law and not struggle against law'. He then intervened in the debate on the remarks made by Charles Caesar reflecting on the lord treasurer, to support those MPs who wished to make an example of such conduct. On 19 Jan. 1706 he returned to the debate on the regency bill to back a proposal that the interim council be composed of the seven great officers of state at the Queen's death plus an unlimited number nominated by the Hanoverian heir. He was also active on 21 Jan., when the 'place clause' in the bill was debated, warning diehard Country Whigs not to press their cause too strongly for fear of causing the bill's defeat. Hartington reaffirmed this attitude on 18 Feb. when, although he acted as a teller to add the word 'secretary' to a Lords' amendment, thus excluding more officers in the Prize Office from the Commons, he nevertheless voted against the so-called 'whimsical' clause. The following day he managed the conference at which the bill was returned to the Lords with amendments. His last recorded intervention of the session again related to the succession, when he joined in the general condemnation of Sir Rowland Gwynne's* published letter to the Earl of Stamford, which had suggested that the Electress Sophia had countenanced the 'Hanover motion'. Hartington's concentration on national matters did not mean that he ignored more parochial concerns, James Lowther* reporting on 12 Jan. 1706 that he was among the MPs supporting the Parton Harbour bill.[14]

Hartington's reward for staunchly supporting both Whig and ministerial causes was a place on the commission to negotiate the Union with Scotland in April 1706. However, not all Yorkshire Whigs were pleased with his conduct during the previous session. In the debate on the 'whimsical' clause he had clashed with John Aislabie, and a rumour began circulating in April 1706 that some of Hartington's most enthusiastic supporters had decided to set up Aislabie against him at the next election. Such manoeuvres were overtaken by the death of his fellow knight of the shire, Sir John Kaye, although the long-term threat to his interest remained. As sole Member for Yorkshire he presented an address from the county to the Queen in August 1706, after which Sunderland wrote to him to suggest that a journey into Yorkshire was advisable in order to influence the choice of Kaye's successor. At the opening of the 1706-7 session, Hartington was appointed to the committee on the Address, which he reported to the House on 4 Dec. On 20 Dec. he presented a bill to add the enrolment of bargains and sales within the West Riding to the register set up by the Act of 1704. On 11 Feb. he was appointed to prepare the bill to enact the treaty of Union, an obvious choice as he had been a commissioner. His efforts during this session seem to have been appreciated, for on 25 Mar. 1707 he could write, 'I am very well pleased to find I have got new friends, since my desire is to be as serviceable as I can to every part of the county, as well as to represent it in general.' On a list of the post-Union Parliament he was classed as a Whig.[15]

On 18 Aug. 1707 Hartington succeeded his father as 2nd Duke of Devonshire. His political status in the Commons was such that Hon. James Brydges* could write, 'we lose by his removal to the House of Peers a very considerable member of the House of Commons, and whose loss will not easily be repaired'. Two days after his father's death he was admitted into the Privy Council and three weeks later appointed lord steward of the Household. Thus he embarked upon a long career in the Upper House. He died on 4 June 1729 and was buried in All Saints church, Derby.[16]

[1] IGI, London; *CSP Dom.* 1689-90, p. 559; Devonshire mss at Chatsworth House, Berand to Devonshire, 6 Aug. 1690; Beds. RO, Lucas mss L30/8/14/2, Cavendish to Ld. Grey, 23 Dec. 1691; Luttrell, *Brief Relation*, ii. 13; *HMC Rutland*, ii. 118. [2] *Beverley Bor. Recs.* (Yorks. Arch. Soc. rec. ser. lxxxiv), 192; Hants RO, Winchester bor. recs. ordnance bk. 7, f. 166; Somerville, *Duchy of Lancaster Official Lists*, 162, 170. [3] Devonshire mss, Berand to Devonshire, 6 Aug. 1690; Rachel, Lady Russell to Thomas Owen*, 23 Oct. 1691; Luttrell, 462; J. Grove, *Lives of Dukes of Devonshire*, 1. [4] Devonshire mss, Hartington to his wife, [25 Feb. 1696]; Northants. RO, Montagu (Boughton) mss 46/59, Vernon to Shrewsbury, 26 Jan. 1697; *CSP Dom.* 1697, p. 513; 1698, p. 170. [5] *Vernon-Shrewsbury Letters*, ii. 226, 246, 286, 288, 290; HLRO, HC Lib. 12, Salwey Winnington's notes, f. 101; Centre Kentish Stud. Stanhope mss U1590/O59/7, Robert Yard* to Alexander Stanhope, 10 Jan. 1698[-9]; *CSP Dom.* 1699-1700, pp. 5-6, 28; Bodl. Carte 228, f. 261; Luttrell, iv. 470; Grimblot, ibid. 321. [6] Suff. RO (Ipswich), Gurdon mss mic. M.142(1), John to Thornagh Gurdon, 18 Jan. 1699[-1700]; J. G. Simms, *Williamite Confiscation in Ire.* 90-91, 115; *Cocks Diary*, 55-56; Som. RO, Sanford mss DD/SF 4107(a), notes on debate, 13 Feb. 1700; Montagu (Boughton) mss 48/48, 51, Vernon to Shrewsbury, 21, 28 Mar. 1699[-1700]; *Vernon-Shrewsbury Letters*, iii. 22-23, 82, 94; *Shrewsbury Corresp.* 608, 610-11; New York Pub. Lib. Hardwicke mss 33, p. 41. [7] NMM, Sergison pprs. Ser/103, ff. 63-65; *Cocks Diary*, 62-63, 83; Add. 70272, 'large acct. Revolution and succession'; 17677 WW, f. 177. [8] D. Rubini, *Court and Country*, 226-7; *Cocks Diary*, 91, 130, 136n, 152; PRO 31/1/188, f. 24v; Add. 17677 WW, f. 217. [9] *Cocks Diary*, 113, 130, 132, 140; *HMC Cowper*, ii. 431; Add. 57861, f. 69; Norf. RO, Howard (Castle Rising) mss, Walpole to Lady Diana Howard, 11 Jan. 1701[-2]. [10] SRO, Leven and Melville mss GD26/13/120, [-] to Ld. Leven, 1 Jan. 1702; Luttrell, v. 124; Add. 17677 WW, f. 181; 70075-6, newsletter 30 Dec. 1701; 40803, ff. 25-26; *CSP Dom.* 1700-2, p. 492; *Cocks Diary*, 222-3, 226-7, 246, 283; *Epistolary Curiosities* ed. Warner, ii. 16; Lambeth Palace Lib. ms 2564, p. 407; Boyer, *Anne Annals*, i. 29; *Cal. Treas. Bks.* xvii. 254. [11] Devonshire mss, Whildon pprs. William Grosvenor to James Whildon, 21 July 1702, Robert Revell to same, 3 Apr. 1702; Stanhope mss U1590 C9/31, Sir John Cropley, 2nd Bt.*, to James Stanhope*, 2 Apr. 1706; BL, Lothian mss, William Bromley II* to Coke, 23 July 1702; Rutland mss at Belvoir Castle, no.38, Rachel, Lady Russell to Lady Rutland, 30 June 1702, same to Earl of Rutland (John Manners†), 7 July 1702; Add. 61119, f. 81. [12] Coxe, *Walpole*, ii. 4; Boyer, ii. 226; Howell, *State Trials*, xiv. 732-3, 777; *Top. and Gen.* iii. 149. [13] *HMC Var.* viii. 232; Camb. Univ. Lib. Cholmondeley (Houghton) mss, Hon. Spencer Compton* to Robert Walpole II, 12, 14 Oct. 1704; *Bull. IHR*, xli. 179; Sheffield Archs. Copley mss, CD503/14, memo. on Don navigation n.d.; *Party and Management* ed. C. Jones, 97-99. [14] *HMC Cowper*, ii. 27; Lothian mss, John Beresford to Coke, 14 Dec. 1703, Michael Burton to same, 19 May 1705; *HMC Portland*, iv. 183; Cobbett, *Parlty. Hist.* vi. 450; BL, Trumbull Alphab. mss 53, John Bridges to Sir William Trumbull*, 26 Oct. 1705; *Cam. Misc.* xxiii. 43, 45, 49, 54, 72, 80-81; Stanhope mss U1590 C9/31, Cropley to Stanhope, 26 Mar. 1706; C707/5, Walpole to Horatio Walpole II, 13 May 1706; Cumbria RO (Carlisle) Lonsdale mss D/Lons/W2/1/39, James Lowther to William Gilpin, 12 Jan. 1705[-6]. [15] *Cam. Misc.* xxiii. 81; Stanhope mss U1590 C9/31, Cropley to Stanhope, 2 Apr. 1706; Rutland mss no.64, Lady Russell to Rutland, 18 Aug. 1706; Nottingham Univ. Lib. Mellish mss 157-96/23, Hartington to [?Robert Mellish], 25 Mar. 1707. [16] Huntington Lib. Stowe mss 57(1), p. 255; Boyer, vi. 238-9.

S. N. H.

CECIL, Hon. Charles (c.1683–1726)

STAMFORD 1705–1722

b. c.1683, 3rd s. of John Cecil†, 5th Earl of Exeter, by Lady Anne Cavendish, da. of William, 3rd Earl of Devonshire, and wid. of Charles, Ld. Rich (o. s. *d.v.p.* of Charles Rich†, 4th Earl of Warwick); bro. of John Cecil*, Ld. Burghley, and Hon. William Cecil*. *educ.* privately (Matthew Prior*); travelled abroad (France, Italy), 1699–1700; St. John's, Camb. adm. 20 Oct. 1696, aged 13; I. Temple 1701. *unm.* ?*suc.* bro. William at Snape Hall, Yorks. 1715.[1]

Cecil had accompanied his family to the papal jubilee in Rome in 1699, and may have visited the exiled James II on both the outward and the return journey. Shortly after coming of age, Cecil succeeded his brother William at Stamford on the family interest. He voted on 25 Oct. 1705 against the Court candidate for Speaker and was classified as a Tory in a list of early 1708. He was returned again in 1708, but the presence in the House of Hon. Robert Cecil at the same time makes it difficult to distinguish his parliamentary record. Cecil was recorded as having opposed the impeachment of Dr Sacheverell, and the 'Hanover list' of 1710 classed him as a Tory. In 1711 he was listed as both a 'Tory patriot' voting for peace and a 'worthy patriot' exposing the mismanagements of the previous administration. The compiler of the Worsley list also marked him as a Tory *tout court*. Appointed as a deputy-lieutenant for Rutland in 1713, it seems likely that he was living at one of the Cecil properties in the locality, although by the time of his appointment as deputy-lieutenant for the North Riding, Yorks., in 1722, he was resident at Snape Hall. He continued to represent Stamford as a Tory under the Hanoverians. Dying on 14 Mar. 1726 he was buried in the parish church of Well, near Snape.[2]

[1] *VCH Northants. Fams.* 34–35. [2] Travel diary of Maj. Richard Creed (*ex inf.* Prof. J. M. Black); *CSP Dom.* 1699–1700, p. 259; Luttrell, *Brief Relation*, iv. 564, 569; NRA Rep. 6666, Exeter mss 52/30, deputation 1713; 49/24, deputation 1722; *VCH Northants. Fams.* 35; W. D. Whitaker, *Richmondshire*, ii. 81.

E. C./S. M. W.

CECIL, John, Ld. Burghley (1674–1721), of Burghley House, Northants.

RUTLAND 1695–29 Aug. 1700

b. 15 May 1674, 1st s. and h. of John Cecil†, 5th Earl of Exeter; bro. of Hon. Charles* and Hon. William Cecil*. *educ.* privately (Matthew Prior*); travelled abroad 1692–3. *m.* (1) 9 Feb. 1697 (with £30,000), Annabell (*d.* 1698), da. of John Bennet, 1st Baron Ossulston, *s.p.*; (2) 19 Sept. 1699, Elizabeth (with £10,000 and £1,200 p.a.), da. and coh. of Sir John Brownlow, 3rd Bt.*, and sis. of William Brownlow*, 5s. (2 *d.v.p.*) 1da. *suc.* fa. as 6th Earl of Exeter 29 Aug. 1700.

Freeman, Stamford, 1697–*d*; recorder, Nov. 1697–*d*.; custos rot. Peterborough by 1701–c.1720; ld. lt. Rutland 1712–15; custos rot. 1712–?[1]

Cecil's father, the Earl of Exeter, was a scholar, something of a virtuoso and a frequent traveller on the Continent. He was an early patron of Matthew Prior, whom he employed as private tutor to his three sons. Exeter was a non-juror who was turned out as chief justice north of the Trent after the Revolution. Both sides believed that he was sympathetic to James II in the 1690s. Evidence of anything more than sympathy, however, is generally as nebulous as the report of one Williamite agent, who claimed in 1691 that there was a concentration of 'malcontents' at Stamford, meeting under cover of the apparently innocent pastime of cockfighting. The agent's suspicions were aroused by a trip made by Exeter into Yorkshire, 'about a cock match; and [he] has given money to a plate in that county, and some of the gentlemen of Yorkshire have contributed to that at Stamford. What the meaning of it is, or whether there be any in it or not, you can better guess.' In June 1692 and again in July 1693 Burghley was granted passes to go to Holland to accompany his father's European travels. In 1695, Lord Exeter's instructions to give William III a welcoming reception at Burghley House were somewhat marred by his own absence, which was widely reported at the time, and there is no record that Burghley was present either. The King was said to be delighted with Burghley House and apparently remarked that it was too great a house for a subject. Despite this, on his being returned for Rutland Burghley was described by Roger Martin of Stamford, as 'very hopeful and much in the King's eye since his election'.[2]

However, in Parliament Burghley consistently joined the opposition. He was forecast as likely to oppose the Court in the divisions of 31 Jan. 1696 on the proposed council of trade and refused at first to sign the Association. On 14 Feb. he was given leave of absence for three weeks and was not in attendance at the time of the division on the price of guineas. Charles Bertie I* wrote on 14 Mar. 1696 in reference to the Association, that Burghley 'is expected up, to leap the gulf', but the Speaker reported to the House on 31 Mar. that he still declined to sign. Absent again at a call of the House on 2 Nov. and ordered to be taken into custody, Burghley returned in time to vote on 25 Nov. against the attainder of Sir John Fenwick†.[3]

On 13 Mar. 1697 Burghley was once more granted

leave, having in February married an heiress with a dowry of £30,000, only for her to die in the summer of the following year. On 19 Aug. 1698 a correspondent wrote to Sir Joseph Williamson*:

> My Lord Burghley is to refund £10,000 of his lady's portion (or my Lord of Exeter rather), if one can call that refunding that was never received (nor perhaps never would have been), several of the securities being so defective. When my Lord Burghley marries again, which I presume may not be long (for it is an evidence of a good wife when the husband makes such haste to be happy again), what portion he shall have with a wife will be all his own, except the £10,000 (to be refunded), which my Lord of Exeter is to have. Already they talk of a fair lady with £20,000; and then he will have £3,000 p.a. in possession, £7,000 p.a. in reversion and £10,000 in his purse.

A year later, Burghley duly married another heiress.[4]

In the meantime, on 18 Nov. 1697, the King acquiesced in Stamford's choice of Burghley as their recorder, Exeter having resigned. Returned again for Rutland in 1698, Burghley was listed as a supporter of the Country party. Never an active Member, he received further leaves of absence on 17 Feb. 1698 (14 days), and on 8 Jan. 1699 due to his wife being very ill. He was classed as 'doubtful' in an analysis of January–May 1700 grouping Members into 'interests'. Going up to the Lords on the death of his father, his position as chief butler at Queen Anne's coronation perhaps indicates a *rapprochement* with the court under the new regime. He wielded the family interest at Stamford for the Tories and also enjoyed electoral influence in Northamptonshire. A Whig described him as 'a gentleman who never was yet in business, loves hawking, horse matches and other country sports'. In 1705 he renewed a club founded by his father at Burghley in 1684, the 'order of Little Bedlam', with himself as grand master 'Lion', his brother William as 'Panther' and brother Charles as 'Bull'. Other members included the Duke of Devonshire (William Cavendish†), the Earl of Gainsborough, Charles Bertie I* and Sir Godfrey Kneller. Burghley was in poor health in the winter of 1707–8 and unwilling to 'undergo the danger and inconvenience' of a journey to London in February to attend the Lords on a private bill to break the entail on some of his estates. However, he did not die until 24 Dec. 1721. He was buried in the family vault at St. Martin's church, Stamford, his will directing his executors, his widow, his brother Charles, Sir Thomas Mackworth*, Charles Bertie I, and Joshua Blackwell, to take care of his children, all of whom were still under age.[5]

[1] NRA Rep. 6666, Exeter mss 76/119, freedom of Stamford, 1697; 80/17, custos rot. Rutland, 1712; *CSP. Dom.* 1697, p. 477; Exeter mss at Burghley House, EX76/119/6, confirmation as recorder, 1721; NLW, MS17071E 'Bk. of the Peace'. [2] Bridges, *Northants.* ii. 591; G. R. Dennis, *House of Cecil,* 136–7; *Cal. Treas. Bks.* ix. 1960; Westminster Diocesan Archs. Old Brotherhood mss iii/3/232, memo. by 'Mr Davis', 23 Mar. [1691]; *Orig. Pprs.* ed. Macpherson, i. 459; *Ideology and Conspiracy* ed. Cruickshanks, 125; *HMC Finch,* ii. 309; iii. 74; *CSP Dom.* 1691–2, p. 308; 1693, p. 229; Add 17677 PP, f. 414; Camb. Univ. Lib. Add. mss 2, f. 151. [3] *HMC Rutland,* ii. 159. [4] Rutland mss at Belvoir Castle, Charles Bertie I to Earl of Rutland, n.d.; NRA Rep. 6666, Exeter mss 43/6, mar. settlement 1696; 32/10, settlement of Ld. Exeter's estate on Burghley's mar. 1699; *CSP. Dom.* 1698, p. 376. [5] *HMC 5th Rep.* 309; *HMC Lords*, n.s. vii. 336–7; PCC 70 Marlbro'.

P. W./E. C.

CECIL, Hon. Robert (1670–1716), of St. Anne's, Westminster and King's Walden, Herts.

CASTLE RISING   30 Apr.–11 Nov. 1701
WOOTTON BASSETT   1708–1710

bap. 6 Nov. 1670, 2nd s. of James Cecil†, 3rd Earl of Salisbury, by Lady Margaret, da. of John Manners†, 8th Earl of Rutland. *m.* lic. 28 July 1690, Elizabeth, da. and h. of Isaac Meynell of Meynell Langley, Derbys., wid. of William Hale of King's Walden, Herts. 3s. 2da.[1]

Commr. taking subscriptions to land bank 1696; trade and plantations 1702–7.[2]

On the death of his father, Cecil inherited £6,000 in cash together with £300 p.a., although the annual income was somewhat uncertain because it was to be raised from lands held by his brother James, the 4th Earl, with whom he seems to have been on the worst of terms. Their differences stemmed from Salisbury's conversion to Catholicism in 1688. Cecil, who had himself remained a Protestant, promoted a bill in October 1690 to prevent his brother cutting off the entail of the family estates, to which he was then heir presumptive. In the preamble to the first draft of the bill he claimed that his brother, having made recoveries of part of the estate, and

> continuing a Papist and persisting in his zeal for that party, and having conceived a very great prejudice against and hatred unto your supplicant for no other reason in the world but your supplicant being a Protestant and zealous for their Majesties' service and the present government ... doth intend ... to suffer several other common recoveries of all the residue of the said estate, ... on purpose to bar your supplicant of the said remainder and with a design to settle the said estate upon some person of his own religion or convey the same to the use and service of the Romish party, he the said now Earl, having seriously and publicly declared that he would leave your supplicant a poor Earl and disinherit your supplicant all he could.

During the committee stage, counsel for Salisbury denied the expressions of hatred for his brother, but admitted that the Earl did intend to cut the entail. Consequently the bill was passed but the wording was modified to leave out the sections reciting the state of personal relations between the brothers. The whole proceeding was shortly afterwards rendered void by the birth of an heir to the Earl.[3]

Cecil's parliamentary ambitions originally centred on the county of Hertfordshire, which he unsuccessfully contested in both 1695 and 1697, on the Whig interest. He then switched his attention to Steyning in the January 1701 election, but his bidding came 'too late', and he had to wait for a by-election at Castle Rising in April to enter the Commons, courtesy of the Howard family. During his parliamentary career his activity is obscured by the presence of his Cecil kinsmen in the chamber. He did not stand in the second election of 1701, but in December was appointed a commissioner of trade, with a salary of £1,000 p.a., in which capacity he authored the proposal put before the House in November 1704 for continuing the restraint on trade with France.[4]

In 1702 when Cecil was acting as trustee for his brother, Charles, then living in Rome, he refused to honour his brother's instructions to pay off debts owed to a certain John Wotton. Wotton wrote on 19 Mar. to the 9th Earl of Rutland (John Manners†):

> Mr [Robert] Cecil will not give me anything but abuse me; though he be earnestly desired to do justice by his wife . . . and several other persons, none can prevail. He rails at me and writes me abusive letters . . . I have not seen him these two months, nor his sister Ranelagh [Margaret, Lady Ranelagh], nor will not; they are so abusive. They hate me because they have abused me, and then rail at me because they hate me, and sure there can be nothing more severe and unchristianlike than he is.

In April 1707 he was removed from the commission of trade, but in the following year came in for Wootton Bassett, on the interest of Henry St. John I*. His return was accurately counted as a gain for the Whigs by Lord Sunderland (Charles, Lord Spencer*), since he voted in 1709 for naturalizing the Palatines and in 1710 in favour of the impeachment of Dr Sacheverell.[5]

Cecil did not stand for Parliament again. For much of his adult life he was 'commonly called fat Cecil' and was dogged by ill-health. Lady Cowper reported in 1704 that he 'was so fallen away of his flesh that many scarce know him: from weighing 30 stone, he is now wasted to 23 stone'. Within months another commentator reported that he was 'in so dangerous a condition that [his] physicians despair of [his] recovery'. Cecil drew up his will on 8 June 1714, requesting a private funeral with a hearse and three mourning coaches and leaving all his possessions and estate to his widow, Elizabeth, for whose hand he had once duelled and been wounded, whom he named his executrix. He died on 23 Feb. 1716.[6]

[1] *VCH Herts. Fams.* 118; PCC 94 Exton. [2] *CSP Dom. 1700–2*, p. 475; *Cal. Treas. Bks.* xxii. 141; *CJ*, xii. 508. [3] *HMC Lords*, iii. 141–6; *HMC Egmont Diary*, ii. 333; *CJ*, x. 487, 505. [4] Add. 28886, f.168; *CJ*, xiv. 431. [5] *HMC Rutland*, ii. 170; Beaufort mss at Badminton House, William Walsh* to Earl of Coventry, 24 Apr. 1707. [6] PCC 22 Fox; Northants. RO, Isham mss IC 3314, newsletter 22 July 1690; *HMC Egmont Diary*, 333; Herts. RO, Panshanger mss D/EP F, p. 283; Bath mss at Longleat House, Thynne pprs. 27, f. 447.

P.W.

CECIL, Hon. William (bef. 1682–1715), of Snape Hall, Yorks.

STAMFORD 1698–1705

b. bef. 1682, 2nd s. of John Cecil†, 5th Earl of Exeter; bro. of Hon. Charles* and John Cecil*, Ld. Burghley. *educ.* privately (Matthew Prior*); travelled abroad (Holland, France) 1692–3, (France, Italy) 1698, 1699–1700; ?Padua, ?1696. *unm.*[1]

Cecil, who had earlier accompanied his father and brothers to Europe, may have been on the Continent again in 1696 when a 'William Cecil' is listed as attending the University in Padua. He was returned for Stamford in 1698 on the family interest. At the time of his election he was once more in France, where his old tutor, Matthew Prior, held a diplomatic post. Prior reported to the Earl of Portland that an acquaintance, the Duc de Lauzun, proposed to present Cecil to Louis XIV at Versailles, but Prior had thought this improper, 'considering my Lord Exeter's character in relation to his Majesty's government' and had made Cecil 'excuse himself . . . on pretence of his small stay here'. Prior added that he had given Cecil 'the best notions I could, and will recommend him by letter to Mr [Charles*] Montagu, so that I hope the gentleman may prove a good subject and be right to his Majesty and his country's interest'. Little is known of Cecil's parliamentary career in his first session. His name appears on what was probably a forecast of those likely to oppose a standing army in the 1698–9 session, which is consistent with his classification as a supporter of the Country party in a comparative analysis of the old and new Parliaments in about September 1698.[2]

In the autumn of the following year, William accompanied his family abroad to attend the Pope's jubilee in Rome, passing through France and perhaps visiting Fontainebleau, where the exiled James II was in residence. From Italy, Cecil went on a tour to Malta. On the family's return through France, the English ambassador reported that Exeter intended to see

Versailles and 'I believe he will not come to me and I know it is expected he will go elsewhere; but it may be he will deceive them'. Before they could return to England, Exeter died near Paris, in August 1700.[3]

Re-elected for Stamford in January 1701, Cecil was listed the following month among those thought likely to side with the Court in agreeing with the committee of supply's resolution to continue the 'Great Mortgage', but was 'blacklisted' for opposing preparations for war with France in a list published to influence the second election of 1701. Returned nevertheless, Cecil supported the resolution vindicating the Commons' proceedings in the impeachment of William III's ministers, 26 Feb. 1702. Returned again in the 1702 election, on 13 Feb. 1703 he voted against agreeing with the Lords' amendments to the bill for extending the time for taking the oath of abjuration and in mid-March 1704 was forecast by the Earl of Nottingham (Daniel Finch†) as a government supporter over the 'Scotch Plot' investigations. Cecil was forecast as likely to support the Tack on two lists of 1704, and on 28 Nov. 1704 voted for it, thus earning the designation 'True Church' in a published list of MPs in 1705, and also a minor political martyrdom as one of the Tackers defeated at the general election of that year. He did not stand again, giving way to his younger brother, Charles.

A trustee under his late father's will, Cecil consented to a bill passed in May 1702 enabling the sale of certain lands to pay his father's debts and secured a further Act in March 1709 to sell more of the estate in order to pay off a mortgage of £10,500 raised on the Yorkshire lands. Cecil, who had himself settled on one of the family's outlying properties in Yorkshire, was appointed a deputy-lieutenant for the North Riding in 1712. He died on 6 May 1715 and was buried in the parish church of Well, near Snape.[4]

[1] *VCH Northants. Fams.* i. 34–35; *CSP Dom.* 1691–2, p. 308; 1693, p. 229; 1696, p. 180; 1699–1700, p. 259. [2] *HMC Bath*, iii. 252–3. [3] G. R. Dennis, *House of Cecil*, 137; travel diary of Maj. Richard Creed (*ex inf.* Prof. J. M. Black); Luttrell, *Brief Relation*, iv. 564, 569; C. Cole, *Mems.* 183. [4] PCC 62 Dyer; *HMC Lords*, n.s. v. 32–33; NRA Rep. 6666, Exeter mss 52/5, deputation, North Riding, 1712; W. D. Whitaker, *Richmondshire*, ii. 81.

P. W./E. C.

CHADWICK, James (c.1660–1697), of Lambeth Palace, London; Valentines, nr. Wanstead, Essex; and Enfield, Mdx.

NEW ROMNEY   1689–1690
DOVER   1690–19 May 1697

b. c.1660, 1st s. of James Chadwick, Merchant Taylor, of King Street, London by his w. Elizabeth. *educ.* L. Inn 1693. *m.* lic. 29 July 1682, aged about 22, Mary (*d.* 1687), da. of John Tillotson, dean of Canterbury 1672–91, abp. of Canterbury 1691–4, 2s. 1da. *suc.* fa. 1678.[1]

Freeman, New Romney 1688, Dover 1690.[2]

Member, Mine Adventurers' Co. 1693; commr. taking subscriptions to Bank of England, 1694, Greenwich Hosp. 1695–*d.*[3]

Commr. customs 1694–*d.*[4]

Chadwick's grandfather had been recorder of Nottingham during the Civil War and Interregnum and had sat for that borough in the first and second Protectorate Parliaments. He lost his local offices in March 1659 and died in 1666. His son, James, was a prosperous Merchant Taylor, who paid a £100 fine in 1674 to avoid the mastership, probably for religious reasons, since his will noted four bequests to ministers of local churches, at least two of whom were Nonconformists. He in turn left property in London, Kent and Sussex to his eldest son, James, this Member; the younger, John, received lands in Nottinghamshire, Hertfordshire and some houses in London. Despite the younger James Chadwick's Nonconformist antecedents, he must have conformed to the Anglican church, for in 1682 he married the daughter of a clergyman, albeit one of Low Church inclinations: Dean Tillotson of Canterbury, the future archbishop.[5]

Chadwick began married life in the parish of St. Martin, Ludgate, where his two sons were born in 1683 and 1685. However, after the death of his wife, he seems to have resided with Tillotson in the deanery at Canterbury. He was able to establish himself sufficiently in the county to be considered by the gentlemen of East Kent in September 1688 as a candidate for New Romney. His active role in the Revolution of 1688 no doubt cemented his interest in the borough which duly returned him to the Convention of 1689. Defeated there in 1690, he transferred to Dover.[6]

On an analysis of the 1690 Parliament, the Marquess of Carmarthen (Sir Thomas Osborne†) classed him as a Whig. Chadwick's vote in the Convention for the disabling clause may explain Carmarthen's note on a management list of autumn 1690 deputing Dean Tillotson to speak to him, 'for he gives a very bad example'. Certainly his commitment to the new regime extended to lending £400 on the additional 12*d.* aid. In the Commons he told on 25 Apr. 1690 against a clause offered to a supply bill to extend the time available for Arthur Shallett* and Gilbert Heathcote* to import a cargo of Spanish brandy; and again the following day, against the successful motion rejecting the oath of abjuration. On 28 Apr. he carried up to the Lords a bill regulating elections in the Cinque Ports. On 2 May he was a teller once more in favour of adjourning debate on a pamphlet which printed a list of Members voting against the transfer of the crown. The defeat of the motion led to a vote condemning the pamphlet as a 'false and scandalous libel'. In the following session, he told on 28 Oct. 1690 against going into committee on a supply bill. Finally, he carried back to the Lords a bill transferring a trust to secure the portion of Elizabeth Lucy, and ensure that she was brought up a Protestant.[7]

On 5 Jan. 1691 (the day Parliament was prorogued), Chadwick made his will, 'designing shortly to pass over the seas'. His destination was Holland, Tillotson having asked permission for his son-in-law to wait on the King, where it was reported that Chadwick received 'great civilities' from Viscount Dursley (Charles Berkeley†), the English envoy at The Hague. Tillotson at this point painted an interesting portrait of his son-in-law, as a man who 'considers so well what becomes him and me, that tho' he is still willing to live with me, he will not only take no place from me, but has not so much as spoken to me for any person whatsoever'. Tillotson hoped to see him installed as a customs commissioner, 'for which he is much fitter than for any other place that I know', which may indicate some commercial background, although in the Commons Chadwick had already shown a predilection for matters of that nature. Ambitions for office would certainly tie in with Robert Harley's* assessment of him in April 1691 as a Court supporter. His sojourn abroad did not impede parliamentary duties, for he was present in the Commons on 22 Oct. 1691. On 28 Nov. he was named to draft a bill for repairing Dover harbour, which he presented on 4 Dec. As it was a supply measure, Sir John Trenchard chaired the committee of the whole on the bill, but Chadwick was one of the tellers on 25 Jan. 1692 in favour of its engrossment. On 9 Dec. 1691 Chadwick opened the debate in committee of the whole on the state of the nation, after William Fuller had regaled the House with a series of allegations concerning Jacobite activities. Chadwick was sceptical of Fuller's claims, having earlier been involved (after Tillotson had been approached), in trying to set up meetings between Fuller and the Earl of Portland, only to be thwarted by the informant's prevarication.

> I do believe this fellow may know somewhat of a plot but not so much as he pretends... but whenever you come to fix a time or place for him to come to, he always shuffled and could never be brought to anything. I believe you will find him a shuffling fellow.

After several interventions from Chadwick, Fuller's credibility was sufficiently dented for his demands to be scaled down considerably, and the way prepared for the eventual vote of the Commons on 24 Feb. 1692 that he was a 'notorious impostor, a cheat and a false accuser'. On 5 Jan. 1692 Chadwick opposed giving a first reading to the bill for better regulation and encouragement of the company of fishermen on the Thames, presumably on the grounds attributed by Narcissus Luttrell* to some of the opposers, that the bill would encroach upon the powers of the vice-admiral of Kent and would destroy the fishing industry in the county. On 20 Jan., in a debate in ways and means on a proposed poll bill, Chadwick backed Charles Montagu's* suggestion that every gentleman should pay 30s. a quarter, but limited the liability to those with estates of over £500 p.a. In late April, after the end of the session, Luttrell reported that Chadwick 'stands fair' to succeed Sir Rowland Gwynne*, who had been 'suspended' as treasurer of the Chamber, but the place was kept vacant. Nevertheless, Chadwick's name appeared on two lists of placemen for 1692.[8]

In the 1692-3 session, Chadwick was on hand on 20 Dec. 1692 to back moves by the Whigs to offer the thanks of the House to Admiral Edward Russell*, for his efforts at sea the previous summer, and so ward off Tory attacks on Russell's conduct. Chadwick's concern for the silk industry (important in Canterbury) was seen on 11 Jan. 1693, when he presented to the Commons a petition from several Italian merchants, only for the House to order it to lie on the table since the petition was seeking to 'direct' Members on a bill before them. A motion to engross the bill for the import of fine Italian thrown silk overland was then lost by 89 votes to 85. At the third reading of the land tax bill on 12 Jan., Chadwick offered a rider to ensure that papists should not be allowed to pass on to their tenants the double tax to which their estates were liable. Rather strangely, given his age, but owing no doubt to the influence of his father-in-law, Chadwick was admitted to Lincoln's Inn during this session. He was seen as having influence with Tillotson, for on 8 July 1693 Sir William Trumbull* wrote to Bishop Stillingfleet of Worcester regarding the expected demise of Sir Richard Raines, the judge of the prerogative court of Canterbury: 'I hope also Mr Chadwick is my friend, at least he has promised me.' Chadwick's close association with many leading Whigs such as Hon. Thomas Wharton* and Admiral Russell was emphasized by his membership of the Mine Adventurers' Company, incorporated in September 1693.[9]

In the new session, Chadwick returned to the Lords the bill for the import of Italian thrown silk on 20 Jan.

1694. He was a teller on 7 Feb. in favour of the Whig candidate in the disputed Worcester by-election, and on two further occasions. During this session, in February, he was made a deputy-lieutenant of Kent, a sign of local acceptability. He was also a member of the Rose Club, a contemporary skit noting:

> There's Chadwick is dapper and pert without wit
> Which a place, he sets up for a politic chit
> And 'my Lord, my Father' says for it he's fit.

The place referred to was the customs commissionership mentioned by Tillotson two years earlier. Although as early as April Luttrell had predicted his advancement, the decisive meeting of ministers (Sir John Somers*, Lord Shrewsbury, Lord Godolphin [Sidney†] and Trenchard) called to advise the King on appropriate appointments, occurred in June, with his appointment being made official in August.[10]

The death of Tillotson in November 1694 may well have hit Chadwick's finances hard, for in later years it became apparent that the resources designated by the archbishop to provide for his grandchildren had been eaten up by the needs of his office, particularly in repairing Lambeth Palace. Family affairs, and his new official duties, probably restricted Chadwick's involvement in the Commons for some time. On 14 Mar. 1695 Chadwick told in favour of choosing the Court candidate, Sir Thomas Littleton, 3rd Bt., as a replacement for the disgraced Speaker, Sir John Trevor, and on 22 Apr. he told again, at the report stage on the glass and coal duty bill, in favour of an amendment leaving out the words 'in order to be shipped', which, given the identity of the tellers on the other side, was probably not meant as a concession to the coal lobby. The following day he was elected (in 18th place), to the committee to examine Sir Thomas Cooke*.[11]

Re-elected in 1695, Chadwick was more active in the ensuing session, particularly in matters pertaining to trade and finance, in a way which suggests he was emerging as a government manager. Following his tellership in the previous session on an amendment to the bill levying glass and coal duties, he was appointed on 21 Dec. 1695 to the committee investigating complaints against the resultant act. When this committee reported, on 24 Jan., Chadwick told against a motion to repeal the duty on waterborne coals, except those which were being sent for export. It is not known whether his actions were in accordance with the wishes of his Dover constituents, whose petition (presented on 21 Jan.) the House had declined to read, but it seems from the tellers that the ministry had defeated a proposal promoted by domestic coal-users. Chadwick told on two election cases during the session: on 8 Jan. 1696, in favour of appointing a day to hear the petition of Sir John Guise, 2nd Bt.*; and on 18 Feb., for a resolution that Maurice Thompson* was duly elected for Bletchingley. His official position in the customs made him an obvious choice to manage through the Commons the bill for preventing frauds and abuses in the plantation trade, including chairing a committee of the whole on 9 Mar. Interestingly, in this connexion, he was forecast as likely to support the Court in the divisions on 31 Jan. over the proposed council of trade, that is for a body appointed by the crown. No doubt such an institution would have relieved him of some of the legislative work on colonial trade. Not surprisingly, he signed the Association in February 1696. The problems of the recoinage evidently concerned him, for he spoke in committee of the whole on 13 Feb., seemingly in favour of a reduction in the price of guineas, but a gradual one, as the price of 'gold will hold up for want of silver'. To drop the price by one-third would be 'unjust and unsafe'. His concern over the possibilities for speculation was confirmed by a memorandum he sent to Edward Clarke I*, which detailed the profit made by foreigners; '£100 of milled money sent to Holland would purchase 89 guineas, which exported to London would realize £133 15s., a profit of just over 33 per cent'. In the event he toed the ministerial line, voting in March to fix the price of guineas at 22s. In April 1696 he was a teller on two occasions: on the 23rd, in favour of passing the bill enforcing the laws for restraining marriages without licences and for registering births; and on the following day at the third reading of a supply bill, in favour of removing a clause naturalizing subscribers to the land bank.[12]

During the recess of 1696 Chadwick was prominent in discussions at the Treasury over such diverse matters as whether to appoint William Culliford* inspector-general of imports and exports, and the advisability of taking a bond from the East India Company in lieu of personal bonds. Chadwick's importance as a parliamentary manager to the mainly Whig ministry was brought out by the Fenwick affair, which threatened several important Whigs, including the Duke of Shrewsbury and the Earl of Orford (Russell). Twice in late October Chadwick attended select meetings of prominent government supporters, the first at the home of Lord Keeper Somers, to consider ways in which the ministers could be vindicated before the Commons. In the event the flight to France of one of the witnesses led the Junto to proceed through a bill of attainder, for which Chadwick voted on 25 Nov. 1696.[13]

In parliamentary business Chadwick had a busy

session in the winter of 1696-7. He was active as a teller, usually on trading matters. These included telling in favour of extending the duties of tunnage and poundage and other duties until 1706 (2 Dec. 1696); in favour of going into a committee of the whole the following day to consider the bill encouraging people to bring plate to be coined (31 Dec.); against referring to a committee a petition of some London wine merchants regarding the refusal of the customs' officers to accept hammered money beyond 1 Feb. (15 Jan. 1697); against instructing the committee on the bill encouraging the recoinage to leave out that part of the bill imposing a duty on plate not brought into the mints to be coined (5 Feb.); against the passage of the bill restraining the wearing of wrought silks and calicoes (6 Feb.); in favour of immediately electing a replacement for Lord William Powlett* after Powlett's refusal to serve as a commissioner of accounts (13 Feb.); and in favour of passing the supply bill making good the deficiencies of various funds and enlarging the stock of the Bank of England (26 Mar.). Chadwick had little to do with managing bills, although he was added on 17 Mar. 1697 to the committee drafting a clause for more effectively preventing the export of wool. His importance to the Whig leaders can be shown by two events during the session. James Vernon I* approached him in January 1697 when chasing up Shrewsbury's customs pension (only to be informed that the commissioners' salaries were also in arrears), and on 18 Feb. Vernon reported that Lord Wharton (Thomas) and Chadwick had left for Woburn and would visit Shrewsbury while in the country. In May 1697 Chadwick was listed as subscribing £1,000 to the money to circulate Exchequer bills.[14]

No sooner had a warrant been issued in May 1697 for a new customs' commission, again including Chadwick, than he died on the 19th, 'of a violent fever', having been 'sick not above four or five days', or 'eight days', if Vernon is to be believed. At his death Chadwick may well have been resident in Essex, for not only did he write a letter to Trumbull from Walthamstow in October 1696, but this was also the year in which Sir Thomas Skipwith, 2nd Bt.†, surrendered his estate at Valentines, near Wanstead, to Mrs Tillotson. According to Dr Thomas Sherlock, the dean of St. Paul's, Mrs Tillotson was reduced to 'narrow circumstances' by the 'unexpected death' of Chadwick and the 'less expected condition he has left his family in'. Her complaints included the loss of £300 which she had expended on a life interest in the copyhold of the Essex estate and the building of a house there. Meanwhile Chadwick had apparently 'spent all his estate, but what was settled upon his wife in marriage, which comes to her eldest son'. This left the younger children without 'one farthing to maintain them'. Chadwick's will, written in 1691, confirms that even then his estate was mortgaged, and a codicil signed the day before he died merely altered the list of his trustees to take account of Archbishop Tillotson's demise. After the Hanoverian Succession, the eldest son, George Chadwick, approached Lord Sunderland (Charles, Lord Spencer*) for help, emphasizing Tillotson's use of the money intended for his grandchildren to finance repairs to Lambeth. In the event both younger children fared reasonably well, Chadwick's second son being a merchant at Smyrna, and the daughter 'very well married' to a linen draper, the son of Bishop Fowler of Gloucester. The eldest son, however, was forced to live on the paternal estate in Nottinghamshire.[15]

[1] PCC 93 Reeve, 114 Pyne; *Mar. Lic.* (Harl. Soc. xxx), 102. [2] Centre Kentish Stud. New Romney bor. recs. NR/AC2, p. 1; Add. 29625, f. 122. [3] *CSP Dom.* 1693, p. 207; NLS, Advocates' mss, Bank of Eng. pprs. 31.1.7; Add. 10120, f. 233. [4] *Cal. Treas. Bks.* x. 739. [5] *Nottingham Bor. Recs.* v. 234-5, 301; Jones thesis, 222; C. M. Clode, *Hist. Merchant Taylors' Co.* 348; PCC 93 Reeve. [6] IGI, London; T. Birch, *Life of Tillotson* (1752), 274; Add. 33923, f. 434; *N. and Q.* ser. 3, vi. 2; *Kingdom Without a King* ed. Beddard, 119. [7] A. Browning, *Danby,* iii. 179; *Cal. Treas. Bks.* ix. 2001. [8] PCC 114 Pyne; Birch, 273-4; Add. 70224, Harley to G. Dubourg (*alias* Powell), 9 Apr. 1692; Dubourg to [Harley], 11 Apr. 1692; *Luttrell Diary,* 68, 111, 145; Grey, x. 203, 205; Luttrell, *Brief Relation,* ii. 436; *Cal. Treas. Bks.* x. 114-15. [9] *Luttrell Diary,* 332, 361, 365; info. from Dr D. F. Lemmings; *HMC Downshire,* i. 421-2; *Sel. Charters,* 239. [10] *CSP Dom.* 1694, pp. 20, 179-80, 186; *Poems on Affairs of State* ed. Cameron, v. 432; Luttrell, *Brief Relation,* iii. 300; Nottingham Univ. Lib. Portland (Bentinck) mss PwA 471, notes on customs commrs.; *Cal. Treas. Bks.* x. 739. [11] Add. 61603, f. 60; H. Horwitz, *Parl. and Pol. Wm. III,* 150. [12] Horwitz, 167-8; HLRO, HC Lib. ms 12, f. 115v.; Cobbett, *Parlty. Hist.* vii. 232. [13] *Cal. Treas. Bks.* xi. 33, 45-46, 63; *Vernon–Shrewsbury Letters,* i. 33, 36-38; Northants. RO, Montagu (Boughton) mss 46/13, Vernon to Shrewsbury, 29 Oct. 1696; *Shrewsbury Corresp.* 418. [14] *Vernon–Shrewsbury Letters,* i. 184, 210; Univ. of London mss 65, item 3, list of subscribers. [15] *Cal. Treas. Bks.* xii. 158; *Post Man,* 20-22 May 1697; *CSP Dom.* 1697, p. 162; Montagu (Boughton) mss 46/104, Vernon to Shrewsbury, 20 May 1697; *HMC Downshire,* i. 700; *VCH Essex,* v. 211; Birch, 366-8, 370; PCC 114 Pyne.

S. N. H.

CHAFIN (CHAFFIN), George (1689-1766), of Chettle, Dorset.

DORSET 1713-1754

bap. 7 Jan. 1689, 5th s. of Thomas Chafin I* and bro. of Thomas Chafin II*. *educ.* ?Winchester c.1702-6; Oriel, Oxf. 1707. *m.* lic. 8 Feb. 1714, Elizabeth, da. of (Sir) Anthony Sturt*, 5s. 3da. *suc.* bro. Thomas II 1711.

Having succeeded to the family estates in Dorset, Hampshire, Surrey and Somerset on the death of his elder brother, Chafin served for Dorset in the

Parliament of 1713. No speech or vote by him is known for this period. His party affiliation was nevertheless sufficiently clear for the Worsley list and two other comparative analyses of the 1713 and 1715 Parliaments to classify him as a Tory. Chafin voted consistently with the Tories until 1754, when he retired from Parliament because of increasing financial difficulties. He died on 7 Sept. 1766.[1]

[1] Hutchins, *Dorset*, iii. 565–7.

P. W.

CHAFIN (CHAFFIN), Thomas I (1650–91), of Chettle, Dorset.

POOLE   1679 (Mar.)–1681 (Mar.), 1685–1687
DORCHESTER   9 Dec. 1689–1690
HINDON   1690–17 Jan. 1691

b. 15 July 1650, 2nd surv. s. of Thomas Chafin of Chettle by his 2nd w. Amphillis, da. of Laurence Hyde† of Heale, Wilts. and coh. to her gt.-gdfa. Richard White of Alton, Hants. *educ.* Magdalen Hall, Oxf. 1666. *m.* 23 Jan. 1674, Anne, da. of John Penruddock of Compton Chamberlayne, Wilts., 5s. (2 *d.v.p.*) 6da. *suc.* bro. 1660.[1]
    Freeman, Poole 1679, Salisbury 1683–4, Oct. 1688–?*d.*[2]
    Commr. drowned lands 1690.[3]

Returned for the venal borough of Hindon in 1690, Chafin was classified by Lord Carmarthen (Sir Thomas Osborne†) as a Tory and probable supporter of the Court. Nothing else is known about his brief parliamentary career in this period, apart from a posthumous appearance, as a courtier, in Robert Harley's* analysis of the House in April 1691, Chafin having died on 17 Jan.

[1] Hutchins, *Dorset*, iii. 565, 570; *VCH Hants*, ii. 477; Hoare, *Wilts. Salisbury*, 478, 480, 487. [2] Hoare, 478; Dorset RO, Poole Archs. B17. [3] *Cal. Treas. Bks.* ix. 794.

P. W.

CHAFIN (CHAFFIN), Thomas II (1675–1711), of Chettle, Dorset

SHAFTESBURY   25 Feb. 1699–1701 (Nov.)
DORSET   1702–Mar. 1711

bap. 27 Jan. 1675, 1st s. of Thomas Chafin I* and bro. of George Chafin*. *educ.* Wadham, Oxf. 1693; M. Temple 1693. *unm. suc.* fa. 1691.

Shortly after his coming of age, Chafin was returned as a Tory at a by-election for Shaftesbury in 1699. In February 1701 he was listed as likely to support the Court over the 'Great Mortgage', and was later blacklisted with other Tories for having opposed preparations for war with France. After a brief hiatus in his parliamentary career, Chafin transferred to the county in 1702. Continuing to hold this seat until his death, he remained a staunch Tory. He voted against the Lords' amendments to the bill for enlarging the time for taking the oath of abjuration on 13 Feb. 1703, and was forecast as a supporter of Lord Nottingham (Daniel Finch†) over the 'Scotch Plot' in March 1704. It was predicted that he would vote for the Tack, and he duly did so on 28 Nov. 1704. In a list of 1705 he was classified as 'True Church'. On 25 Oct. he divided against the Court candidate for Speaker. Listed as a Tory in two analyses of the House in 1708, he voted against the impeachment of Dr Sacheverell. The 'Hanover list' of 1710 repeated the classification of Chafin as a Tory, and he was included in the list of 'Tory patriots' who opposed the continuance of the war and that of 'worthy patriots' who detected the mismanagements of the previous administration. He was also a member of the October Club.

Chafin died in 1711 and was buried at Chettle on 16 Mar.[1]

[1] Hutchins, *Dorset*, iii. 565.

P. W.

CHAMBERLAYNE, Francis (aft. 1667–1728), of Stoneythorpe, Warws. and London.

NEW SHOREHAM   1713–1715
                         11 June 1720–26 Sept. 1728

b. aft. 1667, 1st s. of Francis Chamberlayne, Grocer, of St. Lawrence Pountney, London, common councilman of London 1673–82, 1689–*d.*, by Mary, da. and coh. of Richard Smith, Dyer, of All Hallows the Less, London and Islington, Mdx., common councilman of London 1654, 1658–62, 1666; nephew of Samuel Shepheard I*. *unm. suc.* fa. 1695.[1]

Chamberlayne's family had come originally from Warwickshire, and in 1671 his uncle, a London merchant, purchased the manor of Stoneythorpe in that county, which he subsequently left to Chamberlayne's father, a cooper and merchant in the City. Chamberlayne engaged in commerce himself and may have been involved in the slave trade. Either he or his father was added to the London lieutenancy in March 1689, the same year his father recovered his place on the common council. In 1710 Chamberlayne owned at least £4,000 worth of stock in the Bank of England, and three years later he was returned for the venal borough of New Shoreham. He voted against the expulsion of Richard Steele on 18 Mar. 1714, and was classified as a

Whig in the Worsley list, but after returning to Parliament in 1720 was apparently thought of as a Tory. He died, intestate, on 26 Sept. 1728.[2]

[1] J. R. Woodhead, *Rulers of London* (London and Mdx. Arch. Soc.), 44, 153; PCC 91 Irby. [2] *VCH Warws.* vi. 128; *HMC Lords*, iii. 47; Egerton 3359 (unfol.); *Parlty Hist.* xv. 349; PCC admon. Sept. 1728.

P. W.

CHAMBERS, John, of Norwich.[1]

NORWICH   6 Dec. 1705–1710

Chambers' identity has not been established. It is possible that he was the 'John Chambers esquire' buried in 1720 at St. James's church, Norwich, aged 71, whose wife Susan had predeceased him by seven years, having borne him a son (also John) and three daughters, and who in his will declared himself to be 'of Norwich'. This man may be the John Chambers, son of Adam Chambers and Elizabeth Swan, baptised at Marsham, twelve miles from Norwich, on 12 Feb. 1649, who married Susan Bucke at St. Giles, Norwich on 17 Oct. 1671. The Member was at any rate a local man. He stood in 1705 on the Whig interest and with the backing of Charles, Lord Townshend, and he and his partner Waller Bacon* defeated two Tories. Although Chambers was classed in an analysis of the new Parliament as a 'Churchman', his election was marked by Lord Sunderland (Charles, Lord Spencer*) as a gain for the Whigs. Townshend reported at the beginning of October that Bacon and 'Captain Chambers' had promised him 'they would be sure to be in town before the meeting of the Parliament' and that the two men were concerting parliamentary tactics with other Norfolk Whigs. Chambers had to wait to take his seat, however, for there was a double return, and only on 6 Dec. were he and Bacon declared elected. The inclusion of his name in a list of those who had voted for the Court candidate in the division on the Speaker on 25 Oct. 1705 was thus an error.[2]

An undistinguished back-bench Whig, Chambers probably went along with Lord Townshend's friend Robert Walpole II and his followers in the Commons. He voted on the Court side on 18 Feb. 1706 over the 'place clause' in the regency bill. In two lists of 1708 he was classed as a Whig. In 1709 he supported the naturalization of the Palatines, and the following year was listed as having voted for the impeachment of Dr Sacheverell (even though on 9 Mar. 1710 he had been given leave of absence for three weeks). In June Townshend and some supporters agreed that Chambers should be 'promised something for an encouragement' to stand again for Norwich, but he evidently could not be persuaded. A John Chambers subsequently served as treasurer of the county between 1710 and 1714 and again in 1715.[3]

[1] *Compleat Hist. Norwich* (1728), 62. [2] Blomefield, *Norf.* iv. 424; Norf. RO, NCC 348 Blomfield; *Norwich Cathedral Mar. Reg. 1697–1754*, p. 58; IGI, Norf.; Camb. Univ. Lib. Cholmondeley (Houghton) mss, (Sir) Charles Turner* to [Robert Walpole II], 19 Sept. 1705, Ld. Townshend to same, 8 Oct. 1705. [3] G. Holmes, *Pol. in Age of Anne*, 231; Norf. RO, Bradfer-Lawrence mss, Ashe Windham* to [Ld. Townshend], 8 June 1710; *Norf. Rec. Soc.* xxx. 3.

D. W. H.

CHAMPNEYS, Arthur (c.1658–1724), of Raleigh House, nr. Barnstaple, Devon and Love Lane, London.

BARNSTAPLE   1690–1705

b. c.1658, 2nd s. of John Champneys (d. 1682) of Yarnscombe, Devon being 1st by his 2nd w. Anne, da. of Arthur Upton. m. lic. 13 Feb. 1688 (aged 30), Hannah (d. 1693), da. of Sir Arthur Ingram, Spanish merchant, of St. Andrew's, Holborn, Mdx. and Bucknall, Lincs., 1da.[1]

Member, R. Fishery Co. [I] 1691; asst. Glassmakers' Co. 1691, Mines Adventurers' Co. 1693.[2]

Commr. taking subscriptions to land bank 1696.[3]

In 1689 Champneys, a London merchant, purchased from Sir Arthur Chichester, 3rd Bt.*, the manor of Raleigh, which carried the main interest at Barnstaple. Returned for the borough in 1690, he was listed by Lord Carmarthen (Sir Thomas Osborne†) as a Whig on the eve of the new Parliament and as a probable Court supporter towards the end of the second session in December. A list among Robert Harley's* papers drawn up in April 1691 noted him as a Country party supporter. His business activities seem to have prevented him from playing even a moderate part in the proceedings of the House, as his name features only very infrequently in the Journals. He was concerned in several money-making projects with Sir Joseph Herne*, another London merchant representing a Devonian constituency, whose nephew Nathaniel Herne* married Champneys' sister-in-law in 1691. Even so, during the period of Herne's governorship of the East India Company in the early 1690s, Champneys was a member of the interloping syndicate which sought to break the company's monopoly. Marked as a Court supporter by Grascome, he was forecast in January 1696 as likely to vote with the Court on the proposed council of trade, was an early signatory to the Association in February, and in March voted for fixing the price of guineas at 22s. Following the 1698 election he was noted as likely to oppose the Court over the standing army issue, and in another list was classed as a member of the Country party, thus indicating a change in his political allegiance. A year or so later, he sold Raleigh to his fellow MP, Nicholas Hooper, a Tory, but kept his borough seat in the next three parliaments. During these years Champneys' political outlook swung towards Toryism. He was listed as a Tory by Robert Harley in December 1701, and on 26 Feb. 1702 he voted in favour of the resolution vindicating the Commons' proceedings in the impeachment of the King's Whig ministers. Although two years later Harley considered him a probable opponent of the Tack, he in fact supported it in the division on 28 Nov. 1704. He stood down in 1705, eventually dying in London in 1724, his burial at St. Dionis Backchurch, Holborn, taking place on 2 Apr.[4]

[1] Vivian, *Vis. Devon*, 166; Foster, *London Mar. Lic.* 262; *Lincs. Peds.* (Harl. Soc. li), 540; *St. Dionis Backchurch* (Harl. Soc. Reg. iii), 261; *Trans. Devon Assoc.* lxxiii. 182. [2] *CSP Dom.* 1690–1, p. 540; 1691–2, p. 3; 1693, p. 207. [3] *CJ*, xii. 509. [4] *Trans. Devon Assoc.* 181; *Le Neve's Knights* (Harl. Soc. viii), 292; Bodl. Rawl. C.449; Add. 38484, f. 254; *CSP Dom.* 1693, p. 207; Hutchins, *Barnstaple Recs.* i. 82; *St. Dionis Backchurch*, 293.

E. C.

CHAPLIN, John (1657–1714), of Tathwell, Lincs.

GREAT GRIMSBY   1690–1695, 1702–1705

b. 29 Jan. 1657, 1st s. of Sir Francis Chaplin, Clothier, of Thames Street, St. Botolph Billingsgate, London, alderman of London 1668–*d.*, ld. mayor 1677–8, by Anne, da. of Daniel Hutt of Essex; bro. of Sir Robert Chaplin, 1st Bt.† *m.* (1) lic. 13 Mar. 1678, Elizabeth, da. and h. of Sir John Hamby of Lamberhurst, Kent and Tathwell, 4s. (1 *d.v.p.*) 1da.; (2) 3 Feb. 1692, Frances, da. of Thomas Archer† of Umberslade Hall, Tanworth, Warws., sis. of Andrew Archer* and wid. of Sir Francis Rouse, 3rd Bt., of Rouselench, Worcs., *s.p. suc.* fa. 1680.[1]

Sheriff, Lincs. 1689–90; high steward, Grimsby ?–*d.*[2]

Hailing from Bury St. Edmunds, which his uncle Thomas had represented in 1659 and 1660, Chaplin's father became a prosperous London merchant, and served as lord mayor. He left estates in Suffolk, Wiltshire and Jamaica, and over £1,000 in personalty, including stock in the Royal African Company. Chaplin himself does not appear to have entered trade, although one of his brothers took advantage of their father's connexions to become a colonial merchant and administrator. Through his first marriage John acquired Tathwell, which proprietorial interest helped him to fight a successful campaign at Grimsby in 1690. At the beginning of his parliamentary career he was classed by Lord Carmarthen (Sir Thomas Osborne†) as a probable supporter of the Court, though in April 1691 Robert Harley* marked him as a Country Member. He was not active, although in the fourth session he was granted a leave of absence on 13 Dec. 1693, and the following month successfully sued for breach of privilege against two men for arresting one of his servants. In the next session he was reported to be 'very ill' on 22 Feb. 1695 and was granted leave to go into the country. Sickness may thus have been the reason for his decision not to stand at the general election held later that year.[3]

Chaplin did not return to Parliament until 1702, when he emerged at the top of the poll at Grimsby. He soon showed his adherence to Whig principles, voting in February 1703 for agreeing with the Lords' amendments to the bill for enlarging the time for taking the Abjuration. He was classed as a probable opponent of the Tack in October 1704, and duly voted against it or was absent in the division on 28 Nov. Having suffered a resounding defeat at Grimsby in 1705, he did not stand again. He died on 11 Nov. 1714, and was buried at Tathwell. His brother Sir Robert Chaplin, 1st Bt., sat for Grimsby under George I, and the descendants of his youngest son, Thomas, provided many Members for the boroughs and county of Lincoln.[4]

[1] Burke, *LG* (1855), 193; J. R. Woodhead, *Rulers of London* (London and Mdx. Arch. Soc.), 44–45; *Lincs. Peds.* (Harl. Soc. l), 237; *Le Neve's Knights* (Harl. Soc. viii), 221–2. [2] *Letters and Pprs. Banks Fam.* ed. Hill (Lincoln Rec. Soc. xiv), p. xx. [3] Woodhead, 44–45. [4] *Monson's Church Notes* ed. Monson (Lincoln Rec. Soc. xxxi), 371.

P. W./P. L. G.

CHAPMAN, Thomas (1663–aft. 1744). of Caldecote, Newport Pagnell, Bucks.

BUCKINGHAM   1710–1715
AMERSHAM   27 Oct. 1722–1727

bap. 20 Apr. 1663, 1st s. of Roger Chapman of Caldecote by his 1st w. Rebecca, prob. da. of Thomas Catesby of Hardmead, Bucks., sheriff of Bucks. 1659–60. *educ.* Christ Church, Oxf. 1679; I. Temple 1680, called 1687. *m.* lic. 17 July 1682, Elizabeth Goodman of St. Andrew, Holborn, 4s. (1 *d.v.p.*) 5da. (2 *d.v.p.*). *suc.* fa. 1703.[1]

Chapman's father, an attorney, was actively purchasing land in the Newport Pagnell area as early as 1680, including the manors of Sherington (1682) and Caldecote (1695), although the family may have resided at Pindon End. During the 1680s and early 1690s a Thomas Chapman appears regularly on the Buckinghamshire grand jury, and Roger himself appears to have joined the bench in February 1688, and to have acted as a j.p. in the following April. That this did not denote a firm attachment to James II was made clear when Captain Thomas Chapman helped to raise the Buckinghamshire militia and joined its march to Northampton in November 1688 in order to rendezvous with the rebels under Lord Grey of Ruthin. Years later, in a letter to Robert Harley*, Chapman set out his own services in 1688:

> After I had carried a troop of horse to Nottingham upon the Revolution at a very great expense to myself, King William was pleased to order a company of guards in the second regiment, but before the commission was made out (by the influence as I suppose of a great man [Hon. Thomas Wharton*] whose interest I have always opposed in Bucks.), my name was struck out of the roll.[2]

Even before the Revolution parish registers reveal Chapman's residence to have been at Hanslope, near to Stony Stratford and eight miles from Buckingham. Nothing is known of his career in William III's reign. According to his later letter to Harley, his lack of reward following the Revolution was known to the Duke of Marlborough (John Churchill†), and after Queen Anne's accession he 'promised to do me justice, but before that was done an unexpected turn at court put an end to my pretensions, and I believe I am the only man in England whose services upon that occasion, and constant fidelity to the government have been thus rewarded'. The death of his father saw him appointed to the county bench and lieutenancy, but as one of Lord Wharton's 'greatest opponents' in Buckinghamshire elections nothing further came his way.[3]

Chapman's opportunity to enter Parliament occurred with the change of ministry in 1710 and subsequent dissolution. In August Lord Cheyne (William*) wrote to Harley on Chapman's behalf detailing his services at the Revolution and loyalty to the Tories, adding 'if I can, I'll get him into Parliament'. As 'the most popular man in those parts where freeholders are the thickest', Chapman had no difficulty in transferring his popularity to the corporation, being returned by one vote. Marked as a Tory on the 'Hanover list', he was included in the list of 'worthy patriots' who in the 1710–11 session exposed the mismanagements of the previous administration. An active Member, he helped to manage several pieces of legislation through the Commons. After being named on 31 Jan. 1711 to draft the bill continuing the Act for the better preservation of game, he was added to the second-reading committee, acted as a teller on 24 Apr. in favour of its passage and was appointed on 7 May to the conference committee on the Lords' amendments to it. He showed an interest in highway bills, being named on 21 Feb. to draft a bill for the more effectual regulation of waggoners, which he presented on 6 Mar. and then managed through the House, and on 10 Apr. he was named to draft a bill making the laws for the repair of highways more effectual. In the interim he managed the Dunstable to Hockley [Hockliffe] road bill through all its stages in the Commons, including the conference proceedings with the Lords over the bill. His name appears on a broadsheet list of October Club members, but not on Abel Boyer's more accurate list. Certainly in May 1711 he was still seeking patrons from government circles, such as Hon. James Brydges*.[4]

The next session saw Chapman named to two drafting committees including one on the Aylesbury to Buckingham highway. He also managed Owen Bromsall's estate bill through the Commons after it had been brought down from the Lords. He acted as a teller on six occasions: against declaring Sir Henry Belayse disqualified from sitting in the House for becoming a commissioner into the forces in Spain and Portugal (15 Feb.); against postponing the call of the House for a week (28 Feb.); to agree with the amendment from committee to exempt London ships employed within North Foreland from the duties employed for Greenwich Hospital (16 Apr.); against declaring Lord Bellew (Richard*) elected for Steyning (8 May); in favour of declaring William Cotesworth* not elected for Boston (3 June); and in favour of an amendment from committee on the bill allowing Dr Dixon to compound with the Treasury (5 June). In June he presented Buckingham's address upon the peace and in October took the chair at the quarter sessions.[5]

On 18 June 1713 Chapman voted in favour of the French commerce bill. His major legislative role during the session was to manage through the Commons the bill regulating the armed forces, which included chairing the committee of the whole on the bill and acting as a teller on 10 July for a motion that the Speaker leave the chair so that the House could go into committee. At this time he was having to shoulder the financial burden of various suits appertaining to membership of Buckingham corporation, the outcome of which would determine the make-up of the electorate. Some observers felt that this would overwhelm him as 'it is generally said he hath but a small estate, several children and outruns his income'. However, with the suits dragging on he was re-elected for Buckingham in 1713 and keen to make an impression for he went to court on the Queen's birthday (6 Feb. 1714), dressed 'as fine as a prince'.[6]

Chapman continued to be active in the House. He acted as a teller on six occasions: against a motion stating that the commissioners appointed to treat with

France over trade should be classed as a new government office (19 Apr.); against reading for a second time an amendment to the bill to regulate the armed forces that fictitious names on musters might be investigated into by j.p.s (20 May); against postponing the report on the bill explaining the act to encourage wool manufacture (21 June); to agree with the Lords' amendments to the schism bill about not being prosecuted in other courts under the Act while a prosecution was pending (23 June); to engross the bill settling the Earl of Ranelagh's (Richard Jones*) debts (24 June); and to pass the bill relieving poor debtors (28 June). Legislatively he was named to the drafting committee of the bill amending the Dunstable Highway Act and managed through the Commons another bill regulating the armed forces, the bill preserving the navigation of the Thames and was involved in two naturalization bills. Accounted a Tory in the Worsley list, he remained faithful to Lord Oxford (Harley) after the latter's fall from power, writing to him on 10 Aug. 1714 that 'in my opinion (notwithstanding the unreasonable clamours of your enemies), we in a great measure owe to you the peace of our country, and the security of our constitution'. Chapman was defeated in the general election of 1715, petitioning without success. However, he regained his seat in the Commons at a by-election in 1722. The date of his death has not been ascertained, but it was after 1744 when he was obliged to sell Caldecote.[7]

[1] IGI, Bucks.; *VCH Bucks.* iv. 363; *London Mar. Lic.* ed. Foster, 265; Lipscomb, *Bucks.* iv. 178; PCC 24 Dogg. [2] *VCH Bucks.* 348, 417, 454; *Bucks. Sess. Recs.* i. 59, 100, 124, 151, 252, 272, 371, 467; Duckett, *Penal Laws and Test Act* (1883), 153; *Hatton Corresp.* (Cam. Soc. xxiii), 116; Add. 70217, Chapman to Harley, 22 Dec. 1711. [3] Lipscomb, 178; Add. 70217, Chapman to Harley, 22 Dec. 1711; *Wharton Mems.* 30–31. [4] Add. 70217, Cheyne to Harley, 12 Aug. 1710; 29599, f. 119; Huntington Lib. Stowe mss 58(8), p. 161; Huntington Lib. Q. xxxiii. 157. [5] *London Gazette*, 21–24 June 1712; *Verney Letters 18th Cent.* i. 243. [6] BL, Verney mss mic. 636/55, Ld. Fermanagh (John Verney*) to Ralph Verney†, 4 June 1713; *Verney Letters 18th Cent.* 390. [7] *Verney Letters 18th Cent.* 331; Add. 70217, Chapman to Oxford, 10 Aug. 1714; *VCH Bucks.* 417.

E. C./S. N. H.

CHASE, James (c.1650–1721), of Westhorpe House, Little Marlow, Bucks.

GREAT MARLOW 1690–1710

b. c.1650, 1st s. of John Chase of Littlebrook, Kent by Elizabeth, da. of Dr Thomas Soane, canon of Windsor. *educ.* Christ Church, Oxf. matric. 15 Dec. 1665, aged 15. *m.* 17 Nov. 1677, Elizabeth, da. of Sir Ralph Box of Cheapside, London *s.p. suc.* fa. 1690.[1]

Master, Apothecaries' Co. June 1688–Sept. 1689; apothecary to William III, Anne and George I 1690–*d.*; commr. sick and wounded June 1706–May 1707.[2]

Chase's grandfather (*d.* 1665) was court apothecary to Charles I and, after the Restoration, to Charles II. In 1666, Chase's father succeeded him, his patent granting the reversion of the office to Chase himself. Despite holding court office, John Chase gave negative replies to King James's 'three questions' on the repeal of the Test Act and Penal Laws. Chase himself had the honour to serve as master of the Apothecaries' Company both before and after the cancellation of the surrender of the company's old charter in November 1688. He then succeeded his father in the post of court apothecary in June 1690, at a salary of £115 p.a., plus an allowance of £127 p.a. and lodgings in Whitehall.[3]

Chase acquired his estate in Little Marlow in 1684 and built Westhorpe House there during Anne's reign. He appears to have played a part in the election of 1685 at Great Marlow, but was not returned there until 1690. Following his election he was classed as a Whig and Court supporter by the Marquess of Carmarthen (Sir Thomas Osborne†) and as likely to support Carmarthen in December 1690 in the event of an attack on him in the Commons. Chase was also frequently classed as a placeman in lists of this Parliament, including an analysis by Grascome which described him as a placeman but not a supporter of the Court. After nomination on 31 Oct. 1691 to a drafting committee on a bill to regulate abuses in elections, Chase was named on 22 Feb. 1692 to the committee to take the evidence of William Fuller, the informer, in the King's Bench Prison. While there, Chase gave Fuller a medical examination and pronounced him to be 'in a dangerous condition'. In the next session Chase was given leave on 17 Nov. 1692 to attend King's bench to give evidence at Fuller's trial. In the last session of this Parliament he served as a teller on 28 Nov. 1694 against the committal of a place bill. He was also among those listed as 'friends' by Henry Guy*, presumably in relation to parliamentary inquiries into Guy's activities.[4]

The 1695 election marked the beginning of the domination of the parliamentary representation of Great Marlow by Chase and Sir James Etheridge*. In the 1695–6 session Chase was forecast as likely to support the Court in the division on 31 Jan. 1696 over the proposed council of trade. He also signed the Association in February and voted in March for fixing the price of guineas at 22s. In the following session he voted on 25 Nov. 1696 for the attainder of Sir John Fenwick†. The Buckinghamshire by-election of 1696 saw one local commentator regard Chase as a useful person to approach, testimony to his influence in the Marlow area. Returned again in 1698 Chase was classed as a supporter of the Court in an analysis of about September. Although forecast as a likely opponent of the standing army, he voted against the disbanding bill on 18 Jan. 1699. On 20 Feb. he acted as teller against the expulsion of Richard Wollaston for holding an office incompatible with membership of the Commons and on 27 Apr. told for an amendment to the bill suppressing lotteries, extending that for the disposal of Sir Charles Bickerstaffe's estate. In the next session, on 8 Jan. 1700, he was a teller against excusing Ralph Freman II from a call of the House. On 13 Feb., in a debate on a motion aimed at Lord Chancellor Somers (Sir John*), which sought to condemn ministers who procured grants from the crown when they were themselves involved in the passing of such grants, he intervened to support James Vernon I's contention that a minister might have a grant which he well deserved. A list of MPs analysed according to interest compiled between January and May 1700 merely noted that Chase was a placeman.[5]

Returned again unopposed at the January 1701 election, Chase was listed as likely to support the Court in February over the 'Great Mortgage'. His main activity in this session was to chair the committee of the whole House on 20 May on a bill from the Lords to confirm the dissolution of the marriage of his brother-in-law, Ralph Box. Re-elected in December 1701, he was classed as a Whig by Robert Harley*. Although he may have been responsible for a contest in 1702, there was no break in the Chase–Etheridge partnership at Great Marlow. In the new Parliament he voted on 13 Feb. 1703 against agreeing with the Lords' amendments to the bill for enlarging the time for taking the oaths of abjuration. He was forecast in the 1704–5 session as likely to oppose the Tack and did not vote for it on 28 Nov. 1704.[6]

A ballad urging support for Tackers at the 1705 election asserted that 'resentment and want of place' had made Chase talk for the Church and after his return in May he was listed as a 'Churchman'. He was also listed as a placeman and voted on 25 Oct. for the Court candidate in the division over the Speaker. In the debate on the regency bill on 15 Jan. 1706 he declared that it was essential to continue the existing Parliament in the event of the death of the Queen and in the divisions on the place clause of the bill on 18 Feb. he again supported the Court. In June 1706 he was appointed a commissioner for sick and wounded, but resigned the following May. On two lists dating from early 1708 (one after the election) he was classed as a Whig. Returned again in 1708, he voted for the naturalization of the Palatines early in 1709. In the following session he was given leave of absence for ten days on 9 Dec. 1709, but later returned to vote for the impeachment of Dr Sacheverell.[7]

At the general election of 1710, Chase and George Bruere* tied for the second seat and a double return ensued with both men petitioning for the right to sit. Given the Tory majority in the new House, Chase waived his right of election on 8 Dec. 1710, although not before he had been classed as a Whig on the 'Hanover list'. He seems to have remained active in local politics, but never stood again. Chase died on 23 June 1721, the main beneficiaries of his will being his widow and Dr Stephen Chase, the eldest son of his cousin, also Stephen.[8]

[1] *Vis. Kent* (Harl. Soc. liv), 34; *Westminster Abbey Reg.* (Harl. Soc. x), 15; *Cal. Treas. Bks.* xii. 184. [2] C. R. B. Barrett, *Hist. Soc. Apothecaries*, 108; *Cal. Treas. Bks.* xii. 184; xxi. 30; Luttrell, *Brief Relation*, vi. 54. [3] *HMC Pepys*, 256; *N. and Q.* ser. 12, ii. 318–19; *CSP Dom.* 1665–6, p. 227; *Westminster Abbey Reg.* 15; Duckett, *Penal Laws and Test Act* (1883), 144; *Cal. Treas. Bks.* ix. 1953, 1959; xii. 184; Barrett, 108. [4] *VCH Bucks.* iii. 78, 82; *Luttrell Diary*, 199, 201. [5] *Misc. Gen. et Her.* n.s. i. 213–15; BL, Verney mss mic. 636/49, Daniel Baker to John Verney* (Ld. Fermanagh), 5 Dec. 1696; Som. RO, Sanford mss DD/SF 410(a) notes on debate, 13 Feb. 1699[–1700]. [6] *Cocks Diary*, 137. [7] *Bagford Ballads* ed. J. W. Ebsworth, ii. 827; *Cam. Misc.* xxiii. 69; *Cal. Treas. Bks.* xxi. 30. [8] *Hist. Reg. Chron.* 1721, p. 27; PCC 126 Buckingham.

E. C./S. N. H.

CHAUNDLER, Richard (c.1650–1729), of Idmiston, Wilts. and Cams, Hants.

HAMPSHIRE	1701 (Feb.)–1702
ST. IVES	27 July–8 Dec. 1702
HAMPSHIRE	1705–1708
LYMINGTON	1708–1710, 18 Apr. 1715–1722

b. c.1650, s. of Robert Chaundler of Idmiston, Wilts. educ. I. Temple 1661; Trinity Oxf. matric. 23 Mar. 1666, aged 16. m. (1) 23 Feb. 1670, Mary (d.1680), da. of John Palmer, MD, warden of All Souls, Oxf., 2s. d.v.p. 2 da. (1 d.v.p.) 4 other ch. d.v.p.; (2) lic. 15 Sept. 1682, Barbara (d. 1698), wid. of Sir Walter Curle, 1st Bt., of Soberton, Hants; (3) 21 Oct. 1700, Catherine Hobbs.[1]

Sheriff, Wilts. 1686–7; freeman, Wilton by 1692; Winchester by 1701; Lymington 1701, mayor 1706.[2]

The son of a minor Wiltshire landowner, Chaundler gave favourable replies to King James's 'three questions' on the repeal of the Test Act and Penal Laws, and in June 1688 was made a deputy-lieutenant for Wiltshire. Some time before 1701 he bought the estate of Cams in Hampshire and began to enjoy the patronage of the 2nd Duke of Bolton (Charles Powlett I*). He was returned for Hampshire in both the elections of 1701, with Bolton's support, and was classed as a

Whig in Robert Harley's* list of December 1701. At the general election of 1702 he transferred to the Cornish borough of St. Ives, where Bolton had an interest, only to be unseated on petition by a Tory opponent in December that year.³

Chaundler stood successfully for Hampshire in 1705 and was classed as a 'Churchman' in a list of the new Parliament and as a gain for the Whigs by Lord Sunderland (Charles, Lord Spencer*). He duly voted for the Court candidate and fellow Hampshire Whig John Smith I* in the division on the Speaker, 25 Oct. 1705, but otherwise took little part in parliamentary activities. He was twice listed as a Whig in 1708, and at the general election of that year was returned for Lymington, where Bolton shared the representation with a local family, the Burrards. Chaundler supported the naturalization of the Palatines in 1709, and voted for the impeachment of Dr Sacheverell in 1710. He did not sit in Parliament again under Queen Anne, possibly because in the next two elections Bolton was hard pressed by the Tories and could not find him a seat. Returning to the Commons for Lymington in 1715, he continued to support the Whigs. He died in 1729, his will being proved in September of that year.⁴

¹ Hoare, *Wilts*. Alderbury, v. 66; *Wilts. N. and Q.* vi. 99; Wood, *Life and Times*, i. 306–7; ii. 151. ² Pembroke mss at Wilton House, list of burgesses, 1 Oct. 1692; Hants RO, Winchester bor. recs. ordnance bk. 7, f. 166; E. King, *Old Times Revisited, Lymington*, 184, 192. ³ Duckett, *Penal Laws and Test Act* (1882), 214, 228; *VCH Hants*, iii. 214; Surr. RO (Kingston), Somers mss 01/1, Mrs Burnet to Lady Jekyll, [c.Nov. 1701]. ⁴ PCC 242 Abbott.

P. W.

CHERNOCK, Sir Pynsent, 3rd Bt. (by 1670–1734), of Holcot, Beds.

BEDFORDSHIRE 1705–1708, 1713–1715

b. by 1670, 1st s. of Sir Villiers Chernock, 2nd Bt.†, of Holcot by Anne, da. and coh. of John Pynsent of Carlton Curlieu, Leics. and Combe, Surr., prothonotary of c.p. *educ*. I. Temple 1684; Queens', Camb. 1685. *m*. 9 June 1691, Helen (*d*. 1741), da. and coh. of William Boteler† of Biddenham, Beds., 3s. (1 *d.v.p.*) 5da. (1 *d.v.p.*). *suc*. fa. as 3rd Bt. Oct. 1694.¹

Burgess, Bedford 1693.²

Chernock, the son of a moderate Tory squire who had represented the county in the 1685 Parliament, was a distant cousin of the Catholic convert and Jacobite conspirator Robert Chernock (or Charnock), vice-president of Magdalen College, Oxford under James II and later executed for his part in the Assassination Plot of 1696. Sir Pynsent topped the poll for knight of the shire in his first attempt at a parliamentary election in 1705, standing as a Tory and with the particular backing of the local clergy. His success was in part a reflection of the rising fortunes of the High Church interest in Bedfordshire, under the Bruces of Ampthill, with whom Chernock's family had always been on good terms; but it was also due to his having been by some months the first candidate in the field, which had enabled him to collect a substantial number of single votes. He was classed as a Churchman in an analysis of the new House of Commons, and his election was accounted a 'loss' by Lord Sunderland (Charles, Lord Spencer*), so it is no surprise to find him voting on 25 Oct. 1705 against the Court candidate for Speaker. He was subsequently marked as a Tory in two lists of 1708, but he had not been in any respect an active Member, and withdrew at the next election. He may also have been under some financial pressure at this time, for in 1709 he sold one of his Bedfordshire manors, forced into doing so, according to tradition, by the need to meet excessive election expenses. At any rate, it was not until 1713 that he ventured another contest, being returned with John Harvey ahead of two Whigs. This time he was the manager of a bill through the Commons, but it was a measure of strictly local concern, to amend a Bedfordshire highways Act. In the Worsley list he appeared as a Tory. At the next election he canvassed on behalf of Tory candidates in the borough of Bedford as well as standing himself for knight of the shire. Defeat on that occasion marked his last involvement in parliamentary politics, though his name was sent to the Pretender in 1721 as a likely sympathizer.³

Chernock died at Holcot on 2 Sept. 1734, and was buried there. His son Sir Boteler Chernock, 4th Bt., sat for Bedford 1740–7, as a Tory.⁴

¹ Burke, *Commoners*, ii. 104–5; Lipscomb, *Bucks*. i. 132–3; *Beds. N. and Q*. iii. 299; Add. 24120, f. 191; *VCH Beds*. iii. 387; F. A. Blaydes, *Genealogia Bedfordiensis*, 45, 399; *Beds. Par. Reg*. xxix. (Holcot) 9. ² Bedford Bor. Council, Bedford bor. recs. B2/3, corp. act bk. 1688–1718, f. 30. ³ *Bull. IHR*, xlviii. 67–68; *HMC 15th Rep. VII*, 188–9, 217; *Ailesbury Mems*. i. 352; Wilts. RO, Ailesbury mss 1300/998, Ld. Bruce (Charles*) to Ld. Ailesbury (Thomas Bruce†), 30 Jan. 1704[-5]; *VCH Beds*. 436; P. S. Fritz, *Ministers and Jacobitism 1715–45*, p. 151. ⁴ *Beds. N. and Q*. ii. 144; *Beds. Par. Reg*. 9.

D. W. H.

CHETWYND, John (1643–1702), of Ingestre, Maer and Rudge, Standon, Staffs.

STAFFORD   1689–1695
TAMWORTH   1698–17 Mar. 1699
STAFFORD   1701 (Feb.–Nov.), 24 July–9 Dec. 1702

b. 1643, 1st s. of John Chetwynd of Rudge by Susan, da. of John Broughton of Withington, Staffs. *m*. 27 Jan.

1676, Lucy (d. 1738), da. of Robert Roane of Tullesworth, Chaldon, Surr., 3s. 1da. suc. fa. 1674, Walter Chetwynd I* 1693.¹

?Capt. of ft. [I] 1674–8.²

Freeman, Stafford 1689; sheriff, Staffs. 1695–6.³

Chetwynd came from a cadet branch of the Chetwynds of Ingestre, his great-grandfather, Anthony, having settled at Rudge. The main Staffordshire estates of the family descended to him by virtue of an entail after the death in 1693 of his third cousin, Walter Chetwynd I*. It seems probable that he owed his seat to his cousin's decision not to contest Stafford in the election to the Convention of 1689, and subsequent decision to stand for knight of the shire in 1690. At the election for the borough of Stafford in 1690 the corporation appears to have backed him unanimously, leading to his election after a three-cornered contest. The Marquess of Carmarthen (Sir Thomas Osborne†) listed him as a Tory supporter of the Court. Chetwynd's name also appears on a list drawn up in December 1690, probably indicating his support for Carmarthen should he be attacked in the Commons. On Robert Harley's* list drawn up in about April 1691 he was marked as a Court supporter although this was qualified with a 'd', probably meaning doubtful. It is not possible to differentiate his activity in the House from that of his cousin, Walter Chetwynd I, until the latter's death in 1693.⁴

At the county by-election of 1693, called on the death of Walter Chetwynd I, John signed a circular letter in support of Sir Walter Bagot, 3rd Bt.*, which was intended to discourage the pretensions of Hon. Henry Paget*. Indeed, shortly before his death in 1702, Chetwynd was described as Paget's 'greatest enemy in the county' and 'no less' to the Foleys. Thus, it was not surprising that at a by-election for Stafford in 1694 the Foleys and Chetwynds were the main competitors. In the event, Chetwynd's cousin, John of Grendon, withdrew in the face of the superior strength of Thomas Foley III*. At the 1695 election he found himself ousted at Stafford by the Foleys. One report suggested that Chetwynd would then switch to the county, but since the gentry had already agreed upon candidates this was not a serious option. Instead of sitting in Parliament, Chetwynd served as sheriff for the ensuing year.⁵

With the Foleys facing opposition in 1698 at Stafford, and Chetwynd having agreed as early as February of that year to abide by the decision of a gentry meeting for the county, he again faced the possibility of being without a seat. He may well have been the John Chetwynd elected at Tamworth in 1698, but this may equally well have been his cousin and namesake of Grendon, whose seat lay only a few miles from the borough. John of Grendon was the son of Charles Chetwynd of London, the deputy-auditor of the crown revenues in Wales, who was deputy-keeper of the wardrobe at Ludlow Castle. He had acquired the reversionary interest in the Grendon estate by the will of William Chetwynd†, who left it to his sister. Her date of death is unknown but Chetwynd seems to have been residing at Grendon by 1694. In addition, Walter Chetwynd I, by his will, had left him the mortgages on the land and tenements of Edward Slaney, in Baxterley and Bently, just to the south of Grendon. This John Chetwynd was active in local affairs, being a land tax commissioner from 1694 to 1695 for Hemlingford, the northernmost hundred in Warwickshire, sheriff of the county in 1703–4, when he used his position to try to make an interest at Tamworth, and a Whig supporter of George Lucy in the Warwickshire election of 1705. Whichever of the namesakes had been elected in 1698, was unseated on petition in March 1699. During this brief tenure, the Member was classed as a Court supporter on a comparative analysis of the old and new Parliaments, although this was subsequently queried. He voted on 18 Jan. 1699 against the third reading of the disbanding bill. Both John Chetwynds had plausible reasons for supporting the Court: Chetwynd of Ingestre because of his local battles with the Foleys and the aspirations of his second son, John†, to enter the diplomatic service (realized later in 1699 when he was named private secretary to the Duke of Manchester, ambassador in Paris); and Chetwynd of Grendon because his father's office was held at the pleasure of Ralph Grey*, a noted Whig who had forestalled Treasury attempts to oust him in 1694.⁶

By 1700 Chetwynd of Ingestre was as acceptable to the Pagets as a deputy-lieutenant for the county as his son was to the court as a diplomat. With the retirement from politics of Philip Foley, Chetwynd was able to regain a seat at Stafford in January 1701, even though the burgesses 'had no great kindness' for him. However, in 1700 he had given £100 to the borough to endow almshouses. A John Chetwynd also stood at Tamworth at the same election, being easily defeated. The absence of a petition may suggest that John of Ingestre was the candidate and was using the borough as insurance against possible failure at Stafford. In the new Parliament his name appeared on a list of supporters of the Court in February 1701 over the 'Great Mortgage'. He does not seem to have put up in November 1701, but regained his seat at Stafford in the 1702 election. However, on 9 Dec. 1702, being an immodest taker of snuff, and indulging himself even to excess, in his fashionable mode (though he had no visible distemper upon him, and was not an old man and in other things very temperate yet) he died . . . of a fit of sneezing, which was so violent that it could not be allayed by any remedies that were applied to him.[7]

[1] IGI, Staffs, London; J. C. Wedgwood, *Staffs. Parl. Hist.* (Wm. Salt Arch. Soc.), ii. 168–9; H. E. Chetwynd-Stapylton, *Chetwynds of Ingestre*, 224, 226. [2] *HMC Ormonde*, n.s. iv. 84. [3] Staffs. RO, D1323/A/1, p. 355. [4] Chetwynd-Stapylton, 219, 225, ped.; Harl. 7001, f. 396. [5] Hereford and Worcester RO (Hereford), Foley mss E12/F/IV, 'Gents. letter to the country', 4 Oct. 1693; E12/F/IV/BE, John Pershall* to Philip Foley*, 7 Nov. 1702; Add. 70114, [Philip Foley] to Robert Harley*, 29 Sept. 1694; 70018, f. 185. [6] Wm. Salt Lib. (Stafford), Bagot mss D1721/3/291, John Chetwynd to Edward Bagot*, 11 Feb. 1697[–8]; Chetwynd-Stapylton, ped.; *Cal. Treas. Pprs.* 1547–1696, p. 480; PCC 45 Vere, 44 Coker; BL, Dept. of Printed Bks. 816 m.16(36); Bath mss at Longleat House, Thynne pprs. 28, ff. 228–9; Add. 61496, ff. 86–87; *Cal. Treas. Bks.* x. 623, 704. [7] *CSP Dom.* 1700–2, p. 250; *HMC Portland*, iii. 638; *VCH Staffs.* vi. 266; Chetwynd-Stapylton, 226; Add. 27440, f. 141.

S. N. H.

CHETWYND, Walter I (1633–93), of Ingestre, Staffs.

STAFFORD   3 Feb. 1674–1679 (July), 1685–1687
STAFFORDSHIRE   1690–21 Mar. 1693[1]

b. 1 or 9 May 1633, o. s. of Walter Chetwynd of Ingestre by Frances, da. and h. of Edward Hesilrige of Arthingworth, Northants. *m.* 14 Sept. 1658, Anne (*d.* 1671), da. of Sir Edward Bagot, 2nd Bt.†, of Blithfield, Staffs., and sis. of Sir Walter Bagot, 3rd Bt.*, 1da. *d.v.p. suc.* fa. 1669.[2]
FRS 1678.

A renowned antiquary, Chetwynd came from a long line of Staffordshire gentry stretching back into the 13th century. When he regained a seat in the Commons in 1690, it was for the county rather than for the borough of Stafford, situated to the south-west of his principal seat at Ingestre, which he had represented in three previous Parliaments. He had campaigned vigorously for the 'Church' interest in the 1690 election, attending the polls at three boroughs, besides his own unopposed election for the county. At the outset of this Parliament the Marquess of Carmarthen (Sir Thomas Osborne†) classed him as a Tory, with a query as to his stance towards the Court. His name also appears on a list drawn up in December, probably indicating that he was expected to support Carmarthen should the latter be attacked in the Commons. On Robert Harley's* analysis of April 1691 his name was noted with a 'd'. It is impossible to differentiate his activities in the Commons from those of his cousin (and heir), John Chetwynd*. It is clear from the correspondence of his chaplain, Charles King, that Chetwynd led a full life of study and social engagements which may have restricted his political involvement, especially when interspersed with bouts of ill-health. However, it seems likely that he was in London for every session of the 1690 Parliament until his death; and throughout the first two sessions, although he did leave shortly before the prorogation in 1691 to supervise building work on Ingestre church. His enjoyment of social occasions is perhaps most aptly demonstrated in May 1692 at the 'consecration' of his new bowling green, a ceremony attended by one peer and nine MPs. Despite taking precautions, he succumbed to smallpox while in London on 21 Mar. 1693. His body was taken back to Ingestre for burial in his new church. In his will he left £400 for six new bells for this impressive edifice. Most of his landed property was entailed upon John Chetwynd.[3]

[1] *The Commons 1660–90* errs in stating that Chetwynd sat for Stafford after 1690. [2] *Vis. Staffs.* (Wm. Salt Arch. Soc. v, pt.2), p. 84; Harl. 7001, f. 373; J. C. Wedgwood, *Staffs. Parl. Hist.* (Wm. Salt Arch. Soc.), ii. 125. [3] Harl. 7001, ff. 366–8, 371, 373, 396; H. E. Chetwynd-Stapylton, *Chetwynds of Ingestre*, 213; *Vis. Staffs.* 84.

S. N. H.

CHETWYND, Walter II (1678–1736), of Ingestre, Staffs.

STAFFORD   26 Dec. 1702–25 Jan. 1711
                 24 Jan. 1712–1722, 4 Feb. 1725–1734

bap. 3 June 1678, 1st s. of John Chetwynd*, and bro. of John† and William Richard Chetwynd†. *educ.* Westminster c.1692–6; Christ Church, Oxf. matric. 28 May 1696, aged 18. *m.* 27 May 1703 (with £6,000), Mary, da. and coh. of John Berkeley*, Visct. Fitzhardinge [I], maid of honour to Queen Mary, *s.p. suc.* fa. 1702; *cr.* Visct. Chetwynd of Bearhaven [I] 29 June 1717.[1]
Master of buckhounds (jt.) to Prince George of Denmark 1705–9, master (sole) to Queen Anne 1709–by June 1711; ranger of St. James's Park 1714–27.[2]
High steward, Stafford 1717–*d.*[3]

Little is known about Chetwynd's early life, apart from the circumstances of his education. However, the future bishop of Bristol, George Smalridge, did not entertain high hopes for him in 1697:

Mr Chetwynd will take London in his way to Oxford. His long absence from this place, and the fondness after country sports which he brings with him when he comes, will hinder him from making that improvement here which were to be wished, for his own reputation, and the benefit of his country.

Nevertheless, Smalridge expected him to play a significant role in county affairs, and Chetwynd encountered no difficulties in succeeding his father as

Member for Stafford at a by-election in December 1702. Shortly after his entry into Parliament he made a favourable marriage to the daughter and coheiress of the treasurer of the chamber to Queen Anne, Lord Fitzhardinge. It was an advantageous match financially, as his wife's dowry was augmented by the Queen, and politically because of her father's association with the court. These contacts were likely to prove highly valuable to anyone embarking on a political career: Fitzhardinge had been in the service of Queen Anne since 1685, was a kinsman of Lord Treasurer Godolphin (Sidney†) and was well known to the Marlboroughs.[4]

Chetwynd's political stance at the start of his career in the Commons is difficult to determine because of the paucity of evidence. His father had been a Tory, locked in a local battle in the 1690s with the Foley family at Stafford, but the party allegiance of the formerly Whiggish Foleys was now changing. When Lord Nottingham (Daniel Finch†) drew up a forecast of likely supporters over his handling of the Scotch Plot in March 1704, his list contained Chetwynd's name. However, Chetwynd's other activities during the session give little indication of his political predilections. On 14 Jan. 1704 he acted as a teller for committing the wines duty bill, but on 9 Feb. following was given leave for three weeks. In the following session his stance on the Tack was probably indicative of his general attitude to the ministry. On a forecast dated 30 Oct. 1704, he was listed as a probable opponent of the measure. Robert Harley* was taking no chances either, for on his lobbying list Fitzhardinge was deputed to ensure that Chetwynd voted with the Court. However, the ministry was not totally sure of his reliability for on 27 Nov., the day before the crucial division, Godolphin wrote a reassuring letter to the Duchess of Marlborough, 'I believe you may be very sure of Mr Chetwynd for the reasons you have given. He is very desirous of a place, and his friends too, knowing to mistake the road to it.' Not surprisingly, therefore, he did not vote for the Tack on the 28th. On 22 Dec. he was given leave of absence for a month. He had returned to the Commons by 12 Mar. 1705 when he acted as a teller against agreeing with a Lords' amendment to a bill for remedying abuses by revenue collectors, which sought to remove a clause relating to Devon and Exeter.[5]

Chetwynd was returned for Stafford in the election of 1705. Shortly before the new Parliament sat he received his reward for supporting the ministry when he was made joint master of the buckhounds. On one analysis of the 1705 Parliament he was classed as 'Low Church', probably owing to his vote on the Tack. He voted for the Court candidate in the contest for the Speakership on 25 Oct. 1705 and, indeed, seemed to relish the parliamentary duty of a placeman. His enthusiastic support for the ministry was noted by Lord Halifax (Charles Montagu*) in an account to the Duchess of Marlborough of the Whig defeat in the Amersham election case which ended: 'I must not forget to commend Mr Chetwynd and Mr Craggs [James I] who are always right and attend.' For the remainder of the Parliament, Chetwynd seems to have kept a low profile, undertaking no committee work of importance, nor acting as a teller. That he continued to follow the ministerial line is vouchsafed by his appearance on a list of Members supporting the Court on 18 Feb. 1706 over the 'place clause' of the regency bill.[6]

Returned unopposed in 1708, Chetwynd was classified as a Whig on an analysis of the new House. In this Parliament he was more active than before. On 20 Jan. 1709 he told against a motion to adjourn the Abingdon election case, which led directly to the vote to unseat (Sir) Simon Harcourt I. He voted with the Whigs in 1709 in favour of the bill to naturalize the Palatines. He also acted as a teller on quite minor legislative matters, as on 31 Mar. 1709 when he told against bringing up a petition against a clause in the Earl of Clanricarde's estate bill. The death of Prince George eventually saw him appointed as sole master of the buckhounds. This necessitated a by-election at which he was returned unopposed in November 1709. He acted as a teller on 25 Jan. 1710 for a resolution that the town clerk of Beaumaris be taken into custody for contempt over refusing to obey an order of the committee of elections. He also voted for the impeachment of Dr Sacheverell.

Given his own record of support for the Whig ministry, and Sacheverell's triumphant tour through Staffordshire, Chetwynd faced a difficult task in securing re-election in 1710. He was eventually returned amid accusations of malpractice by the mayor of Stafford, and was classed as a Whig on the 'Hanover list'. But he had little time to play an important role in the new Parliament, being unseated on 25 Jan. 1711. The petition was decided at the bar, although it was noted that Robert Harley had voted for a reference to committee (as had one of the Foleys), thus angering the Tories. On the other hand, Thomas Foley III, the second Member for Stafford, was reported to be greatly satisfied by the outcome. Harley's support for Chetwynd possibly recognized his natural inclination to the Court, although in May 1711 Arthur Maynwaring* was surprised that Harley had not been more enthusiastic about sponsoring Chetwynd as a candidate at the New Windsor by-election. Shortly afterwards, in June 1711, Chetwynd lost his place. He was not out of the Commons for long, being returned once more for Stafford in January 1712 at a by-election caused by Thomas Foley III's elevation to the peerage. On 19 Feb. 1712 he showed his opposition to the more extreme Tories, and his continued commitment to the Marlborough circle, by telling against the motion to expel Adam de Cardonnel. Later, on 20 Mar., he acted as a teller against Hon. Philip Bertie* in the Boston election, a non-partisan case which centred on the electioneering of Bertie's brother, Lord Lindsey (Robert Bertie†). After the recess Chetwynd revealed his greater concern for office than party, soliciting Harley (now Lord Oxford) for his old office, since his successor had been promoted. 'I am encouraged to do it because I am not conscious to myself of ever being guilty of any action that at any time could displease her Majesty or any now in the administration.' In the following session, on 21 May 1713, he told in favour of setting the malt tax in Scotland at 6d. per bushel, a measure which embarrassed the Court. His vote might therefore have stemmed from his resentment at failure to regain office. Then on 18 June he voted against the French commerce bill, being noted on one division list as 'very whimsical'.[7]

After re-election in 1713, Chetwynd's opposition seemed to harden. On 16 Mar. 1714 he was a teller for the Whig candidate, (Sir) Thomas Wheate (1st Bt.*), in the New Woodstock election, and two days later voted against the expulsion of Richard Steele. In March and April 1714 he became involved in legislation to control the management of funds raised by turnpike trusts, being named on 10 Mar. to a committee investigating the matter. He reported from the committee three times, and on each occasion a specific bill was ordered. On 20 Apr. 1714 he told for another Whig, Paul Methuen*, in the disputed election for Brackley. In May he was appointed to a drafting committee on a bill to continue the vagrancy laws, which he duly presented and reported from committee, and on the 25th he acted as a teller for the Whig opposition to recommit a supply resolution granting a sum to half-pay officers. The following day he carried up a private naturalization bill to the Lords, possibly as a favour to the bill's manager, Samuel Bracebridge, Member for Tamworth. Chetwynd was marked as a Whig on the Worsley list and on two analyses comparing the Parliament elected in 1715 with its predecessor. Having regained office, he retained his parliamentary seat. He now attached himself to the Earl of Sunderland (Charles, Lord Spencer*) and was rewarded in 1717 with an Irish peerage. He continued in office until 1727, when he joined the opposition Whigs. Dying of a 'consumption' on 21 Feb. 1736, he left most of the property he had purchased and his personalty to be sold towards payment of debts.[8]

[1] IGI, London; H. E. Chetwynd-Stapylton, *Chetwynds of Ingestre*, 227; J. C. Wedgwood, *Staffs. Parl. Hist.* (Wm. Salt Arch. Soc.), ii. 193. [2] Luttrell, *Brief Relation*, v. 598; Add. 17677 EEE, f. 229; *Cal. Treas. Bks.* xxix. 346. [3] Wedgwood, 194. [4] Nichols, *Lit. Hist.* iii. 265. [5] *Bull. IHR*, xli. 183. [6] Luttrell, 598; *Bull. IHR*, lxv. 47 [7] *Post Boy*, 7–10 Oct. 1710; *HMC 5th Rep.* 208; *Wentworth Pprs.* 161; Add. 70144, Mary Foley to Abigail Harley, 25 Jan. 1710[–11]; 61461, ff. 116–17; 70217, Chetwynd to [Oxford], 5 July 1712. [8] L. Colley, *In Defiance of Oligarchy*, 212; Chetwynd-Stapylton, 231, 233, 236.

S. N. H.

CHEYNE, Charles, 1st Visct. Newhaven [S] (1625–98), of Chesham Bois, Bucks.

AMERSHAM	1660
GREAT MARLOW	5 Mar. 1666–1679 (Jan.)
HARWICH	1690–1695
NEWPORT	1695–30 June 1698

bap. 23 Oct. 1625, 4th but 1st surv. s. of Francis Cheyne of Chesham Bois by Anne, da. of Sir William Fleetwood of Great Missenden, Bucks. *educ.* Brasenose, Oxf. 1640; L. Inn 1642. *m.* (1) 1654, Lady Jane (*d.* 1669), da. of William Cavendish†, 1st Duke of Newcastle, 1s. 2da. (1 *d.v.p.*); (2) lic. 8 June 1688, Isabella (*d.* 1714), da. of Sir John Smyth of Bidborough, Kent, and wid. of John Robartes, 1st Earl of Radnor, *s.p. suc.* fa. 1644; *cr.* Visct. Newhaven and Lord Cheyne [S] 17 May 1681.[1]
Commr. customs 1675–87, Mint 1677–8.[2]
Commr. Greenwich Hosp. 1695.[3]

Cheyne was returned for both Harwich and Newport in Cornwall in 1690, choosing to sit for the former after it had been suggested that if he opted for the alternative it would ruin the 'Church interest' in Harwich. No doubt his continued support for the Marquess of Carmarthen (Sir Thomas Osborne†) ensured him the backing of the Court interest in a borough with strong links to the government. Having been a known adherent of Carmarthen in the Cavalier Parliament, he was duly listed by the Marquess as a Tory and probable Court supporter in March 1690. He was also listed as likely to support Carmarthen in the event of an attack upon his ministerial position in December 1690, although Robert Harley* saw him as a Country supporter by April 1691. He was not an active Member. With his son challenging for a seat in the local borough of Amersham in 1695, Cheyne was again returned for Newport. Carmarthen's fall from power may explain why Cheyne was forecast as likely to oppose the government in the division of 31 Jan. 1696 on the proposed council of trade, he refused at first to sign the Association and voted on 25 Nov. against the attainder of Sir John Fenwick†.[4]

Cheyne did not live to see the dissolution of the 1695 Parliament as he died on 30 June 1698 and was buried, according to the provisions of his will, at Chelsea on 13 July.[5]

[1] *Bucks. Recs.* vi. 206; T. Faulkner, *Chelsea*, i. 224, 337. [2] *Cal. Treas. Bks.* iv. 869; viii. 1201; *HMC Lindsey supp.* 170–4. [3] Add. 10120, f. 233. [4] W. Suss. RO, Shillinglee mss Ac.454/816, Luzancy to Sir Edward Turnor*, 17 Mar. 1690; A. F. Robbins, *Launceston*, 237. [5] Faulkner, 225; Lysons, *Environs* (1792–6), ii. 127.

E. C./S. N. H.

CHEYNE, Hon. William (1657–1728), of Chesham Bois, Bucks.

AMERSHAM	1681 (Mar.), 1685–1687
APPLEBY	25 July 1689–1695
BUCKINGHAMSHIRE	24 Feb. 1696–1701 (Nov.)
AMERSHAM	1701 (Dec.)–1702
BUCKINGHAMSHIRE	1702–1705
AMERSHAM	1705–1 May 1707

bap. 14 July 1657, o. s. of Charles Cheyne*, 1st Visct. Newhaven [S], by his 1st w. *educ.* Brasenose, Oxf. 1671. *m.* (1) 16 Dec. 1675, Elizabeth (*d.* 1677), da. of Edmund Thomas of Wenvoe, Glam., *s.p.*; (2) 6 May 1680, Gertrude (*d.* 1732), da. of Robert Pierrepont of Thoresby, Notts. and sis. of Evelyn Pierrepont*, *s.p. suc.* fa. as 2nd Visct. Newhaven [S] 30 June 1698.

Commr. for privy seal 1690–2; clerk of the pipe 1703–6, 1711–Dec. 1727.[1]

Freeman, Hertford 1698; ld. lt. Bucks. June–Dec. 1702, 1712–14.[2]

Cheyne was defeated for the borough of Amersham in the election to the Convention of 1689, being forced to seek refuge at Appleby, where Hon. Thomas Wharton* secured his return at a by-election and at the following general election. Political friendship with Wharton suggests that he did not follow his father in supporting the Marquess of Carmarthen (Sir Thomas Osborne†), and this is reflected in Carmarthen's failure to ascribe a party label to him, while marking him as a Court supporter on a list of the new Parliament. Office quickly followed, when the privy seal was put into commission in February 1690, at a salary of £365 p.a. Thus it was as a placeman that Cheyne made his first recorded speech on 29 Apr. 1690, when the Commons discussed the abjuration oath and the suspension of habeas corpus. He backed the Court unequivocally: 'there is no need of further security, the King's Speech intimates, what he would have us do', which was to forbear reopening old quarrels. Cheyne does not appear on any other lists of Carmarthen's supporters in this Parliament, but Robert Harley* thought him a Country supporter in April 1691. He lost office when the Earl of Pembroke (Hon. Thomas Herbert†) was appointed lord privy seal early in 1692. He was listed as a Court supporter by Grascome, but was not an active Member at this time.[3]

Having again been defeated at Amersham in 1695, Cheyne was returned for Buckinghamshire in the by-election caused by Wharton's elevation to the Lords in February 1696. Cheyne was thus in place to sign the Association. In the following session he voted against the attainder of Sir John Fenwick†, which may denote growing political differences with Wharton. Certainly in December 1696 he was being described in correspondence as a 'Church of England man', and written off as never likely to be chosen for the county again, which, given Wharton's influence, was at least suggestive of a split between the two men. The 1697–8 session saw the first inklings of a more active role in the Commons. As early as May 1698 Cheyne was treating the freeholders in preparation for the shire election, and despite the death of his father at the end of June, he emerged top of the poll in August. He was then able to relinquish his seat at Amersham, where he had been chosen as a precaution against defeat in the county. Most important, the election marked the final breach with Wharton, who opposed his candidature, Richard Steele* later ascribing this quarrel to 'some disgust about a membership . . . a strangeness commenced between them which turned to an emnity on Mr Cheyne's part'.[4]

Two lists from the 1698–9 session would seem to confirm the fact of a breach with the Whigs, both seeming to indicate Country sympathies or opposition to the ministry. A comparative analysis of the old and new Parliaments classed Cheyne as a Country supporter and he was forecast as likely to oppose the standing army. Lord Cheyne (as he was almost invariably styled, except in some official correspondence) was certainly more active in this session, being named on 14 Dec. 1698 to draft a bill for qualifying MPs and regulating elections, which he presented on 28 Feb. On 13 Mar. 1699 he was first-named to the committee on the petition from lace-makers in several counties, including Buckinghamshire, complaining of harassment by officers administering the Act against hawkers and pedlars. Upon his report on 6 Apr. the House resolved that the lace-men did not come under the act. On 14 Mar. he was named to bring in a bill for appointing a commission of accounts, Hon. James Brydges* recording in his diary that Cheyne, Gervase Pierrepont* and one of the Foleys met and 'read over' the old Act 'to make us the better to bring in a bill'. Although Cheyne was not mentioned by Brydges in all the discussions on the bill, he was present at the home of Pierrepont (his wife's uncle) on the 25th when a group of Members agreed on the bill. During this session Cheyne received a legacy of £2,000 from his mother-in-law, who also appointed his wife sole executrix 'by which she will have a great deal'. In the summer of 1699 Cheyne's feud with Wharton culminated in a quarrel at the quarter sessions, over precedency on the bench and a slight which Cheyne felt he had received during the previous election. The resulting duel saw Wharton disarm him. However, at least one observer feared that the reconciliation between the two following the duel might extend to political matters and that Cheyne might prove to be a 'turncoat' and support the Whigs at the impending by-election for Oxfordshire. In the 1699–1700 session, Cheyne put an end to an acrimonious debate by successfully moving a motion for granting a supply to the King. He also managed two private estate bills through the Commons.[5]

Shortly before the 1701 election, Cheyne gave an interesting insight into his motivation as a parliamentarian when he noted 'in truth a seat in Parliament is not worth the pains we undergo to attain, but a place at court with a seat there is most people's aim'. Certainly Cheyne's victory at the 1701 election was not achieved without considerable effort, and he also won a seat at Amersham as an insurance policy. Cheyne was listed as likely to support the Court in February over the 'Great Mortgage'. He was appointed on 2 Feb. to a committee to draft a bill qualifying MPs and regulating elections. On 14 June he was sent to the Lords with a message refusing a conference until the Upper House had proceeded against Lord Haversham (Sir John Thompson, 1st Bt.*) for his denunciation of the Commons over the impeachment of ministers for signing the Partition Treaties. Cheyne was later blacklisted as having opposed preparations for war against France and this may have played a part in his defeat in the county election of December 1701. However, he was returned for Amersham.[6]

Cheyne was listed as a Tory by Harley in December 1701. He played the major role in managing through the Commons the bill to continue the Quaker affirmation Act, which he carried to the Lords on 12 Feb. Likewise, it was Cheyne who at the third reading of the abjuration bill on the 19th 'offered a clause for the Quakers' preachers to be exempted', which was rejected. On the 26th he voted in favour of the resolution vindicating the Commons' proceedings in the impeachment of the King's Whig ministers. On 7 Mar., with the King gravely ill, Cheyne seconded a motion that the Commons should vote to stand by and support Princess Anne, but the suggestion was not taken up. March saw him manage a private estate bill through the Commons. In May Cheyne was again the voice of the Quakers in the House when the abjuration bill returned from the Lords. On the 4th the Meeting for Sufferings decided to leave to Cheyne's discretion 'the timing and indeed the decision on whether to present the clause' they had prepared as a substitute for the Lords' amendment. According to Sir Richard Cocks, 2nd Bt.*, after much lobbying the Lords had added a clause allowing Quakers to affirm to the oath of abjuration, but some Quakers demurred, with the followers of William Penn opposed to the amendment, and it would seem that this was the view Cheyne was asked to represent. In opposing the clause Cheyne divided the House on the 6th and carried his point, being nominated to manage the subsequent conference with the Upper Chamber on the reasons for the Commons disagreement. Rather embarrassingly, Cheyne then attended the conference on 7 May without leave of the House, prompting a short debate as to how to proceed, but the Lords withdrew their amendment. May also saw him manage a second private bill. In June he replaced Wharton as lord lieutenant of Buckinghamshire, although this was a temporary measure until Scrope Egerton, 4th Earl of Bridgwater, came of age.[7]

Helped no doubt by the prestige of his new office, Cheyne was successful for the county in the 1702 election. On the opening day of the session he made a short speech seconding the nomination of Robert Harley to the Chair. His reward was to be named clerk of the pipe in July 1703, an office worth £500 p.a., and which he had been promised during the illness of the incumbent, Lord Robert Russell (Hon. Robert*). In the 1703–4 session 'Lord Shany' [sic] was described by Bonet rather surprisingly as a Whig who played an important role in the debate on the Address on 11 Nov. His other activities in this session included presenting a private bill on behalf of his neighbour in Chelsea, Sir Joseph Alston, 3rd Bt., being first-named to draft the militia bill, and carrying the message inviting Dr Robert Wynn to preach before the Commons on the anniversary of Charles I's execution. In October 1704 he was graciously received by the Queen when he presented a congratulatory address from Buckinghamshire on the victory at Blenheim. Forecast as a probable opponent of the Tack, he was lobbied by Harley, and absented himself from the crucial division of 28 Nov., earning opprobrium as a 'Sneaker', although Dyer later proclaimed him a 'well-wisher' to the Tackers. His other important activities included a drafting committee for the Don navigation bill and the management of an estate bill on behalf of Edmund Waller, presumably the nephew and namesake of the former Member for Amersham.[8]

Cheyne was defeated for the county at the general election of 1705, all the Quakers voting against him, despite (or perhaps because of) his previous role as their spokesman. Returned instead for Amersham, he also took part in the Middlesex election, by virtue of his estate in Chelsea, polling for the two Tory candidates. On 25 Nov. 1705 he was one of the placemen who voted against the Court candidate for the Speakership. His only significant role in the 1705–6 session was to manage a private bill dealing with the estates of his brother-in-law Evelyn Pierrepont* (now Earl of Kingston). No doubt it was Harley's protection which enabled Cheyne to retain his office in the Exchequer until December 1706, despite pressure from Whigs such as Wharton and Archbishop Tenison for his dismissal. In the 1706–7 session his activities in the Commons were limited to managing a bill to sell lands for the payment of the debts of Montagu Garrard Drake*, and for the rebuilding of Humberstone church in Lincolnshire. It was to prove his last session in the House, for as a Scottish peer he became ineligible to sit after the Union. However, he was listed as a Tory on one list of the post-Union Parliament.[9]

Cheyne's removal from the Commons did not affect the level of his political activity. Although he left his proxy for the elections of Scottish representative peers with the Court managers (reserving only one or two votes for particular friends), he continued to play a major role in Buckinghamshire elections on the Tory side. Thus in 1708 he could only bewail the failure to challenge the Whigs for the county and 'wish myself at liberty that I might try my fortune once more'. The 1710 election saw Cheyne presenting an address to the Queen in August and attending a meeting to adopt the Tory candidate from the 'Vale' to partner the man chosen from the Chilterns. Nor was he slow to report his efforts to the head of the new ministry, Robert Harley, hoping for his favour 'towards repairing the suffering I have sustained from a Whiggish ministry'. Cheyne had to wait until September 1711 to be restored to his office of clerk of the pipe, but an even greater honour came in May 1712 when he was named as lord lieutenant of Buckinghamshire.[10]

An indication of Cheyne's importance to the Tories can be seen from the comment by Lord Fermanagh (John Verney*) on hearing a false report of Cheyne's death in February 1713: 'it would be a fatal stroke to the Church party in this county'. From his position as lord lieutenant Cheyne played a pivotal role in securing the election of two Tories for the county in September of that year. August 1714 saw Cheyne engaged in desperate efforts to persuade Fermanagh to join with John Fleetwood† in contesting the general election following Queen Anne's death. Once this prospect had been dashed Cheyne managed to negotiate a compromise with the Whigs whereby the representation would be shared, and then proceeded to ensure that the agreement held. In December 1714 he lost the lord lieutenancy, but seems to have kept his office as clerk of the pipe. Having in December 1707 finally received from the crown the remainder of the purchase price agreed by his father for the lands on which Chelsea Hospital was built, in 1712 Cheyne sold the manor of Chelsea to Sir Hans Sloane. He died on 26 May 1728 'beloved of hospitality, respected for integrity and admired for a well-advised zeal for the true interests of his country'. He left his estate to his wife.[11]

[1] *Cal. Treas. Bks.* ix. 736, 1828; xviii. 353–4; xxi. 118; xxv. 433; xxix. 346. [2] Herts. RO, Hertford bor. recs. 25/100. [3] *Wharton Mems.* 31; Bodl. Rawl. A.79, f. 85v. [4] BL, Verney mss mic. 636/49, W. Bushby to Verney, 6, 19 Dec. 1696; *Verney Letters 18th Cent.* i. 154; *Wharton Mems.* 31. [5] Huntington Lib. Stowe mss 26(1), Brydges diary, 14, 25 Mar. 1699; Bolton mss at Bolton Hall, D37, Ld. Bridgwater (John Egerton†) to [Charles Powlett I*, Mq. of Winchester], 8 Jan. 1698[–9]; Add. 40774, ff. 104–5; Luttrell, *Brief Relation*, iv. 539; Macaulay, *Hist. Eng.* 2938; Verney mss 636/51, Cary Gardiner to Verney, 25 July, 15 Aug. 1699; *Cocks Diary*, 37; *Vernon–Shrewsbury Letters*, ii. 369. [6] H. Horwitz, *Parl. and Policy Wm. III*, 316. [7] Soc. of Friends Lib. Mins. Meeting for Sufferings 15, pp. 337–8; *Cocks Diary*, 220, 237, 284, 286; *CSP Dom.* 1702–3, p.113. [8] Add. 70264, Cheyne's speech, 20 Oct. 1702; *Cal. Treas. Bks.* xviii. 353–4; *Marlborough–Godolphin Corresp.* 227; DZA, Bonet despatch 12/23 Nov. 1703; Rawl. D.863, f. 89. [9] *HMC Portland*, iv. 190; *Mdx. Poll 1705* (IHR), 10; Add. 4743, f. 47; 70217, Cheyne to Harley, 12 Aug. 1710. [10] Add. 61628, f. 153; 70217, Cheyne to Harley, 12 Aug., 23 Sept. 1713; Bodl. Ballard 10, f. 155; *HMC Portland*, iv. 459, 694. [11] *Verney Letters 18th Cent.* 292, 315–19; Huntington Lib. Ellesmere mss EL 10728, John Robartes to Cheyne, 18 Nov. 1713; *Cal. Treas. Bks.* xx. 287; *HMC 7th Rep.* 508; T. Faulkner, *Chelsea*, i. 336, 338; PCC 174 Brook.

E. C./S. N. H.

CHICHELEY, Sir John (c.1640–91), of Southampton Square, Bloomsbury, Mdx.

NEWTON 1679 (Mar.)–1681 (Mar.)
1685–1687
1689–20 Mar. 1691

b. c.1640, 2nd s. of Thomas Chicheley† of Wimpole, Cambs. and Great Queen Street, St. Giles-in-the-Fields, Mdx. by his 1st w. Sarah, da. of Sir William Russell, 1st Bt.†, of Chippenham, Cambs. *educ.* I. Temple 1657. *m.* c.1667, Isabella (*d.* 1709), da. and coh. of Sir John Lawson of Alresford, Essex, wid. of Daniel Norton of Southwick, Hants, 4s. (2 *d.v.p.*) 2da. Kntd. June 1665.[1]

Lt. RN 1662, capt. 1663, r.-adm. 1673–5; envoy, Spanish Netherlands 1670; commr. navy 1675–80, Ordnance 1679–82; ld. of Admiralty 1682–4, 1689–90.[2]

Freeman, Portsmouth 1675, Liverpool 1686; conservator, Bedford Level 1683–*d*.[3]

Chicheley, who had opposed the abdication vote in 1689 as making the crown elective, was nevertheless appointed a lord of the Admiralty by King William. One of the most experienced members of the commission, he was one of three regular attenders who transacted most of the day-to-day business. Returned for Newton by his nephew Peter Legh† of Lyme, a frequent house guest of Chicheley's in Southampton Square, he was classed as a Court supporter by Lord Carmarthen (Sir Thomas Osborne†) in his list of March 1690. On 5 June he resigned from the Admiralty commission, giving no reason for his decision but probably disgusted by the divisions and mismanagement in the navy. At the beginning of the second session of the Parliament Chicheley was listed as a probable supporter of Carmarthen, in connexion with the projected Commons' attack upon Carmarthen's ministerial position, and the session saw him appointed to draft a bill to improve the recruitment of seamen (15 Oct.). In April 1691 Chicheley was listed as a Country supporter by Robert Harley*, but he had long suffered from lung trouble and died very suddenly on 20 Mar. 1691, being buried at St. Giles-in-the-Fields three days later.[4]

[1] *Le Neve's Knights* (Harl. Soc. viii), 234; *Lyme Letters* ed. Lady Newton, 25. [2] *Commissioned Sea Officers of RN 1660–1815* (Navy Recs. Soc. occ. pub. 1), 80; *Cal. Treas. Bks.* vi. 140; *Hatton Corresp.* (Cam. Soc. n.s. xxii), 13; J. Ehrman, *Navy in War of Wm. III*, 639. [3] R. East, *Portsmouth Recs.* 361; Wahlstrand thesis, 58; S. Wells, *Drainage of Bedford Level*, i. 463–5. [4] Ehrman, 279–80, 296–9, 342; Morrice ent'ring bk. 3, p. 155; *Hervey Diary*, 15; *Lyme Letters*, 184.

E. C./R. D. H.

CHICHESTER, Sir Arthur, 3rd Bt. (c.1662–1718), of Youlston, Devon.

BARNSTAPLE   1685–1687, 1689–1690
                   1713–3 Feb. 1718

b. c.1662, 2nd s. of Sir John Chichester, 1st Bt.†, of Raleigh, Devon by his 2nd w. Mary, da. of Theodore Colley of Notts. and wid. of Sir George Warcup of St. Anne, Blackfriars, London. *m.* 15 Apr. 1684, Elizabeth, da. and coh. of Thomas Drewe*, 4s. 6da. *suc.* bro. as 3rd Bt. Sept. 1680.

Freeman, Barnstaple 1684.[1]

Chichester's family had been established in the Barnstaple area since the 14th century. Sir Arthur, a younger son, began his involvement in the town's affairs soon after coming of age, and in 1685 was elected to James II's Parliament. As a Tory, he was blacklisted as having voted during the Convention against the transfer of the crown. He stood down in 1690, apparently without any intention of seeking election in the future, since he promptly sold his manor of Raleigh, with its commanding interest in Barnstaple, to Arthur Champneys*, and thereafter made Youlston his seat. He was dismissed from the commission of the peace in 1696, presumably for refusing to sign the Association. His ostracism in the county seems to have lasted until April 1703 when he was appointed a deputy-lieutenant. In the summer of 1713 he delighted in the prospect of a Tory landslide, declaring that there would not be 'two Whigs in all Devonshire, where all differences are very happily settled', and was himself returned once more for Barnstaple. He was classed as a Tory in the Worsley list; and on 20 May 1714 was granted six weeks' leave of absence. Retaining his seat in the 1715 election, he died on 3 Feb. 1718 and was buried at Pilton, a short distance from Barnstaple.[2]

[1] *Trans. Devon Assoc.* lxxii. 264. [2] Luttrell, *Brief Relation*, iii. 243; *CSP Dom.* 1703–4, p. 278; Bodl. Ballard 18, ff. 49–50.

E. C.

CHILD, Sir Francis (1642–1713), of Hollybush House, Fulham, Mdx. and the Marygold by Temple Bar, London.

DEVIZES   1698–1702
LONDON   1702–1705
DEVIZES   1705–1708, 16 Dec. 1710–1713

bap. 14 Dec. 1642, 6th s. of Robert Child of Heddington, Wilts., by his w. Jane. *m.* 21 Oct. 1671, Elizabeth (*d.* 1720), da. of William Wheeler, goldsmith and banker, of the Marygold, 12s. (9 *d.v.p.*) 3da. (1 *d.v.p.*) Kntd. 29 Oct. 1689.[1]

Apprentice, Goldsmiths' Co. 1656, freeman 1665, livery 1671, asst. 1688, master 1702, prime warden 1690–1; common councilman, London 1682–3, 1689, alderman Oct. 1689–*d*., sheriff 1690–1, ld. mayor 1698–9.

Jeweller to King William 1689–97; receiver, Salt Duty Act 1694; commr. taking subscriptions to land bank 1696. Cttee. Old E.I. Co. 1699–1701; pres. Christ's Hosp. 1702–12; commr. Greenwich Hosp. 1695, 1704.[2]

Child was born in Heddington, Wiltshire, where his family had probably been settled since the mid-16th century. His father was a clothier but he himself, a younger son in a numerous family, was sent to London at the age of 14 to be apprenticed to a goldsmith. The foundation of his fortune was his marriage in 1671 to the daughter of the banker, William Wheeler, who conducted business at the sign of the Marygold by Temple Bar. Wheeler was already dead by the time of the marriage and the firm was currently being run by Robert Blanchard, who had married Wheeler's widow. Blanchard subsequently took Child into partnership, and on Blanchard's death in 1681 the bulk of his estate, including the bank, came to Child. He quickly became one of the capital's leading financiers, and, having been the first banker to give up the goldsmith's trade, he was later heralded as 'the father of the profession'. His wealth and City contacts made him a powerful ally, but his political outlook was less certain, for his allegiance swung from Whig to Tory in the course of an often controversial career.[3]

Child first entered public life in 1682, when he became a common councilman of London. However, having been labelled by one Tory observer as 'indifferent' in politics, he was displaced by another Tory the following year, and only gained greater prominence after the Revolution, when he started making large loans to the government. For a time in 1689 the stability of his bank was threatened by rumours of a run, but he was reportedly helped out of his difficulties by Sarah Churchill (later Duchess of Marlborough). Despite this scare, Child secured rapid advancement in the City and at court, becoming an alderman of London, receiving a knighthood, and gaining appointment as jeweller to the King. Even a Tory like Sir Peter Rich† acknowledged his financial standing, recommending him in March 1690 to Sir Stephen Fox* for the raising of a government loan in the capital. He was clearly identified as a Whig leader in the City, for in May 1690 the Earl of Monmouth rose in the Lords to condemn Child's dismissal as a lieutenant-colonel in the London militia, branding Sir Francis' replacement a 'traitor'. The same month Child successfully stood as a Whig candidate for sheriff.[4]

In December 1690 Child's status as a financier was attested by a summons before the Lords to advise on a bill to prevent the export of bullion. For the next few years the ministry found him a valuable source of credit, and in 1692 he joined Sir Joseph Herne* and Sir Stephen Evance* to advance £50,000 for the maintenance of the government in Ireland. He appears to have remained in Whig ranks until at least November 1693, when he gave evidence against the Tory admirals over the loss of the Smyrna convoy. Moreover, the following March he was chosen a colonel of the City trained bands as the Whigs consolidated their control of the capital, although one source suggests that he may have declined to serve. His Whig allegiance was severely tested after the foundation of the Bank of England in 1694, which, in common with many other private bankers, he opposed. He was subsequently involved in the scandal surrounding the City's payments to secure the passage of the Orphans' Relief Act, but testified to the Commons committee of inquiry in March 1695 that he had never attended the committee set up by the common council to obtain such a bill. In addition, although he had signed the order authorizing the payment of money to the Speaker, Sir John Trevor*, he denied being present when the money was handed over, and claimed he 'could give little account of the matter'.[5]

In 1695 Child conducted his first parliamentary campaign at Devizes, a borough which lay only three miles from his birthplace. His brother John, mayor of Devizes in 1694–5, could boast a strong local interest, but Sir Francis failed to be returned. Most significantly, in preparation for this contest he had sought the aid of the Duke of Leeds (Sir Thomas Osborne†), thereby indicating a further drift towards the Tories. He certainly did not see eye to eye with the ministry during the recoinage crisis, for in May 1696 he and other financiers were summoned to the lords justices and warned 'not to augment the difficulties that are now upon credit'. He was later commended for having weathered the emergency without closing his business, but in August it was reported that his 'head is so turned upon the business of the coin that he hardly knows what he does or what he says'. Given his opposition to the Bank, it was no surprise that in that year he lent his support to the land bank. Furthermore, his alienation from the ministry may even have influenced his resignation as jeweller to the King in 1697. The following year he further identified himself with the Tory financial interest by advancing £3,000 to the subscription which the Old East India Company submitted to the Commons to rival the New Company's proposal.[6]

Having fought a successful campaign at Devizes in 1698, Child was increasingly identified with the Tories. One observer classed him as a likely opponent of the Court on the standing army issue, and even though he was listed as a Court supporter on a comparative analysis of the old and new Parliaments, this assessment was subsequently queried. The ministry clearly did not endorse Child's candidacy for the London mayoralty in September, Robert Yard* reporting to William Blathwayt* that 'many of our friends' were 'indifferent' to any of the competitors. Even less equivocally, James Vernon I* bracketed Child with the Tory Sir Peter Daniel, observing 'there will be no great choice of either of them: the Bank and the New East India Company have spoiled Sir Francis for a good Whig'. Child was elected, and for his inauguration decided to revive the custom of a pageant, held in abeyance for the previous three years. According to one account his was 'one of the finest shows that has ever been seen on the like occasion', but the Whiggish *Post Man* reported that 'the mob was very rude, and threw dirt'.[7]

In the new Parliament Child gave little clue as to his political leanings, although he did gain election to the committee to prepare an address to the King to give thanks for his assent to the disbanding bill. He appeared keen to serve his constituents' interests in the first session, gaining appointment to two conference committees dealing with Blackwell Hall and Billingsgate market respectively. His mayoral duties may have limited his Commons activity, for he proved an active magistrate, paying close attention to the regulation of the price of corn, and distributing charity to London's prisons. He was also reported to have donated £500 in April 1699 for the relief of the Huguenots. Unfortunately for him, 'no place of moment fell to the chair' during his mayoralty, and he finished up some £4,000 out of pocket. Although relieved of the burdens of office, he made little impact in the succeeding session. However, a parliamentary list of early 1700 classed him in the 'interest' of the Old East India Company.[8]

Prior to the general election of 1701 Child emerged as one of the most active Tory campaigners in the City. In September 1700 he clearly backed the Tory (Sir) Charles Duncombe* for the mayoralty, and subsequently led the Tory inquest into Duncombe's failure to achieve a majority in the court of aldermen. The following January he discussed parliamentary elections with Duncombe and Hon. James Brydges*, and, having secured an unopposed return at Devizes, stood unsuccessfully for London in the interest of the Old East India Company. In the new Parliament he proved much more active, and acted as a teller on an amendment to a supply bill. He was duly classed in February 1701 as a likely supporter of the Court in continuing the 'Great Mortgage'.[9]

Perhaps motivated by Sir Francis' desertion of the Whig cause, Child's opponents singled him out for attack, accusing him of Jacobite sympathies. A satire, which has been tentatively dated at around December 1700, provocatively suggested that he was the ideal Member to prepare a bill 'for educating the Prince of Wales in the Protestant religion'. He was subsequently blacklisted as having opposed the preparations for war with France, and it was further alleged that he had 'declared himself for calling home the Prince of Wales'. However, there is no evidence to link Child with St. Germain, and the Tory pamphlet issued to answer such allegations had ample grounds to query whether he 'in every circumstance during the present government have [sic] not signalized himself a wellwisher and a ready assister of his King and country?' It also hailed him as 'a true Churchman, and a hater of popery'. Child's personal accounts suggest that he may even have taken legal advice to clear his name, but he did not feel sufficiently confident to contest London at the general election of November 1701. He again secured an unopposed return at Devizes, and was listed with the Tories by Robert Harley*. He subsequently voted in February 1702 in favour of the resolution vindicating the Commons' proceedings in the impeachments of the preceding Parliament, but made little contribution to the business of the House, only gaining appointment to a committee to draft a bill for the employment of the poor.[10]

In the first general election of the new reign Child was successful at both London and Devizes. Prior to the City poll his standing in the capital had been enhanced by election as a colonel of the Orange regiment of militia, but he needed a scrutiny to beat Sir Robert Clayton* to fourth place in the parliamentary election. Choosing to sit for the City, and turning the Devizes seat over to his son John, Sir Francis was not active in the first session, although he did vote on 13 Feb. 1703 against agreeing with the Lords' amendments to the bill for enlarging the time for taking the oath of abjuration. In the second session he joined with other City figures to speak in the debate on 27 Nov. on the manning of the fleet, and was duly appointed to the drafting committee for a bill to increase the number of seamen. In the next session he was named to draft a bill to redevelop Gresham College, and acted with (Sir) Gilbert Heathcote* to arbitrate between the college and the Royal Society over this measure, albeit with little success. Most significantly, he broke with his party over the Tack, for on 30 Oct. he was listed as a probable opponent of the measure, and before the crucial division on 28 Nov. left the House with the other 'Sneakers'.[11]

Such apostasy may well have influenced Child's decision not to contest London at the general election of 1705. Furthermore, for the first time in a decade he faced opposition at Devizes, where he and his rival Josiah Diston* were reported to have spent some £3,000 a year 'in law and bribes'. In the new Parliament Child resumed the party line, voting on 25 Oct. against the Court candidate for Speaker. In the second session he managed through the House a Devizes highways bill, which he may have viewed as a means to secure his interest in the borough. Sir Francis found himself the victim of Whig advances, being displaced in June 1707 as one of the colonels of the London trained bands. In March 1708, with an imminent threat of French invasion, he and fellow Tory banker Sir Richard Hoare* were accused of promoting a run on the Bank of England by collecting large quantities of bank bills for which they demanded immediate payment in cash. Hoare subsequently published a notice denying any involvement in such a scheme, but Defoe insisted that Child

> carried it with a higher hand and afterwards pretended to refuse the bills of the Bank; but still declared he did it as a goldsmith, and as a piece of justice to himself, in some points in which the Bank had, as he alleged, used him ill. But in general it was looked upon as an open affront to the government, and an abetting and countenancing the invasion of the Pretender from abroad, and the rebellion intended at home.

Two parliamentary lists of early 1708 confirm Sir Francis as a Tory, but his controversial opposition to the Bank did not serve his party well at the ensuing London election. He finished bottom of the poll, and, not having taken the precaution of securing election at Devizes, experienced his first spell outside Parliament in a decade.[12]

The ministerial changes of the summer of 1710 offered Child an entrance back into public life, and he soon established himself as one of the leading financial backers of the new administration, joining with Hoare to advance 'more than they [the ministers] have occasion for this six months'. However, in early August it was reported that he and 'the rest of the monied citizens on the Tories' side' had expressed grave reservations regarding the impending dissolution of Parliament. Evidently such worries were quickly allayed, and Tory election propaganda later praised Child as one of the City figures who could provide 'sufficient' supplies for the government. Despite regaining a colonelcy of the City militia, he did not stand at the ensuing London contest, but voted for the Tory candidates. Shortly afterwards he attended at court for the presentation of an address from the London lieutenancy, on which occasion Robert Harley was said to have been 'very joyous with the rich men', Child and Sir Charles Duncombe. At that time Child was still unsure of his place at Westminster, for he had been involved in a double return at Devizes. One of his opponents, Paul Methuen*, testified to Child's influence at that time, reporting to Harley that Sir Francis 'has made no scruple of telling me himself to my face that he has interest enough in the House to have me turned out'. This boast proved true and he was indeed seated by the House on 16 Dec. 1710.[13]

In the new Parliament Child was generally inactive. Classed as one of the 'worthy patriots' who in the first session helped to detect the mismanagements of the previous ministry, he lapsed from loyalty to the Tory administration on 25 May 1711 by voting against the amendment to the South Sea Company bill, which gave the crown the right to appoint the first directors. However, he subsequently made a considerable investment in the company, and was clearly regarded as a Tory in April 1712, when 'Dutch Whigs' were blamed for having caused a run on his bank. He was not present in June 1713 at the division on the French commerce bill, possibly due to ill-health, for in late August he was prepared to turn the Devizes seat over to his son Robert. Child died on 4 Oct. 1713, and on receiving the news, L'Hermitage described him as a most zealous Tory.[14]

At the time of his death Child was a very rich man, boasting significant stock-holdings in several City institutions. However, he had proved himself an active supporter of charitable projects, including Christ's Hospital, one ward of which he had rebuilt at his own expense. His great wealth ensured that his offspring were able to emulate his achievements: four sons entered Parliament, and one of them, Francis†, also became lord mayor of London. His daughters naturally secured good matches, and in February 1700 one of them had been identified as a possible bride for the Duke of Norfolk. Child himself showed little interest in setting himself up as a country gentleman, although he was mortgagee of Osterley Park, which subsequently became the principal seat of his eldest surviving son, Robert*.[15]

[1] Feret, *Fulham Old and New*, ii. 91, 93–94; IGI, London; *Wilts. N. and Q.* ii. 207–8, 217–18. [2] J. R. Woodhead, *Rulers of London* (London and Mdx. Arch. Soc.), 46; *Cal. Treas. Bks.* ix. 217; x. 549; Add. 38871 (unfol.); 10120, ff. 232–6; Beaven, *Aldermen*, ii. 117; *Daily Courant*, 8 Aug. 1704. [3] *Wilts. N. and Q.* 217–18; Feret, 91–92; T. Pennant, *Some Acct. of London*, 390–1. [4] Woodhead, 46; *Cal. Treas. Bks.* ix. 37, 44, 1652, 1974; F. G. H. Price, *Marygold by Temple Bar* [1902], 43; Dorset RO, Fox-Strangways mss, Rich to Fox, 17 Mar. 1690; *HMC Lords*, iii. 48; *Portledge Pprs.* 73. [5] *HMC Lords*, 183; Luttrell, *Brief Relation*, ii. 395, 538; iii. 283–4; Bodl. Carte 79, f. 488; Grey, x. 337; Beaven, 117; *Debates and Proc. 1694–5*, pp. 11, 13. [6] *Wilts. N. and Q.* 268; Add. 46554–9, bdle. 7, Leeds to Ld. Lexington, 21 Sept. 1695 (Horwitz trans.); *CSP Dom. 1696*, pp. 178–9; E. Settle, *Glory's Resurrection* [1701]; *HMC Buccleuch*, ii. 387; *CJ*, xii. 322, 509; Luttrell, iv. 228. [7] Yale Univ. Beinecke Lib. Osborn Coll. Blathwayt mss, Yard to Blathwayt, 30 Sept. 1698; *Vernon–Shrewsbury Letters*, ii. 186; Settle, dedication; *Post Boy*, 29 Oct.–1 Nov. 1698; *Post Man*, 29 Oct.–1 Nov. 1698. [8] Luttrell, iv. 459, 577; *Flying Post*, 29–31 Dec. 1698; Carte 228, ff. 299–300. [9] Northants RO, Montagu (Boughton) mss 48/126, James Vernon I* to Shrewsbury, 10 Oct. 1700; Huntington Lib. Stowe mss 26(2), Hon. James Brydges'* diary, 26 Jan. 1701. [10] *HMC Portland*, viii. 63; *Answer to Black List* [1701]; R. Bank of Scotland, Child mss CH/199. [11] Luttrell, v. 193; NMM, Sergison mss 103, ff. 450–2; *Newton Corresp.* v. 63–64. [12] *HMC Portland*, iv. 175–6, 244–5;

Luttrell, vi. 186; *Anatomy of Exchange Alley* [1719], 29–31. [13]*HMC Frankland-Russell-Astley*, 202; *Addison Letters*, 229; Boyer, *Anne Annals*, ix. app. pp. 144–5; Boyer, *Pol. State*, i. 10; *London Poll of 1710*; *Wentworth Pprs.* 151; *HMC Portland*, iv. 617. [14]Child mss CH/199; Univ. Kansas Spencer Research Lib. Moore mss 143 Ck, Charles Vere to Arthur Moore*, 9 Apr. 1712; Add. 17677 GGG, f. 358. [15]Child mss CH/199; Add. 30000 D, f. 72; W. Trollope, *Christ's Hosp.* 118; *VCH Mdx.* iii. 109.

P. W./P. L. G.

CHILD, John (c.1677–1703), of the Middle Temple, London.

DEVIZES   14 Nov. 1702–14 Feb. 1703

b. c.1677, at least 2nd surv. s. of Sir Francis Child*; bro. of Francis[†], Samuel[†] and Robert Child*. *educ.* sch. in Fulham; Trinity Coll. Camb. adm. 21 Apr. 1693, aged 15; M. Temple 1694, called 1700. *unm.*[1]

Child, a younger son of the banker Sir Francis Child, inherited houses in Fleet Street, where he was born, and Blackfriars from his mother in 1686. After attending a school in Fulham he progressed to Cambridge in 1693, but left for the Middle Temple in the following year without taking a degree. He was called to the bar in 1700, and his subsequent success as a barrister is suggested by the purchase of several properties, including a manor in Buckinghamshire for which he paid 1,250 guineas. Although he had no property in Devizes, a borough which traditionally elected a member of the local gentry to sit with a townsman, his family had long been established at nearby Heddington, and he was thus a suitable candidate to replace his father at the Devizes by-election on 14 Nov. 1702, caused by the latter's decision to sit for London. Child made little impression on the work of the House, although he may have acted as a teller on 14 Dec. for a motion reviving all committees. His stay at the House was short-lived, however, for on 14 Feb. following he hanged himself from a shutter in his Temple chambers. There was a rumour that his suicide was caused by sorrow for the loss of the occasional conformity bill, but Lady Pye, writing to Abigail Harley 27 Feb. 1703, dismissed this idea as a 'good Derby ale notion, though ... the opinion of some gentlemen'. Dyer's report on the event admitted that 'there is no reason can be given for his committing this violence on himself, being the darling of his father and mother and who amply supplied him with what ever he desired, but his natural temper being hypochondriacal led him to it, though it's said he left two papers containing some reasons behind him'. No will has been found.[2]

[1]J. Feret, *Fulham, Old and New*, 92–94. [2]Wilts. RO, Devizes bor. recs. G20/1/19, min. bk.; Luttrell, *Brief Relation*, iv. 269; *HMC Portland*, iv. 58; F. G. Hilton Price, *Marygold by Temple Bar*, 79–98; Add. 70234, newsletters 16 Feb., 4 Nov. 1703.

P. W.

CHILD, Sir Josiah, 2nd Bt. (c.1668–1704), of Wanstead, Essex.

WAREHAM   24 Nov. 1702–20/21 Jan. 1704

b. c.1668, 3rd but 1st surv. s. of Sir Josiah Child, 1st Bt.[†], of Wanstead, gov. E.I. Co. 1681–3, 1686–8, by his 2nd w. Mary, da. of William Atwood of Hackney, Mdx., merchant, and wid. of Thomas Stone of London, merchant; half-bro. of Sir Richard Child, 3rd Bt.* *m.* 10 Mar. 1691 (with £25,000), Elizabeth (*d.* 1741), da. of Sir Thomas Cooke*, *s.p.* Kntd. 29 Oct. 1692; *suc.* fa. as 2nd Bt. 22 June 1699.[1]

Cttee. E.I. Co. 1687–93.[2]

Freeman, Maldon 1701.[3]

Child's father had acquired a considerable fortune as a merchant and for many years had been regarded as the virtual head of the East India Company, in which he owned over £50,000 of stock. Child, who himself held £6,000, married the daughter of Sir Thomas Cooke, another large shareholder, thus consolidating the family's grip on the company. Child did not take over the leadership of the company after his father's death; instead this passed to Cooke. The terms of his father's will, moreover, indicate that Child was by no means a favourite son. James Vernon I* wrote on 27 June 1699 that

> Sir Josiah Child ... has made such a disposition of his estate as his family is not likely to agree about. He has left his eldest son no more than was settled on him in marriage ... which they reckon about £4,000 p.a. The other son [Sir Richard Child], who is by the present wife, is made heir to the rest and executor. He will have about £5,000 p.a. in land ... They say he does not leave so great an estate as was expected and that he has several accounts depending, which will either take from his estate, or some will be great losers.

Child was nevertheless regarded as a man of sufficient substance to entertain the King to dinner at his house in October 1700.[4]

Child entered Parliament in 1702 at a by-election for Wareham on the interest of George Pitt*. A Tory like his father and brother, he did not stay long enough in the Commons to make any mark. He died of pleurisy on 20 or 21 Jan. 1704 and was buried at Hackney.[5]

[1]Luttrell, *Brief Relation*, ii. 192; W. Letwin, *Sir Josiah Child*, 1, 23. [2]Info. from Prof. H. Horwitz. [3]Essex RO (Chelmsford), Maldon bor. recs. D/B3/1/24, f. 144. [4]*Vernon–Shrewsbury Letters*, ii. 316–17; *Verney Letters 18th Cent.* i. 86. [5]*Frag. Gen.* n.s. i. 120, 128.

P. W.

CHILD, Sir Richard, 3rd Bt. (1680–1750), of Wanstead, Essex.

MALDON 1708–1710
ESSEX 1710–1722, 1727–1734

bap. 5 Feb. 1680, 3rd surv. s. of Sir Josiah Child, 1st Bt.†, being 1st s. by his 3rd w. Emma, da. and coh. of Sir Henry Barnard of Stoke, Salop and Aconbury, Herefs., Turkey merchant of London, wid. of Francis Willoughby of Wollaton, Notts. *m.* 22 Apr. 1703, Dorothy (*d.* 1744), da. and h. of John Glynne of Henley Park, Surr., 3s. 2da. *suc.* half-bro. Sir Josiah Child, 2nd Bt.*, 20 Jan. 1704; to part of estate of Frederick Tylney* and assumed name of Tylney by Act of Parliament 13 June 1733; *cr.* Visct. Castlemaine [I] 24 Apr. 1718, Earl Tylney [I] 11 June 1731.

Freeman, Maldon 1705.[1]
Ld. warden, Essex forest 1709–*d.*[2]

Child inherited wealth and a certain flexibility in politics from his father, who appointed him residuary legatee and executor. Sir Josiah's death in 1699, before Richard's majority, prompted the latter to petition on 12 Feb. 1700 for a bill to vest certain lands in trustees, so that settlements made on his half-brother's marriage could be honoured. In 1704 he inherited the baronetcy and £4,000 p.a., bringing his total annual income to about £10,000. He stood unsuccessfully as a Tory candidate for Essex in 1705, with the backing of Bishop Compton of London, and in 1707 combined his commercial interests and loyalty to the Church by granting the rectory at Wanstead to a Mr Pound, 'who had lately returned a great sufferer from the service of the East India Company'. Child was returned for Maldon in 1708, and was marked as a Tory on a list of Members. In the first session he acted as teller for the minority in favour of an adjournment during the debate on the Whitchurch election, but the House went on to resolve that Frederick Tylney, his wife's uncle, had not been duly elected; and in the second session he voted against the impeachment of Dr Sacheverell. His Tory principles did not prevent him from investing in the Bank of England and at this time he owned some £4,000 worth of stock. He successfully contested the county for the Church party in 1710, with over 90 per cent of his vote consisting of 'plumpers', and was classed as a Tory in an analysis of the returns. In 1711 he was listed as one of the 'worthy patriots' who detected the mismanagements of the last administration, and as a member of the October Club. In June 1711 a rumour that he was about to purchase a peerage for £10,000 prompted Lord Windsor (Thomas*) to complain 'that's beginning too soon to be like the Duchess of M[arlborough] to do anything for money, making a man that's no gentleman a lord'.

Nothing came of the speculation, though the talk of a peerage was renewed in the winter of 1711 and again in early March 1713. Child remained in the Commons, and voted for the French commerce bill on 18 June 1713. He was returned for Essex, again with Compton's support, in 1713, and was classed as a Tory on the Worsley list, though evidently not in the Harleyite mould since Lord Oxford (Robert Harley*) disdainfully referred to him as a jobber who had 'made a prey of the poor'. After Anne's death it was reported that there would be 'great opposition' to him, but he retained his seat, purchasing an Irish peerage in 1718 and becoming a government supporter. By 1722 his mansion at Wanstead had been completed, 'the archetype of the Palladian great house', and attracted so much attention that he felt obliged to shut the grounds for all but one or two days a week to stem the crowds. He died at Aix-en-Provence in March 1750, succeeded by his second son, John, who died unmarried in 1784.[3]

[1] Essex RO, Maldon bor. recs. D/B3/1/24, f. 202. [2] *VCH Essex*, vi. 96. [3] Luttrell, *Brief Relation*, v. 383; Camb. Univ. Lib. Add. mss 5, f. 227; 7, f. 57; Lansd. 1013, f. 112; W. A. Speck, *Tory and Whig*, 23; Add. 70421, Dyer newsletter 26 Oct. 1710; *Wentworth Pprs.* 203; *Verney Letters 18th Cent.* i. 273; Add. 17677 GGG, f. 94; *Secret Hist. of White Staff* (1714), pt.3, p. 38; Bodl. Ballard 31, f. 132; *VCH Essex*, 325; *Essex Rev.* vii. 220; PCC 111 Pett.

P. W./M. J. K.

CHILD, Robert (1674–1721), of Portugal Row, Lincoln's Inn Fields, and Osterley Park, Mdx.

HELSTON 22 Dec. 1710–1713
DEVIZES 1713–1715

bap. 6 June 1674, 1st surv. s. of Sir Francis Child*, and bro. of John*, Francis† and Samuel Child†. *educ.* travelled abroad (Holland) 1697. *unm. suc.* fa. 1713; kntd. 25 Sept. 1714.[1]

Livery, Goldsmiths' Co. 1698, asst. 1709, prime warden 1714–15; alderman, London 1713–*d.*[2]

Treasurer, R. Artillery Co. 1704–8; dir. E.I. Co. 1709–*d.* (with statutory intervals), dep. chairman 1714–15, chairman 1715; commr. building 50 new churches 1712–15; trustee, borrowing £200,000 on S. Sea stock 1713; gov. St. Thomas' Hosp. by 1719; pres. Christ's Hosp. 1719–21.[3]

As heir to his father's great banking house, Child was destined to play a prominent role in the City. By 1702 he was sufficiently independent to purchase a house in Lincoln's Inn Fields, and subsequently joined his father as partner in the family business. He shared Sir Francis' Tory principles, and took advantage of the change of ministry in 1710 to be returned to Parliament at a by-election for Helston. Having also supported the Tory cause at the London contest, in the course of the first session he was identified by Abel Boyer as one of the 'High Church' candidates standing at the elections for the East India Company. Child, in fact, was the only candidate put forward by both the ministry and its opponents, a unique status which may be attributed to the influence of his father, who was at this time both a leading City figure and a close ally of the Tory administration.[4]

Most surprisingly, in his first session Child acted as a teller against a Tory motion condemning the conduct of the mayor of Weymouth at a recent parliamentary election. However, he was classed as one of the 'worthy patriots' who in this session helped to detect the mismanagements of the previous administration, and was cited as a member of the October Club. If he did join the club, it must have been only for a short time, since his name did not appear in the list of members published by Boyer in February 1712. Certainly, both he and his father showed strong support for the ministry's commercial initiatives, investing heavily in the South Sea Company. In the second session Child jnr. displayed a natural interest in fiscal affairs, acting as a teller in favour of imposing a duty on all imported soap. Most significantly, he even maintained the party line over the French commerce bill, ignoring the opposition of many of his City colleagues to vote with the administration in the division of 18 June 1713.[5]

By 1713 Child was acting as a leading government creditor in his own right, and in the general election of that year took over the family seat at Devizes. In the new Parliament, his only significant appointment was to the committee to draft a bill to enforce a contract drawn up by the commission for 50 new churches, of which he was an active member. On his father's death in October 1713 he succeeded as head of the family bank, as an alderman of London, and as colonel of the Orange regiment of trained bands. In April 1714 he was elected deputy governor of the East India Company after a struggle with the Bank of England interest headed by (Sir) Gilbert Heathcote*, and soon afterwards Lord Treasurer Oxford (Robert Harley*) 'took particular notice' of Child when a delegation from the company attended the minister.[6]

Following the accession of George I Child gained recognition at court, significantly as one of the few City Tories to be honoured with a knighthood by the new King. His allies may have resented such preferment, for the *Secret History of the White Staff* (1714) identified 'Sir R. Ch.' as one of the 'jobbers and monied men' who had grown rich at the nation's expense. However, he did not convert to the Whigs, and soon afterwards lost his colonelcy of militia. He chose not to contest the general election of 1715, but his Tory pedigree was confirmed by the Worsley list. In the years after 1715 banking and commercial affairs consumed his energies until his death at Osterley Park on 6 Oct. 1721. His brother Francis inherited his estate, and became the new head of Child's bank.[7]

[1] IGI, London; *CSP Dom*. 1697, p. 181. [2] W. T. Prideaux, *Wardens, Members and Liverymen of Goldsmiths' Co.* 8, 40; Beaven, *Aldermen*, ii. 123. [3] J. Aubrey, *Surr*. v. 310; *Cal. Treas. Bks*. xxvii. 7. [4] *Survey of London*, iii. 56; Boyer, *Pol. State*, i. 263; Huntington Lib. Stowe mss 58(8), p. 73. [5] R. Bank of Scotland Archs. Child mss CH/199. [6] *Cal. Treas. Bks*. 83, 92; *London Rec. Soc*. xxiii.178; Add. 70273, Mathew Decker to Thomas Harley*, 5/16 Mar., 2/13, 16/27 Apr., 30 Apr./11 May 1714. [7] *Secret Hist. of White Staff*, pt. 3, p. 38; Beaven, 123; PCC 177 Buckingham.

P. W./P. L. G.

CHISENHALL, Sir Edward (1646–1727), of Chisnall Hall, Coppull, Lancs.

WIGAN   1689–1690
PRESTON   5 Dec. 1690–1695

b. 14 Oct. 1646, 3rd but 1st surv. s. of Edward Chisenhall of Chisnall Hall and Gray's Inn by Elizabeth, da. of Alexander Rigby of Layton, Lancs. *m*. (1) bef. Apr. 1665, Anne, da. of Thomas Atkinson of Blew Hall, Essex, 1da.; (2) 25 Apr. 1671, Elizabeth, illegit. da. of Sir William Playters, 2nd Bt., of Sotterley, Suff., 2s. 1da.; (3) 21 Sept. 1683, Elizabeth, da. and coh. of Hon. Richard Spencer† of Orpington, Kent, *s.p. suc*. fa. 1654; kntd. 24 Apr. 1671.[1]

Burgess, Wigan by 1684; freeman, Preston 1702.[2]

Chisenhall had extensive landholdings in Lancashire and had acquired the manor of Billingford, Norfolk by his second marriage. Having served for Wigan in the Convention, he stood for the borough in 1690 but was unable or unwilling to force a poll, losing the second seat to Peter Shakerley. The chance to revive his parliamentary career came with the summons of the Preston Member, and chancellor of the duchy of Lancaster, Lord Willoughby de Eresby (Robert Bertie*) to the Lords in April 1690, but although Chisenhall began treating in the spring of 1690 a petition against Willoughby's return prevented the issuing of a writ. Despite this delay Chisenhall was in London in October to hear 'so gracious a speech as the King has made, and especially in that all accounts are ready to be laid before you [the Commons] – a sure way for his Majesty to be supplied by all of you, and, by all you represent, will be most cheerfully paid'. When a writ for the Preston by-election was finally issued in December Chisenhall, standing with the support of Lord Willoughby, the corporation and the 9th Earl of Derby, 'carried it by 57 votes', and in April 1691 Robert

Harley* thought him a likely Country party supporter, though marking this classification as doubtful, presumably due to Chisenhall's recent return to the House.[3]

Chisenhall did not, however, prove an active Member. In October 1694 he was one of the Tory gentlemen removed, at the insistence of the prosecution, from the jury at the trial of those implicated in the Lancashire Plot, but once the case against the accused had collapsed Chisenhall was required to return to the jury, after which it proceeded to an acquittal. He described his experiences at Manchester to the Commons on 22 Nov., being one of the Members who highlighted 'the scandalousness of the evidence and of the judges suffering all the gentlemen to be challenged and none but ordinary freeholders left on [the jury]'. His endeavours at Manchester led to his removal from the Lancashire bench in March 1695. During the final session of the 1695 Parliament Chisenhall was included on Henry Guy's* list of 'friends', compiled in connexion with the Commons attack upon Guy, and on 6 Mar. 1695 he was granted a leave of absence by the House. Although thought a likely victor should he stand at Preston in 1695, Chisenhall instead attempted to regain his seat at Wigan, but was comprehensively defeated at the poll, having ceased to campaign some time beforehand. He twice more figured in Wigan elections, in 1698 and 1702, but it appears that he campaigned actively on neither occasion, and it may be that the small number of votes he received in both elections were merely protests against the candidates on offer. Though restored to Lancashire's commission of the peace in 1702, Chisenhall ceased to play an active role in Lancashire politics, but such inactivity did not prevent his being displaced from the bench after the Hanoverian succession. He was buried at Standish, Lancashire on 1 Apr. 1727 and was succeeded by his son. Following the death of Chisenhall's only grandson in the 1730s his lands passed to his daughter's husband, Stephen Hamerton of Hellifield Peel, Yorkshire.[4]

[1] *Standish Par. Reg.* (Lancs. Par. Reg. Soc. lvi), 104; *Le Neve's Knights* (Harl. Soc. viii), 247–8; *Harl. Soc. Reg.* lxiv. 182; lxxxiv. 63; *VCH Lancs.* vi. 226–7. [2] NLS, Crawford mss 47/3/78, list of Wigan burgesses, Dec. 1684; W. A. Abram, *Mems. Preston Guild*, 72. [3] Cumbria RO (Kendal), Le Fleming mss WD/Ry/3740, R. Fleming to Sir Daniel Fleming†, 16 Feb. 1689[–90]; *Bellingham Diary* ed. Hewitson, 106, 117, 119; Lancs. RO, Kenyon mss DDKe/HMC/749, Chisenhall to Roger Kenyon*, 10 Oct. 1690; 754, Thomas Hodgkinson to same, 5 Dec. 1690; DDKe 9/131/36, Thomas Winckley to Derby, 27 Apr. 1690. [4] *Jacobite Trials Manchester 1694* (Chetham Soc. ser. 1, xxviii), 64, 102; Bodl. Carte 130, f. 353; L. K. J. Glassey, *Appt. JPs*, 281, 285; Kenyon mss DDKe/HMC/967, Charles Rigby to Kenyon, 17 Sept. 1695; DDKe 9/71/42, Sir Roger Bradshaigh, 3rd Bt.*, to same, c.1695; Devonshire mss at Chatsworth House, Finch-Halifax pprs. box 4 bdle. 12, j.p.s put out of commission, c.1715.

E. C./R. D. H.

CHIVERS, Henry (c.1653–1720), of Quemerford, nr. Calne, Wilts.

CALNE 1689–1695, 1698–1700, 23 Mar. 1702–1705

b. c.1653, o. s. of Seacole Chivers of Quemerford and Leigh Delamere, Wilts. by Eleanor, da. and coh. of John Roberts of Fiddington, Ashchurch, Glos. *m.* by 1693, Bridget (*d.* 1724), da. of Duke Stonehouse† of Stock House, Great Bedwyn, Wilts., sis. of Francis Stonehouse*, 1da. *suc.* fa. 1657.[1]

Sheriff, Wilts. 1677–8; alderman, Malmesbury 1685–7.[2]

Capt. of ft. Duke of Beaufort's regt. 1685–7, Queen Dowager's regt. (later 2 Ft.) 1687–9; lt.-col. 1 Ft. Gds. 1689–90.

Chivers' family had occupied a leading position in the cloth trade at Calne since the mid-16th century, and had acquired considerable property in Wiltshire and Oxfordshire. Although Chivers was an infant when his father died, the latter's connexions ensured that he was early associated with the leading local gentry; he had two guardians during his minority, and the family estate was administered by Thomas Hungerford of Blackland and William Duckett† of Hartham, both in Wiltshire. These connexions were strengthened by his own marriage, and that of his sister to John Methuen*. In addition, his estate centred upon Calne was worth about £1,000 p.a. in 1680, and gave him a strong interest in the borough. Returned again in 1690, he was classed as a Tory, and possibly a Court supporter in Lord Carmarthen's (Sir Thomas Osborne†) analysis of the new Parliament. Although he left his regiment in 1690, he was still included among the Court party in Robert Harley's* list of April 1691. Never a particularly active Member, he was granted leave of absence three times during this Parliament: on 7 Feb. 1693, for a fortnight, to attend his sick wife; and again on 26 Dec. 1693 and 25 Jan. 1695 because of his own ill-health. He does not appear to have put up in 1695, when his parliamentary seat was taken by George Hungerford, but after Hungerford's death he came in again at the 1698 general election, probably without opposition. Listed as a member of the Country party in a comparative analysis of about September 1698, he was also forecast as likely to support the disbanding bill, and seems to have voted for it. Following the bill's success in the Commons, he wrote to friends in Calne and Chippenham giving an account of the crucial vote of 18 Jan. 1699, which, he said, 'God be praised, we carried'. In one letter he enclosed a copy of a list of the minority in this division. What brought these letters to public attention, and conferred on Chivers some notoriety, were the comments he made on the conduct of some of his fellow Wiltshire MPs who had voted against the bill. His colleague at Calne, Henry Blaake, was denounced as a Court stooge, and even his own brother-in-law, Francis Stonehouse, did not remain unscathed: Stonehouse 'had his share of the colonel's scandal', it was reported. These attempts at blackguarding political opponents misfired badly. In Wiltshire they did not win him either 'interest' or 'reputation', and one local explanation of the quarrel between Chivers and Blaake was that it was caused by nothing more than the fact that 'one man can't serve two masters'. The matter was brought before the Commons on 4 Apr. 1699 when a complaint was made against Chivers for having 'reflected on' and 'misrepresented' Members. He had taken the precaution of securing a month's leave of absence on 25 Feb., and was thus ordered to attend on 14 Apr. On that day the Speaker read a letter in which Chivers referred to an illness, but also his intention to attend the House. Given a day's grace, he still failed to appear and a motion to send for him in custody was lost by 134 votes to 99. Ordered to attend on the 22nd, he again pleaded ill-health. The Commons then debated the complaint in his absence, voting that the publishing the names of Members, 'reflecting' on them and misrepresenting the proceedings of the House was a breach of privilege and 'destructive of the freedom of Parliament', but put off considering Chivers' role in the matter until the 26th. The matter was then quietly dropped. He made little further impression on this Parliament, and on 9 Feb. 1700 was given leave of absence once again, to recover his health.[3]

Perhaps for reasons of health, or because of the blow his reputation had suffered over the affair of the disbanding bill, Chivers did not stand at either of the two elections in 1701, though he was returned again at a by-election in March 1702 and held his seat, without opposition, in the general election later that year. Twice forecast as a probable supporter of the Tack, he duly voted for it on 28 Nov. 1704. He was again in trouble the following year, when at about the time of the general election he made repeated slanderous allegations against Bishop Burnet, that 'on many occasions, and in many companies', he 'with some others' had seen Burnet 'in an infamous place, and in a scandalous deportment'. Whether or not these incidents had any connexion with the election, Chivers does not seem to have been a candidate himself. In November 1705, however, Defoe reported to Harley that, following the death of Walter White*, a campaign had been set on foot by some Wiltshire Tories to bring in Chivers, 'that scandal to all good manners' and 'the profoundest rake and bully in the county' at the ensuing by-election at Chippenham, the main purpose of the manoeuvre being to 'shelter' him from the action for *scandalum magnatum* which Burnet had begun. Defoe thought that the best way 'to prevent this project' would be to have Chivers removed from the commission of the peace,

> to which he is really a horrible scandal, for by being in that power he influences the town, sits diligently at every petty sessions, and awes the people. He was at this work when I was in Chippenham . . . his character will most clearly justify it, and no man can object.

Presumably on this recommendation, Chivers was displaced from the commission before the by-election. He was then defeated, and, denied this way of escape, was obliged swiftly to seek terms with the bishop. On his agreeing to publish an abject recantation and apology, and to give £50 'for the use of the poor', Burnet dropped the suit. Thereafter little was heard of Chivers, and he did not again stand for Parliament.[4]

Chivers made his will on 26 Apr. 1720, aged 67, and died four days later. He left most of his property in Wiltshire and Gloucestershire to his wife, and other specified lands to a number of local gentry. He was buried at Leigh Delamere, where he had inherited land from his father.[5]

[1] PCC 85 Buckingham, 541 Ruthen; *Wilts. N. and Q*, iii. 520; *Wilts. Arch. Mag.* xxiv. 218. [2] *CSP Dom.* 1685, p. 64. [3] A. E. W. Marsh, *Hist. Calne*, 119; Aubrey and Jackson, *Wilts. Colls.* 38; Bath mss at Longleat House, Thynne pprs. 24, f. 164; *Wilts. Arch. Mag.* 46, 73–74, 77; Bodl. Carte 228, f. 302; Cobbett, *Parlty. Hist.* v. 1198. [4] *London Gazette*, 22–26 Nov. 1705; Luttrell, *Brief Relation*, v. 565, 614; *Defoe Letters*, 103–4, 110; L. K. J. Glassey, *Appt. JPs*, 167; Speck thesis, 310–11. [5] PCC 541 Ruthen.

D. W. H./H.J.L.

CHOLMLEY, Hugh (1684–1755), of Abbey House, Whitby, Yorks.

HEDON 1708–Nov. 1721

b. 3 Aug. 1684, 1st s. of Nathaniel Cholmley of St. Martin's-in-the-Fields, London, merchant, by Mary, da. and h. of Sir Hugh Cholmley, 4th Bt.†, of Abbey House. *educ.* Enfield g.s.; Magdalene, Camb. 1700. *m.* 16 Mar. 1717, Katherine, da. of Sir John Wentworth, 1st Bt., of North Elmsall, Yorks., 8s. (4 *d.v.p.*) 4da. *d.v.p.* suc. fa. 1727.[1]

Surveyor-gen. crown lands 1715–22; commr. victualling Nov. 1721–Mar. 1722.[2]

Sheriff, Yorks. 1724–5.

Cholmley inherited Abbey House through his mother, whose family had long represented Scarborough in Parliament. In 1707 he was appointed by

Lord Keeper Cowper (William*) as a justice of the peace for the North Riding. When he was returned for Hedon in 1708, apparently with the support of William Pulteney*, Cholmley's election was reckoned a 'gain' for the Whigs by Lord Sunderland (Charles, Lord Spencer*). This was an accurate classification, as in 1709 he supported the naturalization of the Palatines, and the following year he voted for the impeachment of Dr Sacheverell. Cholmley had intended to stand for Scarborough in 1710 but, not finding enough support, had been returned for Hedon. He was marked as a Whig in the 'Hanover list', and it was probably Hugh rather than John Cholmley who told on 15 Dec. for the motion to add four names to the land tax commission for Kent and on 27 Jan. 1711 against John Boteler's* election for Hythe, and who was given leave of absence on 5 Mar. for one month. However, Hugh Cholmley was back in the House on 25 May, when he sided with a hard core of Whigs in opposition to the administration, and voted against the amendment to the South Sea bill.[3]

The death of John Cholmley in 1711 makes it easy to identify Hugh henceforth in the proceedings of the House. During the 1711–12 session he told on 19 Feb. 1712 against a motion accusing the Duke of Marlborough's (John Churchill†) secretary, Adam de Cardonnel*, of corruption in relation to provisions for the army. In the following session Cholmley told on two occasions in May 1713 against suspending the duties on imported French wines. On 9 June he acted as a teller in favour of recommitting the report on the French commerce treaty of 1674, while in the debate of the 18th on the bill for confirming the 8th and 9th articles of the new commercial treaty he spoke and voted against the bill, being listed as a Whig. The following day he reported from the committee appointed to consider the petition of some army officers for payment of arrears. Noted as a Whig in the Worsley list, in the 1714 session he voted on 18 Mar. against the expulsion of Richard Steele. On the 31st Cholmley told in favour of discharging from custody Thomas Glascock, who had been arrested for refusing the Tory Nicholas Corsellis* access to Colchester borough records while the latter had been preparing for a disputed election case. Cholmley also told on 6 Apr. for a motion to allow Lord Barrymore (James Barry*) to present a new petition relating to the Wigan election of 1713, and on the 19th in favour of making the commissioners to treat with France ineligible to sit in the House. The following month he told for a motion to include Roman Catholics within the schism bill (12 May), and on 16 June against a motion to instruct the elections committee to proceed with hearing the merits of the Harwich election.[4]

Re-elected for Hedon in 1715, Cholmley was noted as a Whig in a list which compared the 1715 Parliament with its predecessor. He was appointed to government office at the accession of George I, replacing Alexander Pendarves* as surveyor-general. Subsequently he moved from Abbey House to Howsham Hall in the North Riding, a Jacobean house he had acquired by marriage. He died there on 25 May 1755 and was buried at Whitby.[5]

[1] *Dugdale's Vis. Yorks.* ed. Clay, ii. 256–7. [2] *Cal. Treas. Bks.* xxix. 338. [3] J. Taylor, *A Journey to Edinburgh*, 71; Clay, 253–7; Herts. RO, Panshanger mss, D/EP F152, list of j.p.s put in or put out by Ld. Cowper, [1707]; *EHR*, lxxxii. 483; *Hist. Jnl.* iv. 197–8. [4] SRO, Cromartie mss GD305 addit./bdle. 15, [?] to [Earl of Cromarty], 20 June 1713. [5] F. R. Pearson, *Abbey House, Whitby and Cholmley Fam.* 29–30.

E. C./C. I. M.

CHOLMLEY, John (c.1661–1711), of Morgan's Lane, St. Olave's, Southwark, Surr.

SOUTHWARK   1698–10 Nov. 1702
                 25 Nov. 1702–24/25 Oct. 1711

b. c.1661, 1st s. of John Cholmley of St. Olave's, Southwark by his wife Mary. *m.* 25 July 1687, aged 26, Alice, da. of John Standbrook of St. Margaret's, Westminster, 2s. 3 da. *suc.* fa. 1685.

Freeman, Brewers' Co. 1686, master 1706; commr. taking subscriptions to S. Sea Co. 1711.[1]

The family brewery had been established in Southwark for at least two generations by the time Cholmley came to inherit it in 1685. His father's prominence in the trade was attested by the royal custom he enjoyed under Charles II, and, when attending a Nonconformist meeting in December 1681, Cholmley senior was actually identified as 'the King's brewer'. Cholmley himself remained a staunch Whig throughout his political career, faithfully reflecting the views of a constituency which boasted a significant Dissenting interest. His support for the Revolution was indicated by several loans which he made to the crown in 1689–90, amounting to £7,500. Having advanced another £3,500, in July 1694 he became one of the first subscribers to the Bank of England. His professional status was confirmed in March 1697 when he led a deputation of brewers to the Treasury to protest against the debts owed by the victualling office, at which time he probably owned one of the largest breweries in the capital.[2]

The subsequent run of electoral success which Cholmley enjoyed at Southwark alongside his fellow brewer and parishioner Charles Cox* was principally based on the strength of the brewing industry in the constituency. Moreover, by 1698 he had already cultivated local support by several benefactions to St. Thomas' Hospital. His first election victory was comfortably achieved, and though a list of 1698 described his political allegiance as doubtful, by early 1700 an analysis of the House listed him with the Junto interest. In the House Cholmley proved an inconspicuous figure. In November 1701, after achieving their most conclusive election victory to date, Cholmley and Cox were presented with an instruction in the name of 'the inhabitants of Southwark' which was strongly in support of the war. The very next day the two Members led a crowd of 'about 500 liverymen' to vote for the Whig candidates at the London election and in the following month Robert Harley* listed Cholmley with the Whigs. In contrast to such vigorous campaigning at the polls, Cholmley's only significant action in the ensuing Parliament concerned a tellership on 27 Feb. 1702 in favour of adjourning all committees.[3]

The first Southwark election under Anne proved the most testing electoral hurdle of Cholmley's political career. Having achieved a convincing victory over John Lade* in mid-July, the sitting Whig Members were then forced to contest the seat again after the House had declared the election void in response to reports of a 'great tumult and riot' at the poll. However, on 25 Nov. the Whig brewers prevailed at the second election, and in the ensuing session Cholmley's politics were confirmed by his support on 13 Feb. 1703 for the Lords' amendments to the bill to extend the time for taking the abjuration oath. In addition, on 30 Oct. 1704 he was forecast as a probable opponent of the Tack, and on 28 Nov. either voted against this measure or was absent from the House. Having enjoyed an uncontested victory at the Southwark election of 1705, at the outset of the new Parliament he was classified by a parliamentary list as 'No Church', an assessment perhaps reflecting his father's influence. He certainly maintained his political principles, voting Whig at the Surrey election of 1705, and supporting the Court over the choice of Speaker on 25 Oct., as well as in February 1706, when the House considered the regency bill's place clause. In that session he was also involved in a division of 17 Dec. 1705 relating to a land tax bill, telling against an amendment affecting the Marshalsea court, whose prison lay in St. George's, Southwark.

His political outlook confirmed by two parliamentary lists of 1708, Cholmley was returned for Southwark unopposed at the election of that year. However, in the wake of the election he was joined in the House by his namesake Hugh, Member for Hedon, whose presence confounds any attempt to ascertain the subsequent Commons activity of the Southwark brewer. Cholmley clearly remained a loyal party man in the ensuing sessions, voting for the naturalization of the Palatines in early 1709, as well as for the impeachment of Dr Sacheverell a year later. Both issues helped to deepen divisions within his Southwark constituency, but the strength of his local support was highlighted by the election of 1710 when both the sitting Members were returned, thereby defying the Tory tide sweeping the nation. Having voted in an accustomed vein at both the Surrey and London polls, he was classed as a Whig in the 'Hanover list' and duly voted against the amendment to the South Sea bill on 25 May 1711, his last significant act in the House before he died. Some confusion remains concerning the date of Cholmley's death, Boyer recording it as 24 Oct., while Le Neve suggests that Cholmley passed away the following day. It may well have been a sudden demise, given his probable age and the fact that he died intestate. Although one of his two sons did emulate him by entering the Brewers' Company, neither chose to follow their father into politics.[4]

[1]W. Rendle and P. Morgan, *Inns of Old Southwark*, 53; IGI, London; *Mar. Lic. Vicar-Gen. 1687–99* (Harl. Soc. xxxi), 6; Guildhall Lib. ms 5445/23, p. 106; 5445/24, p. 471; Pittis, *Present Parl.* 348. [2]PCC 170 Aylett, 83 Cann; *Cal. Treas. Bks.* vii. 1406; ix. 644, 1980, 2001; x. 720; xi. 361; *CSP Dom.* 1680–1, p. 630; DZA, Bonet's despatch 6/16 July 1694; P. Mathias, *Brewing Industry*, 9. [3]J. Aubrey, *Surr.* v. 296; *Advice of Inhabitants of Southwark* [1701]; Add. 70075, newsletter 27 Nov. 1701. [4]*Surr. Polls of 1705, 1710*; *London Poll of 1710*; Boyer, *Anne Annals*, x. 384; Le Neve, *Mon. Angl.* 1700–15, p. 233; PCC Admon. 7 Dec. 1711, f. 224; Guildhall Lib. ms 5445/25, p. 53.

E. C./P. L. G.

CHOLMONDELEY, Charles (1685–1756), of Vale Royal, Cheshire.

CHESHIRE 1710–1715, 1722–30 Mar. 1756

b. 12 Jan. 1685, 1st surv. s. of Thomas Cholmondeley† of Vale Royal by Anne, da. of Sir Walter St. John, 3rd Bt.*, and sis. of Henry St. John I*. *educ.* St. John's, Camb. 1701; M. Temple 1709. *m.* 22 July 1714, Essex, da. of Thomas Pitt I*, 3s. (2 *d.v.p.*) 5da. *suc.* fa. 1702.[1]

The Cholmondeleys of Vale Royal were a junior branch of Cheshire's leading family the Cholmondeleys of Cholmondeley, the family having been settled in the county since the 13th century. In contrast to the political vacillations of the senior branch of the family, the Cholmondeleys of Vale Royal were loyal Tories. Cholmondeley's father and uncle, who had both sat during the Restoration, became non-jurors after the Revolution and both were suspected of involvement in Jacobite plotting during the 1690s. Little is known of Cholmondeley's early life, and he made no impact upon the public stage until his opposition to the Weaver navigation bill of 1709–10. At the 1710 election he stood on Cheshire's Tory interest against the county's 'two impeaching Members' and was returned after a contested election. He was classed as a Tory in the 'Hanover list'.[2]

Cholmondeley was an active parliamentarian and his Tory sympathies were confirmed in the 1710–11 session. He was appointed on 9 June 1711 to take a message to the Lords to remind the Upper House of the bill sent from the Commons for the better qualification of j.p.s. The session also saw Cholmondeley tell for referring a petition against an enclosure Act passed in the last session to committee (3 Feb.), and carry to the Lords a bill repealing part of the act encouraging trade to America (4 June). He was also listed as a 'worthy patriot' who had helped detect the mismanagements of the previous ministry and as a member of the October Club.

Cholmondeley's willingness to support policies which, while close to Tory hearts, were opposed by the ministry, appears to have concerned Harley at the end of the 1710–11 session, and in a list of June 1711, Harley linked Cholmondeley's name with that of the 4th Earl Rivers (Richard Savage*). Rivers' support in the Cheshire election of 1710 had been an important factor in Cholmondeley's victory, and it may be that Harley hoped that pressure from Rivers would be sufficient to prevent Cholmondeley from involving himself any further in attempts to force more partisan policies on the ministry. If this was the case, then the attempt was unsuccessful, as the 1711–12 session saw Cholmondeley increasingly involve himself in the attempts of Tory back-benchers to influence policy. This was evident in his enthusiastic participation in the Tory attack upon the conduct of Robert Walpole II* and Adam de Cardonnel*, when he was teller in favour of the expulsion of both men (17 Jan., 19 Feb. 1712). Cholmondeley was also an advocate of the Tory-sponsored crown grants resumption bill, and on 10 May the Commons' ballot for commissioners to serve under this bill put Cholmondeley in fourth place. A combination of partisan and Country sentiment also explains Cholmondeley's advocacy of the bill to prevent 'fraudulent conveyances, in order to multiply votes' in county elections, a practice blamed by Cheshire Tories for their defeat in 1705. The first-named Member of the committee appointed on 18 Feb. to draft this bill, he guided the measure through the Commons, chairing the committee of the whole upon it on 4 Apr. In the course of the bill's passage the question of whether Quakers willing to affirm should be entitled to vote was raised, and on 4 Apr. and 15 May Cholmondeley told in favour of amendments in favour of Quaker voting rights. One modern historian has explained Tory support for Quaker affirmation as the consequence of the concern of March Club members to support Protestant unity, and by 1712 Cholmondeley had transferred his allegiance from the October to the March Club. Indeed, when Cholmondeley was elected a commissioner for the resumption of crown grants, Kreienberg included him among the five members of the March Club successful in this ballot. However, Cholmondeley's support for Quaker voting rights probably had its roots in less exalted motives, as Quakers formed a small but significant group in the Cheshire electorate, and in 1710 Cholmondeley had approached William Penn, through Harley, for their votes. Cholmondeley was keenly aware of the need to promote and defend Cheshire interests, and this attention to local interests explains his telling against the imposition of an additional duty on imported hides (22 May), a measure which Chester's tanners opposed strenuously, though in vain.[3]

In the following session Cholmondeley remained a proponent of Country Tory measures. He supported enthusiastically the equalization of the malt tax throughout Britain in order to allow a 2s. reduction in the land tax, and in the crucial division of 21 May 1713 told in favour of retaining the clause in the bill imposing the 6d. a bushel duty on Scottish malt. His concern for the conduct of county elections was again apparent in May as he managed a bill to make 'more effectual' the Act he had guided through the Commons in the previous session to regulate county elections, and his continued support for Quaker voting rights was evident in his telling in favour of confirming the Quaker Affirmation Act (28 May). The bill brought before the House in this session to confirm the 8th and 9th articles of the French commercial treaty saw Cholmondeley's first demonstration of the Hanoverian sympathies associated with membership of the March Club. Although Cholmondeley had presented, in July 1712 and May 1713 respectively, Cheshire addresses thanking the Queen for the peace preliminaries and the Treaty of Utrecht, it was clear once the French commerce bill came before the Commons that he was unhappy with its provisions. When the bill was considered by the Commons on 18 June Cholmondeley spoke and voted against it, being classed as a 'whimsical' in the printed division list. This session also saw Cholmondeley manage a Cheshire estate bill through the Commons in June and early July.[4]

Cholmondeley was unopposed in the 1713 election, and in the ensuing Parliament his sympathy for Country measures and his Hanoverian loyalties were again evident. On 11 Mar. 1714, Cholmondeley seconded the motion for a place bill proposed by Sir Arthur Kaye, 3rd Bt., expressing the hope that 'we should give no money [until] we saw the success of this bill'. Cholmondeley was appointed the same day to draft this measure. His support for Country measures also explains his telling, with Kaye, against the motion of 14 June that existing commissioners of public accounts who wished to continue serving should be reappointed. His concern for the Hanoverian succession led him to speak against the Court in the debate of 16 Apr. upon this issue, but his attitude towards the schism bill demonstrates that he had not abandoned his Tory beliefs. When the Commons considered the introduction of this measure on 12 May, Cholmondeley told against a Whig amendment to extend the bill to include Catholics and was then included among those appointed to draft this measure. He told on two more occasions: against an address asking that papers concerned with the demolition of Dunkirk be laid before the House (15 Mar.), and for bringing in a petition for repealing an act of the Irish parliament (12 Apr.). Not surprisingly, given his attitude during the session, he was classed in the Worsley list as a Tory who had often voted with the Whigs in the 1713 Parliament.[5]

In stark contrast to his unopposed return in 1713, Cholmondeley was abandoned by a number of his Tory supporters in the Cheshire election of 1715. Ostensibly because of the loss of the support of a number of local magnates and a desire to prevent further conflict, a compromise between Whig and Tory interests, to exclude Cholmondeley, had been agreed at the county meeting of August 1714. After much prevarication, and after Peter Legh[†] had vetoed an offer by John Ward III* to stand aside for him at Newton, Cholmondeley decided to take the issue to a poll. His 'whimsical' voting record appears to have counted against him with a number of the county's Tories, and the perception of his unreliability would not have been lessened by his marriage in the summer of 1714 to the daughter of his fellow 'whimsical' Thomas Pitt I*. Despite assurances that he 'remain[ed] a true friend to the establishm[en]t in Church and State', Cholmondeley was defeated at the poll in February 1715. He returned to the Commons in 1722, voting consistently with the opposition. As late as 1743 he was included in a list of those who might be expected to support the calling of a free Parliament after a French-supported Stuart restoration. Cholmondeley died on 30 Mar. 1756, when he was succeeded by his son in both his estates and his parliamentary seat.[6]

[1] G. Ormerod, *Cheshire*, ii. 157–8 [2] *Cheshire Vis. Peds.* (Harl. Soc. xciii), 26–28; Westminster Cathedral Archs. Old Brotherhood mss iii/3/232; *Orig. Pprs.* ed. Macpherson i. 475; *HMC Kenyon*, 293; T. S. Willan, *Navigation of R. Weaver in 18th Cent.* (Chetham Soc. ser. 3, iii.), 11. [3] Add. 70332, memo. 4 June 1711; Grosvenor mss at Eaton Hall, pprs. of the 4th Bt., Peter Shakerley* to city of Chester, 2 Dec. 1714; D. Szechi, *Jacobitism and Tory Pol.* 98, 108; Cobbett, *Parlty. Hist.* vi. 1130; NSA, Kreienberg despatch 16/27 May 1712; *Jnl. of Chester and N. Wales Architectural, Arch. and Hist. Soc.* ser. 2, xliv. 41–44. [4] Szechi, 130; *HMC Portland*, iv. 551; Chandler, v. 41. [5] Szechi, 174; *Bull. IHR*, xxxix. 64; NLS, Advocates' mss, Wodrow pprs. letters Quarto 8, ff. 64, 95. [6] Grosvenor mss, pprs. of the 4th Bt., Robert to Sir Richard Grosvenor, 4th Bt.[†], 3 June 1714; *Bull. John Rylands Lib.* lxxvi. 141–7; E. Cruickshanks, *Pol. Untouchables*, 116.

E. C./R. D. H.

CHOLMONDELEY, Hon. George (1666–1733), of Cholmondeley, Cheshire.

NEWTON 1690–1695

b. 1666, 3rd s. of Robert Cholmondeley (d. 1681) of Cholmondeley, 1st Visct. Cholmondeley of Kells [I], by Elizabeth, da. and coh. of George Cradock of Caverswall Castle, Staffs. *educ.* Westminster; Christ Church, Oxf. matric. 1680, DCL 1695; I. Temple 1680. *m.* Apr. 1698, Elizabeth (d. 1722), da. of Col. Albert van Ruytenburg van Vlaardingen, gov. of Sas van Ghent 1685–9, 3s. (1 d.v.p.) 3 da. *cr.* Baron Newborough of Newborough [I] 12 Apr. 1715, Baron Newburgh [GB] 10 July 1716; *suc.* er. bro. Hugh as 2nd Earl of Cholmondeley 18 Jan. 1725.[1]

Cornet, indep. tp. of horse June 1685; capt. of horse, Ld. Dover's regt. Sept. 1685, Queen Consort's regt. 1686; lt.-col. 1 tp. Life Gds. 1689; col. tp. of horse, Gren. Gds. 1693–Feb. 1715, 1 tp. horse Gren. Gds. (3 tp. Life Gds.) Feb. 1715–*d.*; brig.-gen. 1697, maj.-gen. 1702, lt.-gen. 1704, gen. of horse 1727; gov. of Tilbury and Gravesend 1702–Feb. 1725, Chester ?1705, by 1710–?16, 1725–*d*, Hull Feb. 1725–Oct. 1732, Guernsey Oct. 1732–*d*.[2]

Groom of bedchamber to William III 1691–1702; PC 21 May 1706.[3]

Steward of Richmond, Surr. 1702; ld. lt. and custos rot. Cheshire 1725–*d.*; ld. lt. and vice-adm. N. Wales 1725–*d*; freeman, Chester 1725.[4]

FRS 1715.

Established in Cheshire by the 12th century, the Cholmondeleys of Cholmondeley had become one of the county's leading families, owning extensive lands thought in the 1670s to be worth £5,000 p.a. The family's rise was acknowledged with the award of an Irish peerage in 1628, and Cholmondeley's elder brother had succeeded to the title and estates in 1681. During James II's reign Cholmondeley began to make his career in the army, and in 1688 he took up arms for the Prince of Orange, joining the Earl of Devonshire (William Cavendish†) at Nottingham. The Cholmondeleys' political loyalties were, however, anything but straightforward. Cholmondeley's brother combined support for the Revolution, a moderate court Whiggery and a courtier's instincts when active in central politics, but with an inclination towards the Tories in Cheshire. Cholmondeley's own loyalties were similarly complex, allowing him to accumulate offices and grants under both William and Anne and to continue his rise under the first two Hanoverians.[5]

Cholmondeley's loyalty to Cheshire's Tories was evident in his attempts to enter Parliament. This was first mooted in January 1690 when his cousin Francis Cholmondeley, Member for Newton, was expelled from the Convention for refusing to take the oaths, but the Convention was dissolved before a writ could be issued for a by-election. The general election saw Cholmondeley enter the lists in Cheshire in alliance with the non-juror Sir Philip Egerton†, but he withdrew before the county meeting in March and was instead returned for Newton on the interest of his non-juring cousin Peter Legh† of Lyme, being classed by Lord Carmarthen (Sir Thomas Osborne†) in March 1690 as a probable Court supporter. Cholmondeley's responsibilities as a soldier restricted his parliamentary activity, and his only significant act in the 1690 session came in the debate of 24 Apr. on the Abjuration when he intervened in defence of Sir Thomas Grosvenor, 3rd Bt., who had been accused of using seditious words at the Chester election of 1690. Cholmondeley informed the Commons that Secretary Shrewsbury had told him that Grosvenor 'need not trouble himself, for this was some quarrel only about elections'. Cholmondeley served in Ireland in the summer of 1690, leading his regiment at the Boyne, and in September rumours circulated that he had been killed in action. These reports proved to be false. In December he was listed by Carmarthen as a likely supporter in the event of an attack on the lord president in the Commons, and the following April Robert Harley* classed him as a Court supporter. Cholmondeley received a Household post worth £500 p.a. at the end of 1691, and the following year again distinguished himself on the field of battle, at the cost of personal injury, at Steenkerk. He continued to serve in Flanders until the Treaty of Ryswick. Cholmondeley's contribution to parliamentary business was slight, though he regularly appears in lists of placemen compiled in the last three years of the Parliament, and in 1693 Grascome had classed him as a Court supporter with a place. Despite this inactivity Cholmondeley was keen to remain in the Commons, but his brother's failure to aid Peter Legh when accused of Jacobite conspiracy in 1694 led to Cholmondeley being dropped from Newton in 1695, despite his own willingness to assist Legh. An attempt was made by the Junto Whigs the Earl of Macclesfield (Charles Gerard*) and Earl Rivers (Richard Savage*) to have Cholmondeley stand for Cheshire in order to keep out the Country Whig Sir Robert Cotton, 1st Bt.*, but these suggestions received little support in the county and Cholmondeley was unable to take the shire to a poll.[6]

Out of Parliament, Cholmondeley concentrated on his military career. Marriage in 1698 to a Dutch connexion of the King's brought him favour at court, and Cholmondeley later claimed that at this time King William promised him a gift of £10,000 'or the value thereof in some grant'. Though the money was never forthcoming, Cholmondeley did subsequently obtain various grants, and his standing at court may explain his appointment to oversee the breaking up of regiments while his own troop was specifically excepted under the terms of the Disbanding Act of 1699. His soldiers were not perhaps so fortunate as their officers, for Cholmondeley did not pass his accounts promptly and foreign Protestants who had served under him in the Flanders campaigns complained to the Commons that they had been paid neither arrears nor subsistence. Cholmondeley showed no interest in returning to the Commons but appears to have continued to support the Tory interest in Cheshire: in the county election of December 1701 he advocated the return of Sir George Warburton, 3rd Bt.*, and Sir Roger Mostyn, 3rd Bt.* Marks of official favour continued to be bestowed upon him following the accession of Queen Anne. In 1702 he was granted a lease of lands in, and the stewardship of the manor of, Richmond, and in May the same year was named, through the influence of the Duke of Marlborough (John Churchill†), governor of Tilbury. The commander-in-chief hoped in vain that the appointment would persuade Cholmondeley not to press his claims for promotion to major-general, but in June Marlborough acquiesced in Cholmondeley's promotion. Narcissus Luttrell* reported in 1705 that Cholmondeley had succeeded Peter Shakerley* as governor of Chester, following the latter's support for the Tack, and the following year Cholmondeley was granted forfeited estates at Catterick in Yorkshire, worth £818 p.a., belonging to the Jacobite exile Sir Roger Strickland†. In 1707 Cholmondeley petitioned for a 50-year lease of Old Palace Yard in Richmond, and the following year this request was granted.[7]

The fall of the Marlborough–Godolphin ministry in 1710 led Cholmondeley, at least initially, to emphasize the Tory sympathies that had been evident in his activities in Cheshire politics. In January 1711 he lobbied Earl Rivers for a place for Peter Legh's impecunious brother Thomas II*. Cholmondeley's identification with the Tories at this time was reflected in a report of the Commons' proceedings he sent to Peter Legh the same month. He wrote that when the Commons considered the 'scandalous proceedings' of the previous ministry 'we carried our point', and expressed the fear that the place bill 'will be thrown out by the Lords'. That summer Cholmondeley petitioned Lord Treasurer Oxford (Robert Harley) for a grant of the whole of the manor of Richmond, pointing out that he had had 'the honour to serve the crown these 30 years' and had been passed over for military advancement despite being one of the oldest lieutenant-generals, as Marlborough had preferred 'to make room for his own creatures'. He also claimed to have spent great sums on this manor and that he was owed large arrears by the crown, but Oxford did nothing for him. In 1713 the ministers of the Elector of Hanover were informed that Cholmondeley was 'attached to the Protestant succession' and was one of the officers who 'might be depended upon', and following the Hanoverian succession he found great favour, being the first to obtain a coronation peerage from George I and rising steadily in honours. He died at Whitehall on 7 May 1733, having succeeded his elder brother to the earldom of Cholmondeley in 1725, and was buried at Malpas, Cheshire, ten days later. He was succeeded by his elder son George, who had sat for East Looe and Windsor since 1724 as a Court Whig.[8]

[1] IGI, Cheshire; F. J. G. ten Raa, *Het Staatsche Leger*, vi. 257, 299; vii. 404. [2] Luttrell, *Brief Relation*, v. 255–6. [3] *Cal. Treas. Bks.* x. 19; xvii. 953. [4] *Cal. Treas. Bks.* xvii. 237; xxix. 619; *Chester Freeman Rolls* (Lancs. and Cheshire Rec. Soc. lv), 272. [5] Ormerod, *Cheshire*, ii. 682; *VCH Cheshire*, ii. 103, 107; *Bull. John Rylands Lib.* lxiv. 376; *HMC 9th Rep.* pt. 2, p. 460; G. Holmes, *Pol. in Age of Anne*, 226–8. [6] Chester RO, Earwaker mss CR/63/2/691/71, 73, Sir Willoughby Aston, 2nd Bt., to Sir John Crewe, 18, 26 Feb. 1689[–90]; John Rylands Univ. Lib. Manchester, Legh of Lyme mss, Francis Cholmondeley to Peter Legh, 11 Jan. 1689[–90], 12 Oct. 1695, George to Ld. Cholmondeley, c.1690, Thomas† to Peter Legh, 6 Sept. 1690, Legh Bowden to same, 28 Sept. 1690, Thomas Bankes to same, 8 June 1695, c.1695, Legh to [?], c.1695; Grey, x. 79; *Cal. Treas. Bks.* x. 19; Challinor thesis, 182–7. [7] BL, Trumbull Add. mss 107, newsletter 7–17 June 1697; *CSP Dom.* 1697, p. 493; *Cal. Treas. Bks.* xvii. 202, 205, 237, 440; xx. 276, 450; xxi. 156; xxii. 373; *CJ*, xii. 627; Cheshire RO, Arderne mss DAR/F/33, acct. of Cheshire co. meeting, 1 Dec. 1701, list of new justices for Cheshire, July 1702; *Marlborough–Godolphin Corresp.* 72, 76, 84; Luttrell, 532; *HMC Portland*, v. 255–6. [8] *Lyme Letters* ed. Lady Newton, 233–4; *HMC Portland*, v. 18; *Orig. Pprs.* ed. Macpherson, ii. 478; *HMC Stuart*, iv. 40–41.

E. C./R. D. H.

CHOUTE (CHUTE), Sir George, 1st Bt. (1665–1722), of Surrenden, Bethersden, Kent.

WINCHELSEA 2 Nov. 1696–1698

bap. 10 Feb. 1665, posth. and o. s. of Sir George Choute of Hauxhill and Surrenden by Cicely (*d*. 1675), da. and coh. of Ralph Freke of Hannington, Wilts. *unm. suc.* fa. at birth; *cr.* Bt. 17 Sept. 1684.

Freeman, Hastings 1695, Winchelsea 1696.[1]

Choute's Kentish forebears could be traced back to early Tudor times. His grandfather and namesake had been an ardent Royalist and one of the Cavalier promoters of the 'Kentish Petition' of 1642, while his father, knighted in the early weeks of the Restoration, had seemed destined for a promising career in the service of the court before smallpox killed him at the age of 23. Born after his father's death, Choute was still a minor in 1684 when created a baronet, an honour which both recalled his family's past loyalty to the crown and sought his goodwill. The new status assured him also of a position in the forefront of county affairs, yet he had to wait until 1689 before being nominated to the lieutenancy and to the bench. His opportunity to enter Parliament came in August 1696 when the corporation of Winchelsea invited him to succeed his recently deceased (maternal) uncle, Colonel Robert Austen I*, as one of their representatives. His family ties with the previous Member and the proximity of his estate to the borough promised a degree of continuity and made him an appropriate choice. After he was elected unopposed in November, his sojourn in the House proved brief and unremarkable. A consistent pro-Court stance was retrospectively noted in a comparative listing of the new and old Houses of Commons drawn up shortly after the 1698 election. The only specific occasion on which he is known to have given the administration his support, however, was in the attainder of Sir John Fenwick† on 25 Nov. 1696. The sole reference to him in the Journals records a fortnight's leave of absence granted on 23 Dec. 1697. He made no apparent effort to stand for re-election in 1698.[2]

Choute's Whiggish sympathies are most clearly seen in his approbation of the celebrated Kentish petition of May 1701 urging the Commons to fulfil its obligation of supporting the war. In early July, upon the release of the five signatories who had been arrested on Tory initiative, Choute and Sir Thomas Roberts, 4th Bt.*, headed a delegation of local gentlemen and freeholders to welcome their return. Two of the five, William and Thomas Colepep(p)er, were in fact Choute's distant kinsmen through his grandmother's family. Well in advance of the 1705 election he was known to be harbouring 'pretensions' to one of the county seats but abandoned these thoughts in June 1704 as stronger Whig candidates began staking their claims. Thereafter, he showed no further interest in re-entering Parliament, but confined his attentions to parochial and magisterial chores. He is recorded as having voted Whig in the 1713 contest in Kent. He died unmarried on 4 Feb. 1722 and was buried at Bethersden, having bequeathed his estate to Edward Austen, his first cousin once removed. A monumental inscription praises him as a gentleman of archetypal virtue: 'a true lover of the interest of his country, a generous neighbour, a kind master and a faithful friend'.[3]

[1] Hastings Mus., Hastings ct. bk. C/A(a)2, f. 289; E. Suss. RO, Winchelsea ct. bk. WIN 60, p. 50. [2] *Arch. Cant.* xviii. 55–57, 67–70; A. M. Everitt, *Community of Kent and Gt. Rebellion 1640–60*, 95–107; *CSP Dom.* 1689–90, p. 206; info. from Prof. N. Landau; BL, Althorp mss, box 3, R. Crawford to Ld. Halifax (William Savile*, Ld. Eland), 22 Aug. 1696; box 8, Sir George Rooke* to same, 27 Aug., 3 Sept. 1696. [3] Add. 57861, f. 69; J. Cave-Browne, *Story of Hollingborne*, 35; Hasted, *Kent*, ii. 174–5; Bath mss at Longleat House, Thynne pprs. 17, f. 294; Centre Kentish Stud. Q/Rpe1; PCC Marlbro' 177; *Arch. Cant.* xviii. 70.

A. A. H.

CHUTE see CHOUTE

CHOWNE, Thomas (1679–1724), of Alfriston, Suss.

SEAFORD   27 Jan.–2 July 1702, 1710–1713

bap. 22 Apr. 1679, o. surv. s. of Thomas Chowne of Alfriston, by Elizabeth (*d.* 1688), da. of James Foice, yeoman, of Horsham, Suss. *educ.* Wadham, Oxf. matric. 1696; I. Temple 1696. *m.* 29 June 1703, Phoebe (*d.* 1713), da. and coh. of William Westbrook* of Ferring, Suss. 1s. 2da. *suc.* fa. 1688.[1]

Chowne's family had been settled at Alfriston since the early 17th century, having previously been established in Kent at Fairlawn, near Wrotham. It was his great-grandfather, Thomas, son of Sir George Chowne, MP for Rochester in 1593, who had brought the family to Alfriston. His grandfather, Henry, had served for Horsham in the Cavalier Parliament and enjoyed links with London's trading community. Chowne himself was still a minor when he inherited his father's estate in 1688. As soon as he came of age he began to assume the local responsibilities of a squire, becoming in 1701, for example, a surveyor of highways. In January the following year he landed himself the more exalted role of parliamentarian almost by chance. When one of the Seaford MPs, Sir William Thomas, 1st Bt., opted to sit for the county, Chowne, who held property in the port and whose Alfriston estate was only a short distance away, was a convenient replacement, and in the circumstances his return was a mere formality. Nothing is known of his political conduct in the House, though it is known that his sympathies were Tory. In the general election in the summer of 1702, Sir William reclaimed his old seat, and Chowne, apparently in deference to Sir William's seniority and long service in county affairs, stood down.[2]

Chowne attempted unsuccessfully to regain the seat at a by-election in December 1706 following Sir William Thomas' demise. Having avoided the election of 1708, he evidently saw his chances ripen with the improvement of Tory fortunes in 1710, and his candidacy at Seaford in that year forced a contest in which he displaced one of the sitting Whigs. He was marked as a Tory on the 'Hanover list' of the new Parliament and during the first session featured as a 'worthy patriot' who assisted in revealing the mismanagements of the old Whig ministry. He also became a member of the October Club. But he was equally preoccupied at this time with the affairs of his parish, serving in the offices of churchwarden and overseer of the poor in 1712.[3]

Chowne stood down at the 1713 election, and made no subsequent attempt to re-enter Parliament. He died on 16 Sept. 1724 and was buried at Alfriston, having made bequests of £2,000 each to his two daughters, while the bulk of his estate passed to his only son.[4]

[1] *The Gen.* n.s. xxiv. 78–80; Berry, *Sussex Genealogies*, 133. [2] *The Gen.* 73–79; E. Suss. RO, AMS 5567/1, Alfriston church bk. (unpag.). [3] Ibid. [4] Berry, 133; *The Gen.* 79.

A. A. H.

CHRISTIE, Thomas (1622–97), of Bedford.

BEDFORD   1685–1687, 1689–1690
            12 Apr. 1690–1695

bap. 30 Jan. 1622, 1st s. of Thomas Christie of Bedford by Jane, da. of William Faldo of Bedford. *m.* (1) aft. June

1646, Alice (d. 1666), da. and h. of John Poole, Brewer, of London, wid. of Charles Bainbrigge, Brewer, of Clerkenwell, Mdx., 1s. 2da. d.v.p.; (2) 15 Oct. 1667, Anne (d. 1709), da. of Oliver Luke of Woodend, Cople, Beds., s.p.[1]

Dep. steward, honor of Ampthill by 1662–?d.; burgess, Bedford 1673.[2]

A local attorney, Christie had played a prominent part in the political life of Bedford since the mid-1670s, always as an exponent of the High Church cause and more particularly as an agent for the Bruce family, earls of Ailesbury, in whose service he appears to have enlisted as early as 1646. But he possessed enough influence of his own to secure his return to Parliament even when his patrons were beset with difficulties, as was the case in the years after the Revolution. Moreover, unlike Lord Ailesbury (Thomas Bruce[†]) he seems to have been able to reconcile himself to the new regime fairly speedily: by 1690 he was lending money (some £500) to the crown. In 1690 Christie was seated by the House after a double return for Bedford, Lord Carmarthen (Sir Thomas Osborne[†]) listing him as a supporter of the Court in an analysis of the new Parliament, and despite his age Christie was soon as busy in the House as he had ever been. In the 1690 session he was named to four drafting committees, presenting a bill on 8 May for the easier recovery of small tithes and to facilitate the repairing of churches. He was also a teller twice: on 12 May, on the Tory side on an adjournment motion, and the following day against an amendment to a rider to the bill for confirming the privileges of the Hudson's Bay Company. In the 1690–1 session, Christie was particularly busy on legislative matters, being named to seven drafting committees and presenting two bills, including a revived measure dealing with the recovery of small tithes. He was also active in managing bills originating from other Members, reporting from seven second-reading committees as well as an inquiry committee into abuses in the collection of the aulnage duty. In addition, when Lord Ailesbury sought to pass a private estate bill in December 1690, Christie was naturally included on the committee that discussed the measure and seems to have diligently discharged this obligation. Also in December Lord Carmarthen listed Christie as a probable supporter in the event of a Commons attack on his ministerial position. Following the end of the session his name appears on Robert Harley's* list of April 1691, classed as 'd[oubtful]'.[3]

The session of 1691–2 was Christie's busiest. He was active in the promotion of legislation, especially private bills. He reported from 14 second-reading committees (no less than ten relating to estate bills, including one on behalf of Lord Ailesbury). On general legislation, he finally managed to get through the House a bill for the easier recovery of small tithes, and following his report from a committee on a petition from the Feltmakers' Company (2 Feb. 1692), introduced a bill to amend the Hudson's Bay Company Act (5th). He also reported from the committee on the bill to confirm the charters of Cambridge University (13 Feb.), in favour of which he spoke on 19 Feb. His only other recorded speech occurred earlier in the session, on 6 Nov. 1691, when he successfully moved for the revival of all committees. Christie was less active in the 1692–3 session, but in November turned his attention again to the affairs of the Hudson's Bay Company. On 30 Nov. he brought in a further petition 'from the feltmakers', and three days later presented a bill to prevent fraudulent sales by the Company and to curtail the exporting of rabbit and hare fur. He presented one further bill, on 7 Jan. 1693, to prevent profanity on the sabbath, and also in January reported two private bills from committee. Towards the end of this session he and his parliamentary colleague Thomas Hillersden were thanked officially by Bedford corporation for their 'readiness' to be of service 'by their votes in Parliament in point of trade'. That he was now firmly settled in the 'Country' camp was demonstrated by his speech on 22 Dec. 1692 in favour of the place bill, arguing 'that this would settle the government on the English foundation and preserve the fountain in this House clear'. Ironically, Grascome's list in the spring of 1693 marked him as a placeman, though noting at the same time that he was not a Court supporter. In fact, other than his local office as deputy steward of the honor of Ampthill, he does not appear to have had any connexion with government.[4]

In the 1693–4 session, Christie was named to draft five bills, presenting the legislation against hawkers and pedlars on 29 Nov. 1693. He was involved in the management of five other bills, only one of which was a general measure, the bill to facilitate the recovery of bankrupts' estates. He acted as a teller on three occasions: on 8 Mar. 1694 against a clause proposed to be added to the bill for the relief of the London orphans, and the remaining two on the Country side in divisions on supply legislation (5, 14 Apr.). Later, however, Christie became a substantial stockholder in the Bank, and he was not involved in Country party schemes for an alternative land bank.[5]

In the following session Christie again had numerous committee appointments. He was named to five drafting committees, including another bill to suppress profanity, but his subsequent involvement in the resultant legislation was limited to reporting from committee the bill for the better recovery of debts from heirs who were minors. However, he was involved in the management of seven other bills, most of them relating to private estates. His single tellership during the session, on 7 Feb., was in favour of a rider offered to the land tax bill exempting empty houses.

Christie retired from parliamentary service at the 1695 election, receiving an official expression of Bedford corporation's gratitude to him in the form of a resolution of the common council. He died in July 1697 and was buried in St. Paul's church, Bedford, on 9 July. By his will he returned to the vicar of St. Paul's the great tithes of the parish, charged only with a rent to be paid to some almshouses he built in the town. There was also a bequest to provide a weekly gift of bread to the poor in two Bedford parishes.[6]

[1] *Beds. Par. Reg.* xxv. 9; PCC 93 Lee, 97 Twisse; *St. James Clerkenwell* (Harl. Soc. reg. xvii), 291; F. A. Blaydes, *Genealogia Bedfordiensis*, 345, 352, 368, 376; *Beds. N. and Q.* iii. 110–11. [2] Add. 33590, f. 158; *Beds. Hist. Rec. Soc.* lix. 12. [3] *Beds. Hist. Rec. Soc.* 12–13; *VCH Beds.* iii. 58; *HMC 6th Rep.* 129; *Cal. Treas. Bks.* ix. 645; Wilts. RO, Ailesbury mss 1300/856/A2, cttee. list. [4] *Luttrell Diary*, 5, 194, 271, 336; Ailesbury mss 1300/856/A4, cttee. list; N. Beds. Bor. Council, Bedford bor. recs. B2/3, corp. act. bk. 1688–1718, f. 29. [5] Add. 42593, f. 40. [6] Bedford bor. recs. B2/3, f. 45; *VCH Beds.* 29, 32–33; C. F. Farrar, *Old Bedford*, 230.

D. W. H.

CHURCHILL, Awnsham (1658–1728), of the Black Swan, Paternoster Row, London and Henbury, Dorset.

DORCHESTER 1705–1710

b. 2 May 1658, 1st s. of William Churchill, bookseller, of Dorchester by Elizabeth, da. of Nicholas Awnsham of Isleworth, Mdx.; bro. of Joshua† and William Churchill*. unm. suc. fa. 1706.[1]

Freeman, Stationers' Co. 1681; Dorchester 1705.[2]
Commr. taking subscriptions to land bank 1696.[3]

Churchill was distantly related to the Duke of Marlborough (John Churchill†), but preferred to carve out a strongly independent Whig career. The son of a Dorchester bookseller, he was apprenticed in 1676 to George Sawbridge, one of the principal booksellers in London and Master of the Stationers' Company. In January 1680 Churchill signed, alongside a number of radical printers and publishers, a mass petition calling on Charles II to allow Parliament to sit, subscribing only a few sheets away from John Locke, with whom he was to have a long friendship and business partnership. Although the first surviving letter between the two men is dated June 1688, they knew each other by 1685 and perhaps as early as their participation in the petitioning campaign of 1680. After the Revolution, Churchill published many of Locke's works, including the *Two Treatises*, *Letter Concerning Toleration* and *Considerations of the Consequences of the Lowering of Interest*. By the end of the 1690s he was acting as Locke's financial agent and book dealer in London, holding close to £1,300 of his money in 1701. In 1704 Locke summoned Awnsham to Oates (the home of Sir Francis Masham, 3rd Bt.*, where he had taken up residence) to speak to him before he died. Churchill received £10 in Locke's will, and he and Peter King* were made responsible for the money Locke left in trust for Francis Cudworth Masham.[4]

Churchill's other publications indicate his own strongly Whiggish views. One of his earliest pamphlets was Samuel Bold's *Plea for Moderation towards the Dissenters* (1682), which praised Nonconformist divines as 'shining lights in the church of God' and for which the author was prosecuted and fined for writing 'a scandalous libel'. Churchill published many of Bold's subsequent works, and may have encouraged his vindications of Locke's *Essays on Human Understanding* and *Reasonableness of Christianity*. In 1699 he approached on Bold's behalf the Duke of Newcastle (John Holles†), who held a strong interest at Dorchester, to request (albeit unsuccessfully) a benefice. In 1682 Churchill had also published another tract sympathetic to Dissent, Daniel Whitby's *Protestant Reconciler*, which urged concessions for Nonconformists with a view to their comprehension within the Church. Churchill may have been responsible for urging 'Whigby', as the divine was called, to publish *An Historical Account of Some Things Relating to the Nature of the English Government* (1690), a strongly Lockean pamphlet that upheld the idea that a king's tyranny broke the contract with his people.[5]

In 1685 Churchill and his brother William were in contact with Monmouth rebels who had fled to the Netherlands. According to a well-informed double agent, Churchill 'was in a great conference' with (Sir) John Trenchard* and others, and lodged with Locke's landlord (a radical bookseller named Vandervelde). Although he returned to London, Churchill remained an important link between the exiles and the press in England, for in 1687 he was arrested for printing and selling Fagel's *Letter*, which outlined William's position on toleration. Churchill was active at the Revolution as the co-publisher (in partnership with his brother William) of William of Orange's declarations, by which he made a handsome profit: he was able to invest £500 in Bank stock by 1694. He acted as a land bank commissioner in 1696, and subscribed £200 the following year for the circulation of Exchequer bills. By 1704, the year of the first volume of his publication of Rymer's *Foedera*, he was wealthy enough to buy the manor of Henbury in Dorset. His trade continued to flourish, and his publications included Bishop Burnet's sermons. Fellow bookseller John Dunton noted that the partnership of Awnsham and another brother, John, who joined him in 1690, was

> of an universal trade. I traded very considerably with them for several years; and must do them the justice to say that I was never concerned with persons more exact in their accounts and more just in their payments.⁶

As well as acting as one of Locke's book dealers and financial agents, Churchill also sent him occasional pieces of news which reveal an intense interest in political affairs. In January 1701 he reported that he believed 'the Parliament generally speaking is better than the last', and in March made acerbic comments about Convocation, in which he could see 'no great difference in the knavery of either side'. In August 1701 he sent Locke 'Sir Humphrey Mackworth's* silly book' against occasional conformity, and a few months later was surprised to find himself chosen as 'printer for the Church' when he published Edmund Gibson's *Right of the Archbishop to Continue or Prorogue the Whole Convocation*, though his professional relationship with Gibson dated from much earlier. Justifying himself, he wrote that 'the Church is, or may be made useful to the public at this time, now they think themselves in danger'. The association with Whig clergymen was to continue, for Churchill published works by White Kennett and William Nicolson, and worked actively in support of the latter over the cathedrals bill in March 1708, which involved him in a degree of co-ordination with leading Whig managers of the House. Churchill supported Locke's host Sir Francis Masham in his decision to stand alone at the second Essex election of 1701, and canvassed on his behalf. He reported in December that Masham had 'much the greater appearance at Chelmsford', and hoped he would have 'the same success at the poll'.

As a peripheral member of Locke's 'college', and possessed of a finely tuned political awareness, Churchill may only have been deterred from seeking a seat in Parliament by the pressure of his business interests and a debilitating lameness in one leg; but in 1705 he no longer felt content to spectate on public affairs. His first thought was to stand for Poole, where he sought the aid of the 3rd Earl of Shaftesbury (Anthony, Lord Ashley*), one of the leaders of the Dorset Whigs and a pupil of Locke. Shaftesbury wrote to him on 29 Jan. 1705 that it was 'with very great satisfaction that I hear from you of your intentions to appear in the service of your country. 'Tis what I have much wished for and would contribute to all that in me lay'. However, since previous disappointments at Poole prevented Shaftesbury's intervention there, Churchill, with the Earl's approval, shifted his attention to Dorchester, where he himself owned property. On 1 Feb. 1705 he wrote to Shaftesbury, expressing his gratitude for a promise of support, and adding 'I have had long experience of your good opinion and goodness towards me'. Churchill nevertheless took the occasion to reprimand Shaftesbury's own 'unwillingness to act'; while he admitted that the Earl had suffered 'ill usage by our own friends' he urged his patron to put the past behind him

> when the welfare of the public requires it. I am of your lordship's opinion, that the managers have mistook their own interest in putting into power the enemies of England. I hope England will not suffer by it, but I never expect to see a Court fall into Whig measures by inclination. I believe they will always prefer men of other principles if they can be able to support each other. I cannot but tremble at the thought of a Tory House of Commons... I cannot but think it the interest of England to wish it otherwise, especially at this time. If the honest gentlemen will not act, the honest commonalty must be trampled on, and it's not impossible that the gentlemen may one time or other find the want of them as much as they want protection from them. I shall not think it very comfortable living in Dorset when the T[ories] have got possession of the country, and can let loose the C[our]t or Ch[urch] on those they please at pleasure.⁷

Churchill appears to have encouraged the Whig Thomas Erle* to stand for the county. His own forebodings about a Tory Parliament proved unfounded, and he was himself successful at the polls, though one disgruntled Tory claimed he had been chosen only 'for want of a better'. He had become a freeman of the town in May, when he 'voluntarily gave 10 guineas'. His return was classed by the Earl of Sunderland (Charles, Lord Spencer*) as a gain for the Whigs, and he was described as 'Low Church' on a list of the new Parliament. He voted on 25 Oct. for the Court candidate for Speaker, but was probably on the Country wing of the Whigs, since his name is absent from the list of those who supported the Court in the proceedings on the 'place clause' of the regency bill. Classed as a Whig in the 1708 returns, his activity is difficult to distinguish from that of his brother William, and (until 1709) from that of John Churchill*, though Awnsham's earlier low profile may suggest that he again took a far from active role. Certainly, he was not mentioned as having participated even in the passage of the Copyright Act of 1710. Nevertheless his recorded votes, in favour of naturalizing the Palatines in 1709 and the impeachment of Sacheverell in 1710, were enough to alienate the High Churchmen of Dorchester, who in 1710 procured an address from the borough which pointedly condemned 'republican principles and anti-monarchical notions'. The commentator John Oldmixon thought that because Churchill 'did not give satisfaction to the addressers, they kick at him by saying they'll take care to be represented in future Parliaments by such as shall after their own hearts be eminently loyal and perspicuously zealous'. Churchill was defeated at the poll, and again in 1713, whereafter he made no further attempts to enter Parliament.[8]

Despite his strongly Whig sympathies, Churchill remained on friendly terms with his Tory kinsman George Churchill*: he was the first to break the news of the admiral's death to the Duke of Marlborough, who thanked him for the 'kind concern' he had shown, and he was appointed an executor of George's will. Awnsham had nevertheless always shown a reluctance to approach Marlborough for patronage, preferring the independence his trade gave him. He died on 24 Apr. 1728, leaving £100 to his brother William, the same sum to William's son-in-law Francis Negus†, and his property and extensive library to his nephews. Further evidence of his non-partisan friendships is a legacy of £50 to the Tory Lord Stawell, who had been a gentleman of the bedchamber to Prince George. Awnsham's will referred to £4,000 of stock in the Bank of England, and he left £25 to the poor of local parishes.[9]

[1] Soc. of Geneal. St. Peter's Dorchester par. reg. trans.; Hutchins, *Dorset*, ii. 384. [2] C. H. Mayo, *Dorchester Recs.* 429; *Stationers' Co. Apprentices 1641–1700* ed. McKenzie, 30; info. from Dr M. Treadwell. [3] *CJ*, xii. 509. [4] Hutchins, iii. 352; Plomer, *Dict. Booksellers and Printers 1668–1725*, p. 69; *Past and Present*, cxxxviii. 106; M. Cranston, *John Locke*, 311, 463, 474–5; *Locke Corresp.* vii. 292–3, 385. [5] *DNB*. [6] Ibid.; *Locke Corresp.* vi. 598; Add. 41818, f. 79; R. Ashcraft, *Revolutionary Pol.* 462–3, 486; Wing A4057, H280, W2323, W2326, W2497; Plomer, 69; Hutchins, iii. 352–3. [7] *Locke Corresp.* vii. 468–9, 500, 575; viii. 333, 410; *Nicolson Diaries* ed. Jones and Holmes, 412, 454–5, 459, 461, 463, 466; PRO 30/24/22/2/156, 30/24/20/208/214. [8] Churchill Coll. Camb. Erle mss 2/2, Duke of Bolton (Charles Powlett I*) to Erle, 10 May 1705; Bodl. Ballard 21, f. 222; *Dorchester Recs.* 428; J. Oldmixon, *Hist. of Addresses* (1711), ii. 227. [9] Add. 61367, f. 151; *Marlborough Dispatches* ed. Murray, v. 42; PCC 142 Brook.

M. J. K.

CHURCHILL, Charles (1656–1714), of Minterne Magna, Dorset.

WEYMOUTH AND MELCOMBE REGIS 1701 (Feb.)–1710

b. 2 Feb. 1656, 4th but 3rd surv. s. of Sir Winston Churchill† of Minterne Magna by Elizabeth, da. of Sir John Drake† of Ashe, Devon; bro. of George* and John Churchill†, 1st Duke of Marlborough. m. 9 Feb. 1702 Mary. da. and h. of James Gould*, s.p.; 1s. illegit. (?by Elizabeth Dodd). suc. fa. 1688.[1]

Gent. of bedchamber to Prince George of Denmark 1672–1708; ensign of ft. Duke of York's regt. 1674, lt. 1675, capt. 1678, capt.-lt. of drags. 1679, lt.-col. of ft. Charles Trelawny's† regt. 1682 (Duke of York's 1684, Queen Consort's 1685, Queen's 1687), col. 3 Ft. 1688; brig.-gen. by 1690, maj.-gen. 1694, lt.-gen. 1702, gen. 1703, acting c.-in-c. 1703.[2]

Gov. Kinsale 1690, Brussels 1706, Guernsey 1706; lt. Tower of London 1702–6; master of buckhounds 1702.

Freeman, Portsmouth 1684, Kinsale 1690, Hertford 1703.[3]

'After many battles fought with great bravery and conduct, [Churchill] was esteemed one of the best commanders of foot in Europe.' His promotion to the highest ranks was thus due to personal merit as well as to the pre-eminence and influence of his brother, the Duke of Marlborough. Churchill's favour at the court of Queen Anne was also predetermined by fortuitous service in early life with the royal family of Denmark: he became a page at the age of 13, and three years later a gentleman of honour to Prince George, Anne's future husband. A young hothead who was involved in a duel in 1681, Churchill subsequently served in the Duke of York's troop, and left in 1682 for Tangier. He fought at Sedgemoor in 1685, but followed Marlborough's example at the Revolution by joining the Prince of Orange. Thereafter 'his martial genius led him to the wars', where his 'distinguished conduct' attracted the attention of the new King. He fought with his brother in Ireland in 1690, showing particular resourcefulness and resilience at the siege of Cork, where he and four regiments under his command 'passed the river up to his armpits into the east marsh in order to storm the town'. James II was informed in the autumn that 'the Danish Churchill, now governor of Kinsale, swore God damn him, he would lose his life than ever draw his sword for your Majesty', and Charles claimed that he had 'never got a penny' from the exiled King. Money was evidently very much on his mind at this time, for he was alleged to have embezzled the stores at Kinsale. Still on active service in 1692, when he distinguished himself at the battle of Steenkerk, Churchill avoided suspicion of involvement in Marlborough's dealings with Jacobites, and was rewarded with the grant of 20,000 guilders (£1,205) ransom for his nephew, the Duke of Berwick, whom he captured at the battle of Landen in 1693. That autumn Churchill invested £1,000 in government loans, having three years earlier lent a fifth of that sum, presumably the proceeds from his father's estate, which he had inherited. His was one of the regiments not to be disbanded in 1699, and he was appointed that year as the Duke of Newcastle's (John Holles†) deputy-governor of Hull.[4]

Although his military career under William was pursued almost independently of Marlborough, Churchill was prepared in Anne's reign to play second fiddle to his brother, with whom he worked in close co-operation on the battlefield. Their collaboration on campaign was particularly successful in 1703, when Charles, promoted to general, temporarily took over command of the army during his brother's absence; and in 1704 Churchill 'had a great and honourable share in the memorable battle of Blenheim', for which he was given the honour of escorting the captured French general Tallard back to England. His loyalty to Marlborough was again evident the following year when he challenged General Slangenberg 'to meet him and have satisfaction' after the Dutchman had made disparaging remarks about the Duke. Charles was present at Brabant and stormed Liège in 1705, thereby preparing the way for victory at Namur, and the following year he fought at Ramillies, captured Brussels (of which he was made governor), and directed the siege of Dendermonde. Churchill's military success and his family's return to favour were reflected in the perquisites bestowed on him. In 1702 he became lieutenant of the Tower of London, a post he surrendered in 1706 in order to take up the governorship of Guernsey, which he had long been promised by his brother and which paid an annual salary of £1,200. Despite the reservations of both the Queen and Lord Treasurer Godolphin (Sidney†), Marlborough successfully obtained the appointment for his brother's life because, the Duke explained, 'should I die I know him so well that he would be turned out'.[5]

Although he has been called an uncertain ally for Marlborough in the Commons, Churchill's outlook usually reflected the position of the Duke, who may on occasion have seen advantage in Charles's natural Tory inclinations and willingness to deviate from the Court position. Churchill's day-to-day activity in the House needs to be distinguished from that of his brother George, who is often confusingly called by his military title of colonel, as well as from that of his distant relative Major William Churchill*, who sat in the House after 1708. In contrast with both men, Charles's parliamentary record is meagre and he made no known contribution from the floor, so that his allegiances are only discernible from a number of contemporary analyses of his conduct. Correctly predicted as likely to win a seat at Weymouth in February 1701, he was listed that month among the likely supporters of the Court over the 'Great Mortgage'. He was blacklisted as having opposed preparations for war with France, a surprising categorizaton given his background but evidence of his increasingly obvious sympathy for the Tories, with whom he was listed by Robert Harley* in December. In January 1702 he voted in the Speakership election in favour of Harley, an action interpreted by Lord Shaftesbury (Anthony, Lord Ashley*) as against the King's interest; but although Churchill's vote on that occasion does appear at first sight to show the limits of his loyalty to the Court, the fact that Marlborough had pressed Harley to accept the Chair means that Charles's actions were entirely at one with his brother's views. Moreover, Charles's behaviour may also have owed something to internal rivalries within the Admiralty, where his brother George was a lord and Sir Thomas Littleton, 3rd Bt.*, the Court candidate for Speaker, was treasurer. No doubt as Marlborough and George Churchill wished, their brother Charles favoured the motion on 26 Feb. 1702 vindicating the Commons' proceedings in the impeachments of William's ministers, and in December 1703 he was offered the freedom of Hertford, where a faction within the corporation sought Tory support, though he does not appear to have taken up the privilege of voting there. Although categorized as a 'High Church Courtier' in 1705, he had been forecast as an opponent of the Tack, and did not vote for it on 28 Nov. 1704. Such loyalty to the Court appears to have come under increasing pressure as the administration drifted towards increasing reliance on the Whigs, although once again it is possible that Marlborough was not unhappy to indulge the expression of his brother's Toryism. Charles deliberately avoided the division on the Speaker on 25 Oct. 1705 so as not to have to vote against William Bromley II*, but once more toed the official Court line on 18 Feb. 1706 over the proceedings on the 'place clause' of the regency bill. He, George Churchill and other MPs connected with Marlborough, absented themselves from the vote that month on the Bewdley election. In doing so, it is difficult to prove whether he was showing his true Tory colours or revealing Marlborough's reluctance to join with Godolphin over party issues. Whatever his motives, Churchill was marked unequivocally as a Tory on an analysis of the 1708 Parliament.[6]

Churchill's military and parliamentary careers were curtailed from late March 1708 onwards when he was 'seized with an apoplectic fit' and 'lay ill of it a great while'. Marlborough was sufficiently concerned to delay his departure for the Continent until confident that his brother was out of danger, but then suspected that Charles 'had no mind to serve with' him that summer. Churchill therefore wrote on 17 Apr. assuring the Duke that he was 'perfectly recovered' and begging to be allowed to join him. Charles also refuted the insinuation made against him, declaring that the Duke's informant 'lies like a villain, for I will never leave you and I would rather serve under you than any man breathing'. It was this continuing devotion to Marlborough, rather than the acceptability of his own political views, that saved him his parliamentary seat in the 1708 election.[7]

It is unlikely that Churchill's attendance at Westminster was assiduous, for ill-health dogged him for the rest of his life. At Christmas 1708 he had 'a fit of the palsy in his tongue and one side'; was thought to be 'a dying' in November 1709; and suffered a further attack in the spring of 1710 which left him 'speechless for three or four days'. Always 'a lover of wine' he increasingly turned to the bottle, prompting gossip in 1710 that he never stirred from the country and drank 'from morning till night'. He did not stand again at Weymouth, and in 1712 the search was made for another commander of his regiment prepared to pay the asking price of £10,000; Churchill had by then already invested £3,000 in the Bank of England. He died 'much lamented' on 29 Dec. 1714, leaving his property in the first instance to his wife, whose dowry had enabled him to complete the building of his house. An inscription on the monument she erected declared that his

> known bravery, generous spirit and friendly temper made him esteemed and beloved by all that knew him; and his unalterable affection for the Church, his fidelity to the Crown and love of his country have justly recommended him to posterity.

Churchill also provided in his will for an annuity of £50 to be paid to one Elizabeth Dodd, probably the mother of his illegitimate son Charles† (to whom he left £2,000).[8]

[1] IGI, Dorset. [2] *DNB*. [3] R. East, *Portsmouth Recs.* 367; *Council Bk. of Corp. of Kinsale* ed. R. Caulfield, 192; Herts. RO, Hertford bor. recs. 25, p. 105. [4] Hutchins, *Dorset*, iv. 482; A. L. Rowse, *Early Churchills*, 365; Clarke, *Jas. II*, ii. 225; Boyer, *Wm. III*, ii. 216, 334; HMC Finch, ii. 471; Luttrell, *Brief Relation*, iv. 553; Bodl. Carte 228, f. 321; Add. 30000 C, f. 174. [5] *DNB*; Rowse, 366–8; Hutchins, 482; HMC Portland, iv. 255; Add. 70075, Dyer's newsletters 3, 6 Apr. 1703; *Marlborough–Godolphin Corresp.* 171–2, 701, 703, 707, 717, 722, 724. [6] *Parlty. Lists Early 18th Cent.* ed. Newman, 66; HMC Portland, iv. 11; SRO, Leven and Melville mss GD26/13/120, [–] to Ld. Leven, 1 Jan. 1702; PRO 30/24/20/129–30; Add. 70272, 'Large Account, Revolution and Succession', p. 18; *Bull. IHR*, lxv, 48–9. [7] Luttrell, vi. 284; Egerton 2378, f. 33b; Add. 61163, ff. 174–5. [8] SRO, Hamilton mss GD406/1/7267, Earl of Selkirk to Duke of Hamilton, 21 Nov. 1709; Egerton 2378, f. 33b; Cunningham, *Hist. GB*, ii. 200; Add. 31143, f. 556; Folger Shakespeare Lib. Newdigate newsletters 5 Feb. 1712, 20 Dec. 1712; Hutchins, 482; Rowse, 370–1.

M. J. K.

CHURCHILL, George (1654–1710), of Windsor Little Park.

ST. ALBANS 1685–1708
PORTSMOUTH 1708–8 May 1710

b. 20 Feb. 1654, 3rd but 2nd surv. s. of Sir Winston Churchill† of Minterne Magna; bro. of Charles* and John Churchill†, 1st Duke of Marlborough. *unm.* 1s. illegit. (?by Mary Cooke).

Lt. RN 1666–8, 1672–4, capt. 1678–93, adm. 1702–8; ensign of drags. Duke of York's regt. 1676, lt. 1678–9; capt. King's Drags. 1685–8; cornet and maj. 3 Life Gds. 1691–2; lt.-col. by 1692; groom of bedchamber to Prince George of Denmark 1689–1708; commr. management of Prince's revenue 1704; ld. of Admiralty Oct. 1699– Jan. 1702, member of council May 1702–28 Oct. 1708.

Freeman, Hertford 1698, Portsmouth 1702.[1]

Dep. ranger, Windsor Little Park 1702–*d.*; ranger, Greenwich Park 1707–*d.*; elder bro. Trinity House 1704–*d.*, master 1705–7.

Overshadowed by his brother's achievements, Churchill has traditionally been regarded by admirers of Marlborough as a thorn in the Duke's side, and as a liability at the Admiralty or in the House; only naval historians have admired his administrative talents and successes. Concentration on major character flaws, such as his haughtiness and undoubtedly sharp tongue, as well as his increasingly strident Toryism, have obscured both the admiral's contribution to the war effort and the true nature of his relationship with Marlborough, which seems to have been a good deal closer than is sometimes assumed. Unfortunately Churchill still remains something of an enigma, because his actions were often deeply ambiguous and because the Blenheim archive contains none of his private papers: he can often be assessed only through the unflattering and perhaps distorting evidence of his numerous enemies.[2]

Despite an assertion that he never held any command in the army, Churchill's early military career straddled both naval and land forces, and he was usually referred to by the rank of colonel, which may be recognition of either his rank in the militia or his lieutenant-colonelcy in the regular army. Indeed, his dual career may explain his later advocacy of the utility of marine troops. He fought in the second and third Dutch wars, and was subsequently given a commission in his brother's regiment, though this may have been primarily an honorary appointment. If he did serve on land he must have led an amphibious existence, for during the 1670s he returned periodically to the sea and was therefore excused from annual army musters. Although recommended as a Court candidate for James II's proposed Parliament in 1688, he was one of the first to join William at the Revolution, going so far as to read the Prince's declaration to his crew, and was described as 'much devoted' to William's service. He was nevertheless sent to the Tower in 1689 for having charged a price for convoying merchantmen.[3]

Returned again for St. Albans in 1690 on his brother's interest, Churchill was marked by Lord Carmarthen in March (Sir Thomas Osborne†) as a Tory and a Court supporter, and later that year probably as a supporter of Carmarthen in the event of a Commons' attack upon his ministerial position. Churchill commanded ships at the battles of Bantry Bay and Beachy Head, and came up for promotion as a flag officer: both he and Matthew Aylmer* were recommended by Edward Russell* because, Queen Mary reported to William, 'he says nothing has been done for them, tho' they both were trusted when you came over and have been ever very true to your interest'. Churchill's was the first name on the list of candidates, but his advancement was blocked by Carmarthen who, hostile to Russell and resentful of Marlborough, protested that George 'would be called the flag by favour as his brother [Charles] is called the general of favour'. Marlborough in turn complained that everything was decided 'by partiality and faction'. Churchill accordingly received no preferment, prompting accusations in 1691 that the King had failed to protect 'the first sea officer that gave up his ship to him . . . against the partialities of party in the House'. According to one report, however, Churchill did not go entirely unrewarded: in February 1692 it was said that he had the promise of a lieutenancy in his brother's regiment, but that the King subsequently decided to 'give him a pension of £300 a year and he is in consideration thereof to quit the land service and betake himself wholly to his command at sea'. If this is so, and his future dedication to the navy as well as his army pension suggests that it was, his categorization by Robert Harley* in April 1691 as a Country supporter may have owed less to personal resentment of his own treatment than to his brother's alienation from Carmarthen's administration, which itself derived in part from a feeling of being undervalued. The analysis may in any case have been rather academic, for Churchill was on active service (in May recapturing 16 merchant ships previously lost to French privateers).[4]

By early 1692 Marlborough's discontent and frustrations had pushed him into secret dealings with the Jacobites, and the government's discovery of the intrigues threatened to unhinge his brother's career. It was reported in January that George had surrendered his commission, though Churchill was in fact promoted at this time to first lieutenant, and in May Secretary Nottingham (Daniel Finch†) wrote to Russell to 'encourage [Churchill] in his duty notwithstanding the misfortune of his brother' and to tell him that his good behaviour would increase the Queen's 'good opinion of him'. Russell duly passed on the message and Churchill in turn assured Mary that he would never 'give the least cause to bring himself under any suspicion of want of duty and loyalty, but will prosecute her Majesty's interest while he lives'. Yet despite this profession of allegiance, a few days later Mary ordered Russell to discharge him because the government had received 'such evidence against my Lord Marlborough . . . that the Queen could not think fit to continue Churchill in so great a post'. Russell replied with a glowing testimonial on Churchill's behalf:

> I confess I have a great tenderness for the gentleman as my friend, but that does not in the least way [influence] me in this matter; whatever his brother's faults are . . . I will answer for Capt. Churchill he knows nothing of them, and will as much disapprove of them. Thus far I will venture to say and engage for him, if her Majesty will please to employ him, that his integrity and duty to her Majesty's government will be equal to the faithfullest subject in England, which upon the knowledge and long experience I have had of him makes me very ready to pawn the little credit I have for his performance of what I write.

Fortunately Russell had 'not said anything to him of his misfortune', for Nottingham consequently revoked Churchill's notice of dismissal. Given his own conversations with Jacobite agents at this time, Russell's support can hardly be considered in retrospect to have been a ringing vindication, but it was evidently enough to excuse Churchill on this occasion and he continued on active service. His part in the victory at La Hogue in May, under Russell's command, can therefore only have strengthened his position, and he was accordingly rewarded with the grant of a wreck in the Shannon. Even so, Churchill was still sensitive about his lack of promotion, and Nottingham was warned in July that he and other commanders would be 'highly disgusted' at the promotion of the junior David Mitchell over their heads.[5]

Russell and Churchill's friendship at this time is remarkable in the light of their later antipathy and divergent political views. Yet they had similar forthright characters and were tied by bonds of naval camaraderie and experience; moreover, Russell shared Marlborough's antipathy to Carmarthen, making George a natural ally against the administration. These factors, rather than allegiances of party or place, explain Churchill's conduct in the 1692–3 session. His co-operation with Russell is clearly evident from their both having drafted schemes for ensuring adequate convoying for merchant shipping, and naval historians have pointed to the similarity between Churchill's ideas and those which were finally adopted. The fact that Paul Foley I was the third Member to write a proposal suggests that Churchill may have been close to leading Country critics of the conduct of the war, and in a position to supply them with information concerning the misconduct of naval affairs after La Hogue. Churchill certainly helped to spearhead the attack. On 21 Nov. he referred to the 'strange' management of the fleet, alleging that men had been 'preferred to commands in it no ways fit for it'. This scarcely veiled outburst of resentment against the system of preferment met with a snide remark from Sir Robert Rich, 2nd Bt., about Churchill's earlier extortion for convoying merchants, though George replied that the House should now be equal in its punishments, and he clearly favoured an address requesting the King to put the Admiralty into able and loyal hands. Such self-advertisement irritated the Admiralty lords, who summoned him on 25 Nov. to explain his charges against unsuitable commanders and his expression that 'some persons in the fleet were cowards'. The following day Churchill therefore complained to the House about what he regarded as an infringement of the privilege of free speech. 'I know not that I am to answer anywhere for what I say here but to the House', he remarked, declaring that he had denied the Admiralty's right of questioning him on oath until he had the direction of his fellow Members. Churchill was an unlikely victim of oppression and when it emerged that the Board had not insisted on an oath, and that he may well have repeated his remarks outside the chamber, MPs of all shades began to wonder what the fuss was about. The Tory Sir Edward Seymour, 4th Bt.*, could 'hardly understand the accusation', while the Whig Richard Hampden I failed to 'see how privilege is concerned at all', and although Foley stood up to suggest there was a principle at stake, the mood of the House was clearly bemused, restless and unsympathetic. Churchill wisely let the matter drop, though not before Sir Robert Rich had shot another barbed remark in his direction.[6]

On 20 Dec. the simmering rivalry between Russell and Nottingham boiled over at a joint conference, to which Churchill was named. Churchill supported Russell's explanation of his actions with a convincing first-hand account, assuring the House that he knew the admiral's protestations to be true, 'he being near Mr Russell in the time of action'. On 2 Jan. 1693 Churchill was appointed to the conference committee relating to the failure the previous summer to follow up the victory at sea, presumably with the intention of further clearing Russell's name and renewing his own attack on the Admiralty. Nine days later he again supported the idea of an address advising the King to constitute a commission comprised of men of 'known experience in maritime affairs'. Luttrell noted Churchill to have been

very zealous for it and reflected much on the understanding of the commissioners of the Admiralty and their want of experience, and plainly said they did not understand their business and instanced several particulars, and therefore they ought to be turned out.

He also charged the Admiralty with having 'broken the public faith of the nation' for 'not observing the King's proclamation which promised that seamen should not be turned over'. Although Lord Falkland (Anthony Carey*) answered some of the charges, and Rich suggested that Churchill himself was 'faulty', he pushed his point to division, telling in favour of such an address. Despite his failure to win over the House on that occasion, he maintained the attack, securing (along with Russell, who had now joined Marlborough's faction at the 'Cockpit') nomination to the committee to inquire into the lack of orders to intercept the French fleet. On 11 Feb., listed as Capt. Churchill, he was also the first-named to the second-reading committee for the bill to prohibit trade with France.[7]

Although preferment was one of Churchill's principal aims, neither his opposition to the Admiralty commissioners nor his defence of Russell advanced his career. Indeed, Churchill may have feared that Russell had simply used him for his own ends, for he now blamed Russell for hindering his advancement. According to George Byng*, himself a one-time friend of Churchill who became a rival because of friendship with Russell, William requested the admiral to recommend a new flag officer: Marlborough was out of favour and the King had 'resolved not to make his brother the admiral' even though Churchill was the most senior officer. But Churchill resented the snub and

was extremely disappointed not to be the flag and thought it entirely owing to Admiral Russell as having recommended Mr Aylmer to his prejudice, and tho' he was made sensible how much he was out of the question, yet from that time they had a dislike to each other.

The incident was important in shaping Churchill's future conduct. In the short term, it prompted his resignation in February 1693 from the fleet, beginning a five-year period of political exile. In the longer term, his own discontent ironically forced him into closer alliance with Marlborough, even though it had been his association with Marlborough that had spoiled his career. Churchill's resentment against Russell and Aylmer was thereafter to fester into a desire for revenge that would erupt on several occasions. The affair also shows how easily political groupings in the early 1690s could be affected by personal antipathies and frustrated ambitions, for the announcement of Aylmer's appointment was made after Russell's dismissal as admiral, so that Churchill's misfortune was as much a reflection of the admiral's impotence and declining influence as a sign of hesitant support.[8]

Churchill's sense of outrage at his treatment by King, ministers and friend alike, as well as his loyalties to his brother and the 'Cockpit interest' around Prince George and Anne, encouraged him to adopt the politics of protest. He was marked on a list compiled by Samuel Grascome in the spring of 1693 as a placeman but not a Court supporter, though he preferred to adopt a position of sullen inactivity rather than outright opposition. During the 1694–5 session Churchill was included upon Henry Guy's* list of 'friends', probably in connexion with the Commons' attack upon Guy. Still listed in 1696 as likely to oppose the Court on 31 Jan. over the proposed council of trade, and as having voted in March against fixing the price of guineas at 22s., he nevertheless rallied to the King's cause after the assassination attempt, and signed the Association. Indeed he followed Marlborough's lead in pushing for the attainder of Sir John Fenwick† (who had made accusations against the Duke), and, with an unseemly haste to prevent the prisoner from revealing any embarrassing secrets, cried 'Damn him! Thrust a billet down his throat. Dead men tell not tales.'[9]

By 1698 Marlborough had patched up relations with William, and in September Churchill, who was expected to follow his brother's lead, was included in a list of placemen and marked as a Court placeman in a comparison of the old and new Commons. Yet George also had his own agenda to pursue against Russell, now Lord Orford. On 2 Feb. 1699 he attacked Orford's friend Henry Priestman* by exposing the differences between the latter's corrupt attempts to obtain a salary and the legitimate rewards for those who had commanded large squadrons; and L'Hermitage noted him to be Orford's most zealous critic. On one occasion Churchill sneered that 'he had known other ad[mirals] take diet [and] drink but not set in on the public account', and though magnanimous to admit that Orford had 'done a great deal of good' he also pointed out that he had 'got himself great riches'. Although Churchill was persuaded by his brother to absent himself from the close vote on 15 Mar. against Orford, L'Hermitage observed the effect of his return to the House on 22 Mar. 'en faisant changer ce qui avait été décidé', for the committee of the whole passed resolutions critical of Orford's joint tenure of the navy treasurership and a place on the Admiralty commission. The incident shows both Marlborough's influence over his brother when the occasion demanded, and the advantage for the Duke to have Churchill firing at one of the Junto leaders without himself having to descend to the level of open party warfare. Given this alliance of interest between George and his brother, the appearance of Churchill's name on what was probably a list of those opposed to a standing army seems problematic, and though he did not oppose the disbanding bill in the crucial division of 18 Jan. it may be that he had once more merely abstained on the issue rather than positively cast his vote against the Court. Moreover, it may have suited Marlborough's purposes for his brother to be seen in alliance with Harley and Godolphin, especially at a time when the Junto administration was beginning to disintegrate. Unfortunately, Churchill's other activity in the House sheds little light on his political views at this time. On 21 Feb. he was named to a drafting committee for a private naturalization bill, which he guided through the Commons on behalf of the Boscawen family; and on 14 Mar. he was named to a drafting committee for a bill to repeal a clause in the Act prohibiting trade with France, concerning penalties for the embezzlement of prizes. He presented the bill on 21 Mar. but took no further recorded part in the session after being granted leave of absence on 4 Apr. for the recovery of his health.[10]

Having earlier suffered because of his brother's disgrace, Churchill benefited in 1699 from Marlborough's return to favour. By mid-July the lords justices received orders 'to report their opinions how G. Churchill may retrieve his post in the fleet without injury to those in command'. As Vernon explained to the King, the problem was one of precedence and longstanding ill-will, for Churchill would

> pretend to be admiral of the blue, which gives a rank above Aylmer and Mitchell, who are only vice-admirals of the red. His pretensions are well grounded, so far as he was a senior captain to the other two, and perhaps had a hardship put upon him that kept him from rising gradually and younger officers were preferred before him.

Mitchell therefore offered to allow Churchill to take precedence, but Aylmer was not so compliant and threatened to resign. Vernon discussed the matter with Marlborough, and assured him that his brother would 'have right done him', though the secretary of state feared the likely 'clamour' should Churchill be preferred, for he did not know how 'the Admiralty would be able to answer it if they did so unprecedented a thing as to make one admiral of a squadron who had never had any inferior flag before'. Vernon suggested the compromise that Churchill might have a place on the Admiralty commission instead, and Marlborough agreed, though he 'wished that his brother might not be disgusted when he expected to be preferred'. Vernon thought it prudent that while the King made up his mind he should tell Churchill 'that the delay was not out of unkindness to him, but he may hope for your Majesty's favour, which will likewise engage him to deserve it'. The King agreed to Vernon's expedient, perhaps because the Secretary warned that Marlborough thought it would be 'the utmost mortification to his brother if it be given away from him', and Churchill was appointed as a commissioner of the Admiralty in October 1699, much to the chagrin of Orford.[11]

Churchill was uncharacteristically quiet for the next two years. Though marked as a placeman on a list of interests drawn up in early 1700, his Toryism still prevented him, on occasion, from following his brother's public policy. On 14 Dec. 1699, for example, he slipped out of the House to avoid voting in favour of Burnet, even though Marlborough appeared to be actively concerned for the bishop, but it is difficult to know how far Marlborough resented or even encouraged such independence. Certainly the Duke cannot have been unduly concerned to see Churchill continuing to cause problems for Orford and Somers over the Kidd affair. In early April 1700, when William perhaps had already decided to dismiss the lord chancellor, Churchill wrecked the scheme hammered out by the parliamentary managers to avoid discussion of the manner of Kidd's examination. No sooner had Vernon announced the ministry's plans to ensure that Kidd was examined privately than Churchill stood up to request specific directions for how the Admiralty should act when Kidd was in their custody. 'The House thought there was some trick at first in laying this before them', and Vernon 'thought they would have taken no notice of it at all, and certainly they would not if Churchill had not been talking with some of them beforehand.' It was the first indication of Churchill's real skill as a parliamentary tactician in his own right, and ominous for the Junto because he was part of the Admiralty's inquiry into the Kidd affair.[12]

In February 1701 Churchill was listed among those thought likely to support the Court in agreeing with the committee of supply's resolution to continue the 'Great Mortgage'. During the 1701 Parliament Churchill continued his attack against Whig interests in the navy, being appointed on 28 Mar. to the inquiry into the conduct of Edward Whitaker, a former political radical who had obtained the post of Admiralty solicitor. Churchill also used his credit to shift responsibility for securing the navy from the Admiralty to the Ordnance office 'because it could not be defended without a great land force', and was listed by Harley with the Tories on an analysis of the 1701–2 Parliament. In January 1702 he voted for Harley in the Speakership election, and although Lord Shaftesbury (Anthony, Lord Ashley*) considered this to be an act against the King's interest, Churchill may simply have been following Marlborough's instructions since the Duke appears to have supported Harley's candidature, and the admiral probably needed little encouragement to desert the Court candidate Sir Thomas Littleton, 3rd Bt., the Whig treasurer of the navy. It was reported that when Churchill was struck by illness shortly before the election of Speaker he declared that he would go to the House to vote for Mr Harley [even] if 'he should die in the way'. Yet his opposition had serious repercussions. Later that month Lord Pembroke (Thomas Herbert†) was appointed lord admiral, thereby depriving Churchill of his post; indeed some suspected that Pembroke's promotion had been urged by the Whigs with this result particularly in mind. Returned to the back benches, it is not surprising that Churchill favoured the motion of 26 Feb. 1702 vindicating the Commons' proceedings in the impeachments of William's ministers.[13]

Churchill's political eclipse did not last long. King William died on 8 Mar. and Anne's accession ushered in Churchill's own reign of power, for he had long served as a groom of the bedchamber to Prince George, and had considerable personal influence over him. The combination of this unassailable interest at court, together with the favour shown to Marlborough, ensured Churchill's promotion on 13 May as admiral of the red, replacing Aylmer who duly resigned. Contemporaries saw a certain rough justice in this, but sympathy was less forthcoming when Churchill became involved in a dispute over precedence with Mitchell, who was also destined for a place on the council, advising the new lord high admiral, Prince George, on naval affairs. Godolphin had

> no sort of patience to think that a brother of Lord Marlborough's should put the least difficulty or stop anything that is for the Queen's service and the good of the country for any senseless pretension or interest of his own, which without knowing the particulars of I am inclined to believe he has no just right to.

Even the Queen seems to have thought Churchill unreasonable, but, 'taking the opportunity of the influence he had over the Prince he was in an extraordinary manner preferred to be admiral of the blue' on 6 May, and was thereby raised above Mitchell. Having achieved predominance, Churchill quickly assumed control of the newly constituted (and some thought unconstitutional) Admiralty council, for although a quorum of two was required, day-to-day business devolved into his hands. Respect for the Prince, who nominally headed affairs, and the unparliamentary nature of the council meant that Churchill was also in the enviable position of exercising power without apparent accountability.[14]

This did not mean, however, that before his official appointment on 22 May 1702 Churchill was above being questioned in the House as sharply as he had once probed the Junto. On 8 May he had delivered his department's vindication in response to an inquiry into the discharge of seamen without pay, which he justified as a cost-cutting exercise designed to save the Treasury £300 a day. Sir Richard Cocks, 2nd Bt.*, nevertheless believed 'this barbarous inhumanity was committed in order to disparage my Lord Halifax (Charles Montagu*) by reflecting on the Exchequer bills' which the chancellor had set up. When he heard the full report on 24 May Cocks was sure that

> Churchill and the Admiralty had discharged them in that base disgraceful manner on purpose if possible to bring more disgrace upon the author of the Exchequer bills by pretending that was the occasion they could not pay them off because there was no money, only Exchequer bills.

But the plan backfired when the committee concluded that money had been available and that Churchill had added dishonesty to his cruelty by lying about the instructions the Admiralty had received from the King. Finding he had been 'betrayed' by some members of his own board, Churchill made a clean breast of the affair, and though he insisted that no rules had been broken he agreed that in future seamen 'should be discharged and paid at the same time and place'.[15]

Although increasingly enjoying the freedom for independent action, Churchill aided Marlborough's land campaigns by his strong direction of the Admiralty, and still held his brother's trust. Thus when, in late 1702, the proposal to grant a pension to Marlborough and his heirs ran into difficulties, Churchill was employed to help extricate the government from further embarrassment, a detailed piece of management with Harley and Godolphin that was successful in limiting the damage to the administration when Churchill conveyed the Duke's willingness to accept a favourable address instead. Marlborough did, however, worry about Churchill's ability to upset his colleagues, demonstrated by his quarrels with Sir Stafford Fairborne* and Byng, whose advancement he opposed because of the latter's friendship with Orford. Thus when Rooke fell ill in May 1703, it was with some trepidation that the Duke contemplated his brother assuming command of the fleet. He was not 'pleased at [George's] going abroad. Not that I think he will do anything but what he should but that I am afraid there will be no opportunity for him to do anything that is good and then his enemies will attribute it to his want of will.' Churchill went down to Portsmouth and raised his flag there, and although Rooke's recovery meant that he 'had an uneasy journey to no purpose', Churchill continued to harbour ambitions to take control. Marlborough, however, confided that he would be 'very much troubled' to see his brother in charge, 'for I know him to be of so violent a temper that he would disoblige everybody, which in my opinion would be very prejudicial to her Majesty's service, which shall always be an argument with me against it'.[16]

Churchill's offensive manner was beginning to cause embarrassment. In October 1703 Marlborough felt it necessary to apologize to his wife for the disrespect his brother had shown her, though he added somewhat disingenuously, 'I do not flatter myself with having much power over him'. In February 1704 the Duke thought him 'full of dissimulation' and believed that 'the advancement he desires would be to his own prejudice'; in the summer Marlborough was still warning the Duchess that she could not 'be too much on your guard' against his brother, 'for he loves to do everything rather by a trick than by a plain, honest way'. Yet, despite his negative tone, the Duke may have been deliberately pointing to his brother's faults in order to placate his wife, with whom George must have had very little in common apart from their ability to harbour grudges, and it may have continued to suit both Marlborough and Godolphin to exploit Churchill's links with the High Tories. Certainly the admiral was still useful to them, and appears to have played a significant part that autumn in the management of the opposition to the Tack. Godolphin tried to ensure that Prince George's servants attended for the vote, and had

> likewise spoken to Mr Churchill to speak to him; he answers for Mr [Edward] Nicholas*, but not G[eorge] Clarke* [even though the latter described himself as the admiral's good friend] nor Tom Conyers* . . . He has promised me also to speak to [Thomas] Hopson*, George St. Loe* and to William Gifford*.

He was also detailed to lobby his fellow MP for St. Albans, John Gape*, and the seaman Hon. Algernon Greville*. Godolphin was particularly anxious that Churchill should be present at a meeting of the managers to be held by Sir Charles Hedges*, 'where they may concert who should be more spoken to and by whom'. Forecast as a probable opponent of the Tack, he duly voted against it or was absent from the House on 28 Nov. 1704.[17]

Perhaps in expectation of reward for his loyalty, Churchill was reported in January 1705 as likely to succeed Rooke, and, when he did not, to be about to resign. He nevertheless remained in his posts, and in June received orders 'to sail with a strong squadron and cruise off Brest', though he appears to have sent his ships to join those under Byng's command. On an analysis of the 1705 Parliament he was categorized as a High Church courtier, and curbed his Tory principles sufficiently to vote on 25 Oct. for the Court candidate as Speaker; indeed, he appears to have canvassed at least one Member, Colonel (Henry) Lee*, on behalf of the government, even though Lee did not relent in support for William Bromley II. On 9 Jan. 1706 he was given leave to attend the Lords' committee investigating the fleet's manpower. On 26 Jan. he was duly named to the drafting committee of the bill to encourage and increase the number of seamen. The following month he again supported the Court over the proceedings on the 'place clause' of the regency bill, but the same month absented himself from the vote on the Bewdley election, perhaps because Marlborough was still reluctant to join Godolphin in favouring the Whigs over purely party matters. As more Whigs began to be taken into office, the lord treasurer was evidently unsure about Churchill's reliability, for while he admitted that the admiral had often asked him 'what commands he had for him . . . and that he had contributed to make some things easy . . . at the same time [Prince George] has shown uneasiness in some other things which nobody can tell how to impute to any other influence'. On 20 June 1706 Marlborough therefore informed the treasurer that he had received a letter from his brother

> in which he assures me that he would behave himself in everything as you should like. I do not say that I am persuaded that his heart is just as I could wish, but I verily believe he would take pains not to offend, and that there must be somebody else that does mischief besides himself.

In July Marlborough tried to play down the bad influence exerted by his brother, claiming rather implausibly that the Duchess laid a 'great deal more to [George's] charge than he deserves, for [the Queen] has no good opinion nor never speaks to him'. Indeed, a false report in November 1706 that George had resigned his flag suggests that Churchill was not expected to retain his position for long because of the increasingly Whig complexion of the administration.[18]

The attack did not materialize until October 1707, though it had been brewing throughout the summer. In late June Godolphin informed Marlborough that the Whigs intended to 'disturb [Churchill] as soon as ever they have an opportunity', a decision which the Duke regarded as a mortification to himself and the Court: 'I have done [the Whigs] the best office I can, but I shall think it a very ill return if they fall upon [George]. I do with all my heart wish he would be so wise as to quit his place, but I hope nobody that I have a concern for will appear against him.' Marlborough lamented his brother's indiscretions, but was 'very sure he would not say or do anything that he thought might prejudice the Queen or the government'. Yet it was no longer possible to contain the mounting hostility. Halifax, whom Churchill had earlier tried to discredit and whom Marlborough had refused to nominate as a plenipotentiary for the peace negotiations, sought revenge and ignored a letter from the Duke requesting restraint. The Junto as a whole threatened the offensive in order to force the Queen to give way over the appointment of the bishop of Norwich, an issue which had become a test of faith, and may also have sought to pursue Marlborough's brother in order to menace the Duke into greater alliance with the Junto, whose dominance he appeared to fear. At a personal level Churchill had also irritated the Whigs by criticizing the conduct of the war in Spain under Lord Galway, to whom he offered a 'sarcastic toast' at a public dinner, and by declining to take the usual oaths when Robert Walpole II* was added to the Prince's council, a hesitation which was 'construed as proof of his attachment to the exiled family', though it seems clear from a letter written by Godolphin that Churchill's reservations stemmed from doubts about whether to resign from the council in order to defuse the crisis rather than from scruples about the oath itself. Churchill may also have been suspected of acting as a drag on the employment of the Whigs, through his influence at Court and on Marlborough himself. For all these reasons the Whigs were said in October to 'continue their averseness to George Churchill and have within these four or five days sent a message to him, that if he doth not quit the Prince's council of his own accord they will find means to make him do it in spite of all he can do to keep himself in'. Since it was the place on the Prince's council that provided Churchill's best protection, he did not resign, forcing the conflict into Parliament. The inquiry into the conduct of the Admiralty was launched in the Commons by a petition from Russian merchants, including the son of (Sir) Gilbert Heathcote*, who complained about the lack of convoys for merchantmen, the very issue over which Churchill had earlier made some of his reputation as a capable naval administrator. The merchants 'spoke very boldly and stuck not to charge the managers of the navy with fraud, malice and ignorance, which all bore hard on Admiral Churchill'. A motion, proposed by Sir Gilbert Heathcote and John Ward II, that the petitioners had proved their point, was almost carried,

> but Mr Churchill saying they had indeed made proof of their losses, but it did not yet appear whether those happened through neglect in those that were entrusted in the Admiralty or by misfortune only; that they hoped to satisfy the House there had been no care omitted, which they were preparing and would have been ready before now to do, but that the House were every day sending for new papers and they did not expect it would come to a question till they had the whole before them.

Churchill successfully called for a slight delay, though he 'desired they would take the shorter day for it, since he could not but acquaint them that such an inquiry depending must needs be a great hindrance to their sea preparations'. For all its heralded bitterness, the showdown on 6 Dec. proved an anti-climax. The Whigs were divided over the attack, the Tories increasingly shied away from it, and the 'complaints were feebly managed at the bar of the Commons, for it was soon understood that not only the Prince but the Queen likewise concerned herself much in this matter and both looked upon it as a design levelled at their authority'. Anne personally told Archbishop Sharp that 'the design was against Admiral Churchill who was one of the ablest men for that service that could be found'. After such intervention, the Admiralty had only 'to justify their board and to show they had employed all the ships they had in reach', though this was not quite the end of the matter, for a parallel and more stringent inquiry had been set up by the Lords. On 19 Nov. 1707 the peers held a debate about the losses suffered by the merchants, and although Marlborough did not speak in defence of his brother, he was seen expostulating with Lord Wharton (Hon. Thomas*) directly afterwards. On 8 Jan. 1708 the Admiralty repeated its justification, though its vindication concluded with a reflection on the state of the navy in William's reign, a phrase attributed to Harley and which prompted not only a refutation but also careful and demanding scrutiny of the case. On 25 Feb. 1708 an address from the Upper House contained thinly veiled criticisms of the admiral, who was said to have made 'the worst use imaginable' of the Prince's trust, to have screened himself from criticism, and to have insulted the legislature by a vindication which failed to promise future amendment. The address concluded that the Lords hoped to see 'a new spirit and vigour put into the whole administration of the navy'. To make matters worse, part of the aim of the attack had been to replace Prince George with Churchill's old enemy Orford, and rumours again circulated that the admiral was about to lay down his flag, especially in the light of the promotion of his junior, Sir John Leake*, to command the fleet. The one redeeming feature of the session was the address, which Churchill helped draft, thanking the Prince for his great care in sending out the fleet under Byng to prevent the intended Jacobite invasion, though even then Churchill had not been able to refrain from talking 'loud against Sir George Byng for letting the enemy slip him'.[19]

The Whigs' other principal target in the winter of 1707–8 was Harley, and Churchill played a minor part in the crisis leading to the secretary's dismissal. From an inference in a letter written by Sir Godfrey Copley, 2nd Bt.*, it seems likely that the conversation between Harley and the Queen, news of which affronted Godolphin, became known to Marlborough via Churchill, who had presumably heard a report from the Prince. If this is correct, it suggests that Churchill was acting against Harley, despite their earlier cooperation, and that ironically he was giving the administration a push in the direction of the Whigs. It is likely that he did so on his brother's behalf, since both Swift and Edward Harley* believed that Churchill was employed by Marlborough to persuade the Prince, and hence the Queen, 'that she must use either part with the Duke of Marlborough or Mr Harley'. It is also possible that this act against Harley was the price Churchill had to pay to buy off the opposition to his administration of the navy, and may consequently explain why the attack on him fizzled out. Certainly in early February 1708 the Queen was still trying to save Harley by 'canvassing whatever support she could against the Churchills, who had left town'. An alternative, contradictory and less plausible explanation has also been offered that Churchill was acting in Harley's interest, because by spreading news that the secretary would be sacrificed he might embarrass Marlborough and detach him from Godolphin. This view assumes that Churchill was by now closer to Harley than to his brother, and is only supported by the rumour that after the duumvirs had tendered their resignations, Prince

George 'was said to press [Harley] in and sent to Lord Marlborough and Lord Godolphin again. If that was so, it must be Mr George Churchill that did it.' Given the ambiguous evidence it seems impossible to be certain about the admiral's position, but it seems likely that loyalty to his brother proved stronger than that to party.[20]

Churchill's Toryism, recognized in an analysis of the Commons dating from early 1708, nevertheless posed a problem for Marlborough and Godolphin. In mid-April the lord treasurer told the Duke that he found the Queen very difficult to manage, and blamed Prince George's awkwardness, which in turn he considered was

> much kept up by your brother George, who seemed to me as wrong as is possible when I spoke to him the other day. And finding him, I spoke so freely and so fully to him, of what we must all expect next winter, and himself in particular, if things go on at this rate, he appeared to be much less resolute after I had talked a while to him, and thanked me for speaking so freely.

Godolphin suspected that Churchill may have appeared humble 'out of cunning', and suggested that the Duke act to deter his brother from putting the Prince 'upon the wrong measures'. Marlborough agreed that Churchill's conduct was 'unaccountable', and promised to write to him 'very freely', but he still ordered his wife to smooth the way for George's re-election, though George decided to switch from St. Albans to Portsmouth.[21]

It was soon apparent that Churchill was playing a double game of private remorse and submission to Godolphin on the one hand and open hostility to the Whigs on the other. In May the admiral reported to the Queen that Walpole had declared that an army commission had been granted on Harley's recommendation. Anne understandably 'resented this very highly' and Walpole was forced to explain the affair to Marlborough. The matter revealed just how slippery Churchill could be, for he had deliberately misreported conversations of his Whiggish kinsman, William Churchill*, who seems to have acted as a go-between with Thomas Hopkins*, the under-secretary of state responsible for issuing the commissions. Walpole refrained from drawing conclusions about the admiral's behaviour, perhaps because Churchill's motives are once again very hard to fathom. Besides showing ingratitude to Walpole, who had come to his aid the previous winter in the House, Churchill was presumably attempting to embarrass the Whigs, though how far he was genuinely attempting to boost Harley's reputation or use it for his own ends remains a matter of speculation. The incident once again confirms Churchill's talent for lying for political gain, and backs up the Earl of Westmorland's claim to have been deliberately misrepresented to the Prince by the admiral, who disliked Westmorland's Whig principles. Certainly Godolphin, who thought Churchill 'very much to blame' in the Walpole affair, still suspected his influence, and told Marlborough on 13 June that while his brother was 'not, or at least seems not to be, without his own uneasiness too . . . he had great animosities and partialities and he either cannot or will not prevail with [the Prince] to do any good'. Matters had not improved by the following month when Godolphin complained that the admiral

> does certainly contribute very much to keep up both in [Prince George and the Queen] the natural but very inconvenient averseness they have to [the Whigs] in general, and to Sir George Byng in particular . . . and nothing is more certain than that the general dislike of [Churchill] in that station is stronger than ever and much harder to be supported.

Ostensibly Marlborough shared these misgivings. He told his wife that he wished his brother would retire 'for I have been convinced it would be for his service and everybody else', and in early August he again expressed regret that Churchill was 'so violent' for the Tories. But although the Duke may have been genuinely angered by his brother's tactics, and 'condemned' his actions, his reluctance to take firm action against him betokened regard for and loyalty to George, perhaps strengthened by a belief that his brother was being made a scapegoat for the difficulties caused by the rising favour of Abigail Masham; more deviously, the Duke's softness stemmed from a reluctance to sever links entirely with the High Tories. It may be significant that in July Churchill journeyed to Oxford to meet Harley, and although the Duke told his wife that he feared his brother would do 'what I shall not like', he may again have been placating the Duchess, who was becoming an increasingly shrill critic of George. In any case, Marlborough delayed any reprimand. On 30 Aug. he excused himself from doing 'anything ill-natured to convince [George] that I do not approve of his actions . . . for I shall content myself in letting him know and see that he shall have no assistance from me'. A stiff letter was nevertheless drafted by Arthur Maynwaring* for Marlborough to copy to his brother. It warned George that

> it will be extremely difficult, if not impossible, for you to support yourself next winter in your present station. You know that even in the last session when the Tories were all for you, and the Whigs divided and the power of the

Court exerted to the utmost, you and the rest of the Prince's council were not so well cleared as I could have wished, though you avoided a direct censure. And the struggle was then so great and the public business so much obstructed by it, that I can by no means think of enduring the same uneasiness and trouble again that I underwent last winter upon that single point. And you yourself must own that a good deal of the assistance you then had from the Whigs was owing to the personal friends of Mr Walpole, and to the defence he made in the House, from whom I fear you must expect no such service now, but rather the contrary, after what passed between you this summer ... There is not one man that I can hear of who does not positively declare for a change in the Admiralty as a thing absolutely necessary to carry on the service. And your own foolish journey to Oxford, there to meet Mr Harley, and your declaring so frequently and publicly that you could and would support yourself, has made this load still more heavy upon you. Therefore ... I must be so plain to tell you that as I think 'tis certain you cannot find friends enough of your own to prevent the storm that is coming upon you, so it will be impossible for the lord treasurer and me to give you the assistance you might hope for, without ruining ourselves, and therefore you must not expect it.

The letter promised Marlborough's help to secure an easy retirement,

but if you lose the opportunity, 'tis probable you will never have such another, and therefore I hope you will now seriously weigh this matter, and compare the advantage, ease and security which you may certainly enjoy one way, with the trouble, danger and even ruin which will probably fall upon you the other; and not only upon you only, but upon your nearest relations and friends, the government itself and the public.[22]

This letter has been provisionally dated to 23 Aug. but is more likely to relate to mid-October when Godolphin was trying to arrange a deal with Lord Wharton about Churchill's retirement. On 19 Oct. Marlborough told his wife that he would write 'whatever you and [Godolphin] shall think proper to send me', and the letter certainly reads as though it was dictated by Sarah. A variant and more measured version, endorsed as 'a letter from Mr Freeman [Marlborough] to his brother', confirms the later dating, since it is marked as 19 Oct. 1708. Yet neither copy was ever sent. The draft appears to have been delayed in the post – or at least so the Duke claimed – and arrived at the same time as another from the Duchess requesting that it should not be sent after all. Circumstances had rendered the whole problem obsolete, for when the Prince died on 28 Oct. his council was automatically dissolved and Churchill's appointment terminated.[23]

Churchill continued in town until the Prince's funeral was over, and then retired to Windsor, 'with an intention not to appear this winter in Parliament', though an analysis of the 1708 Parliament listed him, incorrectly, as a Tacker. These categorizations meant little, for though he did not resign his seat he 'retired from business' and made no further recorded contribution in the House. His health declined and he suffered frequent and violent fits of gout until he died 'with great resolution and resignation' on 8 May 1710. He was buried in Westminster Abbey. Churchill was said in a contemporary obituary to have performed his offices 'with so great honour and integrity that he left a very inconsiderable estate behind him'. In fact, he had been receiving a salary of £1,000 p.a. as a member of the council, a further 1,000 guineas from the Admiralty, on top of £400 a year as groom of the bedchamber, and a further £400 in army pension: a report in 1705 put his total income at £3,142. Moreover, he is known to have invested £500 in Bank stock by 1694, and £2,600 in the Old East India Company, though he had sold the latter investment by May 1698. Indeed, his total bequest was 'about £20,000', divided equally between his nephew Francis Godfrey* and George Churchill, his natural son (presumably by Mary Cooke, who was left a £27 annuity). As further proof that loyalty to family overrode political prejudice, Churchill appointed as his executors his Whig kinsmen William and Awnsham Churchill*. The latter informed Marlborough of George's death, claiming that 'no man left a better name or is more lamented by his friends', and Awnsham's publication of *A Collection of Voyages* may have owed something to the admiral. Churchill's will was witnessed by fellow seamen William Gifford and Sir Thomas Hardy*, the latter being one of his protégés. No contemporary left a detailed assessment of his career, but the most fitting epitaph is the praise of Lord Pembroke, who found the admiral had 'a very just and quick apprehension of naval affairs', and could find 'no body so able to assist the Prince and the Queen as Mr Churchill in cases of dispatch and difficulty'.[24]

[1] Herts. RO, Hertford bor. recs. 25, p. 100; R. East, *Portsmouth Recs.* 373. [2] *DNB*; *Parlty. Lists Early 18th Cent.* ed. Newman, 66; A. L. Rowse, *Early Churchills*, 352–3; J. H. Owen, *War at Sea*, 3–4. [3] *DNB*; *CSP Dom.* 1687–9, p. 364; 1698, p. 128. [4] Dalrymple, *Mems.* iii(2), 120–1, 124–5; Centre Kentish Stud. Stanhope mss U1590/059/1, Robert Yard* to Alexander Stanhope*, 2 Feb 1691[–2]; *CSP Dom.* 1690–1, p. 383. [5] *Portledge Pprs.* 129; Luttrell, *Brief Relation*, ii. 343; Hatton Corresp. (Cam. Soc. n.s. xxiii), 170; Add. 37991, ff. 69b-70; *HMC Finch*, iv. 120–1, 131, 136–7, 142, 151, 305; PRO NI, De Ros mss D/638/13/171, John Pulteney* to Thomas Coningsby*, 7 July 1692. [6] *Mariner's Mirror*, xxxv. 339; Cobbett, *Parlty. Hist.* v. 734–7; *Luttrell Diary*, 248, 261. [7] *Luttrell Diary*, 330, 363–4; Cobbett, v. 753. [8] Add. 31958, f. 45. [9] *Ailesbury Mems.* 413. [10] *Vernon–Shrewsbury Letters*, ii. 260; Add. 17677 TT, ff. 81, 130; *Cocks Diary*, 3–4; H. Horwitz, *Parl. and Pol. Wm. III*, 254. [11] BL, Althorp mss box 3, R. Crawford to Mq. of Halifax

(William Savile*), 18 July 1699; Add. 40774, ff. 53-54, 205-6; Northants. RO, Montagu (Boughton) mss 47/248, Vernon to Shrewsbury, n.d. [12]Montagu (Boughton) mss 47/148, Vernon to Shrewsbury, 22 Feb. 1700; *Marlborough–Godolphin Corresp.* 3; *Vernon–Shrewsbury Letters*, ii. 389; iii. 11, 117. [13]HLRO, HC Lib. mss 12, f. 58v; PRO30/24/129-30; Add. 70272, 'Large Account', p. 18; Annandale mss at Raehills, bdle. 828, George Wisheard to [Ld. Annandale], 1 Jan. 1702; DZA, Bonet despatch 16/27 Jan. 1702. [14]*Verney Letters*, i. 107; *Marlborough–Godolphin Corresp.* 62, 66; Add. 31598, f. 46; *Bull. IHR*, xvii. 15. [15]*Cocks Diary*, 113-14, 147-8. [16]*HMC Portland*, iv. 54; *Huntington Lib. Q.* xxx. 252; Add. 17677 WWW, f. 9; 31958, ff. 47-50; Luttrell, v. 256, 272, 313; *Marlborough–Godolphin Corresp.* 181, 187, 240. [17]*Marlborough–Godolphin Corresp.* 256, 267, 338; *HMC Popham*, 284; *Bull. IHR*, xxxiv. 92; Bath mss at Longleat House, Portland misc. pprs. f. 196, Godolphin to Harley, 25 Nov. [1704]. [18]Luttrell, v. 505, 523, 559, 562, 563; vi. 4, 234, 237; *Bull. IHR*, xxxvii. 28; lxv. 48-49; *Marlborough–Godolphin Corresp.* 583, 594-6, 628. [19]*Marlborough–Godolphin Corresp.* 834, 845; *EHR*, lxxxii. 739; Coxe, *Marlborough*, ii. 93, 187; *Huntington Lib. Q.* xv. 36; Cobbett, vi. 603; *Vernon–Shrewsbury Letters*, iii. 283-7; Tindal, *Hist. Eng.* ii. 41-42; T. Sharp, *John Sharp*, i. 302; Stanhope, *Reign of Anne*, 321; Luttrell, vi. 251; 7th Duke of Manchester, *Court and Soc. Eliz. to Anne*, ii. 319. [20]*EHR*, lxxx. 678; *HMC Portland*, v. 647; *Swift Works* ed. Davis, viii. 113; *Huntington Lib. Q.* xxx. 270. [21]*Marlborough–Godolphin Corresp.* 957, 966, 972. [22]Coxe, *Walpole*, ii. 9-11; SRO, Ogilvy of Inverquharity mss GD205/36/6, Grey Neville* to William Bennet*, 11 July 1708; *HMC 10th Rep. IV*, 50; *Marlborough–Godolphin Corresp.* 975, 1009, 1027-8, 1035, 1049, 1052, 1073, 1082-4, 1089. [23]Coxe, *Walpole*, ii. 9-11; Ogilvy of Inverquharity mss GD205/36/6, Grey Neville* to William Bennet*, 11 July 1708; *HMC 10th Rep. IV*, 50; *Marlborough–Godolphin Corresp.* 975, 1009, 1027-8, 1035, 1049, 1052, 1073, 1082-4, 1089, 1132; Add. 61430, f. 60. [24]*HMC Portland*, 510; Boyer, *Anne Annals*, ix. 415; *Marlborough–Godolphin Corresp.* 490; Luttrell v. 177; Bodl. Rawl. A.302, ff. 224-7; *Cal. Treas. Bks.* i. 321; Rowse, 364; PCC 106 Smith; Add. 61367, f. 151; Owen, 3.

M. J. K.

CHURCHILL, John (1657-1709), of Colliton House and Fordington, Dorchester, Dorset.

DORCHESTER 1708-24 Apr. 1709

bap. 10 Feb. 1657, 2nd s. of William Churchill† of Muston, Dorset by his w. Grace. *educ.* Trinity, Oxf. 1676; I. Temple 1675, called 1683. *m.* settlement 8 July 1693, Anne (d. 1722), da. of Roger Clavell of Smedmore, Dorset, wid. of John Darrel, s.p.[1]

Both Churchill's father and uncle had represented Dorchester, where the family owned property, and John inherited part of an estate nearby, at Fordington. A practising lawyer, Churchill was returned for the borough in 1708, alongside his distant kinsman, the bookseller Awnsham Churchill*. There was also a more tenuous connexion between the two men, since John's wife was the daughter of a cousin of a prominent stationer of London. John should not, however, be confused with Awnsham's brother and publishing partner of the same name. The presence of other members of the Churchill family in the House also makes it difficult to be certain about John Churchill's activity in Parliament, for the very short time that he was there. He was probably a Whig, for he was marked by Lord Sunderland (Charles, Lord Spencer*) as a gain for the party, and although another list has the label 'Court Tory' written near his name, this may have referred to Sir Nathaniel Napier, 2nd Bt.*, whose seat he had taken. Another clue to Churchill's political sympathies is that he appears to have been recommended in 1689 for a place as collector of excise for Dorset. He died on 24 Apr. 1709, leaving his estate in the first place to his wife, and upon her death to his brother Charles. He was buried in the Temple Church, London.[2]

[1]Hutchins, *Dorset*, i. 57; ii. 414. [2]*Cal. I. Temple. Recs.* iii. 201, 401, 415; *Cal. Treas. Bks.* ix. 104; *Reg. Temple Church*, 1628-1853, p. 33.

P. W./M. J. K.

CHURCHILL, William (1661-1737), of Dallinghoo and Woodbridge, Suff.

IPSWICH   21 Nov. 1707-1 Apr. 1714
          1715-8 Dec. 1717

bap. 11 Aug 1661, 2nd s. of William Churchill of Dorchester; bro. of Awnsham* and Joshua Churchill†. *m.* Rose, da. of John Sayer of Woodbridge, Suff., 1 da.[1]

Freeman, Stationers' Co. 1684.[2]

Bookseller, bookbinder and stationer to Crown 1689-d.; cashier, Ordnance office 1699-1702; commr. sick and wounded 1704-7, salt 1732.[3]

Like his brother Awnsham, with whom he appears to have been in partnership until 1690, Churchill was active in the 1680s as a radical Whig publisher. In 1685 the government received information that he had 'printed or had a hand in printing Monmouth's *Declaration*'; he had apparently been asked to lend his press to a Quaker, who actually ran off the sheets, though it was probably William rather than his brother who 'furnished the paper for the printing the said *Declaration* after that it was declared to him for what use it was to be employed'. Churchill fled to Amsterdam, where he lodged with 'a notorious bookseller for the rebels' interest' named Vandervelde, who also harboured John Locke; and a spy reported that Churchill 'was going to print some of the archtraitors' letters writ since he went hence'. The first surviving publication in his name (jointly with Awnsham) is dated 1683, but he was most active at the Revolution when he published many of William of Orange's *Declarations* and also the *Association*. It may also have been in 1688 that he acquired the epithet of Major, by which he was thereafter known, though he may also have had some military expertise, for in 1690 he was one of those approved to be field officers in the auxiliaries of the London lieutenancy. In 1689, possibly to promote the passage of the toleration bill, he issued Samuel Blackerby's *An Historical Account of Making the Penal Laws*, dedicated to Charles Mordaunt, Earl of Monmouth, in which the author argued that differences between Anglicans and Dissenters were promoted by papists, and that the Protestants ought to unite. In February 1689 Churchill was rewarded for his services at the Revolution by appointment as stationer to the King, a post which he held throughout his life, and at the beginning of Anne's reign took his brother-in-law Edward Castle into partnership at the stationer's office. Although the number of prints issued in his name declined after 1690, Churchill retained an interest in publishing ventures: in 1711, for example, he acted as an agent for one of his brothers, probably Awnsham, concerning an account of the campaign in 1704, which he said Richard Steele* and others had agreed to correct.[4]

Churchill tried to build on his early success and to exploit his kinship with the Marlboroughs, but although he had his family's eye for the main chance, he was usually unable to follow his schemes through successfully. His own fiercely Whig principles did not prevent a close friendship with the High Tory admiral George Churchill*: on 29 Nov. 1693 William was one of the witnesses examined about the miscarriage of the fleet the previous summer, which George was attacking; and it may have been on his advice that in 1694 William was providing ships for the transport of prisoners of war. A project to supply the army's clothing may also have owed something to George Churchill, who had begun an apprenticeship with the Drapers' Company, though William had himself been active as a clothier since at least 1684. To obtain contracts, William exploited his relationship with Marlborough's other brother, Charles*, for whom he was acting as a financial agent by 1698, presumably supplying the regiment. A man of diverse interests, he later listed his various services as having included officiating for Colonel Hon. Harry Mordaunt* (Monmouth's brother) when he was treasurer of the Ordnance 1699–1702. Churchill, who was said to have acted as Mordaunt's deputy or cashier, had apparently been given a promise to succeed to the post, though this undertaking was never honoured and William's claim to have saved the public thousands of pounds went unrecognized. It was only in Anne's reign, with George Churchill's rise to favour, that he gained office. Although a report at the beginning of the new reign that he was to be added to the reformed prize commission proved unfounded, he was made a commissioner for sick and wounded seamen in April 1704 with the special charge of inspecting accounts and mustering prisoners at the great ports. He later claimed that he had 'discovered great frauds and proposed a method to the Prince of Denmark which was approved; and the public were saved some thousands of pounds by it and he was promised an additional salary' of £200, though once again this was never paid, despite a petition for its issue in 1707. By 1704 he was also supplying clothes to the army in Portugal and Spain in partnership with Richard Harnage*. Both fields of activity, as commissioner and clothier, were later to be investigated by anti-corruption inquiries in the Commons.[5]

Churchill was invited to contest a by-election at Ipswich in 1707 and he accordingly resigned his office on the sick and wounded board, which was incompatible with a seat in Parliament, on the tacit understanding that a place would soon be found for him in some other branch of the naval service; he later claimed that he lost £500 a year by quitting, but had never been rewarded with office. He was successful both in the by-election and the following general election, when supported by the town's recorder, William Thompson III*. In return he backed Thompson's candidacy at Orford, whence he had himself received 'very large promises'. Churchill's return was marked by Lord Sunderland (Charles, Lord Spencer*) as a gain for the Whigs, but in spite of their political differences George Churchill offered him a place on the victualling board if he felt able to keep his seat at the necessary by-election. Nothing came of this, but William's relationship with George was soon to get him into difficulty. In June the admiral was spreading rumours that the recently dismissed Robert Harley* still carried influence at court, citing as proof the appointment of one of Harley's nominees to a military commission and naming William as his source, who in turn was said to have heard it from Robert Walpole II's* secretary. Walpole's account of the affair to Marlborough shows how close the Churchills were, and how the admiral was prepared to use his relation as a pawn in a political struggle to embarrass the Whigs, for George Churchill must deliberately have distorted what William had reported to him of his investigative missions. Although relations between the two Churchills were not seriously damaged, George was no longer in a position to offer patronage after the death of Prince George in October 1708. William's career as an army clothier also seems to have ended about this time: he and Harnage received no further contracts after the end of 1707, although the partnership continued for another two years, possibly supplying individual regiments. With the loss of George's influence, William turned to Marlborough himself. As early as 1705 he had begun zealously petitioning the Duke to advance the military careers of his brother Joshua and son-in-law Francis Negus†, and in 1709 wrote to congratulate Marlborough on his victories and to offer his services. In April 1710 he sent the Duke an account of George Churchill's illness, but was unable to miss even that opportunity to put in another request for an army post. In Parliament he gave further evidence of his Low Church sympathies in 1709 when he supported the naturalization of the Palatines. On 5 Feb. 1709 he told for a resolution about the franchise at Dunwich which favoured the Whigs, and the following year voted in favour of the impeachment of Dr Sacheverell, whose trial he observed to have plunged the nation into 'ferment'.[6]

Again successful for Ipswich in 1710, Churchill was marked as a Whig on the 'Hanover list' and on 7 Dec. 1711 voted for the motion of 'No Peace without Spain'. Earlier that year he had intervened on behalf of the tax receivers of Suffolk, whose only offence had been 'their voting for Sir Philip Parker [3rd Bt.†, the defeated Whig candidate] for the country [sic], which was upon the account of the right of the guildable part to have one Member and not party, whatever may have been represented'. On three occasions during the Parliament he told for Whigs in divisions over disputed elections: on 3 Feb. 1711 in the Ipswich case, on behalf of William Thompson; on 7 Apr. 1711 in favour of James Stanhope's* return for Cockermouth; and on 7 Feb. 1712 in support of Edmund Halsey* in Southwark. On 22 Mar. 1711 he was also 'comforting' to Bishop Nicolson, probably in relation to the Commons' censure on the bishop's having used the Queen's name when electioneering in Carlisle for (Sir) James Montagu I*. Churchill's experience in transporting captives made him a natural addition on 10 Feb. 1711 to the committee investigating the exchange of prisoners, and on 30 May 1711 as a teller on a motion concerning the transport of naval stores. By 1712 he was running into financial difficulties, though he resisted the temptation of investing £15,000 which had come into his hands on the death of Dr Richards (deputy to Hon. Edward Russell* as treasurer of the chamber) by which he 'might have obtained a considerable estate'. He sent a memorial to the Treasury requesting an office 'on any commission in which he might be useful' or, at least, payment of £2,048 owing to him from the government. He was perhaps on the lookout for a post as a stamp duty commissioner, for he also claimed to have 'proposed the [1712] Act for stamping paper and parchment and spent on it £470'.

If his boast is true, the scheme was a strange one for a man whose brothers were friendly with John Locke, a staunch advocate of a free press, and who in 1708 was reported to have a 'share' in the *Daily Courant*, the type of newspaper which suffered by the Stamp Act.[7]

Instead of obtaining payment or office, Churchill found himself increasingly under fire in the House, perhaps because his readiness to subordinate party to personal considerations had lost him friends among the Whigs and made him a relatively easy target. Indeed, an inquiry by the commissioners of public accounts into the state of the sick and wounded service produced an unexpected ally in Viscount Bolingbroke (Henry St. John II*), who wrote on 24 Mar. 1713 to recommend to the Duke of Shrewsbury's favour 'a very hard case ... Mr William Churchill, who has had the honour of your Grace's patronage formerly and for who I have long had a deep kindness, is deeply concerned in it'. Shrewsbury replied that he would assist him, but the report made to the House on 16 Apr. 1713 was still highly critical, and claimed that Churchill had procured transport contracts for the merchant Robert Michell and William's brother-in-law John Pearce, at excessively high rates in order to share in the profits. Both contractors had admitted this, and Pearce's rate of pay had been unnecessarily increased at a meeting of the commissioners attended by Churchill, though Pearce later tried to retract his statement and suggest that because Churchill had bailed Pearce out financially his share was therefore repayment rather than a true partnership. The report was considered on 7 May, when the House, having heard further evidence and Churchill's defence, resolved

> that for any commissioner or other person entrusted by her Majesty in making contracts for public services, to be a partner in such contract, or to reserve a share for any other person, is a high breach of trust and a notorious corruption.

Since his offences had been committed before the Act of Pardon of 1709 it was resolved to take no further action against him, though Churchill had taken the precaution the night before the vote of vindicating himself to Harley, now Lord Treasurer Oxford.[8]

Oxford may not have been very sympathetic: Sir Robert Davers, 2nd Bt.*, approached him for assistance in unseating Churchill, and, although successful at the poll for Ipswich in 1713, Churchill was duly unseated on petition on 1 Apr. 1714, when he and Thompson saw the House so set against them that they 'walked out and gave up their cause'. Shortly afterwards he travelled to France, carrying a letter of recommendation from Bolingbroke to Matthew

Prior*, a journey which allowed him to escape the further embarrassment of another inquiry conducted by the commissioners of accounts, this time into the army clothing contracts he and Harnage had won in 1706. Bolingbroke's helpfulness may well have been inspired by the desire to prevent damaging revelations concerning his own close friend, Arthur Moore*, who had been comptroller of army accounts at that time, particularly as the commissioners were more interested in censuring the army administrators than the contractors. The report, presented to the House on 13 Apr. 1714, claimed that the contract with Churchill and Harnage had been irregular in that it had been made through an agent, who did not himself supply any of the goods and was at that time a government employee. The inquiry may also have been designed to smoke out damaging evidence against the previous ministry, since the report stated that the contract had first been ordered by Marlborough, and concluded under the direction of Lord Godolphin (Sidney†); it was also noted that Harnage and Churchill had been in partnership with Marlborough's confidant James Craggs I*, whom Churchill may have known at the Ordnance office. When questioned, Churchill claimed that since ending the partnership three years earlier he had burnt all his papers; and he left the country before the commissioners could question him on a second set of charges relating to two gratuities, each of £1,000, paid to secure the contracts. He returned to England only after the expiry of the commission for taking public accounts, and no action was taken on the report before the prorogation on 9 July.[9]

Churchill was re-elected for Ipswich in 1715, when he was ranked as a Whig on all lists which categorized Members, and continued to support the Whig party in the House. In 1717 he obtained a patent for supplying stationery to the crown, and vacated his seat in favour of his son-in-law Francis Negus. Churchill also took over Negus' debts, which may partly account for the provision in his will to raise £7,000 to pay creditors. Churchill also left £300 to Negus' son William, though upon his death in February 1737 the estate passed to William Castle, perhaps because Churchill felt guilty about having hindered one of Edward Castle's chancery suits, an intervention which, he regretted, had brought 'a very great loss' to the Castle family.[10]

[1] Soc. of Geneal., St. Peter's Dorchester par. reg. trans.; Hutchins, *Dorset*, ii. 384; Plomer, *Dict. Booksellers and Printers 1666–1725*, p. 70. [2] *Stationers' Co. Apprentices 1641–1700*, ed. McKenzie, 112. [3] *Cal. Treas. Pprs.* 1731–3, p. 229. [4] Add. 41814, ff. 79, 80; 41812, f. 226; 61368, f. 27; Wing A4057, W2323, W2324, W2326; *CSP Dom.* 1690–1, p. 74. [5] *CSP Dom.* 1694–5, p. 91; *Cal. Treas. Bks.* vii. 1272; xiii. 247; xxv. 411; *Cal. Treas. Pprs.* 1708–14, p. 456; Luttrell, *Brief Relation*, v. 182; Watson thesis, 316. [6] Camb. Univ. Lib. Chomondeley (Houghton) mss, Churchill to Walpole, 12 May 1716; W. Suss. RO, Shillinglee mss Ac.454/857, Ld. Dysart (Lionel Tollemache*) to Sir Edward Turnor*, 6 Feb. 1707–8; 1060, John Hooke to same, 12 Apr. 1708; 1166, Thomas Palmer to same, 6 May 1708; *Cal. Treas. Pprs.* 1708–14, p. 40; *HMC Portland*, iv. 494; Coxe, *Walpole*, 9–11; Add. 61292, ff. 119, 121, 123; 61293, ff. 3–5; 61366, f. 189; 61367, f. 139. [7] *Nicolson Diaries*, ed. Jones and Holmes, 562; *Cal. Treas. Pprs.* 1708–14, p. 456; Shillinglee mss Ac. 454/861, Turnor to mayor of Ipswich, [?11] May 1708. [8] *Bolingbroke Corresp.* iii. 515; Cobbett, *Parlty. Hist.* vi. 1198–1200, 1207; Add. 70217, Churchill to Harley, 6 May 1713. [9] *HMC Portland*, v. 377; *Bull. IHR*, xxxiv. 212; *Bolingbroke Corresp.* iii. 516; Boyer, *Pol. State*, vii. 345–51. [10] Cholmondeley (Houghton) mss, Churchill to Walpole, 12 May 1716; PCC 21 Wake.

P.W./M.J.K.

CLARGES, Robert (c.1693–c.1726), of St. James's, Westminster, Mdx. and Stoke Poges, Bucks.

READING 1713–30 May 1716

b. c.1693, 3rd but 2nd surv. s. of Sir Walter Clarges, 1st Bt.*, being 1st s. by his 3rd w.; half-bro. of Sir Thomas Clarges, 2nd Bt.* *educ.* St. Paul's sch.; Trinity Coll. Camb. adm. 22 July 1708, aged 15. *unm.*[1]

Clarges was still a minor when his father died in 1706. In accordance with the testamentary wish of his grandfather, Sir Thomas Clarges*, the family manor and rectory of Stoke Poges in Buckinghamshire descended to him in trust until he came of age. In 1713, Clarges was put up as a Tory candidate at Reading, which lay within easy striking distance of his Buckinghamshire estate. His mother had an important interest within the borough in the form of the crown lease of extensive lands and fisheries which she had inherited from her husband, Sir Walter, and renewed in 1715. The family also owned other property in the borough, most notably the former monastic lands. More significantly, young Clarges' political credentials were assured by his impeccable Tory pedigree. Despite protestations about his age at the time of the election, he was returned by the mayor. A subsequent petition from the defeated Whig candidate, Owen Buckingham*, questioning Clarges' qualification to stand, was never reported. He was identified as a Tory in two lists of the 1713 Parliament, one of which was the Worsley list. His inactivity as a Member obviously stemmed from his youth and inexperience. Although he was re-elected in 1715, his return was declared void the following year, whereupon he made no attempt to regain his seat. He died c.February 1726, at which time an administration of his property was granted to his mother and elder brother, Sir Thomas.[2]

[1] Kimber and Johnson, *Baronetage*, ii. 384; Prob. 10/1401; Admon. Feb. 1726. [2] Prob. 10/1401; *VCH Bucks.* iii. 309–10; *CJ*, xvii. 480; *Cal. Treas. Bks.* xxix. 491; xxx. 426; PCC 170 Irby.

A. A. H.

CLARGES, Sir Thomas (c.1618–95), of Piccadilly, Westminster and Stoke Poges, Bucks.

SUTHERLAND, ROSS AND CROMARTY	1656–1658
ABERDEEN BURGHS AND LAUDER BURGHS	1659
WESTMINSTER	1660
SOUTHWARK	13 Mar. 1666–1679 (Jan.)
CHRISTCHURCH	1679 (Mar.)–1681 (Mar.)
	1685–1687
OXFORD UNIVERSITY	1689–4 Oct. 1695

b. c.1618, o. s. of John Clargis, farrier, of Drury Lane, Westminster by Anne Leaver. *educ.* G. Inn 1662; Wadham, Oxf. matric. 1689. *m.* 29 Sept. 1646, Mary, da. of George Proctor, yeoman, of Norwell Woodhouse, Notts. and coh. to her bro. Edward, 1s. *suc.* fa. 1648; kntd. 8 May 1660.[1]

Commissary-gen. of musters 1660–71; clerk of the hanaper Mar.–June 1660; commr. for maimed soldiers Dec. 1660–1; PC [I] 1663.[2]

Dep. keeper, Hampton Court, Mdx. 1660–70; commr. for recusants, Mdx. and Surr. 1675; freeman and bailiff, Oxford 1687–Feb. 1688.[3]

Commr. public accts. 1691–d.

By the beginning of the 1690 Parliament the elderly Clarges was the doyen of the Country Tories, with a substantial record as an outspoken critic of government. He was pre-eminent among the diminishing stock of 'old Parliament men' whose service in the Commons dated back to the 1650s, and could claim seniority over all the major Country party figures with whom he would be actively associated in his final years. A 'bigoted' High Churchman, Clarges, with his modest London origins, could hardly be regarded as an archetypal country gentleman. Though he later came to own much land in the home counties, his chief interests and links were always metropolitan. He bought and built extensively in the St. James and Piccadilly areas and his distinguished rent-roll included such court figures as the Duke of Shrewsbury and Lord Ranelagh (Richard Jones*). Even in the last years of his life he showed little inclination for the steadier life of a country gentleman and seldom left the capital. Self-conscious of his acquired genteel status, he was attached to the 'succession of posterity' which he regarded as 'one of the greatest blessings and felicities of this life'. Clarges' rise from obscurity took effect after 1653 when his sister married General Monck (George†). It was as one of Monck's close confidants that in the 1650s and 1660s he made some headway as a public servant, mainly in the army administration. Yet he proved to be no natural-born servant of the Court. In the 1660s, he emerged as an articulate man of principle: a severe judge of ministerial conduct; a defender of the rights and liberties of the subject before the law and of the concept of habeas corpus; an earnest upholder of Commons privilege over the Lords and the crown; a rabid anti-papist; and a hater of foreigners, above all the French. Devoted to monarchy in its traditional form, and loyal to the person of the King, he nevertheless frequently criticized the later Stuarts for their religious inclinations, financial demands, and choice of ministers. Alongside these prejudices were clear-minded notions of responsible government. Clarges looms large in the debates of the earlier 1690s, though very little is known of his personality. Much truth, however, can be discerned in Bishop Burnet's description of him as 'an honest but haughty man', his constant emphasis on economy in public expenditure suggesting an austere and conceited character.[4]

During the Convention Clarges was regarded by Court managers as one of a number of 'commoners eminent in Parliament, useful men but not to be trusted'. However, in the early days of 1690 Lord Nottingham (Daniel Finch†) courted him in his endeavours to establish the Church party in the good opinions of the King. He was one of several High Churchmen to whom Nottingham offered the prospect of senior posts in the administration. Quite how Clarges viewed this possibility is not on record, but it is doubtful if office held any real appeal for one who had been so long a back-bencher and who, as reported at the time of his death five years later, had long repented of his associations with Charles II's court. But for all his subsequent criticism of royal policies he retained a £500 pension payable from duties on Newcastle coals with which he had been rewarded in 1661. In February 1690 he was re-elected for Oxford University alongside Nottingham's brother, Hon. Heneage Finch I. Such was their popularity as stalwart Churchmen that they were unanimously acclaimed by convocation at the election. The continuing possibility that Clarges might still prove a trusty servant of the Court was reflected in Lord Carmarthen's (Sir Thomas Osborne*) classification of him on the eve of the new Parliament as a Tory and probable Court supporter. Indeed, at the outset of proceedings on 20 Mar., Clarges seconded the Court

Tory candidate for the Speakership, Sir John Trevor, who was duly selected. Two days later, Clarges and Sir Joseph Tredenham obtained the censure of the House upon several 'libellous' anti-Tory pamphlets and blacklists hawked in the elections by the Whigs. On the same day, when the King's Speech was debated, Clarges cautioned against embarking too hastily upon matters rightfully belonging to the supply committee before other parts of the speech had been considered. His only other recorded speech this session on supply-related business was on 31 Mar. in connexion with the army, but its tenor was wholly consistent with his abiding scepticism towards the workings of government. In the midst of this debate he declared himself 'puzzled' by the revenue accounts and could only surmise that there had been 'great mismanagement' of public money owing to the 'unskilfulness of the managers'. He wondered why as many as 36,000 men were needed for the army when the treaty arrangements with the States General required only 20,000. In a typical aside, he recalled his own experience in army administration, which he saw as a golden era when greater care was taken, and slender public revenues could be stretched to support much larger forces. The ministers, he felt, were obliged 'to explain what condition we are in'. But, confessing weariness at finding fault, he concluded somewhat loosely by moving 'for what sum shall be necessary, and what sum we can have towards this out of the revenue'. Clarges was echoing the general anxiety of Country Members over the difficulties of obtaining reliable figures on which they could adequately assess what money to grant, or indeed whether the sums granted had been sufficient or properly expended. Not surprisingly, he was prominent in the efforts this session to pass a bill establishing a commission of public accounts, being named first to a committee for drafting the bill on 14 Apr.[5]

Much of Clarges' attention in the course of the 1690 session was directed upon the range of measures generated to stabilize William III's accession. He can be seen as a Tory trying anxiously to square his unalloyed attachment to dynastic principle with the facts and implications of the Revolution. The Lords' 'recognition' bill sought to recognize William and Mary as 'rightful and lawful' rulers and to declare the Acts of the Convention Parliament 'of full force'. When the bill reached the Commons, Clarges was one of several Tory MPs who found it necessary to scruple over limitations over William's right by disputing the key phrase devised by the Lords that William and Mary 'were and are' King and Queen. When the bill was debated at its second reading on 9 Apr. he could not accept that they had been monarchs before the Convention had made its formal offer in February 1689. His belief was that the Crown had devolved automatically on Princess Mary as the next Protestant heir, and he had thus voted against the transfer of the crown to William and Mary jointly. He had, however, declared his acceptance of the majority decision that the throne was 'vacant', and that in consequence the new monarchs owed their title to parliamentary vote. The present Parliament, Clarges averred, owed its existence not to the old Convention, but to the oaths framed under the 'original contract' whereby William and Mary had in February 1689 taken upon themselves the government. Only in that context could he 'give them all the authority that may be', but he would not declare that they 'were and are' King and Queen. He thus spoke for committal with a view to changing this formula. Clarges seemed keen to emphasize that it had been a parliamentary act to make them King and Queen, a 'vacancy' having occurred in the succession which Parliament had correctly taken upon itself to supply. This clearly marked an advance on his previous thinking, that parliamentary intervention on matters concerning the succession threatened to make the throne elective, evoking apprehensions of 'a commonwealth'. On 24 Apr. the House debated Hon. Thomas Wharton's* motion for a bill requiring all office-holders to abjure King James. Clarges was naturally concerned at the suggestion that such a bill should contain permanent provision to suspend offenders from their rights of habeas corpus. As the leading promoter of the 1679 Act, Clarges condemned its 'hasty repeal' in the Convention and reasserted his old attachment to 'liberty of speech' as 'a right inherent in us'. 'I value liberty more than life, or estate', he concluded, 'that's my passive obedience; I cannot consent to it.' Despite these fundamental objections he was named to the committee to draft the bill, though it is doubtful if this body ever sat, for Wharton introduced his bill the very next day. Clarges spoke against the bill at its second reading on the 26th. He considered that the 'short' oath of allegiance and the new Recognition Act constituted a perfectly adequate 'renunciation' of King James. Further oaths would weaken rather than strengthen the new King's 'interest': 'to put a buttress to a building is a sign the building is weak, and he builds ill that does so, and worse, that shows the weakness.' He was, of course, only too well aware of the difficulties which such an oath would place in the way of ministerial Tories, many of whom in conscience would be bound to refuse, thus jeopardizing their positions in government. Desirous of seeing more positive steps devised to ensure the security of the new regime, and to demonstrate that Tories were not irresponsible backsliders in time of crisis, he advocated the appointment of a select committee to produce an outline bill for these purposes. To the Whig Edward Harley* Clarges' drift seemed to be 'that the providence of God ought not to be limited', an insinuation that Clarges and his kind wished to keep their consciences clear for King James. The opposition to Wharton's bill secured its narrow defeat. Clarges' proposal that alternative means be found for securing the government was debated on 28 Apr., though he was unable to offer a blueprint of his own for the problems of 'security', limiting himself to a general review of the nation's circumstances. Indicating that the problem was one of degree, he expressed his belief that the nation's predicament was not so acute as to disable the government from obtaining funds from the City, though at the same time he felt that the ministers' lacklustre performance 'will make despondency in the lenders'. The invasion of Ireland might not have been necessary, he told MPs, had the ministers acted more promptly upon his advice the previous session to field an army there. Despite his sturdy defence of the habeas corpus principle a few days earlier, he admitted the need for its possible 'suspension' in present circumstances, though he added, 'our distraction is so great, and our condition so doubtful, I know not what to move'. When the security issue was considered further on the 29th, Clarges merely pointed out, in answer to Sir Edward Jennings' suggestion that greater use be made of the militia, that lords lieutenant already had adequate powers of muster. Even so, having been the instigator of these proceedings, he was named to the select committee to prepare a bill according to the resolutions. On 1 May Clarges spoke somewhat equivocally on the Lords' regency bill. He told the House that if reports were true, the situation in Ireland did not necessarily warrant the King's presence there. While there could be no real objection to such a measure, he was anxious for some provision for ensuring 'the public peace'. The real stumbling block, in his view, was that if William could not quickly reconquer Ireland 'we shall not hope to keep England long'. He thus advised the House not to postpone the matter to some distant date but to sit '*de die in diem*' until we have settled the thing'. Clarges' equivocation on the regency issue was more obvious when the committee resumed on 5 May, though with reluctance he admitted that a regency was the only way of saving Ireland and ultimately of preserving England from the Jacobite threat. His speech exemplifies the delicately balanced attitudes of which he was so capable:

'tis plain we are in great exigency, and the King, as now advised, resolves to go for Ireland. I would not be hasty in advising. I would not raise such a heap of difficulties, that we know not which way to turn. The French king has committed such great cruelties; scarce such since the Roman persecutions. I would rather endure anything than that. Is Ireland in such a condition that his presence is so necessary there, or Ireland will be lost? What if the King does not go, and we advise him to it, and Ireland is lost, and he tells you, 'By your advice I did not go.' You are moved to give the Queen more power, the administration jointly in King and Queen, and to the Queen, in the King's absence; shall the Queen's hand be enough to warrants in the King's absence? There are perplexities every way, all will be of no effect. If the King goes not out of England, or if the King goes into Scotland it relates to both purposes. I wish we apply the debates to amend the bill as well as we can; if he does go, that he may go. I see no great hurt of adding 'administration' to it. Something must be done that the King may be in a possibility of saving that kingdom.

At the report on the regency bill on the 6th there were continued misgivings that its terms seemed to allow for the potentially conflicting situation of 'two co-operative powers'. Clarges, however, could perceive no such contradictions and hoped that if any others were apparent the wisdom of the House would prevail to amend them. He was subsequently a member of the committee appointed on 13 May to confer with the Lords on the matter.[6]

The forthcoming campaign in Ireland led the House to debate on 13 May the motion proposed by Sir Edward Seymour, 4th Bt., to consider measures for the preservation of peace and security in the King's absence. Seymour's main intention, abetted by Sir Christopher Musgrave, 4th Bt., and others, was to question who would counsel the Queen in the King's absence, and thereby throw further opprobrium upon Carmarthen. According to Roger Morrice, Clarges stood out as a moderating influence in the midst of some heated exchanges. He tried to steer the debate away from Carmarthen (for which he was later chided by Seymour), declaring there was no point in the motion, the House having already considered means of putting the militia on the alert and for disarming Papists. He did, however, feel there was more scope for action against Catholics, 'the persons most likely to endanger us', whom he had heard now formed 'confederacies' in northern parts. But on the 14th he warned against excessive persecution and criticized the lord lieutenant of Gloucestershire's high-handedness in raising a force of 'auxiliaries' – 'I say it is levying war and no better' – while on the 15th, when a Lancashire Papist appeared at the Commons' bar to testify concerning Catholic subversion in various parts of the country, Clarges tried to divert inquiry 'and was so fervent therein, diverse Members took notice of it'. Far from being a Jacobite, Clarges was principally concerned with the avoidance of the kind of unsettling extremes witnessed in late years. Clarges' prominence as a wealthy property-owner in and around Westminster gave him notable influence in City politics. As a Tory he took a prominent part in the eradication of Whigs from City government. On 8 Apr., the Tories having defeated a radical Whig attempt both to nullify the 1683 quo warranto judgment and to restore 'ancient rights' to the City's governors, Clarges was one of several Tory MPs named to a committee to prepare a bill that simply reversed the judgment. Clarges' pre-eminence in this work is indicated by his report from the committee and his presentation of the resultant bill on the 14th. A few days later, on the 17th, he condemned a petition from leading Whig citizens which requested the restoration of 'ancient liberties', and welcomed the King's recent remodelling of the militia command which, had this not been undertaken, would have made it impossible for William to venture out of London. Not surprisingly, his remarks angered Whig Members, and during the hearing of counsel against the bill on 24 Apr. several clashed angrily with Clarges. As soon as the committee proceedings closed, Clarges pursued his point by moving to thank the King for his care of the Church in the recent removal of Whigs from the City lieutenancy, inciting a furious response from Paul Foley I*. He spoke much to the same purpose on 12 May in connexion with the Lords' request that two Members, Sir Robert Clayton and Sir George Treby, attend them with a list of the reconstituted lieutenancy, 'to know whether the King has done well or no', and sternly denied that the Lords had any right to cross-examine MPs about the correctness of the King's actions. But far from achieving for City Toryism an acceptably conceived measure for reversing the quo warranto, he was blamed after the bill passed for a misdrafting which enabled the Whigs to retain control over the offices of lord mayor and chamberlain.[7]

Throughout the session Clarges' attention was engaged in a variety of other matters. He was, for example, a particularly assiduous champion of several Tories in disputed election proceedings, in which, as Paul Foley noted, he stood out as one of the 'old Parliament men' who 'commend their zeal for the Church by their diligence and constancy to effect what they desire': for instance, in opposing the Whig attempt to unseat the Tories returned for Plympton Erle (24 Mar., 14 Apr.). Similarly, he allowed his anxieties about popery to intrude into issues not directly concerned with internal security. A clause offered to the poll bill on 14 Apr. to compel the commissioners intended under the bill to take the new oaths to William and Mary provided him with the opportunity to fulminate upon what he saw as an unchecked growth of Catholicism. He also took it upon himself to defend his fellow Tories from Whig innuendoes of disloyalty. On 2 May he became embroiled in a debate on Anthony Rowe's* pamphlet reflecting against the government and naming Tories opposed to the declaration of William and Mary as King and Queen, in which he unsuccessfully attempted to add words of censure to the proposed motion to adjourn. His wide knowledge of affairs was reflected in the heavy demands made of him as a committee-man. On 2 Apr. he was first-named to a committee on the regulation of the East India trade, and on 8 May was also the first appointee to the second-reading committee on the bill for confirming the Company's charter. On 21 May Clarges was selected a commissioner under the bill establishing a commission of accounts, taking fourth place in the ballot with 133 votes. The bill was lost, however, with the close of the session two days later. During the summer recess Clarges conscientiously prepared for the next session by monitoring military and naval developments. He felt that the King's victory at the Boyne was 'in some sort qualified' by the earlier defeat of the allied fleet at Beachy Head. He attended the adjournment meeting of the House on 7 July at which, he noted, the intelligence from Ireland 'was received (as it ought to be) with inexpressible joy'; and despite a report towards the end of the month that the French were at anchor in the English Channel, he was cautiously optimistic of English superiority.[8]

In the autumn of 1690 Lord Carmarthen nursed hopes that Clarges, as one of a number of key Members across the political spectrum, might be encouraged to become a 'manager of the King's directions' in a coalition of Whigs and Churchmen. Similarly, Lord Sydney (Hon. Henry Sidney†) and Lord Coningsby (Thomas*) were under no misapprehensions about his pre-eminence among High Churchmen, and thought it imperative to include him in the cross-party managerial team which they proposed to Lord Portland as essential to the transaction of business during the coming session. They presumed his co-operation could be secured 'by honour ... or otherwise by giving the promise of some considerable employment either to himself or [his] son, together with an assurance of the King's supporting the Church to which he is the greatest of all bigots'. However, Clarges' behaviour during the course of the

1690–1 session would suggest that he disappointed all ministerial hopes of his becoming a Tory manager for the Court. On 6 Oct. he headed the list of nominees to the committee to prepare the Address. It was probably at his prompting two days later that a committee was appointed to prepare a bill to reform the procedures involved in treason trials, Clarges being the first-named appointee. Similarly, his continued advocacy of an accounts commission is highlighted in his nomination on the 11th to the committee ordered to prepare a new bill for that purpose. He spoke for a reduction of the land forces on the 13th, while a few days later, in the debate on meeting the £4,000,000 voted for the supply, his proposals were adopted for increased customs duties. He was also first-named on 20 Oct. to the committee to prepare an address requesting the forfeiture commissioners' report on the Irish rebels' estates. However, the terms of the address which he reported on the 22nd were rejected by the House, and instead the more forthright course was adopted of a bill to attaint rebels in both Ireland and England and to apply their forfeited property to the cost of the war, Clarges being included on the drafting committee. Another important committee on which it was evidently felt that Clarges would serve with effect was that of 25 Oct. to examine the navy and army estimates: in the list of appointees, his name immediately followed Paul Foley's. The work of this committee anticipated the accounts commission, and seems to have marked the beginnings of Clarges' close association with Foley, whose 'Country' notions on matters pertaining to supply and government finance were similar to Clarges' own. Their respective business interests may also have helped to consolidate their friendship. The fact that Clarges may have been critical at this time of the effectiveness of naval power, particularly in view of the summer's setbacks, is suggested by his appointment on 10 Nov. to a committee to prepare an address urging the King to ensure that steps be taken to ensure that the fleet was sufficiently manned. On 8 Dec. Clarges spoke in favour of the City common council's petition (presented on the 3rd) for a bill to amend the shortcomings of the recent quo warranto measure. The principal source of complaint was that the recent Act had facilitated the election for a second year running of Sir Thomas Pilkington† as lord mayor, an 'independent' who, it was said, 'never went to the public Church'. However, the matter was postponed, and afterwards lapsed. On 26 Dec., following the ballot for the accounts commissioners, Clarges was declared elected in joint second place with Foley. At the announcement of the result, Clarges tried to demur on grounds of age and infirmity, but his excuses were overruled by the House. He may possibly have flinched at the prospect of serving with a predominantly Whig set of men, a difficulty which was apparent to such contemporaries as Roger Morrice, who noted that, as High Churchmen, Clarges and a fellow commissioner, Sir Benjamin Newland*, were 'of a sense different from all the rest', the others having Nonconformist backgrounds. Clarges' political standpoint during this session is best described as equivocal. In the early weeks of the session it was apparent that leading Country Tories and Country Whigs were moving towards a more amicable relationship. This had been obvious when Clarges, Seymour and Sir Joseph Williamson had lent their support to the rising Country Whig star Robert Harley in his efforts to unseat Sir Rowland Gwynne* at New Radnor. Clarges' liking for young Harley stemmed from his 'personal respect' for Harley's father, Sir Edward*, while Harley may well have seen in Clarges the model of a government opponent from whom there was much he could learn. Towards the close of the session in December, Carmarthen still regarded Clarges as a government supporter, designating him as such in two lists, while in April 1691 Robert Harley identified him as a Country supporter. Clarges affected to be unenthusiastic about his new role as an accounts commissioner, writing to his friend George Clarke*, the secretary at war in Ireland, 'I have the ill luck to be a commissioner . . . to take the public accounts of the kingdom, which is a very invidious employment. I endeavoured to avoid it but could not, and now I am in it I will do the best service I can in it both to the King and his people.' Undoubtedly the most experienced parliamentarian on the commission, and well practised in the scrutiny of government accounts, Clarges quickly emerged at the forefront of proceedings alongside Harley and Foley, who both admired and valued his industry. Though he found the work onerous, he was mindful of its significance. Far from envisaging the commission as an instrument of criticism of the Court, he saw it as crucial to the processes of government:

> if it be not executed the Parliament and the whole kingdom will be much dissatisfied for after greater subsidies and supplies than ever were given in so short a time, if there be not some accounts taken and examined to justify the occasions of them, men may be discouraged at another season to make the like concessions.

Clarges, it seems, was less interested than Foley in the pursuit of deliberate opposition towards the government. His overriding objective was the improvement of the Commons' ability to scrutinize ministerial action. The commission commenced its proceedings at the beginning of March 1691, and Clarges rarely missed a meeting. When he finally allowed himself a retreat to his Buckinghamshire estate late in the summer, he and Harley maintained their new-found political relationship in an amicable correspondence about current affairs.[9]

The 1691–2 session saw Clarges become more distinctively oppositionist in his attitudes, as his association with the new Country leaders grew closer. Among the leading Country Tories, Clarges and Musgrave were at this juncture particularly notable for their willingness to co-operate with Country Whigs. Robert Harley commented at the end of December 1691 that Clarges and Musgrave 'have got the character of Commonwealthmen'. Clarges' sights were, as usual, trained upon a multifarious range of business, though his involvement with the accounts commission ensured that concern with supply and 'frugal management' were uppermost. The influence of his work for the commission, with its concentration upon the minutiae of administration and expenditure, is evident from many of his speeches. On 27 Oct. he spoke against Sir Charles Sedley's motion to proceed next day on the King's Speech, knowing that many MPs were still en route to Westminster. Initial acquiescence in William's requirements soon evaporated. As part of a pre-arranged plan, Paul Foley and his associates blocked ministerialists from proceeding immediately upon supply business by insisting that attention first be given to shortcomings in the administration of the army and navy which had been found by the accounts commissioners. An immediate outcome of this initiative came on 3 Nov. when Clarges and several of his colleagues supported the proposal for a bill to prevent false musters in the army. The same day he also seconded an unsuccessful attempt at a measure designed to inform the King of incompetent naval officers. When supply business was allowed to begin on 6 Nov. Clarges moved that the House be apprised of next year's war plans before arriving at any binding resolutions. In so doing, he stressed the need for trusting relations between King and Parliament, mentioning how James I's courtiers had 'filled his head with odd notions about his prerogative'. Later in the same debate he opposed giving any consideration to the army until the fleet had first been considered, and was supported by Harley and Foley. Clarges also supported Foley's call for a statement of the nation's military obligations under existing treaties. Though the King had intervened to forestall the Whigs' attack on the ministers over naval 'miscarriages', projected for the 7th, Clarges was not deterred from launching his own full-scale condemnation of Admiral Russell's (Edward*) conduct, telling the House that his capacity as an accounts commissioner required it of him. He delivered a step-by-step exposé of events, drawing upon a log book made available to him by the Tory Admiral Henry Killigrew*, which showed how the fleet had failed to engage and destroy the French fleet in the English channel when opportunity presented. He concluded, 'be it knavishness or ignorance, it is all one to me'. An hour's heated exchange then took place between Russell and Clarges, in which Clarges demanded that the fullest written evidence be produced before a select committee. While denying any wish to 'injure' the admiral personally, he stressed 'it is the wisdom of Parliament to see through things': 'discourses are transient'. His subsequent motion that Russell be required to present his 'journal' of the fleet's actions was subjected to further dispute, it being thought 'unparliamentary' for Members to interrogate their fellows in the House. But his desire that the House probe more deeply into the miscarriages, to investigate suspicions that Russell's apparent incompetence arose from orders he received from higher authority, was put in motion with the scheduling of a committee on the 'state of the nation'. In the meantime, consideration of the naval estimates began two days later, on 9 Nov. Clarges opened the debate by stating that the King, in expecting aid from his people, should be prepared to accept their 'advice', though this could not be tendered until the House was in possession of fuller accounts. The only effective way, in Clarges' view, of examining estimates was methodically, item-by-item, and in a select committee rather than in the more unruly committee of the whole, in accordance with 'the ancient parliamentary way', which he said had been the practice until the last Parliament. He reiterated his point with effect later in the debate with a simple analogy: 'it is very hard that we must give our money and yet must not inquire how it is to be disposed, but must lump it as we pay bills at eating-houses, without inquiring into particulars'. He gave short shrift to Musgrave's view that too much detailed attention would cause delay with possible 'fatal' results, observing that it was 'for the King's service, and not delay, to examine these things'.

These arguments carried weight and a select committee on the naval estimates was appointed, with his own name heading the list. The report made by Harley on the 14th set out the items of naval expenditure agreed by the committee, which were immediately referred to the supply committee. The most controversial proved to be the expenditure of £28,864 on four new fourth-rate ships, which Clarges opposed with other Country MPs on grounds of cost. The plans made earlier at his behest for a comprehensive Commons inquiry into ministerial culpability in Admiral Russell's failings were superseded when fresh developments seemed to cast the direction of naval strategy in an even more sinister light. The contents of papers captured from the French by Admiral Delaval (Sir Ralph*) were thought to suggest that the Tory ministers, Lord Nottingham especially, had been engaged in some form of collusion with the French. On 23 Nov., when Delaval was examined by the House, Clarges hinted that these innuendoes might well bear an element of truth as it certainly seemed to explain why English ships were required to engage the French only when instructed to: 'We are strangely unhappy in the management of our sea affairs. When our ships meet with the enemy's, they are not to fight without orders. This seems to me very strange, for if matters be thus managed our naval war will signify very little.' Though investigations went on until mid-December, Clarges had little more to say on what became a confused and low-key business ending in Nottingham being exonerated.[10]

The army estimates were not so easily despatched. Clarges played his part in tactics which succeeded in dragging out proceedings for the next seven weeks or so. In supply on 12 Nov. he opposed a Court motion to refer the estimates for a total force of 65,000 men to the same select committee examining the navy estimates, believing that progress would be slowed. On the 18th, when the Court in some desperation anxiously tried to initiate consideration of the army estimates, Clarges, supported by Foley, called for further 'light into the alliances, and what men are designed for England, [and] what for Ireland'. He also supported the Country Whig Sir John Thompson, 1st Bt., in a later, though abortive, motion to address the King for an account of how the forces were to be distributed. The Court, anxious to proceed on the army, assured MPs that this information would be forthcoming, and the committee finally embarked upon the estimates the next day, the 19th. In his first intervention in this debate Clarges repeated his oft-stated opinion that the war strategy was misconceived and that 'the only way for you to oppose France is to strengthen yourselves by sea ... I think your main care ought to be that of your fleet'. Later in the debate he refuted insinuations that it was men such as he who 'hindered' the King's business: 'we are all here to advise what is to be done'. The cost of maintaining an army of 65,000, he declared, was 'half the current cash of the nation'. Military requirements on this scale, he argued, would seriously hamper the nation's future ability to defend itself, owing to the crippling and lasting effects of the present loss of specie in deploying almost 40,000 men abroad. He condemned once more the restrictive practice of considering the estimates *in toto*, which effectively dictated the overall sum to be voted, a procedure which he compared with that of the *Parlement de Paris*, and which gave little scope for economies. The 'naming' of a sum commensurate with the entire estimate took away, he believed, the Commons' right to 'advise'. He intervened at least seven times on 25 Nov. when the supply committee resumed, on the first occasion stating that since the Revolution military 'establishments' cost a third part more than formerly, and that the estimate given for 65,000 men was sufficient for 200,000. In a mild way he took issue with Paul Foley's motion to impose the cost of forces serving in Ireland on the Irish, believing the House 'not yet ripe for the question'. But what 'scandalized' him above all else, he declared, was that the House had resolved on 64,500 men without subjecting the estimates to itemized scrutiny. On the subject of the Irish establishment, he contrasted its present extravagance with the regimental economies achieved in Charles II's reign; and was especially puzzled by the fact that only 20,000 of the 39,000 men deployed in Ireland had actually been present at the recent battle of Aughrim. When Richard Hampden I proposed to address for reductions in the Irish establishment to the levels in force during Charles II's reign, Clarges urged the more forthright course of passing an immediate resolution to this effect, which was accordingly done. At a later point he caused ministerial grief by inquiring whether the overall troop figure also included officers, and forced them to concede that it did not. This led him to propose that the 12,960 men intended for Ireland in 1692 include both men and officers, which after some debate was approved. The ministry was also forced to accede to his proposal for a select committee (to which he was named in second place) to establish the cost of the army in Ireland for 1692 and how much revenue would be forthcoming from the Irish. When, on 28 Nov., Lord Ranelagh (Richard Jones*) presented lists of officers and schedules of garrisons, Clarges made the grave charge that the ministry would, as it had the previous year, attempt to secure additional cash under the pretence of paying for extra troops, while the accounts showed that in fact considerably less had been employed. On the 30th he gave vent to his irritation that the Commons was not being allowed a free hand to consider the various military estimates, on which he believed a saving of £150,000 might be made, and demanded the appointment of a 'private' or select committee whose special purpose would be to compare the present with previous establishments. After much debate such a body was appointed, with Clarges among the nominees. It is almost certain that he spoke in the next supply proceedings on 4 Dec., when the land tax was sanctioned, being the first of five Members named to prepare the bill. On the 14th the report was made from the select committee on the army estimates, and his objection that vital information had been omitted was exposed as short-sighted. In supply on the 15th he argued that regimental companies could be increased in size from 50 to at least 80 men so as to economize on the cost of officering them. On 30 Dec. he spoke against the employment of foreign officers as being 'a great discouragement to the English', and put forward an alternative establishment for the Irish forces in which the reduction of officers was a prominent feature, reducing costs to 1682 levels and saving £360,000. These proposals were adopted in a thin House in place of those worked out in the select committee. Agreement on Clarges' proposals was reached in the supply committee on 1 Jan. 1692, but at the report the next day they came under heavy fire from the Court, particularly over the disbandment of officers. Despite efforts by Clarges himself, Foley and Musgrave, the most salient elements of his proposals for a cheaper army in Ireland were lost. His disappointment is apparent in the fact that he made no recorded intervention on the 4th when the charge of the Irish forces received further attention. He did, however, make several interventions in supply on 12 Jan., in which he supported Foley's proposals to allocate £200,000 for war expenditure, and criticized the proposed civil list, 'the highest that ever was', hoping that Household expenses might be as strictly regulated as they were under Charles II. He was guarded about Foley's suggestion to take advantage of the bankers' willingness to lend £1,000,000 at 5 per cent if steps were taken to liquidate the debt to them arising from Charles II's Stop of the Exchequer. 'The seizing of their money was a most wicked thing and the keeping it from them now is I think as bad', but certain 'difficulties' stood in the way of what Foley had now proposed, which required the attention of a select committee. Clarges' advice was followed, and a committee 'to receive proposals for a fund of perpetual interest' towards raising supply was appointed on which he himself was included.[11]

Quite apart from his ingrained 'Country' instincts in supply matters, Clarges' activities as an accounts commissioner could only have enhanced a strong sense of public duty and responsibility. He quickly emerged as a leading spokesman for the commissioners. It was he who on 9 Nov. notified the House of a satirical tract against the commission entitled *Mercurius Reformatus* and moved for its author and printer to be taken into custody as a breach of privilege. Country Members were clearly in a state of high anticipation about the commissioners' report, for the next day Sir Edward Seymour moved that the commissioners be ordered to present their audited accounts with little further delay. Clarges replied immediately, stressing the lack of co-operation they had encountered from 'several' officials and the patent inadequacy often found in the accounts they had examined. He promised that an account of receipts and disbursements, 'but not the truth of them', would soon be presented. Accordingly, the accounts were ordered to be laid before the House on 23 Nov., but when that day arrived he had to report that work was still unfinished: 'ever since you made the order for bringing them in, we have spent two hours every morning and three hours in the afternoon to prepare them'. 'A book of the state of incomes and issues of public revenues' was finally presented on 1 Dec. by Paul Foley, and received consideration on the 3rd. Clarges testily defended the commission on the latter occasion when Sir John Lowther, 2nd Bt. II, highlighted certain 'material' omissions and mistakes: 'I did expect after what that honourable gentleman had said . . . we should have been called to the bar as delinquents.' He then outlined the problems and obstructions which the commissioners had faced and the difficulties in obtaining 'particular accounts' relating to the army, navy, Ireland and the Ordnance. Though admitting that his failing memory prevented him from dealing with every objection Lowther had raised, 'we cannot', he continued, 'be wiser than God has made us, nor, I believe, that gentlemen neither'. He asked Members to give their attention to the 'observations' accompanying the accounts. Answering later complaints about the incompleteness of the accounts, he explained that the commissioners had no powers of coercion over government officials, and in the case of several government departments had had to grapple with chaotic accounting procedures. In these circumstances, the accounts were as perfect as could be reasonably expected. Clarges apparently did not participate in the debate that day, or on 12 Dec. on the more controversial 'observations' such as those concerning the disposal of secret service money, pensions and allowances. Thereafter, interest in the commissioners' findings lapsed. On 28 Jan. 1692, however, when the bill for renewing the commission was returned by the Lords, amended with the names of four additional commissioners, Clarges cited precedents to show 'that the Lords have nothing to do in the matter of money' and 'have no foundation of right to name commissioners'. Consequently he was named to the committee to prepare a statement of disagreement to the Lords. During the ensuing stalemate over the bill, Clarges was prevented by lameness from attending, though when the possibility arose of tacking a clause to renew the commission to the poll bill, he was able to advise Harley of a precedent in William Hakewill's treatise on procedure. It was only through this device that the commission was renewed for a second consecutive year.[12]

One of the more controversial measures to employ Clarges' attention during the 1691–2 session, and one by which he set great store, was the reform of the procedures in treason trials. This notorious area of abuse had been highlighted in the preliminary draft of the Declaration of Rights. The attention which Clarges gave to the issue during the session makes it seem probable that he had supported Sir William Whitlock's* previous bill for reform. On 9 Nov. he seconded the motion for the second reading of the new bill, and on 11 Dec., after its return from the Lords, spoke in favour of an amendment allowing persons impeached for treason by the Commons to have the same advantages as those indicted for treason. He was also placed on a committee to state the Commons' disagreement with other amendments made by the Upper House. The main bone of contention was the peers' desire to be free of the crown's arbitrary power of empanelling juries in the lord steward's court when Parliament was not in session. Whereas many were opposed to a move which seemed to entail the strengthening of the Lords' power against the monarch's, Clarges was keen to promote a spirit of greater co-operation between Lords and Commons in the interests of constitutional well-being. Speaking on 13 Jan. 1692 in support of the Lords' amendment embodying this change, he saw the opportunity to ensure that peers were accorded the same justice as 'the rest of the people of England', a move which would make them 'honest', free from Court influence, and ready to defend English liberties. He recalled the fact that the peers had been of great assistance in passing the Habeas Corpus Act, and had taken a 'brave' stand against King James. At further discussion of the bill on 25 Jan. Clarges restricted his comments to a procedural technicality. As in the previous session, the measure failed amid disagreement between peers and Commons. Clarges took the opportunity on 19 Feb. to indicate his continuing attachment to reform, when the House was upon the Lords' bill to outlaw collusion with the King's enemies, declaring that he saw little point in establishing new treasonable offences when there was still a pressing need for the reform of treason law and trial procedure. Another measure which closely engaged his attention was the bill appointing new oaths of allegiance in Ireland. He had been named on 27 Oct. to the drafting committee, and on the 30th was placed on the second-reading committee. After the bill's return from the Lords, he spoke on 30 Nov. in favour of an important new clause allowing Catholic lawyers to practise on taking only the oath of allegiance. Although he was no friend to popery, Clarges' subsequent efforts to preserve and perfect the bill underline his belief that a conciliatory attitude in Ireland was essential in securing the entrenchment of the Protestant 'interest' there. None the less, despite his enlightened views, he evidently felt that the Lords had gone too far in their phrasing, and became the chief mover in efforts to settle the 'variance' on the matter between the two Houses. He reported back on 5 Dec. from the second of two conferences, that the Lords insisted on a wording which threatened the integrity of the Treaty of Limerick by seeming to give latitude, not only to Catholic lawyers, but to 'all the popish priests in Ireland'. His proposal that the conference delegation which he had led might examine the difference between the Lords' clause and the treaty article was brushed aside, but his adjournment motion later, as an alternative means to facilitate further consideration, was accepted. On the 8th he offered a fresh amendment expunging the dubious wording inserted by the Lords, and at further conferences on 9 and 10 Dec., in which he led for the Commons, an acceptable formula was agreed, the bill eventually receiving the Royal Assent. On another measure concerning Ireland, the bill for vesting forfeited estates in the King and Queen, Clarges made a series of interventions in late January and early February, having already been added on 20 Jan. to the committee to receive proposals for raising money on the estates. At the committal of the forfeitures bill on 28 Jan. he proposed extra provision for a body of commissioners to deal with the claims of 'several pretenders' to estates, as allowed under the articles of Limerick; and later proposed that forfeited tithes, impropriations and appropriations be used to augment the pitifully inadequate livings of the Protestant clergy, in order to combat the spread of popery. This second proposal was adopted. He made several more interventions in committee, on 1, 2 and 5 Dec., provoking a lengthy debate on the 2nd when he offered a clause to exempt from the bill Protestants not in arms on 1 Sept. 1689, which was also accepted.[13]

In the proceedings on the East Indian trade Clarges featured as a defender of the East India Company. Its preservation, he told MPs on 27 Nov. 1691, was all the more essential since whenever the subject arose in the House he saw 'so many foreigners [i.e. members of the new syndicate of interlopers] in the lobby'. He spoke on 2 Dec. against Sir Edward Seymour's proposals for the establishment of the East India Company's stock, and again in favour of the company on 18 Dec. By the 23rd, however, he seems to have accepted that the flotation of an adequate joint stock, as originally proposed by Seymour, would best preserve the operation of the existing company, but criticized as insufficient the £744,000 which they had proposed as security for the £1,300,000 claimed as the value of their stock. Even so, eager to see conciliation, he felt this 'a good ground to work on to make sufficient security'. From these proceedings a bill emerged for establishing an East India company which, at first reading on 22 Jan. 1692, Clarges and others criticized as having been covertly drafted, and which effectively dissolved the existing company. Not surprisingly, on the 26th, when the bill reached its committee stage, he seconded Sir Thomas Littleton's motion to allow any alterations which might subsequently be proposed. Clarges spoke on a variety of other occasions and topics. On 9 Dec. he opposed the payment of expenses to an informant who claimed he could reveal the identities of several Jacobite conspirators. On the 12th he brought to MPs' notice that the roof of St. Stephen's was in a perilous condition and moved that the King's surveyor be ordered to report on the matter forthwith. Four days later he spoke in favour of a measure for the encouragement of privateering against France and to guard against collusion between English and French traders. Cautioning that such a proposal ought to receive preliminary consideration in committee of the whole, he proceeded to advocate the imposition of 'a great duty' on all French goods, and was consequently included among the Members appointed to oversee the bill's preparation. Shortly after the Christmas recess, on 7 Jan., he and Sir Christopher Musgrave took the Speaker (Sir John Trevor*) to task for 'debating' the privileges of the House concerning conferences with the Upper House, both maintaining that the Chair had no right to debate 'any matter whatsoever'. He spoke briefly on 15 Jan. against a minor addition to the mutiny bill, which he had helped to draft, and the same day opposed as procedurally irregular Hugh Boscawen I's motion in the supply committee to provide more convoys for the protection of merchant shipping. When on 18 Feb. it was noted that the Irish forfeitures bill was still pending in the Lords, Clarges backed a motion to withhold the poll tax bill while a formal reminder was conveyed, insisting that it was 'very regular and usual' to hold back money bills until the peers had sanctioned 'some good bills'. He was also involved in a number of matters which engaged his concern as a prominent London citizen. On 3 Dec. he spoke in support of a bill for the relief of London orphans, while on the 15th he presented a bill to furnish the recently created parish of St. Anne with its own church, and was first-named to the bill's second-reading committee on the 18th, though it was his son Sir Walter who reported on the 24th. The problems suffered by the small traders of Westminster in the recovery of debts also preoccupied him so far as to induce him to present a bill on 19 Dec. to simplify the process at law. He reported from its second-reading committee on the 31st. As Member for Oxford University, he also supported the interests of the universities. On 7 Dec. he successfully offered a clause exempting both institutions from the payment of excise. Similarly, on 19 Feb 1692, having earlier espoused the statutory confirmation of his own university's charters, he spoke in favour of a similar measure to confirm those of Cambridge.[14]

Clarges' routine from late February onwards, when the House stood in recess, was again dominated by his work on the accounts commission. Not until August did he allow himself a period of leave from otherwise almost daily attendance. He continued to work closely with Foley and Harley, and when Harley fell ill in September and retired to the country, Clarges kept him supplied with 'foreign prints and intelligence'. It was with a sense of gloom that Clarges regarded the approaching session. The summer's actions at sea and on land had been limited yet expensive, and left him feeling 'perplexed' and downcast. 'There never was more need of wise heads and stout hands since I knew England', he lamented to Harley on 20 Sept. He was especially concerned as to whether the enormous subsidies paid to the allies were yielding value for money, thinking this a matter to which the House should devote attention. At the beginning of October he wrote with much the same despondency to Harley's father, Sir Edward: 'we have been unfortunate in our land campaigns this year; how we shall be next year, God only knows. Our main affair at sea was successful, and might have been more if we could have pushed it better.' Family concerns had perhaps contributed to these forebodings. At the end of August he had been 'much troubled' when his only son's young family had been visited with smallpox. His vain, if understandable, fear, was the extinction of his line. On the first day of the new session, 4 Nov. 1692, he was 'sorry to see so thin a House when we are like to have affairs of such weight come before it': his by now customary motion to adjourn for a few days was carried. His several interventions on the 10th during consideration of the King's speech saw him very much at the forefront of the opposition offensive, and successfully dictating the course of subsequent proceedings. Though he supported an address of thanks which congratulated the King on his return from campaign, he did not accept Thomas Neale's proposal to stand by the King in his prosecution of the war, with its implication of an automatic promise of supply:

> I am for any congratulation you shall think fit but I am against the latter part; it is engaging the House beforehand in the matter of money, which I like not. I desire to see first how matters are and then we will give our advice and assistance as we are able. And in order to this I desire we may address to his Majesty that he will be pleased to order the leagues and alliances he has with any foreign princes [to be laid before the House], for this nation is in a very bad condition and great sums of money have gone out of it already, which impoverishes you mightily. I am for preserving order and method and going upon your address of thanks, leaving out the latter part of your question.

An assurance that the Commons would be ready 'to advise and assist' in the King's crusade against the enemy was resolved upon none the less, and Clarges, presumably mollified by this wording, was included on the committee appointed to draft the address. In the same debate he replied to Hon. Goodwin Wharton's motion for the accounts commission to present their auditings of government expenditure promptly, expressing hope that the House would not impose unreasonably upon the overworked commissioners, and assuring Members that the accounts were almost ready. Later on, at his further insistence, and supported by others, all current alliances were ordered up as a necessary foundation for deliberations upon war expenditure. Finally, Clarges moved to consider 'the state of the nation', invoking the time-honoured principle that the Commons should proceed upon grievances before supply. It was an attempt to open an inquisition into the shortcomings of Admiral Russell's command of the fleet, a move that may have been preconcerted by the accounts commissioners since he was seconded by a fellow commissioner (and neighbour), Sir Peter Colleton. The next day, 11 Nov., Clarges was again seconded by Colleton, in a motion requiring Russell to attend the committee. He justified the inquiry by stating that 'two general questions' were 'very material': first, why the victory at Barfleur in May had not been followed up; and secondly, why mercantile shipping was given such inadequate protection. Responding to efforts by the Court to deflect the attack on Russell, Clarges observed that whereas a portion of the previous year's supply, some £100,000, had been earmarked for a descent on France, the plans had been abandoned by a 'council of war' in favour of a descent upon Ostend, and called for the Admiralty to produce documentation showing who had advised this decision. The inquiry which Clarges had requested, scheduled to open on 12 Nov., was effectively sidestepped that day by the presentation of papers relating to the fleet's summer actions. Clarges none the less persisted in attacking the Court over the conduct of the naval high command, with repeated demands for an explanation of why no attempt to launch a descent was made until July. He wanted to know who had been responsible for ordering the descent, and more pointedly, what instructions had been received by the commanders from Secretary Nottingham whose orders to the fleet were widely felt to have been misconceived. Moreover, he made no secret of his deep pessimism about the ministers' ability to conduct the war, proclaiming that there was 'not that zeal now to the Government, as there was then [viz. during the naval campaigns of Charles II's reign]'. Clarges' initial hopes of a major Commons inquest into the late naval campaign were further set back amid MPs' calls for additional papers, though ironically these requests were probably inspired by Clarges' own insistence on ministerial accountability. By 15 Nov. it was apparent that the leading commissioners of accounts, Foley, Harley and Clarges, had settled on a change of tactic. On the ministry's motion to consider the King's Speech, Clarges repeated earlier calls for the alliances to be examined first, as an essential prerequisite in providing the 'advice and assistance' which the King had requested: 'and since his Majesty has been so very gracious in his speech to ask our advice, which is more than your kings of late have been used to, I desire we may with all duty give him the best we can'. Extreme though Clarges' proposition was, the principle behind it obtained wide support, and Foley and other members of the Country party succeeded in delaying supply proceedings until after a day had been spent upon the King's request for advice.[15]

The first of a series of committee sittings on 'advice' took place on 21 Nov. 1692, with Clarges opening the debate with an agenda-setting speech. He began by demanding clarification of the nation's obligations in the war. So 'deplorable' did he find the nation's condition that he expressed himself at a loss 'to know in what particular to advise the King'. He could only recount, as on many previous occasions, the mishaps and mismanagements of the fleet, the harm done to trade, and the ineffectiveness of the land war over the previous three years; and question the wisdom of placing a massive confederate army in Flanders 'where you draw all the strength of France'. Furthermore, in the King's absence, administration and decision-making had been 'very loose', as nothing could be done by the Queen without directions from the King among his 'foreign' (Dutch) advisers. He hoped, having thus 'opened some matters', that Members would 'touch upon a particular head to go upon'. Inevitably, the subsequent debate dwelt on the mismanagement of the navy, during which Clarges called Lord Falkland (Anthony Carey) to order for his aspersions upon the recent committee on the merchants' complaints about inadequate convoys; accused the Admiralty of being careless of trade; and advocated a change of personnel throughout the naval establishment from the Admiralty commissioners downward, reflecting once more on Russell in saying that the entire fleet was 'too great a trust to be lodged in one man's hands'. The following day, 22 Nov., the Commons passed a general resolution for the supply, though typically, when translations of the treaties were afterwards presented, Clarges attempted to disrupt the unanimity with his observation that England's financial obligations considerably exceeded those of the Dutch. When the House proceeded again on 'advice' on the 23rd, attention turned to army affairs. Clarges broached the problem of indiscipline among the Irish forces, which he attributed to an unclear division of responsibility between civil and military authorities there. In a lengthier intervention he drew attention to the administrative efficiency which had prevailed in Ireland in the early 1660s, when he had himself served on the Irish privy council. Widening the focus of his assault, he amplified the objections of other Country MPs against foreign generals and officers in the English army. Though there were highly experienced English officers available, he doubted if the King's foreign advisers were sufficiently informed to vouch for their suitability: 'from this ingratitude to the officers you have lost the discipline of the army'. He was able to draw upon detailed intelligence, received shortly before the session, about how the cowardice of Dutch commanders, led by Count Solmes, had resulted in the wholesale butchering of English troops at Steenkerk: 'if we had an English general at Steenkerk, 6,000 English had not been lost'. The army and navy estimates, totalling some £4,200,000, were presented two days later, on 25 Nov. Whereas in the previous session the estimates had been severally referred to select committees, preventing discussion in the House, Harley now moved for their referral to the committee of the whole, which, as one scholar has suggested, 'reflected the learning experience of the previous sessions and a belief that the estimates should become a part of the general indictment of the war'. Clarges pitied the fact that 'poor England' had to bear the cost of forces in Ireland and on the Continent and proposed that MPs be allowed several days to scrutinize the demands; otherwise there was the risk that the entire sum would, as in the previous session, be voted 'all in a lump'. Accordingly, the supply committee was put off until the following week. When proceedings on advice resumed next day, 26 Nov., Clarges felt Sir William Strickland's motion condemning the operation of a 'Cabinet council' did not go far enough, and ought to 'name' ministers against whom impeachments might be brought. On 29 Nov. he opened the debate on the navy estimates, regretting the 'prodigious sum' required but advising the House to proceed 'head by head'. At his instance it was resolved that the first item, the ordinary of the navy, be financed from the civil list. Despite his advocacy of a more vigorous naval strategy in the war, he thought the number of seamen proposed excessive. Similarly, he opposed the government's request for new bomb vessels and fourth-rate ships, repeating his objections on this score at the report on 1 Dec. On the 2nd he opposed the Court motion to proceed upon the army estimates until ways and means for the navy had first been settled. When the army estimates were reviewed on the 3rd he intervened several times, expressing apprehensions that 'Dutch advice' had demanded larger English forces than were required by treaty, and in the first instance would only support Harley's motion to approve the force of 20,000 men designated for home defence. Sir Edward Seymour's counter-argument, that the burden would have been so much the greater if England had stood alone, compelled Clarges to state his objections more forcefully. He warned that the Dutch and German allies regarded England as 'an inexhaustible fountain' and that the nation would soon be incapable of its own defence, so deprived would it be of manpower and specie. His work for the accounts commission doubtless reinforced his awareness of abuse and waste in the Ordnance and in the payment of officers, and in further supply proceedings on the 6th he suggested ways of reducing costs in these areas. He preferred, in particular, to see a lump sum granted for the payment of generals rather than the continuance of easily abused daily rates. He objected also to sums intended for foreign princes: 'the Parliaments of England used to give supply to their own princes but never to strangers'. In the proceedings on advice on 8 Dec. he advised MPs that the drain of specie through foreign payments could only be partially rectified by the purchase of army stores at home, as much larger sums were required to subsidize foreign troops. Returning to this theme the following day, he enlarged upon the disparities between English and Dutch subsidy payments to the confederate powers, pointing out that the States General and the Emperor were 'more concerned' in the war than England. In some anger he bluntly suggested that responsibility for this sorry state of affairs lay with the King's Dutch confidant, the Earl of Portland. When the army resolutions were reported on 10 Dec. he targeted another attack on the 'extravagant' establishments allowed the generals. As a result of his recent apprehensions about foreign payments he was on the 12th appointed to a select committee to consider how the English army abroad might be provisioned so as to minimize the export of coin. In the final sitting on 'advice' four days later, he repeated his prejudices against foreigners employed in the garrisons and other military establishments as being an encouragement to soldierly indiscipline.[16]

From mid-December the committee of supply turned to ways and means. In these proceedings Clarges combined his scepticism with a more constructive attention to such details as the revenue-raising capacity of various taxes and duties. Though the supply and 'advice' debates had seen him a strident critic of the conduct and cost of the war, on the ways and means side he showed a statesmanlike commitment to ensuring the sums agreed could be raised. On 13 Dec. he, unlike Harley, opposed a 4s. rated land tax in favour of a monthly assessment which would yield a more 'certain' revenue and was not liable to inequalities. He was apprehensive, too, that the pound rate, requiring the appointment of commissioners, would lead to a multiplication of oaths, an altogether unacceptable prospect to a High Churchman, and that it would increase the King's reserves of patronage. It was the fiscal advantages of a rated tax, however, that prevailed with the House. On the 15th, he and Harley led the way in according warm approval to Paul Foley's 'million project', though it was typical of Clarges that he should caution 'great care' in the penning of a bill for the scheme. Appropriately, he was later included among the five Members ordered to bring in the measure, the others being his fellow commissioners Foley and Musgrave, and the attorney- and solicitor-general. He was at the forefront of further proceedings on the 17th when he proposed a comprehensive set of additional duties on a wide range of commodities which he had devised with the assistance of several merchants, believing they 'would raise a considerable sum'. On 21 Dec. he also suggested levying higher duties on French commodities, especially brandy, which he felt would raise an extra £80,000, and that steps might be taken to encourage effective privateering against French commerce. Most of these proposals, enshrined in 85 separate resolutions, were agreed by the House on 27 Jan. 1693 and a bill 'for impositions on merchandises' was ordered which Clarges was directed to draft with the attorney- and solicitor-general. On 23 Dec., when the Speaker himself took the initiative in scheduling committee proceedings on the land tax bill, Clarges upbraided him for a serious breach of correct procedure, though his outburst was just as likely to have been occasioned by his strong objections to the pound rate intended by the measure. In deliberations on the bill a fortnight later, on 6 Jan. 1693, he felt that the regulations should be changed to allow county commissioners to act within boroughs if no inhabitants met the property requirements. At the report on the 10th, Clarges took the lead in attaching an additional clause, 'une condition désagréable' as Bonet recorded, to suspend the grant of pensions during the war. But though initially accepted, it was rejected on reconsideration later in the debate. The land tax bill was returned from the Lords on 17 Jan. with a new clause to appoint a commission of peers to administer the tax on themselves. It was probably on account of his recent championship of the Upper House over the bill to regulate treason trials that Clarges was entrusted with the sensitive task of leading a conference to state the Commons' objection that the Lords had no right to 'meddle' with money bills.[17]

The committee on 'advice' finally reported on 11 Jan. 1693, but surprisingly Clarges contributed nothing beyond a brief procedural observation. In ways and means on 4 Feb. he gave short shrift to Thomas Neale's idea to lay taxes on all persons who married, the inheritors of legacies, and on burials. Indeed he saw a moral objection to Neale's first proposal, preferring to see a tax on unmarried persons, 'for marriage itself is already too much out of fashion'. On 6 Feb. he prompted the House to consider how much more was needed for the current year's supply in the light of the £4,757,000 already provided, and which left no more than £200,000 still to raise. Sir Edward Seymour immediately took issue, doubting the revenue-raising capacity of the various proposals so far approved, many of which had come from Clarges, and concluded that the sum still needed should more realistically be estimated at £1,300,000. Responding, Clarges assured the House that the duties he had proposed in former sessions 'have fully answered what I valued them at'. But, seeming to acknowledge Seymour's warning that receipts might not meet expectations, he proposed that the 'additional duties' he had proposed back in December, which he calculated at £170,000 p.a., be turned into a three-year fund to raise £510,000 for the current year. However, when Sir John Lowther expressed concern about the dependability of this example of credit finance, Clarges advised the House that they might do well first to consider and estimate if any further revenue sources remained untapped. Two days later, however, on 8 Feb., he again outlined his scheme. So attractive was it to MPs that Charles Montagu's* and Seymour's scepticism about this and a similar scheme, funded on 'continued impositions', failed to impress. It only remained for Lord Ranelagh to point out that Clarges' overall estimate was 'neat money' with no allowance for 'interest and the charge of collecting it'. Clarges' fund scheme was none the less eventually resolved upon, but for a term of four, instead of three, years. On 10 Feb. he took up John Grobham Howe's proposal of a tax on hackney coaches, believing 'a good sum' might be raised from it, but preferred that such a tax be used 'forever' in the establishment and maintenance of a naval hospital 'which will be a noble foundation for this kingdom which is an island and should give some encouragement to seamen on whom they [sic] so much depend'. On the 13th he advocated applying 'a clause of credit' to 'a review of the poll' in the event of a shortfall in anticipated receipts, though he was against extending it to deficiencies in the land tax. In the same debate he opposed as procedurally 'irregular' Sir John Lowther's last-minute attempt to propose another £500,000 on East India goods as 'collateral security'. Clarges was appointed on the 15th to draft bills based on the committee's final resolutions which included his own scheme for 'additional duties'. Although a stickler for procedure, Clarges' own observance could be neglectful when it suited his own purposes. On 18 Feb., at the report on the 'bill of impositions on merchandises' (which he himself had done much to originate), his attempt to introduce a duty on an omitted commodity was overruled, money proposals being the exclusive preserve of the committee of supply. His move the same day to introduce a clause to appropriate £1,200,000 to the navy without prior leave was also deemed improper, though on the 20th he insisted on his point with a tenacious use of precedent. Clarges could thus hardly be considered an old-school Tory on financial matters, one with innate suspicions of the 'monied interest'. On the contrary, his long-standing involvement in the metropolitan business world, and his own particular interests in property speculation, accustomed him to the benefits of credit finance, not least of which were the possibilities of limiting the burdens of direct taxation upon the landed classes.

Although the accounts commission's latest report (presented on 15 Nov. 1692) had been given no specific attention by the House, it was plain in the debates on 'advice', estimates, and ways and means that the commission did not miss the opportunity to make use of the insights and information accumulated in the course of their inquiries. It was as much for this advantage as for the original purpose of overseeing government expenditure that a bill for renewing the commission was sought in January 1693. Clarges benefited from his service as a commissioner in ways that differed from his more opposition-minded colleagues Foley and Harley. His involvement with the commission as a seasoned back-bencher gave added weight to his parliamentary role as a guardian of good government, and ensured for himself the continuing respect of Country MPs of both parties. At the second reading of the renewal bill on 14 Feb. he defended the commission's *raison d'être* against Court detractors, asserting that its annual cost was no more than £5,000, and not £10,000 as Seymour had alleged. He admitted to MPs, 'I find it is a sore place and I do not wonder that some gentlemen are angry at it', but reminded them of their approbation of the commission's first report and its accompanying 'observations'. The commissioners, he also intimated, were willing to provide similar commentary on their second report, indicating somewhat tantalizingly that in unravelling 'the mystery of the Exchequer' they had uncovered matters needing urgent attention. It was also desirable, he said, that government departments, especially the Treasury, be made to release their accounts for inspection, but such a provision was not adopted. In the meantime MPs were invited to submit their observations on the accounts in writing, to which on 18 Feb. Clarges presented the commission's written response. On 17 Feb. he skilfully deflected a clause put up by several courtiers, abetted by Seymour, requiring the commissioners to review the debt to the bankers occasioned by the 1672 Stop of the Exchequer, a move probably calculated to endanger the bill's passage and the commission's existence by seeming to encumber Parliament itself with the debt. Clarges condemned the attempt to reopen the affair as 'very unreasonable', the authenticity of the debts having already been established in the law courts.[18]

Unlike his prominent fellow commissioners, Foley and Harley, Clarges was not an active exponent of mainstream 'Country' measures in this session. The simple explanation, however, may have been his preoccupation with supply business when the place and triennial bills were pending during December and January, for his intervention at the first reading of the

Lords' triennial bill on 28 Jan. 1693 shows a deep sympathy with the impulse to purify the body politic. In his opinion, triennial Parliaments stood alongside the proper regulation of treason trials as a constitutional necessity: 'I should be unworthy to sit here', he said, 'if I did not give my testimony to this bill. It is the best bill that ever came into this House since 25 Edward III of treasons, etc.'

> The worst of Parliaments – even that which is so much run out against, that long pensionary parliament (as it was called) in King Charles II's time – took care to regulate their privileges and keep out officers, the two scandals of Parliament. And if we must do nothing of that matter and have long parliaments, we shall become 500 grievances. And as to the objection that the bill came from the Lords I think it none at all for they may send you down any bill but one for money, nor do I think it any entrenching upon the prerogative, and therefore I am for it.

Of much more immediate concern to him, however, was the renewed attempt to pass a bill for the reform of treason trials. He seems to have hoped that its passage could be eased by cutting procedural corners. Seconding Sir William Whitlock's motion on 11 Nov. 1692 for leave to introduce the bill, Clarges asked that the copy used the previous session might be presented immediately. Though the Speaker objected, Clarges prevailed in his rejoinder that the 'asking of leave is but a new way and an innovation in the House', upon which the measure was brought in and, on Clarges' further motion, given a first reading. He seconded Whitlock again at committal on the 18th, though he could see no need to re-examine a measure which the Lower House had in effect already endorsed. In committee on the 28th he argued forcefully for the bill as 'necessary... for the preservation of the government and the King's person'. Its aim, he told MPs, was to rationalize and define 'treason' in order to prevent perversions of justice, a problem which had become acute in the preceding reign. Moreover, in their unreformed state the procedures for treason trials easily facilitated arbitrary rule: 'the hardships the nation endured in constructive treason was one of the greatest inducements to the late change'. At the end of December, when the bill was under consideration in the Lords, there were differences over whether the Commons should accede to the peers' request for a 'free' conference, or whether the more formalized conference procedure should be followed. Though Clarges supported the idea of a free conference, 'he could not have the managers debate any matter but hear what the Lords will say and then acquaint them you will report it to the House'. Once more, however, the bill failed.

Clarges also gave attention to a series of other matters which touched upon questions of liberty and fairness. One was the case of the moderate Tory MP (Sir) Carbery Pryse (4th Bt.), who was troubled with legal suits in the court of Exchequer in efforts to prevent him exploiting the lead mines discovered on his estates on the grounds that the ore belonged to the crown. Clarges presented the case to the House on 26 Nov. and moved that Pryse have protection from further harassment. He supported the royal mines bill introduced to guarantee Pryse's rights, and on 20 Jan. 1693 indicated the impropriety of hearing King's counsel against the bill, 'for the Commons are his counsel'. The intention, Clarges claimed, was to maintain a prerogative 'that is in no way useful to the crown but very grievous to the people and prejudicial to the kingdom in general'. Somewhat paradoxically with regard to Pryse's predicament, but quite in accordance with his own principles, he supported John Howe's proposal on 12 Dec. that the House consider facilitating private prosecutions against MPs. He recalled that before the Restoration no Member was allowed any privilege 'but for his own person'. Named to the committee appointed, he spoke again when it reported on the 23rd: 'as we pretended to remedy grievances, we should hereby prevent ourselves from being the greatest grievance by hindering our fellow subjects from their just rights'. He spoke to a more popular outrage against personal liberty on 2 Feb. when breach of privilege was alleged on behalf of Bussy Mansel* (or his cousin Thomas I*) regarding the impressment of a servant. Clarges condemned as 'a great oppression to the subject' the increasingly 'common' practice of 'pressing for land service... under colour of pressing seamen for sea service', and later moved for a 'declaratory vote' that impressment generally 'was against the rights and liberties of the subject'. A further complaint, raised by Clarges on the 7th concerning a servant of the parliamentary diarist Narcissus Luttrell*, prompted the appointment of a committee to investigate abuses by pressmasters. Unusually, however, Clarges himself was not among those named. Among other privilege cases during the session, Clarges espoused (on 14 Nov. 1692) the cause of Christopher Musgrave, MP for Carlisle and son of Clarges' friend and fellow commissioner Sir Christopher, who had been peremptorily disenfranchised and stripped of his freedom by Carlisle corporation. Such was Clarges' advocacy that a breach of privilege was immediately declared, *nemine contradicente*. On the other hand, he saw no justice in the Whig Sir John Guise's complaint of privilege on 18 Nov. regarding the mistreatment of his chaplain, who being the holder of a rectorship could not be considered a menial servant.[19]

Of Clarges' remaining activity in the 1692–3 session, several matters are worthy of note. He continued, for example, to support the East India Company, arguing on 17 Nov. in favour of a bill to correct defects in its charter. But when the company's future was debated on 25 Feb. 1693 he refrained from openly aligning with those who argued for its preservation. His Country aversion to 'corruption' came into play on the subject of abuses in military organization. On 2 Jan. he complained, with reference to the militia bill, that muster-masters often issued call-outs unnecessarily 'for their profit', and proposed the restriction of such powers to the King and Council. Similarly, on the mutiny bill, he spoke on 25 Jan. against the purchase of regimental commissions as a practice which adversely affected the well-being of 'the poor soldier'. Clarges took part in the proceedings on 20–23 Jan. against Charles Blount's *King William and Queen Mary Conquerors* (1693) and Bishop Burnet's *Pastoral Letter* (1689) both of which expounded a view of William and Mary's authority as being by right of 'conquest'. Though Clarges was vaguely stated by Luttrell to have 'inveighed' against Blount's pamphlet on the 20th, the substance of his objection is not clear. It is possible, however, that given his concern with the maintenance of liberty, he was keen to echo the terms of the initial complaint by Hon. John Granville that the notion of conquest undermined libertarian principles as guaranteed by law, and left them at the whim of the conqueror. While Edmund Bohun, the Tory licenser of the press, and a known exponent of 'conquest theory', was specifically targeted for allowing the two tracts to be published, the attack was also implicitly aimed at Bohun's administrative senior, Lord Nottingham, for whom Clarges' respect had waned in recent years. Even so, rather than commit the works to an immediate public burning, as desired by Foley and Musgrave, Clarges, with his usual propriety, felt that no censure would be valid until there had been proper inquiry by a parliamentary committee. His views in this respect, however, were overridden. Considering the interest Clarges had previously shown in Ireland, and the pride he took in his own administrative experience there, it is surprising to find him intervening only once when the House inquired into maladministration in the Irish government in late February. Even so, it was he, as an accounts commissioner, who set the tone of the first day's proceedings on 22 Feb. by revealing that though forfeited lands and goods to the value of £167,000 had so far been seized, only £4,000 had accrued to the crown, a deficiency he left to the Treasury lords to explain. Widening his focus, he criticized the recent dissolution of the Dublin parliament, whose Protestantism he had previously hailed as an essential factor in securing the kingdom. He doubted, furthermore, that the 7,000-strong army in Ireland was capable of repelling a French invasion force, in consequence of which it 'may cost you some millions before you beat them out'. Certain matters of secondary or local import also drew Clarges' attention: on 6 Dec., a bill to provide the City with 'convex lights'; on 15 Dec., a bill for preventing abuses by cheese and butter weighers; and on 2 Feb. 1693, a bill for outlawing hawkers which he opposed, thinking it 'would establish monopolies by act of Parliament'. A greater local preoccupation, however, was with an initiative to reduce the City corporation's debt to the orphans' fund. Clarges presented a petition from the orphans' agents on 17 Dec. though it was not given parliamentary attention until 16 Feb. He began the proceedings by outlining a scheme for a fund established from the surpluses of City revenues, and it was a refinement of this which the House accepted. Authorization for a bill was given next day, and Clarges and others were ordered to prepare it. He supported the second reading on 23 Feb., though on the 27th he was unable to fend off the corporation's petition against the bill. In any event the measure lapsed shortly afterwards with the end of the session.[20]

With the cessation of Narcissus Luttrell's diary at the end of the 1692–3 session the frequency and wide range of Clarges' speeches in the House are no longer so readily apparent. But from the information available his vigour was plainly undiminished. Seconding Foley's motion on 13 Nov. 1693 for an inquiry into the summer's naval miscarriages, he set an angry tenor to the debate on supply. In one of his most blistering and impatient onslaughts against the Court, he condemned the ineffectiveness of the ministers' direction of the war, a failing tantamount to a betrayal of the country. He lamented the decline of trade, the loss of £1 million of capital stock in the City, the continued destruction or capture of merchant shipping, and above all the inferiority of the nation's maritime strength. These grievances, he insisted, demanded the urgent attention of the House before money was given. He drew, in conclusion, a provocative comparison between those by whom he believed the nation had been betrayed and 'the first Christianity, where there were twelve apostles, and one of them was a devil; he kept the purse; for thirty pieces of silver he betrayed his master'. On the 16th, when Foley delivered the accounts commission's report on the disposition of money given for the maintenance of the fleet, Clarges supposed that an important factor in the misapplication of resources was the Treasury's inability to resist superior commands, and that the Treasury commissioners were not upon oath. This theme he pursued in proceedings on the army on 28 Nov. and 5 Dec., complaining in his usual fashion of the 'vast sums' spent on both English and allied forces in Flanders. As in previous sessions the mainspring of his general criticism of the conduct of the war was his suspicion that 'foreign counsels' had forced England to bear a disproportionately large share of the financial burdens. On the 28th he responded to Seymour's accusation that he 'spoke little to the purpose':

> I am so used to reflections that I take little notice of them. When Lord Ranelagh brought up the forces to be 60,000 men, I thought it my duty not to let that go so. I observe that when the Apostles spoke the truth of the word, it was opposed by the silversmiths that made the shrines for Diana's Temple.

He was appalled on 5 Dec. when Ranelagh presented estimates for an unprecedented 93,635 men, costing £2,881,194, and moved for the papers to be signed by the lords of the Council, 'that we may know whether this be Dutch or English counsel'. It was necessary, as he saw it, to inquire what new alliances necessitated such an increase, and insisted that 'if aid be called from us, we must judge of the treaties'. Under considerable pressure, Sir Thomas Littleton, for the Court, was obliged to try and refute Clarges' arguments. 'Clarges is an able Member, and always speaks to instruction. He tells you of precedents etc. But was a kingdom ever in such a condition, the enemy stronger than you?' Nevertheless, Clarges' reasoning prevailed and an address for the alliances was ordered. These, together with a schedule of the proportion of forces furnished by the allies, were reviewed in the supply committee on 12 Dec. (not, as stated by Grey, on the 11th), at which Clarges elaborated upon the disparities between the English and Dutch provision of troops, and resented allied assumptions that England was 'inexhaustible in treasure'. He also took the lead in raising the accounts commission's charge of peculation against Lord Falkland (Anthony Carey*), a member of the Admiralty board. It was Clarges who notified the House on 4 Dec. that one of Falkland's staff had refused to explain to the commission several discrepancies in his accounts. When the commission's further report was debated on the 7th, Clarges deplored Falkland's misconduct as a Privy Councillor in having obtained the issue of the money in question through an 'order' signed by the King rather than through the privy seal. In the supply debates on ways and means we find him on 18 Jan. 1694 proposing without success to exempt liability for non-rented or empty town-houses from the provisions of the land tax bill, having identified a need to alleviate the burden of the tax upon individuals like himself whose property lay mainly in the heavily assessed metropolitan area. Following the royal veto of the place bill, Clarges was first in the committee proceedings of 26 Jan. to open fire upon the King's advisers:

> I am sorry for the occasion of this committee. I will not say anything of his Majesty, only of the evil counsellors that presumed to advise the King . . . Formerly, just bills and grievances were first passed; and after that the money given. Now, in great respect to his Majesty, the order is inverted, and our grievances denied redress. I cannot think the King to blame, since his declaration hath been to concur with us in anything to make us happy. I should have been glad if the counsellors, or some of them, would have given some reason for the rejection of this bill. I believe that the people who sent us up will hate us for doing nothing but giving away their money, in effect, one to another, as in the Rump, which was their ruin and may be ours.

His concluding motion 'that the advisers of the rejection of this bill are enemies to the King and the kingdom' was set aside, however, in favour of Harley's less bellicose motion to represent to the King 'how few the instances have been to deny assent'. Notwithstanding, he was named in third place to the committee appointed to prepare this address, and was appointed to another the following day to redraft the conclusion in softer terms. Clarges pursued his interest in the London orphans issue. Even before the session opened he was involved with other leading City dignitaries in preliminaries for a new bill, which on 17 Feb. he and others were ordered to prepare. From then until the end of the session in April there is no further record of Clarges' parliamentary activity. But it was a sure sign of his lasting popularity with Country MPs that he was re-elected to the accounts commission in the ballot declared on 12 Apr., taking third place with 131 votes, and only 14 votes behind Harley in first place.[21]

Clarges' contribution to proceedings in the 1694–5 session is even less well documented, and in the main it is only from references in the Journals that we can discern something of the continuing pattern of his preoccupations. What seems to have been a painful circulatory disorder kept him from his commissioner's work during the latter part of September and throughout October 1694, and his condition was serious enough to have induced him to draw up his will. Though he had recovered by the beginning of the session, he may thereafter have been in decline. On the first day of business, 12 Nov., he as usual took note of the thinness of attendance, declaring to those present that 'the country would take it very ill that they should dispose of their money till the rest of the Members were up', whereupon an adjournment was agreed until the 19th. He presented two reports from the accounts commission: on 5 Jan. 1695, a state of the debt due on transport ships; and on 12 Feb. a state of the Irish arrears due to the army. In the ballot for new commissioners announced on 21 Mar. Clarges achieved second place after Harley with 183 votes. His old concern with corruption among army officers was exhibited anew in deliberations on the mutiny bill, as shown by his appointment on 2 Apr. to a small committee entrusted to draft an extra clause prohibiting officers from accepting bribes to excuse the quartering of men on public houses, which he himself reported next day. The accounts commissioners took their oaths at Clarges' Piccadilly residence in May, and throughout the summer months he attended meetings with few intermissions. With the onset of the general election by September, he showed no resolve to retire from Parliament despite his recent ill-health and advanced years, while at Oxford University his re-election was regarded as a foregone conclusion. It was fitting that he should remain active in the service of the House almost until the day of his death. He presided in the chair of the commission on 1 Oct., but on either that or the day following suffered 'a kind of apoplectic fit', in all probability a serious stroke, which rendered him 'insensible', and, in the opinion of his physician John Radcliffe*, beyond all hope of recovery. He died on the 4th and was buried at Stoke Poges, bequeathing a considerable estate to his only son, Sir Walter (1st Bt.*), comprising land and property in Westminster, Middlesex, Berkshire, Buckinghamshire and Lincolnshire reckoned at £6,000 p.a.[22]

Clarges had distinguished himself as an energetic and tenacious keeper of Country consciences. Some onlookers dismissed him as an aged and pernickety troublemaker, too fond of harking back to a better age of 'good husbandry' in government. Bishop Burnet accurately recalled that 'he had Cromwell's economy ever in his mouth, and was always for reducing the expense of war to the modesty and parsimony of those times'. There was, too, an irksome incongruity about him. Having enriched himself with public money he seemed constantly anxious that no one else should do the same. Yet, despite his obvious self-importance, the trenchant expression he gave to the instinctive grievances of many MPs made him a much-respected figure, and as Burnet had to admit, 'very popular'. To the debates of the 1690s he brought warnings and strictures which he had enunciated since the 1660s, epitomizing Country values absorbed from older and more traditional precepts of good governance. But his rigorous approach to parliamentary politics undoubtedly appealed to a younger generation of Country MPs, and helped to educate them in the proper exercise of their responsibilities. As a critic of government his purpose was usually constructive. In the debates on supply he avoided party faction, preferring the role of disinterested commentator. During the early years of the post-Revolution settlement, he was an active spirit behind the ad hoc and often uncertain initiatives to establish and formalize the Commons' lead in financing the requirements of government. He continually emphasized the importance of full information and thorough, methodical inquiry in proceedings on supply, an essential objective of which was to bring ministers to account; and often he had the satisfaction of seeing the House defer to his advice. Of no less significance was his enterprise in devising fiscal schemes to realize the appropriations granted. Quite apart from whether or not his own proposals were taken up, he set a vital example of senatorial responsibility. As one of the last of his generation, he epitomizes the class of parliamentarian who strove to guide the Commons through the more complex demands of the immediate post-Revolution years.

[1] *Bull. IHR*, vi. 189; IGI, London. [2] *CJ*, vii. 828, 873; viii. 213; *CSP Dom*. 1660–1, p. 432. [3] Mdx. RO, MJP/CP5a; *Cal. Treas. Bks.* iii. 1161; *Oxf. Council Acts* (Oxf. Hist. Soc. n.s. ii.), 191, 196. [4] PCC 170 Irby; *HMC Portland*, iii. 498. [5] Devonshire mss at Chatsworth House, 'Devonshire House notebook', 3 Jan. 1689[–90]; *CSP Dom*. 1689–90, pp. 384–5; H. Horwitz, *Parl. and Pol. Wm. III*, 41, 52; DZA, Bonet's despatch 8/18 Oct. 1695; Add. 10119, f. 82; PCC 170 Irby; Wood, *Life and Times*, iii. 325; Northants. RO, Isham mss IC2254, John Isham to Sir Justinian Isham, 4th Bt.*, 20 Mar. [1690]; Add. 33923, f. 481; Morrice ent'ring bk. 3, pp. 126–7; Bodl. Ballard 22, f. 15; Grey, x. 4, 26. [6] Grey, ix. 55; x. 45, 46, 73, 83, 94, 96, 107, 116–17, 128; A. Browning, *Danby*, ii. 470; Bodl. Rawl. A.79, ff. 75, 83–86; Add. 42592, f. 137; 70014, f. 322. [7] Grey, x. 55, 64, 65, 67, 133–4, 136, 141a; A. I. Dasent, *Hist. St. James' Square*, 5; Dasent, *Piccadilly*, 56–57; PCC 170 Irby; Morrice ent'ring bk. 3, pp. 146–7, 151; G. S. De Krey, *Fractured Soc*. 65–66. [8] Add. 70014, f. 321; Morrice ent'ring bk. 3, pp. 127, 135; Grey, x. 53, 109, 112–13; Trinity, Dublin, Clarke mss 749/1/62, 76, 81, Clarges to George Clarke*, 10, 22, 24 July 1690. [9] *CSP Dom*. 1690–1, p. 211; Nottingham Univ. Lib. Portland (Bentinck) mss PwA 299a, Sydney and Coningsby to Portland, 27 Sept. 1690; Horwitz, 62; Dorset RO, Lane (Trenchard) mss D60/F56, Sir John Trenchard* to Henry Trenchard, 21 Oct. 1690; Add. 70114, Thomas Foley I* to Sir Edward Harley, 29 Oct. 1690; 70014, f. 391; 70015, f. 19; Morrice ent'ring bk. 3, pp. 222, 224; Clarke mss 749/2/488, 619, Clarges to Clarke, 24 Feb., 3 Apr. 1691; Harl. 1488, 1489 passim. [10] Add. 70015, f. 272; Centre Kentish Stud. Stanhope mss U1590/059/1, Robert Yard* to Alexander Stanhope, 27 Oct. 1691; *Luttrell Diary*,

4, 9, 10, 35–37; Bodl. Carte 130, ff. 326–8; Grey, x. 167, 168, 182–3; A. Browning, *Danby*, i. 493–4. [11] *Luttrell Diary*, 6, 7, 15, 26, 31, 32, 36–37, 39–43, 47–48, 51–52, 81, 97, 98, 105, 107, 122, 123; Grey, x. 163–4, 165, 167, 177–8, 180, 184–6; PRO NI, De Ros mss D638/13/63, John Pulteney* to Lord Coningsby, 7 Nov. 1691; Add. 70015, f. 240; Horwitz, 70; *Brit. Lib. Jnl.* xv. 177; Browning, i. 492; Stanhope mss U1590/059/1, Yard to Stanhope, [c.5 Jan. 1692]. [12] *Luttrell Diary*, 8, 12, 37, 59, 60, 161–2; Grey, x. 194–5; *HMC Portland*, iii. 489. [13] *Luttrell Diary*, 8, 49–50, 62–65, 75, 128, 154, 159, 167–9, 172–3, 194–5; Grey, x. 189, 200, 201–2, 238–9; Carte 130, f. 336. [14] *Luttrell Diary*, 46, 56, 64, 69, 75, 83, 88, 91, 115, 131, 148, 156, 193, 194. [15] *EHR*, xci. 39; Add. 70260 (unfol.) George Tollet to Harley, 20 Sept. 1692; 70016, f. 124; *HMC Portland*, iii. 498, 499, 500, 502; *Luttrell Diary*, 214–19, 222, 229; Grey, x. 244–6; Carte 130, f. 341. [16] *Luttrell Diary*, 242, 246, 249–50, 260, 263, 266–7, 269, 279, 284, 288, 290, 297, 299, 302, 304–7, 324–5; Grey, x. 253, 256, 270, 271–2; Carte 130, ff. 339–40; Nottingham Univ. Lib. Portland (Bentinck) mss PwA 2385, acct. of debate 23 Nov. [1692]; PwA 2387, acct. of debate 26 Nov. 1692; PwA 2792a, — to Ld. Portland, [1 Nov. 1692]; *Brit. Lib. Jnl.* xv. 182. [17] *Luttrell Diary*, 312, 322–3, 326–7, 333, 353; Ranke, vi. 201. [18] *Luttrell Diary*, 362, 369–73, 401–5, 410–11, 417, 419–21, 431–5; Horwitz, 113. [19] Grey, x. 249, 285, 289, 299; *Luttrell Diary*, 218, 225, 236, 238, 261, 309, 338, 342, 346, 376, 397, 405. [20] *Luttrell Diary*, 234, 296, 320, 326, 345, 376, 379, 381, 386, 396–7, 425–6, 438–9, 444, 449; *N. and Q.* ccxxiii. 527–32. [21] Grey, x. 313, 317, 332–3, 339, 342, 349, 358–9, 375; Add. 29578, f. 444; 17677 NN, f. 369; Ranke, vi. 232; *CSP Dom.* 1693, p. 360. [22] Add. 70217, Clarges to Harley, 24 Sept., 9 Oct. 1694; 70225 (unfol.), Foley to same, 23 Oct. 1694; 17677 PP, f. 151; Harl. 1494 passim; Carte 76, f. 531; 236, ff. 72, 74; Folger Shakespeare Lib. Newdigate newsletters 5, 8 Oct. 1695; Ballard 24, f. 92; Wood, *Life and Times*, iii. 490; *HMC Portland*, iii. 570; PCC 170 Irby.

A. A. H.

CLARGES, Sir Thomas, 2nd Bt. (1688–1759), of Aston, nr. Stevenage, Herts.

LOSTWITHIEL 1713–1715

b. 25 July 1688, 2nd but 1st surv. s. of Sir Walter Clarges, 1st Bt.*, being 2nd s. by his 2nd w., and half-bro. of Robert Clarges*. *educ.* St. Paul's sch. *m.* (1) May 1706, Katherine (d. bef. 1720), da. and coh. of John Berkeley*, 4th Visct. Fitzhardinge [I]; (2) by 1720, Frances (d. 1745), 1s. (*d.v.p.*), 1 o. da. *suc.* fa. as 2nd Bt. c.31 Mar. 1706.[1]

Gent. of privy chamber by 1734–d.[2]

Clarges' early marriage to the daughter of one of Queen Anne's senior Whig courtiers may have struck some as slightly unusual, but it clearly did not detract from the Tory views he absorbed from his family and their milieu. Among his own associates he could count such eminent Tory publicists as his brother-in-law Anthony Hammond*, and Dean Swift. When in 1711 Hammond wished to be relieved of his post as commissioner of the navy, Hammond's brother James sought the views of their mutual friend Hon. James Brydges*, the army paymaster, suggesting that approaches might be made to Secretary St. John (Henry II*) and George Granville*, the secretary at war, with a view to appointing Clarges as Hammond's replacement. The proposition came to nothing, however, probably because of Clarges' youth and inexperience in public business. But Granville seems not to have forgotten Clarges' political aspirations, for it was apparently through Granville's intercession as the government's manager of Cornish boroughs that Clarges entered Parliament for Lostwithiel in 1713. In the Worsley list of the 1713 Parliament he was marked as an undeviating Tory. In ecclesiastical matters he appears as staunchly Anglican. On 6 July 1714 he served as teller against a motion supported by other Tories, including William Shippen*, imposing on the Lords bill against popery a clause to allow Catholics owning advowsons to sell them to Anglicans 'for valuable considerations'. The precise circumstances of the division are unclear, but it would appear that Clarges disapproved of the retention of Church livings in the hands of papists. Beyond this, no further activity can be credited to him. At the 1715 election the Whig management of the Cornish boroughs evidently precluded his continued representation of Lostwithiel and he did not on this occasion seek re-election elsewhere. He made further attempts to re-enter Parliament in 1722 and 1747, however, standing both times unsuccessfully as a Tory candidate for Westminster, formerly represented by his father. Despite the persistence of his Tory outlook he appears none the less to have been sufficiently acceptable to the Whig establishment to merit appointment as a gentleman of the privy chamber under George II. He had already served in the Middlesex lieutenancy under the Duke of Newcastle since 1716. Clarges died on 19 Feb. 1759, and, as decreed in his will, was buried in St. George's Chapel, Windsor. His son having predeceased him in 1753, he was succeeded by his only grandson, Thomas†, in the baronetcy and estates, chief of which were the manors he had inherited from his father in the vicinity of Kesteven, Lincolnshire.[3]

[1] Kimber and Johnson, *Baronetage*, ii. 384; *Reg. St. Paul's Sch.* 332; Luttrell, *Brief Relation*, vi. 46; IGI, London; Clutterbuck, *Herts.* ii. 250. [2] Info. from Prof. R. O. Bucholz. [3] *Swift Stella* ed. Davis, 618, 646; Huntington Lib., Stowe mss 58(9), p. 260, James Hammond to Brydges, 12 Oct. 1711; PCC 85 Arran; S. M. Bond, *Monuments of St. George's Chapel*, p. xvi.

A. A. H.

CLARGES, Sir Walter, 1st Bt. (1653–1706), of Piccadilly, Westminster and Ashley, Surr.

COLCHESTER 1679 (Mar.)–1681 (Jan.), 1685–1687
WESTMINSTER 1690–1695, 1702–1705

b. 4 July 1653, o.s. of Sir Thomas Clarges*. *educ.* Merton, Oxf. matric. 1671. *m.* (1) Jane, da. of Sir Dawes Wymondsold of Putney, Surr., 1 da.; (2) by 1682, Jane (d.

1690), da. of Hon. James Herbert† of Tythrop House, Kingsey, Bucks., 2s. (1 *d.v.p.*) 2da.; (3) 15 Dec. 1690, Elizabeth (*d.* 1728), da. and coh. of Sir Thomas Gould, Draper, of Aldermanbury, London, wid. of Sir Robert Wymondsold of Putney, 6s. 3da. *cr.* Bt. 30 Oct. 1674; *suc.* fa. 1695.[1]

Capt. Duke of Monmouth's Ft. 1678–9, R. Dgns. 1679–81; maj. 1 Horse Gds. 1681–9.[2]

Freeman, Maldon 1679, Oxford 1687–Feb. 1688.[3]

Clarges possessed none of his august father's enthusiasm for the parliamentary arena. He had emerged in the later 1680s as an opponent of James II's religious policies, while his attendance on William of Orange at Exeter in November 1688, at his father's direction, put his loyalties beyond question. With the backing of Sir Thomas' considerable proprietorial interests and personal influence in the metropolis, he was elected in 1690 for Westminster. Before the new Parliament met, Lord Carmarthen (Sir Thomas Osborne†) classed him as a Tory and regarded him as a probable Court supporter. Clarges' approbation of the new regime was whole-hearted. In the summer of 1690 the recent manifestations of radicalism among the City Whigs made him question the veracity of Whig adherence to the Revolution. Writing to his friend George Clarke*, the new secretary at war in Ireland, concerning the recent 'miscarriages' of the fleet, the culpability of the English command, and the consequent threat of French invasion, he contrasted the principles of 'honest' Tory gentlemen with the conniving duplicity of Whigs who, despite their pretended patriotism, seemed more intent upon undermining the Revolution settlement:

> for those honest gentlemen who ever loved a Protestant monarchy do so still under this gallant prince, and generally those who used to call themselves patriots, and pretend to be most afraid of the French and popery, and most jealous of the honour and interest of their country, even to the degree of calling honest men criminals, are now making excuses for those, who most people think guilty of the basest and most dishonourable action that was ever done in this nation. And one thing more is pretty remarkable; those sort of men, as if they had bespoke the miscarriages here, and doubted of your better fortune in Ireland, begin to insinuate that if nobody would defend us, we must defend ourselves, and you guess well what that means; but I hope there is no more danger in them, if they should now join with our enemies, than there was when most of them did before.[4]

At the end of the year Carmarthen classed Clarges as a probable adherent in the light of the projected attack on him; the following April Robert Harley* had seen sufficient evidence in his parliamentary conduct to mark him as a Country supporter. At the close of 1691 his attention was engaged in a bill for clarifying the provisions of earlier legislation establishing the parish of St. Anne out of that of St. Martin-in-the-Fields, where the Clarges family owned much property. Though it had been initiated by his father, Clarges reported the bill from committee on 24 Dec., supervised its remaining stages in the House, and conveyed it to the Lords on the 30th. This apart, however, he was largely inactive.[5]

With the death of his father early in October 1695, Clarges inherited a considerable estate, comprising property in St. James's, Westminster, and in Berkshire and Buckinghamshire, yielding some £5,000 per annum. His third marriage in 1690 to a 'very rich' widow had already placed him in a financially advantageous situation. In October he stood singly for re-election at Westminster, but from the outset his chances of retaining the seat were severely hampered by the death of his father earlier in the month and his own recovery from serious illness. Leading City figures who had promised the late Sir Thomas their interest for his son now considered themselves relieved of their obligation and transferred their allegiance to Clarges' two opponents, the Court candidates Charles Montagu* and Sir Stephen Fox*. On the day of nomination Clarges desperately tried to secure votes by distributing £2,000. The collapse of his electoral support, however, was confirmed after several days' polling in which he achieved a paltry third place. In July 1696 he was removed from the Middlesex lieutenancy, in which he had served since March 1692, presumably for failing to subscribe the Association. At the 1698 election it was anticipated that he might attempt to recapture his old seat, but he did not in fact venture to stand.[6]

Clarges appears to have developed ties of acquaintanceship with several of the Grecian Tavern set, of whom one was his son-in-law Anthony Hammond*, a regular guest at Clarges' Surrey residence. At the first election of 1701 he campaigned anew for his former seat but was again defeated. He may have found small compensation in readmission to the Middlesex lieutenancy in February. In March he petitioned for a bill to confirm repossession of land in the Piccadilly area which he had leased years earlier to the speculator Thomas Neale* on condition that it was developed at an outlay of £10,000. Neale had defaulted on these terms, and died insolvent at the end of 1699 owing Clarges £800 in rental arrears. A bill was duly authorized, its sponsors being named as Clarges' friend Sir Joseph Tredenham*, son-in-law Hammond and Morgan Randyll*, another close family friend who had married Clarges' sister-in-law. But on 2 May the bill was defeated when the question for its second reading was put to a division, a move probably forced by Neale's friends. Clarges seems none the less to have secured the lease through other means and developed the property himself.[7]

At the election of 1702 Clarges regained his Westminster seat. On 6 Nov., soon after the new Parliament assembled, he initiated a privilege complaint regarding the 'fraudulent entry' perpetrated on his Yorkshire manor of Sutton-upon-Derwent by his arch-enemy William Sherwin. Sherwin's intrusion upon the estate was another episode in the ongoing inheritance dispute with which he had plagued Clarges during the past five or so years. The estate to which Sherwin laid claim, worth about £1,000 per annum, was Clarges' legacy from his cousin the 2nd Duke of Albemarle (Christopher Monck†) who had died in 1688. The Duke's mother, Clarges' aunt, had been previously married to one Thomas Radford, from whom she became estranged. The fact of Radford's death was never established, and it was the basis of Sherwin's case that Radford had been still alive at the time of Anne Clarges' marriage to the 1st Duke (George Monck†), and that their son, the eventual 2nd Duke, was thus technically illegitimate. On this premise, Sherwin maintained that his own wife, a great niece of the 1st Duke, was rightful heir. Despite several court verdicts in Clarges' favour, Sherwin took possession of the estate in 1701 and ran it as his own. None the less, the committee of privileges declared him in breach of Clarges' privilege on 8 Dec. and ordered Sherwin into custody.[8]

In the same early weeks of the new Parliament Clarges was also involved in the investigation of complaints about excessive coal prices in the metropolis. The investigating committee, from which Clarges reported on 7 Nov., took little time to become convinced that profiteering 'combinations' of Newcastle coal-owners and lightermen, the main suppliers of London's coal, were chiefly responsible for the escalating prices. The matter concerned Clarges, not only as a problem affecting the London environs, but also because he was the recipient of a £500 pension, originally granted to his father, payable from a duty of 12d. per chaldron on coal shipped from Newcastle. Whatever his motives, Clarges' continued close attention to the issue is evident from his being first-named among the MPs appointed to draft a bill for regulating the shipment of coal from Newcastle. He introduced the resultant measure on 2 Dec., but inexplicably it was pursued no further after second reading. In the spring of 1703 Clarges was forced to combat yet another attempt by Sherwin to bastardize the late Duke of Albemarle. Once more, the verdict went in Clarges' favour, though he condemned the legal system for allowing the matter to be pursued so relentlessly, to the dishonour of his noble cousin's name. He fell dangerously ill in June, prompting speculation about a possible successor to him at Westminster. In mid-March 1704 Lord Nottingham (Daniel Finch†) listed him as a probable supporter in the event of an attack on him over the Scotch Plot, while in November Clarges voted, as predicted, in support of the Tack.[9]

Clarges' decision not to stand for re-election in 1705 was dictated by declining health. He died at Ashley at the end of March 1706 and was buried at Stoke Poges. In his will he distributed his manors and lands in Buckinghamshire, Lincolnshire, Middlesex, Surrey, Wiltshire and Yorkshire among his extensive offspring, with the exception of his eldest son and successor, Sir Thomas, 2nd Bt.*, who had already been well provided for under Clarges' marriage settlement and under the 2nd Duke of Albemarle's will.[10]

[1] Bodl. Rawl. A.245, f. 71; Kimber and Johnson, *Baronetage*, ii. 384; Prob. 10/1401; Boyer, *Pol. State*, xxxv. 415. [2] Luttrell, *Brief Relation*, i. 509. [3] Essex RO, D/B3/1/24, ff. 5–7; *Oxford Council Acts* (Oxford Hist. Soc. n.s. ii), 191, 196. [4] Trinity, Dublin, Clarke mss 749/1/63, Clarges to Clarke, 10 July 1690. [5] PCC 170 Irby. [6] Clarke mss 749/2/414, Peter Birch to Clarke, 24 Jan. 1691; Luttrell, iii. 534, 541; iv. 89; Centre Kentish Stud. Stanhope mss U1590/059/4, Robert Yard* to Alexander Stanhope, 8 Oct. 1695; Folger Shakespeare Lib. Newdigate newsletter 8 Oct. 1695; Add. 70018, f. 98; Macaulay, *Hist. of Eng.* 2556–8; *CSP Dom.* 1691–2, p. 164; Northants. RO, Montagu (Boughton) mss 47/52, James Vernon I* to Duke of Shrewsbury, 2 July 1698. [7] Moyle, *Works* ed. Hammond (1727), p. 15; Rawl. D.174, f. 35; *HMC Cowper*, ii. 415, 432, 435; Bodl. Carte 228, ff. 341–2, 335–6; *CSP Dom.* 1700–2, p. 269; *Evelyn Diary* ed. Wheatley, iii. 118. [8] *Post Man*, 23–25 July 1702; Luttrell, iv. 243, 642, 643, 708; *Evelyn Diary* ed. de Beer, v. 410–11. [9] PCC 85 Arran; *HMC Portland*, ii. 183–4; Luttrell, v. 294; BL, Trumbull Add. mss 134, Thomas Bateman to Sir William Trumbull*, 20 June 1703. [10] Prob. 10/1401; Luttrell, vi. 33.

A. A. H.

CLARKE, Edward I (1650–1710) of Chipley, Som.[1]

TAUNTON 1690–1710

b. 14 Sept. 1650, o. s. of Edward Clarke of Chipley by Anne, da. and coh. of Mark Knight of West Buckland and Oake, Som. *educ.* Taunton sch.; Wadham, Oxf. matric. 1667; I. Temple 1670, called 1673, reader Lyons Inn 1689. *m.* 13 Apr. 1675 Mary (*d.* 1706), da. of Samuel Jepp of Sutton Court, Chew Magna, Som. 5s. (3 *d.v.p.*) 6da. (2 *d.v.p.*). *suc.* fa. Sept. 1679.[2]

Commr. inquiry into recusancy fines Som. 1688, receiving subscriptions to Bank 1694, excise 1694–1700, leather duty 1697.[3]

Auditor-gen. to Queen 1690–94.

Recorder, Taunton 1695.[4]

Clarke was by nature a back-room politician, an earnest, conscientious and cerebral man of integrity, known as the 'grave squire'. Yet he was thrust into the limelight by his friendship with John Locke and kept there by his overwhelming sense of duty to God, friends, party and nation. Although probably more comfortable in private conversation than holding the floor of the House (MPs were said to have left 'to make water' when he rose to his feet), he became the philosopher's mouthpiece in the Commons and consequently the most important member of Locke's 'college', a policy-making and parliamentary pressure-group that was particularly active in the mid-1690s. Yet Clarke was also much more than a dependable cog in an effective lobby machine, for he was a formidable expert in his own right on finance and the drafting of legislation. Devoted to William III and to the Whigs, his loyalties were to the Court that had given him office, but he was also a stout defender of his 'country' and a fierce opponent of corruption, as his sponsorship of several election bills and tireless promotion of constituency interests make clear. Indeed, the numerous and diverse calls on his energies and abilities rapidly wore him out, both physically and mentally, and overwork pushed him after 1699 into a depression and sickness that overshadowed his early promise as a Junto manager.[5]

Clarke's Chipley estate was brought into his family by his stepmother Elizabeth Lottisham, heiress of Edward Warre. The union of Lottisham and Clarke snr. was childless, so Edward inherited his stepmother's estate. The year after his father died, Clarke began altering the manor house in the latest architectural fashion: Chipley's 120-foot-long north–south front with an ashlar doric frontispiece distinguished its owner as a man of means anxious to stamp his taste and status on a parish that was shared uncomfortably with the Tory Sanford family.[6]

The origins of Clarke's friendship with Locke are obscure. According to his tutor, Clarke made 'laudable progress in learning' at Oxford, where he behaved 'very civilly towards all men', but there is no evidence that he was taught by Locke or that he drew the latter's attention by intellectual distinction. It was probably marriage to Mary Jepp that created the bond. After the early death of her father she lived with her half-uncle John Strachey at Sutton Court, in the parish of Chew Magna, where Locke's grandparents had lived and near to the philosopher's estate at Beluton. Strachey had been educated with Locke at both Westminster and Oxford and remained a friend. Moreover, Locke referred to Mary as his 'cousin', though the precise relationship is difficult to establish. The ties between Strachey, Locke and Mary were nevertheless close enough for Strachey to consult his friend in 1673–4 about potential husbands for Mary, whose own income amounted to a legacy of £400 p.a. as well as her father's property in Westham, Essex. On Strachey's death in February 1675, Mary came under the guardianship of her uncle, John Buckland[†], whose friendship with William Clarke, Edward's 'cousin', may have brought about the necessary introduction that led to marriage. Locke claimed 'without flattery or compliment' that Mary's blend of 'wit and good nature' gave her the 'resemblance of an angel', and the close marriage of minds with Clarke resulted in constant, and often highly revealing, correspondence whenever they were parted.[7]

Clarke's interest in politics and finance predated his association with Locke, since as a law student he reported parliamentary news to his father and managed familial business affairs, but it cannot have been long before Locke's patron, the 1st Earl of Shaftesbury (Anthony Ashley Cooper[†]), noticed the rising young lawyer. Certainly by 1676 Clarke was known in the Earl's household, for his secretary Thomas Stringer informed Locke about Mary's first child. That year also marked the introduction of another key figure in Clarke's life, John Freke, a fellow lawyer. Clarke struck up a lifelong friendship with Freke, whose financial and political shrewdness was to make him an invaluable member of the 'college' and who may have introduced Clarke to the future Junto leader (Sir) John Somers*. By the late 1670s Clarke was thus mixing in circles critical of the Court and, in a gathering that foreshadowed Whig summits held there in the 1690s, frequented the spa at Tunbridge Wells with Freke, Sir Walter Yonge, 3rd Bt.*, and another west-country friend, Richard Duke*, all of whom were intimates of Locke. The final link in Locke's circle came in 1681 when the Clarkes took London lodgings with Lady King; their neighbour was Damaris Cudworth, future wife of Sir Francis Masham, 3rd Bt.*, who was to play hostess to Locke in the 1690s. Both Locke and Clarke were trustees for Mrs Cudworth, Damaris' mother, a duty which was to create a good deal of work because of the legal suits filed by Lady Masham's brother. By 1682, the date of the first surviving letter between Locke and Clarke, the fundamental relationships that were to shape Edward's life had already been formed.[8]

Shaftesbury made Clarke one of his trustees, and when Locke too was forced into exile he also entrusted his affairs to Edward. Locke sent him 'many papers' with power to burn whatever he disliked and Clarke was apparently one of the few to know about the manuscript of the *Two Treatises*. At the same time Locke's will made his friend 'legally entitled to whatsoever' he left. Throughout Locke's five-year stay in Holland, Clarke looked after the philosopher's concerns with a diligence that prompted Locke's profession that he loved him 'above all other men'. Clarke's intimacy with Locke was personal, political but also intellectual. Locke, for example, sent him drafts of his *Essay Concerning Human Understanding* and thought enough of Clarke's judgment to let him decide 'whether it be new or useful'. Edward later helped oversee the publication of some of Locke's philsophical works, and during his exile Locke sent the Clarkes advice on the education of their son, correspondence which he later revised and published in 1693 as *Some Thoughts Concerning Education*, with a dedication to his friend. Indeed, Locke was so fond of Clarke's children that he habitually referred to one of their daughters, Elizabeth, as his 'wife'.[9]

Association with Shaftesbury, Locke and Green Ribbon Club men rendered Clarke politically suspect and in the spring of 1684 he was 'presented as dangerous' by a jury. Kinsman William Clarke could not understand what Clarke 'ever did to beget enemies', but suspected that Clarke's neighbour and rival, John Sanford*, had been the prime mover. Sanford was later described by Clarke as being 'at [Sir William] Portman's* command', an indication that local rivalries were also part of national ones, since Portman was the cousin of one of the Tory leaders, (Sir) Edward Seymour* (4th Bt.). In 1685 Clarke was taken into custody on the suspicion that he 'held correspondence with traitors' but petitioned the King on the grounds of his father's royalism and that he himself had not done or said anything to incur the King's displeasure. He was released on bonds and took no part in Monmouth's rebellion, staying at Tunbridge rather than returning to Chipley.[10]

Clarke's parliamentary ambitions can be traced back to 1679, when he was considered to have Shaftesbury's ear. In July 1679 it was reported that if he could obtain the Earl's recommendation he was thought to stand a good chance at Taunton. Clarke got as far as drafting a letter to (Sir) John Trenchard* in which he referred to his having 'received great encouragements from the Earl of Shaftesbury, my noble friend, and diverse considerable men of that place'. Clarke evidently hoped to join interests with Trenchard: 'I hope you will not deny it me, especially since I can with great sincerity assure you that it is not any private ambition of my own but the persuasion of friends and the earnest desire I have to serve faithfully the public that hath induced me to offer myself thus to you.' Clarke, however, was 'resolved not publicly to appear' without assurance of Trenchard's support and he did not openly contest the election. It was not until Trenchard's imprisonment in 1683 that it was reported that 'the Taunton men would choose the two Clarkes', William and Edward, if Trenchard died. When Edward finally stood for Parliament in 1685, on behalf of what the mayor of Taunton called the 'damnable crew' of 'Grindallizing self-willed humourists', he was unsuccessful.[11]

Ironically Clarke's electoral chances seemed to improve once James II began wooing the Whigs. The King's electoral agents reported in December 1687 that he would 'probably' be chosen at Taunton and he was still thought the likely victor in reports submitted in April and September 1688. But although the King's agents regarded him as 'right' and he was nominated both as a deputy lieutenant and commissioner to enquire into recusancy fines in the county, there is no evidence that Clarke complied with James's policies. Indeed, he was privy to Locke's irritation at unauthorized attempts to secure a pardon and visited Locke in Holland in the summer of 1688, perhaps too sensitive a time to be entirely politically innocent. Certainly Clarke was an enthusiastic supporter of William of Orange and contested Taunton in the elections for the Convention, though his and Trenchard's voters were attacked by men wielding 'great cudgels or clubs'. It was this violence rather than, as has been claimed, association with James's agents, that probably prevented his election. He petitioned, unsuccessfully, but was finally returned in 1690 and remained MP for Taunton until his death.[12]

Almost immediately after the 1690 election, 'general reflections' were made on Clarke in his locality to the effect that he was 'so much for the K[ing]s interest that it should incline [him] to oppress the people'. Clarke was so strongly identified with the Court interest because in 1689 he had been appointed auditor to the Queen, a post officially worth about £100 p.a. but about the same again in perquisites. It was obtained for him, without his prior knowledge, by Locke (with the assistance of Richard Coote*, Earl of Bellomont) because of 'the entrance it g[ave] him into the Court and the countenance it g[ave] him in the country'. But favour at Court had done nothing to dent Clarke's animus against the Tories. In his first session he reported and carried up a bill relating to the estate of the Earl of Essex, whose 'murder' in the Tower in 1683 had provoked a pamphlet of which Locke was accused of being the author. On 24 Apr. Clarke acted as teller in support of an amendment to an address of thanks for the recent alterations in London's lieutenancy which had favoured the Tories, since the Whigs wanted to except those involved in the recent persecutions and arrests. Indeed, the issue prompted Clarke's maiden recorded speech, in which he declared that he was 'as much for the innocent Church of England men as any man; but not for the guilty of innocent blood lately shed'.[13]

The same day he was appointed to the drafting committee of the abjuration bill. An undated draft speech in Clarke's own hand was probably intended for delivery on that issue, since it argued forcibly that religion, liberty and security would all 'be lost if we hold not now together united in this government'. All who recognized William as king should thus 'join in a solemn and public renunciation' of the divine right doctrine 'that annuls his title'. The occasion also offered an opportunity for Clarke to display his uncompromising view of the Revolution:

> The Prince of Orange came with armed force to redeem us. Those who will not own this to be done of right must take it for an invasion of an enemy whom they are willing to be rid of again . . . and how ready they will be to join with the king of France . . . is easy to judge. That which makes such a Declaration as this more necessary is that many among us publicly declared against the vacancy of the throne which opinion I never heard they have publicly recanted but 'tis necessary they should . . . the emissaries of Rome and France [are] busy everywhere to increase our want of union into a breach which will be sure to let in France and his dragoons upon us; I ask any the warmest Whig or Tory . . . what he proposes to himself when he has let in a foreign force that are enemies to our nation and religion and thereby made his country the scene of blood and slaughter.

He was appealing to both republican Whigs and *jure divino* Tories to curb their excesses and unite behind the rightful king against France and popery. Clarke's first actions in Parliament thus thoroughly justified his being ranked with the Whigs by Lord Carmarthen (Sir Thomas Osborne†), albeit on the Court or pragmatic wing of the party. Shortly before the end of the session Clarke acted as teller on 13 May over a proviso to the bill to encourage the manufacture of white paper.[14]

After the naval setback at Beachy Head he observed that the French had been allowed to gain the upper hand 'by treachery and cowardice in the great officers of our fleet'. In a letter written in August to a member of Queen Mary's court, Clarke outlined his hostility to what he saw as the irresponsible activity of High Churchmen in Somerset:

> before the extremity of our danger of the French was over the High Tory party began to show their resentments that so many honest gentlemen were made deputy-lieutenants of this county and other of a different character left out etc and immediately made their application to the bishops who (as if the Church were as much concerned in the establishment of our militia officers as in settling of tender consciences) taking Sir Edward Phelips*, notwithstanding all his notorious characters more black than the ink I write with, to be a pillar of this Church, they presently espoused his cause [and purged the commission, matters] of as ill consequence to the Church as even the landing of the French would have been could they have made good their church upon it . . . I have by this post written to my Lord Monmouth, hoping by his lordships interest to prevent any mischief or inconvenience that so malicious a party may endeavour to do me with the Queen.

Clarke felt vulnerable and urged that if necessary Locke should be brought in to vindicate his reputation to the Queen, whose good opinion he valued 'more than any other favour her Ma[jes]ty can bestow'.[15]

Clarke survived the whispering campaign against him, but the letter is indicative of the bitterness of local disputes that were to plague much of his career, as well as of his lifelong distrust of meddling High Churchmen, whose actions he saw as a cover for more sinister designs. The need to counter-attack may explain Clarke's 'perpetual hurry and vexation' when Parliament reassembled in October 1690. Such busyness is nevertheless not reflected in numerous committee nominations, although Clarke was named to a few inquiry committees. He also made notes of the resolutions passed between 17 and 22 Oct. as part of the attempt to raise money either by sale, or upon the security, of Irish forfeitures. Unsurprisingly, Robert Harley* classed him as a Court supporter in April 1691, an analysis duplicated on six further lists of this Parliament.[16]

It was the session of 1691–2 that really marked the beginning of Clarke's active parliamentary career and the emergence of an embryonic 'college'. The first issue to demand his attention was the treason trials bill. On 18 Nov. he 'spoke against several particulars of it' and returned to his theme more fully on 11 Dec., when he appears to have started the debate about the Lords' amendments. Clarke 'strongly opposed' what he saw as an attempt to weaken the power of parliamentary impeachment. Although what he actually said was subsequently disputed, Clarke certainly objected to one witness being sufficient in cases of 'declaratory treason'. He acted as teller against the Lords' amendment and was accordingly named to the conference committee. On 31 Dec., when the report was debated, Clarke again opposed another of the Lords' amendments, which allowed a majority verdict from the whole Upper House rather than from a panel chosen by the lord high steward.[17]

Although Clarke's critical attitude was not shared by Locke, he remained firm in his opposition, proof of his independent mind, for on 5 Jan. 1692 he returned to the attack, condemning the amendments as leaving 'the government destitute of all means to preserve itself against any conspiracy of the Lords or of any considerable number of the Lords of ancient families'. He even felt it worthwhile to record speeches made by peers at the free conference. The following day Locke again wrote to him to try to change his mind. Clarke nevertheless put principle above party consideration and resisted Locke's argument that the amendments favoured Whig peers (such as Locke's friend Monmouth) who would be the likely victims of any prosecution. On 13 Jan. 1692, in the debate on the report from the conference about the amendments, Edward argued that it was 'not parliamentary for the Lords to prescribe rule' to the Commons and he acted as teller on the issue on two further occasions that session.[18]

The difference of opinion between Locke and Clarke over the Lords' amendments to the treason trials bill should not, however, mask the very considerable co-operation between them on other matters. On 22 Jan. Locke asked his friend to send him a copy of the heads of the proposed bill to regulate the East India Company and Clarke had earlier acted as teller against a motion concerning the consideration of a petition from the company. Indeed, a manuscript among his papers rebutted each of the points made in the company's petition. From Locke's point of view, however, the most important issue was probably the coinage, which had been heavily debased by clipping. Clarke corrected the proofs of Locke's ensuing tract, *Some Considerations of the Consequences of the Lessening of Interest*, which was printed by another of Locke's associates, Awnsham Churchill*, and was ready for distribution in early December. On the 15th Clarke reported that he had given a copy to Sir Francis Masham and

> disposed of four or five more so advantageously in the House that it is already a doubt whether the bill for lowering the interest of money will ever be read a second time or not, and all that have read the *Considerations* are clearly of opinion the arguments therein are abundantly sufficient to destroy that bill and all future attempts of the like kind; I hear the whole treatise generally much approved of and commended.[19]

Although the bill was introduced, Clarke spoke on 8 Jan. 1692 against it, suggesting that 'money was a commodity and would rise or fall in interest according to the plenty or scarcity of money and was not able to be restrained'. He spoke again a week later but for all his effort he was, as Locke put it, 'toiling to no purpose', since the bill passed the House. Clarke reported that 'all imaginable reasons were used' to try to defeat it and that the debates had echoed many of the arguments used in Locke's tract, 'but I am satisfied if an angel from heaven had managed the debate, the votes would have been the same as now, for 'tis not reason but a supposed benefit to the borrower that hath passed the bill . . . I wish we may have better success upon the bill of coinage'. This bill aimed to raise the value of money in order to prevent its export, which was draining England of bullion; but, Clarke argued in notes for an intended speech, the value of silver could not be artificially raised because the coin would only be worth its intrinsic value abroad, 'for 'tis not the denomination but the quantity of silver that gives the value to any coin'. The cause rather than the symptom of the problem therefore had to be tackled and 'standard silver was and eternally will be worth its weight in standard silver'. The experience on both pieces of financial legislation indicated, however, that lobbying by Clarke and Locke would in future have to be stepped up.[20]

Clarke's activity in the 1691–2 session also revealed three other abiding concerns. One was the freedom of the press. On 12 Nov. 1691 he moved that the House receive the petition of the Whig publisher Richard Baldwin. A second campaign was to promote civil toleration for Quakers by removing the requirement to take oaths. Thus, on 30 Nov. he joined others in offering a clause to excuse Quakers from the oaths intended in the bill for Irish oaths (though on 9 Feb. he moved that no one should benefit from the Irish Forfeitures Act 'without taking the oaths and subscribing the declaration') and on 22 Feb. 1692 spoke in favour of the Quaker affirmation bill (support he continued to give in the next session, being nominated on 26 Nov. to the committee established to consider the sect's petition for a new bill and reporting on 5 Dec. in its favour). His prominent involvement in a conference on 20 Feb. 1692 concerning the passage of the bill for the easier recovery of small tithes, which he reported two days later, is nevertheless a reminder that although strongly sympathetic to toleration of Dissent, Clarke remained a member of the Church of England and was seemingly a pious one, for verses composed on his death claimed he was 'scoffed at . . . because he loved his lord and saviour dear' and called him 'an instrument' that prevented danger to 'the Church of Christ'. The purpose of the bill was to transfer jurisdiction over tithe disputes from clerical to secular jurisdiction, but support for the bill also came from Churchmen who sought to bolster parochial finances. The third issue provoking Clarke to action was electoral reform. On 2 Dec. 1691 he reported a bill to prevent false and double election returns and acted as teller ten days later in favour of its passage.[21]

Clarke was also anxious about the Jacobite threat. He made notes about Lord Preston's (Sir Richard Grahme†) conspiracy, and on 4 Jan. 1692 spoke in favour of addressing the King about providing protection for two of William Fuller's witnesses. Clarke rejoiced at the Earl of Marlborough's (John Churchill†) disgrace for corresponding with the exiled James: 'experience will convince', he told Locke, 'that there ought to be no medium between turning him out and putting him in the Tower'. Perhaps because of the pressure of public business, Clarke joined in the condemnation on 14 Jan. of the number of private bills introduced and supported a suggestion to bar their being moved until after 11 a.m., although no formal resolution resulted. Ironically, he was himself ordered on 9 Feb. to carry up Lord Villiers' private estate bill.[22]

The closeness between Locke and Clarke was again evident on the eve of the 1692–3 session when Clarke was asked to liaise with Awnsham Churchill about the publication of Locke's *Third Letter for Toleration* and subsequently to distribute copies. Co-operation on political matters was also ongoing. Locke wrote to Clarke asking him to spend Christmas with him because he longed to talk with him and on 2 Jan. 1693 wrote a long letter of advice about the Licensing Act, requesting Clarke to talk with Churchill about its deficiencies and to consider the coinage. Locke added that he hoped to see Clarke at the contested Essex by-election and is likely to have done so, for on 14 Feb. Clarke acted as teller in favour of the return of John Lamotte Honeywood*, on whose behalf Clarke 'spoke at large'. If the meeting did take place, it would seem likely that Clarke discussed the coinage bill with Locke.[23]

Clarke had, in fact, already spoken on 31 Dec. 1692 against the bill to melt the coin, arguing that 'it would be of no advantage to this nation, because as much as we lessened our coin so much would the exchange abroad rise against us . . . and it would be no good but put people and things in confusion'. He duly acted as teller against the passage of the bill. Locke assisted Clarke's campaign in January by writing his *Short Observations on a Printed Paper*, which may have been prompted by Clarke, who had sent his friend a copy of the tract to which it replied. Locke certainly authorized Clarke to make use of his work as he saw fit. Clarke in return was helpful over the private concerns of Locke's friends. He steered through the House a bill to convey land in Fulham owned by the bishop of London to the Earl of Monmouth, and assisted in the private concerns of Locke's host at Oates, Sir Francis Masham.[24]

One of Clarke's first actions of the 1692–3 session had been to obtain leave on 11 Nov. 1692 to present a new elections bill. He duly did so two days later and subsequently guided its passage through the House, carrying it up to the Lords on 28 Feb. 1693, where it was nevertheless defeated. Clarke's main preoccupation in the session, however, was the conduct of the war and the mismanagement of the navy. Notes, apparently for a speech, suggest that he contributed to the debate on 11 Nov. in defence of Edward Russell*, evidence of his readiness to defend members of the future Junto. On 19 Nov. he was one of the MPs who wanted to question Sir John Ashby further about the conduct of the fleet after La Hogue and four days later upheld the Court's position about the conduct of foreign generals. At the same time he attacked the organization of the failed descent and the transportation provision, a speech aimed at George Churchill*. Clarke was prepared to believe that all the accusations against Churchill were true 'if the objections [we]re not answered' and on 30 Nov. attacked the 'great mistakes' in the orders given the navy.[25]

When the debate on the descent was resumed on 5 Dec. 1692 Clarke seconded Yonge's motion for the House to decide on whom to 'fix this fault', a deliberate attempt to undermine the position of Secretary Nottingham (Daniel Finch†), against whom Clarke made a number of notes and draft resolutions. When Nottingham counter-attacked, the Whigs responded with an abjuration bill and Clarke and Yonge again worked in tandem on its promotion, speaking and acting as tellers on 14 Dec. in favour of its committal. Indeed, a document in Clarke's hand suggests that it was he who was responsible for the insertion of the oath acknowledging that William and Mary were 'the only lawful and rightful King and Queen'. Since Somers had drafted the bill, Clarke's involvement in this and in the attacks on Nottingham confirm his close alliance with the ministerial Whigs, while his frequent alliance with Yonge suggests that the 'college' was already operating to effect on the floor of the House.[26]

The 1692–3 session also witnessed the emergence of Clarke as an energetic constituency MP. On 14 Nov. 1692 he 'took notice that several Members were abroad upon other services' and that their constituents were not represented. He was accordingly named to the committee of inquiry established to search for relevant precedents and on 8 Mar. proposed 'that if any person shall accept of any place or employment that requires his attendance from the service of this House new writs shall go to choose other persons in their places'. Clarke was also specifically concerned to promote his local economy. He was no novice about how this should be done, for in October 1691 the mayor of Taunton had written to him 'in the name of the whole town to acquaint you of the unavoidable ruin of our trade if the woollen manufactures be not some way stopped in Ireland'; the town sought the expansion of the Irish linen industry instead, since that would leave the market clear for English woollens while also damaging French interests. Later that year a joint letter from Taunton had also praised Clarke for his

> great care and pains in prosecuting all public and private business for us [and] also for your favour of communicating the same to us. We have daily letters and application made unto us from Londoners to desire us to write to you [that] if possible a clause might be inserted in the bill ag[ain]st hawkers and pedlars to prevent their travelling w[i]th horse packs as well as foot and that they may be bound within the compass of their own towns or markets.[27]

Mounting local pressure for action may thus explain some of Clarke's activity in 1692–3. On 24 Nov. 1692 Clarke presented a petition from the Blackwell Hall factors against the bill for encouraging woollen manufactures and on 1 Dec. he acted as teller in favour of referring a petition from Gloucestershire clothiers to the committee examining the cloth dealers' petition. The following day he presented a further petition from the clothiers of Wiltshire and Somerset and on 15 Feb. 1693 was teller on a motion about the decay of the wool trade in towns. Five days before, he had tried unsuccessfully to have a clause inserted in a revived bill for the export of wool to allow the import of wool from Ireland to Bridgwater, though even without his clause Clarke was an enthusiastic supporter of the bill. At its third reading a week later he again refuted its detractors in the free-trade terms he had used about the movement of bullion: 'it is very strange that an open trade and a free exportation of any commodity should not be for the interest of the nation', he argued, since it boosted trade. Clarke and Yonge acted as tellers in favour of the bill's passage, though they were defeated.[28]

Despite this setback Clarke continued to be careful to promote any measure that would encourage the principal industry of his locality. On 28 Feb. he thus successfully added a clause to the bill to encourage privateers to give them 'a full moiety of all such ships as they shall take carrying wool into France' (though he ultimately opposed the bill when the Lords amended it because he was against 'allowing the Lords a power to order the manner of disposing of money'). On 11 Mar. he opposed a tithes bill that he believed would discourage the planting of hemp and flax. Local economic rivalry with Ireland also seems to have sharpened his anxiety about its government: he spoke at least twice about the miscarriages and discontent there, and on 24 Feb. was named to the committee drafting an address about the abuses of the Irish administration.[29]

The 1692–3 session also witnessed the start of what was to be a protracted struggle to secure a bill to make the Tone navigable between Bridgwater and Taunton. On 29 Dec. 1692 he found himself in the unlikely company of Sir Edward Seymour in opposing a petition from the Earl of Sandwich for a navigation bill which Clarke believed 'would only benefit some part of Wales'. Perhaps in response, Roger Hoar* mooted the idea of the inhabitants of Taunton paying for the river project (and also at this time requested assistance in obtaining a house of correction established at Bridgwater). Clarke appears to have responded positively and promised to do all he could to promote it. Concern about local reactions may also have inspired a number of interventions in the House. On 13 Dec. 1692 he argued in the debate on supply that levying money by the poor rate was 'very unequal' and that a monthly assessment was fairer. He also favoured stiff penalties for tax commissioners who acted without taking the oaths and successfully moved to restrict appointments of commissioners to those rated as gentlemen in the poll tax. He supported an amendment to the game bill to allow every Protestant to keep a musket in his house. By the end of the session therefore Clarke had established himself as a Court Whig, vehemently anti-Jacobite but with an independent mind and a concern for popular and local opinion.[30]

Those qualities made Clarke useful to the government in the parliamentary recess. In August, Sir John Trenchard asked him to investigate those at Bath who rejoiced 'at whatsoever they hear to the disadvantage of their Majesties' interest' and in November Clarke was informed by Hoar that clippers of coin joined with Jacobites in and around Bridgwater. But the significance of the period between sessions lay in the strengthening relations between Locke's circle and Somers. Somers was clearly on intimate terms with Clarke, who informed Locke about the new lord keeper's state of health. Clarke was also included in policy discussions about the reform of the court of Chancery and Locke's proposal that he, Clarke and Freke should meet to formulate ideas to put to Somers was a further step towards the more permanent formation of the 'college'.[31]

The activity of the 'college' in the next session is, however, less well documented. Clarke's concern for the propriety of elections and MPs' behaviour may explain his being first-named on 7 Nov. 1693 to the committee for elections and privileges and also his subsequent appointments on 21 Dec. to a free conference about the place bill, and on the 23rd to a drafting committee for a new elections bill. It was perhaps such activity that earned him praise at the end of the month as a 'worthy patriot'. Certainly the King's veto of the place bill alarmed him, despite his own position as an officeholder. Clarke had been appointed on 21 Dec. to a committee managing a conference on the bill and when on 26 Jan. 1694 Yonge proposed to widen the wording of the proposed address on the veto to include other public bills he found a seconder in his old ally Clarke.[32]

Yet Clarke essentially remained a courtier and participated in the rivalry within the ministry which expressed itself in the inquiry into the misconduct at sea. On 27 Nov. and 6 Dec. 1693 he acted as teller for motions pressing for condemnation of the Admiralty, at a time when moderate Country MPs were frightened off by the partisan nature of the attacks, indicating that he was first and foremost a Whig. This was also apparent in his interventions over disputed elections when he told with Whigs over Somers' replacement at Worcester and on the franchise favouring the Whig candidate at Arundel and in his masterminding of the attack on two clerics who had slandered his friend Masham. Moreover, partisanship was clearly apparent in Clarke's role in business relating to the East India Company. On 8 Jan. 1694 he acted as teller against the recommittal of a motion which signalled the opening of an attack by the interlopers on the company; and on 26 Mar. he was a teller in favour of adjourning the debate on the proposed loan from the company.[33]

Less controversial activity nevertheless took up most of Clarke's time. On 25 Nov. he was first-named to the drafting committee on the bill for the registration of deeds, which he duly presented on 19 Dec. and later reported. Once again Clarke devoted attention to economic matters that affected his constituents, showing how easy he was with mercantile affairs even though he was a country gentleman. On 14 Nov. he was appointed to the drafting committee for a bill to encourage the clothing trade; on 12 Dec. he acted as teller in favour of bringing in a bill to promote woollen manufactures. He also worked behind the scenes, for in January the mayor of Taunton thanked him for his 'constant endeavour' on behalf of the town, especially in 'getting one company of soldiers to be removed from us and procuring money for payment of their quarters', and was appreciative of Clarke's 'pious inclination of helping the poor'. At the end of the session he was once more active in disputes with the Lords about amendments to the bill for the recovery of small tithes.[34]

Whatever the nature of his earlier reservations, Clarke ended the 1693–4 session closely associated with Whig ministerialists. This is particularly apparent in his willingness after Christmas to aid the treasury team, acting as teller on 17 Jan. 1694 against a restriction on the land tax, on the following day in favour of an amendment to the land tax bill and again on 14 Feb. in favour of a motion about the consideration of ways and means. Six days later he was a teller once more on a motion in favour of retaining a clause in the supply bill relating to rock salt and again on 5 Apr. in favour of discounts for lump-sum payments of the poll tax. Such activity may have been designed to advertise his usefulness to the emerging new ministry but it may also have been a response to overtures made to him. Certainly, even while Parliament sat it was reported that he expected to be made an excise commissioner and Francis Gwyn* was to sneer, when their appointments to office were confirmed in August, that Clarke and Yonge 'at least had their bargain made good to them', with the clear insinuation that some compact had been made earlier.[35]

Clarke himself, however, in private correspondence with his steward, protested in early May that the rumours of new office stemmed only from 'the King and Queen speaking very favourably and kindly to me on several occasions; but I know of no such employment as yet designed for me as hath been reported'. Clarke owed his promotion, when it came, in part to royal favour, in part to Shrewsbury, who in June endorsed him as the 'most acceptable and proper person', and in part to his old ally Trenchard, who believed that with Clarke and Yonge in posts the King's revenue would 'be always well explained and the debate concerning it well supported'. It is clear that Yonge was reliant on his friend's expertise, glad of assistance 'in every step' he made, but Clarke probably relied on Yonge's better oratorical skills to convey their message. Indeed, a satire of 1701 jibed that Clarke spoke only at the end of debates 'with a parcel of such knotty and convincing reasons, as made both sides call out, "The Question, The Question", before [he] had a quarter finished'.[36]

Clarke's selfless conscientiousness must also have counted in his favour. He had reported to his agent as early as 4 Jan. 1694 that 'the fatigue of a constant attendance on the House, sitting so unseasonably as they do', disabled him from attending to almost anything else and his devotion to his duties was paramount over personal interest. Such an attitude may explain his reluctance to accept a directorship of the Bank of England. An enthusiastic supporter, he subscribed £2,000 and had acted as a commissioner for receiving other subscriptions but, despite being chosen by ballot on 11 July, he excused himself 'and desired them to choose another director in [his] place'. Locke was flabbergasted but Clarke refused to change his mind and the deliberate shunning of honours and status was to make him something of an oddity among the rapacious Junto Whigs. His diffidence may also explain why his career has never been accorded its due significance. His refusal of the directorship did not, however, diminish his support for the Bank. Indeed, he did not share Locke's doubts about the wisdom of creating a 'monopoly of money' in the Bank and later made notes about how beneficial it had been both financially and politically, raising money 'cheaper than otherwise it would have been done, tying the people faster to the government'.[37]

Despite their occasional differences, Locke and Clarke remained very close. Indeed, Locke's 'college', with Clarke as its parliamentary representative, seems to have taken firm shape. On 29 Nov. Freke wrote the first in a series of letters on behalf of himself and Clarke, who from then on took the name of the 'college'. Clarke lodged with Freke, who wrote the main body of the letters because, he explained, 'Mr Clarke's attendance in Parliament and at his offices keeps him so continually employed that he has scarce time to eat'. Freke believed Somers needed Locke's 'opinion and advice' on a variety of matters 'but one of them I take to be concerning a project for raising money this session'. Freke outlined the scheme Somers had in mind, and concluded that 'Mr Clarke and I shall take it as no small favour if you would bestow some thoughts on this subject and communicate them to us'.[38]

Consideration of money led inevitably to the state of physical money and the need for recoinage. On 8 Jan. 1695 Clarke was appointed to the committee of inquiry into the clipping of coin and the export of silver. Locke published *Short Observations on a Printed Paper* in February in order to criticize attempts at a devaluation, but the 'college' was concerned that the members of the committee, even some 'who should be chiefly concerned', were ignoring its message. Clarke and Freke did all they could to encourage MPs to read it and Edward worked tirelessly in the House to put its message across. On 14 Mar. 1695 Freke reported that his friend had attended the committee 'till he had obtained the resolution that the crowns and half crowns hereafter to be coin shall be of the present weight and fineness and then he left them to themselves knowing that when it came to be considered in the House that resolution would destroy all the rest'. But he was still unable to persuade 'those that are chiefly concerned to take any care in' the bill (see MONTAGU, Charles).[39]

Besides the revenue, the 'college' was also actively involved during the 1694–5 session on electoral reform. A draft bill among Clarke's papers (though not in his hand) and apparently annotated by Locke, outlined in detail how returning officers should act after receiving the writ, how to conduct the poll and how to make the return, providing for penalties for failure to comply. For the moment, however, there was the more pressing concern of the bill to regulate the press. On 11 Feb. 1695 Clarke was nominated to the drafting committee and on the 28th Freke and Clarke wrote to Locke that although the bill, which was 'new drawn very unlike the old one', would be introduced it was unlikely to pass that session 'for those that desire an act will not be content with what is reasonable'. On 2 Mar. Clarke presented the bill, which was 'so contrived that there is an absolute liberty for the printing everything that 'tis lawful to speak'. The bill had approval from Sir Thomas Trevor*, the solicitor-general, 'and several other honest and able men', including Somers, and it passed the House; but it ran into opposition from vested interests, such as the bishops and the Stationers' Company. On 17 and 18 Apr. Clarke reported the reasons offered by the House against the Lords' amendments at the conference and in doing so encapsulated many of Locke's ideas. However, as the chances of the bill's passage faded, Somers virtually torpedoed any remaining hope by reviving the old Licensing Act for a further year.[40]

Hard work during the 1694–5 session on these bills did not preclude other activity, such as appointment to other drafting committees. Most revealing was Clarke's attitude to 'public' bills. On 19 Nov. 1694 he was named as the sole drafter of the bill for the registry of land deeds and duly presented it three days later, but the bill failed to reach the statute book even though Clarke thought it one of the measures acceptable to the Court. He also thought the triennial bill 'not . . . an unacceptable bill because we that are in their Majesties' service come into the promoting it'. Clarke appreciated that the treason trials bill was far less 'relished at Kensington', but felt that there was 'a great need' for such a bill, even though the draft before the House was 'not what an honest man would desire it should be'. On 8 Feb. 1695 he was duly appointed to the conference on the Lords amendments and among his papers is a list of 'argum[en]ts to be used' as well as the bill 'and proceedings thereupon'. Clarke's role as a Court manager – such as when he acted as teller in favour of imposing an excise tax – thus did not totally remove his independent stance on frequent elections and fair treason trials, but it did incline him to oppose the place bill, against which he acted as teller on 26 Jan., having earlier confidently predicted its rejection.[41]

Clarke's office had nevertheless compromised his status in the House. At the beginning of the session there had been 'occasions . . . to give Mr Clarke a rub for taking a place contrary to an Act of Parliament', because the Tonnage Act included a clause limiting the number of excise commissioners sitting in the House and Clarke's appointment had exceeded the previous figure. Yet having tied his colours to the Court's mast Clarke had to recover from a devastating blow to his hopes of patronage. In August the Queen had received him 'with more than ordinary favour' after his appointment as excise commissioner but on 27 Dec. 1694 he wrote to his wife in tears about the Queen's illness and her death left him 'disconsolate':

'tis an irreparable loss to this nation and all Europe and I have too much reason to say 'tis greatest to me and my family in particular than to most of her servants or subjects, having lately received repeated assurances of her Majesty's grace and favour towards me and my children, of which number poor Jack is most immediately concerned, he being within a few days before her Majesty's sickness promised some particular mark of her Majesty's favour upon the next vacancy.

The tragedy prompted Clarke to express his strong belief in providence: 'let us all submit with all humility to the disposal of that Almighty Providence, who in his great wisdom, does always what is best for us, and 'tis upon his mercy and goodness that we must hope for protection and deliverance from all our difficulties and sorrows'.[42]

Clarke's identification with the Court ensured a vigorous defence of his Whig ministerial friends. On 6 Feb. 1695 he acted as teller on a motion to defend the Lancashire Plot witnesses, a further indication of loyalty to Somers in particular. On 22 Jan. he acted as teller against appointing a further day to hear petitioners against the Bank, signifying his support of Montagu's pet scheme. But Clarke also went on the offensive. On 16 Feb. he was named to the inquiry into the abuses committed by regimental agents, established in the wake of the accusations against Tracy Pauncefort*. The real aim may have been to get at those whom Pauncefort could accuse of bribery, most notably Henry Guy, who was identified that day as the recipient of bribes, for on 26 Feb. Clarke was a teller on a motion which sought to strengthen the charges against the secretary to the Treasury and on 17 Apr. Clarke acted as teller in favour of Guy's expulsion from the House. Since Guy identified his chief persecutor as Charles Montagu, it seems likely that Clarke took part in the latter's campaign to flush out the remaining Tories in government, a view endorsed by his appointment on 15 Mar. to the committee drafting proceedings of the House in relation to the Speaker, Sir John Trevor, who was Montagu's second victim of the session.[43]

Clarke's own dislike of the East India Company and of corruption, together with his alliance with Montagu against the Tories, explain his election (with 96 votes) to the committee established to question Sir Thomas Cooke* and his tellership on 13 Apr. concerning bills of punishment against Cooke. Clarke made a number of notes about the evidence offered by Sir Basil Firebrace* and other witnesses; but he may also have scented a more important scalp, since a fortnight later he was appointed to the committee drafting the articles of impeachment against the Duke of Leeds (formerly Carmarthen) for his part in the scandal. On 18 May he wrote to his wife that he would tell her about corruption in politics and in the coinage when they next met 'because the subject matter of them is not so proper for a letter'.[44]

Clarke returned to Chipley as recorder of Taunton, an honour which prompted a congratulatory address from the corporation and the town's innkeepers who acknowledged Clarke's 'pain and trouble' to serve his constituents. Clarke also spent £3 in July on treating the mayor and his aldermen at his swearing in, and such bolstering of his position in the locality stood him in good stead when an election was called in the autumn. On 3 Sept. 1695 he drafted a letter to the new mayor assuring him that 'if your corporation and town shall think fit to entrust me, I shall diligently and faithfully serve them even to the utmost of my powers', though, somewhat ironically in view of his attitude to electoral bribery, he still found it necessary to spend £60 in 'expences in relation to the election'.[45]

During the summer of 1695 the 'college' intensified discussions about how to tackle the coinage problem. They met and no doubt discussed a paper, written by William Lowndes*, advocating a devaluation. Whether Clarke assisted Locke in drafting his submission to the Treasury is unknown but Lowndes's private lobbying of MPs on their assembly for the new Parliament required the 'college' in turn to redouble its own efforts. On 29 Nov. Clarke was 'deserted' when he attempted to secure an address 'to make clipped money go by weight', even though the King had 'commanded the courtiers to press that matter and if possible carry it'. At Clarke's and Freke's request, Locke began writing what would shortly be published as *Further Considerations Concerning the Raising the Value of Money*; but, he told them, 'in the meantime you have my papers on that subject, which you may communicate or give copies of to all those who would be serviceable in the debate'. Freke assured Locke that 'there is not one question in your catechise that [Clarke] had not asked in proper time and place'.[46]

The correspondence between Locke and the 'college' implies that the credit for the management of the devaluation issue should go to Clarke, who bore almost 'the whole burden' because others were unwilling, unable or too inexperienced to help him, though he was aided behind the scenes by Locke and Freke. This impression may nevertheless be misleading, for although there is little doubt that Clarke played a pivotal role in the recoinage drama, the sense of isolation felt by the 'college' was probably due to a difference of tactics among the ministerial Whigs rather than one of principle. The idea of a fundamental rift between Somers and the 'college' on the one hand, and Montagu and the devaluers on the other can be discounted. Clarke generally worked with, rather than against, the chancellor of the Exchequer, though the latter had a much more pragmatic and less ideological stance.[47]

The coinage crisis came to a head in mid-February 1696, when proposals to allow gold guineas to pass at a rate higher than the silver standard threatened to reintroduce devaluation by the back door. On the 15th an exhausted Clarke reported to his wife:

If I had not been quite worn out with an attendance of 13 hours together without stirring out of the House on Thursday last, I had then acquainted you with the result of the longest debate I ever yet saw in Parliament, the subject matter whereof was the then current price of guineas, wherein gentlemen's reasonings were very different, as you may well imagine by the length of the debate, which lasted from about 12 at noon till 10 at night, in which debate 'twas generally agreed that unless gold and silver be brought and kept near to a proportion in value to each other, that which exceeds will eat out and carry away the other, and that unless gold be reduced to its real intrinsic value, as well as silver, as it has already devoured a great part of the riches of the nation, so it will certainly ease you of the poor remains of the wool and woollen manufactures, and of the silver likewise, and in a little time effectually carry away more of the treasure and wealth of the kingdom than all the expense both of the fleet and army together doth amount unto; and yet notwithstanding, the reducing that exorbitant imaginary value, which hath been for too long time past permitted to be set on gold all at once by a vote of Parliam[en]t, was thought to be of such consequence as to prevail so far against the arguments on the other side, that by a small majority there was a vote obtained in the committee and this day agreed to by the House, viz. that no guineas be allowed to pass in any paym[en]t above the rate of 28s. which 'tis hoped will prevent their rising higher; and I hope the true interest of the nation will soon reduce them to their real intrinsic value, for without that we must in a little time be all undone, and the nation ruined, therefore I desire that nobody concerned for me may receive any guineas at more than 21s. 6d. or 22s. at most.

He had spoken in favour of fixing the rate at 21s., and Montagu advocated 24s., a compromise figure which has been taken as proof that the chancellor sought a high level for gold and was thus at odds with the 'college'. Such an interpretation rests on the assumption that the main point of the debate was to fix the rate for guineas. Yet Clarke's letters to his wife and to Locke, as well as Locke's reply, suggest that he was prepared to see a temporarily higher level than he wanted in order to establish the principle that the denomination of gold should be reduced from its current value of 30s. in accordance with the silver standard. The reduction of the rate to an acceptable level was a battle for another day. Indeed, in a series of votes between 15 Feb. and 26 Mar. the value of guineas was reduced to 22s. and both Clarke and Montagu are recorded as having voted for that lower rate.[48]

Clarke and his allies were therefore responsible for outflanking those who sought devaluation through an artificially inflated value of gold. Indeed, Locke congratulated his friend for fighting 'so bravely' and for having 'carried the point about guineas and clipped money'; he believed that the nation was 'extremely obliged' to him for having saved it from ruin. Clarke may also have been responsible for the passage of the window tax bill, which helped raise the necessary taxation to fund the recoinage, since a draft preamble in his hand is among his papers. Locke was still concerned that people would hoard the clipped coin and needed to be encouraged to pass it by weight to avoid a stop of trade after 4 May, when the Coinage Act came into force. He urged the 'college' to consider the matter, though they replied that they did not think 'a legislative way' was appropriate. They did, however, in early April exhort all tradesmen to refuse clipped money and 'employed some' to lead Smithfield market. At the end of the month they made a third attempt in the House 'to make clipped money go by weight', but perhaps because the previous defeats had shaken Clarke's credibility on the point, the motion was entrusted to another MP, who failed to act on cue. This incident may explain Clarke's draft clause 'for clipped money to pass by weight after 4th May 1696' which he endorsed as 'not accepted'. Nevertheless, the 'college' did secure an order from the lords justices to prosecute anyone who tendered illegal money and Clarke pressed for a 'useful' proclamation about clipped sixpences.[49]

Although money matters had preoccupied Clarke during the 1695–6 session he was also responsible for two other major pieces of legislation. On 3 Dec. he was first-named to the drafting committee of a bill to prevent double returns and presented it on the 6th, being nominated the same day to a committee to inquire into frivolous petitions. Both of these were measures on which he and Locke seem to have been working. On 19 Dec. Clarke carried his legislation up to the Lords, and on 20 Jan. 1696 the King passed the bill to prevent expenses in elections, which incorporated two of the major provisions outlined in the heads of a draft bill drawn up by Clarke and amended by Locke. More effort, however, was needed to push through the new bill to regulate the press. Clarke presented the bill on 29 Nov. 1695. On 2 Dec. Locke remarked that it had 'been taken care of to the utmost and I thank you it is lodged and that's well'. Locke's correspondence reveals that the bill nevertheless raised greater clamour than its forerunner and that Clarke was 'attacked on all sides on account of that bill'. The archbishop of Canterbury 'treated with him' about how to allay the worries of the bishops, while 'the Dissenters are likewise alarmed and ... deputed one of their party to apply to the Squire'. Clarke appears to have amended the bill to take account of the anxieties of both delegations, but it still ran into opposition from the Stationers and other vested interests. The bill's failure did not, however, mean a return to licensing since a provision to revive the old act was rejected by the House. Clarke thus played a major part in ushering in a new era of press freedom. One other long-standing concern was also resolved during this session. On 7 Feb. 1696 Clarke acted as teller in favour of granting leave to bring in the Quaker affirmation bill and again on 10 Mar. in favour of its engrossment. Clarke's tenderness towards Dissenters was again apparent in the 'direction' he gave for the circulation of the Association in Wellington, for which he was thanked by a Dissenting minister. Clarke immediately signed the Association himself.[50]

During the summer of 1696 Clarke urged his wife in Somerset to offer a lead over clipped coins, especially since, as she wrote, money was 'the beginning or end of all discourses'. But it is clear that his high profile in Parliament over the recoinage had damaged his position locally where money had become very short. Indeed, the hostility was such that Clarke was forced to beat a hasty retreat from his own neighbourhood until tempers cooled: the story circulated that he had been forced to flee to a tavern for shelter from an angry mob and was then 'conveyed out the back way' to save his life. He himself lamented to his wife the 'cruel separation forced upon us by the pride and malice of the most wicked and revengeful men living', a clear indication that he believed the crowd had been deliberately misled by his local rivals; but he remained confident that 'in a little time God Almighty will bring us happily together again in peace and prosperity to the confusion of those who, without any just cause, seek our ruin to the utmost of their power'.[51]

Mary Clarke was determined to clear her husband's name in Taunton, particularly because she believed that the rumour spread against her husband 'was the forerunner of another Parliament'. When visited by an influential Taunton alderman she

> said I thought they need not use any such methods for that I had heard you say ever since they thought fit to make choice of you you had served them faithfully and honestly and had not failed to give them an account by every post during the session of Parliament and had not acted in any thing without their consent and as long as they thought to entrust you you would continue to do so ... to which Mr Byrd answered he believed the town now was very well satisfied in relation to money and that a month or so hence they would all give you thanks, he was sure the most sensible part did already; then I told them I hoped that part would take care to set the rest right that they might not be ready to kill the man that would advise them not to take 3*d*. instead of 6*d*. I thought that was very hard, in answer to which some of the company said that if Mr Clarke had spoke what he said to some of his friends privately and not in the public coffee house they would have taken it more kindly and it would not have been so soon carried out among the rabble.

The letter shows how heavily public opinion could weigh on an MP and how invaluable a loyal and active wife was to resurrect a husband's credit in his locality. Even so, when Clarke was prevented by a recall to London from attending the assizes, where he might have vindicated himself, she heard it reported that 'Clarke the highwayman was ran away, which at first hearing indeed I thought they had meant some padder of the roads; but it seems it was a title they had given you for concerning yourself as much in mending the highways; but now I hear you go by the name of Standard Clarke'. Mary was even threatened that a rabble would be lured by a bull-baiting 'and so come and plunder and pull down the house and frighten your wife and children out of doors and pull you in pieces if y[ou] had been here'. She also noted that 'when I pay money they expect better from me than anybody being Standard Clarke's wife'.[52]

Clarke threw himself into his work on his return to London, perhaps in an effort to forget his problems, for Mary wrote to him of her concern 'that you still toil and labour so hard and will tire and wear your self out before your time for those that will not thank you'. But the effort was not entirely in vain, since Clarke had regained much of his position by the time Parliament reassembled. On 20 Oct. 1696 he described the resolutions to support the war and not to 'alter the standard of the gold or silver coin of this kingdom, neither in weight, fineness or denomination' as 'a very good beginning and I hope a happy presage of a prosperous session for the support of this government'. He had even more cause to hope so because he was now acting as a parliamentary manager for the Court. On 29 Oct. he met with others to discuss how to handle Sir John Fenwick's[†] accusations against the Duke of Shrewsbury and attended further meetings to hammer out a common line. He accordingly took an active role in support of Fenwick's attainder, including the division on 25 Nov.[53]

Although victory on the coinage issue was guaranteed, the work was not yet over. On 16 Nov. John Cary of Bristol wrote to Clarke about the danger of a monetary crisis that recent votes on accepting milled money might cause: 'I wish', he wrote, 'you may settle the credit of the nation for us to ensure the ends intended . . . [and] the little acquaintance I have had with you hath given me full satisfaction that you are an honest English gentleman.' On 30 Nov. Clarke was appointed to the conference on the amendments to the bill to remedy the state of the coin further and in early December he supported Somers in attempts to encourage bringing wrought plate to the Mint for coining. On 31 Dec. he acted as teller in favour of the consideration of such a scheme, and on 14 Jan. 1697 was appointed to the committees established to investigate abuses in the Mint and to draft a bill to explain the recoinage acts. Although co-ordination between Clarke and Locke over these measures was on a much lower scale than before, they maintained a close friendship. Thus, when in January 1697 Locke threatened to resign from the Board of Trade, Somers spoke with Clarke to press his mentor to remain in office. Clarke's attention was also diverted during the session by the Chancery case of Locke's hostess, Lady Masham, which prevented him attending Montagu's foray into the City to convince the directors of the Bank to agree to his new engrafting scheme.[54]

Locke is likely to have approved of his friend's efforts to relieve the poor. Clarke received frequent accounts from his wife of the distress and unrest caused by the recoinage process and approved of her establishing a local serge-making relief scheme. But he also received letters from his borough about the dangerous situation and his own damaged political reputation there made it incumbent on him to heed them. Clarke was certainly being made aware of local grievances at this time, for on 18 Nov. nine men signed a petition requesting him to use his interest to prevent the imposition of a £200 landed qualification for candidates, which they described as 'so unkind a dealing with the trading part of the nation and which will conduce to the breaking of the ancient privileges of the subject'.[55]

Pressures such as these may explain Clarke's enthusiasm for measures to protect and foster trade, as he was named to several committees drafting such legislation during the session. He presumably favoured the bill to restrain the wearing of imported silks, though on 21 Jan. the 'college' sent Locke an account of the 'tumultuous' silk weavers who besieged Parliament and Clarke was duly appointed to the committee to investigate the disturbance. A tract was later to accuse Clarke and Freke of having deliberately stirred them into disorder. On 3 Mar. he acted as teller in favour of a resolution concerning the duty on woollen and silk goods. Concern to protect the domestic textile industry even brought Clarke in April into conflict with the Court and into the King's displeasure, for both he and Yonge opposed the bill to increase duties on wine and textiles. Clarke in particular 'had all along opposed the duty and shown the House unanswerably that it would be no supply and yet endanger the ruin of our woollen manufacture'. The King urged their removal from office as a penalty but Somers defended his friends, arguing for a distinction 'between persons who had done wrong only once, through ignorance, and those who, in the whole course of business, were continually opposed'. The argument 'met with so cold a reception' that Shrewsbury felt it necessary to add his voice in favour of the pair, stressing 'we are obliged (I am sure I think myself so) to stand by them'. They were retained in post but Clarke's action shows that even the most loyal and diligent of the King's supporters could deviate from the Court line when it conflicted with local and personal interests.[56]

Despite all his care for his constituents, however, rumours about Clarke's activity in Parliament were once again used to damage his reputation, for in May his wife warned him that she had heard 'that the brewers in London was so angry with you upon account of this malt tax that they was resolved to do you a mischief'. Clarke protested that there was no foundation to the story, 'the brewers here very well knowing that I neither proposed or in the least promoted the duty upon malt, but upon all occasions opposed it' and believed the story was promoted by his long-standing enemy Sanford 'in order to have his former false inventions upon me the better credited'. Indeed, when Clarke finally returned home his wife planned that he should not

> hurry out of Taunton so as you did last time, that the gentlemen may have time to pay you all the respect they have for you and pray put on a cheerful and familiar countenance and let us order the matter so as to go together to Nynehead and the neighbouring parishes and appear before all congregations and look them out of countenance after all their scandalous reports.

Mary certainly knew how to electioneer and in October she dined with Taunton's mayor as part of her drive to revive her husband's fortunes.[57]

Aspersions on Clarke's reputation were, however, being cast at the national as well as the local level. In October he defended his actions as an excise commissioner by showing 'how (since his coming in) the hearing of causes are more expeditious', vindicating his conduct over Exchequer bills (to which he had subscribed £1,000 in May) and claiming that he had instituted a system of checking which excise officers had sworn allegiance to the government. Clarke found backing from Thomas Pelham*, who pointed out that it was 'chiefly' Edward who had begun a reform process. Clarke later made notes on Charles Davenant's* allegations of financial incompetence, arguing that the increase in excise in the 1680s had not been due, as his critic claimed, to 'skill and conduct . . . but [achieved only] by a stretching of the law and taking more than the King's due'.[58]

Nevertheless it was the end of the war which seemed to offer the prospect of a revival of Clarke's reputation, for, as he told his wife,

> the conclusion of the peace has broke all the Jacobite-Tory plots and contrivances in the kingdom . . . the peace seems to have totally broke all their measures and even their whole party too in pieces for the present and I hope they will never be able so to unite again or succeed in any thing.

But peace brought about division in his own party, too, even between Clarke and Yonge over the standing army. As draft notes for a speech make clear, Clarke remained circumspectly loyal to the Court position, arguing that the militia and the navy were insufficient for defence against an invasion, as the failure in 1688 of Lord Dartmouth (George Legge†) had shown. Remodelling the militia was a work which he wanted to see

> well done and when it is done shall be unwilling to have any other forces kept on foot, but till then I confess I think it necessary to maintain a competent number of well-disciplined soldiers, for I doubt we should not sit safe here long enough to frame a scheme to render the militia useful were it not for the disciplined soldiers that are yet in pay for our security.

Clarke's fear of France thus outweighed his fear of arbitrary power and he believed the forces were a safeguard for, not a threat to, Parliament's security. These factors kept him loyal to the Court at a time when many Country Whigs, including Lord Ashley (Anthony*) and John Toland, who had been satellites of Locke's circle, were defecting. Indeed, in March he was 'heartily concerned' at the management of the disbanding of the soldiers, who he thought were in a 'miserable condition'.[59]

Much of the first half of the 1697–8 session was again taken up by the recoinage issue, which reactivated the close alliance with Locke. On 30 Dec. the latter advised the insertion of a clause in the bill concerning hammered money designed to prevent the nation being 'overrun very quickly with false and clipped coin'. Clarke replied that he would do all he could

> to make such a provision as you suggest for the cutting and destroying of all base, counterfeit and unlawfully diminished money and for obliging the tellers in the Exchequer, and all other receivers of the King's revenue and taxes to receive and pay by weight as well by tale, and do hope for better success than in the several attempts I have formerly made to the same purpose.

This time his hopes were realized. On 2 Feb. he presented the bill to prevent counterfeiting and clipping coin, which he carried up to the Lords on 14 May, though his attempt to have it committed to a select committee rather than the whole House had backfired on 7 Mar. when he was deemed to have 'irregularly moved' the idea.[60]

Locke also corresponded with the 'college' about provision for poor relief, sending them in February a copy of his own scheme with the recommendation that Clarke 'might make use of it [if] it should suggest to you anything that you might think useful in the case'. Clarke, who on 8 Dec. had been named to the committee established to consider provision for the poor, promised to do so whenever he could 'find ingenuity, honesty and industry enough to make a proper law for the putting it in execution', though apparently those criteria were lacking, since he did not introduce the measure. Indeed, rather than work at a national scale, his concern about the poor seems to have driven him to promote local schemes. He was appointed on 6 May to the conference about the Colchester workhouse bill but most of his energy was directed into the Tone navigation bill, a project that would both encourage trade and generate profits for charity. On 7 Mar. the Taunton projectors thanked him for his 'indefatigable care and constant endeavours to do all acts of kindness for the good of this town', and enclosed general instructions for the bill. Five days later Clarke was duly named as the bill's drafter, but he evidently believed that the timing was not yet right and although he offered to get the bill 'framed and carried on as far as' he could, he was unwilling to see the backers throw their money away. On 28 Mar. the projectors declared themselves 'fully satisfied that the difficulty will be too great to get an act of Parliament this session . . . so we acquiesce in your former judgment of the thing and will wait till another session'. Further evidence of his concern about trade came in his nomination on 28 Apr. to the drafting committee of the Royal Lustring Company bill, the heads of which are among his papers.[61]

Besides sharing Locke's concern about the coinage and poor, Clarke also shielded his mentor from the House's condemnation of William Molyneux, Locke's friend who had used some of the philosopher's arguments in a book which attacked English parliamentary sovereignty over Ireland and which named Locke as the reputed author of the *Two Treatises*. Deeply embarrassed, Locke thanked his friend at the end of May for a promise of protection against Molyneux's 'indiscretion' and Clarke was true to his word, though 'some inferences' were made from the fact that he 'chiefly pushed on' an investigation into the conditions in Ireland in order to divert the attack. Drafts of the resolutions against Molyneux among Clarke's papers in his own hand, as well as notes on the offending tract, confirm that Clarke took on much of the management of the affair. Locke is also likely to have approved Clarke's nomination on 9 Feb. 1698 to the committee drafting a bill for the suppression of profaneness and immorality, and Clarke's papers include a manuscript 'bill for the more effectual suppressing of vice and immorality' as well as printed *Reasons . . . for Passing the Bill against Vice and Immorality*. Nevertheless, despite these areas of common interest, the bond between Locke and Clarke was gradually weakening as the philosopher drew closer to his cousin and heir, Peter King*, who had more time to take over the personal business that Locke imposed on his favourites.[62]

Clarke in turn was becoming increasingly preoccupied with party wrangles. Despite his profession of help to the Earl of Sunderland at the beginning of the year, he joined the hunting of the lord chamberlain's allies. In March he was named to the conference on the bill to punish Montagu's long-standing enemy, Charles Duncombe*, and there is a draft of the Commons' statements to the Lords about Duncombe among Clarke's papers. Clarke was also waging his own war inside the excise office, where Duncombe had been cashier. The 'long feud' there centred on a split between Clarke and Foot Onslow*. The previous year all the commissioners had been appointed as commissioners of the leather duty and were required to take the oaths and sacrament. Clarke and his allies duly qualified themselves but the others failed to do so. In 1698 a bill was therefore introduced to indemnify them, but the House refused to pass it 'unless it were general', prompting Somers to condemn it in the Lords as an attempt to undermine the Test Acts. Clarke said that he himself 'would have voted against and opposed the bill if he were not one of the commissioners and would be publicly censured'. That he restrained himself is further evidence that he had become a fully fledged Court manager, assiduous in his attendance at important committees and even taking it upon himself in June to chide less experienced men for their 'errors'. In July he was retained as an excise commissioner when others lost their places and was duly marked as a Court supporter or placeman in contemporary assessments of MPs.[63]

Clarke was understandably anxious to ensure his return at the next election and kept his horse ready so that he could ride to Taunton as soon as the dissolution was announced, though he told his agent that he could not meddle in the election 'further than to tend my service'. His name appeared alongside that of Montagu and other Court managers in *The True Englishmen's Choice of Parliament Men*, and it was perhaps because of this close association with the Court that the poll at Taunton became complex. Having tied with Speke in second place, Clarke was belatedly returned by the mayor, and for part of the next session feared a petition against his return from his erstwhile partner. The precariousness of his seat no doubt reminded Clarke of the importance of rewarding local supporters, and may help explain his devotion to constituency work, and to the promotion of the Tone navigation bill in particular, when Parliament met in December 1698. On the 7th the bill's projectors wrote to Clarke thanking him for his care of the bill, the draft of which they approved, though with some amendments. They requested that it be presented at 'the first opportunity', adding that the bill's main aim was to raise funds to build a hospital for the poor who had become 'exceeding burdensome and like to be more . . . if some care be not taken'. Nine days later he was granted leave to present the bill, his prompt action earning him the thanks of its backers 'for putting it into the House so soon'. They also informed him of how they themselves intended to lobby by sending 'letters to many Parliament men to desire their assistance in passing the bill' and that they understood that 'those members that were concerned in the House the last session for passing the bill for making the rivers Wye and Lugg navigable promised their assistance for passing this bill, as a requital of your assisting them in that affair', an indication that Clarke's managerial skills had been employed to effect. The projectors also allowed Clarke to choose a 'solicitor' to 'attend the committees' and thanked him for having presented a petition concerning woollen manufacture, activity not recorded in the Journals but which explains his being first-named on 17 Dec. to a committee of inquiry into the wool trade.[64]

Two pamphlets among Clarke's papers advocating support of the navigation bill indicate how carefully he co-ordinated the lobbying process. He presented the bill on 5 Jan. 1699 and reported it only 20 days later. The bill passed its third reading by a 'great majority' and Clarke reported how he 'carried it up to the Lords for their concurrence and by my particular interest there got the bill immediately read and ordered a second reading'. Clarke spent some £40 on the bill and liaised with its backers to procure four petitions from the locality in its support; he also worked with Sir Rowland Gwynne, George Crane and the Bristol MPs. The bill's rapid passage, together with the fact that he obtained the assizes for the town, reversed Clarke's ebbing popularity in Taunton. On 6 Feb. there were 11 signatures to a letter of thanks which reported that over 40 townsmen had drunk his health and asked him to convey 'their humble services to the Earl of Stamford and the Earl of Tankerfield [Tankerville]' for their assistance. Clarke had evidently been busy since Lord Lisburne (John Vaughan I*) and Lord Sandwich had also all been approached to use their interest. In return, Clarke's supporters promised to 'endeavour to improve' his interest in the town.[65]

Celebrations appeared premature, however, when it became apparent that some sought to put 'clogs' on the bill in the Lords, forcing Clarke to take extra care to guide it through the Upper House. He predicted that 'the difficulties will be great' but emerged triumphant. Twenty-three petitioners therefore thanked him for his 'extraordinary diligence, faithfulness and ingenuity in preparing and carrying the same thro[ugh] both Houses of Parliament notwithstanding the great opposition it met with', which included obstruction from the majority of Taunton's corporation, though not, apparently, Portman himself. When the bill received the Royal Assent the news was greeted in the town with bell-ringing and rejoicing. At a time when Whig fortunes were ebbing at the centre, Clarke thus resurrected his political fortunes in his own town, to the chagrin of his opponents, some of whom now shamefacedly courted his favour and help. ''Tis remarkable the scene is much altered', he commented sardonically at the end of January 1699.[66]

Perhaps to counter or prevent the reviving effect of the successful promotion of the navigation bill, the Tories sought to undermine Clarke in two ways. First, Sanford, who was a member of the Hamburg Company, promoted a petition to be presented to the House to request the encouragement of the export of wool to Germany, and Clarke's friends had to counter-attack with 'another petition against it'. An undated document in his hand, endorsed 'Reasons for the free exportation of the woollen manufacture', may have been drafted at this time, since it opposed any attempt to restrict trade to the Hamburg Company, which was condemned as 'very arbitrary' in its government and monopolistic. Second, on 2 Jan. 1699, as Clarke himself explained to his steward,

> Sir Edward Seymour, having a mind to put (if possible) a flourish on [the] last cause of his brother's party in the town of Taunton, offered a petition to the House from Mr Speke against my election there, which he well knew, by the standing rules and orders of the House, could not be received, yet their malice was such that they hoped thereby to have cast a blemish on me and my election, though they did well know they could receive no benefit thereby, but Sir Edward failed so much of obtaining what he designed against me that his motion was rejected and his attempt served only to expose himself and his party thereby.[67]

Despite this success, it appears that Clarke's supporters at Taunton requested a further £60, on top of the £60 he had spent at the time of the election itself, to keep the electors happy. This 'surprising news' provoked a blistering response:

> 'tis a great sum and much more than I could have imagined my friends would ever have suffered to have been expended by me, considering all the public and particular services I have done for that ungrateful town in general, and almost all the chief and leading men of the town in particular; but it seems those services are now forgotten and I am now to be punished instead of being thanked by

them and that I am now to have so considerable a sum of money taken out of my pocket for having been at so great an expense already of money and time in their service; these things if considered by men that would be industriously and well and faithfully served hereafter in Parliament and not betrayed by such as will always be ready to buy their favour and sell their liberty and all else that's valuable to them would not be put upon me to such a weighty degree as 'tis and I hope the prudent conduct of Mr Frend and the rest of my friends in that town may yet upon [second] thoughts prevent the greatness of the expense designed to be put upon me . . . but (as matters stand) I am now in their power.

The success of the navigation bill had, at this stage, not been secured and Clarke was still in a vulnerable position; but as the bill progressed through Parliament his hand strengthened and he noted with satisfaction on 17 Jan. that 'a good part' of the £60 was likely to be returned to him. Resentment at the tricks played with election returns by party rivals, sharpened by a sense of the ingratitude of grasping, fair-weather electors may nevertheless explain Clarke being first-named on 6 Feb. to the drafting committee of a new elections bill and his subsequent steering of the bill through all its stages in the House. On 3 Mar. he was also appointed to another drafting committee, for a new bill to prevent clandestine elections.[68]

Although Clarke concentrated on the local consequences of his activity at Westminster, he did not neglect his other responsibilities. Work at the excise office had become particularly burdensome. As his wife explained, having joined him in London in the vain hope of spending some time with him, there were 800 excise posts to fill and all the candidates and their patrons were 'importunate and troublesome to the commissioners'. Clarke reckoned 'no less than 20 Parliament men in a day' spoke to him 'for some or other that they have to recommend [but] 'tis impossible to answer all people's expectations'. Such a role did, however, increase Clarke's usefulness to the Court as a manager and he continued to provide a government lead. On 23 Dec. 1698 he made a speech on the committal of the disbanding bill in which he argued, as before, that 'the militia consists of troops and therefore an army if insurrection or invasion [was] no remedy'. On 4 Jan. 1699 he pointed out that a 'standing army will enslave us but this [was] not the question'. He privately wrote that Parliament intended to leave the King 'with a guard of 7,000 men only' and prayed 'God we do not soon see and feel the ill consequences of it', an indication that his support for the standing army was sincere and not merely the result of Court pressure. The day before writing he had voted on the 18th in favour of maintaining the army and on 20 Mar. acted as teller in favour of amending what William regarded as an offensive address concerning the Dutch guards. There was also the defence of the Junto to be secured, by fair means or foul. On 15 Mar. Orford (formerly Edward Russell*) was, as James Vernon I* explained, 'acquitted by one voice only and Ned Clarke, who was our teller against Colonel Granville, says he got two by an over-reach in the counting'.[69]

The punishing workload stretched Clarke to breaking point. Locke thought his friend had 'scarce time to eat or sleep' and Clarke himself admitted he was 'almost worried out of my life with business of one kind or another'. At the end of April a concerned Locke told Clarke to 'remember, doing of business will end in the grave and before [long] too if you neglect your health'. The prediction proved remarkably accurate, though it was his son's serious illness that tipped Clarke into a downward spiral. The young man's illness, he wrote, had 'greatly reduced and dispirited' him and he fell into a state of pious melancholy: "Tis our duty to submit with patience and humility to the Great Disposer of all things, which I shall endeavour to perform, and constantly pray for His assistance, as I do for the continuance of the health of the rest of my children and friends.' Returning to Chipley in the summer did not restore his own failing health and in September he set off for a rest-cure at Tunbridge, in the company of Freke, though the stay can hardly have been a refuge from politics, for Locke sent Clarke a letter to hand to Somers. Meanwhile, the clouds which had been dispersed at the beginning of the year were beginning to gather again in Taunton, where the corporation ominously made 'new members' and early in the new year rumours were being spread against him, 'promoted by the clergy and countenanced by the bishops, to injure me', alleging that he had secured a prohibition against a local schoolmaster 'by my interest in my lord chancellor [Somers]'. The incident must have heightened Clarke's anticlericalism, which three years earlier had expressed itself in a comment to his wife that he hoped 'one time or other that sort of gentleman will find it to be more their interest to meddle only with their own business, than to be so busy upon all occasions in secular affairs'.[70]

Clarke's activity in the 1699–1700 session showed a marked decline but he was still made use of by the Court and was recognized as a probable Junto adherent in an analysis dividing the House into interests. On 18 Jan. 1700 he joined with Vernon to speak on behalf of the Court to reserve a third of the Irish grants for the King's disposal, though they 'were pretty well rapped over the fingers' for their pains. On 17 Jan. 1700 he acted as teller in favour of John Bright's* election at Pontefract, and again on 7 Feb. in favour of retaining the wording on a motion to go into a committee of the whole on the state of the nation. The next day he told against the adjournment of a debate on the bill to prevent papists disinheriting Protestant heirs, a measure on which he had acted as teller as early as April 1696 and for which there are two drafts among his papers. Although the last of the joint letters from Freke and Clarke to Locke was written in March, Clarke was also still in contact with the philosopher, who in January asked him to warn Somers about the weapon which the Darien fiasco offered his enemies, and Clarke himself was urged to keep an 'eye upon that business'. He duly made notes of the debate on 13 Feb. about Somers, which ended in a resolution proclaiming the lord chancellor's faithful services, and it would even appear that at the end of the session the college 'composed' an unidentified 'printed letter' that vindicated Somers. Locke also exhorted his friend to defend Lord Bellomont (Richard Coote*), governor of New York, who 'ought to be supported by all those who would not abandon the plantations'.[71]

Increasingly Clarke was forced to fight his own corner, as he found himself caught up in the attacks on his patrons. On 18 Dec. 1699 and again on 5 and 17 Feb. 1700 he submitted the excise accounts to the House, only to find that they encouraged critics to 'fall upon the mismanagement of the excise and drive at putting it into a farm. They think elections are more influenced by those officers than any others and they would mortify Ned Clarke as a friend of my lord chancellor's.' In committee on 27 Feb. Robert Harley claimed that the excise revenue had declined ever since the Revolution, provoking Clarke to reply with a characteristically technical speech that gave facts and figures to show how higher excise rates had led to fraud and 'forced people upon private brewings, adding to the people being impoverished by the war and the victuallers being burthened with quartering soldiers'. His spirited defence was also aided by a 'tumult' erupting in Westminster Hall directed against Harley, and although on 29 Feb. the committee agreed that the excise revenue had decayed, it refused to include Seymour's clause 'that it came by the mismanagement of the present commissioners'.[72] Even so, farming the excise remained on the agenda and on 2 Mar. Clarke tried to spoil the design by moving a self-denying clause in the supply bill that no MP should be concerned in either farming or managing the excise, arguing no doubt from personal experience that commissioners, 'being obliged to attend the service of the House, they cannot so well discharge the duties in their offices'. This fuelled speculation about his future role, with some reports suggesting that he was 'to be kicked upstairs and some down', but in June Clarke and three other commissioners 'laid down' their offices in order to retain their seats. Clarke thought himself 'indispensably obliged to discharge his trust in Parliament reposed in him' and the *Post Boy* declared that Clarke and his colleagues had resigned 'like true Patriots' who scorned such 'profitable employment' in favour of serving King and country. Resignation must, however, also have come as a blessed release. Still in uncertain health, Clarke was invited by Locke to go to Oates 'to wipe off the fatigue of so long a service' in the session 'and mix some fresh air with so much smoke, some mirth with your chagrin'.[73]

Clarke had joined the ranks of the Junto, who had given up their posts to avoid further attack, but his health and spirits were never properly to recover. He benefited from the waters at Tunbridge in July but even from there he wrote his wife 'melancholy' letters and fell ill again in August, continuing in a poor state for the rest of the year. In November Locke wrote that his friend's health would improve 'if those strong principles of life which are in you were a little roused and excited'. There were family worries, too, in persuading the Quaker (and Locke's friend) Benjamin Furley to accept his second son as an apprentice merchant and in finding a husband for his eldest daughter, Elizabeth. In June 1700 Locke suggested that his 'wife' marry his own heir, Peter King, but the match foundered in July when King's father was unable to meet the contract's demands. Nor was Clarke's peace of mind eased by what was going on in his locality.[74]

By early June 1700 the Tory gentry were meeting to turn out any j.p. 'they did not like' and, as Mary informed him, Clarke's decision to resign as excise commissioner was being misconstrued by his enemies,

for it was concluded if you chose the Parliament you had a pension from the King for so doing more than the income of the excise office came to, so that they will allow you no honour or credit for what you do, especially in your own country. I suppose at the next election there will be a great bustle again for fear of the Church, for most of the persons that I hear preach seem to intimate as if it was in much danger of falling into the hands of the Dissenting party as ever it was into the popish, and many are possessed that you are a meeter though I tell all that I hear say so that I have often heard you say you never was at a meeting in your life and that your father it is well known was a very severe man against them and you being a moderate man gave them such thoughts and that I must needs say this for the Dissenters that though you had done a hundred times more to oblige the Church than ever you did the Dissenting party, yet they was much more civil to you and yours and it would be very ill natured as well as ill breeding to be rude to those that was civil and kind.'

Clarke was no Dissenter – he had been 'sorry' the previous summer to hear that Yonge's daughter 'had been preached into marrying herself to a Nonconformist parson that is worth little or nothing and without the knowledge or consent of Sir Walter', an act that might have strengthened his earlier resolve to promote a bill to prevent elopements – but he certainly had a Low Church outlook. In 1698 he had compared repairs to his local church, which had left a 'breach' in its fabric, to attempts by the Churchmen 'in another sense' to bring down the national structure if they did not 'become more moderate than at present', adding that the 'unnecessary superstitious' rebuilding had been designed only 'for the pride and glory of the priest'. Such an attitude was now an electoral liability.[75]

Clarke therefore had to tread warily when, in late August 1700, he received a request on behalf of the 1,200 serge and worsted weavers of Taunton for help in procuring an act either to incorporate them or to exclude 'foreigners' or women traders, who they saw as swamping the labour market and bringing more poor to the town. The trade was Taunton's principal industry yet the demands cut against Clarke's belief in free trade. Edward replied that incorporation would involve 'a vain attempt to get a special act of Parliament in the case', though he assured them he was prepared to 'pursue in Parliament anything that may be thought by him and them proper for the relief of the poor men'. He received a letter of thanks for his 'intentions', but the representatives of the weavers pointed out that his answer was 'not altogether agreeing with our interest' and they continued to insist on restrictive practices. Clarke responded on 19 Nov. that obtaining such an act would be costly and to little effect and that an act to relieve the weavers would similarly fail, though he was prepared to try if they wanted him to do so. On 27 Dec. the weavers told him that they expected him to work with Portman to procure their act and also required his assistance at the sessions where they had indicted some for intruding on their trading privileges.[76]

The weavers held the whip hand because the election had finally been called. In December Freke notified Clarke's chief local ally of the impending dissolution, 'to the end he may prevent any of the electors of Taunton visiting [Clarke] at Chipley', thereby avoiding any chance of forfeiting the election for 'treating after the date of the writ, as I am afraid many will for want of timely notice'. Freke, who advised Clarke about this and other elections from London, also recommended that Clarke stand with Sir Edmund Harrison and assured him of the support of Lord Spencer (Charles*). In fact, the electorate entered into a 'unanimous agreement' to choose Portman and Clarke, who accepted the arrangement, promising to serve them 'with that diligence and integrity as becomes a true lover of his country'.[77]

Clarke was active at the assembly of the new Parliament in securing the Court's candidate as Speaker, arguing that if MPs really wanted unity they should 'come over to us' rather than propose a rival candidate. The 'college' was 'very sanguine' about the composition of the new House and the success at the beginning may have given a false sense of security. As the Junto came under increasing pressure, party politics dominated Clarke's activity. He was named to several committees inquiring into maladministration, where he no doubt hoped to shield his Whig allies. But it was the attack on Somers that really stung Clarke into action. On 20 Mar. 1701 he was appointed to the committee to investigate the Kidd affair and the following day to the committee to draft an address to the King about the Partition Treaty, the two main issues being used against the lord chancellor. According to Henry St John II*, Somers composed all the messages from the Lords about his own impeachment 'with the assistance of [Sir Joseph] Jekyll* and Clarke'. He also played an active part in the Whig counter-attack. On 6 May he was appointed to a similar committee established to investigate how seamen came to be discharged without pay, a move directed against an old enemy, George Churchill, and 12 days later to a committee to draft an address about the endeavours of the 'ill disposed' to create unrest.[78]

The party wrangling and the truncated nature of the Parliament inevitably squeezed more routine parliamentary business, though Clarke's activity showed continuing commitment to long-standing concerns. He was first-named on 19 Feb. 1701 to the committee of inquiry into the laws regulating woollen manufactures; appointed on 1 Mar. to the drafting committee of a bill to set the poor to work; and on 10 Apr. to the committee to receive proposals for the payment of public debts and the advancement of credit. Clarke was still being lobbied by his constituents about local trade and the poor, who were, he was told, wholly dependent on his attempts to obtain relief.[79]

Perhaps as a result of the renewed pressures in Parliament, Clarke's health again became poor. In July 1701 he was reported to be 'much out of order' and when he returned to Chipley he was 'hardly able to hold [his] pen . . . by reason of excessive pain and weakness' in his shoulder and wrist. When he recovered, he spent his time 'in catching carps'. But Harley certainly did not consider him a spent force, for he appears to have drafted a spoof 'letter', dated 3 Sept., ostensibly from Clarke to Freke, in which the activities of the 'college' were made public. Clarke and his colleagues were alleged to have spread lies in print and to be about to revive the college's meetings. Clarke was accused of having headed rebellion at Oxford and of being in charge of the distribution of *The True Patriot Vindicated*, a tract which attacked Lord Rochester (Laurence Hyde†) and Sir Bartholomew Shower*. Clarke's design, it was insinuated, was 'to make any Parliament impracticable' and Harley's propaganda, if it was his work, was intended to counter the Whig campaign to secure a new Parliament. The pamphlet sought to explain Clarke's 'melancholy' in terms of the 'ill breeding' he had met with in the previous three sessions which, it was alleged, had made him 'almost resolve to speak no more' and turn instead to writing to 'lay the new ministry as flat as a flounder'.[80]

Clarke received news of the dissolution from his 'worthy friend Mr [Thomas] Hopkins*' and was successfully returned again at Taunton. His health, however, was continuing to cause him problems, though Locke clearly thought much of the lack of strength of which his friend complained was psychosomatic, since in December he urged him to 'bestir' himself. Effort was certainly required to maintain Whig fortunes once the House had picked what Edward called 'an ill chosen Speaker' [Harley], but it is significant that Clarke hardly features in the parliamentary diary of Sir Richard Cocks, 2nd Bt.*, and that his activity was limited to his perennial concerns, though the presence in the House of George Clarke makes positive attribution of many speeches and much parliamentary activity impossible. Trading issues continued to preoccupy him, with appointments on 10 Jan. to the drafting committee of a bill to encourage privateers and on the 11th to an inquiry into the Greenland trade. Ten days later he was appointed to an inquiry into libels and scandalous papers written by William Fuller. Clarke's days as a manager of the House were clearly long past, though on 29 Jan. he moved that Lord Peterborough, Locke's ally, be heard in his defence over allegations of misconduct at the Malmesbury election. On 7 May he moved that sales of Irish forfeitures should be restricted to Protestants.[81]

Clarke's relatively low profile in the Commons in 1702 matched his low spirits. At the end of January he wrote to Locke that his 'indisposition and ... constant attendance upon the service of the House' had prevented him from writing, and although he rejoiced at the discontent of the High Churchmen over the abjuration bill, by 14 Feb. he thought 'the conclusion of this session will not be much unlike the proceedings of the last Parliament'. The death of the King to whom he was so devoted appears to have sunk him lower still, for on 23 May Locke implored him 'for my sake, for the family's sake, for your country's sake, not to neglect' his health. Although some of the pension owing to him was now paid, nothing could compensate for the exclusion from Court favour that now became inevitable.[82]

Clarke feared a contest at the polls which, he told his steward and electoral agent,

I believe will prove very injurious to the town as well as prejudicial to myself ... but am perfectly at a loss how to behave myself therein, I am sure I have nothing more at heart than the peace and prosperity of the town, but if both are interrupted and hazarded by mistaken judgments in the present juncture of affairs, I can only bewail the misfortune and must submit to the judgments of those who think their interest stronger in this than in the glorious reign of the great King William, but when 'tis too late I doubt they will find themselves fatally mistaken in the determination what will be made hereupon at my contested election. I shall submit all to providence and the conduct of my friends.

Despite his fears of failure, Clarke was re-elected, though his interest was insufficient to bring in another Whig alongside him to oust the Tory Sir Francis Warre. He returned to London in November 1702 in better health, and on 18 Feb. 1703 carried up the bill to prevent abuses in the manufacture of textiles. He voted on 13 Feb. to agree with the Lords' amendments to the bill for enlarging the time to take the oaths of abjuration and relished signs of division among the Tories, comparing them to cocks 'who though all of a side being left at liberty together fought with and destroyed one another'. Private rather than public matters increasingly preoccupied him, for in June 1703 the possibility that his daughter would marry King was again revived, though once more this came to nothing, ironically, because King was now wealthy enough to look for a more advantageous alliance. Disaster also struck Chipley, in the form of autumn storm damage, and Clarke personally, when he fell victim to a highway robber on his way back to London in early December: 'but since providence has preserved my wife, my children and my whole family from any personal hurt', he wrote, 'I bless God and am thankful whatever other damage I may have sustained'. In the summer he had met up with Locke, who had been shocked to find only 'the outside and shell' of his friend, since 'the better half was away and wanting'.[83]

Clarke rallied at the end of the year to meet the challenge posed by the occasional conformity bill and was in a 'constant hurry' as a result of his 'steady attendance on the House'. On 7 Dec. he reported to his steward: 'We have been so fatigued with this day's debate and the opposition we made against the occasional conformity bill, which after many hours' debate and a division of the House was carried by 223 against 140 of us that opposed the bill.' A relieved and joyful Clarke reported to Locke a week later that the bill had been rejected by the Lords and he was even more gleeful, though with less cause, on 13 Jan. 1704 when he thought the address voted by the Lords so directly contradicted that of the Lower House that 'it will be rendered impracticable for this Parliament ever to meet again'. Once again, Clarke's recorded activity is negligible, though he was added on 11 Mar. to the committee investigating two tracts, having earlier expressed the hope that the new bill to restrain the liberty of the press would be thrown out.[84]

Clarke's health suffered a reverse in May 1704 and Locke invited him to Oates to prevent him spending 'too much time of persecuting' himself with 'melancholy thoughts'. Although the illness was protracted, it was Locke who died first, leaving his friend a £200 legacy, though the loss appears to have deepened Clarke's depression. Forecast as an opponent of the Tack in October 1704, he is unlikely to have attended the House for the vote because of his state of health, being listed among those voting against or absent. On 29 Dec. his wife reported to their steward that her husband would 'do nothing in his own private affairs neither great nor little but spend[s] his whole time in a manner as is enough to w[eary] out any mortal as is so nearly concerned for him as I am'. Clarke appears to have passed on the depressive tendency that he himself had inherited from his father to his own son, who in April drowned himself in the Thames 'upon some discontent'.[85]

Despite his debilitated state, Clarke was re-elected in May 1705 and marked as Low Church on an analysis of the House. On 25 Oct. 1705 he voted for the Court candidate as Speaker but no other parliamentary activity can be ascribed to him with certainty. Indeed, when his wife died in January 1706 Clarke was a broken man. He was absent from the regency bill division in February and does not appear to have attended the next session, for in December 1706 there was a possibility that he would be taken into custody for absence without leave. Yonge had to write to his friend 'earnestly' desiring his 'assistance in the remaining business of the session' and both Henry Lyddell* and Sir Joseph Jekyll wrote in a similar vein. But the call to duty fell on deaf ears, for Clarke replied to Yonge:

> If extremity of weakness and excess of grief and trouble may be thought a reasonable excuse for not answering y[ou]r very kind letter sooner, let that load of both under which I labour plead mine, and I implore the further favour of y[ou]r interest with our friends in the House to get my attendance excused at this time, since for over two months past I have been and still am confined to my chamber and mostly to my bed.

Clarke festered in a state of chronic depression until, fittingly, business of a local kind stirred him into his swansong parliamentary activity. On 12 Dec. 1707 he was appointed to the drafting committee of another Tone navigation bill, which he subsequently guided through all its stages in the House, despite 'violent opposition'. He was classed as a Whig on two lists of early 1708.[86]

Re-elected in 1708, Clarke remained totally inactive in this Parliament, not supporting the naturalization of the Palatines nor appearing on the division lists of the Sacheverell impeachment. By the end of 1709 he began to settle his affairs, though he did not die 'of a fit of apoplexy' until 1 Oct. 1710 (the parish records suggest a date of 20 Oct., but that appears to refer to his burial), shortly before the poll at Taunton where he was once again standing as candidate. According to one report, his death saved him from the final humiliation of being ousted from his seat by the Tories. His will, dated 15 June 1710, bequeathed his estate to his eldest surviving son, Jepp, and his wife's lands were settled on his youngest son, Samuel; each of the daughters received a £4,000 portion. Yonge and Freke were appointed as executors and also received bequests. Accounts drawn up shortly after Clarke's death show that £17,460 was paid in legacies, including £9,000 to a trust fund, and that he owned almost £4,000 of Bank stock, £6,600 of East India stock, £2,160 of million bank shares, £3,000 of East India bonds and £1,700 in mortgages, as well as annuities. The total assets were estimated as being worth about £18,000, though another calculation put the figure at over £21,000.[87]

The contrast between the man of energy, dedication and competence who had to be restrained from overworking in Parliament in the 1690s and the sick, melancholic one who had to be chivvied into attending the House in the 1700s is very marked. His later torpor nevertheless appears to have been ignored, or tolerated, by the Taunton electorate, even during the Tory revival at the beginning of Anne's reign. Yet Clarke's rapid decline in health and importance after the turn of the century should not obscure his very busy and important career during William's reign. Indeed, his papers and correspondence with Locke reveal a much higher level of activity than that recorded in the Journals, putting informative flesh on the bare bones of what might otherwise have appeared as the unspectacular career of a minor Junto associate. It is an irony that those papers survived among the archives of the neighbouring Sanford family, into which Clarke's daughter married, even though the Tory John Sanford had been one of Edward's most bitter enemies.

[1] Bridget Clarke and Priscilla Flowers-Smith kindly provided some of the information in this biography, and what follows owes much to Bridget Clarke's transcripts of the Sanford papers from which a number of quotations have been taken. [2] Som. RO, Sanford mss SF 4057, ped.; SF 851, notes on ped.; *Locke Corresp.* ii. 479; *Harl. Soc.* n.s. xi. 132; Sanford mss, Ursula Venner to Clarke, 10 June 1678 (Clarke trans.). [3] *Cal. Treas. Bks.* viii. 1804, 1982–3; xii. 120. [4] *CSP Dom.* 1694–5, p. 464. [5] *Poems on Affairs of State* ed. Cameron, v. 434; *The Taunton Dean Letter* (1701). [6] Info. from Bridget Clarke; B. Rand, *Corresp. of John Locke and Edward Clarke*, 8. [7] Sanford mss, George Fletcher to Edward Clarke snr. 30 Aug. 1668 (Clarke trans.); Rand, 2–8; *Locke Corresp.* ii. 511. [8] *Locke Corresp.* i. 453; Sanford mss, Clarke to John Buckland, 15 May 1676 (Clarke trans.); subscriptions at St. Charles the Martyr, Tunbridge Wells (*ex inf.* Bridget Clarke); Rand, 13, 57. [9] *Two Treatises* ed. Laslett, 63–64; *Locke Corresp.* ii. 512, 600–3; iii. 77, 107; iv. 221; Rand, 15, 29–31; M. Cranston, *John Locke*, 319. [10] Sanford mss SF 1678(15); Braddon to [–], 30 May 1679; SF 3109, William Clarke to Clarke, 5 Apr. 1684; SF 1749, list of j.p.s, c.1689; SF 3928, Clarke to Mary Clarke, 18 Jan. 1680; *CSP Dom.* 1685, p. 178. [11] Sanford mss SF 3109, William Clarke to Clarke, 20 Jan., 11, 14 Feb., 5 Apr., 28 July, 6 Aug. 1679; SF 3074, Aldred Seaman to Clarke, 30 July 1679; Clarke to [?Trenchard], 2 Aug. 1679; Ursula Venner to Clarke, 23 July 1679 (Clarke trans.); *CSP Dom.* 1685, p. 54. [12] Duckett, *Penal Laws and Test Act* (1883), 17, 229, 243; *CSP Dom.* 1687–9, p. 116; *Bull. IHR*, xlvi. 64; *Locke Corresp.* ii. 672; iii. 201, 455, 494, 501; Sanford mss SF 1084; *DNB Missing Persons*. [13] Sanford mss, Mary Clarke to Clarke, 28 Mar. 1690 (Clarke trans.); *Locke Corresp.* ii. 664; iii. 603; Grey, x. 73. [14] Sanford mss SF 3868. [15] Ibid. Clarke to John Spreat, 8 July 1690 (Clarke trans.); Sanford mss SF 3902, Clarke to ?Lockhart, 25 Aug. 1690. [16] *Locke Corresp.* iv. 148; Sanford mss Mary Clarke to Clarke, 22 Dec. 1690; SF 1678(5). [17] *Luttrell Diary*, 25, 75, 100; Grey, 206–7. [18] *Locke Corresp.* iv. 347–8, 358; Sanford mss SF 2765; SF 2891; *Luttrell Diary*, 128, 154, 177. [19] *Luttrell Diary*, 87; *Locke Corresp.* iv. 322, 339, 340, 343, 368; Sanford mss SF 1678(50). [20] *Luttrell Diary*, 117, 130; *Locke Corresp.* iv. 340, 373; Sanford mss SF 2928. [21] *Luttrell Diary*, 14, 50, 178, 198, 293; Sanford mss SF 1348. [22] Sanford mss SF 1678(7); *Luttrell Diary*, 110, 130, 194, 220; *Locke Corresp.* iv. 373. [23] *Locke Corresp.* iv. 564, 588, 603, 614–15; *Luttrell Diary*, 422. [24] *Luttrell Diary*, 343; *Locke Corresp.* iv. 632, 634, 643–4. [25] Sanford mss SF 1678(11); *Luttrell Diary*, 240, 257, 272; Grey, 284; Cobbett, *Parlty. Hist.* v. 732, 736. [26] *Luttrell Diary*, 294, 319; Sanford mss SF 1678(8), (9); SF 2935. [27] *Luttrell Diary*, 225, 472; Sanford mss mayor of Taunton to Clarke, 30 Oct. 1691 (Clarke trans.); SF 3087, letter from Taunton to Clarke, 16 Dec. 1691. [28] *Luttrell Diary*, 258, 282, 417, 429; Sanford mss SF 2755, draft clause. [29] *Luttrell Diary*, 440, 448, 454, 462, 476–7. [30] Ibid. 339, 353, 444; Sanford mss SF 3092, Hoar to Clarke, 4 Jan., 8 Feb. 1693; SF 3092, Hoar to Clarke, 4 Jan. 1693. [31] *CSP Dom.* 1693, p. 272; Sanford mss SF 3092, Hoar to Clarke, 11 Nov. 1693; *Locke Corresp.* iv. 654, 672–4, 678–9. [32] Sanford mss SF 3092, Hoare to Clarke, 31 Jan. 1694; Grey, 379. [33] *Locke Corresp.* v. 27. [34] Sanford mss SF 3874, Aldred Bickham to Clarke, 22 Jan. 1694. [35] H. Horwitz, *Parl. and Pol. Wm. III*, 126, 212; Harley mss at Brampton Bryan (Hereford and Worcester RO (Hereford), photocopy C64/117), Gwyn to Robert Harley, 23 Apr. 1694. [36] Sanford mss SF 136 Clarke to Spreat, 5 May 1694; *Shrewsbury Corresp.* 43; *CSP Dom.* 1694–5, p. 186; Sanford mss, Yonge to Clarke, 6 Aug. 1694; *The Taunton Dean Letter* (1701). [37] Sanford mss SF 3109 Clarke to Spreat, 4 Jan. 1694; SF 2764; NLS, Advocates' mss, Bank of Eng. pprs. 31.1.7, f. 146; *Locke Corresp.* v. 92, 107, 263. [38] *Locke Corresp.* iv. 769, 774; v. 29–30, 35, 40, 199, 200. [39] Ibid. v. 278–9, 282, 292, 543. [40] Ibid. v. 278, 282, 291, 294, 358; Sanford mss SF 2890; SF 3257; *The Library*, ser. 5, xxxiii. 307, 313. [41] Sanford mss SF 2980, Clarke to Lord Capell (Hon. Sir Henry Capel*), 4, 15 Dec. 1694; SF 2765. [42] Add. 46527, f. 22; Sanford mss, Clarke to wife, 25 Aug., 27, 29 Dec. 1694, 5 Jan. 1695. [43] Horwitz, 147. [44] Add. 70306–9; Sanford mss SF 3314, 25 Apr. 1695; SF 2702 minutes of proceedings, 25, 26 Apr. 1695; SF 2737, notes about Firebrace and Cooke; SF 284, Clarke to wife, 18 May 1695. [45] Sanford mss SF 1088 (1), address; SF 3305, acct. bk. 9 July, 19 Sept. 1695; SF 1089, on reverse of Ben Smith to Clarke, received 2 Sept. 1695. [46] *Locke Corresp.* v. 380, 415, 423–4, 440, 442, 469–70, 471. [47] Ibid. v. 478. [48] Sanford mss SF 284, Clarke to wife, 15 Feb. 1696; Horwitz, 168; *Parlty. Hist.* vii. 228–240. [49] *Locke Corresp.* v. 552, 561–2, 584, 590, 592–3, 620, 632; Sanford mss SF 3869, draft preamble; SF 2095, draft clause. [50] Sanford mss SF 3842, draft bill; SF 3087, Malachi Blake and others to Clarke, 22 Apr. 1696; *The Library*, 317–22; *Locke Corresp.* v. 471, 475, 482. [51] Sanford mss, Mary Clarke to Clarke, 18 June, 18 Aug. 1696, Clarke to wife, 12, 17 Aug. 1696 (Clarke trans.). [52] Sanford mss SF 4515, Mary Clarke to Clarke, 18 Aug., n.d. c.29 Aug., 6 Sept., 9 Nov. 1696. [53] Sanford mss, Mary Clarke to Clarke, 9 Sept. 1696, Clarke to wife, 20 Oct. 96 (Clarke trans.); *Shrewsbury Corresp.* 417, 418, 419; *Vernon–Shrewsbury Letters*, i. 49, 149; Cobbett, v. 1008, 1056. [54] Sanford mss, Cary to Clarke, 16 Nov. 1696 (Clarke trans.); *Locke Corresp.* v. 730, 731, 751. [55] Sanford mss, Mary Clarke to Clarke, 9 Dec. 1696 (Clarke trans.); SF 1088(2), Richard Snowe to Clarke, 6 Dec. 1696; SF 1088 (3), joint letter to Clarke, 18 Nov. 1696. [56] *Locke Corresp.* v. 755; vi. 81; *The Taunton Dean Letter* (1701); *Shrewsbury Corresp.* 479. [57] Sanford mss, Mary Clarke to Clarke, 17 May, 24 July, 4 Oct. 1697, Clarke to wife, 20 May 1697 (Clarke trans.). [58] Univ. of London mss 65, item 3, list of subscribers; *Cal. Treas. Bks.* xiii. 14, 29, 38, 42; Sanford mss SF 2618, notes. [59] Sanford mss, Clarke to wife, 5 Oct. 1697; SF 3868, 'For Land Forces 1697'; SF 3906, 12 Mar. 1698. [60] *Locke Corresp.* vi. 283, 285–6, 301; *CSP Dom.* 1698, p. 134. [61] *Locke Corresp.* vi. 328, 329; Sanford mss SF 1093 (32), (33); SF 3334, heads of a lustring bill 1698. [62] *Locke Corresp.* vi. 410; *Vernon–Shrewsbury Letters*, ii. 83, 93; Sanford mss SF 3839, SF 2909 'notes on the report'; SF 3166, 'the Irish Pamphlet'; SF 1678(136), draft bill; SF 3877, *Reasons*. [63] *Vernon–Shrewsbury Letters*, i. 456; Sanford mss SF 2095, draft; Northants. RO, Montagu (Boughton) mss, 46/78, Vernon to Shrewsbury, 11 Mar. 1698; 47/21, same to same, 28 Apr. 1698; *Cal. Treas. Bks.* 1697–1702, p. 161; *CSP Dom.* 1698, p. 310. [64] Sanford mss SF 3109 Clarke to Spreat, 2, 7 July 1698; SF 290, diary of John Spreat, 28, 29 July, 2, 3 Aug. 1698; SF 3833, Clarke to Ursula Venner, 1 Aug. 1698; SF 1093 (27) joint letter to Clarke, n.d.; SF 1093(47), joint letter to Clarke, 7 Dec. 1698; *The True Englishmen's Choice* (1698), 10–11. [65] Sanford mss SF 1093 (4), joint letter to Clarke, 6 Feb. 1699, Clarke to Spreat, 4 Feb. 1699; SF 1093 (14) petition, 8 Feb. 1699; SF 1093 (20), (22), (23), John Parsons to Clarke, 16, 23, 25 Jan. 1699; SF 1093 (48) tract, (49) tract. [66] SF 1093 (3), (10), (11), Thomas Baker to Clarke, 15, 22 Feb., 29 Mar. 1699; SF 1093 (15), joint letter to Clarke, n.d.; SF 1093 (20), Parsons to Clarke, 25 Jan. 1699; SF 1093 (21), joint letter to Clarke, 30 Jan. 1699; SF 1093 (22), Parsons to Clarke, 23 Jan. 1696; SF 1093 (24), Baker to Clarke, 14 Jan. 1699, Clarke to Spreat, 28 Jan. 4 Feb. 1699. [67] Ibid. SF 1093 (2), Thomas Whinnell to Clarke, 1 Mar. 1699; SF 4511, 'Reasons'; Clarke to Spreat, 3 Jan. 1699. [68] Ibid. Clarke to Spreat, 5, 17 Jan. 1699. [69] Sanford mss, Mary Clarke to Spreat, 4 Mar. 1699, Clarke to Spreat, 19 Jan. 1699 (Clarke trans.); *Cam. Misc.* xxix. 379, 383; Montagu (Boughton) mss 47/157, Vernon to Shrewsbury, 16 Mar. 1699. [70] Sanford mss Clarke to Spreat, 11 Feb., 3, 29 June, 30 Sept. 1699, 17 Feb. 1700, Clarke to wife, 5 Oct. 1697

(Clarke trans.); *Locke Corresp.* vi. 554, 607, 671, 683. [71] *Vernon–Shrewsbury Letters*, ii. 412; Sanford mss SF 2883, draft bill dated 1695; SF 2883, draft bill, n.d.; SF 4107(a), notes; Mary Clarke to Clarke, 15 Apr. 1700; *Locke Corresp.* vi. 771; vii. 20. [72] *Vernon–Shrewsbury Letters*, ii. 439, 448–9, 451. [73] Ibid. ii. 453; iii. 92; Sanford mss, Mary Clarke to Clarke, 22 Apr. 29 Apr. 1700 (Clarke trans.); *Cal. Treas. Bks.* xv. 96; *Post Boy*, 13–15 June 1700; *Locke Corresp.* vii. 25–26. [74] *Locke Corresp.* vii. 109, 129, 139, 187; Sanford mss, Mary Clarke to Clarke, 12 June, 6, 20 July 1700 (Clarke trans.). [75] Sanford mss, Mary Clarke to Clarke, 1, 18 June 1700, Clarke to Spreat, 6 June 1699 (Clarke trans.); SF 3109, same to same, 7 Oct. 1698, Clarke to wife, 4 Apr. 1696. [76] Ibid. SF 1088 (8), joint letter, 30 Aug. 1700; SF 1102 (1), Clarke's draft reply, c.Oct. 1700; SF 1102 (3), 'state and condition', n.d.; SF 1102 (5), weavers to Clarke, 27 Dec. 1700; SF 3108, E. Middleton to Clarke, 12 Sept. 1700; SF 1098, joint letter to Clarke, 20 Sept. 1700; SF 1100, Clarke to 'Gentlemen', 19 Nov. 1700. [77] Ibid. SF 3110, Freke to Clarke, 17, 24, 27 Dec. 1700; SF 1088 (6), Clarke to electors, c.24 Dec. 1700. [78] NMM, Sergison mss Ser/103, f. 64, acct. of Speaker election; *Cocks Diary*, 63; *Locke Corresp.* vii. 245–6, 251; *HMC Downshire*, i. 803. [79] Sanford mss SF 1102 (4), joint letter to Clarke, 24 Mar. 1701; SF 1088 (11), joint letter to Clark, n.d. [80] *Locke Corresp.* vii. 372, 426, 434; Add. 70295, draft; *The Taunton Dean Letter* (1701). [81] Sanford mss, Clarke to Vernon, 15 Nov. 1701, Ward Clarke to Clarke, 3 Jan. 1702 (Clarke trans.); *Locke Corresp.* vii. 523; *Cocks Diary*, 194. [82] *Locke Corresp.* vii. 549, 566, 617; *Cal. Treas. Bks.* xvii. 1048. [83] Sanford mss, Clarke to Spreat, 23 May 1702 (Clarke trans.); SF 3928, Thomas Whinne to Clarke, 20 May 1702; SF 2091, Clarke to Furly, 18 May 1703; *Locke Corresp.* vii. 718; viii. 5, 11, 136, 141. [84] *Locke Corresp.* viii. 135, 145, 162, 163; Sanford mss SF 3837, Clarke to Spreat, 7 Dec. 1703. [85] *Locke Corresp.* viii. 283, 419; Sanford mss, Mary Clarke to Spreat, 29 Dec. 1704 (Clarke trans.); Luttrell, *Brief Relation*, v. 544. [86] Sanford mss SF 3110, Yonge to Clarke, 24 Dec. 1706, with Clarke's response; SF 3077, Lyddell to Clarke, 24 Dec. 1706; SF 3109, Jekyll to Clarke, 24 Dec. 1706; SF 3903, A. Clarke to Spreat, 17 Jan. 1708. [87] Strathmore mss at Glamis Castle box 74, bdle 8, newsletter 7 Oct. 1710; Add. 70421, Dyer's newsletter 7 Oct. 1710; Rand, 72; PCC 242 Smith; Sanford mss, Spreat's accts.

M. J. K.

CLARKE, Edward II (*d.* c.1723), of Norwich.

NORWICH   1701 (Dec.)–1702

m. by 1675, Hannah, da. of Samuel Parmenter, merchant, of Norwich, 5s. (3 *d.v.p.*) 2da.[1]

Common councilman, Norwich 1688, sheriff 1693–4, alderman by 1700, mayor 1700–1.[2]

A worsted cloth manufacturer, Clarke was the father of Samuel Clarke, the theologian and Newtonian philosopher, and was described in biographical memoirs of Samuel as 'a person of an excellent natural capacity and of an untainted reputation for probity and all virtue', one 'whose most excellent character . . . recommended him so to the citizens of Norwich, that they chose him without, nay against, his own inclination to represent them in Parliament'. In fact Clarke was only elected in 1701 after a stiff contest. He stood as a Whig, and his election was reckoned by Lord Spencer (Charles*) as a gain. At no point is it possible to distinguish his parliamentary career from that of his namesake, the Whig Member for Taunton. After being defeated in 1702 and at a by-election in 1703, Clarke withdrew from political life. His will, dated 10 Sept. 1723, was proved 20 Jan. following. He left property in St. Andrew's, Norwich, and at Griston in Norfolk, together with a personal estate of some £800, the bulk of it in Bank stock.[3]

[1] Norf. RO, NCC 195 Megoe; *DNB* (Clarke, John; Clarke, Samuel); Samuel Clarke, *Works* (1738). i. p. i. [2] *Norf. Rec. Soc.* xxiii. 26, 64, 65; *CSP Dom.* 1687–9, p. 270; Blomefield, *Norf.* iii. 426, 431. [3] *HMC Lords*, n.s. iii. 133; W. Whiston, *Mems. Samuel Clarke* (1748), 4; Clarke, p. i; NCC 195 Megoe.

D. W. H.

CLARKE, George (1661–1736), of All Souls, Oxford.

OXFORD UNIVERSITY   23 Nov. 1685–1687
WINCHELSEA   1702–1705
EAST LOOE   1705–1708
LAUNCESTON   29 May 1711–1713
OXFORD UNIVERSITY   4 Dec. 1717–22 Oct. 1736

b. 7 May 1661, o. s. of Sir William Clarke, sec. at war, of Pall Mall, Westminster by Dorothy, da. and coh. of Thomas Hilyard *alias* Hall of Hebburn, co. Dur. *educ.* Jermyn Street academy (Mr Gordon) to 1672; Brasenose, Oxf. 1675, BA 1679, MA 1683, BCL 1686, DCL 1708; I. Temple 1676. *unm. suc.* fa. 1662.[1]

Fellow of All Souls, Oxford 1680–*d.*

Judge-advocate-gen. 1682–1705; sec. at war [I] 1690–Mar. 1692; chief sec. [I] 1690–Mar. 1692; jt. sec. at war Mar. 1692–Mar. 1702; jt. sec. of Admiralty May 1702–5; sec. to Prince George of Denmark May 1702–5; ld. of Admiralty 1710–14.[2]

Gov. and freeman, R. Fishery Co. [I] 1692; commr. building 50 new churches 1712–15.[3]

Freeman, Winchelsea 1702.[4]

Clarke has been described as one of the 'virtuosi' of his age. An urbane and congenial personality, he was a man of versatile ability and interests who was equally at home in the company of scholars and men of letters as with administrators and politicians. As a young man his intellectual prowess earned him a fellowship at All Souls, Oxford, but he was unable to resist the greater attractions and stimulus of a governmental career. Clarke entered the public arena soon after coming of age, succeeding his stepfather, Dr Samuel Barrow, as judge-advocate of the army in 1682. He soon found himself having to resist attempts by the then secretary at war, William Blathwayt*, to absorb the functions of judge-advocate into his own department, and went so far as to put his case before the King. Clarke won his point, and subsequently earned the King's approbation for his astute conduct of court martial proceedings. Soon after the accession of King James he applied for, and obtained, an increase in his judge-advocate's salary on the grounds that the recent augmentation of forces had swelled the volume of business. In November 1685 he was returned for Oxford University at a by-election, but Parliament was prorogued before he could take his seat. An ardent opponent of the King's religious policies, he managed to avoid the three questions ('my mind was well known upon these points', he recalled) and preserved his office, serving the King until he could see it was no longer practicable to do so. In November 1688 he and Dr John Radcliffe* joined the King briefly on his journey from Salisbury to Andover but, finding the court in 'confusion' as the desertion became general, they made their departure, Clarke returning to Oxford.[5]

Clarke's commission was renewed following the declaration of William and Mary as King and Queen, and in the summer of 1689 he accompanied the commissioners for the regulation of the army in a tour of inspection which took him as far as Edinburgh. Early in 1690 the King appointed Clarke to attend him as secretary at war in Ireland. Having heard that Blathwayt had excused himself from going on the expedition, Clarke assumed he was to succeed Blathwayt, his *bête noire*, in the more senior role of secretary at war in England. The King subsequently led Clarke to believe that he would have the English post once he had fulfilled his purpose in Ireland. On taking up his position in Dublin, Clarke also performed the office of chief secretary, which he claimed was his by right of being secretary at war, and established his lodgings at Dublin Castle. He remained in Ireland until early December 1691, following the conclusion of the Treaty of Limerick, when he sought his recall to England. As the King prepared to go on campaign in Flanders in February 1692, Clarke's expectations of becoming sole secretary at war in place of Blathwayt were thwarted as instead he was asked to serve only as a deputy secretary 'in the King's absence'. He remonstrated, first with Lord Athlone, the former commander of forces in Ireland, and then with the King himself, that 'this was not what I had reason to expect'. Determined to be 'no man's deputy', he insisted he would only serve if given a proper commission, whereupon one was immediately issued. Clarke remained in what was only intended as a temporary position until the King's death in 1702, a situation which he later reflected upon with bitterness: it 'was all the King did for me as long as he lived'. In July 1694 he asked the Duke of Ormond and Lord Athlone to intercede on his behalf for the wardenship of the Mint on hearing that the then incumbent, Benjamin Overton*, was close to death. 'I don't know', he wrote to Athlone, 'if the King may have altered the intention he had once of giving me some settled employment, but humbly hope he will not think this too great a recompense for one of three times the value, if ever he designs to do anything for me.' Overton survived his illness, however. Looking back on these years Clarke was apt to hold Blathwayt, and the 'methods' Blathwayt used with Lord Portland, primarily responsible for barring his advancement.[6]

Clarke was spoken of in October 1695 as a possible successor to Sir Thomas Clarges* as Member for Oxford University, but it is unlikely that he had any intention of standing, having himself broken the news of Clarges' imminent demise to Secretary Trumbull* (Sir William), a more obvious favourite for the seat. Though for so long disappointed of promotion, Clarke nevertheless proved himself an able and shrewd army administrator. Despite his resentment towards Blathwayt, and their political differences, the two men seem to have enjoyed an effective working relationship in the running of the war office during the 1690s. When Blathwayt was re-elected for Bath in December 1701 Clarke could warmly congratulate him, 'the only means to prevent foreboding miseries, being placed in the breasts of men of so much honour and zeal for their country's good as yours'. One of Clarke's letters to Blathwayt in 1699 shows him as a typical government servant, concerned to avoid the inquisitorial tactics of MPs and prevent the Commons starving the army of necessary funds: 'the paymaster has given out accounts to the first regiment of guards and has charged £8,000 for the regiments. I am afraid if the House of Commons finds this to be so much less than the account given them, they will save the money.' To this end he found his acquaintanceship among the Members useful in enabling him to detect possible lines of parliamentary attack.[7]

Although he was asking Blathwayt at the end of 1701 'to think of some other place for me', he was, according to his memoir, resolved by this stage to retire altogether from public business, and had made arrangements to sell his judge-advocate's place. However, his career suddenly took a new turn with the accession of Queen Anne in March 1702, and, after some persuasion by his friends, he accepted in May the post of secretary to Prince George of Denmark, the lord high admiral. Clarke had become well acquainted with the Prince during the Irish war and may well have been George's personal choice. He assisted the Prince not only in Admiralty business but in all other official and private affairs: one particular area which Clarke specifically mentioned in his memoir as 'having under my care' was 'the business of the Cinque Ports, whereof his royal highness was warden'. Although he was also appointed joint secretary to the Admiralty council with a salary of £800, regular attendance on the Prince, often requiring his absence from London, prevented him from serving the council as fully as did his colleague, Josiah Burchett*. In the general election held in the summer Clarke was elected for the Cinque Port of Winchelsea. His impeccable Tory credentials, strong Oxford background and friendship with the High Church leaders Lords Nottingham (Daniel Finch†) and Rochester (Laurence Hyde†) and other prominent Tory figures would certainly have endeared him to the new administration. He was not, however, a man in whom political emotion ran high. Rarely did he find the need to air his views in the extensive correspondence he kept up with friends and acquaintances, a sign, perhaps, of the fixity of his convictions. In the Commons he was never more than a passive observer of proceedings, and the presence of others of his surname in the chamber makes it impossible to assign to him with any certainty actions recorded in the Journals. At first Clarke was a loyal Harleyite, adopting the same path of moderation as taken by his other Tory friends now in office such as (Sir) Simon Harcourt I*. Nottingham had marked him as a possible supporter over the 'Scotch Plot', and although his support for the Tack was considered 'doubtful' in October the following year, he did not vote for it in the division of 28 Nov. 1704.[8]

With the approach of the general election of 1705 Clarke accepted the offer of a seat at East Looe from his great friend Bishop Trelawny of Exeter, one of the lord treasurer's (Sidney Godolphin†) chief electoral managers in the west. He had also been in the running for one of the Oxford University seats until shortly before the election, when he withdrew. In the weeks which followed, however, as the ministry was refashioned along Whig lines, friction arose between Clarke and his political masters over the proposed removal of the Tory admiral Sir George Rooke* from the Prince's council. Clarke, clearly anxious to protect Tory brethren, and in a sense following the Queen's known dislike of the new Whig appointments being forced upon her, surreptitiously obtained the Prince's signature to a new commission in which Rooke was retained. Having inquired of her husband as to how Rooke's name had come to be included, the Queen apprised Godolphin on 6 June that

when it was brought to him to sign, Mr Clarke told him it was the same as the old one, only with the name of Mr Walpole (Robert II*) in instead of Mr Brydges (Hon. James*), which the Prince says he did not then reflect upon, always looking upon Sir G. Rooke to be entirely out of service, but remembering since he signed the commission what Mr Clarke had said, he intended if I had not spoke to him to have inquired into this matter and ordered a new commission to be drawn, leaving out Sir G. Rooke.

In conclusion the Queen promised Godolphin that she would use her 'utmost endeavours' to induce the Prince to dismiss Clarke. The Rooke affair was apparently not the only reason for royal and ministerial dissatisfaction with Clarke's conduct in office. A few days later the Duke of Marlborough (John Churchill†) wrote to his wife indicating there were other sources of irritation: 'If [Clarke] commits so many unreasonable things, why is not [the Queen] acquainted with them, for she told [Godolphin] and myself that she would take the first occasion of putting him out.' In the preparations for the election Clarke had tried to urge the Prince to dissuade the Whig deputy lord warden from displacing three Tory MPs from their Cinque Port constituencies. Similarly, his own recent candidacy at Oxford University, apparently without the ministry's blessing, may have suggested that he was aligning himself more overtly with the forces of High Toryism with whom he was known to have some sympathy. Clarke remained in office, though it was clear he was by now a depreciating asset. Recrimination against him continued. Marlborough wrote to his Duchess on 20 Aug. denying any responsibility for Clarke's appointment as the Prince's secretary and adding, 'I always though[t] him a dangerous man'. Ill-feeling between Clarke and the Duke surfaced in the early summer months of 1704 when Clarke sought permission to sell the judge-advocate's place. A combination of procrastination and mislaid correspondence had stretched Clarke's patience to the point where he had written testily to the Duke in a way that reflected against the ministers: 'I am unfortunate enough to be denied what is granted every day to others who have not been longer in the service of the crown, nor served it with more faithfulness and diligence.' Towards the end of September 1705, as the lines were drawn for the contest over the Speakership, Anthony Hammond* heard that Clarke 'will quit his place, some say that he may be free in his vote upon that question, but I have not any certain grounds that this is the motive'. As the new session drew near, Clarke made no secret of his intention to oppose the Court and support William Bromley II*. Nothing, it seems, could induce him to follow the Harleyites. Five days before the opening of Parliament he wrote to his old friend and drinking companion, Colonel (Sidney) Godolphin*: 'I am afraid whoever is here will meet with uneasiness enough to make them wish themselves away, though perhaps one would be vexed as much to be absent when one could contribute to the helping a friend out of difficulty.' A day or two later, when approached by the Prince for his vote, Clarke refused to promise it. It was generally assumed that his dismissal from the Prince's service came swiftly after his vote against the Court on 25 Oct. But according to his own account, and one or two contemporary reports, he had actually received the first intimation of his dismissal that morning, beforehand, in the lobby of the House from the Prince's treasurer, Edward Nicholas*, another Tory friend. The drama was complicated by the arrival of a second, countermanding, message just as Clarke was being acquainted with the first. However, when urged by Nicholas soon afterwards to confirm the rescission, the Prince merely 'sat silent for some time, and then said since it was done it could not be helped'. It can be seen in retrospect that Clarke had been deliberately distancing himself from the Godolphin ministry as increasingly it looked to the Whigs for support. Whether Godolphin had wished to appease the Prince in retaining a faithful servant is uncertain, but Clarke's opposition to the Court over the Speakership was the last straw for the lord treasurer, whose intention was clearly to use Clarke, currently the most conspicuous of Tory dissidents, as a scapegoat while other errant office-holders were proceeded against more cautiously.[9]

Thereafter, Clarke always refused to wait upon the Prince, and in fact they never saw each other again. It was not until 1710 that he resumed his attendances at court on reappointment to office. During the intervening years he was able to settle more permanently in the house he had had built for himself in the grounds of All Souls. Having also sold his post as judge-advocate, he now enjoyed being 'entirely my own master'. Greater leisure did not encourage his more active participation in parliamentary affairs, however. In the summer and autumn of 1706 he undertook an extensive tour of the Low Countries, arriving in the midst of celebrations of Marlborough's recent victory at Ramillies. He resumed his studies in civil law, obtaining the degree of DCL in 1708. His estrangement from the Godolphin ministry effectively precluded Bishop Trelawny from nominating him again to the East Looe seat in the 1708 general election, and he made no attempt to secure re-election elsewhere. In the next election, he was again widely tipped as a suitable successor to the aged Sir William Whitelocke* at Oxford University. But as was observed by Dr Gardiner, the warden of All Souls, it was Clarke's 'modesty', his unwillingness to be the cause of electoral strife between the colleges, that kept Whitlock in place.[10]

An experienced administrator and a much respected Tory figure who had been a martyr to his principles, Clarke was assured of a place in Robert Harley's* new ministry. In December 1710 he was brought back into office as a lord of the Admiralty, the appointment being made, as he recalled, 'without my asking or knowing of it till it was done'. It seems that he had been earmarked by Harley for the post some time before, and reports had circulated prior to the dissolution that Clarke was to be included in a newly constituted Admiralty board. When the appointment was announced, his old friend Harcourt, the new lord keeper, declared, 'I rejoice that Dr Clarke is made one of the Admiralty. I wish all other offices were filled with as good men.' Abel Boyer later noted that in view of the circumstances of Clarke's ejection from office by Godolphin, 'his preferment was now thought to be a piece of justice'. Clarke remained without a seat in Parliament until the death of his old patron and friend Lord Rochester in May 1711 allowed him to succeed Rochester's heir, Lord Hyde (Henry*), at Launceston. His regard for the Earl had been strong, and in his memoir he observed that, had Rochester lived, the last years of the Queen's reign 'would have passed more to her satisfaction and her people's than they did'. At the Admiralty he shouldered much of the burden of work owing to the absenteeism of the other commissioners. He saw a simple irony in the current political difficulties of ending the war and obtaining a satisfactory peace, remarking to Colonel Godolphin in October: 'we have a great many people who can't bear the mention of a peace, and yet are endeavouring to make it impossible for us to carry on the war'. Involved as he was in these larger concerns, the unseemly manoeuvrings begun at Oxford at the end of 1712 to ensure that the lord keeper's son, young Simon Harcourt III*, was chosen at the next election did not win his approval. He trenchantly stated his position to Dr Charlett, the master of University College:

I am not much concerned at anybody's mortification when a worthy man is chosen; I rather congratulate my friends, that they will neither suffer themselves to be driven, nor led, but follow their own judgments and inclinations. I have all my lifetime hated a trick and think nothing worth playing one, which makes me a stranger to the practices which you say begin very early. I wish the peace of Europe, the peace of my country, and of the university in particular, and can never bring myself to be fond of those who would disturb any of them.

In Parliament he voted on 18 June 1713 in favour of the French commerce bill.[11]

For reasons which are unclear Clarke was not re-elected for Launceston in 1713, and seems to have shown no interest in pursuing alternative seats. He gave only fleeting attention in his memoir to the heady party clashes of the last years of the reign, and scarcely mentioned the change of dynasty. Perhaps, on looking back, his dismissal from the Admiralty soon after George I's accession assumed an inevitability amid the sweeping reversal of party fortune inaugurated in the autumn of 1714, and as such hardly worth comment. Although his intentions were 'to live quietly and out of public business', his description of himself in December as an 'exile' hinted at regret at no longer having a place at the centre of events. Apart from a two- or three-month spell in France in the summer of 1715, when he frequently visited Lord Bolingbroke (Henry St. John II*), he spent the next two or so years mostly at Oxford. There he found more time for involvement in various projects for the restoration and architectural enrichment of his college. Even while at the Admiralty he had taken the opportunity to acquire marble from Genoa for the adornment of the college chapel. But his most significant long-term work for the university was undertaken as an executor, along with Sir George Beaumont, 4th Bt.*, and Bromley, of Dr John Radcliffe's* will, which provided for a new library and other buildings.[12]

In December 1717 Clarke was finally elected for the University at a by-election following the death of Whitlock. Confinement at Oxford had become 'less agreeable' to him, and his new duties were a welcome respite. As a moderate Tory he was a consistent, if quiescent, opponent of the Whig regime. In these later years he was afflicted by the deaths of many of his old friends: 'it is a taking away of comfort and assistance when one most needs them'. In July 1727 he mourned the passing of Lord Harcourt (Simon I), 'one of the oldest acquaintances I had in the world'. He and Clarke had intended later that year to dine together in celebration of their 50 years' acquaintanceship, 'but it pleased God to order it otherwise'. Clarke died on 22 Oct. 1736 and was buried in the chapel of All Souls. He left a large part of his fortune and collections to Worcester College, with generous bequests to All Souls and Stone's Hospital.[13]

[1] *HMC Popham*, 259–60. [2] Ibid. 262, 278, 282–3, 285; *CSP Dom.* 1690–1, p. 20; 1691–2, p. 165; *Bull. IHR*, xiv. 183; Luttrell, *Brief Relation*, vi. 666. [3] *CSP Dom.* 1691–2, pp. 112–13; E. G. W. Bill, *Q. Anne Churches*, p. xxiii. [4] E. Suss. RO, Winchelsea ct. bk. WIN 60, p. 81. [5] *HMC Popham*, 261–8; *Cal. Treas. Bks.* viii. 289. [6] *HMC Popham*, 268–82; Centre Kentish Stud. Stanhope mss U1590/053/1, James Vernon I* to Alexander Stanhope, 1 Apr., 27 May 1690; Trinity, Dublin, Clarke mss 749/2/194, Thomas Coningsby* to Clarke, 23 Sept. 1690; *CSP Dom.* 1691–2, p. 165; Boston Pub. Lib. Mass. ms K. 5. 4, Clarke to Athlone, 3 July 1694. [7] Bodl. Carte 79, f. 663; *HMC Downshire*, i. 559; Add. 9732, ff. 238, 262. [8] Add. 9732, f. 262; *HMC Popham*, 282–3; *Bull. IHR*, xiv. 169; *Cal. Treas. Bks.* xvii. 86; Luttrell, v. 176; Ranke, v. 325. [9] Egerton 2618, f. 191; 'Collectanea Trelawniana', p. 283, Atterbury to Bp. Trelawny, 21 Apr. 1705 (Speck trans.); Add. 28052, f. 110; 28070, f. 8; 61285, ff. 56–62; *Marlborough–Godolphin Corresp.* 447, 481; E. Gregg, *Q. Anne*, 200; *HMC Cowper*, iii. 64; *HMC Popham*, 283; Bodl. Ballard 17, f. 86; Luttrell, v. 605; *HMC Portland*, iv. 268; Univ. Kansas Spencer Research Lib. Simpson–Methuen corresp. C163, John Methuen* to Sir William Simpson, 30 Oct. 1705; BL, Trumbull Add. mss 98, John Bridges to Trumbull, 31 Oct. 1705; *Bull. IHR*, xxxvii. 29–30. [10] *HMC Popham*, 283–4; Add. 28052, ff. 133–4; Ballard 20, f. 22. [11] Luttrell, vi. 633, 666; Add. 28052, f. 146; 70421, newsletters 19 Aug., 16 Dec. 1710; *HMC Popham*, 283, 285; Ballard 10, f. 123; 20, f. 78; Boyer, *Anne Annals*, ix. 279; *Bull. IHR*, xvii. 17. [12] *HMC Popham*, 285–6; *DNB*; *VCH Oxon.* iii. 180, 184, 190; I. Guest, *Dr John Radcliffe and His Trust*, 132–4, 136. [13] *HMC Popham*, 286–9; Egerton 2540, ff. 568, 610; E. Craster, *MIs All Souls'*, Oxford, 21.

A. A. H.

CLARKE, Sir Gilbert (c.1645–1701), of Somershall Hall, Brampton, and Chilcote, Derbys.

DERBYSHIRE 1685–1687, 1689–1698

b. c.1645, o. surv. s. of Godfrey Clarke of Somershall by 1st w. Elizabeth, da. of Sir Thomas Milward of Eaton Dovedale, Derbys. *educ.* Univ. Coll. Oxf. matric. 12 July 1661, aged 16; I. Temple 1667. *m.* (1) 20 Apr. 1661, Jane (*d.* 1667), da. and h. of Robert Byerley of Hornby, Yorks., 1da. (*d.v.p.*); (2) 6 July 1671, Barbara (*d.* 1687), da. of George Clerke† of Watford, Northants., 2s. 2da.; (3) 1691, Frances, da. of Richard Legh† of Lyme, Cheshire, wid. of Robert Tatton of Wythenshawe, Cheshire, sis. of Peter† and Thomas Legh II*. *s.p. suc.* fa. 1670; kntd. 2 Mar. 1671.[1]

Sheriff, Derbys. 1675–6.

Clarke's parents married on 26 Apr. 1644, making plausible a birth date, based on university admission, of 1645. By 1690 Clarke had sat in two Parliaments and had gained wide experience, especially in the Convention of 1689, of which he had been an active Member. He was well placed to be knight of the shire, possessing large estates in the north of Derbyshire, near Chesterfield, and a seat in the south of the county, on the border with Leicestershire. Furthermore, he was well versed in local affairs, having first been appointed to the commission of the peace in 1672. A consensus seems to have emerged in local politics in 1690, highlighted by an agreement to regulate the shrievalty which was signed by all shades of gentry opinion, including Clarke. In such a climate, Clarke had many qualities which appealed to the freeholders, not the least being that he represented continuity and stability. Hence he was returned with Henry Gilbert* in the election of 1690.[2]

On a list of the new Parliament, annotated by Lord Carmarthen (Sir Thomas Osborne†), Clarke was classed as a Tory with a query as to whether he was also a supporter of the Court, although another list made no quibble on this point. In the session of 1690, he was appointed to three drafting committees during April, and then on the 26th given leave to go into the country for three weeks. In the next session, on 1 Nov. 1690, Clarke was teller against a motion that two men arrested for breach of privilege should be heard by counsel. His name also appeared on a list of supporters drawn up by Carmarthen in December 1690, probably in case an attack was made on his ministerial position. Robert Harley* classed him as a Country supporter in April 1691. On 2 Feb. 1692 he was a teller in favour of adding a proviso at the report of the bill preventing gunpowder from being stored near the Tower. The session of 1692–3 saw the first positive evidence that Clarke had become disenchanted with the ministry: on 18 Nov. 1692 he acted as a teller for committing a Country measure, the treason trials bill. On 18 Feb. 1693 his request for leave of absence for three weeks was only granted after a division by 113 votes to 72. Presumably he did not return, as the session ended on 14 Mar.

In the following session of 1693–4 Clarke was granted leave for a fortnight on 18 Dec., only six weeks after the beginning of the session. However, he was back in attendance by 17 Jan. 1694, when he told for an attempt to omit from a clause in the land tax bill words relating to hospitals. A letter he wrote on 27 Jan. 1694 emphasizes his commitment to the Country opposition. His comment on the resolutions of the previous day, criticizing the royal veto of a place bill, was that 'some of the Commons that be dissatisfied propose it in another shape than it is now in – being now meek and [?–] good boys', a reference to the subsequent watering down of the address. On 28 Feb. he was again granted leave of absence, this time for three weeks. The reason for these increasingly frequent requests was ill-health. On 21 Mar. Clarke wrote from Derbyshire to Robert Harley* to acknowledge the great favour 'you did me in being instrumental to save my life' by supporting his application for leave due to 'my cold and indisposition'. The letter concluded with the hope that he would soon be recovered sufficiently to wait 'on you once more into the lobby against an excise'. Harley was probably crucial in securing Clarke's leave, for on the day it was granted the Commons ordered a call for 14 Mar. in hopes to increase the opposition vote against the ministerial proposals for an excise. During the summer of 1694 Clarke ventured northwards to offer moral support to his brother-in-law, Peter Legh, who was standing trial on treason charges in Chester. The subsequent collapse of the trial encouraged the opposition to attack the ministry's handling of the whole affair. On 22 Nov. 1694, in a debate on the state of the nation, Clarke provided first-hand evidence of the scandalous proceedings of the judges. He then told against the motion that the chief prosecution witness, John Lunt, be ordered to attend the following day. Later in the session he was still corresponding with Henry Prescott, registrar of Chester, on the matter of witnesses in the case.[3]

In 1695 Clarke was re-elected for the county, this time in company with the Marquess of Hartington (William Cavendish*). In the opening session Clarke was appointed in second place to the committee of elections and privileges on 25 Nov. 1695. He was forecast as a likely opponent of the Court in the divisions on 31 Jan. 1696 over the proposed council of trade, was blacklisted for having refused the Association at first, and was recorded as voting against fixing the price of guineas at 22s. This pattern suggests that he had become a solid Country Tory, and indeed on 1 Feb. Clarke wrote to Lord Huntingdon to report with pleasure the rejection of the Abjuration and election of a new commission of accounts, expressing the hope that 'this Parliament will appear good Englishmen'. On 2 Apr. 1696 he was given leave of absence, it being near the end of the session. However, after only a month of the next session he was ready to state his disappointment about the proceedings of the House: 'By the votes you will see that there is a great majority who choose rather to be courtiers than neglected country gentlemen.' Not surprisingly, he voted on 25 Nov. 1696 against the attainder of Sir John Fenwick†. On 17 Dec. he was granted leave of absence for three weeks, covering the Christmas recess. He returned to Westminster in the new year, but was inactive in Parliament. Possibly he was already weary of attendance, for on 27 Feb. 1697 he predicted that he would be in the country before Easter, and was granted leave again on 18 Mar. His attendance in the last session of this Parliament is confirmed by a letter of 25 Dec. 1697 to inform Hartington of the bill to prevent correspondence with King James, which was before the Commons. It is likely, however, that illness severely curtailed his activities in this session as he was granted leave of absence on 13 Apr. 1698 in order to recover his health. The last comment on his parliamentary career may be left to a contemporary, who on a list drawn up around September 1698 classed him as a supporter of the Country party.[4]

Although Clarke did not stand for election again, his interest and advice were eagerly sought after. He was instrumental in ensuring that Thomas Coke* succeeded him as knight of the shire, helping Coke and his agents in the organization of their campaign, and seeking the withdrawal of John Curzon* in order to create a united Tory interest. Clarke was not averse to offering the new Member advice on local legislation like the Derwent navigation bill and on the constitution of the county commission of the land tax. Moreover, the real extent of his political interest in Derbyshire was only revealed by the evidence surviving from the shire election of January 1701. Initially, many friends hoped that he could be persuaded to join Coke in opposition to Lords Hartington and Roos (John Manners*). Ill-health prevented this from being a realistic option. Nevertheless, Clarke was an indefatigable correspondent in Coke's interest, especially in sending agents into Scarsdale hundred. After Coke's defeat, he tried to find him another seat, by acting as an intermediary with Peter Legh in case a vacancy arose at Newton. Clarke died on 30 May 1701. At a crucial meeting called to adopt his son Godfrey* as a candidate in opposition to Coke in 1710, Sir John Harpur, 4th Bt., noted with approval that 'the country never was better served than by Sir Gilbert Clarke'. Most of Clarke's estate passed to his son, Godfrey, although the Kentish property inherited from Francis Clerke I* went to his second son, Gilbert.[5]

[1] *Fam. Min. Gent.* (Harl. Soc. xxxvii), 335–6; *Vis. Northants.* (Harl. Soc. lxxxvii), 53; info. from Dr D. F. Lemmings and Derby Local Stud Lib.; E. Newton, *Lyme Letters*, 200; E. Newton, *House of Lyme*, ped. [2] *VCH Leics.* iii. 185; Sir G. Sitwell, *Letters of Sitwells and Sacheverells*, ii. 17–19. [3] *Lyme Letters*, 200; Add. 70217, Clarke to Harley, 21 Mar. 1693–4; H. Horwitz, *Parl. and Pol. Wm. III*, 127, 129; Bodl. Carte 130, f. 353; *Prescott Diary*, 903, 907, 909. [4] Add. 70018, f. 103, Lady Anne Pye to Abigail Harley, 4 Nov. 1695; Huntington Lib. Hastings mss HA 1449, 1451–2, Clarke to Huntingdon, 1 Feb. 1695[–6], 27 Feb. 1696[–7], 25 Dec. 1697; *HMC Cowper*, ii. 367. [5] BL, Lothian mss, Clarke to Coke, 21 July 1698, 8, 23, 25 Dec. 1700, 4 Jan. 1700[–1], Robert Harding to same, 21 Oct., 15, 25 Nov. 1700; *HMC Cowper*, ii. 383, 396, 410, 411, 413, 421–2; iii. 89; PCC 110 Dyer.

S. N. H.

CLARKE, Godfrey (c.1678–1734), of Chilcote and Somershall, Derbys.

DERBYSHIRE 1710–25 Mar. 1734

b. c.1678, 1st s. of Sir Gilbert Clarke* by his 2nd w. *educ.* Rugby 1690; Magdalen, Oxf. matric. 25 June 1695, aged 16. *m.* c.13 June 1706 (with £8,000), Lady Catherine Stanhope (d. 1728), da. of Philip, 2nd Earl of Chesterfield, *s.p. suc.* fa. 30 May 1701.[1]

Sheriff, Derbys. 29 Nov.–6 Dec. 1708.

There are several dates of birth for a Godfrey Clarke in the registers of Old Brampton, Derbyshire, but none tallies with his age at matriculation. Clarke's first foray into county politics was as an agent for his ailing father in the election of January 1701. He was sent to rally the family's tenants in Scarsdale hundred in support of Thomas Coke's* candidature. In the election held in December 1701 he was again active, this time in support of Coke and John Curzon* against the Whig Lords Hartington (William Cavendish*) and Roos (John Manners*). For the next few years Clarke consolidated his position among the Derbyshire elite, being named as a deputy-lieutenant in 1702, nominated as sheriff for 1705–6 (he had the influence to avoid being pricked), and contracting a favourable marriage in 1706 which connected him with the peerage.[2]

The opportunity for a career in Parliament came in 1710. Clarke's brother-in-law, Coke, had alienated a wide section of county opinion by his conduct in the Commons, and among Tories resentment was running particularly high against him after he had supported the impeachment of Dr Sacheverell. At a meeting held at the time of the assizes in early August Clarke was nominated to stand with John Curzon. He 'seemed to decline it some time, but soon stood up and said, since it was the unanimous desire of the gentlemen he would serve them'. Despite some opposition, he did not back down. There were differing reports as to whether Clarke had planned to replace Coke as the county Member, but all agreed on his ambition. As Coke's sister put it, 'it suits much with his inclinations, and I doubt he is too far engaged to withdraw'. Eventually, Coke gave up the fight and Clarke and Curzon were returned without a poll.[3]

Not surprisingly, given the circumstances of Clarke's election, the 'Hanover list' classed him as a Tory. In his first session in the Commons he twice acted as a teller: on 10 Jan. 1711, in company with the Country Whig Edward Wortley Montagu*, for referring to committee the Tregony election petition; and on 26 Jan. on a procedural motion that all committees be adjourned. His commitment to the Tory cause was reaffirmed when he signed a circular letter inviting Sir Thomas Cave, 3rd Bt.*, to stand for the vacant Leicestershire seat occasioned by Lord Granby's succession in February 1711 to the dukedom of Rutland. Clarke also appeared on a list of 'worthy patriots' who had detected the mismanagements of the late ministry.

The election of George Clarke* in May 1711 makes it difficult to distinguish his activities for the remainder of this Parliament. Re-elected in 1713 with Curzon, Clarke was classed as a Tory on the Worsley list. On two further lists, drawn up in 1715, he was classed as a Tory, and he continued to sit as such until his death on 25 Mar. 1734, which occurred after he had been adopted as a candidate for the forthcoming election. His estates in Derbyshire and Staffordshire, valued at £6,000 p.a. fell to his nephew Godfrey Clarke, son of his deceased brother, Gilbert, of Ulcombe, Kent.[4]

[1] IGI, Derbys.; Luttrell, *Brief Relation*, vi. 56; Add. 15556, f. 37. [2] BL, Lothian mss, Sir Gilbert Clarke to Coke, 25 Dec. 1700, Godfrey Clarke to same, n.d., John Beresford to same, 25 Nov. 1701. [3] *HMC Cowper*, iii. 86, 89–98, 170; Add. 70421, Dyer's newsletter 8 Aug. 1710; Bagot mss at Levens Hall, William Bromley II* to James Grahme*, 13 Aug. 1710; *HMC Portland*, iv. 612. [4] Leics. RO, Braye mss 2842, Ld. Denbigh to Cave, 6 Feb. [1711]; Add. 15556, ff. 34–35; *Derby Mercury*, 28 Feb., 28 Mar. 1734; *Gent. Mag.* 1734, p. 165; PCC 79 Ockham.

S. N. H.

CLARKE, Thomas (c.1672–1754), of Brickendon, Herts.

HERTFORD   1705–1710, 24 May 1715–1722
                   22 Jan. 1723–1741

b. c.1672, 1st s. of Sir Edward Clarke of St. Vedast's, London, ld. mayor of London, by his 2nd w. Jane, da. of Richard Clutterbuck. *educ.* St. Catharine's, Camb. 1689; M. Temple 1690, called 1706, bencher 1723, treasurer 1731. *m.* 9 Jan. 1699, Elizabeth, da. of Alexander Pinfold of Hoxton, Mdx., *s.p. suc.* fa. 1703; kntd. 24 July 1706.[1]

Freeman, Hertford 1704; commr. charitable uses, Hertford 1708.[2]

Clarke's father was elected sheriff of London in 1690, when he was described as 'of the same temper with the mayor' Sir Thomas Pilkington†, an indication of strong Whig and possibly also Dissenting sympathies. Sir Edward, whose first wife was the daughter of a Puritan divine, himself became lord mayor in 1696. In 1655 he bought the estate at Brickendon, just three miles from Hertford. According to a contemporary historian of the county, the manor was 'reckoned one of the delightful seats of this neighbourhood, having to the front a dry pleasant soil towards Hertford, and on the contrary view woods at half a mile distance, with vistas all pointing to the House'. Thomas Clarke thus inherited the mantle of the country gentleman, and took a prominent role in promoting charitable works in his locality. His neighbour Lady Cowper recorded that he 'built a gallery in the church, set up chimes in the steeple, puts 90 poor children to school, gives bibles, catechisms etc, at Christmas distributes half-peck loaves and two oxen among the poor'. Such philanthropy is reminiscent of that of his brother-in-law, Maynard Colchester*, and Clarke may be the 'Thomas Clerk' who was named with Colchester in 1701 among the founding members of the Society for the Propagation of the Gospel. The two men also shared an interest in landscape gardening, and had also both been educated at the Middle Temple. Unlike Colchester, however, Clarke seems to have been active at the bar and to have played a leading role at his inn of court. His legal training at the Middle Temple may well have brought him into contact with William Cowper*, with whom he evidently had much in common, and it was on the old Cowper interest of the inhabitant and Nonconformist vote at Hertford that Clarke stood for election in 1705 against the Tackers Charles Caesar* and Richard Goulston*. Clarke petitioned against the latter's return, and after a hearing by the elections committee was declared by the House on 6 Dec. to have properly carried the election. Lady Cowper observed that his enemies had been unable to find any 'matter to upbraid him with, unless his good works', and that when the House's decision reached the borough there was rejoicing with bell-ringing and bonfires, even though at the election itself some of the 'brutes' who partook of his charity had 'set up a cry "no gallery, no chimes, no beef, no bread"'.[3]

In the House Clarke acted with the Court, supporting it in February during the proceedings on the 'place clause' of the regency bill, though it is difficult to distinguish his activity from that of the other Clarkes sitting at this time. He was knighted on 24 July 1706, after presenting an address from his borough congratulating the Queen on the Duke of Marlborough's success in arms. His new title makes identification thereafter more easy, but the fact that he made no impact upon the records of the House other than to be granted leave of absence on 9 Dec. 1707 suggests that he was far from being a prominent or active Member. In early 1708, and again after his re-election later the same year, Clarke was listed as a Whig, and during the 1708 Parliament he followed the party line, supporting in 1709 the naturalization of the Palatines and voting a year later for the impeachment of Sacheverell. He served as a teller on 10 Mar. 1709 for committing the bill for restraining buildings on new foundations. He was defeated by the resurgent Tory interest in 1710, despite attempts to poll 'occasional inhabitants' by sending 'his own wagon down with goods to furnish houses and rooms for such voters two or three days before' the election, and he did not regain his seat until after the Hanoverian succession, when he generally acted with the government.[4]

Clarke died on 26 Oct. 1754, and 'whereas I am likely to depart this life without leaving any issue of my body behind me', bequeathed his estate to his niece Jane, wife of Thomas Morgan† of Ruperra, Glamorgan. He had owned stock in the Bank of England (of which his father had been a director) worth at least £2,000 by 1710, and left the same sum, together with the rest of his estate, in the hands of two trustees, one of whom, his 'cousin' Bostock Toller, was a prominent Hertford alderman who had given and gathered evidence on his behalf during the election dispute of 1705. Clarke also left other minor property to his cousin William Freke of Warmington, Wiltshire, who was possibly a kinsman of Thomas Freke II* of Hannington, Wiltshire.[5]

[1] J. R. Woodhead, *Rulers of London* (London and Mdx. Arch. Soc.), 47; Guildhall Lib. ms 1103/1 (unfol.), MI of Sir Edward Clarke. [2] Herts. RO, Hertford bor. recs. 21/39, 5/35. [3] *Portledge Pprs.* 73; Salmon, *Herts.* (1727), 40; Clutterbuck, *Herts.* ii. 188; Luttrell, *Brief Relation*, iii. 195; Herts. RO, Panshanger mss D/EP F31, Lady Cowper's commonplace bk. pp. 106, 167; *CSP Dom.* 1700–2, p. 358. [4] *London Gazette*, 22–25 July 1706; Hertford bor. recs. 23/363, 'defence of the mayor', 1715. [5] PCC 37 Paul; *CJ*, xv. 54; Hertford. bor. recs. 23/317, order by Clarke, 15 Nov. 1705.

M. J. K.

CLAVELL, Edward (1676–1738), of Smedmore, Dorset.

WEYMOUTH AND MELCOMBE REGIS 24 Jan. 1709–1710

b. 19 Jan. 1676, 1st s. of Walter Clavell, merchant, of Bengal, India by his 2nd w. Martha, da. of Thomas Woodruff, merchant, of London. *educ.* St. Paul's 1686–93. *m.* (1) Jane, da. and h. of Sir Edward Littleton, merchant, of London, pres. of Bengal, *s.p.*; (2) settlement 10 Nov. 1717, Elizabeth, da. of George Damer of Dorchester, Dorset and aunt of Joseph Damer†, 1st Earl of Dorchester, 4s. 4da. *suc.* fa. 1678.

Sheriff, Dorset 1702–3.

Clavell was born in India, where his father, a younger son of an old Dorset family, had gone to make his fortune. Although Clavell's father inherited the family seat of Smedmore in 1671, he showed no desire to leave India, where he remained till his death. The family later returned to England and Clavell was sent to school in London. He stood unsuccessfully for Corfe Castle in 1698, but is not known to have made another attempt to enter Parliament until the general election of 1708, when he was narrowly defeated because the Earl of Shaftesbury (Anthony Ashley*) gave his interest to George Churchill*, a Tory. But Clavell took the seat without a contest at a by-election the following year. He made little mark in Parliament, apart from voting for the impeachment of Dr Sacheverell in 1710, and stood down at the general election of that year. He was buried at Winfrith on 9 Sept. 1738.[1]

[1] Hutchins, *Dorset*, i. 566–7.

P. W.

CLAYTON, Sir Robert (1629–1707), of Old Jewry, London and Marden Park, Godstone, Surr.

LONDON	1679 (Mar.)–1681 (Mar.)
	1689–1690
BLETCHINGLEY	1690–1695
LONDON	1695–1698
BLETCHINGLEY	1698–1700
LONDON	1701 (Feb.)–1702
BLETCHINGLEY	1 Dec. 1702–1705
LONDON	1705–16 July 1707

b. 29 Sept. 1629, 1st s. of John Clayton, carpenter, of Bulwick, Northants. by Alice, da. of Thomas Abbot of Gretton, Northants. *m.* 26 Dec. 1660, Martha (d. 1705), da. and coh. of Perient Trott, merchant, of London, 1s. *d.v.p. suc.* partner John Morris† in Bucks. estate 1682; kntd. 30 Oct. 1671.

Member, Scriveners' Co. 1658, asst. 1670, master 1671–2, transferred to Drapers' Co. 1679, master 1680–1; alderman, London 1670–83, 1689–d., sheriff 1671–2, ld. mayor 1679–80; gov. Irish Soc. 1692–1706.

Member, Hudson's Bay Co. 1676, treasurer 1678; asst. R. African Co. 1681; dir. Bank of Eng. (with statutory intervals) 1702–d.[1]

Member, New England Co. 1683; gov. Bridewell Hosp. 1689; pres. Hon. Artillery Co. 1690–1703; St. Thomas' Hosp. 1692–d.; vice-pres. London corp. of poor 1698.

Commr. customs 1689–97, taking subscriptions to Bank of Eng. 1694, Greenwich Hosp. 1695; trustee, receiving loan to Emperor 1706.[2]

Lauded by John Toland as 'the best and bravest of citizens that ever lived', Clayton retained a pre-eminent stature among City politicians. His reputation principally rested on the 'vast riches' he had built up as a banker, since he had risen from humble beginnings as 'a poor boy' of provincial origins to become a 'prince of citizens'. However, such success was not achieved without controversy, for he had been accused of defrauding his clients, most notably the Duke of Buckingham. Even though impartial observers such as John Evelyn respected his professional integrity, Clayton's leadership of the City Whigs ensured him further opprobrium, the Tory scribes deriding him as 'extorting Ishban'. Such slurs did not check his political activity, as he played a key role in the upheavals of the 1680s, moving for an Exclusion bill in the Oxford

Parliament, and taking steps to block the return of James II in December 1688. It was thus inevitable that after the Revolution he should be generally regarded as the father of the Whig cause in the capital.³

Such prominence brought Clayton early recognition from William III, who in April 1689 appointed him a customs commissioner. However, his relationship with the court had cooled before the end of the year, and on several subsequent occasions he was reported to have failed to represent the King's interests in the City. Moreover, in contrast to his prominence before the Revolution, after 1690 he rarely took centre stage at Westminster. Indeed, he appeared an advocate of moderation, particularly in religious affairs, and was attacked by Defoe for failing to give a stronger lead to the Nonconformist cause:

Nor's his religion less a masquerade,
He always drove a strange mysterious trade,
With decent zeal to church he'll gravely come
To praise that God which he denies at home.

However, Dissenter John Dunton was more sympathetic towards Clayton's stance, observing that

he is very much for unity and peace in the Church, but his opinion is that they might be preserved by a mutual forbearance in matters of ceremony, without a rigid imposition of them, for he knows it is equally superstitious to show too much zeal, either for or against them.

Clayton's politique position may have helped to marginalize him in party circles, but as the City's premier private banker, the patron of freethinkers such as Toland, Thomas Firmin and Matthew Tindal, and one of London's greatest philanthropists, he retained an undeniable influence on the affairs of the capital.⁴

Although Clayton and his Whig allies had enjoyed an unopposed return the year before, the City election of 1690 saw them unable to defeat their Tory challengers. Clayton actually obtained an adjournment of the poll so that he could travel to Bletchingley to ensure his return there. Ever since his purchase of the manor of Bletchingley in 1677 he had enjoyed a decisive influence over elections in the Surrey borough, but on this occasion he still had to overcome opposition from local Tories. His decision to travel to Bletchingley was subsequently vindicated by his poor performance at the London poll, where he could only manage sixth place. Further proof of Tory superiority in the capital came later that month when Clayton was removed as colonel of the City militia. Despite this disappointment, his financial standing in the capital was acknowledged by the Tory Sir Peter Rich†, who cited him as one of 'the men of interest . . . in common council and elsewhere'. However, he also noted that on a recent occasion Clayton and other Whig financiers had been slow to support a government loan, and hoped that their reticence might gain the Tories an advantage at court. Clayton in fact advanced loans totalling £1,500 in March 1690, but a banker of his stature was evidently expected to set a better example for his City colleagues.⁵

At the outset of the new Parliament Lord Carmarthen (Sir Thomas Osborne†) duly identified Clayton as a Whig, and in the ensuing first session party tensions prompted Sir Robert to play a prominent role in the Commons. On 8 Apr. controversy arose over his appointment to the committee to draft a bill to reverse the judgment of quo warranto against the London charter, a selection which recalled his role in the early 1680s as a member of the City committee to oppose the surrender of the charter. He subsequently spoke on 17 Apr. in favour of receiving a petition from the London sheriffs, and five days later sought to 'obviate all scandal' on that petition by asserting that it had been drafted in accordance with City procedures. He also took that opportunity to point out several 'defective' features of the bill, and warned that not all former officers should regain their places, observing that 'if all be restored that were before, you may see King James here again if the King go into Ireland'.⁶

Recent changes in the City lieutenancy caused further friction between the parties, and gave Clayton cause to vent his anger over his dismissal as militia colonel. On 24 Apr. he opposed a motion from Sir Thomas Clarges* to address the King with thanks for the recent alteration of the London lieutenancy, arguing that 'neither the ablest nor best men were added' and that 'many have had a hand in the worst things'. However, this attack was accompanied by a call for reconciliation, for he warned that 'divisions and parties never did good, nor ever will, of any church or party whatsoever'. Despite this plea, Clayton's dismissal continued to be a point of contention between rival factions, the Earl of Monmouth drawing attention to it on 7 May when the Lords sat in a committee of the whole on the City lieutenancy. Most significantly, Monmouth identified Clayton as a communicant of the Church of England, and lauded his actions in December 1688 as the man who 'went and prevented the body of the court of aldermen in waiting on the King [James]'. Such was the outcry over the dismissal that on 12 May the Lords requested the Commons to permit Clayton to appear before them to declare his 'knowledge' of the present lieutenancy.⁷

Only a few days after the end of the session Clayton

stood alongside Sir Thomas Pilkington† as a Whig candidate for the mayoralty. Clayton failed to be returned to the court of aldermen, but Pilkington emerged victorious as the London Whigs regained some of the ground recently lost to their rivals. However, in the absence of controversy over City politics, in the second session Clayton played a less prominent role, his significant activity being confined to appointment to a committee to draft a bill to regulate treason trials. His politics were subsequently confirmed in April 1691 by Robert Harley*, who identified him as a Court supporter.[8]

Having hitherto revealed only limited interest in investing in overseas commerce, prior to the third session of the 1690 Parliament Clayton attended meetings of the interlopers in the East India trade, and on 17 Oct. 1691 was appointed to their committee to draw up a bill for the establishment of a new company. Moreover, in the same month his proprietorial influence in the island of Bermuda was also highlighted, for its governor complained of rumours that 'Sir Robert orders and disposes everything here, even to the putting in and turning out of governors'. Clayton's first important action in the new session of Parliament was a motion on 20 Nov. for the reading of the petition of Richard Baldwin, a printer taken into custody for publishing an advice to the House on supplies. He subsequently proved a stubborn opponent of the Old East India Company, speaking 'strongly' against it on 27 Nov., and supporting on 2 Dec. the establishment of a new joint-stock company to regulate the trade. He opposed the company again on 18 Dec., and five days later spoke against its proposed security. A bill for the relief of the London orphans predictably received his steady support: he spoke in favour on 3 Dec., and on 29 Jan. 1692 assured a committee of the whole that the City was 'very willing' to satisfy the debt to the orphans. Moreover, on 11 Feb. he successfully moved that the City's waterbailage duty be applied to the fund for orphan relief. He was also concerned for the welfare of impoverished Huguenot refugees, reporting on 13 Feb. from the committee inquiring into their plight, and acting on 24 Feb. as chairman of the committee of the whole to consider a motion to address the King to secure aid for them. His only other significant parliamentary action was a tellership on 16 Feb. for the second reading of a clause to levy a duty on hunting.[9]

In 1692 Carmarthen included Clayton in his working list of government supporters, and Clayton was certainly active in promoting City loans, making personal advances totalling £3,000 in March and June of that year. Moreover, on 22 Feb. 1693 he loaned a further £2,000 in response to a direct appeal from the ministry to the London common council. On 27 Feb. he acted as a teller in support of hearing the City's counsel against another bill to relieve the London orphans, the party significance of which was indicated by the opposition of rival teller Sir William Prichard*, a City Tory. He did not feature prominently again in that session, and in the next his only important action was an appointment to the committee to draft another London orphans' bill. However, acting in his capacity as president of St. Thomas' Hospital, in January 1694 he lent his support to a petition to the Lords against the Southwark waterworks bill.[10]

In the course of 1692–3 no fewer than four parliamentary lists cited Clayton as a placeman, while another marked him as a Court supporter who held an office. Further evidence of his support for administration came in June 1694 when, despite the threat to his own City interests, he invested £2,000 in the newly founded Bank of England. Despite such backing, and his appointment as one of the commissioners to take the first Bank subscription, his position at the customs was threatened by a government review. After a meeting of ministers on 14 June, Sir John Somers* reported to the King that Clayton was regarded as of 'very little use' as a customs commissioner, a verdict endorsed by Sir John Trenchard* and the Duke of Shrewsbury. However, his value as a financier was acknowledged, Shrewsbury citing him as one of the 'eminent citizens . . . who all do, or should, promote loans and other services you may expect from the City'. Such utility ensured that Clayton's name did appear in the new commission issued in August, but his relationship with the Court continued to be a matter for speculation.[11]

Although Clayton had survived a major test of his political interest, he encountered further difficulties in the subsequent session. On 12 Mar. 1695 the Commons committee inquiring into allegations of bribery concerning the Orphans' Relief Act of 1694 presented their report, implicating him heavily in the scandal. Most damagingly, he was reported to have been present on 22 June 1694 when 1,000 guineas of City money was paid to the Speaker Sir John Trevor*, and 100 guineas passed to clerk of the House, Paul Jodrell. The committee had been unable to interview Clayton, for he was reported to be 'ill and out of town', and on 16 Mar. the House accordingly ordered him to attend to answer these charges. His testimony on 18 Mar. was reported to have only implicated a dead Member, and he subsequently escaped the censure of the House. However, his involvement in such corruption is further suggested by his will, for he bequeathed

£50 to Paul Jodrell, describing him as his 'loving friend'.[12]

Clayton was given little breathing space before the Upper House called him to account for his actions concerning the Orphans' Relief Act. The Lords were keen to investigate allegations that the corporation had secured the support of the Marquess of Normanby for the measure by a grant of City property, and that Normanby had also agreed to obstruct the Southwark waterworks bill. As chairman of the City lands committee, Clayton had evidently played an important role in the transaction, and on 10 and 11 Apr. the Commons granted the Lords permission to interview him. He subsequently put up a stubborn defence before the Upper House, declaring that the contract with Normanby had been signed to no other end than 'that they should make a bargain that should be for the interest of the City'. Although Clayton again escaped punishment, the damage inflicted on his reputation may have led to renewed reports in mid-April of the possible loss of his customs post. However, just before the end of the session, on 20 Apr., he appeared in the House in his official capacity, to present an account of gold and silver exports. Moreover, his appearance on a list drawn up by the beleaguered Treasury official Henry Guy* in this session suggests that at least some government officials regarded him as an ally.[13]

Despite these attacks Clayton could derive some satisfaction from the current strength of the City Whigs, whose growing influence had been demonstrated in March 1694 when he and other Whig leaders had been reappointed as militia colonels. At the parliamentary election of October 1695 the Whigs overcame all Tory opposition, thereby obviating any need for Clayton to seek election at Bletchingley. He subsequently failed to make any significant contribution to Commons business in the first session, although he was forecast as a likely supporter of the Court on 31 Jan. 1696 on a division concerning the proposed council of trade. In addition, he signed the Association on 27 Feb. and later voted for fixing the price of guineas at 22s. He was more conspicuous in the next session in connexion with fiscal matters, appointed to draft clauses to explain legislation for the prevention of abuses in the minting and circulation of public money. In addition, it was reported that he had brought in a petition calling for greater protection for trade, and in an official capacity on 11 Feb. 1697 he presented an account of informations concerning wool exports.[14]

At the very end of the 1696–7 session the Duke of Shrewsbury reported that the King was impatient with his financial backers, and had 'particularly named Sir Robert Clayton as one who neither attended the board, nor encouraged his service in the City by loan or subscription'. Within a few weeks Clayton had been dismissed from the customs commission, after having reportedly 'given great offence by his appearing to discourage the Exchequer bills'. However, the loss of his office appears to have galvanized his support for William, rather than created any antipathy towards him. In October he informed the lords justices that the City was prepared to advance the government £120,000, and also advised them how to allay mercantile concern for the repayment of the loan. Moreover, he was ready to employ £30,000 of his own fortune to pay off the troops, and in November was actively involved in preparations for the King's return to London. Despite such activity, the court still dragged its heels when he sought to extend his lease of the royal manor of Kennington, deferring its decision for nearly two years.[15]

In the third session of the 1695 Parliament Clayton distinguished himself as a supporter of the freethinkers by acting as a teller alongside Robert Molesworth* on 30 Mar. 1698 to defeat a motion to pass a bill for the suppression of blasphemy and profanity. His presidency of the Irish Society seems to have dictated other contributions to Commons business, for on 9 Apr. he reported from committee on a petition from the citizens of Derry requesting compensation for the town's losses during William's Irish campaigns. Moreover, after the House had agreed to seek the crown's support for the Derry petition, he twice reported, on 2 May and 23 June, from the committee to draft the address to the King. However, his principal concern at that time was undoubtedly the newly founded London corporation of the poor, of which he was the vice-president. One historian has suggested that his concurrent support for the Lustring Company was also motivated by a desire to employ the poor. Such concern was clearly demonstrated by a report on 16 Apr. that Clayton had taken part in an inquiry to establish the superior quality of domestically manufactured lustrings.[16]

Clayton's standing in the City was highlighted in May by his appointment as acting mayor in place of the ailing Sir Humphrey Edwin, and later that year he was praised by Toland, who observed that 'without your advice the most eminent of your fellow citizens will not administer their own share of the magistracy'. However, Clayton did not contest the City poll of 1698, resting content with an unopposed return at Bletchingley. His decision to stand aside may have been taken to allow other Whig candidates the opportunity to gain election, or may even have stemmed from weariness with politics. Ever since the

Revolution he had suffered from a kidney infection, and only a few months after the contest he confessed to his nephew that 'I grow old and cannot bear the fatigue of business as formerly'. On the other hand, political tensions within the Whig party may have forced him to step down. Despite his endeavours to rebuild his interest at court, observers still thought him estranged from the ministry, for at the outset of the first session a parliamentary list identified him as a Country supporter, and another forecast that he would oppose the standing army. On 17 Dec. he was appointed to the committee to draft the disbanding bill, but there is no record of his having voted against the Court in the key division of 18 Jan. 1699. During the session he was reported to be 'very busy' in support of the Irish Society in a property dispute with the bishop of Derry. As governor of the Society, he had petitioned the Lords on the matter in the previous Parliament, and did so again on 26 Apr., although with little success. Soon after the end of the session he was charged with 'peevishness' over the affair, and James Vernon I* thought him 'more inclined to provoke and embarrass, than do anything obliging'. He was also belligerent in the cause of the London corporation of the poor, clashing with Sir Francis Child* in May for allegedly discouraging the collection of the rate for its workhouse.[17]

Clayton remained largely inconspicuous in the next session. More industriously, in March 1700 he clearly supported the introduction of a bill to relieve the London poor, since his surviving papers include various drafts of that legislation. A parliamentary list of early 1700 suggested that he had yet to be reconciled with his former Whig allies, identifying him with the interest of the Old East India Company. Later that year he was reported to have backed the candidacy of the Tory (Sir) Charles Duncombe* for the City's mayoral contest, having been canvassed by an agent claiming to act in the name of the 2nd Earl of Sunderland. This rumour was regarded as highly suspect, and at the subsequent general election Clayton removed any doubts concerning his politics by standing for London alongside three Whig candidates. He managed to secure fourth place in the poll, but, as had been the case in 1695, his name featured at the head of the return. Further evidence of his support for the Whig cause had been supplied by the preceding Bletchingley election, when John Ward II* was returned, almost certainly on Clayton's interest. Some electors stubbornly voted for Clayton, but it was clear that he had wished to concentrate his efforts on the City contest.[18]

In the new Parliament Clayton's *rapprochement* with his former allies was quickly acknowledged, for his name appeared on a list of 22 Feb. 1701 as a likely supporter of the Court in agreeing with the resolution of the committee on supply to make good the funding on the 'Great Mortgage'. Returning to a favourite issue, on 25 Mar. he presented a bill to set the poor to work. More controversially, he was also bracketed with the Court in opposition to the Kentish Petitioners, and was accused of having suppressed a City address in their support. On 14 May he sought to play down the importance of a printed attack on the Commons on that issue, observing that the House 'did it too much honour to take notice of it', and that 'if he had had it, he would have dropped it in a place fit for it'. On 23 May he spoke against the 'inconveniences' of mortgaging public supplies to raise supplies for the civil list, and was praised by the Tory Sir Edward Seymour, 4th Bt.*, for speaking against his 'own interest' as a banker.[19]

At the election of November 1701 Clayton again appeared confident of standing in the City, since he did not seek a seat at Bletchingley. However, a controversy subsequently arose from reports that he had promoted John Toland as a candidate for the Surrey borough, an allegation which Toland vigorously denied. Toland actually thought that the story had been spread to impair Clayton's electoral chances in the capital, and insisted that his patron had given his interest at Bletchingley to 'an eminent citizen', i.e. John Ward II. The dispute appeared to have little impact on Clayton's City campaign, for he finished fourth, over 1,000 votes ahead of his nearest Tory rival. In the ensuing session he was named to the drafting committee on yet another bill to set the poor to work, and was the only Member appointed on 24 Jan. 1702 to prepare legislation to penalize 'incorrigible and dangerous rogues', which he subsequently presented as a bill to punish felons and their accessories. He also reported on 16 Mar. on a petition of six London parishes for a bill to oblige Jews to maintain their Protestant offspring, and later that day was appointed to the committee to draw up the measure.[20]

Clayton's identification with the City Whigs was confirmed by the Bank of England elections of 1702, when he became a director for the first time. However, he experienced several disappointments after Anne's accession, beginning with the loss of his colonelcy in the militia. He then seriously miscalculated when deciding not to secure a seat for himself at Bletchingley in the general election of 1702, for he could only manage fifth place at the parliamentary contest for London. Pre-election forecasts had predicted his return, but the scrutiny which followed the poll disqualified a sufficient number of his votes for

Sir Francis Child to finish ahead of him. This defeat proved particularly frustrating, for Clayton was evidently eager to promote the London corporation of the poor in the ensuing session. Among his papers is a short history of the workhouse, dated 5 Nov. 1702 and perhaps in his own hand, which sought to gain exemption for its governors from the penalties of the occasional conformity bill currently under consideration. The account concluded that the bill could 'prove of very fateful consequence to so good a work', thereby suggesting that Clayton was not totally insensitive to the Dissenting cause.[21]

Fortunately for Clayton, one of the Bletchingley seats was soon vacated on the death of John Evelyn I*, and in December 1702 he was back in the House after a convincing by-election victory. He failed to make any contribution to Commons business in the first session, but on 13 Feb. 1703 showed his Whig colours by voting to agree with the Lords' amendments to the bill to extend the time for taking the abjuration oath. The same month he was reported to have interceded on the City's behalf with Whig magnate Lord Wharton (Hon. Thomas*). In the second session he was active in sponsoring a bill to establish more corporations of the poor in the capital, presenting it to the Commons on 10 Jan. 1704. However, having faced increasing opposition for his workhouse scheme since its foundation in 1698, he met with further disappointment, for the bill was lost on a motion for its second reading. On a more successful note, in the third session he lent his support to a bill to separate the parishes of Horne and Bletchingley. His politics were consistent, since on 30 Oct. 1704 he was forecast as a probable opponent of the Tack, and on 28 Nov. he voted against the measure.[22]

At the ensuing general election Clayton initially sought a seat at Castle Rising, backed by the interest of the Howard family of Ashtead, Surrey. He himself owned lands in Norfolk, and he secured an unopposed return on 14 May 1705. He had already spurned the luxury of a victory at Bletchingley, allowing John Ward II to take his seat there, but campaigned hard in London, where he finished in fourth place as the Whigs gained full revenge for their electoral reverse of three years before. He chose to sit for the City rather than Castle Rising. The 3rd Lord Sunderland (Charles, Lord Spencer*) regarded his success as a gain for the Whigs, and Clayton accordingly voted on 25 Oct. 1705 for the Court candidate in the division for the Speakership. Moreover, the compiler of a parliamentary list alluded to his association with freethinkers such as Toland by citing him as 'No Church'.[23]

Clayton made little impact in the new Parliament, probably owing to ill-health. In early November he was reported to be 'so ill that his physicians have no hopes of his recovery', and in the following month he suffered the loss of his wife, who had been a constant source of care and support. Her death was said to have left him 'truly destitute', and his only ensuing political act of any significance was to support the Court on 18 Feb. 1706 during proceedings on the 'place clause' in the regency bill. However, while his Commons activity remained of little moment, right up until his death he was heavily involved in charity work, urging on the completion of building work at St. Thomas' Hospital only months before his demise. He died on 16 July 1707 at his country residence at Marden, the estate which he had transformed from being 'a despicable farmhouse' to a 'pretty house' with justly famed gardens. He was buried at Bletchingley, where he had ordered the erection of a sumptuous memorial in honour of his family.[24]

At his death Clayton's reputation was still largely determined by his activities before 1689. The epitaph composed by his nephew and heir William Clayton[†] celebrated the 'great share' he had borne of the campaign to preserve the constitution, and his monument bore the legend 'non vultus instantis tyranni'. Most significant, William also stressed that his uncle had 'lived in the communion of the Church of England, and in the most perfect charity with all good men, however divided among themselves in opinions'. Clayton himself showed that generosity of spirit in his will, for the deist Matthew Tindal figured among the beneficiaries, and actually signed one of the codicils. Moreover, several years earlier Clayton had testified to his close friendship with the Socinian philanthropist Thomas Firmin by erecting a monument in Firmin's honour at his Marden estate, having worked closely with him to promote Christ's Hospitals in Hertford and London, and the workhouse established by Firmin at St. Botolph Aldersgate. In return, the charities duly acknowledged Clayton's favour, helping him to rebut charges of avarice which continued to be levelled against him by critics such as Defoe. As early as 1701 St. Thomas' Hospital had erected a statue of him, its inscription declaring him 'a just magistrate and brave defender of the liberty and religion of his country'. However, it was his vast fortune which maintained the Clayton name in political circles, and his proprietorial control of Bletchingley which ensured that his successors dominated the representation of that borough for the rest of the century.[25]

[1] J. R. Woodhead, *Rulers of London* (London and Mdx. Arch. Soc.), 48; Bodl. Rawl. D.51, ff. 31–32; Beaven, *Aldermen*, ii. 105; K. G. Davies, *R. African Co.* 379. [2] NLS, Adv. 31.1.7, f. 146; Add.

10120, ff. 232–6; Boyer, *Anne Annals*, iv. 126; W. Kellaway, *New England Co.* 292; F. T. Melton, *Sir Robert Clayton and Origins of English Deposit Banking*, 4; Macfarlane thesis, 362. [3]*Misc. Works of Toland*, ii. 288–9; *Evelyn Diary*, iv. 185; *Le Neve's Knights* (Harl. Soc. viii), 270; Beaven, ii. 191; Grey, viii. 309–10; Beddard, *Kingdom without a King*, 54, 173. [4]Luttrell, *Brief Relation*, i. 523; G. S. De Krey, *Fractured Soc.* 61; *Poems on Affairs of State*, vi. 408; J. Dunton, *Life and Errors*, 353; M. C. Jacob, *Newtonians and English Rev.* 220–2, 226. [5]BL, Verney mss mic. 636/44, John Verney* (Visct. Fermanagh) to Sir Ralph Verney, 1st Bt.[†], 24 Feb. 1690; Manning and Bray, *Surr.* ii. 302; Luttrell, ii. 25; Dorset RO, Fox-Strangways mss D124, box 235, bdle. 4, Rich to Sir Stephen Fox*, 17 Mar. 1690; *Cal. Treas. Bks.* ix. 1993, 2005. [6]SP 29/22, f. 26; Luttrell, *Brief Relation*, i. 158; Grey, x. 57–58. [7]Grey, x. 67–68; *HMC Lords*, iii. 48. [8]Luttrell, ii. 47. [9]Rawl. C.449; *CSP Col.* 1689–92, pp. 554–8; *Luttrell Diary*, 33, 44, 56, 58, 88, 92, 163, 181, 184, 191, 205. [10]*Cal. Treas. Bks.* ix. 1652; 1752; Bodl. Carte 79, f. 488; *HMC 10th Rep.V*, 65; *Luttrell Diary*, 452; *HMC Lords*, n.s. i. 309. [11]*Poems on Affairs of State*, v. 430; Melton, 210; *CSP Dom.* 1694–5, pp. 179, 181, 185. [12]Add. 17677 PP, ff. 198–9; PCC 165 Poley. [13]*LJ*, xv. 551–2; Add. 46527, f. 82. [14]Luttrell, iii. 283; iv. 151. [15]*Shrewsbury Corresp.* 478; Centre Kentish Stud. Stanhope mss U1590/053/7, James Vernon I to Alexander Stanhope, 4 May 1697; Luttrell, iv. 286, 293; *Cal. Treas. Bks.* xiii. 3, 162; xv. 131; *CSP Dom.* 1697, pp. 432, 438, 448, 466. [16]Macfarlane thesis, 265–6, 362. [17]Luttrell, iv. 386; *Misc. Works of Toland*, ii. 322; Melton, 208; TCD, Lyons (King) mss 1999/588, [–] to Bp. King, 20 Dec. 1698; *HMC Lords*, n.s. iii. 18, 21, 23; Add. 40774, ff. 34–36; Macfarlane thesis, 330. [18]Macfarlane thesis, 332; *Vernon–Shrewsbury Corresp.* iii. 138. [19]Cobbett, *Parlty. Hist.* v. p. clxxv; *Cocks Diary*, 127–28, 145. [20]*Modesty Mistaken* [1702], 6–7; *Misc. Works of Toland*, i. pp. liii–liv. [21]Luttrell, v. 193; *HMC Portland*, iv. 43; BL, Trumbull Alphab. mss 50, Thomas Bateman to Sir William Trumbull*, 24 July, 17 Aug. 1702; Guildhall Lib. ms 20484, acct. of workhouse, 5 Nov. 1702. [22]*Nicolson Diaries* ed. Jones and Holmes, 200, 253, 273; Macfarlane thesis, 341. [23]PCC 165 Poley. [24]Folger Shakespeare Lib. Newdigate newsletters 6 Nov. 1705, 17 July 1707; *Misc. Works of Toland*, ii. 288–9; E. M. McInnes, *St. Thomas' Hosp.* 68; *Evelyn Diary*, iv. 121–2, v. 425–6; *Archaeologia*, xii. 187; PCC 165 Poley. [25]Manning and Bray, 310–11; PCC 165 Poley; A. U. M Lambert, *Godstone*, 287; F. M. Page, *Christ's Hosp. Hertford*, 24–26; E. H. Pearce, *Annals of Christ's Hosp.* 55, 100, 169; Macfarlane thesis, 247–8, 257; *Poems on Affairs of State*, vi. 408; J. Aubrey, *Surr.* v. 292–4.

P. L. G.

CLAYTON, William (aft.1650–1715), of Fulwood, nr. Preston and Water Street, Liverpool, Lancs.

LIVERPOOL   1698–1708, 1713–1715

b. aft. 1650, 2nd s. of Robert Clayton of Fulwood by Eleanor, da. of John Atherton of Atherton, Lancs. m. 7 Aug. 1690 (with £1,000), Elizabeth, da. of George Leigh of Oughtrington, Cheshire, 2s. (1 *d.v.p.*) 7da. (4 *d.v.p.*). *suc.* fa. ?1664.[1]

Freeman, Preston 1662, 1682; common council, Liverpool 1687–95, 1705–*d.*, merchant appraiser 1688, mayor 1689–90, alderman by 1694–5.[2]

Trustee, Liverpool grammar school 1709.[3]

?Commr. for taking subscriptions to S. Sea Co. 1711.[4]

Clayton's family hailed from Preston, but his uncle, Alderman Thomas Clayton, traded from Liverpool from 1672 and served as the borough's mayor in 1680. Clayton followed his lead, becoming a prominent tobacco and sugar merchant and serving as mayor in 1689. Apart from the difficulty in distinguishing between the two aldermen, his activity in the early 1690s is hard to disentangle from that of his namesake 'Captain William Clayton'. Nevertheless, it seems likely that it was the future MP who provided ships to assist in the reduction of Ireland and who supplied tobacco to the army in Ireland in 1689. When a vacancy occurred at Liverpool in 1694 Thomas Norris* hoped to persuade 'Alderman Clayton' (either William or Thomas) to stand as 'he has hitherto been a zealous friend to this government and always gone along with me as a justice of the peace and deputy lieutenant in all those things which (for fear of disobliging the Popish party) few others would join in'. Norris was, however, unable to persuade him, attributing Clayton's rejection to the government's failure to reimburse Liverpool's merchants for their provision of ships in 1689, and to Clayton and his fellow merchants 'having lost so many of their richest ships lately taken by French privateers'. When attempts were made in 1695 to replace Liverpool's charter of 1676 Clayton signed the condemnation of these efforts, and, though the reasons for his opposition are unclear, it led to his exclusion from the bench of aldermen in the new charter of 1695. It was Clayton's namesake (the captain) who stood unsuccessfully for the borough in 1695.[5]

By 1698 Clayton appears to have mended his differences with the advocates of the 1695 charter and was returned for Liverpool unopposed. In a comparison of the old and new Houses in about September he was classed as a Court supporter. A month later he was forecast as a likely opponent of the standing army, but though he did not vote against the disbanding bill on 18 Jan. 1699 his support for the Court in this session is suggested by his telling, on 14 Feb., against the expulsion of Samuel Atkinson. Clayton was to prove a diligent representative of local interests throughout his parliamentary career, and soon after his election Liverpool corporation ordered him and his fellow Liverpool Member William Norris to obtain a bill to establish Liverpool as a separate parish from Walton. Leave was granted to introduce such a bill, and on 16 Dec. Clayton and Norris were appointed to the drafting committee. His concern for local interests was also apparent at the end of this session, when he spoke against an attempt by London merchants to prohibit tobacco imports unless transported in hogsheads, cases or chests, a measure thought to be potentially damaging to the small traders of the out-ports. In the following session he was granted a leave of absence on

9 Mar, and in early 1700 was classed as a Court supporter.[6]

At the first election of 1701 Clayton was returned on a joint interest with Norris, but the latter's absence in India had encouraged Sir Cleave More, 2nd Bt.*, to challenge Norris' election. Much of Clayton's time was spent defending against More's petition, and in March he wrote to Richard Norris* that he was 'forced to [at]tend every day and night to mind it', and that 'I dare not be absent one half day for fear'. The prospect of war and its consequences for trade, given the losses he had suffered in the 1690s, was uppermost in his thoughts early in the session. On 11 Feb. he optimistically forecast that 'we shall have no war but to get a good fleet and to make terms for ourselves', but by the 18th he was writing that 'I fear an embargo'. A week later he was resigned to the renewal of hostilities with France, writing that 'we shall strive all we can to keep off the war, but if the French will not enter into a negotiation then a war must arise'. His lack of enthusiasm for the conflict led him to vote against the preparations for the war in this session and to his subsequent appearance on a black list, but on 22 Feb. he still wrote that 'I praise God we are very unanimous about the business of the nation and the King is very well pleased at what we do'. In March Clayton diligently reported the settlement of the succession in approving terms to Liverpool's mayor. Clayton's care for the economic interests of his constituency was emphasized in this session by his efforts between April and June to protect the emerging rock salt industry. Producers of brine salt petitioned the Commons in April 1701 for a bill to prevent frauds and abuses in the salt duties, a measure provoked by what brine salt producers saw as the favourable interpretations of these duties as they related to rock salt producers. Several Liverpool merchants, including Richard Norris and Thomas Johnson*, were heavily involved in the rock salt industry, and in the three months until the end of the Parliament Clayton closely monitored, and reported upon, this bill. His concern for local matters was further indicated by his sensitivity in May to proposals to require that land tax commissioners had themselves paid £100 p.a. in land tax, feeling that the clause exempting Lancashire from these provisions 'will look like disparagement on the county', and in his appointment on 10 June to draft a bill to prevent abuses in the transporting of slaves to the American plantations. Although matters of local interest took up a great deal of his time, his attention was engaged in other matters such as the Speaker's reading of Defoe's *Legion Memorial* on the 'endeavours of several ill-disposed persons to raise tumults and sedition', upon which he wrote to Richard Norris the following day that 'some ill people . . . would fain raise a civil war among us', while his own sole prayer was 'God send peace'. Clayton's hostility throughout this session to the enthusiastic advocates of war appears to have affected his view of the Whigs generally. On 29 May he wrote condemning the denial by Lord Somers (Sir John*) that the Commons articles of impeachment against him 'be any fart', and proposed to 'let the world judge whether we had not reason when such things was done and our poor nation brought so much in debt'. This hostility to Somers was again evident in a hostile report of his acquittal on 17 June in the Lords. Clayton also fully endorsed the Commons' laying of the blame for the delay in the passing of supply on the determination of the Whig Lords 'to procure an indemnity for their own enormous crimes'. His final act of significance in the Parliament was a nomination on 24 June to confer with the Lords on their amendments to a bill continuing several duties.[7]

Hostility to the renewal of war and distaste for the behaviour of the Whig Lords heralded a political shift by Clayton. Having been considered a Whig and returned for Liverpool with the support of the borough's Whig interest, Clayton allied himself with the Tories at Westminster from this point on and became the leader of the Tory interest at Liverpool. Despite this change he was unopposed at Liverpool in December 1701. He was nominated on 6 Jan. 1702 to draft a bill to provide for the relief of the poor, and four days later was appointed to draft a bill to encourage privateers. On the 20th he was added to the committee preparing the bill to prevent bribery and corruption at elections. On 6 Mar. he was nominated to draft a bill to encourage this trade. He was appointed on 10 Feb. to draft a bill to prevent the making of clothes from short threads, and on the 21st presented the resulting bill to make more effectual the act for preventing abuses in the manufacture of linen. Given his views of the previous session it is not surprising that he was listed among those who had favoured the motion of 26 Feb. vindicating the Commons' proceedings against William's former ministers. On 21 Mar. Clayton reported from the committee considering a petition relating to the shipping of unqualified servants to America, a trade in which a number of Liverpool merchants were involved, leading to his appointment the same day to draft a bill to prevent such occurrences. He presented the bill on the 30th, but the following day was given leave of absence, apparently in order to resolve a dispute at Liverpool between the borough's tobacco merchants relating to the terms of a clause which some of these merchants intended to submit to the Commons, for preventing the repacking of tobacco for re-export.[8]

Clayton's altered political allegiance led to some disquiet in the borough before the 1702 election, but he was nevertheless returned unopposed, and his new political loyalties were emphasized in this session when he preferred to work through the new Tory chancellor of the duchy of Lancaster, Sir John Leveson Gower, 5th Bt.*, rather than the Whig 10th Earl of Derby (Hon. James Stanley*), when attempting to obtain a lease of Liverpool Castle for the corporation. After he had been appointed on 9 Nov. 1702 to draft an estate bill, his concern with matters of trade was quickly demonstrated by his nomination on the 18th to prepare a bill to encourage privateers, a measure he presented on 16 Jan. 1703. Concern for trade and manufacturing also explains his appointment on 18 Jan. to draft a bill to prevent the export of wool, and his management through the House of a bill to prevent abuses in the manufacture of textiles. His appointment on 20 Jan. to draft a bill to lay at the charge of the hundred the costs of transporting poor felons to gaol is most easily explicable in terms of a desire to remove from Liverpool's corporation the cost of transporting prisoners to Lancaster. Though Clayton was less active in the following session, he did speak in the debate of 4 Dec. 1703 upon the navy, when he urged the House that 'seamen must have good usage', and later the same month he was appointed to draft two estate bills (16, 22 Dec.). That his political loyalties remained with the Tories was indicated by his inclusion in mid-March 1704 in a list of probable supporters of the Earl of Nottingham (Daniel Finch[†]) over the Scotch Plot. His concern for trade was demonstrated in his letter of May congratulating Robert Harley* on his appointment as secretary of state, Clayton encouraging Harley 'to promote the trade of the nation and not let it be neglected nor run down by foreigners'. Impressions of the moderation of Clayton's Toryism are confirmed by his failure to vote on 28 Nov. for the Tack. The 1704–5 session again saw Clayton's significant parliamentary activity subdued, though he was appointed on 14 Dec. to draft a bill to allow Thomas Whitley of Cheshire to compound with the Treasury. His concern for local interests was again evident in his opposition to the bill to allow the export of Irish linen to the plantations, a measure thought likely to threaten Lancashire's linen industry and against which Liverpool's corporation petitioned the Commons on 31 Jan. 1705. Although the bill passed the Commons, Clayton and Johnson, his fellow Liverpool Member, appear to have been the prime movers behind the clause added to the bill to limit its validity to 11 years.[9]

By 1705 Clayton's Toryism had provoked enough resentment in Liverpool to cause a contested election, but his status as a representative of trading interests in the Commons is suggested by a letter to his challenger from a London merchant confiding that 'I am heartily concerned you stand in opposition to Alderman Clayton, who is a very necessary man in Parliament, and therefore I shall long to hear some means may be found to set your houses together'. Such appeals went unheeded, but Clayton emerged victorious at the poll and in an analysis of the new Parliament was classed as 'Low Church', probably owing to his stance on the Tack. He divided against the Court candidate for Speaker on 25 Oct., but after telling on 10 Nov. for setting a date on which to hear the petition of the Tory Sir George Warburton, 3rd Bt.*, on the Cheshire election, he was granted, on 23 Nov., a seven-week leave of absence. The following month he and a kinsman, Richard Clayton, obtained confirmation of a grant of a plantation of 200 acres on St. Kitts. Returning to the Commons after Christmas, Clayton concerned himself in the attempts of Liverpool and Bristol merchants to raise with the Treasury the question of the interest due upon their bonds. On 24 Jan. 1706 he was nominated to consider the Newfoundland trade. Having reported from this committee on 12 Feb., he was appointed to draw up an address embodying its conclusion that the French had been allowed to gain too large a share of the trade, presenting the address to the Commons four days later. His concern for trade was further demonstrated by his managing through the Commons a bill in February to enlarge Parton harbour in Cumberland, and his appointment on 18 Feb. to a conference with the Lords on their amendments to the bill allowing the import of a cargo of French wine contracted before the ban upon such imports.[10]

Given his trading interests, it is unsurprising that Clayton became involved in the debates in the 1706–7 session surrounding the passage of the Union. News reached Clayton that Johnson had recommended that Liverpool's merchants re-export tobacco from England to Scotland, claim drawback on the customs duties, and bring it back again after the Union came into force on 1 May, thereby undercutting competitors. Clayton's disapproval of Johnson's machinations led him, on 11 Jan., to 'acquaint the House what the revenue was like to suffer' from such schemes, but by February Clayton's allies in Liverpool were following Johnson's lead in shipping tobacco to Scotland. On 4 Feb. Clayton spoke against the section of the 4th article of the Union that provided for exceptions to be made to the removal of obstacles to free trade within the new kingdom. He remained angered by the existence of the customs loophole, attempting to embarrass his fellow Member by informing the ministry of Johnson's plans to take advantage of the loophole, and spoke to William Lowndes* about the bill introduced to close it, towards which Clayton was sympathetic. Clayton also took a keen interest in the effect of the Union upon the salt industry. English salt producers, including the rock and brine salt producers of Cheshire, feared having their domestic market undermined by foreign salt, imported into Scotland before the Union, where there were no salt duties, and then brought to England freely, following the removal of internal customs on 1 May. Clayton was appointed on 27 Feb. to draft a bill to equalize the export allowances of England and Scotland, a bill which when passed allowed the seizure by the government of all stocks of foreign salt in Scotland. Although the Union dominated Clayton's parliamentary activity in this session it did not prevent his pursuing his interest in trade more widely. On 20 Jan. he acted to preserve Liverpool's status as Lancashire's leading port by telling against committing a bill to make Lancaster a staple port for the import of Irish wool, and his chairing on 19 Mar. of a committee of the whole upon trade may indicate a growing respect in the House for his opinion on this matter.[11]

A list compiled early in 1708 classed Clayton as a Tory, and on 17 Jan. 1708 he was approached in the Commons by Robert Harley, who took Clayton behind the Speaker's chair and offered him the nomination to the post of collector of customs at Liverpool in what may have been part of Harley's attempts to gain Commons support for his intended ministerial coup. Four days later Clayton was nominated to draft a bill to regulate linen manufacture. On 5 Feb. he was nominated to draft a bill to encourage fisheries, and, after being appointed on 2 Mar. to draft a bill to revive the Act for better discipline in the navy, he was granted leave of absence on 19 Mar. for an unspecified period, leading to complaints from Johnson that Clayton always left London before the end of a parliamentary session.[12]

Defeated at Liverpool in 1708 and 1710, Clayton remained active in borough politics and was returned unopposed in 1713. His enthusiasm for matters of trade and manufacture had not diminished. On 9 Mar. he was nominated to draft a bill to curb wool smuggling, and six days later to prepare a bill to regulate the armed forces. Having been appointed on 12 May to draft a bill to preserve shipwrecked vessels and goods, he managed this measure through the Commons. This concern for trade can also be seen in his appointment on 14 May to draft a bill to preserve the navigation of the Thames; his nomination six days later to draft a bill to allow a drawback on the export of silver and gold thread; and his management in May and June of a bill to offer a reward for establishing a method of ascertaining longitude. The session also saw him carry a naturalization bill to the Lords. Classified as a Tory in the Worsley list and in a further comparison of the 1713 and 1715 Parliaments, Clayton did not stand in 1715. He died on 7 July at Chester, being buried four days later at St. Nicholas', Liverpool. His monument described him as 'a great encourager of trade', to which might be added Thomas Johnson's comment, written in 1702 when the two were still on cordial terms, that Clayton was 'very sensible, I must always do him that justice, and has a very good notion of most business, and a great memory'.[13]

[1] *Vis. Lancs.* (Chetham Soc. ser. 1, lxxxiv), 85; info. from Prof. J. M. Price; H. Peet, *Liverpool in Reign of Q. Anne*, 127–8, 144–5; W. Gregson, *Fragments Relating to Co. Lancaster*, 165, 167; *The Gen.* n.s. xxvi. 136–42. [2] *Preston Guild Rolls* (Lancashire and Cheshire Rec. Soc. ix), 142, 165; J. Picton, *Liverpool Mun. Recs. 13th–17th Cents.* 271, 288, 290; info. from Dr M. Power. [3] J. Picton, *Liverpool Mun. Recs. 1700–1835*, 75. [4] W. Pittis, *Hist. Present Parl.* (1711), 348. [5] R. Stewart-Brown, *Tower of Liverpool*, 20–28; Picton, *Liverpool Mun. Recs. 13th–17th Cents.* 297; R. Muir and E. M. Platt, *Hist. Mun. Govt. Liverpool*, 204–5; info. from Prof. Price; *HMC Kenyon*, 263; *Cal. Treas. Bks.* x. 646; Add. 70017, f. 319; 28879, f. 264; Liverpool RO, Liverpool bor. recs. 352 MIN/COU I 1/4, p. 346. [6] Liverpool bor. recs. 352 MIN/COU I 1/4, p. 829; Cumbria RO (Carlisle), Lonsdale mss D/Lons/W2/2/2, James* to Sir John Lowther, 2nd Bt. I*, 2 May 1699. [7] *Norris Pprs.* (Chetham Soc. ser. 1, ix), 57; Liverpool RO, Norris mss 920NOR 1/81, 86, 88, 91, 94, 108–9, 118–9, 122, Clayton to Richard Norris, 11, 22, 25 Feb., 1, 15 Mar. 1700[–1], 12, 15 Apr., 15, 17 May, 12 June 1701; 2/182, 220, 212, 215, 218, same to same, 11 Mar. 1700[–1], 20, 29 May, 5, 19 June 1701. [8] *Norris Pprs.* 92–93. [9] Ibid. 104–5, 110–13, 126–7; NMM, Sergison mss ser./103, f. 455; Add. 70161, Clayton to Harley, 27 May 1704; *Parlty. Hist.* xvi. 175–80. [10] Norris mss 920NOR 1/226, Samuel Shepheard I or II* to Richard Norris, 27 Mar. 1705; 2/412, Johnson to same, 31 Jan. 1705[–6]. [11] Norris mss 920NOR 1/303, Ralph Peters to Norris, 15 Feb. 1706[–7]; 1/329, Johnson to same, 1 Apr. 1707; 2/439, 446, 452, 453, 460, 462, same to [same], 11 Jan., 4, 23, 27 Feb., 18, 22 Mar. 1706[–7]; *SHR*, lxiii. 3–4; E. Hughes, *Studies in Admin. and Finance*, 241–2. [12] *Norris Pprs.* 161–2; *EHR* lxxx. 685, 690; Norris mss 920NOR 1/377, Johnson to [Norris], 25 Mar. 1708. [13] *Prescott Diary*, 451; *Norris Pprs.* 89–91.

E. C./R. D. H.

CLEIVELAND (CLEVELAND), John (1661–1716), of Chapel Street and Cleveland Place, Liverpool, Lancs.

LIVERPOOL 1710–1713

b. 3 Aug. 1661, s. of Joseph Cleiveland of Hinckley, Leics. by his w. Dorothy. *m.* bef. 1693, Anne Williamson of Liverpool, 2s. (1 *d.v.p.*) 1da.[1]

Common council, Liverpool 1693–*d.*, bailiff 1691, merchant appraiser 1693, alderman by 1703–*d*, mayor 1703–4.[2]

Descended from a family of Leicestershire Royalists, most notably John Cleveland, a popular poet in the reign of Charles I, Cleiveland was adopted by his uncle Richard Cleiveland, a Liverpool merchant. Cleiveland followed his uncle's lead and by the first decade of the 18th century had become a prominent tobacco importer, as well as possessing a small interest in the sugar trade and engaging in the refining of rock salt, prospering enough to buy the manor and priory of Birkenhead in 1700 and to build a fine town house in Liverpool. Involved in corporation affairs from the early 1690s, Cleiveland was one of those who in 1695 opposed the replacement of the charter of 1676, but despite this opposition he was reappointed a common councilman in the new charter of October 1695. He remained allied at Liverpool with the opponents of the new charter, and in October 1703 the supporters of the new charter forced him to assume the mayoralty against his will. Although he continued to take a keen interest in corporation affairs, supporting the advocates of the old charter in the mayoral election of 1705, Cleiveland did not stand for Parliament until 1710, when he was returned following a contested election.[3]

Classed as a Tory in the 'Hanover list', Cleiveland was an inactive Member, his only appointment of significance being on 27 Feb. 1711 to draft a bill for the navigation of the Weaver. He was granted leave of absence for five weeks on 26 Mar., but despite his apparent inactivity was still included in the list of 'worthy patriots' who during the 1710–11 session had exposed the mismanagements of the previous ministry. The 1711–12 session saw him given a six-week leave of absence on 3 May 1712. His only significant action in the 1713 session was to vote on 18 June against the French commerce bill, though he was surprisingly classed as a Whig in this list. His vote was no doubt influenced by the opposition to the treaty prevalent in Liverpool, and his frequent absence from Parliament may be explained by his activities on behalf of the Tory interest in the borough. Choosing not to stand in 1713, Cleiveland was one of the few Tories left on the Lancashire bench following its regulation after the Hanoverian succession. He died on 1 Aug. 1716, and was buried at St. Nicholas', Liverpool. His only surviving son, William, sat for Liverpool as a Court Whig between 1722 and 1724, and on his death the family estates went to Cleiveland's daughter Alice, who had married the Liverpool Whig, Dr Edward Norris†.[4]

[1] Nichols, *Leics.* iv. 707. [2] J. Picton, *Memorials of Liverpool*, i. 186; info. from Dr M. Power. [3] Nichols, 707; info. from Prof. J. M. Price; Picton, 186; Liverpool RO, Liverpool bor. recs. 352 MIN/COU I 1/4, p. 346; R. Muir and E. M. Platt, *Hist. Mun. Govt. Liverpool*, 249; *Norris Pprs.* (Chetham Soc. ser. 1, ix), 132–4, 144–5; Liverpool RO, Norris mss 920NOR 1/248, William Squire to [Richard Norris*], 15 Oct. 1703. [4] Hamilton mss at Lennoxlove, bdle. 4407, George Tyrer, John Cleiveland and William Clayton* to Duke of Hamilton, 1 June 1711; L. K. J. Glassey, *Appt. JPs*, 293; Nichols, 707.

E. C./R. D. H.

CLERK, John (1676–1755), of Penicuik, Midlothian.[1]

SCOTLAND 1707–1708

b. 8 Feb. 1676, 1st s. of Sir John Clerk, 1st Bt., MP [S], of Penicuik by his 1st w. Elizabeth, da. of Dr Henry Henderson of Elvingston, Haddington. *educ.* Penicuik sch. (Alexander Strauchan) 1686–93; Glasgow Univ. 1693–4; Leyden 1695, J. Dr. 1697; travelled abroad (Italy, France, Low Countries) 1697–9; adv. 1700. *m.* 6 Mar. 1701 (with £2,000), Lady Margaret (*d.* 21 Dec. 1701), da. of Alexander Stewart, 3rd Earl of Galloway [S], sis. of Hon. John Stewart*, 1s. *d.v.p.*; (2) 15 Feb. 1709 (with 14,000 merks), Janet (*d.* 1760), da. of Sir John Inglis, 2nd Bt., of Cramond, Midlothian, 9s. (4 *d.v.p.*) 7da. (1 *d.v.p.*) *suc.* gdfa. at Elvingston bef. 1710, fa. as 2nd Bt. 10 Mar. 1722.[2]

Burgess, Edinburgh 1700, Whithorn 1702, Wigtown, Ayr 1705, Dumfries, Aberdeen, Montrose, Dundee, Stirling 1708, Queensferry 1716, Glasgow 1720, Sanquhar 1729, Musselburgh 1739.[3]

MP [S] Whithorn 1703–7.

Commr. public accts. [S] 1703–5.

Commr. union with England 1706, Equivalent [S] 1707–9; baron of exchequer [S] (for life) 1708; Prince's commr. [S] 1724, 1731, 1742; trustee, fisheries and manufactures [S] 1727–*d.*[4]

Extraord. dir. R. Bank of Scotland 1727–8.[5]

FRS 1729.

'A name celebrated both in the civil history and literature of Scotland . . . Sir John Clerk, from the great extent of his learning, his cultivated taste, and numerous personal accomplishments, joined to his active share in the important national transaction of the union with England, would have held a distinguished place in the history of any country.' Later generations held the first great Scottish *virtuoso* of the 18th century in high regard as a polymath who nurtured a modern ideal of patriotism, grounded in polite scholarship, in which a preserved sense of 'Scottishness' could be 'sublimated . . . into a comprehensive

Britishness'. A consistent advocate of union, Clerk was instrumental in negotiating the treaty and putting it into effect, but in the capacity of a bureaucrat rather than a parliamentarian. Once the Union was accomplished he retreated rapidly into 'an easy life of limited legal opportunity' as a baron of the Scottish exchequer, reserving his real interest for antiquarian studies and extensive cultural patronage, which made him appear a worthy successor to Sir Robert Sibbald and resulted in such sobriquets as 'the Lord Burlington of Scotland' and 'the Maecenas of his age'.[6]

'Having nothing to boast of as to the antiquity of my family, which, by the by, I have always laughed at in others, I shall trace my mean progenitors no farther back than about 1568.' So begins Clerk's autobiography (pp. 3–4), which located his ancestry in a feuar of the Duke of Gordon, whose son became a merchant in Montrose. The family's name was made by Clerk's grandfather: as a factor in Paris he amassed a 'considerable fortune' (p. 4), with which, on his return to Scotland, he purchased the Penicuik estate. Sound commercial principles survived the acquisition of gentility in the next generation, and were reinforced by the Presbyterian piety which made Clerk's father, the first baronet, both a frugal manager of his business affairs and an austere moral guardian. 'Though I be not descended of noble parents', pronounced Clerk with pride, 'yet I am the son of those who bore deservedly a very great name for religion, virtue, honour and honesty' (p. 10).

After a miserable experience under a harsh dominie in the local school at Penicuik, Clerk endured an unhappy spell at Glasgow University. His tutor reported that

> he has not idly spent his time, but made a considerable proficiency in his studies, and besides has been an exemplary pattern in matter of discipline to all his condisciples, and has endeared himself to all the masters here as a very hopeful gentleman.

Sent to Leyden in 1694 to study civil law, he also read widely in ancient history, indulged his passion for music, learned to draw, and took instruction in French and Italian in order to equip himself for the journey to Italy on which he had set his heart:

> the vast desire I had to see a country so famous for exploits about which all my time had been hitherto spent in reading the classics, likewise a country so replenished with antiquities of all kinds, and so much excelling all other countries in painting and music, I say these things created such a vast desire in me to see it, that I am sure nothing in life had ever made me happy if I had denied myself this great pleasure and satisfaction.

Such was his enthusiasm that he was prepared to suffer his father's disapproval and the privations imposed by a niggardly allowance of £100. These slender resources he eked out over two years to fund a Grand Tour in which he made the acquaintance of the Austrian Emperor and the Grand Duke of Tuscany, who took Clerk under his 'protection' and appointed him a gentleman of his bedchamber. At Rome, where his 'two great diversions . . . were music and antiquities' (p. 28), he founded a long-standing friendship with the 2nd Duke of Bedford, whom he accompanied on sightseeing trips to the Bay of Naples. He may also have enjoyed the unusual privilege, for a Scots Presbyterian, of a papal audience. Cutting short his stay in a belated response to paternal expostulations, he returned to Holland via Paris, which he found agreeable but 'far from giving me that entertainment I had at Rome' since everything there appeared but a pale imitation of the Roman original (p. 35); and embarked for Scotland to resume his legal studies, with a view to a career as an advocate.[7]

Clerk was temperamentally unsuited to the law. A 'natural bashfulness' lamed his oratorical powers; indeed, he declared in later life that whenever he had spoken in public it had been 'against my natural inclinations' (pp. 36–37). In typically priggish fashion he added: 'the talent of copiousness and loquacity I abominated in all my acquaintances, and therefore could never think to practise it myself'. To begin with, however, he had little choice but to look to the bar: the epic scale of his Grand Tour had not been contrived without incurring debts that subsequently snowballed. By 1703 he owed nearly £12,000 Scots, with little immediate prospect of being able to pay off his creditors.

> To pay these debts I have but a small stock, seeing my father will retain my annuity of £1,000 Scots till he be paid; and of the rents of Elvingston and the lodging in Edinburgh I cannot make above £1,000 . . . Wherefore I shall bless God if I can maintain myself and my son and hinder my debts to increase.

What saved his prospects at this time was his first marriage, which, despite the tragic death of his wife soon after the birth of their only child, had brought him enduring advantages through her brother Lord Galloway's connexion with the Duke of Queensberry. In 1702 the recently widowed Clerk had accompanied Galloway to Edinburgh to be introduced to the Duke, who

> made his compliments of condolence . . . with great civility and humanity . . . and from that moment he took a resolution to advance me to every station in the government of Scotland that he thought proper for me.

His grace was a complete courtier, and . . . had brought himself into a habit of saying very civil and obliging things to everybody. I knew his character, and therefore was not much elated with his promises. However, I found afterwards that there was nothing he had promised to do for me but what he made good [p. 44].

Clerk, who in politics followed his father's somewhat simplistic adherence to the Presbyterian and 'Revolution' interest, and to Court parties of whatever complexion, now found himself taken up by Queensberry. He responded to this kindness with unconditional loyalty, accepting without question the Queensberry line on every issue and often acting as an apologist for the Duke, to a degree that must indicate a pathological self-interest, an excess of personal devotion, or extreme naivety. A clue can perhaps be found in the self-importance and Panglossian optimism surviving into the autobiography, which suggests that in his immaturity Clerk may well have been even more of an innocent.[8]

To begin with, however, the power of Queensberry's patronage remained to be proved, and Clerk quickly realized that he also required some leverage of his own. On Galloway's nomination he was returned to the Scottish parliament for Whithorn in 1702, and immediately enlisted in the Court party, being appointed a commissioner of accounts on Queensberry's recommendation. As the Duke's principal agent on the commission he naturally became part of the inner group upon whom the business devolved. Its first report in 1704 was Clerk's handiwork alone. As much as anything else, it was probably his literary skills which had first attracted Queensberry's attention: Clerk claimed to have contributed two pamphlets to the previous year's constitutional debates, one a polemic against any diminution of royal prerogatives, the other an essay on the 'limitations' proposed by the Country party. The two grants of £200 which parliament made to the accounts commissioners as reward for their efforts would certainly have helped towards rescuing his embarrassed finances, but he required some more substantial and permanent provision. At first he had harboured designs upon an unnamed 'clerkship' but abandoned these in favour of something grander. At last, on Queensberry's recommendation to the Duke of Argyll, he found himself named as one of the Scottish commissioners to treat for a union with England.[9]

Agreeing to serve on the Union commission was a decision over which Clerk agonized, largely because his father, 'whom I always considered as an oracle seldom mistaken' (p. 58), had expressed grave reservations about the wisdom of such a step. Clerk himself, expecting that the negotiations would come to naught, regarded the prospect with neither pleasure nor satisfaction. When at last his father 'grew passive', however, and at the same time Queensberry 'threatened to withdraw all friendship . . . I suffered myself to be prevailed upon' (p. 58). The case he put to his father was that appointment to the commission might be a first step towards obtaining legal office, whereas a refusal would inflict embarrassment on Queensberry; at the same time Clerk would be placed in a position to perform a vital service for his country, since union would constitute 'the only barrier we can have for keeping out popery and preventing our falling into confusion at the Queen's death'. Forearmed with a battery of detailed advice from his father on the political, ethical and practical implications of the appointment, and determined, or so he said, to act as prudently and live as cheaply as he could while a member of the commission, he travelled to London in March 1706. Once again he found committee work his *métier*, and distinguished himself by diligence in routine affairs, being one of those responsible for compiling the minutes, and entrusted with the particular duty of scrutinizing the calculations of the Equivalent. During the negotiations he made 'three formal speeches' on the settlement of the Kirk, but disparaged their effect. Meanwhile he lost no opportunity to 'cultivate' Queensberry's favour, and on several occasions accompanied the Duke into Queen Anne's presence. Once the treaty had been settled, Clerk receded from prominence. In the debates in the Scottish parliament over ratification he was 'entirely passive' (p. 66), though he naturally added his vote to the Court side, and published two pamphlets: *Some Considerations on the Articles of Union* and *An Essay upon the XV. Article*, the latter concentrating on the question of the Equivalent, and putting the somewhat specious argument that the distribution of the Equivalent among the wealthier and more influential elements of Scottish society was less a political bribe than a necessary stimulus to a depressed economy. One aspect of the issue impinged on him directly: the payments that were to be made to the Union commissioners, which in his case amounted to £500. Squadrone members made two separate attempts at sabotage, first moving for a lesser sum and then opposing priority of payment out of the Equivalent. Clerk was furious at what he considered to be an instance of mere malice and even after these manoeuvres were defeated continued to be concerned that the allowance should be paid.[10]

Queensberry made sure that his protégé was included on the Court slate as one of the Scottish

Members of the first Parliament of Great Britain. 'I had no hand in the honour', Clerk recalled, 'but the Duke of Queensberry insisted that I should be one on the list . . . and as an incitement to me he offered me a place in one of his coaches to London, which I accepted of, and set out with his Grace on the 2nd of April 1707' (p. 67). Once again he was obliged to explain himself to his father, who evidently disapproved of his election on grounds of expense. In anticipation of this objection Clerk stressed that attending the Parliament was probably the only means by which he might secure the £700 due to him from the crown; that he only intended to remain a Member for one session, until the dissolution; and that if he did secure his money he would make a handsome profit, since he intended to live as frugally as possible while in London. He pointed out that it would be 'silly' for him to 'bear the odium' of having played such a part in the Union while others 'carry away the prize'. When he arrived in London other possibilities opened, especially since he found himself given access to the ministry at the highest level, being among those called upon to advise Lord Treasurer Godolphin (Sidney†) on Scottish affairs; and while he protested again that he had 'only one plot' in view, namely to 'make the public pay the expense and debt I contracted upon my education abroad', he was faced with the choice of living for the future 'in a public or a private capacity'. Though his monetary ambitions were modest, requiring a steady income of no more than £1,000 p.a. (something, he was quick to point out, that he had never had the happiness of enjoying), he clearly had his eye once again on a legal office, and insinuated the prospect into his correspondence with his father with sufficient skill to induce Sir John to send more 'suitable advices', this time 'on the nature of preferments, and such as are agreeable to the word of God', a prize example, apparently, being the post of Queen's solicitor, which his father assumed would be a step towards a seat in the court of session. 'For my own part', Clerk wrote, showing more than a suspicion of hypocrisy,

> though I very industriously shun the opportunity of being offered some preferment, yet if it be offered I cannot tell how to refuse it, the duty I owe to my country on the one hand may press me to accept something which requires more of honesty and application than any other qualification, and upon the other hand the regard I ought to have for myself will not allow me, because of the danger there is in meddling, when governors are not like to fall upon such an administration as will be acceptable to these people among whom I am to live.

Eventually, after his return to Scotland, the Duke of Queensberry named him, allegedly without his knowledge, to the commission for the Equivalent. In his autobiography Clerk claimed that a more lucrative post, in customs or excise, would have been his to command, but the Equivalent commission 'requiring persons of known fidelity, I was in some measure compelled to accept of it, not without a positive promise from the Duke that I should be afterwards better provided for' (p. 68). He entertained serious reservations about the appointment because of the poor remuneration to be expected (no more than £100–200 p.a.). There was some consolation in the prospect of making himself an indispensable expert on public finance. The duties of the new office prevented his leaving Edinburgh to attend Parliament until 29 Jan. 1708, and even then he arrived at Westminster suffering the discomfort and handicap of a fractured collarbone. As expected, he attached himself to the Court, and seems to have made a number of new acquaintances among Court Whigs like Hon. Spencer Compton*. On 28 Feb. he reported to his father:

> Our debates upon the state of the war with Spain gave me wonderful satisfaction, and as a blessing to the common cause we defeat[ed] the Tories and the Squadrone by 55 votes, which will give great stroke to the encouragement our enemies once took in our divisions. So we carried an address to her Majesty against them all, justifying her conduct in the Spanish war.[11]

Before returning to Scotland Clerk was vouchsafed an audience with the Queen. Her attention and the promises of his patron proved enough to decide him against seeking election to the new Parliament:

> 1. Because there are about 147 offices above £500 yearly which Parliament-men are capable of and actually do enjoy in our House, to which I might be as much entitled as another.
> 2. I should in that case be in a condition both to assist myself and friends, and in all events to be able to make an honourable capitulation for myself.

Shortly afterwards he was appointed a baron of the Scottish exchequer, at a salary of £500 a year. As a life patent, this satisfied Clerk's worldly ambitions better than the post of solicitor for Scotland, which had apparently also been on offer, but of which he would have had a more precarious tenure. The comparative slowness of the work also made it more attractive than the prospect of a place in the court of session.[12]

Although his father still felt that the new baron's circumstances were 'rather honourable than rich', Clerk was sufficiently emboldened by his preferment to embark on the purchase of an estate of his own, at Cambo in Midlothian, costing 50,000 merks. He seems to have been content to take little further part in politics, at least at national level, retaining an unusual detachment from the bitterness of faction. He claimed that in 1708, of all the appointments to the exchequer bench 'I'm the only man there's no dispute about'; and in 1710 the Earl of Mar, on behalf of the incoming Tory administration, tried, albeit unsuccessfully, to tempt him with an offer of promotion to the court of session. He was prepared to accept the notion of a toleration for episcopalians, which would be 'found to be a better thing for the Presbyterian interest than it appears at first sight', though he refrained from giving a vote to George Lockhart* in Midlothian, and in fundamentals remained stoutly Whiggish. If the Union were to be broken, he wrote in 1713,

> it will be impossible to keep up a good correspondence hereafter between the two nations, whereby it is ten to one but our malt drying trade, linen trade and West India trade will go to ruin; we fall again under the oppression of our own great men; the fundamental security of the Protestant succession will be broken; and it is a great question if Presbytery would be continued.

On the death of the Queen he was a signatory to the proclamation of King George I in Edinburgh. He did not make any efforts to seek a new patron after Queensberry's death, and while his friendship with Lord Justice Clerk Ormiston led him to be described in 1716 as Ormiston's 'creature', he seems to have steered a course between the rival political interests, and it was as an independent rather than an Argathelian that he was nominated to the fisheries and manufactures board in 1727. There was relatively little official business to transact, and with 'a great deal of time on my hands' he returned to the scholarly and artistic pursuits that were his first love: music, antiquarian scholarship, and the plantation and improvement of his estate. Among his most frequent correspondents was the noted English antiquary Roger Gale*, and among those who benefited most from his patronage was the painter Allan Ramsay, for many years a permanent house guest at Penicuik. Clerk's later writings, which were frequently of a historical nature, and for the most part unpublished, included 'Methods for Making a Man Happy and Easy in His Circumstances' (c.1730), a subject in which he must be considered something of an expert; and some lengthy advice to his sons, which featured a set of rules, discovered by experience, 'for enabling a country gentleman to make a considerable figure in life'. Clerk died on 4 Oct. 1755.[13]

[1] Unless otherwise stated this article is based on Clerk's 'History of My Life' (*Scot. Hist. Soc.* ser. 1, xiii), to which specific reference is occasionally made in the text. The only full-scale modern biography, I. D. Brown, 'Sir John Clerk of Penicuik (1676–1755): aspects of a virtuoso life' (Camb. Univ. Ph.D. thesis, 1980), focuses on the intellectual development of its subject. [2] *Album Studiosorum Academiae Lugduno Batavae* ed. Du Rieu, 738; SRO, Clerk of Penicuik mss GD18/1875. [3] Clerk of Penicuik mss GD18/2046–8, 2052–6, 2059, 2061–2, 5246/1/13, burgess tickets; *Scot. Rec. Soc.* lvi. 353. [4] P. W. J. Riley, *Eng. Ministers and Scotland*, 214–15. [5] N. Munro, *Hist. R. Bank of Scotland*, 406. [6] Brown thesis, 3, 116–20, 125–7, 130, 137; H. Fenwick, *Architect Royal*, 75. [7] Clerk of Penicuik mss GD18/5193/2, James Kimble to Sir John Clerk, 20 June 1693; GD18/5201, Sir John Clerk to Clerk, [c. 1696]; GD18/5230, Cosimo Clerk to same, [c. 1698]. [8] Clerk of Penicuik mss GD18/2207, lists of debts 2 Feb. 1702, 1 Jan. 1703; GD18/5238/17/2, Clerk to father 28 July [1702]; GD18/2092/2, Sir John Clerk's 'moral jnls.', 21–26, 28–30 Sept. 1702; *APS*, ix. 26; x. 247; info. from Dr P. W. J. Riley on members of Scot. parl; P. W. J. Riley, *King Wm. and Scot. Politicians*, 170. [9] Clerk of Penicuik mss GD18/5238/17, 38, Clerk to fa. 28 July [1702], 3 Oct. [1704]; *HMC Mar and Kellie*, i. 240. [10] Clerk of Penicuik mss GD18/3131/4, 20, 22, 25, Clerk to fa. 23 July 1706, 12 Mar. [1706], 14 Dec. [1705], Sir John Clerk to Clerk, 11 Mar. 1706; P. W. J. Riley, *Union*, 239–40, 295, 331; *Baillie Corresp.* 181–2. [11] Clerk of Penicuik mss GD18/3135/4, 9, 12, 18, 20, Clerk to fa. 17 Feb., 29 Mar., 24 Apr., 13 May, 10 June 1707; GD18/2092/2, Sir John Clerk's 'moral jnls.', 10 June 1707, 13–29 Jan. 1708; GD18/3139, Compton to Clerk, 14 Dec. 1708; GD18/3140/25, Clerk to father 28 Feb. 1708; Riley, *Eng. Ministers*, 36. [12] Clerk of Penicuik mss GD18/3140/22, 25, Clerk to fa. 2, 4 Mar., 28 Feb. 1708; *Cal. Treas. Bks.* xxii. 237. [13] GD18/3140/3, 22, Sir John Clerk to Clerk, 27 Aug., 2, 4 Mar. 1708; GD18/5269/2, Clerk to fa. 3 Mar. 1710; GD18/3140/11, same to same, 24 Apr. 1708; GD18/5274/37, same to same, 2 June [1713]; GD18/2319, 'Methods'; GD18/2325, Clerk's advice to his sons; *Lockhart Letters* ed. Szechi, 70, 220; NLS, ms 14499, ff. 164–5; J. S. Shaw, *Management of Scottish Soc.* 69, 74; Brown thesis, 106.

D. W. H.

CLERKE, Francis I (c.1665–1691), of Ulcombe, Kent and Restoration House, Rochester.

ROCHESTER 1690–by Sept. 1691

b. c.1665, 1st s. of Sir Francis Clerke† of Ulcombe and Rochester by his 2nd w. Elizabeth, da. and h. of John Cage of Brightwell Court, Bucks., and wid. of John Hastings of Woodlands, Dorset. *educ.* Magdalen Coll. Oxf., matric. 10 Nov. 1681, aged 16; M. Temple 1683, called 1688. *unm. suc.* fa. 1686 or half-bro. 1687.[1]

?Cornet indep. tp. horse 1685.[2]

Both Clerke's father and grandfather were lawyers, so it was natural that as the son of a second marriage he, too, should gravitate towards the law. Having entered the Middle Temple he appears to have broken off his studies in June 1685 to volunteer against Monmouth, since a 'Francis Clerke' was listed as a cornet of horse. The death, in quick succession, of his father and half-brother, John, enabled him to take control of Ulcombe and his family's political interest in Rochester. For all that his father had been a staunch Tory, Clerke's own attitude to the Revolution of 1688 is unknown, and he did not stand for election to the Convention of 1689. In 1690 he defeated Sir John Banks, 1st Bt.*, who, although also a Tory, was the Clerke family's old rival for the parliamentary seat.

Clerke's own Toryism was implied by his description as 'indifferent' by Edward Harley*, his contemporary at the Temple. Other commentators may have been confused by his victory over Banks; thus, although the Marquess of Carmarthen (Sir Thomas Osborne†) marked Clerke as a possible Court supporter in March 1690, he failed to categorize him by party. In December 1690, faced with a need to identify allies in case he was attacked in the Commons, Carmarthen again could not decide Clerke's position with any certainty. To compound matters, in April 1691 Robert Harley* classed Clerke as a Country supporter, although this was modified by the letter 'd', which may of course indicate 'dead'. Clerke may have spoken on 24 Apr. in the debate over the alterations made in the London lieutenancy, but the 'Mr Clarke' referred to by Grey was probably Edward Clarke I*. Clerke died during the summer recess of 1691, making his will on 23 June, when he described himself as 'weak in soul and body', but it was not proved until September. His Kentish estates ultimately passed to Gilbert Clarke, second son of Sir Gilbert Clarke*. Restoration House was bought by William Bokenham*.[3]

[1] *Vis. Kent* (Harl. Soc. liv), 36; PCC 93 Lloyd, 46 Exton. [2] *CSP Dom.* 1685, p. 209. [3] Add. 70014, Edward to Sir Edward Harley*, 22 Feb. 1689–90; Grey, x. 73; PCC 128 Vere; Hasted, *Kent*, v. 392; *Arch. Cant.* xiv. 119.

S. N. H.

CLERKE, Francis II (c.1655–1715), of North Weston, Oxon. and Hillingdon, Mdx.

OXFORDSHIRE   1710–2 May 1715

b. c.1655, 4th s. of Sir John Clerke, 1st Bt., of Shabbington and Hitcham, Bucks. and North Weston by Philadelphia (*d.* 1698), da. and coh. of Sir Edward Carr of Hillingdon. *educ.* Magdalen Coll. Oxf. (demy) matric. 31 July 1671, aged 16, BA 1675, MA 1678, fellow 1676–82. *m.* (1) 23 Mar. 1698, Eleanor Reynardson, *s.p.*; (2) Grace (*d.* 1726), *s.p.* suc. fa. at North Weston 1667, mother at Hillingdon 1698.[1]

Cornet of horse, Capt. Hon. Henry Bertie's (I)* indep. tp. 1685.[2]

Clerke's family had been established at North Weston, on the borders of Oxfordshire and Buckinghamshire, since at least the early 16th century. His father was created a baronet in 1660 in apparent acknowledgment of support rendered to the Royalist cause during the Civil Wars. Until his later twenties, Clerke, a younger son, led a scholarly existence at Oxford University, afterwards settling down as a country gentleman on the North Weston estates he had inherited from his father as a boy. In 1685 he was commissioned a junior officer in a volunteer troop raised against Monmouth by Hon. Henry Bertie, an Oxfordshire neighbour who was soon to marry Clerke's niece. There is no indication, however, as to whether he saw action at Sedgemoor, after which the troop was soon disbanded. He has been identified as the 'Mr Clarke' who stood unsuccessfully against Sir William Whitlock* in the Oxford University by-election of November 1703. Dr William Delaune, the president of St. John's College, described him to Robert Harley* as 'a very worthy gentlemen of our county, related to my Lord Abingdon [Montagu Venables-Bertie*, Lord Norreys] and well known to Mr Solicitor [Simon Harcourt I*]'. At the general election of 1710 he was returned unchallenged as knight of the shire for his native county, his brother-in-law and near neighbour, Sir Edward Norreys*, having retired from one of the seats in 1708.[3]

Classified in the 'Hanover list' as a Tory, Clerke featured in the first session as a 'worthy patriot' who detected the mismanagements of the previous Whig ministry, and in another listing as a 'Tory patriot' opposed in 1711 to the continuance of war. Because of the common mis-spelling of his surname, most parliamentary activity by Clerke is indistinguishable from that of two other Tories, Godfrey* and George Clarke*, the former being returned in 1710, the latter at the end of May 1711. On 18 June 1713 he voted against the French commerce bill. In the preparations for the 1713 election, he volunteered to stand down in favour of the son of Lord Chancellor Harcourt (Simon I), Hon. Simon Harcourt III*, but so prejudiced were the Oxfordshire gentry against Harcourt that Clerke was persuaded to remain. His continuing Tory allegiance was recorded both in the Worsley list and in a later analysis comparing the 1713 Parliament with that of 1715. Re-elected in 1715, he died at Hillingdon a few months later, on 2 May, and was buried, as requested, at 'my chapel at North Weston'. His chief beneficiary was his nephew Francis Carr Clerke, the son of his younger brother Richard, who served the county of Oxfordshire from 1697 to 1716 as clerk of the peace. Clerke also left money towards the completion of a 'house of correction' at Thame. There were, however, debts and legacies still owing from the estates in 1720, totalling £6,000.[4]

[1] F. G. Lee, *Hist. Thame Church*, 290, 311–14; IGI, London; PCC 71 Pott, 85 Fagg; *VCH Oxon.* vii. 173. [2] *CSP Dom.* 1685, p. 209. [3] Ibid.; *Hist. Oxf. Univ.* ed. Sutherland and Mitchell, 72; Add. 70223, Delaune to Harley, 26 Nov. 1704. [4] *HMC Portland*, vii. 118, 139; Le Neve, *Mon. Angl.* 1700–15, p. 304; PCC 85 Fagg; *VCH Oxon.* vii. 173; Lee, 313–14.

A. A. H.

CLERKE, Sir John, 4th Bt. (aft. 1683–1727), of Shabbington, Bucks. and St. Martin-in-the-Fields, London.

HASLEMERE 1710–1713

b. aft. 1683, 1st s. of Sir William Clerke, 3rd Bt., of Shabbington by Catherine, da. of Sir Arthur Onslow, 2nd Bt.† (and sis. of Sir Richard Onslow, 3rd Bt.*) of Knowle and West Clandon, Surr. *unm. suc.* fa. as 4th Bt. 1699.

The Clerkes were ultimately of Warwickshire origin, but had settled on the Buckinghamshire–Oxfordshire border in the early 16th century. Although the family had been honoured with a baronetcy by Charles II at the Restoration, its local political impact after the Revolution was confined to the modest parliamentary career of Clerke's great-uncle, Francis Clerke II*, MP for Oxfordshire between 1710 and 1715. Clerke's father, identified by Dalton as the commander of a troop of horse in the Scottish campaign of 1689, did most to secure an interest in Surrey by obtaining a match with the influential Onslows of West Clandon. In addition, Clerke's great-great-grandfather had married into the Woodroffe family of Poyle, a long-established household in the west of the shire. However, such familial ties were clearly insufficient to promote the young baronet's participation in Surrey politics before his candidacy at Haslemere in 1710.

Although proving a politician of inconsistent allegiance during his subsequent parliamentary career, Clerke clearly stood as a Tory in his only electoral contest. His running mate, Theophilus Oglethorpe*, represented the most influential Tory family in the area, and in election year Clerke sought to establish his interest in the strongly Anglican borough by donating £80 to recast the bells of the local chapel. At the polls he performed extremely well to finish the clear winner, as the Tories scored a notable victory over both Whig candidates. He was duly identified as a Tory in the 'Hanover list' of the new Parliament and was later cited as a 'worthy patriot' for helping in the first session to discover the mismanagements of the previous administration. In the next session he was identified by Boyer as a member of the October Club, but he later broke with his party by voting against the French commerce bill in June 1713, a dramatic switch of political loyalties which was perhaps influenced by his Onslow connexions. His actual contribution to the business of the House was limited, however.

There is no evidence to suggest that Clerke tried to contest the election of 1713, at which the Haslemere seats were shared between the two parties. His opposition to the French commerce bill may have alienated Tory supporters in Haslemere, and it almost certainly played a part in his dismissal from the Oxfordshire commission of the peace in early 1714. Thereafter he slipped back into political obscurity, and the sale of the manor of Shabbington in 1716 indicates that financial difficulties may also have influenced his decision not to seek re-election. On his death on 20 Feb. 1727 his brother William succeeded to the baronetcy, but Clerke left the bulk of his estate to his sister Elizabeth. He was buried in Hanwell church in Middlesex, where his monumental inscription cited his age at death as 31, almost certainly an error, since he should have reached his majority by 1710 to have become eligible for election at Haslemere.[1]

[1] PCC 33 Farrant; G. Lipscomb, *Bucks.* i. 446–7; *VCH Bucks.* iv. 102–3; J. Aubrey, *Surr.* iv. 35; L. K. J. Glassey, *Appt. JPs*, 225; Lysons, *Environs* (1792–6), ii. 553.

P. L. G.

CLOBER(R)Y, John (c.1645–99), of Bradstone, Devon.

TRURO 1695–1698

b. c.1645, 1st s. of Christopher Clobery of Bradstone by Johanna, da. of Hugh Fortescue of Filleigh, Devon. *educ.* Exeter, Oxf. matric. 14 Mar. 1663, aged 18; I. Temple 1663. *m.* 29 Sept. 1673, Elizabeth (*d.* by 1695), da. of Sir William Courtenay, 1st Bt.†, of Powderham Castle and Ford House, Devon, 2s. (1 *d.v.p.*) 9da. (1 *d.v.p.*). *suc.* fa. 1677.[1]

Common councilman, Plymouth 1696.[2]

Clobery came from the senior branch of the Cloberys of Bradstone. His father's younger brother was Sir John Cloberry† (father of the first wife of William Bromley II*), who had settled in Hampshire. Politically, however, the two branches had parted company, with Sir John ready to support the Court under Charles II and James II. Indeed, he married his two eldest daughters to prominent Tories. John, on the other hand was a Whig. Returned for Truro in 1695, presumably on the interest of his cousin Hugh Fortescue*, he was forecast as likely to support the Court in the divisions of 31 Jan. 1696 over the proposed council of trade and signed the Association. Most noticeably, however, he was named as a common councilman in the new charter acquired by the Whigs for Plymouth in October 1696. The following month he voted for the attainder of Sir John Fenwick†. On 16 Dec. 1697 he was absent at a call of the House and was ordered to be sent for into custody. However, there is no mention of his release and on 4 Apr. 1698 he was again absent and ordered to attend in a fortnight. He did not stand in 1698 when listed as a Court supporter 'left out' of the new Parliament. He died in 1699 and was buried at Bradstone on 27 Mar. In the 1699–1700 session a private bill was passed to enable the trustees named in his will to sell part of his estate, in order to provide portions for his eight surviving daughters, amounting to a total of £10,000, and to settle debts worth almost £24,000.[3]

[1] Vivian, *Vis. Devon*, 201–2. [2] *CSP Dom.* 1696, p. 424. [3] PCC 69 Noel; *HMC Lords*, n.s. iv. 56–57.

E. C./S. N. H.

COCHRANE, William (aft. 1659–1717), of Kilmaronock, Dunbarton.

WIGTOWN BURGHS 14 Dec. 1708–1713

b. aft. 1659, 2nd s. of William Cochrane, *styled* Ld. Cochrane (1st s. *d.v.p.* of William, 1st Earl of Dundonald [S]), by Lady Katherine, da. of John Kennedy, 6th Earl of Cassillis [S]. *m.* Lady Grizel, da. of James Graham, 2nd Marquess of Montrose [S], 2s. (1 *d.v.p.*) 5da. *suc.* gdfa. to Kilmaronock 1679 (via disposition); bro. to Powkellie 1694.[1]

Burgess, Dumbarton 1682, Glasgow 1696, Edinburgh 1712.[2]

Lieut. Lord Ross's indep. tp. of horse, 1689–by 1691; commr. justiciary for the Highlands [S] 1693; jt. keeper of signet [S] 1711–13.[3]

MP [S] Renfrew 1689–95, Dunbartonshire 1702–7.

The career of William Cochrane of Kilmaronock illustrates the difficulties in classifying Scots Members in this period. He supported the Revolution, but later joined the cavalier wing of the Scottish Country party. A vigorous opponent of Union, he entered actively into Jacobite conspiracy, only to become a placeman under Lord Oxford (Robert Harley*). After his activities were investigated by the commissioners of public accounts in 1712, he narrowly escaped expulsion from the House, thereafter retiring from political life and not stirring during the rebellion of 1715. While at Westminster, he had acted with the Tories, but the route to this association was not straightforward. The Cochrane family had earned a reputation for extreme Presbyterianism by the late 17th century, despite the royalist vigour which had earned William's grandfather a peerage as 1st Earl of Dundonald. Cochrane's mother had insisted that Presbyterian ministers attend her husband's deathbed in 1679, one of whom reportedly prayed for the success of the western rebels. The mother's fervour, however, did not transmit to her daughters, one marrying the notorious John Graham of Claverhouse, another the 9th Earl of Eglintoun, a prominent episcopalian. The most influential marital connexion, however, was that between Cochrane's elder brother, the 2nd Earl of Dundonald, and a daughter of the 3rd Duke of Hamilton: in due course Cochrane became a firm adherent of the 4th Duke. Cochrane himself married into the family of Graham, marquesses (later dukes) of Montrose. The proximity of his family's estates to those of Montrose resulted in a degree of co-operation on legal, estate and political affairs. But, during the greater part of his Westminster career, Cochrane was estranged from the Duke of Montrose because of the latter's association with the Squadrone.[4]

Cochrane was returned for Renfrew to the Convention of Estates in 1689 and signed the act declaring its legality and the letter of congratulation to William III. A member of the 'Club' opposition of 1689–90, he continued to represent Renfrew in the Scottish parliament until 1695, also serving on several occasions as commissioner to the convention of royal burghs. Cochrane, indeed, had taken up arms in support of the Revolution, though there was a strong element of self-preservation involved. His estate, which bordered Loch Lomond, was a prime target for Highland raiders. Despite some successes, such as the capture of Lieutenant-Colonel MacGregor, a Jacobite officer and 'one of the greatest robbers and plunderers that this nation has seen', Cochrane was unable to prevent a serious devastation in November 1689, for which he later claimed damages of 34,000 merks. In the aftermath of repeated attacks, Cochrane and other landowners sought permission from the Scottish privy council in 1691 to establish a watch to guard against 'the incursions of thieves and broken men from the Highlands'. The watchmen subsequently employed, however, were themselves MacGregors, and in the estimation of one local historian ran a virtual protection racket, using one half of their band 'to recover stolen cattle, and the other half of them to steal to make blackmail necessary'. These difficulties had determined, to a great extent, Cochrane's loyalty during the establishment of the Williamite regime in Scotland. Having lost £1,000 in the Darien scheme, he stood as a Country candidate for Dunbartonshire in 1702. For his part in a bitter contest, Cochrane was deemed to have rekindled animosity between Montrose and the Duke of Argyll. In order to avert threats of imprisonment, he not only paid off some of his supporters' debts, but also brought £1,000 with him on election day. In the Scottish parliament he acted with the cavaliers, signing Country protests and following the lead of the Duke of Hamilton, whose motion in 1704 for deferring a decision on the succession he supported.[5]

Cochrane did not greatly involve himself in the management of his estates, preferring instead to lease them out and channel his resources into commercial and speculative ventures. In January 1705 he made an unsuccessful bid as part of a consortium for the 'roup of the customs'. This plan was blocked by the Marquess of Annandale, who set the public price at £31,000 in order to deter Cochrane and his partners but privately offered the contract to a group of Court supporters for £2,500 less. This action prompted George Lockhart* to complain about the 'scandalous, barefaced seducing of members of parliament'. In the face of such hostility from the Court Cochrane continued to act with the opposition. Although bitterly opposed to union with England, he helped persuade Lockhart to attend the negotiations in London, arguing that 'if he sat quiet and concealed his opinion' the other commissioners 'would not be so shy, and he might make discoveries'. Throughout the Union debates Cochrane took an extreme opposition line, signing numerous protests and only once voting with the Court, over the disposal of the Equivalent money. He tried to make political capital out of the anti-Union disturbances in Edinburgh and, as an episcopalian, opposed legislation to protect the status of the Kirk. Not content with parliamentary opposition, Cochrane and Lockhart were intent on fomenting rebellion in the western shires. In response to an initiative from Major James Cunningham of Aiket, they advanced 50 guineas for an exploratory mission and attempted to secure magnate approval. The Duke of Atholl proved a wholehearted convert, promising Highland support, whereas Hamilton was 'somewhat shy' and later 'thwarted and broke the measure' without consulting Cochrane and his co-conspirators. Since Cunningham was apparently a double agent, Hamilton's caution may have saved Cochrane from disaster.[6]

Having failed to prevent the Union, Cochrane determined nevertheless to derive from it the best advantages for Scotland and for himself. The rationalization of English and Scottish customs duties inevitably created short-term anomalies that were an encouragement to sharp practice and smuggling. In July 1707 Cochrane led a pressure group of merchants against a government crackdown on smuggling and succeeded in forcing some minor concessions from Lord Seafield. On 13 Dec. Cochrane wrote to Montrose, soliciting support on the question of drawbacks on salt-cured fish:

> The great drawback on our fishes would be allowed us, though cured with salt brought in here before 1 May last and did not pay the great duties, if it were not opposed by our own Scots Members. This is most confounding and astonishing to every man ... Is not this declared by the articles of Union and pled in our parliament as a vast encouragement to our fishing? ... Is there not the same reason for giving us the drawback as was in allowing us to bring in wines and brandy into England? ... If this be the way to engage our nation cordially to this Union, then I own I do not understand common sense. I am sure, be the Scotsmen who they will that does oppose this just and reasonable drawback to us, they must own they do not value whether they oblige or disoblige their friends and countrymen.[7]

Cochrane's involvement with Jacobite conspiracy continued. He was contacted by Colonel Hooke prior to the invasion attempt of 1708, but found himself compromised by the equivocal behaviour of Hamilton, who was accused of double-dealing by other Jacobites. Cochrane may well have shared Hamilton's fears that the intended force was insufficient. Montrose was keen to have Cochrane arrested during the invasion scare, but he remained unmolested on his estate, where he received the Stuart emissary Charles Fleming. Described by Fleming as 'very zealous in the King's interest', Cochrane was spared the dangers of armed rebellion by news of the invasion's failure.[8]

Cochrane thought of standing for Renfrewshire in 1708, hoping to secure support from Sir John Schaw, 3rd Bt.*, in return for his own interest in Dunbartonshire. He turned down Schaw's suggested reversal of this arrangement, and, after briefly canvassing in Stirlingshire, decided to wait until a convenient vacancy occurred at Wigtown Burghs in December 1708, where he was returned on the interest of his kinsman and fellow anti-unionist, the Earl of Galloway.[9]

Cochrane's activities at Westminster have left little trace in the Journals. This impression of inactivity is somewhat misleading, however, for he helped secure the Act enforcing payment of the drawbacks on salt-cured fish. Customs officers had refused to pay the stipulated drawback to which Scots merchants were entitled under the Union treaty. Cochrane was sent up to London with a specific commission as a lobbyist and was paid for his services. Lockhart also testified to Cochrane's general activity at this time, naming him as one of those who 'stood firm by the Tories'. According to an undated report, he joined five or six Scotsmen in criticizing the 'ministry's proceedings against the Scots after the invasion last year'. This debate can be provisionally attributed to 10 Mar. 1709 on a motion congratulating the government for 'timely and effectual' action. The following year he was listed as having voted for the impeachment of Dr Sacheverell, which seems intrinsically unlikely and was specifically refuted by Lockhart. In the summer of 1710 Cochrane campaigned for addresses in favour of a dissolution, believing with Hamilton that 'her Majesty is very timorous and needs to be supported'. Re-elected for Wigtown Burghs in 1710, Cochrane was classified as an episcopal Tory by the Duchess of Buccleuch's chaplain Richard Dongworth. On another occasion Dongworth praised Cochrane and his family for their support of episcopalian clergy and laity.[10]

Cochrane proved a loyal supporter of the new Tory administration and in 1711 was made joint keeper of the Scottish signet, an office worth about £700 p.a. This appointment was, in part, a friendly gesture towards Hamilton. In an attempt to stretch patronage a bit further Lord Treasurer Oxford negotiated a private agreement by which the joint keepers, Cochrane and John Pringle*, were instructed to share the profits of the signet with an unofficial participant, Sir Alexander Areskine, 2nd Bt.* They reneged on this deal, however, and Areskine whistled in vain for his money. Cochrane gradually assumed a self-ordained role as adviser to Oxford on Scots affairs, particularly over the management of the customs. He was consulted over the appointment of j.p.s in Renfrewshire and secured valuable forage contracts for the army in Scotland.[11]

In January 1711 Cochrane presented a petition against the return of Patrick Vans for Wigtownshire, favouring the case of Galloway's brother, Hon. John Stewart*, and, with Lockhart, harrying the sheriff of Wigtown for his conduct during the election. He also acted against Mungo Graham*, a client of Montrose, in the disputed election for Kinross-shire, his particular animosity being attributed to resentment at the Duke's earlier attempts to secure his arrest as a suspected Jacobite. Thomas Smith II* described Cochrane at this time as one of those who had never 'spared one Whig in their votes since coming hither'. On a social level, however, he was not averse to mixing with Whigs and frequently attended Lord Ossulston's Anglo-Scottish dining group. He strongly favoured peace negotiations, and thought a successful outcome was essential for the survival of the ministry. He naturally voted for the Scottish toleration bill on 7 Feb. 1712.[12]

Cochrane's attention to political issues in the remainder of this Parliament was overshadowed by an unexpected personal attack upon him by the commissioners of public accounts, chaired by his former ally Lockhart. The commissioners' second report, presented to the House on 17 Mar. 1712, stated that those responsible for implementing the 1709 Act enforcing payment of the drawbacks on salt-cured fish 'had not applied all the money . . . to the uses therein mentioned'. Gilbert Stuart, one of those responsible, deponed that Cochrane, 'who was concerned in trade with Stuart and others', had been sent to London on a dual mission. He was to 'dispose of a quantity of goods they had sent thither', for which he was paid expenses of £300, but at the same time he was to lobby for an act enforcing payment of the debentures. It was agreed beforehand that, in recognition of the agreement to pay his expenses, he would refund to his trading partners 'whatever sum should be given as a gratuity from the proprietors of the salt and debentures'. Accordingly, when Cochrane was paid £195 'he gave his receipt for it', but 'Stuart retained the money and afterwards divided it betwixt himself and partners in trade'. This amounted to a bribe, according to Lockhart, who nevertheless maintained that there was no vindictiveness in these proceedings, for 'though we heard a surmise that bribes had been given, we did not in the least expect or know anything of Mr Cochrane. But since he was accused, we could not help reporting it to the House.' Lockhart's description was somewhat disingenuous, for there had been a distinct cooling in relationships. He referred to 'indignities received, without any reason', from Cochrane and 'many instances of his hearty goodwill to have ruined me'. One consequence of the immediate crisis was that mutual friends manufactured a reconciliation. In Lockhart's version of events, this involved Cochrane becoming convinced of his 'error (to give it no worse term)' and presenting himself at Lockhart's house, 'where he acknowledged the same'. To Cochrane this was no more than a 'seeming friendship' brought about at the 'earnest desire of some of my good friends'. Among his other Scottish persecutors, Cochrane mentioned John Carnegie*, Alexander Murray*, Sir Alexander Cumming, 1st Bt.*, and John Houstoun*, noting that the last had taken the trouble to 'draw up some comparisons . . . between Mr Walpole's [Robert II*] case and mine (of which without saying any more) I am glad I was not here when he was sent to the Tower'. In his defence Cochrane mustered a wide range of support, including such obvious figures as Hamilton, Mar and Dundonald, but also, surprisingly, Montrose, to whom Cochrane wrote 'with all imaginable sincerity':

> It is a true saying that friends are never better known than when one is in trouble . . . and if it had not been for all our countrymen (except six or seven) and the generality of Englishmen, I had been expelled our House long ere now, with all the ignom[in]y their malice could invent . . . The spring of all this affair proceeded without any manner of cause, unless it be because I have the honour and

happiness to be married to one of your Grace's family... I must say never man could have acted a more kindly and friendly part. You have done more for me than I could ask.

The notion that hostility to Montrose lay at the root of this affair is utterly unconvincing, despite the fact that Argyll and his brother Lord Ilay had been active behind the scenes. Although they had no great love for Montrose, they also had sufficient grounds to dislike Cochrane in his own right. There is no doubt, however, that Montrose's influence turned the tide. Cochrane believed that it was the Duke's influence which obliged Carnegie 'to be altogether silent' on 17 May, when consideration of the report was further deferred. No more proceedings took place during this Parliament and the question was never revived. Cochrane's gratitude was fulsome and his apology abject. 'I never sit down to write to your Grace', he told him the following year, 'but I blush when I look back on the past time and how unkindly by, yea and unjustly, I have lived with you, which was unpardonable in me.' His physical and mental health was suffering from the ordeal. Even his involvement with the forage contracts was scrutinized, and in panic he consulted Lockhart for advice, receiving the sarcastic reply that

> I take it a little ill [that] you should banter me so much as to desire my assistance... Did you offer me your friendship in assisting me to get a good place, 'twould be more natural, than for me to pretend to do service to one whose court is so well established and interest so great with the rulers of the land.

A more helpful response was forthcoming from John Pringle, who promised to be active on his behalf. In the event Cochrane suffered no repercussions from this inquiry and was on the way to recovering his health by June 1713. He did not stand at the general election and made no notable impact on public affairs thereafter. The surviving correspondence of his wife indicates the existence of financial difficulties, though their severity remains unclear. Cochrane died in August 1717 and was succeeded by his eldest son, Thomas, who later succeeded his cousin as 6th Earl of Dundonald. In the consequent process of consolidating his estates, Kilmaronock was sold to the Duke of Montrose.[13]

[1] K. Parker and J. Anderson, *Ped. of Cochranes*; *Hist. Scot. Parl.* 127; *Scots Peerage* ed. Paul, iii. 344–52; *Retour of Heirs*, ii. Inquisitiones Gen. 7529. [2] *Scot. Rec. Soc.* lxxiii. 16; lvi. 238; lxii. 40. [3] *APS*, ix. 54. [4] Lauder of Fountainhall, *Decisions of Ct. of Session*, i. 299; M. Napier, *Mem. Dundee*, ii. 386; *HMC Laing*, i. 343; *HMC Mar and Kellie*, i. 216; *DNB* (Cochrane, Sir John; Cochrane, Sir William); *Scots Peerage*, iv. 382; vi. 258. [5] *Hist. Scot. Parl.* 127; info. on members of Scot. parl. from Dr P. W. J. Riley; P. W. J. Riley, *King Wm. and Scot. Politicians*, 175; *Bk. of Dumbartonshire*, ii. 222, 287; *Reg. PC Scotland*, 1689, pp. 530–1; 1690, p. 5; 1691, pp. 124–5; P. A. Hopkins, *Glencoe*, 201; *Scot. Hist. Soc.* ser. 3, xlvii. 62, 86–87; *Darien Pprs.* (Bannatyne Club, xc), 373; Atholl mss at Blair Atholl, box 45, bdle. II, nos. 169, 248, Hamilton to [Tullibardine], 20 Aug. 1702, John Haldane* to [same], 26 Oct. 1702; Buccleuch mss at Drumlanrig Castle, bdle. 1151, no. 23, [–] to [Queensberry], 25 Sept. 1702; *HMC Hamilton suppl.* 157; Boyer, *Anne Annals*, iii. app. 41. [6] *Bk. of Dumbartonshire*, 223; J. G. Smith, *Strathendick and its Inhabitants*, 354; SRO, Seafield mss GD248/571/6/11, Annandale to Seafield, 2 Jan. [1705]; SRO, Breadalbane mss GD112/39/211/19, Polton to [Breadalbane], 18 Jan. [1705]; *Lockhart Letters* ed. Szechi. 10; info. from Dr Riley; P. W. J. Riley, *Union*, 333; *Lockhart Pprs.* i. 142, 166, 182, 186, 189, 204, 211, 221; *Scot. Hist. Soc.* ser. 5, vi. 109; *APS*, xi. 321–2, 415. [7] *HMC Mar and Kellie*, 409, 411; SRO, Montrose mss GD220/5/113/6, Cochrane to Montrose, 13 Dec. 1707. [8] *Orig. Pprs.* ed. Macpherson, ii. 12; *Hooke Corresp.* 141, 543–4; *Lockhart Pprs.* 197–200, 232, 235; Wodrow, *Analecta*, i. 320–1; *Hooke's Negotiations Scot.* 182; Riley, *Union*, 286. [9] Montrose mss GD220/5/250/3, John Grahame to Montrose, 28 Feb. 1708; GD220/5/154/2, Linlithgow to same, 1708. [10] P. W. J. Riley, *Eng. Ministers and Scotland*, 120–1; *Lockhart Mems.* ed Szechi, 287; *Lockhart Pprs.* 36, 301; Scottish Cath. Archs., Blairs College mss BL2/158/3, James Carnegy to Scots Coll. [1709]; Breadalbane mss GD112/39/243/27, Cochrane to [Breadalbane], 29 Aug. 1710; *SHR*, lx. 66; Christ Church Oxf. Wake mss 5, f. 13. [11] SRO, Hamilton mss GD406/1/5755, John Hamilton to Duke of Hamilton, 4 Sept. 1711; NLS, Advocates' mss, Wodrow pprs. letters Quarto 6, f. 19; Riley, *Eng. Ministers*, 168–70; *HMC Portland*, x. 156, 165–6, 239–40, 275–6, 324; Add. 70166, list of Renfrew j.p.s; 70278, Cochrane to [Oxford], 29 Oct. 1711; SRO, Smythe of Methven mss GD190/3/282/6, A. Symmers to Cochrane, 1713; *Cal. Treas. Bks.* xxv. 234, 542; xxvi. 78, 149, 159; *Cal. Treas. Pprs.* 1708–14, p. 351. [12] SRO, Mar and Kellie mss, Hon. Sir James Dunbar, 1st Bt.*, to Ld. Grange (Hon. James Erskine[†]), 20 Jan. 1711; Wodrow pprs. letters Quarto 5, f. 128; Montrose mss GD220/5/808/17, 18a–b, Graham to Montrose, 10, 13 Feb. 1711; *SHR*, lxxi, 116, 125; Wodrow, *Analecta*, 348. [13] Cobbett, *Parlty. Hist.* vi. 1118–19; *Lockhart Letters*, 57; Wodrow pprs. letters Quarto 6, f. 174; *HMC Portland*, 239; Montrose mss GD220/5/283/1–3, Cochrane to Montrose, [April], 17 May 1712, Montrose to Cochrane, 2 May 1712; GD220/5/295/4, Cochrane to [Montrose], 7 May 1713; Atholl mss box 45, bdle. 11, John Douglas to Atholl, 6 June 1713; Smythe of Methven mss GD190/3/282/3, 7, 9, Lockhart to Cochrane, 8 Nov. 1712, Pringle to same, 16 June 1713, same to [–], 25 June 1713; GD190/3/279, corresp. of Grizel Cochrane; *Scot. Rec. Soc.* vii. 104; *Services of Heirs*, i. 1710–19, p. 6; *Scots Peerage*, iii. 351; Parker and Anderson, *Ped. of Cochranes*.

D. W.

COCKBURN, John (c.1679–1758), of Ormiston, Haddington.

SCOTLAND 1707–1708
HADDINGTONSHIRE 1708–1741

b. c.1679, 1st s. of Adam Cockburn, MP [S], of Ormiston, Ld. Ormiston SCJ and lord justice clerk, by his 1st w. Lady Susan Hamilton, da. of John, 4th Earl of Haddington [S]. *educ.* Glasgow Univ. 1695. *m.* (1) 1700, Lady Beatrice (d. 1702), da. of John Carmichael, 1st Earl of Hyndford [S], *s.p.*; (2) Arabella, 3rd da. and coh. of Anthony Rowe*, 1s. *suc.* fa. 16 Apr. 1735.[1]

Burgess, Glasgow 1694, Ayr 1706, Edinburgh 1708, Dunbar 1710.[2]

MP [S] Haddingtonshire 1703–7.
PC [S] 1704, 1707; commr. exchequer [S] 1704, 1707; ld. of Trade 1714–17, of Admiralty 1717–32, 1742–4.[3]

Better known as the 'father of Scottish husbandry', Cockburn also pursued a long and successful career both in the Scottish and British Parliaments. Like his father he was a Presbyterian, staunch to the Revolution interest, though predisposed to look towards the court for rewards. At the Scottish general election of 1702 Cockburn was doubly returned as the fourth commissioner for Haddingtonshire, but succeeded in carrying the consequent by-election in June 1703. He immediately joined the Country party's attack on the ministry from which his father had recently been purged. On his own initiative, he joined the 'New Party' in 1704, seceding from the opposition with his future Squadrone colleagues. Ormiston had taken care to be abroad during this uncertain period, but upon his return successfully manoeuvred his way back into office as lord justice clerk, a return to favour which was unaffected by the subsequent collapse of the 'New Party' experiment. Both father and son supported the Union, although Ormiston's conduct was more Court-orientated than Cockburn's, which conformed strictly to the Squadrone line. He was therefore included in the Squadrone contingent of representatives to the first Parliament of Great Britain. The contemporary historian Cunningham later stigmatized Cockburn as one of those who 'made a specious pretence of the public good' in supporting the Union 'with an eye, in the midst of the public affairs, to their private interest'. This harsh verdict was not without foundation, but the safety of the succession was a paramount consideration, and Cockburn saw the unification of the Scottish and English Parliaments as the surest means to this end.[4]

At Westminster Cockburn rapidly established himself as one of the leaders of the Squadrone in the Commons. He was appointed on 4 Dec. 1707 to the drafting committee to repeal the Scottish act of security and on the 11th he spoke 'very handsomely' in favour of the abolition of the Scottish privy council, being appointed to the resultant drafting committee for a bill to complete the Union. He also featured among those appointed to prepare a bill to deter disloyal clan chiefs. Although he took a strongly anti-Jacobite stance over the invasion, he supported the idea of a political alliance between the Squadrone and the cavalier leader the Duke of Hamilton. Cockburn's hostility to the Scottish Court party was also evident on 25 Feb., when he 'spoke reflectingly and scurvily of the parliament of Scotland' upon an unsuccessful Squadrone motion to invert the classes of the Equivalent. At the 1708 election Cockburn was returned for Haddingtonshire after an awkward contest. He was praised by the cavalier and Squadrone leaders for his work in co-ordinating their joint electoral efforts and was given responsibility for reporting on these matters to the Junto.[5]

In the 1708 Parliament Cockburn continued to take a leading role in parliamentary affairs, though surviving reports of his contributions to debate are few. He was assiduous in his attendance, reporting to Lord Tweeddale on 22 Jan. that, since the recess, he had been 'almost every night' in the Commons, where some sittings had lasted into the early hours of the morning. He also reported that there was 'a project on foot here for erecting an African Company, which if it takes will really prove a West Indian Company too; how prejudicial these companies are to us [in Scotland] every unbiased thinking man must easily see'. He recommended that petitions be started locally both on this topic and on another of purely local interest, namely a harbour bill in favour of William Morison*. Cockburn's successful neutralization of this measure demonstrated a keen eye for the details of parliamentary procedure. Having obtained amendments which considerably reduced the bill's impact, he gave this account of his motives to Lord Tweeddale, the hereditary sheriff of Haddington: 'I hope while I represent the county I shall always be able to answer that I do to the best of my knowledge to serve them [sic] in all their concerns from such as Mr Morison's bill to those of greater consequence.' He also courted favour with the town of Dunbar, writing to the council in late 1709, 'representing that he had been instrumental in getting all the coals brought to the port and harbour of Dunbar exempted from that duty laid on coal waterborne', for which service he was made a hereditary burgess of the town. Cockburn spoke and voted on 10 Mar. against the ministry's conduct during the recent Jacobite invasion attempt, thereby keeping faith with the Hamilton pact; and on 5 Apr. spoke on behalf of 'the dying laws of Scotland', during a debate on the treason bill. He voted for the impeachment of Dr Sacheverell in 1710. In the wake of the trial, as the balance of power shifted strongly towards the Tories, Cockburn's father was dismissed as lord justice clerk and replaced by a nominee of Robert Harley*.[6]

Cockburn was re-elected for Haddingtonshire without a contest in 1710, receiving support from his friend Hon. William Kerr*, who deemed him 'as good a friend and as honest a man as is in the world and I am sure loves my brother [the Duke of Roxburghe] and me to a degree, and also respects my lord Marquess [of Tweeddale] with very much sincerity'. Listed as a Whig both in the 'Hanover list' of 1710 and in the analysis of Scottish elections by the episcopal chaplain Richard Dongworth, Cockburn voted on that side over the Bewdley election on 19 Dec. After the recess he continued to be active on election cases, opposing George Lockhart's motion regarding the sheriff of Wigtown on 20 Jan. 1711, and told in support of Mungo Graham* over the disputed return for Kinross-shire on 10 Feb. Although no doubts should be entertained about Cockburn's loyalty to the Hanoverian succession, he continued to maintain communication with Hamilton and the cavaliers.[7]

On 7 Dec. 1711 Cockburn voted with the Whigs on the motion for 'No Peace without Spain'. In February 1712 he was convinced that the conduct of foreign policy was being mismanaged by Lord Oxford (Harley), who 'seems to divert himself with bamboozling all Europe'. Oxford's policy threatened to increase the power of France and the danger from Jacobitism. Cockburn argued that

> things are gone so far and the interest of the one [France] seems by the measures taken to be so strengthened abroad, and the friends of the other [the Pretender] so encouraged and strengthened at home that he will appear an able minister indeed if he keeps all out of their hands.

The increasing pressure on the ministry from the High Tories was evident in their successful promotion of measures favouring Scottish episcopalians during this session. Cockburn naturally opposed these, voting against the Scottish toleration bill on 7 Feb. 1712 and telling on a procedural motion against the patronages bill on 13 Mar. The following year, he nevertheless found sufficient common ground to unite with the Scottish Tories, albeit temporarily, during the malt tax crisis. Participating fully in the united Scottish opposition, he was one of the four deputies who informed the Queen on 26 May 1713 that the Scots would move for a dissolution of the Union unless their grievances were redressed. Lord Balmerino somewhat grudgingly admitted that Cockburn 'seemed hearty enough', comparing him with George Baillie*, who was 'full of shifts'. Indeed, their divergent reaction to the crisis created some tension. But Baillie, as the senior figure within the Squadrone, appears to have overborne his colleague's enthusiasm. Cockburn was probably the unnamed friend whom Baillie reported to his wife as having 'talked so wildly' about dissolving the Union that he had been 'forced to check him'. The readiness with which Cockburn fell into line indicated that there was no fundamental disagreement: neither expected the motion to succeed in the first instance, nor intended inadvertently to assist the Jacobite cause. After the Hanoverian succession, when both Cockburn and his father were restored to favour at Court, the family was active in suppressing attempts to dissolve the Union. In 1713 Cockburn had also opposed, on Whig principles, the commercial aspects of the peace with France, as a teller against the suspension of duty on French wine on 6 May and by voting against the French commerce bill on 4 and 18 June.[8]

Prior to the 1713 election Roxburghe had made it clear that if Cockburn were to be defeated in Haddingtonshire, this would be 'an affront to all [the] Squa[drone]'. Although there was a contest, Cockburn defeated his Tory challenger, and was classified as a Whig on the electoral analysis sent by Lord Polwarth to Hanover. He opposed the expulsion of Richard Steele on 18 Mar. 1714, speaking in defence of Steele's request to defend his writings paragraph by paragraph, and rejecting Tory attempts to draw unjust parallels with the Sacheverell case. Cockburn was also active on election cases, recording four tellerships hostile to Tory interests. As the likelihood of the Queen's death increased, he played a leading role in concerting the Squadrone's preparations for the succession, and afterwards was rewarded with appointment to an office worth £1,000 p.a., his father also being reappointed lord justice clerk.[9]

Cockburn supported the government until 1733, when he joined the opposition to Walpole (Robert II*). He continued to represent Haddingtonshire until 1741; but local interests, particularly agricultural improvement, occupied much of his attention in later years. Cockburn also developed other enterprises, including a linen manufactory, a brewery, a distillery, and a bleaching-field. These initiatives proved financially ruinous, resulting in the sale of his estates in 1747 and 1749. Cockburn died on 13 Nov. 1758 and the direct line ended with his only son, George, who died without male issue.[10]

[1] *Hist. Scot. Parl.* 131–3; R. Cockburn and H. A. Cockburn, *Recs. Cockburn Fam.* 134–5; *Scots Peerage* ed. Paul, iv. 593; W. Robinson, *Hackney*, ii. 10–11. [2] *Scot. Rec. Soc.* lvi. 232; lxii. 41; Carnegie Lib. Ayr, Ayr burgh recs. B6/18/8, council mins. 23 Apr. 1706; SRO, Dunbar burgh recs. B 18/13/2, f. 269, council mins. 3 Jan. 1710. [3] *Hist. Scot. Parl.* 131–3; SP 55/27, warrant, 23 June 1707. [4] *Hist. Scot. Parl.* 131–3; *DNB* (Cockburn, Adam); info. from Dr P. W. J. Riley on members of Scot. parl.; *APS*, xi. 102; *Crossrigg Diary*, 140; Boyer, *Anne Annals*, iii. app. 43; P. W. J. Riley, *Union*, 45, 327, 334; Cunningham, *Hist. GB*, ii. 60. [5] Roxburghe mss at Floors Castle, bdle. 1069, Hon. William Kerr to Countess of Roxburghe, 4 Dec. 1707; bdle. 739, William Bennet* to same, 16 Dec. 1707; Cunningham, 135; *HMC Mar and Kellie*, i. 428–9; *Duchess of Marlborough Corresp.* ii. 254, 258, 262; Add. 9102, ff. 72–73; 61629, ff. 120–1. [6] NLS, ms 14415, ff. 174–5, 184; Dunbar burgh recs. B18/13/2, f. 269; Scottish Catholic Archs. Blairs Coll. mss

BL2/158/3, James Carnegy to Scots College, n.d. [1709]; *Nicolson Diaries* ed. Jones and Holmes, 493; P. W. J. Riley, *Eng. Ministers and Scotland*, 171. [7] Roxburghe mss, bdle. 1074, Kerr to his mother, 11 Aug. 1710; *SHR*, lx. 64; SRO, Mar and Kellie mss GD124/15/1024/11, Sir James Dunbar, 1st Bt.*, to Ld. Grange (Hon. James Erskine†), 5 Dec. 1710; GD124/15/1020/4, 7, same to same, 19 Dec. 1710, 20 Jan. 1711; Scot. Hist. Soc. *Misc.* xii. 134. [8] *Lockhart Pprs.* i. 113; *Lockhart Letters* ed. Szechi, 74–9; Cobbett, *Parlty. Hist.* vi. 1215; Aberdeen Univ. Lib. Duff House (Montcoffer) mss 3175/2380, 'Resolution of the Commons to Call a Meeting of the Lords', [23] May 1713; Scot. Hist. Soc. *Misc.* 153; Haddington mss at Mellerstain, 5, Baillie to wife, 28 May 1713 (Jones trans.); SRO, Hamilton mss GD406/1/8806, [?Selkirk] to [?Hamilton], n.d. [aft. Aug. 1714]; *Parlty Hist.* i. 69. [9] Douglas diary (Hist. of Parl. trans.), 18 Mar. 1714; SRO, Montrose mss GD220/5/32/a, Squadrone circular letter, [aft. 18 Mar. 1714]; Roxburghe mss, bdle. 756, Roxburghe to his mother, 9 Dec. 1714; Riley, *Eng. Ministers and Scotland*, 258. [10] T. H. Cockburn-Hood, *House of Cockburn*, 158; *Scot. Hist. Soc.* ser. 1, xlv. pp. xvii–xliv.

D. W.

COCKS, Charles (1646–1727), of Worcester and Powick, Worcs.

WORCESTER 7 Feb. 1694–1695
DROITWICH 1695–1708

bap. 9 Sept. 1646, 1st s. of Thomas Cocks of Castleditch, Herefs. by 2nd w. Elizabeth Gower. *m.* bef. 1685, Mary, da. of John Somers of Worcester, sis. and event. h. of Sir John Somers*, 2s. 4da. (2 *d.v.p.*).[1]
  Clerk of the patents 1699–?[2]
  Asst. Worcester workhouse 1705.[3]

As the son of his father's second marriage, Cocks could not hope to inherit a landed estate. He turned to the law, practising as a solicitor in Worcester, for such influential clients as the Worcester clothiers' company. Cocks must be distinguished from his many namesakes, who included a cousin admitted at the Middle Temple in 1667; an uncle (*d.* 1691) who became a barrister at Furnival's Inn; and a second cousin (the brother of Sir Richard Cocks, 2nd Bt.*) who became rector of Dumbleton in Gloucestershire. The mainspring of his political career was no doubt his marriage to Mary Somers, sister of the future lord chancellor. When Somers was raised from attorney-general to be lord keeper of the great seal in March 1693 Cocks sought to replace him as Member for Worcester. The election was no formality, however, and a bitter contest ensued, in which he was defeated. Cocks petitioned, and was eventually seated on 7 Feb. 1694.[4]

During his first session in the House Cocks acted as a teller on 15 Mar. 1694 in favour of an unsuccessful motion that Sir Jonathan Raymond* be granted leave of absence to attend his mother-in-law's funeral. In the 1695 election he retired from the contest at Worcester to come in instead for Droitwich, possibly in a move to avoid adding to the animosities engendered by the Worcester by-election. Henceforth his appearances in the Journals are difficult to distinguish from those of Charles Cox (Southwark) and, later on, from Charles Coxe (Cirencester). In the 1695–6 session Cocks was forecast as a likely supporter of the Court in the divisions of 31 Jan. 1696 over the council of trade. He signed the Association, and in March 1696 voted for fixing the price of guineas at 22s. In the following session, he voted on 25 Nov. for the attainder of Sir John Fenwick†. A Mr 'Cox' or 'Cocks' acted as a teller three times during this Parliament and received leave of absence for three weeks on 9 Jan. 1697 and again on 21 Mar. 1698.[5]

Despite the possibility of a contest at Droitwich in 1698 if the Foleys, Thomas I* and Thomas III*, were defeated for Worcestershire and Stafford respectively, Cocks was returned unopposed with the backing of both Shrewsbury and Somers. Given his close association with Somers, it is not surprising that on a comparative analysis of the old and new Parliaments compiled in about September 1698 he was classed as a Court supporter. During the 1698–9 session Cocks may have been a teller twice. A 'Mr Cox' received leave of absence on 14 Mar. 1699. At the end of the session, in May, Cocks's relationship to Somers bore fruit, with his appointment as clerk of the patents, an office in the court of Chancery in the lord chancellor's gift, and he was appropriately ascribed to Somers' and the Junto's interest in an analysis of the House undertaken between January and May 1700.[6]

Cocks does not seem to have been troubled at Droitwich in the election of January 1701. The possibility of a contest at Droitwich in November again depended on the disposition of the other seats. However, with the election of Sir John Pakington, 4th Bt.*, for the county, this threat receded and Cocks was duly returned unopposed with Edward Foley*. On Robert Harley's* analysis of the new Parliament, he was listed with the Whigs, and he may have acted as a teller twice during the session.[7]

Cocks was returned unopposed at Droitwich at the 1702 election. On 2 Nov. 1702, he may well have told against the motion that the Commons had not had right done them by the Lords over the impeachments. He also followed a predictably Whiggish line on 13 Feb. 1703, when voting for the Lords' amendments to the bill enlarging the time to take the Abjuration. On the main issue of the 1704–5 session, Cocks was listed on 30 Oct. 1704 as a probable opponent of the Tack, may have been on Harley's lobbying list (although this is unlikely), and he did not vote for the Tack on 28 Nov.

Cocks was again returned for Droitwich in 1705, and his name appears on a list of placemen, by virtue of his position as clerk of the patents, and as 'no Church' on an analysis of the new House. In the two extant division lists for 1705–6 he voted on 25 Oct. 1705 for the Court candidate for Speaker, and on 18 Feb. 1706 he supported the Court on the proceedings over the 'place clause' in the regency bill. In between, a 'Mr Cox' had received leave of absence for a month on 15 Dec. 1705. In 1706–7 Cocks seems to have been deeply involved in the manoeuvring around a bill to better preserve the ancient salt springs in Droitwich and the rights of proprietors. On 14 Feb. he and William Bromley I* were ordered to prepare it. Cocks, it seems, favoured a return to the position whereby the corporation rather than the proprietors had ultimate control over the salt industry. In the event the bill ran into opposition and lapsed in committee. The last session of the Parliament was again dominated by the bill to preserve the Droitwich salt springs. Cocks was the main parliamentary manager of the bill. On 15 Jan. 1708, James Vernon I* reported to Shrewsbury that 'Mr Cox [sic] intends to move tomorrow for bringing in the Droitwich bill'. He presented it on the 17th, but it was again opposed and came to grief in committee on the issue of the corporation's assent. As this had not been signified in writing, and at least one burgess was there to dissent, 'Mr Cox [sic] the chairman thought it advisable to adjourn for a fortnight, that in the meantime the corporation might signify their consent to it if it was their intention'. Vernon regarded this as a defeat, and it seems highly likely that the fiasco cost Cocks his seat. Certainly Cocks's colleague Edward Foley succeeded in distancing himself from the debacle and in the 1708 election was joined in Parliament by his relative Edward Winnington. National considerations are unlikely to have played any part, for Cocks had remained a Whig, as is shown in an analysis of early 1708, and the election was in general something of a Whig triumph.[8]

Cocks did not stand again, although he was probably the 'Mr Cocks' touted as a possible partner for Thomas Wylde* at Worcester in 1710. He probably died early in 1727, as his son, James*, wrote to Philip Yorke† on 27 Feb. about taking out an administration for the will. James Cocks eventually inherited all the Somers estates in Worcestershire and Reigate, but it was his grandson by his second son, John, for whom the Somers barony was revived in 1784.[9]

[1] IGI, Herefs.; J. V. Somers Cocks, *Hist. Cocks Fam.* 87–88; Add. 45094 M; Clutterbuck, *Herts.* i. 457; Manning and Bray, *Surr.* i. 286. [2] *CSP Dom.* 1699–1700, p. 191. [3] Hereford and Worcester RO (Worcester, St. Helen's), Cal. Wm. Lygon letters, 127, Thomas Bearcroft to Lygon, 7 July 1705. [4] Hereford and Worcester RO (Worcester, St. Helen's), Worcester clothiers' co. mss 705:232/BA 5955/7/V, receipt for legal services, 1686; Hooper, *Reigate*, 32; Somers Cocks, 76–77, 96–97; info. from Dr D. F. Lemmings; Surr. RO (Kingston), Somers mss 371/14/B5, 6, 8, Cocks to Somers, 11, 13 Nov., 9 Dec. 1693. [5] W. L. Sachse, *Ld. Somers*, 107–8. [6] Somers mss 371/14/E14, Shrewsbury to Somers, 11 May 1698; *Vernon–Shrewsbury Letters*, ii. 119; A. Browning, *Danby*, iii. 214; *CSP Dom.* 1699–1700, p. 191. [7] Somers mss 371/14/B20, William Walsh* to [Somers], 26 Oct. 1701. [8] Northants. RO, Montagu (Boughton) mss 77/81, Talbot to [Shrewsbury], 25 Feb. 1706–7; 48/177, 193, Vernon to same, 15 Jan., 24 Feb. 1707–8. [9] Add. 35359, f. 131.

S. N. H.

COCKS, James (c.1685–1750), of the Middle Temple.

REIGATE   29 Nov. 1707–1710, 1713–1747

b. c.1685, 1st s. of Charles Cocks*. *educ.* Trinity, Oxf. matric. May 1700, aged 15; M. Temple 1702, called 1708. *m.* (1) Sept. 1718, Lady Elizabeth, da. of Richard Newport*, 2nd Earl of Bradford, 1s. *d.v.p.*; (2) May 1737, Anne (d. 1739), da. of William, 4th Baron Berkeley of Stratton, 1s. *suc.* fa. 1727; aunt, Lady Jekyll, to Reigate, Surr. and Brookmans, Herts. 1745.[1]

Trustee, Reigate par. lib. 1708–?d.[2]

James Cocks was remarkably fortunate in his legal connexions, which made a career at the bar almost inevitable. His father was a provincial attorney, who married the sister of Sir John Somers*, the lord chancellor. His uncle, Sir Joseph Jekyll*, was a Welsh judge and master of the rolls, and in 1719 his sister married Philip Yorke†, another man destined for the woolsack. In common with all three, Cocks was educated at the Middle Temple and cannot have found his connexions a hindrance to his career, for he was called to the bar in 1708. The relationship with Somers also helped him to find a seat in the Commons. In 1697 Somers had received a grant of the manor of Reigate, to help maintain the dignity of his recently acquired peerage, and this carried a preponderant influence in the borough, which allowed Cocks to acquire the seat on the death of Stephen Hervey* in 1707. Contemporaries were clear about his political affiliations, and on an analysis of the Commons early in 1708 he was classed as a Whig.[3]

Re-elected for Reigate in 1708, Cocks was again classed as a Whig on a list of that year. In the first session of the new Parliament he supported the naturalization of the Palatines. The presence of two namesakes, Members for Southwark and Cirencester, although they spelt their surnames differently, makes it difficult to identify him. He may have acted as a teller on 14 Apr. 1709 against a motion that the Speaker leave the chair, to allow the committee stage of the bill providing for surveys preparatory to the purchase of land to improve the fortifications at

Portsmouth and Chatham. In 1710 he was listed as voting for the impeachment of Dr Sacheverell and in consequence lost his seat in the Tory backlash at the general election of that year. Returned for Reigate in 1713, he continued to support the Whigs, voting on 18 Mar. 1714 against the expulsion of Richard Steele and was classified as a Whig on the Worsley list and on two further lists of the Members re-elected in 1715.[4]

Although the Reigate property fell to the Jekylls after the death of Somers in 1716, Cocks continued to represent the borough until 1747, by which time he had inherited the Jekyll property himself. By the time of his death, on 26 May 1750, he was a very wealthy man, with over £17,000 due to him on mortgages, £6,000 in South Sea Company annuities, and over £2,500 worth of household goods. His will made provision for his only son and heir, Charles (d. 1758), whose education was to be 'liberal in all respects'. The barony of Somers was revived in 1784 for the eldest son of his brother John.[5]

[1] J. V. Somers Cocks, *Hist. Cocks Fam.* 88–89; *Hist. Reg. Chron.* 1718, p. 34; Manning and Bray, *Surr.* i. 285–6; W. Hooper, *Reigate*, 32; *VCH Herts.* ii. 256. [2] Hooper, 63. [3] W. L. Sachse, *Ld. Somers*, 124, 234. [4] Ibid. 260, 310. [5] Hooper, 121; Add. 36228, f. 214; PCC 290 Greenly; Collins, *Peerage*, viii. 24.

S. N. H.

COCKS, Sir Richard, 2nd Bt. (c.1659–1726), of Dumbleton, Glos.[1]

GLOUCESTERSHIRE 1698–1702

b. c.1659, 1st s. of Richard Cocks of the Middle Temple, (*d.v.p.* o. s. of Sir Richard Cocks, 1st Bt., of Dumbleton), by Mary, da. of Sir Robert Cooke† of Highnam, Glos., and sis. of William Cooke I*. *educ.* M. Temple 1667; Oriel, Oxf. 1677–by 1680. *m.* (1) lic. 6 Oct. 1688, Frances (d. 1724), da. of Richard Neville† of Billingbear, Binfield, Berks., sis. of Richard Neville*, *s.p.*; (2) by Nov. 1724, Mary (d. 1764), da. of William Bethell of Swindon, Yorks., *s.p. suc.* fa. 1669; gdfa. as 2nd Bt. 16 Sept. 1684.[2]

Sheriff, Glos. 1692–3; freeman, Evesham by 1697.[3]

Tradition, upheld by the Member himself, located the common origin of the Cocks family in Kent, but the Gloucestershire branch can be traced back no farther than the mid-16th century, to a Thomas Cocks of Bishop's Cleeve. The manor of Dumbleton was acquired through marriage by Thomas Cocks's daughter, from whom it passed in two removes to the 1st baronet, a staunch adherent of King Charles I and 'a great sufferer for his love to the royal family and for his zeal for the laws and established religion of his country'. This cavalier heritage meant little to the 2nd baronet, his grandson, who took the path of Whiggery, perhaps influenced by his wife's family or even by his cousin Charles Cocks*, a brother-in-law of Lord Somers (Sir John*). In other respects too, the succession of the 2nd baronet marked a new departure: he was responsible for the rebuilding of Dumbleton, which he had returned to occupy after the death of his grandmother in 1690; and his ambitions to play a part in local and national politics were soon realized. He was involved in the manoeuvring that preceded the county election in 1690, at first active in support of Sir John Guise, 2nd Bt.*, and later making promises of goodwill, perhaps genuine, to Lord Weymouth's brother James Thynne*. Sheriff in 1692, and chairman of the Gloucestershire quarter sessions from at least 1696, he stood unsuccessfully against Sir Francis Winnington* in the neighbouring borough of Tewkesbury in 1695, and at the next election was returned as knight of the shire on the Whig interest, receiving a sour tribute from one opponent, who dubbed him 'an ill-favoured orator of that county'.[4]

Cocks's parliamentary career is unusually well documented, thanks to the survival of his memoranda-books. Beginning as a record of some of his own letters and speeches (prepared if not always delivered), his views on matters of theology, morality and politics, and interesting facts culled from the *Votes* and from papers laid before the House, these notes extended into a parliamentary diary comparable in length to that of Narcissus Luttrell*, though much more vivid and personal, covering parts of the sessions of 1698–9 and 1699–1700, and forming a near-continuous record of proceedings in the 1701 and 1701–2 Parliaments. In September 1698 he was listed, probably in error, as a placeman and classed in a comparison of the old and new Commons as a supporter of the Court, presumably on account of his connexion with Somers. However, this latter classification was later queried and Cocks was, in fact, a consistent and enthusiastic Country Whig. His 'first speech in Parliament' delivered on 4 Jan. 1699, was in favour of the disbanding bill. Pointing out that it was not troops but 'the people's affections' which provided the best 'security' for the monarch, he warned that a future King might not be as trustworthy as William III: 'if the throne should be again filled with a weak and impotent prince, and he should have an army at his command, does anyone think he would be mended by his power?' In another speech on the same topic, he dwelt on Cromwellian precedent, drawing on the recent edition of Ludlow's memoirs. The maiden speech also took up more general themes that were to recur in Cocks' speeches and writings: 'the frailty and imbecilities of human nature [and] how many unthinking creatures there are over the virtuous and wise'; the destructive self-interest of 'proud and ambitious' place-seekers; and his own disinterested patriotism – 'I am guided by reason not party'. During this session he also spoke, on 24 Feb., at length, 'extempore', in favour of the place bill:

> Sir, there are two families I always opposed from sitting within these walls, the one I have heard in other Parliaments is the family of the obliged, the other the family of the disobliged: the one by fawning and flattery does everything he is bid and more to get preferment; the other brays and bawls against the government in order to be bought off. If places were not to be the rewards of our actions here men of small or no estates would never try to get in and the chief aim of everyone would more probably be the true interest of their country since they could propose to make no other advantage to themselves.

An even lengthier and more rambling discourse in support of the resumption of Irish forfeitures, delivered on 19 Apr., contained several injudicious passages. Although attacking those who 'aggravate matters by railing and by hot, satirical, witty speeches' (probably a sideswipe at John Grobham Howe*, his *bête noire*), he himself indulged in similarly offensive remarks:

> I have often thought with myself how foolishly those unthinking creatures about court generally live: they invite, keep great tables, have many attendants, liveries and other innumerable fineries; those they entertain scarcely think themselves beholding to them, they think it is on the public. Those that entertain oftentimes do it more to show their grandeur than to show any particular respect to their guest.

Such lapses of judgment were common to Cocks's character: in speaking to the place bill on 8 Mar. he had opposed the exemption of the treasurer of the Ordnance with a personal condemnation of the then incumbent, Charles Bertie I*, which had found no seconder; on another occasion he proposed to move for a bill to disable Sir John Trevor* from 'executing any place of profit or trust', and arranged a meeting of 'those I thought zealous in the matter', to which only two Members turned up (one of them his brother-in-law Neville). In the case of his speech for the Irish forfeitures resumption, his enthusiasm led him not just beyond good manners but beyond the principles of Whiggism and even his own prejudices. He began with a statement of (Country) Whig orthodoxy – 'if this land had been divided among the conquering army they would there have planted colonies and bred up people in the religion and interest of England and would have defended Ireland but without the charge of a standing army' – but went on to show a remarkable sympathy for the deprived Irish Catholics and even for James II. Dismissing the complaints of the 'poor Protestant purchasers', he declared:

> it is less hard for them to pay some years' purchase in acknowledgment of the advantages they have received; than for the poor Irish who stood by their natural prince, whose chiefest fault and misfortune was his being of their religion, of their understanding and being extremely favourable and partial to them on all occasions. Methinks it is a great hardship to be reckoned a traitor for only adhering to one's natural prince . . . but I had almost forgot that the traitor is still he that is beaten; well then, since the Irish are traitors it is more reasonable that they should be traitors to the . . . people of England than to a few court minions.

At other times Cocks showed his party colours, when putting forward an additional clause to the place bill 'to exclude some few . . . that did refuse . . . the voluntary Association from sitting in the next Parliament'; when opposing, on 5 Jan., Tory efforts to displace all foreign-born army officers, 'these outlandish men that came over with the Prince of Orange to assist us . . . to recover our liberties, our religion and properties'; and when speaking for a general naturalization bill against 'the Jacobite party'. He was also prepared to desert the Country side if he felt its conduct to be merely factious, as over the Tamworth election and the East India bill; or if he clashed with 'Jack' Howe. Most of his speeches in his first session, however, reflected Country concerns. A good example was his advocacy of legislation for 'moral reform'. Obsessed with the upkeep of morality in public and private life, he believed strongly in the duty of a civil magistrate to 'punish vice and discountenance immoralities'. A magistrate 'should like a schoolmaster correct faults, punish idleness and instruct all under our care'. Named to the committee of 23 Dec. 1698 to bring in the unsuccessful 'immorality' bill, Cocks vainly proposed another such bill, to the consideration, as he put it, of 'the beaux of all ages . . . the wits, the halfwits, and those that know no lawmaker'. Throughout his parliamentary career the Journals show him to have been an assiduous attender, nominated to numerous committees, especially on private bills or on measures connected with trade and manufacture. Family connexions with commerce; the local importance of the woollen industry in Gloucestershire; and a personal interest in the problem of poverty as an aspect of social regulation: all helped to focus his interests. In this session he introduced the bonelace importation bill (14 Apr.), and reported and carried to the Lords the bill to prevent the production of cloth buttons (11, 13 Jan.). He presented three other bills: the defective titles bill

(7 Jan.); a bill to prevent Catholics from disinheriting their Protestant heirs (16 Feb.), which reflected his fierce antipathy to popery; and a bill to prevent jury corruption (6 Mar.), another element in the Country campaign to purify public institutions. He was appointed one of the drafters of the disbanding bill on 17 Dec. 1698. The essential corollary to disbandment was reform of the militia, and on 6 Feb. 1699 he was named to a committee to bring in such a bill. At the end of the session he set down his first impressions of Parliament and the Members, whose behaviour, seen at close quarters, had disappointed even so determined a jeremiah as himself:

> before I was one among them . . . I fancied the fools were awed, governed and had respect for those that were famous and renowned for their worth and parts, and that the knaves, for indeed I knew some such there were, would disguise themselves and be in fear of being censured . . . upon these considerations I expected, if not a judicious, honest, sober and grave assembly, at least in appearance, I mean one that would seem to be such: instead of judicious and honest I found them all upon parties, in so much that if they did not totally banish judgment I am sure they did honesty . . . then as for the gravity and sobriety it is intolerable, there is such a noise one can scarce hear or mind what is said, and indeed what is particularly minded is private business, to make parties, to make court etc. . . . There [are] few that mind or understand the true integrity of the nation; in most of our public business men are biased by private ends.[5]

The second session of the 1698 Parliament saw Cocks as busy as before, though his most frequent nominations were to committees on private bills and petitions, or uncontroversial items of legislation. His particular interests were again well represented, his committees including those of 6 Mar. 1700, on the j.p.s' qualification bill, 12 Mar., on the London poor bill, and 26 Mar., to draft reasons for a conference over the Lords' amendment to the bill removing duties on the export of woollens. Two failed bills from the preceding session he now reintroduced: the defective titles bill, presented on 8 Dec. 1699, and the bill to stop Catholics disinheriting Protestant heirs, brought up ten days later. He chaired the committee on the Protestant heirs' bill, and his commitment to 'no popery' also earned him a place on the committees to inquire into the recusancy laws (7 Feb. 1700), and on the superstitious uses bill (12 Mar.). His other bill, introduced on 7 Feb., had as its purpose the fixing of the 'water-measure' of fruit. Having seconded the motion for a bill to resume all crown grants since 1684, he was one of the three Members ordered on 13 Feb. to bring it in. He believed this measure would 'yield more than the Irish forfeitures'. His diary records that he spoke regularly, and in some of the more important debates, though there are indications that he was not always taken seriously. When he had prepared a lengthy reproof of Members' unparliamentary habits to be delivered on 13 Feb. 1700, the Speaker 'pulled off his hat as I rose up to speak and so prevented me by speaking to order himself; I believe he partly knew what I intended to speak to'. On another occasion, a debate of 6 Dec. 1699, Sir Bartholomew Shower* seems deliberately to have dropped the name 'Dumbleton' into a speech in order to provoke Cocks into a customary harangue. Possibly it was Cocks's pursuit of his two vendettas, against Howe and Trevor, that encouraged the picture of him as a man with bees in his bonnet. Early on in the session, on 28 Nov., he took up the subject of bribery in order 'to set himself loose against' Trevor but his performance proved a damp squib, concluding only with a motion that Trevor's commission as master of the rolls be laid before the House, which nobody seconded. The speech itself had, at one point, raised 'a quarter of an hour's laugh' in the House. On 13 Mar. 1700 Cocks dragged Trevor's name into a debate on the purges in the commission of the peace: 'vice and immorality' had been mentioned, and on this subject Cocks commented, 'I am afraid . . . all is true; I hear without doors of those entertainments and clubs and caballing of some within doors at the master of the rolls; I fear vice and immorality will find some patrons within doors'. But it was Howe, more than anyone, who could be guaranteed to bring him to his feet. Time and again he rose in response, particularly if any speech from Howe had referred to conditions in Gloucestershire. When, on 13 Feb. 1700, Thomas Stringer*, who was sitting next to Cocks, himself launched a vigorous answer to Howe's attacks on the ministry, 'they said merrily in the House that I had planted my great gun opposite to Jack Howe and discharged it full at him'. Such personal animosities may have made Cocks more of a Whig in this session. In the debate on 6 Dec. 1699 on Captain Kidd he claimed to have changed his mind after Howe and various prominent Tories had denounced the patent, for then

> I had time to consider and strip truth stark naked from the dregs of oratory and filth of satire with which she was defiled and disguised, [and] I found no more in it than that these gent[lemen], when the government was in distress for men, ships and money, set out a ship at their own cost, not to get . . . treasures but to serve the nation at their own loss and hazard.

A similar conversion occurred on 13 Dec., over the proposal to address the King to remove Bishop Burnet from being tutor to the Duke of Gloucester. Howe had 'thirded' the motion, but Cocks spoke directly in answer to Sir Bartholomew Shower. Before the debate, Cocks said, he had thought Burnet to be 'the fittest' to be addressed against 'except one'. However, after 'the incomparable character I have heard of him from . . . gent[lemen] who I am sure know men and on whose judgment I much rely I own I have altered my opinion and believe [him] the fittest man in the world for the place he is in'. There were still issues, of course, on which he followed a Country line.

> Upon Sir Charles Hotham's moving for a supply just after the King's Speech was read . . . I said 'Sir, I have heard that it was the ancient method of Par[liament] to redress grievances before they gave money. I am sure there is nobody more truly loves K[ing] W[illiam] than I do, but . . . I am not for making a bad precedent in a good reign. I desire, therefore, that things may go in their ancient channel.'

The return to the question of the Irish forfeited estates found him again arguing forcefully for resumption. He 'thirded' Simon Harcourt I on 15 Dec. 1699 in moving for the bill, and spoke at its second reading on 14 Jan. 1700, in opposition to a Court-inspired proposal to instruct the committee 'to set apart a proportion for the King'. On each occasion his arguments were derived from Charles Davenant's* pamphlet on the subject, though in the second-reading debate he did take pains to praise King William and register his detestation of King James, whom 'we hate and abominate because he did by an arbitrary power invade our rights, liberties and properties, and because he would have introduced a ridiculous, strange and detestable religion among us'. While in favour of resumption in general terms, 'for the public service', he was nevertheless unhappy with the opposition tactic of singling out for criticism the individual grants to Charles Montagu* and Lord Somers: 'I will not do anything that has any private look or end in it.' As for the Junto ministers, 'I own I like them better than I did. I know no way to judge of men but by comparing them, nor no way of judging of ministers but by comparing them. They are good or bad only comparatively as they are better or worse than others.' Such an attitude may explain why an analysis of the House dating from early 1700 listed Cocks as in the interest of Montagu.[6]

Re-elected for Gloucestershire as a Whig in January 1701, supposedly following an agreement under which he agreed not to stand at the next election, Cocks was up in town early to pledge his vote to Sir Thomas Littleton, 3rd Bt.*, for Speaker. He also attended a meeting of Whigs at the Rose tavern, 'in order to oppose Mr [Robert] Harley*, because we did not like the preceptor [Rochester] at all nor the pupil very well'. Privately, however, he did not despair of Harley: 'for all the opinions of many I cannot believe Mr Harley in the main to be in any interest but that of the country, though I confess I do not approve of many of his words and actions.' Littleton having absented himself from the House on 10 Feb. when the Chair was to be filled, under orders from the King (or so many Whigs suspected), and in order to smooth the way for Harley, Cocks spoke in support of a second Whig candidate, Sir Richard Onslow, 3rd Bt. The climax of his oration, which included an illustration from 'Romish history', was that 'whoever shall by bribe, menaces or any other art persuade a Member to absent himself from the House . . . does pollute the *sacra* of the House'. This emphasis on purification of parliamentary and governmental processes was then reflected in his appointment to committees on 20 Feb. 1701, to bring in a bill to regulate elections and the qualification of MPs, and on 27 Feb., to prepare a further bill to prevent the corruption of juries. Another echo of past battles was the ordering on 21 Feb. of a bill to resume crown grants since 1684, and again he was included in the drafting committee. But in this Parliament Cocks, as a Whig, was becoming even further alienated from erstwhile Country Tory allies, some of whom, in forming a new Court party, had shown themselves to be men who 'prefer the rising sun before God, country, friend and everything'. Cocks's enduring capacity for vigorous Country rhetoric was demonstrated on 10 May, over the 'place clause' of the bill of settlement:

> There is nothing has occasioned so much flattery, so much railing envy and satire as this thing place, which is often the bane of the kingdom and ought to be avoided above all things . . . we all know that those in places generally vote in matters of state all one way, and this can hardly proceed from conscience, to have a body of men entirely all of one mind; it must have something more than chance, and we have seen men vote and talk one way before they have places, another way when in places, and then alter again when they have been out. It gives a handle to gent[lemen] to reflect to people out of doors to believe, there is a separate interest between the King and the country.

He was thus led to oppose the Tories by his own devotion to the Country interest, speaking twice early in May in support of the proposal to trim the civil list, which Tory 'courtiers' were attempting to suppress. On the second occasion, on 5 May, he added a rustic touch, recalling a conversation prior to the election with 'several of my country neighbours', in which they had urged him to 'make war with France and pay our just debts' and ensure that 'poor working horses', rather than courtiers and pensioners, should be fed. So powerful was his conviction that he found himself in the unlikely position of seconding Jack Howe, as he had done once before, earlier in the session, in a debate on the bill of settlement. Cocks also objected to the sheer factiousness of the Tories. On 28 Mar., defending the patent to Captain Kidd's bankers, he deplored the fact that this had become 'a party cause'. Similarly, in May he denounced attacks on Lord Stamford as 'guided' in the main by 'party'. Tory partisanship in election cases was a recurrent grievance. Considering the role of the Commons as judge of elections, he once wrote that 'never was a more corrupter place than this fountain of justice'. In contrast, he was himself capable of a degree of objectivity, as on 13 May, when he moved the taking into custody of the election agent of the Whig Reynolds Calthorpe I*, after bribery had been proved by a Tory petition. But more usually he seems to have excused Whig corruption by focusing instead on that of the Tories. In the prolonged debates in March on the case of Samuel Shepheard I*, his obvious reluctance to condemn, in spite of his often-trumpeted aversion to bribery, led to difficulties. His speech of 14 Mar. began with a *faux pas*, in that he mistakenly named Sir Stephen Fox* as having once before been ordered to name Members in receipt of secret service money; carried on with the obligatory jab at Trevor, for which he was rebuked from the Chair; and ended with an unwilling vote for 'guilty':

> I really believe the bribery of the Old Company to be the occasion of this corruption of the New, for the New found that the Old had bribed Members, and the New were in a manner forced to bring some in by bribery to make a balance to the interest of the Old.

The next day he was prepared to excuse the Shepheards on some charges:

> Sir, I am not New East Indian enough to acquit them when I believe them guilty, nor am I Old East Indian enough to find them guilty when the evidence is not sufficient. Shepheard was undoubtedly guilty in hindering the evidence from . . . Bramber . . . he and his two sons were turned out: himself and one justly enough, the other to bear them company because his name was Shepheard. There were more things, I believe, proved upon him than he was guilty of, and yet he was too guilty to sit there.

When the case of the Great Grimsby election, another scene of conflict between the Old and New East India companies, was heard at the bar on 6 Mar., he acknowledged that the New Company man, William Cotesworth*, had 'come in by bribery' but reserved the severer judgment for Cotesworth's opponent, Arthur Moore*, largely because Moore's case had been argued so 'partially' by the Tories:

> I was truly, Sir, very uneasy to see this House show so much partiality . . . how was everything reflecting on Cotesworth contrary to reason and rules all lost in debates magnified; how was everything relating to Mr Moore after the same partial manner extenuated.

The Old Company, whom he decried as 'the tools of the present ministry', remained an object of his enmity, and on 17 May he spoke against a move to settle the East India trade in their interest. In these and other respects Cocks's one-sided censure of the Tories for factiousness and 'private' motives reveals his own implicit partisanship. In seconding Howe's proposal, on 1 Apr., for a clause in the bill of settlement 'that no foreigner should be capable of a grant or place in this kingdom', he went out of his way to insert a thrust against Lord Rochester, showing that he regarded Rochester's being 'prime minister of state' as just as great a grievance as the making of 'grants to foreigners'. His view of the composition of the House at the opening of this Parliament is an interesting one. He divided the Membership into three 'parties': 'the honestest', 'the Jacobites' and 'the Commonwealthmen'. The two latter, he wrote, 'join in everything', adding, 'many that wished for a commonwealth could not trust the virtue of their party and feared the designs of the Jacobites in conjunction with them'. His own return to the ranks of the 'honestest' party was largely determined by the priority he accorded to the Protestant succession and foreign policy. On 16 Apr. he spoke for amending the address to the King to include a promise to endorse action 'in preventing the union of France and Spain'. 'If we say we will have no war', he told the House, 'we shall be forced to have a war. If we say we will engage in a war if we cannot without it have what we think necessary for our preservation it is very probable our terms may be complied with, and I don't see these words intend further.' Hatred of France and sympathy for the plight of the Dutch led him to acquiesce in the giving of any assistance required by the allies, even by the land tax. In the debate of 24 Apr. he opined that although 'all my small fortune is in land and I believe everyone that knows me knows that I will not easily part with my money', and therefore 'I am against charging land, I mean for charging it with as little as possible', he could not accept the fixing of a maximum rate for the land tax by the committee of ways and means:

> We are threatened and in danger abroad from a malicious and potent enemy . . . [and] though I shall not be willing

to raise more upon land, nor do I well like what is done, yet since there is a possibility that we may be forced into a war I would not give such great encouragement to our enemies ... if there is a necessity, I would willingly part with one half to secure the other.

Subsequently he revised his view in accordance with Country orthodoxy, arguing instead that 'money' rather than land should bear the weight of taxation. Taxes in general were 'odious and grievous to the people', the land tax most of all because of its inequality. Land had 'in a manner borne the whole charge' of the previous, ruinously expensive, war. Of the other alternatives, 'trade' (which was 'the life of England' while land was 'England itself') was 'in most parts sufficiently charged' already, and the idea of an excise was particularly 'odious'. On the great party struggle of the session, over the impeachments, Cocks proved himself uncompromisingly Whiggish, standing for 'moderation and justice' against the factiousness of the prosecution. His family connexion with Somers may well have brought him close to the former lord chancellor: he records being 'with Lord Somers, Orford [Edward Russell*] and Halifax [Charles Montagu]' on 26 Apr. and hearing their own explanations of the Partition Treaty. On 16 May, speaking on the articles of impeachment, he paid Somers this tribute:

> I live in the neighbourhood near him, I have known him as long as I have known anybody, in all the parts of his life he has merited esteem from good men and been honoured ... in the reign of King James he behaved himself as an Englishman, he defended the Church and the bishops for nothing when others betrayed our liberties and attacked them for profit and preferment, and after this Revolution he was deservedly made attorney-general ... lord keeper and afterwards ... chancellor, in no way possible to increase or advance his fortune but by the favour of his prince, and since he has left his business and dedicated himself wholly to the public.

When Somers and Orford were finally cleared he wrote:

> were those little, villainous, poor wretches that hatched these evils against the lords tried for their former ills in Westminster Hall, there would have been as many demanding justice and rejoicing at their condemnation as were at these lords' acquittal.

He reported and carried to the Lords a private estate bill (9, 23 May), and on 3 June was given a fortnight's leave of absence, but to judge from the evidence of the diary, he did not take it up.

Having 'voted well' in the 1701 Parliament, Cocks was able to secure the backing of the entire Whig interest in Gloucestershire in the general election of November 1701, despite any previous pledge to step down. Sir John Guise, 3rd Bt.*, yielded his 'pretentions' and Cocks joined Maynard Colchester* in a ruthless and successful campaign to ditch Jack Howe. The absence of his great enemy robbed parliamentary exchanges of some of their spice, though from time to time Sir Christopher Musgrave, 4th Bt.*, threatened to prove an adequate substitute. Predictably, Cocks was included with the Whigs in Robert Harley's list of this Parliament, and in his diary Cocks was quite open about his antagonism towards 'the Speaker and his party', meaning the Tories. When the accounts commissioners were balloted for, on 17 Mar. 1702, he wrote of 'their list' and 'our list'. As in the preceding Parliament, the judging of election disputes showed as clearly as anything else the conflicting pressures of party and conscience. A lover of justice, who could denounce the elections committee as 'certainly the most corrupt court in Christendom, nay the world', he regularly spoke and voted in favour of Whigs and against Tories. To take three of the most notorious cases in this Parliament: in the debate of 29 Jan. on the Malmesbury election he might have disapproved of the petition from the Whig voters against the Tory Hedges – 'only to put a blemish upon Sir Charles Hed[ges]* now turned out of his employ of secretary of state. S[o in]solent and unmanlike to run a man quite down that was going down before' – and regarded the defence of the Whig Parke as 'artificial', but his conclusion was that Hedges must have bribed harder than Parke. His insinuations to this effect, that 'had I not known the modesty and virtue of the gent[lemen] that were elected I should have thought them the best bidders', aroused Tory anger; and for all his contempt for the petitioners, he felt their prolonged imprisonment by the House to be 'unjust'. He was again an object of Tory fury for remarks on the decision of 24 Feb. in favour of the election of Sir Christopher Hales for Coventry: 'I ... said ... I did not see any right, any colour of a majority, unless that his being one of the black list ... This made all the black-listed buss [sic] all over the House ... and some of the fools cried "to the bar".' During the hearing of 7 Feb. concerning the Maidstone election, where the 'Kentish Petitioner' Thomas Colepeper had been a candidate, he admitted that Colepeper had been 'guilty of bribery' but still argued on his behalf. Later that same day, in a debate arising from Colepeper's 'silly reflecting letter on the last House of Parliament', he seconded a motion to have the affair of the 'Poussineers' inquired into, another merely party cause. In terms of parliamentary business, this, his last session, was one of Cocks's most important. He was named to prepare a bill for taking public accounts (6 Jan.), a measure to which he subsequently 'brought up a clause' in committee 'to inquire into the briberies and corruptions used among the officers concerned in managing the King's treasure'; and to draft a bill to prevent bribery and corruption at elections (17 Jan.). The rest of his work covered mainly private bills and legislation concerning trade and industry, with now and then a local flavour, as when he was nominated to a committee to bring in a bill, along the lines of one of his own previous bills, to regulate the 'water-measure' of fruit, in response to a petition from the Gloucestershire grand jury, or when he presented a petition from Gloucestershire clothiers. He took a special interest in the difficulties of the Quakers over oath-taking, speaking on 28 Jan. in favour of committing the affirmation bill. The subject of oaths had preoccupied him, and he had already spoken twice on the question when in April the bill to 'explain' the Abjuration was read. Now, acting as the Quakers' parliamentary agent, he brought in a clause on their behalf. The attempt proved something of a fiasco, however. On 13 Apr. he and others had suggested that the Quakers seek 'a liberty to affirm the same words', while they themselves 'had a mind to have a shorter way':

> at last we agreed that they should prepare two clauses, one as I directed and one that they liked themselves: but they were so long consulting, so long preparing, that the bill was read before they brought either and at last the short one, so in I went into the House and opened it as if it had been the long clause, and there was a debate and a question put, whether I should bring it up; that was carried and when it was read and it differed a pretty deal from what I had opened it . . . I told the truth which was the haste, and when I saw the House would not receive and that some were for rejecting I asked leave to withdraw it.

On Cocks's further advice, the clause was introduced 'by way of amendment' in the Lords, but some among the Quakers were still unsure that this was the best way to proceed, and were 'soliciting us not to agree'. On the great issues of war and the succession, Cocks made several speeches. In committee of supply on 31 Jan. he refuted the comment by Sir Godfrey Copley, 2nd Bt.*, that 'we must accommodate the war to our conveniences', and later, on 19 Mar., he warmly supported an Anglo-Scottish union as the best 'bulwark to our liberties', extending the idea to include Ireland as well. King William's death was a heavy blow:

> he . . . was . . . engaged in the quarrel of Europe, to defend them against France and . . . to defend us from the pretended Prince of Wales. He was the supporter of the Protestant religion, of the liberty of Europe, and an enemy to France . . . he was the justest, wisest and bravest prince of his age, and his faults were as few as any, his virtues more than any, King now reigning . . . had he lived longer it may be he might have lived more to our good than to his own glory.

Cocks's Country sympathies could still make him an irritant to Whig party leaders. On 11 Feb. he reverted to a topic of former sessions, in moving for the resumption of 'all the grants made since the Revolution', which he thought would raise £700,000. Not for the first time, he was bereft of a seconder. And after Anne's accession he resurrected another pet project, moving on 13 Mar. for an inquiry into the yield of duties given to support the civil list. This time Sir Edward Hussey, 3rd Bt., a man after Cocks's own heart, seconded the motion. Indeed, Cocks's ungracious verdict on Hussey might not unjustly have been applied to himself: 'very honest, but has no great judgment, and [such] a great opinion of his own abilities that he thinks nobody able to advise him'. Cocks persisted in the scheme, vainly approaching several Whig Members, but suspected 'that the impeached lords were against our going on with such a debate lest it might be insinuated that they had promoted it'. The question of the administration of the resumed Irish forfeitures, which took up much of the time of this Parliament, presented him with a dilemma, spelled out by Irish Whig protests, of whether to adhere to the public over private interest, or to uphold the rights of Protestants against Papists. The changed international and political scene now inclined him more to the latter course. Early on in the session he referred to the 'rogueries' of the Irish Catholics, and took a hard line against accepting petitions from those whose 'ancestors were attainted after death, though they had been slain in battle'. He seemed impressed by the arguments of the Irish Protestants' 'national remonstrance'. While not closely involved in the solicitation of any individual case, he did vote on 9 Apr. to commit a Protestant petition. One of his only two interventions in debate on the subject occurred on 30 Apr., when he proposed a measure to 'oblige' Church of Ireland clergy 'to a residence'. The other was more significant, and marks the survival of his faith in the resumption principle: on 7 May he supported the 'public' against the 'poor Protestant purchasers', attacking a move to allow those who had bought from the grants to Lords Albemarle and Romney two-thirds of the 'purchase money' instead of the customary one-third. 'We must not consider persons', said Cocks, 'but what is fit for us to do.' Towards the end of the session he took the opportunity to reaffirm other convictions.

On 2 May he once again defended the foreign army officers. Then two days later, on the deficiency bill, he was able to make his last statement of principle to the House:

> I hope, Sir, you will not let us spend our time . . . in unnecessary reflections. We are engaged in a war with France, and I hope we shall reserve all our malice and envy for France, and not spend it upon one another. I know the hopes and desire to get places has been the only thing that has so long supported party among us and I hope that those that have had the places so long will be satisfied with their so long enjoyment of them, and those that have them now will be satisfied with the possession of them, and that we that never had nor expected places shall all of us join to support our common country. I am sure for my part, though my estate is not a great one, yet it serves my turn, and I don't spend it all every year; if other gent[lemen] would do so too there would not be such hunting after places . . . I am of opinion that it will be more dangerous to our constitution not to reward those that have served us faithfully, and much more not to pay those that have shed their blood for us in a former war . . . I will therefore preserve that part of the constitution, and venture the other as the less dangerous.[7]

With the accession of the Queen came a change of political fortunes in Gloucestershire. A straw in the wind was Howe's clear victory in an election for foreman of the grand jury in March 1702. Already Cocks was preparing to abandon the county and put up at Tewkesbury, but in fact he contested neither constituency in the 1702 election, and found himself out of the House. Robbed of this platform for his views, he began to write in earnest and at greater length than hitherto. In 1704 he sent his great friend and correspondent Lord Hervey (John*) an 'Answer to Faction Displayed' and a 'Vandyke-like picture of Westminster Hall', in which the Duchess of Marlborough was eulogized under the character of 'Sempronia'. Soon afterwards came a 'discourse of religion', a subject on which Cocks was never slow to pick up his pen. Hervey was greatly impressed: 'though I always took you to be an honest good man, I should never have believed you so able a divine, so skilful a merchant, and so general a statesman as I find by your writings'. In retirement, however, Cocks was giving full rein to his various *idées fixes*, especially his overpowering fear of popery. Robert Harley was the recipient of a curious letter in 1704 congratulating him on his elevation to secretary and adding 'an account of the fears and uneasiness of many of the best affected to her Majesty's government at the unusual grandeur of the papists'. Cocks allowed that he had no actual evidence from Gloucestershire of Catholics arming themselves: he was merely keeping Harley informed of what fellow Protestants were thinking. The real aim of the letter was to protest against purges of Whigs from the commission of the peace. Out of Parliament, Cocks seems to have become an even firmer partisan. According to Hervey, Lord Somers was anxious to see Cocks return to the House, agreeing with Hervey 'with respect to the unhappy competition' between Cocks and Sir John Guise for the Whig interest in Gloucestershire in 1705, that while Guise would

> act upon the same honest bottom, yet we can neither of us come up to allow him near the usefulness you'll be of in Parliament, who not only can but will speak those bold and timely truths we all want to hear again uttered there . . . and we jointly agree . . . that there is nobody we had rather have in the H[ouse] of C[ommons] than Sir Richard Cocks.

In the event Cocks stood at Evesham, presumably with the assistance of his kinsmen there and possibly thanks to the intercession of Somers himself, but was defeated in a contest marred by much 'foul play'. He determined to try his popularity in his own county again, and by 1707 had announced himself a candidate for knight of the shire at the next election. He persisted, even though this meant opposing two Whigs, Guise and Matthew Ducie Moreton*, but a further defeat ended his hopes of re-election. The Sacheverellite fever of 1710 found him either in his study, writing circular letters to freeholders in support of Guise and Moreton and composing further unpublished papers in support of the Hanoverian succession, or at quarter sessions, where his own Whiggish address 'had too much of the antidote in it to pass with so poisoned a people'. There followed some further exposition of 'true old Whig principles', culminating in a manuscript history of the reign of Henry III of France, which ran 'almost parallel with more recent transactions'. Of this Cocks entertained quite sanguine literary hopes. He resisted Matthew Ducie Moreton's 'persuasions' to stand for the county in 1713, contenting himself with behind-the-scenes efforts to urge a motion to invite over the Hanoverian heir to the throne, but once the 'happy accession' was accomplished, he reconsidered Moreton's earlier offers. 'Truly, Sir', he wrote, 'I have a desire to appear once more in public in order to take leave of my old friends, and to put my helping hand to part with some enemies to my country.' Unfortunately, he had missed the boat.[8]

Cocks's service in the cause was now restricted to his writings and to his charges to Gloucestershire grand juries. Hervey had recommended publishing the 'excellent discourse you entertained your countrymen with at the quarter sessions in 1715', and two years later a charge did find its way into print. This was in the main a defence of the Hanoverian succession and the right of resistance, as exercised at the Revolution, and a denunciation of the Pretender, who had been 'educated in arbitrary French principles, instructed in all the cruel arts of Popery'. Papists received a verbal lashing, but so too did the 'High Church plotters' whose arguments were seen as no more than a cover for self-interest, the advancement of 'arbitrary power', and even popish sympathies. Subsequently, as he wrote, 'the great infirmities of my body forced me for some years to decline all public business'. He even ceased to act as a j.p. in Gloucestershire. Then in 1721 he returned to print with a belated postscript to the Bangorian controversy, *A Perfect Discovery of Longitude* (1721), in which he claimed to 'prove' that Parliament was 'the fittest body of men to be entrusted with the government of the Church'. In order to do so he was prepared to believe that all parliamentary legislation was for the 'public good' and that there could be no possibility of 'private views', a contrast to his impressions while a Member. The 'High Church' party were the principal objects of his scorn, for neo-papist ambitions. Cocks expanded some of his ideas the following year in *The Church of England Secured*, which judged the established church by the standards of rationality and the pattern of primitive Christianity. In a two-pronged attack, he denounced on the one hand authoritarianism and persecution and on the other the notion of an apostolic succession. Both were derived from popery, and showed the 'High Churchmen' seeking to emulate 'Antichrist'. The pamphlet developed into a swingeing condemnation of 'horrid impudent priestcraft', and concluded with a call for 'another Reformation' in the hearts of men, to be encouraged by specific reforms enacted by Parliament: a change in ordination procedure; prevention of genuflection at communion; outlawing of pluralism and non-residence; abolition of ecclesiastical courts; and lastly, the appointment by the secular authorities of teachers and overseers to instruct people in the principles of true religion and morality. Some passages were frankly abusive. This tone, combined with his accusations that the Church of England clergy were crypto-papists, and his explicit sympathy for Dissenters, whom he hoped to see brought back into 'one sheepfold', naturally provoked replies from High Churchmen, one of which, *The Knight of Dumbleton Foiled at His Own Weapon*, was a scholarly demolition of his shaky theology. Undaunted, he fired off a sequel to *The Church of England Secured*, entitled *Over Shoes, Over Boots*. This was a prolix revisitation of previous arguments, in which he became even more scurrilous and offensive, and at one point criticized his own brother Charles, whom he had presented to the living of Dumbleton: 'my parson is not inspired; I was bred up with him, and I had then as much learning as he had'. By this time he was acquiring notoriety. Tories regarded him as 'a whimsical, crazed man' or a 'peevish elf', but his tracts went through several editions, more rejoinders appeared, and in 1723 he published yet another restatement of his views, cast as a *Farewell Sermon*, the formula emphasizing his conviction that he was as good as any parson. The basis of the work was a paper written at the time of the schism bill in 1714, to demonstrate that 'the Christian religion was not introduced by power and force'. Farewells were premature, since, in the wake of the Atterbury Plot, he returned to the Gloucestershire quarter sessions in 1723 to deliver another charge warning his hearers of the perils of popery and Jacobitism, exonerating the ministry from any criticism over the South Sea Bubble, and pleading for all to 'leave off faction', that is to say to become Whigs.[9]

In his last years Cocks became even more determinedly eccentric. When his wife died in 1724 he erected a monument on which was inscribed his gratitude for the years she had lived 'in peace, harmony and tranquillity with her husband, as far as human imbecilities common to the best of mortals would permit'. He immediately remarried, and in a new will gave his second wife a life interest in his estate. His last pamphlet, published posthumously, purported to be an inquiry into the so-called 'bloody execution' at Thorn, together with 'a vindication of some of the tenets of the Quakers', but was in fact nothing more than a stale reprise of past polemics against popery and High Church priestcraft, the flavour of which is conveyed by his description of Anglican ordination:

> We often see an ignorant, immoral dunce, because he was a relation of the bishop's or his wife's, or for marrying a poor relation or an old servant maid, or sometimes without that drudgery, by making a present to the wife or steward, it will open a way, and prevail upon an old, doting fellow to lay his hands on him, and by that means imprint on him an indelible character, and give him credentials to be from thenceforth an ambassador of Heaven.

After spending some time at Bath in 1726, afflicted by the gout, he died about 21 Oct. of that year, and was buried at Dumbleton. Predictably, in the preamble to his will he gave vent to his natural self-opinionated verbosity, on the worthlessness of deathbed repentances. Under the terms of the will, which took some 11 years to prove, the estate passed directly to a nephew and on his death without issue in 1765, to a kinsman from Herefordshire, who demolished the greater part of the house. The baronetcy had already become extinct.[10]

[1] Unless otherwise stated, this biography is based on the evidence of Cocks's own diary and commonplace books (Bodl. mss Eng. hist. b.209-10, published as *The Parliamentary Diary of Sir Richard Cocks, 1698-1702* ed. D. W. Hayton). [2] J. V. Somers Cocks, *Hist. Cocks Fam.* pt. 3, pp. 96, 99, 111; info. from Mrs Elizabeth Boardman, Archivist, Oriel Coll. Oxf. [3] C 219/81. [4] Add. 21420, f. 208; Somers Cocks, pt. 1, pp. 6-7; pt. 2, pp. 38, 45-46, 56; pt. 3, pp. 76-79, 97-100; Bath mss at Longleat House, Thynne pprs. 13, ff. 256-7; *CSP Dom.* 1694-5, p. 234; *Guise Mems.* (Cam. Soc. ser. 3, xxviii), 140. [5] *Cam. Misc.* xxix. 381; Ludlow, *A Voyce from the Watch Tower: Part V* ed. Worden (Cam. Soc. ser. 4, xxi), 47, 50, 73; *Party and Management* ed. Jones, 62; Add. 34730, f. 250; W. A. Speck, *Stability and Strife*, 6; *Whig Ascendancy* ed. Cannon, 63. [6] Add. 34730, ff. 238-9; *Vernon-Shrewsbury Letters*, ii. 369; Beaufort mss at Badminton House, 503/1/2, Charles Hancock* to Beaufort, 1 Jan. 1700[-1]; *HMC Portland*, iv. 14. [7] Surr. RO (Kingston), Somers mss 0/1/1, Mrs Burnet to Lady Jekyll, [c.Nov. 1701]; *Guise Mems.* 243. [8] Add. 70254, Robert Price* to Robert Harley, 30 Mar. 1702; 70421, Dyer's newsletter 24 Aug. 1710; Hervey, *Letter Bks.* i. 182, 199-200, 205-7, 215-20, 229-30, 262-6, 270-5, 302-3, 335-9, 389-90; *HMC Portland*, iv. 86-87; *Defoe Letters*, 111; Bodl. Ballard 31, f. 50; *Post Man*, 15-18 May 1708; Glos. RO, Ducie mss D340a/C22/10, Cocks to Moreton, 17 Aug. 1714. [9] Hervey, ii. 12; Cocks, *Charge to Glos. Grand Jury 30 Apr. 1717* (1717); *A Perfect Discovery of Longitude* (1721); *The Church of England Secured ...* (1722); *Over Shoes, Over Boots ...* (1722); *Sir R—-d C—-ks His Farewell Sermon* (1722); *Charge to Glos. Grand Jury Midsummer 1723* (1723); [Z. Grey], *The Knight of Dumbleton Foiled at His Own Weapon* (1722); Anon. *A Pair of Clean Shoes and Boots for a Dirty Baronet ...* (1722); Ballard 48, f. 212; Atkyns, *Glos.* 212; *Hearne Colls.* vii. 372. [10] Somers Cocks, pt. 3, pp. 101, 110-11; Cocks, *A True and Impartial Inquiry Made into the Late Bloody Execution at Thorn...* (1727); *Hist. Reg. Chron.* 1726, p. 40; Rudder, *Glos.* 420-1; info. from Mr J. V. Somers Cocks.

D. W. H.

CODRINGTON, John (1677-1754), of Codrington, Glos. and Wraxall, Som.

BATH 1710-1727, 1734-1741

bap. 10 Jan. 1677, 1st s. of Robert Codrington of Codrington and Didmarton, Glos. by Agnes (*d.* 1717), da. of Richard Samwell of Upton and Gayton, Northants. *educ.* Univ. Coll. Oxf. 1695. *m.* (1) Jane (*d.* 1702), da. of one Giffard of Cannington, nr. Bridgwater, Som., wid. of Fortescue Tynte (2nd s. of Sir Halswell Tynte, 1st Bt.) and Hopton Wyndham*, *s.p.*; (2) lic. 24 Sept. 1709, Elizabeth (*d.* 1740), da. and h. of Samuel Gorges of Wraxall, Som., 4da. (3 *d.v.p.*). *suc.* fa. 1717.[1] Freeman, Bath 1702.[2]

Codrington was descended from an old Gloucestershire family which had lived at Codrington since Edward I's reign and acquired the manor in the mid-15th century. Financial misfortune had forced his father to sell off extensive estates in the county including his large house at Didmarton, although Codrington himself went some way to repair this mishap through an advantageous second marriage, which brought him several Somerset manors, including Wraxall. He contested Bath in 1702 and 1705, but could make no headway against the two strongly entrenched sitting Members, Alexander Popham and William Blathwayt. Codrington's chance came in 1710, however, when his near neighbour the Duke of Beaufort, anxious to extend his political influence in Bath, put Codrington forward as his own candidate. In view of the offence Blathwayt had given the corporation by his alleged vote against Dr Sacheverell, Codrington's task, aided by Beaufort, of winning over the majority of the corporation was not difficult, although the result was by no means unanimous. Classed as a Tory in the 'Hanover list' of the new Parliament, he figured as one of the 'worthy patriots' who in the 1710-11 session detected the mismanagements of the previous administration, and was a member of the October Club. In 1712 he helped Beaufort secure the passage through Parliament of a bill to make the Avon navigable between Bristol and Bath, seconding his co-Member Samuel Trotman's motion for the bill on 23 Jan., and taking responsibility for its later stages in the House. Re-elected for Bath in 1713 and 1715, he was classed as a Tory in the Worsley list and again in a further list comparing the 1713 with the 1715 Parliament. In the winter of 1718-19 he was dismissed as a Somerset j.p. for discouraging zeal against sedition, but retained his constituency seat at each subsequent election, except that of 1727, until 1741. He died on 17 Apr. 1754.[3]

[1] *Trans. Bristol and Glos. Arch. Soc.* xxi. 328-32; Collinson, *Som.* iii. 159; A. J. Jewers, *Mar. Lic. Bath and Wells*, 82. [2] Bath AO, Bath council bk. 3, p. 329. [3] *Trans. Bristol and Glos. Arch. Soc.* 330-1; L. K. J. Glassey, *Appt. JPs*, 257.

P. W./A. A. H.

COKE, Thomas (1674-1727), of Melbourne, Derbys.; Melton Mowbray, Leics.; and St. James's Place, London.

DERBYSHIRE 1698-1700, 1701 (Dec.)-1710
GRAMPOUND 1710-1715

bap. 19 Feb. 1674, 1st s. of John Coke† of Melbourne by Mary, da. and h. of Sir Thomas Leventhorpe, 4th Bt., of Shingehall, Sawbridgeworth, Herts. *educ.* Rotterdam (M. Chauvois) 1688; New Coll. Oxf. 1693; travelled abroad (Low Countries) 1696, 1697. *m.* (1) c.June 1698 (with £8,000), Lady Mary Stanhope (*d.* 1704), e. da. of Philip, 2nd Earl of Chesterfield, 2da.; (2) 15 Oct. 1709 (with £6,000) Elizabeth (*d.* ?1722), da. of Richard Hales of King's Walden, Herts., 1s. 1da. *suc.* fa. 1692.[1]

Commr. public accts. 1702; teller of Exchequer May

1704–Dec. 1706; vice-chamberlain of Household Dec. 1706–d.; PC 1708–d.

Coke was a fourth-generation parliamentarian, a sequence begun by his great-grandfather, a secretary of state under Charles I. Little is known of his early years except that in 1688 he was under the tuition of a Frenchman in Rotterdam. Upon his father's death in Geneva on 7 Jan. 1692 Coke seems to have been left under the guidance of Walter Burdett of Knoyle Hill, a Derbyshire barrister (one of his father's executors and the third son of Sir Francis Burdett, 2nd Bt., who had been his father's guardian). His education was completed by two trips to Europe which became very much a rake's progress. In the summer of 1696 he disappeared from London, telling his sister that he intended to see the north of England, but in fact crossed the Channel to Antwerp and Rotterdam. The following summer he again slipped away to Holland causing great alarm to his sister when he visited King William's camp. However, the motivation for these trips had less to do with the army than the charms of a mistress about whom several correspondents kept him informed when he returned to England.[2]

In the early summer of 1698 Coke increased his standing in Derbyshire by contracting a prestigious marriage with the eldest daughter of the Earl of Chesterfield. The fact that his new father-in-law had a seat at Bretby clearly strengthened Coke's interest when he stood for knight of the shire in the election of July 1698. The possibility of a contest was averted when John Curzon* declined to stand, thus allowing Coke to share the representation with the Marquess of Hartington (William Cavendish*). The two families were probably on good terms at this time because Coke's father had been the lieutenant-colonel of the regiment raised in 1688 by the Duke of Devonshire (William Cavendish†), and under Hartington's nominal command. Coke's early parliamentary career is difficult to disentangle from that of John Cooke*, Member for Arundel 1698–1702, although the survival of some of his papers allows a few insights into measures in which he had a particular interest. Contemporaries entertained few doubts about his political views. Two lists were compiled before the new Parliament met: on the first he was noted as a Country party supporter and on the second as a likely opponent of the standing army. Coke's position as a county Member also ensured that he carefully scrutinized two of the navigation schemes which were considered by the House during this session. On 3 Jan. 1699 leave was given to bring in a bill to make the Derwent navigable from Derby to the Trent. The bill was promoted by the corporation of Derby, but it faced considerable opposition from Derbyshire landowners and rival corporate towns such as Nottingham and Leicester. Coke seemed genuinely undecided on the merits of the bill, even asking the advice of Hon. Anchitell Grey*, who had been involved in a similar scheme in the 1670s. In truth, Coke was in an invidious position because he possessed an estate at Wilne Ferry, close to the confluence of the two rivers, which would increase in value as a communications centre if the status quo were maintained. On the other hand, to oppose the bill risked alienating freeholders in the town of Derby who constituted a substantial proportion of the shire electorate. In the end Coke seemed to avoid committing himself to the bill, an ambiguous attitude which his opponents at the next election attempted to use to their advantage. Coke's attitude to the other navigation bill, to make the Trent navigable to Burton, also caused him problems. Initially, as one of the three Members appointed to bring in the bill, his views appeared clear-cut. However, after he received some criticism for his stance he appeared to lapse into a studied neutrality, especially as the Burton promoters were accused of deceiving the riparian landowners. Coke may have been involved in one further piece of legislation during this session. On 27 Feb. 1699 a 'Mr Cook' was ordered to prepare a bill in response to a petition from the Old East India Company requesting a bill to secure its right to trade as a separate entity until the end of the royal charter of 1693. 'Cook' presented the bill on 3 Mar., but it was rejected at its second reading. Although there is no evidence from this session to identify Coke positively as the Member involved, the measure was widely interpreted as an attempt to distress the government, something to which he would not have been averse at this time.[3]

Coke missed the beginning of the 1699–1700 session, possibly owing to a fall in which he hurt his leg. Indeed, it is possible that he did not take an active part in proceedings until after the Christmas recess. He may have been responsible for piloting through to the statute book a bill punishing vagrants, given that his correspondence shows him as interested in the problem. This time he was certainly involved in legislation to incorporate the Old East India Company. According to James Vernon I*, 'Mr Coke of Derbyshire' presented the bill on 24 Jan. 1700 and managed it through the Commons. He may also have acted as a teller twice during the session in favour of adding clauses to the land tax and Irish forfeitures bill. Coke took an active part in one of the contentious debates which was recorded during this session, on the conduct of Whig ministers with reference to royal grants. On 13 Feb. 1700 he attacked Thomas Stringer* for words spoken in defence of Lord Somers (Sir John*) and then seconded a resolution, moved by his friend Hon. James Brydges*, that any minister obtaining estates from the crown was guilty of a violation of trust. Two days later Coke continued the attack along similar lines, moving to take into consideration a grant to one Railton, allegedly an agent for Charles Montagu*. When Robert Harley* interceded to deflect the attack a frustrated Coke reacted violently, declaring that 'he would never trust a Presbyterian rogue more' and threatening that 'this should be the last motion he would ever make' before storming out of the House 'cursing all house meeting dogs, meaning Robert Harley'. On 28 Mar. 1700 he was apparently willing to support Jack Howe's proposal for seven rather than five (and unpaid) commissioners of accounts. In an analysis of the Commons into 'interests' in the first half of 1700, Coke was marked with a 'Q', which probably denotes a query, or perhaps opposition.[4]

When the new Parliament assembled in February 1701, Coke was missing, having been defeated for Derbyshire through the combined efforts of the Whig Lords Hartington and Roos (John Manners*). He also refused the offer of a possible seat at Newton if Thomas Brotherton* died. However, in the year that followed, Coke was able to persuade John Curzon to join with him in a campaign to recapture the shire representation, an ambition they quickly achieved in the election of December 1701. Lord Spencer (Charles*) marked his return as a loss for the Whigs, while another list compiled in December 1701 by Harley included Coke among the Tories, an assessment which ties in with the requests of his friends that he be in London in time to vote for Harley in the election for Speaker. On 2 Jan. 1702 Coke seconded the motion for the Address and was duly appointed (as 'Mr Cooke') to the committee ordered to draft it. He was probably named to four drafting committees in January 1702, including the bill re-establishing the public accounts commission. On 24 Jan. 1702 he was a teller against an amendment to a procedural motion that the next meeting of the committee of the whole on the abjuration bill should be after the committee on supply. The tactical considerations surrounding this vote are difficult to disentangle, but Coke was certainly involved in the proceedings on the bill. Indeed, his advocacy of the Tory line in favour of a compulsory oath of abjuration embroiled him in difficulties with some of his less sophisticated constituents, who did not realize that a voluntary oath might hand the Whigs a propaganda victory, and that many Tories regarded oaths taken under duress as not binding. On 26 Feb., when Henry St. John II* proposed that the Commons had not had right done them in the late impeachments, Coke seconded him, albeit 'in a weaker insipid dreaming way'. Not surprisingly, on that day he was listed as having voted in vindication of the Commons' proceedings. His interest in economy and accountability led him on 2 Mar., in committee of the whole on the public accounts bill, to propose a clause to provide that the officers in the Dutch regiments should not be paid until their accounts had been stated. On the 4th he dined with Brydges, Sir Christopher Musgrave, 4th Bt.*, and others where he was included on a slate for elections for the commission of accounts. On the 7th he told against the committal of a bill to prevent frauds by workers in the woollen, linen and cotton trades. On 12 Mar., when the House took into consideration the Queen's Speech, he 'commended the word entirely English and moved to have it [the speech] considered tomorrow'. On 18 Mar. his reputation as a leading Country Member was confirmed by his election as a commissioner of accounts, albeit in seventh place. To the Earl of Chesterfield, this new employment appeared laborious, temporary and ill-paid. However, Chesterfield added, 'I hope this will be an introduction to something that will be much better'. Coke was probably the 'Mr Cooke' who acted as a teller on 28 Mar. in favour of a motion that the Coventry alderman Edward Owen be taken into custody for threatening a messenger of the Commons sent to apprehend several people guilty of malpractice during the Coventry election. He was probably a teller on 8 Apr. against a motion to complete the blanks in the bill for making provision for the Protestant children of the Earl of Clanricarde and Lord Bophin. On 2 May, he moved for an address that no person be an officer in England or Ireland in the new regiments unless born in England, Scotland, Ireland or the dominions, and of English parents, unless currently on the half-pay list: 'he enforced this by saying it was a shame to have our own want employments and foreigners advanced over their heads', backing up his motion with the example of a half-pay captain who had had a foreigner advanced over him, but this example was comprehensively rebutted by the secretary at war, William Blathwayt*. Coke then attempted to draw Hon. Harry Mordaunt* into the debate, claiming that almost all the officers in his regiment were French. At the end of the debate he told for his motion, which was only narrowly defeated. Part of the session was taken up with lobbying support for a private bill to give legal force to an agreement Coke had negotiated with the bishop of

Carlisle concerning the rectory of Melbourne, adjacent to his seat. The bill was introduced into the Lords on 4 Feb. but was allowed to lapse after its first reading, either owing to the illness of Bishop Smith, who died on 12 Apr., or to shortage of money. Coke's correspondence suggests that he was kept busy in this session. He invited comments on current legislative proposals through his widespread distribution of the *Votes* to important constituents and centres of population. For the 1701–2 session he received advice on the land tax; the abortive bill for the ease of sheriffs; the forfeited estates of Vesey and Vernon; poor debtors (from whom he received a petition but did not present); and the bill to prevent perjury, on which he received several clauses relating to barmote courts and the lead trade.[5]

Coke remained in London until early July 1702, before returning to Derbyshire to attend his election, where he was returned unopposed. By early August he was back at Spring Garden, the office of the commissioners of accounts, where he remained until Parliament opened in October. On 11 Dec., he was a teller against a motion to take into consideration the Queen's message requesting a grant of £5,000 p.a. out of the Post Office revenue to the Duke of Marlborough (John Churchill†). On 16 Dec., when the House agreed to inform the Queen of the reason for not complying with her request, Coke told for rejecting a proposed Whig amendment which would have extended a criticism of exorbitant royal grants to those made by Charles II and James II as well as King William. His stance on the controversial first occasional conformity bill can be inferred from a letter from a constituent who informed him that the bill had 'so envenomed all the Presbyterians that they are making all imaginable interest underhand against you and Mr Curzon against the next election'. On 7 Jan. 1703 his continued rise to prominence in the Commons was emphasized by re-election to the commission of accounts, this time in second place. On 18 Jan. he was ordered to prepare a bill augmenting small vicarages, which never emerged from committee. The only vote recorded for him in this session came on 13 Feb., when he divided against agreeing with the Lords' amendment to the bill enlarging the time for taking the Abjuration.[6]

After the first session of the 1702 Parliament Coke was in a position to exploit his growing influence in the House. In company with St. John, Brydges and Harley, he was one of a group of rising men who looked forward to the exercise of office and its rewards. The session of 1703–4 opened quietly enough. During the debate on the contents of the Address, Bonet reported that Coke, a Tory, favoured a general assurance to the Queen rather than specific mention of the treaties with Portugal and Savoy. On 26 Nov. Bonet reported that, on the previous day, Coke had opposed the motion for leave to bring in a second occasional conformity bill, a view which filtered into Derbyshire prompting one of Coke's correspondents to report to him a rumour that he had voted against the bill. This was perhaps the first indication that Coke was trimming his sails in the hope of preferment. He presented a bill on behalf of his relatives, the Cokes of Trusley, but did not manage the bill because in January 1704 his wife died of a fever a few days after a miscarriage, causing a prolonged absence from the House. On 7 Feb. he wrote to Speaker Harley to ensure that he was not re-elected to the commission of accounts, 'which in the circumstances I am now in I must of necessity decline, being incapable in person to perform it'. Thus, Coke's life was thrown into turmoil at the very moment when opportunities were opening up for his circle. He was forced to follow events from afar, but kept in close correspondence with his friends and may have exploited his inaccessibility in order to avoid accepting uncongenial posts. The ministry was certainly keen to accommodate him: on 3 Apr. 1704 Marlborough wrote to him on the subject of employment that 'I could not leave England with any ease to my mind till I had turned my thoughts to every thing that is possible for placing you in the Queen's service to your satisfaction'. Coke was spoken of in connexion with a place at the Board of Trade and certainly refused an offer of joint-controller of the army before finally securing 'a fat sinecure' as a teller of the Exchequer. By early May he had returned to the capital to obtain his patent and find sureties worth £7,000 to enable him to take up office. Henceforth he regularly appeared on lists of placemen.[7]

Acceptance of office produced a profound change in Coke's political attitude. From being a staunch upholder of the Country tradition, he became an archetypal courtier. Possibly the rewards of office were essential to his plans to rebuild Melbourne Hall. The change was noted by contemporaries, one of whom forecast in October 1704 that Coke would oppose the Tack. He was not listed as voting for it on 28 Nov. 1704. His main concerns in this session seem to centre upon three private bills, the most important being the reintroduced bill to confirm his agreement with the bishop of Carlisle in 1701 over the rectory of Melbourne. Although the bill had an uninterrupted passage through both Houses, Coke had to work hard behind the scenes to ensure the agreement of the new bishop, William Nicolson. In January 1705 Coke undertook one of his duties as knight of the shire when he presented a bill to enable a Derbyshire gentleman to settle a jointure on his wife. He also took over from the secretary at war the management of a bill to naturalize the wife of one of Marlborough's favourites, William Cadogan*, duly reporting the bill on 25 Jan.[8]

An imminent move by Coke towards the Court had been suspected by some in Derbyshire as early as January 1704, and there were rumours that he would again join forces with Lord Hartington for the county at the 1705 election. In the event Coke was returned again with Curzon. However, there were murmurings of discontent: on 25 July 1705 Lady Anne Pye recorded that since the election Coke 'is not so revered by the High Church because he had so much declared against it. It is thought they will endeavour to oppose him against next choice, but that is a great way off.' None the less, there was still some confusion among contemporaries as to his exact political stance: on a list of Members elected to the new Parliament he was classed as a 'Churchman'. The confusion was probably dispelled on 25 Oct. when he joined many Tory placemen in supporting the Court candidate for Speaker. On 19 Dec. in a debate on the regency bill he intervened in the discussion over some ill-judged comments made by Charles Caesar*, to counsel moderation unless the words were deemed so 'exaggerated' as to warrant exemplary punishment. Then on 21 Jan. 1706 he spoke in support of Harley's suggestion that the debate on the 'whimsical' clause be deferred for a day. However, he was not recorded as voting for the Court over the regency bill proceedings on 18 Feb.[9]

Early in December 1706 Coke exchanged offices with Hon. Peregrine Bertie II*, the vice-chamberlain of the Household. This appointment not only strengthened his ties to the Court, but provided a plausible excuse for staying away from the Commons. Indeed, as Coke discharged his duties conscientiously his post often necessitated his absence. 'An able, assiduous, and highly versatile vice-chamberlain', he was awarded £1,000 out of the privy purse owing to his 'constant waiting and attendance' on the Queen. Coke's name appears among 18 names sent by Lord Godolphin (Sidney†) to Harley, dated 26 Oct. 1707, clearly a list of the government managers in the Commons for the coming session. However, Coke was inactive in the 1707–8 session. He was still classed as a Tory on a list compiled early in 1708, but on the dismissal of Harley in February 1708, he failed to resign along with St. John and (Sir) Thomas Mansel I*, despite expectations that he would do so.[10]

Coke was again returned unopposed for Derbyshire in 1708. After December 1706, he had customarily been referred to in the Journals as 'Mr Vice-Chamberlain'. However, the mention on 15 Jan. 1709 of a 'Mr Coke' as teller for William Hale* in the Bramber election may have been a reference to the vice-chamberlain, since Coke was later in the year to marry Hale's sister. On 28 Jan. Coke voted for (Sir) Simon Harcourt I when Harcourt was unseated for Abingdon. On 1 Feb. he was a teller again, this time for Crewe Offley* in another election case. On 29 Jan. he was named to a committee to prepare a bill to bring the treason laws in Scotland into line with those in England, but the bill was dropped in the face of Scottish opposition. The Lords then took up a similar bill, which was amended by the Commons to restrict the forfeiture of estates on attainder to the lifetime of the person attainted. The Lords in turn added a further amendment so that the forfeiture would apply to heirs until the death of the Pretender. On 18 Apr. 1709 Coke told for agreeing with this counter-amendment. His one recorded vote in the session was also in support of the Whigs, being in favour of the general naturalization bill. In 1709 Coke was described as 'that dapper squat gentleman with a tolerable face, poring on a book, and feigning to read it . . . He would willingly be thought a wit: not one of the writers, but brisk at repartee.' The same writer referred to Coke's adventures with various women, but in October he married one of the Queen's maids of honour.[11]

In the session which began the following month, Coke again seemed to keep a low profile, the only legislation with which he was concerned being a bill to facilitate the passage of sheriffs' accounts, which he introduced on 14 Jan. 1710. On 15 Feb., during the debate on the address to hasten Marlborough to the peace negotiations, Brydges described Coke's role as 'a part that he can best account for', which suggests that he had acted differently from the rest of the Duke's friends. Coke himself explained to Brydges that he had opposed the address 'very early in the debate', and when 'the debate turned from being a point of decency to the Queen to the merit of the Duke of Marlborough' he could not join the rest of the Court in voting for the address, 'tho' I was very much provoked to it by the unmannerly behaviour of the Tories'. He then laid down a rule of conduct which was 'to support the prerogative of the crown', even though on this occasion he was 'in bad company'. On the major issue of the session he voted for the impeachment of Dr Sacheverell.[12]

Coke's voting record in the 1708–10 Parliament, although explicable in terms of the need to retain his office, nevertheless did not endear him to his Tory constituents. Indeed, they were particularly indignant over his attitude to Sacheverell. He was reported not only to have been against the Doctor, but to have taken 'several opportunities to show yourself, and to speak, and that very hotly, and when you need not have done it, against him'. He compounded his faults by refusing to leave his post at Court to solicit his election, with the result that his erstwhile partner, Curzon, joined Coke's own brother-in-law Godfrey Clarke* to oppose him. When Coke did finally travel to Derbyshire to survey the situation at first hand, he declined to force a poll and took refuge in the Cornish borough of Grampound.[13]

Coke's new electoral patron was George Granville*, a friend of Harley, a fact which, together with his proven malleability, seems to have enabled him to make a successful transition from a Whig to a Tory ministry and retain his place at court. It is probable that he felt more at ease under a Tory administration. The 'Hanover list' of the new Parliament certainly marked him as a Tory. He does not appear to have engaged in much parliamentary activity in the early part of the session, possibly owing to attendance on the Queen, but managed an estate bill when it came down from the Lords, reporting it on 10 May 1711. On 14 May Coke chaired the committee of the whole on the bill for raising the militia, reporting it on 16 May. His Tory stance in this session was confirmed when he was listed as one of the 'worthy patriots' who detected the mismanagements of the late ministry. He chaired a committee of the whole on 26 May on a bill for clearing a regiment's accounts. Continuing ill-health during the summer of 1711 gave rise to doctor's orders to refrain from drink. He spoke for the Court in the motion of censure against Marlborough in January 1712, although the Duchess had appealed to his wife (whom she claimed to have made a maid of honour) to speak to Coke, who had 'very many great' obligations to the Duke, not to be against him in the Commons. During this session he sent a number of letters to Harley (now Lord Treasurer Oxford) concerning the payment of his salary, an incessant importunity that suggests some financial embarrassment at this time, possibly deriving from expense in the refurbishment of Melbourne Hall. In the 1713 session the only important issues which occupied him in the Commons related to the peace. On 18 June he voted in favour of the French commerce bill and in debate exhorted Tory Members to withdraw their opposition since they were only being made the pawns of a faction.[14]

At the election of 1713 Coke was returned for Grampound, being classed as a Tory on the Worsley list. Nothing of importance was recorded of his activities in the 1714 session, probably owing to his attendance on the Queen at Windsor. However, he did submit a petition to the Lords in June against a bill seeking to amend the Trent Navigation Act of 1698 because he perceived it would prejudice his estate adjoining the river. After the death of the Queen Coke attended the Privy Council which proclaimed George I. He was continued in his office by the new monarch, much to the unease of many Whigs, but did not stand for Parliament in the new reign. He retained his post until his death on 16 or 17 May 1727. In his will of 1722 he made provision for his daughters, with most of his estate going to his son, George Lewis Coke.[15]

[1] *HMC Cowper*, iii. 156–7; Add. 19253, f. 189b; Beaufort mss at Badminton House, Coventry pprs., Ld. Bindon (Henry Howard*) to [Lady Anne Coventry?], 4 Oct. 1709; *Cal. Treas. Bks.* xxiii. 413. [2] *HMC Cowper*, ii. 361–4, 369–70; iii. 156–7; J. T. Coke, *Coke of Trusley*, 72–73; Cottrell-Dormer mss at Rousham, Charles Caesar's jnl.; PCC 139 Fane; *CSP Dom.* 1696, p. 262; 1697, p. 141. [3] *HMC Cowper*, ii. 348–52, 383–4, 385; BL, Lothian mss, Sir Gilbert Clarke* to Coke, 21 July 1698; Robert Harding to same, 20 May 1700; John Beresford to same, 17 Dec. 1700; W. Woolley, *Hist. Derbys.* (Derbys. Rec. Soc. vi.), 58; H. Horwitz, *Parl. and Pol. Wm. III*, 254. [4] *HMC Cowper*, ii. 392–4; *Vernon–Shrewsbury Letters*, ii. 421; *Cocks Diary*, 50, 53–54; Som. RO, Sanford mss DD/SF4107(a), notes on debate, 13 Feb. 1699[–1700]; Northants. RO, Montagu (Boughton) mss 48/51, Vernon to Shrewsbury, 28 Mar. 1700. [5] Lothian mss, Ld. Stanhope to Coke, 24 Feb. 1700[–1], Lady Mary Coke to same, [n.d.]; *HMC Cowper*, ii. 421–2, 443–4, 453–7; iii. 2, 4–5; *Cocks Diary*, 225, 231, 243, 278–9; Huntington Lib. Stowe mss 26(2), James Brydges*' diary, 4 Mar. 1702. [6] *HMC Cowper*, iii. 20. [7] DZA, Bonet despatches 12, 26 Nov. 1703; *HMC Cowper*, iii. 29, 31–32, 34–36, 163; G. Holmes, *Pol. in Age of Anne*, 263; *Marlborough–Godolphin Corresp.* 288; Luttrell, *Brief Relation*, v. 414; *HMC Portland*, iv. 84; *Cal. Treas. Bks.* xix. 231, 240. [8] N. Pevsner, *Buildings of Eng.* Derbys. 278; *Nicolson Diaries* ed. Jones and Holmes, 218–19, 236, 247, 249, 252, 271, 274–5. [9] *HMC Cowper*, iii. 29–30, 54–55; *HMC Portland*, iv. 212; *Cam. Misc.* xxiii. 53, 81. [10] Staffs. RO, Paget mss D603/K/3/6, R. Acherley to Ld. Paget, 3 Dec. 1706; *Daily Courant*, 5 Dec. 1706; R. Bucholz, *Augustan Court*, 45; Add. 70328, list 26 Oct. 1707; *EHR*, lxxx. 697; Stowe mss 57(2), p. 98; *Swift Corresp.* ed. Williams, i. 69. [11] *Bull. IHR*, xl. 160; P. W. J. Riley, *Eng. Ministers and Scotland*, 119–20; Stowe mss 57(3), p. 153; D. Manley, *Secret Mems.* 183. [12] Stowe mss 58(5), pp. 124–7. [13] Lothian mss, Elizabeth Coke to Coke, 9 Sept. 1710; *HMC Cowper*, iii. 84–98, 170–1; *HMC Portland*, iv. 591, 612; Holmes, 264. [14] Stowe mss 57(5), p. 85, James Brydges to Mr Cartwright, 1 June 1711; Add. 70218, Coke to Oxford, 4 Nov. 1711, 16 Feb, 3 Sept. 1712; 17677 GGG, f. 230; 61474, f. 186; Oldmixon, *Hist. Eng.* 488. [15] *HMC Lords*, n.s. x. 370; Boyer, *Pol. State*, viii. 117; xxxiii. 528; Norf. RO, Ketton-Cremer mss, Mrs Katharine Windham to Ashe Windham*, [n.d.], James Windham to same, 28 Sept. 1714; *Hist. Reg. Chron.* 1727, p. 19; PCC 133 Farrant.

S. N. H.

COLCHESTER, Maynard (1665–1715), of Westbury Court, Westbury-on-Severn and the Wilderness, Abbinghall, Glos.

GLOUCESTERSHIRE 1701 (Dec.)–1708

b. 4 Mar. 1665, 1st s. of Sir Duncombe Colchester† of Westbury Court and the Wilderness by Elizabeth, da. of

Sir John Maynard*. *educ.* Exeter, Oxf. 1681; M. Temple 1682, called 1689. *m.* 28 Jan. 1690, Jane (*d.* 1741), da. of Sir Edward Clarke, Merchant Taylor, of St. Peter Cheap and Gutter Lane, London, ld. mayor 1696, sis. and h. of Thomas Clarke*, 2s. *d.v.p.* 3da.; other ch. *d.v.p. suc.* fa. 1694.[1]

Commr. superstitious lands, Glos. 1692; verderer, Forest of Dean ?1709–*d.*; ?dep. constable, St. Briavels Castle, Glos. 1710–*d.*[2]

Member, SPCK 1699, SPG 1701.[3]

It is likely (and if so would be fitting) that the most powerful influence on the young Maynard Colchester was exerted by his maternal grandfather Sir John Maynard, after whom he was named, and whose anti-Catholicism and devotion to 'good works' he shared. Attending Sir John Maynard's inn of court, Colchester was called to the bar in April 1689 at his grandfather's express wish. (He does not, however, appear to have practised.) He accompanied Sir John to a royal audience in 1690, and was appointed an executor and trustee in his will. An enthusiastic supporter of the movement for the reformation of manners, Colchester was one of the founders of the very first society established for this purpose, in 1691, and subsequently served with fellow reformers on the commission of the peace for Middlesex, where he was active in putting into practice the programme of the society. The other face of the reforming coin was represented by his nomination in 1692 to a commission to inquire into estates in Gloucestershire which had been 'conveyed to popish uses'. Typical of his character was his speech to a House of Lords committee in February 1694 discussing a private bill to settle the Maynard estate, in which it was proposed to compensate him handsomely for his work as a trustee. Pecuniary considerations, he declared, were quite beneath him: 'I value not the money; I will give it to the poor. It is my reputation I stand upon.' His most spectacular achievement was probably the deathbed repentance of his father after a life of debauchery. Sir Duncombe, at his son's urging, composed a solemn confession of past sins, to be read in local parish churches 'as a warning to all'.[4]

Succeeding to 'a large house and seat' and 'a great estate', Colchester was quickly added to the county lieutenancy, and in 1697 was given the colonelcy of one of the two militia regiments in Gloucester. A man of means even before his father's death, able to subscribe £500 to a government loan on the poll tax in 1692, he was now wealthy enough to indulge in a variety of philanthropic projects, including the setting up of charity schools, 'the instruction and conversion of Quakers', and poor relief, often disbursing his money 'in secret'. It was almost inevitable that he should be one of the founder-members of the Society for Promoting Christian Knowledge in 1699 and the Society for the Propagation of the Gospel in Foreign Parts two years later.[5]

Colchester is not recorded as taking a significant part in politics until January 1701, when he appears as one of the 'chief supporters' of the Country Whig Sir Richard Cocks, 2nd Bt.*, in the county election. By the autumn he seems to have resolved to be a candidate himself, for at quarter sessions he publicly denounced the other sitting Member for Gloucestershire, John Grobham Howe*, in terms which anticipated a contest at the polls; and indeed, he was returned with Cocks in December at Howe's expense. Lord Spencer (Charles*) calculated his election as a gain for the Whigs. Named with Cocks and other Members of the 'Country' persuasion on 17 Jan. 1702 to bring in a bill to prevent bribery and corruption at elections, he made his maiden speech on 26 Feb. in a debate on the Kentish Petition: according to Cocks he spoke 'very well'. He had also been nominated on 28 Jan., following a petition from the Gloucestershire quarter sessions, to prepare a bill 'for settling the water-bushel for measuring fruit'. On 31 Mar., and again on 6 May, Colchester was ordered to carry this measure to the Lords. Keeping his seat at the 1702 election, he voted on 13 Feb. 1703 in favour of agreeing with the Lords' amendments to the bill for enlarging the time for taking the oath of abjuration. Having been forecast as a probable opponent of the Tack, he did not vote for it on 28 Nov. 1704. During the 1704–5 session Colchester assisted in the management of a private bill. At his re-election in 1705 his fellow Whig candidate Sir John Guise, 3rd Bt.*, described him as 'a very worthy man and a true friend to his country'. Classed as 'Low Church' in a list of the new Parliament, Colchester voted for the Court candidate in the division on the Speaker, 25 Oct. 1705, but his name was missing from the list of the Court side in the vote on 18 Feb. 1706 on the 'place clause' of the regency bill, possibly an indication that he was one of the 'whimsical' Whigs who had inspired the original clause, or perhaps an early example of the valetudinarianism which was to mark his later years. His presence at meetings of the SPCK on 31 Jan. and 21 Feb., however, suggests that he was almost certainly in town on the day in question. By the following year his attendance at Westminster was much less regular, and his determination to withdraw from politics was known as early as July 1707. He was still marked as a Whig in two lists dating from early 1708.[6]

As predicted, Colchester did not put up again in

1708. His epitaph tells how he 'was exercised, for many years, with almost constant sickness, and the most acute pains, which he bore with exemplary patience'. He was incapacitated in the summer of 1709, for instance, by a sharp attack of gout. There was nevertheless time for improvement to his estate, especially the gardens at Westbury and the Wilderness, where he is said to have benefited from the advice of John Evelyn, and above all for works of charity. Moreover, he did not abdicate from what he saw as his duty as a magistrate, crossing swords with local Tory justices so often that in 1712 the Duke of Beaufort unsuccessfully pressed Lord Keeper Harcourt (Simon I*) for his removal from the bench. Colchester died on 25 June 1715, and was buried at Westbury. His will, dated 1706, named Thomas Stephens II* as a trustee. The estates, upon which some £15,000 was to be raised in portions for his daughters, passed eventually to a nephew, another Colonel Maynard Colchester.[7]

[1] *Trans. Bristol and Glos. Arch. Soc.* vi. 189–90; li. 32–33; Morrice ent'ring bk. 3, p. 105; J. R. Woodhead, *Rulers of London* (London and Mdx. Arch. Soc.), 47; PCC 73 Whitfield. [2] *Cal. Treas. Bks.* ix. 1909; xxiv. 567; Add. 61596, ff. 55–58, 63; Le Neve, *Mon. Angl.* 1700–15, p. 305; *Trans. Bristol and Glos. Arch. Soc.* iii. 364. [3] W. K. Lowther Clarke, *Hist. SPCK*, 54; W. O. B. Allen and E. McClure, *Two Hundred Years*, 13, 17–18. [4] *M. T. Recs.* iii. 1388; Morrice ent'ring bk. 3, p. 156; PCC 121 Vere; *HMC Lords*, n.s. i. 340–2; viii. 363; Craig thesis, 26, 61, 64–66, 297; *CSP Dom.* 1691–2, pp. 165, 220; J. Stratford, *Good and Great Men of Glos.* 404. [5] Atkyns, *Glos.* (1768), p. 420; *CSP Dom.* 1694–5, p. 234; 1700–2, p. 357; *Old Wales*, i. 87; *CJ*, x. 724; Lowther Clarke, 54, 57; *Trans. Bristol and Glos. Arch. Soc.* xix. 376–7; Stratford, 405; Allen and McClure, 13, 17–18; SPCK Archs. min. bk. 1, p. 336; min. bk. 4, p. 70; CR1/5, abstract letterbk. 1713–15, no. 3870; Le Neve, 1650–1718, pp. 264–6; Bodl. Rawl. C.933, ff. 25, 27, 29, 35. [6] *HMC Portland*, iv. 14; *Vernon–Shrewsbury Letters*, iii. 158; *Cocks Diary*, 227; *Guise Mems.* (Cam. Soc. ser. 3, xxviii), 145; SPCK Archs. min. bk. 1, pp. 366–70; Bodl. Ballard 31, f. 50. [7] Allen and McClure, 16–17; Add. 61596, f. 57; Rudder, *Glos.* 790; Beaufort mss at Badminton House, Beaufort to Harcourt, 10 Nov. 1712; *Trans. Bristol and Glos. Arch. Soc.* vi. 190; xxviii. 213; PCC 73 Whitfield; SPCK Archs. min. bk. 8, p. 40.

D. W. H.

COLCHESTER, Richard Savage, Visct. *see* **SAVAGE**

COLEMORE, William I (c.1649–1723), of the Old Deanery House, Warwick.

WARWICK 1689–1695

b. c.1649, 3rd s. of William Colemore, merchant, of Birmingham, Warws. being 1st s. by 2nd w. *educ.* Magdalen Coll. Oxf. matric. 3 May 1667, aged 18; I. Temple 1669. *m.* Jan. 1676, Elizabeth (d. 1731), da. and coh. of Edmund Waring† of Humphreston Hall, Donnington, Salop, 10s. (6 *d.v.p.*) 3da. *suc.* fa. 1675.[1]

Alderman, Warwick; commr. rebuilding Warwick 1695; sheriff, Warws., 1699–1700.[2]

Colemore was a senior member of Warwick's aldermanic bench and a trustee for managing the borough's finances and property. He was re-elected for Warwick in 1690, probably with backing from Lord Brooke (Fulke Greville†), and classed by Lord Carmarthen (Sir Thomas Osborne†) as a Tory and likely Court supporter. In December Carmarthen identified him again as an adherent of the Court, but the following April Robert Harley* saw him as a supporter of the 'Country' viewpoint. That he subsequently retained this political outlook is suggested by his involvement in the Country Tory attack on Bishop Gilbert Burnet's *Pastoral Letter* in January 1693: he told on the 23rd with William Bromley II, the Tory Member for Warwickshire, that the *Letter* be publicly burnt by the common hangman. Following the disastrous fire at Warwick in September 1694, he and his parliamentary colleague, Lord Digby (William*), initiated a bill on 7 Dec. to rebuild the devastated western part of the town. Although it was Digby who managed the bill, Colemore was naturally included on the second-reading committee, and was named in the bill as a commissioner for taking subscriptions. On 11 Feb. 1695 he told in favour of allowing three weeks' leave to Salwey Winnington* to attend a sick wife. He did not stand at the 1695 general election, having previously agreed to make way for Lord Brooke's eldest son, Hon. Francis Greville*. Brooke's later inclusion of Colemore in his will is a mark of the cordiality that existed between them. Colemore continued to play his part in Warwick's civic affairs for some years after his departure from the House. He was also active at county level and held the shrievalty in 1699–1700, while in September 1700 he was invited to become a 'lay correspondent' for the county to the recently formed Society for Promoting Christian Knowledge. In a letter to one of the Society's officials in January 1701 he promised to bestir the neighbouring magistrates into enforcing the laws 'for promoting reformation' although he felt that the only matter in which reform was especially needed was absenteeism from church. In 1707 the bishop of Lichfield was anxious to see him included among the commissioners for building the new church at Birmingham, recognizing that his close involvement in the rebuilding of Warwick following the 1694 fire had 'given him a good deal of experience in the building and contriving of a church and he is upon all accounts a very fit person to be advised with and entrusted in this affair'. His will, dated 14 Mar. 1723, contains a suggestion that all was not well between himself and his wife, whom he described as 'unkind and unjust'. He died later that year on 16 July, having requested a private burial at night, his coffin to be borne by 'ordinary tradesmen and labourers' of Warwick.[3]

[1] A. L. Reade, *Johnsonian Gleanings*, vii. 122–4. [2] *Trans. Birmingham Arch. Soc.* lix. 50, 59–60; *Great Fire of Warwick* (Dugdale Soc. xxxvi), 121. [3] PCC 239 Smith; *Luttrell Diary*, 382; *Warws. Recs.* ix. p. xxix; Bodl. Ballard 25, f. 20; *Chapter in Church Hist.* ed. McClure, 79, 302, 320; Warws. RO, Mordaunt mss CR 1368/iii/63, Bp. of Lichfield to Sir John Mordaunt, 5th Bt.*, 12 Mar. 1706–7; PCC 223 Bolton; Reade, 123.

A. A. H.

COLEMORE, William II (1682–1722), of the Old Deanery House, Warwick.

WARWICK 1713–1 Nov. 1722

bap. 24 Jan. 1682, 1st s. of William Colemore I*. *educ.* Magdalen Coll. Oxf. 1699; M. Temple 1699. *unm.*[1]

Little has been ascertained about the younger William Colemore. Returned for his native town in 1713, presumably with backing from the Greville interest, he was almost certainly a Tory, but the indications are that he was a very moderate one: the Worsley list describes him as a Tory who often voted with the Whigs, while in an analysis of Members of the 1713 Parliament re-elected in 1715 he appears somewhat equivocally as a 'whimsical Whig'. In a third list he is identified simply as a Tory. Indeed, his moderate Toryism was noted by one senior Whig who observed that 'Mr [Andrew] Archer* and Mr Colemore in your county are with us in most of the questions'. He evidently made sufficient impression on proceedings to be included on the 'Speaker's list' of moderate Tories canvassed in June 1714 for places on the new commission of accounts. Although not elected he obtained a creditable total of 144 votes. He continued to represent Warwick until his death on 1 Nov. 1722, his father outliving him by eight months.[2]

[1] A. L. Reade, *Johnsonian Gleanings*, vii. 123. [2] Fitzwilliam Mus. Lib. Camb. Perceval mss A21, James Craggs I* to Anne Newsam, 22 Apr. 1714; NLS, Advocates' mss, Wodrow pprs. letters Quarto 8, f. 138; BL, Verney mss mic. 636/55, William Capps to Ld. Fermanagh (John Verney*), [18 June 1714].

A. A. H.

COLEPEPER (CULPEPER), Sir Thomas, 3rd Bt. (c.1656–1723), of Preston Hall, nr. Maidstone, Kent.

MAIDSTONE 1705–1713, 1715–18 May 1723

b. c.1656, o. s. of Sir Richard Colepeper, 2nd Bt., of Preston Hall by Margaret Reynolds. *educ.* Magdalen Coll. Oxf. matric. 15 June 1672, aged 15; *m.* 23 Aug. 1704, Elizabeth, da. of Sir Thomas Taylor, 1st Bt., of Park House, Maidstone, Kent, sis. of Sir Thomas Taylor, 2nd Bt.*, and wid. of (Sir) Francis Wythens† of Southend, Eltham, Kent and the Middle Temple. *s.p. suc.* fa. as 3rd Bt. Jan. 1660.[1]

Sheriff, Kent 1703–4.

The Colepepers were a well-established Kentish family, having been resident in the county since the 12th century. Beginning with Sir Thomas Colepeper of Bayhall, many branches of the family had flowered, so that by the 17th century identification can be very difficult. Thus Colepeper must not be confused with Sir Thomas Colepeper of Hollingbourne (*d.* 1697), or the latter's son Thomas (one of the Kentish Petitioners), nor with Colonel Thomas Colepeper, the hot-tempered engineer and inventor who pursued a quarrel against the Earl of Devonshire (William Cavendish†) after 1685. Having succeeded to the baronetcy at an early age, this Member was left in the capable care of his mother, her deceased husband having provided in his will for the education of his children. In the early 1670s, Sir Edward Dering, 2nd Bt.†, thought a marriage for his son to Colepeper's sister worth pursuing, since the young lady was of 'a very considerable family in our country', but financial constraints prevented a match. Indeed, by 1671, when Lady Colepeper was considering this alliance, she estimated that the cost of her son's education, presumably at Oxford, would be £100 p.a., which would prove a severe constraint on the options available for her daughter, Alicia. In 1681 John Tillotson (the future archbishop of Canterbury) drafted a letter to Colepeper offering moral counsel, having 'known you from your tender years', in which he warned the young man, 'you are now in the slippery and dangerous part of life, exposed to many and powerful temptations, especially in so licentious an age', adding, 'I have good hope you are not yet entangled in any very bad course'. In this Tillotson was unsuccessful, for at some point Colepeper took as his mistress the wife of Sir Francis Wythens. Conflict inevitably arose. In 1693 Lady Wythens tried to have her husband incarcerated in a debtors' prison and in November 1696 Wythens himself entered an information against Colepeper and Sir Thomas Taylor, 2nd Bt. (brother-in-law to both Wythens and Colepeper), for assault. He failed to gain a conviction after Lord Colepeper, Sir Philip Boteler, 3rd Bt.*, Sir George Rooke* and Sir George Choute, 1st Bt.*, all testified to Colepeper's 'great worth and honour'. After Wythens' death on 9 May 1704,

Colepeper wasted no time in marrying his widow. Thereafter it was reported that he never lived with her as a husband.[2]

Considerable difficulty attaches to following Colepeper's career in local office because central government records do not always distinguish between the Member and his namesake of Hollingbourne. One of these men was a j.p. before 1679, almost certainly Sir Thomas Colepeper of Hollingbourne, who also became a deputy lieutenant in November 1679. It was the baronet who was appointed to the lieutenancy in 1685, but it was his Hollingbourne relative who as a 'Whig collaborator' was named as such in February 1688. After the Revolution, it seems likely, on grounds of age alone, that the Sir Thomas Colepeper who served as a deputy-lieutenant and militia colonel was the baronet. In 1701 Colepeper was one of the men suggested for the shrievalty, but he was not pricked until 1703–4. He was elected to Parliament for Maidstone in 1705, although he 'could not be prevailed upon to stand till the alteration was made in Kent', a reference to Lord Rockingham (Hon. Lewis Watson†) replacing the Earl of Winchilsea as lord lieutenant of the county. Despite the fact that one analysis of the 1705 Parliament classified him as a 'Churchman', Colepeper was undoubtedly a Whig. The Earl of Sunderland (Charles, Lord Spencer*) considered his election in 1705 as a gain for the Whigs, and on 25 Oct. he voted for the Court candidate for Speaker. He failed to support the Court on 18 Feb. 1706 over the 'place clause' of the regency bill, which may indicate sympathy with Country Whig views, but on a list of early 1708 he was again classed as a Whig. Returned once more in 1708, Colepeper was marked as a Whig on a list of that year with the election returns appended to it. In 1709 he supported the naturalization of the Palatines and the following year voted for the impeachment of Dr Sacheverell. Not surprisingly, on the 'Hanover list' of 1710 he was again listed as Whig. He was returned at the top of the poll in the 1710 election, but his name does not appear on any division list for the ensuing Parliament. Not having stood as a candidate in the Tory landslide of 1713, he was returned in 1715, being described as a Whig on a comparative analysis of the old and new Parliaments.[3]

Colepeper continued to sit for Maidstone until his death on 18 May 1723. Perhaps the suddenness of his demise accounts for the fact that his will had not been updated since February 1711. The major beneficiary was Sir Thomas Taylor, 3rd Bt., the son of his sister, Alicia, although Catharine, Lady Twisden (née Wythens), whom some would have as Colepeper's natural daughter, benefited to the tune of 500 guineas, and mistress Swayne, 'her woman', by 100 guineas for faithful service.[4]

[1] IGI, Kent. [2] C. W. Martin, *Hist. and Description of Leeds Castle*, 174; Add. 5520, ff. 13–16; 4236, f. 12; *DNB* (Colepeper, Thomas); *Dering Pprs.* ed. Bond, 113; PCC 242 Nabbs; Stowe 745, f. 60; *Arch. Cant.* v. 40; Luttrell, *Brief Relation*, iv.144; *Post Man*, 26–28 Nov. 1696; J. R. Twisden, *Fam. of Twysden*, 296–7. [3] Info. from Prof. N. Landau; *CSP Dom.* 1679–80, p. 286; 1685, p. 165; 1687–9, pp. 141, 228; 1693, p. 212; 1694–5, p. 19; 1700–2, p. 250; Duckett, *Penal Laws and Test Act* (1882), 348, 354, 360; Add. 61458, f. 160; L. K. J. Glassey, *Appt. JPs*, 176; *Party and Management* ed. C. Jones, 80. [4] Boyer, *Pol. State*, xxv. 570; PCC 94 Richmond.

S. N. H.

COLLETON, Sir Peter, 2nd Bt. (1635–94), of Exmouth, Devon and Golden Square, Westminster.

BOSSINEY   1681 (Mar.), 1689–24 Mar. 1694

bap. 17 Sept. 1635, 1st s. of Sir John Colleton, 1st Bt., of Exeter, Devon and London by Catherine, da. of William Amy of Exeter. *m.* c.1669, Elizabeth, sis. of John Leslie of Barbados, wid. of William Johnston, 1s. 3da.; 1s. illegit. *suc.* fa. as 2nd Bt. c.Mar. 1667.[1]

Member of council, Barbados 1664–84, pres. of council 1672–?77, dep. gov. 1673; ld. proprietor, Carolina 1666–*d.*, high steward 1669, chancellor 1670–*d.*; ld. proprietor, Bahamas 1670–*d.*[2]

Member, R. Adventurers to Africa 1667–72, Hudson's Bay Co. 1670–*d.*; asst. R. African Co. 1677–9, 1683–5, 1688–90.[3]

FRS 1677.

Freeman, Exeter 1678.[4]

Commr. public accts. 1691–*d.*[5]

Owner of extensive plantations in Barbados and a former associate of the 1st Earl of Shaftesbury (Sir Anthony Ashley Cooper†) in the proprietorship of Carolina, Colleton was one of the most important representatives in the Commons of transatlantic trading interests, and a staunch adherent of Country Whiggism. Re-elected in 1690 for Bossiney, a borough in which he enjoyed an interest through his mother's family, he was listed as a Whig by Lord Carmarthen (Sir Thomas Osborne†). In the first session of this Parliament he was named to two drafting committees: to settle the East India trade (2 Apr.), and to prevent the export of coin (8 May). When Parliament resumed in the autumn, he reported on 26 Nov. 1690 from the inquiry into the African trade, and was then named to the drafting committee of the resultant bill to settle the trade, which he presented on 5 Dec. On 26 Dec., he was elected a commissioner of accounts, in sixth place, and went on to be one of the most active members of the commission, keeping a detailed record of its proceedings. Not surprisingly, Robert Harley* classed him as a Country supporter. He appears to have been absent from the commission between 24 July and 26 Aug. 1691, but was very regular in his attendance in September and October.[6]

Colleton was very active in the 1691–2 session. He was quickly to the fore when Parliament reassembled, and on 31 Oct. 1691 was appointed to two drafting committees, and to another such committee on 3 Nov. A further four drafting committees followed before the end of the session, including one of more personal interest on 2 Feb. 1692, to prepare a bill which would allow English ships voyaging to the West Indies to be crewed by foreign seamen, which he duly presented on the 5th. Colleton was also prominent in Country party manoeuvres over estimates and supply. He seconded Sir Thomas Clarges' motion on 6 Nov. 1691 requesting army estimates, and on the 9th supported moves to take into custody the author and printer of a libel reflecting on the proceedings of the House. On 30 Nov. he sought to include a clause exempting Quakers from the requirements of the bill to appoint new oaths in Ireland, and the same day seconded another proposal from Clarges, to refer the army estimates to a select committee. On 3 Dec. he was one of four public accounts commissioners who informed the House of the ill management of accounts. Then on 1 Jan. 1692 he supported the estimate that £17,000 might be raised from the Irish hearth tax, and later was one of those who moved successfully for the establishment of a committee to receive proposals for the raising of money on forfeited estates in Ireland, to which he was duly nominated. In the debates on 8 and 23 Jan. 1692 he opposed the bill to lessen the rate of interest. Following the adjournment of the House in February Colleton appears to taken a cure for his health at Epsom. On 22 Mar. he wrote to Harley: 'since I came hither I have found some amendment but so little that I am still dubious whether I shall get the better of my distemper or it of me.'[7]

In September 1692 Colleton was in London, and again attending the commission of accounts regularly. In this session he undertook significantly fewer legislative initiatives, but he continued to speak regularly in debates. At the beginning of the parliamentary session, on 10 Nov. 1692, he seconded Clarges' motion to go into committee of the whole on the state of the nation, rather than supply. The next day in committee of the whole he proposed that Admiral Edward Russell* attend the House to face questions about the fleet's actions that summer, but later in the debate seconded a motion from Hon. Goodwin Wharton that Russell be thanked for his conduct. On 12 Nov. he moved that the Admiralty's account of the summer's expedition be read, and later in the debate supported those who wished to know who was in charge of the descent. On the 15th, in order to solve a procedural wrangle, he suggested reading the orders of the day to determine the order of business. Following the presentation of a book of accounts, he then suggested that the House consider alliances before going on to the King's Speech. On 23 Nov., in the committee of the whole on the advice to be given to the King, he launched a bitter attack on the behaviour of foreign officers in the battle of Steenkerk, concluding,

> I think it is not consistent with the interest of this kingdom for to have foreign officers over an English army when we have so many brave, courageous men among us . . . I think it is a head worthy of your advice that our English armies may be commanded by natives of our own.

On the following day, in a debate in the committee of the whole considering the heads of a bill to regulate the East India trade, he declared himself to be 'against the old and against the new company, and a joint stock as pernicious to trade, but was for a regulated company, being most for the interest of the nation'. He supported Harley's proposal of 3 Dec. that the Commons vote the 20,000 men suggested for domestic defence, before going on to consider the total number of men suggested for the service. On 10 Dec., together with Goodwin Wharton, he opposed the resolution which favoured George Balch* at Bridgwater. On the 15th he supported Paul Foley I's proposal in the committee of supply for raising £70,000 p.a. That this was his last speech recorded in the session suggests that ill-health henceforth limited his activities.[8]

Colleton was clearly not a well man a year later, for on 23 Dec. 1693 Narcissus Luttrell* reported his death the previous day. However, on the 27th Colleton wrote to Harley about ordering some wine from Alicante. On 2 Jan. 1694 Colleton was reported to be 'dangerously ill of an asthma'. Although probably absent from the Commons he kept a close watch on proceedings. At some point following the presentation of a petition on 24 Jan. 1694 from the Royal African Company for a bill establishing the trade by a joint-stock company, he wrote to Harley, the chairman of the select committee inquiring into the petition. Specifically, he was worried that 'if the committee have voted to settle that trade in a joint-stock exclusive to others and there be not sufficient care taken to supply the English plantations with negroes at moderate rates in a little time there will be an end of your plantation trade'. Colleton died on 24 Mar. 1694.[9]

[1] PCC 72 Box; *CSP Dom.* 1666-7, p. 575. [2] *CSP Col.* 1661-8, p. 195; 1669-74, pp. 43-44, 52, 122, 478, 481; 1681-5, p. 938; V. Harlow, *Barbados*, 212; K. H. D. Haley, *Shaftesbury*, 233, 242. [3] K. G. Davies, *R. African Co.* 379; P. C. Newman, *Co. of Adventurers*, i. 320; B. Willson, *Gt. Co.* i. 47. [4] *Exeter Freemen* (Devon and Cornwall Rec. Soc. extra ser. i), 169. [5] *EHR*, xci. 36. [6] *Caribbeana*, iii. 299; PCC 91 Carr; *EHR*, 33, 39; Harl. 6837. [7] *Luttrell Diary*, 4, 8, 50, 52, 60, 102-3, 117, 150; Add. 70218, Colleton to Harley, 22 Mar. 1691[-2]. [8] Add. 70218, Colleton to Harley, 17 Sept. 1692; Harl. 6837; *Luttrell Diary*, 217-20, 224, 228, 252, 258, 290, 308, 322; Grey, x. 253. [9] Luttrell, *Brief Relation*, iii. 244; Add. 70218, Colleton to Harley, 27 Dec. 1693; 70307, same to same, n.d. [Jan.-Mar. 1694]; Nat. Archs. Ire. Wyche mss 1/99, William Ball to Sir Cyril Wyche*, 2 Jan. 1694.

E. C./S. N. H.

COLLIER, William (c.1687–1758), of Hatton Garden, London.[1]

TRURO 1713–1715

b. c.1687, 1st s. of William Collier of Bristol, Glos. *educ.* M. Temple 1708. *m. suc.* fa. bef. 1708.

?Gent. of privy chamber 1702–14; solicitor to Treasury and surveyor of coasts Sept. 1710–14.[2]

Collier's origins are obscure. Nothing is known of him until his admission to the Middle Temple in 1708, when he was described as the son of William of Bristol. Collier was later described by Abel Boyer as 'a petty-fogging attorney . . . hardly worth £30 a year', but Colley Cibber's assessment of Collier was more favourable, describing him as 'a lawyer of an enterprising head and a jovial heart'. Given his obscure origins and apparently modest background it is questionable, though not impossible, that the future Member was the William Collier who served as a gentleman of the privy chamber throughout Queen Anne's reign. In November 1709 Collier, a lesser shareholder of the Drury Lane theatre, took advantage of a conflict between the lord chamberlain and the holders of Drury Lane's patent in order to obtain a licence for a new company to act at the theatre. During this company's first season, however, the trial of Dr Sacheverell attracted larger audiences 'of the better sort' than did his plays. That Collier's role in the cultural life of London led to friendships with leading Tories is suggested by a letter of 1709 from George Granville* to Robert Harley*, in which Granville wrote that 'I can't say Collier is entirely in the land of the living, for it is his hour of being very drunk, but as much of him as live is entirely devoted to you'. In the 1710s Boyer claimed that Collier also formed a friendship with Henry St. John II*, describing Collier as 'an obsequious companion' in St. John's 'nocturnal debauches'. Boyer asserted that this relationship led St. John to 'advance him to a brighter station', presumably a reference to Collier's appointment in September 1710 as solicitor to the treasury and 'surveyor of the coasts to prevent owling [i.e. smuggling]'. In the following two years Collier, according to Cibber, used his ministerial connexions to secure a settlement of disputes which had arisen concerning Drury Lane, an agreement which secured for Collier revenues of £700 p.a.[3]

According to Boyer, Collier was returned unopposed for Truro in 1713 thanks to Bolingbroke's (St. John) prompting of the Duke of Beaufort, but more probably it was on the recommendation of his own friend Granville, now Lord Lansdown. Shortly before his election Collier had written to Oxford (Harley) to inform him of his 'zeal and welfare for your person and welfare', and in a further letter to the lord treasurer Collier put his name forward for the place of surveyor-general of the crown lands, now vacant because of the death of John Manley*. Collier assured Oxford that, should such an appointment be made, the consequent by-election would see either his own return or that of 'a more worthy man'. However, Oxford chose to overlook him. On 12 Apr. 1714 Collier told against receiving a petition from an Irish peer requesting the repeal of an act passed by the Irish parliament. On 14 May he was appointed to prepare a bill to enable the development of the harbour at Whitesand Bay, near Land's End, Cornwall. Later that month he clearly demonstrated his Toryism, telling on the 25th in favour of hearing at the bar the petition of the Bolingbroke-sponsored candidate defeated at the Harwich by-election. Two days later he told against agreeing with an amendment to the schism bill, from the committee of the whole, which would have removed from the bill those Dissenters who taught only writing. Collier's support for this measure was made clear during the debate of 1 June upon the third reading of the bill. Boyer reported that Collier

took this solemn occasion to signalize his zeal for the cause he was to serve. With this intention . . . in order to expose the Dissenters, he desired leave to read to the House a collection of absurdities and impious expressions, which he pretended to have taken from their writings. After reading part of this impertinent legend, he fell on a passage extracted from the nonsensical rhapsodies of the late Mr Hickeringhill, minister at Colchester wherein Mr Collier said, he averred 'that our blessed Saviour was the son of a w[hore]'. At these shocking expressions, Mr

Bromley [William II] interrupted him, saying 'such impious words ought not to be repeated in that assembly'. On the other hand, some other Members observed that Mr Hickeringhill was not a Dissenting teacher, but a minister of the Church of England, and that he was known to be crack-brained, and therefore his extravagances and blasphemies proved nothing against any set of men, much less against Dissenters.

On 22 June Collier told for agreeing with the resolution from ways and means to levy a duty on all imported buckrams, save those that came from Ireland, and three days later he told against a Whig attempt to adjourn consideration of the Southwark election case. The Worsley list duly classed Collier as a Tory. The Hanoverian succession brought an end to ministerial favour as far as Collier was concerned, and in addition to being removed from his offices his Drury Lane patent was assigned to Richard Steele*. Little is known of his later life. He may have been the Mr Collier who was solicitor to Viscount Perceval (John†) in the 1730s. Collier died at Bath on 24 May 1758, aged 70, leaving £100 to the Foundling Hospital.[4]

[1] *Coke Pprs.* 216. [2] R. O. Bucholz, *Augustan Court*, 262; Cobbett, *Parlty. Hist.* vi. 1350; Luttrell, *Brief Relation*, vi. 630. [3] G. Holmes, *Pol. in Age of Anne*, 182, 270; Boyer, *Anne Hist.*, 702–3; *Apology for Life of Colley Cibber* (1740), 249–53; info. from Dr P. A. Hopkins; *HMC Portland*, iv. 527. [4] Boyer, 702–3; Wilts. RO, Suffolk and Berkshire mss 88/10/93, [Thomas Hare*] to Berkshire, 12 Sept. 1713 (*ex inf.* Dr C. Jones); Add. 70218, Collier to Oxford, 1 June, 21 Dec. 1713; *Bull. IHR*, xxiv. 215; Cobbett, 1350; R. H. Barker, *Mr Cibber of Drury Lane*, 100; info. from Dr Hopkins; *HMC Egmont Diary*, i. 142, 198, 200; *Gent. Mag.* 1758, p. 292.

E. C./R. D. H.

COLSTON, Edward I (aft. 1672–1719), of Bristol.

WELLS 1708–1713

b. aft.1672, 4th but o. surv. s. of Robert Colston of Bristol, by Ann, da. of Robert Waters of Bristol. *m.* lic. 4 Aug. 1704, Mary De Bert (*d.* 1733), 1da.[1]

Gov. city of London workhouse by 1708.[2]

Hon. freeman, Merchant Venturers' Soc., Bristol 1708.[3]

Colston was the oldest surviving nephew of the wealthy Bristol philanthropist Edward Colston II*. His uncle, having never married, regarded him as his heir, and settled a considerable fortune in land on him when he married in 1704. Colston himself appears to have pursued a business career of sorts in London, probably under the aegis of his uncle. In the general election of 1705 he was put up by the Tories for Bristol as part of a strategy to break the hold on the city's representation which the Whigs had maintained since 1695. For this important task, it is highly unlikely that the Tories would have ignored Colston's prominent High Tory uncle who, though demurring, probably on grounds of age, was able to nominate his nephew. Despite the 'mighty stir' created on Colston's behalf, however, the Whigs retained both seats.[4]

In 1708, Colston was elected unopposed for Wells. He had a connexion with the city in so far as his uncle's Somerset lands included the nearby manor of Lydford West. More important was the Colston name which no doubt held considerable attraction to Wells's Tory corporation. He was duly classed as a Tory in an analysis of the new Parliament, but was an inactive Member. During the 1709–10 session he voted against the impeachment of Dr Sacheverell, and was again listed as a Tory after the 1710 election. In 1711 he figured among the 'Tory patriots' who supported peace, and among the 'worthy patriots' who detected the mismanagements of the previous administration, while on 18 June 1713 he voted for the French commerce bill. Upon the dissolution of Parliament he stood down. He died on 5 Apr. 1719, predeceasing his uncle, and was buried in the Colston vault at All Saints church, Bristol. Administration of his estates was granted in June of that year. In May 1720 Colston snr. named Colston's only child, Sarah, as his chief legatee, but in consequence of her death early in 1721 the bulk of his fortune passed to his niece, the wife of Thomas Edwards*.[5]

[1] Phelps, *Som.* i. 470; *Vis. Som.* (Harl. Soc. n.s. xi), 188; *Mar. Lic. Fac. Off.* (Brit. Rec. Soc. xxxiii), 207; *Bristol Mar. Lic. Bonds* (Bristol and Glos. Arch. Soc. Publns. i), 64; W. Barrett, *Hist. Bristol*, 443. [2] E. Hatton, *A New View of London* (1708), 755. [3] *Pols. and Port of Bristol 18th Cent.* (Bristol Rec. Soc. xxiii), 191. [4] H. J. Wilkins, *Edward Colston*, 128; H. J. Wilkins, *Edward Colston: Supplement*, 16; Bodl. Rawl. D.863, f. 90; J. Latimer, *Annals of Bristol 18th Cent.* 66; Collinson, *Hist. Som.* ii. 84. [5] Barrett, 443; Wilkins, *Colston*, 128–35.

A. A. H.

COLSTON, Edward II (1636–1721), of Mortlake, Surr.[1]

BRISTOL 1710–1713

b. 2 Nov. 1636, 1st s. of William Colston, merchant, of Bristol, sheriff of Bristol 1643, by Sarah, da. of Edward Batten of the Inner Temple. *educ.* ?Christ's Hosp. *unm. suc.* fa. 1681.

Appr. Mercers' Co. 1654–62, freeman 1673; freeman, Bristol 1683; freeman, Merchant Venturers' Soc., Bristol 1683; hon. guardian, Bristol corporation of the poor 1696.

Member, R. African Co. 1680, asst. 1681–3, 1696–8,

1691, dep. gov. 1689–90; commr. taking subscriptions to S. Sea Co. 1711.[2].
Gov. Christ's Hosp. 1681–?*d*.
Member, SPG 1704.

Colston is celebrated in his native city as a philanthropist *par excellence*. In his day he was revered by Bristol's corporation as 'the highest example of Christian liberality that this age has produced, both for the extensiveness of his charities and the prudent regulation of them'. Stories about Colston's life and good deeds abound, many of them seemingly apocryphal, but beneath the eulogy was an austere man of unbending High Church principles whose charitable ventures were initiated and pursued with the same tough, businesslike vigour with which he made his fortune. Though Bristol became the primary focus for his attention in later years, he never made his home in or near the city, and was disdainful of the factious local politics in which his charitable activities inevitably involved him. None the less, it gratified him to devote the power of his wealth to the larger interests of Church and state, and his influence in Bristol was strongly felt.[3]

The Colston family had flourished in Bristol since the late 13th century. Several of Colston's more immediate forebears had been prosperous merchants with a firm footing in the city's civic life. His father, a pillar of the Merchant Venturers' Society, had been a staunch Royalist who was installed as a councillor and sheriff in 1643, when the city was taken by Prince Rupert, but deprived of his local offices by Parliament in 1645. Much uncertainty surrounds Colston's early years and his rise to fortune, although the outlines of his career are available from official and mercantile records. The family's insecure position during the Interregnum would account for his being educated in London, possibly as a private pupil at Christ's Hospital (of which he was later a governor), and then in 1654 apprenticed in the Mercers' Company. After the Restoration his father resumed civic office in Bristol while Colston himself, having finished his apprenticeship, seems to have spent some time abroad, possibly looking after his father's interests in Spain, although there is no evidence to support claims that he amassed a vast fortune there.[4]

By 1672 Colston had resettled in England and established himself in London as a merchant. From 1680 he became heavily involved in the slave trade, from which he made the bulk of his fortune, and was an active member of the Royal African Company, becoming deputy-governor briefly during 1689–90. At the time of his admission to the Merchant Venturers' Society in 1683 he was also described as a West Indian merchant. The 1680s were undoubtedly his most lucrative years in business, and according to one account he was said to have owned over 40 ships. For a few years after the death of his brother Thomas in 1684, he ran his father's mercantile business in Bristol, though continuing to reside in London. By 1682 he was using profits from the slave trade for money-lending. In addition to a loan of £500 to the government, he loaned £2,000 to Bristol corporation, the repayment of which he demanded in 1687, apparently when the corporation offended his High Church principles by accepting James II's Declaration of Indulgence. It may have been for the same reason that he severed his trading connexion with Bristol at about this time and sold off his ships. He welcomed the Revolution of 1688 and quickly established his position with the new administration, first by advancing several loans to the new government, and second by selling King William £1,000 worth of stock in the Royal African Company. In 1689 he purchased a modest residence at Mortlake in Surrey, evidently with the intention of separating himself from the hubbub of commercial life in London, while the end of his association with the African Company in 1692 indicates that he was by then no longer engaged in the the slave trade.[5]

During the 1690s and 1700s he funded a series of major projects in Bristol to augment several of the city's schools and almshouses, complementing these with a regular flow of gifts for the repair and adornment of its parish churches. His neighbourhood in Surrey and several London charities also benefited from his munificence. He made no secret of his hatred of Dissent, and his charitable settlements were laced with clauses requiring Anglican devotion and practice. In establishing the rules for one foundation he desired pupils 'to be staunch sons of the Church, provided such books are procured for them as have no tincture of Whiggism'. In time, Colston's overpowering High Church philanthropy irritated the Whiggish corporation of Bristol, so much so that in 1705, when he proposed an arrangement with the corporation to enlarge Queen Elizabeth's Hospital, the main boys' orphan school, they declined. He obtained backing for a new school from the more Tory-oriented Merchant Venturers' Society, explaining that he had been 'hardly censured . . . even by some of the magistrates'. However, Colston was equally concerned that a rigid Anglican message 'which combined a catechetical purpose with a call to penitence' be propagated among a wider parochial audience, and from 1708 he funded a yearly series of 'Lent sermons' preached in turn by members of the city's clergy. The force of his pious temperament and devotion to the Church of

England emerges strongly from a grand jury speech he delivered in May 1710:

> My intentions of doing what I have done there [Bristol] were only for the public good; and chiefly, by the Lent sermons, to revive the primitive zeal for the Church government as by law established; and since I understand, to my unspeakable comfort, that it hath the success I aimed at, I bless God for inclining my heart thereto, and shall pray to him to increase daily, more and more, the spirit of piety (that at present seems to be among you) and zeal for the best of churches, I mean that of England, as now established by law, whose holy doctrines, if we follow, will teach us obedience to our governors, as well civil as ecclesiastical, and to support the rights of both, to which that God will incline us all.

Colston's devoted local representative since the 1680s was his Bristol lawyer, Thomas Edwards. Their connexion became a family one when, in the early 1700s, Edwards' son (Thomas*) married Colston's niece and eventual heiress.[6]

By virtue of his good works and reputation in the city, Colston had become an obvious Tory choice of candidate in the election of 1710. July of that year had seen the opening amid great festivity of 'Colston's Hospital', the most costly of his gifts and foundations, involving an outlay of £30,000, which provided for the education and maintenance of 100 boys. He had in fact refused to stand for election on grounds of age, being by then aged 74, but was put up *in absentia* by 'some persons who were well-affected' and who demanded a poll on his behalf. After achieving first place he arrived in Bristol a few days afterwards to attend a dinner on 2 Nov. in celebration of both his triumph and his birthday. The Tory brethren present subsequently constituted themselves into the 'Loyal Society' whose annual dinners were held in Colston's honour each 2 Nov. until the death of Queen Anne. Despite his success, however, Colston had been mortified not to have had the support of his chief associate in several recent charitable projects, Rev. Arthur Bedford, vicar of Temple church whose latitudinarian views were well known, and he publicly denounced Bedford as 'no son of the Church, but rather inclined to, and a favourer of fanaticism'. Colston was classified as a Tory in the 'Hanover list', and was included among the 'worthy patriots' who in the 1710–11 session detected the mismanagements of the previous administration. Age and infirmity seem to have prevented him from taking much part in Commons proceedings other than occasionally to present petitions on behalf of his constituency. He did not stand for re-election in 1713 and in November was too frail to attend the Loyal Society dinner, being represented instead by the Duke of Beaufort. Towards the end of 1714, a Whig pamphlet condemning the recent 'Jacobite' riots in Bristol sought to undermine both his political integrity and his morals:

> The Tories could never have carried any point here [Bristol] but by the interest of a very great Tory and till lately, a nonjuror, Mr C[olston], who has shown how far he prefers good works to purity of life, by laying out some thousands of pounds in building hospitals here, while himself lived very much at his ease with a Tory, though of a different sex, at M[ortla]ke. The appearance of such good deeds acquired him so general a name here, that the people forgot he was a Jacobite and everyone agreed that Mr C[olston] was the best man to represent them and his countenancing the Jacobite interest, made the faction rampant in a place to which he had been so great a benefactor.

Though Colston had been listed in 1691 as one of several prominent 'Citizens' (i.e. of London) then 'inclined' towards King James, his Jacobite leanings appear to have been a thing of his distant past. He was never under government suspicion and remained on the Somerset commission of the peace after the accession of George I. The mystery lady in his life was probably none other than his housekeeper.[7]

Colston died at Mortlake on 11 Oct. 1721 and was buried after a grand funeral at All Saints church in Bristol. It was characteristic that his principal charitable bequest should be a large gift of £6,000 to augment Queen Anne's Bounty, with many of the 'poor cures' which were to benefit being nominated by either himself or his acquaintances. His will also contained provision for small yearly payments to 18 charity schools. His main intended legatee had been the only daughter of his recently deceased nephew Edward Colston I*, but since she had died in January 1721, his niece Mary Edwards became the chief beneficiary.

[1] Unless otherwise stated this biography is based on H. J. Wilkins, *Edward Colston*. [2] Pittis, *Hist. Present Parl.* 349; K. G. Davies, *R. African Co.* 379. [3] S. G. Tovey, *Colston the Philanthropist* (1863), 143, 145. [4] *Glos. N. & Q.* ii. 365–6; J. Latimer, *Annals of Bristol in 17th Cent.* 185, 207. [5] Wilkins, *Edward Colston: Supplement*, 9. [6] W. Barrett, *Hist. Brist.* 443; Tovey, 85, 96; *Reformation and Revival in 18th Cent. Bristol* (Bristol Rec. Soc. xlv), 11–13. [7] J. Latimer, *Annals of Bristol in 18th Cent.* 84–86; Wilkins, *Supplement*, 21; Westminster Diocesan archs., Old Brotherhood mss iii/3/232, memorandum by Capt. Lloyd, 23 Mar. 1691; L. K. J. Glassey, *Appt. JPs*, 250.

A.A.H.

COLT, Sir Henry Dutton, 1st Bt. (c.1646–1731), of St. James's, Westminster.

NEWPORT (I.o.W.)   2 Dec. 1695–1698
WESTMINSTER   1701 (Dec.)–1702, 1705–1708

b. c.1646, 4th s. of George Colt of Colt Hall, Cavendish, Suff. by Elizabeth, da. and coh. of John Dutton† of Sherborne, Glos.; bro. of John Dutton Colt*. *m*. lic. 26 May 1704, Cecilia (*d*. 1712), da. of Francis Brewster of Wrentham, Suff., wid. of William Nuthall of Kingston-upon-Thames, Surr. and Sir Robert Hatton of Thames Ditton, Surr., *s.p. cr*. Bt. 2 Mar. 1694.[1]

Cornet, Barbados drag. 1672–4; corp. yeomen of the gd. 1673–?86, ensign 1685–6; adj. of drag. Prince Rupert's regt. 1678; ensign, R. Regt. Drag. 1678, capt. 1679.[2]

Colt's military career was not markedly successful. By the time he reached 40 he had not progressed beyond the rank of captain, and his financial circumstances, as an officer on the Irish establishment, were then described as 'very sad', possibly a consequence of the fondness for gaming which was certainly to characterize his later years. Nevertheless, in 1687 he was able to stand bail for his brother John in the sum of £2,000. Although he lost his place in the yeomen of the guard by 1686, and perhaps too his dragoon troop, he avoided the more serious dangers to which his family's opposition to King James's policies rendered them subject. He did spend some time in custody in November 1688 but was released when Lord Middleton (Charles†) expressed a belief in his innocence. Unlike his brothers, who received offices or promotion at the Revolution, he obtained no tangible rewards for his apparent fidelity to the Protestant cause. A warrant for the grant of a baronetcy was ordered in June 1690 but the honour was not actually conferred for four years. By then Colt had established an unenviable reputation, not only as a gambler and a 'cheat' who would be 'worth nothing if his debts were paid', but as an ageing rakehell: he had already been fined for one duel, and was subsequently lampooned as a 'satyr', with the hint of a scandal between himself and his own niece.[3]

Colt was returned to Parliament for Newport, Isle of Wight, at a by-election in December 1695, to fill a place left vacant by the island's governor, Lord Cutts (John*), and presumably at Cutts's recommendation. He was soon active in the House, managing a bill through the House in February–March 1696 for facilitating the recovery of servants' wages. The measure had arisen from a celebrated case involving Colt in his capacity as a Middlesex justice: he had signed an order for the arrest of one Feilding, a Catholic and returned Jacobite exile, at the request of a servant of Feilding who had not been paid his wages, whereupon Feilding, enraged at this affront, had attacked him and inflicted a serious wound. During his first session Colt reported on 3 Apr. from a committee investigating a petition over arrears of pay to troops on the Irish establishment, the first of many such committees to which he, as a former soldier and the brother of a serving officer, was to be nominated. He was twice a teller: on 12 Mar., against adding to the bill for the suppression of hawkers and pedlars a clause to provide against street-traders selling 'fresh provisions' in London and Westminster, a clause which had been requested by the Poulterers' Company; and second, on 17 Apr., against receiving the report of the committee on the bill to regulate abuses in the garbling of spices. Meanwhile he was demonstrating his loyalty to the Whig administration: he was listed as likely to support the Court in a forecast for the division on the proposed council of trade on 31 Jan. 1696, signed the Association promptly and voted in favour of fixing the price of guineas at 22*s*.[4]

The volume of parliamentary business undertaken by Colt increased rapidly during the following session, and it would not be unfair to assume that this hyperactivity reflected a determination to attract the attention of ministers, even though many of his committees concerned matters that were beneath governmental responsibility. It would appear that Colt had also by this time embarked upon the second strategy that he would employ in order to try to make his mark, the exposure of Jacobite disaffection, which would enable him to revenge himself on his enemies and simultaneously prove his own loyalty and earn the gratitude of the King. When Lord Bellew, an Irish peer, found his petition for reversal of outlawry blocked as a result of a report that he had not yet taken the oaths, Colt was the person he blamed for informing against him. In the House Colt acted as a teller on 26 Oct. 1696, alongside a Court Whig, in favour of a motion to go into a committee of supply. He was active in forwarding the bill of attainder against Sir John Fenwick†. A teller twice on 16 Nov. in proceedings on the bill, in favour of reading the record of the trial of Peter Cook and the written statements made in custody by the absconded conspirator Goodman, he intervened in the debate to refute Tory arguments against the further examination of witnesses to Goodman's testimony. Needless to say, he voted for the bill at its third reading on 25 Nov., having told against a motion to clear the Speaker's chamber and lock the door of the House before this vote was taken. Of his many tellerships in this session, a number were in divisions on matters concerning the supply and recoinage: on 31 Dec. against adjourning the committee on the bill to encourage the bringing in of plate; on 9 Jan. 1697 in favour of a resolution of ways and means to lay a duty on all plate not brought in; on 21 Jan. for a clause to be added to the land tax bill, to exempt Queen Catherine of Braganza's annuity; on 17 Feb. in favour of a tax on leather; on 30 Mar. and 3 Apr. in favour of committing, then engrossing, the wine duties bill; and on 7 Apr. for agreeing with a resolution of ways and means for an additional tax on land. One of his tellerships on the land tax bill seems at first glance to reflect Country rather than Court sympathies: on 26 Jan. 1697, for an additional clause to prevent excise officers being named as commissioners under the Act. But almost immediately afterwards he served as a teller on the Court side that the bill pass. Three tellerships concerned elections: on 21 Dec. 1696 against (Sir) Arthur Kaye* (3rd Bt.) in the Aldborough election; on 4 Feb. 1697 on the Tavistock case; and on 21 Nov. 1696 on a more general question, albeit arising from a petition from a particular borough, that of Exeter against the land qualifications for Members proposed in the current elections bill, which the petitioners claimed would exclude many 'prudent' and wealthy citizens, a protest Colt endorsed. In each of these cases Colt was demonstrating his loyalty to fellow Whigs, as he also did on 28 Nov. 1696, when he told in favour of upholding a complaint of breach of privilege against (Sir) Isaac Rebow*. His opposition to the bill to restrain the wearing of East Indian cloth, against which he told on 1 Feb. 1697, extended as far as acting as a teller again on 20 Mar. for naming Sir Samuel Barnardiston, 1st Bt., as the Member guilty of speaking against the bill at a conference between the two Houses. It may have reflected a more general dislike of measures restricting freedom of trade. The two public bills that he himself managed through the House during this session, for paving and otherwise regulating the streets near the Haymarket, and a similar measure to explain the Act of 1689 for paving and cleaning the streets within the bills of mortality, exemplified his concern for local interests, but not those of his constituency so much as of his place of residence. He also managed a private bill in March. His one remaining tellership, on 22 Feb., was in support of a general naturalization bill, a subject which was subsequently to interest him greatly.[5]

During the summer and early autumn of 1697 Colt became heavily involved in an attempt to peddle information to the government about reputed Jacobite conspiracies. He was said to have been the 'conduit pipe' for the fantasies of a pair of informers, the experienced rogue William Chaloner and his youthful accomplice, Aubrey Price. Their original approach to Colt coincided with an unsuccessful petition by him to the King for some unspecified grant, a fact that probably explains his heightened zeal in pursuing the affair. He first broached the subject to the lords justices in June 1697, bringing forward a proposal from Chaloner to obtain intelligence of Jacobite plots from Price, who had succeeded, as he put it, in infiltrating the cabals of the disaffected. As a token, Colt exhibited a list of Northamptonshire Jacobites. The lords justices were unimpressed, and particularly dubious of the participation of 'Chaloner the clipper', as they remembered him, but ordered Colt to carry on. Over the next two months the business proceeded slowly, until late in August Colt brought things to a head by presenting plans for what purported to be a plot to seize Dover Castle. Again the lords justices were scornful, telling him it was 'all stuff', but they allowed him to proceed with the arrest of the so-called conspirators. They were especially annoyed at information implicating the Duke of Shrewsbury. Colt, taking his cue from his audience, admitted that this was a 'very impertinent' allegation. But he had earlier tried to make use of it to blackmail Shrewsbury, acquainting the Duke with the details before the Council meeting and offering to suppress them, a proposal Shrewsbury wisely declined. James Vernon I* even suspected Colt of helping to invent the tale himself. After the arrest of Price, Chaloner and one or two unfortunates that they had incriminated, the 'plot' was revealed to be a 'foolish' invention, and Colt, temporarily abashed, acknowledged that he had been 'ill used and imposed upon'. Within days, however, he was bringing forward other informers, and was even publicizing the claims of Price and Chaloner that they had been imprisoned in order to cover up treachery in high places. 'I think we are never to have done with Sir Harry Colt', observed a weary Vernon in September 1697, and indeed in the ensuing session of Parliament the affair was raised again, by Colt and his associate John Arnold*. Chaloner petitioned the House in March 1698 to complain of his imprisonment, and his petition was referred to a committee. Colt 'busied himself for Chaloner' and was regarded by Vernon as the moving spirit behind the entire exercise. At one point, in a debate on 15 Mar., he

> came out with an expression that some things were material to Chaloner's defence which he had advised him to waive for reasons he should acquaint the committee with, intimating as if it were in relation to some services Chaloner had done, without naming what they were.

This deliberately mystifying manner of speech, for which Colt was 'taken up' by the House, was calculated to prolong the agony for ministers, and possibly to encourage them to give Colt a reward of some kind, but presumably because the actual weakness of his hand was well known, no plums were forthcoming.[6]

Besides following up Chaloner's case, Colt was in general highly active in the Commons in 1697–8, with the exception of ten days in April during which he enjoyed leave of absence. Throughout the session he was prominent in helping to forward Court business. He was a teller on 11 Dec. 1697 for recommitting the report on the King's Speech after the reading of a resolution to disband all the land forces raised since 1680; and on 8 Jan. 1698, when the issue of the standing army was raised again, he was a teller for a Court-inspired amendment to the instruction to the committee of supply about guards and garrisons, which would have omitted any reference back to the earlier resolution for disbandment. He also acted as a teller on 20 Jan. in support of a ministerial riposte to the nascent Country campaign over land grants, a motion to lay before the House an account of all crown grants since the Restoration; on 14 Feb., to prevent the adjournment of the bill of pains and penalties against Charles Duncombe*, a measure instigated by Charles Montagu*, and again on 26 Feb., that the bill should pass; and on 22 Feb., against an opposition motion of censure, arising from the disclosure of the Exchequer bill scandal, directed against the receipt of Exchequer bills in payment of excise. Several other tellerships arose from supply measures: against giving leave for a bill to explain the law relating to the drawback on rock-salt (29 Jan.); against a clause in the tunnage and poundage bill to save the debt due to the bankers (9 June 1698); against leave for a clause to be inserted into the bill to impose the salt duties and incorporate the New East India Company, to enable the tellers of the Exchequer to accept Bank bills in payment of the duties (18 June); and for engrossing the latter bill (23 June). In a related case on 3 May he reported from the committee examining a petition from the glovers' company of Chester against the effects of the Leather Duty Act. Much of his activity in this session followed up subjects which had engaged his attention before. On 7 Jan. he reported on a bill to regulate the marriages of minors, and was a teller (on 3 May) for the reintroduced bill to facilitate the recovery of servants' wages. Naturalization bills were a particular interest: he managed four separate bills through the House, including a measure to naturalize foreign-born offspring of serving soldiers. Questions of army pay and arrears engaged him similarly: he reported on petitions concerning regimental agents and unpaid arrears, and another which dealt with the general problems of disbandment. As for questions of trade, he was a teller against a further bill to restrain imports of East Indian stuffs (24 Jan.), and showed once again his dislike of restrictive legislation and privileged commercial interests in two tellerships: on 23 Feb., against committing the bill for the encouragement of trade to Russia, and on 1 June, against a clause to be added to the bill to encourage the Lustring Company, to exempt the looms of alamode and lustring weavers from distraint in civil cases. At the same time he was ordered on 4 June to bring in a bill for the relief of some Virginia merchants, one of whose ships had been unavoidably detained in America and was now prevented from returning to England by the stipulations of the recent Act regulating the Plantations trade. A teller on 9 Mar. for the bill to prevent abuses in weights and measures, he took a similarly constructive approach to economic and social problems with his bill, presented on 20 Apr., for draining part of the Lindsey level, and his support for the bill for the relief of insolvent debtors, on behalf of which he acted as a teller on 17 May. Another bill he presented, 'to prevent mischiefs by squibs and other fireworks', should possibly be regarded in this light, as correcting a social evil. It is likely too that it represented a particular grievance to Colt's Westminster neighbours. His involvement in private bill legislation, covering some five bills, included drafting a bill on behalf of his connexion, Sir Ralph Dutton, 1st Bt.*, and chairing a committee on another, on behalf of Sir Edward Fitzharris, 2nd Bt., father of the executed Whig conspirator, Edward Fitzharris. Opposition to the bill for the suppression of blasphemy and profaneness, against which he stood as a teller three times (on 12, 24 and 30 Mar.), was perhaps only to be expected from someone of Colt's moral outlook and social habits, even though one of his closest parliamentary colleagues, John Arnold, was an ardent supporter of the movement for the reformation of manners. Colt did share some of the other preoccupations of such reforming Members, however; he was active in the field of electoral reform, for example. Having acted as a teller on 19 Apr. against a clause proposed to be added to the elections bill to modify the landed qualification proposed for some borough electorates, he presented the first bill for the prevention of false returns (21 May), and, after it had been lost by the clerks, served on the committee of inquiry into its disappearance (17 June) and then brought in a replacement bill (18 June). His determined anti-popery was another trait shared with Arnold and 'moral reformers'. Colt acted as a teller on 17 June in favour of the bill to vest in Greenwich Hospital and similar charities estates that had formerly been given away to 'superstitious uses'. In promoting inquiries into Catholic landed endowments he was also motivated by financial interests. By the summer of 1698, hunting out forfeited lands had become his main money-making enterprise. He petitioned in August for a grant of several properties in Kent brought to his notice by a professional informer, and then went into partnership with Lord Fairfax (Thomas*) in the revival of an old commission of inquisition, which within a year or two had 'discovered' more forfeited estates in Kent and Essex, to the value of over £5,000 p.a.[7]

The driving force behind Colt's actions at this point in his career was his need for money. He had supported the Whig ministry throughout the 1695 Parliament in order to earn reward, while putting pressure on individual ministers by raking over the embers of Jacobite conspiracies. As late as April 1698 he had begun 'searching at the Signet Office' through the registers of licences issued to returning exiles from France, in the hope of unearthing some scandal with which to embarrass James Vernon I. He took the matter before the King, who remarked to Vernon of 'the behaviour of men out of business towards those that are in it, which would, in great measure, be cured if they themselves were employed, and put into the same dangers they have raised against others'. When these efforts came to nothing, his gambler's instinct prompted him to challenge two leading Court Whigs, Vernon and Charles Montagu, in their campaign for re-election in the Westminster constituency. Colt came third in the poll in what was a very acrimonious contest, which continued in the Commons following his petition. Colt found few supporters in the House, while the full revenge of the ministers came shortly afterwards, when he was put out of the Middlesex commission of the peace. The pretext was that 'among other things' Colt had 'discouraged public houses from quartering of soldiers', possibly in retaliation for the participation of regular army officers in violence directed against his voters at the poll in Westminster. The real motive for his exclusion was, however, political. As Vernon wrote, 'I think it will be for the peace of mankind if we can get rid of such a disturber of it'.[8]

Over the next two or three years Colt worked his way back into the good graces of the Whig Junto, benefiting from their increasing suspicion of, and impatience with, Vernon, his perennial opponent at Westminster. In the first general election of 1701 Colt and Vernon were confronted by three Tory candidates but still did not join interests. Indeed, Colt seems at one point to have regarded Vernon as his principal adversary, though after his defeat he was rumoured to be contemplating a petition not against Vernon but against the successful Tory, Thomas Crosse*. In the following November Colt and Vernon were again the Whig representatives in a large panel of candidates, one of them the prominent High Tory Sir John Leveson Gower, 5th Bt.*, whose 'warm behaviour' in Parliament had 'made the Whigs in general great sticklers against him'. Leveson Gower's presence, and Vernon's surprising decision to join with Crosse rather than Colt, prompted the Junto lords to take up Colt's cause 'very warmly'. Soon after the dissolution Lords Somers (Sir John*), Orford (Edward Russell*) and Halifax (Charles Montagu*) declared for him, the latter evidently forgiving Colt's behaviour in 1698, and a mere matter of days before the election he was restored to the Middlesex bench. At the poll he comfortably took first place. A fourth member of the Junto, Lord Spencer (Charles*), marked his election as a 'gain'. Colt repaid his fellow Whigs for their electoral support by actively assisting in the prosecution of any partisan cause in the House. With regard to election cases, he acted as a teller on 5 Jan. 1702 to appoint a day for hearing the Norwich dispute; on 29 Jan. to put off a vote of censure on the Earl of Peterborough over his conduct in the Malmesbury election; and on 28 Mar. against convicting an alderman of Coventry of breach of privilege in an incident arising from the election. He was also a teller on the Whig side on 23 Jan. on a motion to adjourn all committees, and twice subsequently in divisions connected with the supply: on 4 May to add a rider concerning the transport service to the bill for making good the deficiencies in public funds; and on 13 May against an amendment to the salt duties bill. He also presented two bills. One was a further attempt to facilitate the 'discovery' of lands granted to 'superstitious uses' and to apply them to the support of Greenwich Hospital (3 Mar.); the other was for the relief of insolvent debtors (2 Feb.). His many other activities included managing two multiple naturalization bills, which were still a prime concern of his in spite of the personal opposition he had endured from Huguenot voters in 1698, and reporting on 9 Mar. on the laws relating to woollen manufactures, which as a former opponent of protectionism he might have been expected to examine critically. He served as a teller on 13 Mar. in favour of the bill for the more effectual punishment of felons. But the subject which most frequently engaged his attention in this Parliament was the settlement of the Irish forfeited estates. He told on 23 Feb. against receiving a petition from Patrick Megawley and Pierce Nugent in connexion with Irish forfeitures, and on 26 Mar. against giving leave for a bill to relieve the Jacobite banker Sir Daniel Arthur from the effects of the Resumption Act. However, he was actively involved in the management of no fewer than eight similar relief bills: five for private individuals; two on behalf of the 'Protestant purchasers' and 'Protestant tenants' of forfeited estates, whose cause the English Whigs had adopted; and the last a measure sought by the Church of Ireland, for making provision from the forfeitures for the rebuilding of churches and the augmenting of small vicarages.[9]

Having reportedly 'chosen' Lord James Cavendish* for his partner in the 1702 general election, Colt suffered the mortification first of seeing two Tories returned for Westminster, and then of being struck off the Middlesex commission of the peace by the incoming Tory administration. His bitterness was such that not long afterwards he began legal proceedings on another pretext against Sir Walter Clarges, 1st Bt.*, one of the victorious Tory candidates at Westminster. Nothing came of the suit, and the following year saw Colt seeking fresh fields in which to advance his career. He attempted to ingratiate himself with the electoral court at Hanover, protesting his and his family's 'zeal' for Hanoverian interests, while at the same time cultivating an old Tory connexion, the Duke of Ormond. In March 1703 he wrote of having received 'an encouragement' from Ormond, 'to whom and his family I owe very many obligations', to 'attend him in Ireland', where the Duke had been appointed lord lieutenant. 'If it be my fortune to serve there in Parliament', he told the Hanoverian minister Robethon, 'I shall embrace all opportunities whereby I may any way show my devotion to the illustrious house of Hanover.' In fact, the opportunities did not arise, and in 1705 Colt was contesting Westminster again in the Whig interest, partnered by Hon. Henry Boyle*. In the aftermath of the Tack the two Whigs were able to turn the tables on their Tory opponent. Lord Sunderland (Charles, Lord Spencer) again calculated Colt's return as a 'gain', while another analysis listed him as a 'Churchman'. True to form, Colt voted on 25 Oct. for the Court candidate as Speaker, while his inclinations to the Court, which by the spring of 1706 were prompting him to appeal to Robert Harley* to assist his nephew's search for a suitable military commission, manifested themselves in his support for the Court on 18 Feb. 1706 in the proceedings over the 'place clause' of the regency bill. The author on 1 Nov. 1705 of a motion to print the votes of the Commons, Colt quickly resumed an active parliamentary career. Among his many tellerships, he acted on 1 Feb. 1706 against an instruction to the committee on the tunnage and poundage bill to regulate Exchequer fees; and on 13 Feb., against a clause proposed to be added to the recruiting bill. He also managed through the House a bill to enable the Treasury to compound with Thomas Tomkins over a debt to the crown. Partisan loyalties were evident in his extensive involvement in election cases. He was a teller on 10 Nov. against instructing the elections committee to hear the Cheshire dispute in two weeks; on 24 Nov. against John Gape* in St. Albans; and on 1 Dec. on the Whig side in the Amersham case. Two other tellerships, at the report of the land tax bill on 14 Dec., were probably motivated solely by party sentiments, since they concerned the nomination of commissioners under the Act in Suffolk and in Coventry. Naturalization bills were becoming a major issue between the parties, and Colt again managed a measure providing for the naturalization of a large number of Protestant immigrants. Bills for the relief of claimants to Irish forfeited estates also remained a preoccupation, and he was actively involved in four such cases before the House. Another old interest to resurface was the payment of arrears to soldiers and officers on the Irish establishment. On 26 Nov. 1705 Colt presented a bill for the relief of Colonel Samuel Venner, formerly governor of military hospitals in Ireland. He was also actively involved in the progress of five other bills relating to regimental arrears before bringing in a bill on 6 Mar. to tackle the problem in a more general way, by enlarging the time for registering debentures on Irish forfeited estates. He presented on 25 Jan. a bill for widening the passage into the palace yard at Westminster; on 6 Mar. told for a rider to the bill to prevent frauds by bankrupts; and two days later reported from a committee considering several petitions concerning public mourning. Otherwise his parliamentary activity in this session related to four private bills.[10]

Colt's participation in parliamentary business became noticeably less intense after the 1705–6 session. He brought in three bills in January 1707: for suppressing various industrial premises erected since 1705 in the vicinity of Westminster and St. James's palaces (7 Jan.); for widening the passage into Westminster palace yard (24 Jan.); and a private naturalization bill (28 Jan.). He was also actively involved in four other bills, three of which were on matters of Irish interest: a private bill on behalf of Sir John Mead, an Irish baronet and a member of the Irish parliament; a bill enabling the English holder of the office of remembrancer of the exchequer in Ireland to take the oaths in England; and a measure to improve the Acts to apply the forfeited impropriations in Ireland to the erection of new churches and the augmentation of poor vicarages, a subject in which he had shown some interest previously. He was a teller too against a bill for the relief of Francis Sarsfield from the effects of the Irish Forfeitures Resumption Act (28 Mar. 1707). Another tellership was in opposition to an amendment to the bill repealing the Acts prohibiting the importation of foreign lace (27 Feb.). In the following session Colt seems to have sympathized with the plight of John Asgill*, as would have been natural in one who had opposed earlier blasphemy legislation, for on 18 Dec. he acted as a teller in the minority to adjourn the debate on Asgill's expulsion. He was a teller again on several occasions over supply legislation: on 12 Dec. for a clause to be added to the land tax bill relating to local arrangements in Monmouthshire; on 5 Feb. 1708 against an additional clause offered for the annuities bill; on 25 Feb. against instructing the committee drafting the bill on the Equivalent to ensure payment on a *pro rata* basis to all those on the Scottish establishments; and on 27 Mar. against an amendment to a supply bill. He also acted as chairman of the committee of the whole on 2 Dec. 1707 on the East Indian goods duties bill. Of equal interest to the ministry were the bills for the encouragement of seamen, for which he told on 26 Jan. 1708, and the bill for raising the militia, which he presented on 4 Mar. He presented, on 16 Feb., another bill for the relief of insolvent debtors, a subject not far from his own heart, and managed through the House three more private bills. He was classified as a Whig in two lists from 1708, before and after the general election, at which he lost his seat at Westminster to the Tory Thomas Medlycott*. Colt's petition of 24 Nov. was rejected, to the surprise of many observers. In the Tory landslide of 1710 Colt and James Stanhope* were defeated by two Tories in a 'riotous' election at Westminster, in which Colt finished bottom of the poll. He had evidently been restored to the bench since 1702, for in 1711 he was purged once more. He did not stand for Parliament again. At the Hanoverian succession he was restored as a j.p. and a deputy-lieutenant in Middlesex, and was granted a pension of £200 p.a., which he was still receiving in 1718. His final removal from the commission of the peace in 1721 was presumably because of advanced age. Colt died on 25 Apr. 1731, in his 85th year, and was succeeded by a great-nephew.[11]

[1] Howard, *Vis. Suff.* ii. 36; *Mar. Lic. Fac. Off.* (Brit. Rec. Soc. xxxiii), 205; *Mar. Lic. Vicar-Gen.* (Harl. Soc. xxx), 232; *Le Neve's Knights* (Harl. Soc. viii), 317. [2] *CSP Dom.* 1673, p. 414; 1673–5, p. 603; 1679–80, pp. 324, 349; 1685, p. 35; 1686–7, p. 113; *HMC Ormonde*, ii. 212. [3] *CSP Dom.* 1686–7, pp. 90–91, 385; 1687–9, p. 347; 1690–1, p. 27; 1694–5, p. 9; 1695, p. 247; *Letters from the Living to the Living* ... (1703), p. 24; *Hearne Colls.* ii. 110; *Cal. Treas. Pprs.* 1697–1702, p. 261; Luttrell, *Brief Relation,* iii. 289; Bodl. Carte 79, ff. 521–2; *Poems on Affairs of State* ed. Ellis, vii. 480–6. [4] *HMC Astley*, 93; Add. 17677 QQ, f. 229; *Portledge Pprs.* 219; *CSP Dom.* 1696, p. 17; Luttrell, iv. 5, 7. [5] *Vernon–Shrewsbury Letters*, i. 66–67, 69; J. Oldmixon, *Hist. England* (1735), p.152; Cobbett, *Parlty. Hist.* v. 1050. [6] Nottingham Univ. Lib. Portland (Bentinck) mss PwA 1264, 1468a, 1471, Sunderland to [Portland], 20 July [1697], Vernon to same, 3, 14 Sept. 1697; *Vernon–Shrewsbury Letters*, i. 268–70, 306, 314–15, 319, 322–4, 328–9, 332–3, 337, 350, 352, 361, 385, 405; *CSP Dom.* 1697, pp. 202, 235, 239, 252, 291, 297, 326, 337, 344, 350, 355, 359, 362, 367, 380, 389, 391, 396–7, 472; *Shrewsbury Corresp.* 172, 491, 493; *HMC Buccleuch*, ii. 451–2, 539–40, 549; Northants. RO, Montagu (Boughton) mss 46/78–79, 81–82, Vernon to Shrewsbury, 11, 14, 15 Mar. 1698. [7] *Recusant Hist.* xv. 276; *Cal. Treas. Bks.* xiii. 435; *Cal. Treas. Pprs.* 1697–1702, p. 359. [8] Montagu (Boughton) mss 47/21, 59–60, 122–3, Vernon to Shrewsbury, 28 Apr., 21, 23 July, 20 Dec. 1698; Luttrell, iv. 400, 465; Ranke, v. 184; *Vernon–Shrewsbury Letters*, ii. 138–40, 142, 230; *CSP Dom.* 1698, pp. 365–6, 368, 430, 434; *HMC Astley*, 94; *Cam. Misc.* xxix. 368–9; Add. 30000 B, f. 182; L. K. J. Glassey, *Appt. JPs*, 130–1. [9] Bodl. Ballard 6, f. 35; Carte 228, f. 356; *Vernon–Shrewsbury Letters*, iii. 160–1; Glassey, 149. [10] *Vernon–Shrewsbury Letters*, iii. 223; Luttrell, v. 204; *Verney Letters 18th Cent.* i. 167; Stowe 222, f. 189; *HMC Portland*, viii. 225; Add. 70038, Colt to [Harley], 2 May 1706. [11] Luttrell, vi. 324; Boyer, *Anne Annals*, vii. 272; *Addison Letters*, 124; *Lockhart Pprs.* i. 297, 517, 531; Boyer, *Pol. State*, i–ii. 13, 160; *Brit. Mercury*, 6–9 Oct. 1710; *Cal. Treas. Bks.* xxix. 674; xxx. 229; xxxii. 545; *HMC Laing*, ii. 213; *Hist. Reg. Chron.* 1731, p. 21.

D. W. H.

COLT, John Dutton (1643–1722), of Dutton House, Leominster, Herefs. and St. Augustine's, Bristol.

LEOMINSTER   1679 (Mar.)–1681 (Mar.)
       1689–1698, 8 Mar.–3 Apr. 1701

bap. 16 Mar. 1643, 1st s. of George Colt of Colt Hall, Cavendish, Suff.; bro. of Sir Henry Dutton Colt, 1st Bt.* *educ.* Hayes, Mdx. (Dr Thomas Triplett). *m.* (1) 31 Aug. 1671, Mary (*d.* 1703), da. and h. of John Booth† of Letton, Herefs., 5s. (2 *d.v.p.*) 4da.; (2) lic. 6 Feb. 1705, Margaret, da. of William Cooke I*, wid. of John Arnold*, *s.p. suc.* fa. 1659.[1]

Alderman, Leominster c.1673–85, 1689–*d.*, bailiff 1680–1.[2]

Collector of customs, Bristol 1689–1700, commr. for port regulation 1690; commr. taking subscriptions to land bank 1696; paymaster of first classis lottery 1715–*d.*[3]

Even though Colt married an heiress, he did not fully repair the losses to his family's fortune incurred by his father's support for the Royalist cause in the Civil War, and the award of £10,000 damages against him in 1684 after an action for *scandalum magnatum* brought by the then Duke of York left him in a precarious financial position at the Revolution. Unlike his father and brother he did not turn to gambling as an occupation, but pressed the new regime to recognize his merits and 'sufferings in the Protestant cause' and successfully petitioned for a potentially lucrative post in the customs at Bristol, granted under peculiarly favourable circumstances, the customs commissioners being instructed to make no changes in the establishment of the port without his approval, a rare privilege for a collector. He did, however, in his administrative and political career show something of the gamester's cast of mind: extravagant and reckless, with an eye to the main chance and an eagerness to take risks to secure it. Indeed, the indiscretion which had led to his conviction in 1684 and subsequent imprisonment had been characteristically wild, a declaration in front of witnesses that 'I will be hanged at my own door before such a damned popish rascal as the Duke of York shall ever inherit the crown of England'.[4]

His party credentials thus firmly established, Colt was returned in a contest in 1690 at Leominster, where his wife's inheritance gave him a strong interest. Colt was listed as a Whig by Lord Carmarthen (Sir Thomas Osborne†) in an analysis of the new Parliament. At this stage in his career his closest political friend was still his cousin, the Monmouthshire Whig John Arnold (whose widow he was much later to marry), together with whom he had fought a long campaign against the influence of the Duke of Beaufort in the Welsh marches. He was also on good terms with the Harley family, commiserating with Sir Edward Harley's* general election defeat in Herefordshire; with the Foleys of Stoke Edith; and with Lord Macclesfield, the lord lieutenant of both Herefordshire and Bristol in 1689–90. Despite his office, he seems to have adhered to the Country opposition in the early stages of this Parliament. His tellership on 12 Apr. 1690, to recommit the report of the Bedford election, displays no more than Whig partisan loyalty. His other tellership in this first session was on 30 Apr. in support of going into a committee on the bill to discourage the importation of thrown silk, an issue to which he may have been drawn because of his position in the customs and unofficial role as a spokesman of some of Bristol's commercial interests. It may well have been during the following session that he came to align himself more closely with the Court. In local affairs he continued to do what he could to assist the Foleys and Harleys, backing Thomas Foley II* in the by-election at Weobley in 1691, and as late as January 1693 joining in the almost unanimous invitation from Herefordshire gentlemen to Sir Edward Harley to put up for a vacant seat as knight of the shire. But he was now counted by Paul Foley I*, Robert Harley* and other leading Country Whigs as a follower of the ministry. Harley's list of April 1691 classed him first as a 'Country' Member but then, on second thoughts, as a Court supporter. This change of allegiance may have been prompted by events in his collection at Bristol, which resulted in his becoming involved in negotiations with the Treasury over a monetary reward. During 1690 he had received information of a 'sensational conspiracy', between land-waiters in the port and a large group of merchants, to defraud the crown of tobacco duties. His investigations enabled the Treasury to force the merchants concerned to a composition, from which Colt eventually received a grant of over £1,250 in December 1691.[5]

At the beginning of the 1691–2 session Colt appeared on the Court side, seconding on 30 Nov. 1691 a motion of Sir John Lowther, 2nd Bt. II*, to 'agree to the whole list' of estimates for general officers of the army 'as brought in without alteration'. He spoke on 3 Dec. against the orphans' relief bill, and acted as a teller on 11 Dec. against agreeing with a Lords' amendment to the treason trials bill. On 16 Dec. he was involved in two items of business concerning overseas trade: he told for the bill to register servants going to the Plantations, and joined in moving for leave for a bill to encourage privateers against France. When it was moved on 12 Dec. that a moiety of the profits of all offices worth over £500 p.a. be taken for the expenses of the war, he remarked: 'if offices of £500 p.a. shall not be rated, I shall have no share in it, but if keeping no tables, I am willing to pay my share'. His speech on 1 Jan. 1692 in the committee of supply pushed him to the forefront. The Irish forfeited estates were under consideration and he relayed an optimistic proposition from some Cork merchants staying in Bristol. A committee was appointed the same day, including Colt, to receive proposals for raising money on the forfeitures, and Colt was ordered to 'send for the persons by him named to the House'. When the resultant bill was reported on 5 Feb. he was a teller against the committee's amendment to leave out a clause 'for vesting estates tail in their Majesties in fee simple', and a week later he presented, and told for, an unsuccessful rider on behalf of Colonel Henry Luttrell. Long-term Treasury interests may have coincided with commercial interests in his contribution to a debate on 2 Jan., when he seconded a motion to appoint a committee to inspect the book of rates, arguing that the duties on exported goods were too high and in consequence a discouragement to trade. Of more direct assistance to the financial needs of the crown were his two interventions in committee of supply on 20 Jan.: he put forward one motion, that 'all persons that found foot arms to the militia might be charged for every foot soldier 4s. a quarter'; and seconded another, 'to lay a tax on all persons keeping coaches'. The tone of a ministerial man-of-business may also perhaps be heard in his complaint to the House on 15 Jan. 'Upon the message from the Lords with several private bills', he denounced 'the multiplicity of them which the Lords sent down, for cutting off entails and unsettling of settlements, as if this

House had nothing else to do.' As for the commission of accounts, which he may well have supported earlier, he was now found voting in February 1692 to put an end to its work, though as his erstwhile colleagues in the Country party noted, 'his wishes and words outside the House run another way'. In other respects, however, he retained his old ties: on 22 Jan. he acted as a teller for a resolution condemning the 'bribery' of the Tory Sir Basil Firebrace* in the Chippenham election; on 6 Feb. 1692 he spoke against the Old East India Company and in favour of an address for a new company, although admittedly this was not yet a clear-cut party cause; on 17 Feb. he followed several 'old Whigs' in moving that the House go into committee on the King's message recommending the 'distressed' French Protestants, whose plight attracted the sympathy of Presbyterians like the Harleys; and on 24 Feb. he backed a proposal to urge the prosecution of the informer William Fuller, an early instance of the obsessive interest with spies and informers that was to grip him in subsequent years.[6]

In the meantime Colt's success in detecting customs evasion in Bristol was making him many powerful enemies there, both among his own subordinates and among the aggrieved merchants whom he had caught out, including the Bristol MP Sir John Knight. Early in 1692 the Treasury received a lengthy set of accusations of corruption against Colt, instigated by these vested interests but not necessarily to be discounted for that reason. The collector was charged with personal involvement in frauds, with extorting money from some traders and colluding with others in flouting the law. It was also alleged that

> some time since, being in company where King William and Queen Mary's health were drunk under the title of our sovereign lord and lady King William and Queen Mary's health, he answered in words to this effect, 'to our sovereign lord the people, for we can make a king and queen when we please', and also has been heard to say in discourse . . . that if he gave the King but an ill look he durst not turn him out, or words to that effect.

The flavour of Tory polemic in this last accusation appears to bear out Colt's claim that the attack on him was prompted by party animosity: 'the truth of all this malice is Whig and Tory and a trial of skill'. On the other hand, the charges were countenanced by local Whigs like the pamphleteer John Cary, and were supported by a number of Bristolians who cannot all have had personal or factional grievances against Colt. There was general resentment at the 'sudden grandeur' the collector had assumed, and the investigating customs commissioners found plenty of ready witnesses if little in the way of sensational evidence.

Colt mobilized his political allies, writing to Harley for help in putting his case to the commissioners. 'Sir Richard Temple [3rd Bt.*] is my mortal enemy in it', he wrote, 'which I shall make appear.' And on this occasion the commissioners, and the Treasury lords, did stand by him. 'The articles and witnesses, being each about 40 . . . are come to nothing', reported Luttrell, 'the lords of the Treasury having found them frivolous and partial.'[7]

Colt was twice listed as a placeman during 1692, but despite holding an office, and keeping it through the goodwill of the ministry in the teeth of a sustained effort to have him removed, he did not begin the 1692–3 session as a loyal Court supporter. On 2 Dec. he joined Sir Christopher Musgrave, 4th Bt.*, in raising complaints over the administration of the army in Ireland, especially concerning arrears of pay. He acted as a teller on the 31st against committing the bill to prevent the export of gold and silver and melting down the coin of the realm. His rediscovered commitment to Country causes produced a further tellership on 9 Jan. 1693 for a clause to be added to the land tax bill stipulating a landed qualification of £100 p.a. for commissioners. He took an active part in the investigations into maladministration in Ireland which were being prosecuted both by Country party leaders like Harley and the 'new Whigs' of the Junto. On 21 Jan. Colt presented a petition from one of the prominent Irish oppositionists, James Hamilton, against the royal mines bill, as it related to Ireland. At the committal of the bill appointing commissioners of accounts he moved that they be instructed to consider the accounts of the Irish army. Then on 22 Feb., when the House was debating 'the state of Ireland', he drew attention to an item in the report of the accounts commissioners, to the effect that while £135,000 worth of forfeited goods had been seized in Ireland, only £4,000 had been accounted for: this was, he said, a discrepancy 'worth your consideration'. Much of his other activity in this session was related to trading concerns: he was a teller on 15 Feb. against an amendment to a proviso to the bill to prevent the decay of trade in towns; spoke on 6 Feb. in favour of the bill prohibiting the import of foreign buttons, and on 22 Feb. acted as a teller against a rider offered to this bill; and on 2 Mar. told against a clause proposed to be added to the bill to prohibit trade with France. While he was still put down as a placeman in three lists from 1693 his relationship to the ministry was at this stage somewhat equivocal. His problems with the Bristol merchants and his ambition for greater things combined to enhance his dissatisfaction with his collectorship, and in May 1693 he applied to Lord Sunderland for help in advancing his pretensions. He may already have been trying to improve his prospects through the encouragement of informers, a tactic that both demonstrated his own devotion to the Williamite regime and threatened to make trouble for ministers. Jacobite sources suspected that Colt had been one of the Whig MPs who in 1693 had planted in the mind of a convicted highwayman, Whitney, the idea of claiming that his gang had been hired to assassinate King William.[8]

In the 1693–4 session Colt acted as a teller on 28 Nov. 1693 in favour of passing the triennial bill, and again on 20 Dec. against an amendment to a resolution of the committee of supply relating to the army estimates, which would have stipulated the retention of one regiment for the service of Barbados. After a three-week leave of absence granted on 19 Jan. he returned to the House to act as a teller three times on matters of supply: for an instruction to the committee on the salt duties bill to prepare a clause 'of credit' to make good any deficiencies (13 Mar.); against agreeing with a resolution of the committee of supply for a further imposition on wine (22 Mar.); and in favour of agreeing with the committee of ways and means to lay a tax on coastal shipping (26 Mar.). He was also a teller on 30 Mar. against the Country-inspired bill for the disfranchisement of Stockbridge (30 Mar.). This reorientation towards the Court was even more pronounced in the next session, for on 7 Jan. 1695 he told against a motion to hear the report of the committee on the place bill. He acted as a teller on the 15th against engrossing the bill to exempt apothecaries from the burdens of parish office, and was twice a teller in divisions relating to questions of security: on 6 Feb., for a motion to declare that the Lancashire Plot had truly constituted a danger to the government; and on 11 Mar., for the second reading of a bill requiring 'certain persons' to take the oaths. Colt was re-elected unopposed at Leominster in 1695, despite the fact that he had antagonized his constituents by voting in favour of the leather duty, and by neglecting to correspond with the corporation. Colt acted as a teller on 14 Dec. on the Whig side in a division over the Mitchell election and was listed as likely to support the Court in a forecast for the division on the proposed council of trade on 31 Jan. 1696. He also signed the Association promptly and in March voted in favour of fixing the price of guineas at 22s. A further tellership in this session reflected his and his brother's interest in the acquisition of forfeited Catholic estates: he told on 18 Apr. against an amendment to the bill preventing Papists from disinheriting their Protestant heirs, that there should be no hindrance on the disposal of estates away from the heirs to relations who were Protestants.

No sooner had Parliament been prorogued than Colt was seeking to capitalize on his good behaviour in the House, pressing Secretary of State Sir William Trumbull* to intercede with the King for some preferment.[9]

Failure to secure promotion rapidly soured Colt and made him a danger to the Whig ministers, to whom his loyalty was always conditional. In August 1696 he wrote to Trumbull, 'the kingly promises are at an end for me, unless he [William III] will advance my salary till a better place falls'. In order to force the ministers' hand, or even that of the King, he adopted a two-pronged strategy. Occasional deviations from the ministerial line in the Commons reminded government of his importance, while outside the House he and his associates continued to patronize informers as a means of threatening or even blackmailing those in high office who might have something to hide, especially the former secretary of state, the Duke of Shrewsbury, and Shrewsbury's protégé, deputy, and eventual successor, James Vernon I*. As early as September 1696, for example, Colt was encouraging one 'Captain Fisher', a witness to the Assassination Plot, who claimed to have been told that Shrewsbury and other leading Whigs were implicated in treasonable correspondence with the Jacobites. In the 1696–7 session Colt voted on 25 Nov. in favour of the bill of attainder against Sir John Fenwick†, and was twice a teller in December on the Court side: on the 3rd, against engrossing the bill for further regulating elections; and on the 10th, on an adjournment motion. By March, however, he was becoming distinctly restive. He was a teller on the opposition side on 3 Mar., against an amendment to a resolution of the committee of ways and means, to extend the scope of the cider duties; and on 20 Mar. told in support of the Country Whig Sir Samuel Barnardiston, 1st Bt.*, in a motion arising from an indiscretion committed by Barnardiston at a conference with the Lords over the East India silks importation bill. Notwithstanding these flashes of independence, Colt was still recommended to Sunderland by Sir William Trumbull in April 1697 as someone who had performed 'good service' in the Commons and was deserving of reward. Colt's first ambition was a customs commissionership. When that proved impossible he set his heart on succeeding Thomas Neale* as master of the Mint, on rumours of Neale's illness. Those who solicited on his behalf, among whom Trumbull was probably prominent, emphasized his peculiar 'humour', and that 'disappointments would make him ungovernable'. Even Vernon admitted the truth of this, that frustration would 'enrage him', but Colt's association with John

Arnold and with the mercurial Earl of Monmouth damned him in Shrewsbury's eyes as one who 'would rise by accusations', and Shrewsbury's opposition was enough to keep him from preferment. Colt's reaction, as communicated to Trumbull, promised further difficulties for the ungrateful ministers, both inside and outside the House. He openly threatened that 'the time draws on that friends may be wanted, and though the former plot has been hushed, and some executed of the smaller rank, the time draws near that the bigger shall not be hid'. As for his likely political stance when Parliament resumed, he hinted at a more critical attitude, describing the sad state of affairs in the country at large:

> I find necessities are nowhere fit to be thought for, but supplying an army, and filling the pockets of insatiable men, till a resumption be to help all. I find a very great loss of the hearts of most of our friends, by the heavy taxes and decay of trade, and want of money and increase of beggars, so these taxes cannot be continued. God send peace . . . All things look like confusion in the country through necessities for want of money and trade.[10]

At the same time as his hopes for higher and more lucrative office were being repeatedly thwarted, Colt faced a sudden crisis in his affairs in Bristol, where he seems to have been guilty of a number of abuses and irregularities, both in the administration of his collectorship and, more recently, in connexion with the recoinage there. A serious problem arose with the bankruptcy and subsequent abscondment of his deputy, Daniel Ballard, whom he had entrusted with considerable responsibility for some of his more dubious transactions, and who had in effect served as a 'front man' for a number of improper commercial speculations. Obliged to sacrifice Ballard to save himself, he feigned ignorance of his deputy's activities and seized all Ballard's effects under an extent from the Exchequer in order to satisfy his debts, including a bond for £2,000 that Ballard had given him for security in the performance of his duties. Thanks to the 'singular generosity' of the Treasury commissioners, as one modern historian has put it, he was permitted to add the £2,000 to his own account, but the potential dangers posed by the alienation of such a well-informed accomplice as Ballard, who knew enough to ruin his former master, were very grave. Early in 1698 came the first alarm: another 'information' laid against Colt, setting out various charges of corruption. Although the investigation of a customs commissioner, Robert Henley*, again cleared his name, his anxiety to be out of Bristol and removed to higher things can only have increased.[11]

Colt now turned his attention back to Lord Sunderland as the patron who would put the case to King and Treasury for his advancement, not a particularly happy choice in the circumstances of 1697–8, with Sunderland's increasing distance from the Whig Junto. Simultaneously, he intensified his involvement with the informers who could bring pressure of a different kind to bear on leading ministers. In December he resumed his dealings with Captain Fisher, whose proffered testimony was now directed towards sowing animosity between Trumbull, Shrewsbury and Lord Chancellor Somers (Sir John*), more particularly towards making Shrewsbury suspicious of the lord chancellor. Even though Colt ostensibly broke with Fisher over this information, he was still suspected of having put the captain up to it, and the following May tried to play with the same cards again, claiming to Vernon that he had succeeded in dissuading Fisher from bringing his case, and his stories against Shrewsbury, before the House of Lords. In fact, when Vernon investigated the matter, he found that the truth was quite otherwise, that Colt had in fact been urging Fisher to lay his information 'before Parliament' lest an indemnity bill be suddenly passed. Colt was also trying to make use of the spy Matthew Smith, who presented an additional threat to Shrewsbury since Smith had offered Shrewsbury information about the Assassination Plot in its early stages, information that Shrewsbury had then mistakenly ignored. In December 1697 Colt wrote to Vernon claiming to have further papers of Smith's and asking Vernon to read them and give his opinion as to whether Colt and Arnold should pursue the allegations they contained. Vernon did not take the bait, and very soon after was able to report that the 'mystery' of these various approaches from Colt had been 'unriddled'. Evidently Sunderland had succeeded in 'settling' his appointment to a commissionership of excise, with the additional provision that Arnold was to succeed him as collector of Bristol. But, as Vernon reported, 'Colt hath desired me to excuse him from accepting a commissioner's place in the excise . . . since he would rather wait for a vacancy in the customs, but added that his cousin Jack Arnold had rather be in the excise than anywhere'. The reason for this preference was not far to seek: 'no doubt but he hath more mind to the customs, as having the higher salary, and that he might have the £400 in the meantime . . . This is the reformation and zeal for the public that these rogues ever designed.' To insist, however, proved unwise. The King was adamant that Colt 'must be in the excise', and further solicitation for a place in the customs commission proved in vain. Colt attempted to promote his cause in this way in Parliament too, where in March 1698 he seconded a motion of Sir Rowland Gwynne* for an address to the King to 'cause a list to be printed of the persons who have leave to stay in England, pursuant to the late Act'. This was another contrivance to put pressure on Vernon, as the intended victim himself recognized:

> They pretend to mean no more by it [he wrote to Shrewsbury] but to know those who have no leave, that they may be taken up . . . but I must always suspect these gentlemen, and I rather imagine that they have more mind to be finding fault with the licences that have been given.

More often in the Commons Colt sought to demonstrate his usefulness to the Court, as in several tellerships: on 11 Feb. 1698, against a resolution of the committee of supply concerning the debt due to the king of Denmark; on 29 Mar., against adjourning the debate on the clause in the land tax bill appointing commissioners; on 4 Apr., against excusing the Tory James Praed* for defaulting in attendance; on 20 Apr. (just 11 days after being granted a three-week leave of absence), against receiving a petition relating to the coal duties bill; on 26 May, against an amendment to the resolution of ways and means for the establishment of the New East India Company, which would have deprived the Company of privileged trading status; and twice more in support of the bill setting up the Company, to read the bill (10 June) and to agree with a committee amendment (22 June). His other tellerships occurred on 6 May, against receiving a petition against the power of forcible entry upon property conferred on sheriffs' officers by the Act against prison corruption; on 18 May, against the blasphemy bill, which his brother also opposed; and on 28 May, this time dividing from his brother, in favour of the bill to encourage a newly invented pumping system for shipping. He also brought in a measure for the relief of insolvent debtors (telling for its committal on 17 May). It was therefore with some justification that he wrote to Trumbull in July 1698 to set forth his claim to the long-promised preferment: 'I have served now nine years in Parliament, which has caused an expense that I am £2,000 in debt. I have been a true drudge, and waked while others slept.'[12]

By this time Colt had lost his seat in Parliament, forced to 'resign' at Leominster rather than face inevitable defeat at the hands of Robert Harley's brother Edward*. Exclusion from the House deprived him of one means of levering himself into higher office, though it did not stop him from trying more straightforward approaches. Vernon was soon sending on to Shrewsbury more begging letters from 'John Colt, who never fails to put in his claim when there is a vacancy in the custom house'. Worse still, he was now vulnerable to renewed accusations of corruption in his customs collectorship. These originated with his former deputy, Ballard, who via a third party wrote privately to Charles Montagu* at the Treasury in January 1699 with a string of new charges. Colt, who was here described as 'almost illiterate, and ignorant of custom house business', was said to be 'wholly directed and governed' in his office by his 'wife's gallant', one Robert Barnes, himself 'formerly an A.B.C. schoolmaster' and ill-versed in customs business but covetous and willing to make false seizures in order to line his own pocket. The charges against Colt were that he had violated the rules against private trading by underwriting insurance and speculating in commercial ventures in his wife's name; had accepted bribes for turning a blind eye to customs fraud and for receiving clipped money at the customs house for the recoinage; and had diverted receipts from the customs to his own family's needs. It was even alleged that he had brought up from London to a post in the custom house a 'pickpocket' (upon whose wife Colt entertained carnal designs), who had subsequently been caught stealing from official funds. In April 1699 Ballard's attorney appeared before the Treasury commissioners and elaborated these allegations, adding a claim that Colt had cheated his client of some £1,700 in making up the accounts when Ballard absconded in 1697. Finally Ballard himself appeared at the Board and Robert Henley was again despatched to Bristol to investigate. The hearings dragged on through 1699, with Colt retreating a little further in his defence at every stage, until at last, after the affair had been referred to the King, a warrant was issued for his dismissal in February 1700. Later that year his name was removed from the Somerset commission of the peace. Vernon wrote that he had done what he could to prevent, or at least defer, Colt's removal from his collectorship, and that the King was sympathetic, but 'the lords of the Treasury thought they could not withstand the clamour that would be raised upon this occasion'. Vernon was unable, however, to resist pointing the moral: 'I can't but reflect on the just ways of Providence, when I see a man fall under a criminal accusation who I must say has been too busy in fomenting accusations against innocent persons.'[13]

Colt was still not entirely in the clear, even after his dismissal, for there was £3,166 owing to the crown from his collection, and in 1702 the Treasury began a legal process against him to recover it. He was thus under some compulsion to seek election again to

Parliament, and during 1700 mounted a counter-attack against the Harley interest in Leominster, putting together a powerful 'party in the magistracy' there to influence votes by various, largely irregular, means. His faction, reported Edward Harley in May 1700, 'stick at nothing to serve their designs'. Colt may also have enjoyed the tacit support of Lord Coningsby (Thomas*), with whom he was co-operating in electoral contests elsewhere in the county in January 1701. Having succeeded in defeating Harley by some 30 votes at the poll, he faced two petitions, one from his opponent and another from 'divers inhabitants' of the borough complaining of the practices of Colt's friends in the corporation. Harley's confidence of carrying the case in Parliament because he was 'better beloved' there than Colt, proved amply justified. Moreover, besides unseating Colt, the House also committed to custody one of his leading supporters in Leominster, an action which effectively overawed the pro-Colt faction in the town. There was even a motion, by John Grobham Howe*, that the affair between Colt and Ballard at Bristol, 'heard and determined before the lords of the Treasury', might be re-examined in Parliament. Despite the novelty of this procedure a committee was appointed for the purpose. The aim, according to Sir Richard Cocks, 2nd Bt.*, was to pass a censure on Lord Tankerville (first lord of the Treasury during the final stages of the investigation) or 'to oppress Colt, to oblige the Speaker [Robert Harley] and his brother', but here the matter rested, for the committee made no report. Colt's party in Leominster was so demoralized that he was able to make only a token effort in the second general election of 1701, and although he petitioned following another defeat by Edward Harley the petition was unheard. In 1702 he did not stand at all, and began to pay his debt to the crown in order to stave off the Treasury process. Once this had been settled he made a counter-claim of his own, alleging that the £3,166 had in fact been embezzled by Ballard during Colt's absences from Bristol attending to parliamentary duties. In a derisory response a warrant was issued in June 1703 for £100 as payment 'in full for his losses and services' in the collectorship. Colt followed up with yet another petition for an allowance, on the grounds of his having remitted Exchequer bills as collector: this was ignored.[14]

After failing again to shake the Harleian ascendancy in the 1705 election at Leominster, Colt did not put up in 1708, although his hand seems to have guided the unsuccessful challenger in that year, Farley Osborne. In 1710 he tried surprise, announcing his candidature at the last minute. This was no more successful, and finding the Leominster voters disposed against him, he withdrew in high dudgeon, announcing that 'he would not poll one man to expose his friends to double taxes'. In 1712 along with Sir Herbert Croft, 1st Bt.*, he stood out against the general trend of Herefordshire opinion by refusing his vote to the Tory Sir Thomas Morgan, 3rd Bt.*, in the by-election for knight of the shire, and the following year made a final attempt to recover his seat in Leominster, only to suffer the worst of his defeats. He did not stand for Parliament after the Hanoverian succession, but was able, once more, to cash in on his loyalty to, and sufferings for, the 'Protestant cause', receiving the office of paymaster of the first state lottery, at a salary of £500 a year which he held until his death on 19 Apr. 1722.[15]

[1] *Bristol Rec. Soc.* xxv. 41; Howard, *Vis. Suff.* ii. 37; *Mar. Lic. Fac. Off.* (Brit. Rec. Soc. xxxiii), 211; Copinger, *Suff. Manors*, i. 65; *Cal. Clarendon SP*, iv. 138. [2] G. F. Townsend, *Leominster*, 149, 151, 156. [3] *CJ*, xii. 509; *Cal. Treas. Pprs.* 1720–8, p. 383. [4] *CSP Dom.* 1689–90, p. 25; J. M. Price, 'Tobacco Trade and Treasury 1685–1733' (Harvard Univ. Ph.D. thesis, 1954), pp. 572–3. [5] Add. 70014, f. 311; 70015, f. 73; 70218, Colt to Robert Harley, n.d.; 70114, Paul Foley I to Sir Edward Harley, 10 Jan. 1691[–3]; 70017, ff. 5, 22; *HMC Portland*, iii. 446; Price thesis, 574–6. [6] *Luttrell Diary*, 51, 58, 83, 102, 104, 130, 145, 175, 182, 191, 204; Grey, x. 216; Add. 70016, f. 30. [7] Price thesis, 577–9; Add. 5540, ff. 23, 52–53; 70218, Colt to Robert Harley, 11 Apr. 1692; Luttrell, *Brief Relation*, ii. 415, 515. [8] *Luttrell Diary*, 285, 378, 402, 421, 439, 446; Nottingham Univ. Lib. Portland (Bentinck) mss PwA 1212, Sunderland to Portland, 3 May [1693]; *Ideology and Conspiracy* ed. Cruickshanks, 101, 109. [9] *HMC Downshire*, i. 664. [10] Ibid. 683, 693, 743–4; Hopkins thesis, 218, 222, 225; H. Horwitz, *Parl. and Pol. Wm. III*, 192–3; Luttrell, iv. 213; *Vernon–Shrewsbury Letters*, i. 242–3, 405; Northants. RO, Montagu (Boughton) mss 46/104, Vernon to Shrewsbury, 20 May 1697. [11] Price thesis, 579–80; Add. 70159, info. to Robert Harley, [1697]. [12] *HMC Downshire*, i. 768, 781; *Vernon–Shrewsbury Letters*, i. 434–5, 438; ii. 27, 69–71; Montagu (Boughton) mss 46/158, 162, 181, 195, Vernon to Shrewsbury, Dec., 9 Dec. 1697, 18 Jan., 19 Feb. 1697[–8]. [13] Montagu (Boughton) mss 47/23, 48/38, Vernon to Shrewsbury, 3 May 1698, 29 Feb. 1699[–1700]; Add. 70117, Abigail to Sir Edward Harley, 26 Apr. 1698; *Vernon–Shrewsbury Letters*, ii. 161, 250; iii. 106; Price thesis, 580–3; *Cal. Treas. Pprs.* 1697–1702, pp. 260–1; Luttrell, iv. 529, 532, 535, 618; *Cal. Treas. Bks.* xv. 279; L. K. J. Glassey, *Appt. JPs*, 141. [14] Price thesis, 583–4; Add. 70236, Edward to Robert Harley, 3 May 1700; Bath mss at Longleat House, Thynne pprs. 25, f. 55; *Cocks Diary*, 98–99; *Cal. Treas. Bks.* xvii. 22, 210, 276; xviii. 265, 311; *Cal. Treas. Pprs.* 1702–7, p. 158. [15] Add. 70236, Edward to Robert Harley, 25 Apr. 1708; 70216, James Caswall to same, 9 Oct. 1710; 70226, Thomas Foley II to same, 19 Aug. 1713; Huntington Lib. Stowe mss 58(12), pp. 131–2; *Cal. Treas. Bks.* xxix. 758.

D. W. H.

COMPTON, James, Ld. Compton (1687–1754).

WARWICKSHIRE   1710–28 Dec. 1711

b. 2 May 1687, 1st s. of George Compton, 4th Earl of Northampton, by his 1st w. Jane, da. of Sir Stephen Fox* and sis. of Charles Fox*. *educ.* privately; Eton c.1696–1700; travelled abroad (Holland, Germany, Italy)

1707–9. *m.* 3 Mar. 1716, Elizabeth (*d.* 1741), da. of Hon. Robert Shirley of Staunton Harold, Leics., sis. and h. of Robert Shirley*, Visct. Tamworth, *suo jure* Baroness Ferrers, 3s. *d.v.p.* 5da. (4 *d.v.p.*). *summ.* to the Lords in his fa.'s. barony as Lord Compton 28 Dec. 1711; *suc.* fa. 13 Apr. 1727; uncle Hon. Spencer Compton* 1743.[1]

Compton came back to England in July 1709 from a grand tour in which among other things he had developed a dislike of the Dutch for their 'natural inclination . . . of requiring money in every place'. The following year his father, as lord lieutenant of Warwickshire, successfully persuaded the gentlemen of that county to select Compton as knight of the shire. He was classed as a Tory in the 'Hanover list', and was included among the 'worthy patriots' who in the first session exposed the mismanagements of the previous ministry. A teller on 3 Feb. 1711 in a division on the Honiton election, he also managed through the House the bill to prevent abuses in textile and iron manufacture. He was a member of the October Club, acting as 'steward' at one of its feasts in April 1711 which Swift was invited to join, but was not listed by Boyer, presumably because he had left the club by February 1712, having been called to the Upper House as one of Harley's 'dozen' to secure the ministry's majority there. Compton died on 3 Oct. 1754.[2]

[1] W. G. Compton, *Comptons of Compton Wynyates*, 167, 169; Add. 38507, ff. 1–78. [2] Add. 38507, ff. 9, 17; *Swift Stella*, i. 241–2; *Huntington Lib. Q.* xxxiii. 157.

D. W. H.

COMPTON, Hon. Spencer (c.1674–1743) of Compton Place, Eastbourne, Suss.

EYE	3 June 1698–1710
EAST GRINSTEAD	1713–1715
SUSSEX	1715–8 Jan. 1728

b. c.1674, 6th but 2nd surv. s. of James Compton†, 3rd Earl of Northampton, by Mary, da. of Baptist Noel†, 3rd Visct. Campden. *educ.* St. Paul's; M. Temple 1687; Trinity, Oxf. 28 Feb. 1690, aged 15, DCL 1730. *unm.* KB 27 May 1725; *cr.* Baron Wilmington 8 Jan. 1728; Earl of Wilmington 14 May 1730; KG 12 June 1733.

Chairman, cttee. of privileges and elections 1705–10; Speaker of House of Commons 1715–27.

Paymaster of Queen's pensions 1707–13; treasurer to Prince George of Denmark 1707–8; treasurer to Prince of Wales 1715–27; PC 6 July 1716; paymaster-gen. 1722–May 1730; ld. privy seal May–Dec. 1730; ld. pres. of Council Dec. 1730–Feb. 1742; first ld. of Treasury Feb. 1742–*d.*

A solitary Whig in a family of High Church Tories, Compton stood unsuccessfully at East Grinstead in 1695, on the interest of his kinsman the Earl of Dorset (Charles Sackville†). He was eventually brought into Parliament three years later by Lord Cornwallis (Hon. Charles Cornwallis*) at a by-election for Eye, in all likelihood as a favour to Cornwallis' grandfather Sir Stephen Fox*, one of whose daughters had married Compton's elder brother, and who had thereafter taken a close and avuncular interest in the family's affairs. It may have been through Cornwallis that Compton became connected at about this time with Lord Somers (Sir John*), to whose electioneering efforts at Reigate in 1698 Compton lent his assistance, acquiring a burgage there shortly before the poll. Classed as a Court supporter and for no accountable reason as a placeman in lists of the new Parliament in 1698, and also in early 1700 as being in the Junto interest, Compton took some time to make his mark in the House. On 13 May 1701 he appeared as a teller on the Whig side against addressing the King for an answer to the previous address for the removal of Somers and the other three Whig lords, and on 3 June 1701 was given leave of absence for three weeks to recover his health. Classed with the Whigs in Robert Harley's* list of the 1701–2 Parliament, he was again a teller on 12 Feb. 1702, for leave for a bill to permit the poll for the Somerset county election to be held at Taunton and Wells. In the first session of the 1702 Parliament he managed a private bill, and voted on 13 Feb. 1703 in favour of agreeing with the Lords' amendments to the bill for enlarging the time for taking the Abjuration. In the next session, he told on 10 Jan. 1704 against the wine duty bill. By now he had established himself among the more prominent Whigs in the Commons, his circle of political friends including John Smith I*, Lord Hartington (William Cavendish*), and not least Robert Walpole II*, to whom he was particularly close. It fell to Compton in October 1704 to press Walpole to come up to Parliament for the start of the session. Compton was also a member of the Kit-Cat Club. Forecast as likely to oppose the Tack, he duly voted against it or was absent on 28 Nov. In a list of about June the following year he was classified as a 'Churchman'.[1]

Compton naturally voted for Smith in the division on the Speakership on 25 Oct. 1705, and was himself the Court Whig candidate for the chair of the elections committee on 7 Nov., when he defeated the Tory (Sir) Gilbert Dolben, subsequently reporting many election cases to the House. He supported the Court in the proceedings of 18 Feb. 1706 on the regency bill, acting as a teller in favour of one of the Lords' amendments to the 'place clause'. He was also a teller, with Henry St. John II, on 8 Mar., in favour of a Court-inspired motion to censure the pamphlet, *A Letter from Sir Rowland Gwynne**, and reported from a conference with the Lords on this matter on 11 Mar. Some advice that he offered at about this time to the Earl of Dorset, then bound for Hanover, illustrates his own characteristic caution: warning Dorset to 'tread carefully', he suggested that because of recent parliamentary 'differences' over the 'Hanover motion' the best way to safeguard his position would be to 'avoid making acquaintance with the agents of any party or faction here, or with any busy, intriguing person there'. Whether or not Compton followed his own counsel, he continued to make himself useful to government in the next session, and was first-named on 3 Dec. 1706 to the committee to give the thanks of the House to the Duke of Marlborough (John Churchill†). Soon afterwards he was spoken of as probable successor to John Grobham Howe* as paymaster of guards and garrisons. A teller on 27 Jan. 1707 for a motion vindicating the ministry's conduct of the war in Spain, he also played a key role in carrying through the legislation to put into effect the union with Scotland. In February, he chaired the committee of the whole on the articles of union; was first-named to the drafting committee for the bill of union itself and subsequently chaired the committee of the whole on the bill; and was a teller against a Tory move for an additional clause to prevent the future imposition in England of any 'oath, test or subscription' inconsistent with the 'government, worship and disciplines' of the established Church (22 Feb.). The following month he was appointed paymaster of the Queen's pensions and treasurer in the household of the Prince of Denmark. There were even rumours that ministers were considering him as a candidate for Speaker should Smith step down. Listed as a Whig in early 1708, he was one of the 'Lord Treasurer's Whigs' who in the winter of 1707–8 stood by Godolphin and Marlborough against attacks from the rest of the Whig party. Included with Walpole and Hon. Henry Boyle* among those consulted by Godolphin and Robert Harley about forthcoming parliamentary business early in the session, he later joined in defending the Admiralty, and of course Prince George, from Junto-directed criticism. In November and December 1707 he chaired committees appointed to consider a Scottish merchants' petition on the Union and those parts of the Queen's speech concerning the Union. He was also a teller on 31 Jan. 1708 against an opposition attempt to adjourn discussion of a resolution to accept an advance from the New East India Company in return for an extension of its charter; on 24 Feb. against a Tory motion of censure on the ministry over the management of the army in Spain; and again on 17 Mar. in favour of passing the bill for the encouragement of trade with the plantations. During the session he also managed a private bill. On the resignation of the Harleyites in February 1708 Compton was talked of as a possible secretary at war. Although no new appointment materialized, he was involved in Godolphin's schemes to set up a Court Whig candidate for Speaker in November 1708, which earned him the enmity of Lord Wharton (Hon. Thomas*) who said he believed Compton to be 'of Mr Harley's [party]'. When these schemes fell through, one Whig MP wrote:

> now those that were engaged, as Smith, Compton and others, to be heads of a new ministry, and the managers of this Parliament, are prettily dropped, and can't . . . be so well pleased in coming under those they had set at defiance.

Indeed, Compton was one of the slowest of the 'lord treasurer's Whigs' to make his peace with the Junto. He was again classed as a Whig in a list compiled after the election.[2]

Whether because he remained a 'Lord Treasurer's Whig' for another session, or out of a desire to atone for previous behaviour and impress the Whig Junto with his zeal, Compton was particularly active in the 1708 Parliament. Continued as chairman of the committee of privileges and elections, he was also a teller on the Whig side in a division on the Westminster election (24 Nov. 1708) and in December chaired the committee of the whole considering methods of recruiting the army, subsequently being appointed to prepare a recruiting bill which he introduced on 10 Jan. 1709 and managed through the House. On 29 Jan. he told in favour of William Thompson III* in the disputed election for Orford. He spoke on 5 Feb. in support of the motion for the general naturalization bill, and was listed as having voted for it. He was a teller four more times in this session: on 8 Feb. in a division over the Bewdley election; on 26 Feb. for a Court party amendment to a proposed address about the arrears of the land tax; on 8 Mar. for the Whig Thomas Meredyth* in the disputed Midhurst election; and on 10 Mar. with Walpole in favour of another Court motion, to declare that 'timely and effectual care' had been taken against the threatened invasion in 1708. In March and April he managed through the Commons bills to preserve parochial libraries, to preserve the privileges of foreign ambassadors, and for improving the Union. He also managed two private bills, one on behalf of Lord William Powlett*. In the following session Compton was nominated to the committee of 14 Dec. 1709 to draw up the articles of impeachment against

Dr Sacheverell, later reconstituted as the committee to manage the impeachment. He told on 2 Feb. 1710 for agreeing with the 'replication' drafted by the committee appointed to consider Sacheverell's answer. Other tellerships in this session were on 28 Jan. against committing, and on 2 Feb. against passing, the place bill, and he also managed the bill for the encouragement of learning through the House. In the proceedings against Sacheverell, he spoke on 1 Mar. 1710, seconding William Thompson III's presentation of the case for the 'Church in danger' article. Compton 'ran a long encomium' on the Parliament which in 1705 had voted that the Church was not in danger, and in answer to Sacheverell's comparison of this resolution with one in 1648 declared that 'there was no resemblance between those times and these, but that the ministers, who should preach peace, turn trumpeters of rebellion, and incendiaries'. A Whig pamphleteer claimed that the speech was delivered 'with skill and fidelity', but a less sympathetic witness noted that Compton 'showed so much inveteracy, and so much passion, that he trembled every joint, and almost foamed at the mouth', at one point going so far as to refer to Sacheverell as 'the criminal at your lordships' bar'. Naturally, he was later listed as having voted for the impeachment.[3]

Compton was dropped by Lord Cornwallis at Eye for the 1710 election, either as a belated reprisal for his disloyalty to the Junto in 1707–8 or because of local difficulties in the constituency. In common with other managers of Sacheverell's impeachment, he preferred not to risk his reputation in an electoral contest elsewhere. Under the new ministry of Robert Harley he kept his office of paymaster of pensions and in January 1711 was granted an annuity of £400 (backdated to September 1710) in consideration of past service as treasurer to Prince George. This he enjoyed until the summer of 1713, when he gave it up 'voluntarily', shortly before being replaced as paymaster by the man he had succeeded in 1707, his cousin Edward Nicholas*. He had himself acquired an estate in Sussex by this time, and in 1713 was returned for East Grinstead. He voted on 18 Mar. 1714 against the expulsion of Richard Steele, with whom he had previously been associated in the Prince's household, and was classed as a Whig in the Worsley list and in two lists of the Members re-elected in 1715. After Queen Anne's death he demonstrated his support for the new regime, moving a bill on 11 Aug. to continue the royal revenue and being named to the consequent drafting committee. The arrival of the new king did not bring immediate gratification, and he was said in October 1714 to have gone off into the country 'dissatisfied'. The following year, however, he came into office and was chosen Speaker. Compton died on 2 July 1743.[4]

[1] Horsfield, *Suss.* i. 388–9; *CSP Dom.* 1700–2, p. 250; W. L. Sachse, *Ld. Somers*, 138; Camb. Univ. Lib. Cholmondeley (Houghton) mss, Compton to Walpole, 14 Oct. 1704; J. Carswell, *Old Cause*, 91; Coxe, *Walpole*, ii. 4–5. [2] *HMC Portland*, ii. 191; Add. 17677 AAA, f. 510; 70284, Godolphin to Robert Harley, n.d.; W. A. Speck, *Birth of Britain*, 91; Luttrell, *Brief Relation*, v. 609; vi. 267; Speck thesis, 45–46, 148–9; *HMC Stopford-Sackville*, i. 33–34; Folger Shakespeare Lib. Newdigate newsletter 12 Dec. 1706; Huntington Lib. Stowe mss 57(2), p. 18; Boyer, *Anne Annals*, vi. 222–3; Cholmondeley (Houghton) mss, Ld. Townshend to Walpole, 26 Apr. 1707; Huntington Lib. Q. xv. 38; *Duchess of Marlborough Corresp.* i. 156–7; Centre Kentish Stud. Stanhope mss U1590/C9/31, Sir John Cropley, 2nd Bt.*, to James Stanhope*, 22, 27 Nov. 1708. [3] Boyer, vii. 290; *Impartial View*, 185; Yale Univ. Beinecke Lib. Osborn mss, 'Acct. of the Trial of Dr Sacheverell', 1 Mar. 1710; G. Holmes, *Trial of Sacheverell*, 147. [4] G. Holmes, *Pol. in Age of Anne*, 311; *Trial of Sacheverell*, 253; *Cal. Treas. Bks.* xxv. 142; xxvii. 312, 330; W. G. Compton, *Comptons of Compton Wynyates*, 164; *Steele Corresp.* 255–6; BL, Trumbull Add. mss 136, Ralph Bridges to Sir William Trumbull*, 11 Aug. 1714; *Wentworth Pprs.* 427.

D. W. H.

COMYNS, John (c.1667–1740), of Hylands, nr. Chelmsford and Writtle, Essex.

MALDON (Nov.) 1701–1708,
1710–20 May 1715
1722–7 Nov. 1726

b. c.1667, 1st surv. s. of William Comyns, barrister, of L. Inn by Elizabeth, da. and coh. of Matthew Rudd of Little Baddow, Essex. *educ.* Felsted sch.; Queens', Camb. 1683; L. Inn 1683, called 1690. *m.* (1) lic. 21 Apr. 1693, Anne (*d.* 1705), da. and coh. of Dr Nathaniel Gurdon, rector of Chelmsford, 1s. *d.v.p.*; (2) 21 Nov. 1708, Elizabeth Courthorpe of Kent, *s.p.*; (3) Anne Wilbraham (*d.* 1758), *s.p. suc.* fa. 1686; kntd. 8 Nov. 1726.[1]

Gov. Chelmsford g.s.; treasurer, SPG 1701; freeman, Maldon 1699, recorder 1699–1736.

Serjeant-at-law 1705; counsel to George II as Prince of Wales; baron of Exchequer 1726–Jan. 1736, j.c.p. Jan. 1736–July 1738, c. baron July 1738–*d*.[2]

'A man of great abilities and integrity', Comyns nevertheless claimed that he was 'not ambitious of honour or riches; my sole ambition hath been to do what good I could in my passage thro' the world, and not seem unworthy of the station I was in'. He went through life avowing aversion to public office, while finding that Providence thrust it upon him. 'I am fully persuaded', he wrote, 'that promotion comes neither from the east nor the west, but God almighty disposes it as he sees fit.' Such piety encouraged him to join the Society for Promoting Christian Knowledge shortly after its foundation, and to subscribe money for parochial libraries throughout England and the plantations. In April 1700 his lawyer's eye proved useful in considering proposals to incorporate the society, and to audit its accounts. As a further demonstration of his commitment to the suppression of vice and immorality he helped in June 1701 to draft the charter for the Society for the Propagation of the Gospel in Foreign Parts. A year earlier his friends, including the philanthropist John Philipps*, had advised him to seek a post in Ireland, which he regarded 'as a means to advance religion and the divine glory', but he was not unhappy to find that his destiny lay in England: 'I believe it is best for me as it is, and perhaps it will become me rather to continue in a private than a public station.'[3]

Yet within a year Comyns found himself in one of the most public of offices. He later claimed that his election at Maldon had been 'without [his] seeking, without expense, and contrary to [his] express desire'. Early in 1700 he had acted on behalf of the town over a mandamus, and his election must have been at least partially in recognition of this service, though he had probably been promoted also in order to oppose the Whig Irby Montagu*, brother of Charles*. Consequently, as Comyns reminisced, although the latter had 'professed himself much obliged to me, I was violently opposed by the then ministry'. Colonel Montagu's petition against him was the first to be considered by the committee of elections, making the case a test of Court strength. No doubt as a pointed gesture to highlight Montagu's electoral corruption, Comyns was among the appointees named on 17 Jan. 1702 to draft the bill to prevent bribery at elections. Later that day an extremely full committee of elections upheld his own return. After a 'great debate' and marshalling of Comyns' support, the House narrowly voted on 27 Jan. to accept the resolution. He was listed by Robert Harley* with the Tories, and his election had been noted by Lord Spencer (Charles*) as a loss for the Whigs. On 26 Feb. he duly voted for the motion vindicating the Commons' proceedings in the impeachments of William III's ministers. He was a teller on the 28th on a division over Irish forfeitures.[4]

Re-elected in July 1702, Comyns entered the most active period of his parliamentary career. His zealous Anglicanism made him a natural nominee on 10 Dec. to the committee considering amendments to the first occasional conformity bill, and he maintained a strong interest in such a measure, voting in favour of the Tack on 28 Nov. 1704. He had been one of the opponents of the Lords' amendment to the 1703 bill for enlarging the time for taking the abjuration oath, and was listed by Lord Nottingham (Daniel Finch†) in mid-March as a likely supporter in the event of a parliamentary attack over Nottingham's handling of the Scotch Plot. On 12 Dec. 1702 Comyns reported from the committee considering the repair of Aberystwyth harbour, a scheme promoted by his SPCK colleague Sir Humphrey Mackworth*. He was also diligent on behalf of his own locality. The following month, on 21 Jan. 1703, he reported from the committee considering the state of the roads in Essex, and in June of that year obtained a mandamus from the Queen's bench with the aim of forcing the Whig mayor of Colchester to register Prince George, rather than Sir Isaac Rebow*, as the borough's high steward. He took the chair of the House on 21 Nov. 1704 during its deliberations on Mackworth's bill for the relief and employment of the poor, and subsequently reported on the progress made. He was appointed on 28 Feb. 1705 as one of the managers of the conference with the Lords over the Aylesbury election case.[5]

Despite the fact that the ceremony calling him to be a serjeant-at-law was deliberately deferred until after the election, Comyns was returned without opposition in 1705. Marked as 'True Church' and Tory during the following sessions, his party allegiance ensured his dismissal as a deputy-lieutenant of Essex in 1705. He voted against the Court candidate as Speaker on 25 Oct. On 4 Dec. he spoke in a debate about the succession, in favour of leaving to the Queen the decision to bring over the Electress Sophia, but he was much less active than he had been in the previous Parliament. He did not stand for re-election in 1708, but was returned again in 1710, ranked as a Tory on the 'Hanover list', and counted as one of the 'worthy patriots' who in the first session detected the mismanagements of the previous administration. Yet although he assured Harley of his service, he obtained no place from the new ministry, in marked contrast to his bounty-hunting colleague, William Fytche*. Indeed, as he later complained, throughout Anne's reign, 'when I might have expected better, I was by every ministry successively treated with disregard, not to say despite; tho' I am not conscious of [having given] any just offence'. On 29 Jan. 1712, presumably on account of his animus against the Montagus, he was chosen as substitute for the ill Ralph Freman II* as chairman of the elections committee, to hear James Montagu* defend his return against a petition from the Tory Samuel Gledhill. Unrestricted by office, Comyns retained an independent spirit, but normally shared the views of the administration. His name appears on one of Oxford's canvassing lists, possibly in connexion with the 1712 attack on Marlborough (John Churchill†), and on 18 June 1713 he voted in support of the French commerce bill. Lord Chancellor Cowper (William*) retained him on the commission of the peace in October 1714, despite his categorization as a Tory on the Worsley and other lists.⁶

After 1715 Comyns was employed in two separate lawsuits in defence of men accused of having Jacobite sympathies, although his activity in each case can be accounted for by ties of locality, friendship or religious views rather than his own political disaffection. The first was in early 1716 when he successfully moved for a writ of habeas corpus for the release of Anthony Bramston, with whose cousin he had represented Maldon since 1712. On the second occasion, Comyns was one of the counsel representing a schoolmaster and a clergyman, thought to be 'seditiously disposed to the government', who were accused of taking children from London to beg at a charity sermon in Kent. The 'harangue upon the virtue of charity' which the Court heard from one of the lawyers smacks of the pious advocacy of Comyns, whose interest in alms and education are both well attested. A successful lawyer, he rose to become chief baron of the Exchequer, and wrote two important legal treatises, one of which was hailed as being 'exceedingly clear and perspicuous, and at the same time, remarkably concise and exact'. He rebuilt Hylands, which he had inherited from his father, on a Greek temple design, and remodelled Guy Harlings in New Street, Chelmsford, in white brick. Since he also bought the manor at Writtle, and owned land in Kent, his failure in 1715 to take the oath for the £600 property qualification is puzzling. He died on 13 Nov. 1740, the year after he had acquired the advowson of a living which he intended for the use of poor clergymen, but he failed to provide for this in his will and it, and the rest of his property, passed after the death of his wife to his nephew, John Comyns, who had followed him into the legal profession.⁷

¹IGI, London; *Gent. Mag.* 1758, p. 292. ²*Essex Review*, lv. 70; *Chapter in Eng. Church Hist.* ed McClure 24; *CSP Dom.* 1700–2, p. 358; Bodl. Ballard 7, f. 100; Essex RO, Maldon bor. recs. D/B3/1/24, f. 112; D/B3/1/25, f. 584. ³*Gent. Mag.* 1740, p. 571; Add. 35585, f. 309; NLW, Picton Castle mss 1489, Comyns to Philipps, 1 Apr. 1700; *Chapter in Eng. Church Hist.*, 1, 4, 7, 23, 59; *CSP Dom.* 1700–2, p. 358. ⁴Add. 35585, f. 309; 70305, (m); Essex RO, Maldon bor. recs. D/B3/3/555, Comyns to William Carr, 5 Jan. 1699–1700; Luttrell, *Brief Relation*, v. 131, 135; BL, Lothian mss, folders of election papers, case of Maldon; Cumbria RO (Carlisle) Lonsdale mss D/Lons/W2/2/5, James Lowther* to Sir John Lowther, 2nd Bt. I*, 22, 27 Jan. 1702; G. Harris, *Life of Ld. Chancellor Hardwicke*, i. 188. ⁵Luttrell, v. 303. ⁶Speck thesis, 315; Essex RO, Winterton (Turnor) mss D/Dkw/o1/37; *Cam. Misc.* xxiii. 41; Add. 70197, Comyns to Harley, c.Oct. 1710; 35585, f. 309; Luttrell, vi. 720; L. K. J. Glassey, *Appt. JPs*, 240. ⁷*Essex Review*, xxv. 151; xxix. 103; xlix. 49; lviii. 43; *State Trials*, xv. 1407–22; *VCH Essex*, ii. 535; iv. 200; *A Digest of the Laws*, preface; Morant, *Essex*, ii. 64; *Gent. Mag.* 1740, p. 571; PCC 290 Browne.

M. J. K.

CONINGSBY, Thomas (1657–1729), of Albemarle Street, Westminster and Hampton Court, Herefs.

LEOMINSTER   1679 (Oct.)–1681 (Mar.)
                  1685–1687, 1689–1710
                  1715–18 June 1716

b. 2 Nov. 1657, o. s. of Humphrey Coningsby† of Hampton Court by Lettice, da. of Sir Arthur Loftus of Rathfarnham, co. Dublin. *educ.* L. Inn 1671. *m.* (1) lic. 18 Feb. 1675, Barbara (div. 1697), da. of Ferdinando Gorges, merchant, of St. Bartholomew by the Exchange, London and Eye, Herefs., sis. of Henry Gorges*, 3s. *d.v.p.* 4da.; (2) Apr. 1698, Lady Frances (*d.* 1717), da. and coh. of Richard Jones*, 1st Earl of Ranelagh [I], 1s. *d.v.p.* 2da. *suc.* fa. 1671; *cr.* Baron Coningsby of Clanbrassil [I] 7 Apr. 1692; Baron Coningsby of Coningsby 18 June 1716; Earl of Coningsby 30 Apr. 1719.¹

Commr. appeals in excise 1689–June 1690; jt. receiver- and paymaster-gen. [I] July 1690–July 1698, sole July 1698–1710; ld. justice [I] Sept. 1690–Mar. 1692; vice-treasurer and treasurer at war [I] Dec. 1692–1710; PC [I] 1692–*d.*; PC 13 Apr. 1693–7 Nov. 1724; gamekeeper of Ireland and ranger of Phoenix Park by 1696–1702.²

High steward, Hereford 1695–*d.*; custos rot. Herefs. 1696–1721, Rad. 1714–21; ld. lt. Herefs. and Rad. 1714–21; steward of crown manors, Rad. Nov. 1714–21.³

Commr. taking subscriptions to land bank 1696, Queen Anne's bounty 1704, taking subscriptions to S. Sea Co. 1711.⁴

Chairman, cttee. of ways and means 6–9 Jan. 1697.⁵

Coningsby represented what many opposition critics came to consider the true picture of a Court Whig: greedy, unscrupulous and probably corrupt. Accustomed to fawn upon the powerful and bully the powerless, he naturally gravitated to government and, except for one brief interval, succeeded in keeping on good terms with every administration from the Revolution until the fall of his friend Lord Treasurer Godolphin (Sidney†) in 1710, when he himself temporarily retired from Parliament and from national politics. Wealth and titles accrued to him from a career in office, but he also acquired a pack of enemies, many of them political opponents who had run foul of his notorious ill-temper. As one put it, Coningsby 'was ever a hot and violent man'. A more charitable assessment was that of a local historian, for whom Coningsby was always

> contending against the disadvantages of a neglected education, although he never overcame the evil effects of a want of early discipline and self-control . . . Upright, courageous, and high-principled, though vain, impulsive and impatient of control, Lord Coningsby's greatest enemy was himself.⁶

Coningsby's father and grandfather, both Royalists, had successively represented Herefordshire in the early years of the Long Parliament, before seclusion. Mortgages and fines, aggravated by his grandfather's indescribable negligence, as Coningsby himself termed it, reduced an estate of £4,000 a year to a mere £800, and both his parents were imprisoned as debtors. Recovery was solely due to Coningsby's marriage to the daughter of a parvenu merchant, Ferdinando Gorges, while he was still a minor. The marriage itself was a failure, but Coningsby's father-in-law took over the management of the estate and restored financial solvency. Unfortunately, Coningsby seems to have been emotionally scarred by the episode: he suspected Gorges of having defrauded him, and relations between the two were always strained. It is indeed possible that early insecurity and the sense of being his father-in-law's pawn may have contributed in large measure to the almost desperate ambition and avarice which characterized his later behaviour. From his entry into the Commons in the second Exclusion Parliament Coningsby had shown himself to be a busy, if not especially eloquent, Member, and a stout Whig. It was as a Whig that he was returned to the Convention, for his own borough of Leominster, and during the first session he 'carried himself very worthily', in the eyes of the doyen of Herefordshire Whiggery, Sir Edward Harley*. However, his appointment as commissioner of appeals in excise seems to have worked a change in him. In the second session he several times acted as a teller for the Court side, and probably voted against the disabling clause of the corporations bill. This shift towards administration placed Coningsby in an awkward position at the 1690 election, at which he managed to fall out with the Harleys, the most powerful Whig family in Herefordshire, over both the county election and his own return in a contest at Leominster. He was, however, unhappy at the thought of burning his boats, and by the following winter had effected a reconciliation with Sir Edward Harley, but it is doubtful whether any of the Harleys were prepared to trust Coningsby again.[7]

Classified as a Court supporter in Lord Carmarthen's (Sir Thomas Osborne[†]) list of the new Parliament, Coningsby regularly spoke and acted for the government in the first session: his appearances as a teller on 10 and 15 May (with Tory colleagues) in favour of the bill vesting certain forfeited estates in the crown are probably cases in point. This sometimes involved him in a pragmatic departure from old Whig principles: over habeas corpus, for example, on which he spoke on 26 Apr. and 5 May. 'For some time I would repeal that law', he stated on the latter occasion, 'it does not so much save you, as that your enemies, that would destroy the government, may not have the benefit of the government.' In a further debate on the security of the kingdom, on 29 Apr., he made the case against relying solely on the militia to resist invasion: 'I am for having an army and the militia, not the militia to defend us against the army, but that both defend us.' In each instance he was not abandoning his former beliefs so much as arguing priorities: the maintenance of the Revolution settlement demanded the suspension of constitutional niceness. The voice of the Exclusionist might still be heard in his speeches. Later in the debate on 29 Apr. he declared that 'all papists are enemies to this government' and moved for an order 'that they shall not come within five miles of a market town, if so to be esteemed papists convict'. Some other interventions showed the continued functioning of partisan reflexes. He was a teller on 26 Apr. in favour of the bill imposing an oath of abjuration and made a trenchant speech on the 17th on the changes that had been made in the London lieutenancy in which he expressed the hope that the new lieutenants included 'no murderers' and that 'those that will not qualify themselves will be turned out'. However, in a division the same day on whether to call in the sheriffs of the City to present their petition he told for the Tories against admitting, and in other divisions, especially over election cases, he figured as a teller for the Tory rather than the Whig side: on 12 Apr. on the Bedford election; on 30 Apr. against permitting Quakers to vote without taking the oaths, a question arising out of the Hertford petition; and on 2 May on a procedural point, effectively supporting the motion to censure Anthony Rowe* for publishing his election 'black list' against Tories, the *Letter to a Friend*. Coningsby's name had not appeared on Rowe's list of the division of 5 Feb. 1689 on the transfer of the crown, but had figured on an unpublished manuscript version of the same vote. His remaining tellerships in this session took place on 25 Apr. for an additional clause to the tunnage and poundage bill to extend the time given in a former Act to allow Gilbert Heathcote* and Arthur Shallett* to import brandy from Spain, and on 3 May to engross the bill for the erection of a court of conscience in Southwark.[8]

Coningsby's connexions with the Court were already stronger than the bonds of his office, for he had been borrowing money on the security of his estate in order to make loans to the crown, and apparently had been soliciting an army paymaster's place. He had probably been promised the post of receiver- and paymaster-general in Ireland, which he was granted in

July 1690 jointly with Charles Fox*, some time before the issue of the warrant, for he accompanied King William's expedition to Ireland that summer, and had the good fortune, at the battle of the Boyne, to be at hand with a bandage when the King required one, thereby performing the kind of personal service that guaranteed royal gratitude. When William returned to England in September Coningsby was appointed to the commission of lords justices who were to head the civil government in the King's absence. His colleague was Lord Sydney (Henry† Sidney), with whom he quickly established a close rapport, gaining a new, though somewhat indolent, patron. Taking as their excuse the critical posture of affairs in Ireland and Europe, the two men sent the Earl of Portland a long letter of advice in late September 1690 concerning the management of the forthcoming Parliament at Westminster, on which depended 'not only his Majesty's happiness, but the fate of England, of this poor country [Ireland], and consequently of the Protestant interest in Christendom'. The main thrust of their comments was that it was vital for the King to have 'a formed management' in the Commons.

> By that we mean, a number of men on whom the King may confidently rely, joined with the Speaker [Sir John Trevor*] (who now is most certainly yours) and they to meet privately every night, and there to resolve how and by what methods they will oppose anything which may obstruct his Majesty's affairs, or propose anything that will further his interest the next day. Amongst these there ought to be had at any rate two or three men who have fair reputations in the House, such as Sacheverell [William*], Leveson Gower [Sir John, 5th Bt.*] and Sir Tho. Clarges*, who must by no means have any employments during the session but be rewarded afterwards, and we look upon these three to be those that have the greatest influence over the three parties of the House that are not for King James; Sacheverell of the Whigs, Leveson Gower of the middle party, and Sir Tho. Clarges of the High Church; the first of these . . . it may be a matter difficult enough to secure . . . but the other two may most certainly be had, the one by honour, the other by . . . a promise of some considerable employment . . . together with an assurance of the King's supporting the Church.

It was also vital that the King remind Parliament what he had done for his subjects, especially in the reduction of Ireland. 'Pray, my lord, don't let the King forget that nine tenths of the common people of England are firmly his, which is more than could be said by any of his predecessors this many ages.' Moving on to Irish affairs, Coningsby and Sydney argued strongly against permitting the English Parliament to interfere with the forfeited estates of Irish rebels, and in particular to 'sell' them 'towards the supply':

> It would be very hard upon the King if he should not have the disposing of some of those lands to such who he thinks deserves his favour, and whenever the King has any such thoughts if he pleases to let us have his commands therein we'll take care according to the value he designs to bestow, to pick out the choicest and best situated estates in the kingdom, of which a large account is preparing and shall be suddenly sent.

As for the domestic government of the kingdom, they urged the advantages of calling an Irish parliament quickly, not from any devotion to representative institutions but in order to forestall any outbreak of disaffection or even independent-mindedness on the part of the Anglo-Irish Protestant landowners, many of whom had spent 1689–90 in exile in England and were yet to return. A parliament called in the near future, the lords justices argued, could effectually be packed with Williamite army officers and other officials. Coningsby seems to have spent most, if not all, of the next two years in the chief government of Ireland, first in commission with Sydney and then with an English Tory lawyer, Sir Charles Porter*, who also became not only a congenial colleague but a close friend. An Irish observer in December 1691 bracketed Coningsby and Porter together as assiduous servants of the Court interest. Coningsby 'kept in the old trade of revelling' while in Dublin, according to one crony, but his post nevertheless carried considerable responsibility and brought with it a heavy workload, especially when combined with the paymastership of the forces. The lords justices were responsible for the maintenance of public order in areas under Williamite control, and for completing the negotiations with the Jacobite forces in Connaught and Munster which ended the war. Coningsby and Porter signed the final Treaty of Limerick, and indeed Coningsby himself had been responsible for much of the draftsmanship. Although ultra-Protestant critics denounced the treaty and its architects as too favourable to the Catholics, it is clear that Coningsby's own preference was for severity. Sydney wrote to him in June 1692 to thank him for giving an account

> of the behaviour of the papists upon the hopes of a descent; I confess you have been all along in the right in your opinion of these gentlemen, and I was in the wrong, for I thought they might have been made good subjects, but now I see 'tis impossible, and they must be used accordingly.

Coningsby did not, however, believe in the universal application of harsh measures. Another criticism of the lords justices was that they had been willing to favour individual papists, allegedly in return for bribes or other considerations. Such rumours may have found their way to England as early as October 1690, for in that month Coningsby's intimate friend Lord Ranelagh sent him a copy of a pamphlet in which the lord justice was depicted in an unflattering light. 'The author hath not yet been beaten', added Ranelagh in a sinister postscript, and 'if you have any service of that kind to command me, I will do my utmost to obey you.' None of this made any difference to the high regard in which Coningsby seemed to be held by some at least of the English ministers. On hearing in March 1691 that he had been taken ill in Dublin, Lord Godolphin expressed not only fear for his health but anxiety for the future good government of Ireland if his services should be 'lost', while in the following October he was being spoken of as a likely deputy in the event of Sydney being given the viceroyalty. Politically he remained strictly faithful to administration. During his absence in Ireland the compilers of parliamentary lists regularly included him among the adherents of the ministry: he figured in the list of probable supporters of Carmarthen in December 1690 in the event of an attack on the minister in the Commons; in Robert Harley's* analysis of the Commons in April 1691, on the Court side; and in two lists of placemen drawn up in 1692. In return for loyalty, and service in Ireland, Coningsby expected further rewards. He had espied for himself a choice parcel of forfeited estates, approximately 6,000 acres in and around Dublin, and was granted a custodiam in January 1692. The rental amounted to less than £100 p.a. and the property was encumbered with a mortgage of £100, but the potential resale value was over £2,000, and to this end Coningsby pressed to be given the freehold. However, his 'prodigious gettings' had 'made such a noise' that the King thought it would harm both himself and Coningsby to do anything immediately on that score. Coningsby was assured that 'the King hath promised you that estate under his hand, and if he hath but £100 a year in Ireland you must have it by virtue of that promise'; only not just yet. He was also informed that 'your place is in no manner of danger, and your Irish friends, though they have done you all the harm they could, have not lessened you at all in the King's good opinion'. At some point he also obtained the sinecure of ranger of Phoenix Park, and in September applied for the even more lucrative post of vice-treasurer of Ireland, vacant following the death of William Harbord*, which indeed had often been held in conjunction with the paymastership, and which he received before the year was out. Meanwhile in April 1692 he had been raised to the Irish peerage, though he had to accept a barony instead of the viscountcy he had at first expected.[9]

When the Irish parliament for which the lords justices had helped prepare the way was eventually convened in Dublin in October 1692, under Sydney's lord lieutenancy, Coningsby attended its upper house, where he presumably acted as a linchpin of the Court interest. He soon came under fire because of his participation in the peace settlement at Limerick, regarded by the opposition factions in Ireland as their greatest grievance. According to one observer, many members 'were averse from doing the Irish . . . justice' and thus 'aspersed Lord Coningsby' for his role in 'signing the articles'. The Irish house of commons in particular began to inquire into allegations of administrative corruption, which threatened to involve office-holders at the highest level, so that in order to protect his own reputation and those of his friends Sydney prorogued the parliament after little more than a month. Coningsby then sailed for England where he threw himself immediately into the business of the English parliamentary session. On 18 Nov. he spoke against the committal of the treason trials bill, arguing that the moment was inopportune to embark on reforms which in practice would 'only be a benefit to the enemies of this government, those that will not own it, and give them an advantage to bring back a government which, I'm sure, will make traitors of all of us'. He was particularly hard on the Catholics, condemning them as 'public enemies', an opinion that was doubtless heartfelt but was out of harmony with the rumours concerning his conduct in Ireland. As a corollary to his stand against the treason trials bill, he appeared in support of the abjuration bill, speaking for it in the debate of 14 Dec. His commitment to the Court was reflected in a series of contributions on matters of supply. On 25 Nov. Coningsby joined Charles Montagu* in opposing a Country-inspired motion to delay referring the army and navy estimates to the committee of supply. Four days later he rebutted opposition criticisms that England was spending a disproportionate amount on the continental war, especially in comparison to the Dutch. 'I am not for letting in an exasperated, abdicated King', he declared, 'and therefore I think we are engaged deeper in the war and are more concerned therein than they are.' Further speeches in the committee of supply occurred on 2 Dec., when he stressed the need for promptness in tackling financial questions and dismissed an opposition proposal which would have deferred consideration of the army estimates to a later date, and on 3 Dec., again over the army, when he observed, 'I think the question properly before you is whether you will have so many men for the defence of England'. Always his argument for granting whatever the King asked was that domestic security depended on effective military strength. He repudiated any suggestions that the army could be reduced, or that its administration required improvement, and, as befitted one who had first-hand experience in Ireland of the successful leadership of foreign-born general officers, resisted demands to restrict such appointments to native Englishmen. He was equally vehement in opposing attempts to remove naval officers, speaking on 21 Nov. 1692 in defence of the Admiralty Board. In all this he was complying with the wishes of the Court rather than fellow Whigs, as was the case too in his dogged opposition to the triennial bill. He first used the pretext that the bill had originated in the Upper House. 'I am not afraid to have the Parliament dissolved', he said, 'but would not have it from the Lords. If the Lords will make themselves temporary, I will consent to do it in this House.' In committee on 7 Feb. 1693 he spoke against the first clause, providing that a Parliament be held every year, 'for that it is unnecessary, being the law already', and at the third reading on 9 Feb., when he acted as a teller against the bill, he made a passionate, if not particularly cogent or rational, attack on the measure as a whole:

> He thought it tended to the alteration of the ancient government, and the next step to that is anarchy and confusion. There was a bill of this nature in King Charles II's time, and when that was passed the next step was to sit as long as they pleased. I will not say this will be, but what has been may be, and therefore I am against this bill.

However, his other parliamentary activity was more localized in scope. On 4 Feb. he presented a petition from one Robert Fitzgerald, possibly an Irish acquaintance, against a private bill; and on 13 Jan. 1693 he was a teller for committing the bill to improve the navigation of the Wye and Lugg, a measure directly affecting his own county, and in the introduction of which he had been consulted. His anxiety to repair relations with Whig interests in Herefordshire is evident from the eagerness with which he entered into schemes to bring Sir Edward Harley into the Commons in January 1693 for a vacant county seat. He was also keen to demonstrate his friendship for another Whig ally, Bishop Burnet, even though the bishop regarded him with contempt as a 'vicious' and unprincipled opportunist. When Burnet's *Pastoral Letter* was denounced in the Commons in January 1693, Coningsby was 'among those who signalized their favour to Dr B[urnet] by speaking in his behalf ... very zealously'. He commented that 'though there were some expressions which might give offence, yet there were many excellent things in that book, and therefore he hoped they would censure the passages which gave offence and not burn the book'. Not for the last time, he found himself the butt of another Member's wit, as this unguarded speech was taken up by Colonel Silius Titus*, who observed that 'in the beginning of King James I's reign, the Bible was printed, and the word "not" being left out of the seventh commandment, the whole impression was burnt, and yet no man can deny but there were many good things in it'. Afterwards 'Coningsby sought out Titus to shake hands, and make friendship with him', but only gave the colonel a further opportunity to twit him, by asking 'why he fell so foul upon [him]'. Titus answered that 'he could not help it . . . but did assure him if he had any occasion to name a commandment, if it were possible he would endeavour to name one he [Coningsby] had not broken'.[10]

Coningsby's obvious desire to maintain good relations with old Whig confrères like Titus and Sir Edward Harley almost certainly stemmed from his apprehension that the accusations made against him in Ireland would be raised again at Westminster, as indeed they were during the 1692–3 session. Some notice had in fact already been taken of ministerial trafficking in forfeited estates in the proceedings of the accounts commissioners in 1691–2 and in the report of the committee of 1 Jan. 1692 to receive proposals for raising money on the Irish forfeitures. Various charges were levelled against Coningsby in the committee 'but they being trivial and the evidence of them amounting to no more than hearsay' nothing of them appeared in the report, which picked out the revenue commissioner William Culliford* as a scapegoat. Then in April 1692 Sir Rowland Gwynne* had unsuccessfully brought allegations against Sydney before the Privy Council. There were 'bitter' remarks made in private against Coningsby at that time, but nothing came of them. Less than a week after Coningsby's reappearance at Westminster in the following November, the grievances of Irish Protestants were raised in a Commons debate. Hon. Harry Mordaunt* noted that tales of extortion by the army in Ireland were current and referred the subject for comment to 'the gentlemen that came lately out of those parts'. Coningsby was quick to excuse himself and his colleagues in the civil administration from responsibility for military matters, and there the inquiry rested. But in January came a report that a petition against Coningsby was in preparation in Ireland. Leading oppositionists from the Irish parliament were proposing to bring over to the English Parliament their case against Sydney, Coningsby and Sir Charles Porter. In debates in the Commons on 22 and 24 Feb. Irish affairs came under scrutiny, and Coningsby was obliged to defend himself against a series of allegations pressed by Lord Bellomont (Richard Coote*) and other Irish politicians, and backed by a temporary alliance of English Tories, Country Whigs and Junto Whigs. The Harleys in particular seem to have been closely associated with the Irish petitioners. Coningsby's defenders were a similarly heterogeneous collection, prominent among whom was Sir Edward Seymour, 4th Bt.* Many of the charges were levelled against the Irish administration in general, which was held responsible for the economic dislocation of the kingdom and the demoralization of the Protestant interest. Coningsby was specifically accused of corruption in securing grants of forfeited estates for himself and to oblige 'favourites'; in permitting his deputy-paymaster to embezzle funds; and in acting arbitrarily to seize the property of a Protestant landowner at the behest of a Catholic claimant. But the most serious charge concerned the summary execution of one Gaffney, servant to a Catholic landed gentleman named Sweetman and the principal witness to his master's involvement in the murder of some Williamite soldiers. It was claimed by more than one witness to the proceedings that Sweetman had obtained his acquittal by bribing members of the administration (although not Coningsby personally), and that to silence Gaffney Coningsby had ordered the provost marshal to take him and 'hang him up immediately', on a gun-carriage if there should be no gallows ready. The story was to haunt Coningsby throughout his political career: indeed, he was often referred to as 'Gaffney's hangman', sometimes to his face. During the inquiries into mismanagements in Ireland, undertaken by both Houses of Parliament, Coningsby made two speeches: a general justification of the conduct of the Irish government since 1690 (22 Feb.), and two days later a more personal defence. 'I do not think things are so bad in Ireland as some gentlemen have represented them', he said on the 22nd,

> or that there are so many miscarriages as you are told. As to the army's free quarter, I cannot excuse all their actions, but they were not so well paid as they ought ... As to the disarming of the papists, it is a difficult matter to do it ... As to the forfeitures, I never was concerned in them, and for the decrease of the forfeited lands from £31,000 to £10,000 that arises from the articles of Limerick, into which the Council there are inquiring.

His remarks on the 24th seemed 'weak and silly' to one side; 'satisfactory' to the other. Fortunately for Coningsby, who at this crisis had appeared 'paler than a criminal on the scaffold', the majority held the latter view, so that although an address was ordered, to set forth the various abuses that had been perpetrated in Ireland, none of the lords justices was mentioned by name. The King chose this moment to underscore his confidence in Coningsby by advancing him to a seat on the English Privy Council, not the most tactful of promotions, since the parliamentary inquiries had aspersed rather than effectively vindicated Coningsby's reputation. It was, observed Lord Sunderland, 'as if care had been taken that that business should not die'. This outcome was rendered even more likely by a decision to grant Coningsby and Porter a pardon for any crimes committed in Ireland. News of this move prompted Bellomont and an Irish party colleague, James Hamilton, to enter a caveat in June 1693 against the passing of the warrants, followed by a petition to the English Privy Council to put a stop to the pardon. On 3 Aug. Bellomont and Hamilton delivered a paper to the Council 'containing the effects of what they had to offer, as if they designed to impeach' the two lords justices in the next session of the Westminster Parliament. The Council, however, requested the presentation of formal charges and appointed a date on which they themselves would hear the matter. Prompted by Robert Harley and other 'Country' politicians, the two petitioners stuck to their guns. They submitted a second paper, recapitulating the evidence given to Parliament in the preceding February, and the subsequent address, but declined to accept a conciliar determination, protesting that this would constitute a breach of parliamentary privilege: 'by the late bill of rights ... [it] is expressly declared that proceedings in Parliament ought not to be questioned in any court or place out of Parliament'. This point the Councillors reluctantly accepted, leaving the way clear for an impeachment. The role played by the Harley interest in the affair was of considerable importance, and it was not to Coningsby's advantage in this respect that he had been 'meddling' once more in Herefordshire elections, to the Harleys' disgust.[11]

During the late summer and autumn of 1693 Bellomont and his friends were busy seeking out further information to support their accusations, and when Parliament resumed at Westminster the procedure of impeachment was quickly set in motion. On 16 Dec. 1693 Bellomont presented articles against both Coningsby and Porter, alleging 'high treason, and other high crimes and misdemeanours'. Some of the articles against Coningsby sought to blame him for policies which had been decided by his superiors, the restrictions applied to the militia, for example, or the allowance of free quarter to the army; others were unsubstantiated, such as the claim that Coningsby 'did ... settle and maintain a correspondence ... with the subjects of the French King' while a lord justice, or that he had 'favoured and supported the papists in their . . . outrages committed upon the Protestants'. A few, however, struck home, notably that Coningsby had enriched himself through the acquisition of forfeited estates and that he had acted arbitrarily and tyrannically in ordering the execution of Gaffney. In his own defence Coningsby had 'several things' to say, presumably a repetition of his statements in February. The main thrust of his speech in reply to the presentment was in fact to recall that the matter had been aired before and decided, or so he said, in his favour. He added, somewhat disingenuously, that neither he nor Porter had sought to avoid the renewal of the accusations (whereas in fact their friends on the Privy Council had tried to settle the matter during the summer). The House proceeded to take evidence during December from a number of witnesses, most of whom had already appeared the previous February, and after several adjournments Coningsby and Porter were themselves heard formally on 20 Jan. 1694. By all accounts they stood together, and a lengthy debate ensued that day, which seems to have been decisive, although the final judgment was not given until the 29th. The impeachments were defeated, but resolutions were accepted declaring the impositions by the lords justices of a new oath on Irish militiamen to have been 'illegal' and the order for Gaffney's execution to have been 'arbitrary and illegal'. Opposition noises about pursuing the affair in the Lords, or obtaining Coningsby's dismissal from the Irish paymastership, came to nothing. Instead, in May 1694 Coningsby and Porter received the royal pardons they had been promised a year before. Moreover Coningsby was able to forestall an attempt by the former proprietor of one of the forfeited estates he held *in custodiam* to have the outlawry lifted, and in June the custodiam itself was extended for a further three years. Preoccupation with the lengthy impeachment process probably accounts for Coningsby's relative inactivity in this session. His one major committee, that of 1 Jan. 1694, to receive proposals concerning the Irish forfeited estates, was on a subject of close personal interest to him, and as paymaster in Ireland he was an obvious choice as chairman of the committee of the whole on the mutiny bill. Apart from defending himself against impeachment, his only recorded speech occurred on 18 Dec. 1693, in committee on the reintroduced triennial bill, which he opposed with as much vigour and with mostly the same arguments as before. He again exploited hostility towards the Upper House, which he professed to regard as possessing a vested interest in the institution of more frequent sessions: 'the Lords will infallibly proceed upon their judicature, and draw all the causes of England before them'.[12]

Having ridden out the storm, Coningsby found himself not only safe but in high favour at court. He was in the close counsels of leading ministers, attending some Cabinet meetings, and had the self-confidence to send William a memorandum after the 1693–4 session, 'to make several observations that may prove for your service to know'. Noting that he had himself 'made it my business not only to give a constant attendance in the House at this sessions, but at all meetings to which I was called to carry on your affairs . . . and it being generally discoursed as if you had a peace in prospect', Coningsby emphasized the importance of concluding that peace before Parliament met again. 'The two great points' that required William's 'care' were 'how to manage the parties as to maintain yourself against the enemies abroad, and at the same time to preserve your authority at home'. He took it for granted that 'the Tories who are friends to prerogative are so mingled with Jacobites that they are not to be confided in during the war'. As for the Whigs, although 'for the reason of necessity' they had perforce 'to be employed to support your cause against the common enemy' they would certainly

> endeavour all they can to make use of the opportunity to lessen your just power; and, let them pretend what they will to you, the several instances they have given this sessions of their intentions that way puts this matter out of all doubt to any person who has taken the least pains to observe them, and it is beyond all dispute manifest, that they will give money to keep out King James, yet they never give you one vote to support your just right in any point where (what they please to call) the interest of your people is concerned.

The exigencies of war, he observed, would throw the King upon the mercies of these Whigs, for royal finances were too weak to maintain present levels of expenditure without parliamentary subsidies, and in any case it was 'manifestly the designs of some people to keep necessities always upon you'. In an aside that sounded strange coming from a Whig, he enunciated the principle that 'it ever was, and ever will be, impracticable for any King of England to be the least happy, who must depend upon a Parliament every year, to give him a million of money for his common and necessary support'. The dissolution of the Parliament would probably avail little, 'for let who will be the giver, there will remain still the same ways of giving; and let which sort of men be chosen, I dare say but a majority of them will be much rather for mortgaging the revenue of the crown than their own land'. Indeed, it was likely that 'the Whigs', who 'pressed' so hard for a new Parliament, would achieve their expected majority, which would leave the King worse off. The only answer, Coningsby argued, was to keep the present Parliament in being, end the war 'honourably' and then 'set up for a party of your own', based upon the loyal courtiers who in the previous session had made an offer of supply of unparalleled generosity, only for this to be 'refused by those that pretended to be your friends'. William should

> let all people see that if they expected your favour they must depend upon you for it, and not let anyone hope for promotion for being true to a faction but by serving of you. I presume to say that, the war being ended, a new Parliament called, and such measures pursued, you would quickly find that the Jacobites would turn moderate churchmen and loyal subjects, and the Whigs much more obsequious courtiers and easy servants than they now are.

In the following September Coningsby travelled over to Holland to attend the King, being primed before his journey by Godolphin with details of the fiscal expedients Godolphin proposed for the ensuing parliamentary session. While there he also raised the subject of changes in the government of Ireland. The necessity of a new parliament in Dublin brought up the question of a viceroy to succeed Sydney. Favourite was the Whig Lord Capell (Hon. Sir Henry Capel*), already a member of the commission of lords justices, but Coningsby, fearful of Capell's close connexions with leaders of the opposition in the Irish parliament of 1692, tried to persuade the Earl of Shrewsbury to let his name go forward, and may have spoken to the King on Shrewsbury's behalf. Certainly Shrewsbury was obliged to deny to Capell that any intrigue had taken place:

> As to my Lord Coningsby, he is a man who owns some former obligations to me, and told me, when he went into Flanders he would say upon the business of Ireland the words I should put in his mouth . . . In all the discourses I ever had with him, unless sometimes when he has wished I might go [as viceroy of Ireland], which I took as a courtier's compliment, at all times it has been taken for granted that your lordship must stay. But it matters not much what his opinion is.[13]

Coningsby returned from Holland just before Parliament resumed and was quickly involved in defending the King from Country Tory complaints that William had spent too long out of England that summer to be fully aware of the needs of his kingdom. His speech, however, was considered to be 'weak' by the Prussian resident. Then in a wide-ranging contribution to the debate on the motion for a supply he 'spoke somewhat in excuse of the . . . witnesses' brought by the government to prove the Lancashire Plot, adding 'that we had a gracious King who would redress all the just grievances'. It may have been in this debate that the affair of Gaffney's execution was raised again and Coningsby received a 'rap'. Later, on 5 Feb. 1695, he acted as a teller for the Court side in a division arising from the inquiry into the Lancashire Plot. He was also a teller on several occasions on questions relating to supply: on 2 Jan., for the Court, in favour of a motion to go into ways and means the following day; on 2 Feb. against an opposition amendment to the land tax bill; and on 19 Apr., once more on behalf of the Court, on a procedural motion relating to the glass duties bill. His other tellership this session was on 20 Feb. against passing the place bill. On 27 Apr. he was ordered to carry a message to the Lords concerning Sir Thomas Cooke's* ineligibility for indemnity. This time his reward for service to the Court during the session was in the form of a gift of two Herefordshire manors, formerly granted in trust for Queen Catherine of Braganza, and worth about £75 p.a.[14]

In the 1695 general election Coningsby was re-elected again for Leominster without opposition, despite the fact that he had offended voters by neglecting to correspond with the corporation in the customary way. Their displeasure had been compounded by his support for the leather duty, which adversely affected two important interest-groups in the town, the glovers and tanners, so that, although his influence was strong enough to intimidate potential opponents in the parliamentary election, he failed to carry the subsequent election to the recordership, when his offer to the corporation was refused. He was rather more successful at Hereford, where he challenged the High Tory Lord Chandos for the high stewardship left vacant by the failure of the previous incumbent, Lord Scudamore (John†), to take the oaths. That contest became a party cause, and emotions ran so high that the two principals became involved in a duel, in which neither was seriously hurt. It is possible that this championing of the Whig interest did something to repair Coningsby's local standing. He sought to improve matters further in this respect by taking a leading part in Parliament in the promotion of the Wye and Lugg navigation scheme. Named to the drafting committee for the enabling bill on 12 Dec. 1695, he presented the bill himself five days later, and lobbied hard for it behind the scenes. His success in transferring his allegiance to the new administration of the Whig Junto was evident from his prominence in the proceedings on several issues with which the ministry was intimately concerned. When the scheme for a recoinage got under way he made a speech on 19 Mar.

1696 to propose adding a clause settling the price of guineas to the bill for encouraging the bringing in of plate to the Mint. This was rejected the following day but on the 26th Coningsby reintroduced it successfully, acting as a teller in favour of the clause when the opposition divided against it. Naturally he was listed among those who favoured fixing the price at 22s. Having been classed as likely to support the Court in the division on the proposed council of trade on 31 Jan. 1696, he spoke and acted as a teller in favour of the imposition of an oath of abjuration on the councillors. He signed the Association promptly, and on 7 Apr. was a teller for a motion to oblige all Members of Parliament to subscribe on pain of disqualification from sitting. As Irish paymaster, he presented the militia bill on 8 Feb. and chaired the committees on both this measure and the mutiny bill. His Irish connexions, and his own personal vested interest in Irish forfeitures, made it almost impossible for him not to speak in the debate on 11 Feb. on the bill to make void grants of forfeited estates in England and Ireland which had been or were to be made without parliamentary consent. As much for his own benefit as anything else, he moved 'to have a bill to attaint those who had forfeited their estates' but received a stinging and not unfamiliar reply, 'that since attainders were to follow forfeitures and not forfeitures attainders, it was desired Gaffney might be expressly attainted, for that lord's sake that moved'. Among his other tellerships, one was related, albeit indirectly, to the business of supply: on 7 Apr., on the Court side, against referring to the committee on the wines and spirits duty bill a petition from those entitled by patent to annual payments on the hereditary excise. He also told on 15 Feb. for a clause to exempt the university constituents from the provisions of the electoral qualifications bill, and on 21 Apr., against the bill for enforcing the laws against unlicensed marriages, and was responsible for introducing, on 22 Feb., a bill to encourage the trade of gardening. As had often been the case before, he sought and received some post-sessional largess from ministers and King: at Shrewsbury's recommendation, he was made custos of Herefordshire; at his own request, he received a grant in fee simple of the Irish property he had hitherto held *in custodiam*. There was even a rumour in Dublin that Coningsby might go back to the Castle as lord deputy in the place of Capell, now mortally ill. At this, however, Portland commented that 'a great part of the people of Ireland are prejudiced against him and would I fear be very uneasy under his government'. That much had been apparent during the 1695–6 session of the Irish parliament, when the opposition factions from 1692 had resumed their pursuit of those they considered guilty of betraying the Protestant interest at the Treaty of Limerick and thereafter. In September the Irish commons had passed a resolution deploring 'the countenance and favour which the Irish papists have had in this kingdom during the late governments here since the year 1690', and it had been 'mentioned in the House that the governments were during the time of my Lord Romney [as Sidney had now become], Sir Charles Porter and Lord Coningsby'. Some observers actually interpreted the vote as a condemnation of the three men, who themselves had feared some such attack ever since the appointment of Capell as deputy and the decision to call a new parliament. They had observed the advance into favour and eventually into office in Ireland of their former enemies, especially the brothers Alan[†] and Thomas Brodrick[*], and had accordingly taken steps for their own protection. In May 1695 Lord Portland had instructed Capell to do what he could to prevent the Irish commons from falling upon Romney and those who had 'counselled' the former lord lieutenant during the 1692 parliament, Coningsby in particular. When the Irish commons passed its resolution against pro-Catholic policies, Capell was able to report that 'I used the best endeavours I could that my Lord Romney and my Lord Coningsby should not be brought on the stage, and indeed most of the leading men promised me not to meddle with them'. Neither Romney nor Coningsby was prepared to rely solely on Capell's goodwill, however, and both deployed what interest they possessed in the Irish parliament on their own behalf. The course of events which followed the first vote is not entirely clear. Impeachment proceedings were brought by some of Capell's supporters against Porter alone, with the deputy's tacit encouragement. They were defeated by an alliance of High Churchmen, 'country gentlemen' and interests associated with the old ministry, among whom may have been numbered 'Lord Coningsby's friends'. Relations between the deputy and Coningsby were still difficult, and in January 1696 Portland wrote again to Capell to relay Coningsby's anxious protestations of friendship. News that Capell had given orders for an inquiry into the validity of Coningsby's patent as ranger of Phoenix Park had excited Coningsby's suspicions, and Capell was politely warned off. The deputy's subsequent illness and death removed what was potentially a serious obstacle to Coningsby's full integration into the Junto ministry.[15]

According to a Jacobite agent's report, Coningsby was one of the leading spokesmen for the Court party in the 1696–7 session of Parliament. Before the session opened he paid a visit to Lord Sunderland at Althorp, and he made friendly overtures to the Harleys, possibly on his own account. He was not slow to offer King William his advice, in particular over the contentious case of Sir John Fenwick†. Under-Secretary James Vernon I* recorded a meeting with Coningsby shortly before Parliament opened in which he

> told me that, finding how much people are set upon having Sir John Fenwick before the Parliament, and that it is not to be avoided, though it shall be thought inconvenient, it came into his head that it was for the King's service, he should make the advances himself, and mention it in his speech, somewhere towards the latter end, which he thinks will prevent its being called for, in the first place to the disturbance of matters of greater moment, and then it will come on only in its course, after the intentions of the House are seen upon the chief points laid before them, and by that means it might be better managed to the King's satisfaction. He is so well persuaded he is right in his notion, that he proposed it to my Lord Portland yesterday.

Coningsby's first reported intervention of the session was on 28 Oct. 1696 in a debate on the Address. He replied to a comment by John Grobham Howe* that the King had been misinformed as to the extent of 'disorder' in the country, saying 'all was quiet where he lived, but perhaps it was that the pamphlet writ to incense the mob against part of the Members was not then come down'. Otherwise his recorded participation in debates mostly concerns the proceedings against Fenwick. On 6 Nov. he 'stood . . . resolutely' in favour of a bill of attainder. At one point, according to Vernon, he 'very dexterously moved that Fenwick might be sent for, and prevented the others doing it'; then to the resolution that Fenwick's 'informations' were 'false and scandalous' he successfully moved the amendment 'and a contrivance to undermine the government, and create jealousies between the King and his subjects, in order to stifle the real conspiracy'. On the 13th he argued in favour of allowing Fenwick 'a short time to make his defence', though he added that he would not oppose granting 'longer time' if 'gentlemen do insist upon it', in order to make it clear that the fate of the bill depended 'upon the guilt of Sir J.F.' and not merely 'upon the bare suggestions of the bill'. Four days later he felt himself impelled to speak in defence of his friend and patron, Godolphin, implicated in Fenwick's allegations. Godolphin ought to be informed before Fenwick was questioned, he argued, 'and then you will do injustice to nobody'. Naturally, he voted in favour of the bill of attainder on 25 Nov. He was active on the Court side on numerous other occasions: on 18 Nov., for example, he moved that the petition presented by the English wife of the Brandenburg trooper Conrad von Griebe, arbitrarily deported to Holland at the time of the discovery of the Assassination Plot, should lie on the table until it could be properly answered by Secretary Trumbull (Sir William*), then absent from the House; and on 8 Dec., in a committee on the state of the nation, he exploited a report of the French king's willingness to recognize William's title to the English throne to 'put the committee in good humour'. He was a teller no less than four times against the bill to introduce a landed qualification for Members of Parliament, and on 18 Jan. 1697 acted as a teller for the Court against a motion to proceed with a call of the House. On 2 Feb. he reported the King's reply to an address from the House on the Newfoundland trade. But his most significant contribution to the ministerial cause was in the business of supply, when he often worked alongside his old friend, the English paymaster Ranelagh. He acted as a teller on 3 Nov. 1696 for the administration, against a motion to refer to the committee of supply the returns from the accounts commissioners which gave an account of the deficiencies of funds, while in January and February 1697 he chaired the committee on the bill to encourage the bringing in of plate to the Mint, and for a brief spell from 6 to 9 Jan. took over the chair of ways and means, making one report on the 9th. Four tellerships arose directly from supply debates: for engrossing the land tax bill (23 Jan.); for going into the committee of supply (16 Feb.); against an opposition attempt to prevent consideration of provision for the civil list (25 Feb.); and for agreeing with ways and means to lay a duty on cider (3 Mar.). On the last occasion, local Herefordshire interests had prevailed over the wishes of ministers. Coningsby was also responsible for chairing the committee on the paper duties bill in February, and for introducing on 26 Feb. the bill for continuing the additional duties on several classes of goods. On related matters, he was a teller on 17 Dec. 1696 against passing the bill for the relief of creditors and, having told on 15 Jan. 1697 for adjourning consideration of the bill to prohibit the importation of East Indian stuffs, figured as a teller in favour of passing the bill on 6 Feb. By virtue of his office he took the chair in March of the committee on the annual bill for raising the militia. His role in this session as an auxiliary Treasury minister, and in particular his close parliamentary co-operation with Ranelagh, seemed to be reflected in his personal life: after the ending of his first, unhappy, marriage (through divorce in 1697 and the subsequent death of his wife) he married one of Ranelagh's daughters. However, his new father-in-law had been too long and too well acquainted with Coningsby's character to approve the match. There is a story that Ranelagh disinherited his daughter, but if he did so at all this can only have been a temporary punishment for his will left much of his real and personal estate to her daughters by Coningsby, a bequest that was to lead Coningsby himself into characteristically bitter litigation, since Ranelagh's affairs at his death were in great confusion. A further twist to the tale is given by the contemporary rumour that, some time before the marriage, Ranelagh had discovered Coningsby and Lady Ranelagh *in flagrante delicto* in his own bed, not the first time that Coningsby had been surprised in this way by an injured husband. Ranelagh's reaction, however, had been far from outraged. Rather, he 'said nothing, but withdrew very civilly and went about his business'. If the friendship between the two men was at all affected by these events, the interruption did not last long, for within 18 months of the marriage Coningsby was being employed by Ranelagh as an intermediary in the purchase of property which had to be acquired under an assumed name. Relations with the ministry in general do not seem to have been in the least fraught. Coningsby was one of the subscribers for circulating Exchequer bills, and in April 1697 asked for and was given a grant in reversion of property in England to the value of some £215 p.a., another part of Queen Catherine's jointure, to make up for the amount by which his share of the Irish forfeitures allegedly 'fell short of' the King's 'intentions'.[16]

Coningsby's substantial Irish interests were still vulnerable, however, since even after Capell's death the administration in Dublin continued to be influenced by those Irish politicians, like the Brodrick brothers, closely associated with the Whig Junto in England, who had long-standing grudges against him. His interest at court and with some ministers was enough to ensure that he was one of an inner group called upon by the King to 'devise a scheme for raising the money necessary in Ireland' before a parliamentary strategy was decided upon. But he needed friends in Dublin Castle, and when Capell's successors were eventually named in May 1697, a commission of three lords justices from England, Coningsby lost no time in worming his way into the confidence of the one he considered the most influential, Lord Winchester (Charles Powlett I*). At the same time he emerged as a spokesman for the 'Irish lobby' at Westminster, presumably with an eye to advancing his prestige in Ireland. At a meeting of 'the gentlemen of Ireland' in June 1697 to discuss possible responses to the proposed English legislation against the Irish woollen industry he advised strongly against proceeding by petition, saying

he verily believed that Ireland had in that House so few friends that such a petition, instead of preventing, would forward the bill, and that they had better take no notice at all of the matter, for that he was sure he could put off the reading the bill for that day, and afterwards their time of sitting would be so short that it must fall of course.

The bill did indeed fall, though what credit Coningsby could claim for its demise is not clear. The purposes of his machinations were twofold: to help him stave off further attacks in the Irish parliamentary session that began once the English Parliament was prorogued; and to obtain legislative confirmation in Ireland of his grant of forfeited lands. Old grievances were rehearsed briefly in August when the Irish parliament debated a bill to ratify the Treaty of Limerick, and Coningsby and Romney were criticized again in the same month when their patent to coin copper money in Ireland, granted some years previously, came under scrutiny. It was their deputy, Roger Moore, who was 'prosecuted against', but Coningsby was informed that the real motive of those who had raised the issue was to 'strike at your lordship's interest'. Then in October further remarks were passed concerning the favour Coningsby had allegedly shown to papists in 1690–2 over the selling of forfeited lands. Much more serious than these minor irritations was the prospect of opposition to the measures being proposed to safeguard his own grant, which had been his prime personal objective for some time. A general bill of attainder to confirm outlawries was supplemented, at Coningsby's insistence, by a private bill confirming the particular outlawries upon which his grant depended. He had already been promised Winchester's support, but made sure of it by assiduous solicitations for the passage of the Irish bills through the English Privy Council, which gratified the lords justices. He might also have hoped that the friendship he was endeavouring to forge with Charles Montagu, by collaborating on fiscal measures in Parliament and by 'taking care of' Montagu's Irish concerns, would have contributed to the muzzling of Irish Whig interests. But while no voice was raised against Coningsby's bill in the Irish privy council, where Winchester and his fellow lord justice, Lord Galway, presided, the Brodricks and their followers opposed him strongly in the Irish parliament, aided and abetted by the Tory faction led by the Duke of Ormond, and the bill was lost. Coningsby could reassure himself that at least the Treaty of Limerick had been ratified, in an amended form, which gave him some small security, but the potential remained for difficulties in the future. He therefore made some efforts to conciliate his Irish Whig enemies over the winter of 1697–8, using English as well as Irish contacts and evidently doing little to assist those Irish friends who appealed to him for protection against the Brodricks. There were rumblings of criticism against him in the Irish parliament in March 1698 for having stopped prosecutions for the seizure of forfeited estates, but by the following June, when another bill to confirm his grant was being contemplated, the attitude of the Brodrick brothers towards him had changed significantly. Alan Brodrick gave 'all the assurances he can give that he will in all things serve your lordship'.[17]

It may have been anxiety over the fate of his Irish bill and resentment at the behaviour of the Irish Whigs in the autumn of 1697 that led Coningsby to attend a meeting at the house of Lord Rochester (Laurence Hyde†) prior to the 1697–8 session of the English Parliament, at which Country Whigs like his cousin Hon. Henry Boyle* were to be found. However, he was also present at a subsequent ministerial conference and, as the session got under way, he settled into his customary round of duties as a Court manager. On the 7th he moved that the House go into committee the next day to consider only the supply and not the King's Speech as a whole, which was the opposition's preference. In his official capacity he laid before the House during this month various accounts of the arrears due to Irish regiments, and in the debate on the army on 10 Dec. he followed Ranelagh and Charles Montagu in unavailingly opposing the Country party motion to disband all the forces raised since 1680. When the struggle over disbandment was resumed after the Christmas recess he acted as a teller for a Court amendment to the instruction to the committee of supply relating to the army estimates, which would have omitted all reference to that earlier vote. On 16 Feb. 1698 he was sent by the Commons to know when the King could be waited upon, and much later in the session, on 29 June, reported William's answer to the address concerning the Londonderry garrison. He was twice a teller in divisions arising out of the inquiry into Exchequer bills: on 22 Feb., for the Court, against a motion condemning the receipt of bills by excise officers; and on 18 June, for leave for a clause to be added to a supply bill to permit the tellers of the Exchequer to accept bills in payment of taxes. Three of his speeches were on fiscal issues. In the debate on 8 Mar. on whether to reconsider the level of subsidies paid to the Allies, Coningsby proposed that a sixth of the sum agreed upon might be remitted as a sign of good faith, a suggestion that won support from Charles Montagu among others. On 13 Apr., in ways and means, he moved for 'a quarterly poll', and was seconded by Montagu – this being only a few days after the Treasury spokesmen had met together at the Cambridgeshire house of Lord Orford (Edward Russell*). Then, in the same committee, on 19 May, when the renewal of the sugar duty came under consideration, Coningsby answered opposition objections against reimposition by advancing the compromise solution of renewing for two years only. He continued his advocacy of Irish interests as the woollen bill was reintroduced. At the committal on 12 Feb. he argued strongly against the measure but made no impression. Surprisingly, perhaps, his other recorded speech in this session was in support of the blasphemy bill. With his rakish reputation, this expression of piety sounded strange to contemporaries, but it is worth remembering that Coningsby was a generous benefactor to the cause of the Huguenot refugees, a favourite charity of many 'reforming' MPs such as the Harleys, with whom Coningsby may still have wished to ingratiate himself for local reasons. At the end of the session he was included in two lists of placemen, and in August he succeeded finally in manoeuvring his erstwhile colleague Charles Fox out of the Irish paymastership, which he now had entirely to himself. Fox and his father, Sir Stephen*, were bitter at what they viewed as Coningsby's intrigues, which went back at least two years, Coningsby refusing to assist Fox in his difficulties in the office and simultaneously misrepresenting Fox's parliamentary conduct by 'treacherous insinuation'. Nor was this development popular with opinion in England generally: a parliamentary report the preceding January had revealed that in May 1697 Coningsby had received an addition to his vice-treasurer's salary of £1,000 a year 'in consideration of his good services', and many observers, including some who were themselves Court party men, felt it to be improper that he 'should be so insatiable as to have some new grant every session'. One common explanation was that 'this is given as a portion to his lady, and that it is to be the means of accommodating matters between the father[in-law] (Lord Ranelagh) and the son'. An alternative interpretation appeared in the autumn. Coningsby went over to Ireland in September 1698 to assist the Irish lords justices and lord chancellor, John Methuen*, with the management of the parliament there. A scheme was laid by Methuen, and it was said that Coningsby 'came into this counsel at last; and, that his agreeing to go over, and make it effectual, got him to be sole paymaster'.[18]

Coningsby had returned from Ireland before the 1698 Parliament opened. He had been re-elected at Leominster easily enough despite previous difficulties: the 'leather mob' at Hereford had again in 1697 expressed their disapproval of the support given to the leather duty by local MPs, and in October of that year

Coningsby had endured various 'slights' while canvassing in his borough. A comparative analysis of the old and new Parliaments classed him as a Court supporter, and on the first day of the session he stood as a teller for Sir Thomas Littleton, 3rd Bt.*, in the division on the Speakership. On 16 Dec. Coningsby laid before the House some official papers relating to the Irish army, as he did again on 11 Jan. 1699. He was less active than before in financial business, but made up for this by his prominence in Court party moves in defence of a standing army. The first occurred on 19 Dec., at the report of a resolution of the committee of supply that would have limited the army in Ireland to 12,000 men. A clarifying amendment was moved to declare that the number included officers, but William Cowper* noted that 'this was indiscreetly opposed by the paymaster of that army . . . who by that means had like to have renewed the debate and reduced that army to yet a lesser number, some beginning thereupon to debate if so many were necessary'. Despite Coningsby's efforts, the amendment passed. The struggle then centred on the disbanding bill. On 22 Dec. the second reading was adjourned for a day 'on motion of Lord Coningsby and [Charles] Montagu, with design as believed to get time to solicit against it'. He then spoke against committal, arguing the ministerial line that in the event of an invasion the kingdom would be left 'without remedy'. King James would not be prevented from returning 'if he hath a mind'. During Christmas Coningsby participated in a conclave of Court politicians presided over by Lord Chancellor Somers (Sir John*) at which the prospects for retaining a substantial standing force were ventilated, and tactics settled. One outcome of this meeting was the motion of 4 Jan. 1699 for an instruction to the committee on the disbanding bill to increase the numbers retained, to which Coningsby spoke. He also intervened twice in the crucial debate of 18 Jan. at the bill's third reading, first to reiterate the usual comment that disbandment would 'expose us to slavery by lessening our security', and later, when a rider was proposed by a ministerialist to exempt the Dutch guards,

> which probably would have been complied with by the House, but Lord Coningsby beginning to express himself against the bill itself, and being heard with more quiet and attention than had been usual for the House to give to such as before spoke against the provision of the bill, it encouraged him and others to debate at large against the bill.

His name was of course included in the black list of those who had voted for a standing army. He spoke twice for the Court in the committee of supply, on 3 Feb. and 2 Mar., and in the committee of inquiry into naval mismanagements on 10 Mar. he sprang to the defence of Lord Orford and the Navy Board. Opposition to the East India bill, against which he was a teller on 9 Mar. 1699, was another political stance dictated for him by his involvement with the Court. The same could not be said of his support for the immorality bill, which many courtiers opposed but which was of a piece with his backing for the previous year's blasphemy bill; unless it was part of a tactical move to dissociate the ministry from opposition to the bill. On issues relating to Ireland he was certainly at greater liberty. Busy again in the 'Irish lobby', he presented on 4 Apr. 1699 a bill to take off the duty on Irish linen imported into England, as a compensation for the textile industry in Ireland should the woollen bill pass, a measure against which he also 'laboured' hard. The fact that two of his daughters either had married or were about to marry Anglo-Irish squires with property in woollen-manufacturing districts gave him something of a personal interest in the subject, besides his general concern to cultivate some influence in Irish political circles and, it may be conjectured, a role for himself in English politics as an expert on Irish affairs.[19]

Ireland, however, remained Coningsby's Achilles' heel where the question of the forfeited estates was concerned. The matter had been brought up again, this time at Westminster, with the appointment of a parliamentary commission of inquiry; the report of this commission was submitted in December 1699, and the tremulous Coningsby found that not only was his own grant detailed, together with the fact that he had recently sold the property, but that he and Romney were accused of receiving goods during their governorship for which they had not accounted. To draw the sting from possible criticism, Coningsby spoke up in favour of a bill of resumption when the Commons considered the report, on 15 Dec. A subsequent motion, on 13 Jan. 1700, that the report be printed, touched a tender spot: he appeared 'very pathetic in their expostulations, not to be proclaimed criminals . . . upon false suggestions'. At the committal of the resumption bill, on 18 Jan., he supported a motion that a third of the forfeited lands still be reserved to the King's disposal. He was doubtless encouraged by the thought that this stand would be gratifying to William, and in his speech 'said the King had ventured and exposed himself for the reducing of Ireland, and repeated the history of Ireland'. Even so, his remarks were observed by the Prussian resident to be noticeably muted, except when it came to protesting that neither he himself nor any other of the grantees had broken a law by receiving the properties in question. He became a little bolder as the opposition increased the vehemence of its attack. On 13 Feb., the day after the House had been informed of grants of forfeited estates in England, including those he had himself received, he acted as a teller against the motion, chiefly aimed at Somers, condemning those ministers concerned in procuring grants for themselves. Then on 26 Feb., when the King's answer to the Commons' address over the Irish forfeitures was reported, and opposition Members protested that those who had advised William as to his response were guilty of 'endeavouring to create a misunderstanding' between King and people, Coningsby reverted to his previous timidity, denying that, as a Privy Councillor, he had taken any part in the advice. This drew the observation that all Councillors would now have to 'make their confessions'. Coningsby had been classified as a placeman in a list of the interest-groups in the House compiled early in 1700, and several of his contributions to debates show him continuing to support the Court on financial business. On 31 Jan. he joined other ministerial spokesmen in opposing a resolution of the committee of ways and means for a duty on imported East India stuffs, and on 24 Mar., when the deficiencies of funds were being considered, he supported Ranelagh and Montagu in the proposition to dock half-pay officers a quarter of their salaries to make up the shortfall, a speech which may have led to an incident shortly afterwards in which he was insulted by a half-pay officer in the court of requests. Challenged to a duel, Coningsby refused to give satisfaction and instead complained of a breach of privilege. The aggrieved officer was not the only person to be angered by Coningsby's manner of discharging his official responsibilities. In common with other office-holders he proved deliberately unco-operative when called upon by the commissioners for taking army accounts. In the House his remaining tellership this session was in a party cause, on 14 Dec. 1699 in favour of Charles Montagu's brother, Irby Montagu*, in the disputed election for Maldon.[20]

In his 'History of Parties', presented to King George I after the Hanoverian succession, Coningsby described the circumstances leading up to the ministerial reconstruction late in 1700. It was, he said, the consequence of a deep-laid plot by 'the Jacobite interest' in the Commons, who by 'cramping the public credit' had prolonged the Nine Years War and thus made the Junto Whig ministry unpopular in the country. The Tory party having attained a majority in Parliament, King William was forced to 'throw himself into the Tories' hands'. Possibly Coningsby believed this at the time. But, scenting a change in the wind, he also sought to rebuild his relations with leading Tories, notably Godolphin, with whom he renewed an amicable correspondence as early as the summer of 1700. Hon. James Brydges*, visiting the Duke of Marlborough (John Churchill†) on 31 Oct. 1700, found Marlborough in the company of Godolphin, Henry Guy* and Coningsby. A correspondence was also renewed with Rochester. Robert Harley was another important figure for Coningsby to conciliate, and he seems to have tried to do so. But electoral politics in Herefordshire made for difficulties. Coningsby had entered into an alliance there with Henry Cornewall*, a maverick local Tory, to challenge established Tory interests in the county and at Weobley. He was even accused of trying to secure for himself a monopoly over the parliamentary representation of the county. The alliance with Cornewall brought Coningsby into conflict with the Harleys whether or not he himself wished it. In fact, both Coningsby and Harley professed to want no more than the peace and quiet of the county and a consensual choice of candidates by 'gentlemen'. Coningsby's real motives may have been different. He claimed that he would have preferred to assist Harley's brother Edward in the three-cornered contest that arose at Leominster and involved Coningsby himself, Edward Harley and another Whig, John Dutton Colt*. It was only Cornewall's connexion with Colt, and his own engagement to remain neutral, that prevented him; or so he said. But Coningsby's attitude to the Harleys was always ambivalent, and envy was never far from his mind. He may have relished the chance to see Edward dished at Leominster while taking advantage of Robert Harley's evident detachment from local political struggles to make himself the arbiter of Herefordshire elections. At any rate, the apologies and forced cordiality between the two men that followed the January 1701 election rang hollow, as in 1690. When the Parliament met, Coningsby was moderately active. He presented the Irish army accounts to the House on 28 Mar., while the first speech attributed to him in this Parliament was on 15 Apr., at the report of the Partition Treaty address. An amendment was proposed to declare Members' readiness to support King William's government against all its enemies, at home and abroad. Coningsby 'would have the words insisted' but feared what would happen if the amendment was put and not carried – 'it might be a thing of dangerous consequence to England' – so himself moved the previous question. A week later, when the subject of Exchequer bills was under discussion, he protested at the irregularity of a motion made by John

Grobham Howe for going immediately upon ways and means. As befitted one who still held an important office, his approach to important political questions was careful and moderate, and calculated to appeal to the sentiments of the King. On 5 May he spoke against a proposal to appropriate part of the civil list for public expenditure. Recalling an earlier theme, and professing the greatest concern for the fate of William's foreign policy, he stressed that 'it would sound ill abroad' to seem to show disrespect to the King. He was therefore happy to be able to join Robert Harley and other Court Tories in endorsing the compromise proposal put forward by Sir Edward Seymour, to preserve the civil list funds and underwrite them by anticipating future taxation. He was still the object of High Tory animosity, as was shown by yet another reference in a debate on 30 May to the affair of Gaffney. On this occasion Coningsby was fortunate that the baiting was done by the notorious eccentric Sir John Bolles, 4th Bt.*, possibly one of the few Members against whom Coningsby could be confident of scoring a point, as indeed he did, if somewhat clumsily, noting that 'Bolles might do anything in any place safely, for he always carried his privilege about him'. However, the impeachments controversy in this Parliament placed Coningsby in a delicate situation, given his partisan identification and his close association with the old ministry. When on 4 June he spoke against sending a message to the Lords and in favour of continuing with conferences in the usual manner, he felt himself obliged to say that he was 'as much for the honour and dignity of the House as anybody'. The skill with which he performed his balancing act is evident from his absence from any of the electoral 'white' or 'black' lists published at around this time, and Robert Harley's inability to classify him with the Whigs or the Tories in his analysis of the Members returned at the second general election of 1701. Sunderland, however, had accurately judged Coningsby's shift of position. The Earl's considered opinion in the aftermath of the 1701 Parliament was that the King should turn back to the Whigs, but he added that William 'would do well to propose none of this to . . . Coningsby'. In the November election Coningsby would seem to have done nothing to harm the Harleys, and was returned at Leominster with Edward Harley. In Parliament the abjuration bill drew Coningsby's particular interest: he clashed with the Tory Hon. Heneage Finch I* in a debate on the bill on 9 Feb. During their exchange Coningsby observed that 'the bill looked as if it was made in another place [and] fitted for the humour and palate of those that could not digest the abjuration oath'. Another Tory Member vainly called for him to be brought to the bar, but the quarrel was made up. He was a teller once, in a party matter, over the East Retford election on 17 Mar., where he supported the Whig candidates, and himself introduced two bills: the routine bill to raise the militia (31 Mar.), and a bill for the relief of Sir Redmond Everard, 4th Bt., a convert from Catholicism and the scion of an Irish Jacobite family, whose cause he may have taken up as a favour to the Duke of Ormond, or the then viceroy of Ireland, Rochester. His two remaining speeches show him abetting the Court. Both occurred on 2 May, over the Queen's message concerning the declaration of war; and in the second of them he moved an amendment to the address against foreign officers, to exempt from objection those on half-pay.[21]

Coningsby's memoirs depict Queen Anne's first ministry as entirely dominated by the Tories, and thus, as far as he was concerned, intolerable. In fact, he was able to work with the Godolphin–Marlborough administration from the very first, even while it was predominantly Tory in complexion. He based himself on his close personal relationship with Lord Treasurer Godolphin, and his burgeoning friendship with the Duke of Marlborough, whose favour he courted in a succession of flattering letters. He also tried to force a friendship with Robert Harley, though predictably with less success. As early as November 1702 he had been admitted to the small circle of parliamentary managers to whom Godolphin looked 'to adjust what shall be opened to the House'. On 7 Dec. Coningsby acted on behalf of the ministry, and more particularly on behalf of his father-in-law, when he told for the adjournment of a debate on Ranelagh's accounts, in order to forestall a motion of censure against him. For some reason he quarrelled bitterly in the House on 15 Jan. 1703 with the Tory Henry Fleming* and the two men had to be prevailed upon not to pursue their quarrel outside. The dispute may have arisen from a debate on Coningsby's motion to add to a supply bill a clause to remove customs duty on imported linen yarn and thread from Ireland. Fleming, as a west-country Member, could well have taken part in the political conflicts over the Irish weaving industries. In the division of 13 Feb. 1703 regarding the Lords' amendments to the bill for enlarging the time to take the oath of abjuration, Coningsby again differed from the Tories by voting for the amendments. But when he went over to Ireland in April 1703 it was to assist the new Tory viceroy, Ormond. Admittedly, his real purpose was to curry favour with the 'duumvirs'. He wrote to Marlborough, 'I hope I may be serviceable to her Majesty's affairs in that kingdom, and thereby to show your Grace I will always endeavour to deserve that favour and protection I have received from you.' To Robert Harley he declared he would follow advice given him by Harley's father 'when I came first into this country, not to forget I was an Englishman'. He stayed for the early stages of the Irish parliamentary session, supporting the Court interest there and suffering 'ill usage' from Ormond's Whig opponents, before hastening back for the opening of the English session. Back at Westminster, he did what he could to solicit the passage of Irish bills through the Privy Council, and was an especially vehement advocate of the notorious 'bill to prevent the further growth of popery'. His contribution to the 1703–4 session of the English Parliament was unusually small, with no tellerships, and only one private bill that he himself brought in on 5 Jan. 1704.[22]

The removal of the High Tory element from the administration in early 1704 made the atmosphere of government rather more congenial to Coningsby. He reappeared as a leading Court spokesman in the Commons in the 1704–5 session. Forecast as a probable opponent of the Tack, he was employed by Robert Harley to canvass Members, and not only voted but acted as a teller for the Court in the crucial division on 28 Nov. Privately he described the Tack as 'a most desperate attempt of an angry squadron'. He was a teller against passing the place bill on 27 Jan. 1705, and brought in the bill for raising the militia on 1 Feb., before succumbing to ill-health – 'a violent defluxion of his eye' – and absenting himself from the House in March as a result. A supporter of the bill to promote the linen industry in Ireland, he had earlier taken the chair of the committee on a private bill on behalf of various Protestant Irish landowners, and had done his best to ease the passage through the Privy Council of legislation from the Irish parliament. He remained on good terms with the Duke of Ormond and advised on the conduct of the second parliamentary session in Ireland, in 1705. In England the general election of May 1705 saw him re-elected at the top of the poll in Leominster, apparently for once co-operating effectively with the Harleys in Herefordshire. Lists of the new Parliament classed him as a placeman and as 'Low Church'. His own view of the prospects that the election result opened up was conveyed in a letter to the Duke of Marlborough. 'This is such a Parliament', he wrote,

> as all that truly love the Queen and her government in our present circumstances would wish for. Neither party can pretend to govern the House, by which means it will naturally follow that the Queen's servants may, with right management, be able not only to prevent the mischiefs designed by the angry Tories, but to lead the Whigs in carrying on the public business, and there is a very comfortable difference between having the Queen's interest at the head of a party and being obliged to follow it.

This was precisely the political analysis being expounded by Robert Harley, though Coningsby saw the practical implications somewhat differently. He began the 1705–6 session by voting on 25 Oct. for the Court candidate as Speaker, and was a teller on 24 Nov. for the courtier Henry Killigrew* in the St. Albans election case. Grey Neville* recorded numerous speeches by him. On 4 Dec. he spoke on the bill to repeal the Alien Act and then argued against the 'Hanover motion' as 'a disrespect' to Queen Anne. He intervened three times on 8 Dec. over the Lords' resolution condemning those who declared the Church of England to be 'in danger'. Strongly supporting the resolution, he observed that 'pulpits were the greatest danger to incite the people', and that the only purpose of the occasional conformity bills had been to 'garble elections'. Responding to remarks by Hon. Arthur Annesley*, he went on to justify the continuance of the *regium donum*, the annual pension paid to Presbyterian ministers in Ulster. Having acted to protect the lord treasurer from being exposed during a debate on the regency bill on 19 Dec., when the Tory firebrand Charles Caesar* spoke of the Jacobite contacts of a 'certain lord' and some cried for the peer to be named, Coningsby spoke several times to the bill in its later stages. Most notably he supported on 10 Jan. 1706 the clause that imposed the penalties of praemunire on anyone who 'by preaching, teaching or advised speaking' cast aspersions upon the legitimacy of the Queen's rule; and on 12 Jan. he opposed the motion to insert clauses to safeguard the provisions of the Act of Settlement, in particular the 'place clause'. On 21 Jan. the 'place clause' was debated at length, and three speeches of Coningsby are recorded, all of which were against it, chiefly because the contentions the clause provoked were delaying what was a vital measure. On 18 Feb. he voted, on the Court side, against the clause. In the following session he was the Member who, on 28 Jan. 1707, laid before the House the Articles of Union with Scotland. Later, on 11 Feb., he was nominated to the committee to prepare the bill of Union, and argued strongly for its acceptance. When a proposal was made to prevent the re-importation from Scotland after the Union of wine previously exported from England, he rounded on the Member concerned and barked out, 'What? Are you mad? You will destroy the Union. You had as good throw it out of the window as move any such thing.' Evidently as a favour to Shrewsbury, he supported the bill for preserving the salt springs at Droitwich, speaking on 6 Mar. to 'expose' the irregular proceedings of the petitioners against the bill. He was a teller on 10 Mar. for the bill for the better preservation of game. Otherwise his significant parliamentary activity concerned Irish business. It was reported to Archbishop King of Dublin in January 1707 that Coningsby was full of good intentions towards the Church of Ireland, and that he was of opinion a bill should be brought into the English Parliament 'to quieten church livings' there. On 18 Feb. Coningsby presented a measure to make more effectual the Acts for appropriating forfeited impropriations in Ireland to the building of churches and the augmentations of small vicarages. A week earlier he and Francis Annesley* had successfully moved for a private bill on Archbishop King's behalf. Then on 27 Mar. Coningsby was a teller with Robert Molesworth* to enable the committee on the salt duties bill to receive a clause to explain 'some doubts' relating to the re-exportation to England of Portuguese and Spanish wines imported into Ireland. With a change of lord lieutenant in Ireland in 1707, and the appointment there of the Court Whig Lord Pembroke (Thomas Herbert†), Coningsby had seen the opportunity to set himself up as the ministry's principal adviser on Irish affairs. He travelled to Dublin with Pembroke in the summer of 1707 and tried to act as a broker between the viceroy and the leading Irish politicians, though no one there really trusted him.[23]

The turn of political events in the winter of 1707–8 raised Coningsby to prominence in the Commons as one of that group of 'Lord Treasurer's Whigs', or as he himself put it 'the moderate Whigs', who worked to 'carry on the public business . . . in opposition to the wild embroilments attempted by the Junto, and the open opposition given by the Jacobite faction'. Until the fall of Robert Harley in February 1708 the 'Lord Treasurer's Whigs' were allied to Harley's faction of Court Tories, but always kept a distance from them. Coningsby in particular was regarded as 'a mere creature of lord t[reasure]r, and what he said in the House of Commons was always looked upon as the sense of lord t[reasure]r'. His name appeared in a list of Court party managers sent to Harley in October 1707. A teller on 17 Nov. against giving leave for a bill to repeal the Game Act, Coningsby presented to the House on the following day an account of the pensions paid on the Irish establishment. In a committee on 4 Dec. he opposed the motion, put forward by the Squadrone and backed by the Junto, that j.p.s in Scotland be invested with the same powers as their counterparts in England. Coningsby moved an amendment, in the words 'as far as was consistent with the twentieth article of the treaty, which is very express for preserving all heritable rights and jurisdictions as they were at the time of framing the treaty'. His argument was simply that the original motion contravened the Union. If the proposal was to be accepted in any form, he suggested it might be added to the bill to repeal the Scottish acts of security and anent peace and war. Subsequently he acted as a teller on 12 Dec. against entrusting the repeal bill to a committee of the whole. He was also a teller the same day on the Court side for an amendment to the land tax bill. When the political storm broke over the inquiry into the conduct of the war in Spain, Coningsby was to the fore. With another 'Lord Treasurer's Whig', Robert Walpole II*, he served as a teller on 29 Jan. 1708 in favour of adjourning debate. Then on 18 and 23 Feb. it was Coningsby who reported the Queen's answer to Commons' addresses on the disparity between the number of troops paid for and the number actually present at the battle of Almanza. In the immediate aftermath of the Harleyites' loss of office (for which, in later years, he unconvincingly claimed responsibility himself), he was highly active in support of the ministry. He acted as a teller on 22 Mar. against giving a second reading to the bill to prevent the importation of woollen and worsted yarn. However a bout of ill-health, apparently eye trouble again, kept him out of public notice for much of the remainder of the session. In the delicate political circumstances of the time it is not inconceivable that this outbreak was diplomatic in origin.[24]

Coningsby was still described as a Whig *tout court* in parliamentary lists compiled in early 1708, but he was now generally recognized as a Court Whig. Like other 'Lord Treasurer's Whigs', he was uneasy at his estrangement from the Junto lords, since it was increasingly likely that they would come to dominate the administration. Instinct for self-preservation led him to reopen lines of communication. In October 1708, for example, he and the 3rd Earl of Sunderland (Charles, Lord Spencer*) 'dined . . . at Pontacks with their City friends'. There 'they took Lille and raised six millions in a trice without the assistance of any but their own party', as Coningsby 'declared . . . in all the public places, adding that lord treasurer had promised to drop the Duke of Queensberry, and to surrender himself up entirely to the sage advices of the Junto'. More significantly, Coningsby tried to identify himself with the latest change of policy in Ireland, where Junto pressure brought about the replacement of Pembroke by Lord Wharton (Hon. Thomas*) in December 1708. Turning with the prevailing wind, Coningsby, who had once argued strongly against Wharton's appointment, now submitted to the ministers a paper critical of Pembroke's management, and sought to ingratiate himself with Pembroke's successor, offering his services as an intermediary between Wharton and the Irish Whig politicians. As before, however, neither viceroy nor Irish 'undertakers' would trust him. Indeed, in the early stages of Wharton's lord lieutenancy in the spring of 1709, Coningsby complained that he was disregarded, and he may even have been threatened with the loss of his paymastership. It was only when Wharton needed his good offices with the 'duumvirs' to prevent interference with Irish appointments or with Irish legislation that friendly relations were established, but this was never more than a cynical collusion of mutual vested interests. In a way that he cannot fully have intended, Coningsby had come to be dependent upon Godolphin and Marlborough, whom he had been cultivating for many years and more recently had been plying with advice on political strategy in England, the burden of which was to continue with 'steady management', not to 'gratify' the Whigs in their 'designs' and to lead 'the party' rather than being led by it. With other 'Lord Treasurer's Whigs' he kept close to Godolphin during the 1708–9 session. He opposed the Scottish treason trials bill, on the grounds that 'no traitor could now forfeit either life or estate', and moved an amendment 'for attainting the Pretender in Scotland as he is already in England'. In the debate, probably on 10 Mar. 1709, over the attempted invasion of the preceding year he made an odd intervention. George Lockhart* reported:

> I must observe what fell from . . . Lord Coningsby . . . who spoke last. Everybody knows he's a person of great capacity, and so much confided in by the ministry that without doubt he must be thoroughly acquainted with the inclinations and temper of her Majesty's subjects in all her dominions, and since his lordship was pleased to assert that there were ten times more disaffected persons in Ireland than Scotland, I am ready to believe it.

He evidently assisted the Court over the recruiting bill, and proved his party loyalties by supporting the naturalization of the Palatines and by opposing (Sir) Simon Harcourt I* in the bitterly contested election dispute at Abingdon, which led to 'very high words' with Robert Harley. During the summer he took part in various intrigues set on foot between Godolphin and Marlborough and individual Junto lords, with a view to dividing the Junto and thus holding them in check. He himself believed that 'there was no confidence between any two of them but my Lord President [Somers] and my Lord Sunderland'. Later, in a letter to Marlborough, he recalled a meeting with Godolphin, the Duke and Duchess, at which

> it was considered how the majority we then held in the House of Commons could be best maintained, considering the different views the leaders of the two sorts of Whigs which made the majority had at that time, and which I [?presumed] to [?affirm] from the observations I had made . . . to be so precarious that it was not possible it should through the continuance of that Parliament [?hold] unless some [?breach] were made upon the best sort of Tories, which, as it lessened . . . that party so by adding to those Whigs which had listed under your grace and my lord treasurer would have kept the Junto and their small party . . . in awe. But my lord treasurer replied such a method would create jealousy to the lords with whom we had then joined and there was no way but to go on in conjunction with them.

The appointment of Orford to the Admiralty commission in November 1709 reunited the Junto, however, and accelerated the drift of 'Lord Treasurer's Whigs' back to their ranks. Coningsby at this stage resurrected the notion of a 'middle scheme' in order to 'recover this near-lost game' and in some desperation urged Marlborough that 'my lord treasurer must be prevailed upon not to prefer any of their [the Junto] wretched dependents preferable [sic] to the other Whigs that opposed them'. But in the absence of any such initiative, although he continued to give Godolphin his counsel, he was himself obliged to act in Parliament with the Junto Whigs. In the impeachment of Dr Sacheverell, the action which would certainly have wrecked any 'middle scheme', he secured for himself a leading part. On 13 Dec. he supported the motion to condemn Sacheverell's sermons, and on the 14th, when the impeachment was moved, proposed calling in the doctor and his publisher. On 11 Jan. he told against a Tory motion to recommit the report of the committee for drawing up the articles. At the trial he was given the easiest article to speak to, as he himself admitted, somewhat ingenuously; that is to say, the third article, that Sacheverell had 'falsely' and 'maliciously' asserted the Church to be in danger under Queen Anne's government. One Whig propagandist claimed that he had 'discharged his part with skill and fidelity', but evidently found his speech so unmemorable that none of it was quoted. A more acerbic commentator, biased against him, wrote that Coningsby

> spoke so indifferently, and seemed to have taken so little pains, that some of his friends said he spoke like one that expected a change of affairs. He said the doctor's answer was from beginning to end one false and malicious misrepresentation of everything, and that he endeavoured to draw a scheme of a church as tyrannical as his state.

During the trial Coningsby found himself once more the butt of an opponent's wit, when 'with great passion' he declared in conversation that '"I was always against the father and will be against the son" (meaning the Pretender)' only to be answered, '"Aye, my lord, and against the Holy Ghost too"'. Naturally, he was blacklisted as having voted for Sacheverell's impeachment. Meanwhile, he had told on 15 Feb. 1710 in favour of a motion for an address that Marlborough be sent over to attend the peace negotiations. He also presented, on 18 Feb., a turnpike bill for his neighbouring county of Gloucester.[25]

The high political manoeuvres of the summer and autumn of 1710 saw Coningsby allying himself rather more closely with Marlborough, whom he may have regarded as indispensable to any new ministry, than with Godolphin, who appeared certain to fall victim to Robert Harley's ministerial coup. His memoirs claim that at one point he had alerted Marlborough to an intrigue Godolphin had begun with the Tories, which would have sacrificed the captain-general, and that he subsequently acted the role of a messenger between the 'duumvirs'. However, no part of this story is borne out by strictly contemporary evidence. As far as Harley was concerned, Coningsby was a marked man, despite, or perhaps because of, their old acquaintance. On 7 July 1710 he received notice of dismissal from his Irish offices. Godolphin expressed his sorrow for 'poor Lord Coningsby, who has never done one single act since the Queen came to the crown, but with the greatest duty imaginable', adding, 'he seems to think some great lie has been told of him'. The Earl of Mar, on the other hand, noting that the vice-treasurership in particular was worth some £7,000 p.a., observed that Coningsby's 'character . . . was none of the best with all sides, everybody knowing him to be a knave', and a similar judgment came from one of the Irish Whigs with whom he had frequently crossed swords in the past. It is not clear whether Coningsby was ever involved in any of the negotiations between Harley, Godolphin and several of the 'Lord Treasurer's Whigs', but if he did figure briefly in them his participation ended when, in an interview with the Queen, he allegedly

> laid before her the inevitable dangers that must attend her making any . . . change in her ministry (till after a peace with France) to the credit of the nation; to herself, with regard to her civil list; and even to the safety of her person and government, and the whole Protestant interest of the world.

Her anger was predictable, and closed off Coningsby's prospects for rehabilitation. To the dismay of Godolphin and many Whigs, he announced that he would not seek re-election in 1710. Several other Members who had also been among the managers of Dr Sacheverell's impeachment reached the same decision, but although fear of a popular reaction against them on this score may have been an inhibiting factor, it is perhaps more significant that all were former 'Lord Treasurer's Whigs' experiencing a common disillusionment with party politics. Coningsby, in particular, seems to have devoted the last four years of Anne's reign to the improvement of his estate at Hampton Court, Herefordshire, in which he was able to invest substantially. He continued to cultivate the Marlboroughs, and even sought to resume his once cordial relations with Ormond, now reappointed Irish lord lieutenant. A letter to Ormond's chief secretary in March 1711 urged the recipient to 'let my lord duke know that I ever was to him a faithful servant'. To the Harleys, however, he remained bitterly antagonistic, opposing their interest in Herefordshire constituencies even though he was not standing himself. After the Hanoverian succession he reappeared on the national stage as one of the most vindictive critics of the outgoing Tory ministers, and especially of Robert Harley, now Earl of Oxford, in whose impeachment Coningsby was a prime mover. He referred to the Harleys as 'the authors of all our miseries'. Returned again for Leominster as a Whig in the 1715 general election, he sat in the Commons for a little over a year before being raised to the British peerage.[26]

Coningsby's later years were darkened by the failure of his various vendettas and by a plethora of troublesome lawsuits. He even spent some time in the Tower in 1720–1 for 'reflections' made upon the lord chancellor in connexion with litigation over the manor of Marden in Herefordshire, where he had convinced himself that his rights as lord had been infringed by the copyhold tenants. In his own justification he collected and published a set of documents concerning the history of the manor, made up into a large, disorganized and tedious volume. His political utterances, ever more violently Whiggish, were on occasion so wild as to suggest a degeneration in his mental powers, an impression that his vain resolve to court the widowed Duchess of Marlborough does not do a great deal to dispel, for all her vast riches. Coningsby died at Hampton Court on 1 May 1729, and was buried at the nearby church of Hope-under-Dinsmore. Of his three titles, the Irish peerage was inherited by a grandson of his first marriage; the British barony, from which the descendants of his first wife had been debarred, and which was confined to the male heirs of subsequent unions, became extinct; but the earldom went, through a special remainder, to his elder daughter by his second wife, who had already been created Viscountess Coningsby in her own right, and now succeeded him as Countess of Coningsby.[27]

[1] PRO NI, De Ros mss D638/55/11, Henry Boyle to Coningsby, 11 Aug. 1711; C. J. Robinson, *Mansions and Manors of Herefs.* 148–9. [2] *Cal. Treas. Bks.* ix. 110, 684; xxv. 321; xxix. 161; *Liber Munerum Publicorum Hiberniae* ed. Lascelles, i(2), p. 47; A. B. Beaven's list of Irish PCs, Hist. of Parl.; SP 63/362/10, 69; Japikse, *Correspondentie,* ii. 55; *Cal. Treas. Pprs.* 1697–1702, pp. 550–1. [3] *Arch. Camb.* (ser. 3), iii. 189. [4] *CJ,* xii. 508; A. Savidge, *Foundation and Early Years of Q. Anne's Bounty,* 124. [5] *CJ,* xi. 652, 654–5. [6] Add. 47128, f. 53; Robinson, 147. [7] Add. 70252, James Powle to Robert Harley*, 23 Feb. 1689[–90]; 70064, Coningsby to Sir Edward Harley, 9 Mar., 7 Nov. 1690, Sir Edward Harley to Coningsby, 11 Dec. 1690; 70233, same to Robert Harley, 18 Nov. 1690; *HMC Portland,* iii. 443, 446; v. 645. [8] Bodl. Rawl. A.279, ff. 82, 88; Grey, x. 57, 141; *Bull IHR,* lii. 43. [9] Add. 70270, Robert to Elizabeth Harley, 29 May 1690; 30149, passim; Macaulay, *Hist. Eng.* iv. 1876, 2068–9; Trinity, Dublin, Clarke mss 749/13/1266, William Robinson to George Clarke*, 17 Oct. 1691; Trinity, Dublin, Lyons (King) coll. 2008a/190, Bp. King to James Bonnell, 4 Dec. 1691; S. B. Baxter, *Wm. III,* 277–8; Nottingham Univ. Lib. Portland (Bentinck) mss PwA 299b, Coningsby and Sydney to Portland, 27 Sept. 1690; De Ros mss D638/6/8, 14, Ranelagh to Coningsby, 27 Oct. 1690, 17 Sept. 1692; D638/11, Ld. Nottingham (Daniel Finch[†]) to lds. justices [I], 25 Nov. 1690–30 July 1692; D638/12, Ld. Athlone to same, 2 Dec. 1690–20 Oct. 1692; D638/14, Sydney to same, 24 Jan. 1691–13 Dec. 1692; Bodl. Carte 130, f. 324; *CSP Dom.* 1697, pp. 269–70; 1695, p. 167; J. G. Simms, *Jacobite Ire.* 188–9, 193, 212–14; J. G. Simms, *Williamite Confiscation in Ire.* 56, 58; Luttrell, *Brief Relation,* ii. 381; *HMC Lords,* n.s. iv. 46, 52. [10] *CSP Dom.* 1695, pp. 210, 220; *HMC Leyborne-Popham,* 280–1; *Penal Era and Golden Age* ed. Bartlett and Hayton, 10–23; Luttrell, ii. 617–18; Grey, x. 251–2, 304; *Luttrell Diary,* 237, 248, 254, 260, 268, 282, 289, 317, 393, 401, 406, 414; Add. 70017, ff. 5, 22; 70114, Paul Foley I* to Sir Edward Harley, 10 Jan. 1692[–3]; 70235, Sir Edward to Robert Harley, 14 Jan. 1692[–3]; 70126, Ferdinando Gorges to Sir Edward Harley, 17 Jan. 1692[–3]; Burnet, *Supp.* ed. Foxcroft, 352; *Hatton Corresp.* (Cam. Soc. n.s. xxiii), 187–8; Bodl. Tanner 25, f. 7. [11] *HMC Portland,* iii. 476, 482, 511, 534, 539, 542; viii. 35, 37; De Ros mss D638/13/112, John Pulteney* to Coningsby, 13 Feb. 1692; D638/18/11, [?Francis Gwyn*] to same, 24 June 1693; D638/27/1, John Edgworth to same, [c.Aug. 1693]; *Luttrell Diary,* 237, 439–40, 446; Portland (Bentinck) mss PwA 2385, notes on debate, 23 Nov. [1692]; *Penal Era and Golden Age,* 23–27; H. Horwitz, *Parl. and Pol. Wm. III,* 111; *HMC 7th Rep.* 220; Macaulay, iv. 2033; *Gallienus Redivivus . . .* (1695), pp. 14–16; Huntington Lib. Ellesmere mss EL9918, 9985; Carte 130, f. 345; Ranke, vi. 214; Tanner 25, ff. 33, 58; Egerton 2540, f. 56; *EHR,* lxxi. 583; Luttrell, iii. 121, 123, 153, 164; Add. 70064, 70264, 70278, drafts of answer by Bellomont and Hamilton to PC, [17 Aug. 1693]; 70017, ff. 149, 157; *CSP Dom.* 1693, p. 295. [12] De Ros mss D638/18/14, Porter to Coningsby, 22 Aug. 1693; D638/27/3, John Edgworth to same, 2 June [1694]; Grey, x. 364–5, 368; Add. 17677 OO, f. 160; Nat. Archs. Ire. Wyche mss 1/103, Sir William Russell[†] to Sir Cyril Wyche*, 23 Jan. 1693[–4]; Luttrell, iii. 279, 310; *CSP Dom.* 1694–5, pp. 115, 134. [13] *EHR,* lxxviii. 102; Horwitz, 200; *CSP Dom.* 1694–5, pp. 307, 310, 362; *HMC Buccleuch,* ii. 145–6, 153; Japikse, ii. 44; *HMC Portland,* iii. 557. [14] Add. 70017, f. 337; Ranke, vi. 249; *HMC Portland,* iii. 559; Carte 76, f. 531; 130, f. 355; *Cal. Treas. Bks.* x. 996, 1031–2, 1102–3. [15] Add. 70118, Edward to Sir Edward Harley, 19 Jan. 1693[–4]; 70017, f. 234; 70257, Henry Seward to Robert Harley, 31 Dec. 1695; 70235, Sir Edward Harley to same, 18 June 1694; 70018, f. 35; Folger Shakespeare Lib. Newdigate newsletter 1 Oct. 1695; Carte 239, f. 71; 130, f. 359; 79, f. 663; Luttrell, iii. 532; *CSP Dom.* 1696, pp. 79, 182; *Acct. of Procs. in House of Commons, in Relation to Recoining . . .* (1696), p. 9; *HMC Hastings,* ii. 253; *Shrewsbury Corresp.* 117; *HMC Buccleuch,* ii. 229, 235, 361; Portland (Bentinck) mss PwA 2522, Portland to the King, 29 May 1696; PwA 240, 246, 252, Capell to Portland, 27 May, 28 Sept., 6 Nov. 1695; *HMC Portland,* iii. 569–70; Wyche mss 1/136, bp. of Kildare to Wyche, 28 Sept. 1695; *HMC Downshire,* i. 574; De Ros mss D638/18/18, 39, 41–42, 48, 52, 56, 56–57, Porter to Coningsby, 15 Jan., 17, 27 Feb., 11 Mar., 15 May, 8, 24 Oct., 1, 9 Nov. 1695; Japikse, ii. 49, 55; Surr. RO (Guildford), Midleton mss 1248/1, ff. 274, 278–9, Alan to St. John Brodrick, 21 Sept., 17 Dec. 1695. [16] BN, Renaudot mss NAF 7487, f. 337; Add. 70113, Coningsby to Sir Edward Harley, 22 Sept. 1696; *Vernon–Shrewsbury Letters,* i. 20–21, 49, 64, 110; Northants. RO, Montagu (Boughton) mss 46/13, 24, Vernon to Shrewsbury, 29 Oct., 19 Nov. 1696; Macaulay, vi. 2662; Cobbett, *Parlty. Hist.* v. 1020, 1052; *CSP Dom.* 1697, p. 464; 1698, p. 207; 7th Duke of Manchester, *Court and Soc. Eliz. to Anne,* ii. 75; Devonshire mss at Chatsworth House, 135/0, Coningsby to his cousin, 6 July 1713; *HMC Hastings,* ii. 288; De Ros mss D638/6/19, Ranelagh to Coningsby, 28 Dec. 1699; *Cal. Treas. Bks.* xii. 7, 85, 95–96, 111–12. [17] *CSP Dom.* 1697, pp. 138, 471; *Vernon–Shrewsbury Letters,* i. 237–8; Bodl. Shelburne mss mic. Henry Petty to James Waller, 9 June 1697; De Ros mss D638/1/10, 14–16, 19–22, John Hely to Coningsby, 19 Sept. 1696, 2, 28 Aug., 6 Sept., 23 Oct., 1 Dec. 1697, 26 Mar., 7 June 1698; D638/30/6, Sir Thomas Southwell to same, 22 Oct. 1697; D638/18/86–87, Porter to same, 20 Oct. 1696, n.d.; D638/35/1–2, Winchester to same, 6, 13 Nov. 1697; D638/137/12, Ld. Drogheda to same, 11 Oct. 1697; Lyons (King) coll. 1999/547, Ld. Clifford (Charles Boyle I*) to Bp. King, 30 Oct. 1697; Montagu (Boughton) mss 46/155, Vernon to Shrewsbury, 21 Oct. 1697; Add. 57861, f. 41. [18] Montagu (Boughton) mss 46/156, Vernon to Shrewsbury, 23 Oct. 1697; Horwitz, 208, 226; *CSP Dom.* 1697, pp. 501, 506; 1698, pp. 134–5, 193, 195, 207, 258; *Vernon–Shrewsbury Letters,* ii. 9, 143; Carte 130, f. 389; Add. 70083, Jacob [?Rouffiona] to Sir Edward Harley, 9 Aug. 169[–]; 51324, ff. 50, 53, 57–59; Luttrell, iv. 430; *Post Boy,* 8–11 Oct. 1698; *Shrewsbury Corresp.* 557–8. [19] Add. 70114, Thomas Foley II* to Sir Edward Harley, 16 July 1698; *HMC Downshire,* i. 743; Bath mss at Longleat House, Thynne pprs. 24, f. 331; *Cam. Misc.* xxix. 367, 370, 376, 379, 381, 384, 390, 393, 398; *Shrewsbury Corresp.* 573; De Ros mss D638/33/1, Ld. Albemarle to Coningsby, [Jan. 1699]; *HMC Lonsdale,* 111; Carte 130, f. 399; Cumbria RO (Carlisle), Lonsdale mss D/Lons/W2/2/2, James* to Sir John Lowther, 2nd Bt. I*, 15 Apr. 1699; *Irish Econ. and Soc. Hist.* vii. 41–42. [20] Boyer, *Wm. III,* iii. 420, 426, 428; *HMC Lords,* n.s. iv. 46, 49, 51–52; Horwitz, 262; Add. 30000 C, f. 283; 30000 D, ff. 19, 69, 112, 128–9, 198; 17677 UU, f. 209; Montagu (Boughton) mss 48/19, 27, Vernon to Shrewsbury, 13 Jan., 1 Feb. 1699–1700; *Cocks Diary,* 45; Baxter, 376. [21] *Archaeologia,* xxxviii. 5; Add. 57861, ff. 53, 59; 70019, ff. 259, 302, 309; 70020, ff. 35–36; 70064, Robert Harley to Coningsby, 26 Dec. 1700; Horwitz, 278; De Ros mss D638/3/2, Rochester to Coningsby, 19 Dec. 1700; L. K. J. Glassey, *Appt. JPs,* 139; Thynne pprs. 25, ff. 29, 55, 58; 26, ff. 287–9; *Cocks Diary,* 101–2, 110, 140, 164, 220, 277; *State Pprs.* ed. Hardwicke, ii. 458. [22] *Archaeologia,* 5–6; Add. 61363, ff. 49–50, 157–8; 57861, f. 75; 21553, ff. 63–64; 38847, f. 190; *HMC Portland,* iv. 49, 69, 71, 75, 85; Liverpool RO, Norris mss NOR1/214, Thomas Johnson* to Richard Norris*, 16 Jan. 1702[–3]; *HMC Ormonde,* n.s. viii. 129–30; J. G. Simms, *War and Pol. in Ire.* ed. Hayton and O'Brien, 270–1. [23] *Bull. IHR,* xxxiv. 96; xxxvii. 31; *HMC Ormonde,* n.s. vi; n.s. viii. 122, 135–6, 138, 148, 151; De Ros mss D638/48/2, Ormond to Coningsby, 24 Nov. 1704; Add. 21553, f. 65; 70221, Sir Herbert Croft, 1st Bt., to Robert Harley, 16 Feb. 1704[–5]; 70064, Coningsby to [?Edward Harley], 1 July 1706; 61634, ff. 40–41; 57861, f. 92; 61635, ff. 151–2; *Cam. Misc.* xxiii. 40–41, 44–45, 48, 51–52, 58, 61, 64, 69, 74, 77, 79, 81; Norris mss NOR2/453, Thomas Johnson to [?Richard Norris], 27 Feb. 1706[–7]; Montagu (Boughton) mss 77/59, 80, Vernon to Shrewsbury, 6 Mar. 1706[–7], M. Talbot to same, 11 Feb. 1706–7; Lyons (King) coll. 2002/1238, 1241, Francis Annesley to Abp. King, 11 Jan., 11 Feb. 1706[–7]; Hayton thesis, 153–4; *Duchess of Marlborough Corresp.* ii. 251–2; *HMC Portland,* iv. 452; *Cal. Treas.*

Pprs. 1702–7, p. 525. [24] *Archaeologia*, 7–8; G. Holmes, *Pol. in Age of Anne*, 228–9, 309–10; Speck thesis, 165, 187, 225; Add. 57862, f. 45; 70334–8, list of names, 26 Oct. 1707; P. W. J. Riley, *Eng. Ministers and Scot.* 92–93; *Vernon–Shrewsbury Letters*, iii. 295; *HMC Mar and Kellie*, 424; Huntington Lib. Stowe mss 58(2), p. 243; *Marlborough–Godolphin Corresp.* 994–5. [25] *HMC Portland*, iv. 508, 518, 533; De Ros mss D638/147, notes by Coningsby [1708]; T1135/11, [Coningsby] to [Ld. Wharton], 21 May 1709; Hayton thesis, 153–4; Add. 57861, ff. 83, 100, 107–8, 110, 114, 117–18, 133; 57862, ff. 39–40, 45, 47–48, 52–57; 61367, ff. 44–45; 70420, Dyer's newsletters 8 Mar., 7 Apr. 1709; 61366, ff. 145, 187; *Wentworth Pprs.* 78; *Marlborough–Godolphin Corresp.* 994–5, 1116–17, 1260, 1417; *Nicolson Diaries* ed. Jones and Holmes, 496; *Lockhart Pprs.* i. 502; *Bull. IHR*, lv. 206–14; *Duchess of Marlborough Corresp.* ii. 389–90; Holmes, *Pol. in Age of Anne*, 190; G. Holmes, *Trial of Sacheverell*, 89, 91, 147, 253; *HMC Lords*, n.s. viii. 341; *Impartial View*, 185; Yale Univ. Beinecke Lib. Osborn mss, 'Acct. of Trial of Dr Sacheverell' (4 Mar. 1710). [26] *Archaeologia*, 12–18; De Ros mss D638/63, Ld. Dartmouth to Coningsby, 7 July 1710; *Marlborough–Godolphin Corresp.* ii. 1563; *HMC Mar and Kellie*, 484; Midleton mss, Lawrence Clayton to Thomas Brodrick, 12 Sept. 1710; Add. 57861, ff. 146–7; 70084, Coningsby to bailiff of Leominster, 11 Dec. 1714; 70147, Martha Hutchins to Abigail Harley, [1715]; 61494, f. 132; Stowe mss 57(4), p. 161; Holmes, *Trial of Sacheverell*, 253; Robinson, 147; *Duchess of Marlborough Corresp.* ii. 85; *HMC Ormonde*, n.s. viii. 330; *HMC Portland*, iv. 607; *Addison Letters*, 321–2, 340. [27] *Manor of Marden* (1722–7); Coxe, *Marlborough* (1848), iii. 428.

D. W. H.

CONWAY, Francis Seymour (1679–1732), of Ragley, Warws.

BRAMBER 18 Mar. 1701–17 Mar. 1703

b. 28 May 1679, 4th s. of Sir Edward Seymour, 4th Bt.*, by his 2nd. w. *educ.* Eton c.1691, Christ Church, Oxf. 1698. *m.* (1) 17 Feb. 1704, Lady Mary (*d.* 1709), da. of Laurence Hyde†, 1st Earl of Rochester, ?4da. *d.v.p.* (2) 1709, Jane Bowden of Drogheda, co. Meath (*d.* 1716), ?1s *d.v.p.* 1da. (3) July 1716, Charlotte, da. of John Shorter of Bybrook, Kent (another da. *m.* Robert Walpole II*), ?2s. ?1da. surv. *suc.* bro. Popham as h. to estates of Ld. Conway, and took name of Conway, 1699; *cr.* Baron Conway of Ragley 17 Mar. 1703; Baron Conway and Killultagh [I] 16 Oct. 1712.[1]

Ranger of Hyde Park 1703–6; PC [I] 1728.

Gov. Carrickfergus 1728–*d.*

Seymour's inheritance of the Conway fortune, worth about £7,000 a year, was an unexpected windfall. In 1683 Lord Conway had left his estates to his wife and thereafter to the sons of his first cousin, wife of Sir Edward Seymour, 4th Bt., on the condition that the heir change his name to Conway. In 1697 Popham Seymour, Francis' elder brother, duly inherited, but died two years later from a wound received in a duel. Francis, thereafter styled Mr Conway, succeeded to the inheritance but had still not yet reached the age of majority, and continued to live with his father until the following May, when he left with Sir Edward on a tour of the newly acquired Irish estates. The young man made a favourable impression there, perhaps because in comparison to his father he was thought 'more to be depended upon'. He was marked out as one of the most eligible young bachelors in England but despite various marriage proposals he did not in fact marry until 1704, to the daughter of his father's political ally, the Earl of Rochester.[2]

As that marriage suggests, Conway was a political cipher for his father's ambitions and designs. Francis was brought into Parliament in 1701 for Bramber, one of the boroughs where Sir Edward's enemy, Samuel Shepheard I*, had unsuccessfully tried to corrupt voters. Like his father, Conway was blacklisted as having opposed preparations for war with France in 1701, and listed by Robert Harley* with the Tories in an analysis of the December 1701 Parliament; but it was a measure of Sir Edward's status and influence, rather than of Conway's own merit, that Francis was created an English peer in March 1703 as part of the High Tories' plan to achieve a majority in the Upper House. Expectation of this transfer to the Lords may explain why he and Sir John Cope* offered no evidence in January 1703 in support of the petition which they had lodged against the return at Andover.[3]

In February 1706 a bill was introduced in Parliament for the exemplification of the 3rd Lord Conway's will, perhaps because it had been disputed by Sir John Rawdon, who claimed to be the rightful heir. As might have been expected, Lord Conway proved a solid High Churchman over the occasional conformity and schism bills, and the impeachment of Dr Sacheverell. Although he was possibly a 'whimsical' deserter of the Court over the French commerce bill, there is insufficient evidence to label him a Hanoverian Tory, and there is no record of his activity in the Upper House after 1714. He died on 3 Feb. 1732 at Lisburn, co. Antrim, and was succeeded by his son, Francis, who became the 16th Earl of Hertford on 3 Aug. 1750. Despite his earlier fortune, Conway appears to have died leaving debts of over £22,000 to English creditors, with the result that one of his estates in Gloucestershire had to be sold in order to fund the generous legacies, which included a life pension of £200 to his brother Charles*.[4]

[1] H. St. Mawr, *Annals of Seymours*, 517, gives 2s. and 1 da. by third marriage, but Lodge, *Peerage of Ire.* iv. 198, gives 4s. 2 *d.v.p.* 3da. [2] *Evelyn Diary*, v. 331; Add. 30000 C, f. 129; 22186, f. 190; *CSP Dom.* 1699–1700, p. 226; 1700–2, pp. 112, 114; Luttrell, *Brief Relation*, iv. 524; v. 715; Bagot mss at Levens Hall, Ld. Weymouth (Thomas Thynne†) to James Grahme*, 6 July 1699; Bodl. Carte 228, ff. 335–6; BL, M/799, Dyer's newsletter 28 Jan. 1703. [3] *Atterbury Epistolary Corresp.* iv. 384–5; Luttrell, v. 257. [4] G. Holmes, *Pol. in Age of Anne*, 427; *Party and Management in*

Parliament ed. C. Jones, 154; Add. 34743, ff. 142–3; 34738, ff. 128–45.

M. J. K.

CONWAY, Sir John, 2nd Bt. (c.1663–1721), of Bodrhyddan, Flints.

FLINTSHIRE	1685–1687, 1695–1701 (Nov.)
FLINT BOROUGHS	2 Feb.–2 July 1702
FLINTSHIRE	1705–1708
FLINT BOROUGHS	1708–1713
FLINTSHIRE	1713–1715
FLINT BOROUGHS	1715–27 Apr. 1721

b. c.1663, 1st s. of Sir Henry Conway, 1st Bt.[†], of Bodrhyddan by Mary, da. and coh. of Sir Richard Lloyd[†] of Esclus Hall, Denb. *educ.* Eton 1678; Christ Church, Oxf. matric. 10 June 1679, aged 16, DCL 1683. *m.* (1) c.1688, Maria Margaretta or Maria Theophila (*d.* 1690), da. and coh. of John Digby of Gayhurst, Bucks., 1s. d.v.p. 1da.; (2) c.Sept. 1701 (with about £20,000), Penelope (*d.* 1745), da. of Richard Grenville of Wootton Underwood, Bucks., 2da. *suc.* fa. as 2nd Bt. 4 June 1669.[1]

Freeman, Denbigh 1679, 1685; sheriff, Flints. Jan.–Nov. 1688.[2]

As a young man Conway had accompanied the Duke of York to Oxford in 1683, receiving a doctorate as a member of the Duke's retinue. He sat in the 1685 Parliament as a Tory, but despite marrying into a Catholic family was pricked as sheriff in 1688 so that he could not stand in the projected general election. There was a wild streak in his nature: in 1691 he and some other gentlemen of the town, 'rambling in the night, fell upon the watch and beat them severely', while the following year Conway and some friends were reprimanded by the Privy Council for dancing one night 'in the painted chamber next to the House of Lords'.[3]

The Flintshire representation rotated between several leading families, and it was not until 1695 that Conway's turn came again. Chosen knight of the shire without opposition, he was forecast as likely to oppose the Court in the divisions of 31 Jan. 1696 on the proposed council of trade, and, having joined the Welsh petition against the grant to Lord Portland, refused the Association, for which he was subsequently purged from the commission of the peace. He was also listed as having voted against fixing the price of guineas at 22*s.*, and on 4 Apr. 1696 was given leave of absence on health grounds. In the following session he voted, on 25 Nov. 1696, against the attainder of Sir John Fenwick[†]. It is possible that he was already showing signs of the self-assertion that would later cause disruption to the consensus among the Tory interests in Flintshire: in 1697 his kinsman Thomas Ravenscroft* had successfully challenged Sir John Hanmer, 3rd Bt.[†], in a by-election for the Boroughs, and at the general election Conway himself was re-elected knight of the shire. A comparative analysis of the old and new Parliaments in about September 1698 marked him as a supporter of the Country party, and the following month he was forecast a likely opponent of the standing army. In 1700 Conway joined the Denbighshire Tory Sir Richard Myddelton, 3rd Bt.*, in protesting at the Treasury against a grant to James Isaacson* of all the sea marshes in the counties of Denbigh and Flint. Having secured his return at the first 1701 election, Conway was listed in February 1701 with those likely to support the Court in agreeing with the committee of supply's resolution to continue the 'Great Mortgage'. But he was no more active in the Commons than he had been before: he was again granted leave of absence to recover his health, for a term of ten days, on 14 Apr. 1701. He was in all probability in serious financial difficulties, for in 1701 he was busy trying to raise the sum of £15,000 on his estate, to pay his debts and his sister's marriage portion. His marriage later that year to a Buckinghamshire heiress, a feat regarded in her locality as a considerable coup, proved at best only a temporary relief.[4]

Conway stood down in the second election of 1701, but in the course of the 1701–2 Parliament he filled a vacancy in the Flint Boroughs constituency, during which he was listed as having favoured the motion of 26 Feb. 1702 vindicating the Commons' proceedings of the previous Parliament in the impeachments of the four Whig lords. He refused to 'withdraw' again at the next election, forcing a contest for the county with (Sir) Thomas Hanmer II* (4th Bt.). The aggrieved Hanmer wrote, 'if Sir John Conway will not be content to be out of Parliament once in ten years, when other gentlemen require to have their turn of serving, it must be disputed with him'. Defeat presumably brought Conway into line. He was chosen for the county in 1705, for the Boroughs in 1708 after humbly offering to defer to Hanmer, and for the county again at the last two general elections in this period. Classified as a 'Churchman' in a list of the 1705 Parliament, he voted against the Court candidate for Speaker in the division of 25 Oct. 1705, was described as a Tory in two lists from 1708 and voted in 1710 against the impeachment of Dr Sacheverell. In the 1710–11 session he was included among the 'Tory patriots' listed as voting for peace, and among the 'worthy patriots' who exposed the mismanagements of the previous ministry. By this time, however, Bodrhyddan, which he had earlier rebuilt, was let. Parliamentary bills had been introduced in 1704 and 1706 to allow him to pay off debts by selling his share of his first wife's estate, and, more specifically, to enable him to settle his Flintshire property (worth £1,200 p.a.) on his son and provide a portion of £3,000 for the daughter of the marriage. These had run into opposition from mortgagors and had failed, giving rise to a court case which went against Conway on appeal in January 1711. By August of the following year he was applying directly to Lord Treasurer Oxford (Robert Harley*) for money to stave off 'the vexatious clamours ... every day from my creditors', a holding operation, he claimed, 'until I can sell two estates that lie in Rutlandshire and Leicestershire'. He hoped to raise £1,000 by a sale of pictures to the Queen, whose evident lack of interest in these 'family pieces' was not communicated by Oxford for some time. Placed in the position of a supplicant, Conway was a weak advocate for the Irish clergyman Francis Higgins (the so-called 'Irish Sacheverell'), a protégé of his friend Sir William Glynn, 2nd Bt.†, and recommended by Conway and Glynn for an Irish bishopric in November 1712. Nor could he afford to be a 'whimsical', voting on 18 June 1713 in favour of the French commercial treaty. Promised £300 from 'cousin Tom Harley*' at the Treasury in the autumn of 1713, he was kept waiting for the money for the duration of Oxford's ministry. The defaulting of a receiver-general for Cheshire and north Wales for whom he had unwisely stood surety also left him owing the crown some £1,600, and here Oxford at least arranged a stay of process. Predictably, Conway had still not paid up by December 1714, pleading disappointment 'in selling an estate'. Oxford had eventually lent him £100 in November of that year, but the £300 from the Treasury remained unpaid. In the light of these circumstances his political record is interesting: classed as a Tory in the Worsley list and in one list of the Members re-elected in 1715; and as a 'whimsical Whig' in another. Nothing further is known of his finances, other than that in his will he was able to leave £2,000 to the daughters of his second marriage, and the remnant of his landed property to the daughter of his first. Under George I he recorded no parliamentary votes. Conway died at Bath 27 Apr. 1721, aged 58, the last of his line, and was buried at Rhuddlan.[5]

[1] *Jnl. Flints. Hist. Soc.* xx. 1–5; A. N. Palmer, *Country Townships of Wrexham*, 4–5; J. E. Griffith, *Peds. Anglesey and Caern. Fams.* 260; Luttrell, *Brief Relation*, v. 92. [2] *Chirk Castle Accts. 1666–1753* ed. Myddelton, 239; J. Williams, *Recs. of Denbigh*, 139–41. [3] Wood, *Life and Times*, iii. 46, 54; Luttrell, ii. 238; PRO NI, De Ros mss D683/13/149, John Pulteney* to Thomas Coningsby*, 14 May 1692. [4] Chandler, iii. 10; L. K. J. Glassey, *Appt. JPs*, 122–3, 131; *Jnl. Flints. Hist. Soc.* 4; *Verney Mems.* i. 115; Luttrell, iv. 603. [5] *HMC Kenyon*, 428; NLW, Bettisfield mss 81, Conway to [Hanmer], Mar. 1708; *Jnl. Flints. Hist. Soc.* 4; *CJ*, xiv. 337, 339, 345, 353, 357, 367; *HMC Lords*, n.s. vi. 345–8; ix. 12–13; *HMC Portland*, v. 210; Add. 70219, Conway to [Oxford], 'Wednesday morning', 'Friday noon', 'Saturday morning', 5 Sept. 1713, 'Monday morning', 21 Nov. 1714; 70269, same to same, 23 Aug. 1712; *HMC Ormonde*, n.s. viii. 333–4; *Cal. Treas. Bks.* xxviii. 329; xxix. 192; *Jnl. Flints. Hist. Soc.* 5, 35–36; *Arch. Camb.* (ser. 1), i. 340.

D. W. H.

CONYERS, John (1650–1725), of Hoe Street, Walthamstow, Essex.

EAST GRINSTEAD   1695–1708
WEST LOOE   1708–1710
EAST GRINSTEAD   1710–10 Mar. 1725

b. 6 Mar. 1650, 1st s. of Tristram Conyers†, serjeant-at-law, of Hoe Street by Winifred, da. of Sir Gilbert Gerard, 1st Bt.†, of Flambards, Harrow-on-the-Hill, Mdx. educ. Merchant Taylors' 1663–5; Queen's, Oxf. 1666; M. Temple 1666, called 1672, bencher 1702. m. lic. 16 Jan. 1681, Mary (d. 1702), da. and h. of George Lee, fellow of Lincoln Coll. Oxf., of Stoke Milborough, Salop. 1s. 2da. (12 other ch. d.v.p.) suc. fa. 1684.[1]

Dep. steward, Havering, Essex 1676–Apr. 1688, high steward Apr. 1688–1715.[2]

KC May 1689.[3]

Commr. taking subscriptions to land bank 1696.[4]

Chairman, cttees. of supply and ways and means 1700–8, 1710–14.

The grandson and son of a lawyer, Conyers followed the family tradition of training in the law and by the 1680s was acting as lawyer to the 1st Marquess of Halifax (Sir George Savile†), through whose intercession he obtained the stewardship of the manor of Havering in April 1688. His appointment, he claimed, would bar that of a Catholic and, in any case, he felt himself entitled to the office having served for 12 years as deputy-steward. Later that year King James's election agents reported their anxiety lest Conyers be brought in for East Grinstead on the interest of his mother-in-law's family, the Goodwins of Rowfant, since he was someone of whom they could give 'no good account'. In October he declined an offer of the recordership of London.[5]

After the Revolution Conyers was made King's Counsel and continued as an active barrister. Successful for East Grinstead in 1695 he proved 'but a poor orator' in the Commons, but was one of the most diligent committee-men of the period, leaving a monumental official record of parliamentary activity mirrored by an almost complete lack of personal detail. He was particularly prominent in drafting legislation. Forecast as likely to oppose the Court in the divisions of 31 Jan. 1696 on the proposed council of trade, he signed the Association promptly and in March voted against fixing the price of guineas at 22s. He was named to drafting committees for bills to repair the highway between London and Harwich (1 Jan. 1696); to proclaim fines levied on lands in ancient demesne and making them a bar to titles (31 Jan.), managing this bill through the Commons in February; and for a land bank (6 Mar). On 5 Mar. he was first-named to the committee to draft a bill for licensing hackney carriages, and on 7 Mar. he was named to the drafting committee for a bill to regulate the Africa trade, presenting the resulting bills later in the month. In February and March he was also involved in four private bills, managing one through all its stages in the Commons.[6]

In the next session Conyers voted against the attainder of Sir John Fenwick† on 25 Nov., but when Lord Ailesbury (Thomas Bruce†), another of the accused, was brought for trial early the following year, Conyers appeared as counsel against him. Ailesbury recalled in his *Memoirs* that Conyers seemed to be 'out of countenance' in his pleading, whereupon a mutual friend, Viscount Weymouth (Thomas Thynne†) 'whispered him in the ear, "Conyers, hold your tongue; you speak against your heart"'. Conyers then 'left off and no one could make anything of what he had begun'. None of this prevented his being chosen to chair the committee of the whole on a bill to attaint various of the alleged Assassination plotters on 5 Jan. 1697, from which he reported the next day. On 18 Feb. he reported on a bill for repairing roads in Sussex and Surrey. He was given leave of absence on 5 Mar. for 21 days, presumably to go on circuit.[7]

Conyers returned early to Westminster at the beginning of the next session and through the efforts of his friend Robert Harley* was placed in the chair of the committee of the whole on the King's Speech on 10 Dec. 1697, thereby enabling Harley to move for disbanding the army. His increasing importance in the House was recognized with his appointment to two conferences with the Lords concerning the bills against corresponding with James II and for the punishment of Charles Duncombe*. On 19 Apr. 1698 he told for agreeing to an amendment to the elections bill which modified the proposed landed qualification by allowing the election of freemen who were resident within five miles of the respective parliamentary borough and possessed £200 worth of movable property. He was also named on 4 June to the committee for impeaching Jean Goudet.[8]

Although a placeman, and listed as such in July and September 1698, Conyers was also forecast as likely to oppose a standing army and was correctly classed in a comparative analysis of the old and new Parliaments as a Country supporter. Henceforth it becomes difficult to distinguish his parliamentary activity from that of his cousin and friend, Thomas Conyers, newly elected for Durham, and also a Tory, who sat for the remainder of the period with the exception of the 1701–2 Parliament. In general, John Conyers appears to have been the more politically important and active of the two. In December Conyers chaired the committee of the whole on the King's Speech. He was also named to the drafting committee for a bill to disband the army (17 Dec.), and subsequently managed it through all its stages in the Commons. A 'Mr Conyers' was also named to several other drafting committees and told on 25 Apr. 1699 in favour of a clause making illegal any public playing of basset, a card game.

In the next session, Conyers again chaired the committee on the King's Speech, and this time was also named to the committee on the Address (28 Nov. 1699), from which he reported on 30 Nov. On 5 Dec. he was appointed chairman of supply and on 25 Jan. 1700 chairman of ways and means, consequently chairing every subsequent meeting of these committees, and reporting their resolutions to the House. In his capacity as chair of ways and means he was closely involved with many supply bills and attendant financial matters. In February and March he chaired the committee of the whole on the Irish forfeitures resumption bill, managing the bill through the House in April, and telling on 1 Apr. against a second reading for a clause in favour of a private estate. In February Speaker Littleton fell ill and James Vernon I* thought the House might choose a replacement *pro tem.*, with the Country party voting Conyers or Simon Harcourt I into the Chair on a permanent basis, but nothing came of this stratagem. In the summer Conyers acted as legal counsel for the Old East India Company in a case before the Exchequer.[9]

Returned again for East Grinstead in the first 1701 Parliament, Conyers continued to chair the committees of supply and ways and means. He was also, on 1 Mar. 1701, put in the chair of the committee to consider that part of the King's Speech concerning the succession. During the subsequent debate it was presumably Conyers who quashed the motion by Lord Spencer (Charles*) to name the house of Hanover, on the grounds that the initial resolutions of the committee to settle the crown in the next Protestant line, and further secure the rights and liberties of the subject, had first to be passed by the House. On 12 Mar. Conyers was first-named to the drafting committee for a bill to settle the succession, which eventually became the Act of Settlement. He may have been the 'Mr

Conyers' named in March to the committee drafting a bill to prevent corruption at elections, appointed in April to the committee to draft the impeachment of the Earl of Portland, which later included the impeachment of the other Whig lords, and who chaired the committee of the whole on the nation's trade and public debts. On 20 May Conyers was in the chair of a committee of supply and consequently had the deciding vote in passing a clause exempting vicarages worth less than £40 p.a. from the land tax. On 2 June he raised the question of changes in the land tax commission in Denbighshire on behalf of fellow Tory Edward Brereton*, who wished to complain about changes to the commission. In the summer Conyers was rumoured to want the post of attorney-general, but was not appointed.[10]

Blacklisted as having opposed preparations for war in 1701, Conyers was classified as a Tory in Harley's list of the second Parliament of 1701, and on 26 Feb. 1702 supported the resolution vindicating the Commons' proceedings in the impeachments of the Whig ministers. He was re-elected as chairman of supply and ways and means, but was prevented from carrying out his duties for some days in March because of the death of his wife. Although recorded in the Journals as chairing the committee of ways and means and carrying up the malt tax bill on 6 Mar., a contemporary report maintained that Hon. Henry Boyle performed the latter duty, and certainly by the following day Boyle had temporarily replaced Conyers as the chairman of supply. Boyle apparently declared that he had Conyers' consent for this, but his actions may have been part of behind-the-scenes manoeuvring to place Boyle, a Court Whig, in the chair permanently. When Conyers returned on 20 Mar. there were some cries for Boyle to take the chair of the land tax committee, but Conyers prevailed. As the only Conyers in the House, he was named to the drafting committee for a clause to be added to the bill to explain the oath to the crown, and managed this bill through the House in March and April. Although himself a Country Tory, Conyers appears to have continued his father's sympathy for Dissenters and when the abjuration bill came back from the Lords on 6 May he supported an amendment to permit Quakers to affirm, as the only way to 'preserve them from ruin', and was named to the committee to manage a conference on the bill.[11]

Conyers was returned again for East Grinstead in 1702, whereupon he was once again elected chairman of the committees for supply and ways and means. He also probably took the chair of the committees to make provision for Prince George and for the Duke of Marlborough (John Churchill†), and to draft the counter-address against the alienation of crown revenues. 'Mr' Conyers was involved with two items of legislation to facilitate church-building: the bills for the finishing of St. Paul's Cathedral and for the easier recovery of monies for the repair of parish churches. In other business, 'Mr Conyers' told on 10 Dec. in favour of hearing a petition from the Merchant Taylors' Company; was named to drafting committees for a bill to strengthen discipline in the army and navy (26 Nov.), which he presented on 8 Dec. and 11 Jan. 1703; and another to revive the act appointing commissioners to examine the debts of the army (12 Jan.), which he subsequently managed through the House. 'Mr Conyers' also chaired the committees on the Irish forfeitures and on frauds in the stamp duties in January and February.

In the 1703–4 session, in addition to his usual work on supply measures, Conyers was in the chair of committees of the whole on the Queen's Speech concerning the navy and the army (27 Nov. 1703, 5 Jan. 1704), and took a leading role in managing the resulting bill for the recruitment of marine and land forces through the House. He was forecast by Secretary Nottingham (Daniel Finch†) as a probable supporter over the Scotch Plot in mid-March 1704. He was also named to draft the bill to resume crown grants, which he presented on 24 Jan., chairing subsequent committees in February. In the 1704–5 session Conyers continued to be very active. He was forecast in October as a probable opponent of the Tack and, after being lobbied by Harley, he did not vote for it on 28 Nov., a list of 1705 classing him as a 'Sneaker'. In December 1704 Conyers chaired the committees of the whole considering the Scottish acts of security, and in January reported the English response, known as the aliens bill. In February 1705 'Mr Conyers' took the chair of the committees for the bill to prohibit trade with France, and managed a conference with the Lords on the Aylesbury case.[12]

Listed again as a placeman in 1705, in the new Parliament Conyers absented himself from the division on the Speaker, 25 Oct. 1705, rather than vote for the Court against his old friend William Bromley II. It was reported on 31 Oct. that for this both Whigs and Tories threatened to keep him out of the chair of supply, but he was re-elected as usual on 9 Nov. There was still the chair of ways and means, however, and a displeased Lord Treasurer Godolphin (Sidney†) wrote to Harley on 11 Jan. 1706: 'I hope there will be no great difficulty today in fixing Mr Conyers in his throne, though at the same time his behaviour shows we ought not to have taken such pains in the matter but for [our] own sakes.' Safely reinstalled as chairman of ways and means, Conyers was not in general quite so active as before in Commons' business. Apart from the usual supply measures, little other significant activity can be assigned to him in the 1705–6 session. After Ramillies, Conyers seems to have rejoiced at a newfound unanimity in public affairs, informing Lord Cutts (John*) in June, that the face of politics had changed dramatically and 'you will scarce believe you knew the men you formerly were acquainted with'.[13]

In the 1706–7 session 'Mr Conyers' was named to the committee for drafting a bill to prevent customs frauds by means of the Scottish drawbacks (14 Mar. 1707), managing the consequent bill through the House. In a related issue, in March Conyers chaired four committees of the whole on equalizing English export allowances with those of Scotland, reporting and carrying the resulting bill up to the Lords. The drawbacks bill met with objections in the Lords and following a short prorogation, Conyers chaired the committee of the whole on 15 Apr. to consider the Queen's Speech calling for the resolution of the issue, then reintroduced the bill and again managed it through the House. 'All things go as they did', commented one observer, 'Lowndes [William*], Conyers and my Lord William Powlett* manage the House.'[14]

In the 1707–8 session Conyers' activity in the House was again largely taken up with his position as chairman of supply and ways and means. 'Mr Conyers' was named to drafting committees for bills to repeal the Scottish act of security (4 Dec. 1707); to prevent French wine smuggling (13 Dec.); and to extend the time allowed the New East India Company to raise £1,200,000 for carrying on the war (2 Feb. 1708), presenting this bill on 19 Feb. He was no doubt the 'Mr Conyers' appointed to the drafting committee for a bill to reform Sussex elections, which he presented and reported to the House. He may also have been the 'Mr Conyers' first-named to a drafting committee for a bill to enforce the Act for completing St. Paul's Cathedral on 8 Jan., subsequently managing the bill through all its stages in the Commons, and was possibly named to draft the bill for the relief of Scottish Quakers (27 Feb.). Listed as a Tory in early 1708, he may have been the 'Mr Conyers' who told on the Tory side on 28 Feb. 1708 against committing the cathedrals bill.

In 1708 Conyers was defeated at East Grinstead but was returned for West Looe, probably following an agreement between Bishop Trelawny and Godolphin. In a list of 1708 Conyers was classified as a Court Tory, but it was soon shown that he was not indispensable to the Court when on 24 Nov. he lost his place as chairman of the committee of supply to the Whig William Farrer, defeated by 50 votes, a result which apparently 'hath almost broke his and poor Lowndes's heart'. One report suggested that Conyers was voted out because he was 'the Treasurer's man', but a letter of Hon. James Brydges* explained that 'there was no avoiding it, the Whigs were bent on having favour and the Court thought it not worthwhile to make a division among themselves upon it'. 'Mr Conyers' was first-named on 11 Mar. 1709 to the drafting committee for a bill to explain the acts relating to sewers, managing the resulting bill through the House. The 1709–10 session appears to have been one of the least active of Conyers' career. In addition to carrying a message to the Lords requesting that they clear the public from MPs' seats in Westminster Hall and reporting back their agreement (2 Mar. 1710), 'Mr Conyers' was named to a drafting committee for a bill for the relief of the creditors of the Mine Adventurers' Company (13 Mar.) and was involved in three private estate bills. In March, he voted against the impeachment of Dr Sacheverell.[15]

Returned for East Grinstead without a contest in 1710, Conyers was regarded in the 'Hanover list' as 'doubtful' but he was re-elected to the chair of supply and ways and means by the Tory majority. Conyers' activity in Parliament increased accordingly. 'Mr Conyers' chaired committees of the whole on that part of the Queen's Speech concerning public debts (10 Jan. 1710), and for the repeal of the General Naturalization Act (27 Jan.). He was also of course involved in all supply bills, which took up much of the session, including (in May) that for establishing a South Sea Company. 'Mr Conyers' also acted as a teller against Hon. John Noel's* election for Rutland (23 Jan. 1711); as the first-named to drafting committees for repealing parts of the Acts for encouraging trade with America (9 Dec.), a bill he presented on 16 Mar.; and as the first-named to drafting committees for prohibiting the import of French wines (8 Feb. 1711). He was also listed with the 'worthy patriots' who in this session exposed the mismanagements of the previous administration.

In the 1711–12 session, from 31 Jan. 1712 Conyers was chairman of the committee of the whole considering the conduct of the war, which culminated in a series of resolutions criticizing the allies, and of the committee for an address to the Queen on the state of the war. In the following April and May he chaired the committee on the lottery fund and the bill for the resumption of crown grants. He may have also told on 10 Apr. in favour of the election of George Hamilton* for Anstruther Easter Burghs. In the next session 'Mr Conyers' told on 2 June against engrossing the bill to establish the African trade. John was almost certainly the Conyers involved closely in the proceedings on the treaty of commerce with France, telling on 9 June against recommitting the report of the committee inquiring into the precedents of the 1674 treaty, and voting on the 18th for the French commerce bill. The next day he was probably first-named to drafting committees on bills to encourage the tobacco trade and the manufacture of sail-cloth. In August 1713, he was paid his arrears of 11 years' salary at £40 p.a. as Queen's Counsel.[16]

Re-elected for East Grinstead in 1713, Conyers was rumoured at one stage as a possible Speaker of the 1714 Parliament, but instead was reappointed chair of supply and ways and means. He may have acted as a teller against (Sir) Thomas Wheate* in the election for New Woodstock (16 Mar.), against Paul Methuen* at Brackley (20 Apr.), and for referring the Harwich election case to committee (28 May). In all probability in March he was the chairman of the committee of the whole on the tobacco and silk drawbacks in Ireland, subsequently reporting a bill in April to lessen the drawbacks on exports to Ireland. Two further tellerships may well be ascribed to him in this session: on 1 June, in favour of passing the schism bill; and on 8 July, against an address for an inquiry into army debts. He was described as a Tory in the Worsley list and in another list comparing the 1713 Parliament with that elected in 1715, although a similar list described him as a 'whimsical Whig'. When Parliament was recalled after the death of the Queen, some Tories tried to intrude Sir William Wyndham, 3rd Bt., into the chair of ways and means on 7 Aug., but Robert Walpole II intervened to represent 'that Mr Conyers had for so many years so well discharged that office, that it were inconsistent with gratitude, good manners and prudence to choose another'. As chairman, in August he steered through the House the vote of supply for George I's Household. The new King at first renewed Conyers' grant as high steward of Havering, but in February 1715 he was replaced. Conyers remained in opposition as a Tory until his death on 10 Mar. 1725. His monumental inscription in St. Mary's church, Walthamstow, declared him to have been

> truly virtuous and of a kindly disposition, wise in counsel and constant in deed, a servant of the state and devoted to the Church, for more than 30 years a Member of Parliament, diligent, faithful, energetic . . . his reputation unspotted, his health good, his fortune whole.

He was succeeded by his son Edward†.[17]

[1] *Walthamstow Antiq. Soc. Publns.* xxvii. 18; *Mar. Lic. Vicar-Gen.* (Harl. Soc. xxx), 51. [2] Devonshire mss at Chatsworth House, Finch-Halifax pprs. Conyers to Halifax, 13 Apr. 1688; *Cal. Treas. Bks.* xxix. 93, 372. [3] *CSP Dom.* 1689–90, pp. 18, 66; Luttrell, *Brief Relation,* i. 529. [4] *CJ,* xii. 509. [5] G. E. Roebuck, *Walthamstow,* 56; Finch–Halifax pprs. Halifax to [–], n.d., 8 Oct.; Conyers to Halifax, 13 Apr. 1688; Duckett, *Penal Laws and Test Act* (1882), 441; Luttrell, i. 471. [6] *Ailesbury Mems.* 428. [7] *Ibid.* 423–8. [8] H. Horwitz, *Parl. and Pol. Wm. III,* 226. [9] *Vernon–Shrewsbury Letters,* ii. 436–7; Luttrell, iv. 658. [10] Horwitz, 283; Add. 29568, f. 9; *Cocks Diary,* 138, 158; Cumbria RO (Carlisle), Lonsdale mss D/Lons/W2/2/4, James* to Sir John Lowther, 2nd Bt. I*, 1 July 1701. [11] *Cocks Diary,* 235, 253, 284. [12] Add. 17677 ZZ, f. 531. [13] *Bull. IHR,* xxxvii. 23; Add. 4743, f. 47; Univ. Kansas Spencer Research Lib. Methuen–Simpson corresp. C163, [?John Methuen*] to Sir William Simpson, 30 Oct., 12 Nov. 1705; BL, Trumbull Add. mss 98, John Bridges to Sir William Trumbull*, 31 Oct. 1705; *HMC Portland,* iv. 278; *HMC Astley,* 194. [14] Northants. RO, Isham mss IC 2729, William Cary to Sir Justinian Isham, 4th Bt.*, 3 Apr. 1707. [15] Luttrell, vi. 377; G. Holmes, *Pol. in Age of Anne,* 42; Huntington Lib. Stowe mss 57(3), p. 122; Trumbull Misc. mss 53, Lord Johnstone (James*) to Trumbull, 24 Nov. 1708. [16] *Cal. Treas. Bks.* xxvi. 315. [17] Lonsdale mss D/Lons/W2/3/13, John to James Lowther, 30 July 1713; Boyer, *Anne Annals* viii. 153–4; *Cal. Treas. Bks.* xxix. 93, 372; *Walthamstow Antiq. Soc. Publns.* 18.

E. C./S. M. W.

CONYERS, Thomas (c.1666–1728), of Eelemore, nr. Durham.

DURHAM 1698–1701 (Nov.), 1702–1727

b. c.1666, 5th s. of Nicholas Conyers of Boulby, Yorks. and South Biddick, co. Dur. by his 3rd w. Margaret, da. and coh. of Nicholas Freville of Hardwick, co. Dur., wid. of Thomas Lambton, gov. Leeward Is. *educ.* Trinity, Oxf. matric. 13 May 1684, aged 17; M. Temple 1686. *m.* lic. 25 June 1690, Elizabeth (*d.* 1725), da. and h. of Thomas Hall of Eelemore, 1da.[1]

Freeman, Durham 1697.[2]

Equerry to Prince George of Denmark 1704–6.[3]

Conyers had acquired lands in county Durham by marriage, and a year after being made a freeman of the county borough he was returned for Durham at the 1698 election. A comparison of the old and new Commons in about September classed Conyers as a Country supporter and at this time he was also forecast as a probable opponent of a standing army. It is impossible to distinguish Thomas' activity in the Journals from those of his cousin John, who was the more prominent of the two in the House. Both men were Tories, and such sympathies were amply demonstrated following Thomas Conyers' return to the first 1701 Parliament. In February 1701 Conyers was forecast as likely to support the Court over the 'Great Mortgage', and later the same year he was blacklisted as having opposed the preparations for war with France. Conyers did not stand at Durham in the second election of 1701, and suggestions that he contest Morpeth also appear to have come to nothing. In 1702, however, he was returned unopposed for Durham, a seat he was to hold until the accession of George II.[4]

Conyers' Tory principles were evident in his vote of 13 Feb. 1703 against the Lords' amendments to the bill to enlarge the time for taking the abjuration oath, but in February 1704 he was given a post in the household of the Prince of Denmark and this appointment was important in determining his attitude to the Tack. In October 1704 he was forecast as doubtful on this measure, and shortly afterwards appeared on Robert Harley's* lobbying list. In the days before the crucial division of 28 Nov. the ministry endeavoured to ensure that the Prince's household would not support the Tack, and Harley himself was deputed to lobby Conyers. The success of Harley's efforts was evident on the 28th when Conyers failed to vote for the Tack. This led to an analysis of the 1705 Parliament classifying Conyers as a 'Sneaker', but on 25 Oct. he was one of the Tory office-holders who voted against the Court candidate for Speaker, a vote which led to his dismissal in June 1706 from the Prince's household. A list of early 1708 classified Conyers as a Tory, and though one list states that in 1710 he voted for the impeachment of Dr Sacheverell numerous other analyses of this division class Conyers as an opponent of the measure. The ministerial revolution later that year led Conyers to write to Harley to stress his 'just pretensions' to a place, but these aspirations were not to be fulfilled. The 'Hanover list' of 1710 classified him as a Tory and the veracity of this judgment was confirmed in the 1710–11 session, Conyers being listed among both the 'Tory patriots' who had opposed the continuation of the war and the 'worthy patriots' who had detected the mismanagements of the previous administration. His loyalty to the ministry was evident in his vote of 18 June 1713 in support of the French commerce bill. Conyers' partisan loyalties remained constant in the 1713 Parliament, the Worsley list and two further comparisons of the 1713 and 1715 Parliaments classing him as a Tory. He died on 4 Oct. 1728, his estates descending to his only surviving daughter and her husband, George Baker*.[5]

[1] *The Gen.* n.s. xiv. 57–58; Surtees, *Dur.* ii(2), 121. [2] Surtees, iv(2), 22. [3] Luttrell, *Brief Relation,* v. 386; vi. 62. [4] Surtees, 120; N. Yorks. RO, Worsley mss ZON13/1/248, J. Gibson to Lady Strickland, 14 Dec. 1701. [5] *Bull. IHR,* xli. 182, 184; xxxvii. 30; Add. 4743, f. 47; *HMC Portland,* iv. 575.

E. C.

COOK, Sir William, 2nd Bt. (c.1630–1708), of Broome Hall, Norf.

GREAT YARMOUTH 1685–1687
NORFOLK   1689–1695, 1698–1700

b. c.1630, 1st s. of Sir William Cook, 1st Bt., of Broome Hall by his 1st w. Mary, da. of Thomas Astley of Melton Constable, Norf. *educ.* Emmanuel, Camb. fell. comm. 1647; G. Inn 1648. *m.* settlement 1664, Jane, da. and coh. of William Steward of Barton Mills, Suff., 7da. *suc.* fa. as 2nd Bt. 1681.[1]

Freeman, Great Yarmouth 1685.[2]

Although Cook was not listed as having voted in the Convention to agree with the Lords that the throne was not vacant, his name appeared on the black list of Tories published before the 1690 election. He was returned, with his kinsman Sir Jacob Astley, 1st Bt.*, a moderate Tory, having defeated two Whigs. Lord Carmarthen (Sir Thomas Osborne†) classed him as a Tory supporter of the Court. Despite the fact that he is not recorded as having made a speech, Cook contributed to the preparation of several bills. On 9 May, for example, he was nominated to prepare the bill for the regulation of wines. In the following session he was appointed to prepare the militia bill (10 Oct.) and to draft a poor relief bill (7 Nov.). In April 1691 Robert Harley* listed him as a doubtful supporter of the Country party. He was appointed the following session (2 Dec. 1691) to draft the bill to encourage the manufacture of saltpetre in England, but on 18 Jan. 1692 was granted leave of absence for a month because of ill-health (and again on 9 Jan. 1693 and 27 Feb. 1695).

Cook did not stand for re-election in 1695, but put up again with Astley in 1698, and was returned at the top of the poll. He was listed in about September 1698 as a member of the Country party, and was forecast as likely to oppose the standing army. His personal correspondence bears out this assessment. In January 1699 he wrote approvingly of (Sir) John Phillips' (4th Bt.) immorality bill, describing its probable failure as a 'scandal of the government'. At the same time he hoped that a bill against distilling brandy from corn would meet with sufficient opposition that 'we may throw it out, for it will be a vast prejudice to our rents, and is driven on chiefly by the brewers and the plantation merchants in regard to their molasses'. On 23 Feb. he wrote:

On Saturday last we had a long tug with the courtiers ... upon the report from the committee of the whole House upon the article of the 15,000 men voted in the committee. We first moved the number should be reduced to 12,000, but upon the question they carried it against us by five; then we moved the addition of these words to the question 'to be seamen only according to the ancient usage of the navy', and we carried that by nine ... We are now coming upon ways and means for raising the money and 'twill be very difficult without a great burthen still upon the land, and I pray God they do not get the excise upon malt continued.

He reported with delight on 9 Mar. that 'we have damned the malt tax I hope for ever in the committee'. On 4 Jan. 1700 he lamented that he had been unable to attend a call of the House having been badly stricken with gout. His attendance a few days later caused him a great deal of discomfort. During February his condition improved somewhat, only to worsen in March with pain from the stone being added to that of gout. Not a candidate in either of the general elections in 1701, he seems to have been prepared to support the two Whigs who put up in December, Sir John Holland, 2nd Bt.*, and Hon. Roger Townshend*, until he heard that Astley was intending to stand as well, whereupon he was forced to reconsider: 'so near and honourable a relation as Sir Jacob Astley concerning himself at this time', he informed Roger Townshend, 'I must beg your pardon if I stand neuter'.[3]

Cook contested the county in 1702, together with Astley, at the urging of Lord Nottingham (Daniel Finch†), but was defeated and retired from active politics. He sold the manor of Broome at about this time and went to live at Mendham in Suffolk, where one of his daughters and her husband resided. He died in January 1708.[4]

[1] *Vis. Norf.* (Harl. Soc. lxxxv), 54; *Vis. Norf. Notes* (Norf. Rec. Soc. xxvii), 64. [2] Norf. RO, Gt. Yarmouth bor. recs. assembly bk. 1680-1701, p. 84. [3] *HMC Townshend*, 329; Suff. RO (Ipswich), Gurdon mss mic. M142(1), Cook to Thornhagh Gurdon, 5 Jan., 16, 23 Feb., 9 Mar., 1698[-9], 4, 11 Jan., 1 Feb. 1699[-1700]. [4] Add. 29588, f. 115; C. J. Palmer, *Gt. Yarmouth*, 214; PCC 158 Alexander; *Vis. Norf.* 54.

D. W. H.

COOKE, Bryan (1684–1734), of Wheatley, Yorks.

EAST RETFORD 11 Jan. 1711–1713

bap. 17 Dec. 1684, 1st s. of Sir George Cooke, 3rd Bt.* *educ.* Clare, Camb. 1703. *m.* c.1712 (with £8,000), Priscilla (*d.* 1731), da. and coh. of Robert Squire*, 2s. 3da. *suc.* fa. as 4th Bt. 18 Oct. 1732.[1]

Cooke's family came from the Doncaster area where his family's seat 'lies low by the river side'. He stood together with Willoughby Hickman* as a Tory candidate for East Retford in 1710, but was defeated. Seated on petition on 11 Jan. 1711, he was included among the 'worthy patriots' who in the first session of the new Parliament helped to detect the mismanagements of the previous ministry, and was also a member of the October Club. He was not, however, an active Member. On 18 June 1713 he voted against the French commerce bill. Cooke did not stand in the 1713 election and it was not until 1732 that he succeeded his father to the baronetcy. He died at the Hotwells, near Bristol, on 25 Oct. 1734.[2]

[1] NRA Rep. 9996 (Cooke of Wheatley), p. 232; *HMC Var.* viii. 259; *Gent. Mag.* 1734, p. 703. [2] *HMC Var.* viii. 259.

E. C./S. N. H.

COOKE, Sir George, 3rd Bt. (1662–1732), of Wheatley, Yorks.

ALDBOROUGH 1698–1700

bap. 16 May 1662, 2nd but 1st surv. s. of Sir Henry Cooke, 2nd Bt., of Wheatley by Diana, da. of Anthony Butler of Coates, Lincs. *m.* 19 June 1683 (with £2,000), Catherine (*d.* 1703), da. of Sir Godfrey Copley, 1st Bt., of Sprotborough, Yorks., sis. of Sir Godfrey Copley, 2nd Bt.*, 7s. (2 *d.v.p.*) 2da. *suc.* fa. as 3rd Bt. 16 Dec. 1689.[1]
Commr. Aire and Calder navigation 1699.[2]

Cooke was descended from Brian Cooke (*d.* 1653), an alderman and mayor of Doncaster, whose son, the 1st baronet, settled at Wheatley. A Royalist in the Civil War, he died unmarried in 1683, leaving Cooke's father to succeed to title and estates. Although rumoured to be a candidate in the 1696 by-election at Aldborough, Cooke did not stand until the 1698 general election. Having a good interest of his own, and also having the support of the Wentworth family, who were lords of the manor, he topped the poll in a contested election. In late 1698 he was forecast as a likely opponent of a standing army, and at around the same time a comparison of the old and new Commons described him as a supporter of the Country party. In an analysis of the House into interests in January–May 1700 he was noted as doubtful or of the opposition.[3]

Cooke retired from politics at the next election in order to devote himself to his Yorkshire estates and to the development of his coal mines at Batley, where he was also a trustee of the local grammar school. As early as 1700 it was rumoured that he intended to sell his lands, and his electoral interest, at Aldborough, but this did not occur until 1702 when the lands were sold for £1,750 to the Duke of Newcastle (John Holles†). Despite his retirement from public life, in July 1713 it was reported that Cooke had been deputized by the leading Yorkshire manufacturers to thank the Queen for the 'great advantages' she had procured for the country by the French commercial treaty. Cooke died in 1732, being buried at Arksey, Yorkshire, on 12 Oct. In his will he recorded that he considered three of his sons, Bryan*, Henry and John, and one daughter, Elizabeth, to be 'already well provided for', and therefore desired that his manor at 'Adwick upon the street in the county of York' and the 'mansion house wherein I live' be sold by trustees in order to make a provision for his son Alexander and daughter Diana. His remaining son, George, who was also made executor, was left 'all those my houses in Doncaster in St. George'.[4]

[1] *Dugdale's Vis. Yorks.* ed. Clay, iii. 200–1; Sheffield Archs. Copley mss CD18–19, settlement 12–13 June 1683. [2] *HMC Lords*, n.s. iii. 204. [3] E. Miller, *Hist. Doncaster*, 206; Thoresby, *Ducatus Leodiensis*, 75; N. Yorks. RO, Swinton mss, Danby pprs. ZS, particulars of the several interests in Aldborough, [n.d.], John Wentworth to Sir Abstrupus Danby*, 12 May 1698. [4] M. Sheard, *Recs. Batley*, 12; Swinton mss, Danby pprs. ZS, Edward Morris to Thomas Johnson, 2 Sept. 1700, Lady Wentworth to Danby, 21 Sept. 1700; Notts. RO, Portland mss DD3P 10/1, Newcastle acct. bks. 30 Mar. 1702; PRO 31/3/201/62; Clay, 200–1; Borthwick Inst. York, prerog. ct. wills, Doncaster, June 1733.

E. C./C. I. M.

COOKE, John (1649–1726), of Petworth, Suss.

MIDHURST 1681 (Mar.)
ARUNDEL 22 Feb. 1694–1695, 1698–1702

bap. 21 Jan. 1649, 1st s. of Edward Cooke of Field Place, Goring, Suss. by his 1st w. Katherine, da. of Thomas Fry of Battlehurst, Kirdford, Suss. *educ.* M. Temple 1667. *m.* lic. 17 Oct. 1671, Susan (*d.* 1707), da. of John Whitehead of Clandon, Surr., wid. of her cos. George Stringer of the Middle Temple and coh. to her uncle Richard Stringer of Petworth, 2s. (1 *d.v.p.*) 1da. (*d.v.p.*) *suc.* fa. 1662.[1]

Sheriff, Suss. 17 Nov.–30 Nov. 1693.

Cooke, whose family had lived in Sussex since the 16th century, acquired his estate at Petworth, near Midhurst, by marriage. Probably an Exclusionist, and a Whig collaborator under James II, Cooke stood as the Whig candidate at a by-election for Arundel in 1694, and was returned on petition. Until 1695 his activities in the Commons are difficult to distinguish from those of William Cooke I. Three tellerships were recorded for a 'Mr Cooke' in this period, including two on 30 Apr. 1695: for recommitting the bill to reverse the attainder of Jacob Leisler, the radical who had taken power in New York in 1689, and then for reading the bill. As these votes appear to have been along party lines, it may be that both Members were tellers, William Cooke I, a Court Tory, telling in the first division and John Cooke in the second. Cooke's defeat at Arundel in 1695 was greeted with relief by Robert Middleton, the vicar of Cuckfield, who wrote to Bishop Simon Patrick of Ely that 'Mr Cooke of Petworth ... is happily shut out ... he being, as divers worthy persons that know him have told me, a derider of all religion, and so of the clergy, and little better than an atheist'.[2]

Cooke's 'atheism' did not prevent his being returned for Arundel in 1698, a seat he held until 1702. However, except for the 1701 Parliament, the presence of Thomas Coke* makes identification from the Journals difficult. Although classed as a Court supporter in a comparative analysis of the old and new Parliaments of about September 1698, Cooke was not listed as voting against the disbanding bill on 18 Jan. 1699. On 12 Apr. 1699 he introduced a clause to the land tax bill for appointing county sheriffs as receivers of the tax, with the exception of London and Middlesex. According to James Vernon I*, 'Mr Cooke of Sussex' proposed the clause which was designed to prevent the dismissal of sheriffs for political reasons and consequently the 'angry gentlemen', that is, the Country party, had supported it. He was listed as being in the Junto interest in an analysis of the House of January–May 1700.[3]

Cooke continued to represent Arundel in both 1701 Parliaments. In the first he acted as a teller on 16 June 1701, against an additional clause for the excise appropriation bill. In the second he was included with the Whigs on Robert Harley's* list of December 1701. He was defeated at the general election of 1702 and did not stand again. A John Cooke appears in a list of stockholders in the Bank of England in 1710 with stock worth £2,000. Cooke was buried at Goring 1 Oct. 1726, and was the only member of his family to sit in Parliament.[4]

[1] *Suss. Arch. Colls.* lxxviii. 66–67; Add. 5699, ff. 66, 67; *London Mar. Lic.* ed. Chester, 322; PCC 16 Laud. [2] *Suss. Arch. Colls.* cvi. 155. [3] Northants. RO, Montagu (Boughton) mss 47/168, Vernon to Shrewsbury, 12 Apr. 1699. [4] Egerton 3359 (unfol.); Add. 5699, f. 67.

P. W.

COOKE, Sir Thomas (?c.1648–1709), of Lordshold, Hackney, Mdx.; Salisbury Court, Fleet Street; and Fenchurch Street, London.

COLCHESTER 19 Nov. 1694–1695, 1698–1705

b. ?c.1648, s. of Thomas Cooke of Lambeth Marsh, Surr. *educ.* adm. and called L. Inn 1694 (hon.) *m.* 7 Feb. 1672, Elizabeth Horne of Exeter, 2s. 4da. Kntd. 15 Sept. 1690.[1]

Appr. Goldsmiths' Co. 1664, freeman 1672, rentor 1689, prime warden 1691; cttee. E.I. Co. 1683–90, 1695–6, 1698–1700, 1702–4, 1706–8, dep. gov. 1690–2, 1694–5, gov. 1692–4, 1700–2, 1704–6, 1708–9, manager, united trade 1702–8; asst. Royal African Co. 1690–2, 1701–2, 1705–9, sub. gov. 1703–4; cttee. Royal Fishery Co. of Ire. 1691; member, New England Co. ?1680.²

Alderman, London, 1692–d., sheriff 1692; vice-pres. Hon. Artillery Co. 1704–7; col. blue regiment 1702–7; freeman, Colchester 1694.³

Commr. Million Act 1694, taking subscriptions to land bank 1696.⁴

Cooke was known as the 'dictator' of the Old East India Company on account of his autocratic and domineering style of administration as its governor, and his name became a byword for corruption and bribery. Yet he had risen to this position of wealth and influence from obscure and humble origins. The son of a hat maker, he was born about 1648 (assuming that he was 16 at the time of his apprenticeship), and first made his fortune as a goldsmith and banker, establishing himself between 1675 and 1684 at the Griffin in Exchange Alley in partnership with Nicholas Carey*, with whom he also owned property at Hackney. He was elected as prime warden of the Goldsmiths' Company in 1691, but presided over only half of the company's courts that year, preferring instead to foster his career in the East India Company, of which he had been elected a committeeman in 1683 and deputy-governor in 1690. He supplied it with bullion, but also traded in saltpetre, fabrics, chinaware and turmeric, and rapidly amassed a fortune: by 1689 he held £12,000 of stock, and in January 1691 Cooke, lately knighted, married off his daughter, with a £25,000 portion, to Sir Josiah Child, 2nd Bt.*, whose father was the company's largest single shareholder. 'He thrives prodigiously', noted one contemporary in 1691, when he owned £40,850 of stock. A year later he was rich enough to lend £15,000 to the government while still accepting a bill of £100,000 from Dutch merchants without experiencing serious cash-flow problems. By the end of 1692 he was even in a position to offer to farm the land tax for £3 million. Having fought, bought and married his way into a dominant position within the East India Company it always remained his deepest concern, but he nevertheless reduced his investments towards the end of his life, selling £30,000 of his holdings in 1700 alone, and by 1703–4 he held only £14,000 in stock.⁵

Apart from the East India Company, Cooke's other main sphere of influence was the City of London. In May 1690 he was nominated 'by the Church party' as sheriff, and although defeated on this occasion he was successful in 1692, having been chosen alderman of Queenhithe ward earlier in the year. He ostentatiously 'laid by £10,000 to spend in his shrievalty' and, no doubt hoping to capitalize on this purchase of good-will, the Tories put him up as a mayoral candidate in 1693 with Sir Jonathan Raymond*, only to see him trail last in the poll, a defeat only partly compensated for by his being chosen an honorary bencher of Lincoln's Inn in February 1694. In 1700, having once more briefly contemplated standing himself, Sir Thomas joined with fellow alderman and East Indiaman Sir Francis Child*, who had been won over by the Tories, to back (Sir) Charles Duncombe's* candidature in the mayoral election. Cooke remained a supporter of Duncombe the following year, but just before the election Sir Thomas and six other East Indies merchants had caused a minor stir at common council by opposing the City's address against Louis XIV's recognition of the Pretender, on the far-fetched grounds that the French king might regard it as a declaration of war and seize English ships; but the Prussian ambassador remarked that since this suggestion came from people 'qui ont fait profession constante de Jacobitisme' little attention had been paid to them and the Whigs' address had been agreed on. Although Cooke could be ignored in 1701 when the Whigs were in the ascendancy in London, he benefited from their purge in 1702, being appointed colonel of the City's blue regiment. The following year he was up for election as mayor again, but James Craggs* observed that the 'Summerites' were all for Sir John Parsons*, who shared political influence at Reigate with Lord Somers (Sir John*), and Cooke lost it. His election as mayor the following year was nevertheless much easier than Craggs had predicted, since Sir Thomas was the senior alderman and regarded as 'a gentleman who will support that dignity with great honour and magnificence'. The obstacle to his holding office was only a self-imposed one, 'not being able to go through the great fatigue of the lord mayoralty, because of his great indisposition'. By taking the unprecedented step of asking to be excused on health grounds, even though he was fit enough to serve as governor of the East India Company, he gave a snubbing demonstration of his priorities and the City proceeded to a new election.⁶

Cooke's early career is difficult to reconstruct, partly because his name makes positive identification difficult. He was sometimes confused with Thomas Coke, MP for Derbyshire, and it is difficult to establish his relationship, if any, to the Thomas Cooke of Hackney, whose sons Charles and James later sat as MPs, the latter owning land in Epsom in Surrey where Sir Thomas also owned an estate. A John Cooke of Hackney, who first sat as a committeeman of the East India Company at the same time as Sir Thomas, may have been his brother, though later references to John in the company records may refer to Sir Thomas' son of that name. It may also have been a namesake who contested Truro in March 1681, though it does seem to have been the goldsmith Cooke who took his family to Holland on private business in April of that year. If so, he may have returned soon after since it is possible that he was the 'Cook' who played a vital role in Algernon Sidney's trial in 1683 by identifying the latter's handwriting, thereby establishing proof of Sidney's authorship of the manuscript treatise being used as evidence against him: the testimony was given alongside that of a Mr 'Cary' (possibly Cooke's goldsmith and banking partner) and related to Sidney's hand to bills of exchange, with which Cooke and Carey would naturally have dealt. If it was the future MP who testified, he kept an unusually low profile in the ensuing years of Tory reaction, making his mark only after the Revolution by unsuccessfully contesting Southwark with the Tory Sir Peter Rich[†] in 1690, and by donating £1,500 that spring for the relief of fugitive Irish and French Protestants, with a further £500 in the autumn to finance the repatriation of the Irish. The same year he was elected an assistant of the Royal African Company, and, more importantly, sub-governor of the East India Company, a position that earned him his knighthood and prepared him for the governorship in 1692.[7]

By 1694 Cooke had achieved all his ambitions: having been elected sheriff of London that year, he was brought in at a by-election at Colchester, possibly through the influence of the Childs. Yet within a year the bubble of his success had burst and he found himself in the Tower, temporarily unable to trade and castigated by Parliament for corruption. The roots of this crisis lay in his zealous, some thought overzealous, protection of the Old Company against interlopers, whose challenge of the monopoly had begun in earnest after the Revolution. In December 1691 Cooke and other leading East Indiamen had attended the Commons to satisfy MPs about their ability to fund the trade, which was to be newly regulated. Sir Thomas himself had been prepared to act as security for £100,000 of stock, and throughout January 1692 had acted as spokesman for the Company, finally conveying to the House on 4 Feb. its rejection of the securities that had been demanded. MPs had responded two days later by passing a resolution to address the King to dissolve the Old Company and establish a new one, although it had been saved from immediate ruin by the provision in its charter of three years' notice before any revocation. Another bill along the same lines as that of 1691 had been introduced in November 1692, and when this had met with further obstruction from the company the House had passed an address on 25 Feb. 1693 asking the King to give the requisite notice. It seems to have been at this stage that Sir Josiah Child[†] had learnt of 'a committee of 25 persons, that sat *de die in diem* to destroy the company', and had shared his apprehensions with Cooke who, it later emerged, had consequently sought to buy off a number of the most prominent interlopers, including Sir Basil Firebrace*, and their supporters, distributing over £80,000 of 'private service' money in 1693 alone.[8]

In the short term this policy had been successful, for on the eve of the parliamentary session the King had granted a new charter, which Cooke presented to the House on 30 Dec., and on 6 Jan. 1694 Sir Thomas showed MPs that subscriptions since then had totalled £744,000. But although the immediate prize had been won, it had only been gained at the cost of greater hostility on the part of those interlopers who had resisted the enticements, as a vote on 19 Jan. showed, and at the cost of mounting suspicions, even among some of the Old Company, that funds had been misappropriated. In what can be seen as a power struggle within the company, its general court initiated on 14 Nov. 1694 an internal inquiry, headed by Sir Benjamin Bathurst*, which produced a report on 12 Mar. 1695 that was highly critical of Cooke's management, and condemned the 'irregular' payments that had been made to Firebrace. This fuelled speculation that money had 'gone among the Members of the House of Commons' to obtain a new charter, especially when 'it was observed that some of the hottest sticklers against the company did insensibly not only fall off from that heat, but turned to serve the company, as much as they had at first endeavoured to destroy it'. Since such converts included Sir Edward Seymour, 4th Bt.*, and the Duke of Leeds (Sir Thomas Osborne[†]), and 'nothing was so likely to convince the people of England of the wicked designs of the Tory faction, as showing what mercenary creatures they were', there was also a strong political motive in pursuing the allegations of corruption in Parliament. Hon. Thomas Wharton* 'got complaints against several Members for taking of bribes to be given into the House, who upon hearing of them appointed a committee', largely composed of Country Whigs and 'mortal enemies of the Duke of Leeds', to inspect the East India Company's books. Cooke found himself the focus of the bribery charges when Paul Foley I* reported the committee's findings on 12 Mar. 1695, revealing largely what the Company's own investigation had discovered, namely that three huge payments, two of over £20,000 and one of £30,000, had been made to unknown persons between April

1693 and January 1694; that this 'was a new course since Sir Thomas Cooke came to be deputy governor or governor'; that five MPs, Sir Samuel Dashwood, Sir John Fleet, John Perry, Sir Joseph Herne and Cooke, had been present when these were sanctioned; and that Sir Thomas had refused to reveal who had received the money, even to fellow committeemen of the company, claiming that he was bound by oath to keep its secrets. Sir Basil Firebrace did, however, admit to the committee that he had used some of the money to win over to the company interlopers like himself, and Members also learned that Sir Edward Seymour's friend, Thomas Coulson*, had been granted an extraordinarily favourable saltpetre contract. Although L'Hermitage reported on 22 Mar. that several MPs understood Cooke's reluctance to make any revelations and that the matter might not therefore be pushed further, Cooke was ordered on 26 Mar. to give an account of how some £87,342 had been spent. He refused, and did so in such an antagonistic manner that MPs, already riled by Sir Thomas' friends 'disant perpetuellement qu'il ne craignoit rien', sent him to the Tower until a bill could be brought in to force him to declare what he knew. This allowed Sir Thomas until 1 June to give his information, or face disablement from holding any office, and imposed heavy financial penalties. Cooke was to have been brought immediately before the House for questioning, but one Member pointed out that if he spoke without some legal measure against him he would have to be allowed to take his seat again. He was therefore sent back to the Tower unheard and the bill against him was presented on 28 Mar. and rushed through the Commons, despite a protesting petition submitted by Cooke on the 30th. On 6 Apr. the bill was sent up to the Lords, who heard Cooke's counsel, Sir Thomas Powys*, succinctly state his client's dilemma: 'by his office he is under a trust; and by this bill he is to disclose his trust and destroy the company', though many suspected the less principled reason for hesitation was that Cooke had embezzled large amounts of the money himself. The following day Cooke was examined by the Lords and, in a histrionic performance that included weeping, declared himself 'ready and very willing' to make a discovery if he received indemnity from 'all actions and suits, except the East India Company, whom, if he had injured, he would be bound to undergo the greatest rigour'. The Upper House clearly felt that Sir Thomas might make the necessary revelations if treated with greater leniency than his colleagues in the Commons had been prepared to show, and resolved to proceed instead with a bill offering the indemnity, though Cooke very nearly lost this concession when he informed the peers via 'a reverend prelate who appeared zealous for him' that it would be three or four months before he was in a position to give a full account. Seeing the furious reaction of several lords angered by his 'trifling and prevaricating', Sir Thomas hurriedly 'engaged to discover within a fortnight', though in the end he was only allowed a week. The indemnity bill received the Royal Assent on 22 Apr. when William warned that he would end the session in a few days, and on 23 Apr. a joint committee set about examining Cooke, who tried to spin out proceedings by submitting a written account that the committee found unsatisfactory. It had been reported 'qu'il avoit parlé en secret que tant qu'il pourroit il ne feroit aucune découverte, mais que s'il étoit poussé à bout il declareroit tout, ne voulant être victime pour personne', but under further questioning he showed that he was prepared to shelter the Company by drawing all the fire on himself. He revealed only that £10,000 had been paid to the King, funded by himself as a well-timed traditional gift, and that the same sum had been paid, for the purposes of influencing MPs, to Richard Acton, whose information he must have hoped would be of limited value since a fall had left the go-between 'distracted'. However, in the event Acton did testify that Henry Goldwell* and two later MPs, James Craggs and Paul Docminique, had received money. Annoyed by Cooke's 'vapouring' evidence, MPs sent him back to the Tower and turned instead to Firebrace's more interesting confession. Sir Basil admitted that three payments of £10,000 had been made to Sir John Trevor*, Seymour, and Henry Guy*, and that he had paid 5,000 guineas to Charles Bates, a friend of the lord president, because Cooke had feared that the new charter 'stuck with the Duke of Leeds'. Here was the smoking gun that the promoters of the investigation had been looking for. Leeds had already twice drawn attention to himself, first on 6 Apr. by speaking 'vehemently' against the Commons' bill against Sir Thomas, when he had 'introduced what he was about to say with a solemn protestation of his [own] cleanness and innocence', and second, a week later, when he urged that Cooke should clear all the lords of taking money. Although proof that he had pocketed the money was not clear-cut, Leeds had panicked and had clumsily offered on 23 Apr. to return the money to Sir Thomas, 'who did scruple to take his money back at first but did afterwards consent to it', an offer that subsequently became public knowledge. On 24 and 27 Apr. the Commons heard reports of, and debated, the witnesses' examinations and on 29 Apr. voted to impeach Leeds, thereby effectively ending the latter's ministerial career. That same day the

Commons, which by now had a very thin attendance, rejected Cooke's plea for the benefit of the indemnity bill and instead read a bill to keep him and the other witnesses in custody. On 30 Apr. an amendment was debated to release all but Cooke on bail, but the two Houses were unable to agree and the clause was eventually rejected. Having made an unsuccessful appeal to the Lords, in which he protested that the bill to imprison him took away 'all his credit and reputation, which is as dear to him as his life' and that 'if he had seven years' time he could make no further discovery', Sir Thomas found himself at the prorogation confined to the Tower until the end of the next session. His desire for release evidently concentrated his memory, since on 28 Aug. he sent a letter to the commission of accounts asking them to examine him fully, and telling them that, while he had the satisfaction of knowing that what he had done 'was faithfully designed for the benefit of the East India Company, and the preserving the trade of the nation', his plight 'had a natural tendency to the utter ruin' of himself and his family. Since examining him would have reopened the old sores, the commission resolved, by a single vote, not to proceed, largely because Robert Harley* and Paul Foley I* no longer wished to pursue the matter, though ostensibly because it was a parliamentary concern. It had in fact already become a national one, with copies of Cooke's examination being printed so that 'patriots' could read 'how the country may be bought and sold by those which should preserve us'.[9]

The lengthy investigation into what one MP described as 'a blemish if not a scandal to the Revolution itself' had important consequences for national politics. It had successfully smeared a number of leading Tories, including Cooke, and produced a resolution on 2 May that offering bribes to any Member was a high crime and misdemeanour. Moreover, since MPs had deliberately delayed supply bills to prevent William from declaring a prorogation before they had had an opportunity to question Sir Thomas, the King was reluctant to risk reassembling them and therefore dissolved Parliament on 11 Oct. 1695. Despite his continued imprisonment and sullied reputation Cooke 'was invited to stand for Colchester, having been a benefactor there', and came remarkably close to being re-elected. Indeed on one of the three polls taken he had a majority, and Luttrell at first recorded the election as a victory for him; but the mayor had returned Sir John Morden, 1st Bt., against whom Cooke petitioned on 29 Nov. 1695, and the House decided in favour of Morden on 28 Mar. 1696. A month later Parliament was prorogued and Cooke duly regained his freedom, but the next two years were to be the nadir of his career, without even a place on the East India Company's committee. In 1697 he sold his Hackney manor, on which he had lavished £3,000 to improve the garden, and, just when he must have thought that the corruption scandal had died down, proceedings in the Commons on 5 May 1698 threatened to revive it. Following an offer by the Company to loan £700,000 in return for exclusive trading rights, it was moved, with the express intention of resurrecting 'the remembrance of what the company was formerly guilty of', to read the letter which Cooke had written in 1695 to the accounts commission. On 6 May this was opened, but was found to contain 'nothing to satisfy anyone's curiosity, since there were no particulars in it but what was known and talked of before', though James Sloane* wanted to use the occasion to 'fall on' Leeds again. The letter was referred to committee on 2 June, with Cooke being summoned to attend, and although it was not pursued there were further ominous investigations that month into the company's business activities. But although his fortunes were low during 1696–8 Cooke was irrepressible. In May 1696 his financial expertise was evidently considered too important for him not to be appointed to the committee for negotiating the land bank with the Treasury, and he used the opportunity to restore some confidence in his abilities, emerging in his favourite role as the group's spokesman. Nor did he neglect his own interests, submitting a petition in December 1696 that Sir John Fenwick† owed him £3,000, which he successfully requested to be paid out of the latter's forfeited estate. Moreover, in 1698 he regained a place on his company's ruling body, and in June of that year was in a position to subscribe £2,000 for the service of the government, a tenth of the Company's proposed loan.[10]

When Parliament was dissolved in July 1698 Cooke felt confident enough to stand again at Colchester, and was this time elected without a contest. Although marked as a Court supporter on a comparative list of old and new MPs, he was forecast as a likely opponent of a standing army, and duly found himself in the incongruous position of supporting the Country Whigs in January 1699 in their attempt to limit the number of troops, speaking twice in debates on the disbanding bill. During the Parliament's lifetime he also presented a bill on 27 Jan. 1700 for prolonging the time for prohibiting the export of corn, and acted as teller on 8 Feb. in favour of an adjournment of the debate about the bill hindering papists from disinheriting their Protestant heirs. It was nevertheless as a champion of the Old East India Company that Cooke primarily acted. After the interlopers' success in 1698 in obtaining parliamentary and Court recognition, the Old Company sought confirmation in 1699 of the 21-year term of its 1693 charter, and on 27 Feb. 1699 Sir Thomas acted as teller, with Francis Gwyn*, on a successful motion for leave to bring in such a bill. Cooke was appointed to the committee to prepare and introduce it, though John Cooke, MP for Arundel and possibly a relative of Sir Thomas, presented the bill on 3 Mar. It was supported by 'those who were for distressing the government', but was defeated at its second reading six days later, when Sir Thomas acted as teller in favour of its commitment. Undeterred by this temporary setback Sir Thomas and John Cooke were again active on the company's behalf when MPs reassembled for the second session, being granted leave on 19 Jan. 1700 to bring in a bill for continuing the Old Company. Sir Thomas had become its principal defender after the death in June 1699 of Sir Josiah Child, and proved an able leader, since on 9 Feb. the bill to reincorporate the company for the remainder of its 1693 charter was ordered to be engrossed. He also acted as teller on 4 Apr. against an amendment to a bill adding duties on East Indies commodities and, despite his losing a Chancery action against the crown over disputed pepper exports, the year marked his restoration to power and influence with re-election to the company's governorship. Not surprisingly Cooke was categorized in early 1700 as being in the East India Company interest.[11]

Cooke's re-election as the Company's governor could hardly have come at a more important time. In December 1700 he was able to inform Secretary Vernon (James I*) that the Old Company had resolved to join with the New if 'it may be effected upon just and honourable terms'. However, by January 1701 it was reported that he had rejected all proposals made thus far as unsatisfactory, a degree of obstruction to the King's wishes that caused Bonet to refer to him as a Jacobite, a charge no doubt made more credible by the financial connexion with his Hackney friend Sir John Freind† that Cooke had revealed the previous session when petitioning for the repayment of debt. Sir Thomas was again returned to Parliament at the first election of 1701 and in the ensuing session was mainly active on the Company's behalf. He was predicted in February as likely to support the Court in agreeing with the committee of supply's resolution to continue the 'Great Mortgage', and on 28 Apr. presented to the committee concerned with ways of redeeming the public debt a proposal from the Old Company to pay the £2 million advanced by the New. This was not debated until 17 May when it was 'ordered to lie on the table, lest, if it should pass, it should destroy the public credit'. Cooke was re-elected as governor in April 1701, with Sir Samuel Dashwood as his deputy, and over the next few months the two men headed the Old Company's delegation for negotiating terms of union with the New, although John Dolben* feared that they would place their private interests first. Agreement was nevertheless reached in December 1701, and from 1702 until the formal union of 1709 the trade was under a joint management committee, of which Cooke was naturally a member.[12]

The dissolution of the short-lived 1701 Parliament forced Cooke to seek re-election at Colchester. The experience was not a comfortable one, since the corporation had received a letter from Sir Thomas Abney* which vilified Sir Thomas' activities as a London alderman, and although Cooke was in fact elected without a contest the matter was observed to have created 'ill blood'. He was listed with the Tories in an analysis made by Robert Harley in December, and on 26 Feb. 1702 favoured the motion vindicating the Commons' proceedings in the impeachment of the King's ministers, no doubt eager to join any condemnation that encompassed the New Company's patron Charles Montagu*, now Lord Halifax. However, he was a teller only once, on 17 Apr. 1702, in a very thin House of 47 MPs, on an amendment to the supply bill which related to the East India Company's saltpetre contract with the Crown. Soon after, on 27 Apr., the Company voted him a free gift of £12,000 'for his good services' as governor when he temporarily stepped down from the post.[13]

Blacklisted as having opposed the preparations for war with France during the previous year, Cooke stood at the election in August 1702 with John Potter, Colchester's Tory mayor. Potter was unsuccessful and petitioned against the return of the Whig Sir Isaac Rebow, who in turn fostered a petition against Cooke's election, though this was rejected by the Commons on 21 Nov. Cooke's chief concern during the subsequent sessions was once more with the East India Company. He obtained special leave on 4 Feb. 1703 to bring in a bill for prolonging the time for exporting foreign goods, and on 14 Jan. 1704 presented to the House an account of the bullion exported by the Company. He was forecast by Lord Nottingham (Daniel Finch†) in mid-March as a likely supporter in the event of a parliamentary attack on him over his handling of the Scotch Plot. Despite his reputation as a staunch Churchman, Cooke was nevertheless listed in October as a probable opponent of the Tack, and on 28 Nov. either voted against the measure or was absent from the House, possibly in order to ingratiate himself with the government. At a local level, however, Cooke had become drawn into Colchester corporation's internal feuding when in 1703 he opposed Rebow's campaign for election as the borough's high steward. The Tories, led by John Potter, nominated the Prince of Denmark instead, and Cooke, coming to the aid of his former running-mate, twice waited on Prince George to inform him of the borough's inclinations. Rebow had not forgotten this opposition by the time of the 1705 election, and the Whigs secured both seats, Cooke being defeated by Edward Bullock, another East Indiaman with marital ties to the Child family but one who had deserted the Tories. When Bullock died, only a few months later, Sir Thomas contested the vacant seat, but local animosities still worked against him. Defeated at the poll, Cooke petitioned on 10 Jan. 1706 against the return of Sir Thomas Webster*, complaining that the mayor had made a large number of Webster's supporters freemen so that they could vote in the election. His petition was accompanied by another, which supported his case, from some of the borough's inhabitants, and the latter was resubmitted on 11 Dec. 1706, only to be rejected on 10 Feb. 1707, while Cooke's own petition seems never to have been pursued.[14]

The defeat left him free to devote his energies to the affairs of the company. In September 1707 he was warned by Lord Treasurer Godolphin about the company's large-scale purchase of silver for export, reminding a man who surely was in little need of such advice that 'a great many' MPs were hostile to the company; and the following year Cooke defended Thomas Pitt I*'s position, and was active in negotiations about union. Although these talks proved fruitful they also provoked a feud between him and (Sir) Gilbert Heathcote*, who headed the New Company's interest, a rivalry that came to a head in the election for governor of the United Company for 1709. Preparations for the contest had started the previous autumn when 'both sides had begun to put in practice all possible arts and contrivances to promote their interests', and John Dolben believed in October 1708 that

> Sir Thomas would have been too hard for Sir Gilbert, having all the party of the Old [Company] to a man secure to him . . . but a fatal accident has given a terrible blow to all those designs. The last week poor Sir Thomas was seized all at once with a violent fit of apoplexy or palsy, I think both, and though 'tis hoped his life is not at present in danger, yet I much fear he will never recover his limbs or understanding, so as never to be a man of business again; he was the very soul of the Old Company, and I conclude without him they cannot so much as make a stand, but that unless he recovers his vigour before the election the majority will certainly fall on the other side, and new measures will be taken all over India.

Although Cooke continued to live for almost another year it was evidently only in an incapacitated state since he was unable to attend the company's meetings, and he failed to draw up a detailed will. It is one of the ironies of his career that Cooke's forceful style of management, intended to maintain the company's strength, had in fact left it weakened and unable to throw up a new leadership after him. On 18 Jan. 1709 Dolben wrote that Cooke's collapse had

> entirely broke the power and interest of the Old Company. He was so absolute a dictator that upon his fall they were all in confusion, and had neither spirit or knowledge to keep themselves any longer in a united body, but gave way in all contests to the superiority of the New.

He suffered a second and fatal fit of apoplexy on 6 Sept. 1709, leaving his son John and wife as executors of his undefined property, though it is known that he had bought estates in 1692 in Hertfordshire, in 1705 at Epsom, Surrey, and in America.[15]

[1] Info. from M. Havlik and Dr D. F. Lemmings; *Le Neve's Knights* (Harl. Soc. viii), 434; *London Mar. Lic.* (Index Lib. lxvi), 23. [2] Info. from M. Havlik and Prof. H. Horwitz; K. G. Davies, *R. African Co.* 380; W. Kellaway, *New England Co.* 292. [3] Beaven, *Aldermen of London*, ii. 118; *Oath Bk . . . of Colchester* ed. W. G. Benham (1907), 248. [4] *Cal. Treas. Bks.* x. 552; *CJ*, xii. 508. [5] *Le Neve's Knights*, 434; C 110/28, John Dolben* to Thomas Pitt I, 20 Oct. 1708, 18 Jan. 1709; Huntington Lib. Ellesmere mss 9930, satire; A. Heal, *The London Goldsmith*, 129; info. from M. Havlik; Add. 22185, ff. 12, 53; Luttrell, *Brief Relation*, ii. 192, 395, 404; Hereford and Worcester RO (Hereford), Foley mss, box E12/F/IV, Richard Normansell to [–], 12 Mar. 1690; *Cal. Treas. Bks.* ix. 1653; Bodl. Rawl. D.747, ff. 268, 276; Rawl. A.303, ff. 56–57. [6] Luttrell, 47, 357, 493, 590; iii. 194–6; v. 193, 343; Beaven, i. 195; info. from Dr Lemmings; Huntington Lib. Stowe mss 26 (1–2), James Brydges'* diary, 13 Aug. 1700; Yale Univ. Beinecke Lib. Osborn coll. Blathwayt mss, box 20, Robert Yard* to William Blathwayt*, 2 Oct. 1701; Univ. Kansas Spencer Research Lib. Moore mss 143Cc, Craggs to Arthur Moore*, 29 Sept. 1703; Folger Shakespeare Lib. Newdigate newsletters 28, 30 Sept. 1704. [7] *CSP Dom.* 1680–1, p. 233; Luttrell, i. 290; ii. 112; Beaven, i. 303; Foley mss, box E12/F/IV, Richard Normansell to [–], 12 Mar. 1690. [8] *Luttrell Diary*, 90–93, 96, 118, 158; Cobbett, *Parlty Hist.* v. 915, 929; *Jnl. Brit. Studies*, xvii (2), p. 5. [9] *Debates and Proceedings 1694–5*; Burnet, iv. 260; *Wharton Mems.* 24; *Ailesbury Mems.* 349; Add. 17677 PP, ff. 202, 210, 220, 233–4, 253–4; *HMC Lords 1693–5*, pp. 548–51, 573; Cobbett, v. 911–3, 917, 921, 927; *Lexington Pprs.* 81; *CSP Dom.* 1695, pp. 324–5; H. Horwitz, *Parl. and Pol. William III*, 156; *Portledge Pprs.* 204. [10] Cobbett, v. 931; Add. 17677 PP, f. 237; 70155, list of 'recommended' lottery commissioners; *Norris Pprs.* 27; *Essex Review*, ii. 226; Luttrell, iv. 51; W. Robinson, *Hist. of Hackney* (1842), i. 200, 304; *CSP Dom.* 1698, p. 227; Northants. RO, Montagu (Boughton) mss 47/25, Vernon to Shrewsbury, 7 May 1698; *Cal. Treas. Bks.* xi. 17, 26, 30, 35; *CSP Dom.* 1696, pp. 259, 456. [11] *Cam. Misc.* xxix. 381, 387; *Cocks Diary*, 19–20.

[12] *English Post*, 27–30 Dec. 1700; Add. 30000 E, f. 9; 70284, Ld. Godolphin (Sidney†) to Robert Harley, 22 Aug. 1701; *CJ*, xii. 675; Luttrell, v. 51; *Post Boy*, 29 Apr.–1 May 1701; C 110/28 John Dolben to Thomas Pitt I, 19 July 1701; *Jnl. Brit. Studies*, xvii (2), pp. 16–17. [13] Add. 70075, newsletter 27 Nov. 1701; Luttrell, v. 168. [14] *Wharton Mems.* 23; Rawl. C.441, ff. 1–2, 'Case of the Town of Colchester' [1703]; L. C. Bullock, *Mem. of Fam. Bullock* (1905), 38. [15] C 110/28, Dolben to Pitt, 1 Mar. 1708, 20 Oct. 1708; Thomas Marshall to Pitt, 23 Jan. 1708; *Cal. Treas. Bks.* xxi. 44; xxii. 41, 44; Newdigate newsletter 14 Oct. 1708; Luttrell, vi. 364; Add. 70420, Dyer's newsletter 8 Sept. 1709; PCC 240 Lane; D. W. Jones, *War and Econ.* 330; *CJ*, xiv. 522; Luttrell, v. 82.

M. J. K.

COOKE, William I (c.1620–1703), of Highnam Court, nr. Gloucester.

GLOUCESTER 1679 (Mar.–July), 1689–1695

b. c.1620, 1st s. of Sir Robert Cooke† of Highnam by his 1st w. Dorothy, da. of Sir Miles Fleetwood† of Aldwinkle, Northants.; bro. of Edward Cooke†. *educ.* G. Inn 1636. *m.* lic. 30 Mar. 1648, Anne, da. and coh. of Dennis Rolle of Stevenstone, Devon, 9s. (5 *d.v.p.*) 7da. (3 *d.v.p.*). *suc.* fa. 1643.[1]

High sheriff, Glos. 1663.

Verderer, Forest of Dean 1668–?*d*.; freeman, Gloucester 1672, alderman 1672–*d*., mayor 1673–4, Nov. 1688–9, Apr.–Sept. 1699; commr. of inquiry, Forest of Dean 1673, 1679, 1683, 1691.[2]

Cooke's family had been established at Highnam since 1597. Highnam, 'a large beautiful seat', was situated only two miles west of Gloucester and commanded a 'pleasant prospect' over the city. Initially, Cooke's public preoccupations had been with county politics, and only subsequently did he become immersed in Gloucester's civic affairs, having been nominated a freeman and alderman under the charter of 1672. A Tory in the first Exclusion Parliament, he fought and lost his next election as an Exclusionist, though his flirtation with the Country party soon afterwards lapsed. In November 1688 he commenced a second mayoral term during which he oversaw the removal of the Jacobite faction from the corporate body and played a leading part in restoring political stability to the city. Elected to the Convention in January 1689, he took a principled Tory line in voting against the motion declaring the throne vacant. In 1690 he successfully contested Gloucester, and in the preparations for the opening session Lord Carmarthen (Sir Thomas Osborne†) reckoned him a probable supporter of the Court but without ascribing a party label. These predictions were evidently confirmed since in December Carmarthen was able to mark him as pro-Court in two further lists, and he was similarly classified in Robert Harley's* list of April 1691. Cooke appears to have been fairly busy in legislative matters, and in the Journals his name can be found associated with a variety of measures tackling social and commercial problems. On 9 May 1690 he was appointed to a committee both to investigate the wine trade and produce a regulatory bill, and in the next session, on 1 Dec., was named one of the drafters of a bill to prevent exports of wool. He was granted leave of absence on the 16th. In November 1691 he was included on the drafting bodies of bills concerning the manufacture of saltpetre and the supervision of the poor. On 14 Nov. 1693 he was among those appointed to draft legislation to stimulate the clothing trade. However, with his namesake John Cooke joining him in the Commons on 22 Feb. 1694, it is no longer possible to be certain of his parliamentary activity, though given his earlier assiduity, he may have been the 'Mr Cooke' intended in three tellerships in the period remaining before the 1695 election. Cooke's name appears on a list of Henry Guy's supporters during the 1694–5 session. It is not known for certain if he stood for re-election: if he did, he either withdrew or was defeated. He continued his involvement in corporation affairs, however, and in April 1699, aged almost 80, was called upon to take the mayoral chair for a third time in place of a deceased incumbent. He died early in 1703. His grandson William II was elected for the city in 1705.[3]

[1] IGI, Glos.; *Vis. Glos.* ed. Fenwick and Metcalfe, 47–48; *London Mar. Lic.* ed. Foster, 324. [2] *Cal. Treas. Bks.* ii. 594; iii. 262; iv. 156; vi. 196; vii. 962; ix. 1156; *Gloucester Freemen* (Glos. Rec. Ser. iv), 27; *VCH Glos.* iv. 378; Rudder, *Glos.* 117; Glos. RO, Gloucester bor. recs. GBR/B3/7, f. 215. [3] Atkyns, *State of Glos.* 176; Gloucester bor. recs. GBR/B3/7, f. 215.

P. W./A.A.H.

COOKE, William II (1682–1709), of Highnam Court, nr. Gloucester.

GLOUCESTER 1705–June 1709

b. 18 Dec. 1682, 2nd but 1st surv. s. of Edward Cooke (*d.* 1724) of Highnam, Glos. by Mary, da. of Rowland Newborough of Berkley, Som.; gds. of William Cooke I*. *educ.* M. Temple 1702. *unm.*[1]

Freeman, Gloucester 1705.[2]

The grandson of one of Gloucester's leading civic figures and MP for the city in William III's reign, Cooke was only in his early twenties when put forward and chosen for the city in 1705, whereupon Lord Sunderland (Charles, Lord Spencer*) noted his election as a gain for the Whigs, while in another list he was noted as a 'Churchman'. He voted on 25 Oct. for the Court candidate in the division on the Speaker, and on 18 Feb. 1706 again supported the Court on the 'place clause' in the regency bill. Inactive in the House, he was, however, observed to have been 'very pressing' in 1707 for the appointment of his uncle as dean of Gloucester, though his efforts in this regard came to nothing. He was incorrectly classed as a Tory in a list of early 1708 but accurately marked as a Whig in another analysis of about the same time. He was returned again in 1708 but died, predeceasing his father, in June 1709, aged 26.[3]

[1] IGI, Glos.; *Vis. Glos.* ed. Fenwick and Metcalfe, 47–48; W. R. Williams, *Glos. MPs.* 206. [2] *Gloucester Freemen* (Glos. Rec. Ser. iv), 61. [3] Luttrell, *Brief Relation*, vi. 457; *Hist. Reg. Chron.* 1724, p. 52; Williams, 206.

P. W.

COOKES WINFORD, Sir Thomas, 2nd Bt. *see* **WINFORD**

COOTE, Richard, 1st Earl of Bellomont [I] (c.1655–1701).

DROITWICH 1689–1695

b. c.1655, 2nd but 1st surv. s. of Richard, 1st Baron Coote of Coloony [I], by Mary, da. of Sir George St. George of Carrick Drumrusk, co. Leitrim. *m.* lic. 19 Aug. 1680, aged about 25, Catherine (d. 12 Mar. 1738), da. and h. of Bridges Nanfan† of Birtsmorton, Worcs., 3s. *suc.* fa. 10 July 1683 as 2nd Baron Coote; *cr.* Earl of Bellomont [I] 2 Nov. 1689.[1]

Capt. of horse, Dutch army 1687–Mar. 1688; capt.-gen. Massachusetts, New York, New Hampshire, Connecticut, Rhode Is. and the Jerseys 1697; capt. ind. coy. New York 1697–d.[2]

Treasurer to Princess Mary of Orange Mar. 1688 (as Queen) 1689–93; gov. co. Leitrim 1689–93; gov. Massachusetts, New York, New Hampshire 1697–d., v.-adm. 1698–d.[3]

Gov. Saltpetre Co. 1692.[4]

Member, New Eng. Co. 1697; commr. for Indian affairs 1701.[5]

Bellomont, an Irish peer, left England in 1687 for the United Provinces, and, once there, accepted a commission in the English regiments serving in the Dutch army. Although summoned to return by James II, he entered into the service of Princess Mary, eventually sailing with her husband in the invasion fleet of 1688. At the Revolution he retained his post in the Queen's household, secured an Irish county governorship and a promotion in the Irish peerage. He was returned to the Convention of 1689 for Droitwich, probably on the recommendation of the Earl of Shrewsbury, and with the support of the Foleys. Although his main estates lay in Ireland these Worcestershire connexions were sufficient to secure his re-election at Droitwich in 1690. His own land-holding in the county appears to have been slender, hence his comment in 1689 that he was 'not satisfied whether I rightly account myself a freeholder of England'. However, his wife was a Worcestershire heiress and he had the power to bequeath the manor of Pendock just to the south of Birtsmorton in his will in 1697, possibly as part of the marriage settlement. In general his economic circumstances were difficult: he was in financial straits even before the war in Ireland, his father-in-law excusing his removal into Holland on the grounds that it was a 'cheaper' country in which to live. No doubt this condition contributed to an abiding interest in two issues throughout his political career: the mismanagement of Irish affairs and the search for additional sources of income.[6]

The Marquess of Carmarthen (Sir Thomas Osborne†) classed Bellomont as a Whig in an analysis of March 1690. In April 1691 Robert Harley* listed him as a Country supporter, albeit with the caveat of 'doubtful', which may well point to the contradictions of Bellomont's position, as a placeman deeply mistrustful of the crown's chosen servants in Ireland and committed to the principles of Country Whiggism. Harley was certainly acquainted with him, possibly through the Foleys. In 1692 he became interested in a new money-spinning project, to take advantage of the speculative boom of the early 1690s. Luttrell reported in October that a charter of incorporation had been granted to 'Lord Bellomont and 20 others' to manufacture and supply the King with saltpetre. This was probably the company for making saltpetre in England, which raised a considerable amount of capital only to fold in 1694. Bellomont's role may have been to smooth the passage of the charter, which was the responsibility of a Worcestershire Whig, the attorney-general, Sir John Somers*, whom Bellomont had known since at least 1684. Unfortunately, involvement in this project can only have worsened his financial predicament.[7]

Bellomont's name appears on three lists of placemen from the years 1692–3, drawn up by Carmarthen and by Samuel Grascome. Events were to show that office-holding and support for the Court were not necessarily compatible, especially if Irish issues were involved. On 7 Jan. 1693 Edward Harley* reported to his father a petition from Ireland aimed at Lord Coningsby (Thomas*), 'which is likely to be followed with vigour. Lord Bellomont is concerned in it. I am told that country is under great oppression and misery.' This agitation prompted the Commons to conduct an investigation into the state of Ireland, which in turn led to the appointment on 24 Feb. of a committee (of which Bellomont was a member) to draft an address to the King. Bellomont was undoubtedly to the fore in attempts to punish the Irish administration and this, together with his advocacy of the triennial bill and criticism of the use of the royal veto, led to his dismissal from the Queen's service for having 'behaved himself impertinently'. Indeed, the Queen having 'spoke to him in that matter', she sent him a message that 'he was not put out of his place for any misbehaviour in it, but for the reason he knew himself'. It was Lord Sunderland's view that his post should be left open until the King's return, 'that my Lord B[ellomont] might have more than is intended, for that matter sticks and was most extremely unreasonable'. He was probably referring to some kind of financial compensation in the form of a pension, which Bellomont refused in response to Coningsby's elevation to the Privy Council, an event described by Sunderland 'as if care had been taken that that business should not die, he being the man in whom all that matter centred'. The opposition response was a paper published in November 1693 by Charlwood Lawton, which described Bellomont as a 'gallant lord' who had been turned out 'merely for giving his vote in the House of Commons according to his conscience'.[8]

The response of Coningsby and Sir Charles Porter*, the lord chancellor of Ireland, was to solicit during the summer recess a pardon for their actions as lords justices of Ireland. A counter-petition from Bellomont and Colonel James Hamilton, another Irish landowner, claimed that since Parliament had taken cognizance of mismanagements in Ireland, and given notice that they would be pursued in the next session, no pardon should be granted, as it would be a breach of the Bill of Rights – an argument which neatly precluded the Privy Council's attempt to pre-empt Parliament by inquiring into events in Ireland and vindicating the accused. It was suspected that Bellomont 'is put upon it by some members of the House of Commons w[h]ere he expects to be supported. Some think that one or both of them may have an eye to some recompense or employment if that open not a way to too many.' There is some evidence of Bellomont receiving advice from prominent opponents of the Court, chief among them Robert Harley, whose papers contain draft replies of arguments used and advice to Bellomont on questions of tactics. On one occasion Bellomont invited Harley to dinner with James Sloane* (an Irish MP sitting on the Hamilton interest), the Earl of Monmouth (a noted troublemaker and Hamilton's brother-in-law) and Hamilton himself. Bellomont duly took up the attack on Irish mismanagements in the following session, presenting articles of impeachment against Coningsby and Porter on 16 Dec. 1693. Harley was again active behind the scenes in preparing the charges, being asked by Bellomont to 'take the pains to illustrate them with all the advantage you please (which you are well able to do) that each article may have a sting in the tail', and to 'polish' them, 'my credit being engaged in the effectual and speedy carrying on the impeachment'. Bellomont seems to have been tenacious in pursuit of his enemies, for on 22 Dec., when the Commons 'showed a disposition . . . not to prosecute them', he announced his readiness to produce further witnesses. However, after several more hearings at the bar, Coningsby and Porter were cleared on 29 Jan. 1694. Bellomont was also disappointed in a plan to mobilize the Commons against his dismissal from office, writing somewhat plaintively to Harley of a promise he had made 'of consulting some of our friends what were proper to be done in the House about my being so turned out of my employment as I was, to the breach of the privilege of Parliament'.[9]

Nevertheless, Bellomont's fate did elicit some sympathy from those Whig friends who had received honours and office following the 1693–4 session. Shrewsbury (once again secretary of state) persuasively put Bellomont's case to William III in June 1694 for a grant of Irish forfeited estates:

his condition I really believe is necessitous to a great degree, and there are several persons, Members of Parliament, who lay great weight, and think his friends obliged to see him taken care of. He seems to the world to have been displaced, for a reason that would do your Majesty great prejudice to have it believed that it sticks with you.

Sunderland, too, was employed in an approach to the Earl of Portland. For the moment nothing came of this pressure. In the meantime the 1694–5 session had opened with Members debating the so-called Lancashire Plot and the ensuing treason trials at Manchester. Investigations revealed that Bellomont had been in contact with the two informers, John Taaffe and John Lunt, to discover lands put to superstitious uses, which could be the basis of allegations of treason. No doubt Bellomont's interest was in lands which would thus fall forfeit to the crown.[10]

There is no evidence that Bellomont expressed any wish to contest the 1695 election at Droitwich; no doubt a wise course in view of his parlous financial position. Indeed, he appears now to have favoured a classic escape-route from penury, namely emigration as a colonial official. In April 1695 he appears to have been appointed governor of Massachusetts, but the question of his salary held up his commission: a vexed question as it concerned not only his desire to clear his debts, but the more general problem of the financial independence of royal governors from colonial assemblies. His friends suggested an Irish grant, through the friendly auspices of Lord Capell (Hon. Sir Henry Capel*), now lord deputy of Ireland, and in July 1695 Bellomont duly petitioned for a grant of the forfeited estates of Sir Valentine Browne (Lord Kenmare) and Sir Nicholas Browne. In April 1696 he was allowed £1,000 p.a. from the estate. The Whigs had contrived an additional plan to augment his salary, while scoring a political point. In July 1695 Shrewsbury had outlined a proposal to the King that Bellomont be made governor of New York as well as Massachusetts, an appointment which would have involved the removal of the Tory incumbent in New York, Benjamin Fletcher, and to that end the Whigs exerted pressure on the Board of Trade. Eventually, Bellomont was appointed governor of both colonies in March 1697, although he did not sail for America until November.[11]

Parliamentary controversy pursued Bellomont across the Atlantic in the person of Captain Kidd, and yet another scheme based on the suppression of piracy in the seas around Madagascar. Bellomont was instrumental in drawing in the Duke of Shrewsbury, and Lords Orford (Edward Russell*) and Romney (Henry Sidney†) as financial backers, as well as Somers, who procured the patent. However, all the participants were vulnerable to attack when Kidd himself turned pirate. Bellomont protected himself by having Kidd arrested as he returned to New York, then sending him to England and scrupulously accounting for all the captured treasure (although this did not prevent him from claiming a share of one-third as vice-admiral). The Tories, however, exploited the grant and it formed the 13th article of impeachment against the former lord chancellor in May 1701. By then Bellomont had died in New York of gout in the stomach, on 5 Mar. 1701. His wife and sons were left destitute in New York where he had to be buried at public expense. In his will he ordered his debts to be paid from the estates bequeathed to him by his father in five Irish counties, provided for the education of his sons, and left his estate to two noted Whigs, Somers and Robert Molesworth*, to sell or mortgage in order to pay his debts and annuities. His long-suffering wife, to whom he paid tribute in his will, remarried successively Captain (later Rear-Admiral) William Caldwell, Samuel Pytts* and Alderman William Bridgen. She died in 1738, leaving Birtsmorton, to which she had succeeded in 1704, to her son, Richard Coote, 3rd Earl of Bellomont.[12]

[1] *Mar. Lic. Vicar-Gen.* (Harl. Soc. xxx), 39. [2] Add. 41820, f. 273; *HMC Downshire*, i. 286; *CSP Dom.* 1697, pp. 59–60, 298. [3] Add. 41821, f. 74; Luttrell, *Brief Relation*, i. 435, 515; *CSP Col.* 1693–6, p. 506; *Publns. of Col. Soc. of Mass.* ii. p. xxix. [4] *Sel. Charters*, 235. [5] W. Kellaway, *New Eng. Co.* 290. [6] Add. 41820, f. 273; 41821, f. 74; 70014, f. 290; *CSP Dom.* 1689–90, pp. 31–32, 456, 464; *HMC Hastings*, ii. 184; *HMC Lords*, ii. 139–40; *CJ*, xiii. 192. [7] Add. 70233, Sir Edward* to Robert Harley, 11 Nov. 1690; 70015, f. 211; 34720, f. 93; *Econ. Hist. Rev.* ser. 2, xxxix. 552, 558–9; Luttrell, ii. 585; W. R. Scott, *Jt.-Stock Cos.* ii. 473–4. [8] Add. 70017, f. 1; Ranke, vi. 212; *Mems. Mary Queen of Eng.* 59; Centre Kentish Stud. Stanhope mss U1590/O59/2, Robert Yard* to Alexander Stanhope, 11 Apr. 1693; H. Horwitz, *Parl. and Pol. Wm. III*, 115, 121; Nottingham Univ. Lib. Portland (Bentinck) mss PwA 1211, 1219, Sunderland to Portland, 25 Apr. [1693], [c. June 1693]; Cobbett, *Parlty. Hist.* v. p. cii. [9] PRO NI, De Ros mss 638/9/7, Lord Nottingham (Daniel Finch†) to Coningsby, 24 June 1693; D638/18/11, [?Francis Gwyn*] to same, 24 June 1693; Huntington Lib. Ellesmere mss 9885, Bellomont's charge against Coningsby and Porter, 17 Aug. 1693; Trinity, Dublin, Lyons (King) mss 1997/284, George Tollet to Bp. King, 24 June 1693; Add. 70264, drafts of Bellomont and Hamilton's answer to the Council; 70219, Bellomont to Harley, 'Wed. morning' [7 Aug. 1693]; 70282, same to same, Thurs. night, Sun. night; *HMC Portland*, iii. 542; Grey, x. 364; Cobbett, 819; Stanhope mss U1590/O53/2, James Vernon I* to Stanhope, 18–27 Dec. 1693. [10] *Shrewsbury Corresp.* 40; Portland (Bentinck) mss PwA 1240, Sunderland to Portland, 5 Aug. 1694; Add. 70017, f. 345; Boyer, *Wm. III*, 7; *HMC Kenyon*, 333–4. [11] Yale Univ. Beinecke Lib. Osborn Coll. Blathwayt mss, Ld. Godolphin (Sidney†) to William Blathwayt*, 3 June 1695; *Cal. Treas. Bks.* x. 1116, 1178, 1405; xi. 95; *CSP Dom.* 1696, pp. 134, 407, 459; 1697, p. 441; *CSP Col.* 1696–7, p. 313; *Shrewsbury Corresp.* 94; *Wm. and Mary Q.* ser. 3, xx. 532–8. [12] G. B. Nash, *Urban Crucible*, 90; M. Kammen, *Col. New York*, 141; R. C. Ritchie, *Capt. Kidd and War Agst. Pirates*, 48–54; D. M. Hinricks, *Fateful Voyage of Capt. Kidd*, 138; *HMC Portland*, viii. 69; PCC 23 Gee.

S. N. H.

COPE, Sir John, 5th Bt. (1634–1721), of Hanwell, Oxon. and Chelsea, Mdx.

OXFORDSHIRE 1679 (Mar.)–1681 (Jan.)
                 1689–1690
BANBURY   23 Feb. 1699–1700

b. 19 Nov. 1634, 3rd but 2nd surv. s. of Sir John Cope, 3rd Bt., of Hanwell by 2nd w. Lady Elizabeth, da. of Francis Fane†, 1st Earl of Westmorland; bro. of Sir Anthony Cope, 4th Bt.† *educ.* Queen's, Oxf. 1651; travelled abroad (France) 1654, (Italy, Germany, Low Countries). *m.* 2 Nov. 1672, Anne (d. 1713), da. of Philip Booth, of ?Dunkirk, 7s. (3 *d.v.p.*) 1da. *d.v.p. suc.* bro. as 5th Bt. 11 June 1675.[1]

Lt. of ft. Visct. Falkland's (Henry Carey†) regt. July 1660–2, capt. of ft. 1667.[2]

Freeman, Oxford 1679–June 1688; asst. Banbury by 1699.[3]

Dir. Bank of Eng. (with statutory intervals) 1695–1702.[4]

A younger son, Cope was unfortunate in receiving only a life interest in the family estates owing to his brother's disapproval of his marriage. Prior to his inheritance he had travelled widely in Europe and served as a soldier. As a considerable landowner he represented Oxfordshire in all three Exclusion Parliaments and the Convention of 1689. Thereafter, his efforts to return to the Commons were usually thwarted.[5]

Cope clearly welcomed the Revolution of 1688, invested heavily in the new regime and served as a deputy-lieutenant for Oxfordshire from 1689. However, he was well able to afford this outlay, his accounts suggesting expenditure in excess of £2,000 p.a. in the early 1690s. At the 1690 election he was defeated for the county despite the appearance of a broadsheet accusing his Tory opponents of having opposed the transfer of the crown. It is difficult to determine if at this point he was residing at Hanwell, or indeed in Oxfordshire at all, because he was engaged in a dispute over the custody of his sister-in-law, who had been certified a lunatic. Furthermore, within a few years, his involvement in setting up the Bank of England, and then his appointment as a director, probably saw him spending most of his time in London. It is not known if he attempted to regain his Oxfordshire seat in the 1695 election, but he had been expected to 'make an interest' there. He did stand in 1698, only to finish bottom of the poll in a four-cornered contest despite enjoying the support of the Dissenters. However, he succeeded in finding a seat in that Parliament at a by-election in 1699 for Banbury, only three and a half miles from his principal seat at Hanwell, the vacancy having occurred when James Isaacson*, a Whiggish friend, was expelled from the Commons for holding an office of profit under the crown. During his short stay in the House his name appears on an analysis of the Commons as a member of the Junto interest, probably an accurate assessment given his long connexion with the Whigs.[6]

Henceforth Cope's career becomes difficult to disentangle from that of his eldest son, another Sir John Cope* (who had been knighted in 1696). It seems likely that Cope snr. continued to be active in Oxfordshire politics, but that any electioneering outside the county was undertaken by his son, established at Bramshill, Hampshire from 1700. Cope became a magistrate of Banbury under the corporation's 1718 charter. He died on 11 Jan. 1721. His will includes a long justification of the actions which had provoked his brother to settle most of the estate on another branch of the family. Written in 1717, it passed most of his personal estate to his heir, while providing the younger sons with £5,000 each in Bank stock, less any money that might be laid out for them in the purchase of public employment.[7]

[1] *Misc. Gen. et Her.* n.s. i. 240; ser. 3, iv. 214; T. E. Sharpe, *Royal Descent*, 57; IGI, Cheshire; PCC 93 Plymouth. [2] *HMC Portland*, iii. 228; *CSP Dom.* 1661–2, p. 278; 1667–8, p. 38. [3] *Oxford Council Acts* (Oxf. Hist. Soc. n.s. ii), 117; *Banbury Corp. Recs.: Tudor and Stuart* (Banbury Hist. Soc. xv), 256. [4] *N. and Q.* clxxix. 41. [5] PCC 93 Plymouth. [6] *Cal. Treas. Bks.* ix. 1971, 1976, 1980–1, 1987; x. 910, 915; *CSP Dom.* 1689–90, pp. 125, 9, 122; *Sotheby's Cat.* 21 July 1980, acct. bks.; Bodl. Top. Oxon. 41b(2); Tanner 22, f. 119; *HMC Portland*, 553; Luttrell, *Brief Relation*, iii. 357; Add. 18675, f. 39; Bodl. Carte 233, f. 73a; *VCH Oxon.* x. 89. [7] A. Beesley, *Hist. Banbury*, 517; PCC 93 Plymouth.

S. N. H.

COPE, Sir John (1673–1749), of Bramshill, Hants.

PLYMPTON ERLE	1705–1708
TAVISTOCK	1708–1727
HAMPSHIRE	1727–1734
LYMINGTON	1734–1741

bap. 1 Dec. 1673, 1st s. of Sir John Cope, 5th Bt.* *educ.* Oriel, Oxf. 1689; travelled abroad. *m.* 18 July 1696, Alice, da. of Sir Humphrey Monoux, 2nd Bt.†, of Wootton, Beds., sis. of Sir Philip Monoux, 3rd Bt.*, 3s. (1 *d.v.p.*) 2da. (1 *d.v.p.*). Kntd. 26 Jan. 1696; *suc.* fa. as 6th Bt. 11 Jan. 1721.[1]

Dir. Bank of Eng. (with statutory intervals) 1706–21; commr. Equivalent 1707–15.[2]

Despite having been effectively disinherited by virtue of his grandfather's will, Cope seems to have managed to circumvent the consequences of his misfortune. In 1696 as 'a pretty gentleman young and hath travelled', he married Alice Monoux who was 'lame, looks sickly, a very coarse skin, low and plain, so I suppose her fortune is large'. By 1700 Cope was able to borrow £5,500 from his father to assist in his purchase for £21,500 of the manor of Bramshill, an estate to which he subsequently added. It was in his adopted county, at Andover, that his parliamentary ambitions initially settled. In November 1701, challenging Francis Shepheard*, he declared his determination to act in concert with the gentlemen of the county and to preserve the independence of the corporation. In fact, in this and the following general election he championed the freeman franchise against the closed oligarchy of the corporation. Defeated on both occasions, he switched his attention to the venal borough of Stockbridge, where his friend Thomas Jervoise* offered assistance. But Jervoise was informed that 'they don't much like Sir John Cope'. As a consequence Cope wisely retreated to Plympton Erle, where he was elected on Sir George Treby's* interest in 1705.[3]

Although on one analysis of the 1705 Parliament Cope was classed as a 'Churchman', he was clearly a Whig, his election being recorded as a gain by Lord Sunderland (Charles, Lord Spencer*). He voted for the Court candidate in the division on the Speaker on 25 Oct. 1705, and in 1706 was elected a director of the Bank of England. He does not seem to have been active in parliamentary business until the 1706–7 session when Anglo-Scottish affairs caught his attention. On 19 Apr. 1707 he acted as a teller against a bill to prevent fraudulent commerce with Scotland, a last-minute attempt to plug several loopholes in the Act of Union, and a measure which outraged the Scots. This attitude probably made him one of the Bank's more obvious nominees for their four places on the commission of the Equivalent, and he seems to have played an important role during the commissioners' expedition to Edinburgh in August 1707 and in subsequent attempts to propitiate Scottish opinion. For some reason he was classed as a Tory on a list compiled early in 1708, but there is no other evidence for such a view.[4]

In the general election of that year Cope migrated to Tavistock, where he was elected unopposed with the support of the Bedford interest. A letter in June to his fellow Equivalent commissioner, Sir Andrew Hume*, made some interesting comments on Scottish politics, when he expressed the hope that the Scots would 'send up those who are for settling North Britain upon the same foot as we are here' and then analysed the English in party terms: 'I think we are much mended in South Britain, for by a moderate computation the Whigs will be 299 and our friends, upon occasion, the Tories 214.' His own election was perceived as a gain by Sunderland, and another list of early 1708 with the returns added, confirmed him as a Whig. In the opening session he acted as a teller on two occasions: on 12 Feb. 1709, in the Hindon election, in favour of Reynolds Calthorpe*, an associate of Jervoise; and on 15 Apr. against taking into consideration the Lords' counter-amendments to the bill for improving the Union. The clause at issue restricted the forfeiture of estates to the lifetime of the person attainted, the effect of which the Lords had nullified by postponing its applicability until after the death of the Pretender. Whether this tellership demonstrated Cope's empathy with Scottish feelings or a preference for discussing another measure it is impossible to tell. Also during this session he was listed as a supporter of the naturalization of the Palatines. At the beginning of the following session he backed the attempt of Jervoise to secure election as knight of the shire for Hampshire, although he hoped that 'men of business' such as himself might be excused attending the poll unless an opponent appeared, whereupon 'neither the distance, business or the dangers of the sea shall prevent my waiting on you when I can serve you'. On the major issue of the session he remained true to the Whigs, voting in 1710 for the impeachment of Dr Sacheverell.[5]

Having retained his parliamentary seat at Tavistock in the difficult circumstances of 1710, Cope seems to have survived allegations of bribery merely because no petition was presented against his election; his Whig partner, Henry Manaton*, on the other hand, was unseated. The 'Hanover list' classed Cope as a Whig. On 3 Apr. 1711 he acted as a teller against a successful motion that counsel be heard on the Cockermouth election. That same year he was re-elected a director of the Bank, his name having appeared on the Whig slate. There is also evidence that he continued to follow Scottish affairs closely, having been reappointed a commissioner for the Equivalent in 1709. In February 1711 he reported to Hume that Scottish Members were uninterested in matters which did not affect them directly, a malaise which extended to the distribution of the remaining Equivalent. In the 1713 session he was a teller on 14 May against giving leave to bring in the French commerce bill and was duly noted as a Whig who voted against the bill on 18 June.[6]

Re-elected in 1713, Cope acted as a teller on 22 June 1714 against a resolution from ways and means to place a duty on all imported buckrams except those from Ireland. He also voted on 18 Mar. 1714 against the expulsion of Richard Steele. He was listed as a Whig on the Worsley list and on two comparative analyses of the 1713 and 1715 parliaments. Cope sat in the Commons until 1741, becoming a committed supporter of Robert Walpole II*. He died on 8 Dec. 1749, leaving estates in Hampshire, Oxfordshire and Wales to his eldest son, Monoux Cope†.[7]

[1] Berry, *Hants Gens.* 302–3; *Misc. Gen. et Her.* ser. 3, iv. 214–15; IGI, London. [2] *N. and Q.* clxxix. 60. [3] BL, Verney mss mic. 636/49, John Verney* (Ld. Fermanagh) to Sir Ralph Verney, 1st Bt.†, 30 July 1696; PCC 93 Plymouth; *VCH Hants*, iv. 36–37; Hants RO, Jervoise mss 44M69/08, Cope to [Jervoise], n.d., 2 May 1704; 43M48/2570, election case; 44M69/08, Ellis St. Jervoise to [?Jervoise], 21 Feb. [1705]; Luttrell, *Brief Relation*, v. 257. [4] *Cal. Treas. Bks.* xxi. 410; P. W. J. Riley, *Eng. Ministers and Scotland*, 210. [5] G. Holmes and W. A. Speck, *Divided Soc.* 29–30; Jervoise mss 44M69/08, Cope to Jervoise, 17 Dec. 1709. [6] G. Holmes, *Pol. in Age of Anne*, 478; *Cal. Treas. Bks.* xxiii. 17; Riley, 218. [7] PCC 368 Lisle.

S. N. H.

COPE, Jonathan I (1664–94), of Ranton Abbey, Staffs.

STAFFORD 1690–14 Sept. 1694

b. 9 July 1664, 3rd s. of Jonathan Cope of Ranton Abbey by Anne, da. of Sir Halton Farmer of Easton Neston, Northants. *educ.* Christ Church, Oxf. 1681. *m.* settlement 19 Oct. 1688, Susannah, da. of Sir Thomas Fowle*, 3s. *suc.* bro. 1675.[1]

Sheriff, Staffs. 1685–6.

Cope's father, a younger son of Sir William Cope, 2nd Bt.†, of Hanwell, Oxfordshire, had inherited the family's Staffordshire estates: Cope himself, also a younger son, succeeded his elder brother in 1675 to this property and then became the likely heir of the main branch of the family following the decision of his cousin Sir Anthony Cope, 4th Bt.†, to disinherit any children born to Sir Anthony's brother John (Sir John Cope, 5th Bt.*). He was thus a man of considerable actual and potential standing, the estate in Staffordshire being estimated at £800 p.a. (plus another £300 after his mother's decease), in a court case in 1698–9.[2]

Cope was elected to the 1690 Parliament after a sharp contest with Philip Foley* at Stafford. The Marquess of Carmarthen (Sir Thomas Osborne†) was in no doubt of his political affiliation, marking him as a Tory and a probable Court supporter on a list of the new House. His name appears on another list drawn up by Carmarthen in December 1690 probably denoting likely support for the minister in the event of an attack upon him in the Commons. In April 1691 Robert Harley* marked his name with a 'd', denoting doubtful or dead. Cope did not play a significant role in the House, acting as a teller only once, against an adjournment motion on 14 Apr. 1694, in order to allow discussion of a clause in the tunnage and poundage bill to limit the trading activities of the Bank of England. Cope died on 14 Sept. 1694, although reports of his impending death had reached Foley by the 11th. His will, dated 15 July 1694, made provision for his three sons, and directed that his body be buried in Ellenhall church, where it was interred on 22 Sept. His eldest son was created a baronet while a Member for Banbury and inherited the Hanwell estates in 1721.[3]

[1] *Ellenhall Par. Reg.* (Staffs. Par. Reg. Soc. 1944–5), 17, 20–21; *Misc. Gen. et Her.* ser. 3, iv. 222; T. E. Sharpe, *Royal Dissent*, 15. [2] Sharpe, 15; A. Beesley, *Hist. Banbury*, 261; PCC 12 Bence; *HMC Lords*, n.s. iii. 270. [3] BL, Verney mss mic. 636/47, John Verney* (Ld. Fermanagh) to Sir Ralph Verney†, 15 Sept. 1694; Hereford and Worcester RO (Hereford), Foley mss, Foley to 'Mr P.', 11 Sept. 1694; PCC 217 Plymouth; *Ellenhall Par. Reg.* 30.

S. N. H.

COPE, Jonathan II (c.1692–1765), of Bruern Abbey, Oxon.

BANBURY 1713–1722

b. c.1692, 1st s. of Jonathan Cope I*. *educ.* Eton 1706; Christ Church, Oxf. matric. 18 Feb. 1708, aged 16. *m.* ?1717, Mary (d.1755), da. of Sir Robert Jenkinson, 2nd Bt.*, 1s. *d.v.p.* 5da. *suc.* fa. 1694; Sir John Cope, 5th Bt.*, to Hanwell, Oxon. 1721; *cr.* Bt. 1 Mar. 1714.[1]

Freeman and bailiff, Oxford 1714.[2]

Under his father's will, Cope was to be left under the charge of his mother unless she remarried. When she did so the provisions of the will, which appointed Sir Thomas Pershall, Sir Robert Jenkinson [?2nd Bt.*] and Henry Farmer as guardians, presumably came into effect. Little is known about Cope's early life, although by the time of his election he was probably residing at Bruern Abbey, Oxfordshire. His election for Banbury in 1713 probably owed much to his presumptive interest in the Hanwell estates of the Cope family, just two and a half miles from Banbury, plus the backing of the Norths. During the 1713 Parliament his only significant action was to act as a teller on 23 Mar. 1714 against setting a date for hearing the London election petition. He was considered a Tory on the Worsley list, although another list comparing Members elected in 1713 and 1715 classed him as a Whig. This latter assignation must have been erroneous, as Lord Guildford backed him at the 1715 election with reference to 'my certain knowledge he acquitted himself as an honest gentleman, with due regard to the true interest of his country'. Cope continued to sit for Banbury until 1722 when his third cousin, Monoux Cope†, was elected, something of an irony since the previous year Cope had inherited the Hanwell estates, which would have come to Monoux's father, Sir John Cope, 6th Bt.*, had the latter not been disinherited. Cope died on 28 Mar. 1765, and was buried at Hanwell.[3]

[1] Baker, *Northants.* ii. 51. [2] *Oxford Council Acts* (Oxf. Hist. Soc. n.s. x), 87. [3] PCC 217 Box; 175 Rushworth; *VCH Oxon.* x. 89; *Cake and Cockhorse*, iii. 55; *Gent. Mag.* 1765, p. 198.

S. N. H.

COPLEY, Sir Godfrey, 2nd Bt. (c.1653–1709), of Sprotborough, Yorks. and Red Lion Square, London.

ALDBOROUGH 15 May 1679–1681 (Mar.)
THIRSK 1695–9 Apr. 1709

b. c.1653, 1st s. of Sir Godfrey Copley, 1st Bt., of Sprotborough by his 1st w. Eleanor, da. of Sir Thomas Walmesley† of Dunkenhalgh, Lancs. *educ.* L. Inn 1674; I. Temple 1681. *m.* (1) lic. 15 Oct. 1681, Catherine, da. and coh. of John Purcell† of Nantribba, Mont., 3s. *d.v.p.* 3da. (2 *d.v.p.*); (2) settlement 31 May 1700, Gertrude, da. of Sir John Carew, 3rd Bt.*, *s.p. suc.* fa. as 2nd Bt. Feb. 1678.[1]

Sheriff, Yorks. Feb.–Nov. 1678.
FRS 1691–d.[2]
Commr. taking subscriptions to land bank 1696, public accts. 1702–4.[3]
Commr. Aire and Calder navigation 1699.[4]
Comptroller of army accts. Apr. 1704–d.[5]

Copley, described as 'ingenious', 'worthy' and a man who 'judged very well of the interest of his own estate and his country', was a keen and active member of the Royal Society from 1691 onwards, serving on the Society's council on several occasions. His interest in science and antiquities was accommodated by healthy finances and a good estate in Yorkshire. When in London, besides attending to Society matters, Copley regularly frequented taverns such as the Thatched House, the Vine, and the Grecian, acquiring in the process a wide circle of friends and acquaintances, including political figures such as Robert Harley* and men of letters such as Dr Hans Sloane, Ralph Thoresby and John Toland. Copley's political stance, which was that of a prominent Country Tory back-bencher, was concomitant with the mixed views of his associates. Copley's earlier parliamentary career had been short-lived and mostly uneventful, though a contested election for Aldborough in 1679 had resulted in rumours being spread by his opponent that he was a Roman Catholic. Although the rumours were unfounded, his connexion with Catholic interests in Lancashire, through his maternal grandfather, remained significant on his return to politics. Having been defeated at Pontefract in 1690, in the 1695 election Copley chose not to stand at Aldborough where he retained an interest, and initially considered standing in Clitheroe, as the Earl of Derby, a 'friend', was prepared to propose him as a colleague to Ambrose Pudsay*. Derby thought Copley a good candidate because 'Mr Walmesley and Mr Townley and all the popish gentlemen's interest he will probably have, because they are his relations, so that if . . . he resolves to spend a great deal of monies, in all likelihood he may carry it'. Copley supposedly only wanted to stand in order 'to keep out a worse' candidate, and to serve 'his country and his Church'. However, he did not contest the seat, and was returned instead for Thirsk, seemingly on the interest of Ralph Bell*.[6]

Copley was active in the Commons from the outset. On 29 Dec. 1695 he wrote:

> I confess my attendance on the House has in a manner taken up all my time, and yet I think it is but a slender excuse for a man's not writing to his friend, especially since we are scarce able to talk of much service we have done our country as yet . . . I wish our public affairs go on well. We stand great need of management and good husbandry, great sums are to be paid and I doubt the money is very hard to be found.

His involvement in business relating to coinage and public revenue continued during the rest of the session. On 23 Jan. 1696 he was appointed to a committee concerned with the shortages of halfpennies and farthings. His heavy workload and concern over money matters were evident when he wrote on 15 Feb.:

> I have had such a cold with sitting up at committees of elections till one and two in the morning that I have been forced to bleed twice to save me from the honour of dying in my country's service. I am as apprehensive as anybody can be of the want of money in the country, and of the vast mischiefs and ill consequences of the high value of guineas. We have laboured as for life, to have had Mints in the country, and cannot obtain it as yet. That very thing alone would cure both evils and all the ill consequences depending thereon, but we are overpowered by the traders in money and guineas and those who send out silver and import gold, who are afraid they shall not cheat the nation six months longer.

Copley demonstrated a certain flexibility in his political stance, and, despite having been forecast as likely to oppose the Court on 31 Jan. over the proposed council of trade, in a debate in committee on 17 Feb. it appeared that he and several other back-benchers were prepared to support the Court on the issue of the value of guineas, and 'were now ready to alter their earlier votes for a 28s. ceiling'. The following day he was appointed to inquire into the number of guineas coined at the Mint the previous year. When the coinage issue came to a head on 26 Mar., he told against fixing the price of guineas at 24s. However, despite his activity in relation to coinage, he was not listed as voting on the motion for fixing the price at 22s. He was one of the majority of MPs who signed the Association promptly. He also told for a motion that the right of election at Dunwich was in non-resident as well as resident freemen (12 Feb.), thereby favouring the Whig candidate in the borough.[7]

Prior to the 1696–7 session Copley was still expressing concern over the money matters raised in the previous session, and the failure of the land bank, writing on 4 June:

> I have been endeavouring to serve some of my friends in the country in helping [?them] of [?off] with clipped money, but we have been in expectation of a new bank which I think comes to nothing and so disappoints us, and the goldsmiths are in such favour that they are admitted to fill up the funds by their knavish subscriptions and by that means cheat poor country gentlemen according to their old prescription time out of mind.

When Parliament reconvened, Copley was prominent among the opposition to the Court-sponsored bill of attainder against Sir John Fenwick†. On 16 Nov. he warned of the consequences of dispensing with the legal requirement of evidence from two witnesses, by allowing a written testimony instead:

> Some have said, that it should be read as evidence. Some others are for reading of this paper, but yet at the same time tell us, it is not to be looked upon as evidence, at least not equivalent to a witness. If the paper be . . . read at all, I would know for what reason? If it be to have any sway upon our judgment, if it hath any effect upon my judgment, then in some measure it is equivalent to a witness, when it is in the nature of a witness. And if it should be read to supply the defect of a witness, then I would know, what the consequence of this might be? I do very well understand, that the court of Parliament does take no precedent from Westminster Hall, nor am I afraid of any precedent they should give to Westminster Hall. But I am afraid of a precedent to future Parliaments. Suppose the information of . . . Fenwick, that has been delivered in here, should be produced as evidence against any of those honourable persons that are charged in it, though I believe they are very innocent, and some knaves and rascals in future reigns should come in against them, and this paper should be brought to supply another witness, what a consequence would that be!

He again emphasized the danger of setting precedents in a later contribution to the debate:

> I must confess, it would weigh with me, if it had been made appear, that . . . Fenwick had taken off any evidence, and I should be ready to apply it as well as I could. But I must needs take notice of what was said in this debate, that we had done as much as this comes to already. This makes me a little more apprehensive, and to take care what we do now, since what this House does hath so quick an operation. We are citing precedents of this very day already, and make one thing a hand to draw on another. And so they may easily be made use of in after Parliaments.

On 25 Nov. he rejoined the debate in a long and impassioned speech, which detailed his objections to the proceedings. He pointed out that there was 'something in duty incumbent upon every man, especially upon me, who can't concur with the general sense of the House, to give my reasons for my disagreement'. While many speakers had said 'they would not speak as to the power of Parliaments, yet the greatest part of their arguments have touched upon your method of proceedings, and to show you how they interfere with the rules of Westminster Hall; so great is the force of custom and education'. He went on to point out that 'it is the custom of our nation, to have two positive witnesses to prove treason', but acknowledged that this rule was alterable, as Parliament had the 'power to abrogate all laws that they have passed, if they think good'. However, this did not mean that they could ignore 'the eternal rules of equity, and justice, and right reason, and conscience' which were unalterable, and needed to be considered in relation to Parliament's proceedings:

> it is a rule agreeable to what I speak of, that no man shall be accused by he knows not whom, and that no man shall be accused, but that the evidence against him, and he, should be confronted, and brought face to face. I am one of those that believe . . . Fenwick to be guilty, and there is clear proof of it by one witness, and you have added to this an indictment that is found. But I must needs own, that I think that to be so far from giving any addition or strength to the evidence, that when that is brought in, I look upon the scales to be lighter than they were before. For if any record or writing that is sworn to behind a man's back, shall be brought here to supply another part of the evidence (and if not so, why is it brought here?), and if that be to be interpreted to make up a part of the evidence, I do, by parallel reason, argue, that the like may make up the whole at one time or another.

He then stated that he wished the case had never come before the House, and proceeded to argue that Fenwick was no threat to King or government while he was in prison, though the proceedings in Parliament were dangerous 'for the nation in general, and for our posterity'. He did not argue for Fenwick's life, as he did not think it worthy of 'a debate in this House, nor the consideration of so great an assembly; but I do say, if this method of proceeding be warranted by an English Parliament, there is an end to the defence of any man living, be he never so innocent'. His final endeavour was to remark that it had been 'mentioned on the other side' that

> King James attainted a great number of persons in a catalogue, in a lump . . . I am not afraid of what arbitrary princes do, nor an Irish parliament. But I am afraid of what shall be done here. I am concerned for the honour of your proceedings, that it may not be a precedent to a future Parliament in an ill reign.

Following a rejoinder from Lord Cutts (John) over the 'small value' Copley put on Fenwick's life, he explained that his intention was to point out that Fenwick, 'considered in his single capacity', was not worth 'the whole of this House to act in their legislative capacity upon him'. In keeping with the sentiments expressed in his speeches, Copley voted against the attainder, and on 28 Jan. 1697 attended Fenwick to the scaffold. On 7 Nov. 1696 he told for a motion that the Bank of England lay its accounts before the House, while on the 9th he was nominated to examine abuses by receivers-general in paying more clipped coin into the Treasury than they actually received from the collectors. On the 30th he was appointed to prepare reasons for disagreeing with the Lords' amendments to the bill to remedy further the ill state of the coinage. These financial interests continued in the new year, with his appointment on 14 Jan. 1697 to a committee for drafting a clause or clauses for better explaining the recoinage Acts, and to inquire into any miscarriages by patent officers at the Mint. On 26 Jan. he told against a motion to pass the amended supply (land tax, subsidy and duties) bill, while on 13 Feb. he was nominated to a committee of inquiry into the abuses of Exchequer officers and receivers of taxes.[8]

In the 1697–8 session Copley's attention shifted to local issues, and the economic interests of his county. On 30 Dec. 1697 he was given leave to bring in a bill for making the Don navigable. On 1 Jan. 1698 he wrote to his regular correspondent, Thomas Kirke, informing him that

> I find by a letter I received from Leeds that the same is intended for their river [Aire and Calder]. I pray tell them I will do them all the service I can, but I desire you would show them the list of Members of Parliament and they would consider what friends they can make, be they of what county they will, and that they would not fail to write to any of their correspondents in town that are well acquainted with Members to solicit for them. I will engage all that are for our river to be for both, but here is Mr Lister of Bautree [Bawtry] solicits as it were for his life.

Copley presented the bill on 21 Jan., though its passage was disrupted by petitions from Doncaster, both for and against, and by the influence of Lister. Despite Copley's efforts to lobby support, the bill was thrown out on 1 Feb., on which occasion he told for the bill's committal. By March his attention had turned to the bill for punishing (Sir) Charles Duncombe* for making false endorsements of Exchequer bills. On 3 Mar. he reported to Kirke that 'the Lords are to be upon Duncombe tomorrow and if they throw out the bill I shall not wonder. They sent down a bill against blasphemy, atheism and profaneness, but it is so crude and indigested that there never was a bill of less goodness with so pious a title.'[9]

Copley was returned again for Thirsk in 1698, though he was unsuccessful in using his interest to get his close friend Cyril Arthington* returned for Aldborough. His involvement in the Aldborough election may have been the cause of his intention of delaying his journey to London until after the 1698–9 session opened. Robert Molesworth* tried to convince him otherwise, writing on 1 Nov. to hasten his friend up to London, and again on 10 Nov., having heard of Copley's intention of deferring his journey to London until 10 Dec:

> I hope when you consider that the Parliament certainly meets on the 29th instant and that perhaps there will be the greatest struggle that ever was known about the choice of a Speaker, that you will not only take [?post] to be here before that day . . . but also that you will encourage all the Members of Parliament that are within your call to accompany you. The Court persist strongly in their standing for Sir Thomas Littleton [3rd Bt.], and perhaps through the negligence of the country gentlemen will carry it. If they do, assure yourself nothing will be able to stand before them.

Although it is unclear whether Copley attended the House when Littleton was elected Speaker on 6 Dec., Molesworth's correspondence was in keeping with the fact that Copley was listed as a Country supporter in a comparative analysis of the old and new Parliaments. Copley appears to have been inactive in December, though on the 28th he received a letter from Leeds recalling his support in the previous Parliament for the Aire and Calder navigation, to which he gave 'very great encouragement', and requesting his assistance for a petition for a second bill. However, Copley became more active in the new year, becoming involved in the standing army issue, and again in matters of public finance. In late 1698 he had been forecast as likely to oppose a standing army, and was not recorded among the MPs who voted against the disbanding bill. As part of the preparations for disbandment he was appointed to a committee on 17 Jan. 1699 to prepare a bill to allow discharged soldiers to exercise trades in cities and corporations. In keeping with his opposition to a standing army, on 18 Mar. Copley was nominated to the committee of address against the Dutch guards remaining in England. On the 19th Hon. James Brydges* recorded in his diary that Copley met with various Members at Sir Richard Onslow's, including Sir Christopher Musgrave, 4th Bt., and Sir John Leveson-Gower, 5th Bt., 'about drawing up the address'. On the 20th Copley told against recommitting the resultant address. On 6 Apr. he presented the bill for allowing disbanded soldiers to carry on trades, which he managed through all its stages in the House. Another issue in which Copley identified himself with the Country party concerned the legality of revenue officials sitting in Parliament, and in mid-February he chaired and reported from a committee appointed to scrutinize returns of revenue officials which the House had called for. Copley also continued to figure in the considerations on coinage. On 15 Feb. he chaired the committee of the whole to consider the price of gold and silver, which sat twice that day. The following day he reported that it was the committee's opinion that no person was obliged, by the two recent coinage acts, to take guineas at 22s. Although not appointed to the committee of 14 Mar. for preparing a bill for a commission of accounts, Copley was deeply involved in the behind-the-scenes activity of the Country interest in preparing this bill. On 17 Mar. Brydges, a member of the committee, recorded in his diary that he dined with Harley, Gervase Pierrepont* and Copley, 'upon account of bringing in the bill for the commission of accounts'. On the 20th Brydges met Copley and Pierrepont again, in order to draw up the bill. Having dined together on the 22nd, Copley and Brydges went to Pierrepont's on the 25th to meet Sir Bartholomew Shower* and Lord Cheyne (William*), the third and final member of the committee, who both agreed on the bill. He was also active on other issues, telling on 7 Feb. for (Sir) Thomas Lee* (2nd Bt.) not being duly elected for Aylesbury, and on 9 Mar. against rejecting the East India Company bill.[10]

In the 1699–1700 session Copley was as active as ever in relation to the public revenue, and as part of the Country interest. He was nominated on 15 Dec. to the committee for drafting the bill to apply the Irish forfeitures to public use. On 12 Jan. 1700 he told against referring the report on the state of the fleet to a committee of the whole. The next day Brydges noted that he had gone with Copley to the Goat, where they stayed till 11 o'clock 'concerting about Lord Ranelagh's [Richard Jones*] accounts'. On the 26th Copley had further discussions about Ranelagh's accounts with Brydges. He also spoke in favour of putting to a vote Brydges' convoluted resolution of 13 Feb. about the obtaining of land grants by government officials, which was ostensibly related to the Commons' earlier resolutions on the Irish forfeitures, but was in reality a thinly veiled attack on Lord Chancellor Somers (Sir John*). Copley's active participation in the preparation of the Irish forfeitures bill, and his consistent attitude to placemen, was demonstrated on 18 Mar. when he told for including a clause in the forfeitures bill for preventing Members from serving on the excise commission. On the 22nd he again acted as a teller for a clause to be included in the forfeitures bill for protecting the grant bestowed on the children of Sir Charles Porter*. Copley's abilities in the area of public finance became more apparent on the 25th, when he was made chairman of the committee of the whole on the bill appointing commissioners of accounts. He reported these proceedings on the 27th, and joined in the ensuing debate to agree that the commissioners should be paid. With the bill for appointing commissioners of accounts approaching completion, Copley went with Brydges on 4 Apr. to the Vine tavern, where they 'met several Members and agreed upon a list for commissioners for the accounts'. The next day Copley was appointed to scrutinize the ballot to choose public accounts commissioners, while on 6 Apr. he carried the bill up to the Lords. Copley was also kept busy during the session dealing with other issues. He had a particular interest, of a more personal nature, in the passage of a private bill for confirming the sale of Thomas Barlow's lands in Yorkshire, as his cousin Lionel Copley was involved in purchasing the lands. On 20 Jan. 1700 he informed Lionel that 'the bill hath passed the House of Peers and is come down to us, and I have moved for a day for the first reading'. He subsequently managed the bill through the House, while keeping his cousin informed of its progress. Thus on the 29th he wrote

> I could never yet have an opportunity to report the bill, but it wanting now nothing at all but one reading I think it is out [of] danger quite. As for the amendments which you mention, you stood in no need of them, for they will not suffer any private bill to create new settlements, but this bill doth supply the want of good title in Mr Barlow when he conveyed to you, [and] secures you against all in remainder after him, which is as much as any private bill doth ... I hope to get the bill reported next week.

Copley was true to his word, and on 4 Mar. reported on the bill to the House, carrying it to the Lords on the 30th. He reported on 23 Mar. from a committee for inquiring into precedents for Members returned to multiple constituencies. An analysis of the House into interests classed Copley at this time as a follower of the Duke of Leeds (Sir Thomas Osborne†).[11]

Copley was returned once again for Thirsk in January 1701, and also succeeded in securing Arthington's return for Aldborough. Probably in keeping with the changing face of the Court party, Copley was forecast in February as likely to support the Court in agreeing with the supply committee's resolution to continue the 'Great Mortgage'. On 21 May, when Sir Edward Seymour sought to placate the Court by retrieving an earlier vote for reducing the civil list, John Howe stood out for the original scheme, receiving support from Copley and a number of Whigs. However, on the 23rd Howe was shown the 'inconveniences' that would follow, so that he and Copley retreated on the issue. The result of the ballot for new commissioners of accounts on 17 June saw Copley elected in first place alongside Howe. This new parliamentary commission was instigated by Tory back-benchers, including Copley, who hoped to make good the repeated charges that millions of pounds of public money granted for the war remained unaccounted for. However, their plans were frustrated by the Lords, whose attempt to alter the composition of the commission, plus other amendments made to the returned bill, made it unacceptable to the Commons. In consequence, Copley was ordered to take part in a conference with the Lords on this issue. Copley was also kept busy during the session with his involvement in the endeavours to take proceedings against certain ministers. He was nominated on 1 Apr. to draw up the articles of impeachment against the Earl of Portland, and later against Orford (Edward Russell*) and Halifax (Charles Montagu*). As part of these proceedings he was among those appointed on the 12th for translating the Vernon–Portland letters relating to the Partition Treaty in 1698, reporting from this committee on the 14th. In a debate on 4 June on the impeachments, Copley stated that 'if we insist on more than what is our right' the House might be accused of delaying proceedings for reasons other than the impeachments. He also pointed out that

> sometimes Lords have been impeached and articles never exhibited, and there may . . . be reason for it as particularly when my Lord Portland was first impeached it was because he did, being a foreigner, make treaties to the prejudice of England without consulting [?of] English council, and so it did then appear. But looking further into matters upon these other impeachments it does appear he has acted nothing but by and with the directions and advice of English councils, so that it does appear that he is not so guilty as at first we had reason to believe him.

In a debate on the war on 9 May, Copley 'was for sending the army out of Ireland that they were ready raised and disciplined and we might presently recruit if occasion'. The next day, in a half-empty House, when Whig placemen moved to throw out the clauses in the bill of settlement excluding office-holders from Parliament, he successfully moved to send the serjeant-at-arms to summon Members, thereby causing the placemen to retreat on the issue. In what was a very active session for Copley it was hardly surprising that he 'made a positive resolution not to be concerned with any petitions at all'.[12]

Following the end of the session Copley opposed the Whig-inspired pressure for a dissolution of Parliament. On 12 Aug. the King was informed that an address 'is set on foot in Yorkshire' in favour of a dissolution, and that 'all the gentlemen that were at the assizes' had signed it, except for Copley and Arthington. However, although included in the 'black list' of those who had opposed the preparations for war with France, Copley was returned once again for Thirsk in the November election, and successfully 'set up' Arthington at Aldborough, despite support from the Duke of Newcastle (John Holles†) for the other two candidates. In the new Parliament Copley was listed with the Tories by Harley. His parliamentary activity followed its usual pattern, with nomination to the committee for drafting the bill of accounts on the 6th. On 31 Jan. he intervened in a debate on the war, saying 'we must accommodate the war to our conveniencies since we cannot accommodate our conveniencies to the war'. Copley and Sir Richard Cocks, 2nd Bt., clashed on 14 Feb. in a debate on the Malmesbury election, when Copley spoke against 'reflections' being made on the conduct of gentlemen, 'and said we should not say things that would look ill one upon another. Would that gentleman take it well to say that Sir Richard Cocks did not bribe the county but was chosen for his great merit and virtue?' Angrily, Cocks declared that

> my country knows me better than his borough I believe does him . . . he is chose 40 miles from the place where he lives and so ill beloved in his own country that his house was lately on fire and his neighbours got about it and said 'a bonfire' and would hard[ly] help to put it out.

In keeping with his earlier stance, Copley was listed among those who favoured the motion of 26 Feb. vindicating the Commons' proceedings on the impeachments of the King's ministers in the previous Parliament. He was also nominated to the committee for drafting a bill relating to the Irish forfeitures. Copley continued to be active in relation to the revenue and at a meeting of Tory MPs at the Thatched House tavern on 4 Mar. was included in a list of six names agreed upon to be commissioners of accounts. Not surprisingly, he was appointed to the committee to scrutinize the ballot. The next day he was declared elected in fifth place, his lower placing on this occasion being due to the fact that the Whigs, having failed to select a list of their own commissioners, chose to 'blemish their [Tory] commissioners by naming the least of theirs, and, by putting him in our list, make him first of the commission'. On the 19th Copley seconded a successful motion that the commissioners should not take any other office, though it was thought that several of his fellow commissioners disagreed with him on this point. It is also worthy of note that Copley's close associate, Brydges, acted as a teller for a motion on the petition of the Jacobite banker Sir Daniel Arthur, for a bill to reverse his outlawry, which was defeated by 148 votes to 16 (26 Mar.). Although

Copley appears to have had no direct involvement in this issue, he was a business associate of Arthur's, and had received a letter from him the previous August 'about his case in Ireland'.[13]

Although continuing to figure as one of the significant men in Yorkshire politics, Copley appears to have ceased taking an active part in Aldborough affairs after 1702, as Arthington did not contest the election following Queen Anne's accession. In view of the fact that Copley sold his landed interests in Aldborough to the Duke of Newcastle in 1703, it is possible that the land deal was preceded in July 1702 by Copley allowing Newcastle's two candidates to be returned in an uncontested election. However, Copley continued to receive Bell's support at Thirsk, and was returned to the first Parliament of the reign. In the 1702–3 session most of his time was consumed by the concerns of the commission of accounts and their inquiries concerning Lord Ranelagh's army accounts. He was re-elected as a commissioner on 7 Jan. 1703, on this occasion in third place. Copley noted on 16 Feb., as the session drew to an early close, that

> I thought we should have seen an end of this session some time ago, though it will be much sooner than ever we used to be at liberty. All the money bills, which is now reckoned the chief, if not the only public business of a House of Commons, are passed our House. We have sent up the qualification bill to the lords, who finding it thwarts the privilege of obliging us to trust men of their putting in with our estates, who they dare not trust themselves with any estate at all, have adjourned it to a long day, and so put the negative upon it.

Cunningham observed that, around this time, when the Commons were debating on ecclesiastical questions, and Members maintained the excellence of the Church of England, Copley, 'who was a man of wit', stated:

> Everyone admires his own church, and we are fond of ours: for my part, I admire it chiefly for this reason, that it is fit for the people, subject to the laws, and most suitable to the clergy. For here, without care, without thought, and without trouble, honour and ease are enjoyed at once, which is a state that most men wish for. But we are not here disputing about churches, but about the common good of the kingdom.[14]

Following the end of the 1702–3 session it was rumoured that Copley had 'deserted' the Tory party, though there was no evidence to substantiate such a claim. He was kept busy during the following months with the work of the commission of accounts. On 2 Mar. he wrote to Kirke, telling him

> I will not say a word of state affairs, nor the public accounts. You are better employed in planting and walling, and other country diversions, and you have all the little lampoons of *The Golden Age*, and *The Golden Age Reversed* . . . and there is to come out in print, when the Lords please, a most severe something upon us poor commissioners.

Thoresby, on visiting Copley at Sprotborough in March, noted that although Copley received him kindly, 'he is obliged to return [to London] in a very few days, being a chief commissioner for taking the public accounts'. However, Copley did find time to show Thoresby, who was also a fellow of the Royal Society, his 'new canal', his 'noble and spacious house' with the gallery adorned with original Van Dykes 'and other great masters', plus other 'choice curiosities', including mathematical instruments in which Copley was 'well versed'. Copley also wrote to Thoresby reassuring him that 'I would by no means have you to be afraid of interrupting my business as a commissioner . . . by your correspondence: that would be to make me a greater sufferer for the public than in reason I ought to be'. However, although he tried to keep up a regular correspondence while in London, he found himself struggling against a weight of business:

> I must own my friends may well think they have good reason to complain of my silence or rather rudeness to them. I have failed writing to everybody. My mistress (if I may be allowed to have any), I mean my borough, would have reason to blame me unless she would call to mind that I am every day sore employed in her service, and I believe it will be very visible in divers places about Sprotborough how much I have been forced to neglect what I love to take care on.[15]

In the 1703–4 session Copley's standing among the Tory party back-benchers was highlighted by his inclusion by Sir William Trumbull* in a list on 17 Dec. of the 'secret committee' of the Commons. As in previous sessions Copley was actively involved in revenue matters, and on 25 Feb. 1704 was again among the successful candidates in the ballot for the accounts commissioners, though now down to the penultimate place. The work of the commission became even more time-consuming than before, as two of his colleagues were prevented from attending due to family bereavements, while, as Copley put it, 'the House hath, for fear we should want employment, given us the examination of the whole account of the 12 commissioners of the Irish forfeitures, which consist of abundance of volumes, and multitudes of vouchers'. On 29 Feb. he delivered the commission's reply to Orford's answer to an earlier unfavourable report, and on 11 Mar.

delivered their favourable report on the Irish forfeitures material. In keeping with his commissioner's role, he was nominated on the 21st to prepare reasons for disagreeing with the Lords' amendments to the public accounts bill, arising from the Lords' endeavours to remove Robert Byerley* from the commission. His attention was also taken up with supply legislation. At some point in January or February he informed Kirke that it was

> with much ado that we save 12*d*. out of the 4*s*. upon land this year. If you know how many there are here who make it their business to charge us deep with debts and deficiencies in order to bring on heavy taxes, you would think a country gentleman had but an ill time of it, and you will find I doubt in a short time their discouragement to be so great that they will most of them come down, and then I know how it will be. I hope to ask leave to come down myself, since I can do some service though it be but little in the country. I am sure if the next House of Commons be like us, it will deserve to be commended as much as we do.[16]

Following the session Copley was appointed comptroller of army accounts in April 1704. However, he continued to express his Country instincts on occasion, although he also became less active in Parliament and the 1704–5 session was a quiet one for him. He was forecast in October 1704 as a probable opponent of the Tack, and was listed by Harley as one of the MPs who could assist in lobbying against it. He did not vote for it on 28 Nov.[17]

Returned for Thirsk once again in 1705, Copley was described as 'Low Church' in an analysis of the new House. He voted on 25 Oct. for the Court candidate in the division on the Speaker. He played a significant role in the naturalization bill for a French Protestant, Peter Silvester, managing its progress through the Commons. On 4 Dec. he chaired the committee of the whole for considering the proceedings of the Scottish parliament relating to the Union and the succession. He contributed to the debate on the 8th about the resolution of the Lords on the 'safe and flourishing condition' of the Church, which the ministry and Whigs wanted the Commons to endorse. He spoke of 'ecclesiastical [inclination?] to ruin moderation', of a 'man in Convocation' who 'preached a scandalous sermon', and concluded that 'the nation may see that groundless ... imaginery by both Houses'. He also participated in the debates on the regency bill in January 1706, though the content of his contribution is unclear. On 4 Feb. he was nominated to prepare reasons for disagreeing with the Lords' amendments to the clauses added by the Commons to this bill and, despite being a placeman, he appears to have remained true to the Country interest by failing to support the Court on 18 Feb. on the 'place clause' of the bill.[18]

Although still taking an interest in election activity in Yorkshire, Copley became less active in the 1706–7 session. On 19 Apr. 1707 he told against a motion for agreeing with an amendment to the bill for preventing customs frauds. Following the session he appears to have suffered a bout of illness, writing to his agent at Thirsk, on 16 July, in order to apologize for his lack of attention to the borough-men, though he had been 'much indisposed' since coming to Yorkshire, and intended to send 'a buck for them this summer'. It appears that Copley also took more time to attend to matters on his estates, though he still maintained an interest in state affairs, expressing concern over the 'deadness of trade and want of money' due to the war. In the first Parliament of Great Britain his visible activity was now mainly concerned with parochial issues relating to his county, although he was also prominent in leading a conference with the Lords over amendments to legislation for the completion of St. Paul's Cathedral. In two lists dating from this period he was marked as a Whig. This classification, although inconsistent with Copley's Country Tory affiliations, may have been due to his support for the Court following his appointment to office in 1704.[19]

Returned again for Thirsk in 1708, Copley was noted in the 1708–9 session for opposing certain expedients suggested by the Court party in the debates, following the Queen's Speech, on proposals for completing the Union. On 29 Jan. 1709 he was appointed to draft the bill to standardize the treason laws within the Union, and on 9 Mar. to draft a bill for the more effectual prohibition of the importation of French wine and other goods. On 12 Mar. he told for a motion that all papers laid before the House in relation to the invasion of Scotland be printed. He died while Parliament was still sitting, on 9 Apr., 'after four or five days' indisposition'. The cause of death was 'the quinsy', an inflammation of the throat (considered a rare ailment in England). He was lamented by Dyer, the Tory newsletter-writer, as 'an honest, loyal gentleman that served his country faithfully'. In his will, dated 14 Oct. 1704, he made substantial financial provision for his second wife and for his only surviving daughter, Catherine, as well as leaving £100 to the Royal Society. This sum became the basis for an annual gold medal award named after Copley, which in time was to be regarded as 'the highest scientific distinction' bestowed by the Society. His close friends Arthington, Sloane and Hon. Sidney Wortley Montagu* were among the trustees appointed under the will, by which the estates were put in trust for

Copley's cousin, Lionel Copley of Wadsworth, on the failure of whose issue they descended to Sir Godfrey's grandson Joseph Moyle (son of Joseph Moyle* by Copley's surviving daughter), who assumed the name Copley by Act of Parliament.[20]

[1] Yorks. Arch. Soc. Copley mss DD38 box H–J, Copley ped.; Sheffield Archs. Copley mss CD246, CD75, marriage settlements, 23 Feb. 1682, 31 May 1700; *The Gen.* n.s. xvi. 110–11; Clay, *Dugdale's Vis. Yorks.* ii. 52–53. [2] *Rec. R. Soc.* 386, 527. [3] *CJ* xii. 508. [4] *HMC Lords*, n.s. iii. 204. [5] Luttrell, *Brief Relation*, v. 417. [6] *Thoresby Diary*, i. 308, 373; ii. 6, 38; Nichols, *Lit. Hist.* i. 478; iv. 74–76; Stowe 747, f. 8; Huntington Lib. Stowe mss 26(2), James Brydges' diary, 12 Feb. 1698, 21 Dec. 1699, 4 Mar. 1702; NLW, Mackworth diary, mss 14362E, 22 Dec. 1701; Add. 70248, Robert Monckton* to Harley, 23 Apr. 1705; Sheffield Archs. Copley mss CD503/14, acct. of Don navigation bill, n.d.; CD75, marriage settlement, 31 May 1700; CD338, memo. 1690; CD246, marriage settlement, 23 Feb. 1682; CD468, acct. of rents, 1691; CD473, ff. 4, 7; *HMC Var.* ii. 394–5; Sloane 4038, f. 95; Lancs. RO, Kenyon mss DDKe/HMC/969, Thomas Wilson to Roger Kenyon*, 24 Sept. 1695. [7] Stowe 747, ff. 56, 62; H. Horwitz, *Parl. and Pol. Wm. III*, 168. [8] Stowe 747, f. 66; Cobbett, *Parlty. Hist.* v. 1039–40, 1050, 1115–17, 1120; Chandler, iii. 58–60; Ralph, *Hist. Eng.* ii. 696, 700; Clarke, *Jas. II*, ii. 558; *Vernon–Shrewsbury Letters*, i. 193; Oldmixon, *Hist. Eng.* 152. [9] Sheffield Archs. Copley mss CD503/14, acct. of Don navigation bill, n.d.; Stowe 747, f. 84. [10] Yorks. Arch. Soc. Copley mss DD38 box B–C, Molesworth to Copley, 1, 10 Nov. 1698, Caleb Askwith to [same], 28 Dec. 1698; *Cam. Misc.* xxix. 387; Stowe mss 26(1), Brydges' diary, 17, 19, 20, 22, 25 Mar. 1699; Luttrell, iv. 484. [11] Stowe mss 26(2), Brydges' diary, 13, 26 Jan. 1700; Som. RO, Sanford mss DD/SF 4107(a), notes on debate on Ld. Chancellor, 15 [sic] Feb. 1700; Northants. RO, Montagu (Boughton) mss 48/51, Vernon to Shrewsbury, 28 Mar. 1700; Yorks. Arch. Soc. Copley mss DD38 box H–J, Copley to Lionel Copley, 20 Jan., 29 Feb. 1699[–1700]. [12] Sloane 4038, ff. 95, 115–16; Yorks. Arch. Soc. Copley mss DD38 box H–J, poll for election for commrs. [1701]; *Cocks Diary*, 118, 120, 140, 147, 163, 179; Horwitz, 284, 290, 292; Luttrell, v. 61; *HMC Portland*, x. 34; *HMC Cowper*, ii. 424–5. [13] Add. 40775, f. 67; 24475, f. 134; 7078, f. 78; Stowe mss 26(2), Brydges' diary, 4 Mar. 1702; *Cocks Diary*, 198, 213, 248–50, 256; Sheffield Archs. Copley mss CD473, f. 9. [14] *Thoresby Diary*, i. 373; Notts. RO, Portland mss DD3P10/2/2, Newcastle acct. bk. 30 June 1703; Sheffield Archs. Copley mss CD473, f. 16; Cobbett, vi. 97–104; *HMC Lords*, n.s. v. 63; Yorks. Archs. Soc. Copley mss DD38 box D–G, Copley to [Molesworth], 16 Feb. 1702[–3]; Cunningham, *Hist. GB*, i. 315. [15] TCD, King letterbks. ms 1489/2, p. 178; Nichols, iv. 74–75; *Thoresby Diary*, i. 411–15, 441–2; Stowe 748, f. 9. [16] *HMC Downshire*, i. 817; Nichols, iv. 76; Stowe 748, f. 21. [17] Luttrell, v. 417; *Bull. IHR*, xxxiv. 93, 95. [18] Luttrell, 620; *Duchess of Marlborough Corresp.* ii. 221–2; *Cam. Misc.* xxiii. 32, 47, 67. [19] Sloane 4040, ff. 225–6; 4041, f. 12; Sheffield Archs. Copley mss CD473, f. 20; *Party and Management* ed. C. Jones, 110; Boyer, *Anne Annals*, vi. 356–7. [20] Cunningham, ii. 137; Add. 70420, Dyer's newsletter 12 Apr. 1709; Bank of Eng. Morice mss, Sir Nicholas Morice, 2nd Bt.*, to Humphrey Morice*, 15 Apr. 1709; Luttrell, vi. 428; PCC 70 Lane; Nichols, i. 478; *Rec. R. Soc.* 53, 112–13; Yorks. Archs. Soc. Copley mss DD38 box H–J; *The Gen.* n.s. xvi. 110–11; Clay, ii. 52–53; *Misc. Gen. et Her.* ser. 5, ix. 350.

E. C./C. I. M.

CORBET, Richard (1649–1718), of Shawbury Park, Salop.

SHROPSHIRE 1701 (Dec.)–1705

bap. 15 Jan. 1649, 1st s. of Richard Corbet of Shawbury Park and Moreton Corbet, Salop by Grace, da. of William Noel of Kirkby Mallory, Leics. *m.* settlement 2 Apr. 1692 (with £3,500), Judith (*d.* 1700), da. of Sir John Bridgeman, 2nd Bt., of Castle Bromwich, Warws., and sis. of Orlando Bridgeman I*, 4s. 1da. *suc.* fa. 1691.[1]

Freeman, Much Wenlock 1680.[2]

Corbet's father had inherited in 1688 the principal family estate of the Shropshire Corbets, at Moreton Corbet, on the death without issue of his great-nephew Sir Vincent Corbet, 3rd Bt. The Member himself first appears in 1694 when, through the influence of the Earl of Bradford (Francis Newport†), the leading Whig in the county, and of Bradford's son, Lord Newport (Hon. Richard Newport I*), he was able to avoid being pricked as sheriff for the ensuing year. He was included in the lieutenancy in March 1701, and at the general election in December was 'prevailed on by Lord Newport . . . and his friends' to stand for knight of the shire on the Whig interest. He and Sir Humphrey Briggs, 4th Bt.*, were opposed by two Tories, one of whom, Robert Lloyd I*, was Corbet's wife's brother-in-law. John Bridgeman of Blodwell, Shropshire, who was brother-in-law to both Corbet and Lloyd, was placed in an awkward position by the opposition of the two men to one another: before the election Bridgeman noted that 'both my brothers to my great satisfaction seemed fair so in their proposals to each other but the other candidates not agreeing I believe will occasion a poll'. In the event Corbet and Lloyd were both returned, Corbet heading the poll. He was re-elected in 1702, after having again stood in opposition to Lloyd. He made no speech in Parliament, as far as is known. On 18 Jan. 1703 he was granted leave of absence in order to recover his health. Considered in 1704 a likely opponent of the Tack, he figured on Harley's lobbying list, and voted against the Tack or was absent on 28 Nov. His brother-in-law Bridgeman, himself a Whig, wrote to him on 19 Dec.: 'I am one of those who rejoice that your opposers lost their point of forcing the sovereign to what they would think a hardship in their own case.'[3]

Corbet did not stand for re-election in 1705, possibly on grounds of ill-health, his place as Whig candidate for the shire being taken by his kinsman Sir Robert Corbet, 4th Bt.*, and in 1708, racked by gout, he again cried off, declining invitations to stand as knight and on the Whig interest at Shrewsbury, and giving over his own interest in the county to Sir Robert Corbet and Hon. Henry Newport*, who were returned unopposed. In 1710, however, although his health was still poor, he joined Henry Newport in opposing a strong Tory challenge in the county election. The two Whigs were defeated, Corbet coming bottom of the poll. He seems to have taken no further part in politics. As one of the nominees for the shrievalty of Shropshire in 1711 he wrote in November of that year to Lord Oxford (Robert Harley*), to whom he was distantly related, begging not to be pricked

> for these reasons following. My estate is much impaired and a great deal in debt and younger children to provide for, but this is not all. I grow old and very infirm, being now confined to my chamber with the gout and stone, in so much that I am fitter for the grave than a white staff.

He was excused. In March 1713 he wrote in despair to Bridgeman: 'I have been confined to my chamber ever since you saw me, with a great deal of pain; and God knows when I will go off . . . in so much misery.' Corbet died in April 1718, after having been bedridden a long time, and was buried at Moreton Corbet.[4]

[1] *Trans. Salop Arch. Soc.* ser. 1, vii. 311; *Salop Par. Reg. Soc.* Lichfield dioc. i. Moreton Corbet, 22. [2] Salop RO, Forester mss, copy of Much Wenlock corp. bk. [3] *Trans. Salop Arch. Soc.* ser. 4, xii. 8; Bradford mss at Weston Park, Corbet to Orlando Bridgeman, 5 Nov. 1694, 5 Jan. 1695; John to Sir John Bridgeman, 19, 25, 29 Nov. 1701; same to Corbet, 19 Dec. 1704; *CSP Dom.* 1700-2, p. 249. [4] Bradford mss, Sir Edward Leighton, 1st Bt.*, to Corbet, 22 Jan. 1708; Sir Robert Corbet to same, 29 Jan. 1708; John Bridgeman to Sir Robert Corbet, 10 Feb. 1708; same to Richard Corbet, 10 Feb. 1708, 17 July 1710; Sir John Bridgeman to (Sir) Arthur Owen II*, 1 Nov. 1710, 25 Apr. 1718; Corbet to Sir John Bridgeman, 3 Mar. 1713; Add. 70219, Corbet to Ld. Oxford, 9 Nov. 1711; A. E. C[orbet], *Fam. Corbet*, ii. 358.

D. W. H.

CORBET, Sir Robert, 4th Bt. (c.1670–1740), of Adderley and Stoke, Salop.

SHROPSHIRE 1705–1710, 1715–1722

b. c.1670, o. surv. s. of Sir John Corbet, 3rd Bt., of Stoke by his 1st w. Theophilia, da. and h. of John Campbell of Woodford, Essex and gdda. of John Mohun†, 1st Baron Mohun of Okehampton. *educ.* Christ Church, Oxf. matric. 6 July 1687, aged 17; I. Temple 1688. *m.* lic. 21 June 1693, Jane, da. of William Hooker of St. Clement Danes, Mdx., 3s. 4da. *suc.* fa. as 4th Bt. 1695.[1]

Sheriff, Salop 1700–1; freeman, Shrewsbury 1721–*d*.[2] Clerk of Green Cloth 1720–1727; commr. customs 1735–*d*.[3]

Corbet belonged to a cadet branch of a prominent Shropshire family, and his mother was a wealthy heiress. Like his grandfather, who had sat for Shrewsbury in Charles II's reign, he was a Whig in politics. Returned unopposed for the county in 1705, in place of his kinsman Richard Corbet*, who was in poor health, he was classified as a 'Churchman' in a list of the new Parliament, but on 25 Oct. 1705 voted for the Court candidate for Speaker and in 1708 was twice listed as a Whig. At the election of that year he was again returned without opposition, having previously made sure of the interest of Richard Corbet and of other leading Whigs in the county, in case of a contest, and in 1709 voted for the naturalization of the Palatines. Although given leave of absence for a month on 18 Feb. 1710, he was included in a published list of those who had voted for the impeachment of Dr Sacheverell. In April 1710 he joined some other Whig gentlemen of Shropshire in signing an open letter to the lord lieutenant of the county, complaining against the way in which Shrewsbury's Tories had gone about drawing up an address to the Queen in Sacheverell's favour. He did not stand in the 1710 general election, Richard Corbet resuming his place as one of the Whig candidates for the shire; nor did he stand in 1713.[4]

Corbet died on 3 Oct. 1740.

[1] A. E. C[orbet], *Fam. Corbet*, ii. 357; *Mar. Lic. Fac. Off.* 208; *Adderley Reg.: Lichfield Dioc.* iv (Salop Par. Reg. Soc.) 8, 9, 14–15, 17, 19, 22. [2] *Shrewsbury Burgess Roll* ed. Forrest, 65. [3] *Cal. Treas. Pprs.* 1735–8, p. 149; 1739–41, p. 624. [4] *HMC 5th Rep.* 152; Staffs. RO, Bradford mss at Weston Park, Corbet to Richard Corbet, 29 Jan. 1708, John Bridgeman to Corbet, 10 Feb. 1708; Boyer, *Anne Annals*, ix. 185–9.

D. W. H.

CORDELL, Sir John, 3rd Bt. (1677–1704), of Melford Hall, Long Melford, Suff.

SUDBURY 1701 (Feb.–Nov.)

bap. 11 Nov. 1677, o. s. of Sir John Cordell, 2nd Bt.†, of Melford Hall by Elizabeth, da. of Thomas Waldegrave† of Smallbridge, Bures, Suff. *m.* 24 Dec. 1701, Eleanor, da. of Joseph Haskins Stiles*, *s.p. suc.* fa. as 3rd Bt. Sept. 1690.

Freeman, Sudbury by 1703.[1]

Probably returned on his own interest at Sudbury in January 1701, Cordell was included in the 'black list' of those who had opposed the preparations for war against France, and in December stood down in favour of his prospective father-in-law, Joseph Haskins Stiles, acting as an 'agent' for Stiles in the borough and continuing to support him actively in the 1702 election.[2]

Killed by a fall from his horse on 8 May 1704, Cordell was buried at Long Melford. The baronetcy became extinct and his estate was divided between his two sisters. Melford Hall passed eventually to his nephew, Sir Cordell Firebrace, 3rd Bt.[3]

[1] Suff. RO (Bury St. Edmunds), Sudbury bor. recs. EE501/4/3. [2] *CJ*, xiv. 120, 245. [3] Howard, *Vis. Suff.* i. 247.

D. W. H.

CORNBURY, Edward Hyde, Visct. *see* **HYDE**

CORNEWALL, Henry (c.1654–1717), of Moccas Court and Bredwardine, Herefs.

WEOBLEY	1685–1687
HEREFORD	11 June 1689–1695
HEREFORDSHIRE	1698–1700
WEOBLEY	1701 (Feb.–Nov.), 1702–1708
	1710–1713

b. c.1654, 1st and o. surv. s. of Edward Cornewall of Moccas Court by Frances, da. of Sir Walter Pye† of the Mynde, Much Dewchurch, Herefs., wid. of Henry Vaughan of Moccas Court and Bredwardine. *m.* (1) 11 Oct. 1683, Margarita Laurentia (*d.* 1692), da. and h. of Laurentius Huyssen, Lord of Weelde, Zeeland, 2s. (1 *d.v.p.*); (2) lic. 27 Apr. 1695, Susanna, da. and coh. of Sir John Williams*, 3s. (1 *d.v.p.*) 1da. *suc.* fa. 1709.[1]

Page of honour to Duke of York c.1669; equerry to Princess Mary 1677; master of the horse by 1683–5.[2]

Ensign of ft. Duke of York's regt. 1672, lt. 1676–7, capt. 1677–82; capt. R. Eng. Regt. (French army) 1672–6; capt.-lt. R. Horse Gds. 1682–5; col. of ft. 1685–Nov. 1688.[3]

Cornewall's lengthy career of personal service both to James II and Princess Mary left him with divided loyalties at the Revolution, but his doubts over James's policies, and perhaps also the Dutch connexions he had forged by his first marriage, overcame any habits of deference. He had determined to give up his regiment in 1687, and, though his resignation was not accepted until after the Prince of Orange's landing, he may well already have been active in the army on William's behalf. The absence of any tangible reward from the new King and Queen, on whom Cornewall had made a poor impression in earlier days, seems to have accentuated his Tory sympathies, and to have pushed him rapidly into opposition. Prior to the 1690 election he was blacklisted as having voted in the Convention against the transfer of the crown, and after an unopposed return for Hereford was classed as a Tory in Lord Carmarthen's (Sir Thomas Osborne†) analysis of the new Parliament. Reports that he would oppose the veteran Whig Sir Edward Harley* in the county proved unfounded. In April 1691 he was classed by Robert Harley*, Sir Edward's son, with the Country opposition.[4]

Not particularly active in the first two sessions of the 1690 Parliament, Cornewall made his mark in the winter of 1691–2. On 28 Nov. 1691 he acted as a teller in the committee on the East India trade, against a motion to proceed to a regulation of the trade 'by a joint-stock'. Then on 9 Dec. came his first recorded speech, when he proposed that the House interrogate the messenger who had apprehended the informer William Fuller. Subsequent contributions reflected his continuing interest in military matters, in which he could of course claim some expertise. On 15 Dec. he spoke in favour of agreeing with the committee on the army estimates, in their resolution to grant extra pay to the two regiments of foot guards, on the grounds that these were 'always attendant on the King's person' and were therefore 'generally here in town at a dearer expense'. Later in the same debate he showed the first sign of that animus against the Allies, especially the Dutch, which was to become even more pronounced after the death of his first wife in April of that year. Opposing the allowance of English rates of pay to Dutch troops in England, he deplored the 'mischievous' practice of giving 'different pay to soldiers of the same nation in one and the same army'. He twice acted as a teller on the subject of the Irish army estimates: first in committee, on 30 Dec., against accepting the estimate provided by the paymaster of the forces in Ireland (Thomas, Lord Coningsby*); and on 2 Jan. 1692, on the report against the sum resolved upon for the maintenance of infantry. Regarding the army generally, he made two attempts to add a clause to the poll tax bill to appropriate 'such a part' of the revenue to the support of the 'land forces': on 10 Feb., when it was rejected as a breach of procedure, and, more successfully, on the 15th, when it was accepted by the House after a division in which Cornewall was a teller. The very next day, however, he withdrew it, saying that 'since the House had agreed to continue the commissioners of accounts for one year longer, he thought there was no great need of this clause'. The connexion between the two issues was tactical. On the 15th, before reviving his appropriation clause, Cornewall had supported another proposed addition to the bill, to continue the accounts commission, the threat of appropriation being used to extort from ministers acceptance of this first demand. His evident hostility to the Court had been manifested again only a few days earlier, on 12 Feb., in a debate on the bill to vest the Irish forfeitures in the King and Queen. Here it was to some degree masked by an affected concern, which appeared natural in an old soldier, for the interests of army veterans. He offered a clause 'that the third part of the estate forfeited . . . shall be given to such officers and soldiers as served in person in Ireland'. It was lost on a division. His other recorded speeches in this session occurred on 16 Feb., in opposition to a clause of Sir Christopher Musgrave, 4th Bt.*, to enable the King to borrow money on the security of future parliamentary grants in order to make up any shortfall in receipts from taxation; and on 20 Feb., in committee on the bill to prevent correspondence with enemies of the King and Queen, when he 'tendered a clause that no one should be prosecuted on this Act without two witnesses, but the law being so already it was laid aside'.[5]

In the 1692–3 session Cornewall made a strong speech on 23 Nov. in the debate on advice to be tendered to the King. Following up attacks on 'foreign officers', he directed his fire particularly at Count von Solms, for his failure to assist the English troops at Steenkerk: 'Reduce the question singly to Solms; put it upon him. He is a man very haughty, and puts officers under such hardships, that I am sure the service will be ill done as long as he is general of the foot.' His own preference was for Thomas Tollemache* to be given the command, 'a better soldier and one who has done you extraordinary service and is well beloved by the soldiers, which the other is not'. The speech also contained some more general remarks of a xenophobic nature – 'I am sorry to see that your English officers are so fond of foreigners; I doubt not but they will make their hearts ache before they have done' – and these were pursued a little later in the same debate, when he observed that 'you have all the foot under Dutch general officers, and the cannon too. I hope they will not play foul play, but if they should, you have a scurvy business of it.' An active member of the 'Country' opposition, Cornewall spoke against the Court on 25 Nov., when he advocated the postponement of consideration of the army and navy estimates until the House had the opportunity to 'look over them'; acted as a teller in committee of supply on the 29th against allowing £11,000 in the navy estimates for the construction of 'bomb vessels'; and on 1 Dec. was a teller against a ministerial amendment to the treason trials bill. He intervened twice on the 'Country' side in committee of supply on 3 Dec. and acted as a teller in the committee on 6 Dec., against a proposal to triple the salary of the secretary at war. In the committee to consider advice to be offered to the King, he first of all defended the lower rate of pay allowed to soldiers when in Holland, in a debate on 8 Dec., explaining that 'things were cheaper there', and subsequently, on the 16th, returned to a familiar theme: 'I think it a proper head for you to advise his Majesty upon', he declared,

> that no foreigners, but only natives of England, be employed in your Tower of London or any other of your garrisons nor in the office of Ordnance, stores, etc., for I think it dangerous that the Dutch should be acquainted so well wherewith, with whom you have had wars and may again.

However, after this date he ceased to make significant contributions to the opposition cause for this session, a fact which may largely be explained by ill-health. He was unable to vote for the triennial bill in February 1693, because he had been obliged to 'keep his chamber for four weeks'. For all his parliamentary co-operation with the Harleys at this time, he was one of the very few Herefordshire gentlemen whose party sentiments and personal antipathies prevented them from joining in the general clamour in the county for Sir Edward Harley to stand for the vacant place of knight of the shire in the by-election of February 1693.[6]

A rumour was current in Herefordshire in November 1693 that Cornewall had been 'secured for compounding with enemies', the only suggestion that he possessed Jacobite sympathies or connexions, and one which was without foundation. When Parliament reassembled he was again prominent among opposition speakers. On 22 Nov. 1693, when the miscarriages of the fleet were under scrutiny, he inquired why no attempt had been made to 'hinder the enemy from coming out', a failure he took to be 'the ground of all'. As before, his special contribution was to debates on supply and the maintenance of the armed forces. He spoke in the debate on supply on 28 Nov., and on 5 Dec. turned his attention to the Allies, and the inequity of England's financial burden in carrying on the war. Why, he asked, had 'the confederates . . . not their numbers complete'? The consequence would be that 'we shall pay above double, and they not above half'. The same argument appeared in his speech on 11 Dec.: 'we are at the charge of the whole war, and they [the Allies] go away with the money'. He also renewed his attacks on the general staff, claiming, 'we have not want of numbers of men, nor officers, but general officers', a point he reiterated the following day, when in a debate on the question of augmenting the land forces he remarked that the House would only be mocking itself if it discussed augmentation, while the main topic at issue remained 'the generals'. Anti-Dutch feeling surfaced again in his intervention on 23 Feb. 1694 on the report of the committee of ways and means. With other Members, he opposed the suggested duty on leather, on the grounds that it resembled too closely the dreaded inland excise and that at this rate Englishmen would find their condition worse than that of the Dutch, in whose country no article was exempt from taxation. He opposed the salt tax too, acting as a teller on 16 Mar. in favour of a motion to adjourn the debate on the salt duty bill. Little is known of his parliamentary activity in the following session, during which he remarried, but he had not lost interest in remaining a Member, and after contemplating a move to Gloucestershire, where a large estate was on the market, he set himself to challenge for the county seat in Herefordshire. In doing so he ignored both his existing constituents at Hereford and the voters of Weobley, 'many' of whom had 'applied themselves' to him to stand there. The venality of the Weobley electorate, however, made any candidature in that borough an expensive proposition. In the county Cornewall made an approach to the Harleys, offering to 'join with' Sir Edward. Rebuffed, he displayed considerable pique, telling Paul Foley I* that Sir Edward Harley's decision to partner instead the Whig Sir Herbert Croft, 1st Bt.*, was an affront he took 'very ill'. His friends, he said, had assured him his chances of carrying the county were good, and although 'he did not much care for standing, but upon a provocation he might do Sir Ed[ward] an unkindness'. This was mere bravado, for the alliance of Harley and Croft was secure. Cornewall then belatedly turned his attention back to the borough of Hereford, but his inquiries there evoked no response and he left without the prospect of a parliamentary seat and entirely 'out of humour'. He did half-heartedly challenge Croft for the county but withdrew before the poll.[7]

Spurning the support he could have secured among the Hereford electors 'if he would be commonly civil to them', Cornewall aimed once more at the county in the 1698 election, where this time he was successful in a contest. He was classed as a supporter of the Country party in a comparative analysis of the old and new Commons. At the crucial vote of 18 Jan. 1699 on the standing army, however, he would seem to have sided with the Court, for three out of four witnesses recorded that he had spoken and voted against the disbanding bill and his name was included in the ensuing black list. Despite his own military background, this appearance in favour of a standing army did represent an unexpected change of heart. Not long afterwards, on 10 Feb. 1699, he was granted a fortnight's leave of absence. He may have striven during the next session to restore his reputation with the Tories. Certainly by autumn 1700 he had convinced Lord Weymouth (Thomas Thynne†) that he had repented his 'wrong step about the army' and become once again an 'honest man'.[8]

Cornewall's efforts to curry favour with Weymouth were part of a tortuous, duplicitous and ultimately corrupt campaign to procure his election for the venal borough of Weobley in January 1701. He had moved over from the county to make room for his cousin Charles Corn(e)wall*, and the manoeuvrings of the autumn and winter of 1700–1 had a dual purpose: to bring in Charles as knight of the shire while safeguarding his own candidacy in the borough. By August 1700 he had made an alliance of convenience with the Court Whig Lord Coningsby to promote his cousin's chances in the county, to offset the opposition of three Tory magnates, Lords Chandos, Kent and Scudamore (James*). Coningsby's backing was insufficient by itself, however, and Cornewall was obliged to approach the Harleys once again. This time he did not go cap in hand but gave himself a bargaining counter by interfering in Radnorshire, where he canvassed apparently on his own behalf against Thomas Harley*, the outgoing knight of the shire and cousin of Robert. In an obscure episode, Cornewall then announced his intention to withdraw, in return, he said, for a promise from the Harley family to support cousin Charles in Herefordshire. This arrangement with the Harleys is not confirmed by any other source, however, and it may well have been an invention of Cornewall's, in order to dupe the Herefordshire electors into believing that his cousin did enjoy the Harleys' support, a trick he was not above trying on other occasions. Such an explanation is suggested by the fact that Cornewall subsequently intervened again in Radnorshire, in favour of another anti-Harley candidate, and then backed off for the second time, appealing directly to Robert Harley:

> I confess I was never so surprised in my life as when my cousin Charles told me you would not promise him your interest . . . I thought we were hardly dealt with, and in the heat of it spoke to two gentlemen at Presteigne assizes [in Radnorshire] in order to oppose your kinsman, but since I have reflected that our enemies may improve this difference to both our prejudices, I am willing to make the first step towards an accommodation, which is, if you think I can be serviceable to your kinsman . . . I will be ready to serve him with my interest.

When this too failed, the Cornewall family and their agents were reduced to bare apology and the hope that the Harleys would 'use Capt. Cha[rles] tenderly': neither stance was of any avail, a fact which largely accounted for Charles Cornewall's failure at the poll. Henry's own election at Weobley, though successful, was an equally arduous and serpentine affair.[9]

Cornewall was included on a list of those MPs likely to support the Court on 22 Feb. 1701 in agreeing with the supply committee's resolution to continue the 'Great Mortgage', which may indicate an endeavour to ingratiate himself with Robert Harley, or with the King. Other evidence suggests a determination to be all things to all men. In October he even dined with the ex-Weobley MP, Robert Price, who reported 'all honour done me and good nature shown by Colonel

Cornewall... Not a word of elections.' However, this did not prevent Price from contesting Weobley in November and effectively ousting Cornewall. The following year, recovering his seat at Weobley, Cornewall gave his interest to the candidate for knight of the shire supported by the Whigs Lord Coningsby, Sir Herbert Croft and John Dutton Colt*. With the Tories temporarily in the ascendant at Westminster, he voted on 13 Feb. 1703 against agreeing with the Lords' amendments to the bill for enlarging the time for taking the oath of abjuration. After the ministerial reshuffle of 1704, however, he was considered a moderate Tory. Forecast in October of that year as a probable opponent of the Tack, he was included in Robert Harley's lobbying list, to be contacted by Lord Treasurer Godolphin (Sidney†). Cornewall did not vote for the Tack on 28 Nov. 1704. An analysis of the Commons following the 1705 election classed him as 'Low Church', although he subsequently voted on 25 Oct. against the Court candidate for Speaker. By this time he had established what he evidently considered a sure route to patronage. He had begun to send flattering letters to the Duke of Marlborough (John Churchill†) in 1704, playing on their 'very long acquaintance' in order to obtain favours, posts and promotions for relations and friends. Marlborough's achievements 'struck your... enemies dumb'; 'the better half of mankind are preserved by the great actions you have done; all the world must know that since Alexander and Caesar no man ever did as much'; the Duke's 'glorious victories and successes... has [sic] struck us all dumb with admiration'. On at least one occasion Cornewall asked for something for himself, the governorship of a garrison, but without success. How far this campaign of ingratiation affected his conduct in Parliament is unclear. A list from early 1708 even marked him as a Whig. What can be said about him with confidence is that he was increasingly inactive, and it was no surprise when he did not seek re-election in 1708.[10]

Two years later Cornewall did an abrupt *volte-face* and decided to contest Weobley again, and in the Tory interest. One Tory rival begged Robert Harley to persuade Cornewall to desist and thus prevent any damage to the party cause. He added,

I can't see why the colonel should deny, for I am well satisfied he does not much care for the fatigue of attending, and there will be as many Members for this county [Herefordshire] firm to the interest which I suppose he befriends as there will be if he comes in.

Classified as a Tory in the 'Hanover list', Cornewall, though, as predicted, almost totally inactive during the 1710 Parliament, meant to use his presence in the Commons as a lever to preferment. Given that he had made two advantageous marriages, had at long last succeeded his father, and besides considerable property owned at least £6,000 in stocks, it is unlikely that even his excessive election expenses at Weobley had reduced him to the level of a parliamentary pauper. None the less his appetite for office, for himself and his family, was undiminished. In February 1711 he was reported to be 'very fond' of purchasing the colonelcy of a regiment, and one letter to Robert Harley, as lord treasurer, bluntly requested appointment as 'master of the Queen's household'. Harley's procrastinations and refusals may account for Cornewall's appearance among the Tory rebels on 7 Dec. 1711 in the division on 'No Peace without Spain', although as an old soldier and an associate of Marlborough it is conceivable that he might have stepped out of character to take a principled stand. He finally abandoned Parliament at the 1713 general election, but his son Henry†, another career army officer, was given the place of groom of the bedchamber to King George I in May 1715, thus resuming, after a long intermission, the family tradition of royal service. Cornewall died on 22 Feb. 1717, aged 63, and was buried in Westminster Abbey.[11]

[1] C. G. S. Foljambe and C. Reade, *House of Cornwall*, 102, 104–5; C. J. Robinson, *Castles of Herefs.* 24, 107; C. J. Robinson, *Mansions and Manors of Herefs.* 119. [2] *CSP Dom.* 1677–8, p. 532. [3] *CSP Dom.* 1676–7, p. 412; J. Childs, *Nobles, Gent. and Profession of Arms* (Soc. for Army Hist. Res. Sp. Pubn. xiii), 21. [4] *Correspondentie* ed. Japikse, iv. 303; *HMC Portland*, iii. 421. [5] Grey, x. 204; *Luttrell Diary*, 46, 81, 98, 180, 182, 187–8, 190, 197. [6] Grey, x. 259, 261, 280; *Luttrell Diary*, 254–6, 260, 270, 287, 290, 298, 302, 324; Nottingham Univ. Lib. Portland (Bentinck) mss PwA 2385, notes on debate, 23 Nov. 1692; Add. 70017, ff. 5, 22. [7] Add. 70115, Abigail to Robert Harley, 11 Nov. 1693; 70116, same to Sir Edward Harley, 28 June 1695; 70226, Thomas Foley II* to Robert Harley, 31 July 1695; 70018, ff. 67, 81; Grey, x. 321, 333, 343, 358; Ranke, vi. 226, 240; D. Rubini, *Court and Country*, 58–59. [8] Bath mss at Longleat House, Thynne pprs. 24, f. 331; 26, ff. 287–9; Add. 70113, Sir Edward Harley to Edward Cornewall, 24 Feb. 1697[–8]; 70019, ff. 58–59; Huntington Lib. Stowe mss 57(1), p. 22; *Cam. Misc.* xxix. 387; *Vernon–Shrewsbury Letters*, ii. 253. [9] Add. 70019, ff. 168, 235, 259, 277, 302; 70056, [–] to [?Robert Harley], 24 Sept. 1700; 70239, Thomas Harley to same, 28 Sept. 1700; 70219, Cyriac Cornewall to same, 10 Nov. 1700; Henry Cornewall to same, [1 Dec. 1700]; 70298–9, [–] to same, 28 Dec. 1700; 70064, Robert Harley to Coningsby, 26 Dec. 1700; 70226, Thomas Foley II to Robert Harley, 20 Sept. 1700; 70020, f. 38; Thynne pprs. 25, ff. 10, 13, 21, 23–25, 27–29, 37, 40, 55–58; 26, ff. 285–9; *HMC Portland*, iii. 635; iv. 11. [10] Thynne pprs. 26, ff. 291–2; Add. 70168, James Brydges to Robert Harley, 4 Feb. 1700[–1]; 70254, Robert Price to same, 11 Oct. 1701; 70256, H. Seward to [?same], 13 Apr. 1702; 61289, f. 125; 61363, ff. 86–87, 117–18, 135–6, 165–6; 61286, f. 26; 61364, f. 144; 61296, f. 72; *Bull. IHR*, xxxiv. 96; *Marlborough–Godolphin Corresp.* 468; *HMC Ormonde*, n.s. viii. 60. [11] Add. 70278, Henry Gorges to [Robert Harley], 3 Aug. 1710; 70219, Cornewall to same [aft. May 1711]; P. G. M. Dickson, *Financial Rev.* 297; *Wentworth Pprs.* 181; *Bull. IHR*, xxxiii. 226–7; *Cal. Treas. Bks.* xxix. 499; J. M. Beattie, *Eng.*

Court in Reign of Geo. I, 62; Le Neve, *Mon. Angl.* 1650–1718, pp. 279–80; *Westminster Abbey Reg.* (Harl. Soc. x), 289.

D. W. H.

CORNISH, Henry (c.1659–1724), of St. Lawrence Jewry, London and Sherrard Street, Westminster.

SHAFTESBURY   1698–13 Feb. 1699

b. c.1659, 1st s. of Henry Cornish of St. Lawrence Jewry, alderman of London, by his w. Elizabeth. *m*. 7 Apr. 1688, Catherine, da. of Sir Robert Henley* and sis. of Anthony Henley*, 1s. 3da. *suc*. fa. 1685.[1]

Cttee. R. Fishery Co. [I] 1691; asst. R. Mines Co. 1693; dir. million subscription to Bank of Eng. 1695, Bank of Eng. 1695–1700, E.I. Co. 1711–12; trustee, loan to Emperor 1706, poor Palatines 1709.[2]

Agent, 2nd tp. Horse Gds. and Col. Churchill's Ft. 1694–5.

Commr. stamp office 1694–1708.[3]

Receiver of taxes, London, Mdx. and Westminster 1696.[4]

Cornish's father, a wealthy London alderman, had been executed on somewhat dubious charges of treason in 1685, but the estates, forfeited to the crown, were returned to the widow to pay her husband's debts and to support her children, and the attainder itself was reversed by Act of Parliament in 1689. Two children were baptised to Henry and Elizabeth Cornish in London in September 1660 and December 1662 respectively, but neither corresponds with Cornish's alleged age at marriage, 24, nor his age at death. Described as a 'factor' on his marriage licence, Cornish prospered after 1690 when he started making loans to government in partnership with Sir William Scawen*, and then, with (Sir) Stephen Evance*, obtained several army clothing contracts. By 1694 he was acting as agent to two regiments. In May he secured appointment as a commissioner of the stamp office and in 1695 replaced Scawen as a director of the Bank of England. The following year he received further evidence of Court favour when he was appointed receiver of taxes for London and Middlesex. Having stood unsuccessfully for Shaftesbury in the 1695 election, he carried the seat at the second attempt in 1698.[5]

Cornish, a Whig, was listed as a Court placeman in September 1698. He voted against the third reading of the disbanding bill on 18 Jan. 1699. On 10 Feb., during a debate on the place bill, Sir John Bolles, 4th Bt., drew attention to the presence in the House of a number of office-holders ineligible to sit under the terms of the 1694 Lottery Act, including Cornish, as a commissioner of the stamp office. Cornish was duly expelled three days later. He thought about standing for Shaftesbury in February 1701, but gave his interest instead to Sir Edmund Harrison, one of the directors of the New East India Company (to which Cornish and his brother-in-law Sir Theodore Janssen† were among the largest subscribers).[6]

At the beginning of Anne's reign, Cornish and Evance presented a petition for £1,482 due to them for supplying clothes to a marine regiment in Ireland in 1691–2. The marines presented special problems, as they were not considered part of the army establishment and the paymaster refused to issue money for them in the usual way. Eventually the two clothiers had to seek relief by means of a bill in Parliament, which received the Royal Assent on 16 Feb. 1706. In common with most government contractors, Cornish experienced difficulty in securing payment for goods supplied to the army, having to accept settlement in unpopular South Sea stock. This did not deter him from tendering, however, and in 1708 he secured a contract to supply the Duke of Savoy's army. That same year he sold his place in the stamp office to contest Shaftesbury, but after causing considerable alarm to the existing Whig interest in the town he eventually withdrew. In March 1710 Cornish was listed as possessing sufficient stock in the Bank of England to entitle him to a vote. Despite an apparent willingness to spend lavishly at the 1710 election, he was unable to find a seat, standing unsuccessfully at Westbury and Whitchurch. He is not known to have made any subsequent attempt to return to Parliament. He died, aged 65, at his house in Sherrard Street on 25 Mar. 1724.[7]

[1] J. R. Woodhead, *Rulers of London* (London and Mdx. Arch. Soc.), 52; IGI, Hants; *Mar. Lic. Vicar-Gen.* (Harl. Soc. xxxi.), 53; *The Gen.* n.s. vi. 103. [2] *CSP Dom.* 1691–2, pp. 3–4; 1693, p. 207; *N. and Q.* clxxix. 41; Pittis, *Present Parl.* 349; Boyer, *Anne Annals*, iv. 127; *English Courant*, 25 May 1695; *Post Boy*, 30 June–2 July 1709. [3] IGI, London; *Cal. Treas. Bks.* x. 618; xxii. 213. [4] *Cal. Treas. Bks.* xi. 67 [5] *HMC 6th Rep.* 463; *CSP Dom.* 1685, pp. 371, 423; Howell, *State Trials*, xi. 382–466; *Cal. Treas. Bks.* viii. 1361; ix. 354, 524, 548, 716, 1635, 1981, 1987, 1998; x. 103, 124, 129, 618; xi. 67, 300. [6] *EHR*, lxxi. 233–4; Add. 28886, ff. 184, 202, 213, 217, 223, 228. [7] *Cal. Treas. Bks.* xvii. 333; xxi. 46; xxii. 22; xxvi. 370; xxviii. 140; Egerton 3359 (unfol); *The Gen.* 103.

P. W./D. W.

CORN(E)WALL, Charles (1669–1718), of Berrington, Herefs.

BEWDLEY   2 Mar. 1709–1710
WEOBLEY   1715–7 Oct. 1718

bap. 9 Aug. 1669, 1st s. of Robert Cornewall of Berrington and Ludlow, Salop by Edith, da. of Sir Francis Cornwallis of Abermarlais, Carm. *m*. (1) *s.p.*; (2)

aft. 1696, Dorothy, da. of Thomas Hanmer I*, 8s. (5 *d.v.p.*) 7da. (1 *d.v.p.*). *suc.* fa. 1705.¹

Ens. RN 1683, capt. 1692, c.-in-c. Dunkirk squadron 1710, r.-adm. 1716, c.-in-c. Mediterranean 1716–18, v.-adm. 1717–*d.*; comptroller of storekeeper's accts. Navy Board Nov. 1714–16; plenip. to emperor of Morocco 1717–18.²

Cornwall, who dropped the 'e' from his name in order to distinguish his branch of the family from his cousins the Cornewalls of Moccas, was a naval officer who had seen action during the Nine Years War, serving with some distinction in the Mediterranean under Edward Russell* and Sir Clowdesley Shovell*. He may well have been on half-pay, however, when he made his first, unsuccessful, attempt to enter Parliament in the general election of January 1701. At this early stage in his political career he seems to have been under the tutelage of his cousin Henry Cornewall*, although he may not have shared Henry's Tory sympathies: another Tory, Robert Price*, wrote to Lord Weymouth (Thomas Thynne†), 'as to Captain Cornwall voting well, I hope he may, but I fear it, and the gentry are of a different opinion'. In March 1700 he announced his intention to put up for Herefordshire, and during the summer of that year he and Henry Cornewall, who proposed to stand for Weobley, gave a 'great entertainment' for the Herefordshire gentry. In the long run his candidature suffered through this association with his cousin, largely because of Henry Cornewall's serpentine intrigues, which alienated several major interests in the county, especially the Harleys. Cornwall himself had begun by flattering Robert Harley*. In November he wrote to acknowledge Harley's right to adjudicate as to who should have the honour of the county representation, 'being assured that from so great a patriot of our country's as you have upon all occasions proved yourself to be, we should still be a happy people if continued under the care and direction of . . . just such a great man'. However, Henry Cornewall managed to alienate both Harley and Lord Weymouth, although he tried (not very truthfully) to answer Weymouth's newly manufactured objections to a serving naval officer with a 'small' estate:

> I told you he had quitted the service when the peace was made, and that I would be answerable for him; that there was not in England a man that would be more hearty and zealous for his country and the Church of England than he; that he was resolved never more to be employed; that as to his estate it was between 5 and £600 a year; that he had between £10,000 and £12,000 in money, which he intended to lay out in land when he could find a convenient purchase in our country.

As the election approached, Charles and his kinsmen strove desperately to mend relations with the Harleys. An apology from one member of the Cornwall clan to Robert Harley imputed 'the ill management of our knight of the shire' to 'Charles's influencers'. The writer added, 'I am sure (were he at liberty) he would not accept it without your approbation, but since he is so far engaged I hope . . . you'll cover him in an honourable retreat'. Cornwall made a last-ditch effort to comply with Harley's preferred solution to the imbroglio, by endeavouring to reach an agreement with his opponent to leave matters to the decision of a county meeting, and then blamed his principal opponent, the Tory Sir John Williams*, and Williams' backer, Lord Chandos, for the failure of the negotiations. Harley would still not support him, but Cornwall had committed himself too far to withdraw and was obliged to go to a poll, where he was defeated. He did, however, receive four votes at the Weobley election, where his candidacy was announced shortly before the poll in the hope of drawing votes away from candidates opposing the election of his cousin Henry. Cornwall's election petition was never reported. Thereafter he did all he could to conciliate Harley, who was now not only the arbiter of local politics but also a leading man at court. In October 1701 he wrote to Harley for help in obtaining command of a ship should war be declared. A month later he wrote again to ask for advice as to whether to put up a second time for knight of the shire. By way of establishing his political credentials on this occasion he stated his fear 'lest the consequences' of a dissolution 'at this critical juncture might in any way retard the glorious designed ends the late [Parliament] seemed resolved to pursue'. In the event, he did not stand. Undeterred, he was quick to congratulate Harley on the latter's re-election as Speaker the following January.³

By the summer of 1702 Cornwall's temper had worsened. Resentment at continued exclusion from Parliament was exacerbated by a professional grievance. On Anne's accession he was superseded in the command of the ship he had been given, now intended for the Newfoundland expedition, and interpreted the decision as 'a modest way of terming me a blockhead, and consequently not fit to command on that service'. So angry was he that he refused the offer of a transfer to another vessel, upon which he was given 'liberty to quit the service'. At about the same time he appeared at the county meeting in Herefordshire to select candidates for the 1702 general election, 'full of complaints upon all the mismanagements of sea affairs' and criticisms of the way in which county elections had been managed. According to one observer, he 'said there had been very indirect practices used . . . the gentlemen at London choosing the knights there, and insinuated that the meeting of the gentlemen was to exclude the freeholders. This created some heat.' He and his cousin promised their interest to John Prise* and Sir John Williams. By 1704, however, he had returned to the practice of writing begging letters to Harley to intercede for him with the Admiralty for reappointment to a naval command.[4]

Cornwall was off the half-pay list and back on active service by February 1708, though it is unclear whether his recall should be attributed to Harley's influence or to the good offices of the Whig Junto, whose preferences carried increasing weight with the ministers. Cornwall's hopes of securing his own return at Weobley in 1708 came to nothing, and rather than advance his own claims at the December 1708 by-election he backed the candidacy of the carpet-bagging Whig Sir John Germain, 1st Bt.* He was instead returned for Bewdley at a by-election in March 1709, and the support he received at this election from the Whig interest suggests that his own party affiliations were becoming more pronounced. Naval duties appear to have kept him away from the House, especially in 1710 when he was placed in command of the Dunkirk squadron, but he seems to have been able to establish his loyalty to the ministry, for in October 1709, after the appointment of Lord Orford (Edward Russell) to the Admiralty, he was confidently forecast for preferment. The redoubtable Whig Anne Clavering predicted that a 'vacant flag' would be given to 'that notorious Whig C[harles] Cornwall, which I sincerely wish'.[5]

The ministerial and political changes of 1710 left Cornwall without a seat in Parliament and without friends at court. He therefore set about repairing his relationship with Harley, the new chief minister. Given command of a squadron detailed to convoy some merchant ships to Turkey, he wrote to Harley in December 1710 to offer whatever assistance might be required by Harley's brother Nathaniel out in the Levant, and at his return conveyed family news, accompanied by a request for personal assistance:

> A hardship has been done me during my service abroad in having a younger officer made a flag before me. I have served almost 30 years, above 20 of them in command, and was never charged with neglect of duty. I hope you will take me into your protection; I might urge the honour you have done me heretofore in owning me as a poor relation, but I shall desire that no other thing but my services may determine you in my behalf.

Further requests followed, some of which met with promises from Harley (now Lord Oxford), but no action; Cornwall was placed on half-pay and remained 'labouring under the uncertainty of not knowing whether he is to be employed again or not'. His party sympathies were well known enough for him to be classed as a Whig in a list of naval captains submitted to Oxford in 1711, and more specific evidence of his political sentiments had come to the chief minister's notice, evidence that may have prejudiced his chances of having his pretensions satisfied. Another voyager recently returned from the Levant wrote to Harley:

> I could not but the other day admire to see Mr Cornwall at your levée professing a profound respect for you, who when at Smyrna did lately declare on his arrival, to the council and the rest of the merchants, that it was the High Church intentions to bring in the Pretender and wipe off the nation's debts with a sponge. I acquaint you with this that you may not countenance such an enemy to the present ministry and yourself.[6]

On the Hanoverian succession Cornwall was brought into an office under the Navy Board, restored to a command and within two years advanced to the rank of admiral. He was returned for Weobley, though once more his parliamentary attendance was probably curtailed by his naval duties. He died at Lisbon on 7 Oct. 1718, and was buried at Westminster Abbey.[7]

[1] Add. 70091–3, extracts from par. reg.; C. J. Robinson, *Mansions and Manors of Herefs.* 118; J. Hanmer, *Par. and Fam. of Hanmer*, 137–8; C. G. S. Foljambe and C. Reade, *House of Cornewall*, 94. [2] Add. 61585, ff. 174–5, 215; *Cal. Treas. Pprs. 1714–19*, pp. 366, 405; *Cal. Treas. Bks.* xxxi. 573–4; xxxii. 161–2. [3] Foljambe and Reade, 93; J. Charnock, *Biographia Navalis*, ii. 410–11; Bath mss at Longleat House, Thynne pprs. 25, f. 13; *HMC Portland*, iii. 616, 634; iv. 12, 32; viii. 91–92; Add. 70019, ff. 168, 235, 272, 301–2, 311; 70226, Thomas Foley II* to Harley, 15 May 1700; 70219, Harley to Cyriac Cornwall, 7 Nov. 1700, Cornwall to Harley, 10 Nov. 1700, Cornwall to same, [1 Dec. 1700], Cornwall to same, 1 Dec. 1700, Harley to Cornwall, 11 Jan. 1701; Add. 70298–9, [–] to Harley, 28 Dec. 1700. [4] *HMC Portland*, viii. 102–3, 116–17; Add. 70236, Edward* to Robert Harley. 15 [?July] 1702; 70256, H. Seward to [?same], 13 Apr. 1702. [5] Add. 61582, f. 65; 61585, ff. 132, 150, 174–6, 215; PRO NI, De Ros mss D638/58/1, Cornwall to Ld. Coningsby (Thomas*), 29 July 1708; Luttrell, *Brief Relation*, vi. 284; *CJ*, xvi. 225; *HMC Portland*, iv. 513; *Cal. Treas. Bks.* xxiv. 360; xxv. 356, 369; *Clavering Corresp.* (Surtees Soc. clxxviii), 50. [6] Add. 70219, Cornwall to Robert Harley, 23 Dec. 1710, 25 Oct., 29 Dec. 1711, 30 Mar. 1711–12; 70310–1, 'General list of the captains of her Majesty's fleet', 22 Aug. 1711; *CJ*, xvii. 374; *HMC Portland*, v. 98, 140. [7] Boyer, *Pol. State*, xvi. 386; Foljambe and Reade, 93.

D. W. H.

CORNWALLIS, Hon. Charles (c.1675–1722).

EYE   1695–29 Apr. 1698

b. c.1675, 1st s. of Charles, 3rd Baron Cornwallis, by his 1st w. Elizabeth, da. of Sir Stephen Fox*, and sis. of Charles Fox*. *educ.* Eton c.1690–4; Camb. Univ. LL.D. 1717. *m.* 6 June 1699 (with £3,000), Lady Charlotte

Butler (*d.* 1725), da. and h. of Richard, 1st Earl of Arran [I] (*d.* 1686), 9s. 3da. *suc.* fa. as 4th Baron Cornwallis 29 Apr. 1698.[1]

Capt. 4 Drag. Gds. 1694–7; jt. postmaster gen. 1715–Apr. 1721; paymaster of forces Apr. 1721–*d.*; PC 11 Nov. 1721.[2]

Ld. lt. and custos rot. Suff. 1698–1703; recorder, Eye 1697–*d*; freeman, Bury St. Edmunds 1705.[3]

Cornwallis was brought up in the household of his grandfather Sir Stephen Fox, who paid for his education (to the tune of at least £4,000) and tried to safeguard his inheritance from the effects of his father's extravagance. Cornwallis saw action as a volunteer in the Low Countries before being returned on the family's interest for Eye, participating altogether in four campaigns. His father was a strong Whig, and he himself was forecast as likely to support the Court in the divisions on 31 Jan. 1696 over the proposed council of trade. He signed the Association promptly, and voted for fixing the price of guineas at 22s. in March. In 1697 he was granted a pension of £1,000 p.a. for life, to begin in 1701. On 31 Mar. 1698 he was granted ten days' leave of absence, presumably on account of his father's failing health. After succeeding to the barony he voted consistently with the Whigs in the House of Lords, for which he was deprived of his local offices in 1703. 'A gentleman of sweet disposition, a great lover of the constitution, and well esteemed in his native county', was how he was characterized in Macky's *Memoirs*, while his physical appearance was described as 'inclining to fat, fair complexion'. As a peer he associated himself with the Whig Junto, although maintaining his close relationship with Fox, who not only continued to provide him with a home, and found for him a wealthy bride, but by various other means and at further considerable expense guided him to financial solvency. In return, until 1710 Cornwallis reserved one seat at Eye, now more or less his pocket borough, for Fox's connexion, Hon. Spencer Compton*.[4]

Cornwallis died 'of gout in the stomach' on 20 Jan. 1722.[5]

[1] *Eton Coll. Reg.* ed. Sterry, 86; Add. 51326, f. 118; *CSP Dom.* 1699–1700, p. 221. [2] *Cal. Treas. Bks.* xxix. 390. [3] *CSP Dom.* 1698, pp. 277–8; *HMC 10th Rep IV*, 521; Suff. RO (Bury St. Edmunds), Bury St. Edmunds bor. recs. EE500 D4/1/3(a), p. 216. [4] G. C. A. Clay, *Public Finance and Private Wealth*, 275–94; Add. 51325, ff. 5–6; L. K. J. Glassey, *Appt. JPs*, 115, 158; *Cal. Treas. Bks.* xii. 128; *Macky Mems.* 105. [5] Boyer, *Pol. State*, xxiii. 232.

D. W. H.

CORRANCE, Clement (c.1684–1724), of Parham Hall, Suff.

ORFORD 1708–1722

b. c.1684, 1st s. of John Corrance of Rendlesham, Suff. and Parham Hall by Elizabeth, da. of Nicholas Vilett, BCL, of Oxford. *educ.* Bury St. Edmunds g.s.; St. John's, Oxf. matric. 11 May 1702, aged 17; I. Temple 1703. *m.* 20 Oct. 1705, Mary, da. of Sir Robert Davers, 2nd Bt.*, sis. of Sir Jermyn Davers, 4th Bt.†, 3s. 3da. *suc.* fa. 1704.[1]

Freeman, Dunwich 1705, Orford 1709.[2]

Corrance's father had settled in Suffolk, purchasing the Parham estate in 1687. He himself began to 'make an interest' at Orford as early as the winter of 1706–7 and by spending 'a considerable amount of money' quickly established a strong position there. In February 1708 the corporation formally agreed to choose him in place of the Tory Sir Edmund Bacon, 4th Bt.*, who had announced his intention to retire at the next election; Bacon's colleague Sir Edward Turnor* approved the arrangement; and the two men stood together in 1708. Despite the corporation's 'pre-engagement', a third candidate put up, the Whig William Thompson III*, but he was easily defeated. Corrance, who was also busy on the Tory side in other boroughs, had resisted Whig pressure to break his compact with Turnor, and continued to stand by his partner when Thompson petitioned, acting as a teller on 29 Jan. 1709, in the minority, against declaring Thompson elected in Turnor's place. He voted against the impeachment of Dr Sacheverell in 1710. On 29 Mar. he reported the reasons for the Commons' disagreements with the Lords' amendments to the bill explaining the Eddystone Lighthouse Act. He carried a message to the Upper House, and reported the following day that the Lords had agreed to a conference on this issue.[3]

Returned again with Turnor after another contest in 1710, Corrance was classed as a Tory in an analysis of the Parliament. A teller on the Tory side on 3 Feb. 1711 on a motion that a petition on the Ipswich election had been frivolous and vexatious, he was listed among the 'Tory patriots' who opposed the continuation of the war and among the 'worthy patriots' who in the 1710–11 session exposed the mismanagements of the old ministry. He was a member of the October Club, but at the same time actively sought government office, resting his hopes on the friendship his father-in-law enjoyed with Robert Harley*. In June 1711 Corrance wrote to Harley, now Lord Treasurer Oxford:

> The favourable answer your lordship was pleased to give to Sir Robert Davers makes me presume to trouble you again, and to beg of your lordship, since the place of treasurer of the Ordnance is promised, you would be pleased to bestow on me Mr Edwin's place in the Exchequer.

The fact that he received only promises from Oxford does not seem to have affected his allegiance to the ministry. He was not particularly active in this Parliament until the session of 1713. Then on 6 May 1713 he moved for leave for a witness to attend the House when the affairs of the commissioners for sick and wounded were to be discussed, a manoeuvre intended to discomfort a Suffolk enemy, William Churchill*, and on 28 May he acted as a teller for an instruction that the bill being drafted for the renewal of the Quakers' Affirmation Act should not extend to parliamentary elections. On 2 June he reported on a petition from the Jamaican planters and merchants; was again a teller on 11 June, against a bill to free the cargoes of two former prize ships; and voted on 18 June in favour of the French commerce bill. He was a teller twice in 1714: on 14 June, for a motion to instruct the committee on the public accounts bill to reappoint the previous commissioners; and two days later, for an instruction to the committee of privileges to hear the Harwich election. As late as 12 July Davers was still pressing Oxford in vain to convert his many promises to Corrance into something more substantial, 'when the Parliament is up'. According to the Worsley list he was a Tory who had sometimes voted with the Whigs in the 1713 Parliament and might do so in the next. In another comparative analysis of the two Parliaments he was listed as a Tory pure and simple.[4]

Corrance was buried at Rougham on 30 Mar. 1724.[5]

[1] Add. 19125, ff. 2–3; Copinger, *Suff. Manors*, v. 156; *Wilts. Arch. Mag.* xxx. 227–8; PCC 197 Pett; *Bury St. Edmunds G.S. List* (Suff. Green Bks. xiii), 88. [2] Suff. RO (Ipswich), Dunwich bor. recs. EE6/1144/14; W. Suss. RO, Shillinglee mss Ac.454/1083, John Hooke to Sir Edward Turnor, 28 Sept. 1709. [3] Copinger, 156; Shillinglee mss Ac.454/1049, 1053, 1056, 1061, 859, John Hooke to Turnor, 23 Jan. 1706–7, 23 Oct. 1707, 23 Feb. 1707–8, 8 May 1708, Turnor to mayor of Orford, 17 Feb. 1707–8. [4] Add. 70219, Corrance to Oxford, 10 June 1711, 29 Oct. 1712; 70222, Davers to same, 12 July 1714. [5] Add. 19125, ff. 2–3.

D. W. H.

CORSELLIS, Nicholas (1661–1728), of Wivenhoe Hall, Essex and Layer Marney, Essex.

COLCHESTER   6 May 1714–1715

b. 21 Sept. 1661, o. surv. s. of Nicholas Corsellis of Wivenhoe and St. Mary at Hill, London by Martha, da. of Maurice Thompson, East India merchant, of Haversham, Bucks., and sis. of Sir John Thompson, 1st Bt.* (subsequently 1st Ld. Haversham). *educ.* Eton 1678; Linc. Coll. Oxf. 1679; L. Inn 1682; called 1687. *m.* 12 May 1694 Elizabeth Taylor, da. of Richard Taylor of Turnham Green, Chiswick, and vintner of the Devil Tavern, Temple Bar, sis. of Mary, wife of Sir Thomas Rawlinson, ld. mayor of London 1706, 1s. 2da. (1 *d.v.p.*). *suc.* fa. 1674.[1]

A 17th-century myth claimed that a Corsellis, rather than Caxton, had been responsible for introducing the art of printing into England, but the family fortunes were in fact laid in less novel ways by Michael Corsellis, a Flemish merchant who had settled in London by 1570. Succeeding generations followed a mercantile tradition, acquiring sufficient wealth to purchase a manor at Wivenhoe for £10,000 in 1657 from Sir Horatio Townshend, 3rd Bt.†, and Layer Marney for £7,200 a decade later. Nicholas Corsellis snr., who bought the latter estate, traded in Colchester bays, Spanish and American tobacco, had extensive dealings with the East India Company, and narrowly escaped ruin in the Great Fire, having to move his papers and money three times before finding them a safe haven. Perhaps wishing to complete the transformation from a London trading family to a professional and landowning one, he sent his son to Eton, where Nicholas jnr. carved his name on a pillar, and then on to Oxford and the bar. Thomas Marshall, the rector of Lincoln College at the time of his admission, may have impressed his ardent royalist views on his pupil, though in any case the family had strong loyalist connexions: it was related to the Tory Essex family of the Abdys; Nicholas was the nephew of Sir John Thompson, who had become a zealous Tory and in 1696 was created Lord Haversham; and Corsellis knew Arabella Savage, daughter of the Tory convert Earl Rivers (Richard Savage*, Viscount Colchester). Moreover, his family had abandoned their adherence to the Dutch Church, and Nicholas' father-in-law was the vintner at the Devil Tavern in London, where many of the 'Church Party' met between 1689 and 1690. With such an impeccably Tory pedigree it is not surprising that Nicholas was reported, in December 1712, to think himself 'highly neglected' for being omitted from a list of new deputy-lieutenants that had been drawn up by Sir Edward Turnor† to effect a purge of Whigs in Essex. William Fytche* warned Turnor that if Corsellis was not included there was a danger that he 'would not come to Chelmsford again. You know his temper so I hope will take care and appease him by giving his name to Lord Bolingbroke [Henry St John II*]', who had been recently appointed lord lieutenant of the county.[2]

It is no surprise, therefore, that Corsellis should have stood for Colchester in 1713, at a time when the Tories had secured the dominance of local offices: the borough was near his estate, and he had been employed in 1709 to resolve a legal dispute there. Although not returned by the mayor, Corsellis and his partner William Gore* petitioned against the return of the Whig candidates, and on 6 May the Commons voted in the petitioners' favour. Shortly afterwards, on 28 May, Corsellis came to the aid of fellow Tory Hon. Benedict Leonard Calvert* by acting as a teller for hearing the Harwich election. During June and July Corsellis handled a private naturalization bill, and more importantly a bill for 'quieting' corporations, a subject on which the turbulence and corruption of Colchester's affairs undoubtedly gave him first-hand knowledge. According to the genealogist Foster, though the evidence for the claim is unclear, he was also the author of a bill offering a reward of £100,000 for the capture of the Pretender if found in the British Isles, a reference either to the address ordered on 24 June 1714 in thanks for the Queen's proclamation of 21 June, or to the bill for the security of the King drawn up in July 1715, which contained such a clause. Corsellis' involvement would be hard to explain in either case since he held no official legal post in 1714, and in 1715 failed to secure re-election, although he and his colleague Samuel Rush[†] were reported to have demanded a scrutiny 'to give all the trouble they can', and unsuccessfully petitioned the House on 30 Mar. 1715. Corsellis was marked as a Tory on the Worsley list but, surprisingly, seems to have appeared against the Tory William Harvey I* at an Essex by-election later that year, when it was reported that 'his bailiff, self and man have all had a short drubbing'. Corsellis did not stand again, and his electoral efforts may have over-reached his income since in 1726 his estates were mortgaged for £1,845. He died on 25 Jan. 1728, at Chelsea. His son Nicholas followed his father's footsteps to Oxford and the bar, though not to Parliament, and married the granddaughter of Sir Josiah Child[†].[3]

[1] *Misc. Gen. and Her.* ser. 5, i. 22–23; Morant, *Essex*, ii. 188. [2] *Misc. Gen. and Her.* 1–23; *Essex Rev.* xviii. 138–145; li. 132–33; lviii. 5; *Trans. Essex Arch. Soc.* xiv. 185; W. Suss. RO, Shillinglee mss, Ac.454/275 Fytche to Turnor, 15 Dec. 1712. [3] Essex RO (Colchester), assembly bk. 6, f. 397; Boyer, *Pol. State*, vi. 257; *Al. Ox. 1500–1714*, p. 331; *Essex Rev.* xx. 183; li. 135; *Verney Letters 18th Cent.* i. 336.

M. J. K.

CORYTON, Sir John, 2nd Bt. (1648–90), of Newton Ferrers, nr. Callington, Cornw.

NEWPORT   1679 (Mar.–July)
CALLINGTON   6 May–17 Nov. 1685
                 1689–July 1690

bap. 21 Jan. 1648, 1st s. of Sir John Coryton, 1st Bt.[†], of Newton Ferrers by 1st w. Elizabeth, da. and h. of John Mills of Colebrooke, Devon; bro. of Sir William Coryton, 3rd Bt.* *educ.* Exeter, Oxf. 1666. *m.* lic. 22 Feb. 1672, Elizabeth, da. and coh. of Sir Richard Chiverton, Skinner, of Clerkenwell, Mdx., ld. mayor of London 1657–8, 2s. *d.v.p.* 2da. (1 *d.v.p.*) *suc.* fa. as 2nd Bt. Aug. 1680.[1]

Sheriff, Cornw. 1683–4; freeman, Saltash 1683; mayor, Callington 1684–5, alderman 1685–Oct. 1688; alderman, Liskeard 1685–Oct. 1688; stannator, Foymore 1686.[2]

Coryton, who in the Convention had voted against the transfer of the crown, was again returned for Callington in 1690. He was classified as a Tory in Lord Carmarthen's (Sir Thomas Osborne[†]) analysis of the House, but he made no significant contribution to the 1690 session and died during the recess. Coryton was buried at St. Mellion, Cornwall on 30 July and was succeeded in his baronetcy by his younger brother. Shortly after Coryton's death his widow, who had brought 'a great jointure', married his steward, James Tillie, with whom, according to a contemporary, she had been 'too familiar before'.[3]

[1] Vivian, *Vis. Cornw.* 101; Boase and Courtney, *Bib. Cornub.* supp. 1136. [2] *CSP Dom.* 1685, pp. 66, 257; *HMC Var.* i. 328; J. Tregoning, *Stannary Laws*, 57. [3] Polsue, *Complete Paroch. Hist. Cornw.* iv. 79–81; *CSP Dom.* 1687–9, p. 323.

E. C.

CORYTON, Sir John, 4th Bt. (1690–1739), of Newton Ferrers and Crocadon, Cornw.

CALLINGTON   1713–1722, 1727–1734

bap. 3 Feb. 1690, o. s. of Sir William Coryton, 3rd Bt.*, by his 1st w. *educ.* Rugby 1698; Christ Church, Oxf. matric. 14 Oct. 1708, aged 18. *m.* 31 Oct. 1715 (with £4,000), Rachel, da. of William Helyar[†] of East Coker, Som., *s.p. suc.* fa. as 4th Bt. 6 Dec. 1711.[1]

Though the estates Coryton inherited in 1711 brought with them an interest at Callington, he did not stand at the by-election consequent upon his father's death. Coryton was added to Cornwall's commission of the peace in April 1713, and at the election later that year was returned unopposed for Callington. He made little impact on the records of the House, but the Worsley list and two other comparisons of the 1713 and 1715 Parliaments classed him as a Tory, and he continued to sit as such after the Hanoverian succession. Coryton died on 22 May 1739, being buried on 9 June, and was eventually succeeded in his estates by his first cousin once removed.[2]

[1] IGI, Kent; Vivian, *Vis. Devon*, 102. [2] L. K. J. Glassey, *Appt. JPs*, 217.

E. C.

CORYTON, Sir William, 3rd Bt. (1650–1711), of Newton Ferrers and Crocadon, Cornw. and the Middle Temple.

BOSSINEY	1679 (Mar.–July)
NEWPORT	1679 (Oct.)–1681 (Jan.)
CALLINGTON	1681 (Mar.), 1685–1687
MITCHELL	18 Sept.–12 Dec. 1689
CALLINGTON	1695–1701 (Nov.)
	30 Nov. 1703–6 Dec. 1711

bap. 24 May 1650, 2nd s. of Sir John Coryton, 1st Bt.†, of Newton Ferrers; bro. of Sir John Coryton, 2nd Bt.* *educ.* Exeter, Oxf. 1666; M. Temple 1669, called 1675. *m.* (1) lic. 11 Dec. 1688, Susanna (*d.* 1695), da. of Sir Edward Littleton, 2nd Bt.†, of Pillaton, Staffs., 1s. 1da.; (2) Sarah (*d.* 1719), wid. of Thomas Williams, banker, of Lombard Street, London, *s.p. suc.* bro. as 3rd Bt. July 1690.[1]

Freeman, Saltash 1683, Bodmin and Callington 1685; alderman, Callington and Lostwithiel 1685–Oct. 1688.[2]

A professional lawyer, Coryton had been an opponent of Exclusion and was to be a life-long Tory. Though he had sat for Cornish seats in the previous five Parliaments, Coryton did not stand at either the 1690 election or the Callington by-election later that year occasioned by the death of his elder brother. His brother's death brought Coryton the family title and estate, but he continued his legal practice and rather than settle at Newton Ferrers he purchased the manor of Crocadon, in St. Mellion, and made this his principal seat. Little is known of Coryton's political activity in the early 1690s, though Kingston later claimed that in 1694 he was numbered among Cornwall's chief Jacobites. Coryton was returned for Callington at the 1695 election, and his contemporaries soon noted his opposition to the ministry as he was forecast as likely to oppose the Court in the divisions of 31 Jan. 1696 over the proposed council of trade. On 20 Feb. Coryton was nominated to prepare a bill to establish a joint stock East India Company, and later the same month reported and carried to the Lords a private bill concerned with Devon estates. Coryton initially refused to sign the Association. On 4 Mar. he was granted a three-week leave of absence, presumably to attend the assizes, though the following day he was appointed to draft a bill to explain the Act for the regulation of Hackney carriages, and he was subsequently listed as having voted later in the month against fixing the price of guineas at 22s. Coryton's Tory sympathies were evident in the early part of the 1696–7 session. During the passage of the bill of attainder against Sir John Fenwick† he spoke, on 13 Nov., against admitting Goodman's evidence against Fenwick, and on the 25th he voted against the bill. The next month he was appointed to draft, and subsequently presented, a bill for the easier partition of lands held in coparcenary (8, 18 Dec.). Coryton was also nominated to prepare the bill to prevent abuses in prisons (30th), but otherwise made little impact upon the records of the House before obtaining, on 10 Mar. 1697, a leave of absence. He was also granted a month's leave of absence on both 24 and 25 Mar. 1698.[3]

Coryton retained his seat unopposed in 1698, following which he was included upon a forecast of likely opponents of a standing army and was classed as a Country supporter in a comparison of the old and new Commons. He twice acted as teller in this session, in favour of receiving the report on the Corfe Castle election (6 Apr. 1699) and against considering the report on the Newfoundland trade (1 May). Appointment to, and reporting from, the committee to inspect the ballot for trustees of Irish forfeitures was Coryton's only recorded significant contribution to the 1699–1700 session. An analysis of the House into interests, dating from early 1700, classed him as 'doubtful', or possibly as opposition. During the first 1701 Parliament Coryton was appointed to draft four bills, most notably the measure for qualifying Members and regulating elections (20 Feb. 1701) and a bill concerned with Cornish estates (16 Apr.), and was also among those ordered to draw up the impeachment of Lord Portland.

Coryton did not stand at either the December 1701 or 1702 elections. Though he was listed as having voted on 13 Feb. 1703 against the Lords' amendments to the bill enlarging the time for taking the Abjuration, Coryton did not return to the Commons until the Callington by-election in November 1703. Though he held this seat until his death Coryton was an inactive Member. On 28 Nov. 1704 he did not vote for the Tack, and consequently an analysis of the 1705 Parliament classed him as 'Low Church'. He voted on 25 Oct. 1705 against the Court candidate for Speaker, and was evidently still attending the Commons in December as he spoke on the 3rd against referring to committee the petition for a bill for the improvement of Parton harbour in Cumberland. It appears, however, that ill-health subsequently limited his parliamentary activity, and he was granted leave of absence on grounds of ill-health on 16 Jan. 1706 and 27 Feb. 1707. In early 1708 an analysis of the House listed Coryton as a Tory. It seems that illness also limited his contribution to the 1708 Parliament, as he was granted a leave of absence on 4 Mar. 1709 and did not make any other impression upon the records of this Parliament. Coryton nevertheless retained his seat in 1710, following which the 'Hanover list' classed him as a Tory. The new Parliament witnessed something of a resurgence in Coryton's parliamentary activity and on 10 Mar. 1711 he told against bringing up a petition, from Exeter, against the bill ending the prohibition upon importing French wines. He was granted, on 16 Mar., a seven-week leave of absence. Coryton was listed among the 'worthy patriots' who in this session had detected the mismanagements of the previous administration, a list which also identified him as a member of the October Club. It is uncertain if Coryton returned to London for the following session, and he died on 6 Dec. 1711. He was succeeded by his son, Sir John Coryton, 4th Bt.*[4]

[1] Vivian, *Vis. Cornw.* 101. [2] *CSP Dom.* 1685, pp. 211, 256–7; *HMC Var.* i. 328. [3] Polsue, *Complete Paroch. Hist. Cornw.* iii. 305, 308; R. K[ingston], *True Hist. of Several . . . Conspiracies* (1698), p. 85; Add. 28879, f. 128; Cobbett, *Parlty. Hist.* v. 1036–7. [4] Cumbria RO (Carlisle), Lonsdale mss D/Lons/W2/2/8, James* to Sir John Lowther, 2nd Bt. I*, 6 Dec. 1705; Vivian, 101.

E. C.

COTES, John (1682–1756), of Woodcote, Salop.

LICHFIELD 1708–1715

bap. 29 June 1682, 1st s. of Charles Cotes of Woodcote by Lettice, da. of Kildare, 2nd Baron Digby of Geashill [I]. *educ.* Magdalen Coll. Oxf. matric. 1698. *m.* ?1706, Lady Dorothy (*d.* 1721), da. of Robert Shirley, 1st Earl Ferrers, 6s. (at least 1 *d.v.p.*) 2da. *suc.* fa. aft. June 1706.[1]

Although the family had been settled at Woodcote since the reign of Henry VIII and before then at Cotes in Staffordshire, Cotes spent his early years at Coleshill, Warwickshire, in a house belonging to his mother's family. By 1704 his father had taken over the Woodcote estate to which he succeeded in due course.[2]

Cotes may have received some help in electioneering at Lichfield in 1708 from his father-in-law, a committed Tory with local connexions. His return was marked by the Earl of Sunderland (Charles, Lord Spencer*) as a gain for the Whigs, probably because he had replaced Sir Henry Gough*. However, evidence of parliamentary activity suggests that Sunderland was incorrect. On 1 Feb. 1709 Cotes acted as a teller in favour of adjournment during the debate on the report of the Newcastle-under-Lyme election. The failure of the motion led to William Burslem*, a Tory agent, being found guilty of bribery and ordered into custody. In the following session Cotes voted against Dr Sacheverell's impeachment. Indeed, he was able to bolster his electoral fortunes by dining with the Tory champion during his triumphant pre-election tour through Staffordshire in the summer of 1710. Archdeacon George Newell described him in August 1710 as 'nephew to my Lord Digby [William*], a gentleman of extraordinary character and very good estate, and one who I am sure is well inclined to put an end to the war abroad'. Not surprisingly, Cotes was then re-elected, in partnership with Richard Dyott.[3]

Classified as a Tory in the 'Hanover list', Cotes was noted in the 1710–11 session as both a 'Tory patriot' who opposed the continuance of war, and a 'worthy patriot' who had helped to detect the mismanagements of the previous ministry. On 25 Jan. 1711 he acted as a teller on the Stafford election, in support of a resolution concerning the franchise which favoured Henry Vernon I*, a Tory candidate who was seated on petition. Five days later he was ordered to prepare a bill relating to the local estate of Theophilus Biddulph, 3rd Bt. (son of Sir Michael Biddulph, 2nd Bt.*), which he managed through the Commons. In the next session he acted as a teller twice: on 4 Apr. 1712 against a clause to save the rights of Quakers to vote during the period covered by the Act preventing the fraudulent multiplication of votes in elections; and on 11 Apr. in favour of taking into custody the printer Samuel Buckley in connexion with a libel on the peace in the *Daily Courant*. In the 1713 session he appears to have been inactive, and indeed may not have been in attendance as he failed to register a vote on the French commerce bill. Nevertheless he was returned unopposed at the general election of that year. In the 1714 session he was a teller on 29 June in favour of the Tory candidate in the Harwich election, and was classified as a Tory on the Worsley list. Cotes was defeated in the election of 1715, but he was not removed from the commission of the peace in 1715 even though he may have been preparing to join the Jacobite field army. In December 1721, Sir Theophilus Biddulph suggested that Cotes would be cheerfully received as a candidate at Lichfield by the 'better sort' of electors. Cotes outlived at least one of his sons, Charles†, but was survived by at least four others, two army officers and two Anglican clerics. He died on 12 May 1756 and was buried in Woodcote parish church.[4]

[1] IGI, Warws.; J. C. Wedgwood, *Staffs. Parl. Hist.* (Wm. Salt Arch. Soc.), ii. 202; *List and Index Soc.* sp. ser. xxii. 227. [2] A. T. Lee, *Town and Par. of Tetbury*, 249; *Hist. Pirewell Hundred* (Wm. Salt Arch. Soc. n.s. xvii), 52. [3] Christ Church, Oxf. Wake mss 2, f. 62. [4] *HMC Townshend*, 229; L. K. J. Glassey, *Appt. JPs*, 245; RA, Stuart mss 216/111, 'Mr Carte's paper given to the King in July 1739'; Staffs. RO, Sutherland mss D593/P/16/1/17b, Biddulph to [Ld. Gower], 25 Dec. 1721; PCC 161 Glazier.

S. N. H.

COTESWORTH, William (1665–1730), of St. James Clerkenwell, Mdx.

GREAT GRIMSBY	10 Jan.–6 Mar. 1701
	1701 (Dec.)–1702
	1705–1710
BOSTON	20 Dec. 1711–20 Mar. 1712
	2 Apr. 1712–1713
GREAT GRIMSBY	1713–1715

b. 26 Sept. 1665, 4th s. of Michael Cotesworth of South Shields, co. Dur. by 1st w. Elizabeth, cos. and h. of Edward Heslop of South Shields and the Hermitage, West Acomb, Northumb. *m.* 18 Oct. 1692, Sarah (*d.* 1736), wid. of James Wallis of St. Gabriel's Fenchurch, London, 1s. 1da.[1]

Freeman, Newcastle 1689, Boston, 1711, Barber-Surgeons' Co. bef. 1710; asst. and 'examiner' 1717; warden, 1718, 1721, 1722; master, 1723.[2]

Dir. New E.I. Co. 1704–8, manager, united trade 1708; dir. E.I. Co. 1710–13.[3]

The Cotesworths were of relatively humble, even obscure, origins, and the connexion between Cotesworth the MP and his namesake, the rather more well-known merchant of Gateshead Park, has not been fully elucidated, although it is probable that they were cousins. Cotesworth's grandfather had been a yeoman at Egglestone, county Durham, and his father was apprenticed in Newcastle, became a hostman and freeman of that city and, in 1657, made a fortunate marriage. Little is known of Cotesworth's mother except that in 1682 she and her husband were presented as recusants, and her cousin Heslop's will, made in 1689, left his whole estate to her and the Cotesworth children. This inheritance included interests in two salt pans and a ship, the *Fortune*. Cotesworth's elder brother, John, was master of this ship and in 1689 was 'credibly reported to be in King William's interest'. Although Cotesworth was described as a hostman on his admission to the freedom of Newcastle in 1689, there is no record of any involvement with the Hostmen's Company; rather it is the Barber-Surgeons' Company in London with which he may be associated, although no date for his admission to the freedom has been discovered. Cotesworth followed his brother Caleb to London and in 1681 was apprenticed to him as a surgeon, later working alongside him as a doctor for St. Thomas' Hospital, Southwark. He continued to live with, or close, by Caleb for some years as in 1695 they were both living in the parish of St. Gabriel's Fenchurch, Cotesworth being then worth at least £600 in personalty. He was probably the William Cotesworth who was one of the original subscribers to the Bank of England in 1694 and contributed £1,000 to the first instalment of £200,000 of the Old East India Company's loan to the government in 1698.[4]

By 1701 Cotesworth was firmly associated with the New East India Company, being one of the candidates put up by the company to fight the first general election of 1701. He contested the notoriously corrupt borough of Great Grimsby as a Whig against Arthur Moore*, a Tory and one of the directors of the Old Company. Although 'never heard of there until he was actually on the road thither', Cotesworth secured his return by an extensive use of bribery but was unseated after Moore petitioned the Commons and on 6 Mar. was sent to the Tower for being 'notoriously guilty of bribery and other indirect practices'. The hearings were widely reported and at least one commentator thought that several Tory Members behaved 'very partially' and that Moore was 'undoubtedly as criminal as Cotesworth'. Moore escaped a bribery charge but no new writ was issued before the dissolution. Perhaps recognizing in each other a certain ruthlessness, and undaunted by their experiences with the committee of elections, Moore and Cotesworth, despite political and commercial differences, combined successfully to contest Grimsby in the following election. Having survived another accusation of bribery, this time in a petition from disappointed candidate Thomas Vyner* on 5 Jan. 1702, Cotesworth retained his seat. Most ironically, he was included among those named on 17 Jan. to bring in a bill to prevent bribery at elections.[5]

Defeated at Grimsby in 1702, Cotesworth continued to prosper commercially and by 1704 held 40 shares in the New East India Company and had been chosen as one of the company's directors. He regained his seat at Grimsby in 1705, was listed as a 'Churchman' in an analysis of the new Parliament and voted on 25 Oct. for the Court candidate for Speaker. A petition against his election, again on the grounds of bribery, was presented on 12 Nov. by several Great Grimsby freemen, but had no repercussions. He both spoke and voted for the Court, on 15 Jan. and 18 Feb. 1706, during the proceedings on the regency bill. In July he was granted a secret service pension of £500 p.a. during the Queen's life at the request of the 2nd Earl of Clarendon (Henry Hyde†) 'for the better accommodation of his [Clarendon's] affairs', the money to come out of Clarendon's own pension of £1,500 p.a.[6]

In the next session Cotesworth was a teller on 5 Dec. 1706 against bringing up a petition from the attorneys and clerks of Chancery and in early 1707 was one of a number of MPs who sought to protect their own interests by opposing any advantage Scottish merchants might gain from the Union. In March Cotesworth was described as 'a mighty hot man' who 'says positively we would not allow them [the Scots] drawbacks'. He was also a teller on 27 Feb. for the question of agreeing with an amendment to the bill for the better preservation of game. Cotesworth's next notable parliamentary action was in March 1708, when he managed a bill to limit the time for claims to forfeited Irish estates through all its stages in the Commons.[7]

Classed as a Whig in two lists of early 1708, Cotesworth was returned unopposed for Grimsby in May and appointed in June to the Whig-dominated London lieutenancy commission. He supported the naturalization of the Palatines early in 1709. In the following session he told on the Whig side on 6 Feb. 1710 for levying a perennial duty on candles, and later that month was appointed to three drafting committees for bills to prevent bribery and corruption in elections, to regulate select vestries within weekly bills of mortality, another anti-corruption measure, and for the relief of the Royal African Company's creditors. He also voted for the impeachment of Dr Sacheverell. Defeated at Grimsby in 1710, Cotesworth was back in London in time to vote for the Whig candidates in the London election. Despite the alterations in 1710 to the London lieutenancy in favour of the Tories, Cotesworth retained his place, and indeed remained on the commission until at least 1716.[8]

Cotesworth returned to the Commons, successfully contesting the Boston by-election in December 1711, but then lost his seat when the election was declared void on 20 Mar. 1712, bribery being proved against both candidates. During the committee hearings it was alleged that Cotesworth was unknown in Boston until a few days before the election. At least one historian has taken this allegation from a hostile witness at face value, describing Cotesworth as a 'carpet-bagger', but it is possible that the allegation was malicious, Cotesworth having acquired by 1706 the manor of Coningsby, about 15 miles from Boston. Cotesworth stood successfully at the resultant by-election held on 2 Apr. 1712 and this time retained his seat, despite another petition against him from the defeated candidate. As a long-standing director of the East India Company and an MP, Cotesworth was an obvious choice in May 1712 to lay before Lord Treasurer Oxford (Robert Harley*) a petition which the company planned to present to the Commons, for perpetuating the company and asking that the debt owing to it from the crown be paid. He voted on 18 June 1713 against the French commerce bill. On 9 July he told against an amendment (in favour of the merchant,

Samuel Shepheard I*) to the bill for encouraging the tobacco trade. At the 1713 election he contested both Boston and Grimsby, being returned for the latter. He voted for the Whig candidates at the London election that year and in the new Parliament divided against the expulsion of Richard Steele in March 1714. Surprisingly, given that all his known votes were on the Whig side, he was described in the Worsley list as a Whig who would often vote with the Tories. Having failed to retain his seat at Grimsby in 1715, Cotesworth retired from active parliamentary politics, although at the time of his death he was a j.p. for Middlesex. He died on either 8 or 12 Dec. 1730, leaving his property, which included lands in Lincoln, Essex and Norfolk, and a lease of London wharves from the Fishmongers' Company, to be divided among his wife and children.[9]

[1] *Soc. Antiq. Newcastle-upon-Tyne Procs.* ser. 4, i. 263–5; PCC 4 Isham, 127 Derby. [2] *Soc. Antiq. Newcastle-upon-Tyne Procs.* 264; *Boston Corp. Mins.* ed. Bailey, iv. 726–7; Guildhall Lib. mss mic. 5257/7, p. 163; S. Young, *Annals of the Barber Surgeons*, 11. [3] *London Post*, 14–17 Apr. 1704; Add. 38871 (unfol.); C. Prinsep, *Madras Civilians*, p. xi. [4] J. Ellis, *Business Fortunes of William Cotesworth*, 2; J. C. Hodgson, *Hist. Northumb.* iv. 143–5; *Soc. Antiq. Newcastle-upon-Tyne Procs.* 264–5; Morrice ent'ring bk. 3, p. 184; Add. 33084, f. 112; Guildhall Lib. mss mic. 5266/1, pp. 14, 115; *CSPDom.* 1699–1700, p. 350; *London Rec. Soc.* ii. 65; DZA, Bonet despatch 6/16 July 1694; *CJ*, xii. 322. [5] Liverpool RO, Norris mss 920NOR 1/93, William Clayton* to Richard Norris*, 6 Mar. 1700–1; Cumbria RO (Carlisle), Lonsdale mss D/Lons/W2/2/4, James Lowther* to Sir John Lowther, 2nd Bt. I*, 6, 11 Mar. 1700[–1], 3 Apr. 1701; *Cocks Diary*, 79–80. [6] Bodl. Rawl. A.303, f. 58; *Cam. Misc.* xxiii. 69; *Cal. Treas. Bks.* xxiii. 491. [7] Norris mss 920NOR 2/452, 462, Thomas Johnson* to Norris, 23 Feb., 22 Mar. 1706–7. [8] *London Poll Bk.* (1710), 10. [9] W. A. Speck, *Tory and Whig*, 55; *Lincs. Rec. Soc.* iv. 35; *Cal. Treas. Bks.* xxvi. 36; xxviii. 51, 200; *London Rec. Soc.* xvii. 77; Boyer, *Pol State.* xl. 649; *Hist. Reg. Chron.* 1730, p. 67; PCC 4 Isham.

P. W./S. M. W.

COTTON, Sir John, 2nd Bt. (c.1648–1713), of Madingley Hall, Cambs.

CAMBRIDGE   1689–1695, 8 Nov. 1696–1702
                1705–1708

b. c.1648, 1st s. of Sir John Cotton, 1st Bt., of Landwade, Cambs. by Jane, da. and h. of Edward Hynde of Madingley Hall. *educ.* Trinity Coll. Camb. matric. 1663. *m.* 14 Jan. 1679, Elizabeth (*d.* 1714), da. and coh. of Sir Joseph Sheldon, Draper, of St. Paul's Churchyard, London, alderman of London and ld. mayor 1695–6, 2s. (1 *d.v.p.*) 8da. (2 *d.v.p.*). *suc.* fa. as 2nd Bt. 25 Mar. 1689.[1]

Freeman, Cambridge 1679, recorder 1702–*d.*, conservator 1709.[2]

Gamekeeper, Newmarket 1689–*d.*[3]

The son of a sequestrated Royalist, Cotton had repaired his fortune by a shrewd marriage to a local heiress, so that he enjoyed a landed income of some £2,000 a year. He seems to have been a staunch Churchman. His appointment to the commission of the peace in 1680 suggests opposition to Exclusion, but he was evidently just as hostile to James II's religious policy and was removed from local office in 1687. Returned in 1689 as a Member for Cambridge, only three miles distant from his seat at Madingley, he attended William III, soon after the Convention opened, with his county's solemn engagement of loyalty, and was rewarded with the grant of a crown dignity in his own neighbourhood as gamekeeper on the royal estate at Newmarket. However, he was listed by Lord Ailesbury (Thomas Bruce[†]) as having voted against the transfer of the crown. Re-elected in 1690, he was classified as a Tory and a probable Court supporter in Lord Carmarthen's (Sir Thomas Osborne[†]) analysis of the new Parliament. In the next session, he told on 12 Nov. 1690 in favour of Sir John Darell's election in the Rye election case, and in December figured on another list by Carmarthen, which probably enumerated those Members whose loyalty could be relied upon in the event of an attack on him in the Commons. He was granted leave of absence on 14 Feb. 1693 for three weeks and on 19 Dec. 1693 for two weeks. In the meantime his name had been added to the Cambridgeshire lieutenancy in 1692. His poor record of parliamentary attendance continued, for he was ordered into custody after having been absent on 12 Feb. 1694 at a call of the House, and was then given leave of absence for three weeks on 23 Feb. He was granted another leave of absence on 6 Mar. 1695, for two weeks. He and the other outgoing Member for Cambridge, Granado Pigot, were replaced by two aldermen of the borough at the general election of 1695, but Cotton regained his own seat at a by-election the following year, and in December 1697 presented the corporation's loyal address on the peace. On 20 Apr. 1698 he was given leave of absence yet again, for a fortnight. Marked as a supporter of the Country party in a comparative analysis of the old and new Parliaments in about September 1698, and forecast as likely to oppose a standing army, he was accorded leave of absence once more on 22 Mar. 1699. In the next Parliament he was listed in February 1701 as likely to support the Court in agreeing with the committee of supply's resolution to continue the 'Great Mortgage'. After the second general election of that year, Robert Harley* listed him with the Tories, and indeed he was named as supporting the motion of 26 Feb. 1701 to vindicate the Commons' proceedings in the impeachments of the Whig lords. That he stayed in London after this division is evident from a letter he sent to Cambridge corporation in March describing the events leading up to the King's death.[4]

Chosen recorder of Cambridge in 1702, Cotton seems not to have attempted to secure re-election that year. In 1705, when Queen Anne visited Cambridge prior to the general election, Cotton, as recorder, 'made her Majesty a speech and presented her with a purse of gold'. At the election itself he reappeared as a candidate and was returned at the head of the poll, being described by Thomas Carte in his account of the return as 'an honest gent.', that is to say a High Church Tory. Indeed his election was listed by Lord Sunderland (Charles, Lord Spencer*) as a loss for the Whigs and he was also classified as a 'High Church courtier' in an analysis of the new Parliament. In the House he voted against the Whig John Smith I* in the division on the Speaker on 25 Oct. 1705. Having received a further leave of absence on 11 Jan. 1707, he was classed as a Tory in two lists of 1708, and at the next general election stood down in favour of his son John Hynde Cotton*, who had recently come of age. Sir John died on 15 Jan. 1713, aged 65, and was buried at Landwade.[5]

[1] *MI Cambs.* ed. Palmer, 115; J. R. Woodhead, *Rulers of London* (London and Mdx. Arch. Soc.), 146; Cambs. RO (Cambridge), Madingley par. reg. P114/2. [2] C. H. Cooper, *Annals of Cambridge*, iii. 582; iv. 52, 110; Cambs. RO (Cambridge), Cambridge bor. recs. common day bk. 1681–1722, p. 449. [3] *CSP Dom.* 1689–90, p. 148. [4] Cambs. RO (Cambridge), Cotton of Madingley mss 588/E40; *Bull. IHR*, lii. 42; Bodl. Tanner 25, f. 339; Add. 70018, f. 83; C. H. Cooper, *Annals of Cambridge*, iv. 38; *Diary of Samuel Newton* (Camb. Antiq. Soc. xxiii), 112–13. [5] Cambridge bor. recs. common day bk. 1681–1722, p. 343; Bodl. Carte 244, f. 58; Stanhope, *Anne*, 173–4; *E. Anglian*, i. 344; MI Landwade par. ch.

E. C./D. W. H.

COTTON, Sir John, 4th Bt. (c.1680–1731), of Conington Castle, Hunts. and Stratton Park, nr. Biggleswade, Beds.

HUNTINGDON   1705–22 Jan. 1706
HUNTINGDONSHIRE   30 Dec. 1710–1713

b. c.1680, 1st s. of John Cotton (*d.v.p*, 1st surv. s. of Sir John Cotton, 3rd Bt.[†], of Cotton House, Westminster and Stratton Park) by Frances, da. of Sir George Downing, 1st Bt., of East Hatley, Cambs. *m.* 4 July 1708 (with £6,000), Elizabeth, da. of Hon. James Herbert*, 2da. *d.v.p. suc.* fa. 1681, gdfa. as 4th Bt. 12 Sept. 1702.[1]

Cotton was descended from the antiquary Sir Robert Cotton, 1st Bt.[†], whose great library of manuscripts at Cotton House, situated between the House of Commons and the Painted Chamber, had been used by Members throughout the 17th century, and especially during the early Stuart Parliaments, as an archive of historical and parliamentary precedents. Indeed, Speaker Harley (Robert*) described it in 1701 as 'the repository of the records that preserved our liberties', the occasion for this tribute being a request from Cotton's grandfather, the 3rd Baronet, conveyed to the Commons by the Speaker, for a bill to settle the library 'inalienably' on the public. Despite strenuous opposition from some members of the family, whose 'private interests' would naturally have been compromised by the loss of an asset valued at some £15,000, and who represented the baronet as 'old, capricious and unsteady in his resolutions', the library, though not the house itself, was duly placed by statute in the hands of trustees 'for the benefit of the public'. The house formed part of Cotton's substantial but disputed inheritance. He had an income from property variously estimated at between £4,000 and £9,000 a year. The ancestral seat of Conington Castle had, however, fallen into dilapidation, and he later pulled down part of the castle and converted what remained into a more modest dwelling. Other property, including lands worth a reputed £8,000 p.a. left under the will of the 2nd baronet, became the subject of litigation, initiated by the 3rd baronet's younger children, which continued until at least 1710.[2]

Cotton's grandfather was a staunch Anglican and in politics a practitioner of the doctrines of passive obedience: 'a very worthy, honest gentleman that understood and loved the constitution of his country'. A Court loyalist during the 1670s, and a Member of James II's Parliament, he gave succour in 1687 to one of the ejected fellows of Magdalen, Oxford, and despite carefully equivocal replies to the King's questions on the repeal of the Test Act and Penal Laws, was dismissed from his local offices in 1688. The Revolution he accepted fatalistically, writing that, 'as for public affairs, I desire wholly to acquiesce in God's providence', though he took no further part in political life. His children seem to have reacted more strongly. A daughter Mary, briefly married before her death in 1714 to a Jacobite physician, was said to be 'as good a Jacobite' as her husband, while a younger son, Robert, of Steeple Gidding in Huntingdonshire, became a non-juror and later participated more actively in the Jacobite cause. Out in the Fifteen, he was captured at Preston and later escaped to France, where he was a pillar of the community of exiled non-jurors at Angers. How much of this advanced loyalism rubbed off on the 4th baronet is unclear. His relations with his impoverished Jacobite kinsmen seem, in this period at least, to have been confined to crossing swords with them in various lawsuits over family property, while his connexions on his mother's side were countervailingly Whiggish. Certainly he espoused the Tory interest when he contested a parliamentary seat in 1705, invited to put up at Huntingdon by a faction among the freemen there, and successful, despite the fact that he was opposed by two Whigs, in an election marred by wholesale bribery on both sides. Marked as a 'High Church courtier' in an analysis of the new Parliament, he voted against the Court candidate in the division on the Speaker, 25 Oct. 1705. Also returned to the 1705 Parliament was Sir John Cotton, 2nd Bt., and either may have been the Member granted a fortnight's leave of absence on 9 Jan. 1706. At the hearing of a petition against him by the defeated Whig candidate, although Cotton's witnesses testified to bribery by the Whigs the elections committee declared against him, and on 22 Jan. he was unseated by the House. Later that year he agreed to the sale of Cotton House, to be taken into public hands along with the library, settling on a compromise price of £4,800 for the freehold. Evidently the fabric was in ill repair, and this, coupled with Cotton's determination to drive a hard bargain, hints at financial problems, the existence of which was confirmed during the negotiations in 1708 for Cotton's marriage to a granddaughter of the Duke of Leeds (Sir Thomas Osborne†). Inquiries elicited the information that there was an encumbrance of £4,000 charged upon Cotton's estate by his grandfather, and a current mortgage of £2,500. Leeds therefore proposed a provision of £2,000 a year for the eldest son of the marriage and £1,000 each for any younger children, and in return the bride's portion was to be settled at £6,000. However, playing on the Duke's affection for the 3rd baronet, Cotton succeeded in reducing this to £1,800 for the heir, clear of all taxes, out of which £800 would come to the bride as her jointure with no further settlement for younger children, and the marriage duly took place at Leeds's house at Wimbledon, Surrey, in July 1708. Three days afterwards, the young couple were presented to Queen Anne. In the 1708 election Cotton had decided not to put himself forward as a candidate, but in the more favourable circumstances of 1710 his brother Thomas stood for the borough of Huntingdon, possibly with the backing of the Jacobite Lady Sandwich, while he himself mounted a late and, probably for that reason, unsuccessful challenge for the county. He petitioned, but on the death of one of the newly elected Members withdrew his petition and was returned unopposed at the by-election. Given leave of absence for three weeks on 9 Apr. 1711 because his wife was ill, he proved in general an inactive Member, and his only recorded vote was on 18 June 1713 in favour of the French commerce bill. No speech of his is recorded. At the general election of 1713 he stood down in favour of Lady Sandwich's son, Viscount Hinchingbrooke (Edward Richard Montagu*).[3]

Cotton died on 5 Feb. 1731, at a house in North Street, Red Lion Square, Middlesex, owned by a 'Mr Hanbury', a Bedfordshire neighbour, and was buried close by in Lamb's Conduit Fields. Besides personal bequests amounting to over £4,000 in money, he left lands in Bedfordshire for various charitable purposes, including the establishment of charity schools at Biggleswade and Holme, to teach poor children reading, writing, arithmetic and the 'principles of the Christian religion as practised in the Church of England'. The bulk of his property went to his cousin John, son of uncle Robert of Steeple Gidding, who inherited the baronetcy. Father and son were both in France at the time but had come back to reside in England by 1742. However, either John or his son went abroad again subsequently and took part in Charles Edward Stuart's abortive expedition from Dunkirk in 1744.[4]

[1] F. A. Blaydes, *Genealogia Bedfordiensis*, 110–11; *Mar. Lic. Vicar-Gen.* (Harl. Soc. xxx), 228; *Beds. N. and Q.* i. 217. [2] *Nicolson Diaries* ed. Jones and Holmes, 79–80; K. M. Sharpe, *Sir Robert Cotton*, 48–83; *Lib. Chron.* xl. 208; *HMC 5th Rep.* 383; *Cocks Diary*, 84; Ballard 38, f. 131; *Statutes*, vii. 642–3; Yorks. Arch. Soc. Leeds mss, B. Osborne to Ld. Danby, 11 June [1708] (*ex inf.* Dr C. Jones): VCH *Hunts.* ii. 145; Cambs. RO (Huntingdon), Cotton of Conington mss Con2/1/1, 5/3/1–15. [3] *HMC Kenyon*, 454; Cotton of Conington mss Con2/4/5/1; VCH *Hunts.* 59–60; H. Broxap, *Later Non-Jurors*, 86, 88, 146–223, 230–1; Boyer, *Pol. State*, x. 543; *Wren Soc.* xi. 48–59; Egerton 3385B, ff. 113, 122, 124; A. Browning, *Danby*, i. 56; Add. 28041, ff. 15, 17; Add. 70201, E. Lawrence to Robert Harley, 8 Aug. 1710; 70421, Dyer's newsletter 23 Nov. 1710. [4] *Gent. Mag.* 1731, p. 82; Boyer, xli. 213; *DNB* (Cotton, Sir Richard); Cotton of Conington mss Con2/1/4, 2/4/5/2; Broxap, 230–1; SP 34/36, p. 37; E. Cruickshanks, *Pol. Untouchables*, 57–58; VCH *Hunts.* ii. 59–60, 117.

E. C./D. W. H.

COTTON, John Hynde (1686–1752), of Madingley Hall, Cambs.

CAMBRIDGE	1708–1722
CAMBRIDGESHIRE	1722–1727
CAMBRIDGE	1727–1741
MARLBOROUGH	1741–4 Feb. 1752

bap. 7 Apr. 1686, 1st and o. surv. s. of Sir John Cotton, 2nd Bt.* *educ.* Westminster; Emmanuel, Camb. 1701, MA 1705. *m.* (1) 24 May 1714 (with c.£8,500), Lettice (*d.* 1718), da. of Sir Ambrose Crowley*, 1s. 1da.; (2) 3 June 1724, Margaret (*d.* 1734), da. and coh. of James Craggs I*, wid. of Samuel Trefusis*, 1da. *d.v.p. suc.* fa. as 3rd Bt. 15 Jan. 1713.[1]

Freeman, Cambridge 1707, Chester 1737; burgess, Edinburgh 1744, Glasgow 1744, Hamilton 1744.[2]

Ld. of Trade 1712–14; treasurer of the chamber 1744–6.[3]

As soon as he came of age Cotton took his father's place as a parliamentary candidate for Cambridge, and topped the poll at the first attempt in 1708, despite the fact that this was in general an unpropitious time for a new champion of the Church interest to make his debut. He was classified a Tory in a parliamentary list of that year. A tall and handsome young man, with an imposing physical presence in the years before excessive eating and drinking caused him to run to fat, he was inhibited from making long speeches by a persistent stammer, but in due course developed a technique for controlling the impediment which enabled him to contribute effective, if necessarily crisp and brief, interventions to debates. In other respects his ability and vigour were sufficient to bring him rapidly to notice. Because of the presence in the House of his namesake and fellow Tory Rowland Cotton*, it is not always easy to distinguish his participation in parliamentary business, but it may well be significant that his arrival in the Commons coincided with a sharp increase in the number of tellerships ascribed to 'Mr Cotton', and that later these decreased just as strikingly when he succeeded to his father's baronetcy. Thus he was probably one of the tellers on the Tory side in a division on 2 Dec. 1708 on the Reading election. Certainly he told on 20 Dec. 1709 for John Kynaston* and Richard Mytton* in the Shrewsbury election, and on 9 Feb. 1710 was a natural choice as teller for declaring Samuel Shepheard II* elected for Cambridge. Having voted against the impeachment of Dr Sacheverell, he again acted as a teller on 24 Mar. 1710, for a motion to adjourn, before a complaint was entered against a recently published edition of selected passages from the doctor's most celebrated (or notorious) sermons.

Added to the Cambridgeshire commission of the peace after the fall of the Godolphin administration, Cotton was re-elected for Cambridge without opposition. He was classed as a Tory in the 'Hanover list' and included in the first session of the new Parliament among both the 'Tory patriots' who favoured a peace and the 'worthy patriots' who exposed the mismanagements of the old ministry. He also belonged to the October Club, even though he and his father expressed a somewhat cynical view of that society, at dinner with Bishop Nicolson of Carlisle in February 1711, as 'made [up] of old beer-drinkers etc.' A tellership recorded to the account of 'Mr Cotton' on 3 Apr., against admitting as evidence in the Cockermouth election a document produced by the sitting Member, James Stanhope*, concerned an affair in which the Octobermen were making their presence felt. Cotton seems to have been one of the prime movers for another pet project of the club, the bill to resume crown grants since 1689, aimed at what High Tories regarded as William III's extravagant rewards to his favourites. He was chosen in third place in the ballot for commissioners but was not called upon to act, as the bill was thrown out by the Lords. Subsequently he may have been a teller on 7 May for an amendment to the game bill. In the following session, during which he remained a member of the October Club, five tellerships ought probably to be added to his account. Two occurred in the course of the proceedings for corruption against Robert Walpole II*, perhaps prefiguring the personal enmity which marked their later careers: 'Mr Cotton' told on 17 Jan. 1712 in favour of including the words 'notorious corruption' in the motion of censure against the former secretary at war for taking bribes to pass forage contracts, and then on 6 Mar., after Walpole's expulsion, for the motion to disqualify him from sitting again in that Parliament. A Cotton told on 17 May in opposition to two other Tories, Henry Campion and Thomas Paske, against adjourning the debate on supply, and on the 23rd, for going into a committee of the whole to consider the affairs of the Royal African Company; while the last tellership of this batch took place on 6 June, against reading the Lords' bill to continue the Quakers' Affirmation Act. When the attack on King William's grants was renewed, Cotton was once more elected, but this time in first place, in the ballot on 13 May for commissioners of resumption, only for this renewed bill to prove abortive. During the summer of 1712 his talents were recognized by the lord treasurer, when he was given a commissionership of Trade, with a salary of £1,000 a year. In that capacity he was involved in the preparation of papers relating to the treaty of commerce with France, and it seems peculiarly appropriate, given his life-long addiction to claret, that he was a teller on 6 May 1713 in favour of the bill to suspend duties on French wines. On 18 May he presented an address of thanks from Cambridge corporation for the conclusion of such an 'advantageous and honourable peace', and for 'securing the Protestant Succession in the illustrious house of Hanover, and of consequence the Protestant religion', an address which also went out of its way to deplore 'factious and party rage'. On the 28th he told against another attempt to renew the Quakers' Affirmation Act. He naturally voted on 18 June in favour of the French commerce bill. After its surprising rejection by the House, he supplied Parliament with reports on trade with Cape Breton and with Flanders, being nominated on 23 June to the committee to prepare an address to request the appointment of commissioners to settle the French trade.[4]

Returned unopposed for Cambridge once again in the 1713 general election, Cotton spoke on 18 Mar. 1714 in favour of the expulsion from the Commons of Richard Steele, following a speech by John Carnegie and possibly in answer to some previous comments by George Baillie on events in Scotland. On 17 June he reported from the committee to scrutinize the lists in the ballot for a new set of public accounts commissioners. He was classified as a Tory in the Worsley list and two other lists of the 1713 and 1715 Parliaments.[5]

By May 1714 Cotton had joined the Duke of Beaufort's political-cum-drinking club, the Board of Brothers, which by this time may have developed Jacobite associations, but it does not appear that he was himself as yet a supporter of the Pretender's cause. According to a story retailed by the 19th-century editor of Bishop Burnet's *History*,

> Sir John Cotton, who was a leading Member among the Tories in the last Parliament of Queen Anne, used to declare, as a person of undoubted credit long since dead often mentioned, that he had been privy to no design of bringing in the son of King James upon the Queen's death, but said that when he returned to London after that event, he found his old friends turned Jacobites.

Jacobite or not, Cotton was dismissed from the Board of Trade in December 1714. He was returned again on the Tory interest to George I's Parliaments, but seems not to have immediately resumed his former prominence in the Tory party. In the list of 'well-wishers' prepared for the Pretender in 1721 he did not appear by name but was subsumed under a collective designation of 'the Cottons in their various branches'. He was not removed from the Cambridgeshire bench until 1726. By 1733 Lord Perceval (John†) could write of him as one of 'the leaders of the Tories' and in fact 'esteemed the very head and knitter together of the violent (some will say the Jacobite) party', but he seems to have avoided Jacobite intrigue until the 1740s, when he took part in negotiations for an invasion but showed caution in committing himself to action. He participated in the Broad-bottom administration from 1744 to 1746, 'the size of his backside' giving rise to obvious witticisms, and subsequently co-operated with the Leicester House party, though still suspected by Court Whigs of harbouring Jacobite sympathies.[6]

Cotton died on 4 Feb. 1752 and was buried with his ancestors at Landwade, where the inscription on his monument praised his 'integrity and manly conduct', his 'eloquence in debate', and successful avoidance of 'faction' and 'invective', an improbable combination of virtues given his role in the politics of the 1740s. It was also observed that 'in his private life, the character of the country gentleman was embellished by a knowledge of the world, by polished manners, and by various and extensive reading'. The obituary in the *Gentleman's Magazine* stressed his incorruptibility rather than his moderation, but in similarly extravagant terms. He had been, it said, a man

> whose lively genius and solid understanding were steadily devoted to the service of his country ... Without any views of venal reward; above the desire of ill-gotten power; untainted with the itch of tinsel titles. He lived, he died a patriot.[7]

[1] Cambs. RO (Cambridge), Cotton of Madingley mss 588/F43, W. Cole, 'Gens Cottoniana Cantabrigiensis', pp. 59–63; 588/T99; 588/L88, p. 8; Madingley par. reg. P114/2; *MI Cambs*. ed. Palmer, 78. [2] Cambs. RO (Cambridge), Cambridge bor. recs. common day bk. 1681–1722, p. 404; Cotton of Madingley mss 588/F56–58; Chester RO, A/B/4/8ov. [3] *Cal. Treas. Bks*. xxvi. 351–2; xxix. 633. [4] *Diary of Samuel Newton* (Camb. Antiq. Soc. xxiii), 122; *HMC Portland*, iv. 579–80; L. K. J. Glassey, *Appt. JPs*, 232–3; *Nicolson Diaries* ed. Jones and Holmes, 543; *Cal. Treas. Bks*. xxvi. 351–2; C. H. Cooper, *Annals of Cambridge*, iv. 112. [5] Cambridge bor. recs. common day bk. 1681–1722, p. 510; Douglas diary (Hist. of Parl. trans.), 18 Mar. 1714; NSA, Kreienberg despatch 19 Mar. 1714. [6] Glos. RO, Beaufort mss 100/5/2; Burnet, iii. 356; *Cal. Treas. Bks*. xxix. 633; RA, Stuart mss 65/16 (cf. P. S. Fritz, *Ministers and Jacobitism 1715–45*, p. 151); Glassey, 250, 259; *HMC Egmont Diary*, i. 361, 365, 371. [7] *E. Anglian*, i. 344; *Gent. Mag*. 1752, p. 92.

E. C./D. W. H.

COTTON, Sir Robert, 1st Bt. (c.1635–1712), of Combermere, Cheshire.

CHESHIRE   1679 (Oct.)–1681 (Mar.), 1689–1702

b. c.1635, 2nd but 1st surv. s. of Thomas Cotton of Combermere (d.v.p., s. of George Cotton of Combermere), being 1st s. by his 2nd w. Elizabeth, da. of Sir George Calverley of Lee and coh. of her bro. Sir Hugh Calverley. *educ*. travelled abroad (France) 1651–5. *m*. c.1666, Hester (d. 1710), da. of Sir Thomas Salusbury, 2nd Bt.†, of Llewenni, Denb., and h. to her bro. Sir John Salusbury†, 5s. (4 d.v.p.) 11da. suc. gdfa. 1649; kntd. 25 June 1660; cr. Bt. 29 Mar. 1677.[1]

Commr. for corporations, Cheshire 1662–3, loyal and indigent officers 1662; alderman, Chester by 1664–84; freeman, Denbigh 1665, common councilman 1700–d.; steward, lordship of Denbigh 1689–1702; custos rot. Denb. June–Oct. 1689, 1699–1702.[2]

Cotton's family had come to prominence in Cheshire in the 16th century and in 1649 he inherited a considerable estate which was to form a sound basis for his political aspirations. A Royalist in the 1650s, Cotton came to prominence in Cheshire politics during the Exclusion crisis as a close political ally of the radical Whig Lord Delamer (Henry Booth†). Like Delamer, Cotton proved himself to be a staunch Whig with a strong Country sensibility. His parliamentary career after the Revolution, which he welcomed with the prayer that 'God restore us our religion, liberties and properties', demonstrated his independent nature and one modern historian has described him as one of the dwindling number of members of 'Shaftesbury's Whig party' who remained in the Commons after the Revolution and were willing to support Country measures on the floor of the House. This adherence to the Country strain of Whiggery did, on occasion, lead Whigs of a less independent nature to question his actions and opinions, but there is no suggestion that Cotton found himself being drawn into Tory circles. His experiences in the bitterly partisan politics of Cheshire had led him to identify himself as an opponent of Toryism so that, unlike some Whigs who co-operated with Tories in Country measures in the 1690s, Cotton remained loyal to the Whig party.[3]

Although allegations that Cotton had voted, contrary to Cheshire interests, in the Convention for raising the land tax by pound rate complicated his campaign for the county in 1690, he nevertheless defeated a Tory opponent to take Cheshire's second seat, and in an analysis of the new Parliament Lord Carmarthen (Sir Thomas Osborne†) listed him as a Whig. Cotton's appearances in the Journals are often impossible to disentangle from those of his namesake Sir Robert Cotton of Hatley St. George, Cambridgeshire. Both men were active Members of the 1690 Parliament, but the contrast between the Cambridgeshire knight's Court Toryism and the Cheshire baronet's Country Whiggery does make it possible to differentiate some of their activities. It seems likely, for example, that it was Cotton of Combermere who twice told on the Whig side in divisions upon the bill to restore the corporation of London, and that it was he who contributed to the debates upon the Abjuration in April, supporting the charges of Jacobitism, made on the 24th, against the Cheshire Tory Sir Thomas Grosvenor, 3rd Bt.*, and three days later advocating a proclamation to oblige all papists to remove out of London or 'be convicted as traitors'.[4]

In 1689 Cotton had been appointed steward of the lordship of Denbigh, where he had gained extensive lands in 1684 by marriage, and his support for the Revolution was again recognized in June 1690 when William III spent a night at Combermere en route for

Ireland. Although Cotton was reported to be 'dangerously ill of a fever' in September, he had recovered in time to attend the 1690–1 session: on 22 Oct. he was appointed, along with his namesake, to draft the bill attainting and confiscating the estates of rebels in England and Ireland. It seems likely that Cotton acted as teller three times in this session: against hearing a Tory petition alleging malpractice in the corporation of London; in favour of adjourning the debate upon this petition; and for an amendment to the bill for the speedier determination of elections, that all disputed elections heard by subsequent Parliaments should be heard at the bar. In April 1691 Cotton was classed as a Country supporter by Robert Harley*. It is possible to be more certain of his activity in the 1691–2 session. He took, for example, a keen interest in the debates of the committee of supply, and his interventions in these debates indicate his sympathy with those Whigs prepared to work with Tories in order to ensure 'good management'. On 9 Nov. he spoke in support of Harley's motion that the naval estimates be referred to a select committee, and three days later it seems likely that it was the Cheshire baronet who told in favour of a proposal for a bill to reduce interest rates, a Country proposal. It was definitely Cotton of Combermere who, when the army estimates came before the committee of supply on the 30th, supported Sir Thomas Clarges' proposal that these estimates be referred to a select committee, pointing out that this would allow the members of the committee to consider 'the condition of the nation and ... whether [it is] able to bear such a charge'. Concerns about military expenditure again surfaced on 15 Dec. when, during consideration of the report of the committee investigating the charge of the army in Ireland for 1693, Cotton echoed the sentiments of Sir Christopher Musgrave, 4th Bt., that the number of men in each Irish company should be increased, a measure which it was thought would reduce the cost of the army in Ireland for 1692 by £100,000. This concern with the burden of taxation was again apparent on 1 Jan. 1692 when Cotton questioned whether the yield of £50,000 p.a. estimated for the inland Irish excise was realistic. Supply was not, however, the only issue in which he took an interest in this session. On 3 Dec. 1691 he spoke in favour of leaving the bill for the relief of London orphans upon the table, and on the 31st told against the Lords' amendment to the treason trials bill, which would have ended the crown's power of empanelling the juries of the lord steward's court, where peers were tried when Parliament was not in session. Cotton also made known his opposition to the renewal of the charter of the East India Company, telling on 17 Dec. against the Commons' moving two days later into a committee of the whole to consider further petitions on the East India trade, and on 6 Feb. 1692 speaking in favour of the Commons' addressing William for the dissolution of the Company. Cotton's Country stance in the debates over supply did not, however, indicate any weakening of his Whig loyalties. On 4 Feb., for example, he moved that a vote of thanks be sent to General Ginkel for his services in the reduction of Ireland, and five days later he told against a Lords' amendment to the tithe bill which would have forced justices to 'execute sentences of the spiritual courts', thereby strengthening the power of the church relative to the authority of the state. The end of this session saw Cotton take a keen interest in the examination of the allegations of Jacobite intrigue by William Fuller. He spoke on 22 Feb. in favour of his immediate examination on oath, moving the following day that he be given a date to produce witnesses for his allegations, and on the 24th argued in favour of declaring Fuller an impostor for not having met this deadline. It can also be said with certainty that in February Cotton managed an estate bill through the Commons.[5]

Despite Cotton's willingness to support Country measures in the 1691–2 session, in the summer of 1692 he was classed as a placeman and government official in two separate lists, on account of his position as steward of the lordship of Denbigh. Cotton's equally independent line in the 1692–3 session indicates that he felt that this place had little relevance to his parliamentary conduct. On 23 Nov., for example, he was one of the Members who, in the second sitting of the committee of the whole upon 'advice' to the King, argued that English troops should be led by English general officers, and, when the army estimates were reviewed on 3 Dec., he argued for separate estimates for Scotland due to its 'being an independent kingdom having a revenue of their own', with the consequence that the Scots should 'maintain their own troops'. The only other parliamentary actions which can be attributed with any certainty to him in this session are carrying an estate bill to the Lords (9 Jan. 1693), and tellerships in favour of granting the Tory Sir Gilbert Clarke a leave of absence (18 Feb.) and for an amendment to a game bill (23 Feb.). That Cotton's parliamentary behaviour led him to make enemies at Westminster is indicated by the comment of one of his Cheshire friends that 'he has enemies where he should not', a comment which may indicate that some Whigs were unhappy with Cotton's Country sympathies.[6]

Cotton's grant of the stewardship of Denbigh

meant that in November 1693 he was again included in a list of placemen. It seems likely that it was Cotton of Combermere who piloted a Welsh estate bill through the Lords in February and March 1694. He demonstrated his political independence early in the 1694–5 session when, on 22 Nov. 1694, he, along with his fellow Cheshire Member Sir John Mainwaring, 2nd Bt., spoke in defence of the prisoners in the Lancashire Plot, being one of the Members who informed the House of the 'scandalousness of the evidence' against the accused. He was reported in early December to be ill, but was present in the House on 12 Mar. 1695 when he took notes on the debate concerning Speaker Trevor's acceptance of a bribe in connexion with the London orphans' bill. It was later alleged that in the same month Cotton had opposed 'the bill for disabling to plead at the bar such counsel as had not or would not take the oaths to the government'. A week after the final prorogation of the 1690 Parliament Cotton appeared before the Treasury lords, with a number of Welsh gentlemen including Sir William Williams, 6th Bt.*, and Sir Roger Puleston*, in opposition to the proposal to grant the lordships of Denbigh, Bromfield and Yale to the Earl of Portland. Combining his Country sensibilities and a concern to preserve his interest in Denbighshire, Cotton pointed out that a similar grant of Welsh lands by Elizabeth I to the Earl of Leicester (Sir Robert Dudley†) had caused such resentment in the principality that Leicester had eventually returned the grant of his own volition. As a result of such complaints the grant was recalled eventually in January 1696.[7]

Cotton's support for independent behaviour in the 1690 Parliament meant that he found some Cheshire Whigs unwilling to countenance his re-election as knight of the shire in 1695. However, the Cheshire Whigs in general were unwilling to give him up, one declaring that although Cotton 'might give a wrong vote, yet [he] be an honest man', so that Cotton was returned without a poll. The only significant appointment in the 1695–6 session that can be attributed to him with any confidence came on 26 Feb. 1696, when he was named to the committee to draft a bill to improve the common at Nantwich in Cheshire in order to raise a stock to maintain the poor. The opposition Cotton had encountered in the 1695 election did not lead him to temper his independent nature. He was forecast as a likely opponent of the Court in the division of 31 Jan. 1696 on the proposed council of trade, and the following day received two votes in the ballot for commissioners of accounts. His continued loyalty to the new regime is evident in his prompt signing of the Association, but in March he voted against fixing the price of guineas at 22s. The summer of 1696 saw him bring to the attention of the lords justices the problems caused in Cheshire by clipped money, and it seems likely that it was he who told in favour of the motion of 3 Nov. 1696 that the report of the commissioners of accounts on the coinage be referred to a committee of the whole. The early stages of the 1696–7 session were, however, dominated by the attainder of Sir John Fenwick†, and the debates revived Cotton's memories of false accusations of his own complicity in the Monmouth rebellion. It therefore comes as no surprise that when Cotton spoke in the third reading debate of 25 Nov. he counselled caution and advocated the maintenance of due procedure. He told the House that

> I do find that gentlemen do very much insist in this case, that if a gentleman does believe that Sir John Fenwick is guilty, he must give his vote for the passing of this bill. If that be so, I am glad that opinion did not take place in the last reign; if it had, I am of opinion I should not have been here now, and I believe my Lord Warrington [the former Delamer], who was very instrumental in promoting this Revolution, would not have died in his bed. My lord and I were [in 1685] accused of a crime, which I believe, if proved by two witnesses, had been treason. I have heard some gentlemen say in this House, they did believe my Lord Warrington was guilty (though he was not guilty of the fact as it had been laid) . . . Now if the same fact was treason when proved by two witnesses, and but misdemeanour when proved by one, methinks we are doing an extraordinary thing; we are going after the fact committed, to make that which is but a misdemeanour to be treason. And for these and other reasons, I can't agree with the passing of it.

After these remarks it was inevitable that Cotton should vote against the attainder. It seems likely that it was he who told on 2 Dec. against the resolution extending the Tunnage and Poundage Act until 1706, and guided a Cheshire estate bill through the Commons in January 1697. Although problems of identification remain, it seems that his parliamentary activity was declining at this time, and it is impossible to attribute any significant activity to him in the 1697–8 session.[8]

Cotton's return for Cheshire in 1698 was uncontested, though he spent a great deal of time and effort attempting to establish an interest at Denbigh Boroughs in opposition to that of the Tory Sir Richard Myddelton, 3rd Bt.* On a comparison of the old and new Commons he was classed as a member of the Country party. Cotton's reputation as an independent Member no doubt explains his inclusion, in October

1698, on what was probably a forecast of the Members likely to oppose a standing army. His local links suggest that he was the Sir Robert Cotton who managed through the Commons between January and February 1699 the bill to establish Liverpool as a separate parish, possibly assuming this task due to the absence (on an embassy for the New East India Company) of Liverpool's senior Member Sir William Norris.

Cotton was re-elected unopposed for Cheshire in the first 1701 election, though again failing in his attempts to gain a seat at Denbigh Boroughs. The absence of his namesake from this Parliament allows a closer examination of his parliamentary activity. On 15 Mar. he was named to draft a Cheshire estate bill, and in May reported from a committee examining allegations that brine salt producers in Cheshire were evading the salt duties. His name appeared on a list of those likely to support the Court over the 'Great Mortgage', which may indicate a sympathy towards the recent ministerial changes. Cotton's most eventful contribution to the session came, however, in the debate upon the land tax bill on 2 June. His Tory opponent in Denbigh politics, Edward Brereton, complained that a number of Denbigh's land tax commissioners had been replaced by outsiders and a servant of Cotton's, on the advice of the baronet, who himself had been appointed custos of the county in 1699. Cotton replied sharply that the new commissioners 'were men of account and recommended to him by men of estates', and when the Commons rose Cotton 'struck Brereton over the head with a little cane', only for Brereton to respond 'with two hard blows over the face with the head of his great cane'.[9]

Despite claims that Cotton had become too keen to support the Court following his appointment as custos of Denbighshire in 1699, he successfully defeated a challenge to his return for Cheshire in the second election of 1701, and was listed as a Whig by Harley. He was named on 6 Jan. 1702 to draft a bill to provide for the poor. This was, however, to be his last significant parliamentary act. Faced with a strong challenge from Cheshire's Tories, he was defeated in the 1702 election, and left the political stage. He remained a wealthy man despite being deprived of the stewardship of Denbigh, so that he was able to give one of his daughters a portion of £6,000 on her marriage to Thomas Lewis II*. His final recorded interest in parliamentary affairs came in early 1706, when he urged Peter Legh† to have his brother Thomas II* ensure the successful passage of the Whitworth–Chester road bill. It seems that Cotton aspired to a peerage, but this desire was not satisfied and he died at his house in Westminster on 18 Dec. 1712. He was succeeded by his son Thomas. Cotton's grandson went on to sit for Cheshire and Lostwithiel as a Whig under George II.[10]

[1] Ormerod, *Cheshire*, iii. 405, 414–15; *Verney Mems.* i. 502; ii. 28. [2] Chester RO, Chester bor. recs. assembly bks. A/B/2, ff. 137, 150; J. Williams, *Recs. of Denbigh*, 136, 143, 145; *Cal. Treas. Bks.* x. 181. [3] A. L. Cust, *Chrons. of Erthig*, i. 68–69; *Party and Management* ed. Jones, 53. [4] Liverpool RO, Sir Willoughby Aston diaries, 920MD 173, 13, 14 Mar. 1690; Grey, x. 80; Bodl. Rawl. A.79, f. 87. [5] Morrice ent'ring bk. 3, p. 161; Chester RO, Earwaker mss CR63/2/691/88, 102, Sir Willoughby Aston, 2nd Bt., to Sir John Crewe, 4 Sept. 1690, 7 Jan. 1691[–2]; *Luttrell Diary*, 10, 52, 58, 87, 100–1, 109, 175, 177, 192, 199, 203–4. [6] *Luttrell Diary*, 252, 291, 355, 431, 444; Earwaker mss CR63/2/691/117, Aston to Crewe, 22 Feb. 1692[–3]. [7] Bodl. Carte 130, f. 353; BL, Verney mss mic 636/48, John Verney* (Ld. Fermanagh) to Sir Ralph Verney†, 5 Dec. 1694; *Cal. Treas. Bks.* 1201–2; Chandler, iii. 17; Sir Willoughby Aston's diaries, 920MD 174, 4 Oct. 1695. [8] Challinor thesis 187; Harley mss at Brampton Bryan bdle. 117, ballot list, 1 Feb. 1695–6. [9] *Cocks Diary*, 158; L. K. J. Glassey, *Appt. JPs*, 138. [10] *Jnl. of the Architectural, Arch. and Hist. Soc. of Chester*, o.s. i. 109–10; John Rylands Univ. Lib. Manchester, Legh of Lyme mss corresp. Cotton to [Legh], 12 Jan., 14 Feb. 1705[–6]; NRA report 16683 (Cotton mss), p.24; *Wentworth Pprs.* 111; Boyer, *Pol. State*, iv. 371; PCC 230 Barnes.

E. C./R. D. H.

COTTON, Sir Robert (1644–1717), of Hatley St. George, Cambs.

CAMBRIDGESHIRE	1679 (Oct.)–1681 (Mar.)
	1685–1687
	1689–1695
NEWPORT (I.o.W.)	1695–1700
TRURO	12 Feb.–2 July 1702

bap. 2 May 1644, 3rd s. of Sir Thomas Cotton, 2nd Bt.†, of Conington Castle, Hunts., being 1st surv. s. by his 2nd w. Alice, da. and h. of Sir John Constable of Dromanby, Yorks.; half-bro. of Sir Joseph Cotton, 3rd Bt.†, of Conington Castle. *m.* lic. 4 July 1663, Gertrude (*d.* 1701), da. of William Morice† of Werrington, Devon, 1s. *d.v.p.* 1da. Kntd. 3 June 1663.[1]

Freeman, Cambridge 1679; sheriff, Cambs. and Hunts. Jan.–Nov. 1688.[2]

Jt. postmaster-gen. 1691–1708.[3]

Commr. taking subscriptions to land bank 1696.[4]

In 1662 Cotton had been granted the manor of Hatley by his half-brother, and his family's status in Cambridgeshire society provided him with the platform from which to launch his parliamentary career. Although his views on Exclusion are obscure, after the Revolution the Marquess of Carmarthen (Sir Thomas Osborne†) pressed, unsuccessfully, his claims for office, and it became apparent in the Convention that Cotton shared the Toryism of his half-brother. As one modern historian has pointed out, in the early 1690s

Cotton was 'among Carmarthen's most faithful followers' and in 1691 he was rewarded with the profitable post of joint postmaster-general. Following this appointment, Cotton was a conspicuous supporter of the ministry in the Commons for the remainder of the 1690 Parliament, and loyalty to the Court quickly took precedence over his Toryism, so that Cotton was able to retain this place, unaffected by the vicissitudes of party conflict, until his retirement in 1708.[5]

Returned unopposed for Cambridgeshire in 1690, Cotton was classed as a Tory and a Court supporter in Carmarthen's analysis of the new House. Although Cotton was active throughout the 1690 Parliament, analysis of his parliamentary activity is complicated by the failure of the Journals and some contemporaries to differentiate him from the Cheshire Member Sir Robert Cotton, 1st Bt., whose parliamentary service overlapped with that of the Cambridgeshire knight. However, the contrast between the knight's Court Toryism and the baronet's Country Whiggery does, in a number of cases, allow the attribution of some of these references. It seems likely, for example, that it was this Member who twice intervened in the committee of the whole on supply, on 27 Mar. 1690 urging that the committee 'answer the King's ends' and settle a fund, and informing the committee, on 1 Apr., that although he was aware 'of the treasure given, and the little effects of it' the business of the committee was 'to consider how this supply may be raised'. It is, however, impossible to attribute with any confidence any further parliamentary activity in this session to Cotton.[6]

Cotton's continued loyalty to Carmarthen was indicated early in the 1690–1 session, when the Marquess included him upon what was probably a list of supporters drawn up in December in preparation for a parliamentary defence of his position as lord president, but, though 'Sir Robert Cotton' appears frequently in the Journals this session, the only appointment that can be definitely attributed to Cotton of Hatley St. George was that of 22 Oct. to draft a bill to attaint rebels, as both namesakes were included in the committee. There is, however, no mistaking the identity of the Cotton appointed joint postmaster-general on 27 Feb. 1691. The place of postmaster had previously been held by one man, but William III chose at this time to split the post between the Tory Cotton and the Whig Thomas Frankland I*, at a salary of £750 p.a. each, a compromise that was condemned by Carmarthen as 'the most destructive method your Majesty can take'. It nevertheless seems likely, though there is no direct evidence of it, that Carmarthen had a hand in Cotton's preferment, and the lord president's concern for the potential difficulties consequent upon dividing the post between rival parties proved to be misguided. Upon their appointment Lord Sydney (Hon. Henry Sidney[†]) described Cotton and Frankland as 'very moderate men', and they worked well together, Cotton being the more active for the Court in the Commons and Frankland shouldering more of the administrative burden. The division of the office was maintained until 1823. Cotton and Frankland had displaced the radical Whig John Wildman[†], and John Hampden[†] commented that Wildman's removal was due not to 'the least intimation of miscarriage on his part' but rather 'to make way for another sort of man', more inclined to follow the Court. Cotton's and Frankland's previous parliamentary behaviour certainly makes such an interpretation of their appointments plausible, and within a month the new postmasters-general had refused to handle the post of the recently established commissioners of public accounts, aiding the Court campaign to harass the commission. His classification as a Court supporter by Robert Harley* in April therefore comes as little surprise.[7]

Cotton's new place reinforced his previous loyalty to the ministry, and in the difficult 1691–2 session he spoke regularly in support of the ministry's supply measures. In the committee of the whole on 9 Nov., for example, he argued against the suggestion that the naval estimates be considered by 'a particular committee', and when such objections were rejected Cotton was named to the committee considering these estimates. Three days later he proposed to the committee of supply 'that the estimates for the land forces might also be referred to the committee that considered that for the fleet', and it appears that some Members, most notably Sir Thomas Clarges, felt that Cotton's proposal was an attempt to frustrate consideration of the naval estimates. When a committee of the whole considered the army estimates, Cotton supported the Court's attempts to frustrate any attempts by the Commons to secure reductions. On 19 Nov. he urged the committee to 'consider how ready the Dutch and other confederates were to assist you in a time of need, how they lent their armies and fleets to deliver you when your laws, your religion, and all were in danger' and asked, 'shall we be so ungrateful to leave them when they have most need of our help?' It also seems likely that he was the Cotton who spoke on 30 Nov. in favour of continuing the general officers as they had been the previous year. It was definitely the joint postmaster-general who, on 15 Dec. 1692, argued in favour of paying Dutch troops on the Irish establishment the English rate of pay rather than the lower, Dutch rate, and given his previous advocacy of the Court case on supply it seems likely that it was he rather than the Cheshire Member who, on 2 Jan., opposed the resolution of the committee of the whole for reducing the Irish establishment. When, ten days later, the committee of supply moved to consider establishing 'a fund for perpetual interest' to carry on the war, he supported the measure. The 18th saw the committee of supply consider the proposal that placemen receiving over £500 p.a. should apply the surplus to the cost of the war, and Cotton's response made his fondness for the emoluments of office clear. He contended that the sum raised by such a scheme 'will not be very considerable', and instead proposed that 'all gentlemen having an estate over £500 p.a. shall contribute the same above that sum to the carrying on the war', a suggestion he had previously made on the 11th. Cotton's intervention in the committee of supply debate on the poll bill on the 20th would seem, however, to indicate that this advocacy of an additional financial burden upon the landed interest was merely a nervous reaction to the attack upon placemen rather than a serious proposal. During this debate Charles Montagu proposed that the poll bill should make no distinction 'between all of the degree of a gentleman and under the degree of a peer' and Cotton opposed this suggestion on the grounds that it would make the poll bill 'a second land tax', thereby demonstrating some sensitivity to the financial demands the war was making on the landed interest. Cotton's support for the Court on supply was mirrored in other areas during this session. When, on 7 Nov., the committee of the whole considering the naval miscarriages of the previous summer was able to lay no direct charges, Cotton supported Montagu's motion that the Speaker resume the chair, and 11 days later he backed a motion by Sir John Lowther, 2nd Bt. II, that the Commons move into a committee of supply rather than consider the third reading of the treason trials bill. Cotton's zealous support of the Court was also evident in his speaking for Richard Hampden I's motion of 28 Jan. that William III be granted £30,000 p.a. from the proceeds of the sales of forfeited Irish estates to reward those who had served him in Ireland. On 15 Feb., he spoke in a similar vein against tacking the legislation to revive the commission of accounts to the poll bill. Cotton's acquisition of office had clearly cemented his allegiance to the ministry, and his Tory feelings were only evident in this session from his telling, on 9 Feb., for an amendment to the tithe bill requiring justices to 'execute the sentences of spiritual courts'. Although he appears to have spent most of his time in this session defending the ministry, he still found opportunities to promote local interests, telling on 8 Dec. for an amendment excluding ale brewed at Cambridge University from the double excise, and speaking on 22 Feb. in favour of the bill to confirm the university's charter.[8]

Given his office, and his staunch support for the Court in the 1691–2 session, it comes as little surprise that Cotton was included on a list of Court supporters drawn up by Carmarthen during the 1692 prorogation, and in a list of placemen dating from 1692. The new session saw him continue in the same vein. On 10 Nov. he moved the Address and was presumably the Cotton appointed the same day to the committee to prepare it. This session saw him less active in matters relating to supply, though on 15 Nov. he spoke against the motion that the nation's alliances be laid before the Commons before supply was considered, and on 13 Dec. argued that the land tax be raised by the pound rate. However, his support for the Court remained undimmed, and was shown in his contribution to the defence against Whig attacks on the management of naval affairs by Lord Nottingham (Daniel Finch†). When on 21 Nov. the committee of the whole considered the attack upon the Admiralty commissioners contained within the report of the committee upon the losses of merchants ships, Cotton argued that 'it is very hard to make a vote against these gentlemen [the commissioners], who are men of credit . . . without hearing them'. It also seems likely that it was the Cambridgeshire Cotton who on 5 Dec. supported the argument by Sir John Lowther, 2nd Bt. II, that criticisms of the Admiralty commission concerning the descent of the previous summer should not be made until the relevant papers had been considered. Cotton's support extended to speaking, on 11 Jan., in opposition to the motion that William III be advised to appoint Admiralty commissioners 'of known experience in maritime affairs'. Cotton's support for the ministry was not, however, limited to this subject. It seems probable, for example, that it was he who, in a committee of the whole of 28 Nov., supported the Court line that the implementation of the treason trials bill be delayed until the end of the war, and it was certainly the joint postmaster-general who spoke in support of the army estimates for 1693 on 3 Dec. He also spoke against the triennial bill in a committee of the whole on 7 Feb., and on the 24th expressed his opposition to calling the Irish parliament. Cotton's only deviation from his pro-Court stance came in the debate of 14 Feb. on the renewal of the commission of accounts, when he supported the measure 'because it gives satisfaction to the nation'. That this was a rare aberration was confirmed later the same day when he spoke in favour of the Whig gentleman of the privy chamber James Honywood* in the Commons' debate upon the disputed Essex by-election. Cotton's official responsibilities led him to complain to the Commons on 2 Feb. about the 'great abuse put upon the King' by newsletter writers who had 'counterfeited the hands of divers Members and franked letters to be sent by the post in their names'. It also seems likely that he told against a proposal to reduce the rate of flax duty (26 Jan.).[9]

Cotton was included upon three separate lists of placemen compiled in 1693, and in the 1693–4 session his loyalty to the ministry continued unabated, though from this time it becomes more difficult to identify his parliamentary activity. It was the Cambridgeshire knight who entered the debate upon William's answer to the Commons' representation upon the royal veto of the place bill, informing the House 'the King's answer tends to full satisfaction', and Hon. Anchitell Grey* recorded that Cotton proceeded to 'read each paragraph, and with strained inferences descants thereon, like a courtier'. Given this clear indication of Cotton's continued support for the ministry, it seems likely that it was he who told on 28 Dec. against the triennial bill, spoke in defence of Lord Falkland (Anthony Carey*) on 7 Dec. when the Commons considered allegations of his misuse of monies as a lord of the Admiralty, and told on 20 Dec. against an amendment which would have committed William III to deploying in Barbados four of the 15 new regiments of foot agreed to be raised by the committee of supply. The joint postmaster-general also seems likely to have reported upon a Cambridgeshire estate bill on 5 Jan. 1694. The problems of identification continue for the 1694–5 session, but it seems likely that he told on 28 Nov. against committing the place bill, and on 16 Apr. in favour of the Speaker leaving the chair so that the glass duties could be considered.[10]

Cotton decided against standing for Cambridgeshire in 1695, resigning his interest to Lord Cutts (John*) and Admiral Russell (Edward*). Instead, he was returned upon the government interest for Newport, Isle of Wight, and the remainder of his parliamentary career was to remain dependent upon the interest of the crown. He was forecast as likely to support the Court in the division of 31 Jan. on the proposed council of trade. He was, however, one of a number of Tory placemen who voted against the Court in this division. This was, however, a rare lapse, as he signed the Association in February and the following month supported the Court's motion that the price of guineas be fixed at 22s. His official responsibilities explain his appointment on 3 Apr. to draft a bill to improve the Post Office, and four days later he presented the bill. The summer saw him involved in the seizure of Jacobite correspondence relating to the Assassination Plot, and on 25 Nov. he voted for the attainder of Sir John Fenwick†. Mention of 'Sir Robert Cotton' in the Journals declines in the remainder of William's reign, and it may be that the Cambridgeshire knight began to keep a low profile in view of the ascendancy of the Junto, though there was no move to dismiss him despite the designs of James Vernon I* upon his profitable office.[11]

Cotton's election at Newport in 1698 was secured with government support, and in September he was classed as a placeman, and as a Court supporter in a comparison of the 'old' and 'new' Commons. He voted, on 18 Jan. 1699, against the disbanding bill, but the only other activity in this session that can be attributed to him with certainty was his action in a complaint for breach of privilege he brought with Frankland against John Woodgate, postmaster at Canterbury, for distributing a libel on their administration of the Post Office. In the early 1690s the postmasters-general had reprimanded Woodgate for not clearing his arrears and for detaining the Dover and Deal post in Canterbury, and by 1699 such inefficiency had led to Woodgate's dismissal. Woodgate had responded, however, by publishing a paper which claimed that he had been turned out for having discovered smugglers and a Jacobite correspondence with France. The matter came before the Commons on 22 Apr. 1699 when Woodgate's paper was voted a 'false, scandalous and malicious' libel. In early 1700 an analysis of the House into interests classed Cotton as a placeman.[12]

Given his support for the ministry in the Commons it is surprising that there is no evidence of Cotton standing at either of the 1701 elections, but in May 1701 he attended the Commons to observe the early stages of the bill to preserve for the public the family library, established by his grandfather Sir Robert Cotton, 1st Bt.†, and now in the possession of his half-brother. On the 8th he wrote to Robert Harley to thank him for his 'assistance to preserve a library by bill, which beside the usefulness to the public, will remain to posterity so great an honour to our family'. In February 1702 Cotton was returned to the Commons at a by-election at Truro, but appears to have made no impact on this Parliament. Following the July dissolution he and Frankland informed the Duke of Marlborough

(John Churchill†) of their intention to go 'into the country to make us further capable of serving her Majesty and the government', but in Cotton's case this appears to have been limited to supporting the candidacy of John Ellis* at Harwich, as there is no record of Cotton having stood at this election.[13]

Cotton's parliamentary career had ended but, despite the rumours circulating in 1702 that John Grobham Howe* was about to replace Cotton and Frankland as postmaster-general, he remained in office for a further six years. One of his more intriguing actions during this time was to write from Hatley St. George to Lord Nottingham on 20 Apr. 1704. The secretary of state's discontent with the lack of support he had been receiving from Marlborough and Lord Godolphin (Sidney†) had brought him to the brink of resignation, and on the evening of the 20th Nottingham informed Queen Anne that he could no longer serve in the Cabinet. Cotton's letter thanked Nottingham for his 'many favours and particular civilities . . . which could have no foundation but in your own innate principle of virtue and integrity, and an unshaken honesty in all your actions as a minister of state, to the Church and to the crown', and finished by expressing the 'wish' that Nottingham 'continue in your present station for the public good'. Whether Cotton was acting on his own initiative, prompted by an affinity with the Tory Nottingham, in urging him to continue in office, or whether he was pressed by a more senior government official to lobby Nottingham to remain in office, is unclear. What became clear later in the year is that Cotton did not share the frustration felt by Nottingham and other High Tories at the failures in Queen Anne's first Parliament of the occasional conformity bills, as in the autumn of 1704 Harley detailed Cotton to lobby his son-in-law Samuel Trefusis* on the forthcoming division on the Tack. Cotton remained in his place until August 1708 when he resigned in favour of Godolphin's nephew John Evelyn II*, on the understanding that he receive £500 p.a. for the remainder of his life out of Evelyn's salary. Cotton's pension from the Post Office ended following the 1711 Post Office Act, and in 1712 he felt obliged to call upon his relationship with Harley, now Earl of Oxford, to request its renewal. Cotton died on 17 Sept. 1717, leaving his daughter as his heir.[14]

[1] F. A. Blaydes, *Genealogia Bedfordensis* 110; *London Mar. Lic.* ed. Foster, 337; *Le Neve's Knights* (Harl. Soc. viii), 171; *Top and Gen.* iii. 40. [2] C. H. Cooper, *Annals of Cambridge*, iii. 582. [3] *Cal. Treas. Bks.* ix. 1037; xxii. 345. [4] *CJ*, xii. 508. [5] *VCH Cambs.* v. 89–90, 107–8; A. Browning, *Danby*, i. 486; ii. 160. [6] Grey, x. 10, 32. [7] H. Horwitz, *Parl. and Pol. Wm. III*, 66; *CSP Dom.* 1690–1, p. 283; H. Robinson, *British Post Office*, 79–80; *EHR*, xci. 41–43. [8] Grey, 162, 226; *Luttrell Diary*, 10, 14–15, 24, 32, 51, 66, 82, 105–6, 125, 137, 144, 159, 177–8, 187, 193, 200. [9] *Luttrell Diary*, 215, 217, 227, 229, 247, 265, 290, 295, 312, 395, 406, 421–2, 447; Grey, 294. [10] Grey, 353, 382. [11] Devonshire mss at Chatsworth House, Edward Russell* to Lady Russell, 12 Oct. 1695; *HMC Buccleuch*, ii. 246; Horwitz, 165; Centre Kentish Stud. Stanhope mss U1590/059/5, Robert Yard* to Alexander Stanhope, 11 Feb. 1695–6; Add. 17677 QQ, f. 500; *Vernon–Shrewsbury Letters*, i. 376. [12] *HMC Astley*, 93, 95; Add. 42586, ff. 184, 221, 233; *Cal. Treas. Pprs.* 1557–1696, pp. 441–2; *Cal. Treas. Bks.* x. 1376. [13] *DNB* (Sir John Cotton, 3rd Bt.); Add. 70270, Cotton to Harley, 8 May 1701; 61363, ff. 38, 40; 28889, f. 20. [14] W. Yorks. Archs. (Leeds), Temple Newsam mss TN/C9/241, Christopher Stockdale* to 3rd Visct. Irwin [S] (Arthur Ingram*), 28 Apr. 1702; Add. 29589, f. 414; H. Horwitz, *Revolution Politicks*, 197–8; *Bull. IHR*, xxxiv. 96; *Cal. Treas. Bks.* xxii. 345; Boyer, *Anne Annals*, vii. 348; BL, Evelyn mss, Anne to John Evelyn II, 13 Sept. 1708; *Cal. Treas. Pprs.* 1708–14, pp. 335, 363; Boyer, *Pol. State*, xiv. 303; PCC 27 Tenison.

E. C./R. D. H.

COTTON, Rowland (1674–1753), of Etwall, Derbys. and Bellaport, Salop.

NEWCASTLE-UNDER-LYME 28 Nov. 1699–27 Feb. 1706
1708–1 Feb. 1709
1710–2 June 1715

bap. 8 Dec. 1674, 1st s. of Ralph Cotton of Bellaport by Abigail, da. of James Abney of Willesley, Leics., and sis. of Sir Edward* and Sir Thomas Abney*. *educ.* Wadham, Oxf. 1691. *m.* 27 May 1695, Mary (*d.* 1761), da. and coh. of Sir Samuel Sleigh of Etwall, 2s. (1 *d.v.p.*) 3da. *suc.* fa. 1693.[1]

Burgess, Newcastle-under-Lyme 1695, capital burgess 1696–1707, mayor 1697–8; sheriff, Salop 1697–8; steward of manor of Newcastle 1702–6.[2]

Member SPCK, SPG.

Cotton inherited estates in Shropshire and supplemented them by the acquisition of Etwall, Derbyshire through marriage. His grandfather, William Cotton, had a considerable interest in Newcastle-under-Lyme, having in 1692 endowed the local school with sufficient funds to be granted the nomination of the schoolmaster in three out of every four vacancies. This supplemented the legacy left by William Cotton's own uncle, Sir Rowland Cotton†, Member for Newcastle under both James I and Charles I and mayor in 1614. It seems likely that the Member's father also resided in Newcastle while waiting to inherit Bellaport.[3]

Cotton's return in a closely fought by-election in 1699 was interpreted as a snub to the Court, not least because his opponent, John Lawton*, was the brother-in-law of Charles Montagu*. The belief that Cotton inclined towards the Country party is given further credence by the support he offered to Thomas Coke*, a noted critic of the Court, during both elections for Derbyshire in 1701. On each occasion his engagement of freeholders and friends in Etwall was not without danger to his own position, for one of his opponents was Lord Roos (John Manners*), brother-in-law of Sir John Leveson Gower, 5th Bt.*, 'who principally supports Mr Cotton's interest at Newcastle'. However, these fears proved unfounded, and he was returned unopposed at each election in 1701. His contribution to events inside the House appears to have been negligible at this time. He maintained interests outside politics, including membership of both the SPCK and SPG as well as the pursuit of antiquarian research in the Cotton library. Despite parliamentary inactivity, his views were well enough known for Robert Harley* to class him as a Tory in an analysis of the House in December 1701 and his name also appeared on a 'white list' of Members who had voted on 26 Feb. 1702 for the motion vindicating the Commons' proceedings over the impeachment of William III's Whig ministers.[4]

Re-elected in 1702, Cotton seems to have been inactive in the first session of the Parliament. On 1 Feb. 1704, he acted as a teller in a division over the wording of an address to the Queen thanking her for communicating to the House papers on the Scotch Plot: he favoured describing their contents as 'relating to' treasonable correspondence with the courts of France and St. Germain rather than the stronger phrase 'wherein are contained', proposed by the Whigs. In March Nottingham (Daniel Finch†) considered him a likely supporter of the government's actions in relation to the conspiracy. He was forecast in October as a probable supporter of the Tack, but did not vote for it on 28 Nov. The reason for this apparent change of mind is unclear, and his name does not appear on Harley's lobbying list; perhaps Leveson Gower's (now Lord Gower) place in the ministry may have influenced his attitude. On 14 Dec. Cotton received leave to go into the country to recover his health.

At the general election of 1705 Cotton was returned with Sir Thomas Bellot, 3rd Bt., after the two men had given assurances of 'their firm adhesion to the Church in this day of danger'. Despite his failure to vote for the Tack, he was described as a 'Churchman' in an analysis of the new Parliament and confirmed his commitment to the Tories by voting against the Court candidate for Speaker on 25 Oct. 1705. However, his contribution to this Parliament was cut short when both he and his partner were unseated on petition on 27 Feb. 1706. Despite being discharged as a capital burgess in 1707, he regained his seat in the 1708 election, a result which the Earl of Sunderland (Charles, Lord Spencer*) accounted a 'loss' for the Whigs. However, Cotton was unseated again on 1 Feb. 1709.[5]

In the more auspicious circumstances of 1710 Cotton was returned with William Burslem*. Perhaps more revealing of his political attitudes was his support for Coke in Derbyshire when the latter was threatened by two Tories critical of Coke's attitude towards Dr Sacheverell. Cotton was not disposed to join their cabal, although he eventually suggested that Coke desist rather than suffer a defeat at the polls. Although this conduct may reveal an affinity with 'moderate' men, Cotton was definitely a Tory, having been reported by Thomas Jervoise* to be 'mightily pleased that the Duchess of Marlborough is out of favour'. His political stance was confirmed by the appearance of his name among the Tories on the 'Hanover list', and by his being listed as one of the 'worthy patriots' who had helped to detect the mismanagements of the previous administration during the 1710–11 session. Although he is difficult to identify in the Journals between 1708 and January 1713, owing to the presence in the House of John Hynde Cotton*, he was involved in one piece of legislation in the 1711–12 session. On 3 Apr. 1712 Cotton was deputed by the SPCK to remind (Sir) Thomas Hanmer II* (4th Bt.) of his promise to assist a measure for the more easy recovery of small legacies to pious uses that had been misapplied. On the 16th 'Mr Cotton' was one of three Members ordered to prepare a bill for these and similar purposes, and on 14 May 'Mr Rowland Cotton' duly presented the bill to the Commons afterwards managing it through the House. However, the bill fell in the Lords. In February 1713 Cotton was desired by the SPCK to recommend a similar bill to the bishops in the hope that such legislation might be introduced in the Lords.[6]

Cotton was re-elected in 1713, and was again approached by the SPCK to offer advice on the measures necessary to revive the pious uses bill which had been lost in the 1711–12 session. He was classed as a Tory on the Worsley list and on two comparative analyses of the 1713 and 1715 Parliaments. Although returned again at the 1715 general election he was unseated on petition on 2 June and never stood again. Very little is known about his subsequent life but he appears to have prospered as his will notes several land purchases in Shropshire. Cotton died on 26 Apr. 1753, being buried in the family vault at Norton-in-Hales, Shropshire.[7]

[1] IGI, Staffs., Derbys.; J. P. Yeatman, *Feudal Hist. Derbys.* v. 52–53, 65; W. Woolley, *Hist. Derbys.* (Derbys. Rec. Soc. vi), 105; Add. 6695, f. 283; NRA Rep. 10882 (Cotton of Etwall), citing 286/M/F/13. [2] R. W. Bridgett, 'Hist. of Newcastle-under-Lyme, 1661–1760' (Keele Univ. MA thesis, 1982), 174; T. Pape, *Educational Endowments of Newcastle-under-Lyme*, 33; idem, *Newcastle-under-Lyme from Restoration to 1760*, p. 31; Somerville, *Duchy of Lancaster Official Lists*, 168. [3] Woolley, 105; *VCH Staffs.*

vi. 161. [4]Add. 70019, f. 143; BL, Lothian mss, Cotton to Coke, 2 Dec. 1700, 14 Nov. 1701, Ellis Cunliff to same, 21 Dec. 1700; Harl. 3778, f. 96; *CSP Dom.* 1700–2, p. 358. [5]Dyer's newsletter 15 May 1705 (Speck trans.). [6]*HMC Cowper*, iii. 87, 90–91, 93, 97; Bodl. mss Locke C38, f. 7; SPCK Archs. minute bk. 5 (1709–12), p. 270; 6 (1712–15), p. 62. [7]SPCK Archs. minute bk. 6, p. 148; PCC 264 Searle; *Gent. Mag.* 1753, p. 248.

S. N. H.

COULSON, Thomas (1645–1713), of Tower Royal, London.

TOTNES 14 Dec. 1692–1695, 1698–1708
1710–2 June 1713

bap. 1 Oct. 1645, o. s. of William Coulson of London and Greenwich, Kent, by Ann, da. of Thomas Rhode of London, citizen and draper. *unm.* ?1da. illegit. by Jane Radcliffe. *suc.* fa. 1664.[1]

Cttee. Old E.I. Co. 1697–8, 1702–9, manager, united trade 1702–4, 1705–8, dir. united co. 1709–13.[2]

Commr. taking subscriptions to land bank 1696; Greenwich Hosp. 1704.[3]

Coulson's grandfather, a yeoman or possibly a minor gentleman, had been in possession of property at Ayton Magna, Yorkshire and South Mimms, Middlesex, while his father appears to have operated as a small-scale businessman in the capital. Coulson followed a more ambitious course and his involvement in the East India trade made him wealthy, though he did not rank among the richest of the City elite. By the early 1690s he was a prominent figure in the City and known for his Tory politics. Indeed, his standing was such as to warrant his nomination in July 1690 as a colonel in the remodelled City militia, but he declined to serve. Having aligned himself with the interloping faction in the East India trade, he became 'treasurer' in October 1691 of a standing committee, which included his close friend Thomas Pitt I*, whose concern was to re-establish the East India trade 'upon a new national joint-stock clear of all encumbrances'. It is from this point that his particular friendship can be charted with one of the foremost parliamentary advocates for the establishment of a new company, Sir Edward Seymour, 4th Bt., and their connexion was to prove a lasting one politically. As one commentator was to observe years later: 'Tom Coulson never had any friendship with anybody but Sir Edward Seymour.' His business activities at this time also extended to the advance of a number of short-term loans to the government, with the amounts outstanding totalling almost £30,000 in July 1692.[4]

In November 1692 Seymour arranged Coulson's election for the vacant seat at Totnes, less than two miles from Seymour's country seat at Berry Pomeroy.

He informed the mayor on the 22nd that Coulson was 'a considerable merchant of this city who is qualified with very good abilities and integrity' whom he was certain would 'not only prove a good patriot to his country, but a benefactor to your town'. Seymour's brother Henry Portman, the other Member for Totnes, also commended him as being 'very much for the Church of England' and would 'always own it as a great obligation . . . to be joined with one that is so deserving'. As parliamentary discussion on the future of the East India Company began to warm up, Seymour had good reason to desire Coulson's election to Parliament. Coulson had been appointed by the interlopers on 18 Nov. to a three-man delegation to meet with the Company's governor, Sir Thomas Cooke*, in order 'to debate the matters in contest before Sir Edward Seymour', though nothing productive was seen to emerge. Once elected, however, Coulson failed to answer any expectation that he might act as a spokesman for the interloping syndicate and there is no record of his ever having spoken in the House on this or any other subject. In March 1695 Coulson's name featured in the parliamentary investigations into the underhand dealings of the East India Company. It emerged that soon after entering Parliament he had been offered £10,000 from Sir Basil Firebrace*, one of the principal East India directors, to 'come over' to the Company, but had turned it down. Of great potential damage, however, was the revelation that he was the probable beneficiary of a transaction involving the sale of a cargo of saltpetre, worth £2,000 to the Company, for the vastly inflated price of £12,000. It was widely thought that Seymour had received a large share in the profits of the deal, having, as the inquiry found, deserted his former friends the interlopers at about this time, and that the saltpetre transaction had been contrived to facilitate the Company's payment to Seymour of a large cash inducement. Though Coulson obeyed the Commons' instruction to provide copies of the relevant contract documents, nothing could be proved against him. During the course of the session the Treasury secretary Henry Guy* had included him on a list of 'friends', probably in connexion with the threatened attack on Guy himself, although if later assessments of Coulson's behaviour are any indication, he could not necessarily be relied upon to support the Court.[5]

Seymour's need for the Totnes seat in the 1695 election in the wake of his difficulties at Exeter gave Coulson little option but to stand down. He was allowed to resume the seat in 1698, however, when he was classed as a supporter of the Country party, and early in the opening session was forecast as likely to oppose the Court over the question of a standing army. By this time Coulson had thrown in his lot with the East India Company and was now a member of its directorial board with a shareholding which stood at £4,000 in 1703–4. His continuing close association with Seymour is clearly stated in a list analysing the House in terms of 'interests' and 'connexions', produced sometime between January and May 1700. He helped to pave the way for his and Francis Gwyn's election at Totnes in January 1701 by promising financial assistance to the corporation for repairing the weir from which the town's mills were powered and to provide an organ for the local church. Seymour involved him in his efforts to preconcert measures for the forthcoming session. During proceedings on the question of war or peace, Coulson's opposition to renewing hostilities with France led to his being blacklisted along with Seymour and other Tory allies. In February, however, he was listed as likely to support the Court in agreeing with the committee of supply's resolution to continue the 'Great Mortgage'. A complaint against Coulson and Seymour for having used threats and bribes at the recent election at Totnes, originally referred to the elections committee, was dismissed by the House on 19 May, though not before Members had been apprised of the contents of letters to the corporation from both Seymour and Coulson, the production of which at this juncture was clearly intended to incriminate. Coulson's letter, which he acknowledged as authentic, 'talked of a dissolution of the Parliament and of persuading them to be reconciled to Sir Edward Seymour and persuading them to bring in Frank Gwyn and promising them to do the town a kindness in relation to the buing [sic] mills that did incommode them'. It was Seymour, however, the instigator of earlier inquiries into electoral corruption, rather than Coulson, who was the main object of the attack. Accordingly, the House ordered the recipient of this correspondence into custody for endeavouring to 'promote reflections'. Despite this unpleasantness, Coulson fulfilled his word to his corporation regarding the weir and subscribed £300 towards its repair.[6]

In December 1701 Coulson was classified by Robert Harley* as a Tory. Succumbing to serious illness in January 1702, he was at one point thought to be close to death. On 26 Feb. he voted for the resolution vindicating the Commons' proceedings in the impeachments of the former Whig ministers, and on 13 Feb. 1703 against agreeing with the Lords' amendments to the bill for enlarging the time for taking the Abjuration. In mid-March 1704 he featured in a list of Lord Nottingham's (Daniel Finch†) supporters, probably in connexion with proceedings concerning the Scotch Plot. On 28 Nov. 1704 he fulfilled earlier expectations that he would vote for the Tack, was noted as 'True Church' in a list drawn up in the aftermath of the 1705 election, and voted against the Court candidate for the speakership on 25 Oct. During the years 1706–8 he played an active part in the lengthy negotiations overseen by Lord Treasurer Godolphin (Sidney†) to secure the merger of the Old and New East India companies and in 1709 became a director of the united company.[7]

Coulson was classed as a Tory in a list of early 1708, but Seymour's death in February weakened his position at Totnes and he failed to retain the seat at the May election. A very different situation obtained in the run-up to the 1710 election, however, when it was reported that he and Gwyn had placed Seymour's son (Sir Edward, 5th Bt.*) in a difficult position, having since the previous contest 'contrived an interest' of their own. Strangely, Coulson's strong Tory credentials eluded the compiler of the 'Hanover list' of the new Parliament and he was marked 'doubtful'. However, his inclusion in a list of 'worthy patriots' who took part during the 1710–11 session in exposing the mismanagements of the previous administration confirms there had been no change in his political colouring. Indeed, in the elections to the board of the East India Company in April 1711 his name was canvassed on a list 'favoured by the Tories'. Coulson died 'after one day's sickness' at his house at Tower Royal on 2 June 1713. His funeral was attended by several peers and he was buried at St. Michael Royal in the vault of the Fellowes family, the merchant clan into which his sister had married. In his will he left £500 and his two houses in Friday Street to his 'entirely beloved friend' Jane Radcliffe, perhaps a relation of his crony Dr John Radcliffe*, and £10,000 and a house in Kensington to her 'reputed daughter', presumably by himself. He was stated by an obituarist to have sired several illegitimate children to whom he had given 'good portions'. The rest of his property devolved upon his nephew John Fellowes, a London merchant to whom he also left £10,000.[8]

[1] IGI, London; info. from Dr P. L. Gauci; Hutchins, *Dorset*, ii. 565; PCC 125 Leeds. [2] Add. 38871, ff. 9–17. [3] *Daily Courant*, 8 Aug. 1704; *CJ*, xii. 509. [4] Info. from Dr Gauci; *CSP Dom.* 1690–1, p. 70; Luttrell, *Brief Relation*, ii. 77; Bodl. Rawl. C.449; Add. 22851, ff. 105, 107, 145; 22852, ff. 4, 6; *Wentworth Pprs.* 97; *Cal. Treas. Bks.* ix. 1743. [5] *HMC 3rd Rep.* 347, 349; Rawl. C.449; *Debates and Procs.* 1694–5, p. 9; *EHR*, lxxi. 227; *HMC Lords*, n.s. i. 556; *Cocks Diary*, 51–52. [6] Rawl. A.303, f. 57; *Cocks Diary*, 135–6; Add. 30000 E, ff. 202–3; 17677 WW, f. 265; NLW, Sir Humphrey Mackworth's* diary ms 14362E, p. 130 [3 Jan. 1701]; *Trans. Devon Assoc.* xxxii.

443. [7]Add. 22851, f. 71; *Cal. Treas. Bks.* xxi. 5; xxi. 44; xxii. 41–42. [8]C 115/110/8929; Boyer, *Pol. State*, i. 263–4; info. from Dr Gauci; *Top. and Gen.* iii. 508; PCC 125 Leeds.

A. A. H.

COURTENAY, Francis (1652–99), of Powderham Castle, Devon.

DEVON 1689–1 Apr. 1699

bap. 27 Feb. 1652, 2nd s. of Sir William Courtenay, 1st Bt.[†], of Powderham Castle by Margaret (*d.* 1694), da. of Sir William Waller[†] of Osterley Park, Mdx.; bro. of George* and Richard Courtenay[†]. *m.* settlement 26 Nov. 1670 (with £4,000), Mary, da. of William Boevey, merchant, of Little Chelsea, Mdx. and Flaxley Abbey, Glos., 3s. (2 *d.v.p.*) 9da.[1]

Courtenay, who was reported to have joined the Prince of Orange after the landing in 1688, took over the representation of Devon when his father's health failed. He was classed as a Tory by Lord Carmarthen (Sir Thomas Osborne[†]) shortly after being re-elected in March 1690, and in another of Carmarthen's lists at the end of the year as a supporter of the Court. A list compiled by Robert Harley* in around April 1691 classified him as a Country party supporter. An inactive Member, he was granted leave of absence for six weeks on 23 Jan. 1692, and was accorded a further grant on 13 Jan. 1694 on the death of his mother. He appears to have displayed consistent support for the opposition, as evident from his recorded behaviour in 1696, being forecast in January as a likely opponent of the Court over the proposed council of trade, and, unlike his father, refusing the Association the following month. During March he voted against the government on the question of fixing the price of guineas at 22*s.*, and on 25 Nov. voted against the attainder of Sir John Fenwick[†]. He was again granted leave of the House on 6 Mar. 1697. In the aftermath of the election in 1698 he was classed as a Country supporter in a list comparing the old and new Parliaments and was forecast as likely to oppose the government on the standing army question. He predeceased his father in London on 1 Apr. 1699, and was buried at Chelsea, the press reporting that he was 'much lamented, he being a gentleman worthy of a good character'.[2]

[1]Vivian, *Vis. Devon*, 248–9; A. W. Cawley-Boevey, *Mems. Boevey Fam.* 19, 156. [2]Bodl. Fleming newsletter 3334; *Cal. Treas. Bks.* ix. 1767; Luttrell, *Brief Relation*, iv. 500; *Post Boy*, 1–4 Apr. 1699.

E. C.

COURTENAY, George (1666–1725), of Ford, Devon.

EAST LOOE 4 Feb.–2 July 1702
TOTNES 1708–1710
NEWPORT 1710–1713

bap. 13 May 1666, 7th but 4th surv. s. of Sir William Courtenay, 1st Bt.[†]; bro. of Francis* and Richard Courtenay[†]. *educ.* M. Temple 1684. *unm.*[1]
Ensign, 1 Ft. Gds. 1689; commr. victualling 1711–14. V.-adm. Devon and Exeter 1689–*d.*[2]

Courtenay joined the Prince of Orange at Exeter in November 1688, and was rewarded 'in consideration of Sir William Courtenay's deserts' with appointment as vice-admiral of Devon and Exeter in May 1689. In this capacity he raised 1,300 men annually in the period 1692–6, receiving £650 on each occasion. On his mother's death in January 1694 he inherited Ford, which had belonged to his maternal great-grandfather Sir Richard Reynell. A Tory, Courtenay was returned for East Looe at a by-election in 1702, presumably by his kinsman Bishop Trelawny. He voted on 26 Feb. for the resolution vindicating the Commons over the impeachment proceedings against the King's Whig ministers in the previous session. Representing Totnes in the 1708 Parliament, he told on 28 Feb. 1709 in favour of a clause to be added to the general naturalization bill, to retain the provisions of a Jacobean statute requiring that all persons naturalized should take the sacrament and oaths of allegiance and supremacy. In 1710 he voted against the impeachment of Dr Sacheverell. Although defeated at Ashburton in the general election of that year, Courtenay was brought in for Newport by Sir Nicholas Morice, 2nd Bt.* Marked as a Tory in the 'Hanover list', he was one of the 'worthy patriots' who detected the mismanagements of the previous administration. A member of the October Club, he was given a place in the victualling office in 1711, but did not stand in 1713. He was removed from office on the accession of George I, and had died before May 1725, when his will was proved.[3]

[1]Vivian, *Vis. Devon*, 248. [2]SP 44/165/285. [3]*HMC 7th Rep.* 416; *CSP Dom.* 1689–90, p. 122; *Cal. Treas. Bks.* ix. 1553; x. 46, 901, 1290; *Brit. Mercury*, 7–9 Nov. 1711; PCC 108 Romney.

E. C.

COURTENAY, William (1676–1735), of Powderham Castle, Devon.

DEVON 1701 (Feb.)–1710, 22 July 1712–6 Oct. 1735

b. 11 Mar. 1676, 1st s. of Francis Courtenay*. *educ.* Exeter, Oxf. 1695. *m.* 13 July 1704, Lady Anne, da. of

James Bertie, 1st Earl of Abingdon, and sis. of Hon. Henry II*, Hon. James* and Hon. Robert Bertie*, and Montagu Venables-Bertie*, Ld. Norreys, 5s. 8da. *suc.* fa. 1699, gdfa. as 2nd Bt. 1 Aug. 1702.[1]

Ld. lt. Devon 1714–16.

Courtenay's grandfather, Sir William Courtenay, 1st Bt.*, who had lost the lordship of the manor of Honiton after the remodelling of the charter in 1684, was given it back by King William in 1697 in a somewhat belated acknowledgment of his services at the Revolution. In an effort to recover the family's electoral interest in the borough, Courtenay stood for one of its parliamentary seats in February 1701, but was defeated. Later in the month, he was able to take the grander prize of a county seat without encountering opposition. He was not deterred, however, from petitioning afterwards against the maltreatment he felt he had suffered at Honiton, but his case was not successful. He was listed with those who in February 1701 were thought likely to support the Court in agreeing with the committee of supply's resolution to continue the 'Great Mortgage', and later was blacklisted as having opposed preparations for war. In Robert Harley's* list of December 1701 he figured as a Tory, and he voted on 26 Feb. 1702 in favour of the resolution vindicating the Commons' proceedings on the impeachments of William III's Whig ministers. He succeeded to his father's baronetcy on 4 Aug. 1702, just three days after having secured his return at the general election of that year. He acted as a teller twice in the 1703–4 session: on 21 Feb. 1704, in favour of committing the bill to encourage manufacturing in England and settle the poor to work, and on 24 Mar., in support of a motion that the commissioners of accounts present their accounts forthwith. In mid-March 1704 he was noted as a probable supporter of Lord Nottingham (Daniel Finch†) in connexion with the attack anticipated over his handling of the Scotch Plot. A moderate in his Toryism, Courtenay voted against the Tack (or was absent) on 28 Nov., for which he was classed as 'Low Church' in a list of the next Parliament. However, he voted against the Court candidate in the division on the Speaker, 25 Oct. 1705. On 8 Feb. 1707 he was given leave of absence. In a debate on 21 Jan. 1708, on restoring the various regiments to their full complement, Courtenay was reported to have 'made a notable speech, in relation to the unfair methods by which several young officers, both by sea and land, were advanced, to the prejudice of others of longer standing, and more experience'. He was again granted leave of absence on 24 Mar. 1708. An analysis of the post-Union House compiled at this time duly noted him as a Tory, and early in 1710, despite his previously moderate tendencies, he voted against the impeachment of Dr Sacheverell.[2]

At the general election of 1710, Courtenay agreed to stand down as knight of the shire in favour of (Sir) William Pole* (4th Bt.). However, in July 1712 when Pole sought re-election after appointment to office in 1712, Courtenay stood against him by popular demand of the county's 'regulating' gentry and was chosen in his place. 'Misrepresentations' against him by Pole and his supporters forced Courtenay to defend his conduct to Lord Treasurer Oxford (Harley) and to deny strongly that he himself had initiated any prior canvassing. Now back in Parliament, he was a member of his brother-in-law Lord Abingdon's (Montagu Venables-Bertie) personal 'clan' and as such attached himself to the Hanoverian wing of the Tory party, voting against the French commerce bill on 18 June 1713. Unsuccessful at Honiton in 1713, but returned for the county, he remained a 'Hanoverian Tory', being classed in the Worsley list as a Tory who often voted with the Whigs, and even as a 'whimsical' Whig in another list of this Parliament. After the Hanoverian succession he retained the county seat until his death on 6 Oct. 1735.[3]

[1] Vivian, *Vis. Devon*, 247–9; Luttrell, *Brief Relation*, v. 445. [2] *CSP Dom.* 1697, pp. 115–16; Boyer, *Anne Annals*, vi. 312. [3] G. Holmes, *Pol. in Age of Anne*, 282.

E. C./A. A. H.

COURTHOPE, John (1673–99), of Danny Park, Suss.

BRAMBER   24 Feb.–Mar. 1699

bap. 27 Nov. 1673, 1st s. of Peter Courthope (*d.* 1725) of Danny Park by Philadelphia, da. of Sir John Stapley, 1st Bt., of Patcham, Suss. *educ.* Lewes sch.; Trinity Coll. Camb. 1691. *unm.*

Courthope's family had been settled in Sussex since the mid-17th century, his great-grandfather having bought Danny Park, which became their principal seat. Returned at a by-election for Bramber on 24 Feb. 1699, Courthope died a few days later, *v.p.*, and was buried on 12 Mar. 1699 at Hurstpierpoint, Sussex.[1]

[1] Comber, *Suss. Genealogies (Lewes)*, 85; *Danny Archs.* ed. J. A. Woolridge, xiv–xv; Luttrell, *Brief Relation*, iv. 494.

P. W.

COURTNEY, Humphrey (1641–96), of Tremeer, Cornw.

MITCHELL   17 Dec. 1689–1690
                12 Nov. 1690–1695
                14 Dec. 1695–Mar. 1696

bap. 4 Aug. 1641, o. s. of Richard Courtney of Tremeer by Philippa, da. and coh. of Humphrey Prouze of Chagford, Devon. *educ.* Balliol, Oxf. matric. 1659; I. Temple 1659, called 1677. *m.* 27 Dec. 1666, Alice (d.1684), da. of Sir Peter Courtney† of Trethurfe, Cornw. and h. to her bro. William Courtney of Trethurfe, 2s. 9da. (4 *d.v.p.*). *suc.* fa. 1660.[1]

Commr. for recusants, Cornw. 1675; freeman, Bodmin 1685–Sept. 1688; stannator, Blackmore 1686.[2]

Courtney had inherited in 1660 substantial estates in Cornwall and Devon, worth £1,200 p.a., but financial difficulties forced him to sell the manor of Tregear in 1690, and the remainder of the estate was mortgaged for £10,000. These debts may have been occasioned, at least in part, by the cost of repeated contested elections at Mitchell. He had been returned to the Convention at a by-election for this borough, and though defeated at the 1690 election his petition was successful and on 12 Nov. the Mitchell return was amended in his favour. The following month he was listed by the Marquess of Carmarthen (Sir Thomas Osborne†) as a probable supporter in the event of an attack upon Carmarthen's ministerial position. In April 1691 Robert Harley* classed Courtney as a Country supporter. At the 1695 election Courtney was involved in a double return, but on 14 Dec. the Commons resolved that the return naming him was valid. In the new year he was forecast as likely to oppose the Court in the divisions of 31 Jan. upon the proposed council of trade, but the following month he signed the Association promptly. He died shortly afterwards, and was buried at the Temple Church on 25 Mar.

[1] Vivian, *Vis. Cornw.* 115; Polsue, *Complete Paroch. Hist. Cornw.* iii. 11, 19. [2] *Cal. Treas. Bks.* iv. 695; J. Wallis, *Bodmin Reg.* 169; PC 2/72, p. 235; J. Tregoning, *Laws of Stannaries*, 57.

E. C.

COURTNEY, William (1678–1716), of Tremeer and Trethurfe, Cornw.

MITCHELL   1701 (Dec.)–1702

bap. 24 Nov. 1678, 2nd but 1st surv. s. of Humphrey Courtney*. *educ.* I. Temple 1695. *m.* 19 June 1704, Susannah (d. 1716), da. of John Kelland† of Painsford, Devon, wid. of Moses Gould of Hayes, Mdx., sis. of Charles Kelland†, coh. of nephew John Kelland (d. 1712), 3s. 1da. *suc.* fa. 1696.[1]

Stannator, Foymore 1703.[2]

Courtney succeeded his father to heavily indebted estates. On 2 Dec. 1696 he petitioned the Commons, stating that unless these debts were satisfied his estate would 'be swallowed up with interest' and requesting a bill to allow his trustees to sell enough land to satisfy his father's debts. A committee was appointed to prepare such a measure, and though the bill was committed on 14 Jan. 1697 it was never reported, the complications raised by three petitions to the House by Courtney's creditors (30 Dec. 1696, 18 and 26 Jan. 1697) presumably causing the bill's failure. In May 1700 the £10,000 mortgage upon Courtney's estates was transferred to John Williams* and Hugh Boscawen I*, but despite his continuing financial problems Courtney was returned for Mitchell to the second 1701 Parliament. Lord Spencer (Charles*) classed his election as a 'loss' and Robert Harley* listed him with the Tories. Both assessments were borne out when Courtney voted in favour of the motion of 26 Feb. 1702 vindicating the Commons' proceedings in the previous Parliament against the Whig lords. Nothing more is known of his activity in the Commons, and, having lost the support of Sir Richard Vyvyan, 3rd Bt.*, he was defeated at Mitchell at the 1702 election. His petition against this return was never reported from committee. The remainder of Courtney's involvement with Parliament concerned his financial affairs. On 14 Nov. 1704 the Commons received a petition requesting an estate bill to allow the executors of the estate of his wife's first husband to pay the £5,000 portion due to her. A second petition was entered from a man who described Courtney's marriage as 'pretended', alleging that the widow had contracted a marriage to him prior to her arrangement with Courtney and that a case concerning this matter was pending in the court of Arches. However, the bill received the Royal Assent in January 1705. In the following session a bill was introduced to allow all Courtney's estates in Cornwall and Devon to be vested in trustees and sold for the payment of debt. It passed in March 1706, and after the consequent sales Tremeer was one of the few manors to remain in Courtney's possession. However, in 1712 his fortunes were enhanced by his wife's inheritance of a fourth part of her family's Devon estates. Courtney died in 1716, his will being proved on 8 Apr. He was succeeded by his elder son William, and his wife married a third time, to Arthur Champernowne†. In

1719 Courtney's younger son Kelland† succeeded to the family estates.³

¹Vivian, *Vis. Cornw.* 115; Polsue, *Complete Paroch. Hist. Cornw.* iii. 19; Vivian, *Vis. Devon*, 508–9. ²J. Tregoning, *Laws of Stannaries*, 118. ³*HMC Lords*, n.s. vi. 248, 391–2; Vivian, *Vis. Devon*, 164, 422, 508–9.

E. C.

COVENTRY, William (c.1676–1751), of London.

BRIDPORT 1708–27 Oct. 1719

b. c.1676, 1st surv. s. of Walter Coventry, Haberdasher and merchant, of St. Peter-le-Poer, London, common councilman of London 1688–92, by Anne, da. of Humphrey Holcombe, merchant, of St. Andrew's Holborn, Mdx. *educ.* Pembroke, Camb. matric. 13 Apr. 1693, aged 16. *m.* 1720, Elizabeth, da. of John Allen of Westminster, 3s. *suc.* fa. 1692; cos. as 5th Earl of Coventry 27 Oct. 1719.

Keeper, bailiwick of Frisham, New Forest by 1717–?d.; ld. lt. Worcs. 1720–d.; high steward, Bridport 1727–d.¹

Jt. clerk comptroller of green cloth 1717–19; PC 22 Mar. 1720.

Coventry's grandfather, a younger brother of Thomas, 1st Lord Coventry, became a merchant in London. His son, the Member's father, followed him into trade, acquiring a personal fortune of some £9,000 and serving as common councilman of the City from 1688 until his death in 1692. Although living in London himself, Coventry broke the family's connexion with commerce. He had expectations from his cousin, the 5th Lord Coventry (Thomas Coventry†), who in 1697 was created Earl of Coventry with a special remainder first to his uncle and then to William.²

Returned for Bridport in 1708, Coventry voted for naturalizing the Palatines and for the impeachment of Dr Sacheverell. He was thus classed as a Whig in the 'Hanover list', subsequently voting in favour of the amendment to the South Sea bill on 25 May 1711 and the motion for 'No Peace without Spain' on 7 Dec. He probably voted against the French wines duty bill on 6 May 1713, also voting as a Whig against the French commerce bill on 18 June. In the 1714 session, on 18 Mar. he voted against the expulsion of Richard Steele, and told on the 27th against the Tory, John Gape*, in the St. Albans election case. He was classed as a Whig both in the Worsley list and in another comparative analysis of the two Parliaments. Coventry continued to represent Bridport after 1715 until he succeeded to the peerage. He died on 18 Mar. 1751.

¹*Cal. Treas. Bks.* xxxii. 231; Hutchins, *Dorset*, ii. 8; J. R. Woodhead, *Rulers of London* (London and Mdx. Arch. Soc.), 53. ²Woodhead, 53; *CSP Dom.* 1697, p. 115.

P. W.

COWARD, William I (1634–1705), of Chamberlain Street, Wells, Som. and Totteridge, Herts.

WELLS 1679 (Mar.)–1681 (Mar.)
17 Jan.–6 Feb. 1690, 1695–1705

bap. 19 July 1634, 1st s. of William Coward of Wells, and East Pennard, Som. by Catherine, da. of John Dodington of Som. *educ.* Lyon's Inn; L. Inn 1655, called 1662, bencher 1680, treasurer 1689–91. *m.* (1) by 1666, Bridget (d. 1683), da. of Sir Thomas Hall of Bradford-on-Avon, Wilts., 1s. 1da.; (2) bef. 1692, Lady Philippa, da. of Arthur Annesley†, 1st Earl of Anglesey, wid. of Charles, 3rd Baron Mohun of Okehampton, 1s. *suc.* fa. 1664.¹

Commr. for appeals in excise Oct. 1660–79; serjeant-at-law 1692–d.; commr. for taking subscriptions to land bank 1696.²

Dep. recorder, Wells 1663, recorder by 1670–83, Aug.–Oct. 1688, 1689–d.³

An Exclusionist who afterwards became a Whig 'collaborator' under James II, Coward was defeated at Wells in 1690, despite his strong interest there conferred by his property-holding in the town and his holding the office of recorder. He was, however, successful in 1695 and retained the seat until his death. By this time he had become a Tory, and, as his attitudes in 1696 indicate, he was a regular member of the Country opposition to the government. In January 1696 he was forecast as a probable opponent of the Court over the proposed council of trade, and in March voted against fixing the price of guineas at 22s., but showed no hesitation in his subscription to the Association the previous month. In the next session, on 25 Nov., he voted against the attainder of Sir John Fenwick†. Following the 1698 election, he was listed as a placeman on account of his legal rank as a serjeant-at-law, but also as a supporter of the Country party, and in another list was considered likely to oppose the government on the standing army issue. In February 1701 he was listed as a probable supporter of the Court on the question of agreeing with the committee of supply's resolution to continue the 'Great Mortgage', and on 26 Feb. 1702 voted for the motion vindicating the proceedings of the Commons in the impeachments of William III's ministers. As a lawyer he occasionally undertook the supervision of private legislation, and it was perhaps due to legal commitments that he was at various times granted leave of absence, as on 4 Mar., 30 Dec. 1697, 13 Jan. 1700, 24 Apr. 1701, 3 Jan. and 22 Dec. 1704.

On 28 Nov. 1704 Coward fulfilled an earlier prediction that he would vote in support of the Tack, despite being lobbied on the ministry's behalf by Nathaniel Palmer, one of the knights for Somerset. He died shortly after the dissolution of Parliament, on 8 Apr. 1705, and, in accordance with the terms of his will, was buried in St. Cuthbert's church, Wells, near his first wife. This direction, together with the assertion that his second spouse, Lady Philippa, 'will not permit me to have anything out of her estate though I have paid £1,500 in debts for her before my intermarriage with her', suggests that his second marriage had been unhappy. He further ruled that if his widow attempted to dispute the will the grants to her and her son would be annulled.[4]

[1] A. J. Jewers, *Wells Cathedral*, 132–4. [2] *Cal. Treas. Bks.* i. 75; v. 1263; *CSP Dom.* 1691–2, p. 247; *CJ*, xii. 509. [3] Wells corp. mss, act bk. 1662–5, f. 33; roll of recorders. [4] Jewers, 134; PCC 133 Gee.

P. W./A. A. H.

COWARD, William II (1666–1716), of Chamberlain Street, Wells, Som. and Totteridge, Herts.

WELLS 1708–1710, 30 May–16 June 1716

bap. 16 Apr. 1666, 1st s. of William Coward I*, by 1st w. *educ.* Merchant Taylors' 1676–81; Magdalen, Oxf. 1682; L. Inn 1682. *unm. suc.* fa. 1705.[1]

Coward's father had been a Tory, but he himself was a Whig and in consequence never achieved the same degree of prominence in Wells. He was returned in 1708, his election being reckoned a gain for the Whigs by Lord Sunderland (Charles, Lord Spencer*). Voting in 1709 in favour of the naturalizing bill and the following year for the impeachment of Dr Sacheverell, it was hardly surprising that he was not readopted at the 1710 election. When he did stand again in 1715 he was defeated. Though subsequently awarded the seat on petition at the end of May 1716, he died shortly afterwards on 16 June.

[1] *Vis. Som.* (Harl. Soc. n.s. xi), 75.

P. W.

COWPER, Henry (1668–1707), of Strood Park, Slinfold, Suss.

HORSHAM 1701 (Feb.–Nov.), 1702–22 Mar. 1707

bap. 30 Oct. 1668, s. of Edward Cowper of Slinfold by Martha, da. of Lancelot Johnson of the Inner Temple, and Lambeth, Surr. *educ.* New College, Oxf. 1685; I. Temple 1687. *m.* lic. 20 June 1693, Sarah, da. of James Smith of St. Benet Gracechurch Street, London, 3s. 2da. *suc.* fa. 1678.[1]

The Cowpers of Slinfold were the root of the family from which Sir William*, Spencer* and William* were descended, though the politics of the two branches diverged. The father of this Member had served as a gentleman pensioner to Charles II, and unlike his kinsmen, his political sympathies lay with moderate Toryism. Slinfold was a 'small seat surrounded with woods', which lay only three miles north-west of Horsham and gave Cowper an influence over the borough. This had been enhanced by his service there as an active magistrate at least since the Revolution; but it may have been the failing health of the Whig lord of the manor, the 7th Duke of Norfolk, that gave Cowper the opportunity to stand for election in January 1701. Although the presence of his kinsman William in the House makes positive identification difficult, Cowper was clearly not an active Member in this or subsequent Parliaments. He was blacklisted as having opposed the preparations for war with France, though his name appeared in a published reply which suggested that his zeal in settling the Protestant succession and readiness to waive privileges for prosecution from debt were enough to merit his re-election. Nevertheless, Cowper failed by one vote to be chosen again in the autumn, and petitioned on 3 Jan. 1702 against the return of the Whig, John Wicker*. Although the case was never heard, Cowper seems to have won the friendship of Robert Harley*, since an undated letter to Adam de Cardonnel* referred to a recommendation on behalf of a relative 'given to you in my fight in the House of Commons by Mr Speaker', who had 'promised to speak again in it'. He regained his seat at the election in 1702, when he initially stood with Charles Eversfield*, the pair probably enjoying the support of the Gorings, to whom Cowper was related. He was forecast as a probable supporter of the Tack, but on 28 Nov. either voted against the bill or was absent from the House. Cowper was re-elected in 1705 by the narrowest of margins, and was subsequently listed as 'Low Church' in an analysis of the new Parliament. On 25 Oct. 1705 he voted against the Court candidate as Speaker. He was given leave of absence from the House on 28 Feb. 1707 to recover his health and died on 22 Mar. His will, dated two days earlier, made provision for his children, all of whom were minors. He left marriage portions of £1,800 for each of his daughters, appointing his 'trusty and well beloved' friend Lawrence Alcock* as one of their guardians, and the bulk of the estate was eventually to pass to the eldest son, Edward. Cowper ordered that mourning gloves be given to each of Horsham's burgage-holders and their wives in gratitude 'for their past kindness'. His last request was that 'my kinsman Spencer Cowper Esq. will be pleased to take care that this my last will be performed', an indication that he valued his more prominent relative's legal expertise and trust, even if he did not follow his politics.[2]

[1] D. Elwes and C. Robinson, *Hist. of Castles, Mansions of Western Suss.* 205–7; IGI, Suss.; *Mar. Lic. Vicar-Gen.* (Harl. Soc. xxxi), 261; Comber, *Sussex Gen.* (Horsham), 77. [2] *VCH Herts. Fams.* 133; *Suss. Arch. Colls.* lxix. 136; *Vis. Suss.* (Harl. Soc. liii), 148; W. Albery, *A Millennium of Facts*, 114; *Answer to the Black List* (1701), 4; Albery, *Parl. Hist. Horsham*, 41–45; Add. 61284, ff. 91–92; PCC 137 Poley.

M. J. K.

COWPER, Spencer (1669–1728), of Hertingfordbury Park, Herts.; Lincoln's Inn; and Bridge House, St. Olave's, Southwark.

BERE ALSTON   1 Dec. 1705–1710
TRURO   1715–1727

b. 23 Feb. 1669, 4th but 2nd. surv. s. of Sir William Cowper, 2nd Bt.*; bro. of William Cowper*. *educ.* Westminster (Dr Busby); Christ's, Camb. 1686; M. Temple 1687, called 1693, bencher 1719; L. Inn 1713, bencher 1715, treasurer 1716. *m.* (1) lic. 4 Feb. 1688, Pennington (*d.* 1727), da. of John Goodere, 4s. (1 *d.v.p.*) 1da; (2) 25 July 1728, Theodora (*d.* 1750), wid. of John Stepney, *s.p.*[1]

Clerk of the Bridge House estates, Southwark 1690–?*d.*[2]

Attorney-gen. to Prince of Wales 1714–27; KC 1715; c.j. Chester 1717–27; j.c.p. 1727–*d.*; serjeant-at-law 1727. Keeper L. Inn lib. 1717, dean of chapel 1718; gov. St. Thomas' Hosp. 1719.[3]

Spencer Cowper was advised as a young man to begin each day with a prayer, to 'be humble and obedient' to his tutor, and to 'be courteous of gesture and affable to all men, [for] there is nothing that winneth so much with so little cost'. He was also told to delight in cleanliness, to think before he spoke, and that 'only by a virtuous life and good actions' might he 'become valuable'. However, the first public notice of him came amid scandal and allegations of an indecent and murderous nature. In 1699 a rich Hertford Quaker heiress named Sarah Stout had been found floating face down in a local pond: Cowper had the misfortune to have been the last person with whom she was seen, and he was known to have been involved in her financial dealings. When local doctors concluded that she had not drowned but had been murdered, Cowper was charged with the crime. The accusation nevertheless had political connotations, since her father had 'at all elections promoted the interest of the Cowpers to the utmost of his power; through which a great intimacy was created between the families'; Sarah Stout had fallen in love with the married Cowper, who may have acted as her tutor and who regularly visited the town for the assizes. It was later claimed by Mrs Manley that Cowper was morally weak, and 'never saw a woman he could not have bestowed some of his favours upon', though even she admitted that Sarah Stout was 'the aggressor' in the affair. It emerged during the trial, which became a *cause célèbre*, that she had sent him a love letter in which she proposed cohabitation, and, when he refused, had probably killed herself for unrequited love. Prosecution resulted when the Quakers, unable to accept that one of their sect had turned away from the inner spirit of God, allied with local Tories who allegedly sought revenge for the 'feuds that have arisen at the elections' in the town, in which Cowper's brother and father had taken part. Describing himself at his trial as 'of some fortune in possession ... in a good employment, thriving in my profession, living within my income, [and] never in debt', he defended himself and produced expert medical witnesses to prove that Stout had died from drowning. Sir William Ashurst* and Sir Thomas Lane also gave evidence on his behalf, declaring Cowper to be 'a gentleman of singular humanity and integrity' and 'altogether untainted' character, who performed his job for the corporation well. Charles Cox, MP for Southwark and Cowper's neighbour there, also testified that he was 'a person of integrity and worth, all the neighbours court his company'. At the original inquest Cowper had foolishly denied any knowledge of why Sarah Stout should have committed suicide, perhaps, ironically, in order to avoid scandal, and although he was acquitted of murder the trial destroyed his family's local standing with the Quakers, and with it their electoral influence, despite Cowper's protestation of sympathy for the sect and declaration 'that if he ever changed his religion he said it should be for theirs'. In 1700 an appeal was lodged against his acquittal, but, under suspicious circumstances, the writ was burnt, and after the lapse of legal time-limits it became impossible to proceed with the case. The whole proceeding had stimulated great public interest, including the publication of a number of tracts, one of which was distributed to MPs, and on 13 Mar. 1701 Stout's mother petitioned the Commons for a new writ of appeal. No action was taken, however, before the Commons was prorogued. The affair finally ended on 16 Nov. 1702, when a complaint for deprivation of justice was made to the Commons against the under-sheriff, who was believed to be Cowper's friend, 'but the House thought not fit to do anything thereupon'. The affair may have sent Cowper into a temporary depression, for his brother wrote in September 1701 that Spencer threatened 'to bespeak a vessel to trip beyond seas'.[4]

Cowper's first attempt to enter the Commons may have come at the Totnes election of January 1701. His brother William had initially been proposed by Lord Somers (Sir John*) and the Duke of Bolton (Charles Powlett I*) in opposition to the outgoing Tory Members. William had, however, declined to take the election to a poll, and it may be that following this withdrawal Spencer was suggested as a possible candidate, for a week after the election Bishop Trelawny wrote that he had declined to support Bolton's candidate as 'I look on Cowper as a murderer'. However, the Totnes election of January 1701 was not contested and Spencer did not enter the Commons until December 1705, when he was returned for the seat at Bere Alston vacated by his brother's appointment as lord keeper. As a lawyer, on 10 Jan. 1706 he voiced reservations in the House about the wording of the treason clauses of the regency bill. Warning that it 'may have some ill consequences to [the] people and the constitution', he wanted provisos included to require two witnesses and a tighter formula for prosecution for spoken and written words. Five days later he spoke on the bill's arrangements for summoning Parliaments, but nevertheless concluded 'for the whole bill', and was noted as having supported the Court during February's proceedings upon the 'place clause' of the bill. His legal practice thrived, and in June 1706 it was rumoured that he would be made a Queen's Counsel, but perhaps his brother again barred his promotion, for he had to wait for this honour until after the Hanoverian succession. He was marked as a Whig on two analyses of Parliament in 1708, and on 30 Mar. successfully moved for an address for the accounts of the armed forces to be presented as part of an attempt by the 'Lord Treasurer's Whigs' to bring the troops up to strength, indicating that he followed his brother's political allegiance to Lord Godolphin (Sidney†). That month he and other lawyers looked over the archbishop of Canterbury's copies of cathedral statutes before they were presented to the House of Commons in connexion with the cathedrals bill.[5]

In April 1708 William, now Lord Cowper, wrote requesting Lord Stamford's continuing support for Spencer at Bere Alston, where he was duly re-elected in May at the general election. On 29 Jan. 1709 he was appointed to prepare a bill for improving the Union by unifying the laws for treason, and, following the failure of this bill, told on 30 Mar. for the committal of a similar measure which had been initiated in the Lords. On 5 Apr. he spoke, as Bishop Nicolson said, on the subject in favour of oyer and terminer. During this session he also supported the naturalization of the Palatines. It was the impeachment of Dr Sacheverell that allowed him to display his lawyer's eloquence at its best. Despite his brush with the Hertford Quakers, he evidently retained his sympathy for Dissent, and on 13 Dec. 1709 seconded John Dolben's* motion to take Sacheverell's sermon into consideration as a libel, being duly appointed the following day to draw up the articles of impeachment. On 22 Dec. he told against granting the doctor bail. In March 1710 he was appointed to the committee to manage the ensuing trial, over which his brother, the lord chancellor, presided, and at which he spoke to the second article which accused the doctor of declaring the toleration to be unreasonable and unwarrantable. Defending the Toleration Act as 'a legal Indulgence' he accused Sacheverell of having represented it

> as an open violence ... Mr Cowper was far from saying that sentences ratified in Heaven could be reversed by the power of this world, but he desired to be excused from thinking any of his curses upon persons who enjoyed the toleration, meaning the Doctor's, were ratified there; and as to any ecclesiastical censure, not ratified there, he thought it downright insolence to say there was no power on earth could reverse it.

He 'spoke with so fine and deliberate a cadence and so soft and engaging a tone' that one observer 'had not time to mind the sense of his speech, only that he maintained that religion had nothing at all to do with the state'. In summing up on 10 Mar. 1710, he again attacked Sacheverell's pedantic distinction between the legal toleration and a universal toleration, implying that the doctor had invented it since the impeachment, and

> the better to enforce what he had said before, in the same elegant way of delivery repeated it, and was very smart upon the whole sermon ... then pretended to prove the doctor had raised this late mob because this seditious libel (as he all along called the sermon) had produced an actual rebellion; and that the meeting-houses were burnt etc. at the instigation of one at the same time stickling for passive obedience; he said the doctor, for maintaining all schismatics damned, wanted to be sweetened by that gentle spirit of moderation he ridicules in his sermon and that he wanted even Christianity itself ... and to his reflecting upon men in high stations he said his words were too big and mighty to mean any little subordinate powers.

Cowper duly voted for the impeachment, but his prominence in the prosecution caused him electoral problems at Bere Alston where his brother quarrelled with Lord Stamford, and Cowper was dropped in favour of a moderate Tory. Even before the trial, Sir Francis Drake, 3rd Bt.*, who had an important electoral interest in the borough, had advised Cowper 'to get an easy discount of a bill' owed to one of the voters there who was a servant of Lord Stamford and who had 'suffered for not complying with his landlord's folly', an indication that trouble had been brewing there for some time.[6]

Cowper was unable to regain his seat before 1715, and although he 'had a great deal of wit and attempt, [and] understood well his business, [he] had not the good fortune to be born an elder brother', and his legal career was overshadowed by that of the more illustrious William, whose scruples about nepotism actually counted against Spencer's appointment as solicitor-general in 1716. Cowper followed his brother into opposition in 1718, and shared his hostility to the South Sea Company, but on the succession of George II was appointed justice of the common pleas. He died on 10 Dec. 1728, though the year is sometimes given in error as 1727. Ironically for a lawyer, he died intestate, and it is therefore difficult to establish how wealthy he had become, though from other sources it is known that he had possessed £4,000 of Bank of England stock in 1710, enough to qualify him as a director. His second wife left £200 for the erection of a funeral monument by Roubillac, so 'that as long as marble can endure, his memory might be preserved, whom living she so much honoured, so tenderly loved, [and] whose loss she so deeply lamented'.[7]

[1] Herts. RO, Panshanger mss D/EP F25, Sir William Cowper's commonplace bk., entry for birth date; *VCH Herts. Fams.* 145. [2] Corp. London RO, Rep. 95, f. 145. [3] J. Aubrey, *Surr.* [1719], v. 312. [4] Cobbett, *Parlty. Hist.* ix. 115; Add. 17677 TT, f. 218; *State Trials,* xiii. 1109–249; *CJ,* xiv. 35; *Post Man,* 8–10 June 1699; *London Post,* 27–29 May 1700; *HMC Portland,* iii. 606; Panshanger mss D/EP F81, f. 96, William Cowper to wife, 3 Sept. 1701; D/EP F29, Lady Cowper's commonplace bk. pp. 67, 71–72, 107. [5] Panshanger mss D/EP F99, f. 1, Somers to [William Cowper], n.d.; f. 2, William Cowper to Bolton, n.d.; ff. 4, 7, Bolton to William Cowper, 28 Dec. 1700, n.d.; f. 6, Robert Symons et al. to Bolton, 24 Dec. 1700; D/EP F31, Lady Cowper's commonplace bk. p. 205; Devon RO, Exeter dioc. archs. Bp. Trelawny to Adn. Cook, 11, 18 Jan. [1701]; Staffs. RO, Paget mss D603/K/3/6, R. Acherley to R. Paget, 13 June 1706; Speck thesis, 221; *Nicolson Diaries* ed. Jones and Holmes, 458. [6] Panshanger mss D/EP F100 (unfol.) Cowper to Ld. Stamford, 14 Apr. 1708; D/EP F54, f. 77, Drake to Ld. Cowper, 15 Dec. 1709; *Nicolson Diaries,* 494; BL, Trumbull Alphab. mss 53, Ralph Bridges to Sir William Trumbull*, 14 Dec. 1709; Cobbett, vi. 825; *Impartial View,* 182–3, 214; Yale Univ. Beinecke Lib. Osborn mss box 21/22, 'Acct. of trial of Dr. Sacheverell', ff. 6, 18–19; G. Holmes, *Pol. in Age of Anne,* 320. [7] D. Manley, *Secret Mems.* (1709), 227–30; *VCH Herts. Fams.* 145.

M. J. K.

COWPER, Thomas (1670–1718), of Chester, Cheshire.

CHESTER 12 Jan.–7 July 1698

bap. 3 Nov. 1670, 2nd but 1st surv. s. of Thomas Cowper of Overlegh by Elizabeth, da. of John Baskerville of Old Withington Hall, Cheshire. educ. Brasenose, Oxf. 1688; I. Temple 1689. m. 18 Aug. 1693, Martha, da. of Robert Callis of Lincs., 2s. (1 d.v.p.) 2da. (1 d.v.p.). suc. fa. 1695.[1]

Freeman, Chester 1696; burgess, Wigan 1697.[2]

Cowper's family had become established Chester merchants by the mid-17th century. His grandfather and namesake had served as the corporation's mayor in 1641–2, remaining loyal to Charles I in the first Civil War; his father, who purchased Overlegh in 1660, had served as an alderman of the borough under Charles II. Having been admitted to the freedom of Chester in 1696, Cowper was returned for the borough in January 1698, but made little impact upon the records of the Commons, though in February 1698 he assisted Peter Shakerley* in attempts to expedite payment of arrears due to Chester for the quartering of invalids in the borough. On 19 May Cowper was granted an indefinite leave of absence, thereby marking the end of his Commons career, since at the 1698 election he stood aside to allow the election of Shakerley. In September that year he was classed as a Country supporter left out of the new House. Little more is known of him, though in January 1713 he was unsuccessfully lobbied to vote for George Kenyon* at the Wigan by-election. Cowper died on 13 Aug. 1718 and was buried five days later at St. Peter's, Chester, with Shakerley and Sir Richard Grosvenor, 4th Bt.†, serving as two of the coffin bearers.[3]

[1] Ormerod, *Cheshire,* i. 375. [2] *Freemen of Chester* ed. J. H. E. Bennet (Lancs. and Cheshire Record Soc. li), 194; Wigan RO, Wigan bor. recs. AB/MR/10. [3] Ormerod, 374–5; *HMC 8th Rep. I,* 389; Chester RO, Chester bor. recs. mayor's letters M/L/4/538, Cowper and Shakerley to William Allen, 8 Feb. 1697[–8]; *HMC Kenyon,* 450; *Prescott Diary,* 648, 649.

E. C.

COWPER, Sir William, 2nd Bt. (1639–1706), Hertford Castle, Herts. and Ratling Court, Kent.

HERTFORD 1680–1681 (Mar.), 1689–1700

bap. 14 Dec. 1639, o. s. of John Cowper (d.v.p. s. of Sir William Cowper, 1st Bt., of Ratling Court, Nonington, Kent) of Hertford Castle by Martha, da. of George Hewkley, merchant, of London. educ. G. Inn 1659. m. lic. 8 Apr. 1664, Sarah (d. 1720), da. of Samuel Holled, merchant, of London, 4s. (2 d.v.p.). suc. fa. 1643; gdfa. as 2nd Bt. 20 Dec. 1664.[1]

Freeman, Hertford 1679; commr. inquiry into recusancy fines, Herts. 1687–Oct. 1688.[2]

Commr. Greenwich Hosp. 1695; gov. Christ's Hosp. c.1678.[3]

A zealous follower of the 1st Earl of Shaftesbury (Sir Anthony Ashley Cooper†), to whom he may have been related, Cowper had been a strong supporter of the exclusion bill, and consistently sympathetic to Dissent. After James II's issue of the 1687 Declaration of Indulgence he was named as a commissioner to inquire into recusancy fines, and was said to have been active in inquiring about fines levied on Dissenters; yet the degree to which he co-operated with the Court was probably very limited, for he published a tract at the Revolution (probably at the time of the elections to the Convention) in which he spat invective against 'the late corruption of affairs' and against those 'small agents in every little corporation' who had helped to invade liberty and religion. Although his anger was directed chiefly against those nominated by Hertford's 1685 charter, by which honorary freemen had been created largely in order to exclude him from Parliament, the tone of the pamphlet betrays no sign of complicity with James' regime. Indeed, Cowper spoke in glowing terms of the Prince of Orange's endeavours to secure Protestantism and restore liberties, and he regarded William as providentially placed at the helm of government as a great example of 'wisdom, justice, humanity and candour'. The tract is also indicative of Cowper's independent Whiggery: he attacked invasions of civil rights and liberties, railed against encroachments on the right of inhabitants to vote at elections, and declared that he 'always esteemed it more honourable to suffer, than to be a tool to any power or interest whatsoever'. This sense of virtuous independence was buttressed, and may have partly derived from, pride in his family's achievements. His wife recalled one evening in 1700 when he 'fell to magnify himself, boasting of the riches in his family . . . and made it out that among 'em they are possessed of £2,500 a year, besides what his sons now get'.[4]

Cowper was far less prominent in Parliament after the Revolution than he had been in Charles II's reign. Classed by Lord Carmarthen (Sir Thomas Osborne†) in March 1690 as a Whig, he was one of four Members sent on 5 Apr. to search the chambers of the Jacobite lawyer Richard Stafford, who had delivered a seditious libel to MPs as they waited in the lobby, and on 25 Apr., as a trustee of the 1st Earl of Shaftesbury's estate, he carried up the 2nd Earl's estate bill, which provided for Shaftesbury's offspring. Marked as a Court supporter by Robert Harley* in April 1691, Sir William was appointed on 2 Nov. to draft a bill to revive the Hertfordshire Highways Act. He may have expressed a special interest in the cost of the armed forces, for a week later he was named to inspect the estimate of the navy for the following year, and on 25 Nov. he seconded Paul Foley I's* proposal that the charge of forces in Ireland should be borne by that kingdom. On 6 Jan. 1693 he presented a bill to revive the acts for the repair of Hertfordshire roads, and on 6 Mar. he reported a private estate bill, which he carried up the following day. In the spring of 1693 Grascome marked him as a placeman but not a Court supporter, but the first categorization was inaccurate and the second needs some qualification, for although concerned with Country measures, particularly those against corruption at court or at elections, his support for Revolution principles seems generally to have placed him in the Court ranks, a stance of independent Whiggery that he passed on to his son William*. In the following session Sir William was ordered on 13 Feb. 1694 to bring in the bill for raising the militia, which he presented four days later and carried up to the Lords on 16 Apr. He appears to have been most active at Westminster during the sessions either side of the 1695 general election. On 13 Nov. 1694 he seconded Hugh Boscawen I's* motion to consider the King's Speech, which urged the need for supply to fight the war, 'both urging that the matters recommended to them were of importance and no time to be lost'. During this session he was included upon Henry Guy's* list of 'friends', probably in connexion with the Commons' attack upon Guy. Between December 1694 and February 1695 he was nominated to two drafting committees, and on 25 Mar. reported on the private bill of another Whig noble family with which he had been intimate, the Russells. On 23 Apr. he was the last MP to be voted on to the committee to examine Sir Thomas Cooke* about corruption by the East India Company, and four days later was named to prepare articles of impeachment against his old adversary Carmarthen, now Duke of Leeds.[5]

When the new Parliament met, Cowper seems to have been concerned to induct his son into committee procedure, and to mould William's political beliefs. Father and son were named on 7 Dec. 1695 to the committee for the bill to prevent charges at elections, though Sir William alone was appointed on 4 Feb. 1696 to another bill to regulate elections, and the pair were both named on 12 Dec. 1695 to the bill to regulate the coinage, and on 17 Jan. 1696 to the debtors' relief bill. Forecast as likely to support the Court in divisions of 31 Jan. upon the proposed council of trade, Sir William signed the Association, and in

March voted with the Court for fixing the price of guineas at 22s. At the start of the next session he voted for the attainder of Sir John Fenwick†. On 20 Feb. 1697 he spoke against the grants of large pensions being made to courtiers, but, perhaps unwilling to give any ground to the Country Tories, included a barbed comment against their leader Hon. John Granville*. Disliking in equal proportions Court corruption and the Tories, he duly tacked on to a vote in April 1700 against exorbitant grants a clause 'that it should be the like crime in any one who was a Privy Councillor in any reign', which was evidently aimed at both Granville and Sir Edward Seymour, 4th Bt.* He had been listed as a Court supporter on a comparative list of the old and new Commons in September 1698, and in early 1700 as in the interest of the chancellor, Charles Montagu*, perhaps because of his activity over the coinage or his son Spencer Cowper's* friendship with the Junto.[6]

The destruction of the Cowper interest at Hertford, as a result of the trial of his son for the murder of a Quaker woman, ended Sir William's career in Parliament. In December 1700 he dodged questions about the family's intentions to be at the next election, having found the town greatly changed 'for the worst'. Determined to brazen out the embarrassment, he confided to his wife that, although he would much rather be at home: 'I must thrash through, be the consequence as 'twill, to please a few friends, but believe I shall hardly be catched any more when once at liberty.' He soon cheered up, for in late January 1701 he 'came home full of glee with the news that Mr Filmer his antagonist for the election at Hertford was dropped down suddenly dead'. His macabre sense of humour was symptomatic of an increasing eccentricity and cantankerousness. Although he wished to go back to Hertford for the 1702 election, his wife feared the family was already 'contemptible enough there', and would be the subject of ridicule when it was known that he had taken over responsibility for household domestic arrangements. She lamented that he 'restrains me in all my due privileges' and believed that since she was given no responsibility or control over the family she had 'been kept as a concubine not a wife'. Always cold and formal, his relationship with his wife became increasingly strained as he grew older. On 31 Jan 1702 she calculated that she had lived 'almost 14,000 days' with Sir William, 'and from the bottom of my soul do believe I never past [sic] one without something to be forgiven him'. The letter he had written her in December 1700, though friendly in tone, had been addressed simply to 'dear Cowper', and she claimed that it was the first he had written to her in 35 years of marriage, leaving her at a loss as to know how to reply. In September 1705 she found his 'exquisite provocations' too much and, as she put it, 'escaped out of gaol, for dwelling with Sir W[illiam] at Hertford castle is not living but a sort of civil death'. Although she returned, he 'provoked and teased her with an ugly air he does not, dare not, use to the worst of servants', and after he had picked a quarrel with her about her 'courtesy and affability' to people pursuing recommendations for offices, Lady Cowper confided to her commonplace book in 1706 that 'never any two disagreed like Sir William and I. The few virtues I have he dislikes.' She may have had good grounds for complaint, for on one occasion he called her 'a liar and a whore, saying pride was a worse sin than either, and a chaste woman that over-valued herself was in greater fault'. Ostensibly the Cowpers shared religious preoccupations: she was described on her funeral monument as 'a great example of industry, virtue, wisdom and piety', and a commonplace book in which Sir William noted the births of his sons includes a number of prayers and meditations, one of which thanked God in a strongly Calvinistic tone 'for electing us before the beginning of the world' and for 'the continual effects of thy gracious providence'. Yet here too, they disagreed, for Sir William was, at the very least, anticlerical. He was a 'Protestant of the true blue', Lady Cowper remarked when he refused to celebrate his birthday or other 'ceremonies', and held an almost mathematically rational view of religion, telling his wife that 'all things hang by geometry'. Lady Cowper's love of order and ceremony – she confessed she was 'prone to superstitious fancies' – seems to have particularly irritated her husband, who lectured her 'sharply against the Church and priests'. When she complained about disobedient servants he 'replied we might thank the Church of England for that neglect, in former days such order was observed, but laid down since that came in'; she retorted that if he went to church he 'might meet with frequent exhortations to the performance of' obedience, though he answered that 'he found no body the better that went so much there, nor for making a stir against whoring, which he thought the least of sins. I could not forbear', Lady Cowper noted, 'to say that he ought not to reproach religion, but love the effects, which 'twas like had prevented him knowing to his last the difference between a chaste wife and a whore as he very well deserved to have done.' Thus although the notes in Sir William's commonplace book attacked 'atheistical libertines', the allegation made after his death that he was 'an old debauchee, given to irregular pleasures, not such as the laws of nature seem to dictate', may have had some foundation. Cowper's freethinking also informed his political views. Lady Cowper found the conversation at Hertford Castle, where Dissenters were frequent guests,

> wretched stuff, ever of one theme, election [?corranto] etc. If I talk of virtue and goodness, Sir W[illiam] calls it preaching. It grieves me I no oftener comply with his sentiments about government, being inclined to love order and obedience, I think him too much a favourer of licentious liberty.

She marvelled 'to hear him talk how much he is for liberty of conscience and setting people at ease to do as they list, when there is not a more absolute tyrant ... than himself'.[7]

In November 1706 Sir William was seized with 'an apoplexy and dead palsy over one side, struck speechless and never spoke more'. In his last days he had not 'shown the least fear, nor bemoaned himself as had power to do in his whole sickness', dying with 'courage and constancy of mind' on the 26th. His death was regretted by his friend Sir Francis Drake, 3rd Bt.*, who had helped to secure the election of Sir William's sons at Bere Alston. Cowper's will requested his burial at St. Michael Cornhill, London, near his ancestors, and left £12 'unto the poor of the town of Hertford to be distributed as I was wont to my Christmas gift', although, to the disgust of his wife, he left nothing to Christ's Hospital, of which he was a governor and where he had placed several children. Such parsimony can have had nothing to do with straitened circumstances, for he is known to have invested some £3,000 or so in the Bank of England during his life, and his personal estate was worth about £2,500, including land and tenements in Kent, London and Hertford, all of which passed to his eldest son, William, though debts and legacies reduced this sum to only £700. A sum of £1,000 was bequeathed to Spencer Cowper, and, mindful of the strained familial relations, Sir William charged his sons and his 'beloved wife' to be kind to each other.[8]

[1] *VCH Herts. Fams.* 138; *Index Lib.* lxvi. 9. [2] Herts. RO, Hertford bor. recs. 25/88; *Cal. Treas. Bks.* iv. 1695–6. [3] Add. 10120, f. 233; Herts. RO, Panshanger mss D/EP F32, Lady Cowper's commonplace bk. p. 174. [4] *Bull. IHR*, lxvi. 62; Hertford bor. recs. 23/331, *The Case of the Ancient Burrough of Hertford in Relation to their Electing Burgesses*, endorsed 'Sir William Cowper's reflections conc[erning] the charter and corporation of Hertford'; D/EP F29, Lady Cowper's commonplace bk. p. 15. [5] Morrice entr'ing bk. 3, p. 130; K. H. D. Haley, *First Earl of Shaftesbury*, 430, 614, 727; *Luttrell Diary*, 41; Add. 46527, f. 22. [6] *Vernon–Shrewsbury Letters*, i. 215; iii. 14. [7] Panshanger mss D/EP F23, f.1, Cowper to his wife, 31 Dec. 1700; D/EP F29, Lady Cowper's commonplace bk. pp. 13, 35, 53, 60, 162, 185, 195, 230; D/EP F31, pp. 133, 135, 183–4, 204; D/EP F25, commonplace bk. (unfol.); *VCH Herts. Fams.* 138; D. Manley, *Secret Mems.* (1709), 213. [8] Panshanger mss D/EP F193, f. 24,

William to Mary Cowper, 26 Nov. 1706; D/EP F32, pp. 1, 174; D/EP F54, Drake to William Cowper, 13 Dec. 1706; D/EP F50, acct. of personal estate; Luttrell, *Brief Relation*, vi. 111; Add. 42593, f. 40; PCC 4 Poley.

M. J. K.

COWPER, William (1665–1723), of Hertford Castle and Colne Green, Hertingfordbury, Herts. and Ratling Court, Kent.

HERTFORD 1695–1700
BERE ALSTON 7 Mar. 1701–11 Oct. 1705

b. 24 June 1665, 2nd but 1st surv. s. of Sir William Cowper, 2nd Bt.*; bro. of Spencer Cowper*. *educ.* St. Albans sch. 1672; M. Temple 1682, called 1688. *m.* (1) 9 July 1686, Judith Booth (*d.* 1705), da. of Sir Robert Booth of London, 1s. *d.v.p.*; (2) settlement 10 Sept. 1706, Mary (*d.* 1724), da. and coh. of John Clavering of Chopwell, co. Dur., 2s. 2da.; 1s. (*d.v.p.*) 1da. illegit. by Elizabeth Culling. *suc.* fa. as 3rd Bt. 26 Nov. 1706; *cr.* Lord Cowper of Wingham, Kent, 14 Dec. 1706, Earl Cowper 18 Mar. 1718.[1]

KC 1689; ld. keeper and PC 11 Oct. 1705, ld. chanc. 4 May 1707–23 Sept. 1710, 21 Sept. 1714–Apr. 1718; ld. justice Aug.–Sept. 1714.

Chairman of supply and ways and means 1699.

Commr. union with Scotland 1706, trade and plantations 1707; trustee, poor Palatines 1709.[2]

FRS 1706.

Gov. Charterhouse by 1710.[3]

Ld. lt. Herts. 1710–12, 1714–*d.*; recorder, Colchester 1714–?*d.*[4]

Cowper's contemporary friends and admirers believed that he was 'the most accomplished lawyer, civilian and statesman that England bore for many ages past'. He had 'a bright, quick, penetrating genius; an exact and sound judgment', but it was his 'manly and flowing eloquence' that really attracted admiration, for he had 'a clear sonorous voice, a gracious aspect, an easy address, in a word all that's necessary to form a complete orator'. He apparently always chose the right moment to speak, and then did so 'from the bottom of his heart without any secret reservation'. His skilful style made him 'much the finest speaker of all the lawyers in England', and he became 'highly renowned for his masterly eloquence'. Rather than weaken his powers of persuasion, his disdain for the formal etiquette normally used in the courts and his natural diffidence may have given his rhetoric even greater credibility. Certainly he was 'considered the man who spoke the best in the House of Commons', despite Lord Chesterfield's subsequent assertion that Cowper often 'hazarded' a weak line of reasoning.[5]

According to the gossip of Mrs Manley, Sir William

Cowper 'did not bestow a liberal education upon his son, but bred him to the practice of the law in that manner that is the least generous and most corrupt'. It is true that, unlike his younger brother, he was not schooled at Westminster, but his father evidently instilled in him the independent Whig sympathies that were to be the hallmark of his career. On his father's death, he wrote that Sir William's 'care' of his education had set him beyond the reach of monetary considerations, protesting (perhaps too much) that he found no consolation for the loss of his parent 'from any increase it brings or may the sooner bring my estate', and a letter of advice preserved by his mother exhorted him to be moderate in all things, to despise vice, and neither 'to affect nor neglect popularity'.[6]

Cowper's rise in the legal profession was, in his own words, 'with the blessing of heaven on my own industry', though his early promotion was hardly unaided by other powers. Having 'set his love and delight on the profession of the law', he found powerful patrons in Lady Russell and Lady Shaftesbury, who in 1689, together with his mother, influenced the Marquess of Halifax (Sir George Savile†) to persuade the King to appoint Cowper as a King's Counsel. Sir Robert Howard* also pressed Secretary Shrewsbury on his behalf. Despite this concerted pressure, Halifax, a fitting model for Cowper's later trimming activity, 'found the King something difficult in respect of Mr Cowper's age, and . . . said he would take time to think of it'; but William eventually gave his consent, albeit 'with some unwillingness', for he said he could only 'justify such an irregularity' as a compliment to the ladies. Even then, the attorney-general's office stopped the warrant's passage, until Lady Russell renewed her entreaties. Yet Cowper's own actions may also have pleaded his cause. As he later wrote, he had constantly 'adhered to that opinion for excluding a popish successor even when it was unfashionable and decried by those that were in authority' and had been active in arms for William at the Revolution, meeting the Prince's army at Wallingford. An account of the expedition records both his valour and his pleasure 'in seeing the fountain of this happy revolution', and he may also have been the author of *A Poem upon his Highness the Prince of Orange's Expedition into England*, for a printed copy among his papers is endorsed as having been written 'by WC'.[7]

Despite, or perhaps because of, Cowper's later stance of embodying the politics of virtue, contemporaries were keen to play up scandal in his apparently dissolute early life, focusing particularly on stories that he had formed a bigamous marriage. Mrs Manley tells a story that

there was an orphan left to his care, her fortune not large, but her person very agreeable; [Cowper] was amorous; he hated his wife, tho' he lived civilly with her, and had the art of dissembling so natural, that it cost him nothing to appear a good husband.

According to Manley, Mrs 'Cullen' had been brought up in the same house as his wife, who had taught her chastity and devotion, and Cowper therefore thought it 'would be a sort of triumph over his wife, whom he hated', to seduce her. He persuaded her to agree to a false marriage, at which his brother Spencer Cowper allegedly presided, dressed as a priest. His new 'bride' became pregnant and had borne two children by 1699. Manley was not alone in thinking of Cowper as 'Will Bigamy'. Hearne described him as having 'very bad principles and morals, being well known to have had two wives at a time', and a tract on bigamy in the Blenheim papers was endorsed as alluding to him. Bishop Nicolson also made a note in 1703, 'Mr Cowper's persuading his Mrs to think herself his *other wife*'. There was some factual basis to the allegations. Elizabeth Culling, whom he seems to have housed at Hertingfordbury, gave birth to two of Cowper's illegitimate children. His natural son died in 1719, but Cowper provided a trust fund of £2,000 in his will for his daughter Mary, who married one Isaacson, a friend of Henry Grey*. Grey acted as an intermediary between the couple and Cowper, who had doubts about the suitability of the match.[8]

Throughout his life Cowper remained susceptible to a pretty face. He was attracted to his second wife because, he declared, she was 'the most beautiful woman and the least conscious of it herself that ever I had met with', and had apparently asked to see her 'undress' before their marriage. The wedding took place secretly in September 1706, and Cowper protested that he

was not induced to the choice by any ungovernable desire; but I very coolly and deliberately thought her the fittest wife to entertain me and to live as I might when reduced to a private condition, with which a person of great estate would hardly have been contented.

Indeed, the marriage was not consummated for several months, though Cowper's own suggestion that this experiment in celibacy was to test whether or not the marriage had been merely 'to satisfy an ungovernable appetite' hides more complex motives centring on his relationship with his cantankerous, and by now ill, father. Sir William had apparently been pressing him to marry a local Hertfordshire woman, but William wanted to conclude the marriage with Mary Clavering so that he could tell his father that further pressure was simply 'too late'. To entice Mary into the match he offered her generous terms: 'that is', he told her,

> for whatever your fortune is, to lay down twice that sum in money in the hands of any friend of yours in trust, that the interest should be your jointure... [which was] about a third more than is usual.

Mary was financially a woman of 'an inconsiderable fortune', though one report claimed that her marriage settlement was to be £2,000, but had charms of wit and conversation as well as virtue imbued by her pious father, for before she met her future husband she had copied an 'encomium' on Parliament in 1699 which referred to the need for MPs to reform their manners and lives.[9]

Yet despite Cowper's profession that his 'heart when once chosen for itself . . . will never more be guilty of wandering', he found it difficult to lead a totally reformed life. In 1710 his wife intercepted a letter from one of his female admirers, and immediately dispatched a furious letter to her rival telling her that her husband had never thought of her 'in the way you wish any more than if you were his grandmother', though privately she wrote a distraught letter upbraiding Cowper for his inconstancy. 'I now live to see that all those assurances were only to keep me silent', she wrote, 'for now I live to see you keep correspondence with people not at all fit for you if you design to be faithful to me.' She suggested that they separate, an idea which Cowper himself had apparently suggested 'several times', but no breach occurred and thereafter the marriage seems to have settled on to a more steady and affectionate footing. The details of Cowper's amorous intrigues warn that the life of virtue was for him as much an ideal as a reality, and that a passionate nature was hidden beneath the easy rhetoric and diffident nature. His lifestyle also casts doubt on his religiosity. Indeed, Hearne described him as 'a man of no religion', and Mrs Manley thought him a man who had 'religion in pretence, none in reality'. Yet, in later life at least, Cowper was touched by a deep sense of providentialism, reflecting the strong Calvinistic beliefs of his family. Reviewing his career, he wrote that even at its height he had

> begged of God that he would preserve my mind from relying on the transient vanity of the world, and teach me to depend upon his providence, that I might not be lift[ed] up with the present success, nor dejected when reverse should happen . . . and I verily believe I was helped by his holy spirit from my sincere dependence upon his good providence in this present undertaking. Glory be to God who has sustained me in adversity, and carried me through the malice of my enemies.

This sense of a favoured destiny may explain his later declaration 'that if he had happened to be at Geneva he would not have scrupled to have communicated with the Protestants there'. Although such sentiments were accompanied by a tender regard for Dissenters, he viewed the Test and Corporation Acts 'as the main bulwark of our excellent constitution in church or state'.[10]

Cowper's glittering career at the bar soon brought him to the attention of Charles Montagu* and Sir John Somers*, who in January 1693 urged that the King's Counsel be heard on the royal mines bill. Cowper was accordingly employed and in February 1693 made notes about the arguments he had used to persuade William not to agree to the measure. The account of the conference reveals Cowper's belief in a balance between the strength of the crown and the rights of the subject, as well as contempt for the self-interest of many MPs, whose activity he had evidently been scrutinizing. 'Those Members that were indifferent and [whom] we might hope would be influenced by reason', he sourly observed, 'did not think it their interest to attend it so closely' as those who had a stake in the outcome, for there was 'private interest fomenting at the bottom of this business'. Believing that the mines bill aimed at profit for a few individuals at the expense of the crown and the nation's good, Cowper told the King that

> a great part of the strength and security of all government consists in a reverential awe towards the governor created in the minds of the people as much by those ornaments and decorations of the royal majesty as by its intrinsic power and authority. The crown ought to be shining as well as weighty. Sir, this prerogative and royal property now sought to be taken from you is one of those public fineries of the ancient English majesty which has been worn by our king as long as the crown itself.

Begging pardon for his 'heat and eagerness', he repeated his outrage that 'so ancient and venerable a part of the royal English majesty' was going to be taken away 'for so sordid and pitiful a reason as the profit of a few projectors'. The interview reveals a number of features of Cowper's personality and principles. Beneath the flowing, passionate rhetoric there lay a deep commitment to public interest above all petty selfish motives, and a utilitarian view of royal prerogative, with a conviction that a strong crown served the country best. The speech may also have been designed to impress the King, for Cowper was still a young, ambitious lawyer. He proudly reported to his wife in August 1693 how the lord chief justice and other prominent barristers complimented him, though he confided that 'at bottom they mean to suppress me as civilly as they can and that the first real kindness I shall receive from any of them will be at their death; and yet I do not blame their doings, but pretensions to the contrary'. His sense of frustration at being held back by established interests in his profession, even Whig ones, led him to complain publicly that Sir George Treby* refused to accord him the usual privileges of a King's Counsel. Yet such impatience did not alter his political leanings. In the summer of 1694 he reported to his wife 'the good news of our getting a King' by the death of the Queen, and, in a remark that suggests that he fully endorsed the land war, added that a prince's power was 'more effectual than his religion for carrying on a war, and I had rather have his armies than his prayers in a right way'.[11]

In October 1695 Cowper was elected for Hertford with his father, who appears to have introduced him to the ways of the House. In both this and the second session Cowper evinced a concern, shared by his father, for electoral reform. He was named on 7 Dec. 1695 to the committee for the bill to prevent election expenses, a measure which prompted his earliest recorded speech. According to his obituary, 'the very first day he sat in the House of Commons he had occasion to speak three times, and came off with universal applause'. In what was seen as a provocative plea against a landed qualification, he argued that 'an active industrious man who employed £5,000 in trade was every whit as fit to be a Member there as a country gentleman of £200 a year who spent all his time hawking and hunting, and was over head and ears in debt', though Lord Norreys (Montagu Venables-Bertie*) returned the jibe by declaring 'himself as fit to sit there as those who were used to take money for their opinion'. Cowper's position, ironic in view of his later protestation that he wished to be thought of 'as a country gentleman with a competent, not great but very clear estate', may have been influenced by the nature of his own seat, a trading borough, and no doubt on account of the electoral support he had enjoyed from the Quakers at Hertford, he acted as teller on 3 Mar. 1696 in favour of the committal of the affirmation bill. He was forecast as likely to support the Court in the divisions of 31 Jan. on the council of trade, and on 13 Mar. again served as a teller, against the third reading of a private estate bill. Although this outline of his activity does not suggest unusual application, Cowper evidently made a very strong mark at Westminster, and on 5 Apr. presented one of the most important measures of the session, the Association bill, thereby establishing his Court Whig credentials. The next day he chaired the ensuing committee of the whole, and reported on the 7th, being ordered to carry the bill to the Lords the following day; on the 14th he again carried the Association to the Upper House after it had been returned with amendments. He naturally signed the Association, both at Westminster and in his county.[12]

The conspiracy against the King provided Cowper with a chance to further both his legal and his political career. As a young King's Counsel, whom the Earl of Ailesbury described as 'very pert, talkative and a fop', he was determined to play, and in some respects overplay, his part in the prosecution of the plotters. At Ailesbury's own trial he 'rose up with a sprightly, modish air' and began speaking beyond his brief, for which he was reprimanded by the judge: according to the Earl, Cowper was 'convinced of his error and asked my pardon on my going out of the court . . . [and] was ever after my friend'. This unusual mixture of zeal for a cause on the one hand, and personal diffidence and geniality on the other, was perhaps the reason for his success both at the bar and in Parliament. When MPs reassembled in November, Cowper's desire to convict the plotters was undiminished, for he attacked Sir John Fenwick's† defence as 'trifling with the House', and supported the bill against him, arguing that far from creating a bad precedent which others might later use to justify arbitrary proceedings, the attainder served 'to protect the innocent' because Fenwick had been heard personally as well as by his counsel. When he suggested that without the bill there would be no discovery of who else had been involved in the plot, and that a man deserved to die for his crimes unless he made a confession, Cowper's speech was interrupted 'by the noise of some gentlemen showing dissatisfaction at that way of arguing'. His arguments were nevertheless thought to have 'had the greatest weight in attainting Sir John', and on 25 Nov. he duly voted in favour of the bill. Besides the security of the state, Cowper was again involved with a bill to regulate elections, being named on 28 Oct. 1696 to prepare this measure, and with the nation's financial crisis. In the last session, on 12 Dec. 1695, he had been appointed to the committee for the bill to regulate the coinage, and on 14 Jan. 1697 he was one of those named to draw up clauses to explain the recoinage acts. After being granted a three-week leave of absence on 5 Mar., probably to attend to legal business, he told on 15 Apr. in favour of the bill against counterfeit coin, and this activity signalled his allegiance to the chancellor, Charles Montagu*, with whose moderate Whig principles he identified. Indeed, in March 1696 Cowper had supported the Court (and Montagu) on fixing the price of guineas at

22s., and he later claimed to have proposed imposing customs duties in vindication of Montagu's maxim of 'raising the supplies within a year'.[13]

The themes of anti-Jacobitism, electoral reform and the problem of the coinage also characterized Cowper's activity in the 1697-8 session. He chaired the committee of the whole on 18 Dec. 1697 discussing the bill to prevent correspondence with King James, and reported two days later, carrying up the consequent bill to the Lords on the 21st. On 22 Jan. 1698 he was granted leave to bring in a bill to regulate elections, which he duly presented on the 25th. On 11 Apr. he took the chair of the committee of the whole which discussed the bill, and reported from it on the 19th. He also chaired, and reported from, a committee of the whole on the issue of counterfeit coin (26 Mar., 15 Apr.), and on 27 Apr. told in favour of a motion to pass the bill to prevent fraudulent currency. He had again been granted a leave of absence, on 23 Dec. 1697, during the session, but had returned by 10 Jan. 1698, when he told in favour of granting leave for a bill to restrain the wearing of silks and calicoes.

In May 1698 Cowper acted as counsel for the King in the prosecution of Peter Cook, another Jacobite involved in the Assassination Plot, before being chosen again at Hertford at the election in July. He was included upon two lists of placemen at this time, and in September a comparison of the old and new Commons classed him as a Court supporter, but he nevertheless displayed strong Country sensibilities. The notes he took of proceedings in the House in the following session reveal nothing about his own speeches, breaking off on 3 Feb. 1699 just as he himself took the floor, and therefore suggest that at this time Cowper was chiefly observing rather than participating in debates. Indeed, the jottings reveal an apparently detached impartiality, since they record the arguments made by both sides of the House without comment as to which Cowper himself believed to be the stronger. This detachment from the Court was chiefly the result of his concern about the maintenance of a standing army in peacetime, an issue over which he parted company with the ministry. He later recalled that he had supported the Junto only when they were for the 'true interest of England', leaving them when 'they were for armies', and throughout his future career he was to repeat the rhetoric of remaining faithful to his principles and to the good of the nation, no matter what the government line. He accordingly chaired the committee of supply to fund the disbandment, and his conscientiousness is evident in notes he made of the committee's debates. Yet his identification with the Court was temporarily blurred, rather than overturned. Even during this session, when he was most alienated from the ministry, he supported the legality of Montagu's election to the Commons. Moreover, on 6 Apr. he served as a teller in favour of the courtier William Culliford's* election at Corfe Castle. As chairman of supply and ways and means, a responsibility he first assumed on 9 Jan. 1699, Cowper was zealous in procuring supply, and in addition to chairing, and frequently reporting from, these committees, he also told, during a debate of 25 Apr. 1699 on lotteries, against a motion to suppress the playing of basset, a card game. Such concerns do not account for all his significant activity in this session: on 14 Jan., for example, he was appointed to draft the bill to hinder Catholics from disinheriting their Protestant heirs. On 25 Mar. he took the chair of the committee on the bill to retain in prison those involved in the Assassination Plot.[14]

In March 1699 Cowper's credit was increased by his performance at the murder trial of Lord Mohun, when he was asked to sum up the evidence in preference to the solicitor-general, (Sir) John Hawles*, whose dullness and mumbling made him difficult to hear and understand. But just as Cowper was beginning to establish a reputation as a first-class lawyer, disaster struck. In July 1699 he had to assist his brother Spencer, who had been indicted on a murder charge which owed much to the feuds at Hertford engendered by William's own election in 1698. Perhaps finding it prudent to adopt a lower profile, Cowper took a much less active part in the new session. Though he was appointed on 28 Nov. 1699 to draw up the Address, and two days later chaired the first sitting of the supply committee, he thereafter featured little in the records of the House, though on 26 Mar. 1700 he told in favour of an address about appointing to the commission of the peace only those 'well affected to the King and government', an important indication of an approach that he himself would one day employ as lord chancellor. Yet Cowper did lend his eloquent voice in support of Lord Somers, defending on 5 Dec. the latter's commission to Captain Kidd, calling for all the papers and facts to be placed at Members' disposal, and again two days later when he declared that just

> as nobody ought to be influenced by great names, so neither should there be any envy or prosecution against men because they were great; the flattering and maligning of them being equally base, and they, as well as all other people ought to have their actions weighed in equal balances.

He spoke 'likewise very well to the legality of the patent'.[15]

The full text of the wide-ranging speech was recorded in shorthand and transcribed with secret pride by his mother, and is one of the best examples of Cowper's powers as a public speaker. He saw 'a cloud' hanging over the reputations of some of the Junto

> and all arising from an action which to the best of my understanding was attended with all the care and caution that could be, both in the rise and progress of it, and it is justifiable by the strictest sense of the law. Nay, I will say further, I believe it was done with a good and honourable intention.

He argued 'how little was affected by this grant that is thought to be such an invasion of property', and, speaking from 'notes of authority' in his hand, proceeded with an analysis of the intricate legal aspects of the case, concluding with a statement of his own political philosophy:

> I have often observed in my own reflections (and there are abundance of examples of it) that the liberties of a people have been as often endangered and ruined by an injudicious and intemperate way of asserting them, as by adulation or the most sterile compliances in the world . . . if this doctrine should prevail upon the king's grants which is now contended for, 'twould be the greatest blow to property that can be imagined . . . Gentlemen do not see how far the consequences of such proceedings will carry them, while they think to assert the liberties of their country by arguments and constructions which are not to be justified upon a foot of right reason. However some gentlemen may flatter themselves and decry others, I can truly say that I have nothing mercenary about me . . . I will not by any reproaches be induced to be against the Court, yet when I have but suspected them I have gone from them, nor valued their discipline on the other hand; and while I do so I think myself in a better way to contribute towards preserving the liberties of England, than if I should be always running upon the ministry.

This somewhat priggish speech is a clear enunciation of Cowper's belief in the virtue of independent Whiggery in the pursuit of the interest of the nation. For the moment, England's interest, a vague concept that he never elucidated, lay primarily with the Junto. Yet ironically, Cowper's speech may not have been in Somers' interest, for Burnet believed that it initiated a damaging debate rather than allowing the House to move to a swift vote. On 11 Apr. James Vernon I* again reported that Cowper 'made a very handsome defence of my Lord, and gave very genteel and satisfactory answers to everything that had been alleged'. This support of the lord chancellor, together with his earlier adherence to the chancellor of the Exchequer, explains his categorization in early 1700 as belonging to the Montagu interest, and suggests that his difference with the ministry over the army had not permanently or deeply affected his loyalties. His only other recorded speech of the session related to a point of law rather than party, and indeed to the supremacy of law over party. Still interested in the proper determination of elections, his opinion prevailed on 9 Jan. 1700 when the House considered the election at Dartmouth, where the mayor had died on the eve of the poll. Cowper 'thought there was not ground enough for a new writ', and that it was up to the sheriff to make a return 'or to show why none could be made by certifying it into Chancery'.[16]

Cowper faced the prospect of losing his seat at the general election because his family's interest at Hertford had been undermined by the trial of his brother. Although in December 1700 Sir William Cowper assured William Monson* that both his sons would be present at the election, he found the chances of success there virtually negligible. Somers therefore wrote to the Duke of Bolton (Charles Powlett I*) to secure a seat for Cowper at Totnes. Despite Bolton's recommendation that he should ride post haste to canvass the electorate personally, Cowper replied that

> if want of exercise had not made it impossible for me to perform such a journey in that manner . . . I fear my presence there would add nothing to what your power and interest has done for me in that place, especially being hindered by the Act of Parliament from using the only means a stranger can on a sudden recommend himself by,

though he was willing to have it made known that he would 'be a benefactor to the town as soon as I safely may'. This letter suggests on the one hand a desire to remain within the letter of the law, and on the other, a wish to go against its spirit in order to procure his return, and may hint that Cowper did not think a seat at Westminster at this time to be worthy of superhuman effort, and perhaps also that such unseemly electioneering was unworthy of him. Certainly his protestation to Somers that the poor state of his health rendered impracticable such energetic electioneering seems a feeble excuse, and it is significant that he also failed to attend later polls. But despite failing to secure the seat, he was not out of the House for long, winning a by-election on 7 Mar. 1701 at Bere Alston on the recommendation of Lord Stamford and Sir Francis Drake, 3rd Bt.* A letter from Drake informed Cowper that

> the same consideration which induced my Lord Stamford to recommend you at Bere Alston, to wit, your integrity and great abilities for the service of his government and the saving poor England, obliges me to serve

you likewise with all my little interest in that borough ... I am heartily sorry the House of Commons should be so long without your assistance in this needful time.

No significant activity in the 1701 session can be ascribed to Cowper with any certainty because of the presence in the House of other kinsmen. Yet the diary of Sir Richard Cocks, 2nd Bt.*, shows William to have been a frequent and effective speaker on behalf of the Junto, and Somers in particular. On 28 Mar. he again defended the commission to Kidd, citing the precedent of the Roman Caesar who had used a privately armed fleet to capture pirates: 'this, says he, Caesar did when a public man and nobody questioned him for it ... Mr Cowper spoke very finely about piracy and the distinction between the rules of law in piracy and felony'. On 16 Apr. he spoke in favour of the wording of an address relating to the preservation of trade and commerce, which opponents said would lead to war, and on 17 May clarified a procedural point during a debate on the Old East India Company, though he professed not to have intended to speak. On 26 May he defended his electoral patron Lord Stamford against accusations about the management of the duchy of Lancaster's woods, and again 'spoke finely ... a great deal very well', so much so that even a political opponent of equal rhetorical skill, Sir Edward Seymour, 4th Bt.*, 'commended his great parts and oratory and said [Cowper] could make a bad cause a good one, and that he hoped he would not take it ill if he showed how he came to espouse my Lord's cause viz. to express his gratitude for bringing him into the House'. Seymour no doubt enjoyed emphasizing how Cowper, the man of independent virtue, was pleading a cause out of self-interest.[17]

Stamford must have been sufficiently impressed by his client's performance to recommend him at the second election of 1701, which was enough to secure Cowper's return without any opposition, 'tho' he never appeared in person but made his application to the town by proxy'. Cowper was listed with the Whigs on Harley's analysis of the new Parliament. Cocks recorded another 'finely' worded speech on 10 Feb. 1702, arguing that the failure of oaths to ensure certain behaviour in the past should not prevent their present use. For the remainder of the session, following the King's death early in March, he was largely concerned with the abjuration bill. Once more to the admiration of Cocks, he opposed a motion on 2 May for the employment only of English officers in the army, pointing out that 'we should take it unkindly if we should hear that the Dutch had made such an order in relation to the English and that we had reason to expect the same from the Dutch if we made such an address; he finely exposed the question'.[18]

In July 1702 Cowper was employed by Montagu in the latter's dispute with Lord Carmarthen (Peregrine Osborne†) over the auditorship of the Exchequer; but Cowper's career mirrored the Junto's ebbing fortunes. Although he retained his seat at the 1702 election, he made little mark on the Journals in the new Parliament, and without diary evidence of his speeches it is difficult to assess his role. On 13 Feb. 1703 he voted for agreeing with the Lords' amendments to the bill for enlarging the time for taking the oath of abjuration. In January 1704 he spoke for the Whigs in the Aylesbury election case, 'as learned and hearty as any of the House against the said encroachments of the Lords in meddling with original causes'. Cowper contended that while the Commons must decide election returns 'we ought not, out of zeal to our own jurisdiction, to go one step further than that known law and custom of Parliament will warrant us to do'. It was thus no violation of rights to allow an elector whose vote was refused to maintain a private action against the returning officer. He feared that the Commons was 'seeking to reverse a legal judgment given in the subjects' favour'. The following year, on 28 Feb. 1705, he was named as a manager of the conference with the Upper House over the writs of error issued in the case. In mid-November he was attacked by the Hertfordshire High Tory MPs Ralph Freman II and Charles Caesar, who moved for him to be sent to the Tower for having acted as counsel to Lord Halifax 'without their leave', even though the Queen had given him permission to do so. Seymour and the 'other little dragons' spewed 'their innate venom' against Cowper, but he 'came off triumphantly with flying colours'. Despite their partisan assault on him, Cowper was sufficiently above party considerations himself to join Freman and Caesar on 13 Jan. 1705 on the drafting committee of a place bill, though the union of Country ideals may soon have dissolved, for William may have been the 'Mr Cowper' who was granted a fortnight's leave of absence on 5 Feb. 1705, possibly on account of his still-thriving legal practice or possibly because he thought it prudent to distance himself from his unusual allies. He had certainly parted company with them earlier, over the Tack, for which he was forecast as a likely opponent. He duly voted against the bill, or was absent from the House, on 28 Nov. 1704.[19]

Having been chosen again for Bere Alston in 1705, Cowper wrote a letter in which he not only agreed to pay £15 towards election expenses but also tried to reassure his patron, Drake, that he would not be corrupted by any place he might be given:

I am sure my resolution is sincere and firm not to depart in the least from acting by those true English principles which you have always approved, either in regard to their power or prevalency or any sort or party of men whatsoever of a contrary opinion or for any offers whatsoever that have been made or may be made to try my constancy in that particular.

Such reassurance was necessary, for on the eve of Parliament's assembly Cowper accepted promotion to the highest legal office, rendering him incapable of sitting any longer in the Lower House, though not before he had been categorized on lists of Members as a placeman and a 'Low Church courtier'. Rumours had circulated as early as 1701 that he would be chosen as solicitor-general, but without even filling this post he was tipped in June 1705 as the next lord keeper. Cowper himself appeared 'indifferent' about the job, though his mother ascribed this to a 'diffidence within himself about accepting', and in August she wrote that if her son gained office it would 'happen to him without his seeking'. As his earlier electioneering showed, Cowper always preferred to be courted rather than to do the courting himself. Halifax may have appreciated this, for in mid-August he took Cowper to a Junto gathering at Boughton, from which Lady Cowper inferred that William's promotion would follow. Certainly he returned 'laden with caresses', although the appointment was not formally announced until October because of opposition from the Queen. Anne preferred to find 'a moderate Tory for this appointment', though her scruples had eventually been overcome by Godolphin, who insisted that Cowper 'was generally thought most proper' for the job. Cowper was thus the first Whig to enter upon an important state office after the party's electoral gains in the spring, and was 'the youngest lord keeper ever known'. 'Wearing his own hair made him appear yet more so; which the Queen observing obliged him to cut it off, telling him the world would say she had given the seals to a boy.' It has been suggested that Somers worked closely with Godolphin and Montagu, now Lord Halifax, to promote Cowper, but at the time it was noted that 'some suspect my Lord S[omer]s is not so hearty as he seems and that he will not be pleased to see an abler man than himself in that post'. Indeed, Cowper himself acknowledged the assistance not so much of the Junto as of Godolphin, the Duke of Marlborough (John Churchill†) and Sarah Churchill. He wrote to Marlborough that he owed his advancement 'to the sole favour and goodness of my lord treasurer', and thanked the Duke for his

unseen hand . . . without the concurrence of which I think I may certainly conclude it had not been. I have always to the best of my little capacity and power steadily pursued what seemed to me the true interest of England, and was consequently (without hopes of reward) as serviceable as I could to that of the present ministry when it was so plainly struck at in the last Parliament, for which reason I need not use words to assure your Grace I must continue firm to those measures to which I am obliged as well by the dictates of my own judgment as by the strongest ties of gratitude and interest. Your Grace and my lord treasurer are the only persons living I ever received any benefit from: the title of Counsel to the crown was procured for me by Sir Robert Howard* in the late reign, and continued in this as of course to me, not having forfeited so unprofitable a mark of respect only in my profession, and what ever I was else in it was wholly owing to my own industry; so that I was found free from all engagements to any one, when your Grace and lord treasurer were pleased to lift me up and make me not only faithfully and zealously but most entirely yours. And as I left a course of life tending more surely and quickly to increase my estate than the present, and have no satisfaction in the state of this, so I assure your Grace nothing in it is so valuable to me as this privilege of drawing a little nearer to these great men I have always loved and admired at a distance.

This revealing letter suggests that Cowper was no longer prepared to acknowledge the Junto as his patrons. Indeed he claimed never to have received anything from them, and that he had always been an independent Member owing allegiance only to his principles. To some extent of course, as his opposition to the standing army had made plain, this was true; but Cowper was also deliberately distancing himself from the Junto, who had after all tried to find him a replacement seat in the Commons, in order to ingratiate himself with the new dominant political power and to rank himself as a 'Lord Treasurer's Whig'. By 1706 it was observed that he was 'not as tractable nor has that deference for my Lords Somers and Wharton [Hon. Thomas*] as was expected, and is very great with my lord treasurer'. The rhetoric of impartiality, selflessness and interest of the state was a piously and sincerely held political philosophy, and no doubt Cowper was ideologically close to the duumvirs' design of non-party government for the good of the nation; but it was also a doctrine that promoted Cowper's own interest. Even financially, Cowper's move was less selfless than he pretended. While admitting that Cowper's predecessors extorted huge sums, John Evelyn noted that the total value of the post was still £7,000 a year, and that Cowper had negotiated a £2,000 a year pension whenever he should be dismissed, 'in compensation of his loss of practice'. The chancellor's own account books confirm that the profits of the post were generally in excess of £7,000 a year, and chart his growing fortune. He had £4,000 invested in the Bank of England by 1710, and a principal capital of £27,160 two years later, which had grown to £29,100 by December 1714, besides further investments in mortgages, annuities and stocks in the Million Bank and East India Company. The letter to Marlborough is also important because Cowper's subsequent actions do not show him to have been quite so 'entirely' the creature of Godolphin and Marlborough as he professed, or as Swift insinuated when he described Cowper as subservient to all their designs. In 1710 he incurred his patron Godolphin's indignation as a result of his doubts about the sincerity of France in seeking peace, and, while defending Marlborough the following year, opposed the Duke's design to be appointed general for life. In any case, he retained his friendship with the Junto, and Somers in particular, employing two of the former chancellor's clerks, turning to Somers when considering how to reform Chancery, and commissioning Kneller to paint Somers' portrait. In 1713, when political circumstances had again changed, he referred to Somers as 'that truly great man'.[20]

As lord keeper, Cowper gained control over ecclesiastical appointments worth less than £40 a year and became the Speaker of the House of Lords, though without a capacity to debate there until his elevation to the peerage in 1706, when he took the title of Wingham, where his family had held land since the time of his great-grandfather. Cowper also stopped the custom of receiving new year gifts from Chancery lawyers because he thought it 'looked like insinuating themselves into the favour of the court, and that if it was not bribery it came too near it; and as lord chancellor brought the Chancery into the concisest method, by narrowing all unnecessary harangues, and had the bench like an oracle'. He was also responsible for the regulation of the commission of the peace, of which his management has been called an 'inconspicuous' policy to give the Whigs a preponderance without proscription for their rivals. Cowper's career as a peer was far more important than his role as a Commoner. A steadfast supporter of the Protestant succession, he told the elector of Hanover in 1706 that it was 'impossible to be in the true interest of England, and not to be a fast friend to that succession'. That year his assimilation at Court seemed complete when he deviated from his Country principles far enough to oppose the 'whimsical clause' of the regency bill which would have restricted the number of placemen in the Lower House. He played an important part in negotiating the Union with Scotland, 'the whole weight of which arduous affair he sustained almost alone'. In 1710 he presided over the trial of Dr Sacheverell, and, at the time of the Junto's dismissal from power, Cowper refused to be drawn by Harley to remain in his post, despite personal pleading by the Queen. Cowper believed that the new ministry would make a bad peace and weaken the Protestant succession 'which he ever had firmly at heart', and go 'high with hereditary right and passive obedience'. His resignation shows his continuing loyalty to the Junto, and to Somers in particular, even though he resolved to 'be of no party', and he penned *A Letter to Isaac Bickerstaffe* in reply to Henry St. John II's* account of the change of ministry, in which Cowper saw 'a real conspiracy, not of the Whigs to enslave their sovereign, but of the Tories to enslave the nation'. In 1711 he supported an offensive war in Spain, and in 1714 attacked the treaty of peace and commerce with France as well as the schism bill, which he believed would introduce superstition and irreligion. George I reappointed him as lord chancellor, but by 1718 he was increasingly voting with the Tories, disgusted by the power-lust of some of his colleagues. He resigned that year partly out of fatigue, partly because of factional manoeuvres against him, and partly because of his 'inviolable attachment to all the royal family not permitting him to act with those who had lately made an unhappy division among the King's best friends'. He attacked the South Sea scheme, and the enemies he created in doing so accused him of Jacobitism, more as a design to blacken his credit than as an accurate description of his views, though he appears to have come to believe that Parliament was now oppressing the liberties of the subject. In his later years he therefore headed, and to some large degree organized, a cabal of discontented peers who sought to attack and embarrass the administration of the Earl of Sunderland (Charles, Lord Spencer*).[21]

Cowper died on 10 Oct. 1723 at Colne Green, where he had built a house (begun in 1694) and laid out a park, which he directed to be kept 'as near as may be to the condition they are in when I am absent'. His will thanked God for giving him worldly wealth and 'for his goodness in supporting me as well against the evil consequences of my sins and follies as against the malice of my enemies and raising me to a condition much better than I have deserved'. He directed that he should be buried at Hertingfordbury 'with as much privacy as possible, particularly without escutcheons which always cause an undecent tumult'. He left portions of £5,000 and £6,000 for his two legitimate daughters, £200 for Christ's Hospital, and £100 for the erection of monuments to his father, to his first wife and to himself. He was succeeded by his eldest son, William, and the younger entered holy orders. His second daughter married James Edward Colleton†. His wife died only a few months later, and stated in her own will Cowper's belief that their son was not to travel because this would involve 'weeding the vices of foreign countries'.[22]

Cowper always justified his actions on the grounds that he was giving impartial advice to serve his country. Yet behind the rhetoric of public interest, no matter how deeply or sincerely the idea was held, there was a close identification of the nation's good with his own actions and a hint of self-justification for a worldly success which part of him both feared and despised. Swift shrewdly, if partisanly, observed that Cowper's 'way of managing an argument . . . made him apt to deceive the unwary and sometimes to deceive himself'. The best example of the different levels at which his rhetoric can be taken is his far from 'impartial history of parties', in which he made it clear to the new Hanoverian King how valuable Cowper himself had been in former ministries, and how reliance on the Whigs alone was the only sensible course for King George to adopt. The history's moderation lay only in its recommendation of how the Tory losers were to be treated. Indeed, some notes in Cowper's almanac for 1714 (perhaps forming an 'addendum' to his impartial history) warned that the Tories wanted to abrogate the Toleration Act, make Convocation a spiritual Parliament and put the Church before the King. The documents suggest that Cowper wished his statements to be taken at face value, but that, with all the instinct and skill of a professional lawyer, he was often working to a hidden brief, however sincerely held. Yet Cowper's 'integrity, moderation, candour, humanity [and] disinterestedness gained him the esteem of all good men'. Certainly Arthur Maynwaring* thought he had 'an integrity very rare in his corrupt age', and contemporaries described him as a man of learning, meekness, humility and probity,

By no superiors awed, no interest led,
with him, not party, but his conscience swayed.[23]

[1] Herts. RO, Panshanger mss D/EP F25, Sir William Cowper's commonplace bk.; D/EP F213, mar. settlement; Campbell, *Lives*, iv. 259; *VCH Herts. Fams.* 138–9. [2] *Post Boy*, 30 June–2 July 1709. [3] *Al. Carth.* 71. [4] Panshanger mss D/EP F179, f. 1, Sir Isaac Rebow* to William Cowper, 3 Nov. 1714. [5] *Hist. Reg. Chron.* 1723, p. 43; Cumbria RO (Carlisle), Lonsdale mss D/Lons/W2/2/8, James Lowther* to Sir John Lowther, 2nd Bt. I*, 11 Oct. 1705; D/EP F34, Lady Cowper's commonplace bk. p. 20; Cunningham, *Hist. GB*, i. 458; Campbell, 262; Cobbett, *Parlty. Hist.* vi. 444. [6] D. Manley, *Secret Mems.* (1709), 213; Panshanger mss D/EP F37, Lady Cowper's commonplace bk., pp. 49–53; D/EP F193, f. 24, William to Mary Cowper, 26 Nov. 1706. [7] Foxcroft, *Halifax*, ii. 215; *Letters of Lady Russell*, 195–9; Stowe 222, f. 380; Campbell, 265. [8] Manley, 214–44; *Examiner*, 4 Jan. 1710; Add. 61360, ff. 174–81; *Nicolson Diaries* ed. Jones and Holmes, 200; Panshanger mss, D/EP F85, ff. 57–8, William Culling to Cowper, n.d.; f. 61, Mary Culling to same, 20 July [–]; ff. 57, 71–72, Grey Neville to same, 16 July, 1 Sept. 1720; Foss, *Judges*, viii. 26; PCC 108 Bolton. [9] Panshanger mss D/EP F193, ff.1–2, 7, 9, Cowper to Mary Clavering, n.d, 19 Sept. 1706; BL, Verney mss M636/53, R. Palmer to Ld. Fermanagh (John Verney*), 19 Nov. 1706; *DNB*; Manley, 246; Add. 17677 BBB, f. 38; Stowe 747, f. 138. [10] Panshanger mss D/EP F37, Lady Cowper's commonplace bk. f. 143; D/EP F59, f. 6, Mary to William Cowper, n.d.; Burnet, v. 225; Campbell, 394. [11] Panshanger mss D/EP F26, 'a sudden recollection'; D/EP F81, ff. 51, 56, 58, 62; *M. Temple Recs.* iii. 1431, 1437. [12] *Hist. Reg. Chron.* 1723, p. 43; Panshanger mss D/EP F193, ff. 1–2, William Cowper to Mary Clavering, n.d.; *Vernon–Shrewsbury Letters*, i. 86. [13] *Ailesbury Mems.* ii. 424, 428, 431; Cobbett, v. 1007, 1141; Boyer, *William III*, iii. 233; *Hist. Reg. Chron.* 1723, p. 43; Campbell, 424. [14] Luttrell, *Brief Relation*, iv. 470; *Cam. Misc.* xxix. 346–7, 364–5, 368–9, 371, 378–9, 392–401; *Post Boy*, 21–24 May 1698. [15] Foss, viii. 20; *CSP Dom.* 1699–1700, p. 244; *Vernon–Shrewsbury Letters*, ii. 375, 379. [16] Panshanger mss D/EP F36, Lady Cowper's commonplace bk., 'the speech of William Cowper'; Burnet, iv. 492; *Vernon–Shrewsbury Letters*, iii. 22; Northants. RO, Montagu (Boughton) mss 48/17, Vernon to Shrewsbury, 9 Jan. 1700. [17] Campbell, 284; Panshanger mss D/EP F99, f. 1, Somers to [Cowper], n.d; f. 2, Cowper to Ld. Bolton, n.d.; ff. 4, 7, Bolton to Cowper, 28 Dec. 1700, n.d.; f. 6, Robert Symons et al. to Bolton, 24 Dec. 1700; D/EP F54, f. 57, Drake to same, n.d.; D/EP F23. f. 1, Sir William Cowper to his wife, 31 Dec. 1700; *Cocks Diary*, 73–74, 76, 100, 134, 149. [18] *Cocks Diary*, 209, 279. [19] Chandler, iii. 363–9; Campbell, 288–9; *Cal. Treas. Bks.* xvii. 51; Add. 70075–6, Dyer's newsletter 29 Jan. 1704; Panshanger mss D/EP F30, Lady Cowper's commonplace bk. pp. 312–13. [20] Panshanger mss D/EP F100 (unfol.), draft letter by William Cowper, n.d.; D/EP F31, Lady Cowper's commonplace bk. pp. 101, 110, 113, 117; D/EP F73, 74, annotated almanacs; G. Holmes, *Pol. in Age of Anne*, 204, 489; Campbell, 294, 341; Bodl. Ballard 33, f. 58; W. L. Sachse, *Ld. Somers*, 231; Add. 61135, f. 1; Univ. Kansas Spencer Research Lib. MS C163, Sir William Simpson to Paul Methuen*, 30 Apr. 1706; *Evelyn Diary*, v. 611; Cowper, *Diary*, 1; Cobbett, vi. 908. [21] L. K. J. Glassey, *Appt. JPs*, 171, 197, 261; *HMC Portland*, iv. 363; Stowe 222, f. 380; G. Holmes and W. A. Speck, *Divided Soc.* 150; *Hist. Reg. Chron.* 1723, pp. 43–44; *Hamilton Diary*, 34, 51; Cowper, *Diary*, 43–44, 58; *Somers Tracts*, xiii. 80; Cobbett, 955, 963, 971, 1146, 1344, 1351; Burnet, iv. 7–8, 13; v. 250; vi. 12, 26; *Albion*, xxiii. 681–96; *Hist. Jnl.* xxxvi. 309–29. [22] Panshanger mss D/EP F71, almanac for 1711, annotated with notes on building costs; PCC 108 Bolton; *VCH Herts. Fams.* 139. [23] Cobbett, vi. 908; Campbell, 421–29; Panshanger mss D/EP F75; *Hist. Reg. Chron.* 1723, p. 44; Oldmixon, *Life of Mainwaring* (1715), 174–5; *A Poem on the Death of Earl Cowper* (1724), 4; *A Poem Humbly Dedicated to . . . Cowper* (1711).

M. J. K.

COX, Charles (*d.* 1729), of Hay's Wharf, Mill Lane, St. Olave's, Southwark, Surr.

SOUTHWARK   1695–10 Nov. 1702
                 25 Nov. 1702–1713

s. of Thomas Cox of St. Margaret's Hill, Southwark; *m.* Jane. Kntd. 21 Sept. 1709.

Freeman, Brewers' Co. 1686, master 1708; sheriff, Surr. 1717–18; gov. St. Thomas' Hosp. by 1719–?*d.*[1]

By the time of his death Cox had established for himself a reputation as an 'eminent brewer', but his origins remain obscure. The identity of his father has been traced from the marriage licence of Cox's sister Susanna, a source which accords Cox senior with the dignity of a gentleman in 1681. However, Cox may well have been brought up in the West Indies, for he later revealed that he had 'resided' in Jamaica, and a survey of the island in 1670 indicates that a 'Thomas Cox' owned a 300-acre estate there. Even though Cox's presence in England can be plausibly assumed from the time of his admission to the Brewers' Company in 1686, he maintained an active interest in colonial affairs throughout his career. He traded to Jamaica, and also acted as London agent for his brother Samuel, who held a succession of posts in the Barbadian administration from 1697. However, it was Cox's success as a brewer which paved the way for his political career, for brewing was the dominant industry in Southwark. Moreover, although opponents often accused him of unscrupulousness at the polls, he proved a beneficent patron to his constituents, sponsoring public lectures in applied mathematics, and dispensing charity to St. Thomas' Hospital.[2]

Cox's success at the Southwark poll of 1695 gave clear proof of his status in the borough, although the agent who informed Robert Harley* of the result felt it necessary for Harley's benefit to identify Cox as 'a brewer'. Lacking such helpful instruction, any attempt to discern Cox's ensuing activity in the House cannot overcome the ambiguity caused by the simultaneous presence of his namesake Charles Cocks*, the Member for Droitwich. In his first session Cox was bracketed with the Court's adversaries in the forecast for the division on the proposed council of trade on 31 Jan. 1696, and he also voted in late March against fixing the price of guineas. He did sign the Association, however, and by the next session was prepared to support the ministry in the division of 25 Nov. concerning the attainder of Sir John Fenwick†. Moreover, Cox's loyalty to the crown had recently been confirmed by his acquittal on charges of obstructing the quartering of royal troops in Southwark. Although failing to steer completely free from local controversy, he proved a loyal adherent of the Court for the rest of his parliamentary career.

At the election of 1698 Cox was returned alongside his fellow brewer and parishioner John Cholmley*, thereby forming an electoral partnership which was to dominate the Southwark constituency for the next 14 years. Soon afterwards a parliamentary observer listed him as a Court supporter, and, after duly voting in favour of the standing army on 18 Jan. 1699, he was bracketed by a list of early 1700 with the Junto interest. In general his activity in the House during this and the next four Parliaments is further obscured by the additional presence of Charles Coxe*, the Member for Cirencester. In the first Southwark election of 1701 he had to campaign hard to meet the challenge of Arthur Moore*, although the poll revealed a comfortable victory for the sitting Members. The electoral contest of November 1701 saw a much more conclusive victory for the two brewers over Edmund Bowyer, the half-brother of Cox's former electoral partner, Anthony*. After their election the Whig Members were presented with an instruction in the name of 'the inhabitants of Southwark', which called upon them to offer vigorous support for war with France. The next day Cox and Cholmley led some 500 liverymen to poll for the Whig candidates at the election for the City of London. Given such party activism, it was little surprise that a month later Cox was identified by Robert Harley as a Whig.[3]

The first election of Queen Anne's reign caused Cox much embarrassment, for in its wake lurid accounts of the violent tactics employed by his supporters were brought before the Commons. He was initially returned on 17 July 1702, but on 10 Nov. the House declared the election void, having blamed the Whig Members for causing 'a great riot' at the polls. Even though the House also decided to restrict the Southwark franchise, at the second election both Cox and Cholmley managed to prevail over their Tory challenger, John Lade*. Cox predictably voted on 13 Feb. 1703 to agree with the Lords' amendments to the bill to extend the time for taking the abjuration oath. However, given his political stance since 1696, he was unlikely to have been the Cox included in Robert Harley's lobbying list in preparation for the vote on the Tack. This assumption is supported by a parliamentary list of 30 Oct. 1704 which forecast him as an opponent of the measure, as well as by Cox's opposition to the Tack in the key division of 28 Nov. In the remainder of the session he may well have been involved with a group of New England merchants lobbying Parliament to encourage the import of potash from North America. In August 1702 a 'Charles Cox' had featured among the petitioners for a charter to supply naval stores from New England and, given his interest in colonial affairs, the Southwark brewer can probably be identified as the 'Mr Cox' whose 'urgent offices' prevented him from presenting the petition to the House on 1 Feb. 1705. Less than a week later Cox's name headed a list of Barbadian estate owners addressing the Board of Trade and Plantations in support of the governor of that island, Sir Bevill Granville*.

In the May election of 1705 Cox enjoyed the luxury of an unopposed return, and dutifully voted for the Whig candidates at the ensuing Surrey election. At the outset of the new Parliament he was described in a list as 'No Church' and proceeded to back the Court in two of the crucial divisions of the first session: on 25 Oct., in favour of John Smith I* as Speaker; and on 18 Feb. 1706, in opposition to the regency bill's 'place clause'. Although the presence of two namesakes in the House continues to obscure his activity, a problem compounded by the return of James Cocks* in November 1707, he can with some confidence be identified as a teller on 24 Apr. 1707 in support of an amendment to a bill to control the import of gunpowder into London and Southwark. Such attentiveness to constituency affairs would have helped him to achieve his unopposed return at the Southwark election of May 1708, although his solid Whig credentials, confirmed by two parliamentary observers earlier that year, remained an enduring basis for his local support. His ruthless campaign to discredit his rival John Lade before the 1708 election, which culminated in Lade's removal as a j.p., aggravated local party bitterness.[4]

In the new Parliament Cox had several opportunities to influence major issues which had a direct bearing on his constituency. Having voted in the first session in favour of the naturalization of the poor Palatine immigrants, Cox sought to alleviate their suffering in the autumn of 1709 by offering temporary shelter in his Southwark warehouses to 'near 1,000' refugees. However, it was for political, rather than charitable, reasons that he earned a knighthood in September 1709, an honour bestowed on the occasion of his presentation of a loyal address at court. Thenceforth his elevated status allows his Commons activity to be differentiated from that of his namesakes. For the rest of the session he was prominently involved in moves against the supporters of Dr Henry Sacheverell, the High Church champion who had procured a chaplaincy at St. Saviour's, Southwark. On 16 Feb. 1710 Cox acted as a teller in favour of a motion to introduce a bill to regulate London's select vestries, a measure coming in response to reports of their corrupting influence in parliamentary elections, and was duly named to its drafting committee. He predictably voted for Sacheverell's impeachment, and also told on 24 Mar. in favour of a motion to burn a pamphlet reporting Sacheverell's answers to the articles of impeachment. Moreover, he signed an address from the London lieutenancy which was severely critical of the outrages committed by High Church mobs.

The Southwark election of 1710 was, inevitably, a keenly contested affair, but the sitting Whig Members managed to repulse the renewed Tory challenge. Cox also voted in the Whig interest at both the Reigate and Surrey contests, thereby displaying a party loyalty which was confirmed by the 'Hanover list' of the new Parliament. Although he had managed to overcome his local adversaries at the polls, in the ensuing session he found himself the target of a vengeful Tory Commons. On 15 Feb. 1711, when the House heard the report of the committee investigating victualling abuses, an information suggested that ten 'embezzled' royal casks had recently been spotted on his premises. Cox was, in fact, a purveyor of beer to the court, and, after a printed paper had been submitted to clear his name, no subsequent action was taken against him. Undeterred, his local opponents petitioned the House soon afterwards in an attempt to discredit Cox for his charity towards the poor Palatines some 18 months before. The committee appointed to investigate the matter reported on 14 Apr., having heard the testimony of parish officials who accused Cox of ignoring their warnings that the immigrants were likely to cause great local hardships, particularly in terms of expense or infection. Although the House later condemned all who had promoted such immigration, Cox defiantly maintained his party loyalty for the rest of the Parliament, voting on 7 Dec. 1711 for the motion of 'No Peace without Spain', and opposing the French commerce bill in the division of 18 June 1713.[5]

Cox's decision to stand down at the election of 1713 was evidently a result of financial hardship rather than any radical shift in his political outlook. A 'calamitous' fire at his Battle Bridge brewery in January 1712 brought him serious financial difficulties, causing him to seek the profits of public office rather than a seat in the House. Although he split his votes at the ensuing London poll, the evidence of an election committee report on 20 Apr. 1714 confirmed that he had used his local influence to aid the Whig candidates at Southwark. He certainly entertained hopes of advancement under the Hanoverians, petitioning the Treasury for 'an appointment' in November 1714. However, having drawn attention to the length of his parliamentary service, as well as to his recent loss of 'some 1,000s of pounds by fire', Cox did not find favour with the ministry. The only significant office which he subsequently held was the shrievalty of Surrey in 1717–18, a position which may have satisfied his desire for status, but one which could only have exacerbated his financial problems.

In the absence of domestic appointment, Cox directed his ambition towards the colonies. In March

1720 he actually sought to become governor of Jamaica, boasting 'the concurrent wishes of the planters and merchants' on the island, but his bid was unsuccessful. However, his petition to the Board of Trade and Plantations suggested that his finances had recovered by this time, for he professed himself concerned only with the prestige of the post, observing that 'without this grant or something equivalent, I am not able to show my head'. His will, written only weeks before his death on 13 June 1729, reveals that he had already provided for his wife 'and all my children more than any law and custom can oblige'. The will provides no clue as to the identity and number of his offspring, but the Cox name ceased to be a significant force in Southwark politics after Sir Charles's death.[6]

[1] W. Rendle and P. Morgan, *Inns of Old Southwark*, 53; *Mar. Lic. Vicar-Gen.* (Harl. Soc. xxx), 73; Guildhall Lib. mss 5449A, f. 4; J. Aubrey, *Surr.* v. 312. [2] Boyer, *Pol. State*, xxxvii. 621; *CSP Col. 1669–74*, p. 101; *1720–1*, p. 1; *APC Col. 1680–1720*, p. 391; E. G. R. Taylor, *Mathematical Practitioners of Tudor and Stuart Eng.* 284; Aubrey, 295. [3] Add. 70070, 70075, newsletters 29 Oct. 1695, 27 Nov. 1701; Luttrell, *Brief Relation*, iv. 120; *Advice of Inhabitants of Southwark* [1701]. [4] *APC Col. 1680–1720*, p. 196; *HMC Portland*, viii. 167–8; Add. 70038, J. Jones to Robert Harley, 1 Feb. 1705; *CSP Col.* 1704–5, pp. 369–70; *Surr. Poll of 1705*; L. K. J. Glassey, *Appt. JPs*, 184–5. [5] Luttrell, vi. 492; Add. ch. 76120; Surr. RO (Kingston), 445/1, Reigate poll 1710; *Surr. Poll of 1710*; *Sir Charles Cox's Case* [1711]. [6] Luttrell, vi. 713; *London Rec. Soc.* xvii. 79; *Cal. Treas. Pprs.* 1714–19, p. 20; Manning and Bray, *Surr.* i. p. xlii; *CSP Col.* 1720–1, p. 1; PCC 162 Abbott.

P. L. G.

COXE, Charles (c.1661–1728), of Lincoln's Inn, and Rodmarton and Lower Lypiatt, Glos.

CIRENCESTER	1698–1705
	1708–10 Dec. 1709
	23 Dec. 1709–1713
GLOUCESTER	1713–1722

b. c.1661, 2nd but 1st. surv. s. of John Coxe of Tarlton, Glos. by Deborah, da. of John Driver of Avening, Glos. *educ.* St. Edmund Hall, Oxf. matric. 10 July 1674, aged 13; L. Inn 1677, called 1684, bencher 1707, treasurer 1711. *m.* lic. 15 Feb. 1693, Catherine, da. and h. of Thomas Chamberlayne of Wanborough, Wilts., 3s. (1 *d.v.p.*) 2da. *suc.* fa. 1692.[1]

Serjeant-at-law 1700; King's serjeant 1701; puisne judge, Brecon circuit 1702–3, c.j. 1703–15.[2]

Coxe's family had been settled at Rodmarton near Cirencester in Gloucestershire since at least the late 16th century. His father set him on what was to prove a successful legal career, and by a fortunate marriage shortly after his father's death in 1692 he augmented his estate with the manor of Lower Lypiatt in the vicinity. He was by the early 1690s a figure of importance in Cirencester as bailiff of the manor, an office which he was said to enjoy 'by purchase for life'. As such he served as returning officer for the town at elections, and in 1690 his actions came under scrutiny when he was accused by the Whig candidate, John Grobham Howe*, of showing blatant partiality towards the Tories. In 1698 he was returned unopposed at Cirencester, having the advantage of the interests of both his kinsman Thomas Master† (whose wife was one of Coxe's cousins) and Sir Benjamin Bathurst*, the lord of the manor. A Tory, he was listed as a supporter of the Country party in a comparative analysis of the old and new Parliaments, and was separately noted as a likely opponent of a standing army. Until the later years of Queen Anne's reign his parliamentary activity is impossible to distinguish from that of Charles Cox (MP for Southwark) and Charles Cocks (Droitwich).[3]

Re-elected in January 1701, Coxe was subsequently blacklisted as having opposed preparations for war, possibly in a division on 14 Feb. 1701. He had recently been appointed a King's serjeant, though Robert Harley's* 'earnest desire' to see him rewarded at this time with a more substantial legal office, as part of the peace offering to the Tories, testifies to his loyalty and usefulness to the Country party. He was duly classified by Harley as a Tory in his list of the December 1701 Parliament, and voted on 26 Feb. 1702 for the motion vindicating the proceedings of the Commons in the impeachment of several of the King's former Whig ministers. On 6 May he carried to the Lords a private bill empowering the bishop of Gloucester to make leases of certain diocesan lands. It was through Harley's continuing friendship that in June 1702, during the Tory appointments that followed Queen Anne's accession, Coxe was appointed a junior Welsh judge, and the next month he was re-elected for Cirencester. On 28 Nov. he was named as a drafter of a bill to establish a workhouse in Gloucester. He followed his party line in voting on 13 Feb. 1703 against agreeing with the Lords' amendments to the bill for extending the period in which the oath of abjuration could be taken. In November Harley secured Coxe's promotion to chief justice of the South Wales circuit. A Court Tory, his name features on a list of probable supporters of Secretary Lord Nottingham (Daniel Finch†) in connexion with the inquiry in mid-March 1704 into Nottingham's conduct over the Scotch Plot. Forecast as an opponent of the Tack in October, Coxe either voted against it on 28 Nov. or was absent.[4]

In the 1705 election Coxe was involved in a double return at Cirencester with Henry Ireton*. Though

Coxe petitioned, he withdrew on 15 Nov., enabling Ireton to be declared duly elected. Defoe told Harley that Coxe had done so in order to prevent the House scrutinizing the extensive bribery that been practised by both sides and which in his case would undoubtedly have harmed his position as a judge. In 1706, while he was no longer an MP, an attempt was set afoot to remove him from the judiciary but this was successfully forestalled by Harley. Deeply appreciative, Coxe told the secretary: 'When I consider that by your favour only, I was made a judge in Wales . . . I must say I have more obligation to you than to all mankind.' The attempt to remove him from office was renewed in April the following year when the Whigs sought to blacken his reputation with the Court by accusing him of having voted for the Tack in 1704. Once more he appealed to Harley:

I cannot forbear taking the first opportunity to clear myself from an aspersion laid upon me as an argument to remove me from the post I have in the Queen's service. If anything were laid to my charge relating to my behaviour in my office I could be content to be silent myself and trust my fate to the report of those counties where I have had the honour to serve. But this, sir, that I hear I am accused of, is most proper to be cleared by myself, that is, that I should vote in the House of Commons for the Tack. Though you were then in the Chair, I cannot suppose you should remember everyone that voted in that question, but I am sure you will remember what I told you (before it came on) was my purpose to do upon that point, and that I should not only vote myself, but do the little I could to bring others to vote against it, and I think I had success therein. I cannot forbear to say, this report is like stabbing a man in the back. The authors might as well accuse me of murder, for as I voted against it, so I find I had like to have been a double sufferer by it. Some misled friends of mine have been my enemies ever since for voting against it; and I perceive somebody or other would have made me suffer under pretence I had been for it. It falls out, I can produce gentlemen who sat near me upon that question, when I voted against the Tack.

Harley's intervention on his behalf was evidently successful and Coxe retained his office.[5]

Coxe recovered his seat at Cirencester in 1708, a result which Lord Sunderland (Charles, Lord Spencer*) recorded as a 'loss' for the Whigs. Although his election was afterwards declared void by the House on 10 Dec. 1709, he was successful in the by-election on the 23rd. He was included on the drafting committee of a bill to remove abuse in the administration of a Gloucestershire turnpike on 25 Jan. 1710. He voted against the impeachment of Dr Sacheverell. Classed as a Tory in the 'Hanover list' of the 1710 Parliament, he featured during the 1710–11 session as a 'Tory patriot' in favour of peace, and as a 'worthy patriot' who detected the mismanagements of the previous administration. He also joined the October Club. On 30 Apr. 1713 he was first-named among the drafters of a bill to simplify the compounding of fines levied on lands in Wales.

At the last election in Anne's reign Coxe was forced to transfer to Gloucester when his former partner at Cirencester, Allen Bathurst, who had recently taken a seat in the Lords, requested him to make way for one of his brothers, while the other seat was wanted by Thomas Master for his son (Thomas Master*). Harley gave backing to an arrangement whereby Thomas Webb, one of the sitting Members for Gloucester, who had initially invited Coxe to stand with him in the forthcoming campaign, was persuaded to relinquish his seat to Coxe. He also accepted the offer of a seat at Helston but, on being returned, made his election for Gloucester. Three lists of the 1713 Parliament identify him as a Tory. In the immediate aftermath of the death of Queen Anne he asked Harley (now Lord Oxford) to recommend him to the new monarch, but must have realized that his professional career as a judge had little future under a Whig regime. Dismissal came in January 1715, though he retained his parliamentary seat until 1722. He died on 17 Oct. 1728 and was buried at Rodmarton. To his eldest son, John, who sat for Cirencester in George II's reign, he left the mansion house which he had rebuilt at Lower Lypiatt and his estate at Tarlton, while to his grandson he left his three manors and various other lands in the vicinity of Cirencester and Stroud.[6]

[1] *Trans. Bristol and Glos. Arch. Soc.* l. 178–9; *Bigland's Colls.* (Bristol and Glos. Arch. Soc.: Glos. Rec. Ser. v. pt. iii), 1028–9; M. A. Rudd, *Hist. Recs. Bisley*, 260–2. [2] *Trans. Bristol and Glos. Arch. Soc.* 178; Luttrell, *Brief Relation*, v. 184, 350; *Cal. Treas. Bks.* xxv. 593, xxix. 343. [3] *Trans. Bristol and Glos. Arch. Soc.* viii. 271; l. 178; *Bigland's Colls.* 1028–30; Rudd, 260–2; *Vis. Glos.* ed. Fenwick and Metcalfe, 59, 120–1; C 219/72; C 219/80; Bodl. 228, f. 110. [4] *HMC Portland*, iv. 24, 74; Luttrell, v. 184, 350. [5] *HMC Portland*, iv. 271, viii. 287; Add. 70220, Coxe to Harley, 10 June 1706. [6] Add. 70319, Coxe to [–], 13 Oct. 1712; 70220, Coxe to Ld. Oxford, 11 Aug. 1714; *Cal. Treas. Bks.* xxix. 343; *Hist. Reg. Chron.* 1728, p. 56; Rudd, 262; PCC 127 Abbott.

P.W./A.A.H.

CRAGGS, James I (1657–1721), of Jermyn Street, Westminster and Charlton, Lewisham, Kent.

GRAMPOUND   1702–1713

bap. 10 June 1657, 1st s. of Anthony Craggs of Wolsingham, co. Dur. by Anne (d. 1672), da. of Rev. Ferdinando Morcroft, DD, of Goswich, Lancs., rector of

Stanhope-in-Wardell, co. Dur. and prebendary of Durham. *educ.* Bishop Auckland g.s., co. Dur. *m.* 4 Jan. 1684, Elizabeth (*d.* 1712), da. of Jacob Richards, corn chandler, of Westminster, 3s. *d.v.p.* 3da. *suc.* fa ?1680.[1]

Sec. to commrs. stating debts due to army 1700; trustee, receiving loan to Emperor 1706; commr. rebuilding Chatham, Harwich and Portsmouth 1709.[2]

Cttee. Old E. I. Co. 1700–1, 1702–5; manager, united trade 1702–4; commr. Greenwich Hosp. 1704.[3]

Sec. to master-gen. of the Ordnance 1702–11; clerk of deliveries 1703–11, 1714–15; jt. postmaster-gen. 1715–20.[4]

Craggs was one of the ablest self-made men of his generation. A shrewd financial operator, he had amassed a considerable fortune by the time of his death. He was remembered by his friend Arthur Onslow† as 'a great instance of the force of natural talents' and as a man of great facility in everything he undertook. Even his detractors acknowledged his superiority in matters of business and finance. Beneath his gruff charm lay acute discernment, a 'talent in reading men' and for 'gaining on the minds of those he dealt with'. He rubbed shoulders with politicians of the first rank but was not overtly ambitious, seeming to be content with the conscientious servitude demanded by his role as the Duke of Marlborough's (John Churchill†) principal intermediary, a position which in any event raised him in the echelons of Whig leadership in the final years of Anne's reign, and yielded its own opportunities for the further acquisition of wealth.[5]

Craggs's penchant for money-making may well have been nurtured by the financial decay which had overcome his family by the last decades of the 17th century. In the later 1680s, even before his rise to fortune and prominence, he was at pains to establish his gentility and right to bear arms. The pedigree drawn up for him and registered at the College of Arms in 1691 cannot entirely be taken on trust. It suggested, but did not prove, his descent from the ancient Scottish family of Craig or Cragg. Craggs's forebears were only properly traceable back to mid-Tudor times, a minor gentry family 'anciently' situated in the parish of Wolsingham, county Durham. In the Civil Wars his grandfather Thomas Craggs, 'a great stickler in the royal cause', apparently suffered grievously from the plunderings of Scots forces. Vital 'deeds and principal writings' relating to the family's past were said to have been destroyed or lost. Thomas Craggs's elder son John settled in Ireland, leaving Anthony in possession of the small and scattered Wolsingham lands. The future MP's family were thus impoverished minor gentry, socially only a little superior to the yeomanry. His father was eventually forced to sell off his meagre estate to settle debts 'he was no ways liable to', obliging Craggs to make his own way in the world.[6]

Craggs was generally understood to be of 'mean extraction', and the early path of his advancement is obscure. When he came to London in 1680 his claim to gentility was enough to gain him employment in several royal and aristocratic households. Beginning briefly in the service of the Duke of York, he became a 'menial servant' to the Earl of Peterborough, passing on to the household of the Earl's son-in-law the Duke of Norfolk, where by 1684 he appears to have been 'steward'. According to Lady Mary Wortley Montagu, he acted as go-between in an amour between the Duchess and James II and in the process 'scraped a great deal of money'. Craggs's wife, a great beauty, was said to have been a maidservant in the employ of Lady Marlborough while Craggs himself was said to have impressed Lady Marlborough as a resourceful manager of money. By the 1690s he seems to have been serving the Earl in the capacity of a private secretary. At the same time he appears to have been set up in business as a financial broker. It was almost certainly under Marlborough's auspices that in the early 1690s Craggs acquired a lucrative army clothing contract. He also became heavily involved in the affairs of the East India Company, particularly as a sturdy defender of its interests against the advocates of a new joint-stock company. By 1695 he was prominent enough as a City businessman to excite the suspicions of the Commons with regard to his dealings as an army supplier and in the East India Company. In March that year he was required by the commission of accounts to produce his books in connexion with their current investigation of army agents, but refused to do so. His forthright answer to the commissioners, read to the House on 6 Mar., stated unequivocally that such demands set a bad precedent since they drew under scrutiny all other members of the trading community supplying the army or navy 'which may expose them to the immediate demands of their creditors to their certain ruin. And will also tend to the general discouragement of all trade and dealing with the government.' Summoned before the Commons on the 7th, he persisted in his refusal and was committed to the Tower. Towards the end of the month Robert Harley*, the chairman of the commissioners, initiated a bill compelling Craggs and several other contractors on pain of punishment to name the recipients of the bribes they were said to have paid. However, late in April, while Craggs was still incarcerated in the Tower, it was revealed in the joint Lords–Commons committee investigating Sir Thomas

Cooke's* 'secret payments' as governor of the East India Company, that Craggs had received £4,540, the largest single amount Cooke had dispersed. Brought from the Tower for questioning by the committee on 26 Apr., he gave in an account showing that he had paid only £1,462 to others, none of whom were MPs, while the remaining sums had been payments to himself including £1,468 alone 'for my own pains and solicitation in the company's affairs, to prevent a new settlement, and endeavouring to establish the old East India Company'. He had also accepted £350 'for encouragement of my friends and self to subscribe £7,000'. Craggs's dubious conduct evidently did not satisfy the joint committee, and under swiftly enacted legislation he was condemned with Cooke and his accomplices to a term of imprisonment in the Tower extending until the end of the following parliamentary session.[7]

Craggs's ardour in business was in no way dampened. Indeed his stout defence of trading interests against the prying eyes of parliamentarians doubtless won him admirers and notoriety. His association with the East India Company continued to flourish. In June 1698, for example, he subscribed £1,000 to the Company's initial advance of £200,000 towards the government's supply needs, while in 1700 he was elected a committeeman, or director, of the Company. Though he was chosen in April 1700 as secretary to the commission for stating debts due to the army, his East India concerns still took priority and prevented him from playing a full part in the proceedings. During the summer and autumn of 1701 he was actively involved in settling 'our squabbles' and in accommodating the differences between the Old and New Companies. Perceiving the great difficulties attaching to the agreement, he stood down from the court of committees in 1702 on being chosen by the general court as a manager of the united trade. The united company was in effect run by Cooke and a small inner cadre of other 'old interest' managers of whom Craggs was one, along with his friend Arthur Moore*, Sir John Fleet* and Charles Dubois. Inevitably, his business interests drew him into the heart of City politics. He was involved, for instance in August 1700, in politicking for a new lord mayor. At the 1702 general election he entered Parliament for the Cornish borough of Grampound, which he represented until 1713. Craggs almost certainly owed his election to the Marlboroughs, through their close connexions with the Boscawens, who exercised formidable electoral influence in the Cornish boroughs. Subsequently, Craggs himself became an intimate of Hugh Boscawen II*. During the formation of the new administration in the months preceding the July elections, Marlborough began to press Lord Treasurer Godolphin (Sidney†) for Craggs's appointment to a senior post in the Ordnance, where his administrative talents could be well deployed. None was readily available, however, and Marlborough expressed concern to the lord treasurer that Craggs was being deliberately overlooked. 'You know', he wrote on 2/13 July, 'I am very desirous of having him there, for he is both honest and able.' In August Marlborough proposed to Godolphin an interim arrangement whereby Craggs was appointed secretary to himself as master-general of the Ordnance, with the prospect of the keepership of the stores if another place could be found for its incumbent, James Lowther*, whom Marlborough regarded as unfit for the post. Nothing was immediately done, however, and at the end of August Marlborough was still urging Godolphin from abroad 'to take some care that Craggs be in good humour for I shall be able to make more use of him than of any other ten'. For the time being Craggs received a pension from the privy purse. At the end of the year, however, Marlborough's original suggestion that Craggs be placed at the Ordnance as his secretary was finally put into effect. Before then, in October 1702, Craggs had taken his seat in the new Parliament. He was never an avid participant in proceedings, though his occasional service in later sessions as a teller may indicate some participation in debates on secondary matters. The first occasion was on 8 Dec. when he told in favour of a motion condemning gross corruption at the Maidstone election, but was not a teller again until 1707. Craggs's Whiggery was made plain in his vote on 13 Feb. 1703 in favour of the Whig Lords' amendments to the bill for extending the time in which the abjuration oath could be taken. He was a thorough courtier, one whom Lord Halifax (Charles Montagu*) regarded as 'always right and attends'.[8]

As soon as the clerkship of the deliveries became vacant in May 1703 Marlborough solicited Godolphin for Craggs's appointment, which took place in June. The post involved Craggs closely in the minutiae of provisioning arms to the theatres of war in the Low Countries, Spain and Italy. But as Marlborough's Ordnance secretary his role was much wider: he was an essential transmitter of information to and from the Duke not only on army matters at home but also upon the course of politics. In addition to his long personal letters, his views also reached the Duke via the Duchess, with whom he consulted regularly. His connexions in the City gave him ready access to all shades of opinion and enabled him to monitor swings of political mood. In particular he kept watch on the Tories, acquiring information from those of his acquaintance such as Moore and Cooke, and duly reported their every move. Some onlookers viewed Craggs disparagingly as an obvious confrère of other low-born, money-minded MPs. In her diary in January 1705 Lady Cowper linked Craggs's name with Moore, lately made army comptroller, and Thomas Boucher*, 'the gamester', as all known to be in the service of 'the great one' [i.e. Marlborough]. Craggs also maintained links with older business associates, most notably Cooke, on whose behalf he handled the concluding stages in the Commons of a private estate bill. In October 1704 Craggs was identified as a likely opponent of the Tack, and was either against or absent in the division itself on 28 Nov. A published list of MPs elected to the 1705 Parliament described him as a 'Churchman'. When the new Parliament assembled in October he duly supported the Court candidate in the Speakership contest on the 25th. In the summer he had remarked to General Thomas Erle* how the contest had been 'blown up to the devil by the Tories', but found by the beginning of October, as he apprised Marlborough, that they had no reason for being 'so cocksure'. His more immediate concerns, however, were the problems imposed on accounting procedures in the Ordnance by the Commons' demand for 'a distinct account upon every head' instead of summarized and abbreviated accounts which previously had been accepted practice. On 18 Feb. 1706 Craggs was one of the courtiers voting against the 'place clause' of the regency bill. The news of Marlborough's victory at Ramillies in May sent him into rapture: 'there is nothing in this world', he wrote to the Duke, 'above your genius nor beyond your reach when your orders are obeyed'. He went on:

> And I hope for the future will never more be contradicted till tyranny and oppression be quite subdued and vanquished and peace and plenty flow in long succession, which all the world will own is due to you when this ungrateful age shall be no more, and truth unenvied shall speak forth your praise, unbiased and uninterested to all future ages.

Not least, victory had immediate effects at home: 'for from growing into all the faction in the world we seem in the space of six days to be the most unanimous, contented, happy people ... your Grace has done wonders here as well as in Brabant'. Craggs's skills as a political intelligencer were clearly displayed in mid-October when he warned Godolphin, apparently before the lord treasurer knew from other sources, that Harley and 'one or two' of Marlborough's 'particular' friends were planning to cause maximum disturbance in the forthcoming session. On the very last day of the pre-Union Parliament, 24 Apr. 1707, Craggs was teller against a minor amendment to a bill for preventing dangers arising from the transport of gunpowder into London from Southwark.[9]

Although Craggs had ceased in 1705 to belong to the Old East India Company's governing body, and was no longer associated with the management of the united trade, he was still in 1707 in the thick of Old Company business as one of Cooke's leading 'agitators'. He was, as one company official observed, 'on account of his intimacy with the Duke of Marlborough, as well as his own merits, in high favour in the City'. To the compiler of an analysis of the Commons early in 1708, he was unmistakably a Whig. On 26 Jan. he served as teller in favour of the bill for the better manning of the fleet. Analysing the May election results for Marlborough, Craggs was circumspect about the new Whig superiority in the Commons and hoped that 'God almighty will bless your Grace's undertakings with a success that will put it out of everybody's power to be troublesome, or I am convinced there can be no dependence upon their pretended majority'. His thoughts were unchanged a month later when he told the Duke that 'there has not been a more ticklish Parliament chosen since the Restoration of King Charles the second'. Only resounding military success could defuse 'this anarchical disposition which rages now among us'. Craggs's prayers were answered the following month with Marlborough's spectacular success at Oudenarde. Proffering his congratulations to the Duke, he was brimming with enthusiastic confidence for the future, his earlier anxieties about the ministry's majority in the Commons now gone: 'it has disconcerted a world of knavish politics and designs here'. But he was even more vigilant for signs of pre-sessional Tory activity, and in late August was feeding information to the ministers via the Duchess of Marlborough concerning recent Tory 'meetings and resolutions'. At the end of September he supervised the transportation of two shiploads of arms and ammunition from the Tower to Ostend, but more important, seems also to have been sent as Godolphin's personal emissary to brief Marlborough on the current round of peace talks. In November, as the new session drew near, his usual preoccupations with army budgeting were especially troubled, for with the year's campaign still unfinished, there was the likelihood of difficulty in raising supply: 'under such circumstances', he wrote, 'people are very loath to part with their money'. His only recorded activity during the session was on 15 Apr. 1709 when he was teller for the Court against a motion that arrears of seamen's wages be paid out of the supply already allotted to the navy. In May Craggs was involved in 'several discourses' with the Junto leaders, who were anxious to have Lord Orford (Edward Russell*) brought into the Cabinet as first lord of the Admiralty. Craggs represented the logic of this arrangement to Marlborough as a means of avoiding Whig 'inquisitions' in the next session when all thoughts should be upon consolidating the peace, now soon expected. Such an obeisance to the Junto Whigs would do service to Marlborough's lofty reputation in Parliament. But Craggs went on, somewhat prophetically:

> Your Grace has so far outdone fame itself in the conduct of the war, that even to name it is far greater praises than the greatest eloquence or poetry can describe, and nothing but the stupendous peace your great merit has alone procured us can bear any comparison with what went before, for which nothing in this world can reward you, only the philosopher's notion that merit is its own reward and one would think envy itself could not find room for complaints; but infallible experience has taught us that not only the whitest innocence, but even the brightest merit may suffer without a prudent guard to attend it, and especially in our noble senate. But which will be the best course, you are the best judge, which is all I shall presume to trouble you on this subject.

It was Marlborough's recent application to be made captain-general for life that prompted Craggs to sound this cautionary note. He had been required by the Duke to investigate the terms of General Monck's (George†) appointment to the office in 1660. In his letter on the 'Admiralty affair', he warned Marlborough that Monck's commission had only been during pleasure, adding, 'all I can learn from my Lord Chancellor's [William Cowper*] opinion is that a commission during life is a new instance and liable to malicious constructions'. The point did not register with Marlborough, however, who broached the subject with the Queen later in the year.[10]

On 20 Dec. 1709, in the proceedings on the Shrewsbury election case, Craggs was teller against allowing reconsideration of a resolution to unseat the Tory John Kynaston*. During February and March 1710 he voted in support of the government's impeachment proceedings against Dr Sacheverell. In May it was becoming clear to him that the Tories were moving in on the ministry. When the Duchess sought his views, he predicted an overwhelming Tory victory if Parliament were to be dissolved: 'as the common people are now set, they will get at least three for one'. Even so, he did not take seriously Marlborough's current thoughts of retiring. 'I agree with you', the Duke informed his wife, 'that [Craggs] wishes us both very well, and has very good judgment, but I know his temper is such that he can't think anybody is in earnest that talks of retiring'. In a long letter to the Duchess on 18 May, Craggs denounced the Junto leaders for their failure to stand by the Duke, 'their very best friend'. He thought it distracting that Harley, Abigail Masham and their 'creatures' should appropriate 'the benefits' of Marlborough's glorious actions in which they themselves 'were no more instrumental than their coach-horses'. He entirely agreed with the Duchess that all would be well if the Duke of Shrewsbury, a Harley associate whom the Queen had appointed lord chamberlain, could be made to accommodate with the ministry, 'but if they [the Junto] force my lord Duke to quit, I believe this will become a very distracted country in a very short time'. As the ministry's situation continued to deteriorate in June, however, Godolphin decided to despatch Craggs to Marlborough in the Low Countries to brief him fully on the current state of affairs, particularly on the government's increasing difficulties in obtaining continued co-operation in the City, and to receive 'his directions'. Godolphin felt that Craggs would be best able to represent Marlborough's views about the need to fight the war to a conclusion 'among all our friends in the City' and thus improve confidence. An ulterior motive for sending Craggs to Marlborough at this juncture may have been a growing sense of isolation on Godolphin's part and an anxiety to ensure that the Duke would not desert him. Craggs embarked for Ostend on 4 July, but not before having conferred with no fewer than 19 leading financiers. Not surprisingly, it was reported that he was sent on the initiative of the 'worthy bankmen' whose interests were now threatened by Tory incursions into the ministry. Shrewsbury's principal creature, James Vernon I*, was resentful of Godolphin's evident ploy to save his ministry. While Craggs was absent, Harley even attempted to secure his dismissal from the Ordnance. Marlborough heard nothing from Craggs that gave him reassurance and above all was concerned that political uncertainty seriously impeded the government's access to credit. Craggs briefed Godolphin when he returned to London in the last week of July. But less than a fortnight later Godolphin's anticipated dismissal had taken place. Shortly before, Craggs had observed to Erle that this event, when it came, would 'be far from giving that general satisfaction which will put a very different face upon all our affairs'. Marlborough was left to find his own way with the new ministers. Shrewsbury was particularly anxious to reach a *modus vivendi* with Marlborough, and met

Craggs at the end of August. Craggs was encouraged by the Duke's conciliatoriness towards Marlborough and by the assurance that there was no intention of dispensing with his services. The main problem, as both men recognized, was the breach between the Duchess and the Queen. Marlborough, as Craggs made clear, would continue so long as no affront was offered his wife. But Shrewsbury indicated that the Queen was unlikely to reform her attitude towards the Duchess. Craggs's discussion with Shrewsbury possibly helped to stabilize Marlborough's position for the time being, but the Duke remained sceptical about the new ministers. In mid-September Craggs was confidently predicting a dissolution when 'great politicians' still believed the contrary, and when the elections were held in October he grieved to see them 'entirely go one way, so that they will have it in their power to do just what they please'. His greatest fear, as he confessed to Erle, was 'a general stop' to the credit and its inevitable crippling of the war effort.[11]

In the 'Hanover list' of the new Parliament, Craggs routinely appeared as a Whig. Towards the end of the first session he twice served as teller: on 22 May 1711 in favour of the Whig candidate William Betts* in the Weymouth election case; and, more importantly, on the 25th at the report on the bill establishing the South Sea Company when he told for the small, mainly Whig minority opposed to the amendment vesting nomination of the Company's first directorate in the crown, and thus in effect in Harley. Craggs's interest in the bill was naturally aroused on account of his East India interests which the new company stood to rival. During the Whigs' wilderness years after 1710, Craggs emerged more distinctively as a senior Whig politician, although he was always seen primarily in the light of his close connexion with Marlborough. His association with the senior Whig grandees, Marlborough's son-in-law Lord Sunderland (Charles, Lord Spencer*) and Lord Halifax (Charles Montagu*), became closer. Throughout the spring and early summer of 1711 Craggs was engaged in a round of consultations, first with Henry St. John II*, and then with Harley. Emerging divisions within the Tory ranks prompted St. John to open a dialogue with Marlborough, via Craggs, with a view to enlisting his future support. These discussions moved cautiously, however, and apparently concluded in April with no deal. Tory commentators such as Dr William Stratford, canon of Christ Church, Oxford, easily saw through St. John's gambit: 'the secretary thinks he has always been able to get secrets out of Craggs, though I am afraid the contrary is true'. Stratford suggested

that Craggs was simply exploiting St. John's need in order to extract advantage of some kind for his son. In July Craggs had a two-hour meeting with Harley, ostensibly concerned with the dispute which had recently erupted over the financing of the construction of Blenheim Palace, and the Queen's insistence, contrary to the Marlboroughs' earlier belief, that she had not promised to meet its cost. The matter had threatened to break the Duke's already strained relationship with the ministry. Harley promised Craggs that he would do what he could but warned that the Queen was 'inexorable'. Craggs was unmoved by Harley's professions of goodwill towards the Duke, and reminded him of the 'difficulties' Marlborough was under and the persistent attacks on him in the Tory press. He could not have been impressed with Harley's dismissive advice that the Duke 'must not mind them'. It was undoubtedly as the Duke's personal representative that Craggs was also from about this time admitted to the inner counsels of the Junto leaders. On the first day of the new session, 7 Dec. 1711, Craggs took his party line in support of the motion of 'No Peace without Spain'. With Marlborough's dismissal at the end of the year came his own removal as chief clerk and secretary at the Ordnance. He had ceased to be clerk of the deliveries in March 1711. At the Commons' proceedings against Marlborough in January 1712, he tried to defend the Duke on the subject of the captain-generalship. According to Swift, Craggs told the House 'with a very serious countenance', though quite disingenuously, that it was the Queen who had pressed Marlborough to accept the commission, 'and upon his refusal, conceived her first displeasure against him'.[12]

Craggs's chief political role as confidant to the Marlboroughs assumed even greater importance from December 1712 when they went into exile. Belatedly, he also participated more actively, if with little distinction, in Parliament. He certainly appears to have had some part in managing the Whig attacks on the peace terms. On 6 May 1713 he voted against the bill suspending the duties on French wine, and on the 14th, in the committee proceedings on the French commercial treaty, contributed to the Whig case that it was potentially ruinous to British trade and markets. On the 30th he told for the minority supporting an opposition motion to print the bill confirming the treaty's eighth and ninth articles, voting against it in the crucial division of 18 June. On 9 May, in an unconnected matter, he had told in favour of a filibustering motion to delay consideration of the committee of public accounts' charge of corruption against Lord Wharton (Hon.

Thomas*). In the supply committee on 25 June, he seconded John Smith I's* abortive motion to prove that the previous ministry's handling of the debt-ridden civil list had been no more maladroit than the present ministry's. At the 1713 election Craggs found himself ousted from his seat at Grampound owing to a rearguard action by an obstreperous local Tory element. He continued, nevertheless, to figure in high-level consultations between leading Whigs, taking part, for example, in the autumn post-mortem discussions on the general election with Sunderland, William Cadogan* and others at Althorp. Despite earlier misgivings about the establishment of the South Sea Company, Craggs had become a shareholder and an active member of the Company's general court by the beginning of 1714. When late in February it emerged that the government was offering the Company only half of the profits accruing from the *asiento* contract, Craggs led a bitter assault against the proposals, which were eventually withdrawn. He watched expectantly as the Tories became increasingly divisive over the succession question. Even 'a great many' High Church Tories, he observed, now apprehended more dangers than they had acknowledged in the past and were voting with the Whigs. In the last weeks of the Queen's life, Bolingbroke, now seeking Whig backing for himself, negotiated with Craggs for Marlborough's support. Craggs viewed with alarm the apparent favour shown the Tories by the Hanoverian court in the early weeks of the new reign. He cautioned the Hanoverian minister Robethon with recent evidence of the Tories' continuing protectiveness towards the Pretender, and argued that Tory proscription was now necessary to overcome the previous exclusion of Whigs; though the King might one day 'succeed in annihilating parties, and in employing without distinction', a wholesale change in office-holders was necessary 'in order to be able to say that you are not governed by a party'.[13]

In December 1714 Craggs was reinstated in his old Ordnance office as clerk of the deliveries. He failed in his bid for another Cornish seat at Newport in the 1715 general election, as also in his application to the Earl of Clare (the future Duke of Newcastle) to be returned for the Earl's Yorkshire borough of Aldborough. Craggs had particularly looked forward to rejoining the Commons in order to play his part in 'bringing to condign punishment all those villains that have betrayed us to France', a privilege, as he told Clare, that would give him 'unspeakable satisfaction'. Very shortly afterwards, however, he was more than adequately compensated by his appointment as joint postmaster-general with Lord Cornwallis. He hoped it would prove 'a very easy office' once its business had been put in order. Indeed, the duties of the post interested him little. His real responsibility was as Sunderland's minister for the City, a field of activity for which his intimate associations with its institutions and personnel suited him well. During the early years of the Whig administration, his membership of the metropolitan Hanover Club provided a vital link between the ministers and the City's political and business interests. It was probably through him, for example, that the government channelled money to finance campaigns against the Tories in common council elections. The monitoring of Jacobite disaffection in the capital also absorbed his attention. The solution to such populist tendencies, as he saw it, was straightforward, if sweeping: 'when the militia, the lieutenancies and the commissions of the peace are put into hands well-affected to the government, we shall not be troubled with such riots for the future'. This concern with the preservation and safety of the new Whig regime was also evident during the passing of the septennial bill in 1716. 'I hope', he wrote to his daughter, 'it will have very good effects in quieting the minds of the people.'

Craggs enjoyed 'the nearest confidence' of Lord Sunderland, and with his own son as secretary at war from 1717, and then as secretary of state, it was natural that he should be 'in the secret and depth of all their designs'. Though he never became a director of the South Sea Company, he was among its foremost proprietors. In November 1719 he and John Aislabie*, the chancellor of the Exchequer, were entrusted to negotiate with company officials the details of the ill-fated South Sea scheme for converting the national debt. Arthur Onslow later heard that Craggs had advised against the scheme at first, fearful of an excessive inflation of stock values. But there is no doubt that he became deeply, perhaps obsessively, immersed in the scheme. His close collaboration with the company's cashier Robert Knight was later used to incriminate him. He himself subscribed to the tune of £6,000. In his enthusiasm to recruit investors he fell foul of his old patroness the Duchess of Marlborough when he tried to bypass her in an attempt to persuade her sick husband to invest. Thwarted, he openly denounced her for deliberately keeping the Duke an invalid and incapable of handling his own affairs. As the company plummeted into ruin in the early autumn of 1720, Craggs anxiously threw himself into the business of devising a viable rescue formula, presiding at the General Post Office over a series of tripartite discussions between representatives of the government, the company and the Bank which, in the third week of September, produced two versions of the 'Bank contract'. Though Robert Walpole II's* name is traditionally associated with the creation of these provisional agreements with the Bank, Craggs may have had a greater share in their conception than has so far been recognized. On 24 Sept. he sent to his daughter the 'heads' of the second, more palatable, agreement drawn up the previous day, 'which', as he remarked, 'I have taken no small pains in. All the negotiations have been at my house and the ministers of state have dined with me every day, and I hope matters will go better than they now appear.' By November, however, the rescue subscription to South Sea shares, whose value the Bank had agreed to peg, was proving a dismal failure. Craggs had argued vigorously, but unavailingly, at a stormy meeting of the general court at the close of September that those who had gained in the summer had a positive duty to subscribe. After September, however, Craggs's involvement in the crisis falls from view. In January 1721 the Commons committee of secrecy found he had applied for, and received, a massive transfer of £30,000 worth of stock for which he had not paid, plus a further £50,000 for Sunderland. Though he vehemently denied the charge when examined before the committee, he seems to have suffered a loss of morale and nerve following the sudden death of his son on 16 Feb. On hearing this news, he was said to have expressed himself in 'the most blasphemous manner'. He died a month later on 16 Mar. of apoplexy, but rumour insisted it was from an overdose of opium. He had been due the following day to be questioned before the Commons about his dealings with the South Sea Company.[14]

By its timing, Craggs's sudden death bespoke his guilt and provided Walpole with a perfect ministerial scapegoat. In the Act passed to compensate the sufferers, he was posthumously declared 'a notorious accomplice and confederate with the said Robert Knight... and did by his wicked influence and for his own exorbitant gain promote and encourage the pernicious execution of the South Sea scheme'. None the less, through Walpole's intercession a minimal confiscation of £68,920 was inflicted on his estate, of which the total value was reckoned at £1.5 million and said to yield £14,000 p.a. Walpole was probably loath to offend the husbands of Craggs's three coheiresses, all of whom were government-supporting Whig MPs: Samuel Trefusis*, Edward Eliot* and John Newsham†. The bulk of Craggs's landed estate lay at Charlton and Kidbrooke in the vicinity of Lewisham and Greenwich, Kent, which he had augmented in 1718 with a £14,000 purchase from the 2nd Duke of Montagu, the husband of the Marlboroughs' youngest daughter. He was buried at Charlton, the monument set up to his memory by his daughters recalling him simply as 'the best of fathers'.[15]

[1] *Misc. Gen. et Her.* ii. 34–39; Stowe 1058, f. 244; IGI, London; *Westminster Abbey Reg.* (Harl. Soc. x), 302. [2] Luttrell, *Brief Relation*, iv. 639; vi. 28; *Cal. Treas. Bks.* xxiii. 224. [3] Info. from Prof. H. Horwitz; Add. 38871 (unfol.); *Daily Courant*, 8 Aug. 1704. [4] H. Tomlinson, *Guns and Govt.* 225–6; *Cal. Treas. Bks.* xxix. 390; xxx. 106. [5] *HMC 14th Rep. IX*, 511; *Misc. Gen. et Her.* 37; Cunningham, *Hist. GB*, i. 209. [6] *Misc. Gen. et Her.* 34–39. [7] Boyer, *Pol. State*, xxii. 442–3; *Lady Mary Wortley Montagu Letters and Works* (1887), i. 129–31; Stowe mss 1058, f. 244; J. Carswell, *S. Sea Bubble*, 20–21; *CJ*, xi. 257; *Debates 1694–5*, pp. 2, 37–38, 45, 52, 56, 60–61; Luttrell, iv. 51. [8] *CJ*, xii. 322; info. from Prof. Horwitz; Add. 70201, Francis Lyn to Harley, 8 May 1700; Huntington Lib. Stowe mss 26(2), James Brydges'* diary, 21 Aug. 1700; Add. 22851, f. 121; 22852, f. 73; Bodl. Rawl. A.303, f. 57; *Marlborough–Godolphin Corresp.* 60, 80–81, 84, 86, 88, 95, 101, 109; Tomlinson, 226; *Bull. IHR*, xlv. 47. [9] *Marlborough–Godolphin Corresp.* pp. xxxiii, 180–2, 247, 715, 929, 1073; Add. 61164, ff. 169, 171, 173; Herts. RO, Panshanger mss D/EP F31, Lady Cowper's diary, 14 Jan. 1705; Churchill Coll. Camb. Erle mss 2/12, Craggs to Erle, 31 July, 28 Aug. 1705. [10] *HMC Fortescue*, i. 30; Add. 61164, ff. 183, 185, 187, 193, 195–7; *Marlborough–Godolphin Corresp.* 1073, 1113, 1116, 1126, 1131; Erle mss 2/12, Craggs to Erle, 15 Nov. 1708; I. F. Burton, *Captain-Gen.* 166. [11] *Marlborough–Godolphin Corresp.* 1492, 1544, 1547, 1549, 1552–3, 1557, 1559, 1566–7, 1568, 1570, 1574, 1577, 1617–19; Add. 61475, ff. 14, 25–26; Bagot mss at Levens Hall, Edward Harvey* to James Grahme*, 12 July 1710; Erle mss 2/12, Craggs to Erle, 5 Aug., 19, 23 Sept., 14 Oct. 1710; D. H. Somerville, *King of Hearts*, 271–2. [12] *Hist. Jnl.* iv. 194–5; *Bolingbroke Corresp.* i. 118, 129, 150, 167; *HMC Portland*, v. 136; vii. 29–30; *Duchess of Marlborough Corresp.* ii. 71; *Parlty. Hist.* x. 177; *Swift Works* ed. Davis, vii. 22. [13] *Hist. Jnl.* xv. 597–8, 614–15; NSA, Kreienberg despatch 15 May 1713; *Wentworth Pprs.* 339; G. S. Holmes, *Pol. in Age of Anne*, 291; Boyer, vii. 176; Carswell, 67–68; Fitzwilliam Mus. Lib. Camb. Perceval mss A21, Craggs to Anne Newsham, 22 Apr. 1714; *Orig. Pprs.* ed. Macpherson, ii. 645. [14] Add. 32686, ff. 29, 31; Perceval mss A23, A27, A29, A55, Craggs to Anne Newsham, 10 Mar. 1714–15, 8 Oct. 1715, 24 Apr. 1716, 24 Sept. 1720; *HMC 14th Rep. IX*, 511; *London Rec. Soc.* xvii. 2, 4–5 and passim; Carswell, 100, 183, 187, 188, 201–5; F. Harris, *Passion for Govt.* 228; *CJ*, xix. 427; P. G. M. Dickson, *Financial Rev.* 95–96, 109, 173, 188; J. H. Plumb, *Walpole*, i. 320–1; Boyer, xxii. 444; *HMC Portland*, v. 618, 619; *Misc. Gen. et Her.* 35. [15] *DNB*; Carswell, 250–1; Hasted, *Kent*, Blackheath, 137, 246; *HMC Buccleuch*, i. 366; Stowe 1058, f. 244.

A. A. H.

CRAGGS, James II (1686–1721), of Jermyn Street, Westminster.

TREGONY 1713–16 Feb. 1721

b. 9 Apr. 1686, 2nd but o. surv. s. of James Craggs I*. educ. M. Le Fevre's sch., Chelsea; travelled abroad (Italy) 1703–4, (Low Countries, Germany) 1706. unm. 1 da. illegit.[1]

Sec. to envoy extraordinary in Spain Apr.–Sept. 1708, resident Sept. 1708–Mar. 1711, envoy extraordinary Mar.–July 1711; commissary of stores in Spain 1710–13;

cofferer to Prince of Wales 1714–17; sec. at war Apr. 1717–Mar. 1718; sec. of state (southern dept.) Mar. 1718–d.; PC 16 Mar. 1718.[2]

The younger Craggs was an ebullient version of his father. Contemporaries were all agreed on his winning social graces and talents which were worldly rather than blessed with learning: eloquence, an excellent memory, and 'a perspicuity scarce to be met with'. A trait which did not endear him to 'cool judges', as Lady Mary Wortley Montagu once observed, was his quick tongue and a juvenile rashness. But from an early age he was marked as a politician in the making. In his own social and political aspirations, Craggs was constantly wracked by uneasiness about his 'want of birth' arising from his father's lowly beginnings.[3] Even so, Craggs's early advancement was due almost entirely to the force of his father's ambitions for him. The elder Craggs originally intended his son to follow him into the world of City business for which he devised an appropriate course of foreign travel combined with directed study. Craggs was put under the supervision of his father's friend Richard Hill, newly appointed envoy extraordinary to Savoy, and accompanied Hill to Turin in the summer of 1703. A paragon of 'dutiful and decent behaviour', he degenerated into waywardness and extravagance once released from his father's tight parental rein. He became involved with the 'top gallantries of the place and at top expense', and outspent even the sons of the Duke of Somerset and the Earl of Jersey. This irresponsibility appalled his father, who in anguished missives to Hill came close to disowning his son, and by September 1704 young Craggs was ordered home in disgrace. In the early part of 1706, however, he was trusted to undertake another educational sojourn abroad, this time in Germany. At Hanover, where he seems to have spent most of his time, he became embroiled in an unspecified, though newsworthy, 'difference' with the British envoy Emanuel Scrope Howe* in which he was considered to have done himself 'a great deal of hurt'. This may have concerned his liaison with the Elector's half-sister Sophia Charlotte, Countess von Platen, by whom he was said to have been seduced. It was through the Countess' recommendation of him as 'a young man of extraordinary merit' that, much to his subsequent advantage, he became acquainted with the Elector. But to Howe, Craggs's prolonged stay in the electorate, where he again proved his ability to incur large debts, was an undoubted embarrassment.[4]

In April 1708 Craggs was appointed secretary to the envoy in Spain, James Stanhope*, almost certainly under the auspices of his father's patron the Duke of Marlborough (John Churchill[†]). In September he was made 'resident', enabling him to deputize in Stanhope's absences on campaign. His real utility was as confidential messenger between Stanhope in Spain, Marlborough in the Low Countries and the ministers in London. During 1708 and 1709 much of this activity concerned Stanhope's ultimately abortive negotiations with Charles III for the cession of Minorca to Britain. Let into the highest counsels at an unusually early age for someone of non-aristocratic birth, Craggs soon came to see the political world for what it was, on one occasion lamenting to Stanhope, 'he that will get rewards and honours here must trust more to his riches, his credit, and his power than to his services and integrity'. He had a special regard for Stanhope, 'my master and best friend', and it was on him more than any other that Craggs seemed to be pinning hopes of advancement by September 1710: 'you know I always declared you heir apparent to the Duke of Marlborough'. In the late summer of 1710 he was fully aware that his continued association with Marlborough 'will entirely ruin me' with the new ministers. He returned to London in October and, as he anticipated, was not sent back to Spain, though technically he remained accredited for a while longer, and was briefly promoted to full envoy in March 1711. Though he found Whig fortunes at a low ebb, he was stoical enough to see the situation as a temporary and necessary aberration: 'we are very nigh a general break . . . and our misfortune is that the evil must be endured before the cure can be applied'. Now lacking suitable employment and with time on his hands, he seems to have reverted to his juvenile ways of indiscipline and profligacy. Early in March 1711 he fought a duel with a Captain Montagu which arose from a difference occurring between them at a playhouse. Wounding his opponent, Craggs was reported to have 'had the right on his side and came off with a great deal of honour'. By contrast, his attempted rape of one of the Duchess of Marlborough's servants in November while staying at her residence at St. Albans earned him the Duchess's undying enmity. Soon afterwards, she received an abusive anonymous letter which she was convinced had come from Craggs, and despite his protestations of innocence she would have no more to do with him.[5]

In April 1713 Craggs contested the by-election for the Cornish borough of Tregony, but was narrowly defeated. He was returned unopposed for the same borough at the autumn general election. He was concerned when Stanhope lost his seat at Cockermouth and made some attempt to secure him an alternative constituency, though not with immediate success. To the compilers of the Worsley list of the 1713 Parliament and of two similar analyses of the House he was easily identifiable as a Whig. Very quickly he was drawn into the Hanover Club, a centre of Whig activism, and by the beginning of 1714 his political activities had taken a propagandist turn. Already a close friend of Richard Steele*, he assisted with the nationwide distribution of *The Crisis*, Steele's controversial pamphlet accusing the ministry of endangering the Protestant succession. On 13 Mar., as prominent Tories launched complaints in the House about the contents of this and several other of Steele's recent publications, Craggs jumped to his defence but was shouted down. His zeal for Steele's cause was demonstrated again on the 18th when he was teller against the motion (which led to Steele's expulsion) that *The Englishman* and *The Crisis* were 'scandalous and seditious libels' damaging to the administration. On 31 Mar. he told in favour of allowing consideration of the unsuccessful Whig candidate's case in the recent Wallingford by-election. During the debate on the safety of the Hanoverian succession on 15 Apr. he offended Tories by 'insolent expressions' wherein he implied that the ministry itself was responsible for jeopardizing the succession. As summarized by the Whig MP Oley Douglas*, Craggs's speech excoriated the government for its naked tolerance of Jacobitism:

> If succ[ession] in danger at all, it must be during her Majesty's government. In danger from pamphlets, Jacobites, Scotch chieftains, levying forces in Ireland, pretend[er's] standard bearing English arms. We are laughed at abroad for not believing it. Our laughing at home at these things increases our danger.

A week later, on the 22nd, he and Robert Walpole II* led an attempt to deflate the Tory defence of the Utrecht peace settlement as 'safe, honourable and advantageous', though they could scarcely be heard above the noise and 'impatience'. According to Douglas' account, however, Craggs argued the favourite Whig line that the peace had been instigated by the allies whose whim the British ministers had blithely followed. Craggs's early eagerness to address the House on topics of the first political magnitude helped establish him in the opinion of his party's rank and file as an able parliamentary performer and as an aspirant to high office. Like most Whigs, he felt that the reconciliation achieved in July between Bolingbroke (Henry St. John II*) and Oxford (Robert Harley*) would not last. 'It would be the first example of sincere reconcilement where men had disputed which should be premier minister.' These ruminations, addressed to the Duke of Newcastle, also contained the first hint of his later discord with the Walpole brothers. Asking Newcastle to convey his 'respects' to Horatio II*, Craggs could not forbear adding that 'he's a cunning, designing shaver. I hope he does none of us ill offices with your lordship.' On 31 July, as the Queen lay dying at Kensington, the Privy Council entrusted Craggs with the task of journeying to Hanover to inform the Elector of the Queen's imminent demise, and to desire his 'immediate presence' in Britain. From London, the Hanoverian envoy Bothmer notified the new King of Craggs's impending mission, advising that he be rewarded with a good post rather than with gold. By the time Craggs arrived at the electoral court on 4 or 5 Aug. the Queen was already dead.[6]

Craggs received as his reward the cofferership of the Prince of Wales's household. His fortune was firmly fixed in the Sunderland–Stanhope orbit, and in the Commons he impressively fulfilled his early promise. Within three years of his vital mission to Hanover he became secretary at war, and shortly afterwards secretary of state. In high office he comported himself, as Speaker Onslow (Arthur†) recalled, with 'a sufficiency that amazed those who knew him, and with candour and frankness that pleased all'. He was certainly implicated in the South Sea scandal in 1720–1, though not as deeply as his father. However, it is impossible to surmise what action Parliament might have taken against him for his comparatively mild crime of procuring stock for the King's mistresses. Just as his name began to feature in the findings of the Commons committee of secrecy, he was struck down by smallpox, dying on 16 Feb. 1721, 11 days after Stanhope, who was by then Craggs's fellow secretary of state. He was buried in Henry VII's Chapel, Westminster Abbey.[7]

[1] *Misc. Gen. et Her*. ii. 37; Boyer, *Pol. State*, xxii. 443; *DNB*. [2] *Cal. Treas. Bks*. xxvii. 451; xxviii. 359. [3] *Misc. Gen. et Her*. 37; *Lady Mary Wortley Montagu Letters and Works* (1887), i. 129–3; HMC *Portland*, vii. 29–30; Burnet, vi. 80–81. [4] Salop RO, Attingham mss 112/1642, 1679, 1681, 1682, 1686, James Craggs I to Hill, 31 Mar., 13, 21 July, 4, 18 Aug., 29 Sept. 1704; Add. 4291, ff. 48, 54–55; HMC *Portland*, iv. 292; *Lady Mary Wortley Montagu Letters and Works*, 131. [5] *Marlborough–Godolphin Corresp*. 1096–7, 1102, 1316, 1321, 1351, 1357–8; Centre Kentish Stud. Stanhope mss U1590/0138/6/67/7, Craggs to Stanhope, 17 Oct. n.s. 1708; U1590/0139/9/71/3, same to same, 9 Aug. n.s., 16, 23 Aug., 1 Nov., 2 Dec. 1709; U1590/0140/12/73/18, same to same, 9, 12 Sept. n.s., 13 Oct., 3 Nov. 1710; *Cal. Treas. Bks*. xxv. 229; xxvii. 451; Huntington Lib. Stowe mss 57(5), p. 23; Luttrell, *Brief Relation*, vi. 699; F. Harris, *Passion for Govt*. 190; Add. 61475, ff. 47, 49, 51–52. [6] Churchill Coll. Camb. Erle mss 2/12, Craggs to Thomas Erle*, 21 Sept. 1713; J. Oldmixon, *Hist. Eng*. 509; *Steele Corresp*. 293; Cobbett, *Parlty. Hist*. vi. 1267, 1369; NSA, Kreienberg despatch 16 Mar. 1714; *Wentworth Pprs*. 370; Douglas diary (Hist. of Parl. trans.) 15, 22 Apr, 1714; Bodl. Ballard 25, f. 113; BL, Trumbull Alphab.

mss 55, Ralph Bridges to Sir William Trumbull*, 23 Apr. 1714; Add. 32686, f. 17; Fitzwilliam Mus. Lib. Camb. Perceval mss A22, James Craggs I to Anne Newsham, 5 Aug. 1714; G. M. Trevelyan, *Eng. under Q. Anne*, iii. 324, 392; *Clavering Corresp.* (Surtees Soc. clxxviii), 128. [7] *Misc. Gen. et Her.* 38; *HMC 14 Rep. IX*, 511.

A. A. H.

CRANE, George (d. 1708), of Somerton and Bridgwater, Som.

BRIDGWATER 1698–1700

s. of Francis Crane of Somerton. *m.* (1) by 1662, Sarah (d.1672), 4da.; (2) by 1673, Anne (d. 1688), da. of Humphrey Blake of Bridgwater, bro. of Adm. Robert Blake, 2s. (1 *d.v.p.*) 2da.[1]

Alderman, Bridgwater, mayor 1679; commr. recusants' fines, Som. 1688.[2]

Crane, a merchant of Bridgwater, may have been the corrupt government agent of that name who, according to John Oldmixon, the Somerset historian, was concerned in the reprisals that followed the failure of the Monmouth rebellion. Despite his earlier support for James II, Crane found no difficulty in accepting the Revolution and when he was returned for Bridgwater in 1698 his fellow Member, Roger Hoar, another local merchant and a Whig, described him as a Court supporter. During his brief spell in Parliament he took little part in proceedings, however, obtaining a grant of leave of absence on 15 Apr. 1699. He died in September or October 1708, his burial at St. Mary's church, Bridgwater, taking place on 6 Oct.[3]

[1] *Som. N. and Q.* iv. 16; J. Oldmixon, *Life of Robert Blake*, 119; St. Mary's, Bridgwater par. reg. (*ex inf.* from Frances Pearce). [2] S. G. Jarmon, *Bridgwater*, 266; *Cal. Treas. Bks.* viii. 1804. [3] J. Oldmixon, *Brit. Empire in America* (1708), i. 337–8; Add. 28883, f. 36; St. Mary's, Bridgwater par. reg. (*ex inf.* Frances Pearce).

P. W.

CRAVEN, Robert (1674–1710), of Combe Abbey, Warws.

COVENTRY 17 Oct.–15 Nov. 1710

b. 3 Dec. 1674, 4th s. of Sir William Craven (d. 1695), of Combe Abbey by Margaret, da. of Sir Christopher Clapham of Beamsley, Yorks. *educ.* Christ Church, Oxf. 1693; M. Temple 1697. *unm.*[1]

From at least the early 16th century Craven's forebears had resided in the Yorkshire parish of Appletreewick, but the family had since come into possession of estate in the vicinity of Speen in Berkshire, where Craven was born. His father moved away from Yorkshire, permanently it would seem, for the Warwickshire visitation of 1682–3 described him as 'now residing at Combe Abbey, Warwickshire'. In 1697 Craven's eldest brother William succeeded the veteran Earl of Craven, his cousin thrice removed, who had died unmarried, in the barony of Craven of Hampstead Marshall. A special remainder to the title had been granted to five of the Earl's relatives in succession, each of whom had predeceased him, the last being Craven's father in 1695. Although sometimes referred to by the title of 'honourable', Craven was never formally granted the rank and style of a younger son of a baron. In the Coventry election of 1708 he stood unsuccessfully as a Tory, and though his petition was heard, the Whig sitting Members 'carried it by a great majority'. After a strenuous campaign in the town in 1710 he topped the poll. Craven was identified as a Tory in the 'Hanover list', but did not live to take his seat. A little more than a fortnight before the Commons was due to assemble he was stricken with smallpox, from which he died on 15 Nov. He was buried at Binley, near Coventry.[2]

[1] *Vis. Warws.* (Harl. Soc. lxii), 72. [2] Luttrell, *Brief Relation*, vi. 413; Add. 70421, Dyer's newsletters 7 Oct., 16, 18 Nov. 1710; *HMC Portland*, iv. 614.

A. A. H.

CRAWFORD, Robert (c.1657–1706), of Duke Street, Westminster.

QUEENBOROUGH 1689–1705

b. c.1657. *m.* (lic.) 27 July 1687, aged about 30, Frances (d. 1693), da. and coh. of Henry Sandford of Bobbing, Kent, wid. of Sir George Moore, 1st Bt., of Maids Moreton, Bucks. and Col. Edward Digges of Chilham Castle, Kent, *s.p.*[1]

Lt. of ft. Admiralty regt. 1673, capt.-lt. 1684, capt. 1686–9; storekeeper, Sheerness 1683–*d.*; lt. gov. Sheerness 1684–Dec. 1690, gov. Dec. 1690–*d.*; brevet col. 1694.[2]

Jurat, Queenborough June 1688–?*d.*; freeman, Portsmouth 1699.[3]

Crawford's origins are obscure. In his will both Hugh Corry and Hugh Montgomery, 2nd Earl of Mount-Alexander [I] are described as his 'kinsmen', suggesting a Scots–Irish connexion. The description was reciprocated by Mount-Alexander in August 1706 when writing to the Duke of Ormond. One of the leading participants in the funeral of the 1st Earl of Mount-Alexander in 1663 had been an Alexander Crawford. The marriage of Crawford's sister to the Reverend Alexander Delgarno of county Meath may also be a significant pointer to his origins. He had at least two brothers: William, a hearth tax collector in London and Middlesex, who fled to Flanders, joined William's invasion fleet and was killed at Killiecrankie; and David, who may have been the long-serving deputy commissary of the musters with whom historians have confused this Member. Crawford's commission in the Duke of York's regiment, under the colonelcy of Sir Charles Lyttleton, 3rd Bt.[†], and in a company captained by Richard Bagot, suggests a Staffordshire link. The association certainly proved enduring, for Crawford served under Lyttleton as lieutenant-governor of Sheerness. Loyalty to James II in 1687–8 seems to have brought him local office as both a justice and deputy-lieutenant, plus the likelihood of entering Parliament in the elections scheduled for 1688. At some point Crawford must have switched sides, for the Revolution saw him keep his post and secure a seat at Queenborough in the Convention of 1689, which he continued to hold until 1705.[4]

No sooner had Crawford been re-elected in 1690 than he was confronted by a Jacobite intrigue designed to secure the surrender of Sheerness to James II. William Fuller visited Crawford with a letter from Mary of Modena hidden inside a hollow key. Crawford arrested the messenger, who thereupon produced a protection from Secretary of State Shrewsbury and was sent up to London. The event caused considerable alarm among the jurats of Queenborough, forcing Shrewsbury to reassure them that Crawford had acted correctly and had received the King's 'good opinion of his loyalty to his service'. In return Shrewsbury hoped that the corporation would 'increase the esteem they have for him'. The Marquess of Carmarthen (Sir Thomas Osborne[†]) classed Crawford as a Court supporter on a list of the new Parliament, and his alertness in Sheerness cannot have harmed his prospects for promotion. Indeed, a memorandum, probably written in September 1690, before the second session of the Parliament, suggested that Crawford wished to succeed Lyttleton as governor. On 31 Oct. 1690 Crawford was granted leave to go to his command, and by early December he had succeeded Lyttelton as governor. Carmarthen felt able to include him on a list later in December, of likely supporters in case of an attack in the Commons against his ministerial position. Paradoxically, Crawford was classed by Robert Harley* as a Country party supporter in April 1691. The 1691–2 session saw his name resurface in connexion with Jacobite intrigues when the Preston Plot was examined by the House, but nothing came of it. Crawford was clearly perceived to be a placeman, classified as such on no fewer than six lists in 1692 and 1693. On 19 Jan. 1694 he was given leave of absence for health reasons, the only time such an order occurs after 1690, although there is plenty of evidence that he spent time in Kent on military business while the House was sitting.[5]

Crawford sold the manor of Bobbing, presumably after the death of his wife in 1693. This did not affect his political interest at Queenborough which was based on his military office, not landownership. It would seem that Westminster was now his main residence. Early in 1696 the vestry minutes of St. James's record him as being particularly involved in a bill to enable the parish to pay off the debts arising from the construction of the church, although he was not responsible for managing the bill through the House. Indeed, Crawford was generally inactive as a Member. He was forecast in January 1696 as likely to support the Court in the divisions over the proposed council of trade. He also signed the Association in February. But he was absent in late March from the division concerning the price of guineas. The by-election at Queenborough in October 1696, caused by the demise of Caleb Banks*, saw Crawford active on behalf of Sir George Rooke*, but in the event the admiral withdrew from the contest. Of greater concern to Crawford were the revelations of Sir John Fenwick[†], which again brought to light the Jacobites' expectations that Crawford would surrender Sheerness to them. When on 6 Nov. Admiral Edward Russell* 'opened the matter' of Fenwick's confession and demanded an inquiry, Crawford was one of the Members who also felt constrained to defend themselves by asking that Fenwick prove his allegations. It may have been this intervention (or a similar one) that the historian John Oldmixon counted as a speech in favour of the attainder bill. Crawford was not listed as voting on 25 Nov. 1696 on the third reading of the bill.[6]

Crawford was classified in September 1698 as a placeman, and on a comparative analysis of the old and new Parliaments he was also grouped with Court adherents. On 18 Jan. 1699 he voted against the third reading of the disbanding bill. In May, he wrote to John Ellis* requesting a letter of recommendation to the bishop of Down on behalf of his brother-in-law Delgarno. On an analysis of the Commons into interests made early in 1700 he was listed as a placeman. He was also listed in February 1701 as likely to support the Court over the 'Great Mortgage'. Crawford appears to have been ill late in 1702, because he wrote on 16 Dec. that he could only go out for an hour or so into Hyde Park. In March 1704 he asked that Delgarno be made an army chaplain, to one of the new regiments being raised, a request he repeated in January 1705 for any of the regiments intended for Ireland. Although Crawford was forecast on 30 Oct. 1704 as a probable opponent of the Tack, and his name was included on Robert Harley's lobbying list, he voted for it on 28 Nov.; a surprising departure, given his previous adherence to the Court. The vote was used against him at Queenborough in the 1705 election, when he was defeated. However, even then he was not removed from the governorship, evidently to the surprise of many, including Lord Halifax (Charles Montagu*). By May 1706 moves were afoot to replace him, but in June correspondence suggests that this was because of illness rather than for political misdemeanours. On 28 June the Duke of Marlborough (John Churchill†) wrote that it was 'apprehended that Mr Crawford could not recover', but he was not reported dead until 19 Nov. His will, made in June and July 1706, ordered his body to be buried next to his wife, 'Lady Moore', in the chancel of Bobbing church, unless he died a long way from London. Tantalizingly, he left £5 to the poor of the parish of his birth, without mentioning this by name. Bequests were made, among others, to his brother David and kinsmen the Earl of Mount-Alexander and Hugh Corry, the chief beneficiary being Crawford's sister, Jane who, with her husband, was named as an executor.[7]

[1] *Mar. Lic. Vicar-Gen.* (Harl. Soc. xxxi), 7; *Canterbury Mar. Lic.* iv. 169. [2] H. Tomlinson, *Guns and Govt.* 233. [3] Centre Kentish Stud. Qb/RPp/1; R. East, *Portsmouth Recs.* 372. [4] PCC 5 Poley; *HMC Ormonde*, n.s. viii. 253; *Montgomery Mss* ed. G. Hill, 248; *Cal. Treas. Pprs.* 1557–1696, pp. 168–9; *Cal. Treas. Bks.* ix. 305, 1093, 1193; Duckett, *Penal Laws and Test Act* (1882), 365. [5] Luttrell, *Brief Relation*, ii. 20; *Hatton Corresp.* (Camden Soc. n.s. xxiii), 172–3; *CSP Dom.* 1689–90, pp. 503, 553, 555; Nottingham Univ. Lib. Portland (Bentinck) mss PwA 2724, memo. [?Sept. 1690]; *Luttrell Diary*, 73, 203. [6] Hasted, *Kent*, vi. 197–8; Huntington Lib. Ellesmere mss EL 9902, St. James's vestry mins.; *HMC Downshire*, i. 629; Add. 28880, f. 70; BL, Althorp mss, Halifax pprs. Crawford to Mq. of Halifax (William Savile*), 22 Aug., 19 Sept., 1, 10 Oct. 1696; *Vernon–Shrewsbury Letters*, i. 47; Centre Kentish Stud. Stanhope mss U1590/059/5, Robert Yard* to Alexander Stanhope, 17 Nov. 1696; Cobbett, *Parlty. Hist.* v. 1051; Oldmixon, *Hist. Eng.* 152. [7] Add. 28884, f. 37; 28889, f. 473; 61298, ff. 145, 147; 61458, ff. 160–1; *Marlborough–Godolphin Corresp.* 548, 574; *Marlborough Despatches* ed. Murray, ii. 648; Folger Shakespeare Lib. Newdigate newsletter 19 Nov. 1706; PCC 5 Poley.

S. N. H.

CRAWLEY, Richard (1666–1713), of Doctors' Commons and Northaw, Herts.

WENDOVER 1701 (Dec.)–1702, 21 Nov. 1702–1705

bap. 29 Aug. 1666, 4th but 3rd surv. s. of Francis Crawley of Northaw, Herts., baron of Exchequer, by Mary, da. of Richard Clutterbuck, merchant, of London. *educ.* ?St. Paul's; Jesus, Oxf. 1683. *m.* settlement 24 Oct. 1699, Sarah, da. of Sir Samuel Dashwood*, 2s. 5da. (1 *d.v.p.*). *suc.* bro. ?1707.[1]

Dep. registrar, ct. of Admiralty 1698–1705; registrar 1705–*d.*; registrar, ct. of Delegates by 1700–*d.*[2]

Crawley's family had been established in Bedfordshire since the 15th century. His grandfather had been a justice of common pleas and his father served as a baron of the Exchequer, with an estate estimated at £1,000 p.a. As a younger son, Crawley entered the legal profession as a 'public notary', probably following in the footsteps of his brother-in-law, Thomas Bedford, who was deputy registrar to the court of the Admiralty from Charles II's reign to his death in 1698. He was probably the Richard Crawley who invested in the Bank of England in 1694. In January of that year Crawley had secured the reversion of the office of registrar of the court of Delegates, after the death of the incumbent, Thomas Oughton, and the reversionary interest of Charles Tucker (which Tucker resigned in 1694). Meanwhile, in 1698, he had acquired the reversion of the same office in the court of Admiralty, serving as Sir Orlando Gee's* deputy after the death of Bedford. He succeeded Gee in 1705.[3]

In 1699 Crawley made a favourable marriage into the Dashwood family, through which he acquired property in Wendover, and also around that time he inherited a half-share in his mother's estate. In November 1701 he was elected for the borough and classed as a Tory by Robert Harley*. He was fairly active in his first session, being appointed on 10 Jan. 1702 to the drafting committee of the bill to encourage privateers, into which his office would have given him an insight, and serving on the conference committee in May after the Lords had returned the bill. On 2 Feb. he provided the Commons with information regarding fees in the court of Admiralty. He also acted as a teller on three occasions: against committing the bill for establishing Worcester College, Oxford; against a clause relating to the transport service being added to a supply bill; and against an amendment to leave out a clause in the bill preventing frauds in the salt duties.[4]

Although defeated at Wendover at the next election, he was eventually seated on petition in November 1702. In this session he acted as a teller on 13 Feb. against the Lords' amendment to the bill extending the time for taking the abjuration oath. This was a crucial political division and his name appeared on the subsequent list of those voting with the Tories. In the following session he acted as a teller on two occasions: on 29 Jan. 1704 in favour of the Speaker leaving the chair so that the House could go into a committee of the whole on a supply bill; and on 18 Feb. against adjourning committees. In the 1704–5 session he was nominated on 11 Nov. to the drafting committee of the bill prohibiting trade with France and two days later provided the Commons with accounts of salvage money and other Admiralty perquisites. On the crucial issue of the Tack he was forecast as a likely opponent, and on Harley's list the Admiralty judge, Sir Charles Hedges*, was deputed to lobby him. He did not vote for the Tack on 28 Nov. A list of 1705 classed him as a placeman by virtue of his legal offices.

At the 1705 election, Crawley stood in partnership with Hedges, but both were defeated. Nevertheless, he continued to attend the Commons on occasion with information from the court of Admiralty. He declined to stand at Wendover in 1708, or in the 1709 by-election, but put up in 1710, when he was defeated and petitioned without result. His brother's will (proved in 1710) made him heir to most of the family property. Crawley died in Doctors' Commons on 21 Mar. 1713. He was buried according to the terms of his will in Someris chapel, near Luton. He left the family estates in the Luton area, including the recently purchased Stockwood estate, to his eldest son, John†. In addition to the provisions of her marriage settlement, his wife received the lands purchased since his marriage in the parish of Wendover and the 'copyhold tenement' at Northaw, Hertfordshire. His younger children received £4,000 apiece, although after the death of one daughter the survivors received an extra £500.[5]

[1] IGI, Beds.; W. Austin, *Hist. Luton*, i. 234–5; PCC 78 Leeds, 177 Smith. [2] *CSP Dom.* 1698, p. 396; 1694–5, p. 14. [3] Austin, 183–4; *Beds. N. and Q.* ii. 274, 321–2; W. Austin, *Hist. of a Beds. Fam.* 209; DZA, Bonet despatch 6/16 July 1694; Luttrell, *Brief Relation*, iv. 412; Add. 28883, f. 80. [4] PCC 166 Noel. [5] PCC 177 Smith, 78 Leeds; Le Neve, *Mon. Angl.* 1700–15, p. 255.

E. C./S. N. H.

CRESSETT, Edward (*d.* 1727), of Cound, Salop.

SHREWSBURY 1710–1715

o. s. of Robert Cressett of Upton Cressett, Salop by Elizabeth, da. of James Huxley of Darnford, Staffs., and cos. of Sir Edward Acton, 3rd Bt.* *m.* 8 Aug. 1695, Elizabeth, da. of John Doughty of Betton, nr. Shrewsbury, Salop, 7s. 5da. *suc.* fa. 1678, gdfa. Robert Cressett at Upton Cressett and Cound 1702.[1]

Freeman, Much Wenlock 1695, Ludlow 1696, Shrewsbury, Bridgnorth by 1719; sheriff, Salop 1702–3.[2]

A sound Shropshire Tory, Cressett came from a family established in the county since at least the 14th century, and during the Civil War his great-grandfather had been one of the leaders of the local Royalists. His first tilt at a parliamentary election was for a vacant seat at Shrewsbury in January 1710, when in spite of the strength of the Tory interest in the borough, and the personal support of a former Member, John Kynaston*, he was defeated by his Whig opponent. He was not deterred, however, and, alongside other prospective Tory parliamentary candidates in Shropshire, soon afterwards placed himself in the forefront of the local agitation on behalf of Dr Sacheverell. Having appeared among the gentlemen who welcomed Sacheverell to Shrewsbury during the celebrated 'progress', he provided an entertainment for the doctor at Cound. Later, when one of Sacheverell's counsel, (Sir) Simon Harcourt I*, arrived at Shrewsbury on circuit he 'was met out of town by 400 horse headed by Mr Owen [Roger*] and Mr Cressett'. The effect of all this stage management was nicely to focus the popular enthusiasm upon the Tory candidates at the general election of 1710, and in Shrewsbury Cressett and his confederates were returned at the top of the poll.[3]

Cressett seems to have been a back-bench Tory of unexceptional opinions: classed as a Tory in the 'Hanover list', he was one of the 'worthy patriots' who in the 1710–11 session detected the mismanagements of the previous ministry. In the same session, on 8 Jan. 1711, he was given leave of absence for one month, owing to his wife's illness. He was a member of the October Club, and on 18 June 1713 voted for the French commerce bill. In the Worsley list he was classed simply as a Tory.

Cressett did not put up for re-election in 1715. Four years later he wrote to Lord Oxford (Robert Harley*), with whom he appears to have been seeking to ingratiate himself, to inform him of an impending vacancy in the parliamentary representation of Bishop's Castle, which he thought would interest Oxford's son Lord Harley (Edward*), adding, 'I am unfortunate in not having a vote for that corporation, as I have in all the rest in Shropshire, otherwise my lord might command it'. His name figured in the list of 'well-wishers' supposedly drawn up for the Pretender in 1721, and the following year he ventured to stand for Much Wenlock in the general election, but came bottom of the poll. Cressett died at his house in Grosvenor Street, Westminster, on 9 Jan. 1727.[4]

[1] Info. from Mr W. Cash M.P.; *Trans. Salop Arch. Soc.* ser. 4, vi. 220; xii. 225; *Salop Par. Reg. Soc.* Lichfield dioc. ii, Cound, 45–46, 53–54; xv. 562, 578, 587, 601, 613, 631; *Ped. Reg.* ii. 31. [2] Salop RO, Forester mss, copy of Much Wenlock corp. bk.; Salop RO, Ludlow bor. recs. admissions of freemen. [3] *Trans. Salop Arch. Soc.* ser. 1, ix.

403–4; A. Fletcher, *Outbreak of Eng. Civil War*, 359–60; Bradford mss at Weston Park, John Bridgeman to (Sir) Arthur Owen ii*, 9 Jan. 1710; Luttrell, *Brief Relation*, vi. 532; Boyer, *Anne Annals*, ix. 203; G. Holmes, *Trial of Sacheverell*, 245; *HMC Portland*, iv. 539. [4]Add. 70221, Cressett to [Oxford], 25 Nov. 1719; info. from Mr Cash.

D. W. H.

CRESSWELL, Richard (1688–1743), of Rudge, Salop and Pinkney Park, Sherston, nr. Malmesbury, Wilts.

| BRIDGNORTH | 1710–1713 |
| WOOTTON BASSETT | 1713–1715 |

b. 1688, 1st s. of Richard Cresswell of Sidbury, Salop by Mary, da. of Edward Moreton of Moreton and Engleton, Staffs., and sis. of Matthew Ducie Moreton*. *m.* (1) 1 Nov. 1709, Elizabeth (*d.* 1717), da. of Sir Thomas Estcourt*, and h. to her bro. Thomas Estcourt (*d.* 1704) of Pinkney Park, 2s.; (2) Roberta, wid., *s.p. suc.* gdfa. 1708, fa. 1723.[1]

'Black Dick' Cresswell was the grandson of a staunch Cavalier, Richard Cresswell (who had served as a page to Charles I), and the son of a roaring Shropshire squire. He inherited his grandfather's loyalism and, to an even greater degree, his father's instability. The atmosphere of the family home is described in a plaintive letter from Cresswell's brother-in-law, who in vain pursuit of a debt was obliged to stay for a time at Sidbury. He called Cresswell's father a 'Judas' and 'a devil incarnate':

in short he is a perfect madman, and to live with him is to live in Bedlam, for he is made up of noise, nonsense, railing, bawling and impertinence, and there is not so much as anything like a gentleman comes near him, but [he] . . . is most honourably entertained by smoking and drinking with his own bailiffs, sheriff's men, tinkers, rat-catchers and such other scoundrels as I would turn my footman away if I should see him in their company.

His father having been disinherited, Cresswell succeeded in 1708 to his grandfather's very considerable estate, comprising several manors in Staffordshire, Shropshire and Herefordshire, worth above £1,200 p.a. Cresswell already enjoyed a reputation as a 'giddy rake' by the time of his marriage 'to a fortune of £2,000 a year', but doubtless his own recent inheritance encouraged his wife's family to overlook any defects in his character. The addition of her property, including the Wiltshire manors of Sherston, Malmesbury and Norton, helped to consolidate Cresswell's status among north Wiltshire gentry, and he was not slow in displaying his wealth more widely. A fellow Salopian reported from London in July 1710: 'On Sunday last I was in Hyde Park, where the most considerable person was our countryman Mr Cresswell, who made his appearance with four footmen in the best liveries that I have seen a great while.'[2]

Cresswell's father threw himself with unaccustomed zeal into county politics in 1710, 'making all his efforts to get High Church Members for next sessions' and originating a 'Tory' address from Bridgnorth in support of Dr Sacheverell. The younger Cresswell stood as a Tory candidate for the borough, where as early as June he was promising to 'spare no money'. His popularity at the time may be gauged from a report of his visit to Hampton, Surrey, in June 1710, where he was selling an estate: 'Mr Cresswell and his lady are come hither . . . with a coach and six, three footmen and all things suitable. The town of Hampton thought it so great a blessing when he came there that the bells rang more than they have done for anything since the doctor's sentence.' Cresswell exploited to the full the propaganda value of the Sacheverell trial. When the doctor's triumphal procession passed through Shropshire in July 1710, he invited him to dine at Bridgnorth. Before Sacheverell arrived, Cresswell set up a printing press in a school yard and invited the neighbouring clergy and gentry to come and pay their respects to 'the idol of the country'. In August he was confident enough to prophesy the imminent dismissal from office of all Whigs, including the lord lieutenant of Shropshire, Lord Bradford (Richard, Lord Newport*), upon which one Court Whig, Sir William Forester*, commented that Cresswell 'may find himself as much mistaken, as his wife was in him'. Cresswell topped the poll at the election, where popular enthusiasm for Sacheverell was combined with efficient organization and financial investment to compensate for the slenderness of his proprietorial interest. The size of his overall outlay presumably contributed to his decision shortly afterwards to sell one of his recently inherited Shropshire manors and remove to Wiltshire.[3]

Cresswell made little impression in the House, and made no recorded speech. He was listed as a Tory on the 'Hanover list' and as a 'worthy patriot' who in the 1710–11 session exposed the mismanagements of the previous ministry. He belonged to the October Club, and in 1711 was arrested on an information which, according to the Dutch agent L'Hermitage, alleged that he 'avait bu à la santé du Prétendant à Bath, et avait dit que le plus grand nombre des autres membres en feraient autant s'ils osaient. Il avait porté cette santé à toute la compagnie qui buvait avec lui, mais chacun l'avait refusé.' No further action appears to have been taken against him. He voted for the French commerce bill on 18 June 1713, and at the following election was returned for Wootton Bassett, a borough lying near his Wiltshire property, where he probably enjoyed the backing of Lord Bolingbroke (Henry St. John II*). He was marked as a Tory in the Worsley list.[4]

Cresswell did not stand for Parliament again after Queen Anne's death. Removed from the county lieutenancy in 1715, it is conceivable that he took some part in the Jacobite rebellion, to which his political principles and financial difficulties (he was obliged to sell Norton manor, Wiltshire, in 1714) would have attracted him. One source hints that he may have been present at the battle of Preston, while in 1716 he was reported to be in France, responsibility for overseeing the education of his children being left to his uncle Matthew Ducie Moreton and his friends Hon. Benedict Leonard Calvert* and Sir Thomas Mackworth, 4th Bt.* Indeed, it is likely that the rest of his days were spent abroad, despite the fact that in 1723 he succeeded his father to an estate worth £1,000 p.a. His mode of life was not salubrious. Soon after his first marriage he began to keep a Miss Wyndham as his mistress, and after her death in March 1714, when he was said to be 'in mourning', he appears to have left for the Continent. In December 1716 he was arrested on 38 separate counts of buggery with 'a young Genoese boy he had lately dressed up'. He had been 'so public in his discourse and actions that they can fix on him the fact . . . in his own house, the streets, in porches of churches and palaces'. He is next heard of in France in 1730, where he had been travelling for four years 'with one Mrs Smith, called his niece'. He had 'run into indiscretions abroad', it was said, and the tutor to the young Lord Harcourt considered him a very unfit companion for his charge:

> Whatever be the gentleman's history, by his equipage it appears that he travels merely for his diversion, as formerly he lived for his pleasure. His fair companion is perfectly well educated, as far as foreigners may judge by her behaviour and appearance. But he, travelling without any female attendance, has on many occasions lost her the respect due to an Englishwoman of family.

His financial situation did not improve, and in 1730 he mortgaged Pinkney Park for £10,000. In his latter years the administration of his affairs was left to his son Thomas Estcourt Cresswell[†]. He died in 1743, although no will or administration of his estate has been found.[5]

[1] *Trans. Salop Arch. Soc.* ser. 4, v. 65–66; Wilts. RO, 403/56C; G. Campbell, *Web of Fortune*, 32–52; Soc. of Geneal. index to par. reg.; M. I. Sherston par. ch. [2] Campbell, 27, 51; Lincs. AO, Monson mss 7/13/132, Gervase Scrope to Sir John Newton, 31 Mar. 1711; *Lady Mary Wortley Montagu Letters* ed. Halsband, i. 19; PCC 110 Barrett; Wilts. RO, 403/52, 56C; Add. 70225, Philip Foley* to Robert Harley*, 3 June 1706; 70298, anon. to [?same], 15 July 1706; NLW, Ottley mss, Sir Thomas Powys* to Adam Ottley, 4 July 1710. [3] Monson mss 7/13/123–4, Scrope to Newton, 26 June, 1 July 1710; Ottley mss, Charles Baldwyn* to Adam Ottley, 30 June 1710; Boyer, *Anne Annals*, xi. 203–4; G. Holmes, *Trial of Sacheverell*, 247–9; Glos. RO, Hardwicke Ct. mss, Lloyd pprs, Daniel Tottis to Dr William Lloyd, 8 July 1710; Salop RO, Forester mss, Forester to George Weld*, 5 Aug. 1710; Surr. RO (Kingston), Somers mss, 371/14/02/98, D. Rogers to Margaret Cocks, 7 June 1710; Add. 70421, 27 July 1710; *CJ*, xvi. 415; *VCH Salop*, iii. 277; *Trans. Salop Arch. Soc.* ser. 4, x. 263. [4] Add. 17677 EEE, ff. 367–8; H. T. Dickinson, *Bolingbroke*, 115; Campbell, 36. [5] Campbell, 27–28, 38, 47, 51–52; Goodenough mss (ex inf. Prof. D. Szechi); Glos. RO, Ducie mss D340a C20/15, Samuel Steward to Matthew Ducie Moreton, 31 Dec. 1716; Monson mss 7/13/131, Scrope to Newton, 17 Dec. 1710; SRO, Stair mss GD135/141/6, Henry Davenant to Ld. Stair, 5 Dec. 1716; BL, Verney mss mic. 636/55, Lord Fermanagh (John Verney*) to Ralph Verney[†], 9 Mar. 1714; *VCH Wilts.* xv. 171; Wilts. RO, 403/52; Harcourt Pprs. iii. 2–3.

D. W. H.

CREWE, John *see* **OFFLEY, John Crewe**

CROFT, Sir Herbert, 1st Bt. (c.1652–1720), of Croft Castle, Herefs.

HEREFORDSHIRE 1679, 1690–1698

b. c.1652, o. s. of Herbert Croft, DD, bp. of Hereford, by Anne, da. of Jonathan Browne, dean of Hereford. *educ.* Magdalen Coll. Oxf. matric. 27 Apr. 1668, aged 16; M. Temple 1668. *m.* c.Oct. 1675, Elizabeth (*d.* 1709), da. of Thomas Archer[†] of Umberslade Hall, Tamworth, Warws., sis. of Andrew Archer*, 6s. (4 *d.v.p.*) 3da. *cr.* Bt. 18 Nov. 1671; *suc.* fa. 1691.[1]

Commr. recusants, Herefs. 1675; sheriff, Herefs. Nov. 1682; high steward, Leominster 1696–*d.*[2]

Croft's brand of moderate Whiggism, and his equivocal relationship with the Harleys in Herefordshire, may be explained at least in part by his immediate family background as the son of a Latitudinarian bishop. A convert from Catholicism, Bishop Croft had become by the 1670s a hammerer of popery in his diocese, and a controversial advocate in print of the comprehension of Protestant Nonconformists within the Church of England. Then under James II he accepted the Declaration of Indulgence. His son was returned to the first Exclusion Parliament as a supporter of the Country party, but appears thereafter to have abated the vigour of his opposition to the Court, except when he was questioned on the repeal of the Penal Laws and Test Act, which, unlike his father, he was not prepared to countenance. He quickly accommodated himself to the Revolution, subscribing the loan to the Prince of

Orange in December 1688, and promoting a loyal address from Herefordshire the following summer. But when he contested the county in 1690 against the veteran Whig Sir Edward Harley* he did so on the basis of opposing a Presbyterian interest. 'Sir Herbert Croft and others', reported Harley's son, 'say that Sir Edward Harley is very worthy, but not for the Church.' His candidature was viewed by the Harleys and their friends as a betrayal, especially after Sir Edward had gone out of his way to recommend Croft for a militia commission. It was stated on the eve of the poll, with heavy irony, that 'Sir Herbert is resolved to show how constant he is to his principles of honour and generosity'.[3]

Lord Carmarthen (Sir Thomas Osborne†) marked Croft as a Tory and probably as a Court supporter in his analysis of March 1690, and Croft was soon being described as 'as base as a Tory' and reported as voting 'to the height for money'. He figured in another list of supporters drawn up by Carmarthen in December 1690, possibly in connexion with the projected attack on the Marquess in the Commons. However, by April 1691 he could be classed by Robert Harley* as a member of the Country opposition. Together with the majority of the greater gentry of Herefordshire, he warmly urged Sir Edward Harley* to stand for the vacant seat in January 1693, and the following month joined most other Herefordshire Members in voting for the triennial bill. He also adopted a strongly 'Country' viewpoint in the debate of 7 Dec. 1693 on the accusations of peculation against Lord Falkland (Anthony Carey*):

> I am sorry to find endeavours to lessen the crime of this lord; I am sorry to find it in an English Parliament. Nothing will more corrupt and destroy us, than this of pensions. It is sufficiently made out, that this money was paid as a pension or gratuity. But I insist upon that offence, that when you had a man before you, after that to withdraw the letter, or stifle your proceeding, you cannot be too severe upon him; and I join in the motion for committing him to the Tower.

Not long afterwards a recurrence of the ill-health which in April 1691 had obliged him to resort to the waters at Tunbridge Wells, had laid him once more 'at death's door'. He was still 'very weak' in March 1694; during the summer he talked of 'laying down' his militia commission; and did not get up to Parliament for the beginning of the next session when, significantly perhaps, it was Robert Harley whom he asked to make his excuses at a call. In reply Harley wrote, 'I hope we shall enjoy the benefit of your assistance against these exorbitant excises and funds, which will quickly destroy all the landed men of England.' This appeal to Croft's interests and instincts as a country gentleman had to compete against party loyalty. According to Grascome's list Croft could already be reckoned a supporter of the 'new Whig' ministry. When he did come up to Westminster his major contribution in the House was in the proceedings over the various bribery scandals and the attempt to impeach Carmarthen, now Duke of Leeds. Elected on 23 Apr. 1695 to the secret committee to examine Sir Thomas Cooke*, Croft was appointed four days later to prepare the articles of impeachment against the Duke, and subsequently chaired the committee on the bill for the imprisonment of Cooke, Sir Basil Firebrace* and others.[4]

Returned again with Sir Edward Harley in 1695, Croft was classed as likely to support the Court in a forecast for the division on the proposed council of trade on 31 Jan. 1696, signed the Association promptly and in March voted for fixing the price of guineas at 22s. He retained an interest in the affairs of the East India Company, taking the chair of the committee appointed on 13 Mar. to audit the Company's accounts. The attainder of Sir John Fenwick† the following November showed him at his most devoutly Whiggish. On 17 Nov., at the committal of the bill of attainder, he spoke 'very zealously' against Fenwick and the 'plot' that had been 'laid for the total subversion of our constitution'. On 25 Nov. he was even more forthright. His conscience, he announced, told him to vote for the bill: 'if there be no such rule that requires two witnesses . . . if I may go upon one witness; if I believe he speaks true, and that the person is guilty; then I am bound to act for the preservation of the nation, and our posterity'. As to the arguments in favour of requiring two witnesses, he took his stand on the supremacy of statute and the right of Parliament to hold itself unbound by precedent: he would not 'subject the freedom of Parliaments' to 'the rules of inferior courts'. This speech was taken up by the Tory Lord Norreys (Montagu Venables-Bertie*), who declared that Croft

> had given arguments that shook him more than all he had heard before, for he said 'there were a great many men who, if they might proceed according to their consciences, would subvert this government, and bring in King James and arbitrary power; and that every precedent in this House is equal to a law, and will justify the like for the future'; and therefore his lordship was very unwilling to make a precedent that should justify men in such ill actions, in saying their consciences prompted them to it.

Naturally, Croft voted for the third reading. However, he was able to show some independence of the Court:

on 1 Dec. he spoke against Sir Charles Sedley's* proposal in ways and means for 'charging the customs', earning a compliment from John Grobham Howe*, 'that the landed men were to be trusted, and would never abandon the interest of their country'. On 17 Mar. 1697 Croft reported from the committee to consider the deficiencies of parliamentary funds. His 'Country' sympathies were again evident in December 1697, when he was one of several Members ordinarily 'firm to the government' who appeared 'very zealous for the question' of disbandment, supporting Robert Harley's motion to reduce the army establishment to the level maintained in 1680. Some clue as to the motivation behind these defections may be found in his involvement with the 'moral reform' lobby, understandable in one from a clerical background. But his prime allegiance was still to the ministry, according to the compiler of a comparative analysis of the old and new Commons after the 1698 election.[5]

Croft did not stand in 1698, nor subsequently. Poor health may have been the cause. In October and December 1700, for example, he reported himself to be 'wholly incapacitated to ride, either by coach or horse'. For some time he remained on good terms with the Harleys. In October 1698 he sent Robert a proposal of his own for a bill to regulate the 'affairs of the spiritual administration', more particularly with regard to bishops' visitations. At the general election of January 1701 he professed himself 'entirely' in agreement with Harley as to the county election, preferring to avoid the entanglements of faction and to leave matters to the decision of 'the gentlemen'. He was happy with Harley's election as Speaker of this Parliament and of its successor, writing in January 1702 to congratulate him, and to express the hope that

> you will compose that diversity of opinion and party, which hath brought us almost to confusion, and which, if not redressed this session, as we now seem to be the balance of Europe, will as certainly render us the most despicable state therein. That this may prove such a healing session . . . is the devout prayer of . . . [etc.].

Although by the following March he was muttering that Harley and 'all' other politicians were 'courtiers' – 'some that would keep and others that would have places' – and that 'the country will have few friends', a disillusionment attributed by one Herefordshire source to Croft's intention to try for Parliament again, he did not oppose the Harley family directly, either by standing himself or by backing others to stand against them. At the general election of 1702 he joined other Herefordshire Whigs in promoting the third Tory candidate, John Prise*, against the outgoing knights of the shire; while in 1705 he canvassed for the Harleys in Radnorshire but sought to make a bargain through which he might advance the interest of the Whiggishly inclined Morgans of Kinnersley. By 1712, however, he was rather more open in his sentiments: with John Dutton Colt* he was the only 'person of consideration' who did not promise his support to the young Tory candidate for the county by-election.[6]

Croft died on 3 Nov. 1720, and was buried at Croft, to be succeeded by his son Archer, an unsuccessful candidate at the 1713 election, who sat for Leominster and Bere Alston 1722–34 as a Court Whig, speaking *inter alia* against a pension bill and against any reduction in the standing army, but following the family tradition in writing (albeit 'unintelligibly') against popery.[7]

[1] O. G. S. Croft, *Croft of Croft Castle*, 104–8. [2] *CSP Dom.* 1696, p. 282; Luttrell, *Brief Relation*, iv. 93; G. F. Townsend, *Leominster*, 291. [3] *DNB* (Croft, Herbert); Add. 70014, ff. 284, 305, 312. [4] Add. 70014, f. 312; 70114, Paul Foley I* to Robert Harley, 10 Jan. 1692[–3]; 70126, Croft to Sir Edward Harley, 10 Jan. 1692[–3]; 70017, ff. 5, 22, 344; 70015, f. 150; 70235, Sir Edward to Robert Harley, 24 Feb. 1693[–4]; same to [Edward Harley], 27 Feb. 1694; 70140, same to same, 13 Mar. 1693[–4]; 70231, Abigail to Robert Harley, 7 Aug. 1694; Grey, v. 354; Bodl. Carte 130, f. 348; *HMC Portland*, iii. 560. [5] *Vernon–Shrewsbury Letters*, i. 63, 91; Cobbett, *Parlty. Hist.* v. 1108–10, 1130–2; Boyer, *Wm. III*, iii. 29–31; *CSP Dom.* 1697, pp. 506–7. [6] Add. 70221, Croft to Robert Harley, 5 Oct. 1698, 15 Oct., 27 Dec. 1700, 2 Jan. 1701–2, 30 Nov. 1703, 10, 16 Feb. 1704[–5]; 70254, Robert Price* to same, 30 Mar. 1702; 70256, H. Seward to [?same], 13 Apr. 1702; 70226, Thomas Foley II* to same, 18 July 1712; *HMC Portland*, iv. 12; Huntington Lib. Stowe mss 58(12), p. 131. [7] Croft, 105.

E. R./D. W. H.

CROKER, Courtenay (1660–1740), of Lyneham, Devon.

PLYMPTON ERLE 1695–1702

bap. 13 June 1660, 1st s. of John Croker of Lyneham by Jane, da. of Sir John Pole, 1st Bt.†, of Shute, Devon. *educ.* M. Temple 1680. *m.* (1) c.1691, da. and h. of Richard Hillersdon, 1da.; (2) 16 Mar. 1696, Katherine, da. and coh. of John Tucker of Exeter, Devon, *s.p.*[1]

Freeman, Plympton Erle 1689, alderman 1692; gov. Dartmouth 1699–?1715.[2]

Croker, a Whig from an old Devon family, had supported the Revolution, which he described to his cousin Sir George Treby* in 1690 as 'our present happy settlement'. He was returned on the Treby interest for Plympton in 1695. Forecast as likely to support the ministry in the division of 31 Jan. 1696 on the proposed council of trade, he signed the Association in February and the following month voted for fixing the price of guineas at 22s. On 25 Nov.

he voted for the attainder of Sir John Fenwick†. He was given leave of absence for five weeks on 15 Jan. 1697. In an analysis of the 1698 Parliament he was classified as a Court supporter, though this was subsequently queried. He was listed as a supporter of Treby and Lord Somers (Sir John*) in early 1700. On 23 May 1701 he was granted leave of absence for the recovery of his health, and Robert Harley* listed him as a Whig in December. He told on 28 Apr. 1702 in favour of bringing in a private bill relating to Irish forfeitures, and on 13 May to grant a drawback on the duty on salt exported to Scotland, but did not stand at the 1702 election. Croker died in 1740.³

¹ *Her. and Gen.* viii. 380; Burke, *LG* (1952), 305; IGI, Devon.
² J. B. Rowe, *Hist. Plympton*, 139, 184, 186; *CSP Dom.* 1699–1700, p. 161; Boyer, *Pol. State*, i. 389; iv. 65. ³ *HMC 13th Rep. VI*, 27; Rowe, 186.

E. C.

CROPLEY, Sir John, 2nd Bt. (1663–1713), of Red Lion Square, Mdx.

SHAFTESBURY 1701 (Dec.)–1710

b. 15 July 1663, o. s. of Sir Edward Cropley (*d.v.p.* 1665) of St. James Clerkenwell, Mdx. by Martha, da. of Robert Wilson, merchant, of London. *educ.* Clare, Camb. 1678; travelled abroad (Italy, France, Germany) 1686–9. *unm. suc.* fa. 1665, gdfa. as 2nd Bt. Nov. 1676.¹

Descended from a London merchant, Cropley was the first member of his family to enter Parliament. The most important relationship in his political life began when he spent three years abroad from 1686, travelling in the company of Lord Ashley (Anthony*). The two became life-long friends. In December 1701 Ashley, now 3rd Earl of Shaftesbury, secured the return of Cropley for the borough of Shaftesbury. His election was reckoned by Lord Spencer (Charles*) as a 'gain' for the Whigs, and Robert Harley* also listed him as a Whig. An opponent of the predominantly Tory ministry of the first years of Anne's reign, he told on 7 Dec. in favour of Lord Ranelagh (Richard Jones*), who was under attack from the commissioners of accounts for alleged corruption. On 13 Feb. 1703 Cropley voted for agreeing with the Lords' amendments to the bill for enlarging the time for taking the oath of abjuration. Forecast as an opponent of the Tack, Cropley did not vote for it on 28 Nov. On 5 Dec. he told against the occasional conformity bill after it had been untacked. Classed as a 'Churchman' in the 1705 Parliament, he voted on 25 Oct. for the Court candidate for Speaker. As the ministry shifted towards the Junto, however, Cropley emerged as one of the members of a group of dissident Country Whigs. In the struggle over the regency bill he was one of the champions of the 'whimsical' clause, which would have disqualified all but about 40 named office-holders from the Commons after the Queen's death. The clause was eventually lost on 18 Feb. 1706. Describing this outcome to James Stanhope*, Cropley wrote that

> We lost it very honourably and advantageously... for... the crown has made the greatest concessions that ever were obtained... However, we had never yield[ed] to this exchange but that Sir Ri[chard Onslow, 3rd Bt.*] fainted at last in the pursuit and Ro[bert] Eyre*, unknown to Peter King* and I, ... had treacherous made at my Lord Halifax's [Charles Montagu*] this bargain... Notwithstanding we lost it but by eight when 440 in the House and many of our friends left us in the division merely, believing we were all parties to the bargain... We had two questions and in the last 14 of those friends, that perceived the treacherous part of R. Eyre, returned to us and I believe their resentment will help their inclination to be firm in the future.

To Shaftesbury he listed those office-holders who would be henceforth excluded from the Commons, adding

> Here comes the best: no man to take any place after his being elected a Member of Parliament, but accepting such a place shall make his election void. This is the equivalent for our clause... 'Tis what we should last year have thought a great deal, but in exchange... a very sorry matter. But our clause being in reversion and this in present makes it go down... There was a real objection and danger in our clause, the unanimous resignation at the death of the Queen. On a whisper if they repealed the act they should be reinstated. However, I would have run the risk... I have made... somewhat of a formidable figure to our Whig lords. I have preferred what I judged right to all hazards... on principle adhering to that and no personal prejudice to them... I am much courted to heal up. I own a Whig ministry running riot makes my blood rise, only I know they are in chains themselves and hazard their all for that already given.

Having demonstrated his principled independence, Cropley was quite willing to co-operate with the Junto on other questions, and indeed did so in the 1706–7 session to secure the Union.²

Meanwhile, the admission to office of some of the Whig leaders encouraged Shaftesbury to try to secure a place for a young kinsman of Cropley's, Thomas Micklethwayte. Application was duly made to the Earl of Sunderland (the former Lord Spencer) and Lord Somers (Sir John*) in 1706. A long delay then occurred, occasioned by annoyance at court over Shaftesbury's supposed patronage of a clergyman who had written a pamphlet attacking the Duke of

Marlborough (John Churchill†), and partly by divisions among the Whigs. In May 1707 Cropley wrote to Shaftesbury that Somers had recently apologized for the delay, but had begged them 'to bear their ill usage longer by reason of the late squabbles had made it necessary for him to keep out of lord treasurer's way'. However, the Junto lords proved unable to make good their promises and their failure opened a door for Lord Godolphin (Sidney†), who in December 1707 was trying to construct a new Court party of 'Lord Treasurer's Whigs' and moderate Tories. Early in December an approach was made through Robert Molesworth*, who arranged a meeting for Cropley with the lord treasurer on 14 Dec. On that occasion Godolphin, having promised a place for Micklethwayte, assured Cropley that 'there is not a man in the kingdom that I more honour than my Lord Shaftesbury'. Cropley wrote excitedly to Shaftesbury that all seemed set for the emergence of a new party. Although flattered by such attention, Cropley did not wish his patron to break openly with the Junto in case the quarrel between the Whigs and Godolphin should be patched up. He therefore urged Shaftesbury to keep a low profile in the forthcoming general election, and not to be seen openly opposing Junto candidates. In his correspondence he adopted the quaint terminology of 'oaks' and 'pines' to distinguish Whigs from Tories, referring to those like himself who supported Godolphin's plans for a new political alignment as 'nymphs'. The main hope of the 'nymphs' was that there would not be 'an overgrown oak Parliament'. At the beginning of 1708 Cropley had received something of a jolt when rumours reached him that the Queen might be prepared to sacrifice Godolphin in favour of Harley. Although this particular fear was laid to rest by Harley's dismissal, Cropley remained uneasy. As Godolphin struggled to reach an agreement with the Junto, Cropley constantly defended the treasurer, whom he described on one occasion as 'the most open, plain man, the freest of art and trick I have ever known'. Conversely, he denounced the Junto's unreasonable demands, claiming that the Whig lords did not make sufficient allowance for Godolphin's difficulties with the Queen. He himself continued to trim, arranging to be out of town in February 1708 in order to miss the debate on the Queen's reply to the address over the number of soldiers present at the battle of Almanza. By the beginning of April he was able to inform Shaftesbury that Godolphin had offered the place of treasurer of transports to Micklethwayte and had promised to accept any of the Earl's recommendations for local offices in Dorset. Moreover, Cropley had himself received indications that an office could be his if he desired, to which he had replied that he thought he could serve the ministry best by remaining a free agent.[3]

Cropley was classed as a Whig both before and after the 1708 election, at which he was eventually returned without a contest after some convoluted pre-election manoeuvring (see SHAFTESBURY, Dorset) that reflected the political uncertainties at Westminster. In this Parliament Godolphin gradually came to terms with the Junto, and therefore Cropley merged back into the reunited Whig party. He voted for the naturalization of the Palatines in 1709, and the following year in favour of the impeachment of Dr Sacheverell. He thought that the failure to obtain more than a token punishment of Sacheverell 'gives us a very sad prospect, for if this is all the ministry and Whigs joined can do against the Tories, I fear we shall soon be overpowered, especially since from the pulpits we shall have all their thunder to depress us'. So closely was he now identified with the Junto that he could write to Stanhope that 'I never was better with them in my life than I am now nor never so much devoted to them as now, for to be sure if they are not supported we are gone indeed'. By June he had come to believe that no more could be hoped for than that the Whigs would be able to delay the expected dissolution till the Duke of Marlborough had made peace. He was also concerned with the fate of the Bank of England, in which he held £2,000 worth of stock. Shortly after Harley acceded to office in 1710, Cropley was invited for an interview with the new minister, who expressed his respect for Lord Shaftesbury and desire to serve him. Cropley duly transmitted these sentiments to his patron, urging Shaftesbury

> to say something in return to me. I'll read it to him. This is what you can't avoid. I would not have you speak of it to anybody living, nor have I done it, for to speak of it as acceptable to you might displease others and to speak of it with slights would be a harsh return.

The response was very cool, however. Cropley's worst fears were realized when he was defeated by a Tory at Shaftesbury in the 1710 election. He spent much of the next three years attending to the affairs of Lord Shaftesbury, who had been forced by illness to settle in Italy, leaving Cropley and Stanhope in charge of his infant son and estates. In May 1711 a correspondent of Lord Strafford described Cropley as one of a group of 'old Whigs' who were 'full as unaccountable and railing as ever'. He did not stand at the general election of 1713 and died shortly afterwards on 22 Oct. 1713, leaving an estate of about £4,000 p.a. to Thomas Micklethwayte.[4]

[1] B. Rand, *Shaftesbury*, pp. xix, 273–4. [2] Centre Kentish Stud. Stanhope mss U1590/C9/31, Cropley to James Stanhope, 19 Feb., 26 Mar. 1706; PRO 30/24/20/280–4. [3] PRO 30/24/20/83, 309, 338–40, 346, 352–7; 30/24/21/1–5, 8, 17–18, 21–30, 33, 45, 52–53; 341–2; W. A. Speck, *Birth of Britain*, 145. [4] Egerton 3359 (unfol.); Stanhope mss U1590/C9/31, Cropley to Stanhope, 21 Mar., 22 Apr., 17 June 1710; Boyer, *Pol. State*, vi. 247; Add. 22236, f. 21; PCC 252 Leeds.

P. W.

CROSSE, Thomas (1664–1738), of Millbank, Westminster.

WESTMINSTER 1701(Feb.–Nov.), 1702–1705
1710–1722

b. 29 Nov. 1664, 1st s. of Thomas Crosse, brewer, of St. Margaret's, Westminster by Mary, sis. of John Lockwood. *educ.* Westminster (Dr Busby). *m.* c.1688, Jane, da. of Patrick Lambe of Stoke Poges, Bucks., 2s. (1 d.v.p.). *suc.* fa. 1682. *cr.* Bt. 11 or 13 July 1713.[1]

Freeman, Hertford 1704.[2]
Commr. building 50 new churches 1711–15.[3]
Dir. S. Sea Co. 1721–4.

Crosse's father was a native of Maulden, Bedfordshire, who moved to Westminster and established a brewery at Millbank. Crosse inherited the business, and his prominence in that trade argues for his identification as the 'Mr Crosse' who was a member of a cartel bidding for the excise farm in June 1695. Moreover, in December 1698 his name headed the list of signatories to a petition of Westminster brewers and woodmongers, who addressed the Lords to amend the time limits imposed on traffic in Parliament's vicinity. His political outlook prior to his candidacy at the Westminster election of January 1701 remains obscure, with namesakes appearing in the lists of subscribers for both the Bank of England and the land bank. One historian has identified him as a stockholder in the New East India Company, but Crosse's subsequent career suggests Tory principles, especially support for the Church. However, in January 1701 he stood alongside the Whig James Vernon I*, whose influence helped to secure Crosse's return. It was reported that the defeated Whig candidate Sir Henry Dutton Colt, 1st Bt.*, would petition against Crosse, alleging bribery on the latter's part, but no such challenge was mounted.[4]

In his first Parliament Crosse did not make a great impact, although he finished 13th in the election of the commissioners of accounts. He proved himself a keen sponsor of local issues, acting as the manager of a bill to develop property in the possession of the parish of St. Martin-in-the-Fields. In addition, his name appeared on a list of the likely supporters of the Court on 22 Feb. to agree with the resolution of the committee of supply to continue the 'Great Mortgage'. Later that year he was blacklisted for having opposed preparations for war with France, and subsequently signed the *Answer to the Vine Tavern Queries* to refute claims of disloyalty. Prior to the general election in November his running-mate Vernon reported that Crosse had 'herded among the Tories' during the preceding session, but the secretary of state was still prepared to stand with him at Westminster, even while regarding him as 'obnoxious'. Crosse performed badly, finishing third, over 1,300 votes behind Vernon in second place. Soon after the contest, his Whig rival Lord James Cavendish* was said to have 'challenged' him, but there is no evidence that any duel was fought.[5]

The accession of Anne saw a swift change in Crosse's electoral fortunes, when he finished top of the Westminster poll as the Tories regained both seats. In the ensuing Parliament he was an active Member, managing several bills through the House. Local matters again appear to have been his principal interest, for he aided the progress of another bill to develop St. Martin-in-the-Fields, and oversaw the passage of a bill to regulate Queen's Bench and the Fleet prisons. He was also appointed to drafting committees for bills concerning London coal prices, and the tolls levied to improve egress from Chancery Lane. His politics appeared consistent, he being listed as voting against the Lords' amendments to the bill to extend the time to take the Abjuration. In the second session he was instrumental in securing the passage of a private naturalization bill through the House, possibly in an attempt to gain support among the many refugees who had settled in Westminster. However, he was forecast by Lord Nottingham (Daniel Finch†) as a supporter, possibly in preparation for proceedings concerning the Scotch Plot. He was appointed with others to prepare a bill to increase the number of seamen, and spoke in a debate concerning a bill on 4 Dec. 1703. Further improving his credentials as a constituency Member, he was appointed on 7 Jan. 1704 as one of the drafters of a bill to regulate the watch within the bills of mortality. In the next session he twice acted as a teller in connexion with trade and supply issues. However, his party loyalties were tested by the Tack, and on 30 Oct. 1704 he was cited as a probable opponent of the High Tory measure. It is unclear how he voted in the key division on the Tack on 28 Nov., although Dyer later cited him as a 'Tacker'. A contrary opinion was supplied by Henry St. John II*, who subsequently commended Crosse to the Duke of Marlborough (John Churchill†) for having 'come very heartily into all the

Queen's measures last session'. On 18 Dec. Crosse featured among the named sponsors of a bill to introduce an alternative judicial punishment to cheek-burning, an initiative prompted by a petition from his constituents. His stance on the Tack may have lost him local support, judging by his poor performance at the Westminster contest of May 1705, when he 'gave over polling' before the books were closed. This crushing defeat possibly influenced his decision not to put up at the Westminster by-election of February 1708 or the ensuing general election.[6]

Following the revival of Tory fortunes in 1710, Crosse stood for Westminster and helped to secure the Tories a resounding victory. Before the election he embroiled himself in controversy by venturing into print to deny that Tory Members had voted in February 1703 against one of the Lords' amendments to the bill to extend the time to take the Abjuration. Whig rivals strenuously contested his claim, asserting that he 'seems principally to intend his own service at the ensuing election of Westminster', but the affair appears to have strengthened his local interest. At the outset of the 1710 Parliament Crosse was identified in the 'Hanover list' as a Tory, and played a full part in pressing home his party's advantage, being celebrated as one of the 'worthy patriots' who in the first session helped to detect the mismanagements of the previous administration, as well as a 'Tory patriot' for opposing the continuation of the war. He was also closely involved with the inquiry into the recent influx of Palatine refugees into Southwark, an issue of much embarrassment to the London Whigs. Of greater personal interest, he was appointed to the committee to assure the Queen that the Commons would provide supplies for the construction of new churches in the capital. He subsequently became one of the commissioners for the 50 new churches, and was a driving force behind the foundation of St. John the Evangelist's church at Millbank.[7]

In the 1710–11 session Crosse distinguished himself as a hard-working Member. His principal achievement was the passage of the bill to continue expiring laws, a measure with which he had been involved in several earlier sessions. He was predictably appointed to the drafting committee for the bill to extend the commission for building the 50 new churches, and sponsored several other bills of local import, including one to erect a court of conscience at Westminster. He was identified as a member of the October Club, and on 18 June 1713 voted in favour of the French commerce bill. Several reports suggested that he had deserted the ministry in this key vote, but his support for the bill was confirmed by Boyer. His activity in the third session betrays little sign of political disaffection, although he did act as a teller on 8 July in opposition to the Tory Sir William Wyndham, 3rd Bt.*, to block a move for the House to go into committee on a bill to regulate the armed forces. More significantly, in that month he was created a baronet, an honour which signified the ministry's desire to secure his loyalty.[8]

At the Westminster election of August 1713 Crosse clearly stood in the Tory interest, and was returned 'without opposition'. In the ensuing session he acted as chairman of the committee of inquiry into government estimates and accounts, reporting on no less than nine occasions. In that capacity he twice motioned the House to consider the army's finances, and was also appointed to the drafting committee for a bill to settle the debts of former paymaster-general Lord Ranelagh (Richard Jones*). On the basis of his contribution to a debate on the succession on 15 Apr. 1714 he was identified as a Court supporter. At the ensuing general election he managed to secure his seat, and an analyst of the new Parliament identified him as a Tory. However, although the Worsley list classed him as a Tory who would often vote with the Whigs, he remained an opponent of the ministry for nearly the whole of the 1715 Parliament. Having been made a director of the South Sea Company, he switched allegiance to fight the Westminster election of 1722 as a Court candidate, but was defeated and did not stand again.[9]

Although retiring from public life, Crosse remained an active Churchman, serving as churchwarden at St. John the Evangelist's. He had already established a reputation as a local philanthropist by supporting charity schools, and after his death on 27 May 1738 he was eulogized as a benefactor 'preferring the silent testimony of his own conscience to the thanks and good wishes of a multitude'. His only surviving son, John†, succeeded to the baronetcy and brewing business, having already emulated his father's success by gaining election as a ministerial candidate at Wootton Bassett and Lostwithiel.[10]

[1] J. P. Malcolm, *Londinium Redivivum*, iv. 125; IGI, London. [2] Herts. RO, Hertford bor. recs. 25/106. [3] E. G. W. Bill, *Q. Anne Churches*, p. xxiii. [4] PCC 107 Cottle; *Cal. Treas. Bks.* x. 1384; *HMC Lords*, n.s. iii. 264; DZA, Bonet despatch 6/16 July 1694; NLS, Advocates' mss 31.1.7, f. 95; *EHR*, lxxi. 237; Bodl. Carte 228, f. 356. [5] Yorks. Arch. Soc. Copley mss DD38, box H–J, poll for commn. of accts.; *Vernon–Shrewsbury Corresp.* iii. 160; *Verney Letters 18th Cent.* i. 167. [6] NMM, Sergison mss 103, f. 456; *Dyer's Newsletters* [1706], 1; Add. 61131, ff. 124–5; *Verney Letters 18th Cent.* 226. [7] *Detection of Falsehood* [1710]; *Acct. of Test Offered to Electors of Great Britain* [1710]; *London Rec. Soc.* xxiii. 26, 169, 171, 178. [8] Boyer, *Pol. State*, v. 389; vi. 126–7. [9] Boyer, vi. 126–7; Advocates' mss, Wodrow pprs. letters Quarto 8, ff. 95–96; *HMC Var.* viii. 334. [10] J. E. Smith, *St. John the Evangelist, Westminster*, 135; Malcolm, 125; Hatton, *New View of London*, 781.

P. L. G.

CROW, Mitford (1669–1719), of Isleworth, Mdx.

SOUTHAMPTON 1701 (Feb.)–1702

bap. 18 Apr. 1669, s. of Patrick Crow of the Hermitage, nr. Hexham, Northumb. by Anne, da. of Robert Mitford of Mitford, Northumb. *m.* c.1698, Oriana, wid. of Sir Willoughby Chamberlayne of Barbados and Chelsea, Mdx., 3s.[1]

Gov. Barbados Jan.–July 1702, Sept. 1706–10; special envoy to Genoa and Spain 1705–Aug. 1706; envoy extraordinary to Spain Oct. 1706.[2]

Freeman, Kinsale 1707.[3]

As a young man Crow was apprenticed to a Barbados merchant in London, eventually setting up on his own in the Mediterranean and Levant trades. According to his own account he spent some eight years living in Spain. This was probably during the 1690s, since in January 1697 he wrote to William III from Barcelona enclosing a paper by the Prince of Hesse, extracted from the archives of Aragon, concerning the right to the Spanish throne of the Austrian Emperor. Crow had probably returned to England by 1698, when he married the widow of a Barbadian colonel. By her first marriage settlement she had an annuity of £500 from an estate on the island and, at the death of her first husband in 1697, had been left sole executrix of his will. In December 1699 Crow unsuccessfully contested a by-election in Southampton against the town's recorder, Roger Mompesson*, but was returned after a contest at the first 1701 election, holding onto the seat in the following November, when he was listed as a Whig by Robert Harley*. In February 1702 he was appointed governor of Barbados and had arranged his passage there, but after the accession of Anne, was superseded in favour of Sir Bevil Granville*, without ever having set foot on the island. As his grant was not cancelled until July 1702, his possession of this office may account for his failure to stand for Parliament in that year.[4]

Towards the end of 1704 Crow was invited to give his opinion on the best method of fomenting a rising in Spain in favour of the Archduke Charles. He advised Lord Godolphin (Sidney†) on 12 Dec. that the most effective means would be to send 'a proper person fully empowered from her Majesty to Genoa or some other neutral post' to negotiate with the Catalans. The following year Crow was despatched to Genoa as a special envoy, ostensibly to cover trade matters but in fact to report on the movements of the French fleet and make contact with the Catalans. He arrived in Genoa on 20 May 1705 and throughout June was sending home encouraging reports of the progress of the revolt. When a British force arrived at Barcelona, Crow joined them, remaining there until the following May, sending back what were now increasingly gloomy reports about the mishandling of relations with the Spaniards and the growing alienation of the Catalans. Crow returned to Genoa in May 1706 with a commission to raise money for the Archduke Charles, and remained there through the summer, receiving his salary up to 27 Aug. at the rate of £5 a day, with £500 for equipage and £330 for extraordinaries. In the meantime Godolphin, who had promised to assist Crow's career, wrote to the Duke of Newcastle (John Holles†) on 15 June, in relation to securing for Crow the governorship of Barbados. This he did, and a warrant was issued on 28 Sept. While it was going through, Crow, who had returned to England by October, was appointed envoy extraordinary to Spain, apparently, as Luttrell recorded, 'to settle the accounts of our army there, of which he is paymaster'. It is not clear whether Crow actually went to Spain, but he did set out for Barbados in the spring of 1707 and arrived there on 9 May.[5]

In December 1708 three members of the Barbados council made accusations of maladministration and bribery against Crow. He was ordered on 22 Aug. 1709 to return to England to answer the complaints, but did not embark until 15 May 1710. By the time he arrived the reconstruction of the ministry was in progress and his commission was superseded on 15 Aug. His case was heard by a committee of the Privy Council in November, which reported their opinion that the charges against Crow had not been proved. The report, together with three addresses from 'the general assembly, clergy and inhabitants of Barbados in favour of Mr Crow', led the full Council to dismiss the complaints as frivolous. After this Crow seems virtually to have retired from public life. He died on 15 Dec. 1719.[6]

[1] IGI, Northumb.; PRO, HCA 13/79, testimony of 18 July 1689; *Misc. Gen. et Her.* n.s. iii. 137; V. L. Oliver, *Caribbeana*, iii. 47, 281; *Reg. St. Nicholas Acons, London*, trans. W. Brigg, 41; *APC Col.* 1680–1720, pp. 593–4. [2] *CSP Dom.* 1700–2, p. 524; 1702–3, p. 171; *APC Col.* 1680–1720, p. 792; Boyer, *Pol. State*, vii. 395; Luttrell, *Brief Relation*, vi. 92, 104; *Cal. Treas. Bks.* xxvi. 129; *Brit. Dipl. Rep.* (Cam. Soc. ser. 3, xlvi), 73, 128. [3] *Kinsale Corp. Council Bk.* ed. Caulfield, 209. [4] *New Hist. Northumb.* iii. 65; Oliver, 281; Add. 28056, f. 206; *CSP Dom.* 1697, pp. 5, 37; *APC Col.* 1680–1720, pp. 396, 511, 593–4. [5] Add. 28056, f. 206; 28057, ff. 19, 30; *HMC Lords*, n.s. vii. 361, 364, 378–9, 458, 459, 465, 500; ix. 43; x. 255; *HMC Portland*, ii. 191, 193; *HMC Bath*, i. 108–9, 114–15, 130; *Brit. Dipl. Rep.* 73, 128; Luttrell, 92, 104. [6] *APC Col.* 1680–1720, pp. 577–82; Luttrell, 653, 664; Oliver, 281.

P. W./C. I. M.

CROWLEY, Sir Ambrose (1658–1713), of Greenwich, Kent.[1]

ANDOVER 25 Aug.–7 Oct. 1713

b. 1 Feb. 1658, 1st s. of Ambrose Crowley, ironmonger, of Stourbridge, Worcs. by his 1st w. Mary, da. of Thomas Hall of Chadwich, Bromsgrove, Worcs. *m.* 1 Mar. 1681[–2], Mary, da. of Charles Owen of All Hallows, Honey Lane, London, 4s. (3 *d.v.p.*) 7da. (2 *d.v.p.*). Kntd. 1 Jan. 1707.[2]

Freeman, Drapers' Co. 1684, master 1708–9; common councilman, London 1697–1711, sheriff 1706–7, alderman 1711–*d.*

Dir. S. Sea Co. 1711–*d.*, dep. gov. 1712–13; commr. building 50 new churches 1712–*d.*[3]

Crowley's rise to ownership of what may have been the largest ironworks in Europe and his innovations in industrial welfare have been extensively studied by economic historians. Coming from a Quaker family in the iron manufacturing business, Crowley was apprenticed at the age of 15 to a London Draper, where, according to his own account, he showed great application: 'I never asked for one holiday all my time of apprenticeship except when my father was in town . . . My diligence in my apprenticeship raised me several friends who were always ready to assist me in everything that was needful.' From the 1680s Crowley was in business for himself. He established an ironware factory at Winlaton, near Newcastle-upon-Tyne, from which he gradually expanded until by 1707 he had a whole complex of factories and warehouses, largely designed to service the naval contracts in which he specialized. The Crowley works were unique in having a written constitution, the *Law Book of the Crowley Ironworks*, based on the methods and procedures laid down by Crowley himself. He was also ahead of his time in the insurance scheme he established to pay for many social services for his workers, to which both employer and employees contributed.

In 1704 Crowley moved his London headquarters to Greenwich, where his neighbour was (Sir) Gregory Page, (1st Bt.)*, a Baptist and Whig, who acted as an intermediary in Crowley's buy-out of a rival business in 1707. In December that year he stood godfather to a son of a fellow iron manufacturer, the Whig John Hanbury*. Having achieved success in business, Crowley began to take a closer interest in politics. Here he showed that, while maintaining good relations in his personal and business life with many Nonconformists and Whigs, he himself was a firm though moderate Anglican and Tory. In 1706, when he was nominated as sheriff of London, the *Post Man* described him as a gentleman of 'known loyalty to her Majesty and well affected to the government both in Church and State'. Duly chosen, he received the customary knighthood during his shrievalty. In January 1708, having noticed recent meetings of city Whigs, he wrote to Sir Richard Hoare* offering help in his campaign for the coming general electons, adding, 'you may depend on it that I shall be a steady friend to the Church of England as by law established'. In November that year Crowley was reportedly gathering support to succeed as alderman in Castle Baynard ward, although in the event he did not stand. In 1709 he was a candidate for alderman, unsuccessfully, in three different wards. He lost the election in Queenhithe ward, according to one newsletter, 'by a new whim, by refusing to treat but promised each that should vote for him a chaldron of coals, which the electors disdained'. In the 1710 London elections he voted for three Tory candidates but, interestingly, his fourth vote went to the Whiggish John Ward II*, a champion of merchant interests, rather than to the High Tory John Cass*. He finally achieved his ambition of becoming an alderman in the more favourable political climate of 1711.[4]

As a large naval contractor, Crowley was inevitably affected by the almost constant financial crises troubling the navy. In 1699 he had been a leader of the naval creditors pressing for better methods of payment. In 1710 he again took the lead in pressing for action about naval payments and several times threatened to stop deliveries. He welcomed the new administration established in the summer and autumn of 1710 and was one of the few wealthy City men to support Robert Harley*. However, he continued to press for some settlement of his naval debts, writing to Harley with proposals which were to some extent embodied in the South Sea Company bill. This scheme arranged for the compulsory transfer of all unfunded naval debts incurred before Michaelmas 1710 into South Sea Company stock, but when it came into operation it was not particularly liked by any of the naval creditors, including Crowley, and in 1712 he described it as 'an intolerable hardship'. He eventually held some £56,000 worth of stock, but it appears that through discount on naval bills and South Sea stock (the selling price of which seems to have soon fallen below par) he lost some £15,000. As one of the largest stockholders, Crowley was at least given some control over the company, being appointed one its directors in 1711. The following year he was chosen as deputy-governor and thenceforth chaired nearly all the directors' meetings. In 1712 he also successfully persuaded Harley to appoint him to the commission for building 50 new churches in London, where he succeeded in getting the ruined church at Greenwich placed first in the list of those to be rebuilt. The suggestion that Crowley was the model for the satiric portrait 'Sir Jack Anvil' in the *Spectator*, February 1712, has been discounted by his biographer.[5]

In January 1713 Crowley reaffirmed his support for the Tory administration by joining with three other financiers to lend the government £130,000. Later that year he successfully contested Andover, possibly with the help of the lord lieutenant of Hampshire, the 2nd Duke of Beaufort, who was steward of the borough. He was classed as a Tory in the Worsley list, but never took his seat, his sudden death occurring on 7 Oct. 1713, before the new Parliament assembled. He left to his four unmarried daughters £10,000 each in South Sea stock, and to his only surviving son, John Crowley†, his great ironworks, worth well over £100,000. A funeral poem celebrated his unique contribution to industry,

Great Crowley led,
Not followed, his proud structures all his own,
the founder of his feast himself alone.[6]

[1] Unless otherwise stated this biography is based on M. W. Flinn, *Men of Iron*. [2] IGI, London. [3] Beaven, *Aldermen*, ii. 122. [4] *Wentworth Pprs.* 62; *Post Man*, 20–22 June 1706; Hoare mss at Hoare's Bank, Crowley to Hoare, 28 Jan. 1707[–8]; Folger Shakespeare Lib. Newdigate newsletters 11 Nov. 1708, 26 Mar., 5 Apr., 29 Nov. 1709; Add. 70420, unfol. newsletter, 24 Sept. 1709; *London Poll 1710* (IHR), 50. [5] *Hist. Jnl.* iv. 192. [6] A. Lacrimans, *A Funeral Poem to Sir Ambrose Crowley*.

P. W./S. M. W.

CULLEN, Sir Rushout, 3rd Bt. (1661–1730), of Upton, Ratley, Warws. and Isleham, Cambs.

CAMBRIDGESHIRE   16 Dec. 1697–1710

b. 12 Aug. 1661, 3rd but 2nd surv. s. of Sir Abraham Cullen, 1st Bt.†, of East Sheen, Surr. and Upton by Abigail, da. of John Rushout, Fishmonger, of St. Dionis Backchurch, London and Maylords, Havering, Essex, and sis. of Sir James Rushout, 1st Bt.* *m.* (1) 13 Apr. 1686, his cos. Mary (*d.* c.1694), da. and h. of Sir John Maynard of Tooting Graveney, Surr. and Isleham, wid. of Francis Buller of Shillingham, Cornw. and William Adams (*d.* by 1687) of Sprowston, Norf., 1da. *d.v.p.*; (2) 19 July 1696, Eleanor, da. of William Jarrett, merchant, of St. Dionis Backchurch, *s.p. suc.* bro. John as 3rd Bt. 1677.[1]

Freeman, Cambridge 1689; asst. Banbury 1718.[2]

In three generations the Cullen family, descendants of an early 17th-century Flemish refugee, Bernard Van Cuelen, had transformed themselves from small traders and manufacturers in Norwich and London into wealthy squires with a baronetcy and estates in several counties. Sir Rushout completed the process of rustication on succeeding his brother in 1677, when he sold the Surrey property his father had acquired while in business in London. He did not, however, attempt a parliamentary seat until 1693, when he stood on the Whig interest at a by-election for Cambridgeshire, a county in which his first wife had inherited an estate and in which he had recently been appointed a deputy-lieutenant. His opponent was Lord Cutts (John*), a Whiggish army officer for once enjoying the support of local 'Churchmen', who scraped home by a mere seven votes and then survived a petition from Cullen despite losing the initial decision in the elections committee. At the 1695 general election Cullen tried to follow in his father's footsteps, putting up at Evesham on the recommendation of his brother-in-law, Sir James Rushout, but encountered resistance because he was an 'outsider' to the borough, and was narrowly defeated. There was better fortune in Cambridgeshire at another by-election in 1697. This time he enjoyed Cutts's support, expressed through the active assistance of Cutts's father-in-law, Sir Henry Pickering, 2nd Bt.*, and, probably more important, the backing of the leading Whig magnate in the county, Lord Orford (Edward Russell*). Not only were the Whigs thus united; the Tories were weakened by the fact that their candidate, Granado Pigot*, had only a year before refused the Association. Cullen, recommended by Lord Orford as 'a very fit person, well qualified, both in understanding and estate', was returned after a contest.[3]

Cullen made little impact in his early days as a Member. Indeed on 8 Feb. 1698 he was granted leave of absence to attend the funeral of a 'Mr Butler'. After he and Cutts had defeated Pigot and another Tory, Lord Alington, in the 1698 election, he was classified as a Court supporter in a comparative analysis of the old and new Parliaments, and in a list from early 1700 was put down as a follower of Lords Bedford and Orford. Returned unopposed at both general elections in 1701, he was listed with the Whigs by Robert Harley* in December. On 23 Feb. 1702 occurred the first of his tellerships, in favour of receiving a petition concerning the Irish forfeitures. In the 1702 election the two parties appear to have agreed to share the county representation, and Cullen was returned with Pigot, his candidacy having received support from, among others, the Tory Lord North and Grey. None the less, on 3 Dec. 1702 he told on the Whig side in favour of granting an early discharge to an agent of Sir Isaac Rebow*, committed to custody for breach of privilege as a result of malpractice at the Colchester poll, and on 13 Feb. he voted in favour of agreeing with the Lords' amendments to the bill for enlarging the time for taking the oath of abjuration. Forecast as a likely opponent of the Tack, he duly voted against it or was absent at the crucial division on 28 Nov. 1704, and a week later retired into the country with leave of absence to recover his health. Obliged to fight the 1705 election against a strong Tory challenge, he topped the poll in a close contest. Classed as a 'Churchman' in an analysis of the new Parliament, he voted for the Court candidate, John Smith I*, in the division on the Speaker, 25 Oct. 1705, and on the Court side again on 18 Feb. 1706, over the 'place clause' of the regency bill. On 10 Dec. 1707 he told in a division on a local issue, against including John Brownell in the list of land tax commissioners for Cambridgeshire, at the report of the land tax bill. Listed twice as a Whig in 1708, he was chosen again, unopposed, in the general election of that year and had two tellerships in the first session: on 24 Nov., on the Whig side, against hearing the Bramber election case on a certain day; and on 7 Dec., against a motion to declare the commissioners of the navy disqualified from sitting in Parliament under the terms of the Regency Act, a preliminary to the opposition's successful bid to exclude Anthony Hammond* from the House. Besides being a member of the Court party Hammond was also a Huntingdonshire man and former Member for Cambridge University, and may well have had some local connexion with Cullen. During the remainder of the Parliament Cullen continued to support the Whig ministry, voting in 1709 for the naturalization of the Palatines and the following year for the impeachment of Dr Sacheverell, but he suffered in the popular reaction to Sacheverell's conviction, and did not venture to seek re-election when the Parliament was dissolved. He did not take part in county politics in the more favourable circumstances after the Hanoverian succession, but seems to have retired to his Warwickshire estates.[4]

Cullen died on 15 Oct. 1730, leaving as his heir his nephew Thomas Bedford of the Middle Temple. The estate, which had already been charged with some £7,000 for his widow and son-in-law, Sir John Dutton, 2nd Bt.†, was encumbered by further bequests amounting to almost £6,000. He was to be buried at Upton, 'in a private and decent manner, without any pomp or show'. The baronetcy thereupon became extinct.[5]

[1] *Vis. Surr.* (Harl. Soc. lx), 34; *Mortlake Par. Reg.* 23, 68; *St. Dionis Backchurch* (Harl. Soc. Reg. iii), 45, 111, 114, 264; IGI, Cambs.; *London Mar. Lic.* ed. Foster, 10, 213, 364, 753; *Le Neve's Knights* (Harl. Soc. viii), 73; *Vis. Norf.* (Norf. Rec. Soc.), i. 1; PCC 72 Bond, 300 Auber. [2] *Diary of Samuel Newton* (Camb. Antiq. Soc. xxiii), 104; A. Beesley, *Hist. Banbury*, 516. [3] *VCH Warws.* v. 145; Bodl. Tanner 25, f. 339; Add. 28931, f. 100; C. H. Cooper, *Annals of Cambridge*, iv. 23, 39; Luttrell, *Brief Relation*, iii. 264; iv. 337; *HMC Portland*, iii. 572; *CJ*, xii. 84–85; *Bull. IHR*, xxxvii. 34. [4] Bodl. North d.1, f. 35; Rawl. B.281, f. 199; Camb. Univ. Lib. Cholmondeley (Houghton) mss, corresp. 405, John Turner* to Robert Walpole II*, 19 Feb. 1704–5. [5] PCC 300 Auber.

D. W. H.

CULLIFORD, William (d. 1724), of Encombe, Dorset.

CORFE CASTLE 1690–6 Apr. 1699

4th s. of Robert Culliford† of Encombe by Elizabeth, da. of Sir Edward Lawrence of Creech Grange, Dorset. *educ.* Shaftesbury g.s. 1656. *m.* (1) Honor Ayliffe, *s.p.*; (2) bef. 26 Aug. 1671, Eleanor, da. of Robert Brandling of Leathley, Yorks., 2s. 4da. *suc.* bro. ?aft. 1698.[1]

Surveyor of excise, London 1666; registrar of seizures and forfeitures 1668–85; commr. revenue [I] 1684–8, 1690–2; commr. customs ?1687–9, 1701–12; inspector gen. imports and exports 1696–1703; commr. customs [S] Dec. 1714–15.[2]

Commr. setting out the wharves, Poole 1679; setting out port of Chichester 1680; freeman, Southampton 1708.[3]

Culliford's father had represented Wareham in the reign of Charles II, but as a younger son he himself made a career in the government revenue services. His first appointment, in June 1666, was of short duration and by January 1668 he was re-employed, this time as registrar of seizures, at the request of Sir Edmund Pooley†. After some initial difficulties with the customs farmers, he settled into the office, which he held without a break for 17 years. In 1684 his years of toil were rewarded when he was added to the Irish revenue commission, at a salary of £1,000 p.a. As he was setting out to take up the appointment he was shot by a discharged customs officer, whom he had refused to take with him into Ireland, but he recovered and eventually reached his destination. Culliford retained his Irish post until early 1688, when he was removed, ostensibly in order to join the English customs commission, though Culliford believed it was only done to make way for a Catholic. A newsletter of January 1688 supports this view, stating that 'Mr Trinder, a romanist, is ordered to go for Ireland to be one of the commissioners', while Culliford was to replace the deceased English commissioner, Sir John Buckworth. Culliford does not appear to have been included in this commission, and by May 1689 he was unemployed and petitioning for the post of surveyor-general of the customs, claiming to be a staunch Protestant with 25 years' experience in the customs service, who in Ireland had

discharged his duties with unwearied diligence; and notwithstanding the Lord Tyrconnel's private directions to some of the commissioners in favour of papists, he openly opposed the removal of the Protestant officers; that about 15 months before, whether by the means of Lord Tyrconnel or to make way for a papist, he was removed from Ireland into the commission in England, but was then left out of that commission.

Although Culliford was promised the first vacancy in the customs service, the Treasury commissioners employed him on a temporary basis during the summer of 1689 for visiting the western ports of England, but by August he was being called upon to assist them in their deliberations on the Irish revenue. In February 1690 Culliford was appointed along with Edward May as 'supervisors' of the Irish revenue, which was only a temporary appointment to an unofficial office. However, in May Culliford was appointed to the official Irish revenue commission, with a salary of £600 p.a.[4]

Although Culliford had been defeated in the 1689 election for Corfe Castle, he was returned unopposed for that borough in 1690, on which occasion he was listed by Lord Carmarthen (Sir Thomas Osborne[†]) as 'doubtful' in relation to his party affiliation, though as a probable Court supporter. In December he was noted as a probable supporter of Carmarthen in the event of an attack upon the minister in the Commons, while in April 1691 he was listed as a Court supporter by Robert Harley*. Culliford's first two parliamentary sessions were relatively quiet. However, in the 1691–2 session he achieved an unwelcome notoriety. The session started peacefully enough. On 1 Jan. 1692 he intervened several times in a debate on supply, in an unsuccessful attempt to persuade the House to reduce its over-optimistic estimate of the likely yield of the Irish revenue. Culliford demonstrated his detailed knowledge of the Irish revenue and his adherence to the Court as he protested against each estimate for individual branches of the revenue. He argued for lower estimates on each branch, which, if they had been accepted, would have spoilt the opposition's policy of using the high Irish estimates as one way of reducing the overall supply to be granted to the government. On 13 Feb. he acted as a teller against a motion for applying certain duties to the payment of debts to the London orphans. However, trouble began on the 17th with the presentation of a report from the committee on Irish forfeitures, which contained a stinging indictment of the Irish revenue commission in general and of Culliford in particular. His three principal accusers were Sir Charles Meredith, the Irish chancellor of the exchequer and a fellow member of the revenue board, Colonel Fitzgerald, one of the commissioners for forfeitures and seizures, and Francis Annesley*. The main charges were that Culliford had been the architect of the scheme whereby forfeited estates were disposed of through the Irish revenue commission rather than the Irish exchequer, thereby greatly increasing the opportunities for malpractice; that he had himself taken, either directly or through nominees, the leases of a number of forfeited estates at particularly low rents, which had then been re-let for substantially larger sums; that he had accepted an estate from one Sweetman in return for protecting him from a charge of murder; that after the battle of the Boyne he had connived at the confiscation of the estates of protected persons; and finally that he had had the customs surveyor at Dublin removed to make way for his own brother. Culliford delivered his answer on 23 Feb., denying all the charges, although he did admit he had taken up leases of some of the forfeited estates at what he considered a fair rent and had re-let at higher charges to cover the cost of repairs. He refuted the complaint that he had made £10,000 from corrupt practices, claiming that he was in fact some £300 out of pocket from his dealings in forfeited estates. The House resolved to consider his reply the next day, but was prevented, first by an adjournment and then prorogation. In March the Irish lord lieutenant, Viscount Sydney (Henry Sidney[†]), informed the Irish vice-treasurer, Lord Coningsby (Thomas*), that 'the [Irish revenue] commission . . . is quite altered, and Mr Culliford left out for the present till he can justify himself'. The following month Culliford was called to be heard at the Treasury. The hearing did not go well, and it was noted on 9 Apr. that he was to be replaced as a commissioner, 'as is generally believed', by 'Mr [Samuel] Travers a member of the . . . Commons'. Culliford's dismissal was reported in a newsletter on the 14th. The outcome of the Treasury meeting was clarified by Lord Godolphin (Sidney[†]), when he wrote to the King on the 15th: 'Culliford was heard at the Treasury as to the charge against him, and though there was nothing that could amount to a legal proof, yet the board was of opinion it was not advisable at this time to continue him in that service.'[5]

Culliford's troubles did not end with his dismissal from office, as in October 1692 the issue was taken up by the Irish house of commons. In Ireland the attack was motivated by general grievances over the Treaty of Limerick, the disposal of forfeited estates, and the mismanagement of the country by the government during the previous two years, although in addition Culliford did have personal enemies among the Dublin merchant community. It was reported in October that the Commons' committee of grievances 'had fallen upon Mr Culliford and had summoned him to attend them', as part of their inquiries into government corruption. Culliford worsened the situation by claiming that his privilege as an English MP freed him from any obligation to participate in the committee's investigations, and thereby 'joined personal to political insult'. He was saved from the complete censure of the commons by a timely prorogation on 3 Nov., the day before charges against him were to be discussed in the house. Although Sydney claimed the prorogation was due to an earlier vote by the commons relating to money bills, his real reason was his desire to protect himself, Culliford and other government officials, such as Coningsby and the Irish lord chancellor, Sir Charles Porter*, from possible impeachment over the investigations by the commons' grievances committee.[6]

However, having avoided the attempts of the Irish commons to charge him with embezzlement, Culliford faced another crisis during the investigations into the state of Ireland undertaken by the English Commons in February 1693. The investigation was resumed in the House on the 22nd and 24th, with an attack mounted by the Whigs, Court as well as Country, who used Culliford as a means of discrediting their chief targets, Sydney and Coningsby. Witnesses claimed that evidence laid before the Irish parliament proved that Culliford was guilty of great breaches of trust, which had significantly reduced the value of the forfeited estates. After hearing the report the Commons resolved 'that there have been great abuses and mismanagements in the affairs of Ireland' and ordered an address. Culliford had been absent during these debates and a move to expel him forthwith was rejected on the grounds that he should first be heard in his own defence. When he had still not appeared by 8 Mar. a motion was passed withdrawing his privilege. He finally took his seat on the 13th, when he 'stood up and justified himself and protested his innocence, and assured the House his accusation came only from such persons whom he had hindered from cheating his Majesty'. After 'a silence some time' it was successfully proposed, with his own agreement, that the suspension of his privilege be continued. This mild sentence reflects the relative lack of importance attached to him at this stage by his accusers, who clearly aimed at grander targets. During March a similar investigation took place in the Lords, who also produced a resolution that there had been grave abuses in the administration of Ireland and an address to the same effect.[7]

In the 1693–4 session Culliford's involvement with the alleged murderer, Sweetman, was cited in the articles of impeachment against Coningsby and Porter in December. However, Culliford ceased thereafter to be in the limelight, and was able to participate in parliamentary affairs that did not revolve around himself. During January–March 1694 he played a leading role in endeavouring to get a bill through the House for preventing the sale and export of English bullion. He also acted as a teller on four occasions in relation to supply in March and April. In the 1694–5 session he acted as a teller on 7 Feb. 1695 in relation to supply, on 30 Apr. against the reading of the bill for reversing the attainder of Jacob Leisler, and on 1 May in favour of accepting a clause for bailing the Tory Sir Thomas Cooke*. Despite having left the Irish revenue service under a cloud, Culliford still enjoyed favour at the Treasury and in October 1694 was considered for appointment as surveyor-general of customs, only for the customs commissioners to insist that no such officer was needed. Again in August 1695 Lord Sunderland reported to Lord Portland that the Treasury commissioners were considering Culliford for the post of solicitor of the customs, but that he was a man 'against whom there are many exceptions', which may explain why he was not appointed to the post.[8]

Returned unopposed for Corfe Castle in 1695, Culliford acted as a teller on 23 Dec. against a motion for delaying the report from the committee on regulating coinage, and was listed as 'doubtful' in the forecast for a division on the proposed council of trade on 31 Jan. 1696. He signed the Association promptly, though he was absent from the division in March on the price of guineas. In March–April he played a leading part in managing the bill for prevention of stock-jobbing. His ambiguous voting record suggests the kind of tact born of ambition, and indeed in June 1696 the Treasury lords were still considering employing Culliford as surveyor-general of the customs. Godolphin and Sir Robert Southwell† were in favour of employing him, while William Young pointed out that the previous survey undertaken by Culliford, in 1689, had resulted in the removal of good officers and their replacement by less deserving individuals. James Chadwick*, a customs commissioner, felt the power of the office was too great. However, the Treasury lords had a 'good opinion' of Culliford. On 15 July the customs commissioners recommended that Culliford be employed in a new office, inspector-general of imports and exports, for detecting frauds and debts. The Treasury lords agreed, and in September Culliford was established in the new post at a salary of £500 p.a. Although this signified that Culliford was acceptable in government once again, the Treasury lords' recommendation of him to the King for a vacancy in the customs commission in July 1696 was not successful. In the 1696–7 session he did not vote on the Fenwick (Sir John†) attainder bill. He acted as a teller on 15 Jan. 1697 against a motion to refer the petition of the London wine merchants to a committee. In the 1697–8 session he was granted leave of absence on 29 Jan. 1698 for two weeks in order to bury his father, while on 15 Apr. he acted as a teller against a motion for adjourning the report on the prevention of counterfeiting and clipping of coin. In May it was reported that Culliford's proposal for raising £100,000 p.a. 'by a new impost upon sugar was much liked at first', but it was eventually dropped. On 8 June he reported on the petition of Colonel Michelburne relating to regimental pay arrears for service at Derry in 1689, while on the 22nd and 23rd he reported on and carried up a bill for granting the freedom to trade as English ships to two prize ships. By now he had also set himself up in business selling sailcloth to the navy.[9]

Culliford successfully contested the Corfe Castle election in 1698. In a comparative analysis of the old and new Parliaments he was listed as a Court placeman, and, not surprisingly, he voted with the Court against the disbanding bill on 18 Jan. 1699. However, following a petition against Culliford's election from Richard Fownes*, the election was declared void. At the ensuing by-election Fownes defeated Culliford, who petitioned unsuccessfully. He seems to have considered standing in the first general election of 1701, but was not returned, and did not sit in Parliament again. In November 1701 he was made a commissioner of customs, where he survived for some years despite twice being accused of malpractice. First, in January 1705 John Strangways, a kinsman of Thomas Strangways I*, charged Culliford with attempting to ruin his family because of opposition at an election, but the customs commissioners adjudged the letter to be 'false, scandalous and malicious'. Then, in 1710, he was charged with involvement in customs frauds. Since his accuser admitted the falsehood of the charges, this accusation was dismissed. He eventually lost his job in January 1712, but returned to office for a short spell after the Hanoverian succession, as a commissioner of the Scottish customs, presumably on account of his long experience. Culliford was buried at Corfe Castle on 19 Mar. 1724.[10]

[1] Hutchins, *Dorset*, i. 516; C7/309/17; *Hist. Northumb.* vii. 286; *St. Olave* (Harl. Soc. Reg. xlvi), 79–85. [2] *CSP Dom.* 1667–8, p. 244; 1673–5, p. 406; 1684–5, p. 118; 1686–7, pp. 54–55, 368, 405; *Cal. Treas. Bks.* i. 726; ii. 244; viii. 333, 1689; ix. 607; xi. 264; xvi. 112; xviii. 292; xxvi. 118; *Cal. Treas. Pprs.* 1557–1696, p. 38. [3] *Cal. Treas. Bks.* v. 1207; vi. 637; Southampton RO, Southampton bor. recs. SC3/2, f. 42. [4] *Cal. Treas. Bks.* ii. 222, 244, 297, 333, 336, 395, 523; vii. 620, 667, 670, 1277–8, 1312; viii. 109, 177, 313, 333; ix. 49–51, 484, 607; T64/139–40 (*ex inf.* Dr G. E. Aylmer); McGrath thesis, 14, 128–9, 359; *Cal. Treas. Pprs.* 1557–1696, pp. 38–39, 63, 65; *HMC Downshire*, i. 285. [5] *Luttrell Diary*, 101–2, 166–7, 185, 191; *HMC Portland*, iii. 476–7; PRO NI, De Ros mss D638/14/34, Sydney to Coningsby, 8 Mar., D638/13/132, John Pulteney* to same, 9 Apr. 1692; Bodl. Carte 76, f. 193; *CSP Dom.* 1691–2, p. 238; McGrath thesis, 129–30. [6] *CSP Dom.* 1691–2, pp. 485–6; *Penal Era and Golden Age* ed. Bartlett and Hayton, pp. 21–22; Add. 28876, ff. 245–8; 28877, f. 376; *Analecta Hibernica*, xxxii. 102; Dalrymple, *Mems.* iii(3), p. 29; McGrath thesis, 130–1, 258–62. [7] *Luttrell Diary*, 438, 442, 446–8, 462, 471–3, 478–9; *LJ*, xv. 253–5, 256–71, 274, 283; *CJ Ire.* ii. 589–90, 627–9; Harl. 4892, ff. 127–31, 153–9; H. Horwitz, *Parl. and Pol. Wm. III*, 111. [8] *Cal. Treas. Bks.* x. 800; Nottingham Univ. Lib. Portland (Bentinck) mss, PwA 1227, [Sunderland] to Portland, 2 Aug. [1695]; BL, Trumbull Misc. mss 51, Sir William Trumbull* to William Blathwayt*, 2–12 Aug. 1695. [9] *Cal. Treas. Bks.* xi. 30, 33, 37, 44, 54, 65, 264, 358; xiii. 93, 304; *Cal. Treas. Pprs.* 1557–1696, pp. 395–6, 527–8; Trumbull Add. mss 98, John Bridges to Trumbull, 22 May 1698; McGrath thesis, 131–2. [10] PRO 30/24/20/35; *Cal. Treas. Pprs.* 1702–7, p. 317; 1708–14, pp. 200, 213, 216.

P.W./C.I.M.

CULLUM, Sir Dudley, 3rd Bt. (1657–1720), of Hawstead Place, Hawstead, Suff. and Hardwick House, nr. Bury St. Edmunds, Suff.

SUFFOLK 1702–1705

b. 17 Sept. 1657, 1st s. of Sir Thomas Cullum, 2nd Bt., of Hawstead Place and Hardwick House by Dudleia, da. of Sir Henry North, 1st Bt.†, of Mildenhall, Suff., coh. of her bro. Sir Henry North, 2nd Bt.† *educ.* Bury St. Edmunds g.s. by 1668; St. John's, Camb. 1675. *m.* (1) 3 Sept. 1681, Anne (*d.* 1709), da. of John Berkeley†, 1st Baron Berkeley of Stratton, *s.p.*; (2) 12 June 1710, Anne, da. of James Wicks of Bury St. Edmunds, *s.p. suc.* fa. as 3rd Bt. Oct. 1680.[1]

Freeman, Ipswich 1714.[2]

Cullum's grandfather, the younger son of a long-established Suffolk family, made his fortune as a draper in London, and purchased Hawstead and Hardwick in 1656. A 'Presbyterian' in City politics during the Civil War, he was one of the aldermen imprisoned in 1647–8 for opposition to the army, and subsequently removed from office; at the Restoration he was created a baronet. Cullum's father stood unsuccessfully on the 'Country' interest at Bury St. Edmunds in the election to the first Exclusion Parliament. Cullum himself was assured while at Cambridge by his old schoolmaster of 'the good signs you already give of being an honest and sober gentleman, such as may both support the honour of your family and promote also the good of your country', but to begin with he had little taste for public life: he refused to serve when pricked as sheriff in 1689. Instead he devoted most of his time to horticulture and botany, pursuits in which John Evelyn was his mentor.[3]

Although he had many Tory connexions through his mother and first wife, including his first cousin Thomas Hanmer II*, Cullum followed his father's politics and was returned as a Whig for Suffolk in 1702. He told on 17 Feb. in favour of a clause on behalf of Colonel Luke Lillingston to be added to the bill continuing the commission of inquiry into the debts of the army, navy and transports. On 17 Mar. he reported from the committee appointed to examine two 'irreligious' books, the *Second Thoughts Concerning Human Soul* and *Vindication of Reason*, by William Coward. Forecast in October 1704 as a likely opponent of the Tack, he did not vote for it on 28 Nov. He managed two private bills through the House in January and February 1705. Cullum was defeated twice in the 1705 election, when he again stood for Suffolk as a Whig, and was also put up at Bury St. Edmunds on the interest of Lord Hervey (John*). He dropped his candidature in a subsequent by-election for Bury, probably in favour of a nominee of Hervey, and thereafter retreated from politics to his gardens and greenhouses, where as 'honest, innocent Sir Dudley Cullum', he lived the rest of his life in rural retirement.[4]

Cullum died on 16 Sept. 1720 and was buried at Hawstead, having enjoyed the distinction of being the only member of his family to enter Parliament.

[1] G. G. Milner-Gibson-Cullum, *Cullum Fam.* 91–92; Muskett, *Suff. Manorial Fams.* i. 171; *E. Anglian*, n.s. iii. 217; Sir J. Cullum, *Hist. Hawstead* (1813), pp. 77, 184. [2] G. R. Clarke, *Ipswich*, 83. [3] Copinger, *Suff. Manors*, vii. 39–40; *DNB*; V. Pearl, *London and Outbreak of Puritan Revol.* 314–15; Cullum, 187–8. [4] W. Suss. RO, Shillinglee mss Ac.454/1162, Thomas Palmer to Sir Edward Turnor*, 26 Feb. 1704–5; Camb. Univ. Lib. Cholmondeley (Houghton) mss, R. Short to Robert Walpole II*, 25 Oct. 1705; *Hervey Letter Bks.* ii. 83.

D. W. H.

CUMMING, Sir Alexander, 1st Bt. (c.1670–1725), of Culter, Peterculter, Aberdeen.

ABERDEENSHIRE   18 Jan. 1709–1722

b. c.1670, 1st s. of Alexander Cumming of Culter by Helen, da. of James Allardice of Allardice, Kincardine. *educ.* adv. 1691; Leyden 30 Dec. 1695, aged 25. *m.* c.1690, Elizabeth (*d.* 1709), da. of Sir Alexander Swinton, Lord Mersington SCJ, 1s. 2da.; (2) 10 Sept. 1710, Elizabeth (*d.* bef. 1739), da. and coh. of William Dennis (*d.* 1701) of Pucklechurch, Glos., 1s. 5da. *cr.* Bt. 28 Feb. 1695. *suc.* fa. c.1715.[1]

Commr. justiciary for Highlands [S] 1701, 1702; capt. of ft. Earl of Mar's regt. 1702–4; conservator, Scottish staple at Campvere 1707–11.[2]

Burgess, Edinburgh 1704, Arbroath 1708, Old Aberdeen 1710, Anstruther Easter 1720.[3]

Cumming, whose grandfather had been penalized by the Scottish parliament in 1645 as a 'malignant', held to the episcopalian principles of his forebears (his library included, among other theological works, a copy of the *Book of Common Prayer*) and when excitement over ecclesiastical issues reached a peak he took on many of the characteristics of a Scottish Tory, except for any perceptible Jacobite sentiment. At the same time, he was also a pragmatist with a strong concern for material advancement, a wide acquaintance, and a clear eye for the main chance, as indeed the relatively modest extent of his patrimony obliged him to be. Moreover his distant relationship with the house of Argyll, his first marriage into a prominent Covenanting family, to the godly daughter of Sir Alexander Swinton, 'the fanatic judge', and his sister's marriage into a dynasty of Presbyterian merchants in nearby Aberdeen, furnished him with numerous connexions of a different kidney.[4]

Presumably through his father-in-law's influence, Cumming entered the faculty of advocates when no more than 21, before he had even begun to study the law, which he then undertook in Holland, returning to Scotland in 1696 to take the oaths and be admitted to practise. His clients soon included such prominent Court magnates as the Duke of Queensberry and, more significant in the long run, the 1st Duke of Argyll, to whose family he became closely attached. Argyll pressed hard, but without success, for his appointment to the Edinburgh commissariat in 1701, and in 1702 Cumming unsuccessfully contested the Scottish parliamentary election for Aberdeenshire, at which he suffered the accusation of being an apprentice courtier. Although he obtained a captain's commission in a Scottish regiment in 1702 (and yet another potential patron in the shape of his colonel, the Earl of Mar), he could not afford to regard this as adequate: he began to search for a more lucrative post, and relinquished the commission to his son in 1704 even before he had found an alternative for himself. Eventually, the following year, the patronage of the 2nd Duke of Argyll secured for him the place of conservator of the Scottish staple in the Low Countries. Worth about £800 p.a., this was given as 'the best the Queen had then in her grant'.[5]

The circumstances of the appointment were, however, far from straightforward. Technically the incumbent, Sir James Kennedy, shared the patent for life with his son Andrew, whose interest extended thereafter at the sovereign's pleasure. Under Sir

James's stewardship the administration of the staple left much to be desired, and merchants' complaints of the infringement of their privileges were cited in justification of his removal. But there was still unease in government circles at the abrogation of the younger Kennedy's rights, on both legal and moral grounds, and Lord Seafield for one 'shunned the doing it'. Furthermore, confirmation by the convention of royal burghs was required, and proved difficult to obtain, Kennedy's own protests finding an echo in complaints that the convention's rights were being violated. Cumming thus became involved in a prolonged dispute, carried on in the law courts, in the convention and at the staple port of Campvere. In December 1707 the lords of session finally affirmed the legality of his grant. He seems to have taken this decision as investing him with authority to act, though it lacked any confirmation from the burghs, and indeed he found himself in 1708 the object of the convention's censure for exacting fines 'unwarrantably'. The fact that the complainant in this case was the Duke of Hamilton's baillie may well have had some political significance, given Cumming's association with Argyll. Even the Treasury felt unable to decide between the rival claimants to the office, suspending payment of the salary in January 1709 until a legal resolution.[6]

During one of his visits to the Low Countries, Cumming was involved in an incident which was to be enshrined in family tradition. After visiting a nephew who had been wounded at Oudenarde, he 'fell in with the ... retinue' of the Electoral Prince of Hanover, and through his influence as conservator at Campvere was able to assist the Prince on his journey home. An even greater opportunity then presented itself. As his heir was to record many years later, Cumming

> had the good fortune to be the instrument of providence to save the Electoral Prince ... from being drowned in his highness's returning to Germany ... and being aboard the same ship with his highness, from Ostend to Zeeland, his highness was pleased to give the said Sir Alexander an invitation to Hanover and to assure him at the same time that if his highness should happen to live to have power in England the said Sir Alexander should be distinguished by the first honours of this kingdom.[7]

At this point in his career Cumming's association with Argyll may still have been strong enough to determine his political conduct. His son went over to Flanders in 1709 to attend the Duke, and fought at Malplaquet, where several members of Lady Cumming's family fell. Certainly, it would seem likely that at his first return to Parliament, in a by-election for Aberdeenshire earlier that year, Cumming was a supporter of the ministry, not least because he needed government backing in order to pursue his claim to the conservatorship: indeed, failure to resolve his dispute with the Kennedys probably accounts for his sudden desire to enter the House. But there were other sources of ministerial influence than Argyll, in particular the Earl of Mar, who seems to have given support to Cumming's parliamentary ambitions in Aberdeenshire. Cumming also cultivated the favour of another Court Tory, Lord Leven, and, as if to demonstrate the eclecticism of his political friendships, went out of his way to make professions of service to Lord Marchmont's son, Hon. Sir Andrew Hume*, though Hume felt that the best service Cumming could do would be to secure for him the interest of the Duke of Argyll.[8]

Cumming came up to Westminster in 1709 armed with detailed instructions from his constituents: he was to use his 'utmost endeavours to procure a division of the [court of] session and settlement of a branch thereof at Aberdeen'; to 'take away all superiorities of subjects and that the whole lands of the nation may hold of his Majesty'; and to 'have a good correspondence with the Member of Parliament for the town of Aberdeen [John Gordon] for advancing the good of the shire and town'. It may well have been with these instructions in mind that he obtained appointment to draft bills to discharge Scottish freeholders from attendance on the lords of judiciary on circuit (18 Jan. 1710), and to explain the Act for better securing the Queen's person and government (16 Feb.). He was also active on behalf of Aberdeen in soliciting the Treasury for the council's claim to the property of one James Douglas, a bastard who had died intestate, and in assisting Scottish merchants in general in their requests for convoys for their coastal shipping.[9]

To begin with, Cumming voted with the ministry, dividing in 1709 in favour of the naturalization of the Palatines. But the following year his party-political allegiance was transformed, and he subsequently claimed that he had been 'the first, if not the only, Commoner of my country that expressed my sentiments to her Majesty in relation to the late administration', that is to say his revulsion from it. The impeachment of Dr Sacheverell may have been a watershed. Cumming was listed (apparently in error) as having voted for the impeachment. George Lockhart* noted Cumming among a number of Scottish Members wrongly classified, who in fact had adhered 'constantly in all votes to the Tories'.[10]

Having become a widower in 1709, Cumming immediately began chasing fortunes, and in the following September 'carried off from the ring in Hyde Park Madam Dennis, and married her'. His sexual mores were questioned by the Edinburgh presbytery in September 1710, when a formal charge was presented relating to a 'scandal' of adultery that had been first raised in December 1708. Although Cumming had formerly condescended to present himself for scrutiny, he now refused to appear to answer the accusation. It is impossible to say whether there was any truth in the charge, or whether it was simply a product of the partisan malice that subsequently produced denunciations in the Edinburgh press of Cumming's 'vicious' character. His remarriage undoubtedly facilitated a less restrained political expression of his episcopalianism. With his new bride he had gained an estate in Gloucestershire, including various coal mines, but although rumour estimated his windfall at £16,000, in terms of rental value the land was worth no more than about £3,700, or some £320 p.a., and parcels were soon being sold off.[11]

In 1710 Cumming was successfully re-elected after a contest in Aberdeenshire, in which he had enjoyed the interest of both Argyll and Mar. The episcopalian clergyman Richard Dongworth described Cumming in an analysis of the new House as an 'episcopal Tory, rather Court', an assessment borne out by events, for in the first session he participated in attacks on the old ministry, being included in the list of 'worthy patriots' who had helped to detect their mismanagement. In a specifically Scottish context, he voted against the Duke of Montrose's factor, Mungo Graham*, in February 1711 over the disputed Kinross-shire election, and was a member of the informal 'steering committee' of Scottish episcopalian MPs, consisting, apart from himself, of George Lockhart, Sir Alexander Areskine, John Carnegie and Hon. James Murray. These men were prepared to urge the episcopalian cause in the Commons irrespective of any restraint attempted by magnates like Hamilton and Atholl who had hitherto claimed leadership of the cavalier faction. Yet at the same time Cumming maintained his connexions with members of the old Court party in Scotland, and his more moderate approach to the issue of toleration gave Lockhart reason to suspect him of being a Court stooge. When the proposal was made to press for a Scottish toleration bill, Cumming and some other members of the informal committee endorsed the idea in principle but produced the same 'scruples and objections' to implementation that Mar had brought forward. Lockhart concluded that they must have 'imparted the design' and been 'instructed to thwart it'. In March 1711 Cumming received a memorial from some 'gentlemen' in his constituency complaining of the 'tediousness' of Scottish legal procedure in relation to insolvency and urging him to move for the extension of the English bankruptcy laws to North Britain: his response is unknown, but nothing came of the initiative. The only speech he recorded during this session was on 19 May 1711 in favour of the bill to regulate the Scottish linen industry, when, in common with all Scotsmen, of whatever political persuasion, he answered the objections raised by the Irish lobby to the clause prohibiting the export of Scottish linen yarn to Ireland. Throughout this Parliament Cumming numbered such particular economic interests among his preoccupations. Fisheries were another recurring theme: in 1711 he helped draft several memorials and cases on behalf of Scottish fishing interests and was appointed to the committee of 16 May on one such petition, concerning imports of foreign salt. Given his experience over the conservatorship he was also an inevitable choice to assist in the preparation of yet another memorial from the Scots merchant community, this time for a removal of the restrictions on Scottish exports to the Continent via the staple port, in order to bring trading practices into line with the requirements of the Act of Union.[12]

In April 1711 Cumming's long struggle to retain his office was effectively ended when an appeal from the Kennedys was upheld by the Lords. Even then Cumming did not let the matter rest, claiming that the verdict declaring his grant invalid applied only to the original commission issued in 1705 and not to a renewal in 1708. At length, in 1713, the Queen withdrew the second commission and reappointed the Kennedys, the last instalment of the saga occurring in the following year when the question of repayment of salary advanced in 1708 was settled against Cumming. These various judicial codas notwithstanding, Cumming conceded in 1711 that he had lost the conservatorship, and although, as he said, the grant had cost him more in expenses than he had received in salary, he bewailed its loss and applied for compensation to Lord Treasurer Oxford (Robert Harley*), in a series of letters beginning in January 1712 and continuing until Oxford was removed as lord treasurer in 1714. Education for the law and experience in administering the staple fitted him for any office, he wrote, and his own 'little fortune', together with the small amount his second marriage had brought him, 'makes it indifferent to me where I am employed'. In justification he cited his services in Parliament, claiming never to have 'opposed' Harley's interest, nor 'trimmed', and to have been constant in his attendance in each session. In June 1712 he recalled having acted as an intermediary between Harley and the Argyll interest, though his use of language makes the chronology obscure: 'I had the honour to be entrusted by that noble Duke to receive your lordship's commands by your nephew last Parliament to be communicated to his friends.'[13]

Circumstantial evidence suggests that in the 1711–12 session Cumming may have become rather less amenable to Court direction. Admittedly his active involvement in Commons business was principally confined to Scottish affairs. The steering committee of Scottish Tory Members having been reconstituted, he played a key role in its promotion of the Scottish toleration bill, in the face of Oxford's disapproval, and was listed as voting for the bill on 7 Feb. 1712. He also joined Lockhart, Carnegie and Murray in harrying the former Scots MP William Cochrane, who was labouring under accusations of corruption, and acted as a teller in two divisions: on 13 Mar., against the Squadrone Whig Sir John Anstruther, 1st Bt.*, in the disputed election for Anstruther Easter Burghs; and on 13 May, in favour of an additional clause to the soap and paper duties bill, to permit a drawback on the paper used by Scottish university presses (including, of course, Aberdeen) for printing books on classical, oriental and 'northern' languages (a proviso which attracted opposition from English Tories, probably acting on behalf of Oxford University). But his chief concern was to protect the burgh of Aberdeen from an increased contribution under the land tax. Acting in conjunction with Thomas Smith II, Member for Glasgow Burghs, Cumming was involved in bringing this matter before Parliament. He was responsible for drafting a clause that was inserted into the Land Tax Act of 1711 stipulating that the quota of cess payable by each burgh ought to be determined by its valued rent. The apportionment of the land tax (or cess) between the burghs had become a matter of some controversy in the convention of royal burghs in 1711, when it was asserted that Court influence had forced tax rises on a number of burghs for wayward votes in the last general election. This political dimension was paralleled by rivalry between Edinburgh and other prosperous burghs such as Glasgow and Aberdeen (see GLASGOW BURGHS). In the interest of improving his reputation locally, Cumming willingly courted the displeasure of 'some leading men in the burghs'. His scheme was rendered unworkable, however, by Edinburgh's influence in the convention, and the clause was discarded in the Land Tax Act of 1712. Cumming failed in his attempts to have it reinstated in 1713, not least because of opposition from his customary ally, Lockhart, a situation which was caused by a divergence in their respective local interests.[14]

The two addresses which Cumming presented in December 1712, from Aberdeenshire and from the burgh of Brechin, were supportive of the Court: both thanked the Queen not only for giving the royal assent to the Scottish Toleration and Patronage Acts, but also for the peace, and in doing so praised ministers and damned their critics. Then at the outset of the 1713 session Cumming joined other Scottish peers and MPs in a circular letter to Lord Dun SCJ to urge non-juring episcopalian clergymen to take the oaths, in order to qualify themselves for the benefits of the toleration, and to disprove the insinuations of disloyalty made against them by their Presbyterian enemies. He may have taken part in a Scottish Tory scheme to impose on the parliamentary electorate in Scotland an oath abjuring the Covenant, since a copy of the draft survives in his papers. Although Cumming clashed with some Scottish Members and incurred the displeasure of the Earl of Findlater (the former Seafield) for his continued support for legislation on burghal taxation, he stood shoulder to shoulder with his fellow countrymen when Anglo-Scottish relations reached a crisis over the malt tax and the motion to dissolve the Union. He drafted various papers against the imposition of the malt duty, signed the letter from Scottish MPs which called for a general meeting of the kingdom's parliamentary representatives to concert a response, and indeed was one of the four Members sent for by 'a great man', presumably Oxford, in an attempt to stifle opposition, but who resisted all blandishments to let the motion fall. It is conceivable that Cumming's stiffness on the issue may have owed something to Argyll's support for the motion, but the greater likelihood is that he simply could not afford to appear lukewarm in defence of the vital interests of his country. Any thought that he was still acting as Argyll's client should be dispelled by his subsequent support for the administration on issues of trade. On 2 June Cumming told for the bill to open up the African trade, a move from which Scottish merchants as well as ministerial allies would benefit. Two days later he voted for the Court over the French commerce bill, dividing from Lockhart and many Scottish Tories in so doing. He supported Oxford again in the crucial debate on the commerce bill on 18 June, both speaking and voting in favour of the treaty as 'advantageous to Scotland', and after the rejection of the bill was appointed on 23 June to prepare an address to request the Queen to appoint commissioners to renew negotiations. This defence of the treaty was continued outside the House, for he drafted various papers setting out the ministerial case against criticism from Scottish trading interests, and published two lengthy anonymous essays with the same message in the *Mercator* on 18 and 27 Aug. In his letters to Oxford he plumed himself on his contribution to the ministry's propaganda campaign:

> As for the commerce bill which I was so much blamed about, as being the author of all those *Mercators* said to be writ from Scotland, and the procurer of the letters signed by the merchants there, approving of our conduct in relation to that bill, though it was not fit for me to own those facts, yet I ventured to assert that those who afterwards opposed the commerce bill would be looked upon as enemies to Scotland.

Offsetting the loss of the treaty, to some small degree, was a minor triumph achieved some five days after the division of 18 June, when a modified version of a resolution originally devised by Cumming, calling for the Board of Trade to consider ways of advancing the fishing industry, was adopted by the House.[15]

Once the session was over Cumming renewed his applications to the lord treasurer for employment. The acquisition of his wife's property had not cleared the problem of indebtedness into which his own personal extravagance constantly propelled him, and his circumstances were now desperate enough for his aspirations to extend to a governorship in the West Indies, where he would willingly have risked health for profit. That nothing came forth, in spite of his considerable services to the lord treasurer, he attributed to a 'design' framed by his enemies to make Oxford believe that he had 'placed my dependence upon some other great men (in whose interest I was said to be)', an accusation he vehemently denied:

> I will never change my principles, desert my party, nor contribute towards the overturning a ministry who have done so glorious things [sic] for their country . . . though I have been told I have not only injured their party, but sullied the characters of several great men, in my voting within, and conversation without, doors, and laid myself out to make converts of others, and yet still may make my peace whereas I would find myself neglected by those I have served. Yet those things were so far from having weight with me, that I very frankly owned my resolutions to support the ministry in the public service.

The assumption must be that he had been suspected of following his friends Lockhart and Murray into the interest of Lord Bolingbroke (Henry St. John II*), rather than that he had turned back to Argyll, although it is unlikely that he had completely lost touch with the Duke at this stage.[16]

In the absence of any alternative employment, Cumming sought re-election for Aberdeenshire in 1713, in the hope that the next Parliament would 'be more auspicious to me than this has been'. He defeated a powerful challenge from Findlater's protégé Alexander Reid*, and was listed as a 'Jacobite' in an electoral analysis sent to Hanover by Lord Polwarth (whose categorization should not be taken literally). In contrast, Lockhart complained of his continued truckling to a Court interest, now specifically Lord Bolingbroke, with whom Cumming and others had allegedly been at 'a good deal of pains to ingratiate themselves'. He and his parliamentary colleagues had as their chief project in this session a bill to resume the Scottish bishops' rents, to relieve those episcopalian ministers who were willing to accept the terms of the 1712 Toleration Act: a move inspired by the Court, possibly as an initiative to woo the Scots Tories. Having taken the ministerial cue to promote the measure, and been appointed on 7 June 1714 to the drafting committee for a bill to state the revenues, Cumming then readily abandoned the idea when Lord Mar represented the Queen's alarm at its likely repercussions. How closely Cumming was attached to Bolingbroke is open to question. He was still soliciting jobs from the lord treasurer as well, including once more 'a government in the West Indies', and Oxford was replying with generalized promises of goodwill. His parliamentary activity offers few direct clues, affected as he was by a dangerous illness and, when he did attend, confining himself once more to matters of Scottish interest. Having in the previous autumn sought to promote the linen industry in Scotland (and especially in the vicinity of Aberdeen) by means of a memorial to the Queen advocating the establishment of a network of charity schools to teach spinning, he spoke 'very fully' in the Commons in favour of the reintroduced linen bill, which had again angered Irish Members by a ban on exports of linen yarn from Scotland to Ireland. Towards the end of the session he participated in a Scots protest against a Treasury motion for a clause to be added to the lottery bill to use the drawbacks fund to pay administrative salaries in Scotland. What can be said, however, is that he remained committed to the Tory interest, as demonstrated by tellerships on the disputed elections for Anstruther Easter Burghs (4 Mar. and 29 Apr.) and Linlithgowshire (8 Apr.), and by his vote on 12 May against the extension of the schism bill to cover Catholic education. He was marked as a Tory on the Worsley list. This partisan loyalty, against whatever representations may have been made by Argyll and his brother Lord Ilay, was in all probability what Mar was alluding to when he wrote subsequently that Cumming had 'behaved very well and tight the last session, notwithstanding of pressure upon him, which I confess has much recommended him to me'.[17]

The Hanoverian succession prompted an immediate attempt to recall not only the former pledges of the electoral family, but Cumming's old connexion with Argyll. A petition to King George in November 1714 appealed for the belated fulfilment of a promise allegedly made by Queen Anne to appoint him as governor of the Leeward Islands. He recounted the story of his travails over the conservatorship, and the expenses incurred by a 'close and constant attendance' in Parliament; cited his qualifications by 'education in the study of the civil and municipal laws at home and abroad, his knowledge of trade' and, with rank disingenuousness, 'his service for some years in the army'; concluding with the claim that he had 'very much impaired his small fortune' and that without some crown employment 'his family will be in danger of being extinct'. On meeting a refusal he tried a different route, approaching the Hanoverian minister Bothmer through an old acquaintance of his, the former envoy Kreienberg, and leaning heavily on his own friendship with Argyll, but to no greater effect. However, he seems still to have attempted to resume relations with Argyll. He was classified as a Whig in a list of the Members of the 1713 Parliament re-elected in 1715, and although he himself remained unprovided for and in opposition, despite efforts to have him appointed a lord of session, his son was benefiting from Argyll's patronage by 1719. At the same time Cumming did not abandon his Tory friends. Mar helped him again at the 1715 election and in the following summer he acted as a conduit for correspondence between the Jacobite 2nd Earl of Kintore and Hon. James Murray shortly before the latter's flight to the Pretender. Even though he took no part whatsoever in the Fifteen or in subsequent Jacobite conspiracy, he included men like Kintore and the non-juring 5th Viscount Arbuthnott among a wide circle of correspondents which also encompassed Revolution-men like Sir David Dalrymple*. Arbuthnott for one refused to believe Whig-inspired rumours that Cumming had voted for the peerage bill in 1719 in hope of being made a baron of the Scottish exchequer, and praised his conduct, as 'a man of honour' whom 'the frowns and menaces of the great, nor their undue methods of making votes, could never terrify or decoy . . . into unjust compliances against your country'. In fact he had been forecast by Lord Sunderland (Charles, Lord Spencer*) as a likely supporter of the bill and had tactfully absented himself from the division. What kept his reputation high among Scottish Tories was his staunch adherence to the Anglican cause: he voted in Parliament in January 1719 against the repeal of the Occasional Conformity and Schism Acts, and made strenuous efforts, at considerable legal expense, to assist the episcopalian incumbent of Maryculter (a man allegedly implicated in the Fifteen) to retain the profits of his living. In consequence he was assured of the votes of the 'honest party' in Aberdeenshire should he have wished to put up again at the 1722 election, but, presumably because of deteriorating health, he did not do so.[18]

Once his father's estate had come into his hands in 1715, Cumming's finances took on a rosier complexion. He gave full rein to his zeal for 'improvement', reconstructing the ancestral seat at Culter, and seeking to develop the agricultural and industrial potential of his landholdings and mines. His extensive library contained works on mathematics, natural science, economics and commerce as well as the more usual collections of history, theology and contemporary political pamphlets. Unfortunately, he was also able to overindulge his naturally litigious disposition in a series of expensive suits over property, and, worse still, to develop a new enthusiasm for investment. By some means he was able to realize over £16,000 in capital, with which he purchased South Sea and African Company stock at the height of the speculation in 1720, most of it disappearing when the Bubble burst. These heavy losses, aggravated by legal costs, and the utter 'confusion' which had, perhaps predictably, overtaken the affairs of his eldest son, broke his health. He died at Aberdeen on 7 Feb. 1725, and was buried at Peterculter. The newly built mansion at Culter had to be sold, and the 2nd baronet, in spite of a colourful career, the highlight of which was election as chief of the Cherokee nation in 1730, spent time in the Fleet before dying a 'poor brother' of Charterhouse. Cumming's grandson, the last representative of the direct male line, was an army captain: he went mad, and died in Whitechapel, 'in a state of indigence'.[19]

[1] H. B. Tomkins, *Table Showing Fams. Descended from Sir Alexander Cumming* (1877); *Album Studiosorum Academiae Lugduno Batavae* ed. Du Rieu, col. 739; Luttrell, *Brief Relation*, vi. 628. [2] *CSP Dom.* 1700–2, p. 339; 1702–3, p. 355; J. Davidson and A. Gray, *Scottish Staple at Campvere*, 246–8; *HMC Lords*, n.s. ix. 91. [3] *Scot. Rec. Soc.* lxii. 48; *Recs. Old Aberdeen* (New Spalding Club), i. 280; Aberdeen Univ. Lib. Duff House (Montcoffer) mss 3175/2378, 2375, burgess tickets. [4] *APS*, vi(1), 464; Duff House (Montcoffer) mss 3175/2384, inventory of Cumming's personal estate, 10 Apr. 1725; *Pollable Persons in Aberdeen.* (Spalding Club), ii. 472; *DNB* (Swinton, Sir Alexander); *N. and Q.* ser. 1, v. 279; Tomkins, *Table*. [5] *APS*, x. 53; Duff House (Montcoffer) mss 3175/2376, Cumming to father, 12 July, 26 Aug. 1703, 16 June 1704; 3175/F11/3, commn. 5 May 1702; *Argyle Pprs.* 93–95, 97–98, 101–2, 120; Carstares, *State Pprs.* 704; Add. 39855, f. 11; 28055, f. 41; 70221, Cumming to Oxford, 17 June 1712; SRO, Ogilvy of Inverquharity mss GD205/33/3/10/24, William Jamisone to William Bennet*, 29 Jan. 1705–6. [6] Davidson and Gray, 233, 246–7; Add. 61631, ff. 86–95, 177–9; *Recs. R. Burghs Scotland*, iv. 374–5, 378–9; *Baillie Corresp.* 57, 61, 71; *HMC Lords*, 91; *Cal. Treas. Bks.* xxii. 267; xxiii. 64. [7] Add. 39855, ff. 10, 41–42. [8] Ibid. f. 12; Duff House (Montcoffer) mss 3175/2377, Leven to Cumming, 26 Apr. 1709, Cumming to

Hon. Sir Andrew Hume, 31 Mar. 1709. [9]Duff House (Montcoffer) mss, 3175/F11/3, Mar to Cumming, 'Sunday morning 12 o'clock'; 3175/2377, James Cumming to Cumming, 24 Mar. 1709; *Cal. Treas. Bks.* xxiv. 47–48; Aberdeen City Archs. Aberdeen burgh recs. 8/1/8/145, council to Cumming et al. 27 Feb. 1710. [10]*Lockhart Mems.* ed. Szechi, 287; Add. 70221, Cumming to Oxford, 17 June 1712. [11]*Clavering Corresp.* (Surtees Soc. clxxviii), 50–51; Duff House (Montcoffer) mss 3175/F11/3, Mar to Cumming, 'Sunday morning, 12 o'clock'; 3175/2375, 'A Survey of the Tenants in Glos. . . . 1710', 'Acct. of Purchase Money Due . . . 1714'; Luttrell, 628; Clarke thesis, 299, 522; *The Gen.* iii. 7–8; PCC 170 Romney. [12]Duff House (Montcoffer) mss 3175/2382, 'The Case of Several Merchants and Others Concerned in the Fishery of N[orth] B[ritain]', 1711, 'Representation for Several of the Merchants and Masters of Ships in Scotland, Concerning the Staple Port'; SRO, Mar and Kellie mss GD124/15/1003, Thomas Erskyne to Ld. Grange (Hon. James Erskine†), Aug. 1710; *SHR*, lx. 63; NLS, Advocates' mss, Wodrow Pprs. letters Quarto 5, f. 128; NLS, ms 16503, ff. 1–2; NLS, ms 25276/56, Dalrymple to Cumming, 9 Apr. 1719; *Cromartie Corresp.* ii. 122; *Lockhart Pprs.* i. 329, 338–9. [13]Davidson and Gray, 248; *HMC Lords*, 92–94; n.s. x. 361–2; *HMC Portland*, x. 301–2, 417–18, 474–5; *Cal. Treas. Bks.* xxv. 543–4; xxvi. 388; Add. 70221, Cumming to Oxford, 17 June 1712, 21 Dec. 1713, 8 June 1714. [14]*Lockhart Pprs.* 378; SRO, Montrose mss GD220/5/283/1, Cochrane to Montrose, 1 Apr. 1712; Duff House (Montcoffer) mss 3175/2380, John Ross et al. to Cumming, 3 Aug. 1711, 'Some Reasons for a Clause to be Inserted in the Land Tax Act', 'A Copy of a Clause to be Added Concerning the Tax Roll of the Royal Burghs', 19 Dec. 1711; *Case of the Royal Burghs* [1712]; SRO, Seafield mss GD248/566/84/50, Reid to [Findlater], 27 [Apr. 1713]; T. Pagan, *Convention of R. Burghs*, 64–65. [15]*Scots Courant*, 22–24 Dec. 1712; Spalding Club, *Misc.* iv. 83–87; Duff House (Montcoffer) mss 3175/2380, draft clause against the Covenant, 1713, 'Reasons against Laying a Duty on Malt in Scotland', 'Scrolls Concerning the Malt Tax', 'Resolution of the Commons to call a Meeting with the Lords, [23] May 1713', 'Scrolls in Relation to Trade for the *Mercator*', 18, 27 Aug. 1713; 3175/2382, 'Resolve Fishery, June 1713'; Mar and Kellie mss GD124/15/1099/5, Alexander Reid to Thomas Erskyne, 7 May 1713; *HMC Laing*, ii. 168; SRO, Seafield mss GD248/566/84/50, Reid to [Findlater], 27 [Apr. 1713]; *Parlty. Hist.* i. 65, 69; Chandler, v. 41; SRO, Cromartie mss GD305 addit./bdle. 15, [–] to [?Cromarty], 20 June 1713; Add. 70221, Cumming to Oxford, 21 Dec. 1713. [16]*HMC Portland*, 301–2; Add. 70279, Cumming to Oxford, 13 Aug. 1713; 70221, same to same, 21 Dec. 1713; Duff House (Montcoffer) mss 3175/2376, Cumming to father, 26 Mar. 1708, 26 Jan. 1711–12, tailor's bill, 6 Oct. 1708; 3175/2377, Lockhart to Cumming, 23 July 1713, William Bromley II* to same, 18 Nov. 1713. [17]SRO, Grant of Monymusk mss GD345/1138/2/5, Cumming to Sir Francis Grant, 8 Jan. 1713; *HMC Portland*, 212; Mar and Kellie mss GD124/15/1099/1, Thomas Erskyne to Grange, 4 Apr. 1713; GD124/15/1129/6, Mar to same, 7 Aug. 1714; *Orig. Pprs.* ed. Macpherson, ii. 559–61; *Lockhart Pprs.* 443–5, 447, 449, 536, 542; P. W. J. Riley, *Eng. Ministers and Scotland*, 253; *Lockhart Letters* ed. Szechi, 101; Add. 70221, Cumming to Oxford, 8 June 1714; Duff House (Montcoffer) mss 3175/2382, 'Memorial for Setting up a Linen Manufacture', 1 Sept. 1713, 'Memorial Concerning the Linen Manufacture', 1713. [18]Duff House (Montcoffer) mss 3175/2382, petition to George I, Nov. 1714; Kreienberg to Cumming, 14 Nov. 1714; 3175/F11/3, Mar to same, 18 Jan. 1714–15; 3175/F51/4, Kintore to same, 30 June 1715; Arbuthnott to same, 4 Feb., 18 Dec. 1719, 5 July 1720, Dalrymple to same, 19 Oct. 1719; 3175/2375, Alexander Cumming to Cumming, 25 Apr. 1723; Add. 39855, ff. 9, 13; 61632, ff. 193, 196; *Sir Alexander Cumming, Bart, Appellant, the Moderator and Presbytery of Aberdeen, Respondents: The Respondents' Case* [1721]. [19]Duff House (Montcoffer) mss 3175/2384, inventory, 12 Apr. 1725; 3175/2379, catalogue of Cumming's library, 1718; 3175/F29/4, Cumming's diary and memo. bk. 1715–19; 3175/2375, Alexander to Sir Alexander Cumming, 25 Apr., 31 Dec. 1723; NLS, Crawford mss 47/2/258, John Daye to Sir Roger Bradshaigh, 3rd Bt.*, 2 Feb. 1720; Boyer, *Pol. State*, xxix. 179; Tomkins, *Table*; Rogers, *Scottish Monuments and Tombstones*, 339; *Colls. Aberdeen and Banff* (Spalding Club), i. 42; *DNB* (Cumming, Sir Alexander, 2nd Bt.).

D. W. H.

CUNNINGHAM, Henry (c.1678–1736), of Boquhan, Gorgunnock, Stirling.

STIRLINGSHIRE	11 Jan. 1709–1710
STIRLING BURGHS	1710–1727
STIRLINGSHIRE	1727–1734

b. c.1678, o. s. of William Cunningham of Boquhan by his 1st w. Margaret, da. of David Erskine, 2nd Ld. Cardross [S], half-sis. of John Erskine*. *m.* by 1708, Jean (*d.* bef. 1736), da. of John Lennox of Woodhead, Campsie, Stirling, s.p. suc. mother 1715, fa. 1722.[1]

Commr. justiciary for Highlands [S] 1701, 1702; muster master gen. [S] 1714–16, 1727–Apr. 1734; commr. forfeited estates June 1716–1724, forfeited estates [S] 1724–5; gov. Jamaica Apr. 1734–*d.*[2]

Burgess, Edinburgh 1713, Glasgow 1722; provost, Inverkeithing 1720–*d.*[3]

'A pretty enough fellow', wrote the Earl of Mar of his 'cousin' Cunningham in June 1708, but 'a little hot'. Politically, Mar was reading temperature in terms of zeal for the Presbyterian interest, which had been the bent of the family since the 1640s, when the laird of Boquhan had worked for the Covenanting cause. For Cunningham's father the Revolution was the culmination of a lengthy record of resistance to Stuart policy in Scotland. Having refused the test, he had been arrested in 1684 for 'conversing with rebels', and had spent some time thereafter in exile in Holland. Even though the part he played in the Revolution itself seems to have been confined to his own locality, he was none the less a staunch supporter of both the Williamite administration and the Kirk.[4]

Perhaps because the Cunninghams had traditionally steered away from the chief magnates in Stirlingshire, Lords Linlithgow and Montrose, no member of the family had hitherto been sent as a commissioner to the Scottish estates. Cunningham himself was returned to Westminster in 1708 because the principal electoral interests were divided. He relied on his own reputation, supplemented by the influence of Mar and the belated conversion of the Duke of Montrose to his cause. Although Linlithgow as sheriff seized upon the pretext of Cunningham's late acquisition of a freehold to make a double return, the Whig majority in the new House of Commons made sure that he was seated. As Montrose told the Junto lord, Sunderland (Charles, Lord Spencer*), Cunningham's 'education and principles' afforded strong grounds for believing that, once elected, he would be 'firmly on our side'.⁵

During the summer before the Parliament was to meet Cunningham took himself over to Flanders, 'to serve [as] a volunteer in the campaign', armed with letters of recommendation from Lord Mar which he hoped would enable him to obtain the acquaintance and favour of the Duke of Marlborough (John Churchill*). Nothing is recorded of his performance on the battlefield, always assuming that he reached it, and little is known of his performance in the Commons either, aside from his vote for the impeachment of Dr Sacheverell. He can have done little to impress either Montrose or Mar, however, for as the 1710 election approached it was clear that his efforts to retain the county seat would have to depend entirely on his own interest. Montrose decided to take no part in the contest, and Mar, regarding the cause as hopeless without such help, simply dropped Cunningham. He fell back on Stirling Burghs as an alternative seat, carrying the election after a contest.⁶

Cunningham's earlier connexion with Mar explains his classification as a 'Court Tory' by Richard Dongworth, the Duchess of Buccleuch's chaplain. It proved wide of the mark. Cunningham sided with the Whigs for most of the 1710 Parliament, notwithstanding his vote against Montrose's factor, Mungo Graham*, in the disputed election for Kinross-shire, and his appearance among the 'worthy patriots' who had exposed the mismanagements of the previous ministry. His shift to a more pronounced Whiggism could have been produced by concern for the Kirk and the succession; equally, the marriage of Sir Hugh Paterson, 3rd Bt.* (his electoral rival in the county) to Mar's sister may have convinced him that nothing more was to be expected from that quarter. Cunningham voted on 17 Jan. 1712 against the Tory motion to send Robert Walpole II* to the Tower, a service which, supposedly, was the origin of his later preferment under Walpole's premiership; and on 7 Feb. he voted against the Scottish toleration bill, and twice told against the bill restoring lay patronage in Scotland (28 Mar. and 7 Apr.). Shortly afterwards it was reported to the Presbyterian divine Robert Wodrow that in one of his recent speeches Cunningham had made a stout defence of his nationality and religion:

> He rose up and said, 'Mr Speaker I bless God I was born in Scotland and bred a Presbyterian', upon which the House hissed him. After that was over, he began again, and said 'I was going to say, Mr Speaker, I blessed God' etc. as above; and they hissed again. After silence was commanded, he said, 'Mr Speaker, there are two rules of this honourable House I thought had been inviolable – the freedom and liberty of speech without interruption, and another against duelling!' And laying his hand upon his sword, he said, 'Mr Speaker, if the House thus break the one, I hope they will allow me to break the other'. Upon that there was an entire silence; and he spoke what he had to say.

Cunningham acted as a teller on three other occasions during this session: on 12 Mar. for an address calling for estimates for finishing the fortifications of Stirling Castle; on 19 Mar. for an amendment upon supply to reduce the sum granted for garrisons; and on 13 May in favour of a drawback for Scottish universities on the paper duty. In the next session he presented an address on the peace from Stirling Burgh in March 1713, the tone of which was uncompromisingly Whiggish, and in the wake of the malt tax crisis joined the united Scottish campaign to dissolve the Union. He also voted against the ministry over the French commerce bill (4 and 18 June), being marked as a Whig in the published list.⁷

Re-elected for Stirling Burghs in 1713 and put down as a supporter of the Hanoverian succession in Lord Polwarth's list, Cunningham was reported in the following January to be travelling around the west of Scotland in the company of his uncle Colonel John Erskine* to promote Hanoverian addresses. These were to be communicated to various 'great men', including Polwarth and Ilay, presumably for presentation to the Queen. In the following session Cunningham's party loyalty was immediately apparent: he figured as a teller on the Whig side in two disputed election cases (Anstruther Easter Burghs and Linlithgowshire), voting likewise on 18 Mar. against the expulsion of Richard Steele. On 12 May he divided with other Scottish Whigs in favour of the extension of the schism bill to cover Catholic education. He also co-operated with a cross-party Scottish initiative on the bill discharging the Equivalent commissioners and was a teller on 24 June in favour of a clause that would have imposed interest of 4 per cent upon the £14,000 appropriated for the wool-producing shires unless this money was entrusted in the meantime to the magistrates of Edinburgh. He was himself responsible for the Scottish Members' attempt to amend the 1712 Linen Act, bringing a bill into the House and chairing its second-reading committee. One of the signatories to the proclamation of George I in Edinburgh, Cunningham presented a loyal address from Stirlingshire in October 1714, being introduced at court by the Duke of Argyll. The extent to which he had by now identified himself with the Whig party in Scotland was graphically illustrated in Mar's comment in September 1714, in a letter to Sir

John Erskine concerning preparations for the forthcoming election: 'for God's sake, get Harry Cunningham defeated, carry it who will'.[8]

Listed as a Whig in the Worsley list, Cunningham was re-elected in 1715, and satirized as one who had already 'acquired a lasting fame, by the service he's done to the godly'. He was provided with office and settled himself into the Argyll connexion. He developed a strong electoral interest in county and burghs, becoming by the 1730s a trusted instrument in Lord Ilay's system of electoral management. Cunningham died in Jamaica on 12 Feb. 1736, having arrived there a little over two months before to take up the governorship, in a desperate attempt to shore up his tottering finances. Little or nothing was left for his only surviving close relative, a sister. The Boquhan estate, of which he was said to be 'passionately fond', was subjected to a judicial sale for the payment of his debts; the extensive plans he had prepared for the laying out of the grounds were thus never carried out.[9]

[1] F. Cundall, *Govs. Jamaica 18th Cent.* 166–70; *SRO Indexes*, iii. 213, 502; *Services of Heirs* (ser. 1), i. 1710–19, p. 7. [2] *CSP Dom.* 1700–2, p. 338; 1702–3, p. 353; SRO, Ogilvy of Inverquharity mss GD205/31/1/17, Roxburghe to William Bennet*, 12 Oct. 1714; *HMC Laing*, ii. 185–6; *Cal. Treas. Bks. and Pprs.* 1731–4, p. 549; Boyer, *Pol. State*, xlvii. 420. [3] *Scot. Rec. Soc.* lxii. 49; lvi. 363; W. Stephen, *Hist. Inverkeithing and Rosyth*, 212. [4] SRO, Mar and Kellie mss GD124/15/868/1, Mar to Stair, 20 June 1708; *APS*, vi(1), 28, 53, 204, 560; vi(2), 32, 192; ix. 26, 52, 140; *Reg. PC Scotland*, 1676–8, p. 513; 1684–5, p. 269; 1689, pp. 374–5; 1691, pp. 289–90; *Scot. Hist. Soc.* xiv. 2, 197–8; Lauder of Fountainhall, *Hist. Notices* (Bannatyne Club, lxxxvii), 484–5; *Leven and Melville Pprs.* (Bannatyne Club, lxxvii), 246–7. [5] Sunter thesis, 1–11; Add. 61628, f. 149; 9102, f. 74. [6] Mar and Kellie mss GD124/15/868/1, Mar to Stair, 20 June 1708; GD124/15/975/2, 10, Mar to Ld. Grange (Hon. James Erskine†), 6 June, 27 July 1710; GD124/15/1005/1,2, Cunningham to same, 5 Sept., 13 Oct. 1710; Add. 61136, f. 111; Sunter thesis, 12–20. [7] *SHR*, lx. 65; SRO, Montrose mss GD220/5/808/17, Graham to Montrose, 10 Feb. 1711; Ramsay of Ochtertyre, *Scotland and Scotsmen in 18th Cent.* ii. 120; *London Gazette*, 10–14 Mar. 1712[–13]; Aberdeen Univ. Lib. Duff House (Montcoffer) mss 3175/2380, 'Resolution of the Commons to Call a Meeting of the Lords', [23] May 1713; *Parlty. Hist.* i. 69. [8] *Orig. Pprs.* ed. Macpherson, ii. 540; *Lockhart Letters* ed. Szechi, 106–8; Boyer, viii. 124; *London Gazette*, 9–12 Oct. 1714; NLS, ms 5072, f. 24. [9] *Lockhart Pprs.* i. 593; R. M. Sunter, *Patronage and Pol. in Scotland*, 214–15, 221; Cundall, 170.

D. W. H.

CURZON, John (c.1674–1727), of Kedleston, Derbys.

DERBYSHIRE 1701 (Dec.)–1727

b. c.1674, 1st s. of Sir Nathaniel Curzon, 2nd Bt., by Sarah, da. of William Penn of Penn, Bucks.; bro. of Nathaniel* and William Curzon†. *educ.* Trinity, Oxf. matric. 18 July 1690, aged 16, BA 1693; I. Temple 1692. *unm. suc.* fa. as 3rd Bt. 4 Mar. 1719.[1]

The Curzons had been settled in Derbyshire since the reign of Henry I, their chief residence being at Kedleston on the main Buxton–Derby road, and they had provided Members for the county since the late 14th century. Curzon's grandfather had sat for Brackley in 1628–9, and for Derbyshire in both the Short and Long Parliaments until excluded at Pride's Purge. He had also stood again, unsuccessfully, in 1661. However, the second baronet never entered the fray himself as a candidate, preferring instead to exercise his political influence on behalf of his son.[2]

The first intimation of Curzon's parliamentary ambition occurred during the preparations for the county election of 1698, when there was a strong suggestion that he had been persuaded to withdraw to facilitate the election of Thomas Coke* with the Marquess of Hartington (William Cavendish*). In the confused circumstances pertaining to the representation of the county in the election of January 1701, there were indications that Curzon would stand in partnership with Coke against Hartington and Lord Roos (John Manners*). In all likelihood the rumour, indecision, and consequent recrimination which surrounded this election deterred the Curzon interest from becoming involved. By the next election, however, in November 1701, Curzon had reached an agreement with Coke which was strong enough not only to defeat the two lords but to forestall any further serious dispute over the county seats until 1710.[3]

Lord Sunderland (Charles, Lord Spencer*) was in no doubt that Curzon's election in 1701 represented a loss to the Whigs, a judgment with which Robert Harley*, in another list, concurred, classing Curzon as a Tory. He voted on 26 Feb. 1702 for the motion to vindicate the Commons' proceedings on the impeachments of the previous session, thus confirming his Tory credentials. His one tellership, on 27 Apr., was on a procedural matter. It is also clear from Coke's papers that during his first session his constituents expected activity on their behalf, whether it concerned the promotion of legislation favourable to the county's lead mines or the application of pressure at the Admiralty over convoys at Hull which affected the traders of Chesterfield. Despite persistent rumours, and some Whig activity, Curzon and Coke were returned again, unopposed, at the general election of July 1702. Curzon then turned his mind to securing the removal of Dissenting justices from the bench and even suggested that much trouble would be avoided in the future if the leading Whig deputy-lieutenants were dismissed.[4]

Curzon set out for the new Parliament on 12 Oct.

1702, travelling via his wife's family estate at Penn, and was in London by 27 Oct., when he was named to a select committee. He also acted as a teller twice during the session: on 2 Nov. for a motion that the Commons had not had right done them on the question of the impeachments, and on 23 Dec. against a place clause in the bill to allow the Queen to settle a revenue on Prince George. He also followed the Tory line on 13 Feb. 1703, when he voted against agreeing with the Lords' amendments to the bill for enlarging the time to take the abjuration oath. Soon after the end of the session he was back in Derby, where on 17 Mar. 1703 he attended a dinner at the assizes for the lord chief justice. A few weeks before the next parliamentary session opened, a letter written by a correspondent of Coke suggested that Curzon was not enamoured with life at Westminster, for 'he talks dangerously as if representing us again would be a fatigue to him'. Nevertheless, he was diligent enough to be present on the opening day of the new session, when he was appointed on 9 Nov. 1703 to the committee on the Address. He served as a teller twice during this session: on 18 Jan. 1704 against giving a third reading to the bill establishing a land registry in the West Riding, thereby securing a postponement and enabling the House to receive a report on the Bramber election; and on 8 Feb. against a resolution from the committee of the whole, that the printing and using of calicoes was destructive of the woollen industry and ought to be restrained. Although nominated to two drafting committees on private estate bills, he did not undertake their management. On the major issue of the 1704–5 session, he was forecast as a probable supporter of the Tack, and duly voted for it on 28 Nov. 1704. He acted as a teller on 28 Feb. 1705 against considering the Queen's answer over writs of error in the Aylesbury case, a masterpiece of evasion designed to free the crown from further involvement in the affair. Curzon's stance on the Tack had created a few problems for his partnership with Coke. In March 1705 Coke's electoral agent, Robert Harding, reported that Curzon had written 'to him about some of the populace being angry at him for tacking and some other at you for the contrary'. Harding's concern here was that any delay in declaring the continuation of the joint interest would encourage enemies to sow dissension among their supporters and even put up rival candidates. In the event Harding need not have worried. As the Whig Samuel Pole remarked, 'for the county the devil cannot stir Curzon and Coke'. The two Tories were returned unopposed.[5]

An analysis of the new House in 1705 noted Curzon as a 'True Churchman', presumably because of his vote for the Tack, and he duly voted against the Court candidate for Speaker on 20 Oct. 1705. However, in contrast to the previous Parliament Curzon's activity in the chamber was now much reduced. A list of this Parliament compiled in early 1708 indicates that he remained a Tory. Re-elected without opposition in 1708, the only vote he recorded during that Parliament was against the impeachment of Dr Sacheverell. In June 1710, Curzon presented a loyal address from Derbyshire, a calculated snub to his fellow Member, Coke. This signalled a break with his erstwhile partner at the election later in the year, when Curzon joined with Godfrey Clarke* in a combination which proved sufficiently strong to deter Coke from forcing a poll.[6]

In the first session of the new Parliament Curzon was more active. He was classed as a Tory on the 'Hanover list' and included among the 'Tory patriots' favouring peace, and as a 'worthy patriot' who had helped to detect the mismanagements of the previous ministry. He was also listed as a member of the October Club. In the following session he acted as a teller on 15 Apr. 1712 against adding a clause relating to Cheshire to the bill for more effectively preventing fraud in county elections. During the summer William Bromley II* sent a reminder to Lord Oxford (Harley) commending Curzon as 'a valuable man in his person and fortunes'. If this was a solicitation concerning an office it was ignored by the lord treasurer, and may have led to a lack of enthusiasm for the ministry on Curzon's part. Certainly, a 'Mr Curzon' told on 2 May 1713 against giving leave to bring in a bill to suspend the duty on French wines, but by that date he had been joined in the Commons by his brother, making it impossible to isolate his parliamentary activities. This measure was a precursor to the French commerce bill, and John Curzon (unlike his brother) did not vote on 18 June in the crucial division on this bill. Re-elected unopposed in 1713, either Curzon or his brother was involved in the management through the House of a bill to make more effectual an Act passed in William III's reign for the navigation of the Trent. He was marked as a Tory on the Worsley list and on two lists comparing the 1713 and 1715 Parliaments.[7]

Curzon continued to sit as a Tory for Derbyshire until his death on 7 Aug. 1727, two days after the dissolution of Parliament. The circumstances of his death were unfortunate: he died following 'a mortification in his leg, which he got about three weeks ago, by one of his spurs striking through his boot in a fall he got from his horse while hunting'. His estate, valued at around £10,000 p.a., thereupon descended to his brother, Nathaniel.[8]

[1] Collins, *Peerage*, vii. 298–9. [2] Lysons, *Derbys*. p. lii.; W. Woolley, *Hist. Derbys*. (Derbys. Recs. Soc. vi.), 95. [3] BL, Lothian mss, Sir Gilbert Clarke* to Coke, 21 July 1698, Sir Philip Gell, 3rd Bt.†, to same, 13 Dec. 1700, John Beresford to same, 14 Dec. 1700; *HMC Cowper*, ii. 408, 411–12. [4] *HMC Cowper*, ii. 457; iii. 4, 9, 11–12; L. K. J. Glassey, *Appt. JPs*, 154; Lothian mss, John Fisher to Coke, 28 Mar. 1702. [5] *HMC Cowper*, iii. 23, 54–55; Lothian mss, Walter Burdett to Coke, 30 Oct. 1703, Robert Harding to same, 5 Mar. 1704[-5]. [6] Add. 70421, newsletter 27 June 1710; *HMC Cowper*, iii. 86. [7] *HMC Cowper*, iii. 89–99; Add. 70287, Bromley to Oxford, 26 June 1712. [8] *The Gen.* n.s. vii. 110; PCC 204 Farrant.

S. N. H.

CURZON, Nathaniel (c.1676–1758), of Kedleston, Derbys. and Queen Street, London.

DERBY	25 Apr. 1713–1715
CLITHEROE	1722–1727
DERBYSHIRE	1727–1754

b. c.1676, 2nd s. of Sir Nathaniel Curzon, 2nd Bt., and bro. of John* and William Curzon†. *educ.* Trinity, Oxf. matric. 2 July 1692, aged 16; I. Temple 1694, called 1700. *m.* 19 Feb. 1717, Mary (*d.* 1776), da. and coh. of Sir Ralph Assheton, 2nd Bt.*, 3s. (1 *d.v.p.*) 2da. *suc.* bro. as 4th Bt. 7 Aug. 1727.[1]

As the second son of a prominent landowning family, Curzon followed a legal career, probably spending most of his time in London. One contemporary observed that he already had 'a very great estate' when he succeeded his brother, which suggests that he had found his chosen profession financially rewarding. Certainly, he was still giving legal opinions to clients shortly before his entry into the Commons at a by-election and he continued to practise at the bar during the early part of his parliamentary career. A report of the by-election suggests that his family's loyalty to the ministry was severely tested by the terms of the peace laid before Parliament in 1713. Lady Anne Pye thought 'it was not over handsome for the Curzons to exclaim, as some of the brothers did in the spring when he was chose on the vacancy, and call the peace dishonourable at a public table, when all the gentlemen of the country [were] by'. Curzon voted for the French commerce bill on 18 June 1713, but, significantly, his brother was absent.[2]

Despite rumours of opposition from Lord James Cavendish* and James Stanhope*, and some electioneering by Richard Pye II*, Curzon was returned with his partner Edward Mundy in 1713. His parliamentary activity in this period is impossible to distinguish from that of his elder brother. He was listed as a Tory on the Worsley list and continued to sit as such after his return to the Commons in 1722. In 1731 he was described as a Hanoverian Tory. Despite rumours of his ennoblement (as Lord Charlton), and claims he made to the barony of Powis, he never obtained a title. He gave up his county seat in favour of his son Nathaniel† in 1754 and died on 18 Nov. 1758. His son and heir was raised to the peerage in 1761 as Lord Scarsdale.[3]

[1] Collins, *Peerage*, vii. 299. [2] *The Gen.* n.s. vii. 110; Add. 6686, f. 150; *HMC Portland*, v. 328. [3] Centre Kentish Stud. Stanhope mss U1590/C28, Thomas Gisborne to [James Stanhope], 11 Apr. 1713; U1590/C9/14, Thomas Stanhope* to same, 2 May 1713; RA, Stuart mss 145/175, Andrew Ramsey to [–], 2 June 1731; *HMC 9th Rep. II*, 401–2; *Derby Mercury*, 18–25 Nov. 1758.

S. N. H.

CUTLER, Sir John, 1st Bt. (1607–1693), of Tothill Street, Westminster.

TAUNTON	1679 (Oct.)–8 Dec. 1680
BODMIN	1689–15 Apr. 1693

b. c.1607, 2nd s. of Edward Cutler, Salter, of London by Jane. *m.* (1) 11 Aug. 1642, Elizabeth (*d.* 1650), da. and coh. of Sir Thomas Foote†, 1st Bt., ld. mayor of London 1649–50, 1da. *d.v.p.*; (2) 27 July 1669, Elicia (*d.* 1685), da. of Sir Thomas Tipping of Wheatfield, Oxon., sis. of Thomas Tipping*, 1da. *suc.* bro. 1630; kntd. 17 June 1660; *cr.* Bt. 12 Nov. 1660.[1]

Freeman, Grocers' Co. 1633, asst. 1632–*d.*, warden of the bachelors of the Co., 1640–1, livery, 1649, master, 1652–3, 1685–6, 1688–9, dep.-master, 1691–2; alderman, London 2–5 Aug. 1651, common councilman 1654–5, 1658–9, 1661–2; jt. receiver-gen. Notts. and Derbys. Dec. 1660–75; receiver contributions for rebuilding St. Paul's; sheriff, Kent 1675–6; commr. for recusants, Mdx. 1675.[2]

FRS 1664.

A self-made man, Cutler was a byword for avarice in the 18th century and his thrifty habits became the source of endless, probably apocryphal, anecdotes. Contemporary comment, however, is sparse and his background remains almost completely unknown. His father is traditionally said to have been one Thomas Cutler, also a Grocer, but contemporary sources do not support this connexion. The wills of this family show that neither Thomas Cutler of the Grocers' Company (father and son) had a son John living of the right age. Cutler's father can now be identified as Edward Cutler, Salter, who died in 1613 while his children were still under age, leaving his meagre estate to be inherited by his wife, two sons, Robert and John, and four daughters. Robert died in 1630, leaving his estate at Bradwell, Essex, to his brother.[3]

By this time Cutler was an apprentice Grocer, and beginning to cultivate the connexions which no doubt contributed to his increasing fortune. By 1657 he was rich enough to offer the indebted 2nd Earl of Strafford a mortgage of £5,000 on his estates in Yorkshire. He then apparently reneged on this offer and combined with his brother-in-law Sir John Lewis, 1st Bt., to offer to buy the lands outright instead, for a total of about £28,000. The aggrieved Strafford, who was reluctantly forced to accept, wrote that this was all 'to their own base ends ... here are fine honest people'.[4]

Cutler supported the Restoration with a loan of £5,000 for which he was rewarded with a baronetcy and government office. He became a public figure during the Restoration, disbursing large sums on public works and the rebuilding of the Grocers' Hall after the Great Fire. Although difficulties arose in some of his other public benefactions, Cutler did not fail to look after the members of his family, particularly the Boulters, children of his youngest sister, Susanna. Cutler had business connexions in common with his nephew Edmund Boulter*, a wholesale grocer, in the 1660s and he may have helped Boulter set up in business.[5]

A brief spell in Parliament did not affect Cutler's success in business and in 1686 he bought the estate of Wimpole, Cambridgeshire, from Sir Thomas Chicheley[†], another Grocer. He returned to Parliament in the Convention for Bodmin on the interest of his other son-in-law, the 2nd Earl of Radnor (Charles Bodvile Robartes[†]), and, being appointed deputy-lieutenant for Middlesex in April 1689, became active against popish adherents of the exiled King James.[6]

Elected unopposed for the same seat in 1690, Cutler was appointed to the Tory-dominated London lieutenancy commission in March and was classed in Lord Carmarthen's (Sir Thomas Osborne[†]) list of the new Parliament as a Tory and probable Court supporter. He was further classified in a list of December 1690, as a likely supporter of Carmarthen, and Robert Harley's* list of April 1691 queried him as a Court supporter. In January 1691 'Mr Foley's' scheme for a collection from MPs for the relief of Irish and French Protestants failed when he suggested Cutler be joined with him in advancing the money until the next session. Foley's naming of one of the richest men in the Commons, who might presumably be prevailed on to advance all of the money (£2,000), 'put the House into a laughter and so it went off for the present'. On 29 Dec. 1691 a suit between John, Lord de la Warr and Cutler over a debt of some £35,000 which the latter claimed de la Warr's father had owed him, reached the Commons, when a petition from de la Warr against Cutler's claim of privilege was heard and resolved in the former's favour. A counter-petition from Cutler was presented on the same day, and considered on 6 Feb. 1692 when it was ordered to lie on the table. De la Warr's petition had stressed the urgency of the case, because of Cutler's great age, and his fears proved well founded – shortly after making a loan of £2,000 to the government on the borrowing clauses of the poll tax in November, Cutler fell seriously ill. He died the following year on 15 Apr., aged 85, and was buried in St. Margaret's Westminster. The expected bonanza of charitable bequests did not materialize and, apart from £1,000 to St. Bartholomew's Hospital, his wealth, altogether said to be worth in the region of £300,000, was largely distributed among his relations. The main beneficiaries were Cutler's surviving daughter and son-in-law, the Earl and Countess of Radnor, and his nephew, Edmund Boulter.[7]

[1] *Stepney Mar. Reg.* ed. Ferguson, ii. 28, 136; *St. Margaret's Westminster* (Harl. Soc. Reg. lxiv), 116. [2] Guildhall Lib. mss 11592A, unfol.; *Calendar of Grocers' Co. Ct. Mins. 1616–92*, iii, iv, v, passim.; J. R. Woodhead, *Rulers of London* (London and Mdx. Arch. Soc.), 55; *CSP Dom.* 1660–1, p. 429; 1663–4, p. 115; *Cal. Treas. Bks.* i. 78; iv. 696; v. 350. [3] J. B. Heath, *Grocers' Co.* 298–307; *DNB*; *St. James Clerkenwell* (Harl. Soc. Reg. ix), 50; PCC 78 Bolein, 36 Wingfield, 7 Barrington, 119 Capell, 64 Scroope; Guildhall Lib. mic. 9171/21, f. 383. [4] V. Pearl, *Puritan Revol.* 315; C2/CHAS1/C45/61; *HMC Var.* ii. 378. [5] *Cal. Treas. Bks.* i. 79; *Pepys Diary* ed. Latham, iv. 430; *DNB*; PCC 90 Carr. [6] *HMC 13th Rep. VI*, 22; *VCH Cambs.* v. 265; *CSP Dom.* 1689–90, pp. 53–54. [7] *CSP Dom.* 1689–90, p. 488; PRO NI, De Ros mss D638/13/5, John Pulteney* to Thomas Coningsby*, 2 Jan. 1691; *CJ*, x. 723; Add. 34096, ff. 334, 341, 347; Bodl. Carte 233, f. 97; Bodl. Tanner mss 25, f. 35; Harley mss at Brampton Bryan, bdle. 117, Robert Harley to [–], 18, 25 Apr. 1693; *HMC Ancaster*, 433.

S. M. W.

CUTTS, John, 1st Baron Cutts [I] (c.1661–1707), of Childerley, Cambs.

CAMBRIDGESHIRE   21 Dec. 1693–1702
NEWPORT I.o.W.   1702–25 Jan. 1707

b. c.1661, 2nd s. of Richard Cutts of Arkesden and Matching, Essex by Joan, da. of Sir Richard Everard, 1st Bt., of Much Waltham, Essex. *educ.* St. Catharine's Hall, Camb. 1676, LL.D. 1690; M. Temple 1678. *m.* (1) lic. 18 Dec. 1690 (with £2,500 p.a.), Elizabeth (*d.* 1693), da. and h. of George Clark of London, merchant, and wid. of William Morley[†] of Glynde, Suss. and of John Trevor of Trevalyn, Denb., *s.p.*; (2) abt. 31 Jan. 1697, Elizabeth (*d.* 1697), da. and h. of Sir Henry Pickering, 2nd Bt.*, *s.p.*; ?(3) 12 Mar. 1700, Dorothy (*d.* by Feb. 1708), da. of Sir John Weld, of Arnolds, Mdx., and wid. of Edward Pickering of Lincoln's Inn Fields, Mdx. *suc.* er. bro. by 1690; *cr.* Baron Cutts [I] 12 Dec. 1690.[1]

Lt.-col. of ft. Henry Sidney's[†] regt. in Holland 1688; col. of ft. 1689–94, 2nd Ft. Gds. 1694–*d.*; gov. I.o.W. 1693–*d.*; brig.-gen. 1693, maj.-gen. 1696, lt.-gen. 1703; col. of drag. [I] 1704–*d.*; lt.-gen. of forces in Ire. 1705–*d*; ld. justice [I] 1705; PC [I] May 1705.[2]

Freeman, Southampton 1693, Colchester 1702.[3]

The fortunes of the Cutts family had been made in the 16th century by Sir John Cutts, treasurer of the Household to Henry VIII. The junior branch of the family, from which Cutts was descended, had settled in Essex, where they owned property in Arkesden and Matching, residing principally at the former. The senior branch became extinct in 1670 when their estates at Childerley in Cambridgeshire came to Cutts's elder brother. Cutts came to London in about 1680, when he made the acquaintance of some of the leaders of the more extreme Whigs. He became a follower of the Duke of Monmouth and in 1682 was part of the entourage which accompanied Monmouth's progress to the North. In 1684 he followed the Duke into exile in Holland, but does not seem to have taken part in Monmouth's rebellion, despite later allegations that he had done so only to 'flee away upon his [Monmouth's] discomfiture'. He was, however, a witness for the defence in November 1685 at the trial for treason of Lord Brandon (Charles Gerard*). He probably considered that his close friendship with Monmouth made the England of James II uncongenial and consequently in the winter of 1685–6 went to the Continent, possibly to Holland first and then, no doubt on the advice and with the help of William of Orange, to join the Imperial army under the Duke of Lorraine as a volunteer. He distinguished himself at the capture of Buda in 1686 and at the end of the campaign was made adjutant-general to the Duke. Early in 1687 he published a second volume of verse, *Poetical Exercises*, which was dedicated to Princess Mary. He was back with the Imperialist army in the summer of 1687 for the campaign in Transylvania, during which he sent letters to the Earl of Middleton (Charles Middleton†), the secretary of state, enclosing reports for the King on the progress of the campaign. At this point he was hoping to get a recommendation from Middleton, whom he exhorted 'to do me good offices by the King'. But when he left the Imperial army in the autumn of 1687 and returned to England, he refused the offer of a regiment from James II before leaving immediately for Holland, where William made him a lieutenant-colonel in an English regiment. On 12 Apr. 1688 Cutts wrote to Middleton:

> I am sensible that my coming here and taking an employment in this service will make a great deal of noise in England, and that my enemies will not lose so favourable an occasion to plunge me as deep as they can in the King's displeasure, and therefore I desire your lordship to represent to his Majesty the reasons that have driven me to this resolution.
>
> It is with a great deal of regret that I find myself incapacitated to serve his Majesty in his present designs . . . No man has a greater veneration for his person nor would go further in his service than myself, were not the present measures of state visibly opposite to the principles and interest of that religion which is dearer to me than all things in this world and than life itself. The laws of conscience are sacred and inviolable, and since my principles are such as make me unfit to serve at home and my private affairs in a posture which does not admit of an idle life, I desire your lordship to do me such offices to his Majesty that he may not be angry at my taking service abroad.

His regiment formed part of William's invasion force and it was subsequently claimed that he spent some £8,000 of his own money in furthering the Prince's cause.[4]

By 1690 Cutts had succeeded his elder brother in the family estates, worth then about £2,000 p.a., but he had already incurred debts of £15,000 and for the remainder of his life was plagued by financial troubles, which forced him to sell much of his property. After the Revolution he clearly hoped to improve his position. He was made colonel of a foot regiment and on 5 Apr. 1690 was granted on petition a commission of inquiry into all estates belonging to Roman Catholic priests or being used for superstitious purposes. For the rest of that year he served with the King on the Irish campaign, distinguishing himself at the Boyne and the siege of Limerick, where he was wounded. These services were rewarded at the end of the year with an Irish peerage. He continued to serve in Ireland until 1692 and subsequently fought in every campaign in Flanders during William's reign. In a memorial written after his death, his sister claimed that his service in Ireland, 'was more expensive to him than either the pay of his regiment or the profits of his own estate'. His financial position worsened with the death of his first wife in February 1693, since her jointure ceased. There was some compensation in March when he was promoted brigadier-general and appointed governor of the Isle of Wight, although he did not receive the vice-admiralty which often went with the latter appointment, but which in this case was granted separately to the Marquess of Winchester (Charles Powlett I*), son and heir of the 1st Duke of Bolton, lord lieutenant of Hampshire. Since the vice-admiral was entitled to a share in any prize ship captured near the coast, Cutts was understandably disappointed at this arrangement and the two men were soon on bad terms. The conflict over prizes may explain why, in the quarrel which then took place between Cutts and the Isle of Wight gentry over the conduct of parliamentary elections in the three island boroughs, Powlett sided with the gentry. Difficulties arose in the boroughs as a result of Cutts's determination to transform them into safe government seats, an attack on the traditional influence of the gentry which the governor was unable properly to carry through because his military duties kept him away from the island for much of the time. So although he intervened continually, he found it difficult to establish a personal influence and was obliged to act through the lieutenant governor, Joseph Dudley*. Moreover, his personal financial difficulties meant that he had no money to spend on elections.[5]

At the end of 1693 Cutts gained a narrow victory at a by-election for his home county of Cambridgeshire. One contemporary reported sceptically that despite a 'scurvy rumour' of Cutts being a 'Socinian', he had gained the support of the moderate Churchmen at the election, and 'this is the first time my Lord [Cutts] ever struck in with the Church, and . . . it may prove encouragement to him to keep in it, for interest may do what religion can't'. Having been listed as a placeman after his election, Cutts signalled his support for the Court in his speech on 25 Feb. 1694 in the debate on the treason trials bill, when he smeared opposition speakers as being in the pay of France, remarking that he had heard 'that there were many Members who were French pensioners, and by these long debates perplexed affairs and that they were to have good offers upon King James's return'. Although few speeches of his have been recorded, he clearly intervened regularly in debate, since the anonymous author of *The Club Men of the House of Commons*, published in 1694, wrote of him:

> Lord Cutts, that pragmatical knight of the sun,
> Though he thinks his set speeches are very fine spun,
> Yet whene'er he begins, men wish he had done.

In the summer campaign of that year he took part in the disastrous expedition against Brest. According to Francis Gwyn*, Hon. Thomas Tollemache*, commander of the whole expedition, had complained, before he died of wounds received in the assault, that Cutts had disobeyed orders. But this did not prevent Cutts replacing Tollemache as colonel of the Coldstream Guards the following October. In Parliament he was given leave of absence on 21 Dec. 1694, and left little further trace on the records of that session. He still sought more tangible financial rewards, and in May 1695 successfully petitioned for the grant of an estate in Barbados, whose owner had recently died, intestate and without heirs. In the same month Cutts began a fresh dispute with Lord Winchester over the appointment of a governor for Hurst Castle on the Isle of Wight, which was eventually resolved in favour of Cutts's nominee.[6]

In the 1695 campaign Cutts greatly distinguished himself at the siege of Namur, where his determination to appear wherever the fighting was hottest earned him the nickname of 'the salamander' and possibly inspired the anonymous author of the lampoon, 'Advice to a Painter', to write,

> See, where the florid, warlike Cutts appears,
> As brave and senseless as the sword he wears.

Cutts was less successful in the electoral battles in the Isle of Wight in the following November. He had hoped to return all six Members, but in the event was completely successful only at Newport, where he himself was returned with his nominee, Sir Robert Cotton. In Parliament Cutts continued to support the Court. He was forecast as likely to support the Court in the division of 31 Jan. 1696 on the proposed council of trade; he voted with the Court for fixing the price of guineas at 22s. in March; and he signed the Association promptly. Indeed he himself had been active in uncovering the Assassination Plot and persuading one of the conspirators to turn King's evidence. Cutts was then a witness at the trial of three of the plotters. His zeal in the whole affair was rewarded with the grant of the estate of another of those convicted, John Caryll, worth £2,155 p.a. In the next session, Cutts spoke against Sir Francis Winnington's motion to consider the state of the nation before supply on 23 Oct. 1696, and spoke several times in favour of Sir John Fenwick's[†] attainder. On 13 Nov. 1696 he opposed allowing Fenwick's counsel more time to prepare and on 16 Nov. spoke for admitting as evidence the examination of the absconded witness, Cordell Goodman, and for reading the record of Cook's conviction. On 17 Nov. when those implicated in Jacobite activity charged by Fenwick were pressing that he should be further questioned, he said:

> I have only one question to be asked Sir John Fenwick. It is not a question that relates to any person named in that paper. I think there is no one person that he hath named but is eminently known or believed to be in the interest of the government; and none but what are in some post of trust and employment in it. Then I think it highly necessary to know, how it comes to pass that he hath had so much conversation with persons of that character, and none with those people that he hath been seen daily to converse with? And if he hath, why he hath not discovered them, as he hath done the rest.

He made two further interventions in the debate and finished with a long speech in favour of committing the attainder bill:

> I do consider what a condition we had been in if the contrivance that was laid had taken effect; . . . and though it

was disappointed then, I know not how far off it is at present; ... I would desire those gentlemen that express so much tenderness in this case to have some for the government and themselves. It was told you that the prisoner before you does not stand convicted of any crime ... I think, with submission, the prisoner stands convicted of high treason, with the highest conviction upon earth, and that is the general consent of all mankind.

Cutts added that if Fenwick would but 'tell truth and leave off this dissembling and be plain; I doubt not but he will find favour'. He spoke and told in favour of passing the bill on 25 Nov. and was later summoned to give evidence before the Lords, 'to support Porter's credit, and to give an account in what manner he made his first discovery to him'. Unsurprisingly, he was listed as having voted for the attainder.[7]

About this time Richard Steele*, who had dedicated a poem on the death of the Queen to Cutts in 1695, entered his household as an unpaid secretary and aide-de-camp. He later dedicated to Cutts his *Christian Hero* (1700), although the two were to part company on bad terms in 1701. In September 1697 Cutts was sent to Vienna on a secret mission, probably to explain to the Emperor the terms of the Treaty of Ryswick. He was back for the following session, when it was reported on 10 Dec. 1697 that he had quarrelled with Henry Holmes, MP for Yarmouth, in the Commons, when the latter 'to second a story ... about officers meddling in elections said that my Lord Cutts in the Isle of Wight had displaced several officers of the militia [at Yarmouth in 1695] for voting for him [Holmes], which my Lord Cutts said was not true'. Peace gave Cutts an opportunity to devote himself to the affairs of the island, where his conflict with the local gentry was still simmering. He had written to his friend Joseph Dudley on 12 Aug. 1697:

I shall certainly make my next campaign in the Isle of Wight ... When I can spend a summer in the Isle of Wight, I will make a great alteration both as to persons and things; besides that I doubt not of being vice-admiral of Hampshire before I see you and I hope to see you before the election of mayors in the island.

He then outlined a plan to appoint unpaid governors at Sandham, Yarmouth and Cowes, who should 'not be less than lieutenant-colonels, such as will keep their coaches, and spend their money there during the whole summer', with paid commanders under them, so that all these gentlemen 'will in the island in general, and in their respective stations, a little counterbalance the dead weight of the factious country gentlemen'. He instructed Dudley to inform the three corporations that the coming of peace would enable him

to spend a great part of my time with them. ... You may tell them the very great expense I have constantly been at, in sending an equipage every year into this country [Holland]; and living at very great expense here (of which whole burden I shall now be entirely eased); ... these difficulties have put me under great disadvantage; but that I shall now have my hands more at liberty, not only to pay off all debts contracted in the island upon my score but to do such acts of generosity and charity (both in public and private occasions) as becomes a man of honour and a man of conscience.

It was probably some rumour of Cutts's intentions that caused the leading gentry of the island to draw up a petition against Cutts, which forced him to come to an agreement with them in March 1698 (see NEWTOWN, I.o.W., Hants). In Parliament, to the surprise of many, Cutts was in favour of the Commons' bill against blasphemy and profaneness, and at the third reading on 30 Mar. supported it with 'extraordinary zeal from first to last, and declared he would defend it with his sword in the field as had done [with] his tongue in the House'.[8]

Although Cutts had secured peace with the local gentry in the Isle of Wight, he was becoming increasingly disillusioned with his treatment by the administration. This centred on his ever-growing financial problems. In an effort to clear his debts he had sold the Caryll estate for £8,000 in November 1697 and in February 1698 he, his father-in-law Pickering, and Joseph Dudley developed a plan to profit by making coins for the colonies, but the existing patentees maintained this would infringe upon their rights, so the plan was dropped. Finally, in March 1698 Cutts asked the King for an estate of £3,000 or £4,000 p.a. in Ireland, writing to him on 17 Mar.

I understand ... by the Archbishop and Mr [William] Blathwayt* that your Majesty made a particular remark upon my asking so much as £3 or £4,000 a year in Ireland.

I considered, Sire, how earnestly you desired me (by the Duke of Monmouth) to break my match with Mrs [Elizabeth] Villiers, and what promises you made me upon it; I considered how often you have ... renewed your promise of favour; I considered what you have since done for her and for her relations; and I could never think, that I should be ill-used for trusting to you ... and for waiting with patience. I told your Majesty of my debt before the Revolution; I told you, Sire, if ever you settled in England, I should hope (by your favour) to get clear of it; and you were pleased to encourage me in those hopes.

He claimed that his debts now totalled £17,534. Nothing was done for him. He was also dissatisfied that his attempts to secure a governorship in the American colonies for his friend Dudley had so far proved unsuccessful. James Vernon I* wrote to Shrewsbury on 9 June 1698, that Cutts 'acknowledges your Grace's great civility to him and compares it with the different behaviour of some from whom he says, he had more reason to expect kinder usage. I know not who they are he would reflect on.' It would seem that Cutts had the Junto in mind, his relations with them strained by his long dispute with Lord Winchester in the Isle of Wight. His name appeared on a list of placemen in about July. In August 1698 he further irritated the Junto ministers, in particular the Earl of Orford (Edward Russell*), by putting up his own brother-in-law, John Acton, at a by-election for Newport, at a time when prominent government supporters were looking for a seat.[9]

In the 1698 Parliament Cutts was classed as a placeman on one list, and as a Court placeman on another. Not surprisingly, given his own military career, he spoke several times against the bill to disband the army and voted against it on 18 Jan. 1699. On 16 May he wrote hopefully to Dudley that he had explained his problems to the King, who had given

> a very obliging, positive and determinative answer; and if his affairs are not in such a posture, as that he can do at present what he would, he will (at least) do that which will be honourable and make me easy . . . My Lord Orford is out of all his employments; which has disgusted some of his creatures. Many changes are soon expected, but none yet certain; except that Lord Pembroke [Thomas Herbert†] and Lord Lonsdale [Sir John Lowther, 2nd Bt. II*] (and another friend of mine) do certainly come into business . . . As soon as ever my own life is safe, I'll endeavour to save yours. I shall soon have the vice-admiralty now.

Although he did not get the vice-admiralty he was given a pension of £1,000 p.a. out of the privy purse. An analysis of the House into interests in early 1700 listed him as a placeman, and on 13 Feb. he spoke against an opposition motion, aimed at Lord Chancellor Somers (Sir John*), condemning crown grants. In the first Parliament of 1701, Cutts was listed as supporting the Court with regard to the continuation of the 'Great Mortgage'. On 2 Apr. he embarrassed Tory ministers by suggesting an amendment to an address to the King to the effect that the renewal of the Treaty of Ryswick by France was not sufficient security for Europe. Strong objections from the Tories meant that the amendment was dropped. On the other hand, Cutts had never been on good terms with the Junto and signalled his willingness to work with the Tory ministry, being notable by his absence from the division on the impeachment of Lord Somers on 14 Apr. On 31 May he was named to the drafting committee for a bill for erecting a corporation for the purchase of Irish forfeited estates, presenting the bill two days later. In Robert Harley's* analysis of the December 1701 Parliament he was listed with the Whigs, and this was certainly the public perception of his politics: it was remarked that there was vigorous opposition from the Tories in the Commons on 18 Feb. 1702 when, having been returned for two seats, Cutts communicated his decision to sit for the county via a letter to the Speaker rather than appearing in person. According to his own later account, Cutts was in fact still co-operating with the Tory ministry. In any event he took no part in the December 1701 Parliament, since he accompanied the Earl of Marlborough (John Churchill†) to Holland and remained there through the winter.[10]

Cutts obviously hoped for some reward from the ministry, but on the accession of Anne was offered only the governorship of Jamaica, which he refused. His pension ceased and the arrears due at William's death were never paid. Having transferred from Cambridgeshire to the safer seat of Newport in the Isle of Wight at the general election of 1702, he was generally absent abroad for the first two years of the reign, making him of little value as a political ally, and sent home a stream of letters complaining of neglect. He also found, to his annoyance, that when his commission as governor of the Isle of Wight was renewed the power he had been granted by the previous patent to appoint his own deputy was removed and his nominee replaced by an old enemy, Anthony Morgan*. Although Secretary Nottingham (Daniel Finch†) had instructed Lord Treasurer Godolphin (Sidney†) that 'care should be taken' not to appoint anyone unacceptable to Cutts, a complaint from Cutts after Morgan's appointment merely elicited a reply justifying the new arrangement. Petitions for promotion to lieutenant-general and for financial relief met with no response. He clearly hoped to be rewarded after the capture of Venloo in September 1702, when he led the attack on one of the out forts, writing to Nottingham:

> If her Majesty were put in mind of it, I believe she has too good and great a mind to leave me undistinguished. The Duke of Marlborough has made me great and repeated promises in general, but I'm sensible your lordship's good offices are of weight and you know how to do them . . . I beg your lordship's favour at this critical time. What is done for me will not be a distinction unless done soon.

This produced no immediate result and he spent the winter of 1702–3 in command of the English forces in Holland. In February 1703 he was made lieutenant-general, but continued to beg financial relief, if only in consideration of his extra services as commander-in-chief during the winter. Despite assurances from both Lord Treasurer Godolphin and Secretary Hedges (Sir Charles*), he received nothing. Cutts wrote to James Brydges* in July 1703:

> I have not had the honour to hear one word from you; this together with the Speaker's [Robert Harley] not answering my three letters I wrote him; and Mr Hammond's [Anthony*] being silent too (though I had done myself the honour of writing to him) gave some unpleasant thoughts, especially in an age of uncertainties. I assure you the impression sunk deep with me . . .
>
> I was indeed conscious to myself that I had served and suffered for a cause you are all concerned in; and, with relation to Mr Speaker and Mr Hammond in particular, I had made such steps during the late reign that I was become [more] obnoxious to the ministry then reigning (for so it was) than perhaps any man in England was; whether or no I did them any service I leave to others to determine but the thing I'll venture to say without vanity, and I've credible witnesses to prove it, that when the exorbitant power of the then great triumvirate [Orford, Somers and Halifax (Charles Montagu*)] received its first fatal blow, I determined above 30 voices on the right side by my own personal interest and credit.

The division in question was probably either that of 14 Apr. 1700 on whether the Junto Lords were guilty of high crimes and misdemeanours (although as stated above Cutts himself was absent from that division), or on 15 Apr. for their removal from the King's presence. The ministry seems to have remained unimpressed by these claims. After the 1703 campaign Cutts remained abroad for a third successive winter, writing his usual complaints and begging letters. Eventually, in April 1704, he received a royal bounty of £1,000 in consideration of services rendered.[11]

In the summer of 1704 Cutts played a prominent part in the battle of Blenheim, receiving £240 as bounty. He returned to England at the beginning of November in time to take part in the proceedings against the Tack. Having been forecast as a probable opponent of it, he spoke in the crucial debate on 28 Nov., saying that

> the Duke of Marlborough had lately concluded a treaty with the King of Prussia for 8,000 men, to be employed towards the relief of the Duke of Savoy, who was in most imminent danger. That those troops were actually on their march, upon the credit of the resolution the House had already taken, to make good her Majesty's treaties, and that obstructing the money bills, which the tacking of the occasional conformity bill would infallibly do, would put an immediate stop to the march of those troops and thereby occasion the entire ruin of the Duke of Savoy.

He did not vote for the Tack. He was listed as a placeman in 1705, but his political position at this time was somewhat ambiguous. On 13 Mar. 1705 he wrote enthusiastically to a kinsman of a new accord which he observed between the Country Whigs and the High Tories. He insisted that the party which at present

> prevails at court . . . will not be so long triumphant as they think, and that the same men that I wished well to last winter will be the prevailing side next, with this advantage that they will have a strong party from the other side to join them. And to make you comprehend this, Peter King* and Annesley [Hon. Arthur*] with Bromley [William II*] etc. are reconciled and have shaken hands to stand by each other next winter to oppose the iniquity of the times and promote the public welfare.

At the same time, Cutts's money troubles made it essential for him to remain on good terms with Marlborough and Godolphin, to whom he sent memorials on 11 and 13 Feb. 1705 asking for the payment of his debts. In March he was appointed general of all the forces in Ireland, a post estimated to be worth £6,000 p.a. Ministers probably considered this a more convenient way of helping Cutts than providing him with sums of money, but according to his sister, he went to Ireland most unwillingly. In a letter written to Godolphin after her brother's death she claimed that his going was not, as alleged by his enemies,

> a reward asked by him, but on the contrary a very unwilling act of obedience and submission, as his lordship and Lord Marlborough know well, Mr St. John [Henry II*] having been employed by the Duke to persuade him to undertake the employment.

He was also given a gift of £1,000 as royal bounty to cover the expenses of his removal.[12]

In 1705 Swift presented a very unflattering portrait of Cutts in his 'Ode to a Salamander', in which he wrote:

> So when the war has raised a storm
> I've seen a snake in human form,
> All stained with infamy and vice,
> Leap from the dunghill in a trice,
> Burnish and make a gaudy show
> Become a general, peer and beau,
> Till peace hath made the sky serene,
> Then shrink into its hole again.

Cutts was returned for Newport in 1705, whereupon he was classed as a 'Low Church courtier', but absence in Ireland prevented him from taking part in parliamentary activities and he was duly marked as absent in the division on the Speaker on 25 Oct. 1705. He died in Dublin, on 25 Jan. 1707, still deeply in debt, his hopes of recouping his fortune by means of Dorothy

Pickering, an elderly relation who had inherited a significant amount of the Cutts estate some years previously, remaining unfulfilled. It is unknown whether or not Cutts had actually married Dorothy, aged 77 in 1700 when the marriage was reported by one contemporary, but she managed to outlive Cutts by a few months and changed her will in favour of her own family, to the great disappointment of Cutts's sister. Immediately after Cutts's death, an Irish correspondent informed Sir John Perceval, 5th Bt.[†]:

> His lordship, though he had by his place under the government in England and Ireland, together above £6,000 p.a., is yet dead vastly in debt, insomuch that the poor butchers, bakers and all others that dealt with him are half ruined. His two aides-de-camp clubbed their ten shillings apiece to pay for the embalming his corpse, which is deposited in a vault in St. Patrick's till it be known whether his friends will send for it over to bury it in England.[13]

[1] *HMC 10th Rep. IV*, 334; *Vis. Northants.* (Harl. Soc. lxxxviii), 171; *London Mar. Lic.* ed. Foster, 1057. [2] Luttrell, *Brief Relation*, v. 535. [3] Southampton RO, bor. recs. SC3/1, f. 245; *The Oath Book . . . of Colchester* ed. W. S. Benham. [4] *Monthly Miscellany* (1710), 47; Add. 41842, ff. 41–59; S. S. Swartley, *Life and Poetry of John Cutts*, pp. xii–xviii; *Trans. Essex Arch. Soc.* iv. 25–42; *CSP Dom.* 1682, pp. 398, 408, 413, 429, 537; 1683, p. 70; 1683–4, p. 329; 1687–9, p. 244; Wood, *Life and Times*, iii. 200; *HMC Downshire*, i. 59; *HMC Astley*, 66, 206–7. [5] *Trans. Essex Arch. Soc.* 40–42; *CSP Dom.* 1689–90, p. 447; 1690–1, pp. 144–5; 1693, p. 229; Luttrell, ii. 24, 100, 266, 293; iii. 41, 146, 123; Macaulay, *Hist. Eng.* iv. 1875; *HMC Astley*, 77. [6] Add. 28931, f. 100; Swartley, p. xxii; Bodl. Carte 130, ff. 347–8; *Poems on Affairs of State* ed. Ellis, v. 433; *HMC Portland*, iii. 551; *CSP Dom.* 1694–5, p. 188; *HMC Downshire*, i. 462; *Cal. Treas. Bks.* x. 952, 1001, 1037; *Mass. Hist. Soc. Procs.* ser. 2, ii. 180–1. [7] *HMC Downshire*, i. 542, 635–6; Luttrell, iii. 518; Macaulay, v. 2530–2; *Mass. Hist. Soc. Procs.* 180–1; Burnet, iv. 304–5; *CSP Dom.* 1699–1700, p. 366; *Cal. Treas. Bks.* xi. 177; *Lexington Pprs.* 115; Northants. RO, Montagu (Boughton) mss 46/11, Vernon to Shrewsbury, 24 Oct. 1696; Cobbett, *Parlty. Hist.* v. 1019, 1034, 1043, 1053, 1054, 1056, 1070–3, 1118; *Vernon–Shrewsbury Letters*, i. 48, 108–9; *Poems on Affairs of State*, vi. 21; SP 100/362–4; Howells, *State Trials*, xii. 1424–7; H. Erskine-Hill, *Soc. Milieu of Alexander Pope*, 54. [8] *Steele Corresp.* ed. Blanchard, 18–19, 20–21, 441–2, 430; Luttrell, iv. 272; *CSP Dom.* 1697, p. 512; *Mass. Hist. Soc. Procs.* 185–7; Worsley, *Hist. Isle of Wight*, pp. 161, cxvii–cxviii; Carte 130, f. 389; BL, Trumbull Misc. mss 57, Sir Gilbert Dolben* to Sir William Trumbull*, 31 Mar. 1698. [9] Luttrell, iv. 303; Swartley, p. xxxiv; *APC Col.* 1680–1720, p. 321; *Trans. Essex Arch. Soc.* 40–42; *Vernon–Shrewsbury Letters*, ii. 93, 96–97, 101–2, 145–6; *HMC Astley*, 95, 207–8. [10] *Camden Misc.* xxix. 357, 379, 381, 384; *Mass. Hist. Soc. Procs.* 190–1; Som. RO, Sanford mss DD/SF 4107(a), 'notes of the debate on my Ld. Chancellor, 13 Feb. 1699[–1700]'; H. Horwitz, *Parl. and Pol. Wm. III*, 286, 288; *Cocks Diary*, 83, 95, 219; *HMC Astley*, 98, 101. [11] Add. 29588, ff. 37, 383; 61118, f. 132; Huntington Lib. Stowe mss 58(1), pp. 27, 33; *HMC Astley*, 108–9, 111–12, 114–16, 119, 122, 124, 138, 142, 207; *Wentworth Pprs.* 8–9; Stanhope, *Reign of Anne*, 52; Luttrell, v. 420; *CSP Dom.* 1703–4, p. 47; *Cal. Treas. Bks.* xix. 217; *CSP Col.* 1698, pp. 99–100, 106, 109, 125, 127. [12] Cobbett, vi. 361; *Procs. Occasional Conformity Bill*, 58; *HMC Portland*, iv. 164; *HMC 7th Rep.* 246; *HMC Astley*, 176, 197–8; *Cal. Treas. Bks.* xx. 8. [13] Swift, *Works* ed. Williams, i. 82–85; *HMC Egmont*, ii. 215; *HMC Astley*, 208; Burke, *Commoners*, i. 198; *HMC 10th Rep. IV*, 334; PCC 71 Penn, 28 Poley, 41 Barrett.

P. W.

D'AETH

D'AETH, Thomas (1678–1745), of Knowlton Court and North Cray, Kent.

CANTERBURY   1708–1710
SANDWICH   1715–1722

bap. 4 Dec. 1678, o. surv. s. of Thomas D'aeth of St. Dionis Backchurch, London by Elhanna, da. of Sir John Rolt of Milton Ernest, Beds. *educ.* travelled abroad (Italy) ?1698–1700; Padua Univ. 1699. *m.* (1) 23 Jan. 1701, Elizabeth (*d.*1721), da. and event. h. of Adm. Sir John Narborough of Knowlton Court, 6s. (4 *d.v.p.*) 6da. (1 *d.v.p.*); (2) Jane, da. of Walter Williams of Dingestow, Mon., 1s. *suc.* fa. 1708; *cr.* Bt. 16 July 1716.[1]

Freeman, Canterbury 1708, Sandwich 1715.[2]

Commr. Dover Harbour 1709; member SPCK by 1712.[3]

The D'aeths were of Flemish origin, an ancestor settling in Dartford in the 16th century and becoming prominent in municipal affairs. D'aeth's father, a younger son, also Thomas, was a successful Mediterranean merchant, possibly following in the footsteps of his elder brother Adrian, who was based at the factory at Smyrna in 1661, although Thomas D'aeth snr. appears to have been trading from London at that date. This Thomas D'aeth did spend some time at Smyrna before returning in 1669, and getting married in October of that year. He continued in trade, living in the parish of St. Dionis Backchurch, where this Member, known as Thomas jnr., was born. Thomas D'aeth snr. was a wealthy man, having a personal estate assessed in 1695 at over £600. The D'aeths were large wholesale Italian merchants with widespread commercial interests and trading contacts in France, Germany, Netherlands, Spain and the East Indies. Thomas jnr. was obviously brought up with the idea of joining the family firm, for his father's letterbook indicates that he was abroad in Italy between 1698 and 1700, learning the secrets of the trade. A letter of May 1700 indicated that D'aeth had been taken into a partnership with his father, who had also altered the spelling of his name from Death to D'aeth.[4]

Soon after his return to England, D'aeth married the daughter of Sir John Narborough, bringing him into a close relationship with Admiral Sir Clowdesley Shovell*, her stepfather. Evidence from the poor-rate assessment books indicate that the D'aeths moved from St. Dionis in 1705 because the entry for that year merely has the word 'gone' against their name. Further, the baptism of their daughter Elhanna on 10 Mar. 1705 was the last of the family in that parish. Thomas D'aeth snr. probably remained in London, or residing at his 'country' home in Hackney, because in his will he is still described as of the city of London and his wife was living in Hackney at her death in 1738. His son may well have taken up residence in Kent, for he was named as a justice for that county for the first time in March 1706, and in September 1708 D'aeth snr. expressed the wish to be buried in his son's parish church at North Cray. D'aeth's interest in the county was immeasurably strengthened in 1707 by the fortuitous death of his wife's two brothers (drowned along with Shovell off the Scilly Isles), which brought her the Narborough estate at Knowlton, four and a half miles south-west of Sandwich. However, it is unclear when exactly D'aeth took up full residence at Knowlton because he had two children christened, in 1710 and 1712, at St. Andrew's, Holborn, and in 1714 wrote to solicit a seat at Sandwich with the introductory comment that he had 'now come to settle in your neighbourhood'.[5]

D'aeth's parliamentary ambitions centred on Canterbury, where he was made a freeman on 20 Apr. 1708, preparatory to his return to Parliament in the May election. He was classed as a Whig on a list of early 1708 with the election returns added, and the Earl of Sunderland (Charles, Lord Spencer*) noted his election as a gain for the Whigs. In his first session in the House he voted in 1709 for the naturalization of the Palatines, and acted as a teller on 31 Mar. 1709 against bringing up a petition opposing a clause in the Earl of Clanricarde's estate bill. In the following session he was named to a drafting committee concerned with setting a time-limit to public mourning and voted for the impeachment of Dr Sacheverell. Indeed, on 21 Mar. he acted as a teller in favour of a motion of thanks to the managers of the impeachment. There is no doubt about his position on the Sacheverell affair. In May 1710 he wrote:

'tis strange that people should pretend to show a zeal for our excellent established church by broaching again and supporting those doctrines which entirely ruined both it and the monarchy in the late civil wars and brought us to the brink of losing both our religion and our liberties in King James's time. The doctrine of absolute passive obedience was the occasion of that; and what can it now mean, joined with an indelible hereditary right, but at least to enervate and weaken the Hanover succession?

As the summer of 1710 wore on, his letters betrayed his bewilderment at the swings of political fortune following the Sacheverell trial as well as a concern for their effects in Canterbury. Not surprisingly, he was defeated at the 1710 election.[6]

In the Kent county election of 1713 D'aeth voted for the Whig candidates, citing property in North Cray as his freehold. He re-entered the Commons for Sandwich in 1715, being classed as a Whig on a comparative analysis of the old and new Parliaments. He continued to sit until 1722. According to Josiah Burchett*, his successor at Sandwich, his retirement was prompted by the death of his first wife, a popular figure in Kentish society. D'aeth died on 3 Jan. 1745. In his will he made provision for his son by his second marriage as well as providing for his five surviving daughters. His eldest son, Narborough, inherited the estates; the younger, Thomas, he put out to Charles Smith, a Turkey merchant.[7]

[1] *Archives*, iii. 33–35; Berry, *Kent Gens*. 248–9; Add. 33920, f. 39b; *St. Dionis Backchurch* (Harl. Soc. Reg. iii), 49; IGI, London. [2] *Canterbury Freemen Roll* ed. Cowper, 315; Centre Kentish Stud. Sandwich bor. recs. Sa/Ac8, f. 386. [3] Add. 42650, f. 113; SPCK Archs. min. bk. 5, p. 284. [4] S. K. Keyes, *Dartford Further Hist. Notes*, 312–13; *Archives*, 33–36; *HMC Finch*, i. 148, 398; *Cal. Treas. Bks.* i. 259–60; *London Rec. Soc.* ii. 85; *Markets and Merchants* ed. Roseveare, 100; Guildhall Lib. ms 9563, f. 112. [5] *Archives*, 35; *St. Dionis Backchurch*, 144; PCC 236 Barrett, 59 Brodrepp; *Hist. Reg. Chron.* 1738, p. 10; info. from Prof. N. Landau; IGI, London; Add. 33512, f. 202. [6] Centre Kentish Stud. CC/A/C8, burghmote min. bk. p. 382; U47/16/O6, D'aeth to [John Lee], 23 May, 9, 15, June, 4 July 1710. [7] Centre Kentish Stud. Q/RPe1, 1713 pollbk.; Add. 33512, f. 212; *Arch. Cant.* v. 99, 107; PCC 10 Seymer.

B. D. H./S. N. H.

DAINES, Sir William (1647–1724), of St. Leonard's, Bristol.[1]

BRISTOL 1701 (Jan.)–1710, 1715–1722

b. 1647, s. of William Daines of Norfolk county, Virginia by Phillis, da. of Thomas Bembrigg of St. Giles Cripplegate, London. m. c.1662, Elizabeth (d. 1726), da. of Captain James Harris of Norfolk county, Virginia, 1s. (d.v.p.) 2da. suc. fa. 1687; kntd. 28 Nov. 1694.[2]

Member, Merchant Venturers' Soc. of Bristol 1690, warden 1692–3, master 1698–1700; common councilman, Bristol 1691–1702, sheriff 1694–5, mayor 1700–1, alderman 1702–d.; asst. Bristol corporation of the poor 1696–8, gov. 1705–6.[3]

Daines's parents were resident in London at the time of their marriage at St. Dunstan's, Stepney, in 1636, and emigrated to Norfolk county, Virginia, in around 1645. William Daines snr. soon established himself in the colony as a planter and attorney and became a county commissioner. His son William, the future MP, was born in the colony and contracted an 'under-age' marriage in 1662. In the later 1680s, possibly just after his father's death in 1687, he emigrated to Bristol where his involvement in Virginia's tobacco-growing trade provided him with essential connexions and the basis for a thriving mercantile business. He was undoubtedly a key figure in the expansion of Bristol's engagement in the Virginia and Maryland trade at this time, and his pre-eminence in this field and the local influence which it brought him are clearly indicated by his swift rise during the 1690s in both the city's Merchant Venturers' Society and the corporation.[4]

Elected to the common council in September 1691, Daines aligned himself with the Whig faction in its bitter struggle with the power-holding Tories, and his selection to the city shrievalty in 1694, within a year of the Whigs' success in ending the Tory grip on the corporation, indicates the significance of his own contribution in this process. In November 1694, during his term as sheriff, he and the serving mayor, Thomas Day, were received and knighted by the King. Along with other leading Whig citizens he was involved in the foundation of the Bristol corporation of the poor, and during 1699–1700 received a foretaste of parliamentary life when he assisted the city MP Robert Yate in procuring for the corporation an Act to improve the navigation of the Frome and Avon and for 'cleansing' Bristol's streets. In the election of January 1701, three months into his mayoralty, Daines was returned to Parliament for Bristol and retained the seat until 1710. He was present at the opening of Parliament in February 1701, the former Member Sir Thomas Day deputizing for him as mayor, and remained in attendance until obliged to obtain three weeks' leave of absence on 16 Apr.[5]

For a Bristol MP, Daines was surprisingly inactive and hardly ever featured on inquiry committees concerned with trading issues. During several sessions he was allowed lengthy spells of absence, possibly on account of his extensive business activities. His Whiggish political views were apparent in his vote on 13 Feb. 1703, for agreeing with the Lords' amendment to the bill for extending the time in which the oath of abjuration could be taken. He was forecast in October as a probable opponent of the Tack, and did not vote for it in the division on 28 Nov. After his re-election in 1705 he was classed as 'Low Church' in a list of the new House of Commons and voted on 25 Oct. for the Court candidate for Speaker. On 18 Feb. 1706 he supported the Court against the 'place clause' of the regency bill. He was also listed as a Whig in two lists from 1708, voted in 1709 in favour of naturalizing the Palatines and the following year in favour of the impeachment of Dr Sacheverell. Defeated in two hotly contested elections for Bristol in 1710 and 1713, he returned to Parliament in 1715 and supported the Whig administration.[6]

In 1708 Daines had transferred a large tract of his Virginia lands to his sister Elizabeth Lawson and her son while the remnant appears to have been retained by his only son, William, who continued to manage the plantation until his death in 1717. Daines himself died 'at his residence' in Bristol on 5 Sept. 1724, and was buried at the city church of St. Augustine the Less. The extent of his wealth is indicated by his bequest of £10,000 to the children of his two daughters, one of whom, Anne, the wife of 1st Viscount Barrington [I] (John Barrington†), Daines named as his sole executrix.

[1] *Inhabitants of Bristol 1696* (Bristol Rec. Soc. xxv), 99. [2] IGI, London, and USA; A. Beaven, *Bristol Lists*, 285; PCC 205 Bolton; Boyer, *Pol. State*, xxxi. 228. [3] *Soc. of Merchant Venturers in 17th Cent.* (Bristol Rec. Soc. xvii), 33; Beaven, 116, 125, 187, 209, 225, 285; *Bristol Corporation of the Poor 1696–1834* (Bristol Rec. Soc. iii), 46. [4] Info. from Mr J. Deans, Texas, USA. [5] *CSP Col.* 1702–3, pp. 57, 95; Bristol AO, common council procs. 1687–1702, ff. 171, 205, 219. [6] Info. from Mr Deans; *The Gen.* n.s. vi. 105; *Hist. Reg. Chron.* 1724, p. 41; Beaven, 285; W. Barrett, *Hist. Bristol*, 408; PCC 205 Bolton.

A. A. H.

DALBY, John (c.1651–1720), of the Inner Temple and Reading, Berks.

READING   1698–1700, 1710–1713

b. c.1651, 1st s. of Edward Dalby of the Inner Temple and Reading by Frances (d. 1717), da. of Charles Holloway, serjeant-at-law. *educ.* I. Temple 1669, called 1676, bencher 1699, treasurer 1709. *unm. suc.* fa. 1672.[1]

Recorder, Reading July 1686–7, Oct. 1688–d.[2]

Dalby's father was described in 1686 by the Earl of Clarendon (Henry Hyde†) as a person 'of eminent loyalty and as wise a man as I have known of his rank'. Having been called to the bar in 1641, Edward Dalby married into the Holloway family, becoming recorder of Reading after the Restoration. By his death in 1672, he had set his eldest son on the path towards a legal career, which resulted in his being called to the bar. Upon Dalby's election in turn to the recordership of Reading in 1686, Clarendon wrote to Lord Rochester (Laurence Hyde†) describing Dalby as 'a very honest and ingenious young man, and fit for the situation'. He was dismissed in 1687 when James II attempted to remodel the corporation, but returned as an assistant and as recorder in October 1688. Throughout the period 1690–1715 he appears to have been active both in the corporation and as a member of the Inner Temple, where he kept chambers.[3]

Dalby was elected to Parliament at the 1698 election, although his opponent petitioned against his return, claiming that Dalby had used 'promises and threats' during the campaign. On a comparative analysis of the old and new Parliaments in 1698 he was classed as a Country supporter, and he was also forecast as likely to oppose the standing army. He was given a week's leave of absence on 22 Feb. 1699. Marks in the Reading corporation diary indicate that he was present at a council meeting on 27 Feb., suggesting that he continued to play an active role when necessary as the borough's recorder. In the following session, Dalby managed through all stages in the Commons a private estate bill in favour of the Harrison family of Hurst, Berkshire. In 1719 the manorial courts at Hurst were being held by John Dalby (probably the Member's nephew) who bought the estate three years later. It would seem probable that either Dalby or his brother Edward, an attorney, was steward to the Harrisons by the time the Act passed.[4]

Dalby did not stand at the election of January 1701 and returned to the Commons only in 1710. The 'Hanover list' of the new Parliament classed him as 'doubtful', but this can only have been through unfamiliarity, as he was undoubtedly a Tory, being included on a list of 'worthy patriots' who during the 1710–11 session detected the mismanagements of the previous Whig administration. He was also a member of the October Club, one of only 15 October men with a legal background. Final proof of his party affiliations was his vote, on 18 June 1713, for the French commerce bill.[5]

Dalby did not stand in 1713. His declining years seem to have been spent serving the Inner Temple and making plans for the future. His will of 1717 made generous provision for his brothers Thomas, the vicar of Sutton Courtenay, Oxfordshire, and Edward, the latter's in trust, possibly because of mental illness (Hearne reported him 'crazed' some time before he died). The major beneficiary, however, was his nephew John, already admitted to the Inner Temple at his uncle's request in 1711, who received lands in Caversham, Oxfordshire, and in Berkshire, as well as the reversion to Sunningwell (Berkshire) and Stanton St. John (Oxfordshire) after the death of Dalby's brother, Thomas. The exact date of Dalby's death in 1720 is unknown, but it must have occurred before 20 Oct. when Reading elected a new recorder.[6]

[1] *Vis. Berks.* (Harl. Soc. lvi), 189; C. Kerry, *Hist. St. Lawrence, Reading*, 129. [2] *HMC 11th Rep. VII*, 200; Berks. RO, Reading corp. diary, 30 Oct. 1688. [3] *Clarendon Corresp.* ed. Singer, i. 555; *Cal. I. Temple Recs.* ii. 262; *HMC 11th Rep. VII*, 194. [4] Reading corp. diary, 27 Feb. 1698[–9]; *VCH Berks.* iii. 252 [5] *Huntington Lib. Q.* xxxiii. 158. [6] PCC 229 Shaller; *Hearne Colls.* xi. 299; info. from Dr D. F. Lemmings; Reading corp. diary, 20 Oct. 1720.

S. N. H.

DALRYMPLE, Hon. Sir David, 1st Bt. (c.1665–1721), of Hailes, Haddington.

SCOTLAND   1707–1708
HADDINGTON BURGHS   1708–3 Dec. 1721

b. c.1665, 5th s. of James Dalrymple, 1st Visct. of Stair [S], ld. president ct. of session 1671–81, 1689–95, by Margaret, da. and coh. of James Ross of Balneil, Wigtown., and wid. of Fergus Kennedy of Knockdaw, Ayr. *educ.* Edinburgh Univ. MA 1681; Leyden 1682; adv. 1688. *m.* 4 Apr. 1691, Janet, da. of Sir James Rochead of Inverleith, Edinburgh., and wid. of Alexander Murray of Melgund, Forfar., 3s. (1 *d.v.p.*) 4da. (3 *d.v.p.*). *cr.* Bt. 8 May 1701.[1]

MP [S] Culross 1698–1707.

Jt. solicitor-gen. [S] 1701–9; auditor of treasury [S] 1701; commr. union with England, 1702, 1706; ld. adv. 1709–11, 1714–20; auditor gen. of exchequer [S] 1720–*d.*

Burgess, Edinburgh 1702, Glasgow 1704, Dunbar 1708, Ayr 1709.[2]

Dean, faculty of advocates, 1712–*d.*[3]

Commr. visitation, Glasgow Univ. 1717, 1718, St. Andrews Univ. 1718.

The Dalrymples, by their conduct before and after the Revolution, acquired a reputation for political opportunism and duplicity. The principal targets of opprobrium were the Member's father and eldest brother, who successfully straddled the political fence during the 1680s. Sir James Dalrymple of Stair, a wily survivor under the Commonwealth, transferred smoothly to high office under the Restoration regime and rose to the presidency of the court of session in 1671. Yet his role in ensuring that the Test Act of 1681 included safeguards against Catholicism lost him favour at Court, and (in conjunction with his unwillingness to subscribe to the act) prompted his removal from office. Taking stock of uncertain prospects, Stair chose the safety of exile, leaving his eldest son, Sir John, Master of Stair, in charge of the family estates. While the elder Stair consoled himself with those academic pursuits which earned him enduring fame, the younger suffered a period of vexatious persecution, until he made his peace with James II, being appointed lord advocate in 1687 because of his readiness to condone the crown's dispensing power. His attitude towards conventiclers was nevertheless deemed insufficiently rigorous and he was transferred, the following year, to the post of justice clerk. In the prelude to the Revolution, therefore, the father was at the centre of Williamite planning in Holland, whereas his son held confidential office in Scotland. Sir James was a natural beneficiary of the events of 1688–9, resuming the presidency of the session and securing a peerage in 1690. But, to the outrage of many contemporaries, the King found it likewise expedient to include the Master of Stair in the Scottish administration, appointing him lord advocate in 1689. Such triumphs created an abiding impression that the family was always acting, as Lord Seafield expressed it, 'upon double views'. Inevitably, Dalrymple's own reputation was tarnished by association with his eldest brother, who was created Earl of Stair in 1703. George Lockhart* styled Stair 'the Judas of his country' and deemed Dalrymple as 'equally willing, yet not equally capable of doing so much evil as his lordship'.[4]

Dalrymple had accompanied his father to Leyden in October 1682, an event which coincided with the completion of his legal training. At the Revolution he returned to Scotland and was immediately admitted advocate. The law was his first love, as he later explained when recommending it as a subject of study to his own son: 'the language in which it is written elegantly, the varieties of subjects, the antiquities it partly opens and partly requires to be carried along with it, for company and understanding have in my mind much the preference to all other subjects of study'. His intelligence and application were considerable, but his acquisition of a lucrative private practice owed not a little to the influence of his father as president of the session, and that of his elder brother, Sir Hew, who held the same office from 1698. Dalrymple never allowed others to forget the extent of the financial sacrifice he made by devoting his attention to politics. Entering the Scottish parliament in 1698 as a member of the Stair–Queensberry alliance, he was rewarded with appointment as joint solicitor-general and with a baronetcy in 1701. He supported the Court over the handling of the Darien affair, voting for an address rather than an act of parliament (his political allegiance outweighing his personal loss as an investor of £400 in the Company of Scotland). He remained with the Court under Queen Anne, serving dutifully at the outset of the abortive negotiations for union with England in 1702. His experiences as a commissioner presaged, albeit fleetingly, later dissatisfaction with English attitudes towards Scotland, for he left the negotiations in disgust. During the ministerial changes of 1704, he held aloof, declining to join those of Queensberry's followers who cynically voted in favour of the Duke of Hamilton's motion for deferring a decision on the succession. In this he acted in accordance with his Hanoverian sympathies, while at the same time taking care not to give offence to the English court. He was sufficiently emboldened, however, to conduct a harrying campaign against the beleaguered Marquess of Tweeddale in the tail end of the 1704 session of the Scottish parliament. With the failure of the 'New Party' experiment and the re-establishment of Queensberry's dominance, Dalrymple reverted to his former stance, being aptly described by the Jacobite agent Scot as 'entirely courtier'.[5]

Appointed to the Union commission, Dalrymple played an active role in the negotiations, and his legal expertise was valuable in drawing up the treaty, to which he was a signatory. In August there were strong rumours that he would resign his post as solicitor-general. Dalrymple was concerned about the effects of a parliamentary career on his health and finances, the latter consideration being based on the dual blow of the increased costs of living in London during the session and the loss of profitable legal work in Scotland. He was persuaded to remain in office, however, and played his part in the Union debates in the last Scottish parliament, voting solidly with the Court with very few absences. The untimely death of his brother, the Earl of Stair, in January 1707 was a great personal and political blow. Thereafter, Dalrymple became the effective political head of the family because Sir Hew's legal office prevented him from playing an active part in Westminster politics and the 2nd Earl had already embarked on what would prove a distinguished military and diplomatic career. Although the family remained one of the most important in Scotland, Dalrymple lacked that drive for dominance which had been so evident in the late Earl's political conduct. He merely continued the political attachment to Queensberry, but lacked the desire to develop a personal following in his own right. After the final session of the Scottish parliament, he travelled to London as one of the half-dozen Scottish advisers to the English ministry, and upon returning home was one of those whom the Queen requested to remain in Edinburgh over the summer, both to confer on the legal changes consequent upon the Union and to dispel disaffection in the Scottish capital. Dalrymple reported to the Earl of Mar on 5 Aug. that 'there is indeed great need for a watchful eye upon the people of this country. There arise every day new subjects of complaint.' He lamented the lack of troops, and drew particular attention to the teething problems in assessing excise and customs, citing the hardships inflicted on Scottish brewers. 'These things will be remedied in time', he predicted, 'but in the meantime ill men inflame these broils all they can.'[6]

Dalrymple fell seriously ill prior to the first Parliament of Great Britain and was making 'very small recovery' in early October 1707. As the natural spokesman for the Scottish Court party, it was 'doubted who will make the answer' to the expected speech of welcome from the Speaker to the Scottish Members. Illness did indeed prevent Dalrymple from attending the opening of the session, though not his nomination to the committee on the Address. His absence continued during the early stages of the

Squadrone attack on the Court that culminated in the bill to complete the Union. Dalrymple's arrival from Scotland was eagerly anticipated by ministerial supporters, James Vernon I* reporting on 6 Dec. 1707 that this 'eminent pleader' would 'open things clearer as to their constitution than we understand of it at present'. He arrived in time to participate on 11 Dec. in the debate upon the report from the committee of the whole on those aspects of the Queen's Speech relating to the Union. Dalrymple proposed an amendment to the third of the five resolutions reported, moving that the unification of the powers of j.p.s should be rendered consistent with the articles of union preserving hereditary jurisdictions. Although his motion was defeated, the point of attack was well chosen and contributed to the alienation of the Duke of Argyll from the Squadrone's agenda. Dalrymple maintained that that Scottish heritors would resent any infringement upon the 15-day period reserved under Scottish law to the heritable jurisdictions prior to the interference of any other authority, and also denied the validity of any parallels with the immediate power of intervention which had been exercised by the Scottish privy council. The privy council itself was earmarked for abolition in the first resolution reported from the committee, and the Squadrone argued that it was fitting to transfer that right of intervention to the justices. Dalrymple, however, maintained that the council's 'intermeddling was more *de facto* than *de jure* and the transmitting that power ... to single and inferior persons would be of little use to preserving the peace'. William Bennet* reported that Dalrymple 'showed much dexterity' and influenced 'some eminent lawyers' (including Sir Thomas Parker, Sir Joseph Jekyll and Robert Eyre) into recanting their former declarations in committee. Dalrymple was appointed to the drafting committee for the bill to complete the Union, and was active in an abortive Court campaign to amend it during its passage. He was also critical of the Scottish militia bill, voicing his reservations on 15 Jan. 1708, when both this bill and that relating to the Union received their second reading:

> He made some observations upon each of them to show that the bills would want larger explanations to make them intelligible or practicable. The bill for constituting justices of the peace says only in general [that] they shall have the same power in relation to the peace as they have in England, which he doubts will be easily understood in Scotland or practicable while the heritable jurisdictions subsist, as is provided for by the treaty and not altered by the bill. The same bill sets up assizes and circuits, which he says is a very odious name in Scotland, they having never seen any more of those courts for above 40 years past but to the grievance and oppression of the country and the destruction of many an honest man. As to the other bill of the militia, he observed [that] they were to be put in a new method more to their expense than their advantage. Though a month's cess, which the militia would require, were not great matter, yet being added to the three month's cess they were to pay this year to the land tax it would be felt in a poor country.

He continued his criticisms on the bill to complete the Union in a committee of the whole on 22 Jan., arguing against the Squadrone motion to precipitate abolition of the Scottish privy council. His counter-proposal was to preserve the council beyond the next election but abolish it 'at the end of the next session of Parliament'. According to Vernon,

> he gave many good reasons for it, particularly that nobody could have any prospect of their peace being preserved till they had some experience how the new methods of justices would take ... Enemies to the Union among them desired the dissolution of the council and the friends to it feared it.

He also denied that preservation of the council was sought for the purpose of influencing the coming elections. Leading Scottish supporters of the Court, he argued,

> could have no influence but by their personal interest which would be the same whether they were of the council or not, and they had more to fear of that kind from those who were like to be invested with their new powers of the militias and justiceship added to their superiority and heritable jurisdictions.

Defeated by 34 votes, Dalrymple attempted to reverse the decision the following day by subjecting all parts of the bill to a detailed examination and demonstrating that the provisions 'for preserving the peace were neither of that sufficiency or certainty but that in prudence some trial ought to be made of them before the council be abolished'. He concluded his speech 'with great earnestness', forecasting that the bill would place the security of Scotland in 'imminent danger'.[7]

Dalrymple's prominent role in such important parliamentary proceedings demonstrated that he was the leading Scottish ministerialist in the Commons. One contemporary described him as Queensberry's 'mouth in that House, at least he is said to be wholly his creature and therefore speaks his mind'. In legislative work Dalrymple concentrated principally on matters of Scottish interest, being appointed to draft a recruiting bill (21 Jan. 1708) and two fishery bills (2, 5 Feb.). He spoke on 29 Jan. in the committee of ways and means against William Lowndes's suggestion that the East India Company be given a new monopoly for 21 years, insisting that 'a new grant . . . without a new subscription' put Scotland 'under an inequality as to trade, contrary to the sense of the treaty [of Union]'. He was appointed to the drafting committee on 23 Feb. for a bill directing the payment of the Equivalent and spoke effectively, three days later, against a Squadrone motion to instruct the committee to invert the classes of payment, taking particular exception to adverse reflections on the Scottish parliament, for which he was applauded by the House. He duly presented the bill on 10 Mar. During this period he had also been nominated to draft a harbour bill (13 Feb.). Dalrymple himself presented a petition on behalf of Scottish Quakers on 27 Feb. and was first-named to the drafting committee for a bill to extend the Quaker Affirmation Act to Scotland. This bill had two further objectives relevant to Quakers throughout Britain, namely to alter the official title of the Act (removing any implication that the affirmation was 'an oath, though not in the usual form') and to alter certain 'expressions in the affirmation itself which are too much like an oath'. Also during February, having been lobbied by the bishop of Carlisle on the 24th, he was foremost among the Scots who 'zealously and unanimously' supported the controversial bill to clarify the statutes of cathedrals and collegiate churches, voting for its committal on the 28th. Intimations of the Jacobite descent on Scotland prompted Dalrymple into a further round of parliamentary activity: on 11 Mar. he seconded James Stanhope's motion for a bill to deter disloyal clan chiefs, and was appointed to the drafting committee.[8]

On the basis of this diligent performance at Westminster, Lord Coningsby (Thomas*) deemed Dalrymple 'much the ablest' of the Scottish Court Members, 'indeed of the whole [Scottish] representation'. During the second half of the session, rumours had circulated of Dalrymple's imminent promotion to higher office, and these speculations continued after the dissolution. He was variously tipped as Scottish secretary of state, lord clerk register, lord chief baron of the exchequer, and (accurately though prematurely) as lord advocate. In fact, the secretaryship devolved on Queensberry, the post of lord register fell to Lord Glasgow, and Dalrymple was denied the exchequer, on the grounds that it was inadvisable to place the judicatures of the courts of exchequer and session 'in the hands of one family'. This obvious objection did not impress Dalrymple, who petulantly attributed Lord Seafield's success to the partiality of the Squadrone and the Junto, a mistaken impression which the Duke of Roxburghe and George Baillie* were at pains to dispel. Although personally on good terms with Baillie, his hostility to the Squadrone was evident in his vote against John Cockburn* in the Haddingtonshire election, albeit that this involved voting for a lesser figure from the same party. Dalrymple's own election was secured for Haddington Burghs by the weight of his own influence, bolstered by that of his elder brother. He suffered a life-threatening illness in July, but had recovered sufficiently by the autumn for the Court to express the earnest hope that he would soon arrive in London. On 5 Oct. Lord Mar relayed that 'the Queen asks very often about you and of your coming up . . . and expects that you'll come as soon as possible, and the sooner the better'. Dalrymple was informed that the session would not open until 16 Nov., but instructed that this 'must not stop your coming'. He was also requested to 'acquaint our friends of the adjournment that they may not come too soon, which would make them repine after they come'. Mar's letter also conveyed assurances from Lord Treasurer Godolphin (Sidney†) that financial rewards would be forthcoming. This prompted a sullen reply on 12 Oct., in which Dalrymple expressed mock gratitude at the compliments paid to him, then wrote the following sentence which he crossed through but left legible: 'I cannot forbear saying that I think the great man – to whom your lordship's letter refers has proceeded coldly and backwardly.' The remainder of the letter continued in the same vein:

> I have no better assurances, neither for the past nor for the future, than I have always had, and, even supposing all effectual, I must forgo a way of living which yields me yearly more than ever was proposed for me, and to that must [be] add[ed] the difference of living here and at London and leaving the management of my own affairs . . . I have sometime since resolved that I ought to stay at home on a just reflection of what has happened to me in six years' service, especially last year when at the desire of my friends I came up on the peril of my life and having done to my little capacity the best service I could, I was neglected with something more than ordinary contempt.

Dalrymple was subsequently recompensed for his earlier service as a Union commissioner, received back-pay on his official salary and was granted a lump sum for each of his journeys to London from 1707 to 1709. Such sweeteners, together with a recognition that only co-operation could ensure advancement, overcame his reluctance to attend at Westminster. His nephew, Lord Stair, reassured Mar that Dalrymple 'did not seem averse to coming, though his family were of a very different opinion'.[9]

Dalrymple was appointed to two committees on the opening day of the session, which suggests that he arrived for the start of business, and he was certainly present in London by early December, featuring among those named to draft bills to encourage the fishery (16 Dec.), to prevent embezzlement of shipwrecked goods (20 Dec.), and to improve recruitment (23 Dec.). After the Christmas recess, he was active in presenting the objections of Edinburgh merchants to a harbour bill sponsored by William Morison*. On 17 Jan. 1709 he was first-named to the drafting committee for a bill to ease insolvent debtors, and on the 25th declared in the House that an address advising the Queen to remarry was 'untimely', nevertheless being nominated to the ensuing committee. He was appointed on the same day to search for precedents relevant to the message from the Lords requesting the attendance of three Scottish Members to give evidence in relation to the first-ever Scottish peerage election, and subsequently acted as counsel for the sitting Court peers over the election petitions. He assisted in the formulation of a bill to ascertain allowances for the export from Scotland of fish and flesh cured with foreign salt, being appointed to the drafting committee on 21 Feb., and also indicated his views in memorials on this topic to ministers. He argued against the niggardly English attitude towards the lower duties paid in Scotland on salt imported prior to the Union, which were held to invalidate the current payment of drawbacks. He forecast disaffection if the provisions of the Union were infringed even in such small details. 'We are apt to think', he lectured the lord treasurer, 'that he who offends in one thing sinneth against the whole law.' He acted as a lobbyist on behalf of the Scottish fishing industry and maintained that it was anomalous for these drawbacks to be paid in England but not in Scotland 'which is not only uneasy to the merchants and fishers [as] exporters, but to the whole body of the people of Scotland, who have no better security for the articles of the treaty than the curers and exporters of these merchandises have for their encouragement'. He told on 28 Feb. against a motion to instruct the committee on the general naturalization bill to continue the provisions of former statutes, and was added on 12 Mar. to the drafting committee on the Scottish militia bill. On 13 Mar. he reported a bill to make two ships free.[10]

The issue of greatest significance for Dalrymple in this session was the passage of the Treason Act. This legislation was later viewed as the root cause of Dalrymple's disillusionment, and he 'frequently and publicly declared how much he was grieved, and repented having been so instrumental in promoting the Union'. He contributed to the debate of 28 Jan. 1709 in the committee of the whole on improving the Union, and was appointed the following day to the drafting committee for a bill to standardize treason law throughout Britain. This initiative originated in the recent failure of the lord advocate, Sir James Stewart, to convict several Stirlingshire lairds who were prematurely 'out' in the previous year's invasion scare. Stewart was widely thought to have bungled proceedings (an opinion shared by Dalrymple), and in the previous December it had been in contemplation to remove Stewart and 'send Sir David Dalrymple from this Parliament by making him advocate'. Yet, as Mar explained, he 'would not have accepted on such an occasion', so the idea was shelved. Dalrymple therefore viewed the crisis precipitated by the verdict of 'not proven' on the Stirlingshire lairds as a consequence of human error rather than fundamental flaws in Scottish treason law. Indeed, so great was his reverence for Scottish law and his father's memory as author of the famous *Institutions* that it would have been unthinkable for him to have concluded otherwise. It must be assumed that Dalrymple played a major part in killing off the treason bill in committee; but the determination of the ministry, especially the Junto, to prosecute this initiative resulted in a similar bill being reintroduced via the Lords. Dalrymple spoke against this second treason bill on 5 Apr. on the same side as his erstwhile Squadrone opponents Cockburn and Baillie. The disdain with which Dalrymple's lengthy disquisitions against the treason bill were treated by his English audience was noted by the contemporary historian Cunningham, who recalled that after one speech of some two hours' duration, 'full of many cases collected out of the grounds of the laws and ancient histories', he was answered by an unnamed Member with a few lines from Samuel Butler's mock-heroic poem *Hudibras*, to the great amusement of the back-benchers. Frustration on this issue did not drive Dalrymple into the opposition camp, and it was with him in mind that Lockhart referred dismissively to those Scots who 'pretended to regret the measures they had followed' but 'were in such a state of dependence or so corrupted in their principles . . . that they could not or would not fly heartily in the face of the Court'. Certainly, Dalrymple was eager for a permanent solution to his financial worries. He had set out his case at length to Lord Loudoun on 13 Feb.:

> My attendance here and in Scotland for many years has been extremely prejudicial to my private affairs. I have changed the living cheap to living dear, left the management of my estate to others and have been so much diverted from the pursuit of my employment that out of six or seven years I can scarcely be said to have enjoyed

one usefully . . . [Neither] the expenses allowed for attending the treaty, nor the other sums which have been given me upon extraordinary occasions, [have] any proportion to that loss, which I cannot compute to be less than £6,000 spending and losing over and above what I have got. These things I mention because that affords me a very good reason to propose that either I may retire without offence . . . [and] without the least desire or thought of mutiny, or that I may be provided . . . with a sizeable post in such a way as I may be secure during my life at home, equal to my employment, and if my services be thought of any use here . . . there may be an allowance for the expenses and charges of attending . . . I ask no more than not to be a loser . . . The most natural thing for me is to be chief baron, and not inconsistent with being a Member . . . It was last year upon the matter agreed in my favours . . . If it be not thought proper for me, I submit and desire your lordship to consider . . . the office of auditor to the exchequer in Scotland.

Dalrymple then entered into a lengthy explanation of the different auditors in England, Wales and Ireland, citing relevant reference works and concluding with an analysis of the former functioning of the Scottish exchequer. The crown, he maintained, possessed an undoubted right to create this post, which would 'be of the greatest use and service', and that in financial emergencies requiring speedy intervention 'the administration would be lame without it'. He demurred at suggesting the actual salary, but was apparently expecting about £1,500 p.a. Dalrymple's proposal was taken sufficiently seriously for Lord Yester to report back to Scotland on 19 Feb. that a new auditor's place was to be 'coined' for Dalrymple. Instead of placing a new burden on the Scottish civil list, the ministry reverted to the earlier plan of appointing Dalrymple lord advocate, but with an increased salary and an allowance for London expenses during the session.[11]

The abolition of the privy council had removed the predominant branch of the Scottish executive, but it was felt that the lord advocate would naturally assume some of its former politico-legal functions. There were obvious advantages in associating the post with parliamentary service, not least that this was a logical continuation of the *ex officio* presence of the advocate in the Scottish parliament. The first post-Union advocate, however, had remained out of the House and resided exclusively in Scotland. The appointment of Dalrymple (with a salary of £1,000 p.a., plus a Westminster allowance of £500 per session) apparently augured a change for the better. The high Presbyterians did not view matters in this light, however, and expressed resentment at the replacement of Stewart by one who would not 'be so friendly to the Kirk'. Dalrymple had taken care not to appear too eager, giving out to Baillie that he was only prepared to accept the post 'if the advocate consents to it'. Stewart, somewhat reluctantly, gave way to Dalrymple, but expressed particular concern about the security of the Kirk and portrayed Scottish episcopalians as 'a club of Jacobites', who merited discouragement to the full extent permissible under Scottish law. To this diatribe, Dalrymple replied that he 'was not a *jure divino* Presbyterian', and although a supporter of the Kirk and opponent of Jacobitism, he believed it an injustice that 'some have suffered who had owned and prayed for the Queen'. Privately he reported his dislike of the Presbyterians of Edinburgh and their 'too great passion for persecution'. His early days in office were not made easier by a fallacious press report that the royal chapel at Holyrood House was to be refitted for episcopalian worship. Dalrymple instructed the printer of the newspaper not only to make a formal retraction but to go in person to the principal Edinburgh coffee-house and score through the offensive section in the current issue. There are no grounds for doubting that Dalrymple was, as he put it, 'an honest Presbyterian'. His sympathy for the sufferings of episcopalians did not extend to legal toleration. Upon learning of the controversy in Edinburgh over the minister James Greenshields, Dalrymple did not write to England solely on account of Greenshields' use of the English service, but principally concerning Greenshields' earlier ordination by a non-juring bishop in Ireland. In October 1709 Dalrymple informed the Presbyterian divine Robert Wodrow that, on the Queen's orders, he had instructed Greenshields to desist from his 'encroachment on the privileges of the established church in Scotland'. Dalrymple condoned the imprisonment of Greenshields by the Edinburgh magistracy and remained opposed to the gathering momentum in favour of episcopalian toleration which this case precipitated. Dalrymple's correspondence with the ministry also embraced the continuing problems of Scottish customs and excise. He consistently advocated English leniency as a prerequisite of Anglo-Scottish harmony. On the question of smuggling, he favoured some moderate proposals emanating from the mercantile community, which, if implemented, would

> beget in the minds of the people a better opinion still of the Union and a greater confidence in those that are entrusted in the dispensing of justice . . . The complaints of the populace are not always to be regarded but neither are they to be contemned and in my humble opinion the giving some ease in this matter will be of better use to the government than the profits of these foolish people's goods can be.

To Hon. James Brydges*, on 22 Sept., he outlined his general policy:

We do what we can to make people here have a good opinion of the Union ... We have always said and everywhere that the Union will be improven [sic] by doing us good, raising trade that will employ the poor, ascertain the rents, increase the numbers, strength and wealth of the whole island; and that in making laws that concern us, regard shall be had to our own desires, alterations shall be avoided but where they are necessary. In a word that we shall be used kindly and as becomes freemen. These things would do more real service to Great Britain than 20 new laws with gilded titles.[12]

Dalrymple's appointment having taken place during the prorogation, a new writ was moved and he remained in Scotland until after his unanimous re-election for Haddington Burghs on 15 Dec. He travelled to London in time for the second half of the session, voted for the impeachment of Dr Sacheverell and was made an additional manager of the impeachment on 10 Feb. 1710. However, he never acted in this capacity due to ill-health, a turn of events which provided scope for Tory wits to propose a vote of thanks to Dalrymple and his fellow invalid Hon. Harry Mordaunt on 21 Mar. 'for their faithful management in never appearing'. Understandably, Dalrymple's parliamentary activity in this session was minimal, but he remained in London after the prorogation, giving information and advice to the Treasury on Scottish affairs, during April and May. He was not pleased with the manner in which his suggestions were treated, for Godolphin reported to Seafield in June that Dalrymple 'went down from hence, not very well satisfied ... and some words have been dropped here as if he would be willing to demit'. Mar also sent word to Edinburgh that he wished to be informed of 'how Sir David Dalrymple behaves and talks of affairs since he came down'. Shortly before departing, Dalrymple had apparently persuaded one of his political associates (probably Queensberry) to present a petition on his behalf to the Queen. This argued that he had accepted the post of lord advocate against his inclinations, on the understanding that the additional emoluments and his continuing legal work in Scotland would at least cover his increased expenses:

By the experiment he has made he finds that he cannot pursue his private practice to any advantage if he serves the public thoroughly, and that if he should throw up his private employment he cannot return to it again: and therefore being now about to go home to Scotland he has entreated me to represent to your Majesty with the greatest respect and in the most humble manner that ... he finds himself obliged to retire unless ... for the future his establishment be made up [to] £2,000.

This outrageous demand for a doubling of his salary was partially softened by the explanation that he only expected to have full pay while in office, and that he would content himself on retirement with a pension of only £1,000 p.a. He was also prepared to relinquish the £500 for expenses in London, further arguing that prior to the Union the advocate enjoyed considerable perquisites, and that the net increased charge to government was only £300 p.a. It is by no means certain that Dalrymple's petition was ever formally submitted. No response to it is known, nor was it renewed after the fall of Godolphin.[13]

In the election of 1710 Dalrymple denied hostility towards the new ministry of Robert Harley*, maintaining, for example, that his support for Baillie in Berwickshire did not amount to 'caballing with the Squadrone', but was simply support for a friend from boyhood, whose competitor was a suspected Jacobite. While this was indeed an honest version of events, it did not amount to the whole truth, for the Dalrymples departed from custom to support Cockburn in Haddingtonshire. Sir David also supported his nephew by marriage, Sir James Stewart, 1st Bt.*, against Lockhart in Edinburghshire. Harley's son-in-law Lord Dupplin (George Hay*) had already reported that 'my Lord Stair, president of the session, Sir David and all the Dalrymples, with all the interest they can make are against you'; and Lord Ilay asserted in November that Dalrymple had attempted to suborn the vote of Lord Blantyre in the peerage elections in return for averting a capital conviction upon his nephew for murder. Such intimations damaged Dalrymple's reputation with the English ministry. He himself was returned for Haddington Burghs, once more without a contest, but the description of him as a Court Tory in Richard Dongworth's analysis of the election results was to prove wide of the mark. His hostility to episcopalian toleration was undiminished and his pro-ministerial sympathies, which had been waning under Godolphin, continued to decline. Ill-health further disinclined him towards attendance, and he did not come to Westminster at any point during the first session of the 1710 Parliament. This loss was keenly felt by Baillie, who regarded Dalrymple as the most effective guardian of Scottish interests in the Commons. Before Dalrymple next attended, he had been dismissed from office, and thereafter drew closer to his former Squadrone rivals. Initially, this was in opposition to the emergent Scottish Tory pressure group within the Commons, but increasingly Dalrymple became associated with the broader Whig agenda of supporting the Hanoverian succession and countering the Jacobite threat.[14]

Ironically, it was leniency towards an essentially trivial act of Jacobite propaganda that prompted

Dalrymple's dismissal. The Duchess of Gordon sent a Jacobite medal to the faculty of advocates, which was accepted on 30 June 1711, nominally as a curio of future historical interest. The faculty's proceedings were notable for some inflammatory speeches by several lawyers, led by James Dundas of Arniston. Dalrymple's initial reaction, as conveyed to Queensberry on 3 July, was to treat it as a 'foolish incident' in what he described as a talking-shop for rash and indiscreet young men. He was aware that Jacobites might 'possibly make observations upon it, as if so considerable a body of the lawyers were disaffected', but believed that such assertions would lack all credibility. The death of Queensberry on 6 July created problems for Dalrymple, not simply because he lost an influential supporter at Court, but also because the Dundas case fell into an administrative limbo. Meanwhile the significance of the affair escalated with the publication of Dundas' self-justification, together with misleading reports in the press and diplomatic pressure from Hanover. Dalrymple, who had been aware of rumours of his dismissal prior to this burgeoning crisis, was shocked to discover that Lord Dartmouth (who had assumed responsibility for the correspondence following Queensberry's death) directed his first inquiries to Sir James Stewart, wrongly entitling him lord advocate. Dalrymple put a brave face on this 'oversight', but his friends did not like 'such jests that have so much the appearance of turning to earnest'. Dalrymple's attempt to salvage his reputation foundered because ministers had mistakenly come to believe that they were being subjected to an elaborate subterfuge. Henry St. John II* explained on 4 Sept. that it was now thought that Dundas was playing a role akin to that of Defoe in the publication of the pseudo-High Church pamphlet *The Shortest Way with Dissenters*:

> Many circumstances induce us to this opinion. Among others ... nothing weighs more with me than the behaviour of Sir David Dalrymple. The Queen's advocate he ought to be, and [yet] he proves rather the advocate of the Duchess of Gordon, of Dundas, and of whoever else may appear to have had a hand in sending, receiving, or defending the medal. His excuses are grounded on the weakness of the guilty persons, on the ill-temper of Scotland, and on mistakes in law, which I cannot persuade myself are real; but sure it is, that if the administration should be influenced by that coolness which he endeavours to inspire, he would himself hereafter prove one of the most forward to convert it into a crime ... The Queen is determined to turn his artifice upon his own head, and to remove him from his post, after which the most strict inquiry into this whole matter, and the most vigorous prosecution of it, will be directed.

Such a convoluted scenario was entirely out of character for Dalrymple, but the lingering reputation of his family may explain its credibility. The reasons behind Stewart's reappointment as lord advocate were obvious, and Dalrymple's subsequent alienation from the ministry explains why he failed to regain the post after Stewart's death in 1713. Speculation continued for some time over the true cause of Dalrymple's dismissal, the balance of opinion favouring the view that ministers had predetermined upon this course of action, but then made convenient use of the affair to placate the Hanoverian court. Dalrymple's attempts at self-justification fell on deaf ears, and, after travelling briefly to London, he learnt upon his return to Edinburgh that he was to be accused of malversation in the report by the commissioners of public accounts. It was gleefully reported in certain quarters that when Dalrymple arrived in London he would shortly follow Robert Walpole II* to the Tower.[15]

The report was presented to the Commons on 21 Dec. 1711 by Lockhart, whose role in attacking Dalrymple was far from incidental. The accusation proved identical to the rumours which had been reported to Dalrymple in November, namely that he had obtained £200 as part of 'the bargain for the forage in Scotland'.

> Sir Samuel MacClellan* had proposed Sir Alexander Murray [Dalrymple's son-in-law] to be a sharer in the contract, which the other partners rejected as being too young or not a man of business, but Sir Samuel having gone a great length ... could not come handsomely off without giving him some acknowledgement and that it was agreed to give him £200, which sum for his behalf was given in Scotland to you or your lady; now it seems that there was no transaction relating to that contract or if you had not such a sum ... Mr Walpole is just so concerned but for a greater sum ... he is much concerned about it, and indeed if the commissioners make any report like the town talk [of] nobody knows what sudden vote may pass to a man's prejudice.

Dalrymple's reaction was sanguine. 'I hear at a distance', he wrote to Brydges, that

> little arts are used to wound me, in my reputation, but I will wait patiently till I see what shape the malice of my undeserved enemies takes. I am sure if they charge me with anything that is not very clear, they do it falsely, and I shall be acquitted by such as know me, and especially by my own conscience.

He had no intention of resuming active political life, but contented himself with wishing well to the peace, if it were 'safe and honourable to the Queen', while doubting whether political stability were possible when 'what is done by the authority of the Queen, the government and Parliament today is treated with the utmost disrespect . . . the next. No state can flourish where neither maxims nor ministers have no[t] some established force.' In particular, he viewed English opposition to the Duke of Hamilton's right to a seat in the Lords as destructive to the Union. This stance as a remote commentator on the political fray was shattered by the warnings that he would have to answer the commissioners' charges in person. One friend informed Dalrymple that they 'cannot bring any part relating to you before the House till you are ordered to attend in your place, that being a privilege and form due to every Member', adding that this stigma might be avoided by someone 'making an excuse of the bad weather hindering you'; but he was unsure 'how far one dare venture upon that, considering how resolute you seem to be in not coming'. Another wrote directly to Dalrymple's wife, informing her bluntly that 'all his friends here reflect very much upon him for his not coming up all this time and throw it entirely upon you'. In response to this pressure Dalrymple travelled south, and was heard in his place on 19 Feb. 1712, immediately after the expulsion of Adam de Cardonnel from the House. No details of Dalrymple's speech are known but his defence can be reconstructed from his deposition and supporting evidence. The latter was not entirely convincing, consisting primarily of retrospectives testifying to the existence of a lost note by Murray authorizing Dalrymple to receive £200 on his behalf. The crux of the accusation that Dalrymple himself benefited from the transaction was apparently confirmed by his own deposition that he could not swear that 'the very sum or specie received was paid to the said Sir Alexander', but that he had subsequently given about £150 to Murray, who furthermore was 'debtor to this deponent in about . . . £670'. In other words, Dalrymple had used his influence to obtain an interest in the forage contract for his son-in-law, and then accepted the money himself to help finance loans to him. Dalrymple's conduct was technically legal, however, and he 'did so satisfy the House of his innocency, that no question was put upon him'. It also proved impossible to connect him with another set of accusations against William Cochrane*, despite the fact that Dalrymple had been promised 300 guineas as part of the money authorized under the 1709 Act enforcing payment of the drawbacks on salt-cured fish and meat. Fortunately for Dalrymple, his share of the money had not become available until November 1711, by which time it was apparent how unwise it would have been to accept such a reward while the public accounts commission was making inquiries. Despite pressure from the commissioners, the principal witness (although prepared to admit the original bargain) stuck fast to his story that Dalrymple had refused the money and pretended that he did not remember what Dalrymple's attitude had been when the original warrant for payment had been issued earlier in the year. That Dalrymple expected to profit from his legislative expertise and influence seems clear, but the extent to which this should be viewed as corrupt is a matter of perspective. Certainly, at the time of the agitation over the malt tax, he was legitimately retained by the Scottish brewers as a legal and parliamentary adviser.[16]

Persecution at the hands of the Tories drove Dalrymple into closer co-operation with the Whigs. The virulence with which he opposed the Scottish toleration and patronage bills in 1712 was not just a matter of Presbyterian principle, but amounted to early indications of his personal crusade to expose the latent Jacobitism in Scottish Tories. In his speech on the third reading of the toleration bill on 7 Feb., he declared that since no alterations were to be made 'in the body of the bill, he acquiesced; and only desired that the title might be changed thus: a bill for establishing Jacobitism and immorality in Scotland'. When the Lords' amendments were debated on 21 Feb., Dalrymple joined with Baillie in support of Presbyterian scruples over the wording of the abjuration oath, arguing that the regular clergy should be indulged, and tried to 'explain as far as was fit' the theological basis of the objection. He opposed on 13 Mar. the bill for restoring lay patronages and wrote a pamphlet on this topic, which became one of the standard authorities for 19th-century Presbyterians. In addition to historical and theological analysis, this contained a contemporary political message:

> Providence has delivered us from [lay patronage] . . . and we are as much secured against it, as our own particular laws, founded on the Claim of Right, and the treaty of Union can secure us . . . Many of the patrons in Scotland are neither well affected to the establishment of the church, nor to the civil government; and no doubt such patrons will present men to whom the church cannot agree; and then a division must arise betwixt the church and the patrons upon every occasion of a vacancy . . . the churches will be kept vacant to the great discouragement of religion and piety . . . to the great encouragement of trafficking popish priests.

Dalrymple also opposed, on 12 Mar., the bill for the restoration of the Yule Vacance in the court of session, which was likewise an episcopalian attack upon a sacred cow of Presbyterianism. He made similar objections to those on preceding issues, namely that Scottish rights under the Union were being infringed.[17]

On 27 Mar. 1712 he wrote to the Squadrone peer, Montrose, upon the 'melancholic scene' of Anglo-Scottish affairs:

> What can one think, or conclude? The nobility trampled on, the clergy of all sides set on edge . . . the administration before the Union, and the very circumstances of the Union treaty, exposed by the report of a favourite commission of accounts. The matter of passing of signatures made more strict, and in a view to improve it to be a revenue. No Scotsman that I know of trusted in direction of Scots affairs, nay the troops of our country are withdrawn, and while the sourness of our unhappy country increases towards our southern brethren, who do too visibly despise us, they are sent in greater numbers among us . . . But our last and uncurable [sic] misfortune is that our countrymen lead and encourage all men to hate and condemn us. If they are honoured with a whisper and a smile when a party measure is to be wrought, they are transported to forget themselves. When they are once in, on they dance, and to keep them in countenance they can whip one another and never want assistance. They have interest to set Church against Kirk till both bleed . . . For my part I shut my eyes like one on the brink of a precipice.

After returning home, Dalrymple remained in Scotland until after the malt tax crisis of 1713. His departure from Edinburgh in early June was noted by several observers, one of whom blamed him for having stayed away from Parliament during the preceding crisis, while another believed that he was now intent on bringing in a bill to dissolve the Union. By the time he arrived, this crisis had also passed and he was only able to participate in its after-effects by joining the Scottish opposition to the French commercial treaty, speaking and voting on 18 June against the bill confirming the 8th and 9th articles. In conversation a few days later with Lord Balmerino, who was sympathetic to Jacobitism, Dalrymple flatly denied Balmerino's contention that Scotland's ruin was a natural consequence of the Union irrespective of the malt tax. His campaign against Jacobitism was further evidenced in the general election, when he campaigned against Lockhart in Edinburghshire, eventually standing down prior to the poll. He was returned unopposed for Haddington Burghs.[18]

In the first session of 1714 Dalrymple continued to avoid nomination to select committees, being appointed only to draft two bills relating to the Equivalent (1 May, 14 June). He contributed to debate on major issues, speaking and voting on 18 Mar. against the expulsion of Richard Steele, and against the ministry on 15 Apr. on the question of the danger to the Hanoverian succession. The latter speech, according to Lockhart, was full of alarmist notions about the 'great increase in popery and the power of the Highland clans'. He voted on 12 May for extending the schism bill to cover Catholic education, and after the failure of this wrecking amendment later denounced the bill (presumably on the 24th at its second reading) as 'contrary to the law of nature by which parents had an absolute right to educate their children after what manner and with whom they pleased'. On 24 June he deserted Lockhart over a proposal to add a punitive clause to the bill for discharging the Equivalent commissioners, despite having co-operated with him in its formulation. On the 29th Lockhart reported in alarm that Dalrymple had come into possession of a pirated copy of his manuscript memoirs. Dark threats were made by Dalrymple that Lockhart faced compound actions for *scandalum magnatum*, which might reach a total of £30,000. Dalrymple arranged for the publication of the memoirs, writing an explanatory preface castigating the author's Jacobitism and offering translations of its terminology for a Hanoverian readership: 'When the reader finds the terms cavalier, royal family, prince, king, episcopal, dispersed through these memoirs, he cannot be at a loss for the meaning of them . . . in Revolution dialect [they] go for no more than Jacobite, a spurious issue, Pretender, mock-monarch, and popish persuasion.' Dalrymple was one of the Scottish Members 'expected in town' for the brief parliamentary session following the Queen's death, and was certainly in London during September and October, when he presented loyal addresses to George I from Edinburghshire and four of his constituency burghs. On 9 Oct. he was restored to his post as lord advocate and granted the same salary as previously. Listed as a Whig in the Worsley list and other comparative analyses of the Parliaments of 1713 and 1715, he continued to represent Haddington Burghs until his death. He now abandoned his earlier flirtation with abolishing the Union. His fears about Jacobitism were confirmed by the rising in 1715, which he described in September as having 'gone far enough to confound the impudence of the Tories, who have said and sworn so lately that our fears were imaginary or fictitious, and the silly scruples of the whimsical who fall in with them in a great measure'. He urged the government 'to act with vigour in quenching the flame that may spread and increase by very small accidents'. After the rebellion, however, he favoured clemency towards the rebels, and therefore avoided taking any part in the prosecutions at Carlisle by travelling to the Continent, ostensibly for his health. During his progress from Aix-la-Chapelle to Hanover, which included visits to Paris and Brussels, he met various Jacobites in exile. It was reported that he 'still complains of the measures that are taking, but continues still otherways in his former way of thinking . . . he seems not to be trusted by the present managers nor in any of their measures'. Although he remained in high office, Dalrymple was on indifferent terms with ministers, and at odds with them over major issues of Scottish policy. He opposed the forfeited estates bill in 1718, even publishing a pamphlet against it; privately, he dubbed it 'the damned bill of sale'. He retired from office in 1720, as part of the ministerial reconstruction after the reunion of the Whig party, receiving a sinecure of £1,200 p.a. with a reversion to his eldest son. He died on 3 Dec. 1721 and was buried at Morham in Haddingtonshire, leaving his entire property to his eldest son, James†, but making provision for his wife's annuities and giving her discretionary powers to apportion some money to his second son.[19]

[1] *Scots Peerage* ed. Paul, viii. 143; *Edinburgh Graduates*, 117; *Hist. Scot. Parl.* 174. [2] *Scot. Rec. Soc.* lxii. 51; lvi. 257; SRO, Dunbar burgh recs. B18/13/2 f. 245; Carnegie Lib. Ayr, Ayr burgh recs. B6/18/8, council mins. 4 Oct. 1709. [3] *Scot. Rec. Soc.* lxxvi. 49. [4] *Hist. Scot. Parl.* 174–6; *Stair Annals*, i. 351–2; *DNB* (Dalrymple, Sir James; Dalrymple, Sir John); P. W. J. Riley, *King Wm. and Scot. Politicians*, 16–18; *Anglo-Dutch Moment* ed. Israel, 168–70; *HMC Laing*, ii. 63; *Lockhart Mems.* ed. Szechi, 59. [5] *Stair Annals*, 65–66; NLS, ms 25276/1, Dalrymple to son, 28 Mar. 1712; info. from Dr P. W. J. Riley on members of Scot. parl.; Riley, *King Wm.* 78, 175; *Darien Pprs.* (Bannatyne Club, xc), 377; Boyer, *Anne Annals*, iii. app. 44; *Orig. Pprs.* ed. Macpherson, ii. 15. [6] P. W. J. Riley, *Union*, 176, 182–9; Boyer, v. 65; *HMC Mar and Kellie*, i. 272, 408, 410; *Crossrigg Diary*, 184; info. from Dr Riley; P. W. J. Riley, *Eng. Ministers and Scotland*, 36; SRO, Clerk of Penicuik mss GD18/3134, p. 2, 'Mems. of Affairs of Scot. aft. Adjournment of Parl.'; GD18/3135/12, John Clerk* to fa. 24 Apr. 1707. [7] SRO, Ogilvy of Inverquharity mss GD205/32/2, Robert to [William Bennet], 1 Oct. 1707; *Vernon–Shrewsbury Letters*, iii. 285, 290, 358; Roxburghe mss at Floors Castle, bdle. 739, Bennet to Countess of Roxburghe, 16 Dec. 1707; Cunningham, *Hist. GB*, ii. 138; Northants. RO, Montagu (Boughton) mss 48/177, Vernon to Shrewsbury, 15 Jan. 1707–8; Speck thesis, 168–9. [8] Atholl mss at Blair Atholl, box 45, bdle. 8, no. 7, [–] to [–], 9 Feb. 1708; *HMC Mar and Kellie*, 429; Montagu (Boughton) mss 48/183, Vernon to Shrewsbury, 29 Jan. 1707–8; *HMC Portland*, iv. 478; *Nicolson Diaries* ed. Jones and Holmes, 455; Boyer, vi. 339. [9] Add. 28055, f. 426; SRO, Mar and Kellie mss GD124/768/2, 3, Ld. Grange (Hon. James Erskine†) to Mar, 24 Jan. 1708, David Erskine to same, 20 Jan. 1708; GD124/831/32, 34, Sir David Nairne to same, 3, 6 July 1708; GD124/15/897/1, 2, Mar to Dalrymple, 5 Oct. 1708, Dalrymple to Mar, 12 Oct. 1708; Ogilvy of Inverquharity mss GD205/36/6, Grey Neville* to Bennet, 11 July 1708; Clerk of Penicuik mss GD18/3140/14, Clerk to fa. 13 Apr. 1708; GD18/2092/2, 'Moral Journals', 1 Mar. 1708; Folger Shakespeare Lib. Newdigate newsletter 4 May 1708; NLS, Advocates' mss, Wodrow pprs. letters Quarto, 5, f. 8; *Baillie Corresp.* 192; SRO, Haddington sheriff ct. recs. SC40/68/3, pp. 5–6, Haddington poll, 24 May 1708; *HMC Portland*, x. 455; *Cal. Treas. Bks.* xxii. 113, 120; *Stair Annals*, 239. [10] *HMC Mar and Kellie*, 477–8; NLS, ms 14415, ff. 170–1; 7021, f. 161; DZA, Bonet despatch 25 Jan./5 Feb. 1709; *HMC Lords*, n.s. viii. 3. [11] NLS, ms 16502, ff. 232–3; 17498, ff. 94–101; *Lockhart Mems.* ed. Szechi, 276; *Lockhart Pprs.* i. 300–1, 532–3; *Nicolson Diaries*, 493; Huntington Lib. Loudoun mss 8319, Dalrymple to [Loudoun], 13 Feb. 1709; *Cal. Treas. Bks.* xxiv. 128.

[12] Riley, *Eng. Ministers*, 97; G. W. T. Omond, *Ld. Advocates of Scotland.* i. 282–6; *Wodrow Corresp.* ed. McCrie, i. 18, 20, 69, 79; SRO, Hume of Marchmont mss GD158/1117/2, Baillie to Marchmont, 1 June 1709; Loudoun mss 8343, [Dalrymple] to [Loudoun], 2 June 1709; Douglas-Home mss at the Hirsel, Box 21, folder 4, same to Hume, 22 Oct. 1705; SRO, Stair mss GD135/140 f. 1, same to Godolphin, 4 July 1709; Huntington Lib. Stowe mss 58(4), pp. 196–7. [13] Add. 70421, newsletter 2 Mar. 1709–10; G. Holmes, *Trial of Sacheverell*, 118; *Cal. Treas. Bks.* xxiv. 21, 32, 382; NLS, ms 25276/20–23, 'Some Particulars Humbly Offered to Ld. Treasurer', 26 Apr. 1710; 25276/37–8, 'Petition on behalf of Dalrymple', [c. June 1710]; *HMC 14th Rep III*, 208; Mar and Kellie mss GD124/15/975/11, Mar to Ld. Grange, 29 July 1710. [14] Add. 70222, Dalrymple to Harley, 10 Oct. 1710; *HMC Portland*, iv. 558, 622; Riley, *Eng. Ministers*, 150; Wodrow pprs. letters Quarto 5, f. 70; Haddington mss at Mellerstain, Baillie to wife, 14 June 1711 (Jones trans.); G. Holmes, *Pol. in Age of Anne*, 357. [15] Omond 291–6; SP54/4/15, 20, 26; Boyer, x. 203–12; *HMC Portland*, iv. 695; x. 384, 396; *Stair Soc.* xxix. 293–4; *Bolingbroke Corresp.* i. 343; Add. 17677 EEE, f. 314; Mar and Kellie mss GD124/15/1024/23, Mar to Ld. Grange, 21 Sept. 1711; SRO, Montrose mss GD220/5/256/9, Baillie to Montrose, 16 Oct. 1711; NLS, ms 25276/43, John Montgomery to Dalrymple, 18 Oct. 1711; SRO, Campbell of Balcardine mss GD170/630/10, John to Alexander Campbell, 14 Nov. 1711; NLS, ms 16503, ff. 28–29; Atholl mss, box 45, bdle. 10, no. 2, James Murray to Atholl, 25 Jan. 1712. [16] NLS, ms 16503, ff. 1–2, 28–29, 48; 17498, f. 133; Stowe mss, 58(10), pp. 253–4; NLS, Douglas of Cavers mss, Acc. 7488/1, William Douglas† to Archibald Douglas*, 19 Feb. 1711–12; Wodrow pprs. letters Quarto 6, f. 116; Scot. Hist. Soc. *Misc.* xii. 159. [17] Wodrow, *Analecta*, i. 7; Haddington mss, 5, Baillie to wife, 7 Feb., 13, 29 Mar. 1711–12 (Jones trans.); Boyer, x. 345; *Wodrow Corresp.* 277; Montrose mss GD220/5/268/10, [Baillie] to Montrose, 15 Mar. 1711–12; *An Account of Lay Patronages in Scotland* (1712); NSA, Kreienberg despatch 14 Mar. 1712. [18] Montrose mss GD220/5/278, Dalrymple to Montrose, 27 Mar. 1712; Atholl mss, box 45, bdle. 11, nos. 24–25, John Flemyng to [Atholl], 8 June 1713, John Douglas to [same], 8 June 1713; *HMC Portland*, 296; *Parlty. Hist.* i. 69; Scot. Hist. Soc. *Misc.* 164; Clerk of Penicuik mss GD18/3149/2, Dalrymple to Sir John Clerk, 2 Mar. 1713; *Lockhart Letters* ed. Szechi, 85. [19] Douglas Diary (Hist. of Parl. trans.), 18 Mar., 15 Apr. 1714; *Lockhart Letters*, 98, 106–14; *Lockhart Pprs.* 569; *Lockhart Mems.* 269; *Flying Post*, 12–14 Aug. 1714; *London Gazette*, 28 Sept.–2 Oct., 30 Oct.–2 Nov. 1714; *Memorial concerning the State Prisoners* (1716); *Observations on the Bill for the Sale of Forfeited Estates* (1718); Add. 38507, f. 178; *HMC 10th Rep I*, 148; Stowe 158, ff. 101–8; *Stair Annals*, i. 321–5; ii. 45, 47, 346; *HMC Polwarth*, i. 95; *HMC Stuart*, ii. 129, 231; iii. 176, 190–1, 205–6, 293, 451; vii. 301; *Scots Peerage*, 143; PCC 29 Bolton.

D. W.

DALRYMPLE, Hon. William (1678–1744), of Glenmuir, Ayr.

SCOTLAND	1707–1708
CLACKMANNANSHIRE	1708–1710
WIGTOWN BURGHS	1722–1727
WIGTOWNSHIRE	1727–1741

bap. 11 Oct. 1678, 5th but 2nd surv. s. of John Dalrymple, 1st Earl of Stair [S], by Elizabeth, da. and h. of Sir James Dundas of Newliston, Linlithgow. m. 26 Feb. 1698, his cos. Penelope, *suo jure* Countess of Dumfries [S], da. of Charles, Ld. Crichton (2nd s. *d.v.p.* of William Crichton, 2nd Earl of Dumfries [S]) and sis. and h. of William Crichton (*d.*1694), 3rd Earl of Dumfries, 6s. (3 *d.v.p.*) 2da.[1]

MP [S] Ayrshire 1702–7.

Jt. muster master gen. [S] 1706; commr. Equivalent [S] 1707–19; capt. and lt.-col. 3 Ft. Gds (Scots Gds.) Sept. 1710–1714.²

Sheriff, Clackmannanshire 1708–d.; burgess, Edinburgh 1708, Ayr 1717.³

A Court drudge in the Scottish parliament, as befitted his filial attachment to the Stair–Queensberry alliance, Dalrymple seems to have served there in silence, except for his participation in a Court-inspired protest on 7 Aug. 1703 against an additional clause in the Act of Security. Even in 1704, in the division on the Duke of Hamilton's motion on the succession, he registered his factional allegiance by absenting himself rather than by casting a vote in favour. A nominal attempt was made to gratify him with a half-share in William Bennet's* office of muster master general in 1706, but he derived no real benefit from this gesture, nor did he succeed to the whole when Bennet himself subsequently fell out of favour. Dalrymple voted a straight Court line over the Union, with few absences, thereby earning a place on the Equivalent commission and a seat in the first Parliament of Great Britain.⁴

In the Commons, Dalrymple presented papers to the House on behalf of the Equivalent commissioners on 22 and 31 Jan. 1708, and also signed their memorial to the Treasury complaining of the lack of payment of either salary or expenses. He remained loyal to the Court and was returned in 1708 for Clackmannanshire, where he had been acquiring property since at least 1704. In May 1708, barely three weeks before the meeting of the freeholders' court, a charter was passed to validate his purchase of the sheriffdom of the county (in conjunction with a sleeping partner, Alexander Inglis) at a judicial sale of the estate of the former sheriff, David Bruce. At the election Dalrymple enjoyed the support of Lord Mar, the principal magnate in the shire, who allegedly created some eight or nine 'fictitious votes' for him. Dalrymple was returned following a bitterly fought contest with Hon. Charles Rosse*, and though Rosse petitioned against the return no report was made. In February 1709 Dalrymple was granted a vacant company in the Scots Guards, at his father's express request. He does not appear to have gone to Spain with his regiment, and so avoided its disastrous surrender at Brihuega. Continuing to support the Court in Parliament, he presented further documents from the Equivalent commissioners on 3 Mar. 1709, and the following year voted for the impeachment of Dr Sacheverell.⁵

Clackmannanshire did not elect in 1710, and by 1713 Dalrymple was no longer on good terms with Mar. He was obliged to wait until 1722 before returning to the Commons, this time on his family's interest in Wigtownshire. Having at first settled into his natural groove as a supporter of administration, he went into opposition in 1733 with his brother, the 2nd Earl of Stair, and stayed there. Dalrymple died on 30 Nov. 1744. His eldest surviving son, William, had already succeeded to his mother's title as Earl of Dumfries; the second son, James, inherited the earldom of Stair in 1747, which on his death in 1760 also passed to William.⁶

¹ *Scots Peerage* ed. Paul, iii. 236; viii. 149–50. ² Boyer, *Anne Annals*, vi. 234; *Cal. Treas. Bks.* xxiii. 234; xxix. 342; xxxi. 578–9. ³ J. Wallace, *Sheriffdom of Clackmannan*, 54, 108–11; Carnegie Lib. Ayr, Ayr burgh recs. B6/18/9, council mins. 10 July 1717. ⁴ Info. from Dr P. W. J. Riley on members of Scot. parl.; SRO, Ogilvy of Inverquharity mss GD205/37/8, Bennet to William Nisbet*, 16 Oct. 1708; R. Walcott, *Pol. Early 18th Cent.* 234; *APS*, xi. 73; P. W. J. Riley, *Union*, 93, 331. ⁵ *Cal. Treas. Bks.* xxii. 79; SRO, Alloa sheriffs' ct. recs. SC64/63/24, Clackmannan. electoral ct. mins. 16 June 1708; *SRO Indexes*, iii. 226–7; Wallace, 52–55, 108–11; *HMC Mar and Kellie*, i. 477; SRO, Mar and Kellie mss GD124/10/959, Alexander Rait to Mar, 17 Feb. 1709; Add. 61628, ff. 174–5; 61631, ff. 61–62; Lincs. AO, Yarborough mss 16/7/1, Defoe to Duke of Leeds (Sir Thomas Osborne†), 29 June 1708; *Marlborough–Godolphin Corresp.* 1219. ⁶ *Scots Peerage*, 149–50.

D. W. H.

DANBY, Sir Abstrupus (1655–1727), of Masham, nr. Ripon, Yorks.

ALDBOROUGH 1698–1700

b. 27 Dec. 1655, 1st s. of Christopher Danby, of Farnley, Yorks. by Anne, da. of John Colepeper. m. bef. 1679, Judith, da. of Abraham Moone of Great St. Helen's, Bishopsgate, London, wid. of William Davies of Old Jewry, London, 1s. 2da. suc. fa. 1689; kntd. 30 Aug. 1691.¹

Commr. Aire and Calder navigation 1699.²

Described as 'courteous', 'very obliging' and of an 'ancient' family, Danby was the grandson of Sir Thomas Danby, who owned ten manors and over 2,000 acres as well as coal mines in Yorkshire, and sat as a Royalist in the Long Parliament until being disabled in 1642. Danby himself was well provided for in Yorkshire: in 1685 the rental on his estate stood at £2,714 p.a. In 1687 his kinsman, Thomas, 2nd Lord Colepeper, informed him that he was being considered for inclusion in the county commission of the peace, though this appointment does not appear to have been made. The following year, however, he was listed as one of the justices for the North Riding. It appears that Danby first expressed his political ambitions in 1691, when, following the death of Sir Edmund Jennings, he considered contesting the ensuing by-election at Ripon, where he had an electoral interest.

In the end he decided against it, explaining to Lord Carmarthen (Sir Thomas Osborne†), that he had 'waived the thoughts of standing . . . so that Mr [Jonathan] Jennings* enjoys the fruits of your lordship's favours, none opposing my lord archbishop's [of York] letter'. However, in 1698 Danby was successful at Aldborough, where he had the support of the Wentworth family, who were lords of the manor. However, the election had been keenly contested, and cost Danby a great deal of time and money, as well as presents of free coal for the electors. A satirical poem relating to the election referred to him as 'the weathercock Sir Scrupulous Danby', and admonished the electors for selling their votes 'for ale and smoke':

> What can you gain if you elect a knight
> who built a house yet ne'er did workmen right.
> Perhaps he courts because he stands in dread
> 'tis sometimes payment privilege to plead
> Or like his neighbours he'll your freehold take
> And make you slaves and vassals for his sake
> Pull down your houses and enclose your bound
> Alter your bridges till his neighbours drowned
> Such kindnesses as these he keeps in store
> not to relieve but to destroy the poor.

On 12 Dec. Danby's opponents, Christopher Tancred* and Cyril Arthington*, petitioned unsuccessfully against his return, alleging that Danby and his agents had resorted to bribery. In late 1698 Danby was forecast as likely to oppose a standing army, but he was not active in Parliament. In an analysis of the House into interests in January–May 1700 he was noted as doubtful or of the opposition.[3]

During 1700 it began to become apparent that Danby's interest at Aldborough was not secure. The Wentworths were rumoured to be withdrawing their support and looking to sell the manor of Aldborough. Danby failed to secure the purchase of the manor late in that year, for which reason he appears to have decided against contesting the first 1701 election in the borough. Prior to the second 1701 election, he turned his attention back to Ripon, where he had the support of Sir Jonathan Jennings*. However, with John Aislabie* almost certain of winning one seat, Danby had to fight a campaign against John Sharp*, son of the archbishop of York. Although the archbishop was normally opposed to interfering in Yorkshire elections, he made an exception for Ripon. In October one of Danby's agents tried to come to an accommodation with Aislabie and Sharp, but to no avail. Canvassing became more intense following the dissolution of Parliament. However, Danby's efforts proved to be in vain, for on the day of the poll he came a poor third.[4]

Despite his defeat in 1701, Danby continued to take an active interest in Yorkshire politics, being asked to use his interest in 1713 for Lord Downe [I] (Hon. Henry Dawnay*) and Sir Arthur Kaye, 3rd Bt.*, in the county election, and considering putting himself or his son up at a by-election at Ripon in 1719. He also took a very active role in the management of his estate, noting at one point that 'I never have any money beforehand, and as we have managed thus far, cannot keep out of debt'. However, he must have had a substantial turnover of capital because in 1707 he secured a chancery decree against one Mr Palmes, who owed Danby 'near £20,000'. Thomas Hearne reported that in about 1708 Danby spent some time in Oxford, gaining admission to the Bodleian Library and looking over

> Mr Dodsworth's manuscript collections with great diligence, purely, I suppose, for things concerning his own estate and family, and he and his servant with him extracted many things. He was then a very old, but brisk, regular man and used to rise very early in a morning.

Danby also continued to figure as a prominent character in Yorkshire. In 1715 Lord Burlington, the lord lieutenant of the East and West Ridings, desired that Danby meet him at Leeds with as many men as possible for the defence of the county against the Jacobite rising. Danby died on 27 Dec. 1727. By his will his principal heir was his son, Abstrupus, though he made financial provisions, ranging from £10 to £50, for various relatives.[5]

[1] Thoresby, *Ducatus Leodiensis*, 202; *Thoresby Soc.* xxxvii. 2; J. Fisher, *Hist. Masham*, 244; J. R. Woodhead, *Rulers of London* (London and Mdx. Arch. Soc.), 116–17. [2] *HMC Lords*, n.s. iii. 204. [3] *Thoresby Diary*, i. 352; ii. 220; Keeler, *Long Parl.* 152–3; N.Yorks. RO, Swinton mss, Danby pprs. ZS, estate rental, 28 Jan. 1685, Ld. Colepeper to Danby, 2 July 1687, Danby to Carmarthen, 2 Nov. 1691, same to Lady Wentworth, 5 Aug. 1698, 'Ten rhymes for nine reasons', [n.d.]; Duckett, *Penal Laws and Test Act* (1883), 292; Luttrell, *Brief Relation*, iv. 610, 619. [4] Swinton mss, Danby pprs. ZS, Edward Morris to Danby, 5 May, 26 July 1700, same to Thomas Johnson, 2 Sept. 1700, Lady Wentworth to Danby, 7, 17, 21 Sept., 10 Oct. 1700, Danby to Morris, 17 Sept. 1700, Jennings to Danby, 28 Sept. 1701, John Wastwell to same, 16 Oct. 1701, Robert Bayne to same, 14 Nov. 1701, 'persons to be elected at Ripon', 24 Nov. 1701. [5] Swinton mss, Danby pprs. ZS, Danby to Thomas Johnson, 26 Jan. 1692, 28 Sept., 3 Oct. 1700, 5 July 1707, Aislabie to Danby, 18 Oct. 1713, Burlington to same, 7 Nov. 1715, Danby to Aislabie, 28 June 1719; *Hearne Colls.* ix. 391–2; Borthwick Inst. York, wills, prerog. court, Oct. 1729.

E. C./C. I. M.

DANIELL, William (1665–98), of St. Margaret's, Preshute, Wilts.

MARLBOROUGH 1695–25 Apr. 1698

bap. 29 Jan. 1665, o. surv. s. of Jeffrey Daniel(l)† of St. Margaret's, Preshute by his 2nd w. Rachel, da. of John Ernle of Whetham House, Calne, Wilts. *educ.* Magdalen, Oxf. 1682; M. Temple 1684. *unm. suc.* fa. 1681.[1]

Daniell was a minor at his father's death in 1681, but was provided with a generous maintenance. He also had substantial connexions among north Wiltshire gentry, including his guardians Sir John Ernle*, Sir Henry Goodricke, 2nd Bt.*, and Thomas Fettiplace. This pedigree and local standing helped Daniell regain his father's old seat at Marlborough at the second attempt in 1695, having been defeated by Thomas Bennet* at a by-election in January of that year. Forecast as likely to oppose the Court in the division of 31 Jan. 1696 over the proposed council of trade, he refused the Association, and subsequently voted against fixing the price of guineas at 22*s*. In the next session he voted against Sir John Fenwick's† attainder on 25 Nov. On 13 Feb. 1697 he reported from the committee appointed to scrutinize the ballot for an accounts commissioner.[2]

Daniell died in London on 25 Apr. 1698 and was buried in Preshute church, where a plaque was raised to his memory, on 3 May following. His sister, the wife of Thomas Fettiplace of Fernham, Shrivenham, Oxfordshire, inherited the Preshute estate, which her son eventually sold in 1714.[3]

[1] *Wilts. Arch. Mag.* xxx. 104; *Coll. Top. et Gen.* v. 349. [2] PCC 103 Drax; Wilts. RO, Marlborough ct. bk. 1684–96, G22/1/24, p. 104; *Coll. Top. et Gen.* 349; J. Waylen, *Hist. Marlborough*, 500. [3] *Wilts. Arch. Mag.* xxx. 104; xlvi. 70.

D. W. H./H. J. L.

DARCY, Conyers (c.1685–1758), of Aske, nr. Richmond, Yorks.

YORKSHIRE	3 Dec. 1707–1708
NEWARK	1715–1722
RICHMOND	1722–1727, 14 Mar. 1728–1747
YORKSHIRE	1747–1 Dec. 1758

b. c.1685, 2nd surv. s. of Hon. John Darcy† of Hornby Castle, Yorks. (*d.v.p.* s. of Conyers Darcy†, 2nd Earl of Holdernesse) by Bridget, da. of Robert Sutton†, 1st Baron Lexington. *educ.* ?Eton 1698; King's Coll. Camb. matric. 1703. *m.* (1) Aug. 1714, Lady Mary (*d.* 1726), da. of Hans Willem Bentinck, 1st Earl of Portland, sis. of Henry Bentinck*, Visct. Woodstock, and wid. of Algernon Capell, 2nd Earl of Essex, *s.p.*; (2) 12 Sept. 1728, Elizabeth (*d.* 1741), da. of John Rotherham of Much Waltham, Essex, wid. of Sir Theophilus Napier, 5th Bt., of Luton Hoo, Beds. and Thomas, 6th Baron Howard of Effingham, *s.p.* KB 27 May 1725.[1]

Cornet and maj. 1 Life Gds. 1706–15; gent. of horse 1710–17; avener and clerk martial 1711–17; commr. executing the office of master of the horse 1712–14, 1715–17; master of Household 1720–May 1730, comptroller May 1730–55.[2]

Bailiff and steward of Richmond 1721–*d.*; ld. lt. N. Riding, Yorks. 1727–40.

The Darcys were one of the leading Whig families in the North Riding. In the 1690s Darcy's brother, the 3rd Earl of Holdernesse, obtained the office of bailiff and steward of the liberty of Richmond, with reversion to Darcy himself. The family already held a substantial number of burgages in Richmond, which they gradually increased by purchase.[3]

Although proposed as a potential candidate for Yorkshire prior to a by-election in January 1707, Darcy did not stand for the county until a second by-election in December, at which he was returned unopposed. He was listed as a Whig in an analysis of Parliament in early 1708. At the general election later the same year he stood again, but was defeated in one of the fiercest county contests of the period, and in 1710 refused to stand. Though a Whig, he became gentleman of the horse and a joint commissioner of the office of master of the horse under the new Tory administration, despite protests from Horatio Walpole I*, who claimed that 'her Majesty's person is not safe' in Darcy's hands. Remaining in office, he re-entered Parliament in 1715, when he was listed as a Whig in a comparative analysis with the 1713 Parliament. He continued to sit in Parliament after the Hanoverian succession as a Whig. He died on 1 Dec. 1758.[4]

[1] *Dugdale's Vis. Yorks.* ed. Clay, ii. 84. [2] Info. from Prof. R. O. Bucholz; Boyer, *Anne Annals*, ix. 279; *Pol. State*, i–ii. 54; iv. 31. [3] *Cal. Treas. Bks.* x. 54; xi. 257; xvii. 287; xx. 659. [4] Cumbria RO (Carlisle), Lonsdale mss D/Lons/L1/4/Stray letters (Wharton), Ld. Carlisle (Charles Howard*) to [Thomas, Ld. Wharton*], 13 Dec. 1707; W. A. Speck, *Tory and Whig*, 147; Luttrell, *Brief Relation*, vi. 673; *Swift Stella* ed. Davis, 376; Add. 70262, Walpole to Ld. Oxford (Robert Harley*), [1712]; Clay, 84.

E. C./C. I. M.

DARCY, James (1650–1731), of Sedbury Park, nr. Richmond, Yorks.

RICHMOND 1698–1701 (Nov.), 1702–1705

b. 21 Aug. 1650, 1st s. of Hon. James Darcy† (yr. s. of Conyers, 5th Baron Darcy and 1st Earl of Holdernesse) by Isabel, da. of Sir Marmaduke Wyvill, 2nd Bt.†, of Burton Constable, Yorks. *educ.* Sidney Sussex, Camb. 1668. *m.* (1) Bethia (*d.* 1671), da. of George Payler of Nun Monkton, Yorks., 1da.; (2) Anne, da. of Ralph Stawell†, 1st Baron Stawell of Somerton, 3da.; (3) lic. 19 Oct. 1693, Mary (*d.* 1710), da. of Sir William Hickes, 2nd Bt., of Ruckholts, Essex, *s.p.*; (4) 6 Apr. 1725, Margaret

Garth, of Forcett, Yorks., *s.p. suc.* fa. 1673; *cr.* Baron Darcy of Navan, co. Meath [I] 13 Sept. 1721.¹

Darcy's return for Richmond in 1698 was largely the result of the electoral influence of his Whig cousin, the 3rd Earl of Holdernesse, and presumably for this reason he was classified as a Court supporter in a comparative analysis of the old and new Parliaments. However, he was in fact a political follower of the Tory William Bromley II*, who, like Darcy, had married a daughter of Ralph, 1st Lord Stawell. In late 1698 Darcy was forecast as likely to oppose a standing army. However, he was not an active Member, which may help to account for the fact that in an analysis of the House into interests in 1700 he was classed as doubtful or of the opposition. Having been returned unopposed for Richmond in the first 1701 election, he was listed as likely to support the Court in agreeing with the supply committee's resolution to continue the 'Great Mortgage'.²

Darcy did not contest the second 1701 election, at which time it was reported that John Hutton I*, a Whig, 'turns out of Richmond Mr. Darcy'. However, he was returned unopposed once more in the general election of 1702, though he continued to be inactive in Parliament. In early 1704 he was noted as a supporter of Lord Nottingham (Daniel Finch†) over the Scotch Plot. At the beginning of the 1704–5 session he was forecast as a probable supporter of the Tack, and was included in Robert Harley's* lobbying list. On 28 Nov. Darcy voted for the Tack, an action that provoked the anger of Lord Wharton (Hon. Thomas*), who was actively trying to increase his own interest in Richmond. In December Wharton declared himself willing to serve Lord Holderness' brother and Darcy's cousin, Conyers Darcy*, but that he would oppose James Darcy, whatever the expense. Wharton did not like the behaviour of Darcy, 'who has very much of late increased that dislike'. In the 1705 election Wharton secured the election of one of his own relations, Wharton Dunch*, in place of Darcy. Darcy petitioned, on the grounds that Wharton, as a peer, should not have 'meddled' in the election at all, let alone by corrupt means. However, he was given permission to withdraw his petition on 21 Nov., following a motion to that effect by Bromley, possibly so that Darcy could contest the by-election at Richmond necessitated by Dunch's death. However, Darcy did not contest the by-election the following month. In 1710 Robert Monckton*, a Whig, reported Darcy's dinner conversation to Robert Harley*, stating that he believed that what Darcy had said 'was not his own but the dictates of the [Tory] party'. Aside from his elevation to an Irish peerage in 1721, which argues some modification in his political views, little more has been discovered of Darcy prior to his death on 19 July 1731. The newly acquired title devolved on his grandson, James Jessop, afterwards Darcy, the son of William Jessop* by Mary, Darcy's daughter by his first wife.³

¹ *Dugdale's Vis. Yorks.* ed. Clay, ii. 81–82. ² Fieldhouse and Jennings, *Hist. Richmond and Swaledale*, 263; *HMC Portland*, iv. 574; Bagot mss at Levens Hall, Bromley to James Grahme*, 26 July 1707. ³ Add. 24475, f. 134; G. Holmes, *Electorate and National Will*, 6; Fieldhouse and Jennings, 413–14; L. P. Wenham, *Richmond Burgage Houses* (N. Yorks. publ. 16), 2–3; Robbins thesis, 195–7, 442–3; Quinn thesis, 123–5, 237, 239; *HMC Portland*, 574; Clay, 82.

E. C./C. I. M.

DARCY, Sir Thomas, 1st Bt. (1632–1693), of Braxted Lodge, Essex.

MALDON 1679 (Oct.)–1681 (Mar.)
     1685–1687, 1689–Apr. 1693

b. 1 Jan. 1632, posth. and o. s. of Thomas Darcy of Tiptree Priory, Essex by Mary, da. of Sir Andrew Astley of Writtle, Essex. *educ.* Jesus, Camb. 1650; G. Inn 1652. *m.* (1) c. 1657, Cicely (*d.* 1661), da. of Sir Simonds D'Ewes, 1st Bt.†, of Stowlangtoft Hall, Suff. and h. to her gdfa. Sir William Clopton of Kentwell, Suff., 1 da.; (2) lic. 12 Feb. 1663, Jane, da. and h. of Robert Cole, barrister, of the Middle Temple, 5s. (4 *d.v.p.*) 3 da. *suc.* fa. at birth, gdfa. 1638; *cr.* Bt. 19 June 1660.

Gent. privy chamber (extraordinary) 1660.¹

Freeman, Maldon 1679.²

Darcy, the ward of Sir Thomas Honywood†, was a 'Puritan bred and born' and was returned at the elections of 1679 and 1681 as a Country candidate for Maldon, near his estate. However, his friendship with his neighbour, the 2nd Duke of Albemarle (Christopher Monck†), moderated his views, and it was through the latter's influence that he was re-elected for the borough in 1685. Removed from local office under James II for his unwillingness to comply with the King's religious policy, he was returned for the town in 1689 and again in 1690. After he had been listed as a Tory in 1690 by Lord Carmarthen (Sir Thomas Osborne†), and as one of the latter's followers, Darcy's most significant act in the first session was to serve as teller on a procedural motion. Classed as a Country supporter in April 1691, he served again as a teller on 8 Dec. on a report from the committee of elections in favour of a restricted franchise at Dunwich, thereby securing the return of the Tory John Bence*. He died in April 1693, and stated in his will that he had 'assured hopes of glorious resurrection when this mortal shall put on immortality'. He left his property to his son, George, a minor who died young. The estate then passed to his three daughters, the eldest of whom married a future archbishop of York, Sir William Dawes, 2nd Bt., and the youngest married William Pierrepont*. Their provision may have tipped the family, which had sold Tiptree in 1637, further into debt. Part of the estate was sold in 1690, and a bill was pushed through Parliament in February 1699 to allow the sale of further portions after the baronetcy's extinction.[3]

[1] LC 3/2. [2] Essex RO, D/B3/1/23 Maldon bor. recs., 23 May 1679. [3] *VCH Essex*, v. 273, 294; *Bramston Autobiog.* (Cam. Soc. xxxii), 374; PCC 50 Coker; Morant, *Essex*, ii. 41, 139; F. Chancellor, *Ancient and Sepulchral Mons.* 159.

M. J. K.

DARELL, Henry (aft. 1664–1706), of Chawcroft, Hants and Trewornan, Cornw.

LISKEARD   12 Nov. 1696–1701 (Nov.)

b. aft. 1664, 1st s. of Thomas Darell of Chawcroft (*d.v.p.*, s. of Thomas Darell of Trewornan) by Elizabeth, da. and h. of Henry Bromfield of Chawcroft. *m*. bef. 1697, Anne Sagittary (*d*. 1697), 2s. (1 *d.v.p.*) 3da. (1 *d.v.p.*) *suc*. fa. 1683; gdfa. at Trewornan 1698.[1]
Sub-commr. prizes, Plymouth Apr. 1705–*d*.[2]

Darell was descended from Sir Thomas Darell, MP for East Retford in 1604. His grandfather, a London merchant, had gained Trewornan, near Liskeard, by marriage. Returned unopposed at a by-election for Liskeard in 1696, Darell was again successful in 1698 on the recommendation of the recorder, Bishop Trelawny of Exeter. Shortly afterwards, Darell was forecast as likely to oppose the standing army, and a comparison of the old and new Commons classed him as a Country supporter. Darell was absent at a call of the House on 8 Jan. 1700 and was ordered into custody, not being released until the 22nd. He was an inactive Member, making no recorded speech. Re-elected in January 1701, he does not appear on any subsequent list and after the dissolution no longer figured as a parliamentary candidate. In April 1705 he replaced John Manley* as sub-commissioner of prizes in Plymouth, a post he held until his death on 4 Feb. 1706. Darell died intestate, and on 12 Dec. 1706 his wife petitioned the Commons for a bill allowing the sale of part of his estates, estimated to be worth £600 p.a., in order to satisfy debts amounting to £8,000 and to provide for his younger children. Such a bill was ordered and gained the Royal Assent in March 1707.[3]

[1] Vivian, *Vis. Cornw.* 481; *Vis. Eng. and Wales Notes* ed. Crisp, xi. 122–3. [2] *Cal. Treas. Bks.* xx. 232, 682. [3] *Vis. Eng. and Wales Notes*, 122–3; HMC Lords, n.s. vii. 24–25; Boase and Courtney, *Bibl. Cornub.* 1147.

E. C.

DARELL, Sir John (1645–94), of Calehill, Little Chart, Kent.

MAIDSTONE   1679 (Mar.–July)
RYE   1679 (Oct.)–1681 (Mar.), 1689–c.Jan.1694

bap. 20 Aug. 1645, 1st s. of Edward Darell of Gray's Inn by Dorothy, da. of Robert Kipping of Tudeley, Kent. *educ*. G. Inn, entered 1658; Corpus, Oxf. 1663. *m*. 4 Aug. 1670, his cos. Elizabeth (*d*. 1672), da. and h. of Sir John Darell of Calehill, *s.p. suc*. fa. 1664; kntd. 26 July 1670; *suc*. his uncle Sir John Darell at Calehill 1675.[1]
Member, Soc. of Mines Royal 1666, asst. 1669–74, 1675–7, 1682–3; member, Soc. of Mineral and Battery Works 1667, asst. 1671–7.
Commr. recusants, Kent 1675; freeman, Maidstone 1678; recorder, Canterbury 1687–Oct. 1688.[2]
Chairman. cttee. of privileges and elections Nov. 1693–Jan. 1694.

Darell's father, the younger son of a long-established Kentish gentry family, had made a modest fortune at the bar. From him, Darell inherited in 1664 a small estate in the parishes of Little Chart and Charing, as well as investments in two mining companies, the Mines Royal and the Mineral and Battery Works. He received a more substantial inheritance of land in the same area from his uncle, Sir John, in 1675, by which time he had been knighted and had become a j.p. At the time of the Exclusion Crisis he made himself prominent in his county as a Whig activist, as a result of which he twice lost his place on the bench. He was especially well regarded in Canterbury by the 'fanatics', and it was they who initially recommended him to the corporation of Rye at the second Exclusion election. At the election of 1685, when James II installed his own nominee for the Rye seat alongside another Tory, Darell apparently refrained from initiating any challenge. Within the next few years he emerged as a willing collaborator in the King's religious policies, and in February 1688 was reinstated as a j.p. and appointed to the county lieutenancy. None the less, it pained him that his heir, a young distant cousin, had lately been thrust into a Catholic seminary in France in order, as he later complained, 'to pervert him in his principles of religion'. Unlike the other two Whig contestants at Rye in the election of 1689, Darell himself seems to have encountered no challenge and was returned to the Convention unopposed.[3]

Re-elected in 1690, Darell appears to have been something of an independent. On the eve of the new Parliament Lord Carmarthen (Sir Thomas Osborne†) noted him in general terms as a Whig. In April 1691, Robert Harley* marked him as a Country supporter, subsequently qualifying this notation as 'd[oubtful]'. By 1692 Darell's behaviour appears to have crystallized and Carmarthen felt able to include him in a list of Court supporters under Lord Nottingham's (Daniel Finch†) influence, possibly because of his Kentish connexion. However, this impression of a general leaning towards the Court needs to be treated with caution when his particularly full record of parliamentary activity is examined in detail. He had a strong attachment to 'Country' notions of a purified legislature and governmental thrift, but his prime (almost obsessive) concern was that the Commons should take the initiative to regulate agriculture, trade and industry to beneficial effect. In his speeches he articulated the basic anxieties of country gentlemen about their local economies, in which the preservation of agriculture, and of its markets and outlets in industry, was seen as essential to the buoyancy of rents and land values. In advocating the fundamental interests of traditional, landed wealth it was not surprising that he should regard with suspicion the paper wealth of the new financial interests, especially their tendency to form themselves into monopolistic bodies. He was a conspicuous exponent of an unimpeded domestic market, and was sure that most instances of fiscal and monopolistic restriction upon agriculture, manufacture and other forms of enterprise retarded the nation's prosperity, frequently calling for such obstacles to be removed. As these designs often entailed the removal of government imposts, his regard for Court policy may therefore have often seemed lacking.

During the 1690 session Darell appears to have been disposed towards the idea of establishing a commission of accounts. Early in December 1691 he supervised the passage of a bill (of which he may well have been the initiator) to encourage the sowing of hemp and flax by lifting obstructive and 'vexatious' tithing practices. The bill's preamble stressed that these two new agricultural crops – vital to the production of linen, rope, canvas and netting – were 'exceedingly beneficial to England by reason of the multitude of people that are and would be employed', a statement which could easily have been one of Darell's pronouncements on the virtues of cultivation and manufacture. On 12 Dec. he spoke in favour of the bill to prevent false and double returns of MPs. He opposed on the 29th the first reading of the bill to encourage privateers to operate against France, on the grounds that this measure would facilitate, rather than hinder, trade with the French. On the 31st, he spoke against the Lords' addition of a clause to the treason trials bill, to remove the crown's power of appointing juries in the trial of peers, arguing that in the current circumstances of 'great danger' such a measure was inopportune. When the Irish revenue was considered in supply on 1 Jan. 1692, Darell joined with other Country speakers in disagreeing with the low estimates given by the Irish revenue commissioner William Culliford* of the yield anticipated from 'hearth money'. The following day, at Darell's own instigation, a select committee was appointed to review the book of rates in order to ascertain which goods were being withheld from export owing to the heavy duties they carried. Under Darell's chairmanship the committee worked quickly, and he reported back on 5 Jan. with a recommendation to repeal the tonnage and poundage duties imposed in 1660 on beef, pork, butter, cheese and candles. Though a bill for this purpose was authorized, Darell did not pursue the opportunity. Instead, his attention switched to a bill 'for encouraging the breeding and fattening of cattle', which he introduced on 8 Jan. and which he had seen through all its Commons stages by the 16th. On 15 Jan. he supported a bill for reducing interest rates from 6 to 4 per cent, doubtless in order to encourage trade. He served as teller on the 22nd in favour of granting a second reading to a routine bill enabling the bishop of London to sell off episcopal property in Worcestershire. His antipathy to the privileged status of the livery companies was in evidence on the 29th during a debate on proposals to establish a fund out of City revenues from which the 'orphans' debt' could be liquidated. Objecting to suggestions that new duties be laid on coals and chimneys, he told the House that 'there are diverse companies in the City who have great rents and revenues and little to do with them. They are persons within the City and who have helped towards this debt, and therefore I am for laying 5s. in the pound upon their lands.' However, Darell's intervention, more protest than proposal, was ignored. He evidently sympathized with the approaches made at this juncture by impoverished French Protestants for financial assistance, supporting on 17 Feb. the motion for their cause to be considered in the supply committee in accordance with the King's request. His personal crusade against the powers of privileged bodies was again seen on 19 Feb. when he spoke against the bill for confirming Cambridge University's charter, while on the 22nd he joined Paul Foley I* in voicing 'exceptions' to the bill. It was probably for similar reasons that he opposed the bill to incorporate the proprietors of the waterworks in St. Paul's, Shadwell parish, Middlesex, at the third reading on 20 Feb.[4]

On 10 Nov. 1692, a week after the new session began, Darell spoke in the debate on the King's Speech. Though he felt it 'a very good speech', he considered Thomas Neale's* motion to meet the King's requests in full 'a little too fast'. He suggested instead that the House await the commission of accounts' first report 'and then you will be better able to judge what is necessary'. Paradoxically, however, as the House made preparations the following day for an inquiry into the recent conduct of the naval high command, he appeared as an advocate for the Court in speaking against a motion by one of the commissioners, Sir Peter Colleton*, requiring the attendance of Admiral (Edward) Russell*. On the 17th he resumed his efforts of the previous session for a measure to encourage the exportation of home manufactures. In favour of his proposed bill he told MPs that improved exports would

> raise the value of your land. If you take off the duty on these English commodities at the exportation, there will be more transported . . . and it is but a small loss to the Crown in customs in a year – about £1,500 per annum. The duty I would have taken off on these several commodities are mutton, veal, oats, grafts, raw hides, English soap, tallow and biscuit flour.

However, Sir Edward Seymour's* arguments that demand for these goods already exceeded supply, and that the present circumstances of war made it undesirable that they should be exported in quantity, were convincing enough to forestall consideration of Darell's own proposals. Even so, his initiative clearly succeeded in stirring some anxiety about the state of the nation's 'balance of trade' and the following day a select committee was appointed to re-examine the Book of Rates, with himself as a nominee. In the proceedings on naval 'mismanagements' on 19 Nov. he moved that Admiral Sir John Ashby be admitted to explain his failure to give chase to the French following the English victory at Barfleur; and when Ashby had reassured the House of the propriety of his conduct, it was Darell who moved (unsuccessfully) to pass a vote of thanks for his 'good services'. On 24 Nov. he presented a petition against a bill to renew the term allowed the partnership concerned in supplying 'convex lights' to the City. The bill became a matter of contention, and Darell spoke against it on two subsequent occasions: on 6 Dec. he asserted that it was 'pernicious to the interest of England' in hindering the consumption of tallow, 'which is the concern of all landed men', and that the continuation of fiscal obstacles to its exportation only encouraged its price to fall still further. At the bill's third reading on the 30th, Darell reiterated these objections, adding that the partnership 'was a direct monopoly and had been adjudged so at law'. He found similar opportunities to advertise his protectionist views in relation to other measures. On 3 Dec. he spoke against a bill aimed at preventing the export of rabbitskins and hareskins as setting a limit to prices, while on the 7th he opposed another allowing the importation of Italian thrown silk. Supporting on the 8th a bill to prevent the export of gold and silver, he spoke of the need to curb what had become a 'beneficial trade' among the merchants, defending it again on the 31st at its second reading. The loss of specie was also considered on the 8th in relation to payments abroad for army supplies, Darell seconding Sir Richard Temple's* recommendation that the army be provisioned with home-produced stores. He argued that a buoyant export trade was the key to a stable currency: 'the more of your commodities you export beyond sea, you raise the value here of what is left. The exportation of your money is very pernicious unless it bring in such commodities that being carried out will bring in more money.' On 14 Dec., on one of the comparatively few occasions when he intervened on important matters of state, Darell spoke somewhat reservedly for committing the hotly contended bill 'for preserving their Majesties' sacred persons and government'.[5]

Early in the new year, on 6 Jan. 1693, Darell took up the cause of the London cloth-dyers, presenting a petition from them which called for exports of undyed woollen material to be forbidden in order to preserve their trade. It was referred, however, to the dormant grand committee on trade, and thus received no attention. On the 10th he came to the government's defence over a resolution that the King be advised to replace the present Admiralty board. He believed it ironic that mismanagements had not been found in the aftermath of Lord Torrington's defeat in June 1690, but were now being pursued at a time of improved naval effectiveness. The following day he also opposed a separate motion requesting the King to appoint a new board. On 19 Jan. he was one of several Members whose opposition to a bill for the encouragement of the English woollen industry, 'as a project drove on by the factors of Blackwell Hall for their own interest', blocked its further progress. On the 26th, during report proceedings concerning the levy of additional duties on merchandise, he acted as a minority teller in favour of retaining the high duty proposed on flax, which suggests that he may have tried to safeguard the industries dependent upon flax-growing whose interests he had previously upheld. He was strongly opposed to a bill to outlaw the activities of hawkers and pedlars; as he explained at its report stage on 2 Feb., such a measure would seriously disrupt the infrastructure of internal commerce:

> for it was to take away the living of several thousand people, which consequently would tend to dispeople the nation which he thought not our interest. Then this bill puts it into the inhabitants of corporations to exact upon the country gentlemen as they please. And it tends to spoil and ruin your servants whom you must [send] to a town if you want never so small a thing, whereas before they were brought home to your door.

At the bill's third reading on the 15th, he acted as teller against its passage, albeit for the minority. On 6 Feb. he spoke out against a bill for prohibiting the import of foreign buttons as more likely to stultify than to encourage home manufacture of the item. He was a majority teller on the 10th in favour of allowing Granado Pigot*, a Tory Member, three weeks' leave of absence. A second bill designed to protect the English woollen industry was given a third reading on 17 Feb., but, as with the earlier measure, Darell 'thought it against the interest of the nation to limit and confine trade to companies, who will set the dice upon others and sell at their own price'. On 20 and 24 Feb. he offered further amendments to the 'additional duties' supply bill, one (which was rejected) to exempt from the usual impositions small vessels coming in to London from Kent and Essex; and another with a distinct 'Country' appeal (which was adopted) requiring customs officers to take an oath 'for the due and true execution of their places'. Darell's vision of economic freedom and prosperity seems also to have embraced the holding of lotteries: he was certainly prepared to lay before the House on the 28th a petition on behalf of individuals whose interests were threatened by a bill to ban them. His final recorded act during the 1692–3 session was on 2 Mar., in connexion with the 'privateers bill', when he served as a majority teller in favour of Hon. Goodwin Wharton's clause to give scope to privateers to operate against the French in the East Indies as well as the Mediterranean.[6]

Darell's parliamentary career took a new turn in November 1693 when, during the first week of the next session he was selected to the chair of the committee of privileges and elections. He was an appropriate choice in view of his earlier involvement in legislative attempts to regularize electoral procedure, though a deciding factor in his favour would almost certainly have been the impartiality which characterized much of his performance in the House. On 20 Nov. he chaired the committee of the whole on the bill to permit the importation of brandy, aqua vitae and other spirits from France, which he reported the following day. He presented on the 23rd a bill to facilitate the import of saltpetre, but did not superintend its subsequent stages. He addressed the House at length on 5 Dec. when the paymaster-general, Lord Ranelagh (Richard Jones*), presented estimates for an army of over 93,000 men costing nearly £3,000,000. While 'amazed at this estimate as much as any man', he recognized that it was now imperative to confront the French menace at whatever cost. His typical concern was that such an unprecedented wartime demand should be laid equitably as in other countries: 'this charge is borne by the fortieth part of England. If every shoulder bore part of the proportion, the sum of two millions would be easily borne.' But despite his willingness to acquiesce in the government's requirements, he nevertheless concluded by adding his support to the motion put forward by Sir Thomas Clarges* calling for the names of the ministers who had put their signatures to the estimates. On 6 Dec. he reported from a committee which had examined complaints from small tradesmen of Worcester and Stafford against the oppressions of the farmers of the aulnage duty. The House agreed with the committee that the duty was long since 'unnecessary and obsolete', but the bill which Darell presented on the 7th to effect its removal made no further progress. His only report from the privileges and elections committee was on the 18th and concerned a breach of privilege, but he was one of five Members named on 23 Dec. to prepare a bill for settling the right in elections and for preventing undue returns to Parliament.[7]

Darell appears to have succumbed to serious illness in January 1694. He added a codicil to his will on the 16th, leaving his estate to a kinsman, John Darell, and died towards the end of the month. He was buried at Little Chart on 2 Feb.[8]

[1] *Vis. Kent* (Harl. Soc. liv), 45; *Le Neve's Knights* (Harl. Soc. viii), 240; *Arch. Cant.* xvii. 46–48; *Little Chart Reg.* 50, 113, 116, 146, 148, 153. [2] Centre Kentish Stud. Maidstone burghmote mins. Md/RF2/1, list of freemen, 1598–1721. [3] PCC 14 Bruce; L. K. J. Glassey, *Appt. JPs*, 51; *CSP Dom.* 1691–2, p. 535. [4] *Luttrell Diary*, 76, 78, 94, 101, 102, 104, 130, 148, 164, 169, 192, 194, 196, 200. [5] Ibid. 215, 218, 233, 239, 258, 286, 296, 299, 301, 302, 318, 340, 343. [6] Ibid. 352, 358, 363, 374, 388, 395, 402, 416, 424, 428, 435, 446, 454, 459; Grey, x. 295. [7] Luttrell, *Brief Relation*, iii. 226; Grey, x. 340–1. [8] PCC 30 Box; *Little Chart Reg.* 153.

A. A. H.

DASHWOOD, Sir Francis, 1st Bt. (c.1658–1724), of St. Botolph without Bishopsgate, London, and West Wycombe, Bucks.

WINCHELSEA 1708–1713

b. c.1658, 3rd s. of Francis Dashwood, Saddler and Turkey merchant, alderman of London 1658, by Alice, da. of Richard Sleigh of Derbys.; bro. of Sir Samuel Dashwood*; bro.-in-law of Fulke Greville†, 5th Baron Brooke. m. (1) lic. 13 Apr. 1683, aged 25, Mary (d. by 1695), da. of John Jennings of St. Margaret's, Westminster, 1s. d.v.p. 2da.; (2) lic. 30 May 1705, Lady Mary (d. 1710), da. of Sir Vere Fane*, 4th Earl of Westmorland, 1s. 1da.; (3) 17 June 1712, Mary (d. 1719), prob. da. of Major Charles King (bro. of Thomas King*), 2s. 2da. (1 d.v.p.); (4) 21 July 1720, Lady Elizabeth (d. 1736), da. of Thomas Windsor, 1st Earl of Plymouth, and sis. of Hon. Andrews Windsor*, Hon. Dixie Windsor*, and Thomas, 1st Visct. Windsor [I]*, s.p. Kntd. 29 Oct. 1702; cr. Bt. 28 June 1707.[1]

Freeman, Vintners' Co. 1680, upper warden 1712; asst. R. African Co. 1693–5, 1697–1700, 1704, 1706–7, 1709–12; dir. Old E.I. Co. 1700–2, 1703–5, 1707–9, manager, united trade 1707–8.[2]

Commr. Greenwich Hosp. 1695.[3]

A younger son of a prosperous Turkey merchant of Somerset origin, Dashwood sought a career in the family silk business. Although eclipsed by the success of his eldest brother, (Sir) Samuel, in City circles, he had evidently built up a sizable fortune by the Revolution, as he was able to loan the government £1,000 in March 1690. However, a letter from his brother Sir Samuel only four months later suggested that Francis was unhappy with his share of the family business and was 'making great dispatch' to obtain a government office. He did not succeed in this aim, but his personal fortune was still sufficient for him to establish a residence at Wanstead in Essex. Moreover, by 1698 both Francis and his brother were able to invest £15,000 to purchase the manor of West Wycombe, Buckinghamshire. However, when the Commons was presented on 20 June 1698 with a list of East India Company members willing to subscribe to a government loan, Francis had to rely on his eldest brother to advance £2,000 on his behalf. Similarly, it was at the feast to celebrate Sir Samuel's inauguration as lord mayor of London in October 1702 that Francis was honoured with a knighthood by Queen Anne. His elevated status faithfully reflected his prominence within the African and East Indian companies, but he still declined to seek civic advancement.[4]

Dashwood first became involved in politics prior to the general election of 1705, when his name was cited by a Whig electoral agent, George Lucy, in connexion with the contest at Coventry. Lucy, troubled at the prospect that Dashwood's son-in-law, Sir Orlando Bridgeman, 2nd Bt.*, might not stand, proposed to the Earl of Sunderland (Charles, Lord Spencer*) in February 1705 that Bridgeman be partnered at Coventry by another of Dashwood's sons-in-law, Sir Fulwar Skipwith, 2nd Bt.*, or even by Dashwood himself. Dashwood had no local interest to aid the Warwickshire Whigs, but nearly four weeks later Lucy considered Dashwood an important ally in furthering his own ambitions for the forthcoming county contest. As Lucy reasoned to Sunderland, 'the ill usage Sir Orlando Bridgeman meets with from the Tory party at Coventry' might 'raise Sir Francis Dashwood to such a pitch of resentment as to prevail with Sir Fulwar Skipwith to stand for the county and join his interest with mine'. However, Lucy revealed that Dashwood had already overstepped the mark by attempting to intercede on Skipwith's behalf with his brother-in-law Lord Brooke, the Tory patron of the sitting county Members. Brooke had reportedly 'put off' this approach, and even though Dashwood gave Bridgeman £100 'towards his expenses' for the borough contest, the Whigs were defeated at both the Coventry and county polls.

Although unable to aid his relations, Dashwood became increasingly successful in securing his own advancement. Within a few weeks of the Warwickshire election he had married a daughter of the 4th Earl of Westmorland, a match which brought him both prestige and political interest. In 1706, following the death of his brother Sir Samuel, he paid £15,000 to his nephew George Dashwood II* to assume complete ownership of the manor of West Wycombe, which, having already transferred his Wanstead estate to his son-in-law Bridgeman, he proceeded to develop as the family home. Most significantly, a baronetcy was bestowed upon him in June 1707 in recognition of 'his known loyalty and affection for her Majesty's person and government'.[5]

Such personal success was capped by Dashwood's uncontested election for Winchelsea in May 1708. Although his eldest brother had gained recognition in City circles as a Tory politician, Sir Francis' candidacy most probably reflected the influence of his own Whiggish brother-in-law Thomas Fane, 6th Earl of Westmorland, the deputy warden of the Cinque Ports. The compiler of a list of the new Parliament, possibly misled by Sir Samuel's former reputation, actually identified him as a Tory, but Sunderland cited his return as a Whig gain. Sunderland's assessment proved a more accurate guide to Dashwood's politics in the ensuing sessions, for in February 1709

Dashwood voted for the naturalization of the Palatines, and a year later supported the impeachment of Dr Sacheverell. Moreover, he also signed an address of the London lieutenancy which attacked recent outrages by High Church mobs. In general, however, he proved an inactive Member, failing to make any significant contribution to the business of the House.[6]

At the Winchelsea election of 1710 a Tory challenge was mounted to the sitting Members, and Dashwood's cash-book reveals that he was at some expense to retain his seat. Although the Winchelsea Whigs carried the poll, their opponents petitioned the House, alleging that bribery had proved a decisive influence on the return. The elections committee subsequently heard several witnesses testify that Dashwood had offered financial inducements to voters, but on 7 Feb. 1712 the Commons ruled against the petitioners. Maintaining Whiggish politics, he had voted the party line at the London election of 1710, and was identified as a Whig in the 'Hanover list', but was incongruously cited as he was one of the 'worthy patriots' who in the first session of the 1710 Parliament detected the mismanagements of the preceding Whig ministry. By the third session he had apparently rediscovered his political loyalties, voting on 18 June 1713 against the French commerce bill, a measure of obvious relevance to his trading interests. Having remained an inconspicuous Member during his second Parliament, he did not stand at the Winchelsea election of 1713 and retired from active participation in party politics.

Away from Westminster Dashwood channelled his energies into developing the family estate. In about 1720 he bought the Buckinghamshire manor of Halton, and was 'at great expense' to beautify its manor-house while also adorning his home at West Wycombe. Despite these costly improvements, when he died at his town-house in Hanover Square on 4 Nov. 1724 his personal estate was valued at over £34,000. His will also testified to the social connexions which his four marriages had brought him, for the trustees of the estate included two of his brothers-in-law, Hon. Dixey Windsor*, son of the 1st Earl of Plymouth, and Hon. John Fane†, later 7th Earl of Westmorland. Dashwood's wealth and prestige were instrumental in facilitating the rise of his son and heir, Sir Francis, 2nd Bt.†, who served as chancellor of the Exchequer under Lord Bute and was elevated to the peerage in 1763 as Lord Le Despenser.[7]

[1] IGI, London; *Le Neve's Knights* (Harl. Soc. viii), 388; J. R. Woodhead, *Rulers of London* (London and Mdx. Arch Soc.), 56–57; 'London Inhabitants without the Walls, 1695' (t/s in Guildhall Lib.). [2] Guildhall Lib. ms 15212/1, p. 65; 15202/3, f. 112; K. G. Davies, *R. African Co.* 380; Add. 38871. [3] Add. 10120, ff. 232–6.

[4] *Cal. Treas Bks.* ix. 2006; Bodl. D.D. Dashwood (Bucks.) A1/6, Sir Samuel Dashwood to Dashwood, 5 July 1690; Morant, *Essex*, i. 31; Shaw, *Knights*, ii. 273. [5] Add. 61496, ff. 84, 87; D.D. Dashwood (Bucks.) A2, ff. 9, 34; Boyer, *Anne Annals*, vi. 372. [6] Add. ch. 76120. [7] D.D. Dashwood (Bucks.) A2, f. 124; B14/1, piece 41; *London Poll of 1710*; *VCH Bucks.* ii. 340; PCC 264 Bolton.

P. L. G.

DASHWOOD, George I (1669–1706), of St. Anne Soho, Westminster.

SUDBURY   6 Dec. 1703–1705

bap. 25 Nov. 1669, at least 3rd s. of George Dashwood of Hackney, Mdx. by Margaret, da. of William Perry of Thorpe, Surr.; bro. of Sir Robert Dashwood, 1st Bt.* educ. Trinity, Oxf. 1684. m. 4 June 1698, Algerina (d. 1748), da. of Sir Algernon Peyton, 1st Bt., of Doddington, Isle of Ely, Cambs. 2s. 5da.

Lt.-col. Edmund Soame's* regt. ft. 1705–d.

Dashwood's identification principally rests on the evidence of his proprietorial and familial links with Sudbury and its neighbourhood. Further support comes from a list of placemen in 1705, which cites the Member as holding an army commission, albeit a captaincy of horse. Such a career did not reflect Dashwood's background as the son of an extremely wealthy excise farmer, whose business interests had tied him firmly to the capital. However, from his father Dashwood inherited lands in Suffolk and Essex, and his interest in East Anglia was further improved by his marriage into the Peyton family of Doddington, Isle of Ely. Indeed, his bride may have brought as part of her dowry the manor of Boxford, about six miles from Sudbury. By the time of his candidacy at the general election of 1702 he may have already purchased property within the town itself, for only three years later he voted as a Sudbury freeholder at the Suffolk election. In order to procure Tory votes for the borough contest he promised to fund several local projects, but these inducements were insufficient to enable him to overcome the Whig candidates. However, following Dashwood's petition to the House on 24 Oct., the return of John Haskins Stiles* was declared void, thereby presenting Dashwood with a second opportunity to gain election. At the Sudbury poll of February 1703 Stiles defeated Dashwood by only 21 votes, but, undaunted, the latter petitioned the Commons on 22 Feb. and again on 10 Nov. His perseverance was rewarded when the House ruled in his favour on 6 Dec. 1703, a decision which was widely regarded as a victory for party prejudice.[1]

Soon after taking his seat Dashwood was confirmed as a Tory by the Earl of Nottingham (Daniel Finch†), who listed him as a likely supporter, possibly in connexion with proceedings concerning the Scotch Plot. In the next session he was forecast on 30 Oct. 1704 as probably in favour of the Tack, and two parliamentary lists marked him as voting for the measure on 28 Nov. However, an opponent subsequently accused him of deserting his party, describing him as 'a Tacker in principle, yet turned Sneaker now'. During that session he also featured as a teller in two divisions: on 11 Jan. 1705, to block a resolution to allow Protestants in the North to arm themselves; and on 3 Mar. against a motion to adjourn debate on the Aylesbury case. Having campaigned with such persistency to gain his seat, he revealed that his ambitions lay elsewhere, petitioning the Duke of Ormond in January 1704 for a lieutenant-colonelcy in one of the six newly raised regiments of foot. In the previous reign Ormond had unsuccessfully sought for Dashwood 'a company in the guards', but on this occasion Dashwood was more fortunate, gaining his commission in March 1705.[2]

Even though he had achieved his long-desired military appointment, Dashwood still contested the Sudbury election of 1705, but failed to carry the poll. One report suggested that he had alienated many local townsmen by 'tricking' them over the recent Stour navigation bill, he having been named to its drafting committee, and by failing to pay his local poor rate. He was also accused of falling out with 'his party', but he did vote for the Tory candidates at the succeeding Suffolk election. Undeterred by such allegations, on 2 Nov. 1705 he sought to alert the House to the corrupt electoral practices of his opponents, but then withdrew his petition on 6 Dec. before the case could be heard, a decision possibly influenced by his regiment's posting to Spain. Although out of the Commons, he may have continued to court local voters by promoting the Stour navigation, since on 12 Feb. 1706 a 'Mr Dashwood' submitted clauses to the Lords' committee reviewing that measure. He was never to serve overseas, dying at Torbay in September 1706 as the regiment prepared to embark for the Iberian peninsula. It was reported on 7 Sept. that Dashwood 'is dead on board the fleet at Torbay', and his body was subsequently conveyed to Norfolk for burial. His heir, George, although retaining a proprietorial interest in Sudbury and eventually settling at Bury St. Edmunds, did not endeavour to emulate his father's electoral success.[3]

[1] IGI, London, Norf., Suff.; Add. 19126, ff. 100–3; PCC 112 Vere; Copinger, *Manors of Suff.* i. 26–27; *Suff. Poll 1705*. [2] *London Post*, 23 May 1705; Nat. Lib. Ire. ms 2458, p. 89. [3] *London Post*, 23 May 1705; *Suff. Poll 1705*; *HMC Lords*, n.s. vi. 398; Luttrell, *Brief Relation*, vi. 84; PCC 138 Poley, 191 St. Eloi; Le Neve, *Mon. Angl.* 1700–15, p. 123.

P. L. G.

DASHWOOD, George II (1680–1758) of St. George's, Hanover Square, Mdx.

STOCKBRIDGE 1710–1713

bap. 7 Mar. 1680, 4th but 1st. surv. s. of Sir Samuel Dashwood*; bro.-in-law of Robert Bristow II* and John Bristow†. *educ.* I. Temple 1697; Magdalen Coll. Oxf. 1698; ?travelled abroad (France, Italy, Germany, Austria, Switzerland, Low Countries) 1700–3. *m.* by 1712, Catherine (*d.* 1779), da. of Robert Bristow I* of Michelldever, Hants, 1s. 2da. *suc.* fa. 1705.

Sheriff, Suff. 1731–2.[1]

Given his family's political connexions, the heir of Sir Samuel Dashwood can be identified with some certainty as the George Dashwood 'of London' returned in 1710 as the Member for Stockbridge. Born into a prosperous mercantile household, Dashwood chose not to follow his father's example, declining to seek civic or commercial advancement in the City. However, he may have revealed his empathy with Sir Samuel's Tory principles as early as August 1703, when a 'Mr Dashwood' fought and lost a duel with Lord Wharton (Hon. Thomas*) at Bath. Wharton's challenger was described as 'a hot young gentleman', and at least one report suggested that it was the son of Sir Samuel. Another account thought the duel a deliberate Tory ploy to embarrass the Whig magnate, and the incident evidently brought the young Dashwood much publicity, an observer at Bath describing it as 'the subject of all discourse both here and at London'. In consideration of such newly acquired fame, he may plausibly be identified as the 'George Dashwood' who petitioned the House on 2 Nov. 1705 and 14 Dec. 1706 to contest the return for the Bath election of May 1705. The death of Sir Samuel Dashwood clearly gave him financial independence, particularly after he had received £15,000 from his uncle Sir Francis Dashwood, 1st Bt.*, for the sale of his share of the manor of West Wycombe, Buckinghamshire.[2]

Proof of Dashwood's standing within Tory circles came in February 1710 when he was elected a 'nephew' of the Board of Brothers, the Duke of Beaufort's drinking club. The following September Beaufort was a key figure in Dashwood's election campaign at Stockbridge, a notoriously venal borough which was accustomed to electing outsiders. Dashwood was duly returned unopposed alongside the Earl of Barrymore [I] (James Berry*), a fellow member of the Board of Brothers, and was cited in the 'Hanover list' as a Tory.

Although failing to make any significant contribution to Commons business in his only Parliament, he initially maintained the party line, listed as one of the 'worthy patriots' who in the first session sought to discover the mismanagements of the previous administration. Moreover, on 25 Jan. 1712, the day after the vote of censure against the Duke of Marlborough (John Churchill†), he was one of the eight Members to receive the thanks of the Board of Brothers for their 'good attendance and service' in the House. The following month he was identified as a member of the October Club, but before the Parliament was over he had broken with his party, choosing to vote on 18 June 1713 against the French commerce bill. Only a few weeks before, he had presented at court an address on behalf of his constituents which gave thanks for the end of the war, but his apostasy in that division may have cost him his seat, since he did not appear at the succeeding Stockbridge election.[3]

There is no evidence to suggest that Dashwood pursued any political activity after 1713. However, following his purchase of an estate at Heveningham, Suffolk in 1719, he was eventually prepared to undertake public office as sheriff of that county. He did not completely sever his links with the capital, and even though his fortune was bolstered in March 1738 by his brother Thomas' bequest of 'a considerable estate', he chose to sell his Suffolk holdings in 1745. By the time of his death, on either 10 or 11 Jan. 1758, he had settled in the fashionable area of St. George's, Hanover Square, and further testimony to his wealth was provided by his substantial bequests to his two daughters. His widow subsequently achieved some eminence by serving as a lady of the bedchamber to Queen Charlotte, the consort of George III, but his only son Samuel did not reveal any political ambitions.[4]

[1] IGI, London; Hoare, *Wilts.* Frustfield, 11; *Addison Letters*, 27, 30, 33, 38. [2] Cunningham, *Hist. GB*, i. 351; Add. 28890, f. 401; *Wharton Mems.* 35; Bodl. D.D. Dashwood (Bucks.) mss A2, f. 9. [3] Add. 49360, f. 18; Beaufort mss at Badminton House, Beaufort letter bk. Beaufort to Robert Pitt*, 14 Sept. 1710; G. Holmes, *Pol. in Age of Anne*, 297; *London Gazette*, 30 May–2 June 1713. [4] Suckling, *Suff.* ii. 390; *Survey of London*, xxxiii. 58; *Hist. Reg. Chron.* 1738, p. 13; *Gent. Mag.* 1758, p. 46; *London Mag.* 1758, p. 52; PCC 9 Hutton; Hoare, 11.

P. L. G.

DASHWOOD, Sir Robert, 1st Bt. (1662–1734), of Northbrook, Kirtlington, Oxon.

BANBURY 1689–1698
OXFORDSHIRE 29 Nov. 1699–1700

bap. 6 Nov. 1662, 1st s. of George Dashwood, merchant, of Hackney, Mdx. by Margaret, da. of William Perry of Thorpe, Surr. bro. of George Dashwood*. *educ.* Eton c.1675–9; Trinity, Oxf. 1679; I. Temple 1679. *m.* lic. 9 June 1682, Penelope (*d.* 1735), da. and coh. of Sir Thomas Chamberlayne, 2nd Bt., of Wickham, Oxon., 5s. (4 *d.v.p.*) 4da. *suc.* fa. 1682; kntd. 4 June 1682; *cr.* Bt. 16 Sept. 1684.[1]

Sheriff, Oxon. 1683–4; freeman, Woodstock 1684, Oxford Feb. 1685–Feb. 1688; ?asst. Banbury by 1689.[2]

Gent. privy chamber 1685–1702; commr. for preventing export of wool 1689–95.[3]

Dashwood was one of the wealthiest of Oxfordshire's resident gentlemen. His family were recent arrivals in the county, his father, a London merchant, having been a prosperous revenue farmer. As a young man, Dashwood was probably involved in these business concerns himself. Certainly, at the time of receiving his knighthood he was described as a 'merchant', and his life-long habit of meticulous account-keeping must have originated with an early training in commercial matters. On the death of his father and father-in-law in 1682, he inherited considerable landed wealth, much of it from the Chamberlayne estate in the vicinity of Banbury and Oxford, which he continued to augment until old age. Some sources name him as a commissioner of excise but this is to confuse him with his cousin Sir Samuel Dashwood*. Sir Robert was first elected in 1689 for Banbury, where his interest as lord of the manor of Wickham was substantial enough to give him an important though not a preponderant influence, a fact highlighted when he stood again in 1690 and faced at least four other local contenders, whittled down by the election to only one. A Tory and a devoted Churchman, Dashwood was twice marked by Lord Carmarthen (Sir Thomas Osborne†) as a probable Court supporter in the opening stages of the new Parliament. By April 1691 he was regarded by Robert Harley* as a supporter of the Country opposition. At the beginning of the 1691–2 session he was forced to defend his return for Banbury before the elections committee though the petition against him was rejected. In parliamentary proceedings he was for the most part a spectator: his appearances in the Journals consisted of little more than periodic grants of leave, the first occurring on 14 May 1690, for a week, the second on 19 Dec. 1693, for a fortnight. Following a call of the House on 7 Jan. 1696, he was ordered into custody 'for absenting himself from his service in Parliament' and discharged on the 11th, though was granted leave again, for an unspecified period, on 12 Mar. He was accorded further periods of leave on 16 Dec. 1696, 27 Feb. 1697 (on grounds of ill-health) and 19 Apr. 1698.[4]

The record of Dashwood's political stance in 1696 confirms that he had become an unequivocal Tory: he was forecast in January as an opponent of the Court over the proposed council of trade, refused initially to sign the Association and voted on 25 Nov. against Fenwick's (Sir John†) attainder. In 1698 he was classed as a supporter of the Country party in a comparative analysis of the old and new Houses of Commons, but he was not re-elected. It is not certain whether he simply stepped down at Banbury or was defeated in a contest. The balance of probability is that he initially set up against James Isaacson*, the corporation's Whig nominee, but afterwards withdrew on finding Isaacson powerfully backed by the corporation. When Isaacson was expelled the House in February 1699 Dashwood appears to have contemplated standing once more, but decided otherwise when it became clear that the new Whig candidate was in a far stronger position. In May, however, he put himself forward as a serious contender for the Oxfordshire seat vacated by Lord Norreys (Montagu Venables-Bertie*). He spent the summer months campaigning vigorously against the Whig Sir Thomas Wheate*. Dr Arthur Charlett, master of University College and Oxford University's chief electoral manager, wrote that it was widely thought that Dashwood would be a perfect choice, with 'his vast estate', yielding £6,000 p.a., together with '£40,000 in specie', and 'being also a true member of the Church in opposition to popery and fanaticism'. He was indeed elected knight of the shire at the end of November, but his second spell in the House proved short-lived. On 1 Apr. 1700 he served as a teller for the one and only time, in a minor division on a private clause intended for the Irish forfeitures bill. A 'misunderstanding' with the leader of the Tory interest in Oxfordshire, Lord Abingdon (the former Lord Norreys) forced him to stand down at the January 1701 election. Though Dashwood himself never returned to the House, his family's pretensions to a county seat resurfaced in March 1707 when, with his probable blessing, his son Chamberlayne made interest for knight of the shire in preparation for the election due the following year. But as this candidacy threatened to overset the county grandees' commitment to return Lord Rialton (Hon. Francis Godolphin*), eldest son of Lord Godolphin (Sidney†) and son-in-law of the Duke of Marlborough (John Churchill†), Chamberlayne was quickly prevailed upon to stand for Banbury instead. In the event, however, he did not put up there either. Sir Robert died at his seat at Northbrook, 14 July 1734, to be succeeded by his grandson James, who entered Parliament for Oxfordshire at a by-election in January 1740.[5]

[1] *Eton Coll. Reg.* ed. Sterry, 96; J. Townsend, *Oxon. Dashwoods*, 13–14. [2] Woodstock council acts 1679–99 (17 Sept. 1684); *Oxford Council Acts* (Oxf. Hist. Soc. n.s. ii), 170, 196. [3] Carlisle, *Privy Chamber*, 198; info. from Prof. R. O. Bucholz; *Statutes*, vi. 96, 417. [4] Townsend, 10; *VCH Oxon.* vi. 223; ix. 6, 173, 200; x. 47, 233–4; BL, Verney mss mic. M636/44, John Verney*, (later Visct. Fermanagh) to Sir Ralph Verney, 1st Bt.†, 18 Feb. 1689[–90]. [5] Bodl. Carte 130, f. 396; Tanner 21, ff. 69, 80, 92; Ballard 31, f. 60; Add. 70019, f. 312; *Hearne Colls.* ii. 2; xi. 363.

A. A. H.

DASHWOOD, Sir Samuel (c.1643–1705), of St. Botolph without Bishopsgate, London.

LONDON   1685–1687, 1690–1695

b. c.1643, 1st s. of Francis Dashwood, Saddler and Turkey merchant, alderman of London 1658 by Alice, da. of Richard Sleigh of Derbys., and bro. of Sir Francis Dashwood, 1st Bt.* *m.* lic 17 May 1670, aged 27, Anne (*d.* 1721), da. of John Smith of South Tidworth, Hants, and sis. of John Smith I*, 4s. (2 *d.v.p.*) 10da. (5 *d.v.p.*). *suc.* fa. 1683; kntd. 30 July 1684.[1]

Freeman, Vintners' Co. 1663, master 1684–5; member, Levant Co. 1663, asst. 1680–91; asst. R. African Co. 1672–4, 1677–9, 1682–4, 1687–9, 1692–3, 1698–9, 1701–3, 1705–*d.*; sheriff, London 1683–4, alderman 1683–7, Oct. 1688–*d.*, ld. Mayor 1702–3; dir. E.I. Co. 1684–6, 1690–5, 1698–1703, dep.-gov. 1700–2; pres. Bethlehem and Bridewell Hosps. 1704–*d.*[2]

Jt. farmer of excise 1677–83, commr. 1689–96; commr. preventing export of wool 1689–92, Greenwich Hosp. 1695, taking subscriptions to land bank 1696.[3]

Of Somerset stock, Dashwood's father had established himself as a prosperous Turkey merchant in the capital. Although following him into the silk trade, Dashwood also chose to emulate his uncles William and George by diversifying into excise-farming. Moreover, unlike his father, who had fined for alderman in 1658, he actively sought civic advancement as a loyal supporter of the court. On the surrender of the London charter in October 1683, he was retained as sheriff by a special royal commission, and replaced the Whig magnate Sir Robert Clayton* as alderman for Cheap. Elected a Member for the City when the Tories carried the poll at the election of 1685, he further proved his loyalty by loaning the government £32,500 by September 1686. However, he became increasingly alarmed by the King's policies and was ousted as alderman in August 1687 for failing to support the corporation's address of thanks for the first Declaration of Indulgence. Reinstatement in the final days of the reign did not secure his allegiance, as he was appointed on 11 Dec. 1688 to the City's committee to address the Prince of Orange. Within a year, having made 'great interest and solicitation to great men', he had become a commissioner of excise, his first government office following abortive appointments to the excise commission of December 1688. He was less successful when contesting the London by-election of May 1689, but managed to regain his seat by finishing second in the poll of 1690.⁴

At the outset of the new Parliament Lord Carmarthen (Sir Thomas Osborne†) cited him as a Tory who would probably support the Court, a view endorsed by Sir Peter Rich† when recommending Dashwood as one of 'the persons proper to be consulted with of our side' to raise a government loan. However, although a prominent civic Tory, Dashwood did not relish his parliamentary duties, complaining to his brother Francis in July of 'the great trouble and charge I find therein, it having cost me many a pound'. Indeed, although boasting an annual income of £2,200, he wished that his membership of the House 'may happen but seldom and not long continue', a reluctance reflected in his failure to make a significant contribution to Commons' business in the first two sessions of the 1690 Parliament. However, he was keen to promote the cause of his City allies, presenting to the Commons on 2 Dec. 1690 a petition signed by 124 common councilmen which detailed the abuses allegedly committed by the Whig-dominated corporation since the Act to restore the London charter. Later that month a besieged Carmarthen identified him as a likely ally, and in a separate assessment confirmed him as a supporter of the Court. By contrast, Robert Harley's* list, compiled in around April 1691, noted him as doubtful.⁵

The 'great bustle' attending the contest for the mayoralty of London in October 1691 helped to dispel any lingering worries concerning Dashwood's allegiance, for he stood for the Tories in a losing cause. In the ensuing session he was much more conspicuous, rising to address a variety of issues relating to his professional and personal interests, particularly the defence of the East India Company. On 23 Dec. he sought to convince the House that the company's proposals for offering security for their own stock were 'very good', and a list of the company's sureties six days later revealed that he was willing to stand for £15,000. His responsibilities regarding the excise prompted him on several occasions to intervene in debates concerning taxation, beginning on 21 Nov. with the presentation of two clauses for addition to an excise bill. On 16 Dec. he spoke without success in favour of a motion to render the inns of court liable for the land tax. Increasing concern for the excise yield brought him continuing prominence, and on 6 Jan. 1692 he introduced a bill to regulate the collection of duties on low wines and strong waters. Later that day he clashed with one of the commissioners of accounts, Paul Foley I, over the excise estimates, arguing that 'I really do believe the excise this year will not amount to what it did last year'. Dashwood's plea did not convince the committee of ways and means, and five days later he again failed to carry his point against Foley when arguing for a reduction in the expected yield of the excise due to collection charges. He was more successful when representing the City over its debts to the London orphans, featuring on 29 Jan. as one of the speakers who insisted that the corporation was 'very willing' to pay its debts. In the ensuing debate he proposed that 'a further fund' be raised from a duty on coals imported into the capital, a measure which aroused opposition but which was later carried.⁶

The fourth session saw an even greater prominence for Dashwood, as trade and taxation continued to concern the House. On 17 Nov. 1692 his East India interests prompted him to act strongly against a motion for a bill to establish a new company, rising 'to demand right to be heard against the said bill before my right be precluded'. He was unable to prevent the introduction of the bill, and on 24 Nov. informed the Commons committee that although the East India Company's general court was ready to submit to parliamentary regulation, 'the private committees' were opposed to any such move. He was equally stubborn in defence of the Levant Company when its future was threatened by a bill to allow the importation of fine silk transported overland. On 7 Dec. he opposed the committal of the bill on the grounds that it would 'ruin your Turkey trade' and have an adverse effect on the domestic manufacture of woollens and silk. He failed to prevent the committal, but on 11 Jan. 1693, after he had again expressed his reservations, the bill was defeated at the engrossment stage.⁷

Apart from trade, Dashwood maintained an active interest in London affairs, informing the House on 19 Dec. 1692 that the corporation wished to present a petition relating to a bill to extend the lease for supplying convex lights in the capital. Eleven days later he was one of the Members who attacked the measure openly, and had the satisfaction of seeing it fail. The preceding day, 29 Dec., he had spoken against a bill to regulate the packing and weighing of butter, an initiative which the London cheesemongers had condemned as the design of 'particular interest' of Suffolk farmers. Of more personal significance, on 10 Jan. 1693 he requested that his counsel be heard at the bar when a motion was made for the suspension of pensions during wartime.⁸

For the rest of the session Dashwood concentrated

on mercantile matters. On 17 Feb. he opposed a bill to revive the Act banning the export of wool, and the next day self-interest prompted him to move a clause to allow the importation of Italian silks in foreign vessels. This proposal was rejected as contrary to the Navigation Acts, and he met with further disappointment on 25 Feb. when his speech failed to prevent the passage of a motion for an address to the King to dissolve the East India Company. The cause of the regulated companies was better served on 6 Mar. when Dashwood successfully opposed a clause permitting privateers to export goods, a measure deemed 'absolutely destructive' of the rights of the Levant and other companies. However, his concern to aid the war effort had been demonstrated several weeks earlier when he advanced £2,000 to the government in response to a direct appeal to the London corporation. In addition, later that year he was prepared to be bound for £10,000 to guarantee the export of large quantities of domestic produce to the East Indies. By way of reward, in October 1693 he was co-recipient of a royal grant of a seized cargo of illegally imported silks. His professional link to the court, of course, dominated assessments of his political allegiance, no less than five lists citing him as a placeman in the course of the 1690 Parliament.[9]

In the absence of Narcissus Luttrell's* detailed accounts of debates, Dashwood's activity over the final two sessions of the 1690 Parliament again appears of only limited importance. In the fifth session he appears among the drafters of a bill to encourage the clothing trade, and acted as a teller on 20 Mar. 1694 in order to block the addition of a clause to a bill levying duties on salt and other commodities. Moreover, although his City status was confirmed when he was appointed on 28 Mar. as one of the commissioners for the Million Act, the very next day his name was removed on the orders of the crown. There followed a concerted attempt on the part of several Whig ministers to oust him from the excise commission. Sir John Trenchard* reported to the King on 15 June that Dashwood and other City financiers were 'very little serviceable in that employment', but they did gain some support from Lord Godolphin (Sidney†) and Lord Shrewsbury, the latter observing that the government was well served by having such 'eminent citizens' on the commission. Even Sir John Somers* admitted that Dashwood's aldermanic contacts were useful, and this City influence undoubtedly played a key role in securing his place in the new commission issued in August. In the ensuing session the Commons' inquiry into the East India Company threatened to tarnish his reputation further, but the investigative committee reported on 12 Mar. 1695 that it had decided not to interview Dashwood and other Members who had been directors when serious irregularities within the Company had occurred. He was also listed as a 'friend' of Henry Guy, who was under attack in the Commons during this session. Remaining true to the sentiments he had expressed in July 1690, he retired from parliamentary politics at the end of the session, declining to seek re-election at the London contest of 1695.[10]

Destined never to sit in the House again, Dashwood remained prominent in trading and civic circles for the rest of his career. However, although confirmed as a leading financier in 1696 by his appointment as one of the commissioners to take subscriptions to the land bank, he was removed from the excise commission in May of that year. His dismissal may well have been politically motivated, but it did not form part of a major purge and may simply have reflected a reluctance on his part to serve, he having complained as early as July 1690 of the 'care, trouble and charge' which the office caused him. Significantly, when his name was touted as a potential farmer of the excise duties in February 1700, he was reported not to have 'any great mind to it'. He continued to prove his value as a government creditor, listed by the Commons on 20 June 1698 as a member of the East India Company willing to advance £3,000 for himself and a further £2,000 on his brother Francis' behalf. Political machinations were certainly instrumental in halting his civic advancement, for although he was the senior alderman below the chair, he was defeated by Whig candidates at the mayoral elections of 1698 and 1700. These setbacks did not mirror his fortunes within the Old East India Company, where, having been appointed in February 1699 as one of the commissioners to negotiate with the New Company, he was elected deputy-governor in April 1700. By July 1701 he and Sir Thomas Cooke* were regarded as 'sole dictators' of the Old East India Company, and two months later he confidently predicted that the two companies would merge.[11]

The mayoral elections of 1701 revealed that Dashwood had by no means lost his political zeal, ready as he was to combat the growing calls for war with France. On 25 Sept. he sought to delay an address from the London corporation which drew attention to the French threat, a filibuster which, according to James Vernon I*, was largely responsible for Dashwood's poor performance in the mayoral election held three days later. Although touted as 'altogether qualified and well-affected to the present government', Dashwood finished bottom of the poll and was unable to prevent the return of Sir William Gore by the court of aldermen. The accession of Anne revived the spirits of the City Tories, however, and in July 1702 Dashwood gained a colonelcy in the London militia. Later that year the Whigs were reportedly 'quite down in the mouth' after he had achieved an overwhelming victory in the mayoral contest, the aldermen having given him their unanimous support. The City poet Elkanah Settle praised Sir Samuel's 'attracting merit', and observed that the aldermanic vote had been 'the work of minutes', a great contrast to the manner in which they 'had [for] so many years past so coldly neglected' his qualities as a magistrate. The Queen herself signified her approval of Dashwood by attending the lavish celebrations which accompanied his inaugural feast, on the occasion of which she knighted his brother Francis.[12]

Having achieved the pinnacle of his civic career at the age of about 60, Dashwood might have anticipated leading the City Tories for several more years, but illness curtailed any ambitions. In January 1705 he was already reportedly 'at the point of death', and although there is some confusion surrounding the date, he probably died on 12 Aug. of that year. His commercial success had enabled him to buy properties in Buckinghamshire and Surrey, but he had continued to reside in the capital until his death and was buried at St. Botolph without Bishopsgate. He left an estate reportedly valued at £100,000, which was shared among his surviving two sons and five daughters. His eldest son, George Dashwood II*, employed some of his father's fortune to become the Member for Stockbridge in 1710, but did not seek to emulate Sir Samuel's success in civic politics. The social contacts which Dashwood had made in the course of his career were clearly testified by the marriages of his daughters to Andrew Archer*, Sir Thomas Saunders Sebright, 3rd Bt.†, and Richard Crawley*, the last of whom was appointed an executor of his estate.[13]

[1] *Le Neve's Knights* (Harl. Soc. viii), 388; J. R. Woodhead, *Rulers of London* (London and Mdx. Arch. Soc.), 56–57; *London Mar. Lic.* ed. Foster, 379; IGI, London. [2] Guildhall Lib. ms 15212/1, p. 16; K. G. Davies, *R. African Co.* 380; Add. 38871 (unfol.); E. G. O'Donoghue, *Bridewell Hosp.* 273. [3] *Cal. Treas. Bks.* v. 532, 1250; Add. 10120, ff. 232–6. [4] Luttrell, *Brief Relation*, i. 283, 411; *Cal. Treas. Bks.* vii. 1523; viii. 2137, 2176–9, 2181; ix. 273; R. Beddard, *Kingdom Without a King*, 171; Bodl. D.D. Dashwood (Bucks.) mss A1/6, Dashwood to (Sir) Francis Dashwood, 5 July 1690. [5] Dorset RO, Fox-Strangways mss D124, box 235, Rich to Sir Stephen Fox*, 17 Mar. 1690; D.D. Dashwood (Bucks.) mss A1/6; Add. 70014, f. 371. [6] *Portledge Pprs.* 121; *Luttrell Debates*, 34, 84, 92, 96, 113, 121, 163–4. [7] *Luttrell Debates*, 234, 258, 299, 360. [8] Ibid. 328, 339–40. [9] Ibid. 429, 432, 449, 464; Bodl. Carte 79, f. 488; *Cal. Treas. Bks.* x. 354, 1211. [10] *Cal. Treas. Bks.* x. 552, 556; *CSP Dom. 1694–5*, pp. 180, 186; H. Horwitz, *Parl. and Pol. Wm. III*, 134. [11] *Cal. Treas. Bks.* xi. 155; D.D. Dashwood (Bucks.) mss A1/6; *Vernon–Shrewsbury Letters*, ii. 452; Beaven, *Aldermen*, ii. p. xxvi; Luttrell, *Brief Relation*, iv. 432, 692; *Flying Post*, 21–23 Feb. 1699; *London Post*, 26–29 Apr. 1700; C 110/28, John Dolben* to Thomas Pitt I*, 19 July 1701; Add. 22851, f. 52. [12] Add. 40775, ff. 198, 220–1; *Post Boy*, 16–18 Sept. 1701; Yale Univ. Beinecke Lib. Osborn coll. Blathwayt mss, box 20, Robert Yard* to William Blathwayt*, 2 Oct. 1701; Luttrell, *Brief Relation*, v. 193; Herts. RO, Panshanger mss D/EP/F29, Lady Cowper's commonplace bk. p. 281; Guildhall Lib. ms 15378; Boyer, *Anne Annals*, i. 126. [13] Folger Shakespeare Lib. Newdigate newsletter 30 Jan. 1705; PCC 239 Gee; Bodl. Rawl. D.734, f. 75; F. A. Crisp, *Frag. Gen.* n.s. i. 130.

P. L. G.

DAVALL, Sir Thomas I (1644–1712) of Dovercourt, Essex.

HARWICH 1695–1708

b. 18 May 1644, er. s. of Thomas Davall, merchant, of St. Mary at Hill, London, by Anne, da. of Thomas Potts. *educ.* Merchant Taylors' 1655. *m.* 18 May 1676, Rebecca (*d.* 1714), da. of Daniel Burr, merchant, of Amsterdam, 3s. (2 *d.v.p.*) 1da. *suc.* fa. 1663; kntd. 21 Feb. 1683.[1]

Asst., Haberdashers' Co. 1685, master Nov.–Dec. 1686; member, R. Lustring Co., Levant Co. 1689; cttee. E. I. Co. 1682–6.[2]

Recorder, Harwich 1690–*d.*; freeman, Colchester 1701.[3]

Commr. taking subscriptions to land bank 1696, to S. Sea Co. 1711.[4]

Davall was a Country Tory who became a supporter of Robert Harley*. He was born in Amsterdam, where both his father and father-in-law traded as merchants, and his wife was a member of the Dutch Church in London. He was evidently considered to be 'loyal' by both Charles II and James II since he was knighted in 1683 and served as a commissioner for the London lieutenancy in 1685. Described at the time of his marriage as a merchant living at St. Martin Orgar, he owned £3,700 of East India Company stock by 1689 and was rich enough to offer security for £4,300 for the East India Company on 28 Dec. 1691. In March 1687 he had bought the manor of Dovercourt, which lay within the borough of Harwich, and in 1690 sought to use his interest there to become one of the corporation's MPs, though competition was fierce. If Lord Cheyne had declined to stand, as was reported, Davall and four or five other candidates would have 'put in' for election, with Sir Thomas being thought to have the best chance of winning. In fact Cheyne did stand, and Davall had to wait until the 1695 election for his seat.[5]

Although granted leave of absence on 27 Mar. 1696, after signing the Association, Davall's mercantile interests had already become apparent in the first session, since he was forecast as likely to oppose the Court over the proposed council of trade on 31 Jan. 1696. As a financier he had a special interest in the coinage: he voted in March against fixing the price of guineas at 22s., cut his teeth in committee at the start of the next session over the issue of the importation of money, and told on 3 Jan. 1698 against a motion to amend a bill to prevent hammered coin from entering the currency. On 8 Mar. 1697 he and fellow Levant merchant Thomas Molyneux* were granted leave to bring in a bill to exempt two Turkey merchants from the law that prohibited the import of their goods in foreign-built ships. He told on 30 Mar. with Sir William Ashurst*, a leader of the Presbyterian merchants in the City, on a motion to commit the wine duties supply bill. On 13 Jan. 1698 Davall and his Harwich colleague, Sir Thomas Middleton, were ordered to prepare a bill to prevent the influx of poor people by packet boats at the port, and, after a fortnight's leave of absence granted on 15 Mar., he resumed his concern about the numbers of poor in Essex when he was appointed to the committee for erecting hospitals and workhouses in Colchester. Davall seems to have been one of the underwriters of the Royal Company dealing with lustrings, a glossy silk fabric imported from France; on 16 Apr. 1698 the House heard that one of those accused of illegally importing the French goods was 'bound for the company' to Sir Thomas who 'had double the value of the money lent, in goods, in his hands, as security', and on 19 May he was appointed to the committee examining ways to encourage the trade legally.[6]

Davall was re-elected in July 1698, and the following session was to prove the most active of his career, probably because of his strong sympathies for the Country party at this time, which were noted on one contemporary list. Forecast as a likely opponent of a standing army, he used his local knowledge to attack the administration of the navy, rehearsing in committee on 10 Mar. 1699 the charge that 'preference to particular men' had resulted in 'a great damage to the nation'. On 27 Mar. he pressed home his dissatisfaction by acting as teller with Sir John Bolles, 4th Bt., on an amendment to a resolution on the state of the navy that would have moderated condemnation of its victuallers. On 5 Jan. 1699 he told in favour of a resolution concerning the suppression of vice and immorality, and on 17 Mar. was teller for Country Tory Sir Henry Gough* in the disputed election for Tamworth. On 21 Jan. he promoted Harwich's important fishing industry by presenting a bill to make Billingsgate, in London, a free market for the sale of fish; on 16 Mar. he reported from its committee, and managed a subsequent conference with the Lords over amendments to the bill. He was also one of three Members ordered to bring in a bill for expanding trade with Russia, and on the 25th and 27th chaired and reported on the subject.

A friendship between Davall and Sir George Hungerford, who had also been appointed to the Russia committee and was also interested in the navy, may explain why Sir Thomas was a teller on 21 Apr. on a motion about reflections on the Whig Henry Blaake, who was Hungerford's son-in-law, even though the reflections centred on Blaake's support of Davall's hated standing army. In the next session Davall maintained his Country stance, acting as teller on 4 Mar. 1700 against a motion to consider supply. He also told on 10 Jan. 1700 on an amendment to the bill to restore Blackwell Hall market to the clothiers. He was classed as being in the Old East India Company interest in early 1700.[7]

Davall was re-elected in January 1701 and was listed among the likely supporters of the Court over making good deficiencies in parliamentary funds. On 23 May he asserted that the excise revenues would raise far more in peacetime and that the King could therefore be allowed a very generous settlement of the civil list. This change from hostility to sympathy for the Court reflected William's turn to the Tories, and Davall seems to have felt a diminished need for activity now that the administration seemed to be in more trustworthy hands. He was only active in this and subsequent Parliaments on private estate bills. He was again returned in November 1701, and was marked as a Tory by Harley the following month. As befitted the lord of the manor, he made time for local concerns, being consulted over Harwich's custom house in 1700, and by the captains of its packet-boats in 1703. Despite being blacklisted as an opponent of the war with France, Davall was once more elected in 1702. He was listed as a supporter of the motion vindicating the Commons' proceedings in the impeachment of King William's ministers on 30 Mar. Having been listed as a probable opponent of the Tack, he duly voted against it or was absent from the House on 28 Nov. 1704, though he was marked as 'High Church' on an analysis of Parliament the following year. Preparations for the 1705 election began early, with rumours circulating in May 1704 that Davall intended to put up his son, Thomas II*, as a candidate, perhaps to run alongside him. In July it was thought that he only 'aims for himself, and very coldly for any colleague, having thoughts for his son', but in the event Sir Thomas stood alone, and was successful. Although he voted for the Court candidate as Speaker when the new Parliament met on 25 Oct. 1705, possibly through Harley's influence and not, as has been suggested, because he was a placeman, there is little other evidence of his activities in the House. He was marked as a Tory in early 1708, and was one of those marked as a

Tory loss in the May election of that year, but his defeat can have come as no great surprise. As far back as March 1707 he was reported 'to be in fear for himself' on account of the growing interest of Thomas Frankland I*, a Whig who used his place in the Post Office so successfully that by August 1707 Davall was already thought to have lost the struggle. Indeed in April 1708 the corporation were alleged to be 'unanimously agreed to sink' him. Always determined to stand on his own, to the point of selfishness, Davall was unwilling to join with the courtier John Ellis, though the latter was informed that even if Davall was to do so 'he has not honour enough in his temper not to drop you to preserve himself'. The following spring Frankland and Sir John Leake* joined interests, so that, as one mocking report had it, 'the liberal, magnificent, strong-brained Sir Thomas Davall will no more . . . appear for that corporation. They design to turn him out of his recorder's place.' The end of Davall's parliamentary career was not, however, so clear-cut. When Leake opted to serve for Rochester, a by-election was held on 6 Dec. 1708 at which a double return was made of Davall and Kenrick Edisbury*. On 18 Dec. Davall petitioned that he had one more undisputed vote than his rival, but Edisbury counter-petitioned two days later that Davall's agents had been guilty of malpractice. On 13 Jan. 1709 the Commons voted the by-election void, and ordered a new one, at which Sir Thomas was finally defeated.[8]

Although Davall had been appointed as a commissioner for the London lieutenancy in 1704 and was 'drunk to' in April 1709 by the lord mayor to nominate him for sheriff, his public life was effectively over. He may have sold all his East India stock by 1702, perhaps to his younger son Daniel who first appears as a committee man of the company that year, but must have reacquired it since he was an unsuccessful Tory nominee for a directorship in April 1711. He died the following November, and according to the local historian Taylor, who wrote less than 20 years later, was buried on 7 Dec. 1712 at Ramsey church; Davall's wife stated in her will that he was buried at St. Michael Stone, near Harwich, and bequeathed money for the minister there.[9]

[1] *Merchant Taylors' Sch. Reg.* ed. Hart; *The Gen.* n.s. xxxi. 237–8; *Mar. Lic. Vicar-Gen.* (Harl. Soc. xxxiv), 169; J. H. Bloom, *Her. and MIs Harwich*, ped.; Shaw, *Knights*, ii. 258. [2] Guildhall Lib. Haberdashers' Co. minute bk. 15842/3, ff. 279, 299; info. from Prof. R. R. Walcott and Prof. H. Horwitz. [3] Harwich bor. recs. 98/4, f. 167; S. Taylor, *Hist. and Antiquities of Harwich* (1730), 207; *Oath Bk . . . of Colchester* ed. Benham, 249. [4] *CJ*, xii. 508; Pittis, *Present Parl.* 349. [5] *The Gen.* n.s. xxxi. 237–8; A. W. C. Boevey, *Perverse Widow*, 235; *Mar. Lic. Vicar-Gen.* 169; *CSP Dom.* 1685, p. 56; Taylor, 207; *CJ*, x. 602; W. Suss. RO, Shillinglee mss Ac.454/816, Hippolitus de Luzancy to Sir Edward Turnor*, 17 Mar. 1690. [6] Add. 61611, f. 179; *Cal. Treas. Bks.* xviii. 62; *CJ*, xi. 568. [7] *Cam. Misc.* xxix. 389–90. [8] Add. 28886, f. 158; 28890, f. 358; 28891, ff. 241, 278, 322; 28927, ff. 176, 180, 322; *Cocks Diary*, 144; *Cal. Treas. Pprs.* 1697–1702, p. 420; *Bull. IHR* xlv, 51. [9] Taylor, 207; Luttrell, *Brief Relation*, vi. 43; *EHR*, lxxi. 227; *Daily Courant*, 13 Apr. 1711; Boevey, 237.

M. J. K.

DAVALL, Sir Thomas II (1682–1714), of Burr Street, Wapping, Mdx., Dovercourt and Grays, Essex.

HARWICH 1713–Apr. 1714

bap. 25 Oct. 1682, o. surv. s. of Sir Thomas Davall I*. *m.* c.1713, Lydia Catherine, da. of John Van Hatten, of St. Swithin's, London, 2s. *suc.* fa. 1712; kntd. 17 June 1713.[1]

Davall's career was very much overshadowed by that of his father, and little is known about his early life, or the extent of his involvement in business ventures, although it may have been he who built a wharf for the family's lime kiln at Grays Thurrock. His father had hoped to secure a Harwich seat for him as early as 1704, but it was not until he had inherited the manor of Dovercourt, and been knighted in 1713 for having presented an address of thanks for the peace, that he was successful at the polls. Although three candidates had in fact been returned on two indentures, Davall's name was common to both and on 6 Apr. 1714 the House confirmed his election. He had been marked as a Tory on the Worsley list, but died later the same month leaving no trace of any activity in the Journals. He bequeathed £4,000 to his mother, all his Essex estates passed to his eldest son, Thomas, and all other property to a new-born infant; but, perhaps because he had married his first cousin, the two boys were sickly, the younger dying soon after his father and the elder being buried in June 1718. The deaths of all Davall's direct heirs gave rise to a legal suit over the terminology of his will, in which he, or an amanuensis, had used a confused form of words. The case was heard in Chancery between 1719 and 1722, and judgment was given in favour of Sir Thomas' cousin, Daniel Burr, who thereby gained the Essex and Middlesex properties, though a subsequent settlement gave Davall's widow her jointure of £800, as well as her late husband's personal estate. This was enough to attract the attention of her second spouse, the Duke of Chandos (Hon. James Brydges*) though she was considered to have married above herself, often being 'reproached with her being bred in Burr Street, Wapping'.[2]

[1] IGI, London, and Berks.; *The Gen.* n.s. xxxi. 237–8. [2] *VCH Essex*, viii. 43, 45; Add. 28927, f. 176; *London Gazette*, 16–20 June 1713; Boyer, *Pol. State*, vii. 412; Folger Shakespeare Lib. Newdigate newsletter 29 Apr. 1714; PCC 65 Aston; Morant, *Essex*, i. 492; *Swift Corresp.* ed. Williams, iv. 476.

M. J. K.

DAVENANT, Charles (1656–1714), of Red Lion Square, Mdx.[1]

ST. IVES   1685–1687
GREAT BEDWYN   1698–1701 (Nov.)

b. 17 Nov. 1656, 2nd but 1st surv. s. of Sir William Davenant of Lincoln's Inn Fields, Mdx., being 1st s. by his 3rd w. Henriette Marie du Tremblay, wid. of St. Germain Beaupré of Anjou, France *educ.* Cheam g.s. 1665; Balliol, Oxf. 1673–5; travelled abroad (Holland) c.1673–5; LL.D. Camb. 1675; Doctors' Commons 1675. *m.* ?(1) 1678, da. of Lionel Walden† of Huntingdon, *s.p.*; (2) c.1679, Frances, da. and h. of James Molins, MD, of Shoe Lane, London 3s. (2 *d.v.p.*) 6da. *suc.* fa. 1668.

Commr. excise 1678–89, hearth tax 1684–Jan. 1685, July 1685–9; sec. to commrs. for union with Scotland 1702–3; inspector-gen. of imports and exports 1703–*d*.[2]

The dominant theme in Davenant's life after the Revolution was a constant lack of money. Out of office in 1689, and 'very poor', he put aside his earlier allegiance to James II, swallowed his pride, and began almost immediately to apply to the Williamite government for a revenue post suitable to his talents and experience. 'I must own', he wrote to one leading Whig, 'the hard usage I met with might at first perhaps draw some little anger from me, but I ... quieted those resentments and satisfied myself for my private loss with the good I saw the commonwealth was to receive by the Revolution.' His most important contact in the new administration was Lord Godolphin (Sidney†), who was recommending him to the King as early as 1689. As Godolphin's influence waned and that of the Whig Junto waxed his chances of employment diminished. Failure rankled with him. He suspected some prejudice in the ministry, and this in due course sharpened his satires on the Junto. His early writings, on trade and economic policy, were intended to impress those in power: the *Essay upon the Ways and Means of Supplying the War* in December 1694, its unpublished 'supplement' in November 1695, and the privately circulated 'memorials' on the coinage, public credit and the council of trade in 1696. He argued against heavy taxation, long-term government borrowing ('the new funds for interest') and a recoinage, and in favour of a retrenchment of war expenditure, the 'enlargement of public credit', the establishment of a council of trade, and the replacement of the land and poll taxes by a general excise. A number of central themes of his later political pamphleteering were already present: his support for 'the landed interest' against merely moneyed wealth, his belief that too great a commitment by England to land campaigns in Europe would harm the domestic economy, his preference for the navy over land forces as the principal arm of national defence, and the necessity to pursue competition for trade and colonies. When developed, these would form the basis of the Tory critique of William's and Marlborough's wars. They were never really to the taste of the Whig ministry, and Davenant's cause was not assisted by a style that was long-winded and abstruse, and on occasion too obviously pedagogic. Three times he came close to success in his quest for office: in 1694, when he nearly secured the surveyor-generalship of the salt duty; in May 1696, when John Locke pipped him to a seat on the Board of Trade; and later in the summer of 1696, when he obtained Treasury backing for the post of surveyor-general of the excise but was blackballed by the excise commissioners.[3]

This third disappointment, and Godolphin's resignation in October 1696, appears to have been decisive. Davenant swiftly signalled a radical change of attitude with his 'Essay on Public Virtue', dedicated to Godolphin and the Duke of Shrewsbury, which was an almost hysterical attack on the 'corruption' of the Junto ministers, 'persons weak, ambitious, light, designing, rash, unskilful in the arts of wise administration, versed in nothing but craft and tricks'. He became a kind of unofficial adviser to the 'new Country party' opposition, at first chiefly on economic matters, which were still the main preoccupation of his writing. For remunerative employment he had to look in other directions. One pamphlet, the *Essay on the East India Trade* (1696), which was a defence of the East India trade in general and the Old Company in particular, was useful in forwarding his efforts to enter that company's service. From November 1698 he was paid a retainer of £1 a day in advance of a promised appointment as unofficial 'ambassador' to India for the company (to counteract the embassy of William Norris* for the New Company). In an analysis of the House in early 1700 into interests he was classed with the supporters of the Old Company, and during the session he assisted in the passage of the East India Act. When this measure became law and his travels could begin, he excused himself from the commitment, presumably because he had now, after a long interval, resumed a parliamentary career, and prospects of advancement seemed bright. He had been returned at the 1698 election on the Bruce interest at Great

Bedwyn. A frequenter of the Grecian tavern, along with Anthony Hammond*, Walter Moyle* and other 'Country party' stalwarts, he was classed as a supporter of the Country party in a comparative analysis of the old and new Parliaments, and was forecast as likely to oppose a standing army. The first of his pamphlets to make a significant political impact was the *Discourse of Grants and Resumptions*, written in the summer of 1699 and published late in the year, on the subject of the grants of Irish forfeited estates, then under investigation by parliamentary commissioners. He was in close touch with these commissioners, especially Francis Annesley*, and his aim was to 'endeavour to prepare the town' to give their report 'a kind reception'. In putting the case for resumption on the grounds of financial necessity, Davenant recited historical precedents and also pre-empted the arguments of the 'poor Protestant purchasers' in Ireland by reminding his audience that Ireland had been reconquered at the expense of the English taxpayer and that Parliament had given fair warning of its intentions, thus disposing in advance of the two main props of the Junto Whig case. But his most important service to the Country party was to shift the focus on the subject of the grievance from the King himself to his 'favourites' and to the Junto, and thereby to integrate this issue into the wider campaign against the ministry. There were attacks on Portland, Lady Orkney and Charles Montagu*, and he summarized his position by observing of the forfeitures that 'it would be very hard if all this should be intercepted from the public, and that we should waste our blood and treasure only to enrich a few private persons'. The *Discourse*, selling in great numbers, effectively paved the way for the resumption bill, a measure Davenant himself helped to draft. He was not, however, a candidate for the board of trustees elected under the bill. Indeed, it is likely that he had publicly disavowed any interest, since he received not one vote in the ballot.[4]

Davenant had established himself as the Tories' leading propagandist, writing at the behest of Tory politicians and with the close co-operation of Robert Harley* in particular. It was Harley who made available to him various documents to facilitate his *Essays upon . . . the Balance of Power*, composed in 1700 and printed in February 1701, which was an attack on the Partition Treaty and a warning against any return of the Junto ministers with their self-interested and damaging war policies. This was another *tour de force*, though in the long run it was to leave him open to accusations of favouring the French, and therefore the Pretender, and in the short run it aroused the anger of Convocation, from which he was fortunate to escape lightly, on account of his wild denunciations of Whig bishops as persons that 'almost from their cradles' had professed 'enmity . . . to the divinity of Christ'. Later in the year came his most successful piece of political journalism, *The True Picture of a Modern Whig*, an incisive satire that, in synthesizing his own and other criticisms of the Junto Whig administration, was to have a seminal effect on the development of Tory ideology. His principal character, 'Tom Double', the self-seeking, unprincipled 'modern Whig', was set against 'Whiglove', the embodiment of the old Whig tradition, to emphasize that the Junto represented a mushroom-like political interest, lacking any foundation but corruption. Having been appointed to the abortive commission of accounts on 17 June, he was struck off by a Lords' amendment as a reprisal for his earlier disparagement of the episcopate. He was listed as likely to support the Court in continuing the 'Great Mortgage' in February 1701. Opposed to the idea of a war with France (at least until the death of James II and Louis XIV's recognition of the Pretender) he was well acquainted with the French ambassador, Tallard, and after Tallard's departure stayed in touch with the chargé d'affaires, Poussin, who reported that Davenant claimed to be well disposed towards the Pretender. This friendship with Poussin proved his downfall, as Davenant was one of three Tory Members discovered in September 1701 supping with the Frenchman and the Spanish consul Navarra, another long-standing acquaintance, at the Blue Posts tavern. For all his protests that the presence of Poussin was 'a mere accident' for which he was in no way responsible, Davenant, like the other 'Poussineers', became the victim of a Whig smear campaign. He was blacklisted as having voted against the preparations for war; was taunted in public by Whigs 'mimicking in gibberish speech Monsieur Poussin'; and his *Essays upon . . . the Balance of Power* were declared to have been commissioned by French gold. This last canard was already well established: Navarra related how 'Dr Davenant said at the Blue Posts if it were known he was with them people would swear he had the 7,000 pistoles they had talked of'. However, while the French were well aware of his vulnerability – 'il a une grosse famille avec peu de bien', observed Poussin – they did not take advantage of it. Ironically, the incident had occurred at a time when even Davenant had come round to the feeling that war was inevitable. He attempted a piece 'to make men lay aside their animosities for the good of the public', and 'to show the necessity of a war against France', but abandoned it in the face of a strenuously and bitterly fought election, in which he was a prime sufferer on the Tory side.

Rejected at Bedwyn, he was still hopeful that 'I have done my country so much service that some friend or other will bring me into this Parliament', but such was the effect of the discovery at the Blue Posts, and his inability to explain himself adequately, that no one did.[5]

After the debacle of the Poussin affair and the disappointments of the election, Davenant remained on the defensive for a spell, keeping out of the limelight as far as he could. A sequel to *The True Picture*, entitled *Tom Double Returned out of the Country*, was published anonymously in January 1702, and although the Lords were provoked to inquire into the authorship by an allusion in the pamphlet to a Whig scheme to exclude Anne from the succession, Davenant was not exposed. On behalf of Jane Lavallin he undertook the parliamentary management of a private bill arising from the Resumption Act, running into more trouble with the Lords in the process, when his client's clumsy endeavours to solicit her cause left him open to possible charges of bribery. He stood unsuccessfully at New Shoreham in 1702, and two other efforts to re-enter Parliament also came to grief. He returned to the possibility of an official salary as a means of staving off his creditors. He looked for assistance from Godolphin, Harley and Lord Nottingham (Daniel Finch†), who were all bombarded with offers and schemes. He obtained a diplomatic posting for his son, and for himself the place of secretary to the short-lived union commission, 'a present entertainment' that would suffice until 'something better' and more permanent should 'fall'. Prior to the commission's first meeting it was reported that Davenant was busy 'consulting papers about what was transacted in King James I's and King Charles's reign'. He also declined two offers of an excise commissionership, which was proof to Godolphin that 'vanity and folly well rooted are not to be cured even by necessity itself'. When he missed the vacancy for auditor of the imprest his discontent reached the ears of the newswriters and it was reported that he charged 'a great man [Godolphin] . . . with breach of promise'. Eventually in June 1703 an appropriate niche was found for him as inspector-general of imports and exports, where his self-proclaimed expertise in fiscal matters could be put to good use. He marked his satisfaction with the *Essays upon Peace at Home and War Abroad* (1703) 'the design' of which was 'to recommend moderation' and in particular to oppose the second occasional conformity bill. It was said that Marlborough and Godolphin had personally encouraged him to write it, and that a former victim of his pen, Lord Halifax (Montagu), had read the proofs. For this 'shaking hands with his old friends' and enlistment 'with a new party' he was savaged by Tories in Parliament and in the press, who accused him of emulating his own creation, 'Tom Double'. Sir Edward Seymour, 4th Bt.*, referred to him as 'a profligate scribbler', while a Tory pamphleteer wrote of

> a certain doctor, who after having scribbled himself, and that simple wretch his son, into preferment, has lately appeared in his proper colours, and unsaid what he had formerly urged with so much vehemence and pretended zeal for his country's good.

Davenant regarded himself as having suffered in a good cause: 'I may venture to say, for this last age there has not been so persecuted a martyr to truth, and right sense, as I have been.'[6]

Until the fall of the Godolphin ministry Davenant seems to have been happy to collect his salary and espouse moderation only in his correspondence. The 'changes at court' in 1708 did not affect him, as he still possessed 'some interest with those above', though his creditors were frightened enough to 'come at' him in droves for their money, 'with the utmost rage and violence'. Much of his energy was spent in this way, coping with the 'torments' of debt, dodging the duns and avoiding arrest, a struggle in which he was greatly helped by his friend Hon. James Brydges*. In return he counselled and assisted Brydges in the paymaster's efforts to curry favour with the 'duumvirs', especially Marlborough, to whom Davenant was accustomed to write toadying letters. The essence of Davenant's advice to Brydges was that 'at court they who undervalue themselves, will soon be undervalued by others'. He survived the transition to a Tory ministry in 1710 by virtue of his previous friendship with Harley, and his opportunism in resurrecting the characters of 'Tom Double' and 'Whiglove' to satirize the old ministry and extol the new. In *Sir Thomas Double at Court* (1710) and *New Dialogues upon the Present Posture of Affairs* (1710) his story was brought up to date, with an even stronger emphasis on the clash between the 'landed' and 'moneyed' interests. 'Whiglove' had by now transmuted into a Tory, having supposedly succeeded to the family baronetcy of 'Comeover'. It is worth pointing out, however, that in private Davenant had always been opposed to 'this tedious war' and sceptical of the role of 'the confederates', especially the Dutch. He was soon outpaced as a ministerial polemicist by his 'cousin' Jonathan Swift, who took up many of Davenant's themes and ideas in his own writings. Indeed, Davenant was suspected in some quarters of being the author of *The Conduct of the Allies*, and lost a dinner with the Dutch envoy as a result. His last years saw him in miserable health and even deeper in debt, living mainly off the hospitality of Brydges, to whom he owed at his death several thousand pounds. Davenant died on 6 Nov, 1714 and was buried in the church of St. Bride's, Fleet Street.[7]

[1] *HMC 7th Rep.* 680. Unless otherwise stated, this biography is based on D. A. G. Waddell, 'The Career and Writings of Charles Davenant' (Oxf. Univ. D. Phil. thesis, 1954), summarized in an article by the same author in *Econ. Hist. Rev.* n.s. xi. 279–88. [2] *Cal. Treas. Bks.* v. 1055; vii. 1074; viii. 247; ix. 190. [3] *Macky Mems.* (1733), 132–3; Add. 7121, f. 19; H. Horwitz, *Parl. and Pol. Wm. III*, 93. [4] W. Moyle, *Works* ed. Hammond (1727), 21; Univ. Kansas Spencer Research Lib. Moore mss 143 Cz.3, Annesley to [Arthur Moore*], 5 Aug. 1699; J. G. Simms, *Williamite Confiscation in Ire.* 111, 124–7; Add. 17677 TT, f. 311; 70036, f. 98. [5] Horwitz, 268; Add. 30000 D, f. 225; 17677 UU, ff. 276, 302, 313; 40775, ff. 110–12, 215, 220–1; 17677 WW, ff. 271, 345; 70075–6, newsletter 27 Nov. 1701; *HMC Portland*, iv. 5, 30; *HMC Cowper*, ii. 410, 436; *Vernon–Shrewsbury Letters*, iii. 149–50; J. P. Kenyon, *Revol. Principles*, 177; *Clarendon Corresp.* ed. Singer, ii. 398; Luttrell, *Brief Relation*, v. 100, 116; Huntington Lib. Stowe mss 58(1), p. 26; Wilts. RO, Ailesbury mss, Davenant to Ld. Bruce (Charles*), 20 Nov. 1701; Cumbria RO (Carlisle), Lonsdale mss D/Lons/W2/2/4, James* to Sir John Lowther, 2nd Bt. I*, 29 Nov. 1701. [6] Add. 29588, ff. 70, 177–8; 70225, Nottingham to Harley, 9 July 1702; 70075–6, newsletters 21 Jan., 20 Nov. 1703; 17677 YYY, f. 161; 61459, f. 138; 4291, f. 14; Strathmore mss at Glamis Castle, box 70, folder 2, bdle. 2, newsletter 17 Oct. 1702; *HMC Lords*, n.s. v. 46–48; Luttrell, v. 175; *HMC Portland*, iv. 48, 50, 52; HLRO, Hist. C/5, BRA 833, Abel Boyer to [–], 22 Dec. 1703; Calamy, *Life*, ii. 16; Lansd. 773, f. 8. [7] Lansd. 773, ff. 27, 32–33, 49, 57, 66–67; Huntington Lib. Q. vi. 313–16, 318–19, 328–31; Stowe mss 58(6), pp. 65–66; Add. 4291, ff. 3, 64–65; 70222, Davenant to Oxford, 19 Oct., 10 Dec. 1713; *Swift Corresp.* ed. Williams, i. 13; *Swift Stella* ed. Davis, ii. 429.

D. W. H.

DAVENANT, Thomas (d. 1697)

EYE   1690–25 July 1697

Exon, yeoman of the guard 1697–d.

Thomas Davenant has not been identified. He may have been the younger brother of Charles Davenant* (sixth son of Sir William Davenant by his third wife, Henriette Marie du Tremblay). This Thomas Davenant was admitted to the Middle Temple in 1681. The Member was returned on the Cornwallis interest at Eye in 1690 and was classed as a Whig by Lord Carmarthen (Sir Thomas Osborne†). Robert Harley* listed him as a doubtful Court supporter in April 1691. Forecast as likely to vote with the administration in the divisions of 31 Jan. 1696 on the proposed council of trade, he signed the Association promptly. He voted on 25 Nov. 1696 for the attainder of Sir John Fenwick†. Lord Cornwallis had put forward his name without success in the winter of 1695–6 for a vacancy in the yeomen of the guard, renewing his recommendation the following June. Davenant's pretensions were supported by Lord Somers (Sir John*) and the Duke of Shrewsbury, who both testified to his 'honesty' in Parliament, claiming that he had 'never failed a vote to serve' King William and that he 'would be entirely satisfied with the gift of this place'. He was sworn as exon in the yeomen in April 1697.[1]

Davenant died on 25 July 1697 'of a fever at Moor Park'. Administration was granted to one Robert Cowper.[2]

[1] Hoare, *Wilts.* Frustfield, 86; *M.T. Adm.* i. 204; *HMC Buccleuch*, ii. 353; Nottingham Univ. Lib. Portland (Bentinck) mss PwA 1180, Somers to Portland, 19 June 1696; *Cal. Treas. Bks.* xiv. 143; *CSP Dom.* 1697, p. 125. [2] *CSP Dom.* 1697, p. 268; *Cal. Treas. Bks.* xiii. 378.

D. W. H.

DAVERS, Sir Robert, 2nd Bt. (c.1653–1722), of Rougham and Rushbrooke, Suff.

BURY ST. EDMUNDS   1689–1701 (Nov.)
                               22 Nov. 1703–1705
SUFFOLK   1705–1 Oct. 1722

b. c.1653, o. s. of Sir Robert Davers, 1st Bt., of St. George's, Barbados and Rougham by Eleanor ?Luke. m. 2 Feb. 1682, Mary, da. and coh. of Thomas Jermyn†, 2nd Baron Jermyn, 6s. (3 d.v.p.) 5da. suc. fa. as 2nd Bt. c.June 1685.[1]

Member of council, Barbados 1682–aft. 1695; baron, later chief baron, of exchequer and j.c.p. Barbados 1683–c.1687.[2]

Freeman, Bury St Edmunds 1689.[3]

The son of a wealthy Barbados planter who had bought the manor of Rougham in 1680, Davers himself came back from the West Indies to settle there in about 1687 and was chosen on his father-in-law's interest for the nearby borough of Bury St. Edmunds in the Convention. He stood unsuccessfully for the county in 1690 but was re-elected at Bury. Lord Carmarthen (Sir Thomas Osborne†) listed him in March 1690 as a Tory supporter of the Court. He told on 11 Apr. for an amendment to the poll tax bill; on 12 Apr. on the Tory side in the disputed election for Bedford; twice on 14 Apr., against recommitting a naturalization bill (a type of measure which he was consistently to oppose) and against taking into custody the Tory mayor of Plympton Erle; and on 26 Apr. against the committal of the abjuration bill. Despite being given six days' leave of absence on 6 May, he told the following day against committing the bill for improving the woollen manufacture. Carmarthen forecast in December 1690 that Davers would probably support him in the event of an attack on his ministerial position in the Commons. His five tellerships in the 1690–1 session were: in favour of going into committee on the land tax bill (28 Oct.); in a division on the

Cirencester election (4 Nov.); in favour of Sir Carbery Pryse, 4th Bt.*, in a disputed election for Cardiganshire (28 Nov.); against adjourning the debate on the city of London charter controversy (11 Dec.); and against one of the clauses proposed by the committee on the attainder bill (18 Dec.). Also in December he assisted in the management of a private bill. Robert Harley* listed him as a Country party supporter in April 1691.[4]

On 21 Nov. 1691 Davers presented a bill to remedy abuses in the weighing and packing of butter. He told on 1 Dec. for Sir Basil Firebrace* in the Chippenham election case, and again on 14 Dec. against sending for one Captain Tilford, who claimed to have information about smugglers. He was one of the Members who moved on 16 Dec. for leave for a bill to encourage privateering against French ships. On 5 Jan. 1692 he reported a bill to transfer the collection of the alnage duty to the customs service, and managed it through subsequent stages in the Commons, including its re-committal. Other tellerships in this session were: on 8 Jan. 1692, for an amendment to the East India bill, which aimed at preserving the company's monopoly of trade; on 23 Jan., against the bill to lower interest rates; and on 25 Jan., against adjourning the debate on the Commons' amendments to the treason trials bill. He joined other Members from East Anglia and the south-east of England in arguing in ways and means on 18 Dec. in favour of settling the land tax at a fixed rate of 4s. in the pound. The following day he spoke against the abjuration bill at its second reading, claiming that 'this bill does not agree with the title. The body of the bill is to make words treason, which will in effect make all gentlemen slaves to their servants.' He was also a teller against the bill. From December he managed the reintroduced alnage duty bill, carrying it up to the Lords on 6 Feb. 1693. On 10 Jan. 1693 he had spoken and acted as a teller against a clause proposed to be added to the land tax bill, to suspend for the duration of the war all government pensions except those which the barons of the Exchequer exempted. It was, he said, 'unjust to put it in the power of the barons to determine as they please'. In ways and means on 10 Feb. Davers was reported to have 'proposed a single poll', and four days later he told against John Lamotte Honywood* in an election petition for Essex.[5]

Davers was a teller on 27 Nov. 1693 on a question relating to the victualling of the navy in the previous campaign, and again two days afterwards in support of the Tory admirals during another debate on the conduct of the fleet. He was active in investigations into the woollen industry in Norwich and told on 14 Feb. in condemnation of the practices of the Weavers' Company there. He also told on 20 Dec. 1693 for an amendment relating to armed forces in Barbados in the report on supply; on 4 Jan. 1694 against committing the naturalization bill; on 10 Jan. against going into committee on the petition for a new East India company; and on 24 Jan. against committing the bill to revive the 1689 Woollen Act. In the 1694–5 session he told on 8 Feb. against the bill to permit the importing in English ships of wines and other goods from Portugal, Spain and Italy. He reported a private bill on 20 Mar.

On 13 Dec. 1695 Davers presented a bill to suppress hawkers and pedlars. Forecast as likely to vote against the Court in the divisions of 31 Jan. 1696 on the proposed council of trade, he was a teller in the debate against the resolution that members of the council be obliged to swear that William was 'rightful and lawful King'. He was named to the committee on 4 Feb. on the bill for regulating elections, a familiar topic for him, and on 20 Feb. was a teller against the bill confirming William and Mary's grant to the Earl of Torrington (Arthur Herbert†) of land in the Bedford Level. When Torrington's bill was reported on 18 Apr. Davers was again a teller, this time in favour of agreeing with the committee's amendment that Torrington be obliged to perform all the various covenants and agreements made by King James II. He told on 28 Feb. against an amendment to the wine duties bill. On 16 Mar. he reported the bill to encourage woollen manufactures, and on the 26th presented a bill to encourage the Irish linen industry. In the same month he voted against fixing the price of guineas at 22s. Although Davers had signed the Association, he told on 7 Apr. against making subscription compulsory for Members. He also told on 17 Apr. in favour of receiving the report on the garbling spices bill. A teller twice, on 16 and 17 Nov., in support of Sir John Fenwick†, he voted on 25 Nov. against the bill for Fenwick's attainder. The following February he told against giving leave for a general naturalization bill (8 Feb. 1697) and in favour of the King's Lynn harbour bill (18 Feb.). He was given leave of absence the following month. On 30 Mar. 1698 he told in favour of the bill to suppress blasphemy. Listed in September as a member of the Country party, he was forecast in October as likely to oppose a standing army. On 15 Mar. 1699 he presented a bill to prevent export of wool and encourage woollen manufacture. In the 1699–1700 session he managed the Deal waterworks bill. He told on 26 Feb. 1700 against a bill to make a particular vessel a 'free ship'; on 1 Apr. for a clause to be added to the Irish forfeitures resumption bill; on 2 Feb. against the bill prolonging the time for the export of corn; and twice on 26 Mar., first on a procedural point, and then in opposition to a Whig amendment to the proposed address about the commissions of the peace.

A teller for his friend Robert Harley in the division on the Speaker on 10 Feb. 1701, Davers was forecast later that month as likely to support the Court over continuing the 'Great Mortgage'. On 12 Mar. he reintroduced the Deal waterworks bill, and resumed responsibility for its parliamentary management. In the debate on 9 May on the Dutch request for aid he opposed John Grobham Howe's motion for an address couched merely in general terms, saying

> that he had given great attention to the debate; that he was very sensible of the bad condition the Dutch were in; that we had had general questions enough and that we should particularly say that our ships, our men, our money were ready for the Dutch.

Despite this expression of bellicosity he was among those subsequently blacklisted for having opposed preparations for war. On 12 May he brought to the attention of the House the 'great quantities' of timber being felled in Enfield Chase. On 4 June he spoke 'to maintain the honour of the House' in the debate on the impeachments. The next day he told against the Halifax workhouse bill.⁶

Hitherto Davers had experienced no difficulties at Bury St. Edmunds, sharing the representation by agreement with the borough's Whig patron, John Hervey*, but in the second 1701 election Hervey resolved to turn him out, and Davers, who had not been in good health, was easily defeated. In 1702 he put up for the county as well as at Bury but without success. However, in 1703, after the death of his father-in-law, Lord Jermyn, he acquired the Rushbrooke estate near Bury St. Edmunds, buying the shares of his three surviving sisters-in-law and nephew for £24,000, and thereby strengthened his interest in the constituency. At a by-election in November 1703, after the purchase had been arranged but before it had been completed, he was able to defeat Hervey's nominee. The following year Defoe was to report from Bury that Davers 'rules this town'. Davers had previously been listed in error as having voted on 13 Feb. 1703 against agreeing with the Lords' amendments to the bill for enlarging the time for taking the oath of abjuration. He was chairman of the committee of January–February 1704 on the East Indian trade. He also managed a private bill during February, and presented a bill on the 11th to encourage English manufactures. In May he wrote the first of numerous surviving letters to Robert Harley, congratulating him on his appointment as secretary of state:

> I remembered what you said to me just before I took my leave of you, that the Whigs would not come in, but when Lord Nottingham [Daniel Finch†] laid down it was reported . . . that he was turned out, and the Whigs upon it grew more insolent . . . but when I heard you had that place I was at ease again.

On 13 Nov. he presented a bill to prevent the adulteration of wine. Davers figured in Harley's lobbying list for the Tack and was forecast as likely to support the motion, duly voting for it on 28 Nov. He was a teller on 14 Feb. 1705 against agreeing with the first of the Lords' amendments to the place bill; again on 21 Feb., in favour of retaining in the wine duties bill the clause exempting from poundage sugar imported from the colonies; and the next day, against a naturalization bill. Also in the same month he managed another private bill.⁷

Davers was returned in two constituencies in 1705: at the head of the poll for the county, in an election fought on the issue of the Tack; and also at Bury, despite possible government backing for the Hervey interest there and 'resentment' in the town at his putting up for knight of the shire. He naturally opted to sit as knight, and was marked as 'True Church' in a list of the new House and reckoned a 'loss' by the Earl of Sunderland (Charles, Lord Spencer*). He told Harley in July that he hoped the Duke of Marlborough (John Churchill†) 'will go on with success and beat the French into an honourable peace, not such [a] one as the last was made, for that was a wretched one', but early in the following October was presuming to warn his friend against the course the ministry was taking:

> I hope your interest will not come into choosing Jack Smith [John I] Speaker, for I very well remember what you said to me about him, and desire you may not have Cassandra's fate, for . . . she was ravished at last. Do you not remember that you told me my lord treasurer bid you tell me and all your friends he would not suffer a Whig to come into place nor a 'leagh' Tory. I will not launch out but will say we have been most barbarously used by one that we have not deserved it from. I have often told you that those vile wretches the Whigs only watch for an opportunity to tear you and that lord to pieces . . . and we that have stood by that noble lord and you [are] to be called factious and sent home with a paper on our backs to be torn to pieces by the mob! I do hope nothing of that matter lies at your door.

When Harley defended himself Davers was not really convinced:

> I . . . wish I knew what you mean in your letter where you say if we would but do what was reasonable without making any advances all would be well and the gentlemen

of England restored . . . this much I know, my friends, and that [were] yours once, do think you have left them . . . I can answer for myself, I have a true value for you and am vexed when I hear things that are said of you concerning public matters, for heavy loads are laid upon you.

He voted against Smith in the Speakership election on 25 Oct. 1705. He introduced a private bill on 17 Dec., and a bill for the reconstruction of the Eddystone lighthouse on 22 Jan. 1706, and managed both bills through the House. He told on 14 Dec. 1705, against adding the name of Henry Sparrow to the list in the land tax bill of commissioners for Ipswich, and on 1 Feb. 1706, in favour of a clause proposed for the supply bill (tonnage and poundage) regulating Exchequer fees.[8]

A teller again on 16 Dec. 1706 for an additional clause in the land tax bill, and on 23 Jan. 1707 in favour of Philip Herbert* in a disputed election for Rye, Davers chaired the committee in January–March to consider the state of trade, and presented on 10 Mar. a bill, pursuant to his report, relating to the salt duties. He was an unsuccessful candidate for chairman of the committee to bring in the bill of union. Having been first-named to a committee on a petition of the Royal African Company, he introduced a bill on 3 Mar. to oblige Henry Bishop and his accomplices to surrender themselves and their effects to the Company. He was still friendly enough with Harley to secure in June the approval of both Harley and Lord Chancellor Cowper (William*) concerning some recommendation he had made to the Suffolk commission of the peace, but when no changes were made within two months he wrote in irritation:

> Now, dear namesake, forgive me for being plain with you and thinking you have not been sincere with me. If it be in your power to put these gentlemen in, who is to blame? If it be not in your power, say so, and I will never ask you to do it. I do wish my good friend Mr Harley had never left the Speaker's place.

When Harley explained that it was Cowper who had objected to his nominee, Davers readily forgave the secretary, and by the beginning of the first Parliament of Great Britain the two men were once more on the best of terms, a situation which Harley, at that time constructing his 'middle scheme', was anxious to maintain. Classed as a Tory and as a Tacker in two lists of 1708, Davers presented two bills (29 Jan. and 26 Feb.) and was named to the committee for a bill to regulate the qualifications of governors of the Bank of England (26 Mar.). He told on 17 Mar. in favour of an additional clause to the bill to encourage the American trade.[9]

Davers was a teller on 5 Feb. 1708 on the Tory side for the Dunwich election case. His eldest son Robert was defeated in a by-election for Bury in March, after Davers had declared that he would not 'trouble his head' about the contest and that he would 'never concern himself' with that corporation 'again as long as he lives'. He voted in 1710 against the impeachment of Dr Sacheverell. He was a teller for Lewis Pryse in a disputed election for Cardiganshire (18 Jan. 1710), and against the Barber-Surgeons' Company bill (16 Feb.). On 11 Feb. he brought in a bill to amend his former Eddystone Lighthouse Act, a measure he subsequently guided through the Commons. Delighted at the political revolution which Robert Harley was working, he wrote in August to congratulate him on his 'glorious success' in 'getting over the black gentleman'. He added, 'go on with your blow and restore us'. In September he wrote again, urging the appointment of a Tory lord lieutenant for Suffolk before the expected dissolution; the next month it was the replacement of two 'notorious' receivers of taxes in the county which was urged. Returned without difficulty for Suffolk in 1710, although he once more failed to bring in his son at Bury, he was classed as a Tory in the 'Hanover list'. Listed as one of the 'Tory patriots' who had opposed the continuation of the war, he was a teller on the disputed election for Ipswich (3 Feb. 1711) and presented a bill to exempt the importing of French wines from the Act prohibiting trade with France (13 Feb. 1711), telling against hearing a petition from Exeter against the bill and in favour of a new clause which would allow foreign importers the same advantages as British merchants once the war was over (10 Mar.). A member of the October Club, he was also listed among the 'worthy patriots' who in this session exposed the mismanagements of the previous ministry. He managed three private bills. Having taken the chair of the committee to examine the Acts relating to London 'brokers', he was ordered on 7 May to bring in the resulting bill for the better preservation of public credit by regulating the activities of 'brokers and stock-jobbers'. In the same month he also served as chairman of the committees to repeal part of the Act to encourage the American trade, and to investigate the methods of computing duty on unrated goods from the East Indies.[10]

'Though you do not think of me', Davers wrote to Harley (now Earl of Oxford) at the beginning of November 1711, 'you are in my thoughts.' He had tried to see Oxford before leaving London, though in vain, having 'obeyed you in staying until the South Sea bill was passed'. Oxford replied by requesting his attendance again for the debates on the peace at the opening of Parliament, at which Davers promised to 'stand by you with my life and fortune. I beg of your lordship not to undertake to make the Whigs ashamed of anything they have done. It is washing a blackamoor white. But with your assistance I hope to make them examples.'

Again active in matters of trade and commerce, Davers chaired the committee on the American trade and presented a bill to relieve merchants importing prize goods from America (22 Feb. 1712); introduced a bill to encourage the importing of naval stores from Scotland (11 Apr.); moved for a bill to improve the collection of duty on imports from the East Indies (13 May); and presented another bill, to explain the Act for the relief of the Leeward Islands planters (19 May). He was a teller three times: on 12 May on an extra clause for the soap duties bill; on 14 May against agreeing with the Lords' amendment, on behalf of Quakers, to the bill to prevent fraudulent conveyances (for county elections); and on 3 June in favour of the bill to settle the African trade. Although he was said to have refused a place for himself on the commission of appeals, he had no such scruples when it came to jobs for his children, and in September 1712 wrote twice to remind Oxford of a promise to make young Robert an auditor of the excise, complaining somewhat pathetically that 'my patience is worn out, and my wife and son think it is my fault'. The appointment was eventually completed at the beginning of the following year. At the same time there was an unsubstantiated rumour that Davers was himself to return to Barbados as governor. He acted as teller on 2 May 1713 for leave for a bill to suspend for two months the duties on imported French wines. Having brought in the bill himself, he was again a teller on 4 May for its second reading. He served as a teller three times in favour of the reintroduced African trade bill; and in a debate on the bill on 1 June he moved that the House consider in a week's time the charter of the Royal African Company. Of particular assistance to the ministry was his work on the bill to put into effect the 8th and 9th articles of the French commercial treaty. He chaired the committee on the bill and was a teller for the Court in the crucial division of 18 June.[11]

Davers was returned once more for Suffolk in 1713 after a busy campaign, but he was slow to give assistance to party colleagues in other constituencies. Robert Monckton*, writing to Oxford to ask him 'to speak to Sir Robert Davers for his assistance to me at Ipswich', commented, 'Sir Robert is so heavy that unless you excite him he will not move'. Davers remained loyal to Oxford in 1714, reminding him in letters in March and July of various promises of help and preferment and pledging himself to be 'your faithful friend and servant . . . as long as I live'. He successfully moved on 6 May 1714 for a clause to be inserted into the bill to prevent importation of fresh fish by foreigners, in order to exempt the importing of lobsters. He was a teller on the Harwich election case on 25 May, and he managed a private estate bill during June. He was classed as a Tory in the Worsley list and in two lists of the Members re-elected in 1715, and remained a Tory under George I.[12]

Davers, whose portrait at Rushbrooke apparently reveals him as having been 'a big, red-faced man', died on 1 Oct. 1722, aged 69, 'of a violent fever attended with a dangerous diabetes'. By his will his property in Barbados, including slaves, was to be sold to pay his debts and various legacies. His second son Jermyn, who succeeded in 1723 as 4th baronet, sat for Bury St. Edmunds in the 1722 Parliament and for Suffolk 1727–43.[13]

[1] *Rushbrook Par. Reg.* (Suff. Green Bks. vi), 40, 162–70, 174–6, 352–66. [2] *CSP Col.* 1689–92, p. 146; 1693–6, p. 444; *Cal. Treas. Bks.* viii. 1820. [3] Suff. RO (Bury St. Edmunds), Bury St. Edmunds bor. recs. EE500/D4/1/2, f. 234. [4] *Rushbrook Par. Reg.* 349–54; Bodl. Tanner 27, f. 110. [5] *Luttrell Diary*, 83, 312, 314, 359, 417. [6] *Cocks Diary*, 117–18, 144. [7] *HMC Portland*, iv. 26–27, 86; Camb. Univ. Lib. Cholmondeley (Houghton) mss, Davers to Robert Walpole II*, 13 Dec. 1701; *Hervey Diary*, 35, 37, 40; *Hervey Letter Bks.* i. 175–6; *Rushbrook Par. Reg.* 347–8; *CJ*, xiv. 249; *Defoe Letters*, 58; Speck thesis, 63. [8] W. A. Speck, *Tory and Whig*, 102, 104; W. Suss. RO, Shillinglee mss Ac.454/878, Sir Edmund Bacon, 4th Bt.*, to [Sir Edward Turnor*], 20 Mar. [1705]; Add. 70222, Davers to Robert Harley, 19 July, 11 Oct. 1705; *HMC Portland*, iv. 256, 261. Note that the pet name 'your rosebud', which occurs in Davers' letters to Robert Harley (Add. 70222, 11 Oct. 1705, 12 July 1714), applied not to Davers himself, as stated in G. Holmes, *Pol. in Age of Anne*, 327, but to one of his daughters. [9] Folger Shakespeare Lib. Newdigate newsletter 1 Feb. 1706–7; L. K. J. Glassey, *Appt. JPs*, 182; Add. 70222, Davers to Harley, 10 June, 7 Nov. 1707; *HMC Portland*, iv. 434, 439. [10] *Hervey Letter Bks.* i. 243, 244, 273; *HMC Portland*, iv. 573, 590; Add. 70222, Davers to Harley, 14 Oct. 1710, 2, 29 Sept. 1712; 70217, William Churchill* to same, 19 May 1711; Boyer, *Pol. State*, i–ii. 288. [11] *HMC Portland*, v. 106, 113–14; Add. 70220, A. Cowper to Ld. Oxford, n.d.; *Cal. Treas. Bks.* xxvii. 92; Boyer, v. 359. [12] Add. 70222, Davers to Oxford, n.d. [recd. 10 July 1713], 4 Mar., 12 July 1714; *HMC Portland*, v. 377; P. S. Fritz, *Ministers and Jacobitism 1715–45*, p. 151. [13] *Rushbrook Par. Reg.* 90, 174–6, 363; *Hervey Letter Bks.* ii. 229, 231.

D. W. H.

DAVY, Robert (c.1657–1703), of Ditchingham, Norf.

NORWICH   1698–25 Oct. 1703

b. c.1657, o. s. of Robert Davy of Ditchingham by Margaret, da. of Philip Paine of Halesworth, Suff. *educ.* Exeter, Oxf. matric. 1659; St. John's, Oxf. BA 1662; I. Temple 1663, called 1673. *m.* by 1682, Anne (d. 1701), da. and h. of Francis Bacon (d. 1692) of St. Gregory's, Norwich, 1s. 1da. *suc.* fa. 1679.[1]

Steward, Norwich 1683–8, recorder 1688–d.[2]

Davy was returned for Norwich in 1698, having already held the recordership of the town for ten years. A Tory, he was classed in a list of the new Parliament as a Country party supporter, and it was forecast in October that he would vote against the standing army. In early 1699 the provisions of a private bill for the repair and maintenance of Great Yarmouth harbour concerned him, and (although not specifically appointed to any committee on this measure) he was involved in suggesting changes to it. But a prediction by Sir William Cook, 2nd Bt.*, that a clause devised by Davy would 'cause the bill to be recommitted' proved unfounded. Davy's only recorded parliamentary activity in the Journals was the management of a private bill on behalf of Norwich city corporation in February–March 1700. He was listed in February 1701 among those thought likely to support the Court party in continuing the 'Great Mortgage'. He was granted leave of absence for three weeks on 15 Mar. to attend his dying wife. In April 1701 it was reported by a Norfolk Whig that Davy and Thomas Blofield*, having 'voted for the peace of Europe', had 'mightily lost the good opinion' of their Norwich constituents, and he was included in the black list of those who had opposed preparations for war with France. Davy was re-elected in November, but only after a close contest. He voted on 26 Feb. 1702 for the resolution vindicating the conduct of the Commons in the previous year's impeachments, and in the 1702 election headed the poll at Norwich. Dean Prideaux, whom he had sometimes opposed, described him then as 'a hot-headed, weak man'.[3]

Given leave of absence for three weeks on 22 Dec. 1702, 'for recovery of his health', Davy died on 25 Oct. 1703 and was buried with his wife and her family in St. Gregory's church, Norwich. His son Robert, also a lawyer, figured in 1721 in the Jacobite Christopher Layer's list of the 'loyal gentlemen of Norfolk', with an estate of £800 a year.[4]

[1] IGI, Norf.; *E. Anglian Peds.* (Harl. Soc. xci), 55; *Vis. Norf.* (Harl. Soc. lxxxv), 9; Blomefield, *Norf.* iv. 276–7. [2] *CSP Dom.* 1683–4, pp. 119–20, 204; 1687–9, p. 270; H. Le Strange, *Norf. Official Lists*, 127–8. [3] Add. 27448, f. 78; *CSP Dom.* 1683–4, pp. 119–20; 1702–3, p. 237; *Norf. Rec. Soc.* xxx. 89; Egerton 2719, f. 98; Suff. RO (Ipswich), Gurdon mss mic. M142(1), Cook to Thornhagh Gurdon, 19 Jan. 1698[–9]; Camb. Univ. Lib. Cholmondeley (Houghton) mss, Charles Turner to Robert Walpole II*, 9 Apr. 1701. [4] *E. Anglian Peds.* 55; Blomefield, 276–7; P. S. Fritz, *Ministers and Jacobitism 1715–45*, p. 144.

D. W. H.

DAWNAY, Hon. Henry (1664–1741), of Cowick Hall, Yorks.

PONTEFRACT 1690–1695
YORKSHIRE 1698–1700, 3 Dec. 1707–1727

bap. 7 June 1664, 1st surv. s. of John Dawnay†, 1st Visct. Downe [I], by his 2nd w. Dorothy, da. of William Johnson of Wickham, Lincs. *m.* 29 Sept. 1685, Mildred (*d.* 1725), da. of William Godfrey of Thonock, Lincs., 11s. (2 *d.v.p.*) 2da. *suc.* fa. as 2nd Visct. Downe [I] 1 Oct. 1695.[1]

At the general election of 1690 Dawnay's father stood down at Pontefract, a borough some 12 miles from Cowick and in which the family owned burgages. Returned unopposed, Dawnay was classed as a Tory and a Court supporter by Lord Carmarthen (Sir Thomas Osborne†). In December Dawnay was classed as a probable supporter of Carmarthen in the event of an attack upon the minister in the Commons. However, in April 1691 Dawnay was noted as a Country supporter by Robert Harley*, a classification that was more consistent with his political stance. Initially he was an inactive Member: on 2 Jan. 1693 he was absent from a call of the House, was ordered to be taken into custody of the serjeant-at-arms, and was discharged on paying his fees on the 13th. In the following session he was given leave of absence on 30 Nov. for one month due to his wife being ill. His failure to seek re-election in 1695 may perhaps be ascribed to the poor health of his father, who died that autumn. However, at the 1698 election Dawnay, now Lord Downe, put up unexpectedly for the county, standing with Lord Fairfax (Thomas*) against Sir John Kaye, 2nd Bt.* Having regained his place in the Commons, Downe was forecast as likely to oppose a standing army. On 13 Feb. 1699 he reported from the committee for considering petitions from the merchants and clothiers of Leeds and Halifax relating to the Hamburg Company. Although appointed in 1699–1700 as a deputy-lieutenant of the East, North and West Ridings and the Ainsty and City of York, he was unable to resist a resurgence of county opinion in favour of Kaye. At a poorly attended county meeting in August 1699 Fairfax and Kaye were adopted as prospective parliamentary candidates: so great, indeed, was the concern of the gentlemen at Kaye's previous defeat that a county subscription was raised 'to exclude Lord Downe'. In response, Downe withdrew, 'designing for a country retirement'. Although out of Parliament, Downe's name arose in the House on 27 Mar. 1701 in a report on crown grants made under James II. In 1686 Downe and John Ramsden* had been jointly granted the manor of Coppingthorp in Yorkshire, forfeited for treason by Sir Michael Livesey and Augustine Gaitland. At the second 1701 election Downe was one of many Yorkshire peers and gentry to support the successful candidature of Lord Irwin (Arthur Ingram) for knight of the shire.[2]

Although it was rumoured prior to the 1702 election that Downe intended standing for the county again, he did not endeavour to re-enter politics until an unsuccessful attempt at a by-election for the county in January 1707, but he was returned unopposed at a second by-election in December. On 20 Mar. 1708 the House interposed to stifle a quarrel between Downe and Robert Monckton* (see MONCKTON). Two days later, Downe reported from the committee on a petition of merchants and clothiers from Leeds, complaining about the exportation of wool. He was classed as a Tory in two separate analyses of Parliament, before and after the election in that year, in which he was returned at the top of the poll in one of the fiercest contests in Yorkshire in this period. In the 1709–10 session he was noted as voting against the impeachment of Dr Sacheverell, while on 4 Mar. 1710 he told in favour of recommitting an address of thanks to the Queen, and on the 11th was granted leave of absence for one month.[3]

At the 1710 election, held in an atmosphere of Sacheverellite hysteria, Downe and Sir Arthur Kaye, 3rd Bt., son of Sir John, were triumphant on the 'Church' interest. Downe was classified as a Tory in the 'Hanover list'. In 1711 he was listed as a Tory 'patriot' who had opposed the continuance of the war, and was also noted as one of the 'worthy patriots', who helped to detect the mismanagements of the previous administration. He was also listed on two occasions as a member of the October Club. On 24 Apr. he told against passing the bill for the better preservation of game, while on the 28th he acted as a teller for a motion that the failure to compel revenue officials to pass their accounts was a high injustice to the nation, part of the October Club's attack on the outgoing Treasury ministers. In July he wrote to Harley, now Lord Treasurer Oxford, to say that he would be 'mighty happy' to succeed the recently deceased Duke of Newcastle (John Holles†) as governor of Hull. His claims were supported by the archbishop of York, who urged that 'his being in that place will be of great service for the breaking that interest in the East Riding which has always opposed your lordship's measures'. These solicitations, however, fell on deaf ears. In the 1711–12 session Downe was chosen on 13 May 1712 in the ballot for commissioners for the resumption of crown grants, but the enabling bill was lost in the Lords. On the 14th he told for a motion to agree with the Lords' amendment relating to Quakers in the bill for preventing frauds in parliamentary elections. In the 1713 session he presented a bill for endowing poor vicarages in the West Riding (30 Apr.), and told in favour of its being committed (5 May). On 9 June he acted as a teller for hearing the report of the ways and means committee, while on the 18th he told against the motion for engrossing the French commerce bill.[4]

Returned for the county once more in the 1713 election, in the first session of 1714 Downe acted as a teller on 5 Mar. against hearing the petition on behalf of the Whig candidates in the London election. In keeping with the aims of the March Club, of which he was a member, he seconded a motion by Kaye, his fellow Member, for a place bill, and on the 11th he and Kaye were given leave to bring in such a bill. However, he did not join Kaye and other Hanoverian Tories in attacking the government in the stormy 'succession in danger' debate of 14 Apr. Instead, on 22 Apr. he moved to agree with the Lords' address that the 'peace was safe, honourable and advantageous'. Speaker Hanmer (Thomas II) was accused of partiality in sending Sir William Wyndham, 3rd Bt., to the Lords with this address rather than Downe. At this time it was rumoured that Downe was to be made an English peer. On 12 May he was ordered to bring in the schism bill, a measure designed to unite the Tory party. On 1 June he told for the passage of this bill, while on the 23rd he carried up a private estate bill. He was classed as a Tory in the Worsley list and in an analysis comparing the 1715 Parliament with its predecessor. He may even have shared his son's Jacobitism and been involved with Sir William Blackett, 2nd Bt.*, in preparations for the Fifteen; at any rate Lord Carlisle (Charles Howard*) tried to get Lords Derwentwater and Widdrington to confess to Downe's participation. His name was sent to the Stuart court in 1721 as a probable sympathizer. He died in May 1741 and was buried on the 21st.[5]

[1] *Dugdale's Vis. Yorks.* ed. Clay, ii. 335–6; *The Gen.* n.s. vi. 212.
[2] G. Holmes, *Pol. in Age of Anne*, 143; *Luttrell Diary*, 347; *CSP Dom. 1699–1700*, pp. 310, 399; 1700–2, p. 30; BL, Althorp mss, Halifax pprs. box 4, Gervase Eyre* to 2nd Mq. of Halifax (William Savile*), 19 Aug. 1699; box 10, Ld. Weymouth (Thomas Thynne†) to same, 28 Aug. 1699; Huntington Lib. Stowe mss 58(1), pp. 17–18; W. Yorks. Archs. (Leeds), Temple Newsam mss TN/C9/114, Thomas Lumley to Irwin, 29 Sept. 1701, TN/PO10/4, Downe to same, 16 Nov. 1701. [3] Temple Newsam mss TN/C9/239, Lumley to John Roades, 18 Apr. 1702; W. Yorks. Archs. (Leeds), Vyner mss 5781, 'contested elections'; Cumbria RO (Carlisle), Lonsdale mss D/Lons/L1/4/Stray letters (Wharton), Ld. Carlisle to [Ld. Wharton], 13 Dec. 1707; Bagot mss at Levens Hall, Sir John Bland, 4th Bt.*, to James Grahme*, 25 May 1708; W. A. Speck, *Tory and Whig*, 147. [4] Add. 24475, f. 138; 70421, newsletter 4 May 1710; *Thoresby Diary*, ii. 69; G. Holmes and W. A. Speck, *Divided Soc.* 48, 153–4, 159–60; *Thoresby Letters* (Thoresby Soc. xxi), 214; *Huntington Lib. Q.* xxxiii. 163, 169; *HMC Portland*, v. 50, 58; Cobbett, *Parlty. Hist.* vi. 1130; Boyer, *Anne Annals*, iii. 308. [5] NLS, Advocates' mss, Wodrow Pprs. letters Quarto 8, f. 64; BL, Trumbull Alphab. mss 52, Thomas Bateman to Sir William Trumbull*, 23 Apr. 1714; Douglas diary (Hist. of Parl. trans.), 22

Apr. 1714; *Bull. IHR*, xxxiv. 215; xxxix. 64; *Wentworth Pprs.* 376; *HMC Townshend*, 169; Clay, 335.

E. C./C. I. M.

DAWNAY, Hon. John (1686–1740), of Cowick Hall, Yorks.

ALDBOROUGH and PONTEFRACT 1713–1715
PONTEFRACT 1715–22 Mar. 1716

b. 8 Dec. 1686, 1st s. of Henry Dawnay*, 2nd Visct. Downe [I]. *educ.* Christ Church, Oxf. matric. 1703, MA 1706; travelled abroad (Netherlands and Italy) 1709–11. *m.* 10 Aug. 1724, Charlotte Louisa, da. and h. of Robert Pleydell of Ampney Crucis, Glos., 2s. 2da.[1]

Dawnay, according to the 1st Lord Egmont (John Perceval†), 'was bred at Oxford, from whence he brought away a zeal, without knowledge, for the Church and Pretender'. Following his time at university Dawnay travelled abroad, returning to England in 1711. In November of the following year Lord Downe asked the dowager Duchess of Newcastle to choose Dawnay at Aldborough at the next general election. He was duly recommended by the Duchess against a Whig candidate fielded by Lord Pelham, the late Duke's heir. As a precaution, Dawnay also stood at Pontefract, where his family had an interest, and where he had the support of Lord Strafford. He was successful at both boroughs in contested elections. Although a petition was presented to Parliament against the Aldborough return, and it was reported elsewhere that Dawnay intended to opt for Pontefract, he was not required to make a choice between the two seats as no action had been taken on the petition by the time of the dissolution of Parliament in 1715. Dawnay was not an active Member during this time, though he told on 23 June 1714 against an amendment to the schism bill, which would have extended the Toleration Act to Ireland. Noted as a Tory in the Worsley list, Dawnay was returned for Pontefract in 1715, on which occasion he was classed as a Tory in a comparison of the 1713 and 1715 Parliaments. However, another comparative list recorded him as a Whig, though this would appear to be an error. He was unseated on petition in March 1716, and did not sit in Parliament again.[2]

Considered in later life to be a Jacobite, Dawnay was noted by Egmont in 1731 as a dutiful Anglican who considered the 'church of Rome to be full of errors, in doctrine and practice'. Egmont also recorded that Dawnay took communion in a neighbouring church almost every Sunday due to his belief that hearing sermons, though fitting, is the least of a Christian's duty, when they meet for public worship, but that the essential part is communicating; that the ancient Christians never assembled without doing it, and thought their service otherwise imperfect. He added that commemorating the death of our Lord is not the principal business when we communicate, but the offering up the elements to God, a doctrine he said our Church should have retained, and that when we reformed we went too far.

Dawnay was also reputed to be 'charitable, though careful enough of his money'. He died *v.p.* on 31 July, and was buried on 12 Aug. 1740. His father, Lord Downe, died the following year, at which time Dawnay's eldest son, Henry Pleydell Dawnay†, succeeded as 3rd Viscount Downe.[3]

[1] *Dugdale's Vis. Yorks.* ed. Clay, ii. 335–6; *HMC Hastings*, iii. 1; Grosvenor mss at Eaton Hall, Andrew Forrester to Sir Richard Grosvenor, 4th Bt.†, 10 May 1709; Add. 22229, f. 103; *HMC Portland*, v. 100. [2] *HMC Egmont Diary*, i. 191; Add. 22229, f. 103; 22238, f. 126; *HMC Portland*, 100, 245, 328, 344; T. Lawson-Tancred, *Recs. of a Yorks. Manor*, 258–61, 263, 265–6. [3] P. K. Monod, *Jacobitism and Eng. People*, 273; *HMC Egmont Diary*, 191–2; Clay, 335–6.

E. C./C. I. M.

DAY, Sir Thomas (c.1628–1709), of Tilly's Court, Barton Hill, Bristol.

BRISTOL 1695–1700

b. c.1628; *m.* Anne (*d.* 1722) da. of Capt. Roger Richards, 5s. (2 *d.v.p.*) 2da. Kntd. 28 Nov. 1694.[1]

Common councilman, Bristol 1661–84, 17 Oct. 1688–*d.*, sheriff, 1670–1, alderman Mar.–Sept. 1681, 8 Aug.–17 Oct. 1688, 5 Aug. 1689–*d.*, mayor 4 Feb.–Sept. 1688, 1694–5; gov., corporation of the poor, Bristol 1701–2.[2]

At the height of his public career in the 1690s, Day was one of the most influential Whigs in Bristol's political life, and a model of pious-minded civic virtue. His background and rise remain obscure. According to one corporation chronicler he was by trade 'a soapboiler', but he is also described as a merchant and had considerable interests in the local sugar-refining industry. Despite his wealth, much of which was invested in property in and around the city, he maintained a retail shop on the ground floor of his 'great house' which stood at the south end of Bristol Bridge. His longstanding friendship (and possible kinship) with the philosopher John Locke undoubtedly influenced his Whiggish outlook and his approach to civic affairs.[3]

He was first elected to the Bristol common council in 1661 after a purge of Cromwellians. In March 1681, during a fierce quarrel in the corporation, he was coopted onto the aldermanic body by a faction opposed to the Tory mayor, Sir Richard Hart*. Hart had not forgiven Day for voting against him in favour of the moderate Tory candidates in the recent parliamentary contest, and in September engineered Day's displacement. Under the new charter, obtained for the city in 1684, he was one of 19 Whigs dismissed from the common council. Keeping discreetly out of public life over the next few years, he came back to the centre of Bristol politics in 1688, assuming almost immediately a pre-eminence among the leading Whigs in the city. In accordance with James II's edict of 14 Jan. 1688, he was elected mayor and shortly afterwards was chosen an alderman for a second time. Though he had at first responded in the negative to the King's 'three questions' on the repeal of the Penal Laws and Test Act, he was found by the royal agents in April 1688 to be 'very popular' and 'right' and certain to carry an election. The restoration of the old charter in October of that year simultaneously removed him from the aldermanic bench but restored him to the common council. He was unsuccessful in the election to the Convention in 1689, but was re-elected alderman in August.[4]

In September 1694 Day became mayor, and two months later was received and knighted by the King at Kensington, a token of royal gratitude, it would seem, for the part he had played in breaking down Tory domination over the corporation. In 1695 he successfully contested for Bristol in the general election, and was returned with his 'good friend' and business associate, Robert Yate. In partnership with Yate and others in 1695, Day obtained a lease of the Hot Well in Bristol in order to build a pump-room and lodging-house for visitors to the spa which was completed two years later. Shortly after taking his seat in November, Day expressed pious gratitude that his none-too-robust health had so far withstood the long hours of attendance: 'I trust in the Lord that he will continue it.' Almost immediately, he and Yate became embroiled with Bristol's merchants over the administration's plans for a council of trade, and there was a swift exchange of correspondence on the subject. The Merchant Venturers' Society of Bristol were generally in favour of a council, but were anxious that the new board be fully representative of all the kingdom's main ports, and not dominated by courtiers or by the mercantile interests of the capital. In mid-December they were alarmed at reports that nominations were to be made by the King, and asked to be allowed to recommend one or two names. Day and Yate jointly replied on the 19th that the matter remained to be properly debated, but 'we did not find that the House were inclinable' to nominate anyone but MPs. However, they promised to join with Members from other ports to protect Bristol from the growing dominance of London. On hearing the names of the proposed commissioners, 'men, according to our judgment, altogether improper for such an undertaking', the Bristol merchants sent up a petition on the 28th, asking that the council be filled with men experienced in trade. In their reply the two Members were non-committal, agreeing on the one hand that the council should be 'made up of honest and experienced persons', but pointing out that if the advocates of such a commission insisted on powers to deploy 'all carriers and convoys', not only would the King be unlikely to give his assent, it would be unsafe 'to lodge such a separate power in time of war in any number of persons, however so honest or skilful they may be'. It is not unlikely that Day was influenced in the matter by his friend Locke, whose advocacy of a committee of experts and statesmen, in preference to a board of narrow-minded merchants or parliamentarians, had been instrumental in determining the Court nominees. Having obtained a fortnight's leave on 10 Jan., Day was absent on the 20th when ministerialists attacked the opposition's proposal for a 'parliamentary' council and was therefore saved the embarrassment of displaying to his constituents his pro-Court stance on the issue. However, he was not expected to change his views, being forecast as likely to support the Court on 31 Jan. in a division over the same issue. Day was back in the House by 15 Feb. when he presented a petition from the mayor, aldermen and other city worthies requesting a bill 'for erecting hospitals and workhouses' in Bristol. His concern for the relief of the poor was a long-standing one. Over recent weeks he and Yate had been kept informed of the progress of local discussions on a project 'for the better maintenance of the poor', based upon proposals published at the beginning of the year by John Cary, a prominent Bristol merchant and writer on trade and social problems. The basis of Cary's proposal was to remove responsibility for the poor from the parishes to civic level. The petitioners submitted to Day and Yate their request for legislation, 'not doubting but that you will promote a thing so suitable to the common good of this city and so agreeable to the inclination of all honest men within the same'. It would appear that Day took the lead in securing a draft bill in accordance with the promoters' instructions, he being the only Member ordered by the House to prepare it. On 4 Mar. he duly presented a bill for establishing a 'corporation of the poor'. Although its later stages were managed by Yate and others, Day clearly played a key part in commending to the Commons what was to become a prototype for workhouse institutions in many other localities.[5]

In the Commons, Day's political allegiances remained with the Court. He signed the Association and voted with the administration in March 1696 on fixing the price of guineas at 22s. These pro-government sympathies doubtless helped him to prevail on the Treasury by June 1696 to agree to the corporation's request that Bristol provide the location for one of the new provincial mints. Day himself was a beneficiary in these arrangements, since it was from him that the corporation rented premises for the coining apparatus. In the next session he voted on 25 Nov. 1696 for the attainder of Sir John Fenwick†. On 11 Jan. 1697 he was granted three weeks' leave, the second in a regular pattern of January absences from the House that enabled him to carry out what he described on one occasion as 'my pressing occasions' in Bristol. He spoke in the House on 6 Mar. 1697 against a draft clause intended for the bill for preventing exports of wool. He felt that the proposed impost of 'ten per cent on the woollen manufacture would not proceed by reason . . . it would put a great stop to the work of many poor people these hard times'. In August 1697 his son Samuel was appointed governor of Bermuda 'in consideration', it was minuted by the lords justices, 'of the merit of Sir Thomas Day, his father, and the good service he has done his Majesty at Bristol'. However, Samuel Day's dictatorial rule on the island soon resulted in his dismissal, and subsequently involved the elderly Sir Thomas in lengthy proceedings on his son's behalf before the lords of Trade. It was no doubt in recognition of his previous experience in providing for Bristol's poor that Day was included on the committee appointed on 8 Dec. 1697 to consider how the poor in the nation at large might be 'better provided for and employed', one of the very few such inquiries to which he was appointed. The following month he was forced to obtain three weeks' leave of the House in order to attend his wife during a serious illness. Following his re-election in 1698, he was classed as a Court supporter in a comparative analysis of the old and new House of Commons, though on an associated list this ascription appears to have been questioned, with his name being marked 'q[uery?]'. An analysis of the House according to 'interests', compiled in 1700, identifies Day as a Junto supporter. He was granted a month's leave on 12 Jan. 1699, but minor committee appointments indicate that he was back in the House by 28 Feb., and continued his attendance until April. After the session closed, early in May, he was reported by the London press to be seriously ill. He was well enough to attend the next session, however, and was granted three weeks' absence on 13 Jan. 1700, in order to attend corporation business in Bristol. After briefly attending the House during February, he returned to Bristol a month before the session closed and on 8 Mar. was present at a meeting of 55 leading citizens whose design was to inaugurate a society for the reformation of manners 'out of a sense of duty we owe to almighty God'. Day played a central part in furthering the aims of the society, and, until it ceased in 1705, chaired many meetings of its steering committee.[6]

Advancing years and poor health, coupled with the difficulties of long-distance travel, were probably the chief reasons for Day's retirement at the January 1701 election, though his active involvement in civic affairs continued. As a senior alderman he deputized on several occasions during mayoral absences in London, while in September 1702 he played host to the Queen at his 'great house' at Bristol Bridge during her tour of the West. He also enjoyed a term of office in 1701–2 as governor of the corporation of the poor which he had helped to found in 1696. Day died on 17 Dec. 1709, aged 81, and was buried at St. Thomas' church, Bristol. In addition to his property in Bristol, he left land at Westbury leased from the bishop of Bath and Wells, and a farm at Congresbury in Somerset. He also bequeathed £30 to provide bread for the poor and £50 towards rebuilding an almshouse in his native parish of St. Thomas'.[7]

[1] *Procs. Clifton Antiquarian Club*, iii. 74; PCC 12 Smith. [2] A. B. Beaven, *Bristol Lists*, 186, 187, 201, 207–8, 225, 286. [3] Bristol AO, ms 'calendar hist. of Bristol 1067–1724', [sub. 1697]; J. Latimer, *Annals of Bristol in 17th Cent.* 473, 478; PCC Smith 12; *Locke Corresp.* iii. 752–3; iv. 249–50; vii. 431–2. [4] Latimer, 310, 401, 424, 447, 449, 453–4; Duckett, *Penal Laws and Test Act* (1883), 228. [5] Luttrell, *Brief Relation*, iii. 405; Latimer, 472, 479; ms 'calendar hist. of Bristol', [sub. Sept. 1697]; *EHR*, liv. 58–61; *Wm. and Mary Q.* ser. 3, xiv. 394–5; *Min. Bk. of Men's Meeting of Soc. of Friends in Bristol 1667–86* (Bristol Rec. Soc. xxvi), 85; Add. 5540, ff. 81, 100. [6] Add. 5540, f. 92; Bristol AO, common council procs. 1687–1702, ff. 134, 192; *CSP Col.* 1700, pp. 63–64, 1702, pp. 383–4; *Portledge Pprs.* 253; *CSP Dom.* 1697, pp. 258, 288; *Post Boy*, 13–16 May 1699; *Reformation and Revival in 18th Cent Bristol* (Bristol Rec. Soc. xlv), 15–41. [7] Bristol common council procs. 1687–1702, f. 219; 1702–22, pp. 89, 120; J. Latimer, *Bristol in 18th Cent.* 45; *Procs. Clifton Antiquarian Club*, 74; PCC 12 Smith.

A. A. H.

DEANE, John (1632–1694), of Oxenwood, Wilts.

GREAT BEDWYN	1679 (Jan.–July)
LUDGERSHALL	1689–31 Dec. 1694

b. 1632, 1st s. of James Deane of Deanland, Basing, Hants by his 2nd w. Frances, da. of Thomas Baynard of Lackham, Wilts. *educ.* M. Temple 1650. *m.* (1) Margaret, da. of Thomas Garrard of Lambourne, Berks.; (2) bef. 1665, Magdalene, da. and h. of John Stroughill of Barkham, Berks., 2s. 7da. (1 *d.v.p.*). *suc.* fa. 1652.[1]

Lt. of ft. Sir William Killigrew's regt. 1662. Freeman, Portsmouth 1683.[2]

Deane had petitioned unsuccessfully in 1689 for a customs office, claiming that he had served the crown in a military capacity for nearly 50 years, that under the Commonwealth he had lost an estate worth £10,000, and that James II had turned him out of 'all he had' for not agreeing to the repeal of the Penal Laws and Test Act. Listed as a Tory in March 1690 by Lord Carmarthen (Sir Thomas Osborne†), he obtained the recommendation of Lord Nottingham (Daniel Finch†) in June of that year for the office of housekeeper of the excise, but although Nottingham represented him to the King as one 'who has heretofore been a great sufferer, and is now very zealous in your service', this indirect approach proved no more successful, and in March 1691 Lord Pembroke (Hon. Thomas Herbert†) requested Nottingham once more to 'remember Colonel Deane'. None the less, Deane had been marked by Carmarthen on a list of December 1690 possibly in connexion with an attack on the Marquess in the House and in April 1691 he was classed as a Court supporter by Robert Harley*. So acute had Deane's financial embarrassments become, however, that either during the winter of 1692–3 or later in 1693 he accepted a bribe of a mere £50 to oppose attempts in the Commons to put an end to the East India Company's monopoly (see COOKE, Sir Thomas). On 19 Jan. 1693 a complaint of breach of privilege was brought on his behalf by Henry Goldwell, another Member bribed to defend the East India Company, against one Holt, a solicitor, who had 'abused' him in the lobby that morning. Not until March 1694 did Deane at last receive some compensation from the crown: the sum of £470 was paid him as 'royal bounty'.[3]

In Parliament Deane was not very active. On 27 Nov. 1693, he was granted ten days' leave of absence. He was named to two drafting committees in the final session of this Parliament: on 4 Dec. 1694 for bills to improve the condition of prisons, and on 21 Dec. to suppress hawkers and pedlars in towns, a bill he presented the following day. Any further involvement in the work of the House was cut short by Deane's death from smallpox at Westminster on 31 Dec. 1694, from whence his body was carried for burial at Tidcombe. Soon afterwards his younger surviving son, a clergyman, took ship for the Indies. The elder son, having been settled with the Oxenwood estate at his marriage in 1683, secured in 1701 a private Act for its sale, worth then no more than £150 p.a., together with other land in Tidcombe and Shalbourne. For a further five years Deane's widow enjoyed the profits from land leased in Chute, Wiltshire, but by 1704 she and a daughter were forced to sell Deanland under another Act.[4]

[1] *Vis. Hants* (Harl. Soc. lxiv), 199; *Vis. Berks.* (Harl. Soc. lvi), 291; M. B. Deane, *Bk. of Dene*, 20; *Coll. Top. et Gen.* vii. 188–9; PCC 289 Brent. [2] R. East, *Portsmouth Recs.* 366–7. [3] *CSP Dom.* 1689–90, p. 181; 1690–1, p. 300; *HMC Finch*, ii. 289, 291; *CJ*, xi. 326; Luttrell *Diary*, 373; *Cal. Treas. Pprs.* 1557–1696, p. 341; *Cal. Treas. Bks.* x. 552; *Debates and Procs.* 1694–5, p. 38. [4] Add. 46527, f. 39; Wilts. RO, 212B/1870; Deane, 21.

D. W. H./H. J. L.

DE CARDONNEL see CARDONNEL

DE ERESBY, Peregrine Bertie, Ld. Willoughby see BERTIE

DE ERESBY, Robert Bertie, Ld. Willoughby see BERTIE

DE GREY, Thomas (1680–1765), of Merton, Norf.

THETFORD 1708–1710
NORFOLK 1715–1727

bap. 13 Aug. 1680, 1st surv. s. of William de Grey† of Merton by Elizabeth, da. of Thomas Bedingfield of Darsham, Suff. and coh. of her bro. Thomas. *educ.* Bury St. Edmunds g.s.; St. John's, Camb. 1697. *m.* settlement 10 Sept. 1706, Elizabeth (with £4,500), da. of William Windham of Felbrigg, Norf., sis. of Ashe Windham*, William Windham† and Joseph Windham Ashe†, 3s. (1 *d.v.p.*) 2da. *suc.* fa. 1687.[1]

Freeman, King's Lynn 1712.[2]

De Grey's marriage into the Wyndham family connected him with several of the leading Whigs in Norfolk, and may have been what drew him to the Whig side in politics, his father having been a Tory. However, his wife's family had little to do with his putting up at Thetford in 1708. De Grey relied partly on his own interest in the town: his family seat was only ten miles away and his father had represented Thetford in James II's Parliament. He also enjoyed the support of the Duke of Grafton. When Ashe Windham's anxious mother reproached her son for countenancing such a risky enterprise Windham replied,

> I take my brother Grey to be of an age and sense not to want advice in the conduct of his life, and I take him to have been entirely his own governor in this matter . . . You desire to know whether he is like to succeed; for my

part I cannot judge, but the peer thinks he will certainly. I was in hopes your ladyship would have acquitted me, after knowing I had not the least knowledge of it, till after 'twas past recovery. If any disaster had happened upon their being in town purely, then I might have owned your ladyship had had a shrewd guess; but I cannot upon this unexpensive, reasonable desire of serving his country.

De Grey and his Whig partner Robert Baylis* were returned, defeating two Tories, but Windham was probably wrong about the cost, for Thetford's voters were venal, and their price was high. In a list of the new Parliament de Grey was classed as a Whig. An unimportant back-bencher, he wrote on 3 Mar. 1709 to a Norfolk correspondent:

both Houses joined yesterday in an address to the Queen, of, I think, a very extraordinary nature, as to some parts of it particularly. They have desired her that she will not make peace with the King of France till he has acknowledged her title to these kingdoms and the succession of them in the Protestant line as they are by us established, and till he had banished the Prince of Wales out of his dominions and consented to have the fortifications and harbour of Dunkirk demolished and destroyed ... What was the occasion of the address or whether there be a secret in it or not I cannot tell you.

He was listed in 1709 as a supporter of the naturalization of the Palatines, and in 1710 as having voted for the impeachment of Dr Sacheverell, although on 8 Feb. 1710 he had been granted a fortnight's leave of absence. He did not seek re-election in 1710, possibly because of the expense, and in 1713 resisted a proposal by Robert Walpole II* that he stand for the county with Ashe Windham. In 1715, in more favourable circumstances, he agreed to be put up by Lord Townshend, Windham's cousin and close friend, on the Whig interest. De Grey was described as a Whig in the Worsley list and in another comparative analysis of the two Parliaments; a third list, however, noted him as a Tory. De Grey was buried on 18 Dec. 1765, at Merton.[3]

[1] Norf. RO, Walsingham (Merton) mss XII/8/7. [2] Cal. Freemen King's Lynn, 219. [3] Norf. RO, Ketton-Cremer mss, Mrs Katherine Windham, 6 Feb. 1707[-8], Robert Walpole II* to Ashe Windham, 21 Apr. 1713; HMC 11th Rep. VII, 115.

D. W. H.

DELAVAL, Sir John, 3rd Bt. (1654–1729), of the Lodge, Seaton Delaval, Northumb.

MORPETH   1701 (Dec.)–1705
NORTHUMBERLAND   1705–1708

bap. 7 Nov. 1654, 5th but 2nd surv. s. of Sir Ralph Delaval, 1st Bt.†, of Seaton Delaval by Lady Anne, da. of Alexander Leslie, 1st Earl of Leven [S] and wid. of Hugh Fraser, Master of Lovat. *m.* lic. 28 May 1683, Mary (*d.* 1683), da. of Edward Goodyer of Dogmersfield, Hants, 1da. (*d.v.p.*). *suc.* bro. as 3rd Bt. Aug. 1696.[1]

Ensign, 1 Ft. Gds. 1680, lt. 1686, capt. 1691–1702, brevet col. 1693.

A younger son with little expectation of inheriting the family estates, Delaval chose to pursue the profession of arms. He gained his first commission in 1680 and apparently had little difficulty reconciling himself to the Revolution as he continued to pursue a military career during the 1690s, during which period he served with distinction in Flanders. Delaval's succession to the baronetcy in 1696 was unexpected and followed the early death of his elder brother, but his inheritance was a mixed one. Though he succeeded to the family interests in coal mining, quarrying, salt-panning and the harbour at Seaton sluice, Delaval also inherited sizable debts. Moreover, he did not gain possession of the family seat of Seaton Delaval. The terms of his brother's marriage settlement had granted the house to his wife for her life, and Delaval was therefore forced to live at the lodge rather than the main house. Delaval's parliamentary aspirations became evident soon after he succeeded to the family estate, as in 1698 he stood for Northumberland. Defeated at the poll, in late 1700 he again canvassed the county, on this occasion against an anticipated by-election. He did not, however, pursue his candidacy at the January 1701 election, but was returned for Morpeth at the second election of that year. Delaval retained this seat at the 1702 election before transferring to the county in 1705, his own interest in Northumberland being augmented by that of his kinsman, the 3rd Earl of Carlisle (Charles Howard*). Delaval made no significant contribution to the second 1701 Parliament, his energies appearing to have been concentrated during 1702 upon apparently unsuccessful attempts to alter the settlement of the family estates, and he was only slightly more active in the 1702 Parliament. His Whiggery became clear during this Parliament, when he voted on 13 Feb. 1703 in favour of the Lords' amendments to the bill to enlarge the time for taking the Abjuration. In the autumn of 1704 he was forecast as a likely opponent of the Tack, and on 28 Nov. either voted against or was absent from the division for this measure. His only recorded involvement in legislative matters came the following month (6 Dec.), when he was nominated to draft a bill concerned with Durham and Northumberland estates. In 1705 Delaval was included on a list of placemen by virtue of the captaincy of the foot guards which he had in fact resigned in 1702, and later that year an analysis of the new House classed him as a 'High Church Courtier'. On 25 Oct. Delaval voted for the Court candidate for Speaker, but he was one of the Whigs missing from the list of those who had supported the Court in the proceedings of February 1706 upon the 'place clause' of the regency bill. While he was in the House personal matters appear to have continued at the forefront of his concerns, as in December 1705 he petitioned the Treasury for payment of £1,000 owed to his father in respect of piers built at Seaton, a request which appears to have foundered upon an unfavourable report from the salt duty commissioners. An analysis of the Commons dating from early 1708 classed him as a Whig. He does not appear to have stood at the election of that year, and though he canvassed Morpeth at the 1710 election he withdrew before the poll. Delaval did not retire from public life, being named in 1711 a Northumberland justice and there being a rumour in 1715 that he was to be appointed deputy-governor of Tynemouth. After leaving the Commons he suffered from mounting financial problems. The death of his sister-in-law in October 1713 led him to attempt to repossess Seaton Delaval and Hartley, but his attempts were resisted by the servants of her second husband, Sir Edward Blackett, 2nd Bt.* Blackett's resistance of Delaval's claims stemmed from the failure of Delaval to pay the marriage portion of £8,000 which, by the terms of his deceased brother's marriage settlement, was due to Delaval's niece upon her marriage to Blackett's son. The dispute led to a Chancery case in which Blackett was successful and was awarded £14,624 12s. 7d. (the original £8,000 plus interest). In 1718 Delaval was forced to sell the manors of Horton and Seaton Delaval to his kinsman Admiral George Delaval† in order to satisfy this debt. He remained in possession of the manor of Hartley until his death on 4 June 1729. As he died childless, the baronetcy failed and his remaining estates were left to Francis Delaval†, nephew and heir of George Delaval.[2]

[1] *New Hist. Northumb.* ix. 171. [2] Ibid. 161–3; Northumb. RO (Newcastle), Delaval (Horsley) mss 1De/7/119, poll bk. 1698; Howard mss at Castle Howard, Duke of Somerset to Carlisle, 2 Oct. 1700; *CSP Dom.* 1700–2, p. 492; 1702–3, p. 507; *Party and Management* ed. Jones, 80; *Cal. Treas. Bks.* xx. 488, 633; *Cal. Treas. Pprs.* 1702–3, p. 438; Add. 70248, Edmund Maine* to Robert Harley*, 14 Oct. 1710; L. K. J. Glassey, *Appt. JPs*, 211; *HMC Townshend*, 341.

E. C.

DELAVAL, Sir Ralph (*d.* 1707), of Berkeley Row, Westminster.

GREAT BEDWYN   1695–1698

1st s. of William Delaval of Horton, Northumb. by Mary, da. of Sir Peter Riddell of Newcastle-upon-Tyne, Northumb. *m.* (1) bef. 1670, Hester Major (*bur.* 1700) of St. Martin-in-the-Fields, Mdx., 2s. *d.v.p.* 3da. (1 *d.v.p.*); (2) sis. of Lt.-Col. William Eaton, *s.p.* Kntd. 31 May 1690.[1]

Lt. RN 1666, capt. 1673, v.-adm. and adm., 1690; lt. 1 Ft. Gds. (Grenadier Gds.) 1674–8, capt. 1679–87, lt.-col. 1687–93; capt. King's Holland regt. 1678–9; ld. of Admiralty 1693–4.[2]

Commr. reprisals in Barbados, 1693.[3]

Coming from a cadet branch of an illustrious Northumbrian family, Delaval was a protégé of James, Duke of York. He began as a naval officer, seeing action in the second and third Dutch wars. Then, having been commissioned in the Grenadier Guards, he served as a volunteer in the Virginia expedition of 1676. During the Popish Plot he had been falsely accused of being a Roman Catholic, whereas he was in fact a staunch Anglican. Although ordered in 1688 to oppose the Prince of Orange's invasion at sea, and in receipt of favours from King James as late as 10 Nov., he acquiesced in the Revolution and continued to serve thereafter. In the spring of 1690 he conveyed a loyal address from the flag officers to William and Mary, acknowledging them to be 'undoubted rightful King and Queen of these realms'. On presenting the address Delaval was knighted. He served under Lord Torrington (Arthur Herbert†) in the defeat at Beachy Head, after which Lord Preston (Sir Richard Grahme†) and other Protestant Jacobites entertained hopes that Delaval might join their cause. However Delaval, who blamed the outcome of the battle on the 'disorderly' conduct of the Dutch, was appointed president of Torrington's court martial. He did not approve of the action, believing the admiral to be innocent, and Torrington was duly acquitted.[4]

While on active service in 1691 one of Delaval's ships captured a French sloop carrying intercepted letters from England. On 16 Nov. George Rodney Brydges* informed the Commons that he understood these papers included a letter to Delaval from General Ginkel, a copy of the admiral's orders from Secretary Nottingham (Daniel Finch†), and a letter from Delaval to the secretary. A week later Delaval appeared at the bar of the House and testified that, having no French, he had not been able to ascertain what the papers contained, though his captain perused them and said 'they imported little'. Thereafter he had dispatched them to Nottingham. Following some debate on this matter, Delaval produced the originals of his letters and orders and was allowed to withdraw, 'not appearing faulty in the matter'. Both Houses agreed on 15 Dec.

that 'there was not a copy of a letter from Lord Nottingham to Sir Ralph Delaval taken on board the French vessel', and one commentator concluded that the whole incident had been 'set up by the Duke of Bolton's [Charles Powlett†] contrivance and the Whigs to blacken Lord Nottingham, upon some discovery of letters between him and Sir Ralph Delaval . . . but all was madness and knavery'.[5]

In 1692 Delaval took part in the battle of La Hogue under Edward Russell*, with whom he was not on good terms. Delaval's subsequent request to succeed to a vacant commissionership of the navy was supported by Nottingham, though the post was given to (Sir) George Rooke*. Delaval then complained to Nottingham that Russell had failed to acknowledge his exploits at La Hogue, and had denied promotion to officers serving under him, despite his 'having been every winter at sea these four years and no other flag ever taking their turn'.[6]

At the end of 1692 Delaval was appointed to command the fleet in commission with Killigrew and the Whig Sir Clowdesley Shovell*. The two Tory admirals were in an even stronger position in April, when they were made lords of the Admiralty. The Jacobites had high hopes of them because of their professional debt to King James, and 'moreover, they hate the Prince of Orange on account of his insolence, of which they think he has been guilty, towards the nation'. These hopes were realized when Lord Ailesbury (Thomas Bruce†) made contact with Delaval. The admiral's inclinations were reinforced, Ailesbury recalled, by his mistress (later to be his second wife), a zealous Jacobite on her own account. Delaval supposedly undertook to obtain Killigrew's consent and co-operation. Shovel was to be kept in the dark until the moment came to act when, 'being two to one, he knew what to do in that case'. According to Ailesbury, Delaval's plan was that the two admirals would pretend to have secret orders for taking the fleet 200 leagues out to sea, leaving the coast clear for King James to land with an army at Portsmouth. Delaval's chief motive was said to be his conviction that better terms for the nation could be extracted from James II than from William III. After consulting James at St. Germain, Ailesbury was given an audience with Louis XIV, where he explained Delaval's plan. However, Louis insisted that Delaval and Killigrew wait for James at Portsmouth, under pretence of wanting supplies. This was impossible, since they had only just revictualled. Even more decisive was the fact that the French had already settled plans for a campaign in Flanders and for a naval attack on the immensely valuable Smyrna convoy. Not knowing the upshot of Ailesbury's negotiations, Delaval and Killigrew, waiting for a signal that never came, 'dallied out much of their time', and 'in fine . . . did nothing that summer'.[7]

However, the loss of the Smyrna convoy brought Delaval's career to an end. Together with Killigrew he took the blame for the loss of the convoy. The two admirals suffered further by the fall from power of Nottingham, and the arrest of their secretary Abraham Anselme on a charge of high treason. On 17 Nov. 1693 the Whig majority in the Commons voted that there had been 'notorious and treacherous mismanagement' over the loss of the convoy, defeating Tory efforts to delete the word 'treacherous'. On 6 Dec., after Delaval had been questioned at the bar, a motion was narrowly defeated which would have declared that the admirals were 'guilty of a high breach of the trust that was put in them, to the great loss and dishonour of the nation'. Four days later the King forbade Delaval and Killigrew to attend the Admiralty Board, though they were not removed until the following year. The Lords, on the other hand, carrying out their own investigation, found that a key witness had been lying, and voted to exonerate Delaval and Killigrew.[8]

On Russell's reinstatement to the Admiralty Board in the spring of 1694, Delaval was turned out, never to see active service again. The following year he stood for election at Great Bedwyn, possibly on the interest of Ailesbury, and was returned unopposed. On 4 Jan. 1696 he wrote to Sir William Trumbull* about the consequences of the failure to protect trade:

> I hope the question about the commission [of trade] that was carried at the committee [on the state of the nation] will be some way diverted, and it was and is still my opinion it were much better for the King to [?break] this Admiralty, (though for my own part, I desire not to be one) than to give way to the lessening his prerogative in so dangerous a point as this. For my part I neither can, nor ever will, give my opinion for such a commission, and to avoid being named, think it best not to appear in the House.

He was forecast as likely to oppose the Court in the division on the proposed council of trade on 31 Jan. 1696, though he signed the Association promptly. At this time he was petitioning for arrears of his salary as a lord of the Admiralty, payment of which was ordered in March. There were unsubstantiated rumours in May that he was to command the fleet that summer with Shovel and Rooke. Yet another Jacobite plot was afoot, and Ailesbury noted that Sir John Fenwick† had hopes of Delaval. Fenwick's confession actually implicated Delaval, along with Killigrew and Russell, but speaking in his own defence on 6 Nov. Delaval denied the charge, or indeed 'any knowledge of Sir John'. He appears to have been absent from the division on the 25th on Fenwick's attainder. In the 1697–8 session, in the debate on 8 Jan. 1698 on reducing the army, he spoke in support of the Court when he 'showed what uncertainties a fleet must be subject to, so that they ought not to make it their only reliance'. He was included in July 1698 in a list of placemen, presumably as a half-pay naval officer, and was subsequently listed as a Court placeman 'left out' of the new Parliament. He did not contest the 1698 election, and in May 1699 was granted a yearly pension of £637 as a reward for 'good service at sea'. He lived in retirement at Seaton Delaval until his death in January 1707, and was buried in Westminster Abbey on the 23rd of that month. As he had died intestate, administration was granted to his two daughters by his first wife, his widow renouncing any claim.[9]

[1] *New Hist. Northumb.* ix. 175; *Le Neve's Knights* (Harl. Soc. viii), 432; *Westminster Abbey Reg.* (Harl. Soc. x), 258. [2] Bodl. Don. c.40, f. 158. [3] *CSP Dom.* 1693, p. 216. [4] *DNB*; Charnock, *Biog. Navalis*, ii. 4–10; PRO, Adm. 10/15/37 (*ex inf.* Dr J. D. Davies); Magdalene Coll. Camb. Pepys mss 2856, pp. 269, 273–5 (*ex inf.* Dr Davies); Add. 15903, f. 100; Luttrell, *Brief Relation*, ii. 49; D. Ogg, *Eng. in Reigns of Jas. II and Wm. III*, 326; Howell, *State Trials*, xii. 724; *HMC Downshire*, i. 363, 382–3, 493, 495; J. Ehrman, *Navy in War of Wm. III*, 365–6; *HMC Finch*, ii. 495. [5] *CSP Dom.* 1690–1, p. 289; Luttrell, ii. 118, 217, 344–6; *Luttrell Diary*, 22, 27, 35–37, 79; Grey, x. 171, 175, 181–3, 217; Cobbett, *Parlty. Hist.* v. 657; Chandler, ii. 391; Centre Kentish Stud. Stanhope mss U1590/054/1, Richard Warre to Alexander Stanhope, 24 Nov. 1691; *HMC Downshire*, i. 390. [6] Luttrell, ii. 450, 464; *CSP Dom.* 1691–2, pp. 284, 297; *HMC Finch*, iii. 284, 306; iv. 155, 162, 174, 182, 235; Dalrymple, *Mems.* iii(2), pp. 237–8, 242, 245; *Sir Ralph Delaval's Letter to Earl of Nottingham* (1692). [7] *HMC Finch*, iv. pp. xxiv, xxviii; H. Horwitz, *Revolution Politicks*, 132; Nat. Archs. Ire. Wyche mss 1/67, William Ball to Sir Cyril Wyche*, 24 Jan. 1693; Dalrymple, iii(2), p. 227; iii(3), p. 17; *Evelyn Diary*, v. 131; Burnet, iv. 186; Burnet, *Supp.* ed. Foxcroft, 380; *Orig. Pprs.* ed. Macpherson, i. 457–62; *Ailesbury Mems.* 312–15, 331, 333, 341–2; Hopkins thesis, 118, 217, 344–6; BN, Renaudot mss N. Ac. Fr. 7487, f. 83. [8] *CSP Dom.* 1693, pp. 127–8, 135–7; Add. 35898, f. 65; Egerton 2618, ff. 178–9; Ehrman, 341–67; BL, Althorp mss, Halifax pprs. Robert Harley* to Ld. Halifax [Sir George Savile†], 1 July 1693; Ranke, v. 66–68; Horwitz, *Parl. and Pol. Wm. III*, 125, 132; Horwitz, *Revolution Politicks*, 147–8; Cobbett, 779, 782, 800, 827; Grey, 318, 322, 338, 347–8; Chandler, 418, 422; Macaulay, *Hist. Eng.* 2413; DZA, Bonet despatches 7/17 Nov., 12/22 Dec. 1693; *HMC Lords*, n.s. i. 295, 297. [9] *CSP Dom.* 1694–5, p. 114; 1699–1700, p. 197; BL, Trumbull Misc. mss 29, Delaval to Trumbull, 4 Jan. 1695[-6]; Stanhope mss U1590/059/5, Robert Yard* to Stanhope, 17 Nov. 1696; *Ailesbury Mems.* 376; Luttrell, iv. 52, 109; *Vernon–Shrewsbury Letters*, i. 47; Cobbett, 999, 1052; Chandler, iii. 31; Northants. RO, Montagu (Boughton) mss 46/177, James Vernon I* to Duke of Shrewsbury, 8 Jan. 1697[-8]; *HMC Buccleuch*, ii. 396; *DNB*; *Westminster Abbey Reg.* 258–9.

E. C.

DENTON, Alexander I (1654–1698), of Hillesden, Bucks.

BUCKINGHAM 1690–17 Oct. 1698

bap. 8 Dec. 1654, 2nd but 1st surv. s. of Edmund Denton of Hillesden by Elizabeth, da. of Sir Richard Rogers of Eastwood, Glos. *educ.* Oxford (Mr Finch) 1664–5, Hanwell (George Ashwell) 1665. *m.* 10 Nov. 1673, Hester (*d.* 1691), da. and h. of Nicholas Herman of Middleton Stoney, Oxon., 3s. 2da. *suc.* fa. 1657.[1]

An orphan at the age of three, Denton inherited estates decimated by sequestration during the Interregnum and by his father's financial extravagance. He was brought up under the care of his great-uncle, Dr William Denton, court physician to Charles II, and of his godfather, Sir Ralph Verney, 1st Bt.†, who, between them, saved Hillesden for the family.[2]

Denton was appointed to the Buckinghamshire lieutenancy in March 1680, after being recommended by the lord lieutenant, the 2nd Earl of Bridgwater. He originally intended to stand in 1685 for Buckingham, a borough some three miles from his seat, but, finding Verney was a candidate, desisted and put his 'small interest' at his godfather's disposal. In February 1688 he gave negative replies to the first two of James II's 'three questions' on the repeal of the Penal Laws and Test Act. In March his wife ran off with his intimate friend Thomas Smith (son of Sir William Smith†). After a lawsuit he was awarded £5,000 damages against Smith, and because his wife had taken £500 with her she lost any right to financial support, even though she had previously brought him a fortune. Denton refused to see her, and when news of her death broke in September 1691, John Verney* (Lord Fermanagh) thought it 'no ill news to her husband'. However, Denton did pay for her burial in Spitalfields.[3]

After again being mentioned as a candidate for Buckingham in the elections for the Convention, Denton took advantage of Sir Ralph Verney's lassitude, making a strong interest there in February 1690. He was quickly joined with Sir Richard Temple, 3rd Bt.*, much to the chagrin of Verney who gracefully ceded his interest to his 'cousin', when approached by him on the eve of the poll 'for the benefit and advantage of his affairs', while admitting privately that he did so only because he could not win. Much spleen was vented at this betrayal of his kinsman by Denton, John Verney referring to Denton as 'a silly drunken cuck[old]'. Like the Verneys, Denton was a Tory, even going into Oxfordshire to assist the Tory candidates for that county, and being classed as such on Lord Carmarthen's (Sir Thomas Osborne†) list of the new

Parliament and also on two subsequent lists of Carmarthen's supporters. He was assessed as a Country supporter on Robert Harley's* list of April 1691. Denton seems to have divided his time between London and his estate at Hillesden, often visiting Buckinghamshire while Parliament was in session, and indulging in his passion for the turf. However, the concerns of his constituents, particularly the ongoing battle with Aylesbury to secure the county assizes, could bring him to the capital even at the height of summer.[4]

Denton was re-elected after another contest in 1695, despite the distraction of his courtship of 'Mistress Clarke' from Watford. Denton was forecast as likely to oppose the Court in the division on 31 Jan. 1696 over the proposed council of trade, refused to sign the Association at first (although he quickly changed his mind, subscribing on 16 Mar.), voted against fixing the price of guineas at 22s. and on 25 Nov. voted against the attainder of Sir John Fenwick†. He continued to be an inactive Member, however, obtaining frequent leaves of absence (five times in all during his parliamentary career). Returned again in 1698 and listed as a member of the Country party in a comparative analysis of the old and new House undertaken about September, he died on 17 Oct. before Parliament assembled.[5]

[1] Lipscomb, *Bucks*. iii. 17–18; *Recs. of Bucks*. xi. 246–7. [2] *Verney Mems. 17th Cent.* i. 568; ii. 117; Lipscomb, 17–18; *Cal. Comm. Comp.* 2269, 2878; *VCH Bucks.* iv. 175. [3] *CSP Dom.* 1679–80, p. 416; Duckett, *Penal Laws and Test Act* (1883), 148; *Verney Mems.* 379–80, 453; Luttrell, *Brief Relation*, i. 544; BL, Verney mss mic. 636/45, John to Sir Ralph Verney, 2 Sept. 1691. [4] Verney mss mic. 636/44, William Coleman and J. Churchill to Sir Ralph Verney, 10 Feb. 1689[–90], John Verney to same, 20 Feb. 1689[–90], Dr William Denton to same, 16 Apr. 1690, Sir Ralph to Edmund Verney, 21 Feb. 1689[–90]; 636/46, John to Sir Ralph Verney, 28 June 1693; Huntington Lib. Stowe mss STT 479, 482, William Chaplyn to Temple, 11 Feb., 11 Mar. 1689[–90]. [5] Verney mss mic. 636/48, John to Sir Ralph Verney, 25, 26 Sept. 1695; Luttrell, iv. 30; *Verney Mems.* ii. 493; Lipscomb, 21.

E. C./S. N. H.

DENTON, Alexander II (1679–1740), of the Middle Temple.

BUCKINGHAM 1708–1710, 1715–25 June 1722

b. 14 Aug. 1679, 2nd s. of Alexander Denton I*; bro. of Edmund Denton*. *educ.* Buckingham 1694; St. Edmund Hall, Oxf. 1697; Middle Temple 1698, called 1704, bencher 1720. *m.* 3 Mar. 1716, (with £20,000) Catherine (d. 1733), da. and h. of John Bond of Sundridge, Kent, *s.p. suc.* bro. at Hillesden 1714.[1]

Freeman, Chipping Wycombe 1704, Woodstock 1712; recorder, Buckingham 1708–22; asst. Banbury 1718.[2]

Sec. to Ld. Wharton (Hon. Thomas*) as c.j. in eyre, s. of Trent 1706, as ld. lt. [I] 1708–10; paymaster of ordnance [I] 1709–10; attorney-gen. duchy of Lancaster 1714–22; KC 1715; j.c.p. 1722–*d.*; chancellor to Prince of Wales 1729–*d*.[3]

MP [I] 1709–13.

A younger son, Denton was destined for the law, entering the Middle Temple shortly after his father's death. Despite fears in 1700 that he was falling under the spell of Anthony Rowe*, like his brother, and hence not studying as much as he should, Denton quickly progressed to the bar, being called in May 1704. Despite (or perhaps because of) his relative youth, he came into the public eye almost immediately as one of the four counsel employed by Lord Wharton for the five 'men of Aylesbury' in the case of *Ashby v. White* (see AYLESBURY, Bucks.). Having applied successfully on 5 and 12 Feb. 1705 to Queen's bench for a writ of habeas corpus, he was ordered into custody by the Commons on the 26th for breach of privilege, where he remained until Parliament was prorogued on 14 Mar. This minor martydom in the Whig cause ensured that Lord Wharton looked after his interests, making him his secretary as chief justice in eyre south of the Trent, a place worth over £500 p.a. His legal services were again much in use in party matters and in February and March 1708 he advised Bishop Nicolson of Carlisle in his dispute with his High Tory dean, Francis Atterbury.[4]

With his brother transferring to the county seat in 1708, Denton was returned for Buckingham. In an analysis of the 1708 election returns he was listed as a Whig, and the Earl of Sunderland (Charles, Lord Spencer*) classed his election as a gain for the ministry. In the 1708–9 session Denton voted for the naturalization of the Palatines. On 7 Mar. 1709 he reported from a committee examining the petition of Edward Whitaker, formerly solicitor to the navy, and on the 14th was ordered to draft a bill to oblige Whitaker to submit his accounts, presenting it on the 18th. He was unable to manage it further because by 26 Mar. he was in Buckinghamshire 'in order to his journey into Ireland', as private secretary to the new lord lieutenant, Wharton, and reported to be at sea in mid-April. He returned to England early in July, carrying with him Irish bills for the Privy Council to consider, and a recommendation by Joseph Addison* to Lord Somers (Sir John*) which described him as 'a gentleman of excellent sense, great discretion, and true principles'. Denton returned to Dublin at the beginning of August 1709 to play a role as an Irish MP in support of Wharton's administration. His reward for all this activity was an office in the Irish ordnance worth £500 p.a.[5]

Denton was back in Buckinghamshire by early October 1709 and at Westminster by 5 Dec. when he was added to a committee of inquiry. He voted for the impeachment of Dr Sacheverell in March 1710 and, as if to show his important connexions among the Whigs, secured a recommendation from the Duke of Devonshire (William Cavendish*) to the new lord chief justice, Sir Thomas Parker*. On 18 Mar. he was appointed to a conference committee on the bill explaining the act for rebuilding Eddystone lighthouse. In July, Denton was again sent over to Ireland, returning to England in time to lose his seat at the general election in October.[6]

After his defeat, Denton resumed his legal career, appearing as counsel in several cases before the Lords. He remained active locally, being one of only two Whigs attending the Buckingham quarter sessions in July 1712. In March 1713 it was suggested that he 'may as well burn his books through want of business' as the Whigs preferred to use Nicholas Lechmere*. He did not stand in 1713, relinquishing the Whig standard at Buckingham to his brother, but was conspicuous in joining in Whiggish revelry after the general election campaign. In May 1714 Denton's situation was transformed when he inherited his brother's real and personal estate. Almost immediately he made plans to let the park (off-loading the deer to Wharton), his vigour leading Sir Thomas Cave, 3rd Bt.*, to opine, 'I fear our cousin Alex will appear a more inveterate Whig than his brother except his wings are enough clipped from attempting mischief'. The Hanoverian succession saw Denton richly rewarded by his Whig patrons as he began to ascend the ladder of legal office. He was returned for Buckingham in 1715 and the following year contracted an advantageous marriage, with his bride reported to be worth at least £20,000. He left the Commons in 1722 upon his appointment to the judges' bench, dying on 22 Mar. 1740. As he was childless like his brother, his property ultimately descended to his nephew George Chamberlayne†.[7]

[1] Lipscomb, *Bucks.* iii. 17–18; B. Willis, *Buckingham*, 196, 203; BL, Verney mss mic. 636/47, Sir Ralph Verney, 1st Bt.† to John Verney* (Ld. Fermanagh), 25 Aug. 1694; *Pol. State*, xlv. 633; Foss, *Judges*, viii. 120; *Recs. of Bucks.* xi. 21. [2] *Ledger Bk. of Chipping Wycombe* ed. Newall, 63; Verney mss mic. 636/55, Fermanagh to Ralph Verney†, 6 Aug. 1713; A. Beesley, *Hist. Banbury*, 516. [3] Luttrell, *Brief Relation*, vi. 75, 386; *Swift Works* ed. Davis, iii. 233; Somerville, *Duchy of Lancaster Official Lists*, 22. [4] Verney mss mic. 636/51, Elizabeth Adams to John Verney (Ld. Fermanagh), 22 Nov. 1700; 636/52, Cave to Fermanagh, 6 Feb. 1704-5; 636/53, Fermanagh to Lady Cave, 15 Aug. 1706; *Party and Management* ed. Jones, 98–103; Luttrell, *Brief Relation*, v. 516; Foss, 120; *Post Boy*, 13–15 Aug. 1706; *Nicolson Diaries* ed. Jones and Holmes, 455–6, 459. [5] Verney mss mic. 636/54, Margaret Adams to Fermanagh, 26 Mar. 1709; *Verney Letters 18th Cent.* i. 184; *Addison Letters* ed. Graham, 165–6, 171, 176, 178; *Swift Works*, 233. [6] Verney mss mic. 636/54, Lady to Ld. Fermanagh, 9 Oct. 1709; Stowe 750, f. 13; Luttrell, vi. 601; *Addison Letters*, 228–9. [7] *HMC Lords*, n.s. viii. 354; n.s. x. 273; *Verney Letters 18th Cent.* 243, 247; Verney mss mic. 636/55, Cave to Fermanagh, 14 Mar. 1712–13, Margaret Adams to same, 15 Oct. 1713, Fermanagh to Ralph Verney, 18, 27 May 1714, 1 Jan. 1715–16; PCC 113 Aston, 291 Browne.

E. C./S. N. H.

DENTON, Edmund (1676–1714), of Hillesden, Bucks.

BUCKINGHAM   22 Dec. 1698–1708
BUCKINGHAMSHIRE   1708–1713

bap. 25 Oct. 1676, 1st s. of Alexander Denton I*; bro. of Alexander Denton II*. *educ.* Wadham, Oxf. 1695; M. Temple 1697. *m.* 18 May 1700 (with £10,000), Mary (*d.* 1742), da. and coh. of Anthony Rowe*, *s.p. suc.* fa. 1698; *cr.* Bt. 12 May 1699.[1]

Denton's immediate tasks upon succeeding his father were to gain control of his estate and contest the vacant parliamentary seat at Buckingham. To accomplish the first he had to persuade the trustees named in his father's will (made ten years previously) that there was no need for them to act since the debts on the estate had now been greatly reduced. In addition, because he was now of age, it was possible for the legacies due to his siblings to be raised from the estate already settled on him by his mother's marriage articles. Likewise, Denton had to persuade them that he should act as executor and therefore be able to administer his father's personal estate. This matter was made all the more delicate by the fact that one of the trustees, Sir John Verney, 2nd Bt.* (later Lord Fermanagh), was also his main rival at Buckingham. Nevertheless, Denton achieved both aims, although it was not until 1702 that the legal details transferring the trust were complete.[2]

At the time of the Buckingham by-election in 1698 county opinion viewed Denton's conflict with Verney in terms of a disagreement within an extended family, clearly believing that Denton would take the same Tory line as his father. Since Denton made little initial impact on the Commons, it was not immediately apparent that he held different views from those of his father. On 18 Jan. 1699 he voted against the disbanding bill, and the following day received leave of absence. If this vote indicated his turn towards the Whigs, during the summer of 1699 he caused further unease to his Verney relatives, who gradually realized that he had joined the Whig leader Lord Wharton (Hon. Thomas*) and 'that faction . . . his father abhorred tho' he paid them a civility fit for their qualities'. However, Denton was an irregular attender at

Westminster, often preferring his estate at Hillesden. Thus, in the 1699–1700 session, although he was reported to be arriving in London on 4 Nov., he was absent when the House was called over on 11 Dec. and ordered into custody, being discharged on the 15th. He was allowed leave on 17 Feb. 1700. At this time an analysis of the Commons placed him under the 'interest' of Hon. Henry Boyle*. In May, to almost universal disapproval, he married the daughter of Anthony Rowe, part of her portion being a gambling debt of £6,000 he owed to her father. Much was made of this by contemporaries, and of Rowe's role as an intermediary with Sir Thomas Smith, whereby £3,000 of the money owed by Smith to Denton's father (see DENTON, Alexander I) was paid to Denton, although many thought Rowe the chief beneficiary.[3]

The run-up to the January 1701 election saw Denton treating the corporation amid speculation that gaming and racehorses would ruin his estate, not to mention having such a man as Rowe run his affairs. Denton joined with Sir Richard Temple, 4th Bt., to defeat the Tory candidate: their 'being so much for my Lord Wharton makes them despised by the Church party'. Despite rumours of a rift with Temple in September 1701, they were returned again in November. Denton confirmed his predilection for a wager by offering 50 guineas that Sir Thomas Littleton, 3rd Bt., would be elected Speaker of the new House. Robert Harley* classed him as a Whig in an analysis of the new Parliament.[4]

Returned again in 1702, in September Denton was reported to be out of order, possibly 'in a consumption', and removing to Bath for a cure, and he received leave of absence on 18 Jan. 1703 for health reasons. He was listed on 13 Feb. as voting to agree with the Lords' amendments to the bill for taking the oath of abjuration, but in September was again at Bath. He was in London early in December, but received leave for ten days on 22 Jan. 1704, returning by mid-February. March saw a report of him having 'very rich liveries made', and on the 15th the Commons was informed that a servant of his had been arrested, and on a report from the committee of privileges his release was ordered. Denton did not vote for the Tack on 28 Nov., and, having recovered from an attack of the gout by mid-January 1705, he acted as a teller on 14 Feb. to agree with an amendment from the Lords omitting some words from the bill to exclude MPs in places created since 1685. Also in February he managed through the Commons a bill from the Lords to amend the Act which had allowed Sir Peter Tyrrell, 1st Bt.†, and his son, Thomas, to dispose of lands in Buckinghamshire.[5]

Returned again in 1705, Denton was classified as a 'Churchman' and on 25 Oct. voted for the Court candidate in the division on the Speaker. Very little is known about his activities in this Parliament. On 3 Mar. 1708 he presented a bill to explain the previous session's Smithfield Cattle Act, and in early 1708 he was classed as a Whig. By December 1707 Lord Cheyne (Hon. William*), the outgoing knight, had virtually conceded that Denton would be successful should he transfer to the county seat from Buckingham and Denton was in fact returned unopposed in 1708. In the first session of the new Parliament, he moved on 22 Jan. 1709 that the thanks of the House be conveyed to the Duke of Marlborough (John Churchill†), although somewhat surprisingly on 8 Mar. following the 'solicitation of some great lords', Denton opposed the attempt of the Duke's protégé Thomas Meredyth* to overturn the Midhurst election. However, he voted for the naturalization of the Palatines and was reported to be in London just a couple of days before the session closed in April. During the winter of 1709–10 Denton was ill, but he was reported on 7 Mar. to have gone up to London, where he cast his vote in favour of the impeachment of Dr Sacheverell, although one list has him as an absentee.[6]

Despite a fierce contest for the county seats, Denton emerged victorious at the general election of 1710. He was classed as a Whig in the 'Hanover list', but was reported to be ill and did not attend the Commons before Christmas. Indeed, he may have been absent for much of the remainder of the Parliament. Nevertheless, Denton retained a keen interest in supplying his constituents with news and vigorously contested the county and borough of Buckingham in 1713, going down to defeat in both. In May 1714 he was reported to be 'dangerously ill of the smallpox', and died on the 4th. He left his real and personal estate to his brother Alexander, his widow marrying Viscount Hillsborough [I] (Trevor Hill†), who had 'managed' his funeral on 11 May.[7]

[1] Lipscomb, *Bucks.* iii. 17–18, 21; *Verney Letters 18th Cent.* i. 134. [2] PCC 57 Pott; BL, Verney mss mic. 636/50, Belzial Knight to Verney, 3, 10 Nov., 20 Dec. 1698, Verney to Knight, 8 Nov. 1698; 636/51, Willam Busby to Verney, 17 Jan. 1701[–2]. [3] Verney mss mic. 636/50, Cheyne to Verney, 19 Nov. 1698; 636/51, Lady Gardiner to Verney, 25 July, 29 Aug. 1699; 636/52, same to same, 1 Mar. 1702/3; *Verney Letters 18th Cent.* 48. [4] Verney mss mic. 636/51, Lady Gardiner to Verney, 5, 8 Aug. 1700, 11 Sept. 1701, Ralph Palmer to same, 6 Jan. 1701/2; *Verney Letters 18th Cent.* 89, 160. [5] *Verney Letters 18th Cent.* 115, 173; Verney mss mic. 636/52, Elizabeth Adams to Fermanagh, 14 Sept., 7 Dec. 1703, 28 Jan., 18 Feb. 1703/4, 19 Jan. 1704/5. [6] Add. 33225, f. 17; Centre Kentish Stud. Stanhope mss U1590/O139/2, Hon. James Brydges* to James Stanhope*, 17 Mar. 1709; Verney mss mic. 636/54, Elizabeth

Adams to Fermanagh, 19 Apr. 1709, Ld. to Lady Fermanagh, 7 Mar. 1709[-10]; *Verney Letters 18th Cent.* 208; Speck thesis, 73. [7] *Verney Mems.* i. 305, 308; Verney mss mic. 636/54, Fermanagh to Ralph Verney†, 21 Dec. 1710; 636/55, Lady to Ld. Fermanagh, 28 Apr. 1713, George Fellows to same, 2 June 1713, Sir Thomas Cave, 3rd Bt.*, to same, 1 May 1714, Penelope Viccars to same, ?18 May 1714; Le Neve, *Mon. Angl.* 1700-15, p. 290; PCC 57 Pott.

E. C./S. N. H.

DERING, Sir Chomeley, 4th Bt. (1679–1711), of Surrenden Dering, Pluckley, Kent.

KENT   1705–1708
SALTASH   7 Dec. 1708–1710
KENT   1710–9 May 1711

b. 23 June 1679, s. of Sir Edward Dering, 3rd Bt.†, of Surrenden Dering by Elizabeth (*d.* 1704), da. of Sir William Chomeley, 2nd Bt., of Whitby, Yorks., niece of Sir Hugh Chomeley, 4th Bt.† *educ.* M. Temple 1697, New Coll. Oxf. 1697. *m.* 17 July 1704, Mary (*d.* 1707), da. and h. of Edward Fisher of Fulham, Mdx., 2s. *suc.* fa. as 4th Bt. 1689.[1]

Dering, who came from a well-established parliamentary family, was left in the care of his mother after his father's death. Having 'travelled much about England in 1695', he was entered early in 1697 at both the Middle Temple and Oxford. He seems to have spent some time at the university, for in November 1699 the future Viscount Perceval (John†) wrote to say that Dering had welcomed him to Oxford. Shortly after attaining his majority Dering was appointed in April 1701 to the lieutenancy for Kent, and in February 1702 to the commission of the peace. With his marriage in 1704 to a 'great fortune and pretty young lady', he was well set to reassert his family's claim to one of the Kentish county seats.[2]

Dering was duly returned at the top of the poll at the 1705 election. On an analysis of the new Parliament he was classed as a 'Churchman', and on 25 Oct. 1705 he voted against the Court candidate for Speaker. Having been listed as a Tory early in 1708, he was defeated at the general election of that year, but found refuge at Saltash where James Buller* brought him in at a by-election in December. In the 1708–9 session Dering was arrested by two constables at a tavern near the Royal Exchange in company with the Earls of Denbigh and Craven, Buller and Thomas 'Leigh' (possibly Thomas Legh II*). The first three would become members of the 'Board of Brothers', a Tory club to which Dering was also elected on 31 Mar. 1710. In the 1709–10 session he voted against the impeachment of Dr Sacheverell.[3]

In the 1710 election Dering was returned for both Kent and Saltash. He chose on 4 Dec. to sit for the former, but not before he had written to Buller complaining of the behaviour of his opponent there, and adding, 'I hope this Parliament will take some care to prevent if possible the bribery that is at almost all elections, or the country gentleman will be undone'. He was listed as a Tory on the 'Hanover list', and as one of the 'worthy patriots' who in the 1710–11 session detected the mismanagements of the previous administration. On 15 Dec. 1710 he acted as a teller on a local matter, against a motion to add four names to the list of land tax commissioners for Kent. Similarly, as befitted a knight of the shire, he was first-named on 14 Feb. 1711 to a committee considering a request from Greenwich for £6,000 to rebuild their parish church. He was also a member of the October Club.[4]

Dering's death on 9 May 1711, several hours after a duel with Richard Thornhill of Olantigh, a Kentish neighbour, was the subject of much contemporary comment, and resulted in the Commons ordering on 12 May a new bill to prevent duelling. The original quarrel between Dering and Thornhill had taken place on 27 Apr. at the Board of Brothers' meeting at the Toy Tavern in Hampton Court. Thornhill apparently 'affronted' Lord Scarsdale and refused Dering's suggestion that he apologize. In the ensuing scuffle Dering knocked Thornhill down and kicked or stamped on him, dislodging several teeth. Thornhill subsequently recovered, and challenged Dering. The duel was fought in Tothill Fields, where the participants discharged pistols at a sword's length. Thornhill was found guilty of manslaughter at the Old Bailey on 18 May, after witnesses had given evidence on his behalf that Dering was often 'troublesome in company'. However, on 21 May Thornhill was murdered by two men on Turnham Green. Dering had been due to remarry 'in Whitsun week', the week following the duel, and according to Anne Delaune he made a will the night before his death in which he bequeathed his intended bride £500 p.a. In fact, an examination of his will reveals only a codicil, dated 8 May, in which his 'cousin', Jane Tryor, who may have been the lady in question, was left the use of his mansion house at Surrenden Dering till his heir attained the age of 21, and was made an overseer of his will in place of his deceased mother-in-law. Dering was succeeded by his eldest son, Edward†.[5]

[1] Sloane 1770, f. 136; F. Haslewood, *Pluckley Monuments*, 14. [2] PCC 251 Ash; Egerton 2378, f. 9v.; *HMC Egmont* ii. 191; *CSP Dom.* 1700–2, p. 292; info. from Prof. N. Landau; *HMC Portland*, iv. 113. [3] Add. 70420, newsletter 5 Mar. 1708–9; 49360, f. 21. [4] Speck thesis, 328; Boyer, *Pol. State*, iii. 117. [5] Add. 49360, ff. 52–53; 47026, f. 68; 28569, f. 106; *Top. and Gen.* iii. 381–2; *HMC Portland*,

DES BOUVERIE see BOUVERIE

DEVEREUX, Price (c.1664–1740), of Vaynor Park, Mont.

MONTGOMERY BOROUGHS
18 Nov. 1691–9 Aug. 1700

b. c.1664, o. s. of Price Devereux (*d.v.p.* 1666, 1st s. of George Devereux† of Sheldon, Warws. and Vaynor Park) by his 3rd w. Mary, da. of one Stephens of Bristol, Glos. *m.* 3 Dec. 1683, Mary (*d.* 1729), da. of Samuel Sandys† of Ombersley, Worcs., sis. of Edwin Sandys*, 1s. 1da. *suc.* gdfa. 1682; cos. Edward Devereux as 9th Visct. Hereford 9 Aug. 1700.[1]

Freeman, Welshpool 1678; ld. lt. Mont. 1711–14; steward, manors of Mavon, Card. and Mynydd Mallaen and Talyllychau, Carm. 1713–Dec. 1714.[2]

Devereux, whose father was killed fighting the Dutch, was brought up by his paternal grandfather, a (politically) Presbyterian Member of Parliament in 1647–8. Devereux himself was a staunch Anglican, a great supporter of charity schools in his native county, who in 1688 had given negative answers to King James' 'three questions' on the repeal of the Penal Laws and Test Act. As one of the 'chief of the gentry' in Montgomeryshire, he had apparently entertained some hopes of the Boroughs seat at the 1690 general election, but agreed 'not to molest' the outgoing Member, Charles Herbert*, whom he eventually succeeded the following year at a by-election. He was included in the forecast for the divisions of 31 Jan. 1696 on the proposed council of trade, as likely to oppose the Court, but was 'ill' in the country in March and unable to subscribe the Association. His explanation, accompanied by a declaration that he was willing to sign, was accepted by the House, but he may still have been purged from the Montgomeryshire commission of the peace. He was one of a number of MPs ordered, on 2 Nov. 1696, to attend within a week to be sent for in custody for unlicensed absence, and was up in time to vote on the 25th against the attainder of Sir John Fenwick†, but the following year, on 16 Dec. 1697, he was again ordered into custody for defaulting at a call of the House. He was discharged four days later. Classed as a supporter of the Country party in a comparative analysis of the old and new House of Commons in September 1698, the following month he was listed as likely to oppose the standing army. He was again largely inactive in his last Parliament, before going to the Upper House in 1700 on succeeding a cousin as Viscount Hereford.[3]

A staunch Tory under Queen Anne, and associated with the Earl of Rochester (Laurence Hyde†), Devereux remained loyal to the ministry over the peace in 1711–12, urging the vengeance of God on its enemies. Jacobite intelligence, albeit of dubious provenance, considered him in 1721 'a worthy man and fit to be relied on'. Devereux died at Vaynor, 3 Oct. 1740, aged 76, and was buried at Berriew, Montgomeryshire. His heir (and namesake) had sat as a Tory knight of the shire since 1719.[4]

[1] *Mont. Colls.* xii. 320; xxvii. 196–7, 199–201, 206–7; Duncumb and Cooke, *Herefs.* iv. 70; Nash, *Worcs.* ii. 220; IGI, Worcs. [2] *Cal. Treas. Bks.* xxvii. 295, 325, 327; xxxviii. 209–10. [3] *Mont. Colls.* 199–201, 207; *SPCK Corresp.* ed. Clement (Univ. of Wales Bd. of Celtic Studies, Hist. and Law ser. x), 87; Duckett, *Penal Laws and Test Act* (1882), 384; *Cal. Herbert Corresp.* ed. Smith (Univ. of Wales, Bd. of Celtic Studies, Hist. and Law ser. xxi), 346, 352–3, 355; A. Browning, *Danby*, iii. 213; L. K. J. Glassey, *Appt. JPs*, 123. [4] G. Holmes, *Pol. in Age of Anne*, 276, 428; *HMC Portland*, v. 132; P. S. Fritz, *Ministers and Jacobitism 1715–45*, p. 154.

D. W. H.

DE ZUYLESTEIN see NASSAU DE ZUYLESTEIN

DIBBLE, John (*d.* 1728), of Daniells, Abinger Hammer, Surr.

OKEHAMPTON 20 Dec. 1705–1713

s. of Daniel Dibble of Daniells by his w. Susannah. *m.* by 1685, Alice (*d.* 1712), 4s. 2da; *suc.* fa. 1702.[1]

Dibble inherited a house called Daniells at the foot of the North Downs and a forge held under a lease from the Evelyn family, the local landowners, at a rent of £20 p.a. Much more lucrative, however, were his activities as a merchant in timber. He handled the sale of timber from the Evelyn family estate at Wootton in Surrey, although a major outpost of the business was established in the Okehampton area, and for a while prospered upon government contracts to supply timber to the navy. From the early 1700s, however, he was increasingly beset by cashflow problems, and was complaining, for example, to John Evelyn, the diarist, in January 1702: 'it has been much to my grief, I am sure, that I have not been able to raise your money yet, though I hope I have given you security enough for it and will pay you the interest from the time the principal ought to have been paid to you'. He said he expected £800 from the building of a ship, now ready to launch, which would pay most of the debt. Then in July he offered 'land security for £400' for the unpaid money, pleading to pay the rest by Christmas. At the 1705 election he stood for Okehampton, where he employed many local people, and was caught in a double return which was resolved in his favour on 20 Dec. In the meantime he was listed as a placeman, presumably by virtue of his government contracts, and also, evidently in error, as having voted on 25 Oct. 1705 for the Court candidate as Speaker. Soon after the 1705 election he was added to the Devon commission of the peace. Subsequently he was classed as a Whig in 1708 and voted in 1709 for the naturalization of the Palatines. By this time Dibble had quite overstretched himself financially, having sold Daniells to the Countess of Donegall. Nicholas Morice[†] complained of a debt he owed, adding that 'Mr Dibble hath no habitation nor settlement in London, neither drives he any trade in the City. 'Tis difficult to find where he is and 'twill be extreme hard to squeeze any money from him. He owes much in this county and cannot appear but under the protection of privilege of Parliament.' A little later in 1709 Morice came to the conclusion that he 'might as soon squeeze water out of a pumice stone as get money from Dibble'. Early in 1710 Dibble voted for the impeachment of Sacheverell. He was successful again for Okehampton in the election that year, when as many as 135 new freemen were created on his behalf, mostly his 'servants, waggoners and carters'. Apparently he had originally intended to make an interest at Saltash, against John Buller I*, by scattering guineas among the voters, but desisted before the poll. He was classed erroneously as a Tory in the 'Hanover list' of the 1710 Parliament. In May 1712 he claimed privilege to prevent a servant of his being arrested by the high bailiff of Westminster for a debt of £400. He did not stand in 1713 presumably because, his business having failed, he was in hiding from his creditors.[2]

On 17 Dec. 1723 Dibble wrote to (Sir) John Evelyn II*, complaining that he had been deprived of the lease of his family's forge at Abinger without any allowance for the improvements he had made and was now 'in a starving condition, out of all manner of business whereby to gain a penny'. He was hoping to obtain a place in the customs with Evelyn's help, and added that he was 'sure Mr [Robert] Walpole [II*] will be my friend with the least word from you or my Lord Falmouth [Hugh Boscawen II*]'. As Dibble could not appear in public, Evelyn was asked to reply to him at 'Mr William Rowe's, Hole in the Wall in Lambeth Marsh'. His burial is recorded at Abinger parish church on 26 Jan. 1728.[3]

[1] Manning and Bray, *Surr.* ii. 142–3; *Abinger Par. Reg.* (Surr. Rec. Soc. ix), 20–22, 24, 109, 112. [2] *VCH Surr.* iii. 130; BL, Evelyn mss, Dibble to Evelyn, 25 Feb. 1699, 7 Jan., 4, 6 Mar., 24 July 1702, same to (Sir) John Evelyn II, 3 Jan. 1718, 17 Dec. 1723; Morice mss at the Bank of England, Nicholas to Humphry Morice*, 8 Nov. 1709, same to Joseph Moyle*, 29 Nov. 1709; *Cal. Treas. Bks.* xxv. 409; xxviii. 70, 390–1; L. K. J. Glassey, *Appt. JPs*, 174; Luttrell, *Brief Relation*, v. 626; G. Holmes, *Pol. in Age of Anne*, 314, 358; W. A. Speck, *Tory and Whig*, 49–50; Speck thesis, 328; *CJ*, xvii. 232. [3] Evelyn mss, Dibble to Evelyn, 17 Dec. 1723; *Abinger Par. Reg.* 112.

E. C.

DIGBY, John (1668–1728), of Mansfield Woodhouse, Notts.

NEWARK 1705–1708
EAST RETFORD 1713–1722

bap. 22 Sept. 1668, ?2nd but 1st surv. s. of John Digby of Mansfield Woodhouse by Frances, da. of Leonard Pinkney of Westminster and Mansfield Woodhouse.[1] *educ.* Jesus, Camb. 1684. *m.* (1) prob. *s.p.*; (2) 23 July 1699, Jane, da. of Sir Thomas Wharton, KB, of Edlington, Yorks. (uncle of Hon. Thomas*, Hon. Goodwin* and Hon. Henry Wharton†), 2s. 12da. *suc.* fa. bef. 1697.[2]

Ranger of the deer, Clipstone park 1707–?, verderer, Sherwood forest by 1709–aft. 1722.[3]

The Digbys of Mansfield Woodhouse were a cadet branch of the family of Coleshill in Warwickshire. The Member's grandfather had been in arms for Charles I and in 1661 was receiving orders from the King relating to Sherwood forest, thus placing Digby's later role as a forest official firmly within a family tradition. His father served as sheriff in 1684, and in 1686–7 was being used by the Treasury to conduct a survey into decaying trees in Sherwood. It was probably John Digby who was appointed a deputy-lieutenant in May 1692. This man was removed from both the lieutenancy and the commission of the peace in August 1696 for refusing the Association. However, a letter from the Duke of Newcastle (John Holles†) shows that the man dismissed in 1696 was restored in 1700. By that year he had also been restored to the bench. In 1701 he was suggested as a possible sheriff but managed to avoid that onerous office. It is uncertain when Digby first acquired an office connected to the forest, but his keenness in that regard can be demonstrated in 1700 when Gervase Eyre* solicited the Marquess of Halifax (William Savile*) on his behalf in case the illness of Thomas Hewett, surveyor of the King's woods north of the Trent, should prove fatal. Digby's political views were probably close to Eyre's at this time. He voted for Eyre and Sir Thomas Willoughby, 2nd Bt.*, in the county election of 1698; in November 1701 he wrote to another Member with Country Tory inclinations, Thomas Coke*, to assure him of his interest in the Derbyshire election of 1701; and he subsequently continued his connexion with Willoughby, being described as a 'chief manager' for him during the county by-election of 1704.[4]

Digby's own political ambitions centred on Newark. The management of his election in 1705 was attributed to Willoughby, although his own involvement in the administration of the forest may also have made him acceptable to Newcastle, who was steward of Sherwood. On the list of the new Parliament Digby was classed as a 'Churchman' and Lord Sunderland (Charles, Lord Spencer*) counted his return as a loss. He duly confirmed this analysis by voting against the Court candidate in the division on the Speaker, 25 Oct. 1705. On 6 Dec. he acted as a teller against bringing in candles, in order to forestall a motion to take into custody the Tory mayor of Norwich for proceedings at the recent parliamentary election. Digby was given leave of absence on 20 Dec., to recover his health. His name appears on two later lists of this Parliament, one in early 1708 in which he was classed as a Tory and one which incorporated the returns of 1708, in which he was marked as a Court supporter. He did not seek re-election in 1708.[5]

Attempts by Digby to return to the Commons in 1710 were thwarted when the machinations of the county election led Willoughby to stand at Newark 'in opposition to Mr Digby whom he himself formerly brought in there'. Wisely, Digby did not push his candidacy in such circumstances, nor did he vote in the county contest. In January 1711 Newcastle attempted to exploit Digby's discomfiture over the election by promising to support his quest for employment if he in turn applied to Lord Scarsdale, since Willoughby 'is not so forward to know you as I think he ought to be'. However, Willoughby obviously felt an obligation towards Digby, for on being elevated to the peerage as Baron Middleton, he wrote to Lord Treasurer Oxford (Robert Harley*) to ensure that the Duchess of Newcastle placed her interest at Digby's disposal. Paradoxically, Newcastle's death in 1711 may have strengthened Digby's interest, since he was now in personal correspondence with the lord treasurer over forestry matters. In the ensuing by-election, however, he was overwhelmed by Brigadier Richard Sutton*, a defeat he himself ascribed to the failure of the Duchess of Newcastle's agents to obey their orders and support him. Following this debacle the Duchess wrote to Oxford asking for his favour towards Digby, adding that Middleton concurred with her request. In the 1713 election Digby was persuaded by Middleton to stand at East Retford, on a promise that every endeavour would be used with the lord treasurer 'that he might have something that he might hold with being in Parliament, instead of what was designed him'. Middleton backed up his promise, with a recommendation to Auditor Harley (Edward*), but there is no record of Digby having received any additional offices. Returned unopposed for East Retford in 1713 he may have been incapacitated with gout for part of the session, as he wrote in April 1714 of being 'laid up with the gout in so violent a manner that I have not been able to move across my room'. He was classed as a Tory on the Worsley list and on two comparative lists of the 1713 and 1715 Parliaments.[6]

Re-elected in 1715, probably as a result of an agreement with the Whigs, Digby voted against the impeachments of the Tory ministers. It was on these grounds that he refused initially to sign a loyal address to the King, although he subsequently relented. He continued to act as a j.p. and to serve the new Duke of Newcastle in the forest, paying particular attention to the welfare of the ducal hounds. Nevertheless, he did not modify his Tory views, voting for both Tory candidates in the county election of 1722. He died on 3 Aug. 1728.[7]

[1] Pinkney's son was of Mansfield Woodhouse. [2] IGI, Notts.; *Vis. Notts.* (Harl. Soc. n.s. v), 70. [3] Nottingham Univ. Lib. Portland (Holles) mss Pw2 39a, 43a, Digby to Newcastle, 8 Oct. 1707, 1709; *Cal. Treas. Pprs.* vi. 143. [4] Burke, *Commoners*, iv. 461; C. Brown, *Annals of Newark*, 114–15; *HMC 8th Rep.* pt.3 (1881), 23; Add. 70501, ff. 637–8; 33084, f. 165; L. K. J. Glassey, *Appt. JPs*, 125; *Notts. Co. Recs. 18th Cent.* ed. Meaby, 112; *CSP Dom.* 1702, p. 524; 1702–3, p. 396; *HMC Portland*, ii. 179; BL, Althorp mss, Eyre to Mq. of Halifax, 6 May [1700]; Harl. 6846, f. 339; BL, Lothian mss, Digby to Coke, 18 Nov. 1701; Portland (Holles) mss Pw2 167, J. Neale to Newcastle, 6 Mar. 1703–4. [5] W. A. Speck, *Whig and Tory*, 106; Add. 70026, f. 110. [6] Add. 70026, f. 110; 70263, Willoughby to [Oxford], 31 Dec. [1711]; 70223, Digby to same, 5 Sept. 1711; 70502, ff. 491, 496; 70382, Middleton to [Edward Harley], 23 Sept. [1713]; 70375, Digby to Edward, Lord Harley, 17 Apr. 1714; Davies thesis, 292. [7] Add. 70388, William Levinz* to Edward, Ld. Harley, 9 Sept. 1714; 32686, ff. 45–46; Meaby, 27, 211; *Notts. Pollbk.* 1722 (IHR), 36.

S. N. H.

DIGBY, William, 5th Baron Digby of Geashill [I] (1661–1752), of Coleshill, Warws.; Sherborne, Dorset, and Southampton Square, Mdx.[1]

WARWICK 1689–1698

bap. 20 Feb. 1661, 4th but 3rd surv. s. of Kildare, 2nd Baron Digby [I], by Mary, da. of Robert Gardiner of London; bro. of Hon. Robert† and Hon. Simon Digby†. *educ.* privately; Winchester Coll. 1677; Magdalen Coll. Oxf. matric. 1679, BA 1681, DCL 1708; travelled abroad (France) 1683–4. *m.* lic. 22 May 1686 (with £8,000),

Lady Jane (d. 1733), da. of Edward Noel†, 1st Earl of Gainsborough, 4s. (3 d.v.p.) 8da. (6 d.v.p.). suc. bro. Simon as 5th Baron Digby 19 Jan. 1686, cos. John Digby†, 3rd Earl of Bristol, in Dorset estate Sept. 1698.[2]

Gov. King Edward's sch. Birmingham 1687, pres. 1688–91; commr. rebuilding Warwick 1695; gov. St. Bartholomew's hosp. 1729–d.[3]

Member, SPG 1704, common council, Georgia 1733.

In the later years of his life 'the good Lord Digby' was revered as a paragon of Christian virtue. From early manhood he wore his Anglican conscience heavily, living by the maxim which he urged upon an acquaintance in 1686 to keep 'always a sense of religion in your thoughts'. Indeed, religion had a central place in his thought and action. As an MP his conscience lingered painfully over William III's accession, which he came to accept only by degrees, and it seems to have been his inability to resolve his mind firmly upon the issue that drove him to turn his back on Parliament while still in his early maturity. Once free from the clutches of political life he was for the rest of his life able to maintain a dignified reputation through a life of semi-retirement, much occupied in the patronage of numerous charitable and religious projects and in regular contact with those whom he most respected, the pious and the scholarly. One of the foremost influences on Digby's religious and intellectual development was John Kettlewell, who was appointed to the living of Coleshill in 1682 by his brother Simon, 4th Lord Digby. Kettlewell was a forthright and uncompromising exponent of the doctrine of passive obedience, and it is clear from Digby's later utterances in Parliament that these theological precepts assumed a dominant place in his thinking on the Revolution.[4]

Having in 1686 succeeded his elder brother to the Digby barony, Digby was elected to the Convention of 1689 for Warwick, with the backing of Lord Brooke (Fulke Greville†) whose daughter Katherine had recently married Digby's brother-in-law, the 2nd Earl of Gainsborough (Wriothesley Baptist Noel†). In February 1689 he had given his vote against the proposition that the throne was vacant, thus (with other Tories) indicating his belief that the hereditary line remained unbroken. Soon afterwards Kettlewell resigned the Coleshill living, having refused to take the oaths. Digby's attainder *in absentia* by James's Irish parliament on 7 May may have inclined him more favourably towards William and Mary, although according to one account an anonymous nobleman attempted to reinstate him in James's esteem, in the belief that Digby was still sympathetic to the Jacobite cause. However, Digby reconciled himself so far as to take the oath of allegiance, acknowledging the fact of William's accession, if not his right. Writing in February 1690 to his friend Lord Weymouth (Thomas Thynne†), whose attitudes were similar and who was also a patron of non-jurors, Digby expressed the 'zeal I have to see the next H[ouse] of C[ommons] well filled' with men of Tory heart. Early on in the new Parliament he was classed by Lord Carmarthen (Sir Thomas Osborne†) as a Tory and as a probable Court supporter. He was one of the first to speak on 26 Apr. against the committal of the bill for establishing an oath of abjuration, but did so with circumspection:

> It is a tender point that I am going to speak to; and, before I enter into the debate, I desire I may speak freely, without prejudice. Whatsoever concerns the constitution of the present government, I would not be thought to speak against; not for King James, if I speak against the bill. The foundation of the government is the present Bill of Rights; wherein the King promises his part etc., and we swear fealty. This is our original contract; if there be any, I am of opinion that is it. This oath I took with a good conscience, and will keep it. Till the King enlarges his part of the contract, I think we should not enlarge ours. I have heard of enemies against kingly government, and I fear this will create many more. This will not distinguish the enemies from the friends of the government. If this be, now the King is going into Ireland, it may be of dangerous consequence. These considerations weigh with me against the bill.

While wishing to avoid the imputation of Jacobitism, Digby was not prepared to deny James's right to the throne. The resort to an argument for a contractarian balance between King and Parliament, though on the surface highly unusual for a Tory, was calculated to appeal to Whig sections of the House in order to widen the scope of opposition. Much more like a Tory, he denied the existence of any 'contract' before the Bill of Rights, and implied thereby the possibility of continued loyalty to James II. His fears of dangerous consequences if the bill passed into law, from an inevitable sharpening of the distinction between firm and dubious supporters, were probably genuine. It may have appeared to Digby that James's attempt to recover his right indicated that he had not 'abdicated', and it is perhaps possible to surmise from his initial rejection of the Association in 1696 that had the bill been passed Digby would not have abjured. Years later, in Anne's reign, he wrote:

> There is hardly any precept in the Bible more plainly, more frequently, more earnestly enforced than that of obedience to governors and I do not see how a man can take up arms against his prince without rebelling against God himself.

On 29 Apr., three days after the defeat of the abjuration bill, another measure was ordered for the greater security of the government, and for providing new oaths, with Digby as one of the drafting committee. At the beginning of June King William passed through Warwickshire on his way to Ireland, stopping to dine with Sir Clement Fisher, a friend of Digby. William evidently used the occasion to try to reconcile influential opinion, for Digby and one or two other doubters were among those present, while a group of loyal Whigs were excluded.[5]

That Digby continued to feature as an adherent of the Court is confirmed by further lists drawn up by Lord Carmarthen at the end of the year, but in April 1691 he was marked by Robert Harley* as a Country supporter. His appointment to a series of important committees, together with the occasional surviving reference to contributions in debate, shows him to have been an active and prominent parliamentary performer. He presented a bill on 1 Dec. 1691 to explain a proviso about royal mines in the 1689 Act repealing a medieval statute against 'the multiplying of gold and silver', though he afterwards took no further part in the proceedings on the bill. His active interest in this measure is explained by his partnership in Sir Carbery Pryse's* lead and silver mines in Cardiganshire. Though granted a month's leave on 20 Jan. 1692, Digby was back in the House before the end of February. On 5 Dec., in the next session, he spoke against the King's proposal to retain 20,000 troops in England for defence, and on the 14th opposed the second reading of the bill for 'preservation of their Majesties' sacred persons and government' on account of its 'multiplying of treasons, which he thought not safe at this time'. On the 29th he obtained a fortnight's leave to attend his mother's funeral. In a working list of Court supporters compiled by Lord Carmarthen between March and December 1692, Digby was listed as one who might be influenced in favour of the Court by Sir Edward Seymour, 4th Bt.* He took an interest in the game bill introduced at the beginning of February 1693: having been nominated to the drafting committee on the 8th, he was ordered on the 23rd to convey it to the Lords after third reading. Following the King's rejection of the place bill in January 1694, Digby was named to the committees ordered to draft, then redraft, a 'representation'. When the King's response was considered on 1 Feb. he echoed the sentiments of Paul Foley I and Robert Harley in criticizing it as 'so general, that the answer will serve anything' and called for further elucidation. He prefaced these remarks, however, by saying that if a representation had not been ordered by the House, he would have been content himself for the question of the King's conduct to have rested.[6]

During December 1694 and January 1695 Digby managed a bill through the House for the rebuilding of Warwick, following the fire which had destroyed the western part of the town in the previous September. The bill, in which he was named as one of the 'commissioners or judges', duly received the Royal Assent on 11 Feb. On 5 Feb., during proceedings on the Lancashire Plot, he told against taking a suspect into custody. A clear sign of Digby's closer association with the Country party was seen on 14 Mar. when he seconded Sir Christopher Musgrave's (4th Bt.) nomination of Paul Foley I for the Speakership. His services to Warwick, in quickly procuring the legislation necessary to begin rebuilding in the town was probably the uppermost consideration behind his unopposed re-election in the autumn. Forecast as likely to oppose the Court in the division of 31 Jan. 1696 on the proposed council of trade, he voted against fixing the price of guineas at 22s. In the wake of the Assassination Plot he refused at first to sign the Association and was reported at the end of February to be one of the 'ringleaders' of the non-subscribers. However, in common with the other Warwickshire MPs who refused to sign, he was not dismissed from the bench. Indeed, he was unusually active at this time in issuing warrants against Catholics and others suspected of disaffection, but his sudden resignation from the lieutenancy on 15 June clearly indicates that his conscience was troubled. Lord Northampton, the lord lieutenant, was 'sorry that you still persist in the same mind, and that you will not consider your own and [your] country's good but leave them both exposed to the pleasure and disposal of other men'.[7]

On 17 Nov. Digby spoke on the attainder of Sir John Fenwick[†], cautioning against the misuse of Parliament's judicial power. His theme was that 'the just power of Parliament' should be exercised only in situations 'wherein the government is nearly concerned', and he questioned whether the allegations against Fenwick amounted to such a threat. In the division on the 25th he voted against the attainder. On 8 Mar. 1697 he was granted an unspecified period of leave. His final undertaking in the House before standing down at the next general election was the management of a private estate bill, originating in the Lords, to enable his Noel in-laws to sell off land towards settlement of debts left by his father-in-law, the 1st Earl of Gainsborough, who had died in 1689. In the comparative analysis of the old and new House of Commons drawn up soon after the 1698 election he was classified as a Country supporter 'left out'. A combination of political and private factors appear to have influenced his decision to retire. His behaviour over the Association in 1696 had probably made him less acceptable to Lord Brooke, who at this time effectively controlled Warwick's two seats. At the same time Digby was weary of London and with the demands of parliamentary attendance. On 9 July he wrote to his friend Edward Nicholas, the Member for Shaftesbury: 'I fancy you will now be looking towards Shaftesbury: I cannot heartily wish you success, but rather that you would turn country gentleman, and live quietly after the example of your old friend.' Again on 14 Sept.: 'You are pleased with the country as a mistress, I wish you would make it a wife.' Even so, he was anxious for details about the composition of the new Parliament, asking Nicholas to provide him with lists, 'marked' if possible. Commenting on these, he observed, 'I fear we are not much mended' but confessed that party distinctions were now of no concern to him. It is possible that he felt somewhat ostracized by his former colleagues in the House: he had confided to Nicholas on 16 Aug., 'I have no parliamentary friend at present I can be so free with'.[8]

Within a few months Digby had succeeded to the estates of his cousin the 3rd Earl of Bristol at Sherborne in Dorset. The monument to the Earl which Digby commissioned includes an epitaph, composed by his old Oxford friend Dr John Hough, which might equally well refer to Digby's own aspirations: 'He was naturally inclined to avoid the hurry of a public life, yet was careful to keep up the post of his quality.' Much of the remainder of Digby's life was taken up with religio-charitable activity. During the late 1690s he extended his mining interests by investing in Sir Humphrey Mackworth's* lead mines, attracted no doubt by the philanthropic intentions with which Sir Humphrey cloaked his scheme. Digby must also have known Mackworth through their common association with the Society for Promoting Christian Knowledge, which had been established in 1698. Though Digby was not himself especially active in the society, he was a patron and a close friend of one of its founders, Dr Thomas Bray. Digby had first appointed Bray to the living of Over-Whiteacre, a short distance from Coleshill, and in 1690 to that of nearby Sheldon. Subsequently he took a close interest in many of Bray's varied projects, particularly the establishment of parochial libraries. These were set up initially on an experimental basis in the neighbourhood of Coleshill, but soon afterwards Bray took the idea to Maryland. In September 1700 Digby agreed to become the SPCK's 'lay correspondent' for Warwickshire, and in June 1701 ranked among the founding members of Bray's Society for the Propagation of the Gospel.[9]

Digby's letters to Edward Nicholas show that withdrawal from the Commons by no means extinguished his appetite for news of parliamentary proceedings, albeit only 'for diversion', and, just as on religious matters, he could not refrain from offering detailed encouragement and advice to acquaintances on the political topics of the day. In the competition for the Speakership at the beginning of December 1698, Digby agreed that Sir Thomas Littleton, 3rd Bt., was most likely to succeed, though not without paying tribute to Hon. John Granville as an able committee chairman. Typically, at the end of the same month, he delighted 'to hear the disbanding bill goes on so merrily', and complained of the continuation of too large a military establishment in Ireland which he found unpopular among 'the countrymen'. In January 1699 he was concerned about a newly introduced game bill and apprehended that 'mischief rather than good' was likely to come from it. There were some reports in January 1701 that he was ready to re-enter Parliament. Whatever the truth of these, he was subjected to considerable pressure during the summer of 1703 to stand for a vacancy at Oxford University, having the previous year appeared to Lord Nottingham as 'yielding, though not desirous to do it then'. His original intentions remained unshaken, however, and he was 'universally despaired of' by Dr Charlett and other High Tory eminences within the university. Following the 1705 election, Nicholas' confession to Digby that as a Court Tory he would be obliged to vote against William Bromley II for the Speakership met with a characteristic warning against acting merely out of 'a wrong notion of gratitude or some other false argument':

> a great deal more depends upon this than the having a Speaker our friend. All the world sees now which way things are tending . . . and there is nothing so likely to stop this cancer as a majority of the House of Commons appearing early against it.[10]

Throughout Anne's reign Digby took an active interest in the affairs of his native county, and was often present at meetings of county gentry for purposes electoral or otherwise. A major preoccupation during these years was the project for providing Birmingham's expanding population with a new church, a project of which he was a principal promoter, having in 1703 been one of the earliest subscribers. When by February 1707 the scheme was ready for legislative sanction he forwarded a petition to the county Members, 'to whom the people of Birm[ingham] do commit your management of this good work in the H[ouse] of C[ommons]', and issued detailed instructions on how they should proceed. To William Bromley II he delegated the task of securing support in the House from 'other friends'. The bill failed to emerge from the Lords, and it is probable that Digby was involved in the second, successful attempt in 1709. His vigorous attachment to Anglican doctrines shone through in a set of 'rules for your conduct' which he compiled for his son Robert, in about 1708, in which he warned against 'some Calvinistical opinion . . . particularly the doctrine of predestination which cannot possibly be true if God be just':

> Upon a just and impartial inquiry I dare answer that you will not find a better constituted church than the Church of England and therefore you [ought] not only to profess yourself a faithful member of it, but to be an advocate for it upon all occasions and endeavour to support it by all lawful means. She has at this time (as in most times she had had) many open and secret enemies, many false and lukewarm friends and will need all the assistance of her true sons. But remember that passion and ill language will support no cause.

Digby could therefore find no stomach for the Arian views of his old friend William Whiston, a leading proponent of 'primitive Christianity'. Whiston's intellectual questings led him to doubt Trinitarian doctrine and condemn the Athanasian creed as a 'dangerous heresy', and in November 1712 he tried to interest Digby in the founding of a society for promoting these opinions. Digby urged his friend to 'consider well what you are a-doing', and, while he couched his advice with professions of impartiality, it was clear that his orthodox mind was quite closed to Whiston's thinking.[11]

Following the Hanoverian succession, Defoe reported in his Tour that Digby 'is at present a little on the wrong side as to the government, not having taken the oaths to King George', and that most of the market-town of Coleshill were 'eminently that way too'. At the time of the Atterbury Plot in 1721 he was mentioned in a list, supposedly of sympathizers to the Jacobite cause, as 'old though well-affected'. Digby's philanthropic achievements in the vicinity of his estates in Warwickshire and Dorset were prodigious and he received a glowing tribute from his friend Bray in a work published in 1728. He had settled the tithes of Coleshill and Over-Whiteacre; provided land and money for 'a very fine parsonage-house' at Coleshill; rebuilt a ruined chapel at Sherborne; founded two libraries at Coleshill and Over-Whiteacre; contributed 'bountifully' to others at Warwick and Sherborne; built a parochial library and rectory at Sheldon; and founded charity schools at Coleshill and Sherborne. Furthermore, on his Irish estates he rebuilt a church and founded a charity school. In later years at Sherborne he helped to enlarge the vicarage, founded a school for poor girls, and shortly before his death gave £1,000 to the almshouse of St. John the Evangelist. In 1733 he became a member of James Oglethorpe's† Georgia Society, originally established to settle newly released debtors in America, which had been founded from a trust fund set up by Bray. Three of Digby's sons predeceased him; his second and third sons, Hon. Robert and Hon. Edward, later successively represented Warwickshire as Tories. His elder son's violent insanity forced him in 1715 to secure an Act of Parliament disinheriting him. Digby died at Coleshill on 27 Nov. 1752, aged 90, and was buried at Sherborne, the barony and estates passing to his grandson Edward Digby†. Under his will, which contained only a single charitable bequest (of £100 towards the discharge of 'poor prisoners' in Warwick county gaol), he left a personal estate of £23,000, and an additional £12,000 for the purchase of land to be settled on his younger grandsons.[12]

[1] Unless otherwise stated, this biography is based on H. Erskine-Hill, *Social Milieu of Pope*, 132–65. [2] IGI, Warws.; *Winchester Long Rolls 1653–1721* ed. Holgate, 27, 30. [3] *Dugdale Soc. Publns.* vii. 108, 114, 118; *Great Fire of Warwick* (Dugdale Soc. xxxvi), 121. [4] Birmingham Central Lib. Wingfield-Digby mss 'B', 159, 'Some few rules for your conduct'. [5] Bath mss at Longleat House, Thynne pprs. 26, f. 310; Bodl. Rawl. A.79, f. 70; Ballard 25, f. 16; Add. 42592, f. 136; Cobbett, *Parlty. Hist.* v. 595; Wingfield-Digby mss 'B', 159, 'Some few rules for your conduct', p. 5. [6] BL, Dept. of Printed Bks. 695. 1. 14(.5); Luttrell Diary, 290, 319; Cobbett, v. 829, 832–5, 838; H. Horwitz, *Parl. and Pol. Wm. III*, 127. [7] *Warws. Recs.* ix. pp. xxix–xxx; HMC Kenyon, 405; L. K. J. Glassey, *Appt. JPs*, 122; Add. 29578, f. 579. [8] Cobbett, v. 1101; Egerton 2540, ff. 100, 109, 113, 115, 117. [9] *DNB* (Bray, Thomas); *Hist. Mag. of Prot. Episcopal Church*, xxxiii. 18; *Chapter in Eng. Church Hist.* ed. McClure, 79; H.P. Thompson, *Thomas Bray*, 23; *CSP Dom.* 1700–2, p. 358. [10] Egerton 2540, ff. 132–3; SRO, Hamilton mss GD406/1/4657, Gawin Mason to Hamilton, 2 Jan. 1700[-1]; Bodl. Rawl. lett. 92, f. 153; Add. 29589, ff. 109–10. [11] Warws. RO Mordaunt mss CR/iii/98, 21, 16–20, 'List of . . . Gentlemen who met at the Swan, Warwick, 25 Nov. 1701', Digby to Mordaunt, [1705], 13 Jan., 12, 21, 26 Feb., 10 Mar. 1706–7; CR/iv/55, William Clerke to same, 18 Aug. 1712; Egerton 2540, f. 136; Thompson, 83; Wingfield-Digby mss 'B', 159, 'Some few rules for your conduct', p. 2; 80, 81, Whiston to Digby, 6, 18 Dec. 1712; 146, 147, Digby to Whiston, 29 Nov., 15 Dec. 1712. [12] Defoe, *Tour* ed. Cole, 481; P. S. Fritz, *Ministers and Jacobitism 1715–45*, p. 152; *LJ*, xx. 39; Add. 32730, f. 299; Hutchins, *Dorset*, iv. 254.

A. A. H.

DILLINGTON, Sir Tristram, 5th Bt. (c.1678–1721), of Knighton, I.o.W.

NEWPORT I.o.W. 3 Mar. 1707–1710
                22 July 1717–7 July 1721

b. c.1678, 3rd s. of Sir Robert Dillington, 2nd Bt.†, of Knighton by his 2nd w. Hannah, da. of William Webb of Throgmorton Street, London; half-bro. of Sir Robert Dillington, 3rd Bt.† *educ.* I. Temple 1694. *unm. suc.* bro. Sir John Dillington as 5th Bt. 5 Mar. 1706.

Ensign 1 Ft. Gds. 1701; cornet, 1 Drag. Gds. 1703, brevet capt. 1707; lt.-col. 17 Ft. 1708; capt. and lt.-col. Coldstream Gds. 1709, 2nd maj. 1717; gov. Hurst Castle 1716–d.

As a younger son, Dillington made his career in the army and was present at Blenheim. Shortly afterwards, on the death of his half-brother, he inherited the family baronetcy and estates. Returned for a borough on the Isle of Wight at a by-election in 1707 he was listed as a Whig in early 1708 and again after being re-elected for the same borough that year. He voted for the impeachment of Dr Sacheverell, although having been granted a fortnight's leave of absence on 9 Feb. 1710 he had been absent for some of the proceedings. He did not stand in 1710 or 1713. In August 1714 his name appeared on a list of army officers to be turned out as part of a planned Tory purge. He returned to Parliament in the reign of George I, continuing to support the Whigs until his death on 7 July 1721, aged 43.[1]

[1] Boyer, *Pol. State*, viii. 170.

P. W.

DISTON, Josiah (1667–1737), of Bakewell Hall, Basinghall Street, London and Woodcote Grove, Epsom, Surr.

DEVIZES   11 Dec. 1706–1710, 1715–1722

b. 1667, 2nd s. of Josiah Diston of Chipping Norton, Oxon. by his w. Mary.[1]

Dir. Bank of England 1701–21 (with statutory intervals), dep. gov. 1721–3; dir. New E.I. Co. 1706–7, 1708, 1711; trustee for taking loan to the Emperor 1706.[2]

Freeman, common councilman and capital burgess, Devizes 1707–May 1708, Sept. 1709–?*d.*; freeman Oct. 1708–June 1709.[3]

Receiver-gen. of taxes for Westminster and Mdx. 1721–6.

Diston came from a Dissenting family, and although his father was still living in 1697 little further has been ascertained of his pedigree. He evidently had relations in London, one of whom was a member of the Skinners' Company, and he himself became a leading factor at Blackwell Hall, the London cloth market. He was successful enough to build a country house near the increasingly fashionable spa of Epsom, and to make considerable improvements to the extensive grounds, such as 'delighted' John Toland, who nicknamed the estate 'Mount Diston'. As he dealt with west-country clothiers, it was presumably through trading connexions that he first became involved in Devizes elections. Although defeated in 1705, he was successful at a by-election the following year, with the support of the Whig faction in the borough. Diston was no doubt helped by his increasing local prominence; he had been added to the Wiltshire commission of the peace shortly before the election and was also made a municipal j.p. in Devizes. Some of his few committee appointments in the Commons suggest a personal interest. In the 1706–7 session he was named to prepare a bill for the repair of highways through the parishes of Rowde and Bishops Cannings, Wiltshire, having himself recently purchased the mortgage of tolls in that vicinity. In December 1707 he managed through the House a bill to remove the embargo on the export of white cloths, a bill promoted by petitions principally from Gloucestershire and Wiltshire producers. He was listed as a Whig in early 1708. Having secured his entrée into the constituency, he used his wealth to consolidate his interest. Sparing 'no pains or cost', he was said to have spent some £3,000 by the spring of 1708 'in law and bribes'. He also took an active part in the violent party struggles within the corporation. The result was that he headed the poll in the 1708 election. He was named to the drafting committee of a bill encouraging woollen and iron manufacturers in November 1708, and in March 1709 voted for the naturalization of the Palatines. In the 1709–10 session, in response to a petition from the Marlborough quarter sessions that freehold land in Wiltshire was being conveyed to 'ill-disposed persons', Diston was named to draft a bill for the public registering of deeds, wills and conveyances made in the county. Most important, he voted for the impeachment of Dr Sacheverell.

Diston was dislodged at Devizes after a double return at the 1710 election, the Commons deciding in favour of the Tory candidates. While he was re-elected a director of the Bank in 1710, on the Whig slate, Diston's ejection from the Commons was followed in 1712 by his removal from the Wiltshire commission of the peace. He retained an interest in local affairs, for on 13 May 1713, with the French commercial treaty in mind, he sent a petition to the House from several Wiltshire clothiers appealing for the trade in wool not to be discouraged by high duties. Nevertheless, he was defeated at Devizes at the 1713 election.[4]

Despite the fact that he regained his seat in 1715 little has been ascertained of Diston's last years. Having failed as receiver in 1726, he spent the rest of his life in debt and receiving royal bounty, dying at Hampstead on 7 Nov. 1737.[5]

[1] *Cal. Treas. Bks.* xxix. 545; T. Phillipps, *Collectanea*, 374, 379.
[2] *N. and Q.* clxxix. 59; *Daily Courant*, 9 Mar., 16, 25 Apr. 1706;

Boyer, *Anne Annals*, iv. 127. ³Wilts. RO, Devizes bor. recs. G20/1/19, min. bk. ⁴Crosby, *Hist. Baptists*, ii. 258–9; PCC 122 Noel; *Bd. Trade Jnl.* 1708–15, p. 409; 1715–18, pp. 95–96; *Works of John Toland* (1747), ii. 98–99; Bath mss at Longleat House, Thynne pprs. 25, f. 428; L. K. J. Glassey, *Appt. JPs*, 140; *HMC Portland*, iv. 175; Wilts. RO, 212A/36/23; Devizes bor. recs. G20/19, min. bk., grand jury presentment 22 Apr. 1707; *Daily Courant*, 14, 16 Apr. 1711. ⁵*Gent. Mag.* 1737, p. 702.

D. W. H.

DIXWELL, Sir Basill, 2nd Bt. (1665–1750), of Broome, Barham, Kent.

DOVER   1689–1690, 1695–24 June 1700

b. 11 Dec. 1665, o. s. of Sir Basill Dixwell, 1st Bt., of Broome by Dorothy, da. and coh. of Sir Thomas Peyton, 2nd Bt.†, of Knowlton, Kent. *educ.* Christ Church, Oxf. 1682; travelled abroad (France), 1684. *m.* (1) ?c.1688, Dorothy (*d.* 1718), da. of Sir John Temple of East Sheen, Surr., Speaker, house of commons [I], 1661–7, sis. of Henry Temple†, Visct. Palmerston [I] *s.p.*; (2) 25 Apr. 1720, his cos. Catherine, da. of William Longueville of the Inner Temple, *s.p. suc.* fa. as 2nd Bt. 7 May 1668.¹

Freeman, Dover 1689, ct. of lodemanage Cinque Ports 1689.²

Auditor of excise June 1691–Feb. 1713, Dec. 1714–*d.*³

Capt. Sandgate Castle, 1694–6; lt.-gov. Dover Castle 1696–1702, 1714–bef. *d.*⁴

Commr. taking subscriptions to land bank 1696.⁵

Dixwell's grandfather, Mark, a Parliamentarian colonel, left his estates at his death in 1643 in trust to his brother John, charging him with payment of £13,000 for his children when they reached the age of majority. John Dixwell subsequently sat in the Long Parliament from 1646, became a regicide, and re-emerged into prominence as an advocate of the republican cause in 1659–60. Consequently, at the Restoration he fled abroad, eventually arriving in New England, where he remained undetected until his death in 1689. Before his flight he seems to have sold part of his estate to Sir Thomas Peyton, whose daughter married Basill, Mark Dixwell's son and heir, and the Member's father, in March 1660. This connexion with the staunchly loyal Peyton seems to have ensured either that the Dixwell estates were not forfeit to the Duke of York, or, if they were, that Peyton was allowed to buy them back. Basill Dixwell was created a baronet in 1660 and died in 1668. His mother had meanwhile married Sir Henry Oxenden, 1st Bt.†, of Deane, thereby beginning a close association between the two families. This was continued in 1693 when the Member's sister, a maid of honour to Queen Mary, married Oxenden's third son, George*, by a previous wife. Little is known about the second baronet's early upbringing other than that his mother and Peyton served as guardians, that he received a conventional education at Oxford, and went to France in 1684. He came to prominence at the Revolution, as a partisan of William of Orange. Indeed, Dixwell's conduct at Faversham was violently criticized by the Earl of Ailesbury (Thomas Bruce†) on the grounds that the Duke's generosity towards Peyton had saved the Dixwell family, which made his ingratitude doubly pernicious.⁶

At a meeting of the East Kent gentry held in September 1688 to consider candidates for James II's intended Parliament, Dixwell had been recommended for Dover. In the event he was returned for Dover at the elections for the Convention Parliament and was present at a meeting of Kentish gentlemen convened in January 1689 to discuss the method of presenting the county association. Dixwell appears to have stood down in 1690, supporting instead the candidature of James Chadwick*. Following the death in May 1691 of John Birch I*, Dixwell was appointed to the office of auditor of the excise, which he performed by deputy, receiving the salary of £500 p.a., plus £200 p.a. for clerks. In April 1692 he was exempted from the pardon issued prior to James II's attempted invasion. Having been a j.p. since the Revolution, he was appointed a deputy-lieutenant in 1694 and given added responsibility as captain of Sandgate Castle. As such he was active in matters of internal and external security, a role amplified by his promotion to lieutenant of Dover Castle, under the lord warden of the Cinque Ports, the Earl of Romney (Henry Sidney†). Significantly, it was Dixwell and 'Colonel Oxenden' (probably Sir James, 2nd Bt.*, his brother-in-law) who in February 1695 presented to the King the county's address of condolence upon the Queen's death. In March 1695 Dixwell characterized himself to the Earl of Portland as 'so truly and zealously a most affectionate subject (as well as a faithful servant to your lordship)'.⁷

A correspondent of Sir William Trumbull* described Dixwell as a man with 'a great hand in placing and displacing of offices of all sorts', and this was no doubt one reason why he was able to regain his seat at Dover in the 1695 election. In terms of electioneering, however, he seems to have been more active in the county, soliciting votes at Sandwich for Hon. Philip Sydney*, with the argument that 'by principle and extraction' Sydney was a friend of the government; nor did he neglect to mention that Sydney was also the lord warden's nephew. Later in November, it was noted that Dixwell and Sir James Oxenden were organizing a 'great party' to ride from Deal to the county poll. Dixwell's name was on Grascome's list of placemen of 1693, which included a few members of the 1695 Parliament. He was forecast as likely to support the Court on 31 Jan. 1696 in the divisions on the proposed council of trade; signed the Association promptly; and in March voted to fix the price of guineas at 22s. October 1696 saw him engaged, presumably in his capacity as a deputy-lieutenant or as lieutenant of Dover, in apprehending Frenchmen and intercepting French correspondence. However, he was reported on 6 Nov. to be in London and was present on the 25th to vote for the attainder of Sir John Fenwick†. Also in 1696 he was listed as a subscriber (of over £3,000) to the land bank. The £50 p.a. he received in April 1697 for the better support of his office as lieutenant of Dover Castle was the first of many attempts to augment the salary of the various posts he held. In the Dover by-election of December 1697 Dixwell adopted a pose of studied neutrality, apparently at the behest of both Philip Papillon* and the corporation. On 20 Jan. 1698 he received leave of absence from the Commons, 'having been lately very ill'.[8]

At the same time Dixwell and Papillon were concerned about the electioneering of their opponents at Dover. Philip Papillon, who had joined with Dixwell, clearly saw his partner as an asset in the campaign, believing 'the town is easier under him than under any governor they have had these many years', and that Dixwell had been a diligent constituency representative, 'having always appeared for the good of the corporation and . . . very ready in serving them on their least application to him'. Possibly because of this record, Dixwell was returned in the general election while Papillon was defeated. Indeed, almost Dixwell's first task was to enter into a correspondence with James Vernon I* over a debt owed by a company of marines for quarters in the town. He also managed to claim an additional £60 p.a. for a clerk to deal with the new duties on leather. Dixwell was listed as a placeman in September, and as a Court placeman in a comparative analysis of the old and new Parliaments. He duly voted on 18 Jan. 1699 against the third reading of the disbanding bill. On 12 Feb. 1700 Dixwell was appointed to the committee drafting a bill for repairing Dover harbour and told on 26 Mar. in favour of receiving the report on the bill. He resigned his seat at Dover in June 1700 in order to retain his place as auditor of the excise. This did not presage a complete retreat from electioneering, however, for in the subsequent election he was active in bolstering the interest in the borough of Sir Charles Hedges*, who as an outsider was much in need of local support. In the second election of 1701, Dixwell was still prepared to recommend Hedges to the town, but, given the resistance of the freemen to his re-election, was not prepared to press Hedges upon them.[9]

Although deprived of the lieutenancy of Dover upon Anne's succession, Dixwell was reappointed as auditor of the excise. For most of the reign he kept a low profile, but was not averse to the occasional burst of activity on matters of security and intelligence. He also expended energy in flattering his superiors. In 1707 he ended a letter to Secretary of State Sunderland (Charles, Lord Spencer*) with a reference to his own knowledge of the Earl's 'merit in Parliament' and worthiness for the office of secretary. Dixwell also found it expedient to refer to his parliamentary career in September 1710, when lobbying Robert Harley* in the hope of retaining his place in the excise: he hoped for the new minister's protection following 'the civility I received from you, on another occasion when I had the honour to sit with you in the House of Commons, in an affair that afflicted me (upon the then resumption bill) on account of my great-uncle, Colonel John Dixwell'. Since Dixwell had no Irish lands, this would appear to be a reference to a failed bill ordered on 7 Feb. 1698 for vacating all grants in England and Ireland during Charles II's reign. Whether the appeal touched Harley or not, Dixwell retained his office until January 1713, when Robert Davers, son of the leading Tory, Sir Robert Davers, 2nd Bt.*, replaced him. Evidence exists to show that Dixwell continued to take a close interest in parliamentary affairs. He voted for the Whig candidates in the 1713 election for Kent, and in the 1714 session Philip Papillon kept him informed of the progress of the schism bill, of which both men clearly disapproved, and it seems that Dixwell was the originator of a clause rejected by the Commons on 26 June, which was designed to help Dover deal with its vagrancy problem in the wake of the disbandment. The Hanoverian succession saw Dixwell restored to his post in the excise and to the lieutenancy of Dover. In 1720 he wrote a revealing letter to Philip Yorke†, in which he complained that the Tories at Dover were attempting to invoke an Act passed in William III's reign prohibiting excise collectors from involvement in elections, in order to curtail his own electioneering activities. Dixwell claimed that since his appointment in 1691 he had been concerned 'in every one of our county elections (and others near me) during that whole time without the least thought that that clause could at all concern me'.[10]

Although Dixwell had relinquished the lieutenancy of Dover 'some years' before, he retained the auditorship of the excise until his death on 26 or 28 Mar. 1750. Many codicils had been appended to his will but the basic terms remained unaltered from the draft signed in 1732. In it he lamented the 'disappointments and misfortunes' which had left him unable to pay all his debts, and expressed his desire for a monument to be erected in Barham church. With no male heirs, he left his estate, or what remained of it after debts had been paid, to the youngest son of his nephew, Sir George Oxenden, 5th Bt.†, with a remainder to his godson and cousin, Basill Dixwell, the grandson of John Dixwell the regicide, and his brothers, and a further remainder to the right heirs of the Dixwells of Coton, 'from whence my great great uncle Sir Basill Dixwell came'.[11]

[1] *Pol. State*, xvi. 198; Centre Kentish Stud. Papillon mss U1015/C33/3, Lady Dixwell to [?Philip Papillon], 29 Jan. 1684–5. Dixwell's will (PCC 145 Greenly) refers to his first wife, to whom he had been married for 30 years. [2] Add. 29625, f. 120; *CSP Dom.* 1689–90, p. 210. [3] *Cal. Treas. Bks.* ix. 1202; xxvii. 92; xxix. 35; P. Parsons, *Monuments and Painted Glass Chiefly in E. Kent*, 313. [4] *Arch. Cant.* xxi. 254, 256; *CSP Dom.* 1696, p. 152; 1702–3, p. 162; Papillon mss U1015/C41, p. 353; Parsons, 313. [5] *CJ*, xii. 508. [6] E. Styles, *Three Judges of Charles I*, 125, 140; L. A. Welles, *Regicides in Connecticut*, 26–27, 29–30; A. Everitt, *Community of Kent and Gt. Rebellion*, 55, 117, 181, 310; Add. 40717, ff. 169, 175–81; Papillon mss U1015/C33/3, Lady Dixwell to [?Philip Papillon], 29 Jan. 1684–5; *N. and Q.* ser. 3, vi. 2, 23, 42, 81; *Kingdom Without a King* ed. Beddard, 104; *Ailesbury Mems.* 210–11. [7] Add. 33923, ff. 434, 462; 35512, f. 147; 42586, f. 227; Papillon mss U1015/O24/6; *Cal. Treas. Bks.* ix. 1202; Clarke, *Jas. II*, ii. 485; info. from Prof. N. Landau; *CSP Dom.* 1694–5, pp. 20, 25; *London Gazette*, 14–18 Feb. 1695; [8] BL, Trumbull Misc. mss 29, [–] to Trumbull, [?July 1695]; Add. 33512, f. 147; 70081, newsletter 16 Nov. 1695; Luttrell, *Brief Relation*, iv. 131; *Vernon–Shrewsbury Letters*, i. 51; NLS, Advocates' mss 31.1.7; *CJ*, xii. 49; *Cal. Treas. Pprs.* 1697–1702, pp. 128–9; Sevenoaks Pub. Lib. Polhill-Drabble mss U1007/C13/2, Dixwell to David Polhill*, 27 Oct., 23 Nov. 1697. [9] Papillon mss U1015/C44, pp. 66–67, 70; *CSP Dom.* 1698, p. 414; *Cal. Treas. Bks.* xiv. 24; Add. 28886, ff. 119, 200; 28887, f. 374; Northants. RO, Chibnall (Thorpe Malsor) mss CTM 107b, newsletter 9 Nov. 1700. [10] *Cal. Treas. Bks.* xvii. 38; xxvii. 92; Add. 61607, f. 93; 70196, Dixwell to Harley, 15 Sept. 1710; 35584, f. 200; H. Horwitz, *Parl. and Pol. Wm. III*, 231; Papillon mss U1015/C45, pp. 253, 265; C41/6, Dixwell to Papillon, 12 May 1714. [11] Parsons, 313; PCC 145 Greenly.

S. N. H.

DOCMINIQUE, Paul (1643–1735), of St. Martin-in-the-Fields, London and Chipstead, Surr.

GATTON   1705–17 Mar. 1735

bap. 15 Jan. 1643, 1st s. of Paul Docminique of Lille, France and Stepney, Mdx. by Marie Tordereaux of Valenciennes, France. *m.* (1) 22 Dec. 1674, Alice, da. and coh. of William Edwards, Clothworker, of London and Newbury, Berks. *s.p.*; (2) by ?1686, Margaret (*d.* 1734), da. of Rev. Robert Edwards of Kibworth Beauchamp, Leics., cos. of his 1st w. 3s. (1 *d.v.p.*) 1 da. *d.v.p. suc.* fa. aft. 1667.

Dir. Co. of Scotland 1695–6; commr. taking subscriptions to land bank 1696; gov. White Paper Makers' Co. 1697; pres. Soc. of New Jersey proprietors 1711–12.

Ld. of Trade 1714–*d.*[1]

Docminique was raised in the French Huguenot community in London, his family having established itself in the capital a good while before their naturalization in 1662. His father, a merchant of some means, had served as a deacon in the Threadneedle Street congregation, but Docminique more readily integrated himself with his native country, twice marrying into the same English family. Soon after the Revolution he had become sufficiently wealthy to loan the Exchequer over £9,000, and he provided further financial aid to the government in 1691 by acting as the agent for supplying a troop of horse guards for Ireland. It was thus no surprise that he first came to the attention of Parliament on 29 Dec. 1691 as a surety for the stock of the East India Company, pledging for £5,000.[2]

Docminique's next appearance in the Commons Journals, however, was of a far more contentious nature, for his contacts with the East India Company led to his implication in the scandal surrounding Sir Thomas Cooke*. On 24 Apr. 1695 it was reported that Docminique had received £350 from Cooke 'for soliciting the Company's affairs to prevent a new company' and had also sold Cooke over £1,200 stock at a tidy profit. Two days later Richard Acton deposed that he had given £500 to Docminique in the belief that he 'had interest with Members' and could help the Company's cause. Before the year was out Docminique's name had been cited in another controversy on account of his recent appointment to a directorship of the fledgling Company of Scotland trading to Africa and the East Indies. Having invested £20,000 in the scheme, in November 1696 Docminique was one of the six English merchants elected by the company in an attempt to make the venture more acceptable to its English rivals. However, on 9 Dec. he found himself before the Upper House, testifying alongside several other directors that prior interest in Scottish trade had led them to join the company. The Commons was outraged by the manner in which the Scottish parliament had authorized the foundation of the new company, and, having been also grilled by a Commons committee on this matter, on 21 Jan. 1696 Docminique was impeached alongside his fellow directors for their 'high crimes and misdemeanours'. The charges were dropped after the Commons' chief witness absconded, but Docminique's recent experiences no doubt impressed upon him the need to invest more circumspectly.[3]

Docminique's commercial contacts gained him further recognition in 1696 when he was appointed a commissioner to take subscriptions to the land bank.

In March 1697 he petitioned the House on behalf of the Company of White Paper Makers against an amendment to a bill to levy duties on parchment and vellum, but was unable to overcome the opposition of the Stationers' Company. He gained further publicity by representing the proprietors of both East and West New Jersey when they surrendered their governing powers to the crown in early 1702, although the links which he forged with William Penn in the course of his colonial dealings were less likely to win him allies at court. His actual entrance into Parliament came as a direct result of the wealth he had amassed from commerce, since it was achieved by his purchase of the mansion of Upper Gatton from Lord Haversham (Sir John Thompson, 1st Bt.*) in 1704, one of several landed investments which he made in Surrey at that time.

When he took up his seat at the election the following year, Lord Sunderland (Charles, Lord Spencer*) regarded it as a Whig loss, a view endorsed by another parliamentary observer who described Docminique as a 'Churchman'. This attachment to the Church belied his Huguenot upbringing, and can probably be attributed to the influence of such City contacts as his father-in-law, William Edwards. At the outset of his first parliamentary session he voted against the Court candidate for the Speakership, and subsequently showed his political colours in dramatic fashion, nearly fighting a duel with Lord William Powlett* in December 1705. Although he twice contributed to the stormy debate on the second reading of the regency bill on 19 Dec., he proved an inactive Member in his first Parliament, his only other appearance of note coming on 24 Feb. 1708 when he acted as a teller to engross a private bill. His politics must have been more in evidence, since two parliamentary lists bracketed him with the Tories in early 1708. In the Parliament of 1708–10 he was only slightly more active, although in the first session he confined himself to two tellerships: on 11 Dec. 1708 to uphold the election of fellow Tory Anthony Blagrave* for Reading, and on 24 Feb. 1709 to carry a motion to adjourn the House. Another tellership followed in the second session when he acted on 25 Jan. 1710 in support of a motion to recommit the report of the election committee which had condemned the obstructive behaviour of the Tory town clerk of Beaumaris. He was also a predictable nominee for the drafting committee on a Surrey land registry bill. The trial of Dr Sacheverell gave him a further opportunity to publicize his support for the Church, and he was accordingly classed with the Tories in the 'Hanover list' of the 1710 Parliament.[4]

The Tory triumphs at the general election of 1710 seem to have galvanized Docminique into activity in the House. In the first session he featured as a teller in two more divisions: on 16 Dec. to return the Tory Sir Francis Child* as the duly elected Member for Devizes, and on 13 Mar. 1711 against a motion to disable persons from simultaneously holding directorships of the East India Company and the Bank. He was lauded as one of the 'worthy patriots' who had prosecuted the mismanagements of the preceding ministry in that session, and was cited as a 'Tory patriot' for voting to put an end to the war. However, given his status as a leading Tory financier, it is particularly surprising that he showed no apparent interest in the South Sea Company, a reticence which contrasted sharply with his prominence in the second session of the 1710 Parliament. In 1712 Docminique featured as a teller in four divisions, all of which saw success for his cause. On 22 May he supported the resolution of the committee of ways and means to place an extra duty on hides and vellum, and the next day backed a motion for the House to go into committee on a bill to reach agreement between the Royal African Company and its creditors. He was then instrumental on 3 June in defeating a bill to regulate the African Company at its engrossment stage. Four days later he helped to ensure the addition of a clause to a bill to facilitate the recovery of small gifts for charitable purposes.

In the course of the second session Docminique was identified as one of the few merchants within the ranks of the October Club. There was little cause for his colleagues to doubt his politics in the early part of the third session, since he served as a teller on 7 May 1713 to block a motion for adjournment when the House sought to censure the past conduct of the Whig William Churchill*, a former commissioner for sick and wounded. However, after showing consistency in his opposition to the African Company by acting as a teller on 12 May to block the committal of a bill to establish that trade, he then distanced himself from High Church hard-liners on 28 May when telling to reject an instruction that Quakers could not qualify for the franchise by making a solemn affirmation instead of taking an oath. An open breach with the ministry came when debate turned to the French commerce bill. In the key debate of 18 June he denounced the ministry for misunderstanding and intransigence, and, having confessed that he 'would never gratify a rising party for sinking the trade of the nation', voted against the bill later in the day. This opposition resulted in his being identified as one of the 'whimsical' Tories of the March Club.[5]

Uncertainties surrounding Docminique's political allegiance were underlined in the succeeding Parliament when his fears for the succession and for trade drove him ever further from the administration. On 16 Mar. 1714 he actually spoke in defence of the Whig pamphleteer Richard Steele*, arguing that there was a real threat to the Protestant line, and declaring that he would soon reveal 'some great transactions' to prove it. Two days later he featured as one of the few Tories to vote against Steele's expulsion from the Commons. If any further proof of his disaffection from the ministry were needed, on 15 Apr. he launched a bitter attack on its preparations for repulsing the Pretender, mockingly suggesting that 'the Highlanders and Jacobites would join to protect us'. Docminique was subsequently one of the MPs chosen on 5 Aug. to offer condolence on the death of Queen Anne and to congratulate George I on his accession, confirming a shift to the Whigs which was further endorsed by three parliamentary lists at the beginning of the new reign. Before the end of the year, his loyalty to the Hanoverians had been rewarded with the post of commissioner of trade and plantations, an appointment recommended by his active participation in the government of New Jersey.[6]

Docminique remained a steady supporter of the administration for the rest of his parliamentary career. He also proved a most loyal servant of the Board of Trade, attending his final meeting only days before his death on 17 Mar. 1735. His longevity was evidently more celebrated than his public profile, for one obituarist reported that Docminique could recall watching the procession of Oliver Cromwell† en route to Parliament. He was succeeded in both fortune and parliamentary seat by his son Charles†, and having channelled much of his wealth into Surrey properties in the course of his life, was buried at Chipstead.[7]

[1] PCC 96 Ducie; IGI, London; *London Mar. Lic.* ed. Foster, 727; Blore, *Rutland*, 182; *CSP Col.* 1711–12, pp. 2, 282. [2] *CSP Dom.* 1661–2, p. 286; *Publns. Huguenot Soc.* liv. 92; *Cal. Treas. Bks.* ix. 621, 1698; xvii. 309. [3] *Debates and Procs. 1694–5*, pp. 25, 27, 38; J. Prebble, *Darien Disaster*, 20, 38; *HMC Lords*, n.s. ii. 5. [4] *HMC Lords*, n.s. ii. 517; *New Jersey Archives* ii. 459–60; I. K. Steele, *Pol. of Colonial Policy*, 151–2; Manning and Bray, *Surr.* ii. 237, 243, 245; *Cam. Misc.* xxiii. 55–56; Luttrell, *Brief Relation*, v. 623. [5] *Huntington Lib. Q.* xxxiii. 158; SRO, Cromartie mss GD 305 addit./bdle. xv, acct. of debate, 18 June 1713; Boyer, *Pol. State*, v. 389; D. Szechi, *Jacobitism and Tory Pol.* 137. [6] NSA, Kreienberg despatch 16 Mar. 1714; NLS, Advocates' mss, Wodrow pprs. letters Quarto 8, f. 64; Douglas diary (Hist. of Parl. trans.), 15 Apr. 1714; *Cal. Treas. Bks.* xxii. 395. [7] *Jnl. Commrs. Trade and Plantations, 1735–41*, p. 10; *London Mag.* 1735, p. 160; Manning and Bray, 441–2.

P. L. G.

DODINGTON, George (c.1662–1720), of Dodington, Som. and Eastbury, Dorset.

WINCHELSEA 1705–1708
BRIDGWATER 1708–1713
WINCHELSEA 1713–1715
BRIDGWATER 1715–28 Mar. 1720

b. c.1662, 1st s. of John Dodington of Dodington by Hester (d. 1691), da. of Sir Peter Temple, 2nd Bt.†, of Stowe, Bucks. m. lic. 12 Feb. 1697, aged 35, Eleanor (d. c.1714), da. and coh. of Henry Bull*, *s.p. suc.* fa. 1673.[1]

Commr. appeals in excise 1679–1705; paymaster to treasurer of navy 1695–June 1699; trustee for Exchequer bills 1697–1700, for loan to Emperor 1706; commr. Greenwich Hosp. 1695, taking subscriptions to land bank 1696, taking subscriptions to S. Sea Co. 1711; sec. to English commrs. for union with Scotland 1706; chief sec. [I] 1707–8; ld. of Admiralty 1709–10, 1714–17; PC [I] Sept. 1714; clerk of the pells [I] 1715 (for life of his nephew George Bubb Dodington†).[2]

Dir. Old E.I. Co, 1695–8; New E.I. Co. 1702–5.[3]

Freeman, Winchelsea 1705, Dublin 1707; ld. lt. Som. 1715–d.[4]

MP [I] 14 July 1707–13.

Dodington was descended from an ancient Somerset family which claimed to have been settled at Dodington since the 13th century. His grandfather, Sir Francis Dodington, had suffered for his loyalty to Charles I during the Civil War and at the time of his father's death the estate was heavily encumbered with debt and worth only £300 p.a. His father, who had filled several diplomatic and secretarial posts under Charles II, died in 1673, whereupon his mother successfully petitioned the Treasury against the counter-claims of Sir Francis Dodington's second wife that the profits of a commissionership of appeals in excise, granted in trust to Sir Francis and his eldest son, should still be paid to her and her five children. When their trustee was omitted on a reshuffle of the commission in 1678, she again petitioned and was this time rewarded with the appointment of her eldest son to the commission, with a salary of £200 p.a. Establishing himself in London, Dodington set about making his fortune, and by 1688 was part-owner of four ships; but it was after the Revolution that he really began to prosper. On 12 Apr. 1689 the Earl of Shrewsbury successfully recommended his continuation on the excise appeals commission, and in 1690 Dodington and his partners secured a lucrative clothing contract for 21 regiments in Ireland. As early as 1687 he had been acting as occasional 'agent' or cashier to the navy, latterly during the treasurership of Admiral Edward Russell*, and when in 1695 Russell's cashier fell ill and died, Russell made Dodington his paymaster, presumably to run the office during his absences at sea. Dodington's connexion with Lord Orford (as Russell became), and through him his close affinity with the Whig Junto, was to be the keynote of his subsequent political career.[5]

Dodington continued his money-making ventures in government service throughout the 1690s, and also became a significant figure in the commercial sphere, joining the board of the East India Company in 1695. A measure of his rapidly increasing wealth was his subscription in 1694 to the Bank of England of a sum in excess of £4,000, and in 1697 of another £2,000 to the subscription for funding Exchequer bills. Towards the end of the decade, however, he not surprisingly became a target for his patron's enemies. Dodington's main perquisite as cashier or paymaster to the navy treasurer was 12d. in the pound of all deductions from the seamen's pay in respect of slop clothes, dead men's clothes, tobacco and the like, but suspicions about the enormous sums he was thought to be making, and threats to bring the matter under parliamentary scrutiny, compelled him in July 1698 to seek Admiralty confirmation of his entitlement. The opposition attack during the next parliamentary session resulted in Orford's exoneration on 15 Mar. 1699 by a single vote, but as the diarist Sir Richard Cocks, 2nd Bt.*, recorded, 'when they could not hurt Lord Orford they fell foul upon Dodington'. It was claimed that Dodington had made as much as £30,000, and when the matter was referred to the committee of the whole on the state of the navy, 'my lord's friends, to save him, gave up Dodington to shift for himself'. On 27 Mar. the House, besides resolving that his deduction of poundage was 'without warrant and ought to be accounted for', also found him errant in having made several payments by privy seal without vouchers. It was clear that Dodington was being sacrificed in order to save Orford, the belief being that it would be easy to 'retrieve' Dodington on a subsequent occasion. Following Orford's resignation in May, Dodington was dismissed from the paymastership by the incoming navy treasurer, Sir Thomas Littleton, 3rd Bt.*, but he was left with the responsibility of clearing Orford's accounts, a task which occupied him for the next five years. An attempt to resume the attack on both Orford and Dodington was made on 2 Feb. 1700, when Robert Byerley moved for the previously requested accounts of poundage deductions, and there was some expectation that pressure would be brought to have the money paid back and applied to public use. This, as James Vernon I* observed, would be 'a sensible mortification, both to my Lord Orford and Dodington'. The accounts were duly delivered on 5 Mar., but Parliament was prorogued and then dissolved before further action could be taken. It was probably due to the smear of financial impropriety that Dodington was soon afterwards taken off the commission for Exchequer bills. At the end of May 1701 Byerley raised the question of Dodington's administrative conduct once again in ways and means, and accordingly it was resolved to charge him with the deductions, now allegedly amounting to £17,000. Extenuating circumstances were pleaded on Dodington's behalf, however, centring on the fact that 'he had but £3,000 per annum salary' from his perquisites, which he claimed had hardly covered the cost of running his office. At the report on 3 June the Whigs rescued him from a resolution which would have required him to return all his takings to the public coffers.[6]

By 1704 Dodington had cleared Orford's accounts, and in the following year the new Whiggish current in politics enabled him to direct his career towards Parliament. Since becoming involved with the New East India Company, he had joined its board in 1702 and during his final year as a director, 1704–5, rated as the board's second largest shareholder. Although left out of the commission of excise appeals in 1705, he received government help, almost certainly through the auspices of Lord Orford, in obtaining a seat for the Cinque Port town of Winchelsea at the general election. His election was reckoned by Lord Sunderland (Charles, Lord Spencer*) to be a gain for the Whigs, and at the assembling of the new Parliament on 25 Oct. he voted for the Court candidate for Speaker. He also supported the Court in the proceedings on the 'place clause' of the regency bill on 18 Feb. 1706. Soon after the end of the session, he was pressed into service by the Junto over the proposed union with Scotland. Sunderland wrote to Lord Wharton (Hon. Thomas*) on 2 Apr. 1706: 'Lord Orford [one of the commissioners] has spoke to Mr Dodington about his being secretary to the Scotch commission, who made several objections to it, but Lord Orford would not take a denial, but desired him to consider of it; I fancy he will accept of it at last.' The Junto evidently set great store by this appointment, which was settled shortly before the commissioners met. No salary was allocated to him for his secretarial assistance to the English commissioners, although many years later in 1716 he was allowed £628. Meanwhile, in May 1707, his time on Orford's accounts was rewarded with a payment of £1,500. Despite his administrative value to the Junto, in Parliament he did not shine as an active Member. His most substantial act during the 1705 Parliament was to help in proposing a bill for improving the preservation of game (24 Jan. 1707).[7]

Almost as soon as Dodington completed his stint with the Scottish commission, the new lord lieutenant of Ireland, the Earl of Pembroke (Hon. Thomas Herbert†), made him his chief secretary. Dodington went over to Ireland in June 1707 but was soon complaining to Sunderland: 'In truth, I am almost dead with the fatigue I undergo, not having the least assistance from anybody in this family, my lord honouring me with the very least as well as the greatest business.' Overwork did not stop him from plunging incautiously into Irish politics after being returned to the Irish house of commons in July, but he lacked the experience and skill necessary to direct the court party there, a task which invariably fell to the chief secretary. Instead, his tactless advocacy of certain measures, such as the removal of the test, in league with several radicals, proved too much for many Irish Whigs and he was soon regarded as a liability. They were no doubt relieved at his return to England in October for the approaching session at Westminster. At the 1708 election Dodington took a seat at Bridgwater, eight miles from his estate at Dodington. His return for the borough was deemed by Sunderland as a Whig gain. Despite his somewhat unsuccessful Irish interlude he remained high in favour with the Junto, who were now in a strong position to reward his loyalty and industry. In June 1708 he obtained a salary of £400 p.a. for the years he had spent on Orford's accounts, and in August he petitioned for and was granted the reversion of the lucrative clerkship of the pells in the Irish treasury, during the life of his nephew, George Bubb (later Dodington). He was replaced as chief secretary in Ireland in December 1708 when Pembroke was made lord high admiral. In the Commons on 8 Mar. 1709 he strayed from his usual Court allegiance over the disputed Midhurst election and voted with the Tories in company with a number of other Whigs against Marlborough's protégé, General Thomas Meredyth*. This aberration was not repeated, however, in the major questions of the Palatines and the impeachment of Dr Sacheverell in which he voted with his Whig brethren.[8]

In November 1709 Orford, on being appointed first lord of the Admiralty, saw to Dodington's inclusion on the board with a salary of £1,000 p.a. As the holder of £5,000 of Bank of England stock he was at this time involved in several subscriptions to government loans. Early in January 1710 an unfounded rumour arose that he was to become treasurer of the navy, but the Tory appointments in the summer and autumn ruled out any possibility of his advancement for the time being. Orford's dismissal in October was followed by Dodington's in December. He had managed to hold on to the seat at Bridgwater, however, and was classed as a Whig in the 'Hanover list' of the new Parliament. On 25 May 1711 he voted against an amendment to the South Sea Company bill which vested the right to appoint the company's first directorate in the crown; on 7 Dec. for the motion of 'No Peace without Spain'; and on 18 June 1713 against the French commerce bill. He performed his only tellership during the Queen's reign on 27 May 1712, in relation to a minor bill concerning one of the lotteries. His situation at Bridgwater having become politically untenable, he achieved an effortless return at Winchelsea in the September election, where the Tory administration saw fit not to challenge the personal interest he had established there. On 18 Mar. 1714 he voted against the expulsion of Richard Steele even though some years earlier he had successfully prosecuted him for recovery of a £1,000 debt.[9]

Dodington retained his seat in Parliament, switching back to Bridgwater at the 1715 election. The Worsley list and other lists of this period classed him as a Whig. His enduring connexion with Lord Orford had been apparent once again in October 1714 when Orford, back at the Admiralty, included Dodington in the new commission; when the Earl went out of office with the schismatic Whigs in April 1717, Dodington went with him. He died on 28 Mar. 1720. In a vastly complicated will he left land worth about £4,000 p.a. and the clerkship of the pells, yielding some £2,000, to his nephew and heir, George Bubb (who had since assumed the surname Dodington). However, his chief concern was to provide for the completion of the palatial mansion, planned by Vanbrugh, at the Eastbury estate in Dorset which he had purchased in 1709 and intended as a momument to his name and fortune. To this end the sum of £100,000, which he left in cash, company bonds and notes, was placed in trust to be invested in land, and the income to be applied to the cost of construction; only when the work was finished (or 30 years had lapsed, whichever was the earlier) was the trust and mansion to revert to his nephew and heir. Before the will was proved, however, Bubb, having taken his uncle's surname, effectively pre-empted this arrangement by taking possession of the estate and of the securities earmarked for it.[10]

[1] *VCH Som.* v. 66; vi. 329; *The Gen.* i. 27; *London Mar. Lic.* ed. Foster, 409; *CSP Dom.* 1673–5, p. 111. [2] *Cal. Treas. Bks.* vi. 46; x. 1083; xii. 8; xv. 335; xix. 45; xx. 233; xxix. 141; Luttrell, *Brief Relation*, iv. 523; vi. 28, 38, 160; Add. 10120, ff. 232–36; Pittis, *Present Parl.* 349; *CJ*, xii. 509; A. B. Beaven's list of Irish PCs, Hist. of Parl. [3] Info. from Prof. H. Horwitz; Add. 38871, f. 15. [4] E. Suss. RO, Winchelsea ct. bk. WIN 60, p. 104; *Cal. Ancient Recs. Dublin* ed. Gilbert, vi. 369. [5] *VCH Som.* v. 66; *CSP Dom.* 1673–5, p. 111; 1679–80, p. 122; 1689–90, p. 59; 1691–2, p. 456; *Cal. Treas. Bks.* v.

1301; vi. 46; ix. 434, 994, 1039; x. 118, 371-2, 999, 1083; info. from Dr P. J. Lefevre. [6]*CSP Dom.* 1698, p. 356; *Cocks Diary*, 165-7; Luttrell, iv. 523; *Cal. Treas. Bks.* x. 335; xviii. 55; xix. 45; *Vernon–Shrewsbury Letters*, ii. 424. [7] *Cal. Treas. Bks.* xix. 45; xx. 233; xxi. 292; xxx. 612; Bodl. Rawl. A.303, f. 58; Cumbria RO (Carlisle), Lonsdale mss D/Lons/L1/4/stray letters, Sunderland to [Ld. Wharton], 2 Apr. 1706; P. W. J. Riley, *Union*, 109. [8]Add. 61633, ff. 178, 186, 212-15; Hayton thesis, 151; *Cal. Treas. Pprs.* 1708-14, p. 6; *Cal. Treas. Bks.* xxii. 362, 378; Huntington Lib. Stowe mss 57(2), p. 178. [9]P. G. M. Dickson, *Financial Revol.* 263; Add. 70421, newsletter 5 Jan. 1709-10; *Steele Corresp.* ed. Blanchard, 256, 262, 265. [10]*Hearne Colls.* vii. 162, 167; J. Carswell, *Old Cause*, 136-7, 150-1.

A. A. H.

DODSON, Thomas (c.1666–1707), of Hayee, St. Ives, nr. Liskeard, Cornw.

LISKEARD   1701 (Dec.)–by 24 Aug. 1707

b. c.1666, 1st surv. s. of Thomas Dodson of Hayee by Elizabeth, da. and coh. of William Sedley of Digswell, Herts. *m.* 16 May 1684, Mary, da. of John Buller I*, 2s. 5da. *suc.* fa. 1672.[1]

Ensign of ft. Sir Richard Atkins'* regt. 1694-6, Col. George Villiers' regt. 1696; ?cmmdr. Bermuda Castle by Mar. 1702; capt. of ft. Col. Heyman Rooke's regt. 1704–*d.*[2]

The Dodsons had settled in Cornwall in the 16th century, Thomas Tonkin* writing that they were descended from a London family. In 1694 Dodson received a commission in a newly raised regiment intended for service in Ireland. At the election of the following year he stood at Mitchell, and though he was involved in a double return on 14 Dec. 1695 the Commons seated his opponents. In early 1699 Dodson was reported to be claiming that he had been 'reduced to a sorrowful condition for want of his wife's fortune', complaints aimed at his father-in-law, John Buller I. Further, being placed on half-pay on the Irish establishment would have done little to alleviate his financial worries. His relationship with his wife's family had, however, improved sufficiently by December 1701 for them to secure his return at Liskeard. Dodson was classified as a Tory by Robert Harley*, and was also listed as having favoured the motion of 26 Feb. 1702 vindicating the Commons' proceedings of the previous session against the Whig lords. He was re-elected to Queen Anne's first Parliament, and on 23 Nov. was absent from a call of the House and ordered to be taken into custody. On 30 Oct. 1704 Dodson was forecast as a probable supporter of the Tack, but on 25 Nov. he was again absent from a call and was again ordered into custody. Consequently, he did not vote for this measure on 28 Nov. and was not released from custody until 8 Jan.

1705. Later that year he was listed as a placeman, and having retained his seat at the 1705 election was classed in an analysis of the new House as 'Low Church'. On 25 Oct. Dodson voted for the Court candidate for Speaker. Though this may suggest that he had tempered his partisan instincts, perhaps in the hopes of advancement in the army, an analysis of the Commons from early 1708 classed him as a Tory. Dodson had, however, died the previous year. In January 1707 he had been 'dangerously wounded' in a duel with John Manley*, and later that year died from his wounds. He was buried on 24 Aug. 1707. One of his daughters married Thomas Vivian*.[3]

[1]Vivian, *Vis. Cornw.* 57-58, 140, 535. [2]*CSP Dom.* 1694-5, p. 111; *CSP Col.* 1702, p. 118. [3]Polsue, *Complete Paroch. Hist. Cornw.* ii. 244; *Cal. Treas. Bks.* xv. 154; xvi. 442; Cornw. RO, Buller mss BO/23/72/53, P. Lyne to Buller, 11 Feb. 1698-9; Folger Shakespeare Lib. Newdigate newsletter 29 Jan. 1707; Luttrell, *Brief Relation*, vi. 11, 211.

E. C.

DOLBEN, Gilbert (c.1659–1722), of Finedon, Northants.

RIPON   1685–1687
PETERBOROUGH   1689–1698, 1701 (Feb.)–1710
YARMOUTH I.o.W.   1710–1715

b. c.1659, 1st s. of John Dolben, abp. of York 1683-6, by Catherine, da. of Ralph Sheldon of Stanton, Derbys.; bro. of John Dolben*. *educ.* Westminster 1671; Christ Church, Oxf. matric. 18 July 1674, aged 15; I. Temple 1674, called 1680, bencher 1706, reader 1708-9, treasurer 1720-1. *m.* by 1683, Anne, da. and coh. of Tanfield Mulso of Finedon, 1s. *suc.* fa. 1686; *cr.* Bt. 1 Apr. 1704.

?Gent. privy chamber 1689-1702; j.c.p. [I] 1701-20.[1]

Chairman, cttee. of privileges and elections 2 Mar.–27 May 1714.

The offspring of a clerical family, Dolben proved to be a true son of the Church. Unlike his brother John, he was of a priggishly conservative cast of mind, described while in only his late twenties as 'the fustiest old gentleman you ever saw'. He was much exercised by the threats posed to orthodox Protestantism and was responsible for the erection and maintenance of a charity school for girls on his Northamptonshire property. His Anglicanism also made him a staunch Tory, again unlike his brother, though his political partisanship was primarily a product of devotion to the interests of the Church of England rather than any attachment to principles of hereditary right and non-resistance, and he was a tactful enough politician to be able to retain office under ministries of different colours.[2]

Dolben was returned on his own interest at Peterborough in 1690, despite being opposed by some 'whose malice and hatred of my principles much outweighed their strength'. Classed as a Tory and as a Court supporter by Lord Carmarthen (Sir Thomas Osborne†) in an analysis of the new House, Dolben spoke in defence of Carmarthen on 14 May 1690, saying 'I think him as well affected to the government, as any of the Council board'. With other Tories, he supported the bill to 'reverse' the quo warranto against the city of London: named on 8 Apr. to the committee to prepare the bill, he spoke on 22 Apr. in favour of its commitment. On 10 Apr. he told against a motion to bring in a bill for a general naturalization. Throughout his career, Dolben's legal background facilitated a strong interest in legislative projects of many kinds. Apart from bills which he himself steered through the House, he often featured among the groups of MPs formally ordered to prepare and introduce pieces of legislation, a sign of his interest in or involvement at the initiation of various measures. There were, too, many areas of committee business in which he almost certainly played an active part. During the first session of the 1690 Parliament he featured on 2 Apr. among the appointees to draft a bill to confirm the East India Company's charter. Later he was to be one of the counsel retained by the interloping syndicate aiming to overthrow the charter. In the next session he reported and carried to the Lords in December 1690 a private estate bill; acted as teller on 26 Dec. against a motion to hear counsel on a private bill; and reported on 5 Jan. 1691 from a conference with the Lords. In December 1690 Carmarthen listed him as a likely supporter in the event of a Commons attack upon his ministerial position. The lord president also included Dolben upon a further list of Court supporters dating from the same month, and Robert Harley* came to the same conclusion in his own analysis of the House in April 1691. On 31 Oct. Dolben was among those ordered to prepare a bill to secure the rights of corporations. His first recorded speech came in the committee of supply on 6 Nov., and on the 19th he spoke in favour of putting the question generally for a vote of 65,000 for the army. On 12 Dec. he told against passing the bill to prevent false and double election returns. During the debate three days later on the motion vindicating the Earl of Nottingham's (Daniel Finch†) conduct of naval affairs, Dolben made a speech against adding to the motion some notice of the admission of error by the Earl of Danby (Peregrine Osborne†) in his statement that a letter from Lord Nottingham had been found in a captured French vessel. His other reported speech occurred on 31 Dec., when he opposed a Lords' amendment to the treason trials bill. In January 1692 he reported and carried to the Lords an estate bill, and on 2 Jan. told against an opposition motion for reducing the number of regiments from 15 to eight. Although he had loyally supported the administration during this session, approving of its Tory complexion, and was in fact rumoured in September 1691 to be a candidate for a commissionership of the great seal, he was well aware that serious criticisms could be made. 'We extremely want your helping hand in the settling of our disjointed government', he wrote to Sir William Trumbull*, one of his patrons,

for though we are in the hands of ingenious men, yet upon the whole our ministry seems to be so unfortunately constructed and in places so oddly distributed that few act in their natural sphere or have the employment for which their genius or education have intended them ... my great hopes rely upon the King's personal abilities and applications, whose zeal for the depression of the power of France actuates him beyond the strength of his constitution, and the ordinary faculties of a man; to the effecting of which great work the Parliament seems resolved to contribute their utmost assistance, though some particulars of mismanagement which have been laid before them and which justify my observation upon the ministers, have in some measure retarded the supplies and occasioned delay in those proceedings. But this storm seems to be overblown, and the reflections of the Parliament upon some branches of the administration will, I hope, have a good effect in ... the future ... I know it will be a welcome assurance to you that the interest of the Church of England daily gets ground not only in Parliament but in the Cabinet, the King seeming convinced that the present establishment in the Church is the only support of the monarchy.

Despite his connexion with the East Indian interlopers, when the motion to establish a new East India Company was debated on 17 Nov. 1692 he spoke in favour of first hearing the old company before taking action. In the inquiry into the naval miscarriages he refused to defend the largely Whig-dominated Admiralty Board, saying (during a debate on 21 Nov. on a proposal for an address to the King to put the Admiralty into other hands), 'I will not oppose your question, but wish when we change, we may change for the better.' As the attack turned on Lord Nottingham, another of his patrons, he spoke on 20 Dec. against putting the question either for an address for the Earl's removal or for a vote of thanks to Admiral Edward Russell*. On 2 Feb. 1693 he opposed the triennial bill, largely on the grounds that it had emanated from the House of Lords, who never did anything that showed any regard to this House; they have frequently rejected or dogged our bills sent to them . . . They are for the increase of their own powers and diminishing of ours . . . The bill doth certainly entrench upon the prerogative, and every true Englishman ought to keep the true balance.

On 23 Feb. he spoke in favour of a bill for repealing the Act which required those pardoned of a felony to find surety for their good behaviour. When the bill failed to complete all its stages by the end of the session, he reintroduced it on 9 Dec. 1693 and managed it through the Commons before being ordered, on 23 Jan. 1694, to carry it to the Lords. Dolben made little further impact upon the records of this session, though on 21 Feb. he complained to the House that the estate of his deceased uncle, to which he was heir, had been intruded upon. The offender was ordered into custody and was not released until he apologized to the Commons on 10 Mar. In the last session Dolben was included in Henry Guy's* list of 'friends', in connexion with the Commons' attack upon Guy, but of his recorded activity this session, his most noteworthy work was done in connexion with the drafting of a bill for regulating prisons and prisoners (4 Dec.).[3]

Despite the Whig dominance over the administration, Dolben seems to have remained faithful to it for some time. He may even have been spoken of as a likely candidate to be made solicitor-general in 1693, and was listed among the Court party by Grascome. In the new Parliament, however, he joined the opposition. In the forecast for the divisions of 31 Jan. 1696 on the proposed council of trade, he was marked first as 'doubtful' and then as likely to vote against the Court. He refused the Association, for which he was deprived of his place on the commission of the peace, and in late March 1696 voted against fixing the price of guineas at 22s. In the same month he reported a private bill (23rd), and also carried to the Lords the bill for better prevention of escapes and the relief of creditors (28th). An opponent of the bill of attainder against Sir John Fenwick†, he made a long speech on 25 Nov. 1696, at the third reading, arguing that the case ought more properly be tried in the inferior courts, and that in any case Parliament should insist on two witnesses, as required by the recently passed Treason Trials Act, even though that Act was not to come into force for four years. He naturally voted against the third reading of the attainder bill. On 20 Feb. 1697 Dolben carried to the Lords a bill allowing the bishop of London and Lord Nottingham to exchange advowsons, and during the following month chaired committees of the whole on two bills: to continue additional duties on several goods (1, 3 Mar.), and for completing St. Paul's cathedral (10, 12 Mar). In the last session he took a prominent part in the Country campaign over royal grants, being ordered on 7 Feb. 1698 to bring in a bill to vacate all grants of estates in England and Ireland during the reign of Charles II. He also presented on 22 May a bill to repeal the Act for the relief of creditors and chaired the ensuing committee. But the issue which agitated him the most at this time was the challenge offered to the Church by heterodox and sceptical writings, and he was an enthusiastic supporter of the blasphemy bill. He berated Trumbull for failing to attend the House while the bill was under discussion: 'I wonder extremely that your love to [sic] the country could get so much the better of your zeal for religion as to keep you there while the cause of the Trinity wanted your assistance.' In a similar vein, he was ordered on 9 Apr. to prepare a bill to regulate the proceedings of the ecclesiastical courts. After the 1698 general election, at which he failed to secure his continuance in the House, he was classed by the compiler of one list as a supporter of the Country party 'left out'.[4]

Returned once more in January 1701, Dolben was forecast the following month as likely to support the Court in agreeing with the supply committee's resolution to continue the 'Great Mortgage'. Active on the ministerial and Tory side of the House, he was named to the committees of 21 Mar. to draft the address against the Partition Treaty, and 1 Apr. to prepare the impeachment of the Earl of Portland. His legal expertise and concern for the interests of the established church were both evident in his appointment on 8 Mar. to prepare a bill to preserve the rights of Derbyshire's Anglican clergy to tithes from certain lead mines, and he presented this measure on 3 Apr. After the Parliament was dissolved he was blacklisted as one who had opposed the preparations for war against France. Meanwhile, on 13 May 1701, he had received his dividend from revived Tory fortunes when appointed a judge of the common pleas in Ireland. He took up the post in Dublin by July, but in future years generally did not allow his official responsibilities to interfere with parliamentary duties, being frequently excused from going on circuit in order to attend the Commons. At about this time he was also restored to the commission of the peace. Prominent again during the 1701–2 Parliament, he was involved in the production of a bill to prevent bribery at elections (17 Jan. 1702), an area in which he had a long-standing interest. He also made reports from five committees on bills seeking relief from the provisions of the resumption of Irish forfeited estates. As a Tory he supported the motion of 26 Feb. vindicating the Commons' proceedings the previous session in the impeachments of William III's ministers.[5]

Dolben retained his Irish judgeship on Anne's accession, and may even have been considered a possible lord chancellor for Ireland. He also continued to represent Peterborough in the House. In the 1702–3 session he was appointed, on 10 Dec., to prepare amendments to the occasional conformity bill, and in the new year he reported and carried to the Lords a bill relating to the revenues of the Savoy hospital (9, 13 Feb. 1703). An association with the more extreme wing of his party is suggested by his important role, together with Lord Nottingham, in tacking the so-called 'Test clause' onto the Irish popery bill of 1703–4, and thereby imposing a sacramental test on all crown and municipal office-holders in Ireland. Such a conclusion is confirmed by his management during the 1703–4 session of the bill for examining and stating the public accounts, which he guided through all its Commons stages. He also managed the bill enlarging the time for purchasers of forfeited Irish estates to make payment, a matter of Irish, and thus quasi-official, interest, and assumed a managerial role in the passage of bills relating to a specific Irish forfeiture and a private estate. On 24 Jan. 1704 he spoke in the debate on the case of *Ashby* v. *White* (see AYLESBURY, Bucks.), strongly defending the right of the Commons to sole jurisdiction over elections and condemning the intervention of the Lords. Appropriately for a staunch Churchman, he chaired the committee of the whole on 19 Feb. on the bill to restrain the licentiousness of the press. The following month Nottingham listed Dolben as a likely supporter during the proceedings upon the Scotch Plot, but despite his connexions with Nottingham, and with other High Tory leaders like Lord Rochester (Laurence Hyde[†]), with whom he corresponded regularly, Dolben did not leave office when the ministry was reconstructed in the spring of 1704. By the autumn he had become a moderate. Forecast as a probable opponent of the Tack, he was lobbied by the Court, and did not vote for it on 28 Nov. Irish matters figured large in his parliamentary activity in this session. On 8 Dec. Dolben presented a private bill concerning the Ulster Society's estate in Ireland, and on 13 Jan. 1705 he presented, in his capacity as a member of the Irish administration, a bill to permit the export of Irish linen to the plantations. He subsequently managed this bill through the Commons. During this session he also reported from the committee investigating a letter to William Lowndes* in which bribes were offered to secure the passage of a clause to the calico bill (13 Jan.), and reported a bill to divide a chapel from a parish church (9, 14 Feb.).[6]

In the summer of 1705 Dolben was included in a list of placemen, and a list of the new Parliament neatly summed up his political position, describing him as a 'High Church courtier'. Although he had kept his place, and had so far diluted his zeal for the Church as to oppose the Tack, he was far from having abandoned his principles, and seems to have entertained considerable reservations about the direction of ministerial policy. In the division on the Speaker, 25 Oct. 1705, he was one of only five placemen to vote against the Court candidate, John Smith I. The fact that he had done so, coupled with his 'moderation' a year earlier, accounts for his being adopted by the Tories as their candidate in the subsequent contest for the chairmanship of the committee of privileges and elections: he was clearly no extremist, yet neither did he appear a mere time-server. Hearne wrote that he was 'well known to be a man of singular probity, and of an unblemished character in all respects, and of rare abilities for that place'. But after 'several debates' he was narrowly defeated by his Whig opponent, Hon. Spencer Compton. Perhaps chastened by this experience, or its aftermath, Dolben returned to his Court allegiance in the following February, when he voted for government in the proceedings on the 'place clause' of the regency bill. In the same session he reported from three committees managing conferences with the Lords, and assisted in the management of three private bills. His letters in 1707 show him succeeding in keeping on good terms with such varied characters as the arch-placeman Hon. James Brydges*, from whom he was able to obtain a favour for a friend, and the former Tory lord lieutenant of Ireland, the Duke of Ormond. To Ormond's successor in the viceroyalty, the Earl of Pembroke (Thomas Herbert[†]), Dolben expressed himself in revealing terms in April 1707. Writing from Dublin to give the new lord lieutenant an account of the state of parties in Ireland, in which 'almost every person of condition appears to be engaged', he claimed that because of his 'circumstances' (presumably his judicial station) he was 'not obliged' to join with either faction, Tory or Whig, but was able to converse with both. None the less, whenever a question arose which seemed to imperil the established Church, he appeared in his true partisan colours. The failure of an attempt in the Irish parliament to repeal the Test there sent him joyfully to his desk to transmit the good tidings to Lord Rochester. A similar reaction had been visible in the English Parliament too, during the session of

1706–7. When the bill of union with Scotland was under discussion, Dolben made a powerful plea that the Test Act, 'the strongest fortress of the Church', be 'particularly mentioned' in the bill. It was, he pointed out, designed to counter the threat from Catholics,

> and a rock and happy prevention it proved, for when the Church was attacked by a papist that sat on the throne, his first and great endeavour was to get that Act repealed. All his closetings and solicitations were to this sole purpose – give up the Test Act – well knowing that when once the enemies of the Church should be let into office and power by the repeal of the Test, [they might] rid themselves of the Act of Uniformity or any that should stand in their way. So sensible were the nobility and gentry of England of the nature and support of that Test Act that to their eternal honour they chose to be turned out of their commissions, to be disgraced and persecuted rather than part with it. And shall we now show so little regard to a law that has been the chief preservative of our religion and for the sake of which so many of us have suffered, as not to mention it in a bill that is intended for the preservation and security of our religion?

At the same time, he could not resist a dig at the Dissenters: 'I should have been glad if the papists had been the only enemies of the Church who then struck at the Test Act and that some men of another denomination had not concurred with them in that design.' Indeed, as the speech developed, the Scottish Presbyterians inevitably became his principal target: 'They have been very careful in enumerating such Acts as may any way conduce to the security of their Church establishment.' He concluded with a warning 'that if it be not mentioned 'tis very probable we shall in a little time be told that this law is not included in the general words', so that in consequence the Test would be 'exposed to be repealed at any time when a majority of the Parliament shall become better affected to the Kirk of Scotland than to the Church of England'.[7]

In 1708 Dolben was classed as a Tory in two analyses of the Commons, and his predicament, as a Tory office-holder in an increasingly Whiggish administration, was made even more awkward by the ministerial changes of 1708, culminating in the replacement of Pembroke as Irish lord lieutenant by the Junto Whig Lord Wharton (Hon. Thomas*), a situation which was to tax Dolben's powers of diplomacy. In the first session of the 1708 Parliament Dolben managed through the House a bill relating to the estates of Sir Roger Bradshaigh, 3rd Bt.*, and also reported, on 30 Mar. 1709, a bill to preserve the rights of patrons of advowsons. To begin with, his relations with Wharton were surprisingly civil. On arriving in Dublin in April 1709 the new viceroy had been at pains to conciliate potential opponents, including the chief justice, but as that summer's Irish parliamentary session wore on, animosities came to the surface. Dolben, who at first had been 'not so full of complaints' against Wharton 'as other Tories are', began to be critical of the lord lieutenant in his letters to England, circumspectly at first because of the danger that the mail might be tampered with by the Irish postmaster-general, a violent Whig. Nor does he seem yet to have aired his true feelings in conversation with his Irish friends, continuing to urge moderation on the leading Tories in the Irish house of commons. Finally he was driven to exasperation during a debate in the Irish privy council over a factional dispute in a borough corporation. Able to send a letter to England soon afterwards by a trusted hand, he fulminated that Wharton 'sets no bounds to his vileness. His behaviour at the last council was beyond example.' Wharton in his turn denounced Dolben in public, at least according to Swift's satirical *Character* of the viceroy, for having in this matter 'laid down as law, a thing for which a man ought to have his gown stripped off, and be whipped at the cart's a[rs]e'. The quarrel was made up 'some days after' when Wharton 'sent . . . to assure his lordship [Dolben] he said no such thing'. However, on returning to England during the winter of 1709–10, the Earl sought unsuccessfully to have Dolben removed from office, even though Wharton denied subsequently having entertained any such intention. For the remainder of the viceroyalty he and Dolben maintained mutual civilities underneath which resentment and suspicion were barely concealed, while at Westminster Dolben continued to oppose the Court, voting in early 1710 against the impeachment of Dr Sacheverell.[8]

In the 1710 general election Dolben transferred from Peterborough to the Isle of Wight borough of Yarmouth, where he was returned on the interest of the new Tory governor of the island, John Richmond Webb*, and the lieutenant-governor, Henry Holmes*. Classed as a Tory in the 'Hanover list' of the new Parliament, he assisted in the management of four bills, the most important of which were for the better qualification of j.p.s, and to qualify the Earl of Anglesey (Hon. Arthur Annesley†) and the Earl of Rochester (Laurence Hyde) for Irish offices. Dolben's name appeared on the list of those 'worthy patriots' who in this first session exposed the mismanagements of the previous administration. As an Irish judge he was *ex officio* a member of the 'Irish lobby' in the Commons, and on 19 May 1711 spoke against a Scottish MP's bill to regulate the linen industry in Scotland, which would have expressly prohibited the importation of linen yarn from Ireland. His Tory sympathies were clearly evident in the 1711–12 session during the debates on the report from the commission of accounts on the Duke of Marlborough (John Churchill†). On 24 Jan. 1712 he spoke in favour of the motion of censure against Marlborough, and on 29 Feb. supported Henry Campion's motion that the Duke repay the 2.5 per cent he had retained on the army's pay. During this session Dolben continued to make a significant contribution to the business of the House. On 18 Jan. he reported from the committee charged with drawing up an address of thanks for the Queen's message relating to the peace negotiations. He took the chair of the committee of the whole of 3 Mar. on the bill to give further time for enrolling leases from the crown, a measure he carried to the Lords on the 14th. When, on 12 Apr., the Commons set up a committee of the whole to consider 'the great license taken in publishing false and scandalous libels', moved by annoyance at the publication in a newspaper of the Dutch memorial, Dolben acted as chairman, and on 7 June he presented a bill embodying the committee's recommendations. He chaired another committee of the whole on the bill for regulating trade to the South Seas (1, 27 May), and also helped manage three private bills through the Commons. In the final session of the 1710 Parliament Dolben was appointed to draft, and subsequently presented, bills concerned with the estates of the Earls of Thomond and Ranelagh (Richard Jones*) (16, 18 Apr., 6, 11 May). Of greater note, however, was his support for the bill confirming the French commercial treaty. On 14 May he chaired the committee of the whole on the treaty, and later the same day was named to prepare the bill putting the treaty into effect. During the proceedings he wrote on behalf of the ministry to the Northamptonshire Member, Sir Justinian Isham, 4th Bt., to urge him to come up to town 'on account of the trade [with France], which has many enemies'. However, Dolben was himself absent from the crucial vote on the bill on 18 June. In May a correspondent of Trumbull had reported that Dolben was 'a-soliciting' a place on the English bench, and at the beginning of June the same writer noted that it was now thought unlikely that Dolben's hopes would be satisfied. This observer speculated whether such a disappointment would lead Dolben to abandon the ministry over the French commerce bill, but Dolben's absence had in fact been occasioned by the need to leave London for Ireland.[9]

Dolben continued to represent Yarmouth in the 1713–14 Parliament, when he was classed as a Tory in the Worsley list. In September 1713 his name was mentioned as a possible Speaker of the new Parliament, but nothing appears to have come of such suggestions and soon after the general election was over he had begun canvassing for support in what proved to be a successful bid to be chosen as chairman of the committee of privileges and elections, the honour he had narrowly missed eight years previously. Among other tactics, he used his friend Jonathan Swift to secure the backing of the new Speaker, (Sir) Thomas Hanmer II (2nd Bt.). He subsequently reported to the House on ten election cases and two breaches of privilege, but was otherwise inactive and on 22 May 1714 was granted a month's leave of absence. Hoping for promotion, he had earlier presented Robert Harley, now Lord Treasurer Oxford, with a set of ten volumes of papers concerning the Treaty of Nijmegen, and in due course wrote to the treasurer to ask to be made a baron of the Exchequer in England, remarking,

> I am the more emboldened to make this request by your promise to moderate the resentments of the great man who is at the head of our profession [(Sir) Simon Harcourt I*, the lord chancellor] and whose displeasure I have not been able to remove.

In fact, the office did not become available. Dolben did not sit in Parliament after 1715, but through his customary political skill he retained his Irish judgeship until 1720, when he retired after considerably augmenting his wealth by speculation in South Sea stock. 'Labouring under bodily infirmities' when he drew up his will in March 1722, he died, at Finedon, on 22 Oct. Among the various bequests was the sum of £500 to 'the president and governors of the charity for relief of poor widows and children of clergymen'. His only son took holy orders, but a grandson sat for Northamptonshire and Oxford University 1768–1806.[10]

[1] N. Carlisle, *Privy Chamber*, 205; *CSP Dom.* 1700–2, p. 323. [2] *HMC Downshire*, i. 151, 389; *VCH Northants.* iii. 196; *Northants. Past and Present*, vii. 332–3. [3] Northants. RO, Isham mss IC 4704, Dolben to Sir Justinian Isham, 25 Feb. [1690]; Grey, x. 59, 220, 305; Cobbett, *Parlty. Hist.* v. 646, 686, 764–5; Bodl. Rawl. C.449, 10 Oct. 1691; *Luttrell Diary*, 3, 33, 79, 99, 234, 241, 245, 332, 398, 443; BL, Trumbull Add. mss 101, newsletter 11 Sept. 1691; *HMC Downshire*, i. 388–9; BL, Althorp mss box 7, Nottingham to Ld. Halifax (William Savile*), 25 Apr. 1698. [4] Nottingham Univ. Lib. Mellish mss Me 150–89/4, Henry Saunderson to Edward Mellish, 1 Apr. 1693; L. K. J. Glassey, *Appt. JPs*, 123; Cobbett, v. 1123; J. Oldmixon, *Hist. Eng.* (1735), p. 152; BL, Trumbull Misc. mss 57, Dolben to Trumbull, 19 Feb. 1697[–8], 31 Mar. 1698. [5] Add. 29569, f. 156; Isham mss IC 2191, John to Sir Justinian Isham, 8 July 1701; *CSP Dom.* 1702–3, p. 399; 1703–4, p. 286; F. E. Ball, *Judges in Ireland* (1927), ii. 27; *Northants. Past and Present*, vi. 258. [6] Surr. RO (Guildford), Midleton mss 1248/4, ff. 63–64; *Irish Hist. Stud.* xii. 115. [7] Speck thesis, 45–46, 149; Add. 17677 AAA, f. 510; Folger Shakespeare Lib. Newdigate newsletter 8 Nov. 1705; *Hearne Colls.* i. 69–70; *Bull. IHR*, xxxvii. 24–25, 29–30; Huntington Lib. Stowe mss 57(1), p. 106; Bodl. Eng. lett. e.6, ff. 8–12, 20, 22. [8] Bodl. Eng. lett.

e.6, ff. 25–28, 37, 39; *Swift Works*, iii. 236–7; *HMC Downshire*, i. 878. ⁹*Lockhart Pprs.* i. 536; Trumbull Add. mss 136, Ralph Bridges to Trumbull, 25 Jan. 1711-12, 22 May 1713, [1 June 1713]; NSA, Kreienberg despatch 29 Feb. 1712; Isham mss IC 2791, Dolben to Isham, 2 June 1713; *Parlty. Hist.* i. 64, 76. ¹⁰Trumbull Add. mss 136, Bridges to Trumbull, 4, 11 Sept. 1713; *HMC Portland*, v. 146, 474; *Swift Corresp.* ed. Ball, ii. 65–66, 93; *The Gen.* n.s. iv. 166; PCC 47 Richmond.

P. W./D. W. H.

DOLBEN, John (1662–1710), of Epsom, Surr.

LISKEARD   21 Nov. 1707–29 May 1710

bap. 1 July 1662, 2nd s. of John Dolben, abp. of York 1683–6, and bro. of Gilbert Dolben*. *educ.* Westminster 1676; I. Temple 1677, called 1684; Christ Church, Oxf. 1678; travelled abroad (France) 1682–3. *m.* by Dec. 1683, Elizabeth (*d.* 1736), da. and coh. of Tanfield Mulso of Finedon, Northants. 2s. (*d.v.p.*) 4da.¹

Judge-adv. for E.I. Co. in Bengal by 1692–1694; trustee, poor Palatines 1709; dir. Bank of Eng. 1710.²

Dolben's father, perhaps not surprisingly, had originally wished his younger son to study theology. However, Dolben preferred the law, being admitted to the Inner Temple at the special request of his uncle, Sir William Dolben, at that time recorder of London. He then embarked on a journey to France, his arrival in Paris in June 1682 being reported by Lord Preston (Sir Richard Grahme†), the English envoy to France. Upon his return he contracted a favourable marriage (probably by December 1683, and a daughter was baptized in February 1686), and was called to the bar in 1684. With his father's death in April 1686, Dolben's prospects appeared bright. However, his addiction to gambling (some disconcerting reports of which had reached his father during his stay in Paris) led him to dissipate his fortune. The moiety of the manor of Finedon, acquired by marriage, he sold to his brother, Gilbert, around this time. By December 1691 Dolben's circumstances were so bad that Gilbert wrote to Sir William Trumbull*:

> My brother has by profligate gaming wasted so great a part of his wife's fortune and his own that she and her children are obliged to the charity of friends for subsistence. He hopes to amend his condition by going to the East Indies, the company having promised to place him in an advantageous post. This misfortune sits very heavy upon us, not so much for the loss of the estate as of the scandalous means whereby it is lost, which reflects a reproach even upon my father's memory, the enemies of his order saying that it is the effects of his not having educated my brother to better courses.

Dolben went out to Bengal as judge-advocate for the East India Company and subsequently became friendly with Governor Pitt (Thomas I*). Dolben took advantage of the trading opportunities available to him in order to repair his fortune. These included a voyage to China in 1699 in company with one of Pitt's sons. The death of his uncle Sir William in 1694 again brought home to Dolben the folly of his previous conduct. Sir William's will recorded that he had intended to leave his nephew £5,000, but, being 'very unwilling to have so great a part of that which I have gathered together by industry . . . thrown away at gaming houses . . . I give John Dolben no legacy'. The £5,000 was left in trust for Dolben's children.³

By July 1701 Dolben was back in England and writing to Pitt about the politics of the Old and New East India Companies. He seems to have kept Lord Godolphin (Sidney†) informed about events within the ruling councils of the Old Company, for on 11 Sept. Godolphin reported to Robert Harley* that Dolben had told him 'matters sharpen apace in the committee of the Old Company'. By the 24th Sir Samuel Dashwood* was reporting that Dolben was bound for Fort St. George via China. However, it seems likely that he delayed his departure from England until well into the next year, Dashwood writing to Pitt in August 1702 in terms which suggest Dolben's recent departure. This would seem more likely, since February 1702 witnessed the baptism of one daughter and the marriage of another.⁴

Dolben again left the Indies in 1706, and, once back in England, he became one of those trusted by Pitt to conduct his affairs there. Possibly because of his links with Godolphin he appears to have been able to secure a seat in a by-election for Liskeard, at the behest of Bishop Trelawny of Winchester. On the very day of his election, 21 Nov. 1707, he was in London attending the Lords over the issue of privateers in the West Indies. Once he had taken his seat Dolben proved to be very active in the House. He was named to ten drafting committees, including the naturalization bill of John Aleck, who may have come from the Indies with him and which he managed through all its stages in the House; the bill to secure American trade, on which he registered his only tellership in the session on 14 Feb. 1708; and, most important, the bill to extend the East India Company Act. In this he may have been self-interested as his activities certainly aroused the suspicions of Robert Pitt*, who wrote to his father on 3 Jan. 1708,

> Mr Dolben, by means of Lord Halifax [Charles Montagu*] and the lord treasurer [Godolphin], worked himself into the management of the union between the Old and New Companies in the interest of the latter and to the great dissatisfaction of the former. His main object, I believe, is to supplant you in your post, but

while the Old Company stick so close to you, your position is safe.

You may depend on it that the New Company will do you all the hurt they can, and Mr Dolben, notwithstanding his professed friendship, has left no stone unturned to undermine and remove you.

Thomas Marshall concurred with Robert Pitt, writing to Thomas Pitt on 23 Jan. that Dolben had made an interest to replace Pitt, and (Sir) Stephen Evance* may have been making the same point when he wrote that Dolben 'likes Fort St. George better than England, and don't doubt but the first opportunity that offers he will return again, having made a very great interest with both parties in concerning himself very much in uniting the two companies'. Suspicions were perhaps aroused by Dolben's role in Parliament. In ways and means on 26 Jan. Dolben and William Lowndes suggested an alternative to the East India Company's proposals for an extension of their charter, which added £200,000 to the sum to be loaned to the government. On 1 Mar. 1708 Dolben wrote to Thomas Pitt of this bargain: there would not 'be a perfect union [of the Old and New Companies] unless the Parliament force them to it, [although] there will be a fair opportunity this session'. Dolben revealed that his proposal for £1,200,000 'does not yet go down glib with the Company, but if the Parliament seem willing they dare not refuse for fear of a worse bargain'. However, the bill passed into law, perhaps a testament to Dolben's political acumen. In another example of Dolben's perceived influence in legislative matters, Francis Atterbury approached Bishop Trelawny to canvass Dolben, when rallying opposition to the cathedrals bill, as Dolben had 'declared himself to be in suspense because he doth not know your Lordship's opinion'.[5]

Any designs Dolben had on Thomas Pitt's position in India were soon dashed, as he explained to Pitt in a letter of 20 Oct. 1708. After reporting the unification of the two companies following the previous session's Act, he reported that the Company were 'enraged' at the £1,200,000 they had given in the Act,

being almost undone by it, and lay the blame wholly on me, since I moved that sum, which they say was £200,000 more than the House expected or would have taken, and which, they will have it, I prevailed with [Sir Gilbert] Heathcote* and others to consent to as an agent of Lord Treasurer's, many other provocations of the like nature they urge against me in the carrying on of the union.

In these circumstances Dolben denied any design on Pitt's job, affecting to be 'so well settled to my content that no temptation shall ever prevail with me to give up my ease'. In the first session of the 1708 Parliament he continued to be very active. He was named to nine drafting committees, the first being the bill to prevent wagers relating to the public (27 Nov. 1708). Ironically, this was a pastime which still seemed to engage Dolben's attention, according to a correspondent of Trumbull, who only a month previously had reported Dolben a loser by the capture of Lille and that in a separate wager he had contracted to pay a guinea a day while Prince Eugene lived: if so, 'the East India fortune will soon be spent, and we expect to hear of his taking another voyage ere it be long'. Dolben was involved in the management of the bill to establish a regulated company trading to Africa, which he presented on 21 Mar. 1709 and he managed the Earl of Clanricarde's estate bill through all its stages in the Commons. He was a teller on ten occasions in this session, three concerning elections, including the notorious Abingdon case, which saw the defeat of (Sir) Simon Harcourt I. Other partisan tellerships included one on a motion preparatory to the expulsion of Anthony Hammond on 7 Dec. 1708, and another on 9 Apr. 1709 against the passage of the bill improving the Union. Another indication of partisan conduct occurred on 22 Jan. 1709 when 'some words of heat' passed between Dolben and (Sir) Jacob Banks, forcing the House to intervene to compose the quarrel. As might have been expected, he voted in favour of naturalizing the Palatines. When rumours abounded of Thomas Pitt's removal, Dolben again denied making interest to succeed him: 'I have raised such a storm against me about the £1,200,000 given last year by the Company, that their severest resentments are showed on all occasions when my name is but mentioned.' Indeed, Dolben may have been looking to preferment from another quarter, for the death of Lord Herbert (Henry Herbert*) had left a vacancy at the Board of Trade. According to one observer, Dolben, 'a great stickle[r] for [the] lord treasurer in the House of Commons, has the fairest prospect of it', but no appointment was made. Nevertheless, his usefulness to Godolphin and the Whigs was made plain by Lord Johnston's (James*) report that Dolben 'next to [Lord] Coningsby [Thomas*] speaks most' in the Commons.[6]

In the second session Dolben's main preoccupation was with the impeachment of Dr Sacheverell. Dolben was the first to raise the matter of the doctor's printed sermons on 13 Dec. 1709, when he moved, first, that the House should take the matter into consideration, and second, that the sermons should be voted 'malicious, scandalous and seditious libels'. He spoke in the debate the following day and moved that Sacheverell should be impeached. At the end of the debate he was ordered to go to the bar of the Lords and formally impeach Sacheverell, which he could not do till the next day (15 Dec.), since the Lords had adjourned. In the meantime he was appointed to the committee drawing up the articles of impeachment, of which he acted as chairman, making his first report on 22 Dec. on the precedents for allowing bail to those committed for high crimes and misdemeanours. His electoral patron, Bishop Trelawny, was not altogether pleased with Dolben's role in the affair. A correspondent wrote to Robert Harley* on 21 Dec. 1709: 'the Bishop of Winton [Trelawny] storms at Jack Dolben. He sent for him and desired him not to engage in this affair. Dolben excused himself upon a promise he made to great men, I suppose [Lords] Somers [Sir John*] and H[alifax].' Dolben reported the articles of impeachment on 9 Jan. 1710 and carried them up to the Lords on the 12th. Sacheverell's answer was referred to the articles committee, from which Dolben reported the Commons' 'replication' on 2 Feb. At the trial itself he acted as one of the managers, speaking to the third article on 1 Mar. 1710, when he argued that Sacheverell's claim that the Church was in danger could easily be the result of 'malice and envy at its prosperity', at a time when it was so well protected by both Queen and Parliament. He then launched an attack on Sacheverell himself, describing him as

> a trumpeter itinerant of sedition and rebellion . . . an agent detached from that dark cabal whose emissaries appear in all shapes, and almost in all places; an asserter of such pestilential and unparalleled doctrines, as at once overthrow the whole constitution, both of Church and state.

Half-way through his speech, according to one Tory commentator, he 'quitted the article, and ran upon the doctrines of obedience and non-resistance, venting notions that came near, if not up to high treason'. He claimed that the Commons had brought the case 'to obtain an occasion in the most public and authentic manner to avow the principles, and justify the means, upon which the present government and the Protestant succession are founded and established'. He concluded by saying that it would be hard indeed, after 20 years of war against 'tyranny and oppression', to be 'betrayed at home to a perpetual condition of bondage by such false brethren as are at your Lordships' bar'. The use of the plural occasioned Harcourt, one of the defending counsel, to make 'a very low bow, which very much diverted the House'. Immediately, Lord Haversham (Sir John Thompson, 1st Bt.*) moved to adjourn. When the Lords had returned to their own House Haversham explained that, as Dolben's remark reflected on the counsel appointed by the Lords, he thought Dolben should be called on to explain himself. After a two-hour debate the Lords returned to the court and the lord chancellor called on Dolben for an explanation. Dolben arose and after a considerable pause and 'in a great deal of confusion' replied that his words 'had relation only to the prisoner at the bar', which explanation, though according to one commentator 'flat nonsense and a lie, was admitted'. It was subsequently noted in the Commons on 21 Mar. that Dolben had given away 'the right of the Commons by explaining himself . . . without leave of the House'. Nor was this the only moment of discomfort experienced by Dolben during the trial, for the mob threatened to burn down his house and 'were going to hang him upon a tree, till he swore he was not Dolben, nor a Parliament-man'. Further indignity was heaped upon him in Liskeard where the clock he had presented to the town was pulled down by the mob there.[7]

Dolben remained active in other matters apart from the Sacheverell affair. He was named to more drafting committees dealing with a range of private, local or trading legislation, and subsequently played a managerial role in three of these bills and two others. He also acted twice as a teller on disputed election cases. He clashed with Harley on 25 Jan. 1710, during the debate on the place bill, when, commenting on Harley's support for the bill, he told the 'fable of the king of the beasts that had lost his tail, and therefore used all his rhetoric to persuade all the beasts to cut off theirs, but could prevail with none but a few monkeys and jackanapes'. At the end of the session he seems to have retired from the directorship of the Bank of England and taken refuge at his house at Epsom. It was there that he died of a fever on 29 May 1710, 'to the great joy and exultation of Dr Sacheverell's friends'. As one contemporary noted, Dolben 'was worse treated by his physicians a great deal than by the mob, for they mistook his distemper and after three days illness sent him . . . out of the world'. Others attributed a degree of psychological torment to his demise 'as 'tis said for some time discovered a great uneasiness and disquiet in his mind blaming the latter part of his life'.[8]

[1] *DNB*; Bridges, *Northants*. ii. 261; *Le Neve's Knights* (Harl. Soc. viii), 314–15; *HMC Downshire*, i. 22; Add. 28875, ff. 192, 220, 222; *HMC 7th Rep*. 265, 267, 271, 287. [2] *Diary of Sir William Hedges* (Hakluyt Soc. ser. 1, lxxv), 259; C. N. Dalton, *Life of Thomas Pitt*, 142; *Post Boy*, 30 June, 2 July 1709; *N. and Q.* clxxix. 61. [3] *Life and Adventures of John Dolben* (1710), 5–8; *Cal. I.T. Recs*. iii. 111; *VCH Northants*. iii. 198; *Diary of Sir William Hedges* (Hakluyt Soc. ser. 1, lxxviii), 49; *HMC Downshire*, i. 388–9. [4] C110/28, Dolben to Thomas Pitt, 19 July 1701; *HMC Portland*, iv. 22; Add. 22851, ff.

10–11, 52; IGI, London. ⁵*Addison Letters*, 463; C. R. Wilson, *Early Annals in Bengal*, i. 374; *HMC Fortescue*, i. 21, 31, 33–34, 38, 40, 47; *HMC Lords*, n.s. vii. 227; *Vernon–Shrewsbury Letters*, iii. 325; C110/28, Marshall to Pitt, 23 Jan. 1707–8, Evance to same, 31 Jan. 1707[–8], Dolben to same, 1 Mar. 1707–8; *Atterbury Corresp*. iii. 286–7. ⁶C110/28, Dolben to Pitt, 20 Oct. 1708, 18 Jan. 1708–9; *HMC Downshire*, i. 862; *Wentworth Pprs*. 73; BL, Trumbull Misc. mss 53, Johnstone to Trumbull, 4 [Feb. 1709]. ⁷*HMC Portland*, iv. 531–2; *HMC Egmont*, ii. 244; Cobbett, *Parlty. Hist*. vi. 806, 828; *Impartial View*, 185; *Tryal of Dr Henry Sacheverell* (1710), 86–87; G. Holmes, *Trial of Sacheverell*, 89, 91, 94–95, 99, 109–10, 146–9; *State Trials*, xv. 168–9; Calamy, *Life*, ii. 228; *Life and Adventures*, 15. ⁸*Wentworth Pprs*. 106; *Poems on Affairs of State* ed. Ellis, vii. 448; Huntington Lib. Stowe mss 57(4), p. 19; Add. 70421, newsletter 30 May 1710.

P. W./S. N. H.

DONE, Thomas (c.1651–1703), of Park Street, Westminster.

NEWTOWN I.o.W.   1685–1687, 1689–1698

b. c.1651, 7th s. of Sir Ralph Done of Duddon, Cheshire, being 3rd by his 2nd w. Elizabeth, da. of Sir John Savage of Clifton, Cheshire. *educ.* L. Inn 1672; G. Inn 1672, called 1677. *m.* lic. 2 July 1678, aged 27, Jane, da. of Sir Thomas Griffith, merchant, of Bishopsgate, London, 1s. 3da.¹

Auditor of imprests 1677–*d.*; dep. searcher of customs, London 1677–?*d*; commr. inquiry into abuses in the Mint 1678.²

A Court Tory in the Convention, Done was returned again for Newtown in 1690, whereupon he was classed by Lord Carmarthen (Sir Thomas Osborne†) as a Tory and Court supporter. In the first session he was a teller on four occasions: on 8 Apr. 1690, in favour of retaining the word 'reverse' in the motion for a bill to reverse the quo warranto judgment against the city of London; on 14 Apr., in favour of adjourning the House during the hearing of the Plympton election case; on 24 Apr., for the question that the words 'in the lieutenancy of the City of London' should stand in the motion to give thanks to the King 'for the great care he has expressed of the Church of England, in the late alteration of the lieutenancy of the City of London'; and on 10 May, in favour of engrossing the bill for vesting forfeited estates in their Majesties. In December 1690 Done was listed as a probable supporter by Lord Carmarthen in the event of an attack upon him in the Commons. He told on 28 Nov. in favour of Sir Carbery Pryse, 4th Bt.*, in the Cardiganshire election. The following April he was classed by Robert Harley* as a Country supporter. In the next session he spoke on 3 Dec. 1691 during the debate on public accounts, when he claimed that William Harbord*, former paymaster-general, had only accounted for £4–5,000 of the £180,000 granted to him for buying provisions for the army. In a second speech, made on 29 Dec. 1691, he opposed a petition alleging that the Speaker (Sir John Trevor) and Sir George Hutchins*, when commissioners of the great seal, had discouraged a Middlesex j.p. from punishing those who sold produce on Sundays. On 23 Apr. 1694 he was a teller against a clause in the bill for licensing hackney and stage coaches to allow coaches to ply on Sundays. He was named on all the usual lists of placemen in this Parliament, except those by Grascome. Done had an enemy in the Whig chancellor of the Exchequer, Charles Montagu*, who wrote to the Earl of Portland in the summer of 1695: 'I have made a discovery how to humble Auditor Done as much as if he were turned out of place.' The King intended to reduce the fees charged by the auditors and therefore the profits of the post, possibly in reaction to what Montagu claimed was £131,785 unaccounted for by Done.³

By the 1695 Parliament Done had moved into opposition. He was listed as a probable opponent of the Court in the divisions of 31 Jan. 1696 on the proposed council of trade, and voted against fixing the price of guineas at 22*s*. in March, and although his failure to sign the Association caused some surprise, he appears to have been suspected of Jacobite sympathies at this time. Doubtless this was a factor in the King's decision in May 1696 to carry out the previous year's plan to reduce as much as possible 'the profits and exercise' of Done's office. He voted against the attainder of Sir John Fenwick† on 25 Nov. 1696. He did not stand for re-election in 1698, and afterwards was classed in a comparative analysis of the old and new House of Commons as a Country supporter. The appearance of his name on a list of placemen in the same year was without significance, since his patent as auditor of imprests was for life. In 1702 he unsuccessfully tried to surrender the office. Lord Treasurer Godolphin (Sidney†) wrote to Harley on 24 Dec.:

> It's above a month since Auditor Done gave in a petition at the Treasury to resign his place to Mr Drake. I then discouraged the expectation very much, but did not name your brother neither then nor never, but to the Queen and yourself. If I had given the least countenance to the request I am apt to believe they were ready to have made oath there was no money in the case, but I was unwilling to ask that question for fear of bringing the difficulty stronger upon me. By this and by other things I agree it looks as if he were not like to hold out long.

He was still auditor at the time of his death in January 1703.⁴

[1] Ormerod, *Cheshire*, ii. 249; *London Mar. Lic.* ed. Foster, 411; PCC 5 Degg. [2] *Cal. Treas. Bks.* v. 627, 641, 986. [3] *Luttrell Diary*, 59, 94; Nottingham Univ. Lib. Portland (Bentinck) mss PwA 936, Montagu to Portland, 11/21 June 1695. [4] Surr. RO (Kingston), Somers mss 361/14/J14, 'things to be done at council', n.d.; Portland (Bentinck) mss PwA 936, information of Peter Cooke, 12 June 1696; *Cal. Treas. Bks.* xi. 9; *HMC Portland*, iv. 54; PCC 5 Degg.

P. W.

DORE, Thomas (c.1658–1705), of Lymington, Hants.

LYMINGTON   1690–Oct. 1705

b. c.1658, s. of Philip Dore of Lymington. *educ.* Trinity, Oxf. matric. 15 July 1673, aged 15; M. Temple 1676. *m.* by 1681, Elianor, da. and coh. of John Button† of Buckland, Lymington, 1s. 1da. 2 other. ch. *d.v.p.*[1]

Freeman, Lymington 1681, mayor 1683–5; freeman, Winchester by 1705.[2]

Capt. of ft. Duke of Bolton's 2nd regt. 1691–4; capt. and lt.-col. 28 Ft. 1694–8, 34 Ft. 1702–5, 1 Ft. Gds. 1705–*d*.[3]

Dore's family had resided in Lymington since the early 17th century. His father had been mayor in 1652 and 1653 and an assessment commissioner for the county in 1657. Dore himself became prominent in the borough, doubtless helped by his marriage, which made him the brother-in-law of John* and Paul Burrard I*, who together had a strong electoral interest at Lymington. In 1683 he and other members of his family were suspected of complicity in the Rye House Plot, at which time he was described as a 'great' Whig, and one of the small group which dominated elections in the borough. He was mayor at this time, as he was in 1685 during the Monmouth rebellion, when it was reported that he 'and several other rebels to the number of fourscore horse and foot are hovering about New Forest . . . and have committed several robberies in those parts'. The Sussex militia was ordered to march into Hampshire to suppress the rebels, and soon most of them were willing to accept the government's proffered pardon. Dore, however, was excepted. He may have fled abroad or remained in hiding in England. If arrested, he does not seem to have been brought to trial, and a year later, in August 1686, his pardon was procured by the 2nd Earl of Sunderland.[4]

Dore actively supported the Prince of Orange in 1688, according to his own later petition, in which he stated that

> being early acquainted with his present Majesty's great and happy design of rescuing these kingdoms and by an express from Holland having received many of his Majesty's declarations, [he] did carefully disperse the same and afterwards waited on his Majesty in the west, with several men and horses equipped at his own charge.

After the Revolution he received the patronage of the 1st Duke of Bolton (Charles Powlett†), probably obtained through the Burrards, who after 1690 shared their electoral interest at Lymington with the Powletts. In March 1689 Bolton secured Dore's appointment as woodward of the New Forest, of which the Duke himself was warden, but the claims of a previous holder prevented the patent going through, despite assertions that

> Mr Dore hath always showed a steady and constant zeal for the Protestant religion and the laws and liberty of the kingdom and hath exposed himself to great hazards and undergone many real sufferings for the same whereby his estate hath been greatly impaired; that he hath withstood many frequent solicitations (though backed with the offers of great regards and preferment) which have been made him to consent to the taking off the Penal Laws and Test and to engage his interest to be chosen as Member of Parliament to that end.

He was compensated for this disappointment by the grant of a captaincy in one of the Duke's regiments of foot. He unsuccessfully contested Christchurch in 1690 as Bolton's candidate but was returned at Lymington, with his brother-in-law, John Burrard, after a contest. He was classed as a Whig in Lord Carmarthen's (Sir Thomas Osborne†) list of the new Parliament, and as a Court supporter by Robert Harley* in April 1691. Dore was given a fortnight's leave of absence on 17 Dec. 1691 to attend his regiment, and a week's leave on 4 Dec. 1693. He was named on several lists of placemen in this Parliament, and was listed as a friend by Henry Guy* in anticipation of the attack on Guy for corruption during the 1694–5 session. Re-elected for Lymington in 1695, Dore was forecast as likely to support the Court on 31 Jan. 1696 over the proposed council of trade, signed the Association early and voted with the Court in March for fixing the price of guineas at 22*s*. On 25 Nov. 1696 he voted for the attainder of Sir John Fenwick†. Dore was given leave from the House for two weeks on 17 May 1698. Named as a placeman in a list of July 1698 and in an analysis of the new Parliament of September 1698, his regiment was in fact disbanded that year and he spent the next four years on half-pay. He voted against the disbanding bill on 18 Jan. 1699, was again listed as a placeman in an analysis of the House of early 1700, and was classed as a Whig by Robert Harley after the general election of December 1701. Shortly before the King's death he was appointed lieutenant-colonel in a newly formed regiment of foot.[5]

After the accession of Anne, Dore remained loyal to the Whigs, voting on 13 Feb. 1703 for agreeing with the Lords' amendments to the bill on the abjuration oath. He was forecast as an opponent of the Tack and voted against it or was absent on 28 Nov. 1704. Although expected to take over his regiment on the death of the colonel in 1705, he was not appointed, being given a troop in the Guards instead. He was listed as a placeman in 1705, and as a 'Churchman' in an analysis of the new Parliament. Although he was listed as voting for the Court candidate for Speaker on 25 Oct. 1705 and as supporting the Court on the 'place clause' of the regency bill on 18 Feb. 1706, these were only statements of his general sympathies, since he was reported as dangerously ill on 22 Sept. 1705 and had died by 16 Oct.[6]

[1] Berry, *Hants Gen.* 35; S. Burrard, *Annals of Walhampton*, 20–21. [2] E. King, *Old Times Revisited*, Lymington, 184, 191; Hants RO, Winchester bor. recs. ordnance bk. 7, f. 214. [3] *CSP Dom.* 1690–1, p. 507; 1694–5, p. 30. [4] King, 183, 188, 189; *CSP Dom.* July–Sept. 1683, pp. 378, 385–6, 391–2; 1685, pp. 211, 213, 230; 1686–7, pp. 227, 250; SP 31/2/20, 44/164/212. [5] *Cal. Treas. Pprs.* 1557–1696, pp. 58, 64, 143–4; *CSP Dom.* 1689–90, p. 32; T1/4/146, 67, f. 265; T1/11/8, ff. 28, 30, 33; *Cal. Treas. Bks.* xiii. 275; xvii. 1124. [6] Luttrell, *Brief Relation*, v. 514, 534, 594, 602.

P. W.

DORMER, Fleetwood (1657–1723), of Lincoln's Inn and Chipping Wycombe.

CHIPPING WYCOMBE   28 Mar. 1696–1698
                              1701 (Feb.)–1710
MALMESBURY   30 Nov. 1719–1722

bap. 14 Apr. 1657, 3rd s. of John Dormer† of Lee Grange, Quainton, Bucks. by Katherine, da. of Thomas Woodward of Ripple, Worcs.; bro. of Robert Dormer*. *educ.* Trinity, Oxf. 1674; L. Inn 1676, called 1683, bencher 1707, treasurer 1710. *unm.*[1]

Freeman, Chipping Wycombe 1695; recorder 1695–1718.[2]

Commr. of prizes May 1706–7; master in Chancery 1710–21.[3]

A lawyer, like his brother, though less well known, Dormer was appointed recorder of Wycombe in August 1695 and quickly cultivated an interest in the borough, regularly inviting members of the common council to dinner, at Christmas and Easter. Indeed, in 1706 it was noted that 'the chief inhabitant of the town is their recorder and burgess, Fleetwood Dormer', and it is known that he was an active j.p. between 1693 and 1711. His earliest political activity seems to have been in support of the Whig interest at Aylesbury in 1691 and his chance of a seat in Parliament came at the Wycombe by-election of March 1696, presumably with the backing of Hon. Thomas Wharton*. His first act in the Commons was to add his name to the Association before it was presented to the King on 4 Apr. Unlike his brother he was not an active Member, being granted leave of absence on 2 Mar. 1697 for a fortnight and again on 11 Mar. 1698, presumably to go on the spring circuit.[4]

Dormer was defeated at Wycombe in 1698, despite Wharton's efforts, being listed in September as a member of the Court party 'left out' of the new Parliament. He represented Wycombe in the next four Parliaments, but references to 'Mr Dormer' in the Journals have been taken to refer to his elder brother, Robert. Dormer was classed as a Whig by Robert Harley* in December 1701, and voted on 13 Feb. 1703 for agreeing with the Lords' amendments to the bill for enlarging the time for taking the oath of abjuration. He was forecast as likely to oppose the Tack and indeed did not vote for it on 28 Nov. 1704. An analysis of 1705 classed Dormer as a 'Churchman', but in the new Parliament he voted for Smith as Speaker on 25 Oct. 1705 and voted again with the Court on 18 Feb. 1706 over the 'place clause' of the regency bill. Having been rewarded with a commissionership of prizes in May 1706 he was forced to resign this place in November 1707 in order to remain in the House under the Regency Act. Two lists from 1708 classed Dormer as a Whig. In the following Parliament he voted in 1709 for the naturalization of the Palatines and in 1710 for the impeachment of Dr Sacheverell.[5]

Dormer stood for Wycombe in 1710, but withdrew before the poll. At the end of the year he was appointed a master in Chancery, and did not attempt to regain his seat in 1713. In October 1714 he suffered a serious accident on his way from Wycombe to London, being thrown from his horse and breaking a leg. He resigned his recordership of Wycombe in March 1718 and his mastership three years later. He was buried at Quainton on 21 Oct. 1723.[6]

[1] IGI, Bucks.; Lipscomb, *Bucks.* i. 415. [2] *Ledger Bk. of Chipping Wycombe* ed. Newall, 42. [3] Info. from Sir John Sainty. [4] *Ledger Bk. of Chipping Wycombe*, 42; *CSP Dom.* July–Dec. 1695, p. 67; L. J. Ashford, *Hist. High Wycombe*, 168; *Bucks. Dissent and Parish Life 1668–1712* ed. Broad (Bucks. Rec. Soc. xxviii), 255; *Bucks. Sess. Recs.* i. 509; ii. 454; iii. 306; BL, Verney mss mic. 636/45, John Verney* (Ld. Fermanagh) to Sir Ralph Verney, 1st Bt.†, 14 Apr. 1691. [5] *Vernon–Shrewsbury Letters*, ii. 142; *Cal. Treas. Bks.* xx. 647; xxi. 50; Luttrell, *Brief Relation*, vi. 235. [6] *Verney Letters 18th Cent.* i. 302; Verney mss mic. 636/55, Fermanagh to Ralph Verney†, 1, 7 Nov. 1714.

E. C./S. N. H.

DORMER, Robert (1650–1726), of Lee Grange, Bucks. and Lincoln's Inn Fields.

AYLESBURY   22 Feb. 1699–1700
BUCKINGHAMSHIRE   1701 (Dec.)–1702

NORTHALLERTON 23 Nov. 1702–1705
BUCKINGHAMSHIRE 1705–11 Feb. 1706

bap. 30 May 1650, 2nd s. of John Dormer†; bro. of Fleetwood Dormer*. educ. Christ Church, Oxf. 1667; L. Inn 1669, called 1675, bencher 1696, treasurer 1702. m. bef. 1692, Mary, da. of Sir Richard Blake of London, 2s. d.v.p. 5da. (1 d.v.p.). suc. uncle Sir Fleetwood Dormer at Arle Court 1696; nephew Sir William Dormer, 2nd Bt., at Lee Grange and Purston, Northants. Mar. 1726.¹

Attorney-gen. to Bp. Crewe of Durham 1676–?93; chancellor dioc. of Durham 1693–1719; serjeant-at-law 1706; j.c.p. 1706–d.²

Freeman, Chipping Wycombe 1704.³

Dormer's father was a barrister and local landowner. As a second son Dormer was also put to the law, being appointed attorney-general to Bishop Crewe of Durham. Fortune was on his side, too, for in 1675 his elder brother, Sir John Dormer, 1st Bt., died at Leghorn, leaving an infant son, William, aged six, to inherit the family estate at Lee Grange. This child was subsequently declared a lunatic and Dormer, as his uncle and heir, successfully petitioned the crown in 1693 for a grant of the estate to save it from destruction. Meanwhile Dormer's legal career had flourished: in 1680 he was junior counsel in the trial of Sir Thomas Gascoigne for treason and later that year of a Mr Cellier for libel. Nor did he restrict his practice to the law courts, being counsel before the Lords in 1690 for the bill against the export of bullion and appearing as counsel for parties interested in legislation and in legal disputes which came before Parliament. He was appointed chancellor of the diocese of Durham in November 1693. Dormer was at this point a Tory, apparently sending to Aylesbury to make interest for James Herbert I* in 1691 while his brother, Fleetwood, backed the Whig candidate.⁴

Dormer's legal acumen propelled him into local politics as both parties in the disputed election at Buckingham in 1695 sought to retain him as counsel. In February 1698 he acted as counsel for the bill of pains and penalties against Charles Duncombe*. At the general election of 1698 he stood at Aylesbury in the Tory interest, but was defeated. However, he was returned at the by-election in February 1699, after the Commons had declared void the election of (Sir) Thomas Lee (2nd Bt.). In that election he had the support of (Sir) John Verney* (later Lord Fermanagh); however, Dormer was soon to forfeit Verney's affection when he switched sides in the political battle, becoming a client of Lord Wharton (Hon. Thomas*).⁵

The presence in the Commons at various times of his younger brother, Fleetwood, makes it difficult to attribute the activities of 'Mr Dormer'. However, given that important activity only occurs when Robert is in the House, most committee appointments have been attributed to him. He was accorded leave of absence on 6 Mar. 1699 upon extraordinary occasions, but was back in the Commons by 18 Apr. when he was named to a conference committee. Two days later he oversaw the ballot for commissioners of Irish forfeited estates. On the 22nd he reported Cyriac Westlyd's estate bill. In the following 1699–1700 session he was nominated to a drafting committee for a bill to prevent gambling and duelling. His one recorded contribution to debate suggests that he was already turning away from the Tories, for on 6 Dec. 1699 in committee on the grant to Captain Kidd, he spoke 'very strongly for the legality of the grant and answered all objections against it', particularly the view that a felon's goods could not be granted before conviction. An analysis of the House into 'interests' between January and May 1700 marked Dormer's name with a query, as if to underline that his political views were in transition.⁶

By the end of 1700 Dormer was firmly in the Whig camp, Lord Cheyne (Hon. William*) averring that it was the result of 'a friendship contracted in the last sessions, contrary to what brought him thither [to Westminster]'. Verney was appalled that his help at Aylesbury in 1698–9 was now being reciprocated by a challenge for the county, an honour Verney also coveted. However, Verney was not surprised by Dormer's actions, thinking it

> not unlikely for he is of a soaring temper, tho' he hath the management of a good estate in Buckinghamshire by his nephew Sir William's lunacy, yet I think he is no freeholder in this county, this he told me himself, but he hath thought of buying Dorton House [residence of Robert Dormer d.1694] and 200 or 300 acres that might be sold with it.

What irked Verney was Dormer's supposed stance as an independent when Verney was sure that it was merely a tactic to take votes from the Tories to ensure Hon. Goodwin Wharton's* victory. In the event Dormer was unsuccessful, although the 'variance' between Dormer and his brother, Fleetwood, was reportedly healed during the campaign, and he was successful at the November election for both Buckinghamshire and Northallerton, choosing to sit for the former.⁷

Dormer's return was listed as a 'gain' by Lord Spencer (Charles*) and Robert Harley* classed him as a Whig in December 1701. He was also very active in the new Parliament, with much use being made of his legislative abilities. He was named on the 6th to draft the bills establishing a commission of accounts, to regulate the King's bench and Fleet prisons (which he presented on 3 Feb.) and to employ the poor. On the 17th he was appointed to the drafting committee on the bill to prevent bribery and corruption at elections. On the 29th he ensured that the Earl of Peterborough was able to defend his conduct at the Malmesbury election when the House considered the matter. On 7 Feb. he spoke during the proceedings on the Maidstone election, against moves to brand the Kentish petitioner Thomas Colepeper, 'one of the instruments in promoting the scandalous, insolent and seditious petition'. On the 24th he attended the report of the Coventry election to protest that 'he had attended the committee and that he hoped he should never have lived so long as to see such injustice at the committee confirmed at the House', that is the election of the Tory candidate against Henry Neale*, an acquaintance of Wharton. On 12 Mar. he seconded Lord Hartington's motion that the statute of mortmain should be repealed so as to allow people to endow poor vicarages. On the 14th he was named to draft Edgeworth's relief bill relating to Irish forfeited estates (Edgeworth's wife being the heir of Sir Edward Tyrell, 1st Bt.) and on the 21st presented the Earl of Exeter's (John Cecil†) estate bill to the Commons, reporting it on 20 Apr. At the time of his death Dormer was a lessee of the Cecils' property in the Strand. On 16 Mar. he attempted to persuade Sir Richard Cocks, 2nd Bt.*, that it was unwise to promote a debate inquiring into the yield of the duties comprising the civil list. On the 20th he reported from the committee examining the petition on Holder's escape from the Fleet, being ordered on the 28th to draft a bill summoning Holder to justice, which he presented on 8 Apr.[8]

Dormer was defeated for Buckinghamshire at the 1702 election. Lady Gardiner thought 'Mr Dormer can bear an affront as ill as any man by he being accounted a high man, but his generous humours have made him many friends, but being of the party as is going down at present has been a great means of losing it'. Also rumours that he would have been made lord keeper if the King had lived were not considered helpful to his campaign. Almost immediately the search began for another seat. Initially, Aylesbury was considered but in the end he came in at a by-election for Northallerton.[9]

In the 1703–4 session Dormer was the sole Member ordered on 10 Jan. 1704 to prepare a bill to sell the Buckinghamshire estates of Sir Peter Tyrell, 1st Bt.†, subsequently managing it through all its stages in the House. Other legislative activity involved appointment to drafting committees on the bills to extend the time for the import of thrown silk from Italy (13 Jan.) and on the same day a bill for the relief of Captain James Roche over Irish forfeited estates, which he presented on the 24th. On 25 Jan. 1704 Dormer spoke in favour of Ashby in the Aylesbury case, arguing that the question at issue was 'whether a freeholder or freeman, who hath a right to give his vote for his representatives in Parliament, may arbitrarily and maliciously be deprived of that privilege without any redress in any court whatsoever'. Moreover, 'if the Lords have not a right to determine in this matter, which by writ of error is regularly brought before them, we shall be turned into a state of villeinage, and the people will be deprived of choosing their own representatives without relief'.[10]

In November 1704, having been listed as a probable opponent, he was one of the principal speakers against the Tack. He was also at pains to defend his brother-in-law, John Parkhurst*: when MPs inquired as to why Parkhurst had not been prosecuted according to a Commons address, Dormer 'took that occasion to say there had been several commissioners of prizes, who were well enough known, and he saw no reason why two of them only should be obliged to make up their accounts'. By January 1705 it was clear that Dormer would make another attempt to sit for Buckinghamshire, in partnership with Sir Richard Temple, 4th Bt.* He was returned, although he took the precaution of securing a retreat at Northallerton as well. As chancellor of Durham, Dormer generally visited that city 'twice a year, attended with a great number of horse', and in August 1705 he attended the thanksgiving there for the Duke of Marlborough's (John Churchill†) victory.[11]

Dormer was classed as a 'Churchman' on one list of the 1705 Parliament, but the Earl of Sunderland (Lord Spencer) classed his return as a 'gain'. He duly voted on 25 Oct. for the Court candidate as Speaker. Next month, Lord Treasurer Godolphin (Sidney†) praised his services 'in putting an end to a contest about the chair of supply, which would perhaps have been very inconvenient', adding 'that the Queen would not be ungrateful'. On 11 Dec. he reported and carried to the Lords a naturalization bill. On 7 Jan. 1706 Dormer was on the deputation to present the congratulations of the House to Marlborough on the battle of Ramillies. Also during January Dormer was active in the debates over the regency bill. On the 10th he appeared to favour amending the treason laws to include writing; on the 12th and 21st he spoke against the 'place clause' of the regency bill; on the 15th he joined in discussions on convening Parliament on the Queen's demise; and on the 19th he spoke on the composition of the regency.[12]

This proved to be the end of Dormer's services in the Commons because in February 1706 he was made a judge, at a salary of £1,000 p.a., which he celebrated by holding a dinner on the 11th. On the bench Dormer retained his Whiggish reputation, as befitted a member of the Kit-Cat Club, and one bound to attract adverse comment from Tories after the ejection of the Whigs from office in 1710. Thus, on circuit in July he attempted to dispel rumours that Parliament would be dissolved and was criticized for extending his protection to a young kinsman who had killed a gentleman of fortune in a duel. In 1713 he gave a Whiggish charge to the Northamptonshire grand jury in which he contended 'that which was in dispute now was whether papist or Protestant'. Not surprisingly, he was reappointed in 1714 and continued until his death, despite rumours of his retirement from the bench with a pension in December 1725. He died 'at his house in Lincoln's Inn Fields' on 18 Sept. 1726, his only surviving son, Fleetwood, having predeceased him earlier in the year.[13]

[1] Lipscomb, *Bucks.* i. 415; [2] Hutchinson, *Dur.* i. 565; Sainty, *Judges of Eng.* 80. [3] *Ledger Bk. of Chipping Wycombe* ed. Newall, 63. [4] *Cal. Treas. Bks.* x. 93; Foss, *Judges*, viii. 30; *HMC Lords*, iii. 109, 180, 227, 452; BL, Verney mss mic. 636/45, John Verney (Ld. Fermanagh) to Sir Ralph Verney, 1st Bt.†, 14 Apr. 1691. [5] Verney mss mic. 636/48, John to Sir Ralph Verney, 9 Nov. 1695; 636/51, same to Ld. Cheyne, 19 Dec. 1700; Bodl. Carte 103, f. 256; *CSP Dom.* 1698, p. 92. [6] *Vernon–Shrewsbury Letters*, ii. 380. [7] *Verney Letters 18th Cent.* i. 159, 162. [8] *Cocks Diary*, 194, 205, 223, 246, 258–9; Lambeth Palace Lib. ms 2564, p. 407. [9] *Verney Letters 18th Cent.* 167; Verney mss mic. 636/51, Lady Gardiner to (Sir) John Verney, 31 Mar., 30 July 1702. [10] Cobbett, *Parlty. Hist.* vi. 267–8. [11] *Bull IHR*, xli. 179; *Vernon–Shrewsbury Letters*, iii. 274; Verney mss mic. 636/52, Dormer to Ld. Fermanagh, 20 Jan. 1704-5; C. E. Whiting, *Nathaniel, Ld. Crewe*, 239. [12] *Huntington Lib. Q.* xxx. 250; *Cam. Misc.* xxiii. 57, 66, 71, 75, 80. [13] *Cal. Treas. Bks.* xxx. 578; *HMC Portland*, vii. 6, 406; *Nicolson Diaries* ed. Jones and Holmes, 375; *Hearne Colls.* iii. 25–26; G. Holmes, *Pol. in Age of Anne*, 186; Verney mss mic. 636/55, Lady to Ld. Fermanagh, 11 May 1713; *The Gen.* n.s. vii. 46.

E. C./S. N. H.

DOUGLAS, Sir Alexander (d.1718), of Egilsay, Orkney.

SCOTLAND	1707–1708
ORKNEY AND SHETLAND	1708–1713

1st s. of William Douglas, MP [S], of Spynie, by Marjorie, da. and h. of Patrick Mentieth of Egilsay. *m.* 12 Apr. 1688, Janet Scot (d. aft. 1718), wid. of Alexander Cruickshanks of Waristoun, 2s. 3da. *suc.* fa. aft. 1685; kntd. c.1707.[1]

MP [S] Orkney and Shetland 1702–7.
Chamberlain of the bishopric of Orkney 1710.
Jt. lt. Orkney 1715.[2]

An impecunious Orkney laird, Douglas was a thoroughgoing courtier in both the Scottish and British Parliaments. Returned for his native county in 1702, he supported the Duke of Queensberry while in office, but tactfully absented himself from the vote on the Duke of Hamilton's motion in 1704 for deferring a decision on the succession. Aware of Queensberry's hostility to the 'New Party' experiment, Douglas was nevertheless unwilling to join the Duke's hard-line supporters in cynical opposition to the Court. With the fall of the 'New Party' ministry and the return to power of Queensberry, Douglas' difficulties were resolved. His attitude during this period was similar to that of his political patron, the 11th Earl of Morton (James Douglas). The connexion between Morton and Douglas, who were not near relations, may be traced to the Earl's attempts to regain his family's grant of crown lands in Orkney and Shetland, which had been revoked by Charles II. The attainment of this objective in 1707 may be attributed to Morton's support for the Union, activities which had included persuading Douglas, who had registered a hostile vote on the first article of the treaty, to follow the Court line thereafter without demur. Douglas himself was rewarded with a knighthood and a seat in the nominated first Parliament of Great Britain.[3]

An inactive Member, who is not known to have spoken in debate, Douglas found the cost of attendance at Westminster prohibitive. It is uncertain if he made any appearance during his first Parliament. He was elected unanimously for Orkney and Shetland in 1708, but his only known vote was in favour of the impeachment of Dr Sacheverell in 1710 (though his inclusion on this list was queried by George Lockhart*). In the same year he was appointed to a collectorship of the bishopric rents in Orkney, presumably via Morton's influence. It was later asserted by a hostile commentator that this office brought 'a salary or pension of the crown of a thousand pound Scots or thereby'. Prior to the 1710 election, moreover, Douglas was promised £200 from the government to cover the cost of attendance at Westminster. He was duly re-elected, despite local resentment against the Morton interest. Douglas was described as an episcopal Tory in the electoral analysis of Richard Dongworth, chaplain to the Duchess of Buccleuch. A supporter of the new ministry, Douglas was listed as a 'worthy patriot' who helped to detect the mismanagements of the previous administration, and Lockhart later recalled that he had adhered 'constantly in all votes to the Tories'. Douglas was nevertheless dissatisfied at the failure of Lord Treasurer Oxford (Robert Harley*) to provide the promised living expenses. Morton explained to the Earl of Mar that Douglas had been persuaded to 'set up to be a Parliament man contrary to his intentions, he being a gentleman of a very low estate'. His case was taken up in September 1711 by John Pringle*, who forwarded to Oxford the original letter from Morton's agent which had promised the money in Queensberry's name. Pringle added by way of recommendation that Douglas had 'ever since the Queen's accession to the throne served his country in such measures as seemed most agreeable to her Majesty, and is desirous to continue to give further proof of this loyalty and affection to the crown'. No satisfaction was evidently forthcoming. Douglas was listed as absent in Scotland for the vote on 7 Feb. 1712 on the Scottish toleration bill, and likewise for the votes on 4 and 18 June 1713 over the French commerce bill.[4]

Douglas did not stand in 1713, when his own disinclination chimed with Morton's desire that his brother, Hon. George Douglas*, should have a refuge from electoral difficulties elsewhere. He acted, however, in the capacity of *praeses* of the electoral court, using his influence to ensure the election of Morton's nominee. During these proceedings his own right to vote was queried by James Moodie[†], who belatedly drew attention to the fact that the Egilsay estate was of maternal descent. Moodie claimed that this rendered Douglas' entitlement open to question because 'it is in law presumed there is an heir male till the contrary is be proven by a service'. He also attempted to confuse the issue by referring to the inheritances of Douglas' aunts as 'heirs portioners' to the estate. This absurd objection was swiftly dismissed, Douglas having plainly stated that his mother was

> served heir and retoured to Patrick Monteith my grandfather who stood publicly infeft in the lands of Egilsay and others holden feu under the crown which rights were produced in the parliament of Scotland in anno 1703 and my right to vote in the election was determined in the parliament.

Douglas died in January 1718, and Egilsay descended via his eldest son, William, to his granddaughter, Janet, in 1729.[5]

[1] Orkney Archs. Morton mss D38/2505/17, electoral ct. mins. 23 Oct. 1713; *Hist. Scot. Parl.* 194; B. H. Hossack, *Kirkwall in the Orkneys*, 244; *Scot. Rec. Soc.* xxvii. 194; Orkney Archs. unpub. genealogy by R. W. St. Clair. [2] *Hist. Scot Parl.* 194; J. B. Craven, *Hist. Church in Orkney*, 44. [3] Hossack, 244; *Hist. Scot. Parl.* 194; info. from Dr P. W. J. Riley on members of Scot. Parl.; P. W. J. Riley, *Union*, 109, 332; J. N. Ross, *Orkney and the Earls of Morton*, 14. [4] *Edinburgh Courant*, 28–30 June 1708; *SHR*, lx. 65; *Lockhart Mems.* ed. Szechi, 287; *Lockhart Letters* ed. Szechi, 45, 50; Orkney Archs. Morton mss D38/2505/17, electoral ct. mins. 23 Oct. 1713; SRO, Morton mss GD150/3464/10–11, John Ewing to Morton, 21 Sept., 21 Nov. 1710; *HMC Portland*, v. 53; Add. 70292, John Ewing to Douglas, 28 Sept. 1710, Pringle to [Oxford], 21 July 1711; *Parlty. Hist.* i. 69. [5] Orkney Archs. Morton mss D38/2505/17, electoral ct. mins. 23 Oct. 1713; *Hist. Scot. Parl.* 194; unpub. genealogy by St. Clair; *Services of Heirs*, i. 1730–9, p. 10.

D.W.

DOUGLAS, Archibald (c.1667–1741), of Cavers, Roxburgh.

SCOTLAND   1707–1708
DUMFRIES BURGHS   1727–1734

b. c.1667, 2nd s. of Sir William Douglas of Cavers (*d.* 1676) by Catherine, da. of William Rigg of Aithernie, Fife. *m.* Anna, da. of Francis Scott of Gorrenberry, Roxburgh, 4s. *suc.* bro. Sir William Douglas, MP [S], 1698.[1]

Hereditary sheriff, Roxburghshire 1698–*d.*; commr. union with England 1702; exchequer [S] 1703; Equivalent [S] 1707–9; PC [S] 1703–8; receiver-gen. [S] 1704–18; postmaster-gen. [S] 1725–*d.*[2]

MP [S] Roxburghshire 1700–7.

Douglas of Cavers came from an ancient Roxburghshire family with a strong Covenanting tradition. His father had been deprived of the hereditary sheriffdom on account of his opposition to the court, and his mother, the reputed 'good Lady Cavers', was imprisoned in Stirling Castle in November 1682. She was only released permanently in December 1684, when, upon being given the choice of conforming or leaving the country, she took up residence in England. The family's status naturally revived with the Revolution, whereupon the heritable jurisdiction of Roxburghshire was restored, Douglas succeeding his elder brother to the sheriffdom and the estate of Cavers in 1698. In his electoral capacity, he consistently opposed the Roxburghe interest both in the Scottish and British Parliaments. Repeated successes prompted his son William[†] to remark with pardonable exaggeration in 1712 that 'you have it in your hands to make the Member for the county'. Prior to the Union Douglas had been able to return himself as one of Roxburghshire's four representatives to the Scottish parliament. He supported the Court interest of Queensberry, it being asserted by some that he was 'entirely managed' by the Duke, whereas others stressed his indispensability to the Court. He was rewarded in 1703 with appointment to the privy council, supplemented the following year by the lucrative office of receiver general. His predilection in favour of union with England was borne of deep conviction that a strong bulwark was necessary to ensure the Protestant succession. Having served on the abortive commission of 1702, he voted consistently in support of the Union in 1706-7. Acknowledgment of his contribution was made via appointment to the Equivalent commission and selection as a representative to the first Parliament of Great Britain.[3]

At Westminster Douglas was a loyal adherent of the ministry, but little record survives of his parliamentary activities. Grey Neville*, however, later alluded to his propensity for long speeches, so he may not have been a parliamentary mute. Douglas did not stand in 1708 and was dropped from the Equivalent commission the following year. He continued to be active in local politics and successively ensured the defeat of Roxburghe's candidates. Douglas did not exercise a tight rein over his own nominees, but was understandably wary of any conduct which might have repercussions for his own status as an office-holder. His son expressed some alarm in February 1712 that the political 'stiffness and obstinacy' of Sir Gilbert Eliott, 3rd Bt.*, 'in not coming over to the measures of the Court' might 'be of prejudice as to your place'. Douglas retained his office, despite occasional rumours of dismissal, up to and beyond the Hanoverian succession, also taking a lead in the suppression of the Jacobite rebellion of 1715.[4]

Disaster struck three years later at the hands of the Duke of Roxburghe and the Squadrone, when Douglas was removed as receiver-general. Douglas denied that he had given any cause for his dismissal, and this assertion was entirely justified, for his arrears were never exceptional. The nearest he came to parliamentary censure was on 16 Apr. 1713, when the report from the public accounts commission had criticized Lord Godolphin's (Sidney†) system for maintaining invalids in Scotland by depositing nearly £10,000 with Douglas, since 'no interest has been received for it and they are subsisted out of the capital stock, which will in a short time reduce it to nothing'. The accusation was that the receiver-general pocketed the interest, rather than investing the money and using the interest to fund the pensions. he was not a selfless servant of the public, but an astute manipulator of the perquisites of his office, profiting from the large balances which he held. Moreover, he benefited from the revenue reforms of 1709, by which court salaries in Scotland were also channelled through him. He received no immediate compensation for dismissal, but was awarded a pension of £400 p.a. in 1721, obtained the office of postmaster-general in Scotland in 1725 and returned to the Commons in 1727. Douglas retired at the end of this Parliament and died on 3 July 1741, the estate of Cavers passing to each of his four sons in succession.[5]

[1] G. Tancred, *Annals of a Border Club*, 119; *Hist. Scot. Parl.* 190-1. [2] *HMC 7th Rep.* 732; *APS*, xi. app. 145. [3] *HMC 7th Rep.* 727, 732; *Reg. PC Scotland*, 1678-80, p. 377; *Hist. Scot. Parl.* 190-1; Tancred, 119; NLS, Douglas of Cavers mss, Acc. 7570, 'Cavers Barony and Family', pp. 197-213; Acc. 6991, William Douglas to fa., 14 Feb. 1711/12; info. from Dr P. W. J. Riley on members of Scot. parl.; *Crossrigg Diary*, 122, 154; *APS*, x. 247; *Orig. Pprs.* ed. Macpherson, ii. 10; P. W. J. Riley, *Union*, 331. [4] SRO, Ogilvy of Inverquharity mss GD205/36/6, Neville to William Bennet*, 11 July 1708; Douglas mss, Acc. 6991, William Douglas to fa. 14 Feb. 1711/12; Glasgow mss at Kelburn Castle, 3/C11/31, William Boyle to Ld. Glasgow, 30 Aug. 1715; Boyer, *Pol. State*, viii. 124-5; P. Rae, *Hist. Late Rebellion* (1718), 232, 273. [5] Douglas mss, Acc. 7488/1, memorial of Douglas [n.d.]; *HMC 7th Rep.* 732; Cobbett, *Parlty. Hist.* vi. 1190; P. W. J. Riley, *Eng. Ministers and Scotland*, 85, 267; SRO, Montrose mss GD220/5/205/4, Robert Pringle to Montrose, 7 July [1709]; *CJ*, xvi. 636; *Services of Heirs* (ser. 1), i. 1740-9, p. 10; ii. 1770-9, p. 11; 1780-9, p. 13.

D. W.

DOUGLAS, Hon. George (1662-1738).

LINLITHGOW BURGHS	1708-1713
ORKNEY AND SHETLAND	1713-1715
LINLITHGOW BURGHS	1715-1722
ORKNEY AND SHETLAND	1722-22 Jan. 1730

b. 1662, 4th s. of James Douglas, 10th Earl of Morton [S], by Anne, da. of Sir James Hay, 1st Bt., of Smithfield, Peebles; bro. of Hon. Robert Douglas*. m. (1) a da. of Alexander Muirhead of Linhouse, Edinburgh, 1s. *d.v.p.* (2) bef. 1702, Frances, da. of William Adderley of Halstow, Kent, 3s. (1 *d.v.p.*). suc. bro. as 13th Earl of Morton [S] 22 Jan. 1730.[1]

Lt. Ft. Gds. [S] 1685, capt.-lt. 1688; capt. Col. Richard Cunningham's Drag. (7th Hussars) 1692; brevet lt.-col. 1703; maj. 1707; brevet col. 1709; ret. 1709; ld. lt. Orkney and Shetland 1725-*d.*; v.-adm. Scotland 1733-*d*.

Burgess, Edinburgh, Lanark, Linlithgow, Selkirk 1708.[2]

Rep. peer [S] 1730-4.

Douglas entered the army shortly after escaping prosecution for murder in 1685. The dispute which led to the killing originated in the theft of a dog that was later found in the possession of the laird of Chatto. While Chatto accepted Douglas' claim to ownership, this was disputed by one of the laird's footmen, who had the temerity to confront him in public. Dismissing the servant as a mere 'rascal', Douglas was shocked to find the insult returned in kind, 'which being such an indignity and affront to a gentleman' he 'did step back and make to his sword, but the footman before he got it drawn did hit him twice with a cudgel'. Douglas was thus able to claim self-defence. 'Still retiring and with his sword warding the blows' was how Douglas described his own reaction, whereas that of the footman was characterized as 'so earnest and furious that he run himself upon the point of the petitioner's sword and so was killed'. This barely credible account was sufficient to exculpate the son of a peer, though his departure for military service was perhaps an additional insurance against any reprisal. Rewarded for his role in quelling the anti-Union disturbances at Glasgow in 1706 (see CAMPBELL, Hon. James), Douglas otherwise proved a competent but undistinguished soldier. He was passed over for promotion, despite having for 'many years undergone the whole care and charge of managing' his regiment. When the colonelcy was purchased by Hon. William Kerr* in 1709, Douglas retired, merely receiving a non-regimental commission and a pension of 10s. a day. He encountered difficulties in extracting payment: not until 1717 was a retrospective grant made in his favour with effect from December 1710.[3]

Douglas had entered Parliament in 1708 as a supporter of the Duke of Queensberry's Court party. His brothers, the 11th Earl of Morton and Hon. Robert Douglas, were longstanding members of this connexion. Douglas, who had complained of the passivity of the Scottish Court party prior to the general election, secured a seat on his own initiative at Linlithgow Burghs. An inactive Member, Douglas' only known vote in this Parliament was for the impeachment of Dr Sacheverell.[4]

Re-elected for Linlithgow Burghs in 1710, Douglas was described by Richard Dongworth, chaplain to the Duchess of Buccleuch, as a Court Tory. In common with his patron Queensberry, he supported the new ministry. As before, he made little impression in Parliament, apart from being mentioned in the report of the commissioners of accounts on 21 Dec. 1711 in connexion with the allegedly corrupt handling of forage contracts by Robert Walpole II*. Douglas, who had been favoured by Walpole in 1709–10, gave no evidence to the commission and was not subjected to any direct censure. His partner John Montgomerie I* did admit that the contracts had been obtained only after the payment of sweeteners. Douglas spoke in Walpole's defence on 17 Jan. 1712, but his intervention was insufficient to prevent expulsion. The death of Queensberry in July 1711 had left Douglas without an obvious patron among the Scottish magnates. He gravitated towards the Earl of Mar, but later became dissatisfied with what he perceived as his neglect, in particular over a civil case in the court of session. Douglas came gradually into the orbit of the Duke of Argyll and his brother Lord Ilay. He was listed as absent though in town for the vote on 7 Feb. 1712 upon the Scottish toleration bill, though it remains unclear whether this was indicative of scruples or mere indifference. In a letter to Lord Oxford (Robert Harley*), written from Scotland in August, Douglas described himself as a government supporter; but like other Scots, he came to resent the ministry's conduct during the malt tax crisis of 1713. Disillusioned at English unwillingness either to defer the imposition or reduce the burden of this tax, Douglas was active in the ensuing campaign for a dissolution of the Union. He advocated an immediate secession from Parliament and an electoral boycott. This suggestion was rejected at a combined meeting of Scottish parliamentary representatives on 26 May 1713. His aggressive stance, in common with that of Hon. Charles Rosse*, may reflect the influence of Argyll, but no conclusive evidence can be adduced to support this hypothesis. Douglas attended the Lords on 1 June for the debate on Lord Findlater's motion for leave to introduce a bill for dissolving the Union. He thought that Findlater 'made a handsome discourse' and that Mar 'spoke well'. His highest praise was reserved for Argyll, however, who 'spoke like an angel'. Douglas remained disenchanted with the ministry even after the return to the fold of Mar and other Scottish Court supporters in the aftermath of Lord Oxford's narrow victory on this question. Unwilling to oppose the ministry outright, Douglas nevertheless absented himself from the votes on 4 and 18 June over the French commerce bill. He returned to Scotland shortly afterwards, all thoughts of boycott now abandoned, in order to prepare for the coming election. His activities included advising Morton to support Robert Munro* in the election for Tain Burghs, and forwarding the Earl's proxy to Mar for the Scottish peerage election. Morton thus supported the entire Court list, from which Ilay had been excluded because he and Argyll had fallen out with the ministry. Douglas neither endorsed nor condemned Ilay's abortive attempt to obtain Squadrone votes in the peerage election; but, for his own reasons, Douglas came to an electoral pact with Sir James Carmichael, 4th Bt.*, who enjoyed Squadrone support in Linlithgowshire.[5]

Douglas' re-election for Linlithgow Burghs appeared doubtful because of the determination of the 4th Duchess of Hamilton to secure the return of her own nominee. Douglas contented himself, therefore, with a spoiling operation against the Duchess, contriving to support Carmichael in return for a promise of Lanark's vote at the next election. With the family interest in Orkney and Shetland at his disposal, he was able to obtain an alternative seat. He did not attend the election in person, but the contest was managed effectively by his brother, Robert. In return for his speech in 1712, Douglas was promised Walpole's support over the subsequent election case. Although a petition was entered against Douglas, it was never reported.[6]

Little is known of Douglas' conduct in the 1713 Parliament, but Lord Polwarth's description of him as a Jacobite in his analysis of the Scottish returns should not be taken literally. One modern historian has nevertheless compounded the error by stating that Douglas was involved in Jacobite plotting, but the letter cited in support of this assertion was written from France by a Jacobite namesake at a time when Douglas himself was in Scotland. His only known vote, on 12 May 1714, was against the Whig amendment to the schism bill which sought to extend its provisions to Catholics. Douglas was nevertheless listed as a Whig in one comparative analysis of the 1713 and 1715 Parliaments. The Worsley list also classified him as a Whig, but, if an annotation next to the name of James Moodie† (who had never previously sat) was actually intended to apply to Douglas, he should be regarded as a Whig who had sometimes voted with the Tories.[7]

By virtue of the pact made at the previous election, Douglas was returned for Linlithgow Burghs in 1715. He supported the Argathelian interest under George I, and succeeded as 13th Earl of Morton in January 1730, being also elected a representative peer at a by-election later that year caused by the death of Findlater. Douglas was a government supporter in the Upper House, but was not re-elected in 1734. He died on 4 Jan. 1738.[8]

[1] *Scots Peerage* ed. Paul, vi. 380–1. [2] SRO, Morton mss GD150/2627, burgess tickets. [3] *Reg. PC Scotland*, 1685–6, p. 82; *HMC Portland*, x. 449–50; Morton mss GD150/3462/2, Queensberry to Douglas, 1 May 1711; *CJ*, xvii. 116; *Cal. Treas. Bks.* xxxi. 111–12. [4] Morton mss GD150/3461/2, Douglas to Morton, 29 Jan. 1708; *Edinburgh Courant*, 26–28 May 1708; J. W. Buchan, *Hist. Peebles.* ii. 74; iii. 113–17; SRO, Peebles burgh recs. B58/13/3. council mins. 14 Apr. 1708. [5] *SHR*, lx. 65; Norf. RO, Rolfe mss, Walpole to Edmund Rolfe, 18 Jan. 1711–12; Add. 70292, Douglas to Oxford, 17 Aug. 1712; Morton mss GD150/3461/9, Douglas to Morton, 23 June, 16 Oct. 1713; GD150/3458/13, same to same, 25 Mar. 1714; Aberdeen Univ. Lib. Duff House (Montcoffer) mss, 3175/2380, 'Resolution of the Commons to Call a Meeting of the Lords', [23] May 1713; *Lockhart Letters* ed. Szechi, 76–77; *Parlty. Hist.* i. 69. [6] Morton mss GD150/3461/12–13, Douglas to Morton, 27 Aug., 23 Sept. 1713; GD150/3458/12, Morton to Douglas, 31 Oct. 1713; GD150/3464/26, Ewing to Morton, 24 Mar. 1714. [7] D. Szechi, *Jacobitism and Tory Pol.* 18, 201; Add. 70031, C[ount] Douglas to Mar, 30 Sept. 1713. [8] Morton mss GD150/3462/3, Argyll to Douglas, 29 Oct. 1719; W. Robertson, *Peerage of Scotland*, 125–8; *Scots Peerage*, 380–1.

D. W.

DOUGLAS, Oley (1684–1719), of Gray's Inn, London.

MORPETH 1713–1715

bap. 21 Mar. 1684, 5th but 1st surv. s. of John Douglas (*d.* 1727) of Westgate, Newcastle-upon-Tyne, and East Matfen and Halton, Northumb. by Alice, da. of Michael Hutchinson of Leeds, Yorks. *educ.* G. Inn 1703, called 1710. *m.* settlement 24 Jan. 1718 (with £7,600), Mary, da. of Richard Harris, merchant, of London, 1da.[1]

Freeman, Newcastle 1709.[2]

The early life of Douglas' father is obscure. Said to be of Scottish origin, by the 1670s he was closely linked to Newcastle's company of hostmen, a body intimately connected to the region's coal industry. When he was admitted in 1675 to the freedom of Newcastle he was described as a hostman, and four years later was appointed clerk of the company. This appointment may indicate that John Douglas provided some kind of legal services in Newcastle, and in 1682 he was chosen to act for the city's Merchant Adventurers in a dispute concerning the rights of Newcastle's drapers. The following year he was admitted to Barnard's Inn. The 1680s were also notable for Douglas senior's extensive land purchases in Northumberland. Starting with the purchase of Clarewood in 1686 and Halton Shields and Great Whittington the following year, Douglas' father made at least six other large purchases in the next 20 years, at a total cost of over £10,000, and his continuing involvement in the county's coal trade was demonstrated by his ownership of a coal pit at Kenton. John Douglas' rising social and economic status received corporate recognition in September 1699 when he was appointed Newcastle's town clerk, a post he held until 1709 when he resigned in favour of a younger son. Clinching testimony of the family's new importance was seen in 1700 when Douglas' daughter married Hon. Sir Andrew Hume*, a younger son of the 1st Earl of Marchmont.[3]

Like his father and younger brother, Oley Douglas trained for the law, entering Gray's Inn on the same date as his father in 1703 and remaining resident there until his marriage. Elected on the corporation interest for Morpeth in 1713, against the Whig candidate of the borough's dominant patron Lord Carlisle (Charles Howard*), Douglas was classed as a Whig in the Worsley list. An inactive Member, his only significant act in the Parliament saw him confirm his partisan allegiance when he voted, on 18 Mar. 1714, against the expulsion of Richard Steele. His notes of debates upon disputed elections, the expulsion of Steele and the 'succession in danger' debate, reveal nothing of Douglas' own activities but are distinctively Whig in bias.[4]

Defeated at Morpeth in 1715 the following year Douglas stood at the Northumberland by-election against a Whig candidate sponsored by Lord Carlisle, but despite a vigorous campaign he was defeated by 23 votes. Douglas' father claimed that these electoral reverses placed a considerable burden upon the family's finances, writing to Douglas in September 1717 that election expenses of 'above' £3,000 had contributed significantly to family debts of over £7,000. He informed Douglas that 'in case your elections had not been, my debts would have been easy and paid without much trouble', and these financial difficulties led to negotiations for Douglas' marriage to the daughter of the wealthy African trader Richard Harris, who may have been the Richard Harris elected to the capital's common council on the Whig interest in 1716. Negotiations for the marriage were convoluted. Harris was suspicious that Douglas' father had over-valued his lands, and his discovery that part of the indebtedness of the Douglases' Northumberland estate had been concealed during the early stages of negotiations did little to allay such concerns. Douglas' father was also wary of Harris' demands in relation to the marriage settlement. He wrote to Douglas that settling estates upon the marriage of a son had 'proved fatal' for many men, and stated that though 'I will be kind to my children' he was not prepared to 'strip myself for their sakes nor rely or depend on their favours'. Prepared to settle the manor of Halton on Douglas, which he claimed was worth £1,200 p.a., he was determined to retain East Matfen in order to provide for his younger children. The delays occasioned by negotiations for the settlement caused Douglas some concern, as he wrote to his father that 'my fate depends so much on your favourable answer next Monday that I am on the rack till it comes, strange extremes of happiness and misery possess me till you crown it with success'. Articles of agreement, stipulating that a portion of £7,000 would be paid in return for settling Halton upon Douglas, were drawn up on 15 Nov. 1717, but it appears that in the eventual settlement Douglas' father agreed to Harris' demand also to settle East Matfen on Douglas in return for increasing the portion to £7,600. The wedding followed early in 1718, but by winter the following year Douglas had fallen ill and he died on 9 Nov. 1719 with his will, drawn up three days previously, devising his estates to his only daughter. In the early 1720s his widow and father-in-law began a Chancery suit alleging that Douglas had been forced by his father to enter into a number of bonds with the express intention of providing for his younger siblings, amounting to a premeditated undermining of Douglas' marriage settlement. The lands inherited by Douglas' daughter descended, upon her marriage in 1751 to Sir Edward Blackett, 4th Bt.†, to the Newby branch of the Blackett family.[5]

[1] *New Hist. Northumb.* x. 406; Borthwick Inst. York, Prob. reg. lix, f. 434. [2] *Reg. of Freemen* (Newcastle Rec. Soc. iii), 193. [3] *Reg. of Freemen*, 91; *Newcastle Hostmen's Co.* (Surtees Soc. cv), 139; *Newcastle Merchant Adventurers* (Surtees Soc. xciii), 228; *New Hist. Northumb.* iv. 228–9; vi. 135; viii. 411–12; x. 349, 404–5; J. Hodgson, *Hist. Northumb.* pt. ii(1), pp. 81–82; *Clavering Corresp.* (Surtees Soc. clxxviii), 33; *CSP Dom.* 1699–1700, pp. 261, 264; J. Brand, *Hist. and Antiq. of Newcastle*, ii. 215. [4] Douglas diary (Hist. of Parl. trans.), passim. [5] E. Hughes, *N. Country Life*, i. 263–4; Northumb. RO, Blackett (Matfen) mss ZBL 197, John to Oley Douglas, 20 Sept., 1 Oct. 1717, Oley to John Douglas, 2 Nov., 26 Sept., 22 Oct., 12 Nov. 1717, J[oshua] to Oley Douglas, [1717], articles for mar. settlement, 15 Nov. 1717; ZBL 261/9, copy of Oley Douglas' will, 6 Nov. 1719; ZBL 56, brief, 1721; *Jnl. Commrs. Trade and Plantations* 1708–15, pp. 219, 289, 346–8; *London Politics 1713–17* (London Rec. Soc. xvii), 28, 30, 32, 38, 39, 43, 44, 51; *New Hist. Northumb.* x. 406.

E. C./R. D. H.

DOUGLAS, Hon. Robert (*d.* 1730).

TAIN BURGHS 5 May 1709–1710

3rd s. of James Douglas, 10th Earl of Morton [S]; bro. of Hon. George Douglas*. *unm. suc.* bro. as 12th Earl of Morton [S] 7 Dec. 1715.

Steward and justiciar of Orkney and Shetland 1696, 1702.[1]

MP [S] Kirkwall 1702–7.

Douglas owed his seat in the Scottish parliament to the influence of his elder brother, the 11th Earl of Morton, who was a supporter of the Duke of Queensberry's Court party. The Morton interest at Kirkwall originated in a grant of lands in Orkney and Shetland from Charles I as a reward for the extensive financial assistance given to the royalist cause by William, Earl of Morton (*d.* 1648). Although the crown had resumed control in 1669, the harsh manner in which this had been done gave grounds for hope of full redress after the Revolution. The appointment of Douglas as steward and justiciar of Orkney and Shetland in 1696 was a step towards this end. Morton reported in 1701 that William III had recognized the family's 'pretensions to Orkney and Shetland' and that the King was resolved to grant 'an easy tack of these rents'. At the 1702 election to the Scottish parliament, Douglas made use of his influence as a tacksman of crown rents both to aid his own election for Kirkwall and to frustrate the Country opposition in Orkney and Shetland. He proved a loyal Queensberryite in the Scottish parliament, even voting against the Court (when Queensberry was out of office) on the Duke of Hamilton's motion in 1704 for deferring a decision on the succession. Morton himself abstained, however, which may indicate trimming by the family until the Court's intentions became clearer. The fall of the 'New Party' ministry and the return of Queensberry removed any uncertainty. Douglas voted the Court line over the Union, without absence or abstention. Shortly afterwards, the grant of Orkney and Shetland was renewed to Morton.[2]

Douglas was apparently unwilling to accept nomination to the first Parliament of Great Britain, and did not stand in 1708. The following year he was returned at a by-election for Tain Burghs at the instance of Queensberry, who promised 'assistance in what can be for your interest'. He made no mark during his brief tenure. His only known vote was in favour of the impeachment of Dr Sacheverell. Douglas declined to stand in 1710, despite Morton's wishes to the contrary; but he was active in Orkney elections on behalf of Sir Alexander Douglas in 1710 and his younger brother, George, in 1713. He remained on the periphery of national politics even after succeeding to the earldom in 1715. His conduct in Scottish peerage elections nevertheless indicates that, like his younger brother, he became an Argathelian. He died on 22 Jan. 1730.[3]

[1] *Scots Peerage* ed. Paul, vi. 380; *Hist. Scot. Parl.* 202. [2] *Hist. Scot. Parl.* 202; F. J. Shaw, *Northern and Western Isles*, 22; Annandale mss at Raehills, bdle. 827, Morton to Annandale, 17 July 1701; Atholl mss at Blair Atholl, box 45 bdle. II/ no.169, Hamilton to [Earl of Tullibardine], 20 Apr. 1702; info. from Dr P. W. J. Riley on members of Scot. parl.; Boyer, *Anne Annals*, iii. app. 42; P. W. J. Riley, *Union*, 331. [3] SRO, Morton mss GD150/3459/12, Queensberry to [Douglas], 12 Apr. 1709; GD150/3464/10, John Ewing to Morton, 21 Sept. 1710; W. Robertson, *Peerage of Scotland*, 82, 101–2; *Scots Peerage*, 380.

D. W.

DOWDESWELL, Charles (c.1688–1714), of Forthampton, Glos.

TEWKESBURY 1713–c.June 1714

b. c.1688, 1st s. of Charles Dowdeswell of Forthampton by Anne, da. of Timothy Coles of Hatfield, Herefs. *educ.* Balliol, Oxf. matric. 12 Mar. 1706, aged 17. *m.* 29 May 1707, Anne, da. of Robert Tracy, j.c.p., of Coscombe, Glos. by Anne, sis. of Richard Dowdeswell*, 1da. *suc.* fa. 1706.[1]

Dowdeswell's father was the second son of Richard Dowdeswell† of Pull Court (*d.* 1673), who purchased an estate at Forthampton (two and a half miles from Tewkesbury) from the Earl of Essex in 1671, and bought the manorial estate in 1677. A settlement of 1678 noted that he owned 584 acres in Forthampton and nearby Swinley. Relations between the two branches of the family do not seem to have been good at this time, as a dispute over the rectory of Bushley in 1677 had to be settled in favour of the senior line by Chief Justice Scroggs. Any parliamentary ambitions which his father may have had were blocked by Richard Dowdeswell's interest at Tewkesbury, but Charles snr. was of sufficient status to be appointed a deputy-lieutenant in Gloucestershire by 1694. The two branches were presumably reconciled by 1707 when Dowdeswell married the daughter of Justice Tracy, whose uncle was his own cousin, Richard Dowdeswell.[2]

Unlike the senior branch of the family, Charles Dowdeswell was a Tory. Returned with his second cousin William* at the 1713 election, he was described as a Tory on the Worsley list. He made his will on 30 May 1714 and was reported dead on 2 June by Edward Popham*, who had accepted an invitation from 'the gentlemen that were his [Dowdeswell's] friends' to oppose Anthony Lechmere* in the ensuing by-election. Dowdeswell's will made provision for the possibility of an as yet unborn child, providing a portion of £10,000 for his only daughter Anne, and leaving his estates to his brother Richard in case a male heir was not produced. His widow married Thomas Wylde* in 1720. Richard Dowdeswell required a private Act in 1733 to fulfil the terms of his brother's will.[3]

[1] *Vis. Eng. and Wales Notes* ed. Crisp, vii. 66; J. Bennett, *Tewkesbury*, 441; W. R. Williams, *Glos. MPs*, 246; IGI, London. [2] Bennett, 441; *VCH Glos.* viii. 201; *CSP Dom.* 1694–5, p. 235. [3] PCC 173 Aston; Add. 70251, Popham to Ld. Oxford (Robert Harley*), 2 June 1714; Williams, 246.

P. W./S. N. H.

DOWDESWELL, Richard (c.1653–1711), of Pull Court, Bushley, Worcs.

TEWKESBURY 1685–1687, 1689–1710

b. c.1653, 1st s. of William Dowdeswell of Pull Court by Judith, da. of Elkin Wymondsold of Putney, Surr. *educ.* Christ Church, Oxf. matric. 27 July 1669, aged 16. *m.* 1 Jan. 1677, Elizabeth, da. of Sir Francis Winnington*, and sis. of Edward* and Salwey Winnington*, 5s. (3 *d.v.p.*) 3da. *suc.* fa. 1683.[1]

Freeman, Preston 1682, Tewkesbury by 1698; sheriff, Worcs. Nov. 1688–Mar. 1689.[2]

Dowdeswell was the grandson of Richard Dowdeswell, Member for Tewkesbury 1660–73. The family's interest in the borough was based upon the ownership of local property, Pull Court, lying in the next parish. After sitting in the 1685 Parliament, Dowdeswell was suggested as a possible Whig 'collaborator' to be added to the commission of the peace in 1688 and was selected as sheriff of the county in November 1688. He was returned to the Convention of 1689 and again in 1690. There can be little doubt of his adherence to the Williamite regime, as he was active in the lieutenancy, especially in seizing horses from the disaffected, and was even prepared to act as a surety for Worcestershire's receiver of the poll tax. He was also active in the Gloucestershire bench. At the outset of the 1690 Parliament he was classed as a Whig by the Marquess of Carmarthen (Sir Thomas Osborne†). In April 1691 Robert Harley* tentatively assessed him as a Country supporter. In the following session, on 31 Oct. 1691, he was appointed to prepare the bill to secure the rights of borough corporations, an indication perhaps of contemporary problems in Tewkesbury. Indeed, by May 1693 Dowdeswell, together with his fellow Member (and father-in-law) Sir Francis Winnington, had set in train a petition for a new charter which was eventually granted by the crown in 1698. On Grascome's list, compiled originally in the spring of 1693, Dowdeswell was classed as a Court supporter. He was certainly prepared to invest in the regime, lending the government £400 on the security of the parliamentary aid in January 1695. He provided a further indication of this support on 13 Apr. 1695, when he acted as a teller in favour of giving an early hearing to the glass duty bill.[3]

Returned again for Tewkesbury at the 1695 general election, Dowdeswell continued to support the ministry. He was forecast as likely to support the Court on 31 Jan. 1696 on the division over the council of trade, signed the Association and in March voted for fixing the price of guineas at 22s. He acted as a teller twice during April 1696: on the 17th, at the report of the low wines duty bill, against a clause safeguarding the rights of persons with claims on the hereditary excise by virtue of letters patent from Charles II; and on the 24th, in favour of retaining in the bill establishing the land bank the clause naturalizing subscribers. In the following session he voted on 25 Nov. 1696 for the attainder of Sir John Fenwick†. Two days later he acted as a teller against a motion to refer to the committee on the bill regulating elections a petition from Southwark, arguing the right of people to sit in the House with large personal estates but little landed property. On 3 Mar. 1697 Dowdeswell told against a resolution from ways and means for a duty on all goods containing wool, silk or hair, a tax which would have fallen heavily on his constituents. In the last session of this Parliament, he acted as a teller on 21 Jan. 1698 in favour of a clause to a naturalization bill that no person should benefit who removed himself and his family out of England.

With the aid of a new charter, naming him as one of the 24 'principal burgesses', Dowdeswell was re-elected for Tewkesbury in 1698. In Worcestershire politics he appeared at the county election in favour of the Whigs. On a comparative analysis of the old and new Parliaments he was marked as a Court supporter, but a subsequent calculation queried this definition. On 11 Mar. 1699 he told in favour of taking the second reading of the land tax bill on the following Monday (13 Mar.), but this was resolved for Tuesday instead. This tellership probably indicates less enthusiasm for disbandment than an attempt to delay the committee of the whole on the state of the navy, which was criticizing the conduct of the Earl of Orford (Edward Russell*). Such a motivation would have been entirely consistent with a contemporary analysis of the House into interests, which placed Dowdeswell under Charles Montagu's* influence. Modern scholars have agreed that he was a follower of the Junto, but have seen a Worcestershire connexion with Lord Somers (Sir John*) as the decisive link. It would in fact be more accurate to characterize Dowdeswell as a committed Whig who not only owed his seat at Tewkesbury to his own efforts, but also played a significant role in Worcestershire politics. Certainly William Walsh* felt that Dowdeswell should be consulted about the forthcoming county contest in 1701. Walsh faced a dilemma in that he did not want a county meeting to intervene in the run-up to the poll to enforce an electoral agreement. Dowdeswell, together with his friends William Lygon and Edmund Lechmere, favoured a meeting of the freeholders, despite uncertainty as to who had the authority to call one in the absence abroad of the lord lieutenant, Shrewsbury. He acted as a teller on 5 June 1701, when he supported an attempt to get Richard Porter appointed a land tax commissioner for Suffolk.[4]

The election of November 1701 saw Dowdeswell keenly espousing the candidature in Worcestershire of William Bromley I*, and willing to discuss with Lygon and Lechmere the joint disposal of their second votes. In a parliamentary calculation by Robert Harley in December 1701, Dowdeswell was classed either as doubtful or absent. Since it is unlikely that Harley was unsure of his views, it is more probable that he was absent for at least the early part of the session. Although he was named to the committee of elections and privileges on 2 Jan. 1702, his next appointment was not until 13 Mar. He was present for the Queen's speech on 30 Mar. which, as he put it,

> occasioned some very warm ones in our House, some setting it out as a proof of her unparalleled goodness and a heart entirely English; others looked upon these great encomiums to be a reflection upon the memory of our late king and asserted that his heart was as entirely in the interest of England as ever anyone's was and that he had given as good proof of it.

In this letter Dowdeswell again showed himself a committed supporter of Bromley in Worcestershire elections, and an advocate of holding a county meeting to coincide with the quarter sessions to arrange the shire representatives. Returned again for Tewkesbury in the 1702 election, on 19 Nov. he was a teller against declaring John Grobham Howe* elected for Gloucestershire. He also sent detailed parliamentary reports to William Lygon. On 14 Dec. 1702 he discussed in detail the likely composition of the grant of supply. Later the same month, on the 22nd, he sent Lygon a copy of the Commons' address in response to the Queen's desire to reward the Duke of Marlborough (John Churchill†) 'by which you will find the grateful memory we have for King William'. This was no doubt a reference to the phrase in the address about the 'exorbitant grants' of the previous reign and the rejection by the Commons of an amendment describing in the same way the grants of Charles II and James II. On 16 Jan. he informed Lygon of a lengthy debate held the previous day over whether the malt tax bill should be carried up to the Lords. This had been disputed because Members felt 'that there are some bill[s] of moment depending and therefore it was necessary to keep the money bills in our own possession till these matters were adjusted'. The main item was undoubtedly the occasional conformity bill, the subject of a free conference between the Houses on 16 Jan., which Dowdeswell 'attended as a spectator till almost ten o'clock and then I left them not likely to make an end to it'. On 6 Feb. 1703 Dowdeswell reported the defeat of the occasional conformity bill the previous day, as the Commons voted to adhere to their rejection of the Lords' amendments. On 13 Feb. he voted for the Lords' amendment to the abjuration bill enlarging the time for taking the oath. Four days later he acted as a teller for the second time during the session, in favour of adding to the bill reviving the commission of accounts a clause for stating the debts due to several soldiers for attendance at sieges in Ireland.[5]

One of the surviving letters from Dowdeswell to Lygon during the 1703–4 session dealt extensively with the second occasional conformity bill. On 7 Dec. 1703, Dowdeswell reported the passage of the bill in the Commons with the hope that it would be opposed in the Lords. There were grounds for optimism, he believed, as 'a computation is made that it will be flung out by three' and because the Queen and Prince had gone to Windsor, 'which we hope will not encourage the passing of it'. He then gave a detailed justification of the Whigs' actions in opposing the bill even though they were in a minority:

> It has every time been very well debated on our side, as we that are against it are apt to judge. We have divided upon it three times and still increased our numbers, though the division this day was 223 and 140. We do not think ourselves wrong in dividing, though we still lost it, for we have thereby showed faces that everyone may judge of us according to their respective opinions: besides we have given in it encouragement to such of the Lords as are against it that it cannot be said all the Commons of England are for it; besides the Queen will see it is not perfectly agreeable to all the nation.

The question of occasional conformity was revived in the following session. Dowdeswell was forecast as a probable opponent of the Tack on 30 Oct. 1704 and did not vote for it on 28 Nov. Two days later he wrote to Lygon recounting the debate on the Tack, which was espoused

> as being the best and securest way to make the conformity bill pass with the Lords, but it was opposed as a thing of the last consequence in relation to the carrying on of the present war, which is undoubtedly the security of England, for should the Lords, who have generally protested against receiving any bill with a tack to it, have flung out the said bill by reason of the Tack, which I do verily believe they would, our allies would have been startled, our soldiers must have wanted subsistence and our supplies put so far back as would have given a great advantage to the common enemy; at last after a debate of seven hours we divided upon the question and there were for the Tack 134, against it 251.

Given Dowdeswell's views on the Tack, it was not surprising that Lygon was doubtful of being able to draw him into supporting Sir John Pakington, 4th Bt.*, rather than Walsh as a partner for Bromley in the forthcoming Worcestershire county election.[6]

Following Dowdeswell's re-election for Tewkesbury at the 1705 he was listed as 'Low Church'. He was absent from the division over the Speaker on 25 Oct. 1705 but had arrived by 10 Dec., when he provided Lygon with an account of the debate over joining with the Lords' address repudiating the notion that the Church was in danger. Opponents of the resolution pointed out the threats from papists and Dissenters who are its professed enemies; from the occasional conformists who qualify themselves for places of trust yet still continue Dissenters; from the many pamphleteers who so frequently defame the universities and clergy; from the immorality and profaneness of the age; from the Queen's charity to the inferior clergy not being perfected, it being delayed by such persons as are about her Majesty's person; from the Act of parliament which passed in Scotland for their better security; from the many seminaries and schools which are set up by Dissenters.

On 20 Dec. 1705 Dowdeswell received leave of absence for three weeks. However, he was probably back by 24 Jan. 1706 when he was nominated to an inquiry committee. On the 31st he apologized to Lygon: 'I do assure you that attending three nights a week at committees and the other days sitting so very [late?] I have not had time to write to anybody.' He reported that the Commons had added a clause to the regency bill 'to exclude all persons (some only excepted) that at the demise of her Majesty shall have any place or offices of profit under the crown from sitting in the House' and correctly predicted that the Lords would not let the clause stand in that form. By 12 Feb. he was worried that the whole bill would be lost 'by the disagreement of the two Houses concerning a clause which we added'. His own position was made clear by the division list of 18 Feb., which noted him as a supporter of the Court on the 'place clause'. In the following session Dowdeswell remarked to Lygon on 28 Jan. 1707 that the Commons' work was really beginning. He illustrated what he meant with an account of the previous day's report from the committee of supply 'which has agreed to several articles which have been expended the last year and were not contained in the estimate of the expense of the war which was given in and agreed to the last sessions'. The sum involved was about £930,000, which provoked complaints that the Commons had granted all that had been demanded and that 'it was too great a power which the ministry took upon them to engage the credit of the nation without consent of Parliament'. Dowdeswell was of an opposite view, fully supporting the ministry, 'since unexpected occasions offered which the ministry embraced and which were so much for the public advantage'. No doubt he was one of the majority that sanctioned the expenditure retrospectively. Dowdeswell also offered a comment on the Queen's speech recommending the Union: 'I do judge it will be much opposed in our House, yet with numbers that will not come near to a majority.' During the summer of 1707, William Walsh discussed Dowdeswell's possible stance in the by-election for Worcestershire caused by the death of his friend Bromley. Walsh hoped that Dowdeswell could be influenced by his brother-in-law, Judge Tracey, in favour of Sir Thomas Cookes Winford, 1st Bt.*, if it came to a contest. Although no letters survive from Dowdeswell to Lygon for the 1707-8 session, the Journals indicate that Dowdeswell attended at least part of the time. On 15 Dec. his name was added to the committee of privileges (perhaps indicating that he may have been absent at the very beginning of the session, as in 1705). Contemporaries had no difficulty in establishing his political position, two lists of 1708 classifying him as a Whig.[7]

Re-elected yet again in 1708, Dowdeswell does not seem to have been very active in the new Parliament. He was present in 1709 to vote for the naturalization of the Palatines but, significantly, his name does not appear on any lists detailing the division over the impeachment of Dr Sacheverell in the following session. It seems probable that by this time he was ailing, which may have been a contributory factor to his defeat at Tewkesbury in 1710. It was reported in July 1711 that Dowdeswell was 'so very weak that [he] cannot survive the autumn', and on 14 Oct. William Dowdeswell wrote that his father had died 'suddenly, in the space of four hours, on Sunday last' (the 7th). Judging by his will, made in 1708, Dowdeswell was a wealthy man. He left £3,000 or £4,000 to each of his children, including £3,000 to his daughter Elizabeth, who had married without his consent. According to a list of 1710 he also possessed £2,000 in Bank stock. He was succeeded by his eldest son, William, who quickly regained the Tewkesbury seat.[8]

[1] *Vis. Eng. and Wales Notes* ed. Crisp, vii. 64-67; *Glos. N. and Q.* ii. 412; *Temple Church Reg.* (Harl. Soc. Reg. n.s. i), 70. [2] J. Bennett, *Hist. Tewkesbury*, 393; *Preston Guild Rolls* (Lancs. and Cheshire Rec. Soc. ix), 185. [3] Duckett, *Penal Laws and Test Act* (1882), 242; *Epistolary Curiosities* ed. Warner, i. 144-6; *Cal. Treas. Bks.* ix. 604; x. 915; *HMC Portland*, x. 75; *CSP Dom.* 1694-5, p. 325; 1693, pp. 156-7; Bennett, 393. [4] *Shrewsbury Corresp.* 539; W. L. Sachse, *Ld. Somers*, 108, 112, 140; Surr. RO (Kingston), Somers mss 371/14/B18, 20, Walsh to Somers, 4, 7 Dec. 1700. [5] Hereford and Worcester RO (Worcester St. Helen's), Cal. Wm. Lygon letters 40, 55, 64, 67-69, Dowdeswell to Lygon, 16 Nov. 1701, 31 Mar., 14, 22 Dec. 1702, 16 Jan., 6 Feb. 1702-3; *HMC Lords*, n.s. v. 199-200. [6] Cal. Wm. Lygon letters 83, 86, 104, 106b, Dowdeswell to Lygon, 7, 16 Dec. 1703, 30 Nov. 1704, Lygon to [?Wm. Bromley I*], 30 Jan. 1704[-5]. [7] Ibid. 152, 162, 165, 236-7, Dowdeswell to Lygon, 11 Dec. 1705, 31 Jan., 12 Feb. 1705-6, 28 Jan., 15 Feb. 1706-7; Somers mss 371/14/L29, Walsh to Somers, 18 Aug. 1707. [8] Cal. Wm. Lygon letters 434, Roger Tuckfield to Lygon, 28 July 1711; Add. 70375, William Dowdeswell to Edward, Ld. Harley*, 14 Oct. 1711; PCC 6 Barnes; Egerton 3359.

S. N. H.

DOWDESWELL, William (1682–1728), of Pull Court, Bushley, Worcs.

TEWKESBURY   1 Jan. 1712–1722

bap. 18 Aug. 1682, 1st s. of Richard Dowdeswell*. *educ.* ?Eton 1698; Christ Church, Oxf. 1700; travelled abroad. *m.* (1) 13 Mar. 1712, Katherine (*d.* 1716), da. of Charles Cokayne, 3rd Visct. Cullen [I], 1s. *d.v.p.* 1da.; (2) 5 Aug. 1719, Amy, da. of Anthony Hammond*, 4s. (1 *d.v.p.*). *suc.* fa. 1711.[1]

Sheriff, Worcs. 1726–7.

As the heir to a considerable interest at Tewkesbury, Dowdeswell was well placed to embark on a parliamentary career. However, his immediate prospects were put in jeopardy as a result of an unfortunate incident in which he was involved while travelling on the Continent. While journeying through France to England in July 1709, having been granted a safe conduct, he killed a Roman Catholic servant who had robbed him. A letter survives to his uncle, Hon. Robert Tracy, a judge of common pleas, asking that the government demand his return to stand trial in England, but in fact no action was taken against him. It is not certain whether the incident played any direct part in the defeat of his father at Tewkesbury at the 1710 election, but in the year following his father's death, Dowdeswell himself was able to reassert the family's claim to a seat in the by-election to replace Henry Ireton*.[2]

Like his father, Dowdeswell was a committed Whig. He voted on 18 June 1713 against the French commerce bill, being classed as a Whig in the ensuing printed division list. Re-elected in 1713 with his kinsman Charles Dowdeswell, he was classed as a Whig on the Worsley list. In the 1714 session he voted on 18 Mar. against the expulsion of Richard Steele. Returned again in the 1715 election, he was classed as a Whig on two comparative analyses of the old and new Parliaments. After loyally supporting the Whig ministry, he retired from Parliament in 1722. Dowdeswell died on 5 Sept. 1728, being succeeded by his son, William†, chancellor of the Exchequer in the Rockingham administration, 1765–7.

[1] *Vis. Eng. and Wales Notes* ed. Crisp, vii. 64–67.   [2] Add. 61129, f. 36.

P. W./S. N. H.

DOWNE [I], 2nd Visct. *see* **DAWNAY, Hon. Henry**

DOWNING, George (c.1685–1749), of Gamlingay Park, Cambs.

DUNWICH   1710–1715, 1722–10 June 1749

bap. 24 Oct. 1685, o. s. of Sir George Downing, 2nd Bt., of East Hatley, Cambs. by Lady Catherine (*d.* 1688), da. of James Cecil†, 3rd Earl of Salisbury. *educ.* travelled abroad (inc. Holland, Germany, Denmark, Italy) 1700–4. *m.* 1700, Mary (*d.* 1734), da. of Sir William Forester*, *s.p.*; 1da. (*b.* c.1726) illegit. by Mary Townsend. *suc.* fa. June 1711; KB 12 Jan. 1732.[1]

Freeman, Dunwich 1709, common councilman 1710, alderman 1712, bailiff 1712–13.[2]

Downing was the grandson of Sir George Downing, 1st Bt.†, the Restoration bureaucrat who gave his name to Downing Street. His father, the 2nd Bt., was by contrast 'not accounted of sound judgment', and after his mother's death Downing was brought up in the family of his maternal aunt, the wife of Sir William Forester*. When he was 15, 'by the procurement and persuasion of those in whose keeping he was', he married his 13-year-old cousin, Mary Forester. He left her almost immediately to begin a long foreign tour, adjuring her not to go to court, where her noted beauty would be too much admired. Her acceptance in 1703 of the post of maid of honour, therefore, while he was still in Italy, 'filled me with surprise and pain, and shattered the loveliest image man ever cherished in his heart', and on his return to England in the following year he kept apart from her.[3]

Downing's electoral interest at Dunwich was probably established in 1709, when it was reported that he had 'bought most of the houses' there. He was returned unopposed at the next election, having failed to become knight of the shire for Cambridgeshire, where Dyer described him as a 'Whig candidate'. In a list of the new Parliament he was, however, marked as a Tory. He seconded Edward Wortley Montagu's* motion of 6 Dec. 1710 for a place bill, and was named to the committee to prepare the bill. He told on 25 Jan. 1711 against Henry Vernon I* in a disputed election for Stafford. Listed among the 'worthy patriots' who exposed the mismanagements of the previous ministry, and as a member of the October Club, he broke from the Court on 7 Dec. 1711 over the 'No Peace without Spain' motion, and was described as a Whig both at the time of the 1713 election, in the *Post Boy*, and subsequently, in the Worsley list.[4]

Downing endorsed his wife's unsuccessful petition to the Lords in 1715 for a divorce bill, in which it was alleged that the marriage had not been consummated, that they had never lived together, and that now 'such disgusts and aversions have arisen and continue between the two that there is no possibility of mutual agreement'. Defeated in the 1715 election, where he seems to have stood as a Tory, he was removed from the Bedfordshire commission of the peace in the following year. However, regaining his seat in 1722, he was granted soon afterwards a 99-year lease of Dunwich in fee farm, which put the borough in his pocket, and thereafter became a loyal supporter of government. Despite the fact that he was wealthy enough to give his natural daughter a dowry of some £20,000, 'for the latter part of his life he led a most miserable, covetous and sordid existence'.[5]

Downing died on 10 June 1749. His wife having been provided for by a private Act of Parliament in 1717, he left his lands in Cambridgeshire, Bedfordshire and Suffolk to a cousin, Jacob Garrard Downing[†], with remainders to the heirs male of three other cousins. In default of such, the estate was to be applied to the foundation of a college at Cambridge. This provision came into effect in 1764, but because of extensive litigation it was not until 1800 that Downing College was granted its charter.[6]

[1] H. W. P. Stevens, *Downing College*, 18-36, 256, 267; *CSP Dom.* 1702-3, p. 412; *HMC Astley*, 126-31; *Addison Letters*, 47. [2] Suff. RO (Ipswich), Dunwich bor. recs. EE6 1144/14; T. Gardner, *Dunwich* (1754), 86. [3] Stevens, 18-24. [4] W. Suss. RO, Shillinglee mss Ac.454/869, Clement Corrance* to Sir Edward Turnor*, 10 June 1709; Add. 70421, Dyer's newsletters 2 Nov., 7 Dec. 1710; *Bull. IHR*, xxxiii. 228. [5] Stevens, 25-26, 31, 36; *Cases of Divorce for Several Causes* ... (1715), pt. 3, p. 32; L. K. J. Glassey, *Appt. JPs*, 252. [6] Stevens, 28, 37, 49, 256-70.

D. W. H.

DRAKE, Sir Francis, 3rd Bt. (1647-1717), of Buckland Abbey, Devon, and Holborn End, St. Giles-in-the-Fields, Mdx.

TAVISTOCK   26 Mar. 1673-1681 (Mar.), 1689-1695
10 Nov. 1696-1700

bap. 1 May 1647, 2nd but 1st surv. s. of Thomas Drake of Brendon Barton, Week St. Mary, Devon by Susan, da. of William Crymes of Buckland Crymes, Devon. *educ.* Exeter, Oxf. 1663, MA 1663. *m.* (1) 6 Feb. 1665, Dorothy (*d.* 1679), da. of Sir John Bampfylde, 1st Bt.[†], of Poltimore, Devon, 4da.; (2) lic. 21 Oct. 1680, Anne (*d.* 1685), da. of Thomas Boone[†] of Mount Boone, Devon and coh. to her bro. Charles Boone*, *s.p.*; (3) 18 Feb. 1690 (with £5,000), Elizabeth (*d.* 1717), da. of Sir Henry Pollexfen[†] of Woodbury, Devon, 7s. 1da. *suc.* fa. c.1653; uncle Sir Francis Drake, 2nd Bt.[†], as 3rd Bt. 6 Jan. 1662.[1]
Recorder, Plymouth 1696-*d.*; v.-adm. Devon 1715-*d.*[2]

A staunch Whig, Drake had property in and nearby Bere Alston, as well as long leases which gave him a preponderant interest in that borough. He also enjoyed influence for one seat at Tavistock, which, until 1705, he managed for the Russells. This enabled him to provide seats for several leading Junto Whigs, often on the recommendation of Lord Somers (Sir John*), whom he held in great esteem, and his own friend and unpaid legal adviser, Peter King*. Returned for Bere Alston as well as Tavistock in 1690, Drake chose the latter and was classed as a Whig by Lord Carmarthen (Sir Thomas Osborne[†]) in March 1690. On 24 Mar. he served as a teller on the Whig side in connexion with the disputed return for Plympton Erle. A list among Robert Harley's* papers noted him in April 1691 as a Country supporter. In a debate on 4 Jan. 1692 he spoke in favour of granting passports to the 'witnesses' mentioned in the recent disclosures of Jacobite intrigue by William Fuller, asserting that 'Fuller has done service and I hope he may have the countenance of this House in an address to the King for his protection and those to come over'. However, when other MPs pointed to the contradictions in Fuller's statements, Drake urged that these be investigated. His support for the interlopers' plans for superseding the existing East India Company were revealed in tellerships he performed on 8 and 22 Jan.; while also on the 22nd he was teller against a private bill enabling the bishop of London to sell a manor in Worcestershire. On 14 Jan. 1693 he was allowed a month's leave of absence to attend his sick wife, and family commitments led him to speak later in the year of retiring from parliamentary service. From this point on he was certainly less assiduous in the attention he gave his duties at Westminster. In the autumn Drake saw it as his responsibility to intercede with the new sheriff of Devon, Christopher Savery, to dissuade him from appointing as under-sheriff a friend of Sir Edward Seymour, 4th Bt.*: 'if the under-sheriff should be of another kidney, if anything of difficulty should happen – which God prevent – it will be very easy for him to do what you and all your friends will be heartily sorry for'. However, Savery politely reassured Drake that he had reserved for himself both the handling of writs for parliamentary elections and the empanelling of quarter sessions juries, but would make his own nomination. Apologizing for his presumption, Drake commented that 'the plain designs now set on foot against the government may perhaps have transported me into an unnecessary tenderness', and expressed longing 'for such an agreement among us as was in the late King Charles II's time'. He was granted a month's leave of absence on 19 Jan. 1694, but was still absent without leave on 14 Mar. when he was ordered into custody. On 14 Feb. 1695, when his absence was again noted, a motion to excuse him was defeated and he was again ordered into custody. He chose not to stand at the general election of 1695, saying that he would find it 'mighty inconvenient' to serve again, as the London air was 'very prejudicial' to his health.[3]

Early in 1696 Drake busied himself in scotching an attempt by a group of senior county Tories to avoid taking the parliamentary association by drafting instead an address to be presented by the Earl of Bath, the county's lord lieutenant. He pointed out 'the great absurdities and defects' of such a document and was gratified to see it 'somewhat amended'. Commenting to his friend Sir George Treby*, he said that there seemed at first 'an almost universal inclination' for the Association but then

> one night we lost, many having notions put into them that Harrow-on-the-Hill stood in a bottom, for that the word 'rightful' was to break the Act of Settlement. Moreover, they could not consent to the word 'revenge'. So nice are some of us grown since we hunted the poor fellows that followed the Duke of Monmouth after the whole of the design was wholly defeated. This defection is owing to some of our leading Churchmen . . . there was a most abominable grand jury provided, in it many non-jurors, which the judge having notice of discouraged that panel, and we have a new one . . . I am almost ashamed of the condition of our militia. The commissions to the colonels came last week, and they, under the impression of what may happen upon their not signing the Association, are not likely to be very effective in settling their regiments.

The matter was clarified when Parliament passed a bill making the taking of the Association compulsory for all those holding office under the crown and Bath was replaced as lord lieutenant of Devon by Lord Stamford, Drake's Whig associate at Bere Alston. This led to a purge in the county commissions and an open breach between Drake and his Tory kinsman Sir William Drake, 4th Bt.* Sir Francis followed up the success by obtaining a new charter for Plymouth with the help of Somers and the Duke of Shrewsbury, under which he became recorder for life. His filling up the new corporation with Whig friends and contriving to exclude Charles Trelawny* from the command of the town's militia earned him the nickname of 'the regulator'. In November of that year he returned to Parliament at a by-election at Tavistock, where he had put up in order to keep out a Tory, Henry Manaton*. He was granted leave of absence on 6 Mar. 1697. In the following session he was teller on two occasions, but on succumbing to illness early in March 1698 was granted leave of absence. Following the 1698 election he was classed as a supporter of the Court party, and on 18 Jan. 1699 voted in favour of a standing army. On 15 Feb. he was given six weeks' leave on account of a bronchial complaint which appears to have kept him at home for the rest of the Parliament. An analysis of the House according to 'interests' compiled during the first half of 1700 placed him as a supporter of Charles Montagu*.[4]

In later years Drake, who had seven sons to provide for yet continued to indulge in the expense of electioneering for the Whig interest, fell into serious financial difficulties. As trustee of the estates of Sir Henry Pollexfen[†], and guardian to Sir Henry's epileptic heir, he was able to marry off one of his own daughters to the heir and ensure that the Pollexfen estates eventually came into his family. Not surprisingly, Sir Henry's brother, John Pollexfen*, accused him of sharp practice. Drake died during the last week of December 1717 and was buried at Meavy, near Tavistock. A local Tory remarked that 'he died a lingering and tormenting death. I wish he be not punished worse in the other life.'[5]

[1] E. F. Eliott-Drake, *Fam. and Heirs of Sir Francis Drake*, i. 400; ii. 30, 65, 117 [2] Ibid. ii. 113. [3] Eliott-Drake, ii. 86, 89–93, 114, 142–3; Cobbett, *Parlty. Hist.* v. 690; Add. 44058, ff. 75–81; *HMC 13th Rep. VI*, 33–34. [4] Eliott-Drake, ii. 104–10, 113, 126; *HMC 13th Rep. VI*, 40–41; L. K. J. Glassey, *Appt. JPs*, 123; Coxe, *Shrewsbury*, 481. [5] Eliott-Drake, ii. 119–23, 153–6, 207; *Jnl. of James Yonge* ed. Poynter, 229.

E. C.

DRAKE, John (1657–1716), of Marsham Street, Westminster.

AMERSHAM 2 Jan. 1699–1700
19 Feb. 1701–1705
21 Nov. 1707–1708, 1710–1713

bap. Apr. 1657, 5th s. of Francis Drake[†] of Walton-upon-Thames, Surr. being 3rd s. by his 3rd w. Susanna Potts of St. Bride, Fleet Street, London; half-bro. of Sir William Drake*. *educ.* St. John's, Oxf. 1675; M. Temple 1677. *m.* Anne (*d.* aft. 1728), *s.p.*[1]

Ensign, Coldstream Gds. 1678, lt. 1685, capt. Sept. 1688.[2]

An officer in James II's army, Drake left the Coldstreamers after the Revolution. What occupied his time before 1698 is unclear, but it is conceivable that he was the John Drake appointed an ensign in a foot regiment in 1694. As the uncle of Montagu Drake* he was one of the trustees appointed in 1698 to administer his nephew's estate. Another of his roles seems to have been as surrogate for the family's parliamentary interest until his great-nephew Montagu Garrard Drake* came of age. Thus, in 1698, when Lord Cheyne (Hon. William*) opted to sit for the county, Drake was brought in at Amersham by Sir John Garrard, 3rd Bt.*, at the ensuing by-election held in January 1699. Luttrell gave him the title 'colonel', but in the Journals he was referred to as 'Mr Drake' when he was named on 27 Feb. 1700 to a committee of inquiry.[3]

The same arrangement with Cheyne seems to have

operated for the election of January 1701, but before Cheyne could choose to sit for the county, Drake came in as a replacement for the deceased Garrard. Drake was again appointed to a key family role, which probably increased his influence in the area, when he was named overseer of the will of his eldest half-brother, Francis Drake (d. 1701) of Woodstock Park. Indeed, Francis specifically instructed his own son that if he ever came into the estate of Sir William Drake, he was not to break the entail upon it without consulting John first. The election of November 1701 saw Drake hold his seat and he was listed as a Tory by Robert Harley* in December 1701. In the new Parliament he acted as teller on 20 Feb. 1702 in favour of leaving on the table the petition of Lord Haversham (Sir John Thompson, 1st Bt.*) relating to forfeited estates in Ireland preparatory to its being considered with similar requests. Six days later, he voted for the resolution vindicating the proceedings of the Commons in the impeachments of William III's ministers. In March he presented the Amersham address on the accession of Queen Anne, pledging support 'against the pretended Prince of Wales and all other your enemies both at home and abroad'. In preparation for the general election of 1702, he persuaded the widow of Montagu Drake to provide Amersham with 'a convenient inn', and undertook to repay the money involved in case of her son's death. Returned in 1702, Drake made little impact on this Parliament. Although forecast by Harley as a probable opponent of the Tack, he in fact voted for it on 28 Nov. 1704.[4]

Drake appears not to have contested Amersham in 1705. No doubt as a consequence of his stance on the Tack he was removed from the Buckinghamshire commission of the peace. He was also out of the Commons when, as one of the surviving trustees of Montagu Drake's will, he petitioned the Lords in the 1706–7 session for a private Act to sell lands in Kent (acquired through the Garrard marriage) to pay off debts. However, a document from 1709 suggests he was still involved in administering the Drake estates. Drake returned to the Commons at the by-election in November 1707 caused by Lord Cheyne's ineligibility to sit in the House as a Scottish peer. On two lists of the post-Union Parliament he was classed as a Tory. Again stepping down in 1708, Drake was returned in 1710. He may have been the John Drake with over £500 worth of Bank stock at this date. Though classed as 'doubtful' in the 'Hanover list' of 1710, he was a member of the October Club and named in 1711 as one of the 'worthy patriots' who detected the mismanagements of the previous administration. As 'Colonel' Drake he was given leave of absence on 9 Mar. 1711 for three weeks, but had returned by 4 Apr., when he reported from the committee on the bill for ascertaining and establishing the glebe lands and profits of the rectory of Gothurst in Buckinghamshire. Early in January 1712 'Colonel' Drake was included on Lord Treasurer Oxford's (Harley) list of those to be lobbied in support of the attack on the Duke of Marlborough (John Churchill†). In July 1712 he presented the Amersham address expressing hopes for 'a happy peace', which contained severe reflections on the Whigs. In the 1713 session he voted on 18 June for the French commerce bill.[5]

Drake lost his parliamentary seat and his electoral influence when his great-nephew, Montagu Garrard Drake, came of age in 1713. Drake died about 15 Dec. 1716, leaving no will, and letters of administration were granted in 1723 to his widow Anne. She later was provided with an annuity of £50 by the will of Montagu Garrard Drake, no doubt in memory of the services her husband had rendered the Drake family, for according to one rector of Amersham he did not sit in Parliament 'out of choice, but to keep the family interest from sinking'.[6]

[1] *Surr. Arch. Colls.* lxxvi. 94; *St. Paul's Covent Garden* (Harl. Soc. Reg. xxxv), 1; Bucks. RO, D/Dr/9/10. [2] *CSP Dom.* 1687–9, p. 289. [3] *CSP Dom.* 1694–5, p. 68; PCC 263 Lort; Northants. RO, Isham mss 1604, John to Sir Justinian Isham, 4th Bt.*, 3 Jan. 1698–9; Luttrell, *Brief Relation*, iv. 468. [4] PCC 94 Dyer; *London Gazette*, 30 Mar.–2 Apr. 1702; Bucks. RO, D/Dr/9/10. [5] Glassey, *Appt. JPs*, 176; HMC Lords, n.s. vii. 47; D/Dr/9/12; Egerton 3359; Add. 70331, 'canvassing list'; *Post Boy*, 5–8 July 1712. [6] *Hist. Reg. Chron.* 1717, p. 4; PCC 144 Brook; *Bucks. Recs.* xiv. 293.

E. C./S. N. H.

DRAKE, Montagu (1673–98), of Shardeloes, nr. Amersham, Bucks.

AMERSHAM 1695–27 June 1698

b. 13 Sept. 1673, 1st s. of Sir William Drake*. m. 3 Dec. 1691, Jane (d. 1724), da. and h. of Sir John Garrard, 3rd Bt.*, 2s. (1 d.v.p.) 1da. suc. fa. 1690.[1]

Master, chirographer's office in c.p. 1692–d.
Freeman, Hertford 1698.[2]

After Drake succeeded his father around his 17th birthday, the family priority appears to have been to get him married and settled. Not the least reason for this may have been the wish of his mother to remarry: mention in April 1691 of a 'match' between Drake and a Mrs Grenville being 'off' coincided with news of Lady Drake's likely alliance with Samuel Trotman*. Drake did not remain single for long however, marrying into the Garrard family, although a later family historian surmised that 'her father not making her fortune or portions so good as he had promised . . . occasioned some family discontents'. Indeed, although marriage articles exist for 2 Dec. 1691, a post-nuptial settlement of 16 Oct. 1694 was referred to by Drake in his will.[3]

At the first opportunity after his coming of age Drake was returned for his family borough. Though technically a placeman, in that he held a post in the court of common pleas which he exercised by deputy, he followed his father-in-law Garrard's Tory politics rather than his father's Whiggism. He was forecast as likely to oppose the government in the division of 31 Jan. 1696 on the proposed council of trade and refused the Association, for which he was removed from the Buckinghamshire bench. He also voted against fixing the price of guineas at 22s., and on 25 Nov. against the attainder of Sir John Fenwick[†]. Significantly, he was appointed on 1 Feb. 1697 to convey the thanks of the House to the Tory divine Dr William Lancaster for preaching to the Commons. In the Hertfordshire by-election of December 1697 he voted for the Tory Ralph Freman II*. On 15 Mar. 1698 he was given leave of absence for health reasons, but was nominated on 11 Apr. to an inquiry committee. He died on 27 June 1698, John Isham remarking: 'Montagu Drake died last week of convulsions which I fear is in a great measure to be attributed to his drinking strong waters and that in a morning as I am told, Sir John Garrard shews little concern upon the occasion.' Another noted that he had 'made too free with a good constitution' and referred to a fall from his horse on 'the road near Acton', the effects of which contributed to his death. His inventory, mainly of his lodgings in Brewer Street, St. James's, came to £625, with a further £735 being granted to Sir John Garrard, mostly from Shardeloes. In his will Drake appointed Sir John Garrard, his uncle John Drake*, Simon Harcourt I*, William Jennens* and Belzial Knight as trustees to pay his legacies and debts. However, since his estate was encumbered with debts amounting to £14,800, this proved too complex a task and necessitated a private Act in 1707 to enable his widow and his uncle, John Drake, to sell the Kentish property which had come to him at his marriage. The residue of the money, after debts had been settled, went to his son Montagu Garrard Drake*.[4]

[1] Lipscomb, *Bucks*. iii. 155, 169; Burke, *Commoners*, i. 582; BL, Verney mss mic. 636/45, John Verney* (Ld. Fermanagh) to Sir Ralph Verney, 1st Bt.[†], 9 Dec. 1691; *HMC Lords*, n.s. vii. 47. [2] Herts. RO, Hertford bor. recs. 25/100. [3] Add. 70149, Lady Pye to Abigail Harley, 11 Apr. 1691; *Shardeloes Pprs*. ed. Eland, 70; *Bucks. Probate Inventories* (Bucks. Rec. Soc. xxiv), 263; PCC 261 Lort. [4] L. K. J. Glassey, *Appt. JPs*, 123; Bodl. Carte 79, f. 682; Herts. RO, Q/PE/2, f. 3; Lipscomb, 168–9; Northants. RO, Isham mss IC 1579, John to Sir Justinian Isham, 4th Bt.*, 5 July 1698; *Bucks. Recs*. xiv. 352; *Bucks. Probate Inventories*, 258, 262, 271; PCC 263 Lort; Bucks. RO, D/Dr/9/12; *HMC Lords*, 47–48.

E. C./S. N. H.

DRAKE, Montagu Garrard (1692–1728), of Shardeloes, nr. Amersham, Bucks.

AMERSHAM   1713–1722
BUCKINGHAMSHIRE   1722–1727
AMERSHAM   1727–26 Apr. 1728

b. 14 Oct. 1692, 1st and o. surv. s. of Montagu Drake*. *educ.* private tutor (Philip Ayres); St. John's, Oxf. 1706, MA 1709; Padua 1710; travelled abroad (Netherlands, Italy, Switzerland, France) 1710–12. *m.* 13 Oct. 1719 (with £30,000), Isabella (*d.* 1744), da. and h. of Thomas Marshall (*d.* 1712), merchant, of St. Michael Bassishaw, London, wid., 3s. (1 *d.v.p.*). *suc.* fa. 1698.[1]

Master, chirographer's office in c.p. 1698–*d.*

Drake benefited from the private Act passed in 1707 to dispose of the family's Kentish estates, amendments being tabled to ensure that he profited from any surplus gained by the sale after debts had been paid. Coming from an influential Tory family, Drake was thought of as a future candidate for the county as early as December 1707, and he was able to enter Parliament two months before his 21st birthday at the general election of 1713, when his great-uncle John* stepped down from the family seat at Amersham. Thus he was of age when the Parliament sat. However, he made little impact on the 1714 session, with no recorded intervention in debate. He supported the compromise drawn up in October 1714 whereby the county representation was divided between the parties. He was re-elected in 1715, when the Worsley list described him as a Tory, and also appeared as such in a list of the Members returned again in 1715. He voted consistently with the opposition under the Hanoverians and died at Bath on 26 Apr. 1728, being succeeded by his son, William[†].[2]

[1] *HMC Lords* n.s. x. 248; Lipscomb, *Bucks*. iii. 155; *Shardeloes Pprs*. ed. Eland, 70–71, 143; Egerton 3339, f. 111; Add. 22229, f. 103; Bucks. RO, D/Dr/9/16; 10/3; *Westminster Abbey* (Harl. Soc. Reg. x), 44; *Yorks. Arch. Soc*. vii. 97; Burke, *Commoners*, i. 582; *Verney Letters 18th Cent*. ii. 75. [2] *HMC Lords*, n.s. vii. 47–48; Bodl. Ballard 10, f. 155; *Verney Letters 18th Cent*. i. 317; *The Gen*. n.s. vii. 158; Nichols, *Lit. Anec*. i. 206.

E. C./S. N. H.

DRAKE, Sir William (c.1651–90), of Shardeloes, nr. Amersham, Bucks.

AMERSHAM   6 Nov. 1669–1679 (July)
                 18 Dec. 1680–1681 (Mar.)
                 1685–1687
                 1689–Sept. 1690

b. c.1651, 2nd s. of Francis Drake[†] of Walton-on-Thames, Surr., but 1st by his 2nd w. Dorothy, da. of Sir William Spring, 1st Bt.[†], of Pakenham, Suff.; half-bro. of

John Drake*. *educ.* St. John's, Oxf. matric. 22 Nov. 1667, aged 16; M. Temple 1669. *m.* in or bef. 1671, Elizabeth, da. of Hon. William Montagu*, 4s. 3da. Kntd. 2 Sept. 1668; *suc.* uncle Sir William Drake, 1st Bt.†, in Bucks. and Cheshire estates 1669.[1]

Drake was re-elected unopposed in 1690 for Amersham, where he was lord of the manor. A former Exclusionist who seems to have been willing to 'collaborate' with the Jacobite regime, he voted in the Convention for the disabling clause in the corporations bill. He was listed as doubtful in Lord Carmarthen's (Sir Thomas Osborne†) analysis of the Commons in March 1690. He died in September 1690, his remains being interred at Amersham on the 24th. In 1691, his widow married Samuel Trotman*.[2]

[1] Lipscomb, *Bucks.* iii. 154–5; *Surr. Arch. Colls.* lxxvi. 94–95; *VCH Bucks.* iii. 154. [2] *HMC 13th Rep. VI*, 19; Duckett, *Penal Laws and Test Act* (1883), 240; Lipscomb, 155; *HMC Lords*, n.s. x. 247.

E. C./S. N. H.

DRAKE, Sir William, 4th Bt. (1658–1716), of Mount Drake, and Ashe House, Musbury, Devon.

| HONITON | 1690–1713 |
| HONITON AND DARTMOUTH | 1713–1715 |

bap. 12 July 1658, 4th s. of Sir John Drake, 1st Bt.†, of Great Trill, Axminster and Ashe House by Dionyse, da. of Sir Richard Strode† of Newnham, Devon. *educ.* Oriel, Oxf. matric. 1675; Corpus Christi, Oxf. BA 1679, MA 1683. *m.* (1) 5 Apr. 1687, Judith (*d.* 1701), da. and coh. of William Eveleigh of Olcomb, Ottery St. Mary, Devon, 2s. 3da.; (2) 16 Apr. 1705, Mary (*d.* 1729), da. of Sir Peter Prideaux, 3rd Bt.†, of Netherton, Devon and sis. of Sir Edmund Prideaux, 4th Bt.*, *s.p.* Kntd. 13 Mar. 1685; *suc.* bro. as 4th Bt. 1687, sis. at Ashe House and Mount Drake 1694.[1]

Commr. public accts. 1703–4; ld. of Admiralty 1710–14.

A cousin of John Churchill†, later 1st Duke of Marlborough, Drake was knighted shortly after James II's accession. In 1687 his elder brother's suicide unexpectedly brought him the baronetcy given his father. Although he survived a purge of the commissions of the peace in June 1688, he was displaced the following month. He then joined the Prince of Orange at Exeter in November, being noted as a gentleman of 'considerable fortune'. In the election to the Convention in 1689 he stood for Lyme Regis where he owned a manor, but was defeated.[2]

Drake was returned in 1690 for Honiton, another borough in which he owned property, and was classed as a Tory in Lord Carmarthen's (Sir Thomas Osborne†) list. His fellow Member was his kinsman Sir Walter Yonge, 3rd Bt., with whom he shared the representation of Honiton in eight successive Parliaments, though the two men were on different sides of the party-political divide. In December 1690 Carmarthen noted him as a supporter in connexion with a projected attack on his own position. Until the end of the decade, however, Drake was an inactive Member. Grants of leave were given him on 17 Feb. and 21 Dec. 1693, though he did act as teller, on 23 Feb. 1695, on a supply motion. In January 1696 he was forecast as likely to oppose the Court over the proposed council of trade, at the end of February subscribed to the Association without hesitation, and in March voted against fixing the price of guineas at 22s. Although he supported the parliamentary association, he helped to organize a High Church protest against the removal from the Devon commission of the peace of those who had refused to sign. He was apparently absent from the division on 25 Nov. on the impeachment of Sir John Fenwick†. His otherwise blank record of activity in the Commons was only marked by a further grant of leave on 30 Mar. 1697.[3]

During the 1697–8 session Drake took the lead in securing the passage of a bill to prevent the importing of foreign lace, a measure which did much to strengthen his interest at Honiton by wiping out foreign competition to the town's staple industry. Drake's promotion of this bill also marks his transition towards greater involvement in the business of the House, especially in select committee, the value of which was later widely recognized in his election as a commissioner of accounts. Following the 1698 election he was classed as a supporter of the Country party in a comparative analysis of the old and new Parliaments, and in another list was noted as likely to oppose a standing army. Participation in debate on the floor of the House did not come easily to him, however, and while speaking on 14 Jan. 1700 against the allocation of a proportion of the forfeited estates in Ireland to the King's use, he disclosed to MPs: 'upon my word, Sir, it is very uneasy for me and unpleasant to rise up unwillingly in this place to speak'. On 29 Apr. 1701 he was granted leave of absence to attend his dying wife. In the aftermath of the December 1701 election, Robert Harley* listed him as a Tory, and on 26 Feb. 1702 Drake voted for the resolution vindicating the Commons' late proceedings in the impeachments of the King's Whig ministers. Towards the end of the session he took charge of a private bill to enable Exeter's cathedral clergy to grant leases in a Devon manor.[4]

On 7 Jan. 1703 Drake was among the group of prominent Tories balloted by the House to serve on the revised commission of public accounts, and was elected a second time on 25 Feb. 1704, this time achieving first place with 261 votes. However, the bill authorizing the commission's renewal failed to pass. Drake nevertheless continued to be an active presence in the House and maintained his reputation as a willing committee-man. In mid-March he was noted as a supporter of Lord Nottingham (Daniel Finch†) in connexion with the projected attack on Nottingham over his handling of the Scotch Plot. In October he was forecast as a probable supporter of the Tack, an expectation which he fulfilled in the division on 28 Nov. At the end of February 1705 he was actively involved in the proceedings of the Aylesbury case and on the 28th was one of the managers of a conference with the Lords. In the middle of the next month he was chief rapporteur in similar proceedings concerning the Commons' disagreement with the Lords' amendments to the militia bill. Following the dissolution of the Parliament, Drake was accorded a grand reception on his arrival at Honiton on 29 Mar. He was welcomed, so one news writer reported, by

> all the principal gentry and clergy of that part of the country, making a body of 6 or 700 horse; and this honour was paid him from a grateful sense they have of the good service performed by that worthy gentleman during the whole Parliament, and particularly in the last session, for his endeavours for the passing of the bill to prevent hypocrisy in matters of religion.

Early in May, however, he filed a suit against an Exeter man for calling him a 'Tacker' and describing him as a friend to France.[5]

Following the 1705 election Drake was described in a published list of the returns as 'True Church', and at the assembling of the new Parliament he spoke and voted on 25 Oct. 1705 against the Court candidate for the Speakership. In a debate on 4 Dec. on proposals for union with Scotland and protecting the Protestant succession, he opposed going into committee on such a 'dangerous experiment' without first examining precedents. Then on the 19th he spoke in defence of Charles Caesar* for alluding in a speech on the regency bill to Lord Treasurer Godolphin's (Sidney†) alleged correspondence with St. Germain in the previous reign. In a further debate on the bill on 10 Jan. 1706 he did not fully support a Tory 'blocking' proposal to require an immediate summons of Parliament at the Queen's death, but advocated a delay of 20 days to allow west-country MPs time to make their journeys to London. In two analyses of the House drawn up early in 1708 Drake was classed as a Tory. He reported from a select committee on 28 Feb. 1709 on an Exeter petition against imports of Irish yarn, and in February 1710 assisted in the passage of a private bill concerning the Devon estate of the late Sir John Rolle†. On 4 Mar. 1710 the House had to interpose to prevent Drake and Sir William Strickland, 3rd Bt., from pursuing a quarrel which had broken out between them in the House. He was naturally listed as having opposed the impeachment of Dr Sacheverell.[6]

Drake was classed as a Tory in the 'Hanover list' of the new Parliament. After the fall of the Marlborough–Godolphin administration he was rewarded in mid-September with a place on the Admiralty Board, though it appears that some persuasion was needed to induce him to accept. By November, however, John Ward III* was able to inform Lord Nottingham that 'Sir William Drake is come to town, and [I] have prevailed with him (much against his inclination) to act in the Admiralty'. He was one of the few office-holders to vote on 29 Jan. 1711 for committing the place bill. After this session he was listed among the 'Tory patriots' who had voted for peace, and among the 'worthy patriots' who had detected the mismanagements of the previous administration. In the election of 1713 he was successful once more at Honiton, and was also returned for Dartmouth – though in fact he never declared his choice between the two. He was named on 12 Nov. 1713 a commissioner for administering the oaths to Members. The Worsley list classed him as a Tory. By the early months of 1714, however, increasing ill-health from 'dropsy' had prevented him from fulfilling his duties at the Admiralty. Losing his seat at Honiton in 1715, he died on 28 Feb. 1716 and was buried at Musbury.[7]

[1] Vivian, *Vis. Devon.* 297. [2] L. K. J. Glassey, *Appt. JPs*, 88; Bodl. Rawl. lett. 109, f. 115; Luttrell, *Brief Relation*, i. 477. [3] *HMC 13th Rep. VI*, 40. [4] *Cocks Diary*, 45. [5] Strathmore mss at Glamis Castle, box 72, bdle. 3, newsletter 3 Apr. 1705; bdle. 4, newsletter 8 May 1705. [6] Cobbett, *Parlty. Hist.* vi. 450; BL, Trumbull Alphab. mss 53, John Bridges to Sir William Trumbull*, 26 Oct. 1705; *Cam. Misc.* xxiii. 40, 43, 45, 54, 61. [7] Boyer, *Anne Annals*, ix. 242; Leics. RO, Finch mss 4950/23, Ward to Nottingham, 2 Nov. 1710; *Cam. Misc.* xxxi. 329; Add. 31139, f. 92.

E. C.

DREWE, Francis (c.1674–1734), of Exeter, and the Grange, Broadhembury, Devon.

EXETER   1713–1734

b. c.1674, 1st s. of Rev. Edward Drewe, canon of Exeter and adn. of Cornw., by Joan, da. and coh. of Anthony Sparrow, bp. of Exeter; nephew of Thomas Drewe*. *educ.* Corpus Christi, Oxf. matric. 2 Aug. 1690, aged 16; M. Temple 1691, called 1697, bencher 1723. *m.* 7 Jan. 1695, Mary, da. of Humphrey Bidgood of Rockbeare, nr.

Exeter, Devon, 2s. 3da. *suc.* fa. 1714.[1]

Freeman, Exeter 1699, Totnes 1712; dep. recorder, Totnes 1709–18.[2]

Drewe's father, a member of the cathedral chapter at Exeter, had inherited the Grange in 1710 after the deaths of his two elder brothers. He was a staunch High Churchman, who was connected with George Granville*, the leader of the Cornish Tories and had campaigned in Exeter in the 1705 election on behalf of the Tackers Sir Edward Seymour, 4th Bt.*, and John Snell I*. Francis Drewe himself had begun his career as a barrister in the city. His father's influence and his own financial assistance to the corporation presumably played a key part in his being returned unopposed in 1713. An inactive Member in his first Parliament, he was given leave of absence for a month on 10 May 1714. The Worsley list described him as a Tory and he continued to represent Exeter in the Tory interest until shortly before his death on 13 Sept. 1734.[3]

[1] Vivian, *Vis. Devon*, 307; Burke, *Commoners*, iv. 624; IGI, Devon. [2] *Trans. Devon Assoc.* lxii. 212. [3] Ibid. 212; *EHR*, xlv. 26–72; *HMC Exeter*, 88; *Gent. Mag.* 1734, p. 511.

E. C.

DREWE, Thomas (c.1635–1707), of Broadhembury, Devon.

DEVON 16 May 1699–1700

b. c.1635, 1st s. of Francis Drewe of Broadhembury by Mary, da. of Richard Walrond of Illbrewers, Som. *educ.* Oriel, Oxf. matric. 1652; L. Inn 1655. *m.* 14 May 1661, Margaret (*d.* 1695), da. of Sir Peter Prideaux, 3rd Bt.†, of Netherton, Devon, 1s. *d.v.p.* 2da. *suc.* fa. 1675.[1]

Sheriff, Devon 1688–9.

A descendant of Edward Drewe (*d.* 1622), a successful lawyer and recorder of London, who purchased substantial estates in Devon including Broadhembury, Thomas Drewe had been appointed sheriff of the county by James II just before the Revolution. He was adopted and returned as knight of the shire in the Tory interest at a by-election in 1699, but made no impact on the House. Neither did he stand for re-election in January 1701 or at any subsequent election. In April 1703, however, his name was added to the Devon lieutenancy. He died on 10 Aug. 1707. The eventual successor to Drewe's estate in 1714 was his nephew, Francis, who the previous year had been elected for Exeter. His daughter Elizabeth was the wife of the Barnstaple MP, Sir Arthur Chichester, 3rd Bt.[2]

[1] Vivian, *Vis. Devon*, 307; Burke, *Commoners*, iv. 673. [2] Moore, *Devon*, 393–4; *CSP Dom.* 1703–4, p. 278.

E. C.

DRYDEN, John (c.1641–1708), of Chesterton, Hunts.

HUNTINGDONSHIRE 1690–1695
 8 Apr. 1699–3 Jan. 1708

b. c.1641, 2nd s. of Sir John Dryden, 2nd Bt.†, of Canons Ashby, Northants. by his 3rd w. Honor, da. and coh. of Sir Robert Bevill† of Chesterton, Hunts. *educ.* Wadham, Oxf. matric. 1651; M. Temple 1654. *unm. suc.* fa. in Chesterton estate c.1658.[1]

Sheriff, Cambs. and Hunts. 1664–5.

Dryden was a first cousin of his namesake the poet, whose affectionate portrait of the Member in his later years, published in the *Fables* (1700), was probably influenced to some degree by gratitude for generous financial assistance afforded in time of need. Dryden was eulogized as an archetypal country squire, enjoying the pleasures of the chase, dispensing charity to the poor, and settling disputes among his neighbours:

How bless'd is he who leads a country life,
Unvex'd with anxious cares and void of strife!
Who studying peace, and shunning civil rage,
Enjoy'd his youth and now enjoys his age.

Dryden was fitted for the part by his ample means, provided by the fortune that had once been his mother's. Succession to the Chesterton estate placed him among the county elite, and during Charles II's reign he served in a variety of local offices – justice of the peace, commissioner for recusants, deputy-lieutenant and sheriff – without, it would seem, aspiring to the highest rank of the country gentleman's *cursus honorum*, a seat in Parliament. He left few clues to his political opinions at this time, though his answers to King James' 'three questions' on the repeal of the Penal Laws and Test Act suggest that in matters of religion he may have shared some of the sentiments of his father, a keen Parliamentarian during the Civil War and a political 'Presbyterian' under the Commonwealth and Protectorate. If returned to James's projected Parliament, he said, he would listen to the arguments on both sides before making up his mind. At the election he would 'give his voice for none but who are eminent for loyalty and wisdom', but in the meantime he welcomed the King's first Declaration of Indulgence,

and is desirous to live friendly with persons of all persuasions, and heartily wishes that all the subjects of our gracious King may approve themselves good Christians by their holy lives and conversations, and then they cannot fail of being loyal to their sovereign and in charity one with another. And he sincerely promises to venture his life and fortune for the preservation of his Majesty's person, crown and dignity, and prays that the King may reign long and happily over the nation.[2]

For all these professions of loyalty Dryden seems to have had few qualms about accepting the Revolution, retaining his place in the county lieutenancy under Lord Manchester. He and Manchester's brother, Hon. Robert Montagu*, were chosen without opposition as knights of the shire in the general election of 1690, after which Lord Carmarthen (Sir Thomas Osborne†) listed him as doubtful but probably a supporter of the Court. Dryden continued to confuse the compilers of parliamentary lists: in April 1691 Robert Harley* marked him as a member of the Country party, but a doubtful one, and two years later Samuel Grascome included him again among the followers of the Court. Neither his sole speech nor his sole tellership in this Parliament concerned an issue of party politics. Instead, both arose from debates on financial or commercial questions, involving, directly or indirectly, the interests of investors, of whom Dryden was one: at some point after the Revolution he advanced £1,000 as a loan to the government; and later he was to be a substantial stockholder in the various institutions of public credit. Thus on 20 Jan. 1693 he offered a clause to be added to the million fund bill 'to make void any grant of moneys arising by the Act upon the death of any nominee' to the tontine; and on 6 Jan. 1694 he acted as a teller against going into committee on the petition of the interloping East India merchants. His absence from the county election in 1695, when he was in effect replaced by the Tory Anthony Hammond*, led one local historian to believe that he was himself a high-flyer, but it seems more likely that he had temporarily grown tired of Parliament and preferred to devote himself to rural pursuits. Four years later he returned to the House, after a by-election in 1699, and apparently as a supporter of the Country party. As such he was idealized in his cousin's verse:

> Well-born and wealthy; wanting no support,
> You steer betwixt the Country and Court:
> Nor gratify whate'er the great desire,
> Nor grudging give, what public needs require.

The poet admitted, however, that in this sketch he had 'not only drawn the features of my worthy kinsman, but have also given my own opinion of what an Englishman in Parliament ought to be', and his reference elsewhere to the Member's 'sprightly wit' suggests at least some exaggeration. Subsequent parliamentary lists indicate a fairly consistent inclination towards the Whigs. Following the November 1701 election, Dryden was listed by Robert Harley as a Whig. Then in the autumn of 1704 he was forecast as likely to oppose the Tack, and in the division of 28 Nov. he did not vote for it. Classed as 'Low Church' in an analysis of the new Parliament in 1705, to which he was once more returned unopposed for the county, he voted for the Court candidate in the division on the Speaker on 25 Oct. 1705, and in a list from early 1708 was put down as a Whig. His parliamentary activity at this time seems to have focused on private and county business: in January–February 1704 he managed a bill to enable the Treasury to make a composition for the debt of one John Ferrar, surety for a defaulting receiver-general for Cambridgeshire; and in November of the following session he was appointed to the committee investigating various petitions from Huntingdonshire, Bedfordshire and Norfolk against the local duties imposed on coal imported at King's Lynn, reporting from the committee and being first-named on 3 Feb. 1705 to a drafting committee for a bill to reduce coal duties.[3]

Dryden died at Chesterton on 3 Jan. 1708 and was buried there. In his will he constituted his nephew Robert Pigott* his heir (though not to Chesterton, which was entailed, but to the other property in Cambridgeshire, Huntingdonshire and Warwickshire), in preference to Dryden's own childless elder brother, 'being sensible that 'twill be unkindness to load him with greater estate'. His personalty, including considerable 'stock in London', was held to be sufficient to support legacies of between £12,000 and £13,500. Some £800 was reserved for charitable purposes, to be administered at the discretion of the municipal authorities in various Huntingdonshire and Northamptonshire towns. The prodigious benefactions, amounting to some £16,000, which are said to have earned him renown in his county as a philanthropist, must therefore have occurred within his own lifetime.[4]

[1] *Vis. Northants.* (Harl. Soc. lxxxvii), 67; Bridges, *Northants.* i. 226; *VCH Hunts.* iii. 140. [2] Dryden, *Fables* (1700), 93–101; *Letters of John Dryden* ed. Ward, 112; *DNB* (Dryden, John); *Cal. Treas. Bks.* iv. 790; M. F. Keeler, *Long Parl.* 160–1; D. Underdown, *Pride's Purge*, 218; Duckett, *Penal Laws and Test Act* (1883), 69. [3] *CSP Dom.* 1700–2, p. 254; Northants. RO, Dryden (Canons Ashby) mss D(CA)37, Exchequer order, 1703; Luttrell Diary, 378; *VCH Hunts.* ii. 34; Dryden, 98, 100; *Dryden Letters*, 120, 124. [4] *VCH Hunts.* ii. 34; iii. 140, 143; PCC 35, 105 Barrett.

D. W. H.

DUCIE MORETON, Matthew *see* **MORETON**

DUCKETT, George (1684–1732), of Hartham House, Corsham, Wilts. and Dewlish, Dorset.[1]

CALNE 1705–1710, 1722–19 Feb. 1723

b. 19 Feb. 1684, 1st s. of Lionel Duckett† of Hartham House by Martha, da. of Samuel Ashe† of Langley

Burrell, Wilts., sis. of Joseph Ashe*; bro. of William Duckett†. *educ.* Trinity, Oxf. 1700; M. Temple 1703. *m.* settlement 28 Mar. 1711 (with £3,000), Grace (*d.* 1755), da. and h. of Thomas Skinner of Dewlish, 6s. (1 *d.v.p.*) 3da. (1 *d.v.p.*). *suc.* fa. 1693.[2]

Commr. excise 1723–*d.*

Duckett's family had been established in Wiltshire since the 16th century. As lord of the manor of Calne, the youthful Duckett was thus assured of a seat there when he came of age in 1705. He stood as a Whig, despite a sharp contest which created 'a great tumult' in the town. Though marked as a 'Churchman' in one analysis of the new Parliament, his return was accounted a 'gain' for the Whigs by Lord Sunderland (Charles, Lord Spencer*), and he voted on 25 Oct. 1705 for the Court candidate in the division on the Speaker. It would appear that Defoe had recommended him to the ministry for appointment to some local office (as a means of dealing a blow to the Tory interest in Wiltshire) but unavailingly: at least nothing had been done by May 1706, when Defoe complained to Robert Harley* about it.[3]

Duckett spoke on the proceedings against Charles Caesar* on 19 Dec. 1705, probably in favour of the House taking action against Caesar for his remarks during the debate on the regency bill, and was recorded as having voted on the Court side in the proceedings on the 'place clause' of the bill on 18 Feb. 1706. His only other action of note occurred on 6 Mar. when he reported from the committee examining a petition exposing abuses in the administration of the Fleet prison. In the next session he acted as teller on 5 Dec. 1706 for receiving a petition from the six clerks in Chancery, and presented a highway bill relating to Calne which failed to reach the statute book (Duckett owned the mortgage of the turnpike at Calne). He was more active in the 1707–8 session. He reintroduced the Calne highway bill and this time piloted it through the House. He was also named to draft a bill to end the embargo on the export of white woollen cloth, a measure of interest to his constituents. He acted as a teller on four occasions: for adjourning debate on the report of the committee investigating the publication of *An Argument Proving that . . . Man May Be Translated into . . . Eternal Life, without Passing through Death . . .*, written by his friend John Asgill* (9 Dec.); again for the adjournment of a later debate on the book (18 Dec.), in an unsuccessful attempt to prevent Asgill's expulsion from the House; on 12 Dec., with Robert Walpole II, on an additional clause offered to the land tax bill; and on 9 Feb. 1708, on an adjournment motion to put off consideration of a private bill in favour of Francis Annesley*. He was listed as a Whig in an analysis of the House in early 1708.[4]

Returned again at Calne after another contest in 1708, Duckett successfully prosecuted in March 1709 a complaint of breach of privilege against an agent of the former Tory MP Sir George Hungerford, for delivering 'declarations in ejectment' to his tenants at Calne, though he was unable to secure the inclusion in the complaint of Hungerford himself. He voted for the naturalization of the Palatines in 1709, and for the impeachment of Dr Sacheverell in 1710. He contested Calne once more as a Whig in the 1710 election, which cost him at least £58 in legal fees. This time, however, there was a double return, and the Tory majority in the new House decided against him and his Whig partner.[5]

Out of Parliament, Duckett retired to the country to live with his father-in-law in Dorset. As a minor pamphleteer and satirist, he had become a familiar figure in Whig literary circles. He was a close friend of the poet Edmund Smith, and a regular correspondent and collaborator of Thomas Burnet, and was thus on the fringes of the coterie presided over by Joseph Addison*. To Tories, on the other hand, he was little more than a 'rattle-pate'. He devoted his time to his books and to composing occasional pieces of political satire in the Whig cause. These were written, according to his friend Burnet, 'not . . . to turn a penny but to enlighten the darkened part of the British nation'. They included an answer to Swift's *Windsor Prophecy*, 'A Prophecy of Merlin's', printed in the *Protestant Post Boy* in May 1712; a squib on the so-called 'Band-Box Plot', 'A Great Plot . . . or, Mine Ar[s]e in a Ban-Box', published in the *Flying Post* in the following November; possibly a ballad on the same theme; *Dr D[avena]nt's Prophecys* (December 1712), in which he skilfully applied against the present Tory ministry arguments drawn from the early writings of Charles Davenant*; *The Plotter Found Out . . .* (after Nov. 1713); and *John Bull's Last Will and Testament*, in 1713, an attack on the peace, and on the ministers' supposed Jacobitism, in which he displayed a particular concern with the likely damage which the terms would inflict upon the woollen manufactures, a staple industry of his own borough of Calne. There were also other projects which never reached print, including a 'History' which Burnet felt ran the risk of a libel prosecution. He freely gave advice and historical examples to Burnet, who confessed, 'I would not have anything of mine come out without a dash or two of honest George's pen'. Whether or not Duckett wrote for money, there is evidence that his finances were under some strain after 1711: his lease of Hartham and removal to his father-in-law's, where he stayed until 1714, and his decision not to contest the next parliamentary election. Burnet wrote to him in November 1712:

> I must own I think George is in the right to let elections rub on, for, by God, none that stand against a court but are soon either ruined or rascals; the latter my friend can never be, and the former I hope he never will be; and therefore I am glad he does not think of throwing his money into a kennel.[6]

Duckett seems to have given his interest to two other Whigs in 1713, who were well beaten by the Tories. After the succession of George I he entertained some thought of putting up again himself – he had by now returned to the family home at Hartham – but in the end settled for bringing in another Whig instead. When he finally returned to Parliament in 1722, he lasted there less than a year, accepting a post as a commissioner of excise, with a salary of £800 p.a., and thereby disqualifying himself in February 1723. His writing continued, often in collaboration with Burnet, with whom he wrote some verses to the Duke of Marlborough (John Churchill†) and, in 1715, *A Second Tale of a Tub*, intended as a satire on Robert Harley, now Lord Oxford, who was variously characterized as 'Robert Powell the puppet-show man' and 'Oliver Volpone'. But he and Burnet were best known for *Homerides*, their attack on, and parody of, Pope's translation of Homer, earning them a place in the *Dunciad*, in which, in its first edition, Duckett was declared to be 'famed . . . for pious passion to the youth'. Duckett's writings also adumbrate his evident anti-clericalism, for although his father had urged that he be brought up 'in the protestant religion according to the orthodox reformed episcopal Church of England', he was later described as 'an inveterate enemy to the clergy', while a fellow of Oriel College, Oxford, suggested that 'no clergyman will keep him company'. The preface of his *Summary of Religious Houses* (1717), in which work he was partly assisted by Burnet, is strongly critical of monastic excesses.[7]

Duckett died on 6 Oct. 1732 without making a will, and administration of his estate was granted to his widow, then of St. Clement Danes, Westminster. His heir, Lionel, entered into possession of the estates in 1742 but had to convey lands worth £45,000 to cover debts and settle portions for his six brothers and sisters. One of Duckett's sons, Thomas, later sat for Calne.[8]

[1] Unless otherwise stated, this biography is based upon *Letters of Burnet to Duckett* ed. Nichol Smith. [2] *Wilts. Arch. Mag.* xxiv. 218; G. F. Duckett, *Duchetiana*, 40, 46–48, 66, 79. [3] *VCH Wilts.* v. 210–11; Duckett, 59; J. Aubrey, *Wilts. Colls.* 32; *Defoe Letters*, 111, 116. [4] *Cam. Misc.*, xxiii. 54; Duckett, 60. [5] Aubrey, *Wilts. Colls.* 83; Duckett, 46–48, 60, 66, 79. [6] Duckett, 59–60; *Hearne Colls.* vii. 337; *Poems on Affairs of State* ed. Ellis, vii. 576–81; *John Bull's Last Will and Testament* (1713), 16–24. [7] *A Second Tale of a Tub* (1715) passim; Duckett, 59; *Hearne Colls.* 337. [8] Prob. 6/108, f. 208v; Duckett, 48, note 20aa.

D. W. H.

DUDLEY, Joseph (1647–1720), of Cowes, I.o.W. and Roxbury, Massachusetts.[1]

NEWTOWN I.o.W. 1701 (Dec.)–1702

b. 23 Sept. 1647, 4th s. of Thomas Dudley of Roxbury, gov. Massachusetts, by his 2nd w. Catherine Dighton, wid. of Samuel Hackburn of Roxbury. *educ.* free sch., Cambridge, Mass.; Harvard c.1662–5. *m.* 1688, Rebecca, da. of Edward Tyng, judge and member of ct. of assts., Massachusetts, 8s. (6 *d.v.p.*) 5da. (1 *d.v.p.*).[2]

Freeman, Massachusetts Bay Co. 1672; member, gen. ct. Massachusetts 1673–6, ct. of assts. 1676–84; agent for Massachusetts in Eng. 1682–3; v.-adm. New England 1685; pres. Massachusetts, New Hampshire, Maine and Narragansett May–Dec. 1686; member, council of Massachusetts 1686–9; judge of superior ct. New England 1687–9; pres. of council and c.j. New York 1690–2; commr. inquiring into complaints against Gov. Sir William Phipps 1694; gov. and capt.-gen. Massachusetts and New Hampshire 1701–15; capt.-gen. Rhode Island and Narragansett 1702–15, v.-adm. 1702–15.[3]

Lt.-gov. I.o.W. 1694–1701; freeman, Newport 1694; dep. mayor, Newtown, I.o.W. 1694.[4]

Dudley's father, the son of a sea captain, migrated to Massachusetts for religious reasons, rising to be governor of the province. Dudley himself held office in Massachusetts as early as 1673 and his role in colonial government was rather more significant than his short time in the English House of Commons. In 1689, having been imprisoned in Boston on suspicion of opposing the Prince of Orange, his case was considered in England and dismissed. Dudley then rose to become chief justice in New York in which capacity in 1691 he presided at the trial for treason of Jacob Leisler, who had led an uprising in New York in 1690 against the administration appointed by James II. Leisler was attainted and executed. In 1692 New York's new governor removed Dudley from his offices for non-residence, claiming he was 'very unacceptable to the people'. Dudley returned to Boston and in 1693 came to England, hoping to use the influence of his friends to secure another colonial office, preferably the governorship of Massachusetts. His wife and family remained in New England.[5]

In England Dudley gained a new patron in the

person of Lord Cutts (John*), and when Cutts was made governor of the Isle of Wight in 1693, he appointed Dudley as his deputy. Their arrangement was that Cutts supported Dudley for a colonial governorship and in return Dudley would handle the governor's personal affairs in the Isle of Wight and act as his electoral manager for the three parliamentary boroughs on the island, while Cutts was away with his regiment on campaign. In January 1694 Dudley had been appointed one of the commissioners to investigate complaints against the governor of Massachusetts, Sir William Phipps. Giving evidence before the Board of Trade, he affirmed that Phipps 'had not done one good thing since he had been governor'. When Phipps was recalled to London the following year to answer the charges, Dudley had him arrested in an action for £20,000. Before anything was done, Phipps died. Immediately, Dudley, aided by Cutts, tried to secure the office for himself, and on 21 Feb. 1695 it was reported that he 'stood fairest' to succeed. However, the Massachusetts agents in England, aided by Sir Henry Ashurst*, thwarted their plans by supporting attempts by Jacob Leisler's son to have his father's attainder reversed. When the bill came before the Commons in April 1695 Dudley had to give evidence before the committee, which was chaired by Ashurst, thus drawing attention to his part in the trial. After the bill was passed on 30 Apr. it was reported that Dudley was 'not so much talked of to be governor'. Eventually Lord Bellomont (Richard Coote*) was appointed.[6]

Cutts continued to encourage Dudley, writing on 20 Sept. 1696 to congratulate him on the successful handling of affairs at Newtown and Yarmouth:

> If you can carry the point of these two corporations, I'll improve it so much to your advantage to the King and everybody else (and I promise you to do it) that it shall be the best card you ever played ... Whatever expenses you are at (public or private) as far as £200 goes, I'll willingly repay you immediately at my return. This will be a matter of greater moment than you imagine, and you'll have a large share in the advantage of it.

On 1 Apr. 1698, however, Cutts complained of Dudley's neglect, writing:

> Your personal civilities are most certainly your own, and dispose on 'em how much you please; provided you trouble me no more if fortune should chance to smile on me, than you do now, she seems at least to do otherwise. That which I have just reason to complain of is your real neglect of the King's service in your station. For if I neither see nor hear of a lieutenant-governor in a week, I would fain know (when so many things are to be discovered now the spring comes on) what you are paid for. You have the 4s. per diem which I give you gratis; which no other governor ever had (I mean the captain at Cowes, which captain always took some notice of me) and you have 2s. per diem out of my own pocket; both which you know I can stop when I please; and really I can employ 'em better if you treat your employment so remissly.

The quarrel had been patched up by June 1698 when Cutts was pressing Dudley's claim to the governorship of Maryland, but James Vernon I* informed the Duke of Shrewsbury: 'I think the person he recommends is none of the fittest, and those employments at least should not be carried by solicitation only.' Dudley did not get the office.[7]

By 1700 Dudley was experiencing financial difficulties and on 23 Dec. wrote to his son, Paul, who had joined him in England:

> I see no way for my own return [to New England] and think it absolutely necessary that you return this year. I shall lose what I have there and my respects and hopes and family, for want of a head; nor shall I be able to support myself and you here much longer, but shall fall into contempt, and that will be what I cannot bear and live ... If my arrears fail me, I must sell my land under my feet to pay my debts, and that will please those in New England, who do not love my name.

The death of Lord Bellomont the following year at last saw the realization of his hopes, and on 18 June 1701 he was appointed governor of Massachusetts Bay and New Hampshire. He resigned as lieutenant-governor of the Isle of Wight, but before he could take up his new appointment his old enemy, Sir Henry Ashurst, intervened by presenting a memorial against him to the lords justices. When the matter was heard in the Privy Council, the charges were dismissed and Dudley received his commission as governor of Massachusetts in December. While the decision was pending Cutts had secured Dudley's return at Newtown in the November 1701 election. He was listed as a Tory in Robert Harley's* analysis of the new House of Commons, but did not involve himself much in parliamentary proceedings. William III's death delayed his departure for New England, but Anne duly renewed his commission and he sailed for Boston in April 1702.[8]

Dudley's term as governor of New England was somewhat controversial, and his support of the 1711 Quebec expedition was enthusiastic but apparently ineffective. However, he survived several complaints of maladministration from his opponents, only being removed from the governorship after the accession of George I. He died on 2 Apr. 1720.[9]

[1] Unless otherwise stated, this biography is based on E. Kimball, *Public Life of Joseph Dudley*. [2] D. Dudley, *Dudley Gens. and Fam. Recs.* 83–84; G. Adlard, *Sutton-Dudleys of Eng. and Mass.* 61–94;

HMC Lords, n.s. v. 80–81. ³*CSP Col.* 1681–5, pp. 410, 587; 1685–8, pp. 98, 117, 375; 1689–92, pp. 322, 397–8, 699, 714; 1701, pp. 304, 670–1; 1714–15, pp. 512–13; *CSP Dom.* 1690–1, p. 128; 1700–2, pp. 365. ⁴*CSP Dom.* 1694–5, p. 96; *Mass. Hist. Soc. Colls.* ser. 6, iii. 512–13. ⁵*Dict. Am. Biog.* v. 481–3; Adlard, 61–94; *CSP Col.* 1681–5, pp. 587, 610, 628, 669; 1689–92, pp. 33, 102, 111, 206, 246, 251, 322, 397, 612, 699, 714; 1693–6, pp. 20, 141; *Mass. Hist. Soc. Colls.* ser. 6, iii. 502–3. ⁶*Mass. Hist. Soc. Procs.* ser. 2, ii. 172–98; *CSP Dom.* 1695, p. 312; *CSP Col.* 1693–6, pp. 224, 295. ⁷*Mass. Hist. Soc. Procs.* ser. 2, ii. 184, 188–9; *Vernon–Shrewsbury Letters,* ii. 93, 96, 101–2. ⁸*CSP Col.* 1701, p. 610. ⁹*CSP Col.* 1706–7, pp. 234–5; Adlard, 81; *Walker Expedition to Quebec* (Navy Recs. Soc. xciv), 6, 105, 107, 226–8.

P. W.

DUDLEY, Sir Matthew, 2nd Bt. (1661–1721), of Clopton, Northants. and St. James's Street, Westminster.

NORTHAMPTON   1702–1705
HUNTINGDONSHIRE   1713–1715

b. 1 Oct. 1661, 1st s. of Sir William Dudley, 1st Bt.†, of Clopton by his 3rd w. Mary, da. and h. of Sir Paul Pindar of London. *m.* 8 Oct. 1693 (with £12,000), Lady Mary (*d.* 1735), da. of Henry O'Brien*, 7th Earl of Thomond [I], 4s. (3 *d.v.p.*) 1da. *suc.* fa. as 2nd Bt. 18 Sept. 1670.¹

Sheriff, Northants. 1683–4.

FRS 1703.

Commr. customs 1706–12, 1714–*d.*²

The manor of Clopton, Northants., had been in the keeping of Dudley's family since the 14th century. His father had been rewarded with a baronetcy at the Restoration for services to the Royalist cause, a distinction which elevated the family to the forefront of the Northamptonshire gentry. Although Sir William's death in 1670 imposed a long minority, it was an indication of the family's standing that eight months before coming of age in 1682, Sir Matthew was added to the commission of the peace; at the beginning of 1683 he graduated to a deputy-lieutenancy and towards the end of the year, to the shrievalty. In the election of March 1685 he contested Higham Ferrers, though without success. His marriage in 1693 to a daughter of the Earl of Thomond brought him considerable financial benefit. He appears to have been amenable in some degree to James II's religious policies, answering the three questions on the Penal Laws, 'consents, but to others denied', and was entered in December 1687 as one of the deputy-lieutenants to be 'offered to the King'.³

From 1687 Dudley became involved in a project for mining newly discovered deposits of copper ore and other minerals in Massachusetts. A recent visitation by New Englanders had brought over specimens, no doubt with the intention of encouraging English merchants to open trade. Within a short time almost £100,000 was subscribed by merchants and others to found a company with exclusive mining rights, and in March 1687 the subscribers, headed by Dudley, addressed the King for a charter of incorporation. The venture soon broadened to include production of the full range of ships' stores, 'to [the] increase of trade and revenue of the crown'. How Dudley first became involved in such a project is not clear, but, still only in his twenties, he was designated the company's deputy-governor. The Revolution prevented the charter from passing the seal, and in March 1689 Dudley led his fellow subscribers in a renewal of their application, only to be told by the secretary of state, Lord Shrewsbury, that it would not be considered until the King returned from Ireland. When in August 1690 another group of subscribers, represented by (Sir) Joseph Herne*, obtained a patent for similar purposes, Dudley's protest met with a ruling from the attorney-general in July 1691 that there appeared 'no inconsistency between the pretensions of the parties'. But friction between the two merchant cliques culminated in a hearing of their respective claims before the lords of Trade in May 1692, after which Herne's company appears to have ceased to operate. A draft charter incorporating Dudley and his associates into a joint-stock company to work mines and provide naval stores was sent for the attorney-general's scrutiny in May 1693, and in October it was considered by the lords of the Treasury. Strong representations against the proposal had been made by the New England agents, led by Sir Henry Ashurst*, and the projectors were unable to persuade the governors of Massachusetts, Connecticut and Rhode Island that their project would have anything but a ruinous effect on them. The colonists argued that their land rights being limited to 'bare possession' would be threatened by 'so wealthy a body' with superior rights of possession as defined by charter. Although there soon followed a recommendation by the lord chief justice and the attorney-general that the projected company be granted its charter, the scheme lay dormant until July 1696 when the subscribers, headed once more by Dudley, presented their case to the lords of Trade expressing a readiness 'to receive such encouragements as you think meet', but he pursued the project no further.⁴

Dudley boldly displayed his Tory colours in preparations for the Northamptonshire elections of 1701–2. In January 1701 he assumed responsibility for rallying voters in his neighbourhood in support of the Tory–Whig compromise agreed by the gentry, telling the Tory candidate, Sir Justinian Isham, 4th Bt.*, that he would 'spur them up a little' if a poll was necessary.

At the second election, in November, he was perturbed by Isham's seeming obliviousness to the divided state of opinion within the county and his delay in giving notice to Dudley's own locale of his intention to stand jointly with another Tory, Thomas Cartwright*. Then in the spring of 1702 he took a resolute stance in favour of the Tory interest, brimming with indignation at the 'base insinuations . . . on all the Queen's actions' contained in the county address on the accession drawn up under the eye of the Whig chairman of the quarter sessions. In May, having heard that the stamp office commissioners would probably be removed, Dudley requested in vain that Isham use his influence with Secretary Nottingham (Daniel Finch†) or Lord Marlborough (John Churchill†) to recommend his brother for one of the vacancies. At what stage prior to the 1702 election he offered himself for the borough of Northampton is unclear, but against all expectations he and another Tory, Bartholomew Tate*, comfortably defeated the Whig candidates.[5]

Dudley's election was naturally viewed by Lord Spencer (Charles*) as a 'loss' to the Whigs. In the first months of the 1702 Parliament Dudley emerged as an active figure in the House, managing a great deal of minor legislative business. He gained early notoriety from his supervision, between November 1702 and February 1703, of the Tory bill to allow an additional year for taking the abjuration oath, chairing the committee of the whole on the bill on 21 Jan. 1703. At consideration of the Lords' amendments on 13 Feb., Dudley served as a teller in favour of the new Whiggish clause to bar from reappointment those deprived of their offices for refusing the oath. His agreement with the Whigs on this issue marks the beginning of his move away from Toryism. During the early weeks of 1703 Sir Justinian Isham was alerted to the fact that Dudley had been covertly building up a rival 'interest' among leading politicians in London, a rumour which Dudley was understandably anxious to scotch, though his efforts in relation to the abjuration bill leave no doubt of his ambition at this time to make a name for himself.[6]

As the 1703–4 session commenced, Dudley told on 15 Nov. 1703 against the motion to consider the Queen's Speech. In mid-February 1704 he managed a bill to clear the Sword Blade Company of £18,864, certified by the commissioners of accounts to have been an overcharge in its purchase of forfeited estates in Ireland, after which he attended to a private estate bill, begun in the Lords, for selling land in Northamptonshire. On 21 Feb. he told against committing the bill for the encouragement of manufactures and 'setting the poor at work', and on 3 Mar. reported the bill to discharge insolvent debtors who would serve in the army or navy. He chaired a committee appointed on 22 Feb. to investigate arrears of interest on the malt lottery tickets, reporting on 7 Mar., and in mid-March took charge of another private bill.

In the next session Dudley chaired the committee of 11 Nov. 1704 on expiring laws, and later supervised the resulting bill through its stages. In October he had been forecast as a probable opponent of the Tack and did not vote for it in the division on 28 Nov. On 9 Dec. he reported from the committee considering the arrears of £1,050 claimed by the administrators of the 'fixed and moving hospitals' attending the army in Ireland in 1690. He was one of the chief promoters of a bill to improve the regulation of the night watch, which failed after its first reading in January 1705. On 3 Feb. he reported from a second-reading committee on the interest due to the holders of malt lottery tickets, who in the previous session had failed to obtain legislative relief; on the 12th he was teller for an amendment to a supply bill; and on the 21st against the addition to another supply bill of a clause to exempt naval stores.

Towards the end of February Dudley made it known that he would not contest Northampton in the forthcoming general election, expecting instead to be brought in at Higham Ferrers by the outgoing Member, Hon. Thomas Watson Wentworth*. However, Watson Wentworth retained the seat and Dudley did not re-enter Parliament until 1713. By 1705 Dudley had completed his transmogrification from Tory to Whig, and in the election of that year voted for the Whig candidates in the Northamptonshire contest. In the earliest stages of electioneering he was briefly considered a possible Whig candidate. His apostasy earned him appointment in May 1706 as a customs commissioner with a salary of £1,000 p.a., joining a board that was politically mixed. His attachment to Lord Treasurer Godolphin (Sidney†), which was mentioned in 1711 by his friend Jonathan Swift, may have been a result of the appointment, or may have predated it.[7] In 1709 Dudley's sympathy with the plight of the Palatine refugees resulted in his becoming a trustee in June of the brief to oversee their settlement. He even accommodated two Palatine families for a short time on his own estates. The Tory landslide of October 1710 made it unlikely that Dudley would retain his customs post and there were reports in December and in January 1711 that he and several other commissioners were about to be replaced. He prevailed on the Earl of Peterborough, the lord lieutenant of Northamptonshire, with whom he was on good terms, to intercede with Robert Harley*, which

Peterborough did, requesting Harley to see Dudley that he might 'beg . . . to be reckoned one of your servants and [I] believe he is worthy of that favour'. Either as the result of such a meeting, or more simply because he could not be dispensed with immediately, Dudley was kept on. His position was none the less tenuous and he several times unburdened himself on the subject during meetings with Swift. In March, Swift wrote that Dudley was: 'one of those that must lose his employment whenever the great shake comes; and I can't contribute to keep him in, though I have dropped words in his favour to the ministry; but he has been too violent a Whig and friend to the Lord Treasurer [Godolphin] to be kept in'. Calling on 'poor Sir Matthew Dudley' in July, Swift noted 'he is in hopes of continuing: I would not tell him the bad news, but advised him to prepare for the worst'. Dismissal did not come, however, until the middle of January 1712. A month later Swift observed that Dudley 'affects a good heart' but reported that he continued to talk 'in the extremity of Whiggery, which was always his principle, tho[ugh] he was gentle a little while he kept in employ[me]nt'.[8]

Dudley returned to the Commons in 1713 as a knight of the shire, having successfully contested Huntingdonshire through the support of the 2nd Duke of Montagu, whose seat at Boughton was very near his own. He was identified on the Worsley list unequivocally as a Whig, and on 18 Mar. 1714 voted against the motion that led to the expulsion of Richard Steele. On 7 Apr. he told against committing a bill for tightening existing laws to prevent wool smuggling, and, on 6 May, on the Whig side in the disputed Colchester election. During May and June he steered through the House a bill for reimbursing William Paterson for his 'expense and pains' in the service of the Company of Scotland, and another for repairing the road between Royston in Hertfordshire and Wandsford Bridge in Huntingdonshire. Early in November 1714, following the Hanoverian succession, he was reinstated in the customs commission and was thus obliged to quit his parliamentary seat. He died in harness on 14 Apr. 1721, 'about noon', having directed in his will that his body 'be buried among my ancestors in the usual burying place in the church of Clopton'. The baronetcy became extinct on the death of his only surviving son in 1764.[9]

[1] PCC 107 Buckingham; Add. 32500, f. 151; 24120, f. 274; Baker, *Northampton*, i. 21. [2] *Cal. Treas. Bks.* xx. 655; xxvi. 118; xxix. 145. [3] *VCH Northants*. iii. 126; *CSP Dom.* 1682, p. 78; Jan.–June 1683, p. 2; *The Commons 1660–90*, ii. 240; Duckett, *Penal Laws and Test Act* (1883), pp. 84, 275. [4] Egerton 3340, ff. 199–202; *CSP Col.* 1689–92, pp. 612, 678, 701, 751; 1693–6, pp. 75, 95, 158, 165, 168, 242, 246, 253, 258, 266, 297, 307; 1696–7, pp. 42–43; *CSP Dom.* 1691–2, p. 364; *Cal. Treas. Bks.* x. 425. [5] Northants. RO, Isham mss IC 2708–9, 2719, 2721–2, Dudley to Isham, 20, 26 Dec. 1700, 18 Nov. 1701, 21 Apr., 11 May 1702; IC 2720, Edward Stratford to same, 18 Apr. 1702; Add. 29568, f. 114. [6] E. G. Forrester, *Northants. Elections and Electioneering 1695–1832*, p. 31. [7] Isham mss IC 4987, Edward Morpott to Isham, 24 Feb. 1704–5; *Northants. Past and Present*, vi. 262; *Northants. Poll Bks*. 1702–1831, p. 46; *Cal. Treas. Bks.* xx. 655; *Swift Stella* ed. Davis, 226. [8] *Post Boy*, 30 June–2 July 1709; *EHR*, lxxxii. 477; *HMC Downshire*, i. 891; Luttrell, *Brief Relation*, vi. 664, 717; Add. 70409, Ld. Peterborough to Robert Harley, 5 Jan. 1710–11; *Swift Stella*, 68–69, 118, 159, 226, 312, 317, 337, 403, 410, 484; *Post Man*, 19–22 Jan. 1712. [9] *HMC Buccleuch*, i. 359–60; *Cal. Treas. Bks.* xxix. 145; *The Gen.* n.s. iii. 139; PCC 107 Buckingham.

A.A.H.

DUFF, Alexander (1657–1726), of Drummuir, Banff.

INVERNESS BURGHS 1708–1710

b. 1657, 1st s. of William Duff, MP [S], by his 1st wife Christian, da. of Alexander Duff of Kinloss, Elgin. *educ.* ?1673 Aberdeen Univ. (King's Coll.). *m.* 1684, Katherine (*d.* 1758), da. and h. of Adam Duff of Drummuir, 7s. 7da. *suc.* fa. 1715.[1]

MP [S] Inverness 1702–7.
Collector of customs, Inverness 1703.[2]
Provost, Inverness 1706–9, 1712–15.[3]

Duff's father was a wealthy merchant of Inverness, who made his fortune by exporting fish to the Continent and, in return, importing foreign commodities. He was also an excise farmer under the Cromwellian regime and, after paying a fine of £1,800 at the Restoration, was appointed a collector of excise in 1662. Prominent in local affairs as provost of Inverness, he also made his mark in national politics as a commissioner from Inverness to the convention of royal burghs and as the town's representative in the Scottish parliament of 1681, where he served as a lord of the Articles. At the Revolution he took the Williamite side and was rewarded with appointment as King's chamberlain of Ross and Ardmeanach, and farmer of the inland excise for the northern shires. He was then commissioned to purchase supplies for the army, offsetting his costs against the funds under his jurisdiction.[4]

Alexander Duff participated fully in his father's business, both in its mercantile and revenue aspects, frequently acting as his representative. In 1684 the estate of Drummuir was effectively purchased for him by his father, who agreed to clear all outstanding debts as a condition of his son's marriage to its orphaned heiress. This commitment to Drummuir did not, however, extend to the previous owner's widow, who was harshly treated. Not only was she a second wife and not the bride's mother, but she was also an interloping Englishwoman. Denied her due, she sought redress in the court of session, where she received some compensation (being 'a stranger and in a starving condition') but thereafter departed permanently for England. After acquiring Drummuir, Duff continued to participate in the family's commercial activities, but also gradually assumed some of the airs of a landed gentleman. This transformation did not go unremarked, Lord Lovat commenting on one occasion that 'Drummuir's words are rather like Louis XIV than like William Duff's son'.[5]

In many respects Duff's political career mirrored that of his father, not least in its demonstrable trimming. The elder Duff had accommodated himself successively to the Protectorate, the Restoration and the Revolution, whereas the younger supported the Revolution, opposed the Union, served briefly at Westminster, drifted towards Jacobitism and finally settled peacefully under the Hanoverian regime. Also like his father, Duff began his political career as a commissioner to the convention of royal burghs and went on to serve as provost of Inverness. He entered the Scottish parliament in 1702 and joined the cavalier wing of the Country party. He voted in favour of the Duke of Hamilton's anti-succession motion in 1704 and continued in opposition up to and including the Union debates of 1706–7. On the latter question his conduct was marked by a certain independence, as evinced by his support of the Court over such issues as the communication of trade and the preservation of the rights of the royal burghs. But on the major divisions over the Union he was in opposition and therefore excluded from the slate of representatives to the first Parliament of Great Britain.[6]

Duff showed no particular eagerness to serve in Parliament and only stood for the Inverness district of burghs in 1708 after it became clear that the candidacy of Hon. Charles Rosse* would be unsuccessful. Prior to his departure for Westminster, he hosted a lavish feast at Inverness, at which participants drank the health of the Queen, Prince George and the Duke of Marlborough (John Churchill†), toasting also 'prosperity to the Protestant religion and success to her Majesty's arms by sea and land'. In reports of the election, Duff's political allegiance was claimed by Lords Ross and Seafield, both of whom predicted his support for the ministry of Lord Godolphin (Sidney†). In fact, having been returned essentially on his own interest, Duff pursued an independent line. His sympathies were Tory, grounded in both a strong episcopalian faith and his previous association with fellow anti-unionists such as George Lockhart*, who maintained that Duff adhered 'constantly in all votes to the Tories'. No speech by him is known and the evidence of the Journals is minimal. Local economic interests explain his nomination on 16 Dec. to the drafting committee for a bill to encourage the fishery. His only recorded vote, however, contradicts Lockhart's assessment, since Duff was listed as voting for the impeachment of Dr Sacheverell in 1710. His inclusion on this list may simply be an error, but it is also possible that he voted in support of government for self-interested motives.[7]

Duff did not stand in 1710, giving way to another Tory, George Mackenzie, and is not known to have stood at any subsequent election. During the rebellion of 1715, he allegedly connived at the delivery of Inverness Castle into the hands of the Jacobites, who were led by his son-in-law Lachlan Mackintosh of Moy. Duff's wife was a strong supporter of the Stuart cause and her influence was probably crucial. The recapture of Inverness by government forces in November did not result in any known repercussions against Duff and he continued to live prosperously and peacefully until his death on 22 Aug. 1726. Drummuir passed nominally to his eldest son, Robert, who was, nevertheless, deemed too weak-minded to exercise actual control, which remained with Duff's widow.[8]

[1] A. and H. Tayler, *Bk. of the Duffs*, ii. 355, 360, 367, 380; *Recs. Univ. and King's Coll. Aberdeen* (Spalding Club), 493; *Hist. Scot. Parl.* 207–8. [2] Tayler, 367. [3] Ibid. 376. [4] *Hist. Scot. Parl.* 208; Tayler, 356–66. [5] *Reg. PC Scotland*, 1686–9, pp. 580, 587; 1683–4, p. 327; Tayler, 345–53, 366, 371; *Scot. Hist. Soc.* ser. 2, ix. 18, 23, 31, 40, 43. [6] Info. from Dr P. W. J. Riley on members of Scot. parl; Boyer, *Anne Annals*, iii. app. 42; P. W. J. Riley, *Union*, 333; *Lockhart Pprs.* i. 36, 166, 182, 186, 301. [7] Add. 9102, ff. 68–69; 28055 f. 418; *Edinburgh Courant*, 8–10 Sept. 1708. [8] A. and H. Tayler, *Jacobites of Aberdeen. and Banff.* in 1715, 49–51; *More Culloden Pprs.* ed. Warrand, ii. 153–5; M. Mackintosh, *Hist. Inverness*, 117–18; Tayler, *Duffs*, ii. 371–5, 380; *Scot. Rec. Soc.* iv. 4; *Services of Heirs* (ser. 1) i. 1730–9, p. 11.

D. W.

DUKE, Sir John, 2nd Bt. (1632–1705), of Benhall, Suff.

ORFORD   1679–1681 (Mar.), 1689–1690
                 4 Mar. 1697–1698

bap. 3 Jan. 1632, 2nd but 1st surv. s. of Sir Edward Duke, 1st Bt.†, of Benhall by Ellenor, da. and coh. of John Panton of Westminster. *educ.* Emmanuel, Camb. 1649; travelled abroad 1657. *m.* by 1670, his 3rd cos. Elizabeth, da. of Edward Duke, MD, FRCP, of London, 1s. 5da. *suc.* fa. Jan. 1670.[1]

Portman, Orford ?–d., mayor 1677–8; alderman, Dunwich June–Oct. 1688; freeman, Aldeburgh by 1690.[2]

In the 1690 election Duke stood down at Orford in favour of Thomas Felton*, and he continued a strong supporter of the Whig faction in the town, so strong a Whig indeed that in 1695 he vehemently denounced the electoral compact between Thomas and his brother Sir Adam Felton, 3rd Bt.*, saying of the latter that 'they had taken in one to cut their throats'. When Sir Adam developed a fatal illness early in 1697, Duke was soon busy in Orford, making an interest. One local Tory observed, 'I thought there must be something more than ordinary, otherwise he would not have ventured his old, rotten, porky carcase ... in such weather.' Thomas Felton, however, was anxious to bring in a Whig from outside. His efforts to do so turned Duke against him. At first Duke gave his support to the Tory candidate sponsored by Lord Hereford, but when the Tories in desperation asked him to stand himself as the only way to defeat Felton's nominee he accepted, after some hesitation, 'he having professed himself to be so much at my lord's devotion could not deny him and other friends that request'. After his return, Felton's man having backed down before the poll, Duke was reported to have declared that 'he is sensible what party in the House all our calamities are owing to, and he will oppose them while he lives, and will never forsake my lord'. 'This is a wonderful change', commented a Tory, 'and, if it holds, there will good use be made of it.' Another was less sanguine: 'I hope a great use can be made of him, if his quicksilver can be fixed.' He made little impression in Parliament, and on 28 Feb. 1698 was granted leave of absence to recover his health. Probably because of illness he did not put up for re-election in 1698, being listed in about September as a member of the Country party left out of the new Parliament. At Orford, however, he split his votes between (Sir) Thomas Felton (4th Bt.) and the Tory William Johnson, and as late as 1704 seems to have occupied a neutral position between the party factions in the borough.[3]

Duke was buried at Benhall on 24 July 1705, aged 73. His son Sir Edward, 3rd Bt., sat for Orford 1721-2.[4]

[1] Add. 19127, ff. 243-4, 253, 255. [2] W. Suss. RO, Shillinglee mss Ac.454/890, 897, [-] to Sir Edward Turnor*, Sept. [1704], Aldeburgh poll 1690; HMC Var. iv. 269; vii. 104. [3] Shillinglee mss Ac.454/902, 904, 906, 911, 965, 969, 1009, 1013-5, 1020, 1159, 890, Edward Pratt to Turnor, 16 Aug., 12 Nov. 1692, 1 Oct. 1693, 2 Mar. 1696[-7], Nathaniel Gooding to same, 3 Nov. 1695, 27 Jan. 1696[-7], Theophilus Hooke to same, 4 Nov. 1695, 2, 5, 13 Mar. 1696-7, John Hooke to same, 6 Mar. 1696-7, Orford poll 1698, Thomas Palmer to Turnor, 8 May 1704, [-] to same, Sept. [1704]; Add. 22186, f. 99. [4] Add. 19127, ff. 243-4.

D. W. H.

DUKE, Richard (1652-1733), of Essex Street, Westminster and Otterton, Devon.

ASHBURTON 1679 (Oct.), 1695-1701 (Nov.)

b. 2 May 1652, 1st s. of Richard Duke of Otterton by Frances, da. of George Southcote of Buckland Tout Saints, Devon. educ. Colyton sch. 1660; Powderham, Martock, Exeter and Ottery schs.; Exeter, Oxf. 1669-70; I. Temple 1670-1; travelled abroad 1671-2, 1673-5. m. (1) 17 May 1673, Isabella (d. 1705), da. of Sir William Yonge, 3rd Bt.*, 2da. d.v.p.; (2) 28 Feb. 1705, Elizabeth (d. 1726), da. of John Cholwich of Farrington, Devon, 1s. 1da. d.v.p. suc. fa. 1716.[1]

Freeman, Lyme Regis 1680.[2]

A Whig and possibly a Dissenter, Duke wrote a series of hectoring letters in 1693 full of biblical quotations to persuade Christopher Savery to serve as sheriff of Devon. Having succeeded, he then urged Savery unsuccessfully not to choose two non-jurors as his under-sheriffs: 'if you choose such officers, you will be but a Jack Straw and worse than a Tory justice, and will be declined by the true friends of the Government'. Savery took offence and Sir Francis Drake, 3rd Bt.*, who tried to smooth things over, had to admit that Duke 'is a very indiscreet man'. Duke was returned in 1695 for Ashburton, where his father owned a moiety of the manor, and where the outgoing Member was his kinsman, the Irish lord chief justice Sir Richard Reynell, 1st Bt.* He was forecast in January 1696 as likely to support the Court over the proposed council of trade, signed the Association in February, and on 25 Nov. voted for the attainder of Sir John Fenwick†, although he was related to another of the conspirators, Sir John Freind†. Classed as a Court supporter in a comparative analysis of the old and new Parliaments after the general election of 1698, he voted on 18 Jan. 1699 in favour of a standing army, but by February 1701 he was listed as likely to support the Court in agreeing with the committee of supply's resolution to continue the 'Great Mortgage'. On standing for re-election at Ashburton in December 1701 he was either defeated or more probably was brought to desist through the efforts of Sir Edward Seymour, 4th Bt.*, and Sir William Courtenay, 2nd Bt.* A further blow was his removal early in 1702 from the Devon commission of the peace at Seymour's request. In September 1704 Duke wrote to Robert Harley* complaining bitterly that many wealthy and respectable gentlemen had not been reinstated in the commission, and took occasion to berate Seymour as a man 'of many passions and perturbations' whose views about the Resurrection were 'unsound'. Duke made no attempt to regain his seat. He died in February 1733 and was buried at Otterton on the 27th, having devised his estates to his cousin Richard Duke.[3]

[1] *Trans. Devon Assoc.* i. 493–4; *Misc. Gen. et Her.* ser. 4, iii. 31; *Devon and Cornw. N. and Q.* x. 196. [2] Dorset RO, Lyme Regis mss B6/11, f. 321. [3] Add. 44058, ff. 69–74, 149; Som. RO, Sanford mss DD/SF 3068, Elizabeth Duke to Mary Clarke [c.Dec. 1701]; *HMC Portland*, iv. 134–5; L. K. J. Glassey, *Appt. JPs*, 162, 173; *Misc. Gen. et Her.* 31.

E. C.

DUMMER, Edmund (1651–1713), of London.

ARUNDEL 1695–1698, 1701 (Feb.–Nov.) 1702–1708

bap. 28 Aug. 1651, 1st s. of Thomas Dummer of S. Stoneham, Hants by Joane. *m.* by 1679, Sarah, 3da. (2 *d.v.p.*).[1]

Asst. master shipwright, Chatham by 1686–90; asst. surveyor of the navy 1690–2; commr. of navy 1692–9.[2]

Freeman, Southampton 1696.[3]

Dummer's family had been settled at Swaythling in Hampshire since the early 17th century, but he himself was descended from a junior branch and had to make his own way, which he did as a shipwright, learning his craft under Sir John Tippetts, surveyor of the navy from 1672 to 1685. As early as February 1679, Dummer was sending Samuel Pepys ideas for improvements in ship design. From 1682 he spent nearly two years in the Mediterranean in the service of the navy, surveying ports and dockyards there, and on his return was appointed assistant to Robert Lee, the master shipwright at the naval dockyard at Chatham. In 1686, when Pepys was searching for a replacement for Sir Anthony Deane on the navy board, Dummer's was one of the names suggested, but Pepys, clearly considering him too inexperienced for the post, wrote that he was 'an ingenious young man, but said rarely to have handled a tool in his life, a mere draftsman'. Dummer did not get the job. After the Revolution Tippetts returned to his old post as surveyor of the navy and took Dummer with him as his assistant. It was during this period that Dummer gave evidence before the commissioners of public accounts concerning the poor state of the fleet in 1689, which was the responsibility of the special commission for repair of the navy set up in 1686 and dominated by Pepys and Deane. He claimed that while he was assistant master shipwright at Chatham both he and the master, Lee, had been overruled by this commission, which had used its authority to conceal defective repairs. Deane counter-attacked by alleging that Lee was himself corrupt and Dummer so inexperienced that an ordinary shipwright had to be provided to do his work. Their report, he claimed, 'carried on it deeper characters of remissness, ignorance and unfaithfulness, than we believe can be shown to have ever met in any one account of the navy'. The commissioners eventually exonerated Deane. A more fruitful achievement of this period was the friendship that Dummer developed with Robert Harley*, then serving as one of the public accounts commissioners. In 1692 Dummer succeeded Tippetts as surveyor of the navy, and during his tenure of the office made a lasting contribution by designing and supervising the building of the dockyards at Plymouth and Portsmouth.[4]

In 1695 Dummer was returned for Arundel on the Court interest, and was forecast as a probable Court supporter in the division of 31 Jan. 1696 on the proposed council of trade. Naval duties prevented his taking a very active role in the Commons and on 31 Jan. he wrote anxiously from Portsmouth to Robert Harley and Arthur Moore* soliciting their aid in case he should be unable to get back for the call on 3 Feb., which in fact was postponed a week. He signed the Association promptly, voted for the Court in March over fixing the price of guineas at 22s. and, in the next session, on 25 Nov. 1696, voted in favour of the attainder of Sir John Fenwick†. On 7 Jan. 1697 he was given leave to go to Portsmouth on navy business.[5]

Listed as a placeman in July 1698, Dummer did not stand in the general election of that year and was named again in an analysis of the old and new House of Commons of about September as a Court placeman. The following December he received a setback, which began a steady decline in his fortunes. During the building of the Portsmouth dockyard, he had criticized the work of one of the contractors, John Fitch, and thus brought about Fitch's dismissal. Fitch retorted by accusing Dummer of taking bribes. On 24 Dec. Dummer in turn was suspended from his office. The charges were supported by another witness, who wrote:

> With humble submission, how can this surveyor be ever capable to manage the high post of a surveyor of the navy, to examine and judge of other builders' capacity, when this surveyor never built not one ship for his Majesty's service, nor never was an actual warranted master shipwright in any of his Majesty's shipyards ... But doth not such a surveyor's conduct and most sublime management sound like a bell, just like the abominable stone dock at Portsmouth, which falls down almost as fast as they can build it up, because they build the basis of it upon a sandy foundation; so that it is plainly a perfect cheat, and a kind of bottomless gulf (for our hopeful young surveyor to enrich himself by).

The charges were heard by the lords of the Admiralty, who upheld Fitch's complaints, and on 10 Aug. 1699 removed Dummer from the navy board. Dummer then began an action for defamation, which was heard in May 1700. Although Fitch 'brought the Earl of Bridgwater [John Egerton†], Lord Haversham [Sir John Thompson, 1st Bt.*] and the rest of the Admiralty with Sir Clowdesley Shovell* and commissioner of the navy to speak for him', the jury found for Dummer and awarded him £364 damages. Afterwards he successfully petitioned the Treasury for arrears of pay during his suspension, but he was not reinstated in his job. He now had to rely for his living on the packet service he had started between London and Rotterdam.[6]

Dummer successfully contested Arundel in February 1701 but did not stand in the second general election of 1701, concentrating instead on attempts to interest the government in his proposal to run a packet service to the West Indies. With the assistance of Harley and Henry Guy*, who described him as 'so very able a man that the giving assistance to any of his proposals will be a credit to him that gives it', he obtained a contract in August 1702. He was elected once more for Arundel in 1702, possibly in the hope that being in Parliament would facilitate his return to the Navy Board. On 20 Aug., on hearing rumours that Shovell intended to resign as comptroller of the victualling accounts, Dummer wrote to Harley, 'if you think it proper to mention to my lord treasurer any remembrance of me, in case Sir Clowdesley Shovell quits, as is said, it will be seasonable'. However, Shovell did not resign. Later, on hearing that the comptroller of the storekeeper's accounts had died, Dummer wrote again to Harley on 24 Sept. 1702:

> Providence has opened the way wherein if . . . I might succeed, I should be able to do much better service than ever I have done for the navy, and that is not a little if it were accounted to me in justice. I have made bold to move Mr Guy to give a hint to my lord treasurer not to be too precipitate in the disposal of this office. There is none at that board who understands it, nor hath it ever been understood rightly in my opinion. Nevertheless the Navy Board in a body this day recommended one of their members . . . for the same to the council of the lord high admiral. Some time or other there will be a severe reflection upon that board for having too great a balance of clerk-commissioners in that body. They may understand accounts, but the prudential judgement with relation to the bulk of that business is a science they are great strangers to . . . If this occasion be not made use on to show me some countenance for my abuses, I shall never think anything else in the navy worth asking for.

Again, he did not get the job, although in September 1703 he was granted a contract for a packet service to Lisbon. He remained loyal to the Court, and was marked as a probable opponent of the Tack in a forecast of 30 Oct. 1704. Harley still took the trouble to lobby him, and on 28 Nov. he duly voted against the Tack or was absent.[7]

Returned again for Arundel in 1705, Dummer voted for the Court candidate in the division on the Speaker on 25 Oct. Classed as a 'Churchman' in an analysis of the new Parliament, his increasing financial difficulties probably dictated that he follow Harley's political lead and, although not listed among those supporting the Court in the proceedings on the 'place clause' of the regency bill on 18 Feb. 1706, the following day he joined Court Tories in voting against a Whig motion to appoint a day for hearing the Bewdley election. Meanwhile Dummer's debts multiplied. Both his packet services had incurred heavy losses, and he was released from the Lisbon contract in 1707. On the West Indies service the terms of the original contract, which had laid down that £8,000 p.a. should be paid to the crown from the charge of carrying letters and passengers, had proved wildly unrealistic. Profit from letters and freight had only amounted to a few hundred pounds; several of the ships had been sunk or captured; and already Dummer had been allowed several times to defer payment. Eventually a new contract was negotiated and signed in early 1708.[8]

Classed as a Tory in a list of early 1708, Dummer stood down at Arundel in the election of that year, and his financial troubles grew steadily worse. Although it was generally agreed that his packet service was useful, losses of ships, delays in payments from the Treasury and the failure of government credit in 1709–10 combined to ruin him. The appointment of Harley to the Treasury induced Dummer to send a desperate appeal for help on 19 Aug. 1710:

> I have been 12 years to this time contending with misfortunes and the ill-will of some people, who never had more than a groundless jealousy to justify the persecution and malice I have felt from them, which however implacable it hath been, I hope will now have no longer any influence over me . . . I pray you to think of this matter and not to forget as occasion may now offer what I have done and suffered for meaning and doing well according to my circumstances and that this my long suffering may at last (by your protection and favour) become a prevalent argument to redeem me from that prejudice which in some people once offended, admit no appeal to compassion.

Harley was either unable or unwilling to help. On 30 May 1711 Dummer wrote again asking for the treasurer's support for a petition to the Queen to clear his name from the charges made against him by Fitch and accepted by the Admiralty in 1699:

which hath obscured me (to this time) near 12 years, for no other reason that I know of, but either for refusing to yield up my innocence a voluntary victim to false oaths or becoming myself an accuser of my brethren to please the passions and revenge of some power.

Again Harley did not help. By 1711 Dummer was unable to continue the West Indies packet service and the ships were assigned to John Mead*, deputy-paymaster of the forces in Spain and Portugal, one of his most intractable creditors, who was himself desirous of taking over the service. Dummer was declared a bankrupt in April 1712 and died at the end of April 1713. His wife and daughter successfully petitioned for pensions of £150 p.a. each on account of Dummer's services and out of charity for the total destitution in which they had been left. Despite his misfortunes and the accusations of incompetence, Dummer had been highly regarded by many as a shipbuilder and naval architect. Charles Sergison*, clerk of the acts on the navy board, had written a letter in 1705 to the effect that no previous surveyor of the navy had achieved anything like so much, and that the docks at Portsmouth and Plymouth would be lasting monuments to his skill.[9]

[1] IGI, Hants; *The Gen.* n.s. xiv. 172; *Cal. Treas. Bks.* xxvii. 429; *St. Margaret's Westminster* (Harl. Soc. Reg. lxxxviii), 55; (lxxxix), 91. [2] G. F. Duckett, *Commrs. of Navy*, 4–5; *Cat. Pepysian Mss* (Navy Recs. Soc. xxvi), i. 77; *Sergison Pprs.* (Navy Recs. Soc. lxxxix), 12, 147–9. [3] Southampton RO, Southampton bor. recs. SC3/1, f. 248. [4] Wilks, *Hants*, 87, 116–17; Duckett, 71–72; *Cat. Pepysian Mss*, i. 77, 92; J. Ehrman, *Navy in War of Wm. III*, 207–8, 416–17; *Cal. Treas. Bks.* vii. 1410; *Cal. Treas. Pprs.* 1702–7, p. 391; H. Horwitz, *Parl. and Pol. Wm. III*, 202. [5] Add. 70224, Dummer to Harley, 30 Jan., 1 Feb. 1695[-6]. [6] *CSP Dom.* 1699–1700, pp. 59–60, 70, 71, 235; 1700–2, p. 73; 1702–3, p. 61; Add. 70224, Dummer to Harley, 30 May 1711; Luttrell, *Brief Relation*, iv. 576, 645, 658. [7] *CSP Dom.* 1702–3, pp. 90, 146, 213; *Cal. Treas. Bks.* xviii. 394, 468; *HMC Portland*, iv. 45, 47; viii. 90, 104–6, 110–11. [8] *Bull. IHR*, xlv. 48–49; Add. 70224, Dummer to Harley, 17 Apr., 19 June 1704, 3 June, 20 Sept. 1707; *Cal. Treas. Bks.* xx. 744; xxi. 430–2, 455; xxii. 83. [9] *Cal. Treas. Bks.* xxiv. 571; xxv. 102, 395, 487; xxvi. 102; xxvii. 429; xxviii. 98; *Cal. Treas. Pprs.* 1702–7, p. 391; 1708–14, pp. 202, 319, 452, 529; Add. 70267, Sarah Dummer to Charles Sergison, 2 May 1713; 70224, Dummer to Harley, 19 Aug. 1710, 30 May 1711, 30 Apr. 1712.

P. W.

DUNBAR *alias* **SUTHERLAND, Hon. Sir James**, 1st Bt. (aft. 1676–1724), of Hempriggs, Caithness.

CAITHNESS-SHIRE 1710–1713

b. aft. 1676, 2nd s. of James Sutherland, 2nd Ld. Duffus [S] by Lady Margaret, da. of Kenneth Mackenzie, 3rd Earl of Seaforth [S]. *educ.* adv. 1704. *m.* c.1705, Elizabeth (*d.* 1756), da. and h. of Sir William Dunbar, 1st Bt. (*d.* 1711), MP [S], of Hempriggs, and wid. of Sir Robert Gordon, 3rd Bt., MP [S], of Gordonstoun, Elgin, 2s. 4da. Changed name to Dunbar on marriage; *cr.* Bt. 21 Dec. 1706.[1]

MP [S] Caithness-shire 1706–7.
Provost, Wick 1711.[2]

Although Dunbar was to rescue himself by a successful marriage, the calamitous state of his family's finances left its mark, for in some quarters he had the reputation of an unscrupulous opportunist, toadying to the powerful and oppressing the weak. His father had been rendered so desperate by debt that in 1688 he had killed a creditor and had been forced to flee to England in pursuit of a royal pardon. Presumably he obtained some guarantee of indemnity from the Prince of Orange, for he returned to Scotland to subscribe the act declaring the legality of the convention of estates, and in 1690 took the oath of allegiance. He was not a reliable supporter of the Court, despite his poverty. By the time of his death he had lost control of his estates, and his eldest son, a naval officer, inherited no more than the title. His second son, the Member, who had put himself to the law as a profession, made repeated applications to Lords Cromarty and Mar for the grant of an escheat to his family. Dunbar's own circumstances had improved somewhat with his marriage to the daughter (and, after 1707, heir presumptive) of the laird of Hempriggs, and he had changed his surname in expectation of her succession. But he was probably not entirely comfortable financially until his father-in-law's death in December 1711, for there were reports in 1707 that old Hempriggs and Lady Dunbar were 'not at a good understanding'. Indeed, when Sir William was dying his daughter and son-in-law refused to visit him, 'albeit he sent several times for them', they 'having been at variance of a good time'. This uncertainty may explain Dunbar's obstructive response to his brother's efforts to reunite the ancestral lands of Duffus with the title. It may also account for his continued courtship of Mar and his brother Lord Grange SCJ (Hon. James Erskine†). Dunbar supported the Union, though registering one or two protests, most notably against the use of troops to quell the Edinburgh mob.[3]

Dunbar did not find a place in the contingent of Court Members chosen to the first Parliament of Great Britain. He was reluctant to stand in 1708, even though his father-in-law's interest at Wick was at his disposal. While prompt with professions of service to Mar and Grange, he was firm in resisting pressure to step forward himself. He still kept open his lines of communication with Cromarty, supporting his son Sir James Mackenzie as a candidate for Tain Burghs. But in 1710 his attitude was reversed and he pursued a seat eagerly. His purchases of land from Lord Breadalbane in the vicinity of Wick, and the coup he had been able to engineer in that corporation, 'throwing out' one council *en masse* and 'packing' another, might have given him leverage enough to challenge for the district, but instead he took the easier run offered in Caithness-shire, which had not elected in 1708 since it alternated its representation with Buteshire.[4]

Up early to Parliament in December 1710, Dunbar maintained throughout his first session a regular correspondence with Grange, until he was granted what seems to have been a terminal leave of absence, for six weeks, on 7 Apr. 1711. He despatched lengthy reports of Commons debates, written from a ministerial point of view. He had, indeed, been classified as an episcopal Tory in the analysis of Richard Dongworth, the Duchess of Buccleuch's chaplain, and later he was included in the 'white lists' of 'Tory patriots' and 'worthy patriots', who in this session had, respectively, supported peace and exposed the mismanagements of the previous administration. His letters show him sharing Tory scruples over the place bill, which threatened to 'unhinge our constitution' (12 Dec. 1710); voting with the Tories over the Bewdley election (19 Dec.); approving of the speeches of Henry St. John II* in commendation of the landed qualification bill (30 Jan. 1711); and subscribing to the commonly held back-bench Tory assumption that 'by all the examinations yet heard it appears that all in public employment' under the outgoing ministry 'have very much wronged the public'. He also attended the private meetings of Scots peers and Commoners to discuss what measures might be brought forward for the benefit of the Scottish episcopalian clergy. But the enduring theme of the correspondence was his professed devotion to Mar.[5]

His loyalty unrewarded by even a crumb of patronage, it seems unlikely that Dunbar ever came back to Westminster. He was absent in Scotland on 7 Feb. 1712 for the vote on the Scottish toleration bill, and the following year was again absent at both recorded divisions on the French commerce bill (4 and 18 June 1713). Instead, his attention was taken up by the local difficulties he was encountering in Wick, where the Breadalbane interest had reasserted itself. In 1711 there were competing elections for the provostship of the burgh. Dunbar was chosen by one faction; Breadalbane's eldest son, Lord Glenorchy, by another and also with the support of 'the gentlemen of the country', whom Dunbar had in some way alienated. Townsmen then proceeded to bring forward complaints against the 'oppressions' they had suffered at the hands of Dunbar and his wife, who had enclosed common land and encroached on vital harbour and fishing rights. Allegedly the baronet was 'wife-ridden', and observers assumed that it was Lady Dunbar's vindictiveness that drove on the dispute, until her husband found himself the subject of a legal process in the court of session, and a petition to the convention of royal burghs. He did not stand in 1713, when there was no opportunity in the county and the prospect unclear in the burghs district. At least five years later his conflict with the inhabitants of Wick was still simmering, his election as commissioner to the convention controverted, and further complaints being preferred against him for persistent and systematic encroachment on the privileges of the burgh.[6]

While his two brothers and stepson, Sir Robert Gordon, 4th Bt.†, were all 'out' in the Fifteen, Lord Duffus forfeiting the peerage on attainder, Dunbar himself kept a low profile, and little is known of him until his death, presumably at Hempriggs, in 1724. He was succeeded by his second son, William.[7]

[1] *Scots Peerage* ed. Paul, iii. 210–11; J. Henderson, *Caithness Fam. Hist.* 222–3; *Scot. Rec. Soc.* lxxvi. 204. [2] SRO, Breadalbane mss GD112/39/258/13, (Sir) Robert Dunbar (2nd Bt.) to Glenorchy, 22 Oct. 1711. [3] *Scots Peerage*, 209–10; info. from Dr P. W. J. Riley on members of Scot. parl.; P. W. J. Riley, *King Wm. and Scot. Politicians*, 166; P. W. J. Riley, *Union*, 93, 109, 330–1; *Seafield Letters*, 104; *Cromartie Corresp.* ii. 10–11, 77; *HMC Mar and Kellie*, i. 470; *APS*, xi. app. 130; SRO, Breadalbane mss GD112/39/210/5, Duncan Toshach to Breadalbane, 10 Dec. 1707; GD112/39/262/4/1, same to [same], 7 Jan. 1712; *Lockhart Pprs.* i. 166. [4] SRO, Mar and Kellie mss GD124/15/754/1, Mar to Grange, 6 Jan. 1707–8; GD124/15/768/2, Grange to Mar, 24 June 1708; *Cromartie Corresp.* 75, 77; SRO, Cromartie mss GD305 addit./bdle. 12, Royston to [Cromarty], 7 Dec. 1708; bdle. 14, same to [same], 21 Nov. 1710; Breadalbane mss GD112/39/244/18, Toshach to Breadalbane, 19 Sept. 1710; GD112/39/259/6, Glenorchy to Dunbar, 10 Nov. 1711. [5] *SHR*, lx. 64; Mar and Kellie mss GD124/15/1020/1–2, 4–5, 8, 12 14, Dunbar to Grange, 5, 12, 19, 21 Dec. 1710, 30 Jan., 17 Feb., 1 Mar. 1711; *HMC Mar and Kellie*, 485–6. [6] NLS, ms 1392, f. 80; *Parlty. Hist.* i. 69; Breadalbane mss GD112/39/258/13, Robert Dunbar to [Glenorchy], 22 Oct. 1711; GD112/39/259/5–7, 22–3, Glenorchy to Robert Dunbar, 10 Nov. 1711, same to Sir James Dunbar, 10 Nov. 1711, same to [Colin Campbell], 10 Nov. 1711, same to Sir William Dunbar, 26 Nov. 1711, Duncan Toshach to [?Breadalbane], 26 Nov. 1711; GD112/39/260/4, Glenorchy to Campbell, 3 Dec. [1711]; GD112/39/269/22, Sir Robert Dunbar to [?Glenorchy], 26 Oct. 1713; *Recs. R. Burghs Scotland*, v. 92, 189, 172–3, 192–3. [7] Douglas, iii. 211; *Scot. Rec. Soc.* xxxi. 15.

D. W. H.

DUNCH, Edmund (?1677–1719), of Little Wittenham, Berks. and Down Ampney, Glos.

CRICKLADE	1701 (Feb.)–1702, 1705–1713
BOROUGHBRIDGE	1713–1715
WALLINGFORD	1715–31 May 1719

b. 14 Dec. ?1677, o. s. of Hungerford Dunch† of Little Wittenham and Down Ampney by Katherine, da. of

William Oxton, Brewer, of Westminster and Herts. *m.* 24 Apr. 1702, Elizabeth (*d.* 1760), da. and coh. of Charles Godfrey*, and maid of honour to Queen Anne, 4da. *suc.* fa. 1680.[1]

Freeman, Wallingford 1695.[2]
Master of the Household 1708–12, 1714–*d.*

Dunch has often been mistakenly represented as a nephew of Lord Wharton (Hon. Thomas*), in confusion with his third cousin Wharton Dunch*. He did have some association with the Junto lord, through his father-in-law, Charles Godfrey, a crony of Wharton's, and through his own membership of the Kit-Cat Club; but equally, if not more important was Godfrey's connexion with the Churchill family. In his youth, according to Caulfield's *Memoirs* of the Kit-Cat, Dunch 'received and profited by a liberal education', though where this took place has not been ascertained. He enjoyed some reputation for wit, and apparently before his marriage some notoriety as a ladies' man. His parliamentary ambitions may have initially lain in Berkshire, as in 1695 he was admitted as a freeman of Wallingford and four years later he made an unsuccessful attempt to become the borough recorder there. However, his Gloucestershire estate gave him an interest in the nearby borough of Cricklade and it was here that he secured his return, unopposed, in January and again in November 1701, and he was included on the Whig side in Robert Harley's* list of the latter Parliament. However, the beginning of his Commons career was uneventful, and either he or his cousin was given leave of absence for a week on 23 Apr. 1701. Defeated at the 1702 election, he was none the less considered a possible nominee for a peerage that year, presumably as a favourite of the Marlboroughs, and twice in 1704 it was rumoured that he would succeed Godfrey in the jewel office. He won back his seat at the next election, a result marked as a 'gain' by Lord Sunderland (Charles, Lord Spencer*). Despite being labelled a 'Churchman' in one classification of the returns, he voted on 25 Oct. 1705 for the Court candidate for Speaker, and on 4 Dec. told in favour of the House going into committee forthwith to consider the proceedings of the Scottish parliament with regard to union and the succession. In early 1708 Dunch was listed as a Tory, but another list from later the same year more realistically described him as a Whig, and in the feverish speculation in the aftermath of the fall of Harley in February 1708 he was very quickly recognized as a likely appointee to an important Household office, first the comptrollership and later the mastership. When he eventually kissed hands as master in October it was to the Duchess of Marlborough that his wife wrote in gratitude. Before the appointment it was reported that he had been granted a pension of £1,000 a year for life, but almost certainly this was never confirmed. Re-elected without difficulty after taking office, he voted for the naturalization of the Palatines. He supported the impeachment of Dr Sacheverell both inside and outside Parliament, on one occasion becoming involved with other Whig MPs and peers in a fracas provoked by toasts on the subject of the doctor.[3]

Returned at the head of the poll for Cricklade in 1710, and marked as a Whig in the 'Hanover list', Dunch retained his office over two sessions in spite of stout adherence to his party. This again seems in all probability to have been due, directly or indirectly, to the Duke of Marlborough (John Churchill†). Dunch voted on 7 Dec. 1711 in favour of the 'No Peace without Spain' motion. Finally removed from his place after Marlborough's disgrace, in a purge of Whig office-holders in June 1712, he continued in opposition, voting against the French commerce bill on 18 June 1713, as a Whig. It is not clear why he withdrew from Cricklade in 1713: perhaps for financial reasons. Instead he was nominated by Lord Pelham and William Jessop* at Boroughbridge, as 'a gentleman of an estate of at least £4,000 a year . . . a true Whig and a very honest, civil, well bred and good-natured gentleman'. Lord Pelham called him 'a particular friend' and specifically brought to the electors' attention Dunch's relationship to Marlborough and Wharton and his staunch voting record in Parliament, which was further enhanced on 18 Mar. 1714, when he voted against the expulsion of Richard Steele. He was classed as a Whig in the Worsley list and in a list of the Members chosen again in the election of 1715, prior to which he had been restored, along with his father-in-law, to his Household office.[4]

Dunch died on 31 May 1719 and was buried at Little Wittenham, where he left 'a very good estate'. Down Ampney, on the other hand, had to be sold to pay gambling debts of over £6,000. 'He was a very great gamester', wrote Hearne, 'and had, a little before, lost £30 one night in gaming', a vice into which he was supposed to have allowed himself to be drawn 'purely to please his lady'.[5]

[1] Foster, *London Mar. Lic.* 426; *Daily Courant*, 2 May 1702. [2] J. K. Hedges, *Hist. Wallingford*, ii. 239. [3] J. Carswell, *Old Cause*, 45, 90–91; J. Caulfield, *Kit-Cat Club*, 210; W.L. Sachse, *Ld. Somers*, 192; *Materials Hist. Cricklade* ed. Thomson, 156; Add. 47025, f. 57; 61450, f. 224; 61461, f. 63; 70075–6, Dyer's newsletter 2 Mar. 1704; Luttrell, *Brief Relation*, v. 185, 419; vi. 267, 354; Northants. RO, Isham mss, John to Sir Justinian Isham, 4th Bt.*, 17 Sept. 1704; 7th Duke of Manchester, *Court and Soc. Eliz. to Anne*, ii. 280, 336; Folger Shakespeare Lib. Newdigate newsletters 14 Feb., 28 Sept. 1708; *Marlborough–Godolphin Corresp.* 1124; *HMC Portland*, iv.

505. [4]Boyer, *Pol. State*, iii. 387; Add. 17677 FFF, f. 249; Sir T. Lawson-Tancred, *Recs. of a Yorks. Manor*, 249–55, 259–61. [5]*Misc. Gen. et Her.* ser. 3, ii. 46; *Hearne Colls.* v. 380; vii. 17.

D. W. H.

DUNCH, Wharton (by 1679–1705), of Pusey, Berks.

APPLEBY   1701 (Feb.)–1702
RICHMOND   14 May–c.22 Sept. 1705

b. by 1679, 1st s. of Major Dunch of Pusey by Margaret, da. of Philip, 4th Baron Wharton, by his 2nd w., and sis. of Hon. Henry[†], Hon. Thomas* and Hon. Goodwin Wharton*. *educ*. Pembroke, Oxf. matric. 27 Mar. 1697, 'aged 15'. *unm. suc.* fa. 1679.[1]

Freeman, Southampton 1705.[2]

Though Dunch's reported age when he matriculated at Cambridge suggests he was born in about 1682, he must have been born before the death of his father in 1679, for there was another, posthumous son born after Wharton. Dunch's grandfather and great-grandfather had both sat for Berkshire in the Parliaments of the 1650s, but when Dunch himself entered the Commons it was for two boroughs held by his uncle Lord Wharton in the north of England, though he did make an unsuccessful attempt at Abingdon as a Whig candidate in the second election of 1701. He may have been given a week's leave of absence on 23 Apr. 1701, and, not surprisingly, was classed with the Whigs in Robert Harley's* list in December of that year. Though again standing with the support of his uncle, Dunch was defeated at Appleby in 1702. He was also unsuccessful at Southampton, where he stood on his own interest, based upon the possession of a nearby manor which his great-grandfather had gained by marriage. Wharton found an alternative seat for him at the next election, a 'gain' for the Whig party according to Lord Sunderland (Charles, Lord Spencer*). He was also marked as 'Low Church' in a list of 1705, but died before Parliament met, Luttrell reporting the news on 22 Sept. His age was then given as 24. Since he made no will, his heir was his sister, who is supposed thereby to have had 'a vast fortune'.[3]

[1] *Misc. Gen. et Her.* ser. 3, ii. 47; Stowe 639; Wood, *Life and Times*, iii. 465. [2] Southampton RO, Southampton bor. recs. SC3/1/2, f. 41. [3] W. A. Speck, *Tory and Whig*, 70, 154; *VCH Hants*, iii. 464; *CSP Dom.* 1700–2, p. 452; Luttrell, *Brief Relation*, v. 594; *Misc. Gen. et Her.* 47.

D. W. H.

DUNCOMBE, Anthony (aft. 1650–1708), of Barford, Wilts.

HEDON   1698–1702, 23 Nov. 1702–4 Apr. 1708

b. aft. 1650, 4th s. of Alexander Duncombe of Drayton Beauchamp, Bucks. by Mary, da. of Richard Paulye of Whitchurch, Bucks.; bro. of Charles Duncombe*. *m.* Jane, da. and coh. of Hon. Frederick Cornwallis (2nd s. of Frederick Cornwallis[†], 1st Baron Cornwallis), 1s.

Q.m. Earl of Oxford's horse gds. 1683–?90; capt. 2nd marine regt. 1690–?2; commr. transports 1695–9, prizes 1702–7; gov. Scarborough castle 1702–*d*.[1]

Duncombe boasted an impressive Buckinghamshire pedigree, his ancestors having been settled in the county since at least the early 16th century. As a younger son, he entered the army, and in that capacity demonstrated his support for the Revolution, reportedly being 'very instrumental in bringing over several of my Lord Oxford's regiment to the King [William] at Exeter'. He was subsequently 'very useful' in raising a regiment of marines, and gained a captaincy under the Earl of Pembroke (Arthur Herbert[†]). However, he failed to win higher promotion, despite recommendations from Lords Nottingham (Daniel Finch*) and Pembroke. The ministerial connexions of his wealthy brother Charles later secured him a commission at the transport office, for Anthony's candidacy was endorsed by such influential figures as the Earl of Sunderland and Henry Guy*, the latter of whom praised Duncombe as 'in every way well qualified ... both in integrity and understanding'.[2]

Duncombe's advancement was further aided by his brother in 1698, since it was Charles's proprietorial interest at the Yorkshire borough of Hedon which procured a seat for Anthony. At this time the politics of the younger Duncombe were a source of some conjecture, and in spite of his government office, a parliamentary list classed him as a likely opponent of the Court on the standing army issue, while another queried his allegiance. For certain, he had ample cause to feel aggrieved towards the ministry following the attack which Charles Montagu* had launched on his brother during the preceding Parliament. However, his removal as commissioner in 1699 may not have been politically motivated, since several other officers lost their places as the department's operations were scaled down during peacetime. Indeed, he was in all probability the 'Mr Duncomb' who on 26 Jan. 1700 presented a paper from the transport office to the House. His Tory allegiance was more in evidence in the second session, since he was listed as adhering to the interest of the Old East India Company. At the first election of 1701 he enjoyed an unopposed return at Hedon, and was listed in February 1701 as likely to support the Court in agreeing with the committee of supply to continue the 'Great Mortgage'. He was subsequently blacklisted for having opposed the preparations for war, but at the end of the year had no difficulty in securing his seat. In December Robert Harley* bracketed him with the Tories, and the following February he duly supported the motion to vindicate the Commons' proceedings during the impeachment of William III's ministers.[3]

Duncombe's association with the Tories brought him ample reward on the accession of Anne, for he was appointed a commissioner for prizes, as well as governor of Scarborough Castle. He initially declined to stand for Hedon in 1702, in deference to his brother, but after Sir Charles had opted to sit for Downton, Anthony carried the Hedon by-election without opposition. He remained inactive during this Parliament, but his loyalties seem to have wavered in the course of the last session. In November 1704 Robert Harley included Duncombe on his lobbying list in preparation for the division on the Tack, and may well have influenced Duncombe to become one of the 'Sneakers' who on 28 Nov. absented themselves before the crucial vote on the measure.

Such apostasy did not affect Duncombe's return at Hedon in 1705, and at the outset of the next Parliament he was prepared to put place before party, supporting on 25 Oct. the Court candidate for the Speakership. The passage of the Regency Act subsequently forced him to choose between his office and his seat, and in November 1707 he resigned his post at the prize office. He had no apparent difficulty in securing his return at the ensuing by-election, and in early 1708 two parliamentary lists identified him as a Tory. However, he did not live to see the end of the session, dying on 4 Apr. He was succeeded by his only son Anthony[†], who, having inherited part of the vast estate of Sir Charles Duncombe, later became a Member for Downton, and in 1747 was created Lord Feversham.[4]

[1] *Yorks. Peds.* ed. Foster, ii (unpag.); *CSP Dom.* 1695, p. 80; 1702–3, p. 370; *Cal. Treas. Bks.* xvii. 250. [2] Hoare, *Wilts.* Downton, 45; Nottingham Univ. Lib. Portland (Bentinck) mss PwA 502–3, Guy to [Ld. Portland], 31 May, 14 June 1695; PwA 1245, 1248, Sunderland to same, 29 May, 29 July 1695; *HMC Finch*, iii. 253–4. [3] Watson thesis, 261. [4] Hoare, 45.

P. W./P. L. G.

DUNCOMBE, Charles (1648–1711), of Teddington, Mdx. and Barford, Wilts.

HEDON	1685–1687
YARMOUTH I.O.W.	1690–1695
DOWNTON	1695–1 Feb. 1698
IPSWICH	1701 (Feb.–Nov.)
DOWNTON	1702–9 Apr. 1711

bap. 16 Nov. 1648, 2nd s. of Alexander Duncombe of Drayton Beauchamp, Bucks.; bro. of Anthony Duncombe*. *unm.* Kntd. 20 Oct. 1699.[1]

Apprentice, Goldsmiths' Co. 1665, freeman 1672, livery 1674, prime warden 1684; receiver-gen. Bucks. 1670–1, 1676, Hunts. 1670–3, 1676, Beds. 1670–81, London, Mdx. and Westminster 1689–90, Surr. and Southwark 1689–94; alderman, London 1683–6, 1700–*d.*, sheriff 1699–1700, ld. mayor 1708–9; freeman, Portsmouth 1684.[2]

Member, R. Fishery Co. 1677, E.I. Co. 1677; steward, Hon. Artillery Co. 1682, treasurer 1703–4; commr. Greenwich Hosp. 1695, 1704; pres. Corp. Merchant Woolstaplers 1700.[3]

Cashier, excise 1680–97, hearth money 1684–Nov. 1688; commr. for the mint 1680–by 1686, coining tin farthings and half-pence by 1685–8, taking subscriptions to Bank 1694.[4]

Earning both fortune and notoriety in equal measure, Duncombe established himself as one of the leading bankers of his day. His rise in the City was astonishingly quick, particularly considering his modest provincial background, and can largely be attributed to his association with the great financiers Edward Backwell[†] and Richard Kent[†]. Moreover, even though contemporaries censured him for avarice, an opponent grudgingly admitted that Duncombe was 'not use to slip a favourable opportunity'. His banking activities brought advantageous connexions with several noblemen, in particular the 1st Earl of Shaftesbury (Sir Anthony Ashley Cooper[†]), and the 2nd Earl of Sunderland, who proved a most valuable patron at court. As a revenue official under both Charles II and James II, Duncombe was said to have amassed a considerable fortune at the government's expense. However, such profits were insufficient to secure his loyalty to James and during the Revolution he carried an address from the City lieutenancy to Prince William, and further distinguished himself in January 1689 by advancing the government £20,000, thereby becoming the first major creditor to the new regime. Critics saw such generosity as 'intended as security for his place', and he duly retained his office at the excise by making a succession of substantial loans.[5]

Having failed to retain his Hedon seat at the elections for the Convention, Duncombe resurrected his parliamentary career in 1690 by being brought in for the government borough of Yarmouth. At the outset of the new Parliament Lord Carmarthen (Sir Thomas Osborne[†]) classed him as a Tory and probable Court supporter, but Duncombe proved an inactive Member. Such inactivity was in some contrast to his fiscal services for the ministry, and in the course of the Parliament most political commentators assessed his politics on the basis of his office, with five lists classing him as a placeman. In addition, in April 1691 Robert Harley* bracketed him with supporters of the Court, as did Samuel Grascome in 1693-5. However, Duncombe's professional interests made him a reluctant supporter of the Bank of England, and although appointed a commissioner to take the first subscription, he proved one of the Bank's leading opponents. Despite such antipathy, he maintained his place thanks to the support of powerful allies such as Sunderland, who warmly commended Duncombe's advance of £30,000 during the sixth session, observing that he, 'without excepting any man whoever, has been, and will be, more useful than any'. Given this powerful connexion, it was predictable that Henry Guy* in 1694-5 should identify him as a 'friend' and likely supporter against opposition attacks in the Lower House.[6]

Although ready to stand the government credit, in the course of the recoinage crisis Duncombe exhibited a less than public-spirited approach to national finance. In August 1695 he was reported to have sold 'all his effects in the Bank of England, being £80,000', a move which one historian has interpreted as an attempt to increase the Bank's difficulties. Moreover, he subsequently invested a reported £90,000 in the purchase of the Duke of Buckingham's former estate at Helmsley, Yorkshire, perhaps wishing to protect himself against the inflationary impact of the recoinage. This transaction certainly invited much comment at a time of national hardship, and later led Pope to pen the couplet:

And Helmsley once proud Buckingham's delight
Slides to a scrivener or City knight.

This acquisition permitted Duncombe to influence elections at Hedon for the rest of his career, but at the general election of 1695 he preferred to take advantage of his proprietorial interest at Downton, having bought an estate at nearby Barford some five years before. After gaining an unopposed return, he continued to back the Court, being forecast as a likely supporter in a division on 31 Jan. 1696 concerning the proposed council of trade. He also signed the Association, but remained inconspicuous in the House, his only significant appointment in the first session resting with the drafting committee for a bill to explain the Acts concerning highways. He was still valued by the ministry, however, and the following summer was employed by the chancellor of the Exchequer, Charles Montagu*, as an intermediary for negotiations with the land bank. These talks failed to raise the expected supply, but in August Duncombe's name headed a cartel of financiers ready to advance £300,000 to the crown.[7]

Despite Duncombe's forwardness to aid the administration, he remained on uneasy terms with Montagu. Matters came to a head in February 1697, when the banker refused a request to lend the government £50,000. Duncombe appeared before the Treasury on 10 Feb. to give his answer, and, in front of the King, stubbornly defended his record as a government creditor, offering to resign his excise post if anyone else could supply the crown better. Moreover, he firmly denied that he had made any personal gain from his tenure of office, and even claimed to have lost money due to the 'noise' of rumours concerning his future employment. Sir Stephen Fox* was his principal adversary on this occasion, and as soon as Duncombe had left the meeting, he assured the King that other financiers could meet royal needs. The following month it was reported that Duncombe had joined with Fox and others to establish a fund of £400,000 for public supplies, but by April Duncombe had been replaced at the excise by Bartholomew Burton, thereby ending any immediate hopes for reconciliation with Montagu.[8]

Having severed his own ties with the ministry, Duncombe encouraged Sunderland to break with the Junto. Before the end of the year he had warned Sunderland of possible impeachment, and it was later claimed that Duncombe and Guy 'did perpetually alarm him [Sunderland] with stories of his being delivered up by the Whigs'. Sunderland's resignation as lord chamberlain in late December sparked an immediate response from acolytes like Duncombe, who launched an attack on Montagu in the Commons, accusing the chancellor of fraud in connexion with the circulation of Exchequer bills. In particular, Duncombe was said to have charged Montagu with engineering his removal from office so that Burton could aid the conspiracy. Sunderland hastily tried to distance himself from these allegations, confiding to the Duke of Shrewsbury on 15 Jan. 1698:

I am informed that some in the House of Commons, who usually were thought to be influenced by me, have gone wrong of late, in particular Sir William Trumbull*, Mr Duncombe and Mr [John] Methuen*. For the two first, I think people need only consider one moment the difference between men in good places and good humour, and out of them, angry and unsatisfied.

Few believed Sunderland's denials, but after Montagu had cleared his name before the Commons in early January, it was Duncombe who became the principal victim of the minister's counter-attack.[9]

Having helped to broach an investigation into the circulation of Exchequer bills, Duncombe now found himself charged with corruption. On 17 Jan. he 'entertained' the House with his answer to the reasons given by Fox for his dismissal as cashier, and the next day James Vernon I* menacingly observed that Montagu was ready to go on the offensive, although Vernon was unsure whether Duncombe would be the chancellor's target. Most significantly, Vernon remarked upon Sunderland's readiness to abandon his ally, reporting that the peer had 'nothing to say for' Duncombe. On 22 Jan. Montagu openly delivered 'a very severe charge' against Duncombe before the House, but the banker made a spirited defence of his actions, accusing his opponents of trying to screen the real offenders, and it was reported that 'no part' of the allegations against him had been 'made out'.[10]

However, the Commons pursued the matter three days later, focusing attention on a payment of £10,000 in Exchequer bills which Duncombe had made to the Exchequer in May 1697 to clear his account as cashier. The House was particularly keen for him to reveal the name of the person from whom he received the bills, and under such pressure Duncombe cracked, testifying to a central role in a fraud. He had purchased the bills at a 5 per cent discount from a Jew, John da Costa, who was persuaded by Duncombe to endorse them with fictitious names so that it appeared that they had been paid to Duncombe for excise duty. As a result, Duncombe could then pay the bills into the Exchequer at their face value, and pocket the discount himself. Such revelations were considered particularly unwise, for they 'made him appear more guilty than perhaps could ever have been proved'. In response, the House committed him to the Tower for 'having contrived and advised the making false endorsements of Exchequer bills', and ordered him to prepare a written defence of his actions. Vernon gleefully blamed 'Duncombe's imprudence and his friends' obstinacy' for the banker's downfall, observing that Duncombe's 'lavishness of tongue' had implicated him with other disgraced revenue officials such as Burton and John Knight I*.[11]

Over the next few days Duncombe petitioned the Commons for time and counsel to prepare his defence, but on 1 Feb. the House's patience ran out and his testimony of 25 Jan. was ruled as having been tantamount to a confession of guilt. He was accordingly expelled from the Commons, and, on the motion of 'Mr Harley', a committee was appointed to prepare bills to penalize Duncombe, Burton and Knight. Some Members wished to impeach Duncombe for his crime, but others foresaw that 'his money and lordships' tricks might puzzle the cause'. Montagu took the greatest pleasure from Duncombe's discomfort, hoping that it would encourage Sunderland to come into the ministry on the chancellor's terms:

> We have taken away his [Sunderland's] tools and engines. Duncombe's fall will more disable him, and cut off his power to play tricks, than anything else could have done. He was the cement that kept [Lord] Peterborough, [the Duke of] Bolton [Charles Powlett†], [Sir Edward] Seymour [4th Bt.*], and the rest united. He was the Iago of the whole villainy, and nothing can keep them together, but such a busy temper, joined with a faculty of helping those that have money to dispose of it, and those that have none to borrow.[12]

The bill of pains against Duncombe was presented on 7 Feb., by which time speculation was already rife that he would be fined £150,000. His bitterest enemies wished to take nearly the whole of his estate, valued by most sources at £400,000. The first major hurdle for the bill was negotiated on 14 Feb., when the House heard counsel for both sides before the second reading. Duncombe's allies sought to highlight the wide variety of practices permitted by Exchequer bill legislation, stressing that if Duncombe had transgressed, then so had many others. Moreover, they continued to target Montagu, querying why there had been no investigation of Duncombe's transaction when the Treasury had first taken note of it the previous June. Up to this point John Pulteney* had been identified as his 'great advocate' in the Commons, but on this occasion Duncombe also received the support of Court opponents such as Seymour, Sir Christopher Musgrave, 4th Bt.*, and John Grobham Howe*, whose activity highlighted the growing significance of the controversy. Their arguments were brushed aside, however, and after a motion for candles had passed easily, there was no opposition to the bill's referral to a committee of the whole.[13]

That committee sat on 18 Feb., when debate lasted some seven or eight hours, and it was eventually resolved that Duncombe should lose two-thirds of his estate, and never hold public office again. John Ellis* interpreted 'this severity' as retaliation on the part of the ministry's supporters, who had been angered by an attempt to embarrass Montagu by bringing to the House's attention a grant of Irish forfeitures to the chancellor. At the report stage on 21 Feb., Duncombe's allies were still striving to ambush the bill, proposing an amendment that the confiscated estate be appropriated by Parliament. This was probably a thinly disguised attempt to expose the self-interest of Duncombe's opponents, for, as Sir Miles Cooke later observed, 'the getting and keeping of £200,000 will find enemies and friends'. However, the amendment was rejected on the grounds that it would turn the bill into a fiscal measure, and thus run the risk of antagonizing the Lords. Furthermore, the House confirmed its resolve to punish Duncombe by ruling that it was a felony for anyone to aid the concealment of his estate. Indeed, such was the desperation of the Duncombe lobby that Vernon was sure that 'some would be willing to blow the coals to a dissolution of this Parliament'. Other observers also thought that the struggle was far from over, speculating that the banker had allies in the Lords who were ready to come to his rescue.[14]

Duncombe's allies were unable to prevail in the debate on the third reading on 26 Feb., even though Attorney-General Sir Thomas Trevor*, a member of the bill's drafting committee, made an impassioned speech against the House's proceedings. Trevor declared 'little acquaintance and consideration' for Duncombe, but echoed many of the arguments already broached against the bill, highlighting anxieties concerning the novelty of the crime, and questioning the legality of depriving an individual of his estate without a proper trial. Despite Trevor's opposition, and that of Treasury commissioners Thomas Pelham I* and Fox, the bill was subsequently passed by 138 votes to 103. Most significantly, Sunderland's heir, Lord Spencer (Charles*), had been cited as one of Duncombe's fiercest critics. Spencer may have been acting independently of his father over this affair, but his stance can also be interpreted as further proof of Sunderland's desertion of Duncombe.[15]

Duncombe may have lost Sunderland's support, but when the bill was presented to the Upper House, his cause was strongly upheld by Tory leaders such as Nottingham (Daniel Finch†), Rochester (Laurence Hyde†) and Leeds (Carmarthen), as well as Whig dissidents like Bolton and Peterborough. Their principal objection was that the measure was 'a method introduced to intermeddle in their jurisdiction', and even proponents of the bill such as Lord Godolphin (Sidney†) were reportedly concerned over its drafting. The bill passed its first reading on 4 Mar. by 48 votes to 36, but sufficient opposition had been raised for the Lords to hold a conference with the Commons three days later in order to discover 'the matters of fact' on which the Lower House had proceeded. Also on 7 Mar., the Commons took into consideration a pamphlet, *Mr Duncombe's Case*, which claimed that the banker had never made any confession to its Members. Predictably, this was ruled to be 'false and scandalous', and ordered to be burnt in public. Only two days later, the conference sparked another tempestuous debate in the Commons, when some Members argued that the 'confession' should not be represented to the Lords as proof of Duncombe's guilt. Opponents of the bill had consistently asserted that the Lower House had no power to administer an oath to take such testimony, but Duncombe's adversaries, with Lord Spencer again conspicuous among them, prevailed on the Commons to appoint a committee to inform the Upper House that the bill was grounded upon the 'confession' and other evidence. The conference took place the same day, but another was needed on 11 Mar., such was the rift which the bill had created between the Houses. As Cooke wearily observed on 15 Mar., 'hitherto there have happened so many blunders in the matter that I cannot say it [the bill] goes forward'.[16]

On 15 Mar. came the second reading in the Lords, and counsel were again heard for both sides. In a dramatic and unexpected reversal of fortune, the bill was then lost by a single vote on a motion for committal. Some observers attributed the defeat to Duncombe's connexions with such peers as Bolton, to whom the banker had earlier given advance warning of the Stop of the Exchequer. Others credited enmity towards Montagu, with Leeds singled out as casting the decisive vote against the bill, in order to repay Montagu for having 'a few years before accused the Duke himself of corruption'. Furthermore, it was suggested that the result had been 'not without some charge' to Duncombe, who was said to have gained this victory by 'a golden sacrifice'. There were also recriminations on the ministry's side, for several of its supporters had left the House before the vote, 'not thinking there was any danger of losing it'.[17]

However, the surprise result was quickly surpassed in importance by the Lords' decision immediately after the vote to order Duncombe's release from the Tower, which was interpreted by the Commons as a breach of privilege. It was claimed that the Lords had only acted in haste, being 'sufficiently tired after a long debate', but there was great apprehension that Duncombe's 'wonderful good fortune' would cause 'very much ill blood between the Houses'. Moreover, it was not only constitutional issues that were at stake, for Vernon anxiously took notice of the King's impatience with the Duncombe affair, which had delayed discussion of fiscal business. The Commons had no compunction in pursuing the matter, hastily appointing a committee to examine the Lords' proceedings, and later choosing another to search for precedents to assert their rights against the Lords. After both committees had reported their findings, the House resolved on 22 Mar. that its prisoners could not be discharged by 'any other authority whatsoever' during the same session, and that Duncombe should be taken into custody. Even at this late stage, an attempt was made to prolong the dispute by a motion to condemn the Lords for their release of Duncombe, but it was defeated by moderates eager to contain the controversy. There were also reports that 'it has been endeavoured to terrify Mr Duncombe as to make him run away', but the banker wisely surrendered himself to the serjeant-at-arms, and on 31 Mar. was recommitted to the Tower, where he remained until the end of the session.[18]

Even though the Lords had saved Duncombe from immediate punishment, it was inevitable that he would face further arraignment for his crime. On 18 May the Lords addressed the King for Duncombe to be prosecuted, a request to which William readily assented, and informations were filed against Duncombe in both London and Middlesex. Accordingly, he was tried at King's Bench in February 1699, only to be acquitted on a technical error in the information. He was retried in the same court on 17 June, but was quickly acquitted by the jury, whose foreman was the Country Tory Member Warwick Lake*. Provocative as ever, Duncombe treated the jurors to 'a noble dinner' afterwards, and gave them five guineas each, declaring 'the prosecution had cost him £10,000'. However, it was nearly two years before he finally obtained royal approval to quash the second process against him.[19]

The Exchequer bill controversy had obviously precluded any thoughts in Duncombe's mind of standing at the general election of 1698, and even after his acquittal it was reported that 'being out of favour at court, he seemed to retire himself from business'. He did not remain in the political wilderness for long, for in the summer of 1699 he staged a remarkable comeback with the support of the City Tories. His first success came at the London shrieval elections in June of that year, a victory which Charles Davenant* viewed as 'a just rebuke to those invaders of property who had so unreasonably persecuted him the last Parliament'. Davenant also maintained that Duncombe's allies had been planning his candidacy for some time before the election, thereby contradicting other accounts which suggested that the banker had only been put up to raise money for the corporation. In his new office Duncombe embarked on a campaign to win over the London electorate, paying particular attention to the City's prisons. The newspapers avidly followed his philanthropic path, and it was claimed that during his shrievalty he dispensed £5,364 to poor prisoners, and freed some 170 debtors. In addition, he donated £500 to redeem captives taken abroad. Several pamphlets celebrated his generosity in verse, but others viewed him sceptically, insinuating that he 'designs to live very splendidly to wipe off the blemish the late business of the Exchequer bills cast upon him'. His civic dignity even brought him recognition at court, for in October 1699 he was knighted when a City delegation attended the King. He also established himself as a leading Churchman, playing host to some 100 London clergymen on New Year's Day, 1700. Duncombe's popularity had evidently been transformed during his shrievalty, with one observer remarking that only two years before the banker 'was thought to deserve nothing less than the gallows . . . and now is the idol of the mob'. However, another believed that 'his credit is as ill among the best sort of people'.[20]

Duncombe's benevolence was seen to pay further dividends in June 1700 when he was elected as alderman for Bridge ward. In order to curry favour with the local electorate he donated a clock for St. Magnus' church, the magnificence of which was said 'to answer the design of the donor', and he later presented the parish with an organ as well. Once he had been admitted to the court of aldermen, interest was immediately made for his candidacy for the mayoralty, and rumours soon spread of the liberality which would follow his election. Various building schemes were promised, including an armoury for the Honourable Artillery Company, a statue of the King at Cheapside, and a mansion house for the mayor, and it was claimed that he would spend £40,000 for 'the good of the City'. The success of this strategy was demonstrated in September by his resounding victory in the mayoral poll, when he beat his nearest Whig challenger Sir Thomas Abney* by a majority of over 800. However, the court of aldermen ignored the result and voted by 14 to 12 in favour of Abney. The City Tories, who had been confident of securing the support of 13 aldermen for Duncombe, reacted furiously, launching an inquest to overturn the result. The controversy aroused 'great animosities' in the capital, and speculation surrounded the ministry's involvement. One account maintained that Montagu had attempted to influence the current mayor against Duncombe, but another rumour suggested that the Earl of Marlborough (John Churchill†) had endorsed Duncombe's candidacy, although this report was dismissed as 'Lord Sunderland's work'. Furthermore, after Baron of the Exchequer William Simpson had made 'a violent panegyric upon Duncombe' when swearing in the new City sheriffs, the Whig leader Sir William Ashurst* challenged

Simpson whether 'Lord Sunderland had not made him the speech, and Duncombe given him money for pronouncing it'. An anti-Duncombe pamphlet surprisingly claimed that Sir Charles 'did not appear so much concerned at the repulse as his friends were', but all the strenuous efforts made on his behalf proved in vain.[21]

Despite this setback, Duncombe had successfully re-established himself as a major force in City politics, and in October he was cited as a member of a cartel of financiers ready to advance the government £4,000,000 to pay off the Bank and the New East India Company. Earlier in the year he had appeared reluctant to resume the role of government financier when touted as a possible excise farmer, and this most ambitious scheme predictably failed to get off the ground. However, the subsequent dissolution of Parliament gave him ample opportunity to advance the cause of the Old East India Company, and in January he met Hon. James Brydges* and Sir Francis Child* to discuss the elections. He first took the precaution of securing his own return at Ipswich, a victory which he probably gained through his connexions with the Old Company. However, he suffered narrow defeats at both Downton and London. Duncombe's popularity in the capital may well have been adversely affected by attacks in the press (such as Defoe's *True Born Englishman*), which even persisted after the City poll. Most significantly, one pamphleteer censured Duncombe for becoming a tool of party, condemning his rapid rise to civic office, and lambasting him for failing to distance himself from Jacobite supporters. Such themes were also rehearsed in an anti-Tory satire of about December 1700, which suggested that plans were afoot for the introduction of a bill 'to authorize Sir Ch. Dun—b, when he is lord mayor of London, to proclaim the Prince of Wales'. In addition, he was attacked in February 1701 for having attempted a run on the Bank as part of a conspiracy hatched by supporters of the Old East India Company.[22]

In contrast to the showmanship which had salvaged his political career, once back in the House Duncombe proved an inactive Member, failing to make any significant contribution to Commons business. However, he was listed in February 1701 as a likely supporter of the Court in continuing the 'Great Mortgage', and was also blacklisted for opposing the preparations for the war. In response he signed *The Vine Tavern Queries*, which defended the Tories from allegations of crypto-Jacobitism. However, his City adversaries still managed to prevail against him at the mayoral election in September, when he only managed to gain the backing of three other aldermen, a poor performance which was attributed to his absence from the corporation's recent debate on an address to decry Louis XIV's recognition of the Pretender. Equally worryingly, his support among the liverymen had fallen by over 1,000 votes in the space of a year, and it was thus of little surprise that he suffered a heavy defeat at the City's parliamentary contest in November. Further ignominy followed, for not having taken care to secure himself at either Ipswich or Downton, he again faced exclusion from Parliament.[23]

The accession of Anne saw a resurgence in the fortunes of the City Tories, and Duncombe was duly appointed a colonel of the London militia. However, he was the only Tory candidate to fail at the ensuing parliamentary election. Personal notoriety may well have contributed to his defeat, for in the same month Defoe launched a bitter attack on him in his *Reformation of Manners*:

> Duncombe, the modern Judas of the age,
> Has often tried in vain to mount the stage:
> Profuse in gifts and bribes to God and man,
> To ride the City horse and wear the chain.

Fortunately, Duncombe was able to secure his own return at both Downton and Hedon, and chose to sit for the former. He remained generally inactive in the House, although he was appointed in the first session to a committee to investigate London coal prices. Moreover, in February 1703 he acted on behalf of his constituents to petition the crown for an extra market day at Downton. In the next session he was predictably forecast by Lord Nottingham as a supporter concerning proceedings over the Scotch Plot, but by the end of the Parliament had broken with his party over the Tack. On 30 Oct. 1704 he was classed as a probable opponent of the measure, and, having been included on Robert Harley's canvassing list, left the House with the other 'Sneakers' prior to the crucial vote on 28 Nov.[24]

Duncombe's estrangement from his party did not last long, for he backed the Tory candidates at the Middlesex election, and, after retaining his seat at Downton, he voted on 25 Oct. 1705 against the Court candidate for Speaker. He remained inconspicuous in the House, and his activity outside of it during the Parliament for once merited little publicity. Whig advances in the City conspired to undermine his standing: in June 1707 he was removed as a militia colonel, and three months later he was again overlooked for the mayoralty by the court of aldermen. In early 1708 two parliamentary lists confirmed his Tory politics, and in May of that year he had no difficulty in securing his election at Downton. Although failing to make any significant contribution to Commons business, he finally gained the mayoralty in September as the senior alderman below the chair, despite the fact that 'some great men' and 'a furious Whig party' had reportedly opposed his election. Unfortunately, the death of Prince George pre-empted his plans for a spectacular Lord Mayor's Day parade, but he was able to use his new authority to promote the Church interest. In May 1709 he endorsed the candidacy of Dr Henry Sacheverell for the chaplaincy of St. Saviour's, Southwark, but did not attempt to secure Sacheverell any City appointment. However, the following summer he displayed Tory partisanship towards the poor Palatine refugees, reportedly giving only £50 for their relief, 'and would scarce have done that but for the sake of his office'. Such parsimony was in some contrast to his previous support for charitable causes, but in the ensuing parliamentary session he received praise from the poor debtors of the Wood Street compter for assisting them during his mayoralty. He opposed the impeachment of Sacheverell, and later entertained the Tory champion at his Teddington home.[25]

Given such publicized support for the High Church party, it was no surprise that Duncombe was cited as a Tory candidate shortly before the City election of 1710. However, even though he did vote for the Tories at the London poll, he settled for another unopposed return at Downton. Soon afterwards he was greeted most warmly at court by Harley, who, as Tory election propaganda had made out, evidently considered him as a potential government creditor. Duncombe did not live up to such expectations, for despite reports that he 'cries out everything that's now done, is very well done, and talks as if they shall never want money', it was observed that 'the devil a penny does he lend'. Although unforthcoming in financial terms, he clearly maintained support for the ministry, since he was later cited as one of the 'worthy patriots' who in the first session of the 1710 Parliament helped to detect the mismanagements of the previous administration. However, well before the end of the session the Tories had been robbed of his interest by his death at Teddington on 9 Apr. 1711, on the occasion of which he was cited as 'the richest commoner of England'.[26]

Duncombe had undoubtedly made many enemies in the course of a tempestuous career, even if his philanthropy had gained him support among the London populace. Many of his election promises remained unfulfilled, but imprisoned debtors had much to thank him for, and he had also supported the SPCK. However, such charity did not spare him vilification at the hands of critics like Defoe, who portrayed Duncombe as the personification of ingratitude. Moreover, Defoe also cast aspersions on his private life, and other sources allude to the mistresses of the bachelor banker. Towards the end of his life he kept to a more fastidious diet, and preferred the joys of his estates at Teddington and Barford, both of which drew praise for their ornament. He may also have planned to develop his property at Helmsley, for within two years of his death an impressive mansion had been built there. He died intestate and unmarried, and thus his considerable fortune was split between the offspring of his brother and sister. The Wiltshire estates passed to his nephew Anthony[†], who further consolidated the family interest at Downton. Another nephew, Thomas*, who took the name of Duncombe, succeeded him as Member for Downton, but founded a dynasty at Helmsley. In addition, £200,000 was said to have passed to the Duke of Argyll, who had married Duncombe's niece, Mary.[27]

[1] Hoare, *Wilts. Downton*, 45; *Yorks. Peds.* ed. Foster, ii. (unpag.). [2] J. R. Woodhead, *Rulers of London* (London and Mdx. Arch. Soc.), 63; *Cal. Treas. Bks.* iii. 369, 854; iv. 127; v. 210; vi. 725; ix. 129, 570; x. 466, 590; R. East, *Portsmouth Recs.* 367. [3] *Cal. Treas. Bks.* vi. 2; *Cal. Ct. Mins. E.I. Co. 1677–9* ed. Sainsbury, 56; Luttrell, *Brief Relation*, i. 179; Beaven, *Aldermen*, ii. 110; Add. 10120, ff. 232–6; *Daily Courant*, 8 Aug. 1704; *Flying Post*, 29–31 Aug. 1700. [4] *Cal. Treas. Bks.* vi. 580, 612; vii. 1347; viii. 176, 1621, 2125. [5] Hoare, 45; F. G .H. Price, *Handbook of London Bankers*, 108–110; *Liveryman's Reasons* [1701], 6; Burnet, i. 561–2; *HMC Lords*, ii. 307; Le Neve's *Knights* (Harl. Soc. viii), 468; Boyer, *Wm. III*, ii. 325; R. Beddard, *Kingdom Without a King*, 173; E. Hughes, *Studies in Admin. and Finance*, 165–6, 173; *Cal. Treas. Bks.* ix. 369, 999, 1607; x. 883. [6] NLS, Advocates' mss 31.1.7, f.146; J. E. T. Rogers, *First Nine Years of the Bank*, 70; *Cal. Treas. Bks.* x. 906; Nottingham Univ. Lib. Portland (Bentinck) mss PwA 1245, Sunderland to [Portland], 29 May 1695. [7] Luttrell, iii. 513; Rogers, 28; *Evelyn Diary*, v. 246; *Poems of Alexander Pope* ed. Butt, iv. 69; *VCH Wilts.* xi. 34, 45; H. Horwitz, *Parl. and Pol. Wm. III*, 181–2; *Portledge Pprs.* 236. [8] *Cal. Treas. Bks.* xi. 353–4; xii. 5; Add. 17677 RR, f. 261. [9] J. P. Kenyon, *Sunderland*, 299; *Shrewsbury Corresp.* 524, 526; Add. 17677 SS, ff. 136–7. [10] *CSP Dom.* 1698, pp. 34, 41; *Vernon–Shrewsbury Letters*, i. 469–70; Add. 70019, Edward* to Sir Edward Harley*, 22 Jan. 1698. [11] *CSP Dom.* 1698, pp. 33–34; *Vernon–Shrewsbury Letters*, i. 477–8. [12] *CSP Dom.* 1698, pp. 53, 58; *Vernon–Shrewsbury Letters*, i. 487–8; *Shrewsbury Corresp.* 532. [13] Add. 17677 SS, ff. 136–7, 146; 30000 B, ff. 40–41; *CSP Dom.* 1698, p. 89; Bodl. Ballard 39, f. 136; *Vernon–Shrewsbury Letters*, i. 487–8; Yale Univ. Beinecke Lib. 1987. 7. 1, Robert Yard* to Ld. Manchester, 18 Feb. 1698. [14] Add. 17677, ff. 168–9; *CSP Dom.* 1698, pp. 95–96, 102, 144; *Vernon–Shrewsbury Letters*, ii. 19; Ballard 39, f. 136. [15] Stowe 364, ff. 70–79; Yale Univ. Beinecke Lib. 1987.7. 1, Yard to Manchester, 1 Mar. 1698; *Vernon–Shrewsbury Letters*, ii. 19. [16] *CSP Dom.* 1698, pp. 97, 129, 139–40, 144; *HMC Lords*, n.s. iii. 136; Add. 17677 SS, ff. 183–4. [17] Burnet, 561–2; Cunningham, *Hist. GB*, i. 169; Cobbett, *Parlty. Hist.* v. 1171; Bodl. Carte 130, f. 392. [18] *CSP Dom.* 1698, pp. 144, 173; *Vernon–Shrewsbury Letters*, ii. 26–27; Kenyon, 304; Add. 17677 SS, ff. 198–201; BL, Trumbull Alphab. mss 50, Thomas Bateman to Trumbull, 23 Mar. 1698; Luttrell, iv. 399. [19] *HMC Lords*, 224; Luttrell, iv. 480, 528; *CSP Dom.* 1699–1700, p. 229; 1700–2, pp. 136–7, 174. [20] *Liveryman's Reasons*, 4; *HMC Cowper*, ii. 388–9; Yale Univ. Beinecke Lib. Osborn Coll. Blathwayt mss, box 19, Vernon to

William Blathwayt*, 27 June 1699; *Post Boy*, 6–8 Feb., 24–26 Sept. 1700; Ballard 4, f. 44; G. Hogaeus, *Ad Virum Nobilissimum . . . Carolum Duncombum* [1699]; *Poet's Address to Sir Charles Duncombe* [1700]; Centre Kentish Stud. Stanhope mss U1590/059/8, Yard to Alexander Stanhope, 4 July 1699; Luttrell, iv. 574, 599; *Verney Letters 18th Cent.* i. 47. [21] J. P. Malcolm, *Londinium Redivivum*, iv. 34; Luttrell, iv. 660, 667, 692; *HMC Portland*, iii. 631; Trumbull Alphab. mss 50, Bateman to Trumbull, 11 Oct. 1700; *HMC Bath*, iii. 421–2; *Liveryman's Reasons*, 8. [22] Luttrell, iv. 693–4; *Vernon–Shrewsbury Letters*, ii. 452; Huntington Lib. Stowe mss 26(2), Brydges' diary, 26 Jan. 1701; *Poems on Affairs of State* ed. Ellis, vi. 300–8; *Liveryman's Reasons*; *HMC Portland*, viii. 63; Rogers, 134. [23] Blathwayt mss, box 20, Vernon to Blathwayt, 2 Oct. 1701; Add. 40775, ff. 220–1. [24] Luttrell, v. 193; *Poems on Affairs of State* ed. Ellis, 409–10; *CSP Dom.* 1703–4, p. 379. [25] *Mdx. Poll of 1705*; Luttrell, vi. 186, 364, 367; Boyer, *Anne Annals*, vi. 240; *HMC Portland*, iv. 503; Folger Shakespeare Lib. Newdigate newsletter 30 Sept. 1708; E. Settle, *Triumphs of London* [1708]; G. Holmes, *Trial of Sacheverell*, 57–58; *Bull. IHR*, xl. 161; *CJ*, xvi. 321; Add. 70421, newsletter 28 Mar. 1710. [26] Luttrell, vi. 633; *Wentworth Pprs.* 151; Boyer, *Anne Annals*, ix. app. 144; *Le Neve's Knights*, 468; *Post Man*, 10–12 Apr. 1711. [27] *Chapter in Eng. Church Hist.* ed. McClure, 26; *Poems on Affairs of State* ed. Ellis, 300–8, 409–10; *HMC Bath*, 321; *Liveryman's Reasons*, 14–15; *A Common Council Journal* [1701]; Hoare, 40–42; Lysons, *Environs* (1792–6), iii. 512; *VCH Yorks. N. Riding*, i. 486; PCC Admon 1711, f. 93; *VCH Wilts.* 34; *Swift Stella* ed. Davis, 238.

P. W./P. L. G.

DUNCOMBE, Edward (b. 1675–by 1744).

APPLEBY 1708–1713

b. 5 Sept. 1675, 1st s. of William Duncombe*. *m.* Susanna, *s.p. suc.* fa. 13 Apr. 1704.[1]

Duncombe was successful for Appleby on the interest of the Earl of Thanet (Thomas Tufton†) in both 1708 and 1710, but his parliamentary activity is difficult to distinguish from that of Francis Duncombe*, who also sat in the 1708 and 1710 Parliaments. In 1710 Duncombe voted against the impeachment of Dr Sacheverell, and in June the same year presented an address from Appleby which deplored the 'lately revived' doctrine of resistance and promised to return Members at the next election who would support the Queen's hereditary right to the throne. The 'Hanover list' classed Duncombe as a Tory, and he was listed in 1711 as both a 'Tory patriot' who had opposed the continuation of the war and a 'worthy patriot' who had helped detect the mismanagements of the previous administration. Duncombe's friendship with (Sir) Thomas Hanmer II* (2nd Bt.) was evident in January 1712 when the Earl of Oxford (Robert Harley*) listed Hanmer to lobby Duncombe for the Commons' attack upon the Duke of Marlborough (John Churchill†), and on 18 June 1713 Duncombe followed Hanmer's lead by voting against the French commerce bill. He thereby forfeited Lord Thanet's favour and was not recommended for Appleby at the next election. Duncombe's subsequent life is obscure and the date of his death has not been ascertained, though his will, written in 1740, was proved on 12 Jan. 1744. Duncombe, described as being of Southampton, left his house in Southampton and lands in Lincolnshire and Yorkshire to his wife for life, and thereafter to Henry Scott, 3rd Earl of Deloraine [S], grandson of Duncombe's deceased sister.[2]

[1] *Beds. N. and Q.* ii. 45–47; IGI, London; PCC 100 Anstis. [2] *HMC Portland*, iv. 578; R. Hopkinson, 'Elections at Appleby 1701–15' (Newcastle-upon-Tyne Univ. B.A. thesis, 1968), 63, 67, 73, 88; Add. 70331, canvassing list, c. Jan. 1712; PCC 100 Anstis.

P. W.

DUNCOMBE, Francis (c. 1653–1720), of Broughton, Newport Pagnell, Bucks.

AMERSHAM 1708–1713

b. c. 1653, 1st s. of Thomas Duncombe of Broughton by 1st w. Mary, da. of Charles Edmonds of Preston, Northants. *m.* (1) 26 Apr. 1683, Mary (*d.* 1686), da. of Sir Anthony Chester, 3rd Bt.†, of Chicheley, Bucks., 1da. *d.v.p.*; (2) lic. 13 Feb. 1688, aged about 34, Frances, da. of James Baron, linen-draper and alderman of London, 1s. 1da. *suc.* fa. 1672.[1]

Duncombe's family was well established in Buckinghamshire, having acquired the manor of Broughton in 1572. Duncombe himself first appeared as a deputy-lieutenant and j.p. of the county in 1684. There may have been a hiatus in his service in local office consequent upon his refusal to agree to the first two of James II's 'three questions', but this is unclear. His name regularly appears in the quarter sessions records until after the Hanoverian succession. In August 1702 his wife and two children inherited £2,200 from her uncle Arthur Baron (London common councilman, merchant, and uncle to Gilbert Heathcote*), and he himself, as one of the four executors, received two-thirds of the residue of the estate after numerous bequests had been paid. It seems likely that at least some of this windfall was laid out in land, for around this time Duncombe acquired the manor of North Crawley, near Newport Pagnell. His enhanced wealth may also explain his candidature for the county in the Tory interest in the by-election of November 1704, which ended in defeat.[2]

Returned for Amersham in the general election of 1708, Duncombe was classed as a Tory on a list of early 1708, amended to take account of the elections. His career in the Commons is almost impossible to disentangle from that of Edward Duncombe and, after May 1711, that of Thomas Duncombe (formerly

Browne). However, 'Francis Duncombe' was named on 23 Dec. 1708 to the drafting committee on the bill for the more effectual recruitment of the army. In the following session he was almost certainly responsible for managing through the House a local bill from the Lords relating to a Buckinghamshire estate. He also voted against the impeachment of Dr Sacheverell.

Re-elected in 1710, Duncombe was classed as a Tory in the 'Hanover list'. In the first session of the new Parliament, he may have been the 'Mr Duncombe' who managed a bill for the relief of insolvent debtors through all its stages in the Commons. Politically, in the 1710–11 session Duncombe was listed as a 'Tory patriot' who opposed the continuation of the war, a 'worthy patriot' who helped to detect the mismanagements of the previous administration, and a member of the October Club. His name also appears on a canvassing list, probably relating to the attack in January 1712 on the Duke of Marlborough (John Churchill[†]), as one to be spoken to by William Lowndes*, secretary to the Treasury, but, more important in this instance, a Buckinghamshire landowner. In August 1712 William Wotton, rector of nearby Milton, proffered the view that 'whatever his [Duncombe's] skill for speaking may be in the House of Commons, his reputation for integrity is very great in this country'.[3]

In the 1713 session Duncombe was almost certainly the Member who told on 2 May in favour of introducing a bill suspending the duties on French wines, an essential prerequisite for the French commerce bill for which he voted on 18 June. Also in May 1713, he presented to the Queen the Amersham address on the 'glorious peace'. His interest in commercial matters in this session may indicate that he acted as a teller again, on 8 June, against a bill to open up the African trade. Duncombe did not stand at the 1713 election, but was still accounted 'of the right side' by the Tory, Sir Thomas Cave, 3rd Bt.*[4]

In September 1714, preparatory to the expected general election, Duncombe was one of the signatories to an agreement to split the county representation between a Whig and a Tory. He was reported to have been omitted from the Buckinghamshire bench in February 1716. He died on 31 Jan. 1720 in his 70th year. In his will he left charitable bequests, providing for the Church catechism to be taught and for cleaning the parish church. He was succeeded by his son, also Francis (d. 1747), the last of the family.[5]

[1] PCC 43 Pye; Lipscomb, *Bucks*. iv. 82–83; *Mar. Lic. Vicar-Gen.* (Harl Soc. xxxi.), 46; J. R. Woodhead, *Rulers of London* (London and Mdx. Arch. Soc.), 24–25. [2] Lipscomb, 79, 82; *CSP Dom.* 1683–4, p. 358; *Bucks. Session Recs.* ii. 509; iii. 454; iv. 210; Duckett, *Penal Laws and Test Act* (1883), 148; PCC 133 Herne. [3] Add. 70331, canvassing list; Huntington Lib. Stowe mss 58(12), p. 9. [4] *London Gazette*, 12–16 May 1713; *Verney Letters 18th Cent.* i. 244. [5] *Verney Letters 18th Cent.* 317; ii. 38; Lipscomb, 82; *London Mag.* 1747, p. 149.

E. C./S. N. H.

DUNCOMBE (formerly **BROWNE**), **Thomas** (c.1683–1746), of Duncombe Park, Yorks.

DOWNTON   9 May 1711–1713
RIPON   1734–1741

b. c.1683, o. s. of Thomas Browne, merchant, of St. Margaret's, Westminster by Ursula, da. of Alexander Duncombe of Drayton, Bucks.; sis. of Anthony* and Charles Duncombe*. *educ*. Christ Church, Oxf. matric. 27 Apr. 1703, aged 19; I. Temple 1709. m. 18 Aug. 1714, Sarah, da. of Sir Thomas Slingsby, 4th Bt., of Scriven, Yorks., and sis. of Henry Slingsby*, 3s. 2da. *suc*. uncle (Sir) Charles Duncombe in Yorkshire estates and assumed name of Duncombe 1711; fa. 1720.[1]

Sheriff, Yorks. 1727–8.

Duncombe's father had been concerned with his uncle, the banker (Sir) Charles Duncombe, in making government loans in the reign of Charles II and continued to do so on his own after 1690, lending various amounts. In 1711 the Member himself succeeded to his uncle's Yorkshire estates, and was returned unopposed for Downton in the by-election necessitated by his uncle's death. Duncombe was probably a Tory like the rest of his family, although his Commons career is obscured by the presence of namesakes in the chamber. However, he is not recorded as having voted in any of the divisions during his time in Parliament. He did not stand for Parliament in 1713, and was not returned again until 1734. He died on 23 Mar. 1746.[2]

[1] *Yorks. Peds.* ed. Foster, ii (unpag.); *The Gen.* n.s. ii. 147. [2] *Cal. Treas. Bks.* ix. 1923.

P. W.

DUNCOMBE, William (c.1647–1704), of Battlesden, Beds.

BURY ST. EDMUNDS   10 Feb. 1673–1679 (Jan.)
BEDFORDSHIRE   1689–1690
   1695–1698

b. c.1647, o. surv. s. of Sir John Duncombe[†] of Battlesden by Elizabeth, da. of Sir Humphrey May[†] of Carrow Priory, Norf., and sis. of Baptist May*. *educ*. travelled abroad (Flanders) 1666. m. settlement 30 May 1672, Jane, da. of Frederick Cornwallis[†], 1st Baron Cornwallis, 2s. (1 d.v.p.) 3da. *suc*. fa. 1687.[1]

Envoy to Sweden 1689–92; ld. justice [I] 1693–5; joint comptroller of army accounts 1703–d.[2]
Freeman, Merchant Adventurers' Co. 1692.[3]
Member Dublin Philosophical Society, 1693.[4]

Duncombe, a distant kinsman of (Sir) Charles Duncombe*, was appointed ambassador to Sweden in 1689 to try to persuade Charles XI to provide troops against France, and to negotiate treaties of alliance and commerce. He failed in both objectives and was recalled in 1692, supposedly 'at his own desire'. He informed the diplomatist Sir William Dutton Colt that 'I am going out of the ministry, which is too much for me in truth, for I am not able to cope with it'. His absence abroad probably accounts for his failure to stand for Parliament in 1690.[5]

Duncombe had returned to England by September 1692 and the following May was appointed one of the three lords justices of Ireland, with Sir Cyril Wyche* and the Whig Lord Capell (Hon. Sir Henry Capel*). Duncombe arrived in Dublin in July, having travelled over with Capell. Initially the three men enjoyed a successful working relationship, but by 1694 it was clear from their communications with the English ministers that Duncombe and Wyche had fallen into disagreement with Capell. In July 1694 Duncombe and Wyche sent the Privy Council an unfavourable report on the prospects for a successful session of parliament in Ireland, an action which marked the turning point in Duncombe's sojourn in Ireland. Capell's more positive opinion, and the strong support in England he derived from the Whig Junto, ensured that Duncombe and Wych would not remain in office much longer. In May 1695 the conflict was resolved when Duncombe and Wyche were recalled, and Capell was left as lord deputy. At this time there was a rumour, which proved to be false, that Duncombe was to succeed Sir William Trumbull* at the Treasury. The rumour may have prompted Capell to write to James Vernon I* on 12 May 1695: 'I wish Mr Duncombe well, he being my relation; but the King, I presume, will be wary whom he puts in great places, for I doubt he is not sound to this government.' In July, at a Privy Council meeting on the government's bills prepared for presentation to the forthcoming Irish parliament, Duncombe and Wyche 'opened themselves pretty freely' against several of the bills. Their action caused Vernon to express the view that given their opinion, it was a good thing that the calling of parliament had been put off until after they had been removed from office.[6]

Duncombe was returned for Bedfordshire in 1695 in a contested election. He was noted as likely to oppose the Court in a forecast of the division on the proposed council of trade on 31 Jan. 1696, though he signed the Association promptly. However, in March he voted against fixing the price of guineas at 22s. He does not appear to have voted on the attainder of Sir John Fenwick† in the 1696–7 session, and was in general an inactive Member. He was granted leave of absence on 22 Dec. 1696 for recovery of his health, and was probably the 'Mr Duncombe' granted leave again on 6 Mar. 1697 because his family was ill. He unsuccessfully contested Bedfordshire in 1698, when a comparative analysis of the old and new Houses described him as a Country party supporter. He petitioned against the return on 12 Dec., though without success. In October he was nominated as the Old East India Company's ambassador to the Mogul, but in the event was not chosen. After the accession of Anne he was appointed, along with Sir Joseph Tredenham*, as comptroller of army accounts, with a shared salary of £1,500 p.a. Duncombe died of smallpox on 13 Apr. 1704.[7]

[1] *Beds. N. and Q.* ii. 45–47; F. A. Blaydes, *Genealogia Bedfordiensis*, 22, 344. [2] *CSP Dom.* 1693, pp. 134, 175; 1694–5, p. 471; *Cal. Treas. Bks.* xviii. 41, 300. [3] Rutland mss at Belvoir Castle, no. 20, list of freemen, 1621–93. [4] K. T. Hoppen, *Common Scientist in 17th Cent.* 204. [5] *EHR*, xxxix. 571–87; *HMC Finch*, ii. 415; PRO NI, De Ros mss D638/13/106, John Pulteney* to Thomas Coningsby*, 2 Feb. 1692; Add. 36662, f. 388. [6] *CSP Dom.* 1693, pp. 134, 175–6, 238; 1694–5, pp. 236, 471; McGrath thesis, 265, 267, 269, 270–1; Burnet, iv. 284; Coxe, *Shrewsbury*, 58; Centre Kentish Stud. Stanhope mss U1590/059/4, Robert Yard* to Alexander Stanhope, 7 May 1695; H. Horwitz, *Parl. and Pol. Wm. III*, 154; Folger Shakespeare Lib. Newdigate newsletter 1 June 1695; Add. 40771, f. 39. [7] *Vernon–Shrewsbury Letters*, ii. 196; *Cal. Treas. Bks.* xviii. 41, 300; Luttrell, *Brief Relation*, v. 413.

P. W.

DUPPLIN, George Hay, Visct. [S] *see* **HAY**

DURSLEY, James Berkeley, Visct. *see* **BERKELEY**

DUTTON, Sir Ralph, 1st Bt. (c.1635–?1721), of Sherborne, Glos.

GLOUCESTERSHIRE 1679–1681 (Mar.), 1689–1698

b. c.1635, 2nd s. of Sir Ralph Dutton of Standish, Glos. by Mary, da. of William Duncombe, Haberdasher, of London. *educ.* ?Hayes, Mdx. (Thomas Triplett). *m.* (1) settlement 13 Aug. 1674, Grizel (d. 1678), da. of Sir Edward Poole† of Kemble, Wilts., 2da. (1 *d.v.p.*); (2) 14 Jan. 1679 (with £10,000), Mary, da. and h. of Peter Barwick, MD, of Westminster, physician to Charles II, 4s. (3 *d.v.p.*) 4da. *suc.* bro. 1675; *cr.* Bt. 22 June 1678.[1]
Freeman, Gloucester 1689.[2]

Dutton, who was widely renowned for his enthusiasm for greyhound racing, inherited an estate which through carelessness and improvidence he steadily encumbered with extensive debt. Not least among the financial drains on his wealth was his determination to maintain a premier position among Gloucestershire's gentry and provide himself with one of the shire seats in successive elections. Having previously represented the county in the Exclusion Parliaments and more recently in the Convention, he was returned again in 1690. Lord Carmarthen (Sir Thomas Osborne†) classed him as a Whig, and a list compiled the following March categorized him as a Court supporter. A fairly active county Member in the 1690 Parliament, he interested himself in many issues, not least those which bore typically on the interests of his rural constituents, and despite his otherwise consistent support for the Court, showed an enthusiasm for 'Country' measures. In October 1690 he supported the initiation of a bill to regulate Smithfield market and appears to have been the prime mover of a measure to tighten laws against the export of wool. On 18 Nov. 1691 he spoke in favour of the treason trials bill, and on the 25th was included among those ordered to prepare a bill regarding the domestic manufacture of saltpetre. On 8 Dec. he made a spectacle of himself when he insisted that he could prove the existence of an illegal trade between Jersey and France, only for his witness, when questioned by the House, to deny the allegation completely. A week later he supported a move to increase the number of officers in each army regiment, and on 16 Dec. spoke against the bill to encourage privateers. He spoke twice on 19 Jan. 1692 regarding the poll bill, arguing against too high a levy, which he and others feared would lead to 'a rebellion'. In the next session he complained on 8 Dec. 1692 that the committee of the whole House on 'advice' to the King had dissolved itself without ordering a report or a request for leave to sit again, and moved successfully that the committee be revived. He supported the place bill on 22 Dec., and on 20 Jan. 1693 spoke against the bill on royal mines. In the supply debates of that session he was the unsuccessful proposer on 4 Feb. of a tax on all new buildings towards financing the army. He intervened several times on 22 Feb., during the long debate on the state of Ireland, chiefly to condemn the prorogation of the Irish parliament, which he claimed had been done to forestall inquiries into financial irregularities; and to urge that William Culliford*, the Irish revenue commissioner implicated in these allegations, be summoned for questioning. Later, on 13 Mar., when he spotted Culliford in the House, he immediately demanded that Culliford give account of himself there and then, which he did. Dutton had in the meantime, on 25 Feb., spoken in favour of addressing the King to dissolve the East India Company. In the spring of 1693 Grascome classed him as a Court supporter. On 14 Nov., in the ensuing session, he was an appointee to a committee to scrutinize the laws 'concerning clothing' and to prepare a bill for their improvement, and on 2 Jan. 1694 he was required to participate in a similar exercise regarding laws on the assize of bread. He acted as a teller on the 11th in favour of a bill to stimulate woollen manufacture, and on 23 Feb. reported from the second-reading committee on the clothing bill, which he had earlier helped to draft. In the last session of this Parliament, on 17 Dec. 1694, he spoke in favour of the place bill, suggesting an additional clause excluding all holders of office under Charles II and James II. He was a teller on 20 Feb. 1695 against the release of the Tory mayor of Liverpool, in custody for misconduct at a recent by-election for the town. A little later he supervised the report and final stages of a bill concerning locks on the Thames 'westward of the city of London'.[3]

Dutton's personal affairs were not improving and in the summer of 1695 he seriously considered selling off part of his estate to pay his debts. These difficulties did not deter him from securing his county seat again in 1695, but as far as can be determined he was hardly involved at all in the next Parliament's proceedings. He was noted at this time as a 'discontented man' by a group of apparently misinformed Jacobite conspirators who hoped he might join them, though he betrayed no such inclinations in the Commons, where his support for the Court continued unabated: he was forecast in January 1696 as likely to support the Court on the proposed council of trade, was a prompt subscriber to the Association, and in March voted for fixing the price of guineas at 22s. On 25 Nov. he voted for the attainder of Sir John Fenwick†. The only bill which he played any part in initiating was a measure for regulating the local courts of equity, which he and others were ordered to prepare on 5 Dec. 1695. In May 1698 a private bill was introduced to enable him to raise money to pay his debts, but was thrown out at second reading. Declining solvency may have been the primary cause of growing antipathy towards him in Gloucestershire and which led to the loss of his seat in the 1698 election. Though he canvassed, it is not clear whether support was sufficient to encourage him to go through a poll. His desperation to return to Parliament, quite probably in order to immunize himself from the threat of arrest, manifested itself in several more electoral gambits, but his ability to command support was severely cramped by lack of money (see GLOUCESTERSHIRE). At the first election of 1701 he even took some momentary interest in the idea of staking his return on a partnership with the rabid Tory John Grobham Howe*, though in the end he insisted on standing singly, a course which was thought to have caused his defeat. He tried again at the end of the year, but as the weakest of three Whig candidates, he stood down at the last minute. By 1705, it was observed by one prominent Gloucestershire Whig, Sir John Guise, 3rd Bt.*, that Dutton 'having lost his credit in the county by the ill state of his affairs, ... had been laid aside by the gentlemen of that party for two or three elections'. His rancour towards the Whigs ran to such heights that in the election of that year he threw in his lot with the Tories and agreed to partner Howe in the campaign. In so doing, however, he became the unwitting victim of Howe's own mischievous schemes to blacken the Whigs. Howe insinuated himself into Dutton's confidence, it appears, by alerting him to the 'ill management and dishonesty' of his steward John Prinn, a zealous and active figure among the county Whigs. Shortly before the poll was due to commence, Dutton therefore brought a charge against Prinn for having defrauded him of £42,000 in the hope that Prinn's immediate arrest would ruin the Whig campaign. The ruse failed, however, and the two Whigs opposing Dutton and Howe were elected. Ironically, when Dutton's accounts were finally reckoned, he was found to be in debt to Prinn by £1,500.[4]

After this debacle Dutton withdrew from public life. In 1710 he made over his estate to his heir (Sir John Dutton, 2nd Bt.†) and spent his last years in Ireland. His will, in which he described himself as of Rathfarnham, Co. Dublin, was dated 12 Oct. 1720 and proved 21 Mar. 1721.

[1]*PCC* 105 Penn. [2]*Gloucester Freemen* (Glos. Rec. Ser. iv), 43. [3]*CSP Dom.* 1690–1, p. 548; *Luttrell Diary*, 24, 66, 80, 83, 141–2, 303, 336, 376, 402, 438, 440, 442, 449, 478; *Lexington Pprs.* 22. [4]Add. 70117, Abigail to Sir Edward Harley*, 28 June 1695; R. Blackmore, *Hist. of Conspiracy Against . . . King Wm. III* (1723), 117; *Guise Mems.* (Cam. Soc. ser. 3, xxviii), 145–6.

P. W./A. A. H.

DUTTON COLT, Sir Henry, 1st Bt. *see* **COLT**

DUTTON COLT, John *see* **COLT**

DYKE, Sir Thomas, 1st Bt. (c.1650–1706), of Horeham, Waldron, Suss.

SUSSEX   1685–1687
EAST GRINSTEAD   1689–1698

b. c.1650, 2nd but 1st surv. s. of Sir Thomas Dyke† of Waldron by Catherine, da. of Sir John Bramston, c.j. Kb, of Skreens, Essex. *educ.* Westminster 1660–1; Christ Church, Oxf. matric. 1 June 1666, aged 16; M. Temple 1667; travelled abroad. *m.* 1695, Philadelphia, da. and coh. of Sir Thomas Nutt of Selmeston, Suss., 2s. (1 *d.v.p.*) 3da. *suc.* fa. 1669; *cr.* Bt. 3 May 1677.

Commr. public accts. 1696–7.[1]

A High Church Tory, Dyke supported the Revolution and was returned in 1690 for East Grinstead, where he owned property. He was classed as a Tory and probable Court supporter on lists of the new Parliament annotated by Lord Carmarthen (Sir Thomas Osborne†). Carmarthen also identified him in December 1690 as a likely supporter in the event of an attack upon himself in the Commons. By contrast, in April 1691 Dyke was classed in Robert Harley's* list as a supporter of the Country party, and his subsequent parliamentary record seems to confirm this analysis. Granted three weeks' leave of absence on 19 Feb. 1694, he probably did not return to the House until the next session. From 1695 he seems to have become moderately active, and to have been involved in various minor items of legislation. He served as teller three times during the 1694–5 session: on 2 Feb. 1695 for an opposition amendment to the supply bill; on the 8th against a bill for the relief of merchants who had imported foreign goods and were being prosecuted under the Navigation Acts; and on 3 May on a procedural motion during the impeachment of the Duke of Leeds (the former Carmarthen).

Dyke successfully contested East Grinstead in 1695 against opposition from the 6th Earl of Dorset (Charles Sackville†), who had a strong interest there. Sir John Bland, 4th Bt.*, wrote to Roger Kenyon* on 31 Dec. that Dyke had

always behaved himself very honestly and like a lover of his country, all the last Parliament. At his election he met with all the opposition the C[ourt] party could give him, and they did not forget to call him Jacobite and told the town, if he was chose, and 60 more of the old Members of his principles, they would be turned out of the House.

Despite a determined attempt by the Whigs to unseat Dyke on petition, his return was confirmed. Forecast as a probable opponent of the Court in the division of 31 Jan. 1696 on the proposed council of trade, Dyke was elected on 1 Feb. as one of the commissioners of accounts, but his refusal to sign the Association prevented him from serving on the commission. In March he voted against the Court over fixing the price of guineas at 22s.[2]

During the opening months of the next session

Dyke concentrated on the case of Sir John Fenwick†. On 6 Nov. he spoke against proceeding against Fenwick by way of attainder; on 13 Nov. he intervened again in debate, arguing that counsel for the prosecution be confined 'to proofs of the matter contained in the bill'; and on 17 Nov. he made a powerful speech opposing the bill:

> That the Parliament hath a power to make such a law, is agreed, but I think it ought not to be used but upon extraordinary occasions, when great persons are concerned that cannot be otherwise brought to justice, and when crimes do not fall under the denomination of the law, which is not the present case. This case is, that a gentleman is charged with treason and it is proved but by one witness, though the counsel did say that a consult to levy war was not treason. Now either it will not be the crime that is alleged, or it is not proved. Here you are judges, prosecutors, witnesses and jury. I would know in what country it is so? Besides the witnesses are produced here and not sworn, and upon the whole, there is but one witness. Sir, I am against the bill . . . as being of dangerous consequence.

He told against engrossing the bill on 23 Nov., and voted against it in the final division two days later. Earlier he had told twice on the bill for regulating elections: on 19 Nov. for a motion to consider the bill before supply, and on 21 Nov. against receiving a petition from Exeter against the bill. On 24 Nov. he defended the secretary of state, Sir William Trumbull*, from criticism of his actions in office, in such a way that James Vernon I* believed Dyke hoped to turn the attack on to the Earl of Portland. During the winter he was purged from the Sussex commission of the peace for refusing the Association. In the second half of the session he brought into the House on 19 Feb. 1697 a letter from Ostend about the joining of the Brest and Toulon squadrons, but the opposition could make little headway on the matter. He also told on 24 Feb. 1698 for a motion to recommit the resolution granting £515,000 for the civil list; on 3 Mar. against laying a duty on all goods made of wool, silk or hair; and on 10 Mar. for a bill for the repair of Whitby harbour.³

In the 1697–8 session Dyke was one of the opposition speakers who began the attacks on Lord Sunderland, saying on 21 Dec.,

> if it were not time now to talk of ill ministers, and if any were about the King who misled the two last, and that either gave up the rights of the people, or the Protestant religion, he would move for addressing the King, that he might be removed from his councils and his presence for ever.

The attack frightened Sunderland into resigning almost immediately. On 8 Jan. 1698 Dyke spoke in the debate on a motion to grant £500,000 for guards and garrisons, apparently opposing it on the grounds that the debate was irregular. He was teller on 11 Feb. for a resolution of the committee of supply fixing the debt due to the king of Denmark, and on the 16th for the opposition in favour of Charles Montagu's* withdrawing from the House during a debate on Montagu's Irish grant, making on 18 Feb.

> a long and set speech upon the subject of these grants and particularly against Mr [Charles] Montagu, who as one of the lords commissioners of the Treasury, ought to have dissuaded his Majesty from granting them, much less have taken one himself, which he thought a breach of his trust and oath, and that the House could not do otherwise than censure him for it.

He was a teller on 29 Mar. against the Court for adjourning consideration of adding an appropriating clause to the land tax bill. In late March, he was described as one of the leaders of the opposition. In May 1698 it emerged that he had been involved with attempts to discredit the commissioners of excise, encouraging Thomas Webb's* allegations that some members of the board had neglected to qualify themselves by taking the oaths, and in the same month he was reported to be contemplating an attack on Lords Albemarle and Orford (Edward Russell*), exploiting the failure of Norris' squadron to attack the French under Pointis. Vernon wrote that 'if Sir Christopher Musgrave [4th Bt.*] and Sir Thomas Dyke have espoused it, as I hear they have, they will make a troublesome piece of work of it'. However, possibly because of the lateness in the session, little headway was made with the attack. On 1 June he moved that a list of disbanded troops and those to be disbanded be laid before the House, but enthusiasm for disbanding had cooled and Vernon wrote, 'they say it was not intended to be carried further'.⁴

Dyke's continued refusal to sign the Association led to his decision not to stand in the 1698 election, much to the regret of the Tory leader Lord Nottingham (Daniel Finch†). He was classed as a supporter of the Country party in an analysis of the old and new House of about September. In January 1701 a rumour that Dyke would return to Parliament at the next election proved unfounded, and in 1704 Nottingham wanted to put him forward as the candidate for the University of Oxford, but he resisted all requests. A letter to his Oxford friend, Dr Arthur Charlett, on 15 Oct. 1704, suggests that he took a gloomy view of current politics and preferred to remain on the sidelines: 'the whole world seems to be playing at pushpin for their lives. . . . Your statesmen are at cross-purposes and blind man's buff.' Dyke died on 31 Oct. 1706 and was buried at Waldron.[5]

[1] *CJ*, xi. 429. [2] *HMC Kenyon*, 387; H. Horwitz, *Parl. and Pol. Wm. III*, 166, 179; Luttrell, *Brief Relation*, iv. 74. [3] *Vernon–Shrewsbury Letters*, i. 49–50, 76, 213–14; Cobbett, *Parlty. Hist.* v. 1004, 1019, 1059; L. K. J. Glassey, *Appt. JPs*, 123. [4] *Vernon–Shrewsbury Letters*, i. 445; ii. 85–87, 94; *CSP Dom.* 1697, p. 534; 1698, p. 96; *Cam. Misc.* xxix. 358; PRO 31/3/180, f. 150; *Cal. Treas. Bks.* xiii. 94. [5] Horwitz, 239; SRO, Hamilton mss GD 406/1/4657, Gawin Mason to Duke of Hamilton, 2 Jan. 1700[-01]; Add. 29588, ff. 265–6, 281; Bodl. Ballard 11, ff. 54–55, 56.

P. W.

DYMOKE, Charles (1667–1703), of Scrivelsby, Lincs.

LINCOLNSHIRE 1698–17 Jan. 1703

b. 1667, 3rd but 1st surv. s. of Sir Charles Dymoke of Scrivelsby, champion of Eng. by Eleanor, da. of Lewis Watson†, 1st Baron Rockingham; bro. of Lewis Dymoke*. *educ.* Magdalene, Camb. adm. 6 Feb. 1682 aged 14, MA 1682. *m.* c.1696, Jane (*d.* 1744), da. and h. of Robert Snoden of Horncastle, Lincs., *s.p. suc.* fa. 1686.[1]

Champion of Eng. 1686–*d.*

Dymoke's family had been settled in Lincolnshire since at least the 14th century, when by marriage they had acquired the manor of Scrivelsby, which conferred on its owner the dignity of champion of England. The first of his ancestors to sit in Parliament, John Dymoke, had represented the county in 1372. In the late 17th century the Dymokes were still at the forefront of county society, with the Member's father described in 1684 as 'of great fortune and considerable interest in Lincolnshire'. Charles Dymoke first acted as champion at the coronation of William and Mary in 1689, and two months later a warrant was prepared to make him a baronet, although the honour somehow eluded him. In 1696 his estate was estimated at 'almost £2,000 a year', but it was thought that 'he owes more by far than he is worth'.[2]

Despite these financial worries, Dymoke fought a successful campaign for Lincolnshire in 1698. Shortly afterwards his name appeared in a probable forecast of those who were likely to oppose a standing army, but he was classed as a Court supporter by another political observer. The latter assessment may have been assumed from his position as champion, and was subsequently queried by another analyst. He was not prominent in that Parliament, but secured an unopposed victory at the Lincolnshire election of January 1701, and was listed in February as likely to support the Court in agreeing with the committee of supply's resolution to continue the 'Great Mortgage'. The following month he was appointed with two other local Members to draft a bill for the draining of Deeping Fen, Lincolnshire. In the wake of an unopposed return at the second general election of 1701, he made little impact in the House, but voted on 26 Feb. 1702 for the resolution vindicating the Commons' recent proceedings in the impeachments of the King's Whig ministers.

As champion, Dymoke took part in the coronation of Queen Anne, and found little difficulty in retaining his seat at the ensuing general election. However, during the first session he died, 'much lamented', on 17 Jan. 1703, 'of a complication of distempers, which a very gross body brought upon him'. He was buried at Scrivelsby, and left extensive property in its neighbourhood to his younger brother Lewis, who succeeded him as champion.[3]

[1] IGI, Lincs.; *Lincs. Peds.* (Harl. Soc. lv), 1207; S. Lodge, *Scrivelsby*, 89. [2] *Lincs. Peds.* 1203; *HMC 7th Rep.* 298; *CSP Dom.* 1689–90, p. 68; *Pryme Diary* (Surtees Soc. liv), 109. [3] *Lincs. Peds.* 1207; *Post Boy*, 19–21 Jan. 1703; Add. 27440, f. 135; Lodge, 91; PCC 89 Dogg.

P. W./P. L. G.

DYMOKE, Lewis (1669–1760), of Scrivelsby, Lincs.

LINCOLNSHIRE 10 Feb. 1703–1705, 1710–1713

b. 14 Feb. 1669, 4th but 2nd surv. s. of Sir Charles Dymoke and bro. of Charles Dymoke*. *educ.* Christ Church, Oxf. matric. 1685. *unm. suc.* bro. Charles Dymoke 1703.[1]

Champion of Eng. 1703–*d.*

Returned at the by-election for Lincolnshire caused by the death of his elder sibling, Dymoke was commended by one county gentleman as 'fitter for that station than his brother'. A Tory, he voted in February 1703 against agreeing with the Lords' amendments to the bill for extending the time for taking the Abjuration. In the second session he was named to a drafting committee for a private estate bill, and twice acted as a teller: on 23 Dec. against referring to a committee a petition opposing a highways bill; and on 18 Feb. 1704 in favour of adjourning all committees. In the third session his only significant activity was an appointment to a drafting committee on a bill to enforce the Ancholme Level Drainage Act, a matter of obvious local importance. In October he was forecast as doubtful for the vote on the Tack, but did vote in favour of the High Tory measure. His stance on this contentious issue probably played an influential part in his defeat at the Lincolnshire election of 1705.[2]

Dymoke did not stand in 1708, but came top of the county poll two years later. He remained a firm backbencher, his only nomination of note in the whole Parliament resting with the drafting committee on a Boston waterworks bill. At its outset, the 'Hanover list' classed him as a Tory, and he was celebrated as one of the 'worthy patriots' who in the first session detected the mismanagements of the previous administration. He was a member of the October Club, but deserted the government in June 1713 by voting against the French commerce bill. Having failed to put up at the general election in 1713, he retired from active politics but carried out his public duties as champion at the coronations of George I and George II. He died a bachelor on 5 or 14 Feb. 1760, shortly before the accession of the George III, and left his estate to a kinsman, Edward Dymoke, a London merchant.[3]

[1] *Lincs. Peds.* (Harl. Soc. lv), 1207. [2] Lincs AO, Massingberd mss 20/50, Sir William to Burrell Massingberd, 5 Feb. 1705. [3] S. Lodge, *Scrivelsby*, 129; *Lincs. Peds.* 1207; PCC 145 Lynch.

P. W./P. L. G.

DYOTT, Richard (1667–1719), of Freeford, Staffs.

LICHFIELD 1690–1695, 1698–1708, 1710–1715

b. 9 May 1667, o. s. and h. of Richard Dyott[†] by 1st w. Katherine, da. of Thomas Gresley of Lullington, Derbys. *m.* 20 Sept. 1685, Frances (*d.* 1702), da. of William Inge of Thorpe Constantine, Staffs. and sis. of William Inge[†], 2s. (1 *d.v.p.*) 4da. *suc.* fa. 1677.[1]

Member, soc. of loyal youths (bellringers), Lichfield 1686, alderman 1689, senior bailiff 1695, 1699, 1715; asst. linen corp. 1690; trustee, Lichfield Conduit Lands 1700–*d*.[2]

The Dyott family had represented Lichfield in Parliament for most of the 17th century, Dyott's father sitting in the Cavalier House of Commons. They owed their influence to the close proximity of their main residence at Freeford, two miles to the south of the borough. Nothing is known of Richard's education, but he probably lived locally for in 1686 he was a founder member of a society of bellringers, the 'loyal youths', and a year later subscribed £5 to recast the bells, a fund for which he acted as receiver. He was present at a meeting of gentry on 29 Nov. 1688 which considered how to act in the invasion crisis and on 4 Dec. signed an address to James II asking for the removal of all non-qualified officers from civil and military posts. On 28 May 1689 he was chosen as alderman of the city, which entailed regular attendance at council meetings when not in London on parliamentary business. He stood for Lichfield in the election of 1690 with the intention of turning out Sir Michael Biddulph, 2nd Bt.*, a feat he easily accomplished in partnership with the other outgoing Member, Robert Burdett*, and no doubt also with the support of the majority on the corporation. At that election he was already accorded the title 'captain', due to the leadership of the city's trained bands, which he inherited from his father.[3]

From the outset of his parliamentary career Dyott was a stalwart of the Church, as befitted a man who had been baptized by Bishop Hackett. On a list of the 1690 Parliament, the Marquess of Carmarthen (Sir Thomas Osborne[†]) classed him as a Tory and probably as a supporter of the Court. In the first session of the Parliament he was named to one drafting committee before receiving leave of absence to go into the country on 17 Apr. In the following 1690–1 session he acted as a teller on 26 Nov. against the committal of the bill for reducing interest. On a list of December 1690 he was marked by Carmarthen as a supporter, possibly in connexion with a projected attack on the minister himself and in April 1691 Robert Harley* classed him as a Court party supporter. In the 1691–2 session he was appointed to two drafting committees, both on 31 Oct., but his parliamentary activities were curtailed on 19 Dec. when he was given leave of absence for three weeks to attend his sick wife. He had returned by 15 Jan. 1692, for on that day he seconded a motion by Biddulph that the dean of St. Paul's be requested to preach to the House. In the 1692–3 session he acted as a teller on three occasions: on 28 Jan. against giving a second reading to the Lords' triennial bill; on 10 Feb. against granting leave of absence to Granado Pigot*; and on 15 Feb. against a bill to prevent the decay of trade in cities and market towns. On Grascome's list of spring 1693, extended to 1695, he was listed as a Court supporter and a placeman, but this may have confused him with a namesake, who was a Middlesex j.p. and later a stamp commissioner. Certainly, his support was contingent on the ministry retaining a significant Tory element, as was revealed in the Staffordshire by-election of October 1693, when he signed a circular letter backing the candidature of Sir Walter Bagot, 3rd Bt.*, against the more Court-inclined Hon. Henry Paget*. Dyott appears to have been less active in the 1693–4 session, serving as a teller only once, on 16 Jan. 1694, against an amendment to the land tax bill, to limit the assessment on masters of colleges to £30. In the last session of the 1690 Parliament he reported from committee on 9 Mar. 1695 a bill from the Lords relating to Lord Brooke's (Fulke Greville[†]) estates in Shropshire. On 20 Mar. he was granted leave of absence for three weeks.[4]

In the 1695 election at Lichfield, Dyott may have stood down in favour of Biddulph and Burdett in order to serve himself as senior bailiff of the corporation, and hence as returning officer. However, he was returned in 1698, and survived a petition from his opponent. On a comparative analysis of the old and new Parliaments he was marked as a Court supporter, although on a supplementary list this opinion was amended by a query. Inside the chamber he was named to two drafting committees, presenting one of the resultant bills, to encourage the apprehension of felons, on 24 Feb. 1699, but thereafter leaving its management to Thomas Brotherton*. He received leave of absence on 6 Apr. In the following session he was granted leave of absence for a fortnight on 26 Feb. 1700. He faced a strong challenge at Lichfield in the election of January 1701, despite joining forces with Biddulph and receiving unequivocal backing from the corporation. In a remarkably close contest, only 29 votes separated Dyott, who topped the poll, from Biddulph at the bottom. The defeated candidate on each side petitioned without success, although it was thought likely at one point that William Walmisley* would be unseated and a new election ordered. To cover such a contingency Dyott made clear his support for Biddulph, who had promised that he would 'always vote with Dyott', much to the chagrin of local Tories, who favoured putting up Thomas Coke*. Dyott's name appears on a list of February 1701 as a likely supporter of the Court over the 'Great Mortgage'. On 19 May he showed his Tory principles by moving to have Restoration Day, 29 May, 'observed' by the House and a sermon appointed, insisting that he was acting according to statute. However, no one seconded the motion. At the election of November 1701 there seems to have been no opposition to his return, again in partnership with Biddulph. His general political stance is clear from Robert Harley's analysis of the new Parliament, which classed him as a Tory. He was named to a drafting committee, relating to Greenwich Hospital, and on 26 Feb. 1702 he supported the motion vindicating the proceedings of the Commons over the impeachment of the King's Whig ministers.[5]

The agreement between Dyott and Biddulph held firm at Lichfield in 1702, when both were returned, despite Sir Henry Gough* forcing a poll. Dyott does not seem to have been active in the early part of this session and he was granted a month's leave on 16 Dec. following the death of his wife. In the following session he was ordered to attend the Commons, following his absence from a call on 22 Nov. 1703, and was present by 15 Dec., when he was nominated to a drafting committee on an estate bill. In the following session he was forecast as likely to vote for the Tack and did so on 28 Nov. 1704. He was named to draft six bills, including three estate bills and the bill allowing Sir Michael Biddulph to compound his debts with the Treasury. He duly presented the three estate bills and reported one of them from committee. At the 1705 election he was elected unopposed, although he changed partners, being returned this time with Gough. On an analysis of the new Parliament he was classed as 'True Church', probably because of his attitude towards the Tack. His consistent Toryism was underlined by his vote against the Court candidate for Speaker on 25 Oct. 1705. He appears to have been less active in this session, being appointed to two drafting committees, including a measure for the better regulation of Lichfield cathedral. In 1707–8 he was nominated to draft two bills, including a measure for the maintenance of a minister in Tettenhall parish, Staffordshire, and also to one inquiry committee. On a list of early 1708 he appeared as a Tory.[6]

Dyott did not stand at the 1708 election, but was very prominent in the run-up to the 1710 election, escorting a triumphant Dr Sacheverell around the county in his coach. With the endorsement of the High Church champion, Dyott topped the poll at Lichfield and was duly classed as a Tory on the 'Hanover list'. He appeared in the first session of the Parliament among the 'Tory patriots' opposed to the continuance of the war, and the 'worthy patriots' who helped to detect the mismanagements of the previous administration. After being named to a drafting committee (a Biddulph estate bill) on 19 Mar. 1711, he was granted leave of absence for a month. In the following session he acted as a teller on 4 Apr. 1712 against a clause in the bill for preventing the fraudulent multiplication of votes in elections, which sought to save the rights of Quakers to the franchise. He does not appear to have been active in the 1713 session, and did not register a vote on the controversial French commerce bill.[7]

Dyott was returned unopposed at the 1713 election and was again classed as a Tory, this time on the Worsley list. Although defeated at the 1715 election he remained in the commission of the peace despite attempts by Lord Uxbridge (Henry Paget) to have him removed by branding him as a flagrant Jacobite. He did not live to fight another election in the Tory cause, his burial taking place at St. Mary's, Lichfield on 13 May 1719.[8]

[1] Erdeswick, *Staffs.* 310; *Staffs. Peds.* (Harl. Soc. lxiii), 77; Burke, *Commoners*, ii. 425–6; T. Harwood, *Hist. and Antiq. Lichfield*, 464.

[2] Harwood, 71, 430–1; Lichfield RO, D77/5/1, p. 26; Sel. Charters, 213; P. Laithwaite, Hist. Lichfield Conduit Lands Trust, 80. [3] Shaw, Staffs. i. 359; Harwood, 68, 71; Wm. Salt Lib. (Stafford), Bagot mss D1721/3/291; Harl. 7001, f. 350; CSP Dom. 1693, p. 148. [4] Erdeswick, 310; Luttrell Diary, 130. [5] Lichfield RO, D77/5/1, pp. 59v, 101; HMC Cowper, ii. 419, 424–5; Centre Kentish Stud. Stanhope mss U1590 C9/9, Ld. Stanhope to 'my Ld.', 26 Apr. [1701]. [6] Cocks Diary, 136–7. [7] Add. 70421, newsletters 20, 22, 27 June 1710; Glos. RO, Hardwicke Ct. mss, Lloyd pprs. box 74, Dan. Tollie to Dr Lloyd, 8 July 1710. [8] L. K. J. Glassey, Appt. JPs, 245, 250; Harwood, 476.

S. N. H.

DYSART, Lionel Tollemache, 3rd Earl of [S] see **TOLLEMACHE**

EARLE, Joseph (c.1658–1730), of St. Werburgh's, Bristol.

Bristol 1710–1727

b. c.1658, 1st s. of Sir Thomas Earle†, merchant, of St. Werburgh's, Bristol, and Crudwell, Wilts., mayor of Bristol 1681, by Elizabeth Ellinor (d. 1709), da. of Joseph Jackson† of Small Street, Bristol and Sneyd Park, Glos.; bro. of Giles Earle†. m. lic. 18 Nov. 1689, Elizabeth, da. of Sir Thomas Cann, merchant, of Bristol, 1da. d.v.p. suc. fa. 1696.[1]

Member, Merchant Venturers' Soc., Bristol 1697, warden 1709–10, master 1721–2; president Loyal Soc., Bristol 1712–13.[2]

Earle's father, the son of a Wiltshire yeoman, had prospered in Bristol as a merchant and had then risen in civic politics, becoming MP for the city during the Exclusion Parliaments. Earle himself was destined to succeed to the family business and was already the leading member of a mercantile partnership at the time of his father's death in 1696. In February 1693 he had petitioned the government for Admiralty protection of shipping bound for the West Indies, taking command of a privateer for this purpose later in the year. He was also, by this time, a captain in the local militia.[3]

At the election of 1710, having completed his term as warden of the city's Merchant Venturers' Society, Earle took advantage of the strong upsurge of popular Toryism in his native city and stood as a candidate in partnership with the wealthy Bristol philanthropist, Edward Colston II*. Although Colston was undoubtedly the better known Tory, his absence from the city left Earle to front their campaign. Their success marked the end of the 15-year Whig monopoly over the city's parliamentary seats and was hailed as a great victory for the 'Church party'. Enthusiasm still ran high a month later when, during the first few miles of his journey to London, he was escorted by 'above 500 horse'. Earle was classed as a Tory in the 'Hanover list', and was subsequently listed as one of the 'worthy patriots' who in the 1710–11 session detected the mismanagements of the previous administration and was a member of the October Club. On 5 Apr. 1711 he was teller against a minor amendment to the bill preventing bribery at elections. Indications of a weakening in Earle's Toryism in the next session presaged his alignment with the Whigs a few years later. On 7 Dec. 1711 he was one of a handful of Tories who voted with the Whigs in favour of the 'No Peace without Spain' motion, though as would later appear the measure of his disagreement with his party brethren was not confined to the commercial implications of the Tory government's peace policies, but, more fundamentally, involved his attitudes to the Church. It is possible, however, that he was never a committed Tory in the first place. His father was a moderate Tory who had dissociated himself from the extremist Tories in the corporation in the 1680s, and in 1690 found himself at loggerheads with their leaders, who attempted to engineer his expulsion from the corporation. On 1 Mar. 1712 Earle was first-named to a committee on a petition from the copper and brass manufacturers of Bristol and London complaining of unfair advantages given to foreign imports; and on 23 May he was a teller against providing legislative relief to two London wine merchants who claimed they had been overcharged on customs duty. Next session, on 2 May 1713, he was among those ordered to prepare a bill to open up the African trade, almost certainly as a result of a petition from the merchants of Bristol, which Earle may have presented. Two days later his telling against a bill for the temporary suspension of duties on French wine further underlined his disapproval of the new trading relationship with the French, and on 18 June he voted against the French commerce bill. In the printed list of the division he was noted both as a 'whimsical' and as 'concerned in trade'. He was teller on 8 July against a technical amendment to a bill for encouraging the tobacco trade.[4]

Earle, who by now ranked as a colonel of militia, was again successful for Bristol in 1713, though his recent failure to support his party line evidently annoyed the High Tory zealots in the city, giving rise to reports that he had 'underhand encouraged the Whig side, notwithstanding his outward appearance'. So lukewarm had his adherence to the Tory party become by the session of 1714 that he was described by the compiler of the Worsley list as a Whig who often voted with the Tories. In Bristol his relations with the Tory faithful worsened, not least over a bill to provide the corporation of the poor, established in 1696, with a sounder financial base. Tory aversion towards the corporation arose from the way in which it had lessened the autonomy of the city parishes through its assumption of responsibility for poor relief. Moreover, the corporation was regarded as a 'Whig device', the 1696 Act having exempted guardians and poor law officers from the religious test, which had made it a multi-denominational body. Earle's promotion of the corporation's bill, which had the full backing of the Whiggish city council, did nothing for his diminishing credit with Bristol's Tories. Between April and June 1714 he personally supervised the bill through all its Commons stages. His conflict with High Tories over the issue was clearly registered on 8 June during consideration of the second-reading report. When Tory MPs, almost certainly at the behest of Bristol Churchmen, took the opportunity to strike a blow at the corporation by pushing for a clause to end the poor rate when payment of the corporation's debts had been completed, Earle was on the losing side as a teller in the ensuing division. The Tories then added another clause ending the exemption of guardians from the religious test. His only other tellership, on 7 May, had been against a bill concerning imports. He was the same day first-named to a second-reading committee on a private bill. At some point during 1714, a Tory attack on him was published in Bristol, announcing his expulsion from the city's chief Tory venue, the Loyal Society, of which he had lately been president. The author roundly accused him of flagrant anticlericalism, citing his frequent railings 'against the established Church and the ministers of it', and his declaring publicly 'that religion was of very little use, and that there ought to be no more pastors to take care of our souls that there were judges to preside over our laws'. He had refused to pay his parish dues and had profaned Christ's miracles as 'no more than the curing of a Tertian ague':

> He was a man so variable in his temper that though he had in the most solemn manner promised Mr [Edward] Colston [II], and even pawned his salvation upon it, so far as words would suffer him, that he would stand by the society, and persevere on his loyalty to the Church and its government, yet (when he was by the sole interest of that society chosen into the House during the time of his sitting there) he kept no other correspondence in this city than with Quakers, Independents, Anabaptists, and other professed enemies to it.[5]

Earle's defection to the Whigs was complete by 1715, when he successfully defended his seat as a Whig candidate against the Tories. He thereafter established a close rapport with the Hanoverian administrations and could boast of his ability always to fill vacancies in Bristol's customs establishment with his own nominees. At the election of 1727 he chose to stand and lose his seat, rather than retire gracefully. He died on 13 Mar. 1730, aged 72, and was buried at St. Werburgh's church. He left his Bristol property and land at Crudwell in Wiltshire to his younger brother Robert, with remainder to his daughter's son from her marriage to William Benson†.[6]

[1] *Inhabitants of Bristol 1698* (Bristol Rec. Soc. xxv), 133; F. A. Brown, *Som. Wills*, ser. 4, p. 125; W. Barrett, *Hist. Bristol*, 482; *Fac. Off. Mar. Lic.* (Brit. Rec. Soc. xxxiii), 110; *Le Neve's Knights* (Harl. Soc. viii), 338–9; Hoare, *Wilts.* Ambresbury, 105. [2] A. B. Beaven, *Bristol Lists*, 126, 342; *Merchant Venturers of Bristol* (Bristol Rec. Soc. xvii), 33. [3] *Merchants and Merchandise in 17th Cent. Bristol* (Bristol Rec. Soc. xix), 225–6; *Trade of Bristol in the 18th Cent.* (Bristol Rec. Soc. xx), 7. [4] J. Latimer, *Annals of Bristol in 18th Cent.* 85; Strathmore mss at Glamis Castle, box 74, bdle. 9, newsletter 23 Nov. 1710. [5] Latimer, 102–3; Bodl. Ballard 31, f. 119; *Parish, Church and People* ed. S. J. Wright, 168–9; *A Few and True Reasons Why a Late Member was Expelled the Loyal Society* (1714). [6] Bristol Cent. Lib. Southwell mss B1156 (unfol.) Richard Matthews to Edward Southwell†, 14 June 1740; *Hist. Reg. Chron.* 1730, p. 30; Barrett, 482; PCC 93 Auber.

A. A. H.

ECHLIN, Robert (c.1657–by 1724), of Monaghan, Ireland and Purfleet, Essex.

SUDBURY 1710–1715

b. c.1657, 3rd s. of Robert Echlin of Ardquin, co. Down by his 1st w. Anne, da. of Alexander Conyngham of Mount Charles, co. Donegal, dean of Raphoe 1631–d. *educ.* Trinity, Dublin, adm. 9 July 1675, aged 18. *m.* 7 May 1696, Anne (d. 1724), da. of Sir Francis Blundell, 3rd Bt., of Blundell Manor, King's Co., sis. of Sir Montagu Blundell, 4th Bt.†, *s.p.*[1]

Lt. Mountjoy's regt. ft. 1685; lt.-col. 6 Drag. 1689, col. 1691–1715; brig.-gen. 1703, maj.-gen. 1704, lt.-gen. 1707.[2]

MP [I] 1695–1713.

Of Scots planter stock, Echlin was commissioned as lieutenant-colonel in the regiment raised by his uncle Sir Albert Conyngham in Ireland in 1689, known as the Inniskilling Dragoons, and served with distinction at the siege of Derry and at the Boyne, where he came to the notice of King William. On his uncle's death while a prisoner of the Jacobite army in 1691, Echlin was given the regiment. One of the 'Londonderry and Enniskillen officers', he had a long-standing grievance against the government for the non-payment of arrears dating back to the Irish war, a debt which was still outstanding in 1708. Financial difficulties forced the sale of his Monaghan estates in 1705. As a Member of the Irish parliament he strongly supported the administration of the Duke of Ormond, to whom he attributed his belated promotion to general, and whose dismissal from the lord lieutenancy in 1707 he described as 'the greatest misfortune that ever he met'. For this loyalty he was summarily 'struck . . . off the establishment' of general officers in Ireland by the Whig Lord Wharton (Hon. Thomas*) soon after Wharton's nomination as viceroy in 1708, only to be restored again two years later when Ormond was reappointed lord lieutenant.[3]

Returned at Sudbury in 1710, a borough with which he may have had some connexion through the Kekewich family, Echlin was classed as a Tory in the 'Hanover list' and was listed among the 'worthy patriots' who in the first session exposed the mismanagements of the old ministry. His regiment, which had been on the British establishment since 1709, was ordered to the Low Countries in March 1711, but later that year Echlin went over again to Ireland to give his support to Ormond in the Irish house of commons. Back at Westminster, he voted against the Duke of Marlborough (John Churchill*) in the censure motion of January 1712. Resentful that expected advancement was once more being denied him, he petitioned the Queen in 1712 for 'justice'. If he was still to be passed over in favour of younger officers, he requested permission to dispose of his regiment and retire from public service, 'which such usage will make the world believe he is thought unworthy to be continued in'. He had, he said, given 'long and signal services to his country', and shown a 'steady adherence to the Queen and Church, which rendered him obnoxious to the late ministry, and subjected him to their persecutions', and he claimed that

> upon the late happy change of ministry, he put himself to great expense to get into the House of Commons, upon the view only of doing service to the common cause, and last summer was at a further charge, in going for Ireland to attend the service of the parliament there, by his lordship's [Ormond] orders.

Ormond endorsed the petition with the words, 'he is a very honest man; I wish we had more of such in the army, I mean as to his principles'; and in June 1712 Lord Strafford asked on his behalf that his regiment be returned to Ireland. Instead it was brought back to England and reduced, though it suffered less in this respect than other regiments. Echlin's own 'pretensions' were ignored. In January 1713 he begged Lord Treasurer Oxford (Robert Harley*) for swift financial aid or at least 'liberty to sell my troop', predicting that otherwise he would be 'entirely ruined' because of 'executions both on my real and personal estate'. On 18 June he supported the government in the division on the French commerce bill. He resisted overtures to stand at the Irish general election in 1713, but was re-elected on the Tory interest at Sudbury. He was later classed as a Tory in the Worsley list.[4]

Echlin's continuing financial difficulties were reflected in a privilege complaint on 17 Aug. 1714 against a group of creditors who had 'made a forcible entry upon' his Essex estate, 'and do detain the possession thereof, and have arrested . . . [his] agent and servants'. Then early in 1715 he was 'turned out' of his regiment 'without any other charge against him but that of being a Tory . . . and not a farthing paid to him, though he was poor and had not [the] wherewithal to subsist himself and his family'. He went over to France and in June 1715 wrote to the Duke of Berwick from Calais offering his services to the Pretender. Taken into the Jacobite service, he was sent to Scotland during the Fifteen and 'after running great hazard' escaped back to the Continent, having made his way with a group of other Jacobite officers across to the Orkneys, where they 'took a vessel by force'. Thereafter he remained in France, living on a pension from the Pretender, whom he said he would 'contentedly support with the meanest morsel of bread', and awaiting any occasion 'to show my zeal and loyalty' in another invasion attempt. The sum of £300 was paid him 'very privately' on James's instructions in November 1719. The previous August his old patron Ormond wrote to condole with him upon the recent missed opportunity: 'had not the bad weather separated and disabled the fleet', concluded Ormond, 'we might have met in our own country'.[5]

The date of Echlin's death has not been ascertained. His widow died on 19 Nov. 1724.[6]

[1] J. R. Echlin, *Gen. Mems. Echlin Fam.* 39-40; *Dublin Wills Abstracts* ed. Eustace, ii. 128; *CJ*, xviii. 10. [2] *CSP Dom.* 1685, p. 78; 1691-2, p. 46. [3] Echlin, 40; PRO NI, Rossmore mss T2929/2/2, Alexander Montgomery to William Cairnes, 7 July 1705; *HMC Portland*, viii. 311; Add. 9715, ff. 150-1; *HMC Ormonde*, n.s. viii. 80, 97, 153, 299; *Swift Works*, iii. 237-8. [4] *VCH Essex*, vii. 139; Luttrell, *Brief Relation*, vi. 693; Add. 34777, ff. 30, 71-73; 70197, Echlin to Oxford, 23 Jan. [1713]; 70214, Ormond to Oxford, n.d.; *Verney Letters 18th Cent.* i. 309-10; *HMC Portland*, ix. 329; x. 86. [5] *Lockhart Pprs.* i. 459-60; *HMC Stuart*, i. 366, 457, 487, 490-1; ii. 31-32, 202, 329-30, 442; v. 174; vi. 512; vii. 196-7; RA, Stuart mss 45/92; Master of Sinclair, *Mems. Insurrection in Scotland* (Abbotsford Club, xxx), 344-7, 363, 374; Add. 33950, f. 71. [6] *Hist. Reg. Chron.* 1724, p. 49.

D. W. H.

EDEN, John (1677–1728), of West Auckland, co. Dur.

DURHAM CO. 1713–1727

bap. 11 Sept. 1677, 1st s. of Sir Robert Eden, 1st Bt.* *educ.* Queen's, Oxf. matric. 1695. *m.* 31 Jan. 1715, Catherine, da. of Mark Shafto of Whitworth, co. Dur., sis. of Robert Shafto*, 1s. *suc.* fa. as 2nd Bt. 30 Mar. 1721.[1]

Mayor, Hartlepool 1714–15, 1722–3.[2]

In 1713 Eden was returned for the county seat previously held by his father. On 31 Mar. 1714 he told against setting a date to hear the petition of the defeated Whig candidate in the Wallingford by-election, and on 1 May was appointed to prepare a bill for the endowment of poor vicarages. Both the Worsley list and a comparison of the 1713 and 1715 Parliaments listed Eden as a Tory, and his classification as a Whig in a further comparison of these Parliaments was probably an error. Upon his marriage in 1715 he was given Windlestone, and he remained in the House throughout George I's reign. He died at Bath on 2 May 1728.[3]

[1] Hutchinson, *Dur.* iii. 339–40; R. A. Eden, *Notes on Eden Fam.* 31. [2] C. Sharp, *Hist. Hartlepool*, 75–76. [3] Eden, 32.

E. C.

EDEN, Sir Robert, 1st Bt. (c.1644–1721), of West Auckland, co. Dur.

DURHAM CO.   1679 (Mar.–July), 1690–1695
1698–1700, 1702–1713

b. c.1644, 1st s. of John Eden of West Auckland by Catherine, da. of Sir Thomas Layton of Layton, Yorks. *educ.* Queen's, Oxf., matric. 2 Aug. 1661, aged 17; M. Temple 1664, called 1670. *m.* 4 Dec. 1672, Margaret (*d.* 1730), da. and h. of John Lambton of Durham, 8s. (at least 2 *d.v.p.*) 6da. *cr.* Bt. 13 Nov. 1672; *suc.* fa. 1675.[1]

Commr. for recusants, co. Dur. 1675.[2]

Returned for the county in 1690 after a long interval in his parliamentary career, Eden was classed a Tory and Court supporter by Lord Carmarthen (Sir Thomas Osborne†) in a list of March 1690. No significant activity is recorded for him in either of the first two sessions of this Parliament, though Carmarthen included him in a list of December 1690, probably of those likely to give support in the event of a Commons attack on him, and in April 1691 Robert Harley* classed him as a Country supporter. In the 1691–2 session Eden was nominated to draft bills to explain the Acts concerning provision for the poor (7 Nov.) and to encourage the manufacture of saltpetre (25 Nov.). His only recorded speech came at the start of the following session when, on 4 Nov. 1692, he moved the writ for the Morpeth by-election. During the 1693–4 session Eden told in favour of sending Lord Falkland (Anthony Carey*) to the Tower for withholding evidence from the commissioners of accounts (7 Dec. 1693), and for engrossing the bill to make more effectual the Act regulating leather-cutting (21 Mar. 1694). His most significant activity in the final session of the Parliament was his appointment on 4 Dec. to draft a bill relating to prisons and prisoners, and his reporting and carrying to the Lords a private bill concerned with estates in Yorkshire and Durham (26, 29 Mar. 1695). Eden did not stand at the 1695 election, but it seems that his withdrawal was against his inclinations and in 1698 he successfully contested Durham. A comparison of the old and new Commons from about September classed him as a Country supporter, and he was also included in a forecast of those likely to oppose a standing army. His most notable activity in the first session of the Parliament was his appointment on 21 Feb. to draft the bill to make the *Nazareth* a free ship, a measure he presented two days later, and an estate bill which he guided through the Commons during April on behalf of the Northumberland Member William Forster. During the following session Eden managed through the House a bill extending to Wales and the counties palatine, including Durham, the terms of the Act limiting legal costs, as well as carrying to the Lords, on 6 Mar. 1700, the bill to prevent frivolous and vexatious lawsuits.[3]

Eden does not appear to have been a candidate at either of the 1701 elections. He was, however, returned unopposed at the 1702 election, and held the seat unchallenged at the following three elections. During the 1702 Parliament, and afterwards, he was frequently employed in the initiation and passage of estate bills, most of them emanating from his own county. On less parochial matters, he confirmed his Tory sympathies by voting, on 13 Feb. 1703, against the Lords' amendments to the bill enlarging the time for taking the abjuration, but demonstrated that he was not a partisan extremist during the proceedings on the Tack. In October 1704 he was forecast as a likely opponent of the measure, and on 28 Nov. 1704 was not recorded as voting for it. Failure to support the Tack does not, however, appear to have diminished his standing with Durham's Anglican clergy, as it was recorded that in the summer of 1705 Eden was accompanied to the uncontested county election by the prebendaries of Durham Cathedral and other Anglican ministers. Despite this display Eden was classed as 'Low Church' in an analysis of the new Commons, but on 25 Oct. he voted against the Court candidate for Speaker. In December 1705 he supported Thomas Lamplugh's* bill for the improvement of Parton harbour, and his nominations in the new year to draft bills to constitute the mayor of Newcastle-upon-Tyne governor of the hospital for keelmen there (16 Jan.) and to enable a pier to be built at the mouth of the Wear (23 Jan.) denote his concern to further local interests. In the 1707–8 session he managed through their Commons' stages a naturalization bill and a bill to allow a captured French privateer to be sold as a prize. A further area of interest was the regulation of servants: on 10 Feb. 1708 he was appointed to a committee to examine existing legislation on the subject, and after making the committee's report on the 16th, was among those named to prepare a new bill. During this session he was also listed as a Tory. Between December 1708 and January 1709 he managed through its early Commons stages a bill to preserve Plymouth's Catwater harbour, and in February and March he guided through the House the Liverpool waterworks bill. On matters of more national import, Eden was listed as having voted against the impeachment of Dr Sacheverell.[4]

Classed in the 'Hanover list' as a Tory, the most important of Eden's parliamentary actions in the first session of this Parliament were his appointment to draft a bill for the navigation of the Tyne (20 Feb. 1711) and his reporting and carrying to the Lords a bill for the sale of the estates of Sir Philip Monoux, 3rd Bt.* (21, 26 Feb.). He was listed as one of the 'worthy patriots' who had helped to detect the mismanagements of the previous administration, and was also a member of the October Club. Between April and May 1713 he managed a bill to establish a new parish at Stockton, county Durham and on 18 June he voted for the French commerce bill. Eden did not stand at the 1713 election, his seat being taken by his eldest son, John. He died on 30 Mar. 1721.[5]

[1] *Vis. Dur.* ed. Foster, 111; *Pepys Diary*, ix. 512; Collins, *Peerage*, viii. 288; Hutchinson, *Dur.* iii. 348–9; IGI, Durham. [2] *Cal. Treas. Bks.* iv. 740. [3] *Luttrell Diary*, 214; Add. 70019, ff. 94–95; *Six N. Country Diaries* (Surtees Soc. xxviii), 57. [4] Add. 70019, f. 312; 28893, f. 137; Cumbria RO (Carlisle), Lonsdale mss D/Lons/W2/2/8, James* to Sir John Lowther, 2nd Bt. I*, 8 Nov., 6 Dec. 1705. [5] *The Gen.* n.s. iii. 85; Boyer, *Pol. State*, xxi. 340.

E. C.

EDGCUMBE, Richard (1680–1758), of Mount Edgcumbe, Maker and Cothele, Cornw.

CORNWALL	25 June–11 Nov. 1701
ST. GERMANS	1701 (Dec.)–1702
PLYMPTON ERLE	1702–1734
LOSTWITHIEL	1734–1741
PLYMPTON ERLE	1741–20 Apr. 1742

bap. 23 Apr. 1680, 3rd but 2nd surv. s. of Sir Richard Edgcumbe† of Mount Edgcumbe and Cotehele by Lady Anne, da. of Edward Montagu†, 1st Earl of Sandwich. *educ.* Trinity Coll. Camb. 1697; travelled abroad 1699. *m.* 12 Mar. 1715 (with £20,000), Matilda (*d.* 1721), da. of Sir Henry Furnese* by 2nd w., 3s. (1 *d.v.p.*). *suc.* bro. to family estates 1694; *cr.* Baron Edgcumbe 20 Apr. 1742.[1]

Stannator, Tyrwarnhaile 1710; recorder, Lostwithiel 1733–*d.*, capital burgess 1736, mayor 1738, 1742; ld. lt. Cornw. 1742–*d.*[2]

Ld. of Treasury 1716–17, 1720–4; jt. vice-treasurer [I] 1724–42; PC [I] 1734–*d.*; ld. warden of Stannaries 1734–7; chancellor, duchy of Lancaster 1743–58; PC 28 June 1734–*d.*; col. of ft. 1745; maj.-gen. 1755; c.j. in eyre north of Trent Jan. 1758–*d.*

Edgcumbe succeeded his brother, Piers, to the family estates at the age of 14, shortly after his mother married Christopher Montagu*. After a spell at Cambridge, in April 1699 he received a pass and left England to travel on the Continent with his tutor, Isaac Diserete. The death of Hugh Boscawen II saw a vacancy for the county seat, to which he was returned unopposed at a by-election in June 1701. As Parliament had been prorogued the previous day he never took his seat. In December 1701, he switched to St. Germans, presumably on the Eliot interest. Contemporaries may have been unsure of his politics at this stage: his election was classed as a 'gain' by Lord Spencer (Charles*), whereas Robert Harley* classed him as a Tory. Returned at Plympton in 1702, presumably on the Treby interest, Edgcumbe survived a petition. He was forecast as a probable opponent of the Tack, and did not vote for it on 28 Nov. 1704. Re-elected in 1705 after a contest, he was classed as a 'Churchman' in a list of that year. On 25 Oct. he voted for the Court candidate as Speaker. The absence of his name from those supporting the Court over the 'place clause' of the regency bill perhaps suggests a 'Country' slant to his Whiggism, but if so it did not prevent the development of lifelong friendships with Court Whigs like Robert Walpole II*. Early in 1708 he was classed as a Whig, and at the general election of that year he was again returned for Plympton, this time without opposition. Following the election he was classed as a Whig. On 8 Feb. 1709 Edgcumbe was a teller against a Tory motion relating to the Bewdley election, and he told on the 22nd for a motion that the Whig, Robert Balle*, was elected for Ashburton. He also told on 25 Jan. 1710 against the recommittal of a report from the committee of privileges and on the 31st in favour of receiving the report on the place bill the following day. He was absent from the divisions on the impeachment of Dr Sacheverell, possibly being in

Cornwall for the convocation of tinners. However, he was evidently regarded as one of the doctor's opponents and after being mobbed by tinners at the convocation in Truro in April 1710 'said merrily . . . that he was a lucky man to have escaped out of one mob (meaning Dr Sacheverell's) to fall into a new one here, which, he said, he thought really was worse than that'. Perhaps he was correct to comment on his good fortune because, according to Thomas Tonkin*, he was the leader of the 'wardenists' in the convocation. His prominent role in the Whig party in Cornwall was confirmed on 4 Oct. at the county meeting at Liskeard when along with Hugh Boscawen II* he objected to a letter being read from the lord lieutenant, the Earl of Rochester (Laurence Hyde†). He then played a leading role in rallying support for Boscawen in readiness for the county contest.[3]

Safely returned again for Plympton in 1710, Edgcumbe was classed as 'doubtful' in the 'Hanover list', and later was listed as a 'Tory patriot' who opposed the continuance of the war. However, he took a strongly Whiggish line in the new Parliament. On 9 Dec. 1710 he told for a motion that determination of election cases should be decided by ballot, and on the 16th was a teller against the return of Sir Francis Child for Devizes. He voted on 25 May 1711 for the amendment to the South Sea bill. In late November 1711 the government banned a great Whig procession in the city of London, which was to be led by the 2nd Duke of Montagu, Edgcumbe and Richard Steele*, all members of the Hanover Club, during which the devil and the Pope were to be burnt in effigy. On 7 Dec., the opening day of the new session, Edgcumbe voted for the motion 'No Peace without Spain'. On 18 June 1713 he divided against the French commerce bill and was classed as a Whig on the subsequent division list. In the 1713 Parliament, he voted on 18 Mar. 1714 against the expulsion of Steele. He was listed as a Whig on the Worsley list and on two further lists comparing the 1713 and 1715 Parliaments. A pillar of the Whig establishment under the first two Georges, he died on 22 Nov. 1758.[4]

[1] Vivian, *Vis. Cornw.* 143; *The Gen.* n.s. iii. 84; PCC 234 Barnes. [2] R. Inst. Cornw. Thomas Tonkin's ms hist. Cornw. ii. 244. [3] *Top. and Gen.* iii. 152; *CSP Dom.* 1699–1700, p. 148; Tonkin, 246, 251; Add. 70204, 'at the meeting of the gentlemen at Liskeard'; Cornw. RO, Buller mss BO/23/63/7, Edgcumbe to John Buller I*, 24 Oct. 1710. [4] *Wentworth Pprs.* 212; Polsue, *Complete Paroch. Hist. Cornw.* iii. 248.

E. C./S. N. H.

EDISBURY, Kenrick (?1670–1736) of Deptford, Kent (? and Gresford, Denb.).

HARWICH   24 Jan. 1709–1713

bap. ?3 June 1670, 2nd s. of Kenrick Edisbury of Deptford and Gresford by Grace, da. of Mr Cooper of Wrexham, Denb. *m.* aft. 1694 Frances, ?1s. ?3 da. *suc.* fa. 1707.[1]

Clerk of the cheque at Deptford by 1684, to commr. of navy Feb.–Oct. 1688, in ticket office Dec. 1689–Dec. 1694, second chief clerk Dec. 1694–Apr. 1704; commr. victualling the navy Apr. 1704–Dec. 1714, for sick and wounded?–*d*.[2]

Freeman, Portsmouth 1709, Harwich 1710.[3]
Dir. London Assurance Office aft. 1720.[4]

Edisbury's successful career in the administration of the navy emulated that of his great-grandfather and namesake, who had been appointed surveyor to the navy in 1632 and had purchased many of the family's estates near Wrexham in Denbighshire. In honour of these achievements a number of the surveyor's descendants had been named Kenrick, including the Member, his father and two of his cousins, a source for confusion made worse by variant spellings of the surname. It would appear to be the Member's father, who went to Merchant Taylors' school in 1647 and Oxford in 1655, and patented a number of inventions, including carts and wagons designed to run on rollers rather than wheels in order to preserve the highways. Although some of these improbable ideas were taken up, including a horizontal mill, the eccentric Kenrick snr. made no money from the projects and in 1694, convinced that Providence had crossed him, was 'master of but one shilling'. He took refuge at Erddig in Denbighshire, which had been rebuilt by his cousin Joshua, to whom he made over the patents for his inventions, together with two houses in St. James's, Westminster, in partial payment for debts which included the expenses of several lawsuits. He also sold his share in the family estate at Hafod-y-bwch. Kenrick senior spent his time in Wales horse-racing, womanizing, and, to the amusement of those who baited him about his views, in collecting Socinian books. In 1696 he was so poor that he thought it likely he would die in a debtor's prison, though he assured his patient cousin that 'when I grow as rich as I have often fancied, you might come in for a snap'. In fact his luck did turn, though never to win him the fabulous wealth he dreamed of. He was probably the Kenrick Edisbury who was given a commission in 1697 in Sir Clowdesley Shovell's* marine regiment, though he may not have taken up the post, being appointed soon after as agent of the packet boats in Harwich, a job which he performed with surprising diligence until his death in 1707.[5]

It would seem that Edisbury's father knew Dennis Lyddell*, a commissioner of the navy, and that his cousin Richard held a navy office at Plymouth, but Kenrick junior probably owed his place at the Deptford shipyard either to the fame of his ancestor, to the patronage of Sir John Trevor* (who was a neighbour), or, as the tightly knit nature of his extended family might suggest, to Joshua or John Edisbury[†], whose father had held office in the navy and had married the daughter of a navy commissioner. Edisbury rose through the ranks of the navy office, but, although he did not show the family character defects of dissoluteness or financial incompetence, wealth came slowly. In 1694 he wrote to Joshua, whose building projects had overreached his income:

> I could wish my own circumstances would enable me to help you to the sum you desire, but I am so far from it that I cannot procure such a sum from any of my friends or acquaintances, they being people concerned in the government and have so great an advantage for the loan of their money in the service that they will not otherwise dispose of their money.

In 1704, however, having long proved himself in the ticket office, he was appointed a commissioner for victualling the navy, with an annual salary of £400. He took up the post at a time when inefficiency in the service had only partly been tackled: the investigation into the accounts of Philip Papillon* as the office's cashier, for which Edisbury's new office required him to provide information to MPs, revealed the lack of regular accounting methods. A report compiled in May 1711 by Charles Sergison*, clerk of the acts, shows Edisbury to have been at the forefront of attempts at reform. He had joined with two other commissioners, Hunter and Tilghman, to expose the mismanagement, and 'soon drew the hatred and ill will' of some members of his own board who, 'obtaining the ears of great men', alleged that Edisbury and the others were 'unsociable persons, of turbulent and unquiet spirits, not fit to sit with'. In 1706 Hunter and Tilghman were dismissed, 'Edisbury narrowly escaping by the interposition of some friends', and Denzil Onslow* and Thomas Bere* appointed in their stead, 'gentlemen wholly unacquainted' with victualling procedures. The resulting administrative laxity encouraged corruption, and in February 1711 the Commons probed the department's contracts with brewers, concluding that the commissioners had been 'guilty of great negligence and remissness in their duty' and that there had been 'a notorious mismanagement' of the service. The inquiry had helped highlight the financial crisis confronting the commissioners, who were three years in arrears on payments and consequently of such low credit that no contractor would supply 'but at 35 per cent at least above the market price'. Indeed the collapse of the navy's supply lines was only averted by the development of the South Sea Company and the cessation of hostilities.[6]

His father's connexion with Harwich, reinforced by his sister's marriage to the corporation's mayor, Captain Phillipson, together with his own influence as a commissioner of the navy, ensured Edisbury's victory there at a by-election in December 1708, and although a double return prompted the House on 13 Jan. 1709 to declare the election void, he was again returned on 24 Jan. He was a consistent supporter of the Court whatever its political leanings. Thus, in the spring of 1710 he supported the impeachment of Dr Sacheverell and was marked as a Whig on the 'Hanover list' of the 1710 Parliament, presumably on account of his past behaviour, but voted for the French commerce bill in June 1713. He does not seem to have stood for re-election in 1713, perhaps being preoccupied with the task of retrenching the victualling board after the end of the war, a reduction which in any case undermined his interest at Harwich. He was turned out of office in December 1714, perhaps because he was distantly related to Robert Harley*, Earl of Oxford, whose administration he had supported. His maritime expertise was not wasted, however, since he became a director of the London Assurance Office, which was established in 1720 and initially specialized in marine insurance, though it is not possible to say how his fortunes were affected by the collapse of the South Sea Company (which is known to have reduced the value of Assurance stock from £175 to just £5) since he died intestate in 1736.[7]

[1] A. N. Palmer, *Hist. Thirteen Country Townships*, 224; A. L. Cust, *Chronicles of Erthig*, 99; IGI, London. [2] Watson thesis, 297; *London Mag.* 1736, p. 581. [3] R. East, *Portsmouth Recs.* 374; S. Taylor, *Hist. and Antiquities of Harwich*, 233. [4] *London Mag.* 1736, p. 581. [5] Palmer, *Country Townships*, 225, 232; *CSP Dom.* 1676–7, pp. 128, 471, 476; 1690–1, pp. 26–27, 43; 1697, pp. 85, 519; 1702–3, p. 725; *Cheshire Arch. Soc.* xxii. 26–53; Cust, 78–99; Clwyd (Hawarden) RO, Erddig mss D/E/836, letters from Kenrick Edisbury snr. to Joshua Edisbury, 1693–6; Add. 28891, f. 273. [6] Cust, 56, 78–79, 93–95, 98–99; Clwyd (Hawarden) RO, Erddig mss D/E/836, letters of Kenrick Edisbury jnr. to Joshua Edisbury; *Cal. Treas. Bks.* xix. 292; *CJ*, xiv. 431; xvi. 525; Harl. 6287, f. 117, Sergison to Robert Harley*, 15 May 1711; Watson thesis, 349–62. [7] Cust, 114; Speck thesis, 79; Watson thesis, 311, 372–3; Add. 70116, Abigail Harley to Sir Edward Harley*, 28 Dec. 1693; W. R. Scott, *Jt.-Stock Cos.* i. 430; ii. 407; PCC Admon. Oct. 1736.

M. J. K.

EDWARDS, Thomas (c.1673–by 1743), of the Middle Temple and Filkins Hall, Oxon.

BRISTOL   1713–1715
WELLS   14 Dec. 1719–25 Mar. 1735

b. c.1673, 1st s. of Thomas Edwards, attorney-at-law, of Redland, and Broad Street, Bristol by his 1st w. *educ.* Balliol, Oxf. matric. 29 Oct. 1691, aged 18, BCL Hart Hall 1698; M. Temple 1693, called 1698, bencher 1724. *m.* c.1703, Mary, da. and h. of Sir William Hayman, merchant, of Bristol, mayor of Bristol 1684, 1s. (*d.v.p.*) 2da. *suc.* fa. 1727.[1]

Edwards' father was a leading Bristol attorney whose clientele included prominent local gentry and mercantile families. Such was his turnover in fees that in 1690 he was able to purchase for £4,350 the Somerset manor of Clapton-in-Gordano. His prominence as a public figure stemmed in large part from his close association with the wealthy philanthropist Edward Colston II*, whose extensive Bristol interests he managed. Apart from his involvement as legal adviser in Colston's many charitable ventures, he was involved in the setting up of the corporation of the poor in 1696 and was an active member of the Bristol society for the reformation of manners, though he never held civic office. The bond between the two families was strengthened around 1703 when Edwards' son Thomas, the future MP, married Colston's niece.[2]

Edwards jnr. was sent by his father first to Oxford and then to the Middle Temple, qualifying as a barrister in 1698. The details of his subsequent legal career are not clear, but it would seem likely that he was encouraged by his business-minded father to maintain a practice in London. He kept chambers at his inn of court until the mid-1730s. In 1703 he acquired Filkins Hall, Oxfordshire, probably from Edward Colston II as part of his marriage settlement. When in 1713 the elder Colston signified his intention of retiring as MP for Bristol, the choice of a replacement Tory seems to have fallen quite naturally on Edwards, even though he was much less intimately involved in the city's affairs than his father. Colston may even have recommended him to the Tory zealots in the Loyal Society who shouldered much responsibility for their party's campaign in the city. It would appear, however, that Edwards' Toryism was projected largely through his family tie with Colston, since his own background, given his father's past links with Whiggery and Dissent, could hardly be regarded as unimpeachably Tory.[3]

Elected after a stormy and violent contest, Edwards figured in the ensuing Parliament as a Tory who would often vote with the Whigs. On 2 Apr. 1714 he helped promote the corporation's petition for a new Act to place the workhouse established in 1696 on a sounder financial footing, being one of the three Members named to prepare a bill for the purpose, though it is not clear whether he fell in with the Tory initiative, sponsored by Joseph Earle*, to rid the institution of its Whig bias. He was a teller for the Tory side on 25 June on the disputed Southwark election. Towards the end of the session he took charge of a private bill concerning lands in mid-Somerset. Denied his seat in the 1715 election through the partiality of the Whig sheriff, he and his fellow candidate petitioned three years in succession without receiving a hearing. However, a vacancy arising at Wells in 1719, which Edward Colston's nephew and namesake (Edward Colston I) had represented until 1713, afforded Edwards the opportunity to return to the House. The earlier connexion between the city of Wells and the Colston family, reinforced by the elder Colston's possession of the manor of Lydford West, a short distance south of the city, made Edwards an appropriate choice.[4]

Edwards continued as a Tory MP for Wells until unseated in March 1735. Thereafter he appears to have fallen upon difficult times. His wife had inherited much of her uncle's considerable fortune in 1721, but when on her death in or around 1736 it passed to his two daughters in accordance with the terms of Colston's will, he was left in dire financial straits. While his younger daughter, Sophia, was said to be worth £20,000 at the time of her marriage in February 1737, Edwards himself was so deeply in debt that he could no longer afford the £35 rent for his chambers in Middle Temple, and in the same year was forced to sell Filkins Hall. His date of death has not been accurately ascertained but it is clear from an entry in the Middle Temple records that he was no longer alive by May 1743.[5]

[1] *M.T. Adm.* i. 231; Add. 36648, f. 126; W. Barrett, *Hist. Bristol*, 392; *London Mar. Lic.* ed. Foster, 1481; *Vis. Som.* (Harl. Soc. n.s. xi), 188; A. S. T. Fisher, *Hist. Broadwell*, 59; *Bristol and Glos. Arch. Soc. Trans.* xxxviii. 176. [2] Barrett, 392; *Reformation and Revival in 18th Cent. Bristol* (Bristol Rec. Soc. xlv), 11, 58; Add. 18616, f. 35; Collinson, *Hist. Som.* iii. 178; *Bristol Corp. of the Poor* (Bristol Rec. Soc. iii), 174; S. G. Tovey, *Colston the Philanthropist*, 47. [3] Fisher, 58; M.T., mss mins. of parliament, MT.1/MPA, 16 June 1727 passim; Wilkins, *Edward Colston: Supp.*, 21; *Reformation and Revival*, 11, 58. [4] Collinson, ii. 84. [5] H. J. Wilkins, *Edward Colston*, 128–35; MT.1/MPA, 29 Oct. 1736, 13 May 1743; Fisher, 58; *Hist. Reg. Chron.* 1737, pp. 126–7.

A. A. H.

EGERTON, Hon. Charles (1654–1717).

BRACKLEY 1695–27 Jan. 1711

b. 12 Mar. 1654, 4th s. of John Egerton†, 2nd Earl of Bridgwater, by Elizabeth, da. of William Cavendish†, 1st Duke of Newcastle; bro. of Hon. Sir William Egerton*. *educ.* M. Temple 1673; L. Inn 1678. *m.* 30 Apr. 1691, Elizabeth, da. and h. of Henry Murray, groom of the bedchamber to Charles I, wid. of Randolph Egerton of Betley, Staffs., 1s.[1]

Egerton was returned unopposed on his family interest for Brackley in 1695. He was listed as likely to support the Court in the forecast of a division on 31 Jan. 1696 on the proposed council of trade, and he signed the Association promptly. In March he voted for fixing the price of guineas at 22s., while in the 1696–7 session he voted on 25 Nov. for the attainder of Sir John Fenwick†. Returned in a contested election in 1698, he was noted as a Court supporter in a comparative analysis of the old and new Commons. Towards the end of the year he was forecast as likely to oppose a standing army, though he was noted on two lists as having voted on 18 Jan. 1699 against the third reading of the disbanding bill. In 1700, in an analysis of the House into interests, he was classed as an adherent of the Junto. Returned unopposed in the first 1701 election, he was listed among those Members likely to support the Court in agreeing with the committee of supply's resolution to continue the 'Great Mortgage'. Egerton was successful in a contest in the second 1701 election, and again in 1702. However, he remained inactive in Parliament. In the 1702–3 session he voted on 13 Feb. 1703 for the Lords' amendments to the bill for enlarging the time for taking the oath of abjuration. At the beginning of the 1704–5 session he was forecast as a probable opponent of the Tack, and did not vote for it on 28 Nov. 1704. Returned in a contested election in 1705, at which time he was noted as a 'Churchman', he voted on 25 Oct. for the Court candidate as Speaker, and supported the Court on 18 Feb. 1706 in the proceedings on the 'place clause' of the regency bill. In 1708 he was returned unopposed for Brackley, at which time he was noted as a Court Whig in an analysis of Parliament. In the 1708–9 session he supported the naturalization of the Palatines. At the 1710 election he was returned in a contested election, and was classed as a Whig in the 'Hanover list'. However he was unseated on petition on 27 Jan. 1711.[2]

Although Egerton shared in the division of the estates of Aubrey de Vere, 20th Earl of Oxford, who died in March 1703, he nevertheless fell into financial difficulties, and in 1712 he obtained a private Act of Parliament to sell his manor of Marchington in Staffordshire, in order to pay a mortgage of £2,500 and other debts. He did not stand for Parliament again and died on 11 Dec. 1717.[3]

[1] Baker, *Northampton*, 564; Chauncy, *Herts.* ii. 483; Clutterbuck, *Herts.* i. 392; IGI, London. [2] Luttrell, *Brief Relation*, vi. 683. [3] *HMC Lords*, n.s. vi. 363; vii. 44; viii. 284, 301.

E. C.

EGERTON, Hon. Sir William (1649–91).

BRACKLEY 1679 (Oct.)–1681 (Jan.)
AYLESBURY 1685–1687
BRACKLEY 1690–bef. 24 Dec. 1691

b. 15 Aug. 1649, 2nd s. of John Egerton†, 2nd Earl of Bridgwater, and bro. of Hon. Charles Egerton*. *educ.* I. Temple 1673. *m.* 23 Sept. 1674, Honora, da. of Hon. Sir Thomas Leigh of Hamstall Ridware, Staffs., 1s. *d.v.p.* 4da. KB 23 Apr. 1661.[1]

Freeman, Chipping Wycombe 1672.

Egerton was returned unopposed for Brackley on his family's interest in March 1690, at which time he was noted as a Whig by Lord Carmarthen (Sir Thomas Osborne†). He was an inactive Member, though in April 1691 he was noted as a Court supporter by Robert Harley*. Egerton died just before Christmas 1691, a new writ for Brackley being issued on 24 Dec. He was buried at Hemel Hempstead.[2]

[1] Clutterbuck, *Herts.* i. 392; Chauncy, *Herts.* ii. 483; Baker, *Northampton*, 565; IGI, London. [2] Luttrell, *Brief Relation*, ii. 320.

E. C.

EGERTON, Hon. William (1684–1732).

BUCKINGHAMSHIRE 27 Feb. 1706–1708
BRACKLEY 1708–20 Apr. 1714
  1715–15 July 1732

b. 5 Nov. 1684, 4th s. of John Egerton†, 3rd Earl of Bridgwater, by Jane, da. of Charles Powlett†, 1st Duke of Bolton. *educ.* ?travelled abroad (Germany). *m.* Anna Maria, da. of Adm. Sir George Saunders†, commr. of the navy, 3da.[1]

Capt. 6 Ft. 1704; capt. and lt.-col. 1 Ft. Gds. 1705–Mar. 1714, Dec. 1714–June 1715; brevet col. 1711; col. 36 Ft. 1715–19, 20 Ft. 1719–*d*.

Egerton's father tried in vain to obtain for him a place in the Prince of Denmark's household, making use of the interest of the Duke of Marlborough (John Churchill†). Egerton himself appears to have travelled abroad around this time, as it is probable that he was the 'Mr Egerton' who was reported to have made a good impression at the Court in Hanover in March 1704. Still under-age at the 1705 election, his brother, the 4th Earl, who was lord lieutenant of Buckinghamshire, put him up for the county at a by-election in 1706. He was given no opposition by Tories like Lord Cheyne (Hon. William*), or Lord Fermanagh (John Verney*), who 'supposed Col. Egerton to be of the Church side', erroneously as it turned out.[2]

Egerton was classed as a Whig in two separate analyses of Parliament before and after the election in 1708, at which he was returned unopposed for Brackley, where his brother was lord of the manor. Because of service with the army in Flanders he was inactive in the House, being granted leave of absence on 1 Feb. 1709 for 14 days. In the 1709–10 session he voted for the impeachment of Dr Sacheverell. Returned in a contest at Brackley in 1710, Egerton was classed as a Whig in the 'Hanover list'. He was granted leave of absence on 26 Feb. 1711 for 21 days; in May he was accused in a Commons inquiry of making false musters. On 7 Dec. he voted for the motion of 'No Peace without Spain'. In the 1713 session he voted on 18 June against the French commerce bill, on which occasion he was classed as a Whig. He was successful in a contested election at Brackley in 1713, and on 18 Mar. 1714 voted against the expulsion of Richard Steele. Because Egerton was said to have spoken slightingly of the Duke of Ormond, Marlborough's successor, he was informed early in April 1714 by Secretary at War Francis Gwyn* that the Queen 'had no further service for him' and that he would receive 1,000 guineas for his company, for which, according to the Hanoverian envoy, he had paid £3,000. He was then unseated by the House on 20 Apr. Classed as a Whig in the Worsley list and two lists comparing the 1715 Parliament with its predecessor, Egerton recovered his seat in the Commons in 1715, and proved a staunch government supporter until his death on 15 July 1732.[3]

[1] Clutterbuck, *Herts.* i. 392; Baker, *Northampton*, 565. [2] Huntington Lib. Ellesmere mss EL 9991, Electress Sophia to Lady Bridgwater, 3 Mar. 1704, Duchess of Marlborough to same, n.d.; *Verney Letters 18th Cent.* i. 69. [3] *Bull. IHR*, xxxiii. 232; *HMC Portland*, v. 417; Boyer, *Pol. State*, vii. 268, 404; *Orig. Pprs.* ed. Macpherson, ii. 588.

E. C.

EKINS, Thomas (c.1650–1702), of Rushden, Northants.

HIGHAM FERRERS 1698–25 Mar. 1702

b. c.1650, 2nd but o. surv. s. of John Ekins of Rushden by Elizabeth, da. of Nicholas Mason of Bletsoe, Beds. *educ.* M. Temple 1666, called 1674, bencher 1696. ?*m.* ?1s. *suc.* fa. 1677.[1]

Receiver, honor of Higham Ferrers 1691–1702.[2]

Several branches of the Ekins family were extant in Northamptonshire in the later 17th century, but it has proved impossible to determine the one to which this particular Thomas Ekins and his immediate forebears belonged. The manor of Rushden had been acquired by Ekins' father, who gained local notoriety for sturdily resisting the levy of ship-money, and during the Interregnum held Rushden Hall. Ekins himself, probably owing to his position as a younger son, embarked on a legal career, and even after succeeding to his father's estate in 1677 maintained a barrister's practice. In 1698 he was elected without opposition at Higham Ferrers, a mile or so north of his residence. Before the new Parliament convened he was identified as a member of the Country party, and was subsequently forecast as a Country supporter over the issue of the standing army. A period of three weeks' leave of absence was granted him on 28 Feb. 1699. He may have been the 'Mr Ekins' appointed receiver of fines at the end of May 1700 by the new lord keeper, Sir Nathan Wright. At the election of January 1701 he received a message of goodwill from the Tory Sir Justinian Isham, 4th Bt.*, who was seeking re-election for Northamptonshire, and after his own return Ekins commiserated with Isham over the possibility of opposition in the county. After the 1701 Parliament Ekins was blacklisted as an opponent of the preparations for war. At the second election of that year, he mentioned to Isham that he had experienced 'some little difficulty' at Higham Ferrers, 'more than I did at first expect', which may well have been as a result of a challenge from Thomas Pemberton*, one of Ekins' neighbours and his successor in the borough seat. He retained the seat unopposed, however. On 26 Feb. 1702 he voted for the resolution vindicating the Commons' proceedings in the impeachments of the Whig ministers, but died the following month, on 25 Mar., at his chambers in the Middle Temple.[3]

[1] Bridges, *Northants.* ii. 193. [2] R. Somerville, *Duchy of Lancaster Official Lists*, 194. [3] *Vis. Eng. and Wales Notes* ed. Crisp, xiii. 83–91; *VCH Northants.* iv. 45–46; *Post Boy*, 26–28 Mar. 1702; Luttrell, *Brief Relation*, iv. 651; Northants. RO, Isham mss IC 2716, Ekins to Isham, 16 Nov. 1701.

A. A. H.

ELAND, William Savile, Ld. *see* **SAVILE**

ELFORD

ELFORD, Jonathan (1684–1755), of Bickham, Devon.

SALTASH   19 Dec. 1710–1715
FOWEY   1715–1722

bap. 11 Nov. 1684, 1st s. of Jonathan Elford of Bickham by Amy, da. of Matthew Halse of Keynedon and Elford, Devon. *educ.* Christ Church Oxf. 1702; M. Temple 1702. *m.* 23 Apr. 1713, Anne, da. and h. of Sir Thomas Neville, 1st Bt., of Neville Holt, Leics., *s.p. suc.* fa. 1690.[1]
Commr. public accounts 17 June–Oct. 1714.[2]

Elford's father was connected with several of the chief families in Devon. However, the family also possessed land in Cornwall, Jonathan being matriculated at Oxford in 1702 as the son of Jonathan of St. Anthony, deceased. In 1688 his father had been described by James II's regulators as 'a gentleman of good estate and quality, formerly out of commission in this county, and not at present in his Majesty's service'. After an education encompassing both university and an inn of court, Elford was returned for Saltash as a Tory at a by-election in 1710, probably on the Buller interest. He voted on 18 June 1713 for the French commerce bill and in the general election a few months later was returned again for Saltash. In June 1714 he was elected a commissioner of public accounts on the October Club list, coming sixth in the ballot. He was listed as a Tory on the Worsley list and on two comparative analyses of the 1713 and 1715 Parliaments. His Cornish links were confirmed by his appointment in August 1714 as a deputy-lieutenant for that county. He continued to sit as a Tory under George I, and died 10 Dec. 1755. The immediate beneficiary of his will was his sister, Catherine Ilbert, and after her death his kinsman, Lancelot Elford, and his children.[3]

[1] IGI, Devon, London; Vivian, *Vis. Devon*, 329–30. [2] *CJ*, xvii. 689. [3] Duckett, *Penal Laws and Test Act* (1882), p. 377; NLS, Advocates' mss, Wodrow pprs. letters Quarto 3, f. 138; Buccleuch mss at Drumlanrig, bdle. 303, commn. 20 Aug. 1714; *London Mag.* 1755, p. 596; PCC 34 Glazier.

E. C./S. N. H.

ELIOT, Daniel (c.1646–1702), of Port Eliot, Cornw.

ST. GERMANS   1679 (Mar.)–1681 (Mar.)
                       1685–1687, 1689–1700
                       2 Apr.–11 Nov. 1701

b. c.1646, 3rd but 1st surv. s. of John Eliot† of Port Eliot by Honora, da. of Sir Daniel Norton† of Southwick, Hants; bro. of Richard Eliot†. *educ.* Christ's, Camb. adm. 17 July 1663, aged 17; L. Inn 1668. *m.* 13 July 1685, Catherine (*d.* 1687), da. of Thomas Fleming of N. Stoneham, Hants, 1da. *suc.* fa. 1685.[1]

The Eliots had lived at Port Eliot (the former priory of St. Germans) since 1565, a few years before the first family member sat for the borough of St. Germans. Daniel Eliot continued his tenure of one of the seats in 1690, being classed as a Tory by Lord Carmarthen (Sir Thomas Osborne†) in March 1690. In the following December Carmarthen, anticipating an attack by his political enemies in the Commons, listed him as a likely supporter, and in April 1691 Robert Harley* classed him as a Court supporter. He was not active in the Commons, but on 1 Dec. 1691 he was added to the drafting committee on a bill to encourage the manufacture of saltpetre. In the next Parliament he was forecast as likely to oppose the government on 31 Jan. 1696 in the division on the proposed council of trade, refused the Association at first, and in March voted against fixing the price of guineas at 22s. On 25 Nov. he was listed as voting against the attainder of Sir John Fenwick†, even though in another version he was also marked as 'absent' from the same division. He was classed as a member of the Country party in a comparative analysis of the old and new Parliaments in 1698, and forecast as likely to oppose a standing army. Having retired from the Commons at the second general election of 1701, he died on 11 Oct. 1702, and was buried at St. Germans. A will written in 1694 showed Eliot's concern that the estates should remain associated with the name of Eliot, for he left them to his cousin Edward Eliot*, and recommended that Edward marry his only daughter when she reached the age of 16. By the time he made a codicil to his will, nothing remained of this match (she eventually married Browne Willis*), but Edward was confirmed in the inheritance.[2]

[1] Vivian, *Vis. Cornw.* 148; *Vis. Eng. and Wales Notes* ed. Crisp, xiii. 122–5; IGI, Cornw.; *Mar. Lic. Fac. Off.* (Harl. Soc. xxiv), 176. [2] *Jnl. R. Inst. Cornw.* n.s. ix. 324–5; Polsue, *Complete Paroch. Hist. Cornw.* ii. 40; PCC 82 Dogg.

E. C./S. N. H.

ELIOT, Edward (c.1684–1722), of Port Eliot, Cornw.

ST. GERMANS   4 Dec. 1705–1715
LOSTWITHIEL   26 Nov. 1718–11 June 1720
LISKEARD   12 Apr.–18 Sept. 1722

b. c.1684, 1st s. of William Eliot, RN, of Cuddenbeak, Cornw. by Anne, da. of Lawrence Williams of Ireland.

educ. Exeter, Oxf. matric. 9 Mar. 1703, aged 18. *m.* (1) Susan (*bur.* Jan. 1714), da. of Sir William Coryton, 3rd Bt.*, and sis. of Sir John Coryton, 4th Bt.*; (2) Apr. 1718, Elizabeth (*d.* 1765), da. and coh. of James Craggs I*, and sis. and coh. of James Craggs II*, 1s. 1da. *suc.* cos. Daniel Eliot* at Port Eliot 1702.[1]

Receiver-gen. duchy of Cornw. Mar. 1715–20; commr. victualling 1718–June 1720, excise June 1720–Apr. 1722.

Eliot was the grandson of Nicholas Eliot, fourth son of the noted parliamentarian, Sir John Eliot†. He was the beneficiary of Daniel Eliot's determination to retain the link between the family name and Port Eliot. With the Eliot family estates, he inherited the patronage of the borough of St. Germans, for which he returned himself at a by-election soon after coming of age. He was not active in his first Parliament, but was classed as a Tory in a list of early 1708. Re-elected later that year, he acted as a teller on 20 Apr. 1709 against agreeing with a Lords' amendment to the bill explaining a previous Act 'to prevent mischiefs by fire' by regulating practices in London and Westminster. In the next session, on 18 Jan. 1710, he told for the motion that the High Tory Lewis Pryse* was duly elected for Cardiganshire. He voted against the impeachment of Dr Sacheverell, and was inevitably classified as a Tory in the 'Hanover list'. In the first session of the 1710 Parliament he figured in the lists of 'Tory patriots' voting for peace, and 'worthy patriots' who had helped detect the mismanagements of the previous ministry.

Until 1713 Eliot was a Tory but his absence from the division of 18 June 1713 on the French commerce bill may indicate his disillusionment with the ministry over his failure to gain office. Lord Lansdown's (George Granville*) correspondence with Lord Treasurer Oxford (Robert Harley*) about a place for Eliot suggested that he had 'a bargain ready on the other side'. Given that Eliot had been waiting over three months for an answer to a proposal that he should succeed Francis Scobell* as receiver of the revenues of the duchy of Cornwall, Lansdown felt that 'a man less jealous and impatient of neglect might think himself not fairly dealt with by so long a delay'. Eliot's disappointment may also explain his vote on 18 Mar. 1714 against the expulsion of Richard Steele and appearance on the Worsley list as a Tory who would often vote with the Whigs. Following the accession of George I Eliot went over to the Whigs and obtained the duchy post he had coveted. He died on 18 Sept. 1722, aged 39.[2]

[1] Vivian, *Vis. Cornw.* 148. [2] *HMC Portland*, v. 312, 315; Polsue, *Complete Paroch. Hist. Cornw.* ii. 42.

E. C./S. N. H.

ELIOTT, Sir Gilbert, 3rd Bt. (c.1680–1764), of Stobs, Roxburgh.

ROXBURGHSHIRE 1708–1715, 6 July 1726–1727

b. c.1680, 1st s. of Sir William Eliott, 2nd Bt., MP [S], of Stobs by his 2nd wife Margaret, da. of Charles Murray of Hadden, Roxburgh. *m.* 23 Apr. 1702, Eleanora (*d.* 1728), da. of William Elliot, lace-maker of London and Wells, Roxburgh, 10s. 1da. *suc.* fa. as 3rd Bt. 19 Feb. 1699.[1]

The Eliotts of Stobs considered themselves natural political leaders in Roxburghshire, Sir Gilbert Eliott being the fourth generation of parliamentary representatives for the county. Although his grandfather had supported the Royalist cause in the Civil War and his father initially avoided taking the Williamite oath of allegiance, Eliott himself was staunch to the Revolution interest. He succeeded to the baronetcy and estate of Stobs in 1699, but never sat in the Scottish parliament, unlike his namesake and kinsman Sir Gilbert Eliott, 1st Bt., of Minto, with whom he is sometimes confused. Eliott first stood in the 1708 election and, with the support of the hereditary sheriff Alexander Douglas*, was able to defeat the Duke of Roxburghe's brother, Hon. William Kerr*. At Westminster he acted as a Court Whig, even to the extent of deserting his countrymen. He was the only Scotsman who voted with the Court over the Westminster election case on 16 Dec. 1708, his fellow Scots joining with the Tories to victimize Sir Henry Dutton Colt, 1st Bt., for having formerly expressed anti-Scottish opinions. Perhaps unwilling to repeat this transgression, Eliott absented himself for the vote which finally determined the issue on the 18th. The Journals do not indicate that he was a particularly active Member. In January 1710 his return for Roxburghshire was belatedly considered by the committee of elections. During these proceedings, Eliott demonstrated something of the vindictive temperament which would later land him in serious trouble. On 20 Jan. he made insinuations that Kerr's petition was 'frivolous and vexatious', an accusation which created 'a hubbub'. Tempers were therefore already frayed by the 28th, when following the withdrawal of Kerr's petition, 'Sir Gilbert said he ought to have a vote of the House declaring that Mr Kerr had no just pretensions'. Kerr responded to this charge with such vehemence that Eliott initially apologized, claiming he meant

no affront to him by it, but afterwards, whether put on by some other [person] or thinking that he had given too much satisfaction ... he followed Mr Kerr to the door and in the crowd asked him twice if he had anything to say to him, upon which Mr Kerr took him aside and asked him what he meant, he told him he had said what one gentleman ought to say to one another [sic]. Mr Kerr made him a bow and told him he knew his meaning very well.

Kerr's friends assumed a duel must ensue, but were pleasantly surprised when no challenge materialized from Eliott. The latter was keen to keep the matter quiet and did not encourage discussion of the affair. The remainder of the session was uneventful, Eliott demonstrating his loyalty to the ministry by voting in favour of the impeachment of Dr Sacheverell and, on 3 Apr., carrying up the bill to explain the Act for better securing her Majesty's person and government.[2]

Eliott was re-elected after a contest in 1710 and was classified as a Whig in an electoral analysis by Richard Dongworth, chaplain to the Duchess of Buccleuch. His subsequent voting bears out this assessment. He supported the Whigs over two controverted elections, those of Bewdley on 19 Dec. and Rutland on 18 Jan. 1711. He told on 18 Apr. against adjourning consideration of the bill to establish a post office in her Majesty's dominions, and on 7 Feb. 1712 against the Scottish toleration bill. His 'stiffness and obstinacy' in consistently opposing the Court, were reported adversely to his electoral patron, Archibald Douglas. He was granted a two-month leave of absence on 9 Feb., but on returning to the House his opposition increased rather than abated. He joined in the abortive attempt to dissolve the Union in May 1713 and voted against the French commerce bill on 4 and 18 June.[3]

Unopposed at his re-election in 1713, Eliott was classified as a Hanoverian, that is, a Whig, by Lord Polwarth, an assessment repeated in the Worsley list and borne out by his voting behaviour. He voted against the expulsion of Richard Steele on 18 Mar. 1714 and told on 12 May in favour of the Whig wrecking amendment to extend the provisions of the schism bill to cover Catholic education. On certain matters of Scottish interest he was prepared to co-operate with Tories such as George Lockhart*, drafting with him an additional clause to the bill discharging the Equivalent commissioners from liability for money already disbursed. Eliott told in favour of this clause on 24 June, which would have charged the commissioners with 4 per cent interest upon the £14,000 appropriated for the wool-producing shires, unless this money was entrusted to the magistrates of Edinburgh, until 'the application was agreed upon'. His interest in Scottish economic affairs is also evident in his responsibility for carrying up, on 2 July, a bill to explain the Act regulating Scottish linen manufacture. Eliott's willingness to co-operate with Scottish Tories did not extend to those affecting the interests of the Kirk: he told on 3 July against an initiative to appoint commissioners to investigate episcopal revenues in Scotland.[4]

Eliott did not stand in 1715, making way for the sheriff's son William Douglas†, nor did he at the next election, giving his interest to Sir Gilbert Eliott of Minto, 2nd Bt.† But following Minto's elevation to the court of session in 1726, he came in at a by-election. An unfortunate and fateful fracas, however, prevented him from taking his seat. Sometimes dignified with description as a duel, this drunken brawl was a direct consequence of the recent by-election. At a dinner following a meeting to validate the freeholders' roll Eliott complained bitterly of Colonel John Stewart's* failure to vote for him, and the latter responded by throwing a glass of wine in Eliott's face. So incensed that he did not give Stewart the time to rise from his chair, Eliott ran him through with his sword. Though able to rise and strike Eliott twice before the 'combatants' were separated, Stewart's wounds were fatal and his dying statement was that 'he had been murdered sitting in his chair, and that his assailant was Sir Gilbert Eliott'. Under these circumstances a meeting of local magistrates, including Eliott's friends Douglas of Cavers and Lord Minto, could reach no other verdict than to declare him an outlaw. Eliott was not prevented from escaping, however, and he made his way to Holland. Concern for his soul was expressed by the Presbyterian divine, Robert Wodrow, who lamented that such 'a really religious person' had failed to master his 'passionate and violent temper'. But Wodrow was heartened that Eliott was 'exonerated by the generality on account of the provocation he had received'. Lobbying by Lords Minto and Ilay during 1727 secured a royal pardon for Eliott, who returned to live peacefully on his estates, dying at a 'great age' on 27 May 1764.[5]

[1] *Hist. Scot. Parl.* 224–6. [2] Ibid. 224–6; G. Tancred, *Annals of a Border Club*, 167–9; SRO, Ogilvy of Inverquharity mss GD205/34/4, John Pringle* to William Bennet*, 18 Dec. 1708; GD205/35/5/1/1, Robert Wood to Bennet, 21 Mar. 1709–10; *Lockhart Pprs.* i. 297, 531; NLS, ms 7021, f. 199. [3] *SHR*, lx. 66; NLS, Douglas of Cavers mss, Acc. 6991, William Douglas to fa. 14 Feb. 1711–12; SRO, Mar and Kellie ms GD124/15/1020/4, Hon. Sir James Dunbar, 1st Bt.*, to Ld. Grange (Hon. James Erskine†), 19 Dec. 1710; Aberdeen Univ. Lib. Duff House (Montcoffer) mss 3175/2380, 'Resolution of the Commons to call a Meeting of the Lords', [23] May 1713; *Parlty. Hist.* i. 69. [4] NLS, Advocates' mss, Wodrow pprs. letters Quarto 7, f. 177; *Lockhart Letters* ed. Szechi, 106–8. [5] W. R. Carle, *Border Memories*, 147; Tancred, 27; Wodrow, *Analecta*, iii. 318; G. F. S. Elliot, *Border Elliots*, 310.

D. W.

ELLIS, John (1646–1738) of St. James's, Westminster.

HARWICH 1702–1708

b. 1646, 1st s. of John Ellis, fellow of St. Catharine's, Camb., by Susanna, da. of William Welbore of Cambridge. *educ.* Westminster, 1660, aged 14, Christ Church, Oxf. matric. 22 July 1664, aged 18. ?*unm.*[1]

Sec. paper office 1672–4, at Nijmegen Dec. 1675–Sept. 1677; priv. sec. to Thomas Butler† (styled Earl of Ossory) 1678–Aug. 1680, to 1st Duke of Ormond, Aug. 1680–Oct. 1682; sec. to revenue commrs. [I] Oct. 1682–Jan. 1689; priv. sec. to 2nd Duke of Ormond, 1689–91; commr. transports Feb. 1690–5 May 1695; under-sec. of state May 1695–1705; comptroller of Royal Mint May 1701–June 1711.[2]

Gov. sons of clergy 1678; commr. building 50 new churches 1715–d.[3]

Freeman, Harwich 1702.[4]

Ellis came from a notorious family. His father, a propagandist, university proctor and former chaplain to Archbishop Abbot, had sided with Parliament in 1643 and openly supported its religious policy, but in 1659 made a dramatic, printed retraction of his views and was allowed to keep his living in Buckinghamshire at the Restoration. Two of Ellis' brothers were prominent supporters of James II: Sir William served as secretary first to the Earl of Tyrconnel in Ireland and then to the exiled King at St. Germain, while Philip was James's Catholic chaplain and was appointed vicar-apostolic in 1688. Although Ellis harboured the latter for a short time after the Revolution, John jnr. was a Protestant like his third brother, Welbore, a cleric who rose to become Church of Ireland bishop of Kildare and subsequently of Meath. Heavily influenced by his education at Oxford, John maintained strong links with High Churchmen such as the Earl of Rochester (Laurence Hyde†), Sir Leoline Jenkins†, Bishop Fell and Archbishop Dolben. His own early career showed none of the certainty and conviction shown by other members of his family, and was characterized by self-doubt. As an 'ingenious man and a good scholar', he attracted the patronage of Fell, then dean of Christ Church, who recommended him in 1671 to Sir Joseph Williamson* as a man of 'very good parts', but Fell doubted 'whether his radicated melancholy may render him unfit for business, or whether business may not happily cure his melancholy ... he may be more fit for contemplation than action'. Williamson encouraged the young man to go abroad and learn French prior to appointment in the government's paper office, and Ellis duly left the university without taking his degree; but, as a long confessional letter makes clear, he suffered a form of nervous breakdown when in France. Williamson had recalled him to England after six months, but Ellis, fearing that his French was not good enough and 'being of the disposition that [he] had rather not do things at all than not thoroughly', preferred to risk losing his place than be 'cast out for insufficiency'. He had therefore hidden himself away in Paris for six months, taking refuge in the pursuit of botanical studies. It was only when his money ran out that he was forced to face reality, and apologize for his behaviour by asking Williamson's pardon:

> Are there not some, and yet no fools, that reason themselves into inextricable doubts and so entangle their own thoughts that they have need of some help to be freed from themselves ... Am I the only person that suspected himself and called into question his own abilities?

Regretting his 'pertinacious modesty' he also refuted Williamson's suspicions that his absconding had been caused by conversion to Rome: 'Let me be counted blind, inconsiderate, mad rather than be branded with the anathema of apostasy. Let men say I have undone myself, I have spoiled my own fortunes, but not that I sold my belief and mortgaged my conscience.'[5] This unusual display of naivety, sensitivity and honesty seems to have appealed to Williamson, who possessed the opposite characteristics of cynicism and conceit. By July 1672 Ellis was serving under him, and a year later had become such a favourite that he was made responsible for the plenipotentiary's ever-shifting personal belongings as they criss-crossed the Channel. Nevertheless, in January 1674 Williamson suspected his aide of making disparaging comments about him, perhaps in connexion with the peace treaty with the Dutch, though Ellis pointed out that he could not 'encounter your lordship's reputation without at the same time destroying my own', and was restored to favour, possibly having cleared Williamson when he was summoned before the Lords on the 28th. Even so he lost his job later that year on his patron's promotion to secretary of state, and may have taken up legal studies, apparently contemplating taking a place at Doctors' Commons. Indeed, there was talk later of his applying for the chair of law at Oxford, even though he does not appear to have been admitted to an inn of court. Perhaps preparatory to this alternative career, the Duke of Ormond, chancellor of Oxford University, appealed on behalf of Ellis for an MA, stating that the latter's 'engagement to the public service' had prevented his taking a degree at the appropriate time; but it was another Oxford connexion that redirected his life along its earlier lines of state service. In December 1675 Sir Leoline Jenkins†, principal of Jesus College, Oxford, appointed Ellis as his secretary for the peace negotiations at Nijmegen. On his return Ellis became secretary to Ormond's son, the Earl of Ossory, who commanded troops in the Dutch service, and must have joined the latter in the Flanders campaign of 1677–8, since he later boasted of having won the favour of William of Orange at the battle of Mons. On Ossory's death in 1680 Ellis was employed as secretary to Ormond himself. There were rumours that he might secure another diplomatic posting or the clerkship of the Privy Council, but in 1682 he became secretary to the Irish revenue commissioners, through the patronage of Ormond, Jenkins and Lord Arlington (Henry Bennet†). Ellis was not happy in Ireland – his friend Humphrey Prideaux feared that he found the country 'a kind of banishment' – but the post had a salary of £300, as well as £200 p.a. revenue from wool licensing, and one observer thought the two posts 'almost as considerable as a commissioner's place'. Despite his brother Philip's ascendancy at the Catholic court in England, which Prideaux thought might be used to get his friend appointed as a commissioner of the navy, Ellis merely requested that his name be mentioned to James II 'only to try the King's opinion', otherwise distancing himself from the principles of his brothers and thereby earning the reputation that he 'never was inclinable to their interests or to change his religion for interest'.[6]

At the Revolution Ellis returned to England 'with design', he later claimed, 'to serve the King', but once more found it hard to find employment, though Prideaux thought this unsurprising since his friend was 'so bad a solicitor'. Ellis fell back on the support of the Ormond family, acting as secretary to the young 2nd Duke, until his appointment in 1691 as a commissioner for transports, in the capacity of secretary and accountant. He appeared before the Commons on 16 Nov. 1692 as the spokesman of the commissioners, but may have considered resignation in 1693 since Prideaux wrote advising him to temporize 'with them you cannot like'. He was again rescued by his university connexions, for in May 1695 he was appointed under-secretary to another Oxford alumnus, Sir William Trumbull*, a post that he was to fill until 1705. As his voluminous correspondence shows, the office was a demanding one, especially when it meant attending the monarch outside London or when the secretary of state was absent, as was quite often the case with Trumbull. A change of secretary at the top could also create uncertainty and insecurity below, though Ellis survived Trumbull's fall because the new secretary, James Vernon I*, was his 'old acquaintance and friend', and thereafter his experience was probably too valuable to lose. Perhaps the best tribute to his dedication to the job is the comment of another friend, Matthew Prior*, who said that he aspired to be Lord Jersey's 'Ellis' when the latter became secretary of state, an indication that Ellis had made his name a byword for loyalty and hard work. Despite its drudgery, the post was not without its advantages. One of its main duties was to prepare and send out letters of news (a large number of which are printed with the state papers), and to supervise the publication of the *London Gazette*, responsibilities which gave Ellis excellent contacts, including some at the Post Office, which were later to be useful to him in a more personal capacity when he stood for Parliament. The salary of under-secretary was not high: Ellis claimed that 'he hath never made £500 a year since he hath been in it', and deserved 'greater encouragement than what arises from that employment'. In February 1699 he was rewarded with the grant of his brother William's forfeited estate in Ireland, in repayment of a £1,200 loan, and on 11 Apr. 1702 the former secretary of state Sir Charles Hedges* was ordered to introduce a bill confirming the transaction, though it was another High Churchman, Sir Roger Mostyn, 3rd Bt.*, who actually brought in the legislation. Ellis also received a further £500 as comptroller of the mint, to which office he was appointed on 15 May 1701. Additionally, the King recommended him for a post at the Plymouth customs.[7]

The new political and religious climate created by Queen Anne's accession encompassed Ellis' entry into Parliament, about which he had been long labouring. His struggle shows that despite, or perhaps because of, his governmental post his lack of an electoral interest worked against him. In July 1698 he had put himself forward as a candidate for Oxford University by appearing there in person, and procuring about 'near a 100' letters of recommendation to be sent to the electors, including one from the bishop of Winchester, and another from the chancellor, Ormond, to the heads of houses which testified to Ellis' 'long and affectionate services to me and my family'. Ellis seems nevertheless to have withdrawn from the contest, and in January of the following year he asked Williamson 'to do me the honour to put me up at Thetford', though his former employer was probably already engaged to another candidate since the matter was not pursued. In December 1700, having 'met with encouragement' to stand at Steyning, he wrote unsuccessfully to the Duke of Somerset for his interest. Ellis does not seem to have followed up the suggestion that Bramber might be 'a likelier place for a gentleman who is a stranger to succeed at', preferring instead to make inquiries at Harwich, since there was a possibility of joining with

Samuel Atkinson*, whom Ellis knew as a fellow commissioner for transports. He wrote to Atkinson and the agent of the packet boats at the port for further assistance, but was informed that since Dennis Lyddell* had accepted the nomination there it would be 'to no purpose' to stand. After the dissolution in 1701 he may have been involved in promoting the election of Sir Charles Hedges at Dover, as well as unsuccessfully pursuing his own candidature at Harwich. Despite a letter of support from a member of his old college in case he contested Oxford University in 1702, he preferred to wear down opposition at Harwich, this time successfully, partly with the support of Atkinson and Lyddell.[8]

Ellis made very little impression at Westminster, his diffidence possibly overriding his Court loyalties. He was forecast as a probable opponent of the Tack and did not vote for it in the division on 28 Nov. 1704. It was probably on local issues that he was most active. Having received a warning that his constituents expected some return for their choice of him, he worked on behalf of the packet boats at Harwich, and in March 1705 informed the mayor that he had espoused the town's interest 'in all places and upon all occasions' and hoped to have given 'no reason of being dissatisfied'. He certainly needed local support since at about the time of the election in May there had been moves at a national level to discredit him, ironically coming from Hedges. Ellis was dismissed from office that month, according to the Dutch ambassador 'pour avoir eu la facilité de permettre qu'un marchand Irlandois fit venir des lettres sous son couvert d'un autre marchand de Bourdeaux avec qu'il était en commerce'. Sir Henry Sheres, however, had heard that Ellis had been turned out 'on some information of a woman about a French pass and suggestions of his correspondence with France', though admitting that 'the whole matter is a mystery'. Fortunately Ellis left notes, possibly intended for a vindicatory speech to the Commons, that reinforce the rumour heard by Sheres. Ellis had been summoned by Hedges to explain about a French pass he had authorized and the matter might have gone no further had not Ellis not been 'so confident in [his] own innocency and upright intentions' that he refused to admit any mistake. His concern for his reputation, which he 'had always been very careful of', temporarily outweighed his usual meekness, with disastrous consequences. Hedges was 'uneasy and dissatisfied with Mr Ellis' account of the passes', and the matter was laid before the Privy Council, at which the more serious charge was raised that Ellis had corresponded with France. By his own account he

was in much confusion at so unexpected an accident, which was like a blow upon the head that might have astonished a man of greater firmity of mind than I pretend to be. Not long after the elections to the Parliament coming on, I went to Harwich, and was chosen one of the burgesses there.

On his return, Ellis

found it depended on Mr S[ecretary] H[edges] to keep me or drop me, and he did the latter. I was in hopes it was only suspension not a discharge from the office, and so Mr Vernon . . . believed too, because I had served him in that station very diligently and faithfully, as I have always done since I was in it, neither have I discovered directly or indirectly any of the publ[ic] business I was entrusted with to any body whatsoever, or ever had any correspondence with any person in France, though that I find is the mistaken suggestion insisted upon as that which is most to my disadvantage.

Ellis undoubtedly had contacts among the Jacobite community both at St. Germain and in England, for although in 1697 he claimed that he knew 'none of them' he had already admitted the year before that he had 'sounded the hearts of all sorts of ranks and qualities of the discontented party'; but his conduct during the 1680s suggests his extreme caution in becoming involved in uncertain causes, and loyalty to the Court, both under William and Anne, seems to have been one of his guiding principles. More conclusive is a report of 1718 that shows his zealous activity as a Middlesex j.p. against Jacobite conventicles in London, which included making personal appearances at meetings to note down for later prosecution the names and addresses of participants. In July 1705 Prideaux therefore urged his friend not 'to give up the reputation of your integrity', but Ellis preferred private entreaty to public justification, and drafted a begging letter to Hedges, for whom he claimed to have 'a particular honour', in which he reproached himself for having erred in his work and unsuccessfully asked for forgiveness.[9]

Ellis was marked as a High Church courtier and a placeman on an analysis of the new Parliament. Despite his removal from office, he supported the Court over the Speakership on 25 Oct. 1705 as well as the proceedings on the 'place clause' of the regency bill on 18 Feb. 1706. He had always been able to subordinate his own political views to those of the government, serving under secretaries of state of different allegiances, and there was consequently some doubt about his own political affiliation. In 1708 he was marked on separate lists as, respectively, a Whig and a Tory. This ambiguity, coupled with the loss of office, damaged Ellis' electoral prospects. As early as March

1707 he was warned that he was 'in great danger at Harwich', and was advised to approach the Whig Earl Rivers for support. The following month he formally offered himself to the corporation, but was told in August by one local informant that 'whatever ground your great merit and your services to them seem to give you at the next election, I am afraid your share of electors will come into no competition with any of the other' candidates. He decided against standing at the ensuing general election, and it appears that he did not contest a by-election in May 1709, even though it was reported at about this time that he was actively seeking to return to the House. In 1710 he stood unsuccessfully for Rye, and his petition against the result was rejected by the House. Almost immediately afterwards he was removed as a j.p., and four months later was replaced as comptroller of the Mint, perhaps because of his association with Lord Godolphin (Sidney†), who had originally secured him the office.[10]

After the accession of George I Ellis petitioned for the return of his post at the Mint, identifying himself with 'others loyal to the Protestant succession' who had been removed by Harley, but he never again held office higher than that of j.p. He turned instead to providing for what proved to be a prolonged old age, dying 'immensely rich' on 8 July 1738 at the reported age of 95. The date of birth given on his admission to both school and university suggests, however, that he had attained the only slightly less venerable age of 92. For the last 20 years or so of his life he had been cared for by his 'faithful friend' Samuel Seddon. An Irish estate in Seddon's trust was bequeathed to his nephew Welbore Ellis; the will also mentions property in Whitehart Yard, Westminster, and at Cambridge. Ellis gave almost £3,000 in personal bequests, as well as £50 to the building of Peckwater quad at his old college, and £50 to the poor of Westminster. He requested burial in a vault or churchyard rather than inside any church 'which is the house of God and ought not in my opinion to be made a charnel house'. Positive identification is made difficult, in a number of instances, because of possible namesakes. Although he was almost certainly the Ellis who owned £2,000 of Bank stock in 1710, as well as shares in the United East India Company, he was probably not the Ellis 'of Gray's Inn' who was appointed solicitor of the excise in 1710. Assertions made elsewhere that he was the 'epitome of lewdness' or a lover of the Duchess of Cleveland should almost certainly be discounted.[11]

[1] *Rec. Old Westminsters*, i. 308; W. S. Ellis, *Notices of the Ellises*, pt.4, p. 157; Add. 28918, f. 192. [2] *DNB*; *CSP Dom.* 1682, p. 500; *Cal. Treas. Bks.* ix. 197; xvi. 66; xxiv. 281; xxv. 293; Add. 28940, ff. 2–12. [3] BL, Dept. of Printed Bks. 1865 c 13(6); E. S. Bill, *Q. Anne Churches*, p. xxiv. [4] S. Taylor, *Hist. and Antiquities of Harwich*, 233. [5] *DNB* (Ellis, John, Philip, Welbore and William); Add. 28927, f. 27; 46527, f. 89; 28930, f. 320; *HMC Ormonde*, n.s. vi. 135; *Ellis Corresp.* i. 99; *CSP Dom.* 1671, p. 31; *Ellis Corresp.* i, p. xx; SP 29/295/79. [6] *CSP Dom.* 1673, p. 465; 1673–5, p. 150; 1680–1, pp. 75, 395, 421; 1682, p. 500; SP 29/360/47; Add. 28875, f. 10; 28927, f. 21; 28930, f. 179; 46527, f. 89; PCC 173 Brodrepp; *Cam. Soc.* n.s. xv, 25, 125, 134–5, 146; Egerton 929, f. 148; *HMC Ormonde*, n.s. vi. 43, 424; *HMC Downshire*, i. 41; *Ellis Corresp.* i. 82, 116, 125, 239, 243. [7] *Cal. Treas. Bks.* xiv. 272; xvi. 268; xxiv. 282; xix. 198; *Luttrell Diary*, 232; *Prideaux Letters* (Cam. Soc. n.s. xv.) 149, 157; *CSP Dom.* 1697, p. 516; 1699–1700, p. 2; BL, Trumbull Add. mss 58, passim; Add. 28895, ff. 19, 24, 26, 28; 28886, f. 72; *HMC Bath*, iii. 326, 335; *DNB*. [8] Trumbull Add. mss 60, Rev. Ralph Trumbull to Sir William Trumbull, July 1698; Add. 28883, f. 52; 28927, f. 127; 28886, ff. 168, 172, 180, 185, 195, 196; 28887, f. 374; 28889, ff. 13, 20, 30, 38, 40; Egerton 2618, f. 182; *CSP Dom.* 1699–1700, p. 27. [9] Add. 28893, ff. 75, 103, 166; 28890, f. 358; 17677 AAA, f. 295; 28948, ff. 88–91; 70285, f. 27; 28919, f. 1; 61609, f. 191; 28893, ff. 144–6; Luttrell, *Brief Relation*, v. 555; *HMC Downshire*, i. 839; *CSP Dom.* 1697, p. 280; *Prideaux Letters*, 197. [10] Add. 28891, ff. 241, 278; 28948, f. 162; Trumbull Add. mss 132, John Tucker to Trumbull, 11 Jan. 1709; Luttrell, vi. 688; *Post Boy*, 10–22 Feb. 1711; *Cal. Treas. Bks.* xxv. 293; *HMC Downshire*, i. 714. [11] Egerton 929, f. 148; *Gent. Mag.* 1738, p. 380; PCC 173 Brodrepp; Folger Shakespeare Lib. Newdigate newsletter 29 June 1706; *DNB*; *Ellis Corresp.* i, p. xvi; Bodl. Rawl. D.747, ff. 368–74; Add. 28886, f. 100; 28948, ff. 204–6, 207–9; *Cal. Treas. Bks.* xxiv. 298; Boyer, *Anne Annals*, ix. 417.

M. J. K.

ELLYS, Richard (1683–1742), of Nocton, Lincs. and Bolton Street, Piccadilly, Westminster.

GRANTHAM 1701 (Dec.)–1705
BOSTON 7 Dec. 1719–1734

b. 14 Mar. 1683, 4th but 1st surv. s. of Sir William Ellys, 2nd Bt.*; bro. of Thomas Ellys*. *educ.* travelled abroad (Holland) 1694; Padua Univ. 1697. *m.* (1) lic. 21 May 1714, Elizabeth (*d.* 1724), da. and coh. of Sir Thomas Hussey, 2nd Bt.*, *s.p.*; (2) 1 Dec. 1726, Sarah, da. and coh. of Thomas Gould of Iver, Bucks., *s.p. suc.* fa. as 3rd Bt. 6 Oct. 1727.[1]

Surveyor, duty on houses, Leics. 1715–16, Lincs. 1716–17.[2]

Ellys was probably, like his brothers, first educated at a private Dissenting academy, and then in 1694, following in his elder brother's footsteps, went to continue his education in Holland, after which he kept up a correspondence with continental scholars such as Gronovius and Mettaire. Ellys' family had strong connexions with Grantham, where his father was a long-serving MP. At the first election of 1701, objections at having two members of the same family as the borough's MPs stifled Ellys' candidature, but similar opposition in the second election of that year was overcome and Ellys came in as his father's colleague, aged only 18. He continued to represent the borough in Anne's first Parliament, during which he voted on 13 Feb. 1703 in favour of agreeing to the Lords' amendments to the bill for enlarging the time for taking the oath of abjuration, was forecast in October 1704 as a probable opponent of the Tack and did not vote for it in the division on 28 Nov. 1704. An inactive Member, he deferred to the superior interest of the Marquess of Granby (John Manners*) at the 1705 election and did not stand again in this period. It is possible that he was the 'Richard Ellis' who held a mortgage of £8,000 with interest on Richard Minshull's estate in 1708. If so, it does not seem to have prevented financial difficulties, as shortly after his marriage in 1714, it was reported that Ellys was so deeply in debt that he had been forced to take his wife off to Europe and 'now her house and goods and all is seized. Sir William [Ellys' father], answered for her house and goods, but no more.' Subsequently Ellys represented Boston under George I and II.[3]

Outside politics his main interests were theology, on which he published a book in 1727, and book collecting. He built up large libraries at both Nocton and his London house. Henry Newman, secretary to the SPCK, heard that Ellys wished to leave his library 'to any learned seminary among the Dissenters' and attempted to acquire it for Harvard College in the summer of 1741, but failed. Ellys died on 14 Feb. 1742, leaving an estate worth about £5,000 p.a. according to Newman. His lands in Lincolnshire and Leicestershire were bequeathed to his widow for life and then entailed on the Hobart family, who also inherited the books, which were eventually removed to the Hobarts' seat at Blickling in Norfolk.[4]

[1] IGI, Lincs.; *Assoc. Architectural Socs.* xxiv. 365–6; *Lincs. Peds.* (Harl. Soc. l), 326; *CSP. Dom. 1694–5*, p. 317. [2] *Cal. Treas. Bks.* xxix. 415; xxx. 374–5; xxxi. 578. [3] Calamy, *Life*, i. 134; ii. 188; Add. 70083, Richard Stretton to Edward Harley*, 2 Oct. 1697; *CSP. Dom. 1690–1*, p. 116; *Assoc. Architectural Socs.* 365–6; Glos. RO, Newton mss D1844/C/10, H. Solomon et al. to Sir John Newton, 3rd Bt., 18 May 1700; Lincs. AO, Monson mss 7/12/106, Robert Fysher to Newton, 15 Nov. 1701; *HMC Lords*, n.s. viii. 17; Norf. RO, Ketton-Cremer mss, Katherine to Ashe Windham*, n.d. [1714]. [4] *Assoc. Architectural Socs.* 365–6; L. W. Cowie, *Henry Newman*, 193–4; PCC 50 Trenley.

P. W.

ELLYS, Thomas (1685–1709), of Mitre Court, Inner Temple.

WENDOVER 1708–24 May 1709

b. 13 Apr. 1685, 6th but 3rd surv. s. of Sir William Ellys, 2nd Bt.*; bro. of Richard Ellys*. *educ.* I. Temple 1699. *unm.*[1]

Gent. Usher of the Black Rod [I] c.1708–d.[2]

Ellys' early life is obscure, but he may have attended a Dissenting school near London in 1697 on the recommendation of his aunt Hampden. Returned for Wendover on the interest of his cousin Richard Hampden II*, Ellys was classed as a Whig in a list of Parliament of early 1708 with the returns of the election added. He also supported the naturalization of the Palatines early in 1709, and on 10 Mar. acted as teller against committing a bill for regulating building practices. This promising start to a career in the Commons was ended by Ellys' untimely death on 24 May 1709. Despite coming from a wealthy family, he had few possessions, which were left to a creditor to pay a debt of £160.[3]

[1] PCC 168 Trenley; IGI, Lincs.; *Assoc. Architectural Socs.* xxiv, 362; *Lincs. Peds.* (Harl. Soc. l), 326. [2] Luttrell, *Brief Relation*, vi. 445. [3] Add. 70083, Richard Stretton to Edward Harley*, 2 Oct. 1697; PCC 168 Trenley.

E.C./S. M. W.

ELLYS, Sir William, 2nd Bt. (1654–1727), of Nocton, Lincs.

GRANTHAM 1679 (Mar.)–1681 (Mar.), 1689–1713

b. 2 May 1654, 1st s. of Sir Thomas Ellys, 1st Bt., of Wyham, Lincs. by Anne, da. of Sir John Stanhope† of Elvaston, Derbys. *educ.* Lincoln, Oxf. matric. 1670, MA 1671. *m.* 2 Oct. 1672, Isabella (d. 1686) da. of Richard Hampden I*, and sis. of John Hampden†, 6s. (4 *d.v.p.*) 5da. *suc.* fa. as 2nd Bt. 1668, gt.-uncle William Ellys† 1680.[1]

Freeman, Grantham 1676; commr. inquiry into recusancy fines, Derbys., Lincs. and Notts. Mar. 1688, into losses in Fifteen, Lincs. 1716; trustee for rebuilding St. Peter-at-Arches church, Lincoln, 1719.[2]

The Ellyses, 'an ancient family' in Lincolnshire with strong Dissenting sympathies, had long supplied the area with MPs and had built up a formidable political interest. Ellys, himself possibly a Presbyterian, sat for Grantham from 1679 with only one break until his retirement from active politics in 1713, his interest being successfully maintained by many gifts to the town. An Exclusionist, he remained opposed to James II during his reign and, returned again for Grantham in 1690, was classed as a Whig in Lord Carmarthen's (Sir Thomas Osborne†) list of the new Parliament. At the start of the second session Ellys' brother-in-law, John Hampden, wrote to Robert Harley* about the latter's election petition that Ellys 'has desired me to tell you he will solicit for you, and do you all the service he can'. Further letters followed, from Ellys to Harley, over the next 13 years and are witness to a lasting friendship between the two men. On 5 Dec. the House allowed him two weeks' leave after a division. The next year, in April 1691, Ellys was listed as a Country supporter by Harley, who also reported in August that

Ellys had been left out of the lieutenancy in Lincolnshire. In the summer of 1693 he entertained Sir Christopher Musgrave, 4th Bt.*, at his recently completed house, Nocton Hall, where, Musgrave reported, 'he lives like a prince'.³

At the end of August 1695 Ellys wrote to Harley thanking him for some (unspecified) good news, and adding that he needed 'no pretence to say that your productions have always been worth my knowledge, and that I have received great advantage from your instruction'. Harley's news was evidently not about the forthcoming dissolution, which Ellys was mistaken in thinking would not occur. Re-elected unopposed in October, Ellys was forecast in January 1696 as a probable opponent of the Court in the divisions anticipated on the proposed council of trade. He signed the Association promptly but voted against the government in March on setting the price of guineas at 22s. Ellys' letter of 13 May 1696 to Harley referred, somewhat ironically, to Harley's religious views in expressing some reservations over the planned land bank:

I must confess that honesty is a considerable part of my religion, and I shall not pretend to knowledge, because I would not be thought a favourer of that sect which I know you have no opinion of. I have read over your land bank and I can more easily trace you than Solomon could by his ship in the sea. I find you have delivered it of some monsters, but the court has been hard upon you, though you made them own there might be a failure of cash and credit in their project. I'm afraid you can't raise a million in cash and specie before January, but I'll not be wise at this distance.

In November that year, Ellys voted in favour of the attainder of Sir John Fenwick†.⁴

Ellys was again re-elected unopposed in 1698 when the compiler of a comparative analysis of the old and new Parliaments in about September 1698 could only class him as 'doubtful', an unsurprising verdict given his previous pattern of voting. A list of October 1698 probably forecast Ellys as likely to oppose a standing army and he does not appear on lists of those who voted for it in January 1699. An analysis of the House of January–May 1700 suggests that Ellys was associated with the Junto Lords as it listed Ellys as being in the interest of the Duke of Bedford (William Russell†) and Lord Orford (Edward Russell*): a connexion made plausible by the marriage of Orford's heir, Edward Cheeke, to Ellys' eldest daughter in July 1700. The next year the Ellys and Hampden families reinforced their ties when another of Ellys' daughters married her cousin, Richard Hampden II*. In the 1701 Parliament, Ellys appears on a list of those likely to support the Court in agreeing with the committee of supply's resolution to continue the 'Great Mortgage'.⁵

In Anne's reign Ellys did not abandon his Country Whig principles, but none the less was to be found more often giving his vote to the administration. On 13 Feb. 1703 he voted in favour of agreeing with the Lords' amendments to the bill for enlarging the time for taking the oath of abjuration, and on 28 Nov. 1704 did not vote for the Tack. Listed after his re-election in 1705 as a 'Low Churchman', Ellys voted on 25 Oct. in support of the Court candidate for Speaker. Soon afterwards, however, he devoted his energies once more to a 'Country' cause, taking a substantial share in the attempt to secure a 'place clause' in the regency bill. He was appointed one of the managers for a conference with the Lords on 7 Feb. 1706 and after the bill had been lost on 18 Feb., one of its supporters, Sir John Cropley, 2nd Bt.*, reported that Ellys and 'all such were firm to the last'. Harley's offer to Ellys in the summer of 1706 of the power of recommending someone to a particular position may have been related to the former's interference in the alterations being made to the Lincolnshire bench at that time. Ellys, though 'extremely obliged for the great favour', declined the offer, claiming that he did not know anyone worthy of it and, moreover, 'I think the pot boils over everywhere, and if 'twas in my power I would empty it before I put more in'. The next year, in August, action by Harley in favour of the Grantham corporation's petition to be allowed to collect money in Lincolnshire to repair the damage caused by a fire in the town in July, gave Ellys occasion to write to him,

You are the best friend in the world, . . . your generous temper prompts you to do favours for no other reason but to serve your friends. I hope our corporation are sensible of the great favour you have done them, I'm sure the method you've taken makes a greater impression upon me than I'm able to express.

An analysis of the House of early 1708 classed Ellys as a Whig, and in the subsequent Parliament he voted for the naturalization of the Palatines and for the impeachment of Dr Sacheverell. Described again as a Whig in the 'Hanover list' of 1710, he opposed the Tory ministry in the vote on 18 June 1713 on the French commerce bill. He did not stand for re-election that year, and seems to have retired from active politics.⁶

Ellys continued his role as local patron and benefactor, becoming a trustee for the rebuilding of the church of St. Peter-at-Arches, Lincoln, in 1719. He died at Nocton, 6 Oct. 1727, leaving large legacies to his daughters Sarah and Isabella, £100 to Grantham corporation, and the bulk of his estate to his son Richard*.⁷

[1] *Assoc. Architectural Socs.* xxiv, 362–6; IGI, Lincs. [2] *Cal. Treas. Bks.* viii. 1806; xxx. 425; *Lincs. Peds.* (Harl. Soc. l), 326. [3] *Her. and Gen.* ii. 121; D. R. Lacey, *Dissent and Parlty. Pol. 1661–89*, 389–90; W. Marrat, *Grantham*, 24; A. Browning, *Danby*, iii. 160; Add. 70015, f. 86; 70230, Hampden to Harley, 15 Oct. 1690; *HMC Portland*, iii. 536. [4] Add. 70197, Ellys to Harley, 31 Aug. 1695, 13 May 1696; 70224, same to same, 6 Nov. 1695. [5] Luttrell, *Brief Relation*, iv. 665. [6] Centre Kentish Stud. Stanhope mss U1590 C9/31, Cropley to Alexander Stanhope, 19 Feb. [1706]; *HMC Portland*, iv. 314; Marrat, 23–25; Add. 70267 misc. 42, Grantham petition; 70197, Ellys to Harley, 11 Aug. 1707. [7] *Lincs. Peds.* (Harl. Soc. l), 326; PCC 79 Brook.

P. W./S. M. W.

ELSON, William I (1673–1705), of Oving, nr. Chichester, Suss.

CHICHESTER 1695–1698, 1701 (Feb.)–Oct. 1705

bap. 27 Nov. 1673, 1st s. of William Elson of Oving by Jane Austen of Wivelsfield, Suss. *m.* 9 Oct. 1694, Bridget, da. of Daniel German (or Jarman) of Steeple Morden, Cambs., 1s. 2da. *suc.* fa. 1679, gdfa. 1684.[1]

Common councilman, Chichester by 1695–d.

Elson's family had been settled in Sussex since the late 16th century, acquiring the manor of Oving, just over two miles from Chichester, in 1670. Elson himself had been elected a common councilman for Chichester by 1695, when he successfully contested the borough as a Tory. Forecast as a probable opponent of the Court in the division on the proposed council of trade on 31 Jan. 1696, he voted against the ministry in March on fixing the price of guineas at 22s., although in the meantime he had signed the Association. In the next session he voted on 25 Nov. 1696 against the attainder of Sir John Fenwick†, but otherwise was inactive, being sent for in custody twice for absenting himself without leave (7 Jan. 1696, 25 Jan. 1697): indeed in each session he was granted leave of absence, usually for the recovery of his health (21 Feb., 29 Dec. 1696, 26 Feb. 1697, 27 Jan. 1698). Classed as a supporter of the Country party in a comparative analysis of the old and new Parliaments in 1698, he did not in fact stand in the general election of that year. In June 1700 he purchased the manor of Selsey and other lands in Sussex for £8,940 from Sir William Morley*. He returned to Parliament in February 1701 and remained one of the Members for Chichester for the rest of his days. He was classed as a Tory in Robert Harley's* list of the second 1701 Parliament, was blacklisted as having opposed preparations for war in 1701, and on 26 Feb. 1702 supported the motion vindicating the Commons' proceedings in the impeachments.[2]

So delighted was Elson with the accession of Anne that the Chichester corporation only budgeted £25 for the celebrations attending her proclamation as Elson had 'promised the corporation to make the conduit run with wine at his own charge'. In Parliament he was forecast on 30 Oct. 1704 as a probable supporter of the Tack and duly voted for it on 28 Nov., thus earning the description 'True Church' in a list compiled in June 1705. Re-elected in 1705, he was marked as absent in the division on the Speaker on 25 Oct. but in fact had died some days previously, before 23 Oct. His son William II* inherited the estate.[3]

[1] *HMC Lords*, n.s. vii. 68–69; *Vis. Suss.* (Harl. Soc. lxxxix), 41; PCC 97 Cann, 170 Gee; IGI, Cambs. [2] *Suss. Arch. Colls.* xxxiv. 188–90; *HMC Lords*, 68–69. [3] *Suss. Arch. Colls.* 188–90; Luttrell, *Brief Relation*, v. 604.

P. W.

ELSON, William II (1691–1727), of Oving, Suss.

CHICHESTER 1713–1715

bap. 30 July 1691, o. s. of William Elson I*. *educ.* New Coll. Oxf. 1709. *m.* Anne, da. of Sir John Suffield of Portsmouth, Hants, 1da. *suc.* fa. 1705.[1]

Elson, a minor when his father died, was left in the care of his grandmother, who in April 1707 secured the passage of an Act enabling her to sell some of the family estates to pay off debts. On coming of age he was added to the Sussex commission of the peace and successfully contested Chichester in 1713, topping the poll. He was classed as a Tory in the Worsley list. Defeated for Chichester in 1715, he did not stand again and died in 1727. His will, proved on 15 May 1727, left his property in trust for his only daughter, and named his grandmother and Thomas Carr* among the trustees.[2]

[1] W. Suss. RO, subdeanery of Chichester par. reg. (*ex inf.* Dr P. J. Le Fevre). [2] *HMC Lords*, n.s. vii. 68–69; L. K. J. Glassey, *Appt. JPs*, 238; PCC 113 Farrant.

P. W.

ELWES, Sir Gervase, 1st Bt. (1628–1706), of Stoke College, Stoke by Clare, Suff.

SUDBURY	28 May 1677–1679 (Jan.)
SUFFOLK	1679 (Mar.–July)
SUDBURY	1680–1681 (Jan.)
SUDBURY AND PRESTON	1681 (Mar.)
SUFFOLK	1690–1698
SUDBURY	16 Feb. 1700–11 Apr. 1706

bap. 21 Aug. 1628, 1st s. of Sir Gervase Elwes, Merchant Taylor, of Blackfriars, London by Frances, da. of Sir Robert Lee of Billesley, Warws.; bro. of Sir John Elwes†.

educ. travelled abroad (Spain, Italy, France) 1646–51. *m.* 2 Mar. 1652, Amy, da. and h. of William Trigge of Chiswick, Mdx., 6s. (5 *d.v.p.*) 5da. *suc.* fa. 1652; *cr.* Bt. 22 June 1660.[1]

Prothonotary of c.p., duchy of Lancaster Aug. 1660–*d.*; steward, honor of Clare 1661–85, 1691–*d.*; freeman, Preston 1662, 1682.[2]

Elwes joined with Sir Samuel Barnardiston, 1st Bt.*, in the Suffolk election of 1690 and was returned on the Whig interest, 'though with great protestations and much assurance of steadiness and firmness for the Church'. Lord Carmarthen (Sir Thomas Osborne†) listed him as a Whig. On 8 May he was appointed to the drafting committee for a bill to prevent the export of silver and gold. In the second session he was nominated to prepare bills to regulate King's Bench and Fleet prisons (18 Oct.) and to prevent the export of wool (21 Oct.). He told on 1 Nov. in favour of allowing a hearing at the bar of the House to two men who had been charged with a breach of privilege against the Tory Thomas Christie. In a list of April 1691 Robert Harley* classed him as a doubtful Court supporter. He was a teller on 19 Feb. 1692 with Barnardiston, and probably on the Opposition side, on a motion to adjourn. In 1693 he was included in three lists of placemen, but in respect of the office of receiver-general of the duchy of Lancaster held by his brother Sir John Elwes. On 2 Jan. 1694 he was appointed to the drafting committee for the assize of bread, and at the end of that year (4 Dec.) was nominated to draft a bill on prisons and prisoners.[3]

Elwes was returned unopposed with Barnardiston at the 1695 election. He was forecast as likely to vote with the Court in the divisions of 31 Jan. 1696 on the proposed council of trade, signed the Association and on 17 Apr. was a teller against adjourning the report of Barnardiston's garbling spices bill. He voted on 25 Nov. in favour of the attainder of Sir John Fenwick†. Granted eight days' leave of absence on 22 Dec., he was back in the House by 15 Jan. 1697, when he was named to the committee to prepare clauses to explain the Acts for recoinage and to prevent abuses being committed by receivers of public money. On 30 Mar. 1698 he was given another leave of absence.

At the 1698 election in Suffolk Elwes and Barnardiston were on opposite sides, the latter joining with an opposition Tory while Elwes put up as a Court supporter. Elwes and his partner were well beaten. Worse still, Elwes was even defeated by a local Tory in a by-election in his own borough of Sudbury in February 1699, and this after having 'bribed . . . absolutely', according to his opponents. They claimed that it was because he had been 'very free of his money' that he was 'ashamed to appear' and left it to his supporters to petition. The petition was dropped, however, when in the following year another vacancy arose at Sudbury and Elwes was able to secure the seat. Thereafter he gave up all pretensions to the county and was content to be returned for the borough, though not without a contest on each occasion. He was listed by Harley in December 1701 as a Whig. Forecast as likely to vote against the Tack, he did not vote for it on 28 Nov. On 24 Nov. 1704 he had been first-named to the drafting committee on the Stour navigation bill. He took responsibility for its parliamentary management, but the bill did not progress beyond committee. Despite being reported dead in June 1705, Elwes was returned again to the following Parliament, in a list of which he appeared as a 'Churchman'. He voted for the Court candidate as Speaker on 25 Oct. 1705, and for the Court in proceedings on the regency bill on 18 Feb. 1706. He reintroduced his navigation bill on 29 Nov. 1705, again without success.[4]

Elwes died on 11 Apr. 1706 'at Stoke, about three in the morning', and was buried there.[5]

[1] *VCH Northants. Fams.* 66–69; *Evelyn Diary*, iii. 31, 38, 58. [2] Somerville, *Duchy of Lancaster Official Lists*, 110, 123; *Preston Guild Rolls* (Lancs. and Cheshire Rec. Soc. ix), 144, 185. [3] Bodl. Tanner 27, f. 110; Somerville, 18–19. [4] *Vernon–Shrewsbury Letters*, ii. 151; C. F. D. Sperling, *Hodson's Hist. Sudbury*, 83–85; Luttrell, *Brief Relation*, v. 559, 562. [5] *Hervey Diary*, 44.

D. W. H.

ELWES, Sir Hervey, 2nd Bt. (1683–1763), of Stoke College, Stoke by Clare, Suff.

SUDBURY   16 Dec. 1706–1710, 1713–1722

bap. July 1683, 1st s. of Gervase Elwes† of Stoke College (*d.v.p.* s. of Sir Gervase Elwes, 1st Bt.*) by Isabella, da. of Sir Thomas Hervey† of Ickworth, Suff., sis. of John Hervey*. *educ.* Queens', Camb. 1702. *unm. suc.* gdfa. as 2nd Bt. 11 Apr. 1706.[1]

Freeman, Sudbury 1706.[2]

Elwes succeeded to his grandfather's parliamentary seat at Sudbury, but in other respects his inheritance was a disappointment. Although he was 'nominally possessed of some thousands a year', the family property proved so heavily encumbered that at first it yielded only £100. He is said to have vowed on his arrival at Stoke that 'never would he leave it till he had entirely cleared the paternal estate'. His uncle Lord Hervey, who took a close interest in his welfare, advised him either to sell up or seek a rich wife. He did neither, but eventually restored his fortunes by practising extreme parsimony. He was said to be formed of the very materials to make perfect the character of a miser. In his youth he had been given over for consumption so that he had but a poor constitution and no passions; he was timid, shy and diffident in the extreme; of a thin spare habit of body, and without a friend upon earth. As he had no acquaintance, no books, and no turn for reading, the hoarding up, and the counting of his money, was his greatest joy. The next to that was partridge setting.

Despite the failure of Hervey's attempts in 1707 to secure for him a grant of his grandfather's office under the duchy of Lancaster, Elwes seems to have remained a loyal Whig in the family tradition. He was classed as a Whig in two lists from 1708, being re-elected at the general election of that year, and was recorded as having voted for Dr Sacheverell's impeachment in 1710. He was defeated at Sudbury in the 1710 election, and though Hervey was anxious to bring him in at a likely by-election for Bury St. Edmunds in 1712, the anticipated vacancy did not arise. Regaining his seat in 1713, he voted on 18 Mar. 1714 against the expulsion of Richard Steele, and was classed as a Whig in the Worsley list and in two lists of the Members re-elected in 1715. Much of the remainder of his life he spent in solitude at Stoke, 'perhaps the most perfect picture of human penury that ever existed'.[3]

Elwes died on 22 Oct. 1763, said to be worth at least £250,000, and was succeeded by a nephew, John Meggott[†], who took the name Elwes and became as celebrated a miser.[4]

[1] *VCH Northants. Fams.* 68. [2] Suff. RO (Bury St Edmunds), Sudbury bor. recs. EE501/4/1. [3] E. Topham, *Life of the Late John Elwes* (1790), 3–7; *Hervey Letter Bks.* i. 226–8, 304–5, 327; *Hervey Diary*, 45, 51. [4] *VCH Northants. Fams.* 68; Topham, 6, 9–36.

D. W. H.

ELWILL, John (1643–1717), of Polsloe House, nr. Exeter, Devon.

BERE ALSTON 1681 (Mar.), 1689–1690
      1695–1698

bap. 24 Sept. 1643, 1st s. of John Elwill, grocer, of Exeter by Rebecca Pole of Exeter. *educ.* Exeter, Oxf. 1659; Leyden 1664. *m.* (1) lic. 14 Mar. 1676, Frances, da. of Sir John Bampfylde, 1st Bt.[†], of Poltimore, Devon, *s.p.*; (2) 2 Oct. 1682, Anne, da. of Edmund Lee, Saddler, of London or Edmund Leigh of Egham, Surr., 2s. 2da. *suc.* fa. 1675; kntd. 28 Apr. 1696; *cr.* Bt. 25 Aug. 1709.[1]

Jt. receiver-gen. Devon and Exeter 1689–92, 1694–6, 1699–1701; freeman, Plymouth 1696; dep. master of the mint, Exeter 1698; sheriff, Devon Jan.–Nov. 1699; gov. Exeter workhouse 1701.[2]

Trustee, Exchequer bills 1697; poor Palatines 1709.[3]

A Whig and a Dissenter, Elwill had built up a successful business at Exeter exporting Devonshire serges and importing German linens. He had first been returned for Bere Alston during the Exclusion crisis by his first wife's brother-in-law, Sir Francis Drake, 3rd Bt.*, and was subsequently a trustee of the settlement of Drake's third marriage in 1690. A Whig 'collaborator' under James II, he rallied to William of Orange in 1688 and was briefly Member for Bere Alston again during the Convention Parliament. His extensive trading links with the Continent were singled out for attack in the Commons in February 1693 by Sir Christopher Musgrave, 4th Bt.*, who described him as the 'factor for the foreigners' at Exeter who was helping the Dutch to 'run away' with the English woollen trade.[4]

Elwill resumed his seat at Bere Alston in 1695. He quickly re-established himself as an extremely active man of business, and his record of 36 tellerships during the course of the 1695 Parliament testifies in particular to the wide range of issues to which he gave his attention, albeit that the divisions themselves were often on obscure points of detail or procedure. He was teller for the first time on 10 Dec. 1695 in favour of a recoinage of clipped money at the old weight and fineness, and early in January was involved in conference proceedings on the issue with the Upper House. On 17 Jan. 1696 he was teller against agreeing with the Lords' amendments to the treason trials bills. Having been forecast in January as likely to support the Court over the proposed council of trade, he was teller on the 31st in favour of the new commissioners taking the oaths of allegiance to the King. During the debates on the recoinage in February he supported Charles Montagu's* proposals, and on two occasions, on the 18th and 28th, was teller against fixing guineas at a rate at below 28s., but was not listed as having voted in March in favour of Montagu's scheme for setting guineas at 22s. He was teller on 27 Feb. in favour of the Avon navigation bill, reported on a private naturalization bill on 5 Mar., and on the 9th was teller in support of an estate bill on behalf of Sir Coplestone Bampfylde, 3rd Bt.*, a member of his first wife's family. On 2 Apr. he was teller in favour of a petition for expanding the geographical scope of the East India trade.[5]

The day after prorogation, 28 Apr. 1696, Elwill was knighted, a sure sign of the Court's appreciation of his efforts in the Commons on the government's behalf and as an army contractor. On 22 July he wrote to Sir George Treby*, reporting Tory discontent at the purge of non-Associators from the Devon commission of the peace and the lord lieutenant's efforts to manage all the tantivy men . . . who have most scandalously refused to give a necessary security to the government in the day of distress. They may fret and foam until they see the little good they do thereby [but] in a short time they will compound and be as flexible as any.

In November he assisted the Court's management of the attainder of Sir John Fenwick†, serving as teller on the 9th in support of the second reading of the attainder bill, and on the 16th to allow counsel against Fenwick to examine evidence given at another trial, and duly voted for the attainder on the division on the 25th. On the 21st he was teller in two divisions: in favour of receiving an Exeter petition against the elections bill; and in favour of including clipped as well as hammered money in the recoinage bill. On 29 Jan. 1697 he reported from a committee concerning the Newfoundland fishery, which made recommendations for the provision of convoys and garrisons for future protection. He was teller on 3 Feb. in favour of further subscriptions to the Bank of England; on the 10th in support of the bill for better establishing public credit; and on the 24th, for authorizing a bill to open the port of Exeter to Irish woollens, in response to a petition from the town's mercantile community in which he himself was prominent.[6]

In the next session, on 14 Dec. 1697, Elwill and his political opposite, Sir Edward Seymour, 4th Bt.*, were ordered to bring in a bill focusing on their mutual west-country interests to prevent the export of wool to France. Elwill subsequently managed the bill through all its stages in the House, which included chairing two sittings of the committee of the whole. On 21 Dec. 1697 he told on the government side against the recommittal of a resolution to grant the King a £700,000 civil list for life; was teller on 20 Jan. 1698 in favour of a further bill concerning Sir Coplestone Bamfylde's estates; and four days later, for a bill to restrain the wearing of Eastern silks and calicoes. That same month, a report on crown grants revealed that he held a 22-year grant of the post fines of the duchy of Lancaster. On 9 Mar. he was teller against a bill to prevent abuses in weights and measures, and later that month took charge of a naturalization bill. On the 30th he was teller in favour of a rider in the bill for the suppression of blasphemy and profaneness, to include anti-trinitarian writings within its scope, and on 25 June was teller in favour of the supply bill for raising £2m. Elwill had also taken particular interest during the session in issues concerning the poor, particularly as at the time he was involved in initiatives to establish a corporation of the poor at Exeter, of which in 1701 he became governor. At the general election of 1698 he stood down at Bere Alston, but his attempt to secure one of the Exeter seats ended in defeat. A comparative analysis of the old and new Parliaments noted him as a member of the Court party.[7]

In February 1700 Elwill was granted a property in Queen Street in the city of London forfeited for high treason. His friend Richard Duke*, also a Whig and a Dissenter, wrote to Robert Harley* in September 1704, complaining that by Sir Edward Seymour's influence Elwill had been put out of the Devon commission, despite his wealth (he was worth £50,000 in all, with £1,000 p.a., besides some £20,000 in capital, including an investment in excess of £4,000 in the Bank of England) and the fact that he was 'the most necessary justice in the county, living but two miles from Exeter, who stands so fair with the judges that the last assizes they invited him and many of the outed justices to eat with them'. In February 1705 he and Christopher Bale*, another former receiver of taxes for Devon, succeeded in having a particularly arbitrary clause removed from a bill empowering land tax commissioners to scrutinize the accounts of previous receivers which gave harsh powers over their 'properties' with no right of appeal. Although the Commons rejected the Lords' removal of the clause, the bill lapsed. At the 1705 election Elwill, together with his son John, was defeated at Ashburton; and at Honiton, where he also campaigned, Defoe informed Robert Harley* that he endured 'a terrible mob election' and was too 'cowed' to petition. He tried again at Honiton in 1708, and, although defeated, had at least the satisfaction of being restored to the commission of the peace, but lost his place there again after the Tory triumph of 1710. He died on 25 Apr. 1717.[8]

[1] IGI, Devon; *Trans. Devon Assoc.* lxii. 221; *Mar. Lic. Vicar-Gen.* (Harl. Soc. xxxiv), 612; *St. Stephen Walbrook* (Harl. Soc. Reg. xlix), 66; Manning and Bray, *Surrey*, iii. 252. [2] *Cal. Treas. Bks.* ix. 250; x. 934; xiv. 341; xv. 204, 323; *HMC Lords*, n.s. vi. 288; *HMC 9th Rep.* pt. 1, p. 282; *Trans. Devon Assoc.* 221. [3] *Cal. Treas. Bks.* xii. 7; Boyer, *Anne Annals*, viii. app. p.41. [4] *Luttrell Diary*, 429; E. F. Eliott-Drake, *Fam. and Heirs of Drake*, ii. 65. [5] *Account of Procs. in House of Commons, Relating to Recoining* . . . (1696), p. 7. [6] *CSP Dom.* 1697, p. 114; *HMC 13th Rep. VI*, 40–41. [7] *Trans. Devon Assoc.* 221. [8] *CJ*, xiii. 193; L. K. J. Glassey, *Appt. JPs*, 207; *HMC Portland*, ii. 122, 134, 270; Egerton 3359 (unfol.); *HMC Lords*, n.s. vi. 287–8.

E. C./A. A. H.

ENGLAND, Benjamin (1647–1711), of Great Yarmouth, Norf.

GREAT YARMOUTH 1702–1708

bap. 26 Mar. 1647, 3rd s. of Sir George England of Great Yarmouth by Sarah, da. of Thomas Smith of Runton, Norf.; bro. of George England I*. *m.* Jan. 1668, Prisca

Ballow, prob. da. of Henry Ballow of St. Mary Woolnoth, London, *s.p. suc.* bro. 1702.¹

Freeman, Great Yarmouth 1667, alderman 1673–84, Oct. 1688–*d.*, bailiff 1675–6, 1688–9, 1697–8, mayor 1703–4; freeman, Dunwich –1703.²

England's family had acted as the chief supporters of religious toleration at Yarmouth in the 1680s, and his own career in local politics was characterized by a temperate and unprejudiced Anglicanism. A fat and gouty merchant, he took over the family interest on the death of his brother in 1702, and was returned to Parliament at the general election of that year. At Westminster he seems to have been active principally in matters of local concern. In December he assisted in the parliamentary management of a bill to amend the Great Yarmouth Harbour Act in the light of the borough's new charter. He was nominated on 12 Jan. 1703 to the drafting committee for a bill to explain clauses in the Acts concerning linens. Having been listed as a probable opponent of the Tack, he did not vote for it on 28 Nov. 1704. On 3 Feb. 1705 he told against a resolution critical of Yarmouth corporation, which had been passed by the committee investigating restrictive practices in the East Anglian coal trade. Marked as 'Low Church' in a list of the new Parliament in 1705, he voted against the Court candidate for the Speakership on 25 Oct., possibly influenced by his nephew and heir-presumptive George England II* 'and all his friends in Yarmouth'. On 19 Dec. 1706 he was first-named to the drafting committee for a bill to regulate rates paid by non-freemen importing coal into Yarmouth. In two lists of 1708 he was classed as a Tory. Defeated at the general election of that year, he did not stand again for Parliament.³

England died on 30 Apr. 1711. His will, dated 6 Dec. 1706, mentioned various properties in Yarmouth and elsewhere in Norfolk and Suffolk, including 'my brewhouse'.⁴

¹ IGI, Norf.; D. Turner, *Sepulchral Reminiscences*, 111, 113–14; C. J. Palmer, *Perlustration Gt. Yarmouth*, ii. 275; J. R. Woodhead, *Rulers of London* (London and Mdx. Arch. Soc.), 23; J. M. S. Brooke and A. W. C. Hallen, *St. Mary Woolnoth Reg.* 62, 69, 72, 239. ² *Cal. Freemen Gt. Yarmouth*, 98; Norf. RO, Gt. Yarmouth bor. recs. ass. bk. 1662–80, 1680–1701; H. Swinden, *Hist. Gt. Yarmouth*, 951, 952, 953, 954; Suff. RO (Ipswich), Dunwich bor. recs. EE6/1144/14. ³ P. Gauci, *Pol. and Soc. in Gt. Yarmouth*, 208; Palmer, 276; Camb. Univ. Lib. Cholmondeley (Houghton) mss, Ld. Townshend to Robert Walpole II*, 10 Oct. 1705. ⁴ Turner, 110, 113–14.

D. W. H.

ENGLAND, George I (1643–1702), of Great Yarmouth, Norf.

GREAT YARMOUTH   1679 (Oct.)–1681 (Mar.)
                             1689–1701 (Nov.)

bap. 22 Sept. 1643, 1st s. of Sir George England of Great Yarmouth; bro. of Benjamin England*. *educ.* Emmanuel, Camb. matric. 1660; G. Inn 1661, called 1668. *unm. suc.* fa. 1677.¹

Freeman, Great Yarmouth 1663, sub-steward Oct. 1688–91, recorder 1691–*d.*²

England, who was classed by Lord Carmarthen (Sir Thomas Osborne†) in 1690 as a Whig, was an active Member with a particular interest in matters of trade and commerce. In the first session of this Parliament he was nominated to the committees to draft bills on the East India trade (2 Apr. 1690), the commission of accounts (14 Apr.) and the regulation of wines (9 May); and, similarly, shortly after the House reconvened in October, to draft a bill to regulate the militia. In December Carmarthen forecast England as a likely supporter should the Commons proceed with an attack on his ministerial position. Robert Harley*, in April 1691, saw grounds to note him as a doubtful supporter of the Country party. On 25 Jan. 1692 he told against the Dover harbour bill, the provisions of which were considered to be detrimental to the interests of other ports, including Yarmouth. On 18 Nov. he was appointed to the drafting committee on the bill to extend the patent on convex lights. He was marked as a Court supporter in Samuel Grascome's list in 1693. On 26 Jan. 1693 he was a teller in favour of amending a resolution of the committee of ways and means, to lower the rate of duty on spirits, which, it was agreed, would lead to an overall increase in the yield of the duty: in this proposal the interests of merchants and of the Court coincided. He assisted in the parliamentary management of two private bills in January–February. Over the next two sessions he was involved in the preparatory stages of bills to encourage the clothing trade, to regulate the assize of bread, to facilitate the recovery of minors' debts, to improve the administration of prisons, and to regulate printing presses. He told on 15 Mar. against giving leave of absence to Sir Jonathan Raymond, and on 5 Apr. on a clause in the poll tax bill.³

Re-elected in 1695, England was named on 1 Jan. 1696 to the committee to bring in a bill imposing duties for the war against France. Possibly with a view to his concern for local commercial interests, he was forecast as likely to oppose the government on 31 Jan. 1696 over the proposed council of trade. He signed the Association promptly and voted in March against fixing the price of guineas at 22s. In November 1696 he and Samuel Fuller I* were negotiating with the Admiralty on behalf of Great Yarmouth corporation over a claim concerning a captured privateer, and both Members voted on 25 Nov. for the attainder of Sir

John Fenwick†. England, in his capacity as recorder of the borough, inquired in mid-December of the Yarmouth bailiffs 'whether your thoughts are to go on with the quarter sessions, that [I] may dispose of [myself] accordingly', and on 5 Jan. 1697 he was granted leave of absence for three weeks. Almost certainly he did not return to the House before the end of the session, for in early February he had been taken so seriously ill at Yarmouth that he seemed 'to decay sensibly'. On 30 Dec. 1697 he was again allowed leave of absence. He told with Fuller on 10 Mar. in favour of referring to the committee on Anglo-Irish trade a petition from Yarmouth on the local herring trade. England was given another leave of absence on 11 May.

England was listed among the Country party in a comparative list of the old and new Parliaments in 1698. From December to February 1699 he managed the Yarmouth harbour bill through the Commons, while in January he also assisted with the management of an estate and a naturalization bill. He told on 27 Mar. in favour of the Burscott highway bill, and in favour of receiving a grievance petition on 26 Apr. He was forecast in February 1701 as likely to support the Court over continuing the 'Great Mortgage', and on 20 Mar. was named to the drafting committee on the bill to prevent bribery at elections.[4]

England lost his seat at the second 1701 election, and died on 30 June 1702, leaving an estate that included the manor of Billockby in Norfolk to his brother Benjamin, with a remainder to his nephew, George England II*. His memorial in Yarmouth parish church described him as 'a true friend' to the borough and to 'the liberty of his country'.[5]

[1] *East Anglian Peds.* (Harl. Soc. xci), 67–68; D. Turner, *Sepulchral Reminiscences*, 30, 110, 113. [2] *Cal. Yarmouth Freemen*, 95; C. J. Palmer, *Hist. Gt. Yarmouth*, 345, 351. [3] Norf. RO, Gt. Yarmouth corp. mss, letters of England and Fuller to Yarmouth bailiffs, 29, 31 Oct., 7, 12, 14, 24 Nov., 3, 12 Dec. 1696, Richard Ferrier* to Thomas Godfrey, 18, 20 Mar. 1696[–7]; Palmer, 345. [4] *Luttrell Diary*, 387–8. [5] H. Swinden, *Hist. Gt. Yarmouth*, 882; Turner, 113.

D. W. H.

ENGLAND, George II (1679–1725), of Great Yarmouth and Stokesby, Norf.

GREAT YARMOUTH 1710–1722

b. Dec. 1679, 1st surv. s. of Thomas England, merchant, of Great Yarmouth by Ann, da. of Thomas Bulwer of Buxton, Norf.; nephew of Benjamin* and George England I*. *educ.* Great Yarmouth; Caius, Camb. 1694–7; G. Inn 1696. *m.* by 1706 (with £2,500), Alice, da. of John Jermy of Bayfield, Norf., 4s. 1da. *suc.* fa. 1693, uncle Benjamin England 1711.[1]

Freeman, Great Yarmouth 1699, alderman 1715–*d.*, mayor 1715–16.[2]

In 1710 England was returned for Great Yarmouth, a seat which his uncles had represented before him, and was described as a Tory in the 'Hanover list'. He was listed among the 'Tory patriots' who opposed the continuance of the war and the 'worthy patriots' who exposed the mismanagements of the old ministry, and was given a month's leave of absence on 29 Mar. 1711. In April he succeeded to the fortune of his uncle Benjamin, and thus also to that of his other uncle George, to whom he was heir-at-law. He joined the Tory back-bench rebellion on 7 Dec. 1711, voting with the Whigs over the 'No Peace without Spain' motion. On 10 Dec. he was nominated to the drafting committee on the Great Yarmouth causeway bill. In January 1712 Lord Treasurer Oxford (Robert Harley*) wished him to be canvassed by Lord Anglesey (Hon. Arthur Annesley*) prior to the debate on the motion censuring the Duke of Marlborough (John Churchill†). England and his fellow Member for Yarmouth, Richard Ferrier, were among the merchants who provided ships for the Canada expedition. His political affiliation was unclear to a number of contemporary observers. His re-election in 1713 was announced at first by one newspaper as a Whig gain, a report that was later reversed. In the Worsley list he was classed as a Tory who had sometimes voted with the Whigs during the 1713 Parliament and might do so again in the ensuing one. Another comparative analysis of the two Parliaments listed him as a 'whimsical Whig', but he was described as a Tory in a third list and indeed polled for the Tory candidates in the county election in 1715. In the remainder of his parliamentary career he voted consistently against the government. He died on 12 June 1725.[3]

[1] Blomefield, *Norf.* xi. 251; C. J. Palmer, *Perlustration Gt. Yarmouth*, ii. 298. [2] *Cal. Freemen Gt. Yarmouth*, 134; Norf. RO, Gt. Yarmouth bor. recs. ass. bk. 1701–19. [3] Camb. Univ. Lib. Cholmondeley (Houghton) mss, Ld. Townshend to Robert Walpole II*, 10 Oct. 1705; Palmer, ii. 226–7; D. Turner, *Sepulchral Reminiscences*, 113–14; G. Holmes, *Pol. in the Age of Anne*, 282; *Cal. Treas. Bks.* xxvi. 255.

D. W. H.

ERESBY, Peregrine Bertie, Ld. Willoughby de *see* **BERTIE**

ERESBY, Robert Bertie, Ld. Willoughby de *see* **BERTIE**

ERLE, Thomas (c.1650–1720), of Charborough, Dorset.

WAREHAM	1679 (Mar.)–1681 (Mar.), 1685–1687 1689–1698
PORTSMOUTH	1698–1701 (Nov.)
WAREHAM	1701 (Dec.)–20 Mar. 1718

b. c.1650, 2nd but 1st surv. s. of Thomas Erle† (*d.* 1650) of Bindon House, Axmouth, Devon by Susanna, da. of William Fiennes, 1st Visct. Saye and Sele. *educ.* Trinity, Oxf. matric. 12 July 1667, aged 17; M. Temple 1669. *m.* 1675, Elizabeth (*d.* 1710), da. of Sir William Wyndham, 1st Bt.†, of Orchard Wyndham, Som., sis. of Sir Edward Wyndham, 2nd Bt.*, 1da. *suc.* gdfa. Sir Walter Erle† 1665.[1]

Commr. rebels' estates, Dorset 1686; freeman, Poole 1691; commr. Portsmouth and Sheet Turnpike trust 1711–*d.*; commr. R. Hosp. Chelsea 1715–*d.*[2]

Col. of ft. 1689–98, 19 Ft. 1691–1709; brig.-gen. 1693, maj.-gen. 1696, lt.-gen. 1703, gen. of ft. 1711; gov. Portsmouth 1694–1712, 1714–18; PC [I] 1701; c.-in-c. [I] 1701–5, of expedition 1708, land forces in Eng. 1708–12; ld. justice [I] 1702–3, Mar.–Nov. 1704; col. of Drag. [I] 1704–5; lt.-gen. of Ordnance 1705–12, 1714–18; PC 3 May 1705.[3]

MP [I] 1703–13.

After a chequered career under Charles II and James II, Erle had been one of the first to come out in support of William of Orange in 1688. Although he was nearing 40 and had hitherto only served in the militia, he now embarked on a military career and was made colonel of one of the newly raised regiments of foot in 1689. He went to Ireland with his regiment and saw action at the Boyne and at Aughrim. He was rewarded with the colonelcy of another regiment of foot and the grant of an Irish estate. Meanwhile, he had been returned to the 1690 Parliament for Wareham, which was some six miles from his principal seat at Charborough. Lord Carmarthen (Sir Thomas Osborne†) classed Erle as an adherent of the Court, and forecast his support in December 1690 in the event of an attack upon his own ministerial position in the Commons. Robert Harley* also listed Erle as a Court supporter in April 1691. His name occurs on all known lists of placemen in this period. Erle's rare contributions to debate usually related to the armed forces. Thus, on 15 Dec. 1691, in a committee of the whole on the army estimates, he spoke on the question of the numbers of officers and men to be allowed in a regiment. For the next summer's campaign he transferred from Ireland to Flanders, where he was wounded at the battle of Landen. In the 1692–3 session he spoke for the first time in a full debate, against the motion to employ only English officers in the army:

No man is of less sufficiency to speak than myself. I have had the honour to serve in three or four Parliaments and have not troubled you. I was a colonel of foot in the engagement at Steenkerk, where the ground was mistaken, and so we were forced to retreat. As to the question, no man is more pleased than I for English officers to command the English army; but I do not think that three or four years service can make a general. I wish we had men fit; but before you have them, pray do not rid yourselves of all foreign generals. I hope when you come to the question you will not part with all the foreign generals before you can have some of your own to come into their places.

This session saw his first involvement with mutiny bills, and in the following session he carried up the mutiny bill on 27 Feb. 1694, attending a conference on this subject with the Lords on 5 Mar. On 27 Mar. he obtained three weeks' leave of absence. In July 1694 he was made governor of Portsmouth. His only significant activity in the 1694–5 session again revolved around the mutiny bill.[4]

At the 1695 election Erle was returned again for Wareham. He was forecast as a probable opponent of the Court in the division of 31 Jan. 1696 on the proposed council of trade. In February 1696, he was again concerned in the management of the mutiny bill, and, having signed the Association later that month, voted with the Court in March to fix the price of guineas at 22*s*. On 25 Nov. he voted for the attainder of Sir John Fenwick†. In March 1697 he was granted the residue of a debt to the crown amounting to £1,864. On 8 Jan. 1698 he spoke against a reduction of the military establishment, explaining 'the defenceless condition they would be in without some troops to make a stand'. His two legislative initiatives in this session concerned a bill to naturalize the foreign-born children of armed forces personnel, and an estate bill on behalf of his nephew, Sir William Wyndham, 3rd Bt.* On 28 May 1698 he was granted another leave of absence.[5]

By the 1698 election Erle appears to have entered into an agreement with George Pitt*, a Tory, to share the parliamentary representation of Wareham. Under this arrangement he gave his own seat there to his nephew, Thomas Trenchard, and was himself returned on the government interest for Portsmouth. Classed as a Court supporter in a comparative analysis of the old and new Commons, he spoke and voted on 18 Jan. 1699 against the third reading of the disbanding bill. His loyalty to the Court was not strained by the loss of one of his regiments in March 1699, which he was 'willing to lay down'. Later in the same year he successfully proposed the Duke of Bolton (Charles Powlett I*), an ally of the Junto, to be lord lieutenant of Dorset, 'those in the county not having been able to agree'. In the first general election of 1701 Erle was returned for both Wareham and Portsmouth, opting to sit for the latter, and leaving his Wareham seat for his son-in-law, Sir Edward Ernle, 3rd Bt.* He was listed as a supporter of the Court in February 1701 over the 'Great Mortgage'. Reverting to Wareham for the second election of 1701, he was classed as a Whig by Harley. He brought in the mutiny bill on 5 Feb. 1702, and told against an amendment to it on the 16th. He was given leave to go to Ireland on 4 Mar., having been appointed commander-in-chief of the land forces under the lord lieutenancy of the Earl of Rochester (Laurence Hyde†), with whom, despite their political differences, he appeared to be on the best of terms. He was added to the Irish privy council and was one of the three lords justices during Rochester's absence in England. 'I think I cannot appoint a fitter man', Rochester had written on 5 Dec. 1701, adding 'there's no man here but himself to whom the care of the army can be committed'.[6]

Although pressurized by fellow Whigs to stand with Trenchard for Dorset in 1702, Erle declined to do so, apparently out of a desire to retain his places and the good opinion of the new administration. He was returned for Wareham after a contest. On 23 Aug. 1702 he wrote to Rochester:

> I am confident I had never failed of your protection but I must confess it would be a very sensible mortification to me if I thought I served her Majesty so ill in the command of her army under your lordship here that I should deserve to be the very last who had a mark of her favour in a military promotion since her reign.

His promotion did not come through until 11 Feb. 1703, the day after Rochester was replaced by Ormond as lord lieutenant. Erle was shown a further mark of favour when, on the viceroy's recommendation, he was given the command of a newly raised regiment of dragoons in June 1704. He was forecast as a probable opponent of the Tack, and did not vote for it on 28 Nov. 1704.[7]

In April 1705 Erle left Ireland to take up a new appointment as lieutenant-general of the Ordnance. For the election of that year he again considered standing for Dorset, but contented himself with his customary return for Wareham. He was classed as 'Low Church', and supported the Court over the choice of Speaker on 25 Oct. First-named to the drafting committee on the mutiny bill on 23 Jan. 1706, he managed it through the House, including chairing the committee of the whole on 6 Mar. He voted with the government on 18 Feb. over the regency bill. At the end of the session he received a summons to go as second-in-command under Earl Rivers (Richard Savage*) in a descent on the French coast. The Duke of Marlborough (John Churchill†) had insisted that a lieutenant-general go with the expedition and Erle was the only one available. The Duke assured him that the Queen 'will make you sensible how well she is pleased with the zeal you have shown on this occasion and the readiness wherewith you accepted the service'. After the descent had been delayed by contrary winds and then cancelled, Erle stayed with the troops, who were sent to join Lord Galway's army in Spain. He remained there during the winter of 1706–7, sending Marlborough 'a melancholy account' of affairs in January 1707, to which the Duke replied, 'you may be assured I shall omit no opportunity of laying your services favourably before the Queen, that her Majesty may have a just regard for them'. In the disputes between Rivers and Galway, Erle sided with the former. He took part in the battle of Almanza and remained in Spain until the end of September, increasingly dissatisfied and in poor health. Marlborough received a stream of letters depicting Spanish affairs in a gloomy light. Erle repeatedly requested permission to return to England, being anxious about becoming a subject of censure at home. On 20 June Marlborough reassured him that

> the Queen is perfectly well inclined to you, and . . . there are none about her Majesty but what are so much your friends as to do you all good offices imaginable; and if her Majesty thinks fit to continue you abroad, I am certainly persuaded it proceeds from the opinion she has of the services you will be able to do there.

Eventually given leave to return to England, he immediately joined James Stanhope* in defending Galway in the Commons on 24 Feb. 1708, during the debate on the deficiency of English troops at Almanza. He gave this public display of loyalty, despite private misgivings about the generalship of the campaign.[8]

A list in early 1708 classed Erle as a Whig, and after the election he was listed as a 'gain' by Lord Sunderland (Charles, Lord Spencer*) and as a Court Whig in another analysis of the new Parliament. He had been returned for Portsmouth and Wareham, choosing to sit for the latter. While he was still in the country he was informed that he was to be commander-in-chief of a descent on the French coast. This news did not greatly please him, since previous attempts had been unsuccessful. He was also irritated that his field pay as general had been stopped on his return from Spain, whereas that of Lord Rivers had been continued. Replying to his complaint, Lord

Treasurer Godolphin (Sidney†) reassured him that the favour shown to Rivers was the product of 'a sort of bargain with the Duke of Marlborough before he went over'. Godolphin not only emphasized his own high regard for Erle, but also stated that 'you have no reason so much as to imagine that there can be the least competition betwixt you in the opinion of the Queen or of the Duke of Marlborough'. On Marlborough's recommendation his pay was continued from the time he left Spain, and in July he was awarded £1,500 in consideration of his services. The expedition itself was a fiasco. It was late in starting and the original plan of landing at St. Valery to capture Abbeville was abandoned. After one false start the force eventually landed at Ostend. An outpost was then established at Leffingham, but this fell to the French without a fight on 16 Oct. Although Erle had not been personally in command, he came in for criticism in England from 'coffee-house politicians'. Despite his failure, upon returning home in December 1708 he was appointed commander-in-chief of land forces in England. In this Parliament he was involved in various measures relating to Portsmouth harbour and voted for the naturalization of the Palatines in 1709, and the impeachment of Dr Sacheverell in 1710.[9]

Erle was active in the 1710 election, securing his own return at Wareham, but also bringing his influence to bear at Poole and Shaftesbury. He was classed as a Whig in the 'Hanover list'. Despite the ministerial revolution of 1710 Erle retained all his offices and was promoted general of foot in January 1711. In February he was named to draft the mutiny bill, and, moreover, when later that month Harley set up a committee of Council at the war office to run the administration of the army, Erle was included along with Rivers and Argyll. The committee seems to have been an attempt by Harley to circumvent Marlborough. Certainly the Duke was alarmed and on 7 Apr. 1711 asked Erle to endeavour 'at least to screen me from anything that might seem a hardship to me at this committee'. In fact it ceased to function after July 1711, owing to the intrigues of Henry St. John II* and Marlborough himself. In the House Erle spoke on the Court side in the disputed election at Carlisle on 20 Feb., seconding the motion to take the defeated candidate, Samuel Gledhill, into custody for prevaricating as a witness at the bar. Erle abandoned the Court in the next session, voting with the Whigs on 7 Dec. on the motion for 'No Peace without Spain'. In the following June he was removed from all his offices, and since he had already sold his regiment he was, for the first time in many years, without employment. He presented the mutiny bill on 20 Feb. 1712, and on 23 May told against a private bill for the relief of two London wine merchants. He voted against the French wine duties bill on 6 May 1713, but does not appear to have voted on 18 June on the French commerce bill. He told against the ministry on a clause in the bill to encourage the tobacco trade (8 July) and on a procedural question on a bill to regulate the armed forces (13 July). On 18 Mar. 1714 he voted against the expulsion of Richard Steele, and reported on 31 May the bill to enforce the Bristol Workhouse Act. The Worsley list classed him as a Whig, as did two other comparative analyses of the 1713 and 1715 Parliaments. After the accession of George I he was reappointed lieutenant-general of the Ordnance, but his performance in Parliament was considered unsatisfactory and in March 1718 he was dismissed. He received a pension of £1,200 p.a., which obliged him to vacate his seat. In a defence of his conduct, submitted to the King, he maintained that

> I have now served in the House of Commons 39 years, and have always endeavoured to serve my Prince and country there to the best of my judgment. I have often differed in opinion with the ministry in power, which was never laid to my charge but by the late administration some time before your Majesty's accession to the crown. The event has since shown I was then in the right . . . On all occasions I have endeavoured to serve without reproach, and have made it my business in every station to take more care of the public money than my own, so that in the long course of my services I have added very little to my paternal estate.

Erle died at Charborough on 23 July 1720.[10]

[1] Hutchins, *Dorset*, i. 82; iii. 502; Dorset RO, D60/F2; *HMC Portland*, iii. 352; W. D. Christie, *Life of Shaftesbury*, i. p. xlix. [2] *CSP Dom.* 1679–80, p. 61; *Cal. Treas. Bks.* viii. 546; Poole Archs. B17; *Portsmouth and Sheet Turnpike Commrs. Min. Bk.* (Portsmouth Rec. Ser. ii), 169; C. G. T. Dean, *R. Hosp. Chelsea*, 298–9. [3] *CSP Dom.* 1700–2, p. 390; *Cal. Treas. Bks.* xxii. 13; xxvi. 325; xxix. 99, 252; xxxii. 246; *Cal. Treas. Pprs.* 1708–14, p. 49; Boyer, *Pol. State*, iii. 386; Luttrell, *Brief Relation*, iii. 341; v. 545; vi. 725; SP 63/362; Add. 37531, f. 1; *Daily Courant*, 30 Apr. 1705. [4] *CSP Dom.* 1690–1, p. 528; 1691–2, p. 98; 1693, p. 246; *Luttrell Diary*, 81, 254; *Cal. Treas. Bks.* ix. 898, 1602; Grey, x. 258. [5] *CSP Dom.* 1697, pp. 484, 532–3; *Cal. Treas. Bks.* xi. 432; *Cam. Misc.* xxix. 360; Northants. RO, Montagu (Boughton) mss 46/77, James Vernon I* to Duke of Shrewsbury, 8 Jan. 1697[–8]. [6] *Cam. Misc.* 385; *CSP Dom.* 1699–1700, p. 71; Hutchins, i. 82; iii. 502; *Vernon–Shrewsbury Letters*, ii. 301; Add. 15895, ff. 195, 319–20; 40775, f. 304; *Cal. Treas. Bks.* xvii. 180. [7] Add. 15895, f. 276; *HMC 7th Rep.* 768. [8] Churchill Coll. Cambridge, Erle mss 2/2, Bolton to Erle, 10 May 1705; *Marlborough–Godolphin Corresp.* 602, 620, 623, 630, 673, 754, 792, 797, 799, 805, 808, 813, 881, 892–3, 899; *Marlborough Letters and Despatches* ed. Murray, iii. 34, 293–4, 429, 569, 570; Luttrell, *Brief Relation*, vi. 176; *Vernon–Shrewsbury Letters*, iii. 355; *HMC 8th Rep.* ii. 95; Yale Univ. Beinecke Lib. Osborn coll. Manchester mss 1987.1.7, p. 8, Joseph Addison* to Ld. Manchester, 27 Feb. 1707[–8]. [9] *Marlborough–Godolphin Corresp.* 946–7, 1001, 1008,

1017, 1049–51, 1054, 1057, 1066, 1068, 1072, 1076, 1086, 1089, 1091, 1095, 1098, 1101–2, 1113, 1128, 1133, 1135, 1140, 1143, 1156, 1180; Erle mss 2/12, James Craggs I* to Erle, 19, 29 Oct. 1708. [10]Erle mss 2/65, Robert Walpole II* to Erle, 16 Sept. 1710; 2/19, Erle to George I, n.d.; *Hist. Jnl.* iv. 82–83; *Marlborough Letters and Despatches*, v. 301; NLS, Advocates' mss, Wodrow pprs. letters Quarto 5, ff. 138–9; SRO, Montrose mss, Mungo Graham* to Montrose, 22 Feb. 1711; Boyer, iii. 386; Add. 17677 FFF, f. 249; H. C. Tomlinson, *Guns and Govt.* 80; *The Gen.* n.s. ii. 144–5.

P. W./D. W.

ERNLE, Sir Edward, 3rd Bt. (c.1673–1729), of Winterbourne Maddington, Wilts.

Devizes	1695–1698
Wiltshire	1698–1700
Wareham	5 Mar.–11 Nov. 1701
Heytesbury	1701 (Dec.)–1702
Wareham	22 Feb. 1704–1705
Marlborough	10 Dec. 1708–1710
Wareham	13 Dec. 1710–1713
Portsmouth	1715–1722
Wareham	1722–31 Jan. 1729

b. c.1673, 2nd s. of Edward Ernle of Ashlington, Wilts. (1st s. *d.v.p.* of Sir Walter Ernle, 1st Bt.[†]) by Anne, da. of Edward Ashe[†] of Heytesbury, Wilts. *m.* Frances, da. and h. of Thomas Erle*, 2da. *suc.* bro. as 3rd Bt. 1690.[1]

Although his principal seat lay in southern Wiltshire, Ernle successfully contested Devizes on his own interest in 1695 on the strength of his inherited property near the borough, where his cousins, established at Brimslade Park, Wiltshire, also held a number of tenements. His grandfather had also represented the borough. Ernle was forecast as likely to oppose the Court on 31 Jan. 1696 in the division over the proposed council of trade. He signed the Association, and in March voted against fixing the price of guineas at 22s. In the following session, he voted on 25 Nov. against the attainder of Sir John Fenwick[†]. On 4 Mar. 1697 he was sent to the Lords to desire a conference regarding their amendments to the bill preventing the sale of Indian silks, which he reported on the following day. In the next session he was asked by Devizes corporation to deliver their address to the King in respect of the damage the war had done to its cloth industry and the benefits they hoped to gain from the peace. On 11 May 1698, he was granted leave of absence.[2]

By the time of the 1698 election his marriage to the daughter of General Thomas Erle had transformed Ernle into a Whig. At first he intended to stand for re-election at Devizes, but finding his interest in abeyance he challenged successfully for the county seat. He was classed as a Court supporter in a comparative analysis of the old and new Parliaments, but left no mark in the Journals. On a classification of the House into 'interests' in early 1700 he was included under those headed by Henry Boyle*. He did not stand in the first general election of 1701, but when Erle left his own borough at Wareham to sit for Portsmouth Ernle replaced him at the ensuing by-election. At the next election Ernle was returned for Heytesbury, another constituency close to his properties. Classed as a Whig by Robert Harley* in December 1701, he acted as a teller on four occasions in the 1701–2 Parliament. Twice he told on bills relating to Irish forfeited estates, once on proceeding to a choice of public accounts commissioners and once on an election dispute. He failed to find a seat in 1702 and had to wait for Erle to bring him in at a by-election for Wareham in February 1704. He did not vote for the Tack in the following November and acted as a teller on three occasions: on 11 Jan. 1705 in favour of allowing Protestant freeholders in the six northern counties to carry arms; on 21 Feb. against adding a clause to a bill prohibiting trade with France; and on 2 Mar. against clauses to a mutiny bill.

In the 1705 election Ernle unsuccessfully contested Wiltshire, but on this occasion his father-in-law could not provide him with a seat at Wareham. He was invited to contest Marlborough in 1708 by the Duke of Somerset, but was dropped before the poll. At the by-election caused by the Earl of Hertford's (Algernon Seymour*) decision to sit for Northumberland the Duke put him up again and this time he succeeded. In the Commons he acted as a teller on 12 Feb. 1709 in favour of the Whig candidate for Hindon, and voted for naturalizing the Palatines. In the following session, he received leave for three weeks on 22 Dec. 1709, but returned to vote for the impeachment of Dr Sacheverell. Perhaps as a consequence, he seemed to have difficulty finding a seat in 1710 and was eventually brought in at a by-election for Wareham later in the year. He does not seem to have been as active in this Parliament. He received leave for a month on 10 May 1712. On 2 May 1713 he was a teller against suspending for two months the duties on imported French wines, and four days later voted against the French wines duty bill. He did not stand in 1713 but he returned to Parliament after the accession of George I and in 1715 was classified as a Whig in a comparison of the two Parliaments.[3]

On Erle's death in 1720 Ernle inherited the electoral interest at Wareham, for which borough he returned himself in 1722. However, some animosity had evidently developed between the two men, for in his will Erle had stipulated that his estates in Dorset and Devon were to be held by trustees for his daughter, Frances, and that Ernle should 'not intermeddle, have challenge, receive or take any benefit, property or advantage thereby, but shall be wholly excluded therefrom'. Ernle could only acquire the profits of the estates on the condition that his wife predeceased him and that he paid both his daughters £15,000 for their advancement. Ernle's will, made on 10 May 1727, testifies to his growing financial difficulties, for his estates were subject to several jointures with his wife and mother, and most of the profits were siphoned off to pay the £10,000 dowry for his daughter's marriage to his nephew Henry Drax. His wife was left the household goods of the Charlborough and Maddington residences and was asked to ensure that the daughter's dowry was successfully settled. Ernle died on 31 Jan. 1729, the baronetcy being inherited by his cousin, Sir Walter Ernle.[4]

[1] Wilts. Arch. Mag. xi. 192; Prob. 6/105, f. 276. [2] Wilts. RO, Devizes bor. recs. G20/1/19, min. bk. [3] Wilts. RO, Ailesbury mss 1300/1348, Charles Becher to Ld. Bruce, 1708; Walpole mss at Wolterton, Somerset to Robert Walpole II*, 5, 9 Dec. 1708; Churchill Coll. Camb. Erle mss 2/19, same to Erle, 9 May 1708; PCC 71 Abbott. [4] PCC 252 Shaller, 71 Abbott.

P. W.

ERNLE, Sir John (c.1620–97), of Bury Blunsdon and Whetham House, Calne, Wilts.

WILTSHIRE	1654–1655, 1660
CRICKLADE	1661–1679 (Jan.)
NEW WINDSOR	27 Feb.–5 Apr. 1679
GREAT BEDWYN	1681 (Mar.)
MARLBOROUGH	1689–1695

b. c.1620, 2nd but o. surv. s. of John Ernle of Whetham House, by Philadelphia, da. of Sir Arthur Hopton of Witham Friary, Som. m. (1) settlement, 1 Mar. 1646, Susan, da. of Sir John Howe, 1st Bt.†, of Little Compton, Withington, Glos., 2s. *d.v.p.* 7da.; (2) 19 Sept. 1672, Elizabeth (*d.* 1691), da. of William, 1st Baron Allington of Killard [I], wid. of Charles Seymour†, 2nd Baron Seymour, 2da. Kntd. Nov. 1665; *suc. fa.* 1684.[1]

Sub-commr. prizes, Bristol 1664–6; freeman, Windsor 1679.[2]

Commr. navy 1671–6, accounts, loyal and indigent officers 1671; chancellor of the Exchequer 1676–89; PC 10 May 1676–Dec. 1688; ld. of Admiralty 1677–9; ld. of Treasury 1679–85, 1687–9; commr. Tangier 1680–4.[3]

Ernle befriended John Aubrey, and was one of those Wiltshire gentry who in 1659 agreed to assist in the proposed collaborative history of the county, in imitation of Dugdale's recently published *Antiquities of Warwickshire*, although he failed to contribute to the work. An opportunistic courtier under Charles II, he had diligently enforced the Corporation Act in those boroughs neighbouring his county estate, while under James II he was one of those Privy Councillors asked to advise on changes to the county bench to promote Dissenting j.p.s. Having represented Marlborough since 1685, a seat partly owed to connexions through his second wife, he was returned there again in 1690 after a contest. Carmarthen (Sir Thomas Osborne+) classed him as a Tory and Court supporter at the beginning of the Parliament and his name appeared on another list of supporters at about this time. In December 1690 Carmarthen listed him again as a supporter, probably in case of an attack on his ministerial position. He was classed as a Country supporter by Robert Harley* in December 1691 and his name appeared on Henry Guy's* list of 'friends' in the 1694–5 session when Guy was under attack in the Commons. Ernle was not active in the House, and held no offices under William III. Perhaps prompted by age, he chose not to stand in 1695.[4]

Ernle spent his last two years in retirement as a country gentleman at the family's Wiltshire estate. He made his will on 20 Aug. 1696, leaving annuities of £100 to two daughters while they remained unmarried, together with £1,500 portions. A further £84 owed to him from the Exchequer was given to three grandsons. He made additional bequests to the poor of Calne, Highworth and Bury Blunsdon, and allowed a year's wages to each of his servants. Two of his sons-in-law, Hon. Peregrine Bertie II* and Edward Pleydell*, were named executors. Ernle was buried at Calne on 27 June 1697. Having founded a widows' charity in the town, he was further remembered by a memorial inscription in the church set up by his grandson.[5]

[1] *Vis. Wilts.* (Harl. Soc. cv-cvi), 57; *Le Neve's Knights* (Harl. Soc. viii), 200; *Westminster Abbey Reg.* (Harl. Soc. x), 8; *CJ*, viii. 543. [2] *HMC 6th Rep.* 338; *HMC Var.* iv. 132. [3] *CSP Dom.* 1671, pp. 288, 324; 1676–7, p. 71; 1677–8, p. 136; *HMC 6th Rep.* 378; *HMC Ormonde*, n.s. viii. 347; *HMC Finch*, ii. 28. [4] Aubrey and Jackson, *Wilts. Colls.* 3, 39; Add. 32324, f. 149; PC 2/67, pp. 6, 64, 76; PC 2/68, p. 47; PC 2/71, pp. 325, 352, 376. [5] *The Gen.* n.s. xiv. 42; PCC 232 Bond.

P. W./H. J. L.

ERSKINE, Sir Alexander, 2nd Bt. *see* **ARESKINE**

ERSKINE (ARESKINE), Sir John, 3rd Bt. (1672–1739), of Alva, Stirling (now in Clackmannan).

SCOTLAND 1707–1708
CLACKMANNANSHIRE 1713–1715

b. 1672, 2nd s. of Sir Charles Erskine, 1st Bt., MP [S], of Alva by Christian, da. of Sir James Dundas, MP [S], of Arniston, Midlothian, Ld. Arniston SCJ; bro. of Charles Erskine (Areskine)†, Ld. Tinwald SCJ. *educ.* adv. 1700. *m.* by 1708, Catherine (*d.* aft. 1719), da. of Henry St. Clair, 10th Ld. Sinclair [S], and sis. of John Sinclair*, 2s. *suc.* bro. as 3rd Bt. 23 July 1693.[1]

Commr. justiciary for Highlands [S] 1693, 1701, 1702, Equivalent [S] 1707–15.
MP [S] Clackmannanshire 1700–2, Burntisland 1702–7.
Curator, Fac. Adv. lib. 1704.[2]
Dir. Bank of Scotland 1706.[3]
Burgess, Edinburgh 1725.[4]

Erskine, whose tortuous political career was to end in Jacobitism, began from unimpeachable Presbyterian stock. Both his grandfathers had been vigorous opponents of Charles I and episcopacy. Sir Charles Erskine served in the army of the Covenant and as one of the commissioners sent to England in 1644, while Sir James Dundas had resigned as a lord of session in 1663 rather than abjure the Solemn League and Covenant. More recently, Erskine's father (*d.* 1689) welcomed the Revolution, and his elder brother was killed fighting the French at Landen in 1693. An investor of £300 in the Darien scheme, Erskine was returned to the Scottish parliament at a by-election for Clackmannanshire in 1700. He became a prominent supporter of the Country party, making himself heard in debate and consistently voting against the Court. At the beginning of Queen Anne's reign he was heavily involved in the agitation over the calling of the old parliament, and he stayed resolutely in opposition until the votes on the Union, so much so that the Jacobite agent, Scot, considered him in 1706 to be 'honest' and 'well affected'. At some point, however, he had been recruited into the connexion of the Squadrone peer the Duke of Montrose, possibly through the intercession of his brother-in-law John Haldane*. With the benefit of a little hindsight, George Lockhart* listed Erskine as a supporter of the 'New Party' ministry in 1704. Against this testimony should be set his vote in favour of the Duke of Hamilton's motion to postpone settling the succession, but Montrose himself and a number of his adherents, including Haldane, had done likewise. By 1706 Erskine was certainly counted as a Squadrone man, one whom the Earl of Rothes could heartily recommend to Lord Treasurer Godolphin (Sidney†) for a vacant judgeship in the court of session. Erskine's votes on the Union strictly followed the Squadrone pattern, and he was rewarded with a place on the Equivalent commission and a seat in the first Parliament of Great Britain.[5]

Welcomed into the Commons with nomination on 10 Nov. 1707 to the committee on the Address, Erskine proved as energetic and loquacious a Member at Westminster as he had in Edinburgh. With George Baillie* on 29 Nov. 1707 he opened the Squadrone campaign for the abolition of the Scottish privy council. On 12 Dec. he told against the Court, on a motion to refer to a committee of the whole the bill repealing the Scottish act of security and act anent peace and war. He also signed the letter from the commissioners of the Equivalent in January 1708 to complain at the lack of provision for their salaries and expenses. National interests and political expediency combined on 31 Jan. 1708, when, in a debate on the report from ways and means concerning the £1,200,000 to be advanced to the government by the East India Company, he proved the only opposition speaker able to suggest a specific method by which the loan might be increased, arguing that a further £200,000 could be secured 'by admitting a subscription of North Britain, for a proportionable share of the trade'. The poor response of the House to this suggestion doubtless prompted him to tell for a motion to adjourn the debate before a decision on the resolution had been reached. A further tellership two days later may also have had political overtones, despite the fact that it concerned a private bill: again, Erskine's colleague was a Tory while the tellers on the other side of the division were both Whigs. However, on 25 Feb., when he told once again, the context was more obvious. In a division concerning the Equivalent, Erskine favoured an instruction to the committee that was to draft the bill to direct further payment, to include a clause guaranteeing disbursement to all persons on the military list in equal proportion. He was subsequently named on 11 Mar. to the drafting committee on the bill to discharge Highland clansmen of their obligations to disloyal chieftains.[6]

Despite some preliminary moves towards making an interest in Clackmannanshire prior to the 1708 general election, Erskine did not offer himself as a candidate. Instead he gave his support to Hon. Charles Rosse*, acting as his chief agent at the freeholders' court and managing his subsequent petition. His own hopes of election were placed in the adjacent county of Stirling, where Montrose had recommended him.

Unfortunately, the Duke had been slow in deciding whom to support, which had permitted other candidates to steal a march, and eventually Erskine was instructed to support Henry Cunningham*.[7]

The succeeding summer witnessed a concerted effort by Erskine to obtain a judicial post, either in the court of session or as lord clerk register. Neither Montrose nor Lord Ross made headway with their recommendations, probably because of the antagonism of Queensberry's Court party. All that could be obtained was the renewal of his place on the Equivalent commission in June 1709. Impressed by the evident superiority of Mar's interest over that of Montrose and aware that in the changed political circumstances of 1710 Mar was likely to enjoy even greater influence, Erskine decided to rejoin the family 'name' and switch to his kinsman's patronage. A suitable occasion to set in motion a *rapprochement* came with the arrest for murder of Lady Erskine's brother the Master of Sinclair (John Sinclair), after the killing of two of Sinclair's fellow army officers in Flanders. Anxious to obtain clemency, Erskine approached Mar to beg that the Earl would not withhold his favour from the Master 'on my account'. Whether Mar's acquiescence conveyed an obligation sufficient to bind Erskine to him thereafter, as one historian has deduced, is open to question, but it is at any rate clear that in the run-up to the 1710 general election Mar considered himself quite 'sure' of Erskine; so much so that he counted on being able to employ his assistance for Sir Hugh Paterson, 2nd Bt., without even a pretence at consultation. For his part, Erskine declared that he would be 'guided' by Mar, and in other counties besides Stirlingshire did not refuse requests for his interest for High Tory and quasi-Jacobite candidates. Although he informed Mar's brother Lord Grange (Hon. James Erskine†) that he wished to remain 'an honest farmer ... at home, without meddling in politics', the reality was quite otherwise. Far from coveting rusticity, at this stage of his life he avoided Scotland altogether, so he told one of his brothers, unless he 'had occasion for a bill of exchange'. Instead, calculations of personal advantage were the mainspring of his motives. He wrote that he had been deterred from approaching another old friend, Lord Rothes, to put him in for Dysart Burghs, solely on grounds of political propriety:

> It's pretty plain what was my design ... that ... I might in the smoothest and handsomest way have got myself shuffled altogether into my Lord Mar's interest ... it would be the most agreeable thing that could happen for me to be so, but how to bring that about in such a way as would neither be too remarkable nor seem blameable in me was what I resolved to refer to time to furnish me a full opportunity of doing.

None of this prevented him from putting a final squeeze on Mar as the Earl seemed to be running into difficulties in Stirlingshire. Erskine pressed Mar for office and hinted that in the event of a close contest he might well hold the balance. He was easily mollified by promises, and as *praeses* of the electoral court duly supported Mar's candidate at this and the next election.[8]

In 1713 Erskine resumed his place in the Commons, having been unopposed in Clackmannanshire, where Mar's interest was added to his own and proved sufficient to ward off the malevolent designs of the Duke of Argyll. Although chosen as Mar's 'creature', Erskine was classed as a 'Hanoverian', that is a Whig, in Lord Polwarth's list of the new Scottish Members, presumably on the basis of his Squadrone past. His two tellerships on election cases saw him acting with the Tories, however, and he spoke on the ministerial side in the 'succession in danger' debate of 15 Apr. He presented the Equivalent commissioners' accounts on 7 May. When a bill was introduced to discharge the commissioners from liability for money expended, a politically diverse group of Scottish Members sought to add a clause imposing interest on the £14,000 appropriated to the woollen industry. Erskine responded with what Lockhart described as an 'ingenious' riposte that encouraged a number of Scottish Whigs to desert at the vote. Erskine found himself in opposition to Lockhart over two other issues in this session. Following Mar's lead, he disapproved of the sweeping nature of Lockhart's draft bill to resume bishops' rents in Scotland for the relief of the episcopalian clergy. Private interest also affected Erskine's judgment, since his brother Charles and his friend Patrick Haldane† (John's brother) were both paid their salaries as university professors from this fund. Erskine therefore supported the ministerial compromise of a bill merely appointing commissioners of inquiry, telling in its favour on 3 July. This dispute should be understood in connexion with another over the Scottish militia bill during June, Erskine as a courtier taking the opposite side to Lockhart over the abolition of the Duke of Argyll's hereditary rights.[9]

In the crisis following the Hanoverian succession Erskine's fate remained fastened closely to Mar's. Though he does not appear to have considered standing in 1715, he assisted in the campaign to obtain Paterson's re-election for Stirlingshire, in the teeth of vigorous opposition from Montrose and the Haldanes.

Then, as Mar turned towards armed rebellion, Erskine joined him, a decision which the Master of Sinclair, a Jacobite of much longer standing, ridiculed in his *Memoirs* with hearty contempt. No one, Sinclair recalled, had been

> of a more opposite principle to us all his life ... and tho' it were hard to blame him for having a great hand in the Union, because his capacity nor influence was not great, yet he gave his vote to each article of it; for it's not his way to hesitate on those occasions, nor dare the boldest of those who promoted it say he bellowed so loud in that cause as Sir John Erskine ... or maintained so long that the Union was a good thing ... and to my certain knowledge was of that opinion not one year before, and for what I know ... continued so till the very day of joining his friend Mar; for by that time he had lost all expectation of doing his work with the Whigs, both parties of that set being offended at him for his too great levity, and his endeavouring to make up his want of sufficiency by going betwixt them; nor had he ever been constant in anything but being our and his country's enemy. So it may be said that his chief was turned out by the Whigs for being so intolerable a knave, and he thrown out of expectation for being so intolerable a fool.

Erskine's participation in the Fifteen was in an auxiliary rather than a military role. One of his cant names in Jacobite correspondence, 'the Pope', though it was a nickname of long standing, may suggest that his new confederates did not see him as a man of action. In January 1715 he lost a valuable cargo of gold and arms when the ship in which he had sailed from the Continent was stranded on a sandbank near Dundee, and the following month he was sent back again to France by the Pretender. Subsequent diplomatic ventures proved equally unsuccessful, including a mission to Sweden to negotiate a treaty between the Jacobites and King Charles XII; money was short, and when, in the summer of 1716, Erskine was given an inkling that he might be able to make his peace with the Hanoverian regime and return to Scotland, he responded with cautious interest. The key to his rehabilitation was the large deposit of silver ore he had found on his estate some four years earlier, and which he had until 1715 mined in secret, with the help of a servant, and one or two of his 'poorer tenants'. The servant, the only member of the workforce who had understood what it was that they were digging, informed the government of the existence of the mine. Immediately various friends and relations, most notably John Haldane, began to try and exploit the situation to wheedle a pardon for Erskine, provided that he made a full discovery of the whereabouts and extent of the mine, the incentive for the King being the share in the profits which according to Scottish law would fall to the crown. Erskine's own sensitivities in the matter were acute: he mistrusted the Hanoverians, was anxious not to alienate his Jacobite friends, and ultimately feared the loss of his mine. His intense secretiveness on the subject had communicated itself to his wife, with whom he had left orders on his original departure for France to bury the ore he had already extracted, and who now, to Haldane's frustration, disclaimed all knowledge of the existence of the mine. Eventually a kinsman, Sir Harry Stirling, was dispatched to the Continent with a firm offer of a pardon, which Erskine accepted because of lack of funds and the demands of creditors. Mar, in reassuring the Pretender of Erskine's 'honesty', explained the pardon with the gloss that Erskine 'made conditions with them that there should be no oaths nor questions put to him, which they have kept'; and although the Earl's enemies made what play they could of Erskine's defection others continued to regard him as true. Erskine himself kept in touch with the Pretender, occasionally exchanging jocose letters, and, while largely inactive (promising nothing more than help with organizing the collection of money) remained in contact with Jacobite circles, even after Mar's fall from grace. As late as the mid-1720s Lockhart regarded him as 'very honest', though still 'too much attached to the Earl of Mar'.[10]

Granted a licence to work his mine, Erskine failed to make the fortune he had promised himself, largely through his chronic incapacity to resist any opportunity to speculate. Agricultural improvement, in which he showed a love of 'the English husbandry' (though 'he had little partiality for the personal manners of that people'), canal building and further mining enterprises swallowed the profit from the silver. In his later years, when showing a visitor around his estate, he 'pointed out a great hole and remarked, "Out of that hole I took £50,000"; then, presently walking on, he came to another excavation, and, continued he, "I put it all into that hole."' When reproached for the extravagance of his schemes, he was wont to excuse himself by recalling the intoxicating effect of the great wealth the mines had first brought him, with which 'I could not help looking upon the Elector of Hanover as a small man'. At the end, however, he was obliged to sell the entire property to his brother Charles.[11]

Contemporaries recognized in the history of Erskine's life a minor tragedy of overreaching ambition. Ramsay of Ochtertyre considered him to be potentially the ablest of his remarkable family, outshining not only Charles, the lord justice clerk, but also a younger brother Robert, who became court physician to Peter the Great. Unhappily, however, Erskine proved to be 'a man of more genius than conduct, of more wit than wisdom'. The verdict of the Master of Sinclair was essentially the same, though more bitterly expressed:

> I must say that his darling passion, of being fond of desperate projects, was . . . none of his least motives; the force of his imagination hinders the stretching the views of his spirit to make a just judgment of anything . . . He imagines he can put a thing in execution sooner than one who has thrice his sense to conceive it; nor has all the different experiments failing, that he ever tried in his life, convinced him one bit of his own insufficiency. He still has the misfortune to imagine he's born to be a great man, and when all fails, nothing but want of wings can hinder him from undertaking the voyage of the moon.

Erskine died, in his 67th year, after a fall from his horse in the Isle of Man on 12 Mar. 1739. Both sons took army commissions: the eldest, Charles, was killed at the battle of Lauffeld in 1747; the second, Henry, sat for Ayr and Anstruther Easter Burghs, 1749–65.[12]

[1] *Hist. Scot. Parl.* 228–9; *Scots Peerage* ed. Paul, vii. 587–8; Scot. Hist. Soc. *Misc.* ii. 400, 427–8. [2] *Stair Soc.* xxix. 248. [3] C. A. Malcolm, *Bank of Scotland*, 296. [4] *Scot. Rec. Soc.* lxii. 66. [5] *APS*, vi(1), 51, 159; (2), 9, 186; ix. 9, 20; x. 207, 246, 251, 269, 294; xi. 73, 102, 237; *HMC 4th Rep.* 521–3; *Scot. Hist. Soc.* (ser. 4), xviii. 60, 65; Brunton and Haig, *Senators Coll. Justice*, 380–2; info. from Dr P. W. J. Riley on members of Scot. parl.; P. W. J. Riley, *King Wm. and Scot. Politicians*, 171; Atholl mss at Blair Atholl, box 45, bdle. 1, no. 122, John Flemyng to Atholl, 3 June 1700; box 45, bdle. 2, no. 246, Erskine to [Tullibardine], 8 Dec. 1702; *Darien Pprs.* (Bannatyne Club, xc), 375; *Crossrigg Diary*, 19–20, 53, 62, 97–98, 128; Carstares, *State Pprs.* 691; *Orig. Pprs.* ed. Macpherson, ii. 14; *Lockhart Mems.* ed. Szechi, 67; Boyer, *Anne Annals*, iii. app. 42; v. 375; R. Walcott, *Pol. Early 18th Cent.* 235; *HMC Laing*, ii. 135; P. W. J. Riley, *Union*, 334; P. W. J. Riley, *Eng. Ministers and Scotland*, 209. [6] Atholl mss, box 45, bdle. 7, no. 190, James Murray to Atholl, 5 Dec. 1707; *Vernon–Shrewsbury Letters*, iii. 331; *Cal. Treas. Bks.* xxii. 79. [7] SRO, Mar and Kellie mss GD124/15/762/9, George Erskine to Grange, 25 Mar. [1708]; GD124/15/831/12 Mar to Ld. Nairne, 8 June 1708; Add. 61631, ff. 61–62, 80; 61628, ff. 148–50; SRO, Montrose mss GD220/5/154/2, Linlithgow to Montrose, 1708; Sunter thesis, 2–7. [8] Riley, *Eng. Ministers and Scotland*, 111; Add. 61628, ff. 148–50; 61631, ff. 71–72, 75, 80; *Cal. Treas. Bks.* xxiii. 234; Sunter thesis, 12–13, 18–19; Mar and Kellie mss GD124/15/985/2, John Erskine* to Grange, 17 Aug. 1710; 124/15/989/2–4, Erskine to same, [17], 21 Aug., 12 Sept. 1710); Scot. Hist. Soc. *Misc.* ii. 400. [9] NLS, Advocates' mss, Wodrow pprs. letters Quarto 8, ff. 95–96, 133–4; Douglas diary (Hist. of Parl. trans.), 15 Apr. 1714; *Lockhart Letters* ed. Szechi, 107; *Lockhart Pprs.* i. 447–8. [10] Sunter thesis, 30; Master of Sinclair, *Mems. Insurrection in Scotland* (Abbotsford Club, xxx), 174–5; NLS, ms 5073, ff. 81; 5098, f. 6; 5116, ff. 1–8; *HMC Stuart*, i. 476, 486–7; ii. 64, 207, 308, 372, 376, 388–9, 396, 413–14, 422–3, 432, 437, 495–503; iii. 76, 90, 109, 169, 518; iv. 16, 31, 442–3; v. 127, 135, 350, 358; vi. 368–71; *HMC Portland*, vi. 207; *Cal. Treas. Pprs.* 1714–19, pp. 233, 239; Scot. Hist. Soc. *Misc.* ii. 383–5, 309, 414–17; *HMC 8th Rep. I*, 84–86; *HMC 4th Rep.* 521, 525–6; *Lockhart Letters*, 216–17, 251, 298. [11] *Cal. Treas. Bks.* xxx. 44, 442, 537–8; xxxii. 12, 114, 194, 541, 546; NLS, ms 5073, ff. 32–33, 220–222; D. Beveridge, *Between Ochils and Forth*, 258–60; Ramsay of Ochtertyre, *Scotland and Scotsmen in 18th Cent.* ii. 110–11; *Ordnance Gazetteer of Scotland*, i. 46. [12] Ramsay of Ochtertyre, 110–11; Master of Sinclair, 175–6.

D. W. H.

ERSKINE, John (1660–1733), of the Sand Haven, Culross, Fife.

SCOTLAND 1707–1708
STIRLING BURGHS 1708–1710

b. Sept. 1660, 2nd s. of Sir Charles Erskine, MP [S], of Alva, Stirling, being 1st s. by his 2nd w. Helen, da. of Sir James Skene of Curriehill, Midlothian, SCJ, ld. pres. [S] 1626–33, and wid. of Robert Bruce of Broomhall, Dunfermline, Fife, SCJ, ld. of session 1649–52; uncle of Sir John Erskine, 3rd Bt.* *m.* (1) contract 17 Apr. 1682, Jean, da. of John Murray of Polmaise, Stirling, 1s. 2da.; (2) 29 Apr. 1697, Lady Mary (*d.* aft.1708), da. of George Maule, 2nd Earl of Panmure [S] and wid. of Charles Erskine, 5th Earl of Mar [S], *s.p.*; (3) 1714, Euphemia, da. of William Cochrane of Ochiltree, Ayr, 3da. (1 *d.v.p.*).[1]

Ensign of ft. Earl of Mar's regt. (21 Ft.) Mar.–Sept. 1680, coy. ft. Stirling Castle garrison Sept. 1680, capt. 1689, lt.-col. (brevet) 1692; commr. justiciary for Highlands [S] ?1697, 1701, 1702; dep. gov. Stirling Castle 1701–?*d.*; PC [S] 1707–8; commr. exchequer [S] 1707–8.[2]

Burgess, Stirling 1681; provost 1707–9, 1711–13; burgess, Edinburgh 1708, Culross.[3]

MP [S] Stirling 1702–7.

As Defoe observed, the neighbourhood of Stirling contained 'several gentlemen of quality' bearing the surname Erskine, and the problems of identification associated with this Member, who has been confused more often than not with his first cousin once removed, John Erskine (1662–1743) of Carnock, Fife, a younger son of the 2nd Lord Cardross, are considerable. Such confusion is understandable given the unusual extent to which the lives of these two men ran parallel: both reached the military rank of lieutenant-colonel; both were employed, simultaneously, in the garrison of Stirling Castle, Carnock as lieutenant-governor, the Member as deputy; and both held the provostship of Stirling during Queen Anne's reign. What is more, they lived 'cheek by jowl' in adjacent mansions by the shore at Culross. To differentiate between the two, contemporaries resorted to the contrast in their physical colouring: Carnock was 'the black colonel'; his deputy 'the white colonel', or 'the fair'.[4]

The reputation of being 'a thorough-paced courtier', which 'the white colonel' had established by the time of the Union, had been a long time in the making. For all that his father had been staunch to the Covenant, serving as a colonel of horse and being chosen a commissioner to the English Parliament in 1644–5, Erskine himself took a post in 1680 at Stirling Castle, under another first cousin once removed, Lord Mar. The following year he was presented with his burgess ticket at the Duke of York's visit to the burgh, among a batch of loyalist lairds and several officials of York's household. Then in 1683 he was nominated to a local commission to try 'delinquents' on charges of treason. However, he still remained sufficiently uncompromised to be able to embrace the Revolution. In the convention of estates his brother Sir Charles, 1st Bt., signed the Act declaring the legality of the assembly's proceedings and the letter of congratulation to William III. Outside, Erskine himself was 'very early' in showing his support for the Williamite cause, and as a result not only retained his post in Stirling Castle but also gained rapid promotion in three years from ensign to lieutenant-colonel. In 1694 Lord Annandale recommended him (unsuccessfully) for some further, unspecified, military distinction with the recommendation that he had 'always carried himself well towards the government'.[5]

Returned to the Scottish parliament in 1702, Erskine never gave any sign that he was other than a dyed-in-the-wool courtier; and this despite his earlier investment (of some £300) in the Company of Scotland. He even supported the Squadrone managers in 1704, voting against the Duke of Hamilton's motion on the succession. In the Union parliament he voted the complete Court line, with only two absences. Afterwards he was named to the Scottish privy council and to the exchequer commission, both institutions destined to survive only briefly after the Union. He was also included on the Court slate as a Member of the first Parliament of Great Britain.[6]

What little is known of Erskine's conduct and opinions at Westminster comes from his letters to his stepson (and first cousin twice removed), the 6th Earl of Mar, and to other members of the family. Although one historian, confusing him with Erskine of Carnock, had categorized him as a client of the Duke of Queensberry, this correspondence places him firmly in Mar's circle. In November 1707 he reported to the Earl's brother Lord Grange (Hon. James Erskine†) the promising reception the Commons had given to the Scottish merchants' petition against the continued seizure of their goods by English customs officers contrary to the provisions of the Union. Later, after the Christmas adjournment, his response to the proposed abolition of the Scottish privy council, of which he was himself a member, betrayed rather more anxiety:

I doubt not but our new prospects for government for Scotland are both surprising and alarming to most of our people there, and it's no wonder, for we are confounded with the thoughts of it here, for all our folks have letters telling them of the confusion it will certainly occasion in North Britain.

No speech of his is recorded, however. Erskine showed no enthusiasm for re-election in 1708, but agreed to stand at Mar's insistence. He was listed as having voted for the impeachment of Dr Sacheverell. His patron was keen for him to stand again in 1710, but Erskine was even more determined not to, 'for several reasons', not least the difficulty he faced in the two burghs where he himself had some influence, Stirling and Culross. At the same time, he promised to do what he could to secure the return of 'a firm friend' to Mar's interest. Erskine was persuaded out of electoral retirement in 1713, in an unsuccessful attempt to unseat the outgoing Member for the burghs district, Henry Cunningham. He neither contested the 1715 election, nor took any part in the Jacobite rising. Erskine died in 1733, aged 73, his life still intertwined with that of his namesake of Carnock, who was one of the debtors to his estate.[7]

[1] *Hist. Scot. Parl.* 232; *Scots Peerage* ed. Paul, v. 627; viii. 349; D. Beveridge, *Culross and Tulliallan*, ii. 47; *Stewart Soc. Mag.* v. 123–4; *Memorials Fam. Skene of Skene* (New Spalding Club), 113–14; Brunton and Haig, *Senators Coll. Justice*, 253–4, 338. [2] *CSP Dom.* 1679–80, p. 418; 1680–1, p. 11; 1689–90, p. 200; 1697, p. 80; 1700–2, pp. 317, 338; 1702–3, pp. 353, 472; *Cal. Treas. Bks.* xxiv. 249–50; *Scot. Rec. Soc.* lxii. 65. [3] *Extracts Stirling Recs.* 1667–1752, pp. 32, 392, 400–1; *Scot. Rec. Soc.* lxii. 66; Beveridge, 48. [4] Defoe, *Tour* ed. Cole, 756–7; *APS*, xii. 513; Foster, *MPs Scotland*, 128; R. Walcott, *Pol. Early 18th Cent.* 234; *Stewart Soc. Mag.* 125–6. [5] *Orig. Pprs.* ed. Macpherson, ii. 14; *APS*, v. 392, 395, 400; vi(1), 28, 51, 53, 101–2, 141, 159, 202–3, 381, 862; vi(2), 9, 33, 190, 291, 536; ix. 9, 20; *Extracts Stirling Recs.* 32; *Reg. PC Scotland*, 1683, pp. 289–90; *Annandale Fam. Bk.* ii. 79. [6] Info. from Dr P. W. J. Riley on members of Scot. parl.; *Darien Pprs.* (Bannatyne Club), xc), 388; Boyer, *Anne Annals*, iii. app. 43; v. 344; P. W. J. Riley, *Union*, 331. [7] SRO, Mar and Kellie mss GD124/15/510/7–8, Erskine to Mar, 20 Nov., 23 Dec. 1707; GD124/15/829/4–5, same to Grange, 25 Apr., 24 May 1708; GD124/15/868/1, Mar to Ld. Stair, 20 June 1708; GD124/15/975/2, 7–8, same to Grange, 6 June, 20, 22 July 1710; GD124/15/985/1, Erskine to same, 28 July 1710; GD124/15/991/2, Ld. Dupplin (George Hay*) to same, 13 Aug. [1710]; Sunter thesis, 20; *Stewart Soc. Mag.* 124.

D. W. H.

ESSINGTON, John (c.1667–1740), of Gossington Hall, Slimbridge, Glos.

AYLESBURY 1710–1715

b. c.1667, 2nd s. of John Essington of Gossington Hall by Elizabeth, da. of Francis Haslewood of Uphenham, Worcs. *educ.* L. Inn 1691. *m.* (1) 14 Aug. 1697, Margaret

(d. 1702), da. and coh. of John Godfrey, clerk of Mercers' Co., and h. to her bro. Thomas Godfrey, 1da.; (2) aft. 1702, Mary (d. 1763), s.p. suc. bro. 1703.¹

Clerk of Mercers' Co. ?1697–d.; gov. St. Thomas' Hosp. 1719.²

Essington's grandfather (d. 1680) purchased Gossington Hall, Gloucestershire. His father served briefly as an alderman of Gloucester (1687–9), suggesting strong Toryism, and was probably the man who subscribed £3,000 to the land bank. Essington himself gave his age as 30 and his address as of Lincoln's Inn on his marriage licence of August 1697: in fact he was residing with John Godfrey at Mercers' Hall, whose will of that year described him as 'now dwelling with me'. He married Godfrey's daughter seven weeks after her father's death. Through his marriage Essington acquired London property, and in May his wife inherited at least £4,000 from her brother, Thomas. Essington's wife died in March 1702, leaving him by her will of December 1697 her Bedfordshire estates and probably much else besides. Further additions to his estate no doubt followed the death of his father (?1701) and his brother, William, in 1703.³

At some point, possibly as early as 1697 in succession to Godfrey, Essington became clerk of the Mercers' Company. He had property at Chesham and this, combined with his Toryism, made him a credible torch-carrier for the interest of Sir John Pakington, 4th Bt., in Aylesbury. Although defeated in 1708, he was marked as a Tory on a list of early 1708 which detailed the returns of the general election, even to the extent of revealing the size of his vote. He was successful in 1710 and classed as a Tory on the 'Hanover list' and as one of the 'worthy patriots' who in the 1710–11 session detected the mismanagements of the previous administration. His one appointment of note was on 22 Mar. 1712 to draft the Aylesbury to Bicester highway bill. Introduced by Lord Cheyne (Hon. William*), he presented in July of that year the Aylesbury address in favour of peace. He was re-elected in 1713 and was classed as a Tory in the Worsley list. He did not stand in 1715, but was a signatory to the attempted compromise for the shire seats in Buckinghamshire. However, he retained his seat on the Gloucestershire bench.⁴

Essington was clearly a wealthy man, although he may on occasion be mistaken for John Essington of Wandsworth (d. 1729), sheriff of Surrey in 1724, who was involved in copper manufacture. In 1710 a John Essington owned ten shares in the East India Company and stock worth between £500 and £2,000 in the Bank of England. On the marriage of Essington's only daughter to the Irish peer Lord Kinsale in 1725, Hearne wrote that she 'will be a fortune of £100,000', and considered Essington himself to be 'a gentleman that bears a very good character'. At this point Essington appears to have been resident in his property at Berkhamsted in Hertfordshire, where his wife continued to live after his death. He died on 21 Oct. 1740, 'suddenly, after eating grapes', leaving a considerable fortune to his daughter and instructions that his wife should complete 'my house, outhousing, garden walls, planting and any other conveniency or ornaments at Gossington Hall'. His will mentioned lands in Buckinghamshire, Cheshire, Devon and Hertfordshire as well as houses in London.⁵

¹ *Misc. Gen. et Her.* ser. 5, iv. 26–27; IGI, London; PCC 26 Dogg. ² Bank of Eng. Morice mss, Nicholas* to Humphry Morice*, 6 Feb. 1707[–8]; *London Mag.* 1740, p. 510; J. Aubrey, *Surr.* 313. ³ *VCH Glos.* iv. 378; NLS, Advocates' mss, Bank of Eng. pprs. 31.1.7, f. 96; *London Mar. Lic.* ed. Foster, 456; PCC 160 Pyne, 122 Lort, 26, 227 Dogg. ⁴ *London Gazette*, 22–24 July 1712; *Verney Letters 18th Cent.* i. 317; L. K. J. Glassey, *Appt. JPs*, 239. ⁵ *Wandsworth Par. Reg.* 358; Bodl. Rawl. D.747, ff. 368–74; Egerton 3359; *Hearne Colls.* viii. 371; PCC 429 Caesar; *Gent. Mag.* 1740, p. 525; *Misc. Gen. et Her.* 28–32.

E. C./S. N. H.

ESTCOURT, Sir Thomas (c.1645–1702), of Chelsea, Mdx. and Pinkney Park, Sherston Pinkney, nr. Malmesbury, Wilts.

MALMESBURY   3 Nov. 1673–1679 (Jan.), 1685–1687
BATH   1695–1698

b. c.1645, 1st s. of Sir Thomas Estcourt of Sherston Pinkney, master in Chancery 1652–83, by his 1st w. Magdalen, da. of Sir John Browne of East Kirkby, Lincs. *educ.* St. Edmund Hall, Oxf. matric. 24 May 1661, aged 16; L. Inn 1662. *m.* lic. 11 Feb. 1678, Mary, da. of Sir Vincent Corbet, 1st Bt.†, of Moreton Corbet, Salop, 2s. (1 *d.v.p.*) 2da. Kntd. 15 Sept. 1674; *suc.* fa. 1683.¹

High steward, Malmesbury 1671, 1673–7; sheriff, Wilts. 1692–3; freeman, Bath 1693.²

Examiner in Chancery 1674–82.³

Vice-treasurer, Linen Co. 1690; cttee. R. Fishery Co. [I] 1691; asst. Mine Adventurers' Co. 1693.⁴

Estcourt had been a strong Court supporter in the Cavalier Parliament but had later the misfortune to be charged with complicity in the Popish Plot and withdrew to Flanders in the entourage of the Duke of York. Regaining his seat at James II's accession, he was inactive in proceedings and at first showed a non-committal attitude towards the King's religious policies. His influence at Malmesbury, where in the 1670s he had held the key office of high steward, was afterwards increasingly undermined by Hon. Thomas Wharton*, and he was defeated there in 1690. It was evidently this failure which induced him to look towards Bath and forge links with its corporation. He appeared as a candidate there at the by-election in November 1693, withdrawing apparently on finding that the corporation's favourite was William Blathwayt*, the secretary at war, but he was narrowly successful at the 1695 election. Once back in Parliament, his political attitudes proved hard to classify, though in party terms he appears to have been a Tory. In January 1696 his support for the Court was noted as 'doubtful' in the forecast concerning the proposed council of trade, while there is conflicting information as to whether or not he signed the Association. He was then absent from the division on the price of guineas in March. In April the House received a petition against him in which one Robert Hookes claimed that in 1690 he had been appointed treasurer of the Linen Company and had entered into an agreement with Estcourt and Craven Howard, the Member for Malmesbury, whereby Estcourt was to be vice-treasurer, to manage and account for the company's profits. Estcourt had received about £30,000 by this arrangement, but refused to account for it and although Hookes and Howard had taken out a bill in Chancery against him, he had failed to put in a reply and was now protected by privilege. Estcourt agreed to waive his privilege if Howard would do likewise. The House ordered both to do so when Hooke's petition was considered on 15 Apr. Estcourt's absenteeism became increasingly noticeable after this incident. He was not in the House for the vote on Sir John Fenwick† on 25 Nov., and was granted leave on 30 Mar. 1697 to recover his health. His failure to respond to a call of the House later in the year resulted in his being ordered into custody on 16 Dec. 1697, from which he was discharged on the 23rd.[5]

In 1698 Estcourt stood down at Bath in favour of a Wiltshire neighbour, Alexander Popham*. Although one intention, undoubtedly, was to challenge the Wharton interest at Malmesbury, his more immediate aim appears to have been to oust his ex-business partner Craven Howard, who was seeking re-election as one of Wharton's candidates in the borough, and debar him from the legal immunity offered by privilege of Parliament. Estcourt's original desire to stand at Malmesbury was blocked by some complicated last-minute manoeuvring in which he withdrew on the pretext that he was ill. The reasons for this change of heart are not entirely clear, but it seems there may have been some pecuniary quarrel between him and William Adye, Wharton's deputy-steward, who had, in effect, put his own electoral influence in the borough up for sale. The complaint was indeed later made in a petition referred to the elections committee that Estcourt and his brother had paid Adye 'several sums of money on account of this election', but were outbid by Michael Wicks*, a Malmesbury native whose own legal difficulties made it imperative for him to have a seat in Parliament. Estcourt later vented his animus against Adye in a letter to Wharton: 'I will never have more to do with him as long as I live.' The committee did not, however, investigate the accusations of bribery which had been levelled against Estcourt. By 1701 Estcourt's health had broken down and he played no part in the elections of that year. He died between March and October 1702.[6]

[1] Burke, *Gentry* (1952), 1941–2; *Lincs. Peds.* (Harl. Soc. l), 181; *London Mar. Lic.* ed. Foster, 456. [2] *Coll. Top. et Gen.* vi. 297; Bath AO, Bath council bk. 3, p. 171. [3] T. D. Hardy, *Chancery Officers*, 125. [4] *CSP Dom.* 1691–2, pp. 3–4; 1693, p. 207; *Sel. Charters*, 239; PC 2/76/503. [5] H. Horwitz, *Parl. and Pol. Wm. III*, 338. [6] Beaufort mss at Badminton House, 602.1.7, 'Malmesbury election petition, 1698'; PCC 160 Herne.

P. W./A. A. H.

ETHERIDGE, Sir James (1658–1730), of Harleyford, Bucks.

GREAT MARLOW 1695–1715

b. 9 Feb. 1658, 1st s. of James Etheridge of St. Paul's Churchyard, London by Mary, da. of one Mawhood, woollen draper, of Cannon Street, London. *educ.* Ware (Mr Nelson), Watton, Hitchin, Bishop's Stortford (Mr Cudworth and Mr Conway) 1665–73; Trinity, Camb. 1674; I. Temple 1676, called 1682. *m.* (1) 6 Nov. 1683, Katherine (*d.* 1687), da. and h. of Robert Moore of Great Marlow, Bucks., 1s.; (2) 14 Nov. 1689, Frediswed (*d.* 1735), da. of Robert Morris of Abingdon, Berks., wid. of Sir William Gulston† of Fairfield, Kent, 1s. (*d.v.p.*). *suc.* fa. 1664; kntd. 17 Feb. 1682.[1]

Freeman, St. Albans 1686; recorder and alderman, Chipping Wycombe 1688–9.[2]

Etheridge's father was bound apprentice in 1646 to a woollen draper in London. After marrying the daughter of a fellow draper in 1657, he died in 1664 leaving a young family. Etheridge's mother quickly remarried and took up residence in Hertfordshire, where Etheridge went to school. After a spell at Cambridge, he became clerk to William Waltham of Clifford's Inn, staying out his time there and then moving to his own chambers in the Inner Temple. In 1676 he had been entered specially at the Inner Temple by the then treasurer, Sir John King, and was called to the bar in February 1682, 'the house giving me above two years of my time as a mark of their singular favour and regard'. Five days later he was knighted by Charles II, being 'in great favour with him, had not my own affairs crossed my court attendance'. Marriage followed in 1683 and, through his wife, an interest at Great Marlow. Sworn a Buckinghamshire j.p. in June 1684, he contested that borough at the 1685 election only to lose it 'through the knavery of the Chases and Laws'. Nevertheless, he was clearly in tune with the politics of the time, being made a freeman of St. Albans in 1686 and a militia captain in July 1687. Having given favourable replies to James II's 'three questions' on the repeal of the Penal Laws and Test Act, he was named recorder of Chipping Wycombe in March 1688, and would have been Member for the town in the proposed Parliament had not 'the Dutch invasion diverted his Majesty's intentions'.[3]

Whatever Etheridge's views on the Revolution, he felt confident enough of the future to remarry in November 1689. Shortly afterwards he completed the purchase of Harleyford and the manor of Great Marlow for £6,000 from the 5th Viscount Falkland [S] (Anthony Carey*), following the passage of an Act in the 1690 session. This immeasurably strengthened his interest in the borough. Although in 1693 he was still regarded by Simon Mayne* as the chief opponent of the Whig interest at Wycombe, by 1695 it was clear that his parliamentary ambitions had settled on Great Marlow. At the election of that year he was unopposed when he joined interests with James Chase. In the new Parliament he was forecast as likely to oppose the Court in the division of 31 Jan. 1696 on the proposed council of trade, refused to sign the Association, voted against fixing the price of guineas at 22s., and in the following session divided on 25 Nov. 1696 against the bill for the attainder of Sir John Fenwick†. On 27 Jan. 1697 he acted as teller against reading the report from the committee considering abuses in prisons and places of sanctuary. He received leave of absence on 11 May 1698.[4]

Returned again in 1698, Etheridge was classed as a member of the Country party in a comparative analysis of the old and new Parliaments about September of that year and forecast as likely to oppose the standing army. Clearly, he was already feeling the financial strain of electioneering, for in November 1699 he was seeking a loan of £4,000 at 5 per cent upon security of 'an estate of £400 p.a. at Marlow... and a house on it that cost £5,000'. On a list of January–May 1700 he was classed as part of the Old East India Company interest. The most obvious link with the company was his wife, whose first husband owned over £5,000 worth of shares at his death. Returned again in January 1701, he was listed the following month as likely to support the Court over the 'Great Mortgage'. His stance in this session led to his being blacklisted for having opposed the preparations for war with France. Re-elected in November 1701, in December he was classed as a Tory by Robert Harley*, and voted on 26 Feb. 1702 in favour of the resolution vindicating the Commons' proceedings in the impeachments of the King's ministers. After facing opposition in the 1702 election, he was forecast in the 1704–5 session as likely to support the Tack, duly voting for it on 28 Nov. 1704.[5]

Notwithstanding his vote on the Tack, Etheridge was re-elected without opposition in 1705 and classed as 'True Church' on a list of the new House. He voted against the Court candidate for Speaker on 25 Oct. On 24 Jan. 1706 he was named to the drafting committee on the estate bill of Morris Gulston (his wife's son by her first marriage) providing for his sisters' portions and the payment of debts, a bill to which Etheridge had to give his consent at the committee stage in the Lords. On 15 Mar. he acted as a teller on an amendment to a law reform bill which regulated costs in Exchequer suits. In a list of early 1708 he was classed as a Tory. Despite predicting that the 1705 Parliament would probably be his last, he stood again in 1708, and triumphed despite opposition from a Scottish interloper. Again he was classed as a Tory. He voted against the impeachment of Dr Sacheverell, and was returned at the top of the poll in the 1710 election. He was classed as a Tory in the 'Hanover list', and in the 1710–11 session he was marked as both a 'Tory patriot' opposed to the war and a 'worthy patriot' who helped detect the mismanagements of the previous administration. He also joined the October Club. In early 1712 he was named on Harley's (now Lord Oxford) lobbying list regarding the attack on the Duke of Marlborough (John Churchill†), and to be spoken to by William Lowndes*. Financial pressures were again worrying him, for on 29 May 1712 he wrote to Oxford, stressing his 18 years of service in the Tory cause 'which has had so great a share of my estate and services', particularly in the previous election. He asked for his son Charles to be made comptroller of the wine licences at £200 p.a., but without success. Somewhat surprisingly, he voted on 18 June 1713 against the French commerce bill.[6]

At the general election in that year he was opposed

by a candidate supported by Lord Wharton (Hon. Thomas*) and the Whig Richard Hampden II*, and repaid them by intervening in the county election for the first time in seven years against Hampden and (Sir) Edmund Denton* (1st Bt.), and helping to return the two Tory candidates. Successful in his own election, he was classed as a Tory in the Worsley list. However, by October 1713 Sir William Trumbull* was being informed that Harleyford was for sale for £20,000.[7]

In October 1714 Etheridge delivered the Marlow address on the accession of George I, but he did not stand in 1715. He had spent £18,000 on Great Marlow since purchasing the manor there, and had not only to sell Waltham Abbey in Essex, his paternal estate, but to mortgage Harleyford for £6,000 to his son Charles and assignees. In July 1718 he sold Harleyford and the manor of Great Marlow to Sir John Guise, 3rd Bt.*, and so 'got out of the hands of my son Charles and my usurers that might have devoured me up'. He was put out of the commission of the peace at this time by the influence of Wharton's son, Philip, 1st Duke of Wharton, but was restored in 1728. Etheridge was buried at Marlow on 23 June 1730. Clearly his relations with his son had not improved, for in his will Etheridge left him 1s. 'and no more (he having used me with all the inhumanity possible without any regard to the ties of blood or duty and almost if not altogether broke my heart)'. His widow received his real and personal estate, with George Bruere* acting as executor.[8]

[1] Except where otherwise stated, this biography is based on Etheridge's account of his own life in *Misc. Gen. et Her.* n.s. i. 197–200, 211–15. [2] A. E. Gibbs, *Corp. Recs. of St. Albans*, 87; *Ledger Bk. of High Wycombe* ed. Newall, 24, 30. [3] Duckett, *Penal Laws and Test Act* (1883), 143, 155. [4] Bucks RO, D/CE/M/46, 126; *VCH Bucks.* iii. 71; *HMC Lords*, iii. 15; Bodl. Carte 223, f. 276. [5] BL, Verney mss mic. 636/51, Jo. Stewkeley to Sir John Verney* (Ld. Fermanagh), 1 Nov. 1699; Add. 22185, f. 12. [6] *HMC Lords* n.s. vi. 429–30; Add. 70331, canvassing list c. Jan. 1712; 70294, Etheridge to Ld. Oxford, 29 May 1712. [7] BL, Trumbull Alphab. mss 51, Bateman to Trumbull, 30 Oct., 4 Nov. 1713. [8] Bucks. RO, D/CE/M/36–38, 46; PCC 178 Isham.

E. C./S. N. H.

ETTRICK, William (1651–1716), of Holt Lodge, Dorset and the Middle Temple.

POOLE   1685–1687
CHRISTCHURCH   1689–4 Dec. 1716

b. 15 Nov. 1651, 1st s. of Anthony Ettrick† of Holt Lodge by Anne, da. of Edward Davenant, DD, vicar of Gillingham, Dorset. *educ.* Trinity, Oxf. 1667; M. Temple 1669, called 1675, bencher 1699, treasurer 1711. *m.* (1) Elizabeth, da. and coh. of Sir Edmund Bacon, 4th Bt.*, 1da.; (2) Frances, da. of Thomas Wyndham† of Witham Friary, Som., 1da. *suc.* fa. 1703.[1]

Freeman, Poole 1684.[2]

Attorney to Prince George by 1692–1708; commr. taking subscriptions to land bank 1696; counsel to Admiralty 1711–14.[3]

A Tory who had voted in 1689 against the transfer of the crown, Ettrick successfully contested Christchurch in 1690 on the Hyde interest and represented the borough for the rest of this period. At the beginning of the new Parliament, Lord Carmarthen (Sir Thomas Osborne†) classed him in several lists as a Court supporter and also on one list as a Tory. Indeed, throughout his subsequent career, various analyses of the House affirmed his unwavering Toryism. At this time the most important influence in his career was his connexion with Carmarthen, to whom he at times acted as a legal adviser and for whom he was sometimes spokesman in the Lower House. The first such instance occurred on 27 Mar. 1690, when he strongly urged that the regular revenue should be settled on the King for life, saying: 'I cannot, in justice and gratitude, do less for him than his predecessors. In King Charles I's time, the not settling the revenue upon him for life drew on us all the mischiefs that followed.' He pressed the point again when the debate was resumed the following day, saying: 'the question is whether you will show that countenance to the government, as to support the King, or keep him as it were at board wages'. Ettrick continued to assist the Court over supply. Sir John Lowther, 2nd Bt. II, speaking for the Treasury, had recommended a grant of £1,500,000, but when the much lower figure of £700,000 was mentioned, Ettrick on 1 Apr. moved for a compromise figure of £1,200,000, which was eventually accepted. On 24 Apr. he opposed a motion by Hon. Sir Henry Capel, an old rival, to widen the terms of a proposed address thanking the King for his care of the Church of England, as evinced by his recent changes to the London lieutenancy. He opposed Hon. Thomas Wharton's abjuration bill on 26 Apr., saying that it 'is intended not to distinguish who are Churchmen or for this government, but who are of a party, and I like this the worse because it comes from the other side of the House'. He spoke again on 28 Apr. against the suspension of the Habeas Corpus Act, a move he had also opposed in the Convention. On 14 May 1690, when the Whigs tried to move for an address requesting the removal of Carmarthen, Ettrick warmly defended his patron, saying:

I am sorry that, without doors, we are divided into parties. What can be a greater punishment to a man of honour, than to have an old impeachment revived, and an address to the King against him as unfit to be near him, and to remove him?

In the 1690–1 session Carmarthen listed Ettrick in November 1690 as a 'manager of the King's directions', noting him as one of the 'gentlemen that can and have given very great satisfaction to the King's affairs', and in December as a probable supporter in the Commons if there was a further attack on Carmarthen's position. On 13 Mar. 1691 Carmarthen recommended Ettrick to the King to be appointed a baron of the Exchequer, writing that Ettrick 'is a very able lawyer and [has] long practised in that court; he is a Parliament-man and has constantly served you well there'. The suggestion was ignored. Robert Harley's* list of April 1691 queried Ettrick as a Court supporter.[4]

In the third session Ettrick spoke for the East India Company on 18 Dec. 1691, and on 12 Jan. 1692 supported a motion to set up a committee to consider the proposal of the bankers to advance an immediate sum of £100,000 at 5 per cent return for the establishment of a reliable fund to pay interest on the debt owed to them by the crown. On 4 Feb. 1692 he presented a clause on behalf of a fellow Member, Thomas Preston, to the bill vesting forfeited estates in the King and Queen. In the next session, he spoke on 27 Feb. 1693 for the bill to indemnify those who had acted for their Majesties' service in defence of the kingdom, and on 6 Mar. in favour of a bill relating to the estates of the Earl of Pembroke (Thomas Herbert†).[5]

Ettrick was much less prominent in the last two sessions, particularly after the political eclipse of Carmarthen, now Duke of Leeds, in 1694. Ill-health seems to have been a factor, as Ettrick was granted leave of absence on 27 Feb. 1694 and on 22 Feb. 1695, both times for his health. By the beginning of the next Parliament he was in opposition. He was forecast in January 1696 as likely to vote against the Court on the proposed council of trade, though he signed the Association promptly. He was given leave of absence on 27 Feb. for 21 days, but was back in the House in March in time to divide against the government on fixing the price of guineas at 22s. although this meant separating from Leeds himself and most of his followers. Indeed from this time onwards he seems to have followed the lead of Robert Harley, rather than his former patron. In the next session he voted on 25 Nov. against the attainder of Sir John Fenwick†. He was once more given leave of absence on 3 Mar. 1697 to recover his health. Although still a Court placeman and being classed as such in a comparative analysis of the old and new Parliaments in about September 1698, he remained in opposition, being queried as likely to oppose a standing army, and not being listed as voting against the disbanding bill on 18 Jan. 1699. On 18 Mar. 1699 he was given leave from the House for a week. In the Parliament of February 1701, the changes in government brought him back to the Court, and he was listed as likely to support the Court in agreeing with the committee of supply's resolution to continue the 'Great Mortgage', and was blacklisted as having opposed the preparations for war. Classed as a Tory by Harley in December 1701, Ettrick supported the resolution on 22 Feb. 1702 vindicating the Commons' proceedings in the impeachments of William's Whig ministers. On 28 Feb. he spoke in the debate on a petition concerning plantations in the Leeward Islands. In March he reported and conveyed to the Upper House the Lords' bill for explaining the Act for the better security of the monarch's person and government. A rumour in May that he would be made lord chancellor of Ireland proved unfounded. He still retained connexions with the Duke of Leeds and acted as counsel for him in the summer of 1702 when Leeds tried to recover the office of auditor of the receipt then held by Lord Halifax (Charles Montagu*).[6]

After the accession of Queen Anne Ettrick featured as a Court Tory. For some years he had held the office of attorney-at-law in the household of Prince George of Denmark, with a salary of £20 p.a., but when the Prince became lord high admiral his salary was increased to £400 p.a. He was forecast in March 1704 as a supporter of the government's actions over the Scotch Plot, was forecast as a probable opponent of the Tack and did not vote for it in the division on 28 Nov. 1704. In 1705 he was named on a list of placemen and was also classed as a 'Churchman' in a list of about June. In the next Parliament he voted on 25 Oct. 1705 in favour of the Court candidate for Speaker, and on 18 Feb. 1706 he supported the Court on the 'place clause' in the regency bill, although two days earlier he was one of Harley's followers who had voted against the Whigs on the Bewdley election. Ettrick reverted to opposition on the fall of Harley. This did not prevent him in February, in the pre-election manoeuvres at Shaftesbury, from recommending to his brother-in-law, Edward Nicholas*, that he join with the Court candidate, Sir John Cropley, 2nd Bt.* Ettrick himself was returned as usual at Christchurch and was again classed as a Tory in a list of 1708 with the returns added. He voted against the impeachment of Dr Sacheverell in 1710.[7]

In June 1711, under the Harley administration Ettrick was given another legal post, that of counsel-at-law to the Admiralty commission. He was listed as a 'Tory patriot' who opposed the continuance of the war in 1711, and as one of the 'worthy patriots' who 'detected the mismanagements of the late ministry' in the first session of the Parliament, and he voted on 18 June 1713 for the French commerce bill. After George I's accession he continued to sit for Christchurch as a Tory until his death on 4 Dec. 1716.[8]

[1] *Vis. London* (Harl. Soc. xcii), 61; Aubrey, *Brief Lives*, i. 250. [2] Poole archives B17. [3] *Cal. Treas. Bks.* xxiii. 222–3; *CJ*, xii. 509; Boyer, *Pol. State*, i–ii. 381; iv. 58. [4] A. Browning, *Danby*, i. 366, 468; Cobbett, *Parlty. Hist.* v. 557–9, 569–70, 602, 610, 647; Grey, x. 73; Bodl. Rawl. A.79, f. 77; *CSP Dom.* 1695, p. 168; SP 8/8/118. [5] *Luttrell Diary*, 88, 124, 170, 450, 469. [6] *Cocks Diary*, 229; Surr. RO, Midleton mss, 2, ff. 63–64, Alan Brodrick† to St. John Brodrick, 19 May 1702; *Cal. Treas. Bks.* xvii. 51. [7] *Cal. Treas. Bks.* xvii. 343; *Bull. IHR*, xlv. 48; PRO 31/24/21/9. [8] *Vis. London*, 61.

P. W.

EVANCE, Stephen (c.1655–1712), of the 'Black Boy', Lombard Street, London.

BRIDPORT 1690–1698

b. c.1655, s. of John Evance of New England and London, merchant. *unm. suc.* fa. bef. 1669; kntd. 14 Oct. 1690.[1]

Apprentice, Goldsmiths' Co. 1669, freeman 1676, livery 1682, member, ct. of assts. 1691, prime warden 1692; receiver, poll tax, London, Mdx. 1690.[2]

Commr. excise 14 Oct. 1689–98, wine licences 1690–1701; cttee. loans on Poll Act 1693; receiver, contributions on salt and beer duties 1694; commr. leather duty 1697; jeweller to K. William 1697–1702, to Q. Anne 1702–*d.*; receiver, stamp duties 1703; trustee, loan for Emperor 1706; commr. subscriptions to S. Sea Co. 1711.[3]

Asst. R. Corp. Co. 1691; gov. Hollow Sword Blades Co. 1691–2; cttee. R. Fishery Co. [I] 1692; gov. Hudson's Bay Co. 1692–6, 1700–11, cttee. 1696–1700; member, Mines Co. 1693; gov. Bridewell and Bethlem Hosps. 1708–*d.*[4]

Evance's pedigree has not been fully ascertained. His father, possibly the John Evans who emigrated from London to Virginia in 1635, was a merchant based in Newhaven, New England, from where he had been trading to Barbados from at least the early 1650s. Evance was born in Newhaven, but in 1669, aged 14, he was sent to London as an apprentice to the Goldsmiths' Company. In a critical appraisal of his subsequent career, the Earl of Ailesbury (Thomas Bruce†) described Evance as having been 'a poor boy in the goldsmith's shop and at the Revolution [he] went on errands for his master; and in a small number of years he was reputed to be worth £200,000'. In 1681, with his reputation as a banker well established, he became chief cashier of the Hudson's Bay Company, entrusted with much of its financial business. He arranged the sale of the company's annual intake of beaver coats and parchments, and was instrumental in establishing trade with Russia in furs and hemp. In February 1684 he bought company stock, and although he sold out briefly in 1689, he was to enlarge his holdings considerably in later years, owning £4,300 in stock by 1704. Evance's loans to the company in this period were often the only means by which it remained solvent, but they were also precarious – in 1687 alone he signed bills for £10,510 yet received only £5,411. At about this time he also bought stock in the White Paper Makers', Royal African and East India Companies.[5]

Evance was involved in a myriad of other business enterprises. He financed a partnership between Prince Rupert and the 1st Earl of Shaftesbury (Anthony Ashley Cooper†), for making steel and guns. Other interests were to a degree an extension of his involvement with the Hudson's Bay Company. In August 1691 he emphasized his knowledge of New England in a petition for letters patent for a 31-year lease to develop royal copper mines there, in return for paying a tithe to the crown and delivering the copper to the Royal Mint. He also petitioned for letters patent to develop and use a newly invented air pump to allow divers to salvage wrecks, and to establish a company in the north of England for the manufacture of hollow sword blades. He had already paid for 20 families to be settled in the north for this work, and in September 1691 he became the company's first governor. After the Revolution he became more prominent as a government financier. From the summer of 1689 onwards he made substantial loans to the crown, supplying, often in partnership with other leading bankers, money for the armies in Ireland and Flanders, subsidies for the allies in Europe and credit for both the army and navy. In October 1689 he was appointed to a new excise commission, with a salary of £800 p.a., in return for contributing to a loan of £175,000. Ministers were not ungrateful for this service, and he was knighted in October 1690. On several occasions between June and November he was also given as royal bounty sums amounting to £1,368. In September 1690 he was made a commissioner of wine licences as reward for a loan of £30,000, and in 1691 and 1692 various industrial consortia to which he belonged were successful in petitioning for incorporation as chartered companies. In subsequent years he engaged in supplying clothing to troops in Flanders, arms to the garrison at Kinsale and stores to the navy from Maryland, New Hampshire and Sweden, having formed a trading association to make tar, pitch and resin.[6]

Returned to Parliament for Bridport in 1690, Evance was listed as a Whig by Carmarthen (Sir Thomas Osborne†). He was subsequently named as a Court supporter by Robert Harley* in April 1691 and as a placeman on many of Carmarthen's lists from 1692. Grascome also classed him as a Court supporter in this Parliament. In September 1692 he failed in a bid to be chosen an alderman of London. By 1694, although remaining one of the chief suppliers of government credit abroad, he found some of his other business threatened by the Bank of England. Like most of the goldsmiths, he opposed the formation of the Bank. This opposition, together with his poor attendance record at the Excise Board and apparent lack of diligence, led to recommendations that he be removed from the commission. Sir John Trenchard* considered Evance to be 'very little serviceable in that employment', while Lord Keeper Somers (Sir John*) listed Evance among other commissioners 'who are at best so useless . . . that the commissions would certainly be improved by leaving them out, and putting diligent men in their room'. However, Shrewsbury informed the King that Evance was 'very considerable in the City, and very useful to you upon all occasions of loans'. His usefulness as a financier clearly outweighed his negligence as an official, and he retained his place, although there was mounting criticism of his business practices: in November 1693 he had been censured for importing 100 bales of raw silk 'upon pretence' that weavers had need of the material, while in June 1696 a consignment of timber imported by Evance from New England was rejected as unfit for use by the navy, and commissioners examining the bills found a £601 discrepancy in his invoices. In April 1695, during an inquiry into alleged bribery by directors of the East India Company, his name appeared on company documents as having received three small sums, but, as he engaged in overseas trade, this was probably insignificant. In a list of placemen he was described as 'a commissioner of excise, who by melting down the milled money, loans at the Exchequer and remitting our money to Holland has got above £50,000'. He also held securities in trust for foreign investors in English funds, thereby allowing them to evade taxes.[7]

Evance was re-elected after a contest at Bridport in 1695 and continued to support the ministry. He was forecast as likely to support the government in the division of 31 Jan. 1696 on the proposed council of trade, signed the Association in the following month and voted in March for fixing the price of guineas at 22s. However, his loyalty was insufficient to prevent him joining with other goldsmiths in the attack on credit, aimed at destroying the Bank of England. On 15 May 1696 he was summoned before the lords justices and warned against augmenting the government's financial difficulties. He voted for the attainder of Sir John Fenwick† on 25 Nov. 1696, and in the same month (21 Nov.) the Commons read a petition of Sir Francis Wyndham, 3rd Bt.*, complaining that Evance stood upon his privilege and refused to pay £3,000 which had been lodged in his hands. After a debate the House gave the two parties a week to settle the matter, and nothing further was done. A somewhat similar petition from Sir Thomas Peshall, 3rd Bt., concerning £1,400, was presented on 20 Jan. 1697, but despite two orders for Evance to attend to answer the petition the affair petered out. He was also ordered into custody on 25 Jan. for being absent from a call of the House, but was released the following day.[8]

When he succeeded Sir Francis Child* in May 1697 as jeweller to the King, Evance's career seemed to have attained a peak of success. However, as he controlled one of the private syndicates upon which the government depended for financing the war in Flanders, he stood to lose valuable contracts to the Bank of England which, having some of this business transferred to it by the Treasury, was undermining the importance of men like Evance in government finance. Moreover, the following autumn there was more trouble for him in the excise commission. Three members of the board, Edward Clarke*, John Danvers and Thomas Everard, presented to the Treasury a memorial concerning alleged mismanagement. The other commissioners, including Evance, responded with their own report, accusing Danvers and Everard of Jacobitism. The dispute went a stage further in February 1698 when a Tory Member of Parliament, Sir Thomas Dyke, at the instigation of Danvers and Clarke, urged one Thomas Webb to bring in prosecutions against Evance and some other commissioners, telling Webb that 'they had done ill offices to some worthy gentlemen by giving false information'. The grounds of the complaint were that while already on the Excise Board they had been appointed to the commission for leather duties but had failed to retake the oaths. The threat of prosecution led to the introduction of a bill on 2 Apr. to extend the time for such people to qualify themselves. It passed the Commons but was rejected by the Lords as unnecessary, since all those concerned had taken the oaths when first appointed to the excise commission. Although Evance survived this crisis, ministers no longer valued his financial support enough to wish to continue him on the Board, and he was eventually removed in the following July. Indeed by this time he had ceased to make loans to government, his share in public finance taking the form of contracts for providing money overseas. He nevertheless kept his places as commissioner for wine licences, with a salary of £250, and as jeweller to the King.[9]

Evance did not stand in 1698, but was listed as a placeman in July and as a Court supporter 'left out' of the new Parliament. Although his political career was now at an end, he continued to be involved in public life and occasionally made use of Parliament to further his aims. On 26 May 1701 he was one of a number of men who petitioned for a bill to incorporate a company to manufacture woollen goods 'perfect and true according to the laws and statutes in being', through raising a voluntary subscription of £1,000,000. In the 1705 Parliament he pursued a claim for the recovery of £1,482 which had been owed to him and his associate Henry Cornish* since 1691: a restitution bill was introduced by Edward Strode on 1 Dec. 1705 which gained the Royal Assent on 16 Feb. following. Evance continued to be active as a banker and trader, and in 1700 he resumed the governorship of the Hudson's Bay Company, his cash advances helping to carry the company through the difficult opening years of the new war. He also engaged in some private trading on his own account with Governor Thomas Pitt I*, with whom he had been in regular correspondence from at least 1702. He later became one of Pitt's trustees in England, and when the young Robert Pitt* was sent back to England from Madras entrusted with his father's great diamond, it was Evance who met him as he disembarked in London. Evance was for a time custodian of the diamond, which he kept in a trunk at his shop in Lombard Street. He was to show the same service to Pitt in later years, guarding numerous jewels and advising on their relative value and demand. During Anne's reign Evance ceased all part in government funding and went into a speculative type of insurance, providing cover for merchants. This proved disastrous. By 1707 Pitt was hearing rumours of financial difficulties, and his son removed all his jewels from Evance's care after learning that the latter was not only in 'suspicious circumstances' but, perhaps encouraged by these financial difficulties, was insisting on a 5 per cent 'East India' commission on the sale of the jewels. Evance's finances were further strained when, having offered surety to Sir Thomas Littleton, 3rd Bt.*, he was obliged to pay £13,000 to Littleton's widow to satisfy a deficit in accounts due from Littleton's cashier, William Hubbald, and had to depend upon the sale of the latter's estates to recover the money. At the beginning of January 1712 Evance was declared bankrupt 'for above £100,000': Ailesbury commented that 'as ill got money never thrives, he broke . . . by grasping at too much'. On 5 Mar. 1712, no longer being able 'to keep shop', Evance shot himself in the temple, or, according to one report, hanged himself, at the house of Sir Caesar Child, who had married his niece, Hester. One of his numerous creditors, the Hudson's Bay Company, which had often depended upon advances from him, claimed £844 from his estate but was initially only able to recover £11. However, in 1719 Evance's trustees discovered that he had held £500 in Company stock in his own name, together with an additional £3,574 in stock held in trust for him by Thomas Lake, the son of the Company's Governor. In this way Evance was able to leave a substantial estate to pass to his niece.[10]

[1] *Original Lists of Persons of Quality* . . . ed. J. Camden Hotten, 84; *Le Neve's Knights* (Harl. Soc. viii), 435. [2] Goldsmiths' Hall, apprenticeship bk. 2, f. 182; apprenticeship and freedom index; *Wardens and Members of Ct. of Goldsmiths' Co.* 2; *Cal. Treas. Bks.* ix. 718. [3] *Cal. Treas. Bks.* ix. 273, 817; x. 3; xii. 120; xvi. 424; xviii. 456; *CSP Dom.* 1698, p. 366; Luttrell, *Brief Relation*, iv. 228; Boyer, *Anne Annals*, iv. 126; Pittis, *Present Parl.* 349. [4] *CSP Dom.* 1690-1, pp. 422, 522; 1691-2, pp. 3, 112; *Sel. Charters*, 239; E. E. Rich, *Hudson's Bay Co. Bk. of Letters Outward* (Hudson's Bay Rec. Soc. xx), 292. [5] *CSP Col.* 1574-1660, pp. 370, 404; *Ailesbury Mems.* 241-2; E. E. Rich, *Hudson's Bay Co. 1670-1870* (Hudson's Bay Rec. Soc. xxi), 154, 187, 191, 229, 461, 462; P. G. M. Dickson, *Financial Revol.* 491. [6] Rich, *Hudson's Bay Co. 1670-1870*, 100; F. G. Hilton Price, *London Bankers*, 128; *Cal. Treas. Bks.* ix. 40, 123, 366, 419, 595, 817, 1184, 1759; x. 3, 28-29, 205, 222, 424, 1376-7; xvii. 577, 586, 596; *CSP Dom.* 1690-1, pp. 485, 505-6, 522; *CSP Col.* 1693-6, pp. 246-7, 266, 427. [7] Luttrell, ii. 566; *CSP Dom.* 1691-2, p. 437; 1694-5, pp. 179-81, 186; 1696-7, pp. 10, 17-18, 141; BL, Verney mss mic. 636/44, John Verney* (Visct. Fermanagh), to Sir Ralph Verney, 1st Bt.†, 12. Nov. 1693; Dickson, 252. [8] Centre Kentish Stud. Stanhope mss U1590/059/5, Robert Yard* to Alexander Stanhope, 24 Nov. 1696. [9] *CSP Dom.* 1696, pp. 178-9; 1698, p. 207; Luttrell, iv. 143, 173, 228; *Cal. Treas. Bks.* xiii. 18-19, 25, 29-31; *Cal. Treas. Pprs.* 1697-1702, p. 161; *HMC Lords*, n.s. iii. 223-4; Yale Univ. Beinecke Lib. Biscoe-Maunsell newsletters 9 Apr. 1698; Univ. Kansas Spencer Research Lib. Lowther mss, deposition of Thomas Webb, 18 May 1698. [10] *HMC Lords*, n.s. vi. 388; ix. 104; *Cal. Treas. Pprs.* 1705-6, p. 675; C110/28, Evance to Thomas Pitt, 11 Aug. 1702, 11 Jan. 1703, c. Jan. 1705; Rich, *Hudson's Bay Co. Bk. of Letters Outward*, 292, 340, 358, 375-6, 461-2, 467-8; Rich, *Hudson's Bay Co. 1670-1870*, 468; *HMC Fortescue*, i. 5, 26, 30, 33, 64; *Swift Stella* ed. Davis, 462; Add. 22851, ff. 123-8; 22852, f. 11v; *Brit. Mercury*, 5-7 Mar. 1712.

P.W./H.J.L.

EVELYN, George I (1641–99), of Ventris House, Nutfield, and Rooksnest, Tandridge, Surr.

BLETCHINGLEY 1679 (Mar.)–1681 (Mar.)
GATTON 5 Nov. 1696–1698

b. 4 Dec. 1641, 4th s. of Sir John Evelyn† of Godstone, Surr. by Thomasine, da. of William Heynes of Chessington, Surr. *educ.* M. Temple 1657, called 1664; Christ Church, Oxf. matric. 1658; Padua 1664. *m.* (1) 8 Sept. 1664, Mary (*d.* 1673), da. of Richard Longley of Coulsdon, Surr., *s.p.*; (2) 13 June 1673, Margaret (*d.* 1683), da. and coh. of William Webb of Throckmorton Street, London, 3s. 5 da. (1 *d.v.p.*); (3) 15 Aug. 1684, Frances (*d.* 1730), da. of Andrew Bromhall of Stoke Newington, Mdx., 2s. 1 da. *d.v.p. suc.* fa. Jan. 1664, bro. 10 Aug. 1671.[1]

A descendant of the less celebrated Godstone branch of the Evelyn family, George Evelyn was nevertheless blessed with a considerable inheritance founded on his great-grandfather's gunpowder works. Evelyn's irresponsible elder brother, Sir John, 1st Bt., had inflicted great harm on the entailed Godstone estate by the time George succeeded to it in 1671, but this setback did not hinder his political advancement. The manor of Godstone, an Evelyn possession since Elizabethan times, had long enabled his predecessors to influence elections at nearby Bletchingley, and George, emulating his father's success, gained three electoral victories there between 1679 and 1681. An Exclusionist, he predictably failed to gain re-election at the contest of 1685, but his equally poor showing in 1690 must be attributed to a growing antipathy between Evelyn and fellow Whig Sir Robert Clayton*, the influential owner of the manor of Bletchingley. This rivalry largely determined Evelyn's subsequent parliamentary career, for, unlike the Evelyns of Wotton, his political influence was confined to the immediate locality.[2]

Indeed, it was only through the mediation of his kinsman John Evelyn of Wotton, the diarist, that George became a deputy-lieutenant for Surrey. In the spring of 1694 the diarist assured the lord lieutenant, the Duke of Norfolk, of Evelyn's 'abilities and fitness', but both the Duke and Sir Richard Onslow, 3rd Bt.*, still insisted, as a condition of Evelyn's promotion, that the elderly and much respected George Evelyn† of Wotton be continued as a deputy-lieutenant. In August of that year Evelyn had a chance to thank his kinsman in person when the latter visited Nutfield, on the occasion of which the diarist paid tribute to Evelyn's teeming household of ten children, the offspring of 'two most extraordinary beautiful wives'.[3]

At the Bletchingley election of 1695 Evelyn had another opportunity to test his local interest against that of Sir Robert Clayton when the City magnate backed the youthful Maurice Thompson* and the sitting MP, Thomas Howard*. The strength of Evelyn's support within Bletchingley was revealed by the number of block votes registered for himself and Howard, and at the end of polling he stood a clear second, 11 votes ahead of Thompson. However, the returning officer, clearly acting on Clayton's orders, disqualified over half of Evelyn's votes and returned Thompson alongside the outright victor, Howard. Evelyn's petition against the return was read by the House on 25 Nov. and saw initial success when the elections committee reported on 5 Feb. 1696 against Thompson. However, the House then ordered that the case be heard a second time, and Thompson's return was upheld on 18 Feb. after a division. Evelyn was soon presented with an opportunity for revenge when, on the elevation of Thompson's father (Sir John, 1st Bt.*) to a peerage in May 1696, a by-election was called for nearby Gatton. Backed by the considerable support of Thomas Turgis*, the proprietor of the manor of Gatton, and of Sir Richard Onslow, Evelyn managed to secure his return after a closely contested poll on 5 Nov. However, he then had to reappear before the elections committee to rebuff the claims of John South, the Thompson candidate, and it was not until after the committee's report on 15 Dec. that his seat in the House was finally secure.

Although territorial rivalry clearly contributed to these divisions between fellow Whigs, Court and Country tensions were also evident, and in the subsequent sessions Evelyn was identified as one of the ministry's opponents. Even before he knew the outcome of the appeal against his return at Gatton, Evelyn had voted on 25 Nov. 1696 against the attainder of Sir John Fenwick†. He acted as a teller on 3 Mar. 1697 to block an amendment concerning an additional duty on cider, and was named to the drafting committee on a bill to prevent the export of wool. In the next session he was granted a leave of absence on 7 Jan. 1698 to attend to one of his sons, who was said to be 'very ill', and he subsequently guided through the House a bill to curb house-breaking. There is no evidence to suggest that he tried to secure a seat at either Gatton or Bletchingley at the election of 1698, but a political observer, when comparing the new Parliament with its predecessor, confirmed Evelyn's Country sympathies.

Illness may have influenced Evelyn's decision to avoid re-election, but his sudden death, 'of an apoplexy', in June 1699 clearly took his relatives by surprise. His final will was only drawn up on the day of his demise, and the settlement contained therein had been so hastily arranged that a private Act had to be passed in 1704 to ensure that his wishes could be carried out. He bequeathed a sizable estate to his eldest son John I*, but also left as much as £4,500 to be shared between four of his other children. John and two of Evelyn's younger sons, George Evelyn II* and William Glanville† (formerly Evelyn), all followed their father's example by entering Parliament.[4]

[1] Manning and Bray, *Surr.* ii. 328; *Misc. Gen. and Her.* ser. 2, iv. 337–9. [2] J. Aubrey, *Surr.* iii. 88; U. Lambert, *Godstone*, 264–5. [3] BL, Evelyn mss, letterbk. 2, p. 173, John Evelyn to George Evelyn†, 28 Mar. 1694; *Evelyn Diary*, v. 169–70, 187. [4] *Post Boy*, 20–22 June 1699; *Evelyn Diary*, v. 333; PCC 20 Dyer.

P. L. G.

EVELYN, George II (1678–1724), of St. Giles-in-the-Fields, London, and Rooksnest, Tandridge, Surr.

BLETCHINGLEY 1705–18 Oct. 1724

b. 26 Oct. 1678, 2nd s. of George Evelyn I* by 2nd w., and bro. of John Evelyn I* and half-bro. of William Glanville† (formerly Evelyn). *m.* (1) 4 Aug. 1701, Rebecca Rollinson (*d.* 1703), of Covent Garden, Mdx., *s.p.*; (2) 26 Feb. 1707, Anne (*d.* 1716), da. of Hon. Robert Paston, bro. of Ld. Paston (Charles*), *s.p.*; (3) settlement 22 Aug. 1720, Mary (*d.* 1738), da. of Thomas Garth of Morden, Surr., 3 da. *suc.* bro. 8 Nov. 1702.

Clerk of Bd. of Green Cloth to Prince of Wales 1716–*d.*[1]

Evelyn's entrance into public life was aided by the premature death of his childless elder brother John I* in November 1702, which saw him inherit the family's Godstone estate at the age of 24. His first major task was to resolve the ambiguities surrounding his father's will, the terms of which did not give Evelyn's siblings any power to raise the substantial sums which their father had bequeathed to them. A petition requesting Parliament's aid in this matter was read in the House on 14 Jan. 1704, and within a few months a private Act to settle the estate had been secured, guided through the House by Thomas Onslow*, Evelyn's eventual electoral partner. Evelyn was then able to follow up this success by gaining a seat at nearby Bletchingley at the election of 1705, a victory facilitated by his ownership of several burgages in the town.

Although he voted for the Whig candidates at the subsequent county poll, in the House itself Evelyn initially betrayed rather different political sympathies. One analyst described him as a 'Churchman' at the outset of the Parliament, and he subsequently voted on 25 Oct. against the Court in the division on the Speakership. However, he established himself within Whig ranks in the course of that Parliament, acting as teller on 10 Feb. 1707 to block a High Tory instruction to the committee reviewing a bill for the security of the Church of England. He was accordingly identified as a Whig by two parliamentary lists of early 1708, and in the succeeding Parliament proved his party loyalty by voting in early 1709 in favour of naturalizing the poor Palatines, and by supporting the impeachment of Dr Sacheverell a year later. The entrance of John Evelyn II* into Parliament in December 1708 obscures George's activity, although as the more experienced Member he is more likely to have acted as a teller on 24 Feb. 1709 to defeat a motion to adjourn the House, thereby ensuring that a bill to naturalize foreign Protestants was heard. His only certain appearances in the Journals during the 1708 Parliament concerned a predictable nomination to the drafting committee on the Surrey land registry bill, and the grant of a leave of absence on 1 Feb. 1710.[2]

Evelyn's first experience of a contested election came in October 1710, but the strength of his local interest, when combined with the influence of his running-mate Thomas Onslow*, ensured that he did not suffer the disappointment experienced by other Whig candidates in Surrey and elsewhere. Having been cited as a Whig in the 'Hanover list' of the 1710 Parliament, he voted against the French commerce bill in June 1713. Two months later he had to fight off another Tory challenge at Bletchingley, and in the ensuing session rallied to the Whig cause by voting on 18 Mar. 1714 against the expulsion of Richard Steele. His Whig allegiance, confirmed by three parliamentary lists at the outset of the George I's reign, was subsequently rewarded by a post in the Prince of Wales's household. He was prepared to follow Prince George into opposition in 1717, a loyalty which his royal master acknowledged in October 1724 after news of Evelyn's death had reached Leicester House. Dying 'of a spotted fever after many days' illness', he left no will and only three young daughters to succeed him. The entailed Godstone estate thus passed to his younger brother Edward, who, in 1734, sold it for £24,000 to Charles Boone†, an East Indiaman who had married Evelyn's widow.[3]

[1] IGI, London; U. Lambert, *Godstone*, 292. [2] U. Lambert, *Bletchingley*, 541–3; *Surr. Poll of 1705*. [3] BL, Evelyn mss, diary of (Sir) John Evelyn II*, 20 Oct. 1724; Lambert, *Godstone*, 295.

P. L. G.

EVELYN, John I (1677–1702), of Rooksnest, Tandridge, Surr.

BLETCHINGLEY 18 July–13 Nov. 1702

b. 3 Oct. 1677, 1st s. of George Evelyn I*; bro. of George Evelyn II* and half-bro. of William Glanville† (formerly Evelyn). ?*m.* lic. 5 May 1701, Anne, da. and coh. of John Glynne of Ash, Surr. *s.p. suc.* fa. 19 June 1699.

Succeeding to 'a fair estate' at the age of 21, Evelyn had bright prospects which were destined never to be fully realized. Following the example of both his grandfather and father, he managed to secure a seat in an uncontested election at Bletchingley, the borough adjoining the familial estate at Godstone. He was to sit for such a brief period in the House that his politics remain uncertain, although the Evelyns of Godstone were clearly Whiggish in outlook and the borough, under the lordship of Sir Robert Clayton*, had been a Whig preserve since the Revolution. En route to Westminster he visited his kinsman John Evelyn, the diarist, who described him as 'a young and very hopeful gentleman'. However, within three weeks of the opening of his first session and before he had had any opportunity to make his mark in the House, Evelyn died of smallpox on 13 Nov.

Evelyn's premature death not only obscures his political outlook, but also helps to fuel speculation concerning his possible marriage to Anne Glynne 'of Haslemere'. Although a marriage licence was taken out, all secondary sources suggest that both Evelyn and his potential bride died unmarried. Evelyn clearly left no issue, for his family's entailed estate passed to his younger brother George, who, in 1705, also succeeded to his seat at Bletchingley.[1]

[1] U. Lambert, *Godstone*, 291; H. Evelyn, *Hist. Evelyn Fam.* 218–19; *Misc. Gen. and Her.* ser. 2, iv. 338–9; BL, Evelyn mss 219, f. 34, travel diary; *London Mar. Lic.* ed. Foster, 462; Manning and Bray, *Surr.* iii. 72–73.

P. L. G.

EVELYN, John II (1682–1763), of Wotton, Surr., and St. James's, Westminster.

HELSTON 15 Dec. 1708–1710

b. 2 Mar. 1682, 2nd but o. surv. s. of John Evelyn of Deptford, Kent by Martha, da. and coh. of Richard Spencer of London. *educ.* French sch. (Greenwich) 1689, Kings St. (Mr Arbuthnot) 1691, Eton 1692–8, Balliol, Oxf. matric. 1699. *m.* 18 Sept. 1705, Anne (*d.* 1752), da. of Edward Boscawen† of Worthevale, Cornwall and sis. of Hugh Boscawen II*, 6s. (3 *d.v.p.*) 3 da. (1 *d.v.p.*). *suc.* gdfa. 27 Feb. 1706; *cr.* Bt. 6 Aug. 1713.[1]

Receiver of stamp duties 1703–Aug. 1708; commr. prizes 1705–Aug. 1708; jt. postmaster gen. Aug. 1708–15; commr. customs 1721–?1763.[2]

FRS 1722.

Eagerly monitored for signs of genius, Evelyn's early progress became a near obsession for his grandfather and namesake, the celebrated diarist. When Evelyn's father was appointed as a commissioner of the Irish revenue in Dublin, 'little Jack' was sent to Eton in the hope that 'he may be a man useful and ornamental to his country'. However, after the death of his father in 1699, Evelyn became the heir apparent to the Wotton estate, 'one of the best compacted in Surrey', and from that time onwards his social advancement became the diarist's absolute priority. Able to count among his playfellows the offspring of such notable families as the Boscawens and Godolphins, Evelyn had considerable prospects, a view endorsed by Samuel Pepys, who commended the diarist in December 1701 on the abilities of 'your excellent grandson'. Despite such obvious talents, the sheer momentum of Evelyn's early career in public office was only sustained by the patronage of Lord Treasurer Godolphin (Sidney†), a close family friend whom the diarist had bombarded with notices of Evelyn's precocity. Although it took several years of patient negotiation before arrangements were finalized for Evelyn's betrothal to the Treasurer's niece, the wedding, in September 1705, effectively secured the future of the Wotton estate.[3]

From the moment he entered public life, Evelyn appeared content to pursue a career as a government official, betraying an aversion to party politics which closely mirrored the outlook of his mentor. The diarist had taken great care to set down guidelines for his grandson's future conduct in office, and Evelyn's subsequent electoral career largely accorded with his advice 'to be diligent, impartial, studying how to serve the country who chose you and to which you are in conscience to be accountable'. Most significantly, the diarist admonished him to seek electoral success 'without affectation and vainglory . . . or the being carried away by a faction or to serve a party'. Evelyn adhered to this tenet at the Surrey election of 1705, when, in protest against the corrupt methods employed by the Whig financier Sir William Scawen*, he led his family's tenants to poll for the Tory Edward Harvey*. He was fortunate that this action did not sour his relationship with his patron Godolphin, and in the course of his subsequent career Evelyn clearly learnt to pay greater heed to the wishes of his political masters. However, he found that he could not completely distance himself from politics, and even so notorious a figure as Scawen had claims on Evelyn's favour, for Evelyn had been welcomed at Scawen's Haversham estate while attending Eton. Evelyn's friendship with the Finches of Albury rendered him equally susceptible to Tory overtures, but it was Scawen who managed to secure the Wotton interest at the Surrey election of 1708. In the run-up to that contest, Scawen gave some indication of the extensive local influence which the lords of the manor of Wotton enjoyed when informing Evelyn that the town of Dorking 'would very willingly wait on you to the election'.[4]

It was only through a by-election at Helston, the pocket borough dominated by his patron Godolphin, that Evelyn actually gained entrance to Parliament. Having recently been advanced to the lucrative position of postmaster-general, 'one of the most desirable offices there is, both for credit and advantage', Evelyn no doubt took up the seat at the request of the Lord Treasurer. The parliamentary presence of his namesake George Evelyn II* adds confusion to the task of delineating his activity at Westminster, but it is clear that he remained on the back benches. Just as inevitably, he supported the Whigs in early 1709 over the naturalization of the poor Palatines, and then voted in favour of Sacheverell's impeachment a year later. However, he remained characteristically cautious when discussing the great issue of the war on 25 Feb. 1710, remarking to his brother-in-law Boscawen, 'there is very good reason at all times to suspect the intentions of the French, but as long as the negotiations for peace retard not the preparations for an early campaign, we are safe enough'.[5]

At the time of the subsequent general election he appeared more perturbed by the possible loss of his postmastership than of his seat, one of his correspondents finding him 'so indifferent whether you sit in the House or not'. Fortunately for Evelyn, he did manage to retain his office under the new ministry, but there is no evidence to suggest that he mounted any campaign to secure Helston. However, he could not ignore the bitter contest fought between the electoral combatants in Surrey throughout the summer of 1710. In the race to obtain the Wotton interest, Scawen again proved successful, although Evelyn actually confessed to another candidate, his Tory friend Hon. Heneage Finch II*, that it was 'so much my inclination' to back him. Support for Scawen was undoubtedly politically dangerous, and early in 1711 came reports that the Tory Francis Gwyn* was to become postmaster-general. Evelyn survived, and at the next general election was much more openly committed to the Surrey Tories, for he attended one of their election meetings as early as January 1713, some eight months in advance of the actual poll. This switch of allegiance may have been heavily influenced by renewed speculation concerning his postmastership, the cares of office having been no doubt increased by the loss of a 'never-enough-to-be-lamented friend and benefactor' with the death of Lord Godolphin in September 1712. On the day of the poll itself Evelyn rode to Guildford at the head of some 100 freeholders, but was unable to prevent the return of the Whig grandee Sir Richard Onslow, 3rd Bt.*[6]

Even though Evelyn chose to remain in exile from the parliamentary arena, he continued to gain public recognition, capping his high-flying career with a baronetcy in July 1713. Typically, he recorded in his diary that the honour only came to his attention when reading a newspaper and that it was granted 'against my desire'. As postmaster, he was later ideally placed to record the events at court during the final days of Queen Anne, although he was also indebted to his family friend, Lord Chancellor Harcourt (Simon I*), for supplying information concerning her deteriorating condition. In consideration of his connexions with the Oxford (Robert Harley*) administration, Evelyn could expect little favour under the new dynasty, and within a few months had been dismissed from the Post Office. In December 1717 he sought to resurrect his parliamentary career at a Surrey by-election, but failed to overcome the Onslow interest. Not until 1721 did he regain ministerial favour under Walpole, but then managed to retain his new office at the Customs Board until 'a short time before his death' in 1763, a longevity based on his professionalism as well as his accommodating attitude towards successive administrations.[7]

Away from office, Evelyn's energies were principally directed towards scholarly interests and the improvement of the Wotton estate. It was thus entirely appropriate that his most notable personal achievement was the construction of a private library at Wotton to house the collections built up by three generations of Evelyn bibliophiles. Lord Egmont (John Perceval†), with whom Evelyn was on familiar terms, thought him 'a sober and religious man and of modest behaviour', adding that he found him 'a good scholar'. Two of his sons, John† and William†, emulated their father by representing Helston in Parliament, the latter of whom raised a monument to his deceased parents, extolling their virtues as 'worthy the imitation of posterity'.[8]

[1] BL, Evelyn mss 279, travel diary; PCC 377 Caesar; H. Evelyn, *Hist. Evelyn Fam.* 156–9; *Evelyn Diary*, iv. 189. [2] *Cal. Treas. Bks.* xviii. 95, xx. 314. [3] Evelyn mss 667, 685, 1690; *Private Corresp. of Samuel Pepys* ed. Tanner, ii. 242; W. G. Hiscock, *John Evelyn and*

His Circle, 227–36. [4] J. Evelyn, *Memoirs for my Grandson* ed. G. Keynes, pp. 32–33; *Evelyn Diary*, v. 595; Evelyn mss 326–7, 667; Evelyn mss, Scawen to Evelyn, 17 Apr. 1708. [5] *Cal. Treas. Bks.* xxii. 372; Evelyn mss, Anne Evelyn to Mrs. Evelyn, 13 Sept. 1708, Evelyn to Boscawen, 25 Feb. 1710. [6] Evelyn mss, Samuel Thomson to Evelyn, 10, 24 Oct. 1710, Evelyn to Finch, 26 July 1710; diary of John Evelyn II, 29 Jan., 9 Sept. 1713; *Scots Courant*, 8–10 Jan. 1711; Add. 15949, ff. 50–51. [7] Evelyn mss, diary of John Evelyn II, 27 July 1713, 29 July 1714; *Cal. Treas. Bks.* xxix. 390; Manning and Bray, *Surr.* ii. 152. [8] J. Aubrey, *Surr.* iv. 125; *HMC Egmont Diary*, ii. 486; Manning and Bray, 156.

P. L. G.

EVERSFIELD, Charles (1683–1749), of Denne Place, nr. Horsham, Suss.

HORSHAM	1705–1710
SUSSEX	1710–1713
HORSHAM	1713–16 June 1715, 12 June 1721–1741
STEYNING	1741–1747

b. 15 Sept. 1683, o. s. of Nicholas Eversfield† of Charlton Court, nr. Steyning, Suss. by Elizabeth, da. and h. of Nicholas Gildridge of Eastbourne, Suss. *m.* (1) 21 July 1702, Mary, da. and h. of Henry Duncombe of Weston, Surr., 1s. 4da.; (2) 9 Aug. 1731, Henrietta Maria, da. and coh. of Charles Scarborough of Windsor, Berks., wid. of Sir Robert Jenkinson, 3rd Bt.*, *s.p.* 2 da. illegit. *suc.* fa. 1684; uncle Anthony Eversfield† at Denne 1695.[1]

Paymaster and treasurer of Ordnance 1712–14.[2]

Eversfield was the representative of the cadet branch of the Eversfield family of Sussex, and inherited from his uncle the estate of Denne and a number of burgages carrying an electoral interest in Horsham. Taking the first opportunity after coming of age, he successfully contested the borough in 1705, when his return was classed as a 'loss' by Lord Sunderland (Charles, Lord Spencer*) and he was also listed as a 'Churchman'. He voted against the Court candidate for Speaker on 25 Oct. 1705, and was relatively inconspicuous in his first Parliament. Marked as a Tory in a list of early 1708, he was returned again for Horsham in the election of that year. He acted as a teller on 8 Mar. 1709 against the election of the Duke of Marlborough's (John Churchill†) protégé, Thomas Meredyth*, for Midhurst and voted against the impeachment of Dr Sacheverell in 1710.[3]

In 1710, he was returned for both Horsham and Sussex, choosing to sit for the county, and was classed as a Tory in the 'Hanover list'. In this Parliament Eversfield achieved a certain prominence as one of the spokesmen for the October Club. On 5 February 1711 he was reported as saying that

> unless Mr Harley [Robert*] made further discoveries (which if he pleased he would) they must believe that a great man in the late ministry (meaning [Lord] Godolphin [Sidney†]) and a great man in this (meaning Harley) were to direct this House what they were to do in these matters.

On 17 Feb. the club persuaded the House, against the wishes of the ministry, to bring in a bill to appoint a new commission of accounts, Eversfield being named to the drafting committee. On 19 Feb. he raised the question of the disputed election at Carlisle at the request of the defeated candidate, Colonel Gledhill, and complained that the Whig victor, (Sir) James Montagu I, had written and circulated a letter to promote his election, which Eversfield thought, 'reflected on her Majesty's honour'. When the debate was resumed on 14 Mar. Eversfield told in favour of a motion condemning the bishop of Carlisle for circulating Montagu's letter. On 2 Apr. he was involved in a quarrel with Robert Walpole II*:

> Mr Walpole and Mr Eversfield ... were very near a duel for a thing that happened in the House. A young Member [rose] to speak. Mr Walpole, being very attentive, looked earnestly in his face, for which offence Mr Eversfield told him he was very impudent ... Mr Walpole went out without returning any answer and Mr Eversfield followed, but their friends interposed and reconciled them without any bloodletting.

On 18 Apr. Eversfield told in favour of surplus revenue raised by the Post Office going to public use. His election on 20 Apr. as one of the commissioners to carry out the provisions of the resumption of grants bill was another success for the October Club, although the subsequent defeat of the bill in the Lords prevented his acting. Divisions within the October Club were highlighted on 28 Apr. in the debate on a report into the arrears of the imprest accountants. Eversfield and other hard-liners wanted Lord Godolphin to be named in an address criticizing the late government, and were against adjourning consideration of the report on the arrears of the imprest accountants (Eversfield acting as a teller on the latter), but on both counts were defeated by more moderate Octobrists. William Pittis dedicated his account of parliamentary proceedings in this session to Eversfield, who was listed among the 'worthy patriots' responsible for detecting the mismanagements of the previous administration. Boyer included him among the leaders of the October Club.[4]

Eversfield was the recipient of Lord Oxford's (Robert Harley) favour in June 1711 in the form of an office for a friend, but this did not prevent him from challenging the ministry for some months into the next session. On 7 Dec. 1711 it was reported that Eversfield was the only member of the October Club to speak against the Whig motion of 'No Peace without Spain', and he added a warning to the government, saying, according to L'Hermitage that: 'il ne voulait pas insister sur cette clause, sa Majesté n'ayant pas demandé leur avis, mais qu'il était sur qu'aucun membre de la chambre n'entendait par là que les ministres seraient mis à couvert de faire une méchante paix'. When Oxford managed to persuade some October Club Tories to postpone the introduction of an occasional conformity bill, Eversfield refused to acquiesce, and in December joined the Earl of Nottingham (Daniel Finch†) in attempting to force through such a bill. The next year, on 25 Jan. 1712, Eversfield was one of the members of the October Club to support the attack on the Duke of Marlborough, which followed the report of the commissioners of accounts' inquiry into the captain-general's accounts. On 19 Feb. he told in favour of the expulsion of Marlborough's secretary, Adam de Cardonnel*, and on 25 Feb. supported Henry Campion's proposal that Marlborough repay the 2.5 per cent he had retained on the army's pay. Harley needed the support of the October Club to secure the peace and to this end ministerialists co-operated when members of the club, led by Eversfield, accused the allies of not bearing their fair share of the burden of war: on 4 Feb. Eversfield spoke in the debate on the treaties with the allies and on 5 Feb. was a teller for the motion that the Dutch had failed to provide a full quota of forces. On 7 Feb. he was a teller in favour of passing the Scots toleration bill and also told on 12 Feb. against putting the question of giving further consideration to the Queen's Speech. On 21 Feb. he led the club's attack on supply, ostensibly to the surprise of Secretary St. John (Henry II*), who blamed the need for more funds on the commitments made by the Godolphin administration and the failures of the allies. The growing accord between the October Club and the ministry was hastened by the defection of a minority to form the pro-Hanoverian March Club, which expressly excluded Eversfield from membership on the grounds that at one meeting of the October Club he had introduced Secretary St. John and Chancellor of the Exchequer Robert Benson*. Despite this, on 21 Apr., a day St. John was absent from the House, Eversfield was one of the proponents of the October Club's measure of tacking a bill to inquire into crown grants onto a supply bill, thereby endangering the latter. In early April a memorial defending the allies' record was printed in the *Daily Courant*, reportedly provoking Eversfield to utter threats of violence against the newspaper's proprietor. On 8 May he told for the Tories in the Steyning election dispute, and on the same day moved that John Houstoun* be given leave of absence. On the peace, Eversfield became one of the ministry's defenders and on 28 May spoke and told against the Whig motion condemning Ormond's failure to take offensive action against the French in Flanders. He also, on 10 June, supported John Hungerford's motion to censure the *Four Sermons* of Bishop Fleetwood of St. Asaph, which criticized the ministry. Eversfield's reward came in June 1712, when, as part of the ministry's policy of buying off the October men, he was appointed treasurer of the Ordnance.[5]

Before the next session, Eversfield was wounded in a duel with Lord Lumley (Richard*) but had recovered in time to help the Court with the passage through the House of the French commerce bill, for which he voted on 18 June 1713. In 1713 Eversfield once more contested Horsham successfully. On 9 Mar. 1714 he was named to the drafting committee for a bill to curb wool smuggling, the result of a local petition. On 15 Apr., during the debate on the Court motion that the Protestant succession was not in danger under the present government, he fulminated against both the Barrier Treaty and the allies. He also spoke in the debate on the committee's report the next day. A few days later, on 24 Apr., he was reported to be suffering from smallpox and was probably absent for the rest of the session. He was marked as a Tory on the Worsley list and on two other analyses comparing the Parliaments of 1713 and 1715.[6]

The accession of George 1 and the consequent change in the political climate threatened Eversfield's career: it was reported in August that he was courting the favour of the Dukes of Somerset and Argyll, and would not support his 1713 electoral partner, the Jacobite Tory Henry Campion: 'he declares he will keep his place if he can, and that he will not stir for Campion's election in the county of Sussex. Campion and he have had some high words upon that account.' However, Eversfield lost both parliamentary seat and office, and was threatened with prosecution for the recovery of £6,000 which he retained from the Ordnance. His accounts were finally passed in August 1718. Returning to the Commons in 1721, he changed his allegiance entirely and became a supporter of the Whig ministry. He died 17 Jan. 1749, leaving a substantial part of his estate, real and personal, to his natural daughters, Henrietta and Charlotta Forman.[7]

[1] *Suss. Gens. Horsham*, 96; 'Steyning par. reg. baptisms, 1565–1925' (Soc. of Geneal. trans.), 57. [2] *Cal. Treas. Bks.* xxvi. 336; xxix. 189. [3] W. Albery, *Parl. Hist. Horsham*, 42, 46–47. [4] G. Holmes, *Pol. in Age of Anne*, 342, 358; D. Szechi, *Jacobitism and Tory Pol.* 72,

77; *Huntington Lib. Q.* xxxiii. 159, 160, 161; Boyer, *Pol. State*, i–ii. 170; Cobbett, *Parlty. Hist.* vi. 1010, 1014; *Nicolson Diaries* ed. Jones and Holmes, 512–13; NSA, Kreienberg despatch 1 May 1711; *HMC Var.* viii. 251; Pittis, *Present Parl.* [5] Add. 70197, Eversfield to Oxford, 5 June 1711; 17677 EEE, ff. 391–2; Kreienberg despatches 11 Dec. 1711, 22, 29 Feb., 1, 22 Apr., 30 May, 13 June 1712; *Bull. IHR*, xxxiii. 225; BL, Trumbull Add. mss 136, Ralph Bridges* to Sir William Trumbull*, 25 Jan. 1711/12; Szechi, 106–8; *Huntington Lib. Q.* 165, 166–9; *Scots Courant*, 8–11 Feb. 1712; *Letters of Burnet to Duckett* ed. Nichol Smith, 6. [6] Folger Shakespeare Lib. Newdigate newsletter 25 Oct. 1712; Chandler, v. 41; Douglas diary (Hist. of Parl. trans.), 15 Apr. 1714; NLS, Advocates' mss, Wodrow pprs. letters Quarto 8, ff. 95–96; *HMC Portland*, v. 430. [7] *Swift Corresp.* ed. Williams, ii. 121; *Cal. Treas. Bks.* xxix. 189, 248, 268, 303, 307, 339, 749; xxx. 1, 403, 560; *Gent. Mag.* 1749, p. 44; PCC 74 Greenly.

P. W./S. M. W.

EYLES, John (c.1683–1745), of London.

CHIPPENHAM   1713–1727
LONDON   1727–1734

b. c.1683, 2nd but 1st surv. s. of Sir Francis Eyles, 1st Bt., Haberdasher, of London by Elizabeth, prob. da. of Richard Alie, Draper, of London; nephew of (Sir) John Eyles†; bro. of Joseph Eyles†. *m*. by 1708, his cos. Mary (*d*. 1735), da. of Joseph Haskins Stiles*, 2s. (1 *d.v.p.*) 2da. (1 *d.v.p.*). *suc*. fa. as 2nd Bt. 24 May 1716.[1]

Dir. E.I. Co. 1710–14, 1717–21, Bank of Eng. 1715–17; freeman, Levant Co. by 1718; sub-gov. S. Sea Co. Jan. 1721–33; pres. St. Thomas' Hosp. 1737–*d*.[2]

Common councilman, London 1715–16, alderman 1716–*d*., sheriff 1719–20, ld. mayor 1726–7; master, Haberdashers' Co. 1716–17; steward, crown manor of Havering atte Bower, Essex by 1737.[3]

Commr. forfeited estates 1716–25; jt. post master-gen. 1739–*d*.

Eyles's father was the son of a Wiltshire mercer and woolstapler, but like his brother John† (originally a Dissenter) he made his fortune in London and rose to be an alderman of the City, becoming a director and governor of the Bank of England and finally, in 1714, a baronet. Sir Francis Eyles was one of the four Bank directors who in 1710, after the dismissal of Lord Sunderland (Charles, Lord Spencer*), made representations to the Queen of the dangers further ministerial alterations would hold for public credit. His son 'Jack' was entered early into business: in 1698, at only 15, he was able to subscribe £2,000 himself to the Old East India Company's advance loan. By 1710 he had become a director of the united company. Chosen again in the directorial elections of the following year, when he was a candidate on the Whig slate, he was returned to Parliament in 1713 at Chippenham, not far from the Eyles family estates in Wiltshire. A petition from the defeated Tory candidate was subsequently dropped. Eyles voted on 18 Mar. 1714 against the expulsion of Richard Steele*, and was a teller on 25 June in favour of adjourning the hearing of the Southwark election. He was also active from about this time in the Hanover Club in London, which organized the Whig effort at common council elections and in the elections to the major City committees. He was classed as a Whig in the Worsley list and in two comparative analyses of the 1713 and 1715 Parliaments. Eyles died on 11 Mar. 1745 and was buried in the family vault in St. Helen's, Bishopsgate.[4]

[1] Wright, *Essex*, ii. 440; *London Vis. Peds.* (Harl. Soc. xcii), 3; *St. Helen's Bishopsgate* (Harl. Soc. Reg. xxxi), 351, 355, 372; Beaven, *Aldermen*, i. 68, 123. [2] A. C. Wood, *Levant Co*. 137; J. Carswell, *S. Sea Bubble*, 231–2. [3] *Cal. Treas. Bks. and Pprs.* 1735–8, p. 386. [4] *HMC Portland*, iv. 545; Luttrell, *Brief Relation*, vi. 594; *Letters of Burnet to Duckett* ed. Nichol Smith, 50; Boyer, *Pol. State*, i–ii. 263; *London Politics 1713–17* (London Rec. Soc xvii), 11–44; *St. Helen's Bishopsgate* 378.

D. W. H.

EYRE, Gervase (1669–1704), of Rampton and Wheatley, Notts. and Sandbeck, Yorks.

NOTTINGHAMSHIRE   1698–1701 (Nov.)
                      1702–16 Feb. 1704

bap. 20 Aug. 1669, 1st s. of Anthony Eyre† of Rampton by 2nd w. Elizabeth, da. of Sir John Pakington, 2nd Bt.†, of Westwood, Worcs. *educ*. Christ Church, Oxf. matric. 1683; I. Temple 1686. *m*. 26 May 1687, Catherine, o. surv. da. and event. h. of Sir Henry Cooke, 2nd Bt., of Wheatley, 7s. (2 *d.v.p.*) 6da. (1 *d.v.p.*). *suc*. fa. Nov. 1671.[1]

Sheriff, Notts. 1696–7.
Ranger of Sherwood forest.[2]

The Eyres of Rampton were descended from a branch of a prominent Derbyshire family which became established at Laughton, Nottinghamshire. Eyre's great-grandfather sold some of the family's Yorkshire estates to Sir Edward Osborne† and bought a moiety of the manor of Rampton. The other moiety was obtained through the marriage of his grandfather, Sir Gervase Eyre†, to a coheiress of the Babington family.[3]

Apart from the fact that Eyre succeeded his father at the age of two, nothing is known about his early life. However, his status in the county was deemed sufficient to warrant his appointment as a deputy-lieutenant in 1692 and he served his turn as sheriff in 1697, when a warrant was issued permitting him to live outside the county. His political outlook at this time can be gauged from a series of letters he sent to the 2nd Marquess of Halifax (William Savile*), which, among other things, details his criticism of the county Members for Nottinghamshire during the last session of the 1695 Parliament, particularly in relation to their attitudes to a standing army and taxation. In one letter he referred to himself as a 'fellow huntsman' and in another revealed his prejudice against court life after attending a local gathering of courtiers in which he noted

> how unfit I was for court attendance, and when they talked of coming down every year they frightened me almost as bad as [sic] for fear they should debauch the county with formality, as he might fear they would disorder his family.

Eyre took comfort from this prospect: 'when I considered that it was said by courtiers, I recovered my spirits and believed there was no great danger of their performing their promise'.[4]

In the 1698 election Eyre joined with another young Tory, Sir Thomas Willoughby, 2nd Bt.*, to defeat the outgoing county Members by 'a great majority'. Unfortunately, his career in the Commons is obscured by the presence in the chamber of the Wiltshire Members John and Robert Eyre, most of the references to activity in the Journals being ascribed to the latter. Not surprisingly, given his criticisms of his predecessors, an analysis of September 1698 included him as a supporter of the Country party, and he was also forecast as likely to oppose a standing army. Although re-elected in January 1701, with the support of zealous Country Tories like Thomas Coke*, he seems to have lost his place in the county lieutenancy, perhaps because he had alienated prominent Whigs such as the Duke of Newcastle (John Holles†). He was listed as likely to support the Court in February 1701 over the 'Great Mortgage'. However, he refused to sign the Nottinghamshire address promoted to entice the King into a dissolution and perhaps as a consequence lost his seat at the December election after a concerted Whig campaign to keep him out. In January 1702 he wrote to his cousin, Sir John Pakington, 4th Bt.*: 'I should have been tempted to a petition, but the charge of it frightened me.' In the election of 1702, Willoughby refused to stand, allowing Eyre a clear run, which resulted in victory by over 1,000 votes. Judging from two recommendations for military employment that he signed early in Anne's reign, he maintained significant contacts with the Yorkshire and north country Tories, perhaps in consequence of the fact that he resided for part of the year at Sandbeck.[5]

Eyre died in London, probably from smallpox, on 16 Feb. 1704 and was buried in the chancel of All Saints', Rampton. A monument erected by one of his daughters bears an inscription extolling his conduct as 'having always been such as entitled him to the favour of all true friends of our Church and constitution' and including references to his ancestors' loyal service under Charles the Martyr.[6]

[1] Burke, *Commoners*, iv. 235; J. Hunter, *S. Yorks*. i. 289; info. from Dr D. F. Lemmings; IGI, Notts. [2] BL, Althorp mss, Halifax pprs. Eyre to Halifax, 3 Nov. [?1698]. [3] Hunter, 289. [4] *CSP Dom*. 1691–2, p. 277; 1696, p. 472; Halifax pprs. Eyre to Halifax, 8 Jan., 19 Mar. [1698], 21 Dec.; Huntington Lib. Hastings mss HA 6107, p. 42, Earl of Huntingdon to 'Mr Davys', 14 Aug. 1698. [5] *Vernon–Shrewsbury Letters*, ii. 157; HMC *Cowper*, ii. 414; Add. 70501, f. 45; 40775, f. 72; 21553, f. 56; 61283, f. 119; 61291, f. 44; Hereford and Worcester RO (Worcester, St. Helen's), Hampton mss 705: 349/BA4657/ii/29/43, Eyre to Pakington, 17 Jan. [1702]; *Flying Post*, 20–22 Aug. 1702. [6] *Trans. Thoroton Soc*. xxiv. 29; Thoroton, *Notts*. iii. 247–8.

S. N. H.

EYRE, John (1665–1715), of Lincoln's Inn.

DOWNTON   23 May 1698–1701 (Nov.),
1705–2 Nov. 1715

bap. 12 Apr. 1665, 2nd s. of Sir Giles Eyre† of Brickworth House, Whiteparish, Wilts. and Lincoln's Inn, j.Kb, by his 1st w. Dorothy, da. of John Ryves of Ranston, Shroton, Dorset. *educ.* Merton, Oxf. 1682; L. Inn 1682, called 1688, bencher 1715. *m.* lic. 18 June 1687, Mary, da. of one Williams of St. James in the Fields, Mdx., *s.p.s.*[1]

Freeman, Wilton 1706–*d*.[2]

Eyre was descended from the parliamentarian branch of an extensive Wiltshire family, settled at Brickworth since their purchase of the estate in 1605. The estate conveyed considerable electoral influence at Downton, which was effectively at Eyre's disposal after his father's death in June 1695, his elder brother being a 'lunatic'. He made use of it to return himself at a by-election in May 1698 and again at the two succeeding general elections. The family had a long record of opposition to the Stuart monarchy, and it was natural that Eyre should appear in politics as a Whig, and at first as a Country Whig. As the son of a Williamite judge, he was included on the Court side in a comparative analysis of the old and new Parliaments in about September 1698. However, his career in the Commons cannot often be distinguished from that of his third cousin Robert Eyre or from that of their Nottinghamshire namesake Gervase Eyre. Eyre was forecast as a probable supporter of the disbanding bill, and indeed did not figure among those who voted against it on 18 Jan. 1699. Later, in March 1700, he received a substantial vote in the ballot for trustees under the Irish Forfeitures Resumption Act. In the 1701 session he and his partner at Downton, Carew Raleigh*, were reported to have 'behaved . . . like honest men' (in Whig terms) in the foreign policy debates. However, he may have left before the end of the session as he was reported to be in Wiltshire in early June. In November 1701 he stood down for Sir James Ashe, 2nd Bt.*, whose support he had himself enjoyed in the preceding election, and when Ashe offered to 'relinquish' to him in 1702 he was 'positive' in his determination not to stand. At the 1705 election, however, Ashe did succeed in returning the previous compliment by resigning in his favour. Described, oddly, as a 'High Church courtier' in a list of this Parliament, he voted on 25 Oct. 1705 for the Court candidate in the division on the Speaker, and on 18 Feb. 1706 for the Court in the proceedings on the 'place clause' of the regency bill. The only speech of his to have been noticed – in the debate of March 1708 on the motion for a loyal address – did not make his reputation. According to a Tory, who described him as 'one Eyres (not the lawyer)' to distinguish him from Robert, he 'said he thought it very proper to present an address of thanks to the Queen for having removed dangerous persons from her person, etc. Some say he was drunk; perhaps he wanted to make his court.' Listed twice as a Whig early in 1708, he voted for the naturalization of the Palatines in 1709 and for Dr Sacheverell's impeachment in 1710. Although generally inactive in the 1710 and 1713 Parliaments, and once given indefinite leave of absence, on 7 Apr. 1711, he appeared on the lists of Whig voters against the French commerce bill on 18 June 1713 and against the expulsion of Richard Steele on 18 Mar. 1714. He was classed as a Whig in the Worsley list and in two lists of Members re-elected in 1715.[3]

An active lawyer until the end of his life, Eyre made his will on 10 Oct. 1715, leaving all his real estate to his nephew Giles Eyre, £300 of Exchequer annuities to another nephew and niece, and £20 to the poor of Downton and Whiteparish. He died at Lincoln's Inn shortly afterwards, on 2 Nov. 1715. Though greatly overshadowed by his cousin, both in the law and in Parliament, he left a favourable impression, at least among his own party, for staunchness and resolution. A 'person of natural abilities and acquired knowledge in the law of the country inferior to few', Eyre 'showed himself (like many of his ancestors) a lover of liberty and independence', according to the inscription on his memorial at Whiteparish, and 'served his country at his own expense and not . . . himself at the expense of his country'. A more genuine tribute, perhaps, is that of Thomas Burnet, whose versified account of a convivial evening in 1713 included among the Whig toasts one to

John Eyre of Brickworth,
than whom, in all Wiltshire, I know none of like worth.[4]

[1] Hoare, *Wilts*. Frustfield, 56; *Wilts. N. and Q.* v. 101; *Mar. Lic. Vicar-Gen.* (Harl. Soc. xxx), 299. [2] Wilts. RO, G25/1/22, pp. 5, 25. [3] *Wilts. N. and Q.* v. 97; HMC Lords, n.s. vii. 27–28; Add. 70036, ff. 98, 202; Wilts. RO, Radnor mss 490/909, Ashe to John Snow, 30 Nov., Dec., 13 Dec. 1700, May, 2 Dec. 1701, 6 Apr. 1702; *HMC Portland*, iv. 480. [4] *Wilts. N. and Q*, 101; *Letters of Burnet to Duckett* ed. Nichol Smith, 44.

D. W. H.

EYRE, Robert (c.1667–1735), of New House, Whiteparish, Wilts.

SALISBURY 1698–6 May 1710

b. c.1667, 1st s. of Sir Samuel Eyre of New House, j.Kb, by Martha, da. and coh. of Francis Lucy of Westminster and Brightwalton, Berks. *educ.* Lincoln, Oxf. 1683; L. Inn 1683, called 1690, bencher 1707, treasurer 1709. *m.* 6 Dec. 1694 (with £4,000), Elizabeth (*d.* 1724), da. of Edward Rudge* and sis. of John Rudge*, 3s. 1da. *suc.* fa. 1698; kntd. 6 May 1710.[1]

Dep. recorder, Salisbury 1693–5, recorder 1695–*d.*; recorder, Southampton 1703–23; recorder and alderman, Bristol 1704–28; gov. Charterhouse by 1723–*d.*[2]

QC 1707, solicitor-gen. 1708–May 1710; j.Qb May 1710–Nov. 1723, serjeant-at-law 1710; chancellor to Prince of Wales 1714–?27; commr. for building 50 new churches 1715; l.c. baron of the Exchequer Nov. 1723–May 1725; l.c.j.c.p. May 1725–*d.*

Eyre's father had purchased New House, six miles south-east of Salisbury, in 1660, although his family had been established in Wiltshire since before the reign of Edward II. This longstanding association with Salisbury helped Eyre first to the recordership, succeeding his second cousin Sir Giles Eyre†, and then to a seat in Parliament. Like Sir Giles's son John*, who also entered the Commons for the first time in 1698, Eyre began as a Country Whig, classed as a member of the Country party in a comparison of the old and new Parliaments, and forecast as a probable supporter of the disbanding bill, which at any rate he did not vote against. The Journals often fail to distinguish between the cousins, or between them and the Nottinghamshire Member, Gervase Eyre, although most references in the Journals were probably to Robert as a prominent lawyer. The importance of the clothing industry in Salisbury makes Robert the most likely of the three to have managed through the House the bill for the improvement of the woollen manufactures and the restoration of Blackwell Hall which he reported on 4 Mar. 1699. Two days later he was given indefinite leave of absence. When the Blackwell Hall bill was revived in the following session he was again probably the 'Mr Eyre' who managed it through the House, chairing a committee of the whole on 22 Dec. 1699 and, following the report, telling on 10 Jan. 1700 in favour of retaining some words in the bill, but it again fell in the Lords. Also connected with the clothing trade in Salisbury was his appointment to a petition from his constituency on 14 Dec. arguing for the repeal of a recent Act preventing the import of lace, from which he reported favourably on the 20th, only for the House to recommit the report. He spoke on 13 Dec. 1699, his first known intervention, in defence of his friend Bishop Burnet's being continued governor to the Duke of Gloucester.[3]

Surviving a contest in January 1701, Eyre was probably first-named on 21 Feb. 1701 to draft yet another bill restoring Blackwell Hall, which was never presented. Robert Harley* classed him with the Whigs in December 1701. Although he was the only 'Eyre' in the House during this session, his single significant contribution to this Parliament was to present a private relief bill relating to the Irish forfeited estates.

With Gervase Eyre also present during the first two sessions of the Parliament elected in 1702, it is impossible to distinguish him from his namesake in the 1702–3 session. As a parliamentary lawyer with a growing reputation he was probably the 'Mr Eyre' named to the committee of 10 Dec. 1702 to redraw the Lords' amendments to the occasional conformity bill, before being granted a week's leave of absence on 8 Jan. 1703. He was present on 13 Feb. to vote in favour of agreeing with the Lords' amendments to the bill for enlarging the time for taking the oath of abjuration. Three days later a 'Mr Eyre' acted as a teller for a rider to the militia bill. In the following session he was probably the 'Mr Eyre' who presented two bills: to develop properties in Lincoln's Inn Fields (17 Jan. 1704) and to place promissory notes on the same legal footing as bills of exchange (2 Feb.). With the death of Gervase Eyre, his activity is much easier to detail for the 1704–5 session, when his only task of importance was to manage through the Commons the reintroduced bill to extend the security of bills of exchange. An opponent of the Tack, according to a forecast in October 1704, he did not vote for it on 28 Nov.

Classed as 'Low Church' in a list of the 1705 Parliament, Eyre divided for the Court candidate in the contest for the Speakership on 25 Oct. The return of John Eyre to the Commons again makes identification of 'Mr Eyre' uncertain. Robert was one of the foremost Country Whig agitators in the struggle over the regency bill. Believing in the necessity of the measure (he spoke on 15 Jan. 1706 in favour of maintaining the arrangements it laid down for summoning Parliament after the Queen's death), he opposed Ralph Freman II's motion on 12 Jan. for an instruction to the committee to insert a clause to secure the provisions of the Act of Settlement because this would 'obstruct the bill'. In any case, he believed a total exclusion of officeholders too sweeping, and especially in the circumstances for which the bill was designed: there were the consequences of '150 new elections' to consider, as well as the fact that, in a House from which many of the more prominent Members had been purged, they would find 'none to inform you of the state of the nation but burg[esses] not knowing anything'. He supported, however, a modified instruction to 'regulate' the arrangements in the Act, the origin of the so-called 'whimsical clause'. In his view, if 'reason' determined Members' voting a 'self-denying bill' would pass easily, but 'reason [did] not always prevail', and this method was therefore the only way to secure some exclusion of placemen: 'the regency bill has such friends as will see it pass with a reasonable instruction'. He it was who on 21 Jan. brought in the amending clause, and he was busy in that day's debate, speaking for the clause and warding off Court-inspired attempts to adjourn discussion. His principal argument seems to have been that the clause would 'preserve the constitution' and the influence of the 'gent[lemen] of England' from the encroachments of 'pensioners'. So closely was he identified with the clause that his desertion from the 'whimsicals' on 18 Feb. to vote for the Court's compromise provoked Sir John Cropley, 2nd Bt.*, to write to another leading 'whimsical', James Stanhope*, who had already left town:

> Ro[bert] Eyre, unknown to Peter King* and I . . . had treacherous made at my Lord Halifax's [Charles Montagu*] this bargain, and in the most audacious as well as infamous manner that ever was seen in that House gave up his cause, his friends and himself . . . had you been here . . . [he] had preserved his honour.

To Lord Shaftesbury (Anthony, Lord Ashley*) Cropley was equally scathing: 'Ro[bert] Eyre, to his eternal infamy (can never show his face more), gave up the clause, and you know what giving up a question is, in a manner beyond all instances of that kind ever seen in the House'. A case can be made for Eyre as a consistent supporter both of the regency bill and a limited or 'reasonable' exclusion of officers, who colluded at last with the Junto in order to secure at least a partial success for the place clause while at the same time saving the bill, though the evidence of his subsequent career and the critical opinion of his friends, the cooler scepticism of Stanhope as well as Cropley's wrath, would suggest a more cynical interpretation. However, despite Cropley's prognostications, Eyre did not lose his reputation forever among Country Whigs. Indeed, he retained, or won back, Shaftesbury's confidence enough to be named a beneficiary under the Earl's will and one of the guardians of his heir.⁴

The episode of the regency bill may be regarded as a turning point in Eyre's career, though he had been reported in early September as being on the point of death. Perhaps his health was slow to improve, for while he was instructed by Salisbury corporation on the bill to establish a nightly watch there, it is by no means certain that he and not John Eyre was named to other important committees during the session. In May came his first step on the ladder of preferment, as Queen's Counsel, the first fruits of which were doubtless not what he had expected: going the western circuit he sustained a broken arm when his coach overturned. His change of tack in national politics seems to have been paralleled at this time by a similar shift locally. In backing the efforts of the Tory Charles Fox* to obtain a new charter for Salisbury, he came into conflict with his own former supporters, who accused him of neglecting 'his true interests' and dividing the Whig party in the city. Perhaps because he considered the preferment he had received to be inadequate and felt obliged to remind ministers of his capacity for mischief, he began the 1707–8 session in opposition, but came over to the Court in December in the debate on the Scottish privy council. On 20 Dec. he was one of those nominated to invite Dr Eyres to preach before the Commons and on 7 Jan. 1708 he was ordered to draft a bill to alter the Regency Act. By the time of Harley's fall in February 1708 Eyre was numbered among the 'Lord Treasurer's Whigs'. He was thought likely to be made solicitor-general in the consequent ministerial reshuffle, and apropos of his and Henry Boyle's* likely advancement Thomas Johnson* observed, 'the staunch Whigs come in, for you know these were often against the Court in King William's time'. Queen Anne's refusal to sanction the promotion of (Sir) James Montagu I* to be attorney-general obstructed Eyre's ambition, though both Lord Treasurer Godolphin (Sidney†) and the Queen herself would have been happy with his own nomination. In April it was being said that Eyre 'has the first promise of attorney or solicitor, as either shall become vacant', and the following month Anne, in proposing an alternative scheme of legal appointments, pencilled in his name for the solicitor-generalship. Throughout the summer the struggle for Montagu's acceptance continued, with Eyre a frustrated spectator. Meanwhile he was consulted by Bishop Nicolson in February 1708 over Tory objections to the cathedrals bill, was classed as a Whig in two parliamentary lists, and in May secured his re-election at Salisbury unopposed.⁵

Eyre was eventually confirmed as solicitor in October 1708, necessitating another election which passed again without a contest. He was diplomatically absent on one occasion in January 1709 when the controversial Abingdon election case was decided, but was otherwise as active in the House as his official position demanded. Fortunately, he is now identifiable in the Journals, under his official designation, and, as befitted a law officer, was much involved in legislative matters. Thus he was named to 11 drafting committees, but took little part in the management of the resultant bills through the House. He is known to have voted for one of these, the general naturalization bill, and in April he spoke in favour of another, the bill to amend the Scottish treason laws. During 1709 he subscribed some £2,000 to the Bank.

The 1709–10 session was Eyre's most important in the Commons. He was named to nine drafting committees, including five relating to supply. He also managed three other bills through the House: the mutiny bill; a recruitment bill; and the bill to secure the government. Most important, however, was his role in the Sacheverell impeachment. He was included among those ordered to draw up the articles of impeachment, which became the committee charged with prosecuting the case. His initial advice had been against this procedure, and he had advocated instead the 'short way' of summoning the doctor to the Commons on a charge of showing contempt for the resolution of 1705 that the Church was not 'in danger'. By this means Whig MPs could have ensured a vote for 'burning the sermon, and keeping him in prison during the session'. Once impeachment had been decided upon, however, Eyre voted for it and carried out his duties as a manager punctiliously, if without any great zeal. Burnet certainly thought that he had 'distinguished himself' in his two contributions to the presentation of the Commons' case. On 28 Feb. 1710 he spoke to the first article, his task being to show, by close scrutiny of the text of the sermon that Sacheverell had indeed denied that an act of resistance had occurred at the Revolution. When he departed from textual analysis his main concern was to defend not a right of resistance in general but the particular acts of resistance in the peculiar circumstances of 1688, when in his view the very foundations of the constitution had been threatened. Perhaps his most original argument was the one used to counter Sacheverell's claim that resistance was against the laws of the land, when he pointed out, with some sarcasm, that 'it can never be supposed, that the laws were made to set up a despotic power to destroy the laws themselves, and to warrant the subversion of a constitution of government which they were designed to establish and defend'. His main point, though, was that any denial of the right of resistance rendered illegal not just the Revolution but all that had flowed from it. To cast doubt on the legitimacy of the Revolution 'strikes . . . directly at the present establishment' and 'must certainly shake' the authority of 'that Act of Parliament whereby the crown is settled on her Majesty', and, obviously, the Protestant succession as well. He did not accuse Sacheverell and other proponents of non-resistance directly of Jacobitism, but such was the unmistakable innuendo: it was no coincidence, he suggested, following Sir Joseph Jekyll, that the recent revival of these doctrines dated from the invasion attempt of 1708. Nevertheless a Sacheverellite observer noted that his manner had not been offensive to the defendant: 'the doctor afterwards thanked him for using him like a gentleman, which only he did'. Eyre returned on 9 Mar. to reply to Sacheverell's answer, again confined to the first article, and again for the most part relying on a detailed investigation into the intent and meaning of the sermons. According to a Whig observer, he 'took notice of the miserable shifts and evasions resorted to by Sacheverell and his counsel', while a Sacheverellite diarist, admitting that Eyre 'spoke civilly enough', saw his efforts as mere repetition. Where he did go further was in his exposition of Parliament's role in the disposition of the crown. He reaffirmed the Queen's 'hereditary right' but added that her occupation of the throne also enjoyed 'the sanction of an Act of Parliament'. Furthermore, 'we have reason to lay some weight upon a parliamentary title, since the Protestant Succession entirely depends upon it'. This was not as categorical as it sounded. To deny any 'parliamentary title' would not necessarily debar the Hanoverians, for whom some 'hereditary claim' was imputed, but it would lead to 'endless disputes' and bloodshed. His peroration consisted of a strong defence of the resort to impeachment, which in private he had argued against. It was the only 'adequate remedy' for 'these great and growing evils', the public attacks on the legitimacy of the Queen's title and foundations of government, the disturbances in religion which endangered the Church, the 'defamation' of the episcopate and 'vilification' of the ministry, for all of which, he declared, Sacheverell and his ilk were responsible. It was, we may presume, at least partly in recognition of his services in the impeachment that Eyre was knighted and raised to the bench in May 1710. Before he took his place as a judge he was sworn a serjeant, he and the other new serjeant, Thomas Pengelly[†], marking the occasion with a 'splendid' feast attended by Lord Chancellor Cowper (William*) and other peers and judges. The rings distributed bore the motto 'unit et imperat'.[6]

During the Harley ministry Eyre was able as a judge to offer some protection to Whig journalists and pamphleteers who had fallen foul of the administration. Following the Hanoverian succession his career continued to progress. As chancellor to the Prince of Wales he faced Commons' criticism in 1716 for accepting the office while still a judge. Two years later he was obliged to take the Prince's side in the legal dispute over the King's prerogative to interfere in the upbringing of the royal grandchildren, but he did not forfeit George I's favour, and was advanced to be lord chief baron and then lord chief justice of common pleas. Although he was pilloried in print for arrogance, his judicial career was only once touched by controversy, when in 1729 he was cleared of charges of having assisted the sadistic warden of the Fleet, Thomas Bambridge. Eyre became ill by October 1735, when he began receiving treatment from a doctor, and died on 28 Dec., aged 68. He was buried with his forebears in St. Thomas' church, Salisbury. His eldest son, Robert, who succeeded him as recorder of Southampton, sat for the borough from 1727 to 1729.[7]

[1] Hoare, *Wilts.* Frustfield, 56; Burke, *Commoners*, iii. 291; *Vis. Warws.* (Harl. Soc. lxii), 93–94; *Vis. Eng. and Wales Notes* ed. Crisp, xii. 38; *Al. Carth.* 86; Boyer, *Pol. State*, l. 680; PCC 213 Lort. [2] Wilts. RO, G23/1/4, pp. 308, 313; J. S. Davies, *Hist. Southampton*, 186; A. B. Beaven, *Bristol Lists*, 289. [3]*Cocks Diary*, 42; Burnet, vi. 327. [4]*Cam. Misc.* xxiii. 62–63, 66, 71, 79–81; *Bull. IHR.* xxxix. 57–58; Centre Kentish Stud. Stanhope mss U1590/C9/31, Cropley to Stanhope, 19 Feb. 1706; PRO 30/24/20/113, [Stanhope] to [Cropley], 24 Feb. 1706; 30/24/20/114, Cropley to Shaftesbury, Feb. 1706; PRO 30/24/21/224, copy of Shaftesbury's will. [5] Folger Shakespeare Lib. Newdigate newsletter 3 Sept. 1706; Hoare, *Wilts.* Salisbury, 504; Luttrell, *Brief Relation*, vi. 166, 202, 294; Hants RO, Jervoise mss, James Harris to Thomas Jervoise*, 26 May, 23 June 1707; *Vernon–Shrewsbury Letters*, iii. 290–2; G. Holmes, *Pol. in Age of Anne*, 341; *Huntington Lib. Q.* xv. 40; *Norris Pprs.* (Chetham Soc. ix), 167; *Addison Letters*, 91, 110; *Duchess of Marlborough Corresp.* i. 98–99; *Daily Courant*, 24 Apr. 1708; E. Gregg, *Q. Anne*, 265; Stanhope mss U1590/C9/28, Somerset to Stanhope, 24 June 1708; *Clavering Corresp.* (Surtees Soc. clxxviii), 4–5; *Nicolson Diaries* ed. Jones and Holmes, 456. [6] Holmes, 186; *Cal. Treas. Bks.* xxii. 417; *Parlty. Lists Early 18th Cent.* ed. Newman, 81–82; *Nicolson Diaries*, 494; P. G. M. Dickson, *Financial Revol.* 267; Burnet, v. 435, 440; G. Holmes, *Trial of Sacheverell*, 82, 136, 139–40; *Tryal of Dr Henry Sacheverell* (1710), 52–58, 271–80; J. P. Kenyon, *Revol. Principles*, 135; Yale Univ. Beinecke Lib. Osborn mss, 'Account of the trial of Dr Sacheverell', 28 Feb., 9 Mar.; *Impartial View* (1711), 213; Luttrell, vi. 579, 581; Add. 70421, newsletters 9, 11 May 1710. [7]*Diary of Dudley Ryder*, 362; Foss, *Judges*, viii. 221–3; *London Mag.* 1735, p. 687; Sloane 3984, f. 47.

D. W. H.

FAGG, Sir John, 1st Bt. (1627–1701), of Wiston, nr. Steyning, Suss.

Rye	3 Oct. 1645–1653
Sussex	1654–1655, 1656–1658, 1659
Steyning	1660–1681 (Jan.)
Sussex and Steyning	1681 (Mar.)
Steyning	1685–1687
	1689–18 Jan. 1701

b. 4 Oct. 1627, o. s. of John Fagg of Rye, Suss. by Elizabeth, da. of Barnaby Hodgson of Framfield, Suss. educ. Emmanuel, Camb. 1644; G. Inn 1644. m. (1) 19 Mar. 1646, Mary (d. 1687), da. of Robert Morley of Glynde, Suss., 9s. (4 d.v.p.) 5da.; (2) Anne (d. 1694), da. of Philip Weston of Newbury, Berks., wid. of Thomas Henshaw of Billingshurst, Suss., s.p. suc. fa. 1645; cr. Bt. 11 Dec. 1660.[1]

Commr. high ct. of justice 1649; councillor of state 31 Dec. 1659–25 Feb. 1660.[2]

Col. of ft. 1659, Feb.–July 1660.[3]

Commr. for derelict lands, Suss. and Hants 1696.[4]

A wealthy Sussex squire and Presbyterian, Fagg had influence in several boroughs and in 1690 had already a long parliamentary career behind him when he was returned for Steyning, where he retained a strong interest, owning property in the borough in addition to his estate at Wiston, two miles away. Indeed, Fagg was to represent the borough until the end of his career. He was classed as a Whig by Lord Carmarthen (Sir Thomas Osborne†) in March 1690, and as a doubtful but possible Country supporter by Robert Harley* in April 1691. On 29 Dec. 1691 he spoke against a bill to encourage privateers, on the grounds that it would allow trade with France. He spoke on 26 Jan. 1692 against a bill for the repair of highways, as being particularly disadvantageous to Sussex. He was granted leave of absence four times in this Parliament: for 14 days on 29 Dec. 1692; 14 days due to his brother's illness on 22 Feb. 1693; 14 days due to his wife's illness on 15 Mar. 1694; and an unspecified time to recover his own health on 19 Mar. 1695. It was a pattern of absence which continued for the remainder of his career. He was classed as a Court supporter by Grascome in his list of 1693–5. In the next Parliament he was forecast in January 1696 as a probable supporter of the Court on the proposed council of trade, and signed the Association promptly, but on 27 Feb. he was granted leave of absence for the recovery of his health, which must account for his absence from the division in March on the price of guineas. In the next session he voted on 25 Nov. 1696 in favour of the attainder of Sir John Fenwick†. On 24 Feb. 1697 and on 5 Apr. 1698, he was once more granted leave, again because of ill-health.

Classed, somewhat surprisingly, as a member of the Country party in about September 1698, he voted on 18 Jan. 1699 against the bill for disbanding the army, and as before was granted leave of absence for health reasons on 27 Mar. 1699. Listed as being in the Junto interest in an analysis of the House of early 1700, he was granted leave of absence on 23 Mar. 1700 to recover his health. He successfully contested Steyning in the first 1701 election but died shortly afterwards, on 18 Jan. 1701, of apoplexy.[5]

[1] Berry, Suss. Gen. 193, 262; Glynde Par. Reg. (Suss. Rec. Soc. xxx), 18; Suss. N. and Q. xv. 21. [2] CJ, vii. 799. [3] CSP Dom. 1659–60, p. 562. [4] Cal. Treas. Bks. xi. 281. [5] Suss. Arch. Colls. liv. 52; Norfolk mss at Arundel Castle M571, Steyning original presentments; Luttrell Diary, 94, 156.

P.W.

FAGG, Robert I (c.1649–1715), of Wiston, nr. Steyning, Suss.

New Shoreham	1679 (Mar.)–1681 (Mar.)
Steyning	1690–1695, 4 Mar.–10 Apr. 1701
	1701 (Dec.)–1702

b. c.1649, 2nd but 1st surv. s. of Sir John Fagg, 1st Bt.*, by 1st w.; bro. of Thomas Fagg*. educ. Steyning acad. (William Corderoy) 1662–3; St. Catharine's, Camb. 1663; I. Temple 1664, called 1671. m. 21 Sept. 1671, Elizabeth, da. of Benjamin Culpepper of Wakehurst, Suss., 1s. 2da. suc. fa. as 2nd Bt. 18 Jan. 1701.[1]

Educated by a Nonconformist minister, Fagg was an Exclusionist in 1679 and a probable Whig collaborator in 1688. He was returned with his father for Steyning on the family interest in 1690, when he was classed as a Whig in Lord Carmarthen's (Sir Thomas Osborne†) list of March 1690. On 5 Apr. following he wrote to his brother-in-law, Sir Philip Gell, 2nd Bt.†, that when the Commons resumed the debate on the poll tax bill, he intended, if no one else did, to move an amendment to exclude poorer people from its provisions. The bill was taken in a committee of the whole on 10 Apr., but whether or not Fagg moved his amendment is unknown. In April 1691 Robert Harley* listed Fagg, like his father, as doubtful but possibly a Country party supporter. On 15 Feb. 1692 Fagg told on for an amendment to another poll bill, to appropriate part of the money to be raised for the use of the army, and in the next session he proposed in the committee of ways and means on 10 Feb. 1693 that

half the charge of the civil list might be struck off; that officers might have but half their salaries, which was but reasonable; that [if] gentlemen ... were forced to live on half their estates, that officers also should live on half their salaries and this would raise the sum that was wanting.

Despite this, in Grascome's list of 1693–5 he was named as a Court supporter.[2]

Fagg did not stand again until he successfully contested a by-election for Steyning in March 1701, caused by the death of his father. During the hearing of the petition against his return, charges of bribery were proved against both candidates and the election was declared void. At the subsequent by-election he was defeated by two votes. He was returned again in the second general election of 1701 when he was classed as a Whig by Harley. His rather surprising vote on 26 Feb. 1702 in favour of the motion vindicating the Commons' proceedings in the impeachments of William III's Whig ministers might reflect a particularly strong Country sentiment. On 27 Mar. it was reported that he had refused to take the oath of abjuration, perhaps as a result of Dissenting scruples. Consequently he did not stand for Parliament again. He died on 22 Aug. 1715 and was buried at Albourne, Sussex.[3]

[1] *Vis. Suss.* (Harl. Soc. lxxxix), 43; PCC 174 Fagg; D. R. Lacey, *Dissent and Parl. Pol.* 392. [2] *Luttrell Diary*, 417; *HMC 9th Rep.* II, p. 399; *Suss. Arch. Colls.* lxix. 149. [3] H. Horwitz, *Parl. and Pol. Wm. III*, 302; Add. 7074, f. 109.

P. W.

FAGG, Robert II (1673–1736), of Wiston, nr. Steyning, Suss.

STEYNING 1708–1710

bap. 9 Aug. 1673, 2nd but o. surv. s. of Robert Fagg I*. *m.* in or bef. 1698, Christian (*d.* 1765), da. of Sir Cecil Bishopp, 4th Bt.†, of Parham, Suss., 4s. (2 *d.v.p.*) 3da. (1 *d.v.p.*) *suc.* fa. as 3rd Bt. 26 Aug. 1715.[1]

Fagg successfully contested Steyning in 1708 on the family interest. His grandfather, father and uncle were all Members in this period and all were Whigs, and it is thus not surprising that the analysis by the Earl of Sunderland (Charles, Lord Spencer*) of the 1708 returns listed Fagg as of the same party. However, Fagg's political inclinations are indeterminate: he was not listed as voting for the naturalization of the Palatines, and neither is his vote recorded on the impeachment of Dr Sacheverell. Defeated at Steyning in 1710, he did not stand again until the reign of George I, when he unsuccessfully contested the borough in 1722 and 1727, apparently standing as a Tory, on the latter occasion managing to collect only two votes.

Fagg died at Horley, near Reigate in Surrey, on 22 June 1736 and was buried at Albourne, Sussex, his son Robert† inheriting the estate.[2]

[1] *Suss. Arch. Colls.* v. 26. [2] Ibid. xvi. 245.

P. W.

FAGG, Thomas (1665–1705), of Rye and Glynley, Westham, Suss.

RYE 1701 (Dec.)–1705

bap. 12 Apr. 1665, 7th s. of Sir John Fagg, 1st Bt.*, by 1st w.; bro. of Robert Fagg I*. *m.* 1 Dec. 1694, Elizabeth (*d.* 1721), da. of William Hay of Horsted, Suss., wid. of John Meeres of Glynley, 2s. 3da.[1]

Freeman, Rye 1701.[2]

A Presbyterian like his father, Fagg had settled in Rye, whence his family had originated, and there established himself in a modest way as a trader and shipowner. His marriage in 1694 put him in possession of the comfortable estate of Glynley, but he retained his interests at Rye and in 1701 was granted three acres of waterfront there. In December of that year he was returned for the borough in the general election, whereupon he was classed as a Whig by Robert Harley*. On 10 Jan. 1702 he was named to the drafting committee for a bill to repair the harbour at Rye. Later in the session, on 28 Apr., he was granted leave of absence, but his interest at Rye kept him in the House until the next day when he told for an amendment to the bill for encouraging privateers, which was designed to safeguard the rights of the warden of the Cinque Ports and admiralty officials. Successful once more for Rye in 1702, Fagg was forecast as a probable opponent of the Tack and did not vote for it in the division on 28 Nov. 1704. In 1705 Fagg's son stood at Rye while he himself unsuccessfully contested Lewes on the Nonconformist interest. He died a few months later, on 19 Sept.[3]

[1] *Suss. Arch. Colls.* v. 26; Berry, *Suss. Gen.* 255, 262–3; *Suss. Mar. Lic.* (Suss. Rec. Soc vi), 155. [2] E. Suss. RO, RYE 1/17, Rye assembly bk. p. 258. [3] *CSP Dom.* 1703–4, pp. 368–9; Luttrell, *Brief Relation*, v. 590; C. Brent, *Georgian Lewes*, 169.

P. W.

FAIRBORNE, Sir Stafford (1666–1742), of St. Anne's and St. James's, Westminster.

ROCHESTER 1705–1710

b. 1666, 1st s. of Sir Palmes Fairborne of St. Anne's by Margery, da. of one Devereux, and wid. of Mr Mansell. *m.* (1) 24 June 1694, Dorothy Fane (*d.* 1707), 3s. (*d.v.p.*) 1da.; (2) 20 Oct. 1708 (with £10,000), Rebecca, da. of

FAIRBORNE

Hon. Thomas Paston (6th s. of Robert, 1st Earl of Yarmouth), 1s. (*d.v.p.*) 1da. *suc.* fa. 1680; kntd. 3 Nov. 1701.[1]

Ensign, 2 Tangier Ft. 1678–85 (Queen's Ft. 1684–5, Queen Dowager's Ft. from 1685, later 2 Ft.), lt. 1685–Sept. 1687, 2nd lt. grenadier coy. in same regt. 1687–9, capt. by Oct. 1689–1700; lt. RN by 1685, capt. Sept. 1688, r.-adm. 1701–Feb. 1703, v.-adm. May 1703–8, adm. June 1708, adm. of the fleet Dec. 1708–Dec. 1709; commr. forts, Newfoundland 1700 (not taken out), disbanding marines 1713 (not taken out); one of council of ld. high adm. Feb. 1706–June 1708.[2]

Freeman, Portsmouth 1702, Great Grimsby by 1705, Rochester 1705.[3]

Fairborne's father was a soldier who spent most of his career in the defence of Tangier. In 1680, while serving as governor, he was killed during a Moorish attack. By that date Fairborne was himself embarked on a military career, having been commissioned in 1678 as an ensign in a Tangier regiment. Like many military men in Restoration England he held commissions in both the army and the navy, serving as lieutenant aboard the *Bonadventure* in 1685. Evidence suggests that he became a client of Admiral Arthur Herbert[†] (later Earl of Torrington) the naval commander at Tangier, 1679–83. Thus, in 1689–90, Phineas Bowles, secretary to both Herbert and the Admiralty, informed Fairborne that 'the commissioners are jestingly pleased (sometimes) to call you my captain'. Fairborne was also on hand to discredit the evidence of his own ship's master at Torrington's court martial after Beachy Head. Finally, his mother's will of 1694 shows that a house in Lisle Street, Westminster, intended for Fairborne was in fact sold to Torrington in return for an annual payment of £100 p.a. to Fairborne for life. This may explain how Fairborne was able to borrow money from Torrington in later years. Although he was promoted to captain in September 1688, Fairborne's loyalty to James II must have been sorely tried by his mother's attempts to obtain the pension of £500 granted to her in 1681 for her husband's service and to provide for her large family. As the payments were already £1,500 behind by the time of Charles II's death, Lady Fairborne was forced in 1687 to surrender it and to renounce most of her arrears in order to obtain any funds at all. Needless to say, prompt payment was not resumed under the new regime, but the treatment of his mother must have coloured Fairborne's attitude to the Revolution of 1689.[4]

Fairborne was employed at sea during much of William III's reign, being described in a list of captains of 1691 as 'a young man, but a very good man'. His mother's death in June 1694 allowed him to marry later the same month. The precipitate nature of this event suggests that Fairborne was not a rich man, which may in turn explain his sensitivity as regards precedence and promotion. For example, in May 1696, Secretary Shrewsbury attempted to pacify him on the occasion of Admiral Benbow's appointment with the assurance that 'one of your character and service need not doubt that his claims shall be considered'. Fairborne attained his flag in June 1701, being knighted the following November. Queen Anne's reign saw renewed attempts to obtain the arrears for his mother's pension, a total of over £1,000, if calculated at £200 p.a. for five years and 40 days from 13 Feb. 1689 until her death; over £6,000 if calculated at £500 p.a. since 1680. Although 'generally esteemed a bold and brave man' Fairborne proved difficult to manage. In February 1703 he surrendered his flag rather than command a squadron in the West Indies under conditions he felt unfavourable. This refusal gave rise to newsletter reports that he had 'managed his affairs with that haughtiness and indiscretion as to be entered upon the Admiralty books never to serve her Majesty more'. In response, Fairborne waited outside the Admiralty in order to challenge the first commissioner he came upon. George Churchill* accepted, and a duel in Hyde Park was narrowly averted by the arrest of both men. Fairborne was soon back in favour, however, being appointed vice-admiral of the red in May 1703. The Duke of Marlborough (John Churchill[†]) informed his duchess on the 17th that 'I have always had so much good of Sir Stafford Fairborne that I am very glad he is restored'. Further problems occurred the following year when Fairborne clashed over seniority with Vice-Admiral Graydon, the man who had succeeded him in the West Indies command.[5]

By May 1704 Fairborne was beginning to press for an administrative post to supplement his naval duties. In August he asked the Duke of Ormond (under whom he had served at Cadiz) to speak on his behalf to Prince George and Lord Treasurer Godolphin (Sidney[†]) to obtain 'some additional employment, either as a commissioner of the navy, Admiralty or else a pension extraordinary', such as many other flag officers possessed. Fairborne based his case upon his need to support 'the character her Majesty has been pleased to honour me with', the sufferings he had by loss of pay when put out of office in 1703, the expenses attendant upon his being driven into a foreign country in the great storm of 1703, and finally the claims of his family, his mother's unpaid pension and his own zealous services. To further his ambitions Fairborne stood for Parliament, targeting Rochester since the naval interest usually controlled one seat there. As he informed Ormond on 15 Mar., his electoral strategy was to persuade the voters that Sir Clowdesley Shovell* should be accounted a country gentleman, so that he could come in as 'the sea officer'. By 13 Apr. Fairborne was anxiously writing to Arthur Moore*, comptroller of army accounts, about his fear of being ordered to sail before the election. He needed to stay in Rochester to 'keep my friends fast together'. Having secured his election Fairborne wrote from shipboard to Robert Harley* pressing his claims for a place on the 'Prince's Council' in order 'better to support the flag I wear'. Preferment was not forthcoming immediately. Contemporary assessments of his political stance varied: one list classed him as a 'High Church Courtier', but the more reliable Earl of Sunderland (Charles, Lord Spencer*) thought his election in place of Edward Knatchbull* a gain for the Whigs. Fairborne was still absent at sea when the Commons divided on 25 Oct. 1705 over the choice of Speaker. He had returned by 9 Jan. 1706 when he was given leave by the Commons to attend the Lords' committee considering more effective methods of manning the fleet. Although tipped for a place on the Prince's council in succession to Richard Hill in December 1705, he had to wait until 8 Feb. 1706 to be appointed. He then loyally supported the Court on 18 Feb. over the 'place clause' of the regency bill. His name also appears on two lists of 1708, on both occasions as a Whig, and he was duly returned again for Rochester at the general election of that year.[6]

Although he had been reappointed on 19 Apr. 1708, Fairborne was dropped from Prince George's council on 20 June in return for a commission as admiral of the white, dated so as to give him seniority over Sir John Leake*. October 1708 saw Fairborne, aged 41, marry Rebecca Paston, whose uncle Jasper Paston had married Fairborne's mother 25 years previously; her portion was reportedly £10,000. Further honour followed in December when the new lord high admiral, the Earl of Pembroke (Thomas Herbert†), made him one of the admirals of the fleet. In the Commons Fairborne continued to support the Whig ministry, voting in 1709 for the naturalization of the Palatines and a year later for the impeachment of Dr Sacheverell. However, if Fairborne had benefited from the changes attendant upon the death of Prince George, the Queen's decision in December 1709 to employ as lord high admiral the Earl of Orford (Edward Russell*) ruined his career. Whether because of some ancient grudge or a more recent professional rivalry, Orford obtained an order in council setting aside both Fairborne's recent appointments, and allowing him half-pay only as a vice-admiral. Although not a poor man (he had over £500 in Bank stock in 1710), Fairborne saw this as unjust, and appealed in June 1710 to Marlborough to 'become my advocate to my Lord Orford' that 'I should be allowed the half-pay of an admiral of the fleet, till I am employed again at sea', or that he should have an office 'which does not prevent my serving in the House of Commons'. With Fairborne at odds with Orford, the advent of Robert Harley* to power must have given him fresh hope of securing some preferment or a recall to active duty. Arthur Maynwaring* reported rumours that Fairborne would be included in a new Admiralty commission to be headed by the Earl of Peterborough. However, Fairborne was not named in the new commission issued on 4 Oct. nor was he returned to the Commons, being defeated on the 7th at Rochester. He did not give up hope of employment or of a generous pension under the Tories, soliciting Harley at the moments he judged most opportune to stress his '33 years' service and 45 commissions in the service from the lowest to the highest'. Harley relented in 1713, appointing him a commissioner for disbanding the marines, but Fairborne refused to take out his commission, holding out for a place in the Admiralty. With the accession of George I and the return of Orford at the head of an Admiralty commission, Fairborne appears to have settled into retirement. In 1718 Thomas Hearne reported the birth of a son, but little information survives of his other activities. He died on 11 Nov. 1742, aged 76, 'the oldest admiral in the navy'. He was buried in Westminster Abbey.[7]

[1] *London Mar. Lic.* ed. Foster, 468; *London Mag.* 1742, p. 569; *Le Neve's Knights* (Harl. Soc. viii), 268–9; IGI, London; *Westminster Abbey Reg.* ed. Chester, 362; Luttrell, *Brief Relation*, vi. 364; *Top. and Gen.* iii. 40. [2] Charnock, *Biographia Navalis*, ii. 144; *CSP Dom.* 1699–1700, p. 398; *Post Boy*, 8–11 Aug. 1713; *Cal. Treas. Bks.* xxvii. 409. [3] R. East, *Portsmouth Recs.* 373; Univ. Kansas Spencer Research Lib. Moore mss 143 C1, Henry Vincent I* to Arthur Moore, 1 May 1705; info. from Medway Area Archs. [4] *DNB* (Fairborne, Sir Palmes); Charnock, 144; *Navy Recs. Soc.* lx. 249–50; J. Ehrman, *Navy in War of Wm. III*, 293; *Mariner's Mirror*, lxxvi. 345–6; PCC 121 Box; *Cal. Treas. Bks.* vii. 100, 1495; viii. 1305; *Cal. Treas. Pprs.* 1702–7, p. 185. [5] Folger Shakespeare Lib. Rich mss Xd. 451(98), list of capts. 1691; *CSP Dom.* 1696, p. 175; 1702–3, p. 709; *Cal. Treas. Bks.* xvii. 958; *Cal. Treas. Pprs.* 1702–7, p. 185; *HMC Portland*, viii. 302; Add. 70075, newsletters 13, 20, 23 Feb. 1703; Luttrell, *Brief Relation*, v. 272, 295; DZA, Bonet despatch, 19 Feb. 1703; *Marlborough–Godolphin Corresp.* 187; *HMC Ormonde*, n.s. viii. 57; Bath mss at Longleat House, Thynne pprs. 12, f. 127. [6] *HMC Portland*, viii. 117, 175, 183; iv. 94; *HMC Ormonde*, n.s. viii. 110, 147; Moore pprs. mss 143 cd, Fairborne to Moore, 13 Apr. 1705; *Bull. IHR*, xxxvii. 23; Spencer Research Lib. Methuen–Simpson corresp. mss C.163, Simpson to Methuen, 11 Dec. 1705; Luttrell, v. 622. [7] Add. 61164, f. 161; 61116, f. 69; 57861, f. 151; 70292, Fairborne to Harley, 20 June 1711; 70317, same to same, 7 Aug., 8 Sept. 1712, 9 June, 21 July 1713; 70311, same to same, 19 Aug. 1713; Luttrell, vi. 364; Egerton 3359; *Marlborough–Godolphin*

Corresp. 1545, 1557; *HMC Portland*, x. 54, 246; *Hearne Colls.* vi. 246; *London Mag.* 1742, p. 569; *Westminster Abbey Reg.* 362.

S. N. H.

FAIRFAX, Hon. Henry (1659–1708), of Toulston Hall, Yorks.

ALDBOROUGH   Sept.–21 Dec. 1696

b. 20 Apr. 1659, 2nd s. of Henry Fairfax†, 4th Ld. Fairfax of Cameron [S], by Frances, da. and h. of Sir Robert Barwick of Toulston Hall; bro. of Thomas, 5th Ld. Fairfax*. *educ.* G. Inn 1678. *m.* 27 Sept. 1684, Anne, da. and coh. of Richard Harrison of South Cave, Yorks., 6s. (3 *d.v.p.*) 2da.[1]

Sheriff, Yorks. 1691.[2]

Under a settlement made in 1685, Fairfax was given his maternal grandfather's estates at Toulston. He remained close to his elder brother Thomas, taking an active interest in his election campaign in 1690 for Yorkshire. Henry himself sat in Parliament for only a very short period, being returned in a contested by-election at Aldborough in September 1696. Although at first he had feared that Sir George Cooke, 3rd Bt.*, would stand against him, in the end the other candidate was Arthur Kaye, later 3rd Bt.*, son of Sir John, 2nd Bt., who was a knight of the shire along with Fairfax's brother. Fairfax was returned, but on 27 Nov. two petitions, one from the inhabitants of Aldborough and one from Kaye, were read in the Commons. Both petitions protested that Fairfax had 'spent great sums of money in treating the electors', contrary to the Act against bribery at elections. The merits of the case were considered on 21 Dec., and it was resolved that Fairfax was 'disabled and incapacitated' from serving for Aldborough. The election was declared void, though a new writ was not issued until a year later. Although Fairfax initially considered standing again, he did not contest the new by-election. In the short time he spent in Parliament, he did not appear to be active, and was not recorded as having voted on the attainder of Sir John Fenwick†.[3]

In March 1699 it was reported that Fairfax hoped for a receiver's place, though he was not appointed to any such office. In November 1704 he sent a memorandum to the Duke of Marlborough (John Churchill†), urging that his position in Yorkshire and 'his connexions with the best families of that and adjacent counties' qualified him to raise a regiment for the Queen's service and to command it, but the application failed. He did not stand for Parliament again, and died in 1708. He appears to have died intestate, as in September 1711 his estate at Toulston was granted to a creditor, Edward Marshall, of Tadcaster, Yorkshire.

Of Fairfax's children, his second son, William, was the best known, having moved to Virginia, where he became the friend and adviser of George Washington, to whom he was related through his aunt.[4]

[1] *Her. and Gen.* vi. 405; *Dugdale's Vis. Yorks.* ed. Clay, ii. 191–2. [2] *Her. and Gen.* 604. [3] E. D. Neill, *Fairfaxes of Eng. and America*, 31, 41–42, 60; Stowe 747, ff. 30, 43, 60, 68; Add. 17677 RR, f. 149; N. Yorks. RO, Worsley mss ZON 13/1/32, Fairfax to Worsley, 11 Feb. 1689[–90]; N. Yorks. RO, Swinton mss, Danby pprs. ZS, Sir William Hustler* to Sir Abstrupus Danby*, 21 Jan. 1697. [4] Swinton mss, Danby pprs. ZS, Edward Morris to Danby, 7 Mar. 1698–9; *HMC Portland*, viii. 162; Clay, 192; Borthwick Inst. York, wills, prerog. ct. Sept. 1711.

E. C.

FAIRFAX, Robert (1666–1725), of Searle Street, Westminster; Bishop Hill, Micklegate, York; and Steeton and Newton Kyme, Yorks.[1]

YORK   1713–1715

bap. 23 Feb. 1666, 2nd s. of William Fairfax of Steeton and Newton Kyme by Catherine, da. of Robert Stapleton of Wighill, Yorks. *m.* 20 Nov. 1694, Esther (*d.* 1735), da. of Robert Bushell of Ruswarp, Yorks., wid. of Charles Tomlinson of Whitby, Yorks., 2s. (1 *d.v.p.*) 2da. (1 *d.v.p.*). *suc.* bro. 1694.[2]

Lt. RN 1689, capt. 1690, r.-adm. 1708; member, Admiralty council June–Oct. 1708.[3]

Freeman, York 1713, alderman 1714, mayor 1715–16.[4]

A grandson of Sir William Fairfax, a colonel in the Parliamentary army, Fairfax went to sea in 1681 on a merchant ship commanded by Captain Bushell, whose sister he later married. He then studied navigation in Marsh Yard, Wapping, Essex, under John Colson, regarded as the best naval instructor of the time. This brought him into contact with James II, most notably at royal fox hunts, of which events Fairfax wrote that 'he wished many a time as he rode by him that he might have had the privilege to have uttered his mind to his Majesty'. Fairfax obtained a letter of recommendation to Sir Roger Strickland, a Roman Catholic who commanded the fleet, and entered the Royal Navy as a volunteer in January 1688, later serving under Lord Dartmouth (George Legge†), Strickland's successor. No doubt helped in the Revolution by the services of his cousin Lord Fairfax (Thomas*), he obtained a commission as lieutenant under Thomas Hopson* and served at Bantry Bay in 1689. He subsequently took part in the battles of Beachy Head in 1690 and La Hogue in 1692. In the years 1698–1708 he kept a journal of operations under Sir George Rooke*, covering, *inter alia,* the capture of Gibraltar in 1703 (for which he received a silver cup from the Queen), and the battle of Malaga. In 1706 he was ordered to Spithead to serve under Sir

Clowdesley Shovell* in an abortive descent on France. Although he was gazetted as vice-admiral in January 1708, the appointment was cancelled after Shovell's death. Lord Berkeley (John*), who was by some way Fairfax's junior, was appointed instead. In pique, Fairfax refused all further service. Prince George obtained for him half-pay as rear-admiral, and named him a member of his council, but after the Prince's death on 28 Oct. 1708, Fairfax left the navy altogether.[5]

Retiring to Newton Kyme, Fairfax built a house there which became his chief residence. He was much concerned at the extravagance of his cousin, the 5th Lord, on whose death in 1710 he became one of the four trustees of the estates and the guardian of the 6th Lord Fairfax. His uncle, Thomas Fairfax of Steeton, wrote to him on 6 Aug. 1710:

> now ... that the times begin to alter, I hope there may be some hopes for men to come in play again, in order to which, if it were possible, I would have you see to get into the Parliament if you can. I am sure your estate qualifies you for it, and men who have served the crown so long as you have I am sure deserve it well, and that will be a good beginning to be doing.

Fairfax had decided by July 1712 to contest the next election at York. On the 12th he informed Lord Oxford (Robert Harley*) that he had 'for some months prepared for a journey to York, in order to cultivate an interest there against the next election'. Ralph Thoresby assisted Fairfax in his campaign, during which he was associated with several Yorkshire Tories, such as Sir Arthur Kaye, 3rd Bt.*, and Sir Brian Staplyton, 2nd Bt.* At the 1713 election Fairfax was returned in a close contest, following which he was classed as a Tory in the Worsley list. He was not an active Member. In a re-run of the same contest at the York election in 1715, Fairfax was defeated. He did not sit in Parliament again. Fairfax died on 17 Oct. 1725 and was buried at Newton Kyme. By his will his heir was his eldest son, Thomas, who inherited all of the lordship of Steeton not previously settled by indenture on Fairfax's wife and Alderman Charles Perrott. Fairfax's will included a contingency with the requirement that any heir had to be a member of the Church of England and had to adopt the name of Fairfax. He also left £50 to the poor.[6]

[1] Unless otherwise stated, this biography is based on C. R. Markham, *Adm. Robert Fairfax*. [2] *DNB*; York City Archs. list of civic officials ed. Skaife, f. 214. [3] *DNB*; *Commissioned Officers RN*, 149. [4] J. Malden, *Reg. York Freemen*, 157; List of civic officials ed. Skaife, f. 214. [5] *DNB*. [6] Add. 70197, Fairfax to Oxford, 12 July 1712; *Thoresby Diary*, ii. 195–6; York City Archs., E40/54–55, mins. concerning the election of MPs, 1713; Borthwick Inst. York, wills, prerog. ct. Sept. 1727.

E. C./C. I. M.

FAIRFAX, Thomas, 5th Ld. Fairfax of Cameron [S] (1657–1710), of Denton and Cookbridge Hall, Yorks.

MALTON 1685–1687
YORKSHIRE 1689–1702, 1 Jan.–1 May 1707

b. 16 Apr. 1657, 1st s. of Henry Fairfax[†], 4th Ld. Fairfax of Cameron [S]; bro. of Hon. Henry Fairfax*. *educ.* Magdalen Coll. Oxf. 1675. *m.* c.1685, Catherine (d. 1719), da. and h. of Thomas, 2nd Baron Colepeper, of Thoresway and Leeds Castle, Kent, 3s. 4da. *suc.* fa. 9 Apr. 1688.[1]

Capt. indep. tp. 1685–7; lt.-col. 2 Horse Gds. 1689–94; col. 3 Drag. Gds. 1694–5; brig.-gen. 1701–2.

Commr. Aire and Calder navigation 1699.[2]

As colonel of the Yorkshire militia in 1688 Fairfax had been active with the Earl of Danby (Sir Thomas Osborne[†]) in the rising in the north. In February 1690 he was returned unopposed for Yorkshire. Various lists compiled by the Marquess of Carmarthen (as Danby had become) on the eve of the new Parliament and in December 1690 classed Fairfax as a Tory and Court supporter, while similarly, in April 1691, Robert Harley* had no doubts about his Court sympathies. During 1692–5 he was included in further lists of Court supporters and placemen in the Commons. He had previously been inactive in the Convention and continued to be away a great deal, being granted leave of absence on 19 Dec. 1691, 28 Jan. 1693, 19 Feb. 1694 and 7 Mar. 1695.[3]

Returned unopposed once again for the county in the 1695 election, Fairfax was forecast as likely to support the government in the divisions on the proposed council of trade on 31 Jan. 1696. On 10 Feb. he was granted leave of absence for ten days. He signed the Association promptly, but in March was absent from the division on the price of guineas. In the 1696–7 session he voted on 25 Nov. for the attainder of Sir John Fenwick[†]. On the 30th John Pershall*, whose wife was the sister of Fairfax's wife, petitioned the House with a claim that Fairfax was using his privilege to obstruct payment of Charlotte Pershall's portion from the Colepeper estate. The House thereupon resolved *nem. con.*

> that no Member of this House during the continuance of this Parliament, have any privilege, except for his person only against any commoner, in any suit or proceedings in courts of law or equity for any longer time than the House shall be actually sitting for dispatch of business in Parliament.

Fairfax was granted leave of absence once again on 22 Dec., while on 12 Feb. 1697 a bill was brought in to enable him to sell part of his lands in order to pay the portion and discharge other legacies under Colepeper's will. The 3rd Lord Colepeper, Fairfax's uncle by marriage, objected to the bill and on 9 Apr. Fairfax 'at his own desire' waived his privilege in the case. However, the bill itself had already been carried up to the Lords on 17 Mar. In the 1697–8 session he played a leading role in managing two bills, one for making the Aire and Calder navigable and the other for supporting the merchant adventurers' trade to Germany, both of which failed to reach the statute book. On 3 Mar. he was granted leave of absence for one week. Another petition from Colepeper during this session was rejected by the House.[4]

Returned for the county in a contested election in 1698, Fairfax was classed as a Court supporter in a comparative analysis of the old and new Parliaments. At this time he was included in two lists of placemen. In January 1699 he was involved in managing another bill for making the Aire and Calder navigable, and a bill (which later failed) for preventing the export of wool, while in April a bill was passed in the Commons for confirming the grant and settlement by William Forster* of manors and lands in Durham and Northumberland to Fairfax and others, for certain trusts and uses. In the 1699–1700 session Fairfax managed a bill through the House for the repair of Dover harbour. In an analysis of the House into interests in that year he was noted as a placeman.[5]

Before the first general election in 1701 Fairfax agreed at the York assizes to combine his candidacy with Sir John Kaye, 2nd Bt.*, in order to exclude his former partner Lord Downe (Henry Dawney*). By early December 1700 Downe had decided against contesting the election, at which time it was also reported from Yorkshire that Fairfax 'continues here expecting with a Christian application the sentence of dissolution', and that he would 'sooner quit the ten commandments than the strongest side or the prospect of advantage'. At the election Fairfax and Kaye were returned unopposed. In the 1701 Parliament Fairfax played a leading role in managing two bills, one for the relief of poor debtors in prison, which failed, and the other for establishing a corporation for the poor in Halifax, which did reach the statute book. When first delivering the report for the bill for relief of poor debtors Fairfax gave the report 'by word of mouth which was wrong'. His concern for debtors was not altogether disinterested, since he had himself wasted his Yorkshire estates and been obliged to mortgage Leeds Castle. However, his financial problems were alleviated to some extent in July when he was granted a pension of £600 p.a.[6]

Prior to the second 1701 election Ralph Thoresby, the Yorkshire antiquarian who had been a supporter of Fairfax in the past, wrote to Fairfax deploring his failure to attend a county meeting, because,

> as the world goes, notwithstanding the great services your lordship has been so eminent for, there seems to be a necessity to let your friends know that your lordship is willing to stand for the county. I humbly beg your lordship's pardon for this freedom, but I cannot bear that your truly ancient as well as honourable family should be excluded.

Fairfax certainly wished to stand and made a belated (and successful) application to the Duke of Newcastle (John Holles†) on 15 Nov., claiming that he had not expected 'so sudden a dissolution of this Parliament'. Although for a while it looked as if there would be a contest for the county seats, Kaye decided in November not to stand on grounds of ill-health, thereby ensuring that Fairfax would be returned unopposed along with Lord Irwin (Arthur Ingram*). In the new Parliament Fairfax played a leading role in the management of a failed bill for encouraging an invention for fixing colours in cloth, and he also reported and carried up two bills, one for navigation of the Derwent, and the other for reversing the outlawry of Charlotte Talbot. Before the 1702 election it was reported that Irwin, 'as well as others, wonder Lord Fairfax has not intimated his intentions to friends in the county for his resolution to stand again, which many complain they cannot hear from his lordship nor his agents here'. Despite the fact that many of the Yorkshire gentry wanted him to stand, Fairfax eventually desisted in favour of Lord Hartington (William Cavendish*).[7]

While out of Parliament Fairfax lived in Kent or in London. In order to recoup his finances, he took an interest in a Spanish galleon wrecked off the West Indies, said to be worth £2 million. He obtained a grant of an eighth part from Queen Anne, and then chartered a ship and provided diving equipment and a crew. The venture proved to be a financial disaster, and supposedly 'never brought in one farthing'. However, when a by-election came up for Yorkshire in January 1707, Fairfax was persuaded by Newcastle and Lord Wharton (Hon. Thomas*) to stand for election. He was returned in a contest, and during the remainder of the 1706–7 session he managed two private estate bills through the House, telling on 29 Mar. for the engrossment of the second of these measures. In an analysis of the House in early 1708 he was listed as a Whig. However, he had already lost his place in Parliament as a result of the Union, which barred peers of Scotland from sitting in the Commons. Fairfax died in London on 6 Jan. 1710. The servant attending him robbed him of what little money he had left. Fairfax was buried on the 10th at St. Martin-in-the-Fields. In order to save Leeds Castle and her Kent estates, his widow had to sell Denton and other properties in Yorkshire, but did so on very poor terms. Their son, the 6th Lord, went to settle on his mother's extensive plantations in Virginia.[8]

[1] *Dugdale's Vis. Yorks.* ed. Clay, ii. 191–2. [2] *HMC Lords*, n.s. iii. 204. [3] Boyer, *Anne Annals*, ix. 403; Cheshire RO, Shakerley mss, Fairfax to Peter Shakerley*, 15 Dec. 1688; N. Yorks. RO, Worsley mss ZON 13/1/32, Henry Fairfax to [Thomas Worsley I*], 11 Feb. 1689[–90]. [4] Stowe 746, f. 124. [5] *Cocks Diary*, 26. [6] BL, Althorp mss, Halifax pprs. box 4, Gervase Eyre* to Mq. of Halifax (William Savile†), 19 Aug. 1699; box 10, Ld. Weymouth (Thomas Thynne†) to same, 28 Aug. 1699; Huntington Lib. Stowe 58(1), pp. 17–18; Foxcroft, *Halifax*, ii. 327; *Cocks Diary*, 83; *Cal. Treas. Pprs.* 1697–1702, p. 511; E. D. Neill, *Fairfaxes of England and America*, 44. [7] Add. 70501, f. 31; W. Yorks. Archs. (Leeds), Temple Newsam mss TN/C9/160, James Blythman to Irwin, 1 Dec 1701; Glos. RO, Newton mss D.1844/C/10, Timothy Kiplin to Sir John Newton, 23 May 1702; Devonshire mss at Chatsworth House, Whildon pprs. William Grosvenor to James Whildon, 21 July 1702; *Thoresby Diary*, i. 373. [8] *Nicolson Diaries* ed. Jones and Holmes, 242, 437; Add. 37682, f. 155; Luttrell, *Brief Relation*, v. 433; W. Yorks. Archs. (Leeds), Vyner mss 5781, 'contested elections'; Boyer, 403; C. R. Markham, *Thomas, Ld. Fairfax*, 31; Neill, 40.

E. C./C. I. M.

FALKLAND, Anthony Carey, 5th Visct. [S] *see* **CAREY**

FANE, Sir Henry (c.1650–1706), of Basildon, Berks.

READING 1689–1698

b. c.1650, o. s. of Hon. George Fane† of Basildon by Dorothy, da. and h. of James Horsey of Honington, Warws., wid. of Thomas Marsh of Cambridge and Hackney, Mdx. m. 28 Apr. 1668, aged about 18, Elizabeth, da. of Thomas Southcote of Exeter, Devon, and h. to her nephew George Southcote of Calwoodley, Devon, 6s. (2 d.v.p.) 1da. KB 23 Apr. 1661.[1]

Capt. Queen's regt. horse 1678–9.

Freeman, Wallingford 1685.[2]

Commr. excise Apr.–Oct. 1689, forfeited estates [I] 1690; PC [I] 1690–d.[3]

Fane's principal estates lay in Ireland and Berkshire. For the former he had to thank his aunt, the dowager Countess of Bath, who settled on him some Irish estates of the Bourchiers in Limerick just prior to his marriage in 1668. In her will she confirmed the descent of other Irish estates as laid down in a deed of 1677 which probably favoured Fane as well. His Berkshire interest was strengthened by a mortgage of lands in Basildon which she also made over to him. Fane's political sympathies were Whiggish, sufficiently so in 1686 for the Earl of Clarendon (Henry Hyde†) to suggest alternative candidates to Sir William Rich, 2nd Bt.*, and Fane at Reading on the grounds that neither was 'good'. Although Fane lost local office early in 1687 his parliamentary ambitions remained. By September 1688 James II's regulators were reporting that he was making an interest in Reading 'as hoping to carry the mobile', and that he had the backing of Lord Lovelace (Hon. John†). His reward for supporting the Revolution was a seat in the Convention of 1689, a short spell as an excise commissioner and the office of standard-bearer of the gentlemen pensioners for his son, Henry Bourchier Fane.[4]

After securing re-election for Reading in 1690 Fane was well placed to exploit his connexions to obtain in May 1690 a valuable lease of some land adjoining St. James's Park. He was also in receipt of considerable sums of money from the secret service account (payments beginning in February 1690), plus £1,000 as recompense for losing his post in the excise. Fane thus had close ties to the Court, but was still perceived to be a Whig by Lord Carmarthen (Sir Thomas Osborne†) on a list of the 1690 Parliament. He was named during the first short session, on 24 Apr., to prepare the bill to appoint the oath of abjuration. Ireland now appeared as the only feasible outlet for his political ambitions and in July 1690 he was appointed to the commission of inquiry into Irish forfeited estates. In November he was sworn in as an Irish privy councillor. Irish business kept him out of England for most of the next session, although he was on the verge of returning on 28 Mar. when William Robinson reported 'Sir H. Vane [sic] goes next week to England, having sent his equipage (the little whore at the Duke's Head) before him'. In April 1691 Robert Harley* classed him as a Court supporter. Fane appears to have remained in England during the 1691–2 session, as on 14 Jan. 1692 he was granted leave of absence for a fortnight owing to ill-health. On a list of government officials drawn up by Lord Carmarthen between May and November 1692 he was described as a pensioner, a list of placemen for the same year putting his pension at £800 p.a. Similarly, on Grascome's list of spring 1693, extended to 1695, he was classed as a Court supporter with both a place and a pension. On 12 Feb. 1694 Fane was ordered into custody for failing to answer a call of the House. He was excused the following day when the House was informed that he was in London but ill with gout. He missed the beginning of the following session, and did not leave Dublin until mid-December 1694. He was then granted leave of absence on 23 Feb. 1695 to go into the country for the benefit of his health.⁵

After a contest, Fane was returned for Reading again at the 1695 election. He was involved in managing a private estate bill in favour of Lady Katharine Fane, the daughter of his second cousin, the 4th Earl of Westmorland (Vere Fane*), which was sent down from the Lords on 10 Jan. 1696. He reported from committee on 16 Jan. that no amendments were necessary and the bill duly passed the same day. Forecast as likely to support the Court on 31 Jan. over the proposed council of trade, he signed the Association promptly and voted in March for fixing the price of guineas at 22s. In April 1696 tragedy struck when his eldest surviving son, Henry, was killed in a duel. Subsequently Fane was able to secure the succession to the office of standard-bearer of the gentlemen pensioners for his next son, Charles. Fane did not vote on the question of Sir John Fenwick's† attainder on 25 Nov. 1696, possibly because he was absent in Ireland, where he still hoped for political advancement. In July 1697 Lord Winchester (Charles Powlett I*), one of the lords justices in Dublin, wrote to the Duke of Shrewsbury, 'I believe our old friend Sir H. Vane [sic] would accept of being a commissioner of the revenue'. However, no appointment followed. Fane's name appeared on one more parliamentary list, a comparative analysis of the old and new Parliaments in 1698, in which he was described as a Court supporter. He did not stand at Reading in 1698 and, indeed, little is known about his retirement, although he was reappointed to the Irish privy council upon Queen Anne's accession. He was buried on 12 Jan. 1706, leaving his estates to his heir, Charles, who subsequently sat as a Court Whig in the Irish parliament and who was created an Irish peer in 1718. Fane's grandson sat for Tavistock and Reading during the reign of George II.⁶

¹ *VCH Northants. Fams.* i. 112–13; IGI, Kent; *London Mar. Lic.* ed. Foster, 470. ² J. K. Hedges, *Hist. Wallingford*, 239. ³ Luttrell, *Brief Relation*, i. 523; ii. 86, 142. ⁴ *VCH Northants. Fams.* 112–13; PCC 139 Bath; *Clarendon Corresp.* ed. Singer, i. 555; L. K. J. Glassey, *Appt. JPs*, 74; Duckett, *Penal Laws and Test Act* (1883), 237; *CSP Dom.* 1689–90, p. 53. ⁵ *Cal. Treas. Bks.* ix. 527, 627; xvii. 554; Chandler, ii. 426; Trinity, Dublin, Clarke mss 749/6/564, 566, William Robinson to George Clarke*, 28, 31 Mar. 1691; Nottingham Univ. Lib. Portland (Bentinck) mss PwA 2392, list of placemen; *CSP Dom.* 1695, p. 238. ⁶ *VCH Northants. Fams.* 112; Luttrell, iv. 44, 61; *Portledge Pprs.* 227; *HMC Buccleuch*, ii. 510; *CSP Dom.* 1702–3, p. 144; PCC 36 Eedes.

S. N. H.

FANE, Hon. John (1686–1762), of Mereworth, Kent; Apethorpe, Northants. and Hanover Square, London.

HYTHE	1708–27 Jan. 1711
KENT	28 Sept. 1715–1722
BUCKINGHAM	1 Mar. 1727–1734

bap. 24 Mar. 1686, 4th son of Vere Fane*, 4th Earl of Westmorland; bro. of Hon. Mildmay Fane†. educ. Eton 1698; L. Inn 1703; Emmanuel, Camb. 1704. m. 5 Aug. 1716, Mary (d. 1778), da. and h. of Ld. Henry Cavendish*, s.p. suc. bro. Mildmay at Burston, Kent, 1715; cr. Baron Catherlough [I] 4 Oct. 1733; suc. bro. Thomas as 7th Earl of Westmorland 4 July 1736.¹

Capt. of horse, William Cadogan's* regt. (later 5 Drag. Gds.) 1709–10; lt.-col. regt. of William Windress (later 37 Ft.) 1710–14, col. 1715–17; col. 1 tp. Horse Gren. Gds. 1717–33; col. 1 tp. Life Gds. 1733–7; brig.-gen. 1735; maj.-gen. and lt.-gen. 1742, with effect from 1735 and 1739 respectively; gen. 1761.²

Asst. warden, Rochester Bridge, 1737–57, warden 1738, 1748, 1755; ld. lt. Northants, 1737–?d.; warden, East Bailiwick, Forest of Rockingham, 1737–?d.; master forester, Cliff Bailiwick, Forest of Rockingham, 1736–d.³

High steward, Oxford Univ. 1754, chancellor 1759–d.

Fane's life was characterized by luck and longevity. As well as an extensive army and parliamentary career spanning three reigns, he also outlived his three brothers thereby inheriting virtually all of the family property and titles. In 1708, his elder brother, the 6th Earl of Westmorland, the deputy-warden of the Cinque Ports, almost certainly influenced Fane's decision to contest Hythe. Following his return, the Earl of Sunderland (Charles, Lord Spencer*) listed him as a gain for the Whigs, and the compiler of a list of the new Parliament concurred, classing him as a Whig. Fane joined the army as a volunteer for the 1708 summer campaign seeing action at the battle of Oudenarde and the siege of Lille.

Fane returned to England for the opening session of Parliament carrying a letter of recommendation from the Duke of Marlborough (John Churchill†), who wrote to Lord Treasurer Godolphin (Sidney†) that Fane had 'behaved himself very well, so that I am desirous you would do him the honour of presenting him to the Queen. I like him much better than his brother [Westmorland].' Fane showed his support for the Whigs, telling on 29 Jan. 1709 against the question of whether to adjourn the consideration of the Orford election, and voting for the naturalization of the Palatines. Showing rather more interest in his army career than politics, Fane then left for Europe as a captain in General William Cadogan's* regiment of horse and fought at Malplaquet.⁴

A by-election for Hythe was ordered on 23 Dec., necessitated by the place clause in the Regency Act of 1706 which obliged Fane to seek re-election following his receipt of a captain's commission (the exception of army and navy officers from the provisions of the Act not extending to first commissions). Consequently, Fane was re-elected on 7 Jan. 1710, apparently without a contest. On 1 Feb. he told against an addition to an amendment to Edward Wortley Montagu's* place bill, a matter in which he might well have been expected to show some interest. He also supported the impeachment of Dr Sacheverell. Fane contested the 1710 Hythe election successfully, being classed as a Whig in the 'Hanover list', but the defeated Tory candidates presented a petition against them which led to Fane being unseated on 27 Jan. 1711.[5]

Fane then concentrated on his military career. In April 1713 his brother Westmorland wrote on his behalf to the Earl of Oxford (Robert Harley*) asking that Fane be promoted to the rank of colonel. Having 'thrown himself and his fortune entirely into the army', Fane had travelled with his regiment to Flanders, Canada, Inverlochy and Ireland. His fortunes increased with the Hanoverian succession and in 1715, when he inherited a substantial estate from his younger brother, Hon. Mildmay, and again in 1736 when he succeeded to the Westmorland title and estates. He embarked on an ambitious rebuilding programme at Apethorpe and Mereworth and, on a trip to France in 1751 with his wife, commented that the intendant of a particular town was 'no less diligent than myself in stone and mortar'. An opposition Whig in George II's reign, Westmorland later became a Tory and seems to have been involved in Jacobite intrigues.[6]

On his death, on 26 Aug. 1762, Westmorland's estate was split, with his nephew Sir Francis Dashwood, 2nd Bt.†, inheriting the lands in Kent, Middlesex and Sussex, and Thomas Fane†, a second cousin once removed, inheriting the Westmorland title and the property in Bedfordshire, Northamptonshire and Yorkshire.[7]

[1] IGI, Kent; J. R. Woodhead, *Rulers of London* (London and Mdx. Arch Soc.), 29. [2] Bodl. Dashwood C5, lt.-col. commn. for John Fane, 1710; Add. 70775, Westmorland to Harley, 9 Apr. 1713. [3] *Traffic and Politics* ed. Yates and Gibson, 298; Add. 34223, f. 35. [4] *Marlborough–Godolphin Corresp.* 1128. [5] *Statutes at Large*, iv. 281. [6] Add. 42593, f. 135; 70775, Westmorland to Harley, 9 Apr. 1713; *VCH Northants.* ii. 545; Hasted, *Kent*, v. 79–80; *HMC Denbigh*, v, 277. [7] PCC 405 St. Eloi.

S. M. W.

FANE, Hon. Sir Vere (1645–1693), of Apethorpe, Northants. and Mereworth, Kent.

PETERBOROUGH   22 Mar. 1671–1679 (Jan.)
KENT   1679 (Mar.)–1681 (Mar.)
            1689–18 Sept. 1691

b. 13 Feb. 1645, 3rd s. of Mildmay Fane†, 2nd Earl of Westmorland, being 1st surv. by 2nd w. Mary, da. and coh. of Horace, 1st Baron Vere of Tilbury, Essex, wid. of Sir Roger Townshend, 1st Bt.†, of Raynham Hall, Norf.; half-bro. of Charles Fane†, Lord le Despenser, and Sir Horatio Townshend, 3rd Bt.† *m.* 13 July 1671, (with £5–6,000), Rachel (*d.* 1711), da. and h. of John Bence†, Grocer and merchant, of Bevis Marks, London, 5s. (1 *d.v.p.*) 3da. KB 23 Apr. 1661; *suc.* half-bro. as 4th Earl of Westmorland 18 Sept. 1691.[1]

Asst. warden, Rochester bridge 1672–*d.*, warden 1673, 1680, 1687; jt. ld. lt., Kent 1692–*d.*[2]

The Fanes were a prominent family of Kentish origin with a long tradition of providing Members of the House of Commons and, more recently, the Lords. They had increased their fortunes through a series of judicious marriages until, by the time of the Restoration, they owned extensive estates in Northamptonshire, where their main seat was Apethorpe, and in Kent, where they owned Mereworth Castle. During the Civil War, Fane's father had joined the King's army but was imprisoned from 1643 to 1644 and was one of the first lords to take the Covenant and compound for his estates. Thereafter, his resistance took the quieter form of writing lampoons on the Parliamentarian regime. Fane himself was too young to take part in the politics of the Commonwealth and little is known of his early life. During the Restoration he showed himself to be of Country Whig inclinations, voted later for Exclusion and evidently welcomed the Revolution, although his son's recollection that he was 'very active and forward' in it is not backed up by any contemporary evidence and he is not mentioned in the account of events in Kent during December 1688 given by Sir John Knatchbull, 2nd Bt.* In 1689 Fane failed to be elected as the Whig candidate at Maidstone but combined with other Whigs to engineer the defeat of Sir William Twisden, 3rd Bt.* (who would not sign the Association), in the election for knight of the shire. As the Members for Kent, Fane and Knatchbull were accorded the honour of presenting the county Association to Hon. Henry Sidney† for delivery to King William.[3]

In the 1690 election for Kent, Fane was persuaded that Knatchbull need not be opposed by a man with better Whig credentials, and both were returned unopposed. The energy Fane displayed in elections was not translated into much activity in the House. He was classed as a Whig in the Marquess of Carmarthen's (Sir Thomas Osborne†) list of the new Parliament. During the summer of 1690, as a deputy-lieutenant and justice for Kent, he was involved in the pursuit and prosecution of suspected Jacobites and malcontents. Fane was listed as a Country supporter in Robert Harley's* analysis of April 1691.[4]

On 18 Sept. 1691 Fane inherited the Westmorland title and an estate which by all accounts was much encumbered with debts. According to his son, despite getting some £40,000 from his father-in-law, Westmorland lived beyond his means and his mismanagement contributed to the family's financial problems. Westmorland did, however, make some attempts to recoup the family fortunes. In 1689 he, Thomas Mun† and John Farthing had claimed to be able to show that the charges of managing the excise were too high and they petitioned to be appointed as the new commissioners. Although the petitioners were allowed to inspect the accounts, Fane seems to have made no financial gain from this project. He was, however, more successful in 1692–3 in having large debts owed to the crown by John and Sir Alexander Bence assigned to himself. This grant was in consideration of his 'good and faithful services', which may refer to his performance in the Lords as a supporter of the Court.[5]

Westmorland died on 29 Dec. 1693, probably from complications brought on by diabetes. His will, made on 29 Dec., left his children in the guardianship of his wife and his lands to be inherited by his eldest son, Vere. Two of his younger sons, Hon. John* (later 7th Earl of Westmorland) and Hon. Mildmay†, sat in Parliament.[6]

[1] Add. 34223, f. 4. [2] *Traffic and Politics* ed. Yates and Gibson, 296; *CSP. Dom.* 1691–2, p. 155; 1693, p. 212. [3] *VCH Northants. Fams.* i. 100; Add. 33923, ff. 457–9, 462–3; 34223, f. 4. [4] Add. 33923, ff. 470, 477, 480, 481; *HMC Hastings*, ii. 370, 388; *CSP Dom.* 1690–1, pp. 80, 84. [5] *HMC Portland*, iii. 475; *HMC Ancaster*, 435; Add. 34223, ff. 4, 6; *Cal. Treas. Bks.* ix. 28, 30, 61, 121, 278, 298, 324, 1621; x. 83, 114, 841–2; xvii. 510; *Cal. Treas. Pprs.* 1557–1696, pp. 41, 47–48, 69–71, 80–81, 210; *HMC Lords*, iv. 51, 297. [6] *VCH Northants. Fams.* 101; *The Ancestor*, xi. 148–9; PCC 22 Box.

S. M. W.

FARINGTON, Sir Richard, 1st Bt. (c.1644–1719), of South Street, Chichester, Suss.

CHICHESTER   4 Jan.–28 Mar. 1681, 1698–1700
1708–1713, 1715–7 Aug. 1719

b. c.1644, 2nd s. of John Farington† of Chichester by Anne, da. of John May of Lavant, Suss. *m.* (1) lic. 28 Feb. 1671, aged 27, Elizabeth, da. of William Marlott of Itchingfield, Suss., 3s. *d.v.p.*; (2) lic. 24 May 1687, Elizabeth (*d.* c.1739), da. and h. of John Peachey of Eartham, Suss., *s.p. cr.* Bt. 17 Dec. 1697.[1]

Sheriff, Suss. 1696–7.

Some four generations of Faringtons had lived in Chichester, which both Farington and his father had represented under Charles II. Described during the Restoration period as a 'fanatic' in religion, Farington had been a supporter of Monmouth in 1683 and was arrested on Monmouth's invasion 1685. He may have been a Whig 'collaborator' in 1687–8, which would possibly explain his defeats at Chichester in 1690 and 1695, even though on the latter occasion he enjoyed the support of a local magnate, the Earl of Tankerville. Farington did eventually succeed: having married his eldest son to the daughter of local Tory Sir Thomas Miller* in 1697, he stood successfully in the 1698 election with Miller's son, John. Queried as a Court supporter in a comparative list of the old and new Parliaments of about September 1698, he in fact voted for the disbanding bill on 18 Jan. 1699, although in the next session an analysis of the House of early 1700 listed him in the Junto interest. It is not known whether he stood in the first general election of 1701, but he was certainly defeated in the second.[2]

Farington returned to Parliament for Chichester in 1708 after a local agreement had been made between the parties, in which Farington had been involved on the Whig side, to avoid future contests. He was marked as a Tory in a list of 1708 with the returns added, though possibly in error due to his absence from the Commons for some years, but his political position may in general have become less clear for he was classed as both supporting and opposing the impeachment of Dr Sacheverell in different lists from 1710. Otherwise he was not particularly active in the House. He was given leave for one month on 16 Dec. 1709. The 1707 agreement having broken down, Farington was obliged to contest Chichester in 1710 and did so successfully. Although classified as a Tory in the 'Hanover list', if he had temporarily flirted with Toryism Farington had by this time returned to his earlier politics, voting for the Whig candidates in the county election, and for the motion of 'No Peace without Spain' on 7 Dec. 1711. He was given leave of absence on 18 Mar. 1712 for the recovery of his health. On 18 June 1713 he voted against the French commerce bill. He was defeated at Chichester in 1713 but was returned in 1715 when he was classed as a Whig in a comparative analysis of the 1713 and 1715 Parliaments. Thereafter he voted consistently with the Whigs until his death on 7 Aug. 1719.[3]

[1] *Vis. Suss.* (Harl. Soc. lxxxix), 44; J. Comber, *Suss. Gens. Horsham*, 220; PCC 7, 183 Browning. [2] *Dorm. and Extinct Baronetcies*, 192. [3] East Suss. RO, Danny MS 2188, Suss. poll 1710.

P. W.

FARRER, William (c.1656–1737), of Biddenham, Beds. and the Inner Temple.

BEDFORD 1695–1698, 1701 (Dec.)–1702
1705–1713, 1715–1727

b. c.1656, prob. 1st s. of Thomas Farrer of Harrold, Beds., Aylesbury, Bucks. and the I. Temple by Helen, da. of Sir William Boteler of Biddenham and Harrold. *educ.* I. Temple 1667, called 1677; Trinity, Oxf. matric. 16 Feb. 1672, aged 15. *m.* (1) 2 Mar. 1680, his 1st cos. Mary, da. and coh. of William Boteler† of Biddenham, 1s. *d.v.p.* 3da. (1 *d.v.p.*); (2) Elizabeth (*d.* 1734), *s.p. suc.* fa. 1703.[1]

Burgess, Bedford 1690; dep. recorder by 1691–1711.[2]

Member, SPCK c.1699–bef. 1708; master, St. Katherine's Hosp. by the Tower 1715–bef. 1727; commr. for building 50 new churches 1715–aft.1727.[3]

Commr. army, navy and transport debts 1700–5; clerk of the pipe Apr. 1710–July 1711.[4]

Chairman, cttees. of supply and ways and means 1708–10, 1715–27.

Several members of Farrer's family had achieved minor distinction in the practice of the law: his own father had been a bencher of the Inner Temple, while an uncle and namesake, also a templar, had been appointed King's Counsel in 1689 and served after the Revolution as solicitor to Queen Catherine of Braganza. Farrer himself was admitted to the Inner Temple as a ten-year-old, at his father's special request, and called to the bar at the age of only 20. His appointment as deputy-recorder of Bedford under the 3rd Earl of Bolingbroke (Paulet St. John†), himself chosen recorder in 1689, involved him closely in the politics of the borough and enabled him, possibly with the assistance of the St. John interest, to secure his election to Parliament for Bedford in 1695. Although his political sympathies were clearly always with the Whigs, Farrer's early behaviour in Parliament was unpredictable, perhaps reflecting the 'Country' proclivities of Lord Bolingbroke, who had voted in the Lords in 1693 in favour of the place bill. On the other hand, his legal training ensured that he was also very active in managing politically uncontroversial bills through the House, including many private bills. Thus, even in his first session in the House he helped to manage two private bills through the Commons. He was marked as 'doubtful' in the forecast for the division of 31 Jan. 1696 on the proposed council of trade and, returning after a fortnight's leave of absence granted on 12 Mar., he voted against fixing the price of guineas at 22s. He had, however, signed the Association promptly.[5]

By the second session Farrer had aligned himself more closely with the Whig ministry, possibly in order to qualify himself for some employment. He voted on 25 Nov. 1696 in favour of the attainder of Sir John Fenwick†, and was a teller on 18 Jan. 1697 on the Whig side against a motion for a call of the House. He assisted in the management of bills. On 4 Mar. he was given leave of absence for three weeks. The following session he reported two bills from committee, including the bill to give more time to 'divers persons' to 'qualify themselves for their employments'. His opposition to the coal duty bill, against which he told on 3 May, may have been prompted by local concerns, for in a later Parliament Bedfordshire interests were instrumental in reforming the trade in imported coal (see CARTERET, Edward). On the other hand, a more general principle probably lay behind his tellership three days later against receiving a petition from several landlords in Southwark against the Act to regulate the privileges of prisons, which empowered sheriffs' officers to make a forcible entry into various premises without a prior warrant, since this local opposition threatened to hinder efforts to suppress urban crime. An association with the movement for the reformation of manners, for which a society was active in Southwark, is suggested by Farrer's appearance among the earliest subscribers to the Society for Promoting Christian Knowledge, though by 1708 his keenness had waned and he was noted as one of the 'residing members' of the society who neither attended nor paid his subscriptions. In July 1698 he was included in a list of placemen (probably in error, being confused with his uncle the King's Counsel), and in about September he was classed as a supporter of the Court party in a comparative analysis of the old and new Parliaments.[6]

Farrer does not appear to have sought re-election in 1698 and was not returned again until the 1701–2 Parliament. But he was elected (in fourth place out of five) in April 1700 as one of the parliamentary commissioners to examine the debts due for the army, navy and transports, and reported to the House from that commission in February 1701. He was classed as a 'gain' for the Whig party by Lord Spencer (Charles*) when he won back his seat in November 1701, and in Robert Harley's* list of this Parliament he was included with the Whigs. He retained his place on the army debts commission while an MP, presenting accounts to the House on one occasion in his official capacity. He presented a bill to strengthen the Henrician Act for the repair of bridges, and then piloted it through its stages in the Commons. He also chaired the committee of the whole on the mutiny bill during February 1702. After a brief period in the country to attend a daughter's marriage he was back in the House by 28 Apr. to act as a teller against giving leave for a bill to relieve the merchant Ignatius Gould from the effects of the Irish Forfeited Estates Resumption Act.[7]

Farrer was not returned again until the 1705 general election, in which he and Sir Philip Monoux, 3rd Bt.*, a fellow Whig, defeated the Tory Samuel Rolt*. By this time the army debts commission, to which he had given continuous service, was coming to an end. He was listed as a 'Churchman' in an analysis of the 1705 Parliament, and voted for the Court candidate as Speaker on 25 Oct. 1705. He took a managerial role in three bills during the session, and in between was granted leave of absence for three weeks on 20 Dec. In the division of 18 Feb. 1706 on the 'place clause' of the regency bill he sided with the Court. In the 1706–7 session he was named to five drafting committees, four relating to private estates and the other to the repair of a Bedfordshire highway, which he managed through the House. Indeed, his usefulness as a parliamentary lawyer was recognized at about this time by a correspondent of the Duke of Shrewsbury, who had enlisted his assistance with a private bill in January 1707. Farrer was also called upon to manage a conference with the Lords during April 1707 over the bill continuing the vagrancy Acts. In the 1707–8 session he was named to seven drafting committees, and managed one of the resulting bills through the Commons, a bill to continue the Act for ascertaining tithes on hemp and flax. He also contributed to the management of three other bills. In two parliamentary lists of 1708 he was classed as a Whig.[8]

Returned unopposed in 1708, Farrer was named on 24 Nov. as the Whig candidate for the chair of the committees of supply and ways and means, securing a majority of 50 over the Tory John Conyers*. This post saw Farrer chair the committee of the whole on 37 occasions during the session, as supply and related financial business (such as the resettlement of Nevis and St. Christopher's and the allowances for Scottish fish exports) passed through the House. In the only vote in this session for which a division list has survived he supported the naturalization of the Palatines. His involvement in financial legislation clearly limited his availability for other business, but he was concerned to forward several private bills and did manage a Northamptonshire road bill through the House. He voted for the impeachment of Dr Sacheverell, and was rewarded in April 1710 for his services to his party in the House with the office of clerk of the pipe, worth £800 a year. He then survived not only the by-election necessitated by his acceptance of a place, but the general election only a few months afterwards, in which the Whig interest in Bedford encountered a Tory challenge.[9]

Things soon began to go wrong for Farrer in the new Parliament. He lost the chairmanship of the committee of supply, although the Commons did make use of his legislative experience in the management of several private bills. The new lord treasurer, Oxford (Robert Harley*), had marked him down as a prime target for dismissal from office, and in July 1711 he lost the clerkship of the pipe. Worse was to follow: with the death of Bolingbroke late in the year, Bedford corporation elected the Tory Lord Bruce (Charles*), as recorder, and he in turn replaced Farrer with a deputy who conformed to his own principles. Farrer stuck to his political guns, voting on 7 Dec. 1711 in favour of the 'No Peace without Spain' motion. In the 1711–12 session he continued to be active in legislative matters, helping to pilot an estate bill through the House on behalf of the Duke of Bedford, and acting as chair of the committee of the whole when the Commons discussed a bill on the African trade. Rather surprisingly he seems to have been inactive in the 1713 session, although he was recorded as voting on 18 June against the French commerce bill, as a Whig. In the 1713 general election the loss of his local office, combined with a swing to the Tories in Bedford corporation and in the constituency generally, proved too much to overcome, and he was defeated by Samuel Rolt. He petitioned, alleging that Rolt was not duly qualified according to the terms of the 1711 Landed Qualification Act, but the petition was never heard.[10]

Farrer regained his seat, and the chairmanship of supply and ways and means, in the 1715 Parliament, being listed as a Whig in a comparative analysis of the 1713 and 1715 Parliaments. He voted consistently with the Court until he retired from active politics at the 1727 election. A year later he made his will, giving his address as St. George the Martyr, Middlesex, and leaving as his heir a great-nephew, Dennis Farrer, of Cold Brayfield, Buckinghamshire, whom Farrer referred to as his 'grandson': in fact, Dennis had married Farrer's granddaughter, the daughter of William Hillersden*. By the time of his death on 22 Sept. 1737, Farrer was living at Cold Brayfield, and he was buried there.[11]

[1] *Beds. Hist. Rec. Soc.* v. 90–91; Lipscomb, *Bucks.* iv. 48–49. [2] Bedford Bor. Council, Bedford bor. recs. B2/3, corp. act bk. 1688–1718, ff. 12, 17, 116. [3] *Chapter in Eng. Church Hist.* ed. McClure, 2; SPCK Archs. min. bk. 4, pp. 93–94; C. Jamison, *Hist. St. Katherine's Hosp.* 192; E. G. W. Bill, *Q. Anne Churches*, p. xxiv. [4] *Post Boy*, 1–4 Dec. 1711; *Cal. Treas. Bks.* xxv. 433. [5] *VCH Bucks.* iv. 325; Lipscomb, 49; J. C. Sainty, *Eng. Law Officers* (Selden Soc. supp. ser. vii), 89; *Cal. Treas. Bks.* xi. 305; Bedford bor. recs. B2/3, f. 7; *Bull. IHR*, liii. 82. [6] *Bull. IHR*, sp. supp. vii. 25; *Chapter in Eng. Church Hist.* 2; SPCK Archs. min. bk. 4, pp. 93–94. [7] *Cal. Treas. Bks.* xv. 414; Add. 70037, Farrer to Harley, 9 Apr. 1702. [8] Northants. RO, Montagu (Boughton) mss 77/70, M. Talbot to Shrewsbury, 13 Jan. 1706–7. [9] Add. 17677 CCC, f. 649. [10] Add. 70332, memo. by Harley, 4 June 1711; Luttrell, *Brief Relation*, vi. 377, 564;

Huntington Lib. HM 30659, newsletter 4 Apr. 1710; Bedford bor. recs. B2/3, f. 111; Post Boy, 29 Aug.–1 Sept. 1713. [11] PCC 223 Wake; VCH Bucks. 325; Lipscomb, 48–49; Hist. Reg. Chron. 1737, p. 22.

D. W. H.

FARRINGTON, Thomas (c.1664–1712), of St. James's Street, Westminster, and Chislehurst, Kent.

MALMESBURY 1705–7 Oct. 1712

b. c.1664, o. s. of Thomas Farrington of St. Andrew Undershaft, London and Chislehurst, asst. R. African Co. 1672–3, by Mary, da. of John Smith of St. Mary Aldermanbury, London and S. Tidworth, Hants, sis. of John Smith I*. m. lic. 16 Aug. 1687 (with £3,000), Theodosia, da. of Richard Bettenson (1st s. d.v.p. of Sir Richard Bettenson, 1st Bt., of Wimbledon, Surr. and Scadbury Park, Chislehurst), and coh. of her bro. Sir Edward Bettenson, 2nd Bt. (d. 1733), of Scadbury Park, 1s. 2da. suc. fa. 1694.[1]

Capt. 2 Ft. Gds. (Coldstream Gds.) Dec. 1688–93, lt.-col. 1693–4; col. of ft. (later 29 Ft.) 1694–8, 1702–d.; commr. stamp duty 1698–1702; brig.-gen. 1704, maj.-gen. 1706, lt.-gen. 1709.[2]

Farrington's father, a London merchant descended from the Faringtons of Worden Hall, Lancashire, had purchased a 'small estate' at Chislehurst in about 1670. Thomas snr. may well have been the 'Mr Farringdon that lives in Holborn' against whom an information was laid in 1681 for 'speaking treasonable words . . . 'tis said of the same nature as those for which [Stephen] College suffered'. At any rate there can be no doubting the Whig sympathies of his son. The younger Thomas was commissioned by the Prince of Orange as a captain in the Coldstream Guards in December 1688, being promoted to lieutenant-colonel in 1693 under Hon. Thomas Tollemache*. This regimental connexion perhaps inaugurated Farrington's association with Hon. Thomas Wharton*, one of Tollemache's close friends, who was later to provide him with his parliamentary seat. Another valued political contact was his maternal uncle John Smith I, and after he had been given his own regiment in 1694 it was Smith, together with other 'friends', who interceded with the secretary of state, Shrewsbury, to prevent a West Indian posting. Intended at one point for service in Flanders, Farrington's regiment in fact saw no action during the Nine Years War, and was broken after the peace. Farrington himself was compensated with a commissionership of the stamp duty, but this did not stop him from acting as 'captain' of the 'band' of disbanded officers formed under Lord Romney (Hon. Henry Sidney†) to press for re-employment. When his regiment was reconstituted in 1702 he lost the stamp duty commissionership. Obliged to threaten resignation in October 1702 to forestall another proposed tour of duty in the West Indies, he eventually reached the Low Countries in May 1704, by which time he had attained the rank of brigadier-general (his commission backdated, supposedly at the Duke of Marlborough's [John Churchill†] particular insistence), and although his regiment arrived just too late for the Blenheim campaign it was actively engaged in the fighting of the following year, and in 1706 participated in the battle of Ramillies.[3]

Recommended by Wharton at Malmesbury in 1705, and surviving both a contest and a petition, he was classed as a 'Churchman' in a list of this Parliament and, more realistically, his election was reckoned by Lord Sunderland (Charles, Lord Spencer*) as a gain. He voted for Smith in the division on the Speaker on 25 Oct. 1705, and for the Court side over the 'place clause' in the regency bill on 18 Feb. 1706. Following a brief spell in Portugal, his regiment returned to England in 1707. He was an occasional appointee to important committees, and on 24 Apr. 1707 there occurred his only tellership, against agreeing with one of the Lords' amendments to the bill to prevent dangers arising from the bringing of large quantities of gunpowder into London and Southwark. He was marked as a Whig in two lists of early 1708. Later that year he took part in the expedition to Ostend commanded by Thomas Erle*. His connexion with Wharton had been reinforced shortly after the previous general election when his eldest daughter married one of Wharton's nephews, Lord Lindsey (Robert Bertie*, Lord Willoughby de Eresby), and in the 1708 election he was returned again safely at Malmesbury, despite another petition. Now a lieutenant-general, he voted for the naturalization of the Palatines in 1709 and for the impeachment of Dr Sacheverell in 1710. Under the Tory administration his regiment was transferred to the Spanish establishment and stationed at Gibraltar. Whether or not he ever joined it there, he was back at Westminster on 7 Dec. 1711 to support the 'No Peace without Spain' motion.[4]

Farrington died on 7 Oct. 1712, aged 48, and was buried at Chislehurst. He had owned some £3,000 worth of Bank stock in 1710, and his will mentioned property in the City, besides the houses in St. James's Street and at Chislehurst. His mother and John Smith I were named as trustees.[5]

[1] Le Neve, Mon. Angl. 1650–1718, p. 248; 1680–99, pp. 158–9; PCC 187 Barnes, 76 Box; CSP Dom. 1700–2, p. 456; Mar. Lic. Vicar-Gen. (Harl. Soc. xxiii), 97; (Harl. Soc. xxxi), 11; K. G. Davies, R. African Co. 381; Webb, Miller and Beckwith, Hist. Chislehurst, 156.

[2] H. Everard, *Hist. 29 Ft.* 1, 562; *Cal. Treas. Bks.* xiii. 450; xvii. 238; *CJ*, xii. 501. [3] Croston, *Lancs.* (1888–93), iv. 170–1; *Arch. Cant.* xiii. 395; Webb, Miller and Beckwith, 157–8, 269–70; *CSP Dom.* 1680–1, p. 657; Everard, 5–10, 14, 19–23; Luttrell, *Brief Relation*, iii. 376; iv. 440; v. 223; *HMC Buccleuch*, ii. 121, 127, 131. [4] *Wilts. Arch. Mag.* xlvi. 85; Everard, 27–32. [5] Le Neve, 1650–1718, p. 248; Egerton 3359 (unfol.); PCC 187 Barnes.

D. W. H.

FAWKES, Francis (1674–1747), of Farnley, Yorks.

KNARESBOROUGH 15 Mar. 1714–1715

b. 18 June 1674, 2nd but 1st surv. s. of Thomas Fawkes* by 1st w. *educ.* Jesus, Camb. 1690; G. Inn 1692, called 1700, bencher 1724. *m.* 7 May 1700, Margaret (*d.* 1721), da. and coh. of John Ayscough of Osgodby, Lincs., 8s. (5 *d.v.p.*) 3da. *d.v.p. suc.* fa. 1707.[1]

Fawkes was a candidate for Parliament only once, being returned for Knaresborough in March 1714 at a by-election necessitated by the death of Christopher Stockdale. Any time which Fawkes may have spent at the House was cut short by his procuring leave of absence on 3 June. He was classed as a Tory in the Worsley list. He died on 11 Nov. 1747, and was buried at Otley, Yorkshire.[2]

[1] *Dugdale's Vis. Yorks.* ed. Clay, i. 207–8. [2] Ibid. 207.

E. C.

FAWKES, Thomas (c.1640–1707), of Farnley, Yorks.

KNARESBOROUGH 21 Mar. 1689–1690
17 May 1690–1695

b. c.1640, 1st s. of Michael Fawkes of Farnley by his 3rd w. Mary, da. of Sir John Molyneux, 1st Bt., of Teversall, Notts. *educ.* G. Inn 1659. *m.* (1) by 1669, Sarah (*d.* 1674), da. and h. of Francis Mitchell of Arthington Grange, Yorks., 2s. (1 *d.v.p.*) 1da.; (2) lic. 25 Dec. 1677, Mary, da. of William Welby of Denton, Lincs., 1s. *d.v.p. suc.* fa. 1647.[1]

A captain in the West Riding militia, Fawkes had given evasive answers to James II's 'three questions', on the repeal of the Test Act and Penal Laws, and at the Revolution acted locally with Lord Fairfax (Thomas*) on behalf of the Prince of Orange. Involved in a double return for Knaresborough in 1690 with Sir Henry Slingsby, 3rd Bt.†, he petitioned on the grounds of bias on the part of the bailiff, and on 17 May, on the report of the merits of the double return and election, was agreed to have had 'most qualified voices' and was declared duly elected. Classed in March as a Tory and probable Court supporter by Lord Carmarthen (Sir Thomas Osborne†),

Fawkes was included in another list in December as a likely supporter of Carmarthen in case of an attack on the minister in the Commons. In April 1691 Robert Harley* noted him as a Country supporter. However, he was not an active Member, and was twice given leave of absence, on 31 Mar. 1694 and 9 Mar. 1695. Although standing down at Knaresborough in the general election of 1695, he remained active in local affairs, especially in charitable work towards church restoration, as a friend and correspondent of John Killingbeck, the celebrated preacher and vicar of Leeds. Fawkes died on 7 Aug. 1707.[2]

[1] *Dugdale's Vis. Yorks.* ed. Clay, i. 206–7. [2] Add. 15587, ff. 232–4; Stowe 747, ff. 114, 127.

E. C./C. I. M.

FEILDING, Hon. William (1669–1723), of Ashtead, Surr. and Duke Street, Westminster.

CASTLE RISING 29 Nov. 1705–21 Sept. 1723

b. 1669, 2nd s. of William Feilding, 3rd Earl of Denbigh, by his 1st w. Mary (*d.* 1669), da. of Sir Robert King of Boyle Abbey, co. Roscommon, wid. of Sir William Meredith, 1st Bt., of Creenehill, co. Kildare. *educ.* Eton c.1680–6; Queen's, Oxf. 1686. *m.* c.Dec. 1705, Lady Diana, da. of Francis Newport†, 1st Earl of Bradford, sis. of Hon. Richard Newport I* and Hon. Thomas Newport*, wid. of Thomas Howard*, *s.p.*[1]

Lt. yeomen of the gd. 1704–8; 2nd clerk comptroller of Bd. of Green Cloth 1716, 1st clerk comptroller 1717, 2nd clerk 1720, 1st clerk 1723.

Feilding, who in 1704 had bought an office with a salary of £500 p.a., made a highly advantageous marriage the following year to a wealthy widow with a parliamentary seat at her disposal. She had title during her lifetime to the estates of her first husband (with no surviving children to complicate matters) and thereby enjoyed the nomination of one Member at Castle Rising. Feilding obtained the seat in 1705 when a family friend chose to sit elsewhere. It was gossiped before the wedding that 'this old lady, for she is near fifty if not quite, is fallen in love with this young Feilding, and says she only begs he will be civil to her; she fears he cannot love her, though she does him so much'. Although himself the younger brother of a Tory peer, Feilding was now connected with various Court Whigs among his wife's kinsmen and her first husband's friends. He also came into contact with Robert Walpole II*, who controlled the other seat at Castle Rising, but this association was not particularly friendly, as the Howard and Walpole interests co-existed in the borough uneasily and in a constant atmosphere of mutual distrust.[2]

In Parliament Feilding was a Whig, with leanings towards the Court. On 18 Feb. 1706 he voted with the ministry over the regency bill. He was marked as a Whig in two lists of 1708. In the same year he resigned his office of lieutenant of the yeomen of the guard. Having supported the naturalization of the Palatines in 1709, the following year he voted for the impeachment of Dr Sacheverell, and on 7 Dec. 1711 he voted for the 'No Peace without Spain' motion. He opposed the French commerce bill on 18 June 1713 and voted against the expulsion of Richard Steele on 18 Mar. 1714. In the Worsley list he was classified as a Whig.[3]

Feilding was appointed to the Board of Green Cloth in 1716, most probably through the interest of his wife's family, the Newports, both at Court and with the clerk of the Green Cloth, their Shropshire ally Sir William Forester*. Feilding died at Epsom on 21 Sept. 1723 and was buried at Ashtead. 'I regret him prodigiously', wrote his niece, Lady Mary Wortley Montagu, on hearing of his death. His wife outlived him.[4]

[1] *Cal. Treas. Pprs.* 1702–7, p. 459; *Wentworth Pprs.* 51; Nichols, *Leics.* iv. 293. [2] Luttrell, *Brief Relation*, v. 427; *Wentworth Pprs.* 50–51. [3] Luttrell, vi. 319. [4] F. E. Paget, *Recs. Ashtead Estate*, 71; *The Gen.* n.s. vi. 23; *Lady Mary Wortley Montagu Letters*, ii. 31.

D. W. H.

FELTON, Sir Adam, 3rd Bt. (aft. 1637–97), of Playford, Suff.

ORFORD 1695–9 Feb. 1697

b. aft. 1637, 1st surv. s. of Sir Henry Felton, 2nd Bt.†, of Shotley, Suff. and Playford by Susanna, da. of Sir Lionel Tollemache, 2nd Bt.†, of Helmingham, Suff.; bro. of Thomas Felton*. *m.* by 1676, Elizabeth, da. of Sir George Reresby of Thrybergh, Yorks., wid. of Sir Francis Foljambe, 1st Bt.†, of Walton, Derbys., Edward Horner of Mells, Som. and William, Visct. Monson of Castlemaine [I]†, 1da. *suc.* fa. as 3rd Bt. Oct. 1690.[1]

Felton stood with Sir Joseph Williamson on the Tory interest at Thetford in 1690, but after a double return they were declared not elected. Although he originally had no intention of standing at Orford, in 1695 he joined his Whig brother Thomas as a candidate at the eleventh hour, in order to prevent an outsider being brought in and to settle the 'differences' in the borough. Thomas was quite 'cold in the matter and told him he durst not propose him to his party for they looked on him [to be] as great a Jacobite as Sir Edward Turnor*', but Felton 'proposed himself' at a meeting of the local Whig 'cabal' and was accepted. Afterwards, some Whigs expressed strong reservations about the arrangement. Their fears, however, were not borne out. Forecast as likely to support the Court in the divisions of 31 Jan. 1696 on the proposed council of trade, Felton signed the Association promptly and in his dealings with the corporation he did little to satisfy Tories in Orford: in October 1696 one Tory wrote, 'I have reason to believe he is more for them [the Whigs] than us'.[2]

Reported on 27 Jan. 1697 to be 'very sick and not like to recover', he died on 9 Feb.[3]

[1] *Procs. Suff. Inst. Arch.* iv. 33, 55; Add. 19125, ff. 127–9. [2] W. Suss. RO, Shillinglee mss Ac.454/1009, 968, Theophilus Hooke to Sir Edward Turnor, 4 Nov. 1695, Nathaniel Gooding to same, 26 Oct. 1696. [3] Ibid. Ac.454/969, Gooding to Turnor, 27 Jan. 1696[–7]; *Hervey Diary*, 26.

D. W. H.

FELTON, Thomas (1649–1709), of Whitehall, Westminster and Playford, Suff.

ORFORD 1690–10 Feb. 1700
BURY ST. EDMUNDS 1701 (Dec.)–3 Mar. 1709

bap. 12 Oct. 1649, 6th but 2nd surv. s. of Sir Henry Felton, 2nd Bt.†, of Playford; bro. of Sir Adam Felton, 3rd Bt.* *m.* ?(1) lic. 1 Feb. 1677, Elizabeth King of Down Ampney, Glos., *s.p.*; (2) Lady Elizabeth Howard (*d.* 1681), da. and coh. of James, 3rd Earl of Suffolk, 1da. *suc.* bro. as 4th Bt. 9 Feb. 1697.[1]

Page of honour 1665–Mar. 1671; groom of the bedchamber Mar. 1671–by 16 May 1679; master of the hawks (apptd. for life) 1675–1703; master of the Household 1689–Nov. 1708, comptroller Nov. 1708–*d.*[2]

Asst. Mines Adventurers' Co. 1693.[3]

The circumstances under which Felton left his post as groom of the bedchamber to Charles II have not been established. He was a crony of the 2nd Earl of Sunderland and by 1690 at least, unlike his father and elder brother, was a firm Whig. Lord Carmarthen (Sir Thomas Osborne†) classified him as such in his analysis of the 1690 Parliament. In the previous election Felton had been willing to aid his Whig cousin Hon. Thomas Tollemache*, and at Orford had enjoyed the assistance not only of his family, but also of the Whig Sir John Duke, 2nd Bt.* He was listed as a supporter of the Court by Robert Harley* in April 1691, figured in no fewer than four lists of placemen in 1692–3, and was marked by Samuel Grascome as an office-holder and a member of the Court party. But he was never prominent or particularly active in the House. His important political role was behind the scenes as an agent for, and adviser to, Sunderland, and especially as an intermediary between the Earl and the Whig leaders. He also acted for Sunderland in a business matter, undertaking the preliminary negotiations for the marriage of Lord Spencer (Charles*) in 1694. Common knowledge of his part in Sunderland's intrigues probably explains the attack on him in 'The Club Men of the House of Commons' (1694), a satirical ballad against placemen:

> Tom Felton pretends to be wonderful sly;
> Yet sure without taking much labour to pry,
> One may see that, both sober and drunk, he's a spy.

A beneficiary of King William's land grants, he received the lordship of Egham in Surrey, and by the time of the 1695 election his political record had rendered him highly obnoxious to many Tories in Orford. Sir Edward Turnor*, faced with an offer of an electoral compact, snorted, 'I scorn to stand with Mr Felton; Sir Robert Rich [2nd Bt.*] is only fit to stand with him'.[4]

Either for tactical reasons, or to please his family, Felton acquiesced in an accommodation with a Tory candidate in 1695, but 'the heads of his party' repudiated this scheme. In order to forestall the election of an 'outsider' Sir Adam Felton then proposed to stand himself. Thomas 'coldly' refused to recommend him but the local Whigs accepted his candidature and both brothers were returned. Thomas was forecast as likely to back the Court in the divisions of 31 Jan. 1696 on the proposed council of trade. He signed the Association in February and voted the following month for fixing the price of guineas at 22s. He was involved with Sunderland in meetings with the Junto to decide how best to proceed in Parliament in Sir John Fenwick's† case, and voted on 25 Nov. for the attainder. 'Laid up with a fit of the gout' in February 1697, he was none the less able to make efforts on behalf of (Sir) Joseph Jekyll* at the Orford by-election caused by his brother's death. It was rumoured in March and April 1697, and again a year later, that on the promotion of Lord Wharton (Hon. Thomas*) he would be made comptroller of the Household, but Wharton was not promoted. Meanwhile Felton had accompanied the King to the peace negotiations at Ryswick.[5]

Blacklisted as a placeman before the 1698 election, Felton stood for knight of the shire as well as at Orford. In the county he was heavily beaten; at Orford, on the other hand, he was returned with Sir Charles Hedges after a contest that was hotly disputed and made the subject of a petition. Marked as a placeman and as a member of the Court party in lists of the new Parliament, Felton voted on 18 Jan. 1699 against the third reading of the disbanding bill. The Orford election case was finally reported in February 1700 and after a long debate carried against the sitting Members by the narrowest majority. Even a Country sympathizer like Sir Richard Cocks, 2nd Bt.*, admitted that 'Hedges and Felton had a very hard case of it', while James Vernon I* interpreted the outcome as a serious blow to the Court interest. Removal from Parliament did not lessen Felton's value to Sunderland, however, and at the news of the Duke of Gloucester's death he immediately made his way to Althorp to give his counsel. He attempted to regain his seat at Orford at the next election but without success, and a petition was rejected by the House. After his defeat it was reported in the borough that 'Sir Thomas Felton's gang hath declared he will lay down the cudgels', and although during the summer of 1701 he and his supporters went through the motions of keeping up his interest, he did not put up again. Instead he was returned at the next election for Bury St. Edmunds on the interest of his son-in-law John Hervey*, being classed as a 'gain' by Lord Spencer and as a Whig by Harley.[6]

Felton made his only recorded speech on 6 Mar. 1702, when he pointed out to the House that 'the King was very bad and had not slept, and proposed that in case of the King's death we should vote that we would stand by and support the Princess Anne of Denmark'. This was 'not well received' and was 'evaded easily'; but it may have served a purpose, for Felton survived Anne's accession without losing office. On the strength of a reported appointment for Hervey, 'the people' at Orford were inclined to believe for a while that Felton 'can do anything now and that he is as great a man in this [reign] as in the last', and certainly Hervey's peerage in 1703 owed much to his efforts. Felton remained a Whig, voting on 13 Feb. for agreeing with the Lords' amendments to the bill to extend the time for taking the oath of abjuration. It was reported, prematurely, in September 1704 that he was 'dead or dying'. Having been forecast as a probable opponent of the Tack, he did not vote for it on 28 Nov. 1704. He supported the Whig candidates for the county in 1705, when Hervey brought him in again at Bury, and was listed as a placeman and as a 'Churchman' in analyses of this Parliament. Having voted for John Smith I* in the contest for the Speakership on 25 Oct., and with the Court in the proceedings on the 'place clause' of the regency bill on 18 Feb. 1706, he was classed as a Whig before and after the 1708 election.[7]

At last advanced to the comptrollership in 1708, Felton enjoyed the office for only five months, dying on 3 Mar. 1709 'at his lodgings in Whitehall of the gout in his stomach'. He was buried six days later at Playford. Hervey, to whose wife the Playford estate eventually descended after the death in 1710 of Felton's only surviving brother, penned the following panegyric:

> A man so religiously just to his word, that one could not be more sure of the thing he had done than of that which he had once promised; one who never deservedly made any man his enemy; and if he had any . . . they were such as had shown themselves to be no friends either to the liberty or laws of our country, whereof he was always a zealous patriot.[8]

[1] Nottingham Univ. Lib. Portland (Bentinck) mss, Thomas Tollemache to Felton, 29 Apr. [1693]; *Hervey Diary*, 48; *Hervey Letter Bks.* i. 240–1; *Procs. Suff. Inst. Arch.* iv. 55; Add. 19129, ff. 128–9, 148; *London Mar. Lic.* ed. Foster, 479; Wood, *Life and Times*, ii. 561. [2] *Cal. Treas. Bks.* i. 669; iii. 1199; iv. 752; ix. 949; xviii. 263, 328; *CSP Dom.* 1672, p. 662; 1678, p. 299; 1684–5, p. 275; Boyer, *Anne Annals*, vii. 244; R.O. Bucholz, *Augustan Court*, 262. [3] *Sel. Charters*, 239. [4] J. P. Kenyon, *Sunderland*, 15, 241, 253, 260, 267; *EHR*, lxxi. 587; *Ailesbury Mems.* 304; Bodl. Carte 79, f. 300; 130, f. 355; W. Suss. RO, Shillinglee mss Ac.454/902, Edward Pratt to Sir Edward Turnor, 16 Aug. 169[2], Turnor to [?Theophilus Hooke], 18 Aug. 1695; *Poems on Affairs of State* ed. Cameron, v. 437. [5] Shillinglee mss Ac.454/1007, 1009, 1013–14, Theophilus Hooke to Turnor, 19 Oct., 4 Nov. 1695, 2, 5 Mar. 1696–7; Kenyon, 280; *Vernon–Shrewsbury Letters*, i. 30, 36, 45, 195, 205, 221; *Shrewsbury Corresp.* 414, 418, 429; Add. 30000 A, f. 300; *Hervey Diary*, 26; *Verney Letters 18th Cent.* i. 298; Luttrell, *Brief Relation*, iv. 354; Add. 19129, f. 141. [6] Cobbett, *Parlty. Hist.* v. p. clxxii; *Vernon–Shrewsbury Letters*, ii. 151, 262; *Hervey Diary*, 24, 26–28, 31–32, 35–36, 38–39, 41, 46–47; Shillinglee mss Ac.454/1022, 1045, 1063, 1151, 1166, 843, 1183, 1185, 981, John Hooke to Turnor, 22 July 1698, 2 Apr. 1705, 8 June 1708, Thomas Palmer to same, 25 July 1698, 6 May 1708, William Betts to same, 11 Apr. 1701, Leicester Martin* to same, 26 Aug., 5 Sept. 1701, Nathaniel Gooding to Betts, 23 Nov. 1702; Add. 30000 D, f. 47; Luttrell, iv. 612; v. 27; *Cocks Diary*, 48; Kenyon, 318; *Hervey Letter Bks.* i. 175, 181–2. [7] *Cocks Diary*, 237; Shillinglee mss Ac.454/1031, John Hooke to Turnor, 30 Oct. 1702; *Duchess of Marlborough Conduct*, 220; *Defoe Letters*, 58–59; G. Holmes, *Pol. in Age of Anne*, 31. [8] Folger Shakespeare Lib. Newdigate newsletter 28 Sept. 1708; *Hervey Diary*, 48; Copinger, *Suff. Manors*, iii. 91; *Hervey Letter Bks.* 240.

D. W. H.

FENWICK, Roger (c.1662–by 1701), of Stanton Hall, Long Horsley, Northumb.

MORPETH 1689–1695

b. c. 1662, 1st s. of William Fenwick (*d.v.p.* s. of Edward Fenwick of Stanton, Northumb.) of Irthington, Cumb. by Elizabeth, da. of Robert Ellison† of Hebburn, co. Dur. *educ.* St. Edmund Hall, Oxf. matric. 25 June 1678, aged 16; G. Inn 1678, called 1686. *m.* 10 July 1692, Elizabeth, da. and h. of George Fenwick† of Brinkburn, Northumb., 4s. (1 *d.v.p.*) 2da. *suc.* fa. 24 May 1675, gdfa. 14 Aug. 1689.[1]

Re-elected in 1690 for Morpeth, Fenwick was listed as a Tory and Court supporter in Lord Carmarthen's (Sir Thomas Osborne†) analysis of the new House. Though his recorded speeches are few, Fenwick acted frequently as a teller and was often involved in proceedings relating to various bills. In the 1690 session, for example, he assisted in the management of three estate bills, one of which concerned the lands of his kinsman Sir Robert Fenwick, and told on a number of occasions. On 10 Apr. he told against granting leave for a bill for 'the naturalizing of all Protestants', and Fenwick again demonstrated Tory sympathies seven days later when he told against allowing the sheriffs of London to present a petition to the Commons. During the following month Fenwick told on four further occasions: against referring to a select committee the bill for the improvement of woollen manufactures (7th); in favour of reading the engrossed bill concerning the £500 forfeitures (14th); in favour of exempting from the £500 forfeitures bill those who had taken office between 8 Oct. 1688 and 13 Feb. 1689 (15th); and in favour of the resolution that the franchise at Aldborough extended beyond the burgage-holders (17th). Early in the following session Fenwick was listed by Carmarthen as a likely supporter in the event of a Commons' attack upon him, and his Toryism was clearly demonstrated on 2 Dec. when he told in favour of receiving a Tory petition detailing alleged Whig abuses in the corporation of London. Fenwick was less active in this session, his legislative work being limited to assisting in the management of a bill to settle a charity upon London's Haberdashers' Company, and in April 1691 was classed as a Country supporter in an analysis that survives among the papers of Robert Harley*. During the 1691–2 session Fenwick told on 11 Dec. 1691 in favour of accepting, as it had been subsequently altered by the Commons, a Lords' amendment to the treason trials bill, and on 14 Dec. against summoning persons with information relating to illicit trading with France. In the new year he reported and carried to the Lords a bill for the relief of creditors (16, 21 Jan.). Fenwick's only recorded speech came in the 1692–3 session when, on 21 Dec. 1692, he moved for leave to introduce a bill to allow special bail to be taken in the country for cases depending in the Westminster courts. He subsequently managed this measure through the House. Fenwick also took a keen interest in the bill to prevent the decay of trade in towns and cities. Having reported this measure on 2 Feb., he told on the same date against a clause allowing 'any person' who settled in a town, and who paid church and poor rates, to trade there. On 15 Feb. he was a teller in favour of passing the bill and was appointed to carry the measure to the Lords. Eight days later Fenwick presented a petition concerning arrears still owed for the quartering of the army in

1677, and he told on two further occasions in this session: against an amendment to the bill prohibiting the import of hair buttons (22 Feb.), and against what Narcissus Luttrell* described as an attempt by 'the Whig party' to adjourn consideration of the London orphans bill (1 Mar.). Fenwick remained an active Member in the 1693–4 session. On 11 Jan. 1694 he told against the House reading the Act prohibiting the export of woollen manufactures, and in the following weeks assisted in managing Roger Whitley's* estate bill through the Commons. He told on the Tory side in a division upon the Clitheroe election case (2 Feb.) and against committing two clergymen into custody for a breach of privilege against Sir Francis Masham, 3rd Bt. (6 Mar.). Fenwick also carried to the Lords a bill to prevent delays at quarter sessions (15 Mar.), reported from committee the bill to prevent vexatious lawsuits (17 Mar.), and on 23 Mar. was granted an indefinite leave of absence. His parliamentary activity noticeably declined in the following session, though he was appointed to the committee to examine the laws on highway robbery and was subsequently named to prepare a bill on this matter (31 Jan., 12 Feb. 1695). During this session he was included upon Henry Guy's* list of 'friends', probably in connexion with the projected Commons attack on Guy. Fenwick did not stand for Morpeth in 1695, his Toryism perhaps leading to his exclusion by the borough's dominant patron, the Whig 3rd Earl of Carlisle (Charles Howard*), and little more is known of him. He remained a commissioner of assessment for Northumberland until 1698 and his death can be dated no more certainly than before 2 Oct. 1701. He was succeeded by his eldest surviving son, John.[2]

[1] Hodgson, *Northumb.* ii (2), 113–14; *Arch. Ael.* ser. 4, xxiv. 102. [2] G. S. De Krey, *Fractured Soc.* 69–70; *Luttrell Diary*, 333, 443, 457; Hodgson, 114.

E. C.

FERMANAGH, John Verney, 1st Visct. [I] *see* **VERNEY**

FERNE, Robert (c.1690–1723), of Snitterton Hall and Locko House, Derbys.

LUDGERSHALL 1713–1715

b. c.1690, o. s. of Henry Ferne of Snitterton Hall and Butterwick House, Hammersmith, Mdx., receiver-gen. of customs 1700–16, by Elizabeth, da. and coh. of Nicholas Dayrell of Kingsclere, Hants. *educ.* Balliol, Oxf. matric. 1 Feb. 1706, aged 16; M. Temple 1706. *m.* 24 May 1717, Diana, da. of John Turner of Stoke Rochford, Lincs., *s.p. suc.* fa. 1723.[1]

Ferne's grandfather, a Derbyshire gentleman, had been prepared to consent to the repeal of the Penal Laws and Test Act in 1688, while his son, the Member's father, had drawn the line at the loss of the Test, 'for by that means perhaps we may give up our lives and religion too all at once'. Though probably Tory in sympathy, Henry Ferne avoided making a clear commitment to either party, presumably for fear of putting his customs place at risk. Robert Ferne was, however, returned as a Tory on the Webb interest at Ludgershall in 1713, and was classed as such in the Worsley list. He was not put up again in 1715, the Webbs needing both Ludgershall seats themselves, and the following year Henry was removed from office.[2]

Ferne died less than three months after his father, on 6 Oct. 1723, at his house in Bow Street, Covent Garden, where he had recently removed from Derbyshire. His will, written in 1719, had mentioned only some South Sea stock worth about £9,000, the bulk of which was to go to his wife.[3]

[1] Add. 6668, f. 236; 6669, f. 116; 6673, f. 191; PCC 207 Richmond; *Cal. Treas. Bks.* xv. 290; xxvi. 281; xxx. 250; Lysons, *Environs* (1792–6), ii. 405. [2] *William Woolley's Hist. Derbys.* ed. Glover and Riden (Derbys. Rec. Soc. vi), 204; Add. 6672, ff. 250, 253; *HMC 15th Rep. VII*, 211–12. [3] Add. 6668, f. 236; *Hist. Reg. Chron.* 1723, p. 42; PCC 207 Richmond.

D. W. H.

FERRIER, Richard (c.1671–1728), of Great Yarmouth and Hemsby, Norf.

GREAT YARMOUTH 1708–1715

bap. 24 May 1671, o. s. of Richard Ferrier of Great Yarmouth and Hemsby by Judith, da. and coh. of Thomas Wilde of Lowestoft, Suff. *educ.* Great Yarmouth; Sidney Sussex, Camb. 1685; travelled abroad (France) 1687. *m.* 1695, Ellen, da. and h. of Robert Long of Reymerston, Norf., 1s. 5da. *suc.* fa. 1695.[1]

Freeman, Great Yarmouth by 1690, common council 1690, alderman 1694–*d.*; bailiff 1696–7; mayor 1706–7, 1720–1.[2]

Ferrier, whose family had been among the leading merchants of Yarmouth since settling there two generations before, stood as a Tory candidate in 1708 and was returned at the top of the poll. 'A very sensible, understanding merchant' was how Thomas Tanner described him. He was quite active in Parliament, principally on questions of trade and commerce, and especially where the interests of the borough were concerned. He was added to the drafting committees on bills to encourage the fishery (18 Dec.) and on export allowances on Scottish fish cured with foreign salt (23 Feb. 1709). He was granted leave of absence on 17 Dec. 1709 for a month. On 9 Feb. 1710 he was appointed to the drafting committee on the bill for repairing Eddystone lighthouse. He voted against the impeachment of Dr Sacheverell. In the 1710 election he and his relation by marriage, George England II*, were successful on the Tory interest, and he was classed as a Tory in the 'Hanover list'. From February to April 1711 he managed through the Commons a bill on the assize of fuel, also assisting with the management of a bill to encourage the coal trade. He told on 28 Feb., with his fellow Norfolk MP Horatio Walpole I and opposite two other Tories, against an additional clause proposed to the supply bill; and again on 10 Mar. against a bill permitting the importation of French wines. Listed in April 1711 among the 'Tory patriots' who opposed the continuation of the war, he was also included among the 'worthy patriots' who had exposed the mismanagements of the previous ministry. He was one of the merchants who provided ships for the expedition to Canada. On 11 Dec. 1711 he presented the Great Yarmouth causeway bill, and managed it through subsequent stages in the House. Three days later he was nominated to the drafting committee on the Norwich workhouse bill, eventually carrying it up to the Lords, for the second time, on 3 Apr. On 26 Feb. 1712 he had taken the chair of the committee on the African trade, acting in this capacity until 27 Mar. 1712, when he was unable to attend because of illness and a deputy was appointed. The committee resuming in April 1713, he took his place once again in the chair, and thereafter managed the bill, ordered following his report on 2 May, to end the Royal Africa Company's monopoly over the African trade and facilitate the participation of all merchants. Twice he was a teller in divisions on this bill: on 2 June 1713 in favour of an additional clause, and on 8 June that the bill pass. No sooner had it been despatched to the Upper House than he introduced and subsequently managed another for the more local purpose of uniting two parishes in the diocese of Norwich. He voted on 18 June for the French commerce bill. In the same month his son Richard was appointed as a Queen's waiter in the port of London.[3]

Ferrier acted as teller on 31 Mar. 1714 on the Tory side in the disputed election for Colchester. He had been one of the foremost supporters of a scheme in Great Yarmouth to build a new church at the southern end of the town, and on 6 Mar. he was at last able to bring in a bill for this purpose, which he saw through the House. On 22 Apr. he presented another bill, also in the interests of his constituents, to allow a drawback on salt exported for use in curing fish. He chaired committees of the whole House on this bill and on a bill for the relief of wine merchants. He told on 7 May against the bill preventing the covert importation of aliens' goods.[4]

Ferrier, who stood down from his seat in 1715, was marked as a Tory in the Worsley list. The following year, upon hearing that various applications had been made for his son's post (despite the fact that the patent had been confirmed by King George), he wrote to Robert Walpole II* at the Treasury to declare that nobody had 'a truer zeal for his Majesty's service' than his son.

> And if I have had the misfortune formerly to incur your displeasure, I would hope that my late conduct and influence in this town and neighbourhood (by which not only the public peace was eminently preserved, but by which also, had it pleased God to have suffered the rebellion to spread, we should have appeared an example of loyalty to the best of his Majesty's towns) will in some measure atone for me.

Nevertheless the patent was revoked soon afterwards.[5]

Ferrier appeared in the 1721 list of the 'loyal gentlemen of Norfolk', compiled by the Jacobite Christopher Layer, with £600 a year. He died on 4 Dec. 1728 and was buried 'with great pomp and splendour' in Yarmouth parish church. It was said that 'by his profuseness' the family property had been 'greatly injured'. His political enemies circulated a satirical mock-translation of his Latin epitaph, including the lines:

> For his politic skill
> We refer to his votes
> On the French commerce bill,
> The posts he enjoyed
> Though quite varied in kind,
> Could not be more varied
> Than was his own mind.[6]

[1] IGI, Norf.; *Cam. Misc.* ix. 3–12, 15–39. [2] Norf. RO, Gt. Yarmouth bor. recs. assembly bk. 1680–1701; *Cam. Misc.* ix. 6. [3] Bodl. Ballard 4, f. 90; *Cal. Treas. Bks.* xxvi. 255; xxvii. 244. [4] C. J. Palmer, *Hist. Gt. Yarmouth*, 179–80. [5] J. H. Plumb, *Walpole*, i. 210–11; *Cal. Treas. Bks.* xxx. 215. [6] P .S. Fritz, *Ministers and Jacobitism 1715–45*, p. 145; H. Swinden, *Hist. Gt. Yarmouth*, 860–1; C. J. Palmer, *Perlustration Gt. Yarmouth*, i. 237–8; *Cam. Misc.* ix. 11.

D. W. H.

FILMER, Thomas (c.1660–1701), of Great Amwell, Herts. and the Inner Temple.

HERTFORD 3–22 Jan. 1701

b. c.1660, s. of ?John Filmer of Stonehall, Kent. *educ*. M. Temple 1678; I. Temple 1681, called 1685. *m*. (aged 23) lic. 7 Nov. 1683, Susan Fiennes, da. of John Fiennes of St. Giles-in-the-Fields, London, 2da.[1]

Recorder, Hertford 1699–*d*.[2]

Filmer 'died suddenly of an apoplexy without having the honour of ever sitting within the walls of the Parliament House'. The origins of his prematurely curtailed career are relatively obscure. Probably the son of a Kentish gentleman, who also lived in the parish of St. Bride's, London, he first entered the Middle Temple before transferring to the Inner Temple three years later. He became such a successful lawyer that he was able to contract a prestigious marriage with the daughter of the third son of Viscount Saye and Sele. In 1693 he bought the reversion of the manor at Amwell Magna (which lay within the borough of Hertford) from his father-in-law, who died in 1696. The same year he bought Pendley manor, Hertfordshire, for £5,200, though he had to take court action in 1697 to secure possession of the purchase. This wealth reflected his active legal practice. In 1691 he was retained as a barrister by the East Indian interlopers, and in 1694 acted as counsel on behalf of a number of Whig merchants, including Samuel Shepheard I*, Thomas Morice* and (Sir) James Bateman*, who objected to the provisions of the London Orphans Act. He was employed by the New East India Company to plead in favour of an East Indies silks bill in 1696, and in February 1700 for several dealers against the poor relief bill which prohibited the wearing of Persian silks. It has been suggested that it was this association with the East Indian trade that explains his candidature in 1701, when the rival companies fought hard to seat their supporters, and that he stood as candidate for the New Company. Nevertheless, he also seems to have acted in a legal capacity for the Company of Scotland, which neither of the English companies liked, and in 1699 had written about their cause to Thomas Coke*, who was also probably involved in the legislation to incorporate the Old Company. Moreover Filmer's sympathies seem to have been with the local Tories. In August 1698 Hertford's corporation ordered that Filmer be allowed to take up the freedom of the borough whenever he chose to request it, and in February the following year he was elected recorder. In his new office Filmer was intimately involved in the defence of local Tories against a quo warranto, challenging the corporation's right to create non-resident freemen, obtained by the borough's Whigs, and at the first election of 1701 he stood at Hertford on the Tory interest, in alliance with Charles Caesar*. Successful at the poll, Filmer then turned his energies to trying to reconcile the divided Essex Tories, even offering to go down from London 'with a strong party' for Sir Charles Barrington, 5th Bt.*; but, to the macabre delight of the defeated Whig candidate at the Hertford election, Sir William Cowper, 2nd Bt.*, Filmer died on 22 Jan. 1701. He was buried in the vault at the Inner Temple. His unexpected death meant that he did not make a will, and on 23 Feb. 1702 his wife petitioned the Commons for a bill to vest Filmer's estate in trustees, in order to pay his debts and provide for herself and her two daughters. Though a drafting committee was appointed no such measure was presented. Filmer's two daughters eventually succeeded to his estates, which they sold in 1718.[3]

[1] *London Mar. Lic.* ed. Chester, 483; Chauncy, *Herts*. i. 554–5. [2] Herts. RO, Hertford bor. recs. 1/76. [3] Add. 27440, f. 155; Bodl. Rawl. C.449, 12 Oct. 1691; Chauncy, *Herts*. i. 554–5; *HMC Lords*, n.s. i. 372; ii. 240; iv. 94; vi. 339; *EHR*, lxxi. 237; *HMC Cowper*, ii. 395; Herts. bor. recs. 25/99, 23/131–6; Herts. RO, Panshanger mss D/EP F29, Lady Cowper's commonplace bk. p. 53; D/EP F81, Lady Cowper's diary, p. 97; W. Suss. RO, Shillinglee mss Ac.454/1174, Filmer to Sir Edward Turnor*, 28 Dec. 1700; 454/1175, same to Henry Howard, Ld. Walden*, 13 Jan. 1701 (draft); 454/1176, same to Turnor, 13 Jan. 1701; *Post Boy*, 21–23 Jan. 1701; *I. Temple Recs*. iii. 459; Salmon, *Herts*. 20; Clutterbuck, *Herts*. ii. 9, 11.

M.J.K.

FINCH, Daniel, Ld. Finch (1689–1769).

RUTLAND   1710–1 Jan. 1730

b. 24 May 1689, 1st surv. s. of Daniel Finch†, 2nd Earl of Nottingham and 7th Earl of Winchilsea, by his 2nd w. Anne, da. of Christopher Hatton†, 1st Visct. Hatton. *educ*. Westminster; Christ Church, Oxf. 1704; travelled abroad (Low Countries, Germany, Italy) 1708, 1709–10; LL.D. Cambridge, 1728. *m*. (1) 28 Dec. 1729, Lady Frances Feilding (*d*. 1734), da. of Basil, 4th Earl of Denbigh, 1da.; (2) 18 Jan. 1738, Mary, da. and coh. of Sir Thomas Palmer, 4th Bt.*, 8da. (4 *d.v.p.*). *suc*. fa. as 8th Earl of Winchilsea and 3rd Earl of Nottingham 1 Jan. 1730; KG 13 Mar. 1752.

Gent. of the bedchamber to Prince of Wales 1714–16; ld. of Treasury 1715–16; comptroller of Household 1725–30; PC 1 June 1725; first ld. of Admiralty Mar. 1742–Dec. 1744, Apr.–July 1757; ld. pres. of Council 1765–6.

A year or so after matriculating at Christ Church, Oxford, Lord Finch was taken away from university and placed under the supervision of William Wotton, a prebendary of Salisbury, his father Lord Nottingham declaring that he would send no more of his sons to Oxford (a resolution that was abandoned within two years). In 1708, accompanied by a governor, Finch toured the military encampments at Tournai under the hospitable care of Lord Stair, a senior officer in command. Another officer described him as 'a youth of much modesty, virtue and sweetness of temper, and seems to have a good understanding and a good stock of sense'. As part of his foreign itinerary he spent time at the ducal academy at Wolfenbüttel with other young Tories, and in 1710 was preparing to set forward for Italy from The Hague, though at first he protested, 'not caring to ride post haste for three quarters of a year' and preferring an immediate return home.[1]

While still abroad, Finch was returned on his father's interest for Rutland in the general election of 1710. The 'Hanover list' classified him as a Tory, and he appeared in the first session as a 'Tory patriot' favouring peace, and a 'worthy patriot' approving the exposure of the mismanagements of the previous ministry. At the beginning of May, Robert Harley* pondered the possibility of recalling Nottingham to the Cabinet but was strongly dissuaded by Lord Poulett, who argued that Nottingham's inclusion in the ministry would threaten Harley's own supremacy. Poulett pointed out that Nottingham might be just as useful if Lord Finch were given a place instead. Harley thought this 'prudent' but there is no evidence that Finch received any offer, although some of his relations were provided for. Towards the end of the year Finch obediently toed his father's line in opposition, a lone figure at first: he was the only one of his father's close associates among the Tory defectors on the 'No Peace without Spain' motion on 7 Dec. In 1713 he began an early and energetic campaign for the general election, fearful that his father's and his own defection from the ministry was likely to prove a sore point with the freeholders. Harley, now Lord Treasurer Oxford, was informed by a Tory clergyman in Rutland that Finch's chances appeared slim despite his having 'been personally around the county, haranguing the freeholders, and spending liberally among them, endeavouring as well as he can to justify his own and others' proceedings last winter'. Before the dissolution Finch voted on 18 June 1713 against the French commerce bill. Finch's prospects in Rutland improved as the election drew near, and after a stiff contest he headed the poll.[2]

The Worsley list analysing the 1713 Parliament identified Finch as a Whig, though he would have been more accurately described as a 'whimsical' Tory. On 5 Mar. 1714 he told against Thomas Wynn† in the Caernarvon Boroughs election but he made no significant speech aside from his defence of Richard Steele* in March 1714. This intervention was a repayment of a debt of gratitude his family owed to Steele for replying to a public attack on one of the Finch sisters in the *Examiner* of 23 Apr. 1713. When Finch rose on 18 Mar. 1714 to argue against the charge that Steele's *Englishman* was seditious, he was at first supposed to have been so flustered and overcome with nerves that he resumed his seat, uttering 'it is strange I can't speak for this man, though I could readily fight for him', but on being urged, he resumed his speech. As Nottingham's heir, he was assured of attention, and, as one observer recorded, he 'made a very handsome speech in which every sentence pushed at the T[reasure]r'. On the 'tenderest part of the charge', that Steele had insinuated that the Hanoverians were suspicious of royal and ministerial intentions, he gave examples to illustrate how dismissive the English ministers had been towards the electoral court. In justification of Steele's reflections on the peace, he pointed out that 'we may give all the fine epithets we please, but epithets do not change the nature of things', and denied that the peace could be considered universally 'honourable' or uniformly 'advantageous'. In spite of his acknowledged eloquence Finch suffered the mortification of being accidentally shut out of the division that led to Steele's expulsion. Steele none the less publicly demonstrated his gratitude by dedicating to Finch a new work against popery, *The Romish Ecclesiastical History of Late Years*, published at the end of May, which congratulated him 'upon the early conspicuous figure you make in the business of the nation'.[3]

After the Queen's death, Nottingham ranged himself in alliance with the Townshend Whigs, and Finch was among the family members rewarded for their loyalty to the new dynasty, being appointed to the Prince of Wales's household. As a Hanoverian Tory now in office, he naturally puzzled the compilers of lists of the 1715 Parliament, one calling him a Tory, while another assumed that he was now a Whig. Returned again in 1715 he continued to serve for Rutland until succeeding to his father's earldoms in 1730.[4]

Finch died on 2 Aug. 1769.

[1] *Nicolson Diaries* ed. Jones and Holmes, 299; *HMC Portland*, iv. 496–7; BL, Walpole mss, Stephen Poyntz to Horatio Walpole II*, 17 Dec., 27 Dec. N.S. 1709, 10 Jan. 1710 N.S.; *Trans. R. Hist. Soc.* ser. 3, i. 187. [2] H. Horwitz, *Revol. Politicks*, 223, 228, 234; *HMC Portland*, iv. 684; Add. 70251, Thomas Peale to Oxford, 27 Jan. 1712–13, 15 July 1713; Devonshire mss at Chatsworth House, Halifax pprs. Nottingham to Ld. Guernsey (Heneage Finch I*), 26 Aug. 1713. [3] Speck thesis, 88; G. A. Aitken, *Life of Steele*, i. 318; ii. 19, 30; Cobbett, *Parlty. Hist.* vi. 1272, 1274, 1283; NLS, Advocates' mss, Wodrow pprs. letters Quarto 8, f. 69; *Steele Corresp.* 480. [4] Horwitz, 246.

A. A. H.

FINCH, Hon. Edward (1663–1738).

CAMBRIDGE UNIVERSITY 1690–1695

bap. 20 Apr. 1663, 8th but 5th surv. s. of Heneage Finch†, 1st Earl of Nottingham, by Elizabeth, da. of Daniel Harvey, Grocer and merchant, of Lawrence Pountney Hill, London and Croydon, Surr., sis. of Daniel Harvey†; bro. of Daniel Finch†, 2nd Earl of Nottingham, Hon. Heneage Finch I* and Hon. William Finch†. *educ.* Christ's, Camb. 1677, MA 1679, fellow 1680–4; I. Temple 1685. *m.* Mary, da. of Nicholas Stanley, MD, fellow of New Coll. Oxf., *s.p.*[1]

Under-sec. of state 1689–93; preb. of Wetwang, dioc. of York 1704–*d.*, rector of Kirkby in Cleveland 1705–7, of Wigan 1707–14; canon of 2nd preb. dioc. of Canterbury 1710–*d.*; chaplain-in-ordinary to George I by 1715–27.[2]

Freeman, Wigan 4 July 1702.[3]

It proved surprisingly difficult for Finch's family to settle him in any walk of life. At first he had seemed destined to be a Cambridge don. His 'excellent parts' had enabled him to make a favourable impression as an undergraduate: indeed, he had contributed as a freeman to the university's celebratory volume of verses on the marriage of Princess Mary. But after a rapid election to a fellowship in his own college, obtained through a combination of royal influence and the personal intervention of the master, Ralph Cudworth, he became disenchanted with Cambridge, and with Christ's, and was 'resolved' to depart. He then dabbled in the law, a field in which his elder brother Heneage had already achieved outstanding success, and in 1689 was found a minor place in government as under-secretary to his eldest brother Daniel, now Earl of Nottingham, in the office of secretary of state. On Nottingham's recommendation, he was returned as a Member for Cambridge University in 1690. Naturally, he was classed as a Tory and a probable Court supporter by Lord Carmarthen (Sir Thomas Osborne†) in an analysis of the new Parliament, and he figured on a further list by Carmarthen in December 1690, probably of Members who could be relied on for support in the event of an attack on Carmarthen in the Commons. Robert Harley* counted him among the Country opposition in April 1691, but this is the only surviving indication that Finch may ever have behaved in Parliament while under-secretary otherwise than as his brother's faithful servant. Carmarthen included him in a list of government officials sitting in the Commons in 1692, and he was named in two lists of placemen (including that by Grascome) from 1692–3. Generally speaking, it is impossible to distinguish his parliamentary activity from that of the more vociferous and experienced Heneage, though he certainly spoke on 19 Feb. 1692, as indeed his constituents would have expected him to, in support of the bill to confirm Cambridge University's charter. His bitterness at Whig attacks on Lord Nottingham during the inquiries in the 1692–3 session into naval failures may well have been manifest at the time in the Commons, and may have contributed to his decision, taken in the spring of 1693, to leave the 'infectious heat' of politics and the routine of official business and retire to the parsonage of another brother (Henry) at Winwick in Lancashire. He made his departure from London in April of that year hoping, as he said, never to return. His plan was to subsist on a small 'allowance' from Nottingham until 'a *sine cura*' could be found. Clearly he also intended to seek ordination at some point, but was in no haste to make this step and in the meantime eked out his meagre inheritance. It is possible that he stayed at Winwick during the winter of 1693–4, but the ministry's unscrupulous exploitation of perjured informations of a so-called 'Lancashire plot' roused him again to action, implicating as they did men like Peter Legh† of Lyme, who were his and his brother's friends. Not only did he decide to journey up to Parliament himself, he also encouraged other local Tories to attend the House in order to foil 'the game' he was sure the Whigs would endeavour to play:

> I suppose they will convict these people of perjury, to stop inquiry; vote Trenchard [Sir John*], Shrewsbury [Charles Talbot, 1st Duke], Willoughby [Robert Bertie*, Lord Willoughby de Eresby] and Norris [Thomas*] . . . the thanks of the House for their watchful care of the government, in his Majesty's absence, so that their scandalous grafting upon Dodsworth's plot will be looked on as a pardonable over-forward zeal.

Once the affair was ended his rekindled interest in parliamentary matters seems to have expired again, although he was named in Henry Guy's* list of 'friends' in 1694–5 in connexion with the Commons' investigation of Guy for corruption. On 26 Feb. 1695 Finch was given leave of absence, in part for the recovery of his health but also 'upon extraordinary occasions'.[4]

Even before the 1690 Parliament had been formally dissolved Finch had taken holy orders, in September 1695, but it was almost ten years before he could find a benefice. His brother's fall from power, and his own personal unpopularity in ministerial and court circles, occasioned by ill reports of his 'behaviour in the Lancashire plot', presumably account for this, at least until 1702 when King William died and Nottingham returned to office. Even then he had to wait two more years before obtaining a prebend at York, where

Nottingham's old friend John Sharp was archbishop, and then in 1707 was made rector of Wigan, a preferment said to be worth £600 p.a., by Sir John Bridgeman, 2nd Bt., in what was a blatantly party-political manoeuvre to strengthen the Tory interest in the borough. Indeed, he and his brother at Winwick had already been active in Wigan politics for some years. Finch did not disappoint his patron, and was soon involved in disputes with the town's corporation who were hostile to Bridgeman's party, leading eventually to a lawsuit over some renovations Finch had made to the church which had involved pulling down the mayor's gallery. He was given a canonical prebend at Canterbury in 1710 as a move by the incoming Tory ministry to mollify Nottingham, and was even considered for the deanery of Carlisle, a promotion which would have had the additional advantage of removing him from the seat of the disturbances he was fomenting in Wigan. These reached a climax in the 1713 election when Finch took a leading role in promoting the candidature of Bridgeman's son Orlando Bridgeman I* and Lord Barrymore (James Barry*) against two other Tories, Sir Roger Bradshaigh, 3rd Bt.*, and George Kenyon*.[5]

Finch resigned his rectory in 1714 and retired to live in the cathedral close at York, where his brother Henry was now dean, on the income from his two prebends and from property in Yorkshire and Leicester. He benefited from the family's vaunted Hanoverianism in so far as he was appointed a chaplain-in-ordinary to King George I, but his chief enthusiasm was now music, and a number of his compositions survive, mainly of a choral and liturgical nature. He died at York on 14 Feb. 1738, aged 75, and was buried in the Minster.[6]

[1] IGI, London; A. B. I'Anson, *Hist. Finch Fam.* 76; J. Peile, *Biog. Reg. Christ's Coll.* ii. 64. [2] *Nicolson Diaries* ed. Jones and Holmes, 620. [3] Wigan RO, Wigan bor. recs. AB/MR/10. [4] Peile, 64; *CSP Dom.* 1679–80, p. 152; *HMC Finch*, ii. 188; Staffs. RO, Dartmouth mss D(W)1778/I/i/1804, Ld. Dartmouth (George Legge†) to William Legge†, 10 Feb. 1689–90; *Luttrell Diary*, 194; *HMC Kenyon*, 371–2; Northants. RO, Isham mss IC 1474, John to Sir Justinian Isham, 4th Bt.*, 15 Apr. 1693; H. Horwitz, *Revol. Politicks*, 152, 259–60; Bath mss at Longleat House, Thynne pprs. 17, f. 320; Glos. RO, Hardwicke Ct. mss, Sharp pprs. Henry Finch to Abp. Sharp, 3 Nov. 1694; Luttrell, *Brief Relation*, iii. 81. [5] Peile, 64; Luttrell, iii. 529; vi. 140–1; Hardwicke Ct. mss, Sharp pprs. Henry Finch to Sharp, 22 May 1697; *HMC Portland*, iv. 391; *HMC Kenyon*, 441, 447; *Bull. J. Rylands Lib.* 128–9; Horwitz, 222, 240; *Nicolson Diaries*, 523–4; *HMC Downshire*, 890. [6] Peile, 64; *Gent. Mag.* 1738, p. 109.

D. W. H.

FINCH, Hon. Heneage I (c.1649–1719), of Arch Row, Lincoln's Inn Fields, Mdx.; and Albury, nr. Guildford, Surr.

OXFORD UNIVERSITY   1679 (Mar.–July)
GUILDFORD   1685–1687
OXFORD UNIVERSITY   1689–1698
   1701 (Feb.)–15 Mar. 1703

b. c.1649, 2nd s. of Heneage Finch†, 1st Earl of Nottingham, by Elizabeth, da. of Daniel Harvey, Grocer and merchant, of Laurence Pountney Hill, London and Croydon, Surr.; bro. of Daniel Finch †, 2nd Earl of Nottingham, Hon. Edward* and Hon. William†. *educ.* Westminster; I. Temple 1662, called 1673, bencher 1673; Christ Church, Oxf. matric. 18 Nov. 1664, aged 15, DCL 1683. *m.* 16 May 1678 (with £10,000), Elizabeth, da. and coh. of Sir John Banks, 1st Bt.*, 3s. 6da. *cr.* Baron Guernsey 15 Mar. 1703, Earl of Aylesford 19 Oct. 1714.[1]

Attaché to Hon. Henry Coventry† as plenip. congress of Breda 1667; KC 1677; solicitor-gen. 1679–86; groom of bedchamber 1685–89; PC 20 Mar. 1703–May 1708, 13 Dec. 1711–*d.*; chancellor, duchy of Lancaster 1714–16.[2]

Chairman, cttees. of supply, and ways and means 22 May–20 Nov. 1685.

Commr. building 50 new churches 1711–15.[3]

As a leading and able member of the Church party, Heneage Finch was more respected than liked. A gifted and highly successful barrister, he had acquired a reputation for what Bishop Burnet called 'vicious eloquence', and the legal pedantry in which he sometimes seemed to wallow did not readily win him friends: fellow Tories spoke derisively about the 'smoothness of his discourse'. John Macky's description of him as able but 'splenatick', alludes to a sharpness of intellect and a dogmatism which dominated his personality. Comparing him with his elder brother, Lord Nottingham, in 1714, Swift felt that Heneage was by far the more talented. By 1690 he had already emerged as one of the chief spokesmen for the Church Tories, but was almost always in the shadow of such men as Sir Thomas Clarges*, Sir Christopher Musgrave, 4th Bt.*, and Sir Edward Seymour, 4th Bt.* Though Finch tended to speak less frequently than they, and was much less a pillar of 'Country' opposition, the fact that he was Nottingham's brother assured him of a platform. Moreover, his closeness to Nottingham imposed upon him to a considerable degree the routine work of managing the Church interest in the Commons, business for which more senior politicians had no particular inclination. His success at the law, in which he continued to practise, his sophistry in debate, his marriage into considerable commercial wealth, and his being less openly devoted to conventional 'Country' preoccupations of government finance and corruption, all seemed to set him slightly apart from the rank and file of Country Tories.[4]

Appointed solicitor-general in 1679, Finch was at first a loyal courtier. The devastating panache which he displayed in the prosecution of Lord Russell (Hon. William Russell†) was long remembered and was forever a blight on his political record. But after James II's accession it was only a matter of time before fervent defence of the Church brought him into collision with the King's policies, and in 1686 he was dismissed. He was destined to climb no higher on the ladder of legal preferment. In leading the successful defence of the Seven Bishops in 1688 he in effect acknowledged the fallacy behind the notion that the King could do no wrong, though in the months following the King's flight in November he reluctantly came to recognize that the reign was effectively over. His primary concern, as shown in speeches to the Convention in the crucial 'state of the nation' debate on 28 Jan. 1689, was that the traditional pattern of kingship should not be put at risk, and that James be retained at least as titular king. He expressed gratitude to the Prince of Orange 'for so great a deliverance', but felt it would be 'more to his glory to reduce this monarchy to its just and lawful establishment than to be king'. He urged that William be relied upon to recall King James and act as 'arbitrator' between him and his subjects, 'that we may have due limits set to the King's prerogative'. Later in the debate, he acknowledged the important reality that James's 'zeal to popery' had made him unfit to be king of England, and disavowed his earlier plea for him to be recalled. But his proposal for a regency also fell on stony ground. Although he voted against the proposition that the throne was 'vacant', he subsequently displayed the same readiness as his elder brother to accept the new order, though, as his stand over the Association was to show in 1696, he still maintained that William was only king *de facto*. Following Nottingham's appointment as secretary, Burnet suggested that Finch might be made lord chancellor of Ireland, while in April it was confidently reported that he was to be made attorney-general. However, having both brothers in high office was probably giving too much official influence to the Church Tories at a time when cautious moderation was the new king's chief view.[5]

The early weeks of 1690 saw Finch take a leading part in the initiative to establish the Church party as the leading pro-government force in the Commons. On 29 Jan. he was 'a principal person' at a meeting of some 150 Churchmen at the Devil Tavern, which agreed to an address thanking the King for his 'adhesion' to the Church and, in effect, indicating their willingness to support the requirements of supply in a new Parliament. Finch's name was mentioned in connexion with the vacant lord keepership, but the King had already affirmed to Lord Halifax (George Savile†) in the first week of February that he had no thoughts of making such an appointment. Finch had no problem retaining his seat for Oxford University following the dissolution of the Convention. St John Brodrick, a Whig acquaintance and a fellow lawyer, praised him to Dr Charlett of the university for having 'acted as considerable a part on the side which he stuck to as any one in the House'. If the university prided its defence of the Church, Brodrick wrote, "twill be but a justice to yourselves to stick to him, for else 'twill be looked upon as you thought he had taken the wrong side'. Brodrick felt that Finch epitomized 'the fury and indignation of a party who will never be contented till the Church and state be brought to their own mould'. Certain of Finch's continued goodwill in the new Parliament, Lord Carmarthen (Sir Thomas Osborne†) duly noted him as a probable Court supporter. It was reported in the early weeks of the session that Finch had turned down an offer of the lord chancellorship. In the supply debate on 27 Mar. he tried to give the proceedings some direction by urging the House first to proceed on the unresolved question of the hereditary revenues. He appears to have given his support to the idea of establishing a commission of accounts, as on 14 Apr. he was included among those named to prepare a bill for this purpose, though in later sessions he was never involved in the commission's work, possibly due to the burdens of his legal practice. On the 22nd he supported the committal of the bill for reversing the quo warranto judgment against London, having been counsel for the crown when the proceedings were originally instigated. After the enactment of the bill, which had been (according to Roger Morrice) in his 'special care', he was held responsible for a misdrafting which had allowed City Whigs to retain control over the offices of lord mayor and chamberlain. Then in the debate on 24 Apr. Finch dismissed as impossible the suggestion that the London lieutenancy still included men who had not taken the oaths, and reminded his hearers that the purpose of the debate was to approve an address thanking the King for his support to the Church as reflected in his remodelling of the lieutenancy. Although he had been appointed to assist in drafting the bill for an Abjuration, his aversion to oaths and oath-taking was plain. Speaking on the 29th, a few days after the bill's defeat, he showed his disdain for the proposal to impose 'declarations' that oaths already taken would be kept. None the less, it was still deemed essential to include him on the drafting committee of the bill ordered that day for 'securing' the government. He spoke on 2 May regarding Anthony Rowe's* *Letter to a Friend* . . ., insisting that a proposed adjournment motion be so worded as to indicate condemnation of the tract as a 'scandalous libel'. The Lords' regency bill was a focus of Finch's particular concern. He supported its committal on 30 Apr., and in committee on 5 May addressed the complex problem of defining what powers might be specifically vested in the Queen during the King's absence in Ireland without divesting William of 'regal authority'. Finch's solution was a clause which declared 'that during the King's absence, every act of administration by the Queen alone shall be good when the King directs not to the contrary'. By this expedient, he argued, the Queen provided for the immediate 'necessaries' of government and was subject to the King's orders in his absence, while the King retained overall control. When the debate resumed next day his 'nice distinctions' were belittled, but the essence of his proposal was subsequently enacted. On 10 May he was ordered 'to take care' of a bill concerning the conviction of recusants, while in the same month he participated in conferences with the Lords on two measures, of which one was the regency bill.[6]

In preparation for the next session, Finch had been noted as one who might be encouraged to join other prominent parliamentarians as a 'manager of the King's directions', to assist in holding together a coalition of Churchmen and Whigs, chiefly for the prompt dispatch of supply business. Two of Carmarthen's lists, compiled in December 1690, present Finch as a Court supporter, though whether he actually fulfilled some managerial role for the ministry in the House is uncertain. That there were also times when he leaned towards a 'Country' point of view is suggested by Robert Harley's* analysis of the House in April 1691 in which Finch was classed as a Country supporter. In the next session, Finch emerged at the forefront of the supporters of Sir William Whitelocke's* treason trials bill. At its third reading on 18 Nov. 1691 he spoke 'very largely and handsomely' for the bill, rejecting arguments that the improvement of defence procedures in such cases would weaken the government. 'All that is required', he told the House, 'is a just and lawful defence at a man's trial'. When on 11 Dec. the House deliberated on the Lords' amendments, Finch stood by the principle of having two witnesses to prove a treasonable act. He defended the peers' addition of the contentious 'clause A', for establishing procedures for the trial of peers. Some MPs were uneasy about summoning the entire House of Lords to participate in trials when Parliament was not in session, but Finch maintained there was 'no hurt' in the clause, and that there was no implication that the government was less weak when Parliament was not sitting. He was included among the Members appointed at the close of the debate to confer with the Lords over the amendment. But this and later conferences did nothing to resolve the deadlock. Finch argued again on 31 Dec. that the clause did not give the Lords a power of endangering the government, and stressed that it was only reasonable that the methods of proceeding during and outside the parliamentary session be kept uniform. He also spoke concerning procedural aspects of the bill's faltering progress on 7 and 25 Jan. 1692.[7]

Finch was engaged in the lengthy proceedings on the East India trade, in which he represented the interests of the 'interlopers', who employed him as counsel and presumably paid him royally. In the committee of the whole on 27 Nov. 1691 he 'argued very largely' in support of the motion to dissolve the existing company, which he claimed had managed the trade ineptly. On 17 Dec. he supported Sir Edward Seymour's motion for the creation of a new company, in line with the schedule of 'regulations' recently agreed by the Commons, and joined with Richard Hampden I* in condemning the prerogative powers of 'peace or war' which the old company might exercise by virtue of its charter. Given the opportunity to submit proposals for establishing a joint stock, the company presented assurances of their security, but when these came under consideration on 23 Dec. Finch was particularly damning and dismissed the company's response as 'unsatisfactory and indecent and not pursuant in the least to your vote', an opinion which was later put into the form of a motion which Finch seconded. At £744,000, the security offered was only about half the value claimed for the stock. He naturally opposed the decision to allow the company further time to name guarantors, and was against giving them more than a day. When the matter was resumed on 8 Jan. 1692, the House arrived at an accommodation with the company, but the proceedings took a turn when Sir John Lowther, 2nd Bt. II, seconded by Finch, tabled a new motion for an address calling for the company's dissolution. The debate ended in a successful motion for a bill to establish 'an' East India company according to the earlier 'regulations' laid down by the House. Finch was the leading advocate for the bill at its second reading on 26 Jan., and was willing to encourage members of the Old Company to present security for the proper value of its stock (already ascertained at £744,000 in earlier proceedings) with a view to its incorporation in a reestablished company. The Old Company, highly dissatisfied, communicated its feelings to the House on

6 Feb., and in the debate on how to proceed with the bill, Finch supported the idea of an address to dissolve the existing company but thought the King should be left 'to constitute a new one according as his Majesty shall think fit'. With the end of the session approaching, however, little further progress was made. Luttrell's diary suggests that Finch was much less attentive to supply matters, and unlike other leaders of the Church Tories, was not at all innovative in his approach. On 12 Jan. he advised caution in response to the 'million fund' scheme proposed by Paul Foley I*, whereby the bankers would agree to advance £1 million in return for the establishment of a 'good fund', from which the crown's long-outstanding debt to them could be repaid. Finch joined those who were for appointing a committee to investigate and report on the feasibility of the proposal. In so far as the bankers' debt was concerned, he added that this had been judicially proven and they had in fact a right to any money coming into the Exchequer from excise duties. His preference for traditional revenue-raising methods was seen more clearly on the 19th, in his dismissiveness towards a proposal from Sir John Lowther of a fund of perpetual interest at 5 per cent, generated from 'bills of credit', which he said would 'prove a cheat upon the people', and he expressed irritation that the matter had been intruded 'irregularly' in the proceedings on the poll bill. He supported an equitable levy of the tax at parochial level that would excuse 'the poor' but embrace 'the men of estates'. Opposition to speculative finance was also implied on the 23rd in his criticism of a bill for reducing interest.[8]

Finch was not among those of Nottingham's associates who were offered ministerial posts after the 1691–2 session, but his continuing support for the Court was indicated in another list drawn up by Carmarthen in 1692. On 21 Nov. 1692, a fortnight or so after the beginning of the next session, he spoke guardedly in relation to Edmund Waller's* controversial motion that the Admiralty be placed in the hands of more capable commissioners. While admitting that he had heard complaints, and wishing 'things better managed', he insisted, 'when I am to pass a judgment upon men, I must have something to found my judgment on, which I see not in this case'. He laid particular blame on the merchants, whose risk-taking had laid them open to enemy attacks on the high seas, and accused them of being too concerned with profits and with making gains from insurance money. Proceedings on the East India trade began anew on 24 Nov., when Finch made an abrupt intervention to save the debate from trailing off into lengthy disquisitions about whether the trade should be left unregulated: 'I think the first foundation you are to make is for the carrying on this trade, and that by a joint stock.' He spoke in favour of the reintroduced treason trials bill in committee on 28 Nov., arguing that the bill's purpose was no more 'than that an innocent man may have opportunity to make his innocence appear'. Later in the debate he laboured in even stronger terms for the bill, telling the House,

> I think no Englishman can be safe if the King be not safe upon the throne; and in the establishment of him there is the security of every Englishman, and this bill does do it, and it is no hardship upon the government – only without it, it is impossible for an innocent man to make his innocence appear.

The abjuration bill provided him with the opportunity to address another important aspect of internal stability. On 14 Dec., towards the end of the long debate prior to its committal, he spoke with great sagacity on the dangers inherent in the imposition of oaths:

> The more I consider the reasons urged for the commitment of this bill, the more I am against it. In all times when words have been made treason, parliaments have found mischiefs thereby and repealed them in some short time and reduced them to the standard of 25 Edw. III, c. 1. It is said that some men prevaricate with your former oath; perhaps so, but consider if the oaths you have already will not hold them; you will hardly make any oath that can or which they will not easily take. The security of this government lies not in oaths but in the good laws and the regular administration of justice and the law of the people. For my part, I think the oaths you have already are sufficient, and that thereby a man is bound to assist and to do all they can for the security of this government – the oath you have is the old oath of allegiance which was before 3 Jac. I. I did observe one gentleman did in effect tell us the commitment of this bill was not to mend it but to make an oath that some men shall not take, which I am not for, but would not make more enemies to this government – we have too many already. Then for making words treason, I think it at all times very dangerous, for words are liable to be mistaken and misunderstood, and it is not in such cases sufficient to prove by standers-by that they heard no such words spoken because one might hear that another did not.

Speaking on 20 Dec., in a debate on mismanagements in the navy, he began by showing 'all respect and acknowledgment' towards Admiral Russell (Edward*), but then 'reflected what he could, in his fine way, upon him'. Also in this debate, he was forced to defend his brother Nottingham. 'I will be bold to say', he told MPs, 'none was ever more diligent in your service, and he never goes to bed before all orders and despatches are executed and leaves them not till the next morning.' Finch's recorded interventions on economic issues were few, except where matters as fundamental as the currency were concerned: on 31 Dec. he criticized the potentially deleterious effects of a bill for preventing the export of gold and silver and the melting down of coin. He spoke on 10 Jan. 1693 against the damaging intentions of a clause proposed for the appropriation bill, suspending payment of all pensions while the war lasted, as liable to obstruct the bill's passage and bring the public service to a standstill. In the proceedings on Bishop Burnet's *Pastoral Letter*, on 23 Jan., Finch 'spoke much in vindication' of the bishop and his book, refuting allegations that it sought to establish that King William's right to the throne was by right of conquest. During the debate his own position on William's possession of the crown was exposed when the quick-witted Whig MP Hon. Harry Mordaunt* interrupted him with the jesting assumption that his reference to William the Conqueror's being King *de jure* also applied to William III, and wished that all Finch's relations were of the same opinion. When Finch questioned Mordaunt's 'understanding' of his argument, Mordaunt responded with a pointed apology for thinking Finch's opinion was that William was King *de jure*. Finch applied firm Tory thinking in his stand against the Lords' triennial bill, and made at least three major speeches against it: on 28 Jan., at first reading, when he questioned the peers' right to regulate the length of time between elections, and highlighted the 'distrust' it showed towards 'this King in particular and of kingly government in general'; on 7 Feb., in committee, when he pointed out that 'annual Parliaments' were already theoretically permissible under medieval statutes; and on the 9th, at the report, when he outlined the damage the bill would do to the prerogative by taking away 'that inherent power the King hath to preserve his government and his people'. He spoke on at least two more occasions before the close of session: on 14 Feb., in support of the Country Tory Sir Eliab Harvey* in the disputed election for Essex; and on the 25th, in favour of an address to dissolve the East India Company. On the 18th he was named to a committee ordered to draft one of the supply bills.[9]

Finch's activities in the next session are less fully documented, but evidence suggests that Nottingham's dismissal at the beginning of November 1693 goaded him into greater criticism of ministerial failure in managing the war. He was still, of course, constrained to defend Nottingham's name in the continuing attacks over the poor performance of the fleet. During the debate on naval 'miscarriages' on 22 Nov. he adopted a conscientiously neutral line, dealing not with the issue itself but the haphazard and illogical course which the proceedings were taking. This superior courtroom attitude was effectively displayed again at the resumption of the debate on the 27th. When Comptroller Wharton (Hon. Thomas*) posed the question as to whether the naval officers had obeyed orders, Finch answered that it had already been shown that the officers in question had none to obey, and, having no idea of the French fleet's whereabouts, could not organize an attack. He then rounded on another Court Whig, William Palmes*, for speaking 'rubbish'. Neither did he show much sympathy towards Lord Falkland (Anthony Carey*), a member of the Admiralty Board against whom the accounts commissioners had raised charges of peculation. On 7 Dec. when the matter was debated, Finch observed that if the manner in which Falkland acquired the money was 'not according to law', the Commons should not hesitate to punish him. Finch's shift away from the Court was further highlighted in January during the reaction to the King's veto of the place bill, by his inclusion on the committee appointed on the 27th to sharpen the 'representation' in which the Commons expressed its dissatisfaction. Almost nothing can be ascertained of Finch's opinions during the 1694–5 session. On one occasion, in January 1695, he appears to have criticized government speakers for too often referring to individuals by name as if 'to tar men as enemies to the government for not coming up to some people's notions'. The comment drew harsh reflections from Sir John Morton, 2nd Bt.*, who wished that Finch's professions of impartiality had been true of his role as counsel against the Whig martyrs Algernon Sidney† and Lord Russell. Legal business prevented him from appearing in person at his university constituency prior to the general election in October, but he was re-elected in his absence 'unanimously'.[10]

Now that the balance of ministerial power was firmly in the hands of the Whigs, Finch began to feature as one of the leading representatives of the Tory wing of the Country party. On 29 Nov., during the initial proceedings on the coinage crisis, he joined other prominent Churchmen in opposing proposals for a recoinage which they felt would only exacerbate the economic difficulties of wartime. All the while he kept Nottingham abreast of developments in the Commons. When a set of resolutions on the coin began to emerge, Nottingham cautioned that 'you will find more difficulties to obstruct the perfecting those resolutions than barely such as arise from the thing itself' and warned him of the likelihood of future obstruction from Court spokesmen such as Lowther. In supply proceedings, Finch demanded drastic cuts in the size of the army. He was also a leading advocate of the proposed parliamentary council of trade, and was among the principal Tories who contended 'zealously' for it on 2 Jan. 1696. He was forecast as likely to oppose the Court when discussions were resumed on the 31st, as indeed he did, taking a characteristic stand against the ministerial attempts to impose an abjuration oath on those whom the House should nominate as commissioners. In the latter part of February, Nottingham's arrival in London after an absence of nine months, coupled with Whig misfortunes in the Commons, prompted rumours of a ministerial reshuffle in which Finch was tipped to replace Shrewsbury as secretary of state. But these reports were quickly overtaken by news of the Assassination Plot. In the debate on the Association on 25 Feb., Finch and Seymour were the chief objectors to declaring William as 'rightful and lawful' king: according to Burnet, 'they said the crown and the prerogatives of it were vested in him, and therefore they would obey him, and be faithful to him, though they could not acknowledge him their rightful and lawful king'. For the moment at least, Finch's dogmatism at a time of potential danger cast a shadow over his suitability for high office. In his *Memoirs*, Lord Ailesbury alleged that Finch belonged to 'a sort of association' which came into being in around 1695, comprised of such cronies as Seymour, Musgrave, John Grobham Howe* and Simon Harcourt I*, and dedicated to the task of restoring James II. There is no other evidence, however, that Finch was at any time involved in Jacobite activity. Later in the session, on the question of stabilizing the price of guineas, he opposed the ministers' preference for the price to be set at 22s.[11]

In June 1696 Finch became seriously ill with what appears to have been a tubercular condition, and by the middle of the month was not expected to live. Dr Charlett was advised by several London correspondents to prepare for a by-election for the university. Finch had partially recovered by the beginning of October, but was still unwell when the new parliamentary session began a few weeks later. Only his opposition to the attainder of Sir John Fenwick† brought him to the House. Having missed the first day's proceeding on 6 Nov., he spoke on the 13th on the second reading of the bill of attainder, questioning the wisdom of the 'untrodden path' on which the House was bound and the summary nature of the proceedings, particularly as Fenwick now stood indicted by a single witness, whereas the law required two. He felt that the resort to the 'extraordinary authority' of the legislature smacked of a ministerial determination to proceed in disregard of the due requirements of justice, a situation which he found unpalatable. More specifically, he pointed to obvious weaknesses in the manner of proceeding: it was first of all wrong to bring in an instrument of attainder in the expectation that the reasons for it would later appear, while any subsequent amendment to the bill in its progress through Parliament would be an admission that there had originally been insufficient ground for it. He concluded by cautioning against such a dangerous precedent and warned that bills of attainder might become as frequent as they had been during the reign of Richard II. After this, however, Finch made no more recorded appearances in connexion with the bill. Late in December he succumbed again to serious illness, and at one point was reported dead. In April 1697, as he slowly recovered, misfortune of another kind struck when his residence at Albury was gutted by fire. His ill-health continued well into the following year, during which time there are no indications of Commons attendance. In July 1698 he told his kinsman Dr Leopold Finch, the warden of All Souls, of his intention not to seek re-election for the university, quite happy to be succeeded by his old comrade-in-arms in the House, Sir Christopher Musgrave. Although he had not attended Parliament on a regular basis for some time, the compiler of a comparative listing of the old and new Houses of Commons identified him as a Country supporter.[12]

In October 1699, Finch succeeded to the best part of his father-in-law's fortune, an estate at Aylesford in Kent valued at some £200,000, from which the annual income was said to be £5,000. Thenceforward he was to have an electoral interest in the nearby borough of Maidstone. It was also said that he had been left £50,000 'in money'. He was again reported 'very ill' at the end of April 1700, but had recuperated sufficiently towards the end of the year to consider standing again for Parliament in the forthcoming election. On this, Lord Nottingham gave brotherly advice: 'whatever I wish you upon a public account, you must let your health determine you, but pray resolve in due time'. There was a good chance of his being chosen for Surrey, but he was rather more attentive to the efforts of his kinsman of All Souls to secure his former place for the university. Apparently restored in health, he regained the seat in January 1701, and when the new Parliament convened, his former stature and prominence soon reappeared in the reprisals against the King's Whig ministers over the Partition Treaties. On 20 Mar. he featured among the sponsors of a bill to prevent bribery and corruption at elections, a measure beloved by Country Members. On 28 Mar., as one Country Whig reported, he spoke 'long and maliciously' against the ministerial grant to Lord

Bellomont (Richard Coote*) of all rights to the booty captured by Captain Kidd. Next day, as the House in committee proceeded in its investigation of the circumstances under which Britain had signed the Partition Treaties, Finch joined in condemning Lord Chancellor Somers (Sir John*) for completing the ratification, despite professed misgivings, without consulting ministerial colleagues. Although Somers escaped official censure for the time being, the House began impeachment proceedings against Portland for his part in the negotiations, and Finch was named first to the committee of 1 Apr. to draft the articles. The following day, during consideration of the King's request for measures against the French, Finch firmly supported Sir Edward Seymour's cautious line, 'not for declaring against war nor being too forward in it, but for supporting the Dutch according to the treaty, to be seconds, not principals'. Finch moved the question that the House 'assure' William that they would 'effectually enable him to support' the 1678 treaty and advise him to continue peaceable negotiations with France in association with the Dutch. This was agreed 'after many hours' debate'. The presentation of the translated 1698 correspondence between James Vernon I* and Lord Portland two days later reopened the question of Somers' role in the first Partition Treaty, which he was accused of sealing without a warrant. During the debate Finch told the House that if Somers had disagreed with the treaty 'he should plainly have wrote to the King that he could not approve of it, and if that would not do he should rather have given up his seals than have complied'.[13]

Before the second general election of that year, Finch was blacklisted as having opposed the preparations for war with France, an allegation refuted in another pamphlet. Such propaganda did nothing, of course, to affect his standing among his university electorate, who re-elected him without opposition. At the start of supply business on 6 Jan. 1702, he supported Musgrave's contention that the House delay making a formal promise of financial assistance until the King had communicated details of his commitments to foreign powers, although the general consensus was that such a step was unnecessary. Finch was spoken of as a possible successor to Sir Rowland Gwynne* as chairman of the committee of privileges and elections, but on the 9th Gwynne was chosen once more. On 16 Jan. Finch seconded Seymour in a preconcerted attempt to obstruct progress on supply, with a motion proposing that the 7,000 troops garrisoned in England constitute part of England's quota towards the allied war effort. But this, too, proved unpopular. At the second reading of the Lords' abjuration bill on 17 Jan. he put forward a clause against occasional conformity, but it was decided instead to proceed with the Commons' own abjuration measure, so that nothing came of the amendment. On the 28th, when this subsequent measure was considered in committee of the whole, Finch strongly exerted himself in favour of a clause to oblige Dissenting ministers to take an oath to defend the Church, only to see it thrown out by a narrow majority. Finch remained at the forefront of Tory resistance to the Commons' abjuration bill, and was said to have spoken on the subject as many as 17 times in the session. At the third reading on 19 Feb. he declared that he did not oppose the reading of the bill, but offered, in Burnet's words, 'an alteration to the clause abjuring the Prince of Wales, so that it imported only an oath not to assist him'. He pressed this intended compromise 'with unusual vehemence', but found few supporters. After several other clauses had been received, Lord Coningsby (Thomas*), in a piece of sarcasm clearly directed at Finch, commented that the 'new bill' now seemed more palatable to 'those who could not digest the abjuration oath'. Finch, however, ignored the gibe and rose merely to say that 'there was not one equivoking expression in it'. In the meantime, he, along with Seymour and Musgrave, had continued to attack the government on supply issues, and had done so 'mightily' on 2 Feb. when they opposed a proposal for raising 10,000 extra men even though it was to be achieved with little additional charge. He was greatly concerned, too, about the recent scurrilous attacks on the proceedings of the last Parliament, especially those made by Thomas Colepeper, one of the 'Kentish Petitioners', during the recent election campaign at Maidstone, and moved that the House set aside time to consider properly of 'the rights, liberties, and privileges' of the Commons. The matter was debated on 17 Feb., though what took place hardly measured up to Finch's expectations of a wide-ranging consideration of how the endangered privileges of the House might be protected. He began by talking 'at random' against libels and reflections on Parliament, and in a later intervention proposed three motions, one condemning as unconstitutional the assertion that the House of Commons was 'not the only representative of the commons of England'; another that the House had no 'power of commitment, but of their own members'; and a third denouncing printed attacks on MPs, en masse and individually, as 'a high violation' of the rights and privileges of the House. The committee adopted these with very little debate, and the proceedings ended inconclusively in some confusion. Though Finch's resolutions were retained when the matter was resumed on the 26th, the

Whigs, seizing the initiative, added two more. Finch voted in that debate in favour of a Tory motion, which narrowly failed, vindicating the Commons' proceedings in the impeachments the preceding year. It is conceivable that his omission from the committee appointed at William III's death (8 Mar.) to draft the loyal address to Queen Anne was intentional in the light of his well-known views upon William's position as King, though fittingly it was at Finch's residence that members of the committee met to complete the draft.[14]

Finch was not included among the High Tories appointed to office at the start of the new reign, though this may have been a personal choice dictated by his recent poor health. His re-election at Oxford University was a foregone conclusion, however. At the beginning of the new Parliament, on 20 Oct. 1702, he formally proposed Robert Harley as Speaker. Before long, his new proximity to the ministry led to tensions between himself and the Tory back-benchers and their leaders. This was particularly apparent in the question of the Queen's proposed grant of £5,000 to the Duke of Marlborough (John Churchill*). Finch was anxious to find ways of facilitating the grant through an expedient that would mollify Tory squires whose hopes for a new era of 'honest government' were rapidly fading. But his proposal that it be made from prize money was regarded by Lord Godolphin (Sidney†) as impracticable. When the grant was debated in committee on 15 Dec. Seymour and Musgrave spoke for the opposition while Finch defended the Duke and his services to the nation in 'establishing an entire correspondence with the States General' which, he claimed, had been necessary since English envoys abroad had represented 'the gentlemen of England' as happily disposed towards the French. 'Was it not good service,' he asked 'to assure the States [General] that the government of England was misrepresented?' Finch's efforts to support Marlborough were hardly likely to placate Tory gentlemen who knew only too well the Duke's unenthusiastic attitude towards the occasional conformity bill. Still, his concern that Marlborough be rewarded from an acceptable source of finance could be seen on the 16th, when he was named in second place after Seymour to a committee to address the Queen requesting her not to draw upon the crown revenues. There was the greater possibility that Finch would openly oppose the ministry over the large addition of 10,000 troops requested by the Dutch, but Nottingham prevailed on both him and Seymour to hold fire during deliberations on the supply at the end of that month and in early January. Finch was of course able to maintain his high profile among Tories in his advocacy of the occasional conformity bill, and on 16 Dec. was one of the main participants in the conference with the Lords. Predictably, he cast his vote on 13 Feb. 1703 against the bill for extending the time allowed for taking the Abjuration. His involvement, too, in the various recriminatory proceedings against former Whig ministers was also a matter for Tory applause. On 1 Feb. he was named in first place to the committee to draft an address condemning the former paymaster, Lord Ranelagh (Richard Jones*), for misapplying public money, and later that month took a leading part in the Commons' unsuccessful attempt to find Lord Halifax (Charles Montagu*) guilty of a 'breach of trust' as auditor of the Exchequer. A discrepancy in the printed *Votes* of the House regarding these allegations prompted Finch's motion on 25 Feb. to stop the practice of printing the *Votes*, but the House concluded that publication should be kept under closer supervision.[15]

Finch's career in the Commons ended a few weeks later with his elevation to the peerage as Lord Guernsey. There had been reports in mid-February that he would be among several new additions to the Lords, in order, it was said, 'to keep a balance in that House'. His patent, dated 15 Mar., stated that the creation was 'in consideration of his great merits and abilities'; and five days later he was admitted to the Privy Council. The discord between the two Houses over the occasional conformity bill had exposed the need for more influential Church Tories in the Upper House. But Finch's removal from the Commons may also have been intended to prevent his causing future difficulties there for the ministry, and especially for Nottingham, over issues such as military expenditure, matters in which his 'Country' sensibilities had become entrenched during Nottingham's years in the political wilderness. In the presence of his elder brother in the Lords, there was less likelihood that he would deviate from the ministerial line. The connexion of Finch relatives, friends and retainers was, of course, deprived of an obvious representative in the Commons until the election of 1710 brought in Nottingham's son Lord Finch (Daniel*) and Finch's own son Hon. Heneage II*. Once in the Lords, Finch ranked alongside such champions of High Anglicanism as his brother and Lords Weymouth and Rochester. In the summer of 1710 he was one of several considered for the lord chancellorship, but, probably because of his brother's distrust of Harley, was passed over. When Nottingham finally broke with the Tories over the peace in December 1711, Guernsey did not immediately follow suit, continuing to support the ministry. In April 1713, however, after an uneasy period of indecision, he came round to accepting Nottingham's view that a peace settlement which placed Spain and the West Indies in Bourbon hands was untenable. His emergence as a 'Hanoverian' during the final year of the Queen's life earned him reward soon after the accession of George I with the earldom of Aylesford and appointment as chancellor of the Duchy of Lancaster. However, as a member of the new Whig ministry he quickly annoyed his colleagues by failing to uproot the strong Tory element from the Lancashire magistracy, forcing Secretary Townshend to intervene instead. Despite their unequivocal support for the impeachment of Lord Oxford in 1715, the Finch brothers were an incongruous element in the new Whig establishment, and once Nottingham began pleading mercy for the condemned Scottish Jacobite peers in February 1716 the opportunity was taken to secure their dismissal. Finch died at his Surrey seat on 22 July 1719, though he was buried near his Aylesford estate in Kent, his eldest son and namesake, the MP for Surrey, succeeding him in the peerage.[16]

[1] H. Horwitz, *Revol. Politicks*, 259. [2] *HMC Finch*, i. 457, 479; info. from Prof. R. O. Bucholz. [3] E. G. W. Bill, *Queen Anne Churches*, p. xxiii. [4] Burnet, ii. 379; *Macky Mems.* 90; *Swift Works* ed. Davis, vii. 11; Horwitz, 268. [5] Burnet, ii. 379; Stowe 364, ff. 62-69; Horwitz, 74, 82, 84; *HMC Portland*, iii. 436. [6] Horwitz, 107-8; Morice ent'ring bk. 3, pp. 106, 151; Add. 29573, f. 407; 29578, f. 318; Foxcroft, *Halifax*, ii. 249; Bodl. Ballard 11, f. 185; Surrey RO (Guildford), Midleton mss 1248/1, f. 232, Charlett to Brodrick, 13 Feb. 1690; Grey, x. 15, 61, 70, 101, 113, 121, 125-6; Bodl. Rawl. A.79, f. 90. [7] *CSP Dom.* 1690-1, p. 211; Horwitz, 123; Grey, 172, 206-8, 214, 220; *Luttrell Diary*, 25, 99, 115, 154. [8] Rawl. C.449 (unfol.); *Luttrell Diary*, 45, 84, 87, 91-92, 118, 125, 141-2, 150, 166, 175. [9] Grey, 272-3, 287, 290-2; *Luttrell Diary*, 248, 259, 265, 319, 332, 344, 360, 382, 392-3, 407, 414, 422, 449; Chester RO, Earwaker mss CR63/2/691/116, Sir Willoughby Aston to Sir John Crewe, 28 Jan. 1692[-3]; Cobbett, *Parlty. Hist.* v. 759. [10] Grey, 325-6, 328, 352; Add. 46527, f. 47; 28879, f. 219; Devonshire mss at Chatsworth House, Finch-Halifax pprs. box 4, bdle. 12, Finch to Dr Leopold Finch, [Oct. 1695]; Centre for Kentish Stud. Stanhope mss U1590/059/4, Robert Yard* to Alexander Stanhope, 22 Oct. 1695. [11] *Life of Montagu* (1715), 30; Finch-Halifax pprs. box 3, Nottingham to Finch 14 Dec. 1695; K. Feiling, *Tory Party*, 316; Stanhope mss U1590/059/4,5, Yard to Stanhope, 17 Dec. 1695, 6 Jan. 1695-6; *HMC Hastings*, ii. 253, 259; Horwitz, 156; Burnet, iv. 306; *Ailesbury Mems.* 359. [12] Ballard 39, f. 128; 11, f. 135; Bath mss at Longleat House, Thynne pprs. 14, f. 279; 17, ff. 253-4; Cobbett, v. 1017-19; *Vernon-Shrewsbury Letters*, i. 151-2; Stanhope mss U1590/053/6, James Vernon I* to Stanhope, 29 Dec. 1696; Finch-Halifax pprs. box 5, bdle. 3, Sir John Banks* to Finch, 23 Feb. 1697; box 4, bdle. 1, Finch to Dr Leopold Finch, [July 1698]; Luttrell, *Brief Relation*, iv. 209. [13] Luttrell, iv. 573; Thynne pprs. 15, f. 284; Ballard 10, f. 40; Finch-Halifax pprs. box 2, no. 60, Nottingham to Finch, 18 Nov. 1700; no. 63, Dr Leopold Finch to Finch, 18 Dec. 1700; *Cocks Diary*, 76, 94. [14] Add. 17677 XX, ff. 160, 166, 175; 7074, ff. 168, 188; DZA, Bonet despatch 16/27 Jan. 1702; Horwitz, 188; *Cocks Diary*, 220; Strathmore mss at Glamis Castle, box 70, bdle. 1, newsletter 29 Jan. 1701-2; Cumbria RO, Carlisle, Lonsdale mss D/Lons/W2/2/5, James Lowther* to Sir John Lowther 2nd Bt. I*, 3 Feb. 1701[-2]; *Locke Corresp.* ed. de Beer, vii. 567-8; Burnet, iv. 551;

Huntington Lib. Stowe mss 26(2), James Brydges'* diary, 8 Mar. 1702. [15] Add. 70264, misc. 17; *HMC Portland*, iv. 53; *Norris Pprs.* (Chetham Soc. ix), 106; Horwitz, 179; *Nicolson Diaries* ed. Jones and Holmes, 175; *Atterbury Epistolary Corresp.* iv. 380. [16] Add. 22852, ff. 73-76; Horwitz, 222, 234-5, 238, 240-1, 246, 249-50; Bagot mss at Levens Hall, William Bromley II* to James Grahme*, 1 Sept. 1710; L. K. J. Glassey, *Appt. JPs.* 199, 290-4; G. Holmes, *Pol. in Age of Anne*, 331.

A. A. H.

FINCH, Hon. Heneage II (1683-1757), of Albury, Surr.

MAIDSTONE   3 Nov. 1704-1705
SURREY   1710-22 July 1719

bap. 27 Aug. 1683, 1st s. of Hon. Heneage Finch I* and bro. of Hon. John Finch†. *educ.* Westminster; Christ Church, Oxf. matric. 1700. *m.* 9 Dec. 1712, Mary, da. and h. of Sir Clement Fisher, 3rd Bt., of Packington, Warws., 1s. 4da. *Styled* Ld. Guernsey, 1715-19; *suc.* fa. as 2nd Earl of Aylesford 22 July 1719.

Master of jewel office 1711-16.[1]

Finch gave a fine demonstration of his talent at public speaking – and of his promise as a future parliamentarian – when as an Oxford student he 'complimented' Queen Anne in verse during her stay at Christ Church at the end of August 1702. He was returned to Parliament almost as soon as he came of age, a by-election conveniently arising early in November 1704 at Maidstone, where his father had an interest through ownership of the nearby manor of Aylesford. It was appropriate that Finch's entry to the House should occur during the controversy over occasional conformity: as a scion of one of the most influential High Church families in the land he was easily identifiable as a prospective supporter of the Tack, and duly voted for the measure on 28 Nov. At the 1705 election, however, he lost his seat. For the next five years he settled down to the typical existence of a country gentleman, and it was presumably during this period of his life that he made Albury in Surrey, recently rebuilt after a devastating fire, his 'constant residence'. There he occupied his time as a 'very useful' magistrate, indulged a fondness for country sports, and bred pheasants. Only in 1708 do these routines appear to have been disrupted, when he attempted to gain a seat at Wigan on the interest of his uncle, Hon. Edward Finch*.[2]

As Tory fortunes began to revive during the spring of 1710, Finch became more active in Surrey politics where increasingly he was seen as a leader of the Tory interest. In May he was 'graciously received' by the Queen and presented a loyal address signed by over

2,000 of the county's freeholders. But such was the arduousness of the ensuing contest that Finch did not refuse the opportunity of standing also at Maidstone. Ironically, it was for the latter constituency that he was beaten, while in Surrey he obtained second place in a precariously close poll. He was marked as a Tory in the 'Hanover list' of the 1710 Parliament, and was included in a list published after the first session of those 'worthy patriots' who had contributed to the detection of the 'mismanagements' of the Marlborough–Godolphin administration. But his eagerness to see censure heaped upon the previous ministry was more evident in an initiative of his own to expose the public costs involved in resettling the Palatine refugees in Britain, a favourite Whig venture which had received bitter Tory condemnation. Under Finch's chairmanship an inquiry was set up on 15 Jan. 1711 into the circumstances of the invitation and the costs involved, from which he reported on 23 Feb., but it was not until 14 Apr. that the House gave the report consideration. Although the Commons agreed with the committee's findings that there had been a 'scandalous misapplication' of public money in resettling the Palatines, the matter lapsed. The inquiry was part of the attack upon the General Naturalization Act of 1709, whereby foreigners of any Protestant persuasion could become naturalized subjects. Finch was one of the Members authorized to bring in a bill of repeal, but this was later rejected in the Lords. During proceedings on 16 Jan. the House was forced to intercede in a personal quarrel which erupted between Finch and Hon. John Noel, the Whig Member for Rutland. The issue concerned the Rutland election, which was currently under review in the elections committee, and in which the Finches were at odds with Noel for reneging on a pact to exclude any but 'true freeholders' from the poll. A week later, on the 23rd, when the committee's report on the election was received, Finch had the pleasure of telling for the majority against the motion declaring Noel duly elected. Finch was among the members of the October Club whom Lord Treasurer Harley (Robert*) was anxious to bring into the ministry during the summer. As the session drew to its close early in June, Finch was given the Household appointment of master of the jewel office. During the following month he supervised all stages of a second bill for the repeal of the General Naturalization Act, which this time passed into law. It was undoubtedly this personal success which led to his being distinguished as a 'leader' of the October Club in a list of the members published in February 1712.[3]

Though apparently less active in the 1713 session, Finch began to emerge as a 'whimsical' critic of the peace terms, following the line set by his father and his uncle, Lord Nottingham (Daniel Finch†). On 18 June he voted against the French commerce bill. In the general election in the autumn of that year, he was re-elected knight of the shire for Surrey, this time achieving first place in the poll. The 1714 session saw him acting regularly with the Whigs. He was regarded within the ministry, certainly by Secretary Bolingbroke (Henry St. John II*), as a leading figure among (Sir) Thomas Hanmer's (II)* following of 'whimsical Tories', 'the busiest spark among them'. With growing apprehension, Bolingbroke appealed urgently to the lord treasurer on 21 Apr. for Finch's immediate dismissal from the jewel office: 'it will be worth the remove of two Whigs, and more grateful to our friends'. But Finch was kept on. Indeed, his High Anglican loyalties were easily provoked on 12 May when the ministry introduced the schism bill, aimed against Dissenting schools and masters, and designed primarily to paper over the recent cracks in Tory unity. Not only was he included in the cross-section of Tories ordered to produce the bill, but he also acted during the debate as teller against a Whig attempt to broaden it to include Catholics. He also showed unequivocal support for his own party during the hearings on the disputed Southwark election, wherein the defeated Tory candidates attempted to prove corruption against the Whig victors, and on three separate occasions (25 May, 15 June and 3 July) was teller for the Tory side. But these strictly party considerations did not obviate his critical attitude towards the ministry. On 3 June, for instance, he appeared as one of the sponsors of the bill to renew the commission of accounts. The Worsley list, published after the 1715 election, characterized Finch's overall political conduct during the sessions of 1713–14 as being that of a Tory who would often vote with the Whigs. Along with other Hanoverian Tories he attended at St. James's Palace on 1 Aug. 1714 to sign the proclamation of George I. By virtue of his custodianship of the jewel office he was ordered by the lords justices on 12 Aug. to convey the late Queen's jewels to the Tower for greater safety.[4]

Re-elected for Surrey in 1715, Finch enjoyed office only for a short while longer. His father and uncle's relations with the new ministry, already uneasy, deteriorated rapidly towards the end of February 1716 over Nottingham's and Guernsey's desire to save from execution the lords condemned for taking part in the Fifteen. Finch, too, had voted in their favour, and resigned, no doubt sensing that he too would soon be dismissed. Thereafter, both as an MP and subsequently as a peer, he was invariably in opposition to the

Whig establishment. Succeeding his father as Earl of Aylesford in 1719, he also inherited the extensive family estates around Maidstone, where for many years the High Church interest thrived under his patronage. He died on 29 June 1757, and was succeeded as 3rd Earl by his only son, Lord Guernsey (Heneage Finch†).[5]

[1] Info. from Prof. R. O. Bucholz. [2] Boyer, *Anne Annals*, i. 76; Manning and Bray, *Surrey*, ii. 125. [3] Add. 70421, newsletter 4 May 1710; 70332, [memo. by Robert Harley, 4 June 1711]; *Huntington Lib. Q.* xxxiii. 164. [4] *HMC Portland* v. 425, 487; G. Holmes, *Pol. in Age of Anne*, 104, 475; Boyer, *Pol. State*, viii. 118. [5] J. Beattie, *Eng. Ct. in Reign of Geo. I*, 175.

A. A. H.

FIREBRACE, Sir Basil (1652–1724), of London and Enfield, Mdx.

CHIPPENHAM   9 Dec. 1690–1 Dec. 1691, 14 Dec. 1691–22 Jan. 1692

b. 1652, 2nd s. of Sir Henry Firebrace of Whitehall, Westminster and the Old Hall, Stoke Golding, Leics., page of the bedchamber, yeoman of the robes and clerk of the kitchen to Charles I 1647–9, clerk of the kitchen, clerk comptroller and second clerk of the Bd. of Green Cloth to Charles II and James II 1660–89, by his 1st w. Elizabeth, da. of Daniel Dowell of Stoke Golding. *m.* 7 Sept. 1671, Mary, da. of Thomas Hough, milliner, of St. Botolph's, Bishopsgate, 6s. (4 *d.v.p.*) 2da. (1 *d.v.p.*). Kntd. 2 Aug. 1687; *cr.* Bt. 28 July 1698.[1]

Yeoman purveyor of French wines to the Household 1673–85; jt. ranger of Enfield chase by 1694–1714.[2]

Sheriff, London and Mdx. 1687–8; alderman, London 1687–Oct. 1688, freeman Oct. 1688; freeman, Cambridge 1693.[3]

Cttee. E.I. Co. 1694–5.[4]

Firebrace's father was 'Honest Harry', who had attended Charles I after his surrender to the Scots in 1646, had thereafter assisted the King in several abortive escape plans and had been rewarded at the Restoration with a secure Household office. Sir Henry set up his second son as a vintner, a trade his own brother had prospered in. Basil was even more successful than his uncle, privileged as he was with the monopoly of supplying French wines to Charles II's court, an advantage he exploited unscrupulously. He was said to have made

£14,000 in one year besides what he got in other years when French wines were prohibited, by carrying [the wine] down to Whitehall in a barge with a file of musketeers to a cellar of his own that he had provided there, under pretence of carrying it there for the King's own use.

Discovered in this fraud in 1681 he secured a pardon by 'making interest . . . with the Duchess of Cleveland'. A loyal supporter of James II, he was nominated an alderman of London by royal commission in 1681 without ever having been admitted a freeman, and in September 1688 was recommended with Sir John Parsons* as a Court candidate for Reigate in the projected parliamentary election. Despite their close connexions with James's court, Firebrace and his father did not suffer unduly at the Revolution: Sir Henry, accepting the new regime, retired voluntarily from the Green Cloth with a pension, and Basil, though he had been superseded as an alderman of London by the restoration of the old charter in October 1688, was still an active and prosperous merchant. One of a group of Tory citizens considered likely to 'put . . . forward' a proposed loan in March 1690, he personally lent some £5,000 to the crown between 1690 and 1692. Successful at a by-election for Chippenham in December 1690 against another City figure, the Dissenter Sir Humphrey Edwin, Firebrace was unseated on petition a year later, when the House found both candidates guilty of bribery and declared the election void. During this period he was not recorded as having spoken in Parliament. He was listed in December 1690 as among those likely to support Lord Carmarthen (Sir Thomas Osborne†) in the event of a parliamentary attack against him, and he was named in Robert Harley's* list of April 1691 as a Court supporter. At the ensuing by-election he again defeated a Whig, Hon. Thomas Tollemache*, and was again ejected on petition, after wholesale bribery and treating had been proved. The Tories tried in vain to prevent this resolution being printed, because, as they put it, 'the gentleman, being a citizen, this vote would much reflect on him and blast his reputation'. Firebrace survived inclusion in Robert Young's 'sham plot' of 1692, aimed principally at Bishop Sprat and the Earl of Marlborough (John Churchill†), and was confirmed in 1694 in the half-share in the rangership of Enfield chase that he had already acquired from Viscount Lisburne. In the same year he made a final effort at Chippenham, in a third by-election. This time, however, he was defeated, and his own petition was dismissed in January 1695, without a division, in committee or in the House.[5]

Firebrace's subsequent career was shadowed by scandal and a descent into penury. In April 1695 his part in the alleged corruption surrounding the grant of a new charter to the East India Company late in 1693 and the launching of a new subscription was exposed by the joint investigative committee established by the two Houses. It transpired that Firebrace, who although once an investor in the company, was now a member of the interloping syndicate, had been bought off by Sir Thomas Cooke* in the autumn of 1692 and in return for a sizable stake in the company had agreed to act on its behalf in soliciting a new charter and in persuading ex-colleagues among the interlopers to abandon their proceedings and come into the company's terms, an agreement at first kept secret though later discovered: he admitted having been 'turned off by the interlopers' when they began to suspect him. In particular it was shown that he had received at least £10,000 for himself and a further £30,000 to distribute to opponents, including Members of Parliament. In disclosing part of his activities to the company, who promised to 'indemnify him', he may have encountered difficulties: early in April, at a general court, there were 'heats', and Firebrace and another man 'passed from words to blows'. His first evidence to the parliamentary committee, on 24 Apr. 1695, was as discreet as possible in the circumstances, but he returned two days later at his own request (having excused himself one day to 'take physic') to make specific allegations against prominent Parliamentarians. While exonerating his 'intimate' friend Sir Edward Seymour, 4th Bt.*, he accused Henry Guy* and Sir John Trevor* of accepting 'presents', and the Duke of Leeds (formerly Carmarthen) of taking 5,500 guineas via an intermediary, one Charles Bates. These charges formed the basis of an impeachment against Leeds, who angrily denounced Firebrace. He said that he had all along considered Firebrace 'a very ill man' and had warned Bates against him. Now, he claimed, Firebrace had been put up to incriminate him. Firebrace had been 'treated with to discover only this part, and so he should be excused from any other discovery', or even 'excused' altogether for what he had done. Certainly the committee agreed to 'commute with' him 'for a confession of what he was not charged with', and the Commons appeared to be favouring him: they amended the emergency bill, designed to retain Cooke, Firebrace and two others in custody during the parliamentary recess, so that it applied solely to Cooke. When the Lords disagreed, however, the point was not pressed, and the bill passed. As a result Firebrace remained in prison for a year, unable to dispose of any part of his estate, except for the £20,000 he had already agreed on as a portion for his daughter. Despite this he emerged from confinement relatively unscathed, in a material sense: he was able personally to subscribe £3,000 of the Old East India Company's advance loan of £200,000 in 1698, and in July of that year was created a baronet. His reputation, on the other hand, was permanently stained. In 1697 he was accused of profiteering over the sale of timber from Enfield chase, while Ned Ward's *The London Spy* directed its readers' attention to a tavern which had 'ruined almost as many vintners as Sir Base'ill fiery-face'. Evidently it was Firebrace's practice to set up young vintners in business and whenever defaults occurred to take execution against them immediately. The rangership of Enfield led him into various disputes, all reflecting his enmity to Lord Stamford, the chancellor of the duchy of Lancaster: in 1699 he 'fell into a feud' with Sir Henry Belasyse* over a dog belonging to Belasyse that was killed in the chase; in 1700 he was cleared of a breach of privilege in ordering the arrest of a servant of Christopher Lister*; and last, in May 1701, he gave evidence to the Commons against Stamford, who was accused of neglecting his duties at Enfield. In 1701 Firebrace was granted a considerable financial opportunity on being appointed 'broker' for the Old East India Company in the negotiations with the New, for which he was promised £20,000. He discharged the commission but was forced to sue for his fee, settling for £10,000 worth of stock in 1703 but reopening his case a year later with a claim for £100,000 more, which he lost. Eventually in June 1705 a general court voted him £22,500. It was too late, if ever paid, for by now Firebrace was almost ruined. He still functioned as a wine shipper, but his debts mounted, despite a loan of £6,000 from the Earl of Portland. He was rumoured in January 1705 to have gone bankrupt, and within 18 months rumour had become fact. Thomas Hearne reported:

> Sir Basil Firebrace, a noted old sinner of London, has shot himself, but 'tis thought 'twill not prove mortal, as some perhaps could wish, whom he had cheated by odd tricks and shams, from whence he grew rich . . . but notwithstanding he decayed, through crosses and being reduced to some unexpected extremities, was the cause of this violence on himself.

Another contemporary reported that Firebrace had in fact stabbed himself. Still a Tory, Firebrace polled for the Tory candidates in the London election of 1713, and at the accession of George I he sold his half-share in the Enfield rangership. In 1720 he was gaoled briefly after stabbing a half-pay officer who had come to his lodging to demand money.[6]

Firebrace died on 7 May 1724 and was buried at St. Margaret's, Westminster. His elder surviving son having restored the family fortunes by an advantageous marriage, his grandson, Sir Cordell Firebrace, 3rd Bt., sat for Suffolk as a Tory from 1735 to 1759.

[1] J. R. Woodhead, *Rulers of London* (London and Mdx. Arch. Soc.), 69; Folger Shakespeare Lib. Newdigate newsletter 25 June

1695; BL, Lothian mss, 'Abstract of the Case of Sir Basil Firebrace . . .'; C. W. Firebrace, *Honest Harry*, 29, 141–2, 201, 204, 217–18, 220, 224, 226, 229–31, 240, 245; *DNB* (Firebrace, Sir Henry). ² Somerville, *Duchy of Lancaster Official Lists*, 209–10. ³ Beaven, *Aldermen*, i. 31; Cambs. RO (Cambridge), Cambridge bor. recs. common day bk. 1681–1722, p. 221. ⁴Add. 38871 (unfol.). ⁵ Firebrace, 217, 230, 232–3; *CSP Dom.* 1680–1, p. 539; 1687–9, p. 274; 1691–2, pp. 279, 300; *Ailesbury Mems.* i. 227; *Cal. Treas. Bks.* ix. 1636, 1742, 2002; Dorset RO, Fox-Strangways mss, Sir Peter Rich† to Sir Stephen Fox*, 17 Mar. 1690; *Luttrell Diary*, 149–50; *Parl. Hist.* v. 739; Luttrell, *Brief Relation*, iii. 415–16. ⁶*CJ*, xi. 268–9, 288, 317–18, 320–7, 329–32; xii. 321; xiii. 176, 571–2; P. G. M. Dickson, *Financial Revol.* 491; Add. 22185, f. 12; Bodl. Rawl. C.449 (12 Oct. 1691); HMC Lords, n.s. i. 554–62; Newdigate newsletter 2 Apr. 1695; *CSP Dom.* 1695, p. 320; *Lexington Pprs.* 84; Chandler, ii. 465, 468, 470; Cobbett, *Parlty. Hist.* v. 935, 938–9; BL, Althorp mss, Halifax pprs. box 10, Ld. Weymouth (Thomas Thynne†) to Halifax (William Savile†, Ld. Eland), 27 Apr. 1695; Luttrell, iii. 466; iv. 51; v. 43, 284, 487, 566; *Debates and Procs. 1694–5*, pp. 61–62; *VCH Mdx.* v. 236; Firebrace, 234–6; Ned Ward, *The London Spy* ed. Hayward, 238; Northants. RO, Montagu (Boughton) mss 47/201, James Vernon I* to the Duke of Shrewsbury, 22 June 1699; Nottingham Univ. Lib. Portland (Bentinck) mss PwA 1497, Vernon to Portland, 4 July 1699; *Cocks Diary*, 149; W. R. Scott, *Jt.-Stock Cos.* ii. 168–9; PRO, C110/28, John Dolben* to Thomas Pitt I*, 19 July 1701; Add. 22852, f. 74; Horwitz, *Parl. and Pol. Wm. III*, 298; *Cal. Treas. Pprs.* 1702–7, p. 388; *Cal. Treas. Bks.* xx. 184, 472; *Verney Letters 18th Cent.* i. 221; *Hearne Colls.* ii. 18–19; Herts. RO, Panshanger mss D/EP F32, pp. 67–8; *London Rec. Soc.* xvii. 85.

D. W. H.

FITCH *see* **FYTCHE**

FITZGERALD, John, 18th Earl of Kildare [I] (c.1661–1707), of Caversham Park, Oxon.

TREGONY   16 Mar. 1694–1695

b. c.1661, o. s. of Wentworth Fitzgerald†, 17th Earl of Kildare [I], by Lady Elizabeth, da. of John Holles, 2nd Earl of Clare. *educ.* Oxf. Univ. DCL 1683. *m.* (1) aft. Aug. 1682, Mary (*d.* 1683), da. of Henry O'Brien†, Ld. Ibrackan, 1s. *d.v.p.*; (2) lic. 12 June 1684 (with £10,000), Lady Elizabeth (*d.* 1758), da. and coh. of Richard Jones*, 1st Earl of Ranelagh [I], *s.p. suc.* fa. as 18th Earl 5 Mar. 1664.

Succeeding his father at the age of four, Kildare was left to the care of his mother, and then, following her death in 1666, of his grandmother, the dowager Lady Clare. In February 1682 his name was variously linked with a daughter of Lady Clancarty, and with a lady in the west of England who had 'great expectations'. In August 1682 a match was afoot with Lord Chesterfield's daughter, but in fact Kildare married into another Anglo-Irish family. He attended James, Duke of York on his visit to Oxford University in June 1683, when he was made a DCL. A year later, he took as his second wife the daughter of Lord Ranelagh, who brought a fortune as well as valuable political connexions, though her amorous intrigues made her a butt of satirists. At this time, Lord Arran wrote to Ormond:

> my Lord Ranelagh threatened that my Lord Kildare, whom, it seems, he governs now, shall petition the council board there [in Ireland] for recovering a debt at law due to me by the late Lord of Kildare above 20 years ago. I knew the time indeed when, for fear of his lordship, judges durst not do justice, I mean in the exchequer, but I hope his lordship's power is not so great now. I have all my Lord Kildare's estate in my possession.

Evidently Kildare recovered his Irish property, but he preferred to reside at Caversham, and in 1687 he entertained Mary of Modena on her way to Bath. As he did not attend James II's Irish parliament of 1689, Kildare's estates were temporarily sequestered by the Jacobites.¹

In 1694 Kildare was returned for Tregony at a by-election, on the interest of either Hugh Boscawen I*, who had married Kildare's cousin the previous year, or Hon. Francis Robartes*, the husband of Kildare's sister, or perhaps both. Kildare made no recorded speech and did not appear on any parliamentary list. In September 1695 he was summoned to attend the Irish house of lords, and did not stand at the English general election of that year. He travelled to Montpellier, France in December, and was still abroad in April 1700 when he was reported to be keeping 'open house for all the Irish' in Bruges. In March 1705 a private Act was passed to sell part of his estates. Kildare died on 9 Nov. 1707, Lady Rachel Russell reporting eight days later 'no will is found of Lord Kildare, so, as yet the Duke of St. Albans is defeated. He had told him [the Duke] that Saturday at dinner that he was heir to all in his power to give, went home, found himself ill, called for music, made them play till he died.' A will was found, George Rodney Brydges* being one of his executors, and Kildare was succeeded in his title by his cousin Robert Fitzgerald.²

¹ Lodge, *Peerage of Ire.*, i. 105–9; HMC Ormonde, n.s. vi. 321–2, 420; vii. 34, 164, 248; *Poems on Affairs of State* ed. Cameron, v. 347, 358; HMC Downshire, i. 263. ² *CSP Dom.* 1695, p. 138; HMC Bath, iii. 400; HMC Lords, n.s. vi. 249; viii. 275–6; HMC Rutland, ii. 187.

E. C.

FITZHARDINGE, John Berkeley, 4th Visct. [I] *see* **BERKELEY**

FITZHARDINGE, Maurice Berkeley, 3rd Visct. [I] *see* **BERKELEY**

FITZWILLIAM, Hon. John (c.1681–1728), of Milton, Northants.

PETERBOROUGH 1710–28 Aug. 1728

b. c.1681, 3rd but o. surv. s. of William, 3rd Baron Fitzwilliam† of Lifford [I] (*cr.* Earl Fitzwilliam [I] 1716) by Anne (*d.* 1717), da. and h. of Edmund Cremer of West Winch, Norf. *m.* 17 Sept. 1718, Anne (*d.* 1726), da. and h. of John Stringer of Sutton-upon-Lound, Notts., 1s. 3da. *Styled* Visct. Milton 1716–19; *suc.* fa. as 2nd Earl 28 Dec. 1719.[1]

Custos rot. Peterborough 1720–8.

It is probable that Fitzwilliam had either just reached or was soon to attain his majority by the time of the election of November 1701, since it was then rumoured in Peterborough that his father intended him to stand. A few days before the election, however, Lord Fitzwilliam told his steward that he had entertained 'no such thoughts in the least'. At the next general election several leading Tory townsmen seem to have been desirous that young Fitzwilliam should stand, despite his being the scion of a Whiggish family. Loath to provoke a contest, Lord Fitzwilliam declined to allow his son to be put forward but made expressions of obligation towards the gentlemen concerned 'for their kind intentions'. Only when Sir Gilbert Dolben* transferred to another seat in 1710 did Fitzwilliam's father seem prepared to set him on the political stage, possibly because he could see that he might then do so without involving his family in a costly and contentious election. Though the return was indeed disputed, the issue did not touch Fitzwilliam, which suggests his father had taken measures to ensure that the ground was clear in so far as the family interest was concerned.[2]

Fitzwilliam appears in the 'Hanover list' as a Tory but the truth of this ascription needs to be carefully weighed in the light of his background and later consistent support for the Whig party. He and his Tory partner, Charles Parker*, were together described in Dyer's report of their electoral success as 'very loyal gentlemen', the usual description for men of Tory opinion, and it is conceivable that locally he gave an impression of being sympathetic to the incoming Tory ministry. The compiler of the 'Hanover list' may thus have used Dyer's newsletter as his source. Fitzwilliam's name is noticeably absent, however, from the other Tory lists of this period, and it is much more likely he was a moderate Whig. Soon after the new Parliament commenced he associated himself with Edward Wortley Montagu's* initiative to bring in a place bill, an indication that he entered the House in a 'Country' frame of mind: his inclusion on the small committee appointed on 6 Dec. to prepare the measure suggests he had given vocal support to it in the House. On 16 Jan. 1711 he was granted three weeks' leave of absence. He told for the majority on 28 Feb. 1712 against postponing a call of the House, and on 2 Apr. against a motion that a private petition against Arthur Moore*, a ministerial Tory, be deemed 'frivolous and vexatious'. He then voted on 18 June 1713 against the French commerce bill, and in the general election later in the summer was returned unopposed at Peterborough. On 18 Mar. 1714 he voted against the motion leading to the expulsion of Richard Steele, and in the Worsley list and other lists reflecting behaviour in the 1713 Parliament was classified unequivocally as a Whig. On 5 Apr. 1714 he presented a petition from the gentlemen and inhabitants of Peterborough applying to be heard by counsel against the bill for making the River Nene navigable from Northampton to Peterborough. Later in the session, on 28 June, he was a teller against passing the bill to relieve insolvent debtors.

Fitzwilliam continued to represent Peterborough until his death on 28 Aug. 1728. In 1744 his son and successor, William†, the 3rd earl, married a daughter of the 1st Marquess of Rockingham (Thomas Watson Wentworth†), and was created an English earl in 1746.[3]

[1] *Vis. Eng. and Wales Notes* ed. Crisp, 74–77. [2] Northants. RO, Fitzwilliam (Milton) corresp. 1191, 1226, Ld. Fitzwilliam to Francis Guybon, 20 Nov. 1701, 23 July 1702. [3] Add. 70421, newsletter 10 Oct. 1710.

A.A.H.

FLEET, Sir John (1648–1712), of Allhallows Staining, London, and Battersea, Surr.

LONDON 2 Mar. 1693–1700
         20 Mar. – 11 Nov. 1701, 1702–1705

bap. 18 Mar. 1648, s. of Richard Fleet of Bourton, Bucks. *m.* (1) 20 June 1674, Elizabeth Arnold of St. Andrew, Holborn, Mdx.; (2) aft. 1695, wid. of Thomas Newcombe, royal printer, 3s. (2 *d.v.p.*) 4da. Kntd. 11 Oct. 1688.[1]

Freeman, Coopers' Co. 1667, asst. 1685, master 1689, transferred to Grocers' Co. 1692, master 1693–5; alderman, London Oct. 1688–*d.*, sheriff 1688–9, ld. mayor 1692–3; freeman, Colchester 1694.

Cttee. Old E.I. Co. 1692–1708 (with statutory intervals), gov. 1694–1708 (with statutory intervals); manager, united trade 1702; dir. E.I. Co. 1709–10, 1711–*d.*; asst. R. African Co. 1693–4, 1699–1702, 1704, sub.-gov. 1697–8; gov. Battersea Sch. 1700; vice-pres. Hon. Artillery Co. 1703–4, pres. 1704–8; pres. St. Bartholomew's Hosp. 1705–12.

Commr. Greenwich Hosp. 1695, 1704, taking subscriptions to land bank 1696.[2]

Of humble origins, Fleet established himself in the cooping trade, enjoying 'so early and quick an advance to such a mass of prosperity'. Diversifying into colonial commerce, he was actually described by one source as a 'sugar baker', and later acted as a spokesman for the sugar trade before the Treasury Board. His father, a Buckinghamshire innkeeper of possible Cheshire ancestry, had clearly played little part in securing his son's advancement, and Fleet's independent spirit was reflected by his subsequent political career. The sole survivor of a purge of the Coopers' Company in October 1687, he did not emerge as one of James II's supporters in the City, although he achieved rapid civic promotion in the final months of the reign. He even received a knighthood from King James in October 1688, but that did not secure his allegiance, prepared as he was to recognize the post-Revolution regime.[3]

In the early years of the reign of William and Mary, Fleet's politics remained the subject of some debate. In March 1690 the Tory Sir Peter Rich[†] identified him as one of 'the persons proper to be consulted with of our side' over a government loan, but at the mayoral contest of Michaelmas 1691 Fleet actually stood against the 'Church party'. Although unsuccessful on that occasion, at the succeeding mayoral election Fleet emerged triumphant, having been championed by Robert Yard* as 'a person of known affection and firmness to the present government'. Whig pamphleteers gave testimony to his popularity within the metropolis, one citing him as a man 'of unspotted reputation, both to the interest of the present government in general, and to the rights and liberties of this City in particular'. His favour with the London electorate was confirmed at the parliamentary by-election of February 1693, when he prevailed against his only serious challenger, the Whig Sir William Ashurst*. His readiness to stand against Ashurst may have reflected his increasingly close ties with the City Tories, Fleet having joined the East India Company in November 1691 at the behest of Sir Thomas Cooke*. He quickly assumed a prominent position within the company, and by October 1693 was willing to stand £10,000 as a surety to guarantee the company's export of domestic manufactures.[4]

Entering the Commons only eight days before the end of the fourth session of the 1690 Parliament, Fleet had little chance to make any immediate impact, but in the next session he actively represented City concerns. In addition, he served on the drafting committees to the bill to relieve the London orphans, in connexion with which on 2 Mar. 1694 he presented to the House a list of the debts owed to orphans. Having been appointed governor of the East India Company, during the recess he represented the company's fears of government regulation, warning the Duke of Shrewsbury that any change would be 'a great blow to their reputation which is not in a position to bear it'. His close relationship with fellow East Indiaman Sir Thomas Cooke was evident in November, when Fleet became a Colchester freeman only four days prior to Cooke's return at a by-election there. His association with Cooke was embarrassingly highlighted by the Commons' inquiry into the East India trade in March 1695, when the House heard that Fleet had been present at the company meetings which authorized Cooke's lavish bribes to advance their cause. However, as a Member he was not called upon to give evidence concerning such irregularities. In connexion with another scandal examined in this session, he was listed by Henry Guy* as a probable supporter.[5]

The London election of October 1695 proved a personal triumph for Fleet, for he topped the poll, over 2,000 votes ahead of his nearest rival. This result demonstrated the bipartisan support which he enjoyed within the City electorate, one pre-election forecast having suggested that his candidacy had been endorsed by all the competing factions. Not surprisingly, he continued to puzzle political commentators in the succeeding session, being forecast as 'doubtful' in January 1696 for a division concerning the proposed council of trade. More predictably, on 20 Feb. he was appointed to the committee to draft a bill for raising a new joint stock for the East India trade. Seven days later he signed the Association, and in late March opposed the ministry over its proposal to set the price of guineas at 22s. In the course of that year his prominence in the City was attested by his promotion to a colonelcy of a London militia regiment, as well as by his election to the land bank committee. During the next session he was generally inconspicuous, although he exchanged sharp words with Tory Member Thomas Blofield on 21 Jan. 1697 in the aftermath of the invasion of the House by Spitalfields weavers supporting the bill to ban the import of Indian wrought silks.[6]

In the third session of the 1695 Parliament Fleet was most conspicuous as the East India Company fought to maintain its existence. On 4 May 1698 he presented to the House the company's offer to advance a £700,000 loan to the government in exchange for a 31-year extension of its monopoly, an initiative subsequently outflanked by the interlopers' offer to raise a £2 million subscription. Fighting a rearguard action, on 9 June he submitted the company's petition for their counsel to be heard before the second reading of the bill to settle the East India trade. On that occasion he sought to reassure the House of the company's 'ready dispositions' to serve the public interest, and James Vernon I* identified him as one of the directors sympathetic to the new subscription. The next day, 10 June, Fleet actually presented the company's proposal to raise the proposed subscription from their own stock, a move which failed to delay the committal of the East India bill. When the House was informed on 14 June that the company's stock had been fraudulently overvalued, a defensive Fleet could only beg time to take counsel. Six days later he presented to the Commons a list of the subscribers ready to advance £200,000 as a security for the company to raise the £2 million subscription, Fleet's name standing at its head with a personal commitment of £2,000. However, this move was again countered by the interlopers, who demonstrated that £1,350,000 of their own subscription had already been raised.[7]

Although unable to preserve the Old Company's monopoly, Fleet continued to find success as a City politician, finishing first at the London election of July 1698. At the outset of the new Parliament he was identified as a likely opponent of the standing army, and another list confirmed him as a Country supporter. His principal interest remained the fate of the Old Company, for on 19 Jan. 1700 he presented a petition on its behalf and was then appointed to the committee to draft a bill to extend its charter. A parliamentary list of early 1700 duly identified him as a supporter of the Old Company, an association which clearly contributed to his failure at the London election of January 1701. Fortunately, the subsequent expulsion from the House of Gilbert Heathcote* gave him an opportunity to regain his seat, and he managed to achieve a narrow victory over Sir Thomas Stamp, his erstwhile Whig running-mate at the mayoral election of Michaelmas 1691. Having failed to make any significant contribution to Commons' business in that Parliament, Fleet was unable to retain his seat at the second general election of 1701, finishing sixth in the poll.

The accession of Anne brought renewed confidence to the City Tories, and Fleet, in particular, benefited from the change of monarch, regaining a colonelcy in the City militia, and then emerging at the head of the London poll of July 1702. His only noteworthy contribution to Commons' business in the whole of the ensuing Parliament rested with the presentation on 15 Dec. 1702 of a bill to encourage the consumption of malted corn. He was more prominent in East India affairs, being cited in February 1703 as a supporter of Sir Thomas Cooke amid the continuing struggles between Old and New Company factions. His commitment to the trade could not be doubted, however, after his investment in the company's stock had more than doubled to £18,000 in the course of 1703–4. His politics remained less predictable, for although he was forecast by Lord Nottingham (Daniel Finch†) in mid-March 1704 as a probable supporter in connexion with the Scotch Plot, in the next session he was listed on 30 Oct. 1704 as a probable opponent of the Tack. However, he clearly stood with the Tories at the London election of May 1705, albeit in a losing cause which spelt the end of his parliamentary career.[8]

Fleet remained a prominent figure in City politics, even though he suffered a further setback in June 1707 when he was dismissed as a militia colonel. His political outlook evidently remained volatile, Abel Boyer identifying him as 'High Church' after Fleet's election to the board of the United East India Company in April 1711, only to cite him three days later as a candidate of the 'moderate party' at the aldermanic contest for the ward of Bridge Within. Fleet died on 6 July 1712 and was buried at Battersea, his principal residence from perhaps as early as 1689. His epitaph proclaimed him as 'a merciful and just magistrate, constant to the Church, loyal to his prince, and true to his country', and paid tribute to 'a generous benefactor and a faithful friend'. Fleet's favourite charity, St. Bartholomew's Hospital, was a major beneficiary of his will, and he did not neglect his locality, having served as one of the founding governors of the school established by Sir Walter St. John, 3rd Bt.*, at Battersea. His only surviving son, James, did not aspire to parliamentary office, but, having settled at Tewin, Hertfordshire, served in 1718 as sheriff of that county.[9]

[1] IGI, London; *EHR*, li. 681; *London Rec. Soc.* ii. 107; Cussans, *Herts.* Hertford hundred, 16. [2] Guildhall Lib. ms 5602/5, f. 51; 6, f. 165; Beaven, *Aldermen*, ii. 116; Add. 38871 (unfol.); 10120, ff. 232–6; K. G. Davies, *R. African Co.* 381; *Daily Courant*, 8 Aug. 1704. [3] E. Settle, *Triumphs of London* [1692]; G. S. De Krey, *Fractured Soc.* 140–1; Luttrell, *Brief Relation*, i. 468; *Cal. Treas. Pprs.* 1557–1696, p. 213; *EHR*, 681; W. Foster, *Short Hist. Coopers' Co.* 45. [4] Dorset RO, Fox-Strangways mss D124, box 235, bdle. 4, Rich to Sir Stephen Fox*, 17 Mar. 1690; Luttrell, ii. 289; Centre Kentish Stud. Stanhope mss U1590/059/1, Yard to Alexander Stanhope, 27 Sept. 1692; Bodl. Carte 180, f. 106; Add. 59479, ff. 154–60; *EHR*, 684; *Cal. Treas. Bks.* x. 1211. [5] Grey, x. 335; *HMC Buccleuch*, ii. 117, 121, 133; W. G. Benham, *Oath Bk . . . of Colchester*, 248; *Debates and Proceedings 1694–5*, p. 9. [6] Luttrell, iii. 538; Beaven, ii. 116; Add. 70155, jnl. of land bank commn.; Northants. RO, Montagu (Boughton) mss 46/57, James Vernon I to Duke of Shrewsbury, 21 Jan. 1697. [7] *CSP Dom.* 1698, pp. 289–90, 300; *Vernon–Shrewsbury Corresp.* ii. 102. [8] Luttrell, iv. 605; v. 193; Add. 22852, ff. 10–11; Bodl. Rawl. D.747, f. 57. [9] Luttrell, vi. 186; Boyer, *Pol. State*, i. 264, 266; *CSP Dom.* 1689–90, p. 94; J. Aubrey, *Surr.* i. 143; PCC 133 Barnes; J. G. Taylor, *Our Lady of Batersey*, 183; Cussans, 16–17.

P. L. G.

FLEETWOOD, Henry (c.1667–1746), of Penwortham, nr. Preston, Lancs.

PRESTON 1708–1722

b. c.1667, 1st s. of Arthur Fleetwood of Lichfield, Staffs. and St. Margaret's, Westminster, by Mary, da. and h. of Sir Henry Archbold of Abbots Bromley, Staffs., chancellor of Lichfield dioc. *educ.* Brasenose, Oxf. matric. 25 Oct. 1683, aged 16. *m.* settlement 12 Feb. 1714, Sarah (*d.* 1719), da. of Roger Sudell of Preston, *s.p. suc.* fa. 1677, his cos. Edward Fleetwood† at Penwortham 1704.[1]

2nd lt. 7 Ft. 1685, lt. 1688.[2]

Freeman, Preston 1714; burgess, Wigan 1714.[3]

Fleetwood was descended from the Fleetwoods of Vache, Buckinghamshire, and his recent ancestry was impeccably Royalist. His grandfather had been a Royalist chaplain during the Civil Wars and had received ecclesiastical preferment from Charles I and Charles II, culminating in his appointment as Bishop of Worcester in 1675, while his father's political sympathies can be gleaned from his service as secretary to the Earl of Danby (Sir Thomas Osborne†) during the Restoration period. His father's sister had also married Lord Dartmouth (George Legge†), in whose regiment Fleetwood served until Dartmouth was stripped of his offices in 1689, and through this marriage Fleetwood was first cousin once removed of the Cumberland Tory Sir Christopher Musgrave, 5th Bt.* In April 1704 Fleetwood succeeded to the Lancashire estates of his cousin Edward Fleetwood, another veteran of the Royalist cause during the Civil Wars. Given such a background, it is scarcely surprising that having inherited a significant estate near Preston he should use this interest to launch a staunchly Tory political career.[4]

At the Preston by-election of 1706 Fleetwood canvassed support, claiming that despite being 'very ambitious of serving my church and country' he stood only in response to pressure from the corporation and local gentry. Forecasts that he would be defeated proved to be accurate and, despite petitioning against the return of Arthur Maynwaring, the start of his parliamentary career was delayed until 1708 when he was returned unopposed with Maynwaring. Fleetwood was an inactive Member. However, his inclusion among those named to draft a bill for an additional Anglican parish to be established in Manchester (7 Feb. 1709) perhaps reflected a concern for the Established Church. Such concerns are evident from his vote in 1710 against the impeachment of Dr Sacheverell.[5]

Fleetwood secured his return at Preston in 1710 with the support of the Duke and Duchess of Hamilton, and he was classed a Tory in the 'Hanover list'. On 7 Apr. 1711 he told against the election of the Whig James Stanhope* at Cockermouth, and he was listed among the 'Tory patriots' opposed to the war and the 'worthy patriots' who detected the mismanagements of the previous administration. In January 1712 he was included in Lord Oxford's (Robert Harley*) canvassing list for the Commons' attack upon Marlborough (John Churchill†), and on 24 May told against the late paymaster of marines for paying £6,798 to marine officers without any parliamentary sanction. In June he managed through the Commons the estate bill of his niece Barbara Chetwynd, which named her husband Walter Chetwynd† and himself as trustees. Fleetwood's concern to secure his interest at Preston was clear from his pursuit in July 1712 of the complaint that the borough's address, presumably upon the issue of the peace, had not been published in the *London Gazette*. In the autumn of 1712 he declared his intention to stand for Preston at the next election, hoping to benefit from his friendship with the Duke of Hamilton, the lord lieutenant of Lancashire. Fleetwood's relationship with Hamilton was in strong contrast with the legal disputes in which Hamilton was involved at this time with one of the Staffordshire branches of Fleetwood's family. Hamilton's death in November 1712 was perceived as a great loss to Fleetwood, Sir Roger Bradshaigh, 3rd Bt.*, claiming that Hamilton had been applying to the chancellor of the duchy of Lancaster, Lord Berkeley, to 'set him up at Preston as the chancellor's man'. Despite this setback, Fleetwood campaigned assiduously, attending the Preston corporation at the proclamation of the peace, which 'was done with great splendour', and, having voted on 18 June 1713 for the French commerce bill, he was returned at the head of the poll. Although he had made such efforts to retain his seat Fleetwood made no impact upon the records of the 1713 Parliament, though two comparisons of the 1713 and 1715 Parliaments listed him as a Tory. Fleetwood was nevertheless eager to remain at Westminster, and in October 1714 his cousin Sir Christopher Musgrave canvassed the new chancellor of the duchy, Lord Guernsey (Heneage Finch I*), to support Fleetwood at the forthcoming election. Musgrave pointed out that Fleetwood

> has laboured so long in the vineyard without any view but his country's service, for which reason he never received the least civility from the former ministers. He lives within half a mile of the town and seems to have the natural interest of the place with the gentry, who are all entirely his friends.

The request fell on deaf ears, but Fleetwood retained his seat in 1715, his defeated opponent attributing this to Preston 'being one of the greatest Tory or Jacobite towns in England'. He stood aside at the 1722 election, but was an active member of the mock corporation of Walton-le-Dale for the next two decades. He died on 22 May 1746, leaving no heir and debts of £16,000, which necessitated an estate Act in 1748 and the sale of the Penwortham estate the same year.[6]

[1] *N. and Q.* ser. 10, vii. 302–3; *Priory of Penwortham* (Chetham Soc. ser. 1, xxx), p. lxix. [2] *CSP Dom.* 1687–9, p. 294. [3] Lancs. RO, Preston bor. recs. CNP 3/1/1, p. 593; Wigan RO, Wigan bor. recs. AB/MR/11. [4] *DNB* (Fleetwood, William); *N. and Q.* 303; *Priory of Penwortham* pp. lxvii–lxviii; Baines, *Lancs.* ed. Croston, iv. 208. [5] Staffs. RO, Sutherland mss D.593/P/13/10, Fleetwood to Ld. Gower (Sir John Leveson-Gower, 5th Bt.*), 18 May 1706; Lancs. RO, Stanley mss DDK/1683/1, Richard Edge to Mr Worthington, 15 Nov. 1706. [6] Lancs. RO, Kenyon mss DDKe 9/102/14, Thomas Winckley et al. to George Kenyon*, 10 May 1708; DDKe/HMC/1144, Richard Langton to same, 15 May 1713; NLS, ms 8262, ff. 40–42; Add. 70223, Fleetwood to Duchess of Hamilton, 26 Sept. 1710; 70331, canvassing list, c.Jan. 1712; SP 34/19, ff. 17–18; *HMC Kenyon*, 448; Devonshire mss at Chatsworth House, Finch-Halifax pprs. box 5 bdle. 11, Musgrave to Guernsey, 19 Oct. 1714; G. Holmes, *Pol. in Age of Anne*, 118; Leics. RO, Finch mss 4969, John Chetwynd† to Ld. Finch (Daniel), 13 Jan. 1714–15; Harris Museum Preston, min. bk. of mock corp. of Walton-le-Dale.

E. C./R. D. H.

FLEETWOOD, John (1686–1745), of Great Missenden, Bucks.

BUCKINGHAMSHIRE 1713–1722

bap. 9 Mar. 1686, 1st surv. s. of William Fleetwood of Great Missenden, being 1st by 2nd w. Sarah, da. of Thomas Bridgwood, embroiderer, of London, wid. of William Whorwood of St. James Clerkenwell, Mdx. *educ.* Oriel, Oxf. 1702. *m.* 19 Jan. 1724, Elizabeth, da. of Richard Seare of Great Missenden, high sheriff of Bucks. 1712, *s.p. suc.* fa. 1691.[1]

Sheriff, Bucks. 1709–10.

Fleetwood was descended from William Fleetwood, who acquired the abbey of Great Missenden in 1574. The senior branch of the family, the Fleetwoods of The Vache in Chalfont, had represented Buckinghamshire since the reign of James I.[2]

Fleetwood was baptized in St. James Clerkenwell, and presumably spent much of his childhood in the capital, for two of his siblings were also baptized in that parish, and on his admission to Oxford he was listed as the son of William Fleetwood of London. But by 1706 he was residing at Great Missenden and in 1707 his cousin Lord Cheyne (Hon. William*) had to intervene to prevent him from being pricked as sheriff. Cheyne wrote to Secretary Harley (Robert*) asking that Fleetwood be excused as 'his father served not long before he died [1688–9]; he is not 22 years of age, has a younger brother and sisters to provide for, and his mother keeps in jointure half the £1,000 per annum the estate is worth'. Having thus escaped once, he was not so fortunate in 1709. However, this turned to the advantage of the Tories when Parliament was unexpectedly dissolved in 1710, and he was in place as sheriff and able to assist Lord Cheyne in securing the return of Tory candidates for the shire. In 1711 his father's personal and leasehold property, of which his mother had gained control in order to provide for her three younger children, together with her own property, reverted to him, although he had to provide his siblings with £2,000 apiece. Fleetwood now felt able to stand for the county himself, his successful campaign in 1713 being financed by Lord Cheyne. He was classed as a Tory on the Worsley list and in an analysis reclassifying MPs re-elected in 1715, but he does not seem to have been an active Member. Lord Cheyne reported on 27 Apr. 1714 that Fleetwood had left in haste for Buckinghamshire on the previous day, but he appears to have been at Westminster attending a committee on 14 May.[3]

Fleetwood retired from Parliament in 1722. He died on 17 or 19 Aug. 1745. Unlike his father, who had died intestate, Fleetwood left a will in which he confirmed his wife's marriage settlement of £300 p.a. and added a legacy of £500. The chief beneficiary, however, was his young nephew John Ansell, who inherited his estates.[4]

[1] *St. James Clerkenwell* (Harl. Soc. Reg. ix), i. 315; Lipscomb, *Bucks.* ii. 376–7, 386–7; *Vis. Bucks. 1634* (Harl. Soc. lviii), 55. [2] *VCH Bucks.* ii. 351. [3] *St. James Clerkenwell*, 315, 327, 331; *HMC Portland*, iv. 459; PCC 104 Young; BL, Verney mss mic. 636/55, Cheyne to Ld. Fermanagh (John Verney*), 27 Apr. 1714, Mary Lovett to same, 15 May 1714. [4] Lipscomb, 387; *Gent. Mag.* 1745, p. 444; PCC 247 Seymer.

E. C./S. N. H.

FLEETWOOD, Richard (1653–1709), of Rossall Hall, Lancs.

LANCASHIRE 18 Apr. 1704–1705

b. 1653, 2nd but 1st surv. s. of Francis Fleetwood of Rossall Hall, by Mary, da. of Charles Foster of Preesal Park, Lancs. *m.* 16 June 1674, Margaret, da. and h. of Edward Fleetwood of Leyland, Lancs., 3s. (1 *d.v.p.*) 2da. *suc.* fa. bef. 1682.[1]

Freeman, Preston 1662; bailiff, Salford hundred 1709–*d.*[2]

Fleetwood shared a common ancestor with the Fleetwoods of Penwortham, Lancashire, being descended from Thomas Fleetwood (*d.* 1570) of The

Vache, Buckinghamshire, the comptroller of the Mint who purchased Rossall together with the advowson of Poulton-le-Fylde and Bispham in Lancashire, and whose elder brother, John Fleetwood†, acquired Penwortham. Little is known of Richard Fleetwood before he entered Parliament, though in 1693 he was active in taking depositions from Lancashire's Catholics under the authority of a commission for superstitious uses, and he may perhaps have been the 'Mr Fleetwood' talked of as a candidate for the Liverpool mayoralty in October 1702. Fleetwood was incorrectly included on a list as having voted to agree on 13 Feb. 1703 (before he had entered the House) with the Lords' amendments to the bill for enlarging the time for taking the oath of abjuration. He was returned for Lancashire at a by-election in April 1704, and soon after informed Robert Harley*, through a third party, of his intention to 'pay you his respects in person' as soon as he arrived at Westminster. On 30 Oct. 1704 he was listed as a probable opponent of the Tack, was included in Harley's lobbying list on this issue, and did not vote for the measure on 28 Nov. Fleetwood did not stand at the 1705 election, and the only other impression he made in the public sphere was his appointment to a duchy of Lancaster office in July 1709. He held this post, however, for only six months before his death on 21 Dec. 1709. He was buried on the 27th at Poulton-le-Fylde, and was succeeded by his first surviving son, Edward.[3]

[1] Baines, *Lancs.* ed. Croston, iv. 208; *Vis. Lancs.* (Chetham Soc. ser. 1, lxxxv), 111; H. Fishwick, *Hist. Poulton-le-Fylde* (Chetham Soc. ser. 2, viii), 164–5. [2] *Preston Guild Rolls* (Lancs. and Cheshire Rec. Soc. ix) 144, 182; Somerville, *Duchy of Lancaster Official Lists*, 142. [3] E.134 6 W&M/Trinity 9, f. 2; *Norris Pprs.* (Chetham Soc. ser. 1, ix), 95–96; Add. 70213, William Brenard to Harley, 25 Apr. 1704.

E. C./R. D. H.

FLEMING, Henry (c.1663–1713), of Edmondsham, Dorset.

ST. GERMANS 1690–1698, 4 Jan. 1700–1708

b. c.1663, 2nd but 1st surv. s. of Edward Fleming of Edmondsham by a da. of Thomas Fleming of North Stoneham, Hants. *educ.* L. Inn 1682, called 1694; St. John's, Oxf. matric. 6 Apr. 1682, aged 18. *unm. suc.* fa. by 1682.[1]

Fleming was returned for St. Germans by his uncle Daniel Eliot*, the patron of the borough. He was classed as a Tory by the Marquess of Carmarthen (Sir Thomas Osborne†) in March 1690, and in December the same year Carmarthen listed Fleming as a likely supporter in the event of a Commons attack upon his ministerial position. In April 1691 Robert Harley* classed him as a Court supporter. On 28 Dec. 1693 he was granted a two-week leave of absence. His only notable activity in the 1693–4 session was on 26 Mar. 1694 when he told against imposing a duty on the coastal trade in England and Wales. In the following session Fleming was ordered into custody for being absent at a call of the House on 14 Feb. 1695. He was discharged four days later. At the 1695 election he was again returned unopposed, and in early 1696 he demonstrated his opposition to the predominantly Whig ministry. He was forecast as likely to oppose the Court in the divisions of 31 Jan. 1696 on the proposed council of trade, initially refused to sign the Association, and was listed as having voted in March against fixing the price of guineas at 22s. On 25 Nov. he voted against the attainder of Sir John Fenwick†. Granted a leave of absence on 10 Mar. 1697, Fleming made no further contribution to this Parliament and he did not stand at the 1698 election. A comparison of the old and new Commons dating from September that year listed him as a Country supporter 'out' of the new Parliament. He regained his St. Germans seat at a by-election in January 1700, and held it for the four succeeding Parliaments. In December 1701 Harley classed him as a Tory, and he was listed as having favoured the motion of 26 Feb. 1702 vindicating the Commons' proceedings in the impeachments of the Whig ministers. His first significant act in the 1702 Parliament was to tell, on 19 Dec. 1702, against the second reading of an engrossed clause to the land tax bill. On 15 Jan. 1703 the Commons was informed that 'some words of heat' had passed between Fleming and Lord Coningsby (Thomas*), and 'they were enjoined by the House not to prosecute the same'. The following month, on the 13th, Fleming voted against the Lords' amendments to the bill enlarging the time for taking the Abjuration. His previously consistent Tory sympathies were no doubt what led in October 1704 to his being forecast as a probable supporter of the Tack, but he did not vote on 28 Nov. for this measure. However, it was probably the Member for St. Germans (rather than the Westmorland Whig William Fleming) who told on 14 Mar. 1705 for the committee of the whole's amendment to the bill for suppressing the growth of popery, imposing upon occasional conformists a fine of £100 for every time they attended a Dissenting meeting. An analysis of the 1705 Parliament described Fleming as a 'Churchman', and on 25 Oct. he voted against the Court candidate for Speaker. He made little further impact upon the records of this Parliament, but in early 1708 an analysis of the Commons classed Fleming as a Tory. At the election later that year Edward Eliot*, who had succeeded his uncle as patron of St. Germans, chose not to support Fleming. He did not stand for election again, though in 1710 the 'Hanover list' mistakenly noted his return and classed Fleming as a Tory. He died in 1713, his will leaving small bequests to numerous relations and godchildren, including Browne Willis*, who had married Fleming's cousin.[2]

[1] Burke, *LG* (1937), 793; *VCH Hants*, iii. 479; C. S. Gilbert, *Hist. Surv. Cornw.* i. 449. [2] Gilbert, 449; PCC 273 Leeds.

E. C.

FLEMING, Michael (1668–1718).

WESTMORLAND   20 Feb. 1707–1708

b. 12 July 1668, 6th s. of Sir Daniel Fleming† of Rydal, Westmld. by Barbara, da. of Sir Henry Fletcher, 1st Bt., of Hutton Hall, Cumb., sis. of Sir George Fletcher, 2nd Bt.*; bro. of William Fleming*. *educ.* Hawkshead sch. 1683–5. *m.* Dorothy Benson of Yorks., 1s. 1da.[1]

Ensign of ft. James Stanley's* regt. (later 16th Ft.) 1693, lt. 1694–7, 1699–1701, capt. 1697–9, 1701, maj. 1708.

Fleming was the sixth of 11 sons, and from the early 1690s his father was keen to find him some gainful employment which would lessen Fleming's financial dependence upon the family estate. Having failed in attempts to find him employment in both the navy and the excise office, Sir Daniel Fleming succeeded in January 1693 in gaining the promise of an ensign's commission for his son in the regiment of Hon. James Stanley*. Fleming arrived in London in March the same year, accompanied by the 20 men he had raised for the regiment, only to find that no commission had been prepared for him. Following the intercession of Sir John Lowther, 2nd Bt. II*, with William Blathwayt*, and further assistance from his brother William, Richard Kirkby* and Sir George Fletcher, Fleming was informed he would receive the next vacant commission and in May, while in Flanders, was appointed ensign. Fleming served in the Low Countries for the remainder of the Nine Years War, fighting at Landen and Namur, and slowly progressed through the ranks. Fleming's company was disbanded in April 1699 following the Peace of Ryswick, but his hopes for a further commission were satisfied in July when he was appointed a lieutenant in one of the remaining companies of Stanley's regiment. In April 1700 his father was concerned that Fleming would again find his company disbanded, but such fears were groundless and in 1701 Fleming regained the rank of captain; and following the renewal of hostilities in 1702 he again served in the Low Countries, being one of those wounded at Blenheim. Fleming owed his return to the Commons in 1707 to the interest of his brother William. Unable to persuade Daniel Wilson's* grandfather to allow Wilson's candidacy, and unwilling to stand himself due to poor health, William Fleming secured his brother's unopposed return for Westmorland at the by-election of February 1707. Little is known of Fleming's brief parliamentary career. He arrived in London by 4 Mar. 1707 and later that month Bishop Nicolson recorded the congratulations he received from Fleming following the passage of the cathedrals bill. However, he left little mark upon the records of the Commons and an analysis of the House dating from early 1708 was unable, or unwilling, to give him a party label. Fleming did not stand for re-election later that year, making way for his nephew Daniel Wilson, who by this time had secured family approval for his candidacy. Fleming returned to his military career, being promoted to major in May 1708 and a year later, following the efforts of his brother William, to regimental major. He died at Kingston-upon-Hull in about May 1718, leaving a son 'with nothing to maintain him', for whom his brother William claimed to have provided subsequently.[2]

[1] Add. 24120, f. 345; *Fleming Mems.* (Trans. Cumb. and Westmld. Antiq. and Arch. Soc. tract ser. xii) 76; *HMC Le Fleming*, 399, 401–2. [2] Cumbria RO (Kendal), Le Fleming mss WD/Ry 4267, Sir Daniel Fleming to Sir John Lowther, 2nd Bt. I*, 8 Jan. 1691–2; 4275, same to Fletcher, 29 Jan. 1691–2; 4541, same to [–], 18 Jan. 1692–3; 4565, Stanley to Sir Daniel Fleming, 9 Feb. 1692–3; 4590, Michael Fleming to same, 21 Mar. 1692–3; 4609, 4616, Sir Daniel to Michael Fleming, 6, 12 Apr. 1693; 5524, same to William Fleming, 4 July 1700; *HMC Le Fleming*, 331–9, 353; Bagot mss at Levens Hall, William Fleming to Mr Ingesson, 7 Feb. 1706–7; Add. 70197, same to [Robert Harley*], 23 Feb. 1706[–7]; 24120, ff. 329, 345; *Nicolson Diaries* ed. Jones and Holmes, 422, 463, 491.

E. C.

FLEMING, Richard (c.1682–1740), of N. Stoneham, nr. Southampton.

SOUTHAMPTON   1710–1722

b. c.1682, 2nd s. of Edward Fleming† of N. Stoneham by Margaret, da. of Thomas Bland. *educ.* L. Inn 1701. *m.* 1714 (with £10,000), Anne, da. of Sir Ambrose Crowley*, *s.p. suc.* bro. Thomas 1708.[1]

Freeman, Southampton 1709.[2]

Fleming's family had connexions with the town of Southampton dating back to the late 16th century, and his father had represented the borough briefly in the 1689 Convention before losing his seat on petition. Fleming himself, as a younger son, was initially intended for the law, but on the death of his elder brother inherited the family estates in Hampshire and in 1710 was returned for Southampton. A member of the October Club, he was included in 1711 on the list of 'worthy patriots' who detected the mismanagements of the previous administration. However, he appears to have been an inactive Member. On 21 Mar. 1712 he was given leave of absence for three weeks, but voted for the French commerce bill on 18 June 1713. Re-elected for Southampton in 1713, he was classed as a Tory in the Worsley list and on two separate lists which compared the 1715 Parliament with its predecessor. Fleming died on 4 Aug. 1740, aged 58.[3]

[1] Berry, *Hants Gen.* 126; *Top. and Gen.* iii. 510. [2] Southampton RO, SC3/1/2, f. 43. [3] *VCH Hants*, iii. 479; Boyer, *Anne Annals*, iii. 119; *Gent. Mag.* 1740, p. 413.

P. W./C. I. M.

FLEMING, William (1656–1736), of Rydal, Westmld.

WESTMORLAND   12 Nov. 1696–24 June 1700
30 Nov. 1704–1705

b. 25 July 1656, 1st surv. s. of Sir Daniel Fleming† of Rydal; bro. of Michael Fleming*. *educ.* Kendal sch. 1672–5. *m.* 1 Aug. 1723, Dorothy (*d.* 1757), da. of Thomas Rowlandson of Kendal, Westmld., 3da. *suc.* fa. 25 Mar. 1701; *cr.* Bt. 4 Oct. 1705.[1]

Commr. excise 1698–1702.[2]

Fleming, who at the age of two had dislocated his leg and was consequently lame for the rest of his life, was the heir to considerable Westmorland estates, but from at least 1688 was in almost constant conflict with his father. The dispute was financial rather than political in nature, Fleming loyally following his father's decision to give evasive answers in 1688 to James II's questions on the Penal Laws and Test Act. Its roots lay in Fleming's annoyance at his father's refusal to grant him an adequate allowance. By 1692 Fleming was living in London, when his father wrote to chide him that 'every child ... ought to consider his father's obligations, and estate, one must not be allowed to spend all extravagantly in twash and swash, or in vain projects and progresses'. The breakdown in relations was clear the following year when Fleming found that his father was unwilling to satisfy debts that, Fleming claimed, had been built up primarily in search of relief from the pain caused by his lameness. The continuing friction between the two was evident when Fleming was mentioned as a possible candidate at the 1695 Westmorland election, his father making it clear that he would not support this pretension. Further details emerged in a letter Fleming wrote to his father in January 1696, in which he claimed that at the previous year's election Sir Christopher Musgrave, 4th Bt.*, had proposed that Fleming 'assist' or 'not oppose' him at the Westmorland election in return for facilitating Fleming's marriage to one of Musgrave's daughters, but that his father had 'slight[ed] that opportunity'. Sir Daniel Fleming was similarly hostile to the proposal in May 1696 that Fleming stand for the county seat vacated by the elevation of Sir John Lowther, 2nd Bt. II, to the peerage as Lord Lonsdale. When Fleming persisted in declaring his candidacy, with the support of Lonsdale, Lord Carlisle (Charles Howard*) and Sir George Fletcher, 2nd Bt.*, at the Kendal sessions in July, his father publicly condemned the decision, largely on the grounds of the great charges a parliamentary career would make upon the family estates. Fleming was nevertheless elected unopposed in November.[3]

Shortly after Fleming's election his father wrote that 'it will not be for his real advantage; for when young men's heads are filled too full of public politics, it often prejudices their own private concerns', and the frequent parliamentary reports Fleming wrote to his father, emphasizing in particular his attempts to protect Westmorland interests during the passage of Commons business, were probably sent as an attempt to alter such perceptions. Fleming first attended the House on 4 Dec. 1696, and eight days later claimed that he had 'persuaded a Member to withdraw his proposal to tax malt, but could not stop a much worse proposal, viz. a tax on live cattle and those killed in private families'. This proposal was defeated, according to Fleming, due to the proposal of the capitation, but the measure was no more welcome to Fleming who described it as 'an ill way of raising money for our country [?county]'. Of particular concern was the willingness of the House to vest in the crown the power of nominating commissioners, and on 5 Jan. 1697 he went so far as to describe the bill as 'so ill that I hope it will be thrown out', and claimed that he had successfully lobbied a number of other Members. He played a prominent part on 20 Jan. in preventing weavers, who were demonstrating their support for the bill prohibiting the wearing of East India silks, from entering the Commons; and when the capitation bill passed the Commons on 26 Jan. Fleming claimed to his father that he had 'got a good many Members to join with me' in opposing three proposals relating to the qualification of land tax commissioners. He nevertheless maintained that the measure would 'be ill for the north', and claimed that during the bill's passage the 'middle of England men' had been 'all for having the rates of the north raised'. Fleming appears to have spent a great deal of time in the following months on the question of the nominees for Westmorland's land tax commission. Financial matters also interested him in the next session. At the end of December 1697 he wrote of his opposition both to continuing the malt duty and the land tax, but once the land tax bill had been introduced he was concerned to protect Westmorland interests. This was most obvious in the committee of the whole of 11 Mar. 1698 on the land tax bill, Fleming writing that

> Most of the day yesterday was spent upon the land tax bill, whether three fourths of the sum raised in the first 4d. aid should be fixed, but not only upon every county but upon every ward, parish and township. The first was generally agreed to, but the latter was put to the question and carried by 14 that it should not. I, knowing that the barony [of Kendal] would save £98 4s. 2d. by having it placed upon the wards, was for this, but we lost it by many mistaking the question, as they owned after.

When the poll bill was considered on 29 Apr. Fleming opposed a motion that land tax commissioners be rated for the poll tax as gentlemen, and on 14 May he carried an amendment to the bill against house breaking. Two weeks later he and Sir Christopher Musgrave made attempts to protect Westmorland interests affected by the bill to prevent the export of wool to Holland.[4]

In January 1697 Fleming had accompanied a peer to an audience with the King and informed his father that he had stayed with William 'till he went to supper, attended him there, returned with him to his chamber, till he was undressed to go to bed'. This audience was probably facilitated by Lord Lonsdale, and it was Lonsdale who in December 1697 wrote to Lord Portland requesting that Fleming be given a place on the excise commission. The request was granted in July 1698, the salary of £800 p.a. no doubt bringing welcome financial relief for Fleming, but he was determined to remain in the House and was returned for Westmorland unopposed in the election later that year. He was consequently included upon a list of placemen dating from September that year, and a comparison of the old and new Parliaments listed him as a Court supporter. On 18 Jan. 1699 Fleming voted against the disbanding bill, and given his loyalty to the Court and his place he was naturally concerned in February when the opposition began to expel a number of financial officials, claiming that they were ineligible to sit in the House according to a clause of the 1694 Lotteries Act. Fleming reported the confident predictions that as an excise commissioner he too would be expelled, but his belief that the clause of the 1694 Act could not be applied to the excise commission proved well founded.

In February 1699 James Lowther* wrote that Fleming 'is just as he used to be in the House, no manner of difference to his office', and his further comment that Fleming 'pretends to have great interest in the country and has often found fault with my Lord L[onsdale] for being so intimate with the D[uke] of L[ee]ds [Sir Thomas Osborne†], my L[ord] God[olphin] [Sidney†] etc.' suggests that having attained office Fleming had a growing sense of his own importance. He certainly emphasized to his father the high esteem in which he claimed Lord Portland held him, but in February 1700 his combined role of Member and excise commissioner was undermined. An amendment to the bill for the land tax and the resumption of grants of forfeited Irish estates excluded excise commissioners from the Commons, which meant that he had to choose between his seat and his place. Thus on 22 June he appeared before the Treasury lords and informed them of his decision to remain in the excise commission. Unsurprisingly, Fleming's father approved of the choice, writing to his son that 'I think you have done more prudently to stick to the more beneficial employment'.[5]

Despite rumours in May 1701 that he intended to retire to the country, Fleming retained his office until the accession of Queen Anne. He had maintained an interest in Westmorland politics, being consulted by the county's Whigs in August 1701 for advice on how to respond to an unfavourable regulation of the bench, and stood for the shire at the 1702 election, finishing bottom of the poll. Further ignominy followed in 1704 when he was himself removed from the commission of the peace for 'words ag[ain]st her Ma[jes]ty'. He bitterly resented this exclusion, and his candidacy at the Westmorland by-election of 1704 was, he later claimed, motivated by his desire to clear his name of the 'malicious and false information' which had occasioned his removal from the bench. Fleming's return at this by-election was unopposed, due to an agreement with his fellow Whigs, Robert Lowther* and Sir Richard Sandford, 3rd Bt.*, that in return for their support at the by-election he would stand down at the imminent general election. Though not returned until 30 Nov., Fleming was later included upon the list of those who on 28 Nov. had voted against the Tack. By early 1705 he had begun to regret agreeing to stand down at the next general election and as early as January had made an initial canvass against this election. In April 1705 he wrote to Robert Harley* asking if Harley and Lord Treasurer Godolphin were 'in earnest about my standing for the next Parliament', and claiming that he had been 'solicited' to stand for Westmorland. He received a non-committal response from Harley and, his actions having already alienated a section of Westmorland opinion, Fleming did not pursue his candidacy. In the autumn he was created a baronet, when Godolphin obtained for him a discharge of the baronetcy fee of £1,095 normally paid into the Exchequer, and in October the bishop of Carlisle found him 'very brisk in his new honour'. Fleming remained active in Westmorland elections, securing the return of his younger brother Michael at the 1707 by-election and thereafter supporting his nephew Daniel Wilson, and concerned himself with matters of minor local patronage. In December 1713 he wrote to Lord Oxford (Harley) to request a place on the Excise Board, stating that

> it is not the desire of that salary makes me think of or wish it . . . but most of my nearest relations having for some time used me not so well as formerly, and run into measures very opposite to my advice and wishes upon a presumption that I will not now marry and they are secure of what I have, I am the more inclined to disappoint them by marrying. And this country [i.e. county] being furnished with no females worth marrying, I could wish to have such a call to London as would renew my former acquaintance, get me new, and assist me something in doing that to my satisfaction, credit and advantage.
> And as I would thankfully resign it to your disposal again in eight or ten months, or sooner . . . (not liking to continue with a wife in London), so you would soon have it in your Lordship's power again to oblige another friend.

The application was unsuccessful and he stayed in the country, where ten years later he married, at the age of 67, a woman by whom he had no male heir, so that at his death, on 29 Aug. 1736, the baronetcy and his estates passed to a younger brother.[6]

[1] *Fleming Mems.* (Cumb. and Westmld. Antiq. and Arch. Soc. tracts ser. xi), 75; *HMC Le Fleming*, 105, 115. [2] *Cal. Treas. Bks.* xiii. 393; xv. 385; xvii. 227. [3] *HMC Le Fleming*, 331, 343, 366; *Trans. Cumb. and Westmld. Antiq. and Arch. Soc.* ser. 2, xxxviii. 189; Cumbria RO (Kendal), Le Fleming mss WD/Ry 4516, Sir Daniel to William Fleming, 11 Nov. 1692; 4884, [William] to [Sir Daniel Fleming], 27 Jan. 1695–6; 4983, Lowther to same, 14 May 1696; 5845, [William Fleming] to same, 8 Oct. 1696; Bagot mss at Levens Hall, Timothy Banks to James Grahme*, 16 Sept. 1695; *HMC 10th Rep. IV*, 333. [4] *HMC Le Fleming*, 345–52. [5] *HMC Le Fleming*, 346, 352–4; Nottingham Univ. Lib. Portland (Bentinck) mss PwA, Lonsdale to Portland, 5 Dec. 1697; *CSP Dom.* 1698, p. 366; Cumbria RO (Carlisle), Lonsdale mss D/Lons/W2/2/2, James to Sir John Lowther, 2nd Bt. I*, 4 Feb 1698–9; H. Horwitz, *Parl. and Pol. Wm. III*, 253–4; *Cal. Treas. Bks.* xv. 96; Le Fleming mss WD/Ry 5254, Sir Daniel to William Fleming, 4 July 1700. [6] Lonsdale mss D/Lons/W2/2/4, James to Sir John Lowther I, 10 May, 19 Aug. 1701; Add. 29588, ff. 47, 125; 70334, cabinet minutes, 16 July 1704; 61611, f. 115; 21420, f. 240; 70197, Fleming to [Harley], 23 Feb. 1706–7; W. A. Speck, *Tory and Whig*, 81; Bath mss at Longleat House, Thynne pprs. 26, f. 506; 25, f. 142; Cumbria RO (Kendal), Hothfield mss, Thomas Carleton to James Grahme, 2 Dec. 1704, 18 Jan. 1704–5 (Speck trans.); *HMC 10th Rep. IV*, 338; *HMC Portland*, iv. 175, 578; v. 374–5; *HMC Le Fleming*, 355; *Trans. Cumb. and Westmld. Antiq. and Arch. Soc.* ser. 2, iii. 9; *Nicolson Diaries* ed. Jones and Holmes, 293; Bagot mss, Gilfrid Lawson* to Grahme, 24 Apr. 1708.

E. C./R. D. H.

FLETCHER, Sir George, 2nd Bt. (c.1633–1700), of Hutton Hall, Cumb.

CUMBERLAND   1661–1679 (Jan.), 1681 (Mar.)
1689–23 July 1700

b. c.1633, 2nd but o. surv. s. of Sir Henry Fletcher, 1st Bt., of Hutton by Catherine, da. of Sir George Dalston† of Dalston, Cumb. *educ.* Queen's, Oxf. 1651. *m.* (1) lic. 27 Feb. 1655, Alice, da. of Hugh Hare, 1st Baron Coleraine [I], 2s. (1 *d.v.p.*) 3da.; (2) c.1664, Lady Mary Johnston, da. of James, 1st Earl of Hartfell [S], wid. of Sir George Grahme, 2nd Bt., of Netherby, Cumb., 2s. 2da. *suc.* fa. as 2nd Bt. 24 Sept. 1645.[1]

Sheriff, Cumb. 1657–8, 1679–80; commr. for oyer and terminer, Northern circuit 1665, charitable uses, Westmld. 1670, recusants, Cumb. and Westmld. 1675; alderman, Carlisle 1662–87, by Nov. 1689–?*d.*, mayor 1670–1, 1680–1; freeman, Newcastle-upon-Tyne 1680.[2]

Asst. gov. Linen Corp. 1690–?*d.*[3]

The financial success of Fletcher's grandfather, a Cockermouth merchant, had allowed the family to purchase numerous properties in the north and Fletcher succeeded his father to a considerable estate, primarily in Cumberland but including holdings in Westmorland, county Durham and Yorkshire. He assumed a role in county government during the Interregnum which continued after 1660, and his standing in Cumberland is clear: having gained a county seat in 1661, he retained it at all but two of the elections until his death. During the Restoration period Fletcher developed a close political alliance with the Musgraves of Edenhall and at the Revolution assisted the attempts of Sir Christopher Musgrave, 4th Bt.*, to effect the peaceful surrender of the Catholic troops garrisoned at Carlisle, and to frustrate the desire of Sir John Lowther, 2nd Bt. II*, to raise the county's militia. Fletcher served for Cumberland in the Convention, and claimed in February 1690 that he had intended to retire from the House at the next election 'but my friends since have overruled me, having thoughts that the Church and state may have more than ordinary concern in the new Parliament, there being a great party appeared in the last that were not thought friends to either'. Returned unopposed, Fletcher was classed as a Whig in Lord Carmarthen's (Sir Thomas Osborne†) analysis of the new House. In December 1690 Carmarthen included Fletcher as a likely supporter in the event of an attack upon him in the Commons, and an analysis of the House in the papers of Robert Harley*, dating from April 1691, classed him as a Court supporter. During the 1694–5 session Fletcher was listed as one of the 'friends' of Henry Guy* in connexion with the attack upon Guy in the Commons at this time, but he otherwise made little impact upon the House. He appears to have been preoccupied in the early 1690s by the affairs of his stepson, Lord Preston (Sir Richard Grahme†). Following Preston's arrest for treason, Fletcher and Charles Howard* acted as intermediaries in seeking mercy for him. Though initially unsuccessful in obtaining a full confession from him, Fletcher wrote to his own brother-in-law Sir Daniel Fleming† in January 1691 that 'the business has been very bad, though now things have a better face, my lord being endeavouring to make his peace with the government which I hope he may effect, and deserve his life'. At length Preston confessed, though Lord Ailesbury (Thomas Bruce†) wrote of Preston that

> his father-in-law and Dr Wake, his late chaplain and since archbishop of Canterbury, did far from well in conducting him, at late hours to Kensington, and being in drink he said whatever they desired, and the next morning being cool he knew scarce where he had been and denied all.

In 1694 Howard and Fletcher were granted a lease of Preston's forfeited estates in Cumberland and Yorkshire for 99 years at a rent of £800 p.a., with the proviso that £500 p.a. be paid to Preston's wife.[4]

Fletcher was returned unopposed at the 1695 election, and his only recorded involvement in a legislative matter came with his nomination on 5 Dec. to prepare a bill to regulate proceedings in the courts of equity. In the new year Fletcher clearly demonstrated his support for the Court. He was forecast as likely to vote with the Court in the divisions of 31 Jan. 1696 on the proposed council of trade, signed the Association promptly in February and in March voted to support the Court in fixing the price of guineas at 22s. A month into the following session, on 24 Nov., Fletcher wrote of his hope that the proceedings upon the attainder of Sir John Fenwick† would 'make people afraid to commit treason', and the following day he voted for the third reading of the bill of attainder. In December Fletcher confided to Sir Daniel Fleming that he was 'not fond of the capitation', and in the new year appears to have concerned himself with the details of the new land tax assessment, being particularly aware of the attempts of 'the southern men' to alter the geographical distribution of the tax. A concern for the local consequences of land tax legislation was also evident in the final session of the Parliament, as on 11 Mar. 1698 he supported William Fleming's* attempts to have the land tax assessments levied upon wards as well as counties, a proposal intended to benefit parts of Westmorland. Following his return at the 1698 election Fletcher was listed as a Court supporter, and on 18 Jan. 1699 he voted in favour of the standing army. Little more is known of his contribution to this Parliament, though in February 1700 the Commons was informed of the grant of Preston's estates to Fletcher and Howard (now Earl of Carlisle), and that the two owed £1,006 5s. in rent arrears to the Treasury for this estate. Perhaps because of this parliamentary anonymity Fletcher was classed as doubtful in an analysis of the Commons dating from the early months of 1700. He nevertheless made it known in April 1700 that he intended to stand at the next general election, but died on 23 July, and was succeeded in his estates and title by his elder son Henry†, a Catholic.[5]

[1] Hutchinson, *Cumb.* i. 507; *Flemings in Oxford* (Oxf. Hist. Soc. xliv), 358. [2] *Cal. Treas. Bks.* iv. 697, 789; S. Jefferson, *Hist. Carlisle*, 447; Cumbria RO (Carlisle), Carlisle bor. recs Ca/2/2, f. 4; Ca/4/139; *Reg. of Freemen Newcastle-upon-Tyne*, ed. Dodds 101. [3] *Sel. Charters*, 213. [4] *Hist. Jnl.* xxvii. 290–1; Cumbria RO (Kendal), Le Fleming mss WD/Ry 3733–4, Fletcher to Sir Daniel Fleming†, 13 Feb. [1690]; *HMC Finch*, iii. 1, 313; *CSP Dom.* 1690–1, pp. 228, 272; *HMC Le Fleming*, 313; *Ailesbury Mems.* 278; *Cal. Treas. Bks.* ix. 1569; x. 134, 485–6, 763. [5] *HMC Le Fleming*, 344–5, 347, 348, 350; Cumbria RO (Carlisle), Lonsdale D/Lons/W2/2/3, James* to Sir John Lowther, 2nd Bt. I*, 20 Apr. 1700; *CJ*, xiii. 239–40.

E. C./R. D. H.

FLETCHER, George (c.1666–1708).

COCKERMOUTH 1698–1701 (Nov.)
CUMBERLAND 1701 (Dec.)–1702
 1705–by 30 Mar. 1708

b. c.1666, 2nd s. of Sir George Fletcher, 2nd Bt.*, being 1st by his 2nd w.; bro. of Henry Fletcher†. *educ.* Christ Church, Oxf. matric. 23 Nov. 1683, aged 17; I. Temple 1683. *unm.*[1]

Capt. 5 Drag. Gds. 1692, maj. 1702, brevet lt. col. 1704–d.[2]

The younger son of one of the leading members of the Cumberland gentry, Fletcher chose to pursue the profession of arms, gaining a commission in 1692. His first experience of parliamentary elections appears to have come in 1690, when, in the absence of his father, the successful candidate was chaired by those attending the uncontested Cumberland election, and in 1698 he was himself successful at Cockermouth on his father's interest, who owned burgages in the borough. Included on a list of placemen dating from September, Fletcher was classed as a Court supporter in a comparison of the old and new Commons, and on 18 Jan. 1699 voted for the standing army. In January 1700 James Lowther* informed his father that 'Mr Fl[etcher] never speaks either in the House or at committees', and this low profile may perhaps explain why an analysis of the Commons into interests dating from early 1700 classed him as doubtful. Following his father's death in July 1700 the family estates descended to Fletcher's older brother, the Catholic Henry. In January Sir John Lowther, 2nd Bt. I*, wrote of his belief that Fletcher 'has given so good testimony of his ability and conduct at the sessions and at other places, that, had he joined Mr [Gilfrid*] Lawson, they had certainly carried it for the county', but Fletcher was instead returned again for Cockermouth. Little is known of Fletcher's contribution to the first Parliament of 1701, though James Lowther reported that in March and April Fletcher attempted to persuade his fellow army officer Thomas Stanwix* to withdraw his petition against Lowther's return at Carlisle. Somewhat surprisingly, Fletcher was blacklisted as having opposed in this Parliament the preparations for war with France, and the accuracy of this claim is further called into question by the willingness of Cumberland's Whig interest to support his candidacy for the county at the second 1701 election. Having been successful, Fletcher was reckoned a 'gain' by Lord Spencer (Charles*), and classed as a Whig by Robert Harley*. Fletcher again made little impact in the House, James Lowther noting in April 1702 that Fletcher was 'in town but never comes to the House', his poor attendance being due at least in part to 'bad health'. He nevertheless secured the support of the county's Whig interest for the 1702 election but was unsuccessful and for the next three years concentrated on his military career, fighting in the Low Countries and serving at Blenheim.[3]

Fletcher's continuing parliamentary ambitions are clear from the expectation in the spring of 1705 that he would return to contest the Cumberland election, and he was successful without the contest going to a poll, though when comparing the merits of the aspirants for the Cumberland seats James Lowther could only find to recommend him the expectation that Fletcher was 'a man of such an irregular life that he is not like to trouble the country long'. Fletcher's election was again classed as a 'gain' by Lord Sunderland, and an analysis of the new House classed him as a 'Churchman'. He was loyal to the ministry in the opening session of the Parliament, voting on 25 Oct. 1705 for its candidate for Speaker and supporting it during the proceedings of February 1706 on the 'place clause' of the regency bill, but his contribution to parliamentary proceedings appears to have been minimal. James Lowther forecast in late 1705 that Fletcher would support Thomas Lamplugh's* bill for the enlargement of Parton harbour, and on 25 Jan. 1706 Fletcher was indeed the first-named Member appointed to draft this bill. Little more is known of his parliamentary career. An analysis of the House dating from early 1708 classed him as a Tory, but he appears to have suffered increasingly from poor health. In April 1707 Lowther reported that Fletcher 'has been very ill and cannot live long'. This forecast was premature as Fletcher was still alive in early 1708 and had let it be known that he intended to stand at the next election, but his attempts to muster an interest were hampered by ill-health, which prevented him travelling to Cumberland. His condition deteriorated steadily between January and March 1708, and on 30 Mar. Narcissus Luttrell* reported that Fletcher was 'lately dead'. He was buried at St. Martin-in-the-Fields on the 31st, his coffin 'borne by Lord Berkeley, Mr Christopher Musgrave*, Mr James Lowther, etc. in white scarves'.[4]

[1] Hutchinson, *Cumb.* i. 508. [2] *CSP Dom.* 1691–2, p. 105. [3] Cumbria RO (Carlisle), Lonsdale mss D/Lons/W2/1/25, Thomas Tickell to Sir John Lowther I, 9 Mar. 1689–90; D/Lons/W2/2/3, James Lowther to same, 6 Jan. 1699[–1700]; 4, same to same, 18, 22 Mar. 1700[–1], 1 Apr., 15 Nov. 1701; 5, same to same, 14 Mar. 1701[–2], 8 Apr. 1702; D/Lons/W1/21, Sir John Lowther I to Ld. Carlisle (Charles Howard*), Jan. 1700[–1]. [4] Lonsdale mss D/Lons/W2/2/8, same to same, 20 Feb., 3 Mar. 1704[–5], 5, 12 Apr., 22 Sept., 1, 8, 10 Nov. 1705; D/Lons/W1/27, Fletcher to Sir John Lowther I, 21 Apr. 1702; D/Lons/W2/1/40, James Lowther to William Gilpin, 3 Apr., 23 May 1707; 41, same to same, 12, 20, 27, 30 Jan., 12, 14, 17, 21 Feb., 13, 16 Mar. 1707[–8]; Nicolson and Burn, *Cumb. and Westmld.* ii. 390–1; Luttrell, *Brief Relation*, vi. 285; *Nicolson Diaries* ed. Jones and Holmes, 467.

E. C./R. D. H.

FOLEY, Edward (1676–1747).

DROITWICH   1701 (Dec.)–11 June 1711
                15 Apr. 1732–1741

bap. 23 Sept. 1676, 2nd s. of Thomas Foley I*, and bro. of Richard Foley* and Thomas Foley III*. *educ.* L. Inn 1717. *unm. suc.* bro. Richard 1732.[1]

     Asst. R. African Co. 1704–5.[2]
     Freeman, Bewdley 1706.[3]
     Receiver-gen. of leather duty 1711–15; commr. taking subscriptions to S. Sea Co. 1711.[4]

A dabbler in commerce before eventually taking up the law in a similarly desultory fashion, 'Ned' Foley

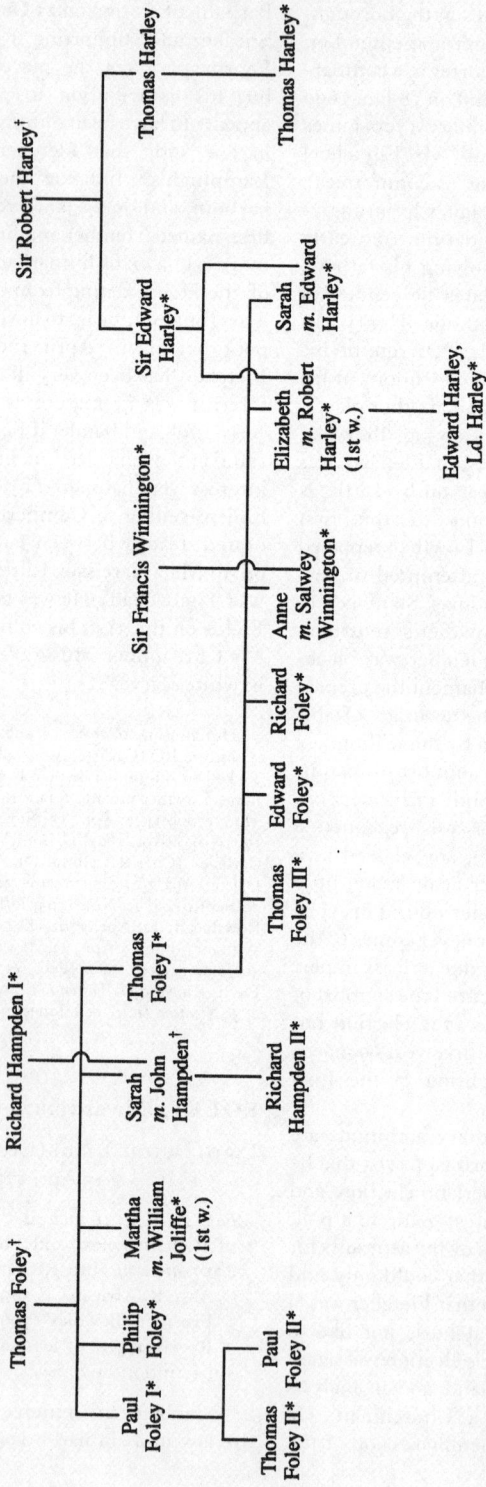

Note: This is not a complete pedigree, nor are children necessarily shown in correct order of precedence by age.

The Foleys and Harleys

was evidently in danger of becoming the black sheep of his highly moral family: in 1704 he was reported to have lost £1,000 'at play in private company' in Tunbridge Wells, and his connexions were being urged to intervene to prevent him from gambling his way to ruin. They may well have succeeded in doing so, since no subsequent references to his gaming have survived. Politically, however, he seems always to have stayed within the fold. Succeeding his father (after a brief interval) to a seat at Droitwich on the family interest in the second general election of 1701, he was classed with the Tories by his brother-in-law Robert Harley* in his list of this Parliament, and voted on 26 Feb. 1702 in vindication of the Commons' proceedings in the impeachment of the four Whig lords. Forecast at the beginning of the 1704–5 session as a probable opponent of the Tack, he did not vote for it on 28 Nov. It is impossible to distinguish his parliamentary activity from that of the many other Foleys in the House, except when he reported a multiple naturalization bill in February 1705. In common with two of his kinsmen he was given the designation 'No Church' in an analysis of the new House of Commons in 1705, and, although he was listed as having voted with the rest of the Foleys on 25 Oct. in favour of the Court candidate for Speaker, his name was queried by the compiler of the list. The family as a whole was uncomfortable with the ministry's turn to the Whigs and the Foleys were reported as intending to reaffirm their party loyalties in December 1705 by voting for the Tory Sir Samuel Garrard, 4th Bt.*, in the disputed election for Amersham. These difficulties continued, and may well have been reflected in Edward's appearance first as a Whig and then as a Tory in two parliamentary lists from early 1708. His relationship with his parliamentary colleague at Droitwich, the Whig Charles Cocks*, was not a happy one, and Foley found himself left out of the preparations in the winter of 1707–8 for a bill to preserve the borough's saltsprings, which Cocks tried to pilot through the House. The exclusion, however, worked in his favour, for the bill failed, and though he was re-elected in 1708, Cocks was not. The ministerial changes of that year had clarified his own political position: he voted in 1710 against the impeachment of Dr Sacheverell, and, following his re-election that year, he was marked as a Tory in the 'Hanover list'. He was subsequently listed among the 'worthy patriots' who in the first session of the Parliament exposed the mismanagements of the old ministry, and the 'Tory patriots' who supported the new administration's peace policy. He was also a member of the October Club, possibly a pro-ministerial infiltrator, for in June 1711 he was nominated by Harley (now Earl of Oxford) to an office under the leather duty commissioners at a salary of £350 p.a. He thereupon gave up his parliamentary seat to his younger brother, Richard. Harley may also have considered him as a potential candidate for a South Sea Company directorship, but nothing transpired.[5]

Although Foley lost office after the Hanoverian succession, he made no attempt to return to Parliament until Richard Foley's death in 1731, when, besides inheriting his brother's property, he recovered the Droitwich seat. Having made his will in December 1746, when he was residing in Carey Street, though still keeping his chambers at Lincoln's Inn, he died 'of a mortification in his foot', on 4 Apr. 1747. His estate passed to his nephew, the 2nd Lord Foley.[6]

[1] Nash, *Worcs.* ii. 464, 468. [2] K. G. Davies, *R. African Co.* 381. [3] *Birmingham Univ. Hist. Jnl.* i. 125. [4] *Cal. Treas. Bks.* xxv. 300; xxix. 488; Pittis, *Present Parl.* 349. [5] Add. 70520, Edward Ashe* to [?Robert Harley], 6 Aug. [1704]; 70145, Elizabeth Foley to Abigail Harley, 10 Aug. 1704; 70284, Ld. Godolphin (Sidney†) to Harley, 'Monday morning' [Dec. 1705]; 70332, memo. by Harley, 4 June 1711; Northants. RO, Montagu (Boughton) mss 48/193, James Vernon I* to Duke of Shrewsbury, 24 Feb. 1707–8; Boyer, *Pol. State*, iii. 19; *Cal. Treas. Bks.* xxv. 300; *Hist. Jnl.* iv. 196. [6] *Hearne Colls.* xi. 48; PCC 96 Potter; *Gent. Mag.* 1747, p. 199.

D. W. H.

FOLEY, Paul I (c.1645–99), of Stoke Edith, Herefs.

HEREFORD   1679 (Mar.)–1681 (Mar.)
1689–11 Nov. 1699

b. c.1645, 2nd s. of Thomas Foley† of Witley Court, Great Witley, Worcs. by Anne, da. and h. of John Browne, gunfounder, of Spelmonden, Kent; bro. of Philip Foley* and Thomas Foley I*. *educ.* Magdalen Hall, Oxf. matric. 19 June 1662, aged 17; I. Temple 1662, called 1668, bencher 1687. *m.* lic. 25 Mar. 1668 (aged about 23), Mary, da. of John Lane, Clothworker, of St. Lawrence Jewry, London, alderman of London 1668, 3s. (1 *d.v.p.*) ?2da. *d.v.p.*[1]

Member, Soc. of Mines Royal 1666, asst. 1667–78; member, Soc. of Mineral and Battery Works 1666, asst. 1673–87.

Freeman, Bewdley 1673.

Commr. public accts. 1691–7.

Speaker of House of Commons 14 Mar. 1695–7 July 1698.

Born into a wealthy Presbyterian family, self-made within two generations, Foley inherited a strong sense of moral purpose and public duty, together with considerable ambition and the resources to finance a serious political career. In religion he seems to have been more of a conformist than his father (a close friend of the Presbyterian divine Richard Baxter), but was himself on good terms with various ejected ministers, several of whom were employed in his family as tutors. His wife, moreover, was of solid Puritan stock, holding a simplistic view of politics as a conflict between 'the people of God' and the ungodly. Foley's own understanding was more sophisticated, but in essence his outlook was much the same. Chief among his characteristics was self-conscious earnestness, which gave him the nickname of 'heavy Paul'. This could make him awkward and opinionated, or as Bishop Burnet put it, 'morose and wilful'. He became addicted to 'particular notions', such as the view he expressed early in his public career that 'all foreign trade was loss, and ruinous to the nation'. Thoroughness became a hallmark: his application to his legal studies, for example, undertaken largely for their own sake and with no view towards a career at the bar, resulted in an impressive command of the law. He was particularly well versed in constitutional precedent, acquiring a sizable collection of books and pamphlets on the subject, and compiling a treatise which, he himself claimed, surpassed the work of previous scholars. He had contemplated standing for Parliament in 1675, but had to wait until the first Exclusion Parliament to be returned. He then quickly established himself as one of the more active Whigs in the Commons. He served his political apprenticeship in the struggle for Exclusion and by 1690 was placed among the leading Country Whigs, 'a man of integrity' with a reputation as a patriot, 'zealous for the present government' but 'much dissatisfied with the administration'. Just as important to his development as a Parliamentarian was his long career as an industrialist. He had been left a substantial share in his father's iron-manufacturing empire, which he was obliged to work in an uneasy conjunction with his brother Philip until 1692, when the two merged their holdings with others in a joint-stock company, 'the ironworks in partnership'. Foley's experience in managing a complex enterprise of foundries and forges, and in raising the capital to maintain them and eventually to float the company, stood him in good stead in Parliament during the detailed debates on governmental accounting and fiscal policy, mastery of which was to be his forte.[2]

At the 1690 general election Foley's prospects for re-election at Hereford were for a while seriously in doubt, but in the event he was returned without opposition. Once in the House, he was his usual forthright self. Classed as a Whig in Lord Carmarthen's (Sir Thomas Osborne†) list of the new Parliament, he made his first recorded speech of the session on 27 Mar. 1690, in the committee of supply, when he vigorously challenged a court motion 'to settle the revenue' on the King and Queen for life. In its determined scepticism of government estimates and its linking of questions of supply to the issue of liberty, this intervention set the tone for Foley's contributions to the political debates of the ensuing sessions. 'What you are now debating is of vast consequence', he began,

> to us, and to England, for ever. I would know what the revenue is, and what it is likely to prove, and not settle a revenue for life, as is necessary in war, but in time of peace. When Charles II returned, it was generally agreed that £1,200,000 p.a. was a sufficient revenue to support the government; in the next Parliament, it was not pretended that more was requisite, but that the revenue came not up to so much. I know not what the revenue is now, but I have heard that in Charles II's time it was two millions, and more in King James's time; therefore I would have you consider, and it is worth your while to consider: if you settle such a revenue, as that the King should have no need of a Parliament, I think we do not do our duty to them that sent us hither. Therefore, I would know what the revenue is.

Later in the same debate he repeated this call for further information, declaring that the House should not agree to give a supply until it had received an account of what had already been given, an interesting pointer to his future involvement with commissions of accounts, and ended with a denunciation of the Court managers' assumption that the crown had a right to a supply, harking back to traditional parliamentary theory: 'I do not think that a good argument to give because the King goes into Ireland . . . I would give this king money, but not by a rule, because we have given other kings.' He reiterated these reservations in further debates in the committee. On 31 Mar., in response to his earlier request, the Treasury presented some accounts of revenue received. Prefacing his remarks with the reminder that although 'it concerns us to give the King a supply . . . it concerns us as much not to give more than is necessary', he proceeded to make his own calculations based on the Treasury papers. These he pronounced to be 'strange': 'I hope our case is not so bad as is represented, and that we are not at a loss for so much money as is represented.' What was needed was 'a fair account', including details of expenditure. Then on 2 Apr. he supported a motion to rule out a land tax, using his knowledge of precedent to refute Court objections against 'putting negatives'. His attitude in the supply debates would make it likely that he actively opposed the bill for vesting the forfeited estates in the crown. A Foley appeared three times as a teller against it: on 9 May, for adjourning the report of the committee; the very next day, against engrossing; and on 15 May, against passing the bill. The survival of some of Foley's old party animosities is shown by the vehemence of his opposition to attempts to restore to office the Tories in London. In the debate on 22 Apr. on the second reading of the bill to reverse the quo warranto against the City, he observed:

> I suppose it is not the design of the House to restore those to their places who have lost them because they would not swear to the government. That is not for the King's interest, nor the City's. 'Tis intimated, that this bill will restore Sir Dudley North† and [Sir] Peter Rich† to be sheriffs. I know not how the House will come up to that . . . I would have them restored to the rights they had before the judgment against the charter.

Two days later, when the changes in the London lieutenancy came under the House's scrutiny, he was even more outspoken:

> I have seen a list, and I must observe many in the lieutenancy that have had their hands in blood several times over . . . Some are there that went to congratulate King James after his return and the landing of the Prince of Orange . . . They have chosen one for colonel who would not qualify himself to be an alderman, and has appeared, by force, to control elections in the City. I believe when you examine many things will be proved upon these persons, and I hope, when the House has a full information of these things, they will not think it for the interest of the King and kingdom, that these men should be continued.

Roger Morrice's report of the debate on Sir Edward Seymour's motion to remove Carmarthen from the Privy Council suggests that Foley was even by this stage accustomed to co-operate with the High Tories in opposition. While most Whigs ignored Seymour's blustering, Foley anxiously 'laboured to hinder it being put to a question, knowing it would not pass'. He spoke on 26 Apr. against the suspension of habeas corpus, while his speeches on the regency bill, in committee on 5 May and at the third reading on the 7th, show him deploying his legal expertise and mastery of detail to pick holes in the bill and eventually to propose ways in which these defects might be remedied, possibly to the embarrassment of ministers and certainly to the enhancement of his own reputation. Then on 14 May, in a committee of the whole to consider ways to preserve the peace and safety of the kingdom during the King's absence in Ireland, he offered a proposal which both appealed to Country notions of accountability and presented a vague threat to those in power, calling for orders of the Privy Council to be 'fairly entered' and that all Councillors present be required to 'notify their assent or dissent', so that 'we may know, for the time to come, who gives advice'. On 23 May he reported on a conference with the Lords over their message accompanying the bill of grace.[3]

Foley's first committee nomination in the following session was one of the most significant: to draft the bill to establish a commission of public accounts (11 Oct. 1690). Because of his prominence in the debates on supply and the agitation for an accounts commission he is almost certain to have been the 'Mr Foley' who on 20 Dec. reported from the committee for examining the naval estimates. When the outcome of the ballot for accounts commissioners was announced, on 26 Dec., he was elected in joint second place behind the Court Whig who headed the poll. A token effort to excuse himself from serving was brushed aside by the House, and on 5 Jan. 1691 the bill embodying the commission received the Royal Assent. Business did not begin immediately, however, and Foley spent some time in Herefordshire in the early weeks of 1691 before the commission started its work in March. Meeting in the Speaker's chambers on an almost daily basis, the commissioners soon developed a sense of comradeship which transcended party differences. This was most pronounced in the case of Foley's nephew by marriage, Robert Harley*, who quickly formed friendships with Country Tory colleagues like Sir Thomas Clarges*. There are indications that Foley's 'morose' temper made it harder for Tories to break the ice with him, and on one occasion Harley attributed some 'hot words' between commissioners to his uncle's 'tenacious humour'. But in due course these barriers too came down. The role of the commission has been the subject of debate among modern historians. The Treasury point of view, put by W. A. Shaw, was that the commissioners were prejudiced against government, that they made the most of any deficiencies in the accounts and ignored mitigating circumstances. An opposing interpretation, favourable to the commissioners, has stressed the obstructionism of officials and has depicted Foley and his colleagues as objective scrutineers whose shabby treatment at the hands of government aroused their resentment and sharpened their criticisms. The truth probably lies in between. Foley, for one, saw himself as open-minded, and there can be no doubt that some officials regarded the commissioners as enemies and treated them accordingly. Sir Robert Howard*, for example, warned the King in the summer of 1691 that the commissioners were 'exceeding their power' and aimed at securing control over the entire management of the war. But it is also clear from Foley's speeches on supply and other issues in the first session of the Parliament that he was hostile to the administration and sought to place difficulties in its path.[4]

During the summer and autumn of 1691, as the accounts commissioners proceeded with their investigations, Foley became embroiled in a local political dispute which at one point even threatened to disturb his close friendship with the Harleys. His efforts to secure the election of his son Thomas (II*) at Weobley brought him up against a fellow Whig, John Birch II*, who himself had designs upon the seat. The dilemma of whether or not to persist with his son's candidature exposed a streak of indecisiveness in Foley's nature that was not usually visible. Robert Harley found him to be 'uncertain and fickle', and his reasonings 'metaphysical'. Foley was inclined to blame the Harleys for a previous decision not to put up his son for Parliament, and Harley believed that he would be quick to blame them again for any 'miscarriages' that now transpired. In a revealing observation Harley wrote to his father that Foley had rejected all outside suggestions: 'I suppose he thinks of some other way, which being his own invention will give more content.' All attempts to head off a contest having failed, the election, in June, resulted in a victory for Thomas Foley over Birch, but the danger did not disappear, since Birch announced his intention to petition. It was then, in about August, that Foley buried his previous resentments towards the Harleys and appealed to them for help in bringing about a compromise which would persuade Birch to withdraw. Robert Harley and his father, Sir Edward*, were both enlisted to negotiate with Birch, and it was Robert who eventually, in October 1691, encompassed the treaty by which Birch dropped his petition. Having imposed some strains on the relationship between Foley and Robert Harley, the affair ended with the two men on more amicable terms than ever.[5]

With the report of the accounts commissioners to be made, the 1691–2 session promised to be an important one for Foley and he began it by opening the debate on 30 Oct. 1691 on the King's speech. 'It was expected that money should be immediately moved for', but Foley argued that consideration be given first to 'the state of the nation, specially in reference to abuses in the navy and army', hinting at revelations to come over the accounts, and secured a priority for grievances over supply. Harley noted that the opposition's attack had 'a little opened the eyes of some gentlemen that came out of the country'. Foley returned to his main theme of scrutinizing accounts and estimates in a debate on 3 Nov. on the conduct of the war at sea, observing that 'two mill[ions had been] misspent by false musters and warrants'. From the brief notes that were taken of this speech it is evident that he also adumbrated the minimalist view of war strategy that was to be a feature of his contributions to parliamentary discussions, declaring that 'the F[rench] k[ing] makes the war defensive'. His frequent interventions in the committee of supply emphasized the advantages of a careful and detailed assessment of the government's actual requirements, so that money should not be wasted (or misappropriated) and taxes raised unnecessarily. On 6 Nov., on a proposal to lay the army estimates before the House, he 'moved to know what alliances we were in, what quota we were obliged to furnish, so that we may see what forces are necessary'. The previous year, he reminded the House, 'we gave and neither considered the state of the nation nor the alliance, nor did we take any measure for what we gave; we lumped it, which cost us near five millions of money'. This was also a delaying tactic; witness his concluding remark that he 'thought this enough at this time'. Three days later the estimates were brought in. He subjected them to withering criticism, claiming that too much money had been granted in previous years and recoiling at the prospect that even these exorbitant sums were to be increased. The amount estimated for each man might, he thought, be trimmed and he could 'see no reason to maintain so many constantly, in summer and winter', thus neatly raising by innuendo the issue of a standing army. Again his final proposition was a means of delay, a motion to refer the question 'to a particular committee to inquire into it'. Further interventions on the subject of the naval estimates were followed on 18 Nov. by the repetition of his call for the committee to take its time in considering the numbers and dispositions of land forces before settling on a grant, with another motion for a 'private committee'. His most important speech on the military estimates was given the following day in the committee, when he challenged Court policy head on. 'You have now before you a great matter', he began:

> It is urged by some that it is necessary to have an army of 65,000 men, but I desire such to consider how they will raise money to pay them. The revenue is already so clogged that will arise thence; the nation is already two millions in debt. I must declare for my part I do not see any necessity for so many men.

By now perhaps over-filled with self-importance, he went on to dispute the strategic arguments which ministers had advanced, particularly that the provision of a large force would make for a speedy end to the war. But, Foley inquired, supposing this force should instead be defeated by the French, in what condition would that leave the war effort? 'What hopes have we', he added, 'if the fleet be in no better hands?' To attempt a landing in France would achieve nothing but the incurring of an unprofitable financial commitment, should a continental port be taken, while a smaller contingent of troops would be ample for a useful diversionary raid. Finally, there were difficulties in raising this revenue: 'consider what our state is, besides land tax and excise, etc. If you find yourself at a loss for money, and must anticipate, you must double your land tax, and at last pay half your revenue.' This was a powerful denunciation of the Court, but in bringing in the wider issues of military strategy Foley had laid himself open to the charge, promptly mounted by a Court Whig, that he himself knew nothing of such matters, and that his attitude to the threat of a French military victory in the Low Countries was altogether too cavalier. Indeed, the Court party proceeded to carry its point. The consciousness that he had made a false move did not, however, weigh heavily upon Foley, and he remained very active and prominent in the Commons' deliberations on supply. He was named to the committees of 9 and 30 Nov. to inspect the navy and army estimates respectively, and spoke again on 25 Nov. in the committee of supply, on the subject of the armed forces in Ireland, which he considered might be supported by 'a tax on that kingdom'. He moved that the cost of the Irish army be borne by the Irish, and was subsequently appointed to the committee to consider the matter. Later in the session he served on the committee to draft bills applying the forfeited estates in England and Ireland 'to the use of the war' (16 Jan. 1692) and was added (on 20 Jan.) to the committee receiving proposals for raising money on the Irish forfeitures. On 1 Jan. 1692, again in the committee of supply, he intervened twice to correct a Court spokesman on the expected yield from the Irish revenue, and on 2 Jan. he spoke in support of a resolution of the committee for the reduction of the Irish regiments. Earlier, in the committee, he had recovered his dignity sufficiently to denounce an attempt on 28 Nov. 1691 by the courtier Sir Henry Goodricke, 2nd Bt.*, to overawe opposition to the army estimates by means of a reference to the King's displeasure. Foley stormed: 'I never saw such things done in a House as has been done this day. To say if we do not comply we shall break the King's measures, this is wholly irregular.' Two days later he criticized the estimate for general officers, though on the relatively safe ground of financial precedent, which showed his capacity for preparation and command of detail:

> Your land army has cost you these three last years as much again as your fleet. The war in general hath been very great and chargeable, occasioned by your great allowances to general officers – the establishments that are now being much advanced, and by comparing them with former you will find they are come to an exorbitant height. The House of Commons in 1677 thought it worth their while to settle an establishment. If you will do so now, money may be saved.

Further speeches in the committee of supply occurred on 15 Dec., when he seconded Sir Christopher Musgrave, 4th Bt., in opposing acceptance of the resolution of the select committee on the army estimates; and on 30 Dec., when, again in the company of Musgrave, he opposed any increase of pay to the army generals, exploiting dislike of 'foreign' officers to make his point. After the committee of supply became ways and means the House saw another side of Foley's talents. Besides his forensic skill in probing for weaknesses in the Court's presentation of its case, he now demonstrated a fertility in inventing expedients of his own. He began in ways and means on a destructive note, disputing government estimates of the likely yield of land tax, customs and excise. Deploying a barrage of statistics, he proved too strong for Court spokesmen like Sir Stephen Fox. Then on 12 Jan., after some sharp exchanges over the excise, he suddenly took a more positive approach, moving 'to put an end to the debate' with a proposal 'that £200,000 be raised upon the revenue for carrying on the war this next year'. Later that day he unveiled his own scheme. He told the House that he was informed the London bankers would agree to lend the government a further £1 million at 5 per cent interest 'if they may have their money now owing to them secured by a good fund to pay a perpetual interest'. Similarly, the East India Company, 'whichsoever you establish by Act of Parliament', would advance £200,000. Not surprisingly, he reported on 18 Jan. from the committee appointed to receive proposals for raising money 'upon a fund of perpetual interest'. The idea showed Foley's originality, his grasp of high finance, and his City connexions. It also revealed him to be no mere negative-minded critic of government but a constructive statesman in his own right; not a back-bench Cato but a professional politician with an alternative scheme of management to offer to the King. However, his last recorded contribution in ways and means this session, on 20 Jan., returned to a more negative approach, arguing against proposals to add a supplementary charge to the poll tax, payable by those liable to provide a horse for militia service.[6]

In the meantime the report of the commission of accounts, on which so many opposition hopes were pinned, had been presented to the Commons. Although the commission had no permanent chairman, its members taking the chair in rotation, nor indeed any gradations of seniority, Foley seems often to have been the principal spokesman. On 1 Dec. he laid before the Commons on behalf of the commissioners a general state of the public revenue since 1688, and two days later, in the debate on taking the report into consideration, he intervened several times to elucidate obscure points, among other things justifying, in the face of objections by courtiers, the inclusion of the secret service accounts in the report, and condemning the increase in the salaries of customs officials. He was again in action on 12 Dec. to explain the commissioners' findings, and had earlier supported Clarges' complaint of a breach of privilege against the commission as a whole perpetrated by the author and publisher of the tract *Mercurius Reformatus*, a satire against the commissioners. With his four oppositionist colleagues on the commission (Clarges, Musgrave, Robert Harley and Sir Peter Colleton*), he was named to the drafting committee on 3 Nov. for a bill to prevent false musters and to reform methods of payment in the army, one by-product of the report. Although the commission had, in fact, produced little else in the way of concrete achievement, it had proved a considerable embarrassment to government, and there was some ineffectual opposition towards the bill that renewed its powers for a second year. Even Foley's two brothers voted against it, probably unhappy at Paul's close co-operation with such High Tories and old enemies of the Presbyterian interest as Clarges, Musgrave and Seymour. But the opportunity for this co-operation constituted one of the greatest benefits Foley obtained from membership of the commission; that and the prominence his role gave him in the Country opposition. As the debates on supply amply demonstrated, the commissioners' official status, their association, and the knowledge they had acquired of the workings of government made them in practice the leaders of the Country opposition on fiscal matters.[7]

While supply and government accounts represented Foley's principal interests during this session, he made contributions on other subjects as well. He spoke on 30 Nov. in a debate on the Lords' amendments to the Irish oaths bill, in favour of the clause allowing Catholic lawyers to practise without taking the oath of supremacy, and on 12 Dec. on an elections bill, he and Musgrave opposing the bill to prevent false and double returns even though the purification of the electoral process was a prime concern of 'Country' Members. More characteristic of the Country party were his speeches early in November about incompetence in the direction of the fleet, and on the 20th of that month on war strategy, when he decried what he claimed was the King's intention to take personal command of a descent upon France, at the risk of capture and the imposition of heavy taxes on his subjects for the payment of a ransom. This argument allowed Foley to parade his knowledge of medieval history and the fates of kings held captive, but, as with his earlier ventures into military matters, it is doubtful whether he was able on this occasion to impress the House. His remaining speeches attracted briefer notice: on 25 Jan. 1692 he made a short contribution to the discussion on the treason trials bill; on 19 Feb. he spoke in favour of committing the bill to prevent correspondence with the King's and Queen's enemies; and on 22 Feb. he offered another comment on a point of detail over the bill to confirm the charter of Cambridge University.[8]

Although the investigations of the commissioners of accounts continued during 1692, their discoveries had been overshadowed by the news of military failures during the summer, or at least the lack of any substantial success, so that the dominant issue in the 1692–3 session of Parliament seemed certain to be the conduct of the war. In September 1692 Foley wrote to Robert Harley to request his presence in London to 'consider' various 'matters' and set out the prospects for what was to be a crucial session:

> Every day brings to town some gent[lemen] but none able to advise what's fit to do . . . As yet only three ways are thought on.
> 1. To reduce the army only, to a defensive at home, making our navy as strong as may be.
> 2. To make our army strong enough by itself to make a descent upon France, so as the command land officers may be by such [sic] as are likely to pursue it to effect.
> 3. The middle between these extremes, to keep off a general excise, and let the Court otherwise get what they can of supply and manage all themselves at their peril as hitherto.
> The first will depend upon the confederacy standing or breaking, the second upon the terms which may be consented unto to encourage it, the third will be the effect of no agreement.

The tone of these remarks suggests that Foley envisaged an important consultative role – perhaps even a participatory one – for the Commons in the determination of war strategy, since everything depended on the size of subsidy, which Parliament would decide. He did not regard the devising of policy as the preserve of ministers, or the duty of those outside the ranks of the Court party as restricted to opposition. Ideally there would be discussion leading to 'agreement'. But he also recognized the improbability of achieving consensus and the major political advantages to be secured by letting the courtiers make the running and making them bear responsibility for failure. Of course, the overall burden of taxation must remain relatively light and in particular a general excise, the bane of 'Country' Members fearful for their liberties, prevented. Further political complications arose from the divisions within the Court party. Ministerial Whigs were threatening some public manifestations of their discontent, and their motives aroused Foley's suspicions. 'Our affairs here make most men very grave and thoughtful', he wrote to Harley's father in October,

> but few or none are able to fix on any resolution. Some, on pretence to please by change of faces, design to fix the foreign interest more completely. Others, who are not free of suspicion of playing a double game, by the like trick hope to get money for the present turn and better places for themselves. Many are very indifferent whether a great deal or a little money be given the next session, hoping for their end both ways; but very few incline to the only probable way, with God's blessing, to save us, and fewer hope to effect it.[9]

On the first day of the new session (10 Nov. 1692), Foley spoke twice in support of Sir Thomas Clarges, who at this stage was heading the opposition's attack, to request more time for the accounts commissioners to prepare and present their papers and, more significantly, to oppose a Court motion to include in the Address a promise to stand by the King in the vigorous prosecution of the war. This general challenge to royal policy was followed on 15 Nov. by the customary attempt on the part of opposition Members to postpone a vote of supply until grievances had been presented. Foley suggested a short adjournment of the committee of supply, effectively giving the House only a day to consider grievances but at least preserving the principle of grievances before supply; the motion was carried. He made a strong speech on 25 Nov. on the army and navy estimates. The sum demanded was, he said, 'greater than ever was asked in this House'. More time was needed 'to recollect what debates were last year' and 'to make just exceptions'. He was careful, however, to ensure that his remarks did not sound entirely negative, adding at the end, 'this will expedite your business better'. The next day, in the committee of supply, the naval estimates were debated again. Foley opposed any augmentation:

> I find the navy is a growing charge; it still increases on you every year, but I see no reason for it to increase now when you beat your enemy the last year, so that I think if you have as good a fleet as you had the last year it is sufficient.

In particular he and Clarges were against giving money to build the bomb vessels and fourth-rate ships the government wished for, and he repeated this opinion in committee again on 1 Dec. He intervened twice in the committee on 3 Dec., first to expose defects in the poll tax, and then to tackle the army estimates, when he returned to the themes he had pursued the year before, pressing for limited strategic objectives, and, as always, asking ministers to supply further details of their plans.

Further contributions in committee on 6 and 9 Dec. again sought to persuade the House to examine these estimates closely and critically. On the latter occasion Foley showed the extent to which he and his opposition colleagues, in particular the commissioners of accounts, were able to influence the direction of debates by proposing a question to resolve differences and carry forward business. He went even further on 15 Dec., in ways and means. He had already been successful in moving an amendment to the land tax – to extend the liability to personality and to income from offices (excluding the army and navy). He then unveiled a novel and ingenious loan scheme to raise £1 million by means of the sale of annuities with a tontine provision, secured in the first place upon 'the hereditary excise', and after three years upon an additional excise on beer. This was in opposition to a project for such a fund put forward by Thomas Neale*. Foley had dismissed the idea of such a fund, 'for you can have no fruit of that unless you will force tallies or paper to go for ready money'. His own proposal did not share this defect, possessed the virtue that it laid no further burden on land, and was, he said, guaranteed to produce £70,000 a year. Despite its novelty, it was scarcely opposed and Foley was named to the committee to draft the bill which would embody both the scheme and the land tax bill. Later, on 8 Feb. 1693, he supported Clarges' proposal to raise £500,000 on the credit of various duties, spread over three years. He liked this idea all the more, he said, because it was 'upon credit' and did not draw further on the limited stock of ready money available. Meanwhile, in the committee of the whole on the million fund bill, on 16 Jan., he found himself for once in tandem with the ministerial Whig Charles Montagu*, when both moved for an instruction to the committee. In all probability he was the Mr Foley who, on 23 Dec. 1692, acted as a teller on the Country side for a long adjournment of the committee on the land tax bill. He also spoke in the committee on 3 Jan. 1693, when he offered a clause to the effect that 'no land should pay less than double what they did to the 2s. Act'. This was no doubt intended to prevent excessive increases in general, as well as limiting the yield from the tax and thus frustrating the Court, but it would also have perpetuated the injustices of the previous Act and for that reason it aroused the antagonism of Members from aggrieved counties, among them Sir Christopher Musgrave. More successful was Foley's next proposal in the committee on the bill: to exempt 'all companies and joint-stocks that shall be taxed by any Act of this sessions, to the end they might be taxed higher than 4s. in the pound, if thought necessary in any other Act this sessions'. Once this had been accepted, he moved in ways and means, on 3 Feb., for a tax of 10 per cent on the stock of the East India Company. Supporters of the company protested that such a punitive charge would ruin it, and bargained the level down to 5 per cent. Further rates were then agreed for the Royal African and Hudson's Bay companies. To soak the great trading companies satisfied some of the resentments of the country gentlemen in the House against the princes of commerce, resentments which had been heightened by the heavy wartime taxation on land. It also attracted support from those interloping mercantile interests who were struggling against the privileged monopolies, especially in the East India trade. Nor should it be forgotten that the blanket exemption which preceded the application of duties had benefited, *inter alios*, Foley's own joint-stock company, 'the ironworks in partnership'. Among his other interventions in debates in ways and means, the following are of interest: on 10 Feb. he proposed a tax on shipping, 'according to their tonnage' and with varying rates for different ports of destination; on 13 Feb. he spoke in favour of 'giving a clause of credit ... in case the land tax and the review of the poll should fall short'; on 16 Feb. he assisted Charles Montagu again, and even more strangely perhaps the courtier Sir John Lowther, 2nd Bt. II, in arguing against setting too high a sum to be raised 'on the continued importations'; and finally, on 23 Feb., he opposed a motion of Sir Edward Seymour to go into committee the next day on the enlargement of the customs debt. Taken as a whole, his contributions to the proceedings on supply could be presented as cautious and constructive, although they cannot have made the job of the Court managers any easier. If an overall coherence can be discerned, Foley's approach would appear to have followed the first of the options he had outlined in the preceding September, to retrench the army while concentrating resources on the navy. He had not so much left the Court to fend for itself as attempted to usurp its position. The commissioners of accounts had appeared less as back-bench auditors than rival front-bench managers. At the same time they had not forgotten their prime function. Foley in particular had twice acted as a spokesman on behalf of the commission, and on 14 Feb. defended its work when the bill to continue it in being a further year was under discussion. Moreover, he returned to an issue highlighted by his previous work as a commissioner on 22 Feb., when at the third reading of the mutiny bill he successfully tendered a rider 'to prevent false rumours and to regulate the pay by the true musters'.[10]

It was in their inquiries into the conduct of the war that critics of the Court showed their teeth. The emphasis placed by Foley and his colleagues on the importance of the navy dictated a close pursuit of tales of maritime incompetence. This was also an issue on which the ministry, and especially Secretary of State Nottingham (Daniel Finch[†]), was peculiarly vulnerable. On 12 Nov. 1692 Foley opened one line of inquiry. During a debate on the naval expedition of the previous summer he observed: 'How true it is I can't tell, but there is a relation printed in France of the fight with Tourville wherein they lay a blame on Sir John Ashby and do in effect say that if he had done his duty their fleet must be ruined [sic].' Then, on 21 Nov., in another debate on naval affairs, Foley widened the scope of the opposition's criticism with an indirect attack on Nottingham:

> I have seen many of your naval orders relating to the descent, and all come from one man and no more sign it. This, I think, is too much for one, for if the French can corrupt him it is in this man's power to render your fleet ineffectual, and therefore I am for changing hands to see what success then you shall have.

Besides Nottingham, and individual naval officers, the members of the Admiralty Board were also under attack, and the opposition exploited on 26 Nov. a complaint brought by George Churchill* of breach of privilege against the lords of the Admiralty who had interrogated Churchill concerning a statement he had made in the House about 'cowards' in the fleet. Foley's opinion was that this was certainly 'a very great breach of privilege'. The various Commons inquiries came to a head on 5 Dec. in a debate on 'advice' to be given to the King. Foley raised the question of the summer's expedition against France. He considered it to be 'apparent' from the report of the investigating committee that 'things were not well managed about that matter', and moved a resolution that 'there hath been an apparent miscarriage in the management of the affairs relating to the descent last summer'. After the House had gone on to vote that one cause of this 'miscarriage' had been the lack of timely and necessary orders, Foley proposed to add a statement that it had been 'the Council that had the management thereof'. Much later, on 3 Feb. 1693, he presented the complaint concerning Captain Robinson's failure to intercept the French fleet. His interest in naval affairs also produced a speech on 28 Feb., in committee on the bill for the encouragement of privateers, when he put forward a clause 'for the privateers to have all the goods taken in French prizes that were not of the growth of France'. As far as the army was concerned, the weight of the opposition's censure fell upon the 'foreign' general officers, whose employment, as Foley claimed in a debate on 23 Nov. 1692, occasioned 'many mischiefs'. He told the House that orders were sent down in Dutch or French, and frequently misunderstood. Furthermore, the very presence of these foreign generals spread 'a great discontent through the army'. Appealing not just to the xenophobia of his audience but also to their distrust of professional soldiers, he went on: 'for my part, I am for Englishmen who are men of estates; they will be for the interest of the nation because they have a stake in the hedge, and will be therefore willing to put an end to this war and make not a trade of war'. In contrast to his remarks during the supply debates, in which he had argued for a defensive military strategy, he now blamed the 'foreign generals' for the failure to put a speedy end to the war, presumably because of their vested interest in its continuance: 'there will be no end of the war but pushing for it. If our men had been seconded last summer, there had been an end of the war, and no need of this debate.' The two prongs of the Country attack, on naval mismanagements and on the inadequacies of the foreign generals, were fused together in Foley's speech on 26 Nov. in the committee on advice, a powerful indictment of war policy since the beginning of the reign. 'We have thought fit to advise as to admirals and generals', he began, 'and must go higher yet.' This time the target was the Privy Council, and the burden of the speech was to move a resolution condemning the management of 'the great affairs of the government, for the time past' and advising the King 'for the future, to employ men of known integrity and fidelity'. After recapitulating the circumstances in which England had entered the war, to assist the Dutch in opposing 'a powerful enemy . . . the king of France' who was on the point of 'enslaving' or indeed 'swallowing up' Europe, he asked his hearers to consider the balance of achievements. The English alone had kept to their determination not to trade with France, thereby impoverishing themselves while other countries (unnamed) had flourished. 'England bears almost the charge of the war and others reap the benefit of it.' Furthermore, prospects were bleak.

Little could be accomplished by land campaigns on the Continent, where the French appeared to have the upper hand; and the recent naval victory at La Hogue had, he claimed, brought no advantage. On the contrary, there seemed every likelihood that Louis XIV would now try to mount an invasion of England. This was a gross exaggeration of King William's military difficulties, but it served the purpose of enabling Foley to cast doubt on the loyalty, as well as the competence, of the ministers, which was his principal objective in the speech as it had been a hidden objective of the naval inquiries. He made no open allegation, but proceeded by innuendo; as one observer wrote, he 'named no particular person, yet . . . did very broadly insinuate the Secretary of State [Nottingham] and the Cabinet Council'.

There must be something to encourage the French king to make a descent . . . 'Tis said, 'the ministers serve you with the best of their skill'. You are the best judges of that; but as to treachery, no man is perfectly good, nor perfectly wicked. No man is so wicked as to bring in the French king; but your orders may be delayed, and intelligence sent him. None doubts but that he is designing a descent, and you are in the dark, and can judge of nothing but by the event. But the French king can take his measures; he knows who are treacherous to you. The last year you were like to have had a great loss by the Smyrna fleet being ordered to come to Ireland, but I observe the French fleet never came to sea till those orders went out. They sent word 'that the French fleet was laid up, and therefore ours must be so'. We kept out, and lost many, though the fleet in pursuit was not windbound, it was order-bound. I know not why they were not at liberty to pursue their victory. From unavoidable evidence, the hands you are in are not safe hands; that is, that the French king should draw so great an army on his coasts, and have transport ships ready for his men, and we should have no notice, and not half forces enough left for our security. I desire you to consider, whether those who have suffered you to be so surprised, will not do it again. 'Tis strange, that we should not know the strength of the French fleet till we had fought them. We know that from all parts of England discontented persons flocked to London, with arms and horses seized, and not one man was discovered of the conspirators . . . A great many instances might be given more, and I might fly higher to take off heads.

His speech played to such effect on the fears of Members and their hostility to the chief ministers that the motion passed *nem. con.* As discussion moved towards the means of making the Privy Council accountable, Foley resurrected his proposal of three years earlier that 'all persons who give any advice in matters of government may set their hands to it by way of assent or dissent', but this did not appeal to ministerialists or would-be ministerialists of either party, and was dropped.[11]

Of Foley's remaining parliamentary activity in this session, much was devoted to the advocacy of 'Country' measures designed to protect the political system from 'corruption'. He was a strong supporter of both the place and triennial bills. At the third reading of the place bill, on 22 Dec. 1692, he spoke heartily in favour, declaring it to be 'the only way to prevent corruption in this House'. He recalled that 'it is no new thing to see a man incline one way and when he is once into place to go another way'. Even after the bill had failed he did not abandon the principle that lay behind it, and during a debate on the triennial bill on 7 Feb. 1693 produced a 'place clause' of his own that went further than the abortive bill had done, 'that no one that was a Member of Parliament should have a place'. The extremism of this provision is typical both of Foley's 'wilfulness' in pursuit of an idea, and of his rather simplistic views on constitutional questions, in contrast to the sophistication of his approach to matters of finance. No fewer than four speeches of his are recorded on the triennial bill. On 28 Jan. 1693, at the first reading, he argued straightforwardly in favour of its acceptance: 'it is necessary for us to have frequent Parliaments, and to take care also that Parliaments be not corrupted, which frequent and fresh are less subject to'. He was also 'for adding something further to it, to prevent corruption if possible, in this House', probably the place clause that he proposed in committee. He spoke on 7 Feb. on behalf of the first clause in the bill, enacting that a Parliament should be held every year, and in a speech shortly afterwards answered Court critics of the bill by linking the issue of regular Parliaments to the wider question of the accountability of ministers:

> Some have objected, what ill laws were made in that Parliament [1661–79] called 'the pensioner Parliament'? What rights of the people gave they up? By the law of triennial Parliaments, as passed and confirmed, they, by implication, perpetuated themselves; by means whereof, the ill ministers of that time were perpetuated. I think it very fit that, if we cannot find out an ill ministry, others should come that may find them out.

Finally, he supported the bill vigorously at its third reading, telling the House point blank that 'if you preserve this government [i.e. the Revolution settlement] you must pass this Act'. Not surprisingly, he then voted for it. Other interventions showed his animosity to the ministry: on 31 Dec. 1692 he denounced as ineffectual the bill to prevent the exportation of gold and silver; and on several occasions he spoke against the indemnity bill, which he considered 'dangerous' because it tampered with habeas corpus, eventually agreeing to vote for its committal 'on condition it should extend to indemnify only such as had acted in the country and not our Privy Councillors here'. On 27 Feb. 1693 he raised popular grievances over impressment, and on 8 Mar. moved to adjourn debate on the expulsion of William Culliford* for abuses committed as an Irish revenue commissioner, for fear of losing the motion for expulsion by forcing it when 'gentlemen' were 'not yet ripe'. Oddly, however, considering his previous interest in the Irish forfeitures, and his family's Irish connexion, he does not seem to have taken any part in the inquiries into maladministration in Ireland. As the session progressed, his ties with Tory colleagues on the accounts commission and in the Country party generally became closer: on 14 Nov. 1692, for instance, he had spoken in support of the claim of breach of privilege made by Christopher Musgrave*, son of Sir Christopher, over Musgrave's disfranchisement at Carlisle. Some vestiges of old Whig loyalties remained, as in his grudging support for the Earl of Pembroke's (Hon. Thomas Herbert†) bill to reverse a judgment made against him before the Revolution in a legal dispute with the former Lord Chief Justice Jeffreys. And in an important debate over 'Revolution principles' Foley adhered to the traditional Whig line. On 20 and 21 Jan. 1693 he joined in Country party complaints against Charles Blount's *King William and Queen Mary Conquerors* and Bishop Burnet's *Pastoral Letter*, even moving that Burnet be impeached (a contribution which may account for the acerbity of Burnet's later description of his character). In part this constituted an attack on Nottingham and, more directly, on the Tory licenser of the press, Edmund Bohun, for having permitted the two tracts to be published. In denying that William and Mary owed the crown to right of conquest Foley and others were also condemning Tory doctrines of non-resistance and passive obedience and reasserting what a modern historian has called 'the ideological purity of old Whig principles', possibly in the hope of attracting 'old Whig' adherents in the same way as they had done with the place and triennial bills. Rather more equivocal was Foley's response to other issues involving traditional party divisions. Of the treason trials bill, which like other Country politicians he favoured, he remarked, 'I am for preserving the government, but I am also for protecting the innocent', and he was similarly concerned over the abjuration bill, which he took the considerable step (for a Whig) of opposing: 'I am sorry to see we are making a law to catch little troublesome fellows', he declared, and yet the great ones will escape, and that this must be by putting honest men in danger. It is very unsafe to make words treason and put it in the power of your servants to ruin you. I am against committing this bill because I do not think it will help you.

Returning to the subject which was rapidly becoming his King Charles's head, he concluded: 'Your disease lies in another place. If you had good ministers, you have good laws enough already and would have no need of this bill.' The unexpected rejection of the bill may have owed something to Foley's stand, and certainly 'some designing men', presumably ministerial Whigs, 'improved' upon the fact to reproach Foley for deserting the Whig interest and endangering the security of the Williamite regime. There were bitter recriminations, even within Foley's own family. Equally significant was the rather different reaction of the Earl of Sunderland, who was acting as a self-appointed broker between the King and those politicians who might be recruited into a reconstructed ministry. During June Robert Harley reported that Foley was 'solicited to meet him', but was confident, and rightly so as it turned out, that care would be taken as in the previous winter 'not to involve us in the inconvenience' of any formal connexion with the administration.[12]

Foley's and Harley's decision to resist the blandishments of the Court in the summer of 1693 possibly marks a turning point in the political history of the period, and certainly in their own fortunes. Only a year before, Foley had, so to speak, committed himself to a political career, or at least committed his energies to the public service, with the foundation of 'the ironworks in partnership' as a vehicle for the management of his industrial interests. And in the 1692–3 session he and his fellow accounts commissioners had taken a leading part in debates on supply. Yet by the 1693–4 session it was not Foley and his friends but the ministerial 'Junto' Whigs who were emerging as the successors to the old Tory Court party of Carmarthen and Nottingham. Foley remained aloof from the Court and seems in this session to have been more determinedly in opposition. Although henceforth the absence of Narcissus Luttrell's* diary hampers generalization, it would appear that Foley's approach became more critical and somewhat less constructive. He was more prominent in his role on the commission of accounts, presenting papers from the commission on six separate occasions, and in the ballot for commissioners under the new Act, announced on 12 Apr. 1694, he took second place, surpassed only by Robert Harley, who had long since advanced in status in their relationship, from protégé to equal. Foley also spoke up in a debate on 7 Dec. 1693 arising from the report of the commission, on a motion to censure Lord Falkland (Anthony Carey*), a member of the Admiralty Board, for peculation. The money concerned, Foley was convinced, had been 'put to an ill use'. In the debates on supply we hear of him supporting, perforce, a reintroduction of his own former proposal for a tax on shipping, and in February 1694 striving in vain to rescue a resolution of ways and means for a loan of £1 million at 8 per cent interest. But he had appeared on the Country side in a division on 20 Dec. 1693 in favour of a resolution of the committee of supply concerning the estimates for army pay and for military hospitals and contingencies, presumably to grant less than the Court required. Moreover, the tenor of his more important speeches on the prosecution of the war was for once wholly negative. In the debate on the King's Speech, on 13 Nov., he moved as usual for grievances to be heard before a supply was voted. Citing both 'the disadvantages our forces have had at land' and 'the miscarriages at sea', he argued that priority be given to an inquiry into the failures of the navy, which had made England 'a scorn and contempt to other nations', and followed up this point with further speeches on 21, 22 and 29 Nov. Among other detailed criticisms, he complained of poor supplies of beer to the fleet, for which the victualling commissioners had been responsible. Later in the session he brought in a bill to improve the discipline of the navy. His more general criticisms of the way the war was being waged, however, developed an interpretation of events first aired in the preceding session, that England was bearing an unfair share of the burden. 'Is England to carry on the war with an unusual proportion', he asked in the committee of supply on 11 Dec., 'and other allies not to come up to it? We ought to have a fair bargain.' He was particularly active in pressing the case for the reintroduced triennial bill, speaking strongly in its favour on 18 Dec. When the royal veto was applied, he was not slow in protesting, and in the debate of 26 Jan. 1694 seconded Harley's motion for an address to the King 'to represent how few the instances have been to deny assent, when so much money has been given'. He served on the committee to draft the representation. The inadequacy of William's reply, as he saw it, provoked Foley to deliver, in the ensuing debate, a broadside against the new style of kingship. 'Since it can be no otherwise done', he proclaimed,

we must tack our grievances to our money bills; for we have just fears and grievances as long as we have a standing army. The King tells us, 'he has a great regard to our constitution', but it appears not that he understands our constitution, which he takes to be to reject our bills of ever so just grievances.[13]

The vigour of Foley's attacks on government, and his continued presence as a force to be reckoned with in the debates on supply, prompted overtures from Court Whigs like the Duke of Shrewsbury, who arranged a meeting during the summer of 1694 to reassure Foley and Harley of his own adherence to Whig principles. Further conferences followed, generally with Lord Godolphin (Sidney†) in attendance, the first lord of the Treasury, presumably to attempt a pre-sessional agreement over supply. Although no definite result was forthcoming, it is possible that the compromise over the triennial bill was at least an indirect outcome of these gatherings, and a temporary lessening of tension between Foley and Harley and the Court Whigs has been detected during the opening weeks of this session. Whether or not he had received the prior approval of the Court, or indeed any encouragement from King or ministers, Foley came up to Parliament for the 1694–5 session armed with another major project for raising revenue, which would help to finance the war while avoiding the hated excise, and also demonstrate his usefulness to the crown. It was once again a loan scheme, underwritten by taxation; in this case, £5 million to be raised on the security of a 1s. land tax voted for ten years. In addition, he proposed to relieve the shortage of specie by striking silver tallies, from the proceeds of the loan, 'each of which should be made to pass for £5 current'. After some discussion, the Commons decided not to adopt the scheme. Moreover, early in December 1694 he made another constructive intervention in the committee of supply, putting forward a compromise (in which he 'engaged for his friends') for the sake of promptitude. Instead of the £2,700,000 the Court had demanded, he offered £2,500,000 and in return to forgo the detailed scrutiny of the estimates 'article by article and regiment by regiment' which had otherwise been intended. Courtiers were only too glad to accept. The *rapprochement* did not last long, however, possibly because of Foley's and Harley's dislike of the ways in which the Lancashire Plot was being pursued, and possibly because their connexions with Tories like Clarges and Musgrave were now too strong to be severed for promises as flimsy as those made by the Court. It is likely, too, that Foley felt the rejection of his fiscal scheme as a personal affront, and that he had already clashed with his rival as a financial strategist, Charles Montagu, now a Treasury lord, who was soon to become his *bête noire*. By January 1695 Foley was helping to organize a petition against the Bank of England, one of the major schemes with which Montagu was identified. Foley was particularly active in this session in his capacity as commissioner of accounts, presenting papers on behalf of the commissioners on 21 Nov. 1694 and on 15 and 25 Jan. 1695. He may also have demonstrated his loyalty to Country principles by acting as a teller for the place bill on 28 Nov., while a Foley told for the Country side on an adjournment motion on 12 Dec. The inquiries into corruption arising from allegations that the East India Company and the City of London had bribed Members to support legislation on their behalf naturally attracted Foley's interest, because they promised to expose the kind of public immorality he detested, and to offer him an opportunity to pay off some old scores. He reported on 12 Mar. from the committee appointed to inspect the books of the East India Company, the object of his suspicion and dislike in previous sessions. The outcome of the inquiries, however, proved of unexpected advantage to him, for when the Speaker, Sir John Trevor, was expelled the House, Foley found himself nominated to succeed to the Chair. According to Burnet, Foley's reputation as a 'great patriot', achieved by his 'constant finding fault with the government, and keeping up an ill humour, and a bad opinion of the Court', had secured him the support of a majority of back-benchers, who believed in his 'integrity'. His proposer and seconders were all Tories – Sir Christopher Musgrave, Lord Digby (William) and Hon. John Granville – but some Whigs voted for him too, 'the Herefordshire and Worcestershire men', for reasons of local loyalty and personal friendship (including his brother Thomas, with whom he was now reconciled), and others, 'purely upon opinion that he had . . . longer experience' than his only rival, Sir Thomas Littleton, 3rd Bt. Another explanation, favoured by the Court Whigs, whose candidate Littleton was, blamed a mistake made by Hon. Thomas Wharton*, the comptroller of the Household, who had proposed Littleton at the same time as he delivered the King's message commanding the election of a Speaker, and thereby had appeared to be seeking to influence Members' choice improperly by implying a royal recommendation. After some debate, Foley's election was voted, *nem. con.* by 'a very full House', the majority in his favour being estimated by one observer at around 35. Whatever may have been Foley's feelings towards the Whig Junto before this incident, their vehement opposition to his candidacy for the Speakership confirmed his antipathy. Once elected, he set out to prove his credentials as an incorruptible patriot, declaring in his acceptance speech that in contrast to his predecessor, 'whatever his failings might be, he would still preserve clean hands'. Shortly afterwards, in an interview with the King, with whom he had not hitherto been personally acquainted, he broke with tradition by refusing a place on the Privy Council, claiming that this would be incompatible with the Speakership. In this way, as one commentator noted, he demonstrated publicly his intention never to take anything from the court. When the elections for the new commission of accounts took place a fortnight later, he was chosen once again, but further down the list than previously. He had also to survive a challenge, presumably from the Court party, that membership of the commission was incompatible with his office as Speaker, an objection rebutted by the argument that although the Speakership was a place remunerated by the crown, the appointment was actually made by Parliament.[14]

Although Foley had been anxious to appear in public as untainted by any connexion with government, in private he lost no time in making contact with the King's 'undertakers', Sunderland and Portland, through their intermediary Henry Guy*, whom he desired to meet on a weekly basis. Guy reported late in May that Foley 'doth zealously profess his resolution of promoting everything for the public, and is considering of the best methods to effect it'. In a month or so he was to confer with Lords Sunderland and Godolphin 'to debate everything'. During these discussions Foley made a highly favourable impression: 'I find no person thinks so much of the means for money', reported Guy to Portland. Foley had 'drawn a scheme for seven or eight millions for the next year, because so much of it must go for bettering the coin of the nation. In my poor judgment it is not an ill one, and Godolphin thinks so too.' One thing Foley would not do, however, was to co-operate with Charles Montagu and the other members of the Junto. From the first, Guy made it clear to Portland and Sunderland that Foley 'in all his discourses declares a wonderful aversion to [Mr Montagu]; and that he neither can nor will communicate with him'. He lost no opportunity to blacken Montagu's reputation, and, through their association with Montagu, to cast doubt on the reliability of Comptroller Wharton and Lord Keeper Somers (Sir John*). This personal enmity made it impossible for Foley to play the part in government to which he seems to have aspired. Guy summed up the situation in a letter to Portland in June 1695:

We must do as well with [Foley] as we can, and keep him easy in some points, since we cannot have him so in all. It will be a very hard matter, if at all possible, to get him ever to communicate with [Mr Montagu], for he says that he hath downright played him a trick twice, after a serious debate and a solemn promise passed between them; and therefore he will never more trust him.

Foley had even threatened, in an oblique way, to make difficulties if the King continued to place reliance on the Junto:

He says ... that the most difficult point [the King] will have will be to have right persons for [management] in the [Parliament], because he believes that the former [insolence of Mr Montagu] will never be forgotten, and that behaviour made more uneasiness to several things than otherwise would have been; and that [Mr (Heneage) Finch (I*)] and [Sir Christopher Musgrave] and several others have often told him so. He says that [Mr Montagu] and [Mr Wharton] do go about to [the Tory party], and assure them that if they will follow their advice, they shall find many things they desire to have effect. He is likewise positive that by a little pains [the Whig party] will finally leave [Mr Wharton] and [Mr Montagu].[15]

The 1695–6 session and its aftermath thus became a prolonged struggle between Foley and Harley on the one side and Montagu and his allies on the other to convince the King and the undertakers as to which of the two political groupings could most effectually carry on the public business. In what was simultaneously a contest both for mastery in the Commons and for the King's favour, Foley's occupancy of the Chair conferred some tactical advantages, but insufficient to compensate for the weakness of his position outside the ministry, and the King's aversion to his Tory friends. Before the Parliament met he had first to surmount some opposition at Hereford, where false rumours had been circulated that he had worked in the Commons against the Wye and Lugg navigation bill: in fact, a 'Mr Foley' had brought in the bill in November 1692. He had also to see off a subsequent challenge for the Speakership. Sir Thomas Littleton was busy soliciting support, only to find that the Court were happy to countenance Foley's re-election. Some royal advisers hoped for his compliance over supply, and perhaps also there was an apprehension that he would be able to continue in the Chair irrespective of the King's attitude. Foley had done well enough in his brief stint to merit another chance, and still carried with him his considerable reputation as a patriot. The Tories were sure to vote for him, and those Jacobite Members in touch with the exiled King James were instructed to 'advance' Foley's election, although he himself is not known ever to have deviated from strict loyalty to King William and to the Revolution settlement. On 22 Nov. 1695 he was proposed by Secretary of State Sir William Trumbull, seconded by another courtier, Lord Ranelagh (Richard Jones), and accepted by the House *nem. con.* As a *quid pro quo*, Foley's 'friends' acquiesced in the election of a Court Whig to the chair of the committee of elections. In his acceptance speech, Foley recommended Members to be 'prompt' in their attendance upon parliamentary business, and, as befitted a student of constitutional law, urged them to pay proper attention to Standing Orders, 'that were made by their predecessors, upon great experience and grounded upon great reason'. In what was a double-edged warning to unruly oppositionists he also pressed them to 'consult' the honour and dignity of the House, 'whereof they owed very much of their liberties and properties in all times, lest by any misbehaviour of theirs they should bring the House into contempt, and thereby endanger the making a way for the overthrow of their constitution'. The deployment of this libertarian rhetoric, perhaps harking back to the controversy surrounding the royal veto of the triennial bill, hints at the constraints on Foley in his response to Court initiatives. He could not afford to alienate his erstwhile Country, in effect Tory, supporters, or to forfeit his standing as a patriot. Thus in the debate of 31 Jan. 1696 on the proposed council of trade, which he had been forecast as likely to oppose, all the Foleys joined in voting against the imposition of an oath of abjuration on the councillors, and Paul, as Speaker, caused the defeated motion to be reported in the published *Votes* in an abbreviated form, so as to disguise the full extent of its anti-Jacobite sentiment and thus protect from Whig innuendo the Tories who had been largely responsible for its rejection. Earlier, the Speaker had also voted with the opposition in committee in favour of a resolution that the names of the members of the projected council be selected by Parliament. Moreover, he was active in at least a consultative capacity in the Country party campaign for electoral reform during the winter of 1695–6, submitting a series of detailed amendments to the Member responsible for drafting one such measure, the landed qualification bill. His success in retaining the respect of Country Members is shown by his re-election as a commissioner of accounts in February 1696. A regular attender at the commission even while occupying the Chair, Foley had remained committed to its work long after it had ceased to be the spearhead of opposition. On this occasion he came second in the poll, behind Robert Harley. At the same time as he maintained credibility with the Country party, however, Foley felt obliged, or more probably actively wished, to respond in a positive way to the overtures the Court had made to him. He distanced himself from High Tory oppositionists on the issue of the Association, to which he himself subscribed promptly, and although differing strongly from Charles Montagu and ministerial Whigs on a variety of questions, ensured that his criticism was of a constructive kind. Over the problem of the coinage, for example, he opposed Montagu's determination to keep to the old standards, and other proposals for a recoinage, arguing at first the advantages of a natural inflation of the currency, and in the later stages of the controversy differed from Montagu on the new value for guineas. The issue which engaged most of his energies, and on which he staked much of his reputation, at court and in Parliament, was the scheme to establish a land bank. Although this was not a project of his own devising, and his name did not figure among the commissioners appointed to collect subscriptions, nor in the committee responsible for the negotiations with the Treasury, he was very busy behind the scenes in promoting the bank. It appealed to his 'Country' prejudices as a means of harnessing the real wealth of the kingdom, the land, and simultaneously of helping the country gentlemen, at risk of exploitation by the rising 'moneyed interest' of City financiers. More attractive still was the role the bank could play as a rival to the Bank of England, and thus as an instrument of Foley's own rivalry with Montagu. Through the summer of 1696 he and Harley pressed upon the King, via Shrewsbury and Portland, the advantages their bank had to offer. Shrewsbury reported to William late in July that 'some of those gentlemen who had procured money for shares in the land bank', naming Foley and Harley in particular, 'seem so convinced of the consequences if your army beyond seas should be reduced to extremity that they promise, and hope to engage others, to lend a considerable sum upon a good premium'. Among the Court's 'undertakers' Sunderland showed a particular warmth towards the project. Foley's identification with the bank, and the political uses to which it was to be put, were part of the common currency of political propaganda during the summer. One lampoon depicted Foley offering the King his service via Sunderland's intermediary, Henry Guy, at the price of royal support for the land bank:

> If the King to my bank and me will be hearty,
> And to some other projects, which I can advance,
> Then I will come over, both I and my party,
> And (I conceive) we can stop the ambition of France.

The failure of the land bank, its backers outmanoeuvred by Bank of England interests, was therefore a serious blow to Foley's reputation, in retrospect perhaps even a catastrophe for his career. 'All that land bank is called a cheat', wrote the Tory Francis Gwyn*, 'that could not perform what they pretended to.' Foley, who prided himself on his probity and personal credit, was said to be in despair. He had lost face in

Parliament, lost the trust of Portland and the King, and been outwitted by his deadly rival, Montagu, who had displayed a degree of nimbleness that 'heavy Paul', shackled to an *idée fixe*, could not match. Significantly, too, it was Foley rather than the more adroit Harley who suffered the odium of association with the failure of the land bank.[16]

The debacle resulted in a hardening of Foley's antagonism towards Montagu and the other Junto Whigs, though he did not abandon hopes of persuading the King of his own superiority as a parliamentary manager. It is probably to the end of 1696 that we should date some meditations on 'faction' in Foley's hand. 'In [the] state', he wrote, faction was called 'parties'. Its cause was 'principally self-interest': for 'honour', 'riches', 'friendship', 'revenge', 'fear', 'security' and 'opposition, in the turbulent'. And its effects were 'distraction in the state, weakening of the government' and eventually 'sowing the seeds of civil war'. The cure was 'the prince's equality', especially in 'preventing occasions', distribution of 'justice, rewards and punishments', the 'discountenancing flatterers and dilators, displacing the turbulent' and 'encouraging the virtuous'. The bitterness of these remarks did not, however, preclude any response at all to advances made by Sunderland and by the King himself before the opening of the following session. In mid-October 1696 Harley reported that 'the Speaker and myself were unexpectedly sent for to the King and kept in discourse two hours and a half'. Some Whigs indeed were 'uneasy about the measures that are like to be taken in Parliament, and at the courtship made to the Speaker and Mr Harley'. The effect of these discussions was evident when the session began. Foley 'declared himself an open enemy of the Bank [of England] in a very long speech, and did not stick to lay the blame upon others that the land bank did not succeed'. He also 'spoke very long' in committee of supply against a proposal made by Montagu. But although to some degree there was a desire to pay off old scores and to confute his chief enemy, he tried to devise some alternative to offer the crown, albeit without the vigour and authority over the subject he had shown before. 'He has a project in his head that is very inconceivable', wrote James Vernon I*; 'as yet I know not what it will appear upon his explaining it'. And Vernon added, significantly, 'whatever he has to propose, he will do well to make the advantages of it very plain and practicable, for otherwise the last year's experience has made men very sharp to distinguish chimeras from realities'. Over Sir John Fenwick's† attainder, Foley was prepared to assist in the protection of some prominent ministers, especially Shrewsbury, with whom he had always enjoyed amicable relations. It was Sunderland who had advised that Foley and Harley be taken into the Court's confidence, and Vernon was able to report more than once that 'the Speaker . . . did his part'. At one point Foley even clashed with a Tory Member, Lord Norreys (Montagu Venables-Bertie), over a point of procedure, in which he himself turned out to be in the wrong. In January 1697 he antagonized other Country Members, in this case the more radical Country Whigs, by intervening to prevent a tack of the landed qualification bill (similar to the bill he had supported a year before) to the capitation bill. Vernon wrote: 'Paul Foley did very good service today against the tacking clause . . . under pretence of speaking to order [he] answered all their precedents, and declared the like never was in Parliament.' That Foley was seeking to present himself as well disposed to the King, if not to some of the ministers, is evident from a remark he made the following month to the Dutch envoy, L'Hermitage, forecasting a rapid conclusion of 'the business of the supply'. Certainly those of his constituents involved in the leather industries regarded him as in some way responsible for the passage of the leather duty and at his return to Hereford in May 1697 paid him an unwelcome visit, abusing him and his family and threatening the 'pulling down his house'. This was not an experience likely to encourage a long stay in the country, but Foley's sojourns at Stoke Edith had in any case been becoming rarer and shorter as the decade had progressed, and a plaintive letter from the country to Under-Secretary John Ellis* shows the extent to which he had become a professional politician more at home in London society than in what he termed 'a barren place which affords little company and no news'. The 1697–8 session followed a similar pattern. After a pre-sessional interview with King William, Foley continued to do what he could to make life difficult for the Junto (so much so that he was considered by a French diplomat to be one of the leaders of the Country opposition) while occasionally producing alternative expedients of his own to advance royal needs. For instance, having in December 1697 'put a rub in the way' of the Junto's plans to settle the civil list, 'by referring . . . the account how the revenue stands charged to the select committee that hath the other accounts before them, and not to the committee of supply', he subsequently 'promoted' a proposal 'that the provision for the civil list may come out of the East India Company upon condition of their being established by Parliament'. In April 1698 his son Thomas even put forward a compromise motion on the issue of the resumption of crown grants that won backing from Charles Montagu. There were drawbacks to this strategy, however. Politically the most serious was that Foley was coming to be isolated from the more militant Country party men, most of them High Tories, who do not seem to have appreciated the subtlety of his approach. The Speakership may in fact have proved a hindrance to his political career, encouraging him to entertain notions of co-operation with sections of the ministry beyond the point at which these were valid. Furthermore, despite the influence he enjoyed, and sometimes exploited, over the business of the House, the Chair was not the best place in which to maintain a high profile as a critic of the Court. And there is some evidence that Foley's tenure of the Speakership was progressively less successful. Symptomatic of his decline in prestige, and inability to exert himself sufficiently as Speaker, was an unsavoury incident in January 1698, in which he quarrelled with the Court Whig John Smith I. 'A little impatient' to put an end to the day's proceedings, Foley had allowed himself a satirical inflexion when repeating the word 'compromise' which Smith had employed in an intervention designed to break a procedural deadlock. Smith took offence and threatened to pull the Speaker's nose. Several Members were in turn outraged at this affront to the Chair but although he had clearly heard the remark Foley was insistent in pretending ignorance and allowing the insult to pass by, to the consternation of many of his friends.[17]

The dissolution of the 1698 Parliament seems to have marked an important final change in the course of Foley's political career, for in the new Commons he was no longer Speaker, and together with Harley took up a stance of uncompromising opposition, even when this involved giving personal offence to the King. Although it was not until the outcome of the contest for the Speakership that he was set free from any connexion with the Court, prior events were already pushing him away. The departure of Shrewsbury and Sunderland from the ministry left few advocates of reconciliation with Foley and Harley in an administration now quite dominated by the Junto. Nevertheless, as the manoeuvring began over the Speakership, there were still some voices at Court willing to recommend Foley as an alternative to a High Tory like Sir Edward Seymour or John Granville, and it was thought that Foley himself might be prepared to stand with ministerial support. In the event his ill-health, against which he had to struggle throughout the session, and the knowledge that few Members had been satisfied with his performance in the Chair, deterred him from putting himself forward as a candidate. More significant still is the fact that the Country party men do not seem ever to have considered him as a possible choice, indicative of the ground he had lost over the preceding two sessions and now needed to make up. He began strongly, appointed to the committee of 17 Dec. 1698 to draft the disbanding bill, and subsequently pressed the resistance against a standing army with vigour. He may have been the Foley who on 23 Dec. joined in demands for a call of the House before the meeting of the committee on the disbanding bill, and on 4 Jan. 1699 he was positively identified as having spoken out against a Court-inspired motion for an instruction to the committee to increase the forces to be retained from 7,000 to 10,000 men: the additional number, he argued, would be of comparatively little importance in the event of an invasion, and in any case fears of such a threat to liberty and property were unduly alarmist – 'there can be no apprehension, for the people are strong enough to defend their liberties and always will do it, though an army may give up our liberties'. Then on 12 Jan., in a committee of supply, he moved that the committee on the disbanding bill be empowered to draft a clause of credit to cover the cost of disbandment, a shrewd tactic since it had the effect of rendering the measure a money bill and inhibiting opposition to it in the Lords, or at the very least making amendment or rejection by the Upper House a major constitutional issue. The previous day in the supply committee he had queried the estimate for general officers, on the grounds that '[a] lesser sum [had been] allowed to general officers during the war as per divers instance[s]'. No doubt as a result of his work in committee, he was among the opposition leaders invited by Montagu to a meeting on the 14th to discuss questions of ways and means. The negotiations had little effect, however, and on 3 Feb. he spoke again in the committee of supply, this time against any increase in the naval estimates. On issues related to disbandment, he was probably the 'Mr Foley' who on 2 Mar. presented a bill for making the militia more useful, and he certainly took a prominent part in the inquiries into maladministration in the navy, which had obvious strategic implications for those opposed to a standing army, besides the party political advantage in exposing the corruption of Lord Orford (Edward Russell*). Foley and Harley together set the inquiries in motion on 20 Dec. 1698, and pursued them strongly throughout the following months. How active Foley was able to be in other respects during this session must be a matter for conjecture. Later in the year he recalled that in the winter his ill-health, from a chest complaint, had so alarmed friends that they had persuaded him to leave the town and spend some time in the cleaner air of Hampstead. Conceivably he was the recipient of a grant of leave of absence (for a fortnight) on 22 Mar.[18]

Foley's health deteriorated as the year progressed. Late in October 1699 he told Harley that he was 'not at present in a condition' to attend the forthcoming session of Parliament. 'I am daily followed with such a cough in my lungs as does often near st[r]angle me, and keeps me that I cannot in the least stir out.' What killed him, however, was gangrene in a foot, after he had been blooded, or alternatively, according to some gossip, after he had 'buckled his shoe too straight and worn it so'. The precise date of his death has been disputed. His monument declared it to have been on 11 Nov. 1699, but family papers, since disappeared, convinced one biographer that this statement had been an error for the 13th. He was buried at Stoke Edith.[19]

Foley's death was a political loss felt keenly by his close friends. 'This is a sore blow to Church and state, to Herefordshire and to all relations', wrote Robert Harley. Robert's brother Edward echoed him: 'the death of so good a friend and person, whose worth and abilities render it a public loss, cannot but be very affecting'. In fact, Foley died at a time when Harley, his one-time political apprentice, was already outstripping him. It is tempting to over-emphasize the difference in generations between uncle and nephew and to contrast Harley's suppler character with Foley's greater solidity and more old-fashioned approach to politics. But this would be to misunderstand Foley's character and thinking. Certainly he was deeper set in his Presbyterian background, and his experience in the Exclusion Parliaments bound him closer to the values of an earlier generation of Country Whigs. But his industrial experience had moulded him into a man of action rather than an armchair constitutionalist. His political principles, a belief in the liberty of the subject and in the right of Parliament to question and if necessary resist royal policy, together with a cynicism of party faction, were based upon commonly held assumptions, often rather simplistic, about the traditional strengths of the English system of government. In speaking on these themes he was short and to the point, as compared with his prolix criticisms of financial mismanagements or other maladministration, when he usually couched his speech in the language of constructive counsel. He was most comfortable in committees of supply and ways and means, devising fiscal expedients that often showed ingenuity and originality, although in the long run he lacked the connexions and the adaptability that made his hated rival Charles Montagu successful. A Treasury minister *manqué*, Foley may have been robbed by death of an eminent place in later Tory administrations, albeit in a subordinate position to Harley. His career must be judged in these terms as a failure. He was, however, a formidable Parliamentarian, who helped to preserve some of the values of the first Whigs and to translate them to the new circumstances of post-Revolution England. It was in one sense ironic that the monument erected by his son should declare the disbandment of much of the army in 1699 to have been Foley's greatest achievement, since this was in essence a negative accomplishment. Yet it was also apt, since his parliamentary career had been spent largely in opposition, seeking to recall governments to what he perceived as traditional, minimalist policies and to the virtues exemplified by the godly and prudent landowner-industrialist.[20]

[1] *Vis. Worcs.* ed. Metcalfe, 46–47; W. R. Williams, *Parl. Hist. Worcs.* 51; *London Mar. Lic.* ed. Foster, 496; MI, Stoke Edith par. ch.; Add. 70225, Foley to Robert Harley, 9 Oct. 1688. [2] D. R. Lacey, *Dissent and Parlty. Pol. 1661–89*, p. 395; W. R. Urwick, *Nonconformity in Worcester*, 91; *DNB* (Oldfield, Joshua); A. G. Matthews, *Calamy Revised*, 373; J. R. Woodhead, *Rulers of London* (London and Mdx. Arch. Soc.), 105; Add. 70114, Mary Foley to Sir Edward Harley, 10 May 1689; Macaulay, *Hist. Eng.* v. 2410; R. North, *Lives of the Norths* ed. Jessop, i. 193; Burnet, iv. 197; Burnet, *Supp.* ed. Foxcroft, 402; *Business Hist.* xiii. 19–38; *Econ. Hist. Rev.* ser. 2, iv. 326–8; *Trans. Bristol and Glos. Arch. Soc.* lxxii. 129–43. [3] Add. 70014, ff. 296, 299, 29594, f. 196; 42592, f. 117; *HMC Portland*, iii. 444; Bodl. Ballard 35, f. 48; Grey, x. 9, 13, 28, 37, 60, 68–69, 117, 132–3, 142; Morrice ent'ring bk. 3, p. 146; H. Horwitz, *Parl. and Pol. Wm. III*, 57; Bodl. Rawl. A.79, ff. 83–84. [4] Add. 70014, f. 391; 70015, ff. 1, 3, 19, 21, 203; *HMC Portland*, iii. 459; *EHR*, xci. 33–51; Horwitz, 69; *Cal. Treas. Bks.* ix. pp. cli–clxxiv; xi. pp. clv–clxxxvi; D. Rubini, *Court and Country*, 69–74, 76; A. McInnes, *Robert Harley, Puritan Politician*, 40–45; B. W. Hill, *Robert Harley*, 26–28; *CSP Dom.* 1690–1, p. 465. [5] Add. 70015, ff. 55, 72–73, 104, 112, 150; *HMC Portland*, iii. 473–4, 478, 485; *Trans. Woolhope Club*, xxxix. 127–9. [6] Add. 70015, f. 30; 42592, f. 175; Horwitz, 70–73; *Luttrell Diary*, 4, 9, 19–20, 26, 30, 39, 41, 48, 51, 80, 97, 101, 105–6, 113, 120–3, 144; Grey, 168, 175–6; Bodl. Carte 130, ff. 326–7; *HMC 7th Rep.* 207, 209. [7] *Luttrell Diary*, 8, 26, 55, 60–61, 77; Grey, 198; Cobbett, *Parlty. Hist.* v. 670; Rubini, 76; McInnes, 42–43; *EHR*, xci. 43–44, 47–51; Add. 70016, f. 30; Horwitz, 77, 98, 100. [8] *Luttrell Diary*, 50, 76, 153, 195, 200; *HMC 7th Rep.* 205, 208; Ranke, vi. 169. [9] Add. 70225, Foley to Robert Harley, 17 Sept. 1692; *HMC Portland*, iii. 502. [10] *Luttrell Diary*, 216, 229, 267, 269, 289, 297, 321–3, 349, 356, 368, 386, 400, 411, 417, 419, 421, 425, 438, 445; Rubini, 96–97; Grey, 280–1; Horwitz, 111. [11] *Luttrell Diary*, 222, 247, 256–7, 261–3, 294, 399, 454; Grey, 245, 262–3, 274–6, 282; H. Horwitz, *Revol. Politicks*, 136; Cobbett, 721–2; Nottingham Univ. Lib. Portland (Bentinck) mss PwA 2385, 2387, notes on debates, 23, 26 Nov. 1692; Suff. RO (Ipswich), Gurdon mss M142(1), p. 17, Sir William Cook, 2nd Bt.*, to Thornhagh Gurdon, 26 Nov. 1692. [12] *Luttrell Diary*, 226, 237, 315, 336, 343, 377, 381, 392, 398, 406, 408, 415, 451, 455–6, 468, 471; Grey, 252, 297, 303, 307; Add. 70017, f. 22; 70016, f. 236; *N. and Q.* ccxxiii. 527–32; Cobbett, 714; Horwitz, *Parl. and Pol. Wm. III*, 109; *HMC Portland*, iii. 528, 536. [13] Grey, 311–12, 317, 320, 350, 362, 368, 378, 382; Horwitz, 130, 132; Add. 17677 NN, f. 354; Ranke, 238; *Hatton Corresp.* (Cam. Soc. n.s. xxiii), 199. [14] Horwitz, 135–8, 144, 149–50, 214; *HMC Bath*, i. 51–52; *CSP Dom.* 1695, pp. 292, 295; Ranke, 253; Burnet, iv. 197, 260; Burnet, *Supp.* 402; Cobbett, 907; Chandler, ii. 456; *Lexington Pprs.* 69; Macaulay, 490; Add. 70017, f. 321; 17677 PP, ff. 196, 201, 203; *Bramston Autobiog.* (Cam. Soc. xxxii), 387; *HMC 13th Rep VI*, 36; Som. RO, Sanford mss DD/SF 290, Edward Clarke I* to Ld. Capell (Hon. Sir Henry Capel*), 23 Mar. 1695; J. P. Kenyon, *Sunderland*,

272. ¹⁵Portland (Bentinck) mss PwA 502, 505–6, Henry Guy to Ld. Portland, 31 May, 25 June, 5 July 1695; G. Holmes and W. A. Speck, *Divided Soc.* 14–15; Kenyon, 274–5; *EHR*, lxxi. 597–8; Horwitz, 155, 215–16. ¹⁶*HMC Portland*, iii. 570; *CJ*, x. 711; xi. 334–5, 429; Add. 70018, ff. 58, 79, 100, 107; 17677 QQ, f. 601; Horwitz, 156, 159, 165, 167–8, 182; *Lexington Pprs.* 148; Burnet, *Supp.* 413; Bodl. Locke c.8, f. 201; Cobbett, 963–4; *Cal. Herbert Corresp.* ed. W. J. Smith (Univ. of Wales Bd. of Celtic Stud. Hist. and Law ser. xxi), 43–44; S. B. Baxter, *Wm. III*, 338, 341, 343; *HMC Kenyon*, 398–9; *HMC Hastings*, ii. 251–2; NLW, Canon Trevor Owen mss 204, 'Mr Foley's amendments . . .'; *EHR*, lxxxv. 697–714; *Shrewsbury Corresp.* 130–1; *CSP Dom.* 1696, p. 296; *Correspondentie* ed. Japikse, i. 181; Burnet, iv. 308; Bodl. Rawl. D.174, f. 103; K. Feiling, *Tory Party*, 322; BL, Althorp mss, Francis Gwyn to Ld. Halifax (William Savile, Ld. Eland*), 3 Aug. 1696. ¹⁷Add. 70225, notes on 'faction' [?1696]; 70114, Foley to [Sir Edward Harley], 16 July 1697; 17677 QQ, f. 259; 28881, f. 221; Horwitz, 183, 189, 232; *HMC Portland*, iii. 580, 593, 596; Northants. RO, Montagu (Boughton) mss 46/7, 19, 72, 167, Vernon to Shrewsbury, 12 Oct., 10 Nov. 1696, 1 Mar. 1697[–8], 8 Dec. 1697; *Vernon–Shrewsbury Letters*, i. 44, 48, 53, 83, 189; Kenyon, 285; Cobbett, 1007; Macaulay, 2661–2, 2689; *HMC Downshire*, i. 743; P. Grimblot, *Letters of Wm. III and Louis XIV*, i. 353–4; Rubini, 191–3; *Jnl. Brit. Stud.* v(2), p. 84; *CSP Dom.* 1698, p. 43. ¹⁸*HMC Portland*, iii. 608; Rubini, 193; *Vernon–Shrewsbury Letters*, ii. 148, 238–9, 251, 257, 271; *CSP Dom.* 1698, pp. 393, 413; Add. 30000 B, f. 251; 70019, f. 44; 70114, Foley to Robert Harley, 30 Oct. 1699; Montagu (Boughton) mss 47/132, 138, Vernon to Shrewsbury, 14, 31 Jan. 1699; *Cam. Misc.* xxix. 380–1, 392–3; Horwitz, 251–2; Huntington Lib. Stowe mss 26(1), James Brydges' diary, 14 Mar. 1699. ¹⁹Add. 70114, Foley to Robert Harley, 30 Oct. 1699; Luttrell, *Brief Relation*, iv. 583–4; *Vernon Letters 18th Cent.* i. 51; *DNB*. ²⁰*HMC Portland*, iii. 611; MI, Stoke Edith par. ch.

D. W. H.

FOLEY, Paul II (1688–1739), of Lincoln's Inn and Newport, Herefs.

ALDBOROUGH   1713–1715
WEOBLEY   1 Feb.–18 June 1715

b. 8 Aug. 1688, 3rd but 2nd surv. s. of Paul Foley I*, and bro. of Thomas Foley II*. *educ.* I. Temple 1693; L. Inn 1706, called 1708; re-adm. I. Temple 1734, bencher 1738. *m.* (1) Susannah, da. of Sir William Massingberd, 2nd Bt., of Bratoft Hall, Gunby, Lincs., sis. of Sir William Massingberd, 3rd Bt.†, *s.p.*; (2) lic. 13 Dec. 1722, Susannah, da. of Henry Hoare, banker, of Fleet Street, London and Stourton Castle, Wilts., sis. of Henry Hoare†, *s.p.*¹

Even though admitted to the Inner Temple at the age of five, presumably as a compliment to his father, Foley was not at that point destined for a legal career. Indeed, while he was still at school in 1702 his mother confessed herself at a loss as to what might be done with him. She feared the moral dangers that lay in wait at university or an inn of court, or in the company of 'prentices', and favoured sending him to Holland to 'improve' himself and to 'fix him in the way of holiness'. His teachers commended his sobriety, and although he was evidently a lazy pupil they considered him to be potentially 'a much better scholar than he pretends to be'. Eventually (it may have been on the advice of his cousin's husband, Robert Harley*) he entered Lincoln's Inn and embarked upon the study of law. Foley was an active barrister, having to make the time from a busy circuit in July 1713 to begin his electoral campaign at Aldborough, where he was obliged to engage in a public disputation with his opponents in order to contradict the various calumnies which, he alleged, were being spread about him. Potentially the most damaging was that he did not possess enough freehold land to qualify him to sit in the Commons under the terms of the Landed Qualification Act. In the event he was able to take the statutory oath, though it is possible that his brother Thomas had come to his rescue with a temporary conveyance. He stood at Aldborough on the Newcastle interest, at that time under the control of the dowager Duchess, to whom Foley had been recommended by Harley. Since the death of Foley's father, Harley had shown an avuncular concern for the family of his old mentor and parliamentary colleague, and since acquiring the leadership of the ministry in 1710 he had taken on the role of a patron to all the Foleys. In the summer of 1713 he was negotiating a marriage between his own son and the Newcastle heiress, and had thus acquired some influence over the Duchess. Not only did she nominate Foley as her candidate, she seems to have entrusted him with the disposal of her interest: applicants for her electoral favour were required to approach Foley first. There was even talk that she intended to appoint him as her steward, though this does not seem to have come to pass. At any rate, Foley was able to report to her in October that 'by the management of what your grace gave me when I went out of town with a considerable addition of my own, being a very expensive election on all sides, I have fixed the interest there in my own power'. After a fierce contest he and his Tory colleague defeated their Whig opponents. With his legal experience, albeit of only a few years, Foley's arrival in the House probably represented a useful addition to the ranks of Harley's followers. It is, however, impossible to isolate his particular role in Commons business (because of the presence there also of his brother and of his cousin Richard) with the exception of a speech on 18 Mar. 1714, in the debate over the expulsion of Richard Steele, when he joined several Tories in arguing that Steele be obliged to withdraw before the charges were discussed. Classed as a Tory in the Worsley list, and in another list from 1715, he was evidently a loyal supporter of Harley, to judge by his comments after the lord treasurer's dismissal. Writing to Harley on 2 Aug. 1714 from Shrewsbury (where he may have been on circuit), he suggested that were I to consider your private interest only, I ought to congratulate your deliverance from the heavy burden you have endured for the good of your country, which I am satisfied was the chief end of all your actions; but when I consider the consequences that may attend this remove, and that it may be the alarm bell to the Protestant religion, to the liberties of our country, and to the Protestant succession in the House of Hanover, both myself and others cannot but be under the greatest concern, and ought to join heartily with your lordship in such measures as you shall think proper.[2]

By the time of the 1715 general election the Harleys and the Duchess of Newcastle had fallen out, and control over her proprietorial interest at Aldborough was in other hands. Foley tried his luck in a constituency nearer home, the notoriously venal borough of Weobley, but after securing his return was unseated on petition on 18 June 1715. He canvassed there again in 1727, and actually contested a by-election in 1732, without success. His inherited wealth, the fruits of his legal practice, and a second marriage into a prosperous banking family had combined to make him a rich man, 'worth above £60,000' if common rumour is to be believed. After his death, on 28 Nov. 1739, administration of the estate was granted to his great-nephew Thomas Foley†, his brother's grandson.[3]

[1] Northumb. RO, Blackett mss, Sir Edward Blackett, 2nd Bt.*, to Foley, 4 Oct. 1713; Add.70114, Paul Foley I to Sir Edward Harley*, 8 Aug. 1688; Nash, *Worcs.* ii. 464; MI, Stoke Edith par. ch. (Paul Foley I); *London Mar. Lic.* ed. Foster, 496; H. P. R. Hoare, *Hoare's Bank*, 32–34. [2] Add. 70225, Mary Foley to Robert Harley, 1 Oct. 1702; 70331, acct. of 'some northern elections', 27 July 1713; 70280, Foley to Duchess of Newcastle, 20 July 1713; T. Lawson-Tancred, *Recs. of a Yorks. Manor*, 247–8, 252, 258–9, 261–2; *HMC Portland*, v. 328, 441; *HMC Bath*, i. 241; G. Holmes, *Pol. in Age of Anne*, 181, 487; Douglas diary (Hist. Parl. trans.), 18 Mar. 1714. [3] Prob. 6/116, f. 17.

D. W. H.

FOLEY, Philip (1648–1716), of Prestwood, Kingswinford, Staffs.

BEWDLEY	1679 (Mar.)–1681 (Mar.)
STAFFORD	1689–1690
DROITWICH	1690–1695
STAFFORD	1695–1700
DROITWICH	25 Feb.–11 Nov. 1701

bap. 12 May 1648, 4th but 3rd surv. s. of Thomas Foley† of Witley Court, Great Witley, Worcs.; bro. of Paul I* and Thomas Foley I*. *m.* 5 Oct. 1670, Penelope, da. of William, 6th Ld. Paget, 4s. (2 *d.v.p.*) 7da. (1 *d.v.p.*).[1]

Freeman, Bewdley 1675, Stafford 1689, Droitwich by 1694, bailiff 1694–5.[2]

Member, Soc. of Mines Royal 1690.

Commr. receiving subscriptions to land bank 1696.[3]

His father's mantle as a capitalist entrepreneur seems to have descended upon Philip Foley. When the great ironmaster's industrial empire had been divided, it had been the two younger sons, Philip and Paul, given their share of the patrimony principally in ironworks rather than land, who had been the more active in developing and expanding their manufacturing interests. Even after the two brothers had eventually merged their holdings with others in 'the ironworks in partnership', the largest iron-manufacturing company in the country, established in 1692 and controlling production in south Staffordshire, Worcestershire and the Forest of Dean, Philip continued to increase his involvement in industrial enterprises, in contrast to Paul, who gave himself up to a career in politics. Philip owned a sixth share in 'the ironworks in partnership' at the company's inception, although this had receded to approximately one-eighth in 1711, when the stock totalled £27,000. He also held a seventh share in the next largest iron-manufacturing company, the 'Staffordshire works', set up in 1693 and incorporating most of the remaining ironworks in the county, north of the Trent valley, and participated in similar partnerships in Derbyshire and Nottinghamshire.[4]

A Presbyterian, Foley retained a Nonconformist chaplain in his family as late as 1706, and was a contributor after the Revolution to the 'common fund' set up for Presbyterian and Congregationalist ministers. His early political sentiments were strongly Exclusionist, though his concern for religious toleration seems for a time in James II's reign to have outweighed other political considerations, since he has been identified as one of the 'Whig collaborators'. He did, however, sign a county address on 4 Dec. 1688 calling for the removal from office of all unqualified persons. In the 1690 election he faced considerable hostility from Tories in Stafford, and was defeated in spite of the strength of his own interest there. His refusal to appear in person in the borough cannot have helped. Fortunately, brother Thomas possessed sufficient influence to secure his return at Droitwich, where Foley in turn defeated a Tory, Sir John Pakington, 4th Bt.* He was classed as a Whig in Lord Carmarthen's (Sir Thomas Osborne†) analysis of the new House. However, instances in which some aspect of parliamentary activity can be specifically attributed to Philip rather than to any of his brothers or nephews, are comparatively rare. One such instance occurred on 31 Oct. 1690, when he was named to the committee on the bill for securing the rights of corporations, a committee he appears to have attended. In April 1691 he was listed by his niece's husband, Robert Harley*, as a supporter of the Country party, but with the addition of 'd[oubtful]', and the following February he and his brother Thomas were said to have voted against 'reviving the powers of the commissioners of accounts'. If there were any fraternal disagreements with Paul, himself an accounts commissioner, these had presumably been resolved by the following April, when Philip offered to back the candidature of Paul's son for a vacancy as knight of the shire in Staffordshire. Philip's involvement in intrigues to bring in his great-nephew Hon. Henry Paget* at by-elections first for the county and then for the borough of Stafford in 1693–4 revealed that the old party divisions in the county still held firm and that Foley was himself still associated in local politics with his former Exclusionist and Whig comrades. When Paget proved unwilling to stand, he recommended his nephew Thomas Foley III* instead. In the House he had returned to his Country party allegiance by March 1694, when he joined in opposition to a general excise, 'so odious to the country, and dangerous', and pressed the ailing Staffordshire Whig John Swinfen* to come up and add his weight to the resistance. Among many possible references to Philip in the Journals, he is most likely to have been the Foley who on 16 Feb. 1694 acted as a teller in favour of allowing a petition from the salt-pit proprietors in his constituency to lie on the table until the salt duty bill received its second reading.[5]

Reverting to his former seat at Stafford in 1695, Philip was almost certainly the 'Mr Foley' who acted as a teller on 24 Jan., with another Staffordshire MP, for leave for a clause to take away the duties on coal transported by water. 'All the Foleys' were recorded as having voted on 31 Jan. against the imposition of an abjuration oath on members of the proposed council of trade, and although Philip signed the Association promptly he divided in March against fixing the price of guineas at 22s., and in the following November against the attainder of Sir John Fenwick†. Marked as a member of the Country party in a comparative analysis of the old and new Houses of Commons in 1698, he was also forecast as likely to vote against a standing army. By this time he seems to have been becoming less conscientious in his parliamentary attendance. In April 1700 one of his nephews wrote to call him back urgently to Westminster:

> I am sorry that what I told you before you left London I feared would happen proved true, that there would be more occasion for you at the latter end of the session than there hath been all the while you were there; I therefore send these to desire you to lay all private business aside, and come to London with the utmost speed, for the Lords have made an amendment to the Irish and land tax bill, and nobody can yet tell what will be the consequence of it . . . by directions from our great men, we have taken several of us with our particular acquaintance to write to, to come up with all speed.

The next general election saw him step down, though only after he had withstood considerable pressure to stay on in the Commons, from his family and especially from Harley, to whom he explained himself as follows in December 1700:

> I have a true zeal for the public, and you know I have attended the service of it many years, to the expense of that which would have provided for divers of my children, which now being grown up puts me to great difficulties. The reflection of my brother Paul's decease and my brother Foley's [Thomas I] indisposition raises great thoughtfulness to provide for my children, and pay my just debts, for doing which I believe I must sell my outlands . . . and leave my son to buy more nearer home with his fortune, and that I needed not to have done if I had avoided public charges sooner . . . It grieves me to deny you anything that you command me. Yet my circumstances being thus I hope you will allow me to stand well in your good opinion and that you and my friends will give me leave now to be excused.

The respite was only brief. On his brother Thomas' death in February 1701 he was pressed to fill the resulting vacancy at Droitwich, at least for the duration of that Parliament. Again he appealed to Harley:

> The loss of my most dear brother is very grievous, which I heartily bewail, and my mind is now so concerned about Wich, what may be my duty therein, that for my own relief I crave leave to chat with you freely. I was use[d] to have a strong appetite, now a strange reluctancy, to appear publicly, and it may be it is the care which possesses me for my numerous family upon these notices of mortality . . . I know the ship is of greater concern than a cabin, but my hopes are that it will be steered by better and fitter men than myself, who am able to contribute so little thereto.

His suggestion, that his nephew Edward Foley*, Harley's brother-in-law, might be drafted instead, was evidently unacceptable, for he was returned himself at the by-election soon afterwards. Little is known for certain of his contribution to the navigation of 'the ship' in this Parliament, other than that he was black-listed among those who opposed making preparations for war.[6]

Foley managed to hand the Droitwich nomination over to his nephew Edward at the next election, and thenceforth retired to devote himself to his estate and to business. He rapidly acquired the reputation of one who did not 'come to town'. But he still offered Harley occasional items of political advice, as in October 1702, when he recommended that Harley find out methods to cure the abominable debaucheries and evil practices in corporations, and why may not those who find the entertainment as well as those who pay for it be equally punished, or what need those who keep public houses at any time be magistrates, whose duty it is to punish disorders and whose interest it is to promote excess.

His electoral influence at Stafford continued to be deployed to benefit his family, though he may not always have agreed with his various nephews in their politics. In particular, there remained in him enough of the old Presbyterian to make him suspicious of the pro-Sacheverell agitation in 1710. Foley died shortly before 11 Dec. 1716, when his nephew Thomas Foley II* was granted leave of absence from duties at the Exchequer on this account. His will was proved ten days later.[7]

[1] *Diaries and Letters of Philip Henry* ed. Lee, 231; Shaw, *Staffs.* ii. 235. [2] *Birmingham Univ. Hist. Jnl.* i. 109-10; Staffs. RO, D1323/A/1/1, Stafford corp. order bk. p. 355; Northants. RO, Montagu (Boughton) mss 77/85, list of Droitwich freemen [c.1697-1702]. [3] *HMC Portland*, iii. 58. [4] *Econ. Hist. Rev.* ser. 2, iv. 326-8, 330; *Business Hist.* xiii. 19-38; *Trans. Worcs. Arch. Soc.* n.s. xxvii. 35-46; *VCH Staffs.* vii. 244; xx. 157. [5] D. R. Lacey, *Dissent and Parlty. Pol. 1661-89*, pp. 395-6; A. G. Matthews, *Calamy Revised*, 132, 267, 383; *VCH Staffs.* xvi. 67; xx. 157; *DNB* (Morton, Richard; Reynolds, John); Duckett, *Penal Laws and Test Act* (1882), 442; Wm. Salt Lib. (Stafford), Bagot mss D1721/3/291; Bath mss at Longleat House, Thynne pprs. 24, f. 172; Add. 70014, ff. 290, 344; 70016, f. 30; 70114, Paul Foley I to Harley, 29 Sept. 1694; 42592, f. 167; 30013, f. 55; *Epistolary Curiosities* ed. Warner, i. 141-2; Hereford and Worcester RO (Hereford), Foley mss, [?Paul I] to Philip Foley, 1 Apr. 1692, Paget to same, 14 June, 25 Sept., 11 Oct. 1693, 18 Sept. 1694, John Swinfen to same, 17 Oct. 1693, Foley to [-], 10 Oct. 1693, same to Sir Walter Bagot, 3rd Bt.*, 17 Oct. 1693, same to Paget, 11 Sept. 1694. [6] *HMC Kenyon*, 398-9; Foley mss, Thomas Foley III to Philip Foley, 6 Apr. 1700; Add. 70225, Foley to Harley, 18 Dec. 1700, 5 Feb. 1700[-1]; *HMC Portland*, iii. 638. [7] Foley mss, John Pershall* to Foley, 7 Nov. 1702, Foley to [-], 13 Mar. 1704[-5]; Add. 70225, Foley to Robert Harley, 28 Oct. 1702; Huntington Lib. Stowe mss 58(6), p. 36; *Cal. Treas. Bks.* xxx. 583; PCC 136 Fox.

D. W. H.

FOLEY, Richard (1681-1732), of Lincoln's Inn.

DROITWICH   18 July 1711-27 Mar. 1732

b. 19 Feb. 1681, 3rd s. of Thomas Foley I*, and bro. of Edward Foley* and Thomas Foley III*. *educ.* L. Inn 1695, called 1702, bencher 1726. *unm.*[1]

Clerk of judgments, c.p. by 1702, 2nd prothonotary 1702-d.

Freeman, Bewdley 1706.[2]

FRS 1708.[3]

Entered like his brothers at Lincoln's Inn, but at a much younger age, Foley took his legal training seriously and made the law a career. After he had begun as a clerk in the prothonotary's office in the court of common pleas, and risen to be clerk of the judgments, his family's financial resources enabled him to purchase for £7,000 the place of second prothonotary (at a salary of £400 p.a.) when it became vacant in 1702, though he required the assistance of his brother-in-law Robert Harley* to persuade Lord Chief Justice Trevor (Sir John*) to admit one so young into the post. In consequence, he did not stand in need of any preferment at Harley's hands when he succeeded in 1711 to the parliamentary seat at Droitwich that was his family's preserve. None the less, he appears to have been a loyal, not to say enthusiastic, supporter of Harley's administration. In October 1712, encountering the bishop of Worcester at Droitwich, he expressed his full confidence that 'we had now great hopes of a very good and lasting peace' and, when the Whig bishop ventured to demur, repeated that 'such a peace there would be, he had reason to believe, for he had it from very good hands', namely Harley himself. He was marked as a Tory in the Worsley list and again in a list of the Members re-elected in 1715.[4]

Foley retained his seat at Droitwich for the rest of his days. Although it is impossible, for the most part, to separate his parliamentary activity from that of his several namesakes in the House, it would be fair to say that he was never an especially active Member. Certainly, by 1729 his colleague in the constituency ascribed his non-attendance at the House to a combination of 'idleness and family affairs'. A staunch Tory, he does not seem to have been implicated at any time in Jacobite correspondence or intrigues; nor was he ever reckoned by the Jacobites as a likely adherent in the event of an invasion, but in his will he left an annuity of £100 to his 'friend', the avowedly pro-Jacobite MP William Shippen, which some contemporaries reported to be a reward 'for services done his country'. He also made elaborate arrangements for the preservation of his 'parliamentary manuscripts', as family 'heirlooms', that is to say 'all my manuscripts of the rolls and journals of both Houses of Parliament' together with all 'office-books, votes, law-books and manuscripts'. Besides a further £2,000 in legacies to his nephews, the remainder of his 'very considerable estate' passed to his elder brother, Edward. Foley died on 27 Mar. 1732.[5]

[1] Nash, *Worcs.* ii. 464, 468. [2] *Birmingham Univ. Hist. Jnl.* i. 125. [3] *Rec. R. Soc.* (1940), 391 [4] Add. 70225, Foley to Harley, 29 Sept., 8 Oct. 1702; Luttrell, *Brief Relation*, v. 226; *HMC Portland*, v. 128. [5] Add. 51396, f. 50; PCC 106 Bedford; *Gent. Mag.* 1732, p. 679; Hearne Colls. xi. 48.

D. W. H.

FOLEY, Thomas I (c.1641–1701), of Witley Court, Great Witley, Worcs.

WORCESTERSHIRE 1679 (Mar.)–1681 (Mar.)
               1689–1698
DROITWICH   14 Jan. 1699–1 Feb. 1701

b. c.1641, 1st s. of Thomas Foley† of Witley Court, and bro. of Paul I* and Philip Foley*. *educ.* Pembroke, Camb. adm. 4 July 1657, aged 16, BA 1660; I. Temple 1657; L. Inn 1698. *m.* bef. 1673, Elizabeth (*d.* 1686), da. of Edward Ashe†, Draper, of Fenchurch Street, London and Halstead, Kent, sis. of William Ashe I*, 4s. 4da. *suc.* fa. 1677.[1]

Member, Soc. of Mineral and Battery Works 1670, asst. 1678–87, dep. gov. 1693–9; asst. Soc. of Mines Royal 1689.

Sheriff, Worcs. 1673–4; freeman, Bewdley 1673, Stafford 1689, Droitwich by c.1697.[2]

Commr. for taking subscriptions to land bank 1696.[3]

Foley inherited the principal share of his father's landed property but only a third part of the ironmaster's massive manufacturing interests, in his case a complex of furnaces, forges and wireworks based at Tintern in Monmouthshire, which he had previously run in partnership with his father. He continued to work them, though, unlike his two younger brothers, made no great attempts at expansion. There were some efforts to deploy his substantial economic resources in public finance, but on the whole he does not seem to have been an especially shrewd manager of his own affairs. His son-in-law Robert Harley*, preaching the wisdom of modesty where personal wealth was concerned, cited him as an example of the ills that could befall a man at the hands of kinsmen and servants when nothing was done to disguise or understate the size of his income:

> I am sure my father Foley suffered sufficiently by tenterhooking his rent-roll, and stretching it to £13,000 a year on paper, when it never answered nine. All his parsimony and swaggering could not hinder them from imposing upon him, so that they made it a common saying, 'God has made him able, and we will make him willing'.[4]

Foley's Presbyterian upbringing had been reinforced by his marriage into the family of a prominent London Puritan. He maintained a Presbyterian chaplain as late as 1687, sent at least one son to a Dissenting academy (and then on to university in Holland), and after the Revolution was a regular benefactor to the 'common fund' set up to assist Presbyterian and Congregationalist ministers. Foley's political creed was resolutely Whiggish. He voted for Exclusion, and seems to have been taken into custody temporarily during Monmouth's rebellion. He was apparently less willing than his brother Philip to lend support to King James's tolerationist policies, even though brought in by the regulators to the remodelled commission of the peace in Worcestershire, and proposed by the royal agents as an acceptable candidate for the county in 1688. At the Revolution he seized Worcester on behalf of the Prince of Orange, and subsequently regained his seat as knight of the shire in the Convention. He was still regarded as a staunch Whig in the 1690 general election, in which he successfully put up brother Philip against the Tory Sir John Pakington, 4th Bt.*, at Droitwich, assisted other Whigs locally and was re-elected himself for the county. Such was his reputation as a loyal party man that he was able to act as an intermediary (albeit without success) in negotiations between the Harleys and Sir Rowland Gwynne* over the representation of New Radnor Boroughs.[5]

Foley was classed as a Whig in an analysis of the new Parliament compiled by Lord Carmarthen (Sir Thomas Osborne†), but it is rarely possible to distinguish his contribution from that of his two brothers, and the situation becomes even more complicated after November 1691, when first his nephew and then his eldest son, both Thomas Foley, entered the House. He did offer, in the continued absence of Robert Harley from the House in October 1690, to introduce the bill Harley had prepared 'for the regulating of sheriffs', but the proposal was not taken up. His son-in-law was in fact causing him embarrassment, by pursuing a petition over the New Radnor election. Foley wrote to Harley's father in late October 1690 that 'many friends do desire him to give way, but he is wilful'. Among other things, Foley was evidently uneasy at the backing Harley was receiving from leading High Tories, although he himself was listed alongside them, and the rest of his family, on the Country side in Harley's analysis of the House in April 1691. At about this time there were rumours of a likely match between Foley and the widow of the veteran MP Sir John Maynard. Harley commented that 'her jointure is not great, but I think it a most suitable and decent match'. The talk came to nothing.[6]

Up until at least November 1691 Foley appears to have been faithfully seconding his brother Paul's attacks on the ministry. In all probability he was the 'T.F.' noted by William Brockman* as having spoken on 3 Nov. in a debate on the conduct of naval affairs and the naval estimates. After sideswipes at the crown's indebtedness and at 'vast pensions', the Speaker proposed a deduction from the 'officers' pay' to meet the interest on the debt, and concluded that 'the establishment' was 'too high'. Foley's later involvement in the raising of the public revenue suggests that these would have been preoccupations of his. During the session, however, relations between the brothers, and between Foley and the leaders of the Country party in general, became strained. First Foley gave 'great offence by soliciting for the East India Company', with which he may have had, or have contemplated establishing, financial connexions. Then in February 1692 he and brother Philip opposed the reviving the powers of the commission of accounts, in which Paul Foley was a leading light. A full-blown quarrel between the Witley Court and Stoke Edith branches of the family broke out the following December: its cause was the abjuration bill, which Thomas Foley had supported, presumably because of the greater strength of his Whig partisan loyalties, and Paul Foley had opposed, claiming that 'the weight would have fallen on many of the Dissenters, who would not have taken the oath'. Thomas had 'not spared to asperse his brother', but had himself been 'reproached' by 'designing men' on the Court side for contributing to the bill's defeat by his unsuccessful defence of it. Even though he had subsequently joined his brother in voting for the triennial bill, and in approaching Sir Edward Harley* to stand for a vacancy as knight of the shire for Herefordshire, the bad feeling continued into the summer. Paul Foley was 'so fixed in his rage' against Thomas, that, it was said, 'he sticks not to charge all the misfortunes of the nation there'.[7]

The divisions within the Foley family seem to have healed by the 1694–5 session. In the 1695 election Thomas found himself the object of some Whig opposition in Worcestershire for the first time, almost certainly inspired by adherents of the new Junto ministry – 'some gentlemen that did pretend to be his friends', as he himself put it. There was, however, no contest at the poll. He was classed as likely to oppose the Court in the forecast for the division on the proposed council of trade on 31 Jan. 1696: in the same debate the Foleys now displayed a united opposition to the idea of imposing an oath of abjuration on the members of the council. They were also united in their willingness to subscribe the Association promptly, and Foley himself took an active part in his brother Paul's abortive scheme for a land bank, serving on the committee elected by the commissioners to undertake negotiations with the Treasury. He did, however, vote in favour of the attainder of Sir John Fenwick† on 25 Nov. 1696, and over the succeeding two sessions seems to have behaved in a friendlier way towards the ministry, perhaps drawn in by his need to maintain amicable relations with the Court Whig magnates in Worcestershire, especially the Duke of Shrewsbury and Lord Chancellor Somers (Sir John*), but more probably motivated by his anti-Catholic and anti-Jacobite prejudices, which would have made him anxious about the political direction his brother Paul and son-in-law Harley were taking. Foley was one of the subscribers for circulating Exchequer bills, though when the subscribers attended the Treasury in April 1697 to choose trustees, he briefly showed his old colours in single-handedly opposing the inclusion of the Bank of England directors as trustees in return for a subscription from the Bank of £50,000. When the proposal was made he instantly 'desired to withdraw his subscription'. But he evidently considered himself to be in a position to make recommendations for preferment to Lord Chancellor Somers, and at the end of April put forward the name of Edward Harley*, Robert's brother and also his own son-in-law, for the office of chief justice of the Chester circuit. Not surprisingly, the post went elsewhere. He seems to have been soliciting a ministerial favour for himself. Negotiating with the Earl of Bath to purchase Bath's offices as keeper of St. James's Park and housekeeper of St. James's Palace, he applied to the Treasury in April for an alteration to the terms of the grants and for an extension to a lease of some lands adjoining the park which he also wished to buy, with building permission and a grant of a market. The Treasury's response is not known, nor whether the purchase went through, although Luttrell recorded its completion some five months later. That Foley remained on good terms with Robert Harley is clear from Harley's report of the journey they shared to Worcestershire in September 1697. Foley seems to have been solicited by the ministry at the beginning of the 1697–8 session not to oppose the standing army, and probably complied. At the end of the session he was able to claim the gratitude of ministers for having 'stuck by the Court and divided from his relations in all votes of consequence, and particularly for supplies'. It was also observed of him that 'nobody is in greater advances to the loan'. A list of the old and new Parliaments drawn up in the following September classified him as a Court supporter.[8]

Service to the administration over the preceding session or two was not enough to protect Foley from Court Whig opposition in Worcestershire in the 1698 election, where he withdrew on the first day of the poll. However his son Thomas III, who was elected at Droitwich and Stafford, duly vacated the seat at the former and Foley came in at the ensuing by-election. This experience seems to have alienated Foley from the Court. When, in March 1699, he went to see the

King to request that Bishop Hall, a Worcestershire man and a Low Churchman from a Presbyterian background, might be translated from Bristol to the vacant see of Worcester, William's tart reply was 'that he should consider it, as much as he and his friends considered any business that related to him'. It still seems most likely, however, that he rather than his son was the Foley who joined another son-in-law, Salwey Winnington*, in unexpectedly dividing with the ministry on 28 Mar. in the committee of supply on a resolution to provide money for disbandment. An important speech was also ascribed to a 'Mr Foley': on 15 Feb. 1700, in support of Hon. James Brydges' motion to condemn 'the procuring or obtaining of grants of estates' by 'any public minister', a scarcely veiled attack on Somers. 'If this q[uestion] passes not', the speech ran, 'there's an end of Parliament'; and the Speaker added that it was the duty of Members of Parliament 'to defend ourselves against all ministers'.[9]

Foley had fallen ill by mid-December 1700, when his son Thomas informed Robert Harley: 'My father continues much as he was, though I fear rather weaker than when you were here. He will take no physic but the Bristol or spa waters, and I cannot persuade him to continue to take Dr Radcliffe's [John*] pills.' Despite his illness, Foley was re-elected for Droitwich in January 1701 but died on 1 Feb., at Witley. Common rumour estimated his estate to have been worth at his death some £10,000 a year. One of his last acts was the foundation of a charity school at Pedmore in Worcestershire. Three of his sons, and three sons-in-law, sat in Parliament in Anne's reign, all voting with the Tories, and his eldest son was raised to the peerage in 1712.[10]

[1] Nash, *Worcs.* ii. 464. [2] Staffs. RO, D1323/A/1/1, Stafford corp. order bk. p. 358; Northants. RO, Montagu (Boughton) mss 77/85, list of Droitwich freemen [c.1697–1702]. [3] *CJ*, xii. 509. [4] *Econ. Hist. Rev.* ser. 2, iv. 326, 330; *Business Hist.* xiii. 22; *HMC Portland*, v. 531. [5] D. R. Lacey, *Dissent and Parlty. Pol. 1661–89*, pp. 396–7; A. G. Matthews, *Calamy Revised*, 80, 549–50; Add. 70083, Richard Stretton to Sir Edward Harley, 4 Sept. 1697; 70014, f. 290; 70225, Paul Foley I to Robert Harley, 16 Oct. 1690; *HMC Portland*, iii. 385, 403–4, 446; A. Browning, *Danby*, iii. 162; Duckett, *Penal Laws and Test Act* (1882), 442; (1883), 255; L. K. J. Glassey, *Appt. JPs*, 86; *HMC Portland*, v. 644; Bath mss at Longleat House, Thynne pprs. 13, f. 259; *Epistolary Curiosities* ed. Warner, i. 141–2; Bodl. Ballard 35, f. 53. [6] Add. 42592, f. 167; 70226, Foley to Robert Harley, 16 Oct. 1690; 70114, same to Sir Edward Harley, 29 Oct. 1690; 70015, ff. 51–52; *HMC Portland*, iii. 463. [7] Add. 42592, f. 175; 70016, ff. 7, 30; 70017, ff. 5, 22; *HMC Portland*, iii. 487, 510, 528, 536; *Luttrell Diary*, 390. [8] Add. 70017, f. 321; 70227, Thomas Foley III to Robert Harley, 25 Oct., 7 Nov. 1695; 70155, jnl. of land bank commrs. 1696; *HMC Kenyon*, 398–9; *Cal. Treas. Bks.* xii. 7, 149; Nottingham Univ. Lib. Portland (Bentinck) mss PwA 1181, Somers to the King, 29 Apr. 1697; Luttrell, *Brief Relation*, iv. 280–1; *HMC Portland*, iii. 587, 593; *Vernon–Shrewsbury Letters*, ii. 118–19. [9] *Vernon–Shrewsbury Letters*, ii. 118–19, 152, 271; *Shrewsbury Corresp.* 541; Som. RO, Sanford mss DD/SF 4107(1), acct. of debate, 13 Feb. 1699[–1700]. [10] *HMC Portland*, iii. 638; Add. 70225, Philip Foley to Robert Harley, 18 Dec. 1700; Folger Shakespeare Lib. Newdigate newsletter 4 Feb. 1701; Luttrell, v. 14; Nash, 240.

D. W. H.

FOLEY, Thomas II (c.1670–1737), of Russell Street, Westminster and Stoke Edith, Herefs.

WEOBLEY	12 Nov. 1691–1698,
	13 Jan. 1699–1700
HEREFORD	1701 (Feb.)–1722
STAFFORD	1722–1727, 1734–10 Dec. 1737

b. c.1670, 1st s. of Paul Foley I*, and bro. of Paul Foley II*. *educ.* at home (Chewning Blackmore, ?Joshua Oldfield); I. Temple 1678; Pembroke, Oxf. matric. 16 Oct. 1685, aged 15. *m.* 12 July 1688, his 1st cos. Anne, da. and h. of Essex Knightley of Fawsley, Northants., 1s. 2da. *suc.* fa. 1699.[1]

Freeman, Bewdley 1704.[2]

Commr. for taking subscriptions to S. Sea Co. 1711, for building 50 new churches 1712–15.[3]

Ld. of Trade 1712–Aug. 1713; jt. auditor of imprests Aug. 1713–*d.*[4]

Although he was probably the ablest of his generation of what was by any reckoning a remarkable political dynasty, Foley did not quite achieve the eminence for which he had seemed to be destined. The heir both to a great estate, augmented by a shrewd early marriage, and to his father's formidable parliamentary prestige, he would have been afforded a seat in the Commons even if he had failed to display any intellectual ability, but in fact his university education marked him out as a young man of promise. His father had it in mind to bring him into Parliament at the general election of 1690, perhaps even before he attained his majority, or at any rate very shortly afterwards, and obtained a promise from one of the outgoing Members for the notoriously venal borough of Weobley, John Birch I, to propose him there. However, Birch went back on his word, and by the time the Foleys began their canvass, vital ground had been lost. Rather than pursue a forlorn hope the candidacy was abandoned. When Birch died in 1691 Foley's father, despite misgivings, quickly put his son up for the vacancy. The ensuing contest, against Birch's nephew and heir, John Birch II*, proved an awkward and unpleasant affair, which resulted in a double return, eventually resolved in favour of Foley.[5]

Because the Foleys sat in Parliament in numbers throughout this period it is for the most part impossible to be certain in ascribing parliamentary activity to individuals, although as a general rule it seems likely that Thomas Foley was initially overshadowed by his father, Paul, and uncles Philip* and Thomas I*, but that after his father's death in 1699 he himself emerged as the most prominent of the covey of Foley cousins in the House. What is clear is that during his first session he 'carried himself very well', presumably adhering to the Country party, in which his father was a leading light. In February 1693 he joined the rest of his family in voting for the triennial bill, and on 20 Feb. acted as teller for agreeing to an amendment to the bill reviving expiring laws. He also added his voice to the clamour of Herefordshire gentlemen pressing Sir Edward Harley* to stand for a vacant seat as knight of the shire, couching his own exhortations in the language of Puritanism, which viewed politics as a godly calling: it was Sir Edward's 'plain duty', he wrote, to undertake 'this good work'. 'Providence hath so ordained it that you can do no otherwise but stand for the county.' He was probably a teller again on 23 Apr. 1695, in favour of engrossing the bill for the better encouragement of privateers. The previous year he had been added to the Herefordshire lieutenancy.[6]

Despite the threat of renewed hostilities with Birch at the 1695 election, Foley was eventually returned unopposed along with Price. At the beginning of the Parliament Foley was named on 12 Dec. 1695 with Lord Coningsby (Thomas), to prepare a bill to improve the navigation of the Wye and Lugg, a matter of considerable concern in Herefordshire. Foley was classed as likely to oppose the Court in a forecast for a division on the proposed council of trade on 31 Jan. 1696, while he and the rest of his family opposed the imposition of an oath of abjuration on the councillors. He signed the Association promptly, but voted in March against fixing the price of guineas at 22s. In the same month, on the 5th, he presented a bill for removing the toll on the bridge at Wilton. In the following November he spoke and voted against the attainder of Sir John Fenwick†. Either he or his cousin Thomas Foley III acted as a teller on 23 Nov. for recommitting the bill for further regulating elections, a subject into which his experiences at Weobley would already have given him a particular insight. But as a Herefordshire Member he is most likely to have been the 'Mr Foley' who acted as a teller on 3 Mar. 1697 against the resolution of the committee of ways and means to impose a duty on cider. His first recorded speech occurred on 8 Jan. 1698 in the debate on the Court-inspired motion for an instruction to the committee of supply to consider the funds required for guards and garrisons, in order to override an earlier resolution for limiting the size of the army. Foley took it upon himself to answer the observations of some naval officer-MPs that the fleet was insufficient to ensure the security of the realm, dismissing their arguments with a joke, and went on to refer to the example of Denmark, where the effects of a standing army in promoting arbitrary government were obvious, turning as he did so to Robert Molesworth, upon whose *Account of Denmark* he lavished praise. He was probably responsible for presenting on 15 Mar. a private naturalization bill, and may have reported on the 18th from the committee on the bill to facilitate the passing of sheriffs' accounts. On 8 Apr. he spoke again on the supply, proposing, as a substitute for the various resumption bills, a levy on all crown grants made since 1660 (in return for giving them legislative confirmation). He was seconded by Edward Harley, a close associate in later years. Although subsequently granted a fortnight's leave of absence, on 26 Apr., Foley may have been back in the Commons in time to have acted as a teller on 10 June for the Country side on a motion for adjournment. In a comparative analysis of the old and new Houses of Commons after the 1698 election he was listed, predictably, among the Country party.[7]

The contest between Foley and Birch at Weobley was fought with its customary bitterness in 1698, resulting in a double return, which was decided in Foley's favour by the House on 13 Jan. 1699, in time for him to vote in the division on the standing army, which he had been forecast as likely to oppose. Although he had intended to be up in town for the beginning of the 1699–1700 session, his father's fatal illness took him back to the country before very long and he seems to have sat out the rest of the session there. In April 1700 Robert Harley wrote to press him to return to the House. Replying, Foley acknowledged that he had already received such requests 'from some of your officers', and would indeed have responded had 'the general', Harley himself, written earlier, but now his wife had also fallen ill, and he was naturally loath to abandon her. This absenteeism probably did not extend to the next Parliament, when he transferred to his father's former seat at Hereford, rejecting overtures to stand for knight of the shire. Possibly he was the 'Mr Foley' who acted as a teller on 16 June 1701 against adding to the civil list bill a clause relating to patentees. He was blacklisted as one who in this Parliament had opposed preparations for war against France, and his name subsequently appeared among those appended to a Tory pamphlet rebutting the accusations in the 'black list'. Robert Harley classed him with the Tories in his analysis of the second Parliament of 1701, during which Foley was listed as favouring the motion of 26 Feb. 1702 vindicating the Commons' proceedings on the impeachments of

William III's ministers. He may have been the Foley who reported on and carried up two private bills (28, 30 Mar., 11, 18 Apr.), and who acted as a teller on 5 Jan. 1702 to hear the Maidstone election petition at the bar of the House, on 3 Feb. to proceed with those petitions on Irish forfeitures which had already been received before admitting others, on 10 Feb. to recommit the abjuration bill, on 8 Mar. to prepare an address of condolence on the death of King William and congratulation on the accession of Queen Anne, on 17 Apr. in a division on an amendment to the land tax bill to determine the price at which the East India Company would supply saltpetre to the crown, and on 28 Apr. in a division on a proposed bill to relieve Ignatius Gould from the effects of the Irish forfeitures legislation.[8]

In the aftermath of his father's death, Foley seems to have been drawn under the wing of Robert Harley, who indeed assumed an avuncular attitude towards the Foley family in general. Sticking by Harley and the ministry after the dismissal of the High Tories in 1703–4, Foley was forecast at the beginning of the 1704–5 session as a probable opponent of the Tack, and did not vote for it on 28 Nov. 1704. He had not been particularly active during this Parliament: the reporting of a private bill on 25 Jan. 1704, and two tellerships the following month, to commit the poor law reform bill (21 Feb.) and against a rider to a bill concerning the Irish forfeitures (26 Feb.), comprised the sum total of significant parliamentary activity which could possibly be credited to him. But after the 1705 general election he may well have become more active. He voted on 25 Oct. 1705 for the Court candidate as Speaker. A 'Mr Foley' acted as a teller on 19 Dec., on the Court side, in favour of a motion to bring in candles, in order that the land tax bill might be passed, and, before being granted three weeks' leave of absence on 21 Dec., made several contributions to debates. On 4 Dec. a Foley was one of several Court Tories to oppose the 'Hanover motion', arguing that the 'future happiness' of the country depended on the Hanoverian succession, that this motion would be 'no inducement to the Scots to settle the succ[ession]', and that it would be best to 'waive the question, leave it to the Qu[een]'. Another such intervention took place four days later, on the question of whether to agree with the Lords' resolution against those who went about declaring the Church to be in danger under the Queen's administration. Although Foley announced that he 'w[oul]d hang no man, but keep wood for building ships', he added that he himself believed that 'all the Qu[een]'s ministers' were 'for the Church' and that he disapproved of 'pamphlets from the pulpit'.

Finally, at the second reading of the regency bill on 19 Dec., a Foley, having argued that the measure was 'by the clamours a bad bill but necessary', led the hue and cry after the High Tory Charles Caesar* for his reference to Lord Treasurer Godolphin's (Sidney†) supposed previous correspondence with St. Germain, urging that a motion of censure be passed. Foley may have voted with the Court in the proceedings on 18 Feb. over the 'place clause' in the regency bill, and served as a teller on 1 Mar. in favour of an alteration to the bill for the amendment of the law. In the following session he was given indefinite leave of absence on 13 Jan. 1707 to go to Bath to recover his health.[9]

Classed as a Tory in two lists in 1708, before and after the general election that year, Foley overcame 'great' opposition at Hereford in 1708, from the higher Tories – 'the Jacobites', as he himself put it – as well as the Whigs. He also followed his mentor Robert Harley in making his peace with his erstwhile Tory colleagues in the House. In a debate on supply on 17 Dec. he moved an opposition amendment to the vote of funds to augment the land forces, to stipulate that 'the same proportion be furnished by the States [General]', and 'exerted himself very much' over the disputed election for Abingdon, acting as a teller for (Sir) Simon Harcourt I* at the report on 18 Jan. 1709. Of course, Harcourt too was closely associated with Harley, but Foley may well have been a teller in other divisions of a partisan nature which did not involve Harleyites and former Court Tories: on 24 Nov. 1708, against the Whig William Farrer being chosen as the chairman of the committee of privileges and elections; and on further election cases, on 2 and 11 Dec. over the Reading election, and on 15 Jan. 1709 over the dispute at Bramber. Another possible tellership was that of 9 Mar., to adjourn for a month the committee of the whole House on the tobacco trade bill. Possibly the Foley who on 8 Dec. 1709 told on the Tory side in a division on the Cirencester election, and on 4 Feb. 1710 for a Tory motion that the Commons attend the trial of Dr Sacheverell as a committee of the whole, he appeared on some division lists on the Sacheverell case as having voted for the impeachment and on others as having voted against it. This may be the reason that he was suspected by local Tories as being only lukewarm in his support for the doctor. At one point during the aftermath of the trial it was rumoured that he disapproved of Hereford corporation's enthusiastically pro-Sacheverell address and had decided to make some excuse rather than remain in London to present it to the Queen. There were fears that 'his Staffordshire uncle [Philip Foley*] had turned him'. These stories proved unfounded, and did not interfere with his prospects for re-election in 1710, but whatever his public protestations it is clear from his private correspondence that he shared Robert Harley's suspicion of the 'hot' men in both parties. During the summer he praised Harley's political initiatives as a 'bold attack, which I believe by what I find in the country is an equal grief to the extremes of Low Church and Jacobite'.[10]

Returned again without serious opposition in 1710, Foley was classed as a Tory in the 'Hanover list', and was included in the lists of 'Tory patriots' and 'worthy patriots' who in the first session of this Parliament respectively opposed the continuance of the war and exposed the mismanagements of the old ministry. His membership of the October Club was presumably a piece of infiltration on behalf of the Court. It is probable that he was the Foley who reported on 11 Feb. 1711 from the committee on the public debts. He may also have been the 'Mr Foley' who was described by Bishop Nicolson of Carlisle as one of the bishop's 'good friends in the House of Commons' over the affair of the Carlisle election. By late May, however, Foley had left Parliament for the country. Sources for the following session show him to have been a prominent Court spokesman in the House from that point onwards. He opposed the 'No Peace without Spain' motion of 7 Dec. 1711 and spoke in favour of the proposed censure of the Duke of Marlborough (John Churchill†) on 25 Jan. 1712. Having on 11 Apr. 1712 seconded Henry Campion's motion of censure against the publisher of the *Daily Courant* for printing the Dutch memorial, he intervened in a later debate on the issue to call for an exceptional punishment. On 13 Apr. he rose on behalf of the ministry to move for a call of the House on 1 May, on the grounds that ministers had weighty matters to put before Parliament, hinting at a statement about the peace negotiations. With other Court Tories, he spoke against the tack of the land grants resumption clause to the lottery bill, despite the fact that in theory he still belonged to the October Club, who were pushing the measure hard. As a reward for his efforts, and in recognition of his status, he received in July 1712 a place at the Board of Trade, with a salary of £1,000 p.a. At this stage he was probably no longer obliged to abstain from office for the purpose of maintaining connexions with the October Club, since his recent speeches in the House would have severed these links in any case. Acceptance of a place, however, did mean the risk of seeking re-election to the House, and at Hereford Foley had to surmount antagonism from disgruntled electors who regarded him as having sold out. The tanners, glovers and shoemakers resented his having supported the imposition of the leather duty, while 'some of the best of the town bore that way', too, 'by his declaring all along he would not accept of a place and that he heed[ed] no other prospect but to serve his country. Now by serving himself in getting a place they say he is not the man they took him to be.' Fortunately for Foley, this opposition fizzled out before the poll.[11]

Even before the next session began Foley had been promised rapid promotion to the post of joint auditor of the imprests, held under a more secure tenure, during good behaviour. A warrant for the appointment was prepared in January 1713, although it was not completed until the following August, presumably to avoid the necessity of another awkward by-election. He spoke on 2 Apr. in support of the bill for the regulation of the press, and on 26 June intervened decisively to defeat a Whig amendment to the bill of commerce, a measure he had voted for in the critical division some eight days previously. He was to the forefront for the Court party on 1 July when the Whig James Stanhope moved that the House concur with the Lords' address for the removal of the Pretender from Lorraine. In order to protect the ministry's reputation, Foley made a point of seconding this motion. He was then named to the committee to prepare the Commons' address, and was even put forward to be its chairman, but was defeated by Stanhope on a division. He was probably the Foley who reported on a private bill on 13 June, and acted as a teller on 28 May in favour of continuing the Quaker Relief Acts, and on 30 May against a Whig motion to publish the bill of commerce.[12]

In 1714 Foley took a leading part in the Tory campaign to secure the expulsion from the House of Richard Steele. On 12 Mar. he made the original complaint against Steele, and together with his friend and colleague as auditor, Edward Harley, 'severely animadverted upon the rancour and seditious spirit conspicuous' in the particular writings cited. Steele, in requesting more time to prepare his defence than the House originally allowed him, replied to the two auditors with a neat stroke of ridicule. Since his accusers were both 'known to be rigid Presbyterians', Steele adopted a 'sanctified countenance' and 'canting tone' and pointed out that unless the date for the motion for expulsion was postponed he would be obliged to break the sabbath in drawing up his answers to the charges. When the debate finally took place, on 18 Mar., Foley began by moving that Steele be required to state whether he acknowledged the writings in question to be his, which he duly did. He then proposed that Steele be obliged to withdraw, which went to another vote, before he himself opened the debate proper, though not with the tirade that had been expected. Instead, he contented himself with saying that

> without amusing the House with long speeches, it was plain that the writings that had been complained of were seditious and scandalous, injurious to her Majesty's government, the Church and the universities, and moved that the question should be put thereupon.

Afterwards Steele vented his spleen on both Foley and Harley in a satire in a number of *The Lover*. Foley was lampooned in the character of 'Peter Brickdust', known as 'the accuser' because of 'his natural propensity to think the worst of every man'. His 'countenance', wrote Steele, 'discovers him a creature of small prey; it is the mixture of the face of a cat, and that of an owl. He has the spiteful eagerness of the former, blended with the stupid gravity of the latter.' More tellingly, Steele commented on the relationship between Foley and Robert Harley, now Lord Treasurer Oxford. Though 'born to a better fortune' than Oxford, Foley was content to be his 'utter slave'. Foley's subsequent speeches certainly demonstrate this close connexion with the lord treasurer. He spoke for the Court on 22 Apr., on the address of thanks for the treaties of peace and commerce with France and Spain, when he answered the 'most material objections to the treaties of commerce' raised by opposition Members, and in the debate of 5 June on paying arrears to the Hanoverian troops he acted even more clearly as an agent of Lord Oxford. In conjunction with Edward Harley he opposed High Tory attempts to withhold payment by reminding those present of their oaths of abjuration (thus insinuating that a refusal to pay the Hanoverians was tantamount to a declaration for the Pretender), and also by defending the conduct of the troops themselves in 1712 in terms which implied some unease at the behaviour of their general, the Duke of Ormond. These remarks prompted a Whig to observe that the 'courtiers' appeared to be falling out among themselves. It is possible that Foley served as a teller on 30 June against a motion put forward by some Scottish Members to set a day for the committee of the whole on the Scottish militia bill. Foley was classed as a Tory in the Worsley list, and in two lists of the Members re-elected in 1715.[13]

'The little captain of Stoke', as Dr William Stratford nicknamed him, retained his office after the Hanoverian succession only because of the terms under which it had been granted. He voted consistently with the opposition. In 1719 he suffered the indignity of dismissal from the Herefordshire commission of the peace. His name does not appear, however, in any lists of sympathizers compiled for the Jacobite court, and no evidence has been cited which would implicate him in Jacobite conspiracy. In a debate on the treaty of Hanover in 1726 he confined his remarks to praise of Lord Oxford's ministry. Foley died at Bath, on 10 Dec. 1737. His son, Thomas Foley†, had already followed in his footsteps as Tory Member for Hereford.[14]

[1] *Vis. Worcs.* ed. Metcalfe, 47; *Mar. Lic. Vicar-Gen.* (Harl. Soc. xxi), 68; D. R. Lacey, *Dissent and Parlty. Pol. 1661–89*, pp. 395, 398; W. R. Urwick, *Nonconformity in Worcester*, 91; *DNB* (Oldfield, Joshua); A. G. Matthews, *Calamy Revised*, 373. [2] *Birmingham Univ. Hist. Jnl.* i. 122. [3] Pittis, *Present Parl.* 349; E. G. W. Bill, *Queen Anne Churches*, p. xxiii. [4] Boyer, *Pol. State*, v. 389; *Cal. Treas. Bks.* xxviii. 318; *Cal. Treas. Bks. and Pprs. 1735–8*, p. 620. [5] Add. 70225, Paul Foley I to Robert Harley, 9 July 1686; 70014, f. 296; 70015, ff. 72–73, 85; 70226, Foley to Robert Harley, 23 May, 9 June 1691; 70234, Sir Edward Harley to same, 27 May 1691; *HMC Portland*, iii. 478. [6] Add. 70016, f. 7; 70017, ff. 5, 22; 70126, Foley to Sir Edward Harley, 10 Jan. 1692[–3]; *Luttrell Diary*, 433; *CSP Dom.* 1694–5, p. 153; 1696, p. 488. [7] Bath mss at Longleat House, Thynne pprs. 25, f. 15; Add. 70018, ff. 50, 62, 82; 17677 SS, ff. 115, 219–20; *HMC Kenyon*, 398–9; Oldmixon, *Hist. Eng.* (1735), p. 152; *CSP Dom.* 1698, p. 184; H. Horwitz, *Parl. and Pol. Wm. III*, 232. [8] Add. 70305, Foley's election case [1698]; 70114, Paul Foley I to Robert Harley, 30 Oct. 1699; 70226, Foley to same, 10 Apr., 15 May, 20 Sept. 1700; *An Answer to the Black-List: Or, the Vine-Tavern Queries* (1701), p. 4. [9] *Cam. Misc.* xxiii. 41, 47, 50–51, 53. [10] *HMC Portland*, iv. 485–8, 518; Add. 70254, Robert Harley to Price, 27 May 1708; 70226, Foley to Robert Harley, 12 Aug. 1710; *Marlborough–Godolphin Corresp.* 1179; Speck thesis, 73; Huntington Lib. Stowe mss 58(2), p. 219; 58(6), pp. 35–36. [11] *Nicolson Diaries* ed. Jones and Holmes, 561; Add. 70226, Foley to Robert Harley, 29 May 1711; 17677 FFF, f. 159; NSA, Kreienberg despatches 7 Dec. 1711, 25 Jan., 11, 15 Apr., 9 May 1712; Oldmixon, 488; Centre Kentish Stud. Stanhope mss U1590/C9/31, Sir John Cropley, 2nd Bt.*, to James Stanhope*, 13 Apr. [1712]; Boyer, iii. 119; *Cal. Treas. Bks.* xxvi. 352; Stowe mss 58(12), pp. 131, 245. [12] *Cal. Treas. Bks.* xxviii. 89, 318; Boyer, vi. 123; Kreienberg despatches 21 Apr., 26 June, 3 July 1713; Add. 17677 GGG, ff. 258–9. [13] Chandler, v. 64, 67, 71, 142; Boyer, vii. 247, 256, 532; Cobbett, *Parlty. Hist.* vi. 1267–8, 1288, 1303; Kreienberg despatches 12, 16, 19 Mar. 1714; Add. 17677 GGG, f. 118; *Steele's Periodical Journalism* ed. Blanchard, 41; *Letters of Thomas Burnet to George Duckett* ed. Nichol Smith, 64; D. Szechi, *Jacobitism and Tory Pol.* 173–4. [14] *HMC Portland*, vii. 216; L. K. J. Glassey, *Appt. JPs*, 257; Nash, *Worcs.* ii. 464.

D. W. H.

FOLEY, Thomas III (1673–1733), of Witley Court, Great Witley, Worcs.

STAFFORD   21 Nov. 1694–1 Jan. 1712

b. 8 Nov. 1673, 1st s. of Thomas Foley I*, and bro. of Edward Foley* and Richard Foley*. *educ*. Sheriffhales acad. (John Woodhouse) 1689; Utrecht 1689–by 1693; L. Inn 1695. *m*. 18 June 1702, Mary (*d*. 1735), da. and h. of Thomas Strode (*d*.1698), serjeant-at-law, of Lincoln's Inn and Beaminster, Dorset, 4s. (3 *d.v.p.*) 3da. *d.v.p. suc*. fa. 1701; *cr*. Baron Foley of Kidderminster 1 Jan. 1712.[1]

Freeman, Stafford 1694, Bewdley 1706, Worcester 1721.[2]
Commr. for taking subscriptions to land bank 1696.[3]
FRS 1696.[4]

Brought up in a milieu of conforming, 'middle-way' Presbyterianism, Foley became in due course a strong Tory, a transformation prefigured in his schoolboy correspondence. One plaintive letter to his father shows him chafing against the narrowness of his Puritan education. Spurred by an exaggerated opinion of his own talents, he was anxious to polish his conversational skill, 'one of my greatest accomplishments', in the cosmopolitan atmosphere of London. Instead, his father despatched him to university at Utrecht, where, among others, he made the acquaintance of Edmund Calamy, the future Nonconformist minister and historian of Dissent. He pursued his studies with a view to some public career, writing in November 1690 to his brother-in-law, Robert Harley*, whose advice concerning classical authors and other elements in the curriculum he was accustomed to seek: 'I suppose you are not ignorant of the advantages I have here of fitting myself to be serviceable to my country.' But, like Harley, he also took a serious, if amateur, interest in matters antiquarian and scholarly. Elected a fellow of the Royal Society after his return to England, he played an active part in the society's business and was responsible for introducing Harley into its ranks. In later life he was known as a book-collector.[5]

Foley was returned at Stafford in a by-election in 1694 'by his uncle Mr Ph[ilip] F[oley's*] interest', after spending 'time and money' in a turbulent, sometimes physically violent, contest against the opposition of 'the gentlemen in general'. As there were four other Foleys in the Commons, two of them (his father and cousin) also named Thomas, it is for the most part impossible to specify his parliamentary activity. Nothing can with certainty be ascribed to him until after the 1695 general election, in which he was re-elected for Stafford, probably without a contest despite some preliminary opposition. He was classed as likely to oppose the Court in a forecast for the division on the proposed council of trade on 31 Jan. 1696, and in the debate that day joined the other Foleys in opposition to the prescription of an abjuration oath for the members of the council. He signed the Association promptly, but voted in March against fixing the price of guineas at 22s., and in the following November against the attainder of Sir John Fenwick†, dividing from his father on the latter occasion. Because of his family's interest in the borough of Droitwich, it is highly probable that he was the 'Mr Foley, jnr.' who on 25 Jan. 1698 presented a bill to oblige all retailers of salt to sell by weight. The threat of opposition to his own re-election and a challenge to his father's position as knight of the shire in Worcestershire led to his being put up at Droitwich in 1698 as well as in Stafford, as an insurance policy for both constituencies. After he and his uncle Philip had defeated their opponents in Stafford, he was able to relinquish the seat at Droitwich, where he had been returned unopposed, and allow his father in. But although father and son were co-operating closely in their electoral manoeuvring, they seem to have been voting on opposite sides in the House, at least in the preceding session. A comparative analysis of the old and new Parliaments, drawn up in about September 1698, classed Foley as a supporter of the Country party and his father as a supporter of the Court. According to an anonymous letter, clearly from a Whig sympathizer, which appears to have been sent to a member of the corporation at Stafford, Foley was at this time 'as violent an actor against the government as any in the House of Commons' and was 'as much [?ruled] by the angry men as 'tis possible to be imagined'. It was not that he was a Jacobite, 'though he ever votes with the rankest of them'; instead, the writer believed that father and son divided their political allegiances because they were 'resolved their new-got wealth shall commit no treason'. Whatever his motive for supporting the Country party, Foley was forecast as likely to oppose the standing army in the 1698–9 session. He did contribute an elliptically reported speech to the debate of 4 Jan. 1699 on a motion to instruct the committee on the disbanding bill. On the other hand, it was later alleged that he was responsible for his family's collective leniency towards Lord Orford (Edward Russell*) in the naval debates of that session, because he was 'courting . . . Lord Orford's niece'. In April 1700 he was directed by the 'great men' of his party to press his uncle Philip to come up to London to oppose the Lords' amendments to the land tax and Irish forfeitures resumption bill.[6]

By this time Foley was well on the way to becoming a typical Tory squire. He wrote from Witley in September of the pleasures of 'the noble sport of fox-hunting in the open country about Stamford and Shelsley', and he was now on the best of terms with local High Churchmen of the kidney of Sir John Pakington, 4th Bt.*, who promised him 'underhand support' if he would stand for the county in the January 1701 general election. Foley preferred, however, to rely on his uncle's interest at Stafford, reinforced by the personal influence he himself had accumulated through serving the town as a Member and through joining his uncle in public benefactions there. Although a strong Tory, he was also loyal to his brother-in-law Harley, later the godfather of one of his sons, and this loyalty seems if anything to have grown stronger rather than weaker after the death of Foley's father in February 1701. He was now the master of a considerable fortune, to be augmented the following year by marriage to an heiress worth some £30,000. But he was not a strong character, henpecked at home by his wife, and seems to have been content to follow his eminent brother-in-law, whose attitude towards him was rather more avuncular than fraternal. Included on a list of those MPs likely to support the Court in February 1701 over the 'Great Mortgage', Foley was blacklisted as having voted against making preparations for war against France. When his father's old borough of Droitwich asked him in November 1701 to prepare an address for them to send up to the King, he turned to Harley for advice: 'having seen none lately but the London one (which I take to be but indifferently drawn) let me beg the favour of you to send one that you think will be proper for me to present'. In the second general election of that year his intervention was said to have been crucial in ensuring Pakington's return for Worcestershire. Harley classed Foley as a Tory in a list of the new Parliament, and he voted on 26 Feb. in favour of the motion vindicating the Commons' proceedings in the impeachments of the four Whig lords. Safely re-elected in 1702, he transmitted to his brother-in-law in September a recommendation from Pakington for the appointment of Dr Sacheverell as Speaker's chaplain. Although he was himself a 'stranger' to the doctor, he was nevertheless prepared to endorse any nomination from such a source.[7]

Foley's appearance in a parliamentary forecast of October 1704 as a probable opponent of the Tack is the final indication that he was aligning himself with the Court Tories rather than with high-flyers like Pakington. The preceding August he had congratulated Sir Edward Seymour, 4th Bt.*, on recovery from illness, so was still at that time on friendly terms with leading High Tories. But he did not vote for the Tack on 28 Nov. In March 1705 his name had cropped up in reports of an intended multiple creation of Court peers, a foretaste of what was to come. Having been re-elected in 1705, at which time he was classed as 'No Church' in an analysis of the new Parliament, he voted on 25 Oct. for the Court candidate as Speaker, and either he or his cousin and namesake was listed on the Court side of the division of 18 Feb. 1706 in the proceedings on the 'place clause' of the regency bill. He may have spoken in an earlier debate arising from this bill, on 19 Dec. 1705, when the House was deciding what action to take against the Tory Charles Caesar for innuendoes in a speech of his concerning the Jacobite correspondence of Lord Treasurer Godolphin (Sidney[†]). While the Foley who first called Caesar to account for his words is perhaps more likely to have been Thomas Foley II, the less violent remarks attributed to a Foley later on seem consonant with what we know of this Member's attitudes. Favouring 'moderation in penalties and inflictions', the speaker argued against sending Caesar to the Tower and proposed only 'a reprimand'. Because of a Worcestershire connexion, two tellerships in this session (16, 23 Feb. 1706) may be ascribed to Foley, both on the Tory side on the Bewdley election case, in which his brother-in-law Salwey Winnington* was a principal. The changing position of the Harleyite faction in the ministerial reconstruction of 1708 probably explains Foley's inclusion first as a Whig and then as a Tory in two parliamentary lists that year, before and after the general election, at which he was returned once more. He was probably a teller in a division on 8 Feb. 1709 on another election dispute at Bewdley, again taking the Tory side. His sympathy for Dr Sacheverell in 1710 is evident both from his vote against the doctor's impeachment and his account of the reception given Sacheverell in Worcestershire during the subsequent 'progress'.[8]

Foley faced a contest at Stafford in the 1710 election, but comfortably survived the challenge, topping the poll. He was marked as a Tory in the 'Hanover list', and was subsequently included among the 'worthy patriots' who in the first session of the new Parliament exposed the mismanagements of the previous ministry. In all probability he was the 'Mr Foley' who acted as a teller on 2 Dec. 1710 in favour of referring to the committee of privileges a petition against the election of his colleague at Stafford. He seems to have been especially close to Harley at this time. Swift's journal contains a note of a dinner, attended by Harley, in April 1711, at which Foley raised the question of a recent indiscretion perpetrated by Harley's junior colleague and rival, Henry St. John II*. His loyalty, and his wealth, made him an obvious candidate for inclusion among Harley's 'dozen' new peers created at a stroke in January 1712 to defeat Whig opposition in the Upper House to the ministry's peace policy. There the new Lord Foley proved a reliable supporter of his brother-in-law's administration: his opposition to the schism bill in 1714, in which he separated once more from his High Tory friends, may have been as much an act of loyalty to Harley (whose attitude to the bill was hostile) as a remembrance of his own Nonconformist education. After 1714 he joined other Harleyites, and

Tories in general, in opposition to the Whig regime. Despite losing heavily in the South Sea Bubble, he remained a very wealthy, and, for that reason, moderately influential, figure in Tory circles. Hearne described him as 'a brave, honest, generous man'. Foley died on 22 Jan. 1733, and was buried at Witley, in the church he had been responsible for rebuilding.[9]

[1] Nash, *Worcs.* ii. 464, 468; MI, Great Witley par. ch.; Add. 70225, Foley to Thomas Foley I, 23 Feb. 1688–9, same to Robert Harley, 26 Dec. 1689; *CSP Dom.* 1689–90, p. 328; Calamy, *Life,* i. 188–9; *HMC Portland,* iii. 482; Hereford and Worcester RO (Hereford), Foley mss, Paul Foley I* to Philip Foley, 20 Mar. 1692[–3]; *Post Boy,* 18–20 June 1702; Hutchins, *Dorset,* ii. 130, 137; H. W. Woolrych, *Lives of Eminent Serjeants,* i. 440–6. [2] Staffs. RO, D1323/A/1/2, Stafford corp. bk. p. 37; *Birmingham Univ. Hist. Jnl.* i. 125; W. R. Williams, *Parl. Hist. Worcs.* 129. [3] *CJ,* xii. 509. [4] *Rec. R. Soc.* (1940), p. 387. [5] Add. 70225, Foley to Thomas Foley I, 23 Feb. 1688–9, same to Robert Harley, 1 May, 26 Dec. 1689, 6 Nov. 1690; *HMC Portland,* iii. 482; M. Hunter, *R. Soc. and Fellows,* 149; *Swift Corresp.* ed. Williams, iii. 440. [6] Add. 70114, Paul Foley I to Robert Harley, 29 Sept. 1694; 70017, f. 321; 70227, Foley to Robert Harley, 25 Oct. 1695; *HMC Portland,* iii. 558; *HMC Kenyon,* 398–9; *Shrewsbury Corresp.* 541; Foley mss, Stafford poll 1698; unsigned letter, n.d.; Foley to Philip Foley, 6 Apr. 1700; *Cam. Misc.* xxix. 381. [7] Add. 70225, Foley to Robert Harley, 12 Sept. 1700, 23 Aug. 1701, Philip Foley to same, 18 Dec. 1700; 70227, Foley to same, 10 Oct. 1701; *HMC Portland,* iii. 639; iv. 26, 45; vii. 280, 450; *VCH Staffs.* vi. 266; Luttrell, *Brief Relation,* iii. 467, 481; iv. 695; v. 185; Foley mss, R. Baker to Philip Foley, 28 Nov. 1701. [8] *HMC Portland,* iv. 108, 550; Folger Shakespeare Lib. Newdigate newsletter 13 Mar. 1705; *Cam. Misc.* xxiii. 50–51, 53–54, 56. [9] *Swift Stella* ed. Davis, i. 253; G. Holmes, *Pol. in Age of Anne,* 428; *HMC Portland,* v. 481; vii. 280–1; L. Colley, *In Defiance of Oligarchy,* 63; Hearne Colls. xi. 154; Nash, 466, 468.

D. W. H.

FOOTE, Francis (c.1681–1730), of Veryan, Cornw. and Gray's Inn, London.

BOSSINEY 1708–1710

b. c.1681, 1st s. of John Foote of Veryan. *educ.* Pembroke, Camb. adm. 7 Jan. 1698, aged 16, BA 1701–2, MA 1714; G. Inn 1713, called 1714. *m.* bef. 1715, Mary, da. and h. of Benjamin Hatley of Cambs. and Beds., 3s. 1da. *suc.* fa. 1702.[1]

Commr. for managing lottery 1711–?12.[2]

Foote's father had been steward of various hundred courts in the duchy of Cornwall, and he himself was a practising lawyer. Returned for Bossiney in 1708, he was appointed, on 29 Jan. 1709, to draft a bill to standardize English and Scottish treason laws, and on 1 Feb. told against bringing in candles in order to continue hearing the Newcastle-under-Lyme election case. This tellership appears to have been an attempt to prevent the House from proceeding further against a Tory election agent, but in 1709 Foote supported the naturalization of the Palatines and the following year he voted for the impeachment of Dr Sacheverell.

Foote did not stand at the 1710 election, and his behaviour in the following two years suggests that he prudently tempered his previous Whig sympathies. In July 1711 he wrote to the Earl of Oxford (Robert Harley*) to thank him for the place he had been given managing the lottery, an office he received following the recommendation of George Granville*. This preferment did not satisfy Foote's ambitions. In the summer of 1711 Sir William Trumbull* expressed a willingness to resign his place of clerk of the signet to Foote, a suggestion put to the Queen by Henry St. John II*. Though the application was unsuccessful Foote pressed for promotion in the lottery or appointment to either the stamp office or victualling commission, citing Robert Benson* and Edward Harley* as men who would testify to his good character. Such applications proved unsuccessful. Foote entered Gray's Inn in 1713 and the following year was called to the bench, 'having taken the degree of Master of Arts in the University of Cambridge and being of more than doctor of civil laws standing there', an entry that may suggest that Foote was an established civil lawyer, though such an intimation cannot be confirmed. Little more is known of Foote before his death on 27 June 1730.[3]

[1] Burke, *Commoners,* i. 372; Berry, *Kent Gens.* 26; *Cal. Treas. Bks.* xvii. 141. [2] Add. 70155, list of lottery commrs. [3] *Cal. Treas. Bks.* xi. 426; Add. 70197, Foote to [Oxford], 21 July 1711, 10 Jan. 1711–12, 18 Apr. 1712; SP 34/16, f. 200; *Pens. Bk. G. Inn,* ii. 160–1; *Hist. Reg. Chron.* 1730, p. 48.

E. C.

FOOTE, Samuel (c.1625–91), of Peter Street, Tiverton, Devon.

TIVERTON 21 Nov. 1673–1681 (Mar.)
1689–26 Mar. 1691

b. c.1625, 1st s. of John Foote of Taunton, Som. *m.* (1) 1657, Mary Keate (*d.* 1678), 4da.; (2) Martha (*d.* aft. 1691), da. of Thomas Mompesson of North Brewham, Som., 1s. *suc.* fa. ?1628.[1]

Alderman, Tiverton 1655–Jan. 1688, Oct. 1688–*d.*, mayor ?1662–3; commr. for recusants, Devon 1675.[2]

?Gent. privy chamber 1671.[3]

Foote was one of the principal merchants in Tiverton, engaged among other things in exporting cloth to Holland and northern Europe. Under the Protectorate he had belonged to an Independent congregation, but quickly conformed at the Restoration, serving as a churchwarden in his local parish in 1662. Indeed, during his mayoralty he became a 'furious persecutor' of his former pastor. An opponent of the Court at the outset of his parliamentary career, and then an Exclusionist, he was even suspected in 1682 of peripheral involvement in armed conspiracy but trimmed his sails sufficiently to retain his place among the Tiverton aldermen until removed in January 1688 for opposing James II's ecclesiastical policy. Although it may well have been a namesake, a London merchant, who lent King William's government over £4,000 in 1689–90, Foote's own standing with the new regime was high enough to guarantee the appointment of his son-in-law John Cruwys as receiver-general for the county. In the Convention he was, not surprisingly, less active than he once had been, though he voted for the disabling clause in the corporations bill (and this despite his own inclusion in the Tiverton charter of 1684). Re-elected unopposed in 1690, he was listed as a Whig by Lord Carmarthen (Sir Thomas Osborne†) in March 1690, and as a supporter of the Country party by Robert Harley* early in the following year. Foote died intestate on 26 Mar. 1691, aged 66, and was buried at Tiverton. His son's inheritance included landed property worth over £500 p.a. and in all probability a considerable personalty, for Foote had already been able to provide a portion of £1,500 for the daughter who had married Cruwys. The estate did not remain intact for long, however, for when his son died childless in 1696 the property was divided among the daughters, another of whom had married Robert Burridge*.[4]

[1] *Trans. Devon Assoc.* lxviii. 326; W. Harding, *Hist. Tiverton*, i. 78; iii. 56, 58; iv. 17; *Taunton Wills* (Index Lib. xlv), 199. [2] M. Dunsford, *Hist. Mems. Tiverton*, 372, 456; *Cal. Treas. Bks.* iv. 695. [3] N. Carlisle, *Privy Chamber*, 189. [4] W. B. Stephens, *17th-Cent. Exeter*, 158–9; *Cal. Treas. Bks.* ix. 130, 508, 568, 1971, 1973, 1979, 1987, 1995, 2004; Dunsford, 316, 372, 443; *Vis. Eng. and Wales Notes* ed. Crisp, vii. 11; *Devon and Cornw. N. and Q.* xviii. 259.

E. C./D. W. H.

FORBES, John (c.1673–1734), of Culloden, Inverness.

NAIRNSHIRE	1713–1715
INVERNESS-SHIRE	1715–1722
NAIRNSHIRE	1722–1727

b. c.1673, 1st s. of Duncan Forbes, MP [S], of Culloden by Mary, da. of Sir Robert Innes, 2nd Bt., MP [S], of Innes, Elgin; bro. of Duncan Forbes†, ld. adv. [S] 1725–37 and ld. pres. ct. of session [S] 1737–47. *educ.* Inverness R. Acad.; privately in Edinburgh 1692; travelled abroad (Low Countries) 1692–c.1693. *m.* c.June 1699, Jean, da. of Sir Robert Gordon, 2nd Bt., of Gordonstoun, Elgin, MP [S], 1s. *d.v.p.* other ch. *d.v.p. suc.* fa. 1704.[1]

Commr. justiciary for Highlands [S] 1701, 1702, Equivalent 1716–17 [S].[2]

MP [S] Nairnshire 1704–7.

Councillor, Inverness 1716, provost 1716–17, 1721; commr. to oversee elections of council at Elgin 1716; visitor, Aberdeen Univ. 1716–17.[3]

'Bumper John' (so called from his enduring belief that 'another bumper' would cure all ills) was something of an oddity in a line of shrewd merchant-lairds and sharp lawyers, whose rise to local and national eminence provoked the envious to disparage them unfairly as a 'mushroom' interest, 'that no man in his senses can call a family'. Although the founder of their fortunes, the Member's great-grandfather, had made his money in trade in Inverness, their descent was in fact from a younger son of the laird of Tolquhon. He and his successors had offset their stiff Presbyterianism with sufficient political skill to bring the family through the trials of Charles II's reign and to recover the serious losses sustained by the estate at the hands of Highland Jacobites during the Revolution, a sum estimated by the Scottish parliament in 1695 at over £46,000 Scots.[4]

Forbes' father, Duncan, had appeared early for the Prince of Orange in 1689 and was active in the convention of estates, where he followed his political mentor Sir Patrick Hume (later 1st Earl of Marchmont), first into the 'Club' opposition and then to the 'Presbyterian' Court party of Lord Melville and Secretary James Johnston*. In return he received a parliamentary grant of a farm of the excise on his lands at Ferintosh in Ross-shire, originally passed in 1690 and confirmed by another act in 1695. In effect, this exempted spirits produced there from any liability for duty beyond the 400 merks p.a. required for the farm, and the Ferintosh distillery became one of the major sources of income for the estate. Following Johnston's dismissal Duncan Forbes moved hesitantly back towards opposition, but remained influential enough to be courted by Lord Seafield in 1701–2, possibly with the assistance of Argyll, and attended the 'rump' parliament alongside other courtiers after Queen Anne's accession, a change of direction which doubtless helped preserve his excise exemption when neighbouring landowners petitioned the parliament against it in 1703: a new act brought in some restrictions but left much of the profit intact.[5]

John Forbes, whose fondness for the bottle was evident in his youth, sadly disappointed his godly parents. Beyond school his education was haphazard and profitless. Having 'shirked' his studies in Edinburgh he was sent to Holland, though without a settled object in view; only, as his father put it, 'to satisfy your own curiosity'. He spent money but read little, and ignored paternal demands that he apply himself to improving pursuits such as fencing and dancing. When he eventually succeeded his father to the estate and to a seat in the Scottish parliament, he put aside political discretion and immediately associated himself with the opposition. Contrary to the view of the Jacobite agent Scot, who may have been thinking of his father in describing him in 1706 as acting 'commonly with the Court', he seems to have stayed with the Country party, at least over the Union, which he denounced as a road to 'inevitable ruin, with regard to Church and state'. It 'wreathes on our neck a perpetual yoke of prelacy and slavery, without any hope of recovery'. In the last session of the Scottish parliament he registered a long list of anti-Court votes. There were some signs of qualification, as for example when he supported the act for the security of religion, and abstained or absented himself over the article of Union settling the succession. Conceivably these may represent Presbyterian scruples; more likely, they were stirrings of more material concern, over the possibility that the Union might terminate his lucrative excise exemption. By October 1707 the issue was before the Treasury, and Forbes's petition for confirmation of the Scottish statutes was rejected on the basis of an opinion given against it by the English attorney-general (Sir) Simon Harcourt I*. He did not admit defeat and, fortified by a favourable report from the Scottish lord advocate, instructed his tenants to refuse payment pending the outcome of legal action. The difficulty of confuting the lord advocate's opinion in a Scottish court deterred the excise commissioners in Edinburgh from going further, and the case hung fire. Meanwhile, an anxious Forbes was exposed to Court blandishments: Lord Ross, for one, approached him in December 1707 with offers of help for his petition to the Treasury and in finding him a seat at the forthcoming general election.[6]

Forbes did not stand in 1708, but his subsequent manoeuvring indicates that he was now determined to add to his stock of political influence by securing a place in the Commons. The disputed election for Ross-shire seemed to offer the best opportunity. The sitting Member, Hugh Rose II (brother-in-law to Forbes's own brother Duncan), had been returned for Nairnshire as well. If successful in retaining Ross-shire, he would probably have freed Nairn for a new election, and Forbes was considered the likeliest candidate: if the Ross-shire election was declared void, the by-election would occur there instead, and again Forbes's local connexions would give him a good chance. His behaviour at this time shows a hitherto unsuspected subtlety, as he reassured courtiers of his willingness to serve the ministry if returned, and determinedly avoided committing himself to any of the rival factions in the localities. Not that this craft availed him in the short term. He was not a candidate when the Ross-shire heritors proceeded to a by-election, nor indeed did he put up at the general election of 1710, for all the assurances he had received. But in 1713 he was at last returned, in succession to Rose as Member for Nairnshire. Lord Polwarth's list classified him as 'Hanoverian', that is, a Whig, and this was how he appeared after the parliamentary session, when English Whigs regarded him as a 'friend' and the compiler of the Worsley list marked him down as a Whig *tout court*. The recruitment of his family into the connexion of their traditional patrons, the house of Argyll, had certainly occurred by the end of the Parliament, and may well have preceded its opening. In the House itself Forbes made little or no impression, not being credited with either an intervention in debate or a significant appearance in the Journals. He was probably late in arriving, but stayed in London until shortly before the Queen's death, his main concern, as he reported to his wife, being to discover whether the electoral prince intended to come over to England in order to thwart what Forbes himself thought would be the inevitable Jacobite invasion. He was in Edinburgh for the proclamation of King George, which he duly subscribed.[7]

Forbes worked hard in the Whig interest in the 1715 election, in which he was chosen for his own county of Inverness, and played a part in the defence of the northern counties during the Fifteen, expending in all some £3,000 in the service of the crown, which was only partly recompensed by his brief tenure of a commissionership of the Equivalent. He remained a loyal Argathelian, though receiving little of the fruits of patronage and increasingly overshadowed by his brilliant brother. Drink took a firmer hold over him, and in 1721 his election as an elder of his local synod excited a protest on the grounds that he was 'a habitual neglecter of family worship' and 'a known drunkard'. To the end 'a friend to a cheerful glass', Forbes died at Edinburgh of 'a complaint in his bowels', 18 Dec. 1734, 'after a tedious illness'. His brother Duncan inherited an estate to which debts had been added but no property alienated.[8]

[1] *More Culloden Pprs.* ed. Warrand, i. 224–32, 259–60; ii. 30–31; *Scot. Hist. Soc.* xxxiv. 231. [2] *CSP Dom.* 1700–2, p. 339; 1702–3, p. 354. [3] *More Culloden Pprs.* ii. 145, 147–9; *Recs. of Elgin* (New Spalding Club), i. 396. [4] *More Culloden Pprs.* i. 4; iii. 100; *Culloden Pprs.* pp. iii–v, ix, xxiii; *Fam. of Innes* (Spalding Club), 191; W. Fraser, *Chiefs of Grant*, ii. 327–8; Ramsay of Ochtertyre, *Scotland and Scotsmen in 18th Cent.* i. 43; A. and H. Tayler, *House of Forbes*, 403–4; *APS*, vi(1), 55, 175, 203, 344, 381–2, 623, 789, 815; ix. 465; *Reg. PC Scotland*, 1684–5, p. 409; 1685–6, p. 498; 1691, p. 349. [5] *Culloden Pprs.* pp. vi–vii, 28–29; *APS*, ix. 9, 20, 51, 220, 458; xi. 64,

87; *Scot. Hist. Soc.* ser. 3, xlvii. 190, 229–30, 266; Fraser, *Melvilles*, 212, 214; *Leven and Melville Pprs.* (Bannatyne Club, lxxvii), 96–97, 103–4, 148, 402–4, 406–8; P. W. J. Riley, *King Wm. and Scot. Politicians*, 29, 57, 118, 171; *SHR*, xlv. 153; Tayler, 404; *Cal. Treas. Bks.* xxi. 460–2; *Cromartie Corresp.* i. 167. [6] *More Culloden Pprs.* i. 224–32; ii. 10–11, 28; info. from Dr P. W. J. Riley on members of Scot. parl.; *Crossrigg Diary*, 140; Boyer, *Anne Annals*, iii. app. 42; *Orig. Pprs.* ed. Macpherson, ii. 17; P. W. J. Riley, *Union*, 333; *Cal. Treas. Bks.* xxi. 460–2; xxii. 120; *Cal. Treas. Pprs.* 1708–14, pp. 1, 469; P. W. J. Riley, *Eng. Ministers and Scotland*, 72–73. [7] *More Culloden Pprs.* ii. 19–25, 37, 40; SRO, Mar. and Kellie mss GD124/15/920/3, Sir John Clerk to Mar, 25 Dec. 1708; NLS, ms 2964, ff. 126, 251; *Culloden Pprs.* pp. iv, 32; Boyer, *Pol. State*, viii. 124. [8] *Culloden Pprs.* pp. xii, xxiii, 33–34; *More Culloden Pprs.* i. 279–80; ii. 48–49, 51, 89; Riley, *Eng. Ministers*, 260, 263; *HMC Stuart*, i. 483; Wodrow, *Analecta*, iii. 301; *Scot. Rec. Soc.* xxxi. 19.

D. W. H.

FORESTER, Sir William (1655–1718), of Dothill Park, nr. Wellington, Salop.

MUCH WENLOCK   1679–1681 (Mar.), 1689–1715

b. 10 Dec. 1655, 2nd but 1st surv. s. of Francis Forester of Wellington by Lady Mary, da. of Richard Newport†, 1st Baron Newport, wid. of John Steventon of Dothill Park. *educ.* Trinity Coll. Camb. 1673, MA 1675. *m.* lic. 23 Apr. 1684, Lady Mary, da. of James Cecil†, 3rd Earl of Salisbury, 2s. 3da. *suc.* fa. 1684; kntd. c.20 Aug. 1689.[1]

Clerk of Bd. of Green Cloth 1689–1717.[2]
Commr. taking subscriptions to land bank 1696.[3]

Closely related to the Newports, the leading Whig family in Shropshire, Forester had been an active Whig conspirator against King James. Implicated in the Rye House Plot, and later, after Monmouth's rebellion, committed to the Tower for a spell on suspicion of 'dangerous and treasonable practices', he had by 1687 taken himself over to The Hague, where he acted as an intermediary between King James's enemies and the Prince of Orange. Having landed with William in November 1688, he was knighted the following year and given a place in the Household, which necessitated residing in Whitehall: he subsequently maintained a 'lodging' there throughout his official career.[4]

After the Revolution Forester was regularly returned for Much Wenlock, where he and the Welds of Willey Park, acting in alliance, enjoyed such influence that they were challenged only once in this period, and then unsuccessfully. He was classed as a Whig in Lord Carmarthen's (Sir Thomas Osborne†) list of March 1690, and as a Court supporter in Robert Harley's* list of April 1691. He also appeared in Grascome's list of 1693–5 as a supporter of the Court, and was repeatedly classed as a placeman. An active Member, he was useful to the administration, though never recorded as speaking. In April 1691, in his official capacity, he stiffly resisted complying with demands for papers from the commission of accounts. He was a teller on 17 Jan. 1693 against a motion that the House debate on the following Friday the report of the committee appointed to consider how the privilege of Members, in regard to suits at law, might be regulated; and again on 4 Feb., in favour of the adjournment of a debate on a report from ways and means. He served as a teller thrice more during the next session: on 28 Nov. 1693, on the Court side, against an amendment to the triennial bill, to provide regular sittings of Parliament; on 22 Jan. 1694, for a clause in the land tax bill; and on 28 Feb., in favour of a resolution from ways and means for collecting £600,000 over and above the land tax. On 13 Feb. 1695 he told in favour of placing a duty on leather, and in March reported and carried up a private bill on behalf of the Earl of Salisbury, his young nephew by marriage. That same year Forester and his wife were together granted a fee farm rent which had formerly belonged to her family, and which they afterwards sold to her sister-in-law, the dowager Countess of Salisbury, for £2,000. On 30 Apr. Hon. John Beaumont* drew to the attention of the Commons that 'upon a division . . . last night [possibly a division on the adjournment], he going out of the House, some words were said to him by Sir William Forester . . . fit for the House to take notice of'. No action having resulted from this complaint before the prorogation on 3 May, the two men shortly afterwards 'meeting accidentally and falling into a heat about the particular words said in the House, which one affirmed and the other denied', settled their dispute by means of a duel, in which Forester was disarmed.[5]

Early in the next Parliament, on 12 Dec. 1695, Forester was named to the committee to bring in a bill for regulating the coinage. He was forecast as likely to support the Court in the division of 31 Jan. 1696 on the proposed council of trade; readily signed the Association; voted in March for fixing the price of guineas at 22*s.*; and on 25 Nov. voted for the attainder of Sir John Fenwick†. Listed in about September 1698 as a Court placeman, he predictably voted on 18 Jan. 1699 against the disbanding bill. On 16 Apr. 1701 he told in favour of a Whig-inspired amendment to the address asking for the removal from office of Lords Portland, Somers, Orford and Halifax. The amendment pledged the Commons' support for the King, should he act to protect the peace of Europe and the interests and trade of England from the dangers posed 'by the present union of France and Spain'.

Forester was one of a number of Whigs listed by Lord Treasurer Godolphin (Sidney†) not long after Anne's accession as to be continued in office. A teller on 9 Dec. 1702 in favour of a motion to enable Thomas Mansel I* to propose the release from custody of one William Mott, detained in connexion with a disputed election for Colchester, he voted on 13 Feb. 1703 for agreeing with the Lords' amendments to the bill for enlarging the time for taking the oath of abjuration, and four days later was again a teller, against a clause in favour of Colonel Luke Lillingston, which was proposed to be added to the bill continuing the Act to appoint commissioners to state the army debts. Forester was commissioned in August 1703 to go to The Hague and wait on the Archduke Charles on the latter's journey to England, and remained as clerk of the Green Cloth in spite of rumours in April 1704 of his dismissal. Indeed, in the following October his daughter Mary was appointed a maid of honour to the Queen. Although he was forecast as a probable opponent of the Tack, and figured on Harley's lobbying list, he appears to have abstained, and was listed in 1705 as a 'Sneaker'.[6]

Having voted for the Court candidate in the election of a Speaker on 25 Oct. 1705, Forester supported the Court over the regency bill on 18 Feb. 1706, and was listed as a Whig in early 1708 and as a Court Whig in another list of 1708 with the returns added. On 28 Jan. 1709 he reported to a fellow Whig that he had been 'laid up of the gout, brought upon me by attending the House to turn out Sir Simon Harcourt [I]* longer than I was able, so you'll say I have suffered in a good cause'. In that year he also voted for the naturalization of the Palatines, and in 1710 for the impeachment of Dr Sacheverell. He felt himself obliged to put up for re-election in 1710 despite having 'grown ... infirm', in order to keep up his interest until his eldest son, William†, came of age and could take over; and out of loyalty to his party's cause, which he was also supporting in other constituencies. When teased about his motives by his partner, George Weld II*, he replied: 'I can assure you 'tis not to secure my place, but all that is dear to an Englishman that I desire to keep up my interest.' In his next letter he added:

> You need not have made the least excuse for what you said in a former letter relating to my place, for I took it only in the friendly sense you intended it, and though Cresswell [Richard*] talks of Lord B[radford (Hon. Richard Newport*)] and some others being out, he may find himself ... mistaken ... But I am not surprised at the rage and malice of that party, for what I did and ventured at the Revolution I find by yours is no more forgotten by some of my friends, than is forgiven by our enemies.

Forester was duly returned, together with Weld, and in the 'Hanover list' was described as a Whig. He retained his place under the ensuing Tory administration. Having been classed once more as a Whig in the Worsley list, and in a list comparing the Parliaments of 1713 and 1715, he decided not to stand for re-election after the Hanoverian succession, and his son William succeeded him as Member for Much Wenlock.[7]

Forester eventually retired from the Board of Green Cloth in April 1717, and was allowed, in consideration of his long service, 'to keep his lodging at Whitehall for the rest of his life'. He died the following year, leaving, besides his estates, stock in the Bank and the East India Company. He was buried at Wellington in Shropshire on 22 Feb. 1718.[8]

[1] *Trans. Salop Arch. Soc.* ser. 2, iii. 167–70; ser. 3, ii. 333–4; *Salopian Shreds and Patches*, vii. 141; Luttrell, *Brief Relation*, i. 572. [2] *CSP Dom.* 1689–90, p. 5; J. M. Beattie, *English Ct. in Reign of Geo. I*, 186. [3] *CJ*, xii. 508. [4] LS 13/231/2; *CSP Dom.* 1694–5, p. 104; *Cal. Treas. Bks.* xv. 26, 209; Beattie, 186. [5] *EHR*, xci. 45–46; Cobbett, *Parlty. Hist.* v. 787; D. Rubini, *Court and Country*, 110; *Cal. Treas. Bks.* xii. 331; *Lexington Pprs.* 86; Luttrell, iii. 468. [6] *Marlborough–Godolphin Corresp.* 64; Luttrell, v. 331–2, 416–17, 477; Cumbria RO (Carlisle), Lonsdale mss D/Lons/W2/2/7, James* to Sir John Lowther, 2nd Bt. I*, 22 Apr. 1704; Hoare mss at Hoare's Bank, Sir Richard Hoare's* letterbk. p. 261. [7] Salop RO, Forester mss 1224/21, Forester to Weld, 28 Jan. 1709, 23 May, 15, 20, 22 July, 5 Aug. 1710. [8] Beattie, 186; *Trans. Salop Arch. Soc.* 170; PCC 58 Tenison.

D. W. H.

FORSTER, Ferdinando (1670–1701), of Bamburgh Castle, Northumb.

NORTHUMBERLAND 16 Jan.–22 Aug. 1701

b. 14 Feb. 1670, 3rd s. of Sir William Forster of Bamburgh, and bro. of William*. educ. Durham sch.; G. Inn 1686; St. John's, Camb. 1686. unm. suc. bro. 1700.[1]

Ensign, Holland Regt. 1685, lt. 1688; capt. 1 Ft. Gds. 1689–91.[2]

Forster gained his first army commission in 1685 aged only 15, but a military career may not yet have been settled upon since the following year he entered Cambridge and Gray's Inn. Two years later, however, he returned to the army, gaining a lieutenant's commission in 1688 and appointment as captain the following year, but he resigned this commission in 1691. Little more is known of Forster until late 1700 when he stood for the Northumberland seat previously held by his elder brother, from whom in September that year he had inherited the heavily indebted family estates. Prior to this Forster does not appear to have involved himself in public affairs. Forster was successful at the election of January 1701, and in February he was listed as likely to support the Court in the supply committee's resolution to continue the 'Great

Mortgage'. At the end of the 1701 session Forster returned to Northumberland, but while attending a dinner on 22 Aug. at Newcastle-upon-Tyne for the grand jury of the county he quarrelled with John Fenwick of Rock. One account relates that Fenwick entered singing 'a favourite party song' to the refrain of 'Sir John Fenwick's† the flower among them' and thereby provoked Forster, while another claims that Forster angered Fenwick by stating that there were 'too many such [i.e. Tories] in the House'. Though the two men were prevented from fighting at the dinner, they met the following day in Newcastle, drew swords and in the resulting skirmish Forster was killed. His murderer was executed later the same year. Forster left his heavily indebted estate to his sister and to Thomas Forster II*, son of his other (deceased) sister. Proceedings in Chancery for recovery of debts forced the sale of this estate, and though this sale yielded £20,679 Forster's debts accounted for all but £1,028 of this sum.[3]

[1] *Arch. Ael.* ser. 4, xxiii. 120; *New Hist. Northumb.* i. 157; Morant, *Essex*, ii. 45. [2] *CSP Dom.* 1690–1, p. 268. [3] *New Hist. Northumb.* 165; Add. 70019, f. 285; J. Scott, *Hist. Berwick-upon-Tweed*, 480; *CSP Dom.* 1686–7, pp. 231–2; PC 2/72, p. 386; R. Welford, *Hist. Gosforth*, 80; Welford, *Men of Mark 'twixt Tyne and Tweed*, ii. 255–60; Mackenzie, *Hist. Acct. Newcastle*, 50; Luttrell, *Brief Relation*, v. 84; E. Hughes, *N. Country Life*, i. 270.

E. C.

FORSTER, Sir Humphrey, 2nd Bt. (1650–1711), of Aldermaston, Berks.

BERKSHIRE   5 Mar. 1677–1679 (July), 1685–1687 1690–1701 (Nov.)

b. 21 Dec. 1650, 1st s. of William Forster (*d.* 1661) of Aldermaston by Elizabeth, da. of Sir John Tyrell† of Heron, East Horndon, Essex. *educ.* Westminster 1663. *m.* 26 Nov. 1672, Judith (*d.* 1720), da. and coh. of Sir Humphrey Winch, 1st Bt.†, of Haynes, Beds. and Harleyford, Bucks., 2s. *d.v.p.* 1da. *d.v.p. suc.* gdfa. as 2nd Bt. 12 Oct. 1663.[1]

Sheriff, Berks. 1703–4.

After an early flirtation with Exclusion, Forster seems to have settled down into the role of a Church Tory. In the 1690 election he defeated the Whig Richard Neville* in Berkshire and successfully fended off a petition. On an analysis of the 1690 Parliament the Marquess of Carmarthen (Sir Thomas Osborne†) declined to describe him as either Whig or Tory (possibly owing to Forster's Exclusionist past), noting his party affiliation as doubtful. During the first session of the Parliament an Act was passed to allow Forster to settle and dispose of some of his estate. By December 1690, Carmarthen had decided that Forster would probably support him in the Commons in the event of an attack by his political enemies. However, just a few months later, in April 1691, Forster was classed as a Country supporter by Robert Harley*. Forster's name also appears in a list of the 1694–5 session which probably identifies 'friends' of Henry Guy*, who was facing attack in the Commons.[2]

In the 1695 election Forster was supported by the Tories as 'a perfect friend to the Church', who was 'so well beloved that . . . he cannot miss of being one'. Somewhat surprisingly, Forster also had the support of the other outgoing knight of the shire, his 'old enemy', Sir Humphrey Winchcombe, 2nd Bt. Although there was much talk of a challenge from Sir William Trumbull*, who thought Forster had been the Member 'too long already', he was returned unopposed. Trumbull may have objected to Forster's uncompromising opposition to the Court, which was to be demonstrated very clearly in the new Parliament. He was forecast as likely to oppose the Court in the divisions of 31 Jan. 1696 over the proposed council of trade. He signed the Association in February 1696, before being given leave of absence on 22 Feb. for two weeks. However, he was back in the Commons by late March when he voted against fixing the price of guineas at 22s. In the following session, on 25 Nov. 1696, he voted against Sir John Fenwick's† attainder. After re-election in 1698, he was marked as a member of the Country party on a comparative analysis of the old and new Parliaments, and his name also appears on what was probably a forecast of those likely to oppose the standing army. Returned again in January 1701, he was listed among those Members likely to support the Court over the 'Great Mortgage'. It seems likely that he stood down at the next election, however, in recognition of the competing claims of Sir John Stonhouse, 3rd Bt.*[3]

In 1702 Forster joined with Stonhouse in an unsuccessful attempt to unseat Richard Neville. He repeated his challenge in 1705, but again met with defeat. Thereafter he appears to have retired from electioneering. He died on 13 Dec. 1711. Following the death of his children (and perhaps with the powers provided in the private Act of 1690) Forster settled Aldermaston on his niece, Elizabeth Pert. He confirmed this settlement in his will of 1699 when she was the husband of William Forster*. She subsequently married William, 3rd Lord Stawell.[4]

[1] Burke, *Extinct Baronetage*, 204–5; *Vis. Berks.* (Harl. Soc. lvi), 208; *Cat. Ashmolean Mss*, 330; *Rec. Old Westminsters*, i. 343; *Mar. Lic. Vicar-Gen.* (Harl. Soc. xxiii), 209. [2] *HMC Lords*, iii. 33. [3] Devonshire mss at Chatsworth House, Finch-Halifax pprs. box 2,

no.13, Hon. Leopold to Hon. Heneage Finch I*, 12 Oct. 1695; BL, Trumbull Misc. mss 30, Trumbull to John Southby†, 15 Oct. 1695. [4] *VCH Berks*. iii. 390; PCC 28 Barnes.

S. N. H.

[1] *New Hist. Northumb.* i. 157, 229. [2] *CSP Dom.* 1687–9, p. 273; R. Welford, *Men of Mark 'twixt Tyne and Tweed*, ii. 254–7; *New Hist. Northumb.* 165, 233; Bodl. Rawl. D.863, f. 90.

E. C.

FORSTER, Thomas I (1659–1725), of Adderstone, Northumb.

NORTHUMBERLAND 1705–1708

b. 6 Aug. 1659, 1st s. of Col. Thomas Forster of Adderstone by Mary, da. of Sir Nicholas Cole, 1st Bt., of Newcastle-upon-Tyne, Northumb. and Brancepeth Castle, co. Dur. *educ*. Durham sch.; St. John's, Camb. 1677. *m.* (1) 27 Jan. 1681, Frances, da. of Sir William Forster of Bamburgh Castle, Northumb., sis. of William* and Ferdinando Forster*, 3s. (1 *d.v.p.*) 3da.; (2) Mary (*d.* 1697), 1s. 1da.; (3) bond 14 Feb. 1701, Barbara Lawes, *s.p. suc.* fa. 1673.[1]

Sheriff, Northumb. 1703–4.

Descended from a family which had been established at Adderstone since the early 15th century, Forster was the son of the proposed Court candidate for Berwick in the abortive general election of 1688. His first marriage to the eventual coheir of Ferdinando Forster led to his son inheriting Forster's heavily indebted estate in 1701. The Forsters of Bamburgh had held one of Northumberland's seats from 1689 to 1701, and having gained this estate the Adderstone branch utilized this electoral interest in 1705. Local and family historians have stated that it was Forster snr. rather than his son and namesake who stood in 1705, but Dyer's account of the election, the only contemporary source, stated that it was 'Thomas Forster jun[ior]' who headed the Northumberland poll. The return simply stated that 'Thomas Forster of Bamburgh' had been elected, and it is difficult to state with absolute certainty whether it was the father or son who had headed the Northumberland poll. Assuming it was Forster snr. who was successful at the poll, he voted on 25 Oct. 1705 against the Court candidate for Speaker but was to prove an inactive Member. His only notable activity was in the 1706–7 session when he guided through the House a private bill concerned with Northumberland estates, though he was classed as a Tory in an analysis of the House dating from early 1708. It was certainly Forster jnr. who was returned for Northumberland in 1708, and Forster snr. does not appear to have stood for Parliament again. He died in 1725, being buried on 25 Oct. In his will he left £1,000 to his only surviving daughter Dorothy and his estates to his younger son John (Thomas II* was by then a Jacobite exile).[2]

FORSTER, Thomas II (1683–1738), of Adderstone, Northumb.

NORTHUMBERLAND 1708–10 Jan. 1716

bap. 29 Mar. 1683, 1st s. of Thomas I* by his 1st w. *educ*. Newcastle sch.; St. John's, Camb. 1700. *unm. suc.* uncle Ferdinando Forster* 1701.[1]

In 1701, when only 18, Forster succeeded, by right of his deceased mother, to half the Durham and Northumberland estates of the Forsters of Bamburgh. Forster was coheir to his maternal uncle Ferdinando Forster, but the inheritance was not a fortunate one. Ferdinando and his brother William* had accumulated considerable debts, and in 1704 the creditors initiated a Chancery case to require the sale of the estates to satisfy these debts. The court agreed with the plaintiffs and in 1709 Forster and his co-heir, his aunt, sold the estates to Bishop Crewe of Durham, husband of Forster's aunt, for £20,679. Once the debts had been settled the coheirs were left with only £1,028.[2]

By the time these matters had come to a resolution Forster had already entered the Commons. The Bamburgh branch had held one of the county seats from 1689 until 1701, and the Forsters of Adderstone appear to have gained this electoral interest with the Bamburgh estates. Previous historians have stated that in 1705 this was used to secure the return of Forster's father, but Dyer's report of this election claimed that 'Thomas Forster jun[ior]' was successful and the return recorded the election of Thomas Forster of Bamburgh Castle. What is certain is that it was the son who secured one of the Northumberland seats in 1708. In 1710 Forster voted against the impeachment of Dr Sacheverell, and in the election later that year assisted unsuccessful attempts to return Tory candidates at the Northumberland boroughs of Berwick-upon-Tweed and Morpeth. He secured his own election for the county after a contest, and was described in the 'Hanover list' as a Tory. Somewhat surprisingly, on 2 Dec. he told in favour of referring to the elections committee the petition of the defeated Tory candidate against the Stafford election, but his continued Toryism was clear from his inclusion in the new year upon both the list of 'Tory patriots' who had opposed the continuation of the war, and of 'worthy patriots' who had helped to detect the mismanagements of the previous ministry. Forster told twice in the following session, in favour of declaring void the election of Sir Henry Belasyse* (15 Feb. 1712) and against hearing counsel for the freemen during consideration of the King's Lynn election case (6 Mar.). The second of these tellerships allowed the House to proceed to declaring Robert Walpole II* incapable of being elected. In the following session Forster told, on 6 May 1713, against adjourning the debate upon the suspension of duties upon French wine, and on 18 June he voted in favour of the French commerce bill. His only other notable activity was to support the endeavours of the Earl of Hertford (Algernon Seymour) and James Lowther, both Whigs, to secure the passage of a bill to regulate trade on the border with Scotland, though Lowther claimed that Forster was 'seldom to be met with' at the House. Forster retained his seat at the 1713 election but was an inactive Member, though the Worsley list and two further comparisons of the 1713 and 1715 Parliaments classed him as a Tory.[3]

Forster was prominent among the English Jacobites in the Fifteen, after which he went into exile in the service of the Stuarts. He died at Boulogne in 1738, being buried there on 27 Oct. A month later, however, his body was exhumed, transported to England and buried at Bamburgh Castle on 7 Dec.[4]

[1] *New Hist. Northumb.* i. 229. [2] Ibid. 165. [3] Bodl. Rawl. D.863, f. 90; *HMC Portland*, iv. 598; Add. 70278, Robert Price* to Robert Harley*, [Aug. 1710]; 70248, Edmund Maine* to [same], 14 Oct. 1710; Cumbria RO, Lonsdale mss D/Lons/W2/1/46, Lowther to William Gilpin, 20, 25 June 1713. [4] *New Hist. Northumb.* 233.

E. C.

FORSTER, William (1667–1700), of Bamburgh Castle, Northumb.

NORTHUMBERLAND 1689–1 Sept. 1700

b. 28 July 1667, 1st s. of Sir William Forster of Bamburgh by Dorothy, da. of Sir William Selby of Twizell, Northumb.; bro. of Ferdinando Forster*. *educ.* Durham sch.; St. John's, Camb. 1682. *m.* settlement 24 June 1693, Elizabeth (*d.* 1748), da. and h. of William Pert of Arnolds Hall, Mountnessing, Essex, *s.p. suc.* fa. 1674.[1]

Common councilman, Berwick-upon-Tweed 1686–7.[2]

The first member of his family to sit in the Commons, Forster was returned to the Convention for Northumberland and retained his seat until his death. In 1689 he had voted to agree with the Lords that the throne was not vacant, and following his return in 1690 was classed as a Tory and Court supporter by Lord Carmarthen (Sir Thomas Osborne†). On 17 May 1690 he told in favour of limiting the right of election at Aldborough to a select number of burgage-holders, and in the following session, around December, Forster was listed by Carmarthen as among those likely to support him in the event of a Commons attack. In April 1691 an analysis of the House among the papers of Robert Harley* listed Forster as a Country supporter. The following year, in February, he was injured while acting as a second for Hon. Thomas Bulkeley* during Bulkeley's duel with Sir Bourchier Wrey, 4th Bt.* He told, on 18 Feb. 1693, against granting Sir Gilbert Clarke a leave of absence, and in the spring of that year was listed by Samuel Grascome as a placeman who was not a Court supporter. On 16 Feb. 1694 Forster told against receiving a petition against the salt duty, and later in the year, in an act which betrayed his growing financial difficulties, he threatened to take legal action in order to recover the £100 he had lost in 1691 when acting as surety for the appearance at the King's bench of Lord Preston (Sir Richard Grahme, 3rd Bt.†).[3]

Having been returned unopposed in 1695, Forster remained an inactive Member. The only trace of any legislative involvement appears when he was named on 17 Dec. 1695 to draft a bill to prevent theft and rapine on the northern borders. His political sympathies were made clear, however, as Forster was forecast as a likely opponent of the Court in the divisions of 31 Jan. 1696 upon the proposed council of trade, refused to sign the Association, and in March voted against fixing the price of guineas at 22*s*. Early in the following session, on 9 Nov. 1696, Forster was ordered into custody for being absent at a call of the House, but he was released eight days later and on 25 Nov. voted against the attainder of his fellow Northumbrian Sir John Fenwick†. On 15 Dec. Forster was granted an indefinite leave of absence on the grounds of his wife's illness, though six days later his name was added to an inquiry committee. Having successfully contested for re-election in 1698, Forster was forecast in the autumn as a likely opponent of the standing army, and was classed as a Country supporter in a comparison of the old and new Commons. He took little discernible part in the proceedings of this Parliament, though in the spring of 1699 a private bill was passed to enable Forster to vest certain of his estates in a trust for the payment of debts, while reserving to his wife an annuity of £350 p.a. after his death. This clause came into effect sooner than would, perhaps, have been expected, as Forster died on 1 Sept. 1700 and was buried at Bamburgh five days later. He was succeeded, in both his heavily indebted estates and his county seat, by his brother Ferdinando.[4]

[1] *New Hist. Northumb.* i. 156–7; Morant, *Essex*, ii. 45. [2] *CSP Dom.* 1686–7, pp. 231–2. [3] Luttrell, *Brief Relation*, ii. 351; Norf. RO, Le Neve mss, [?Peter Le Neve] to John Millicent, 5 Feb. 1691[–2]; *Cal.*

Treas. Bks. x. 647, 686. ⁴*CJ*, xii. 634–5, 645; *HMC Lords*, n.s. iii. 474; *Six N. Country Diaries* (Surtees Soc. cxxiv), 152.

E. C.

FORTESCUE, Hugh (1665–1719), of Penwarne, Mevagissey, Cornw.

TREGONY	1689–1695
GRAMPOUND	1695–1698
TRURO	1698–1700
TREGONY	1701 (Feb.)–1702
MITCHELL	1705–1710
LOSTWITHIEL	1710–1713

bap. 2 June 1665, 1st s. of Arthur Fortescue of Buckland Filleigh, Devon and Penwarne by Barbara, da. of John Elford of Sheepstor, Devon. *m.* (1) settlement 19 Oct. 1692, Bridget (*d.* aft. 1706), da. and h. of Hugh Boscawen I*, 7s. (5 *d.v.p.*) 2da.; (2) c.12 June 1713, Lucy (*d.* 1767), da. of Matthew Aylmer*, 1s. 1da. *suc.* fa. 1693.¹

A Whig in the Convention, Fortescue was returned again for Tregony in 1690 by Hugh Boscawen I*, and was listed as a Whig by Lord Carmarthen (Sir Thomas Osborne†) in March 1690. In April 1690 Lady Clinton told Sir Edward Harley* a story of how Fortescue had been compared favourably to Robert Harley* (who had lately been Member for Tregony) because 'there was no hurt in him, only as to his votes', whereas Harley made speeches and was therefore dangerous. Robert Harley classed him as a Country supporter in April 1691. The observations recounted by Lady Clinton may have proved accurate, as Fortescue was not very prominent in the House. Indeed, on 16 Nov. 1691 he was sent for in custody, having been absent at a call of the House. He was discharged on 17 Dec. In the following session, on 7 Feb. 1693 he was granted leave of absence for ten days owing to ill-health. Likewise, on 4 Dec. 1693 he was excused attendance for 14 days following a call of the House, and given leave again on 7 Feb. 1694. However, on 14 Mar. 1694 he was once more found absent and a motion to send him into custody was carried by 106 votes to 86.²

Meanwhile, Fortescue's marriage to Boscawen's only child, which Luttrell had predicted in August 1692, took place in October and brought him a fortune. His wealth increased further when he succeeded to his own family's estates the following year. In 1695 he was elected for Grampound. He was forecast as likely to support the Court in the division of 31 Jan. 1696 on the proposed council of trade, signed the Association, and voted for fixing the price of guineas at 22s. In the following session, on 25 Nov., he voted for the attainder of Sir John Fenwick†. In keeping with his earlier pattern of inactivity he received leave of absence on 9 Feb. and 16 Mar. 1698, but had returned by 17 June when he was named to an inquiry committee.³

In 1698 Fortescue declined standing again at Grampound, but was returned for Truro on the Boscawen interest. He also stood unsuccessfully for St. Mawes, petitioning against the victors and not withdrawing his petition until February 1700. He was listed as a Court supporter in a comparative analysis of the old and new Parliaments, and confirmed this by voting on 18 Jan. 1699 against the disbanding bill. His main contribution to the work of the House during this session was to manage a bill through the House to make the *Charles* of Exeter a free ship in February–March 1699. He was involved in one further bill this session, as a trustee of the recently deceased John Cloberry*. In the first half of 1700 an analysis of the House rather surprisingly marked him as a placeman. Returned for Truro as well as Tregony in the first election of 1701, he opted to sit for the latter. He was not present for the whole session, however, receiving leave of absence on 15 Apr. for three weeks. On 7 May he was reported to be still in Devon, but by the 17th he was expected in London 'every hour' following the death of Hugh Boscawen I and the expectation that he should 'govern all that related to the funeral' of his father-in-law. He retained his seat in November 1701, when Harley classed him as a Whig.⁴

Fortescue does not appear to have been a candidate anywhere in 1702, so that when he was chosen for Mitchell in 1705 Lord Sunderland (Charles, Lord Spencer*) reckoned his election as a 'gain'. On another list he was classed as a Churchman. Fortescue voted on 25 Oct. 1705 for the Court candidate in the division on the Speaker. On 4 Dec. he seconded the motion of Sir Richard Onslow, 3rd Bt., to go into a committee immediately to consider proposals to secure the succession. He supported the Court on the regency bill proceedings on 18 Feb. 1706. He also told on two occasions on the Whig side in the election disputes over East Retford (17 Jan. 1706) and Bewdley (16 Feb.). Early in 1708 he was classed as a Whig. Returned for Mitchell again in 1708, he voted for the impeachment of Dr Sacheverell. In 1710 he switched to Lostwithiel (where he survived a petition), and was classed as a Whig in the 'Hanover list'. He voted on 7 Dec. 1711 for the 'No Peace without Spain' motion. In August 1712 Ralph Thoresby offered another insight into his character when he told of meeting Fortescue and his brother Joseph at the house of Lord Chief Justice Parker (Sir Thomas*). Both men 'were very conversant in the Holy Scriptures . . . and argued both learnedly and piously against those [Arian] heresies'. Just prior to 12 June 1713 Fortescue married for the second time. Philip Papillon* described him at this point as 'one of the richest commoners we have, his estate being computed to be between eight or ten thousand pounds p.a. besides money'. He stood unsuccessfully at Mitchell at the 1713 election and afterwards seems to have withdrawn from politics altogether. A letter he wrote in November 1715 to Lord Chief Justice Parker offers some insights into his retirement. In his desire to avoid the shrievalty he put forward the 'ill circumstances' of his family brought about by his 'own neglect and easiness'; his dislike of 'pageantry' and 'burble', and his distaste for being 'subjected to the brutal humours of my countrymen'; and lastly 'peace of my conscience' as he did not feel able to 'qualify myself for that office as the law requires with a safe conscience'. The last reason, coupled with the timing of his retirement from Parliament, suggests some scruple over acting in public following the passage of the Occasional Conformity Act, although he may merely have been using it as an excuse to avoid the burden of office. Fortescue died at the end of November or the beginning of December 1719. His eldest son was created Baron Clinton in 1721 (subsequently Earl Clinton); his second son sat for Barnstaple and Devon under George II; and his first son by his second marriage succeeded his half-brother as 2nd Lord Fortescue in 1751.[5]

[1] Vivian, *Vis. Devon*, 355; Centre Kentish Stud. Papillon mss U1015/C45, p. 100; Collins, *Peerage*, v. 346. [2] Add. 70113, Lady Clinton to Sir Edward Harley, 17 Apr. 1690. [3] Luttrell, *Brief Relation*, ii. 541. [4] *HMC Lords*, n.s. iv. 56, 362; BL, Evelyn mss, Lord Godolphin (Sidney†) to Mrs Boscawen, 17 May 1701. [5] *Cam. Misc.* xxiii. 40; *Thoresby Diary*, ii. 158; Papillon mss U1015/C45, p. 100; Stowe 750, f. 137; *Hist. Reg. Chron.* 1719, p. 41; Boyer, *Pol. State*, xviii. 583.

E. C./S. N. H.

FOTHERBY, Charles (1674–1720), of Barham Court, Kent.

QUEENBOROUGH 1713–1715

bap. 7 Apr. 1674, 1st s. of Anthony Fotherby of Barham by Afra, da. of one Aucher of Westwell, Kent. m. 10 Dec. 1706, Mary, da. and coh. of George Elcock of Madekin, Barham, Kent, 2da.[1]

Lt. RN, June 1697; capt. Oct. 1702.

Although the family originally came from Lincolnshire, Fotherby's great-grandfather, also Charles, and his brother Martin achieved high office in the Church in Kent, the former as archdeacon of Canterbury and the latter as a prebendary of Canterbury and later bishop of Salisbury. Early in James I's reign his great-grandfather acquired Barham. His own father was the second son of Sir John Fotherby and from extant correspondence he seems to have been involved in managing the estates of the dowager Countess of Thanet. Fotherby's younger brother went to Eton, but no evidence survives of his own education, with even his date of entry into the navy unknown. Having attained the rank of captain just after the outbreak of the War of the Spanish Succession, he served extensively in the Mediterranean. His marriage in 1706 presumably consolidated his hold on Barham, especially after the death in 1711 of his mother-in-law. He was able to capture a seat at Queenborough at the 1713 election, presumably because he was a naval captain with some local links, and a Tory to boot. Although one of Arthur Charlett's correspondents wrote of two Churchmen being 'over-voted, but not by Whigs' at Queenborough, there is no evidence that Fotherby was anything but a Tory, as he voted for that party ticket in the county election of 1713. He was also classed as a Tory on the Worsley list. However, he was not an active Member and did not stand again after the Hanoverian succession. In August 1715 he was in command of a ship stationed in the Downs in readiness to act against the Jacobites. He died on 1 Aug. 1720, leaving a widow and two daughters, the eldest of whom married, first, Henry Mompesson of Bathampton, Wiltshire, and later, Sir Edward Dering, 5th Bt.†[2]

[1] IGI, Kent; *Vis. Kent* (Harl. Soc. liv), 62; J. R. Walbran, *Antiquities of Gainford*, 87–88. [2] *Vis. Kent*, 62; Hasted, *Kent*, ix. 353; Add. 29551, f. 297; 29554, f. 208; 5440, f. 33; *HMC Lords*, n.s. vii. 430, 433; *Navy Recs. Soc.* lxviii. 193; lxx. 121–2; *Arch. Cant.* cvi. 29; Bodl. Ballard 15, f. 107; Centre Kentish Stud. Q/RPe1, 1713 pollbk.; P. Parsons, *Monuments and Painted Glass Chiefly in E. Kent*, 315.

S. N. H.

FOWELL, Sir John, 3rd Bt. (1665–92), of Fowellscombe, Ugborough, Devon.

TOTNES 1689–Nov. 1692

bap. 12 Dec. 1665, o. surv. s. of Sir John Fowell, 2nd Bt.†, of Fowellscombe by Elizabeth, da. of Sir John Chichester of Hall, Devon. unm. suc. fa. as 3rd Bt. 8 Jan. 1677.

Freeman, Totnes to 1684.

Fowell was re-elected for Totnes in 1690, presumably with the support of Sir Edward Seymour, 4th Bt.* On 30 Apr. he was ordered to attend the House, having absented himself without leave. Lord Carmarthen (Sir Thomas Osborne†) classed him as a Tory supporter of the Court and forecast in December that he would support him in the event of an attack on his ministerial position in the Commons. He obtained a leave of absence on 16 Dec. 1690. Robert Harley* listed him as a doubtful supporter of the Country party in April 1691. On 16 Jan. 1692 he obtained another leave of absence. Fowell died in November 1692 and was buried at Ugborough on the 26th.

E. C.

FOWLE, Sir Thomas (1637–92), of the 'Black Lion', Temple Bar, London.

DEVIZES   29 Mar.–22 Dec. 1690

bap. 22 Jan. 1637, 5th s. of Edward Fowle of Stanton St. Bernard, Wilts. *m.* lic. 9 June 1666 (with £900), Jane, da. of Roger Norton, Citizen and Stationer, of St. Anne Blackfriars, London, 2da. Kntd. 22 Sept. 1686.[1]

Freeman, Goldsmiths' Co. 1660, prime warden 1689; alderman, London 1686–Oct. 1687, 1691–*d.*, common councilman 1688–9; sheriff, London and Mdx. 1686–7.[2]

A younger son of a Wiltshire 'yeoman', Fowle was apprenticed in 1652 to a goldsmith in the City and after becoming a freeman of the Goldsmiths' Company set up on his own as a banker in 1664. He may have returned to his family house in Wiltshire during a quiet trading period following the plague of 1665, but after his shop in Fleet Street fortuitously escaped the fire in the following year he was able to capitalize on the absence of Lombard Street and Cheapside competitors, enabling his profits from the interest of loans to increase from £1,000 p.a. in 1672 to £3,000 p.a. by the end of the decade. This revenue allowed him to invest in property in Wiltshire, notably in Pewsey near Stanton St. Bernard, and Fifield Bavant. His business continued to flourish under King James, to whom he lent £500 in 1686. Having been elected an alderman of London in that year, Fowle was soon after chosen as sheriff and knighted. He was transferred as alderman from one ward to another in July 1687 by royal commission, but four months later was discharged. His Tory sympathies were first evident in 1683 when he offered to give evidence against suspected Whig plotters, and though at the Revolution he was still regarded by Whigs as one of the staunchest Tories in London, he proved willing to co-operate with the Williamite regime, lending some £20,500 to the government between 1689 and 1692, and acting as a member of the committee of City financiers that negotiated further loans in April and May 1690. Supported by Lord Abingdon and other Tories, he stood on the Tory interest in 1690 at Devizes, the borough nearest his birthplace, and where he had recently acquired some property. Despite the fears of friends that his Whig opponent John Methuen* had 'been too forward for him', Fowle was able to secure a double return and when the House considered the merits of the return it decided in his favour. Lord Carmarthen (Sir Thomas Osborne†) had already marked him as a Tory in his list of the new Parliament, and his name appears on one other list of likely Court supporters. Fowle's only important committee appointment, on 8 Apr. 1690, was of local significance, to prepare a bill to reverse the *quo warranto* against London. He was unseated on petition on 22 Dec. 1690.[3]

Although out of Parliament, Fowle was re-elected an alderman in 1691. He died 'of an apoplexy' on 11 Nov. 1692 and was buried in his parish church of St. Dunstan-in-the-West on the 24th, after, as one observer described it, 'the greatest funeral we have had a long time': his remains were

> brought from Stationers' Hall, where he lay in state; the lord mayor and court of aldermen accompanying the corpse, with 120 mourners and 700 other persons: about 1,000 rings were given away of 10s. apiece, 100 of 20s. each: the bishop of London and some of the nobility walked on foot: the dean of St. Paul's preached his sermon.

He was popularly supposed to have died 'very rich': one son-in-law, indeed, put his personal estate at 'upwards of £40,000'. His will referred to his Wiltshire estates and other property in Middlesex and Somerset. The residuary legatee was a nephew, Robert Fowle, who had formerly been his apprentice and now took over his business. Robert had been left, it was 'generally said', £10,000 'to continue that trade, with the house and shop in Fleet Street where he lived, so his dealings seems the same as if Sir Thomas was yet living'. After his death the College of Heralds questioned the coat of arms which he had assumed, and his elder brother Robert, also a goldsmith, was forced to disclaim any right to it.[4]

[1] Wilts. RO, 495/1; *Le Neve's Knights* (Harl. Soc. viii), 407; *Mar. Lic. Vicar-Gen.* (Harl. Soc. xxxiii), 18; C104/115/II/664. [2] J. R. Woodhead, *Rulers of London* (London and Mdx. Arch. Soc.), 72–73; Luttrell, *Brief Relation*, i. 414. [3] Woodhead, 72–73; F. G. Hilton Price, *London Bankers*, 61; Wilts. RO, 727/12/21; C104/120/1; *CSP Dom.* July–Sept. 1683, p. 75; *Cal. Treas. Bks.* viii. 905; ix. 380, 682, 882, 1692, 1979–80, 2002, 2005; Luttrell, 385; Beaven, *Aldermen*, i. 135; Nottingham Univ. Lib. Portland (Harley) mss Pw2 Hy 502, 'Reasons against Sir Bartholomew Shower's* being recorder of London'; PCC 6 Coker; Bath mss at Longleat House, Thynne pprs. 12, f. 97; 24, f. 161. [4] *Portledge Pprs.* 126; Luttrell, ii. 614, 623; Nat. Archs. Ire. Wyche mss, W. Ball to Sir Cyril Wyche*, 15 Nov. 1692, 24 Jan. 1693; BL, Verney mss mic. 636/46, John Verney* (later Ld. Fermanagh) to Sir Ralph Verney, 1st Bt.†, 12 Nov. 1692; *HMC Lords*, n.s. iii. 270; PCC 6 Coker; *Le Neve's Knights*, 407; Hilton Price, 61.

D. W. H./H. J. L.

FOWNES, John (c.1661–1731), of Kittery Court, Devon.

DARTMOUTH   20 Mar. 1714–1715

b. c.1661, 1st s. of John Fownes of Whitleigh, Devon by Mary, da. of Henry Northleigh† of Peamore, Devon, sis. of Henry Northleigh*. *educ.* Exeter, Oxf. matric. 5 May 1679, aged 18. *m.* 23 Aug. 1681, Anne, da. of Edward Yarde† of Churston Ferrers, Devon, sis. of Edward Yarde*, 3s. (2 *d.v.p.*) 3da. (1 *d.v.p.*). *suc.* fa. 1670.[1]
Freeman, Dartmouth 1701.[2]

Fownes, who was descended from a line of aldermen and mayors of Plymouth, moved after his marriage to Kittery Court, a fine house in the vicinity of Dartmouth, and in 1701 was admitted a freeman of that borough (an 'honorary not a trading freeman') as part of a mass creation of freemen to build up a rival interest in Dartmouth to that of the Herne family. But it was not until a by-election in 1714 that he stood for Parliament there, as a High Tory, in opposition to the Hanoverian Tory Frederick Herne*, whom he defeated. His son John succeeded him in the seat in 1715, keeping out on that occasion Frederick's brother Nathaniel Herne*. Fownes himself died on 4 Oct. 1731 and was buried at Brixham.[3]

[1] Vivian, *Vis. Devon*, 373. [2] *Trans. Devon Assoc.* lxxxv. 78–79. [3] Ibid.; Vivian, 373.

E. C.

FOWNES, Richard (1652–1714), of Steepleton Iwerne, Dorset.

CORFE CASTLE   1681 (Mar.), 1685–1687
1689–1698
26 Apr. 1699–July 1714

bap. 25 Aug. 1652, 1st s. of Thomas Fownes of Steepleton Iwerne by Alice, da. of John Mynne of Woodcote, Epsom, Surr. *educ.* Oriel, Oxf. 1668. *m.* (1) aft. 1677, Elizabeth, da. of Gabriel Armstrong of Rempstone, Notts., 2s. (1 *d.v.p.*) 1da.; (2) settlement 21 Nov. 1693, Elizabeth, da. of William Aysh of South Petherton, Som., wid. of Samuel Cabell of Buckfastleigh, Devon, *s.p. suc.* fa. 1670.[1]
Freeman, Poole 1691.[2]
Steward of crown estates, Som. 1705–8.[3]

Fownes, who had represented Corfe Castle since 1681, was returned again for the borough in 1690. In March he was listed as a Tory by Lord Carmarthen (Sir Thomas Osborne†), who also forecast in December that Fownes would probably support him in the event of an attack in the Commons. Robert Harley* marked him as a member of the Country party in April 1691, and Fownes told on the Tory side in the Arundel election case on 22 Feb. 1694. He obtained a fortnight's leave of absence on 21 Dec. Forecast as likely to oppose the Court in the division of 31 Jan. 1696 on the proposed council of trade, he refused to sign the Association at first. He voted in March against fixing the price of guineas at 22*s*. and likewise voted on 25 Nov. against the attainder of Sir John Fenwick†. He obtained another leave of absence on 5 Mar. 1698, and later that year stood unsuccessfully at Corfe Castle and Poole and was consequently listed as a Country Member who had failed to secure re-election. He petitioned at Corfe Castle and succeeded in having his opponent's return declared void; he then carried the ensuing by-election. In February 1701 he was listed as likely to support the Court over the 'Great Mortgage', and in December 1701 Harley listed him as a Tory.

Fownes continued to represent Corfe Castle throughout Anne's reign, voting consistently with the Tories. He divided on 13 Feb. 1703 against agreeing to the Lords' amendments to the bill for enlarging the time for taking the oath of abjuration. In March 1704 he was forecast as a supporter of Lord Nottingham (Daniel Finch†) over the Scotch Plot. Forecast as a supporter of the Tack, he duly voted for it on 28 Nov. 1704. Classified as 'True Church' in an analysis of the 1705 Parliament, Fownes voted on 25 Oct. against the Court candidate for Speaker. During the summer of 1706 he petitioned the Treasury for leave to surrender to his deputy the stewardship of certain crown lands in Somerset, which was eventually allowed in June 1708. Classed as a Tory both before and after the 1708 election, he duly voted against the impeachment of Dr Sacheverell. Likewise noted as a Tory in the 'Hanover list' of the 1710 Parliament, Fownes appears both among the 'Tory patriots' who opposed the continuance of the war and the 'worthy patriots' who detected the mismanagements of the previous administration. On 18 June 1713 he supported the Oxford ministry over the French commerce bill. He stood for Ashburton and Corfe Castle in 1713, but only succeeded in carrying his old seat, and nothing is known about his voting in his final Parliament. His death was reported on 20 July 1714. Although his son, Richard, initially attempted to maintain the family interest at Corfe, he failed to secure his own election in 1715 and made no subsequent attempt to win back the seat.[4]

[1] Hutchins, *Dorset*, i. 299; F. Brown, *Som. Wills*, iv. 98–99. [2] Poole Archs. B17. [3] *Cal. Treas. Bks.* v. 1204; xxii. 270. [4] Ibid. xx. 736; xxii. 270; *HMC Portland*, v. 473.

P. W.

FOX, Charles (1660–1713), of Chiswick, Mdx. and Farley, Wilts.

EYE	8 Dec. 1680–1681 (Jan.)
CRICKLADE	26 May 1685–1687, 1689–1698
SALISBURY	1698–1700
	9 July 1701–21 Sept. 1713

b. 2 Jan. 1660, 3rd s. of Sir Stephen Fox* by his 1st w. *educ.* travelled abroad (France) 1669, (Italy, Germany, Holland, France) 1676–8. *m.* 1679 (with £6,000), Elizabeth (*d.* 1703), da. and coh. of Sir William Trollope, 2nd Bt., of Casewick, Lincs., *s.p.*[1]

Freeman, Salisbury 1680–4, Oct. 1688–?*d.*, Portsmouth 1684–8.[2]

Paymaster of forces 1682–5, (jt.) Dec. 1702–5; jt. paymaster of army in Ireland May–July 1690; jt. receiver-gen. and paymaster-gen. [I] July 1690–8; treasurer to Queen Catherine of Braganza by 1700–aft. 1704.[3]

Commr. R. Hosp. Chelsea 1702–*d.*, taking subscriptions to S. Sea Co. 1711.[4]

An amiable man, but quiet and unremarkable, Fox never outran his father's shadow. Despite marrying a considerable heiress, supposedly worth some £2,000 a year besides her portion, he did not establish a home of his own and was always content to live under Sir Stephen's roof. He was thus an absentee landlord of the Water Eaton estate, near Cricklade, which had been settled on him at his wedding, though this did not impair his management of the family interest in the borough, for which he was returned again in 1690. The only respect in which he differed from his father was that, not having had to make his own way in the world, he was less cautious politically, and on two notable occasions was to allow himself the luxury of placing party principle above personal position. At the outset of this period, he was still following Sir Stephen's lead. The Marquess of Carmarthen (Sir Thomas Osborne†) classified him as a Tory and probably also as a Court supporter in March 1690, when it was already being rumoured that he was to be given office, and he was included in a second of Carmarthen's lists in the following December, possibly a calculation of support in case Carmarthen was attacked in the Commons. Meanwhile, in May Fox had been named with Thomas Coningsby* as joint paymaster of the army in Ireland, the office being transferred to the Irish establishment two months later as joint receiver- and paymaster-general. This appointment was intended less as a recognition of Fox's own abilities than as an inducement to Sir Stephen to return to the Treasury and give his personal financial backing to the war effort. While Coningsby was the man on the spot, Charles Fox stayed in England to take charge of affairs there, or rather to let his man-of-business and deputy in office, Edward Pauncefort*, take charge for him. Fox was in essence a figurehead, and little that was done in his name should actually be credited to him: the paymaster's business was for the most part undertaken by Pauncefort, and the very substantial loans he apparently made to government came in reality from Sir Stephen. As paymaster he was obliged to play some active part in Commons' proceedings, which went against his natural reticence. Even a sympathetic Tory pamphleteer observed that 'notwithstanding he always voted honestly . . . his modesty made him backward in attempting set speeches'. His office accounts for his frequent appointment to committees on Irish army affairs in this period and to the occasional drafting committee. He was as loyal to the administration as his place dictated, being listed as a member of the Court party by Robert Harley* in April 1691, figuring on no less than five lists of placemen in 1692 and 1693, and being included as a Court supporter on Grascome's list. He was also, in the 1694–5 session, listed among the 'friends' of Henry Guy*, then under investigation for corruption. Difficulties arose eventually, almost inevitably, under the Junto ministry. He was at first forecast as 'doubtful' in the divisions of 31 Jan. 1696 on the proposed council of trade, but this was then changed to indicate his likely opposition to the Court, and indeed he voted on the same day with other Tory office-holders against imposing the abjuration oath on council members; and although he made no bones about subscribing the Association, and voted in March for fixing the price of guineas at 22*s.*, he could not acquiesce in the attainder of Sir John Fenwick†, and voted against that bill on 25 Nov. 1696. His father was still too useful to government to permit him to be dismissed forthwith, and Charles retained the paymaster's post for a further 20 months, during which time he frequently appeared in the Commons, reporting on various petitions from Irish army officers for settlement of arrears. Listed as a placeman in July 1698, he was finally replaced just before the 1698 election, though news did not leak out until August and he himself was not told for several weeks. Despite the recognizable party logic behind the move, and the compensation of a pension of £1,500 a year, it was still galling to him. He had carried out his trust honestly, never taking more than his salary; for all the efforts of the accounts commissioners no irregularities had been found; and his father's huge loan in 1693 had extricated the Irish revenue from a desperate predicament. Sir Stephen complained that Charles had been 'made a sacrifice for his steady principles towards the Church and government by Parliament', and blamed Coningsby for what had happened:

Now, after all this most reasonable service, in which my Lord Coningsby could or would not bear any share, by his treacherous insinuation with King William did so represent Mr Fox's proceedings in Parliament against the Whigs that the King at his going to Holland . . . left a warrant to displace Mr Fox and grant the whole office to the said Lord Coningsby, which was not communicated to the lords of the Treasury till after the King was in Holland. So that till his Majesty's return Sir Stephen had no opportunity but by letters not answered to represent to his Majesty the faithful services of Mr Fox, particularly in Parliament, always to forward supplies and to keep steady to the constitution, which he did so effectually that the King granted him a pension of £1,500 per annum.[5]

Although neither Sir Stephen nor Charles himself accepted the pension as adequate, both continuing to press either for reinstatement or for 'the same bounty out of that office . . . as all his predecessors have ever had', to wit a lump sum of £16,000, this gesture, combined with Sir Stephen's continuance on the Treasury Board, seems to have prevented any violent reaction on Charles's part. Chosen at both Cricklade and Salisbury in the 1698 general election, and opting for the latter, he was marked with a 'query' in a comparative analysis of the old and new Houses of Commons, voted against the third reading of the disbanding bill on 18 Jan. 1699, but was classed as doubtful or possibly as opposition in an analysis of early 1700. He was a teller twice in this Parliament: on 29 Mar. 1699, against recommitting a report on the Malmesbury election, in which Edward Pauncefort* was involved; and on 14 Mar. 1700, against receiving the reports of the committee of privileges at that time. Defeated at Salisbury in January 1701, and a petitioner himself, he came in at a by-election after the death of the sitting Member, against whom he had petitioned. He did not figure on the anti-war 'black list', but Harley's list of the December Parliament classed him with the Tories, and on 26 Feb. 1702 he supported the motion in favour of vindicating the Commons' proceedings in the impeachments of the Whig ministers. In April he presented a bill on his father's behalf to extend the deadline for entering Sir Stephen's claim with the trustees for the Irish forfeitures. Through the agency of Lord Treasurer Godolphin (Sidney†), who had been instrumental in his earlier appointment in 1690, and once again principally in order to gratify his father, he was given a share in the English paymastership in December, being responsible for the forces in the Low Countries. Once again it was Pauncefort who did the work, and reaped the unofficial pecuniary benefits, while Fox merely drew his salary – at £1,500 no advance on his pension. As paymaster he appeared before the Commons in November 1703 with his accounts, and was forecast in March 1704 as likely to support Lord Nottingham (Daniel Finch†) in his actions over the Scotch Plot, but otherwise remained in the parliamentary background. In the next session, on 24 Oct. 1704, it was reported that Fox had told his friends he expected trouble from the ministry as he had written to John Methuen*, the ambassador to Portugal, demanding a muster roll of the army currently stationed in that country. Moreover, this time the issue of occasional conformity was to prove his Achilles' heel – although on Harley's lobbying list for the Tack, on 28 Nov. 1704 he voted for it. Thereafter no argument from Sir Stephen could keep him in office:

> I did debate the matter with [Godolphin], representing how hard a case it was that Mr Fox, who never did an unworthy action in his life, should not be permitted to proceed with honour . . . according to the trust reposed in him as a Member of the House of Commons and according to her Majesty's royal words from the throne of giving liberty of speech to the House of Commons, but nothing could prevail, neither old acquaintance, a constant, steady friendship with his lordship, many obligations that he has received of me.

According to this evidence Fox also lost his 'pension of recompense', but there are indications that he was still in receipt of some kind of annuity in 1707.[6]

Fox's dismissal took place in April 1705. At about the same time he was said to have arranged to marry a daughter of Lord Rochester (Laurence Hyde†) but this came to nothing. As in 1698, the loss of office made no difference to his position as an MP, though on this occasion it was not for want of effort by his enemies. Bishop Burnet, who later claimed to have acted only after a clear hint from the Queen herself on the subject, ran a candidate against him in Salisbury. Fox's success in these circumstances was a considerable fillip to the High Church interest not only in that borough but in the country at large. Lord Halifax (Charles Montagu*) considered that it was owing entirely to the delay in announcing his removal as paymaster, and related a story of Fox's having been 'in so much despair when the Parliament rose' that he had spoken to his nephew, Lord Cornwallis (Charles*), 'to bring him in at Eye'. On the other hand, Fox had built up a strong personal interest in the corporation. This he reinforced in 1707, when he was able to secure a new charter. As well as bolstering the ascendancy of the Tory faction in the borough, it was interpreted locally as a demonstration that he was back in favour at court, and he was returned again without difficulty thereafter, and without even having to put in an appearance in the town. Any improvement in his standing with Godolphin's administration was short-lived, however, and did not deflect him from the Tory path. Listed as a placeman and as 'True Church' in 1705, he voted against the Court candidate on 25 Oct. 1705, and was listed as a Tory twice in 1708. He had told against the third reading of the bill to secure American trade on 17 Mar. 1708. In 1710 he opposed the impeachment of Dr Sacheverell. He was quick off the mark in congratulating Harley in August 1710, but, if seeking restitution to office, he came away empty-handed. He appeared on two lists compiled during the first session: the 'Tory patriots' who voted in favour of peace, and the 'worthy patriots' who exposed the mismanagements of the previous ministry. He was also a member of the October Club. He told on 10 Jan. 1711 against an additional clause to the bill to prevent bribery and corruption at elections, saving the Quakers' right to affirm. He was marked as a Tory in the Worsley list of the 1713 Parliament, to which he was returned but in which he was never to sit.[7]

Fox's health had been causing concern since he was a young man, when his early tendency to corpulence had been noticed by John Evelyn, and on one occasion in 1691 news of his death had been confidently given out. In the summer of 1713 he was seriously ill, and he died at Chiswick on 21 Sept. His body was transported to Farley for burial, where over 2,000 were said to have followed the cortège, including 'about 20 clergymen and several of the corporation of Salisbury'. The pall-bearers included John Gauntlett* and Edward Pauncefort, and Pauncefort was also named a trustee in his will. Fox left his finances in an unhealthy state. Election costs have been mooted as one cause, but probably more important was the fact that Fox coupled 'a weakness for speculative investments', especially in the realm of foreign trade, with a surprising lack of judgment and business acumen. By the time of his death he had sold off much of his wife's inheritance, and still faced debts of around £15,000, nearly half of which was owed to Pauncefort alone. His assets were sufficient to cover these, but not to pay the £6,000 he had disposed of in legacies, mostly to members of the family, and his father was obliged to make up the shortfall.[8]

[1] G. S. Fox-Strangways, *Life of Henry Fox, 1st Earl of Holland*, i. 12–14; C. Clay, *Public Finance and Private Wealth*, 266. [2] Hoare, *Wilts*. Salisbury, 477–8, 480, 487; R. East, *Portsmouth Recs*. 367. [3] Clay, 270; *Cal. Treas. Bks*. ix. 678; x. 119; xvii. 425; Add. 43772, f. 36. [4] C. G. T. Dean, *R. Hosp. Chelsea*, 168, 178; Pittis, *Present Parl*. 350. [5] R. Eyre, *A Sermon Preach'd at the Funeral of Charles Fox . . .* (1713), 17; *Evelyn Diary*, iv. 219; Clay, 194–6, 228–9, 237, 242–3, 245, 269–72; Luttrell, *Brief Relation*, ii. 24; iv. 410; Morrice ent'ring bk. 3, p. 127; *Mems. of Sir Stephen Fox* (1717), 77, 88; *CJ*, x. 511, 518–19; *Luttrell Diary*, 101; H. Horwitz, *Parl. and Pol. Wm. III*, 165; *Cal. Treas. Bks*. xiii. 397; *HMC Lords*, iii. 433–4; Add. 51324, ff. 57–59. [6] Add. 51324, ff. 57–59; 51335, ff. 50, 53; 17677 YY, f. 316; Clay, 246, 270–2; Univ. Kansas Spencer Research Lib. Methuen–Simpson Corresp. Ms. C163, [?John Methuen] to Sir William Simpson, 24 Oct. 1704; *Cal. Treas. Bks*. xvii. 425; *Cal. Treas. Pprs*. 1702–7, p. 487. [7] *Cal. Treas. Bks*. xx. 236; Add. 17677 AAA, f. 211; 70227, Fox to Harley, 17 Aug. 1710; 61458, f. 160; Luttrell, v. 536; Burnet, *Supp*. ed. Foxcroft, 513; *HMC Portland*, iv. 213; Bodl. Ballard 21, f. 222; Hants RO, Jervoise mss, Peter Phelps et al. to Thomas Jervoise*, 26 May 1707, James Harris to same, 23 June 1707; Dorset RO, Fox-Strangways mss, William Davis to Fox, 30 Sept. 1710. [8] *Evelyn Diary*, 248; Luttrell, ii. 274; Ballard 31, f. 102; Add. 51336 (unfol.), acct. of Fox's funeral, 30 Sept. 1713; *Mems. of Sir Stephen Fox*, 95–97; Clay, 272–4.

D. W. H.

FOX, Sir Stephen (1627–1716), of Whitehall, Westminster; Chiswick, Mdx.; and Redlynch, Som.[1]

SALISBURY	30 Nov. 1661–1679 (Jan.)
WESTMINSTER	1679 (Mar.–July)
SALISBURY	1685–1687
WESTMINSTER	9 Nov. 1691–1698
CRICKLADE	26 Jan. 1699–1702
SALISBURY	15 Mar. 1714–1715

b. 27 Mar. 1627, 6th but 4th surv. s. of William Fox of Farley, Wilts. by Elizabeth, da. of Thomas Pavy of Plaitford, Hants. *educ*. Salisbury Cathedral sch. 1633–40. m. (1) 8 Dec. 1651, Elizabeth (d. 1696), da. of William Whittle of London, 7s. d.v.p. 3da. (2 d.v.p.); (2) 11 July 1703, Christian (d. 1718), da. of Francis Hopes, rector of Aswarby, Lincs. 1682–1705, 2s. 2da. (1 d.v.p.). Kntd. 1 July 1665.[2]

Gent. of horse to Prince of Wales 1646; master of horse 1649–50; clerk of stables 1653–July 1654, kitchen July 1654–June 1660; clerk comptroller of Bd. of Green Cloth Aug. 1660–Jan. 1661, 2nd clerk Jan. 1661–71, 1st clerk 1671–8, 1679–89; paymaster of forces 1661–76, 1679–80; 1st commr. of stables 1679–82, Apr.–July 1702; ld. of Treasury 1679–85, 1687–9, 1690–1702; treasurer to Queen Catherine of Braganza 1697; commr. trade 1701; receiver of crown revenues, S. Wales 1701–d.[3]

Freeman, Salisbury 1661; recorder, Boston 1682–5.[4]

Commr. Chelsea Hosp. 1691–1703; dir. Greenwich Hosp. 1703–d.[5]

Fox's transposition from the court of James II to that of William and Mary might have seemed merely the latest blessing of that 'wonderful . . . providence' to which he himself, in his moderately Calvinist piety, was wont to ascribe his phenomenal rise from an obscure upbringing in a Wiltshire 'cottage' to the distinction of being 'the richest commoner in three kingdoms'. In reality he owed his continuing prosperity and influence after 1688 just as much to tact, and to the unrivalled expertise and experience in financial administration and in the management of public credit which made his presence at the Treasury indispensable in a period of continental war and fiscal emergency. Moreover, his private banking activities had won for him a number of valuable friends, not least the new King himself, to offset the enduring enmity of his old antagonist Lord Carmarthen (Sir Thomas Osborne†) and the ill-repute clinging to servants of the Jacobite regime. Although at several crises in the past he had courageously, or perhaps obstinately, voted in the Commons according to conscience and against the express desire of his royal master, discretion proved his better part in the circumstances of 1689, and by not seeking a seat in the Convention he escaped the necessity of committing himself publicly on any sensitive political issue. Indeed, even in private he recorded no opinion on the events of the Revolution, though he evidently found little difficulty in transferring his allegiance, a fact that Jacobite agents could put down only to malice, and which impressed King James so forcibly with the enormity of Fox's ingratitude that Sir Stephen was among those excepted by name from the general indemnity promised in James's declaration of 1692.[6]

All was not plain sailing, however. William wished to employ Fox, and did restore him as first clerk of the Board of Green Cloth in February 1689; but Fox wanted more than this. Specifically, he coveted the position of cofferer of the Household, which he regarded as his by dint of his long service and 'by right' of some previous arrangements made under Charles II, claiming in effect a reversionary interest in the office. The appointment of Lord Newport (Richard†) instead cut him to the quick, and set off one of those long-standing grudges to which his *amour propre* made him susceptible: two decades later he was still drafting memorials and petitions detailing this grievance. Apparently in consequence, he formed a resolution to retire from public business, 'excusing himself' on grounds of age from service not only in the Household but also in the Treasury, where his friend and former colleague Lord Godolphin (Sidney†) fretted for his assistance. Eventually he allowed himself to be won over by Godolphin's entreaties. As he himself remembered it, 'his lordship thought it necessary for him to be sometimes out of that commission whose absence could not be well dispensed with, as he told me, unless I would come in'. Thus 'I did weakly alter my resolution of retirement', at the price of a place on the Treasury board for himself and the potentially lucrative office of joint paymaster of the forces in Ireland for his son, Charles*. The effect of the return to the Treasury of the 'grey fox' (as one lampoonist dubbed him), a man renowned both for his wealth and his 'regularity', was soon apparent. Fox was himself willing to lend money to the crown, most notably in 1693 when an advance of £40,000 kept the Irish administration afloat, but his chief value was in the stability he brought to the government's credit, inducing other City financiers to invest, although occasionally he and Godolphin had to resort to 'underhand' methods to secure loans, such as promising higher rates of interest than those stipulated officially. The two men worked closely together, and even if Godolphin seems to have made the running Fox was more than the mere hatchet-man for his younger colleagues, with whom on occasion he publicly disagreed. His role in administration seems to have been to provide prudent, and often severe, judgment rather than ingenuity, and while unfailing courtesy saved him from much of the personal unpopularity attendant upon harsh decisions, his slowness sometimes irritated the impatient.[7]

A return to the Commons was the almost inevitable corollary to Fox's return to office, but it seems that when a suitable opportunity arose, at a by-election in 1691 for Westminster, a constituency in which there was a strong governmental and, more particularly, a Household interest, Fox required considerable persuasion to offer himself as a candidate. This could have been partly on account of the cost, his expenses in the end amounting to over £630; and partly because there were already several other candidates in the field, most of them Whigs, and Fox naturally shrank from factional conflict and too close an identification with a partisan cause. The fact that he had some interest of his own in the constituency, through possession of the Hungerford estate, may have helped him come to a decision. Pre-election manoeuvring had eventually resolved into a straight fight between Fox and the Dissenting lawyer Thomas Owen*, with Fox emerging victorious. Fox's acceptance address was typically laconic:

> I heartily thank you all for the honour you have done me; and if there be any occasions wherein I can serve you, either in relation to the community or a particular capacity, you shall always find me ready and willing to serve you faithfully.

Fox took his seat on 13 Nov. 1691 and his subsequent committee nominations and speeches in this Parliament reflected his position in the Treasury. On 3 Dec., in the debate arising from the report of the accounts commissioners, he began by speaking in his own justification, unnecessarily as it turned out, for neither the commissioners nor Country MPs generally made any complaint against him: 'I only desire to appeal to the commissioners, whether I did not appear according to their summons.' Then, as the attention of the House shifted, he intervened to defend the Treasury as a whole from criticism of its policy of issuing tallies on funds which had not yet come in. It was, he said, not only common practice but essential in this instance of 'unavoidable' necessity: 'we had not done our duties to the nation if we had done otherwise'. On 12 Dec., on the motion that half the income of official salaries be paid towards the cost of the war, he urged the importance of a speedy provision of supply. In what was to become a standard refrain of his commentaries on subsidy debates, he pointed out that 'the necessities of the government are so great, that they make the valiantest men tremble at the consequences of delay'. So often was this theme repeated that it was eventually picked up in popular satire, one ballad depicting Fox's contributions to Treasury board meetings in the same terms:

> Sir Stephen next, in tears, laments our fate,
> And then declares the pinchgut kitchen's state.

After one such speech on 15 Dec., in favour of agreeing with the estimates committee that the Dutch forces on the army establishment be paid at the same rate as the English, he spoke twice in the same committee on 2 Jan. 1692 to support his fellow Treasury lord Sir John Lowther, 2nd Bt. II*, in maintaining the number of regiments on station in Ireland, commenting on the second occasion, 'I hope this House will not make this alteration at this time when the army there are so much in arrear, at least £400,000, that it is not safe to do'. Here and in subsequent debates he set himself to bring fiscal and budgetary reality home to the Members, often expressing himself in a tone of schoolmasterly resignation. On 6 Jan., for example, he spoke twice in ways and means to explain the Treasury's calculation of land tax yields, and again in the same committee to expound another point of detail concerning the liability of the civil list. When the suggested levy on official salaries surfaced again, on 18 Jan., he opposed it, this time deploying the argument from urgency to make a case for doing nothing else that might hinder a prompt subsidy.

> The revenue is already loaded sufficiently. You have now towards this year's war charged it with £200,000. And the crown is also in arrears to the officers under it three quarters, so that if you trust to that nothing will be done and the King's service will be totally disappointed. And I am afraid little of the arrears will be paid. And if the revenue were clear, I would not only give all my pension but a great part of my estate.

His last speech of the session occurred on 15 Feb., once more on the Court side, against the revival of the accounts commission, but his involvement in parliamentary business had not been entirely confined to the province of his office, for earlier in the session (on 17 Dec. 1691) he had presented a bill to divide the parish of St. Martin-in-the-Fields and to 'settle' the various charities by 'Dr Tennison', presumably the future archbishop.[8]

Classed as a placeman in a list compiled between May and November 1692, Fox was a no less frequent speaker in the following parliamentary session. He made a characteristic contribution on 15 Nov. 1692, on a motion from the Country party leader Paul Foley I that the House postpone consideration of supply until grievances had been aired. 'I observe it is the opinion of some gentlemen', he replied,

> that there is no present need of money and that things go on as well as if you gave money. I do assure you it is no such thing, for the Exchequer was never barer than now and we have nothing to live on but the clause of credit given by this House upon the Poll Act and the Act for the double excise, which now expires the 17th of this month. So that all things are at a stand till you set them going.

Ten days later he made the same plea almost verbatim for a speedy vote of supply – 'some cheerful vote', he called it – during a discussion of naval estimates, and on 2 Dec., in committee of supply, he pressed the matter of the army establishment in these familiar terms, that 'money now falls short, and if you cannot pay them you must consider to disband them, else an unsatisfied army will be a dangerous thing'. He even managed to refer to the poverty of the Exchequer in a speech on 10 Jan. 1693 against an additional clause offered to the land tax bill for the suspension of payment of all pensions during the war unless allowed officially 'upon good and valuable considerations'. Fox claimed that this amendment would wreck the bill, since 'all the lords concerned' would be heard by counsel.

> Then upon these pensions there is very little paid, but just enough to keep body and soul together. And for many of them I know they are granted upon good considerations. So that upon the whole matter, if the bill be delayed . . . your service will be neglected and all things stand still. Your weekly payments to the army will cease, which amount to a great sum, and there is already hardly enough money in the Exchequer to carry on this service now.

Apart from an intervention on 22 Nov. 1692, against the opposition's proposed address calling for a reconstruction of the Admiralty Board, all the other occasions on which Fox spoke in this session concerned fiscal issues: on 3 Dec., in a committee of supply, when he gave the Treasury's computation of the likely shortfall in the yield of the poll tax; on 13 Feb. 1693, in ways and means, when he followed Sir John Lowther, 2nd Bt. II, in a motion to add two years to the term of the East Indian goods duties and to make them a collateral security for the continued impositions upon which a fund of £500,000 was being raised; and on 23 Feb., when he supported other Treasury lords in favour of going into committee the next day in order to extend the term of the customs duties beyond Christmas 1694.[9]

Fox was included as a placeman in three lists drawn up in 1693, and was also marked as a Court party man and an office-holder in Grascome's list. In his capacity as a Treasury commissioner he was now attending some Cabinet meetings, but the gradually changing complexion of the ministry was beginning to create difficulties for him, an early indication of which may have been his colleagues' refusal in 1693 to adjudicate between Fox and Lady Dorchester in a dispute over an annuity on the Irish civil list, to which both had a claim by purchase. Without reports of debates, we know little of Fox's parliamentary activity in the sessions of 1693-4 and 1694-5, although he was listed in the latter session by Henry Guy* as one of his 'friends' in connexion with the Commons' investigation of Guy for corruption. He continued to subscribe to government loans, largely to encourage other investors, and was a substantial buyer of stock in the newly established Bank of England, to the tune of between £4,000 and £10,000, but whether or not he played much part in the negotiations preceding the foundation of the Bank is unclear. This and other innovations in the field of public credit represented a striking departure from the traditional techniques employed in his own 'undertaking' of some 20 years before, and there is nothing in Fox's parliamentary speeches or personal memoranda to indicate that he had thought much on the subject. What we know of his role in Exchequer business reflects his reputation as a 'man of accounts' rather than expedients. For example, his Household experience induced the board in May 1695 to require him to take responsibility for a retrenchment in expenditure on the royal gardens, and that same month he spoke strongly in the commission against a proposed grant of the lordship of Denbigh. His motives on this occasion were, however, almost certainly more than administrative, the intended recipient of the grant being the King's Dutch favourite, Lord Portland. The strenuous opposition mounted by Fox, which Portland's friends interpreted as wholly malicious, contrasting it with his own involvement in other such grants, succeeded in holding up the process long enough for Country party activists in Wales to mount a more public campaign. It says much for Fox's force of character that he was prepared to press such a tender point, and much for his continued value to the King that William was prepared to overlook it.[10]

The 1695 general election saw Fox in a politically incongruous partnership with his Treasury colleague Charles Montagu* as Court candidates for Westminster. With strong official backing, the two placemen defeated the Tory oppositionist Sir Walter Clarges, 1st Bt.*, in a bitter contest. Tory electoral propaganda had coupled Fox with Montagu as 'courtly upstarts', but when the Parliament met, the refinements of Fox's position became apparent. He was marked as 'doubtful' in the forecast for the divisions of 31 Jan. 1696 over the proposed council of trade, and in the event joined his son, a much more strongly partisan Tory, in opposing at least the imposition of an abjuration oath on the council's members. He did, however, sign the Association promptly, and voted in March in favour of fixing the price of guineas at 22s., as befitted a Treasury lord and occasional Cabinet councillor. He also continued to give the government his personal financial support, acting as one of the securities for borrowing from the Dutch, and remained unwaveringly loyal to the King, as was demonstrated by his prompt attention to an information sent him of Jacobite intrigues.[11]

Godolphin's snap resignation in November 1696, before the Parliament resumed, placed Fox in a difficult position. Portland's anger at the frustration of the Denbigh grant threatened his own continuance in office, and without his closest ally on the Treasury commission he felt isolated and exposed. He began to be aware once more of his age and infirmity. His chaplain was reported to have announced at a dinner party that Fox was 'unwilling to undergo the fatigue of that station, the whole trouble being like to fall upon him . . . He added, that it was high time for a man of his years to retire from business.' As before, however, he relented; this time on being advanced to the position of acting first lord, where he brought his considerable authority to the task of presiding over the most desperate financial crisis faced by the English government since the Stop of the Exchequer in 1672. Not much is known of Fox's individual contribution to the work of the Treasury in these months, other than that he attended board meetings more assiduously than any of his colleagues. He may well have had to speak more frequently in the House, on questions of supply at least, but no account of a speech survives. After his scruples over the attainder of Sir John Fenwick† had induced him to 'go away' from the House before the crucial vote on 25 Nov. 1696 (his son voting against the bill), he seems to have settled down again into his role as a stalwart of the Court interest. From being anxious to shrug off the burden of office he had become determined by the following spring to hold on to his newly won authority, and when after a struggle the King decided to give the post of first lord to Charles Montagu, Fox showed such pique that he first desired to resign and only permitted himself to be pacified by the promise (never actually fulfilled) of a seat on the Privy Council and a bizarre agreement by which Montagu's promotion was not gazetted. Just as important to the mastering of his disgust, in all probability, was his unwillingness to sacrifice the influence a Treasury commissionership afforded him in matters of patronage, which he was far from shy of exploiting, and his concern too over Charles's position as paymaster in Ireland now that Fox *fils* had openly defied administration in the Fenwick affair. As part of the settlement of May 1697 both father and son remained in office, and Sir Stephen sealed his renewed commitment to the ministry by subscribing £12,000 of his own money towards financing a further issue of Exchequer bills.[12]

For Fox the 1697–8 session was dominated by the Commons' inquiry into the Exchequer bills scandal, in which his protégé John Knight was deeply involved, and in which he himself narrowly escaped being implicated. Knight had been a client of his for many years, and it was on Fox's recommendation that Knight's accomplice, Bartholomew Burton, had been brought into the business. When evidence of the scandal first came to the Treasury's attention in the autumn of 1697, Fox offered himself as a security for Knight and, alone of the commissioners, defended Knight's character at the board, while at the same time being obliged to admit that he himself and his son had given bills. Reginald Marriott's testimony to the House in the following January reflected on him directly, with its claim, denied by Knight, that Fox's name had been used by Knight as a guarantor of security, and in common with his Treasury colleagues Fox was forced to speak in his own vindication. But unlike them he went so far as to defend Knight, this time in public. Having survived this trial he almost perversely involved himself in another, and risked again the wrath of his ministerial colleagues in voting on 26 Feb. against passing the bill of pains and penalties against his old confederate Charles Duncombe*: an act of bravado perhaps, or a deliberate gesture from a man on the point of resignation.[13]

The evidence would seem to indicate that Fox had now made up his mind to leave the public stage. In June 1698 he declared that he would not seek re-election at Westminster, and put his interest there at the disposal of Secretary of State James Vernon I*. Nor at first did he think of standing elsewhere. He was named as a placeman in July, and in August his son's dismissal as Irish paymaster, announced in William's absence without prior warning, provoked him into offering his resignation from the Treasury. It had been a particularly bitter blow, but the King decided that Fox could not for the present be spared and so he returned from sulking in the country to resume his place at the board. Henceforth, however, his attendance became noticeably slacker. Listed as a Court placeman in about September 1698, he re-entered the Commons with ease in January 1699, taking the seat Charles had vacated at Cricklade when he had opted to sit for Salisbury, and without encountering any opposition in a borough his proprietorial interest had come to dominate. But in his obvious disgruntlement his parliamentary activity seems to have slowed almost to a standstill. At the end of the session there were rumours that he would be dismissed. Indeed it seems that Montagu was authorized by the King to canvass suitable replacements. In the absence of an alternative, Fox 'stuck on', and in the 1699–1700 session was roused to speak in the debate of 13 Feb. 1700 on the state of the nation. In reply to the attack launched by John Grobham Howe* upon the 'exorbitant grants' passed in favour of members of the current administration, he 'spoke to Mr Howe's grant, *etc.*'.[14]

The change of ministry, and the recall of Godolphin to high office, seems to have rekindled Fox's zest for politics. He even contemplated a candidature at Westminster in the first general election of 1701, before backing off and settling for another return at Cricklade, though on this occasion at the unprecedentedly high cost of over £250. He was listed, predictably, with those Court supporters thought likely to agree with the committee of supply to continue the 'Great Mortgage'. Meanwhile, he had endured a brief embarrassment on 14 Mar., during an inquiry into the electioneering activities of Samuel Shepheard I*. The Country Whig Sir Richard Cocks, 2nd Bt.*, had harked back to Fox's evidence of secret service payments, given before the Commons in May 1679, in order to illustrate the long history of parliamentary corruption. Fortunately, sufficient Members came to Fox's defence to preclude the necessity for him to respond directly. Chosen again for Cricklade in November 1701, he was classed with the Whigs in Robert Harley's* list of the new House, presumably in reference to his lengthy association with the previous Whig administration, but from rumours of his impending removal from the Treasury in the following February we may infer that his credit with the temporarily resurgent Whig Junto was not especially high.

His principal concern in this Parliament, however, seems to have been the successful passage of a private bill to allow him a longer time to enter his claim with the trustees for Irish forfeited estates for relief from the effects of the Resumption Act.[15]

With Godolphin's appointment as lord treasurer after Queen Anne's accession, Fox was at last able to leave the Treasury. Retirement, he wrote, 'now happily came upon me'. This was an over-simplification. In fact, his reappointment as commissioner of the stables for the first few months of the new reign involved him in various ceremonial duties, some of them, at the coronation in particular, quite arduous for an elderly man. Moreover, he was asked to frame a new establishment for the royal household, with a view, as he thought, to some more permanent post there. But his uncompromising scheme for retrenchment antagonized vested interests. Not only was he disappointed in his renewed ambitions for the cofferership, but three of his dependants were dismissed from Household places and his own long-standing pension from the Board of Green Cloth (title to which he had recently purchased) was stopped. Although Charles Fox's reinstatement as joint paymaster was some compensation, Sir Stephen took his own personal slight as badly as was customary with him. A series of querulous memorials denounced the 'ill manners and . . . great injustice' with which he had been treated, and as late as 1704 Godolphin was complaining that Fox continued to 'persecute' him over the cofferer's place. Charles's dismissal for voting for the Tack in 1704 added insult to injury and produced a further batch of complaints. It is noticeable, however, that Fox continued to exploit his ministerial contacts, especially with Godolphin and the Duke of Ormond (who owed the preservation of his estate to Fox's financial help), to find patronage plums for his numerous relations and dependants. According to the anonymous biography that appeared shortly after his death, he now 'set himself at work to wind up the bottom of his life with acts of piety and charity', including the establishment of a hospital and charity school in his ancestral parish of Farley, other hospitals in Northamptonshire and Suffolk, and a school near his Somerset estate. He had severed one remaining official connexion with his resignation in 1703 from the commission for the Royal Hospital, in protest at having to serve under a younger chairman in an institution he had been principally responsible for inaugurating, but found himself nominated soon afterwards as a founding director of the naval hospital. His banking activities, both public and private, decreased perceptibly, though he remained, for instance, a substantial holder of Bank stock (with some £5,000 in about 1707–9), and he began to purchase real property once more, in order to consolidate the estate he would hand on to Charles. At the same time he proved he was far from his dotage by remarrying in 1703, at the age of 76, and producing four more children in old age, a demonstration of virility that led some envious observers to air doubts over his reputation for 'gravity and wisdom' and others to imply that he had received carnal assistance in the enterprise from his busy chaplain. That he had not forgotten his manifold grievances is clear from his resumed complaints of ill-treatment to Godolphin in the summer of 1710, as the lord treasurer's administration tottered to its fall, and his attendance upon Queen Anne in 1712 in the fruitless pursuit of further petitions over the cofferer's place and Chelsea Hospital, which he doubtless hoped would meet with a more sympathetic response under a Tory ministry.[16]

There was to be a brief coda to Fox's parliamentary career. In 1714, following Charles Fox's death, he allowed his name to be put forward for the vacancy at Salisbury, and, as the preacher at his own funeral remarked, it was a testimony to his reputation, and the local popularity he had for so long cultivated, that even at a crisis of party animosities he was returned unopposed and as 'one with whom all were pleased'. While he is not known to have spoken in this session, 'he was often seen to attend the House, as if not his life only, but his youth had been extended to that length', being spoken of as 'a prodigy for health and age'. He neither sought re-election in 1715, nor any personal advancement under the Hanoverians, but did continue his solicitations over minor matters of Treasury patronage.[17]

Fox died at Chiswick on 28 Oct. 1716 and was buried at Farley, leaving assets estimated by his modern biographer as having a capital value of over £174,000. These included property in five counties, besides his Whitehall apartments. According to a Grub Street panegyrist he

> left behind him a character, by the means of which, the greatest favourite of his prince, the chiefest minister of state, and the wealthiest subject, may read and see with pleasure and advantage an example of the greatest modesty and condescension, the exactest justice, most consummate generosity, and the most extended humanity.

That this was a judgment with which most contemporaries would have concurred is a tribute to Fox's genuine, if somewhat self-regarding, honesty in public affairs, and to the courtesy he invariably displayed towards friends and opponents alike. These qualities, together with a pride in efficient administration, made him an invaluable servant to successive monarchs, even in the Commons, where his contributions to debates on supply compensated in authority for what they lacked in *élan*. Though Fox's greatest services had been performed in previous reigns, King William was fortunate that his continuing appetite for office surmounted for so long the handicap of age and the resentments the Whigs seemed at times to load upon him. Ambitious for influence rather than status, he had always refused a peerage himself. His two surviving sons, however, both obtained titles, the elder, Stephen†, becoming Earl of Ilchester, the younger, Henry†, whom Fox had wished to be 'bred up for some honourable employment', following him as Treasury lord and paymaster (though with a different approach to the ethics of public duty), and eventually being raised to the peerage as Baron Holland.[18]

[1] This article draws heavily on C. Clay, *Public Finance and Private Wealth*. [2] G. S. Fox-Strangways, *Life of Henry Fox, 1st Lord Holland*, i. 3–15. [3] Luttrell, *Brief Relation*, iv. 191; v. 160, 192; *Cal. Treas. Bks.* xxviii. 29; *CSP Dom.* 1700–2, p. 475; 1703–4, p. 463. [4] Salisbury corp. recs. D35, f. 131; P. Thompson, *Hist. Boston*, 458. [5] C. G. T. Dean, *R. Hosp. Chelsea*, 125; *Daily Courant*, 8 Aug. 1704. [6] Westminster Diocesan Archs. Old Brotherhood mss iii/3/232, memo. by David Lloyd, 23 Mar. 1691; Clarke, *Jas. II*, ii. 485. [7] *CSP Dom.* 1689–90, pp. 5, 514; 1690–1, p. 242; *Mems. of Sir Stephen Fox* (1717), 86–87; Dorset RO, Fox-Strangways mss D124/238/25, petition from Fox, [?1704]; Add. 70314–15, Fox to Godolphin, 14 Aug. 1710; Luttrell, ii. 16, 22; DZA, Bonet despatch 18/28 Mar. 1690; Hamilton, *Grammont Mems.* ed. Scott, 209; *Poems on Affairs of State* ed. Cameron, v. 486; Dalrymple, *Mems.* iii(1), pp. 86, 252. [8] Bodl. Carte 79, f. 438; SRO, Breadalbane mss GD112/40/5/30, Countess of Caithness to Mrs Campbell, 10 Nov. 1691; Luttrell, ii. 304; Trinity, Dublin, Clarke mss 749/13/1329, Robert Yard* to George Clarke*, 12 Nov. 1691; Add. 51319, ff. 103–4; *Luttrell Diary*, 16, 77, 82, 105–6, 112–14, 137, 187; Grey, x. 195–6, 217; *Poems on Affairs of State*, v. 502; *Mems. of . . . Fox*, 87–88. [9] *Luttrell Diary*, 230, 248, 260, 283, 287, 360, 420, 445; Carte 130, f. 341; Grey, 281. [10] *CSP Dom.* 1693, p. 310; P. G. M. Dickson, *Financial Revol.* 258; Add. 17677 OO, f. 279; 42593, f. 40; *Cal. Treas. Bks.* x. 1370; Nottingham Univ. Lib. Portland (Bentinck) mss PwA 501, 507, 513, Guy to Portland, 17 May, 19 July, 20 Aug. 1695; *Correspondentie* ed. Japikse, ser. 1, ii. 58, 61–62. [11] Add. 51319, ff. 146–9; K. Feiling, *Tory Party*, 309; H. Horwitz, *Parl. and Pol. Wm. III*, 165; *EHR*, lxxviii. 108; Luttrell, iv. 92; *Portledge Pprs.* 236; *HMC Downshire*, i. 690. [12] Luttrell, iv. 134, 211; Add. 30000 C, f. 242; Bodl. Ballard 5, f. 101; Northants. RO, Montagu (Boughton) mss 46/27, Vernon to Shrewsbury, 26 Nov. 1696; Macaulay, *Hist. Eng.* vi. 2695–6; *Shrewsbury Corresp.* 476, 478, 480; J. P. Kenyon, *Sunderland*, 291; *Vernon–Shrewsbury Letters*, i. 227; *HMC Downshire*, i. 668. [13] *HMC Finch*, iii. 220; *Cal. Treas. Bks.* xiii. 16, 35–36; Add. 70018, f. 234; *CJ*, xii. 24, 27, 35–36; Montagu (Boughton) mss 46/175, Vernon to Shrewsbury, 4 Jan. 1697[–8]; Yale Univ. Beinecke Lib. Osborn coll. Manchester mss, Yard to Ld. Manchester, 22 Feb., 1 Mar. 1697[–8]; *CSP Dom.* 1698, p. 65; Horwitz, 235. [14] Montagu (Boughton) mss 47/49, Vernon to Shrewsbury, 25 June 1698; Add. 51324, ff. 57–59; *CSP Dom.* 1698, p. 331; *Cal. Treas. Bks.* xiv. 2, 109; *Vernon–Shrewsbury Letters*, ii. 143, 175, 293, 297; Luttrell, iv. 431; Horwitz, 258, 272; Som. RO, Sanford mss DD/SF4107(a), notes of debate, 13 Feb. 1699[–1700]. [15] Carte 228, ff. 335, 341, 343; W. A. Speck, *Tory and Whig*, 60; Fox-Strangways mss, election expenses, Jan. 1701 (Horwitz trans.); *Cocks Diary*, 66; Luttrell, v. 140. [16] Fox-Strangways mss D124/237/17, memo. by Fox [c.1706]; *Marlborough–Godolphin Corresp.* 288; *Mems. of . . . Fox*, 90–91; *Cal. Treas. Pprs.* 1702–7, p. 53; *Cal. Treas. Bks.* xxvi. 310; *HMC Ormonde*, n.s. viii. 153; R. Eyre, *Sermon Preached at the Funeral of Sir Stephen Fox* (1716), 6, 12; Ballard 10, f. 118; Add. 70314–15, Fox to Godolphin, 14 Aug. 1710; *Wentworth Pprs.* 250; *HMC Portland*, x. 85. [17] Eyre, 10; Boyer, *Pol. State*, vii. 265; Ballard 31, f. 102; *Cal. Treas. Pprs.* 1714–19, p. 25. [18] Add. 51324, f. 25; Eyre, 11; *Mems. of . . . Fox*, 99; Fox-Strangways, *Henry Fox*, 23.

D. W. H.

FRANK, Robert (1660–1738), of Pontefract, Yorks.

PONTEFRACT 1710–22 Mar. 1716

bap. 2 Feb. 1660, o. s. of John Frank of Pontefract by Mary, da. and coh. of William Harbred of Wistow, Yorks. *educ.* St. John's, Camb. 1676; G. Inn 1678, called 1685, ancient 1704. *m.* 21 Feb. 1699 (with £2,000), Elizabeth (d. 1726), da. of Ralph Lowther (uncle of Sir John Lowther, 2nd Bt. I*) of Ackworth Park, Yorks., 1s. *d.v.p.* 3da. *suc.* fa. 1698.[1]

Recorder, Pontefract 1686–?98, 1703–*d*; commr. Aire and Calder navigation 1699.[2]

The Franks of Pontefract, a junior branch of the Franks of Campsall, were established by Frank's grandfather in the early 17th century. The senior branch of the family had been leading members of the corporation since at least the mid-16th century and the cadet branch continued this tradition, with Frank's father serving as an alderman from the Restoration until his death in March 1698. Having received a legal education, Frank was named recorder of Pontefract in 1686, an appointment confirmed when James II regulated the corporation in May 1688. In August the same year, however, Frank gave evasive replies to the questions concerning the repeal of the Test Act and Penal Laws, and a recommendation was made to the King that Frank be replaced as recorder. This suggestion was not acted upon, but in 1696, in the midst of prolonged political infighting in the corporation, Frank's qualification as recorder was called into question. The then mayor claimed that Frank had failed to qualify himself by taking the necessary oaths when first appointed recorder in 1686, and that his taking of these oaths two years later was not sufficient to qualify Frank as the corporation had subsequently declared illegal James II's regulation of 1688. These claims were accepted by Secretary Shrewsbury and in April 1696 Frank was deprived of his office and a new recorder elected. Frank continued to be active in borough politics, however, and as late as June 1698 he was still exercising the office while his allies refused to swear in Frank's replacement. The case was brought before the Privy Council, which ordered the arrest and prosecution of Frank. This ended Frank's resistance to his removal, but in 1703 he was reappointed borough recorder. He was to retain this post until his death, and in this period became one of the leading figures in Pontefract politics.[3]

At the 1710 election Frank, in alliance with his father's stepson Sir John Bland, 4th Bt.*, gained one of the borough's seats, and was classed in the 'Hanover list' as a Tory. This assessment was borne out by his inclusion in 1711 on the list of 'Tory patriots' who had opposed the continuation of the war, but he was to prove an inactive Member. On 16 Mar. 1711 he was granted a leave of absence on account of his poor health, and the following year, on 17 May, was granted a further month's leave. On 18 June 1713 he voted against the French commerce bill. Successful at Pontefract at the 1713 election, he was granted a month's leave of absence on 31 May 1714. The Worsley list and two further comparisons of the 1713 and 1715 Parliaments all listed him as a Tory. He retained his seat at the 1715 election, due in part to the 20 Pontefract burgages he was said to own at this time, but was unseated the following year upon petition. He died in 1738 and was buried within the ruins of Pontefract Castle on 6 Sept. Frank was succeeded in his estates by his three daughters, one of whom had married Richard Frank of Campsall who succeeded Frank as Pontefract's recorder.[4]

[1] *Dugdale's Vis. Yorks.* ed. Clay, iii. 175; Sheffield Archs. Bacon Frank mss BFM 599, marriage settlement, 17 Feb. 1698–9. [2] *Pontefract Corp. Bk.* ed. Holmes, 165, 209, 211, 252–3; PC 2/77, p. 186; *HMC Lords*, n.s. iii. 204. [3] *Dugdale's Vis. Yorks.* 173–5; J. Foster, *Peds. Yorks. Fams.* i. (Frank); *Pontefract Corp. Bk.* 165, 171–3, 209–12, 216, 252; PC 2/77, pp. 186, 195. [4] Add. 70211, Bland to Robert Harley*, 14 Oct. 1710; Quinn thesis, 210.

E. C./R. D. H.

FRANKLAND, Thomas I (1665–1726), of Thirkleby, nr. Thirsk, Yorks. and Chiswick, Mdx.

THIRSK	1685–1687, 1689–1695
HEDON	3 Dec. 1695–1698
THIRSK	1698–7 June 1711

b. Sept. 1665, 1st s. of Sir William Frankland, 1st Bt.†, of Thirkleby by Arabella, da. of Hon. Henry Belasyse†, of Newburgh Priory, Yorks. *educ.* Trinity, Camb. 1681; L. Inn 1683. *m.* lic. 14 Feb. 1683, aged about 18, Elizabeth (*d.* 1733), da. of Sir John Russell, 3rd Bt., of Chippenham, Cambs., 7s. (2 *d.v.p.*) 3da. *suc.* fa. as 2nd Bt. 2 Aug. 1697.[1]

Commr. excise Apr.–Oct. 1689, customs 1715–18; jt. postmaster-gen. 1691–1715.[2]

Frankland was described by a contemporary as being 'chief of a very good family in Yorkshire, with a very good estate', and as 'a gentleman of a very sweet, easy, affable disposition; of good sense, extreme zealous for the constitution of his country, yet does not seem over forward'. Swift, who dined with Frankland on several occasions, recorded this description as being 'a fair character'. Frankland's wife was a granddaughter of Oliver Cromwell† by her mother, a factor that was believed to have caused his uncle, Thomas Belasyse, Earl Fauconberg, who had married one of Cromwell's daughters and was therefore Elizabeth's uncle also, to settle a considerable estate in Middlesex upon him at the time of his wedding, along with other valuable property in Yorkshire and London. Frankland's marriage and his relationship to Fauconberg were said to have been the factors that 'first recommended him to King William'. They also explain why, in September 1688, Frankland was regarded as 'doubtful' by James II's agents when they reported on the reliability of MPs likely to be returned for Thirsk. He had a strong interest in the borough due to the town's proximity to Thirkleby, his familial ties with Fauconberg, and, most of all, as a result of his ownership of about 40 of the 48 burgages.[3]

Although Frankland's tenure as an excise commissioner in 1689 was short-lived, following the dismissal of John Wildman†, in February 1691 he was appointed as joint postmaster-general with Sir Robert Cotton*, who was a Tory and a follower of Lord Carmarthen (Sir Thomas Osborne†). The post was split in two in an attempt to strengthen the Court party in Parliament, and probably as an endeavour to balance Whig and Tory in a sensitive employment. Almost immediately after their appointment Frankland and Cotton were in conflict with the commission of public accounts over payment of postage costs. The alteration in office did not pass without criticism, though Lord Sydney (Henry Sidney†) informed William that 'the displacing Major Wildman is the discourse of all the town, and people generally are well satisfied with it, and so they are with the choice the Queen has made as his successor'. Of Frankland he stated: 'I do not know him much, but he has such a good character that I do not doubt his deserving the favour that is shown him.' Sydney also noted that Carmarthen did not approve of the choice, his chief objection being that 'one is a Whig and the other is a Tory, which he says is the most destructive method your Majesty can take. I confess I cannot agree with him . . . but besides, this is not the case, for they are both moderate men.'[4]

The office was politically important, and was perceived, in 1702, as making the office-holder 'master of all intelligence', as he could open or withhold mail, and generally control the dissemination of information, while also having first contact with information from abroad. Frankland was the more active of the two postmasters, and during his tenure 'important improvements in the frequency and extension of postal communication were inaugurated', especially in the area of the foreign, Irish and plantation services. A contemporary assessment stated that 'by abundance of application he understands that office better than any man in England', and that, despite the war with France, 'he improved that revenue to £10,000 a year more than it was in the most flourishing years. He was the first that directed a correspondence with Spain and Portugal, and all our foreign plantations, to the great advantage of our traffic.' He supposedly kept 'an exact unity among the officers under him, and encourages them in their duty, through a peculiar familiarity, by which he obliges them, and keeps up the dignity of being master'. Initially, Frankland and Cotton shared an annual salary of £1,500, which was later increased to £1,000 each, and in 1711 to £1,500 each, by which time Frankland shared the office with John Evelyn II*.[5]

Although he was a serving MP from 1690 to 1711, there is not a great deal of evidence to suggest that Frankland was a very active Member. Returned for Thirsk in March 1690, he was listed as a Whig by Carmarthen. On 12 May he acted as a teller in favour of a motion to adjourn proceedings for the day. In April 1691 Robert Harley* noted him as a Court supporter, and at some point between May and November 1692 he was named in a working list of Court supporters in Parliament. In the 1692–3 session he acted as spokesman for his office when a debate on 1 Feb. centred upon the abuse of the Members' privilege of free postage, to the detriment of the revenue. Frankland pointed out that 'anciently there was a book lay open in the Speaker's chamber where every Member set his name and put his seal to prevent any tricks'. However, the House felt that this, and other suggestions made on the subject, were excessive. In the 1693–4 session Frankland was one of several MPs to be identified as having received payments out of the secret service fund. The purpose of these disclosures, on 9 Dec., was to attack the Court party over payments that were perceived as bribes to Members. Frankland, for his part, had received £800 as a 'free gift' in compensation for his removal from the excise commission in 1689. A list originally compiled by Samuel Grascome in 1693 recorded Frankland as a placeman and Court supporter, and on a series of later lists he continued to be noted as a placeman. In the session of 1694–5 Henry Guy* listed him as a 'friend', probably in connexion with the Commons' attack upon Guy.[6]

Though not standing at the 1695 election, Frankland was chosen as Member for Hedon in a by-election on 7 Dec. In a forecast for a division on 31 Jan. 1696 over the proposed council of trade, he was listed as likely to support the Court. The following month he was among the majority of MPs who signed the Association. In March he voted with the Court on the issue of fixing the price of guineas at 22s. On 3 Apr. he and Cotton were nominated as a two-man committee for drafting a bill for correcting several defects in the laws relating to the Post Office. Frankland voted, on 25 Nov. 1696, for the attainder of Sir John Fenwick†. In the 1697–8 session, following a complaint made in the Commons on 30 Apr. about Members' letters being intercepted and taken away at the door of the House, Frankland was first-named to a committee to inquire into the issue. On 27 May he reported the committee's findings and resolutions to the House. Returned for Thirsk in 1698, Frankland was listed as a placeman and a Court supporter in the comparative list of the old and new Parliaments in September of that year. In line with this classification, he voted on 18 Jan. 1699 against the third reading of the disbanding bill. On 23 Feb. he presented a petition to the Commons, from the inhabitants and clothiers of Halifax, relating to the particularly sensitive issue of the woollen manufacture. He hoped that the petition would 'meet with the desired success', and looked upon his action, of 'promoting what may be thought most conducing and effectual to encourage the woollen manufacture', as 'a service to the public' and as beneficial 'to this kingdom'. However, on 6 Apr. Frankland seemed to express a certain boredom with proceedings in a letter to Thomas Worsley I*:

> Our proceedings since you went down have been of so little moment, that I did not think them worth giving you the trouble of a letter, for notwithstanding the great promises you heard of making good the deficiencies, we have hitherto made very slow steps towards it, having only as yet resolved to apply the overplus of the customs, and the 22s. per pound weight laid upon all Indian [wrought?] silks by the last Parliament both which will scarce exceed £500,000 and I cannot hear they have any other ways and means except a single poll which I believe will be the upshot of this sessions.

Despite the reference to events of 'little moment', the letter did demonstrate Frankland's particular interest and understanding of revenue affairs. Proceedings gained more interest for Frankland on 12 Apr., when he and Cotton complained about a printed paper entitled *The Case of John Woodgate, Late Postmaster of Canterbury*, which reflected badly upon their management of the Post Office. A committee of inquiry was appointed, which made a lengthy report on 22 Apr. with which the Commons agreed, finding the paper to be 'false, scandalous, and malicious', and ordering that Woodgate be taken into the custody of the serjeant-at-arms. Frankland was also involved later that month in giving evidence to a committee of inquiry in defence of Daniel Gwyn.[7]

Although Frankland appeared to be inactive during the 1699–1700 session, he watched developments with interest in the lead-up to the new Parliament in 1701. On 5 Sept. 1700 he noted that, although there was little news from London, 'our politicians chiefly entertain themselves without, forming schemes how to enlarge our Act of Settlement. Most agree it is necessary to do something, but the dispute is about what is best.' He was returned once more for Thirsk in 1701, and continued to act in support of the Court. In February 1701 he was forecast as likely to support the Court in agreeing with the supply committee's resolution to continue the 'Great Mortgage'. During a difficult session, in which the balance of power and the disagreements over issues such as the policy towards France led to a certain amount of confusion in Parliament, Frankland described events in a letter to Worsley on 1 Apr.:

> I cannot at all wonder you should think some of our proceedings want explanation for we who are daily witnesses of the transactions can scarce tell how to unriddle many of them, then as to parties they put on such various postures and dresses that they can scarce be always called by the same name. Those in our House who are supposed friends to the present ministry appear the most averse to a war, and those of a contrary party more inclined to it, being more apprehensive of the power of France. I believe Mr [John] Smith [I*] perceived some men in the House had a mind to be picking at him, and his party not in as you imagine, made him rather choose to quit, than to stay in and not have the credit he might expect in his post.

He then told how that day a report from 'the committee [of the whole, on the state of the nation] immediately ordered Sir John Leveson Gower [5th Bt.] to carry an impeachment to the lords against my Lord Portland for high crimes and misdemeanours, and appointed a committee to draw up articles'. However, Frankland, despite appearing in the sentiments expressed in his own correspondence to be non-aligned in terms of party, was still classified as a Whig by Harley in December 1701.[8]

Frankland began to become more active in endeavouring to use his personal interest in Yorkshire, and the Post Office interest elsewhere, to influence elections from 1701 onwards. It appears that Viscount Irwin (Arthur Ingram*), standing for Yorkshire, was advised in November 1701 that, along with needing the support of Fauconberg, Frankland also could 'do my lordship a kindness'. On 13 Nov. it was suggested that Frankland's brother, Henry, believed he could procure 'all the freeholders within his brother Sir Thomas Frankland's lordship to give their votes for my Lord Irwin'. At the same time Frankland was also exploiting his Post Office interest. On 18 Nov. he wrote to David Polhill*, one of the Kentish Petitioners, enclosing a letter which was to inform Captain Lucas, presumably of the packet-boats, that 'in case the Dover election is to be in a little time he may return back again before he comes to London. We thought it better to put it upon that than take any notice of the election at Rochester.'[9]

Frankland was inactive for most of the 1701–2 Parliament, though he did tell on 21 May against a rider for the reversal of the Irish outlawry of Charles Trant. However, he may have had other concerns on his mind, as in April 1702 it was rumoured that he was to be replaced as postmaster-general by John Grobham Howe*. Despite the rumour, he retained his office, and was returned once more for Thirsk in the first of Queen Anne's Parliaments. However, he belonged to a significant group of Whigs in the Commons who 'found their allegiances to a varying extent divided during Anne's reign between party and Court'. During the 1704–5 session he was forecast as a probable opponent of the Tack, and he did not vote for it on 28 Nov. Following the 1705 election, in which he was returned for Thirsk once more, he was listed as a placeman and as 'Low Church' in an analysis of the new Parliament. In the division over the Speaker on 25 Oct., he voted for the Court candidate. His continued support for the Court was demonstrated again on 18 Feb. 1706, in the proceedings on the 'place clause' of the regency bill. He was recorded as a Whig on two lists in 1708.[10]

Frankland continued to utilize the Post Office interest in elections, in 1708 to secure his eldest son's return to Parliament. As early as May 1704 it had been reported that Frankland was thinking of putting up his son for Harwich, and though nothing came of this in 1705 Frankland was able to secure his son's return there in 1708. It was also suggested by Sir John Cropley, 2nd Bt.*, in late April 1708 that Henry Cornish*, in attempting to stand for Shaftesbury, derived 'his expectation' from Frankland.[11]

During the 1708–9 session Frankland, in line with Whig sentiments, was recorded as supporting the naturalization of the Palatines. He also endeavoured to act on behalf of Dumfries Burgh in getting their postal service to Carlisle established by Act of Parliament. On 21 May 1709 John Hutton II, MP for the district, wrote to Dumfries town council giving an account of their affairs at the rising of Parliament. Frankland had had a clause ready to suit their needs, but had fallen ill and could not attend the House for a lengthy period. His son Thomas, and Frankland's associates, had been entrusted with the business, but, because the bill for improving the Union, in which it was intended to insert the clause, was unlikely to be passed that session, it was decided to proceed by a short Act 'to empower the postmasters to transact whatever should be for the interest of the crown and the ease of Her Majesty's good subjects'. However, in view of 'the heats between parties', and especially between English and Scottish Members over the bill to improve the Union, it was thought best to defer the post bill rather than present it just before the prorogation. Frankland apologized for the delay, and expressed his intention to settle the matter the following winter. At the same time Hutton informed the provost that

> Frankland says you need not went [sic] to no trouble any more about the post, because it is solely and only his proper business, and he must have the powers needful by an Act of Parliament; if you can agree to employ a carrier for the summertime, you will in a few months be able to judge of the advantage.[12]

Later that year Frankland advised Worsley on the prospects for getting his son, and Frankland's future son-in-law, returned at a by-election for Malton, following William Strickland II's appointment as a revenue commissioner in Ireland in 1709. Frankland wrote to Worsley snr. on 11 Aug. expressing his views on the likely outcome:

> You judge very rightly of difficulty to succeed against a favourite, and therefore I should choose to have my cause as strong as possible, and if you could have more votes than your son, were it not better to stand yourself? . . . I should endeavour to prevent the matter being disputed in the House of Commons, where considering your late treatment [decision on a double return, 1708] you may expect no little partiality.

In the end Strickland was returned unopposed in November. His desire that 'we shall meet with olive branches this winter in St. Stephen's', for the 1709–10 session, went unfulfilled, primarily due to the turmoil attending the trial of Dr Sacheverell. In line with his Whig affiliations he voted for Sacheverell's impeachment.[13]

Frankland was returned for Thirsk in 1710, and was listed as a Whig in the 'Hanover list' of the new Parliament, though his Court inclinations came to the fore in a Tory-dominated assembly, as his instinct for survival in office dominated his actions. In late 1710 and early 1711 rumours began to circulate that he was to be replaced by Francis Gwyn*. In September Swift recorded that Frankland would 'sacrifice everything to save himself' if the rumours were true. On 7 Dec. Frankland wrote to Harley expressing his concerns:

> I have . . . been told by so many persons that Mr Gwyn was to come into my place in the Post Office . . . I hope you will pardon my giving you this trouble to beg your friendship to me, that after so long and faithful services, as well as successful endeavours in improving this branch of her Majesty's revenue, I may be considered as one who has made it his business to perform the duty of his place, but never to engage himself in those heats and violence which have created these unhappy divisions among us. I am sure I need not acquaint you, how dissatisfied some persons were with me, for the unwillingness I frequently showed to comply with the pressing instances I have met with to put in or turn out purely for the sake of party, and I doubt not but you may now have many complaints that we keep in and support ill men.

However, despite his concern over his office, Frankland continued to participate in Parliament, and on 18 Feb. 1711 he was appointed to the drafting committee for a bill for establishing a General Post Office for Great Britain and the dominions, and for repealing the individual acts for England and Scotland. He told on 18 Apr. against an amendment to the bill, for reserving any surplus of duties over £700 per week to the use of the public. On 25 Apr. he again wrote to Harley in connexion with this bill, and concerning his position as postmaster-general:

> I . . . must observe, it was very hard upon me, to be left almost alone to be baited by some unreasonable gentlemen, when I could have no other interest by my endeavours than to obtain those powers and regulations necessary to secure her Majesty's revenue, especially since, if from the want thereof there should be a deficiency, it will fall upon her Majesty's civil list. The Act is to commence upon the 1st of June. There are many things necessary to be done, to be ready to put it in execution to the best advantage . . . I own I had formed that scheme to myself, as to have the office under as punctual an economy as was possible where so many persons are employed, but being every day told I am not like to continue in the employment, I do not know how to behave myself. I am sure nothing shall prevent me doing her Majesty the best and most faithful service I am capable of, in whatever station I am.

At the same time he pointed out that a clause in the first Lottery Act 'renders those in this office incapable to be Members of Parliament. As you have always been pleased to honour me with your friendship I beg you will let me know how I am to be disposed of, that I may not be perpetually under these uncertainties.' Having voted on 25 May against an amendment to the South Sea bill, Frankland, still being postmaster, ceased sitting as an MP following the issuing of a new writ for Thirsk on 7 June. He did not re-enter Parliament, though his continued interest in Thirsk ensured that his son-in-law, Thomas Worsley II, was returned in the 1711 by-election, while his own son sat for the borough 1713-47.[14]

Despite his concerns in 1711, Frankland retained his position as postmaster-general until the accession of George I, after which he was appointed as a customs commissioner. His continued affiliation to the Whig party was demonstrated by his membership of the Hanover Club, founded in 1712. In 1718 he was granted a pension of £500 a year as he was too infirm to continue his customs commission duties. He took no further part in public life. In 1722 he rebuilt Thirkleby church at his own expense. He died on 30 Oct. 1726, in his 62nd year, leaving all his lands to his eldest son, and more than £13,000 divided between his other four surviving sons, his wife, three daughters, two brothers, one sister, and various servants and tenants.[15]

[1] R. W. Gallwey, *Ped. Frankland of Thirkleby, Yorks.*; *Her. and Gen.* vii. 260-1; *Dugdale's Vis. Yorks.* ed. Clay, ii. 245; M. Noble, *Mems. House of Cromwell*, ii. 418-22; J. Waylen, *House of Cromwell*, 109-10; *CSP. Dom.* 1697, p. 287. [2] *Cal. Treas. Bks.* ix. 82, 273, 1037; xxix. 390, 407; xxxii. 666. [3] Noble, 416-17; Waylen, 109; *Her. and Gen.* 260; Gallwey, *Ped.*; *Swift Stella*, ed. Davis, 12, 131, 157; *Swift Works*, ed. Davis, v. 260; Duckett, *Penal Laws and Test Act* (1882), 103; W. A. Speck, *Tory and Whig*, 47-48; *HMC Astley*, 62. [4] *Cal. Treas. Bks.* ix. 82, 273, 1037; H. Horwitz, *Parl. and Pol. Wm. III*, 66; *EHR*, xci. 41-42; H. Robinson, *Brit. Post Office*, 78-79; *CSP. Dom.* 1690-1, p. 283; A. Browning, *Danby*, i. 286. [5] W. Yorks. Archs. (Leeds), Temple Newsam mss TN/C9/241, Christopher Stockdale* to Visct. Irwin (Arthur Ingram*), 28 Apr. 1702; *HMC Var.* viii. 86; Robinson, 78-79, 99; Noble, 417-18; *Her. and Gen.* 260; J. C. Hemmeon, *Hist. Brit. Post Office*, 31, 115. [6] *Luttrell Diary*, 395, 493; Cobbett, *Parlty. Hist.* v. 808, clxxii; Horwitz, 347, 361; Chandler, ii. 426; Som. RO, Sanford mss DD/SF 4513, secret service money for MPs [n.d.]; Bodl. Carte mss 130, ff. 330-1. [7] Luttrell, *Brief Relation*, iii. 558; iv. 508; Stowe mss 747, f. 109; N. Yorks. RO, Worsley mss ZON 13/1/216, Frankland to Thomas Worsley I, 6 Apr. 1699; *CJ.* xii. 680. [8] Worsley mss ZON 13/1/240, 243, Frankland to Worsley, 5 Sept. 1700, 1 Apr. 1701. [9] Temple Newsam mss TN/C9/93, 139, Thomas Lumley to John Roades, 8 Nov. 1701, Thomas [Story] to Lumley, 13 Nov. 1701; Sevenoaks Pub. Lib. Polhill-Drabble mss U1007/C13/5, Frankland to Polhill, 18 Nov. 1701. [10] Temple Newsam mss TN/C9/241, Stockdale to Visct. Irwin, 28 Apr. 1702; *HMC Var.* viii. 86; G. Holmes, *Pol. in Age of Anne*, 228; *Bull. IHR*, xxxvii. 32. [11] *Hist. Jnl.* iv. 197-8; Add. 28927, f. 176; 28893, ff. 241, 278, 322, 329; PRO 30/24/21/52-53. [12] Dumfries Archs. Centre, Dumfries Burgh Recs. RB2/2/39-41. [13] Waylen, 155; *Her. and Gen.* 261; *Dugdale's Vis. Yorks.* 245; Worsley mss ZON 13/1/303, Frankland to Worsley, 11 Aug. 1709; Bagot mss at Levens Hall, Frankland to James Grahme*, 20 Aug. 1709. [14] *HMC Portland*, iv. 640; Trumbull Alphab. mss 54, John Bridges to Sir William Trumbull*, 5 Jan. 1710[-11]; SRO, Montrose mss GD220/5/808/2, Mungo Graham* to Duke of Montrose, 4 Jan. 1711; *Scots Courant*, 8-10 Jan. 1711; *Swift Stella*, 12; Add. 70227, Frankland to Harley, 7 Dec. 1710, 25 Apr. 1711; Ellis thesis, 16; Boyer, *Anne Annals*, ix. 396; Boyer, *Pol. State*, i-ii. 325; Chandler, iv. 223; Cobbett, vi. 1032; Pittis, *Present Parl.* 322. [15] Boyer, *Pol. State*, i-ii. 380; iv. 56; *Cal. Treas. Bks.* xxix. 61, 390, 407; xxxii. 666; Robinson, 99; Egerton ch. 7654; Holmes, 299; Luttrell, v. 333; *HMC Portland*, 501; *Swift Stella*, 10; *Her. and Gen.* 260; Gallwey, *Ped.*; PCC 256 Plymouth.

E. C./C. I. M

FRANKLAND, Thomas II (c.1685-1747), of Thirkleby, Yorks.

HARWICH   1708-1713
THIRSK   1713-17 Apr. 1747

b. c.1685, 1st s. of (Sir) Thomas Frankland I* (2nd Bt.). *educ.* Jesus, Camb. 1700; travelled abroad (Italy) 1704-5; Padua Univ., 1705. *m.* (1) 5 June 1715, Dinah (*d.* 1741), da. and h. of Francis Topham of Agglethorpe, Yorks., 2da.; (2) 9 July 1741, Sarah Moseley of Worcs., 1s. *d.v.p. suc.* fa. as 3rd Bt. 30 Oct. 1726.[1]

Clerk of deliveries in Ordnance and sec. to muster-master-gen. 1715-22; commr. revenue [I] 1724-8; ld. of Trade 1728-30; ld. of Admiralty 1730-42.[2]

As a young man travelling through Europe Frankland was described in December 1704 as

one of the prettiest young gentlemen I ever saw, and hath a right genius for perfectly understanding architecture, painting, and the curiosities of Rome. The Duke of Shrewsbury says he is the prettiest gentleman he hath seen abroad, because he hath brought more knowledge of his own country and its constitution with him than any of them; he makes a good figure at a small expense.

Such glowing testimony was apt at a time when Frankland's father was said to be having 'thoughts of putting up his eldest son' for election in Harwich on the Post Office interest. These plans gathered momentum by 1707, when John Ellis was warned that his seat was in great danger. On a visit to the borough in April 1708, Frankland was described as 'a pretty sort of a gentleman, and appears to me to have sense above his years, for he seems to me to be very young'. The united interests of Sir John Leake* and the Post Office, based on the packet-boat service, duly secured the election for Frankland.[3]

In an analysis of the returns following the 1708 election Frankland was classed as a Whig. His early parliamentary activity also identified him as a Court supporter, like his father. He supported the naturalization of the Palatines in early 1709, and told on 9 Mar. for a motion to appoint a date one month later for consideration of the bill to encourage tobacco exportation. He also endeavoured to take responsibility for his father's affairs in Parliament while Sir Thomas was absent through illness. In the most significant event of the 1709–10 session he followed the Whig line, and voted for the impeachment of Dr Sacheverell.[4]

Frankland was returned unopposed for Harwich in the 1710 election. As Harwich was considered a 'government borough', Frankland was expected to continue to support the Court. However, he became a member of the opposition to Robert Harley* in the new Parliament, being classed as a Whig in the 'Hanover list'. As he was not yet an office-holder, even though his brother William held the office of cashier of the stamps in trust for him, Frankland did not have to deal with the conflict of interests facing Whig placemen in Parliament. On 16 Dec. he acted as a teller against the Tory Sir Francis Child* being declared duly elected in the disputed Devizes election. On 18 Apr. 1711 he acted as a teller in favour of an amendment to the General Post Office bill, for continuing the present managers during pleasure, one of whom was Frankland's father, who had sat on the drafting committee for the bill. In the 1711–12 session, in line with Whig sentiment, he voted on 7 Dec. for the 'No Peace without Spain' motion. In the 1713 session he again showed his party allegiance when he voted on 18 June against the French commerce bill. For the 1713 election he transferred to the borough of Thirsk, which his father had previously represented in Parliament, and where the family interest was extremely strong. Returned unopposed, he was classed as a Whig in the Worsley list, and, in keeping with this classification, voted on 18 Mar. 1714 against the expulsion of Richard Steele. On 31 Mar. he told in favour of discharging Thomas Glascock from custody, Glascock having been arrested for refusing the Tory Nicholas Corsellis* access to Colchester borough records while preparing for a disputed election case. On 24 June Frankland acted as a teller against the Tory candidate, Hon. Benedict Leonard Calvert*, being declared duly elected for Harwich. Not surprisingly, Frankland was classed as a Whig on two lists which compared the 1715 Parliament with its predecessor, while at the same time he commenced a lengthy period of office-holding which resulted in his eventual description as a 'Walpolian placeman'. Described in his later years as a 'trusted counsellor of Frederick, Prince of Wales', Frankland continued to sit for Thirsk until his death on 17 Apr. 1747.[5]

[1] R. W. Gallwey, *Ped. Frankland of Thirkleby, Yorks.*; *HMC Astley*, 170; *Dugdale's Vis. Yorks.* ed. Clay, ii. 245; *Swift Stella* ed. Davis, 131; *Her. and Gen.* vii. 260–2. [2]*Cal. Treas. Bks.* xxix. 433; M. Noble, *Mems. House of Cromwell*, ii. 422–3; *Liber Munerum Publicorum Hiberniae*, ed. Lascelles, i(2), 134; Add. 36129, f. 200; 36130, f. 91; *Swift Stella*, 131. [3]*HMC Astley*, 170; Add. 28927, f. 176; 28893, ff. 241, 245, 278, 322, 329; *Hist. Jnl.* iv. 197–8. [4]Dumfries Archs. Centre, Dumfries burgh recs. RB2/2/41. [5]G. Holmes, *Pol. in Age of Anne*, 362–3; *HMC Portland*, iv. 501; *Hist. Jnl.* 197–8; Gallwey, *Ped.*; *Her. and Gen.* 260–2, 268; *Swift Stella*, 131; PCC 125 Potter.

E. C./C. I. M.

FREKE, Thomas I (c.1638–1701), of Shroton and Melcombe Horsey, Dorset.

DORSET   1679 (Mar.)–1681 (Mar.), 1685–1687
                1689–1701 (Nov.)

b. c.1638, 3rd s. of John Freke† of Cerne Abbey, Dorset being 2nd s. by his 2nd w. Jane, da. and coh. of Sir John Shirley† of Isfield, Suss., wid. of Sir Walter Covert† of Slaugham, Suss. *educ.* M. Temple 1655. *m.* 19 Sept. 1669, Cicely, da. of Robert Hussey of Stourpaine, Dorset, *s.p. suc.* bro. 1657.[1]

Freeman, Poole 1660, Lyme Regis 1666; sheriff, Dorset 1663–4; high sheriff, Dorchester 1679–*d.*[2]

Freke had inherited property in Dorset worth £4,000 p.a. in 1657, and by subsequent purchases considerably augmented his estate. He represented Dorset from 1679 and never faced a contest there. Initially, he was a follower of the 1st Earl of Shaftesbury (Sir Anthony Ashley Cooper†), but later joined the Court. After the 1690 election he was listed by Lord Carmarthen (Sir Thomas Osborne†) as one of the Court supporters who would probably defend him in the event of an attack in the Commons on his ministerial position. Robert Harley*, however, classified Freke with the Country party in April 1691. Although a Tory, Freke continued to enjoy the friendship of the Whig earls of Shaftesbury, whose electoral interests in various Dorset boroughs he bolstered in return. Thus a kinsman and namesake, Thomas II*, enjoyed Freke's support at Weymouth, despite being a Country Whig. Between May 1691 and April 1700, their activities in the House are often indistinguishable, although it seems 'Mr Freke' was more active when Thomas II sat in the Commons, and most activity has been tentatively ascribed to him. Thomas I was forecast as a probable opponent of the Court in the division of 31 Jan. 1696 on the council of trade, and in February refused to sign the Association. In March 1696 he voted against the Court over fixing the price of guineas at 22s., and also opposed the attainder of Sir John Fenwick† on 25 Nov. He was granted leave of absence on 16 Feb. and 23 Dec. 1697. Listed as a member of the Country party in about September 1698, he was forecast as likely to oppose the standing army the following month. In an analysis of the House into interests in 1700 his name was marked with a query. In the first Parliament of 1701 he was thought likely to support the Court over the 'Great Mortgage', and was later blacklisted as having opposed preparations for war. Having been given leave of absence on 30 May 1701 owing to failing health he agreed to stand for re-election on the understanding that he would not actually attend the House. In fact he died on 5 Dec. 1701, shortly before the election. He left his estate to Elizabeth Freke, the wife of Thomas II, and her father Thomas Pile, with a reversion to the eldest son of George Pitt* in the event of her death without children.[3]

[1] *The Ancestor*, x. 199; Hutchins, *Dorset*, iv. 86–87; Wards 5/11/1951. [2] Hutchins, i. 32; C. H. Mayo, *Dorchester Recs.* 443; Dorset RO, Lyme Regis mss B6/11, p. 26. [3] Add. 28887, f. 403; Luttrell, *Brief Relation*, v. 114; PCC 5 Herne; *CJ*, xiv. 424.

P. W.

FREKE, Thomas II (1660–1721), of Hannington, Wilts.

CRICKLADE	26 May – 10 June 1685
	5 Apr. 1689–1690
WEYMOUTH AND MELCOMBE REGIS	
	22 May 1691–1700
LYME REGIS	1705–1710

b. 17 Jan. 1660, 1st s. of Thomas Freke of Hinton St. Mary, Dorset by his 2nd w. Elizabeth, da. of Sir William Clarke of Ford Place, Wrotham, Kent. *educ.* Wadham, Oxf. 1675; M. Temple 1675. *m.* (1) 10 Oct. 1683, Elizabeth (*d.* 1714), da. and coh. of Thomas Pile of Baverstock, Wilts., *s.p.* and Thomas Freke I*; (2) Dec. 1718, Mary Corbett, *s.p. suc.* gt.-uncle at Hannington 1684.[1]

Freeman, Lyme Regis 1705.[2]

In 1684 Freke, a Whig, had inherited a Wiltshire estate worth £1,000 p.a. After two sharp contests at Cricklade in 1685 and 1689, he transferred to Weymouth in 1691, where he established an interest with the help of his kinsman and namesake, Thomas I. Although the two men differed politically, they appear to have been on excellent terms. Their parliamentary activity as recorded in the Journals cannot always be differentiated, although there is some evidence that Thomas II was the more active. On 12 Nov. 1691, 'Mr Freke' moved for leave to bring in a bill to reduce the rate of interest, presenting it two days later. 'Mr Freke' told on 8 Dec. against a clause in the excise bill to exempt the universities, and spoke on 19 Jan. 1692 in favour of levying a poll tax at four times the former rate. Luttrell has a 'Mr Freke' acting as a teller on 16 Feb. 1692, but the Journals ascribe this to Colonel Granville. On 3 Dec. 1692 'Thomas Freke' opposed moves to continue proceedings on the poll bill instead of considering the army estimates, and on the 30th proposed that the landlord's valuation of his estate for the purposes of the land tax should be the upper limit for the rent he could charge. Luttrell refers to Freke 'junior' as a teller on 23 Dec. 1692, but this time the Journals record a Mr Clarke. Twice in January 1693, 'Mr Freke jnr.' acted as a teller: on the 9th against excluding the universities from the land tax; and on the 26th against a procedural motion on a proposal to reduce the duty on brandy. On 23 Jan. a Socinian pamphlet published by Freke's brother, William, was declared an infamous libel and ordered to be burnt by the common hangman; but Freke himself did not take part in the debate. In the debate on the triennial bill on 28 Jan. Freke 'the younger' equated the role of the Lords in initiating this bill, which did not 'immediately concern them', to that of the Commons in making the Lords 'purge their House of popish recusants and such as would not take the Test, which you did in King Charles II's time'. A 'Mr Freke' acted as a teller on 2 Feb. on the bill to prevent the decay of trade in towns and cities, before being granted three weeks' leave on both 3 and 4 Feb. In the 1693–4 session 'Mr Freke' was a teller on two occasions and received two grants of leave of absence for health reasons.[3]

Continuing to represent Weymouth in the next two Parliaments, Freke was forecast as a supporter of the Court in the division of 31 Jan. 1696 on the proposed council of trade. He signed the Association the following month, and voted for fixing the price of guineas at 22s. in March, a 'Mr Freke' being granted leave on 5 Mar. 1696. He did not vote on the Fenwick attainder, and Freke 'junior' was granted leave of absence on 22 Dec. 1696 and 23 Dec. 1697. He was presumably the 'Mr Freke' also granted leave on 15 Feb. 1698 owing to his mother's illness. In September 1698 he was classed as a supporter of the Court in a comparative analysis of the old and new Parliaments. It was probably Thomas II, rather than his namesake, who brought in a Berkshire highways bill on 18 Mar. 1699, and told on 27 Mar. on a clause relating to the navy victualling board. A 'Mr Freke' was granted leave on 3 Apr. 1699. In an analysis of the House into interests in 1700 he was classified as a follower of Charles Montagu*. Freke declined to stand at the first 1701 election, as he explained to the Earl of Shaftesbury (Anthony Ashley*):

I am ... of opinion that an entire change is intended and that we are to be in the hands of those who formerly managed us very ill, nor do I believe they are by now less violent, insolent or mischievous in their inclinations, as there are beasts and birds, so there are men of prey, and that race for a while must and will prevail.

Those that would oppose them have no cement, nor can they . . . create any sort of confidence among themselves . . . I judge nothing but many years and much suffering can reduce them to any temper.

For my own share . . . I know my ability to be no way correspondent to my inclinations to serve the public. This is one reason makes me resolved not to be concerned in this Parliament, which I think is called to make the friends of the Revolution accountable to those very men that were laid aside with King James. Another indispensable one is that my private affairs by means of these long and constant sessions of Parliament are so disordered that it requires time and application to set them right.

His financial situation improved considerably in November 1701, when his wife and her father inherited the estate of Thomas I. Shortly afterwards Freke took up residence at Shroton. He contemplated standing for Dorchester at a by-election in February 1702, but is not known to have stood a poll. Freke supported the unsuccessful attempt by the Dorset Whigs to persuade Thomas Erle* to contest Dorset at the general election of 1702, but was reluctant to involve himself in electioneering at Shaftesbury on behalf of Sir John Cropley, 2nd Bt.* His experience of the incessant demands of the 100 or so electors at his former constituency of Cricklade made him 'very unwilling to have anything to ask from double the number so near as Shaftesbury'. He set his own sights on Weymouth, but a planned partnership with Anthony Henley* did not materialize. In 1705 he was returned for Lyme Regis, and was classed as a 'Churchman' in an analysis of the new House, also voting for the Court candidate for Speaker on 25 Oct. In January 1706, shortly after the return from the Continent of the Duke of Shrewsbury, it was reported that a 'Mr Freke [possibly Thomas] entertained the company at the Grecian coffee-house . . . with ridiculing his duchess and her conversation, etc.' This display was prompted by the 'great umbrage' felt by the Whigs at reports that Shrewsbury had only been persuaded to return by assurances of appointment to high office. Freke was listed as a Whig before and after the 1708 election, at which he was re-elected for Lyme Regis. The Earl of Sunderland (Charles, Lord Spencer*) classed him as a 'gain'. He told in favour of recommitting a resolution on subsidies to the Allies on 12 Feb. 1709, and voted for the naturalization of the Palatines. The following year he voted for the impeachment of Dr Sacheverell. Freke retired at the dissolution and did not stand for Parliament again, dying in 1721. The Hannington estate passed to his brother, William.[4]

[1] *The Ancestor*, xi. 36–37; Hutchins, *Dorset*, iv. 333; PCC 195 Barnes, 129 Buckingham; C. B. Fry, *Hannington*, 44. [2] Dorset RO, Lyme Regis mss B6/11, p. 41. [3] *Luttrell Diary*, 14, 66, 142, 191, 287, 337, 341, 355, 388, 392, 396; Luttrell, *Brief Relation*, iii. 268, 304, 313, 315; Grey, x. 303; Fry, 42–43. [4] PRO 30/24/20/97–99; Univ. Kansas Spencer Research Lib. Simpson–Methuen corresp. C163, Sir William Simpson to [?John Methuen*], 7 Jan. 1706; PCC 129 Buckingham.

P. W.

FREMAN, Ralph I (1627–1714), of Aspenden, Herts.

HERTFORDSHIRE 1685–1687, 30 Apr. 1690–1695

bap. 29 May 1627, 1st s. of Ralph Freman of Aspenden by Mary, da. of Sir William Hewett† of Pishiobury, Sawbridgeworth. educ. privately (Seth Ward). m. 10 Feb. 1662 (with £4,000), Elizabeth (d. 1720), da. of Sir John Aubrey, 1st Bt., of Llantrithyd, Glam. sis of Sir John Aubrey, 2nd Bt.*, 3s (1 d.v.p.) 7da. suc. fa. 1665.[1]

Freeman, Hertford 1681, Portsmouth 1683.[2]

Freman's devotion to the Church owed much to his tutor and friend, Seth Ward, bishop of Salisbury, whose charitable bequests for the assistance of apprentices in Hertfordshire he administered as trustee. Freman was unsuccessful in February 1679 in his first attempt to be returned for the county, allegedly because freeholders saw a body of Catholics voting for him, perhaps due to his connexion with Queen Catherine, from whom he leased mines at Wirksworth, Derbyshire, in trust for another Catholic, William Montagu. He was returned to James II's Parliament, but was noted as an opponent of the King in 1687. Freman stood again in 1690 against his 'cousin' Sir Charles Caesar†, a source of confusion to James Bonnell, his son's tutor, who thought the dispute between the two Churchmen indicated the existence of 'subordinate factions'. Attitudes towards Dissent may have been one of the dividing factors, for the double return was resolved on 30 Apr. in Freman's favour, when the House decided not to count Caesar's Quaker votes.[3]

In March 1690 Lord Carmarthen listed Freman as a probable supporter of the Court, and in December the lord president thought Freman likely to support him in the event of a Commons' attack upon his ministerial position. However, in April 1691 Robert Harley* marked him as siding with the Country party. The confusion may have arisen from Freman's low parliamentary profile. A concern for local interests is indicated by his nomination on 2 Nov. 1691 to prepare a bill relating to roads in Hertfordshire. Freman presented this measure on 14 Nov. His apparent inactivity may have owed something to his failing health, since on 19 Feb. 1694 he was granted leave of absence for his recovery, though during the 1694–5 session Henry

Guy* included Freman in a list of 'friends', probably in connexion with the Commons' attack upon Guy. In September 1695 it was reported that Freman would not be chosen again at the general election. The following month, however, Sir Edward Turnor* was informed that the 'good men' of the county were supporting 'honest Mr Freman', presumably Ralph snr., and a newsletter dated the day of the poll records his unsuccessful candidature. His partisan sympathies are clear from his subsequent support for Tory candidates at the Hertford elections of 1695, 1701 and 1705, but having left the Commons he appears to have turned his attention mainly from public to private affairs. A particular concern was to improve Aspenden, where he cased the house with brick, 'beautified the gardens with delicious greens, the grove with pleasant walks, and made all things neat and curious to the spectator'. He may also have accumulated an extensive library, primarily of devotional works, and is known to have encouraged Bonnell to translate Erasmus' paraphrases into English. Despite treatment by Dr Sloane for loss of appetite and swollen legs, Freman died on 17 Nov. 1714. Aspenden passed to his eldest son, Ralph II*, who erected a monument to his parents describing them as having been 'amiable and delightful'.[4]

[1] Herts. RO, D/E Cd F40. [2] Herts. RO, Hertford bor. recs. 25/89; R. East, *Portsmouth Recs.* 367. [3] *Trans. East. Herts. Arch. Soc.* iii. 224; *Cal. Treas. Bks.* xi. 436; C 108/63; Camb. Univ. Lib. Add. mss 1, f. 93. [4] BL, Verney mss mic. M636/48, John Verney* (Ld. Fermanagh) to Sir Ralph Verney, 1st Bt.†, 12 Sept. 1695; W. Suss. RO, Shillinglee mss Ac.454/834, M. Blurke to Turnor, 16 Oct. 1695; Folger Shakespeare Lib. Newdigate newsletter 7 Nov. 1695; Hertford bor. recs. 23/99–100, 131, 147, 169, 245; Sloane 4075, f. 154; Chauncy, *Herts.* i. 249; Add. 36246; Camb. Univ. Lib. Add. mss 1, f. 40; Clutterbuck, *Herts.* iii. 358.

M. J. K.

FREMAN, Ralph II (1666–1742), of Aspenden Hall and Ham(m)ells, Herts.

HERTFORDSHIRE 30 Dec. 1697–1727

bap. 10 June 1666, 1st s. of Ralph Freman I*. *educ.* privately (James Bonnell, Daniel Duckfield); travelled abroad (Holland, France, Italy) 1678–?1684. *m.* settlement 17 Feb. 1700 (with £4,000), Elizabeth, da. and coh. of Thomas Catesby of Ecton, Northants., 3s. *suc.* fa. 1714.[1]

Freman, Hertford 1698, St. Albans Sept.–Nov. 1705.[2] Chairman, cttee. of privileges and elections 1710–13. Commr. taking subscriptions to S. Sea Co. 1711.[3]

One of the leaders of the Hanoverian Tories in Queen Anne's reign, Freman nevertheless remains a rather colourless, and in some ways inscrutable, figure. His youth was spent in a hothouse of piety under the influence of his father and of his tutor, James Bonnell, who endeavoured

> to give Mr Freman a right sense of his duty to God, and fix the impressions of religion in his mind. They frequently joined together in prayer, and every day their devotions led the way to their studies, the *Te Deum* and some other psalms being the first business of it.

Freman later admitted that it was Bonnell's 'prudent management and good instructions which kept him from following many ill examples of great looseness and immorality; and hindered him from running into mischiefs he should hardly otherwise have avoided'. Though he was surely free from temptation on the first leg of his European tour, when staying with the pious Sir Leoline Jenkins† at Nijmegen, in France he met the beautiful but poor daughter of Sir John Austen, 2nd Bt.*, and hankered after her on his return. He had in fact been contracted at a tender age to marry Dorothy Dicer, the granddaughter of Richard Goulston† of Wyddial, Hertfordshire, himself the grandfather of Freman's later political ally of the same name. This early match abandoned, Freman told Bonnell that, so far as a wife was concerned, he was 'willing to be pleased with an agreeable face if not beauty'. However, a later match suggested by the bishop of Durham and one with the daughter of Colonel Silius Titus* both failed to come to fruition, and Freman deferred marriage until 1700.[4]

Freman's father had wanted his son to 'be a scholar if he be capable of it', but Ralph jnr. entered Parliament in December 1697 at a by-election for Hertfordshire, a seat he was to hold until the accession of George II. His Country views were noted in September on a list of Members returned to the new Parliament and, having been forecast as likely to oppose a standing army, his first recorded speech, on 23 Dec. 1698, was to request a call of the House before MPs reconsidered the disbanding bill. He twice acted as teller on the issue, once on 11 Mar. 1699 in favour of the second reading of the supply bill needed to pay off the army, and again on 20 Mar. against recommitting the address on the King's request to keep the Dutch guards. Antipathy to the army may also explain his tellership on 20 Apr. against a bill to naturalize a number of officers, since on 19 Jan. he had reported and carried to the Lords a personal naturalization bill and his tutor was the descendant of a Protestant refugee. Freman's abiding passion was the regulation of elections and of the personnel of the House, combining partisan zeal to return Tories with a concern, engendered by an increasing awareness that the system itself needed reform, for impartiality at the polls and independence of Members in the House. He began a long career nurturing these concerns with his appointment on 10 Jan. to the committee on the return of election writs. The subject involved him as a teller on four further occasions this session: on 9 Feb., in favour of declaring 'frivolous and vexatious' a petition by George Rodney Brydges* concerning the Haslemere election; on 10 Feb., against an adjournment of the debate on the expulsion of the Whig James Isaacson*, who had accepted a place of profit; on 1 Mar., on the franchise at Ludlow, in favour of the Country Tory William Gower*; and on 17 Mar., on the franchise at Tamworth. As further demonstration of his own Country views, Freman told on 18 Apr. on an amendment to the bill to include the sheriffs of London and Middlesex as receivers of the land tax. He was equally concerned to prove his allegiance to the Church. Perhaps in response to prompting from Thomas Coke* and from the clergy, who believed him to be their 'great friend', he presented a bill on 17 Mar. for continuing the Act for the recovery of small tithes, reporting this measure on the 23rd and carrying it to the Lords two days later. He was involved in national as well as Church finance, and was active on two supply bills this session, reporting on 1 Apr. from the committee on duties on glass, and on 26 Apr. telling in favour of an amendment to the provisions for a duty on paper. Although not known to have owned shares in the Old East India Company, he told on 9 Mar. against the rejection of its bill. His connexion with the Royal Fishery bill, which he presented on 20 Mar., is also not straightforward. It is possible that he was friendly with fellow Country Tory MP Sir Thomas Davall I*, with whom he acted as teller on 17 Mar. and 21 Apr., and who, as MP for Harwich, had a strong interest in fisheries. Alternatively, Freman's concern may have been to regulate the trade, a suggestion that gains credibility from the fact that he also told on 23 Jan. on an amendment to the bill for prohibiting the distillation of spirit from corn, though that in turn might have stemmed from local pressure from the county's brewing trade or from a personal interest, since a distiller named 'Freeman' was taken into custody after alleging that MPs had been bribed to oppose the bill. Freman also looked after local matters, presenting on 21 Mar. a private bill relating to a Hertfordshire estate, which he was to pursue in subsequent sessions. He was the third named on 16 Nov. 1699 to the privileges and elections committee, but Freman's significant activity in the 1699–1700 session was limited compared with the previous session, though he told on 1 Jan. 1700 against the election of the Whig John Bright*. A week later he was found to be absent from the House, but was excused after a division.[5]

In the new Parliament Freman guided a private estate bill through the House, but his chief concern was the resolution of disputed elections in favour of Country Tories, telling to that effect on three occasions: on 15 Apr., against a delay in receiving the report on the East Retford election; on 10 May, against the adjournment of the report on the Lichfield election (where the Churchmen had been involved in a hard-fought contest); and on 28 May, against the election of the Court Whig Lord William Powlett* at Winchester. Despite his Country credentials, Freman seems to have been sympathetic to the new ministers at Court, being forecast in February 1701 as likely to support the Court in agreeing with the supply committee's resolution to continue the 'Great Mortgage'. His continued Toryism was evident from the fact that he was later blacklisted as having opposed the preparations for war with France early in 1701. On 3 June he was teller for the minority in favour of allowing defalcations by paymasters of the navy to be used for the public good, and served as teller the next day against reading Somers' reply to his impeachment. Although he had failed to gain a seat on the commission of accounts, Freman did attract 20 votes, a modest indication of his steadily growing interest in the House.[6]

Freman retained his seat at the second election of 1701, following which Robert Harley* listed him with the Tories. He had by now established himself as something of a specialist interested in determining controverted elections in favour of Tories. Thus, on 5 Jan. 1702 he told for the minority in favour of hearing the Maidstone election at the bar; on the 29th moved that the Whig petitioners against the Malmesbury election be taken into custody; and on 24 Feb. told against an adjournment during the debate on the Coventry election. Two days later he supported the motion vindicating the House's proceedings in the impeachments of William III's ministers. He was keen to quieten Tory concerns about the abjuration bill, being named on 2 Feb. to the committee to draw up reasons for disagreement with the Lords over a voluntary oath, and on 10 Feb. telling against the omission of a clause which declared support for the established constitution and government.[7]

On his re-election in 1702, Freman immediately wrote to encourage Robert Harley's own hopes of re-election as Speaker. Anne's accession had ushered in a political and religious climate in which Freman's talents could more naturally flourish. On 29 Jan. 1703 he chaired a committee of the whole on brandy running, evidence of his continued interest in the spirit trade, and in January and February assisted in the management of a private bill relating to a Hertfordshire estate. Predictably perhaps, given his earlier record, he voted on 13 Feb. against the Lords' amendments to the bill for enlarging the time for taking the oath of abjuration. In the autumn of 1703 Harley reported to Lord Treasurer Godolphin (Sidney†) that the failure to restore Freman to the Hertfordshire lieutenancy meant that he was 'out of humour', and this dissatisfaction may have been the spur for his renewed zeal in the 1703-4 session. Though he helped guide an estate bill through the House, his concern about the malpractice current in determining the composition of the House again dominated his significant activity, particularly the Aylesbury case. On 21 Jan. 1704 he reported from the committee appointed to search the Journals for precedents, and on the 25th chaired the ensuing debate of the committee of the whole which ended, as he no doubt wished, in a resolution backing the House's power to determine elections. On the 27th and 28th he chaired another committee of the whole which debated the Lords' decision contravening this resolution, resulting in a vote against interference from the Upper House. Having apparently developed a taste for conflict with the Whig-dominated Lords, Freman took the chair on 28 Feb. on the contentious Scotch Plot. The following month he was included in Lord Nottingham's (Daniel Finch†) forecast of likely supporters during the proceedings on the plot.[8]

Freman's handling of these issues encouraged him to become very active during the 1704-5 session, which debated all the issues that most concerned him. He confirmed his animosity towards William III's Whig ministers by telling on 18 Nov. against an adjournment during the proceedings against Lord Halifax (Charles Montagu*) and, as Lady Cowper put it, was one of the 'Hertfordshire enemies' spewing forth venom like a dragon against her son William*, a local rival whom they wished to send to the Tower. Freman's adherence to the Church party was manifest on the 23rd, when he acted as teller in favour of the second reading of the occasional conformity bill. He was forecast as a probable supporter of the Tack, and on the 28th he and his ally William Bromley II told in favour of this measure. On 21 Dec. he told against the second reading for the bill of union with Scotland. He also assisted in the management of two estate bills, and on the last day of the session was sent to the Lords to desire a conference on a naturalization bill. But his primary concern had once again been the determination of the composition of the House. The Commons' resumption of the Aylesbury case prompted his tellership on 26 Feb. in favour of finding Francis Page* (a lawyer for the Aylesbury men) guilty of a breach of privilege, and two days later Freman was appointed as a manager of the conference over the writs of error issued in the controversy. However, his long experience of election cases had convinced him of the need for more general reform, and he embarked on a campaign to promote place legislation. On 13 Jan. 1705 he obtained leave to introduce a bill designed to exclude office-holders appointed since Charles II's death, and with a group of like-minded Church Tories such as Bromley, Francis Annesley and his brother-in-law, Charles Caesar, was named to draft it. Since, as one observer suspected, the bill owed its birth to resentment over the loss of the Tack, this combination of names is significant. The bill was presented on 17 Jan. and three days later Freman chaired the committee of the whole on it. When he reported on the 25th, an amendment was defeated which would have extended the bill to include personnel of the armed forces. Two days later, when Freman acted as teller, his bill failed to pass by only six votes.[9]

Freman had meanwhile been tightening his grip on local politics. By 1704 he had become 'master' of his county, thanks partly to the activities of the local Anglican gentry's Royston Club, and consequently faced no problem at the polls in 1705 despite his prominent support for the Tack. Marked as 'True Church' on an analysis of Members, he told on 25 Oct. against the Court candidate for Speaker. He continued to be preoccupied with the question of who should be allowed to sit in the House. He told on 19 Nov. 1705 in favour of putting a motion that the committee of elections should not sit after midnight, and became involved as a teller in determining elections, two of which were local affairs: twice on 24 Nov., on divisions relating to the election of John Gape* at St. Albans; twice again on 6 Dec. (both with Caesar), in favour of the election of Richard Goulston* at Hertford, where Freman was able to vote consistently for the Tory candidate (including Caesar) after his admission as a freeman in 1698; on 11 Dec., against the return of Charles Mompesson* for Old Sarum; and on 17 Jan. 1706, against a motion declaring that Thomas Powell* had not been duly elected at Ludgershall. Moreover, encouraged by the slim margin by which his first attempt at place legislation had been defeated, he told on 13 Dec. 1705 in favour of bringing in a new bill, this time to restrict rather than to forbid the presence of office-holders in the House, a shift that may explain the subsequent involvement of John Aislabie* and Sir Richard Onslow, 3rd Bt.*, in its drafting. Freman presented the bill on 8 Jan. 1706, but it was displaced from the parliamentary agenda by the succession. At the beginning of the session, during a debate on Scotland on 4 Dec. 1705, Freman had supported the proposal that the Queen be addressed to invite to England the heir presumptive, an early indication of his own Hanoverian sympathies, but he and Caesar nevertheless acted as tellers on 19 Dec. against the second reading of the regency bill. On 10 Jan. 1706, having told against a motion to debate the regency bill, Freman made a speech in support of fixing the length of time Parliament would continue after the Queen's death. Two days later, perhaps with the intention of defeating the whole bill – or perhaps simply wishing to graft onto it the content of his own place bill – he moved to give an instruction to add the clause from the 1701 Act of Settlement which excluded placemen on Anne's death, and for this to remain in force for six months into the new reign. He was teller for his own motion, which was defeated, though he was then gratified to count a majority in favour of the committee to explain or alter the place clause. He repeated his worries during the resumed debate on 15 and 21 Jan., and expressed concern on the 19th for a separation of royal and executive power in a regency. He considered the Church to be in as much danger as the government, having opened a debate on 8 Dec. 1705 about the Lords' resolution rejecting such a notion, and been a teller for the minority in favour of referring the matter to a committee of the whole.[10]

Characteristically, Freman followed this period of intense political involvement with a session in which he figures only occasionally in the printed records, perhaps because by then most of the controverted elections had been decided. The only election dispute on which he was teller was on 23 Jan. 1707, concerning Edward Southwell's* poll at Rye. Freman guided through the Commons a bill for the repair of highways in his county, but was otherwise content to lower his public profile. This may have encouraged ministers to try to engage him for the Court before the 1707–8 session, but his Country principles were too deeply held, and he and the other Tory leaders approached were 'not wrought upon by that management'. Indeed, the growing Whig influence at Court seems to have dispelled his lethargy. Perhaps feeling snubbed from being denied his usual place on the Address committee, he offered an explanation of the text 'which he pretended was to prevent a prejudging of 'em; and to leave 'em free to argue against it if it were their judgment or opinion so to do; but upon hearing the words of his explanation they appeared to be nonsense'. Freman's purpose in this obscure speech was clarified by one of the Annesleys (Arthur or Francis), who 'directly' opposed the clause in the Address relating to the Union. Freman's hostility to the ministry, and to the Scots, was clear enough on 11 Dec. when he was teller against an amendment to the Union allowing a different system of j.p.s north of the border, and the following day in favour of referring to a committee of the whole the bill repealing the Scottish acts of security. On 18 Dec. he told against an adjournment of the debate which led to the expulsion of John Asgill for a profane publication, and the same day joined Bromley in moving for further papers relating to the war in Spain, in preparation for an attack on the government over the deficiency of forces at Almanza, a charge on which he acted as teller on 24 Feb. His own collection of papers relating to the cost of the war shows how well prepared the Tory attack was. Classed as a Tory in a list of early 1708, Freman told, on 31 Jan. 1708, in favour of an adjournment of the consideration of the report on the East India Company's supply of £1 million in return for an extension of its privileges. Once more, he concerned himself with the membership of the House. On 22 Dec. he was first-named to a drafting committee for a bill against electoral bribery and corruption, chairing the committee of the whole on the bill and carrying it to the Lords on 27 Feb. On 17 Feb. he had told in favour of the return of the Tory Frederick Tylney* at Whitchurch, and his lack of success may have prompted him to act as teller again on 21 Feb. in support of a suggestion that controverted elections be decided by ballot.[11]

Immediately after the Queen's speech opening the new Parliament in 1708, Freman, classed as a Tacker in an analysis of the 1708 election returns, renewed attempts to oppose the terms of the Union by calling for the abolition of the Scottish privy council. On 9 Dec. he is reported to have heard a sermon by Bishop Burnet, which was thought to have had such a good effect on him that he bowed to the wife of his local rival William, now Lord, Cowper. On 22 Nov. MPs reversed their decision in favour of determining disputed elections by ballot, a vote for which Freman acted as teller, but he was determined to press on with electoral reform. Having told on 2 Dec. on the franchise at Reading, he pursued his war against corruption by telling on 23 Feb. 1709 in favour of an account of secret service monies detailing all sums disbursed, rather than just those distributed to Members. His support for legislation against bribery and placemen was again evident in the following session, as he told on 27 Jan. and 4 Feb. for the passage of another bill limiting the number of officers in the House.

Appointed on 14 Feb. to prepare a bill against bribery at elections, Freman presented this measure the following day. His Tory sympathies were clearly demonstrated on the 16th when he told against the Whig address to the Queen to send the Duke of Marlborough (John Churchill†) to Holland, and when he voted against the impeachment of Dr Sacheverell.[12]

At the beginning of the 1710 Parliament, Freman acquired the post he probably most desired, the chair of the committee of elections. With 101 petitions before it, the committee was evidently important in determining the balance of parties in the House, but the large number of Tory gains at the polls may have encouraged him to shed some of his pretence of impartiality, for when the Whigs changed their tune and called for balloting on election decisions, the Church party now rejected what they themselves had formerly supported. Freman's own bias was blatant in December 1710, when, perhaps also motivated by local antagonisms, he opened the attack on Lord Cowper's actions over the Bewdley charter, and on 3 Feb. 1711, when he used his position to report, as frivolous and vexatious, the petition of William Thompson III*, a manager in the last session against Sacheverell. In addition to steering this important committee, Freman also guided through the Commons the Members' qualification bill, which stipulated a minimum £600 p.a. landed income as necessary for election as knight of the shire, and £300 for a borough Member. These and other activities during the 1710–11 session earned him inclusion in printed lists of 'worthy patriots' and 'Tory patriot' opponents of the continuation of the war. On 2 Jan. 1711 he spoke immediately after Secretary Henry St. John's (II*) explanation of the Queen's message about the losses in Spain, and moved for an address of thanks to promise her that Parliament would support whatever measures she considered to be necessary to fight the war, but attacked General James Stanhope's* conduct of the campaign, and threatened an inquiry, in order to make 'such an example of the authors of these miscarriages as might put us out of apprehension of being so served again'. He was of course named to the consequent committee, from which he reported on 3 Jan. Six days later he was said to have made general accusations of 'malversations' against the recent ministry, and on 28 Apr. was teller in favour of a motion promoted by the October Club (which he joined in February and of which he became a leading member), which attacked the 'breach of trust' evident in Lord Godolphin's administration. On 24 Apr. Freman told against passing the bill for the better preservation of game. Personal interests may have encouraged his tellership on 3 May against a clause in the Mine Adventurers' Company bill, since his father had leased a lead mine in Derbyshire, and Freman was himself a friend of another Country Tory, Sir Humphrey Mackworth*, who was the company's deputy-governor.[13]

There had been speculation since the end of 1710 that Freman would succumb to Court offers. Edward Wortley Montagu* believed that Freman's qualifications bill had been designed to put off Montagu's own place bill, a suspicion that suggests that the pursuit of independence in the House could have strong party-political connotations. Freman's commitment to pure Country principles was also being tested at this time, for during the 1710 Christmas recess he was offered the treasurership of the navy, either by himself or jointly with Caesar. The fact that Freman resumed his seat on 4 Jan. 1711 was interpreted as a sign that the commission had not yet been settled, but it was reported that the delay was only 'till he has finished his reports as chairman of elections'. Thus, as the session drew to a close in June, there was renewed speculation that the warrant for the post would be made out 'in Mr Caesar's name and Mr Freman to have half pay without having his clear estate subjected for security of great sums which that place requires'. If this was true, which seems likely, given that it was 'generally believed' that Caesar had accepted the post 'upon the foot of an understanding with his brother-in-law', Freman's rejection of the post was not entirely the principled stand it has appeared to be. His activity dropped off markedly in the two remaining sessions of the 1710 Parliament though he remained in the chair of the elections committee. During the 1713 session he assisted in the early stages of the Enfield highway bill. Whatever the exact nature of his agreement with the Court about the profits of office, Freman's support for the Hanoverian succession now pushed him into occasional or 'whimsical' support for the Whigs. He was one of the Tories who voted on 18 June against the French commerce bill. His dislike of the army was once more apparent on 1 July when he told for the majority against officers being paid over and above their salaries. He also assisted in the management of two private estate bills, one on 4 June for the Bydes, a Hertfordshire family that had made its money from brewing, and the other on 20 June for James, 19th Earl of Salisbury, who had long had Freman's political backing and who had been appointed lord lieutenant of Hertfordshire in 1712.[14]

The 1713 election tested Freman's Qualifications Act, and on 6 Mar. 1714 he chaired the committee of the whole which reported on a mechanism for challenging claims about fulfilment of the Act's criteria.

Listed as a Tory in every categorization of the 1713 Parliament, he was one of the leaders of the Hanoverian wing of the party. On 15 Apr. he chaired the committee of the whole on the state of the nation relating to the succession, and the following day reported its resolution that the Protestant succession was in no danger. On 23 Apr. he was listed as one of the 'revolters from the Ch[urch] Party' in his attitude to a similar resolution by the Lords, and on 24 June it was Freman who spoke warmly not only in favour of thanking the Queen for the proclamation offering a reward for the apprehension of the Pretender, but also of increasing the sum, a motion that drew opposition from his erstwhile ally Bromley. His other significant role that session related to economic matters, for on 26 June he chaired the committee of the whole upon the bill to reduce the rate of interest. The Worsley list and two further comparisons of the 1713 and 1715 Parliaments all classed Freman as a Tory.[15]

Following George I's accession, Freman again refused a seat on the Admiralty board, but may have done so only to appease the Hertfordshire gentry of the Royston Club, to whom he had 'so frequently declared [his] opinion that no person who took place could act fairly and candidly for his country's interest'. Some of them also resented his monopoly of the county seat, which he continued to hold as a Tory until 1727. He died on 8 June 1742, when his estate passed to his eldest son, William. He had earlier made provision for his wife by an estate Act, which mentioned lands held in Essex, but Freman disinherited his younger son, Catesby, on account of what he regarded as Catesby's scandalous way of life and disrespect. By an endowment of land, Freman set on a firmer footing the provision of Seth Ward's charity for apprentices, for which Freman's father had acted as trustee.[16]

[1] IGI, Herts.; W. Hamilton, *Life and Character of James Bonnell* (1808), 13–14; Camb. Univ. Lib. Add. mss 1, f. 66. [2] Herts. RO, Hertford bor. recs. 25/100; St. Albans Pub. Lib. St. Albans bor. recs. 299. [3] Pittis, *Present Parl.* 349. [4] Hamilton, 14–15; Camb. Univ. Lib. Add. mss 1, f. 69; *Mar. Lic. Fac. Off.* (Harl. Soc. xxiv), 137. [5] Camb. Univ. Lib. Add. mss 1, f. 42; *Cam. Misc.* xxix. 380; *HMC Cowper*, ii. 387; Luttrell, *Brief Relation*, vi. 487. [6] Yorks. Arch. Soc. Copley mss Box H–J, poll Feb. 1701. [7] *Cocks Diary*, 228. [8] Add. 70197, Freman to Harley 6 Aug. [1702]; Cobbett, *Parlty. Hist.* vi. 298–300. [9] Herts. RO, Panshanger mss D/EP/F30, Lady Cowper's commonplace bk. pp. 312–13; *Huntington Lib. Q.* xxxix. 52. [10] *Cam. Misc.* xxiii. 31, 40, 44, 60, 61–62, 71, 73, 78; Herts. RO, Hertford bor. recs. 23/145, 169, 245, 368, 397, 425; *Huntington Lib. Q.* xxxix. 54. [11] Burnet, v. 339–40; Tindal, *Hist. Eng.* ii. 38; Staffs. RO, Paget mss D603/K/3/6, R. Acherley to Ld. Paget, 6 Dec. [1706]; *Vernon–Shrewsbury Letters*, iii. 298; Add. 35868; G. Holmes, *Pol. in Age of Anne*, 143–4. [12] *Clavering Corresp.* (Surtees Soc. clxxviii), 20; Cunningham, *Hist. GB*, ii. 137. [13] Luttrell, vi. 661; Boyer, *Pol. State*, i–ii. 160; SRO, Mar and Kellie mss GD/15/1020, Sir James Dunbar, 1st Bt.*, to Ld. Grange (James Erskine†), 12 Dec. 1710; *Clavering Corresp.* 105; Holmes, 179; SRO, Montrose mss GD/220/5/808/1a, Mungo Graham* to Montrose, 2 Jan. 1711; BL, Trumbull Alphab. mss 54, Ralph Bridges to Sir William Trumbull*, 19 Feb. 1711; NSA, Kreienberg despatch 9 Jan. 1711; *Huntington Lib. Q.* xxxiii. 163; Northants. RO, Isham mss IC 4864, Freman to Sir Justinian Isham, 4th Bt.*, 15 Mar. [–]. [14] Montrose mss 22/5/808/1a, 2, Mungo Graham to Montrose, 2, 4 Jan. 1711; Holmes, 118; Trumbull Alphab. mss 54, John Bridges to Trumbull, 5 Jan. 1711, Ralph Bridges to Trumbull, 8 June 1711; Huntington Lib. Stowe mss 57 (5), pp. 91–92; Add. 57861, f. 162; *HMC Portland*, iv. 563. [15] Burnet, v. 339; Trumbull Alphab. mss 55, Brydges to Trumbull, 23 Apr. 1714; Add. 47027, f. 133; Cobbett, vi. 1358. [16] Panshanger mss D/EP/F53, f. 38, John Boteler* to Lord Cowper, 10 Oct. 1714; PCC 244 Trenley; *HMC Lords* n.s. vii. 335.

M. J. K.

FREWEN, Thomas (1630–1702), of Cleybrooke House, Fulham, Mdx.; St. James's, Westminster; and Brickwall House, Northiam, Suss.

RYE   1679 (Mar.)–1685, 15 Jan.–1 Apr. 1689
           9 Feb. 1694–1698

bap. 27 Sept. 1630, o. s. of Stephen Frewen, Skinner, of London and Northiam by his 1st w. Katherine, da. and coh. of Thomas Scott of Northiam. *educ.* I. Temple, entered 1648, called 1656; Padua 1649; St. John's, Oxf. BA 1650, MA 1653. *m.* (1) c.1656, Judith (*d.* 1666), da. and h. of John Wolverstone, Fishmonger, of Cleybrooke House, 2s. (1 *d.v.p.*) 1da.; (2) 1671, Bridget (*d.* 1679), da. of Sir Thomas Layton of East Layton Hall, Stanwick St. John, Yorks. and coh. to her bro. Charles, 5s. (3 *d.v.p.*) 1da.; (3) lic. 15 Dec. 1681, Jane (*d.* 1718), da. and h. of Sir Robert Cooke† of Highnam, Glos.; sis. of William Cooke I*, and wid. of Sir Dawes Wymondsold of Putney, Surrey, *s.p. suc.* fa. 1679.[1]

Commr. recusants 1675.
Freeman, Portsmouth 1675.[2]

Frewen's father rose from the modest circumstances of a rector's family and made a comfortable fortune in London as a furrier and Turkey merchant. His wealth was much increased in 1664 when he inherited from his brother, Archbishop Accepted Frewen of York, an immense legacy said to have totalled 27,000 guineas, and soon afterwards he was able to set up as a gentleman in his native Sussex parish of Northiam. Thomas Frewen received all the educational benefits of his father's wealth, and from the early 1660s began to acquire the responsibilities of magisterial, militia and other local offices. In March 1679 he was elected on the family interest for the Cinque Port of Rye, six miles from Northiam. It would seem, however, that after the death of his father and of his second wife, Bridget, at Northiam on almost exactly the same day six months later (both were interred at Northiam on 11 Sept.), Frewen conceived a dislike for the place and spent as little time there as possible, residing instead at

Westminster or at Cleybrooke House, the Fulham seat he inherited from his first wife.[3]

In his politics Frewen emerges as a Country Tory of a strong anti-papist and, later, anti-Jacobite cast. During the Exclusion Crisis Lord Shaftesbury at first regarded him as 'base', but later as 'doubtful', and then as 'honest'. He was no friend of the Whig group in Rye's corporate body and was unequivocally opposed to James II's religious policies. Through his third marriage in 1681 to the widow of Sir Dawes Wymondsold of Putney he enjoyed a connexion with Sir Thomas Clarges*, one of the leading Country Tory figures of the day, whose son Sir Walter (1st Bt.*) had married one of Sir Dawes's daughters and afterwards married the widow of Sir Dawes's son. In March 1690, having been unseated during the Convention Parliament in favour of a Whig, Frewen was warmly commended to his corporation as a 'most worthy and honest gentleman' by Hon. John Beaumont*, a Tory acting as the Court's electoral agent in several of the Cinque Port towns. Again unsuccessful, however, he bided his time until a by-election opportunity occurred at Rye in February 1694, when he was returned unopposed.[4]

Frewen's second period of parliamentary service was inactive, though he seems to have featured as an opponent of the Court. In January 1696 he was forecast as likely to register his opposition in the divisions anticipated over the proposed council of trade, voted in March against fixing the price of guineas at 22s., and voted on 25 Nov. against the attainder of Sir John Fenwick†. He was, none the less, one of the early Tory signatories to the Association. His anti-Court inclinations are further confirmed in an analysis of the House compiled shortly after the 1698 election in which he was classed as a Country supporter. In the election itself, however, Frewen was defeated.

A major source of friction between Frewen and the ministers throughout the 1690s was the non-payment of a considerable debt owed him by the government. The substantial sum which his father had deposited with the leading City goldsmith-banker, Sir Robert Vyner, constituted part of the sizable cash advances which Vyner had made to Charles II's Treasury but which were frozen in 1672 at the Stop of the Exchequer. From 1677 Frewen's father, and then Frewen himself, in common with the other 'patentees', had each received annual 'rents' or payments allocated according to their respective shares out of the hereditary revenues of the excise, but in 1683 these were discontinued. Although the ensuing ten-year legal struggle for judicial recognition of the debts was not conducted in Frewen's name, there can be little doubt that he, as a principal sufferer, was closely involved. In May 1701, on hearing that the government intended to make over the hereditary revenues towards the civil list, Frewen and three other major creditors petitioned the House on behalf of themselves 'and many thousands more' for their own original legal entitlement to the revenues to be observed and enforced. In March Frewen had stated before the Treasury Board that his demand for arrears of interest now totalled £14,661. He was dissatisfied with the provision made in the 1701 Appropriation Act for the hereditary revenues to be charged with annual interest on the debt at 3 per cent. On his deathbed the following year he gave vent in his will to his bitterness over the whole painful affair, regretting that it had prevented him from making the bequests he had intended to his younger sons and his grandchildren, and from repaying money borrowed from his wife: 'it hath pleased God that so considerable a sum is so miserably curtailed.'[5]

Frewen died on 8 Sept. 1702, the day on which he made his will, and was buried in the Wymondsold vault at Putney church. He had already settled his lands on his eldest son, Edward, who, together with his stepson Robert Wymondsold, had been knighted by James II in 1685.

[1] *VCH Yorks. (N. Riding)*, i. 132; *London Mar. Lic.* ed. Foster, 515; C. J. Feret, *Fulham Old and New*, ii. 172–3. [2] R. East, *Portsmouth Recs.* 361. [3] J. R. Woodhead, *Rulers of London*, 74; *Grants of Arms* (Harl. Soc. lxvi), 95; W. Holloway, *Hist. Rye*, 580; Feret, ii. 172. [4] Add. 42586, f. 85. [5] *CJ*, xiii. 597; *Cal. Treas. Bks.* xvi. 55; R. D. Richards, *Early Hist. of Banking*, 65–67; PCC 147 Herne.

A. A. H.

FULFORD, Francis (1666–1700), of Great Fulford, Devon.

CALLINGTON 1690–1695, 1698–26 Sept. 1700

b. 8 Oct. 1666, 2nd but 1st surv. s. of Francis Fulford of Great Fulford by Susanna, da. of John Kelland of Painsford, Devon. *educ.* Exeter, Oxf. 1682. *m.* (1) Margaret (d. 1687), da. of John Poulett†, 3rd Baron Poulett, of Hinton St. George, Som, *s.p.*; (2) 9 Oct. 1690, Mary (bur. 2 Jan. 1729), da. and coh. of John Tuckfield of Little Fulford, Devon, 1s. *d.v.p. suc.* fa. 1674.[1]

Sheriff, Devon 1689–90; mayor, Exeter 1689–90.[2]

Fulford's family claimed to have been resident in the township from which they took their name since the reign of Richard I, and had provided Devon with knights of the shire in the Parliaments of 1553 and 1625. His grandfather, Sir Francis Fulford†, had been a staunch Royalist during the Civil Wars, but the fines levied on him do not appear to have ruined the family fortune, as Sir Francis was able to leave his Dorset estates to Francis Fulford's great-uncle George[†] while preserving for the main branch of the family 'a very great estate' in Devon. In 1687, James II's agents included Fulford on a list of Devon gentlemen 'of good estates and quality formerly out of commission . . . and not at present in his Majesty's service'. Though this may suggest Fulford's willingness to support King James's religious policies, in November 1688 he joined the Prince of Orange. Returned for Callington in 1690, presumably upon the Rolle interest, Fulford was classed as a Tory by Lord Carmarthen (Sir Thomas Osborne[†]). He was an inactive Member, though in December 1690 he was listed by Carmarthen as a likely supporter in the event of a Commons' attack on his ministerial position, and in April 1691 was listed by Robert Harley* as a Country supporter. On 16 Nov. Fulford was placed in custody after failing to attend the House, but was discharged five days later and on 18 Dec. was granted a leave of absence to recover his health. He made no further significant recorded contribution to this Parliament, and at the 1695 election made way at Callington for the election of Francis Gwyn*. He was again returned for Callington in 1698, being included upon a forecast of likely opponents of the standing army and listed in a comparison of the old and new Commons as a Country supporter. He died on 26 Sept. 1700, and was buried on 7 Oct. He was succeeded in his estates by Francis Fulford of London, whose precise relationship to the Member has not been ascertained.[3]

[1] Vivian, *Vis. Devon*, 380; Hutchins, *Dorset*, ii. 698–9. [2] *CSP Dom.* 1689–90, pp. 349, 355; 1690–1, p. 42. [3] Burke, *Commoners*, i. 158; Hutchins, 699–700; Bodl. Rawl. lett. 109, f. 115; Duckett, *Penal Laws and Test Act* (1882), 377; *HMC 15th Rep. VII*, 112–13; Vivian, 380.

E. C.

FULHAM, John (1664–1726), of Compton, Surr.

HASLEMERE 1705–1708

bap. 19 June 1664, 4th s. of Rev. Edward Fulham (*d.* 1694), DD, of Windsor, Berks. by Margaret, da. of Sir Robert Clerke of Oxon. *educ.* Christ Church, Oxf. matric. 1680, BA 1683, MA 1686; I. Temple 1682, called 1689; M. Temple 1694. *m.* 19 May 1687, Anne (*d.* 1720), da. of Robert Waith of Camberwell, Surr., 2s. 6da.(2 *d.v.p.*)

Recorder, Guildford 1703–22, Chichester 1709–12.

A younger son of an eminent royalist divine, Fulham chose not to follow the clerical path taken by three of his brothers, and embarked on a career in the law. His father, an attendant of Charles II in exile, had been the first to establish a family seat in Surrey, and the Compton estate enabled Fulham to seek advancement at nearby Guildford. His first notable appointment, the recordership of Guildford, which he gained in October 1703, highlighted his professional reputation and he later gained further recognition when chosen by the borough of Chichester to the same office. His family background clearly marked him out as a Tory, and his connexions with several of the party's leading households in the west of the shire provided him with an interest sufficient to launch his brief parliamentary career.[1]

In the run-up to the election of 1705 Fulham was cited as one of the likely candidates for the forthcoming contest at Guildford, a prediction which reflected the influence he wielded by virtue of his corporate office. However, he chose to stand at Haslemere instead, taking advantage of a local Tory strategy to rotate the borough's two seats between the party's supporters among the neighbouring gentry. Although suggestions were subsequently made that Fulham and his running-mate George Woodroffe* had rebuffed a challenge from two other local Tories, there is no evidence of a poll having taken place and Fulham certainly voted for the Tory candidate at the ensuing county election. At the outset of his political career he was cited by a printed parliamentary list as 'Low Church', a surprising verdict given his family's strong Anglicanism, but on 25 Oct. 1705 he predictably voted against the Court candidate for Speaker. He did not make any significant contribution to the business of the House in the first session, but thereafter became closely involved in several mercantile matters, beginning on 27 Mar. 1707 with a report from the committee to review a petition complaining of the seizure of an English ship in Scotland. A week later he carried up to the Lords a private estate bill. He reported on another merchant petition on 13 Feb. 1708, in the wake of which he was ordered to prepare a bill to improve Portsmouth harbour and the ballasting of royal vessels. He duly presented that bill to the House on 25 Feb. and his last important duties concerned bills to enable merchants to compound with the Treasury.

Identified as a Tory in early 1708, Fulham seemed reluctant to contest the May general election, at which one of the Haslemere seats was lost to the Whigs. However, although destined never to return to the House, he sought to promote the local Tory cause in November 1712 by acting as one of the co-presenters at court of an address which highly praised the current administration. He played no other prominent political role before his death in April 1726, having been prepared some four years before to resign his recordership at Guildford. He was succeeded in that office by Arthur Onslow†, a political rival who subsequently acted as a patron of the Fulham household, most notably by obtaining for Fulham's son John a chaplaincy at the House of Commons. This proved to be the extent of the family's parliamentary involvement in the 18th century, although Fulham's grandson re-established links with the court by becoming a chaplain to George III.[2]

[1] IGI, Berks., Surr.; PCC 96 Plymouth; Manning and Bray, *Surr.* i. 40; ii. 5–6; *Suss. N. and Q.* xiii. 82. [2] Add. 70335, list of constituencies, 8 Feb. 1705; *Colls. from Dyer's Letters* [1706], 4; *Surr. Poll of 1705*; *London Gazette*, 1–4 Nov. 1712; Manning and Bray, i. 40; ii. 6, 12.

P. L. G.

FULLER, John (1680–1745), of Brightling, Suss.

SUSSEX 1713–1715

bap. 28 July 1680, 1st s. of John Fuller of Tanners, Waldron, Suss. by Elizabeth, da. and h. of Samuel Fowle of London. *m.* 20 July 1703, Elizabeth (*d.* 1728), da. and coh. of Fulke Rose of St. Catherine, Jamaica, 9s. (3 *d.v.p.*) 1da. *suc.* fa. 1722.[1]

FRS 1704.

Surveyor of house duty, Suss. 1708–?1709, 1710–16.[2]

Fuller was descended from a family of yeomen settled in Waldron since the 16th century. His grandfather had held the lease of an ironworks at Chiddingley and his father purchased land for a furnace at Heathfield, but it seems to have been John jnr. who developed this latter site into a successful ironworks in the early 18th century. In 1708 Fuller was appointed as surveyor of the duty on houses in Sussex, a job he had lost by September 1710, when, in response to his petition for a place, the new Treasury lords ordered the commissioners of taxes to appoint him to the first vacancy. He was thus reappointed to his old post on 21 Nov. 1710. Successful for Sussex in the general election of 1713, he was classed as a Tory in the Worsley list. On 3 July 1714 he told in favour of his relation John Lade* in the election for Southwark. He did not stand in 1715 but from 1718 to 1744 served as chairman of the eastern division of the Sussex bench. In 1734 he unsuccessfully contested the county as a Tory. He died on 4 Aug. 1745 and was buried at Waldron. Two of his sons, John and Rose Fuller, sat in Parliament under George II and George III.[3]

[1] *Vis. Eng. and Wales Notes* ed. Crisp, ix. 39–40; *Suss. Arch. Colls.* civ. 66; F. Cundall, *Historic Jamaica*, 114. [2] *Cal. Treas. Bks.* xxii. 197; xxiv. 481, 512, 589; xxix. 350; xxx. 54. [3] *Suss. Arch. Colls.* 63–87; *Cal. Treas. Bks.* xxii. 197; xxiv. 481, 512, 589; info. from Dr P. J. Le Fevre; *Vis. Eng. and Wales Notes*, 40.

P. W.

FULLER, Samuel (1646–1721), of Great Yarmouth, Norf.

GREAT YARMOUTH 1689–1698, 1701 (Feb.–Nov.)

bap. 20 Dec. 1646, 1st s. of John Fuller, merchant, of Great Yarmouth by his w. Elizabeth. *m.* bef. 1679, Rose, da. of Richard Huntington† of Great Yarmouth, 3s. (1 *d.v.p.*) 2da. *suc.* fa. 1673.[1]

Freeman, Great Yarmouth 1672, alderman 1676–84, Oct. 1688–*d.*; bailiff 1679–80, 1698–9, mayor 1707–8; freeman, Dunwich? –1703.[2]

Fuller often acted in Parliament with his Yarmouth colleague George England I*, particularly in proceedings concerning trade and shipping, and followed the same political line. Listed as a Whig by Lord Carmarthen (Sir Thomas Osborne†) in March 1690, he was appointed during the first session to assist in the drafting of bills concerning the East India trade (2 Apr.); to appoint commissioners of public accounts (24 Apr.); and for the regulation of wines (9 May). In December, Carmarthen forecast that Fuller would probably support him in the event of a Commons' attack on his ministerial position. Robert Harley* noted him as a 'doubtful' member of the Country party in April 1691. In August 1691 he was excused the office of bailiff of Great Yarmouth 'by reason of the sickness and infirmity of his body', but he was able to serve on the committee of 30 Oct. 1691, to prepare a bill appointing new oaths in Ireland, and on 25 Jan. 1692 as a teller against an amendment to the Dover harbour bill, most probably protecting the interests of Great Yarmouth. He was among the appointees on 14 Nov. 1693 to prepare a bill to encourage the clothing trade, and at about the same time was noted by Samuel Grascome as a Court supporter. On 5 Apr. 1694 he acted as a teller with George England over a clause in the poll tax bill. He lent the government £1,000 in 1694, and on 1 Dec. was among those named to a committee to prepare legislation for the recovery of minors' debts.[3]

Like England, although he signed the Association he had been forecast as a likely opponent of the Court in January 1696 on the proposed council of trade and later voted against fixing the price of guineas. He and England spent much of November and December 1696 in negotiation on behalf of Yarmouth corporation with the Admiralty Board over a captured privateer, and both men voted on 25 Nov. for the attainder of Sir John Fenwick†. Fuller was included in the committee of 14 Jan. 1697 to prepare clauses to explain the Recoinage Acts and prevent abuses by receivers of public money. A month later, after England had already travelled back to Yarmouth, one of the bailiffs of the corporation went to attend the Admiralty, again on the borough's behalf, to express gratitude for the increase in the numbers of North Sea convoys, and was advised: 'You had best not carry Mr Fuller with you; his deportment is not very pleasing to the board. 'Tis thought . . . he hath done us great disservice by his carriage to those commissioners (but this *inter nos*).' He assisted in the proposal made on 29 Jan. 1698 for a bill to crack down on robbery, and on 10 Mar. acted as a teller with England in support of a petition from Yarmouth for protection of the herring trade. Although he stood down at the 1698 election, in a list of about September 1698 he was classed with England as a member of the Country party.[4]

Resuming his seat in 1701, Fuller was listed in February as likely to support the Court in agreeing with the committee of supply's resolution to continue the 'Great Mortgage'. He remained a Whig under Queen Anne, and co-operated with the followers of Viscount Townshend, who was building up a strong interest at Yarmouth, against a Tory faction which included the heirs of George England I. Either Fuller or, more probably, his eldest son Samuel contested Yarmouth with Townshend's brother in 1708 against Benjamin England* and another Tory. When a vacancy occurred in the following year, Fuller sought the return of his son Samuel and nearly came into conflict with Lord Townshend, who wanted the seat for his secretary. Eventually a compromise was reached. In the 1710 election Fuller seems not to have involved himself in Yarmouth at all, while co-operating with the Townshend interest in the county.[5]

Fuller died 19 May 1721, aged 74. His eldest surviving son, John†, consul at Leghorn, succeeded to his property in Yarmouth and his manor of Langley, Norfolk. His daughter Rose received £2,000 (£1,500 in South Sea and Bank stock), while another £1,000 in South Sea stock went to his grandson Richard. Both John and Richard were to stand unsuccessfully at Yarmouth against the Townshend–Walpole interest: John (MP Plympton Erle 1728–34) in 1727; Richard in 1741, 1754 and 1756.[6]

[1] C. J. Palmer, *Perlustration Gt. Yarmouth*, ii. 149; D. Turner, *Sepulchral Reminiscences*, 35–36; Blomefield, *Norf.* xi. 381. [2] Norf. RO, Gt. Yarmouth bor. recs. assembly bk. 1680–1701, p. 205; Suff. RO (Ipswich), EE6:1144/14. [3] Gt. Yarmouth bor. recs. assembly bk. 1680–1701, p. 205; *Cal. Treas. Bks.* x. 908. [4] Norf. RO, Gt. Yarmouth corp. mss, Fuller and George England I to Yarmouth bailiffs, 29 Oct.–3 Dec., 12 Dec. 1696, Richard Ferrier* to Thomas Godfrey, 15 Feb. 1696[-7]. [5] *HMC Townshend*, 329, 334–6; Norf. RO, Bradfer-Lawrence mss, Ashe Windham* to [Ld. Townshend], 7, 14 June 1709, 8 June 1710; Add. 38501, f. 98. [6] Add. 27967, f. 240.

D. W. H.

FULTHORPE, Robert Raikes *see* RAIKES

FURNESE, Sir Henry (1658–1712), of Waldershare, Kent and Dover Street, Westminster.

BRAMBER   1698–14 Feb. 1699
SANDWICH   3 Jan.–19 Feb. 1701
              1701 (Dec.)–30 Nov. 1712

b. 30 May 1658, 1st s. of Henry Furnese of Sandwich by Anne, da. of Andrew Gosfright of Sandwich. m. (1) 11 Nov. 1684, Anne (d. 1695), da. of Robert Brough, linen draper, of St. Lawrence Jewry, London, 1s.; (2) 1 Dec. 1697, Matilda, da. of Sir Thomas Vernon*, wid. of Anthony Balam, 1da. *suc.* fa. 1672; kntd. 8 Oct. 1691; *cr.* Bt. 27 June 1707.[1]

Apprentice, Drapers' Co. 1672, master 1694–5; sheriff, London and Mdx. 1700–1; common councilman, London 1691–4, alderman 1711.[2]

Member, R. Fishery Co. [I] 1692; commr. taking subscriptions to Bank of England, 1694, dir. 1694–7, 1699–Apr. 1700, Nov. 1700–2; ?commr. Birth, Marriages and Deaths Act 1695, Greenwich Hosp. 1695; trustee, circulating Exchequer bills 1697–1701, receiving loan to Emperor 1706, poor Palatines 1709; dir. New E. I. Co. 1698–1703; member, Russia Co. 1699, Levant Co. 1699.[3]

From humble origins, Henry Furnese rose to be the most important government financier in England between 1705 and 1710. Historians may have exaggerated his low birth: although his father only reached the rank of sergeant in Cromwell's dragoons, on settling in Sandwich, Henry snr. married the daughter of Andrew Gosfright, jurat of the port and mayor in 1636–7. Furnese's alleged early penury appears to have been inferred from his father's bankruptcy, and from the work of Augustan satirists keen to highlight the lowliness of his birth and the vulgarity of his plebeian manners. In fact Furnese's apprenticeship to a London hosier in the year of his father's death may not have been evidence of poverty, but rather the making of him, because his master was one of his Gosfright uncles, many of that family appearing in the records as quite well-to-do tradesmen. Indeed, Furnese was following in the footsteps of two of his Gosfright cousins who were entered as apprentices in 1667 and 1670 respectively. This wider family network may explain how Furnese was able to take the all-important initial steps up the ladder of London commerce. His Gosfright relations certainly traded to Flanders and Italy, where Furnese was to exploit his own trading contracts as a means of remitting money for the allied armies. Moreover his uncle George Gosfright was in 1678 deputy-paymaster to the forces in Flanders under the command of the Duke of Monmouth.[4]

Politically, Furnese was a committed Whig, and this, too, he may have picked up from his own father and his Gosfright relatives. The restoration of Charles II saw his uncle George Gosfright in trouble with the Privy Council and having in March 1661 to post a bond of £500 for good behaviour. In 1668 George was reported to be shipping seditious tracts from Rotterdam to London, and the Exclusion Crisis saw him under suspicion of propagating the myth that the King had been married to the Duke of Monmouth's mother. A friend of Titus Oates, he was arrested at the time of Monmouth's rebellion. Furthermore, he was a Dissenter. This brings us to the question of Furnese's own religious beliefs. He was married by Edmund Calamy snr., the Nonconformist divine, although the ceremony was recorded in the register of St. Lawrence Jewry. Obviously by that date Furnese had prospered sufficiently to set up a separate household, although little is known about his trading activities. That he continued to prosper is indicated in verses describing the parade of the City's volunteer regiment of horse during the lord mayor's show in 1689, where Cornet Furnese's rich trappings were seen as 'mighty presumptuous'.[5]

In the early 1690s Furnese concentrated on the trade to Flanders, even importing fine linen and lace for the use of the King. He also supported the war effort by clothing several regiments and helping to finance a galley for use against the French. His communications network was already second to none, for it was Furnese who brought King William the first notice of the capitulation of Limerick, for which he was rewarded with a jewel reputed at the time to be worth £10,000 (but only valued at £200 when it was stolen in 1695) and a knighthood. In January 1692 three peers voted for him in the Lords' ballot for commissioners of accounts. Furnese's Irish interests extended to subscribing towards the cost of a dinner at Merchant Taylors' Hall in February 1692 in honour of General Ginkel, Lord Cutts (John*) and other officers who had served in the campaign, and to joining the newly incorporated Royal Fishery Company of Ireland. When 300 pieces of his cloth were seized by the customs he attempted to get a grant of the King's moiety for himself, just one incident of many which led to rumours that he was engaged in smuggling prohibited goods. He enjoyed loaning money to the government, but clearly saw that there were many ways in which astute men could make a fortune out of war: in November 1692 Lord Coningsby (Thomas*) was informed from Ireland that Furnese was attempting 'to get a grant for clothing all the King's forces, as well as those here'. Furnese even found time to wager heavily on the outcome of siege warfare in Flanders, his superior information allowing him to increase his chances of success; political bets, such as the failure of the French to take Charleroy, netted him a reputed £2,500 from 'Jacobites' at the end of 1692.[6]

If proof were needed of Furnese's position in London mercantile society, his elevation in February 1694 to the London lieutenancy certainly provided it. Further recognition came in July when he was elected to the first directorate of the Bank of England (in 23rd place), having subscribed £3,000. Evidence uncovered by the Commons relating to the attempt to bribe the Speaker, Sir John Trevor, over the London orphans bill, revealed that Furnese was one of the eight commoners appointed to the committee set up by the City to discover a way in which the debts due to the orphans of the city could be satisfied. No doubt his burgeoning wealth was also a recommendation for his appointment in March 1695 to the first board of governors of Greenwich Hospital. His connexion with the Bank saw him attend the Treasury in May regarding the use of the Bank for transmitting money to pay the forces in Flanders, a development of great significance for the future. All was not well, however, as it was reported to Sir William Trumbull* in June that customs officers at Gravesend had been unfaithful in their trust 'particularly in compliance with the intrigues of Sir Henry Furnese in his smuggling'. Other information suggested that the packet boats had been used by Furnese, particularly when John Wildman[†] ran the Post Office.[7]

The years 1696-7 saw an important change in the method by which money was remitted to the army in Flanders. In March 1696 Furnese was one of the directors who represented to the Treasury the Bank's unwillingness to remit money on the credit of tallies. The following year, he was one of those employed in a private capacity to send funds, his chief collaborator being Sir Theodore Janssen[†]. In April 1697 he was elected a trustee for circulating Exchequer bills, a post worth £200 p.a. initially, rising to £400 p.a. in 1698. In May 1697 he subscribed £2,000 to the fund. The following year saw him heavily engaged in setting up the New East India Company (having sold his stock in the Old Company at some point after 1693), the aim being to raise £2 million for the government in return for a parliamentary charter giving the interlopers a monopoly of the trade for 31 years. Much depended on the ability of men such as Furnese to overcome the scepticism of the King and some of his ministers by demonstrating that a loan of such magnitude could be raised without difficulty. In the event £1,200,000 was pledged within a fortnight and Furnese was the intermediary used by such people as James Vernon I*, when he sought to subscribe on behalf of the Duke of Shrewsbury. In July Furnese's role was recognized by the subscribers, when they elected him a director of the New Company. The same month he was returned for Bramber at the general election. When Parliament sat his return was the subject of a petition on 12 Dec. 1698 and he was accused of bribery. Given the battle between the two East India Companies, his election was bound to be controversial and in the event his enemies were able to secure his expulsion on 14 Feb. 1699, on the grounds, as James Lowther* put it, that he was 'acting as receiver and manager of the subscription of the new East India Company'. At least one contemporary felt that Furnese had welcomed expulsion on these grounds rather than waiting to be thrown out for bribing the electorate. During his short spell in the House he was classed as a placeman on a list of September 1698, as a Court placeman on a comparative analysis of the old and new Parliaments, and on 18 Jan. 1699 he voted against the third reading of the disbanding bill.[8]

In February 1700 Furnese was involved in remitting £120,000 to Holland to pay off a debt to the States General. In June, together with Robert Beachroft, he was set up for sheriff of London, both men 'being gentlemen of known loyalty and ability'. Having been elected, Furnese was then reported at the end of the month to be 'very ill at Bristol, he being gone thither to drink the water of the hot well near that city'. This excursion may account for reports that he had attempted to fine off for the office, but in July he gave bond to perform his duties. Thus, he presided in September over the election of lord mayor, which saw the sheriffs declare the Whig Sir Thomas Abney* and the moderate Tory Sir William Hedges elected, only for Sir Charles Duncombe* to demand and then to top a poll, before the court of aldermen chose Abney as mayor. Furnese was much criticized for his handling of this heated election, but in mitigation Matthew Prior* pointed out that the Court had singularly failed to give any guidance as to which party it favoured. In October the court of aldermen declined to invite the King to a feast, even though Furnese offered '£400 for himself and £400 for his brother sheriff towards the charge'. When Furnese did organize a banquet in Drapers' Hall in November, over 400 attended (L'Hermitage reported the number as 600), including many Whig peers, MPs and the Treasury lords. November 1700 also saw Furnese return as a director of the Bank, replacing one of the two deceased directors, Sir James Houblon* or Thomas Goddard, who both died in late October 1700.[9]

On 3 Jan. 1701, polling day at Sandwich, Furnese was admitted a freeman of the corporation 'by birth' and duly returned as MP for the borough. The defeated Tory candidate, John Michell II*, attempted to unseat Furnese by petitioning. Michell not only alleged bribery, but claimed that Furnese was ineligible to sit by virtue of his office as sheriff of London and because of his interest in managing several parliamentary funds. Upon receipt of the petition, the Commons voted to consider on 17 Feb. the relevant 'place clause', that no Member be concerned 'in farming, collecting or managing any monies, duties or aids' granted to the King. Preparatory to this, on the 15th the House ordered the commission constituting the trustees for circulating Exchequer bills to be laid before them, and when the matter finally came before the Commons on the 19th, the House brushed aside Furnese's defence, that as a trustee for the subscribers' money he did not come within the scope of the clause, and expelled him. Sir Richard Cocks, 2nd Bt.*, saw the matter in party terms, since the Tory Sir Joseph Herne* had escaped a similar fate in the preceding Parliament when he had also been named as a trustee. Outside the House, Furnese was a representative of the Bank when it told the Treasury in June 1701 that it did not wish to 'meddle' in remittances to Holland, but this did not deter him from offering to undertake the business on a personal basis. He was also a subscriber of £100 to the corporation of the poor of the City, an institution dominated by Whig and Dissenting interests.[10]

Furnese resigned his post as a trustee for circulating Exchequer bills on 14 Nov. 1701, three days after the dissolution, and was thus able to put up at Sandwich, appealing to the voters on the grounds of both birth and personal sacrifice, he having 'quitted a trust of £400 p.a. profit for your service'. He was returned at the top of the poll. In December 1701 Robert Harley* listed him as a Whig, and it was no doubt partly because of his political affiliations that an attempt was made to have him expelled the House a third time. Sir John Bolles, 4th Bt., moved on 10 Feb. 1702 that by virtue of being a trustee for the circulation of Exchequer bills Furnese was ineligible to sit in the Commons. However, extracts from the Treasury minutes laid before the House on 21 Feb. showed that Furnese had resigned his post before the election, and any attempt to take the matter further was baulked on 24 Feb. by the presentation of a medical certificate from Furnese claiming that he was too ill to attend in his own defence. Furnese was still in poor health on 8 Mar. when he informed Sandwich corporation of the King's death, although he did promise to attend the Commons 'constantly, health permitting'. Re-elected in 1702, Furnese was a nominee of the New Company on the directorate of the united East India Company, a place he retained for only one year.[11]

In the 1702–3 session, Furnese voted on 13 Feb. 1703 for agreeing with the Lords' amendments to the bill enlarging the time for taking the oath of abjuration. His activities in the Commons were no doubt limited by his increasing involvement in the remittance of funds to the army in Flanders and Portugal. Almost every month in 1703 the Treasury minutes reveal Furnese tendering for contracts to remit money, along with references to loans to the government on various taxes, all of which seems to have yielded him a handsome profit. Such activity continued in 1704, with mention also being made of remittances and a clothing contract for the army in Portugal. However, he did show concern for the needs of his constituents. In February 1704 the corporation wrote to thank him for a gift of coals and 'pulpit clothes', and he responded to requests which saw him waiting on the secretary of state, Sir Charles Hedges*. He was also keen to ensure that the corporation made adequate preparations to celebrate the victory at Blenheim, deputing his brother-in-law Branch to represent him on that occasion. He was forecast as a probable opponent of the Tack, and did not vote for it on 28 Nov. 1704. An important area was indicated on 11 Nov. by his nomination to a committee to draft a bill to restrain commerce with France more effectually, especially in the receipt and negotiation of French bills of exchange, an area in which he was an acknowledged expert. It was also one of his main arguments against some of his rivals in the remittance trade, along with the view that one contractor could obtain better rates of exchange than a multitude. When the Treasury finally heeded his advice, Furnese benefited personally because he signed a contract in February 1705 giving him a six-month monopoly of all remittances to the Low Countries, Germany and Portugal, for which he was allowed a commission of 11s. for every £100 transferred.[12]

Returned again at the 1705 election, Furnese was classed as 'Low Church' in an analysis of the new Parliament, and on 25 Oct. 1705 voted for the Court candidate as Speaker. He was clearly becoming ever more closely identified with a ministry increasingly preoccupied by the war effort, as one might expect given his central role in ensuring that the money to pay the army was actually sent abroad. It was this powerful position which led him to write to the Duke of Marlborough (John Churchill†) in December 1705 about what can only be described as warfare by financial means, and more particularly the need to persuade the Dutch to prevent the French supplying their forces in Italy by bills of exchange drawn on Amsterdam and in Brabant and Flanders by the transfer of specie from thence to Antwerp. Should this continue, Furnese foresaw a shortage of money for the allied forces, with serious consequences for the war effort (and his own business). March 1706 saw him appointed to the commission of the peace in Kent in recognition of his growing estate in the county. Also in March he was appointed a trustee of the £250,000 loan being raised for the Emperor on security of revenues in Silesia, and then one of the seven managers of the subscription. A measure of his importance to government may be gleaned by the fact that he had to seek permission from the Treasury on 3 Sept. to go into the country for two to three weeks. October and November 1706 saw a dispute between Furnese and the paymaster of the forces abroad, Hon. James Brydges*, over remittances, and more particularly Furnese's plans to use Antwerp in addition to Amsterdam as a means of transmitting the funds. Brydges came off second best, and was vitriolic on the subject of Furnese's conduct, writing on 18 Oct. to William Cadogan* (who was Brydges' confederate, along with Adam de Cardonnel* in an alternative scheme), 'Sir Henry hath upon this occasion shown a malice that I could not have imagined anyone could have been capable of, much less one who loves his interest and pursues it by all such sorts of methods as he doth'. The explanation, according to Brydges, was Furnese's anger at not being 'admitted into the partnership as he expected, if the army had marched into Italy'. Perhaps the dispute can best be explained by Furnese's attempts to get a better deal from the Treasury in view of the risks he ran. In December 1706, when Furnese was allowed 12s. per £100, back-dated to August, it transpired that he had been remitting money without a written contract (and hence with no guarantee of repayment) since the previous February.[13]

In February 1707 Furnese renewed his agreement for a monopoly of remittances to the Low Countries for a further six months. In June he was created a baronet and in September was again writing to Marlborough, this time about the iniquities of the East India Company's actions in draining England and Holland of £600,000 of silver when it was needed for other purposes. Late November saw him 'given over by the physicians, his distemper the twisting of the guts', but he soon recovered and the following month Tower Ward elected him and Sir Charles Peers as their nominees to the aldermanic bench, which plumped for the latter. On two lists of early 1708 Furnese was classed as a Whig. His own self-assessment when soliciting votes from the corporation in 1708 was that 'I have acquitted myself with loyalty to her Majesty and faithfulness to my country'. He secured re-election easily and seems to have been employed in trying to convince his neighbour from St. Lawrence Jewry, Henry Cornish*, to withdraw from the contest at Shaftesbury. In the new Parliament he had the pleasure of seeing one of his chief persecutors from 1701, Anthony Hammond, expelled from the Commons under the same place clause by which he himself had suffered. Yet again, however, heavy involvement in financial affairs appears to have precluded active work in the Commons, although he did support the naturalization of the Palatines in the first session. Furnese's influence was now at its apogee: titbits of information from his network of correspondents were traded by others, such as Peter Wentworth, who in June 1709 was keen to tell his brother at third hand what Furnese had said about the prospects for peace. He was still unpopular, even in government circles, Cardonnel writing to Brydges that 'I have known Sir H. a great many years according to the character you give me of him and I reckon it a great misfortune in your business to be obliged to have anything to do with him'. James Craggs II* may have identified the reason when he told James Stanhope* in August 1709 that such was Furnese's credit with Lord Godolphin (Sidney†) that ''tis not only a difficult, but also a dangerous matter to oppose his schemes'.[14]

In the 1709–10 session Furnese's time was taken up in deflecting an attempt by the Bank to regain part of the remittance contract to Flanders and, more important, the fateful decision to impeach Dr Sacheverell. In November 1709 Furnese appears to have been 'promoted' within the Kit-Cat Club, whose rotating chairmanship involved hosting a feast, and he was especially keen to invite Marlborough to his own feast held in December. It was around this time that a Kit-Cat meeting was held at Furnese's house to decide Sacheverell's fate and contemporaries reported Marlborough's recruitment to the club. Not surprisingly, Furnese voted for the impeachment of Sacheverell and signed the address of the London lieutenancy abhorring the tumults of 'Catholics and non-jurors' during the doctor's trial. That Furnese retained his power in the dying days of the Whig ministry is shown by a meeting in February 1710 at the Treasury, attended by Marlborough, Robert Walpole II*, Brydges and Cardonnel, at which Furnese received an undertaking that no money ordered for subsistence would be diverted by Brydges towards extraordinary expenses or other uses, unless the lord treasurer so directed. Furnese maintained his iron grip on government remittances until Godolphin's dismissal, although his early confidence in April about subscriptions to another Imperial loan had lapsed into concern that by June the 'present situation' was retarding the loan. In July he sent Marlborough a present of wine, 'in this melancholy time when all runs counter to what every honest man might reasonably expect', and expressed 'great apprehensions of the failure of our public credit'. Furnese was in a difficult position here, torn between the need to support Marlborough's armies with funds, and the attempt of Whig bankers to coerce the Queen into retaining Godolphin by threatening government credit. In July Marlborough suggested to the lord treasurer that he use Furnese to prevent the haemorrhaging of Dutch money from London. At the first meeting of the new Treasury commission on 12 Aug. 1710, Furnese attended, and both parties agreed to fulfil their existing obligations. However, on the following day Harley wrote to the Duke of Newcastle (John Holles†) that 'it is most certain there has been great labouring with the Bank and Sir Henry Furnese not to deal', and that Furnese 'was turned quite off and pretended to make propositions of accommodation'. On the 14th, Godolphin informed Marlborough that Furnese 'has continued to give bills for some farther subsistence to your army'. What seems clear from the Treasury records for August was that Furnese continued to bid for remittance contracts, but, apart from the funds for Lisbon, others were preferred. Craggs may have offered the most likely explanation of all this manoeuvring, when he noted that after Godolphin's dismissal Furnese and Janssen had threatened to renege on an agreement to lend £300,000, but that Godolphin had persuaded them otherwise. As early as 21 Aug. Brydges was certain that 'the remittances will be taken out of Sir H. Furnese's hands', but John Drummond† may have been more realistic when he advised a period of cohabitation to ensure that Furnese is 'doing something that he may not do mischief till you can do without him'. In the end this was precisely what occurred: the last contract Furnese signed was in November 1710, for remitting money to Portugal, which was not completed until April 1711. This is not to say that Furnese's conduct in the ministerial crisis in 1710 was approved. Brydges for one believed that 'what he did in relation to his stopping at once in all ports his credit is so much resented that I question much whether he will not hear of it in Parliament'.[15]

Furnese's position in Sandwich was unassailable and in the 1710 election he topped the poll. Somewhat surprisingly, he failed to vote in the London election, presumably because the contests in Kent absorbed all his attention. He was classed as a Whig on the 'Hanover list'. In April 1711 he was elected an alderman for Bridge Within, a useful piece of news in the hands of Arthur Maynwaring*, who used it to refute the allegation that the Whigs were hated by the people. The 1711–12 session saw Furnese more active, possibly owing to the reduction in his involvement in public finance. He voted on 7 Dec. 1711 for the 'No Peace without Spain' motion. As a Whig financier, Furnese was an obvious target for Tory attack, and on 26 Feb. 1712 Thomas Harley*, a secretary to the Treasury, was trying to hurry the auditor into processing Furnese's accounts. On 12 June the Treasury laid before the Commons minutes of Treasury proceedings relating to remittances and also the auditor's report on Furnese's remittances to Holland. It was ordered that they should lie on the table until the actual accounts were laid before the House. If this was intended as a prelude to an attack on Furnese, his enemies were thwarted by his death, which occurred before the next parliamentary session. The accounts were eventually cleared in 1717.[16]

Furnese died on 30 Nov. 1712, of a 'violent colic' at his seat at Waldershare, shortly after entertaining the Duke of Marlborough. His will, as might be expected, demonstrated his great wealth, but may also reflect quarrels after 1710 with some of his erstwhile colleagues. Thus a codicil of November 1711 revoked bequests to John Taylor[?*], George Townsend and Moses Berenger (along with a mysterious trust of £1,000 for purposes 'as I have privately directed or shall privately direct'). The poor of Sandwich gained permanent benefit from his will, £500 being allowed the corporation to purchase lands, with the rents so gained being distributed annually on his birthday. St. Bartholomew's and St. Thomas' hospitals, together with the hospital in Bishopsgate street, all benefited by £100. Finally, a monument was to be erected signifying 'God's great goodness to me in advancing me to a considerable estate from a very small beginning', an instruction evidently carried out by his son Sir Robert* in commissioning a 'towering mass of marble, with its seated female figures, cherubs, and ammonite-like volutes'. The inscription not only paid heed to Furnese's humble origins, but revealed that 'being early distinguished by the favour of our great deliverer King William, he faithfully adhered to the cause of liberty and the Protestant interest with a steady and indefatigable zeal'.[17]

Furnese was an obvious target of critics of the new finance. Although his origins were probably less humble than he himself or his detractors made out, his success in trade and especially public finance was spectacular. Nor did he scruple at investing in land: in 1710 it was noted that, like everyone else, he subsisted on credit, as 'all his ready money is laid out on land'. He purchased extensively in Kent, initially at Waldershare in the 1690s and then more extensively in Anne's reign, rebuilding his seat, as well as beautifying local churches in Sandwich and New Romney. All this was based on the ruthless maintenance of his position in the remittance business, which earned him a widespread notoriety: in December 1701 George Petty wrote of the arrival in India of Sir Henry's brother, George, who he said, had 'a little of the blood of the Furneses, and more of their impudence'. None the less, Furnese played a unique and vital role in the war effort during Anne's reign and in the ongoing experiments in public finance.[18]

[1] IGI, London; W. Boys, *Hist. Sandwich*, 484–6; *St. Lawrence Jewry* (Harl. Soc. Reg. lxxi), 97, 193; *Mar. Lic. Vicar-Gen.* (Harl. Soc. xxx.), 181. [2] P. Boyd, *Roll of Drapers' Co.* 71; Beaven, *Aldermen*, ii. 122. [3] *CSP Dom.* 1691–2, p. 112; NLS, Advocates' mss, Bank of England pprs. 31.1.7; Beaven, 122; Luttrell, *Brief Relation*, iv. 709; *London Rec. Soc.* 16. 114; J. Cooke and J. Maule, *Hist. Greenwich Hosp.* 8–30; Add. 10120, f. 234; 38871 (unfol.); Boyer, *Anne Annals*, iv. 127; viii. 41, App.; *Cal. Treas. Bks.* xii. 8; xvi. 110; *Post Boy*, 31 July–2 Aug. 1698; *Trans. Amer. Phil. Soc.* li. 106; info. from Prof. R. Walcott. [4] G. Holmes, *Pol. in Age of Anne*, 156; G. S. De Krey, *Fractured Soc.* 145–6; *EHR*, lxxi. 230; Boyrs, 424, 484; *Swift Works* ed. Davis, iii. 151–2; *Poems on Affairs of State* ed. Ellis, vi. 406–7; Boyd, 78; PCC 86 Cann; *Cal. Treas. Bks.* v. 1032; *CSP Dom.* 1678, p. 294; *Market and Merchants* ed. Roseveare, 650. [5] *CSP Dom.* 1660–1, p. 542; 1667–8, p. 282; 1678–80, pp. 448, 451; info. from Dr M. J. Knights; *St. Lawrence Jewry*, 97, 193; *Poems on Affairs of State* ed. Cameron, v. 95. [6] *Cal. Treas. Bks.* ix. 1086, 1653; x. 124, 205 354, 725; xiii. 300; *CSP Dom.* 1690–1, pp. 495, 548; 1691–2, pp. 3, 112, 210; *HMC Lords*, iv. 50; Trinity, Dublin, Clarke mss 1267, Robert Yard* to George Clarke*, 17 Oct. 1691; Folger Shakespeare Lib. Newdigate newsletter 7 May 1695; Luttrell, ii. 295, 363, 472–3, 593, 595; Add. 57861, f. 15; Oldmixon, *Hist. Eng.* 61. [7] *CSP Dom.* 1694–5, p. 21; 1696, p. 285; Luttrell, iii. 269, 342; Bodl. Carte 79, f. 557; *CJ*, xi. 269; DZA, Bonet despatch 6/16 July 1694; *Cal. Treas. Bks.* x. 1376; Cooke and Maule, 8–30; Add. 10120, f. 234; *HMC Downshire*, i. 483–4. [8] *Cal. Treas. Bks.* x. 1441; xi. 6; xii. 3, 8, 54, 83, 143, 270; xiii. 102, 238, 386; Univ. of London Lib. ms 65, item 3; Bodl. Rawl. A.302, ff. 224–7; H. Horwitz, *Parl. and Pol. Wm. III*, 232–3; *Vernon–Shrewsbury Letters*, ii. 84–85, 88; Carte 130, f. 396. [9] *Cal. Treas. Bks.* xv. 47; *Post Boy*, 20–22, 25–27 June 1700; Luttrell, iv. 660, 662–3, 692, 709, 712; *HMC Bath*, iii. 421–2; BL, Trumbull Alphab. mss 50, Thomas Bateman to Sir William Trumbull*, 25 Oct. 1700; Add. 17677 UU, f. 358. [10] Centre Kentish Stud. Sandwich bor. recs. Sa/Ac 8, f. 375; *Cocks Diary*, 82; *Vernon–Shrewsbury Letters*, ii. 266; *Cal. Treas. Bks.* xvi. 73, 75; *Cal. Treas. Pprs.* 1697–1702, p. 497; E. Hatton, *A New View of London*, 752. [11] *Cal. Treas. Bks.* xvi. 110; Add. 33512, ff. 179, 183; 38871; *Cocks Diary*, 207. [12] *Cal. Treas. Bks.* xviii. 41, 56, 66, 72, 76–77, 89,

364, 390; xix. 4, 17, 19, 29, 43, 49, 59, 72; xx. 76; Sandwich bor. recs. Sa/ZB2/159, corp. to Furnese, 26 Feb. 1703/4; Sa/ZB2/160-2, Furnese to corp., 21 Apr., 10 Aug., 27 Dec. 1704; D. W. Jones, *War and Econ.* 84–85. [13] Add. 61135, ff. 93, 95; info. from Prof. N. Landau; *Daily Courant*, 9, 21 Mar. 1706; Luttrell, vi. 24, 28; *Marlborough Letters and Depatches* ed. Murray, ii. 396; *Cal. Treas. Bks.* xx. 95; xxi. 9; *Marlborough–Godolphin Corresp.* 609–10; Huntington Lib. Stowe mss 57 (1), pp. 4, 40, 47. [14] *Cal. Treas. Bks.* xxi. 18; Add. 61135, ff. 109–10; 33512, f. 190; Luttrell, vi. 237–8; PRO, 30/24/21/52–53; *Parlty. Lists Early 18th Cent.* ed. Newman, 80; Boyer, viii. 41, App.; *Post Boy*, 30 June–2 July 1709; *Wentworth Pprs.* 90; Stowe mss 57 (4), p. 104; Centre Kentish Stud. Stanhope mss U1590/O139/9/71/3, Craggs to Stanhope, 3 Aug. N.S. 1709. [15] *Cal. Treas. Bks.* xxiii. 34; xxiv. 7, 35, 39, 42–44, 99; *HMC Portland*, ii. 209, 215–16; iv. 583; *Duchess of Marlborough Corresp.* i. 172, 279; G. Holmes, *Trial of Sacheverell*, 87; Trumbull Alphab. mss 53, Ralph Bridges to Trumbull, 20 Dec. 1709; *N. and Q.* ccxvi. 48–49; Add. Ch. 76120; Add. 61135, ff. 113–17; *Marlborough–Godolphin Corresp.* 1558, 1603–4; Stanhope mss U1590/O140/12/73/18, Craggs to Stanhope, 9 Sept. N.S. 1710; Stowe mss 57 (4), pp. 3, 150. [16] *London Poll 1710*, 175; Boyer, *Pol. State*, i–ii. 266; *Swift v. Mainwaring*, 384; *Cal. Treas. Bks.* xxvi. 169; xxxi. 242. [17] Boyer, *Pol. State*, iv. 368; Add. 17677 FFF, f. 431; *Wentworth Pprs.* 306; PCC 234 Barnes; *Arch. Cant.* lxii. 69; P. Parsons, *Monuments and Painted Glass in E. Kent*, 401–2. [18] *HMC Portland*, iv. 583; Hasted, *Kent*, vi. 511; vii. 123, 128, 391, 460, 502, 511; x. 53–54; C. W. Chalklin, *17th Cent. Kent*, 203; Add. 59480, f. 66.

S. N. H.

FURNESE, Robert (1687–1733), of Waldershare, Kent and Dover Street, Westminster.

TRURO	16 Dec. 1708–1710
NEW ROMNEY	1710–1727
KENT	1727–14 Mar. 1733

b. 1 Aug. 1687, o. s. of Sir Henry Furnese* (1st Bt.) by 1st w. Anne. *educ.* Eton, c.1697; travelled abroad (Germany, Austria) 1705. *m.* (1) lic. 1 Oct. 1708, his stepsister Anne (*d.* 1713), da. of Anthony Balam, 1da.; (2) 8 July 1714, Arabella (*d.* 1727), da. of Hon. Lewis Watson†, 3rd Baron (later 1st Earl of) Rockingham, sis. of Hon. Edward Watson*, 1s. 1da.; (3) 15 May 1729, Lady Anne Shirley (*d.* 1779), da. of Robert, 1st Earl Ferrers, 2da. (1 *d.v.p.*) *suc.* fa. as 2nd Bt. 30 Nov. 1712.[1]

Freeman, New Romney 1710.[2]

Having been steward of the Eton feast in 1704, Furnese seems to have been sent abroad by his father, although probably for the purposes of receiving a genteel, as opposed to a professional or commercial, education. In 1705 he appears to have been part of the entourage of the Earl of Sunderland (Charles, Lord Spencer*) during Sunderland's embassy to Vienna, the Earl having brought a 'parcel of notable Whigs' with him including Furnese. A letter from the Duke of Marlborough (John Churchill†) in July 1708 informed the Duchess that, as the French would grant no passes to travel by sea, he could not comply with Sir Henry's request for a pass for his son. As a consequence Furnese was abroad during the 1708 general election and had to wait for a by-election in December 1708 to enter the Commons. Even then his opportunity probably owed a great deal to his father's influence, for when Hon. James Brydges* chose to serve for Hereford rather than Truro, the Boscawen interest chose his son as a replacement.[3]

Furnese's first important action in the House was appointment on 21 Jan. 1709 to the drafting committee of a naturalization bill on behalf of Moses Berenger, a business associate of his father. No bill was brought in, however, Berenger presumably being covered by the general naturalization bill which passed that session and which Furnese supported. In the following session, he told on 20 Dec. 1709 in favour of recommitting a resolution from the committee of elections on the franchise at Shrewsbury. In effect Furnese was voting for the sitting Tory Members, subsequently ejected on very weak grounds by the Whigs, which may reflect a desire to see fair play, given his father's earlier experiences before a partisan House. On a more vital party matter, he voted in favour of the impeachment of Dr Sacheverell in this session. Before the 1710 election the Norfolk Whigs exerted considerable pressure on his father to put Furnese forward at Thetford, but a seat was found for him instead at New Romney, and before the election he was added to the Kentish commission of the peace. He was classed as a Whig on the 'Hanover list' and showed his colours in the opening session by telling on 27 Jan. 1711 in favour of the motion that Viscount Shannon [I] (Richard Boyle*) had been duly elected for Hythe, a resolution heavily defeated by the Tory majority. In the next session Furnese voted on 7 Dec. 1711 for the 'No Peace without Spain' motion.[4]

The death of his father in November 1712 left Furnese a very rich man. As sole executor he had many bequests to arrange, some of which proved difficult, including the gift of £500 to Sandwich corporation, which fell foul of corporate prevarication, and which was still bedevilling him in 1727. As heir to his father's political interest he tried to influence the electors of Sandwich in favour of Sir Henry Oxenden, 4th Bt.*, at the by-election called in April 1713. However, despite being recommended as 'a sincere lover of his country and firmly fixed to the present settlement of the Protestant Succession in the House of Hanover', words which might have applied equally well to his father, Oxenden was defeated by the Tory John Michell II* (although he did win the seat at the subsequent general election). It seems probable that family business kept Furnese away from Parliament in 1713, since he even missed the division on 18 June over the French commerce bill, barely a fortnight after the death of his first wife. The careful cultivation of an interest at New Romney, begun by his father, ensured his return at the 1713 election. It was based primarily on acts of public benevolence, for around this time the chancel of the parish church was beautified and gifts of an altar piece and an organ bestowed on the town. These did not make him a Churchman, and his membership of the Hanover club attested to his commitment to the Whig cause, although he did split his vote at the Kent election of 1713, rather surprisingly failing to back his fellow Member for Romney, Hon. Edward Watson. In Parliament, he voted on 18 Mar. 1714 against the expulsion of Richard Steele. A few days after the close of the session Furnese married a daughter of Lord Rockingham and in doing so became Edward Watson's brother-in-law. The social advantages of such a match were made clear by one Kentish lady who wrote, 'I think Sir Robert judges right to get a little quality to so much riches'.[5]

Furnese's closeness to the Duke of Marlborough was revealed following the death of Queen Anne when his residence at Waldershare provided a safe haven for the Duke on the night of his return to England. The minutes of a Whig club in the City of London in December 1714 note that Furnese had influence over at least one voter at the election of common councilmen in Cornhill Ward, but he does not seem to have attended any of the club's meetings himself. Indeed, despite his appointment in 1716 to the London lieutenancy, he did not cut a figure in City politics as his father had done. In reality, Furnese was a country gentleman living off the rents of the estates accumulated by his father, plus his holdings in government stock (he had £36,000 in South Sea stock in 1723). He was returned for New Romney in 1715, being classed as a Whig on the Worsley list and on two analyses comparing the 1713 and 1715 Parliaments. His main task in the aftermath of the Hanoverian succession was to ensure that his father's accounts were accepted by the Treasury. To this end he attended the commissioners in December 1716 and January 1717, and in the following April the accounts were cleared.[6]

Furnese continued to serve in Parliament for New Romney, switching to the county in 1727, a clear sign that he had become well established in county society. He died on 14 Mar. 1733, 'by his own fault, for he had one of those colds hanging on him and he drank so hard that he was not sober for ten days before he was taken ill'. His will left most of his estate to his son Henry (d. 1735) and mourning rings to his three daughters and his cousin George, a captain in Lord Cobham's (Sir Richard Temple, 4th Bt.*) cavalry regiment. His executors were his cousin Henry Furnese† and his brother-in-law through marriage Lord Monson (John†). His monument was fulsome in its tribute to one who, as

> heir to his father's virtues and estate ... after exerting in several Parliaments integrity, zeal and spirit, for the true interest and support of our happy constitution in Church and state, was elected knight of the shire for the county of Kent; a public testimonial of the trust and confidence of his countrymen, whose hearts and affections were naturally engaged by his most affable behaviour and liberal spirit.

The early death of his son saw the estate divided by Chancery between Furnese's three daughters, a decree which was given statutory force by private Act in 1737.[7]

[1] W. Boys, *Hist. Sandwich*, 486; *Eton Reg.* ed. Sterry, 133; *HMC Hare*, 204; *Canterbury Mar. Lic.* v. 182; P. Parsons, *Monuments and Painted Glass in E. Kent*, 402–3. [2] Centre Kentish Stud. New Romney recs. NR/AC3. [3] *Eton Reg.* 133; *HMC Hare*, 204; S. Spens, *George Stepney*, 257; *Marlborough–Godolphin Corresp.* 466, 1039. [4] Norf. RO, Bradfer-Lawrence mss, Ashe Windham* to [Ld. Townshend], 8 June 1710; Walpole mss at Wolterton, Horatio Walpole II* to Robert Walpole I*; info. from Prof. N. Landau. [5] Add. 33512, ff. 194, 122; *Arch. Cant.* xiii. 473; xliii. 279; v. 91; Oldmixon, *Hist. Eng.* 509; Centre Kentish Stud. Q/RPe, poll bk. 1713. [6] Boyer, *Pol. State*, viii. 141; *London Rec. Soc.* xvii. 15; P. G. M. Dickson, *Financial Revol.* 280; *Cal. Treas. Bks.* xxx. 51; xxxi. 1, 242. [7] *HMC Hastings*, iii. 15; Coxe, *Walpole*, iii. 129; Boyer, *Pol. State*, xlv. 312; Parsons, 402–3 (cf. *Gent. Mag.* 1733, p. 157); Hasted, *Kent*, v. 438.

S. N. H.

FYTCHE (FITCH), William (c.1671–1728), of Danbury Place, Essex.

MALDON   1701 (Feb.)–1708
                30 Apr. 1711–Jan. 1712

b. c.1671, s. of Sir Barrow Fytche of Woodham Walter, Essex by Elizabeth, da. of Sir Mundeford Bramston of Little Baddow, Essex. *educ.* Queens', Camb. 1689. *m.* by 1696, Mary (d. 1757), da. and h. of Rev. Robert Corey of Danbury, Essex, adn. of Essex, 5s. (2 *d.v.p.*) 8 da. *suc.* fa. 1673.[1]

    Freeman, Colchester 1701.[2]
    Comptroller of lotteries 1712–15.[3]

Fytche demolished Woodham Walter Hall, 'the ancient seat of the noble families of Fitzwalter and Ratcliffe', preferring to live at Danbury Place, a few miles west of the borough that he represented. His militant Anglican Toryism mirrored that of his grandfather, who had been a colonel in the Royalist army at the siege of Colchester, and that of his mother's family, the Bramstons. Indeed, the influence of the latter was particularly strong because his uncle, Dr George Bramston, acted as his guardian, a service which Fytche sought to repay through his role as patron of another uncle, William Bramston, a man deeply hostile to Dissent, whom he appointed rector of Woodham Walter. It was thus presumably on the Bramston interest that William first contested Maldon in 1698, though he was defeated 'by the folly and ignorance of the bailiff', who returned Charles Montagu's* brother, Irby*, against whom Fytche unsuccessfully petitioned. He does not appear to have contested the by-election the following year, but was returned at both elections in 1701, and William was listed as a Tory by Robert Harley* in December 1701. He voted for the motion on 26 Feb. 1702 vindicating the Commons' proceedings in the impeachments of William III's ministers, and on 28 Mar. acted as teller on behalf of the Tories over the bitterly disputed Coventry election case. Five days later he was again a teller, in favour of a motion exempting Great Yarmouth from the duty laid down by the bill for rebuilding Whitby harbour. Re-elected in July 1702, despite having been blacklisted as an opponent the previous year to preparations for war with France, he acted as teller on three occasions in the new Parliament: on 10 Nov., in support of a motion that the under-sheriff of Merioneth be taken into custody for failing to return a by-election writ; on 9 Dec. 1703, to determine a procedural motion, and on 7 Mar. 1704, in favour of a motion to impress into the army those otherwise liable to be sent to houses of correction. In accordance with his High Tory sympathies, on 13 Feb. 1703 he opposed the Lords' amendment for enlarging the time for taking the oath of abjuration, and in mid-March 1704 was listed by Lord Nottingham (Daniel Finch†) as a likely supporter should he be the victim of a parliamentary attack over his handling of the Scotch Plot. He voted for the Tack on 28 Nov., and, as Dyer jubilantly recorded, was one of the first of its supporters to be returned at the 1705 election, meriting the labels 'True Church' and 'Tory' on two analyses of Members.[4]

Fytche opposed the Court candidate as Speaker for the new Parliament, but, perhaps alerted by his dismissal as deputy-lieutenant to the fact that his political and religious views had made him a marked man, he subsequently adopted a much lower profile. He did not contest his seat in 1708, and in 1710 admitted to being 'so stupid (for I can call it no better) to neglect coming in', though his former colleague, John Comyns*, offered a more benevolent explanation. Fytche's interest, Comyns told Robert Harley, was 'so absolute at Maldon that it is easy for him to be chosen without opposition, but the precept being down almost as soon as himself there was not time to take other measures, and his generosity would not permit him to make any attempt'. Fytche's electoral oversight was not, however, as ingenuous as either he or his friend pretended. Calculating that he could advance his fortunes better out of Parliament than in it, he petitioned, with the support of Henry St. John II*, for a place as a commissioner of salt duties, a post that was 'not consistent with a seat'. He was thus placed in a quandary when, without his having received any firm assurance of office, a vacancy arose in April 1711 to represent Maldon. Having secured the corporation's backing for the impending by-election, he told Harley that it 'would be by much the most convenient for me and my affairs to obtain [the salt commissionership], but if you would have me come in myself, and you think of anything that I may hold within doors of equal value, I shall readily submit and go down and be chosen accordingly'. Harley's reply, if there was one, is unknown, but Fytche evidently thought it safer to have himself elected and continue to lobby from a position of strength. Showing his loyalty to Harley by his activity as one of the 'worthy patriots' who detected the mismanagements of the previous administration, he reminded his patron in November 1711 that 'with the greatest pleasure in the world I shall with equal joy and satisfaction obey your commands in whatsoever station you shall please to place me', and in January 1712 was finally rewarded with the comptrollership of the Two Million Lottery, which carried a salary of £500 p.a. and consequently forced him to resign his seat. Responsible for registering the transactions of the lottery, he employed a large number of sometimes unruly clerks to issue tickets, and, although officially he was to make 'no delay in directing the orders when any money is in the Exchequer or in the paymaster's hands', the possibilities for peculation were clear enough. At any rate, his successor complained that during the three years of Fytche's tenure, the office had failed to keep adequate accounts. Ousted in 1715, Fytche did not re-enter public life before his death on 12 Sept. 1728, aged 57, which he had unsuccessfully tried to avert by a rest-cure at Bath. His eldest son, a naval captain, died unmarried in 1740, and the estate passed to his third son, Thomas; the youngest son later became governor of Bengal.[5]

[1] *Le Neve's Knights* (Harl. Soc. viii), 233; *Bramston Autobiog.* (Cam. Soc. xxxii), 387, 411; BL, Dept. of Printed Bks. 1856.g.6(26); IGI, Essex; *Essex Rev.* i. 101. [2] *Procs. Huguenot Soc. of London*, xii. 130. [3] *Cal. Treas. Bks.* xxvi. 4. [4] Morant, *Essex*, i. 340; *Essex Arch. Soc.* xx, 227; Morrice ent'ring bk. 3, p. 116; *Essex Rev.* i. 96; *Bramston Autobiog.* 404; BL, Dept. of Printed Bks. 1856.g.6(26);

W. A. Speck, *Tory and Whig*, 102. ⁵Essex RO, Winterton (Turnor) mss D/Dkw/01/37; Add. 70197, Fytche to Harley, 31 Oct. 1710, Comyns to Harley, c. Oct. 1710; 70278, Fytche to Oxford, 10 Nov. 1711; *HMC Portland*, iv. 676; *Cal. Treas. Bks.* xxvi. 4, 116, 385; xxvii. 11, 55, 160–1; xxxi. 145; *Cal. Treas. Pprs.* 1708–14, p. 406; BL, Dept. of Printed Bks. 1856.g.6(26); *Essex Rev.* ii. 34.

M. J. K.